KEY TO WORLD MAP PAGES

- Large scale maps
  (> 1:2 500 000)
- Medium scale maps
  (1:2 800 000–1:9 000 000)
- Small scale maps
  (< 1:10 000 000)

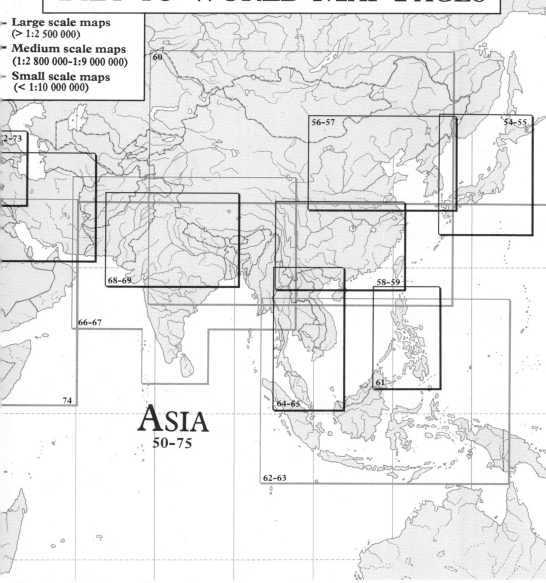

ASIA
50-75

NORTH
AMERICA
98-121

SOUTH
AMERICA
122-128

COUNTRY INDEX

Afghanistan	66	Kuwait	70–71	
Albania	40	Kyrgyzstan	50	
Algeria	78			
Angola	84–85, 128	Laos	64	
Argentina	126, 128	Latvia	46	
Armenia	73	Lebanon	75	
Australia	92–95	Lesotho	88–89	
Austria	26–27	Liberia	82	
Azerbaijan	73	Libya	79	
		Lithuania	46	
Bahamas	120–121	Luxembourg	17	
Bahrain	71			
Bangladesh	67	Macedonia	40	
Barbados	121	Madagascar	89	
Belarus	46–47	Malawi	87	
Belgium	17	Malaysia	62–63	
Belize	120	Mali	78, 82–83	
Benin	83	Malta	36	
Bhutan	67	Mauritania	78, 82	
Bolivia	124	Mauritius	77	
Bosnia-Herzegovina	29, 40	Mexico	118–119	
Botswana	88–89	Moldova	43	
Brazil	124–127	Mongolia	60	
Brunei	78	Morocco	78	
Bulgaria	40–41	Mozambique	85, 87	
Burkina Faso	82–83			
Burma	67	Namibia	88	
Burundi	86	Nepal	69	
		Netherlands	17	
Cambodia	64–65	New Zealand	91	
Cameroon	84	Nicaragua	120	
Canada	100–101	Niger	83	
Central African Republic	84	Nigeria	83	
Chad	79	Northern Ireland	15	
Chile	124, 128	Norway	8–9	
China	56–60			
Colombia	124	Oman	74	
Congo	84			
Congo, Dem. Rep. of the	84–85	Pakistan	68	
Costa Rica	120	Panama	120	
Croatia	29, 42	Papua New Guinea	90	
Cuba	120–121	Paraguay	126–127	
Cyprus	36	Peru	124	
Czech Republic	26–27	Philippines	61	
		Poland	44–45	
Denmark	11	Portugal	34–35	
Djibouti	74	Puerto Rico	121	
Dominican Republic	121	Qatar	71	
		Romania	42–43	
Ecuador	124	Russia	50–51	
Egypt	80	Rwanda	86	
El Salvador	120			
England	12–13	Saudi Arabia	74	
Equatorial Guinea	84	Scotland	14	
Eritrea	80–81	Senegal	82	
Estonia	46	Sierra Leone	82	
Ethiopia	74, 81	Singapore	65	
		Slovak Republic	27	
Fiji	91	Slovenia	29	
Finland	8–9	Somali Republic	74	
France	18–21	South Africa	88–89	
French Guiana	125	Spain	32–35, 37	
		Sri Lanka	66	
Gabon	84	Sudan	79, 81	
Gambia	82	Surinam	124–125	
Georgia	73	Swaziland	89	
Germany	24–25	Sweden	8–9	
Ghana	82–83	Switzerland	25	
Greece	38–41	Syria	72–73	
Greenland	4			
Guatemala	120	Taiwan	59	
Guinea	82	Tajikistan	50	
Guinea-Bissau	82	Tanzania	86–87	
Guyana	124	Thailand	64–65	
		Togo	83	
Haiti	121	Trinidad and Tobago	121	
Honduras	120	Tunisia	78–79	
Hungary	42	Turkey	72–73	
		Turkmenistan	50	
Iceland	8	Uganda	86	
India	66–69	Ukraine	47	
Indonesia	62–63	United Arab Emirates	71	
Iran	70–71	United Kingdom	12–15	
Iraq	70–71	USA	106–117	
Irish Republic	15	Uruguay	126–127	
Israel	75	Uzbekistan	50	
Italy	28–31			
Ivory Coast	82	Venezuela	124	
		Vietnam	64–65	
Jamaica	120			
Japan	54–55	Wales	12–13	
Jordan	75			
		Yemen	74	
Kazakstan	50	Yugoslavia	40, 42	
Kenya	86			
Korea, North	57	Zambia	84–85, 87	
Korea, South	57	Zimbabwe	87	

PHILIP'S

WORLD ATLAS

PHILIP'S

WORLD ATLAS

NEW EDITION

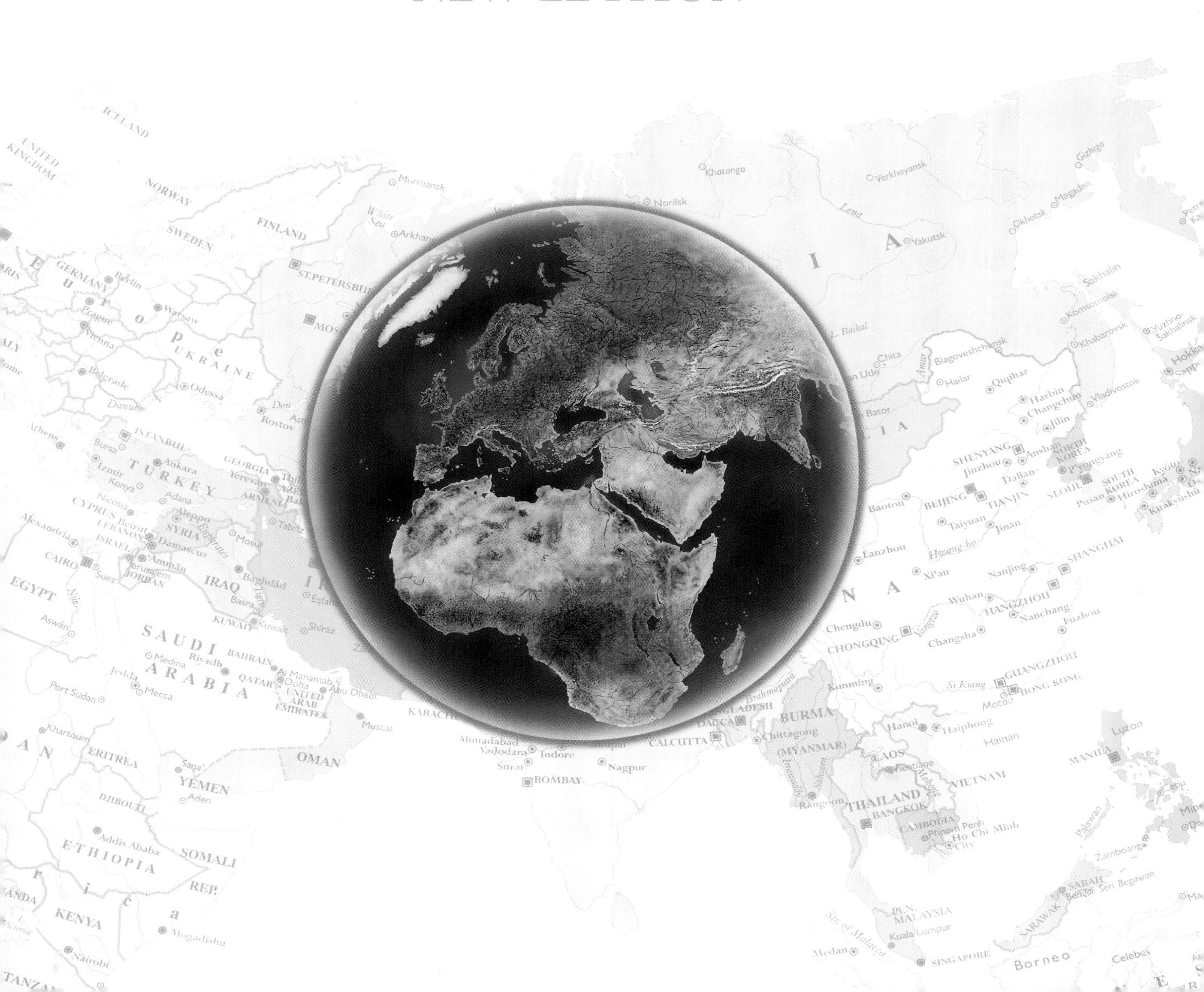
ICELAND
NORWAY
SWEDEN
FINLAND
GERMANY
Berlin
Warsaw
Prague
Vienna
UKRAINE
Belgrade
Odessa
Rostov
Athens
ISTANBUL
TURKEY
Ankara
Izmir
Konya
Adana
GEORGIA
Yerevan
ARMENIA
Nicosia
CYPRUS
Beirut
LEBANON
ISRAEL
Alexandria
SYRIA
Aleppo
Damascus
Mosul
Tabriz
CAIRO
Suez
Jerusalem
'Ammān
JORDAN
EGYPT
IRAQ
Baghdād
Basra
Esfahān
Aswân
KUWAIT
Kuwait
Shīrāz
SAUDI ARABIA
Riyadh
Medina
Jedda
Mecca
BAHRAIN
QATAR
Doha
Al Manamah
Abu Dhabi
UNITED ARAB EMIRATES
Muscat
Port Sudan
Khartoum
ERITREA
OMAN
Sana'
YEMEN
Aden
DJIBOUTI
Addis Ababa
ETHIOPIA
SOMALI REP.
KENYA
Mogadishu
Nairobi
Murmansk
White Sea
Arkhangelsk
ST. PETERSBURG
Khatanga
Norilsk
Verkhoyansk
Lena
Yakutsk
Okhotsk
Magadan
Gizhiga
Sakhalin
Komsomolsk
Khabarovsk
Yuzhno-Sakhalinsk
L. Baikal
Chita
Amur
Blagoveshchensk
Hailar
Qiqihar
Harbin
Changchun
Vladivostok
Jilin
SHENYANG
Anshan
Jinzhou
Dalian
NORTH KOREA
P'yongyang
SEOUL
SOUTH KOREA
Pusan
Hiroshima
Kitakyushu
Baotou
BEIJING
TIANJIN
Taiyuan
Jinan
Hwang-ho
Lanzhou
Xi'an
Nanjing
SHANGHAI
Wuhan
HANGZHOU
Nanchang
Fuzhou
Chengdu
CHONGQING
Yangtze
Changsha
Kunming
Si Kiang
GUANGZHOU
HONG KONG
Macau
Brahmaputra
BURMA (MYANMAR)
Chittagong
Hanoi
Haiphong
Hainan
LAOS
Vientiane
Mekong
VIETNAM
Rangoon
THAILAND
BANGKOK
CAMBODIA
Phnom Penh
Ho Chi Minh City
Luzon
MANILA
Palawan
Zamboanga
SABAH
Bandar Seri Begawan
SARAWAK
PEN. MALAYSIA
Kuala Lumpur
Str. of Malacca
Medan
SINGAPORE
Borneo
Celebes
KARACHI
Ahmadabad
Vadodara
Indore
Surat
BOMBAY
Nagpur
CALCUTTA
DACCA

THE EARTH IN SPACE
Cartography by Philip's

Text
Keith Lye

Illustrations
Stefan Chabluk

Star Charts
John Cox
Richard Monkhouse

PICTURE ACKNOWLEDGEMENTS
Corbis Sygma /Thorne Anderson 47
Robert Harding Picture Library /PHOTRI 13, /Bill Ross 41, /Adam Woolfitt 43
Hutchison Library /John Hatt 46
Image Bank /Peter Hendrie 20, /Daniel Hummel 34, /Image Makers 8 top,
/Pete Turner 39
Images Colour Library Limited 15
Japan National Tourist Organization 45
NASA/Galaxy Picture Library 8 bottom left
NPA Group, Edenbridge, UK 48
Panos Pictures /Howard Davies 35
Chris Rayner 19 top
Rex Features /SIPA Press /Scott Andrews 12
Science Photo Library /Martin Bond 14, /CNES, 1992 Distribution Spot
Image 27 top, /Luke Dodd 3, 6, /Earth Satellite Corporation 25 bottom,
/NASA 9 centre right, 9 top, 22, 23, 24, /David Parker 26, /Peter Ryan 27
below, /Jerry Schad 4, /Space Telescope Science Institute /NASA 9 centre left,
9 bottom right, /US Geological Survey 8 centre right
Space Telescope Science Institute /R. Williams /NASA 2
Starland Picture Library /NASA 8 centre left
Still Pictures /Francois Pierrel 28, /Heine Pedersen 31, 40
Tony Stone Images 33, /Glen Allison 38, /James Balog 16, /John Beatty 21,
/Neil Beer 30, /Kristin Finnegan 11, /Jeremy Horner 42, /Gary Norman 36,
/Frank Oberle 25 top, /Dennis Oda 17, /Nigel Press 37, /Donovan Reese 18,
19, /Hugh Sitton 32, /Richard Surman 44, /Michael Townsend 29, /World
Perspectives 10
Telegraph Colour Library /Space Frontiers 9 bottom left

Published in Great Britain in 2002
by Philip's,
a division of Octopus Publishing Group Limited,
2–4 Heron Quays, London E14 4JP

This edition produced for Lomond Books, 2002

Copyright © 2002 Philip's

Cartography by Philip's

ISBN 0–540–08356–9

A CIP catalogue record for this book is available from the British Library.

Printed in Hong Kong

Details of other Philip's titles and services can be found on our website at:
www.philips-maps.co.uk

Philip's World Maps

The reference maps which form the main body of this atlas have been prepared in accordance with the highest standards of international cartography to provide an accurate and detailed representation of the Earth. The scales and projections used have been carefully chosen to give balanced coverage of the world, while emphasizing the most densely populated and economically significant regions. A hallmark of Philip's mapping is the use of hill shading and relief colouring to create a graphic impression of landforms: this makes the maps exceptionally easy to read. However, knowledge of the key features employed in the construction and presentation of the maps will enable the reader to derive the fullest benefit from the atlas.

MAP SEQUENCE

The atlas covers the Earth continent by continent: first Europe; then its land neighbour Asia (mapped north before south, in a clockwise sequence), then Africa, Australia and Oceania, North America and South America. This is the classic arrangement adopted by most cartographers since the 16th century. For each continent, there are maps at a variety of scales. First, physical relief and political maps

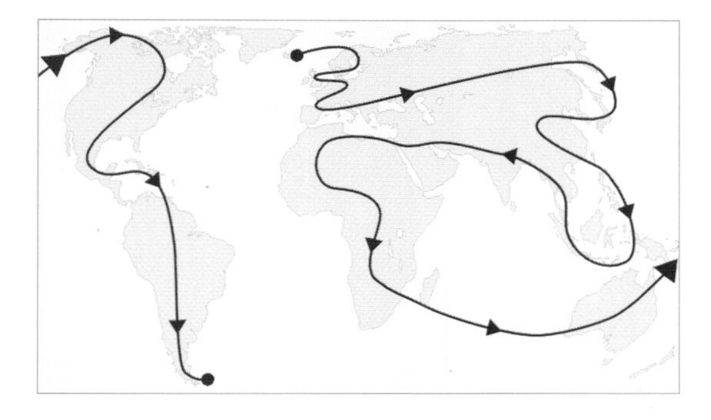

of the whole continent; then a series of larger-scale maps of the regions within the continent, each followed, where required, by still larger-scale maps of the most important or densely populated areas. The governing principle is that by turning the pages of the atlas, the reader moves steadily from north to south through each continent, with each map overlapping its neighbours.

MAP PRESENTATION

With very few exceptions (e.g. for the Arctic and Antarctic), the maps are drawn with north at the top, regardless of whether they are presented upright or sideways on the page. In the borders will be found the map title; a locator diagram showing the area covered and the page numbers for maps of adjacent areas; the scale; the projection used; the degrees of latitude and longitude; and the letters and figures used in the index for locating place names and geographical features. Physical relief maps also have a height reference panel identifying the colours used for each layer of contouring.

MAP SYMBOLS

Each map contains a vast amount of detail which can only be conveyed clearly and accurately by the use of symbols. Points and circles of varying sizes locate and identify the relative importance of towns and cities; different styles of type are employed for administrative, geographical and regional place names to aid identification. A variety of pictorial symbols denote landscape features such as glaciers, marshes and coral reefs, and man-made structures including roads, railways, airports, canals and dams. International borders are shown by red lines. Where neighbouring countries are in dispute, for example in parts of the Middle East, the maps show the *de facto* boundary between nations, regardless of the legal or historical situation. The symbols are explained on the first page of the *World Maps* section of the atlas.

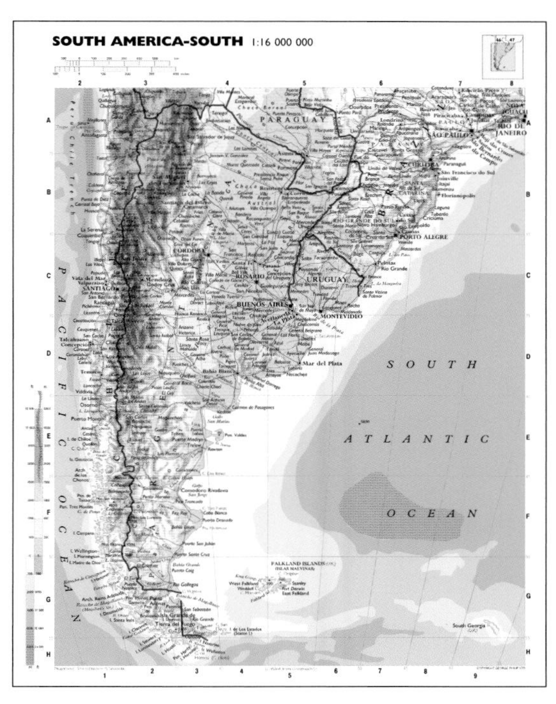

MAP SCALES

1:16 000 000
1 inch = 252 statute miles

The scale of each map is given in the numerical form known as the 'representative fraction'. The first figure is always one, signifying one unit of distance on the map; the second figure, usually in millions, is the number by which the map unit must be multiplied to give the equivalent distance on the Earth's surface. Calculations can easily be made in centimetres and kilometres, by dividing the Earth units figure by 100 000 (i.e. deleting the last five 0s). Thus 1:1 000 000 means 1 cm = 10 km. The calculation for inches and miles is more laborious, but 1 000 000 divided by 63 360 (the number of inches in a mile) shows that 1:1 000 000 means approximately 1 inch = 16 miles. The table below provides distance equivalents for scales down to 1:50 000 000.

LARGE SCALE		
1:1 000 000	1 cm = 10 km	1 inch = 16 miles
1:2 500 000	1 cm = 25 km	1 inch = 39.5 miles
1:5 000 000	1 cm = 50 km	1 inch = 79 miles
1:6 000 000	1 cm = 60 km	1 inch = 95 miles
1:8 000 000	1 cm = 80 km	1 inch = 126 miles
1:10 000 000	1 cm = 100 km	1 inch = 158 miles
1:15 000 000	1 cm = 150 km	1 inch = 237 miles
1:20 000 000	1 cm = 200 km	1 inch = 316 miles
1:50 000 000	1 cm = 500 km	1 inch = 790 miles
SMALL SCALE		

MEASURING DISTANCES

Although each map is accompanied by a scale bar, distances cannot always be measured with confidence because of the distortions involved in portraying the curved surface of the Earth on a flat page. As a general rule, the larger the map scale (i.e. the lower the number of Earth units in the representative fraction), the more accurate and reliable will be the distance measured. On small-scale maps such as those of the world and of entire continents, measurement may only

be accurate along the 'standard parallels', or central axes, and should not be attempted without considering the map projection.

MAP PROJECTIONS

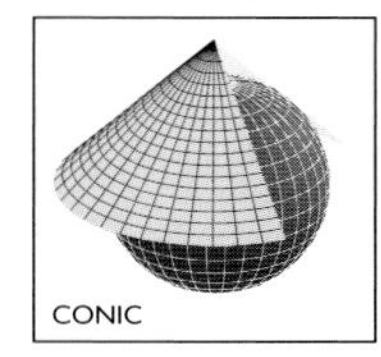

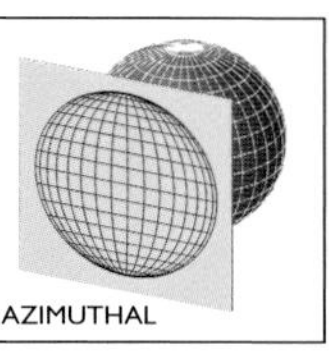

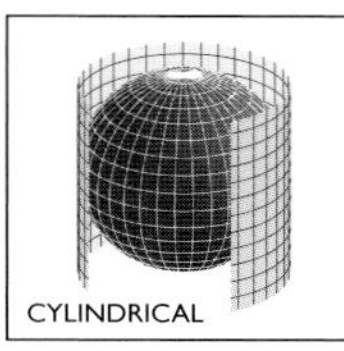

Unlike a globe, no flat map can give a true scale representation of the world in terms of area, shape and position of every region. Each of the numerous systems that have been devised for projecting the curved surface of the Earth on to a flat page involves the sacrifice of accuracy in one or more of these elements. The variations in shape and position of landmasses such as Alaska, Greenland and Australia, for example, can be quite dramatic when different projections are compared.

For this atlas, the guiding principle has been to select projections that involve the least distortion of size and distance. The projection used for each map is noted in the border. Most fall into one of three categories – conic, azimuthal or cylindrical – whose basic concepts are shown above. Each involves plotting the forms of the Earth's surface on a grid of latitude and longitude lines, which may be shown as parallels, curves or radiating spokes.

LATITUDE AND LONGITUDE

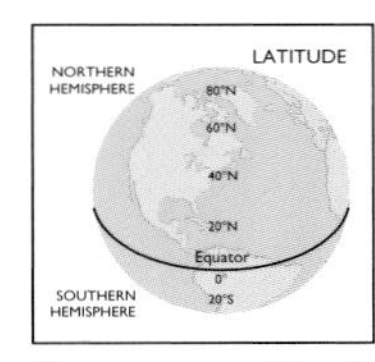

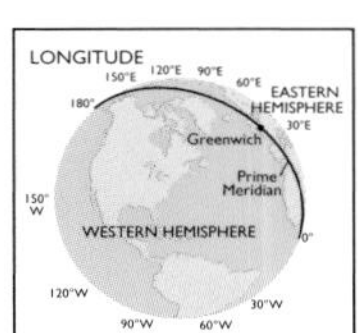

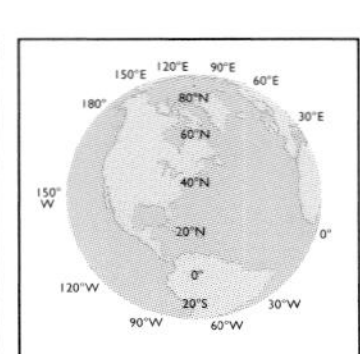

Accurate positioning of individual points on the Earth's surface is made possible by reference to the geometrical system of latitude and longitude. Latitude *parallels* are drawn west–east around the Earth and numbered by degrees north and south of the Equator, which is designated 0° of latitude. Longitude *meridians* are drawn north–south and numbered by degrees east and west of the *prime meridian*, 0° of longitude, which passes through Greenwich in England. By referring to these co-ordinates and their subdivisions of minutes (1/60th of a degree) and seconds (1/60th of a minute), any place on Earth can be located to within a few hundred metres. Latitude and longitude are indicated by blue lines on the maps; they are straight or curved according to the projection employed. Reference to these lines is the easiest way of determining the relative positions of places on different maps, and for plotting compass directions.

NAME FORMS

For ease of reference, both English and local name forms appear in the atlas. Oceans, seas and countries are shown in English throughout the atlas; country names may be abbreviated to their commonly accepted form (e.g. Germany, not The Federal Republic of Germany). Conventional English forms are also used for place names on the smaller-scale maps of the continents. However, local name forms are used on all large-scale and regional maps, with the English form given in brackets only for important cities – the large-scale map of Russia and Central Asia thus shows Moskva (Moscow). For countries which do not use a Roman script, place names have been transcribed according to the systems adopted by the British and US Geographic Names Authorities. For China, the Pin Yin system has been used, with some more widely known forms appearing in brackets, as with Beijing (Peking). Both English and local names appear in the index, the English form being cross-referenced to the local form.

Contents

World Statistics

Countries	x
Cities	xi
Climate	xii–xiii
Physical Dimensions	xiv–xv
Regions in the News	xvi

The Earth In Space

The Universe	2–3
Star Charts and Constellations	4–7
The Solar System	8–9
The Earth: Time and Motion	10–11
The Earth from Space	12–13
The Dynamic Earth	14–15
Earthquakes and Volcanoes	16–17
Forces of Nature	18–19
Oceans and Ice	20–21
The Earth's Atmosphere	22–23
Climate and Weather	24–25
Water and Land Use	26–27
The Natural World	28–29
The Human World	30–31
Languages and Religions	32–33
International Organizations	34–35
Agriculture	36–37
Energy and Minerals	38–39
World Economies	40–41
Trade and Commerce	42–43
Travel and Communications	44–45
The World Today	46–47

World Maps

Map Symbols	**1**
The World: Political 1:71 100 000	**2–3**
Arctic Ocean 1:31 100 000	**4**
Antarctica 1:31 100 000	**5**

Europe

Europe: Physical
1:17 800 000   6

Europe: Political
1:17 800 000   7

Scandinavia
1:4 400 000

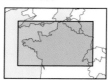

                                            8–9

Denmark and Southern Sweden
1:2 200 000

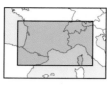

                                            10–11

England and Wales
1:1 800 000

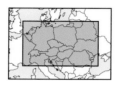

                                            12–13

Scotland
1:1 800 000

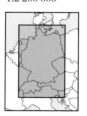

                                            14

Ireland
1:1 800 000

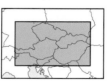

                                            15

British Isles
1:4 400 000

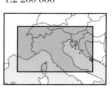

                                            16

Netherlands, Belgium and Luxembourg
1:2 200 000

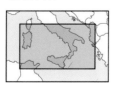

                                            17

Northern France
1:2 200 000

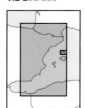

                                            18–19

Southern France
1:2 200 000

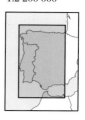

                                            20–21

Middle Europe
1:4 400 000

                                            22–23

Germany and Switzerland
1:2 200 000

                                            24–25

**Austria, Czech Republic
and Slovak Republic**
1:2 200 000

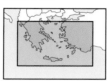

                                            26–27

Northern Italy, Slovenia and Croatia
1:2 200 000

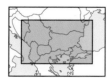

                                            28–29

Southern Italy
1:2 200 000

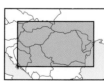

                                            30–31

Eastern Spain
1:2 200 000

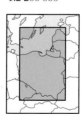

                                            32–33

Western Spain and Portugal
1:2 200 000

                                            34–35

Malta, Crete, Corfu, Rhodes and Cyprus
1:900 000 / 1:1 200 000

                                            36

The Balearics, the Canaries and Madeira
1:900 000 / 1:1 800 000

                                            37

Southern Greece and Western Turkey
1:2 200 000

                                            38–39

Northern Greece, Bulgaria and Yugoslavia
1:2 200 000

                                            40–41

Hungary, Romania and the Lower Danube
1:2 200 000

                                            42–43

Poland and the Southern Baltic
1:2 200 000

                                            44–45

Baltic States, Belarus and Ukraine
1:4 400 000

46–47

The Volga Basin and the Caucasus
1:4 400 000

48–49

Asia

Russia and Central Asia
1:17 800 000

50–51

Asia: Physical
1:44 400 000   52

Asia: Political
1:44 400 000   53

Japan
1:4 400 000

54–55

Northern China and Korea
1:5 300 000

56–57

Southern China
1:5 300 000

58–59

China
1:17 800 000

60

The Philippines
1:6 700 000

61

Indonesia and the Philippines
1:11 100 000

62–63

Mainland South-east Asia
1:5 300 000

64–65

South Asia
1:8 900 000

66–67

The Indo-Gangetic Plain
1:5 300 000

68–69

The Middle East
1:6 200 000

70–71

Turkey and Transcaucasia
1:4 400 000

72–73

Arabia and the Horn of Africa
1:13 300 000

74

The Near East
1:2 200 000

75

Africa

Africa: Physical
1:37 300 000   76

Africa: Political
1: 37 300 000   77

Northern Africa
1:13 300 000

78–79

The Nile Valley and the Nile Delta
1:7 100 000 / 1:3 600 000

80–81

West Africa
1:7 100 000

82–83

Central and Southern Africa
1:13 300 000

84–85

East Africa
1:7 100 000

86–87

Southern Africa
1:7 100 000 / 1:7 100 000

88–89

Australia and Oceania

Australia and Oceania:
 Physical and Political
1:44 400 000

90

New Zealand and Samoa, Fiji and Tonga
1:5 300 000 / 1:10 700 000

91

Western Australia
1:7 100 000

92–93

Eastern Australia
1:7 100 000

94–95

Pacific Ocean
1:48 000 000

96–97

North America

North America: Physical
1:31 100 000

98

North America: Political
1:31 100 000

99

Canada and Alaska
1:13 300 000 / 1:26 700 000

100–101

Eastern Canada
1:6 200 000

102–103

Western Canada
1:6 200 000

104–105

United States and Hawaii
1:10 700 000 / 1:8 900 000

106–107

Eastern United States
1:5 300 000

108–109

North-eastern United States
1:2 200 000

110–111

Middle United States
1:5 300 000

112–113

Western United States
1:5 300 000

114–115

Central and Southern California
 and Western Washington
1:2 200 000

116–117

Mexico
1:7 100 000

118–119

Central America and the West Indies
1:7 100 000

120–121

South America

South America: Physical
1:31 100 000

122

South America: Political
1:31 100 000

123

South America – North
1:14 200 000

124–125

Central South America
1:7 100 000

126–127

South America – South
1:14 200 000

128

Index to World Maps

129–224

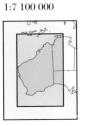

World Statistics: Countries

This alphabetical list includes all the countries and territories of the world. If a territory is not completely independent, the country it is associated with is named. The area figures give the total area of land, inland water and ice.

The population figures are 2001 estimates. The annual income is the Gross Domestic Product per capita† in US dollars. The figures are the latest available, usually 2000 estimates.

Country/Territory	Area km² Thousands	Area miles² Thousands	Population Thousands	Capital	Annual Income US $
Afghanistan	652	252	26,813	Kabul	800
Albania	28.8	11.1	3,510	Tirana	3,000
Algeria	2,382	920	31,736	Algiers	5,500
American Samoa (US)	0.2	0.08	67	Pago Pago	8,000
Andorra	0.45	0.17	68	Andorra La Vella	18,000
Angola	1,247	481	10,366	Luanda	1,000
Anguilla (UK)	0.1	0.04	12	The Valley	8,200
Antigua & Barbuda	0.44	0.17	67	St John's	8,200
Argentina	2,767	1,068	37,385	Buenos Aires	12,900
Armenia	29.8	11.5	3,336	Yerevan	3,000
Aruba (Netherlands)	0.19	0.07	70	Oranjestad	28,000
Australia	7,687	2,968	19,358	Canberra	23,200
Austria	83.9	32.4	8,151	Vienna	25,000
Azerbaijan	86.6	33.4	7,771	Baku	3,000
Azores (Portugal)	2.2	0.87	243	Ponta Delgada	11,040
Bahamas	13.9	5.4	298	Nassau	15,000
Bahrain	0.68	0.26	645	Manama	15,900
Bangladesh	144	56	131,270	Dhaka	1,570
Barbados	0.43	0.17	275	Bridgetown	14,500
Belarus	207.6	80.1	10,350	Minsk	7,500
Belgium	30.5	11.8	10,259	Brussels	25,300
Belize	23	8.9	256	Belmopan	3,200
Benin	113	43	6,591	Porto-Novo	1,030
Bermuda (UK)	0.05	0.02	64	Hamilton	33,000
Bhutan	47	18.1	2,049	Thimphu	1,100
Bolivia	1,099	424	8,300	La Paz/Sucre	2,600
Bosnia-Herzegovina	51	20	3,922	Sarajevo	1,700
Botswana	582	225	1,586	Gaborone	6,600
Brazil	8,512	3,286	174,469	Brasília	6,500
Brunei	5.8	2.2	344	Bandar Seri Begawan	17,600
Bulgaria	111	43	7,707	Sofia	6,200
Burkina Faso	274	106	12,272	Ouagadougou	1,000
Burma (= Myanmar)	677	261	41,995	Rangoon	1,500
Burundi	27.8	10.7	6,224	Bujumbura	720
Cambodia	181	70	12,492	Phnom Penh	1,300
Cameroon	475	184	15,803	Yaoundé	1,700
Canada	9,976	3,852	31,593	Ottawa	24,800
Canary Is. (Spain)	7.3	2.8	1,577	Las Palmas/Santa Cruz	17,100
Cape Verde Is.	4	1.6	405	Praia	1,700
Cayman Is. (UK)	0.26	0.1	36	George Town	24,500
Central African Republic	623	241	3,577	Bangui	1,700
Chad	1,284	496	8,707	Ndjaména	1,000
Chile	757	292	15,328	Santiago	10,100
China	9,597	3,705	1,273,111	Beijing	3,600
Colombia	1,139	440	40,349	Bogotá	6,200
Comoros	2.2	0.86	596	Moroni	720
Congo	342	132	2,894	Brazzaville	1,100
Congo (Dem. Rep. of the)	2,345	905	53,625	Kinshasa	600
Cook Is. (NZ)	0.24	0.09	21	Avarua	5,000
Costa Rica	51.1	19.7	3,773	San José	6,700
Croatia	56.5	21.8	4,334	Zagreb	5,800
Cuba	111	43	11,184	Havana	1,700
Cyprus	9.3	3.6	763	Nicosia	13,800
Czech Republic	78.9	30.4	10,264	Prague	12,900
Denmark	43.1	16.6	5,353	Copenhagen	25,500
Djibouti	23.2	9	461	Djibouti	1,300
Dominica	0.75	0.29	71	Roseau	4,000
Dominican Republic	48.7	18.8	8,581	Santo Domingo	5,700
East Timor	14.9	5.7	737	Dili	N/A
Ecuador	284	109	13,184	Quito	2,900
Egypt	1,001	387	69,537	Cairo	3,600
El Salvador	21	8.1	6,238	San Salvador	4,000
Equatorial Guinea	28.1	10.8	486	Malabo	2,000
Eritrea	94	36	4,298	Asmara	710
Estonia	44.7	17.3	1,423	Tallinn	10,000
Ethiopia	1,128	436	65,892	Addis Ababa	600
Faroe Is. (Denmark)	1.4	0.54	46	Tórshavn	20,000
Fiji	18.3	7.1	844	Suva	7,300
Finland	338	131	5,176	Helsinki	22,900
France	552	213	59,551	Paris	24,400
French Guiana (France)	90	34.7	178	Cayenne	6,000
French Polynesia (France)	4	1.5	254	Papeete	10,800
Gabon	268	103	1,221	Libreville	6,300
Gambia, The	11.3	4.4	1,411	Banjul	1,100
Gaza Strip (OPT)*	0.36	0.14	1,178	–	1,000
Georgia	69.7	26.9	4,989	Tbilisi	4,600
Germany	357	138	83,030	Berlin	23,400
Ghana	239	92	19,894	Accra	1,900
Gibraltar (UK)	0.007	0.003	28	Gibraltar Town	17,500
Greece	132	51	10,624	Athens	17,200
Greenland (Denmark)	2,176	840	56	Nuuk (Godthåb)	20,000
Grenada	0.34	0.13	89	St George's	4,400
Guadeloupe (France)	1.7	0.66	431	Basse-Terre	9,000
Guam (US)	0.55	0.21	158	Agana	21,000
Guatemala	109	42	12,974	Guatemala City	3,700
Guinea	246	95	7,614	Conakry	1,300
Guinea-Bissau	36.1	13.9	1,316	Bissau	850
Guyana	215	83	697	Georgetown	4,800
Haiti	27.8	10.7	6,965	Port-au-Prince	1,800
Honduras	112	43	6,406	Tegucigalpa	2,700
Hong Kong (China)	1.1	0.4	7,211	–	25,400
Hungary	93	35.9	10,106	Budapest	11,200
Iceland	103	40	278	Reykjavik	24,800
India	3,288	1,269	1,029,991	New Delhi	2,200
Indonesia	1,890	730	227,701	Jakarta	2,900
Iran	1,648	636	66,129	Tehran	6,300
Iraq	438	169	23,332	Baghdad	2,500
Ireland	70.3	27.1	3,841	Dublin	21,600
Israel	20.6	7.96	5,938	Jerusalem	18,900
Italy	301	116	57,680	Rome	22,100
Ivory Coast (= Côte d'Ivoire)	322	125	16,393	Yamoussoukro	1,600
Jamaica	11	4.2	2,666	Kingston	3,700
Japan	378	146	126,772	Tokyo	24,900
Jordan	89.2	34.4	5,153	Amman	3,500
Kazakstan	2,717	1,049	16,731	Astana	5,000
Kenya	580	224	30,766	Nairobi	1,500
Kiribati	0.72	0.28	94	Tarawa	850
Korea, North	121	47	21,968	Pyŏngyang	1,000
Korea, South	99	38.2	47,904	Seoul	16,100
Kuwait	17.8	6.9	2,042	Kuwait City	15,000
Kyrgyzstan	198.5	76.6	4,753	Bishkek	2,700
Laos	237	91	5,636	Vientiane	1,700
Latvia	65	25	2,385	Riga	7,200
Lebanon	10.4	4	3,628	Beirut	5,000
Lesotho	30.4	11.7	2,177	Maseru	2,400
Liberia	111	43	3,226	Monrovia	1,100
Libya	1,760	679	5,241	Tripoli	8,900
Liechtenstein	0.16	0.06	33	Vaduz	23,000
Lithuania	65.2	25.2	3,611	Vilnius	7,300
Luxembourg	2.6	1	443	Luxembourg	36,400
Macau (China)	0.02	0.006	454	–	17,500
Macedonia (FYROM)	25.7	9.9	2,046	Skopje	4,400
Madagascar	587	227	15,983	Antananarivo	800
Madeira (Portugal)	0.81	0.31	259	Funchal	12,120
Malawi	118	46	10,548	Lilongwe	900
Malaysia	330	127	22,229	Kuala Lumpur	10,300
Maldives	0.3	0.12	311	Malé	2,000
Mali	1,240	479	11,009	Bamako	850
Malta	0.32	0.12	395	Valletta	14,300
Marshall Is.	0.18	0.07	71	Dalap-Uliga-Darrit	1,670
Martinique (France)	1.1	0.42	418	Fort-de-France	11,000
Mauritania	1,030	398	2,747	Nouakchott	2,000
Mauritius	2	0.72	1,190	Port Louis	10,400
Mayotte (France)	0.37	0.14	163	Mamoundzou	600
Mexico	1,958	756	101,879	Mexico City	9,100
Micronesia, Fed. States of	0.7	0.27	135	Palikir	2,000
Moldova	33.7	13	4,432	Chişinău	2,500
Monaco	0.002	0.001	32	Monaco	27,000
Mongolia	1,567	605	2,655	Ulan Bator	1,780
Montserrat (UK)	0.1	0.04	8	Plymouth	5,000
Morocco	447	172	30,645	Rabat	3,500
Mozambique	802	309	19,371	Maputo	1,000
Namibia	825	318	1,798	Windhoek	4,300
Nauru	0.02	0.008	12	Yaren District	5,000
Nepal	141	54	25,284	Katmandu	1,360
Netherlands	41.5	16	15,981	Amsterdam/The Hague	24,400
Netherlands Antilles (Neths)	0.99	0.38	212	Willemstad	11,400
New Caledonia (France)	18.6	7.2	205	Nouméa	15,000
New Zealand	269	104	3,864	Wellington	17,700
Nicaragua	130	50	4,918	Managua	2,700
Niger	1,267	489	10,355	Niamey	1,000
Nigeria	924	357	126,636	Abuja	950
Northern Mariana Is. (US)	0.48	0.18	75	Saipan	12,500
Norway	324	125	4,503	Oslo	27,700
Oman	212	82	2,622	Muscat	7,700
Pakistan	796	307	144,617	Islamabad	2,000
Palau	0.46	0.18	19	Koror	7,100
Panama	77.1	29.8	2,846	Panamá	6,000
Papua New Guinea	463	179	5,049	Port Moresby	2,500
Paraguay	407	157	5,734	Asunción	4,750
Peru	1,285	496	27,484	Lima	4,550
Philippines	300	116	82,842	Manila	3,800
Poland	313	121	38,634	Warsaw	8,500
Portugal	92.4	35.7	9,444	Lisbon	15,800
Puerto Rico (US)	9	3.5	3,939	San Juan	10,000
Qatar	11	4.2	769	Doha	20,300
Réunion (France)	2.5	0.97	733	St-Denis	4,800
Romania	238	92	22,364	Bucharest	5,900
Russia	17,075	6,592	145,470	Moscow	7,700
Rwanda	26.3	10.2	7,313	Kigali	900
St Kitts & Nevis	0.36	0.14	39	Basseterre	7,000
St Lucia	0.62	0.24	158	Castries	4,500
St Vincent & Grenadines	0.39	0.15	116	Kingstown	2,800
Samoa	2.8	1.1	179	Apia	3,200
San Marino	0.06	0.02	27	San Marino	32,000
São Tomé & Príncipe	0.96	0.37	165	São Tomé	1,100
Saudi Arabia	2,150	830	22,757	Riyadh	10,500
Senegal	197	76	10,285	Dakar	1,600
Seychelles	0.46	0.18	80	Victoria	7,700
Sierra Leone	71.7	27.7	5,427	Freetown	510
Singapore	0.62	0.24	4,300	Singapore	26,500
Slovak Republic	49	18.9	5,415	Bratislava	10,200
Slovenia	20.3	7.8	1,930	Ljubljana	12,000
Solomon Is.	28.9	11.2	480	Honiara	2,000
Somalia	638	246	7,489	Mogadishu	600
South Africa	1,220	471	43,586	C. Town/Pretoria/Bloem.	8,500
Spain	505	195	38,432	Madrid	18,000
Sri Lanka	65.6	25.3	19,409	Colombo	3,250
Sudan	2,506	967	36,080	Khartoum	1,000
Surinam	163	63	434	Paramaribo	3,400
Swaziland	17.4	6.7	1,104	Mbabane	4,000
Sweden	450	174	8,875	Stockholm	22,200
Switzerland	41.3	15.9	7,283	Bern	28,600
Syria	185	71	16,729	Damascus	3,100
Taiwan	36	13.9	22,370	Taipei	17,400
Tajikistan	143.1	55.2	6,579	Dushanbe	1,140
Tanzania	945	365	36,232	Dodoma	710
Thailand	513	198	61,798	Bangkok	6,700
Togo	56.8	21.9	5,153	Lomé	1,500
Tonga	0.75	0.29	104	Nuku'alofa	2,200
Trinidad & Tobago	5.1	2	1,170	Port of Spain	9,500
Tunisia	164	63	9,705	Tunis	6,500
Turkey	779	301	66,494	Ankara	6,800
Turkmenistan	488.1	188.5	4,603	Ashkhabad	4,300
Turks & Caicos Is. (UK)	0.43	0.17	18	Cockburn Town	7,300
Tuvalu	0.03	0.01	11	Fongafale	1,100
Uganda	236	91	23,986	Kampala	1,100
Ukraine	603.7	233.1	48,760	Kiev	3,850
United Arab Emirates	83.6	32.3	2,407	Abu Dhabi	22,800
United Kingdom	243.3	94	59,648	London	22,800
United States of America	9,373	3,619	278,059	Washington, DC	36,200
Uruguay	177	68	3,360	Montevideo	9,300
Uzbekistan	447.4	172.7	25,155	Tashkent	2,400
Vanuatu	12.2	4.7	193	Port-Vila	1,300
Vatican City	0.0004	0.0002	0.89	Vatican City	N/A
Venezuela	912	352	23,917	Caracas	6,200
Vietnam	332	127	79,939	Hanoi	1,950
Virgin Is. (UK)	0.15	0.06	21	Road Town	16,000
Virgin Is. (US)	0.34	0.13	122	Charlotte Amalie	15,000
Wallis & Futuna Is. (France)	0.2	0.08	15	Mata-Utu	2,000
West Bank (OPT)*	5.86	2.26	2,091	–	1,500
Western Sahara	266	103	251	El Aaiún	N/A
Yemen	528	204	18,078	Sana	820
Yugoslavia (Serbia & Montenegro)	102.3	39.5	10,677	Belgrade	2,300
Zambia	753	291	9,770	Lusaka	880
Zimbabwe	391	151	11,365	Harare	2,500

*OPT = Occupied Palestinian Territory   N/A = Not Available

† Gross Domestic Product per capita has been measured using the purchasing power parity method. This enables comparisons to be made between countries through their purchasing power (in US dollars), showing real price levels of goods and services rather than using currency exchange rates.

World Statistics: Cities

This list shows the principal cities with more than 500,000 inhabitants (only cities with more than 1 million inhabitants are included for Brazil, China, Indonesia, Japan and Russia). The figures are taken from the most recent census or estimate available, and as far as possible are the population of the metropolitan area, e.g. greater New York, Mexico or Paris. All the figures are in thousands. Local name forms have been used for the smaller cities (e.g. Kraków).

City	Population
AFGHANISTAN	
Kabul	1,565
ALGERIA	
Algiers	1,722
Oran	664
ANGOLA	
Luanda	2,250
ARGENTINA	
Buenos Aires	10,990
Córdoba	1,198
Rosario	1,096
Mendoza	775
La Plata	640
San Miguel de Tucumán	622
Mar del Plata	520
ARMENIA	
Yerevan	1,256
AUSTRALIA	
Sydney	4,041
Melbourne	3,417
Brisbane	1,601
Perth	1,364
Adelaide	1,093
AUSTRIA	
Vienna	1,560
AZERBAIJAN	
Baku	1,713
BANGLADESH	
Dhaka	7,832
Chittagong	2,041
Khulna	877
Rajshahi	517
BELARUS	
Minsk	1,717
Homyel	502
BELGIUM	
Brussels	948
BENIN	
Cotonou	537
BOLIVIA	
La Paz	1,126
Santa Cruz	767
BOSNIA-HERZEGOVINA	
Sarajevo	526
BRAZIL	
São Paulo	10,434
Rio de Janeiro	5,858
Salvador	2,443
Belo Horizonte	2,239
Fortaleza	2,141
Brasília	2,051
Curitiba	1,587
Recife	1,423
Manaus	1,406
Pôrto Alegre	1,361
Belém	1,281
Goiânia	1,093
Guarulhos	1,073
BULGARIA	
Sofia	1,139
BURKINA FASO	
Ouagadougou	690
BURMA (MYANMAR)	
Rangoon	2,513
Mandalay	533
CAMBODIA	
Phnom Penh	570
CAMEROON	
Douala	1,200
Yaoundé	800
CANADA	
Toronto	4,881
Montréal	3,511
Vancouver	2,079
Ottawa–Hull	1,107
Calgary	972
Edmonton	957
Québec	693
Winnipeg	685
Hamilton	681
CENTRAL AFRICAN REPUBLIC	
Bangui	553
CHAD	
Ndjaména	530
CHILE	
Santiago	4,691
CHINA	
Shanghai	15,082
Beijing	12,362
Tianjin	10,687
Hong Kong (SAR)*	6,502
Chongqing	3,870
Shenyang	3,762
Wuhan	3,520
Guangzhou	3,114
Harbin	2,505
Nanjing	2,211
Xi'an	2,115
Chengdu	1,933
Dalian	1,855
Changchun	1,810
Jinan	1,660
Taiyuan	1,642
Qingdao	1,584
Zibo	1,346
Zhengzhou	1,324
Lanzhou	1,296
Anshan	1,252
Fushun	1,246
Kunming	1,242
Changsha	1,198
Hangzhou	1,185
Nanchang	1,169
Shijiazhuang	1,159
Guiyang	1,131
Ürümqi	1,130
Jilin	1,118
Tangshan	1,110
Qiqihar	1,104
Baotou	1,033
COLOMBIA	
Bogotá	6,005
Cali	1,986
Medellín	1,971
Barranquilla	1,158
Cartagena	813
Cúcuta	589
Bucaramanga	508
CONGO	
Brazzaville	938
Pointe-Noire	576
CONGO (DEM. REP.)	
Kinshasa	2,664
Lubumbashi	565
CROATIA	
Zagreb	868
CUBA	
Havana	2,204
CZECH REPUBLIC	
Prague	1,203
DENMARK	
Copenhagen	1,362
DOMINICAN REPUBLIC	
Santo Domingo	2,135
Stgo. de los Caballeros	691
ECUADOR	
Guayaquil	2,070
Quito	1,574
EGYPT	
Cairo	6,800
Alexandria	3,339
El Gîza	2,222
Shubra el Kheima	871
EL SALVADOR	
San Salvador	1,522
ETHIOPIA	
Addis Ababa	2,316
FINLAND	
Helsinki	532
FRANCE	
Paris	11,175
Lyons	1,648
Marseilles	1,516
Lille	1,143
Toulouse	965
Nice	933
Bordeaux	925
Nantes	711
Strasbourg	612
Toulon	565
Douai	553
Rennes	521
Rouen	518
Grenoble	515
GEORGIA	
Tbilisi	1,253
GERMANY	
Berlin	3,426
Hamburg	1,705
Munich	1,206
Cologne	964
Frankfurt	644
Essen	609
Dortmund	595
Stuttgart	585
Düsseldorf	571
Bremen	547
Duisburg	529
Hanover	521
GHANA	
Accra	1,781
GREECE	
Athens	3,097
GUATEMALA	
Guatemala	1,167
GUINEA	
Conakry	1,508
HAITI	
Port-au-Prince	885
HONDURAS	
Tegucigalpa	814
HUNGARY	
Budapest	1,885
INDIA	
Mumbai (Bombay)	16,368
Kolkata (Calcutta)	13,217
Delhi	12,791
Chennai (Madras)	6,425
Bangalore	5,687
Hyderabad	5,534
Ahmadabad	4,519
Pune	3,756
Surat	2,811
Kanpur	2,690
Jaipur	2,324
Lucknow	2,267
Nagpur	2,123
Patna	1,707
Indore	1,639
Vadodara	1,492
Bhopal	1,455
Coimbatore	1,446
Ludhiana	1,395
Cochin	1,355
Vishakhapatnam	1,329
Agra	1,321
Varanasi	1,212
Madurai	1,195
Meerut	1,167
Nasik	1,152
Jabalpur	1,117
Jamshedpur	1,102
Asansol	1,090
Faridabad	1,055
Allahabad	1,050
Amritsar	1,011
Vijayawada	1,011
Rajkot	1,002
INDONESIA	
Jakarta	11,500
Surabaya	2,701
Bandung	2,368
Medan	1,910
Semarang	1,366
Palembang	1,352
Tangerang	1,198
Ujung Pandang	1,092
IRAN	
Tehran	6,759
Mashhad	1,887
Esfahan	1,266
Tabriz	1,191
Shiraz	1,053
Karaj	941
Ahvaz	805
Qom	778
Bakhtaran	693
IRAQ	
Baghdad	3,841
As Sulaymaniyah	952
Arbil	770
Al Mawsil	664
Al Kazimiyah	521
IRELAND	
Dublin	1,024
ISRAEL	
Tel Aviv-Yafo	1,880
Jerusalem	591
ITALY	
Rome	2,654
Milan	1,306
Naples	1,050
Turin	923
Palermo	689
Genoa	659
IVORY COAST	
Abidjan	2,500
JAMAICA	
Kingston	644
JAPAN	
Tokyo	17,950
Yokohama	3,427
Osaka	2,599
Nagoya	2,171
Sapporo	1,822
Kobe	1,494
Kyoto	1,468
Fukuoka	1,341
Kawasaki	1,250
Hiroshima	1,126
Kitakyushu	1,011
Sendai	1,008
JORDAN	
Amman	1,752
KAZAKSTAN	
Almaty	1,151
Qaraghandy	574
KENYA	
Nairobi	2,000
Mombasa	600
KOREA, NORTH	
Pyŏngyang	2,741
Hamhung	710
Chŏngjin	583
KOREA, SOUTH	
Seoul	10,231
Pusan	3,814
Taegu	2,449
Inch'on	2,308
Taejŏn	1,272
Kwangju	1,258
Ulsan	967
Sŏngnam	869
Puch'on	779
Suwŏn	756
Anyang	590
Chŏnju	563
Chŏngju	531
Ansan	510
P'ohang	509
KYRGYZSTAN	
Bishkek	589
LAOS	
Vientiane	532
LATVIA	
Riga	811
LEBANON	
Beirut	1,500
Tripoli	500
LIBERIA	
Monrovia	962
LIBYA	
Tripoli	960
LITHUANIA	
Vilnius	580
MACEDONIA	
Skopje	541
MADAGASCAR	
Antananarivo	1,053
MALAYSIA	
Kuala Lumpur	1,145
MALI	
Bamako	810
MAURITANIA	
Nouakchott	735
MEXICO	
Mexico City	15,643
Guadalajara	2,847
Monterrey	2,522
Puebla	1,055
León	872
Ciudad Juárez	798
Tijuana	743
Culiacán	602
Mexicali	602
Acapulco	592
Mérida	557
Chihuahua	530
San Luis Potosí	526
Aguascalientés	506
MOLDOVA	
Chişinău	658
MONGOLIA	
Ulan Bator	673
MOROCCO	
Casablanca	2,943
Rabat-Salé	1,220
Marrakesh	602
Fès	564
MOZAMBIQUE	
Maputo	2,000
NEPAL	
Katmandu	535
NETHERLANDS	
Amsterdam	1,115
Rotterdam	1,086
The Hague	700
Utrecht	557
NEW ZEALAND	
Auckland	1,090
NICARAGUA	
Managua	864
NIGERIA	
Lagos	10,287
Ibadan	1,432
Ogbomosho	730
Kano	674
NORWAY	
Oslo	502
PAKISTAN	
Karachi	9,269
Lahore	5,064
Faisalabad	1,977
Rawalpindi	1,406
Multan	1,182
Hyderabad	1,151
Gujranwala	1,125
Peshawar	988
Quetta	560
Islamabad	525
PARAGUAY	
Asunción	945
PERU	
Lima	6,601
Arequipa	620
Trujillo	509
PHILIPPINES	
Manila	8,594
Quezon City	1,989
Caloocan	1,023
Davao	1,009
Cebu	662
Zamboanga	511
POLAND	
Warsaw	1,626
Lódz	815
Kraków	740
Wroclaw	641
Poznań	580
PORTUGAL	
Lisbon	2,561
Oporto	1,174
ROMANIA	
Bucharest	2,028
RUSSIA	
Moscow	8,405
St Petersburg	4,216
Nizhniy Novgorod	1,371
Novosibirsk	1,367
Yekaterinburg	1,275
Samara	1,170
Omsk	1,158
Kazan	1,085
Chelyabinsk	1,084
Ufa	1,082
Perm	1,025
Rostov	1,023
Volgograd	1,005
SAUDI ARABIA	
Riyadh	1,800
Jedda	1,500
Mecca	630
SENEGAL	
Dakar	1,905
SIERRA LEONE	
Freetown	505
SINGAPORE	
Singapore	3,866
SOMALIA	
Mogadishu	997
SOUTH AFRICA	
Cape Town	2,350
Johannesburg	1,196
Durban	1,137
Pretoria	1,080
Port Elizabeth	853
Vanderbijlpark–Vereeniging	774
Soweto	597
Sasolburg	540
SPAIN	
Madrid	3,030
Barcelona	1,615
Valencia	763
Sevilla	720
Zaragoza	608
Málaga	532
SRI LANKA	
Colombo	1,863
SUDAN	
Omdurman	1,271
Khartoum	925
Khartoum North	701
SWEDEN	
Stockholm	727
SWITZERLAND	
Zürich	733
SYRIA	
Aleppo	1,813
Damascus	1,394
Homs	659
TAIWAN	
T'aipei	2,596
Kaohsiung	1,435
T'aichung	858
T'ainan	708
Panch'iao	539
TAJIKISTAN	
Dushanbe	524
TANZANIA	
Dar-es-Salaam	1,361
THAILAND	
Bangkok	7,507
TOGO	
Lomé	590
TUNISIA	
Tunis	1,827
TURKEY	
Istanbul	8,506
Ankara	3,294
Izmir	2,554
Bursa	1,485
Adana	1,273
Konya	1,140
Mersin (Içel)	956
Gaziantep	867
Antalya	867
Kayseri	862
Diyarbakir	833
Urfa	785
Manisa	696
Kocaeli	629
Antalya	591
Samsun	590
Kahramanmaras	551
Balikesir	538
Eskisehir	519
Erzurum	512
Malatya	510
TURKMENISTAN	
Ashkhabad	536
UGANDA	
Kampala	954
UKRAINE	
Kiev	2,621
Kharkov	1,521
Dnepropetrovsk	1,122
Donetsk	1,065
Odessa	1,027
Zaporizhzhya	863
Lviv	794
Kryvyy Rih	720
Mykolayiv	518
Mariupol	500
UNITED ARAB EMIRATES	
Abu Dhabi	928
Dubai	674
UNITED KINGDOM	
London	8,089
Birmingham	2,373
Manchester	2,353
Liverpool	852
Glasgow	832
Sheffield	661
Nottingham	649
Newcastle	617
Bristol	552
Leeds	529
UNITED STATES	
New York	21,200
Los Angeles	16,374
Chicago–Gary	9,158
Washington–Baltimore	7,608
San Francisco–San Jose	7,039
Philadelphia–Atlantic City	6,188
Boston–Worcester	5,819
Detroit–Flint	5,456
Dallas–Fort Worth	5,222
Houston–Galveston	4,670
Atlanta	4,112
Miami–Fort Lauderdale	3,876
Seattle–Tacoma	3,554
Phoenix–Mesa	3,252
Minneapolis–St Paul	2,969
Cleveland–Akron	2,946
San Diego	2,814
St Louis	2,604
Denver–Boulder	2,582
San Juan	2,450
Tampa–Saint Petersburg	2,396
Pittsburgh	2,359
Portland–Salem	2,265
Cincinnati–Hamilton	1,979
Sacramento–Yolo	1,797
Kansas City	1,776
Milwaukee–Racine	1,690
Orlando	1,645
Indianapolis	1,607
San Antonio	1,592
Norfolk–Virginia Beach –Newport News	1,570
Las Vegas	1,563
Columbus, OH	1,540
Charlotte–Gastonia	1,499
New Orleans	1,338
Salt Lake City	1,334
Greensboro–Winston Salem–High Point	1,252
Austin–San Marcos	1,250
Nashville	1,231
Providence–Fall River	1,189
Raleigh–Durham	1,188
Hartford	1,183
Buffalo–Niagara Falls	1,170
Memphis	1,136
West Palm Beach	1,131
Jacksonville, FL	1,100
Rochester	1,098
Grand Rapids	1,089
Oklahoma City	1,083
Louisville	1,026
Richmond–Petersburg	997
Greenville	962
Dayton–Springfield	951
Fresno	923
Birmingham	921
Honolulu	876
Albany–Schenectady	876
Tucson	844
Tulsa	803
Syracuse	732
Omaha	717
Albuquerque	713
Knoxville	687
El Paso	680
Bakersfield	662
Allentown	638
Harrisburg	629
Scranton	625
Toledo	618
Baton Rouge	603
Youngstown–Warren	595
Springfield, MA	592
Sarasota	590
Little Rock	584
McAllen	569
Stockton–Lodi	564
Charleston	549
Wichita	545
Mobile	540
Columbia, SC	537
Colorado Springs	517
Fort Wayne	502
URUGUAY	
Montevideo	1,379
UZBEKISTAN	
Tashkent	2,118
VENEZUELA	
Caracas	1,975
Maracaibo	1,706
Valencia	1,263
Barquisimeto	811
Ciudad Guayana	642
Petare	176
Maracay	459
VIETNAM	
Ho Chi Minh City	4,322
Hanoi	3,056
Haiphong	783
YEMEN	
Sana'	972
Aden	562
YUGOSLAVIA	
Belgrade	1,598
ZAMBIA	
Lusaka	982
ZIMBABWE	
Harare	1,189
Bulawayo	622

* SAR = Special Administrative Region of China

World Statistics: Climate

Rainfall and temperature figures are provided for more than 70 cities around the world. As climate is affected by altitude, the height of each city is shown in metres beneath its name. For each location, the top row of figures shows the total rainfall or snow in millimetres, and the bottom row the average temperature in degrees Celsius; the average annual temperature and total annual rainfall are at the end of the rows. The map opposite shows the city locations.

CITY	JAN.	FEB.	MAR.	APR.	MAY	JUNE	JULY	AUG.	SEPT.	OCT.	NOV.	DEC.	YEAR
EUROPE													
Athens, Greece	62	37	37	23	23	14	6	7	15	51	56	71	402
107 m	10	10	12	16	20	25	28	28	24	20	15	11	18
Berlin, Germany	46	40	33	42	49	65	73	69	48	49	46	43	603
55 m	-1	0	4	9	14	17	19	18	15	9	5	1	9
Istanbul, Turkey	109	92	72	46	38	34	34	30	58	81	103	119	816
14 m	5	6	7	11	16	20	23	23	20	16	12	8	14
Lisbon, Portugal	111	76	109	54	44	16	3	4	33	62	93	103	708
77 m	11	12	14	16	17	20	22	23	21	18	14	12	17
London, UK	54	40	37	37	46	45	57	59	49	57	64	48	593
5 m	4	5	7	9	12	16	18	17	15	11	8	5	11
Málaga, Spain	61	51	62	46	26	5	1	3	29	64	64	62	474
33 m	12	13	16	17	19	29	25	26	23	20	16	13	18
Moscow, Russia	39	38	36	37	53	58	88	71	58	45	47	54	624
156 m	-13	-10	-4	6	13	16	18	17	12	6	-1	-7	4
Odesa, Ukraine	57	62	30	21	34	34	42	37	37	13	35	71	473
64 m	-3	-1	2	9	15	20	22	22	18	12	9	1	10
Paris, France	56	46	35	42	57	54	59	64	55	50	51	50	619
75 m	3	4	8	11	15	18	20	19	17	12	7	4	12
Rome, Italy	71	62	57	51	46	37	15	21	63	99	129	93	744
17 m	8	9	11	14	18	22	25	25	22	17	13	10	16
Shannon, Ireland	94	67	56	53	61	57	77	79	86	86	96	117	929
2 m	5	5	7	9	12	14	16	14	11	8	6		10
Stockholm, Sweden	43	30	25	31	34	45	61	76	60	48	53	48	554
44 m	-3	-3	-1	5	10	15	18	17	12	7	3	0	7
ASIA													
Bahrain	8	18	13	8	<3	0	0	0	0	0	18	18	81
5 m	17	18	21	25	29	32	33	34	31	28	24	19	26
Bangkok, Thailand	8	20	36	58	198	160	160	175	305	206	66	5	1,397
2 m	26	28	29	30	29	29	28	28	28	28	26	25	28
Beirut, Lebanon	191	158	94	53	18	3	<3	<3	5	51	132	185	892
34 m	14	14	16	18	22	24	27	28	26	24	19	16	21
Bombay (Mumbai), India	3	3	3	<3	18	485	617	340	264	64	13	3	1,809
11 m	24	24	26	28	30	29	27	27	27	28	27	26	27
Calcutta, India	10	31	36	43	140	297	325	328	252	114	20	5	1,600
6 m	20	22	27	30	30	30	29	29	29	28	23	19	26
Colombo, Sri Lanka	89	69	147	231	371	224	135	109	160	348	315	147	2,365
7 m	26	26	27	28	28	27	27	27	27	27	26	26	27
Harbin, China	6	5	10	23	43	94	112	104	46	33	8	5	488
160 m	-18	-15	-5	6	13	19	22	21	14	4	-6	-16	3

CITY	JAN.	FEB.	MAR.	APR.	MAY	JUNE	JULY	AUG.	SEPT.	OCT.	NOV.	DEC.	YEAR
ASIA (continued)													
Ho Chi Minh, Vietnam	15	3	13	43	221	330	315	269	335	269	114	56	1,984
9 m	26	27	29	30	29	28	28	28	27	27	27	26	28
Hong Kong, China	33	46	74	137	292	394	381	361	257	114	43	31	2,162
33 m	16	15	18	22	26	28	28	28	27	25	21	18	23
Jakarta, Indonesia	300	300	211	147	114	97	64	43	66	112	142	203	1,798
8 m	26	26	27	27	27	27	27	27	27	27	27	26	27
Kabul, Afghanistan	31	36	94	102	20	5	3	3	<3	15	20	10	338
1,815 m	-3	-1	6	13	18	22	25	24	20	14	7	3	12
Karachi, Pakistan	13	10	8	3	3	18	81	41	13	<3	3	5	196
4 m	19	20	24	28	30	31	30	29	28	28	24	20	26
Kazalinsk, Kazakstan	10	10	13	13	15	5	5	8	8	10	13	15	125
63 m	-12	-11	-3	6	18	23	25	23	16	8	-1	-7	7
New Delhi, India	23	18	13	8	13	74	180	172	117	10	3	10	640
218 m	14	17	23	28	33	34	31	30	29	26	20	15	25
Omsk, Russia	15	8	8	13	31	51	51	51	28	25	18	20	318
85 m	-22	-19	-12	-1	10	16	18	16	10	1	-11	-18	-1
Shanghai, China	48	58	84	94	94	180	147	142	130	71	51	36	1,135
7 m	4	5	9	14	20	24	28	28	23	19	12	7	16
Singapore	252	173	193	188	173	173	170	196	178	208	254	257	2,413
10 m	26	27	28	28	28	28	28	27	27	27	27	27	27
Tehran, Iran	46	38	46	36	13	3	3	3	3	8	20	31	246
1,220 m	2	5	9	16	21	26	30	29	25	18	12	6	17
Tokyo, Japan	48	74	107	135	147	165	142	152	234	208	97	56	1,565
6 m	3	4	7	13	17	21	25	26	23	17	11	6	14
Ulan Bator, Mongolia	<3	<3	3	5	10	28	76	51	23	5	5	3	208
1,325 m	-26	-21	-13	-1	6	14	16	14	8	-1	-13	-22	-3
Verkhoyansk, Russia	5	5	3	5	8	23	28	25	13	8	8	5	134
100 m	-50	-45	-32	-15	0	12	14	9	2	-15	-38	-48	-17
AFRICA													
Addis Ababa, Ethiopia	<3	3	25	135	213	201	206	239	102	28	<3	0	1,151
2,450 m	19	20	20	20	19	18	18	19	21	22	21	20	20
Antananarivo, Madag.	300	279	178	53	18	8	8	10	18	61	135	287	1,356
1,372 m	21	21	21	19	18	15	14	15	17	19	21	21	19
Cairo, Egypt	5	5	5	3	3	<3	0	0	<3	<3	3	5	28
116 m	13	15	18	21	25	28	28	28	26	24	20	15	22
Cape Town, S. Africa	15	8	18	48	79	84	89	66	43	31	18	10	508
17 m	21	21	20	17	14	13	12	13	14	16	18	19	17
Jo'burg, S. Africa	114	109	89	38	25	8	8	8	23	56	107	125	709
1,665 m	20	20	18	16	13	10	11	13	16	18	19	20	16

CITY	JAN.	FEB.	MAR.	APR.	MAY	JUNE	JULY	AUG.	SEPT.	OCT.	NOV.	DEC.	YEAR
AFRICA (continued)													
Khartoum, Sudan	<3	<3	<3	<3	3	8	53	71	18	5	<3	0	158
390 m	24	25	28	31	33	34	32	31	32	32	28	25	29
Kinshasa, Congo (D.R.)	135	145	196	196	158	8	3	3	31	119	221	142	1,354
325 m	26	26	27	27	26	24	23	24	25	26	26	26	25
Lagos, Nigeria	28	46	102	150	269	460	279	64	140	206	69	25	1,836
3 m	27	28	29	28	28	26	26	25	26	26	28	28	27
Lusaka, Zambia	231	191	142	18	3	<3	<3	0	<3	10	91	150	836
1,277 m	21	22	21	21	19	16	16	18	22	24	23	22	21
Monrovia, Liberia	31	56	97	216	516	973	996	373	744	772	236	130	5,138
23 m	26	26	27	27	26	25	24	25	25	25	26	26	26
Nairobi, Kenya	38	64	125	211	158	46	15	23	31	53	109	86	958
820 m	19	19	19	19	18	16	16	16	18	19	18	18	18
Timbuktu, Mali	<3	<3	3	<3	5	23	79	81	38	3	<3	<3	231
301 m	22	24	28	32	34	35	32	30	32	31	28	23	29
Tunis, Tunisia	64	51	41	36	18	8	3	8	33	51	48	61	419
66 m	10	11	13	16	19	23	26	27	25	20	16	11	18
Walvis Bay, Namibia	<3	5	8	3	3	<3	<3	3	<3	<3	<3	<3	23
7 m	19	19	19	18	17	16	15	14	14	15	17	18	18
AUSTRALIA, NEW ZEALAND AND ANTARCTICA													
Alice Springs, Aust.	43	33	28	10	15	13	8	8	8	18	31	38	252
579 m	29	28	25	20	15	12	12	14	18	23	26	28	21
Christchurch, N.Z.	56	43	48	48	66	66	69	48	46	43	48	56	638
10 m	16	16	14	12	9	6	6	7	9	12	14	16	11
Darwin, Australia	386	312	254	97	15	3	<3	3	13	51	119	239	1,491
30 m	29	29	29	29	28	26	25	26	28	29	30	29	28
Mawson, Antarctica	11	30	20	10	44	180	4	40	3	20	0	0	362
14 m	0	−5	−10	−14	−15	−16	−18	−18	−19	−13	−5	−1	−11
Perth, Australia	8	10	20	43	130	180	170	149	86	56	20	13	881
60 m	23	23	22	19	16	14	13	13	15	16	19	22	18
Sydney, Australia	89	102	127	135	127	117	117	76	73	71	73	73	1,181
42 m	22	22	21	18	15	13	12	13	15	18	19	21	17
NORTH AMERICA													
Anchorage, USA	20	18	15	10	13	18	41	66	66	56	25	23	371
40 m	−11	−8	−5	2	7	12	14	13	9	2	−5	−11	2
Chicago, USA	51	51	66	71	86	89	84	81	79	66	61	51	836
251 m	−4	−3	2	9	14	20	23	22	19	12	5	−1	10
Churchill, Canada	15	13	18	23	32	44	46	58	51	43	39	21	402
13 m	−28	−26	−20	−10	−2	6	12	11	5	−2	−12	−22	−7
Edmonton, Canada	25	19	19	22	43	77	89	78	39	17	16	25	466
676 m	−15	−10	−5	4	11	15	17	16	11	6	−4	−10	3
Honolulu, USA	104	66	79	48	25	18	23	28	36	48	64	104	643
12 m	23	18	19	20	22	24	25	26	26	24	22	19	22
Houston, USA	89	76	84	91	119	117	99	99	104	94	89	109	1,171
12 m	12	13	17	21	24	27	28	29	26	22	16	12	21

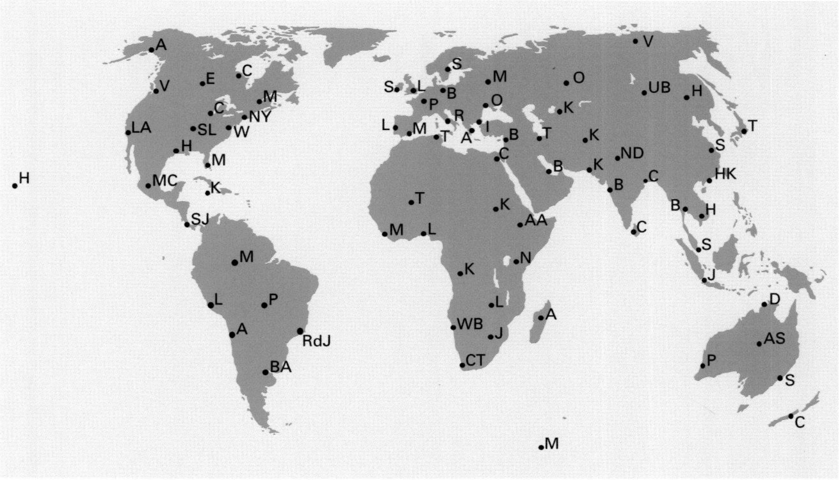

CITY	JAN.	FEB.	MAR.	APR.	MAY	JUNE	JULY	AUG.	SEPT.	OCT.	NOV.	DEC.	YEAR
NORTH AMERICA (continued)													
Kingston, Jamaica	23	15	23	31	102	89	38	91	99	180	74	36	800
34 m	25	25	25	26	26	28	28	28	27	27	26	26	26
Los Angeles, USA	79	76	71	25	10	3	<3	<3	5	15	31	66	381
95 m	13	14	14	16	17	19	21	22	21	18	16	14	17
Mexico City, Mexico	13	5	10	20	53	119	170	152	130	51	18	8	747
2,309 m	12	13	16	18	19	19	17	18	18	16	14	13	16
Miami, USA	71	53	64	81	173	178	155	160	203	234	71	51	1,516
8 m	20	20	22	23	25	27	28	28	27	25	22	21	24
Montréal, Canada	72	65	74	74	66	82	90	92	88	76	81	87	946
57 m	−10	−9	−3	−6	13	18	21	20	15	9	2	−7	6
New York City, USA	94	97	91	81	81	84	107	109	86	89	76	91	1,092
96 m	−1	−1	3	10	16	20	23	23	21	15	7	2	11
St Louis, USA	58	64	89	97	114	114	89	86	81	74	71	64	1,001
173 m	0	1	7	13	19	24	26	26	22	15	8	2	14
San José, Costa Rica	15	5	20	46	229	241	211	241	305	300	145	41	1,798
1,146 m	19	19	21	21	22	21	21	21	21	20	20	19	20
Vancouver, Canada	154	115	101	60	52	45	32	41	67	114	150	182	1,113
14 m	3	5	6	9	12	15	17	17	14	10	6	4	10
Washington, DC, USA	86	76	91	84	94	99	112	109	94	74	66	79	1,064
22 m	1	2	7	12	18	23	25	24	20	14	8	3	13
SOUTH AMERICA													
Antofagasta, Chile	0	0	0	<3	<3	3	5	3	<3	3	<3	0	13
94 m	21	21	20	18	16	15	14	14	15	16	18	19	17
Buenos Aires, Arg.	79	71	109	89	76	61	56	61	79	86	84	99	950
27 m	23	23	21	17	13	9	10	11	13	15	19	22	16
Lima, Peru	3	<3	<3	<3	5	5	8	8	8	3	3	<3	41
120 m	23	24	24	22	19	17	17	16	17	18	19	21	20
Manaus, Brazil	249	231	262	221	170	84	58	38	46	107	142	203	1,811
44 m	28	28	28	27	28	28	28	28	29	29	29	28	28
Paraná, Brazil	287	236	239	102	13	<3	3	5	28	127	231	310	1,582
260 m	23	23	23	23	23	21	21	22	24	24	24	23	23
Rio de Janeiro, Brazil	125	122	130	107	79	53	41	43	66	79	104	137	1,082
61 m	26	26	25	24	22	21	21	21	21	22	23	25	23

World Statistics: Physical Dimensions

Each topic list is divided into continents and within a continent the items are listed in order of size. The bottom part of many of the lists is selective in order to give examples from as many different countries as possible. The order of the continents is as in the atlas, Europe through to South America. The world top ten are shown in square brackets; in the case of mountains this has not been done because the world top 30 are all in Asia. The figures are rounded as appropriate.

WORLD, CONTINENTS, OCEANS

THE WORLD	km²	miles²	%
The World	509,450,000	196,672,000	–
Land	149,450,000	57,688,000	29.3
Water	360,000,000	138,984,000	70.7
Asia	44,500,000	17,177,000	29.8
Africa	30,302,000	11,697,000	20.3
North America	24,241,000	9,357,000	16.2
South America	17,793,000	6,868,000	11.9
Antarctica	14,100,000	5,443,000	9.4
Europe	9,957,000	3,843,000	6.7
Australia & Oceania	8,557,000	3,303,000	5.7
Pacific Ocean	179,679,000	69,356,000	49.9
Atlantic Ocean	92,373,000	35,657,000	25.7
Indian Ocean	73,917,000	28,532,000	20.5
Arctic Ocean	14,090,000	5,439,000	3.9

SEAS

PACIFIC	km²	miles²
South China Sea	2,974,600	1,148,500
Bering Sea	2,268,000	875,000
Sea of Okhotsk	1,528,000	590,000
East China & Yellow	1,249,000	482,000
Sea of Japan	1,008,000	389,000
Gulf of California	162,000	62,500
Bass Strait	75,000	29,000

ATLANTIC	km²	miles²
Caribbean Sea	2,766,000	1,068,000
Mediterranean Sea	2,516,000	971,000
Gulf of Mexico	1,543,000	596,000
Hudson Bay	1,232,000	476,000
North Sea	575,000	223,000
Black Sea	462,000	178,000
Baltic Sea	422,170	163,000
Gulf of St Lawrence	238,000	92,000

INDIAN	km²	miles²
Red Sea	438,000	169,000
The Gulf	239,000	92,000

MOUNTAINS

EUROPE		m	ft
Elbrus	Russia	5,642	18,510
Mont Blanc	France/Italy	4,807	15,771
Monte Rosa	Italy/Switzerland	4,634	15,203
Dom	Switzerland	4,545	14,911
Liskamm	Switzerland	4,527	14,852
Weisshorn	Switzerland	4,505	14,780
Taschorn	Switzerland	4,490	14,730
Matterhorn/Cervino	Italy/Switz.	4,478	14,691
Mont Maudit	France/Italy	4,465	14,649
Dent Blanche	Switzerland	4,356	14,291
Nadelhorn	Switzerland	4,327	14,196
Grandes Jorasses	France/Italy	4,208	13,806
Jungfrau	Switzerland	4,158	13,642
Barre des Ecrins	France	4,103	13,461
Gran Paradiso	Italy	4,061	13,323
Piz Bernina	Italy/Switzerland	4,049	13,284
Eiger	Switzerland	3,970	13,025
Monte Viso	Italy	3,841	12,602
Grossglockner	Austria	3,797	12,457
Wildspitze	Austria	3,772	12,382
Monte Disgrazia	Italy	3,678	12,066
Mulhacén	Spain	3,478	11,411
Pico de Aneto	Spain	3,404	11,168
Marmolada	Italy	3,342	10,964
Etna	Italy	3,340	10,958
Zugspitze	Germany	2,962	9,718
Musala	Bulgaria	2,925	9,596
Olympus	Greece	2,917	9,570
Triglav	Slovenia	2,863	9,393
Monte Cinto	France (Corsica)	2,710	8,891
Galdhöpiggen	Norway	2,468	8,100
Ben Nevis	UK	1,343	4,406

ASIA		m	ft
Everest	China/Nepal	8,850	29,035
K2 (Godwin Austen)	China/Kashmir	8,611	28,251
Kanchenjunga	India/Nepal	8,598	28,208
Lhotse	China/Nepal	8,516	27,939
Makalu	China/Nepal	8,481	27,824
Cho Oyu	China/Nepal	8,201	26,906
Dhaulagiri	Nepal	8,172	26,811
Manaslu	Nepal	8,156	26,758
Nanga Parbat	Kashmir	8,126	26,660
Annapurna	Nepal	8,078	26,502
Gasherbrum	China/Kashmir	8,068	26,469
Broad Peak	China/Kashmir	8,051	26,414
Xixabangma	China	8,012	26,286
Kangbachen	India/Nepal	7,902	25,925
Jannu	India/Nepal	7,902	25,925
Gayachung Kang	Nepal	7,897	25,909
Himalchuli	Nepal	7,893	25,896
Disteghil Sar	Kashmir	7,885	25,869
Nuptse	Nepal	7,879	25,849
Khunyang Chhish	Kashmir	7,852	25,761
Masherbrum	Kashmir	7,821	25,659
Nanda Devi	India	7,817	25,646
Rakaposhi	Kashmir	7,788	25,551
Batura	Kashmir	7,785	25,541
Namche Barwa	China	7,756	25,446
Kamet	India	7,756	25,446
Soltoro Kangri	Kashmir	7,742	25,400
Gurla Mandhata	China	7,728	25,354
Trivor	Pakistan	7,720	25,328
Kongur Shan	China	7,719	25,324
Tirich Mir	Pakistan	7,690	25,229
K'ula Shan	Bhutan/China	7,543	24,747
Pik Kommunizma	Tajikistan	7,495	24,590
Demavend	Iran	5,604	18,386
Ararat	Turkey	5,165	16,945
Gunong Kinabalu	Malaysia (Borneo)	4,101	13,455
Yu Shan	Taiwan	3,997	13,113
Fuji-San	Japan	3,776	12,388

AFRICA		m	ft
Kilimanjaro	Tanzania	5,895	19,340
Mt Kenya	Kenya	5,199	17,057
Ruwenzori (Margherita)	Uganda/Congo (D.R.)	5,109	16,762
Ras Dashan	Ethiopia	4,620	15,157
Meru	Tanzania	4,565	14,977
Karisimbi	Rwanda/Congo (D.R.)	4,507	14,787
Mt Elgon	Kenya/Uganda	4,321	14,176
Batu	Ethiopia	4,307	14,130
Guna	Ethiopia	4,231	13,882
Toubkal	Morocco	4,165	13,665
Irhil Mgoun	Morocco	4,071	13,356
Mt Cameroon	Cameroon	4,070	13,353
Amba Ferit	Ethiopia	3,875	13,042
Pico del Teide	Spain (Tenerife)	3,718	12,198
Thabana Ntlenyana	Lesotho	3,482	11,424
Emi Koussi	Chad	3,415	11,204
Mt aux Sources	Lesotho/S. Africa	3,282	10,768
Mt Piton	Réunion	3,069	10,069

OCEANIA		m	ft
Puncak Jaya	Indonesia	5,029	16,499
Puncak Trikora	Indonesia	4,750	15,584
Puncak Mandala	Indonesia	4,702	15,427
Mt Wilhelm	Papua NG	4,508	14,790
Mauna Kea	USA (Hawaii)	4,205	13,796
Mauna Loa	USA (Hawaii)	4,169	13,681
Mt Cook (Aoraki)	New Zealand	3,753	12,313
Mt Balbi	Solomon Is.	2,439	8,002
Orohena	Tahiti	2,241	7,352
Mt Kosciuszko	Australia	2,237	7,339

NORTH AMERICA		m	ft
Mt McKinley (Denali)	USA (Alaska)	6,194	20,321
Mt Logan	Canada	5,959	19,551
Citlaltepetl	Mexico	5,700	18,701
Mt St Elias	USA/Canada	5,489	18,008
Popocatepetl	Mexico	5,452	17,887

NORTH AMERICA (continued)		m	ft
Mt Foraker	USA (Alaska)	5,304	17,401
Ixtaccihuatl	Mexico	5,286	17,342
Lucania	Canada	5,227	17,149
Mt Steele	Canada	5,073	16,644
Mt Bona	USA (Alaska)	5,005	16,420
Mt Blackburn	USA (Alaska)	4,996	16,391
Mt Sanford	USA (Alaska)	4,940	16,207
Mt Wood	Canada	4,848	15,905
Nevado de Toluca	Mexico	4,670	15,321
Mt Fairweather	USA (Alaska)	4,663	15,298
Mt Hunter	USA (Alaska)	4,442	14,573
Mt Whitney	USA	4,418	14,495
Mt Elbert	USA	4,399	14,432
Mt Harvard	USA	4,395	14,419
Mt Rainier	USA	4,392	14,409
Blanca Peak	USA	4,372	14,344
Longs Peak	USA	4,345	14,255
Tajumulco	Guatemala	4,220	13,845
Grand Teton	USA	4,197	13,770
Mt Waddington	Canada	3,994	13,104
Mt Robson	Canada	3,954	12,972
Chirripó Grande	Costa Rica	3,837	12,589
Pico Duarte	Dominican Rep.	3,175	10,417

SOUTH AMERICA		m	ft
Aconcagua	Argentina	6,960	22,834
Bonete	Argentina	6,872	22,546
Ojos del Salado	Argentina/Chile	6,863	22,516
Pissis	Argentina	6,779	22,241
Mercedario	Argentina/Chile	6,770	22,211
Huascaran	Peru	6,768	22,204
Llullaillaco	Argentina/Chile	6,723	22,057
Nudo de Cachi	Argentina	6,720	22,047
Yerupaja	Peru	6,632	21,758
N. de Tres Cruces	Argentina/Chile	6,620	21,719
Incahuasi	Argentina/Chile	6,601	21,654
Cerro Galan	Argentina	6,600	21,654
Tupungato	Argentina/Chile	6,570	21,555
Sajama	Bolivia	6,542	21,463
Illimani	Bolivia	6,485	21,276
Coropuna	Peru	6,425	21,079
Ausangate	Peru	6,384	20,945
Cerro del Toro	Argentina	6,380	20,932
Siula Grande	Peru	6,356	20,853
Chimborazo	Ecuador	6,267	20,561
Alpamayo	Peru	5,947	19,511
Cotapaxi	Ecuador	5,896	19,344
Pico Colon	Colombia	5,800	19,029
Pico Bolivar	Venezuela	5,007	16,427

ANTARCTICA		m	ft
Vinson Massif		4,897	16,066
Mt Kirkpatrick		4,528	14,855
Mt Markham		4,349	14,268

OCEAN DEPTHS

ATLANTIC OCEAN	m	ft	
Puerto Rico (Milwaukee) Deep	9,220	30,249	[7]
Cayman Trench	7,680	25,197	[10]
Gulf of Mexico	5,203	17,070	
Mediterranean Sea	5,121	16,801	
Black Sea	2,211	7,254	
North Sea	660	2,165	
Baltic Sea	463	1,519	
Hudson Bay	258	846	

INDIAN OCEAN	m	ft	
Java Trench	7,450	24,442	
Red Sea	2,635	8,454	
Persian Gulf	73	239	

PACIFIC OCEAN	m	ft	
Mariana Trench	11,022	36,161	[1]
Tonga Trench	10,882	35,702	[2]
Japan Trench	10,554	34,626	[3]
Kuril Trench	10,542	34,587	[4]
Mindanao Trench	10,497	34,439	[5]
Kermadec Trench	10,047	32,962	[6]

PACIFIC OCEAN (continued)

	m	ft	
Peru–Chile Trench	8,050	26,410	[8]
Aleutian Trench	7,822	25,662	[9]

ARCTIC OCEAN

	m	ft
Molloy Deep	5,608	18,399

LAND LOWS

		m	ft
Dead Sea	Asia	−411	−1,348
Lake Assal	Africa	−156	−512
Death Valley	N. America	−86	−282
Valdés Peninsula	S. America	−40	−131
Caspian Sea	Europe	−28	−92
Lake Eyre North	Oceania	−16	−52

RIVERS

EUROPE

		km	miles	
Volga	Caspian Sea	3,700	2,300	
Danube	Black Sea	2,850	1,770	
Ural	Caspian Sea	2,535	1,575	
Dnepr (Dnipro)	Black Sea	2,285	1,420	
Kama	Volga	2,030	1,260	
Don	Black Sea	1,990	1,240	
Petchora	Arctic Ocean	1,790	1,110	
Oka	Volga	1,480	920	
Belaya	Kama	1,420	880	
Dnister (Dniester)	Black Sea	1,400	870	
Vyatka	Kama	1,370	850	
Rhine	North Sea	1,320	820	
N. Dvina	Arctic Ocean	1,290	800	
Desna	Dnepr (Dnipro)	1,190	740	
Elbe	North Sea	1,145	710	
Wisla	Baltic Sea	1,090	675	
Loire	Atlantic Ocean	1,020	635	

ASIA

		km	miles	
Yangtze	Pacific Ocean	6,380	3,960	[3]
Yenisey–Angara	Arctic Ocean	5,550	3,445	[5]
Huang He	Pacific Ocean	5,464	3,395	[6]
Ob–Irtysh	Arctic Ocean	5,410	3,360	[7]
Mekong	Pacific Ocean	4,500	2,795	[9]
Amur	Pacific Ocean	4,400	2,730	[10]
Lena	Arctic Ocean	4,400	2,730	
Irtysh	Ob	4,250	2,640	
Yenisey	Arctic Ocean	4,090	2,540	
Ob	Arctic Ocean	3,680	2,285	
Indus	Indian Ocean	3,100	1,925	
Brahmaputra	Indian Ocean	2,900	1,800	
Syrdarya	Aral Sea	2,860	1,775	
Salween	Indian Ocean	2,800	1,740	
Euphrates	Indian Ocean	2,700	1,675	
Vilyuy	Lena	2,650	1,645	
Kolyma	Arctic Ocean	2,600	1,615	
Amudarya	Aral Sea	2,540	1,575	
Ural	Caspian Sea	2,535	1,575	
Ganges	Indian Ocean	2,510	1,560	
Si Kiang	Pacific Ocean	2,100	1,305	
Irrawaddy	Indian Ocean	2,010	1,250	
Tarim–Yarkand	Lop Nor	2,000	1,240	
Tigris	Indian Ocean	1,900	1,180	

AFRICA

		km	miles	
Nile	Mediterranean	6,670	4,140	[1]
Congo	Atlantic Ocean	4,670	2,900	[8]
Niger	Atlantic Ocean	4,180	2,595	
Zambezi	Indian Ocean	3,540	2,200	
Oubangi/Uele	Congo (D.R.)	2,250	1,400	
Kasai	Congo (D.R.)	1,950	1,210	
Shaballe	Indian Ocean	1,930	1,200	
Orange	Atlantic Ocean	1,860	1,155	
Cubango	Okavango Swamps	1,800	1,120	
Limpopo	Indian Ocean	1,600	995	
Senegal	Atlantic Ocean	1,600	995	
Volta	Atlantic Ocean	1,500	930	

AUSTRALIA

		km	miles
Murray–Darling	Indian Ocean	3,750	2,330
Darling	Murray	3,070	1,905
Murray	Indian Ocean	2,575	1,600
Murrumbidgee	Murray	1,690	1,050

NORTH AMERICA

		km	miles	
Mississippi–Missouri	Gulf of Mexico	6,020	3,740	[4]
Mackenzie	Arctic Ocean	4,240	2,630	
Mississippi	Gulf of Mexico	3,780	2,350	
Missouri	Mississippi	3,780	2,350	
Yukon	Pacific Ocean	3,185	1,980	
Rio Grande	Gulf of Mexico	3,030	1,880	

NORTH AMERICA (continued)

		km	miles
Arkansas	Mississippi	2,340	1,450
Colorado	Pacific Ocean	2,330	1,445
Red	Mississippi	2,040	1,270
Columbia	Pacific Ocean	1,950	1,210
Saskatchewan	Lake Winnipeg	1,940	1,205
Snake	Columbia	1,670	1,040
Churchill	Hudson Bay	1,600	990
Ohio	Mississippi	1,580	980
Brazos	Gulf of Mexico	1,400	870
St Lawrence	Atlantic Ocean	1,170	730

SOUTH AMERICA

		km	miles	
Amazon	Atlantic Ocean	6,450	4,010	[2]
Paraná–Plate	Atlantic Ocean	4,500	2,800	
Purus	Amazon	3,350	2,080	
Madeira	Amazon	3,200	1,990	
São Francisco	Atlantic Ocean	2,900	1,800	
Paraná	Plate	2,800	1,740	
Tocantins	Atlantic Ocean	2,750	1,710	
Paraguay	Paraná	2,550	1,580	
Orinoco	Atlantic Ocean	2,500	1,550	
Pilcomayo	Paraná	2,500	1,550	
Araguaia	Tocantins	2,250	1,400	
Juruá	Amazon	2,000	1,240	
Xingu	Amazon	1,980	1,230	
Ucayali	Amazon	1,900	1,180	
Marañón	Amazon	1,600	990	
Uruguay	Plate	1,600	990	

LAKES

EUROPE

		km²	miles²
Lake Ladoga	Russia	17,700	6,800
Lake Onega	Russia	9,700	3,700
Saimaa system	Finland	8,000	3,100
Vänern	Sweden	5,500	2,100
Rybinskoye Res.	Russia	4,700	1,800

ASIA

		km²	miles²	
Caspian Sea	Asia	371,800	143,550	[1]
Lake Baykal	Russia	30,500	11,780	[8]
Aral Sea	Kazakstan/Uzbekistan	28,687	11,086	[10]
Tonlé Sap	Cambodia	20,000	7,700	
Lake Balqash	Kazakstan	18,500	7,100	
Lake Dongting	China	12,000	4,600	
Lake Ysyk	Kyrgyzstan	6,200	2,400	
Lake Orumiyeh	Iran	5,900	2,300	
Lake Koko	China	5,700	2,200	
Lake Poyang	China	5,000	1,900	
Lake Khanka	China/Russia	4,400	1,700	
Lake Van	Turkey	3,500	1,400	

AFRICA

		km²	miles²	
Lake Victoria	E. Africa	68,000	26,000	[3]
Lake Tanganyika	C. Africa	33,000	13,000	[6]
Lake Malawi/Nyasa	E. Africa	29,600	11,430	[9]
Lake Chad	C. Africa	25,000	9,700	
Lake Turkana	Ethiopia/Kenya	8,500	3,300	
Lake Volta	Ghana	8,500	3,300	
Lake Bangweulu	Zambia	8,000	3,100	
Lake Rukwa	Tanzania	7,000	2,700	
Lake Mai-Ndombe	Congo (D.R.)	6,500	2,500	
Lake Kariba	Zambia/Zimbabwe	5,300	2,000	
Lake Albert	Uganda/Congo (D.R.)	5,300	2,000	
Lake Nasser	Egypt/Sudan	5,200	2,000	
Lake Mweru	Zambia/Congo (D.R.)	4,900	1,900	
Lake Cabora Bassa	Mozambique	4,500	1,700	
Lake Kyoga	Uganda	4,400	1,700	
Lake Tana	Ethiopia	3,630	1,400	

AUSTRALIA

		km²	miles²
Lake Eyre	Australia	8,900	3,400
Lake Torrens	Australia	5,800	2,200
Lake Gairdner	Australia	4,800	1,900

NORTH AMERICA

		km²	miles²	
Lake Superior	Canada/USA	82,350	31,800	[2]
Lake Huron	Canada/USA	59,600	23,010	[4]
Lake Michigan	USA	58,000	22,400	[5]
Great Bear Lake	Canada	31,800	12,280	[7]
Great Slave Lake	Canada	28,500	11,000	
Lake Erie	Canada/USA	25,700	9,900	
Lake Winnipeg	Canada	24,400	9,400	
Lake Ontario	Canada/USA	19,500	7,500	
Lake Nicaragua	Nicaragua	8,200	3,200	
Lake Athabasca	Canada	8,100	3,100	
Smallwood Reservoir	Canada	6,530	2,520	
Reindeer Lake	Canada	6,400	2,500	
Nettilling Lake	Canada	5,500	2,100	
Lake Winnipegosis	Canada	5,400	2,100	

SOUTH AMERICA

		km²	miles²
Lake Titicaca	Bolivia/Peru	8,300	3,200
Lake Poopo	Bolivia	2,800	1,100

ISLANDS

EUROPE

		km²	miles²	
Great Britain	UK	229,880	88,700	[8]
Iceland	Atlantic Ocean	103,000	39,800	
Ireland	Ireland/UK	84,400	32,600	
Novaya Zemlya (N.)	Russia	48,200	18,600	
W. Spitzbergen	Norway	39,000	15,100	
Novaya Zemlya (S.)	Russia	33,200	12,800	
Sicily	Italy	25,500	9,800	
Sardinia	Italy	24,000	9,300	
N.E. Spitzbergen	Norway	15,000	5,600	
Corsica	France	8,700	3,400	
Crete	Greece	8,350	3,200	
Zealand	Denmark	6,850	2,600	

ASIA

		km²	miles²	
Borneo	S. E. Asia	744,360	287,400	[3]
Sumatra	Indonesia	473,600	182,860	[6]
Honshu	Japan	230,500	88,980	[7]
Sulawesi (Celebes)	Indonesia	189,000	73,000	
Java	Indonesia	126,700	48,900	
Luzon	Philippines	104,700	40,400	
Mindanao	Philippines	101,500	39,200	
Hokkaido	Japan	78,400	30,300	
Sakhalin	Russia	74,060	28,600	
Sri Lanka	Indian Ocean	65,600	25,300	
Taiwan	Pacific Ocean	36,000	13,900	
Kyushu	Japan	35,700	13,800	
Hainan	China	34,000	13,100	
Timor	Indonesia	33,600	13,000	
Shikoku	Japan	18,800	7,300	
Halmahera	Indonesia	18,000	6,900	
Ceram	Indonesia	17,150	6,600	
Sumbawa	Indonesia	15,450	6,000	
Flores	Indonesia	15,200	5,900	
Samar	Philippines	13,100	5,100	
Negros	Philippines	12,700	4,900	
Bangka	Indonesia	12,000	4,600	
Palawan	Philippines	12,000	4,600	
Panay	Philippines	11,500	4,400	
Sumba	Indonesia	11,100	4,300	
Mindoro	Philippines	9,750	3,800	

AFRICA

		km²	miles²	
Madagascar	Indian Ocean	587,040	226,660	[4]
Socotra	Indian Ocean	3,600	1,400	
Réunion	Indian Ocean	2,500	965	
Tenerife	Atlantic Ocean	2,350	900	
Mauritius	Indian Ocean	1,865	720	

OCEANIA

		km²	miles²	
New Guinea	Indon./Papua NG	821,030	317,000	[2]
New Zealand (S.)	Pacific Ocean	150,500	58,100	
New Zealand (N.)	Pacific Ocean	114,700	44,300	
Tasmania	Australia	67,800	26,200	
New Britain	Papua NG	37,800	14,600	
New Caledonia	Pacific Ocean	19,100	7,400	
Viti Levu	Fiji	10,500	4,100	
Hawaii	Pacific Ocean	10,450	4,000	
Bougainville	Papua NG	9,600	3,700	
Guadalcanal	Solomon Is.	6,500	2,500	
Vanua Levu	Fiji	5,550	2,100	
New Ireland	Papua NG	3,200	1,200	

NORTH AMERICA

		km²	miles²	
Greenland	Atlantic Ocean	2,175,600	839,800	[1]
Baffin Is.	Canada	508,000	196,100	[5]
Victoria Is.	Canada	212,200	81,900	[9]
Ellesmere Is.	Canada	212,000	81,800	[10]
Cuba	Caribbean Sea	110,860	42,800	
Newfoundland	Canada	110,680	42,700	
Hispaniola	Dom. Rep./Haiti	76,200	29,400	
Banks Is.	Canada	67,000	25,900	
Devon Is.	Canada	54,500	21,000	
Melville Is.	Canada	42,400	16,400	
Vancouver Is.	Canada	32,150	12,400	
Somerset Is.	Canada	24,300	9,400	
Jamaica	Caribbean Sea	11,400	4,400	
Puerto Rico	Atlantic Ocean	8,900	3,400	
Cape Breton Is.	Canada	4,000	1,500	

SOUTH AMERICA

		km²	miles²
Tierra del Fuego	Argentina/Chile	47,000	18,100
Falkland Is. (East)	Atlantic Ocean	6,800	2,600
South Georgia	Atlantic Ocean	4,200	1,600
Galapagos (Isabela)	Pacific Ocean	2,250	870

World: Regions in the News

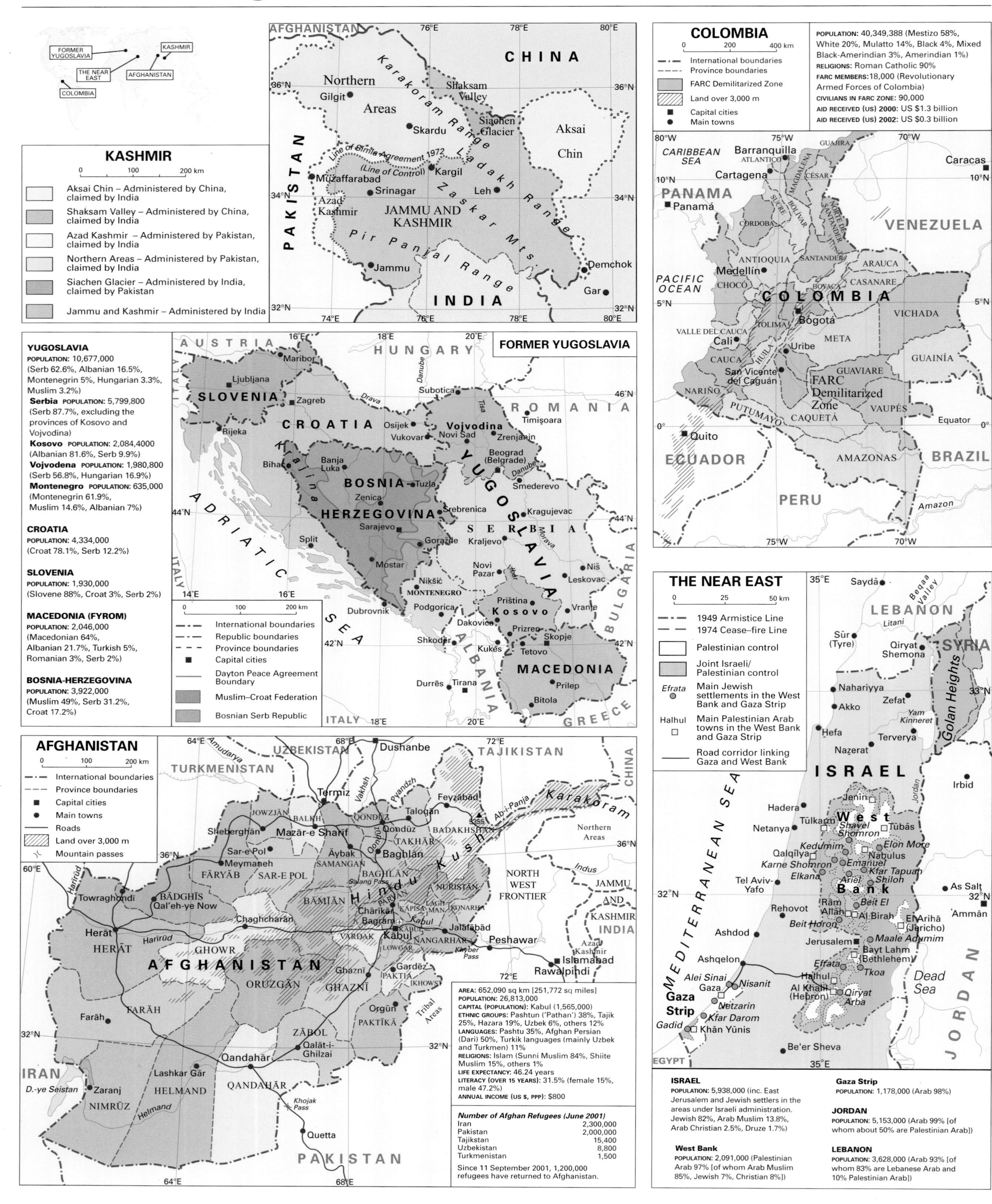

KASHMIR

0   100   200 km

	Aksai Chin – Administered by China, claimed by India
	Shaksam Valley – Administered by China, claimed by India
	Azad Kashmir – Administered by Pakistan, claimed by India
	Northern Areas – Administered by Pakistan, claimed by India
	Siachen Glacier – Administered by India, claimed by Pakistan
	Jammu and Kashmir – Administered by India

YUGOSLAVIA
POPULATION: 10,677,000
(Serb 62.6%, Albanian 16.5%, Montenegrin 5%, Hungarian 3.3%, Muslim 3.2%)
Serbia **POPULATION:** 5,799,800
(Serb 87.7%, excluding the provinces of Kosovo and Vojvodina)
Kosovo **POPULATION:** 2,084,4000
(Albanian 81.6%, Serb 9.9%)
Vojvodena **POPULATION:** 1,980,800
(Serb 56.8%, Hungarian 16.9%)
Montenegro **POPULATION:** 635,000
(Montenegrin 61.9%, Muslim 14.6%, Albanian 7%)

CROATIA
POPULATION: 4,334,000
(Croat 78.1%, Serb 12.2%)

SLOVENIA
POPULATION: 1,930,000
(Slovene 88%, Croat 3%, Serb 2%)

MACEDONIA (FYROM)
POPULATION: 2,046,000
(Macedonian 64%, Albanian 21.7%, Turkish 5%, Romanian 3%, Serb 2%)

BOSNIA-HERZEGOVINA
POPULATION: 3,922,000
(Muslim 49%, Serb 31.2%, Croat 17.2%)

AFGHANISTAN
0   100   200 km

- --- International boundaries
- --- Province boundaries
- ■ Capital cities
- ● Main towns
- —— Roads
- Land over 3,000 m
- ⋈ Mountain passes

AREA: 652,090 sq km [251,772 sq miles]
POPULATION: 26,813,000
CAPITAL (POPULATION): Kabul (1,565,000)
ETHNIC GROUPS: Pashtun ('Pathan') 38%, Tajik 25%, Hazara 19%, Uzbek 6%, others 12%
LANGUAGES: Pashtu 35%, Afghan Persian (Dari) 50%, Turkik languages (mainly Uzbek and Turkmen) 11%
RELIGIONS: Islam (Sunni Muslim 84%, Shiite Muslim 15%, others 1%
LIFE EXPECTANCY: 46.24 years
LITERACY (OVER 15 YEARS): 31.5% (female 15%, male 47.2%)
ANNUAL INCOME (US $, PPP): $800

Number of Afghan Refugees (June 2001)

Iran	2,300,000
Pakistan	2,000,000
Tajikstan	15,400
Uzbekistan	8,800
Turkmenistan	1,500

Since 11 September 2001, 1,200,000 refugees have returned to Afghanistan.

COLOMBIA
0   200   400 km

- --- International boundaries
- --- Province boundaries
- FARC Demilitarized Zone
- Land over 3,000 m
- ■ Capital cities
- ● Main towns

POPULATION: 40,349,388 (Mestizo 58%, White 20%, Mulatto 14%, Black 4%, Mixed Black-Amerindian 3%, Amerindian 1%)
RELIGIONS: Roman Catholic 90%
FARC MEMBERS: 18,000 (Revolutionary Armed Forces of Colombia)
CIVILIANS IN FARC ZONE: 90,000
AID RECEIVED (US) 2000: US $1.3 billion
AID RECEIVED (US) 2002: US $0.3 billion

THE NEAR EAST
0   25   50 km

- --- 1949 Armistice Line
- —— 1974 Cease–fire Line
- Palestinian control
- Joint Israeli/ Palestinian control
- *Efrata* ● Main Jewish settlements in the West Bank and Gaza Strip
- *Halhul* □ Main Palestinian Arab towns in the West Bank and Gaza Strip
- —— Road corridor linking Gaza and West Bank

ISRAEL
POPULATION: 5,938,000 (inc. East Jerusalem and Jewish settlers in the areas under Israeli administration. Jewish 82%, Arab Muslim 13.8%, Arab Christian 2.5%, Druze 1.7%)

West Bank
POPULATION: 2,091,000 (Palestinian Arab 97% [of whom Arab Muslim 85%, Jewish 7%, Christian 8%])

Gaza Strip
POPULATION: 1,178,000 (Arab 98%)

JORDAN
POPULATION: 5,153,000 (Arab 99% [of whom about 50% are Palestinian Arab])

LEBANON
POPULATION: 3,628,000 (Arab 93% [of whom 83% are Lebanese Arab and 10% Palestinian Arab])

THE EARTH
IN SPACE

THE UNIVERSE 2

STAR CHARTS AND CONSTELLATIONS 4

THE SOLAR SYSTEM 8

THE EARTH: TIME AND MOTION 10

THE EARTH FROM SPACE 12

THE DYNAMIC EARTH 14

EARTHQUAKES AND VOLCANOES 16

FORCES OF NATURE 18

OCEANS AND ICE 20

THE EARTH'S ATMOSPHERE 22

CLIMATE AND WEATHER 24

WATER AND LAND USE 26

THE NATURAL WORLD 28

THE HUMAN WORLD 30

LANGUAGES AND RELIGIONS 32

INTERNATIONAL ORGANIZATIONS 34

AGRICULTURE 36

ENERGY AND MINERALS 38

WORLD ECONOMIES 40

TRADE AND COMMERCE 42

TRAVEL AND COMMUNICATIONS 44

THE WORLD TODAY 46

The Universe

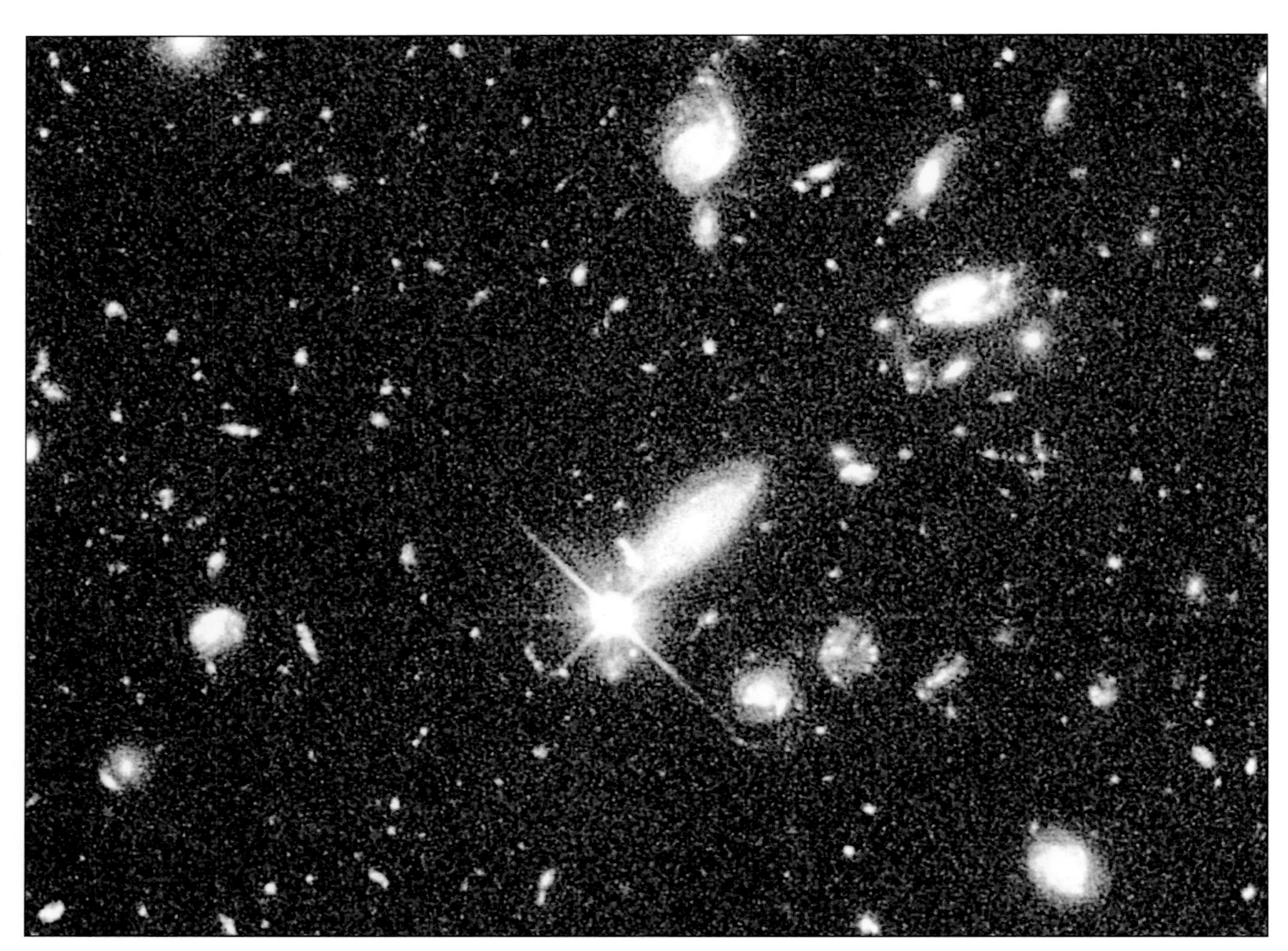

The depths of the Universe
This photograph shows some of the 1,500 or more galaxies that were recorded in the montage of photographs taken by the Hubble Space Telescope in 1995.

Just before Christmas 1995, the Hubble Space Telescope, which is in orbit about 580 km [360 miles] above the Earth, focused on a tiny area in distant space. Over a ten-day period, photographs taken by the telescope revealed unknown galaxies billions of times fainter than the human eye can see.

Because the light from these distant objects has taken so long to reach us, the photographs transmitted from the telescope and released to the media were the deepest look into space that astronomers have ever seen. The features they revealed were in existence when the Universe was less than a billion years old.

The Hubble Space Telescope is operated by the Space Telescope Science Institute in America and was launched in April 1990. The photographs it took of the Hubble Deep Field have been described by NASA as the biggest advance in astronomy since the work of the Italian scien-

tist Galileo in the early 17th century. US scientists described these astonishing photographs as 'postcards from the edge of space and time'.

THE BIG BANG

According to research published in 2001, the Universe was created, and 'time' began, about 12,500 million (or 12.5 billion) years ago, though earlier estimates have ranged from 8 to 24 billion years. Following a colossal explosion, called the 'Big Bang', the Universe expanded in the first millionth of a second of its existence

The End of the Universe
The diagram shows two theories concerning the fate of the Universe. One theory, top, suggests that the Universe will expand indefinitely, moving into an immense dark graveyard. Another theory, bottom, suggests that the galaxies will fall back until everything is again concentrated in one point in a so-called 'Big Crunch'. This might then be followed by a new 'Big Bang'.

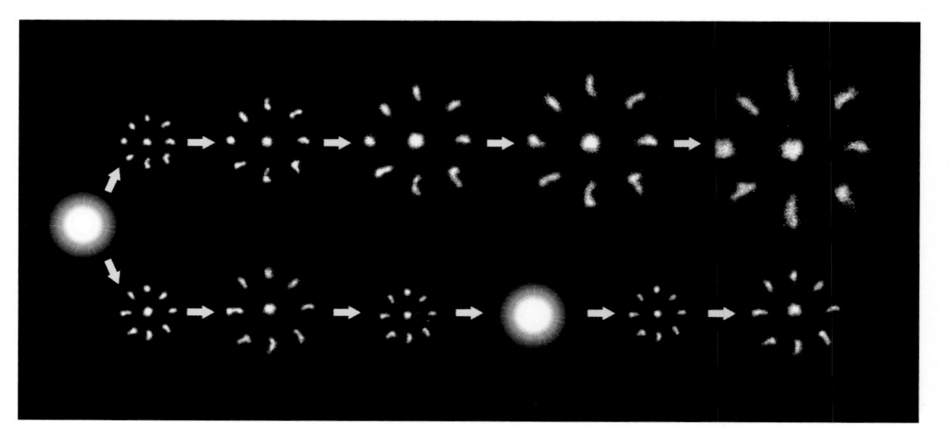

from a dimensionless point of infinite mass and density into a fireball about 30 billion km [19 million miles] across. The Universe has been expanding ever since, as demonstrated in the 1920s by Edwin Hubble, the American astronomer after whom the Hubble Space Telescope was named.

The temperature at the end of the first second was perhaps 10 billion degrees – far too hot for composite atomic nuclei to exist. As a result, the fireball consisted mainly of radiation mixed with microscopic particles of matter. Almost a million years passed before the Universe was cool enough for atoms to form.

A few billion years later, atoms in regions where matter was relatively dense began, under the influence of gravity, to move together to form proto-galaxies – masses of gas separated by empty space. The proto-galaxies were dark, because the Universe had cooled. But a few billion years later, stars began to form within the proto-galaxies as particles were drawn together. The internal pressure produced as matter condensed created the high temperatures required to cause nuclear fusion. Stars were born and later destroyed. Each generation of stars fed on the debris of extinct ones. Each generation produced larger atoms, increasing the number of different chemical elements.

THE GALAXIES
At least a billion galaxies are scattered through the Universe, though the discoveries made by the Hubble Space Telescope suggest that there may be far more than once thought, and some estimates are as high as 100 billion. The largest galaxies contain trillions of stars, while small ones contain less than a billion.

Galaxies tend to occur in groups or clusters, while some clusters appear to be grouped in vast superclusters. Our Local Cluster includes the spiral Milky Way galaxy, whose diameter is about 100,000 light-years; one light-year, the distance that light travels in one year, measures about 9,500 billion km [5,900 billion miles]. The Milky Way is a huge galaxy, shaped like a disk with a bulge at the centre. It is larger, brighter and more massive than many other known galaxies. It contains about 100 billion stars which rotate around the centre of the galaxy in the same direction as the Sun does.

One medium-sized star in the Milky Way galaxy is the Sun. After its formation, about 5 billion years ago, there was enough leftover matter around it to create the planets, asteroids,

The Home Galaxy
This schematic plan shows that our Solar System is located in one of the spiral arms of the Milky Way galaxy, a little less than 30,000 light-years from its centre. The centre of the Milky Way galaxy is not visible from Earth. Instead, it is masked by light-absorbing clouds of interstellar dust.

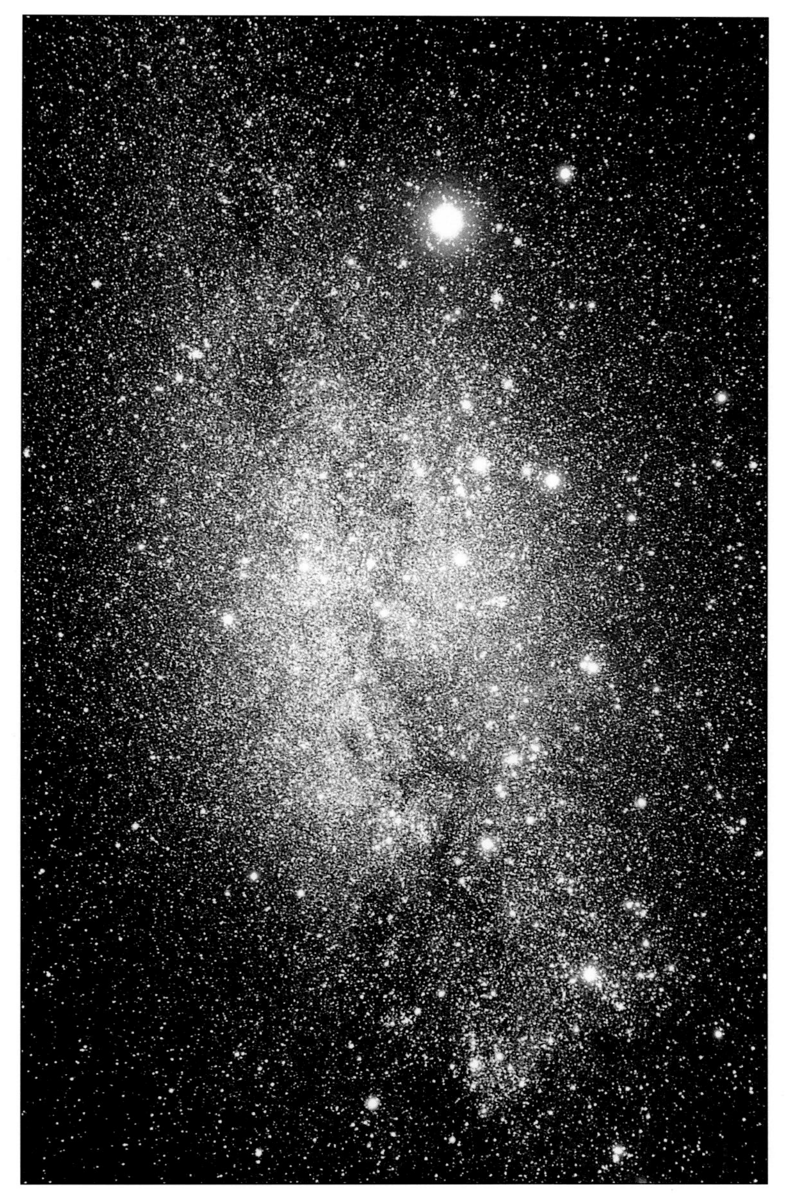

The Milky Way
This section of the Milky Way is dominated by Sirius, the Dog Star, top centre, in the constellation of Canis Major. Sirius is the brightest star in the sky.

moons and other bodies that together form our Solar System. The Solar System rotates around the centre of the Milky Way galaxy approximately every 225 million years.

Stars similar to our Sun are known to have planets orbiting around them. By the start of 2002, more than 70 extra-solar planets had been reported and evidence from the Hubble Space Telescope suggests that the raw materials from which planets are formed is common in dusty disks around many stars. This provokes one of the most intriguing questions that has ever faced humanity. If other planets exist in the Universe, then are they home to living organisms?

Before the time of Galileo, people thought that the Earth lay at the centre of the Universe. But we now know that our Solar System and even the Milky Way galaxy are tiny specks in the Universe as a whole. Perhaps our planet is also not unique in being the only one to support intelligent life.

Star Charts and Constellations

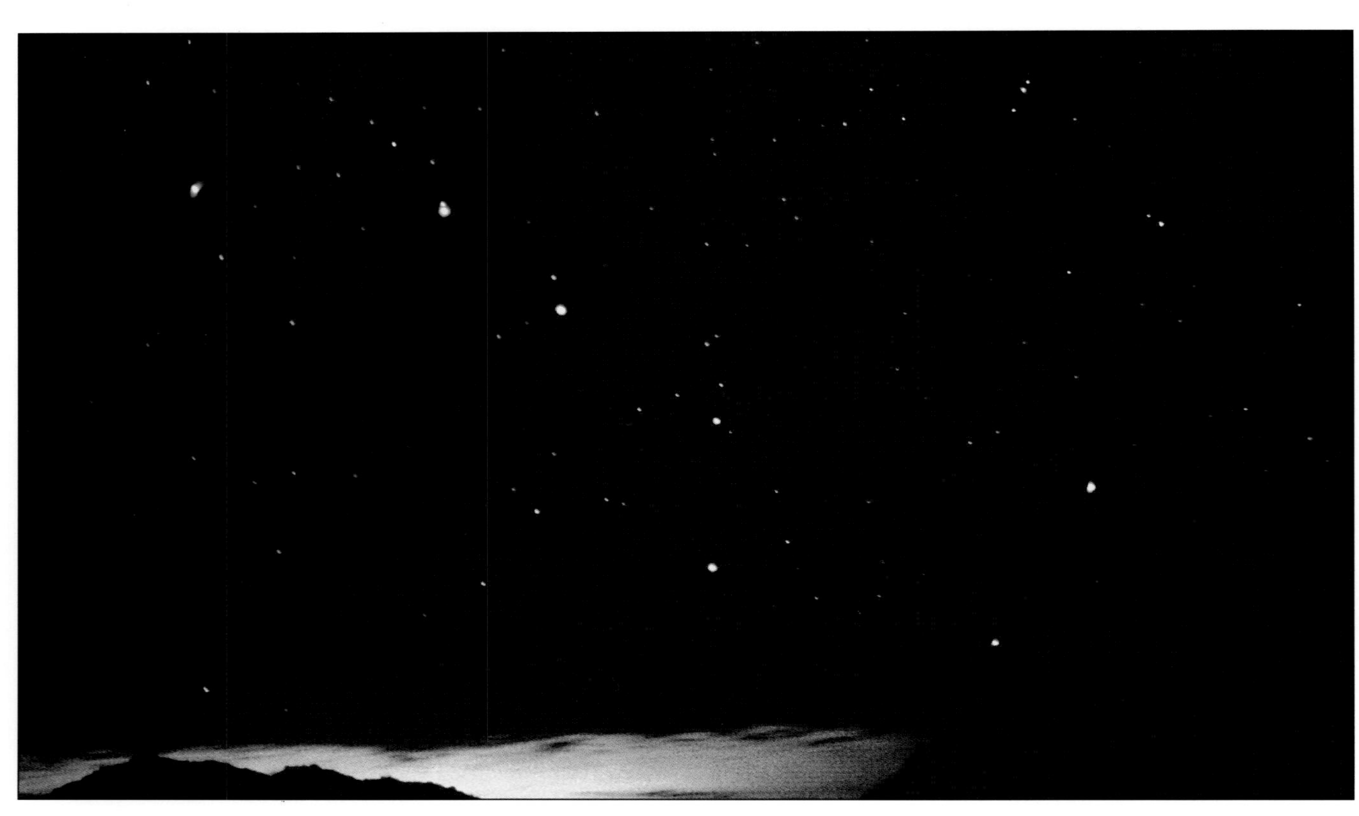

The Plough

The Plough, or Big Dipper, above glowing yellow clouds lit by city lights. It is part of a larger group called Ursa Major one of the best-known constellations of the northern hemisphere. The two bright stars to the lower right of the photograph (Merak and Dubhe) are known as the Pointers because they show the way to the Pole Star.

THE BRIGHTEST STARS

The 15 brightest stars visible from northern Europe. Magnitudes are given to the nearest tenth.

Sirius	−1.5
Arcturus	0.0
Vega	0.0
Capella	0.1
Rigel	0.1
Procyon	0.4
Betelgeuse	0.4
Altair	0.8
Aldebaran	0.8
Antares	1.0
Spica	1.0
Pollux	1.1
Fomalhaut	1.2
Deneb	1.2
Regulus	1.3

On a clear night, under the best conditions and far away from the glare of city lights, a person in northern Europe can look up and see about 2,500 stars. In a town, however, light pollution can reduce visibility to 200 stars or less. Over the whole celestial sphere it is possible to see about 8,500 stars with the naked eye and it is only when you look through a telescope that you begin to realize that the number of stars is countless.

SMALL AND LARGE STARS

Stars come in several sizes. Some, called neutron stars, are compact, with the same mass as the Sun but with diameters of only about 20 km [12 miles]. Larger than neutron stars are the small white dwarfs. Our Sun is a medium-sized star, but many visible stars in the night sky are giants with diameters between 10 and 100 times that of the Sun, or supergiants with diameters over 100 times that of the Sun.

Two bright stars in the constellation Orion are Betelgeuse (also known as Alpha Orionis) and Rigel (or Beta Orionis). Betelgeuse is an orange-red supergiant, whose diameter is about 400 times that of the Sun. Rigel is also a supergiant. Its diameter is about 50 times that of the Sun, but its luminosity is estimated to be over 100,000 times that of the Sun.

The stars we see in the night sky all belong to our home galaxy, the Milky Way. This name is also used for the faint, silvery band that arches across the sky. This band, a slice through our

---

THE CONSTELLATIONS

The constellations and their English names. Constellations visible from both hemispheres are listed.

Andromeda	Andromeda	Delphinus	Dolphin	Perseus	Perseus
Antlia	Air Pump	Dorado	Swordfish	Phoenix	Phoenix
Apus	Bird of Paradise	Draco	Dragon	Pictor	Easel
Aquarius	Water Carrier	Equuleus	Little Horse	Pisces	Fishes
Aquila	Eagle	Eridanus	River Eridanus	Piscis Austrinus	Southern Fish
Ara	Altar	Fornax	Furnace	Puppis	Ship's Stern
Aries	Ram	Gemini	Twins	Pyxis	Mariner's Compass
Auriga	Charioteer	Grus	Crane	Reticulum	Net
Boötes	Herdsman	Hercules	Hercules	Sagitta	Arrow
Caelum	Chisel	Horologium	Clock	Sagittarius	Archer
Camelopardalis	Giraffe	Hydra	Water Snake	Scorpius	Scorpion
Cancer	Crab	Hydrus	Sea Serpent	Sculptor	Sculptor
Canes Venatici	Hunting Dogs	Indus	Indian	Scutum	Shield
Canis Major	Great Dog	Lacerta	Lizard	Serpens*	Serpent
Canis Minor	Little Dog	Leo	Lion	Sextans	Sextant
Capricornus	Sea Goat	Leo Minor	Little Lion	Taurus	Bull
Carina	Ship's Keel	Lepus	Hare	Telescopium	Telescope
Cassiopeia	Cassiopeia	Libra	Scales	Triangulum	Triangle
Centaurus	Centaur	Lupus	Wolf	Triangulum Australe	
Cepheus	Cepheus	Lynx	Lynx		Southern Triangle
Cetus	Whale	Lyra	Lyre	Tucana	Toucan
Chamaeleon	Chameleon	Mensa	Table	Ursa Major	Great Bear
Circinus	Compasses	Microscopium	Microscope	Ursa Minor	Little Bear
Columba	Dove	Monoceros	Unicorn	Vela	Ship's Sails
Coma Berenices	Berenice's Hair	Musca	Fly	Virgo	Virgin
Corona Australis	Southern Crown	Norma	Level	Volans	Flying Fish
Corona Borealis	Northern Crown	Octans	Octant	Vulpecula	Fox
Corvus	Crow	Ophiuchus	Serpent Bearer		
Crater	Cup	Orion	Hunter	** In two halves: Serpens Caput, the*	
Crux	Southern Cross	Pavo	Peacock	*head, and Serpens Cauda, the tail.*	
Cygnus	Swan	Pegasus	Winged Horse		

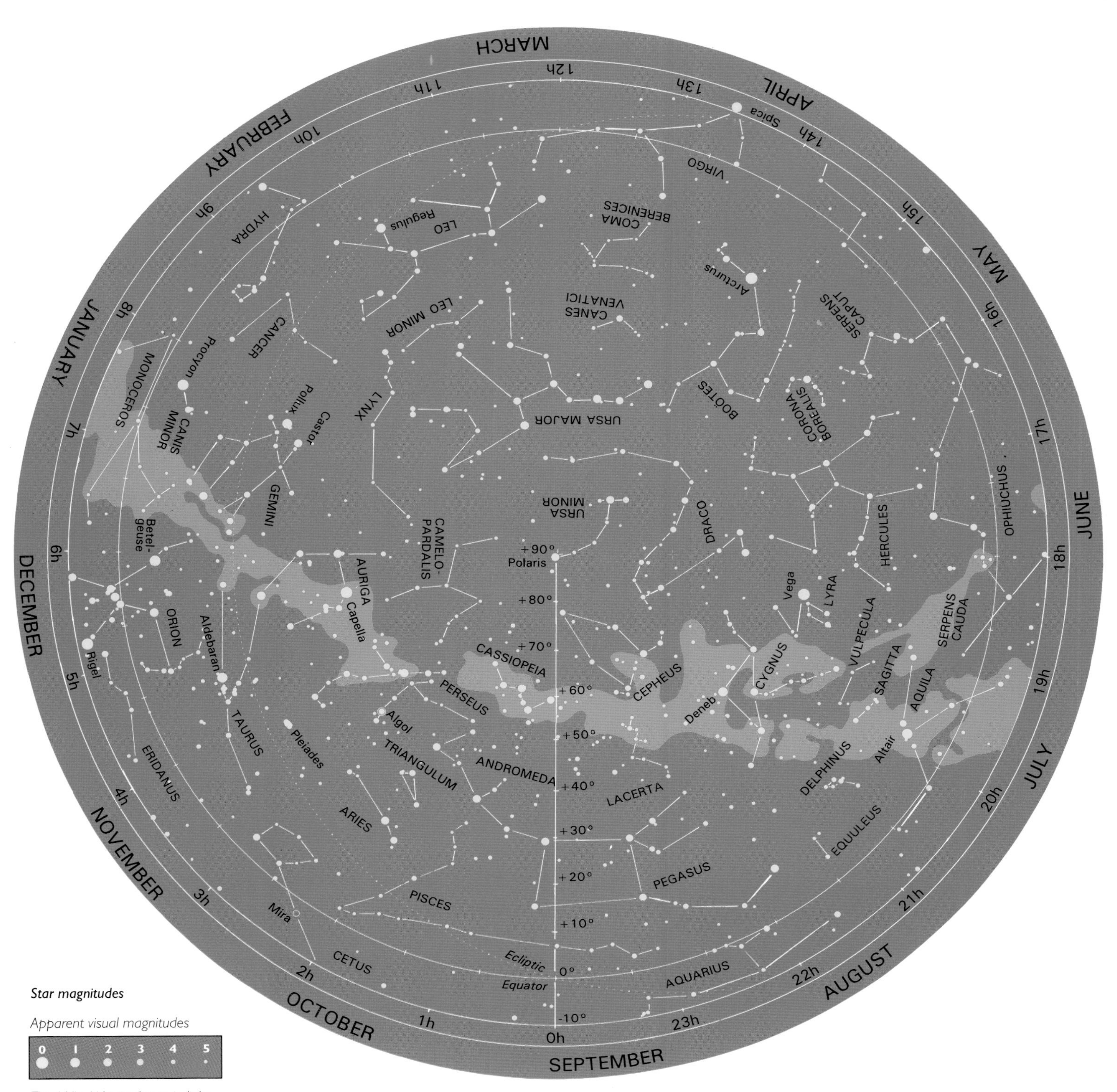

Star magnitudes

Apparent visual magnitudes

0	1	2	3	4	5

The Milky Way is shown in light blue on the above chart.

Star chart of the northern hemisphere

When you look into the sky, the stars seem to be on the inside of a huge dome. This gives astronomers a way of mapping them. This chart shows the sky as it would appear from the North Pole. To use the star chart above, an observer in the northern hemisphere should face south and turn the chart so that the current month appears at the bottom. The chart will then show the constellations on view at approximately 11pm Greenwich Mean Time. The map should be rotated clockwise 15° for each hour before 11pm and anticlockwise for each hour after 11pm.

galaxy, contains an enormous number of stars. The nucleus of the Milky Way galaxy cannot be seen from Earth. Lying in the direction of the constellation Sagittarius in the southern hemisphere, it is masked by clouds of dust.

THE BRIGHTNESS OF STARS

Astronomers use a scale of magnitudes to measure the brightness of stars. The brightest visible to the naked eye were originally known as first-magnitude stars, ones not so bright were second-magnitude, down to the faintest visible, which were rated as sixth-magnitude. The brighter the star, the lower the magnitude. With the advent of telescopes and the development of accurate instruments for measuring brightnesses, the magnitude scale has been refined and extended.

Very bright bodies such as Sirius, Venus and the Sun have negative magnitudes. The nearest star is Proxima Centauri, part of a multiple star system, which is 4.2 light-years away. Proxima Centauri is very faint and has a magnitude of 11.3. Alpha Centauri A, one of the two brighter members of the system, is the nearest visible star to Earth. It has a magnitude of 1.7.

These magnitudes are known as apparent magnitudes – measures of the brightnesses of the stars as they appear to us. These are the magnitudes shown on the charts on these pages. But the stars are at very different distances. The star Deneb, in the constellation Cygnus, for example, is over 1,200 light-years away. So astronomers also use absolute magnitudes – measures of how bright the stars really are. A star's absolute magnitude is the apparent magnitude it would have if it could be placed 32.6 light-years away. So Deneb, with an apparent magnitude of 1.2, has an absolute magnitude of –7.2.

The brightest star in the night sky is Sirius, the Dog Star, with a magnitude of –1.5. This medium-sized star is 8.64 light-years distant but it gives out about 20 times as much light as the Sun. After the Sun and the Moon, the brightest objects in the sky are the planets Venus, Mars and Jupiter. For example, Venus has a magnitude of up to –4. The planets have no light of their own however, and shine only because they reflect the Sun's rays. But whilst stars have fixed positions, the planets shift nightly in relation to the constellations, following a path called

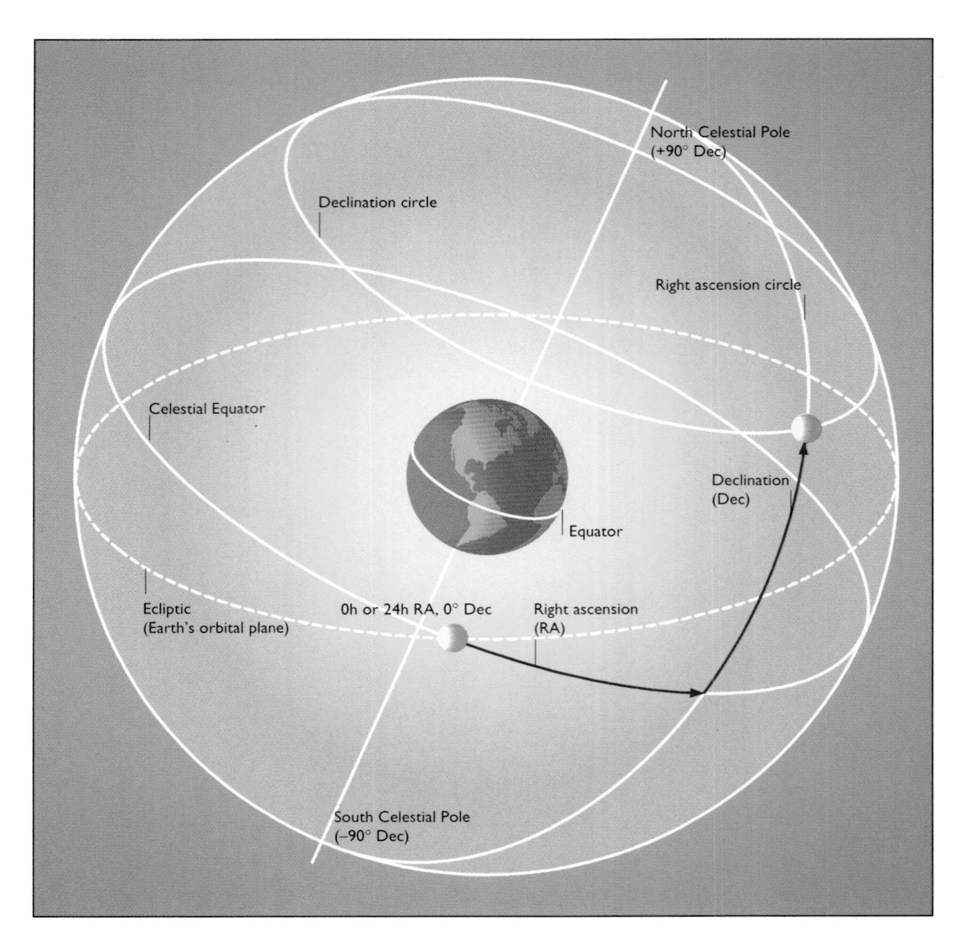

Celestial sphere
The diagram shows the imaginary surface on which astronomical positions are measured. The celestial sphere appears to rotate about the celestial poles, as though an extension of the Earth's own axis. The Earth's axis points towards the celestial poles.

The Southern Cross

The Southern Cross, or Crux, in the southern hemisphere, was classified as a constellation in the 17th century. It is as familiar to Australians and New Zealanders as the Plough (or Big Dipper) is to people in the northern hemisphere. The vertical axis of the Southern Cross points towards the South Celestial Pole.

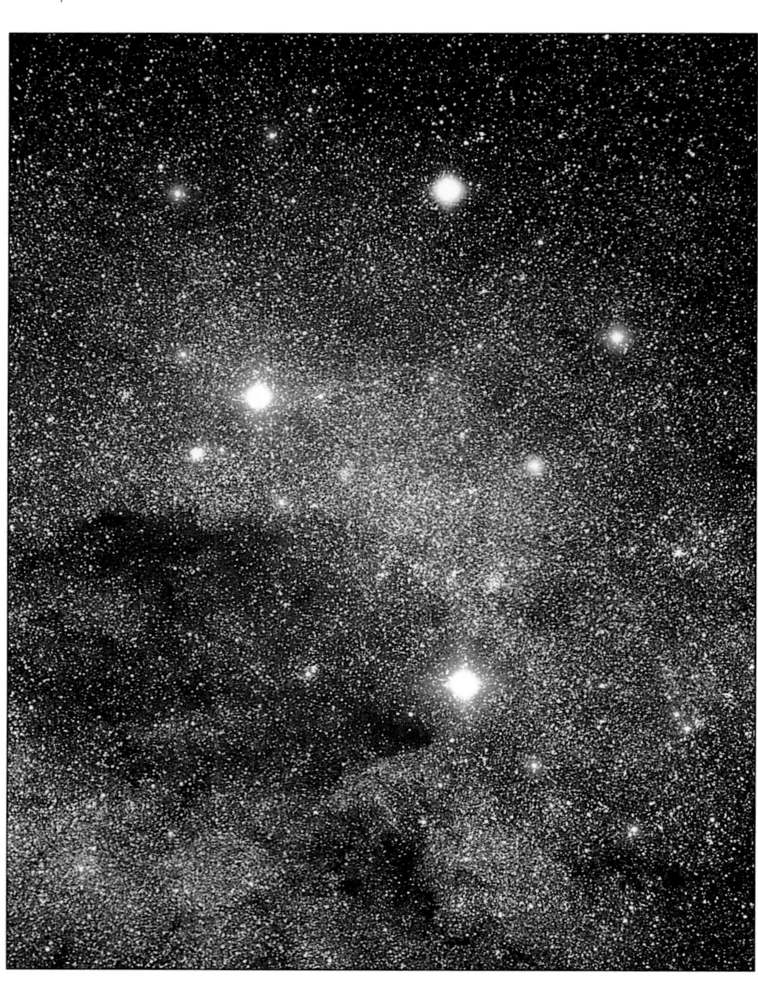

the Ecliptic (shown on the star charts). As they follow their orbits around the Sun, their distances from the Earth vary, and therefore so also do their magnitudes.

While atlas maps record the details of the Earth's surface, star charts are a guide to the heavens. An observer at the Equator can see the entire sky at some time during the year, but an observer at the poles can see only the stars in a single hemisphere. As a result, star charts of both hemispheres are produced. The northern hemisphere chart is centred on the North Celestial Pole, while the southern hemisphere chart is centred on the South Celestial Pole.

In the northern hemisphere, the North Pole is marked by the star Polaris, or North Star. Polaris lies within a degree of the point where an extension of the Earth's axis meets the sky. Polaris appears to be stationary and navigators throughout history have used it as a guide. Unfortunately, the South Pole has no convenient reference point.

Star charts of the two hemispheres are bounded by the Celestial Equator, an imaginary line in the sky directly above the terrestrial Equator. Astronomical co-ordinates, which give the location of stars, are normally stated in terms of right ascension (the equivalent of longitude) and declination (the equivalent of latitude). Because the stars appear to rotate around the Earth every 24 hours, right ascension is measured eastwards in hours and minutes. Declination is measured in degrees north or south of the Celestial Equator.

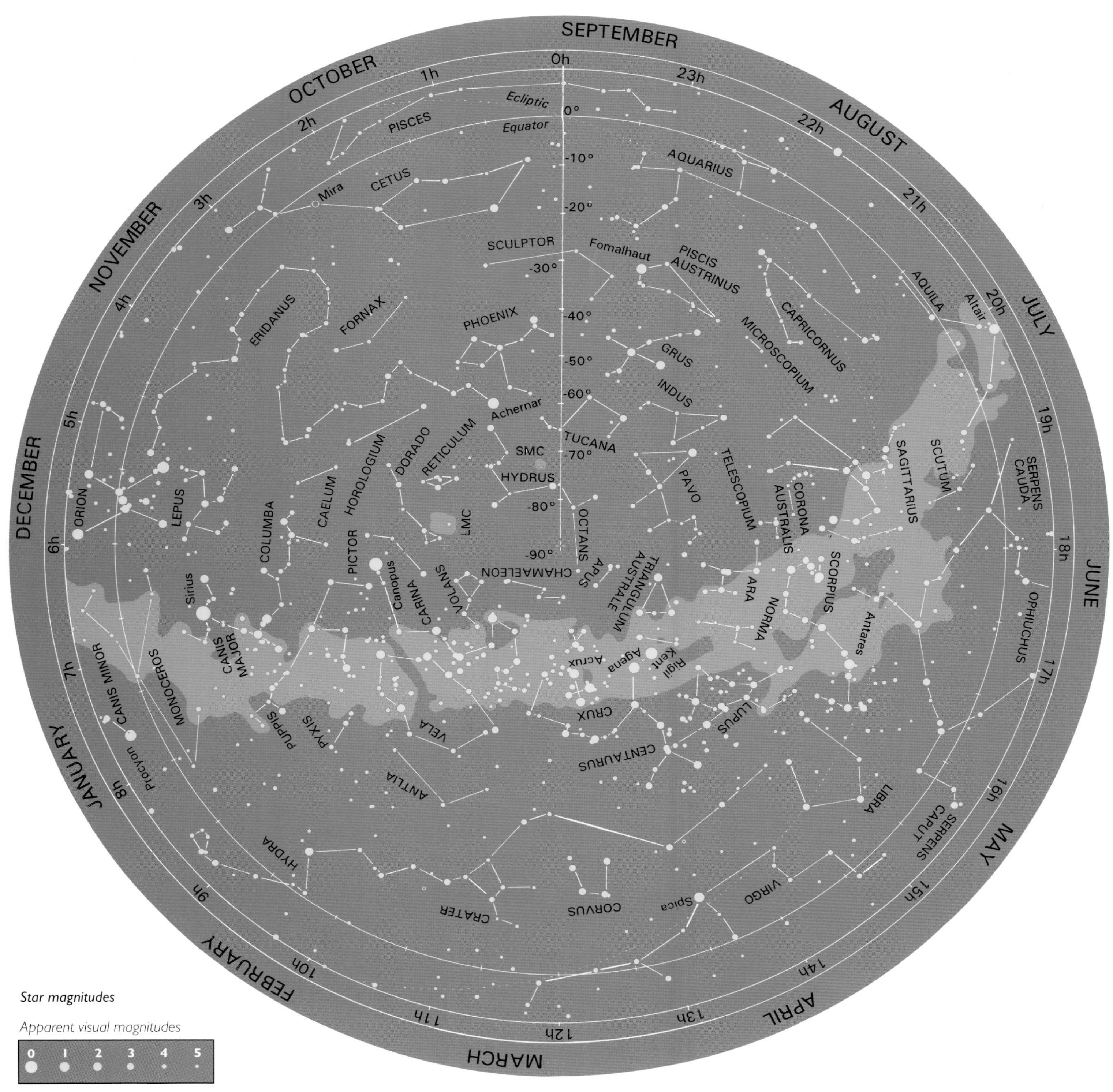

Star magnitudes

Apparent visual magnitudes

| 0 | 1 | 2 | 3 | 4 | 5 |

The Milky Way is shown in light blue on the above chart.

Star chart of the southern hemisphere

Many constellations in the southern hemisphere were named not by the ancients but by later astronomers. Some, including Antila (Air Pump) and Microscopium (Microscope), have modern names. The Large and Small Magellanic Clouds (LMC, SMC) are small 'satellite' galaxies of the Milky Way. To use the chart, an observer in the southern hemisphere should face north and turn the chart so that the current month appears at the bottom. The map will then show the constellations on view at approximately 11pm Greenwich Mean Time. The chart should be rotated clockwise 15° for each hour before 11pm and anticlockwise for each hour after 11pm.

CONSTELLATIONS

Every star is identifiable as a member of a constellation. The night sky contains 88 constellations, many of which were named by the ancient Greeks, Romans and other early peoples after animals and mythological characters, such as Orion and Perseus. More recently, astronomers invented names for constellations seen in the southern hemisphere, in areas not visible around the Mediterranean Sea.

Some groups of easily recognizable stars form parts of a constellation. For example, seven stars form the shape of the Plough or Big Dipper within the constellation Ursa Major. Such groups are called asterisms.

The stars in constellations lie in the same direction in space, but normally at vastly differ-

ent distances. Hence, there is no real connection between them. The positions of stars seem fixed, but in fact the shapes of the constellations are changing slowly over very long periods of time. This is because the stars have their own 'proper motions', which because of the huge distances involved are imperceptible to the naked eye.

The Solar System

Although the origins of the Solar System are still a matter of debate, many scientists believe that it was formed from a cloud of gas and dust, the debris from some long-lost, exploded star. Around 5 billion years ago, material was drawn towards the hub of the rotating disk of gas and dust, where it was compressed to thermonuclear fusion temperatures. A new star, the Sun, was born, containing 99.8% of the mass of the Solar System. The remaining material was later drawn together to form the planets and the other bodies in the Solar System. Spacecraft, manned and unmanned, have greatly increased our knowledge of the Solar System since the start of the Space Age in 1957, when the Soviet Union launched the satellite Sputnik I.

THE PLANETS

Mercury is the closest planet to the Sun and the fastest moving. Space probes have revealed that its surface is covered by craters, and looks much like our Moon. Mercury is a hostile place, with no significant atmosphere and temperatures ranging between 400°C [750°F] by day and −170°C [−275°F] by night. It seems unlikely that anyone will ever want to visit this planet.

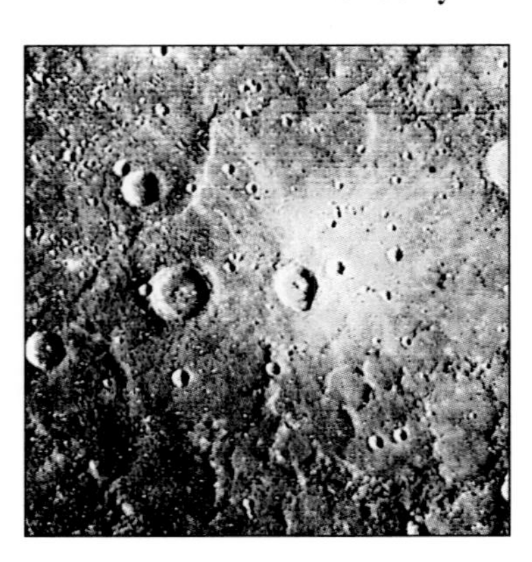

Venus is much the same size as Earth, but it is the hottest of the planets, with temperatures reaching 475°C [885°F], even at night. The reason for this scorching heat is the atmosphere, which consists mainly of carbon dioxide, a gas that traps heat thus creating a greenhouse effect. The density of the atmosphere is about 90 times that of Earth and dense clouds permanently mask the surface. Active volcanic regions discharging sulphur dioxide may account for the haze of sulphuric acid droplets in the upper atmosphere.

From planet Earth, Venus is brighter than any other star or planet and is easy to spot. It is often the first object to be seen in the evening sky and the last to be seen in the morning sky. It can even be seen in daylight.

Earth, seen from space, looks blue (because of the oceans which cover more than 70% of the planet) and white (a result of clouds in the atmosphere). The atmosphere and water make Earth the only planet known to support life. The Earth's hard outer layers, including the crust and the top of the mantle, are divided into rigid plates. Forces inside the Earth move the plates, modifying the landscape and causing earthquakes and volcanic activity. Weathering and erosion also change the surface.

Mars has many features in common with Earth, including an atmosphere with clouds and polar caps that partly melt in summer. Scientists once considered that it was the most likely planet on which other life might exist, but the two Viking space probes that went there in the 1970s found only a barren rocky surface with no trace of water. But Mars did have flowing water at one time and there are many dry channels – but these are not the fictitious 'canals'. There are also giant, dormant volcanoes.

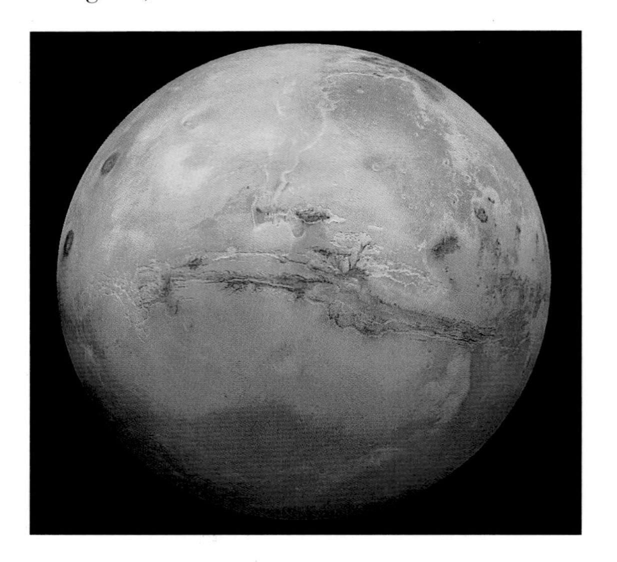

PLANETARY DATA

Planet	Mean distance from Sun (million km)	Mass (Earth=1)	Period of orbit (Earth yrs)	Period of rotation (Earth days)	Equatorial diameter (km)	Average density (water=1)	Surface gravity (Earth=1)	Number of known satellites
Sun	–	333,000	–	25.4	1,391,000	1.41	28	–
Mercury	57.9	0.055	0.2406	58.67	4,880	5.43	0.38	0
Venus	108.2	0.815	0.6152	243.0	12,104	5.20	0.90	0
Earth	149.6	1.0	1.00	1.00	12,756	5.52	1.00	1
Mars	227.9	0.107	1.88	1.028	6,792	3.91	0.38	2
Jupiter	778.3	317.8	11.86	0.411	142,800	1.33	2.69	27
Saturn	1,426.8	95.2	29.46	0.427	120,000	0.69	1.19	30
Uranus	2,869.4	14.53	84.01	0.748	51,118	1.29	0.79	21
Neptune	4,496.3	17.14	164.8	0.710	49,528	1.64	0.98	8
Pluto	5,900.1	0.002	2447.7	6.39	2,320	2.00	0.03	1

Asteroids are small, rocky bodies. Most of them orbit the Sun between Mars and Jupiter, but some small ones can approach the Earth. The largest is Ceres, 913 km [567 miles] in diameter. There may be around a million asteroids bigger than 1 km [0.6 miles].

Jupiter, the giant planet, lies beyond Mars and the asteroid belt. Its mass is almost three times as much as all the other planets combined and, because of its size, it shines more brightly than any other planet apart from Venus and, occasionally, Mars. The four largest moons of Jupiter were discovered by Galileo. Jupiter is made up mostly of hydrogen and helium, covered by a layer of clouds. Its Great Red Spot is a high-pressure storm. Jupiter made headline news when it was struck by fragments of Comet Shoemaker–Levy 9 in July 1994. This was the greatest collision ever seen by scientists between a planet and another heavenly body. The fragments of the comet that crashed into Jupiter created huge fireballs that caused scars on the planet that remained visible for months after the event.

Saturn is structurally similar to Jupiter but it is best known for its rings. The rings measure about 270,000 km [170,000 miles] across, yet they are no more than a few hundred metres thick. Seen from Earth, the rings seem divided

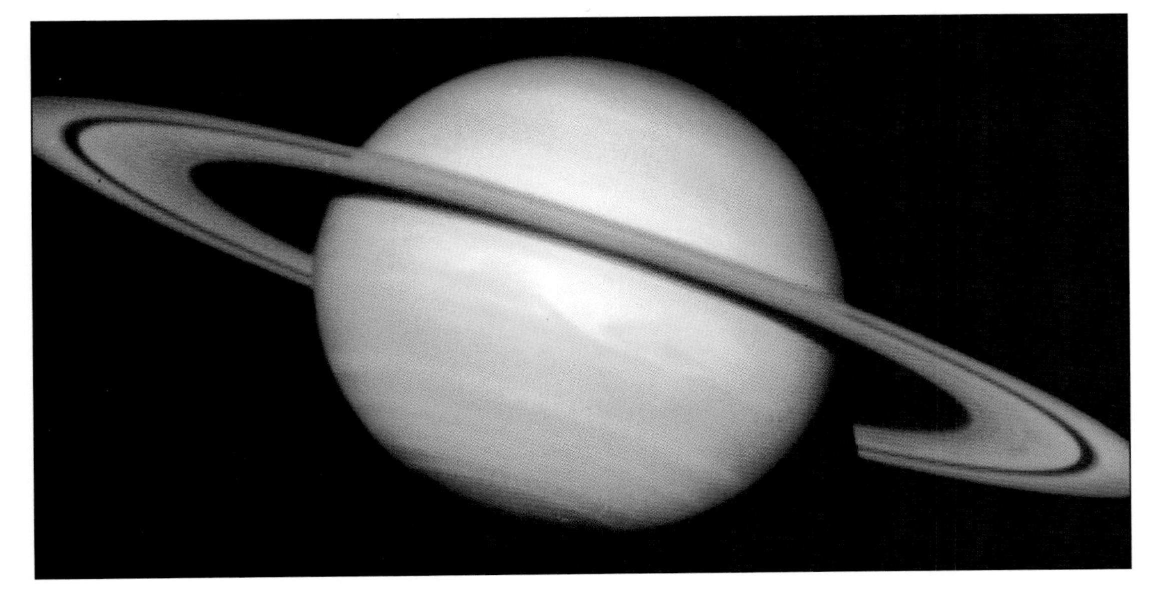

into three main bands of varying brightness, but photographs sent back by the *Voyager* space probes in 1980 and 1981 showed that they are broken up into thousands of thin ringlets composed of ice particles ranging in size from a snowball to an iceberg. The origin of the rings is still a matter of debate.

Uranus was discovered in 1781 by William Herschel who first thought it was a comet. It is broadly similar to Jupiter and Saturn in composition, though its distance from the Sun makes its surface even colder. Uranus is circled by thin rings which were discovered in 1977. Unlike the rings of Saturn, the rings of Uranus are black, which explains why they cannot be seen from Earth.

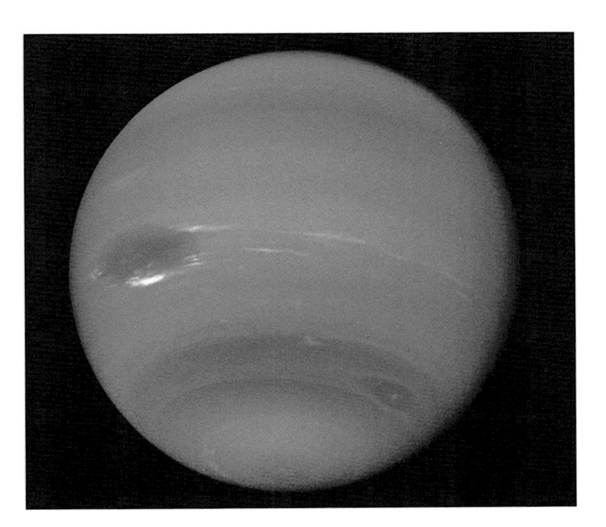

Neptune, named after the mythological sea god, was discovered in 1846 as the result of mathematical predictions made by astronomers to explain irregularities in the orbit of Uranus, its near twin. Little was known about this distant body until *Voyager 2* came close to it in 1989. Neptune has thin rings, like those of Uranus. Among its blue-green clouds is a prominent dark spot, which rotates anticlockwise every 18 hours or so.

Pluto is the smallest planet in the Solar System, even smaller than our Moon. The American astronomer Clyde Tombaugh discovered Pluto in 1930. Its orbit is odd and it sometimes comes closer to the Sun than Neptune. The nature of Pluto, a gloomy planet appropriately named after the Greek and Roman god of the underworld, is uncertain. At Pluto's distance and beyond are many small, asteroid-like bodies the first of which was found in 1992.

Comets are small icy bodies that orbit the Sun in highly elliptical orbits. When a comet swings in towards the Sun some of its ice evaporates, and the comet brightens and may become visible from Earth. The best known is Halley's Comet, which takes 76 years to orbit the Sun.

The Earth: Time and Motion

The Earth is constantly moving through space like a huge, self-sufficient spaceship. First, with the rest of the Solar System, it moves around the centre of the Milky Way galaxy. Second, it rotates around the Sun at a speed of more than 100,000 km/h [more than 60,000 mph], covering a distance of nearly 1,000 million km [600 million miles] in a little over 365 days. The Earth also spins on its axis, an imaginary line joining the North and South Poles, via the centre of the Earth, completing one turn in a day. The Earth's movements around the Sun determine our calendar, though accurate observations of

The Earth from the Moon

In 1969, Neil Armstrong and Edwin 'Buzz' Aldrin Junior were the first people to set foot on the Moon. This superb view of the Earth was taken by the crew of Apollo 11.

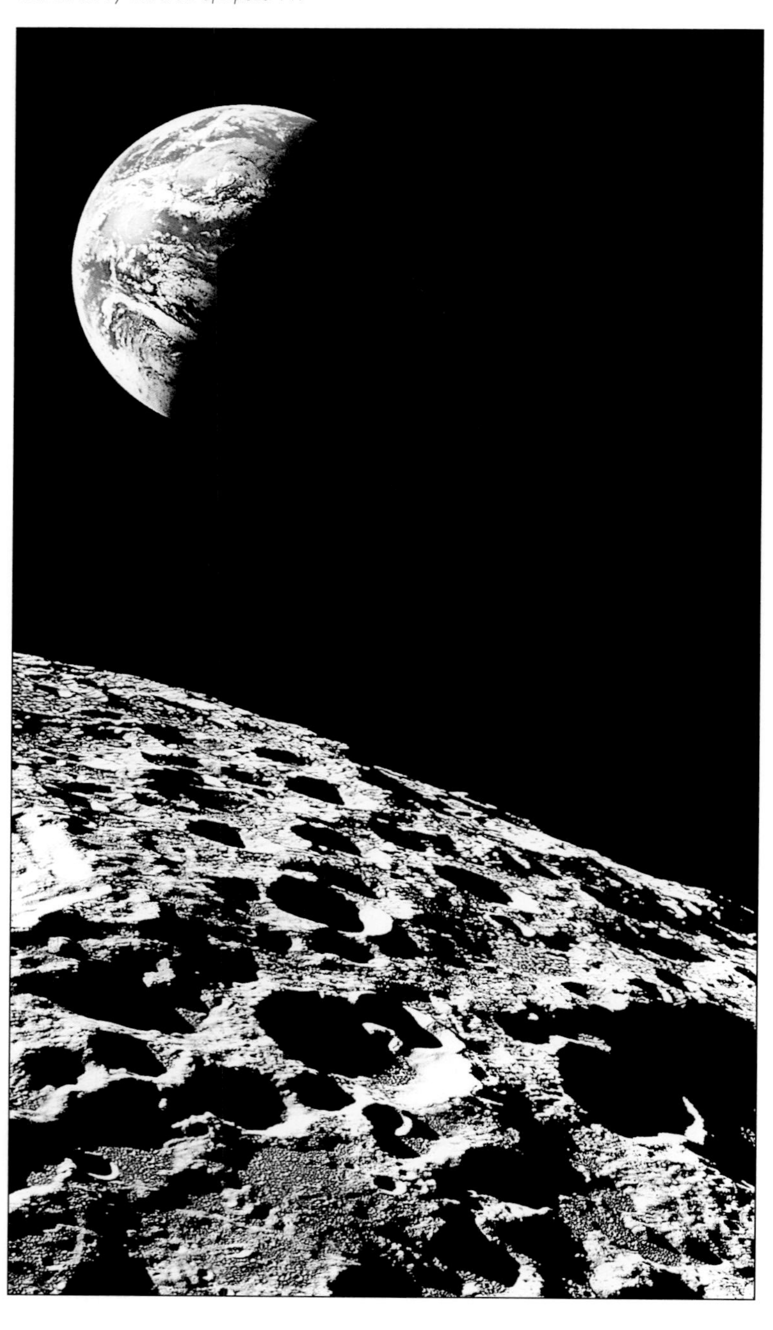

the stars made by astronomers help to keep our clocks in step with the rotation of the Earth around the Sun.

THE CHANGING YEAR

The Earth takes 365 days, 6 hours, 9 minutes and 9.54 seconds to complete one orbit around the Sun. We have a calendar year of 365 days, so allowance has to be made for the extra time over and above the 365 days. This is allowed for by introducing leap years of 366 days. Leap years are generally those, such as 1992 and 1996, which are divisible by four. Century years, however, are not leap years unless they are divisible by 400. Hence, 1700, 1800 and 1900 were not leap years, but the year 2000 was one. Leap years help to make the calendar conform with the solar year.

Because the Earth's axis is tilted by 23½°, the middle latitudes enjoy four distinct seasons. On 21 March, the vernal or spring equinox in the northern hemisphere, the Sun is directly over-head at the Equator and everywhere on Earth has about 12 hours of daylight and 12 hours of darkness. But as the Earth continues on its journey around the Sun, the northern hemi-sphere tilts more and more towards the Sun. Finally, on 21 June, the Sun is overhead at the Tropic of Cancer (latitude 23½° North). This is

The Seasons

The 23½° tilt of the Earth's axis remains constant as the Earth orbits around the Sun. As a result, first the northern and then the southern hemispheres lean towards the Sun. Annual variations in the amount of sunlight received in turn by each hemisphere are responsible for the four seasons experienced in the middle latitudes.

Tides

The daily rises and falls of the ocean's waters are caused by the gravitational pull of the Moon and the Sun. The effect is greatest on the hemisphere facing the Moon, causing a 'tidal bulge'. The diagram below shows that the Sun, Moon and Earth are in line when the spring tides occur. This causes the greatest tidal ranges. On the other hand, the neap tides occur when the pull of the Moon and the Sun are opposed. Neap tides, when tidal ranges are at their lowest, occur near the Moon's first and third quarters.

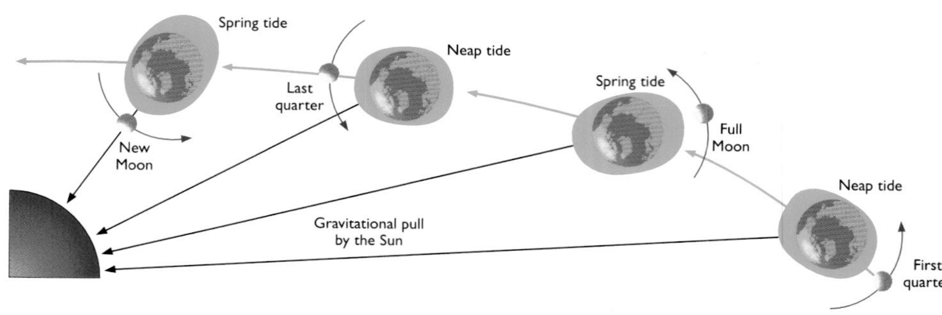

SUN DATA

DIAMETER	1.391×10^6 km
VOLUME	1.412×10^{18} km^3
VOLUME (EARTH=1)	1.303×10^6
MASS	1.989×10^{30} kg
MASS (EARTH=1)	3.329×10^6
MEAN DENSITY (WATER=1)	1.409
ROTATION PERIOD	
AT EQUATOR	25.4 days
AT POLES	about 35 days
SURFACE GRAVITY (EARTH=1)	28
MAGNITUDE	
APPARENT	−26.9
ABSOLUTE	+4.71
TEMPERATURE	
AT SURFACE	5,400°C [5,700 K]
AT CORE	15×10^6 K

MOON DATA

DIAMETER	3,476 km
MASS (EARTH=1)	0.0123
DENSITY (WATER=1)	3.34
MEAN DISTANCE FROM EARTH	384,402 km
MAXIMUM DISTANCE (APOGEE)	406,740 km
MINIMUM DISTANCE (PERIGEE)	356,410 km
SIDERIAL ROTATION AND REVOLUTION PERIOD	27.322 days
SYNODIC MONTH (NEW MOON TO NEW MOON)	29.531 days
SURFACE GRAVITY (EARTH=1)	0.165
MAXIMUM SURFACE TEMPERATURE	+130°C [403 K]
MINIMUM SURFACE TEMPERATURE	−158°C [115 K]

Phases of the Moon

The Moon rotates more slowly than the Earth, making one complete turn on its axis in just over 27 days. This corresponds to its period of revolution around the Earth and, hence, the same hemisphere always faces us. The interval between one full Moon and the next (and also between new Moons) is about 29½ days, or one lunar month. The apparent changes in the appearance of the Moon are caused by its changing position in relation to Earth. Like the planets, the Moon produces no light of its own. It shines by reflecting the Sun's rays, varying from a slim crescent to a full circle and back again.

the summer solstice in the northern hemisphere.

The overhead Sun then moves south again until on 23 September, the autumn equinox in the northern hemisphere, the Sun is again overhead at the Equator. The overhead Sun then moves south until, on around 22 December, it is overhead at the Tropic of Capricorn. This is the winter solstice in the northern hemisphere, and the summer solstice in the southern, where the seasons are reversed.

At the poles, there are two seasons. During half of the year, one of the poles leans towards the Sun and has continuous sunlight. For the other six months, the pole leans away from the Sun and is in continuous darkness.

Regions around the Equator do not have marked seasons. Because the Sun is high in the sky throughout the year, it is always hot or warm. When people talk of seasons in the tropics, they are usually referring to other factors, such as rainy and dry periods.

DAY, NIGHT AND TIDES

As the Earth rotates on its axis every 24 hours, first one side of the planet and then the other faces the Sun and enjoys daylight, while the opposite side is in darkness.

The length of daylight varies throughout the year. The longest day in the northern hemisphere falls on the summer solstice, 21 June, while the longest day in the southern hemisphere is on 22 December. At 40° latitude, the length of daylight on the longest day is 14 hours, 30 minutes. At 60° latitude, daylight on that day lasts 18 hours, 30 minutes. On the shortest day, 22 December in the northern hemisphere and 21 June in the southern, daylight hours at 40° latitude total 9 hours and 9 minutes. At latitude 60°, daylight lasts only 5 hours, 30 minutes in the 24-hour period.

Tides are caused by the gravitational pull of the Moon and, to a lesser extent, the Sun on the waters in the world's oceans. Tides occur twice every 24 hours, 50 minutes – one complete orbit

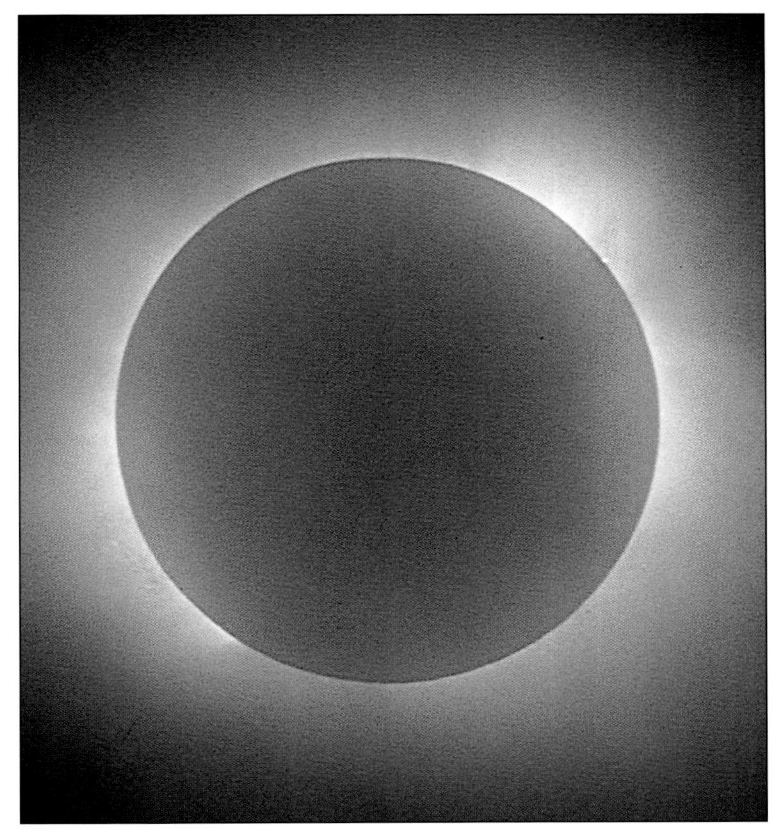

Total eclipse of the Sun

A total eclipse is caused when the Moon passes between the Sun and the Earth. With the Sun's bright disk completely obscured, the Sun's corona, or outer atmosphere, can be viewed.

of the Moon around the Earth.

The highest tides, the spring tides, occur when the Earth, Moon and Sun are in a straight line, so that the gravitational pulls of the Moon and Sun are combined. The lowest, or neap, tides occur when the Moon, Earth and Sun form a right angle. The gravitational pull of the Moon is then opposed by the gravitational pull of the Sun. The greatest tidal ranges occur in the Bay of Fundy in North America. The greatest mean spring range is 14.5 m [47.5 ft].

The speed at which the Earth is spinning on its axis is gradually slowing down, because of the movement of tides. As a result, experts have calculated that, in about 200 million years, the day will be 25 hours long.

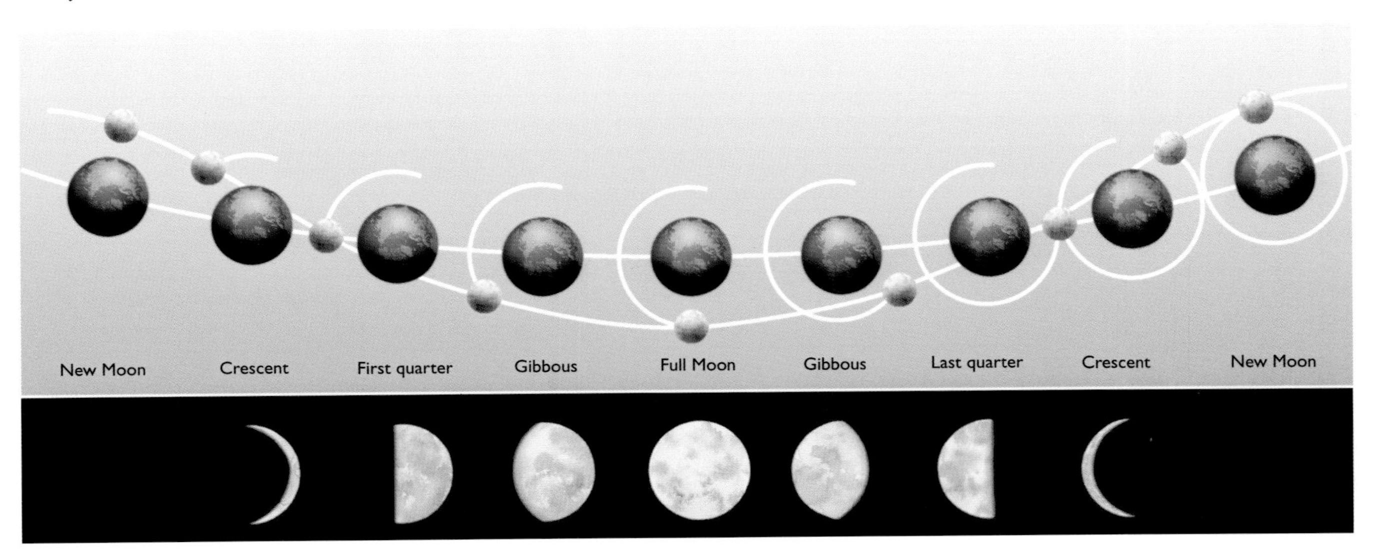

| New Moon | Crescent | First quarter | Gibbous | Full Moon | Gibbous | Last quarter | Crescent | New Moon |

The Earth from Space

Any last doubts about whether the Earth was round or flat were finally resolved by the appearance of the first photographs of our planet taken at the start of the Space Age. Satellite images also confirmed that map- and globe-makers had correctly worked out the shapes of the continents and the oceans.

More importantly, images of our beautiful, blue, white and brown planet from space impressed on many people that the Earth and its resources are finite. They made people realize that if we allow our planet to be damaged by such factors as overpopulation, pollution and irresponsible over-use of resources, then its future and the survival of all the living things upon it may be threatened.

VIEWS FROM ABOVE

The first aerial photographs were taken from balloons in the mid-19th century and their importance in military reconnaissance was recognized as early as the 1860s during the American Civil War.

Launch of the Space Shuttle Atlantis

Space Shuttles transport astronauts and equipment into orbit around the Earth. The American Space Shuttle Atlantis, *shown below, launched the Magellan probe, which undertook a radar mapping programme of the surface of Venus in the early 1990s.*

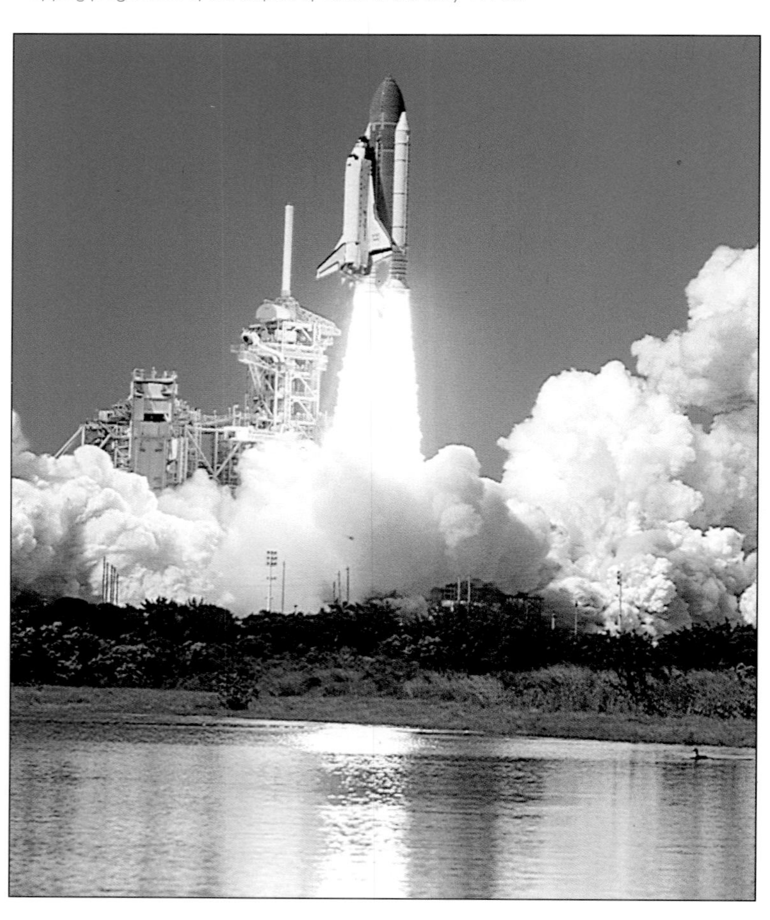

Since the end of World War II, photographs taken by aircraft have been widely used in map-making. The use of air photographs has greatly speeded up the laborious process of mapping land details and they have enabled cartographers to produce maps of the most remote parts of the world.

Aerial photographs have also proved useful because they reveal features that are not visible at ground level. For example, circles that appear on many air photographs do not correspond to visible features on the ground. Many of these mysterious shapes have turned out to be the sites of ancient settlements previously unknown to archaeologists.

IMAGES FROM SPACE

Space probes equipped with cameras and a variety of remote sensing instruments have sent back images of distant planets and moons. From these images, detailed maps have been produced, rapidly expanding our knowledge of the Solar System.

Photographs from space are also proving invaluable in the study of the Earth. One of the best known uses of space imagery is the study of the atmosphere. Polar-orbiting weather satellites that circle the Earth, together with geostationary satellites, whose motion is synchronized with the Earth's rotation, now regularly transmit images showing the changing patterns of weather systems from above. Forecasters use these images to track the development and the paths taken by hurricanes, enabling them to issue storm warnings to endangered areas, saving lives and reducing damage to property.

Remote sensing devices are now monitoring changes in temperatures over the land and sea, while photographs indicate the melting of ice sheets. Such evidence is vital in the study of global warming. Other devices reveal polluted areas, patterns of vegetation growth, and areas suffering deforestation.

In recent years, remote sensing devices have been used to monitor the damage being done to the ozone layer in the stratosphere, which prevents most of the Sun's harmful ultraviolet radiation from reaching the surface. The discovery of 'ozone holes', where the protective layer of ozone is being thinned by chlorofluorocarbons (CFCs), chemicals used in the manufacture of such things as air conditioners and refrigerators, has enabled governments to take concerted action to save our planet from imminent danger.

EARTH DATA

MAXIMUM DISTANCE FROM SUN (APHELION)
152,007,016 km

MINIMUM DISTANCE FROM SUN (PERIHELION)
147,000,830 km

LENGTH OF YEAR – SOLAR TROPICAL (EQUINOX TO EQUINOX)
365.24 days

LENGTH OF YEAR – SIDEREAL (FIXED STAR TO FIXED STAR)
365.26 days

LENGTH OF DAY – MEAN SOLAR DAY
24 hours, 03 minutes, 56 seconds

LENGTH OF DAY – MEAN SIDEREAL DAY
23 hours, 56 minutes, 4 seconds

SUPERFICIAL AREA
510,000,000 km²

LAND SURFACE
149,000,000 km² (29.3%)

WATER SURFACE
361,000,000 km² (70.7%)

EQUATORIAL CIRCUMFERENCE
40,077 km

POLAR CIRCUMFERENCE
40,009 km

EQUATORIAL DIAMETER
12,756.8 km

POLAR DIAMETER
12,713.8 km

EQUATORIAL RADIUS
6,378.4 km

POLAR RADIUS
6,356.9 km

VOLUME OF THE EARTH
1,083,230 × 10⁶ km³

MASS OF THE EARTH
5.9 × 10²¹ tonnes

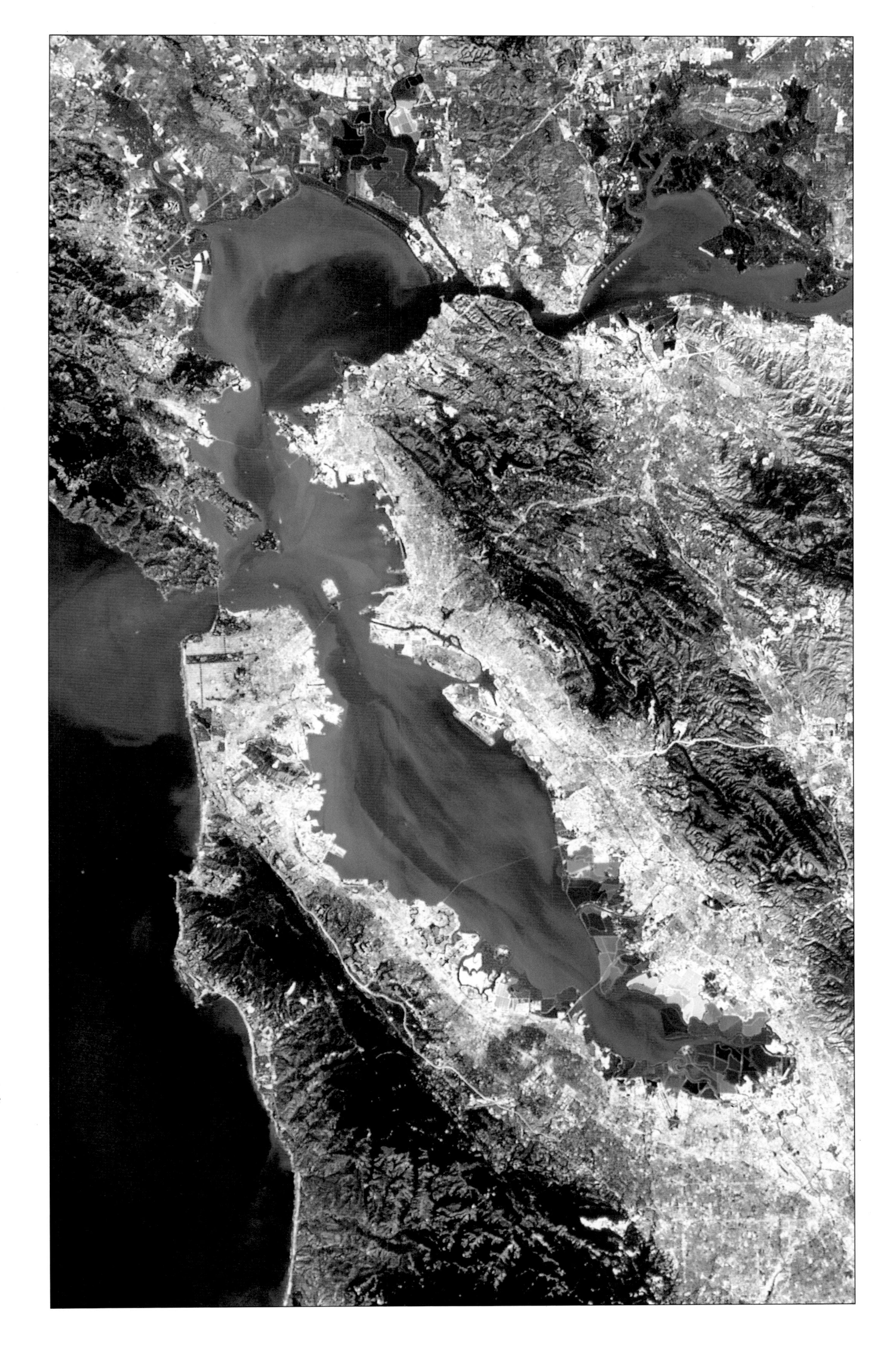

Satellite image of San Francisco Bay

Unmanned scientific satellites called ERTS (Earth Resources Technology Satellites), *or* Landsats, *were designed to collect information about the Earth's resources. The satellites transmitted images of the land using different wavelengths of light in order to identify, in false colours, such subtle features as areas that contain minerals or areas covered with growing crops, that are not identifiable on simple photographs using the visible range of the spectrum. They were also equipped to monitor conditions in the atmosphere and oceans, and also to detect pollution levels. This* Landsat *image of San Francisco Bay covers an area of great interest to geologists because it lies in an earthquake zone in the path of the San Andreas fault.*

The Dynamic Earth

The Earth was formed about 4.6 billion years [4,600 million years] ago from the ring of gas and dust left over after the formation of the Sun. As the Earth took shape, lighter elements, such as silicon, rose to the surface, while heavy elements, notably iron, sank towards the centre.

Gradually, the outer layers cooled to form a hard crust. The crust enclosed the dense mantle which, in turn, surrounded the even denser liquid outer and solid inner core. Around the Earth was an atmosphere, which contained abundant water

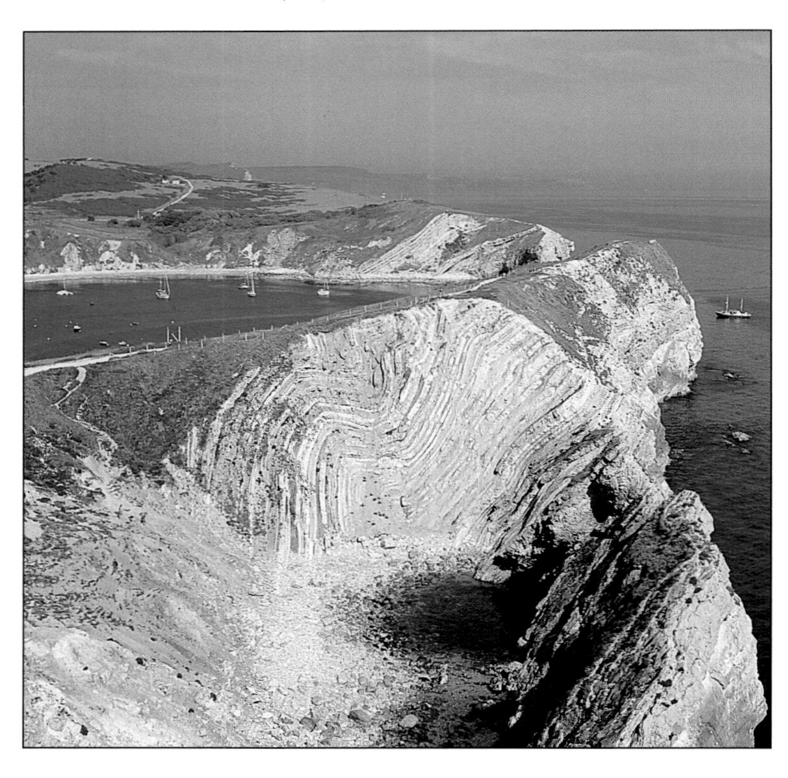

Lulworth Cove, southern England
When undisturbed by earth movements, sedimentary rock strata are generally horizontal. But lateral pressure has squeezed the Jurassic strata at Lulworth Cove into complex folds.

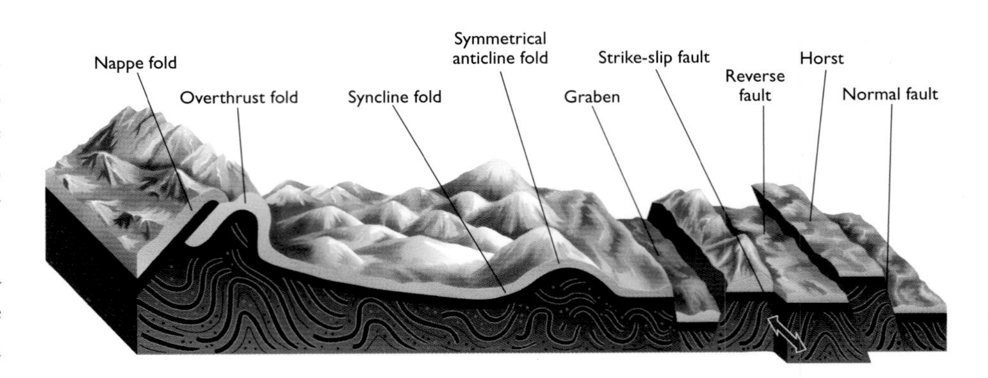

vapour. When the surface cooled, rainwater began to fill hollows, forming the first lakes and seas. Since that time, our planet has been subject to constant change – the result of powerful internal and external forces that still operate today.

THE HISTORY OF THE EARTH

From their study of rocks, geologists have pieced together the history of our planet and the life forms that evolved upon it. They have dated the oldest known crystals, composed of the mineral zircon, at 4.2 billion years. But the oldest rocks are younger, less than 4 billion years old. This is because older rocks have been weathered away by natural processes.

The oldest rocks that contain fossils, which are

evidence of once-living organisms, are around 3.5 billion years old. But fossils are rare in rocks formed in the first 4 billion years of Earth history. This vast expanse of time is called the Precambrian. This is because it precedes the Cambrian period, at the start of which, about 590 million years ago, life was abundant in the seas.

The Cambrian is the first period in the Paleozoic (or ancient life) era. The Paleozoic era is followed by the Mesozoic (middle life) era, which witnessed the spectacular rise and fall of the dinosaurs, and the Cenozoic (recent life) era, which was dominated by the evolution of mammals. Each of the eras is divided into periods, and the periods in the Cenozoic era, covering the last 65 million years, are further divided into epochs.

THE EARTH'S CHANGING FACE

While life was gradually evolving, the face of the Earth was constantly changing. By piecing together evidence of rock structures and fossils, geologists have demonstrated that around 250 million years ago, all the world's land areas were grouped together in one huge landmass called Pangaea. Around 180 million years ago, the supercontinent Pangaea, began to break up. New oceans opened up as the continents began to move towards their present positions.

Evidence of how continents drift came from studies of the ocean floor in the 1950s and 1960s. Scientists discovered that the oceans are young features. By contrast with the continents, no part of the ocean floor is more than 200 million years old. The floors of oceans older than 200 million years have completely vanished.

Studies of long undersea ranges, called ocean ridges, revealed that the youngest rocks occur along their centres, which are the edges of huge plates – rigid blocks of the Earth's lithosphere, which is made up of the crust and the solid upper layer of the mantle. The Earth's lithosphere is split into six large and several smaller

Mountain building
Lateral pressure, which occurs when plates collide, squeezes and compresses rocks into folds. Simple symmetrical upfolds are called anticlines, while downfolds are synclines. As the pressure builds up, strata become asymmetrical and they may be tilted over to form recumbent folds. The rocks often crack under the intense pressure and the folds are sheared away and pushed forward over other rocks. These features are called overthrust folds or nappes. Plate movements also create faults along which rocks move upwards, downwards and sideways. The diagram shows a downfaulted graben, or rift valley, and an uplifted horst, or block mountain.

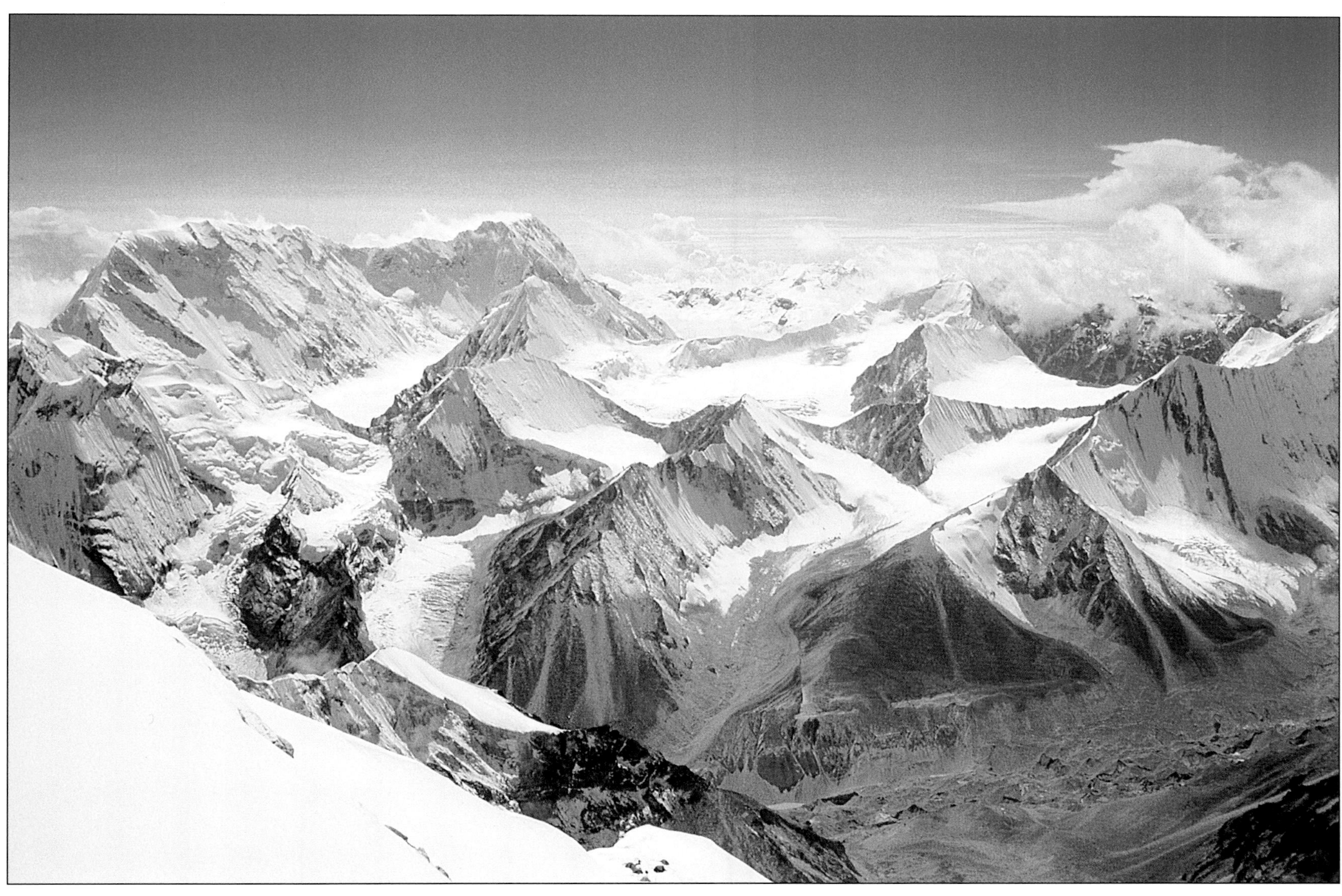

The Himalayas seen from Nepal
The Himalayas are a young fold mountain range formed by a collision between two plates. The earthquakes felt in the region testify that the plate movements are still continuing.

Geological time scale
The geological time scale was first constructed by a study of the stratigraphic, or relative, ages of layers of rock. But the absolute ages of rock strata could not be fixed until the discovery of radioactivity in the early 20th century. Some names of periods, such as Cambrian (Latin for Wales), come from places where the rocks were first studied. Others, such as Carboniferous, refer to the nature of the rocks formed during the period. For example, coal seams (containing carbon) were formed from decayed plant matter during the Carboniferous period.

plates. The ocean ridges are 'constructive' plate margins, because new crustal rock is being formed there from magma that wells up from the mantle as the plates gradually move apart. By contrast, the deep ocean trenches are 'destructive' plate edges. Here, two plates are pushing against each other and one plate is descending beneath the other into the mantle where it is melted and destroyed. Geologists call these areas subduction zones.

A third type of plate edge is called a transform fault. Here two plates are moving alongside each other. The best known of these plate edges is the San Andreas fault in California, which separates the Pacific plate from the North American plate.

Slow-moving currents in the partly molten asthenosphere, which underlies the solid lithosphere, are responsible for moving the plates, a process called plate tectonics.

MOUNTAIN BUILDING

The study of plate tectonics has helped geologists to understand the mechanisms that are responsible for the creation of mountains. Many of the world's greatest ranges were created by the collision of two plates and the bending of the intervening strata into huge loops, or folds. For example, the Himalayas began to rise around 50 million years ago, when a plate supporting India collided with the huge Eurasian plate. Rocks on the floor of the intervening and long-vanished Tethys Sea were squeezed up to form the Himalayan Mountain Range.

Plate movements also create tension that cracks rocks, producing long faults along which rocks move upwards, downwards or sideways. Block mountains are formed when blocks of rock are pushed upwards along faults. Steep-sided rift valleys are formed when blocks of land sink down between faults. For example, the basin and range region of the south-western United States has both block mountains and down-faulted basins, such as Death Valley.

Pre-Cambrian	Lower		Paleozoic (Primary)				Upper	Mesozoic (Secondary)			Cenozoic (Tertiary, Quaternary)					Era
Pre-Cambrian	Cambrian	Ordovician	Silurian	Devonian	Carboniferous	Permian	Triassic	Jurassic	Cretaceous	Paleocene	Eocene	Oligocene	Miocene Pliocene	Quaternary		System
			CALEDONIAN FOLDING		HERCYNIAN FOLDING					LARAMIDE FOLDING	ALPINE FOLDING					Orogeny
600	550	500	450	400	350	300	250	200	150	100	50					

Millions of years before present

Earthquakes and Volcanoes

On 26 January, 2001, an earthquake rocked north-west India and south-east Pakistan. Bhuj, in Gujarat state, suffered the worst damage. The death toll was more than 14,000, and the 'quake was felt as far away as Karachi, Delhi and Mumbai. Earlier that month, an earthquake had struck El Salvador in Central America. Around 1,200 people died, 750 of them being buried by mudslides.

THE RESTLESS EARTH

Earthquakes can occur anywhere, whenever rocks move along faults. But the most severe and most numerous earthquakes occur near the edges of the plates that make up the Earth's lithosphere. Japan, for example, lies in a particularly unstable region above subduction zones, where plates are descending into the Earth's mantle. It lies in a zone encircling the Pacific Ocean, called the 'Pacific ring of fire'.

Plates do not move smoothly. Their edges are jagged and for most of the time they are locked together. However, pressure gradually builds up until the rocks break and the plates lurch forward, setting off vibrations ranging from slight tremors to terrifying earthquakes. The greater the pressure released, the more destructive the earthquake.

Earthquakes are also common along the ocean trenches where plates are moving apart, but they mostly occur so far from land that they do little damage. Far more destructive are the earthquakes that occur where plates are moving alongside each other. For example, the earthquakes that periodically rock south-western California are caused by movements along the San Andreas Fault.

The spot where an earthquake originates is called the focus, while the point on the Earth's surface directly above the focus is called the epicentre. Two kinds of waves, P-waves or compressional waves and S-waves or shear waves, travel from the focus to the surface where they make the ground shake. P-waves travel faster than S-waves and the time difference between their arrival at recording stations enables scientists to calculate the distance from a station to the epicentre.

Earthquakes are measured on the Richter scale, which indicates the magnitude of the shock. The most destructive earthquakes are shallow-focus, that is, the focus is within 60 km [37 miles] of the surface. A magnitude of 7.0 is a major earthquake, but earthquakes with a somewhat lower magnitude can cause tremendous damage if their epicentres are on or close to densely populated areas.

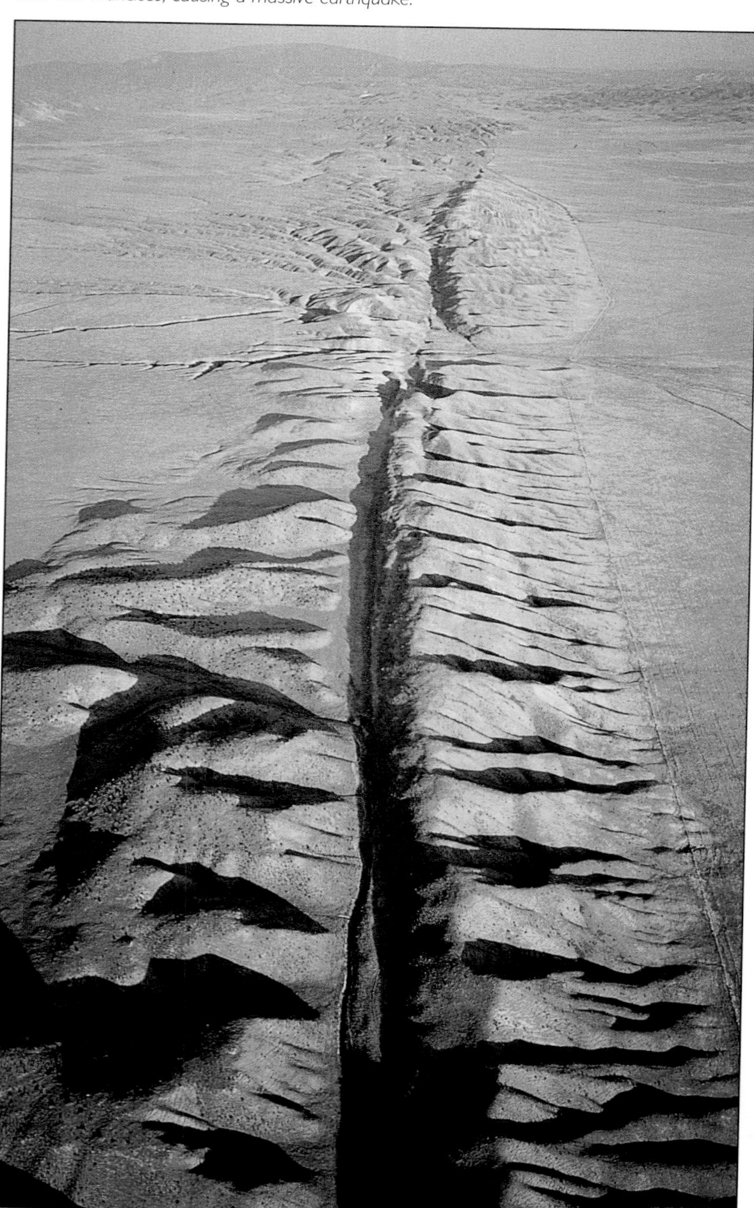

San Andreas Fault, United States
Geologists call the San Andreas fault in south-western California a transform, or strike-slip, fault. Sudden movements along it cause earthquakes. In 1906, shifts of about 4.5 metres [15 ft] occurred near San Francisco, causing a massive earthquake.

NOTABLE EARTHQUAKES *(since 1900)*

Year	Location	Mag.
1906	San Francisco, USA	8.3
1906	Valparaiso, Chile	8.6
1908	Messina, Italy	7.5
1915	Avezzano, Italy	7.5
1920	Gansu, China	8.6
1923	Yokohama, Japan	8.3
1927	Nan Shan, China	8.3
1932	Gansu, China	7.6
1934	Bihar, India/Nepal	8.4
1935	Quetta, India†	7.5
1939	Chillan, Chile	8.3
1939	Erzincan, Turkey	7.9
1964	Anchorage, Alaska	8.4
1968	N. E. Iran	7.4
1970	N. Peru	7.7
1976	Guatemala	7.5
1976	Tangshan, China	8.2
1978	Tabas, Iran	7.7
1980	El Asnam, Algeria	7.3
1980	S. Italy	7.2
1985	Mexico City, Mexico	8.1
1988	N. W. Armenia	6.8
1990	N. Iran	7.7
1993	Maharashtra, India	6.4
1994	Los Angeles, USA	6.6
1995	Kobe, Japan	7.2
1995	Sakhalin Is., Russia	7.5
1996	Yunnan, China	7.0
1997	N. E. Iran	7.1
1998	N. Afghanistan	6.1
1998	N. E. Afghanistan	7.0
1999	Izmit, Turkey	7.4
1999	Taipei, Taiwan	7.6
2001	El Salvador	7.7
2001	Gujarat, India	7.7
2002	Afyon, Turkey	6.0
2002	N. Afghanistan	5.2

† *now Pakistan*

Earthquakes in subduction zones
Along subduction zones, one plate is descending beneath another. The plates are locked together until the rocks break and the descending plate lurches forwards. From the point where the plate moves – the origin – seismic waves spread through the lithosphere, making the ground shake. The earthquake in Mexico City in 1985 occurred in this way.

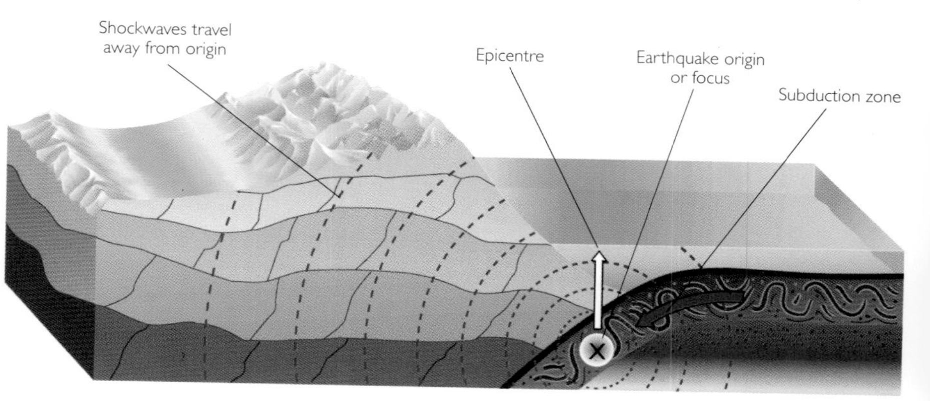

Shockwaves travel away from origin

Epicentre

Earthquake origin or focus

Subduction zone

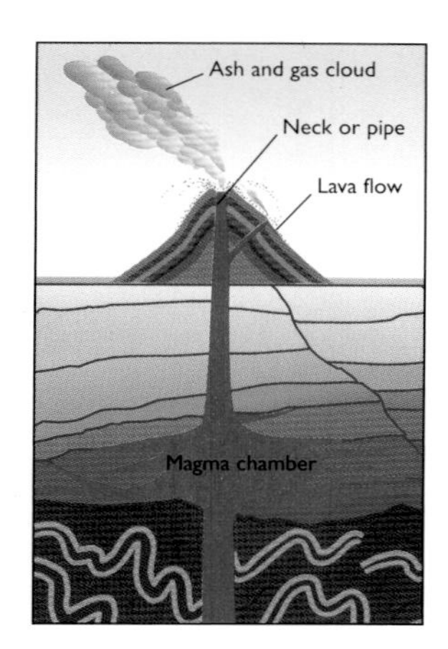

Cross-section of a volcano
Volcanoes are vents in the ground, through which magma reaches the surface. The term volcano is also used for the mountains formed from volcanic rocks. Beneath volcanoes are pockets of magma derived from the semi-molten asthenosphere in the mantle. The magma rises under pressure through the overlying rocks until it reaches the surface. There it emerges through vents as pyroclasts, ranging in size from large lumps of magma, called volcanic bombs, to fine volcanic ash and dust. In quiet eruptions, streams of liquid lava run down the side of the mountain. Side vents sometimes appear on the flanks of existing volcanoes.

Scientists have been working for years to find effective ways of forecasting earthquakes but with very limited success. Following the Kobe earthquake in 1995, many experts argued that they would be better employed developing techniques of reducing the damage caused by earthquakes, rather than pursuing an apparently vain attempt to predict them.

VOLCANIC ERUPTIONS

Most active volcanoes also occur on or near plate edges. Many undersea volcanoes along the ocean ridges are formed from magma that wells up from the asthenosphere to fill the gaps created as the plates, on the opposite sides of the ridges, move apart. Some of these volcanoes reach the surface to form islands. Iceland is a country which straddles the Mid-Atlantic Ocean Ridge. It is gradually becoming wider as magma rises to the surface through faults and vents. Other volcanoes lie alongside subduction zones. The magma that fuels them comes from the melted edges of the descending plates.

A few volcanoes lie far from plate edges. For example, Mauna Loa and Kilauea on Hawaii are situated near the centre of the huge Pacific plate. The molten magma that reaches the surface is created by a source of heat, called a 'hot spot', in the Earth's mantle.

Magma is molten rock at temperatures of about 1,100°C to 1,200°C [2,012°F to 2,192°F]. It contains gases and superheated steam. The chemical composition of magma varies. Viscous magma is rich in silica and superheated steam, while runny magma contains less silica and steam. The chemical composition of the magma affects the nature of volcanic eruptions.

Explosive volcanoes contain thick, viscous magma. When they erupt, they usually hurl clouds of ash (shattered fragments of cooled magma) into the air. By contrast, quiet volcanoes emit long streams of runny magma, or lava. However, many volcanoes are intermediate in type, sometimes erupting explosively and sometimes emitting streams of fluid lava. Explosive and intermediate volcanoes usually have a conical shape, while quiet volcanoes are flattened, resembling upturned saucers. They are often called shield volcanoes.

One dangerous type of eruption is called a *nuée ardente*, or 'glowing cloud'. It occurs when a cloud of intensely hot volcanic gases and dust particles and superheated steam are exploded from a volcano. They move rapidly downhill, burning everything in their path and choking animals and people. The blast that creates the *nuée ardente* may release the pressure inside the volcano, resulting in a tremendous explosion that hurls tall columns of ash into the air.

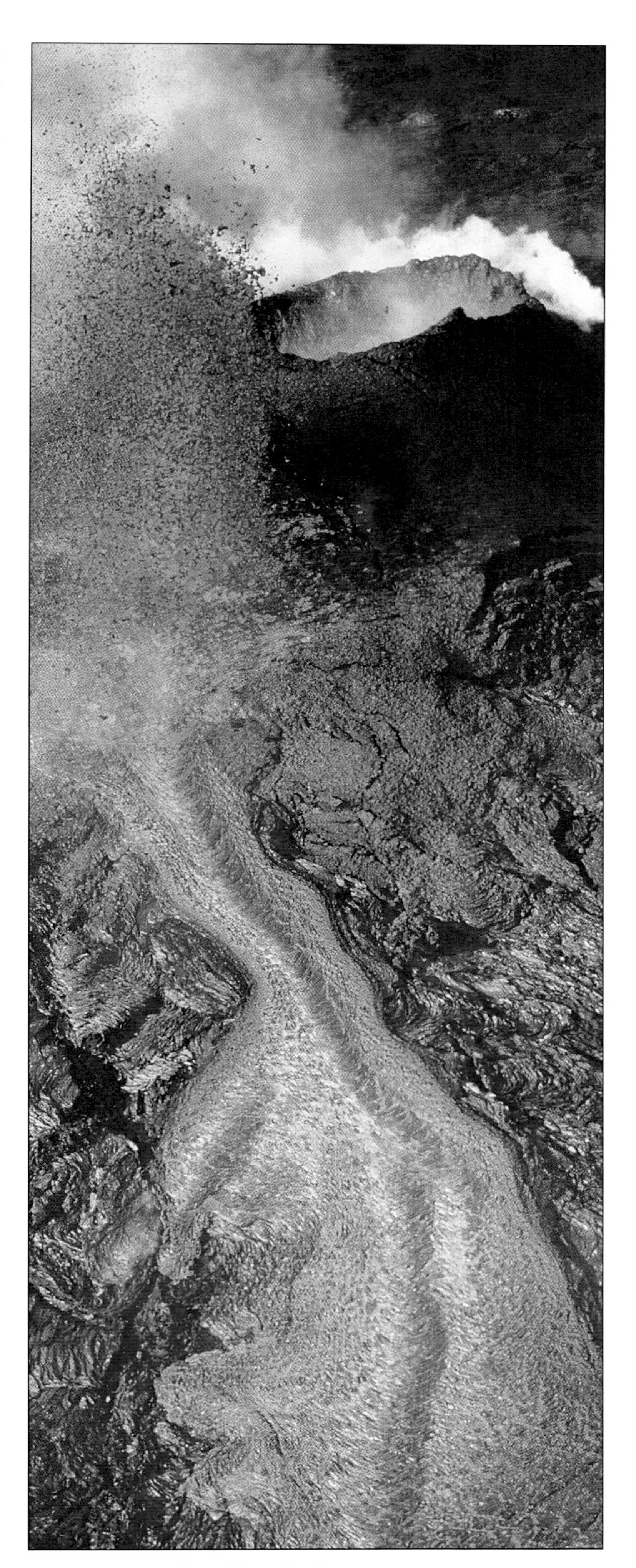

Kilauea Volcano, Hawaii
The volcanic Hawaiian islands in the North Pacific Ocean were formed as the Pacific plate moved over a 'hot spot' in the Earth's mantle. Kilauea on Hawaii emits blazing streams of liquid lava.

Forces of Nature

When the volcano Mount Pinatubo erupted in the Philippines in 1991, loose ash covered large areas around the mountain. During the 1990s and early 2000s, rainwater mixed with the ash on sloping land, creating *lahars*, or mudflows, which swept down river valleys burying many areas. Such incidents are not only reminders of the great forces that operate inside our planet but also of those natural forces operating on the surface, which can have dramatic effects on the land.

The chief forces acting on the surface of the Earth are weathering, running water, ice and winds. The forces of erosion seem to act slowly. One estimate suggests that an average of only 3.5 cm [1.4 in] of land is removed by natural processes every 1,000 years. This may not sound much, but over millions of years, it can reduce mountains to almost flat surfaces.

WEATHERING

Weathering occurs in all parts of the world, but the most effective type of weathering in any area depends on the climate and the nature of the rocks. For example, in cold mountain areas,

RATES OF EROSION

	SLOW ⟵	**WEATHERING RATE**	⟶ FAST
Mineral solubility	low (e.g. quartz)	moderate (e.g. feldspar)	high (e.g. calcite)
Rainfall	low	moderate	heavy
Temperature	cold	temperate	hot
Vegetation	sparse	moderate	lush
Soil cover	bare rock	thin to moderate soil	thick soil

Weathering is the breakdown and decay of rocks in situ. It may be mechanical (physical), chemical or biological.

when water freezes in cracks in rocks, the ice occupies 9% more space than the water. This exerts a force which, when repeated over and over again, can split boulders apart. By contrast, in hot deserts, intense heating by day and cooling by night causes the outer layers of rocks to expand and contract until they break up and peel away like layers of an onion. These are examples of what is called mechanical weathering.

Other kinds of weathering include chemical reactions usually involving water. Rainwater containing carbon dioxide dissolved from the air or the soil is a weak acid which reacts with limestone, wearing out pits, tunnels and networks of caves in layers of limestone rock. Water also combines with some minerals, such as the feldspars in granite, to create kaolin, a white

Rates of erosion

The chart shows that the rates at which weathering takes place depend on the chemistry and hardness of rocks, climatic factors, especially rainfall and temperature, the vegetation and the nature of the soil cover in any area. The effects of weathering are increased by human action, particularly the removal of vegetation and the exposure of soils to the rain and wind.

Grand Canyon, Arizona, at dusk

The Grand Canyon in the United States is one of the world's natural wonders. Eroded by the Colorado River and its tributaries, it is up to 1.6 km [1 mile] deep and 29 km [18 miles] wide.

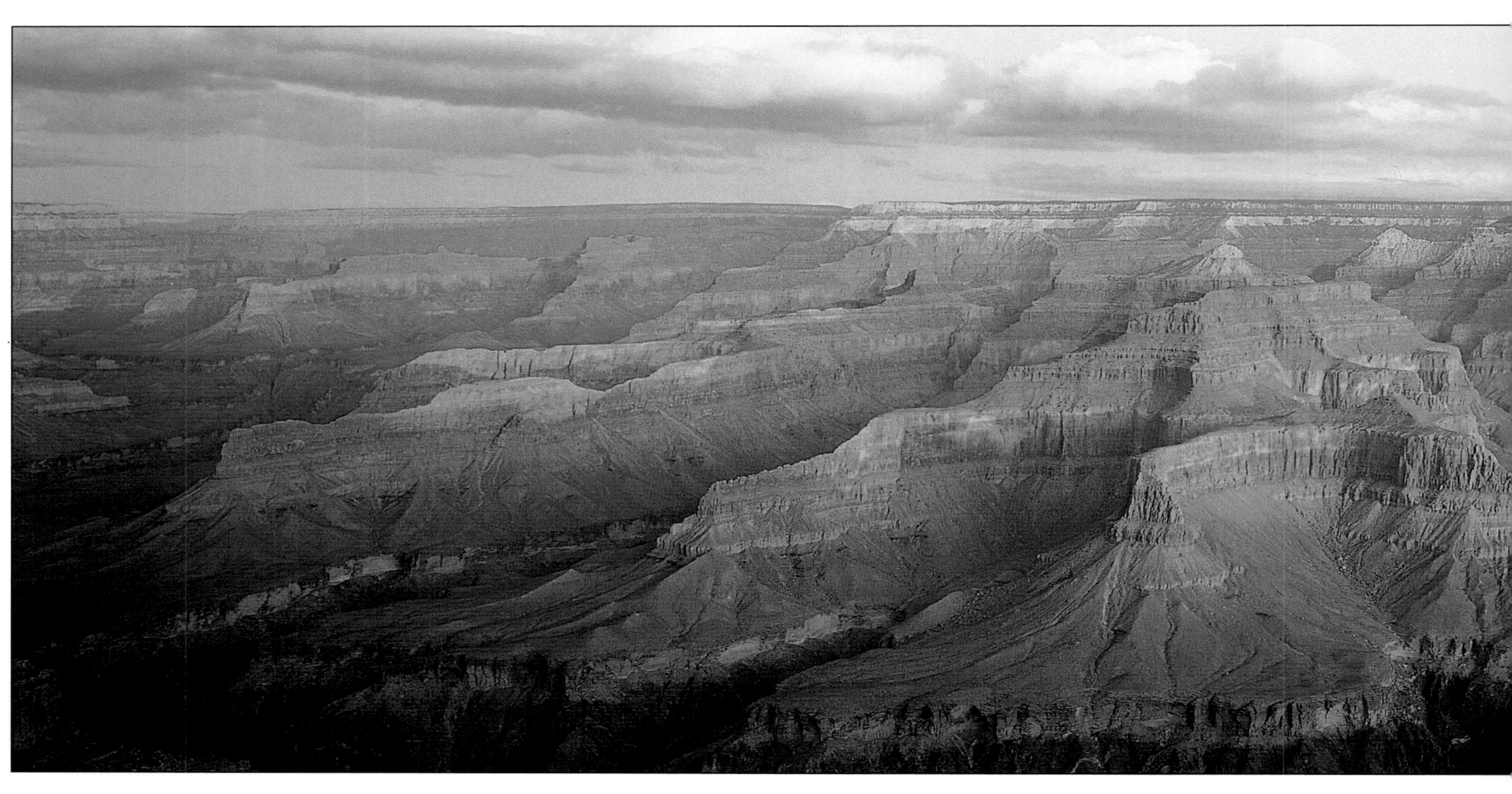

clay. These are examples of chemical weathering which constantly wears away rock.

RUNNING WATER, ICE AND WIND

In moist regions, rivers are effective in shaping the land. They transport material worn away by weathering and erode the land. They wear out V-shaped valleys in upland regions, while vigorous meanders widen their middle courses. The work of rivers is at its most spectacular when earth movements lift up flat areas and rejuvenate the rivers, giving them a new erosive power capable of wearing out such features as the Grand Canyon. Rivers also have a constructive role. Some of the world's most fertile regions are deltas and flood plains composed of sediments

Glaciers

During Ice Ages, ice spreads over large areas but, during warm periods, the ice retreats. The chart shows that the volume of ice in many glaciers is decreasing, possibly as a result of global warming. Experts estimate that, between 1850 and the early 21st century, more than half of the ice in Alpine glaciers has melted.

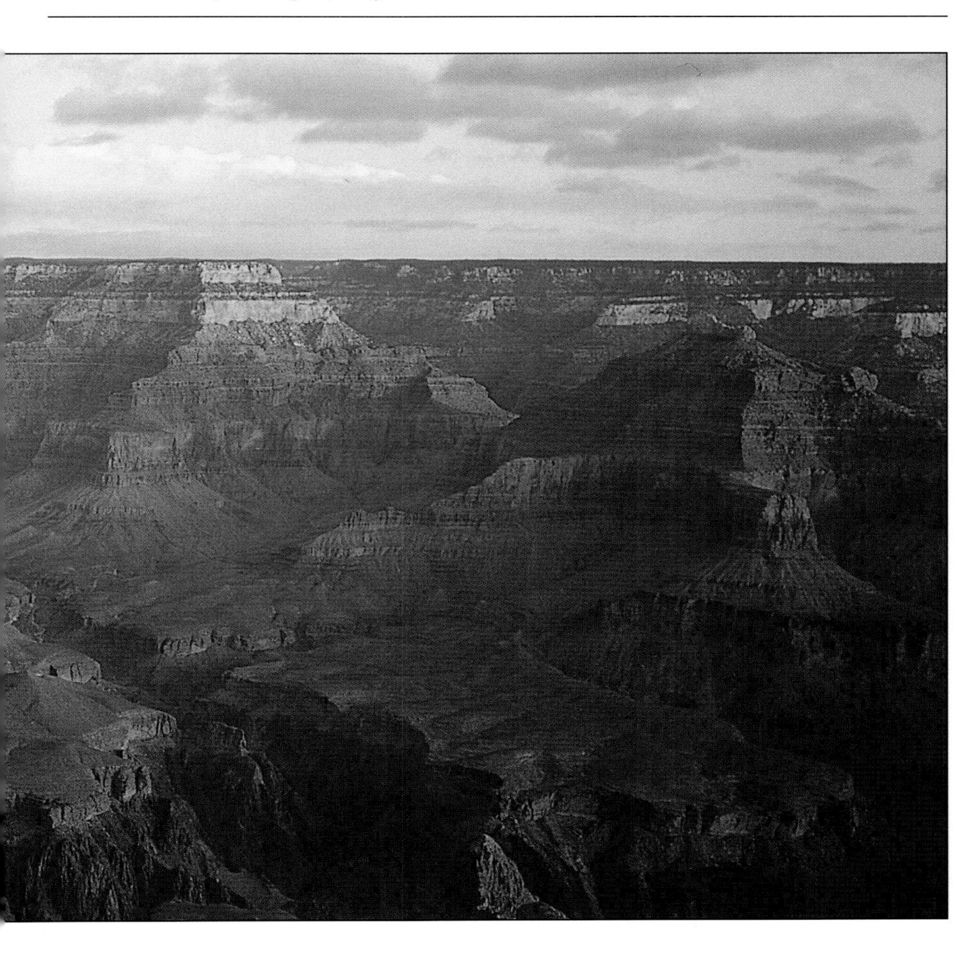

Juneau Glacier, Alaska
Like huge conveyor belts, glaciers transport weathered debris from mountain regions. Rocks frozen in the ice give the glaciers teeth, enabling them to wear out typical glaciated land features.

ANNUAL FLUCTUATIONS FOR SELECTED GLACIERS

Glacier name and location	Changes in the annual mass balance†		Cumulative total
	1970–1	1990–1	1970–90
Alfotbreen, Norway	+940	+790	+12,110
Wolverine, USA	+770	–410	+2,320
Storglaciaren, Sweden	–190	+170	–120
Djankuat, Russia	–230	–310	–1,890
Grasubreen, Norway	+470	–520	–2,530
Ürümqi, China	+102	–706	–3,828
Golubin, Kyrgyzstan	–90	–722	–7,105
Hintereisferner, Austria	–600	–1,325	–9,081
Gries, Switzerland	–970	–1,480	–10,600
Careser, Italy	–650	–1,730	–11,610
Abramov, Tajikistan	–890	–420	–13,700
Sarennes, France	–1,100	–1,360	–15,020
Place, Canada	–343	–990	–15,175

† *The annual mass balance is defined as the difference between glacier accumulation and ablation (melting) averaged over the whole glacier. Balances are expressed as water equivalent in millimetres. A plus indicates an increase in the depth or length of the glacier; a minus indicates a reduction.*

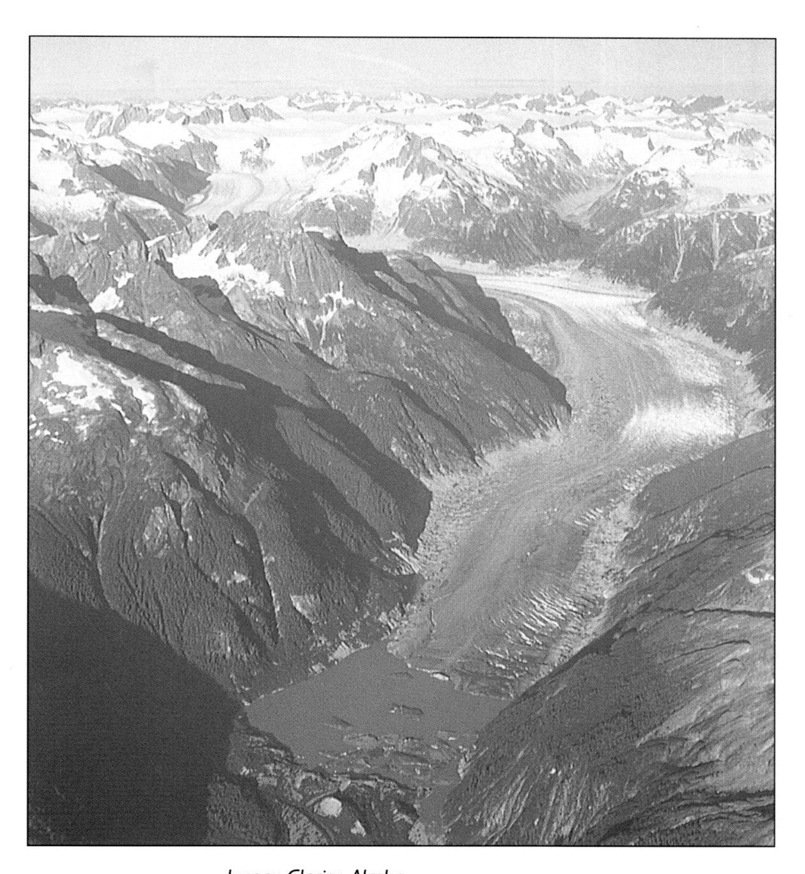

periodically dumped there by such rivers as the Ganges, Mississippi and Nile.

Running water in the form of sea waves and currents shapes coastlines, wearing out caves, natural arches, and stacks. The sea also transports and deposits worn material to form such features as spits and bars.

Glaciers in cold mountain regions flow downhill, gradually deepening valleys and shaping dramatic landscapes. They erode steep-sided U-shaped valleys, into which rivers often plunge in large waterfalls. Other features include cirques, armchair-shaped basins bounded by knife-edged ridges called *arêtes*. When several glacial cirques erode to form radial *arêtes*, pyramidal peaks like the Matterhorn are created. Deposits of moraine, rock material dumped by the glacier, are further evidence that ice once covered large areas. The work of glaciers, like other agents of erosion, varies with the climate. In recent years, global warming has been making glaciers retreat in many areas, while several of the ice shelves in Antarctica have been breaking up.

Many land features in deserts were formed by running water at a time when the climate was much rainier than it is today. Water erosion also occurs when flash floods are caused by rare thunderstorms. But the chief agent of erosion in dry areas is wind-blown sand, which can strip the paint from cars, and undercut boulders to create mushroom-shaped rocks.

Oceans and Ice

Since the 1970s, oceanographers have found numerous hot vents on the ocean ridges. Called black smokers, the vents emit dark, mineral-rich water reaching 350°C [662°F]. Around the vents are chimney-like structures formed from minerals deposited from the hot water. The discovery of black smokers did not surprise scientists who already knew that the ridges were plate edges, where new crustal rock was being formed as molten magma welled up to the surface. But what was astonishing was that the hot water contained vast numbers of bacteria, which provided the base of a food chain that included many strange creatures, such as giant worms, eyeless shrimps and white clams. Many species were unknown to science.

Little was known about the dark world beneath the waves until about 50 years ago. But through the use of modern technology such as echo-sounders, magnetometers, research ships equipped with huge drills, submersibles that can carry scientists down to the ocean floor, and satellites, the secrets of the oceans have been gradually revealed.

The study of the ocean floor led to the discovery that the oceans are geologically young features – no more than 200 million years old. It also revealed evidence as to how oceans form and continents drift because of the action of plate tectonics.

THE BLUE PLANET

Water covers almost 71% of the Earth, which makes it look blue when viewed from space. Although the oceans are interconnected, geographers divide them into four main areas: the Pacific, Atlantic, Indian and Arctic oceans. The average depth of the oceans is 3,370 m [12,238 ft], but they are divided into several zones.

Around most continents are gently sloping continental shelves, which are flooded parts of the continents. The shelves end at the continental slope, at a depth of about 200 m [656 ft]. This slope leads steeply down to the abyss. The deepest parts of the oceans are the trenches, which reach a maximum depth of 11,033 m [36,198 ft] in the Mariana Trench in the western Pacific.

Most marine life is found in the top 200 m [656 ft], where there is sufficient sunlight for plants, called phytoplankton, to grow. Below this zone, life becomes more and more scarce, though no part of the ocean, even at the bottom of the deepest trenches, is completely without living things.

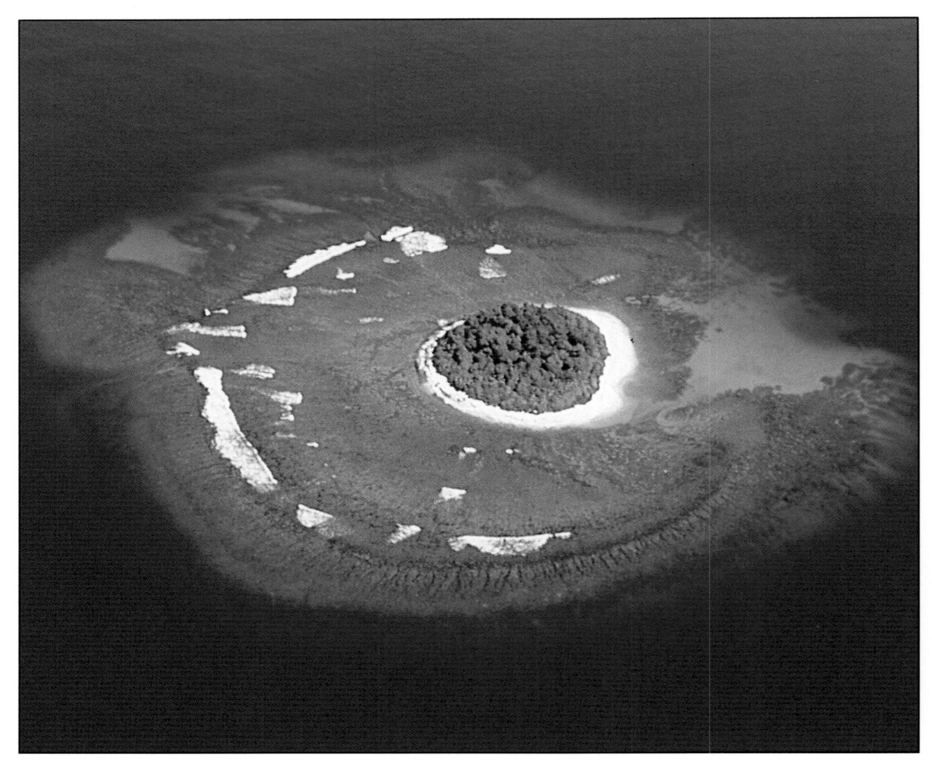

Vava'u Island, Tonga
This small coral atoll in northern Tonga consists of a central island covered by rainforest. Low coral reefs washed by the waves surround a shallow central lagoon.

Continental islands, such as the British Isles, are high parts of the continental shelves. For example, until about 7,500 years ago, when the ice sheets formed during the Ice Ages were melting, raising the sea level and filling the North Sea and the Strait of Dover, Britain was linked to mainland Europe.

By contrast, oceanic islands, such as the Hawaiian chain in the North Pacific Ocean, rise from the ocean floor. All oceanic islands are of volcanic origin, although many of them in warm parts of the oceans have sunk and are capped by layers of coral to form ring- or horseshoe-shaped atolls and coral reefs.

OCEAN WATER

The oceans contain about 97% of the world's water. Seawater contains more than 70 dissolved elements, but chloride and sodium make up 85% of the total. Sodium chloride is common salt and it makes seawater salty. The salinity of the oceans is mostly between 3.3–3.7%. Ocean water fed by icebergs or large rivers is less saline than shallow seas in the tropics, where the evaporation rate is high. Seawater is a source of salt but the water is useless for agriculture or drinking unless it is desalinated. However, land

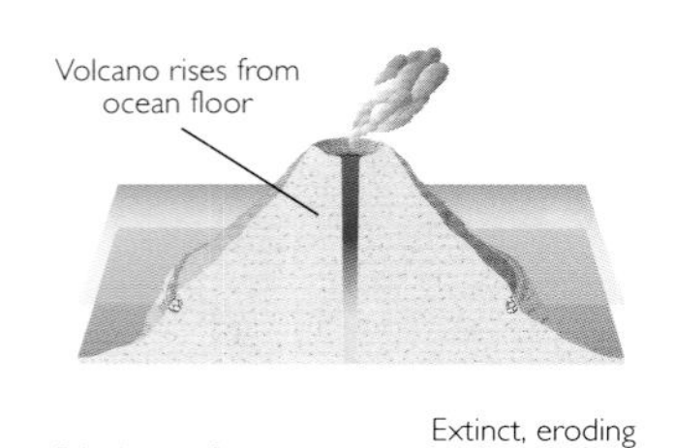

Volcano rises from ocean floor

Fringing reef

Extinct, eroding volcanic island

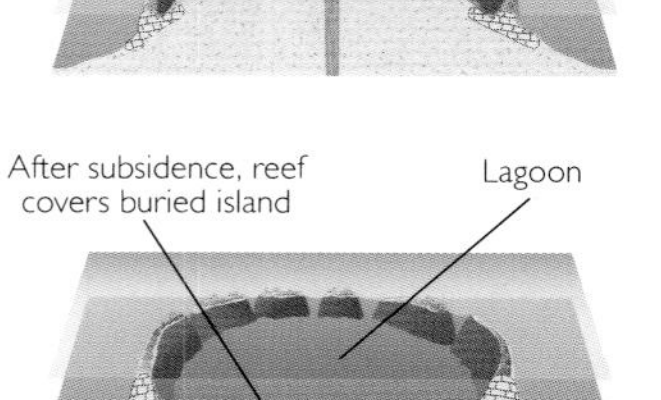

After subsidence, reef covers buried island

Lagoon

Development of an atoll
Some of the volcanoes that rise from the ocean floor reach the surface to form islands. Some of these islands subside and become submerged. As an island sinks, coral starts to grow around the rim of the volcano, building up layer upon layer of limestone deposits to form fringing reefs. Sometimes coral grows on the tip of a central cone to form an island in the middle of the atoll.

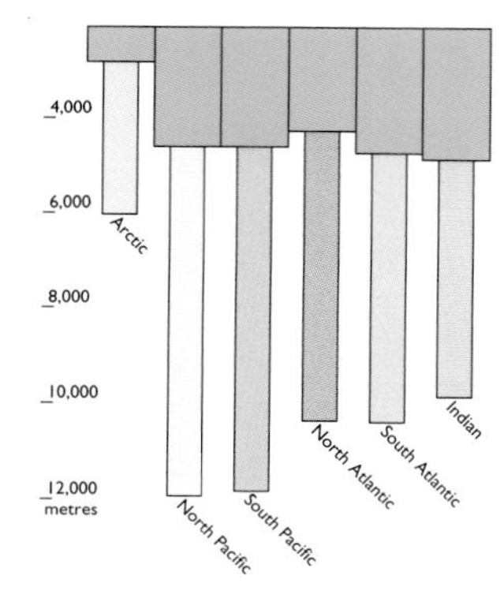

The ocean depths
The diagram shows the average depths (in dark blue) and the greatest depths in the four oceans. The North Pacific Ocean contains the world's deepest trenches, including the Mariana Trench, where the deepest manned descent was made by the bathyscaphe Trieste in 1960. It reached a depth of 10,916 metres [35,813 ft].

Relative sizes of the world's oceans:
PACIFIC 49%   ATLANTIC 26%
INDIAN 21%   ARCTIC 4%
Some geographers distinguish a fifth ocean, the Southern or Antarctic Ocean, but most authorities regard these waters as the southern extension of the Pacific, Atlantic and Indian oceans.

areas get a regular supply of fresh water through the hydrological cycle (see page 26).

The density of seawater depends on its salinity and temperature. Temperatures vary from –2°C [28°F], the freezing point of seawater at the poles, to around 30°C [86°F] in parts of the tropics. Density differences help to maintain the circulation of the world's oceans, especially deep-sea currents. But the main cause of currents within 350 m [1,148 ft] of the surface is the wind. Because of the Earth's rotation, currents are deflected, creating huge circular motions of surface water – clockwise in the northern hemisphere and anticlockwise in the southern hemisphere.

Ocean currents transport heat from the tropics to the polar regions and thus form part of the heat engine that drives the Earth's climates. Ocean currents have an especially marked effect on coastal climates, such as north-western Europe. In the mid-1990s, scientists warned that global warming may be weakening currents, including the warm Gulf Stream which is responsible for the mild winters experienced in north-western Europe.

ICE SHEETS, ICE CAPS AND GLACIERS
Global warming is also a threat to the world's ice sheets, ice caps and glaciers that together account for about 2% of the world's water. There are two ice sheets in the world, the largest covers most of Antarctica. With the ice reaching

maximum depths of 4,800 m [15,748 ft], the Antarctic ice sheet contains about 70% of the world's fresh water, with a total volume about nine times greater than the Greenland ice sheet. Smaller bodies of ice include ice caps in northern Canada, Iceland and Scandinavia. Also throughout the world in high ranges are many valley glaciers, which help to shape dramatic mountain scenery.

Only about 11,000 years ago, during the final phase of the Pleistocene Ice Age, ice covered much of the northern hemisphere. The Ice Age, which began about 1.8 million years ago, was not a continuous period of cold. Instead, it consisted of glacial periods when the ice advanced and warmer interglacial periods when temperatures rose and the ice retreated.

Some scientists believe that we are now living in an interglacial period, and that glacial conditions will recur in the future. Others fear that global warming, caused mainly by pollution, may melt the world's ice, raising sea levels by up to 55 m [180 ft]. Many fertile and densely populated coastal plains, islands and cities would vanish from the map.

Weddell Sea, Antarctica
Antarctica contains two huge bays, occupied by the Ross and Weddell seas. Ice shelves extend from the ice sheet across parts of these seas. Researchers fear that warmer weather is melting Antarctica's ice sheets at a dangerous rate, after large chunks of the Larsen ice shelf and the Ronne ice shelf broke away in 1997 and 1998 respectively. This was followed in March 2002 by the disintegration of the Larsen B ice shelf.

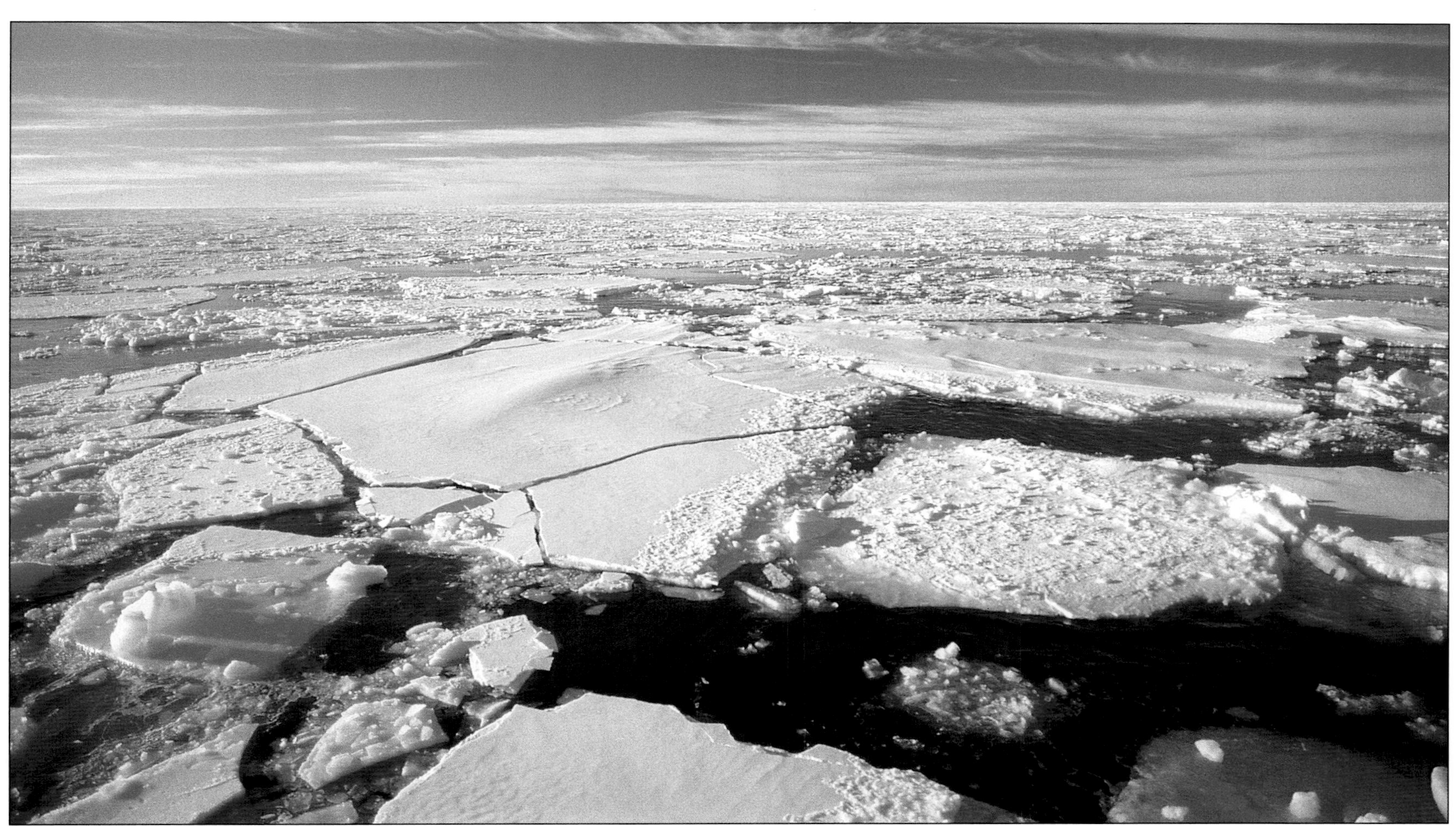

The Earth's Atmosphere

Since the discovery in 1985 of a thinning of the ozone layer, creating a so-called 'ozone hole', over Antarctica, many governments have worked to reduce the emissions of ozone-eating substances, notably the chlorofluorocarbons (CFCs) used in aerosols, refrigeration, air conditioning and dry cleaning.

Following forecasts that the ozone layer would rapidly repair itself as a result of controls on these emissions, scientists were surprised in early 1996 when a marked thinning of the ozone layer occurred over the Arctic, northern Europe, Russia and Canada. The damage, which was recorded as far south as southern Britain, was due to pollution combined with intense cold in the stratosphere. It was another sharp reminder of the dangers humanity faces when it interferes with and harms the environment.

The ozone layer in the stratosphere blocks out most of the dangerous ultraviolet B radiation in the Sun's rays. This radiation causes skin cancer and cataracts, as well as harming plants on the land and plankton in the oceans. The ozone layer is only one way in which the atmosphere protects life on Earth. The atmosphere also provides the air we breathe and the carbon dioxide required by plants. It is also a shield against meteors and it acts as a blanket to prevent heat radiated from the Earth escaping into space.

LAYERS OF AIR
The atmosphere is divided into four main layers. The troposphere at the bottom contains about 85% of the atmosphere's total mass, where most weather conditions occur. The troposphere is about 15 km [9 miles] thick over the Equator and 8 km [5 miles] thick at the poles. Temperatures decrease with height by approximately 1°C [2°F] for every 100 m [328 ft]. At the top of the troposphere is a level called the tropopause where temperatures are stable at around –55°C [–67°F]. Above the tropopause is the stratosphere, which contains the ozone layer. Here, at about 50 km [31 miles] above the Earth's surface, temperatures rise to about 0°C [32°F].

The ionosphere extends from the stratopause to about 600 km [373 miles] above the surface. Here temperatures fall up to about 80 km

CIRCULATION OF AIR

	HIGH PRESSURE
	LOW PRESSURE
	WARM AIR
	COLD AIR
	SURFACE WINDS
	CLOUDS

The circulation of the atmosphere can be divided into three rotating but interconnected air systems, or cells. The Hadley cell (figure 1 on the above diagram) is in the tropics; the Ferrel cell (2) lies between the subtropics and the mid-latitudes, and the Polar cell (3) is in the high latitudes.

Moonrise seen from orbit
This photograph taken by an orbiting Shuttle shows the crescent of the Moon. Silhouetted at the horizon is a dense cloud layer. The reddish-brown band is the tropopause, which separates the blue-white stratosphere from the yellow troposphere.

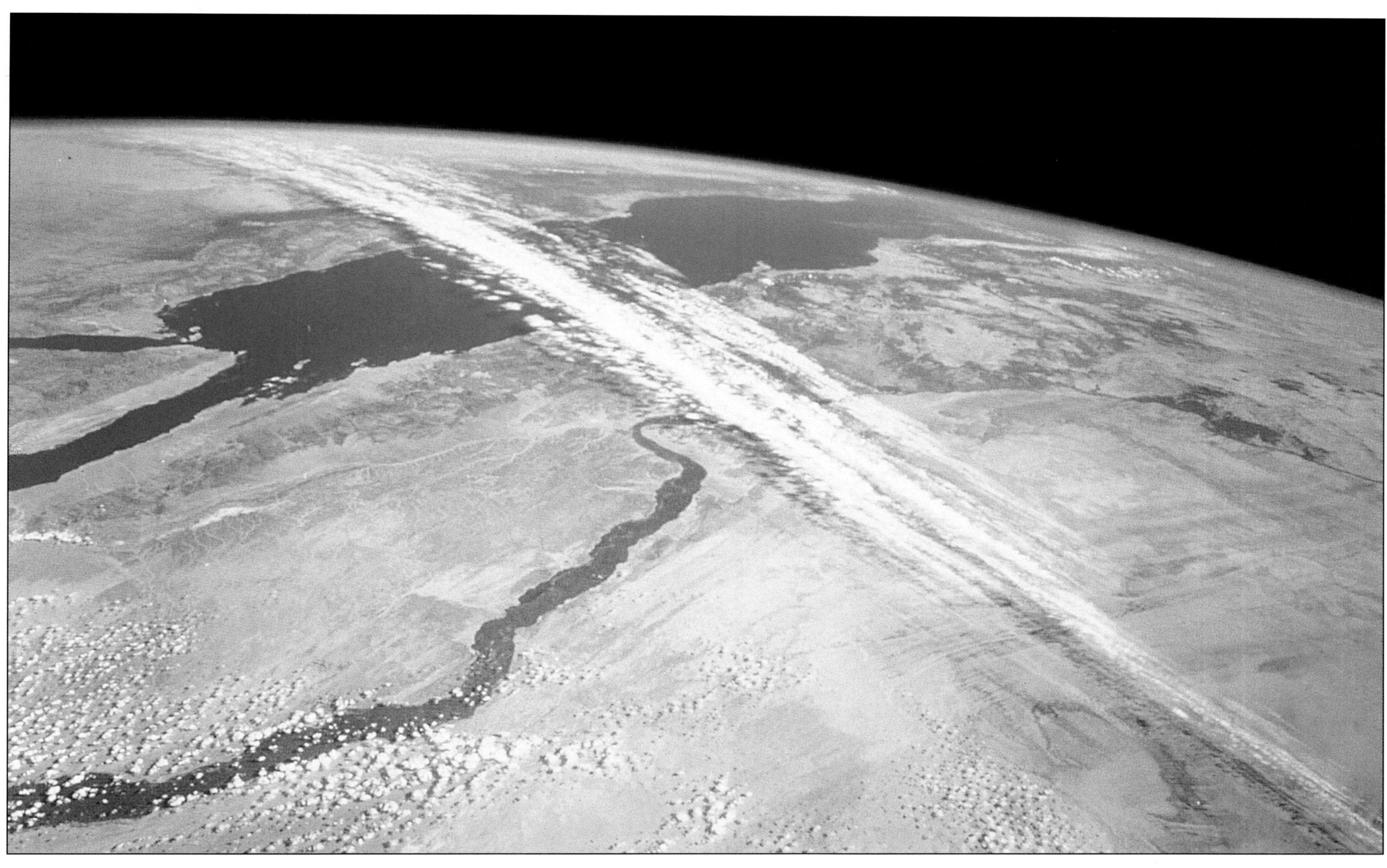

Jetstream from space
Jetstreams are strong winds that normally blow near the tropopause. Cirrus clouds mark the route of the jet stream in this photograph, which shows the Red Sea, North Africa and the Nile valley, which appears as a dark band crossing the desert.

[50 miles], but then rise. The aurorae, which occur in the ionosphere when charged particles from the Sun interact with the Earth's magnetic field, are strongest near the poles. In the exosphere, the outermost layer, the atmosphere merges into space.

CIRCULATION OF THE ATMOSPHERE

The heating of the Earth is most intense around the Equator where the Sun is high in the sky. Here warm, moist air rises in strong currents, creating a zone of low air pressure: the doldrums. The rising air eventually cools and spreads out north and south until it sinks back

to the ground around latitudes 30° North and 30° South. This forms two zones of high air pressure called the horse latitudes.

From the horse latitudes, trade winds blow back across the surface towards the Equator, while westerly winds blow towards the poles. The warm westerlies finally meet the polar easterlies (cold dense air flowing from the poles). The line along which the warm and cold air streams meet is called the polar front. Depressions (or cyclones) are low air pressure frontal systems that form along the polar front.

COMPOSITION OF THE ATMOSPHERE

The air in the troposphere is made up mainly of nitrogen (78%) and oxygen (21%). Argon makes up more than 0.9% and there are also minute amounts of carbon dioxide, helium, hydrogen, krypton, methane, ozone and xenon. The atmosphere also contains water vapour, the gaseous form of water, which, when it condenses around minute specks of dust and salt, forms tiny water droplets or ice crystals. Large masses of water droplets or ice crystals form clouds.

Classification of clouds
Clouds are classified broadly into cumuliform, or 'heap' clouds, and stratiform, or 'layer' clouds. Both types occur at all levels. The highest clouds, composed of ice crystals, are cirrus, cirrostratus and cirrocumulus. Medium-height clouds include altostratus, a grey cloud that often indicates the approach of a depression, and altocumulus, a thicker and fluffier version of cirrocumulus. Low clouds include stratus, which forms dull, overcast skies; nimbostratus, a dark grey layer cloud which brings almost continuous rain and snow; cumulus, a brilliant white heap cloud; and stratocumulus, a layer cloud arranged in globular masses or rolls. Cumulonimbus, a cloud associated with thunderstorms, lightning and heavy rain, often extends from low to medium altitudes. It has a flat base, a fluffy outline and often an anvil-shaped top.

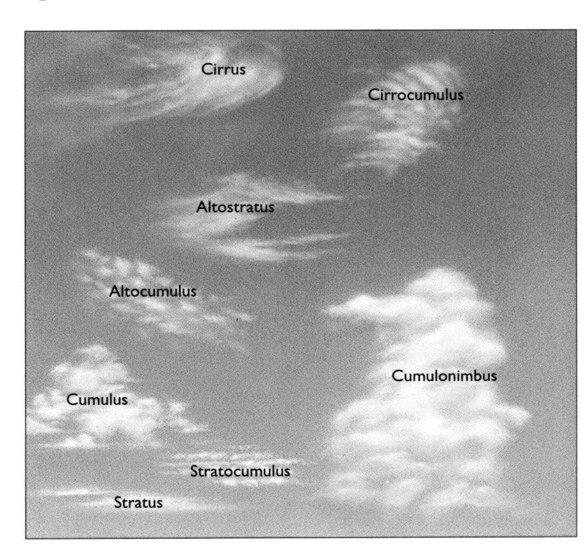

Climate and Weather

In 1992, Hurricane Andrew struck the Bahamas, Florida and Louisiana, causing record damage estimated at $30 billion. In September 1998, following heavy monsoon rains, floods submerged two-thirds of Bangladesh. The same month, in Central America, more than 7,000 people died in floods and mudslides caused by Hurricane Mitch. The economy of Honduras, already crippled by debt, was thought to have been put back by 15 to 20 years. In November 2001, violent storms in Algeria caused the deaths of more than 700 people in floods and landslides.

Every year, exceptional weather conditions cause disasters around the world. Modern forecasting techniques now give people warning of advancing storms, but the toll of human deaths continues as people are powerless in the face of the awesome forces of nature.

Weather is the day-to-day condition of the atmosphere. In some places, the weather is normally stable, but in other areas, especially the middle latitudes, it is highly variable, changing with the passing of a depression. By contrast, climate is the average weather of a place, based on data obtained over a long period.

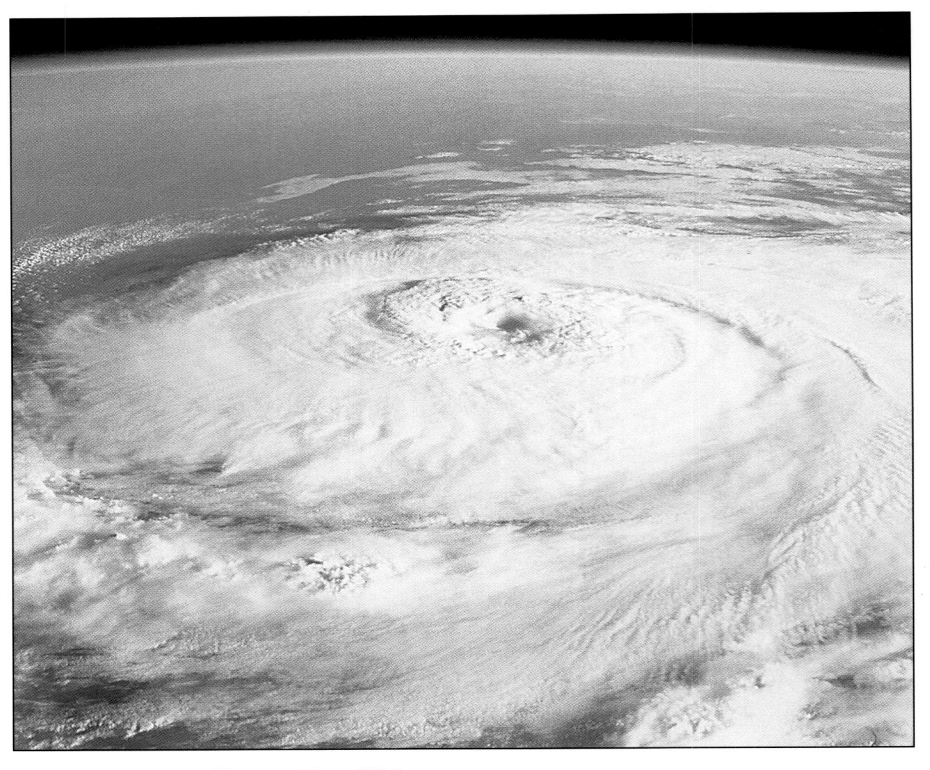

Hurricane Elena, 1995

Hurricanes form over warm oceans north and south of the Equator. Their movements are tracked by satellites, enabling forecasters to issue storm warnings as they approach land. In North America, forecasters identify them with boys' and girls' names.

CLIMATIC FACTORS

Climate depends basically on the unequal heating of the Sun between the Equator and the poles. But ocean currents and terrain also affect climate. For example, despite their northerly positions, Norway's ports remain ice-free in winter. This is because of the warming effect of the North Atlantic Drift, an extension of the Gulf Stream which flows across the Atlantic Ocean from the Gulf of Mexico.

By contrast, the cold Benguela current which flows up the coast of south-western Africa cools the coast and causes arid conditions. This is because the cold onshore winds are warmed as they pass over the land. The warm air can hold more water vapour than cold air, giving the winds a drying effect.

The terrain affects climate in several ways. Because temperatures fall with altitude, highlands are cooler than lowlands in the same

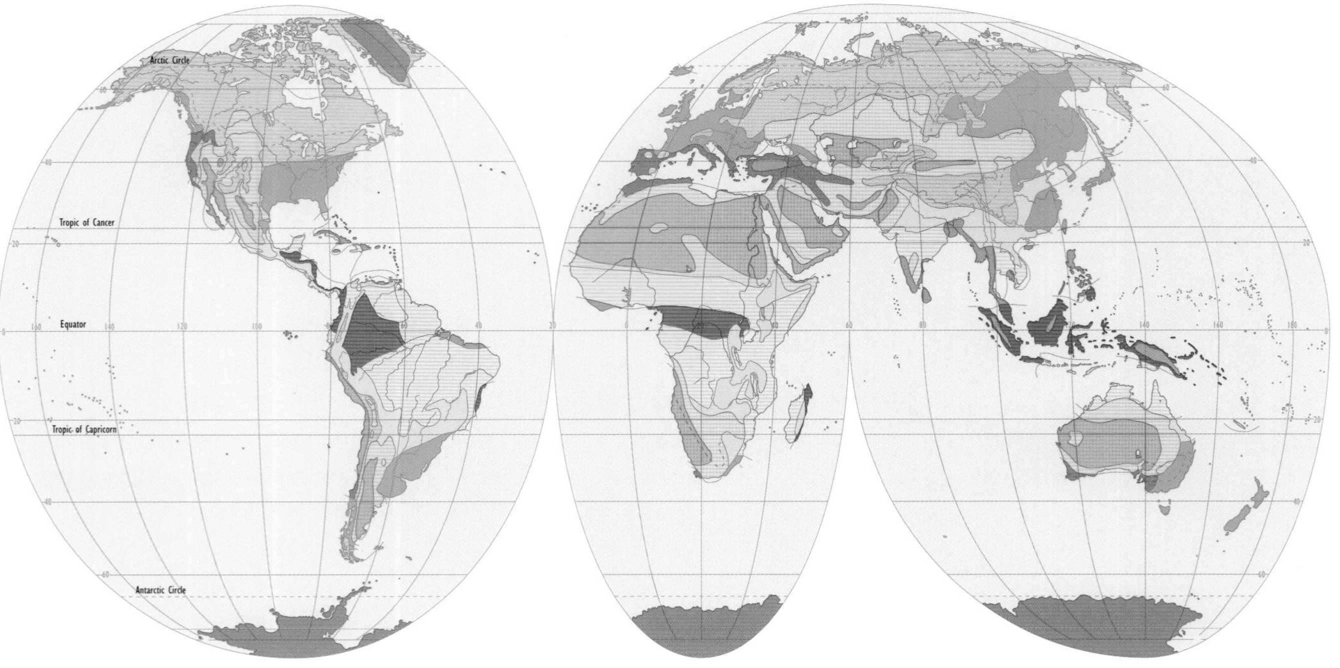

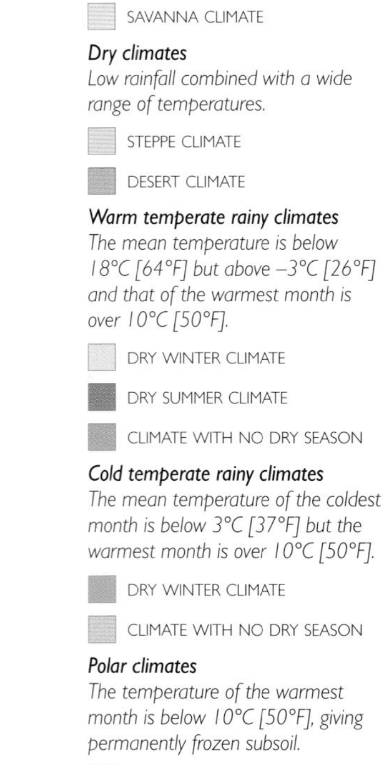

CLIMATIC REGIONS

Tropical rainy climates
All mean monthly temperatures above 18°C [64°F].

◼ RAINFOREST CLIMATE

◼ MONSOON CLIMATE

☐ SAVANNA CLIMATE

Dry climates
Low rainfall combined with a wide range of temperatures.

☐ STEPPE CLIMATE

◼ DESERT CLIMATE

Warm temperate rainy climates
The mean temperature is below 18°C [64°F] but above −3°C [26°F] and that of the warmest month is over 10°C [50°F].

☐ DRY WINTER CLIMATE

◼ DRY SUMMER CLIMATE

◼ CLIMATE WITH NO DRY SEASON

Cold temperate rainy climates
The mean temperature of the coldest month is below 3°C [37°F] but the warmest month is over 10°C [50°F].

◼ DRY WINTER CLIMATE

☐ CLIMATE WITH NO DRY SEASON

Polar climates
The temperature of the warmest month is below 10°C [50°F], giving permanently frozen subsoil.

☐ TUNDRA CLIMATE

◼ POLAR CLIMATE

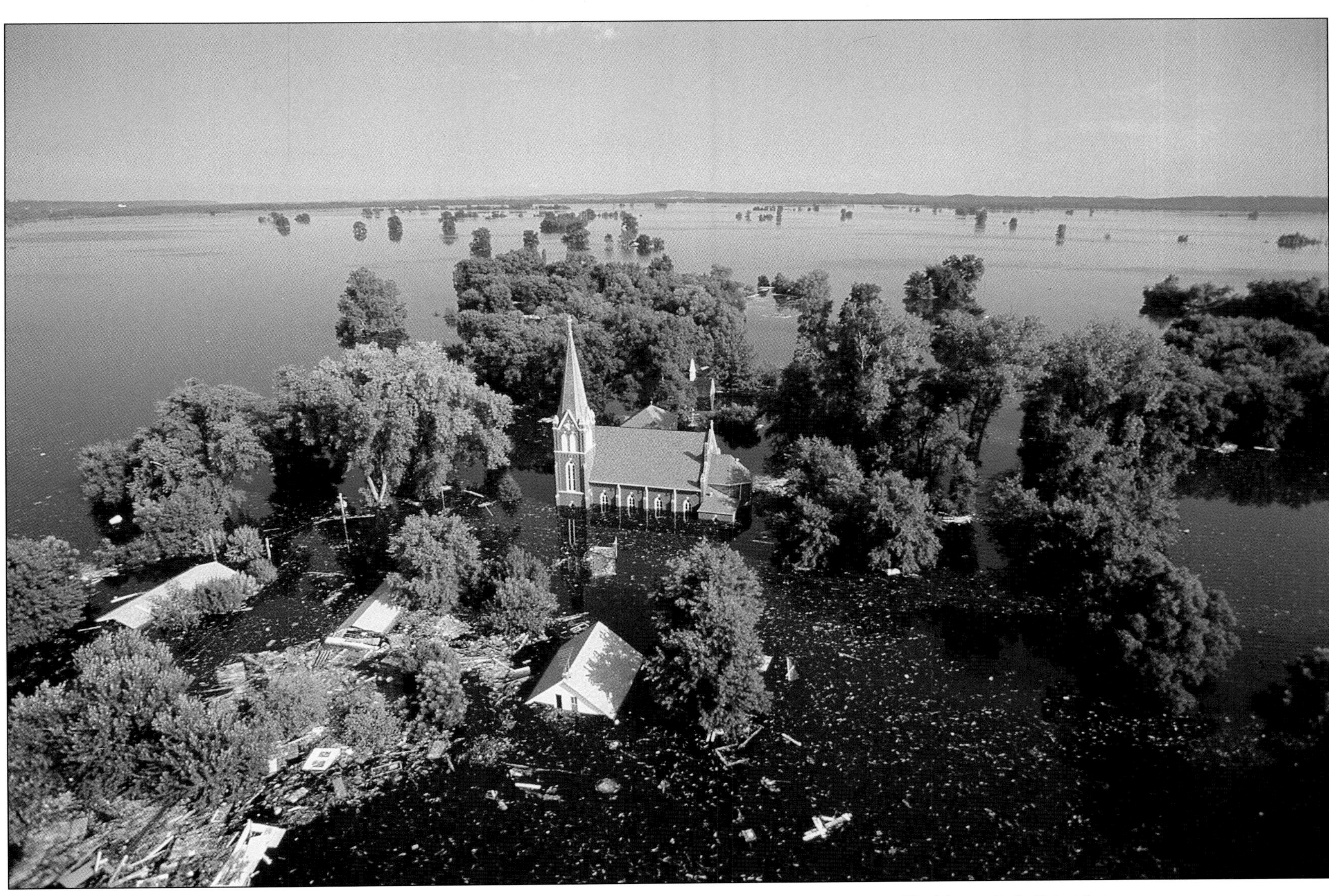

Floods in St Louis, United States
The satellite image, right, shows the extent of the floods at St Louis at the confluence of the Mississippi and the Missouri rivers in June and July 1993. The floods occurred when very heavy rainfall raised river levels by up to 14 m [46 ft]. The floods reached their greatest extent between Minneapolis in the north and a point approximately 150 km [93 miles] south of St Louis. In places, the width of the Mississippi increased to nearly 11 km [7 miles], while the Missouri reached widths of 32 km [20 miles]. In all, more than 28,000 sq km [10,800 sq miles] were inundated and hundreds of towns and cities were flooded. Damage to crops was estimated at $8 billion. The USA was hit again by flooding in early 1997, when heavy rainfall in North Dakota and Minnesota caused the Red River to flood. The flooding had a catastrophic effect on the city of Grand Forks, which was inundated for months.

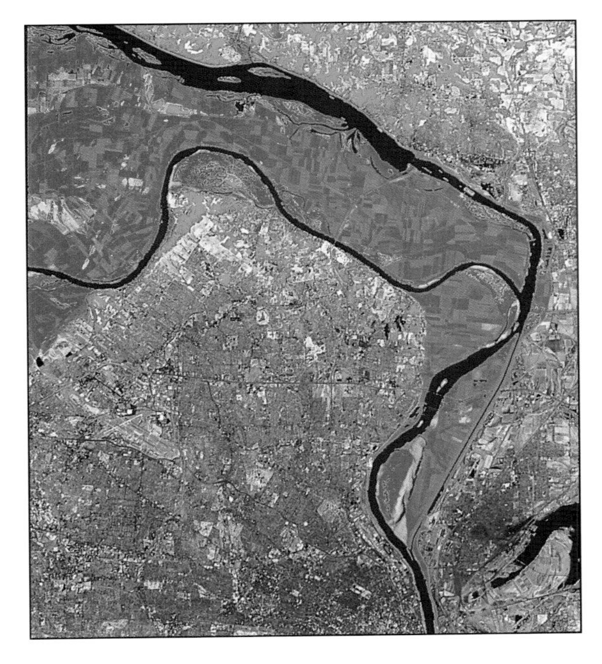

CLIMATIC REGIONS

The two major factors that affect climate are temperature and precipitation, including rain and snow. In addition, seasonal variations and other climatic features are also taken into account. Climatic classifications vary because of the weighting given to various features. Yet most classifications are based on five main climatic types: tropical rainy climates; dry climates; warm temperate rainy climates; cold temperate rainy climates; and very cold polar climates. Some classifications also allow for the effect of altitude. The main climatic regions are sub-divided according to seasonal variations and also to the kind of vegetation associated with the climatic conditions. Thus, the rainforest climate, with rain throughout the year, differs from monsoon and savanna climates, which have marked dry seasons. Similarly, parched desert climates differ from steppe climates which have enough moisture for grasses to grow.

latitude. Terrain also affects rainfall. When moist onshore winds pass over mountain ranges, they are chilled as they are forced to rise and the water vapour they contain condenses to form clouds which bring rain and snow. After the winds have crossed the mountains, the air descends and is warmed. These warm, dry winds create rain shadow (arid) regions on the lee side of the mountains.

Water and Land Use

All life on land depends on fresh water. Yet about 80 countries now face acute water shortages. The world demand for fresh water is increasing by about 2.3% a year and this demand will double every 21 years. About a billion people, mainly in developing countries, do not have access to clean drinking water and around 10 million die every year from drinking dirty water. This problem is made worse in many countries by the pollution of rivers and lakes.

In 1995, a World Bank report suggested that wars will be fought over water in the 21st century. Relations between several countries are

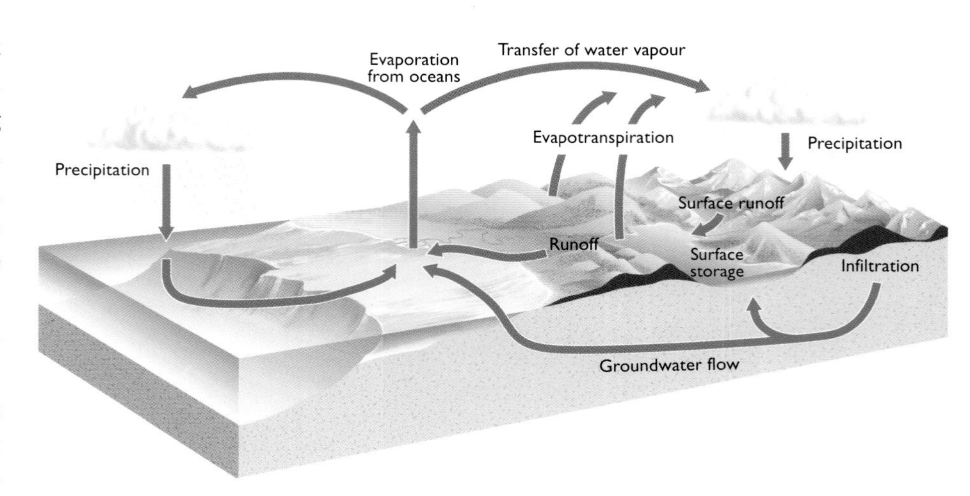

Hoover Dam, United States
The Hoover Dam in Arizona controls the Colorado River's flood waters. Its reservoir supplies domestic and irrigation water to the south-west, while a hydroelectric plant produces electricity.

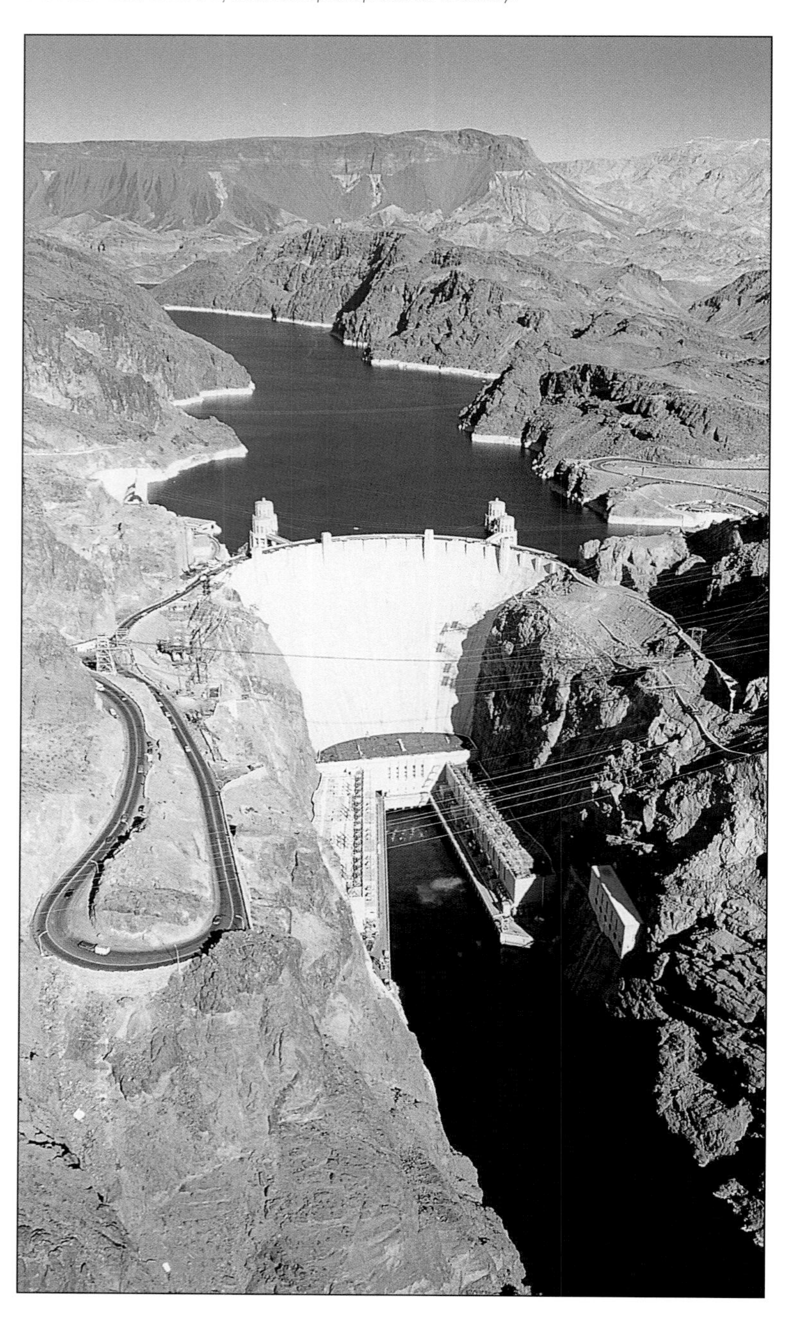

already soured by disputes over water resources. Egypt fears that Sudan and Ethiopia will appropriate the waters of the Nile, while Syria and Iraq are concerned that Turkish dams will hold back the waters of the Euphrates.

However, experts stress that while individual countries face water crises, there is no global crisis. The chief global problems are the uneven distribution of water and its inefficient and wasteful use.

THE WORLD'S WATER SUPPLY

Of the world's total water supply, 99.4% is in the oceans or frozen in bodies of ice. Most of the rest circulates through the rocks beneath our feet as ground water. Water in rivers and lakes, in the soil and in the atmosphere together make up only 0.013% of the world's water.

The freshwater supply on land is dependent on the hydrological, or water cycle which is driven by the Sun's heat. Water is evaporated from the oceans and carried into the air as invisible water vapour. Although this vapour averages less than 2% of the total mass of the atmosphere, it is the chief component from the standpoint of weather.

When air rises, water vapour condenses into visible water droplets or ice crystals, which eventually fall to earth as rain, snow, sleet, hail or frost. Some of the precipitation that reaches the ground returns directly to the atmosphere through evaporation or transpiration via plants. Much of the rest of the water flows into the rocks to become ground water or across the surface into rivers and, eventually, back to the oceans, so completing the hydrological cycle.

WATER AND AGRICULTURE

Only about a third of the world's land area is used for growing crops, while another third

The hydrological cycle
The hydrological cycle is responsible for the continuous circulation of water around the planet. Water vapour contains and transports latent heat, or latent energy. When the water vapour condenses back into water (and falls as rain, hail or snow), the heat is released. When condensation takes place on cold nights, the cooling effect associated with nightfall is offset by the liberation of latent heat.

WATER DISTRIBUTION
The distribution of planetary water, by percentage.

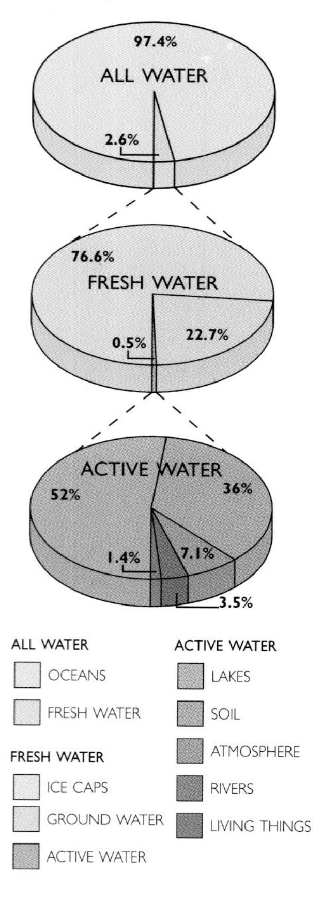

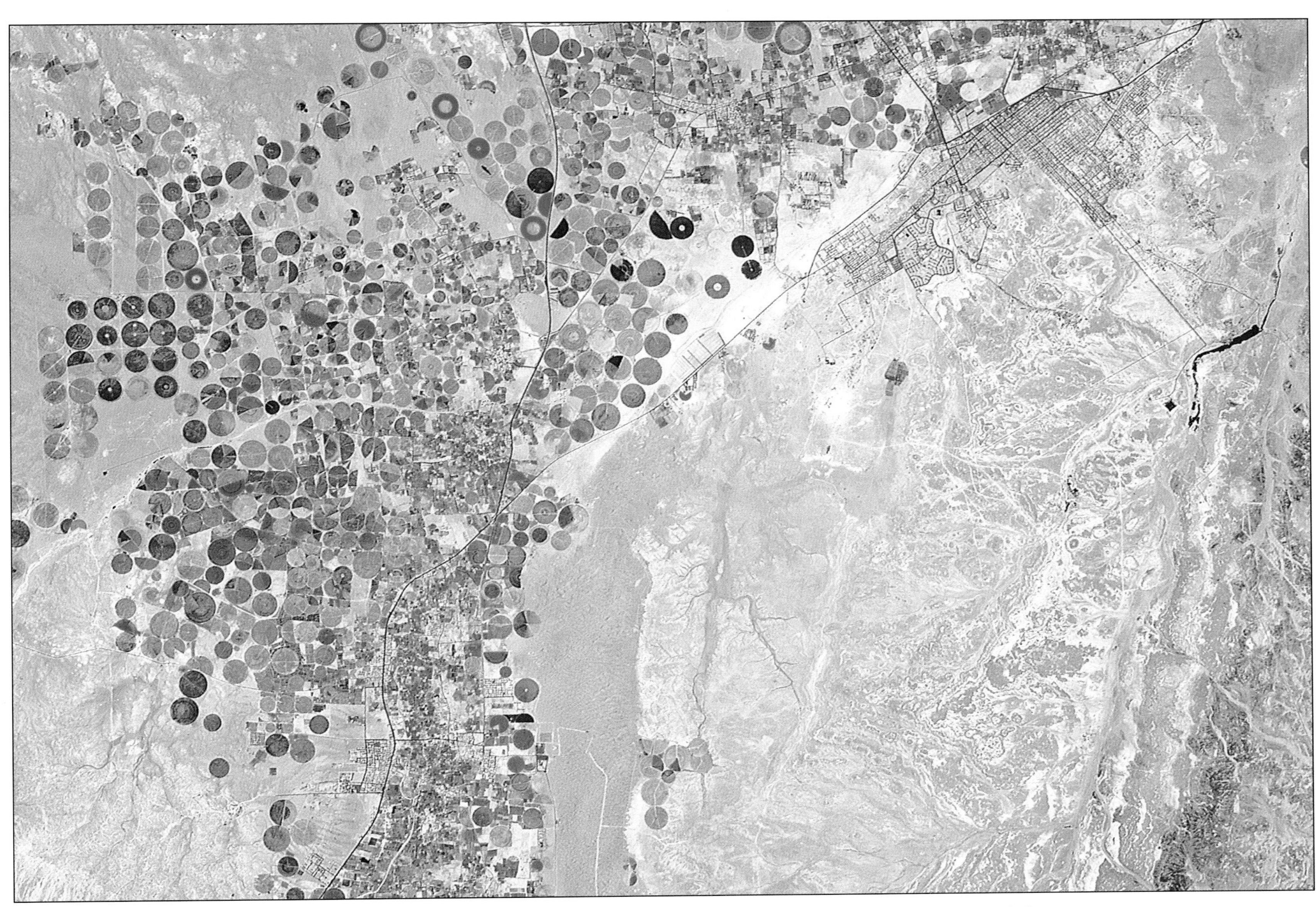

Irrigation in Saudi Arabia

Saudi Arabia is a desert country which gets its water from oases, which tap ground water supplies, and desalination plants. The sale of oil has enabled the arid countries of south-western Asia to develop their agriculture. In the above satellite image, vegetation appears brown and red.

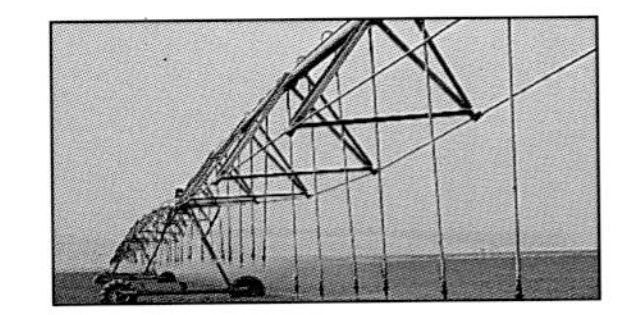

Irrigation boom

The photograph shows a pivotal irrigation boom used to sprinkle water over a wheat field in Saudi Arabia. Irrigation in hot countries often takes place at night so that water loss through evaporation is reduced. Irrigation techniques vary from place to place. In monsoon areas with abundant water, the fields are often flooded, or the water is led to the crops along straight furrows. Sprinkler irrigation has become important since the 1940s. In other types of irrigation, the water is led through pipes which are on or under the ground. Underground pipes supply water directly to the plant roots and, as a result, water loss through evaporation is minimized.

consists of meadows and pasture. The rest of the world is unsuitable for farming, being too dry, too cold, too mountainous, or covered by dense forests. Although the demand for food increases every year, problems arise when attempts are made to increase the existing area of farmland. For example, the soils and climates of tropical forest and semi-arid regions of Africa and South America are not ideal for farming. Attempts to work such areas usually end in failure. To increase the world's food supply, scientists now concentrate on making existing farmland more productive rather than farming marginal land.

To grow crops, farmers need fertile, workable land, an equable climate, including a frost-free growing period, and an adequate supply of fresh water. In some areas, the water falls directly as rain. But many other regions depend on irrigation.

Irrigation involves water conservation through the building of dams which hold back storage reservoirs. In some areas, irrigation water comes from underground aquifers, layers of permeable and porous rocks through which ground water percolates. But in many cases, the water in the aquifers has been there for thousands of years, having accumulated at a time when the rainfall

was much greater than it is today. As a result, these aquifers are not being renewed and will, one day, dry up.

Other sources of irrigation water are desalination plants, which remove salt from seawater and pump it to farms. This is a highly expensive process and is employed in areas where water supplies are extremely low, such as the island of Malta, or in the oil-rich desert countries around the Gulf, which can afford to build huge desalination plants.

LAND USE BY CONTINENT

	Forest	Permanent pasture	Permanent crops	Arable	Non-productive
North America	32.2%	17.3%	0.3%	12.6%	37.6%
South America	51.8%	26.7%	1.5%	6.6%	13.4%
Europe	33.4%	17.5%	3.0%	26.8%	19.3%
Africa	23.2%	26.6%	0.6%	5.6%	44.0%
Asia	20.2%	25.0%	1.2%	16.0%	37.8%
Oceania	23.5%	52.2%	0.1%	5.7%	18.5%

The Natural World

In 2002, a United Nations report identified more than 11,000 plant and animal species known to face a high risk of extinction, including 24% of all mammals and 12% of birds. Human activities, ranging from habitat destruction to the introduction of alien species from one area to another, are the main causes of this devastating reduction of our planet's biodiversity, which might lead to the disappearance of unique combinations of genes that could be vital in improving food yields on farms or in the production of drugs to combat disease.

Extinctions of species have occurred throughout Earth history, but today the extinction rate is estimated to be about 10,000 times the natural average. Some scientists have even compared it with the mass extinction that wiped out the dinosaurs 65 million years ago. However, the main cause of today's high extinction rate is not some natural disaster, such as the impact of an asteroid a few kilometres across, but it is the result of human actions, most notably the destruction of natural habitats for farming and other purposes. In some densely populated areas, such as Western Europe, the natural

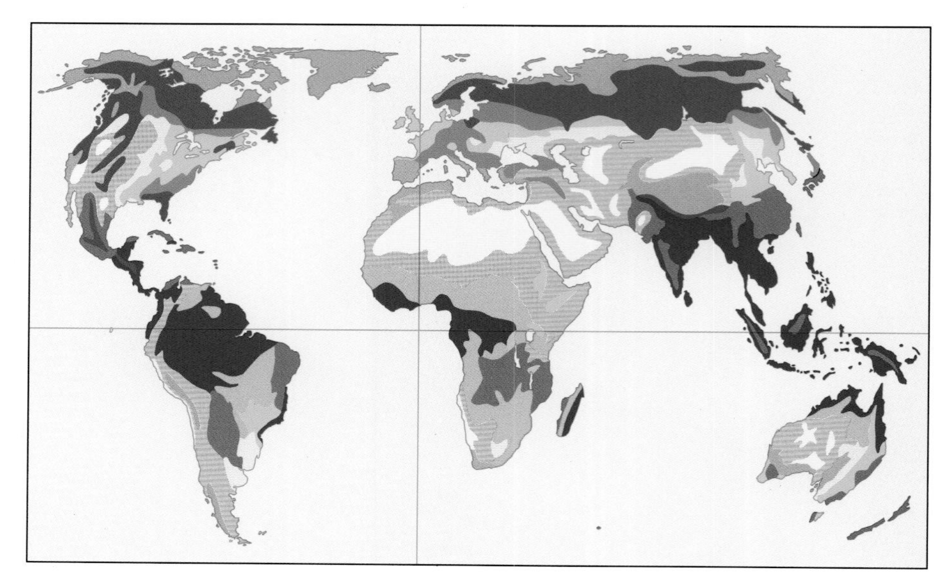

Rainforest in Rwanda

Rainforests are the most threatened of the world's biomes. Effective conservation policies must demonstrate to poor local people that they can benefit from the survival of the forests.

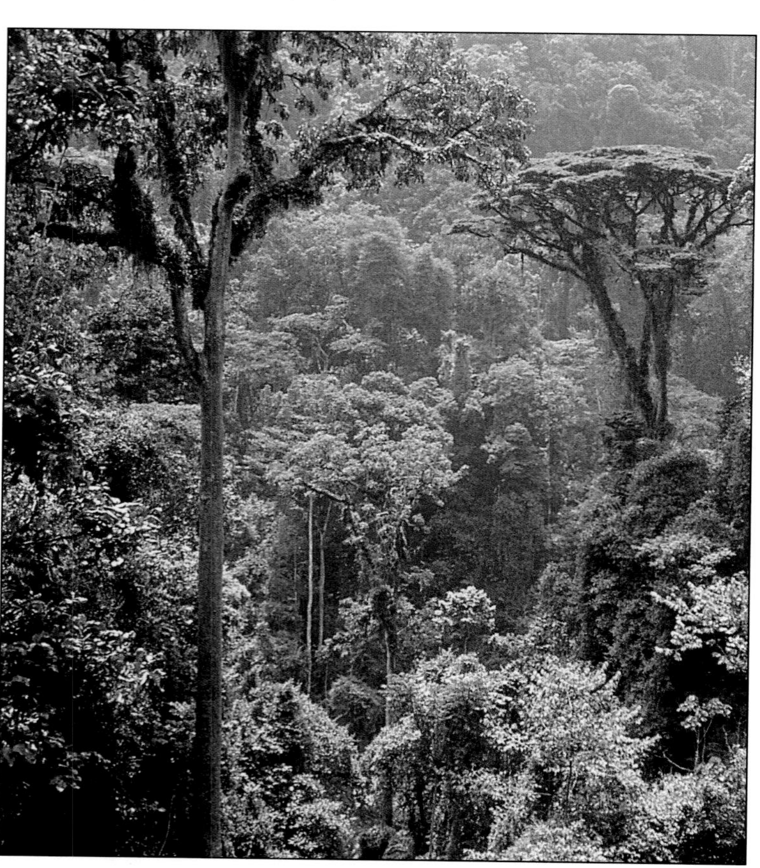

habitats were destroyed long ago. Today, the greatest damage is occurring in tropical rainforests, which contain more than half of the world's known species.

Modern technology has enabled people to live comfortably almost anywhere on Earth. But most plants and many animals are adapted to particular climatic conditions, and they live in association with and dependent on each other. Plant and animal communities that cover large areas are called biomes.

THE WORLD'S BIOMES

The world's biomes are defined mainly by climate and vegetation. They range from the tundra, in polar regions and high mountain regions, to the lush equatorial rainforests.

The Arctic tundra covers large areas in the polar regions of the northern hemisphere. Snow covers the land for more than half of the year and the subsoil, called permafrost, is permanently frozen. Comparatively few species can survive in this harsh, treeless environment. The main plants are hardy mosses, lichens, grasses, sedges and low shrubs. However, in summer, the tundra plays an important part in world animal geography, when its growing plants and swarms of insects provide food for migrating animals and birds that arrive from the south.

The tundra of the northern hemisphere merges in the south into a vast region of needleleaf evergreen forest, called the boreal forest or taiga. Such trees as fir, larch, pine and spruce are adapted to survive the long, bitterly cold winters of this region, but the number of plant and animal species is again small. South of the boreal forests is a zone of mixed needleleaf evergreens and broadleaf deciduous trees, which

NATURAL VEGETATION

- TUNDRA & MOUNTAIN VEGETATION
- NEEDLELEAF EVERGREEN FOREST
- MIXED NEEDLELEAF EVERGREEN & BROADLEAF DECIDUOUS TREES
- BROADLEAF DECIDUOUS WOODLAND
- MID-LATITUDE GRASSLAND
- EVERGREEN BROADLEAF & DECIDUOUS TREES & SHRUBS
- SEMI-DESERT SCRUB
- DESERT
- TROPICAL GRASSLAND (SAVANNA)
- TROPICAL BROADLEAF RAINFOREST & MONSOON FOREST
- SUBTROPICAL BROADLEAF & NEEDLELEAF FOREST

The map shows the world's main biomes. The classification is based on the natural 'climax' vegetation of regions, a result of the climate and the terrain. But human activities have greatly modified this basic division. For example, the original deciduous forests of Western Europe and the eastern United States have largely disappeared. In recent times, human development of some semi-arid areas has turned former dry grasslands into barren desert.

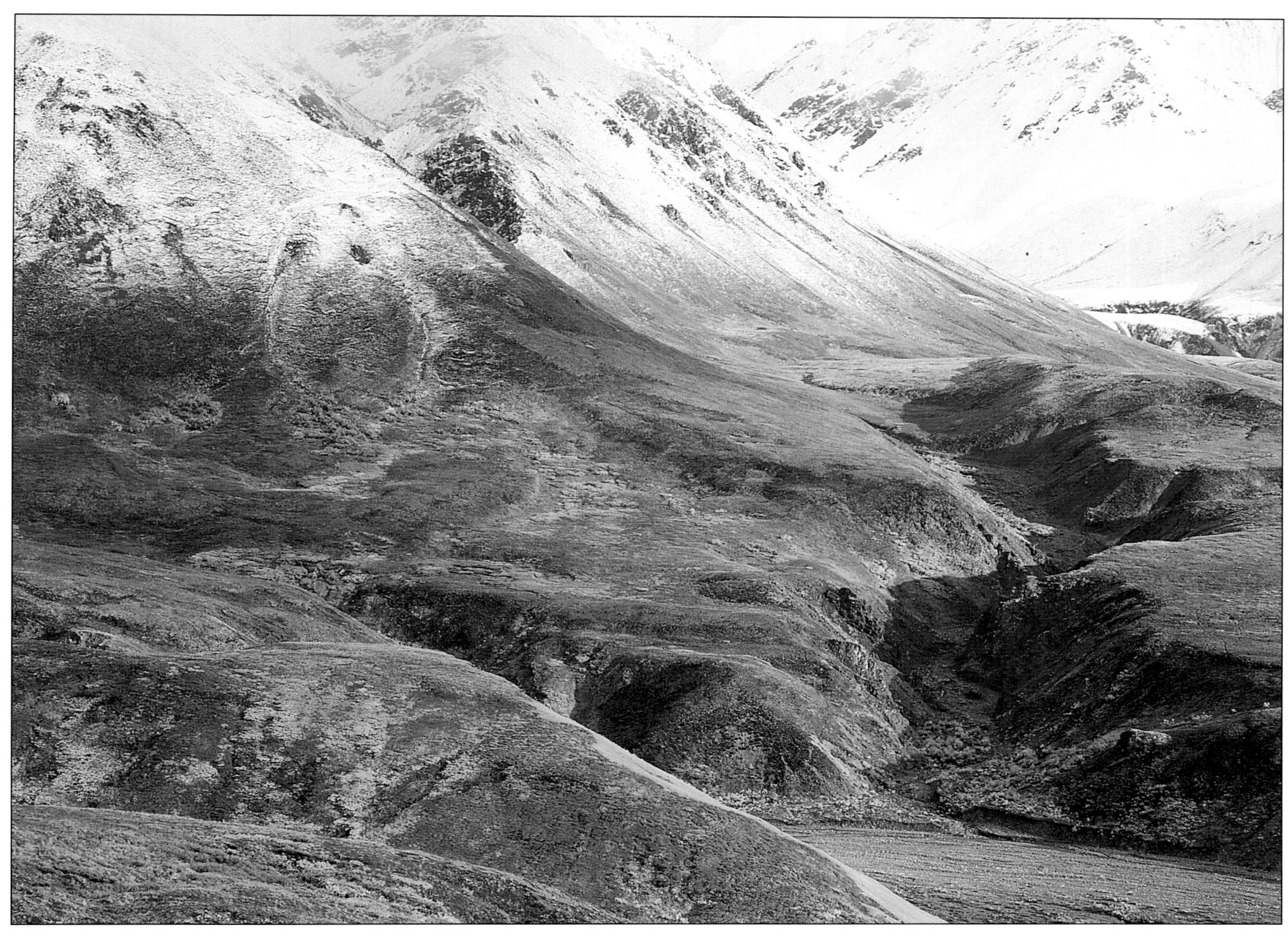

Tundra in subarctic Alaska
The Denali National Park, Alaska, contains magnificent mountain scenery and tundra vegetation which flourishes during the brief summer. The park is open between 1 June and 15 September.

shed their leaves in winter. In warmer areas, this mixed forest merges into broadleaf deciduous forest, where the number and diversity of plant species is much greater.

Deciduous forests are adapted to temperate, humid regions. Evergreen broadleaf and deciduous trees grow in Mediterranean regions, with their hot, dry summers. But much of the original deciduous forest has been cut down and has given way to scrub and heathland. Grasslands occupy large areas in the middle latitudes, where the rainfall is insufficient to support forest

growth. The moister grasslands are often called prairies, while drier areas are called steppe.

The tropics also contain vast dry areas of semi-desert scrub which merges into desert, as well as large areas of savanna, which is grassland with scattered trees. Savanna regions, with their marked dry season, support a wide range of mammals.

Tropical and subtropical regions contain three types of forest biomes. The tropical rainforest, the world's richest biome measured by its plant and animal species, experiences rain and high temperatures throughout the year. Similar forests occur in monsoon regions, which have a season of very heavy rainfall. They, too, are rich in plant species, though less so than the tropical rainforest. A third type of forest is the subtropical broadleaf and needleleaf forest, found in such places as south-eastern China, south-central Africa and eastern Brazil.

NET PRIMARY PRODUCTION OF EIGHT MAJOR BIOMES

- ■ TROPICAL RAINFORESTS
- □ DECIDUOUS FORESTS
- ▦ TROPICAL GRASSLANDS
- ▨ CONIFEROUS FORESTS
- ▤ MEDITERRANEAN
- ▫ TEMPERATE GRASSLANDS
- ▫ TUNDRA
- ▫ DESERTS

The net primary production of eight major biomes is expressed in grams of dry organic matter per square metre per year. The tropical rainforests produce the greatest amount of organic material. The tundra and deserts produce the least.

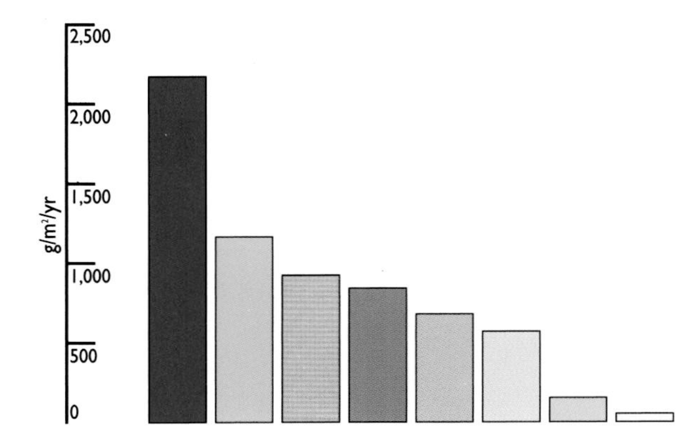

The Human World

Every minute, the world's population increases by between 160 and 170. While forecasts of future growth are difficult to make, most demographers are in agreement that the world's population, which passed the 6 billion mark in October 1999, would reach 8.9 billion by 2050. It was not expected to level out until 2200, when it would peak at around 11 billion. After 2200, it is expected to level out or even decline a little. The fastest rates of increase will take place in the developing countries of Africa, Asia and Latin America – the places least able to afford the enormous costs incurred by such a rapidly expanding population.

Elevated view of Ki Lung Street, Hong Kong
Urban areas of Hong Kong, a Special Administrative Region on the southern coast of China, contain busy streets overlooked by crowded apartments.

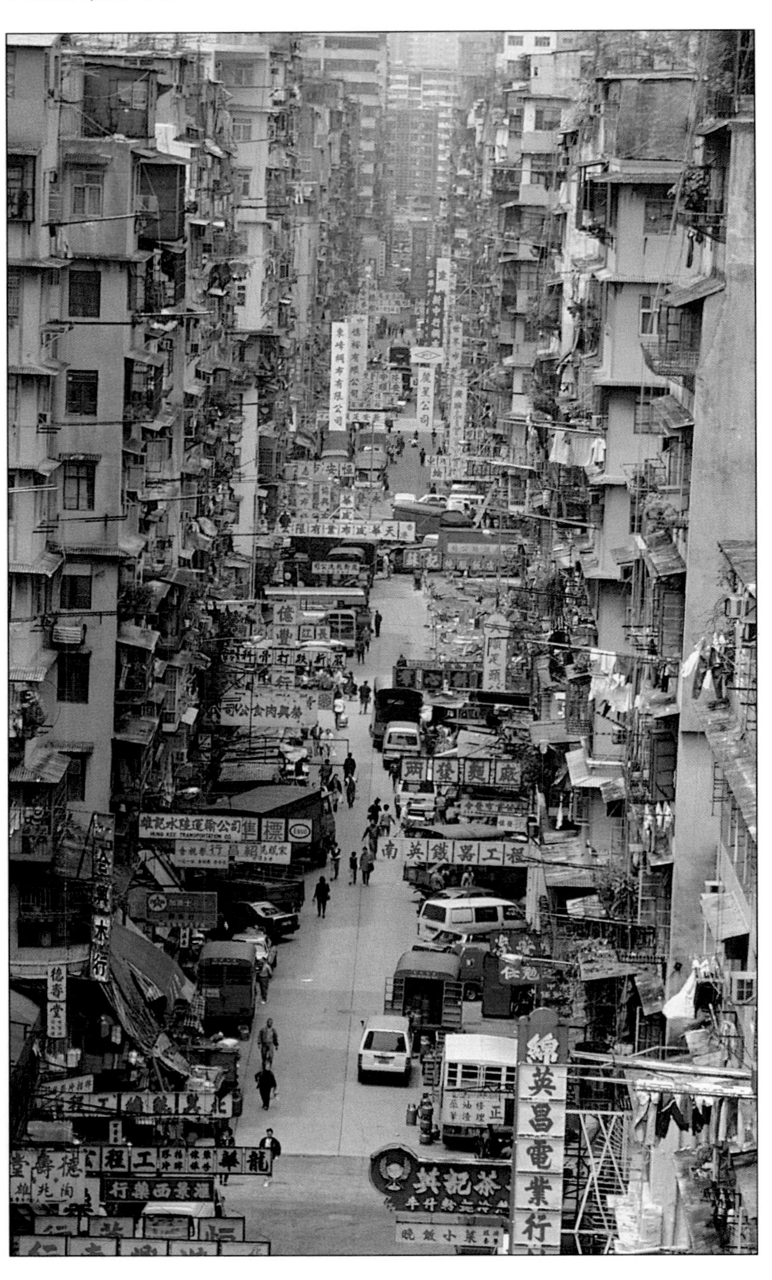

Average world population growth rates have declined from about 2% a year in the early 1960s to 1.4% in 1998. This was partly due to a decline in fertility rates – that is, the number of births to the number of women of child-bearing age – especially in developed countries where, as income has risen, the average size of families has fallen.

Declining fertility rates were also evident in many developing countries. Even Africa shows signs of such change, though its population is expected to triple before it begins to fall. Population growth is also dependent on death rates, which are affected by such factors as famine, disease and the quality of medical care.

THE POPULATION EXPLOSION

The world's population has grown steadily throughout most of human history, though certain events triggered periods of population growth. The invention of agriculture around 10,000 years ago, led to great changes in human society. Before then, most people had obtained food by hunting animals and gathering plants. Average life expectancies were probably no more than 20 years and life was hard. However, when farmers began to produce food surpluses, people began to live settled lives. This major milestone in human history led to the development of the first cities and early civilizations.

From an estimated 8 million in 8000 BC, the world population rose to about 300 million by AD 1000. Between 1000 and 1750, the rate of world population increase was around 0.1% per year, but another period of major economic and social change – the Industrial Revolution – began in the late 18th century. The Industrial Revolution led to improvements in farm technology and increases in food production. The world population began to increase quickly as industrialization spread across Europe and into North America. By 1850, it had reached 1.2 billion. The 2 billion mark was passed in the 1920s, and then the population rapidly doubled to 4 billion by the 1970s.

POPULATION FEATURES

Population growth affects the structure of societies. In developing countries with high annual rates of population increase, the large majority of the people are young and soon to become parents themselves. For example, in Kenya, which had until recently an annual rate of population growth of around 4%, just over half

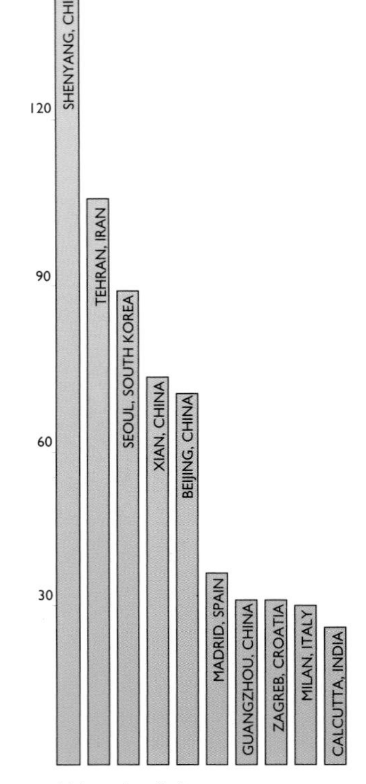

Urban air pollution
This diagram of the world's most polluted cities indicates the number of days per year when sulphur dioxide levels exceed the WHO threshhold of 150 micrograms per cubic metre.

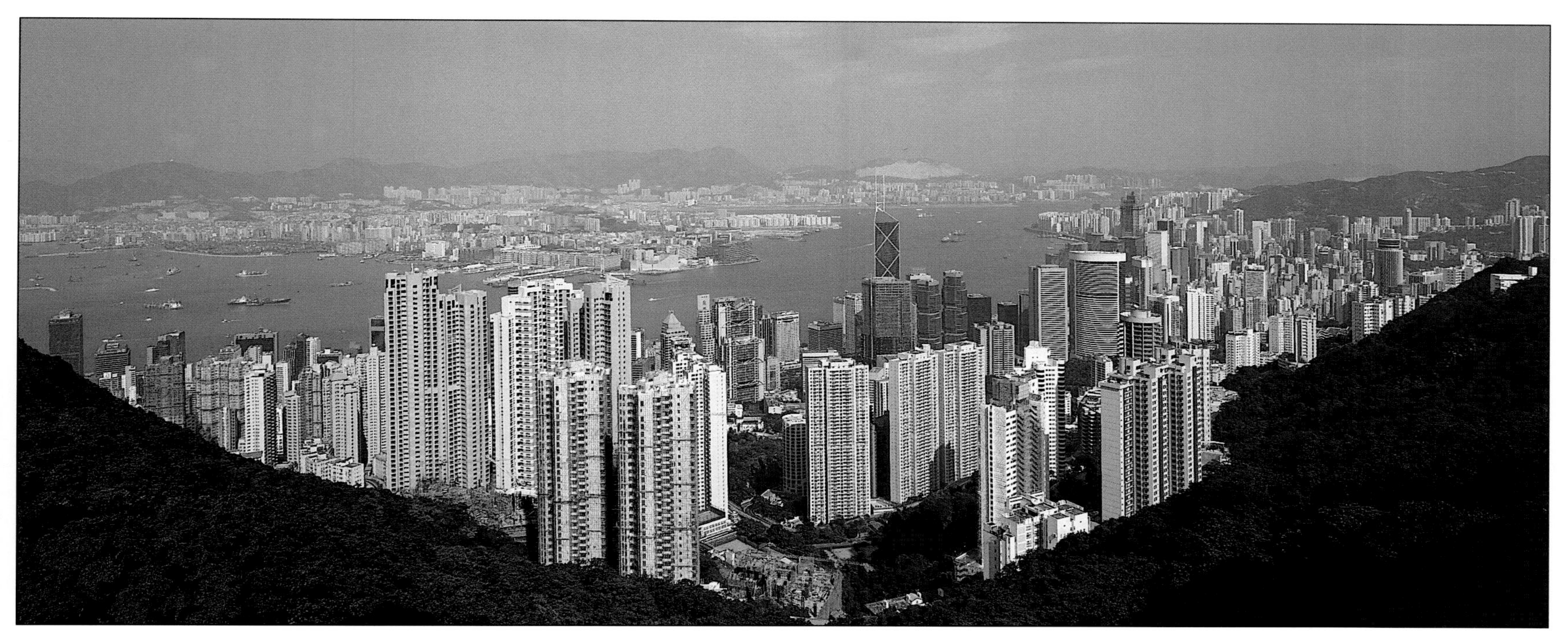

Hong Kong's business district

By contrast with the picturesque old streets of Hong Kong, the business district of Hong Kong City, on the northern shore of Hong Kong Island, is a cluster of modern high-rise buildings. The glittering skyscrapers reflect the success of this tiny region, which has one of the strongest economies in Asia.

of the population is under 15 years of age. On the other hand, the populations of developed countries, with low population growth rates, have a fairly even spread across age groups.

Such differences are reflected in average life expectancies at birth. In rich countries, such as Australia and the United States, the average life expectancy is 77 years (74 years for men and 80 for women; women live longer, on average, than their male counterparts). As a result, an increasing proportion of the people are elderly and retired, contributing little to the economy. The reverse applies in many poor countries, where average life expectancies are below 60 years. In the early 21st century, life expectancies were falling in some southern African countries, such as Botswana, where they fell from nearly 70 to around 40 years because of the fast spread of HIV and AIDS.

Paralleling the population explosion has been a rapid growth in the number and size of cities and towns, which contained nearly half of the world's people by the 1990s. This proportion is expected to rise to nearly two-thirds by 2025.

Urbanization occurred first in areas undergoing the industrialization of their economies, but today it is also a feature of the developing world. In developing countries, people are leaving impoverished rural areas hoping to gain access to the education, health and other services available in cities. But many cities cannot provide the facilities necessitated by rapid population growth. Slums develop and pollution, crime and disease become features of everyday life.

The population explosion poses another probem for the entire world. No one knows how many people the world can support or how consumer demand will damage the fragile environments on our planet. The British economist Thomas Malthus argued in the late 18th century that overpopulation would lead to famine and war. But an increase in farm technology in the 19th and 20th centuries, combined with a green revolution, in which scientists developed high-yield crop varieties, has greatly increased food production since Malthus' time.

However, some modern scientists argue that overpopulation may become a problem in the 21st century. They argue that food shortages leading to disastrous famines will result unless population growth can be halted. Such people argue in favour of birth control programmes. China, one of the two countries with more than a billion people, has introduced a one-child family policy. Its action has slowed the growth of China's huge population.

POPULATION CHANGE 1990–2000
The population change for the years 1990–2000.

- OVER 40% POPULATION GAIN
- 30–40% POPULATION GAIN
- 20–30% POPULATION GAIN
- 10–20% POPULATION GAIN
- 0–10% POPULATION GAIN
- NO CHANGE OR LOSS

TOP 5 COUNTRIES

Kuwait	+75.9%
Namibia	+62.5%
Afghanistan	+60.1%
Mali	+55.5%
Tanzania	+54.6%

BOTTOM 5 COUNTRIES

Belgium	–0.1%
Hungary	–0.2%
Grenada	–2.4%
Germany	–3.2%
Tonga	–3.2%

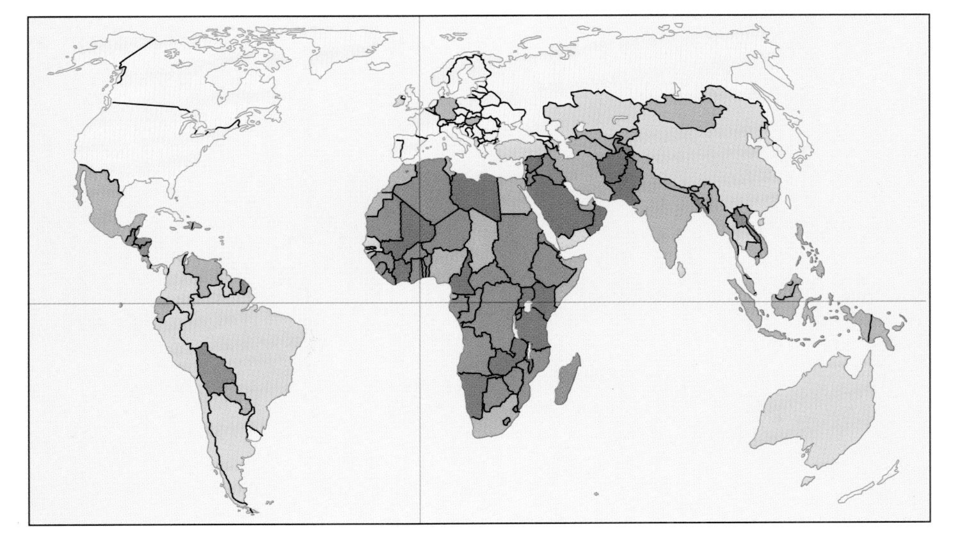

Languages and Religions

In 1995, 90-year-old Edna Guerro died in northern California. She was the last person able to speak Northern Pomo, one of about 50 Native American languages spoken in the state. Her death marked the extinction of one of the world's languages.

This event is not an isolated incident. Language experts regularly report the disappearance of languages and some of them predict that between 20 to 50% of the world's languages will no longer exist by the end of the 21st century. Improved transport and communications are partly to blame, because they bring people from various cultures into closer and closer contact. Many children no longer speak the language of their parents, preferring instead to learn the language used at their schools. The pressures on

children to speak dominant rather than minority languages are often great. In the first part of the 20th century, Native American children were punished if they spoke their native language.

The disappearance of a language represents the extinction of a way of thinking, a unique expression of the experiences and knowledge of a group of people. Language and religion together give people an identity and a sense of belonging. However, there are others who argue that the disappearance of minority languages is a step towards international understanding and economic efficiency.

THE WORLD'S LANGUAGES

Definitions of what is a language or a dialect vary and, hence, estimates of the number of languages spoken around the world range from about 3,000 to 6,000. But whatever the figure, it is clear that the number of languages far exceeds the number of countries.

RELIGIOUS ADHERENTS

Number of adherents to the world's major religions, in millions (1998).

Christian	1,980
Roman Catholic	1,300
Orthodox	240
African sects	110
Pentecostal	105
Others	225
Islam	1,300
Sunni	940
Shiite	120
Others	240
Hindu	900
Secular/Atheist/Agnostic/ Non-religious	850
Buddhist	360
Chinese Traditional	225
Indigenous/Animist	190
Sikh	23
Yoruba	20
Juche	19
Spiritism	14
Judaism	14
Baha'i	6
Jainism	4
Shinto	4

Buddhist monks in Katmandu, Nepal
Hinduism is Nepal's official religion, but the Nepalese observe the festivals of both Hinduism and Buddhism. They also regard Buddhist shrines and Hindu temples as equally sacred.

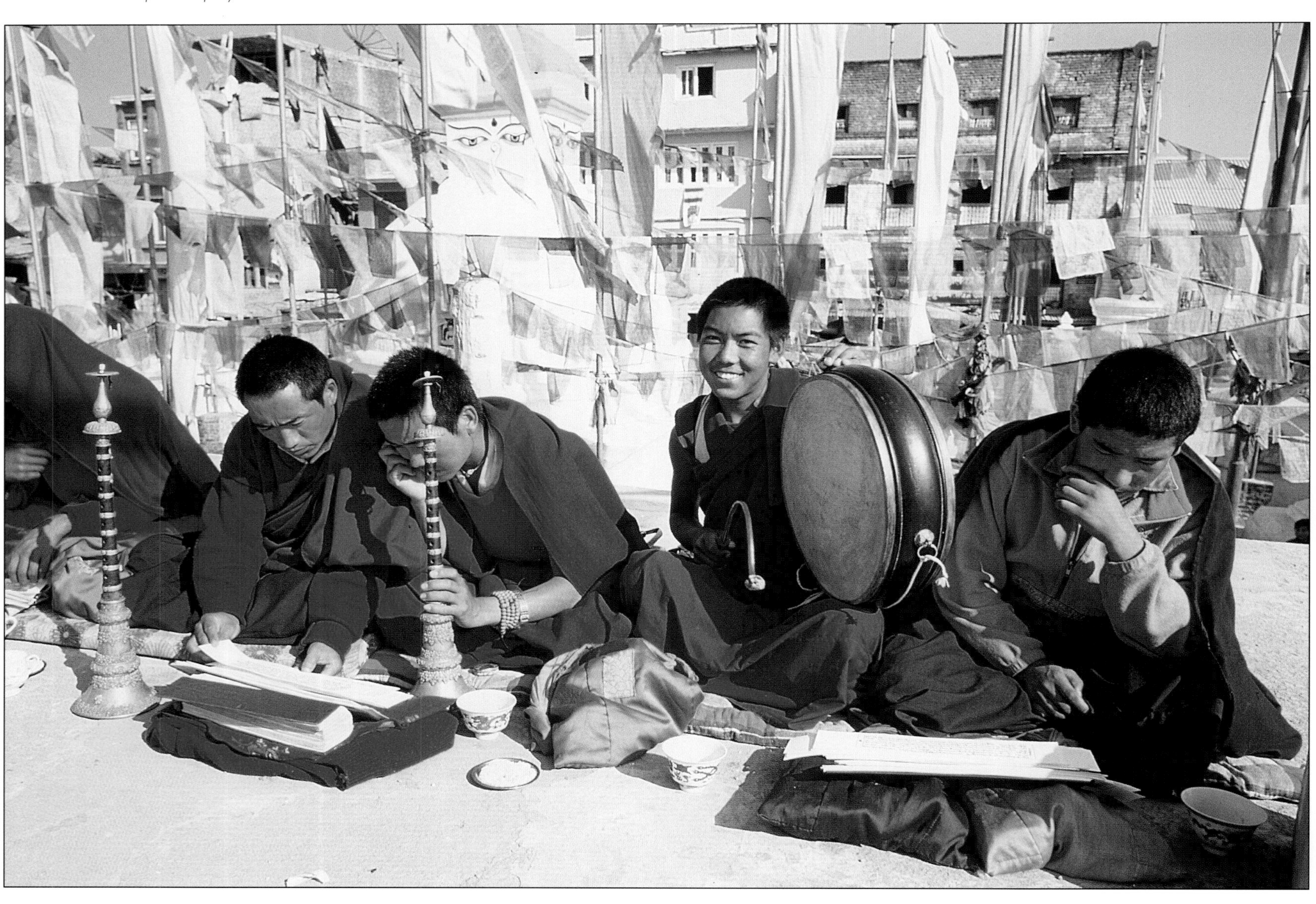

Countries with only one language tend to be small. For example, in Liechtenstein, everyone speaks German. By contrast, more than 860 languages have been identified in Papua New Guinea, whose population is only about 4.6 million people. Hence, many of its languages are spoken by only small groups of people. In fact, scientists have estimated that about a third of the world's languages are now spoken by less than 1,000 people. By contrast, more than half of the world's population speak just seven languages.

The world's languages are grouped into families. The Indo-European family consists of languages spoken between Europe and the Indian subcontinent. The growth of European empires over the last 300 years led several Indo-European languages, most notably English, French, Portuguese and Spanish, to spread throughout much of North and South America, Africa, Australia and New Zealand.

English has become the official language in many countries which together contain more than a quarter of the world's population. It is now a major international language, surpassing in importance Mandarin Chinese, a member of the Sino-Tibetan family, which is the world's leading first language. Without a knowledge of English, businessmen face many problems when conducting international trade, especially with the United States or other English-speaking countries. But proposals that English, French, Russian or some other language should become a world language seem unlikely to be acceptable to a majority of the world's peoples.

WORLD RELIGIONS

Religion is another fundamental aspect of human culture. It has inspired much of the world's finest architecture, literature, music and painting. It has also helped to shape human cultures since prehistoric times and is responsible for the codes of ethics by which most people live.

The world's major religions were all founded in Asia. Judaism, one of the first faiths to teach that there is only one god, is one of the world's oldest. Founded in south-western Asia, it influenced the more recent Christianity and Islam, two other monotheistic religions which

MOTHER TONGUES

First-language speakers of the major languages, in millions (1999).

- MANDARIN CHINESE 885M
- SPANISH 332M
- ENGLISH 322M
- BENGALI 189M
- HINDI 182M
- PORTUGUESE 170M
- RUSSIAN 170M
- JAPANESE 125M
- GERMAN 98M
- WU CHINESE 77M

OFFICIAL LANGUAGES: % OF WORLD POPULATION

English	27.0%
Chinese	19.0%
Hindi	13.5%
Spanish	5.4%
Russian	5.2%
French	4.2%
Arabic	3.3%
Portuguese	3.0%
Malay	3.0%
Bengali	2.9%
Japanese	2.3%

Polyglot nations

The graph, right, shows countries of the world with more than 200 languages. Although it has only about 4.6 million people, Papua New Guinea holds the record for the number of languages spoken.

Brazil (210)
Congo (Z.) (220)
Australia (230)
Mexico (240)
Cameroon (275)
India (410)
Nigeria (470)
Indonesia (701)
Papua New Guinea (862)

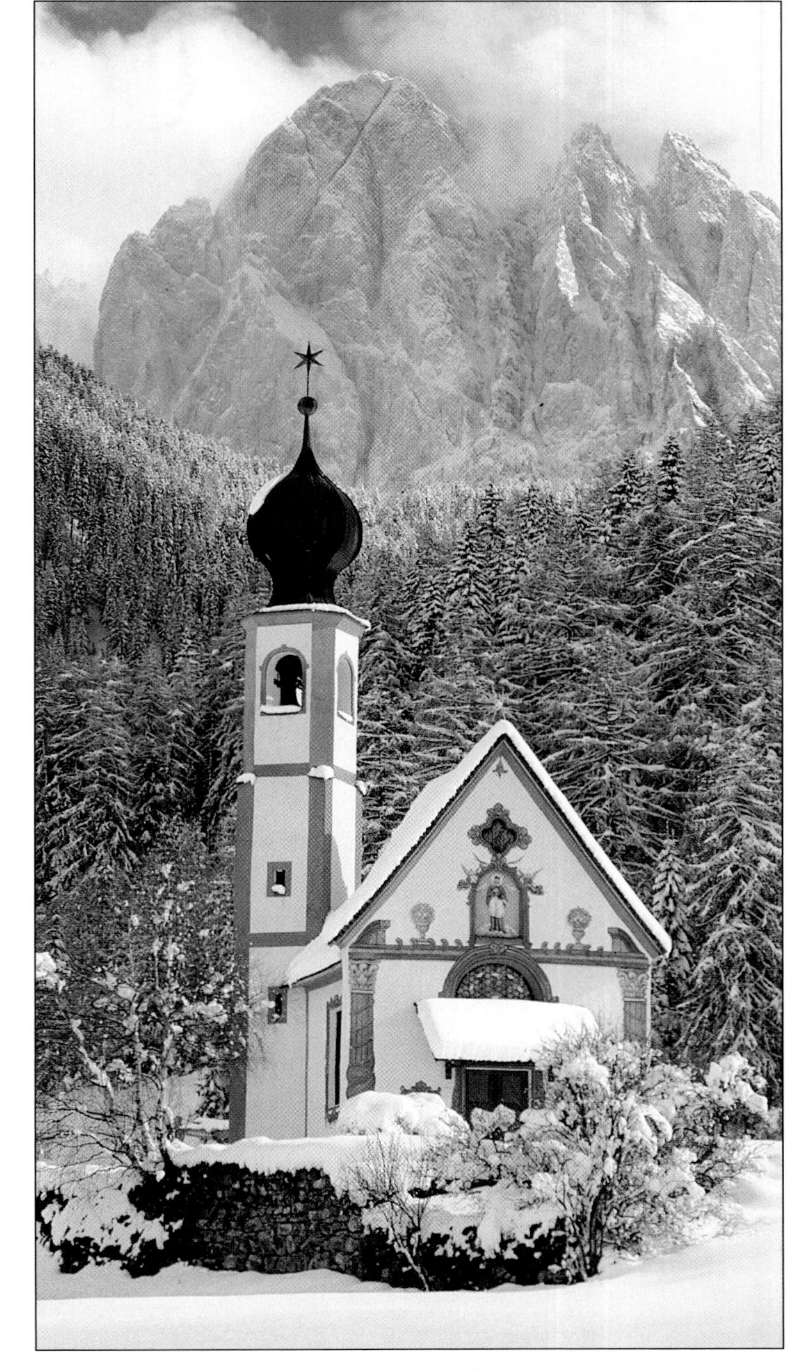

The Church of San Giovanni, Dolomites, Italy
Christianity has done much to shape Western civilization. Christian churches were built as places of worship, but many of them are among the finest achievements of world architecture.

now have the greatest number of followers. Hinduism, the third leading faith in terms of the numbers of followers, originated in the Indian subcontinent and most Hindus are now found in India. Another major religion, Buddhism, was founded in the subcontinent partly as a reaction to certain aspects of Hinduism. But unlike Hinduism, it has spread from India throughout much of eastern Asia.

Religion and language are powerful creative forces. They are also essential features of nationalism, which gives people a sense of belonging and pride. But nationalism is often also a cause of rivalry and tension. Cultural differences have led to racial hatred, the persecution of minorities, and to war between national groups.

International Organizations

Twelve days before the surrender of Germany and four months before the final end of World War II, representatives of 50 nations met in San Francisco to create a plan to set up a peace-keeping organization, the United Nations. Since its birth on 24 October 1945, its membership has grown from 51 to 189 in 2001.

Its first 50 years have been marked by failures as well as successes. While it has helped to prevent some disputes from flaring up into full-scale wars, the Blue Berets, as the UN troops are called, have been forced, because of their policy of neutrality, to stand by when atrocities are committed by rival warring groups.

THE WORK OF THE UN

The United Nations has six main organs. They include the General Assembly, where member states meet to discuss issues concerned with peace, security and development. The Security Council, containing 15 members, is concerned with maintaining world peace. The Secretariat, under the Secretary-General, helps the other organs to do their jobs effectively, while the Economic and Social Council works with specialized agencies to implement policies concerned with such matters as development, education and health. The International Court of Justice, or World Court, helps to settle disputes between member nations. The sixth organ of the UN, the Trusteeship Council, was designed to bring 11 UN trust territories to independence. Its task has now been completed.

The specialized agencies do much important work. For example, UNICEF (United Nations International Children's Fund) has provided health care and aid for children in many parts of the world. The ILO (International Labour Organization) has improved working conditions in many areas, while the FAO (Food and Agricultural Organization) has worked to improve the production and distribution of food. Among the other agencies are organizations to help refugees, to further human rights and to control the environment. The latest agency, set up in 1995, is the WTO (World Trade Organization), which took over the work of GATT (General Agreement on Tariffs and Trade).

OTHER ORGANIZATIONS

In a world in which nations have become increasingly interdependent, many other organizations have been set up to deal with a variety of problems. Some, such as NATO (the North Atlantic Treaty Organization), are defence alliances. In the early 1990s, the end of the Cold War suggested that NATO's role might be finished, but the civil war in the former Yugoslavia showed that it still has a role in maintaining peace and security.

Other organizations encourage social and economic co-operation in various regions. Some are NGOs (non-governmental organizations), such as the Red Cross and its Muslim equivalent, the Red Crescent. Other NGOs raise funds to provide aid to countries facing major crises, such as famine.

Some major international organizations aim at economic co-operation and the removal of trade barriers. For example, the European Union has 15 members. Its economic success and the adoption of a single currency, the euro, by 12

Food aid

International organizations supply aid to people living in areas suffering from war or famine. In Bosnia-Herzegovina, the UN Protection Force supervised the movements of food aid, as did NATO on the borders of Kosovo a few years later.

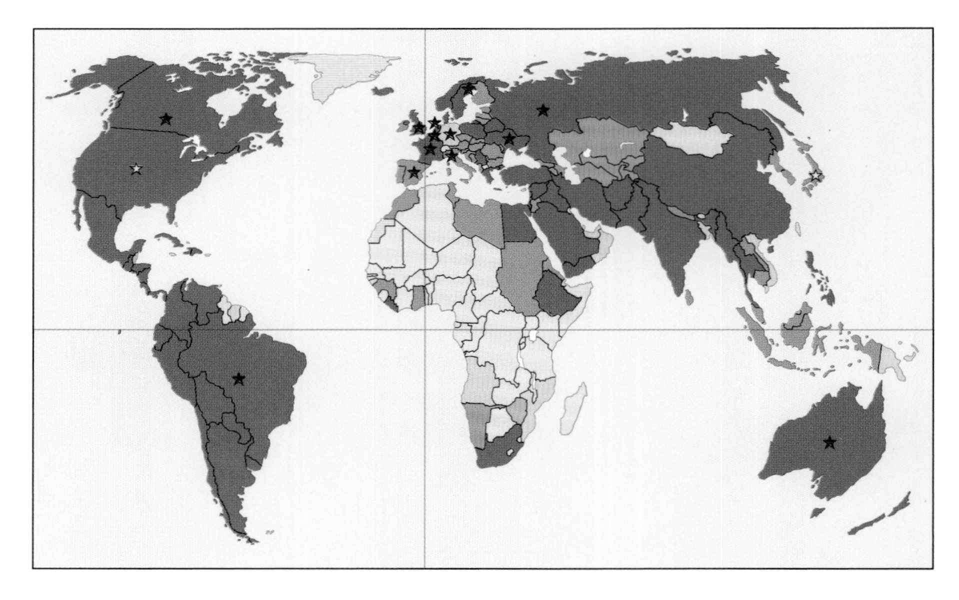

MEMBERS OF THE UN
Year of joining.

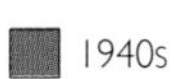

- ■ 1940s
- ■ 1950s
- □ 1960s
- ■ 1970s
- ■ 1980s
- ■ 1990s
- □ NON–MEMBERS
- ★ 1% – 10% CONTRIBUTION TO FUNDING
- ☆ OVER 10% CONTRIBUTION TO FUNDING

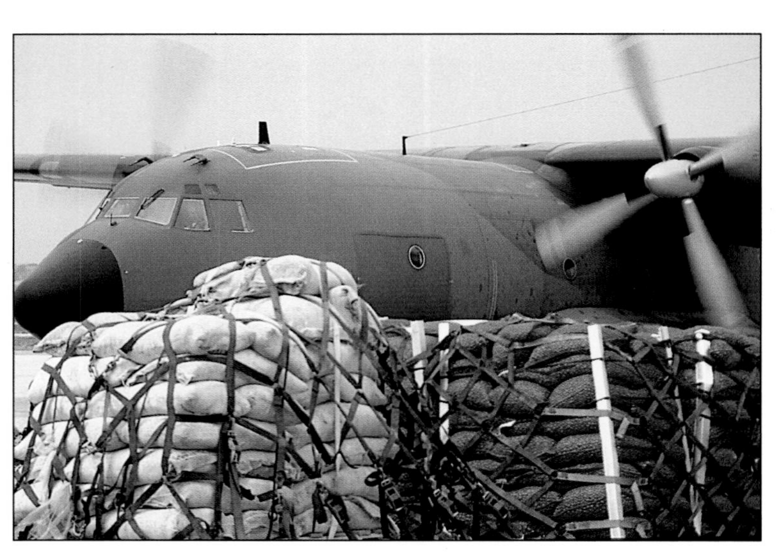

INTERNATIONAL AID AND GNP
Aid provided as a percentage of GNP, with total aid in brackets (1997).

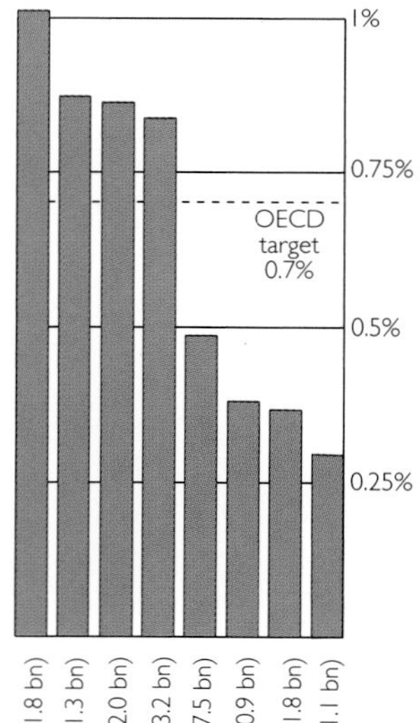

OECD target 0.7%

Denmark ($1.8 bn)
Norway ($1.3 bn)
Sweden ($2.0 bn)
Netherlands ($3.2 bn)
France ($7.5 bn)
Belgium ($0.9 bn)
Canada ($1.8 bn)
Australia ($1.1 bn)

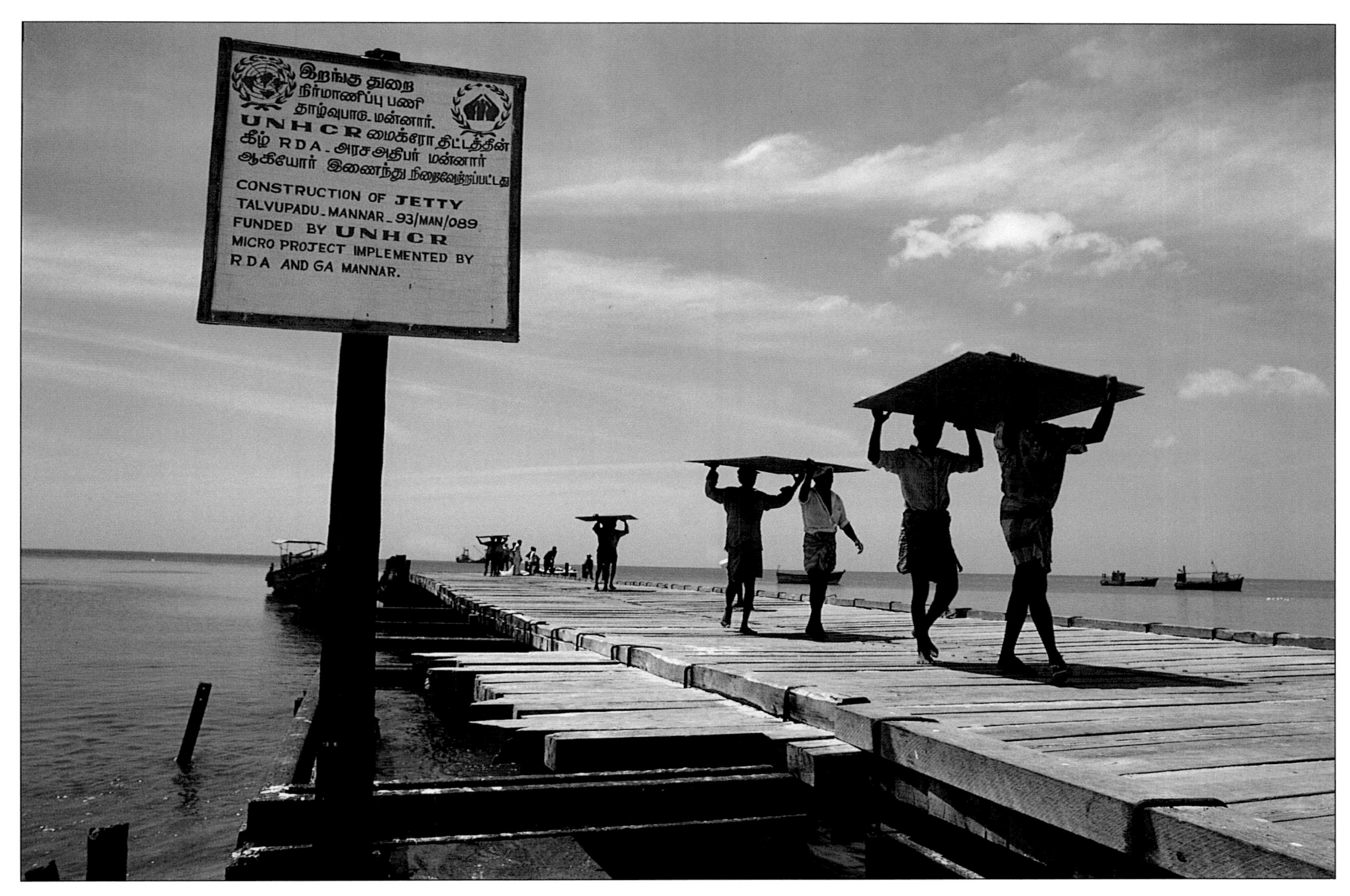

UNHCR-funded jetty, Sri Lanka
At the start of 2000, the number of people 'of concern' to the UN High Commission for Refugees totalled 22.3 million people. Sometimes, it has to provide transport facilities, such as this jetty, to get aid to the refugees.

of its members, has prompted some people to support the idea of a federal Europe. But others fear that political union might lead to a loss of national sovereignty by member states.

Other groupings include ASEAN (the Association of South-east Asian Nations) which aims to reduce trade barriers between its members (Brunei, Burma [Myanmar], Cambodia, Indonesia, Laos, Malaysia, the Philippines, Singapore, Thailand and Vietnam). APEC (the Asia-Pacific Co-operation Group), founded in 1989, aims to create a free trade zone between the countries of eastern Asia, North America, Australia and New Zealand by 2020. Meanwhile, Canada, Mexico and the United States have formed NAFTA (the North American Free Trade Agreement), while other economic groupings link most of the countries in Latin America. Another grouping with a more limited but important objective is OPEC (the Organization of Oil-Exporting Countries). OPEC works to unify policies concerning trade in oil on the world markets.

Some organizations exist to discuss matters of common interest between groups of nations. The Commonwealth of Nations, for example, grew out of links created by the British Empire. In North and South America, the OAS (Organization of American States) aims to increase understanding in the Western hemisphere. The OAU (Organization of African Unity) has a similar role in Africa, while the Arab League represents the Arab nations of North Africa and the Middle East.

COUNTRIES OF THE EUROPEAN UNION

	Total land area (sq km)	Total population (2001 est.)	GDP per capita, US$ (2000 est.)	Unemployment rate, % (2001)	Year of accession to the EU	Seats in EU parliament (1999–2004)
Austria	83,850	8,151,000	25,000	3.9%	1995	21
Belgium	30,510	10,259,000	25,300	6.9%	1958	25
Denmark	43,070	5,353,000	25,500	4.3%	1973	16
Finland	338,130	5,176,000	22,900	9.2%	1995	16
France	551,500	59,551,000	24,400	8.6%	1958	86
Germany	356,910	83,030,000	25,350	7.9%	1958	99
Greece	131,990	10,624,000	23,400	10.3%	1981	25
Ireland	70,280	3,841,000	21,600	3.8%	1973	15
Italy	301,270	57,680,000	22,100	9.4%	1958	87
Luxembourg	2,590	443,000	36,400	2.5%	1958	6
Netherlands	41,526	15,981,000	24,400	2.2%	1958	31
Portugal	92,390	9,444,000	15,800	4.4%	1986	25
Spain	504,780	38,432,000	18,000	13.0%	1986	64
Sweden	449,960	8,875,000	22,200	4.9%	1995	22
United Kingdom	243,368	59,648,000	22,800	5.1%	1973	87

Agriculture

Around the turn of the century, partly because of ongoing turmoil in the Russian economy, the increase in food production was less than the rise in world population, creating a small per capita fall in food production. Downward trends in world food production reopened an old debate – whether food production will be able to keep pace with the predicted rapid rises in the world population in the 21st century.

Some experts argue that the lower than expected production figures in the 1990s heralded a period of relative scarcity and high prices of food, which will be felt most in the poorer developing countries. Others are more optimistic. They point to the successes of the 'green revolution' which, through the use of new crop varieties produced by scientists, irrigation and the extensive use of fertilizers and pesticides,

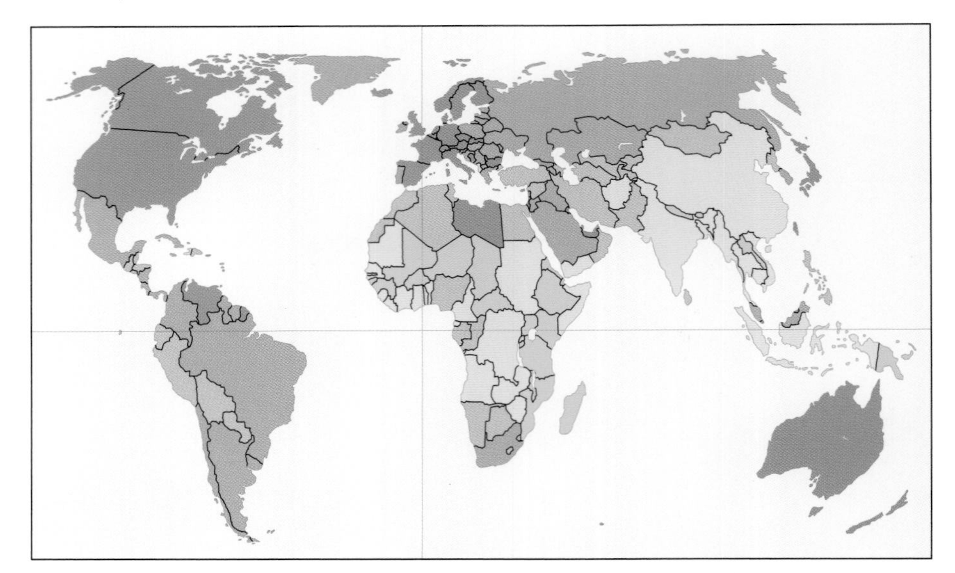

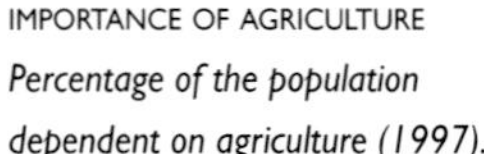

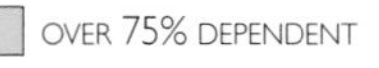

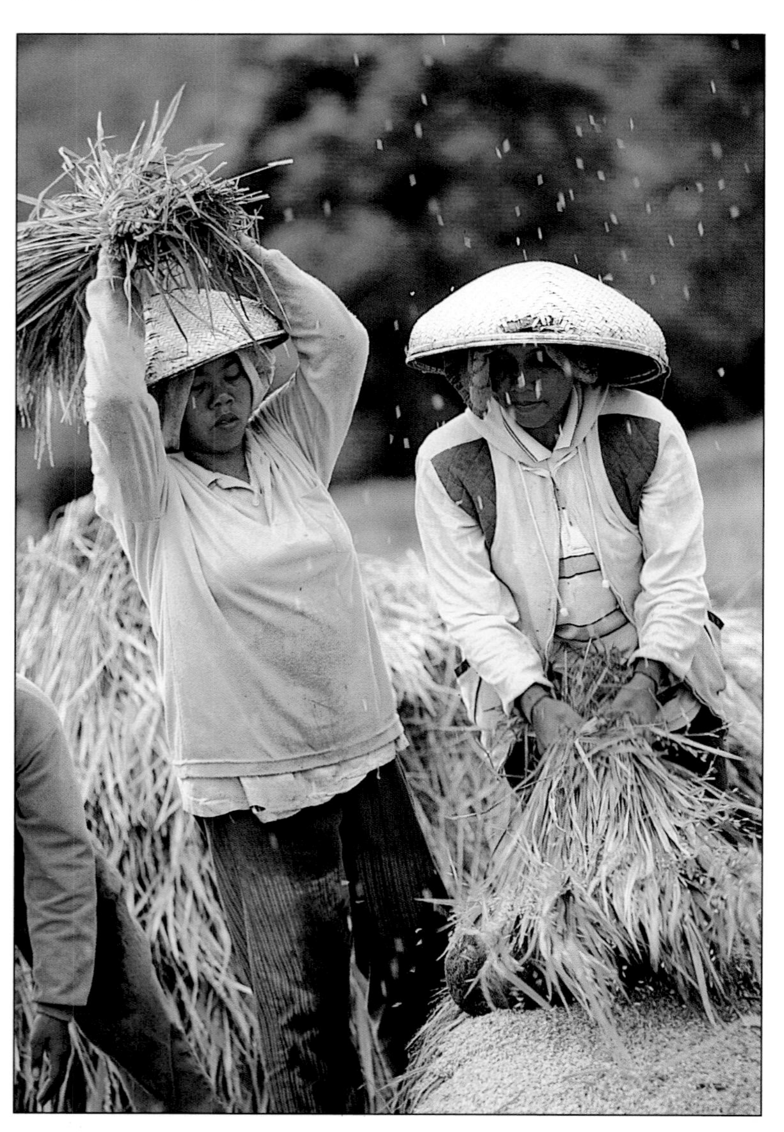

Rice harvest, Bali, Indonesia
More than half of the world's people eat rice as their basic food. Rice grows well in tropical and subtropical regions, such as in Indonesia, India and south-eastern China.

has revolutionized food production since the 1950s and 1960s.

The green revolution has led to a great expansion in the production of many crops, including such basic foods as rice, maize and wheat. In India, its effects have been spectacular. Between 1955 and 1995, grain production trebled, giving the country sufficient food reserves to prevent famine in years when droughts or floods reduce the harvest. While once India had to import food, it is now self-sufficient.

FOOD PRODUCTION

Agriculture, which supplies most of our food, together with materials to make clothes and other products, is the world's most important economic activity. But its relative importance has declined in comparison with manufacturing and service industries. As a result, the end of the 20th century marked the first time for 10,000 years when the vast majority of the people no longer had to depend for their living on growing crops and herding animals.

However, agriculture remains the dominant economic activity in many developing countries in Africa and Asia. For example, by the start of the 21st century, 80% or more of the people of Bhutan, Burundi, Nepal and Rwanda depended on farming for their living.

Many people in developing countries eke out the barest of livings by nomadic herding or shifting cultivation, combined with hunting, fishing and gathering plant foods. A large proportion of farmers live at subsistence level, producing little more than they require to provide the basic needs of their families.

The world's largest food producer and exporter is the United States, although agriculture employs

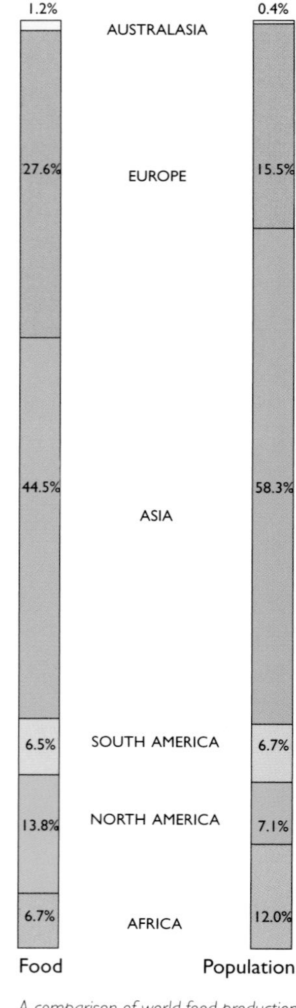

IMPORTANCE OF AGRICULTURE
Percentage of the population dependent on agriculture (1997).

- OVER 75% DEPENDENT
- 50–75% DEPENDENT
- 25–50% DEPENDENT
- 10–25% DEPENDENT
- UNDER 10% DEPENDENT

A comparison of world food production and population by continent.

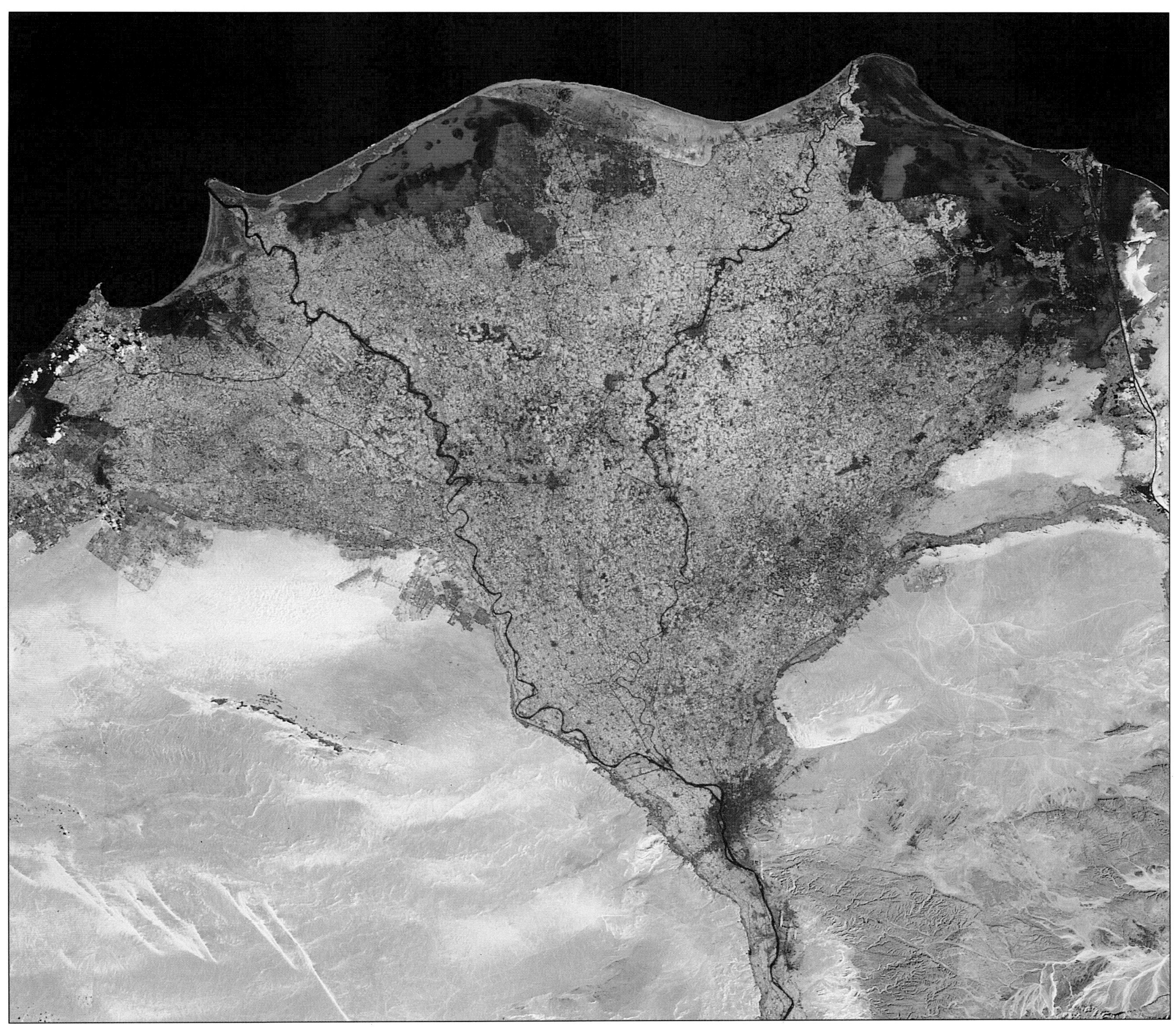

Landsat *image of the Nile delta, Egypt*

Most Egyptians live in the Nile valley and on its delta. Because much of the silt carried by the Nile now ends up on the floor of Lake Nasser, upstream of the Aswan Dam, the delta is now retreating and seawater is seeping inland. This eventuality was not foreseen when the Aswan High Dam was built in the 1960s.

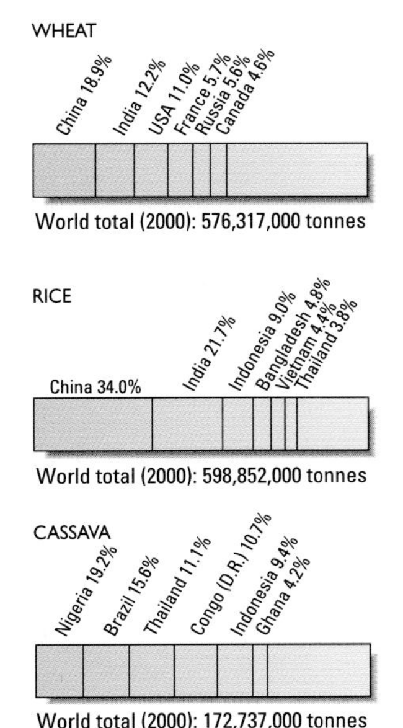

WHEAT

China 18.9% · India 12.2% · USA 11.0% · France 5.7% · Russia 5.6% · Canada 4.6%

World total (2000): 576,317,000 tonnes

RICE

China 34.0% · India 21.7% · Indonesia 9.0% · Bangladesh 4.8% · Vietnam 4.6% · Thailand 3.8%

World total (2000): 598,852,000 tonnes

CASSAVA

Nigeria 19.2% · Brazil 15.6% · Thailand 11.1% · Congo (D.R.) 10.7% · Indonesia 9.4% · Ghana 4.2%

World total (2000): 172,737,000 tonnes

around 2% of its total workforce. The high production of the United States is explained by its use of scientific methods and mechanization, which are features of agriculture throughout the developed world.

INTENSIVE OR ORGANIC FARMING

In the early 21st century, some people were beginning to question the dependence of farmers on chemical fertilizers and pesticides. Many people became concerned that the widespread use of chemicals was seriously polluting and damaging the environment.

Others objected to the intensive farming of animals to raise production and lower prices. For example, the suggestion in Britain in 1996 that BSE, or 'mad cow disease', might be passed on to people causing CJD (Creuzfeldt-Jakob Disease) caused widespread alarm.

Such problems have led some farmers to return to organic farming, which is based on animal-welfare principles and the banning of chemical fertilizers and pesticides. The costs of organic foods are certainly higher than those produced by intensive farming, but an increasing number of consumers in the Western world are beginning to demand organic products from their retailers.

Energy and Minerals

In September 2000, Japan experienced its worst nuclear accident, when more than 400 people were exposed to harmful levels of radiation. This was the worst nuclear incident since the explosion at the Chernobyl nuclear power station, in Ukraine, in 1986. Nuclear power provides around 17% of the world's electricity and experts once thought that it would generate much of the world's energy supply. But concerns about safety and worries about the high costs make this seem unlikely. Some developed countries have already abandoned their nuclear programmes.

FOSSIL FUELS

Huge amounts of energy are needed for heating, generating electricity and for transport. In the early years of the Industrial Revolution, coal formed from organic matter buried beneath the Earth's surface, was the leading source of energy. It remains important as a raw material in the manufacture of drugs and other products and also as a fuel, despite the fact that burning coal causes air pollution and gives off carbon dioxide, an important greenhouse gas.

However, oil and natural gas, which came into wide use in the 20th century, are cheaper to produce and easier to handle than coal, while, kilogram for kilogram, they give out more heat. Oil is especially important in moving transport, supplying about 97% of the fuel required.

In 1995, proven reserves of oil were sufficient to supply the world, at current rates of production, for 43 years, while supplies of natural gas stood at about 66 years. Coal reserves are more abundant and known reserves would last 200 years at present rates of use. Although these figures must be regarded with caution, because they do not allow for future discoveries, it is clear that fossil fuel reserves will one day run out.

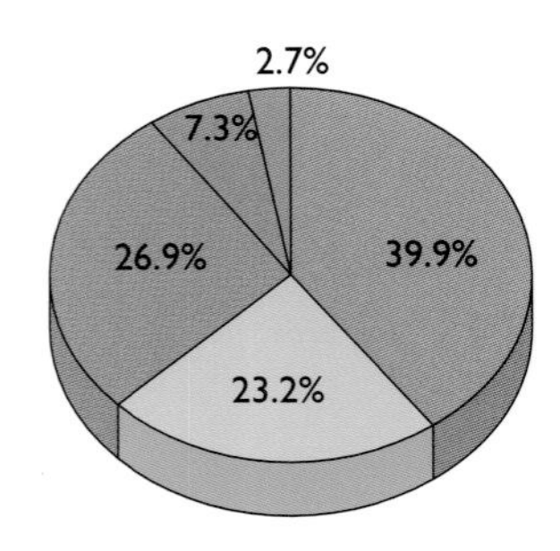

WORLD ENERGY CONSUMPTION

- OIL
- GAS
- COAL
- NUCLEAR
- HYDRO

The diagram shows the proportion of world energy consumption in 1997 by form. Total energy consumption was 8,509.2 million tonnes of oil equivalent. Such fuels as wood, peat and animal wastes, together with renewable forms of energy, such as wind and geothermal power, are not included, although they are important in some areas.

Wind farms in California, United States
Wind farms using giant turbines can produce electricity at a lower cost than conventional power stations. But in many areas, winds are too light or too strong for wind farms to be effective.

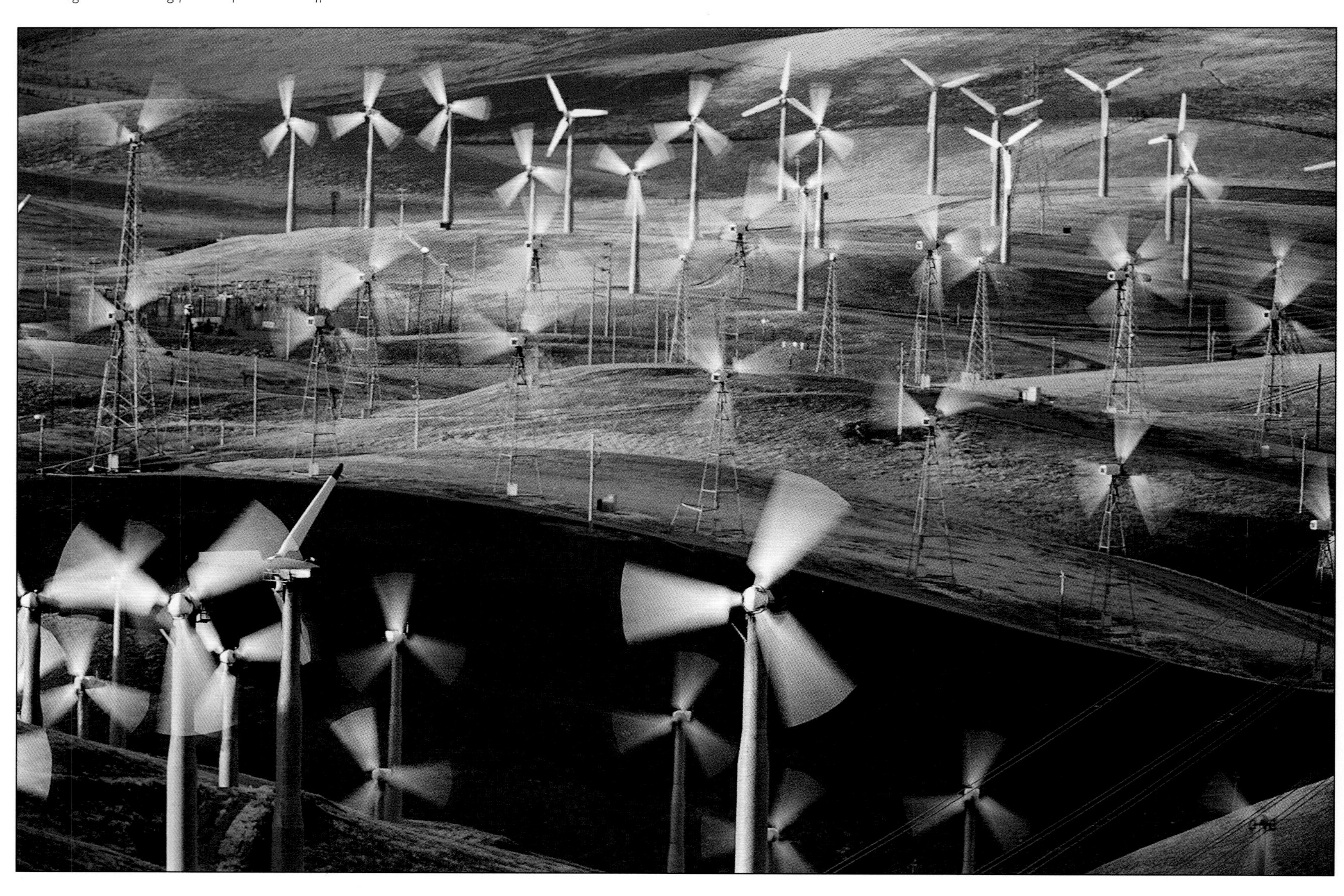

SELECTED MINERAL
PRODUCTION STATISTICS (1997)

Bauxite		Diamonds	
Australia	34.9%	Australia	33.9%
Guinea	15.1%	Congo (D.R.)	18.6%
Brazil	9.8%	Botswana	17.0%
Jamaica	9.4%	Russia	16.1%
China	7.1%	S. Africa	8.5%

Gold		Iron ore	
S. Africa	20.5%	China	22.1%
USA	14.9%	Brazil	17.4%
Australia	13.1%	Australia	14.0%
Canada	7.0%	Ukraine	10.3%
China	6.5%	Russia	6.7%

Manganese		Zinc	
Ukraine	27.0%	China	16.4%
China	25.6%	Canada	14.5%
S. Africa	11.4%	Australia	14.0%
Brazil	8.0%	Peru	11.7%
Australia	7.8%	USA	8.5%

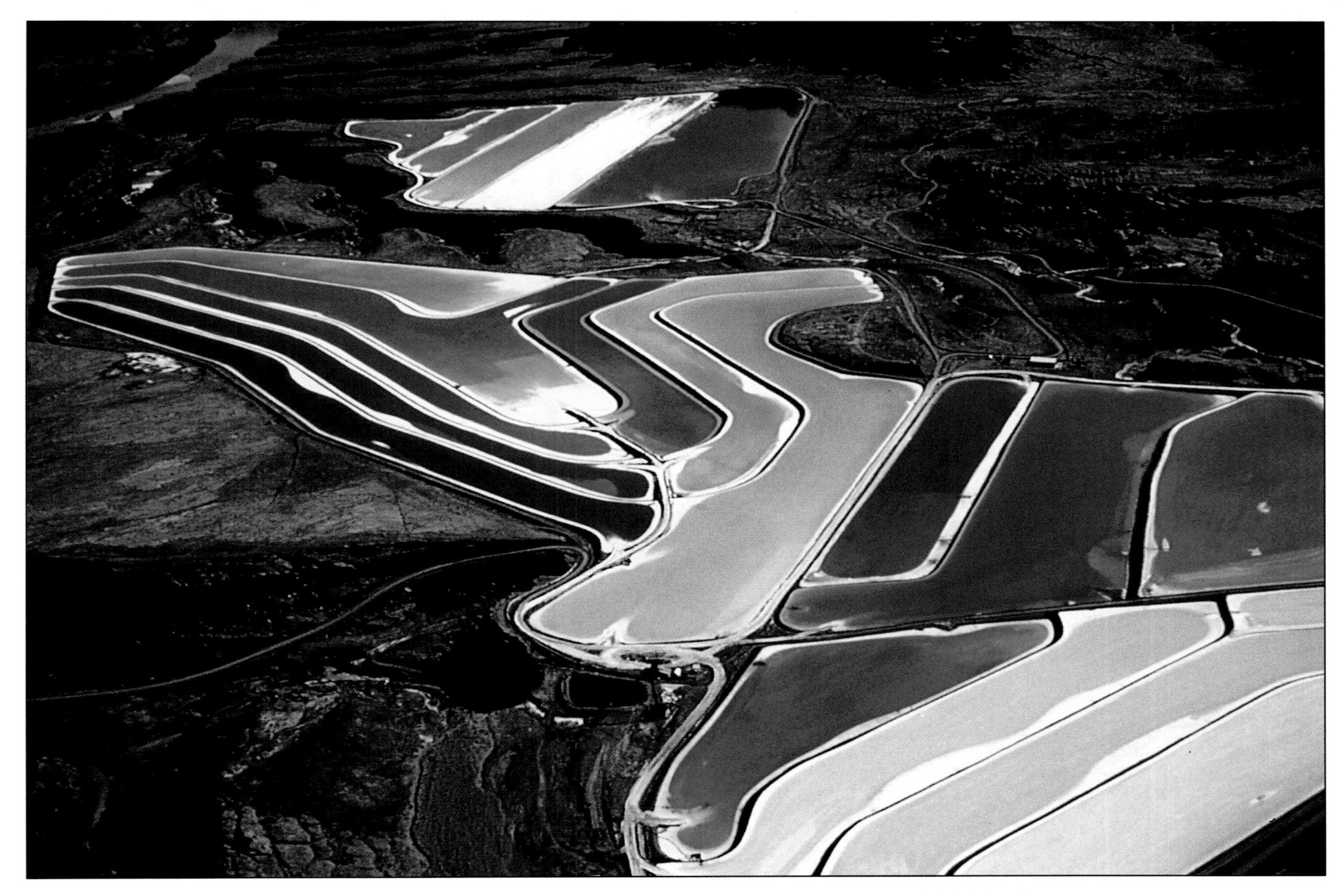

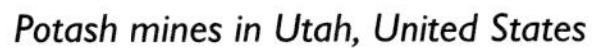

Potash mines in Utah, United States
Potash is a mineral used mainly to make fertilizers. Much of it comes from mines where deposits formed when ancient seas dried up are exploited. Potash is also extracted from salt lakes.

MINERAL DISTRIBUTION
The map shows the richest sources of the most important minerals. Major mineral locations are named. Undersea deposits, most of which are considered inaccessible, are not shown.

▽ GOLD
⬯ SILVER
◆ DIAMONDS
▽ TUNGSTEN
● IRON ORE
▢ NICKEL
▼ CHROME
▲ MANGANESE
▢ COBALT
▲ MOLYBDENUM
▢ COPPER
▲ LEAD
● BAUXITE
▽ TIN
◆ ZINC
▽ MERCURY

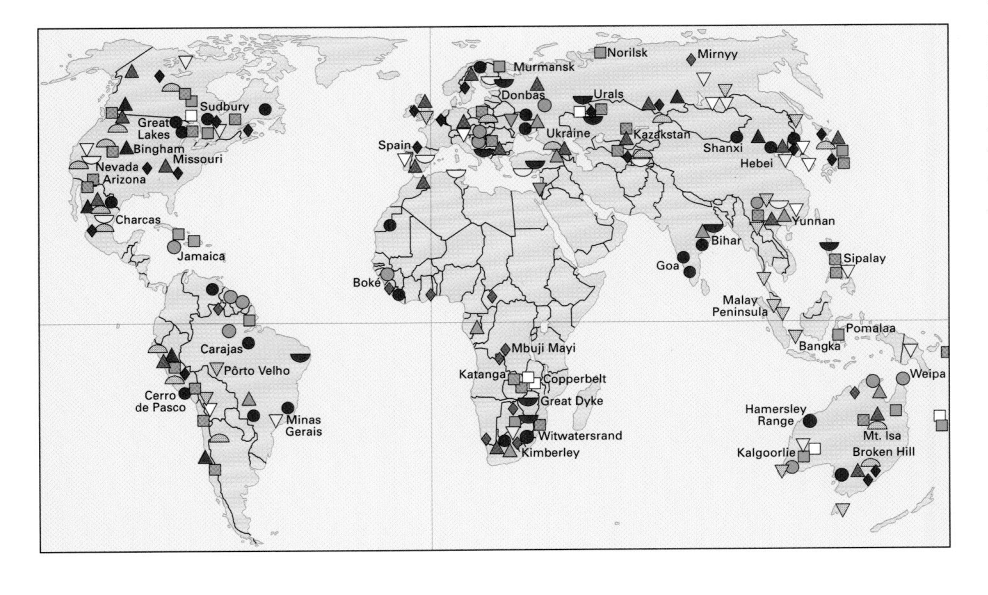

ALTERNATIVE ENERGY

Other sources of energy are therefore required. Besides nuclear energy, the main alternative to fossil fuels is water power. The costs of building dams and hydroelectric power stations is high, though hydroelectric production is comparatively cheap and it does not cause pollution. But the creation of reservoirs uproots people and, in tropical rainforests, it destroys natural habitats. Hydroelectricity is also suitable only in areas with plenty of rivers and steep slopes, such as Norway, while it is unsuitable in flat areas, such as the Netherlands.

In Brazil, alcohol made from sugar has been used to fuel cars. Initially, this government-backed policy met with great success, but it has proved to be extremely expensive. Battery-run, electric cars have also been developed in the United States, but they appear to have limited use, because of the problems involved in regular and time-consuming recharging.

Other forms of energy, which are renewable and cleaner than fossil fuels, are winds, sea waves, the rise and fall of tides, and geothermal power. These forms of energy are already used to some extent. However, their contribution in global terms seems likely to remain small in the immediate future.

MINERALS FOR INDUSTRY

In addition to energy, manufacturing industries need raw materials, including minerals, and these natural resources, like fossil fuels, are being used in such huge quantities that some experts have predicted shortages of some of them before long.

Manufacturers depend on supplies of about 80 minerals. Some, such as bauxite (aluminium ore) and iron, are abundant, but others are scarce or are found only in deposits that are uneconomical to mine. Many experts advocate a policy of recycling scrap metal, including aluminium, chromium, copper, lead, nickel and zinc. This practice would reduce pollution and conserve the energy required for extracting and refining mineral ores.

World Economies

In 1999, Tanzania had a per capita GNP (Gross National Product) of US$240, as compared with Switzerland, whose per capita GNP stood at $38,350. These figures indicate the vast gap between the economies and standards of living of the two countries.

The GNP includes the GDP (Gross Domestic Product), which consists of the total output of goods and services in a country in a given year, plus net exports – that is, the value of goods and services sold abroad less the value of foreign goods and services used in the country in the same year. The GNP divided by the population gives a country's GNP per capita. In low-income developing countries, agriculture makes a high contribution to the GNP. For example, in Tanzania, 40% of the GDP in 1999 came from

Microchip production, Taiwan
Despite its lack of resources, Taiwan is one of eastern Asia's 'tiger'
economies. Its high-tech industries have helped it to achieve fast
economic growth and to compete on the world market.

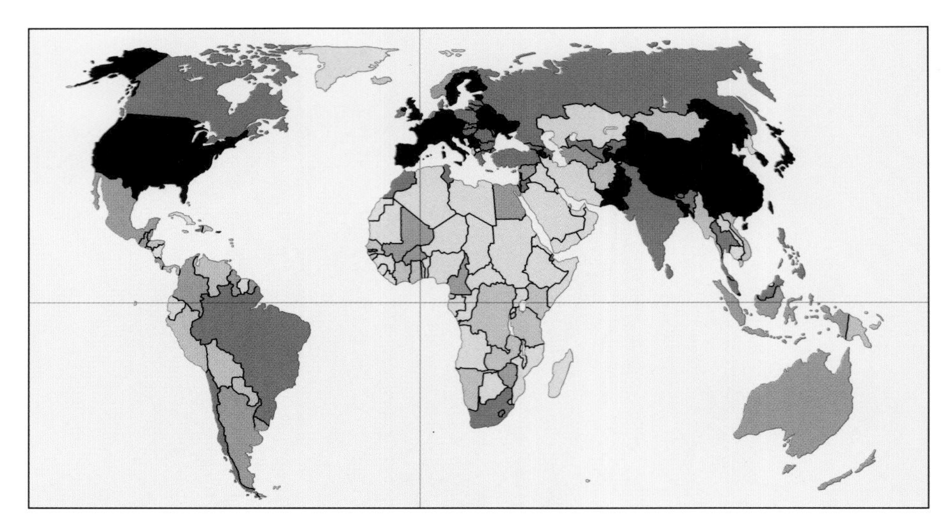

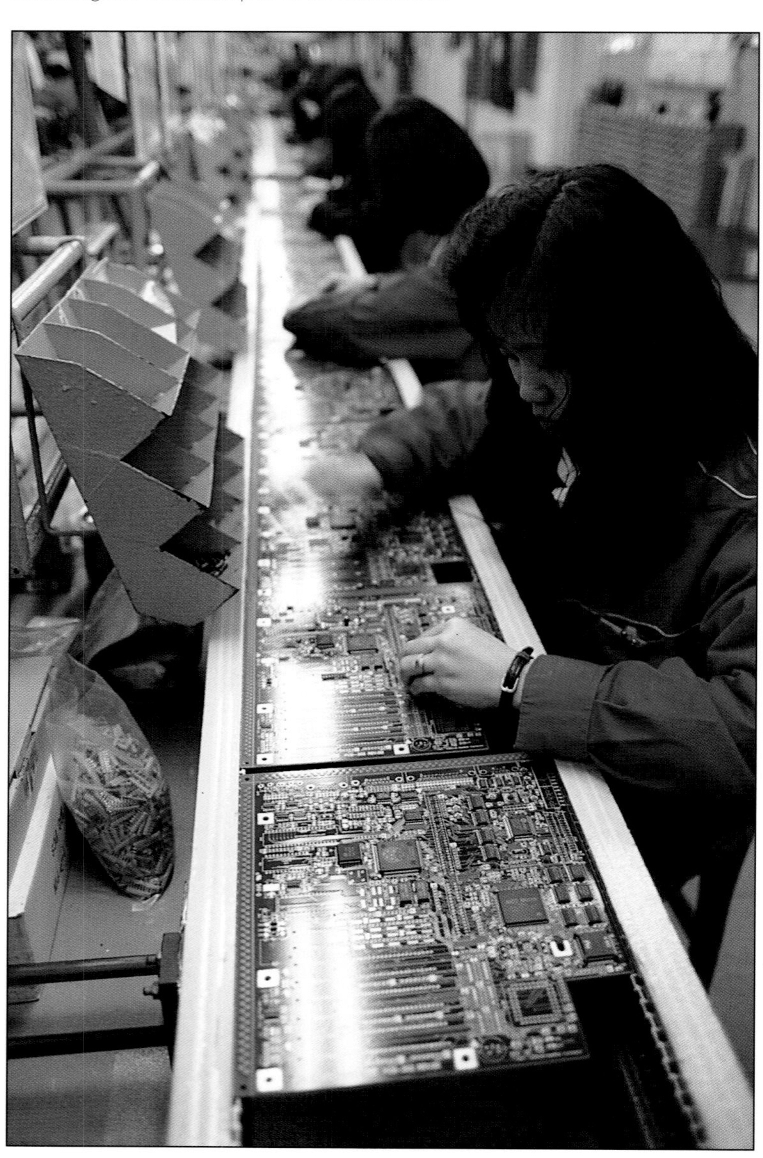

agriculture. On the other hand, manufacturing was small-scale and contributed only 6.6% of the GDP. By comparison, in high-income economies, the percentage contribution of manufacturing far exceeds that of agriculture.

INDUSTRIALIZATION

The Industrial Revolution began in Britain in the late 18th century. Before that time, most people worked on farms. But with the Industrial Revolution came factories, using machines that could manufacture goods much faster and more cheaply than those made by cottage industries which already existed.

The Industrial Revolution soon spread to several countries in mainland Europe and the United States and, by the late 19th century, it had reached Canada, Japan and Russia. At first, industrial development was based on such areas as coalfields or ironfields. But in the 20th century, the use of oil, which is easy to transport along pipelines, made it possible for industries to be set up anywhere.

Some nations, such as Switzerland, became industrialized even though they lacked natural resources. They depended instead on the specialized skills of their workers. This same pattern applies today. Some countries with rich natural resources, such as Mexico (with a per capita GNP in 1999 of $4,400), lag far behind Japan ($32,230) and Cyprus ($11,960), which lack resources and have to import many of the materials they need for their manufacturing industries.

SERVICE INDUSTRIES

Experts often refer to high-income countries as industrial economies. But manufacturing employs only one in six workers in the United

INDUSTRY AND TRADE
Manufactured goods (including machinery and transport) as a percentage of total exports.
- ■ OVER 75%
- ■ 50–75%
- ▦ 25–50%
- ▦ 10–25%
- □ UNDER 10%

Eastern Asia, including Japan (98.3%), Taiwan (92.7%) and Hong Kong (93.0%), contains countries whose exports are most dominated by manufactures. But some countries in Europe, such as Slovenia (92.5%), are also heavily dependent on manufacturing.

GROSS NATIONAL PRODUCT PER CAPITA US$ (1999 ESTIMATES)

1	Liechtenstein	50,000
2	Luxembourg	44,640
3	Switzerland	38,350
4	Bermuda	35,590
5	Norway	32,880
6	Japan	32,230
7	Denmark	32,030
8	USA	30,600
9	Singapore	29,610
10	Iceland	29,280
11	Austria	25,970
12	Germany	25,350
13	Sweden	25,040
14	Monaco	25,000
15	Belgium	24,510
16	Brunei	24,630
17	Netherlands	24,320
18	Finland	23,780
19	Hong Kong (China)	23,520
20	France	23,480

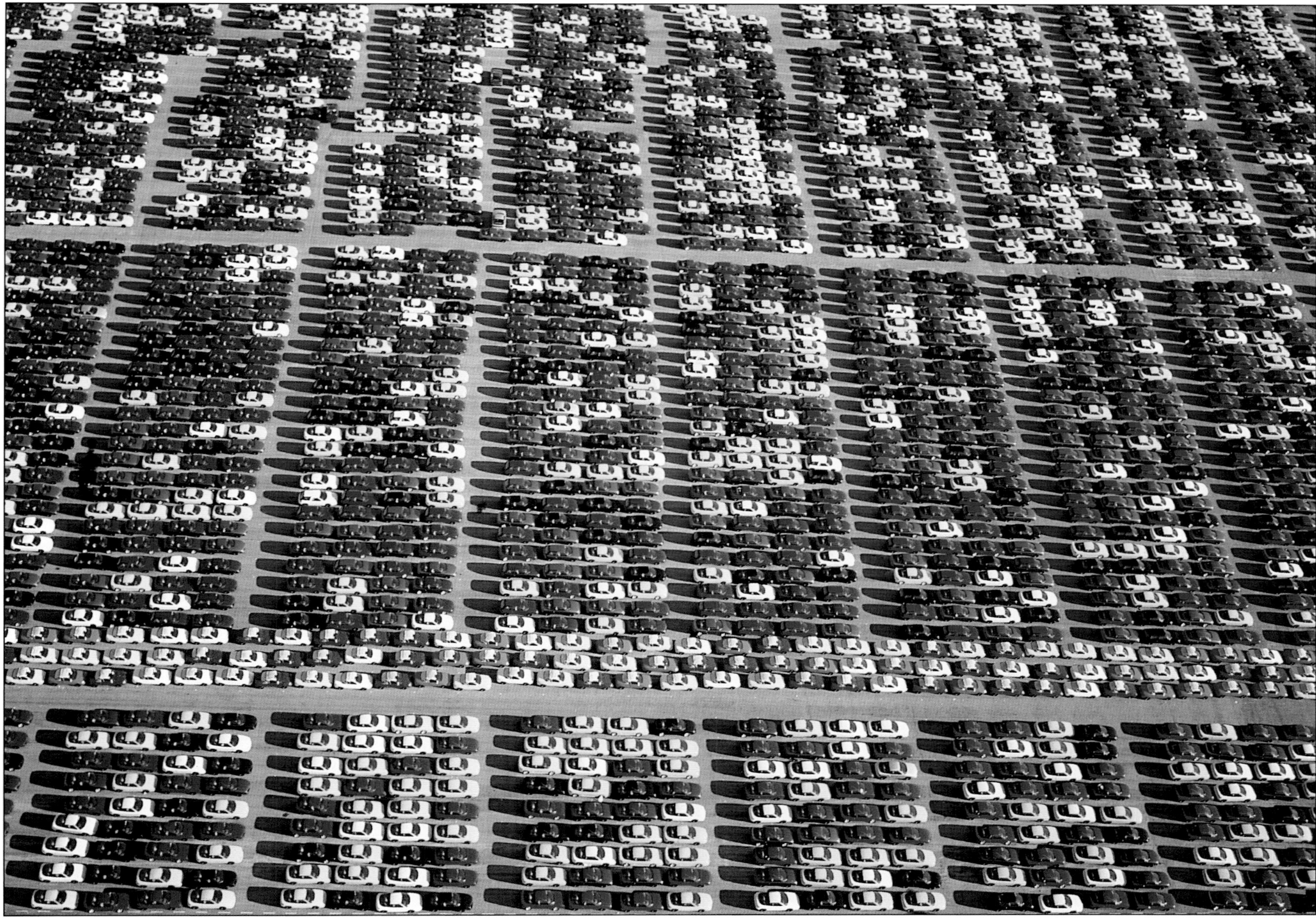

New cars awaiting transportation, Los Angeles, United States
Cars are the most important single manufactured item in world trade, followed by vehicle parts and engines. The world's leading car producers are Japan, the United States, Germany and France.

States, one in five in Britain, and one in three in Germany and Japan.

In most developed economies, the percentage of manufacturing jobs has fallen in recent years, while jobs in service industries have risen. For example, in Britain, the proportion of jobs in manufacturing fell from 37% in 1970 to 14% in 2001, while jobs in the service sector rose from just under 50% to 77%. While change in Britain was especially rapid, similar changes were taking place in most industrial economies. By

the late 1990s, service industries accounted for well over half the jobs in the generally prosperous countries that made up the OECD (Organization for Economic Co-operation and Development). Instead of being called the 'industrial' economies, these countries might be better named the 'service' economies.

Service industries offer a wide range of jobs and many of them require high educational qualifications. These include finance, insurance and high-tech industries, such as computer programming, entertainment and telecommunications. Service industries also include marketing and advertising, which are essential if the cars and television sets made by manufacturers are to be sold. Another valuable service industry is tourism; in some countries, such as the Gambia, it is the major foreign exchange earner. Trade in services plays a crucial part in world economics. The share of services in world trade rose from 17% in 1980 to 22% in the 1990s.

THE WORKFORCE
Percentage of men and women between 15 and 64 years old in employment, selected countries (latest available year).

MEN
WOMEN

Trade and Commerce

The establishment of the WTO (World Trade Organization) on 1 January 1995 was the latest step in the long history of world trade. The WTO was set up by the eighth round of negotiations, popularly called the 'Uruguay round', conducted by the General Agreement on Tariffs and Trade (GATT). This treaty was signed by represent-atives of 125 governments in April, 1994. By the start of 2002, the WTO had 144 members.

GATT was first established in 1948. Its initial aim was to produce a charter to create a body called the International Trade Organization. This body never came into being. Instead, GATT, acting as an *ad hoc* agency, pioneered a series of agreements aimed at liberalizing world trade by reducing tariffs on imports and other obstacles to free trade.

GATT's objectives were based on the belief

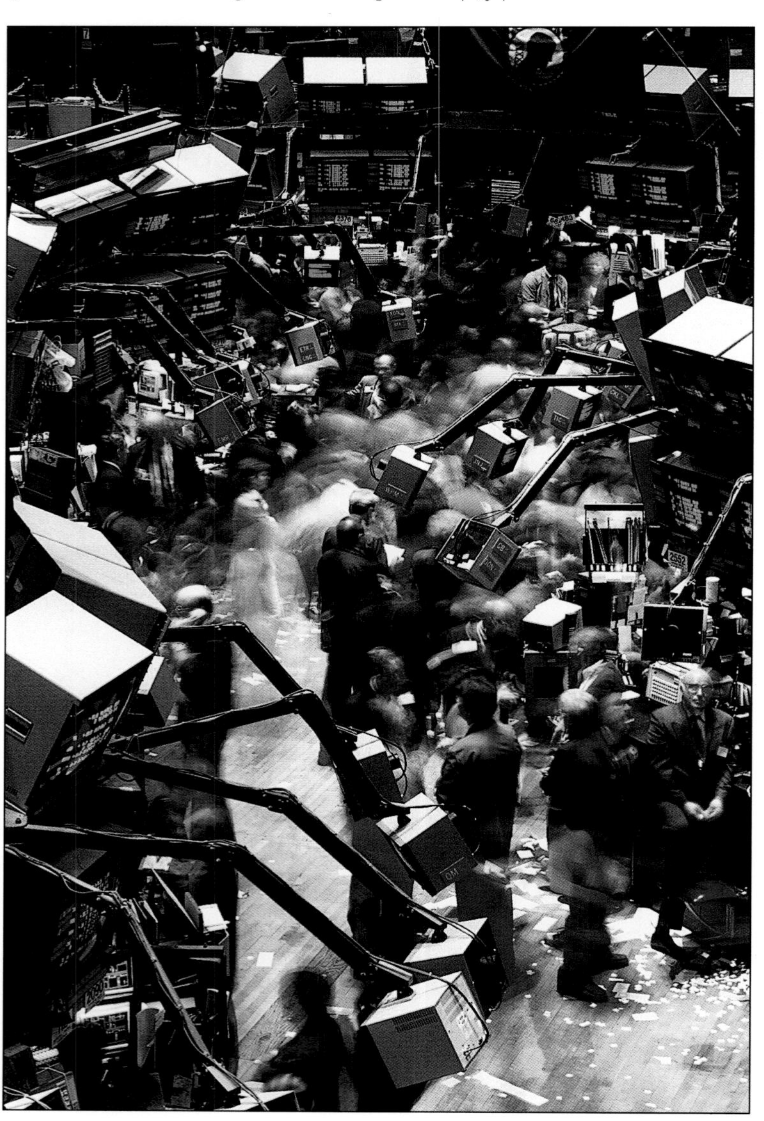

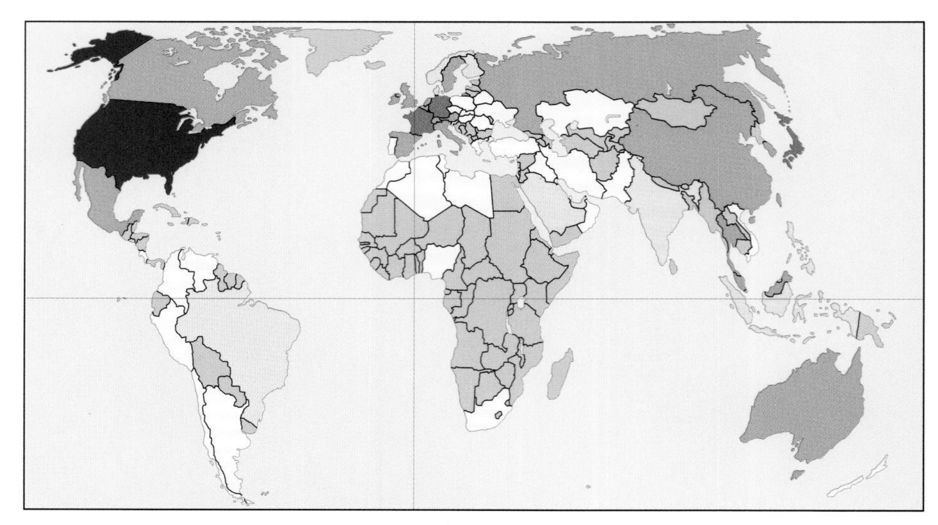

New York City Stock Exchange, United States
Stock exchanges, where stocks and shares are sold and bought, are important in channelling savings and investments to companies and governments. The world's largest stock exchange is in Tokyo, Japan.

that international trade creates wealth. Trade occurs because the world's resources are not distributed evenly between countries, and, in theory, free trade means that every country should concentrate on what it can do best and purchase from others goods and services that they can supply more cheaply. In practice, however, free trade may cause unemployment when imported goods are cheaper than those produced within the country.

Trade is sometimes an important factor in world politics, especially when trade sanctions are applied against countries whose actions incur the disapproval of the international community. For example, in the 1990s, world-wide trade sanctions were imposed on Serbia because of its involvement in the civil war in Bosnia-Herzegovina.

CHANGING TRADE PATTERNS

The early 16th century, when Europeans began to divide the world into huge empires, opened up a new era in international trade. By the 19th century, the colonial powers, who were among the first industrial powers, promoted trade with their colonies, from which they obtained unprocessed raw materials, such as food, natural fibres, minerals and timber. In return, they shipped clothes, shoes and other cheap items to the colonies.

From the late 19th century until the early 1950s, primary products dominated world trade, with oil becoming the leading item in the later part of this period. Many developing countries still depend heavily on the export of one or two primary products, such as coffee or iron ore, but overall the proportion of primary products in world trade has fallen since the 1950s. Today the most important elements in world trade are

WORLD TRADE
Percentage share of total world exports by value (1999).

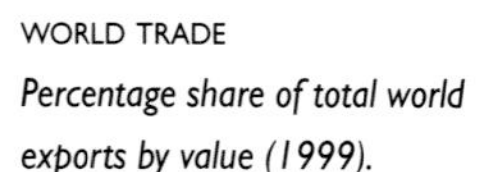

- OVER 10% OF WORLD TRADE
- 5–10% OF WORLD TRADE
- 1–5% OF WORLD TRADE
- 0.5–1% OF WORLD TRADE
- 0.1–0.5% OF WORLD TRADE
- UNDER 0.1% OF WORLD TRADE

The world's leading trading nations, according to the combined value of their exports and imports, are the United States, Germany, Japan, France and the United Kingdom.

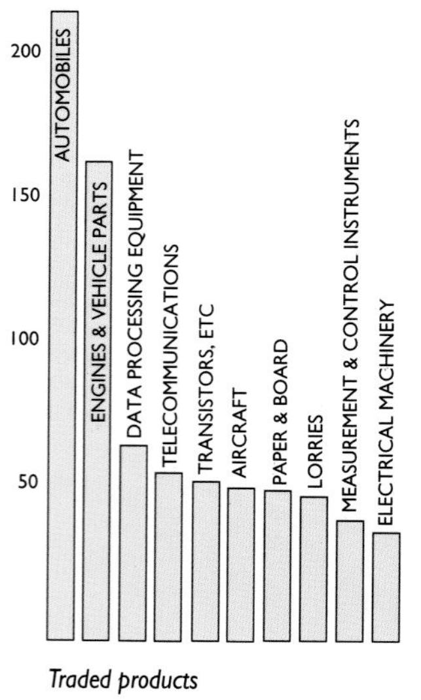

Traded products
Top ten manufactures traded by value in billions of US$ (latest available year).

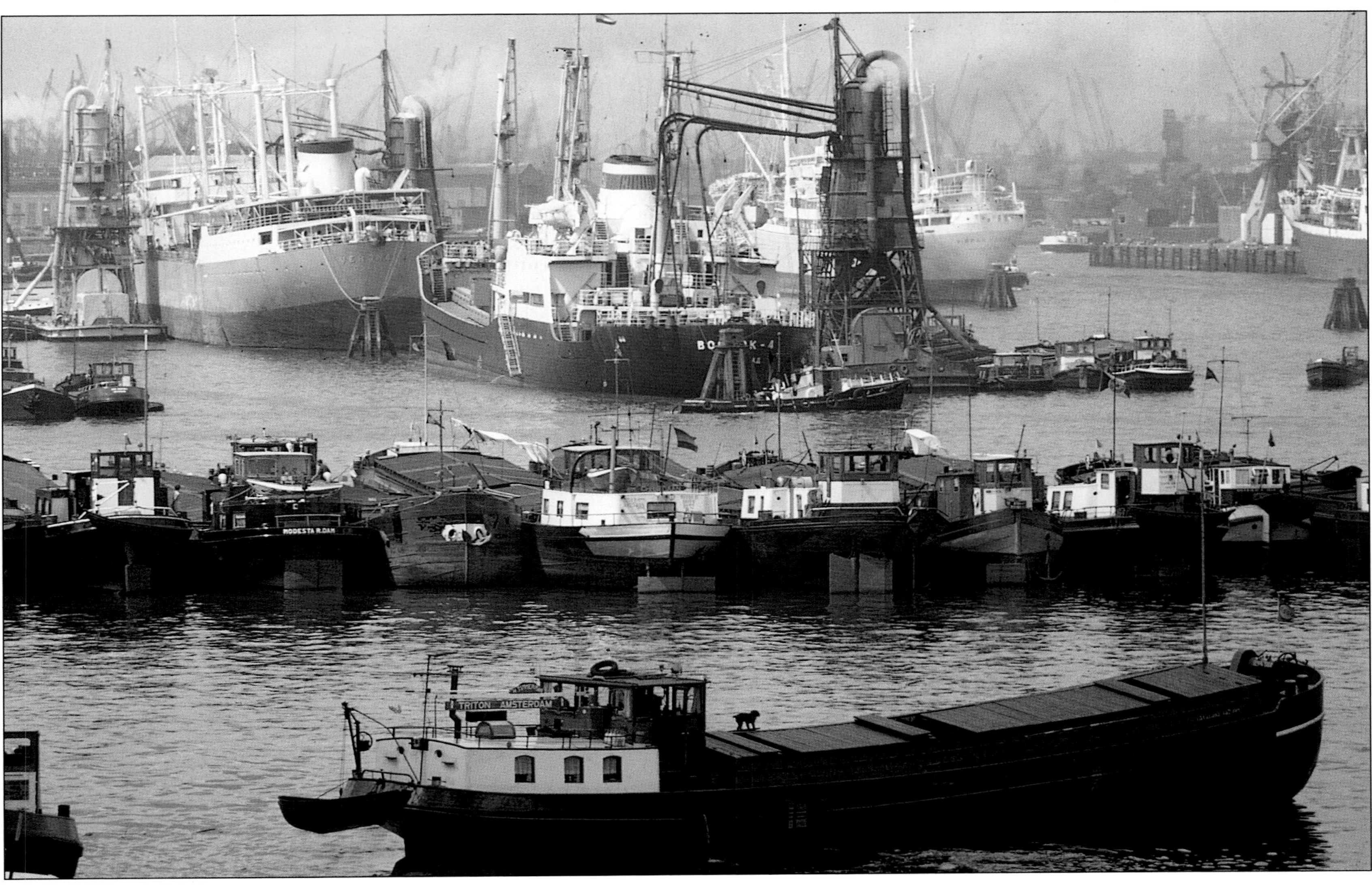

Rotterdam, Netherlands
World trade depends on transport. Rotterdam, the world's largest port, serves not only the Netherlands, but also industrial areas in parts of Germany, France and Switzerland.

DEPENDENCE ON TRADE

Value of exports as a percentage of GDP (Gross Domestic Product) 1997.

- OVER 50% GDP FROM EXPORTS
- 40–50% GDP FROM EXPORTS
- 30–40% GDP FROM EXPORTS
- 20–30% GDP FROM EXPORTS
- 10–20% GDP FROM EXPORTS
- UNDER 10% GDP FROM EXPORTS

○ MOST DEPENDENT ON INDUSTRIAL EXPORTS (OVER 75% OF TOTAL)

● MOST DEPENDENT ON FUEL EXPORTS (OVER 75% OF TOTAL)

◉ MOST DEPENDENT ON METAL & MINERAL EXPORTS (OVER 75% OF TOTAL)

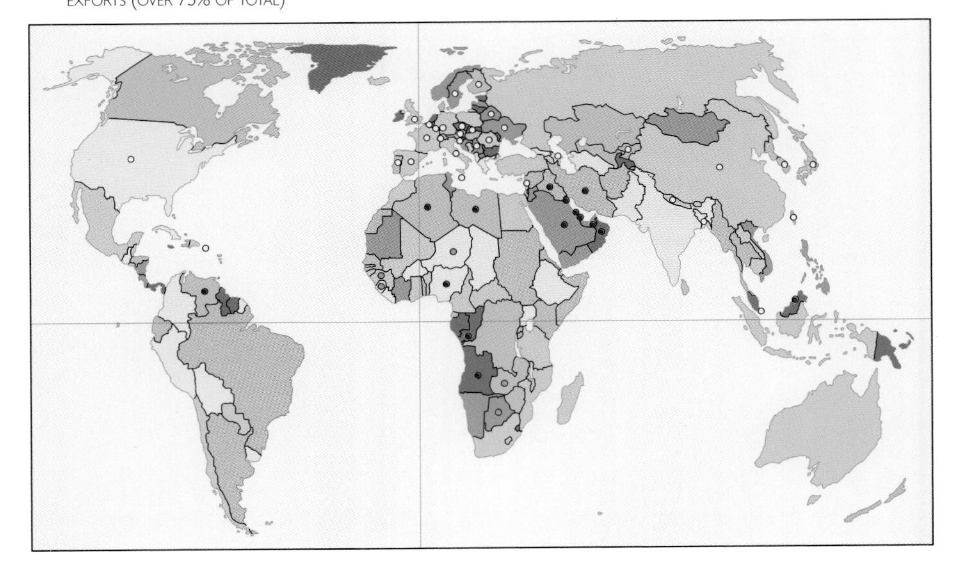

manufactures and semi-manufactures, exchanged mainly between the industrialized nations.

THE WORLD'S MARKETS

Private companies conduct most of world trade, but government policies affect it. Governments which believe that certain industries are strategic, or essential for the country's future, may impose tariffs on imports, or import quotas to limit the volume of imports, if they are thought to be undercutting the domestic industries.

For example, the United States has argued that Japan has greater access to its markets than the United States has to Japan's. This might have led the United States to resort to protectionism, but instead the United States remains committed to free trade despite occasional disputes.

Other problems in international trade occur when governments give subsidies to its producers, who can then export products at low prices. Another difficulty, called 'dumping', occurs when products are sold at below the market price in order to gain a market share. One of the aims of the newly-created WTO is the phasing out of government subsidies for agricultural products, though the world's poorest countries will be exempt from many of the WTO's most severe regulations.

Governments are also concerned about the volume of imports and exports and most countries keep records of international transactions. When the total value of goods and services imported exceeds the value of goods and services exported, then the country has a deficit in its balance of payments. Large deficits can weaken a country's economy.

Travel and Communications

In the 1990s, millions of people became linked into an 'information superhighway' called the Internet. Equipped with a personal computer, an electricity supply, a telephone and a modem, people are able to communicate with others all over the world. People can now send messages by e-mail (electronic mail), they can engage in electronic discussions, contacting people with similar interests, and engage in 'chat lines', which are the latest equivalent of telephone conferences.

These new developments are likely to affect the working lives of people everywhere, enabling them to work at home whilst having many of the facilities that are available in an office. The Internet is part of an ongoing and astonishingly rapid evolution in the fields of communications and transport.

TRANSPORT

Around 200 years ago, most people never travelled far from their birthplace, but today we are much more mobile. Cars and buses now provide convenient forms of transport for many millions of people, huge ships transport massive cargoes around the world, and jet airliners, some travelling faster than the speed of sound, can transport high-value goods as well as holiday-makers to almost any part of the world.

Land transport of freight has developed greatly

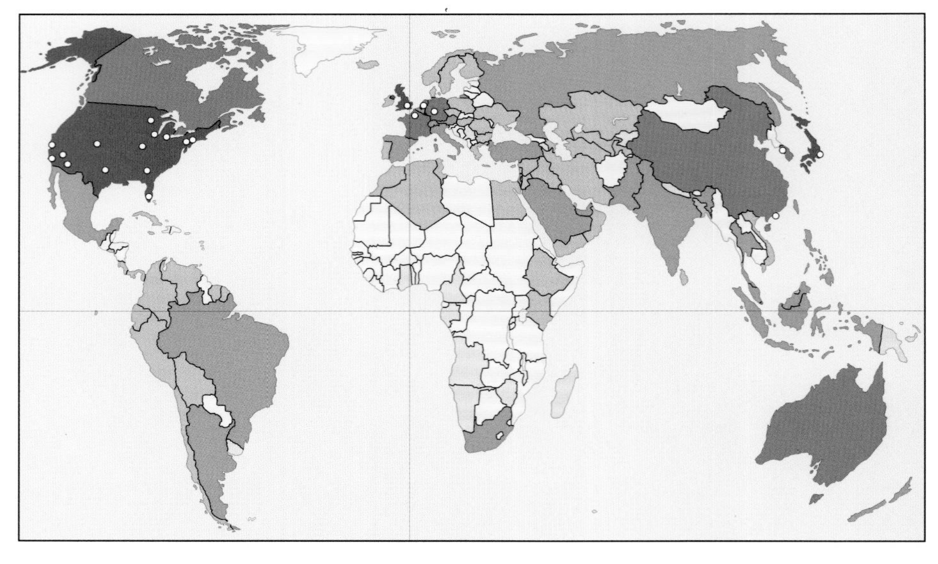

Jodrell Bank Observatory, Cheshire, England
The world's first giant radio telescope began operations at Jodrell Bank in 1957. Radio telescopes can explore the Universe as far as 16 billion light-years away.

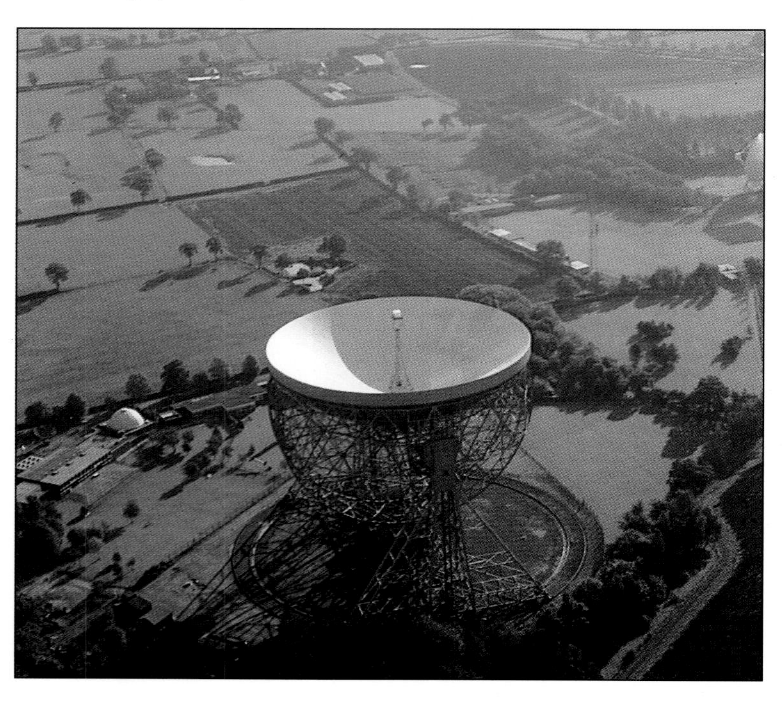

since the start of the Industrial Revolution. Canals, which became important in the 18th century, could not compete with rail transport in the 19th century. Rail transport remains important, but, during the 20th century, it suffered from competition with road transport, which is cheaper and has the advantage of carrying materials and goods from door to door.

Road transport causes pollution and the burning of fuels creates greenhouse gases that contribute to global warming. Yet privately owned cars are now the leading form of passenger traffic in developed nations, especially for journeys of less than around 400 km [250 miles]. Car owners do not have to suffer the inconvenience of waiting for public transport, such as buses, though they often have to endure traffic jams at peak travel times.

Ocean passenger traffic is now modest, but ships carry the bulk of international trade. Huge oil tankers and bulk grain carriers now ply the oceans with their cargoes, while container ships

AIR TRAVEL – PASSENGER KILOMETRES*
FLOWN (1997).

- OVER 100,000 MILLION
- 50,000–100,000 MILLION
- 10,000–50,000 MILLION
- 1,000–10,000 MILLION
- 500–1,000 MILLION
- UNDER 500 MILLION
- ○ MAJOR AIRPORTS (HANDLING OVER 25 MILLION PASSENGERS IN 2000)

* Passenger kilometres are the number of passengers (both international and domestic) multiplied by the distance flown by each passenger from the airport of origin.

SELECTED NEWSPAPER CIRCULATION FIGURES (1995)

France			**Russia**		
Le Monde		357,362	Pravda		1,373,795
Le Figaro		350,000	Ivestia		700,000
Germany			**Spain**		
Bild		4,500,000	El Pais		407,629
Süddeutsche Zeitung		402,866			
			United Kingdom		
Italy			The Sun		4,061,253
Corriera Della Sella		676,904	Daily Mirror		2,525,000
La Republica		655,321	Daily Express		1,270,642
La Stampa		436,047	The Times		672,802
			The Guardian		402,214
Japan					
Yomiuri Shimbun	(a.m. edition)	9,800,000	**United States**		
	(p.m. edition)	4,400,000	New York Times		1,724,705
Manichi Shimbun	(a.m. edition)	3,200,000	Chicago Tribune		1,110,552
	(p.m. edition)	1,900,000	Houston Chronicle		605,343

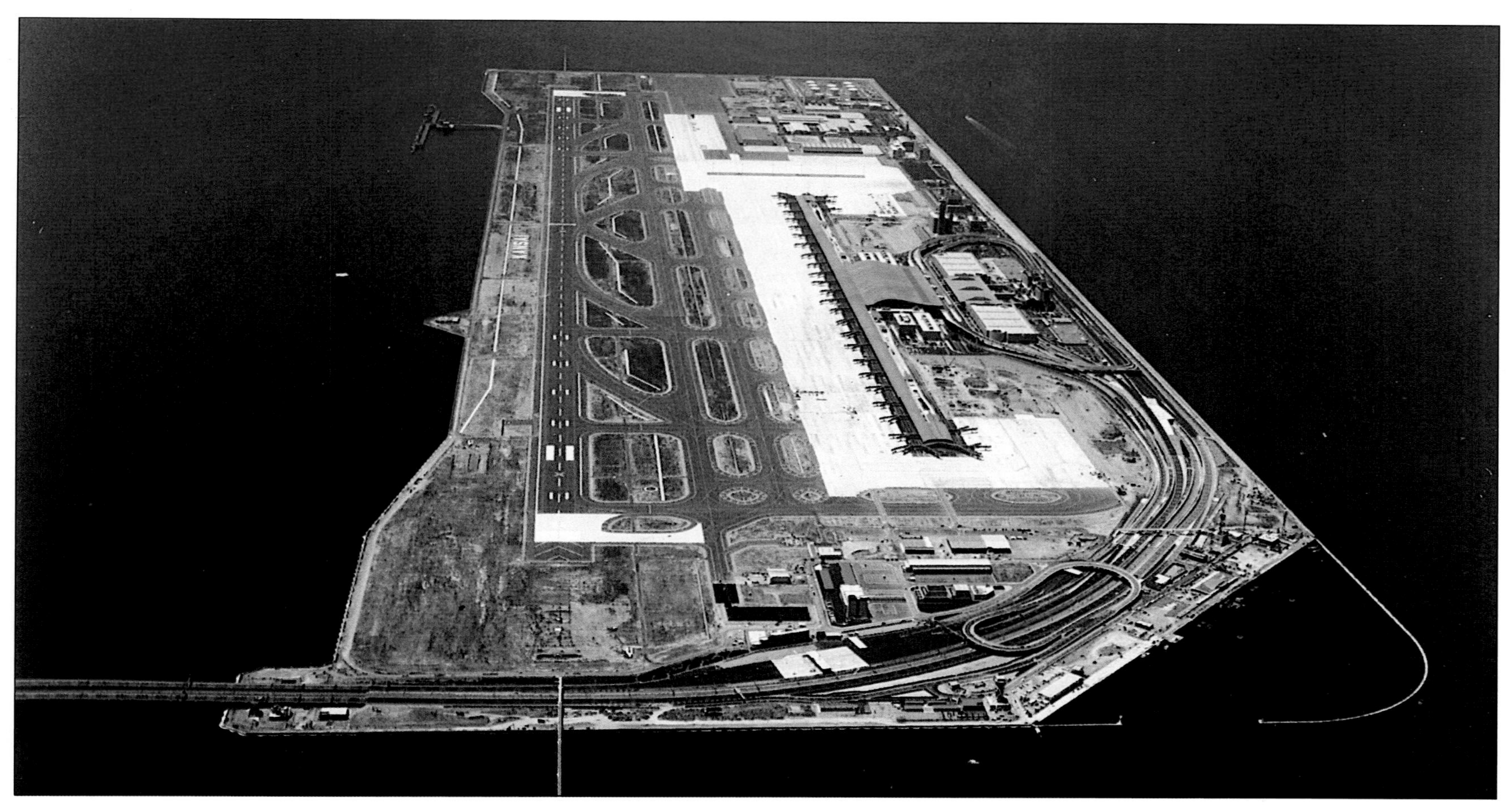

Kansai International Airport, Japan
The new airport, opened in September 1994, is built on an artificial island in Osaka Bay. The island holds the world's biggest airport terminal at nearly 2 km [1.2 miles] long.

carry mixed cargoes. Containers are boxes built to international standards that contain cargo. Containers are easy to handle, and so they reduce shipping costs, speed up deliveries and cut losses caused by breakages. Most large ports now have the facilities to handle containers.

Air transport is suitable for carrying goods that are expensive, light and compact, or perishable. However, because of the high costs of air freight, it is most suitable for carrying passengers along long-distance routes around the world. Through air travel, international tourism, with people sometimes flying considerable distances, has become a major and rapidly expanding industry.

COMMUNICATIONS

After humans first began to communicate by using the spoken word, the next great stage in the development of communications was the invention of writing around 5,500 years ago.

The invention of movable type in the mid 15th century led to the mass production of books and, in the early 17th century, the first newspapers. Newspapers now play an important part in the mass communication of information, although today radio and, even more important, television have led to a decline in the circulation of newspapers in many parts of the world.

The most recent developments have occurred in the field of electronics. Artificial communications satellites now circle the planet, relaying radio, television, telegraph and telephone signals. This enables people to watch events on the far side of the globe as they are happening. Electronic equipment is also used in many other ways, such as in navigation systems used in air, sea and space, and also in modern weaponry, as shown vividly in the television coverage of such military actions as that in Afghanistan in 2001.

THE AGE OF COMPUTERS

One of the most remarkable applications of electronics is in the field of computers. Computers are now making a huge contribution to communications. They are able to process data at incredibly high speeds and can store vast quantities of information. For example, the work of weather forecasters has been greatly improved now that computers can process the enormous amount of data required for a single weather forecast. They also have many other applications in such fields as business, government, science and medicine.

Through the Internet, computers provide a free interchange of news and views around the world. But the dangers of misuse, such as the exchange of pornographic images, have led to calls for censorship. Censorship, however, is a blunt weapon, which can be used by authoritarian governments to suppress the free exchange of information that the new information superhighway makes possible.

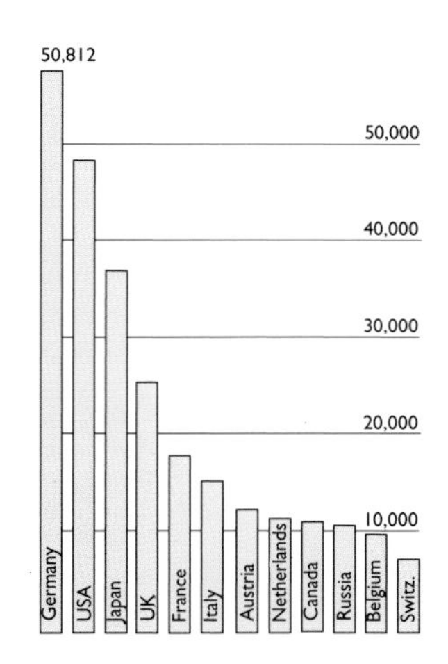

Spending on tourism
Countries spending the most on overseas tourism, US$ million (1996).

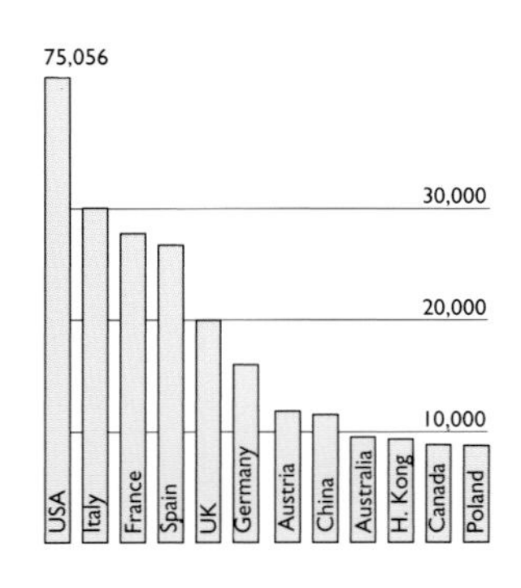

Receipts from tourism
Countries receiving the most from overseas tourism, US$ million (1996).

The World Today

The early years of the 20th century witnessed the exploration of Antarctica, the last uncharted continent. Today, less than 100 years later, tourists are able to take cruises to the icy southern continent, while almost no part of the globe is inaccessible to the determined traveller. Improved transport and images from space have made our world seem smaller.

A Divided World

Between the end of World War II in 1945 and the late 1980s, the world was divided, politically and economically, into three main groups: the developed countries or Western democracies, with their free enterprise or mixed economies; the centrally planned or Communist countries; and the developing countries or Third World.

This division became obsolete when the former Soviet Union and its old European allies, together with the 'special economic zones' in eastern China, began the transition from centrally planned to free enterprise economies. This left the world divided into two broad camps: the prosperous developed countries and the poorer developing countries. The simplest way of distinguishing between the groups is with reference to their per capita Gross National Products (per capita GNPs).

The World Bank divides the developing countries into three main groups. At the bottom are the low-income economies, which include China, India and most of sub-Saharan Africa. In 1999, this group contained about 40% of the

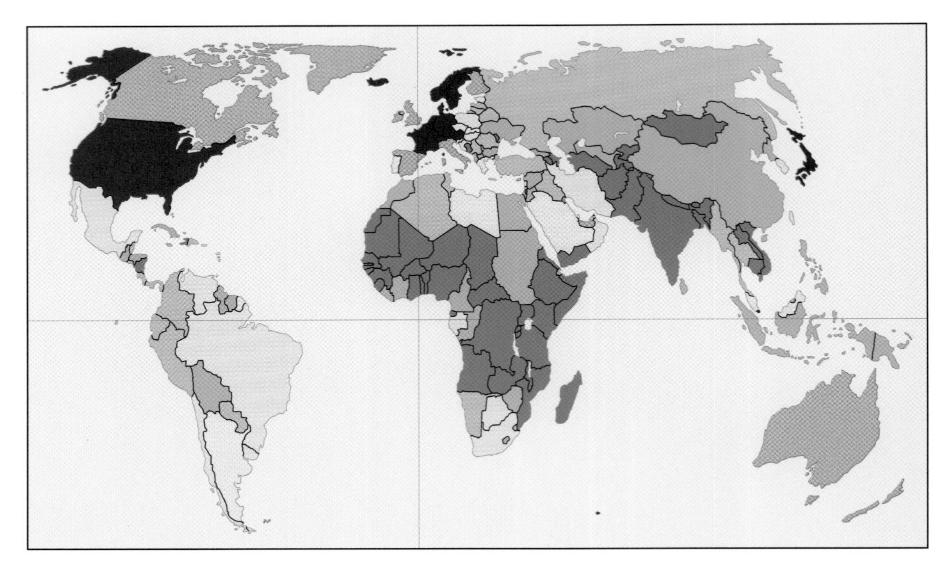

world's population, but its average per capita GNP was only US$420. The other two groups are the lower-middle-income economies, with an average per capita GNP of $1,200, and the upper-middle-income economies with an average per capita GNP of $4,870. By contrast, the high-income economies, also called the developed countries, contain only 15% of the world's population but have the high (and rising) average GNP per capita of $26,440.

Economic and Social Contrasts

Economic differences are coupled with other factors, such as rates of population growth. For example, around the turn of the century, the low- and middle-income economies had a high population growth rate of 1.7%, while the growth rate in high-income economies was around 0.1%. Around 18 countries in Europe experienced a natural decrease in population in 1998.

Stark contrasts exist worldwide in the quality

GROSS NATIONAL PRODUCT PER CAPITA

The value of total production divided by the population (1999).

- ■ OVER 400% OF WORLD AVERAGE
- ▨ 200–400% OF WORLD AVERAGE
- □ 100–200% OF WORLD AVERAGE

[WORLD AVERAGE WEALTH PER PERSON US$6,316]

- ▨ 50–100% OF WORLD AVERAGE
- ▨ 25–50% OF WORLD AVERAGE
- ▨ 10–25% OF WORLD AVERAGE
- ■ UNDER 10% OF WORLD AVERAGE

RICHEST COUNTRIES

Liechtenstein	$44,640
Switzerland	$38,350
Bermuda	$35,590
Norway	$32,880
Japan	$32,230

POOREST COUNTRIES

Ethiopia	$100
Burundi	$120
Sierra Leone	$130
Guinea-Bissau	$160
Niger	$190

Porters carrying luggage for tourists, Selous Park, Tanzania

Improved and cheaper transport has led to a boom in tourism in many developing countries. Tourism provides jobs and foreign exchange, though it can undermine local cultures.

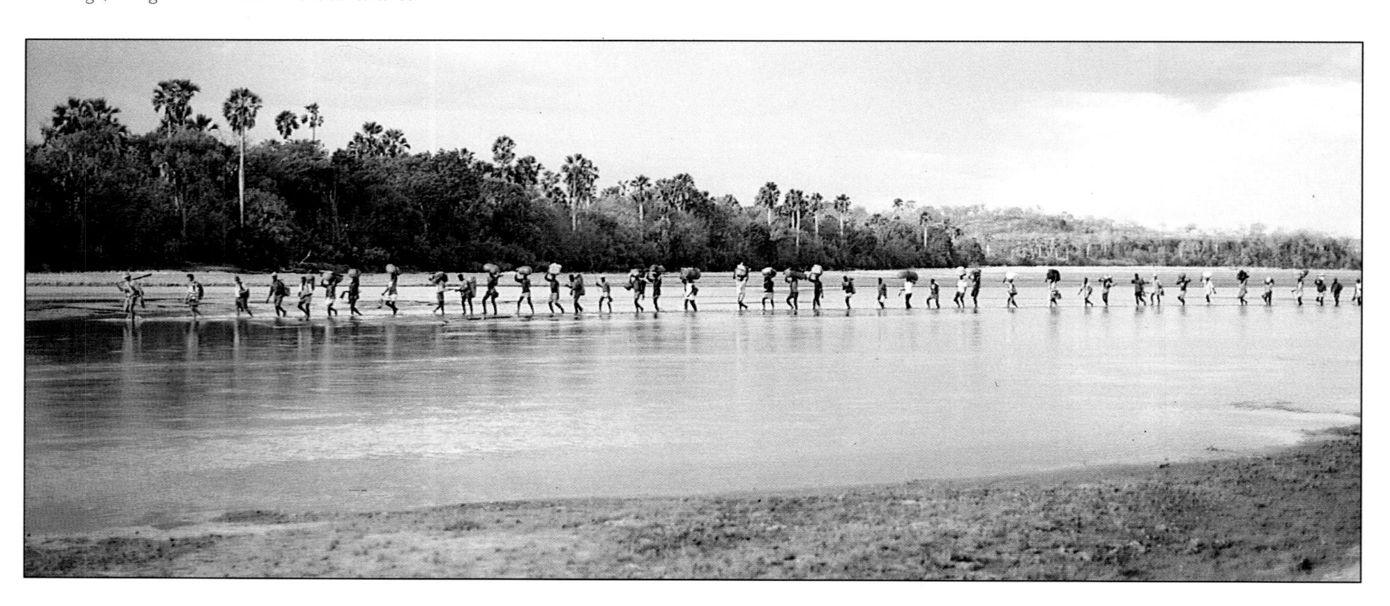

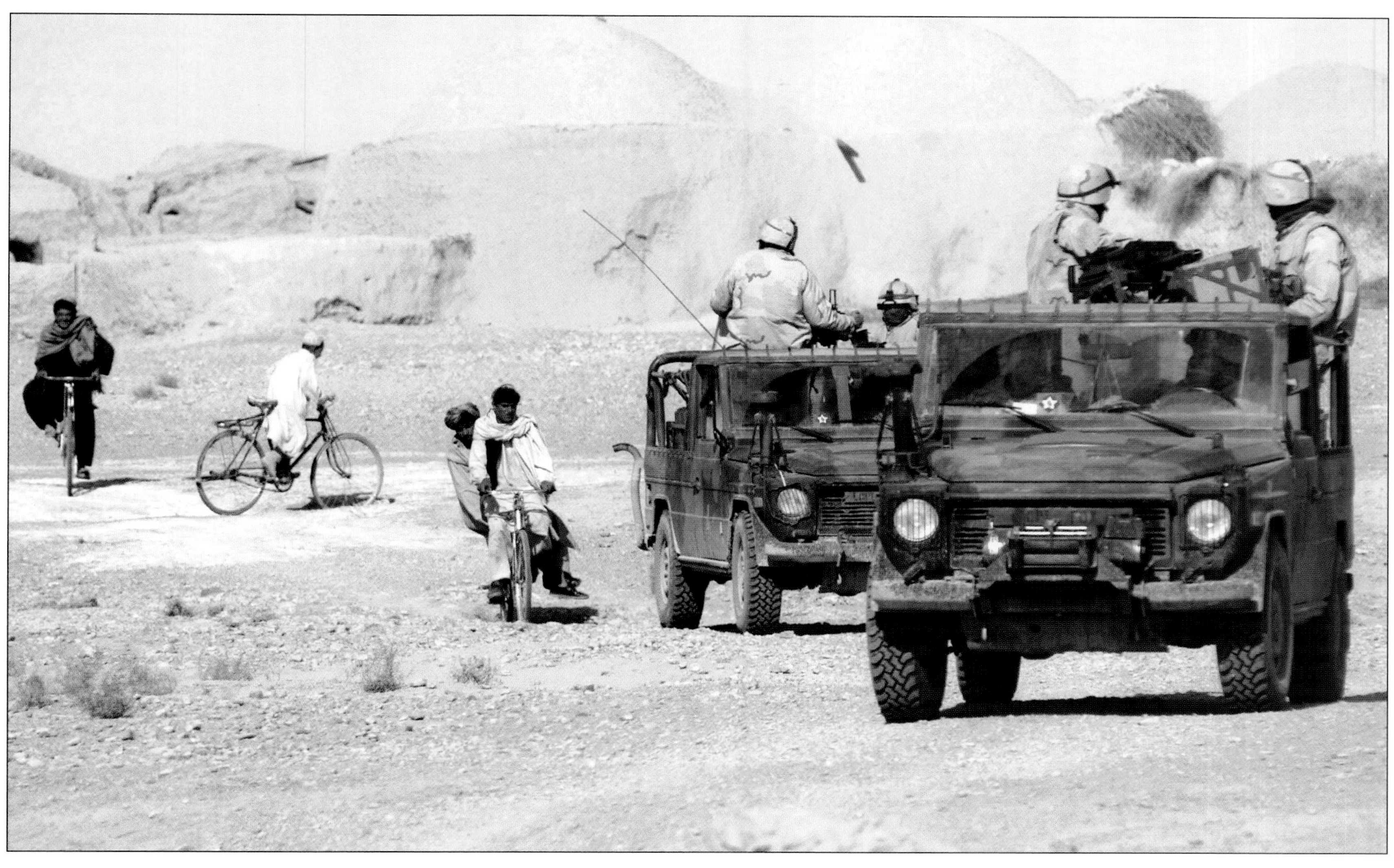

of life. Generally, the people in Western Europe and North America are better fed, healthier and have more cars and better homes than the people in low- and middle-income economies.

In 1999, the average life expectancy at birth in sub-Saharan Africa was 47 years. By contrast, the average life expectancy in the United States and the United Kingdom was 77 years. Illiteracy in low-income economies for people aged 15 and over was 39% in 1999. But for women, the percentage of those who could not read or write was 48%. Illiteracy is relatively rare for both sexes in high-income economies.

FUTURE DEVELOPMENT

In the last 50 years, despite all the aid supplied to developing countries, much of the world still suffers from poverty and economic backwardness. Some countries are even poorer now than they were a generation ago while others have become substantially richer.

However, several factors suggest that poor countries may find progress easier in the 21st century. For example, technology is now more readily transferable between countries, while improved transport and communications make it easier for countries to take part in the world economy. But industrial development could lead to an increase in global pollution. Hence, any strategy for global economic expansion must also take account of environmental factors.

A WORLD IN CONFLICT

The end of the Cold War held out hopes of a new world order. But ethnic, religious and other rivalries have subsequently led to appalling violence in places as diverse as the Balkan peninsula, Israel and the Palestinian territories, and Rwanda–Burundi. Then, on 11 September 2001, the attack on those symbols of the economic and military might of the United States – the World Trade Center and the Pentagon Building – demonstrated that nowhere on Earth is safe from attack by extremists prepared to sacrifice their lives in pursuit of their aims.

The danger posed by terrorist groups, such as al Qaida, or by rogue states, possibly in possession of nuclear or biological weapons, has forced many countries into new alliances to combat the terrorists and the governments that give them shelter. Many people also recognize a pressing need to understand and correct the wrongs, real or perceived, that lead people to acts of martyrdom or murderous destruction.

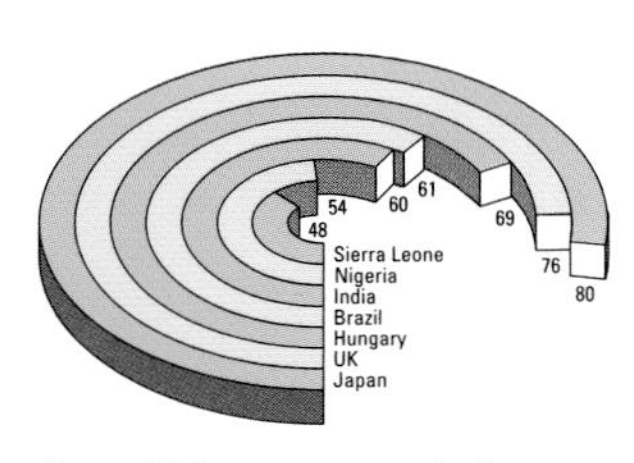

Years of life expectancy at birth, selected countries (1997).
The chart shows the contrasting range of average life expectancies at birth for a range of countries, including both low-income and high-income economies. Generally, improved health services are raising life expectancies. On average, women live longer than men, even in the poorer developing countries.

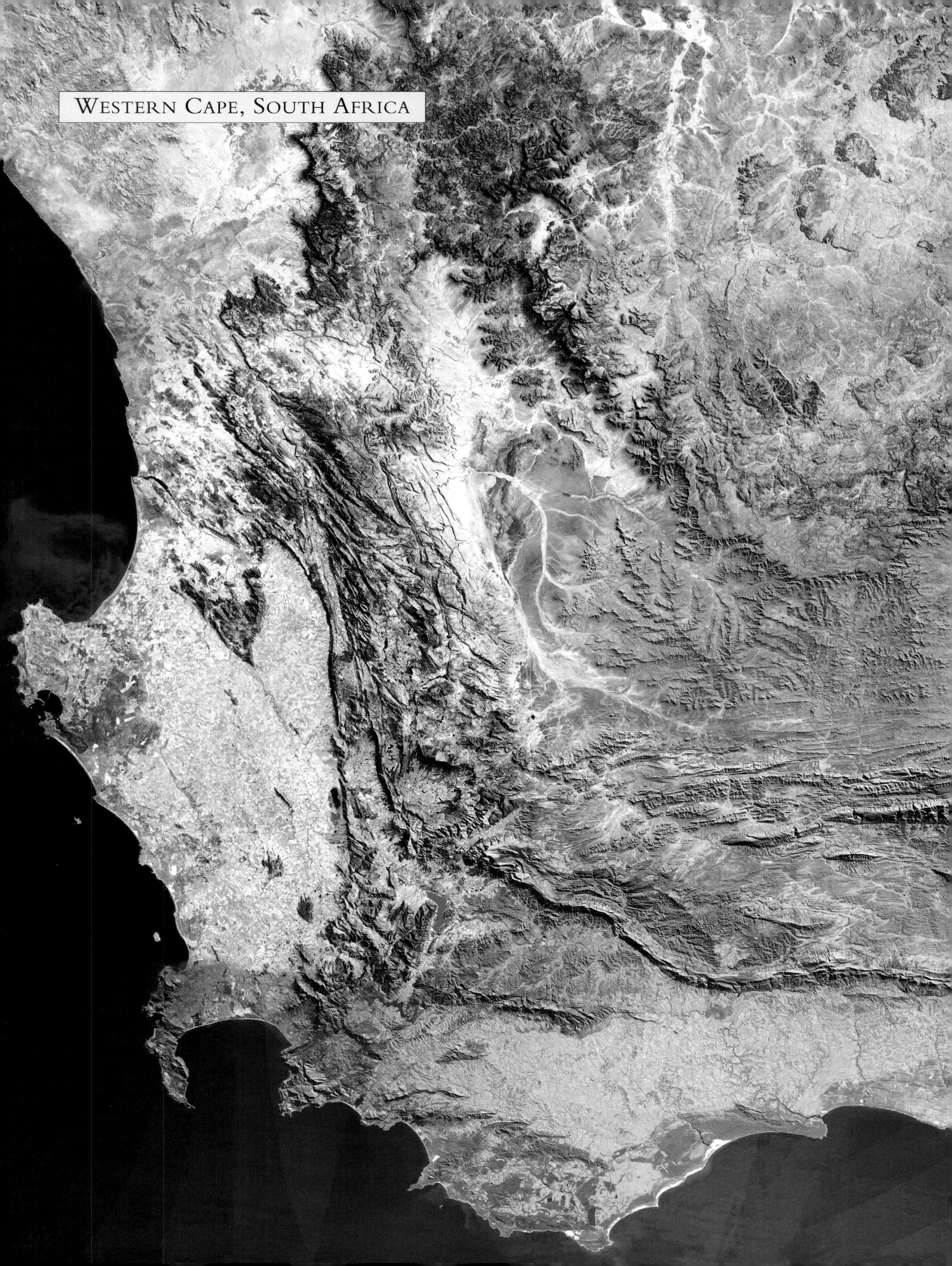

WESTERN CAPE, SOUTH AFRICA

WORLD MAPS

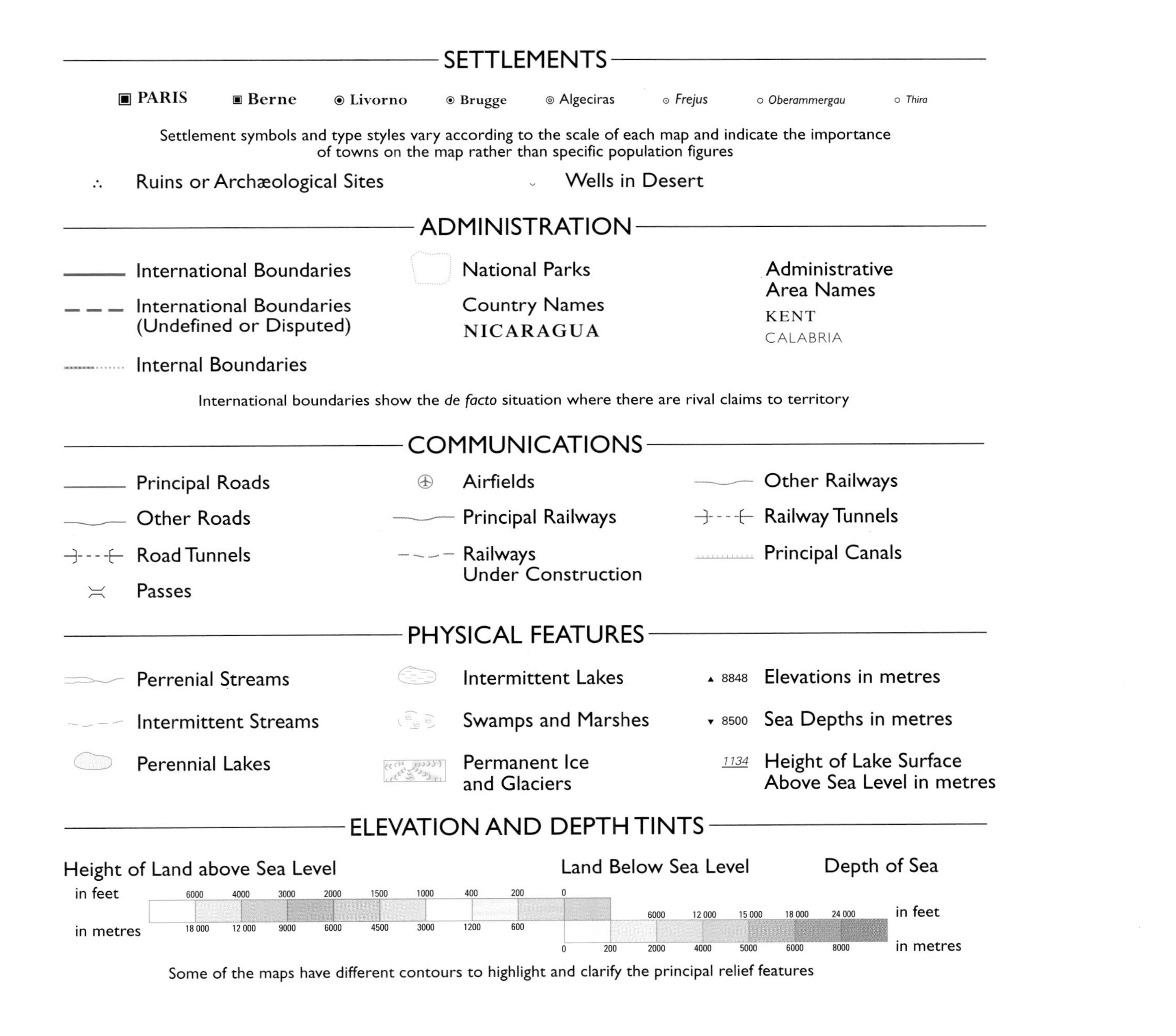

SETTLEMENTS

▣ PARIS   ▣ Berne   ◉ Livorno   ◉ Brugge   ◎ Algeciras   ○ *Frejus*   ○ *Oberammergau*   ○ *Thira*

Settlement symbols and type styles vary according to the scale of each map and indicate the importance
of towns on the map rather than specific population figures

∴ Ruins or Archæological Sites   ◡ Wells in Desert

ADMINISTRATION

————— International Boundaries

– – – International Boundaries
(Undefined or Disputed)

·········· Internal Boundaries

⬭ National Parks

Country Names
NICARAGUA

Administrative
Area Names

KENT
CALABRIA

International boundaries show the *de facto* situation where there are rival claims to territory

COMMUNICATIONS

————— Principal Roads

——— Other Roads

+--+ Road Tunnels

⤢ Passes

⊕ Airfields

——— Principal Railways

– – – Railways
Under Construction

——— Other Railways

+--+ Railway Tunnels

············ Principal Canals

PHYSICAL FEATURES

—⌇— Perrenial Streams

– – – Intermittent Streams

⬭ Perennial Lakes

⬭ Intermittent Lakes

⬭ Swamps and Marshes

▦ Permanent Ice
and Glaciers

▲ 8848 Elevations in metres

▼ 8500 Sea Depths in metres

1134 Height of Lake Surface
Above Sea Level in metres

ELEVATION AND DEPTH TINTS

Height of Land above Sea Level

| in feet | 6000 | 4000 | 3000 | 2000 | 1500 | 1000 | 400 | 200 | 0 |
| in metres | 18 000 | 12 000 | 9000 | 6000 | 4500 | 3000 | 1200 | 600 | |

Land Below Sea Level

Depth of Sea

| | 6000 | 12 000 | 15 000 | 18 000 | 24 000 | in feet |
| 0 | 200 | 2000 | 4000 | 5000 | 6000 | 8000 | in metres |

Some of the maps have different contours to highlight and clarify the principal relief features

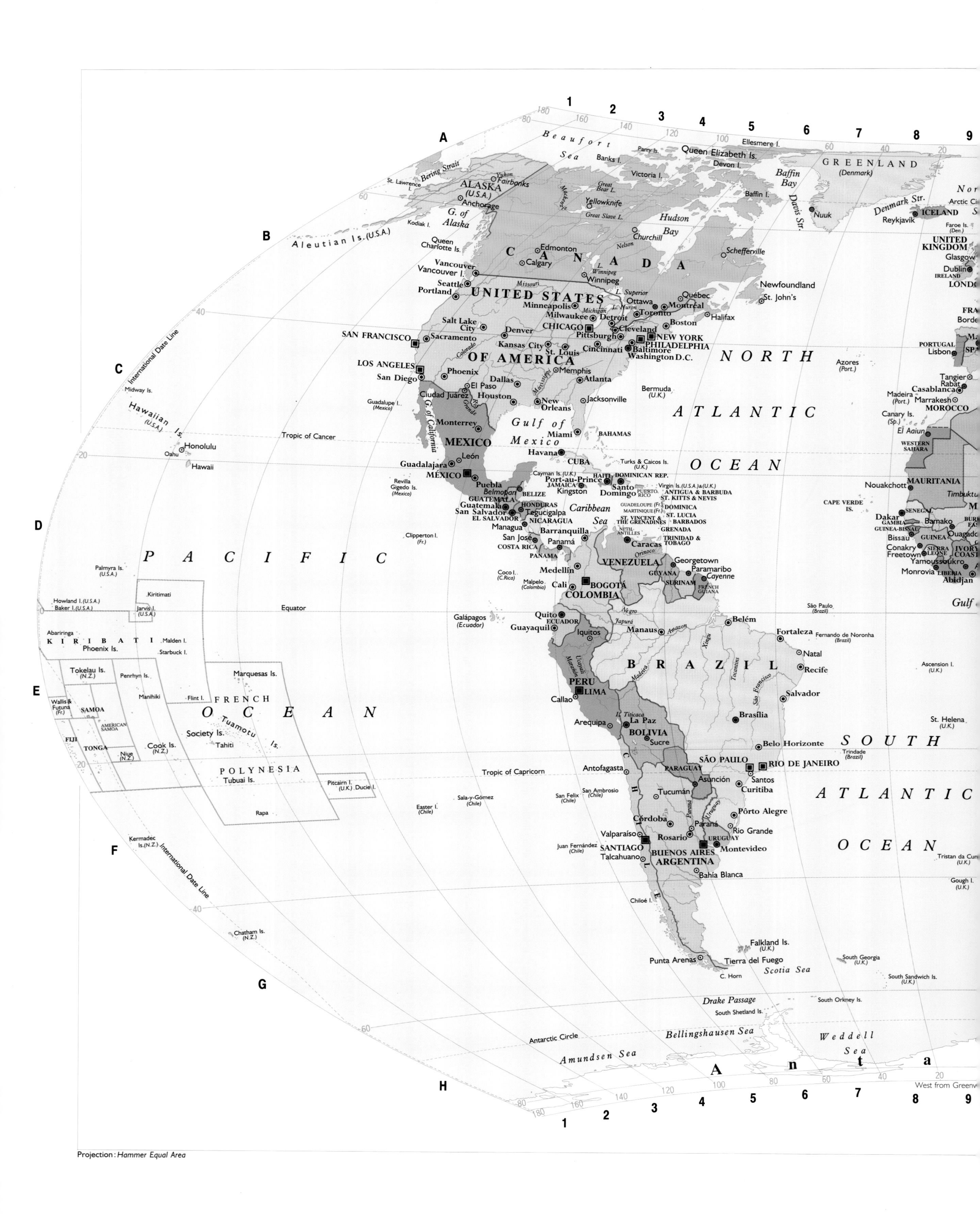

Beaufort Sea
Ellesmere I.
Parry Is.
Queen Elizabeth Is.
Banks I.
Devon I.
Victoria I.
Baffin Bay
Baffin I.
GREENLAND
(Denmark)
Davis Str.
Nuuk
Denmark Str.
Reykjavik
ICELAND
Bering Strait
St. Lawrence I.
Fairbanks
ALASKA
(U.S.A.)
Anchorage
G. of Alaska
Kodiak I.
Yellowknife
Great Bear L.
Great Slave L.
Hudson Bay
Churchill
Aleutian Is. (U.S.A.)
Queen Charlotte Is.
Edmonton
Calgary
CANADA
Schefferville
Vancouver
Vancouver I.
L. Winnipeg
Winnipeg
Seattle
Portland
Newfoundland
St. John's
UNITED STATES OF AMERICA
Minneapolis
L. Superior
Ottawa
Québec
Montréal
Toronto
Halifax
Boston
Milwaukee
Detroit
Salt Lake City
Denver
CHICAGO
Pittsburgh
Cleveland
NEW YORK
PHILADELPHIA
Baltimore
Washington D.C.
SAN FRANCISCO
Sacramento
Kansas City
St. Louis
Cincinnati
NORTH ATLANTIC OCEAN
LOS ANGELES
San Diego
Phoenix
Memphis
Dallas
Atlanta
El Paso
Ciudad Juárez
Houston
New Orleans
Jacksonville
Bermuda
(U.K.)
Azores
(Port.)
International Date Line
Midway Is.
Hawaiian Is.
(U.S.A.)
Guadalupe I.
(Mexico)
G. of California
Monterrey
Gulf of Mexico
Miami
BAHAMAS
Tropic of Cancer
Honolulu
Oahu
Hawaii
MEXICO
Havana
CUBA
Turks & Caicos Is.
(U.K.)
Guadalajara
León
MÉXICO
Revilla Gigedo Is.
(Mexico)
Cayman Is. (U.K.)
Port-au-Prince
HAITI
DOMINICAN REP.
JAMAICA
Kingston
Santo Domingo
PUERTO RICO
Virgin Is. (U.S.A.) & (U.K.)
ANTIGUA & BARBUDA
ST. KITTS & NEVIS
Puebla
Belmopan
BELIZE
GUATEMALA
Guatemala
HONDURAS
San Salvador
Tegucigalpa
EL SALVADOR
NICARAGUA
Managua
Caribbean Sea
GUADELOUPE (Fr.)
MARTINIQUE (Fr.)
DOMINICA
ST. LUCIA
ST. VINCENT & THE GRENADINES
BARBADOS
GRENADA
TRINIDAD & TOBAGO
NETH. ANTILLES
Barranquilla
San José
COSTA RICA
Panamá
PANAMA
Caracas
Clipperton I.
(Fr.)
PACIFIC OCEAN
VENEZUELA
Georgetown
Paramaribo
Cayenne
GUYANA
SURINAM
FRENCH GUIANA
Palmyra Is.
(U.S.A.)
Kiritimati
Medellín
Coco I.
(C.Rica)
Malpelo
(Colombia)
Cali
BOGOTÁ
COLOMBIA
Howland I. (U.S.A.)
Baker I. (U.S.A.)
Jarvis I.
(U.S.A.)
Equator
Galápagos
(Ecuador)
Quito
ECUADOR
Guayaquil
Manaus
Amazon
Belém
Fortaleza
Fernando de Noronha
(Brazil)
São Paulo
(Brazil)
Iquitos
Abariringa
KIRIBATI
Phoenix Is.
Malden I.
Starbuck I.
Natal
Recife
BRAZIL
Tokelau Is.
(N.Z.)
Penrhyn Is.
Marquesas Is.
Manihiki
Flint I.
FRENCH POLYNESIA
PERU
LIMA
Callao
Salvador
Ascension I.
(U.K.)
Wallis & Futuna
(Fr.)
SAMOA
AMERICAN SAMOA
FIJI
TONGA
Niue
(N.Z.)
Cook Is.
(N.Z.)
Society Is.
Tahiti
Tuamotu Is.
Arequipa
La Paz
L. Titicaca
BOLIVIA
Sucre
Brasília
St. Helena
(U.K.)
Belo Horizonte
SOUTH ATLANTIC OCEAN
Trindade
(Brazil)
Tubuai Is.
Pitcairn I.
(U.K.)
Ducie I.
Tropic of Capricorn
Antofagasta
SÃO PAULO
RIO DE JANEIRO
PARAGUAY
Asunción
Santos
Curitiba
Rapa
Sala-y-Gómez
(Chile)
Easter I.
(Chile)
San Felix
(Chile)
San Ambrosio
(Chile)
Tucumán
Pôrto Alegre
Córdoba
Paraná
Rio Grande
Kermadec Is. (N.Z.)
Valparaíso
Rosario
URUGUAY
Juan Fernández
(Chile)
SANTIAGO
BUENOS AIRES
Montevideo
Talcahuano
ARGENTINA
CHILE
Bahía Blanca
Tristan da Cunha
(U.K.)
Gough I.
(U.K.)
Chiloé I.
Chatham Is.
(N.Z.)
Falkland Is.
(U.K.)
Punta Arenas
Tierra del Fuego
South Georgia
(U.K.)
C. Horn
Scotia Sea
South Sandwich Is.
(U.K.)
Drake Passage
South Orkney Is.
South Shetland Is.
Antarctic Circle
Bellingshausen Sea
Weddell Sea
Amundsen Sea
Antarctica
West from Greenwich
UNITED KINGDOM
Glasgow
Dublin
IRELAND
PORTUGAL
Lisbon
Tangier
Rabat
Casablanca
Madeira
(Port.)
Marrakesh
MOROCCO
Canary Is.
(Sp.)
El Aaiún
WESTERN SAHARA
Faroe Is.
(Den.)
Nouakchott
MAURITANIA
CAPE VERDE IS.
Dakar
SENEGAL
GAMBIA
GUINEA-BISSAU
Bissau
GUINEA
Bamako
Conakry
Freetown
SIERRA LEONE
Yamoussoukro
LIBERIA
Monrovia
Abidjan
A
B
C
D
E
F
G
H
1
2
3
4
5
6
7
8
9

Projection: *Hammer Equal Area*

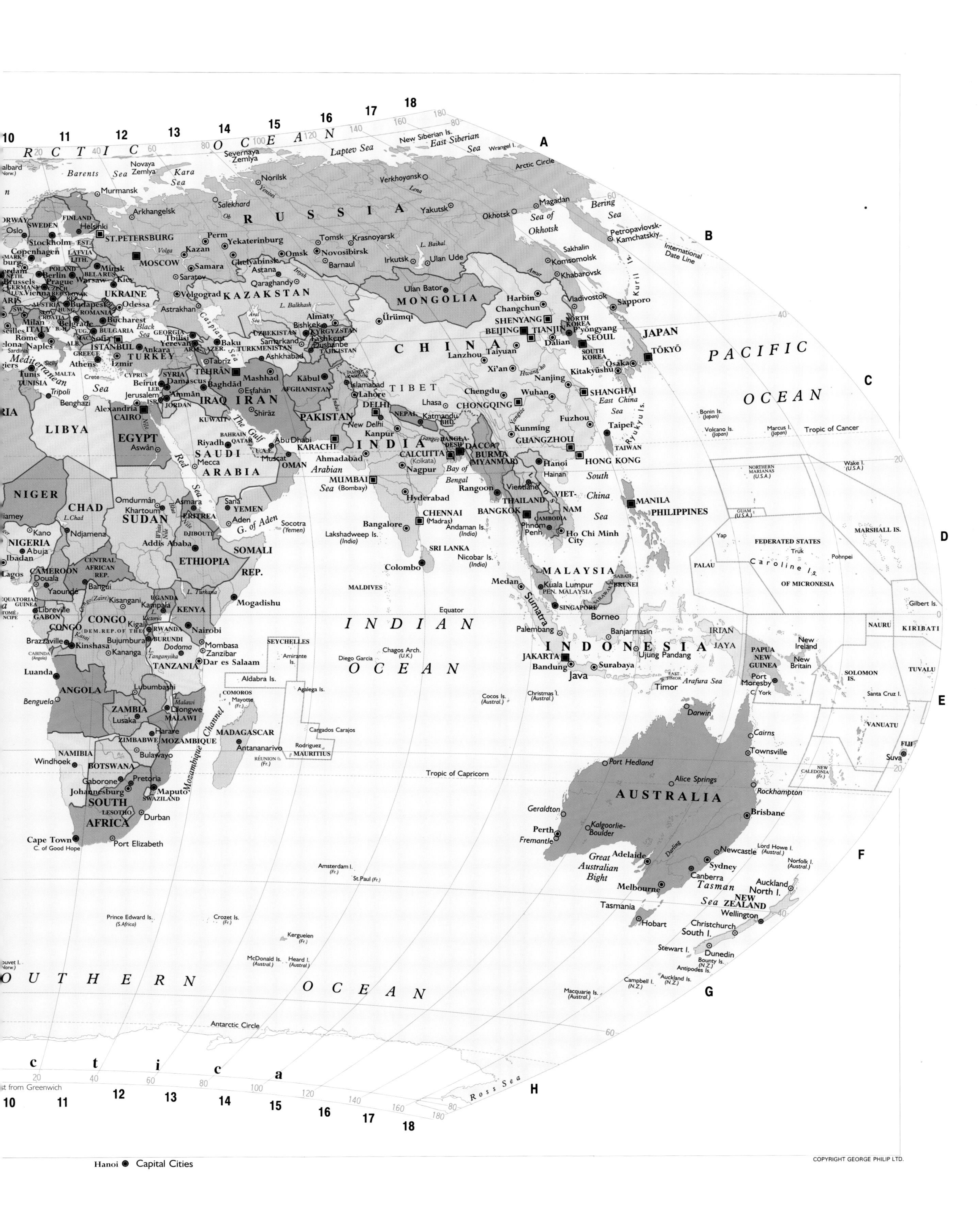

10 11 12 13 14 15 16 18
17

ARCTIC OCEAN

R
20 40
Svalbard
(Norw.)
Barents Sea
Novaya Zemlya
Kara Sea
Severnaya Zemlya
80
100 140
Laptev Sea
New Siberian Is.
East Siberian Sea
Wrangel I.
Arctic Circle

Murmansk
Arkhangelsk
Norilsk
Yenisey
Verkhoyansk
Lena
Yakutsk
Magadan
Bering Sea
A

NORWAY
SWEDEN FINLAND
Oslo Helsinki
Stockholm EST.
Copenhagen LATVIA
burg ST.PETERSBURG
MARK LITH.
Amsterdam POLAND Minsk
Brussels Berlin Warsaw BELARUS
PARIS GERM. Prague Kiev
LUX. Vienna REP.SLOVAK
AUSTRIA Budapest HUNG.
Milan CROATIA ROMANIA
Marseilles ITALY YUG. Bucharest
Rome Belgrade
Naples MAC.
Sardinia ALB. GREECE Sofia
Algiers Sicily Athens
Tunis MALTA Crete İzmir
TUNISIA Mediterranean Sea
Tripoli Benghazi

Perm
Yekaterinburg
MOSCOW Tomsk Krasnoyarsk
Volga Kazan Chelyabinsk Omsk Novosibirsk L. Baikal
Samara Astana Irtysh Irkutsk Ulan Ude
UKRAINE Saratov Barnaul
Odessa Volgograd KAZAKSTAN Ulan Bator
Astrakhan L. Balkhash MONGOLIA
BULGARIA Black Sea Aral Sea Almaty Ürümqi
ISTANBUL GEORGIA Tbilisi UZBEKISTAN Bishkek KYRGYZSTAN
TURKEY Ankara ARM. Baku Tashkent Samarkand
Yerevan AZER. TURKMENISTAN Dushanbe TAJIKISTAN
Okhotsk
Sea of Okhotsk
Komsomolsk
Khabarovsk
Amur
Sakhalin
Petropavlovsk-Kamchatskiy
B
International Date Line
Kuril Is.

Harbin
Changchun
Vladivostok Sapporo
SHENYANG NORTH KOREA
BEIJING TIANJIN Pyongyang
Dalian SEOUL **JAPAN**
SOUTH KOREA TÔKYÔ
Osaka
Kitakyūshū

PACIFIC OCEAN
C

Damascus TEHRAN Mashhad AFGHANISTAN Kabul TIBET
Beirut SYRIA Baghdad Esfahan Islamabad Lahore Lhasa
Jerusalem Amman IRAQ IRAN Shiraz PAKISTAN New Delhi NEPAL Katmandu BHU.
ISR. JORDAN KUWAIT DELHI Kanpur Ganges
Alexandria The Gulf BAHRAIN QATAR Abu Dhabi Ahmadabad CALCUTTA BANGLA- DACCA
CAIRO Riyadh U.A.E. KARACHI INDIA (Kolkata) DESH BURMA
Tabriz OMAN Muscat Nagpur Bay of MYANMAR

Lanzhou Taiyuan Nanjing
CHINA Xi'an Hwang-ho Wuhan SHANGHAI East China Sea
Chengdu CHONGQING Yangtze Fuzhou
Kunming GUANGZHOU Taipei Ryukyus
Hanoi HONG KONG TAIWAN
Hainan

Tropic of Cancer
Bonin Is. (Japan)
Volcano Is. (Japan)
Marcus I. (Japan)
Wake I. (U.S.A.)
20

LIBYA **EGYPT** Aswān Mecca SAUDI Red ARABIA
Omdurmân Khartoum Omdurman
Aden G. of Aden Socotra (Yemen)
MUMBAI (Bombay)
Hyderabad Rangoon
Bangalore CHENNAI (Madras) BANGKOK Phnom VIET-
Lakshadweep Is. (India) Andaman Is. (India) THAILAND CAMBODIA NAM
SRI LANKA Penh Ho Chi Minh City
Nicobar Is. (India) South China Sea
Colombo
MALDIVES
MANILA **PHILIPPINES**
NORTHERN MARIANAS (U.S.A.)
GUAM (U.S.A.)
Yap
D
FEDERATED STATES
Truk Pohnpei
PALAU Caroline Is.
OF MICRONESIA
MARSHALL IS.

NIGER **CHAD** L. Chad Ndjamena **SUDAN** Asmara ERITREA Sana **YEMEN** DJIBOUTI
Niamey Kano CAMEROON CENTRAL Addis Ababa **ETHIOPIA** **SOMALI REP.**
NIGERIA Abuja AFRICAN REP. Bangui
Ibadan Douala Bangui
Lagos Yaoundé EQUATORIAL GUINEA L. Turkana UGANDA KENYA Mogadishu
SÃO TOMÉ GABON Kisangani Kampala L. Victoria Nairobi
& PRÍNCIPE CONGO DEM.REP. OF THE RWANDA Mombasa
Brazzaville Kinshasa Kigali BURUNDI Zanzibar
CABINDA (Angola) Kananga Bujumbura Dodoma Dar es Salaam
Luanda **TANZANIA**
INDIAN OCEAN
Equator
SEYCHELLES
Amirante Is.
Diego Garcia
Chagos Arch. (U.K.)
MALAYSIA
Medan Kuala Lumpur SABAH
PEN. MALAYSIA BRUNEI
SINGAPORE SARAWAK Borneo
Palembang Sumatra Banjarmasin
INDONESIA IRIAN JAYA
JAKARTA Ujung Pandang
Bandung Java Surabaya
East Timor Timor Arafura Sea
Gilbert Is.
NAURU **KIRIBATI**
D
PAPUA NEW GUINEA New Ireland New Britain
Port Moresby C. York SOLOMON IS.
Santa Cruz I.
TUVALU

ANGOLA Lubumbashi COMOROS Mayotte (Fr.) Agalega Is. (Maur.)
Benguela ZAMBIA Malawi MADAGASCAR
Lusaka Lilongwe MALAWI Cargados Carajos
NAMIBIA ZIMBABWE MOZAMBIQUE Antananarivo Rodriguez
Windhoek Bulawayo Harare Mozambique Channel RÉUNION (Fr.) MAURITIUS
BOTSWANA Aldabra Is.
Gaborone Pretoria Maputo SWAZILAND Amsterdam I. (Fr.)
Johannesburg LESOTHO
SOUTH AFRICA Durban
Cape Town Port Elizabeth
C. of Good Hope
St. Paul (Fr.)
Tropic of Capricorn
E
VANUATU
FIJI
Suva
NEW CALEDONIA (Fr.)
20

Darwin
Cairns
Townsville
Port Hedland
Alice Springs
Rockhampton
AUSTRALIA
Geraldton Brisbane
Perth Kalgoorlie-Boulder Darling Newcastle Lord Howe I. (Austral.)
Fremantle Sydney Norfolk I. (Austral.)
Great Australian Bight Adelaide Canberra Auckland
Melbourne Tasman **NEW ZEALAND** North I.
Tasmania Sea Wellington
Hobart Christchurch
Stewart I. South I.
Dunedin
Bounty Is. (N.Z.)
Antipodes Is. (N.Z.)
F
40

Prince Edward Is. (S.Africa)
Crozet Is. (Fr.)
Kerguelen (Fr.)
McDonald Is. Heard I. (Austral.) (Austral.)
Bouvet I. (Norw.)
SOUTHERN **OCEAN**
Campbell I. (N.Z.)
Auckland Is. (N.Z.)
Macquarie Is. (Austral.)
G
60

Antarctic Circle

n t a r c t i c a
East from Greenwich 20 40 60 80 100
Ross Sea
H
80 180

10 11 12 13 14 15 16 17 18

Hanoi ● Capital Cities

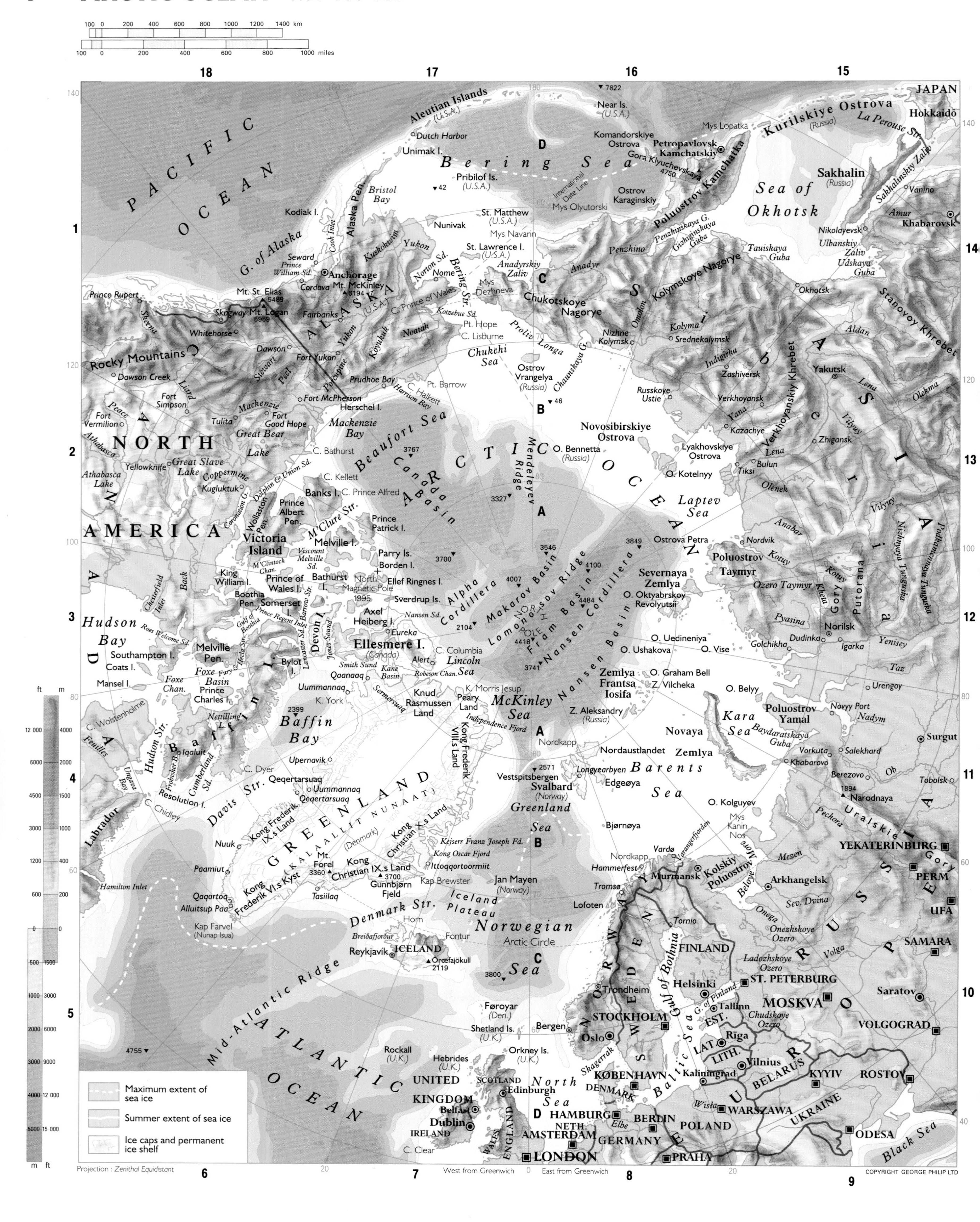

Projection : Zenithal Equidistant

West from Greenwich   East from Greenwich

COPYRIGHT GEORGE PHILIP LTD

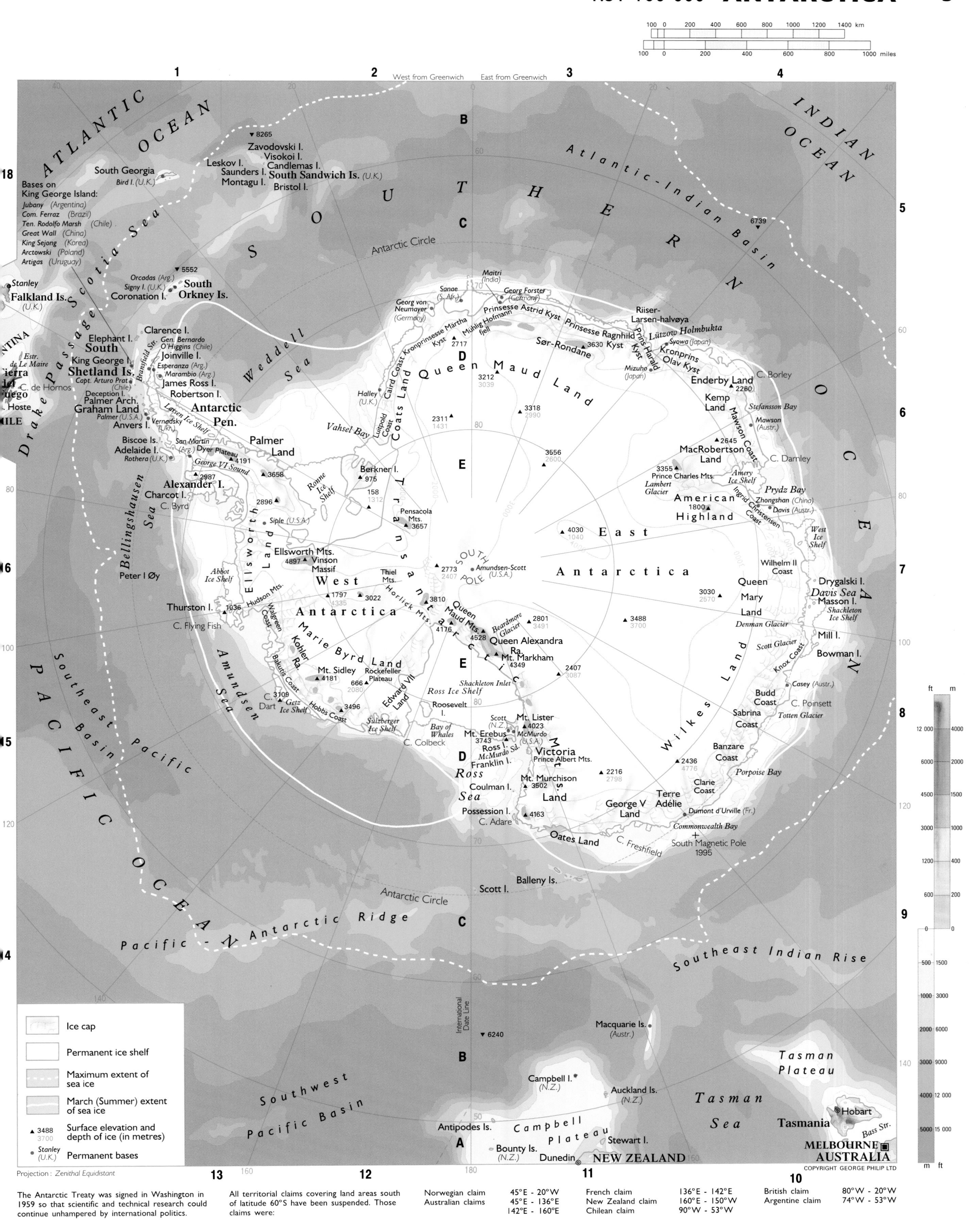

100 0 200 400 600 800 1000 1200 1400 km
100 0 200 400 600 800 1000 miles

Legend:

	Ice cap
	Permanent ice shelf
	Maximum extent of sea ice
	March (Summer) extent of sea ice
▲ 3488 / 3700	Surface elevation and depth of ice (in metres)
● Stanley (U.K.)	Permanent bases

Projection: Zenithal Equidistant

The Antarctic Treaty was signed in Washington in 1959 so that scientific and technical research could continue unhampered by international politics.

All territorial claims covering land areas south of latitude 60°S have been suspended. Those claims were:

Norwegian claim	45°E - 20°W	French claim	136°E - 142°E	British claim	80°W - 20°W
Australian claims	45°E - 136°E	New Zealand claim	160°E - 150°W	Argentine claim	74°W - 53°W
	142°E - 160°E	Chilean claim	90°W - 53°W		

COPYRIGHT GEORGE PHILIP LTD

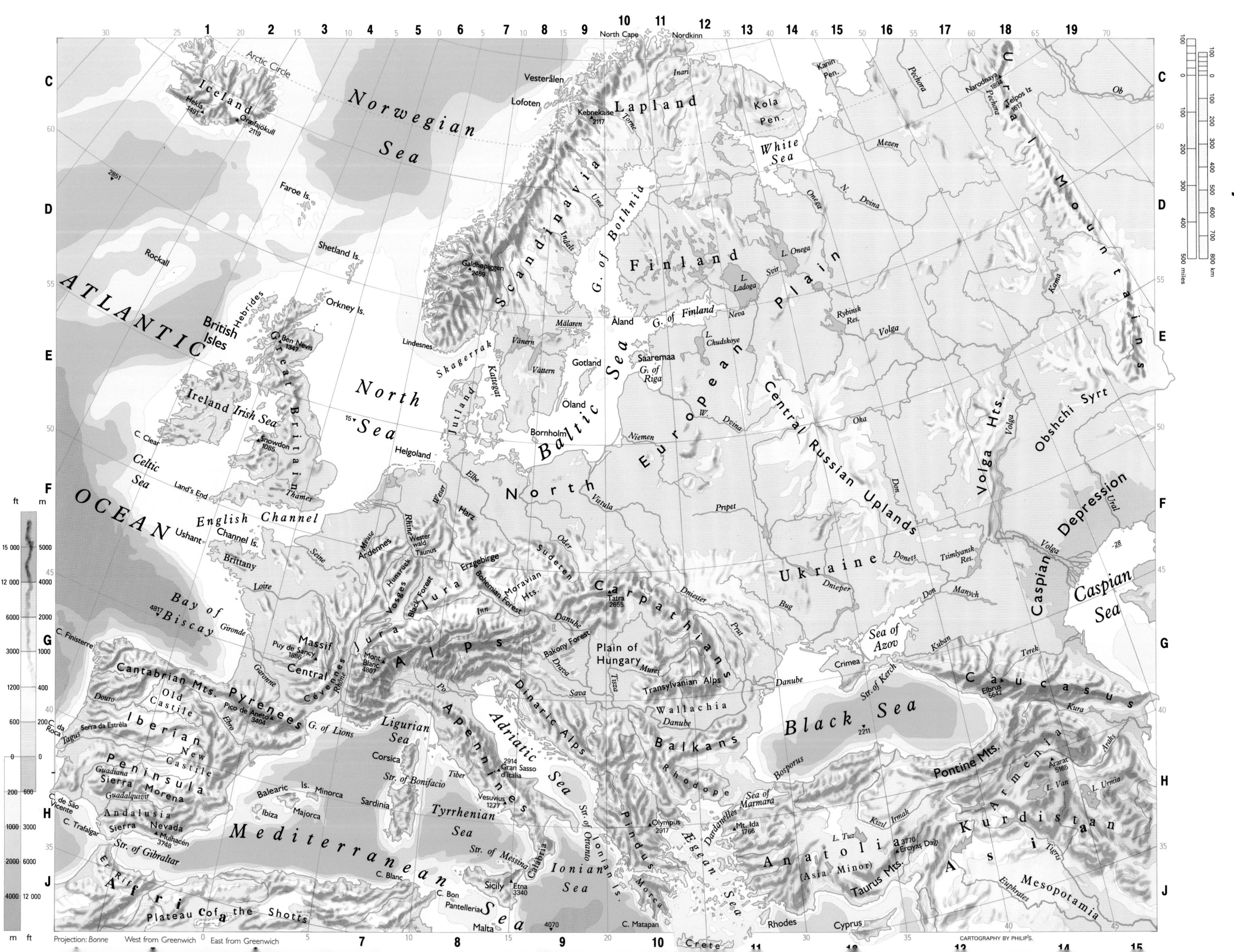

CARTOGRAPHY BY PHILIP'S

Projection: Borne

West from Greenwich 0 East from Greenwich

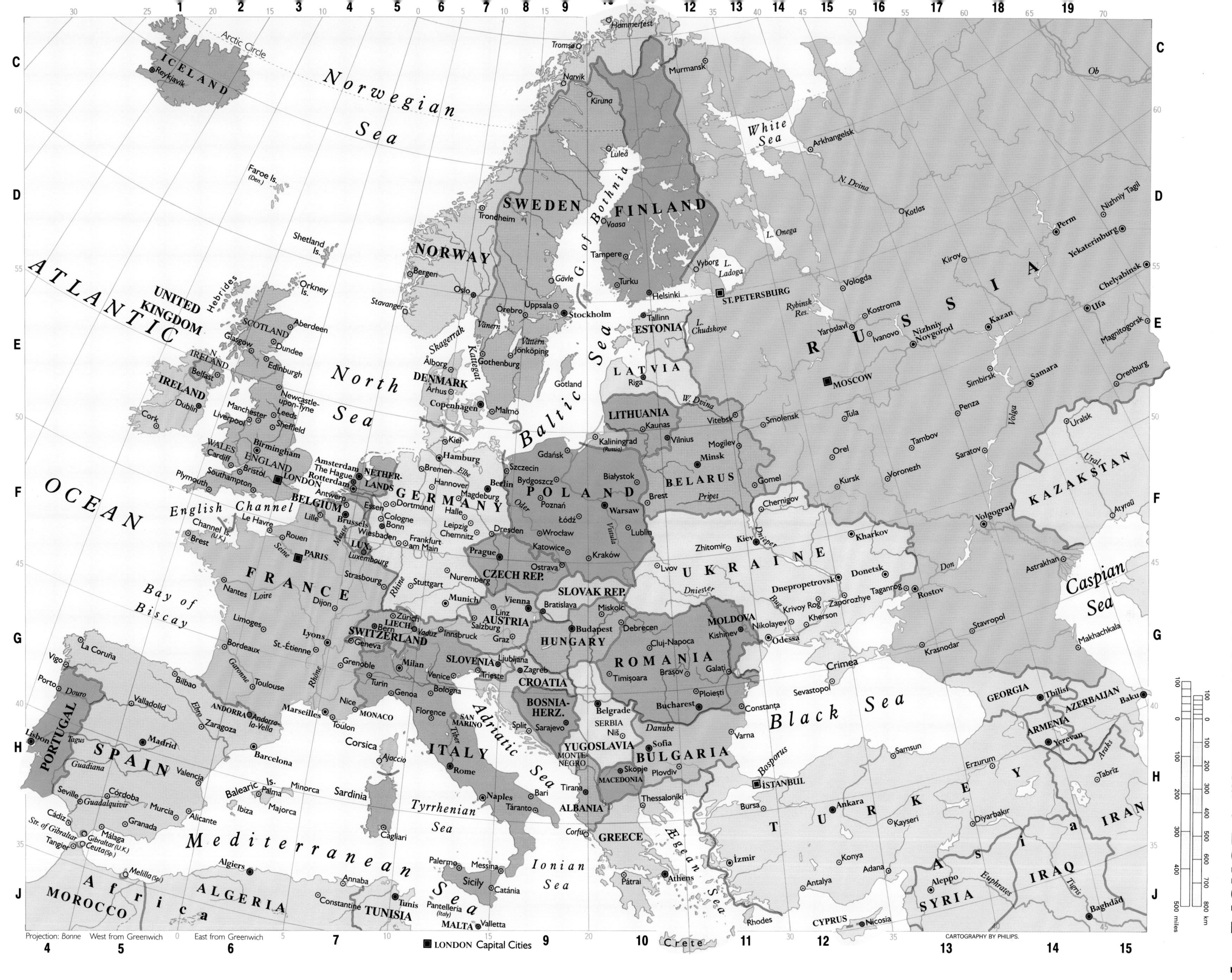

ICELAND
Reykjavík
Arctic Circle
Norwegian Sea
Faroe Is. (Den.)
Shetland Is.
Orkney Is.
Hebrides
ATLANTIC OCEAN
UNITED KINGDOM
SCOTLAND
N. IRELAND
IRELAND
ENGLAND
WALES
LONDON
North Sea
NORWAY
SWEDEN
FINLAND
G. of Bothnia
White Sea
DENMARK
Skagerrak
Kattegat
Baltic Sea
ESTONIA
LATVIA
LITHUANIA
BELARUS
ST. PETERSBURG
MOSCOW
RUSSIA
KAZAKSTAN
Caspian Sea
NETHER-LANDS
BELGIUM
LUX.
GERMANY
POLAND
CZECH REP.
SLOVAK REP.
UKRAINE
MOLDOVA
ROMANIA
HUNGARY
AUSTRIA
SWITZERLAND
LIECH.
SLOVENIA
CROATIA
BOSNIA-HERZ.
YUGOSLAVIA
SERBIA
MONTE-NEGRO
MACEDONIA
ALBANIA
BULGARIA
GREECE
English Channel
FRANCE
PARIS
Bay of Biscay
PORTUGAL
SPAIN
ANDORRA
MONACO
SAN MARINO
ITALY
Adriatic Sea
Tyrrhenian Sea
Ionian Sea
Ægean Sea
Black Sea
Crimea
Bosporus
İSTANBUL
TURKEY
GEORGIA
ARMENIA
AZERBAIJAN
IRAN
IRAQ
SYRIA
CYPRUS
Crete
Mediterranean Sea
MALTA
TUNISIA
ALGERIA
MOROCCO
Africa
Asia
Projection: Bonne
West from Greenwich
East from Greenwich
■ LONDON Capital Cities
CARTOGRAPHY BY PHILIPS.
100 0 100 200 300 400 500 600 700 800 km
100 0 100 200 300 400 500 miles

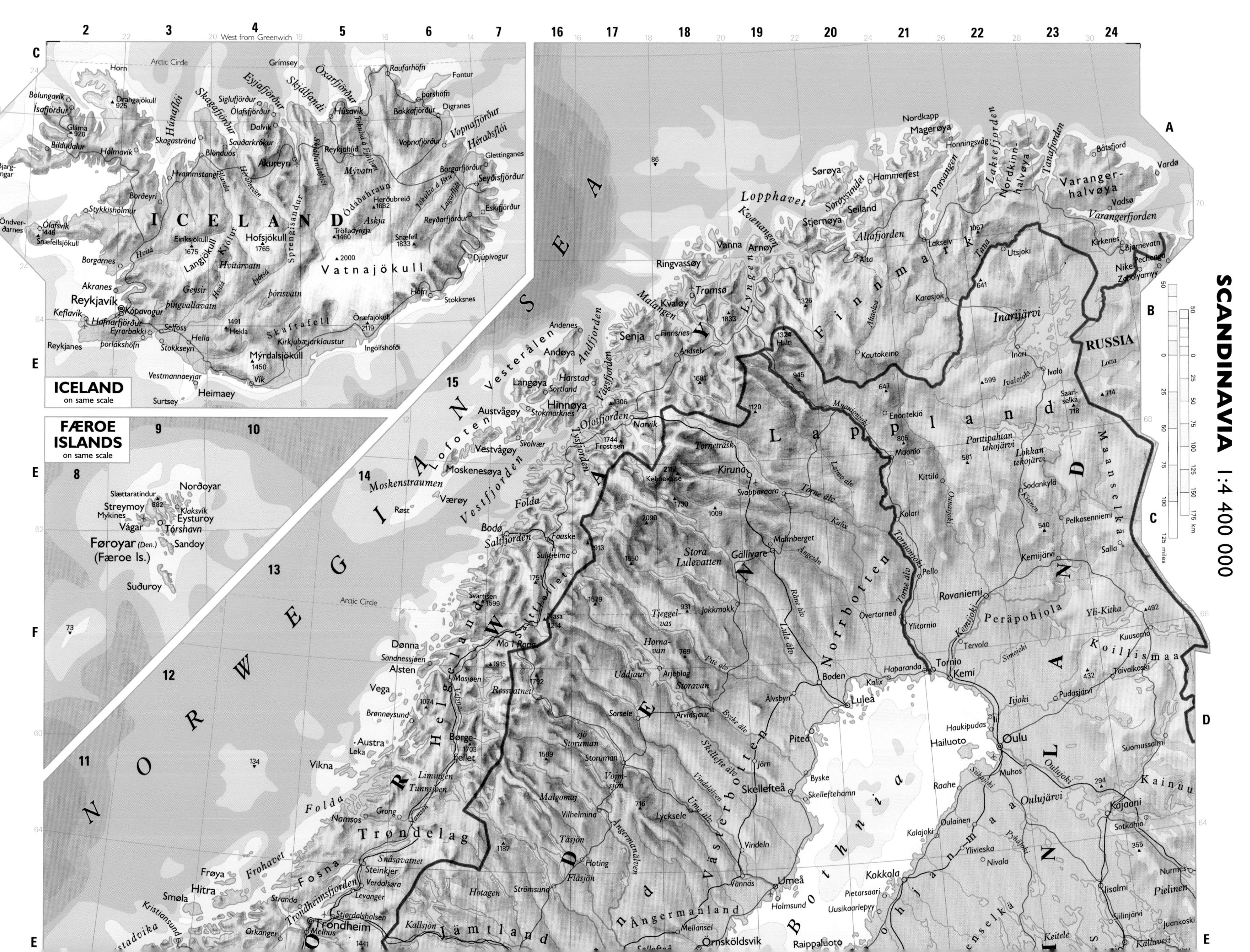

ICELAND
on same scale

FÆROE
ISLANDS
on same scale

F G H J K

Countries and regions: FINLAND, ESTONIA, LATVIA, LITHUANIA, BELORUSSIA, RUSSIA, POLAND, GERMANY, DENMARK, SWEDEN (Sverige), NORWAY

Seas and gulfs: Gulf of Finland, Gulf of Riga, Gulf of Bothnia, BALTIC SEA, Ålands hav, Kattegat, Skagerrak, Øresund, Lille Bælt, Store Bælt, Fehmarn Belt, Mecklenburger Bucht, Kieler Bucht, Deutsche Bucht, Oslofjorden, Sognefjorden, Nordfjord, Hardangerfjord

Selected cities and places:
Helsinki (Helsingfors), Espoo, Vantaa, Tampere, Turku (Åbo), Pori, Rauma, Lahti, Kouvola, Kotka, Hanko, Jyväskylä, Mikkeli, Savonlinna, Varkaus

Tallinn, Tartu, Pärnu, Narva, Haapsalu, Kuressaare, Hiiumaa (Dagö), Saaremaa (Ösel), Muhu, Vormsi

Riga, Jelgava, Jūrmala, Liepāja, Ventspils, Talsi, Tukums, Daugavpils, Rēzekne, Valmiera, Cēsis, Sigulda

Vilnius, Kaunas, Klaipėda, Šiauliai, Panevėžys, Marijampolė, Alytus, Utena, Telšiai

Kaliningrad (Russia), Sovetsk, Chernyakhovsk, Gusev, Baltiysk, Zelenogradsk, Gvardeysk

Gdańsk, Gdynia, Sopot, Słupsk, Koszalin, Kołobrzeg, Malbork, Elbląg, Tczew, Starogard Gdański, Wejherowo, Lębork, Bytów

Rostock, Greifswald, Stralsund, Wismar, Lübeck, Neumünster, Kiel, Flensburg, Schleswig, Rendsburg, Husum, Travemünde, Rügen, Usedom, Fehmarn

København (Copenhagen), Malmö, Lund, Helsingør, Helsingborg, Landskrona, Køge, Næstved, Roskilde, Slagelse, Kalundborg, Odense, Svendborg, Nakskov, Nykøbing, Bornholm, Rønne, Nexø, Møn, Falster, Lolland, Langeland, Sjælland

Århus, Ålborg, Esbjerg, Randers, Horsens, Vejle, Kolding, Fredericia, Herning, Viborg, Skive, Silkeborg, Hjørring, Thisted, Frederikshavn, Skagen, Varde, Ribe, Haderslev, Åbenrå, Sønderborg

STOCKHOLM, Göteborg (Gothenburg), Malmö, Uppsala, Västerås, Örebro, Norrköping, Linköping, Eskilstuna, Jönköping, Gävle, Borås, Helsingborg, Halmstad, Växjö, Kalmar, Karlskrona, Kristianstad, Visby, Gotland, Öland, Karlstad, Falun, Mora, Sundsvall, Härnösand, Hudiksvall, Söderhamn

Oslo, Bergen, Stavanger, Kristiansand, Drammen, Fredrikstad, Sarpsborg, Moss, Tønsberg, Sandefjord, Larvik, Arendal, Hamar, Lillehammer, Gjøvik, Kongsvinger, Hønefoss, Notodden, Porsgrunn, Skien, Haugesund, Egersund, Flekkefjord, Mandal, Førde, Molde

Regions (Sweden/Norway): Uppland, Södermanland, Västmanland, Närke, Dalarna, Värmland, Dalsland, Bohuslän, Västergötland, Östergötland, Småland, Halland, Skåne, Blekinge, Gotland, Gästrikland, Hälsingland, Härjedalen, Telemark, Valdres, Gudbrandsdalen, Østerdalen, Dovrefjell, Jotunheimen, Hardangervidda, Jostedalsbreen

Elevation scale (m / ft):
m: 2000, 1500, 1000, 500, 200, 0
ft: 6000, 4500, 3000, 1500, 600, 300, 150, 0

Scale and grid numbers: 12 13 14 15 16 17 18 19 20 21 22

10 0 10 20 30 40 50 60 70 80 90 km

10 0 10 20 30 40 50 60 miles

Gulf of Bothnia

VÄSTER- NORRLANDS LÄN

JÄMTLANDS LÄN

Östersund
Storsjön

Medelpad

Sundsvall

Hälsingland

GÄVLEBORGS LÄN

Gästrikland

Gävle

Bollnäs

HÄRJEDALEN

KOPPARBERGS LÄN

Siljan
Mora
Falun
Borlänge

Dalarna

DALA LÄN

UPPSALA LÄN

Uppsala

STOCKHOLMS LÄN

STOCKHOLM

Södertälje

VÄSTMANLANDS LÄN

Västerås
Sala

SÖDERMANLANDS LÄN

Eskilstuna

Örebro

ÖREBRO LÄN

Karlstad

VÄRMLANDS LÄN

Klarälven

SØR-TRØNDELAG

Trondheim

MØRE OG ROMSDAL

Dovrefjell

Trollheimen

Kristiansund

HEDMARK

Østerdalen
Rena

OPPLAND

Lillehammer

Gudbrandsdalen

Jotunheimen

Rondane

AKERSHUS

Oslo
Drammen

ØSTFOLD

Fredrikstad
Sarpsborg

VESTFOLD

Tønsberg

BUSKERUD

Hallingdal

Valdres

TELEMARK

Skien

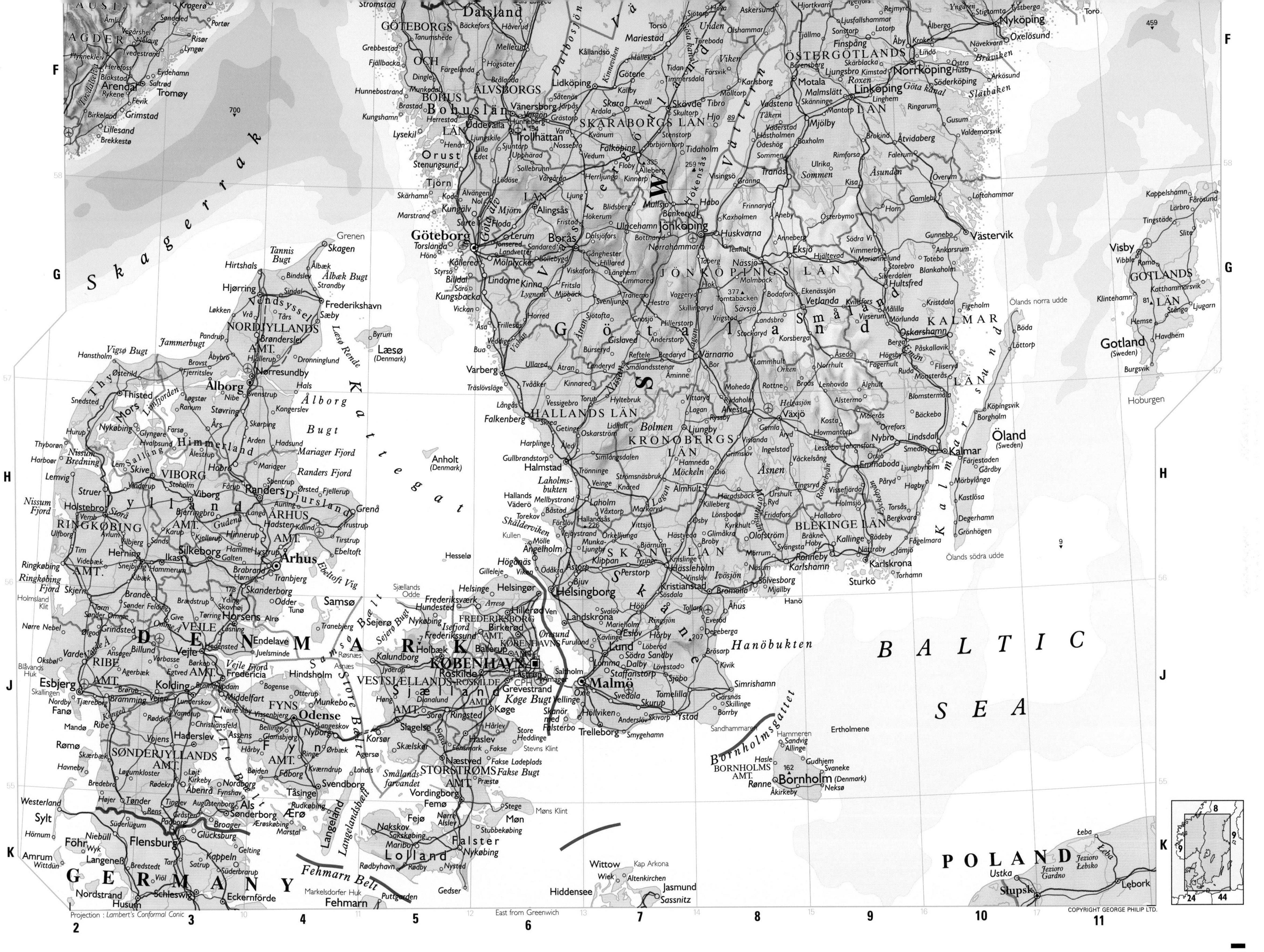

Skagerrak
Kattegat
BALTIC SEA
DENMARK
SWEDEN
GERMANY
POLAND
Jylland
Fyn
Sjælland
Lolland
Falster
Møn
Skåne
Småland
Götaland
Västergötland
Östergötland
Bohuslän
Himmerland
Djursland
Vendsyssel
Salling
Samsø
Læsø (Denmark)
Anholt (Denmark)
Öland (Sweden)
Gotland (Sweden)
Bornholm (Denmark)
Ærø
Als
Langeland
Fehmarn
Sylt
Föhr
Amrum
Rømø
Fanø
Hesselø
Ertholmene
Hanö
Sturkö
Hoburgen
Ölands norra udde
Ölands södra udde
Vänern
Vättern
Sommen
Åsnen
Bolmen
Ivösjön
Limfjorden
Øresund
Store Bælt
Lille Bælt
Fehmarn Belt
Langelandsbælt
Samsø Bælt
Smålandsfarvandet
Kalmarsund
Hanöbukten
Bornholmsgattet
Laholmsbukten
Skälderviken
Køge Bugt
Fakse Bugt
Ålborg Bugt
Jammerbugt
Vigsø Bugt
Tannis Bugt
Ebeltoft Vig
Nissum Fjord
Ringkøbing Fjord
Randers Fjord
Mariager Fjord
Vejle Fjord
Bråviken
Slätbaken
Göta kanal
Göta älv
Dalbosjön
KØBENHAVN
Göteborg
Malmö
Århus
Ålborg
Odense
Esbjerg
Helsingborg
Helsingør
Lund
Jönköping
Norrköping
Linköping
Nyköping
Kalmar
Karlskrona
Växjö
Halmstad
Varberg
Falkenberg
Borås
Trollhättan
Uddevalla
Kristianstad
Ystad
Trelleborg
Landskrona
Karlshamn
Ronneby
Västervik
Visby
Rønne
Flensburg
Schleswig
Husum
Eckernförde
Słupsk
Ustka
Łeba
Lębork
Kristiansand
Arendal
Grimstad
Lillesand
Skagen
Frederikshavn
Hjørring
Thisted
Skive
Viborg
Randers
Silkeborg
Herning
Holstebro
Horsens
Vejle
Kolding
Fredericia
Haderslev
Sønderborg
Svendborg
Nyborg
Slagelse
Roskilde
Køge
Næstved
Vordingborg
Nakskov
Nykøbing
Kalundborg
Holbæk
Hillerød
Skövde
Lidköping
Motala
Mjölby
Vetlanda
Nässjö
Eksjö
Värnamo
Ljungby
Gotland
GÖTEBORGS OCH BOHUS LÄN
ÄLVSBORGS LÄN
SKARABORGS LÄN
ÖSTERGÖTLANDS LÄN
JÖNKÖPINGS LÄN
KRONOBERGS LÄN
KALMAR LÄN
BLEKINGE LÄN
HALLANDS LÄN
SKÅNE LÄN
GOTLANDS LÄN
NORDJYLLANDS AMT.
VIBORG
ÅRHUS AMT.
RINGKØBING AMT.
VEJLE AMT.
RIBE AMT.
SØNDERJYLLANDS AMT.
FYNS AMT.
VESTSJÆLLANDS AMT.
STORSTRØMS AMT.
ROSKILDE AMT.
FREDERIKSBORG AMT.
KØBENHAVNS AMT.
BORNHOLMS AMT.
AGDER
Projection : Lambert's Conformal Conic
East from Greenwich
COPYRIGHT GEORGE PHILIP LTD.

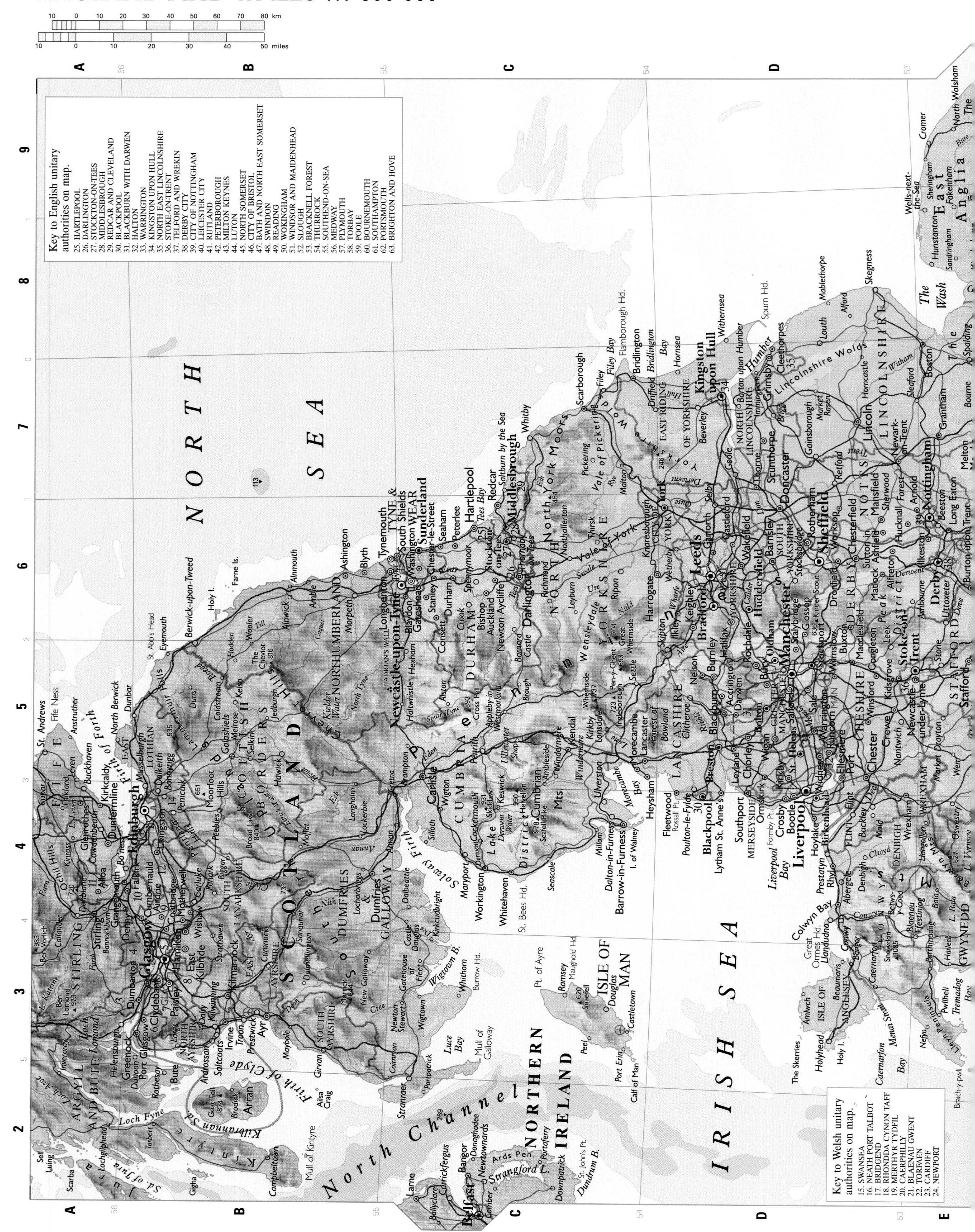

Key to English unitary authorities on map.

25. HARTLEPOOL
26. DARLINGTON
27. STOCKTON-ON-TEES
28. MIDDLESBROUGH
29. REDCAR AND CLEVELAND
30. BLACKPOOL
31. BLACKBURN WITH DARWEN
32. HALTON
33. WARRINGTON
34. KINGSTON UPON HULL
35. NORTH EAST LINCOLNSHIRE
36. STOKE-ON-TRENT
37. TELFORD AND WREKIN
38. DERBY CITY
39. CITY OF NOTTINGHAM
40. LEICESTER CITY
41. RUTLAND
42. PETERBOROUGH
43. MILTON KEYNES
44. LUTON
45. NORTH SOMERSET
46. CITY OF BRISTOL
47. BATH AND NORTH EAST SOMERSET
48. SWINDON
49. READING
50. WOKINGHAM
51. WINDSOR AND MAIDENHEAD
52. SLOUGH
53. BRACKNELL FOREST
54. THURROCK
55. SOUTHEND-ON-SEA
56. MEDWAY
57. TORBAY
58. PLYMOUTH
59. POOLE
60. BOURNEMOUTH
61. SOUTHAMPTON
62. PORTSMOUTH
63. BRIGHTON AND HOVE

Key to Welsh unitary authorities on map.

15. SWANSEA
16. NEATH PORT TALBOT
17. BRIDGEND
18. RHONDDA CYNON TAFF
19. MERTHYR TYDFIL
20. CAERPHILLY
21. BLAENAU GWENT
22. TORFAEN
23. CARDIFF
24. NEWPORT

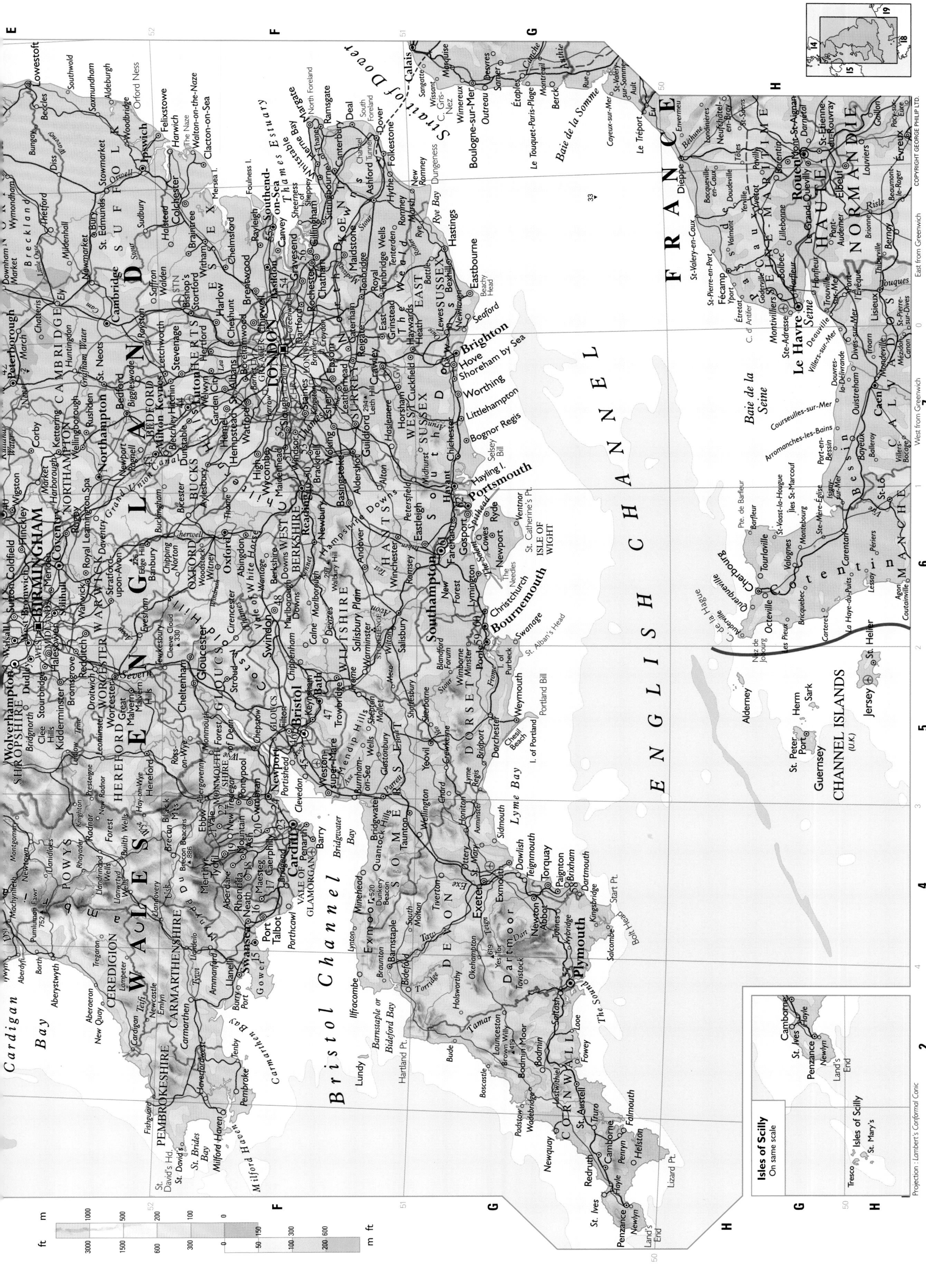

13

ENGLAND

WALES

FRANCE

NORMANDIE

HAUTE-NORMANDIE

SEINE-MARITIME

CALVADOS

MANCHE

ENGLISH CHANNEL

Bristol Channel

Cardigan Bay

Lyme Bay

Baie de la Seine

Baie de la Somme

Strait of Dover — Détroit du Pas de Calais

LONDON

BIRMINGHAM

Bristol

Cardiff

Swansea

Plymouth

Exeter

Portsmouth

Southampton

Bournemouth

Brighton

Hove

Worthing

Rouen

Le Havre

Caen

Cherbourg

Dieppe

Évreux

CHANNEL ISLANDS (U.K.)

Jersey · St. Helier

Guernsey · St. Peter Port

Alderney

Sark

Herm

ISLE OF WIGHT

Newport

CORNWALL

DEVON

DORSET

SOMERSET

WILTSHIRE

HAMPSHIRE

WEST SUSSEX

EAST SUSSEX

SURREY

KENT

ESSEX

SUFFOLK

NORFOLK

CAMBRIDGESHIRE

BERKSHIRE

OXFORDSHIRE

GLOUCESTERSHIRE

HEREFORD

WORCESTER

WARWICK

SHROPSHIRE

POWYS

CEREDIGION

PEMBROKESHIRE

CARMARTHENSHIRE

GLAMORGAN

Isles of Scilly — On same scale
St. Mary's · Tresco

Projection: Lambert's Conformal Conic

COPYRIGHT GEORGE PHILIP LTD.

East from Greenwich / West from Greenwich

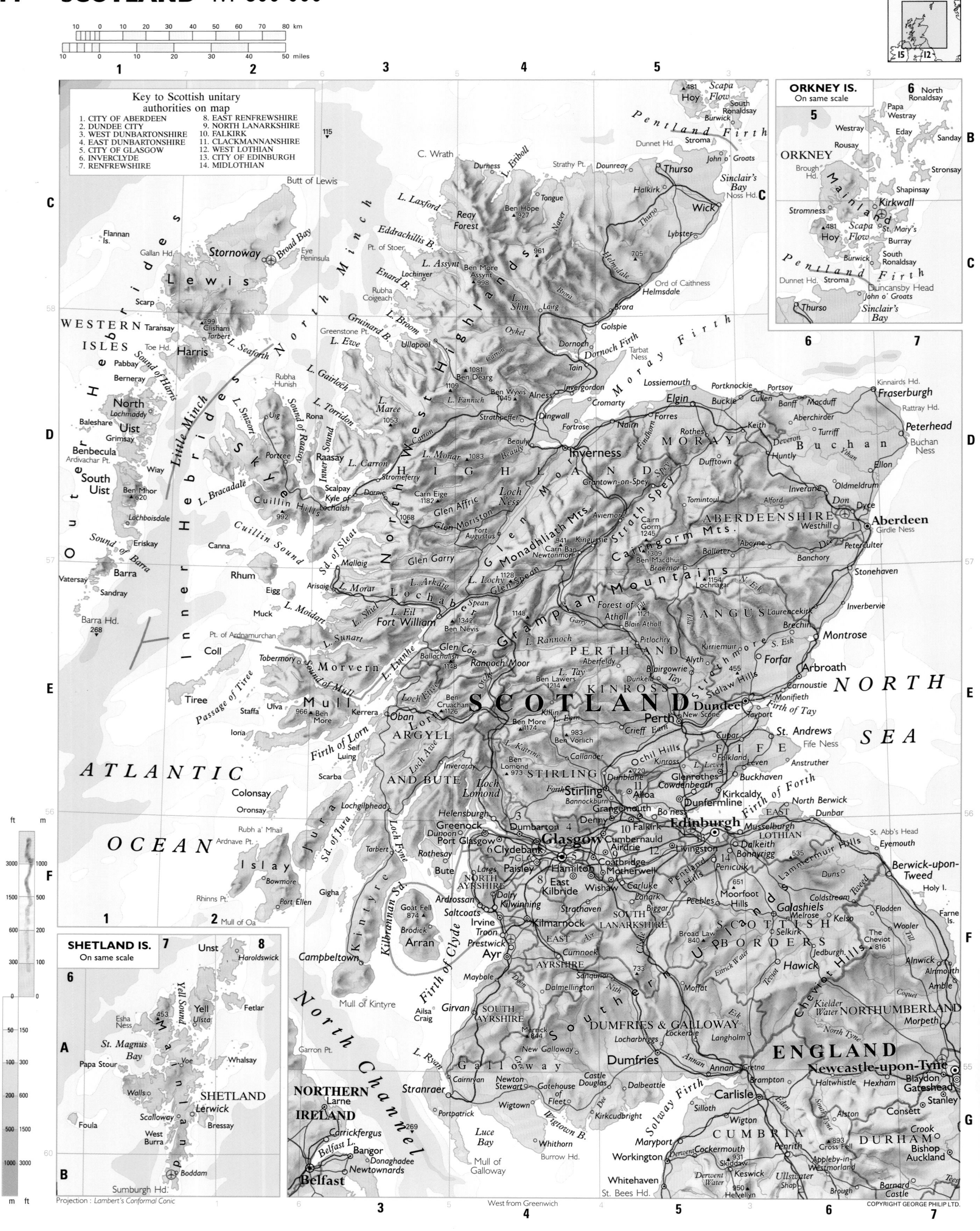

Key to Scottish unitary authorities on map
1. CITY OF ABERDEEN
2. DUNDEE CITY
3. WEST DUNBARTONSHIRE
4. EAST DUNBARTONSHIRE
5. CITY OF GLASGOW
6. INVERCLYDE
7. RENFREWSHIRE
8. EAST RENFREWSHIRE
9. NORTH LANARKSHIRE
10. FALKIRK
11. CLACKMANNANSHIRE
12. WEST LOTHIAN
13. CITY OF EDINBURGH
14. MIDLOTHIAN

ORKNEY IS.
On same scale

SHETLAND IS.
On same scale

SCOTLAND

ATLANTIC OCEAN

NORTH SEA

ENGLAND

NORTHERN IRELAND

Projection : Lambert's Conformal Conic

West from Greenwich

COPYRIGHT GEORGE PHILIP LTD.

10 0 10 20 30 40 50 60 70 80 km
10 0 10 20 30 40 50 miles

ATLANTIC OCEAN

NORTH CHANNEL

IRISH SEA

CELTIC SEA

St. George's Channel

Firth of Clyde
Kintyre
Arran
Brodick
Campbeltown
Mull of Oa
Mull of Kintyre
Ailsa Craig
Cairnryan
Stranraer
Portpatrick

Mull of Oa
Giants Causeway
Portstewart
Portrush
Coleraine
Fair Hd.
Ballycastle
Rathlin I.
Garron Pt.
Trostan ▲554
Ballymoney
Limavady
Larne
Carrickfergus
269
Ballyclare
Randalstown
Ballymena
Carnlough

Malin Hd.
Malin Pen.
Carndonagh
Moville
Buncrana
Inishowen Pen.
L. Foyle
LONDONDERRY
Londonderry
Lifford
Strabane
Sion Mills
Newtownstewart
Sawel Mt. ▲683
Sperrin Mts.
Magherafelt
Cookstown
Coalisland
Dungannon
Moneymore
ANTRIM
Antrim
Lough Neagh
Newtownabbey
Belfast
Belfast L.
Bangor
Donaghadee
Newtownards
Comber
Lisburn
Saintfield
Craigavon
Lurgan
Portadown
Banbridge
Lagan
Tandragee
Ballynahinch
Ards Pen.
Strangford L.
Portaferry
Ballyquintin Pt.
Downpatrick
Dundrum
St. John's Pt.
Dundrum B.
Newcastle
Slieve Donard ▲852
Mourne Mts.
Kilkeel
Greenore
Carlingford L.
Warrenpoint
Slieve Gullion ▲577
Newry
Keady
Middletown
ARMAGH
Armagh
Aughnacloy
TYRONE
Omagh
Castlederg
Derg

Tory I.
Sheep Haven
Horn Hd.
Lough Swilly
Fanad Hd.
Mulroy B.
Rathmelton
Letterkenny
Errigal ▲752
Derryveagh Mts.
Gweedore
The Rosses
Aran I.
Bloody Foreland
Inishfree B.
Crohy Hd.
683
DONEGAL
Glenties
Lavagh More ▲676
Gweebarra B.
Dawros Hd.
Loughros More B.
Rossan Pt.
St. John's Pt.
Killybegs
Donegal
Ulster
Finn
Donegal Bay
Ballyshannon
Bundoran
Erne
Lower L. Erne
FERMANAGH
Enniskillen
Upper L. Erne
Clones
Monaghan
MONAGHAN
Clones
Annalee
Belturbet
Castleblaney
Coatehill
CAVAN
Cavan
Carrickmacross
Kingscourt
Ardee
Dunleer
Dundalk
LOUTH
Dundalk Bay
Ardee
Clogher Hd.
Drogheda
Balbriggan
Skerries
Rush
Lambay I.
Malahide
Swords
Howth Hd.
DUBLIN
Dublin
Dun Laoghaire
Bray
Greystones
123

Downpatrick Hd.
Killala B.
Broad Haven
Erris Hd.
Belmullet
Mullet Pen.
Inishkea North
Inishkea South
Blacksod Bay
Achill Hd.
Achill I.
Corraun Pen.
Clare I.
Clew Bay
Inishturk
Inishbofin
Inishshark
Killary Harbour
Connemara
Slyne Hd.
Clifden
Bertraghboy B.
Kilkieran B.
Slievevemore
L. Conn 806▲
Nephin ▲806
MAYO
Newport
Westport
Croagh Patrick ▲765
Mweelrea ▲819
Ballinrobe
Lough Mask
GALWAY
Oughterard
Lough Corrib
Galway
Galway Bay
Black Hd.
Aran Is.
Inishmore
Inishmaan
Inisheer
Hags Hd.
Liscannor Bay
Mal Bay
Mutton I.
Ennistimon
Milltown Malbay
CLARE
Kilkee
Loop Hd.
Kilrush
Shannon Airport
Ennis
Sixmilebridge
Foynes
Tulla
Killaloe
Mouth of the Shannon
Kerry Hd.
Ballina
Killala
Dromore West
544
Sligo B.
Slieve Gamph
SLIGO
Sligo
Colooney
Ballymote
L. Arrow
LEITRIM
Manorhamilton
L. Allen
Carrick-on-Shannon
Boyle
Ballaghaderreen
Charlestown
Swinford
Knock
Claremorris
Ballyhaunis
ROSCOMMON
Castlerea
Ballinrobe
Glennamaddy
Tuam
Athenry
Loughrea
Ballinasloe
Slieve Aughty
Gort
368
Portumna
Lough Derg
Nenagh
Silvermines
Templemore
Thurles
Keeper Hill ▲694
TIPPERARY
Limerick
LIMERICK
Rathkeale
Foynes
Listowel
Newcastle West
Abbeyfeale
Feale
Golden Vale
Tipperary
Cashel
Kilfinnane
Galtymore ▲920
Galty Mts.
Caher
Mitchelstown
Buttevant
Fermoy
Slievenamon ▲722
Clonmel
Carrick-on-Suir
Suir
Comeragh Mts. ▲792
Knockmealdown Mts. ▲795
Lismore
Dungarvan
Tramore
WATERFORD
Waterford
Tramore
Waterford Harbour
Dungarvan Harbour
Youghal
Youghal B.
Hook Hd.

ROSCOMMON
Roscommon
Strokestown
LONGFORD
Longford
Granard
Castlepollard
WESTMEATH
Mullingar
Castlerea
Athlone
Lough Ree
Moate
MEATH
An Uaimh (Navan)
Trim
Athboy
Ceanannus Mor (Kells)
Oldcastle
L. Sheelin
L. Gowna
Boyne
IRELAND
Connacht
Leinster
Lough Ree
Clara
Edenderry
OFFALY
Tullamore
Daingean
Birr
Slieve Bloom
Arderin ▲528
Bog of Allen
Portarlington
Mountmellick
Port Laoise
Roscrea
LAOIS
Durrow
Mountrath
Abbeyleix
Grand Canal
Royal Canal
Maynooth
KILDARE
Naas
Droichead Nua
Kildare
Monasterevin
Athy
Clondalkin
Kippure ▲
Wicklow Mts.
Lugnaquilla ▲926
WICKLOW
Wicklow
Wicklow Hd.
Rathdrum
Arklow
Mizen Hd.
Poulaphouca Res.
Avoca
Slaney
Shillelagh
Bunclody
Gorey
Cahore Pt.
CARLOW
Carlow
Tullow
Muine Bheag
Mt. Leinster ▲796
Enniscorthy
WEXFORD
New Ross
Wexford
Wexford Harbour
Rosslare
Greenore Pt.
Carnsore Pt.
Saltee Is.
KILKENNY
Kilkenny
Callan
Nore
Barrow
Thomastown
Clonmel

MUNSTER
Smerwick Harbour
Brandon B.
Tralee B.
Brandon Mt. ▲953
853
Slieve Mish
Dingle
Dingle Bay
Dunmore Hd.
Great Blasket I.
Inishvickillane
Valencia I.
Puffin I.
Great Skellig
Cahirciveen
Macgillycuddy's Reeks
Carrauntoohill ▲1041
Killorglin
Killarney
L. Leane
KERRY
Maine
Laune
Kenmare
Kenmare River
Scariff I.
Caha Mts. ▲686
Glengarriff
Dursey I.
Castletown Bearhaven
Bear I.
Bantry Bay
Bantry
Dunmanus B.
Mizen Hd.
Long I.
Skull
Crow Hd.
Baltimore
Sherkin I.
C. Clear
Clear I.
Galley Hd.
Clonakilty B.
Skibbereen
Clonakilty
Old Head of Kinsale
Kinsale
Bandon
Dunmanway
Macroom
Blarney
CORK
Cork
Passage West
Crosshaven
Cork Harbour
Cobh
Midleton
Youghal
Lee
Mallow
Blackwater
Newmarket
Kanturk
Rath Luirc
Charleville
Boggeragh Mts. ▲646
Dunmanway
Newcastle West
Abbeyfeale

NORTHERN IRELAND

Projection : Lambert's Conformal Conic

West from Greenwich

COPYRIGHT GEORGE PHILIP LTD.

ft m
1500 500
600 200
300 100
0 0
50 150
100 300
200 600
500 1500
1000 3000
2000 6000
m ft

115

50   0   25   50   75   100   125   150   175 km
50   0   25   50   75   100   125 miles

1   2   3   4   5   6   7   8   9

ATLANTIC OCEAN

Shetland Is.
Yell
Unst
Fetlar
Foula
Mainland
Lerwick

1224

Fair Isle

316

NORW
Askøy
Bergen
Osøyro
Stord
Bømlo
Haugesund
Kopervik
Åkrahamn
Bok
Stavang
Sand
Bry
Næ

Orkney Is.
Westray
Sanday
Stronsay
Mainland
Kirkwall
Hoy
South Ronaldsay

Pentland Firth

C. Wrath
Thurso
Wick

Outer Hebrides
Lewis
Stornoway
St. Kilda
789
Harris
North Uist
Benbecula
South Uist

North Minch

North West Highlands
Ullapool
Lairg
Helmsdale
Golspie
Tain
Invergordon
Dingwall
Nairn
Elgin
Buckie
Banff
Fraserburgh
Peterhead
Huntly
Inverurie
Aberdeen
L. Ness
1182
Inverness
Aviemore
Don
Stonehaven

Inner Hebrides
Skye
Rhum
Eigg
Coll
Mallaig
Fort William
Ben Nevis
1342
Tobermory
Mull
Tiree
Oban
Colonsay

SCOTLAND
Grampian Mts.
Dee
1311
Ballater
Montrose
1214
Forfar
Arbroath
Perth
Dundee
St. Andrews

Jura
Islay
Greenock
L. Lomond
973
Stirling
Dunfermline
Kirkcaldy
Glenrothes
Glasgow
Edinburgh
Paisley
East Kilbride
Hamilton
Clyde
Dunbar

NORTH SEA

238

Firth of Clyde
Campbeltown
Arran
Kilmarnock
Ayr
Southern Uplands
840
Jedburgh
Hawick
816
Galashiels
Berwick-upon-Tweed

Malin Hd.
Buncrana
Aran I.
Letterkenny
Coleraine
Donegal
Lifford
Londonderry
Ballymena
Larne
Antrim
Bangor
NORTHERN IRELAND
Ulster
Omagh
Lough Neagh
Belfast
Bundoran
Lower L. Erne
Enniskillen
Portadown
Lisburn
Lurgan
Sligo
Leitrim
Clones
Armagh
Newry
Cavan
Castleblayney
Dundalk

North Channel
Stranraer
Kirkcudbright
Girvan
Dumfries
Annan
Carlisle
Workington
Whitehaven
Mull of Galloway
Cheviot Hills
Alnwick

Newcastle-upon-Tyne
South Shields
Sunderland
Hexham
Gateshead
Durham
Hartlepool
Redcar
Darlington
Middlesbrough
Stockton-on-Tees
Scarborough

Cumbrian Mts.
893
978
Barrow-in-Furness
Douglas
I. of Man
Lancaster
Bridlington

UNITED KINGDOM
IRISH SEA

IRELAND
Ballina
Achill I.
Castlebar
Westport
Lough Mask
Connemara
Galway B.
Aran Is.
Galway
Ballinasloe
Roscommon
Longford
Athlone
Lough Ree
Mullingar
Ceanannus Mor
Tullamore
Lough Corrib
Lough Derg
Ennis
Kilrush
Shannon
953
Dingle
Listowel
Tralee
Carrauntoohill
1041
Macgillycuddy's Reeks
Valencia I.
Killarney
Mallow
Blackwater
99

Dublin
Dun Laoghaire
Bray
Birr
Boyne
Kildare
Athy
Carlow
Kilkenny
926
Wicklow Mts.
1085
Arklow
Wexford
Rosslare

Nenagh
Thurles
Tipperary
Clonmel
Carrick-on-Suir
Waterford
Dungarvan
Youghal
Cork
Bandon
Kinsale
Cobh

C. Clear

CELTIC SEA

St. George's Channel

Harrogate
Blackpool
Preston
Blackburn
Burnley
Keighley
Leeds
York
Beverley
Kingston upon Hull
Halifax
Bradford
Huddersfield
Barnsley
Scunthorpe
Grimsby
Bolton
Oldham
Doncaster
Rotherham
Louth
Manchester
626
Sheffield
Lincoln
Liverpool
Warrington
Stockport
Chesterfield
Mansfield
Skegness
Anglesey
Holyhead
Bangor
Colwyn Bay
Chester
Crewe
Nottingham
Boston
The Wash
Snowdon
Wrexham
Stoke-on-Trent
Derby
Grantham
Cromer
Pwllheli
Shrewsbury
Stafford
Trent
King's Lynn
Cambrian Mts.
Welshpool
Telford
ENGLAND
Leicester
Norwich
Great Yarmouth
Lowestoft
Cardigan Bay
Aberystwyth
Nuneaton
Corby
Peterborough
Thetford
Wolverhampton
Coventry
Rugby
Northampton
Ely
Bury St. Edmunds
BIRMINGHAM
Redditch
Royal Leamington Spa
Bedford
Cambridge
Ipswich
Carmarthen
Worcester
Hereford
Milton Keynes
Stevenage
Felixstowe
WALES
Brecon
886
Cheltenham
Gloucester
Cotswold Hills
Oxford
Luton
Harlow
Harwich
Colchester
Merthyr Tydfil
Cwmbran
Hemel Hempstead
Chelmsford
Llanelli
Neath
Rhondda
Newport
High Wycombe
Watford
Basildon
Southend-on-Sea
Swansea
Port Talbot
Barry
Cardiff
Bristol
Swindon
Newbury
Reading
Slough
LONDON
Thames
Chatham
Margate
Bristol Channel
Bath
Basingstoke
Maidstone
Canterbury
Weston-super-Mare
Guildford
Reigate
Ashford
Folkestone
Str. of Dover
Exmoor
Salisbury
Winchester
Crawley
Hastings
Barnstaple
Taunton
Yeovil
Southampton
Fareham
Brighton
Eastbourne
Bude
Dartmoor
618
Exeter
Bournemouth
Poole
Portsmouth
Worthing
Newquay
Truro
Torbay
Exmouth
Weymouth
Isle of Wight
Newport
St. Austell
Falmouth
Plymouth
Land's End
Penzance
Isles of Scilly

English Channel

NETHERLAN
's-Gravenhage
(Den Haag)
Hoek van Holland
ROTTERDA
Dordre
Den He
Haar
Haarl
Alk
T

BELGIU
BRUSSEL
(Bruxelle
Zeebrugge
Oostende
Antwerp
Brugge
Gent
Mech
Vlissingen
Dunkerque
Calais
Gris-Nez
Boulogne-sur-Mer
Béthune
Lille
Roubaix
Bruay-la-Buissière
Lens
Valenciennes
Cambrai
Tournai

FRANCE
Picardie
St-Quentin
Amiens
Dieppe
Abbeville
Le Tréport
Fécamp
Pays de Caux
Rouen
Bolbec
Elbeuf
Seine
Le Havre
Trouville-sur-Mer
Lisieux
Caen
Bayeux
Valognes
Cherbourg
Pte. de Barfleur
C. de la Hague
Alderney
Guernsey
St. Peter Port
Sark
Channel Is.
(U.K.)
St. Helier
Jersey
Cotentin
Le Touquet-Paris-Plage
33
36
16
10

Projection: Conical with two standard parallels

West from Greenwich
East from Greenwich
COPYRIGHT GEORGE PHILIP LTD.

ft   m
3000   1000
1500   500
600   200
0
150
100   300
200   600
500   1500
1000   3000
2000   6000
m   ft

A   B   C   D   E   F   G

60   58   56   54   52   50

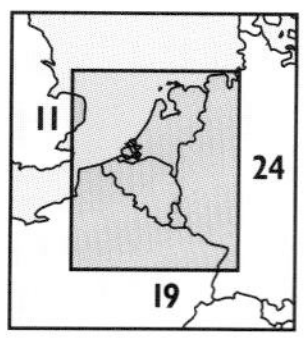

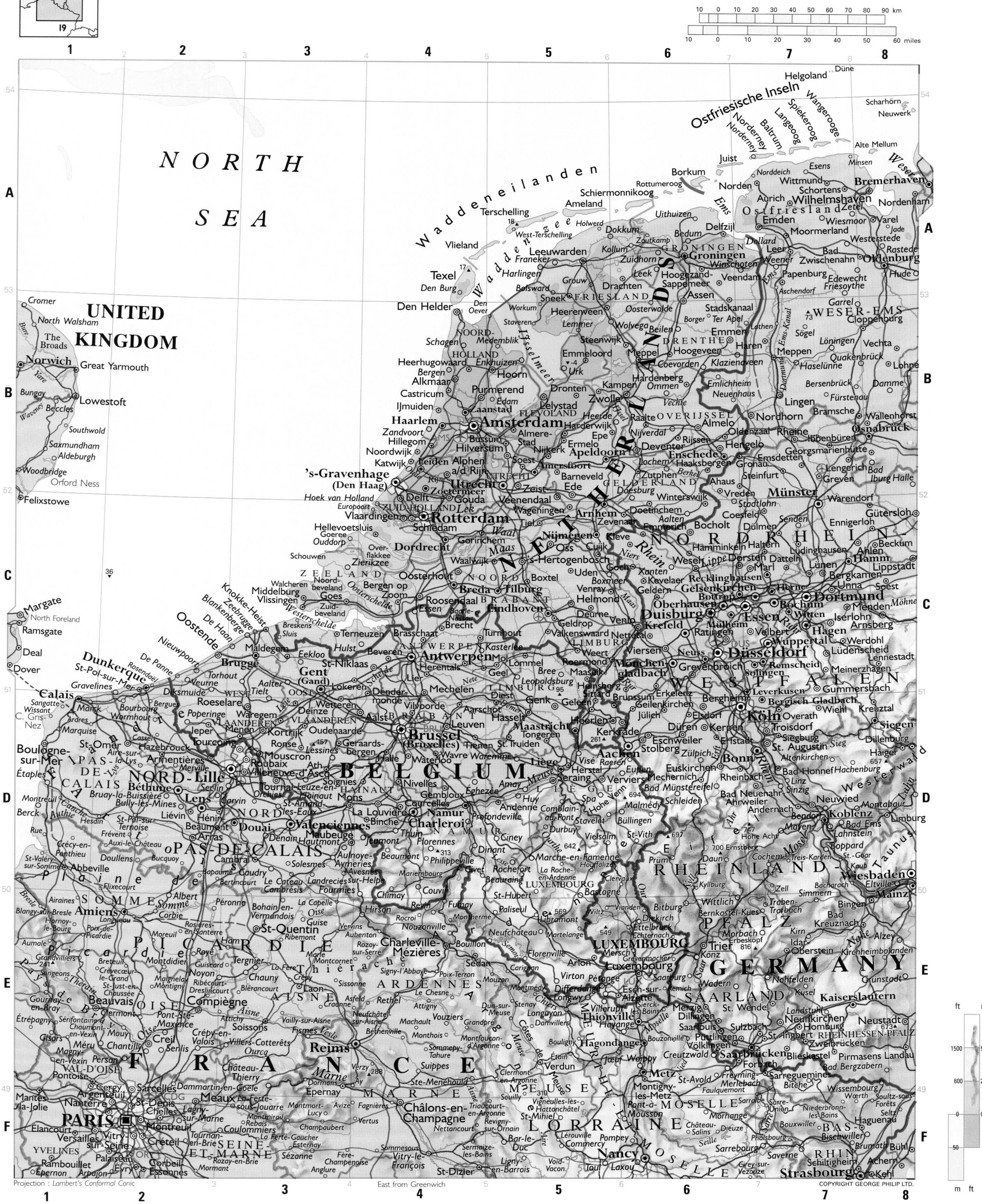

10 0 10 20 30 40 50 60 70 80 90 km
10 0 10 20 30 40 50 60 miles

1 2 3 4 5 6 7 8

N O R T H

S E A

**UNITED
KINGDOM**

Cromer
North Walsham
The Broads
Norwich · Great Yarmouth
Bungay
Beccles · Lowestoft
Southwold
Saxmundham · Aldeburgh
Woodbridge
Orford Ness
Felixstowe

Margate
North Foreland
Ramsgate
Deal
Dover

Helgoland · Düne
Ostfriesische Inseln
Wangerooge
Spiekeroog
Langeoog
Baltrum
Norderney
Juist
Borkum
Scharhörn · Neuwerk
Alte Mellum
Weser

Waddeneilanden
Schiermonnikoog
Ameland
Terschelling
Rottumeroog
Norden · Bremerhaven
Norddeich
Wittmund · Schortens
Aurich · Wilhelmshaven
Wiesmoor · Varel
Emden · Ostfriesland · Zetel
Papenburg · Edewecht · Oldenburg
Leer · Weener · Zwischenahn
Dollart · Hude

Vlieland
West-Terschelling
Harlingen
Texel
Den Burg
Den Helder · Den Oever

Leeuwarden
Franeker
Zuidhorn · Groningen
Dokkum
Kollum · Zoutkamp
Hoogezand-Sappemeer
Winschoten
Veendam
Assen · Stadskanaal
Beilen · Borger · Ter Apel
Emmen · Meppen

N E T H E R L A N D S

Alkmaar · Hoorn
Purmerend · Edam
Zaanstad
Amsterdam
Haarlem · Hilversum · Almere
Zandvoort · Bussum
's-Gravenhage (Den Haag)
Leiden · **Utrecht**
Delft · Gouda · Arnhem
Rotterdam · Nijmegen
Dordrecht
's-Hertogenbosch
Tilburg · **Eindhoven**
Breda · Helmond
Roosendaal · Venlo

Apeldoorn · Deventer
Zwolle · Almelo
Enschede · Hengelo
Zutphen
Münster
Osnabrück
Dortmund
Essen · Bochum
Duisburg · **Düsseldorf**
Krefeld · **Köln**
Bonn · Aachen

N O R D R H E I N
W E S T F A L E N

Z E E L A N D
Middelburg · Vlissingen
Goes · Bergen op Zoom

Oostende
Brugge
Gent (Gand)
Antwerpen
Mechelen
Brussel (Bruxelles)
Leuven · Hasselt
Maastricht
Liège · Verviers

B E L G I U M

Dunkerque
Calais
C. Gris-Nez
Boulogne-sur-Mer
NORD-Lille
Roubaix · Tourcoing
Lens · Douai
Valenciennes
PAS DE CALAIS
Arras · Cambrai

Namur
Charleroi
Mons
LUXEMBOURG
Bastogne
Arlon
Luxembourg
Trier
Koblenz
Wiesbaden · Mainz

GERMANY

R H E I N L A N D
PFALZ
Saarbrücken
SAARLAND
Kaiserslautern
Neustadt
Strasbourg

Amiens
S O M M E
P I C A R D I E
Beauvais
Compiègne
St-Quentin
Laon
Charleville-Mézières
Sedan
A R D E N N E S
Reims
Châlons-en-Champagne
F R A N C E
Verdun
Metz
Thionville
L O R R A I N E
M O S E L L E
Nancy

PARIS
Versailles
SEINE-ET-MARNE
Meaux
Épernay
M A R N E

Projection : Lambert's Conformal Conic

East from Greenwich

COPYRIGHT GEORGE PHILIP LTD.

Underlined towns give their name to the
administrative area in which they stand.

ft m
1500 500
600 200
50

m ft

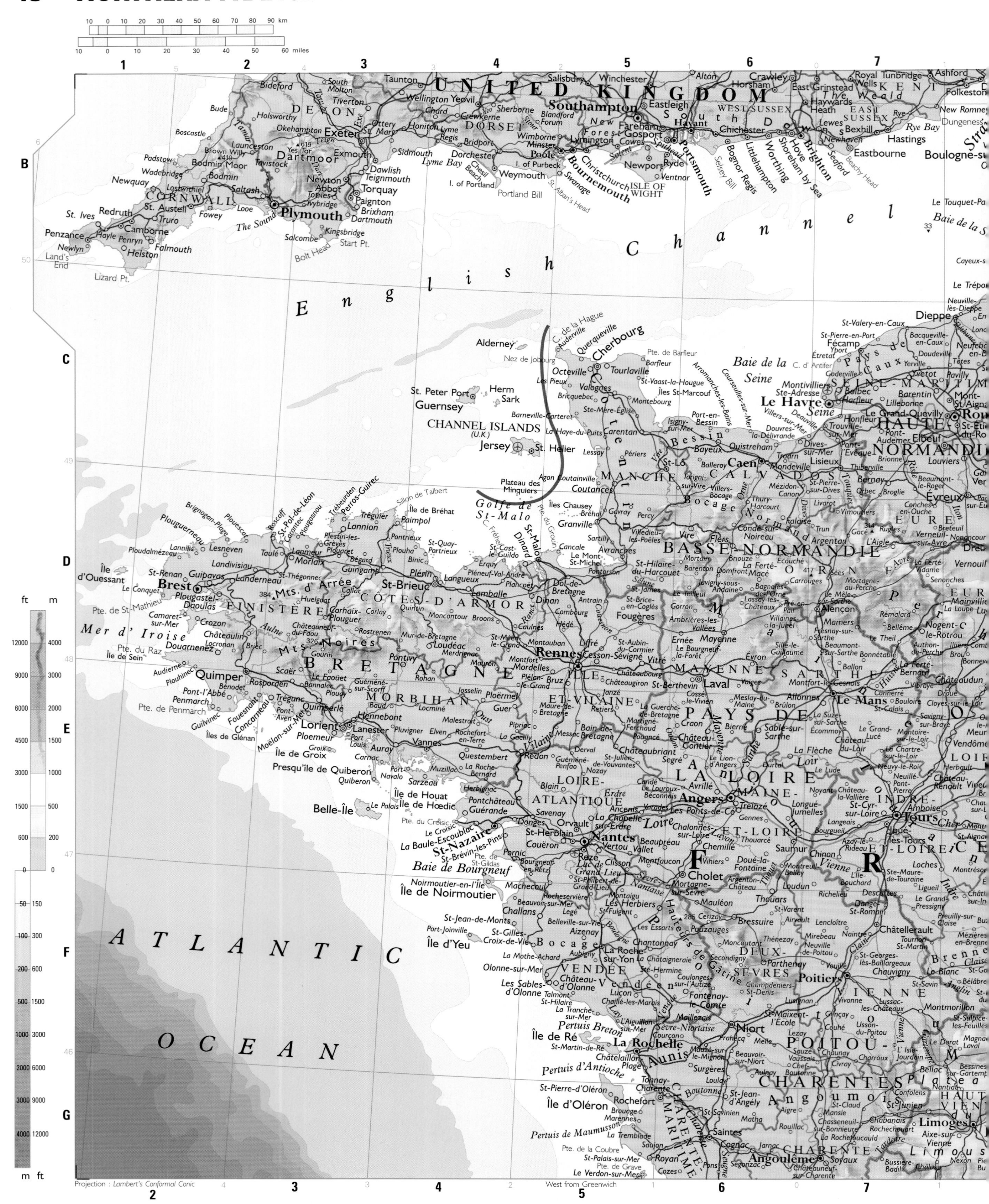

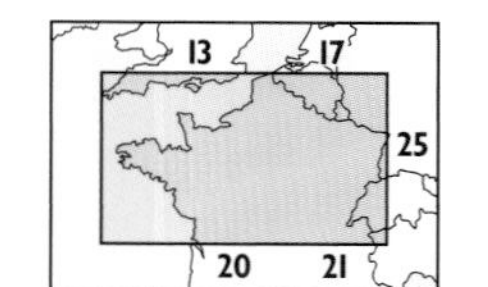

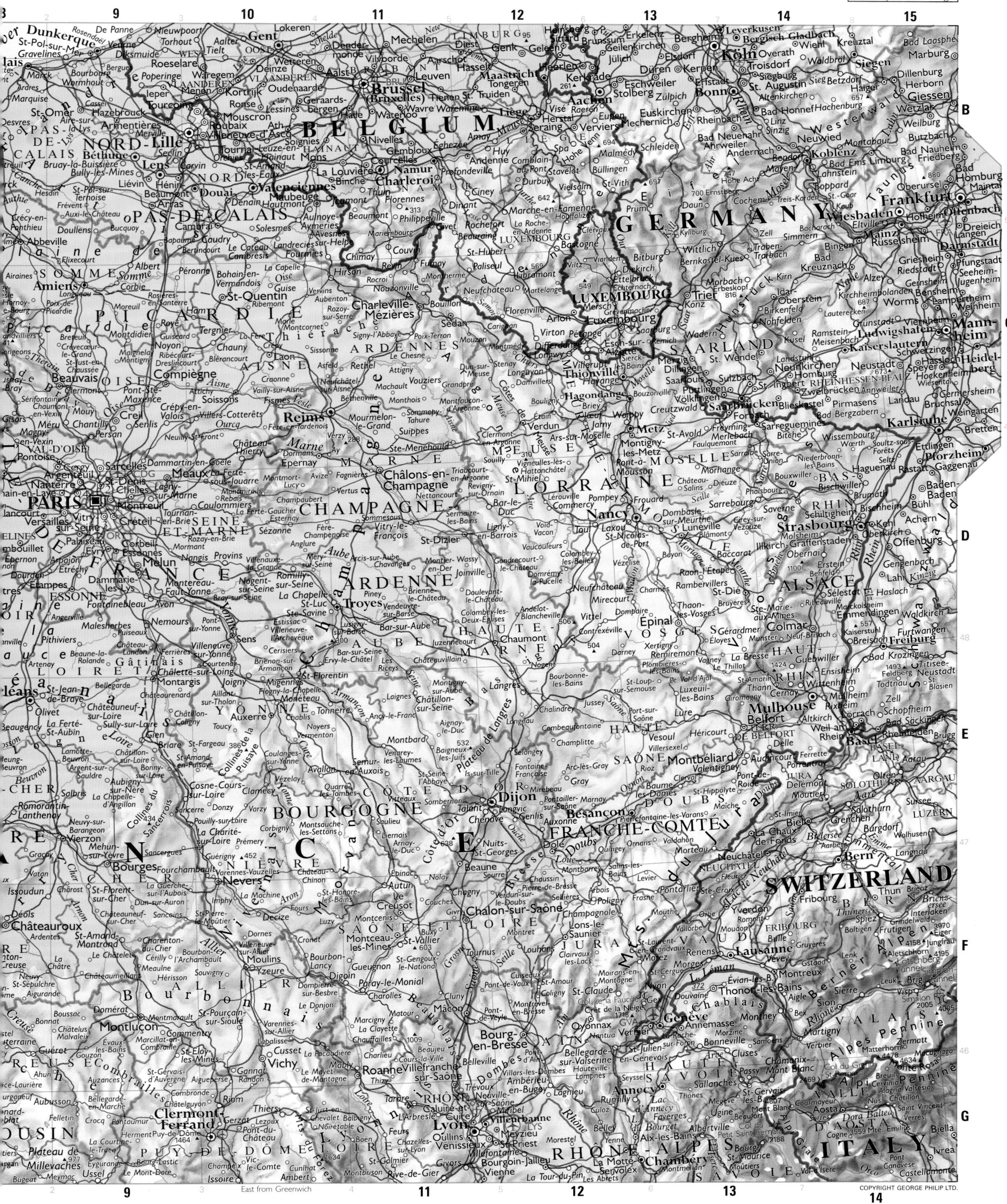

Underlined towns give their name to the
administrative area in which they stand.

COPYRIGHT GEORGE PHILIP LTD.

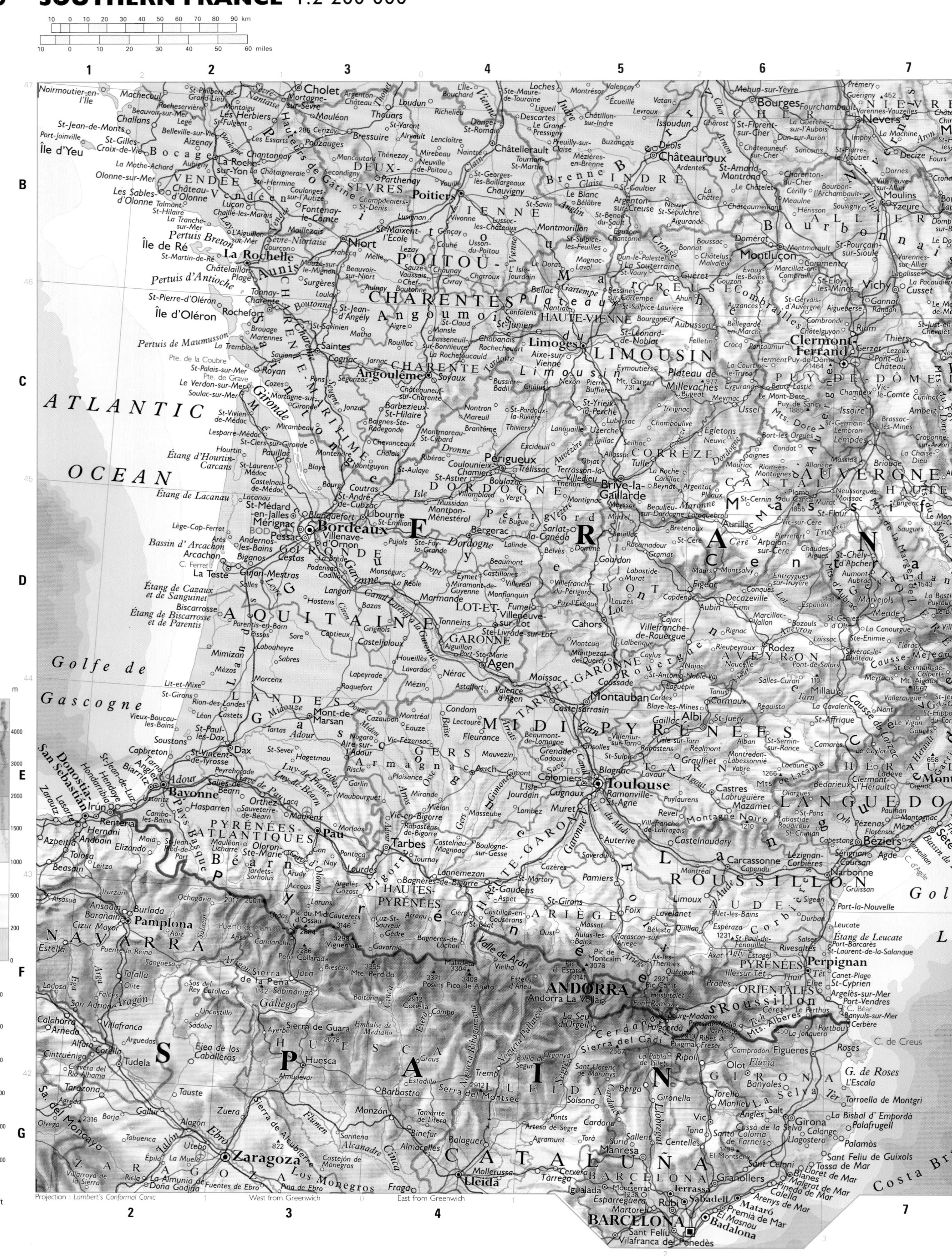
10 0 10 20 30 40 50 60 70 80 90 km
10 0 10 20 30 40 50 60 miles
ATLANTIC
OCEAN
Golfe de
Gascogne
FRANCE
SPAIN
ANDORRA
AQUITAINE
POITOU-CHARENTES
LIMOUSIN
AUVERGNE
MIDI-PYRÉNÉES
LANGUEDOC-ROUSSILLON
NAVARRA
ARAGÓN
CATALUÑA
VENDÉE
DEUX-SÈVRES
VIENNE
CHARENTE-MARITIME
CHARENTE
DORDOGNE
GIRONDE
LANDES
LOT-ET-GARONNE
GERS
HAUTE-GARONNE
ARIÈGE
AUDE
PYRÉNÉES-ATLANTIQUES
HAUTES-PYRÉNÉES
PYRÉNÉES-ORIENTALES
TARN
AVEYRON
CANTAL
CORRÈZE
HAUTE-VIENNE
CREUSE
INDRE
CHER
ALLIER
PUY-DE-DÔME
HUESCA
LLEIDA
GIRONA
BARCELONA
ZARAGOZA
Bordeaux
Toulouse
Limoges
Poitiers
Clermont-Ferrand
Pau
Bayonne
Perpignan
Zaragoza
Pamplona
Lleida
BARCELONA
Montauban
Agen
Périgueux
Angoulême
La Rochelle
Niort
Tarbes
Carcassonne
Béziers
Rodez
Albi
Cahors
Brive-la-Gaillarde
Bourges
Nevers
Vichy
Châteauroux
Montluçon
Huesca
Andorra La Vella
Gol
Projection : Lambert's Conformal Conic
West from Greenwich
East from Greenwich

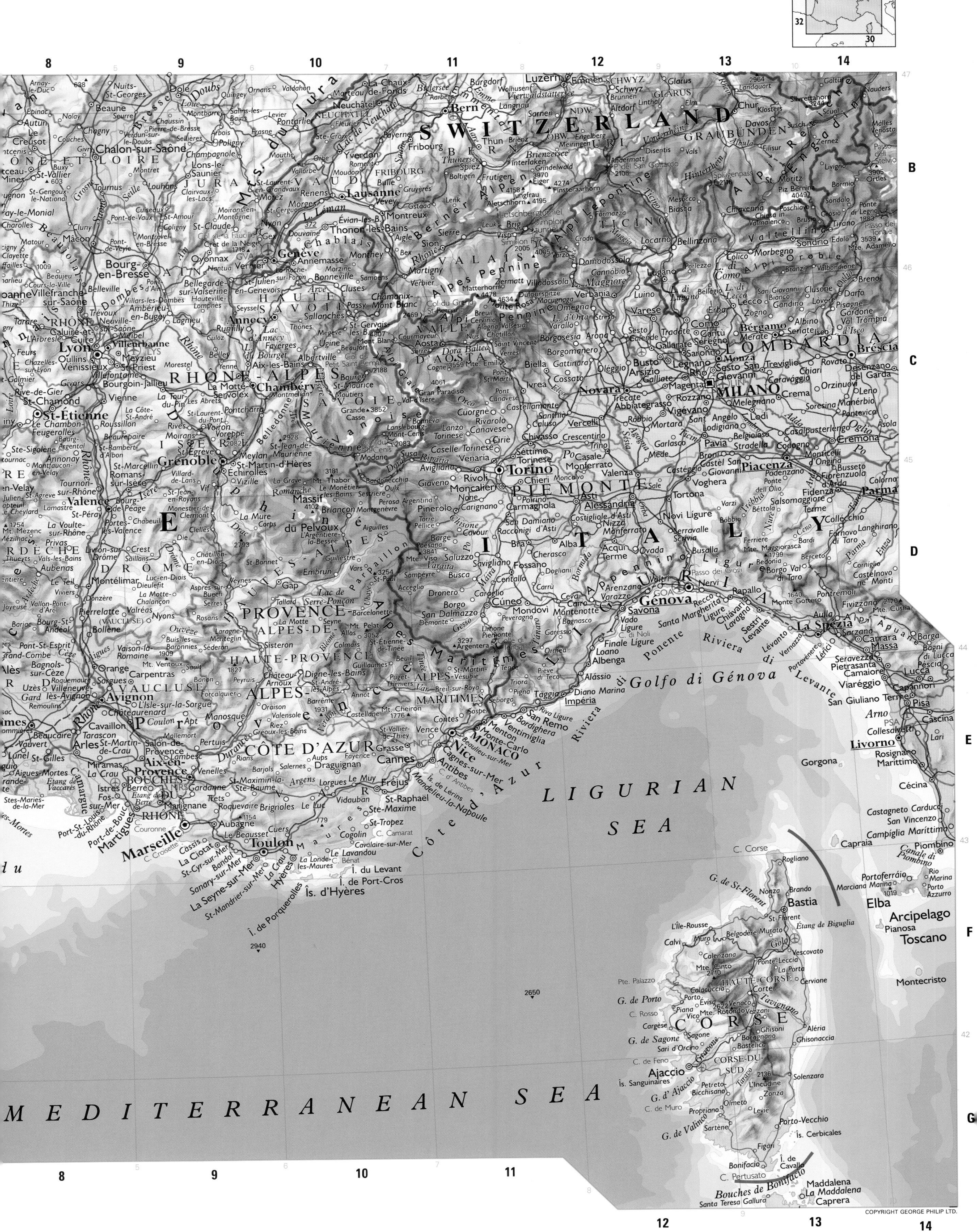
SWITZERLAND
ITALY
LIGURIAN SEA
MEDITERRANEAN SEA
Golfo di Génova
Riviera di Levante
Riviera di Ponente
Côte d'Azur
PIEMONTE
LOMBARDIA
RHÔNE-ALPES
PROVENCE-ALPES-CÔTE D'AZUR
CORSE
HAUTE-CORSE
CORSE-DU-SUD
SAVOIE
HAUTE-SAVOIE
VALAIS
TICINO
GRAUBÜNDEN
VAUD
FRIBOURG
BERN
JURA
AIN
ISÈRE
DRÔME
VAUCLUSE
BOUCHES-DU-RHÔNE
ALPES-MARITIMES
HAUTES-ALPES
ALPES-DE-HAUTE-PROVENCE
VALLE D'AOSTA
MONACO
Alpes Pennine
Alpi Lepontine
Berner Alpen
Alpi Orobie
Alpes Maritimes
Mts. du Jura
Dauphiné
Lyon
Genève
Lausanne
Bern
Luzern
Torino
MILANO
Génova
Marseille
Toulon
Nice
Cannes
Grenoble
Chambéry
Annecy
Avignon
Aix-en-Provence
Valence
St-Étienne
Novara
Alessandria
Asti
Cúneo
Savona
Bérgamo
Brescia
Piacenza
Parma
La Spezia
Livorno
Pisa
Lucca
Bastia
Ajaccio
Bonifacio
Porto-Vecchio
Elba
Arcipelago Toscano
Capraia
Gorgona
Montecristo
Bouches de Bonifacio
Îs. d'Hyères
C. Corse
Mont Blanc
Matterhorn
Lac Léman
L. Maggiore
L. di Como
Rhône
Po
8
9
10
11
12
13
14
B
C
D
E
F
G
18
19
29
30
32

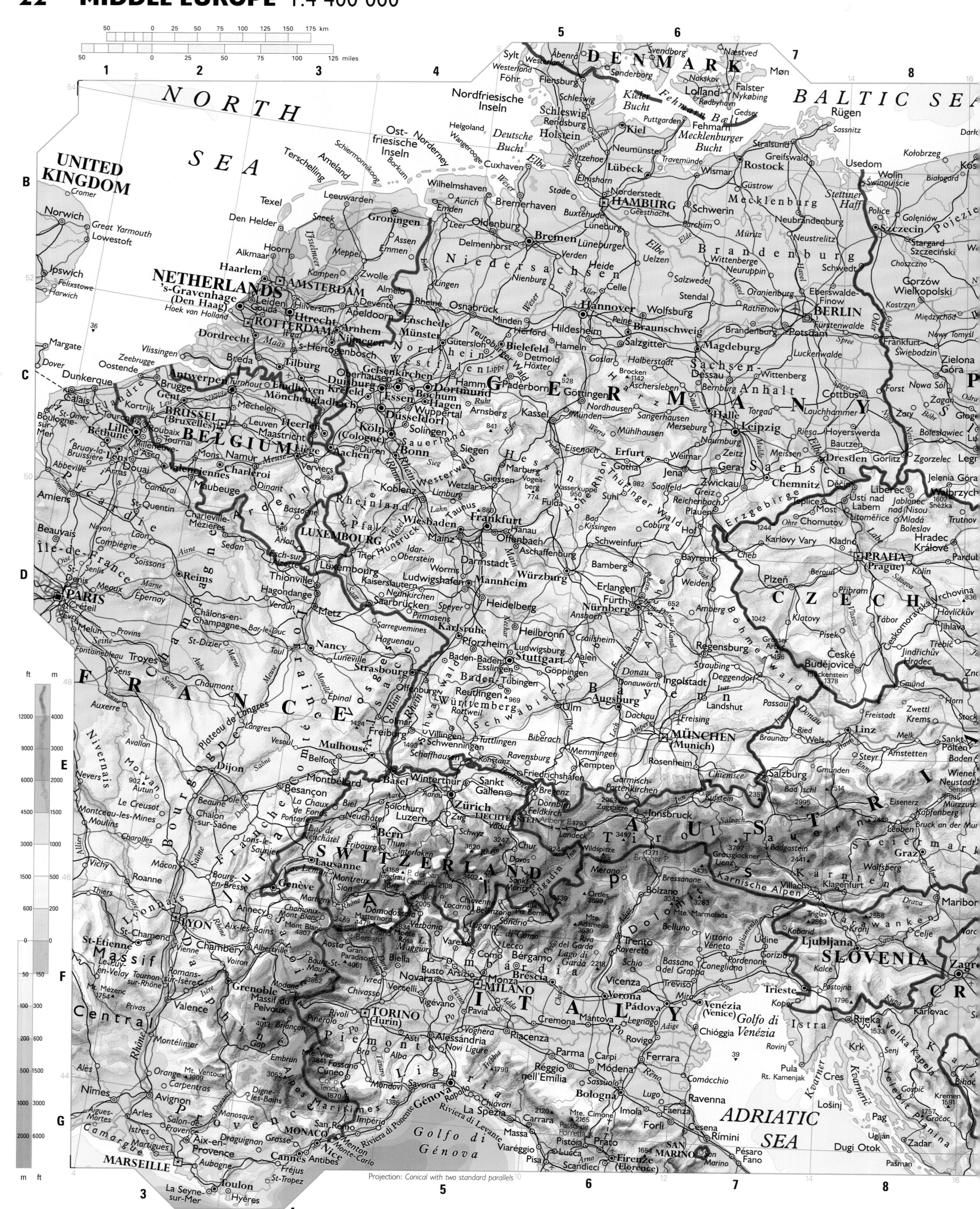

NORTH SEA
BALTIC SEA
ADRIATIC SEA
UNITED KINGDOM
NETHERLANDS
BELGIUM
LUXEMBOURG
DENMARK
GERMANY
FRANCE
SWITZERLAND
LIECHTENSTEIN
AUSTRIA
CZECH
SLOVENIA
ITALY
MONACO
SAN MARINO
AMSTERDAM
BRUSSEL (Bruxelles)
BERLIN
PARIS
PRAHA (Prague)
HAMBURG
MÜNCHEN (Munich)
MILANO
TORINO (Turin)
LYON
MARSEILLE
Golfo di Génova
Golfo di Venézia
Projection: Conical with two standard parallels

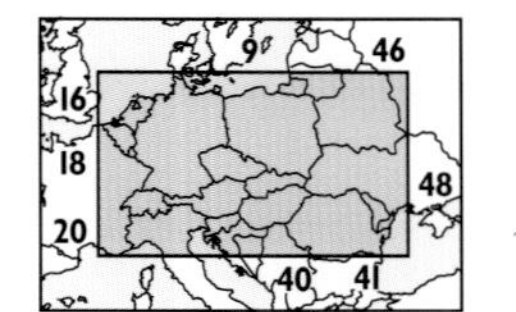
9
46
16
18
48
20
40
41

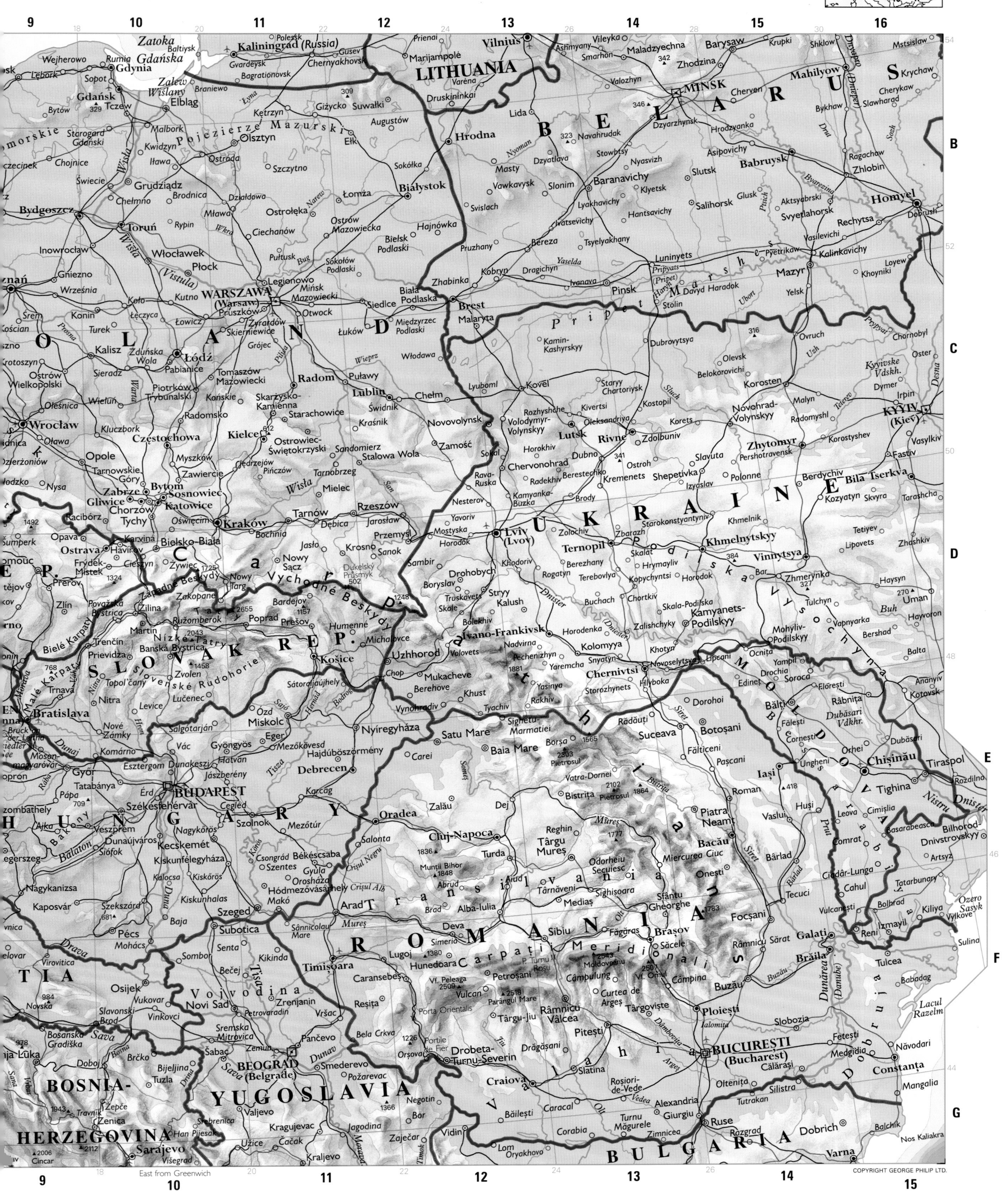
LITHUANIA
BELARUS
UKRAINE
SLOVAK REP.
HUNGARY
ROMANIA
MOLDOVA
BOSNIA-HERZEGOVINA
YUGOSLAVIA
BULGARIA
Vilnius
MINSK
WARSZAWA (Warsaw)
KYYIV (Kiev)
BUDAPEST
BEOGRAD (Belgrade)
BUCUREȘTI (Bucharest)
Chișinău
Sarajevo
Bratislava
Kaliningrad (Russia)
Zatoka Gdańska
Pripet Marshes
Carpathians
Transilvania
Carpații Meridionali
Vojvodina
Podilska Vysochyna
Wisła
Dnister
Dunărea (Danube)
East from Greenwich
COPYRIGHT GEORGE PHILIP LTD.

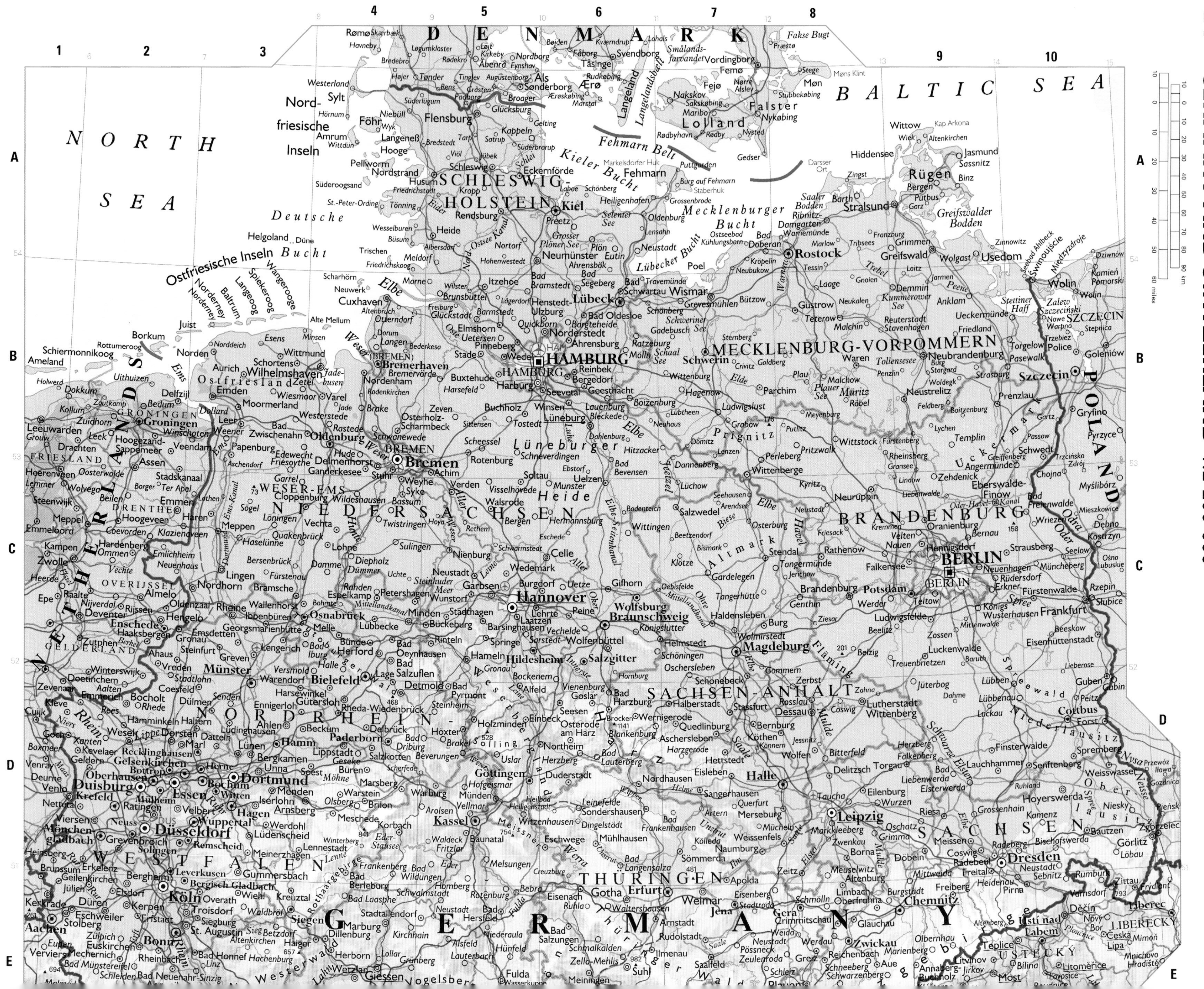

10 0 10 20 30 40 50 60 70 80 90 km
10 0 10 20 30 40 50 60 miles
A
B
C
D
E
1
2
3
4
5
6
7
8
9
10
NORTH SEA
BALTIC SEA
DENMARK
POLAND
NETHERLANDS
GERMANY
SCHLESWIG-HOLSTEIN
MECKLENBURG-VORPOMMERN
BRANDENBURG
NIEDERSACHSEN
SACHSEN-ANHALT
SACHSEN
THÜRINGEN
NORDRHEIN-WESTFALEN
BERLIN
HAMBURG
BREMEN
Kiel
Lübeck
Rostock
Hannover
Braunschweig
Magdeburg
Potsdam
Leipzig
Dresden
Halle
Erfurt
Kassel
Göttingen
Münster
Osnabrück
Bielefeld
Dortmund
Essen
Duisburg
Düsseldorf
Köln
Bonn
Aachen
Wuppertal
Chemnitz
Szczecin
Flensburg
Groningen
Ostfriesische Inseln
Nordfriesische Inseln
Lüneburger Heide
Elbe
Weser
Rhein
Oder

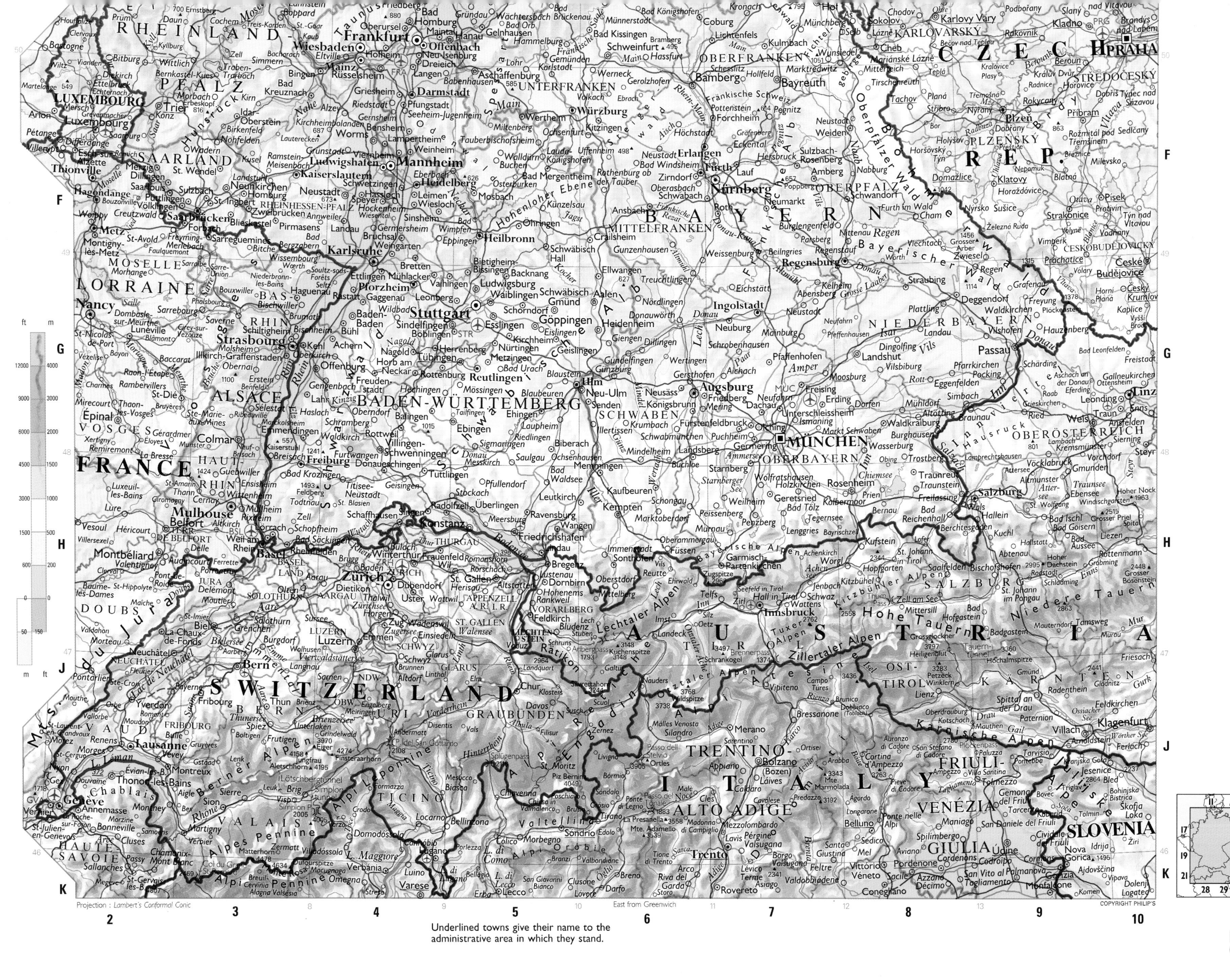

Underlined towns give their name to the
administrative area in which they stand.

Projection: Lambert's Conformal Conic

East from Greenwich

COPYRIGHT PHILIP'S

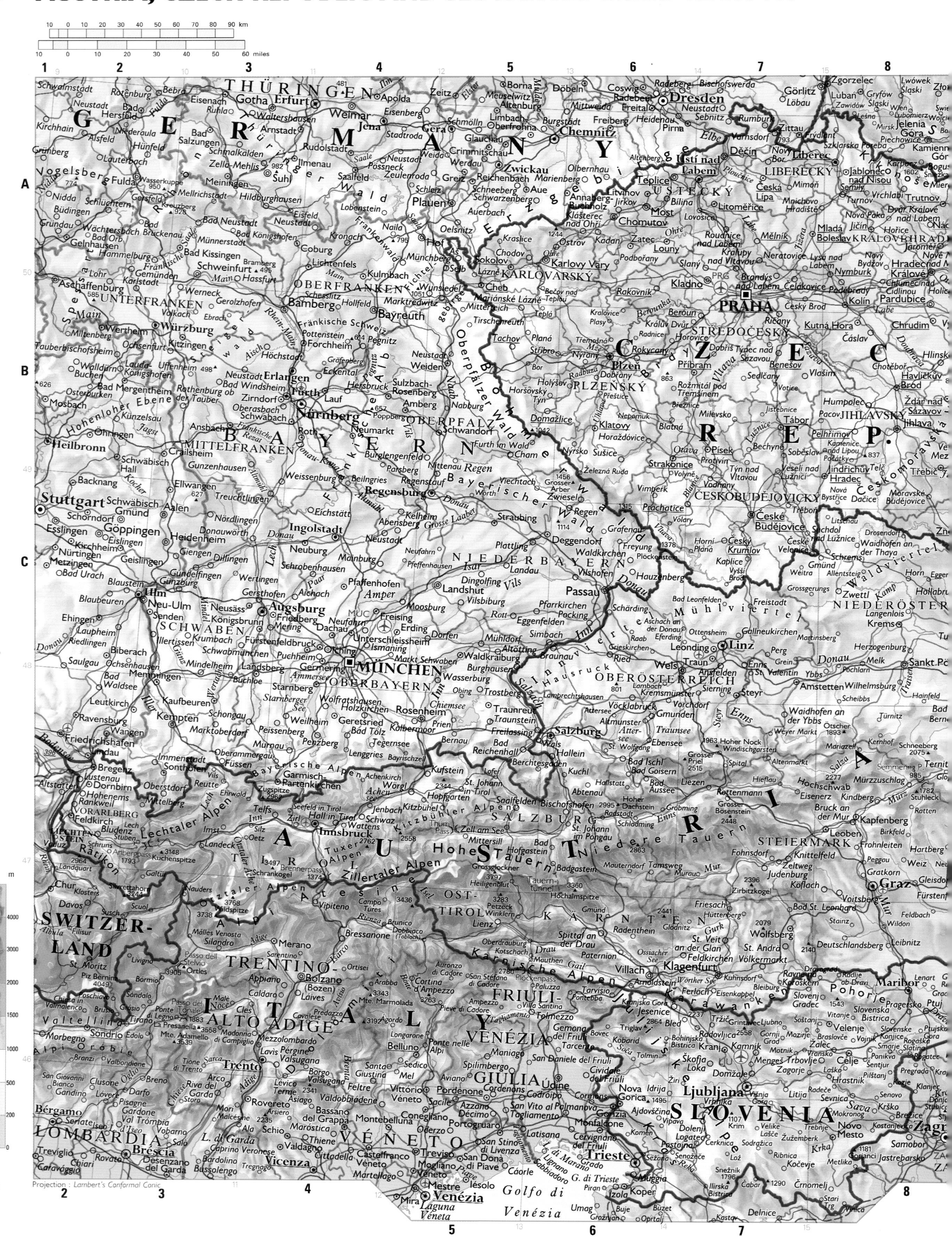
10 0 10 20 30 40 50 60 70 80 90 km
10 0 10 20 30 40 50 60 miles
GERMANY
CZECH REP.
AUSTRIA
ITALY
SWITZERLAND
SLOVENIA
THÜRINGEN
OBERFRANKEN
UNTERFRANKEN
MITTELFRANKEN
OBERPFALZ
BAYERN
NIEDERBAYERN
SCHWABEN
OBERBAYERN
KARLOVARSKÝ
ÚSTECKÝ
LIBERECKÝ
STŘEDOČESKÝ
PLZEŇSKÝ
JIHOČESKÝ
JIHLAVSKÝ
ČESKOBUDĚJOVICKÝ
NIEDERÖSTERREICH
OBERÖSTERREICH
SALZBURG
TIROL
OST-TIROL
KÄRNTEN
STEIERMARK
VORARLBERG
TRENTINO-ALTO ADIGE
FRIULI-VENEZIA GIULIA
VENETO
LOMBARDIA
Erzgebirge
Thüringer Wald
Frankenwald
Fichtelgebirge
Böhmerwald
Oberpfälzer Wald
Bayerischer Wald
Mühlviertel
Waldviertel
Hausruck
Lechtaler Alpen
Kitzbühler Alpen
Hohe Tauern
Niedere Tauern
Zillertaler Alpen
Ötztaler Alpen
Karnische Alpen
Karawanken
Julijske Alpe
Dolomiti
Donau
Inn
Elbe
Vltava
Praha
München
Dresden
Chemnitz
Erfurt
Nürnberg
Würzburg
Regensburg
Augsburg
Stuttgart
Heilbronn
Ingolstadt
Ulm
Passau
Linz
Salzburg
Innsbruck
Graz
Klagenfurt
Villach
Ljubljana
Maribor
Bolzano (Bozen)
Trento
Venézia
Trieste
Údine
Plzeň
České Budějovice
Karlovy Vary
Ústí nad Labem
Liberec
Golfo di Venézia
Projection : Lambert's Conformal Conic

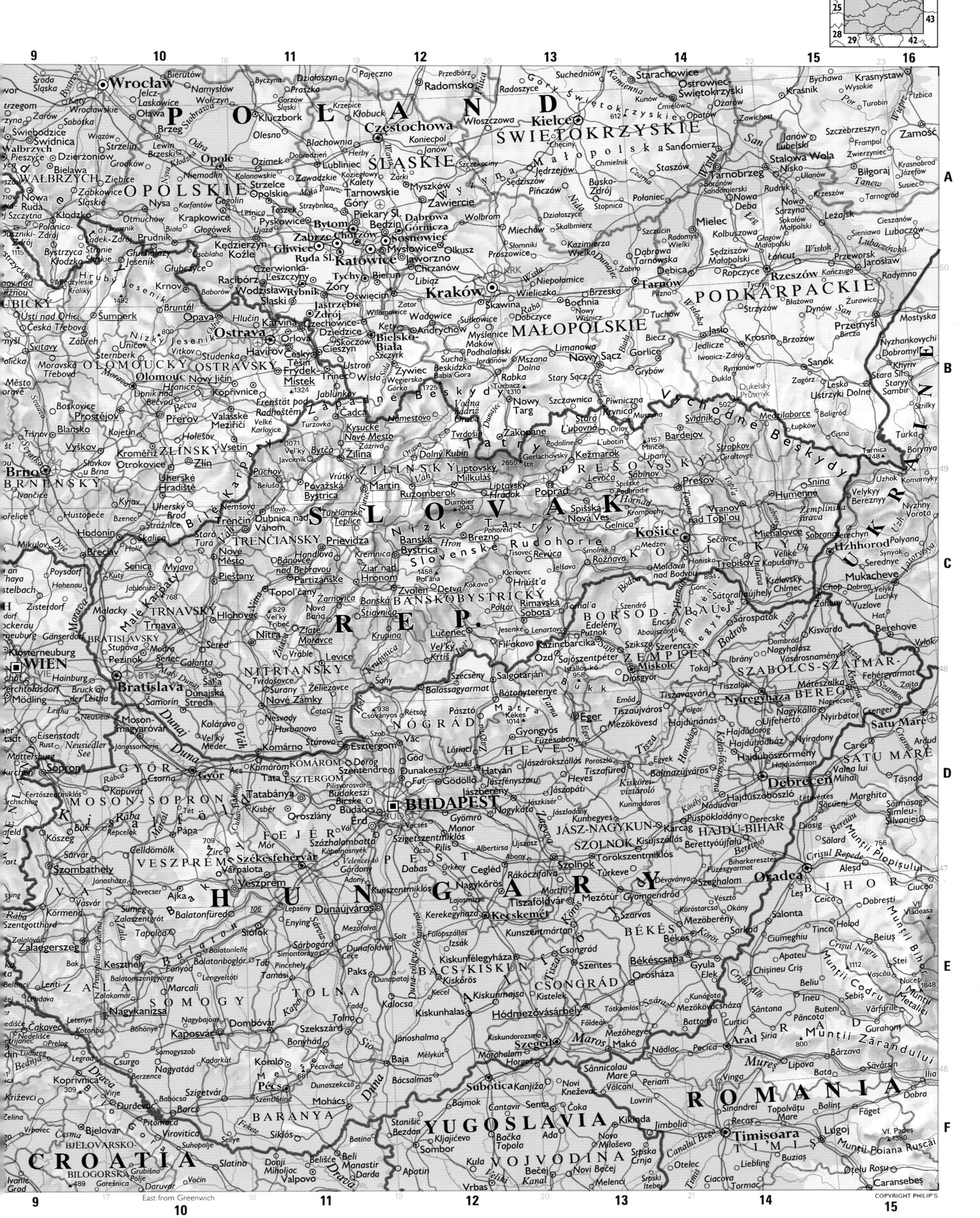

Underlined towns give their name to the administrative area in which they stand.

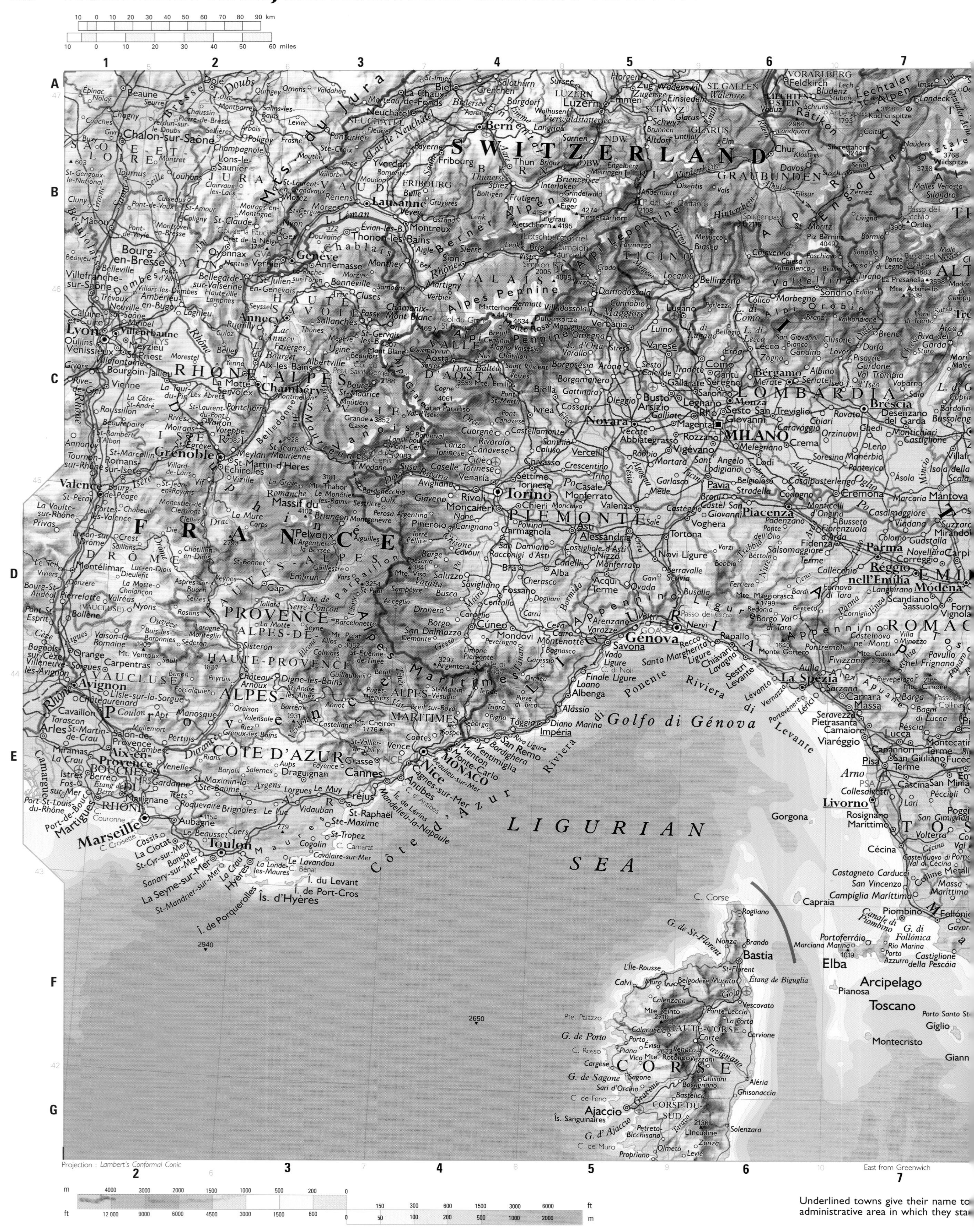

Underlined towns give their name to
administrative area in which they sta

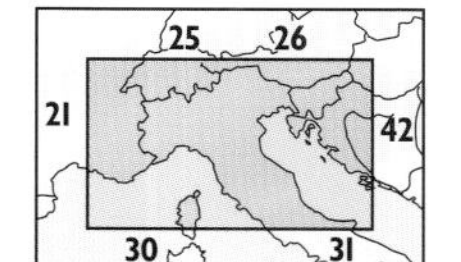

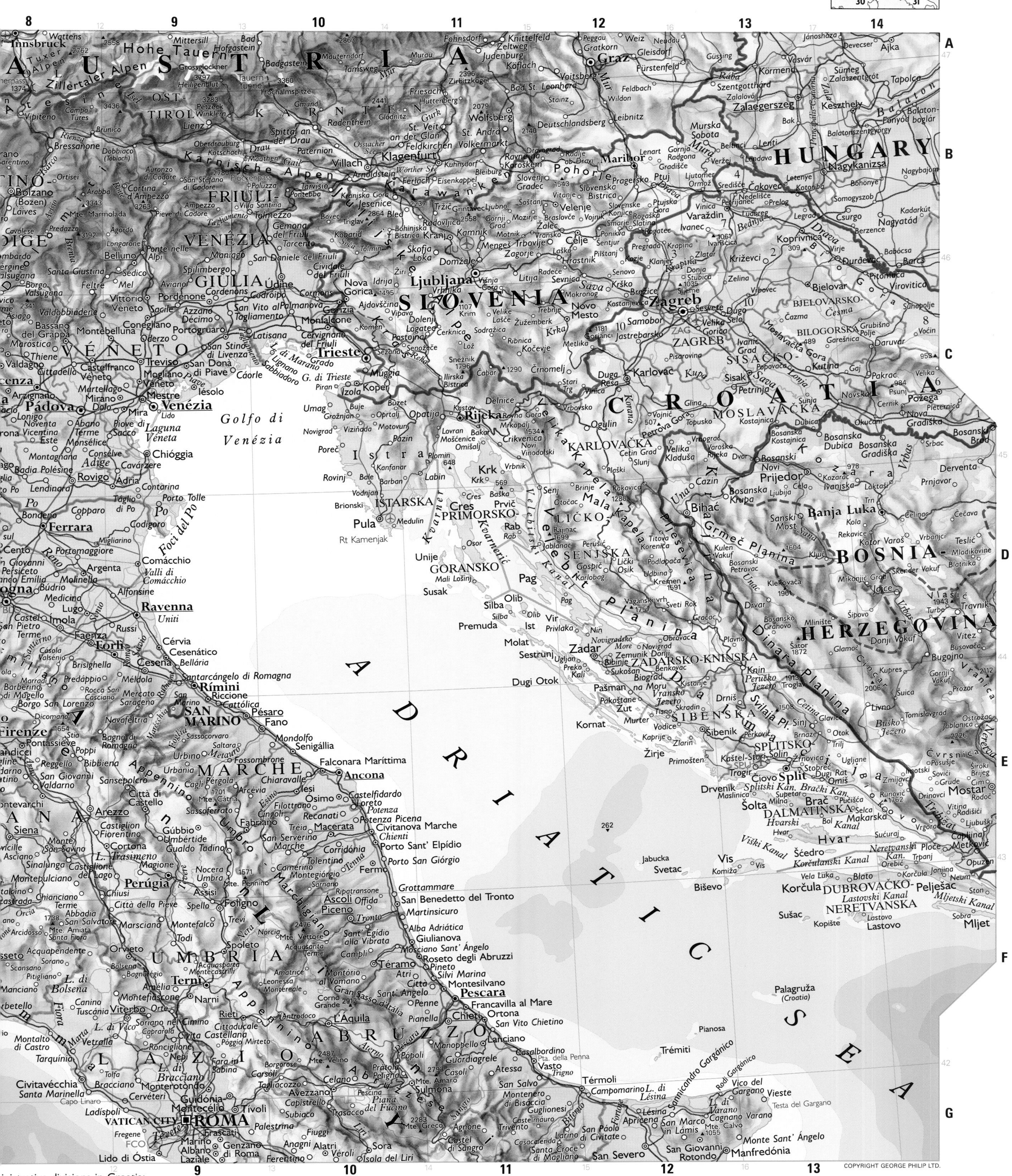

Administrative divisions in Croatia:

...odsko-Posavska	4. Medimurska
...privničko-Križevačka	6. Požeško-Slavonska
...apinsko-Zagorska	7. Varaždinska
8. Virovitičko-Podravska	
l0. Zagrebačka	

Inter-entity boundaries as agreed
at the 1995 Dayton Peace Agreement.

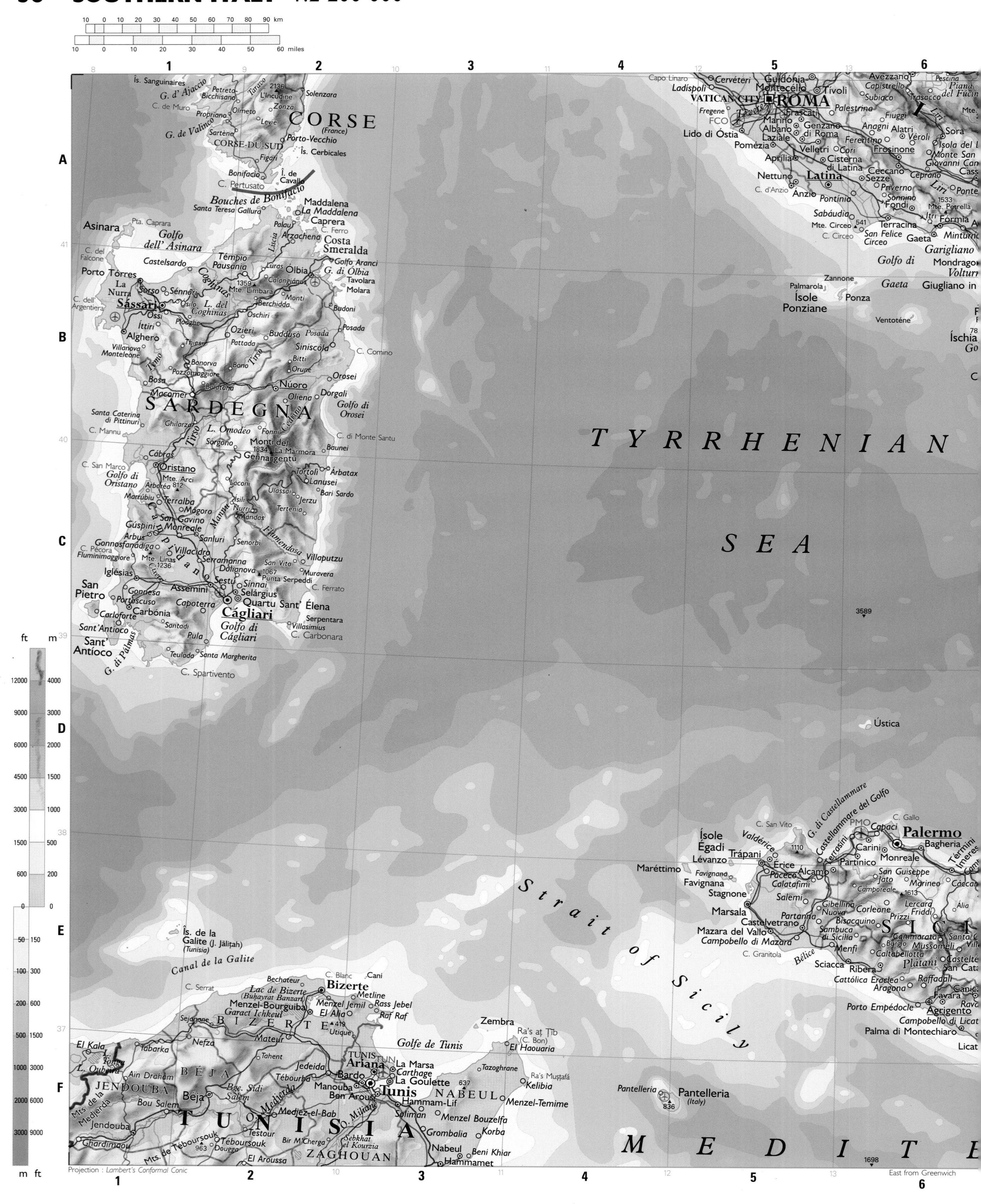

10 0 10 20 30 40 50 60 70 80 90 km
10 0 10 20 30 40 50 60 miles

CORSE
(France)
CORSE-DU-SUD

Ís. Sanguinaires
G. d'Ajaccio
Petreto
Bicchisano
Propriano
G. de Muro
Olmeto
Levie
Zonza
L'Incudine 2136
Sartène
Porto-Vecchio
Figari
Bonifacio
C. Pertusato
Bouches de Bonifacio
Î. de Cavallo
Ís. Cerbicales

Solenzara

Maddalena
La Maddalena
Caprera
Santa Teresa Gallura
C. Ferro
Palau
Arzachena
Costa
Smeralda

Asinara
Pta. Caprara
C. del Falcone
Golfo dell' Asinara

Porto Tórres
La Nurra
C. dell'
Argentiera
Sássari
Sorso
Sénnori
Ossi
Íttiri
Alghero
Villanova
Monteleone

Castelsardo
Témpio
Pausánia
Luras
Calangiánus
Monti
Pattada
Oschiri
Ózieri
Budduso
Posada
Posada

Bono Tirso
Bottida
Macomer
Bosa
Bórore
Ghilarza
L. Omodeo
Sórgono
Fonni
Monti del
1834 Gennargentu
La Marmora

Nuoro
Oliena
Dorgali
Golfo di
Orosei
Orosei
C. di Monte Santu
Baunei

SARDEGNA

Santa Caterina
di Pittinuri
C. Mannu
C. San Marco
Golfo di
Oristano
Oristano
Arborea
Mte. Arci
812
Marrúbiu
Terralba
Mógoro
San Gavino
Monreale
Arbus
Gonnosfanádiga
Flúminimaggiore
Gúspini
Villacidro
Mte. Linas
1236
Iglésias
Gonnesa
Portoscuso
Carbonia
San
Pietro
Carloforte
Sant'Antioco
Santadi
Nárcao
Pula
Sant'
Antíoco
G. di Palmas
C. Spartivento
Teulada
Santa Margherita

Bari Sardo
Tortolì
Árbatax
Lanusei
Jerzu
Ussassai
Locéri
Ísili
Nurri
Tertenia
Mandas
Serpeddì
Senorbi
Dolianova
San Vito
1067
Punta Serpeddi
Muravera
Villaputzu
C. Ferrato
Serpentara
Villasimius
C. Carbonara
Serramanna
Sanluri
Sestu
Assémini
Sinnai
Selárgius
Quartu Sant' Élena
Capoterra
Cágliari
Golfo di
Cágliari

ROMA
VATICAN CITY
Capo Linaro
Cervéteri
Ladíspoli
Fregene
FCO
Guidónia
Montecélio
Tívoli
Capistrello
Avezzano
Pescina
Piana
del Fucin
Subiaco
Palestrina
Fiuggi
Sora
Anagni
Alatri
Véroli
Isola del L
Monte San
Giovanni
Cass
Frosinone
Ceprano
Ponte
Marino
Albano
Genzano
di Roma
Laziale
Velletri
Cori
Ferentino
Pomézia
Aprília
Cisterna
di Latina
Sezze
Priverno
Sonnino
Fondi
1533
Mte. Petrella
Ítri
Anzio
Pontínia
Latina
Nettuno
C. d'Anzio
Sabáudia
Mte. Circeo 541
San Felice
Circeo
Formia
C. Circeo
Terracina
Gaeta
Minturn
Garigliano
Golfo di
Mondrago
Voltur
Palmarola
Zannone
Ísole
Ponza
Ponziane
Ventotène
 Gia
Gaeta
Giugliano in
Íschia
Go

TYRRHENIAN

SEA

3589

Ústica

G. di Castellammare del Golfo
C. San Vito
G. di Castellammare
Capaci
C. Gallo
PMO
Palermo
Bagheria
Ísole
Égadi
Valdérice
Carini
Términi
Trápani
1110
Monreale
Érice
Partinico
Inmeres
Lévanzo
Alcamo
San Guiseppe
Jato
Maréttimo
Paceco
Calatafimi
Campoferra
Marineo
Favignana
Favignana
1613
Corleone
Mineo
Caccan
Stagnone
Salemi
Gibellina
Nuova
Prizzi
Lercara
Friddi
Ália
Marsala
Partanna
Bisacquino
Sambuca
di Sicilia
Bargo
SICI
Mazara del Vallo
Castelvetrano
Campobello di Mazara
Menfi
Caltabellotta
Mussomeli
Vill
Bélice
C. Granitola
Sciacca
Ribera
Plátani
San Cat
Cattólica Eraclea
Aragona
Raffadali
Rav
Porto Empédocle
Favara
Agrigento
Campobello di Licat
Palma di Montechiaro
Licat

Strait of Sicily

Ís. de la
Galite (Tunisia)
(J. Jālīţah)
Canal de la Galite

Cani
C. Blanc
Bizerte
Metline
Rass Jebel
Menzel Jemil
Raf Raf
El Alia
Utique
C. Serrat
C. Serrat
Béchateur
Lac de Bizerte
(Buhayrat Banzart)
BIZERTE
Menzel-Bourguiba
Garaet Ichkeul
Séjenane
Mateur
419

Zembra
Ra's aţ Ţīb
(C. Bon)
El Haouaria
Golfe de Tunis
TUNIS
Ariana
La Marsa
Bardo
Carthage
Tazoghrane
Manouba
La Goulette
Kelibia
Ben Arous
Menzel-Temime
637
NABEUL
Ra's Muştafā

Pantelleria
Pantelleria
(Italy)
836

El Kala
L. Tonga
L. Oubeïra
Tábarka
Nefza
Áïn Draham
Mts. de la
Medjerda
JENDOUBA
Béja
Bge. Sidi
Salem
BÉJA
Jedeïda
Téboursouk
Téstour
TUNISIA
Medjez-el-Bab
Manouba
Soliman
Hammam-Lif
Menzel Bouzelfa
Korba
Jendouba
Bou Salem
963
Bir M'Cherga
Grombalia
Nabeul
Beni Khiar
Ghardimaou
Mts. de Téboursouk
Testour
Sbkhat
el Kourzia
Dougga
El Aroussa
ZAGHOUAN
Hammamet

1698
MEDITE

East from Greenwich

Projection : Lambert's Conformal Conic

ft m
12000 4000
9000 3000
6000 2000
4500 1500
3000 1000
1500 500
600 200
0 0
150 50
300 100
600 200
1500 500
3000 1000
6000 2000
9000 3000
m ft

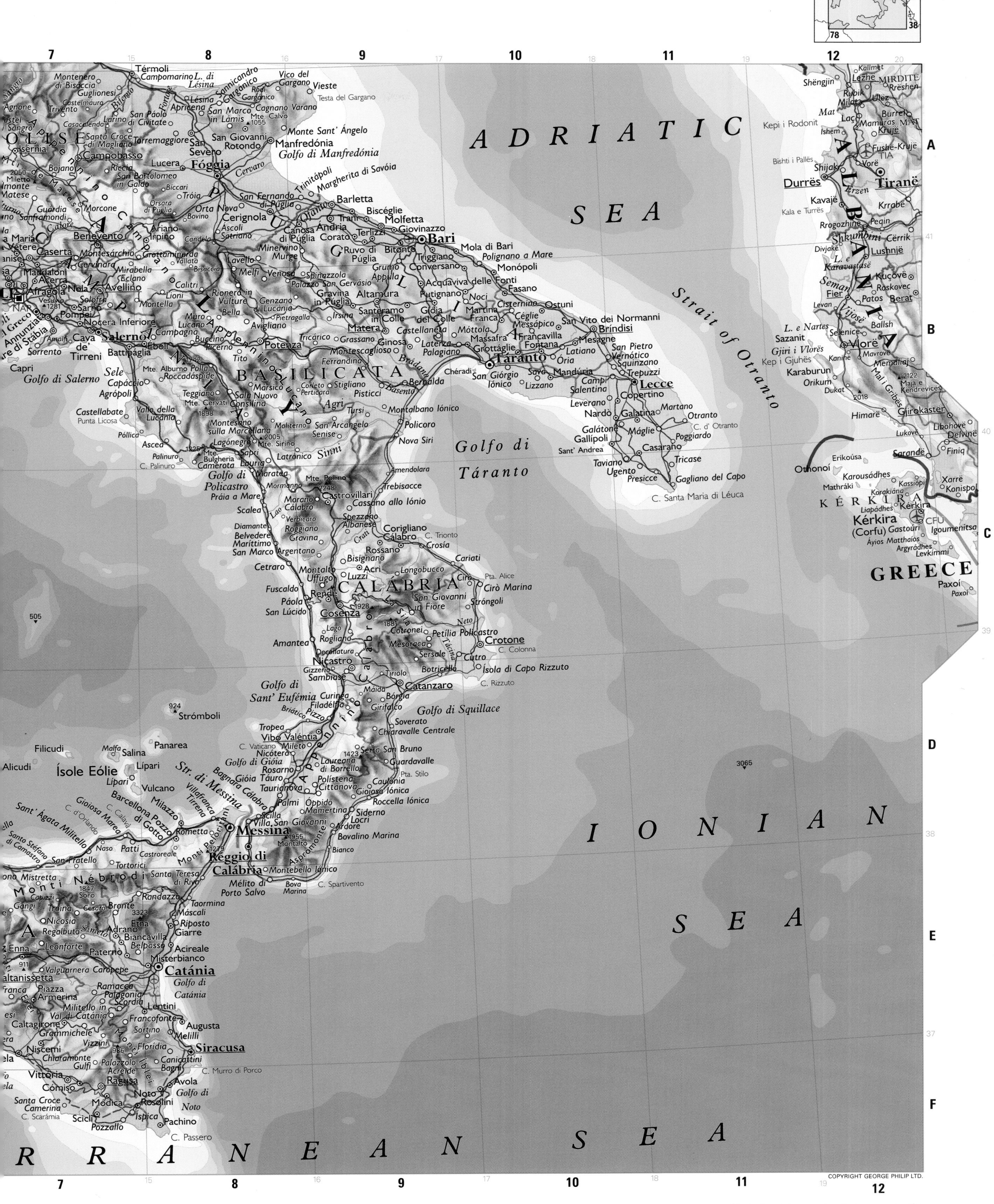

28 29 40
78 38

A D R I A T I C   S E A

ALBANIA

Shëngjin
Lezhë
MIRDITE
Rrëshen
Rubik
Milot
Burrel
Mamuras
Mat
Kruje
Fushe-Kruje
Vore
TIA
Tiranë
Durrës
Kavajë
Krrabe
Peqin
Rrogozhine
Cërrik
Lushnjë
Divjake
Kuçovë
Raskovec
Fier
Patos
Berat
Seman
Sazanit
Vlorë
Gjiri i Vlorës
Kanine
Mavrove
Memdhaj
Karaburun
Orikum
Dukat
Himare
Gjirokaster
Libohovë
Delvine
Finiq

GREECE

K019mét
Shijak
Bishti i Pallës
Kepi i Rodonit
Strait of Otranto
Kep i Gjuhës

Otranto
C. Santa Maria di Léuca

Otonoí
Erikoúsa
Mathráki
Karousádhes
Kassiópi
Korakiána
KÉRKIRA
Liapádhes
**Kérkira
(Corfu)** Gastoúri
Áyios Matthaíos
Argyrádhes
Levkímmi
Igoumenítsa
Xarrë
Konispol
Paxoí
Paxoí

Térmoli
Campomarino
L. di Lésina
Sannicandro Gargánico
Vico del Gargano
Vieste
Testa del Gargano
Montenero di Bisáccia
Guglionesi
Larino
Apricena
San Marco in Lámis
Mte. Calvo 1055
San Severo
Monte Sant' Ángelo
Golfo di Manfredónia
Manfredónia
Cerignola
Fóggia
Lucera
Barletta
Biscéglie
Molfetta
Giovinazzo
Bari
Mola di Bari
Trani
Andria
Corato
Terlizzi
Polignano a Mare
Monópoli
Bitonto
Ruvo di Púglia
Minervino Murge
Canosa di Púglia
Triggiano
Conversano
Fasano
Ostuni
Bríndisi
San Vito dei Normanni
Mesagne
Latiano
Francavilla Fontana
San Pietro Vernótico
Squinzano
Trepuzzi
Lecce
Copertino
Nardò
Galatina
Martano
Maglie
Poggiardo
Casarano
Gagliano del Capo
Presicce
Ugento
Taviano
Tricase
Gallípoli
Galatone
Leverano
Sant' Andrea
Gravina in Púglia
Altamura
Gioia del Colle
Noci
Putignano
Acquaviva delle Fonti
Santeramo in Colle
Gravina
Matera
Castellaneta
Móttola
Massafra
Grottáglie
Manduria
Campi Salentina
Óría
Sava
Lizzano
Táranto
San Giórgio Iónico
Palagiano
Ginosa
Laterza
Bernalda
Metaponto

P U G L I A

BASILICATA

Potenza
Picerno
Tito
Tricárico
Montescaglioso
Pisticci
Montalbano Iónico
Tursi
Policoro
Nova Siri
Rotondella
Scanzano
Ferrandina
Stigliano
Pomarico
Brádano
San Arcangelo
Senise
Latrónico
Rotonda
Chiaromonte

Golfo di Táranto

Trebisacce
Amendolara
Cassano allo Iónio
Castrovillari
Morano Cálabro
Spezzano Albanese
Corigliano Cálabro
Rossano
Crosia
Cariati
C. Trionto
Longobucco
Cirò
Cirò Marina
Pta. Alice
Stróngoli

CALÁBRIA

Cosenza
Rende
Montalto Uffugo
Acri
Bisignano
Luzzi
San Giovanni in Fiore
Petilia Policastro
Crotone
C. Colonna
Cutro
Ísola di Capo Rizzuto
C. Rizzuto
Catanzaro
Botricello
Sersale
Mesoraca
Cotronei
Neto
Tiriolo
Soverato
Chiaravalle Centrale
Golfo di Squillace
San Bruno
Guardavalle
Pta. Stilo
Caulonia
Gioiosa Iónica
Roccella Iónica
Siderno
Locri
Ardore
Bovalino Marina
Bianco
Bova Marina
C. Spartivento
Mélito di Porto Salvo
Montebello Iónico

I O N I A N   S E A

3065

Aspromonte
Bova
Villa San Giovanni
Scilla
Réggio di Calábria
Gallico
Messina
Taormina
Máscali
Riposto
Giarre
Acireale
Misterbianco
Catánia
Golfo di Catánia
Augusta
Melilli
Siracusa
C. Murro di Porco
Avola
Noto
Golfo di Noto
Pachino
C. Passero
Rosolini
Íspica
Pozzallo
Módica
Scicli
Ragusa
Comiso
Vittória
Santa Croce Camerina
C. Scarámia
Chiaramonte Gulfi
Vizzini
Grammichele
Caltagirone
Niscemi
Gela

M E D I T E R R A N E A N   S E A

Underlined towns give their name to the administrative area in which they stand.

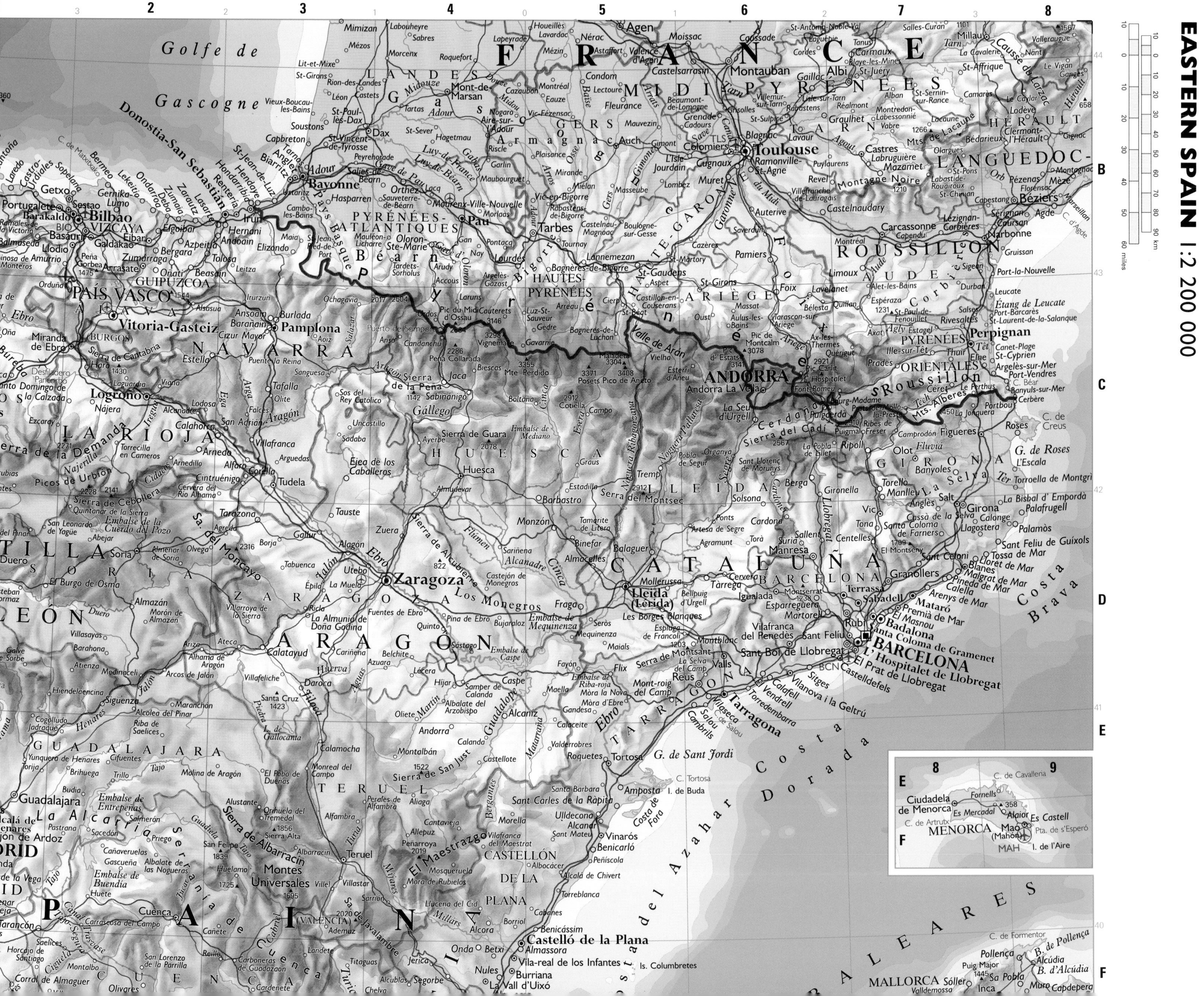
km
miles
FRANCE
SPAIN
Golfe de Gascogne
Donostia-San Sebastián
Bilbao
Vitoria-Gasteiz
Pamplona
Zaragoza
Toulouse
Perpignan
ANDORRA
BARCELONA
Tarragona
Lleida (Lérida)
Girona
MADRID
Guadalajara
Burgos
Logroño
Huesca
Teruel
Castelló de la Plana
Costa Brava
Costa Dorada
Costa del Azahar
MENORCA
MALLORCA

Grid references

F · G · H · J · K
1 · 2 · 3 · 4 · 5 · 6 · 7

Major features and places

MEDITERRANEAN SEA

BALEARIC ISLANDS area
I. des Conills · Cabrera · Palma · B. de Palma · Magaluf · Mogalluf · S. Arenal · C. Blanc · C. de Cala Figuera · Campos del Port · Felanitx · Cala d'Or · Santanyí · C. de ses Salines

EIVISSA (IBIZA) · Sant Joan Baptista · Pta. Grossa · Tagomago · Santa Eulália des Riu · Sant Miquel · San Josep · Sant Antoni Abat · San José · IBZ · S'Espalmador · S'Espardell · Es Vedrà · San Francesc de Formentera · Pta. Roja · C. de Barbària · FORMENTERA · 475 · 191 · 2726 · 2850

Spain (east coast)

VALENCIA · Golfo de Valencia · Valencia de · VALÈNCIA · Costa Blanca · Torrent · Catarroja · Silla · Benetússer · Cheste · Chiva · Buñol · Requena · Utiel · Sueca · Cullera · Alzira · Carcaixent · Algemesí · Vilanova de Castelló · Tavernes de la Valldigna · Gandia · Oliva · Denia · Jávea · C. de San Antonio · C. de la Nao · Benisa · C. Toix · Calpe · Peñón de Ifach · Altea · Villajoyosa · Benidorm · Alfaz del Pi · El Grau · Pego · Cocentaina · Muro de Alcoy · Alcoy · Sierra de Aitana · San Juan de Alicante · ALICANTE · Alicante · ALC · Elche · Elda · Petrer · Santa Pola · Nueva Tabarca · C. de Santa Pola

Almansa · Montealegre del Castillo · Caudete · Yecla · Villena · Banères · Ontinyent · Moixent · Albaida · Xàtiva · Canals · Cárcer · Navarrés · Sierra Martés · Sierra de Enguera · 1104 · 1106 · 1558 · 1583 · 1651 · 1126

Elche · Crevillente · Albatera · Catral · Callosa de Segura · Orihuela · Guardamar del Segura · Torrevieja · La Mata · San Pedro del Pinatar · San Javier · Torre-Pacheco · Mar Menor · C. de Palos · La Manga · Los Nietos · La Unión · Cartagena · Santa Lucía

MURCIA · REGIÓN DE MURCIA · Murcia · Alcantarilla · Molina de Segura · Alhama de Murcia · Archena · Cieza · Calasparra · Caravaca de la Cruz · Cehegín · Mula · Bullas · Totana · Lorca · Águilas · Mazarrón · Puerto de Mazarrón · G. de Mazarrón · Cope · Jumilla · Monóvar · Novelda · Aspe · Fortuna · Abanilla · San Vicente del Raspeig

CASTILLA–LA MANCHA · CIUDAD REAL · ALBACETE
Albacete · Hellín · La Roda · Tobarra · Fuente-Álamo · Peñas de San Pedro · Elche de la Sierra · Yeste · Alcaraz · Sierra de Alcaraz · Socovos · Ayna · Liétor · Chinchilla de Monte-Aragón · La Gineta · Casas-Ibáñez · Casas de Ves · Alcalá del Júcar · Cantos · Tarazona de la Mancha · Madrigueras · Villamalea · Minglanilla · Iniesta · Motilla del Palancar · Sisante · San Clemente · El Bonillo · Munera · Ossa de Montiel · Villanueva de los Infantes · Villanueva de la Fuente · Valdepeñas · La Solana · Manzanares · Daimiel · Membrilla · Tomelloso · Argamasilla de Alba · Campo de Criptana · Alcázar de San Juan · Socuéllamos · Pedro Muñoz · Quintanar · Las Pedroñeras · Los Hinojosos

ANDALUCÍA
GRANADA · ALMERÍA · JAÉN
Granada · Sierra Nevada · Mulhacén 3478 · Veleta 3398 · Guadix · Baza · Caniles · Cúllar · Orce · Galera · Huéscar · Pozo Alcón · Cazorla · Sierra de Cazorla · Quesada · Úbeda · Baeza · Linares · Santisteban del Puerto · Villacarrillo · Beas de Segura · Segura de la Sierra · Sierra de Segura · La Puerta de Segura · La Carolina · Navas de San Juan · Vilches · Bailén · Mengíbar · Jaén · Andújar · Martos · Montefrío · Iznalloz · Loja · Santa Fe · Alhama de Granada · Órgiva · Lanjarón · Las Alpujarras · Motril · Almuñécar · Adra · Berja · El Ejido · Roquetas de Mar · Almería · G. de Almería · Pta. de Almería · Pta. del Sabinar · Níjar · Sierra de los Filabres · 2168 · Vera · Cuevas del Almanzora · Garrucha · Mojácar · Carboneras · C. de Gata · Pta. de la Media Naranja · Sorbas · Tabernas · Gérgal · Macael · Olula del Río · Albox · Serón · Tíjola · Purchena · Alcóntar · Cantoria · Huércal-Overa · Pulpí · Los Gallardos · Bédar · Lubrín · Lucainena

Rivers / features: Río Guadiana Menor · Río Almanzora · Río Andarax · Río Segura · Río Mundo · Río Júcar · Río Cabriel · Río Guadalentín · Río Guadalquivir · Sierra de Alcaraz · Costa del Sol · Costa de Almería

MOROCCO (southwest corner)
Nador · Melilla (Sp.) · Segangane · Sebkha bou Areg · Karlet Arkmane · Azlanen · Ben Tieb · Selouane · Zaio · Pte. Negri · C. des Trois Fourches · Islas Chafarinas · Alborán (Sp.) · Ras el Mar · Kariet Arkmane

ALGERIA
ALGER (ALGIERS) · ALG · Hussein Dey · El Harrach · Birmandreis · Birkhadem · Cheraga · Dély Ibrahim · Kouba · Ain Benian · Bou Ismaïl · Fouka · Koléa · Tipasa · Cherchell · Gouraya · Damous · C. Ténès · Ténès · Béni-Haoua · El Marsa · Bou Maad · Blida · BLIDA · Boufarik · El Affroun · Mouzaïa · Hadjout · Bou Ismaïl · Arba · Bougara · Sidi Moussa · Bougara · El Omaria · Médéa · Berrouaghia · Ksar el Boukhari · Aïn Boucif · Birine · Hassi Bahbah · Guelt es Stel · Chabounia · Aïn Oussera · Ksar Chellala · Hamdia · 1303 · Mahdia · Sougueur · Tiaret · Frenda · Dahmouni · Colonel Bougara · Theniet el Had · Tissemsilt · Lardjem · Khemisti · Bou Kadir · Ech Chéliff · Oued Fodda · El Attaf · Ain Defla · El Abadia · Djendel · Djelida · Miliana · Khemis Miliana · Zaccar · Djebel Zaccar · El Hassan · Sidi Akacha · Oued Sly · Oued Fares · Ouled Farès · Oued Rhiou · Ammi Moussa · Relizane · Mazouna · Mostaganem · Sidi Ali · Aïn Tédélès · Aïn Nouissy · Kheir-Dine · Mohammadia · Tighennif · Mascara · Ghriss · Hacine · Bou Hanifia · Sig · Oued el Abtal · El Bordj · El Hachem · Tizi · Oued Taria · Aïn Témouchent · Hammam Bou Hadjar · El Amria · Aïn Kihal · Béni Saf · Sidi-bel-Abbès · SIDI-BEL-ABBÈS · Oran (Ouahran) · ORAN · Arzew · Golfe d'Arzew · C. Ferrat · Mers-el-Kébir · C. Falcon · Aïn el Turk · Arzew · Bethioua · Oued Tlélat · Sfisef · Telagh · Tessala · Sidi Lahssen · Tizi · Ras el Ma · Cap Noé · Ghazaouet · Oued Mina · Oued Cheliff

Mountain ranges / features (Algeria): TIPASA · DAHRA · MASSIF DE L'OUARSENIS · ECH CHELIFF · AÏN DEFLA · MÉDÉA · DJELFA · RELIZANE · MOSTAGANEM · MASCARA · TISSEMSILT · TIARET · ALGER · ORAN · AÏN TÉMOUCHENT · O. Cheliff · O. Chélif · O. el Malah · O. el Taht · O. Mina · Massif de Tissemsilt

1629 · 1415 · 1041 · 1157 · 1786 · 1982 · 1303

Map credits / projection
Projection : Lambert's Conformal Conic
COPYRIGHT GEORGE PHILIP LTD.
East from Greenwich · West from Greenwich

Elevation scale
m · ft
6000 · 12000
4000 · 9000
3000 · 6000
2000 · 4500
1500 · 3000
1000 · 1500
500 · 600
200 · 300
0 · 0
0 · 50
150 · 300
600 · 1500
1200 · 3000
1800 · 6000
3000 · 9000
m · ft

20 · 34 · 35 · 78

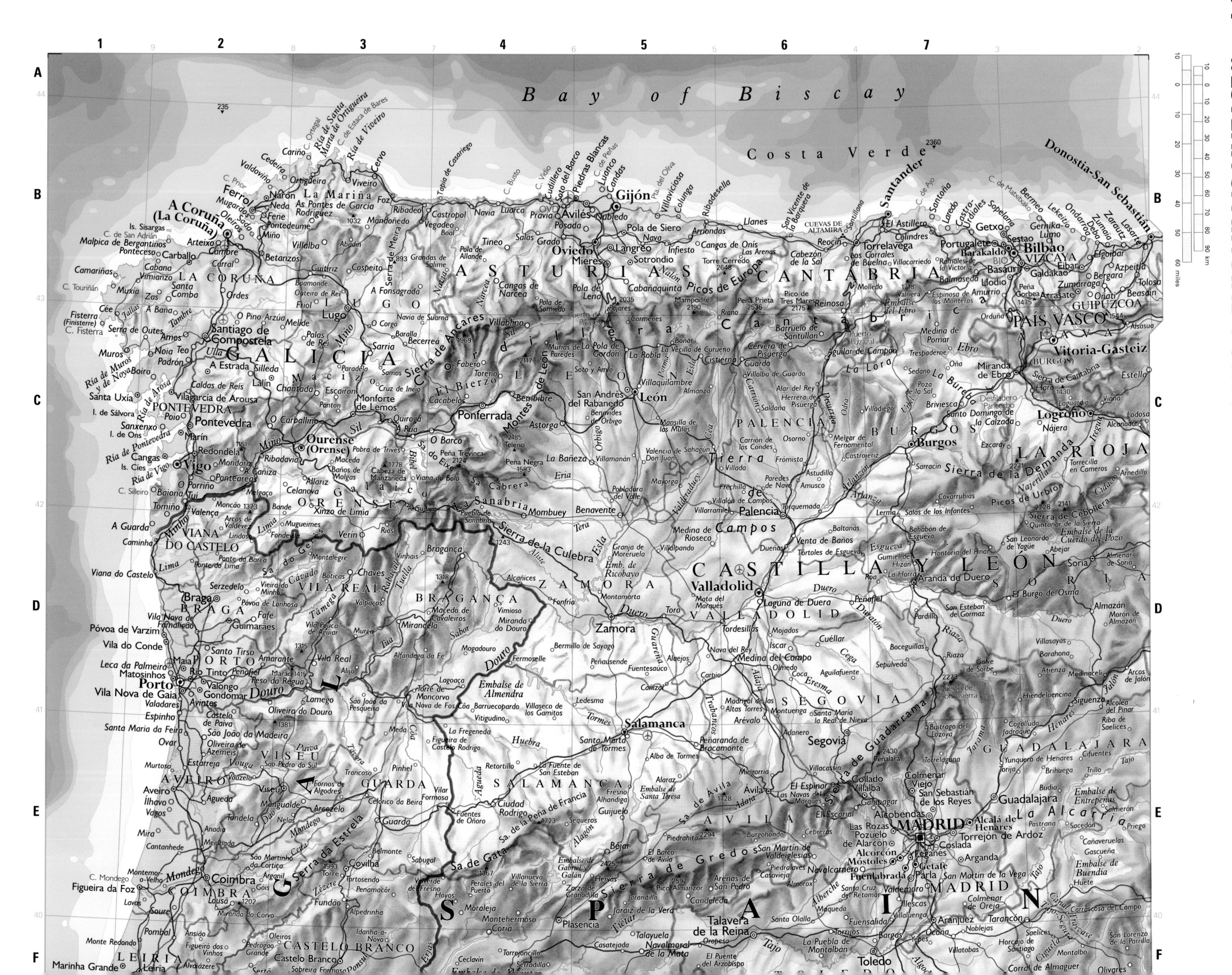
10 0 10 20 30 40 50 60 70 80 90 km
10 0 10 20 30 40 50 60 miles
A
B
C
D
E
F
1
2
3
4
5
6
7
Bay of Biscay
Costa Verde
Donostia-San Sebastián
Bilbao
Vitoria-Gasteiz
PAÍS VASCO
VIZCAYA
GUIPÚZCOA
Santander
CANTABRIA
ASTURIAS
Gijón
Oviedo
Avilés
Picos de Europa
Cordillera Cantábrica
Logroño
LA RIOJA
Burgos
BURGOS
Palencia
PALENCIA
León
LEÓN
Ponferrada
Astorga
Valladolid
VALLADOLID
CASTILLA Y LEÓN
Tierra de Campos
Zamora
ZAMORA
Salamanca
SALAMANCA
Segovia
SEGOVIA
Ávila
ÁVILA
Soria
SORIA
Guadalajara
GUADALAJARA
MADRID
Madrid
Toledo
Talavera de la Reina
Sierra de Gredos
Sierra de Guadarrama
Plasencia
A Coruña (La Coruña)
LA CORUÑA
Ferrol
Santiago de Compostela
GALICIA
Lugo
LUGO
Pontevedra
PONTEVEDRA
Vigo
Ourense (Orense)
ORENSE
Bragança
BRAGANÇA
Vila Real
VILA REAL
Braga
BRAGA
VIANA DO CASTELO
Porto
PORTO
Vila Nova de Gaia
Douro
Duero
VISEU
Viseu
GUARDA
Guarda
Aveiro
AVEIRO
Coimbra
COIMBRA
CASTELO BRANCO
Castelo Branco
LEIRIA
Figueira da Foz
Serra da Estrela
SPAIN
PORTUGAL

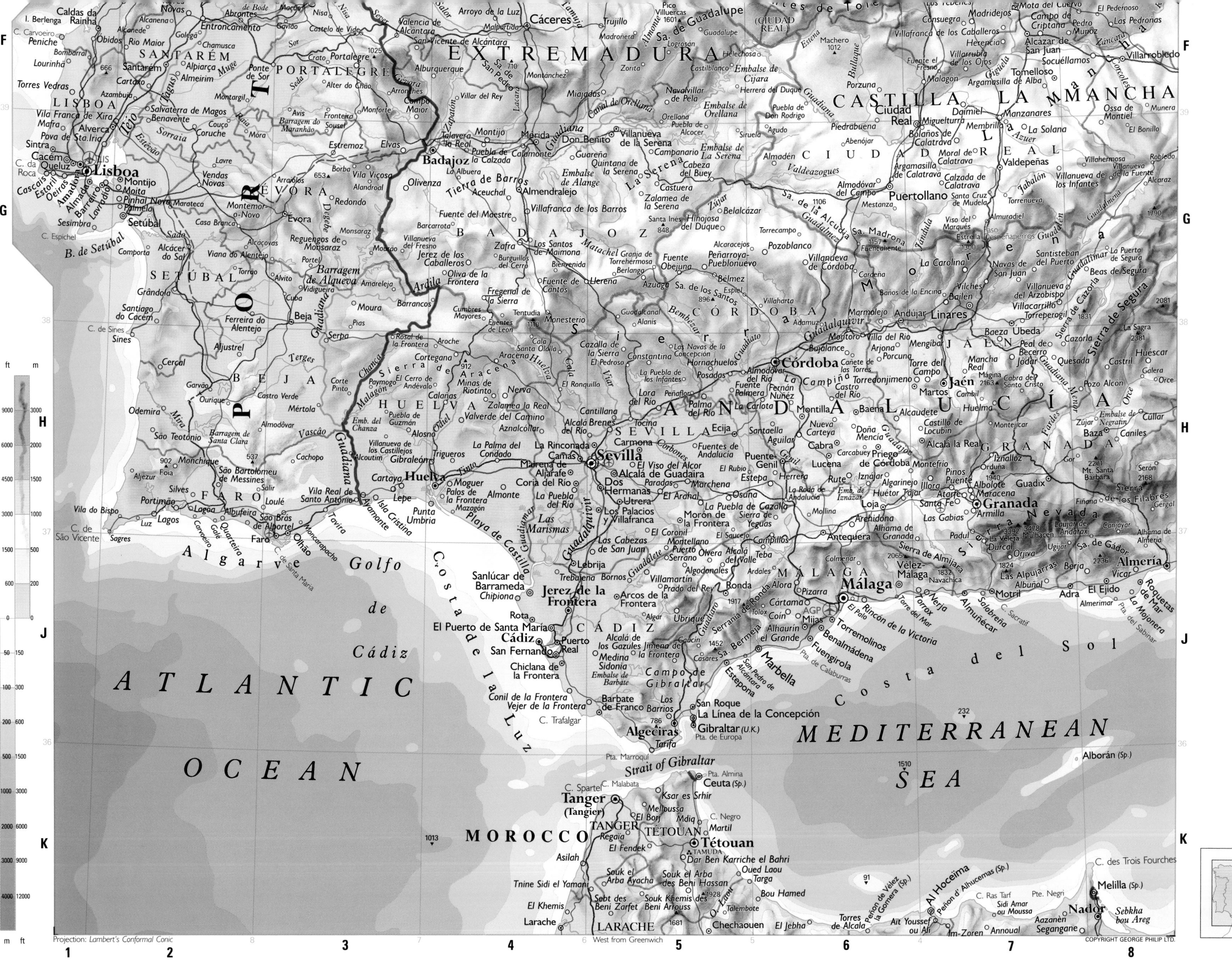
EXTREMADURA
CASTILLA LA MANCHA
ANDALUCÍA
PORTUGAL
ATLANTIC OCEAN
MEDITERRANEAN SEA
Golfo de Cádiz
Costa de la Luz
Costa del Sol
Strait of Gibraltar
MOROCCO
Algarve
Sierra de Aracena
Sierra Nevada
Sierra de Segura
Guadiana
Guadalquivir
Lisboa
Setúbal
Santarém
Évora
Beja
Faro
Badajoz
Cáceres
Mérida
Sevilla
Córdoba
Jaén
Granada
Málaga
Almería
Huelva
Cádiz
Jerez de la Frontera
Algeciras
Gibraltar (U.K.)
Ceuta (Sp.)
Tanger (Tangier)
Tétouan
Melilla (Sp.)
Ciudad Real
Puertollano
Linares
Marbella
Torremolinos
Projection: Lambert's Conformal Conic
West from Greenwich
COPYRIGHT GEORGE PHILIP LTD.

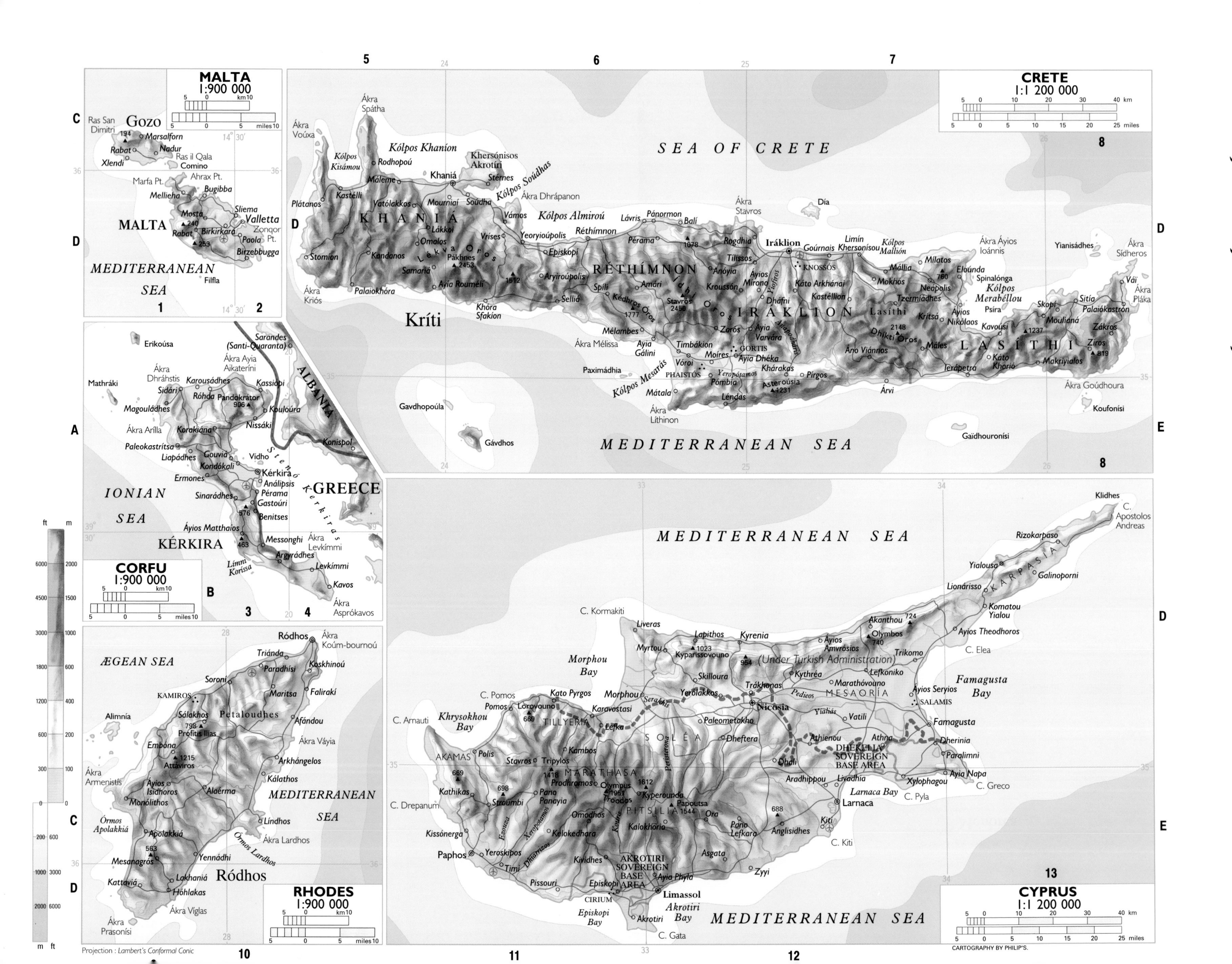
MALTA
1:900 000
Gozo
Marsalforn
Nadur
Rabat
Xlendi
Ras il Qala
Comino
Ahrax Pt.
Marfa Pt.
Mellieha
Bugibba
Mosta
Sliema
Valletta
MALTA
Birkirkara
Rabat
Paola
Zonqor Pt.
Birzebbugga
MEDITERRANEAN SEA
Filfla
CRETE
1:1 200 000
SEA OF CRETE
Kríti
KHANIÁ
Khaniá
RÉTHIMNON
Réthimnon
IRÁKLION
Iráklion
LASÍTHI
Áyios Nikólaos
Ierápetra
Sitía
Knossós
Gortis
Phaistós
Gávdhos
Día
MEDITERRANEAN SEA
CORFU
1:900 000
KÉRKIRA
Kérkira
IONIAN SEA
ALBANIA
GREECE
Erikoúsa
Mathráki
RHODES
1:900 000
ÆGEAN SEA
MEDITERRANEAN SEA
Ródhos
Líndhos
Kamiros
CYPRUS
1:1 200 000
MEDITERRANEAN SEA
Nicosia
Kyrenia
Famagusta
Larnaca
Limassol
Paphos
Morphou Bay
Famagusta Bay
Larnaca Bay
Akrotiri Bay
Episkopi Bay
Khrysokhou Bay
(Under Turkish Administration)
AKROTIRI SOVEREIGN BASE AREA
DHEKELIA SOVEREIGN BASE AREA
Olympus 1951
Troodos
C. Apostolos Andreas
C. Greco
C. Gata
C. Kormakiti
CARTOGRAPHY BY PHILIP'S.
Projection : Lambert's Conformal Conic

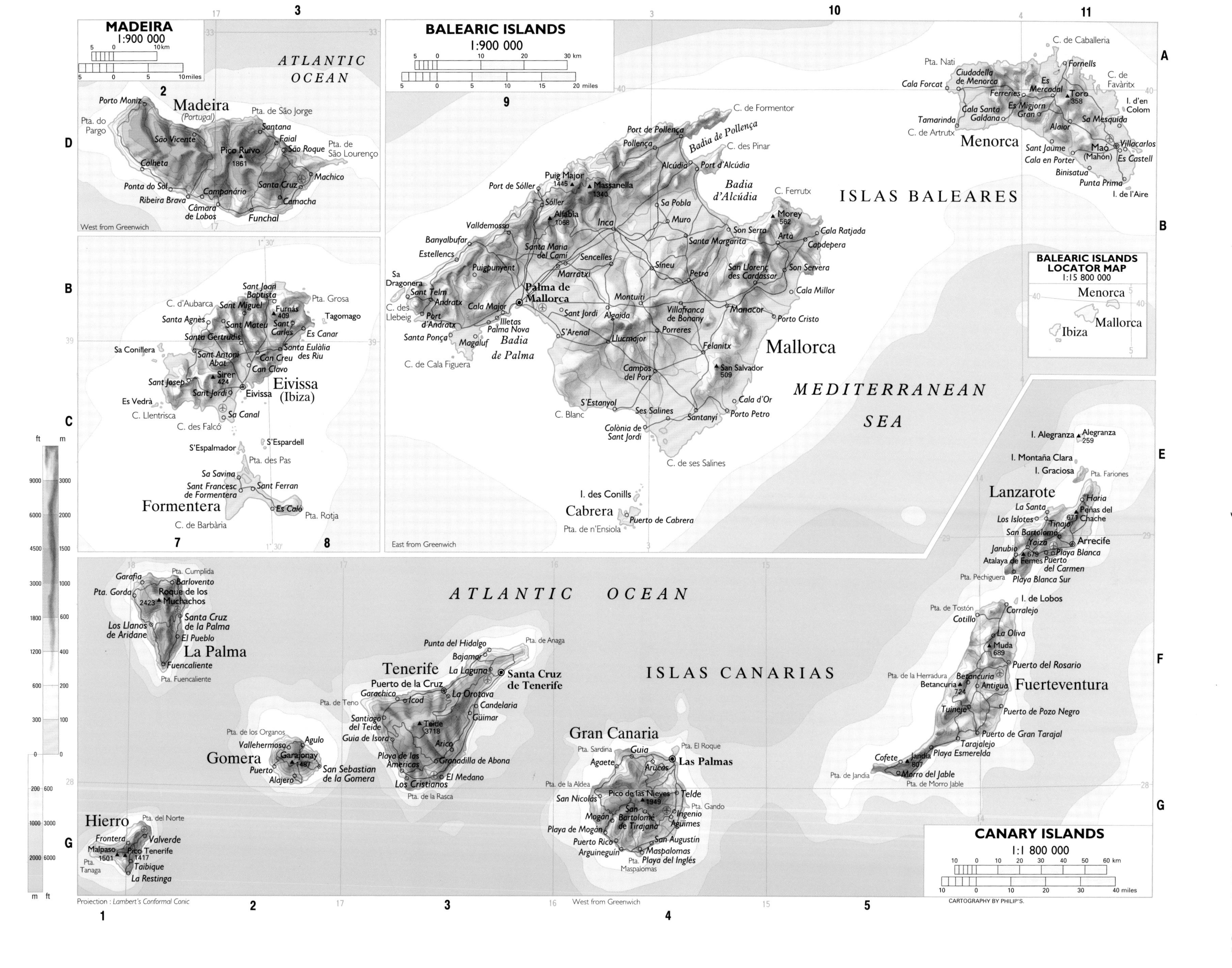

MADEIRA
1:900 000

BALEARIC ISLANDS
1:900 000

BALEARIC ISLANDS LOCATOR MAP
1:5 800 000

Menorca
Mallorca
Ibiza

CANARY ISLANDS
1:1 800 000

CARTOGRAPHY BY PHILIP'S.

MADEIRA

ATLANTIC OCEAN

Porto Moniz
Pta. do Pargo
Calheta
São Vicente
Santana
Faial
Pico Ruivo 1861
Machico
Santa Cruz
Câmacha
Funchal
Câmara de Lobos
Ponta do Sol
Ribeira Brava
Campanário
São Roque
Pta. de São Jorge
Pta. de São Lourenço
Madeira (Portugal)

MENORCA

C. de Caballería
Pta. Nati
Ciudadella de Menorca
Cala Santa Galdana
C. de Artrutx
Tamarinda
Ferreries
Es Migjorn Gran
Es Mercadal
Toro 358
Fornells
Sa Mesquida
Villacarlos
Maó (Mahón)
Es Castell
I. de l'Aire
Punta Prima
Binisatua
Cala en Porter
Sant Jaume
Alaior
I. d'en Colom
C. de Favàritx

ISLAS BALEARES

MALLORCA

C. de Formentor
C. de Pollença
Port de Pollença
Pollença
C. des Pinar
Badia de Pollença
Port d'Alcúdia
Alcúdia
Badia d'Alcúdia
Sa Pobla
Muro
Santa Margarita
Son Serra
Artà
Morey 562
Cala Ratjada
Capdepera
Cala Gat
Cala Millor
Son Servera
Porto Cristo
Manacor
C. Ferrutx
Son Llorenç des Cardassar
Inca
Sineu
Petra
Vilafranca de Bonany
Felanitx
San Salvador 509
Cala d'Or
Porto Petro
Sencelles
Montuiri
Porreres
Santanyí
C. de ses Salines
Lluçmajor
Campos del Port
Ses Salines
Colònia de Sant Jordi
S'Estanyol
Algaida
Marratxi
Sta. Maria del Camí
Santa Eugènia
Alfàbia 1068
Massanella 1340
Puig Major 1445
Sóller
Port de Sóller
Valldemossa
Banyalbufar
Estellencs
Puigpunyent
Palma de Mallorca
Illetas
Palma Nova
Magaluf
Badia de Palma
Cala Major
S'Arenal
Sant Jordi
Blanc
C. Blanc
C. de Cala Figuera
Santa Ponça
Port d'Andratx
Sant Telm
Andratx
Sa Dragonera
C. des Llebeig
Puigpunyent

CABRERA

I. des Conills
Cabrera
Puerto de Cabrera
Pta. de n'Ensiola
I. des Estanyol

EIVISSA (Ibiza)

C. d'Aubarca
Santa Agnès
Santa Gertrudis
Sant Joan Baptista
Portinatx
Pta. Grossa
Tagomago
Sant Miguel
Fruitas 409
Es Canar
Santa Eulàlia
Can Clavo
Sant Carles
Sant Mateu
Sant Antoni
Sant Rafel
Can Creu des Riu
Sant Josep
Sant Agustí
Abat
Sirer 421
Sant Jordi
Eivissa (Ibiza)
Es Vedrà
C. Llentrisca
Sa Conillera
C. des Falcó

FORMENTERA

S'Espalmador
S'Espardell
Sa Savina
Sant Francesc de Formentera
Sant Ferran
Es Caló
Pta. des Pas
Sa Canal
C. de Barbària
Pta. Roija

MEDITERRANEAN SEA

East from Greenwich
West from Greenwich

CANARY ISLANDS

ISLAS CANARIAS

ATLANTIC OCEAN

LANZAROTE

I. Alegranza
Alegranza 259
I. Montaña Clara
I. Graciosa
Pta. Fariones
Haría
Peñas del Chache 670
Arrecife
Los Islotes
San Bartolomé
Tinajo
Yaiza
Teguise
Playa Blanca Puerto del Carmen
Playa Blanca Sur
I. de Lobos
Corralejo

FUERTEVENTURA

Pta. de Tostón
Cotillo
La Oliva
Corralejo
Muda 689
La Muda
Betancuria
Antigua
Janubio
Atalaya de Femes
Pta. Pechiguera
Puerto del Rosario
Puerto de Pozo Negro
Puerto de Gran Tarajal
Betancuria 724
Tuineje
Tarajalejo
Jandía Playa Esmerelda
Cofete
Morro del Jable
Pta. de Morro Jable
Pta. de Jandía

GRAN CANARIA

Pta. El Roque
Las Palmas
Telde
Pta. Gando
Ingenio
Agüimes
San Agustín
Maspalomas
Playa del Inglés
Pta. Maspalomas
Arguineguín
Puerto Rico
Playa de Mogán
Mogán
Bartolomé de Tirajana
Pico de las Nieves 1949
Soria 679
Arucas
Guía
Agaete
Pta. Sardina
San Nicolás
Pta. de la Aldea

TENERIFE

Pta. de Anaga
Santa Cruz de Tenerife
La Laguna
Bajamar
Punta del Hidalgo
La Orotava
Puerto de la Cruz
Candelaria
Güimar
Icod
Garachico
Teide 3718
Granadilla de Abona
El Médano
Arico
Santiago del Teide
Guía de Isora
Playa de las Américas
Los Cristianos
Pta. de la Rasca
Pta. de Teno

GOMERA

Pta. de los Organos
Vallehermoso
Agulo
Garajonay 1487
Puerto
Alajeró
San Sebastián de la Gomera
Pta. de la Aldea

LA PALMA

Pta. Cumplida
Barlovento
Garafía
Pta. Gorda
Santa Cruz de la Palma
Roque de los Muchachos 2423
Los Llanos de Aridane
El Pueblo
Fuencaliente
Pta. de Fuencaliente

HIERRO

Pta. del Norte
Frontera
Valverde
Malpaso 1501
Pico Tenerife 1417
Taibique
La Restinga
Pta. Tanaga

ISLAS CANARIAS

ATLANTIC OCEAN

West from Greenwich

Projection : Lambert's Conformal Conic

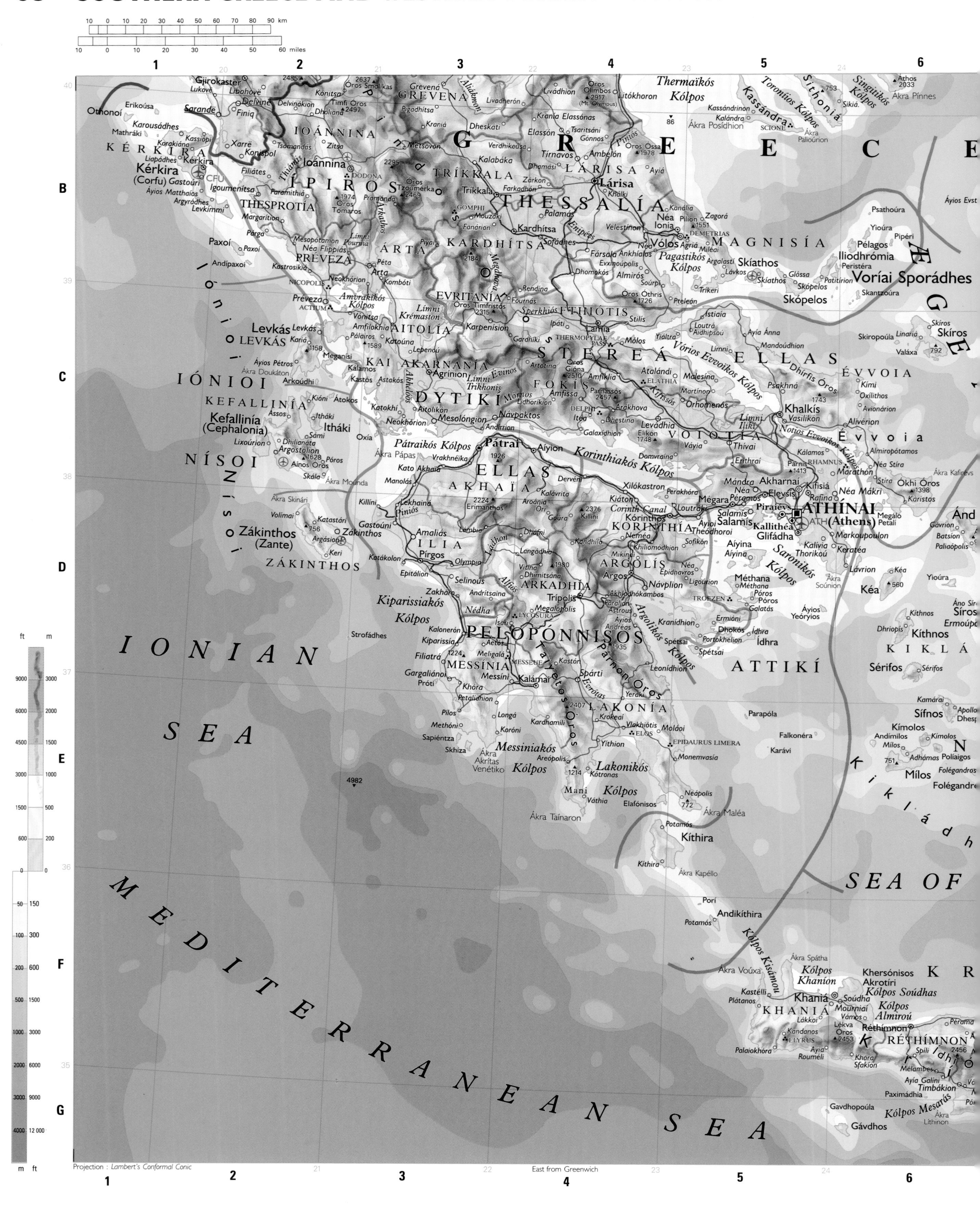
km
miles
IONIAN SEA
MEDITERRANEAN SEA
SEA OF
GREECE
Thermaïkós Kólpos
Toronaíos Kólpos
Kassándra
Sithonía
Singitikós Kólpos
Athos 2033
Ákra Pínnes
Ákra Posídhion
Gjirokastër
Sarandë
Othonoí
Erikoúsa
Mathráki
KÉRKIRA
Kérkira (Corfu)
Paxoí
Andípaxoi
IOÁNNINA
Ioánnina
ÍPIROS
THESPROTÍA
PREVEZA
Préveza
ÁRTA
Árta
Amvrakikós Kólpos
TRÍKKALA
Tríkkala
KARDHÍTSA
Kardhítsa
THESSALÍA
LÁRISA
Lárisa
Vólos
MAGNISÍA
Pagastikós Kólpos
Skíathos
Skópelos
Voríai Sporádhes
Iliodhrómia
Skíros
Olimbos 2917 (Mt. Olympus)
Oros Óssa 1978
Lamía
FTHIÓTIS
EVRITANÍA
AITOLÍA KAI AKARNANÍA
Agrínion
Levkás
LEVKÁS
IÓNIOI NÍSOI
KEFALLINÍA
Kefallinía (Cephalonia)
Itháki
Zákinthos (Zante)
ZÁKINTHOS
STEREÁ ELLAS
FOKÍS
VOIOTÍA
DYTIKI ELLAS
ÉVVOIA
Évvoia
Khalkís
Vórios Evvoikós Kólpos
Pátrai
Pátraikós Kólpos
Korinthiakós Kólpos
AKHAÏA
ILIA
Pírgos
KORINTHÍA
Kórinthos
Corinth Canal
ATTIKÍ
ATHÍNAI (Athens)
Piraiévs
Salamís
Elevsís
Mégara
ARGOLÍS
Árgos
Návplion
ARKADHÍA
Trípolis
Saronikós Kólpos
Argolikós Kólpos
PELOPÓNNISOS
MESSÍNIA
Kalámai
LAKONÍA
Spárti
Kiparissiakós Kólpos
Messiniakós Kólpos
Lakonikós Kólpos
Strofádhes
Ákra Taínaron
Ákra Maléa
Kíthira
Andikíthira
Kólpos Kisámou
Kólpos Khanion
Khaniá
KHANIÁ
Kólpos Soúdhas
Kólpos Almiroú
Réthimnon
RÉTHÍMNON
Gávdhos
Kólpos Mesarás
Kéa
Kíthnos
Sérifos
Sífnos
Mílos
Kímolos
Folégandros
Kikládhes
4982
Projection : Lambert's Conformal Conic
East from Greenwich

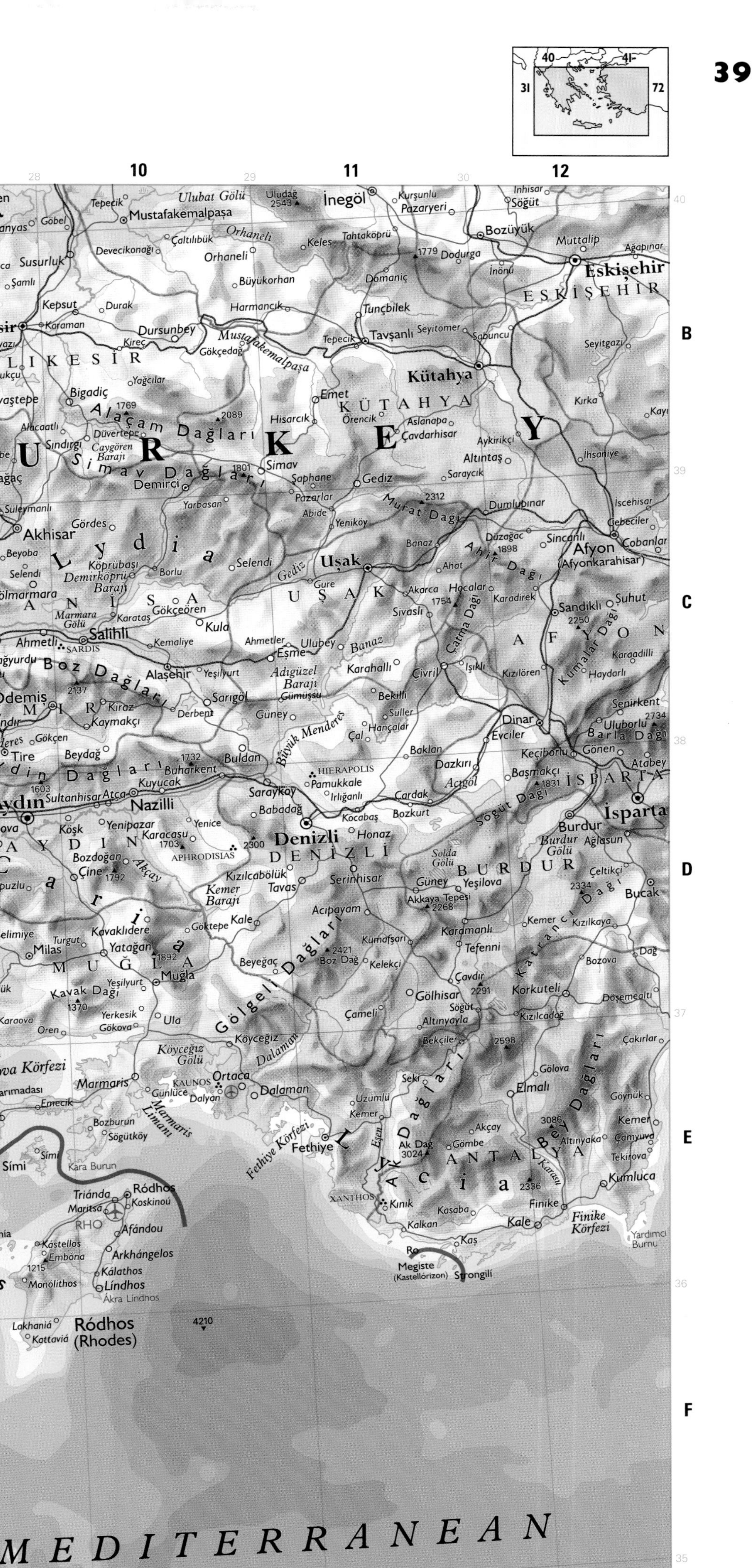

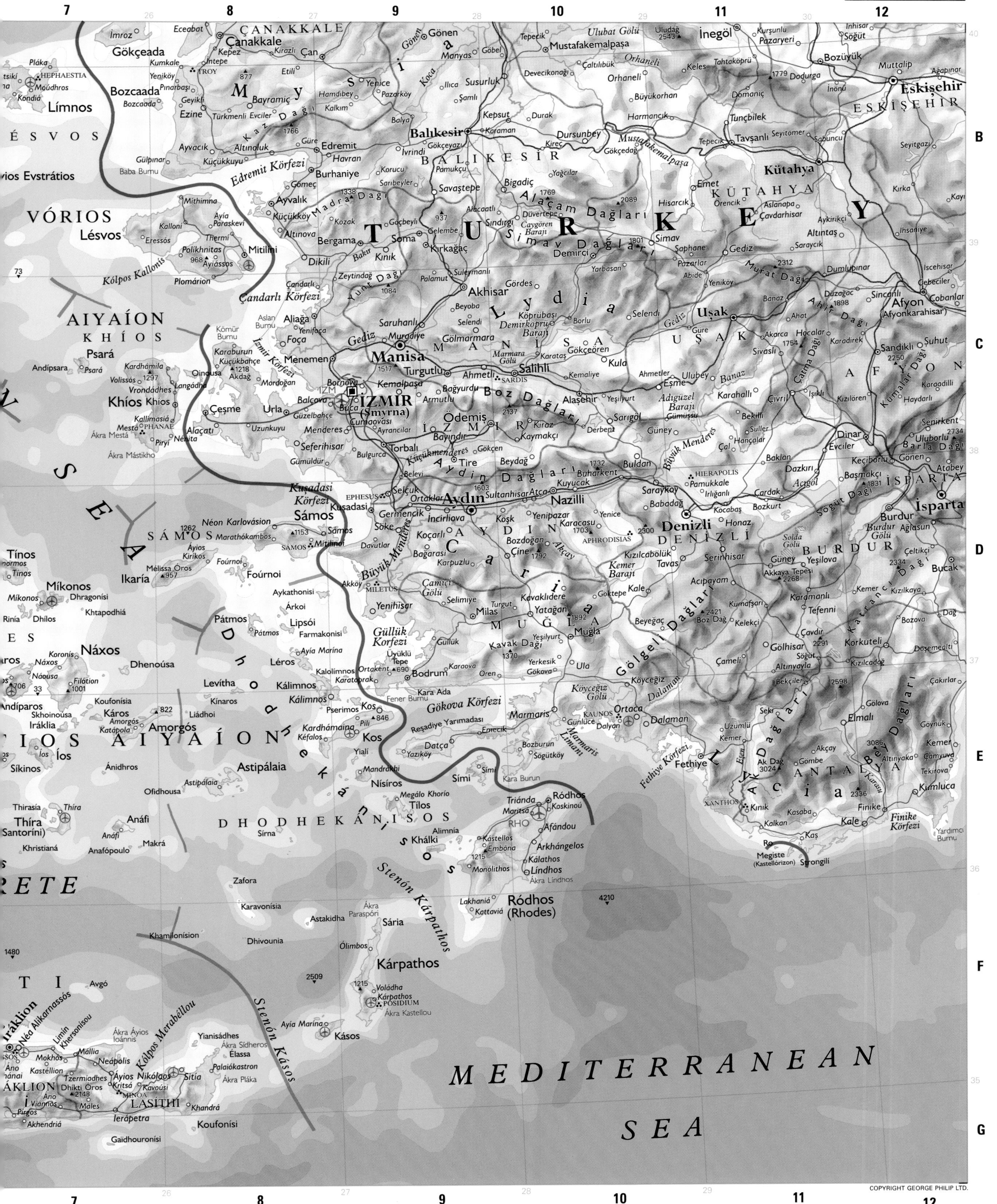
TURKEY
ÇANAKKALE
Çanakkale
Gökçeada
İmroz
Bozcaada
Límnos
LÉSVOS
VÓRIOS
Lésvos
Mitilíni
AIYAÍON
KHÍOS
Khíos
Psará
Sámos
SÁMOS
Ikaría
Foúrnoi
Mýkonos
Náxos
Tínos
Amorgós
Astipálaia
Thíra
(Santoríni)
Anáfi
Pátmos
Léros
Kálimnos
Kos
Nísiros
Tilos
Sími
Ródhos
(Rhodes)
Khálki
Kárpathos
Kásos
Sária
DHODHEKÁNISOS
Stenón Kárpathos
Stenón Kásos
CRETE
LASÍTHI
IRÁKLION
Kólpos Merabéllou
MEDITERRANEAN
SEA
İZMİR
(Smyrna)
Manisa
MANİSA
Lydia
Mysia
Caria
Lycia
Balıkesir
BALIKESİR
Edremit
Edremit Körfezi
Ayvalık
Bergama
Soma
Akhisar
Aliağa
Foça
Menemen
Çeşme
Urla
Seferihisar
Torbalı
Ödemiş
Tire
Kuşadası
Kuşadası Körfezi
Söke
Aydın
AYDIN
Nazilli
Denizli
DENİZLİ
Milas
Bodrum
Muğla
MUĞLA
Marmaris
Datça
Fethiye
Fethiye Körfezi
Gökova Körfezi
Güllük Körfezi
Dalaman
Köyceğiz
Salihli
Turgutlu
Alaşehir
Uşak
UŞAK
Kütahya
KÜTAHYA
Eskişehir
ESKİŞEHİR
İnegöl
Bozüyük
Afyon
(Afyonkarahisar)
AFYON
Isparta
ISPARTA
Burdur
BURDUR
Burdur Gölü
ANTALYA
Elmalı
Kaş
Kale
Finike
Kumluca
Megiste
(Kastellórizon)
Simav
Gediz
Demirci
Gördes
Dursunbey
Bigadiç
Susurluk
Gönen
Kepsut
Tavşanlı
Emet
Mustafakemalpaşa
Ulubat Gölü
Uludağ
2543
Kaz Dağı
Madra Dağı
Yunt Dağı
Alaçam Dağları
Simav Dağları
Murat Dağı
Boz Dağları
Aydın Dağları
Büyük Menderes
Küçükmenderes
Gediz
Sultanhisar
Pamukkale
HIERAPOLIS
EPHESUS
APHRODISIAS
SARDIS
MILETUS
TROY
KAUNOS
XANTHOS
Mediterranean Sea
Baba Burnu
Kólpos Kallonís
Çandarlı Körfezi
İzmir Körfezi
Ák Dağ
3024
Bey Dağları
Gölgeli Dağları
Katrancı Dağı
Barla Dağı
Söğüt Dağı
Ahır Dağı
Kumalar Dağı
4210
2509
1480

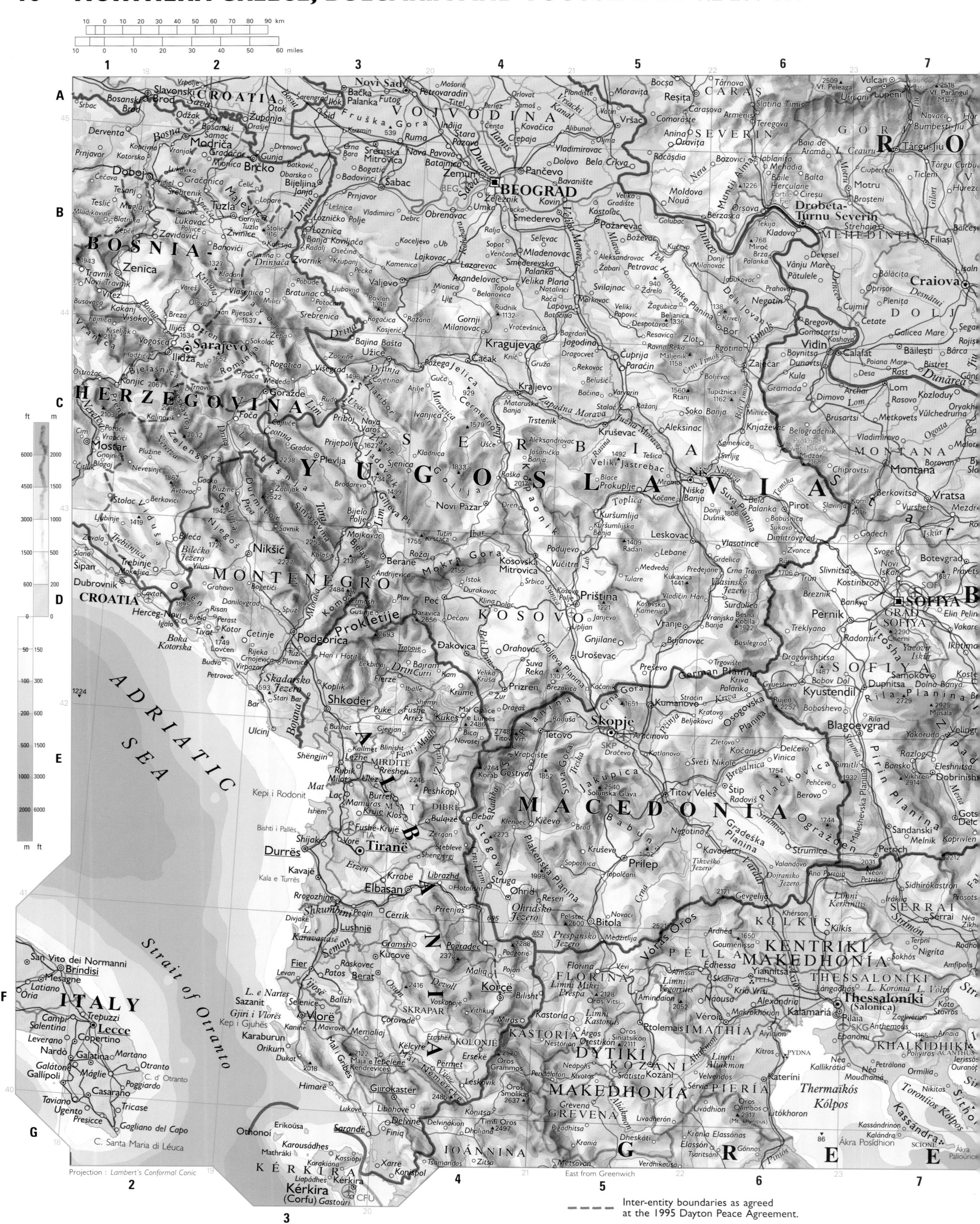

Projection : Lambert's Conformal Conic

East from Greenwich

Inter-entity boundaries as agreed
at the 1995 Dayton Peace Agreement.

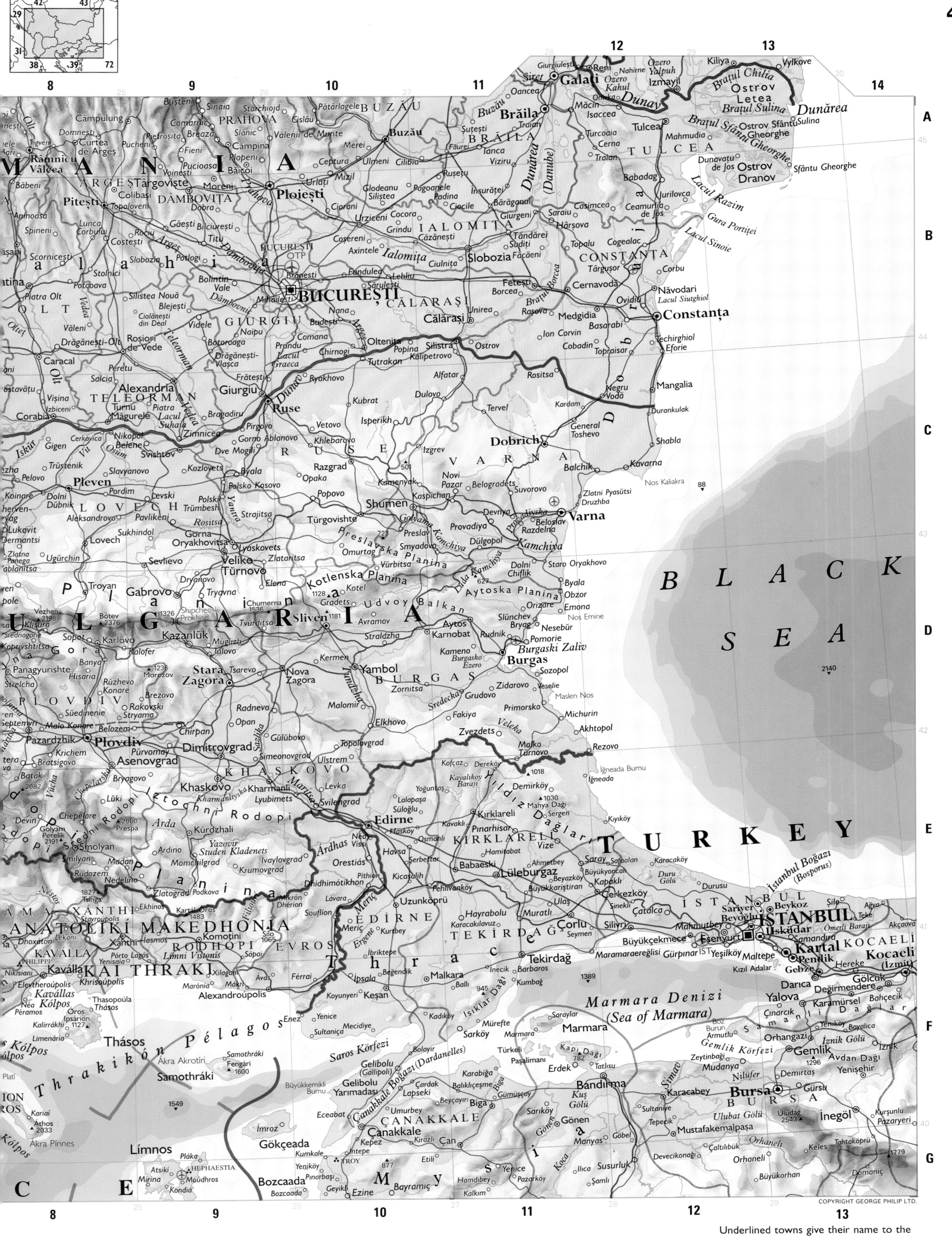

Underlined towns give their name to the
administrative area in which they stand.

COPYRIGHT GEORGE PHILIP LTD.

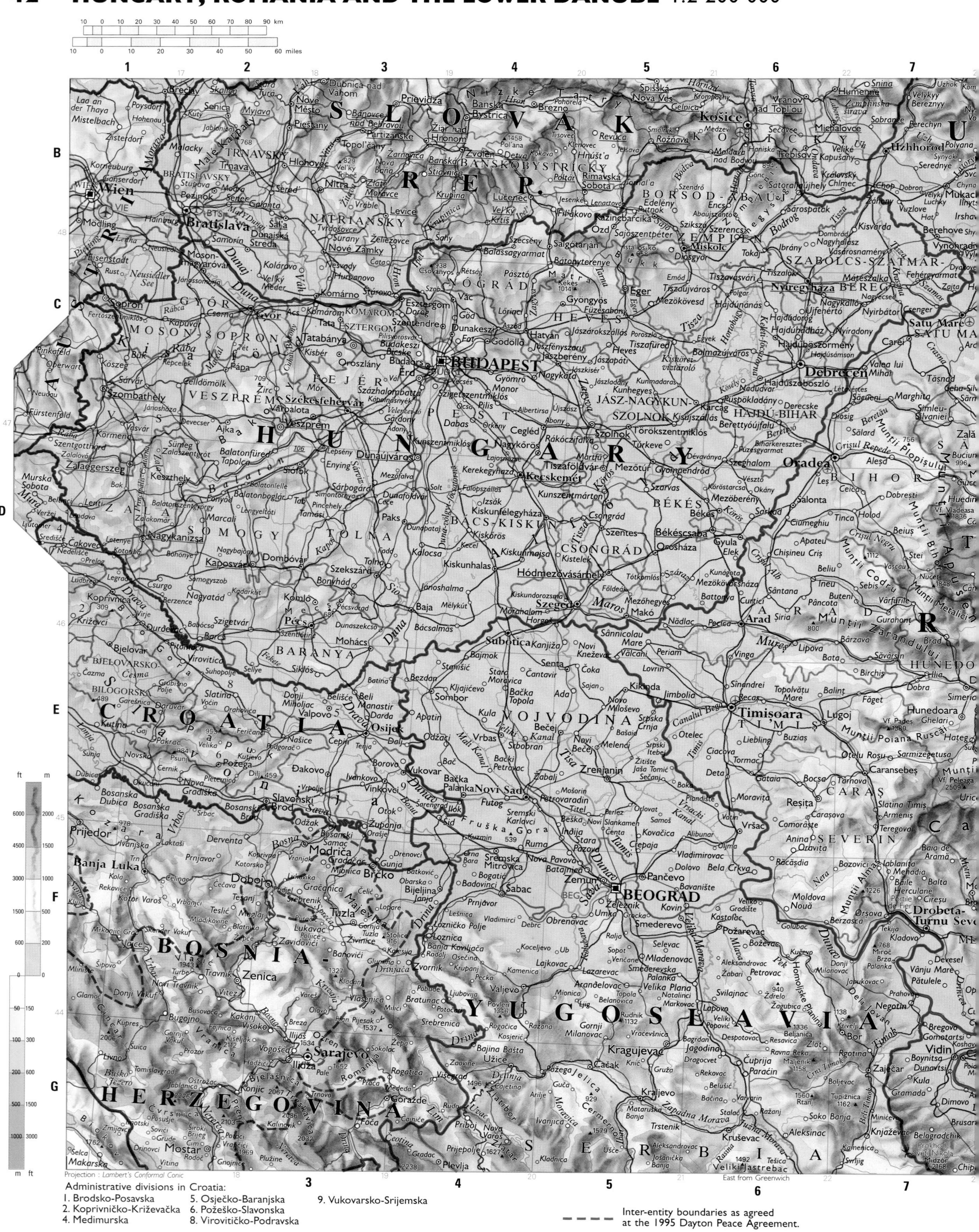

Projection : Lambert's Conformal Conic

East from Greenwich

Administrative divisions in Croatia:
1. Brodsko-Posavska
2. Koprivničko-Križevačka
4. Medimurska
5. Osječko-Baranjska
6. Požeško-Slavonska
8. Virovitičko-Podravska
9. Vukovarsko-Srijemska

– – – – Inter-entity boundaries as agreed
at the 1995 Dayton Peace Agreement.

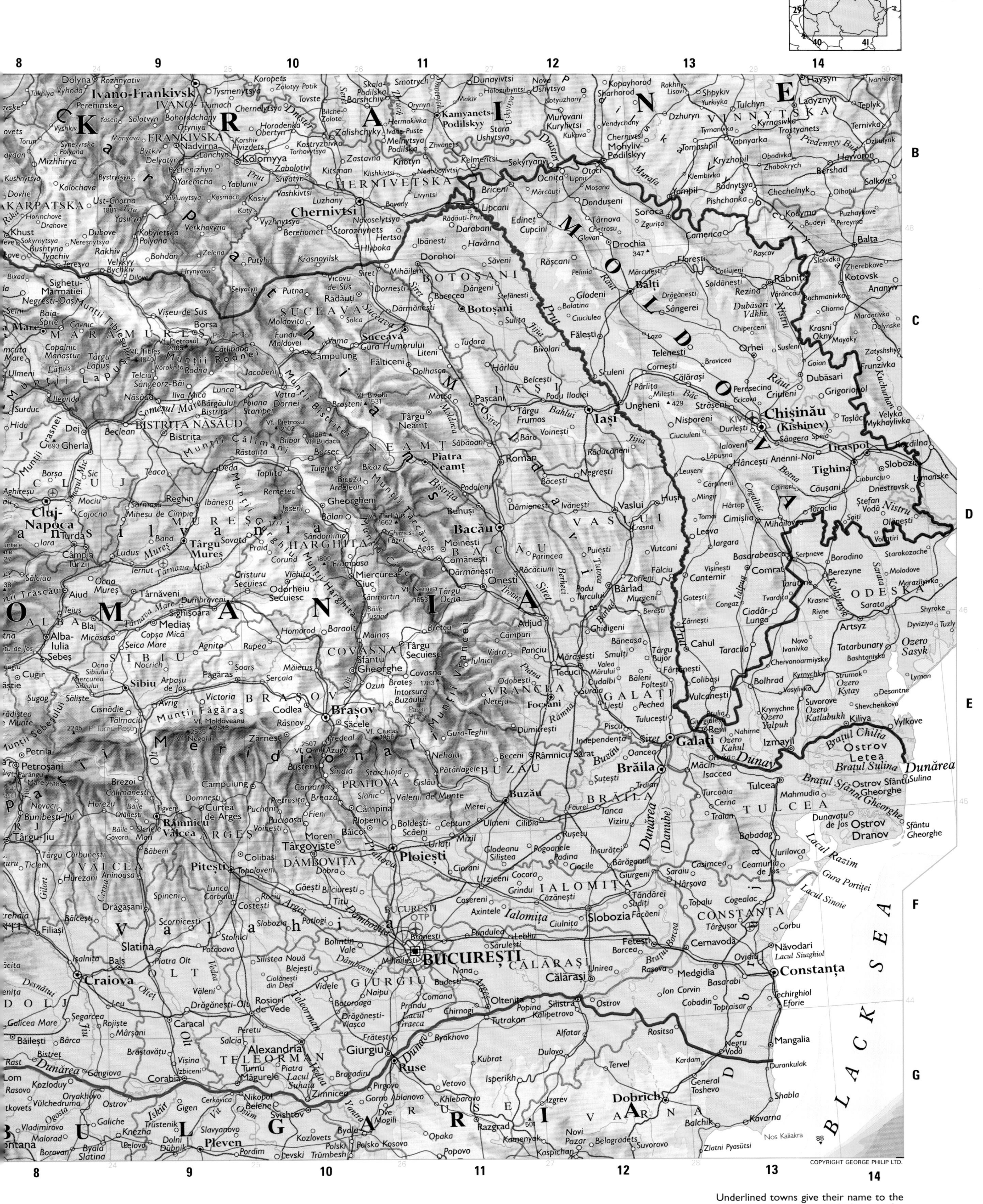

Underlined towns give their name to the
administrative area in which they stand.

COPYRIGHT GEORGE PHILIP LTD.

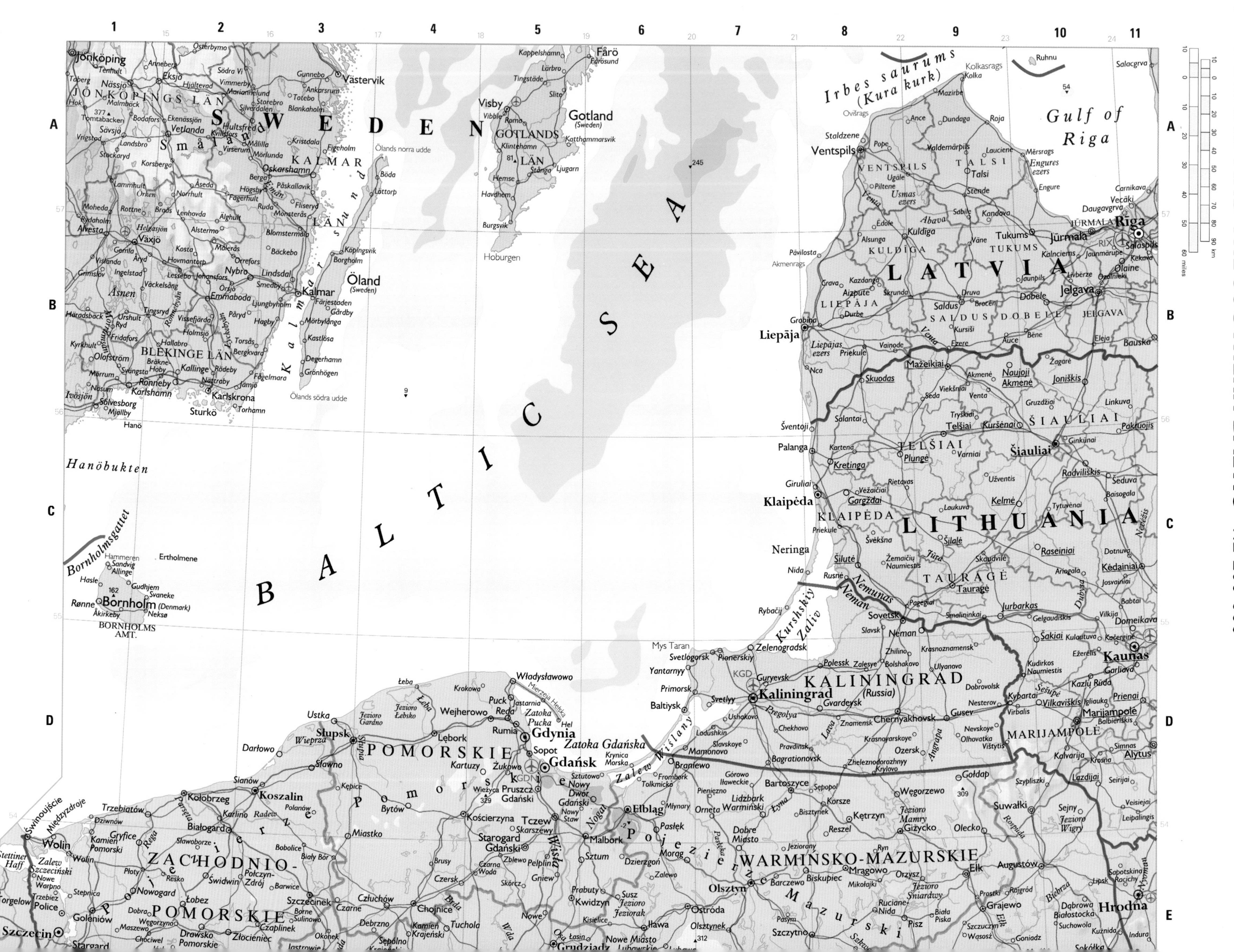

10 0 10 20 30 40 50 60 70 80 90 km
10 0 10 20 30 40 50 60 miles
Gulf of Riga
Irbes šaurums (Kura kurk)
LATVIA
LITHUANIA
KALININGRAD (Russia)
BALTIC SEA
SWEDEN
Gotland (Sweden)
Öland (Sweden)
Kalmarsund
Hanöbukten
Bornholmsgattet
Zatoka Gdańska
Kurshskiy Zaliv
Zalew Wiślany
POMORSKIE
WARMIŃSKO-MAZURSKIE
ZACHODNIO-POMORSKIE
Riga
Kaunas
Liepāja
Klaipėda
Kaliningrad
Gdańsk
Gdynia
Szczecin
Visby
Kalmar
Karlskrona
Bornholm (Denmark)

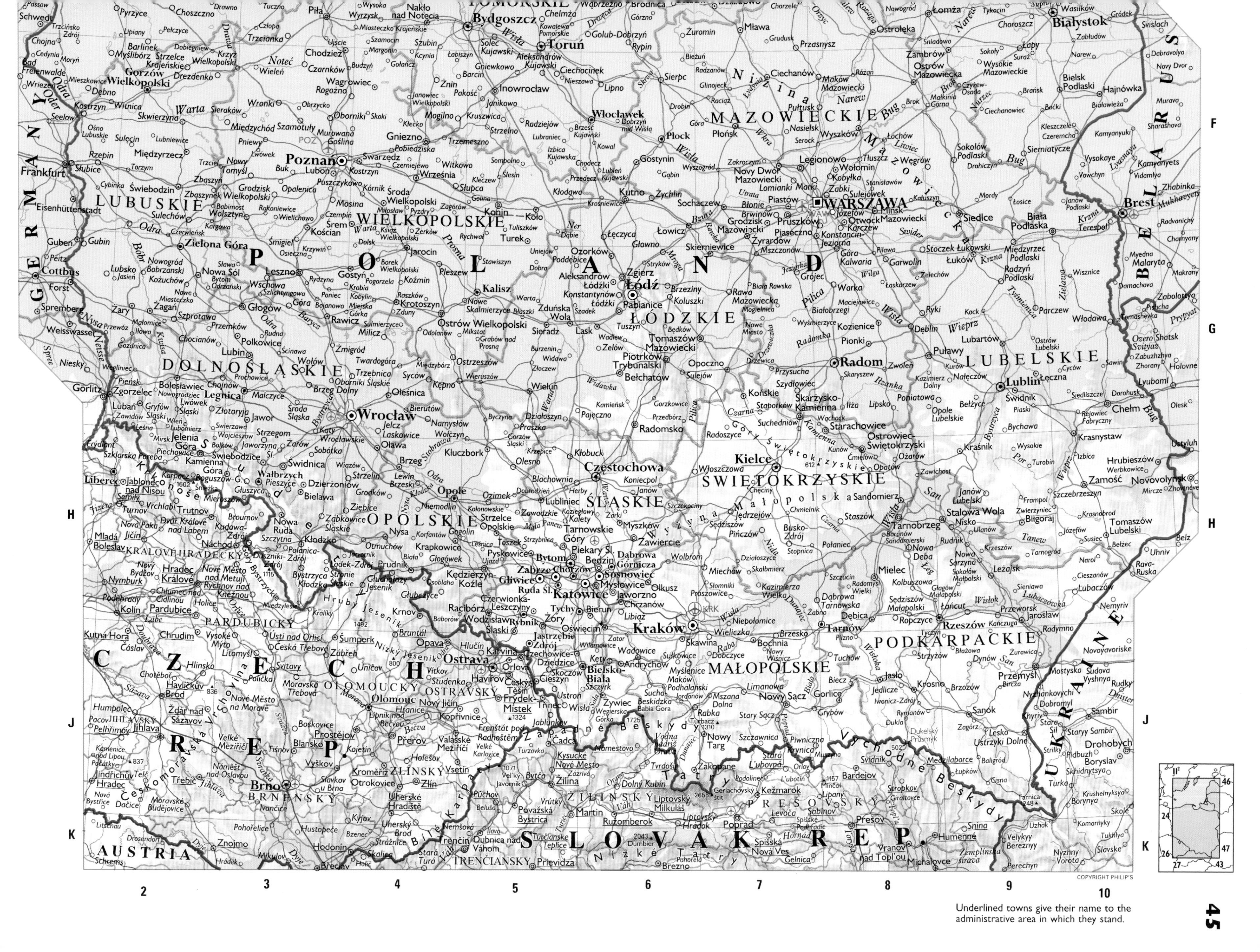

Underlined towns give their name to the
administrative area in which they stand.

BALTIC STATES, BELARUS AND UKRAINE 1:4 400 000

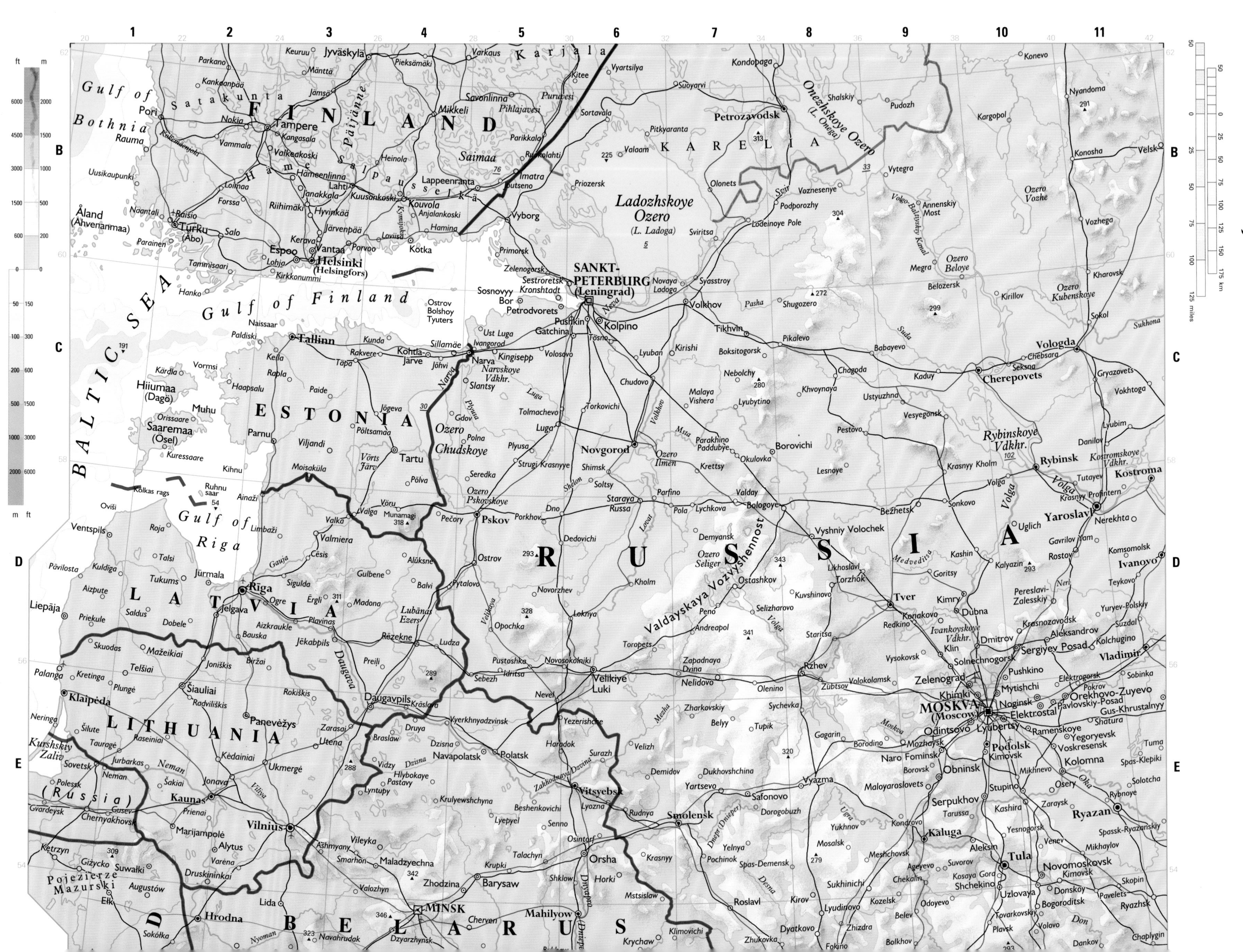

50 0 25 50 75 100 125 150 175 km
50 0 25 50 75 100 125 miles
FINLAND
ESTONIA
LATVIA
LITHUANIA
BELARUS
RUSSIA
KARELIA
BALTIC SEA
Gulf of Finland
Gulf of Riga
Gulf of Bothnia
Ladozhskoye Ozero (L. Ladoga)
Onezhskoye Ozero (L. Onega)
Ozero Chudskoye
Rybinskoye Vdkhr.
SANKT-PETERBURG (Leningrad)
MOSKVA (Moscow)
MINSK
Helsinki (Helsingfors)
Tallinn
Riga
Vilnius
Kaunas
Tartu
Pskov
Novgorod
Tver
Yaroslavl
Vologda
Cherepovets
Petrozavodsk
Smolensk
Vitsyebsk
Hrodna
Daugavpils
Daugava
Valdayskaya Vozvyshennost

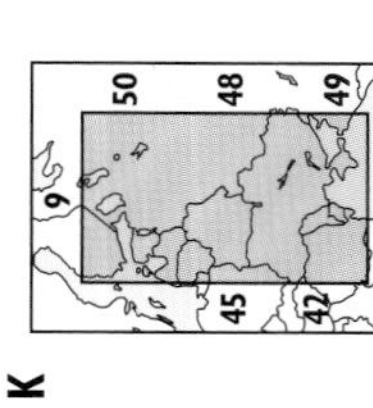

BLACK SEA

Sea of Azov

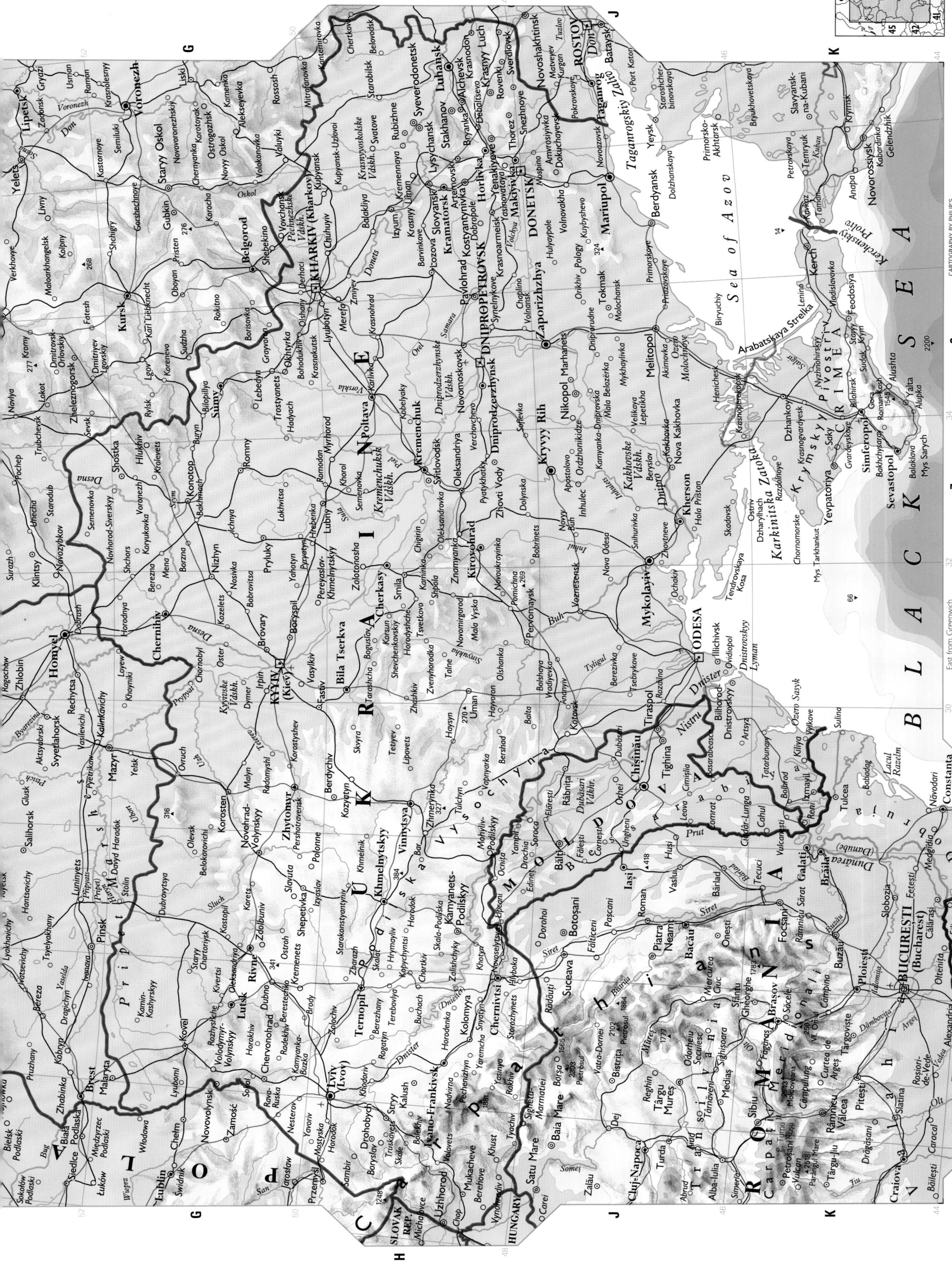

UKRAINE

ROMANIA

MOLDOVA

BULGARIA

HUNGARY

SLOVAK REP.

POLAND

CRIMEA

Carpathians

Major cities (labelled): Voronezh, Lipetsk, Yelets, Kursk, Belgorod, KHARKIV (Kharkov), Luhansk, ROSTOV, Taganrog, Mariupol, DONETSK, Zaporizhzhya, DNIPROPETROVSK, Kryvyy Rih, Poltava, Kremenchuk, Sumy, Chernihiv, Homyel, KYIV (Kiev), Cherkasy, Kherson, Mykolayiv, ODESA, Simferopol, Sevastopol, Yalta, Kerch, Novorossiysk, Berdyansk, Melitopol, Vinnytsya, Zhytomyr, Khmelnytskyy, Ternopil, Rivne, Lutsk, Brest, LVIV (Lvov), Ivano-Frankivsk, Uzhhorod, Chernivtsi, Chişinău, Tiraspol, Tighina, Bălţi, BUCUREŞTI (Bucharest), Galaţi, Brăila, Constanţa, Iaşi, Bacău, Braşov, Sibiu, Cluj-Napoca, Târgu Mures, Ploieşti, Buzău, Piatra Neamţ, Suceava, Satu Mare, Baia Mare, Ruse, Dobrich

Dniester / Nistru

Dnipro

Don

Desna

Prypyat' (Pripet)

East from Greenwich

CARTOGRAPHY BY PHILIP'S

Projection: Conical with two standard parallels

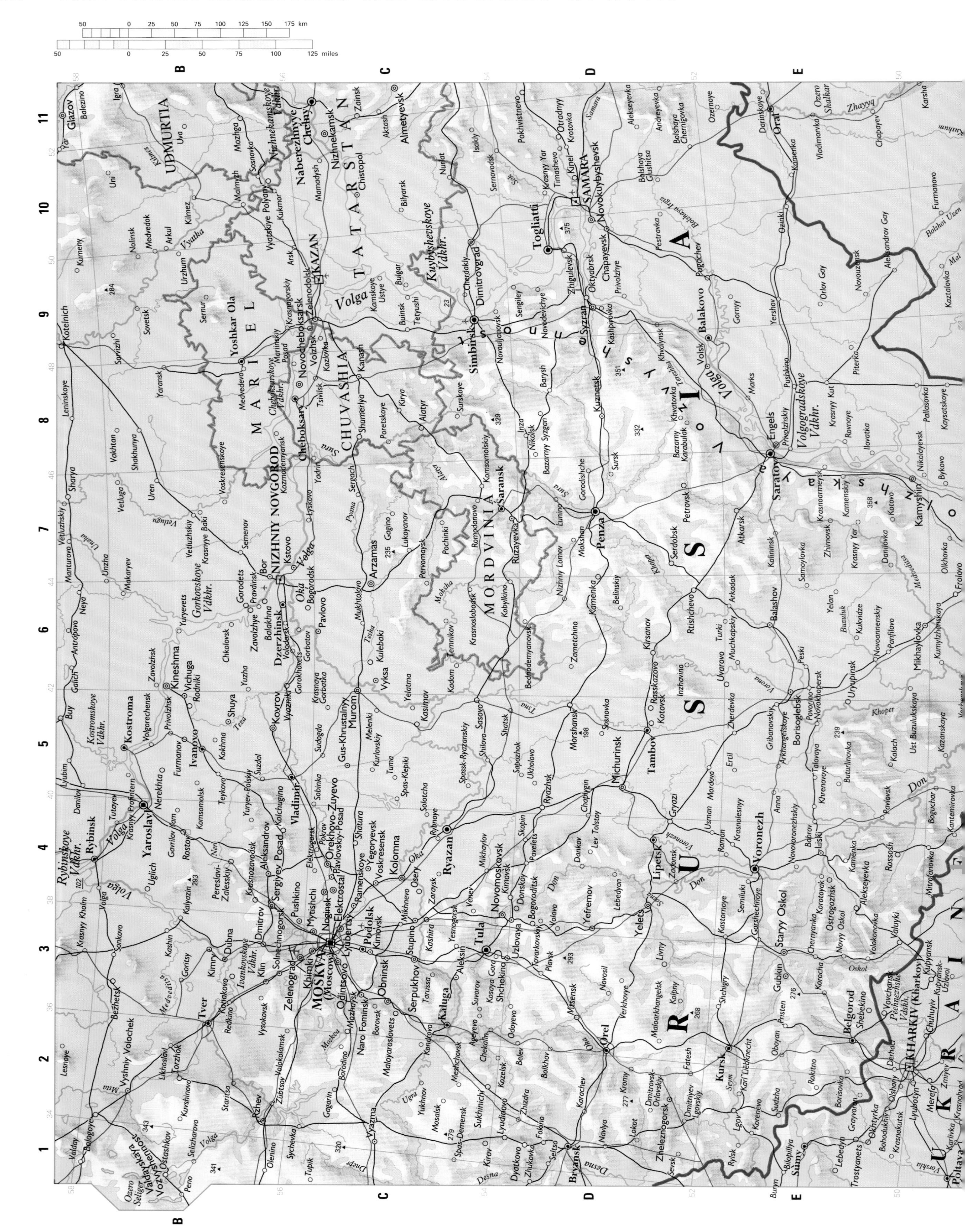
50 0 25 50 75 100 125 150 175 km
50 0 25 50 75 100 125 miles
B
C
D
E
1
2
3
4
5
6
7
8
9
10
11
R U S S I A
UDMURTIA
TATARSTAN
MARI EL
CHUVASHIA
MORDVINIA
U K R A I N E
MOSKVA (Moscow)
NIZHNIY NOVGOROD
KAZAN
SAMARA
Tver
Yaroslavl
Kostroma
Ivanovo
Vladimir
Ryazan
Tula
Kaluga
Bryansk
Orel
Kursk
Belgorod
KHARKIV (Kharkov)
Voronezh
Lipetsk
Tambov
Penza
Saransk
Saratov
Engels
Simbirsk
Togliatti
Cheboksary
Yoshkar Ola
Naberezhnyye Chelny
Volga
Oka
Don
Sura
Rybinskoye Vdkhr.
Gorkovskoye Vdkhr.
Kuybyshevskoye Vdkhr.
Volgogradskoye Vdkhr.
Kostromskoye Vdkhr.
Cheboksarskoye Vdkhr.
Nizhnekamskoye Vdkhr.

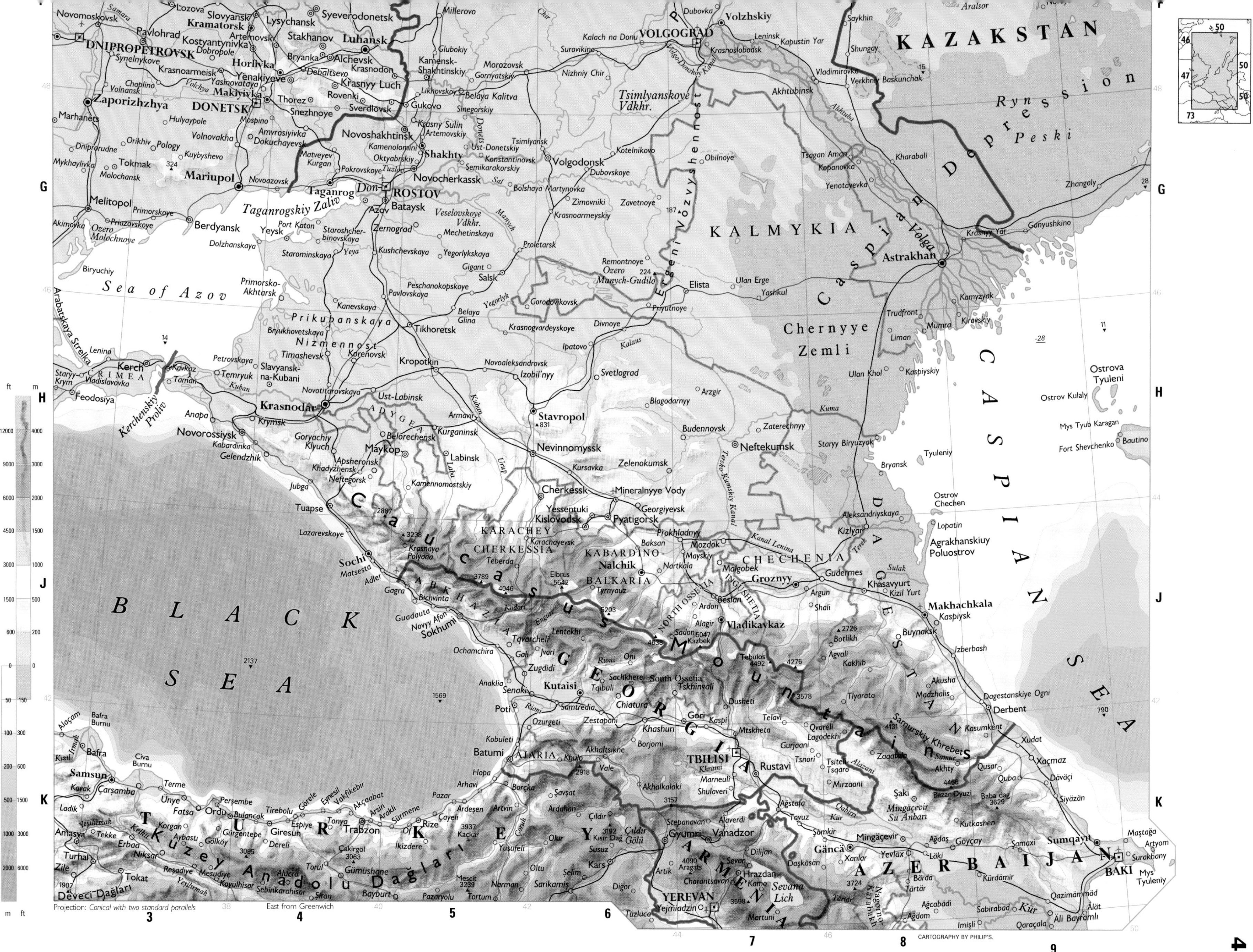
KAZAKSTAN
Ryn Peski
Caspian Depression
KALMYKIA
Chernyye Zemli
CASPIAN SEA
BLACK SEA
Sea of Azov
Taganrogskiy Zaliv
Kerchenskiy Proliv
CRIMEA
Prikubanskaya Nizmennost
Caucasus Mountains
GEORGIA
ARMENIA
AZERBAIJAN
TURKEY
Kuzey Anadolu Dağları
DAGESTAN
CHECHENIA
INGUSHETIA
NORTH OSSETIA
KABARDINO-BALKARIA
KARACHEY-CHERKESSIA
ADYGEA
ABKHAZIA
AJARIA
Nagorno-Karabakh
VOLGOGRAD
ROSTOV
DONETSK
DNIPROPETROVSK
TBILISI
YEREVAN
BAKI
Astrakhan
Krasnodar
Stavropol
Elista
Groznyy
Makhachkala
Vladikavkaz
Nalchik
Sochi
Sukhumi
Batumi
Kutaisi
Trabzon
Samsun
Luhansk
Mariupol
Zaporizhzhya
Taganrog
Volgodonsk
Novorossiysk
Derbent
Gäncä
Sumqayıt
Sevana Lich
Tsimlyanskoye Vdkhr.
Projection: Conical with two standard parallels
East from Greenwich
CARTOGRAPHY BY PHILIP'S

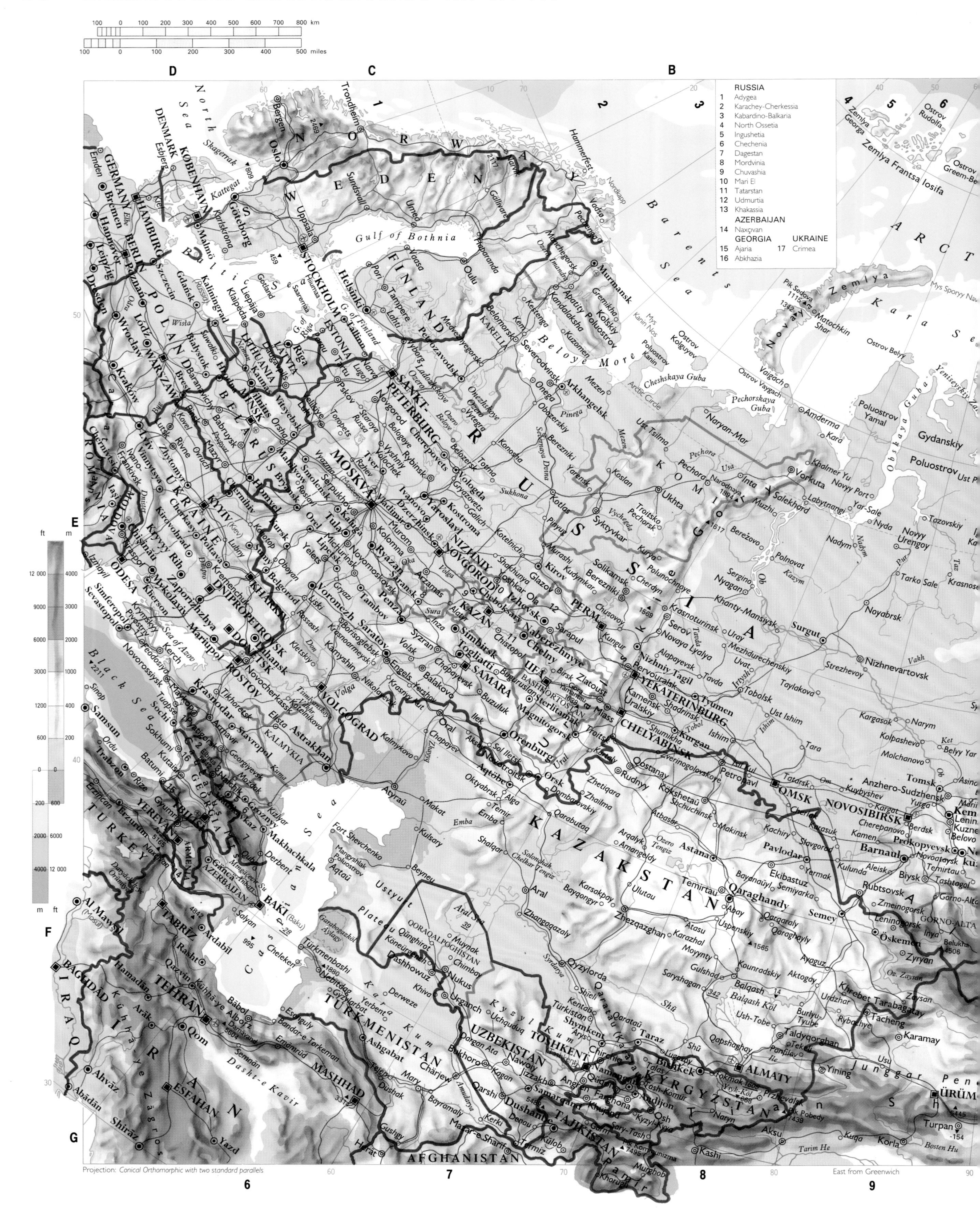

RUSSIA
1 Adygea
2 Karachey-Cherkessia
3 Kabardino-Balkaria
4 North Ossetia
5 Ingushetia
6 Chechenia
7 Dagestan
8 Mordvinia
9 Chuvashia
10 Mari El
11 Tatarstan
12 Udmurtia
13 Khakassia
AZERBAIJAN
14 Naxçıvan
GEORGIA   UKRAINE
15 Ajaria   17 Crimea
16 Abkhazia

Projection: Conical Orthomorphic with two standard parallels

East from Greenwich

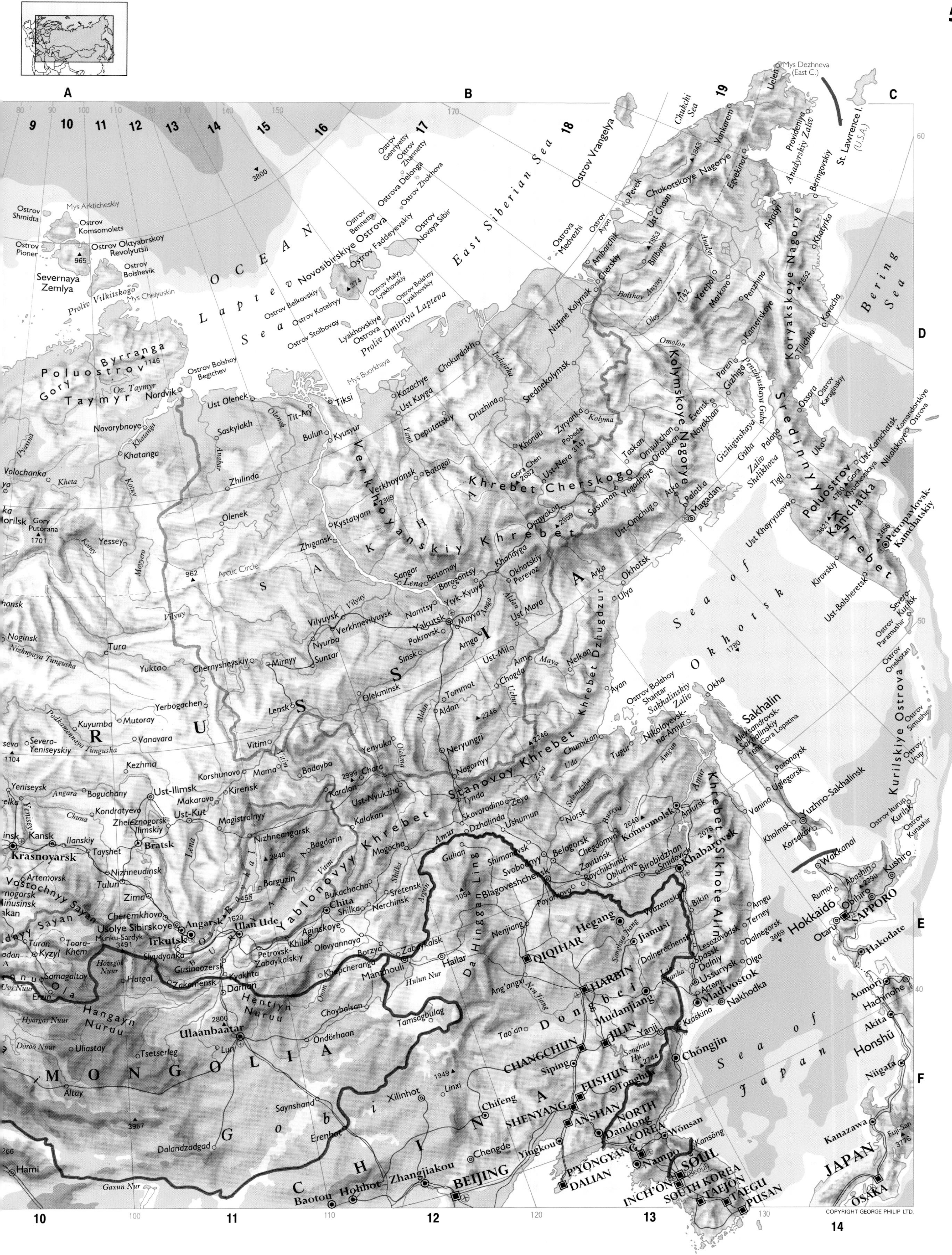

A   B   C

9   10   11   12   13   14   15   16   17   18   19

D

Bering Sea

E

F

10   11   12   13   14

COPYRIGHT GEORGE PHILIP LTD.

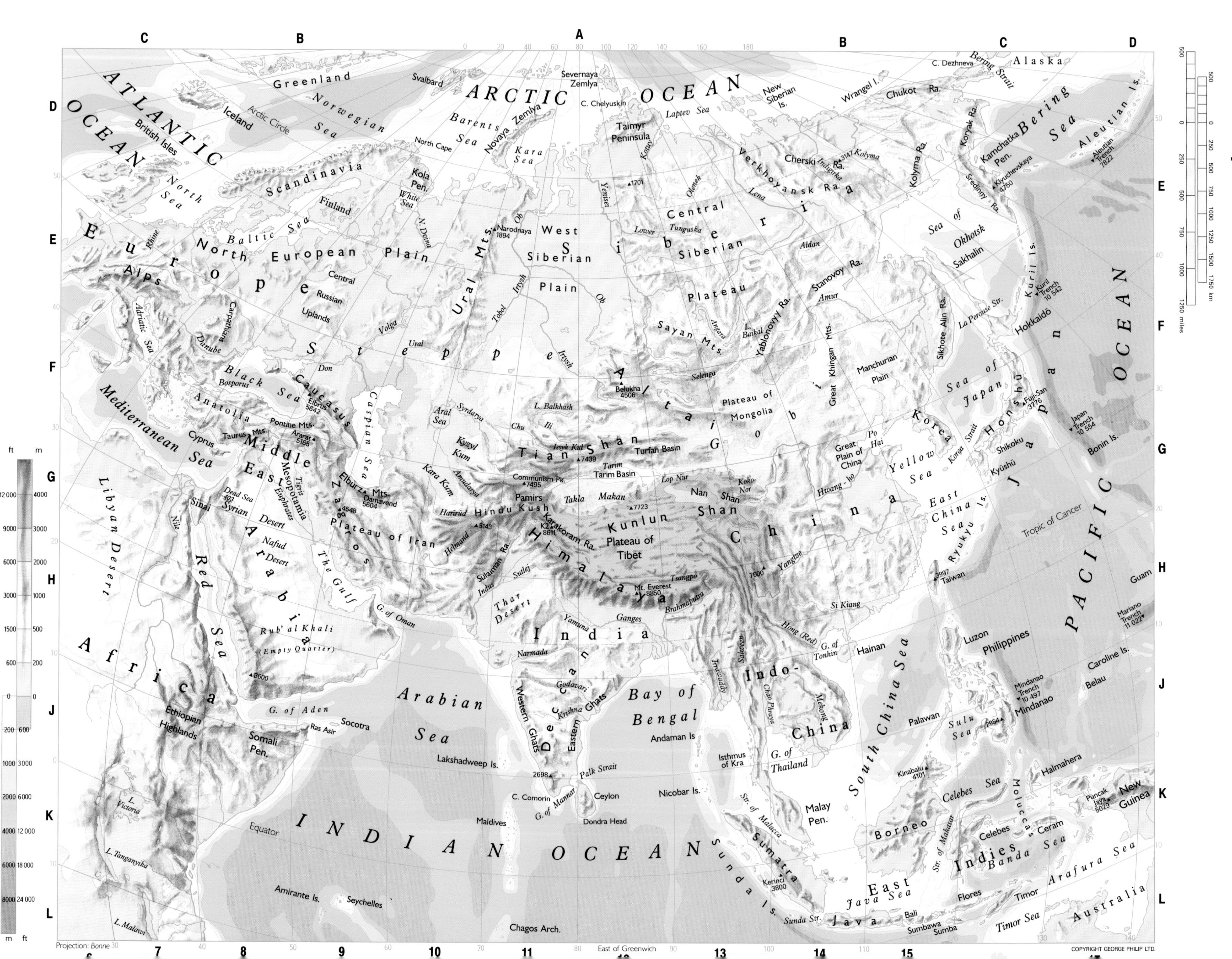
500 0 250 500 750 1000 1250 1500 1750 km
500 0 250 500 750 1000 1250 miles
ARCTIC OCEAN
PACIFIC OCEAN
INDIAN OCEAN
ATLANTIC OCEAN
Bering Sea
Sea of Okhotsk
Sea of Japan
Yellow Sea
East China Sea
South China Sea
Bay of Bengal
Arabian Sea
Caspian Sea
Black Sea
Red Sea
Mediterranean Sea
Barents Sea
Kara Sea
Laptev Sea
Norwegian Sea
North Sea
Baltic Sea
White Sea
Aral Sea
The Gulf
G. of Oman
G. of Aden
Java Sea
Timor Sea
Arafura Sea
Banda Sea
Celebes Sea
Sulu Sea
Siberia
China
Mongolia
India
Arabia
Africa
Europe
Middle East
Indo-China
East Indies
Japan
Himalaya
Tian Shan
Altai
Kunlun Shan
Nan Shan
Hindu Kush
Karakoram Ra.
Plateau of Tibet
Plateau of Iran
Zagros Mts.
Elburz Mts.
Caucasus
Ural Mts.
Steppe
North European Plain
Central Russian Uplands
West Siberian Plain
Central Siberian Plateau
Verkhoyansk Ra.
Cherski Ra.
Kolyma Ra.
Chukot Ra.
Koryak Ra.
Sredinny Ra.
Stanovoy Ra.
Yablonovyy Ra.
Sayan Mts.
Great Khingan Mts.
Sikhote Alin Ra.
Manchurian Plain
Great Plain of China
Plateau of Mongolia
Gobi
Takla Makan
Tarim Basin
Turfan Basin
Pamirs
Kara Kum
Kyzyl Kum
Thar Desert
Rub' al Khali (Empty Quarter)
Nafud Desert
Syrian Desert
Libyan Desert
Mesopotamia
Anatolia
Deccan
Western Ghats
Eastern Ghats
Sulaiman Ra.
Taurus Mts.
Pontine Mts.
Mt. Everest 8850
K2 8611
Communism Pk. 7495
Belukha 4506
Kerinci 3800
Kinabalu 4101
Elbrus 5642
Ararat 5165
Damavand 5604
Narodnaya 1894
Klyuchevskaya 4750
Fuji-San 3776
Puncak Jaya 5029
Kuril Trench 10 542
Japan Trench 10 554
Mariano Trench 11 022
Mindanao Trench 10 497
Aleutian Trench 7822
Kamchatka Pen.
Taimyr Peninsula
Kola Pen.
Malay Pen.
Somali Pen.
Isthmus of Kra
Scandinavia
Finland
Greenland
Iceland
Svalbard
North Cape
Severnaya Zemlya
Novaya Zemlya
New Siberian Is.
Wrangel I.
C. Chelyuskin
C. Dezhneva
Bering Strait
Alaska
Aleutian Is.
British Isles
Alps
Carpathians
Honshu
Hokkaido
Kyūshū
Shikoku
Sakhalin
Kuril Is.
Ryukyu Is.
Bonin Is.
Guam
Taiwan
Hainan
Philippines
Luzon
Mindanao
Palawan
Caroline Is.
Belau
Halmahera
Moluccas
Ceram
Borneo
Sumatra
Java
Bali
Sumbawa
Sumba
Flores
Timor
Celebes
New Guinea
Australia
Ceylon
Dondra Head
C. Comorin
G. of Mannar
Palk Strait
Maldives
Andaman Is.
Nicobar Is.
Lakshadweep Is.
Chagos Arch.
Seychelles
Amirante Is.
Socotra
Ras Asir
Cyprus
Sinai
Dead Sea
Ethiopian Highlands
L. Victoria
L. Tanganyika
L. Malawi
L. Balkhash
L. Baikal
Issyk Kul
Lop Nur
Koko Nor
Bosporus
G. of Tonkin
G. of Thailand
Str. of Malacca
Sunda Str.
Sunda Is.
Str. of Makasar
La Perouse Str.
Korea Strait
Korea
Yenisei
Lena
Ob
Irtysh
Tobol
Amur
Angara
Selenga
Aldan
Kolyma
Indigirka
Olenek
Lower Tunguska
Kotuy
Volga
Don
Ural
N. Dvina
Danube
Rhine
Chu
Ili
Amudarya
Syrdarya
Harirud
Helmand
Tigris
Euphrates
Indus
Sutlej
Ganges
Yamuna
Narmada
Godavari
Krishna
Tsangpo
Brahmaputra
Irrawaddy
Salween
Chao Phraya
Mekong
Hong (Red)
Si Kiang
Yangtze
Hwang-ho
Po Hai
Nile
Tropic of Cancer
Equator
Arctic Circle
East of Greenwich
Projection: Bonne
COPYRIGHT GEORGE PHILIP LTD.

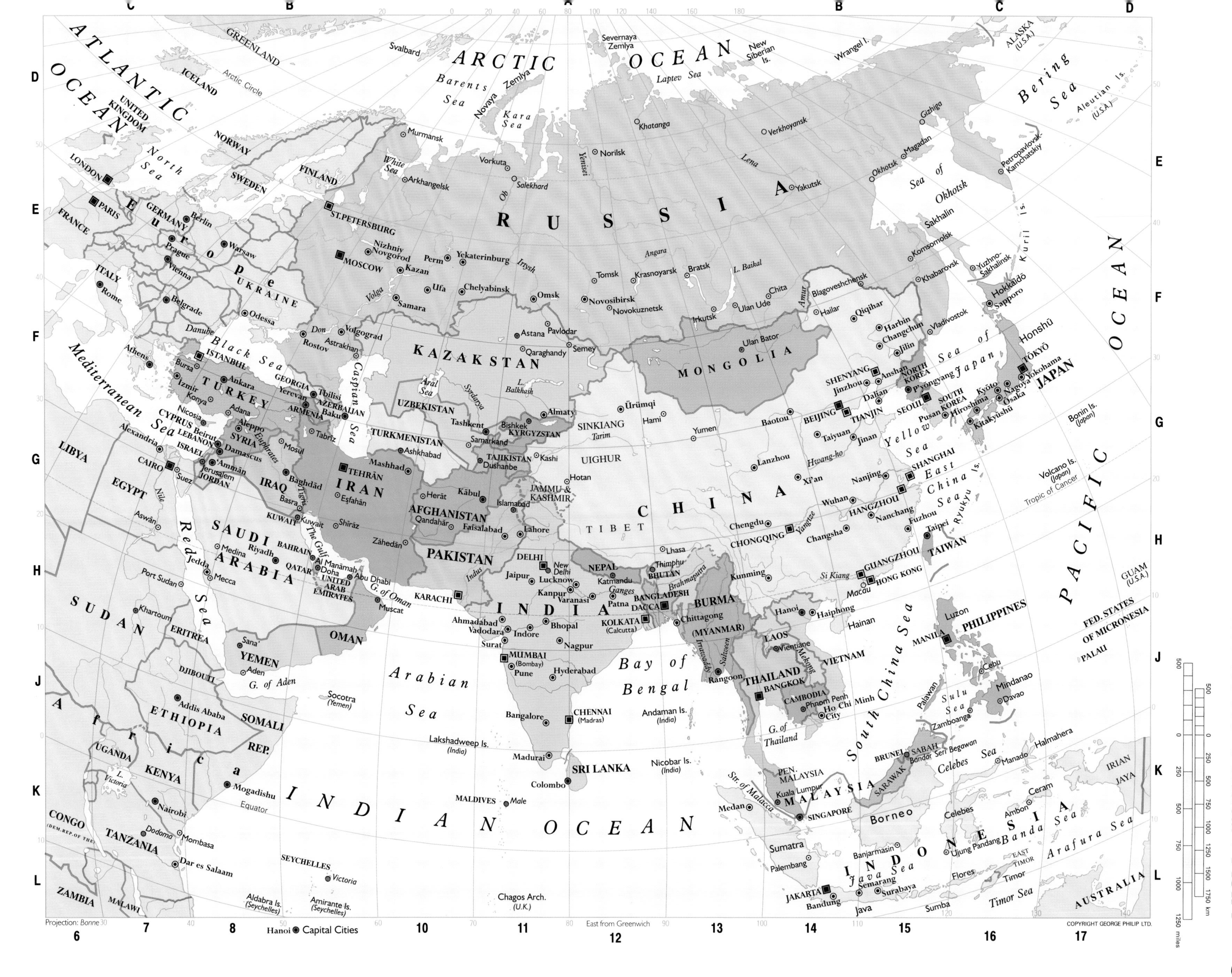

500   0   250   500   750   1000   1250   1500   1750 km

500   0   250   500   750   1000   1250 miles

PACIFIC OCEAN

ATLANTIC OCEAN

ARCTIC OCEAN

INDIAN OCEAN

R U S S I A

C H I N A

K A Z A K S T A N

I N D I A

MONGOLIA

IRAN

SAUDI ARABIA

PAKISTAN

AFGHANISTAN

Bering Sea

Sea of Okhotsk

Sea of Japan

Yellow Sea

East China Sea

South China Sea

Bay of Bengal

Arabian Sea

Caspian Sea

Black Sea

Mediterranean Sea

Red Sea

JAPAN

PHILIPPINES

INDONESIA

MALAYSIA

THAILAND

BURMA (MYANMAR)

VIETNAM

TAIWAN

SRI LANKA

MALDIVES

NEPAL

BHUTAN

BANGLADESH

Projection: Bonne

Hanoi ● Capital Cities

JAPAN 1:4 400 000

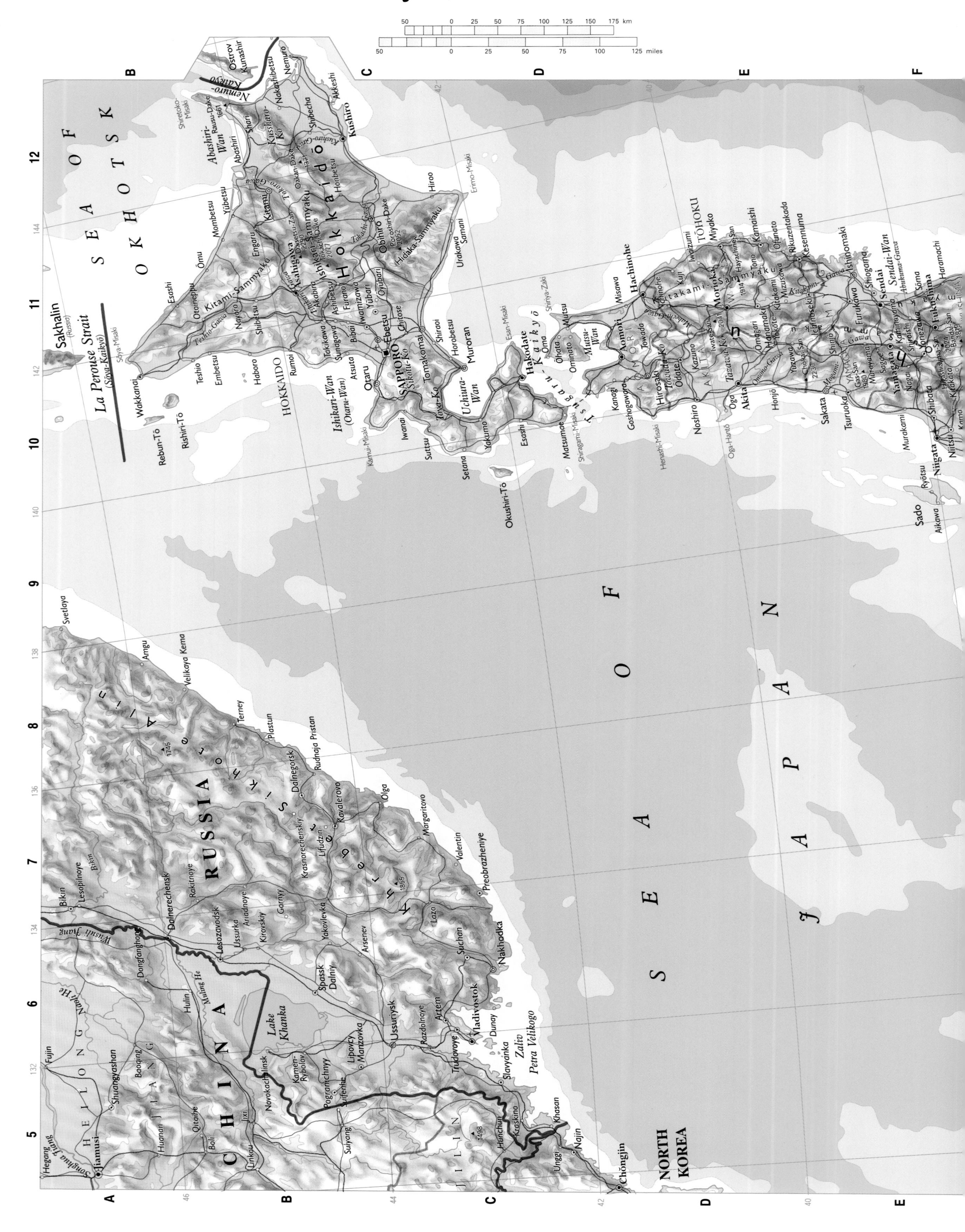

SEA OF OKHOTSK

La Perouse Strait
(Sōya-Kaikyō)

Sakhalin
(Rossia)

Ostrov Kunashir

Nemuro-Kaikyō

Rausu-Dake 1661

Shiretoko-Misaki

Nakashibetsu
Nemuro
Akkeshi
Shibecha
Shari
Abashiri
Abashiri-Wan
Kiritappu-Misaki
Kushiro
Kushiro-gawa
Hiroo
Erimo-Misaki

Akan-Dake
Tokoro-gawa
Teshio-gawa
Kitami-Sammyaku
Asahigawa
Ishikari-Sammyaku
Asahi-Dake 2290
Daisetsu-Dake
HOKKAIDO
Biei-dake 2052
Obihiro
Tokachi-gawa
Hidaka-Sammyaku
Urakawa
Samani

Mombetsu
Yūbetsu
Engaru
Esoshi

Sōya-Misaki
Wakkanai
Rebun-Tō
Rishiri-Tō

Otoineppu
Ōmu

Teshio
Embetsu
Haboro
Rumoi

Kamui-Misaki

HOKKAIDO

Kitami
Takikawa
Ashibetsu
Furano
Yūbari
Iwamizawa
Bibai
Sunagawa
Tōbetsu
Ebetsu
SAPPORO
Shikotu-Ko
Otaru
Ishikari-Wan
(Otaru-Wan)

Nayoro
Shibetsu

Chitose
Tomakomai
Shiraoi
Muroran
Horobetsu
Noboribetsu
Uchiura-Wan
Toya-Ko
Suttsu
Iwanai
Yakumo
Setana
Okushiri-Tō

Esashi

Matsumae
Shiragami-Misaki
Shirakami-Misaki
Tappi-Misaki

Tsugaru-Kaikyō
Esan-Misaki
Hakodate

Ōma
Ōhata
Mutsu
Ominato
Mutsu-Wan
Shiriya-Zaki

Oga-Hantō
Oga

Kanagi
Goshogawara
Hirosaki
Ōdate

Noshiro

Misawa
Hachinohe

TŌHOKU
Miyako
Kamaishi
Ōfunato
Rikuzentakada
Kesennuma

Aomori
Towada
Kitakami-gawa
Morioka
Hachimantai
Kuji
Kuzumaki
AKITA
Akita
Honjō

Kazuno
Hanamaki
Kitakami
Ichinoseki

Kitakami-Sammyaku

Mizusawa

Ishinomaki
Ōshika-Hantō
Sendai-Wan
Sendai
Shiogama

Tazawa-Ko
Tsuchizaki-Kō
YAMAGATA
Yokote
Shinjō
Mogami-gawa

Gassan
Mt. Chōkai 2230
Sakata
Tsuruoka

Furukawa
Shibata
Nagai
Yonezawa
Aizu-Wakamatsu
Bandai-San 1819
Fukushima
Kōriyama
Sōma
Haramachi

Murakami
Niitsu
Niigata

Sado
Ryōtsu
Aikawa

SEA OF JAPAN

RUSSIA

Svetlaya
Amgu
Velikaya Kema
Terney
Plastun
Rudnaja Pristan

Sikhote Alin

Sikhote Alin
1726

Dalnegorsk
Kavalerovo
Olga
Margaritovo

Krasnorechenskiy
Lifudzin
Yakovlevka
Valentin
Preobrazheniye

1855

Bikin
Lesoplinoye
Bikin
Rakitnoye
Dalnerechensk

Gornly
Arkadnoye
Ussurka

Kirovskiy
Arsenev
Lazo
Sichan

Spassk
Dalniy
Nakhodka
Vladivostok
Dunay

CHINA

Songhua Jiang
Wusuli Jiang

HEILONGJIANG

Hegang
Jiamusi
Fujin
Huanan
Boli
Linkou
Qitaihe
Shuangyashan
Baoqing
Dongfangtong

Hulin

Mudan Jiang
Muling He

Lake Khanka

Novokachalinsk
Kamen-Rybolov
Pogranichny
Suifenhe

Razdolnoye
Artem

Ussuriysk
Lipovcy
Manzovka

JILIN

Sulyang

Hunchun

Tudoye
Slavyanka
Zaliv Petra Velikogo

Kaskino

1498

Khasan
Najin
Unggi

NORTH KOREA

Chŏngjin

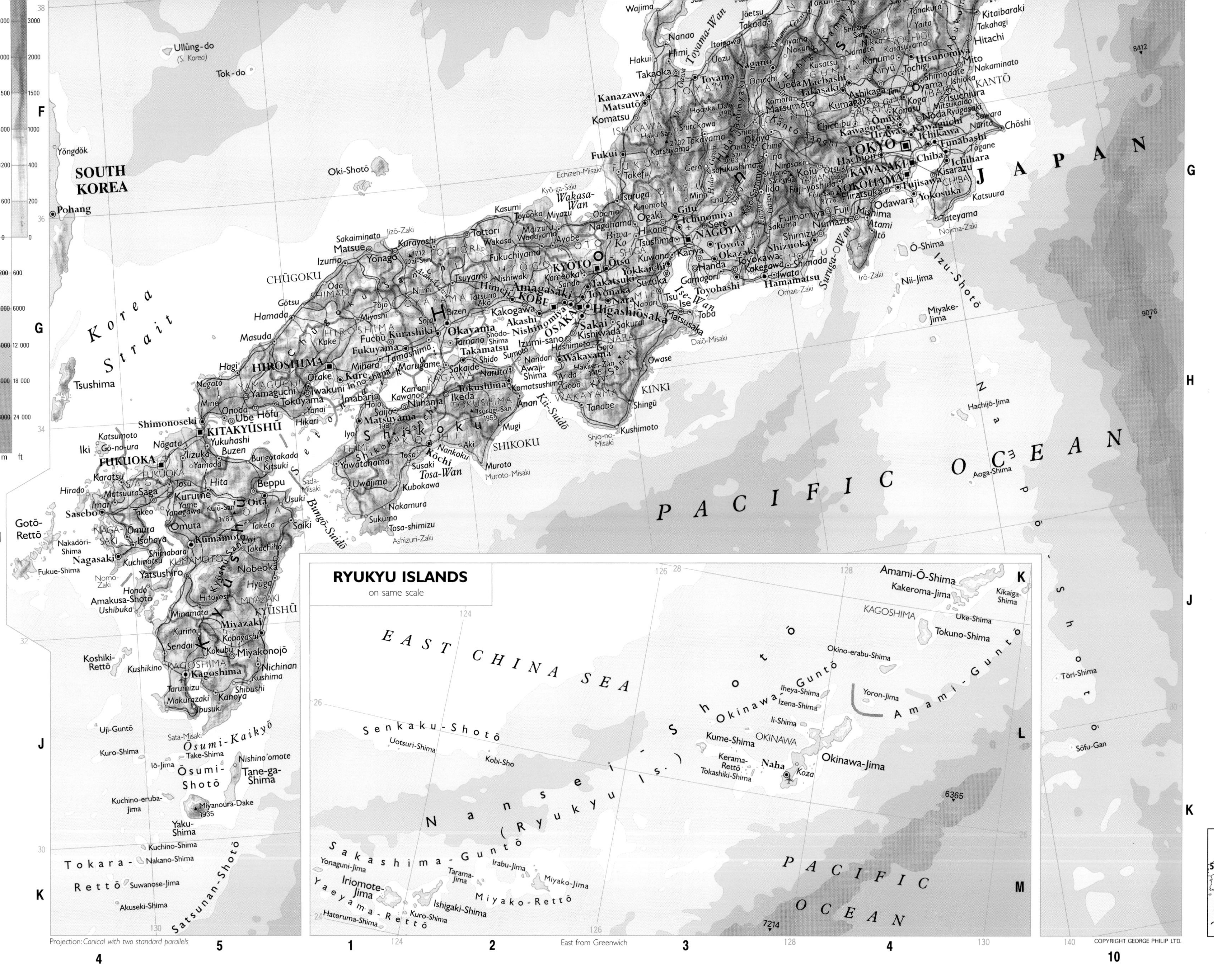

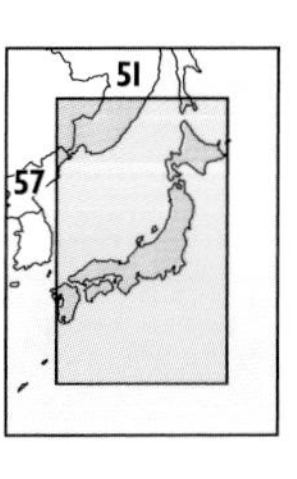

RYUKYU ISLANDS

on same scale

Projection: Conical with two standard parallels

East from Greenwich

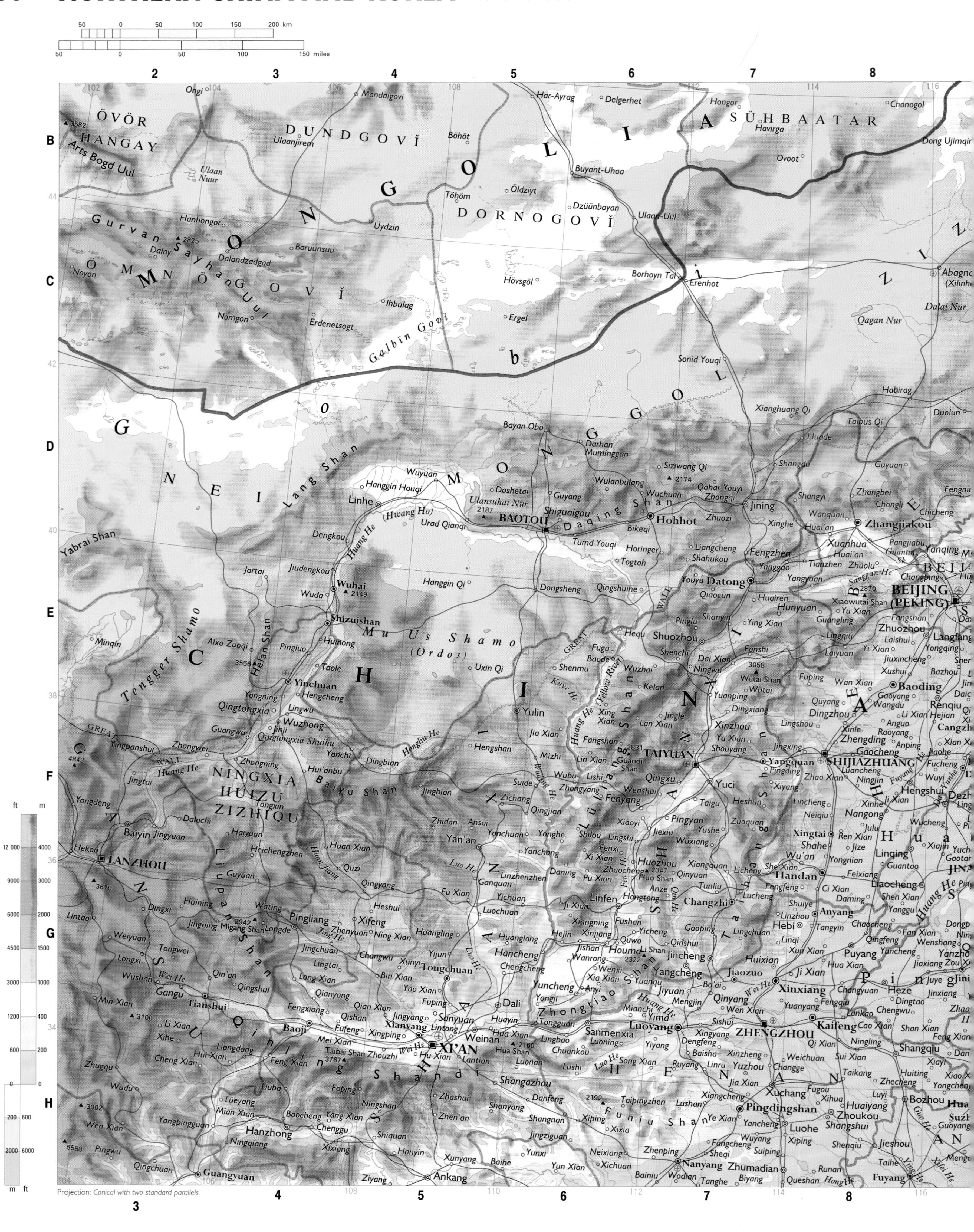
50 0 50 100 150 200 km
50 0 50 100 150 miles
MONGOLIA
ÖVÖR HANGAY
DUNDGOVĬ
SÜHBAATAR
DORNOGOVĬ
ÖMNÖGOVĬ
Gurvan Sayhan Uul
Arts Bogd Uul
Galbïn Govĭ
Gobi
NEI MONGOL
NINGXIA HUIZU ZIZHIQU
GANSU
SHAANXI
SHANXI
HEBEI
HENAN
CHINA
Mandalgovi
Ulaanjirem
Böhöt
Har-Ayrag
Delgerhet
Hongor
Havirga
Chonogol
Dong Ujimqin
Ovoot
Buyant-Uhaa
Öldziyt
Dzüünbayan
Ulaan-Uul
Töhöm
Üydzin
Hanhongor
Dalay
Dalandzadgad
Baruunsuu
Noyon
Nomgon
Erdenetsogt
Ihbulag
Hövsgöl
Ergel
Borhoyn Tal
Erenhot
Abagnar
Dalai Nur
Qagan Nur
Sonid Youqi
Habirag
Xianghuang Qi
Duolun
Taibus Qi
Bayan Obo
Darhan Muminggan
Huade
Shangdu
Guyuan
Siziwang Qi
Wulanbulang
Wuchuan
Qahar Youyi Zhongqi
Jining
Shangyi
Zhangbei
Chongli
Chicheng
Zhangjiakou
Wuyuan
Hanggin Houqi
Linhe
Lang Shan
Dashetai
Guyang
Ulansuhai Nur
Shiguaigou
Daqing Shan
Hohhot
Zhuozi
BAOTOU
Urad Qianqi
Tumd Youqi
Bikeqi
Huang He (Hwang Ho)
Dengkou
Yabrai Shan
Jartai
Jiudengkou
Wuhai
Wuda
Hanggin Qi
Dongsheng
Qingshuihe
Horinger
Togtoh
Liangcheng
Shahukou
Fengzhen
Youyu
Datong
Xuanhua
Huai'an
Yanqing
BEIJING (PEKING)
Shizuishan
Mu Us Shamo (Ordos)
Uxin Qi
Tengger Shamo
Alxa Zuoqi
Helan Shan
Minqin
Pingluo
Huinong
Taole
Yinchuan
Hequ
Shuozhou
Fugu
Baode
Shenmu
Wuzhai
Kelan
Ningwu
Dai Xian
Wutai Shan
Yongning
Hengcheng
Qingtongxia
Lingwu
Wuzhong
Guangwu
Yulin
Jia Xian
Xing Xian
Lan Xian
Jingle
Yuanping
Xinzhou
Dingxiang
Baoding
Dingzhou
Yingpanshui
Zhongwei
Qingtongxia Shuiku
Yanchi
Dingbian
Hengshan
Mizhi
Fangshan
TAIYUAN
Yangquan
SHIJIAZHUANG
Zhengding
Gaocheng
Jingtai
Huang He
Zhongning
Tongxin
Hui'anbu
Baixu Shan
Jingbian
Suide
Wubu
Lishi
Qingxu
Yuci
Yongdeng
Dalachi
Zhichang
Zhongyang
Fenyang
Wenshui
Taigu
Heshun
Hengshui
Baiyin
Jingyuan
Haiyuan
Zhidan
Ansai
Qingjian
Xiaoyi
Pingyao
Xingtai
Shahe
Hekou
LANZHOU
Liupan Shan
Heichengzhen
Huan Xian
Yan'an
Yanchuan
Yonghe
Shilou
Huozhou
Handan
Guyuan
Quzi
Yanchang
Linzhenzhen
Daning
Changzhi
Qingyang
Ganquan
Fu Xian
Linfen
Huining
Heshui
Yichuan
Ji Xian
Anyang
Dingxi
Pingliang
Xifeng
Luochuan
Hebi
Lintao
Jingning
Longde
Ning Xian
Huangling
Houma
Jincheng
Weiyuan
Tongwei
Jingchuan
Changwu
Huanglong
Hancheng
Qinshui
Yangcheng
Jiaozuo
Xinxiang
Longxi
Lingtai
Xunyi
Tongchuan
Jiyuan
Huixian
Wushan
Wei He
Gangu
Qin'an
Qingshui
Long Xian
Yao Xian
Yuncheng
Zhongtiao Shan
Mengjin
Qinyang
Puyang
Min Xian
Tianshui
Fengxiang
Qian Xian
Fuping
Dali
Yongji
Yima
Heze
Li Xian
Baoji
Qishan
Jingyang
Sanyuan
Huayin
Tongguan
Sanmenxia
Luoyang
ZHENGZHOU
Kaifeng
Xihe
Mei Xian
Xianyang
XI'AN
Weinan
Hua Xian
Lingbao
Luoning
Cheng Xian
Hui Xian
Zhouzhi
Hu Xian
Lantian
Hua Shan
Chuankou
Yiyang
Dengfeng
Qinling Shandi
Zhugqu
Feng Xian
Luonan
Lushi
Song Xian
Ruyang
Yuzhou
Xuchang
Shangqiu
Wudu
Liuba
Foping
Shangzhou
Danfeng
Pingdingshan
Zhoukou
Lüeyang
Mian Xian
Ningshan
Zhashui
Shanyang
Funiu Shan
Ye Xian
Luohe
Bozhou
Yangpingguan
Baocheng
Yang Xian
Hanzhong
Chenggu
Zhen'an
Shangnan
Xiping
Xixia
Wen Xian
Ningqiang
Xixiang
Shiquan
Hanyin
Jingziguan
Neixiang
Zhenping
Wuyang
Xiping
Shangshui
Jieshou
Pingwu
Qingchuan
Guangyuan
Ziyang
Ankang
Xunyang
Baihe
Yunxi
Yun Xian
Xichuan
Nanyang
Zhumadian
Runan
Fuyang
Projection: Conical with two standard parallels

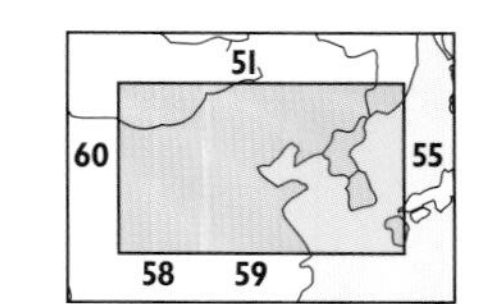
51
60
55
58
59

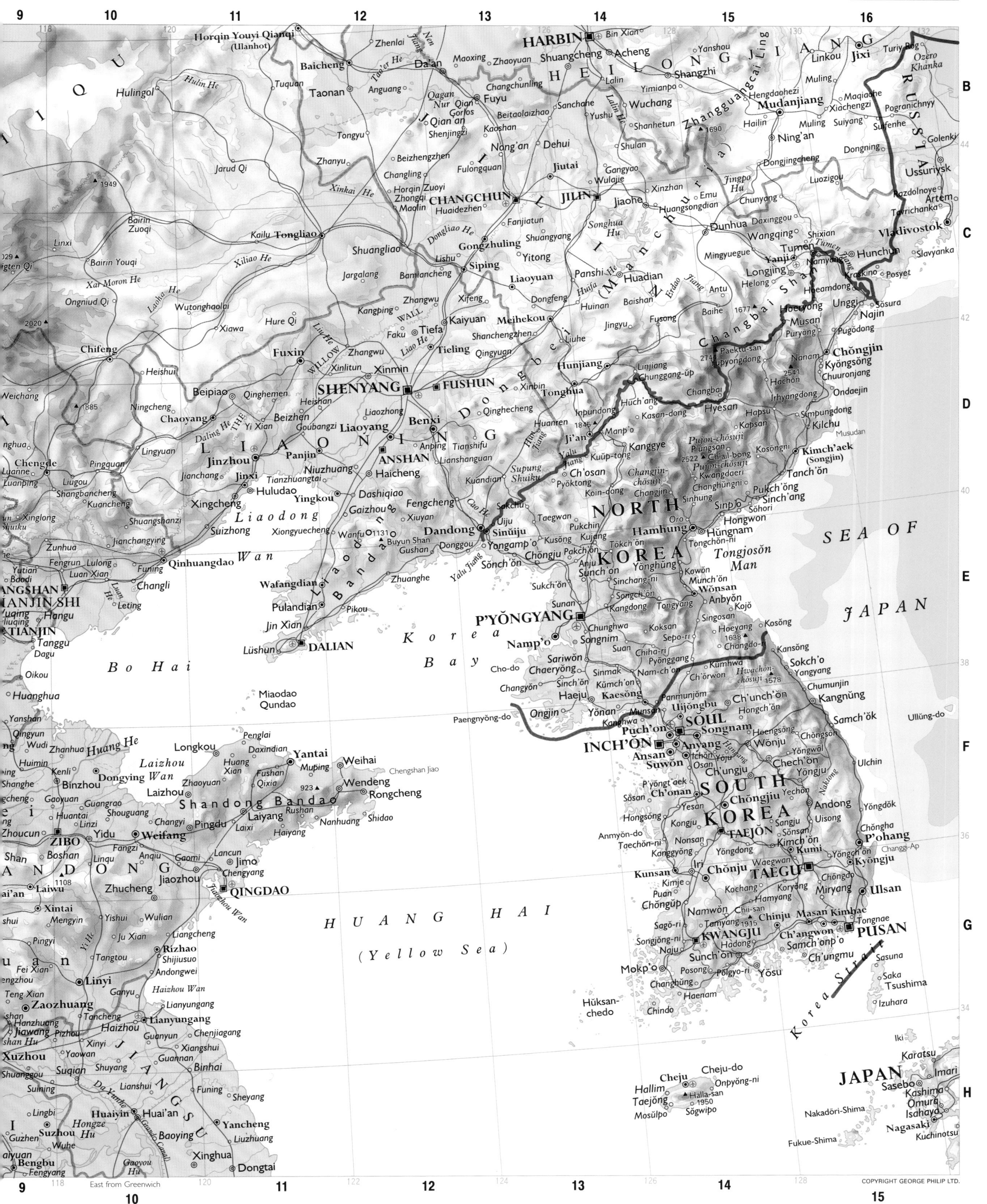
9
10
11
12
13
14
15
16
B
C
D
E
F
G
H
HARBIN
CHANGCHUN
JILIN
SHENYANG
FUSHUN
ANSHAN
DALIAN
P'YŎNGYANG
SŎUL
INCH'ŎN
TAEJŎN
TAEGU
KWANGJU
PUSAN
QINGDAO
ZIBO
TIANJIN
Vladivostok
Ussuriysk
Mudanjiang
Jixi
Yanji
Dandong
Jinzhou
Fuxin
Chifeng
Tongliao
Siping
Benxi
Liaoyang
Yantai
Weifang
Linyi
Xuzhou
Huai'an
Hamhung
Hŭngnam
Chŏngjin
Wŏnsan
Kaesŏng
Suwŏn
Ulsan
Cheju
Sasebo
Nagasaki
H E I L O N G J I A N G
J I L I N
L I A O N I N G
M A N C H U R I A
D o n g b e i
NORTH KOREA
SOUTH KOREA
RUSSIA
JAPAN
Liaodong Wan
Liaodong Bandao
Shandong Bandao
Laizhou Wan
Bo Hai
Korea Bay
H U A N G   H A I
(Yellow Sea)
SEA OF JAPAN
Tongjosŏn Man
Korea Strait
Changbai Shan
Zhangguangcai Ling
Tsushima
Cheju-do
Ullŭng-do
Halla-san 1950
Paektu-san
East from Greenwich

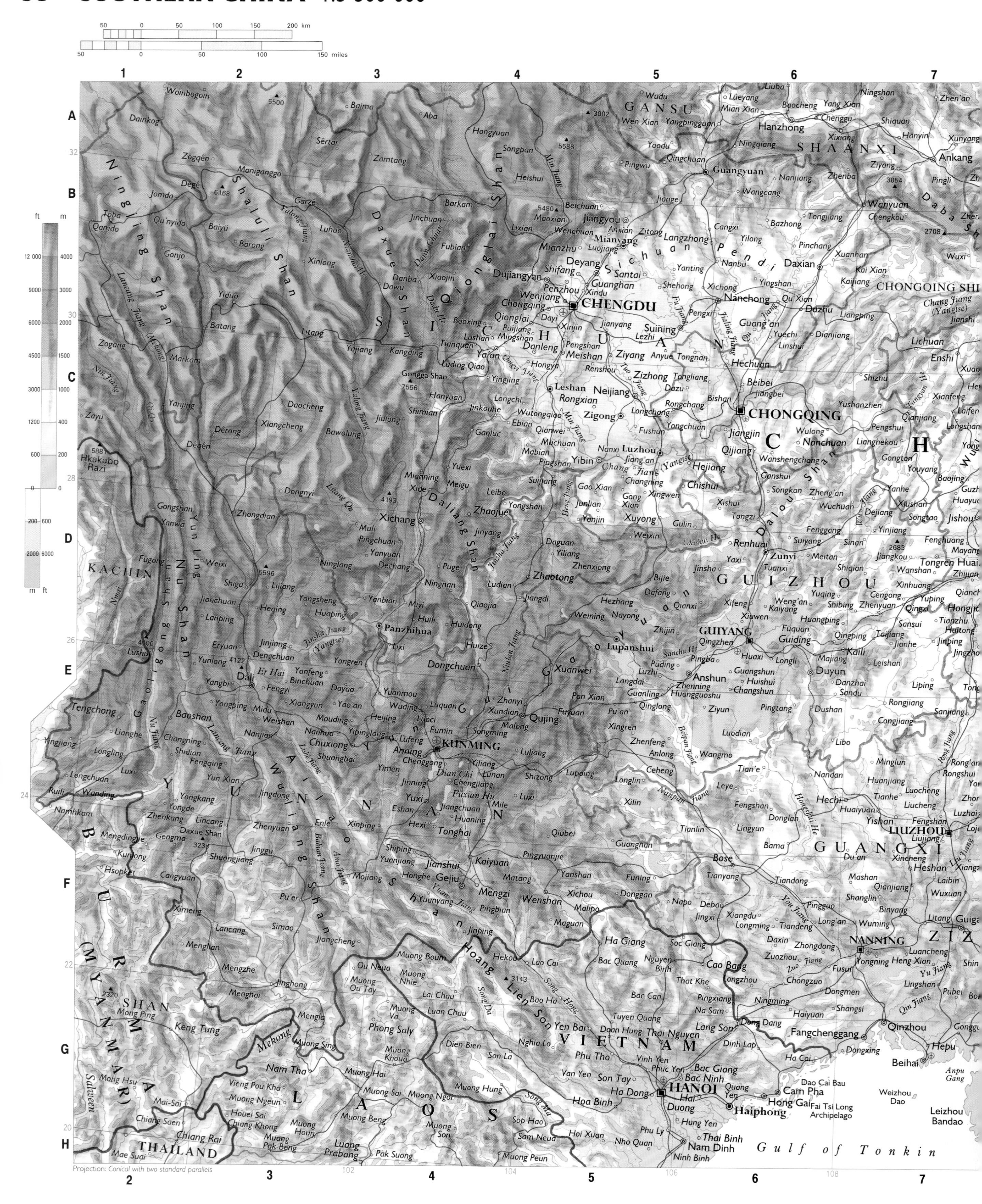
50 0 50 100 150 200 km
50 0 50 100 150 miles
ft m
12 000 4000
9000 3000
6000 2000
4500 1500
3000 1000
1200 400
600 200
0 0
200 600
2000 6000
m ft
GANSU
SHAANXI
SICHUAN
Sichuan Pendi
CHONGQING SHI
GUIZHOU
YUNNAN
GUANGXI
VIETNAM
LAOS
BURMA (MYANMAR)
THAILAND
KACHIN
SHAN
CHENGDU
CHONGQING
KUNMING
GUIYANG
NANNING
LIUZHOU
HANOI
Haiphong
Gulf of Tonkin
Hanzhong
Ankang
Guangyuan
Mianyang
Deyang
Nanchong
Daxian
Leshan
Zigong
Yibin
Luzhou
Neijiang
Xichang
Panzhihua
Zhaotong
Zunyi
Lupanshui
Anshun
Duyun
Kaili
Qujing
Dali
Baoshan
Tengchong
Gejiu
Kaiyuan
Mengzi
Wenshan
Bose
Hechi
Qinzhou
Beihai
Fangchenggang
Lao Cai
Cao Bang
Lang Son
Thai Nguyen
Nam Dinh
Thai Binh
Hong Gai
Cam Pha
Luang Prabang
Chiang Rai
Keng Tung
Ningjing Shan
Shaluli Shan
Daxue Shan
Qionglai Shan
Daliang Shan
Wuliang Shan
Ailao Shan
Nu Shan
Yun Ling
Gaoligong Shan
Dalou Shan
Daba Shan
Hoang Lien Son
Chang Jiang (Yangtze)
Jinsha Jiang (Yangtze)
Lancang Jiang (Mekong)
Mekong
Salween
Nu Jiang
Yalong Jiang
Min Jiang
Jialing Jiang
Wu Jiang
Nanpan Jiang
Hongshui He
You Jiang
Zuo Jiang
Song Da
Song Hong
Song Ma
Dian Chi
Er Hai
Gongga Shan 7556
Hkakabo Razi
Lizhou Bandao
Weizhou Dao
Dao Cai Bau
Fai Tsi Long Archipelago
Projection: Conical with two standard parallels

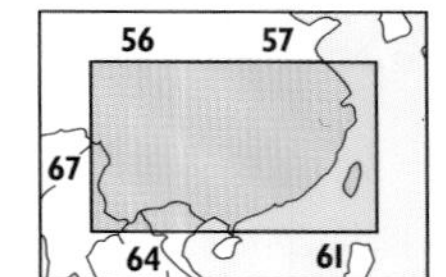
56
57
67
64
61

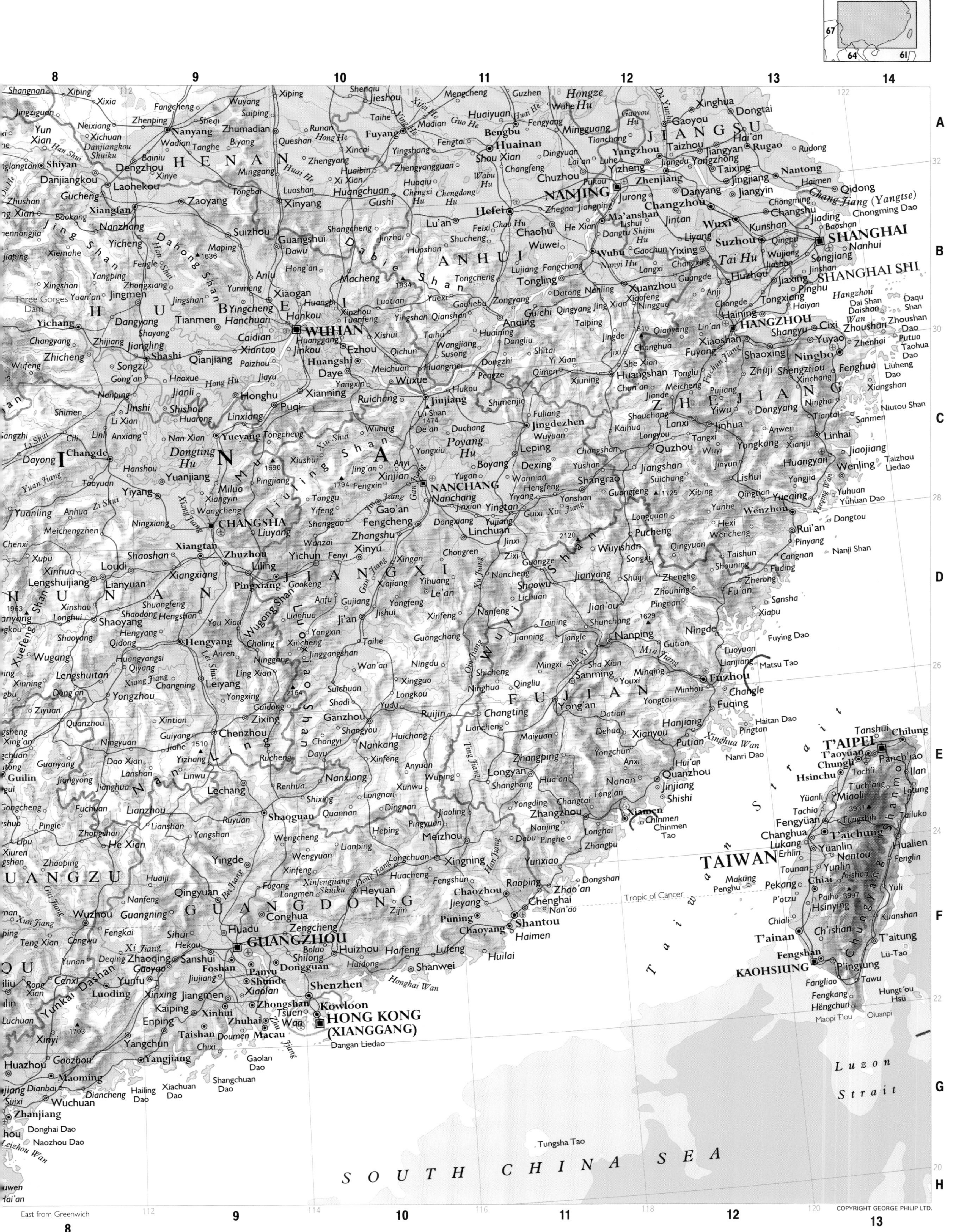
8
9
10
11
12
13
14
A
B
C
D
E
F
G
H
HENAN
HUBEI
HUNAN
ANHUI
JIANGSU
ZHEJIANG
JIANGXI
FUJIAN
GUANGDONG
TAIWAN
SHANGHAI SHI
NANJING
SHANGHAI
WUHAN
HANGZHOU
CHANGSHA
NANCHANG
GUANGZHOU
HONG KONG
(XIANGGANG)
T'AIPEI
KAOHSIUNG
Hefei
Fuzhou
Xiamen
Shantou
Shenzhen
Kowloon
Macau
Zhuhai
Ningbo
Wenzhou
Suzhou
Wuxi
Changzhou
Zhenjiang
Yangzhou
Huainan
Bengbu
Anqing
Jiujiang
Yichang
Shashi
Jingzhou
Yueyang
Changde
Zhuzhou
Xiangtan
Hengyang
Ganzhou
Shaoguan
Zhangzhou
Quanzhou
Putian
Nanping
Sanming
Longyan
Meizhou
Chaozhou
Jieyang
Shanwei
Huizhou
Dongguan
Foshan
Jiangmen
Zhaoqing
Wuzhou
Zhanjiang
Maoming
Yangjiang
Guilin
Shiyan
Xiangfan
Nanyang
Xinyang
Huangshi
Jingdezhen
Shangrao
Quzhou
Jinhua
Taizhou
T'aichung
T'ainan
Hualien
T'aitung
Hsinchu
Chilung
Dongting Hu
Poyang Hu
Tai Hu
Hongze Hu
Chang Jiang (Yangtse)
Dabie Shan
Wuyi Shan
Nan Ling
Luoxiao Shan
Jiuling Shan
Chungyang Shanmo
Taiwan Strait
Luzon Strait
SOUTH CHINA SEA
Tropic of Cancer
Matsu Tao
Chinmen Tao
Penghu
Zhoushan
Three Gorges Dam
1636
1834
1474
1596
1794
1725
1610
2120
1629
2164
1510
1963
1703
3931
3997
East from Greenwich

CHINA 1:17 800 000

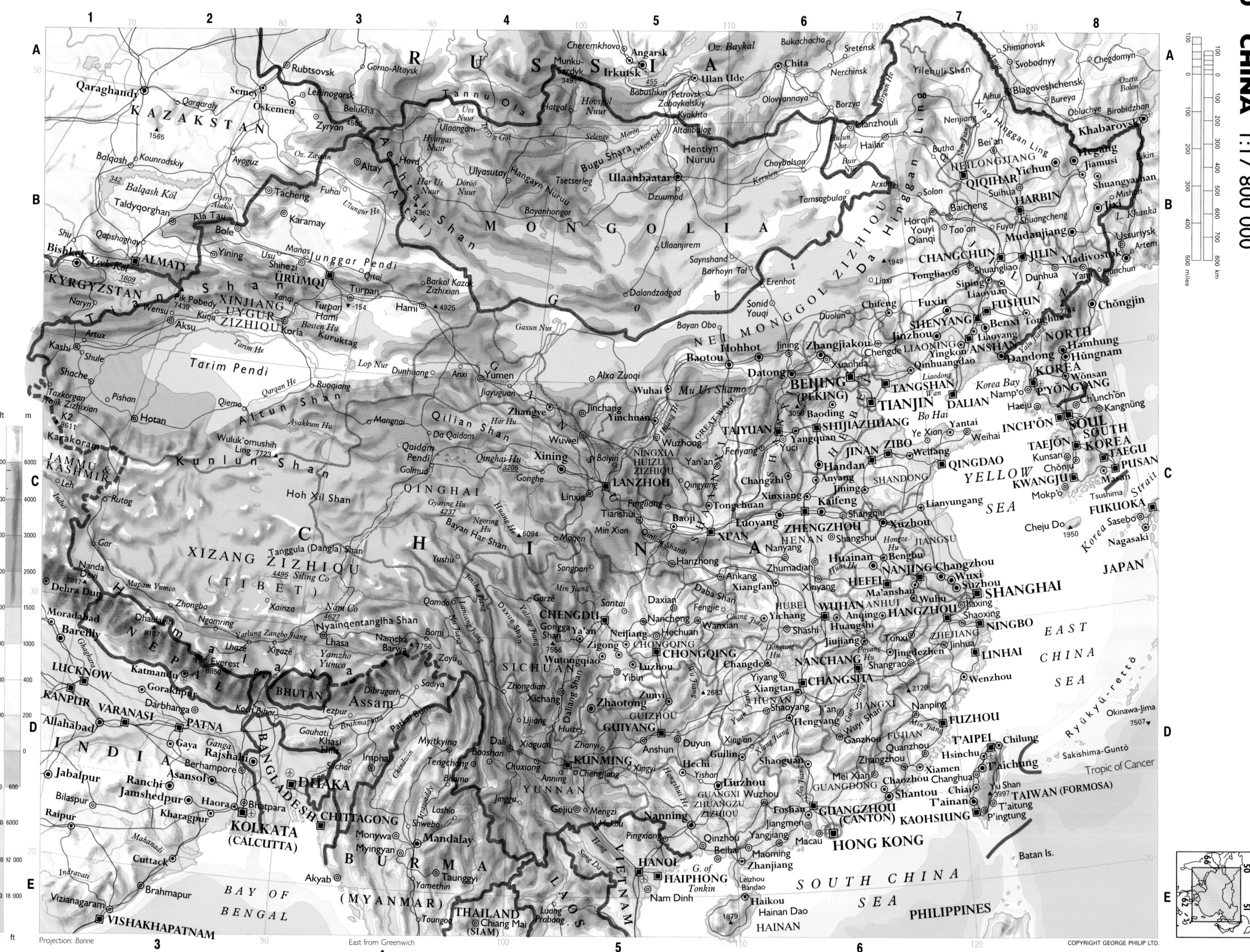
100 0 100 200 300 400 500 600 700 800 km
100 0 100 200 300 400 500 miles
CHINA
MONGOLIA
RUSSIA
KAZAKSTAN
KYRGYZSTAN
JAMMU & KASHMIR
NEPAL
BHUTAN
BANGLADESH
INDIA
BURMA (MYANMAR)
THAILAND (SIAM)
LAOS
VIETNAM
PHILIPPINES
NORTH KOREA
SOUTH KOREA
JAPAN
TAIWAN (FORMOSA)
HONG KONG
YELLOW SEA
EAST CHINA SEA
SOUTH CHINA SEA
BAY OF BENGAL
BEIJING (PEKING)
SHANGHAI
TIANJIN
GUANGZHOU (CANTON)
KOLKATA (CALCUTTA)
Tropic of Cancer
East from Greenwich
Projection: Bonne

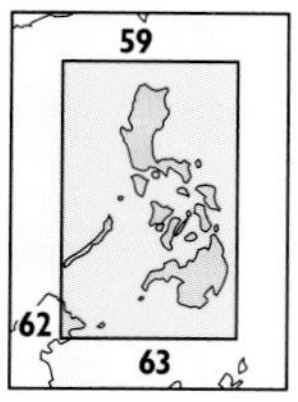

59
62   63

50 0 100 150 200 250 300 km
50 0 50 100 150 200 miles

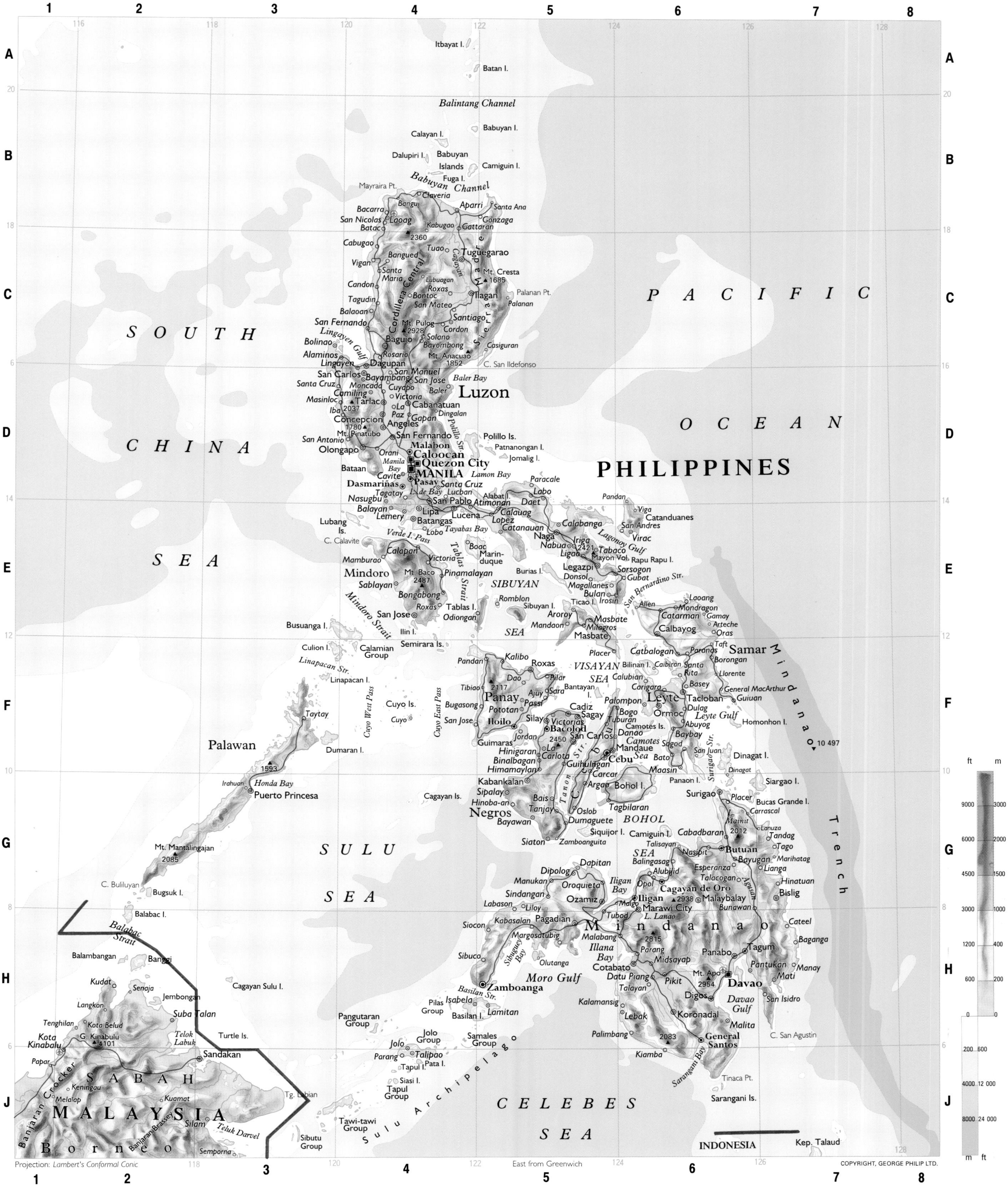

1 2 3 4 5 6 7 8

116 118 120 122 124 126 128

A Itbayat I.
Batan I.

Balintang Channel

B Calayan I.
Dalupiri I. Babuyan I.
Babuyan Camiguin I.
Islands
Fuga I.
Mayraira Pt. *Babuyan Channel*

Bacarra Bangui Santa Ana
San Nicolas Claveria Aparri Gonzaga
Bataca Laoag Kabugao Gattaran
2360

C Cabugao Tuao Tuguegarao
Vigan Bangued Lubuagan Mt. Cresta
Santa Roxas 1685 *P A C I F I C*
Maria Bontoc Ilagan Palanan Pt.
Candon San Mateo Palanan
Tagudin Santiago
Balaoan Mt. Pulog Cordon
San Fernando 2928 Solano Casiguran
Bolinao Baguio Bayombong *O C E A N*
Alaminos Rosario Mt. Anacuao
Lingayen Dagupan 1852 C. San Ildefonso

D San Carlos San Manuel
SOUTH Santa Cruz Bayambang San Jose *Baler Bay* **PHILIPPINES**
Masinloc Camiling Victoria Baler
CHINA Iba 2037 Tarlac *Luzon*
Lo Paz Gapan Dingalan
Concepcion Angeles Cabanatuan
1780 Mt. Pinatubo San Fernando Polillo Is.
San Antonio Patnanongan I.
Olongapo Malabon Jomalig I.
Orani **Caloocan**
SEA Bataan *Manila* **Quezon City** Lamon Bay Paracale Pandan
Bay **MANILA** Labo Viga Catanduanes
Cavite **Pasay** Santa Cruz Daet San Andres
Dasmariñas Lucban Calauag Virac
Nasugbu Tagaytay San Pablo Atimonan Calabanga
Balayan Lipa Lucena Lopez Naga Lagonoy Gulf
Lemery Batangas Tayabas Bay Catanauan Iriga Tabaco
Lubang Lobo Boac Marin- Nabua 2321 Rapu Rapu I.
Is. *Verde I. Pass* duque Ligao Mayon Vol.
C. Calavite Mamburao Calapan Victoria Burias I. Legazpi Sorsogon
Roxas Pinamalayan Magallanes Gubat
Mindoro Mt. Baco Tablas I. Romblon Bulan Irosin
Sablayan 2487 Sibuyan I. Donsol San Bernardino Str.
Bongabong *SIBUYAN* Ticao I. Allen
Odiongan Laoang
San Jose Aroroy Masbate Catarman Gamay
Busuanga I. Ilin I. *SEA* Mandaon Milagros Mondragon Arteche
Culion I. Semirara Is. Masbate Calbayog Oras
Calamian Pandan Placer Catbalogan Paranas Taft *Samar*
Linapacan I. Group Kalibo Bilinan I. Caibiran Santa Borongan
Linapacan Str. Roxas *VISAYAN* Rita Llorente
Taytay Dao Pilar Bantayan Calubian Basey General MacArthur
Tibiao 2117 *SEA* Carigara Guiuan
Cuyo Is. Bugasong Sara Ajuy Cadiz Palompon *Leyte* Homonhon I.
Cuyo *Panay* Silay Bogo Ormoc Dulag
Palawan Cayo East Pass Pototan Passi Sagay Tuburan Abuyog 10 497
Iloilo *Leyte Gulf*
Dumaran I. San Jose Victorias San Carlos Camotes Is. Baybay
Guimaras Jordan 2450 Danao Camotes Sagod
Hinigaran La Bacolod *Sea* Bato San Juan Dinagat I.
Palawan Binalbagan Carlota Mandaue Maasin Siargao I.
Himamaylan Guihulngan **Cebu** Panaon I. Dinagat
Kabankalan Argao Carcar Surigao Str.
Irahuan Sipalay Bais Tanjay Tagbilaran *Bohol I.* Surigao Placer
Honda Bay *Negros* Oslob Bucas Grande I.
Puerto Princesa Cagayan Is. Dumaguete *BOHOL* Carrascal
Bayawan Siquijor I. Camiguin I. Mainit
Mt. Mantalingajan Siaton Zamboanguita Cabadbaran 2012 Tandag
2085 Talisayan Nasipit Togo
C. Buliluyan *SEA* Balingasag **Butuan** Lanuza
Bugsuk I. Dapitan Esperanza Bayugan Lianga
Balabac I. Dipolog Iligan Opol Talacogan Hinatuan
Balabac Strait Manukan Oroquieta Bay **Cagayan de Oro** Bislig
Balambangan Banggi Sindangan Ozamiz **Iligan** 2938 Malaybalay
Balabac Labason Liloy Marawi City Bunawan Cateel
Kudat Kabasalan Pagadian Tubod L. Lanao Panabo Baganga
Senaja Cagayan Sulu I. Siocon *Mindanao* Tagum
Langkon Jembongan Margosatubig 2815 Malabang Parang Panabo Pantukan Manay
Tenghilan Suba Talan Sibuco *Illana* Midsayap Mati
Kota Belud Turtle Is. *Bay* Cotabato Datu Piang Pikit Mt. Apo Digos Davao San Isidro
Kota G. Kinabalu Zamboanga Talayan 2954 **Davao**
Kinabalu 4101 Pangutaran Pilas Basilan Lebak Kalamansig *Davao* Malita
Papar Group Group Str. Koronadal *Gulf*
Sandakan Isabela Palimbang C. San Agustin
Keningau Samales Lamitan
Melalap Jolo Group Kiamba
Silam Parang Talipao Jolo 2083 **General**
Tg. Labian Group **Santos**
MALAYSIA Siasi Sarangani Is.
Kuamat Group Tinaca Pt.
Semporna Tapul I. Tapul *CELEBES*
Borneo Tg. Darvel Sibutu Group
Sembronq *Sulu Archipelago* *SEA* Sarangani Is.
Teluk Darvel Tawi-tawi *INDONESIA* Kep. Talaud
Group Sibutu
Group

SULU *SEA*

SABAH

Banjaran Crocker

Projection: Lambert's Conformal Conic East from Greenwich COPYRIGHT, GEORGE PHILIP LTD.

ft m
9000 3000
6000 2000
4500 1500
3000 1000
1200 400
600 200
0 0
200 600
4000 12 000
8000 24 000
m ft

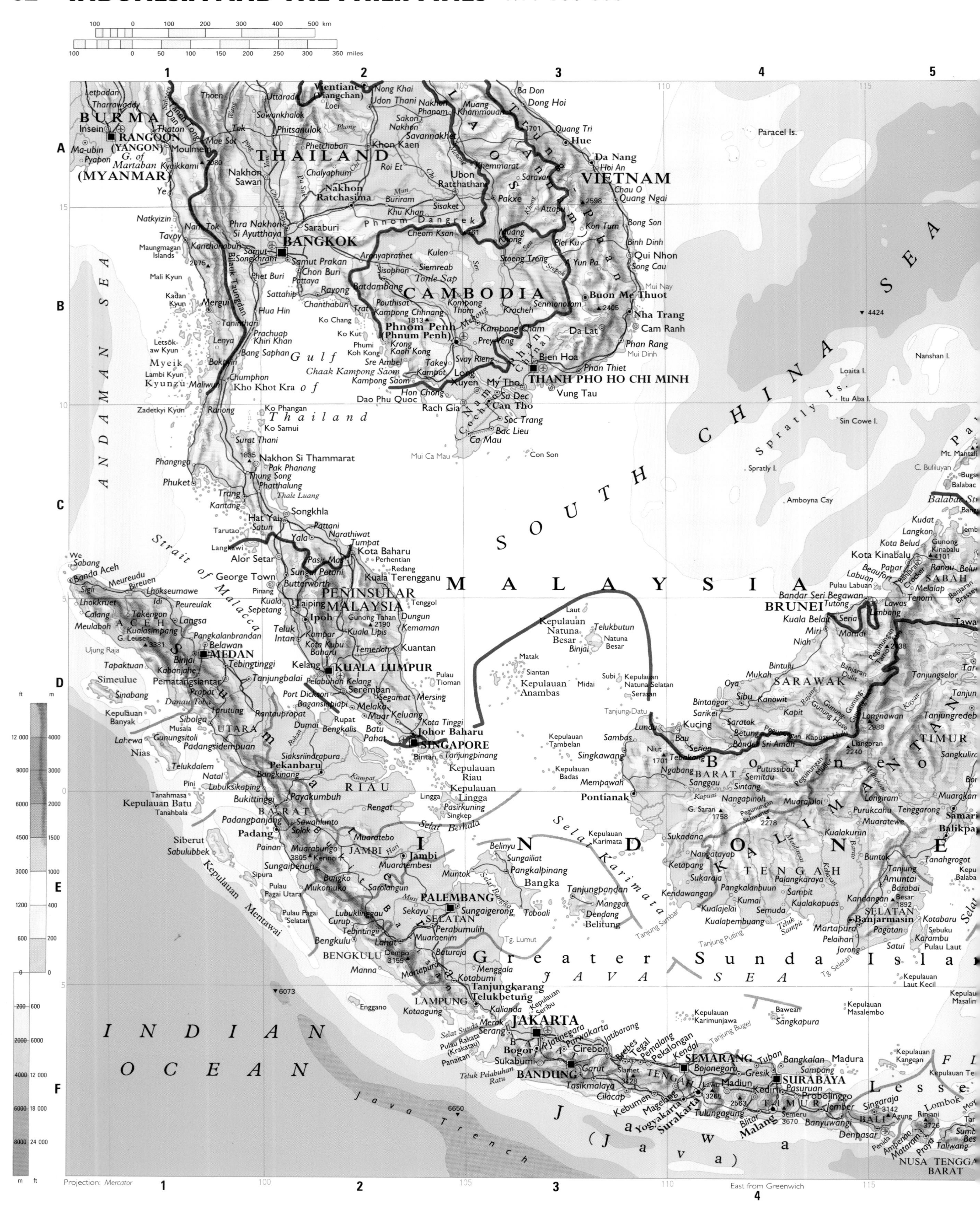

100 0 100 200 300 400 500 km
100 0 50 100 150 200 250 300 350 miles

A

BURMA
(MYANMAR)

Letpadan
Tharrawaddy
Insein
Ma-ubin
RANGOON
(YANGON)
Pyapon
G. of
Martaban
Yapon
Thaton
Moulmein
Kyaikkami
Ye

Thoen
Uttaradit
Sawankhalok
Tak
Mae Sot
Phitsanulok
Loei
Phong
Nong Khai
Udon Thani

VIENTIANE
(Viangchan)

Muang
Khammouan
Nakhon
Phanom
Savannakhet

Ba Don
Dong Hoi

Quang Tri
Hue

Da Nang
Hoi An

THAILAND

Nakhon
Sawan
Saraburi
Phra Nakhon
Si Ayutthaya
Chaiyaphum
Roi Et

Nakhon
Ratchasima
Buriram

Khon Kaen
Sakon
Nakhon

Ubon
Ratchathani
Pakse

Khammarat
Saravan

2598
Chau O
Quang Ngai
Kon Tum
Bong Son

Qui Nhon
Song Cau

B

Natkyizin
Tavoy
Maungmagan
Islands
2075

Mali Kyun

Kanchanaburi
Nan Tok
BANGKOK

Samut Prakan
Chon Buri
Pattaya

Aranyaprathet
Sisophon
Siemreab
Batdambang

Kulen
Tonle Sap

Cheom Ksan
Stoeng Treng

Plei Ku
Yun Pa

Binh Dinh

Buon Me Thuot
2405
Senmonolom

Nha Trang
Cam Ranh

VIETNAM

4424

Nanshan I.

Phet Buri
Samut
Songkhram

Ratchaburi

Sattahip
Chanthaburi
Trat

CAMBODIA
Pouthisat
Kompong Chhnang
Kompong
Thom

Kracheh
Kampong Cham

Da Lat
Phan Rang

Hua Hin
Prachuap
Khiri Khan

Ko Chang
Ko Kut

1813
Phnom Penh
(Phnum Penh)
Krong

Preah Veng

Mui Nay

Phan Thiet
Mui Dinh

Mergui
Tanintharyi

Bang Saphan

Phumi
Koh Kong
Sre Ambel

Takeo
Kampot

Svay Rieng
Long
Xuyen

My Tho

THANH PHO HO CHI MINH
Bien Hoa

Vung Tau

Letsök-
aw Kyun

Chumphon

Gulf
Chaak Kampong Saom
Kampong Saom

Hon Chong

Sa Dec

Myeik
Lambi Kyun
Kyunzu
Maliwun

Ranong

Kho Khot Kra
of
Dao Phu Quoc

Rach Gia
Can Tho
Soc Trang

C

Zadetkyi Kyun

Ko Phangan
Ko Samui

Thailand

Mui Ca Mau
Ca Mau

Bac Lieu

Con Son

Surat Thani

Phangnga
1835
Nakhon Si Thammarat
Pak Phanang

Phuket
Thung Song
Phatthalung

Trang
Thale Luang

Kantang
Songkhla

Tarutao
Satun
Hat Yai
Pattani
Narathiwat

Langkawi
Yala
Tumpat

Alor Setar
Pasir Mas
Kota Baharu
Perhentian

George Town
Sungai Petani
Kuala Terengganu

SOUTH

Paracel Is.

Loaita I.
Itu Aba I.

Spratly Is.

Sin Cowe I.

Amboyna Cay

Spratly I.

Mt. Mantali
C. Buliluyan
Balabac
Balabac Str.

CHINA

We
Sabang
Banda Aceh

Sigli
Meureudu
Bireuen

Lhokseumawe
Idi
Peureulak
Langsa

Kualasimpang
Pangkalanbrandan

Pinang
Butterworth

Taiping
Ipoh

Gunong Tahan
2190
Kuala Lipis

Tenggol

Dungun
Kemaman

MALAYSIA

Kudat
Langkon
Kota Belud
Gunong
Kinabalu
4101
Kota Kinabalu
Papar
Ranau
Beaufort

SEA

Pulau
Labuan
Melalap
Tenom

SABAH

D

Meulaboh
Calang

Lhokkruet

ACEH

G. Leuser
3381

SUMATERA

Takengon

Binjai
MEDAN
Belawan
Tebingtinggi

PENINSULAR
MALAYSIA

Kelang
KUALA LUMPUR
Teluk
Intan
Kampar
Kota Kubu

Kuantan
Temerloh

Pulau
Tioman

Laut
Kepulauan Natuna
Besar
Binjai

Telukbutun
Natuna
Besar

BRUNEI
Bandar Seri Begawan
Kuala Belait
Seria
Miri

Tutong
Lawas
Limbang

Niah
Matudi

2438

Ujung Raja
Tapaktuan

Sinabang
Simeulue

Pematangsiantar
Prapat
Danau Toba
Parapat

Tanjungbalai
Port Dickson
Seremban
Bagansiapiapi
Dumai

Segamat
Melaka
Keluang
Mersing

Rupat
Muar
Batu
Pahat

Kota Tinggi
Johor Baharu

SINGAPORE

Matak
Siantan
Subi
Kepulauan
Natuna Selatan
Serasan

Kepulauan
Anambas
Midai

Tanjung-Datu

Bintulu
Oya
Mukah

Sibu
Kanowit
Kapit

SARAWAK

Kuching
Bau
Serian

1701
Tebedung
Bandar Sri Aman

Niut

Betung

2988

Loagnawan

Tanjungselor

Tanjungredeb

Tanjun

E

Lahewa
Nias
Gunungsitoli
Musala

Sibolga
Tarutung

Telukdalam
Natal

Kepulauan
Banyak

Kepulauan
Batu
Tanahmasa
Tanahbala

Siberut
Sabulubbek

Pulau
Pagai Utara

Pulau
Pagai
Selatan

Sipura

Padangsidempuan

Kabanjahe

UTARA

Bangkinang

Pekanbaru

Siaksriindrapura

Bengkalis
Kampar

RIAU
Rengat

Bukittinggi
Payakumbuh

BARAT
Padangpanjang
Solok
Sawahlunto

Padang
Painan

Muaratebo

Bintan
Tanjungpinang

Kepulauan
Riau

Kepulauan
Lingga

Pasirkuning
Singkep

Tambelan

Singkawang

Sambas
Mempawah

Kepulauan
Badas

Pontianak

Ngabang

BARAT

Sanggau
Sintang

Semitau

Putussibau

KALIMANTAN

Longiram

TENGAH

Muarajuloi
2278

Sukadana

Ketapang

Kualakurun

Purukcahu
Tenggarong

Muaratewe

Samari
Balikpapan

I

N

D

O

N

E

S

F

Muarabungo
JAMBI
Jambi

Kerinci
3805
Sungaipenuh

Bangko

Muaratembesi

Muntok

Belinyu

Sungailiat

Pangkalpinang

Bangka

Selat
Berhala

Kepulauan
Karimata

Nangatayap
G. Saran
1758

Sukadana

Pangkalanbuun
Sampit

Nangapinoh

Kumai

Kendawangan

Semuda

Kualapembuang

Kualakapuas
Sampit

Nangatayap

Barabai
1892
Kandangan

SELATAN
Banjarmasin
Martapura
Pelaihari

Kotabaru
Sebuku
Karamb

E

Lubuklinggau
Curup
Tebingtinggi

Sekayu
Sungaigerong
PALEMBANG

SELATAN
Perabumulih

Lahat
Muaraenim

Sarolangun

Toboali
Belitung

Tanjungpandan
Dendang

Manggar

Belitung

Amuntai
Barabai

Satui
Jorong

Bengkulu

BENGKULU
3159
Dempo

Menggala

Baturaja

Martapura

Greater
Sunda

Tanjung Puting

Teluk
Sampit

Tanjung
Selatan

Kepulauan
Laut Kecil

Kepulauan
Masalima

F

ft m

12 000 4000
9000 3000
6000 2000
4500 1500
3000 1000
1200 400
600 200
0 0
200 600
2000 6000
4000 12 000
6000 18 000
8000 24 000
m ft

6073

Manna

INDIAN

OCEAN

LAMPUNG
Tanjungkarang
Telukbetung
Kotaagung

Enggano

Kotabumi

Kalianda

Merak
Serang

Tanjung
Lumut

Islan

Kepulauan
Karimunjawa

Bawean

Kepulauan
Kangean

Kepulauan
Salembo

Java Trench

6650

Pulau Rakata
(Krakatau)

JAKARTA
Bogor
Sukabumi
BANDUNG

Purwakarta
Cirebon

Teluk Pelabuhan
Ratu

BALI

Garut
Tasikmalaya

Slamet
3428
Cilacap

Kebumen

Magelang

JAVA

Brebes
Tegal
Pemalang
Pekalongan
Kendal

SEMARANG

TENGAH
Bojonegoro
Gresik

Madiun
Surakarta
Yogyakarta
3265
Blitar
2563

Kediri
SURABAYA
Pasuruan
Probolinggo
3670
Malang
Semeru

Tuban
Bangkalan
Sampang
Madura

Pamekasan

Sangkapura

TIMUR
Jember
Banyuwangi

Singaraja
3142
Rinjani
3726
Agung
Denpasar

Lombok
Mataram

Penida
Nusa

Lesse

Fl

NUSA TENGGARA
BARAT

Projection: Mercator

East from Greenwich

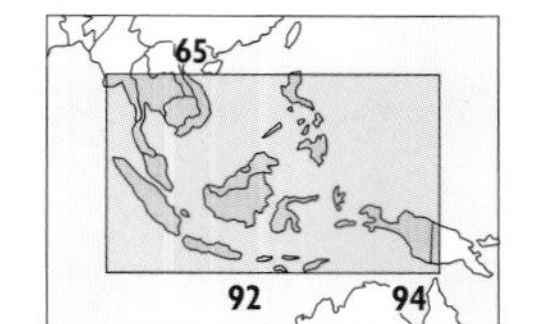

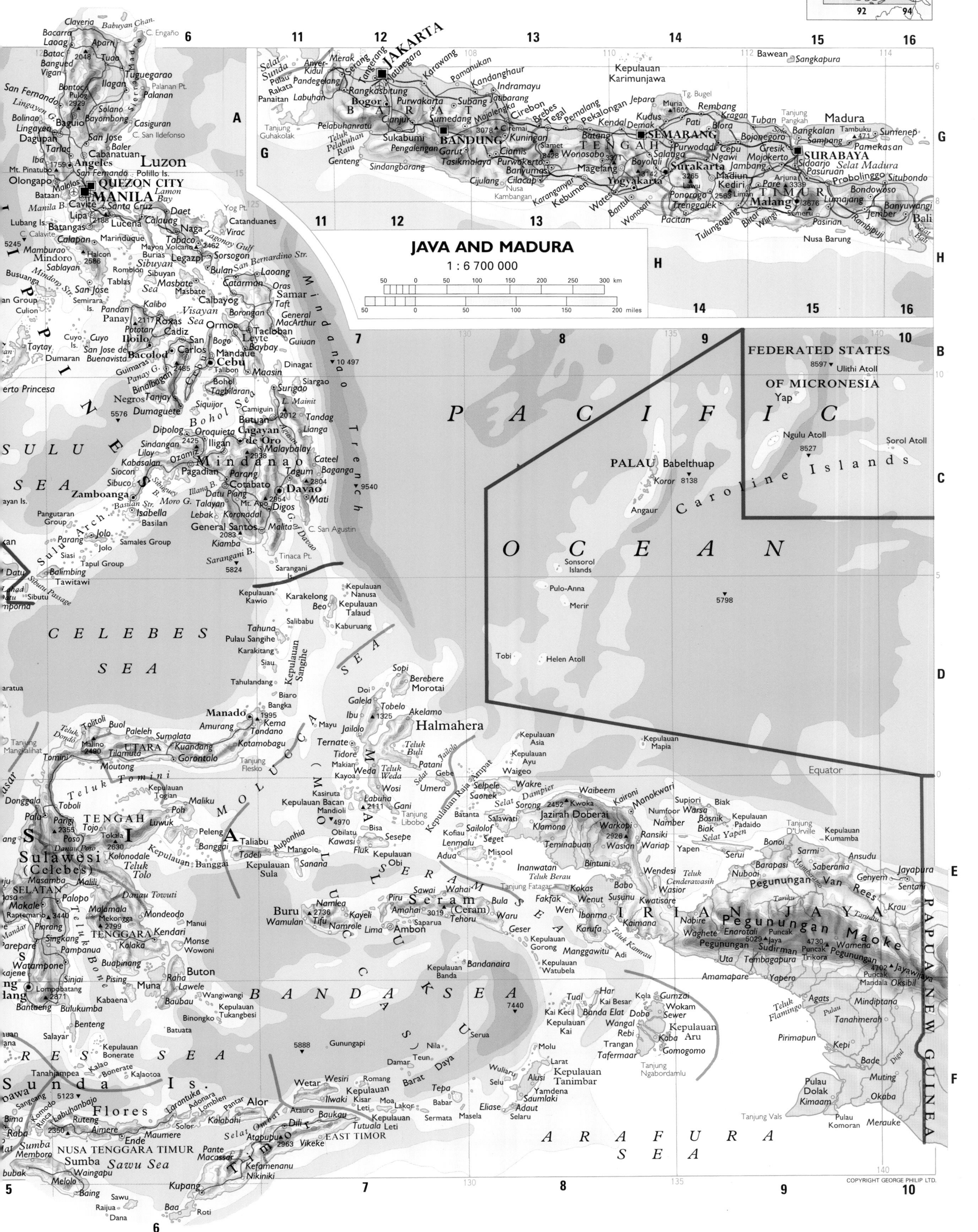

JAVA AND MADURA

1 : 6 700 000

50 0 50 100 150 200 250 300 km

50 0 50 100 150 200 miles

FEDERATED STATES

OF MICRONESIA

COPYRIGHT GEORGE PHILIP LTD.

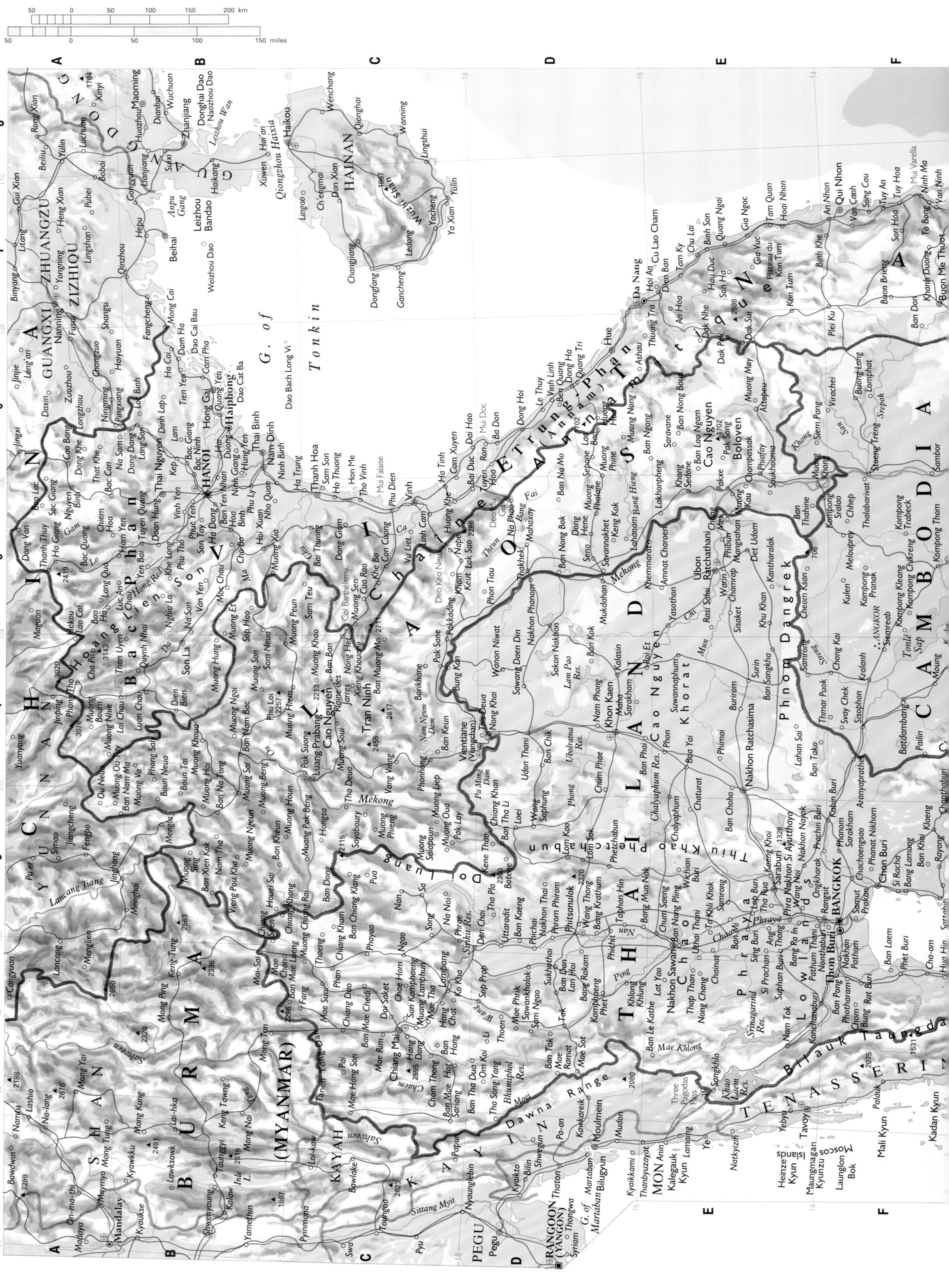

50 0 50 100 150 200 km
50 0 50 100 150 miles
A B C D E F
1 2 3 4 5 6 7 8
GUANGXI ZHUANGZU ZIZHIQU
YUNNAN
GUANGDONG
HAINAN
Haikou
Qiongzhou Haixia
Leizhou Bandao
Zhanjiang
Nanning
G. of Tonkin
HANOI
Haiphong
Hong Gai
Nam Dinh
Thanh Hoa
Vinh
Hue
Da Nang
VIETNAM
LAOS
Vientiane (Viangchan)
Luang Prabang
Tran Ninh
Cao Nguyen
Mekong
THAILAND
Khorat
Nakhon Ratchasima
Ubon Ratchathani
Udon Thani
Khon Kaen
Chiang Mai
Chao Phraya
BANGKOK
Thon Buri
CAMBODIA
Phnom Dangrek
Tonlé Sap
Battambang
Qui Nhon
BURMA (MYANMAR)
SHAN
KAYAH
KAYIN
MON
PEGU
Mandalay
Taunggyi
Moulmein
Martaban
G. of Martaban
RANGOON (YANGON)
Pegu
Salween
Sittang Myit
Dawna Range
TENASSERIM
Bilauktaung
Three Pagodas Pass
Tavoy
Mekong

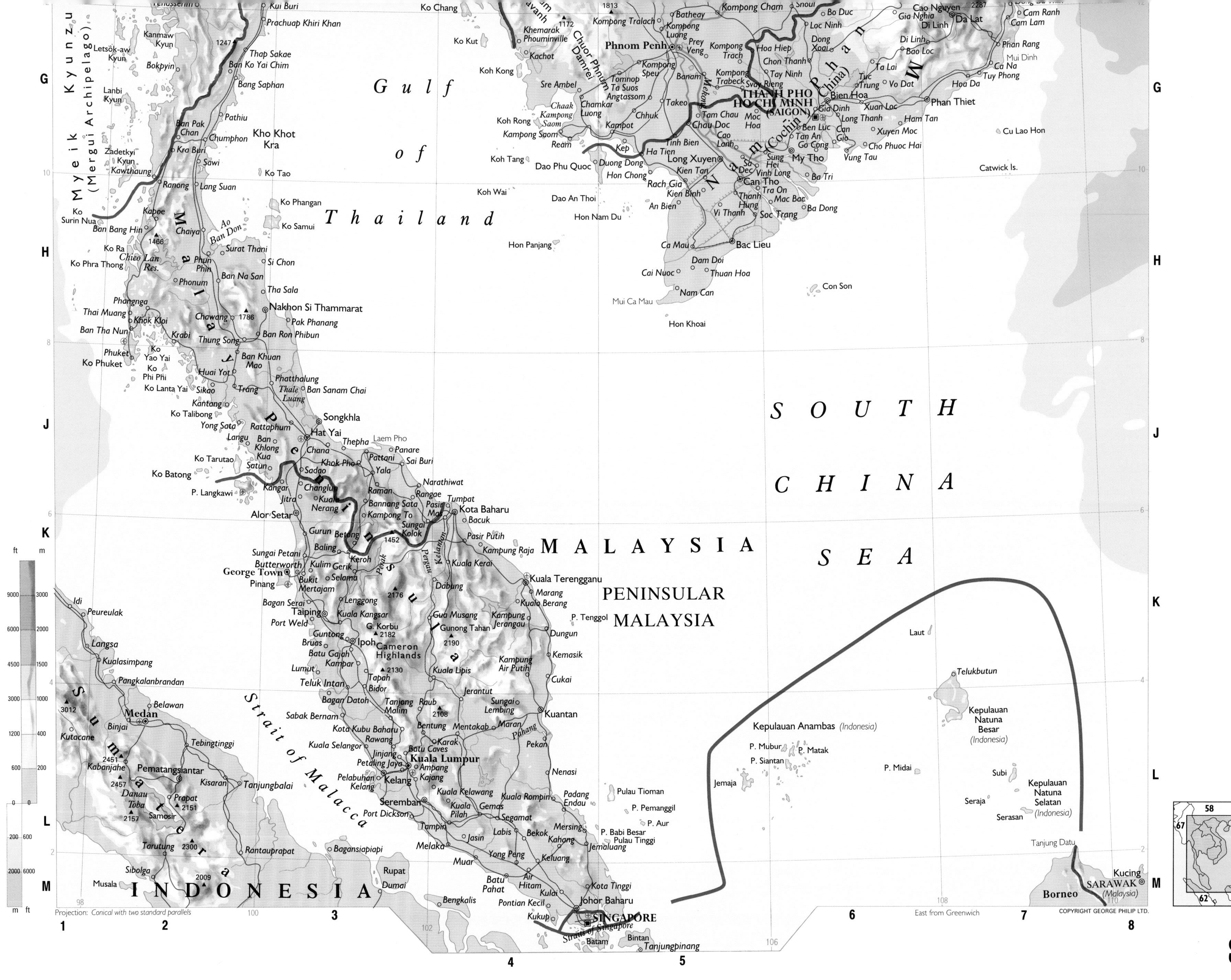

58 62
67 67

SARAWAK®
Kucing
(Malaysia)
Borneo

Tanjung Datu

Serasan

Subi

Kepulauan Natuna Selatan
(Indonesia)

Seraja

Kepulauan Natuna Besar
(Indonesia)

Telukbutun

Laut

P. Midai

Kepulauan Anambas (Indonesia)

P. Mubur
P. Matak

P. Siantan

Jemaja

East from Greenwich

108   106

S O U T H   C H I N A   S E A

Catwick Is.

Cu Lao Hon

Cam Ranh
Cam Lam
Phan Rang
Mui Dinh
Ca Na
Tuy Phong
Hoa Da
Phan Thiet
Ham Tan
2287
Da Lat
Di Linh
Cao Nguyen
Gia Nghia
Di Linh
Ta Lai
Vo Dat
Xuyen Moc
Cho Phuoc Hai
Vung Tau
Ba Dong

M a
Bien Hoa
THANH PHO HO CHI MINH
SAIGON
Long Thanh

Con Son

Kampong Cham
Phnom Penh®
Kompong Luong
Svay Rieng
Kompong Trabeck
Mekong
Takeo
Banam
Prey Veng
Kompong Trach
Tan An
My Tho
Go Cong
Ba Tri
Tra Vinh

Hon Khoai

Ba Duc
Loc Ninh
Dong Xoai
Tuc Trung
Hoa Hiep
Chon Thanh
Tay Ninh
Kampong Speu
Ben Luc
Long An

N a m

Moc Bac
Soc Trang
Bac Lieu
Thanh
Vi Thanh
Thuan Hoa

Dong Dong
Hon Chong
Kep
Ha Tien
Tinh Bien
Chau Doc
Long Xuyen
Kien An
Kien Binh
Rach Gia
An Bien
Ca Mau
Dam Doi
Nam Can
Cai Nuoc
Cai Rong
Can Tho
Sung Hieu
Vinh Long

1813
Khemarak
1172
Chuor Phnum Damrei
Phouminville
Sre Ambel
Kampong Saom
Kampong Som
Ream
Chaak
Kampong Trach
Duong Dong
Dao Phu Quoc
Dao An Thoi
Hon Nam Du
Hon Panjang
Mui Ca Mau

Kachot
Koh Kong
Koh Rong
Kampong Saom
Koh Tang
Koh Wai

Ko Kut
Ko Chang
Ko Kong
Ko Ra
Ko Samui
Ko Phangan
Ko Tao

G u l f   o f   T h a i l a n d

P E N I N S U L A R   M A L A Y S I A

M A L A Y S I A

Kuala Terengganu
Marang
Kuala Berang
Dungun
Kemasik
Cukai
Kuantan
Pekan

Kota Baharu
Bacuk
Pasir Putih
Kampung Raja
Kampung To
Kampung Air Putih
Sungai Lembing
Maran
Kuala Rompin
Nenasi
Padang Endau
Mersing

P. Tenggol
P. Tioman
P. Pemanggil
P. Aur
P. Babi Besar
Pulau Tinggi

Pasir Mas
Tumpat
Kota Baharu
Rangae
Sungai Kolok
Bannang Sata
Kampong To
Kelantan
Dabong
Gua Musang
Gunong Tahan
2190
Kuala Lipis
2130
Jerantut
2108
Raub
Bentung
Karak
Temerloh
Kuala Kerau
Mentakab
Segamat
Labis
Gemas
Jasin
Yong Peng
Batu Pahat
Bengkalis

Pergau
Pengkalan
Yala
Pattani
Saiburi
Ra-ngae
1452
Keroh
2276
Grik
2182
Ipoh
Cameron Highlands
Tanjong Malim
Batu Caves
Kuala Lumpur
Kelang
Port Dickson

Narathiwat
Tak Bai
Sai Buri
Panare
Laem Pho
Thepha
Chana
Khlong
Songkhla
Hat Yai
Sadao
Changlun
Nerang
Baling
Kulim
Selama
Lenggong
Kuala Kangsar
Guntong
Bruas
Batu Gajah
Tapah
Bidor
Teluk Intan
Sabak Bernam
Kuala Selangor
Kuala Kubu Bahru
Rawang
Ampang
Petaling Jaya
Kajang
Sepang
Seremban
Melaka
Muar
Tampin
Tangkak

Nakhon Si Thammarat
Pak Phanang
Phatthalung
Trang
Ban Sanam Chai
Liyang
Thung
Huai Yot
Sikao
Kantang
Ko Talibong
Yong Sata
La-ngu
Satun
Langu
Ko Tarutao
P. Langkawi
Ko Batong

Rattaphum
Phattalung
Ban Khuan
Ban Na San
Ban Don
1786

Alor Setar
Kangar
Sungai Petani
Butterworth
George Town
Pinang
Bagan Serai
Port Weld
Taiping
Lumut
Kampar

Strait of Malacca

Bagansiapiapi
Rupat
Port Dickson
Kelang
Pelabuhan Kelang
Kota Selangor

I N D O N E S I A

Tanjungbalai
Ksaran
Rantauprapat
Tebingtinggi
Pematangsiantar
2151
Prapat
2181
Samosir
Tobu
2457
Kabanjahe
2451
2457
Danau Toba
2157
Medan
Binjai
Belawan
Pangkalanbrandan
Pangkalansusu

Kualasimpang
Langsa
Peureulak
Idi
Musala
Sibolga
Tarutung
2009
230
Kutacane
3012

Sumatera
Sumatera

Bintan
Batam
Tanjungpinang
Johor Bahru
SINGAPORE
Kota Tinggi
Kukup
Pontian Kecil

Hon Thai
Ca Mau

T h a i l a n d

M a l a y   P e n i n s u l a

M y e i k
(Mergui Archipelago)
K y u n z u

Kui Buri
Prachuap Khiri Khan
1247
Thap Sakae
Bang Ko Yai Chim
Bang Saphan
Chumphon
Lang Suan
Ban Pak Chan
Kra Buri
Ranong
Kapoe
1486
Chiao Lan Res.
Khao Phanom
Phangnga
Thai Muang
Phuket
Ko Phuket
Ko Phra Thong

Kra
Kho Khot
Pathiu
Bang Saphan
Sawi
Surat Thani
Phunphin
Chaiya
Ao Ban Don
Ban Ta Khun
Krabi
Ko Lanta Yai
Phi Phi
Ko Yao Yai
Ko Yao
Ban Tha Nun

Surin Nua
Ko
Kawthaung
Zadetkyi Kyun
Lanbi Kyun
Bokpyin
Letsôk-aw Kyun
Kannaw Kyun

Tenasserim

ft
9000
6000
4500
3000
1500
1200
600
400
200
0
200 600
2000 6000
m ft

m
3000
2000
1500
1000
400
200

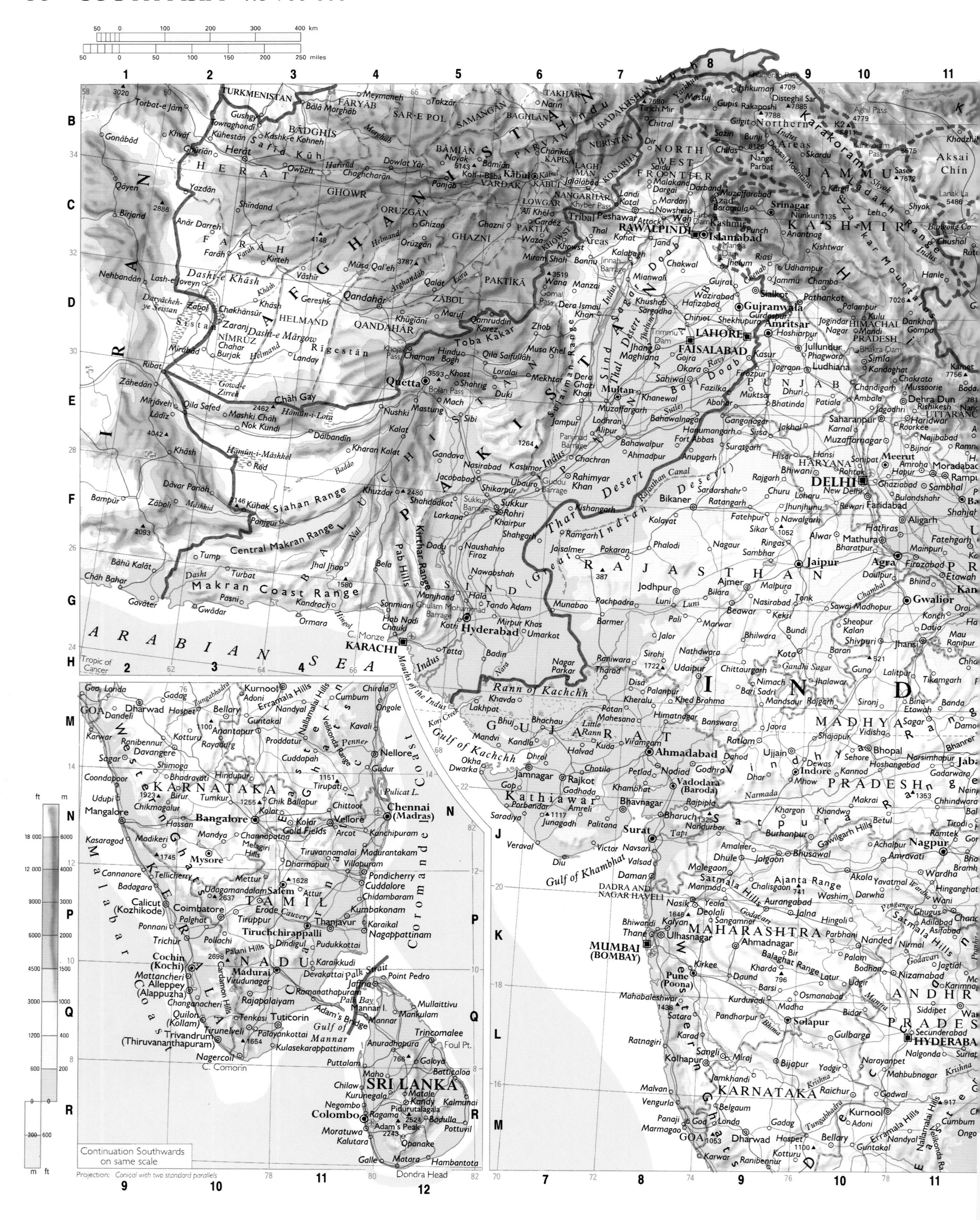

TURKMENISTAN
ARABIAN SEA
AFGHANISTAN
PAKISTAN
IRAN
INDIA
SRI LANKA
BALUCHISTAN
SIND
PUNJAB
RAJASTHAN
GUJARAT
MADHYA PRADESH
MAHARASHTRA
KARNATAKA
TAMIL NADU
KERALA
HARYANA
HIMACHAL PRADESH
JAMMU & KASHMIR
NORTH WEST FRONTIER
Northern Areas
Hindu Kush
Karakoram Range
Thar Desert
Great Indian Desert
Rann of Kachchh
Gulf of Kachchh
Gulf of Khambhat
Kathiawar
Makran Coast Range
Central Makran Range
Siahan Range
Kirthar Range
Sulaiman Range
Toba Kakar
Western Ghats
Eastern Ghats
Satpura Range
Vindhya Range
Malabar Coast
Coromandel Coast
Palk Strait
Gulf of Mannar
Adam's Bridge
Kabul
Islamabad
RAWALPINDI
LAHORE
FAISALABAD
Multan
Quetta
Peshawar
KARACHI
Hyderabad
Herat
Qandahar
DELHI
Jaipur
Agra
Ahmadabad
Surat
MUMBAI (BOMBAY)
Pune (Poona)
Bangalore
Chennai (Madras)
Madurai
Colombo
Srinagar
Amritsar
Gujranwala
Nagpur
Indore
Bhopal
Gwalior
Vadodara (Baroda)
Solapur
Tropic of Cancer
Continuation Southwards on same scale
Projection: Conical with two standard parallels

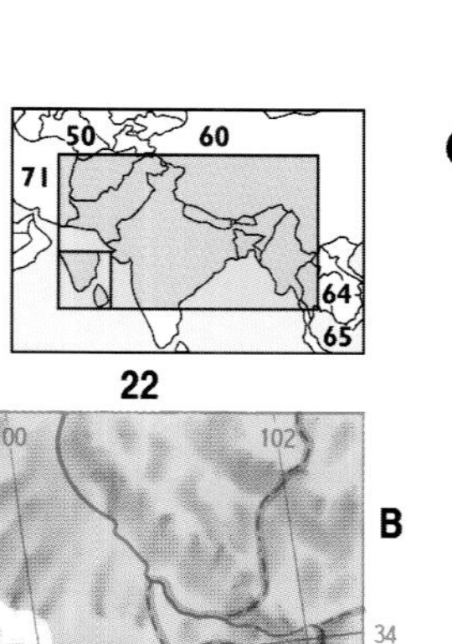

50
60
71
64
65

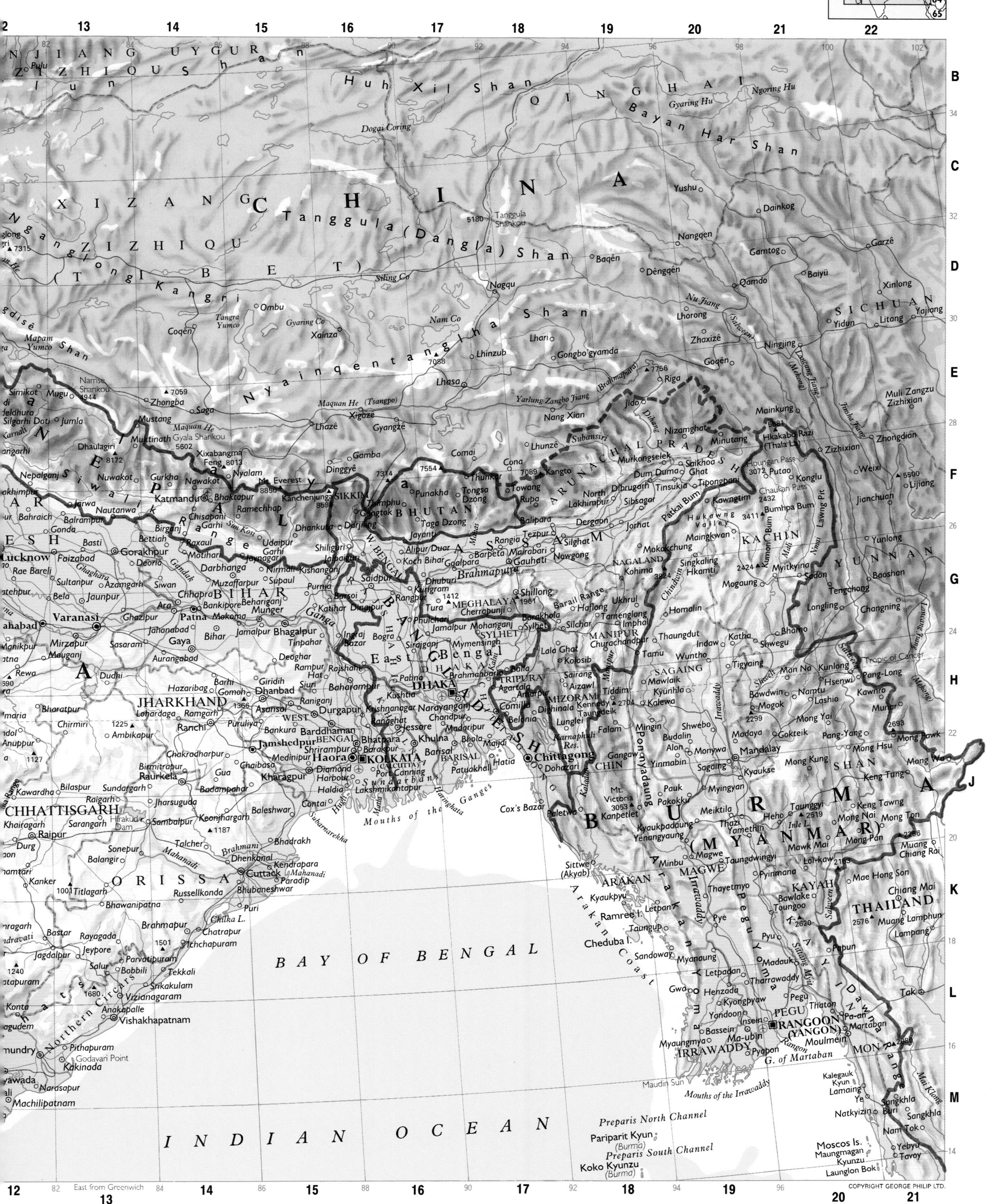

12
13
14
15
16
17
18
19
20
21
22
B
C
D
E
F
G
H
J
K
L
M
C H I N A
XIZANG ZIZHIQU (TIBET)
XINJIANG UYGUR ZIZHIQU
Kunlun Shan
Huh Xil Shan
Q I N G H A I
Bayan Har Shan
Tanggula (Dangla) Shan
Tanggula Shankou
Nganglong Kangri
Gangdisê Shan
Nyainqentanglha Shan
Dogai Coring
Gyaring Hu
Ngoring Hu
Siling Co
Nam Co
Tangra Yumco
Gyaring Co
Mapam Yumco
Yushu
Dainkog
Nangqên
Garzê
Gamtog
Baqên
Dêngqên
Qamdo
Baiyü
Xinlong
Nagqu
Nu Jiang
Lhorong
S I C H U A N
Yajiang
Yidun
Litang
Zhaxizê
Ombu
Coqên
Xainza
Lhari
Gongbo'gyamda
Goqên
Ningjing
Lhinzub
Lhasa
Riga
Mainkung
Muli Zangzu Zizhixian
Zhongba
Saga
Maquan He (Tsangpo)
Yarlung Zangbo Jiang
Xigazê
Gyangzê
Lhazê
Nang Xian
Jido
Nizamghat
Zhongdian
Zizhixian
Lhünzê
Comai
Gamba
Dinggyê
Cona
Weixi
Lijiang
Jianchuan
Simikot
Mugu
Jumla
Dhaulagiri
Mustang
Muktinath
Gyala Shankou
Xixabangma Feng 8013
Nyalam
Mt. Everest 8850
Kanchenjunga 8598
N E P A L
Siwalik Range
Nepalganj
Nuwakot
Gurkha
Katmandu
Bhaktapur
Ramechhap
Balrampur
Bahraich
Gonda
Basti
Gorakhpur
Bettiah
Birganj
Raxaul
Motihari
Dhankuta
Udaipur Garhi
SIKKIM
Gangtok
Darjiling
Thimphu
Punakha
Tongsa Dzong
BHUTAN
Taga Dzong
Jayanti
Thunkar
Towang
Rupa
ARUNACHAL PRADESH
Murkongselek
North Lakhimpur
Dibrugarh
Tinsukia
Putao
Konglu
Hkakabo Razi
Minutang
Balipara
Tezpur
Dergaon
Jorhat
Sibsagar
Patkai Bum
Hukawng Valley
KACHIN
Rangia
Barpeta
Mairabari
Nowgong
Gauhati
ASSAM
Silghat
Brahmaputra
Shiligiri
Jalpaiguri
Alipur Duar
Koch Bihar
Goalpara
W. BENGAL
Dhubri
Shillong
MEGHALAYA
Cherrapunji
Tura
NAGALAND
Kohima
MANIPUR
Imphal
Ukhrul
Tamenglong
Silchar
Haflong
Barail Range
Mokokchung
Singkaling Hkamti
Myitkyina
Mogaung
Bhamo
Katha
Shwegu
Y U N N A N
Yunlong
Baoshan
Tengchong
Longling
Changning
Lucknow
Faizabad
Rae Bareli
Sultanpur
Azamgarh
Deoria
Gandak
Darbhanga
Muzaffarpur
Siwan
Chhapra
B I H A R
Patna
Mokama
Munger
Bhagalpur
Gaya
Bihar
Jahanabad
Varanasi
Mirzapur
Sasaram
Aurangabad
Ganga
Purnia
Katihar
Dinajpur
Rangpur
Saidpur
Kurigram
Bogra
Sirajganj
Mymensingh
Jamalpur
SYLHET
Sylhet
East Bengal
BANGLADESH
Rajshahi
Pabna
DHAKA
Kushtia
Brahmanbaria
TRIPURA
Agartala
Comilla
Chandpur
Narayanganj
Jessore
Khulna
Barisal
BARISAL
Bhola
Hatia
Chittagong
Dohazari
Cox's Bazar
Sundarbans
Mouths of the Ganges
MIZORAM
Aizawl
Lunglei
Tiddim
Falam
Kalewa
CHIN
Mt. Victoria 3053
Kanpetlet
Paletwa
JHARKHAND
Hazaribag
Dhanbad
Giridih
Ranchi
Lohardaga
Ramgarh
Asansol
Durgapur
Barddhaman
Bankura
Purulia
Jamshedpur
WEST BENGAL
Kolkata (Calcutta)
Haora
Shrirampur
Medinipur
Kharagpur
Diamond Harbour
Haldia
Contai
Chakradharpur
Chaibasa
Raurkela
Jharsuguda
Sambalpur
Keonjhargarh
Baleshwar
Bhadrakh
Kendrapara
Paradip
Cuttack
Bhubaneshwar
Puri
Chilka L.
O R I S S A
CHHATTISGARH
Raipur
Durg
Bilaspur
Raigarh
Kawardha
Khairagarh
Sarangarh
Hirakud Dam
Mahanadi
Brahmani
Talcher
Dhenkanal
Sonepur
Balangir
Kanker
Titlagarh
Bhawanipatna
Russellkonda
Brahmapur
Chatrapur
Ichchapuram
Bastar
Jagdalpur
Jeypore
Rayagada
Parvatipuram
Bobbili
Salur
Tekkali
Srikakulam
Vizianagaram
Anakapalle
Vishakhapatnam
Northern Circars
Pithapuram
Godavari Point
Kakinada
Narasapur
Machilipatnam
Bharatpur
Chirmiri
Ambikapur
Anuppur
BAY OF BENGAL
I N D I A N   O C E A N
Preparis North Channel
Pariparit Kyun (Burma)
Preparis South Channel
Koko Kyunzu (Burma)
B U R M A (MYANMAR)
SAGAING
Mawlaik
Kyunhla
Homalin
Thaungdut
Tamu
Indaw
Wuntho
Tigyaing
Mogok
Namtu
Lashio
Hsenwi
Kunlong
Man Na
Tropic of Cancer
Pang-Long
Kawnro
Munar
Mong Yai
Pang-Yang
Mong Hsu
Mong Pawk
Mong Wa
Shwebo
Budalin
Alon
Monywa
Mandalay
Madaya
Gokteik
Sagaing
Kyaukse
Mong Kung
SHAN
Keng Tung
Yinmabin
Pakokku
Pauk
Myingyan
Meiktila
Thazi
Yamethin
Taunggyi
Heho
Inle L.
Mong Nai
Mong Ton
Keng Tawng
Mawk Mai
Mong Pan
Muang Chiang Rai
Kyaukpadaung
Yenangyaung
Minbu
MAGWE
Magwe
Taungdwingyi
Pyinmana
Loi-kaw
KAYAH
Mae Hong Son
Chiang Mai
THAILAND
Lampang
Muang Lamphun
Thayetmyo
Pyu
Bawlake
Toungoo
Sittwe (Akyab)
ARAKAN
Kyaukpyu
Ramree I.
Cheduba I.
Taungup
Sandoway
Arakan Coast
Arakan Yoma
Pegu Yoma
Irrawaddy
Prome
Pye
Myanaung
Letpadan
Tharrawaddy
Henzada
Gwa
Madauk
Sittang Myit
Kyongbyaw
Pegu
PEGU
Yandoon
Bassein
Insein
RANGOON (YANGON)
Thaton
Pa-an
Martaban
Moulmein
Myaungmya
Ma-ubin
IRRAWADDY
Pyapon
G. of Martaban
Mouths of the Irrawaddy
Maudin Sun
MON
Kalegauk Kyun
Lamaing
Ye
Natkyizin
Sangkhla Buri
Nam Tok
Yebyu
Tavoy
Moscos Is.
Maungmagan Kyunzu
Launglon Bok
Tak
Salween
Mekong
Chindwin
Karnaphuli Res.
Ponnyadaung
East from Greenwich

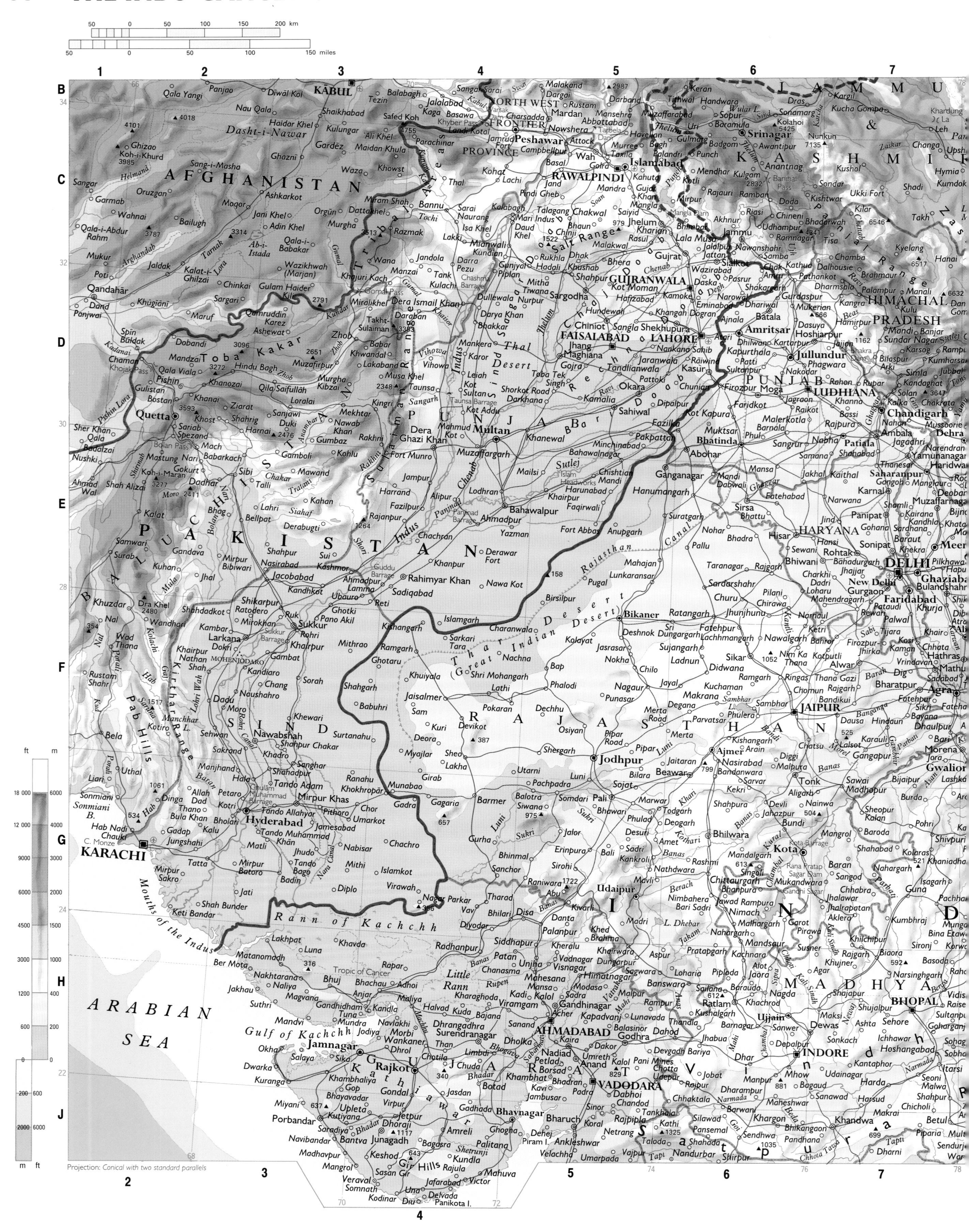

Projection: Conical with two standard parallels

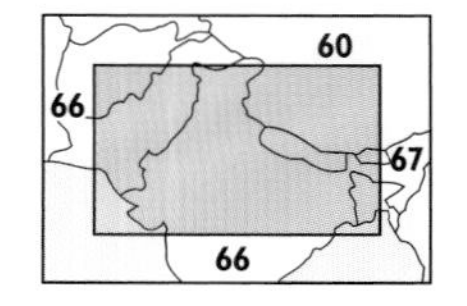

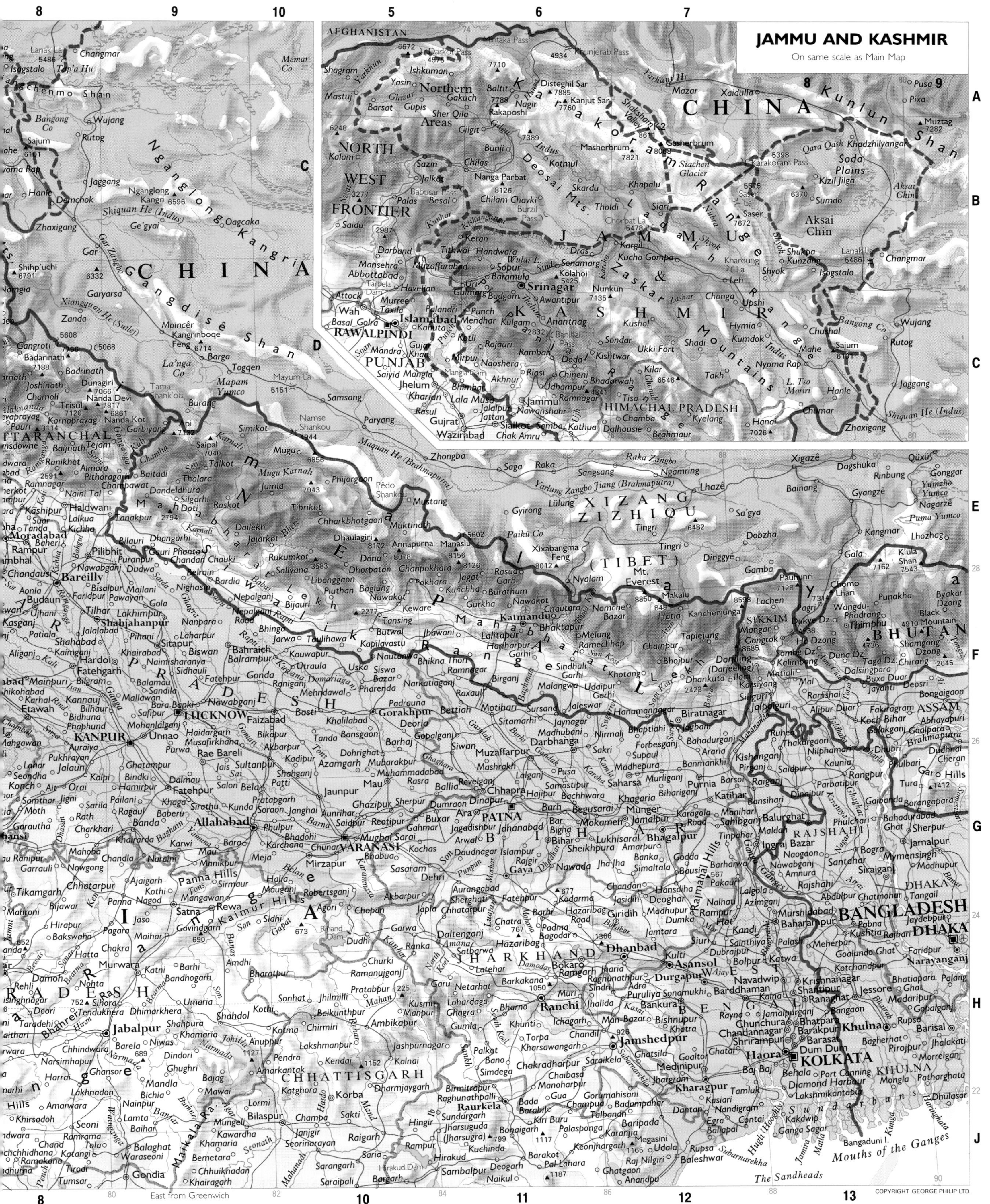

JAMMU AND KASHMIR
On same scale as Main Map

COPYRIGHT GEORGE PHILIP LTD.

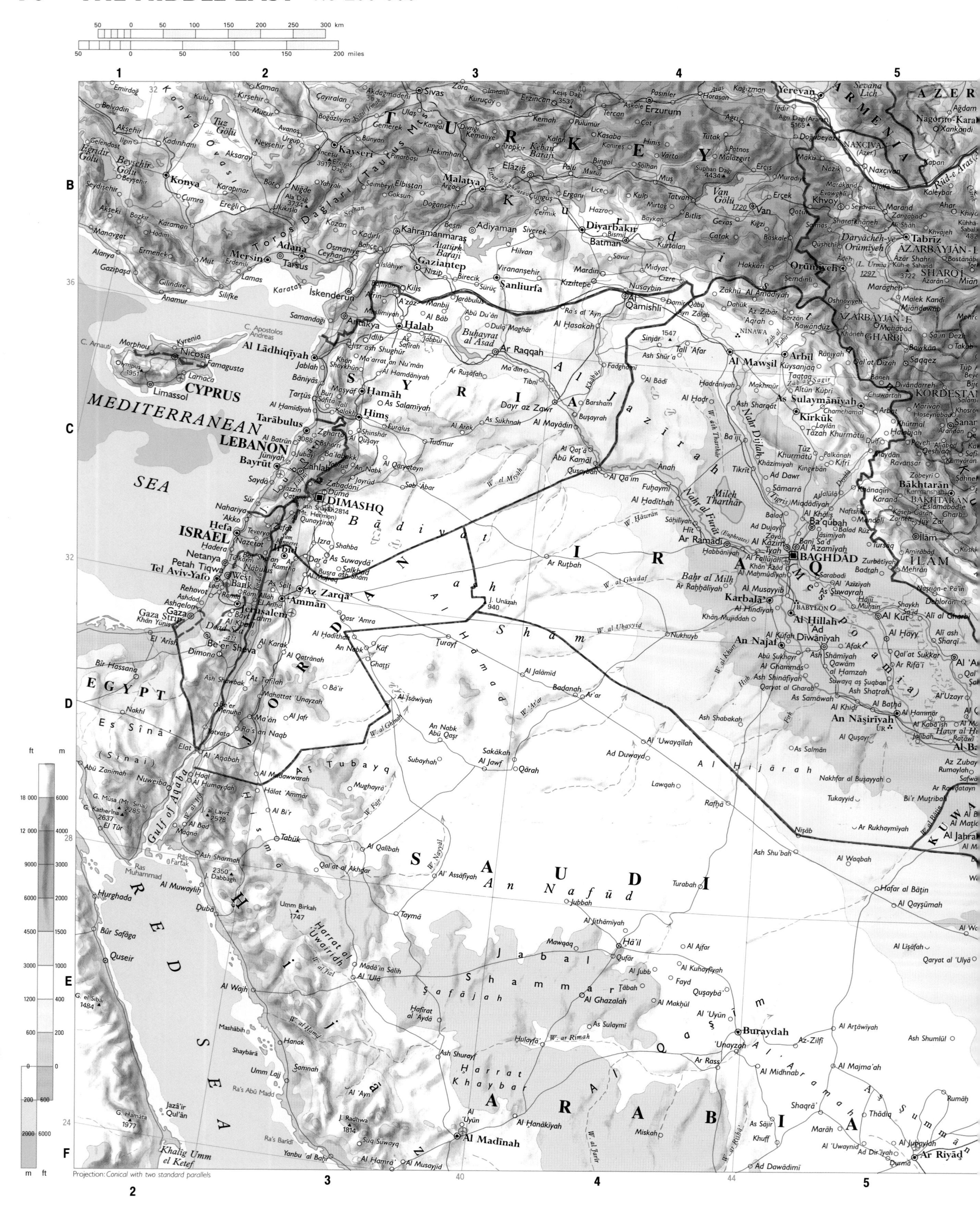

50 0 50 100 150 200 250 300 km
50 0 50 100 150 200 miles
1 2 3 4 5
B C D E F
TURKEY
SYRIA
IRAQ
JORDAN
SAUDI ARABIA
EGYPT
ISRAEL
LEBANON
CYPRUS
ARMENIA
KUWAIT
MEDITERRANEAN SEA
RED SEA
Gulf of Aqaba
Es Sînâ' (Sinai)
Bādiyat ash Shām
Al Jazīrah
Mesopotamia
An Nafūd
Al Ḥamād
Jabal Shammar
Al Ḥijārah
Toros Dağları (Taurus Mts.)
Kurdistan
Ḥijāz
Nicosia
DIMASHQ
BAGHDĀD
'Ammān
Jerusalem
Bayrūt
Halab
Ḥimṣ
Ḥamāh
Al Lādhiqīyah
Tarābulus
Tel Aviv-Yafo
Gaza
Al Mawṣil
Kirkūk
Arbīl
Karbalā'
An Najaf
Al Madīnah
Ar Riyāḍ
Ḥā'il
Buraydah
Tabūk
Al 'Aqabah
Konya
Adana
Mersin
Kayseri
Malatya
Diyarbakır
Erzurum
Yerevan
Tabrīz
Van Gölü
Daryācheh-ye Orūmīyeh
Sanliurfa
Gaziantep
Dayr az Zawr
Ar Raqqah
Ar Ruṭbah
Ar Ramādī
Dead Sea
ft m
18 000 6000
12 000 4000
9000 3000
6000 2000
4500 1500
3000 1000
1200 400
600 200
0 0
200 600
2000 6000
m ft
Projection: Conical with two standard parallels

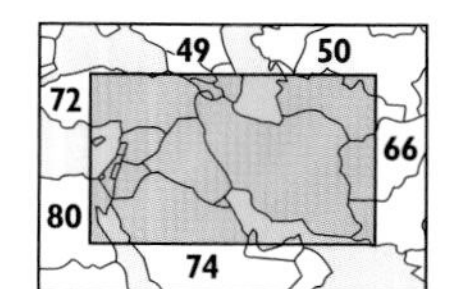
49
50
72
66
80
74

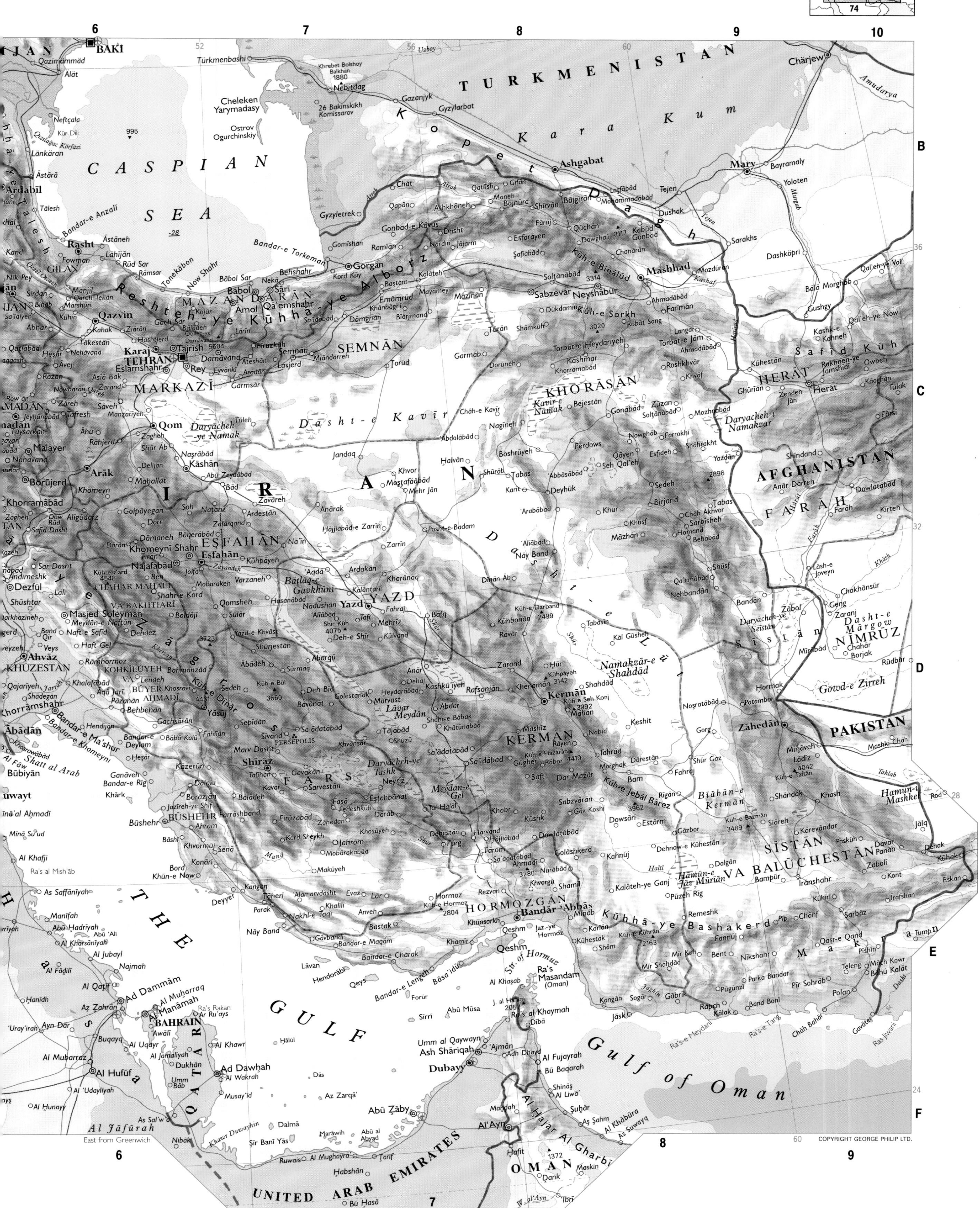
6
7
8
9
10
B
C
D
E
F
BAKI
Türkmenbashi
TURKMENISTAN
Kara Kum
Kopet Dagh
Ashgabat
Nebitdag
Gazanjyk
Gyzylarbat
Chelekan Yarymadasy
Ostrov Ogurchinskiy
Chärjew
Amudarya
Mary
Bayramaly
Yoloten
Tejen
Dushak
Sarakhs
CASPIAN SEA
Ardabil
Rasht
Bandar-e Anzalī
GĪLĀN
Tonekābon
Now Shahr
Bābol
Sārī
Gorgān
Bandar-e Torkeman
Gonbad-e Kāvūs
Bojnūrd
Shīrvān
Qūchān
Mashhad
Neyshābūr
Sabzevār
Reshteh-ye Kūhhā-ye Alborz
MĀZANDARĀN
Amol
Qā'emshahr
Damāvand 5604
Qazvin
Karaj
TEHRĀN
Tajrish
Rey
Eslamshahr
Semnān
SEMNĀN
Dāmghān
Shāhrūd
MARKAZĪ
Qom
Daryācheh-ye Namak
Dasht-e Kavīr
KHORĀSĀN
Torbat-e Heydarīyeh
Kāshmar
Herāt
HERĀT
Safīd Kūh
AFGHANISTAN
FARĀH
Farāh
Arāk
Kāshān
Malāyer
Borūjerd
Khorramābād
I R A N
Eşfahān
EŞFAHĀN
Najafābād
Khomeynī Shahr
Yazd
YAZD
Dasht-e Lūt
Tabas
Ferdows
Bīrjand
Zābol
Daryācheh-ye Sīstān
Dasht-e Mārgow
NĪMRŪZ
Zāhedān
PAKISTAN
Dezfūl
Shūshtar
Masjed Soleymān
Ahvāz
KHŪZESTĀN
Khorramshahr
Ābādān
Būshehr
BŪSHEHR
Shīrāz
FARS
PERSEPOLIS
Kermān
KERMĀN
Rafsanjān
Sīrjān
Bam
Namakzār-e Shahdād
Zagros
Jāsk
Bandar-e 'Abbās
HORMOZGĀN
Qeshm
Str. of Hormuz
SĪSTĀN VA BALŪCHESTĀN
Īrānshahr
Chāh Bahār
Kūhhā-ye Bashākerd
Makran
Gulf of Oman
THE GULF
Al Kuwayt
Ad Dammām
Al Manāmah
BAHRAIN
QATAR
Ad Dawḩah
Al Hufūf
Al Jāfūrah
Dubayy
Abū Z̧aby
Ash Shāriqah
Al 'Ayn
UNITED ARAB EMIRATES
OMAN
Al Hajar Al Gharbī
Ra's Musandam (Oman)
East from Greenwich
COPYRIGHT GEORGE PHILIP LTD.

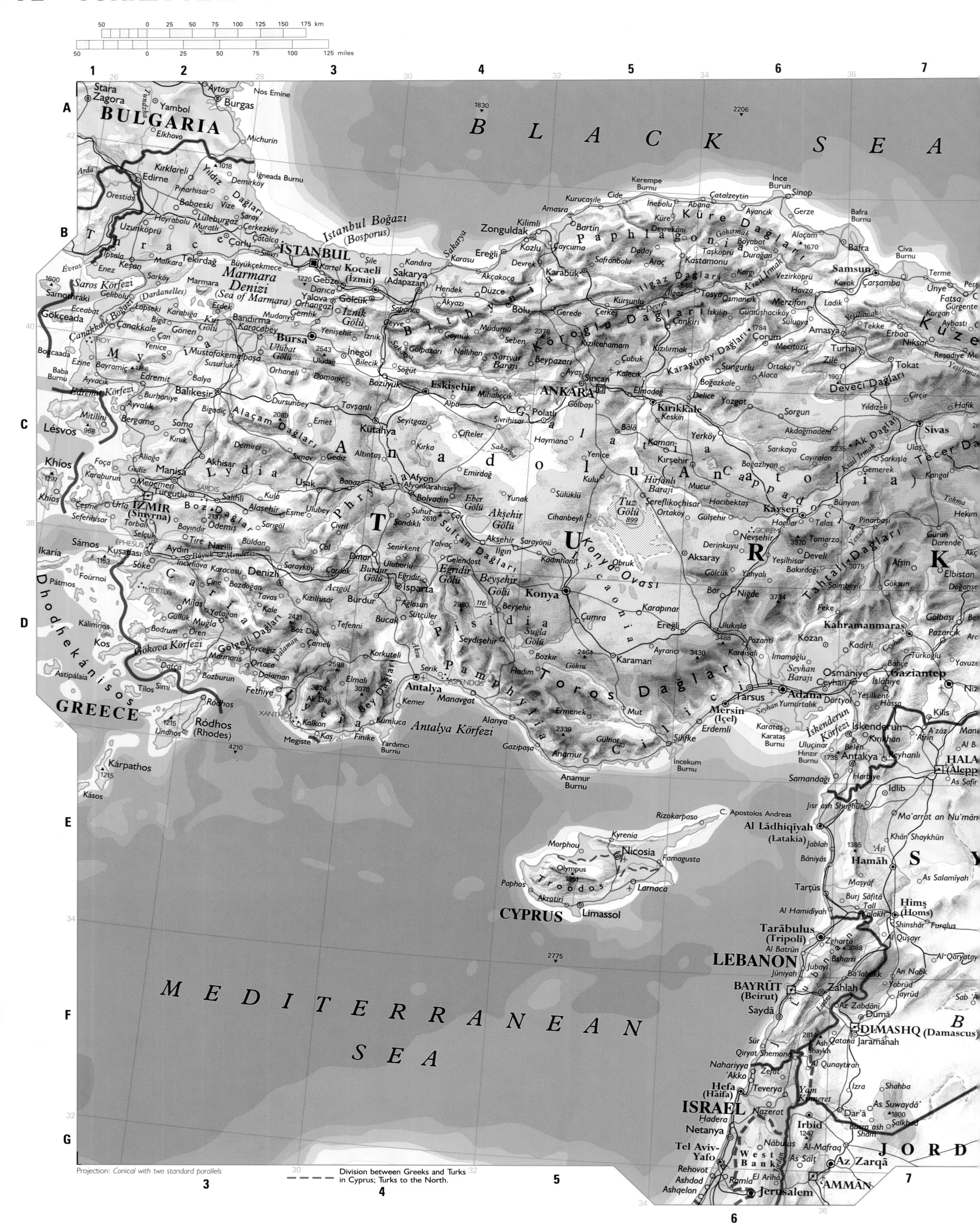

Projection: Conical with two standard parallels

Division between Greeks and Turks
in Cyprus; Turks to the North.

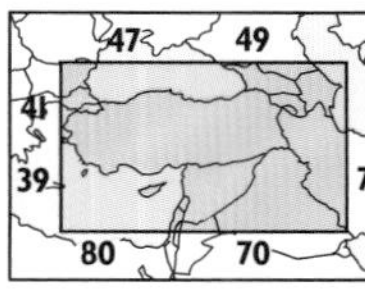

CASPIAN SEA

RUSSIA

GEORGIA

ARMENIA

AZERBAIJAN

IRAN

IRAQ

TBILISI

YEREVAN

BAKI

BAGHDAD

Caucasus Mountains

East from Greenwich

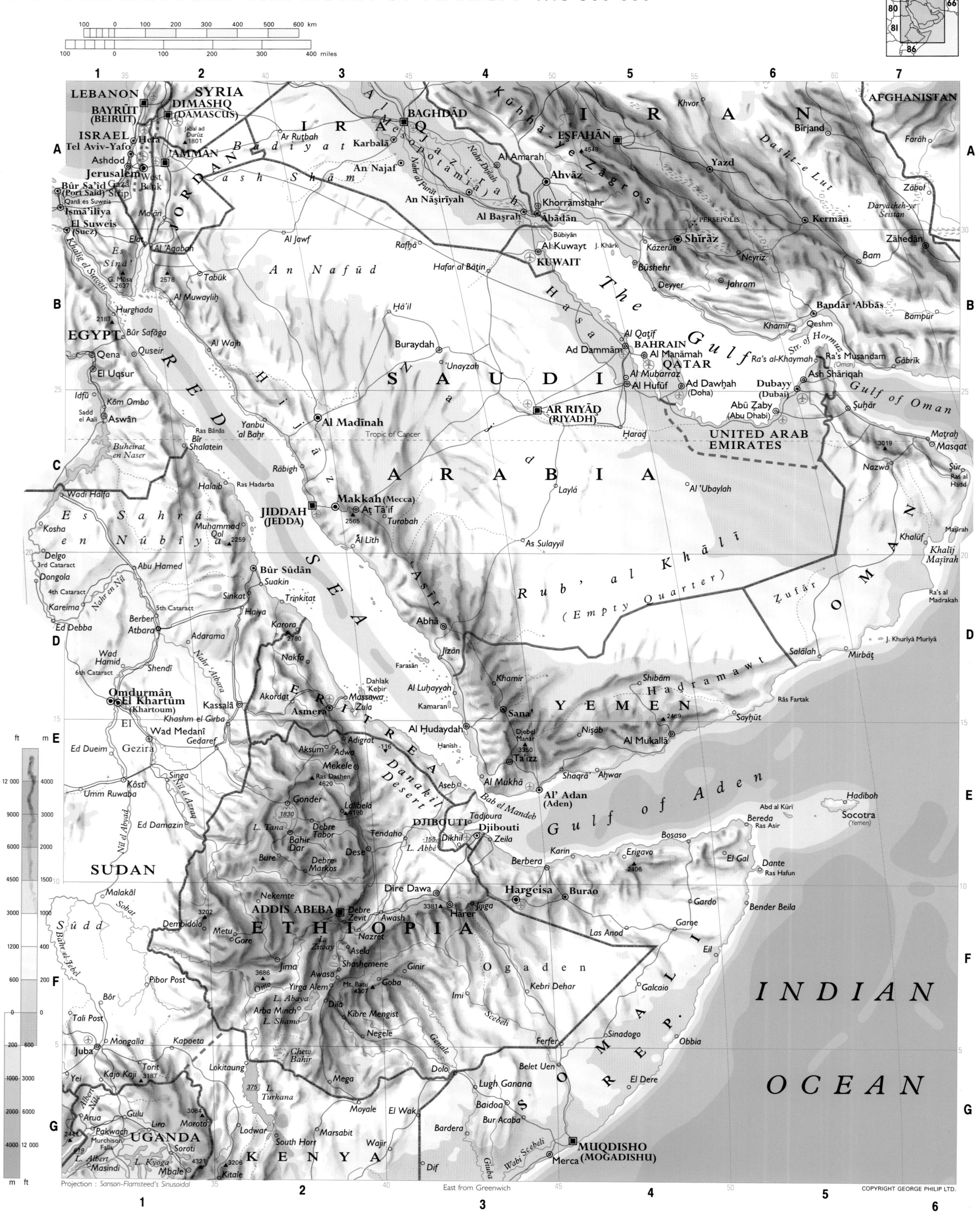

100 100 200 300 400 500 600 km
100 100 200 300 400 miles

1 2 3 4 5 6 7

LEBANON
SYRIA
BAYRŪT (BEIRUT)
DIMASHQ (DAMASCUS)
ISRAEL
Tel Aviv-Yafo
Ḥaifa
'AMMAN
Ashdod
Jerusalem
West Bank
Būr Sa'īd (Port Said)
Gaza Strip
Qanā es Suweis
Ismā'īliya
El Suweis (Suez)
Khalīg el Suweis
Es Sīnā'
G. Mûsa 2637
Elat
Al 'Aqabah
2578
AFGHANISTAN
Farāh
Zābol
Daryācheh-ye Seistan
Birjand
BAGHDĀD
IRAQ
Karbalā
An Najaf
An Nāṣirīyah
Al Amarah
Nahr Dijlah
Al Başrah
Ābādān
Khorramshahr
Ahvāz
ESFAHĀN
IRAN
4548
PERSEPOLIS
Shīrāz
Yazd
Kermān
Bam
Zāhedān
Ar Ruṭbah
Badiyat ash Shām
An Nafūd
Tabūk
Al Muwayliḥ
Hurghada
2187
Būr Safāga
EGYPT
Qena
Quseir
El Uqsur
Idfū
Kōm Ombo
Sadd el Aali
Aswân
Buheirat en Naser
Al Jawf
Rafḥā
Hafar al Bāṭin
Al Kuwayt
KUWAIT
Būbiyān
J. Khārk
Kāzerūn
Būshehr
Deyyer
Jahrom
Neyrīz
Bandar 'Abbās
Khamīr
Qeshm
Bampūr
Gābrīk
Ra's al-Khaymah
Ra's Musandam (Oman)
Str. of Hormuz
Ḥā'il
Buraydah
'Unayzah
Ad Dammān
Al Qaṭīf
BAHRAIN
Al Manāmah
QATAR
Al Mubarraz
Al Ḥufūf
Ad Dawḥah (Doha)
ABŪ Ẓaby (Abu Dhabi)
Dubayy (Dubai)
Ash Shāriqah
Gulf of Oman
Ṣuḥār
Maṭraḥ
Masqat
3019
Ḥasā
The Gulf
SAUDI
Ras Bānās
Bīr Shalatein
Yanbu 'al Baḥr
Al Madīnah
AR RIYĀD (RIYADH)
Ḥaraḍ
UNITED ARAB EMIRATES
Nazwā
Ṣūr
Ras al Hadd
OMAN
Tropic of Cancer
Delgo
3rd Cataract
Dongola
Kosha
4th Cataract
Kareima
Ed Debba
Wadi Halfa
Abu Hamed
Es Sahrâ en Nûbîya
RED
Halaib
Ras Hadarba
Rābigh
Makkah (Mecca)
At Tā'if
Turabah
2565
JIDDAH (JEDDA)
Muhammad Qol
2259
Āl Līth
Laylā
As Sulayyil
Al 'Ubaylah
ARABIA
Rub' al Khālī (Empty Quarter)
Zufār
Ṣalālah
Mirbāṭ
Khalūf
Khalīj Maṣīrah
Maṣīrah
Ra's al Madrakah
J. Khūrīyā Mūrīyā
Būr Sûdân
Suakin
Sinkat
Trinkitat
Haiya
SEA
Karora
2780
Nakfa
Berber
Atbara
Adarama
Nahr el Atbara
Wad Hamid
Shendi
6th Cataract
Omdurmân
El Khartûm (Khartoum)
Kassalâ
Khashm el Girba
Gedaref
ERITREA
Akordat
Asmera
Massawa
Zula
Dahlak Kebir
Adī Luhayyah
Kamaran
Al Ḥudaydah
Farasān
Jīzān
Abhā
Khamir
'Asīr
Sana'
2469
Shibām
Ḥaḍramawt
Sayḥūt
Rās Fartak
Ras 'Al Madrah
EGYPT
Wad Medanî
El Gezira
Ed Dueim
Kôstî
Umm Ruwaba
Singa
Nîl el Azrag
Ed Damazin
SUDAN
Malakâl
Sobat
Sûdd
Bahr el gebel
Pibor Post
Bôr
Tali Post
Juba
Mongalla
Kapoeta
Yei
Arua
Gulu
Lira
Moroto
2434
Pakwach
Murchison Falls
L. Albert (Masindi)
UGANDA
Soroti
4321
L. Kyoga
Kitale
Mbale
Aksum
Adwa
-116
Mekele
Ras Dashen 4620
Adigrat
Gonder
1830
Lalibela 4190
L. Tana
Debre Tabor
Bahir Dar
Dese
Debre Markos
Bure
Danakil Desert
Aseb
Djebel Manar 3350
Ta'izz
Al Mukhā
Shaqrā'
Aḥwar
Nišāb
Al Mukallā
Bab el Mandeb
Al' Adan (Aden)
YEMEN
Gulf of Aden
Abd al Kūrī
Bereda
Ras Asir
Hadiboh
Socotra (Yemen)
-155
Tadjoura
DJIBOUTI
Djibouti
Zeila
Dikhil
L. Abbé
Zayit
Awash
Tendaho
Dire Dawa
Jijiga
Harer
3381
Hargeisa
Burao
Berbera
Karin
Bosaso
Erigavo
2406
El Gal
Dante
Ras Hafun
ADDIS ABEBA
Debre Zeyit
Nekemte
Nazret
Metu
Gore
Dembidola
3202
ETHIOPIA
Asela
Shashemene
Ginir
Ogaden
Kebri Dehar
Imi
Gode
Gardo
Bender Beila
Las Anod
Garce
Eil
Jima
3686
Awasa
Mt. Batu 4307
Goba
SOMALI REP.
Galcaio
Sinadogo
Obbia
INDIAN
Yirga Alem
L. Abaya
Arba Minch
L. Shamo
Dilâ
Kibre Mengist
Negele
Scebeli
Ganale
Dolo
Ferfer
Wabi Scebeli
Belet Uen
El Dere
OCEAN
Omo
375
L. Chew Bahir
Mega
Moyale
El Wak
Baidoa
Bur Acaba
Lugh Ganana
Bardera
MUQDISHO (MOGADISHU)
Merca
Giuba
Dif
KENYA
Lodwar
South Horn
Marsabit
Wajir
L. Turkana
3084
3206
Kajo Kaji
Torit
3187
Lokitaung

Projection : Sanson-Flamsteed's Sinusoidal

East from Greenwich

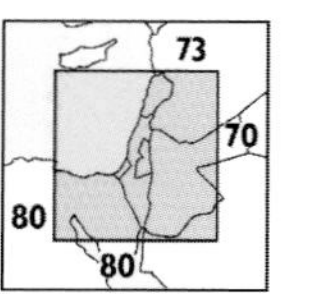

CYPRUS

MEDITERRANEAN

SEA

Paphos
Episkopi
Episkopi Bay
Limassol
Akrotiri Bay
C. Gata

Al Ḥamidiyah
Hims (Homs)
Tall Kalakh
Shinshār
Furqlus
ASH SHAMĀL
Tarābulus (Tripoli)
Zgharta
Al Minā'
Halba
Al Hirmil
Al Quṣayr
HIMŞ
Al Batrūn
Qurnat as Sawdā' 3088
Bsharri
Al Burayj
Al Qaryatayn
Jubayl
Qartaba
Ibrāhīm
AL BIQĀ
2464
Jūniyah
Bikfayyā
2628
Ba'labakk
An Nabk
Bi'r Ghadir
BAYRŪT (Beirut)
Alayh
J. Sannin
Al Labwah
Yabrūd
Ash Shuwayfāt
Zahlah
Sirghāyā
LEBANON
Ad Dāmūr
JABAL LUBNĀN
Hawsh
Al Quṭayfah
SYRIA
1942
Az Zabadānī
Dumayr
Khān Abū Shāmat
Saydā (Sidon)
J. al Bārūk
Barada
Dūmā
DIMASHQ
Jazzīn
Ash Shaykh (Mt. Hermon)
Marj 'Uyūn
Dārayyā
DIMASHQ (Damascus)
An Nabaṭīyah at Tahta
2814
Qaṭanā
Al Kiswah
Al Hājānah
AL JANŪB
Al Khiyām
1197
Al Quṭayfah
Burāq
AŞ ŞAFĀ
Sūr (Tyre)
Qiryat Shemona
Al Qunayṭirah
As Sanamayn
Naḥariyya
Me'ona
Zefat
Ar Rafid
DAR'Ā
'Akko (Acre)
Hagalil
Fiq
Shaykh Miskin
Shahbā
Mifraz Hefa
Qiryat Yam
HAZAFON
Yam -210
Saham al Jawlān
Izra
AS SUWAYDĀ
Hefa (Haifa)
Teverya (Tiberias)
Kinneret
Dar'ā
As Suwaydā 1800
Şalah
HEFA
Qiryat Ata
Nazerat (Nazareth)
Yarmūk
Irbid
Malah
Dāliyat el Karmel
Afula
Taiyiba
IRBID
AL MAFRAQ
Salkhad
Umm el Fahm
Bet She'an
'AJLŪN
Busrā ash Shām
TEL MEGIDDO
Janin
J. Umm ad Dara
Umm al Qittayn
CAESAREA
Shōmrōn
'Ajlūn
Al Mafraq
Pardes
Hanna-Karkur
Tūbās
JARASH
ISRAEL
Tulkarm
SAMARIA
Jarash
Hadera
N. az Zarqā
Netanya
Nāblus
AL BALQĀ
HAMERKAZ
Kefar Sava
Herzliyya
Petah Tiqwa
SHILO
Az Zarqā
Benē Beraq
Ramat Gan
W. al Yābis
AL BALQĀ
Tel Aviv-Yafo
Bat Yam
West Bank
Wādī as Sīr
AMMĀN
Rishon le Ziyyon
Rām Allāh
Karama
Na'ūr
Azraq ash Shishān
Yavne
Rehovot
El Arīḥā (Jericho)
AZ ZARQĀ
Ashdod
Ramla
Lod
AMM
Qiryat Mal'akhi
Bet Shemesh
Jerusalem (Yerushalayim) (Al Quds)
Ma'daba
'AMMĀN
Ashqelon
Qiryat Gat
Bayt Laḥm (Bethlehem)
MA'DĀBA
TEL LAKHISH
N. Shiqma
Al Khalīl (Hebron)
W. al Ḥaydān
Dhibān
Gaza
Az Zāhirīyah
Gaza Strip
Sederot
Dead Sea
Al Ḥadīthah
Khān Yūnis
Rafaḥ
N. Beşor
Arad
W. Al Mawjib
Be'er Sheva (Beersheba)
Sedom
Al Qaṭrānah
El Daheir
Bor Mashash
-411
AL KARAK
Bûr Sa'îd (Port Said)
Bûr Fu'ad
Dimona
Al Karak
W. al Ḥasā
JORDAN
Khalîg el Tîna
Râs Burûn
Sabkhet el Bardawîl
-333
Al Mazār
W. al Makhruq
Râmâni
Bîr el 'Abd
El 'Arîsh
1305
Bîr el Garârât
Bîr Lahfân
HADAROM
AT ṬAFĪLAH
W. Bā'ir
El Qantara
Bîr Qaţia
Bîr el Duweidar
Bîr Kaseiba
-121
At Ṭafīlah
Bā'ir
Wâhid
Bîr Madkûr
Bîr el Jafir
'Arîsh
Qezi'ot
Birein
SHAMÂL SÎNÎ
Sedé Boqér
Ismâ'îlîya
892
El Quṣeima
Jash Shawmari
ISMÂ'ÎLÎYA
Muweilih
1072
Talâta
Bîr Ḥasana
Mizpe Ramon
Mahattat 'Unayzah
Khamsa
El Buheirat el Murrat el Kubra (Great Bitter L.)
Ḥanegev
Nijil
G.Yi 'Allaq 1094
Bîr Beida
El 'Agrûd
Rujm Tal'at al Jama'ah 1736
MA'ĀN
Gineifa
Bîr el Thamâda
W. el Brûk
N. Paran
Wādī Mūsa
Al Jafr
Qa'el Jafr
W. Qiraiya
Ma'ān
EGYPT
E S SÎNÂ' (Sinai)
N. Ḥiyyan
Bîr Gebeil Hisn
W. El Tamarânî
El Suweis (Suez)
Bûr Taufîq
Mamarr Mitla
AL AQABAH
Ra's an Naqb 1435
Adabiya
Uyûn Mûsa
Ra's an Naqb
Mahattat ash Shidiyah
Âin Sudr
Nakhl
El Kuntilla
MA ĀN
Khalîg
Yotvata
948 G. el Kabrît
Bîr Abu Muḥammad
'En 'Avrona
Bîr al Butayyihāt
Bîr al Qattār
Ghubbet el Bûs
Gebel el Tîh
El Thamad
SAUDI
Bîr 1272
W. El Biarât
Batn al Ghûl
Bîr
Abu Sandûq
Râs Matarma
JANÛB SÎNÎ
Elat
Al 'Aqabah
Rum
At Tubayq
EL SUWEIS
W. Abu Ga'da
Bîr el Heisi
Bîr Tâba
Gulf of Aqaba
W. an Nunayrah
Haql
Al Mudawwarah
ARABIA
1165
1592
1754

= = = 1974 Cease Fire Lines

ft m
9000 3000
6000 2000
3000 1000
1200 400
600 200
0 0
200 600
2000 6000
m ft

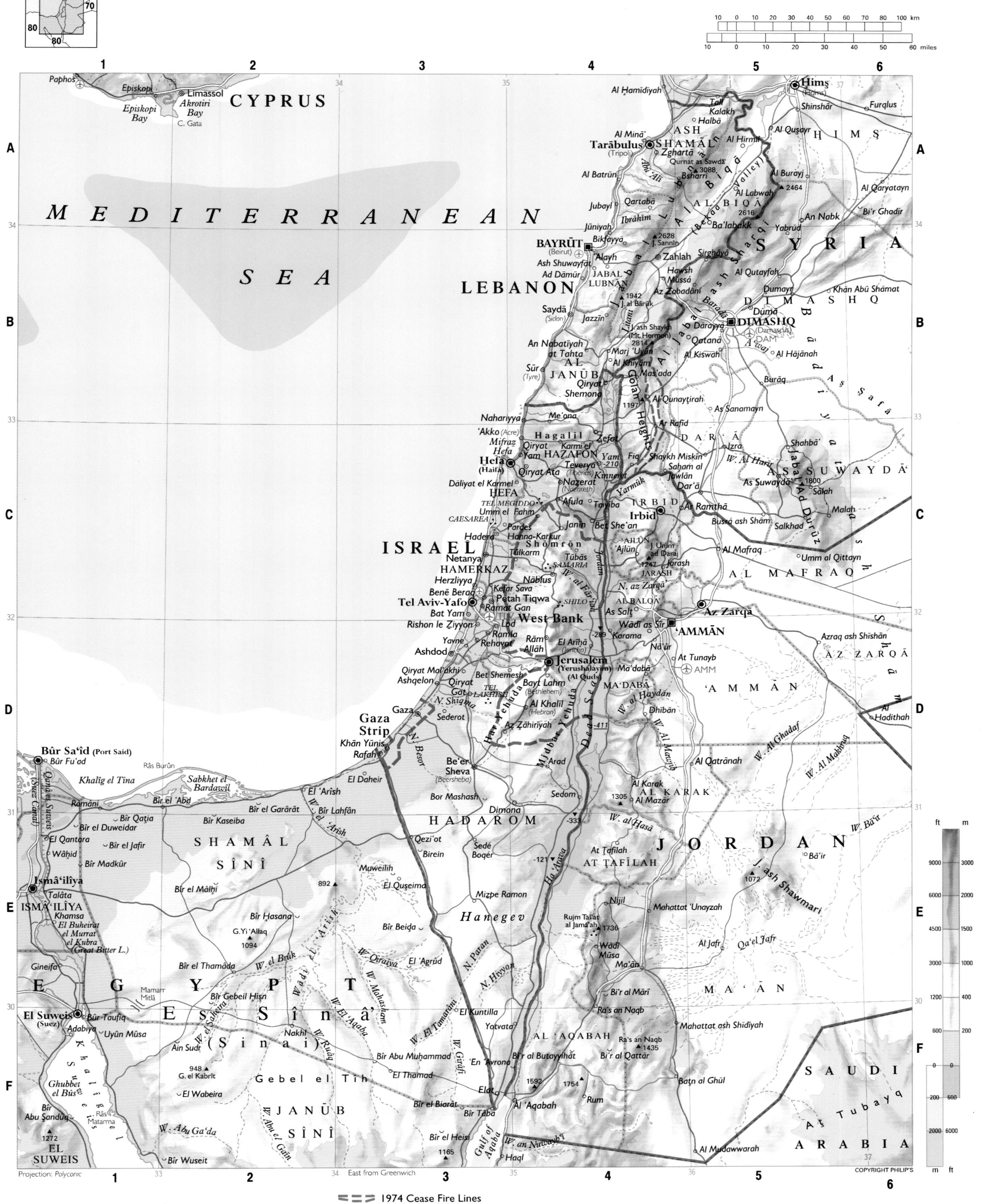

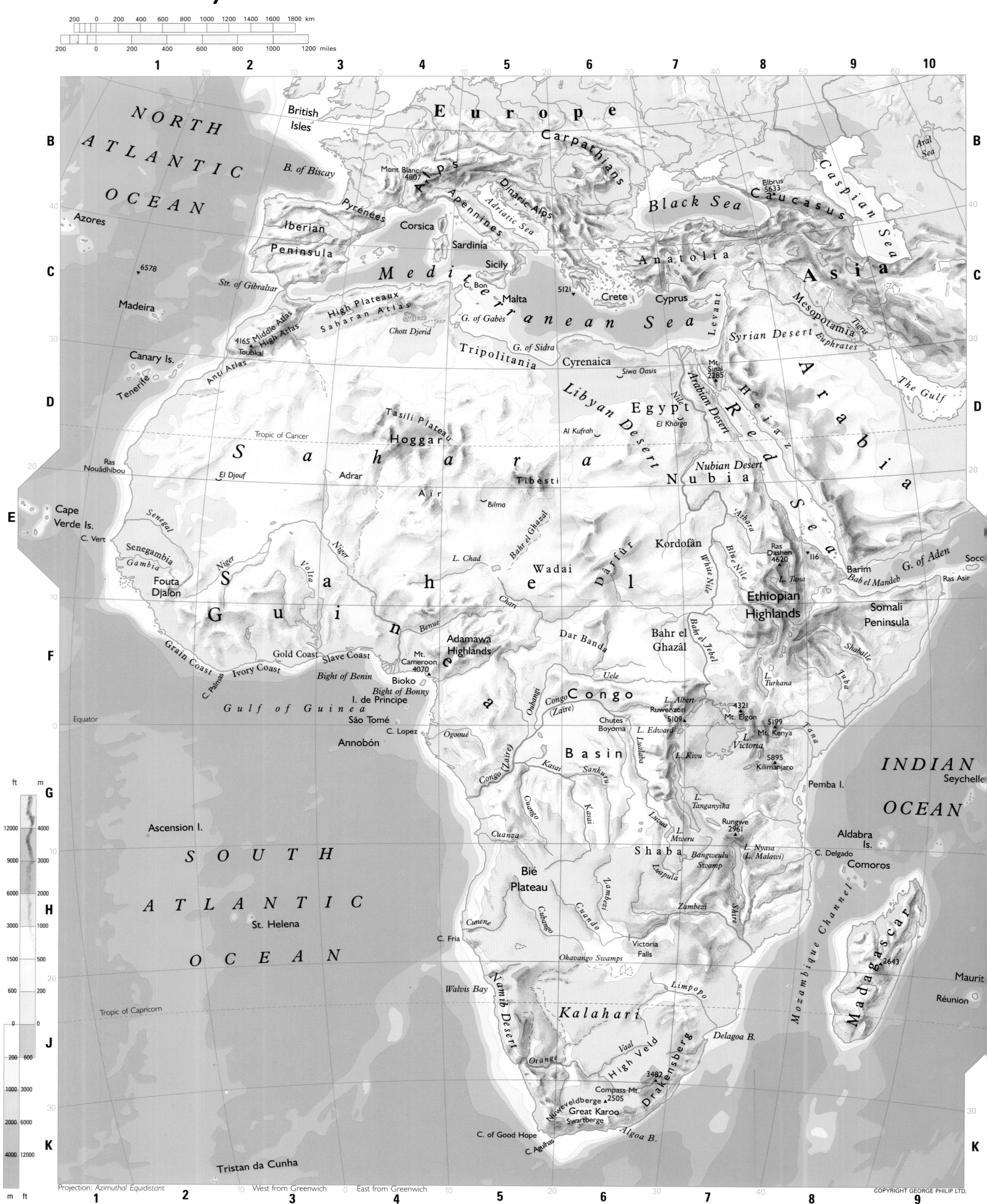
NORTH ATLANTIC OCEAN
SOUTH ATLANTIC OCEAN
INDIAN OCEAN
Europe
Asia
Arabia
Mediterranean Sea
Black Sea
Caspian Sea
Red Sea
Sahara
Sahel
Guinea
Congo Basin
Libyan Desert
Nubian Desert
Ethiopian Highlands
Somali Peninsula
Kalahari
Madagascar
Mozambique Channel
Gulf of Guinea
Iberian Peninsula
Alps
Carpathians
Caucasus
Anatolia
Hoggar
Tibesti
Tasili Plateau
Kilimanjaro
Drakensberg
Great Karoo
Namib Desert
Bié Plateau
Adamawa Highlands
Cape Verde Is.
Canary Is.
Madeira
Azores
Ascension I.
St. Helena
Tristan da Cunha
C. of Good Hope
C. Agulhas
Projection: Azimuthal Equidistant
West from Greenwich
East from Greenwich
COPYRIGHT GEORGE PHILIP LTD.

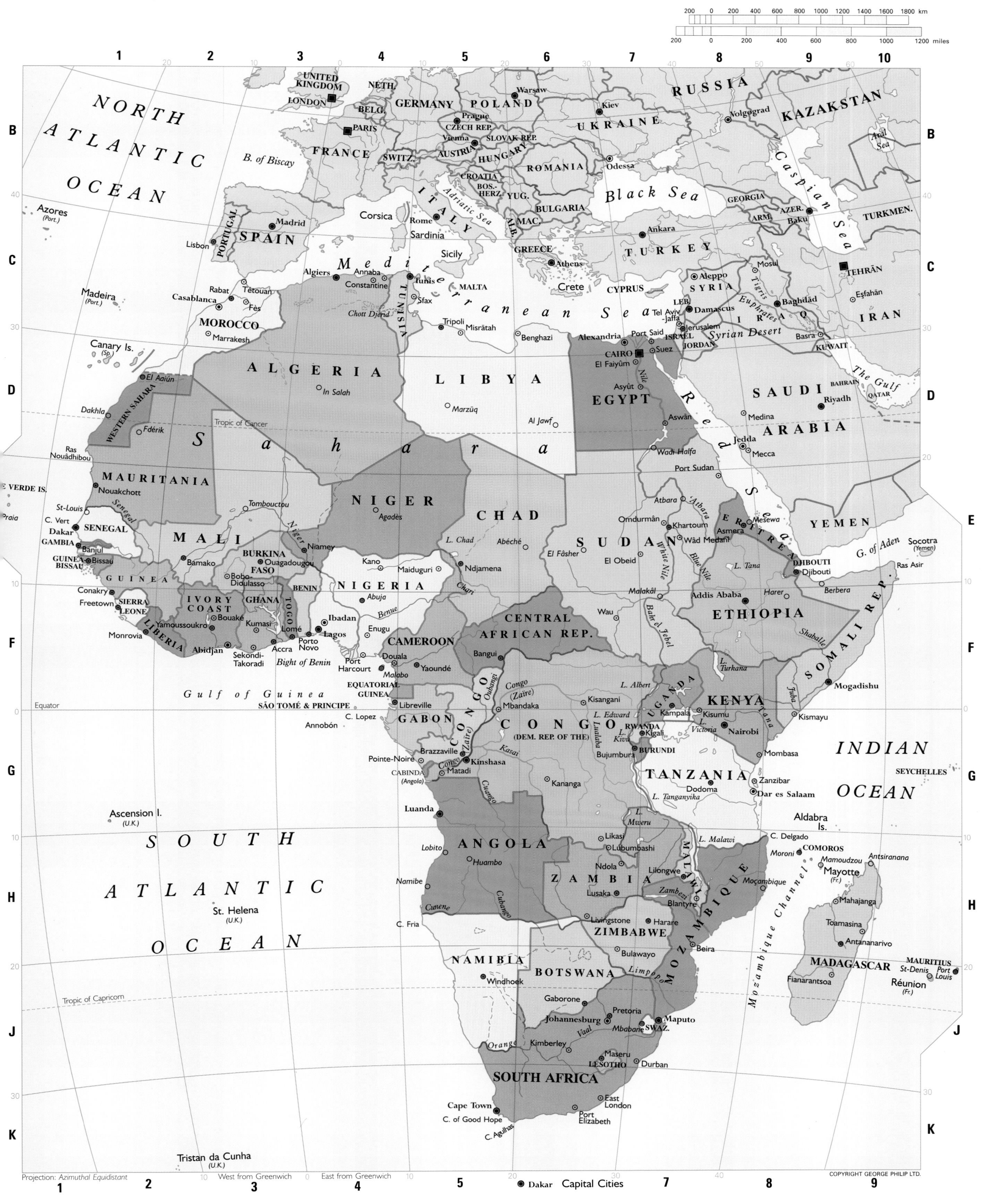

200 0 200 400 600 800 1000 1200 1400 1600 1800 km
200 0 200 400 600 800 1000 1200 miles

NORTH ATLANTIC OCEAN

UNITED KINGDOM
LONDON
NETH
BELG.
PARIS
FRANCE
B. of Biscay
GERMANY
POLAND
Warsaw
Prague
CZECH REP.
Vienna
SWITZ.
AUSTRIA
SLOVAK REP.
HUNGARY
CROATIA
BOS.-HERZ.
YUG.
ITALY
Adriatic Sea
ALB.
MAC.
BULGARIA
ROMANIA
Odessa
Kiev
UKRAINE
RUSSIA
Volgograd
KAZAKSTAN
Aral Sea

Azores
(Port.)

Madeira
(Port.)

Corsica
Rome
Sardinia
GREECE
Athens
Crete
Black Sea
GEORGIA
ARM.
AZER.
Baku
TURKMEN.

SPAIN
Madrid
Lisbon
PORTUGAL

Canary Is.
(Sp.)

Algiers
Tétouan
Constantine
Annaba
TUNISIA
Tunis
MALTA
Sfax
Ankara
TURKEY
CYPRUS
SYRIA
Aleppo
Mosul
LEB.
Damascus
Tel Aviv-Jaffa
ISRAEL
JORDAN
Euphrates
Tigris
Baghdad
Esfahān
Tehrān
IRAN

Rabat
Casablanca
Fès
MOROCCO
Marrakesh

Tripoli
Misrātah
Benghazi
Alexandria
Port Said
Suez
Jerusalem
Cairo
El Faiyûm
Asyût
Syrian Desert
Basra
KUWAIT
The Gulf
BAHRAIN
QATAR

Ras Nouâdhibou
Dakhla

El Aaiún
Fdérik
WESTERN SAHARA

ALGERIA
In Salah
Tropic of Cancer
Marzûq
Al Jawf
LIBYA

EGYPT
Aswān
Red Sea
Wadi Halfa
SAUDI
Medina
Mecca
Jedda
ARABIA
Riyadh

Sahara

MAURITANIA
Nouakchott

St-Louis
C. Vert
Dakar
SENEGAL
GAMBIA
Banjul
GUINEA-BISSAU
Bissau

CVERDE IS.
Praia

Tombouctou
Senegal
MALI
Bamako

NIGER
Agadès
Niamey
Niger

CHAD
Abéché
L. Chad
Ndjamena
Chari

SUDAN
El Fâsher
El Obeid
Omdurmân
Khartoum
Atbara
Wâd Medani
Atbara
Port Sudan

ERITREA
Mesewa
Asmera
YEMEN
DJIBOUTI
Djibouti
G. of Aden
Ras Asir
Socotra
(Yemen)

GUINEA
Conakry
Freetown
SIERRA LEONE
BURKINA FASO
Ouagadougou
Bobo-Dioulasso
Kano
Maiduguri
NIGERIA
Abuja
Benue
Enugu
Ibadan
Lagos
Porto Novo
Accra
Lomé
TOGO
GHANA
Kumasi
Bouaké
IVORY COAST
Yamoussoukro
Abidjan
LIBERIA
Monrovia
BENIN

White Nile
Malakâl
Wau
Bahr el Jebel
Addis Ababa
Harer
Berbera
ETHIOPIA
Blue Nile
L. Tana
SOMALI REP.
Mogadishu

CAMEROON
Douala
Yaoundé
Malabo
EQUATORIAL GUINEA
SÃO TOMÉ & PRINCIPE
Libreville
GABON
C. Lopez
Annobón

CENTRAL AFRICAN REP.
Bangui
Ubangi
CONGO
Congo (Zaïre)
Mbandaka
Kisangani
CONGO (DEM. REP. OF THE)
L. Albert
L. Edward
L. Kivu
UGANDA
Kampala
RWANDA
Kigali
BURUNDI
Bujumbura
L. Turkana
KENYA
Kisumu
L. Victoria
Nairobi
Juba
Tana
Kismayu
Mombasa

Equator

GABON
Brazzaville
Pointe-Noire
Kinshasa
Matadi
CABINDA
(Angola)
Kasai
Kananga
Lualaba
TANZANIA
Dodoma
Zanzibar
Dar es Salaam
L. Tanganyika
SEYCHELLES
INDIAN OCEAN

SOUTH ATLANTIC OCEAN

Ascension I.
(U.K.)

St. Helena
(U.K.)

Luanda
Lobito
Namibe
ANGOLA
Huambo
Cubango
Cunene
C. Fria
Chumbe
Cuando
L. Mweru
Likasi
Lubumbashi
Ndola
ZAMBIA
Lusaka
Livingstone
Kabwe
L. Malawi
MALAWI
Lilongwe
Blantyre
Zambezi
C. Delgado
Moroni
COMOROS
Mamoudzou
Mayotte
(Fr.)
Antsiranana
Mahajanga
Toamasina

NAMIBIA
Windhoek
BOTSWANA
Gaborone
ZIMBABWE
Bulawayo
Harare
Beira
MOZAMBIQUE
Moçambique
Limpopo
Mozambique Channel
Aldabra Is.
MADAGASCAR
Antananarivo
Fianarantsoa
MAURITIUS
St-Denis
Réunion
(Fr.)
Port Louis

Tropic of Capricorn

Orange
Vaal
Kimberley
Johannesburg
Pretoria
Mbabane
SWAZ.
Maputo
Maseru
LESOTHO
Durban
SOUTH AFRICA
Cape Town
C. of Good Hope
C. Agulhas
East London
Port Elizabeth

Tristan da Cunha
(U.K.)

Projection: *Azimuthal Equidistant*
West from Greenwich   East from Greenwich
● Dakar Capital Cities
COPYRIGHT GEORGE PHILIP LTD.

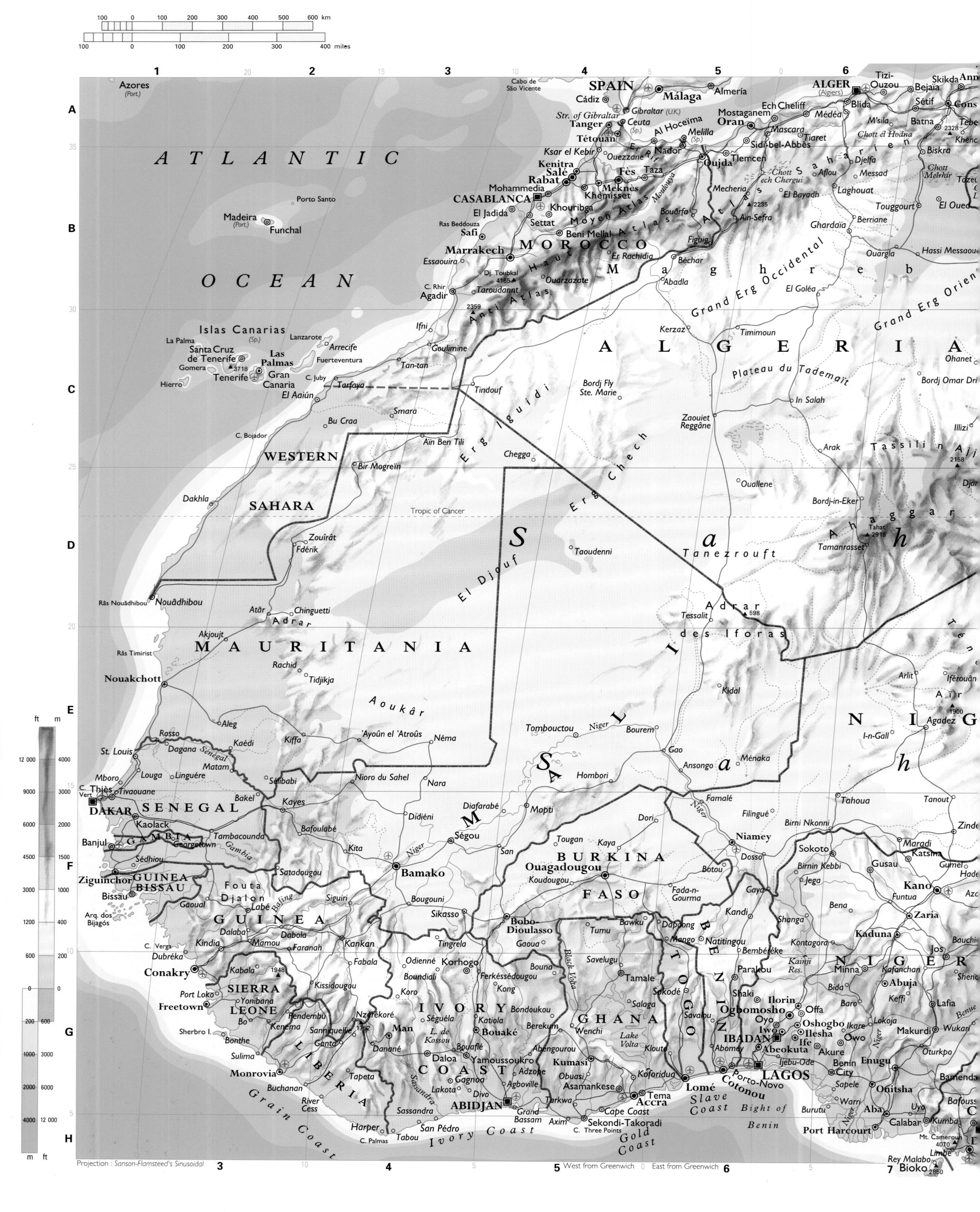

100 0 100 200 300 400 500 600 km
100 0 100 200 300 400 miles
ATLANTIC OCEAN
Azores (Port.)
Porto Santo
Madeira (Port.)
Funchal
Islas Canarias (Sp.)
La Palma
Santa Cruz de Tenerife
Gomera
Tenerife
Hierro
3718
Las Palmas
Gran Canaria
Lanzarote
Arrecife
Fuerteventura
C. Juby
SPAIN
Málaga
Almería
Cádiz
Cabo de São Vicente
Str. of Gibraltar
Gibraltar (U.K.)
Ceuta (Sp.)
Tanger
Tétouan
Al Hoceïma
Melilla (Sp.)
Nador
Ksar el Kebir
Ouezzane
Er Rif
Kenitra
Salé
Rabat
Fès
Taza
Oujda
Meknès
Khemisset
Mohammedia
CASABLANCA
Khouribga
El Jadida
Settat
Moyen Atlas
Haut Atlas
Anti Atlas
Ras Beddouza
Safi
Beni Mellal
Marrakech
MOROCCO
Essaouira
Dj. Toubkal 4165
Ouarzazate
Er Rachidia
Taroudannt
C. Rhir
Agadir
2359
Ifni
Goulimine
Tan-tan
Tarfaya
El Aaiún
Smara
Bu Craa
C. Bojador
Aïn Ben Tili
WESTERN SAHARA
Bir Mogreïn
Dakhla
Zouîrât
Fdérik
Râs Nouâdhibou
Nouâdhibou
Atâr
Chinguetti
Adrar
Akjoujt
Râs Timirist
MAURITANIA
Rachid
Tidjikja
Nouakchott
Aoukâr
Aleg
Rosso
Kaédi
Kiffa
'Ayoûn el 'Atroûs
Néma
St. Louis
Dagana
Sénégal
Matam
Mboro
Louga
Linguère
Sélibabi
Nioro du Sahel
Nara
C. Vert
Thiès
Tivaouane
DAKAR
SENEGAL
Bakel
Kayes
Kaolack
Tambacounda
Banjul
GAMBIA
Georgetown
Gambia
Sédhiou
Ziguinchor
GUINEA BISSAU
Bissau
Arq. dos Bijagós
Fouta Djalon
Labé
Gaoual
GUINEA
Dalaba
Dabola
Mamou
Faranah
Kindia
C. Verga
Dubréka
Conakry
Kankan
Siguiri
Satadougou
Bafoulabé
Kita
Diafarabé
Didiéni
Mopti
Ségou
San
Bamako
Bougouni
Sikasso
Niger
Tombouctou
Bourem
Gao
Ansongo
Ménaka
Hombori
MALI
Sahara
Tindouf
Erg Iguidi
Erg Chech
Chegga
Tropic of Cancer
El Djouf
Taoudenni
Tanezrouft
Adrar des Iforas
Tessalit
598
Kidal
ALGER (Algiers)
Tizi-Ouzou
Bejaia
Skikda
Blida
Médéa
Sétif
Constantine
Ech Cheliff
Mostaganem
Oran
Mascara
Tiaret
Sidi-bel-Abbès
Tlemcen
M'sila
Batna
Chott el Hodna
Biskra
Djelfa
Messad
Chott ech Chergui
Aflou
Saharien Atlas
Mecheria
El Bayadh
2235
Aïn-Sefra
Laghouat
Bouârfa
Figuig
Touggourt
El Oued
Ghardaïa
Berriane
Ouargla
Hassi Messaoud
Béchar
Abadla
Maghreb
Grand Erg Occidental
El Goléa
Grand Erg Oriental
Kerzaz
Timimoun
ALGERIA
Ohanet
Plateau du Tademaït
Bordj Omar Driss
Bordj Fly Ste. Marie
In Salah
Zaouiet Reggâne
Illizi
Arak
Tassili n'Ajjer
2158
Djanet
Ouallene
Bordj-in-Eker
Ahaggar
Tahat 2918
Tamanrasset
Arlit
Iférouân
Aïr
1900
Agadez
I-n-Gall
NIGER
Tahoua
Tanout
Zinder
Birni Nkonni
Filingué
Famalé
Niamey
Dori
Tougan
Kaya
BURKINA FASO
Ouagadougou
Koudougou
Fada-n-Gourma
Botou
Dosso
Gaya
Kandi
Bobo-Dioulasso
Gaoua
Tumu
Bawku
Dapaong
Mango
Natitingou
Bembéréké
Kontagora
Sokoto
Birnin Kebbi
Jega
Gusau
Maradi
Katsina
Gumel
Kano
Funtua
Zaria
Bena
Shanga
Kaduna
Jos
Bauchi
Tingrela
Odienné
Korhogo
Boundiali
Ferkéssédougou
Kong
Bouna
Black Volta
Savelugu
Tamale
Sokodé
Parakou
Kainji Res.
Minna
Kafanchan
Abuja
NIGERIA
Kabala
1948
SIERRA LEONE
Port Loko
Freetown
Yonibana
Kissidougou
Fabala
Koro
Pendembu
Bo
Kenema
Sherbro I.
Bonthe
Nzérékoré
1752
Sanniquellie
Ganta
Man
LIBERIA
Sulima
Monrovia
Buchanan
River Cess
Grain Coast
Tapeta
Harper
C. Palmas
Tabou
IVORY COAST
Séguéla
Katiola
Bondoukou
L. de Kossou
Bouaké
Danané
Bouaflé
Daloa
Yamoussoukro
Gagnoa
Lakota
Divo
Sassandra
Agboville
Adzopé
ABIDJAN
Grand Bassam
San Pédro
Ivory Coast
Berekum
Wenchi
Abengourou
GHANA
Lake Volta
Salaga
Kumasi
Obuasi
Asamankese
Kloute
Koforidua
Tarkwa
Axim
Cape Coast
Sekondi-Takoradi
C. Three Points
Gold Coast
Accra
Tema
TOGO
Savalou
BENIN
Lomé
Cotonou
Porto-Novo
Slave Coast
Bight of Benin
Shaki
Ilorin
Offa
Ogbomosho
Oyo
Iwo
Oshogbo
Ilesha
Ife
Ikare
Owo
Akure
IBADAN
Abomey
Abeokuta
Ijebu-Ode
LAGOS
Benin City
Enugu
Onitsha
Sapele
Warri
Burutu
Aba
Uyo
Calabar
Port Harcourt
Bida
Baro
Keffi
Lafia
Lokoja
Makurdi
Wukari
Oturkpo
Bamenda
Bafoussam
Kumba
Mt. Cameroun 4070
Limbe
Rey Malabo
Bioko
2850
Projection : Sanson-Flamsteed's Sinusoidal
West from Greenwich
East from Greenwich
ft m
12 000 4000
9000 3000
6000 2000
4500 1500
3000 1000
1200 400
600 200
0
200 600
1000 3000
2000 6000
4000 12 000
m ft

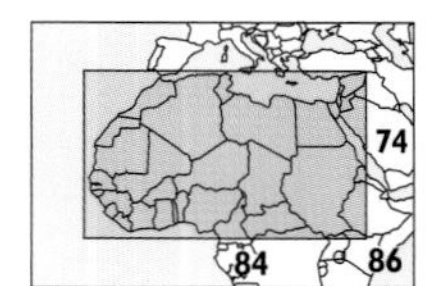
74
84
86

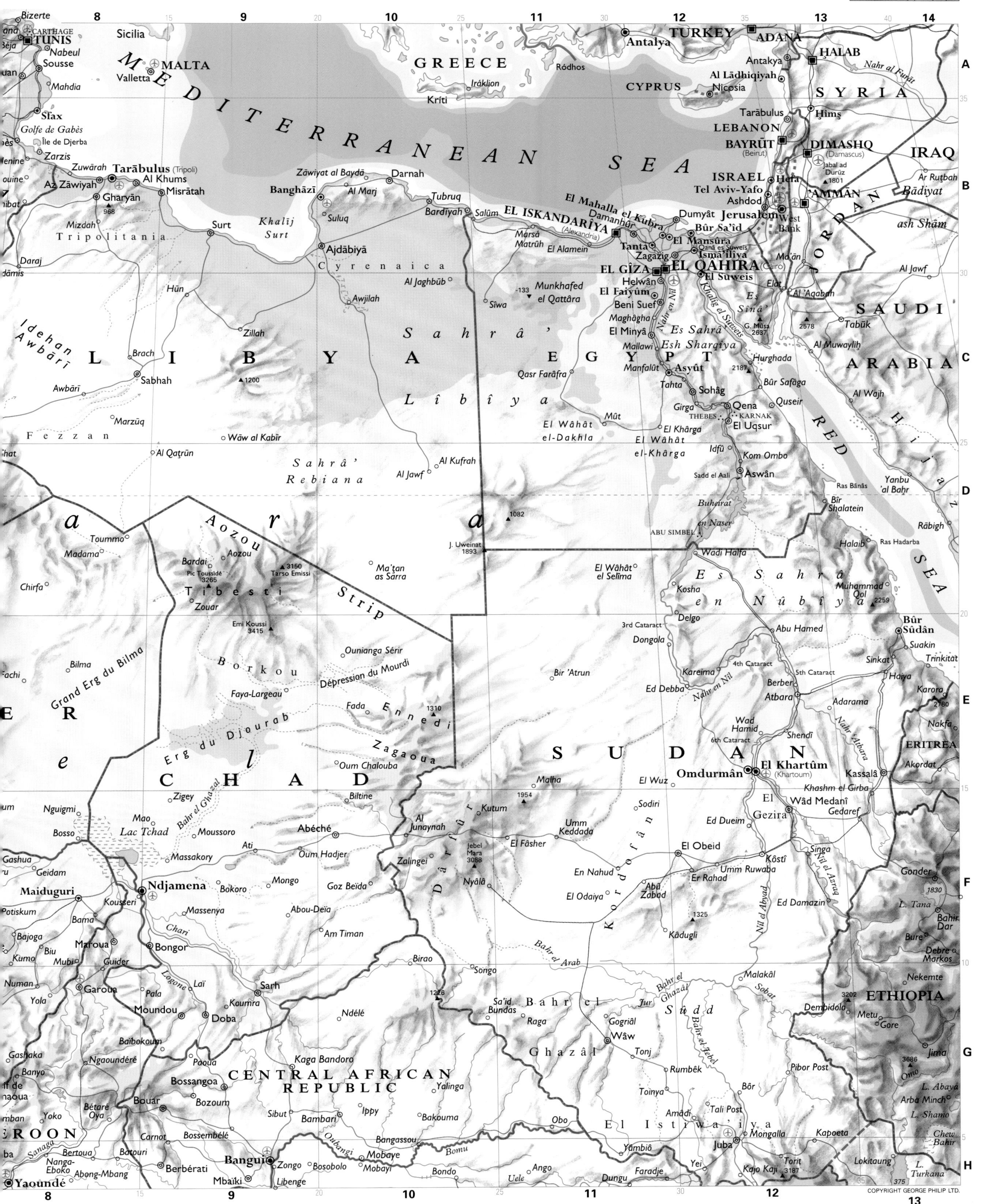
8
9
10
11
12
13
14
A
B
C
D
E
F
G
H
MEDITERRANEAN SEA
Bizerte
CARTHAGE
TUNIS
Nabeul
Sousse
Mahdia
Sfax
Golfe de Gabès
Île de Djerba
Zarzis
Sicilia
MALTA
Valletta
GREECE
Iráklion
Kríti
Ródhos
TURKEY
Antalya
ADANA
Antakya
HALAB
Nahr al Furāt
Al Lādhiqīyah
CYPRUS
Nicosia
SYRIA
Tarābulus
Hims
LEBANON
BAYRŪT
(Beirut)
DIMASHQ
(Damascus)
Jabal ad Durūz
1801
IRAQ
Ar Rutbah
Bādiyat ash Shām
ISRAEL
Haifa
Tel Aviv-Yafo
Ashdod
Jerusalem
West Bank
'AMMĀN
JORDAN
Ma'ān
Al Jawf
Zuwārah
Tarābulus (Tripoli)
Az Zāwiyah
Al Khums
Gharyān
968
Misrātah
Mizdah
Tripolitania
Khalīj Surt
Surt
Zāwiyat al Baydā
Darnah
Banghāzī
Al Marj
Suluq
Tubruq
Bardīyah
Salūm
Ajdābiyā
Cyrenaica
Daraj
Al Jaghbūb
Awjilah
Hūn
Zillah
Idehan Awbārī
Brach
Sabhah
Awbārī
LIBYA
1200
Marzūq
Fezzan
Wāw al Kabīr
Al Qatrūn
Sahrâ' Rebiana
Al Kufrah
Al Jawf
Sahrâ' Lîbîya
EL ISKANDARÎYA
(Alexandria)
El Mahalla el Kubra
Damanhûr
Marsâ Matrûh
El Alamein
Dumyât
Bûr Sa'îd
Tanta
El Mansûra
Zagazig
Isma'ilîya
Qanâ es Suweis
EL GÎZA
EL QÂHIRA
(Cairo)
El Suweis
Helwân
El Faiyûm
Beni Suef
Maghâgha
El Minyâ
Mallawi
Manfalût
Asyût
Tahta
Sohâg
Girga
Qena
THEBES
KARNAK
El Uqsur
Idfû
Kom Ombo
Sadd el Aali
Aswân
Buheirat en Naser
ABU SIMBEL
Wadi Halfa
Nahr en Nil
Khalîg el Suweis
Es Sînâ'
G. Mûsa 2637
Elat
Al 'Aqabah
Es Sahrâ Esh Sharqîya
EGYPT
Hurghada
2187
Bûr Safâga
Quseir
RED SEA
Sîwa
-133
Munkhafed el Qattâra
Qasr Farâfra
Mût
El Wâhât el-Dakhla
El Khârga
El Wâhât el-Khârga
1082
J. Uweinat 1893
SAUDI ARABIA
Tabūk
2578
Al Muwaylih
Al Wajh
Hijaz
Yanbu 'al Bahr
Ras Bânâs
Bîr Shalatein
Râbigh
Halaib
Ras Hadarba
Muhammad Qol
2259
Bûr Sûdân
Suakin
Sinkat
Trinkitat
Haiya
Karora
2780
Nakfa
ERITREA
Akordat
Kassalâ
Sahara
Tummo
Madama
Chirfa
Aozou Strip
Aozou
Bardai
Pic Toussidé 3265
3150
Tarso Emissi
Tibesti
Zouar
Emi Koussi 3415
Ma'tan as Sarra
El Wâhât el Selîma
Es Sahrâ en Nûbîya
Kosha
Delgo
3rd Cataract
Dongola
Abu Hamed
4th Cataract
5th Cataract
Kareima
Ed Debba
Nahr en Nil
Berber
Atbara
Adarama
Nahr Atbara
Wad Hamid
Shendî
6th Cataract
Bir 'Atrun
Ounianga Sérir
Dépression du Mourdi
Borkou
Faya-Largeau
Fada
Ennedi
1310
Bilma
Grand Erg du Bilma
Erg du Djourab
Zagaoua
Oum Chalouba
CHAD
NIGER
SUDAN
El Khartûm
(Khartoum)
Omdurmân
El Wuz
Khashm el Girba
Wâd Medanî
Gedaref
El Gezira
Malha
1954
Kutum
Umm Keddada
El Fâsher
Sodiri
Kordofân
Ed Dueim
El Obeid
Kôstî
Umm Ruwaba
Er Rahad
Singa
Nil el Azraq
Biltine
Al Junaynah
Abéché
Dârfûr
Jebel Mara 3088
Zalingei
Nyâlâ
En Nahud
Abû Zabad
El Odaiya
1325
Kâdugli
Ed Damazin
Nil el Abyad
Gonder
1830
L. Tana
Bahir Dar
Bure
Debre Markos
Zigey
Bahr el Ghazal
Mao
Lac Tchad
Moussoro
Nguigmi
Bosso
Ati
Oum Hadjer
Massakory
Gashua
Geidam
Maiduguri
Potiskum
Ndjamena
Kousseri
Bokoro
Mongo
Goz Beïda
Massenya
Abou-Deïa
Am Timan
Bama
Chari
Bajoga
Biu
Kumo
Maroua
Mubi
Guider
Bongor
Numan
Garoua
Yola
Pala
Logone
Laï
Sarh
Koumra
Moundou
Doba
Birao
Songo
Bahr el Arab
1226
Ndélé
Sa'id Bundas
Raga
Bahr el Ghazâl
Jur
Sûdd
Bahr el Jebel
Malakâl
Sobat
Gogriâl
Wâw
Tonj
Rumbêk
Bôr
Toinya
Pibor Post
Dembidolo
3202
ETHIOPIA
Nekemte
Metu
Gore
Jima
3686
Omo
L. Abaya
Arba Minch
L. Shamo
Chew Bahir
Baïbokoum
Ngaoundéré
Gashaka
Banyo
Paoua
Kaga Bandoro
CENTRAL AFRICAN REPUBLIC
Bossangoa
Bozoum
Bouar
Bétaré Oya
Yoko
Yalinga
Sibut
Bambari
Ippy
Bakouma
Obo
Tali Post
Amadi
El Istiwa'iya
Mongalla
Kapoeta
Carnot
Bossembélé
Bangassou
Bomu
Oubangi
Yambio
Juba
Torit
Kajo Kaji
3187
Lokitaung
L. Turkana
375
CAMEROON
Sanaga
Bertoua
Batouri
Nanga-Eboko
Abong-Mbang
Berbérati
Bangui
Zongo
Bosobolo
Mobaye
Mobayi
Bondo
Ango
Uele
Yei
Faradje
Dungu
Yaoundé
Mbaïki
Libenge

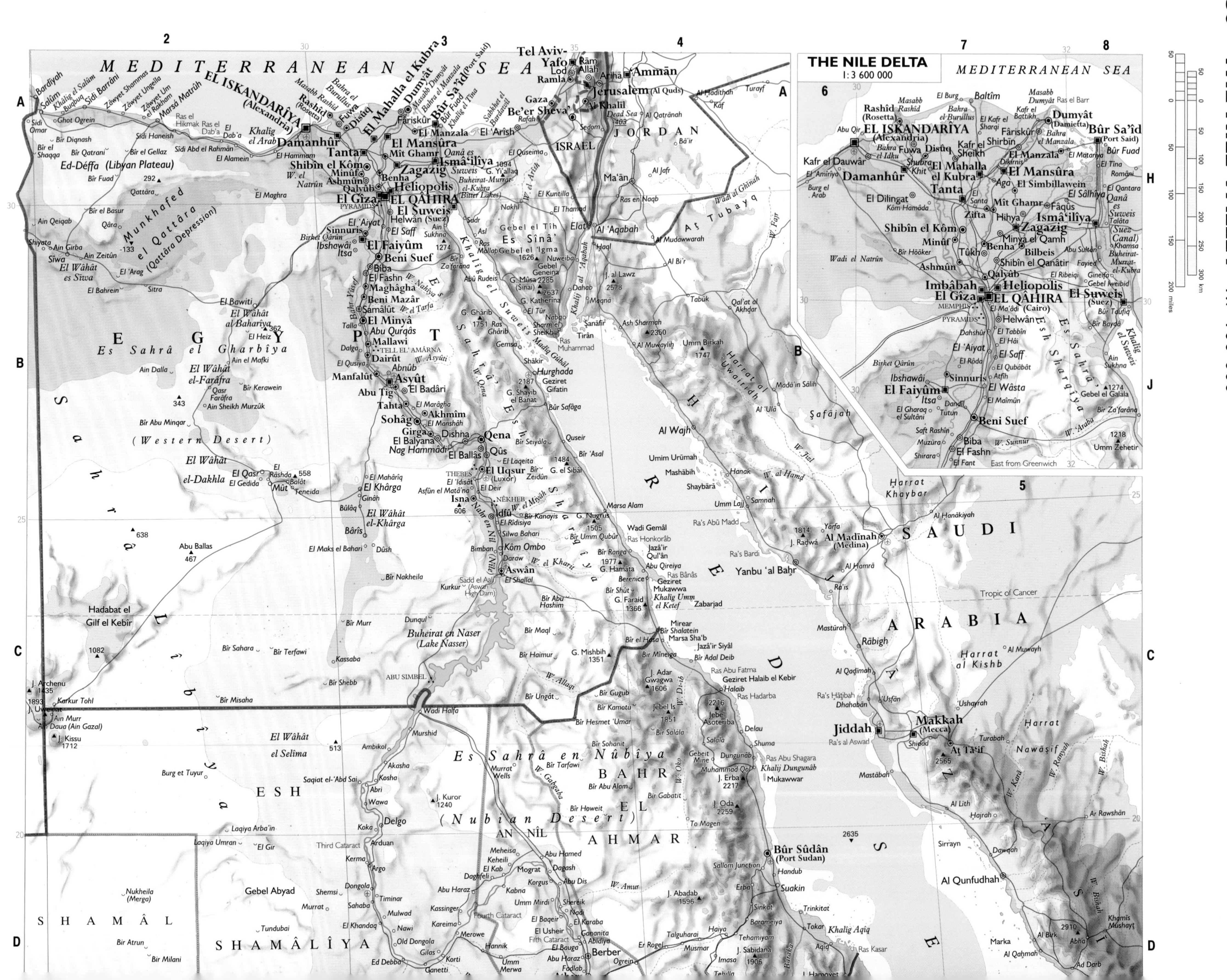
50 0 50 100 150 200 250 300 km
50 0 50 100 150 200 miles
THE NILE DELTA
1:3 600 000
MEDITERRANEAN SEA
EL ISKANDARÎYA (Alexandria)
EL QÂHIRA (Cairo)
Bûr Sa'îd (Port Said)
El Suweis (Suez)
Heliopolis
El Gîza
Damanhûr
Tanta
El Mansûra
Zagazig
Ismâ'ilîya
El Faiyûm
Beni Suef
El Minyâ
Asyût
Sohâg
Qena
El Uqsur (Luxor)
Aswân
Buheirat en Naser (Lake Nasser)
Wadi Halfa
Tel Aviv-Yafo
Jerusalem (Al Quds)
Ammân
ISRAEL
JORDAN
SAUDI ARABIA
RED SEA
EGYPT
Es Sahrâ el Gharbîya
(Western Desert)
Es Sahrâ en Nûbîya
(Nubian Desert)
Munkhafed el Qattâra (Qattâra Depression)
Ed-Déffa (Libyan Plateau)
Hadabat el Gilf el Kebîr
Es Sînâ'
Al Madînah (Medina)
Makkah (Mecca)
Jiddah
Yanbu 'al Bahr
Bûr Sûdân (Port Sudan)
Suakin
Berber
Al Qunfudhah
Tropic of Cancer
East from Greenwich

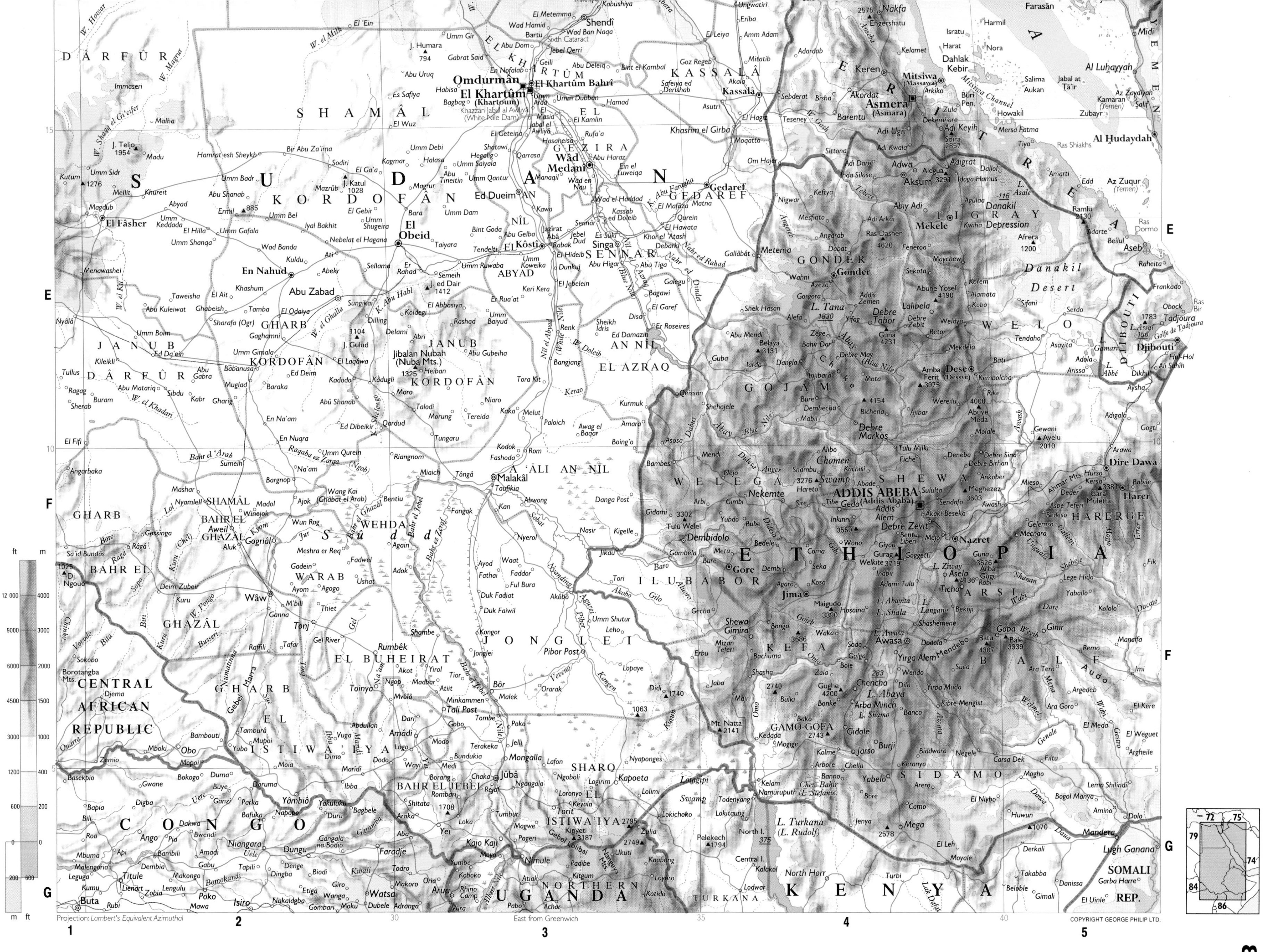

YEMEN

A

Farasān

Al Luḥayyah

Az Zaydah

Jabal at Ṭaʾir

Kamarān (Yemen)

Zubayr I.

Az Zuqur (Yemen)

Harat

Israatu

Nora

Harmil

Nokfa

Engarehatu

Amm Adam

Engeba

Ras Shaikhs

Dahlak Kebir

Massawa)

Mitsiwa

Akkelo

Emni Kwala

DJIBOUTI

Djibouti

Obock

Tadjoura

Gulf de Tadjoura

Ras Bir

Dikhil

ERITREA

ETHIOPIA

Asmera (Asmara)

Keren

Akordat

TIGRAY

Mekele

Aksum

Adwa

Adigrat

GONDER

Gonder

L. Tana

GOJJAM

Debre Markos

Bahr Dar

ADDIS ABEBA (Addis Ababa)

SHEWA

Debre Zeyit

Nazret

HARERGE

Harer

Dirē Dawa

BALE

ARSI

SIDAMO

L. Abaya

GAMO-GOFA

KEFA

Jima

ILUBABOR

WELEGA

Nekemte

Gore

L. Turkana (L. Rudolf)

KENYA

SOMALI REP.

Dolo

El Uinle

Lak Dafat

SUDAN

KHARTÜM

El Khartûm (Khartoum)

Omdurman

El Khartûm Bahri

KASSALA

Kassala

Gedaref

EL GEDAREF

EN NIL EL AZRAQ

SENNAR

Singa

EL GEZIRA

Wad Medani

EN NIL EL ABYAD

Ed Dueim

EN NIL

ABYAD

El Obeid

KORDOFAN

SHAMAL KORDOFAN

JANUB KORDOFAN

Jibalan Nubah (Nuba Mts.)

DARFÜR

SHAMAL DARFÜR

JANUB DARFÜR

El Fasher

En Nahud

Abu Zabad

A'ALI AN NIL

Malakal

JONGLEI

Bör

BAHR EL GHAZAL

Wäw

SHAMAL BAHR EL GHAZAL

WARAB

EL BUHEIRAT

EL WEHDA

WEHDA

SHARQ ISTIWA'IYA

GHARB EL ISTIWA'IYA

GHARB BAHR EL GHAZAL

BAHR EL JEBEL

Jūba

UGANDA

NORTHERN

Imatong Mts.

CONGO

CENTRAL AFRICAN REPUBLIC

Buta

East from Greenwich

Projection Lambert's Equivalent Azimuthal

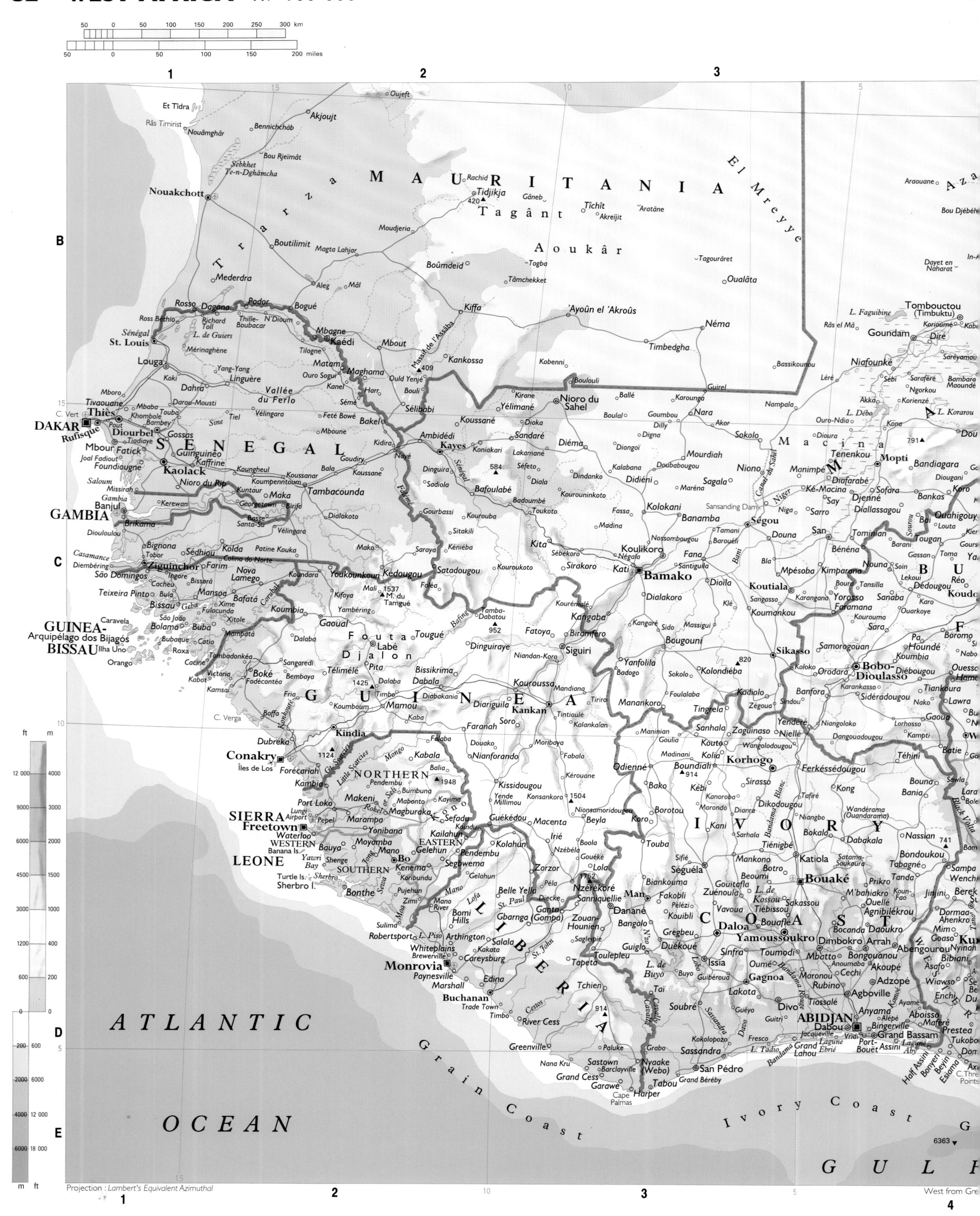
50 0 50 100 150 200 250 300 km
50 0 50 100 150 200 miles
1
2
3
4
B
C
D
E
MAURITANIA
Trarza
Tagânt
Aoukâr
El Mreyyé
Et Tîdra
Râs Timirist
Nouâmghâr
Akjoujt
Bennichchâb
Oujeft
Bou Rjeïmât
Sebkhet Te-n-Dghâmcha
Nouakchott
Rachid
Tidjikja
Gâneb
Tîchît
Akreïjit
Aratâne
Moudjeria
Boutilimit
Magta Lahjar
Boûmdeïd
Togba
Tâmchekket
Tagourâret
Oualâta
Mederdra
Aleg
Mâl
Rosso
Dagana
Podor
Bogué
Kiffa
'Ayoûn el 'Atroûs
Néma
Timbedgha
Araouane
Bou Djébéha
Dayet en Naharat
Ross Béthio
Richard Toll
Thille-Boubacar
N'Dioum
L. de Guiers
Sénégal
St. Louis
Mérinaghène
Mbagne
Kaédi
Mbout
Tilogne
Massif de l'Assâba
Kankossa
Kobenni
Boulouli
Bassikounou
Louga
Yang-Yang
Linguère
Matam
Ouro Sogui
Maghama
Ould Yenjé
Bouli
Sélibabi
Kanel
Harr
Sémé
Koki
Dahra
Vallée du Ferlo
Darou-Mousti
Mboro
Tivaouane
C. Vert
Thiès
DAKAR
Rufisque
Mbaba
Khombole
Touba
Bambey
Diourbel
Pout
Gossas
Tiel
Vélingara
Sine
Mbour
Tiadiaye
Fatick
Joal Fadiout
Foundiougne
SENEGAL
Guinguinéo
Kaffrine
Kaolack
Nioro du Rip
Saloum
Missirah
Gambia
Banjul
GAMBIA
Kerewan
Georgetown
Maka
Kuntaur
Birifo
Basse Santa-Su
Brikama
Diouloulou
Koungheul
Koussanar
Koumpentoum
Tambacounda
Bala
Koussané
Goudiry
Fété Bowé
Mboune
Bakel
Kidira
Ambidédi
Kayes
Nayé
Falémé
Dialakoto
Vélingara
Bignona
Sédhiou
Kolda
Patine Kouka
Casamance
Diembéring
Ziguinchor
Tobor
Farim
Colina do Norte
São Domingos
Ingore
Cacheu
Bissorã
Nova Lamego
Koundara
Youkounkoun
Kédougou
Saraya
Mako
Satadougou
Teixeira Pinto
Bula
Mansoa
Bafatá
Bissau
Xime
Fulacunda
Geba
Corubal
Koumbia
Caravela
Bolama
São João
Buba
Xitole
GUINEA-BISSAU
Arquipélago dos Bijagós
Ilha Uno
Orango
Bubaque
Catio
Roxa
Mampatá
Cacine
Tombadonkéa
Kabot
Victoria
Kamsar
Boké
Fodécontéa
Sangaredi
Bembaya
Fria
Boffa
C. Verga
Konkouré
Dubréka
Conakry
Îles de Los
Forécariah
Kindia
Kambia
Mali
1537
M. du Tamgué
Yambéring
Gaoual
Dalaba
Fouta Djalon
Labé
Tougué
Pita
Télimélé
1425
Timbo
Koumbourn
Mamou
Kaba
Bafing
Tamba-Dabatou
952
Dinguiraye
Bissikrima
Dabola
Diabakania
Niandan-Koro
GUINEA
Kouroussa
Mandiana
Diariguila
Kankan
Tintioulé
Faranah
Soro
Kalankalan
Douako
Nianforando
Moribaya
Fabala
Kérouane
Kissidougou
Yende Millimou
Konsankoro
1504
Nionsamoridougou
Beyla
Guékédou
Macenta
Irié
Nzébéla
Boola
Gouéké
Lola
Zorzor
Kolahun
1752
Nzérékoré
Pela
Diecke
Falaba
Mongo
Kabala
Balia
1948
NORTHERN
Pendembu
Bumbuna
Makeni
Mabonto
Kayima
Port Loko
Rokel
Magburaka
Lungi Airport
Pepel
Marampa
Sefadu
Kono
SIERRA LEONE
Freetown
Waterloo
WESTERN
Banana Is.
Yonibana
Moyamba
Kailahun
Koindu
EASTERN
Gelehun
Pendembu
Bauya
Mano
Bo
Yawri Bay
Shenge
Kenema
Segbwema
Gelahun
Turtle Is.
Sherbro
SOUTHERN
Koribundu
Sherbro I.
Bonthe
Sewa
Pujehun
Zimi
Mano River
Mano
Lofa
Bomi Hills
LIBERIA
Belle Yella
St. Paul
Gbarnga (Gompa)
Ganta
Sanniquellie
Sulima
Moa
Robertsport
L. Piso
Arthington
Whiteplains
Brewerville
Kakata
Salala
Careysburg
St. John
Monrovia
Paynesville
Edina
Marshall
Buchanan
Trade Town
Timbo
Cestos
River Cess
914
Greenville
Paluke
Nana Kru
Sastown
Barclayville
Grand Cess
Garawe
Cape Palmas
Harper
Nyaake (Webo)
Tabou
Grand Bérébi
San Pédro
Sassandra
Grabo
Cavally
Tchien
Zouan-Hounien
Sogleipie
Toulepleu
Tapeta
Danané
Man
Bangolo
Guiglo
Duékoué
L. de Buyo
Buyo
Taï
Soubré
Sassandra
Guéyo
Kokolopozo
Fresco
L. Tadio
Grand Lahou
Ebrié
Divo
Lakota
Gagnoa
Guibéroua
Issia
Sinfra
Daloa
Vavoua
Zuénoula
Gouitafla
Kounahiri
Biankouma
Fakobli
Kouibli
Séguéla
Touba
Koro
Borotou
Odienné
Bako
Kani
Boundiali
Korhogo
Ferkéssédougou
914
Kébi
Sirasso
Dikodougou
Niangbo
Tiénigbé
Mankono
Beoumi
Katiola
Bouaké
Kossou
L. de Kossou
Sakassou
Tiébissou
Bouaflé
Yamoussoukro
Toumodi
Oumé
Tiassalé
Bandama
Bandama Rouge
Moronou
Rubino
Agboville
Adzopé
Akoupé
Cechi
Anyama
Alépé
Bingerville
ABIDJAN
Dabou
Jacqueville
Grand Bassam
Port-Bouët
Assini
Half Assini
Bonyeri
Beyin
Esiama
C. Three Points
Aboisso
Maféré
Prestea
Tarkwa
Tukobo
Dimbokro
Bongouanou
Mbatto
Arrah
Daoukro
Bocanda
M'bahiakro
Prikro
Ouellé
Agnibilékrou
Abengourou
Kong
Tafiré
Nassian
Bondoukou
Tabagné
Tanda
Sampa
Wenchi
Berekum
Dormaa-Ahenkro
Mim
Goaso
Asafo
Bibiani
Wiawso
Enchi
Ayamé
IVORY COAST
Zaguinaso
Tingréla
Kadiolo
Zégoua
Sikasso
Kolondiéba
820
Sokolo
Foulalaba
Manankoro
Sanhala
Kouto
Kolia
Madinani
Manikian
Goulia
Niellé
Yendéré
Niangoloko
Dangouadougou
Banfora
Sidéradougou
Karankasso
Bobo-Dioulasso
Orodara
Diébougou
Samorogouan
Houndé
Koumbia
Boromo
Pa
Sara
Ouarkoye
Faramana
Yorosso
Koutiala
Karangana
Koumankou
Sangasso
Tansilla
Kimparana
Mpésoba
Dioila
Bamako
Kati
Koulikoro
Négala
Siby
Kangaba
Kourémalé
Dialakoro
Birainféro
Siguiri
Yanfolila
Bougouni
Massigui
Sido
Kangaré
Fatoya
Kita
Sébékoro
Sirakoro
Kourouktoto
Kéniéba
Sitakili
Kouroukota
Gourbassi
Toukoto
Badoumbé
Bafoulabé
Sadiola
Dinguira
Sénégal
Koniakari
Lakamané
Sandaré
Séfeto
Diala
584
Diéma
Diongoï
Dindanko
Kalabana
Didiéni
Koussané
Dioka
Yélimané
Kirane
Nioro du Sahel
Ballé
Boulal
Goumbou
Dilly
Digna
Karounga
Nara
Akor
Guirel
Mourdiah
Doubabougou
Maréna
Sagala
Kolokani
Banamba
Fassa
Madina
Nossombougou
Tamani
Barouéli
Ségou
Fana
Santiguila
Bani
Bla
Douna
Niono
Sokolo
Canal du Sahel
Niger
Sansanding Dam
Niga
Sarro
San
Macina
Tenenkou
Mopti
Manimpé
Diafarabé
Ké-Macina
Say
Djenné
Sofara
Diallassagou
Bandiagara
Diougani
Bankas
Koro
Tominian
Bénéna
Nouna
Sourou
Ouahigouya
Tougan
Gassan
Toma
Lekoui
Dédougou
Kouka
Réo
Koudougou
Safané
Nampala
Niafounké
Léré
Sébi
Ngorkou
Koriensé
Akka
L. Débo
Ouro-Ndia
Dioura
Kona
791
L. Korarou
Sarafere
Bambara Maoundé
Goundam
L. Faguibine
Râs el Mâ
Tombouctou (Timbuktu)
Korioumé
Kabara
Diré
Saréyamou
Nampala
Tioulé
Batié
Nako
Gaoua
Lorhosso
Kampti
Téhini
Bouna
Bania
Sawla
Lara
Bole
Black Volta
Wandérama (Ouandarama)
Bokala
Dabakala
741
Wa
Lawra
Tiankoura
ATLANTIC OCEAN
Grain Coast
Ivory Coast
GULF
6363
Projection : Lambert's Equivalent Azimuthal
West from Greenwich
15
10
5
ft m
12 000 4000
9000 3000
6000 2000
4500 1500
3000 1000
1200 400
600 200
0 0
200 600
2000 6000
4000 12 000
6000 18 000
m ft

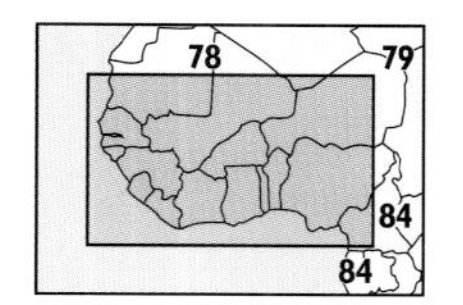
78
79
84
84

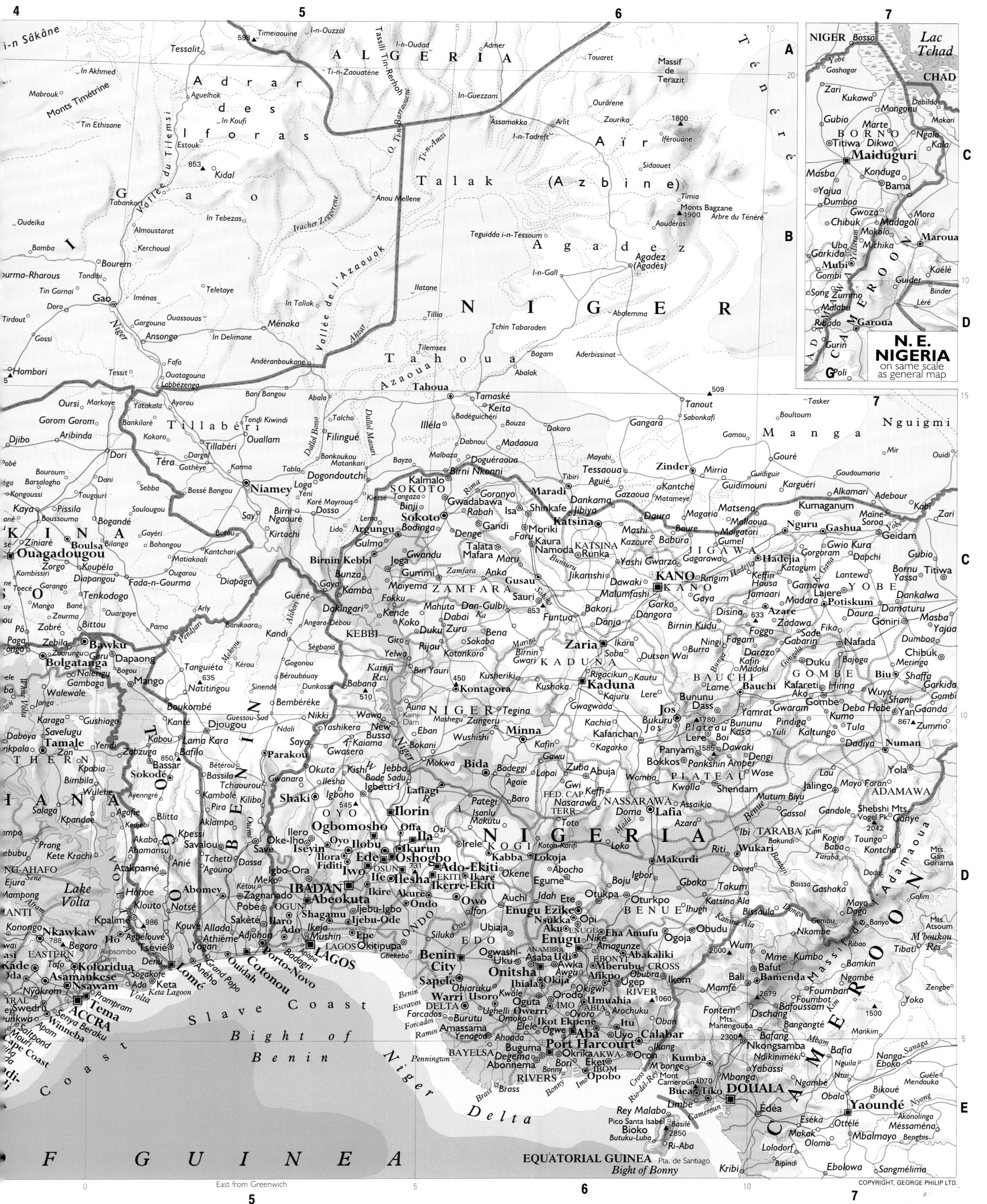
ALGERIA
NIGER
NIGERIA
CHAD
CAMEROON
BENIN
TOGO
GHANA
EQUATORIAL GUINEA
Adrar des Iforas
Aïr
Talak (Azbine)
Agadez
Tahoua
Ténéré
Manga
Tillabéri
Slave Coast
Bight of Benin
Niger Delta
Bight of Bonny
GUINEA
Lake Volta
Lac Tchad
Niamey
Ouagadougou
Sokoto
Katsina
Kano
Zaria
Kaduna
Jos
Bauchi
Maiduguri
Ilorin
Ogbomosho
Oshogbo
IBADAN
Abeokuta
LAGOS
Porto-Novo
Cotonou
Lomé
ACCRA
Tema
Benin City
Onitsha
Enugu
Port Harcourt
Calabar
Aba
Makurdi
Lokoja
Abuja
Minna
DOUALA
Yaoundé
Malabo
Bioko
Zinder
Maradi
Tahoua
Agadez (Agadès)
Gao
N.E. NIGERIA
on same scale
as general map
East from Greenwich
COPYRIGHT, GEORGE PHILIP LTD.

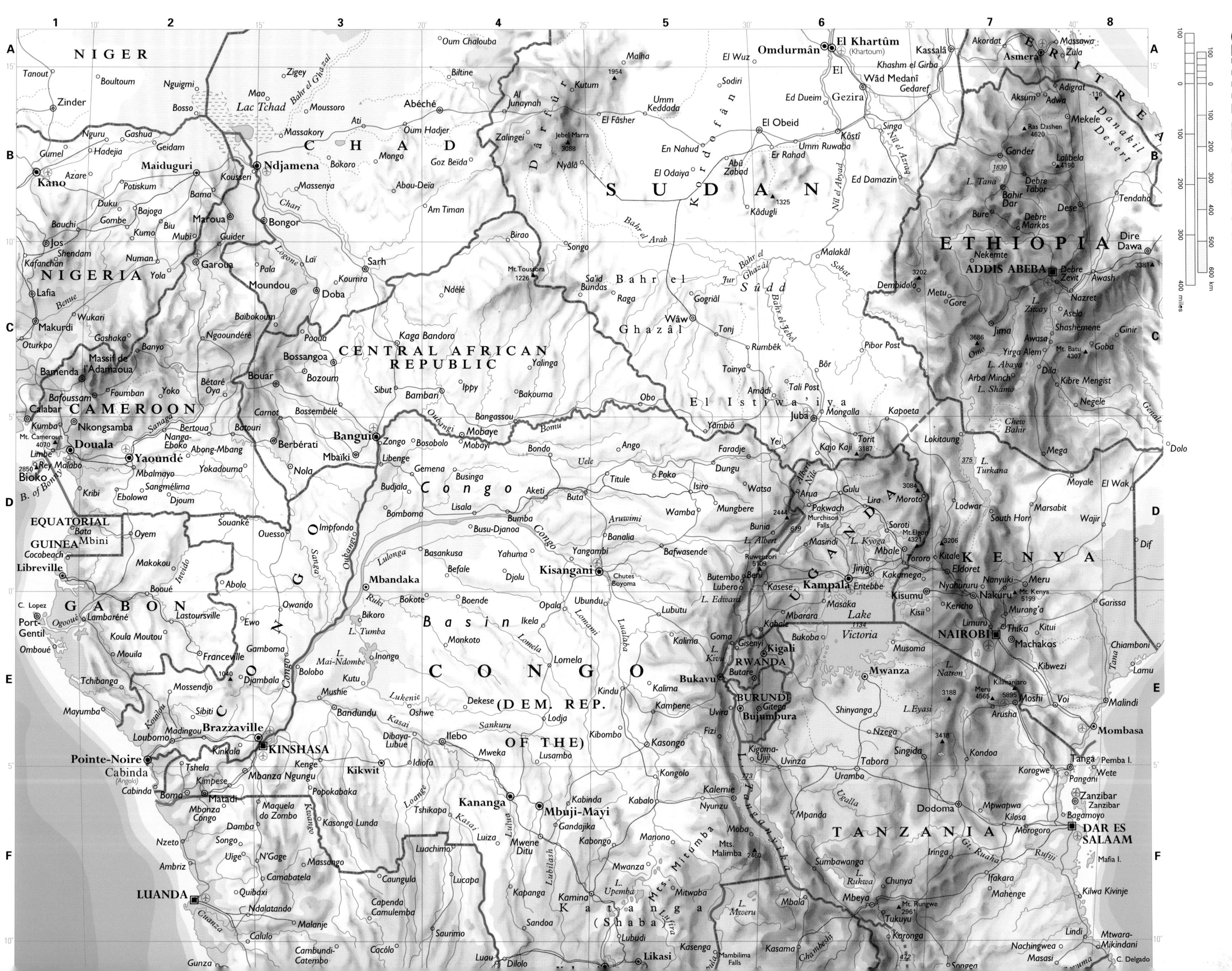
100 0 100 200 300 400 500 600 km
100 0 100 200 300 400 miles
NIGER
CHAD
SUDAN
ERITREA
ETHIOPIA
ADDIS ABEBA
Danakil Desert
Asmera
Massawa
El Khartûm (Khartoum)
Omdurmân
Wâd Medanî
Kassalâ
Gezira
El Obeid
Kordofân
Dârfûr
Jebel Marra 3088
El Fâsher
Bahr el Arab
Bahr el Ghazâl
Sûdd
Juba
Wâw
Malakâl
El Istiwa'iya
Dire Dawa
L. Tana
Ras Dashen 4620
NIGERIA
Kano
Maiduguri
Zinder
Lac Tchad
Ndjamena
CAMEROON
Yaoundé
Douala
Massif de l'Adamaoua
Mt. Cameroun 4070
Bioko
Malabo
CENTRAL AFRICAN REPUBLIC
Bangui
EQUATORIAL GUINEA
GABON
Libreville
Port-Gentil
CONGO
Brazzaville
Pointe-Noire
Cabinda (Angola)
KINSHASA
Matadi
LUANDA
CONGO (DEM. REP. OF THE)
Congo Basin
Kisangani
Mbandaka
Kananga
Mbuji-Mayi
Likasi
Katanga (Shaba)
Mts. Mitumba
UGANDA
Kampala
Lake Victoria
L. Albert
L. Edward
L. Kivu
L. Tanganyika
L. Turkana
RWANDA
Kigali
BURUNDI
Bujumbura
Bukavu
KENYA
NAIROBI
Mt. Kenya 5199
Mombasa
Kisumu
TANZANIA
DAR ES SALAAM
Dodoma
Mwanza
Tabora
Kilimanjaro 5895
Zanzibar
Mafia I.
Pemba I.

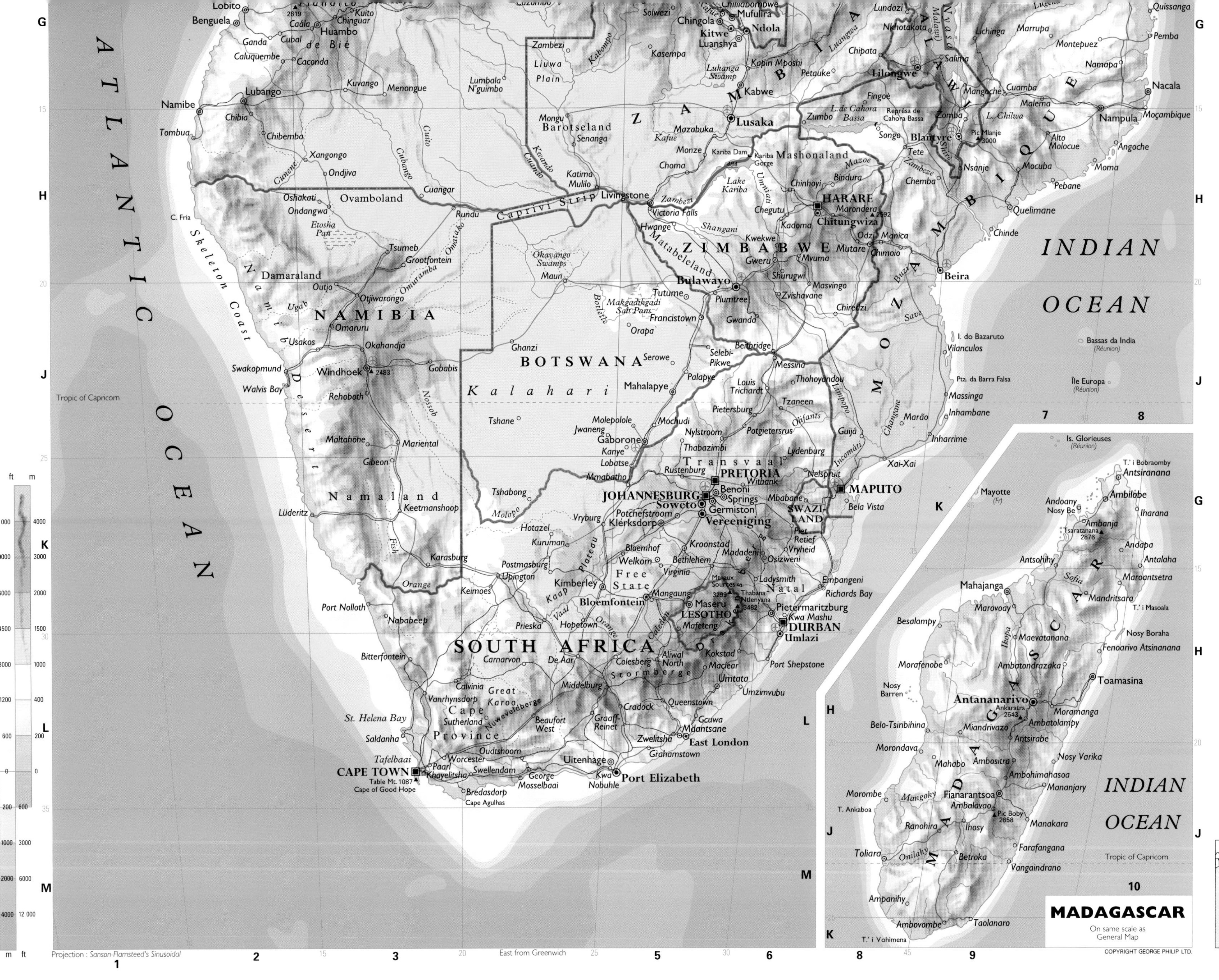

ATLANTIC OCEAN
INDIAN OCEAN
SOUTH AFRICA
NAMIBIA
BOTSWANA
ZIMBABWE
ZAMBIA
MOZAMBIQUE
MALAWI
LESOTHO
SWAZILAND
Kalahari
Namib Desert
Skeleton Coast
Caprivi Strip
Transvaal
Free State
Natal
Cape Province
Great Karoo
Namaland
Damaraland
Ovamboland
Barotseland
Mashonaland
Matabeleland
CAPE TOWN
JOHANNESBURG
PRETORIA
MAPUTO
HARARE
DURBAN
Lusaka
Bulawayo
Windhoek
Gaborone
Bloemfontein
Maseru
Port Elizabeth
East London
Beira
Tropic of Capricorn
East from Greenwich
Projection : Sanson-Flamsteed's Sinusoidal
MADAGASCAR
On same scale as General Map
Antananarivo
Toamasina
INDIAN OCEAN
COPYRIGHT GEORGE PHILIP LTD.

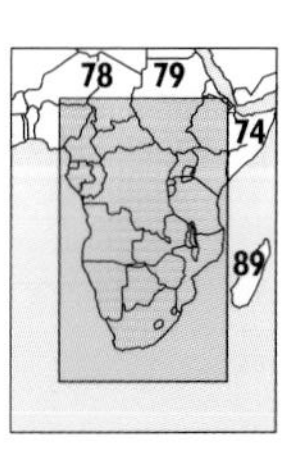

78
79
74
89

SOMALI REP.

ETHIOPIA

KENYA

UGANDA

TANZANIA

RWANDA

BURUNDI

CENTRAL AFRICAN REPUBLIC

Lake Victoria

NAIROBI

MOMBASA

DAR ES SALAAM

Kampala

Kisangani

Zanzibar

L. Turkana (L. Rudolf)

L. Tanganyika

RIFT VALLEY

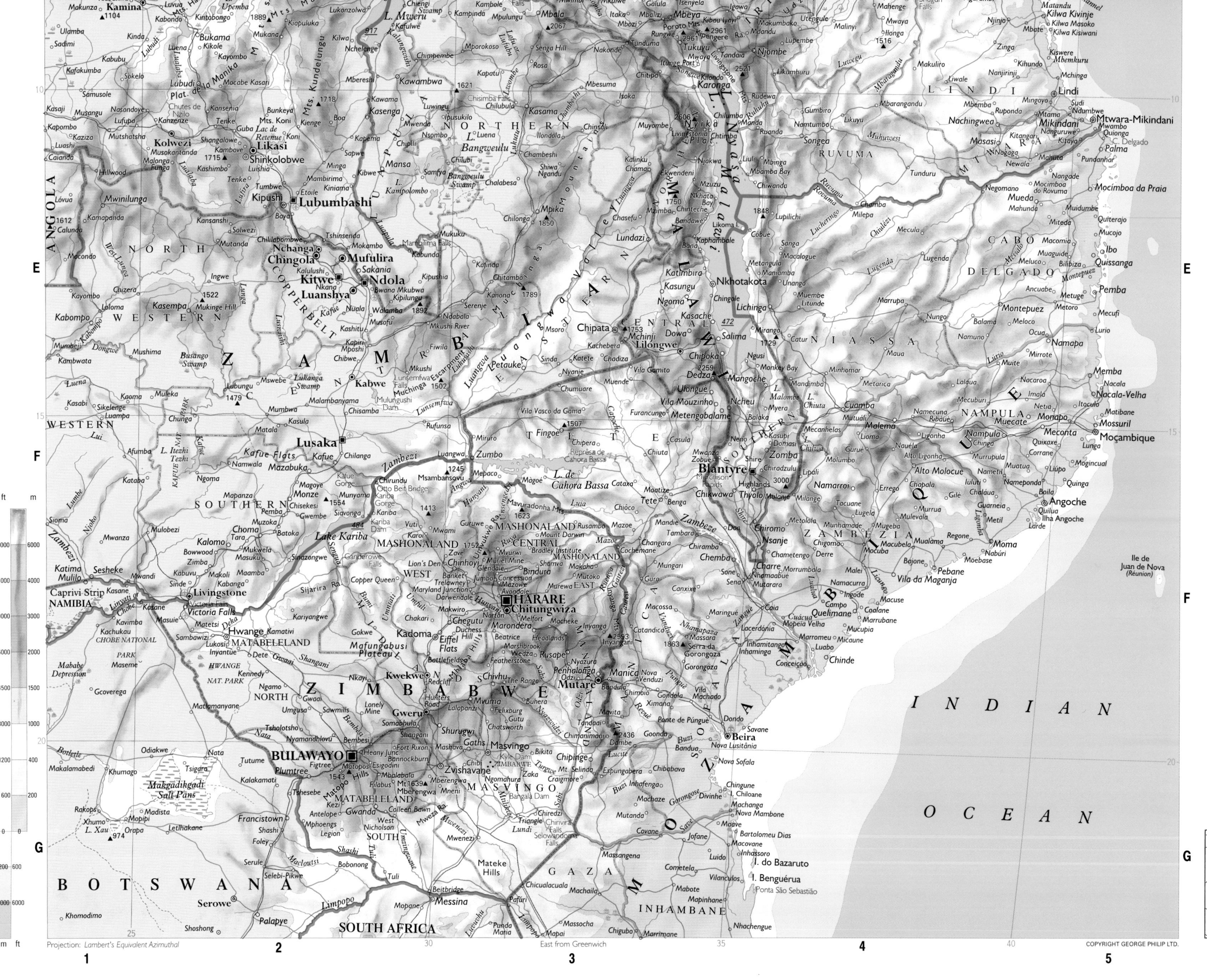

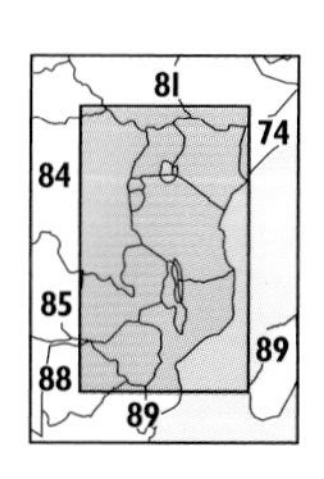

COPYRIGHT GEORGE PHILIP LTD.

Projection: Lambert's Equivalent Azimuthal

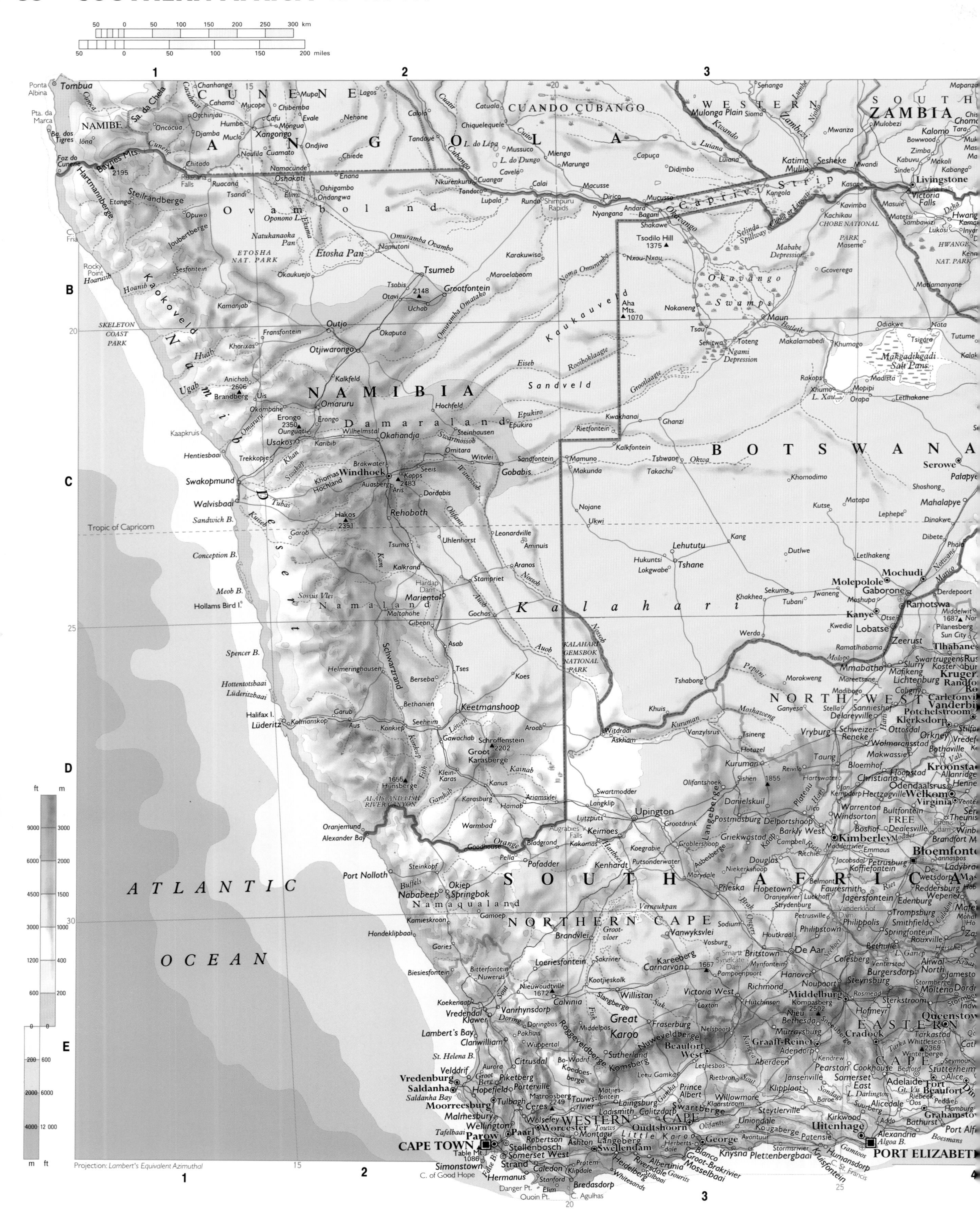

ATLANTIC
OCEAN
NAMIBIA
BOTSWANA
SOUTH AFRICA
ZAMBIA
ANGOLA
CUNENE
NAMIBE
CUANDO CUBANGO
WESTERN
NORTH-WEST
NORTHERN CAPE
WESTERN CAPE
EASTERN CAPE
FREE
Ovamboland
Damaraland
Namaland
Namaqualand
Kaokoveld
Namib Desert
Kalahari
Kaukauveld
Sandveld
Great Karoo
Little Karoo
Okavango Swamps
Caprivi Strip
Etosha Pan
ETOSHA NAT. PARK
SKELETON COAST PARK
KALAHARI GEMSBOK NATIONAL PARK
CHOBE NATIONAL PARK
Makgadikgadi Salt Pans
Tropic of Capricorn
Windhoek
Swakopmund
Walvisbaai
Lüderitz
Keetmanshoop
Rehoboth
Mariental
Tsumeb
Grootfontein
Otjiwarongo
Outjo
Okahandja
Gobabis
Omaruru
Usakos
Oranjemund
Alexander Bay
Port Nolloth
Springbok
Upington
Kimberley
Bloemfontein
Gaborone
Molepolole
Mochudi
Kanye
Lobatse
Maun
Ghanzi
Serowe
Mahalapye
Livingstone
Victoria Falls
Mmabatho
Vryburg
Kuruman
Postmasburg
De Aar
Beaufort West
Middelburg
Graaff-Reinet
Cradock
Queenstown
Grahamstown
Port Alfred
Uitenhage
PORT ELIZABETH
Oudtshoorn
George
Knysna
Mosselbaai
Swellendam
Worcester
Paarl
Stellenbosch
Wellington
CAPE TOWN
Simonstown
Hermanus
C. of Good Hope
C. Agulhas
Saldanha
Vredenburg
Clanwilliam
Calvinia
Carnarvon
Tombua
Ponta Albina
Xangongo
Ondjiva
Oshakati
Ruacana Falls
Katima Mulilo
Sesheke
Tsodilo Hill 1375
Hakos 2351
Brandberg
Anichab 2606
Hunsberge
Groot Karasberge
Schroffenstein 2202
Orange
Kalahari
Projection: Lambert's Equivalent Azimuthal
km
miles

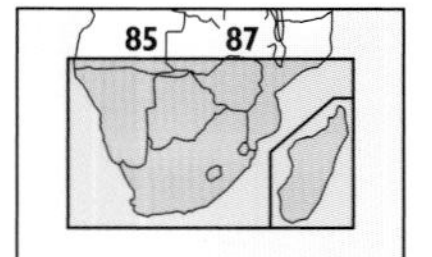

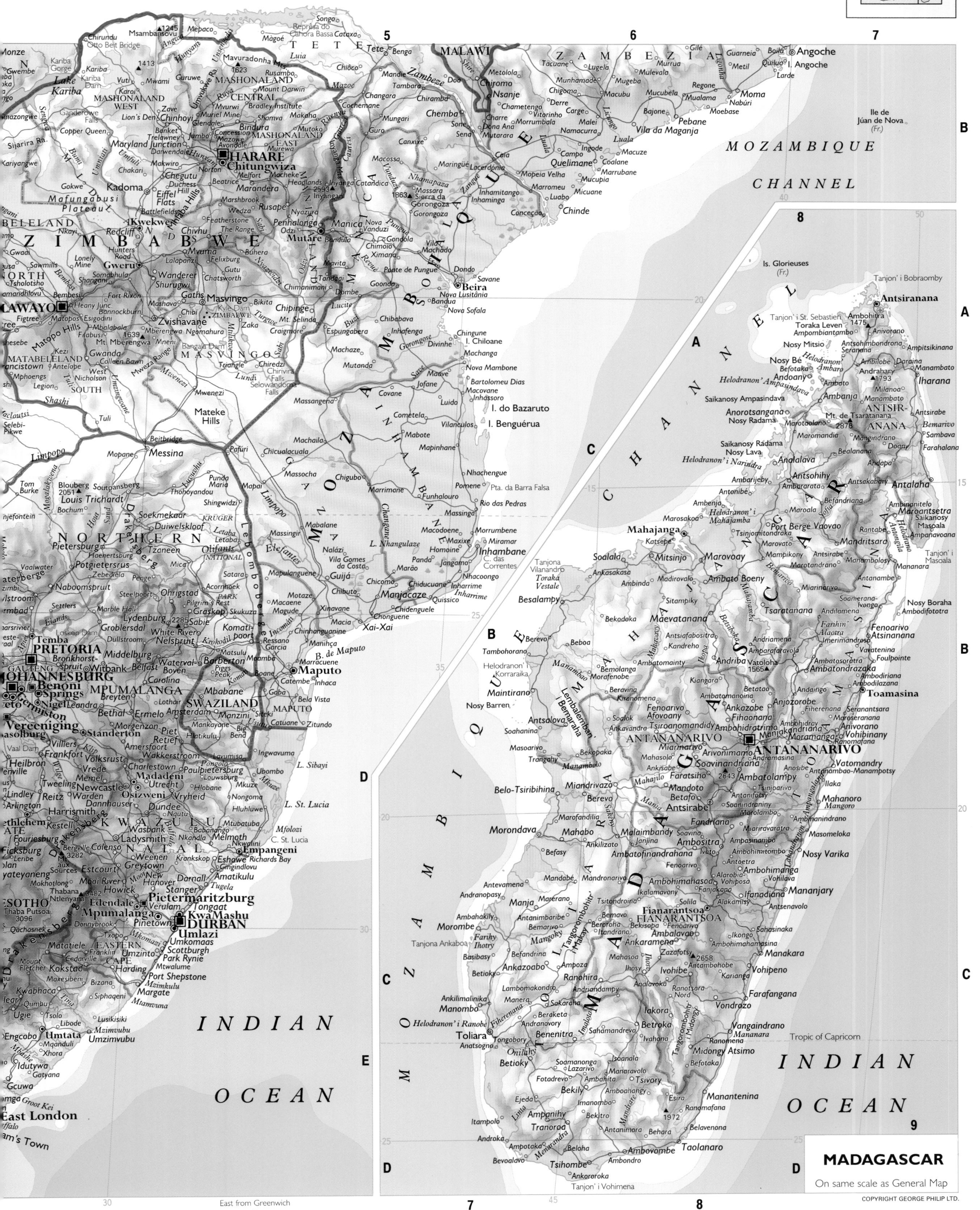

MADAGASCAR

On same scale as General Map

COPYRIGHT GEORGE PHILIP LTD.

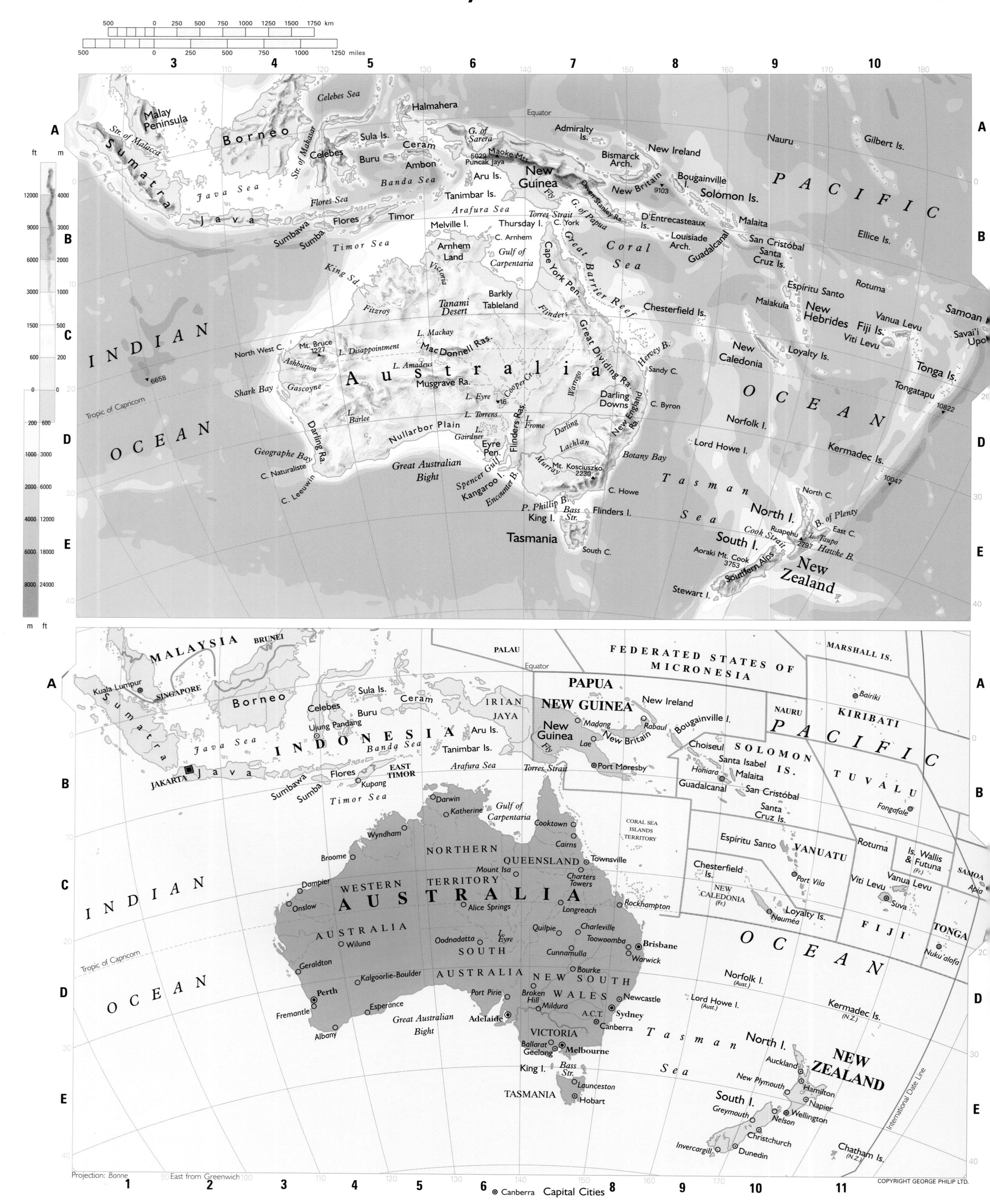

Celebes Sea
Halmahera
Malay Peninsula
Borneo
Sumatra
Str. of Malacca
Str. of Makasar
Celebes
Sula Is.
Ceram
Buru
Ambon
G. of Sarera
Maoke Mts.
5029 Puncak Jaya
Aru Is.
New Guinea
Admiralty Is.
Bismarck Arch.
New Ireland
New Britain
9103
Bougainville I.
Solomon Is.
Nauru
Gilbert Is.
PACIFIC
Java Sea
Java
Banda Sea
Tanimbar Is.
Arafura Sea
Torres Strait
Thursday I.
C. York
G. of Papua
Owen Stanley Ra.
D'Entrecasteaux Is.
Louisiade Arch.
Malaita
San Cristóbal
Santa Cruz Is.
Ellice Is.
Flores Sea
Flores
Timor
Sumbawa
Sumba
Melville I.
C. Arnhem
Arnhem Land
Gulf of Carpentaria
Timor Sea
Coral Sea
Great Barrier Reef
Guadalcanal
Cape York Pen.
King Sd.
Victoria
Barkly Tableland
Tanami Desert
Fitzroy
Flinders
Chesterfield Is.
Espíritu Santo
Rotuma
Malakula
New Hebrides
Fiji Is.
Vanua Levu
Viti Levu
Samoan
Savai'i
Upolu
INDIAN OCEAN
6658
North West C.
Mt. Bruce 1227
L. Disappointment
L. Mackay
MacDonnell Ras.
Ashburton
L. Amadeus
Australia
Musgrave Ra.
Great Dividing Ra.
Hervey B.
Sandy C.
New Caledonia
Loyalty Is.
Tonga Is.
Tongatapu
10822
Shark Bay
Gascoyne
Tropic of Capricorn
L. Eyre
-16
Cooper Cr.
Warrego
Darling Downs
C. Byron
New England Ra.
OCEAN
L. Barlee
L. Torrens
L. Frome
Darling
Norfolk I.
Lord Howe I.
Kermadec Is.
Nullarbor Plain
L. Gairdner
Flinders Ras.
Eyre Pen.
Lachlan
Murray
Darling Ra.
Geographe Bay
C. Naturaliste
C. Leeuwin
Great Australian Bight
Spencer Gulf
Kangaroo I.
Encounter B.
Mt. Kosciuszko 2230
Botany Bay
C. Howe
Tasman Sea
10047
North C.
North I.
B. of Plenty
East C.
P. Phillip B.
King I.
Bass Str.
Flinders I.
Tasmania
South C.
Ruapehu 2797
L. Taupo
Hawke B.
Cook Strait
South I.
Aoraki Mt. Cook 3753
Southern Alps
New Zealand
Stewart I.
Equator
ft m
12000 4000
9000 3000
6000 2000
3000 1000
1500 500
600 200
0 0
200 600
1000 3000
2000 6000
4000 12000
6000 18000
8000 24000
m ft
500 0 250 500 750 1000 1250 1500 1750 km
500 0 250 500 750 1000 1250 miles
MALAYSIA
BRUNEI
Kuala Lumpur
SINGAPORE
PALAU
FEDERATED STATES OF MICRONESIA
MARSHALL IS.
PAPUA NEW GUINEA
Madang
Rabaul
Lae
Port Moresby
Bairiki
KIRIBATI
NAURU
IRIAN JAYA
INDONESIA
Ujung Pandang
JAKARTA
EAST TIMOR
Kupang
Choiseul
SOLOMON IS.
Santa Isabel
Honiara
TUVALU
Fongafale
Darwin
Katherine
CORAL SEA ISLANDS TERRITORY
Cooktown
Cairns
Townsville
Wyndham
Broome
NORTHERN TERRITORY
QUEENSLAND
Mount Isa
Charters Towers
VANUATU
Port Vila
Is. Wallis & Futuna (Fr.)
SAMOA
Apia
Dampier
Onslow
WESTERN AUSTRALIA
Alice Springs
Longreach
Rockhampton
NEW CALEDONIA (Fr.)
Nouméa
Suva
FIJI
TONGA
Nuku'alofa
Wiluna
Oodnadatta
SOUTH AUSTRALIA
Quilpie
Charleville
Toowoomba
Cunnamulla
Brisbane
Warwick
Geraldton
Kalgoorlie-Boulder
Bourke
NEW SOUTH WALES
Norfolk I. (Aust.)
Perth
Fremantle
Esperance
Port Pirie
Broken Hill
Mildura
Newcastle
Sydney
A.C.T.
Canberra
Lord Howe I. (Aust.)
Kermadec Is. (N.Z.)
Albany
Adelaide
VICTORIA
Ballarat
Geelong
Melbourne
Auckland
NEW ZEALAND
New Plymouth
Hamilton
Napier
Wellington
Nelson
Greymouth
Christchurch
Dunedin
Invercargill
Launceston
Hobart
TASMANIA
International Date Line
Chatham Is. (N.Z.)
Projection: Bonne
East from Greenwich
Canberra Capital Cities

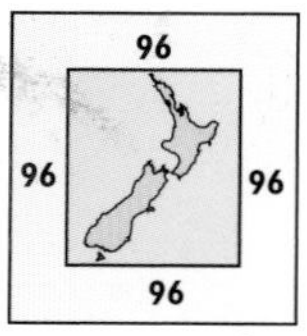

96
96 96
96
1

50 0 50 100 150 200 km
50 0 50 100 150 miles

F

PACIFIC

OCEAN

C. Reinga
C. Maria
van Diemen
North C.
Rangaunu B.
Houhora Heads
Doubtless B.
Mangonui
Whangaroa Harb.
Ahipara B.
Kaitaia
Tauroa Pt.
Okaihau
B. of Islands
C. Brett
Rawene
Kaikohe
Hikurangi
Opua
Hokianga Harbour
Whangarei
Donnelly's Crossing
Whangarei Harb.
Bream Hd.
Dargaville
Bream B.
Little
Barrier I.
Great Barrier I.
Waipu
Warkworth
C. Rodney
C. Colville
Cuvier I.
Kaipara Harbour
Helensville
Hauraki
Gulf
Coromandel
Whitianga
Takapuna Devonport
Mayor I.

G

North
Island

AUCKLAND
Manukau
Papakura
Waiuku Pukekohe
Waikato Mercer
Paeroa
Huntly
Te Aroha
Thames
Waihi
Tauranga Harb.
Mount
Maunganui
White I.
C. Runaway
East C.
Bay of Plenty
Hamilton
Morrinsville
Cambridge
Whakatane
Opotiki
Raglan
Te Awamutu
Kawerau
Taneatua
Hikurangi 1753
Waipiro
Kawhia Harbour
Putaruru
Rotorua
Rotorua
L. Tarawera
Murupara
Motu
Tolaga Bay
Otorohanga
Tokoroa
Te Kuiti
Kinleith
Mokai Wairakei
Taupo
Taumarunui
L. Taupo
Rangitaiki Mts.
Waikaremoana
Ormond
Gisborne
Poverty Bay

H

Mokau
North Taranaki
Bight
Onganie
Ongarue
Turangi
Kaimanawa Mts.
Tarawera
Nuhaka
Waikokopu
Waitara
Whangamomona
Mahia Pen.
New Plymouth
Inglewood
Mt. Taranaki
(Mt. Egmont)
2518
Stratford
Ruapehu 2797
Waioru
Wairoa
C. Egmont
Opunake
Eltham
Ohakune
Bay Hawke Bay
View
Kapuni
Raetihi
Waiouru
Waipawa
Hawera
Taihape
Napier
C. Kidnappers
South Taranaki
Bight
Waverley
Mangaweka
Hunterville
Hastings
Wanganui
Marton
Halcombe
Waipukurau
Bulls Feilding
Dannevirke

40

Palmerston
North
Woodville
C. Turnagain
Foxton
Shannon
Pahiatua
Levin
Eketahuna
Otaki
Paraparaumu
Kapiti I.
Masterton
Carterton
Greytown
Martinborough
Wairarapa
Upper Hutt
Featherston
Petone
Lower Hutt
WELLINGTON
Eastbourne

J

Collingwood
Golden
B.
D'Urville I.
Tasman
B.
Takaka
Tasman
Mts.
Nelson
Havelock
Motueka
Pelorus Sd.
Karamea
Richmond
Picton
Wakefield
Karamea
Bight
Tadmor
Maruia Ra.
Wairau
Blenheim
Seddonville
Seddon
Granity
Murchison
L. Rotoroa
Ward
Westport
Lyell
Inangahua
2885 Tapuaenuku
Reefton
Grey
L. Rotoiti
Spenser
Mts.
Kaikoura
Blackball
Mt. Travers 2338
Hanmer
Springs
Greymouth
Runanga
Stillwater
Kumara
Hokitika
L. Brunner
Jacksons
Waiau
Ross
Culverden
Arthur's
Pass
Waikari
Hurunui
Waipara

K

South
Island
Westland Bight
Abut Hd.
Amberley
Oxford
Rangiora
Pegasus Bay
Aoraki Mt. Cook
Coldridge
Kaiapoi
3753
Springfield
New Brighton
Christchurch
Jackson B.
Okuru
Haast
Mount
Cook
Whitecliffs
Riccarton
Lyttelton
Methven
Lincoln
Staveley
Banks Pen.
Fairlie
L. Tekapo
Southbridge
Akaroa
Mt. Aspiring 3027
Temuka
L. Ellesmere
Milford Sd.
Mt.
L. Pukaki
St.
Lake River
Earnslaw
Wanaka I.
Andrews
Sutherland Falls
2818
Milford
Wanaka
Waimate
Sound
Ohau
Bligh Sound
Arrowtown
Dunstan Mts.
Kurow
George Sound
Queenstown
Cromwell
Tokarahi
Oamaru
Naseby
Maheno
Secretary I.
Kawarau
Clyde
Hampden
Doubtful Sd.
L. Te Anau
Alexandra
Dunback
Kingston
Palmerston
Breaksea Sd.
L.
Garvie
Roxburgh
Manapouri
Mts.
Waikouaiti
Resolution I.
Manapouri
Umbrella Mts.
Lawrence
Port Chalmers
Dusky Sd.
Mossburn
Clutha
Otago Harbour
Lumsden
Edievale
Saunders C.
Chalky
Patearoa
Nightcaps
Fairfield
Dunedin
Inlet
Tuatapere
Winton
Kelso
Preservation
Hedgehope
Tapanui
Milton
Inlet
Te Waewae
Orepuki
Gore
Clinton
Balclutha
Riverton
Mataura
Nugget Pt.
Owaka
Invercargill
Wyndham
Tokanui
Bluff Ruapuke I.
South Invercargill
Tahakopa
Foveaux Str.
Halfmoon Bay
Stewart I.
Southwest C.
Port Pegasus

TASMAN

SEA

SAMOA ISLANDS
1:10 700 000

SAMOA
AMERICAN
SAMOA
Savai'i
Apia
Upolu
Pago Pago
Tutuila
West from
Greenwich
12 13 14

FIJI AND TONGA ISLANDS
1:10 700 000

8 9 Futuna 10 11
Wallis & Futuna (Fr.)
Niuafo'ou
(Tonga)
Thikombia
Labasa
Yasawa Group Vanua Levu
FIJI
Vanua Balavu
Taveuni
Koro
Lautoka 1323
Levuka
TONGA
Nandi Viti Levu
Ovalau
(Friendly Is.)
Suva
Gau
Koro Sea
Lakeba
Vava'u
Lau Group
Moala
Kandavu
Vatoa
Tofua
Tongatapu
Nuku'alofa

50 0 50 100 150 200 km
50 0 50 100 150 miles

East from Greenwich

West from Greenwich

Projection: Conical with two standard parallels

ft m
9000 3000
6000 2000
3000 1000
1200 400
600 200
0 0
200 600
2000 6000
4000 12000
6000 18000
m ft

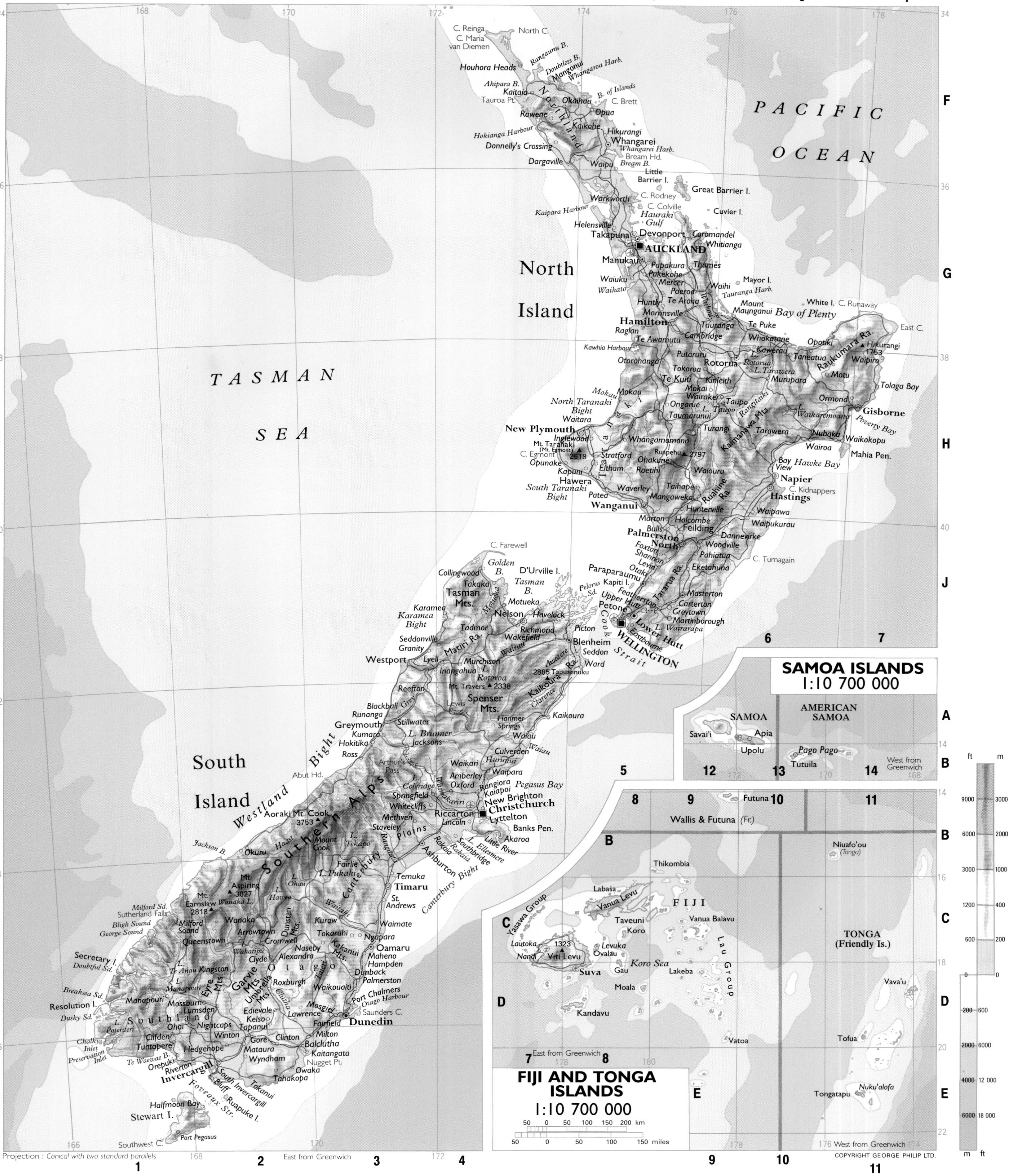

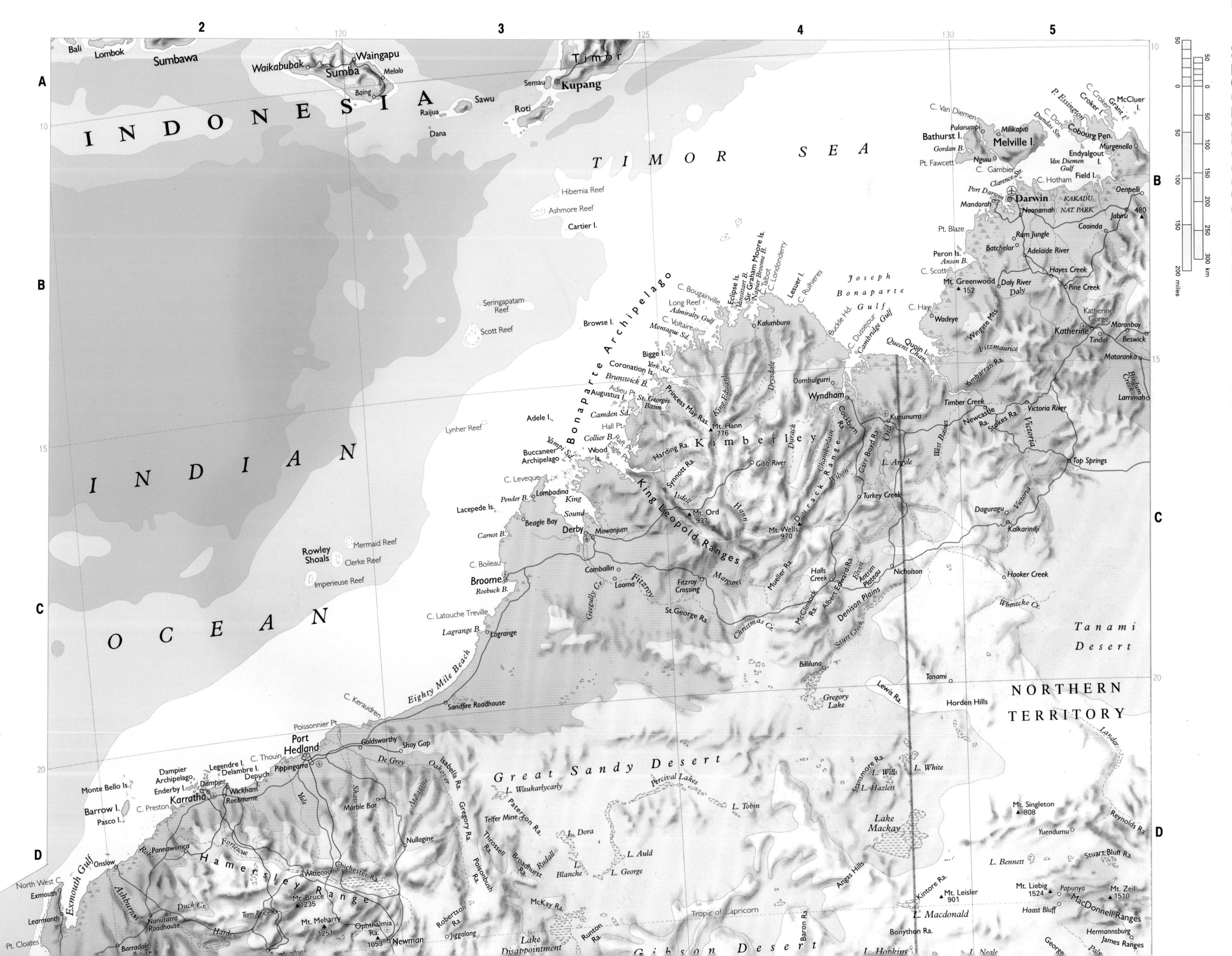
km
miles
INDONESIA
TIMOR SEA
INDIAN OCEAN
NORTHERN TERRITORY
Tanami Desert
Great Sandy Desert
Gibson Desert
Bali
Lombok
Sumbawa
Sumba
Waingapu
Waikabubak
Melolo
Baing
Sawu
Raijua
Dana
Roti
Semau
Kupang
Timor
Hibernia Reef
Ashmore Reef
Cartier I.
Seringapatam Reef
Scott Reef
Browse I.
Adele I.
Lynher Reef
Rowley Shoals
Mermaid Reef
Clerke Reef
Imperieuse Reef
Melville I.
Bathurst I.
Darwin
Katherine
Joseph Bonaparte Gulf
Bonaparte Archipelago
Kimberley
King Leopold Ranges
Wyndham
Kununurra
Derby
Broome
Fitzroy Crossing
Halls Creek
Mt. Ord 937
Mt. Hann 776
Mt. Wells 970
Eighty Mile Beach
Sandfire Roadhouse
Port Hedland
Karratha
Dampier
Barrow I.
Monte Bello Is.
Onslow
Exmouth Gulf
Exmouth
Hamersley Range
Mt. Bruce 1235
Mt. Meharry 1251
Newman
Lake Mackay
Lake Disappointment
Tropic of Capricorn
Tanami
Nicholson
Hooker Creek
Kalkarindji
Top Springs
Victoria River
Timber Creek
MacDonnell Ranges
Mt. Zeil 1510
Mt. Liebig 1524

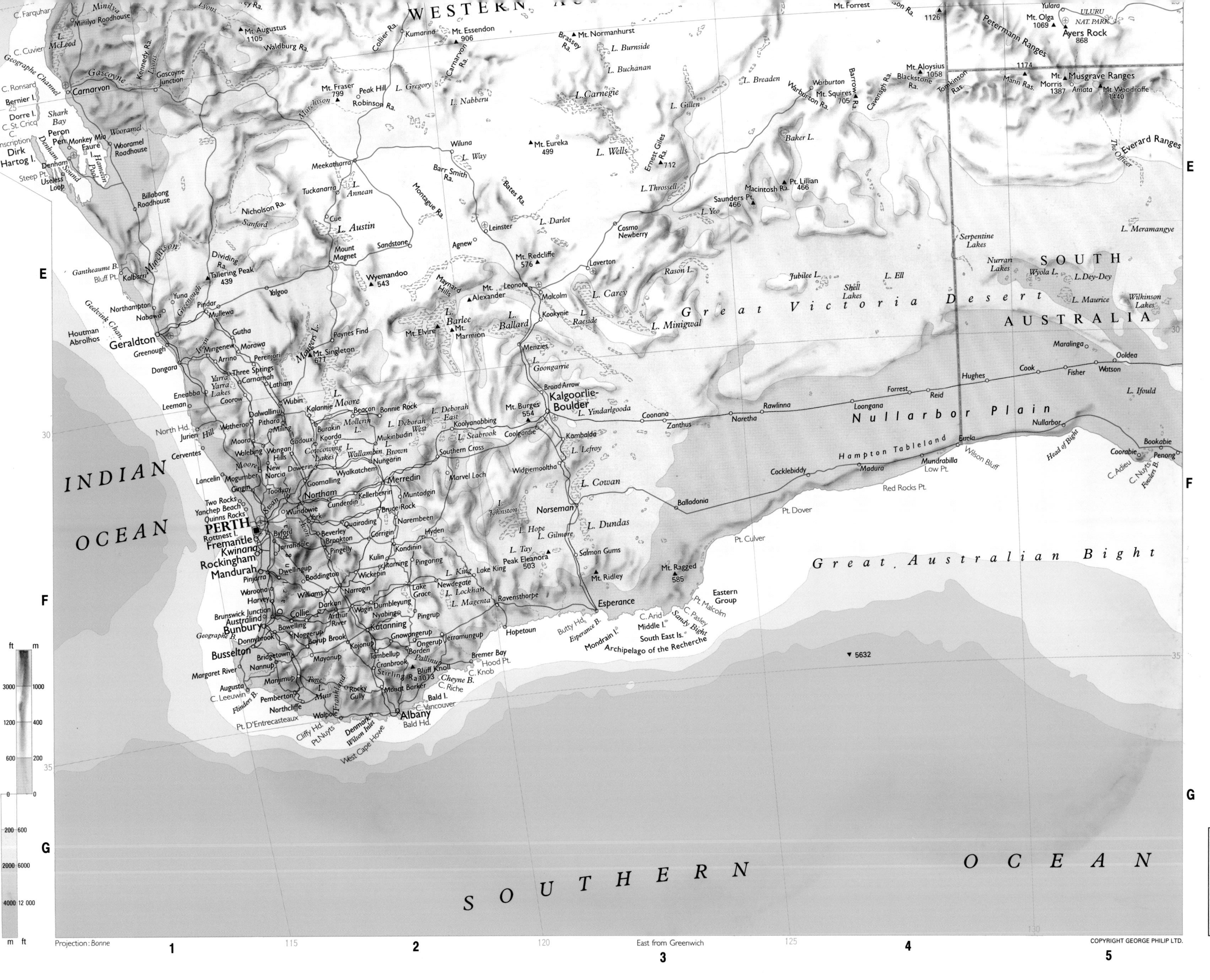

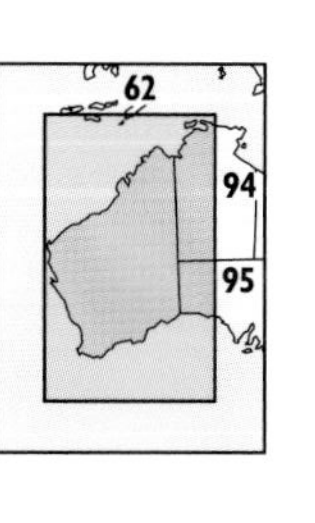

INDIAN OCEAN

SOUTHERN OCEAN

WESTERN AUSTRALIA

SOUTH AUSTRALIA

Great Victoria Desert

Nullarbor Plain

Hampton Tableland

Great Australian Bight

PERTH

Kalgoorlie-Boulder

Albany

Esperance

Geraldton

Carnarvon

Bunbury

Projection: Borne

East from Greenwich

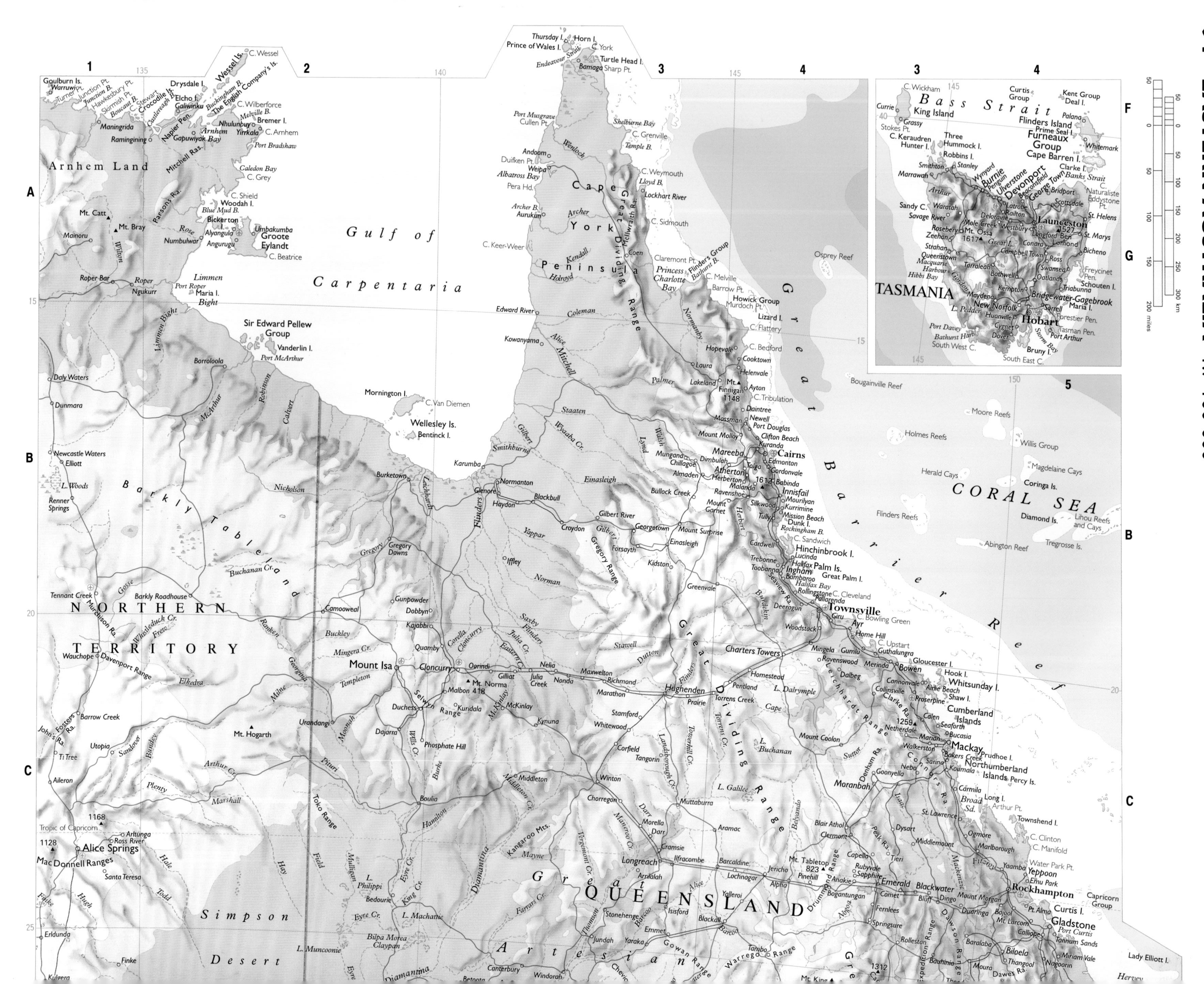

50 0 50 100 150 200 250 300 km
50 0 50 100 150 200 miles
TASMANIA
Bass Strait
Flinders Island
Furneaux Group
Cape Barren I.
King Island
Launceston
Devonport
Burnie
Hobart
New Norfolk
Queenstown
CORAL SEA
Great Barrier Reef
Gulf of Carpentaria
Cape York Peninsula
Great Dividing Range
QUEENSLAND
NORTHERN TERRITORY
Barkly Tableland
Simpson Desert
Great Artesian Basin
Arnhem Land
Groote Eylandt
Wellesley Is.
Mornington I.
Cairns
Townsville
Mackay
Rockhampton
Gladstone
Mount Isa
Cloncurry
Longreach
Charters Towers
Alice Springs
Tennant Creek
Emerald
Hughenden
Cumberland Islands
Whitsunday I.
Tropic of Capricorn

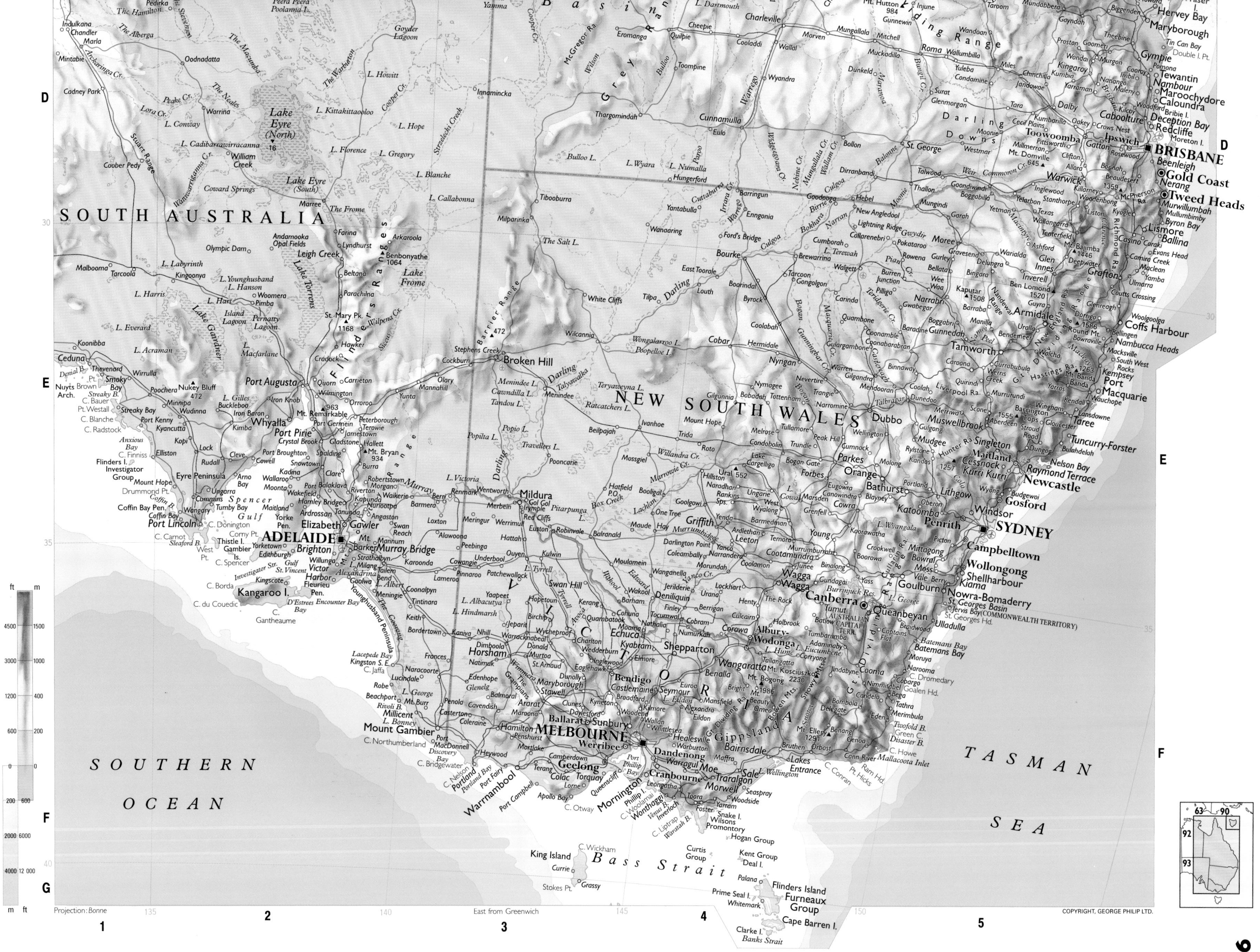

SOUTH AUSTRALIA
NEW SOUTH WALES
VICTORIA
TASMAN SEA
SOUTHERN OCEAN
Bass Strait
Grey Range
Darling Downs
Flinders Ranges
AUSTRALIAN CAPITAL TERR.
(COMMONWEALTH TERRITORY)
BRISBANE
Gold Coast
Tweed Heads
Ipswich
Toowoomba
Maryborough
Hervey Bay
Gympie
Lismore
Ballina
Grafton
Coffs Harbour
Port Macquarie
Kempsey
Armidale
Tamworth
Taree
Newcastle
Maitland
Cessnock
Gosford
SYDNEY
Campbelltown
Wollongong
Nowra-Bomaderry
Goulburn
Canberra
Queanbeyan
Wagga Wagga
Albury-Wodonga
Dubbo
Orange
Bathurst
Parkes
Griffith
Broken Hill
Mildura
Swan Hill
Echuca
Shepparton
Bendigo
Ballarat
MELBOURNE
Geelong
Warrnambool
Hamilton
Horsham
Mount Gambier
Murray Bridge
ADELAIDE
Gawler
Elizabeth
Port Pirie
Port Augusta
Whyalla
Port Lincoln
Ceduna
Kangaroo I.
King Island
Flinders Island
Furneaux Group
Cape Barren I.
Spencer Gulf
Lake Eyre (North)
Lake Eyre (South)
Lake Torrens
Lake Frome
Lake Gairdner
Charleville
Cunnamulla
Bourke
Cobar
Nyngan
Moree
Narrabri
Goondiwindi
Warwick
Roma
St. George
Traralgon
Sale
Bairnsdale
Projection: Bonne
East from Greenwich
COPYRIGHT, GEORGE PHILIP LTD.
ft m
4500 1500
3000 1000
1200 400
600 200
0 0
200 600
2000 6000
4000 12 000
m ft

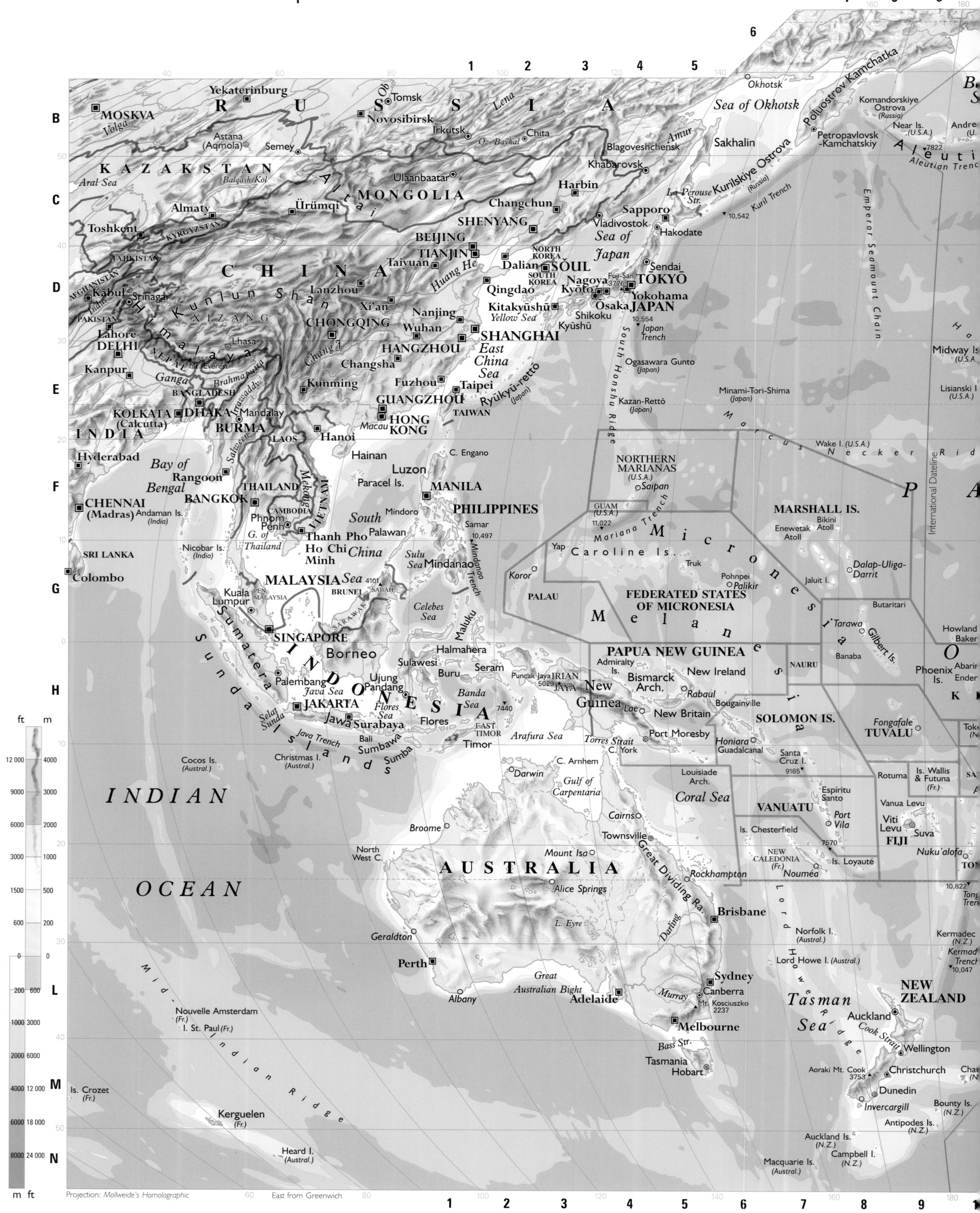

7 8 9

6

1 2 3 4 5

B MOSKVA Yekaterinburg Tomsk R U S S I A Okhotsk Poluostrov Kamchatka
Volga Astana Novosibirsk Ob Lena Sea of Okhotsk Komandorskiye Ostrova (Russia) Andre
(Aqmola) Semey Irkutsk Chita Amur Sakhalin Near Is. 7822
KAZAKSTAN Balqash Köl Oz. Baykal Blagoveshchensk Petropavlovsk Aleuti
Aral Sea Ulaanbaatar Khabarovsk La Pérouse -Kamchatskiy Aleutian Trench
C Almaty Ürümqi MONGOLIA Harbin Str. Kurilskiye Ostrova
Toshkent Altai Changchun Vladivostok (Russia) 10,542 Kuril Trench Emperor Seamount Chain
KYRGYZSTAN SHENYANG Sapporo
TAJIKISTAN Kunlun Shan BEIJING Sea of Hakodate
D Kabul Srinagar TIANJIN Dalian NORTH Japan Sendai Midway I.
AFGHANISTAN C H I N A Lanzhou Taiyuan KOREA SŌUL Nagoya Fuji-San TOKYO (U.S.A.)
PAKISTAN XIZANG Xi'an Huang He Qingdao SOUTH Kyōto 3776 Yokohama
Lahore Himalaya Chang Jiang CHONGQING Nanjing KOREA Kitakyūshū Osaka JAPAN Lisianski I.
DELHI Lhasa 8850 Wuhan Yellow Sea Shikoku 10,554 (U.S.A.)
Kanpur NEPAL Everest Changsha SHANGHAI Kyūshū Japan
Ganga Brahmaputra East Trench
E Kunming Fuzhou China Kazan-Rettō Minami-Tori-Shima H
Hyderabad BANGLADESH GUANGZHOU Taipei Sea Ogasawara Gunto (Japan) (Japan)
KOLKATA DHAKA Mandalay Ryūkyū-rettō (Japan)
I N D I A (Calcutta) HONG Macau (Japan) South Honshu Ridge Wake I. (U.S.A.) Necker Ri
BURMA Irrawaddy KONG TAIWAN Marcus
Hanoi NORTHERN P A
F Hyderabad Bay of LAOS Hainan C. Engano MARIANAS MARSHALL IS.
CHENNAI Rangoon THAILAND VIETNAM Luzon (U.S.A.) Saipan Bikini
(Madras) BANGKOK Mekong Paracel Is. MANILA GUAM Enewetak Atoll
Andaman Is. Salween CAMBODIA South Mindoro PHILIPPINES (U.S.A.) 11,022 Mariana Trench M i c r o n e s i a
(India) Phnom China Samar Yap Caroline Is.
Nicobar Is. Penh Thanh Pho 10,497 Truk Pohnpei Dalap-Uliga-
(India) G. of Ho Chi Palawan Koror Palikir Jaluit I. Darrit
SRI LANKA Thailand Minh Sulu Mindanao PALAU FEDERATED STATES Butaritari
G Colombo MALAYSIA Sea 4101 Sea Mindanao OF MICRONESIA Tarawa Howland
PEN. BRUNEI Trench M e l a n e s i a Gilbert Is. Baker
Sumatera MALAYSIA SABAH Celebes NAURU Banaba Phoenix Abari
Kuala SARAWAK Sea Halmahera PAPUA NEW GUINEA Admiralty Is. New Ireland Is. Ender
Lumpur SINGAPORE Borneo Sulawesi Seram Puncak Jaya IRIAN New Bismarck Arch. Rabaul K
H Palembang Sulawesi Buru 5029 JAYA Guinea New Britain SOLOMON IS.
I N D O N E S I A Banda Lae Bougainville
Java Sea Ujung Flores Sea 7440 Port Moresby Honiara TUVALU Fongafale
JAKARTA Pandang EAST Guadalcanal Santa
Selat Surabaya Jawa Flores TIMOR Arafura Sea Cruz I. Rotuma Is. Wallis
Sunda Bali Sumbawa Flores Timor Torres Strait 9165 & Futuna (Fr.) SA
Cocos Is. Java Trench Sumba C. York Louisiade VANUATU Espiritu Vanua Levu
(Austral.) Christmas I. Sunda Islands C. Arnhem Arch. Santo Viti
(Austral.) Darwin Gulf of Coral Sea Is. Chesterfield Port Levu FIJI
I N D I A N North Carpentaria Cairns NEW Vila Suva Nuku'alofa
West C. Mount Isa Townsville CALEDONIA 7570 Is. Loyauté TO
Broome A U S T R A L I A Rockhampton (Fr.) Nouméa
Alice Springs Great Dividing Ra. Norfolk I.
O C E A N Brisbane Darling (Austral.) 10,822 Tong
Geraldton L. Eyre Kermadec Tren
Great Lord Howe I. (Austral.) (N.Z.)
L Perth Australian Bight Murray Sydney NEW Kermad
Albany Adelaide Canberra ZEALAND Trench
Mt. Kosciuszko Tasman 10,047
2237 Sea Auckland
Melbourne Sea Wellington
M Is. Crozet Bass Str. Aoraki Mt. Cook Christchurch Cha
(Fr.) Tasmania 3753 (N
Hobart Dunedin
Kerguelen Invercargill Bounty Is.
(Fr.) Auckland Is. (N.Z.)
N Heard I. (N.Z.) Antipodes Is.
(Austral.) Campbell I. (N.Z.)
Macquarie I. (N.Z.)
(Austral.)

ft m
12 000 4000
9000 3000
6000 2000
3000 1000
1500 500
600 200
0 0
200 600
1000 3000
2000 6000
4000 12 000
6000 18 000
8000 24 000
m ft

Projection: Mollweide's Homolographic East from Greenwich

1 2 3 4 5 6 7 8 9

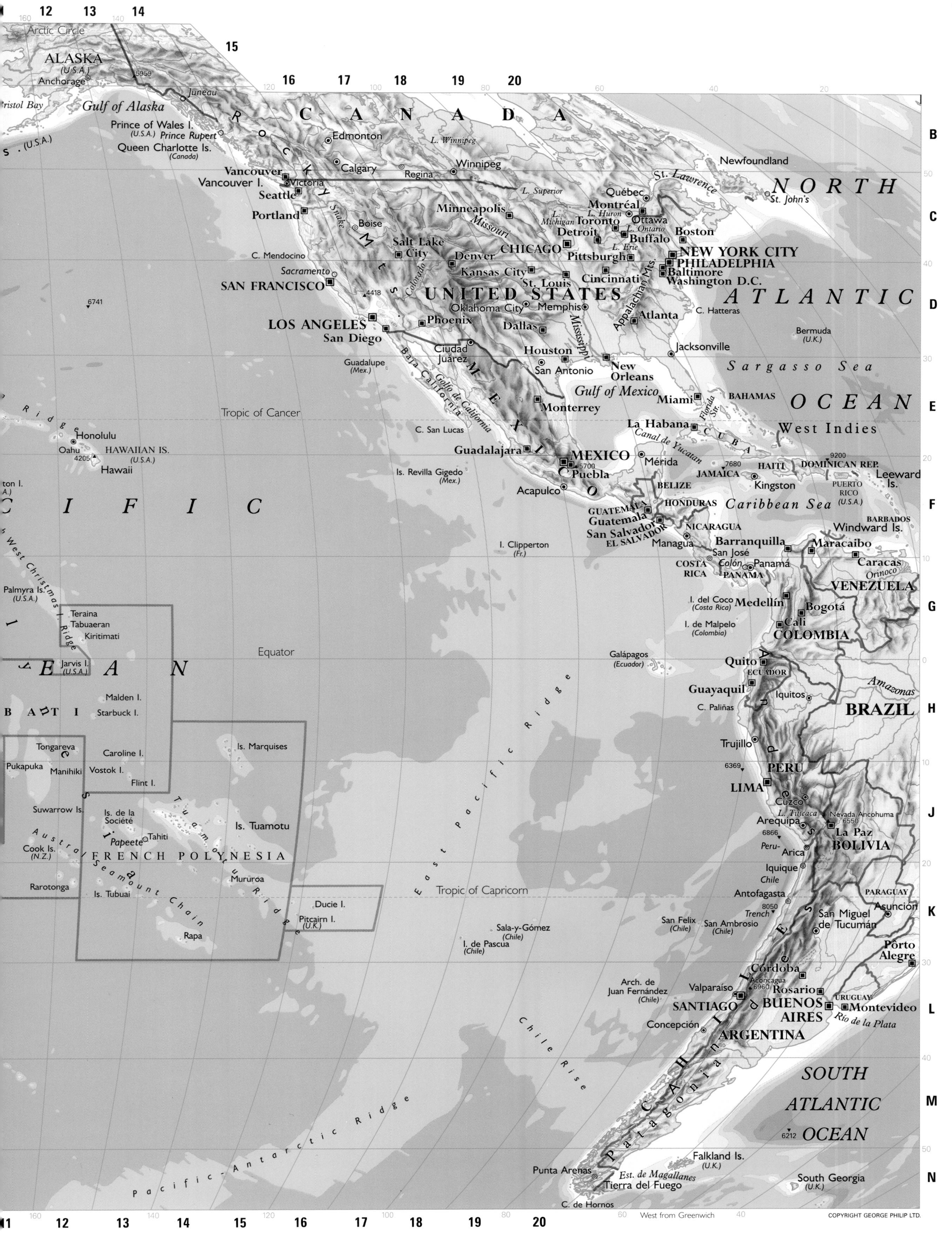

12 13 14

15

16 17 18 19 20

Arctic Circle

160   140   120   100   80   60   40   20

ALASKA
(U.S.A.)
Anchorage

5959

Juneau

Bristol Bay

Gulf of Alaska

C A N A D A

Edmonton
Calgary
Regina
Winnipeg
L. Winnipeg

Newfoundland

N O R T H

B

Prince of Wales I.
(U.S.A.)   Prince Rupert
Queen Charlotte Is.
(Canada)

(U.S.A.)

Vancouver
Vancouver I.
Victoria
Seattle
Portland
Boise

R O C K Y

Snake

Missouri

L. Superior

St. Lawrence

Québec   St. John's

Montréal

L. Huron
L. Michigan   Toronto   Ottawa
Detroit   L. Ontario   Buffalo   Boston
L. Erie

50

C

C. Mendocino

Sacramento
SAN FRANCISCO

Salt Lake
City
Denver

M T S.

4418

Kansas City

CHICAGO

UNITED STATES

Pittsburgh

St. Louis   Cincinnati

NEW YORK CITY
PHILADELPHIA
Baltimore
Washington D.C.

A T L A N T I C

40

D

6741

LOS ANGELES
San Diego

Colorado

Phoenix

Oklahoma City
Dallas

Memphis

Appalachian Mts.

Atlanta

C. Hatteras

Bermuda
(U.K.)

Ciudad
Juárez

Houston
San Antonio

Mississippi

New
Orleans
Jacksonville

30

Tropic of Cancer

Guadalupe
(Mex.)

Baja California

M E X I C O

Gulf of Mexico

Miami

BAHAMAS

Sargasso Sea

O C E A N

E

Honolulu
Oahu   HAWAIIAN IS.
4205   (U.S.A.)
Hawaii

C. San Lucas

Gulfo de California

Monterrey

La Habana

CUBA

Florida Str.

West Indies

ton I.
A.)

6741

I F I C

Guadalajara

5700

MEXICO
Puebla

Mérida

Canal de Yucatán

9200

7680   HAITI   DOMINICAN REP.

JAMAICA   Kingston

Leeward
Is.

20

F

Is. Revilla Gigedo
(Mex.)

Acapulco

BELIZE

GUATEMALA   HONDURAS
Guatemala
San Salvador   NICARAGUA
EL SALVADOR   Managua

PUERTO
RICO
(U.S.A.)

Caribbean Sea

BARBADOS

Windward Is.

Palmyra Is.
(U.S.A.)

West Christmas

Teraina
Tabuaeran
Kiritimati

Ridge

I. Clipperton
(Fr.)

San José
COSTA
RICA   Colón   Panamá
PANAMA

Barranquilla   Maracaibo

Caracas
Orinoco

VENEZUELA

10

G

E   A   N

Jarvis I.
(U.S.A.)

Equator

I. del Coco
(Costa Rica)   Medellín

I. de Malpelo
(Colombia)

Bogotá

Cali

COLOMBIA

0

B   A   T   I

Malden I.

Starbuck I.

Galápagos
(Ecuador)

Quito

ECUADOR

Guayaquil

C. Paliñas

Iquitos

Amazonas

BRAZIL

H

Tongareva
Pukapuka   Manihiki

Caroline I.

Vostok I.

Flint I.

Is. Marquises

East Pacific Ridge

Trujillo

10

Suwarrow Is.

Is. de la
Société
Papeete   Tahiti

Tuamotu

Is. Tuamotu

6369

LIMA

PERU

Cuzco

Nevada Ancohuma
6550

J

Cook Is.
(N.Z.)

Australia

FRENCH POLYNESIA

Ridge

Mururoa

L. Titicaca

Arequipa
6866
Peru-   Arica

La Paz

BOLIVIA

20

Rarotonga

Is. Tubuai

Seamount Chain

Tropic of Capricorn

Iquique
Chile

Ducie I.

Pitcairn I.
(U.K.)

Rapa

Sala-y-Gómez
(Chile)

I. de Pascua
(Chile)

San Felix
(Chile)

San Ambrosio
(Chile)

Antofagasta

8050
Trench

PARAGUAY

San Miguel
de Tucumán

Asunción

K

Pórto
Alegre

30

Arch. de
Juan Fernández
(Chile)

Valparaíso

Córdoba
Aconcagua
6960   Rosario

URUGUAY
Montevideo

SANTIAGO
Concepción

BUENOS
AIRES   Río de la Plata

40

L

ARGENTINA

Chile Rise

Pacific-Antarctic Ridge

SOUTH

ATLANTIC

OCEAN

M

6212

50

Punta Arenas

Falkland Is.
(U.K.)

South Georgia
(U.K.)

N

Est. de Magallanes
Tierra del Fuego

C. de Hornos

1   12   13   14   15   16   17   18   19   20   80   West from Greenwich   40

COPYRIGHT GEORGE PHILIP LTD.

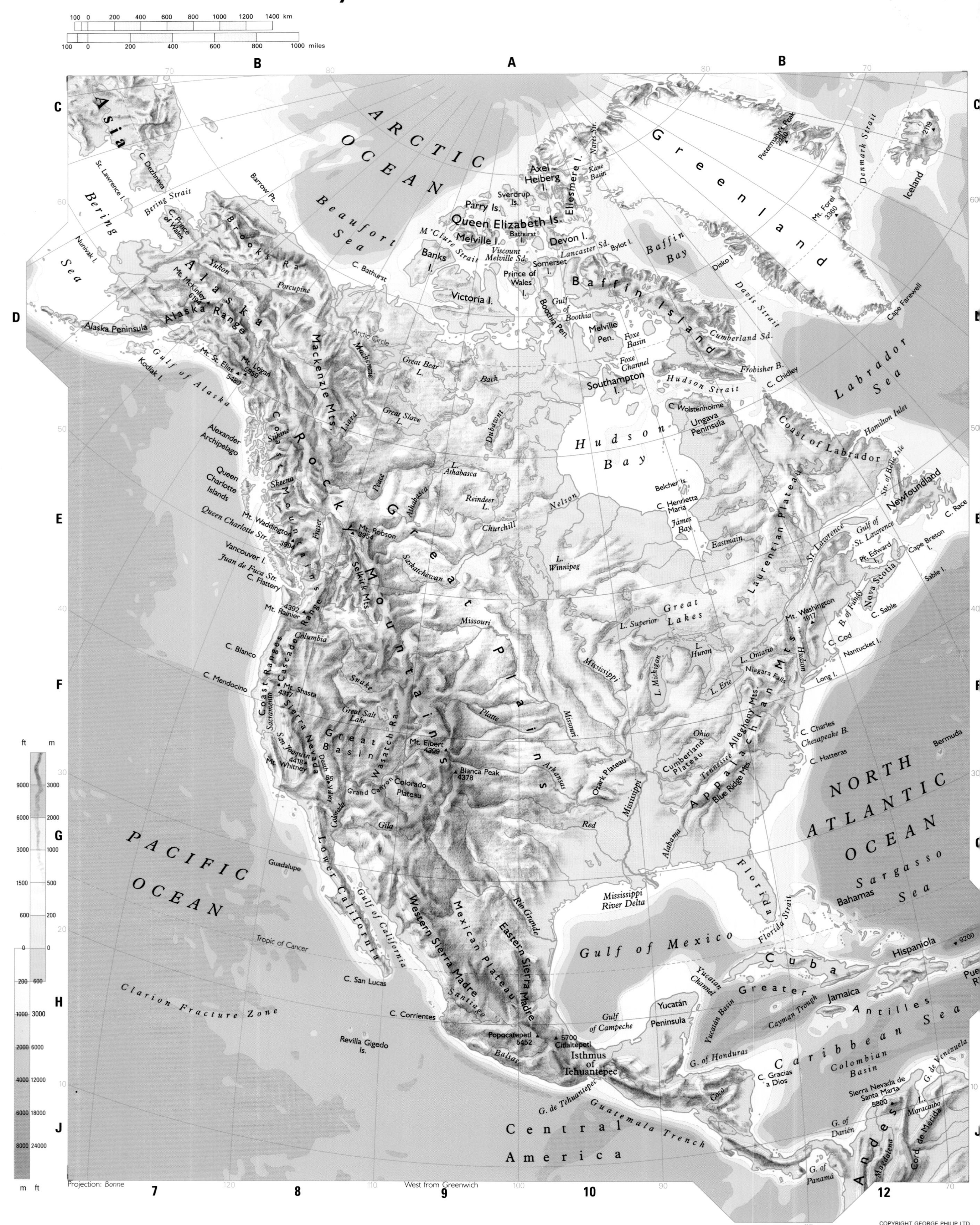
ARCTIC OCEAN
Beaufort Sea
Greenland
Baffin Bay
Baffin Island
Hudson Bay
Labrador Sea
Rocky Mountains
Great Plains
Great Lakes
Gulf of Mexico
PACIFIC OCEAN
NORTH ATLANTIC OCEAN
Sargasso Sea
Caribbean Sea
Central America
Alaska Range
Mackenzie Mts.
Coast Mountains
Appalachian Mts.
Laurentian Plateau
Great Basin
Colorado Plateau
Mexican Plateau
Western Sierra Madre
Eastern Sierra Madre
Mt. McKinley 6194
Mt. Logan 5959
Mt. St. Elias 5489
Mt. Elbert 4399
Mt. Whitney 4418
Popocatepetl 5452
Isthmus of Tehuantepec
Gulf of Alaska
Bering Sea
Hudson Strait
Gulf of St. Lawrence
Gulf of California
Yucatán Peninsula
Cuba
Hispaniola
Jamaica
Greater Antilles
Andes
Projection: Bonne
West from Greenwich

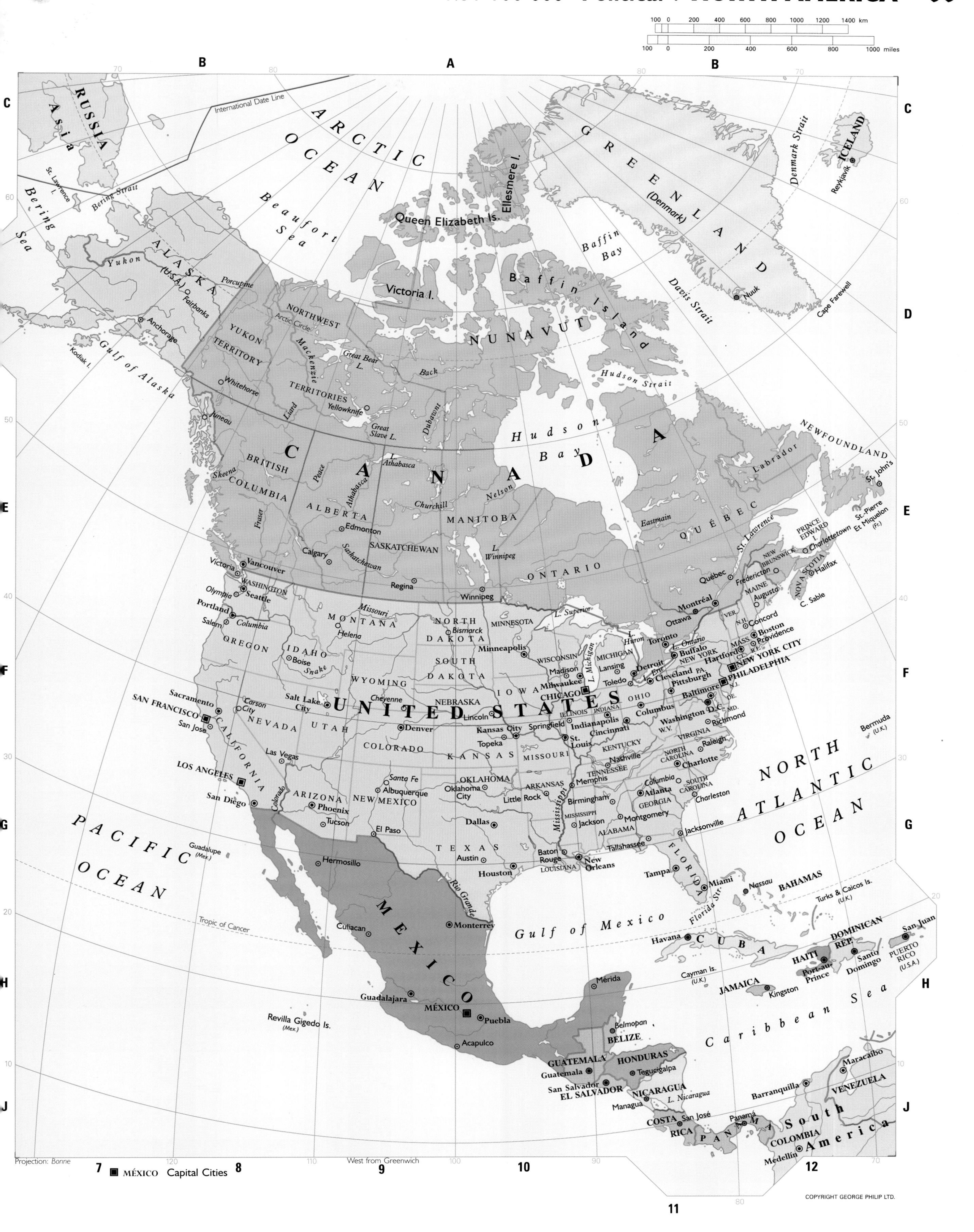

100 0 200 400 600 800 1000 1200 1400 km
100 0 200 400 600 800 1000 miles

B   **80**   **A**   **80**   **B**

C RUSSIA
Asia
St. Lawrence I.
Bering Strait
International Date Line
ARCTIC OCEAN

GREENLAND
(Denmark)
ICELAND
Reykjavik
Denmark Strait

C

Bering Sea
60
Beaufort Sea
Queen Elizabeth Is.
Ellesmere I.
Baffin Bay
Davis Strait
Cape Farewell
60

ALASKA (USA)
Yukon
Porcupine
Fairbanks
Anchorage
Victoria I.
NORTHWEST
Arctic Circle
Baffin Island
NUNAVUT
Nuuk

D

Kodiak I.
Gulf of Alaska
Juneau
Whitehorse
YUKON TERRITORY
TERRITORIES
Mackenzie
Great Bear L.
Back
Yellowknife
Liard
Great Slave L.
Dubawnt
Hudson Strait
D

50
BRITISH COLUMBIA
Skeena
Peace
Athabasca
Athabasca
ALBERTA
Churchill
Nelson
Hudson Bay
Eastmain
NEWFOUNDLAND
Labrador
50

E
Fraser
Victoria Vancouver
WASHINGTON
Olympia Seattle
Calgary
Edmonton
SASKATCHEWAN
Saskatchewan
Regina
MANITOBA
L. Winnipeg
ONTARIO
QUÉBEC
St. Lawrence
St. John's
St-Pierre Et Miquelon (Fr.)
E

CANADA

40
Portland
Salem
OREGON
Columbia
MONTANA
Missouri
Helena
IDAHO
Boise
Snake
WYOMING
Winnipeg
NORTH DAKOTA
Bismarck
SOUTH DAKOTA
MINNESOTA
L. Superior
WISCONSIN
Madison
MICHIGAN
L. Michigan
Lansing
L. Huron
Detroit
Toronto
L. Ontario
Ottawa
Montréal
Québec
Fredericton
NEW BRUNSWICK
MAINE
Augusta
VER.
PRINCE EDWARD I.
Charlottetown
NOVA SCOTIA
Halifax
C. Sable
40

F
Sacramento
San Francisco
San Jose
CALIFORNIA
NEVADA
Carson City
Salt Lake City
UTAH
Cheyenne
Denver
NEBRASKA
Lincoln
IOWA
Minneapolis
Milwaukee
CHICAGO
ILLINOIS
Springfield
INDIANA
Indianapolis
OHIO
Columbus
Cleveland
PA
Pittsburgh
Buffalo
NEW YORK
Erie
Hartford
MASS
Boston
Providence
R.I.
N.Y.
N.J.
Concord
NEW YORK CITY
PHILADELPHIA
Baltimore
F

LOS ANGELES
Las Vegas
San Diego
ARIZONA
Phoenix
Tucson
Colorado
Santa Fe
Albuquerque
NEW MEXICO
El Paso
COLORADO
KANSAS
Topeka
Kansas City
MISSOURI
St. Louis
Cincinnati
KENTUCKY
Nashville
TENNESSEE
Memphis
NORTH CAROLINA
Charlotte
Raleigh
VIRGINIA
Richmond
Washington D.C.
W.V.
MD.
Columbia
SOUTH CAROLINA
Charleston
Bermuda (U.K.)

G
UNITED STATES
OKLAHOMA
Oklahoma City
ARKANSAS
Little Rock
Birmingham
MISSISSIPPI
Jackson
ALABAMA
Montgomery
GEORGIA
Atlanta
Jacksonville
FLORIDA
NORTH ATLANTIC OCEAN
G

PACIFIC OCEAN
Guadalupe (Mex.)
Hermosillo
TEXAS
Dallas
Austin
Houston
Baton Rouge
LOUISIANA
New Orleans
Tallahassee
Tampa
Miami
Nassau
BAHAMAS
Turks & Caicos Is. (U.K.)

H
Tropic of Cancer
Culiacan
MEXICO
Monterrey
Río Grande
Gulf of Mexico
Florida Str.
Havana
CUBA
Cayman Is. (U.K.)
JAMAICA
Kingston
HAITI
Port-au-Prince
DOMINICAN REP.
Santo Domingo
PUERTO RICO (U.S.A.)
San Juan
Caribbean Sea
H

Revilla Gigedo Is. (Mex.)
Guadalajara
MÉXICO
Puebla
Acapulco
Mérida
BELIZE
Belmopan
GUATEMALA
Guatemala
San Salvador
EL SALVADOR
HONDURAS
Tegucigalpa
NICARAGUA
L. Nicaragua
Managua
Maracaibo
VENEZUELA
Barranquilla

J
COSTA RICA
San José
Panamá
PANAMA
COLOMBIA
Medellín
South America
J

7 ■ MÉXICO Capital Cities **8**   **120**   West from Greenwich   **110**   **9**   **100**   **10**   **90**   **80**   **70**   **12**

11

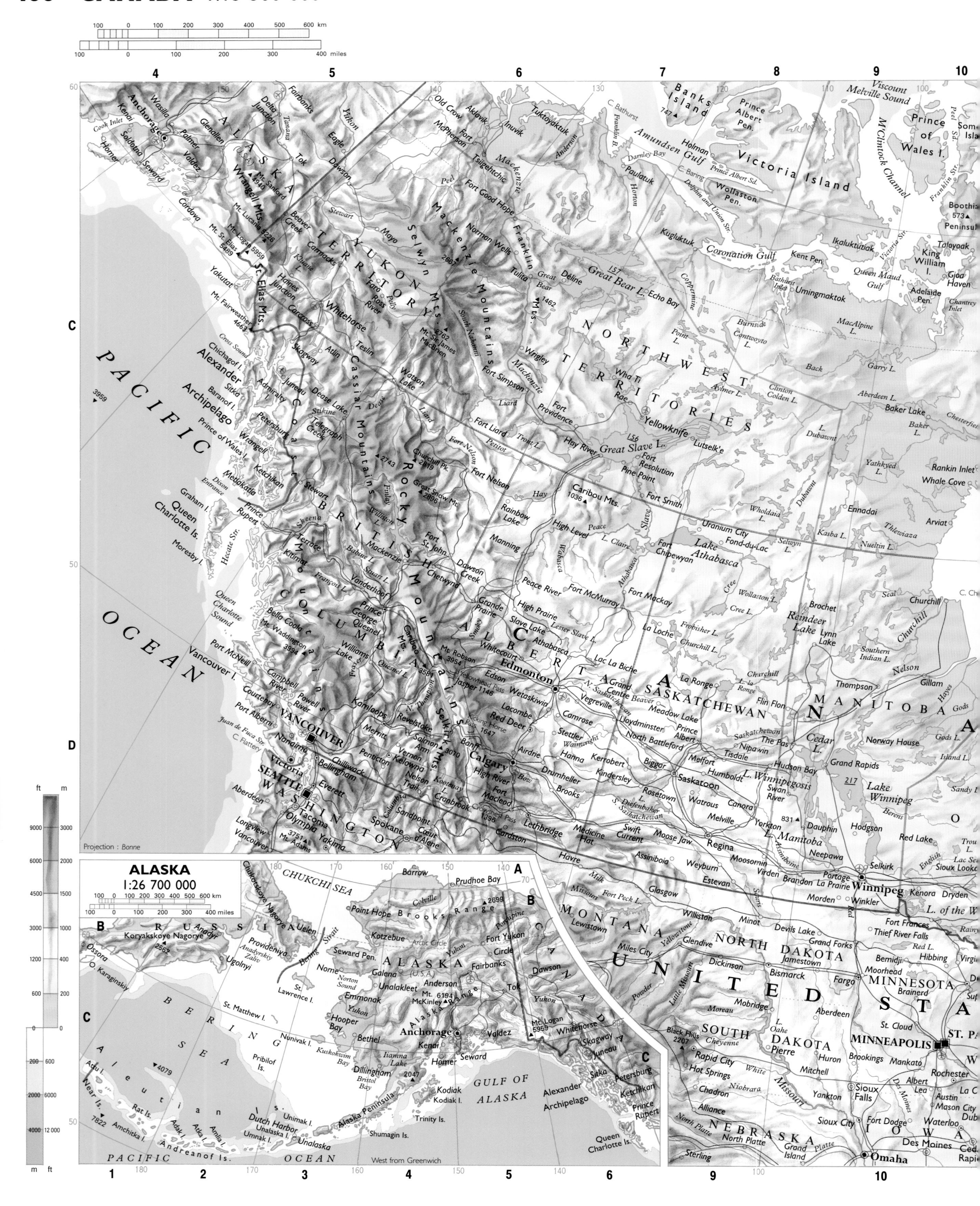

100 0 100 200 300 400 500 600 km
100 0 100 200 300 400 miles

ALASKA 1:26 700 000

100 0 100 200 300 400 500 600 km
100 0 100 200 300 400 miles

Projection : Bonne

West from Greenwich

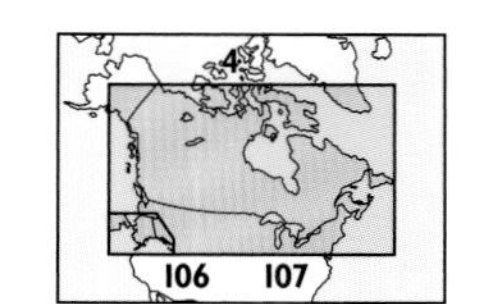
106
107

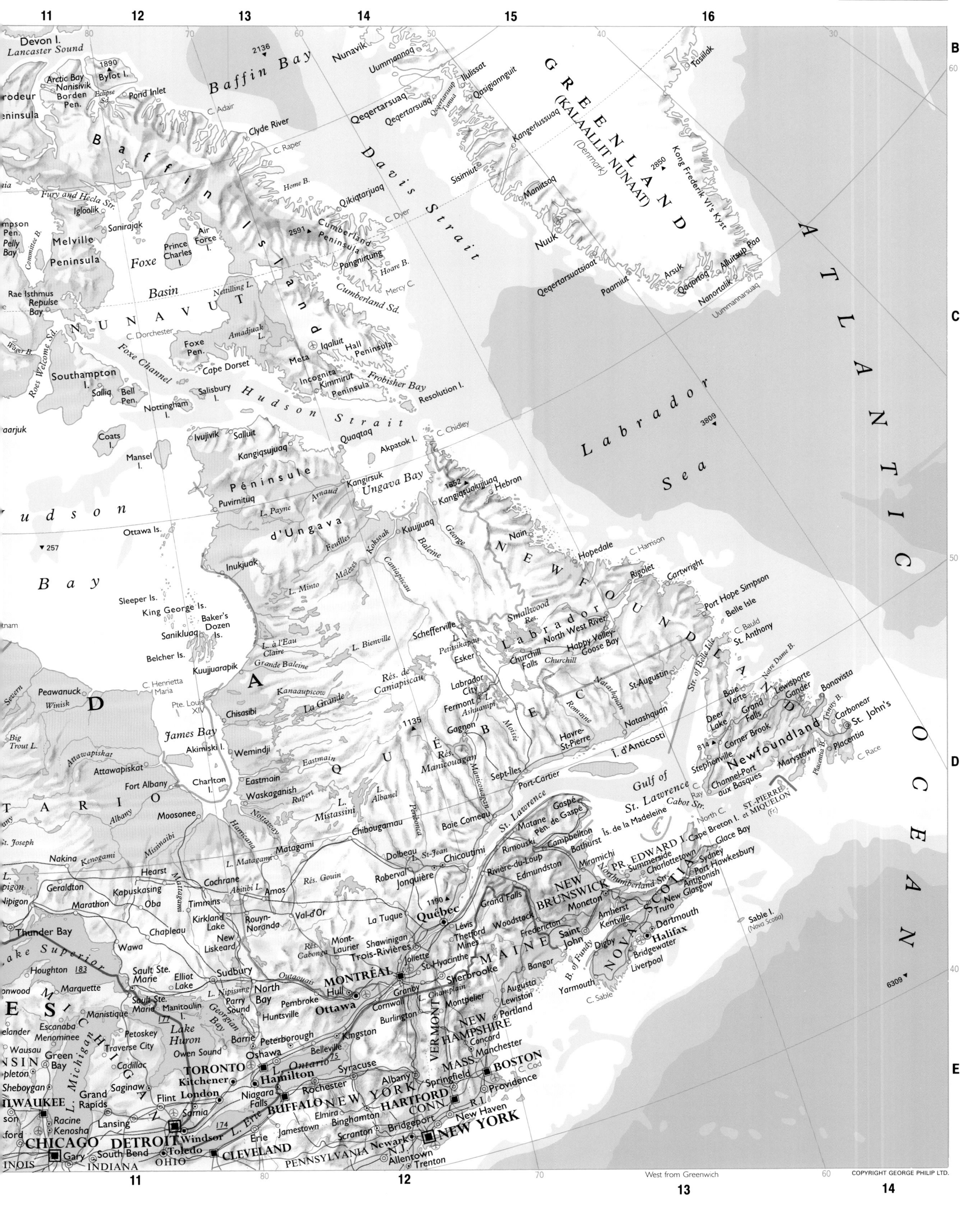
11
12
13
14
15
16
B
C
D
E
Devon I.
Lancaster Sound
Bylot I.
Arctic Bay
Nanisivik
Borden Pen.
Eclipse Sd.
Pond Inlet
Baffin Bay
C. Adair
Clyde River
C. Raper
Baffin Island
Fury and Hecla Str.
Igloolik
Home B.
Melville Peninsula
Sanirajak
Prince Charles I.
Air Force I.
Foxe Basin
Committee B.
Pelly Bay
Rae Isthmus
Repulse Bay
NUNAVUT
Nettilling L.
C. Dorchester
Amadjuak L.
Foxe Pen.
Foxe Channel
Cape Dorset
Wager B.
Roes Welcome Sd.
Southampton I.
Salliq
Bell Pen.
Nottingham I.
Salisbury I.
Hudson Strait
Coats I.
Mansel I.
Ivujivik
Salluit
Kangiqsujuaq
Quaqtaq
Akpatok I.
C. Chidley
Kangirsuk
Ungava Bay
Péninsule d'Ungava
Puvirnituq
L. Payne
Arnaud
Hudson Bay
Ottawa Is.
257
Inukjuak
Feuilles
Mélèzes
Koksoak
Kuujjuaq
Baleine
George
Caniapiscau
L. Minto
Sleeper Is.
King George Is.
Baker's Dozen Is.
Sanikiluaq
Belcher Is.
L. à l'Eau Claire
Grande Baleine
Kuujjuarapik
L. Bienville
Schefferville
Petitsikapau L.
Esker
Rés. de Caniapiscau
Kanaaupscow
La Grande
C. Henrietta Maria
Pte. Louis XIV
Chisasibi
James Bay
Akimiski I.
Wemindji
Eastmain
Charlton I.
Waskaganish
Rupert
Attawapiskat
Fort Albany
Albany
Moosonee
Peawanuck
Winisk
Severn
Big Trout L.
ONTARIO
QUÉBEC
Rés. Manicouagan
Gagnon
Labrador City
Fermont
L. Ashuanipi
Moisie
Romaine
Natashquan
St-Augustin
Havre-St-Pierre
Sept-Îles
Port-Cartier
Î. d'Anticosti
L. Mistassini
L. Albanel
Chibougamau
Péribonca
Manicouagan
Baie Comeau
Nottaway
Harricana
Missinaibi
St. Joseph
Nakina
Kenogami
L. Matagami
Matagami
Hearst
Mattagami
Cochrane
Abitibi L.
Amos
Rés. Gouin
Dolbeau
St-Jean
Roberval
Jonquière
Chicoutimi
Geraldton
Kapuskasing
Oba
Timmins
Marathon
Nipigon
Kirkland Lake
Rouyn-Noranda
Val-d'Or
Thunder Bay
Chapleau
New Liskeard
Wawa
Lake Superior
Rés. Cabonga
Mont-Laurier
La Tuque
Shawinigan
Trois-Rivières
Québec
Lévis
Thetford Mines
Houghton
Sault Ste. Marie
Elliot Lake
Sudbury
Marquette
L. Nipissing
North Bay
Outaouais
MONTRÉAL
Hull
Ottawa
Pembroke
Manistique
Manitoulin I.
Parry Sound
Georgian Bay
Huntsville
Escanaba
Menominee
Petoskey
Lake Huron
Traverse City
Owen Sound
Barrie
Peterborough
Kingston
Belleville
Oshawa
TORONTO
L. Ontario
Kitchener
Hamilton
Green Bay
Cadillac
Sheboygan
Saginaw
Flint
London
Grand Rapids
MILWAUKEE
Lake Michigan
MICHIGAN
Racine
Kenosha
Lansing
Sarnia
DETROIT
Windsor
L. Erie
Niagara Falls
BUFFALO
Rochester
Syracuse
Erie
Jamestown
Elmira
Binghamton
CHICAGO
Gary
South Bend
Toledo
CLEVELAND
INDIANA
OHIO
PENNSYLVANIA
Scranton
NEW YORK
Albany
HARTFORD
CONN.
Bridgeport
New Haven
Newark
N.J.
Allentown
Trenton
Springfield
MASS.
BOSTON
Providence
R.I.
C. Cod
VERMONT
Montpelier
NEW HAMPSHIRE
Concord
Manchester
Cornwall
Burlington
L. Champlain
Granby
St-Hyacinthe
Sherbrooke
Joliette
MAINE
Augusta
Lewiston
Portland
Bangor
Woodstock
Fredericton
Saint John
Grand Falls
NEW BRUNSWICK
Moncton
Edmundston
Rivière-du-Loup
Rimouski
Matane
Campbellton
Bathurst
Miramichi
Gaspé
Pen. de Gaspé
St. Lawrence
Gulf of St. Lawrence
Îs. de la Madeleine
PR. EDWARD I.
Summerside
Charlottetown
Northumberland Str.
NOVA SCOTIA
Amherst
Truro
New Glasgow
Antigonish
Port Hawkesbury
Sydney
Glace Bay
Cape Breton I.
North C.
Cabot Str.
C. Ray
Kentville
Dartmouth
Halifax
Digby
B. of Fundy
Bridgewater
Liverpool
Yarmouth
C. Sable
Sable I. (Nova Scotia)
ST.-PIERRE et MIQUELON (Fr.)
Channel-Port aux Basques
Stephenville
Corner Brook
Deer Lake
Grand Falls
Baie Verte
Lewisporte
Gander
Notre Dame B.
Bonavista
Trinity B.
Carbonear
St. John's
Newfoundland
Placentia
Placentia B.
Marystown
C. Race
Str. of Belle Isle
St. Anthony
C. Bauld
Belle Isle
Port Hope Simpson
Cartwright
Rigolet
Hopedale
C. Harrison
Nain
Hebron
Kangiqsualujjuaq
NEWFOUNDLAND
Labrador
Smallwood Res.
North West River
Happy Valley-Goose Bay
Churchill Falls
Churchill
Labrador Sea
Davis Strait
Cumberland Peninsula
Cumberland Sd.
Pangnirtung
Hoare B.
Mercy C.
C. Dyer
Qikiqtarjuaq
Iqaluit
Hall Peninsula
Meta Incognita Peninsula
Kimmirut
Frobisher Bay
Resolution I.
Nunavik
Uummannaq
Qeqertarsuaq
Ilulissat
Qasigiannguit
Kangerlussuaq
Sisimiut
Maniitsoq
Nuuk
Qeqertarsuatsiaat
Paamiut
Arsuk
Qaqortoq
Nanortalik
Alluitsup Paa
Uummannarsuaq
Tasiilaq
GREENLAND (KALAALLIT NUNAAT) (Denmark)
Kong Frederik VI's Kyst
2850
2136
1890
2591
3809
1652
1135
1190
814
6309
ATLANTIC OCEAN
West from Greenwich
13
14

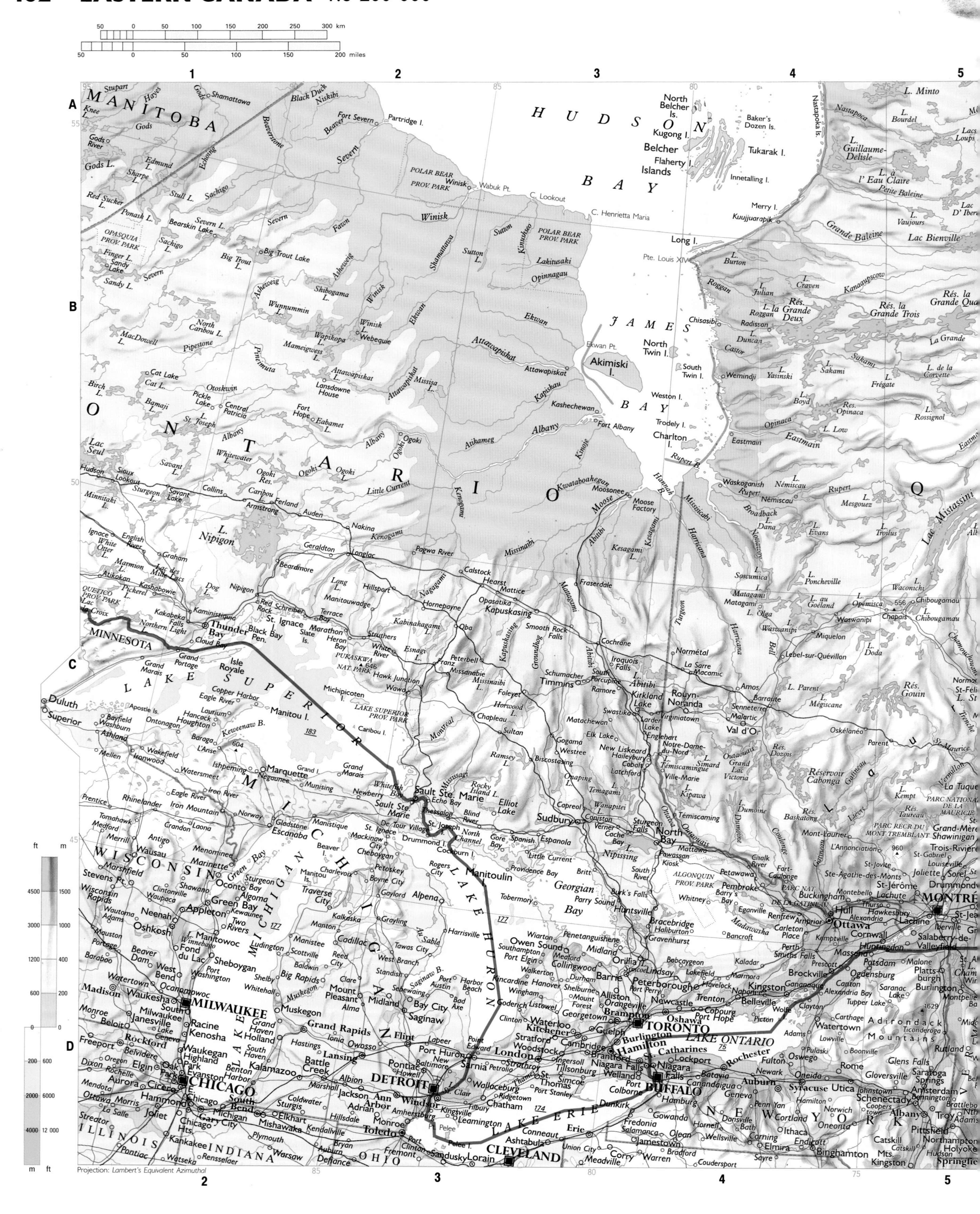
50 0 50 100 150 200 250 300 km
50 0 50 100 150 200 miles
1 2 3 4 5
A B C D
MANITOBA
ONTARIO
MINNESOTA
WISCONSIN
MICHIGAN
ILLINOIS
INDIANA
OHIO
NEW YORK
HUDSON BAY
JAMES BAY
LAKE SUPERIOR
LAKE MICHIGAN
LAKE HURON
LAKE ONTARIO
LAKE ERIE
Georgian Bay
Belcher Islands
Akimiski I.
L. Nipigon
L. Mistassini
Manitoulin
Thunder Bay
Sault Ste. Marie
Sudbury
North Bay
Timmins
Ottawa
Hull
MONTRÉAL
TORONTO
Hamilton
London
Kingston
BUFFALO
Niagara Falls
DETROIT
Windsor
CLEVELAND
CHICAGO
MILWAUKEE
Duluth
Rochester
Syracuse
Moosonee
Chisasibi
Kuujjuarapik
Rouyn-Noranda
Val d'Or
Kapuskasing
Cochrane
Projection: Lambert's Equivalent Azimuthal
ft m
4500 1500
3000 1000
1200 400
600 200
0 0
200 600
2000 6000
4000 12 000
m ft

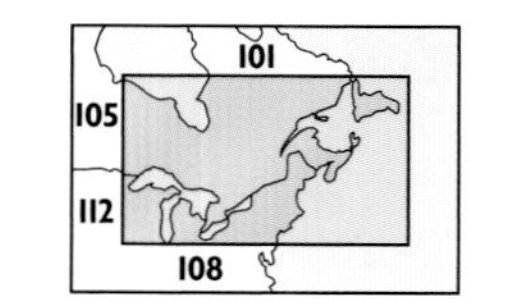

101
105
112
108

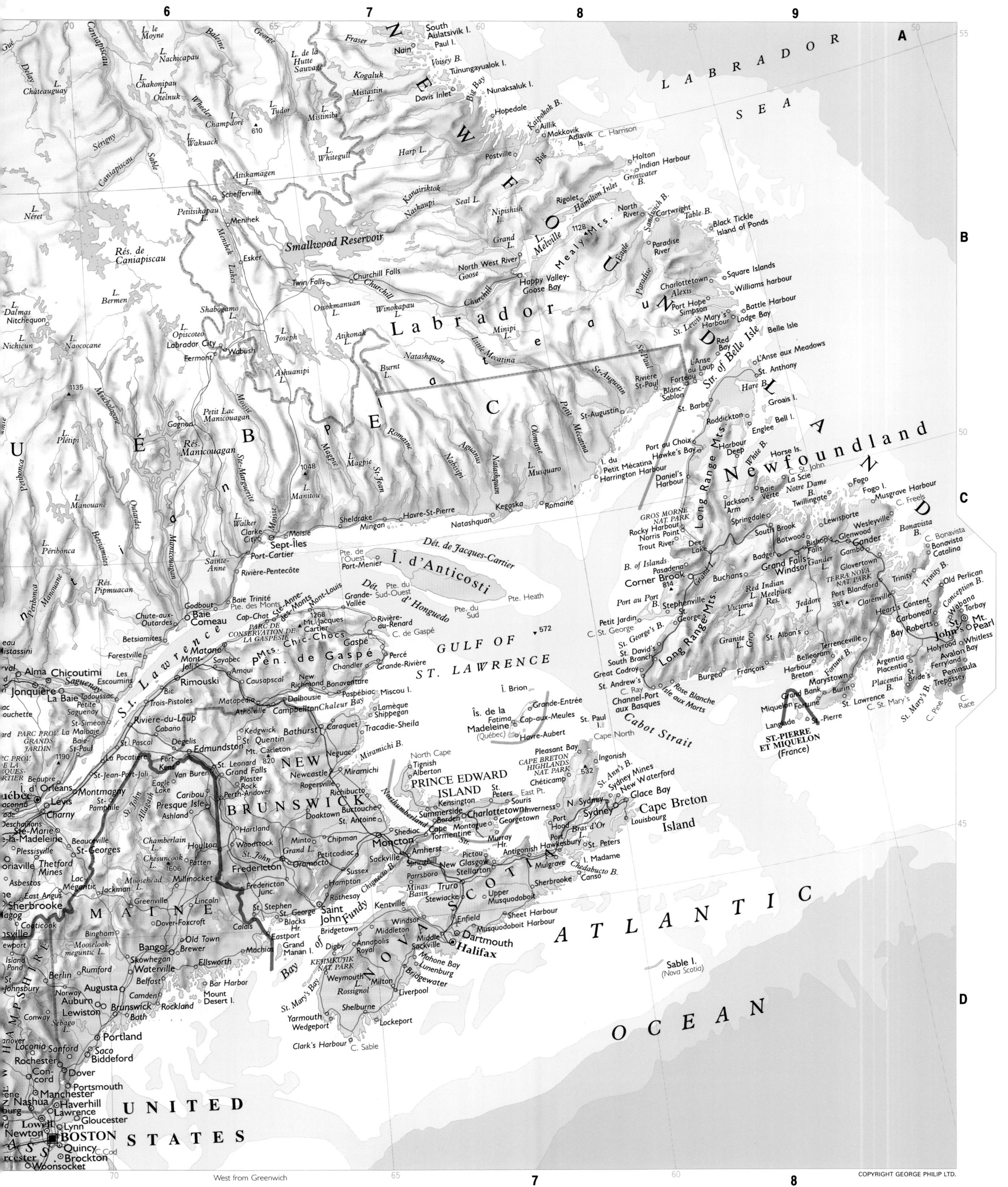

LABRADOR SEA
NEWFOUNDLAND
Labrador
QUÉBEC
Newfoundland
GULF OF ST. LAWRENCE
ATLANTIC OCEAN
UNITED STATES
NEW BRUNSWICK
NOVA SCOTIA
MAINE
PRINCE EDWARD ISLAND
Cape Breton Island
Î. d'Anticosti
Smallwood Reservoir
Rés. de Caniapiscau
Rés. Manicouagan
Pén. de Gaspé
Cabot Strait
Str. of Belle Isle
Bay of Fundy
Dét. de Jacques-Cartier
Dét. d'Honguedo
Îs. de la Madeleine (Québec)
ST-PIERRE ET MIQUELON (France)
Sable I. (Nova Scotia)
Mealy Mts.
Long Range Mts.
Mts. Chic-Chocs
GROS MORNE NAT. PARK
TERRA NOVA NAT. PARK
CAPE BRETON HIGHLANDS NAT. PARK
KEJIMKUJIK NAT. PARK
Nain
Hopedale
Makkovik
Postville
Rigolet
Cartwright
North West River
Happy Valley-Goose Bay
Churchill Falls
Schefferville
Labrador City
Wabush
Fermont
Sept-Îles
Port-Cartier
Baie Comeau
Havre-St-Pierre
Natashquan
Blanc-Sablon
L'Anse aux Meadows
St. Anthony
Corner Brook
Stephenville
Deer Lake
Grand Falls Windsor
Gander
Clarenville
Port aux Basques
Marystown
St. John's
Mt. Pearl
Gaspé
Percé
Rimouski
Matane
Chicoutimi
Jonquière
Rivière-du-Loup
Edmundston
Bathurst
Campbellton
Miramichi
Moncton
Fredericton
Saint John
Charlottetown
Summerside
Amherst
Truro
New Glasgow
Antigonish
Sydney
Glace Bay
Halifax
Dartmouth
Yarmouth
Liverpool
Bridgewater
Lunenburg
Digby
Kentville
Bangor
Augusta
Portland
Lewiston
Sherbrooke
Lévis
Québec
Manchester
Nashua
Concord
Portsmouth
Lowell
BOSTON
Quincy
Brockton
Lynn
Newton
Haverhill
Lawrence
Gloucester
Woonsocket
C. Cod
C. Race
C. Sable
West from Greenwich
6
7
8
9
A
B
C
D

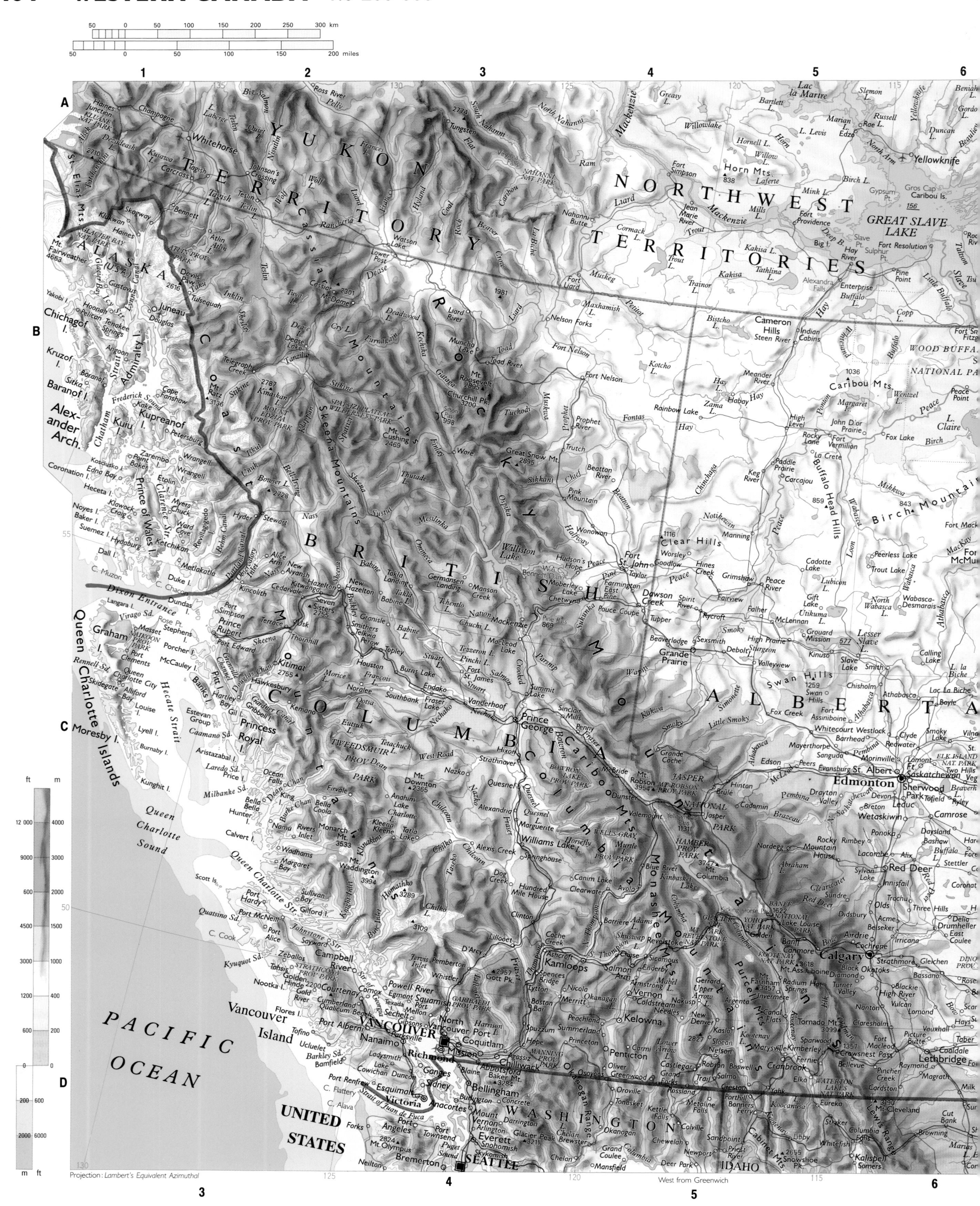
50 0 50 100 150 200 250 300 km
50 0 50 100 150 200 miles
1 2 3 4 5 6
A B C D
YUKON TERRITORY
NORTHWEST TERRITORIES
BRITISH COLUMBIA
ALBERTA
ALASKA (U.S.A.)
WASHINGTON
IDAHO
UNITED STATES
PACIFIC OCEAN
Whitehorse
Yellowknife
GREAT SLAVE LAKE
Fort Resolution
Fort Providence
Hay River
Fort Simpson
Fort Liard
Fort Nelson
Fort St. John
Dawson Creek
Grande Prairie
Peace River
Edmonton
St. Albert
Sherwood Park
Red Deer
Calgary
Lethbridge
Banff
Jasper
Prince George
Prince Rupert
Kitimat
Terrace
Juneau
Skagway
Haines
Sitka
Ketchikan
Kamloops
Kelowna
Vernon
Penticton
Nelson
Cranbrook
Vancouver
Richmond
Coquitlam
Victoria
Nanaimo
Bellingham
Everett
Seattle
Bremerton
Queen Charlotte Islands
Graham I.
Moresby I.
Queen Charlotte Sound
Hecate Strait
Dixon Entrance
Vancouver Island
Alexander Arch.
Coast Mountains
Skeena Mountains
Rocky Mountains
Cariboo Mts.
Monashee Mts.
Purcell Mts.
Caribou Mts.
Swan Hills
Clear Hills
Birch Mountains
Mt. Robson 3954
Mt. Waddington 3994
Mt. Columbia 3747
Mt. Fairweather 4663
Projection: Lambert's Equivalent Azimuthal
West from Greenwich
ft m
12 000 4000
9000 3000
6000 2000
4500 1500
3000 1000
1200 400
600 200
0 0
200 600
2000 6000
m ft

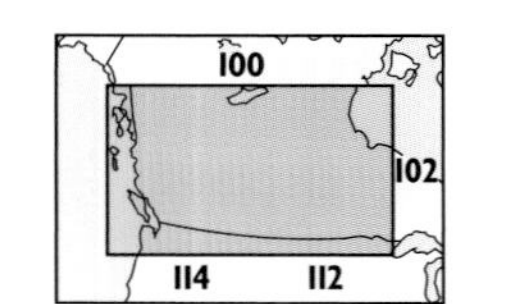

100
102
114
112

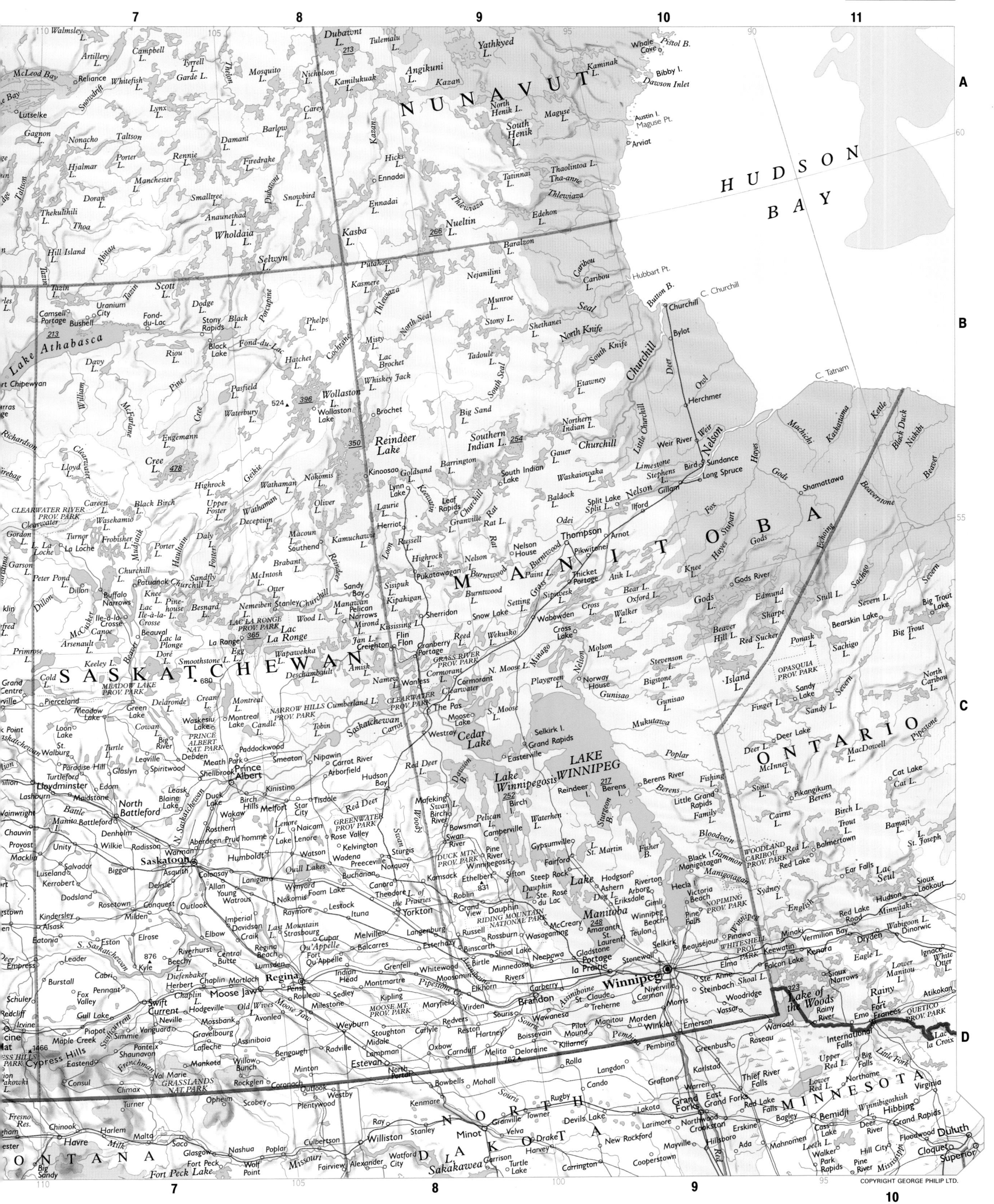

NUNAVUT
HUDSON BAY
MANITOBA
SASKATCHEWAN
ONTARIO
NORTH DAKOTA
MINNESOTA
MONTANA
LAKE WINNIPEG
Lake Winnipegosis
Lake Manitoba
Lake Athabasca
Reindeer Lake
Wollaston L.
Southern Indian L.
Cedar Lake
Lake of the Woods
Churchill
Winnipeg
Regina
Saskatoon
Prince Albert
Moose Jaw
Brandon
Thompson
Flin Flon
The Pas
North Battleford
Lloydminster
Swift Current
Yorkton
Kenora
Dryden
Grand Forks
Minot
Duluth
Williston
Arviat
Whale Cove
La Ronge
Nelson
Churchill
Hayes
Cypress Hills
Big Trout Lake
Lac Seul
RIDING MOUNTAIN NATIONAL PARK
PRINCE ALBERT NAT. PARK
GRASSLANDS NAT. PARK
QUETICO PROV. PARK
WOODLAND CARIBOU PROV. PARK
COPYRIGHT GEORGE PHILIP LTD.

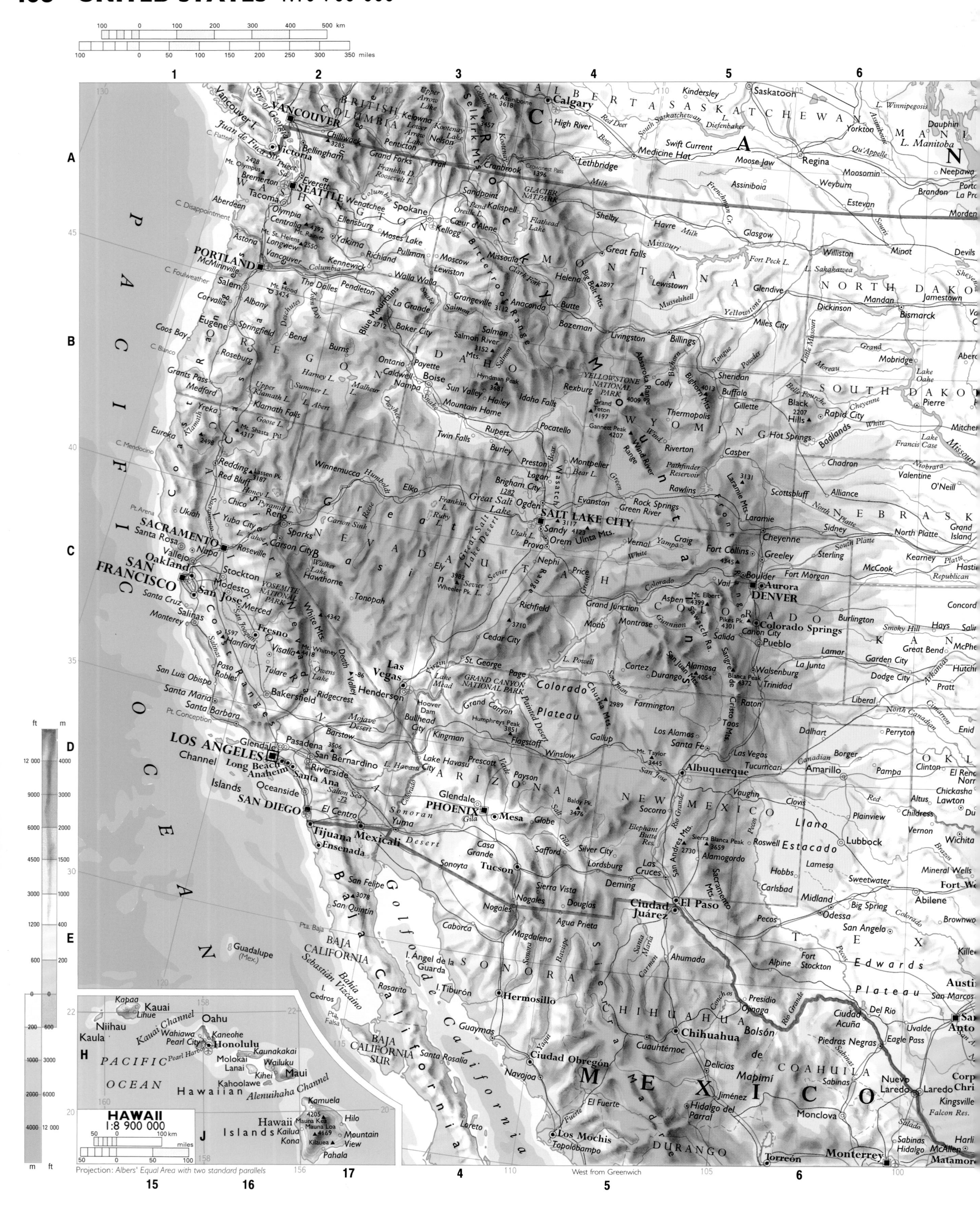

100 0 100 200 300 400 500 km
100 0 50 100 150 200 250 300 350 miles
PACIFIC OCEAN
CANADA
BRITISH COLUMBIA
ALBERTA
SASKATCHEWAN
MANITOBA
WASHINGTON
OREGON
IDAHO
MONTANA
WYOMING
NORTH DAKOTA
SOUTH DAKOTA
NEBRASKA
CALIFORNIA
NEVADA
UTAH
COLORADO
ARIZONA
NEW MEXICO
KANSAS
OKLAHOMA
TEXAS
MEXICO
BAJA CALIFORNIA
BAJA CALIFORNIA SUR
SONORA
CHIHUAHUA
COAHUILA
DURANGO
Rocky Mountains
Great Basin
Sierra Nevada
Coast Ranges
Cascade Range
Colorado Plateau
Front Range
Sierra Madre
Llano Estacado
Edwards Plateau
Bolsón de Mapimí
Gulf of California
Baja California
Vancouver I.
VANCOUVER
Victoria
SEATTLE
Tacoma
Olympia
Spokane
PORTLAND
Salem
Eugene
Boise
Calgary
Lethbridge
Medicine Hat
Swift Current
Moose Jaw
Regina
Saskatoon
Great Falls
Helena
Butte
Missoula
Billings
Bozeman
Bismarck
Pierre
Casper
Cheyenne
Laramie
SALT LAKE CITY
Ogden
Provo
Reno
Carson City
SACRAMENTO
SAN FRANCISCO
Oakland
San Jose
Fresno
Bakersfield
LOS ANGELES
Long Beach
Anaheim
Santa Ana
San Bernardino
Riverside
SAN DIEGO
Las Vegas
Henderson
PHOENIX
Mesa
Tucson
Flagstaff
Albuquerque
Santa Fe
El Paso
Ciudad Juárez
DENVER
Aurora
Boulder
Colorado Springs
Pueblo
Grand Junction
Amarillo
Lubbock
Midland
Odessa
San Angelo
Abilene
Austin
San Antonio
Laredo
Nuevo Laredo
Monterrey
Torreón
Chihuahua
Hermosillo
Ciudad Obregón
Los Mochis
Tijuana
Mexicali
Ensenada
Great Salt Lake
Yellowstone National Park
Grand Canyon National Park
Yosemite National Park
Glacier Nat. Park
Death Valley
Mojave Desert
Sonoran Desert
Mt. Rainier 4392
Mt. Whitney 4418
Mt. Elbert 4399
Gannett Peak 4207
Grand Teton 4197
HAWAII
1:8 900 000
Kauai
Oahu
Honolulu
Molokai
Lanai
Maui
Hawaii
Kahoolawe
Niihau
Hilo
Mauna Kea 4205
Mauna Loa 4169
PACIFIC OCEAN
Hawaiian Islands
Projection: Albers' Equal Area with two standard parallels
West from Greenwich

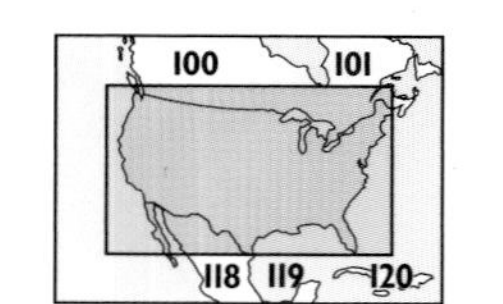
100
101
118
119
120

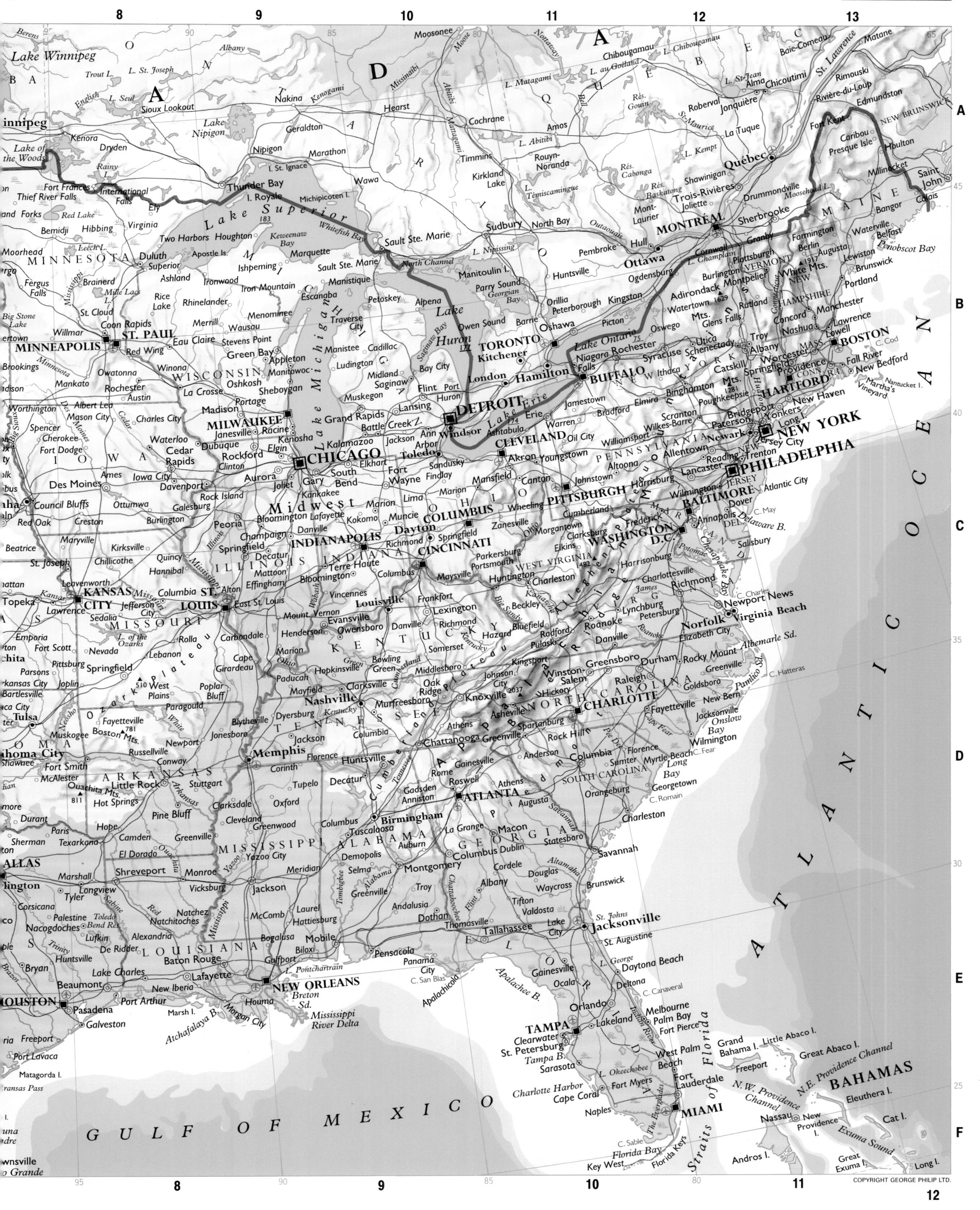
8
9
10
11
12
13
A
B
C
D
E
F
Lake Winnipeg
Lake of the Woods
Lake Superior
Lake Michigan
Lake Huron
Lake Erie
Lake Ontario
Lake Nipigon
Moosonee
Chibougamau
Baie-Comeau
Matane
Rimouski
Rivière-du-Loup
Edmundston
NEW BRUNSWICK
Sioux Lookout
Nakina
Hearst
Cochrane
Amos
Roberval
Jonquière
Alma
Chicoutimi
La Tuque
Québec
Kenora
Dryden
Geraldton
Marathon
Timmins
Rouyn-Noranda
Thunder Bay
Fort Frances
International Falls
Wawa
Kirkland Lake
Shawinigan
Trois-Rivières
Drummondville
MONTRÉAL
Sherbrooke
Sudbury
North Bay
Sault Ste. Marie
Pembroke
Hull
Ottawa
Huntsville
Kingston
Manitoulin I.
Parry Sound
Georgian Bay
TORONTO
Kitchener
Hamilton
London
Windsor
Duluth
Superior
Bemidji
Hibbing
Virginia
Moorhead
MINNESOTA
MINNEAPOLIS
ST. PAUL
Rochester
Eau Claire
Green Bay
Appleton
Oshkosh
WISCONSIN
La Crosse
Madison
MILWAUKEE
Racine
Kenosha
CHICAGO
Rockford
Aurora
Joliet
Gary
South Bend
Elkhart
Fort Wayne
Dubuque
Waterloo
Cedar Rapids
Iowa City
Des Moines
Davenport
Rock Island
IOWA
Council Bluffs
Ottumwa
Burlington
Peoria
Bloomington
Champaign
Springfield
Decatur
ILLINOIS
Quincy
Midwest
Lafayette
Kokomo
Muncie
INDIANAPOLIS
INDIANA
Terre Haute
Evansville
Owensboro
Louisville
Lexington
Frankfort
KENTUCKY
Paducah
Bowling Green
Nashville
Clarksville
Murfreesboro
TENNESSEE
Knoxville
Chattanooga
Memphis
Jackson
Huntsville
Birmingham
Tuscaloosa
Montgomery
ALABAMA
Mobile
ATLANTA
GEORGIA
Columbus
Macon
Augusta
Savannah
Albany
Tallahassee
Jacksonville
St. Augustine
Daytona Beach
Gainesville
Ocala
Orlando
TAMPA
Clearwater
St. Petersburg
Sarasota
Lakeland
Melbourne
Palm Bay
Fort Pierce
West Palm Beach
Fort Lauderdale
MIAMI
Naples
Fort Myers
Cape Coral
Key West
Florida Bay
Florida Keys
Straits of Florida
Lake Okeechobee
The Everglades
DETROIT
Flint
Lansing
Grand Rapids
Kalamazoo
Battle Creek
Saginaw
Toledo
CLEVELAND
Akron
Youngstown
Canton
Mansfield
COLUMBUS
Dayton
Springfield
CINCINNATI
OHIO
Wheeling
PITTSBURGH
PENNSYLVANIA
Erie
Buffalo
Niagara Falls
Rochester
Syracuse
Utica
Schenectady
Albany
Troy
Binghamton
NEW YORK
Scranton
Wilkes-Barre
Allentown
Reading
Lancaster
Harrisburg
PHILADELPHIA
Trenton
Newark
Jersey City
Paterson
Yonkers
Bridgeport
New Haven
HARTFORD
Springfield
Worcester
Providence
BOSTON
Lowell
Lawrence
Manchester
Concord
Nashua
Portland
Lewiston
Augusta
Bangor
Burlington
Montpelier
VERMONT
NEW HAMPSHIRE
MAINE
White Mts.
Adirondack Mts.
Catskill Mts.
Cape Cod
Nantucket I.
Martha's Vineyard
Fall River
New Bedford
Atlantic City
Dover
Wilmington
BALTIMORE
Annapolis
WASHINGTON D.C.
Chesapeake Bay
Delaware B.
C. May
Frederick
Hagerstown
Cumberland
Morgantown
Clarksburg
Elkins
WEST VIRGINIA
Parkersburg
Charleston
Huntington
Harrisonburg
Charlottesville
Richmond
Lynchburg
Petersburg
Roanoke
Norfolk
Newport News
Virginia Beach
C. Charles
Danville
Greensboro
Winston-Salem
Durham
Raleigh
Rocky Mount
Greenville
Goldsboro
Fayetteville
New Bern
NORTH CAROLINA
CHARLOTTE
Asheville
Hickory
Spartanburg
Greenville
Rock Hill
Columbia
SOUTH CAROLINA
Florence
Sumter
Myrtle Beach
Charleston
Wilmington
C. Hatteras
C. Fear
C. Romain
Albemarle Sd.
Pamlico Sd.
Onslow Bay
Long Bay
Appalachian Mts.
Blue Ridge
Cumberland Plateau
KANSAS CITY
Topeka
Lawrence
ST. LOUIS
East St. Louis
Columbia
Jefferson City
MISSOURI
Springfield
Joplin
Ozark Plateau
Tulsa
Muskogee
Oklahoma City
Fort Smith
Fayetteville
Little Rock
ARKANSAS
Hot Springs
Pine Bluff
Texarkana
Shreveport
Monroe
Tyler
Longview
LOUISIANA
Alexandria
Lake Charles
Lafayette
Baton Rouge
NEW ORLEANS
Houma
Beaumont
Port Arthur
HOUSTON
Pasadena
Galveston
Vicksburg
Jackson
MISSISSIPPI
Hattiesburg
Biloxi
Gulfport
Meridian
Pensacola
Panama City
Apalachicola
DALLAS
GULF OF MEXICO
Mississippi River Delta
ATLANTIC OCEAN
Grand Bahama I.
Little Abaco I.
Great Abaco I.
Freeport
N.W. Providence Channel
N.E. Providence Channel
BAHAMAS
Nassau
New Providence I.
Eleuthera I.
Cat I.
Exuma Sound
Great Exuma I.
Long I.
Andros I.
ONTARIO
QUEBEC
CANADA

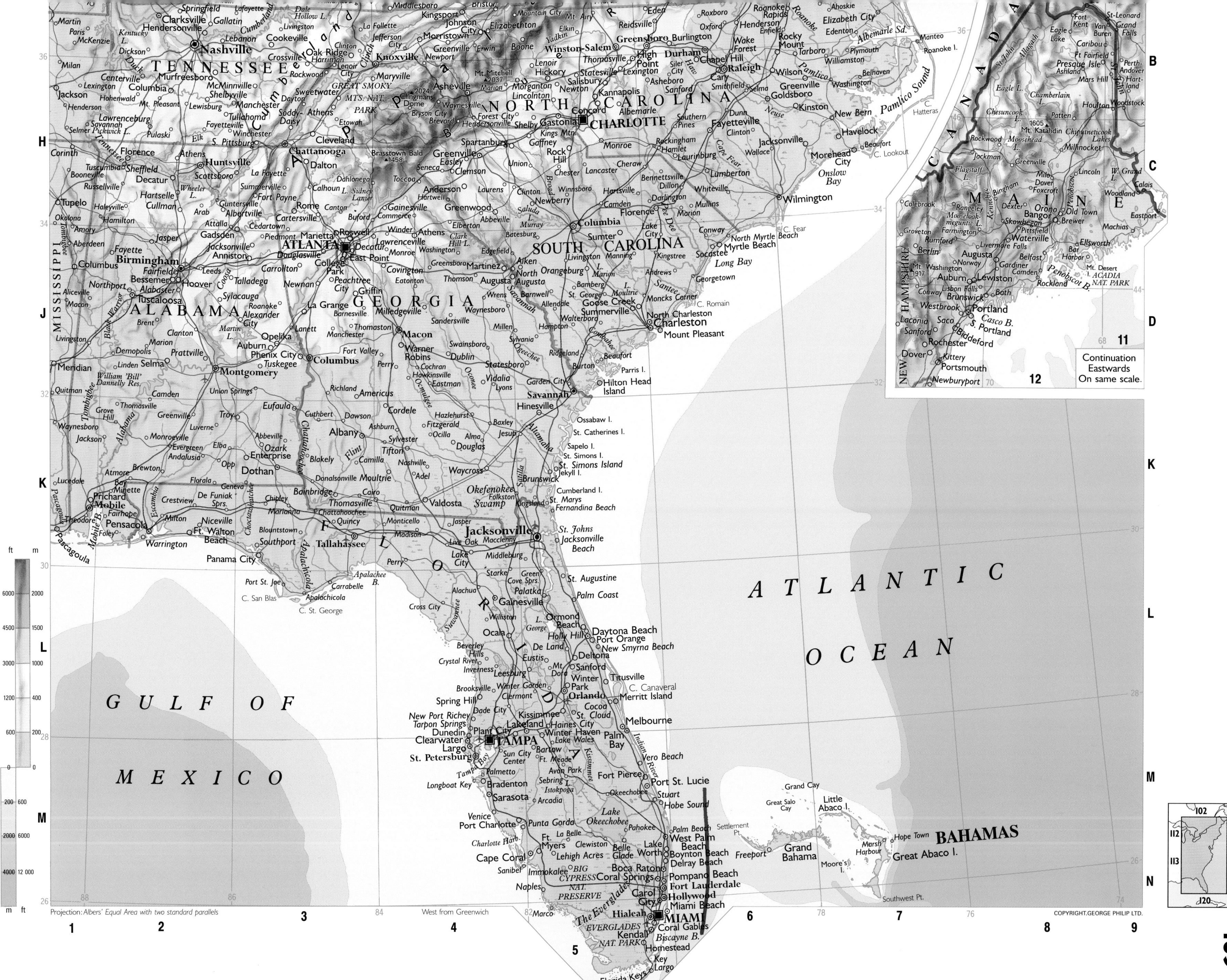

ATLANTIC OCEAN

BAHAMAS

Hope Town
Great Abaco I.
Grand Cay
Little Abaco I.
Great Sale Cay
Moore's I.
Marsh Harbour
Settlement Pt.
Freeport
Grand Bahama
Southwest Pt.

GULF OF MEXICO

TENNESSEE

Nashville

NORTH CAROLINA

CHARLOTTE

SOUTH CAROLINA

Columbia
Charleston

GEORGIA

Atlanta
Macon
Savannah

ALABAMA

Birmingham
Montgomery
Mobile

MISSISSIPPI

FLORIDA

Jacksonville
Orlando
TAMPA
St. Petersburg
MIAMI
Miami Beach
Florida Keys

MAINE

Bangor
Augusta
Portland

NEW HAMPSHIRE

Concord
Portsmouth
Newburyport

Continuation Eastwards
On same scale.

11

12

West from Greenwich

Projection: Albers' Equal Area with two standard parallels

COPYRIGHT GEORGE PHILIP LTD.

ft	m
6000	2000
4500	1500
3000	1000
1200	400
600	200
0	0
200	600
2000	6000
4000	12 000

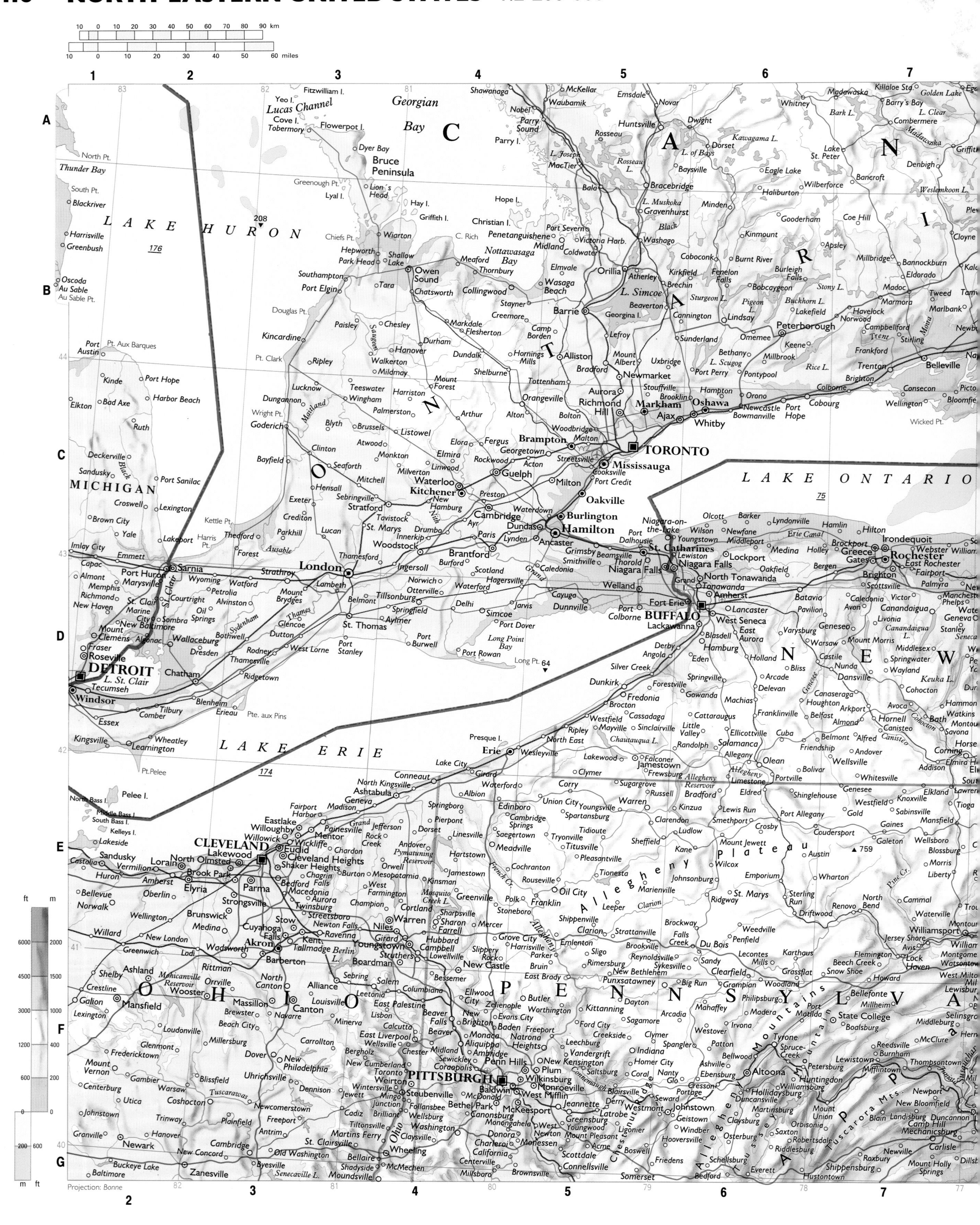
0 10 20 30 40 50 60 70 80 90 km
0 10 20 30 40 50 60 miles
LAKE HURON
LAKE ERIE
LAKE ONTARIO
Georgian Bay
CANADA
ONTARIO
MICHIGAN
OHIO
PENNSYLVANIA
NEW
Bruce Peninsula
Allegheny Plateau
Allegheny Mountains
Tussey Mountains
Tuscarora Mts.
APPALACHIAN
Lucas Channel
Nottawasaga Bay
L. Simcoe
Long Point Bay
Thunder Bay
Saginaw
L. St. Clair
Fitzwilliam I.
Yeo I.
Cove I.
Tobermory
Flowerpot I.
Dyer Bay
Lion's Head
Greenough Pt.
Lyal I.
Hay I.
Griffith I.
Hope I.
Christian I.
Chiefs Pt.
Wiarton
Hepworth
Shallow Lake
Park Head
Owen Sound
Southampton
Port Elgin
Tara
Chatsworth
Meaford
Thornbury
Collingwood
Penetanguishene
Midland
Port Severn
Victoria Harb.
Coldwater
Elmvale
Wasaga Beach
Stayner
Creemore
Orillia
Atherley
Barrie
Georgina I.
Beaverton
Brechin
Douglas Pt.
Kincardine
Paisley
Chesley
Hanover
Durham
Markdale
Flesherton
Walkerton
Mildmay
Ripley
Pt. Clark
Lucknow
Teeswater
Wingham
Dungannon
Goderich
Wright Pt.
Blyth
Brussels
Listowel
Clinton
Seaforth
Bayfield
Mitchell
Exeter
Hensall
Crediton
Stratford
St. Marys
Lucan
Parkhill
London
Thamesford
Woodstock
Ingersoll
Strathroy
Sarnia
Port Huron
Marysville
Wyoming
Petrolia
Watford
Lambeth
Tillsonburg
Aylmer
Port Burwell
St. Thomas
Port Stanley
West Lorne
Dutton
Glencoe
Rodney
Ridgetown
Chatham
Wallaceburg
Dresden
Detroit
Windsor
Tecumseh
Tilbury
Blenheim
Erieau
Pte. aux Pins
Comber
Essex
Kingsville
Leamington
Wheatley
Pt. Pelee
Pelee I.
Kitchener
Waterloo
Guelph
Cambridge
Brantford
Paris
Hamilton
Burlington
Dundas
Ancaster
Oakville
Milton
Mississauga
TORONTO
Brampton
Markham
Richmond Hill
Aurora
Newmarket
Bradford
Ajax
Whitby
Oshawa
Bowmanville
Newcastle
Port Hope
Cobourg
Brighton
Trenton
Belleville
Peterborough
Lindsay
Huntsville
Bracebridge
Gravenhurst
Muskoka
Dorset
Minden
Haliburton
Bancroft
Parry Sound
Shawanaga
McKellar
Nobel
Parry I.
Waubamik
Emsdale
Novar
Dwight
Rosseau
L. Joseph
MacTier
Bala
Baysville
Eagle Lake
Whitney
Madawaska
Killaloe Sta.
Golden Lake
Barry's Bay
Combermere
Denbigh
Coe Hill
Apsley
Norwood
Campbellford
Stirling
Marmora
Madoc
Tweed
Havelock
Frankford
Consecon
Picton
Wellington
St. Catharines
Niagara Falls
Niagara-on-the-Lake
Welland
Port Colborne
Fort Erie
Grimsby
Beamsville
Dunnville
Caledonia
Hagersville
Simcoe
Port Dover
Delhi
Port Rowan
Long Pt.
BUFFALO
Lackawanna
Tonawanda
North Tonawanda
Amherst
Lockport
West Seneca
Lancaster
Hamburg
Angola
Derby
Silver Creek
Dunkirk
Fredonia
Jamestown
Olean
Salamanca
Ellicottville
Batavia
Rochester
Greece
Irondequoit
Brighton
Geneseo
Dansville
Hornell
Bath
Corning
Elmira
Erie
Presque I.
North East
Wesleyville
Conneaut
Ashtabula
Geneva
Madison
Painesville
Mentor
Willoughby
Euclid
CLEVELAND
Lakewood
Parma
Lorain
Elyria
Sandusky
Vermilion
Huron
Norwalk
Oberlin
Medina
Strongsville
Akron
Cuyahoga Falls
Kent
Barberton
Wadsworth
Warren
Niles
Youngstown
Boardman
Alliance
Canton
Massillon
Wooster
Ashland
Mansfield
Galion
Shelby
New Philadelphia
Dover
Uhrichsville
Coshocton
Newark
Zanesville
Cambridge
St. Clairsville
Wheeling
Steubenville
Weirton
East Liverpool
PITTSBURGH
Penn Hills
McKeesport
Washington
Monroeville
Wilkinsburg
Butler
Kittanning
Indiana
Johnstown
Altoona
State College
Bellefonte
Lewistown
Huntingdon
Williamsport
Lock Haven
DuBois
Clearfield
St. Marys
Bradford
Warren
Meadville
Titusville
Oil City
Franklin
New Castle
Sharon
Greenville
Beaver Falls
Latrobe
Greensburg
Uniontown
Somerset
Bedford
Chambersburg
Shippensburg
Carlisle
Projection: Bonne

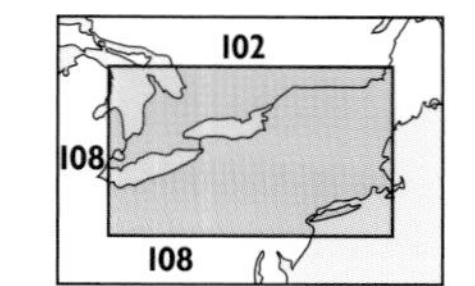

102
108
108

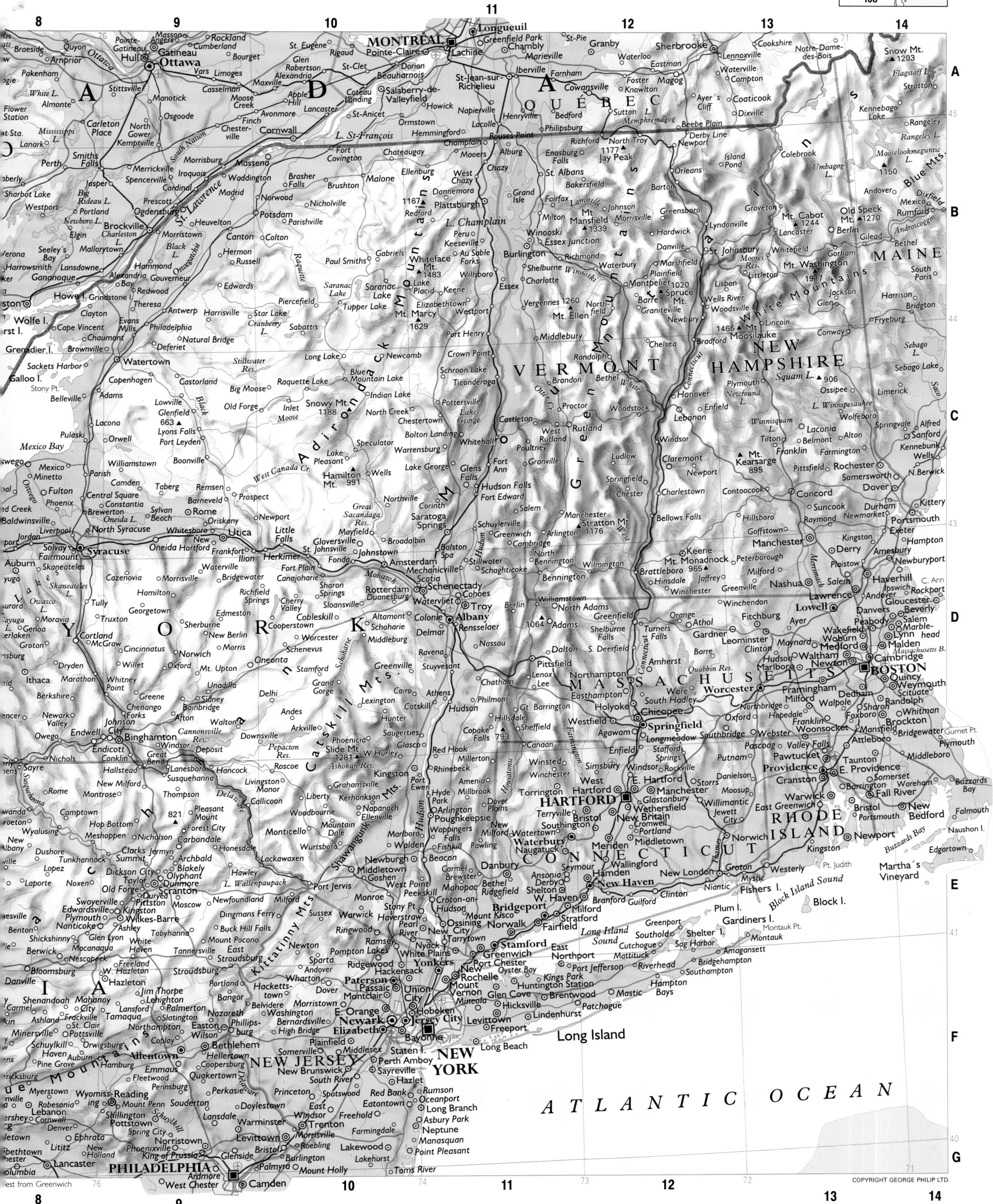

8
9
10
11
12
13
14
A
B
C
D
E
F
G
MONTREAL
Ottawa
QUÉBEC
VERMONT
NEW HAMPSHIRE
MAINE
MASSACHUSETTS
CONNECTICUT
RHODE ISLAND
NEW JERSEY
NEW YORK
BOSTON
HARTFORD
PHILADELPHIA
Adirondack Mountains
Green Mountains
White Mountains
Catskill Mts.
L. Champlain
St. Lawrence
Long Island
Long Island Sound
Block Island Sound
Martha's Vineyard
ATLANTIC OCEAN
Albany
Syracuse
Springfield
Worcester
Providence
New Haven
Bridgeport
Newark
Stamford
Yonkers
Jersey City
Trenton
Camden
Allentown
Scranton
Binghamton
Utica
Schenectady
Manchester
Concord
Portsmouth
Burlington
Montpelier
Plattsburgh
Mt. Marcy 1629
Mt. Washington 1917
Mt. Mansfield 1339
Stratton Mt. 1176
Mt. Monadnock 965
est from Greenwich
76
74
73
72
71

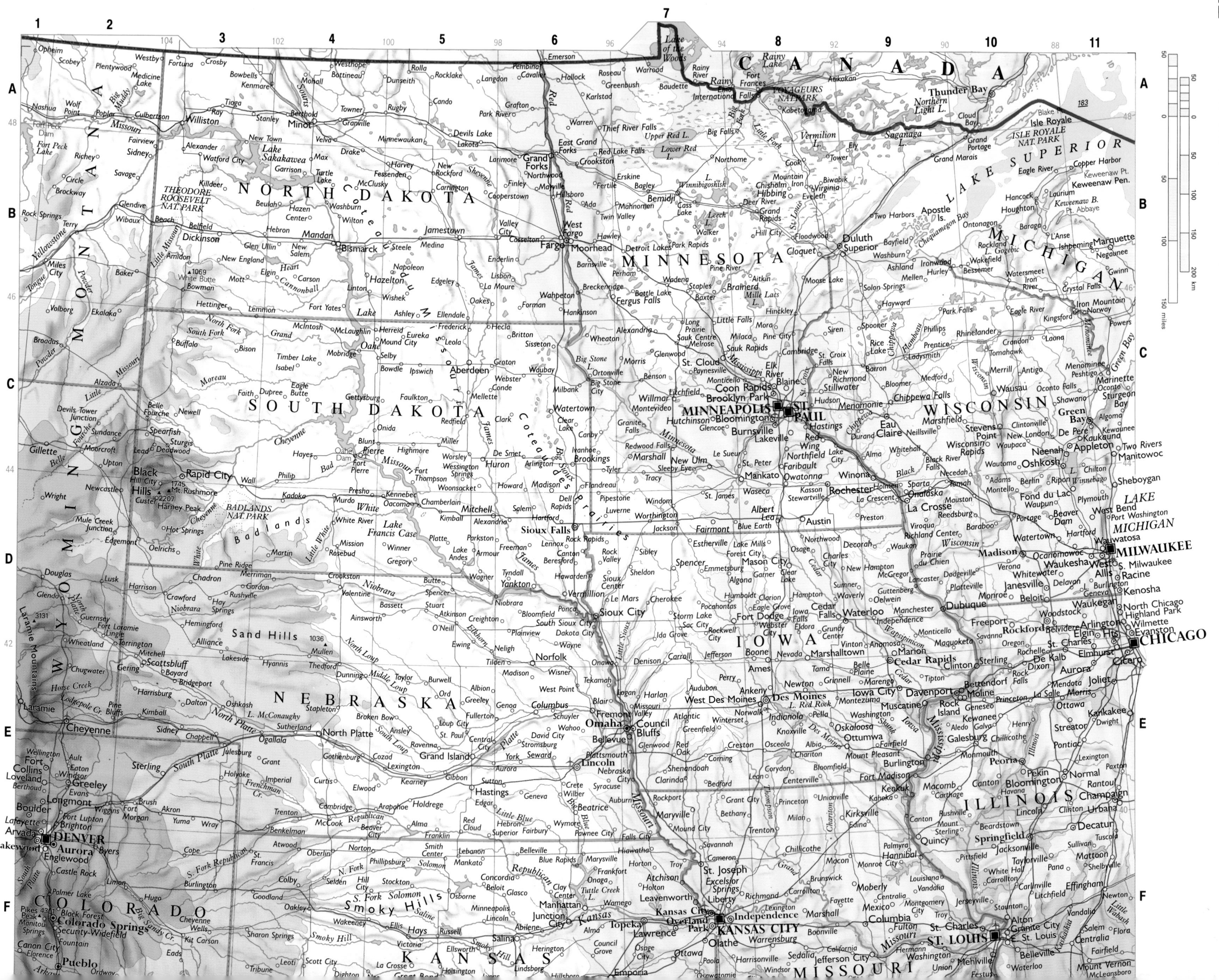

50 0 50 100 150 200 km
50 0 50 100 150 miles
CANADA
LAKE SUPERIOR
LAKE MICHIGAN
NORTH DAKOTA
SOUTH DAKOTA
MINNESOTA
WISCONSIN
MICHIGAN
IOWA
NEBRASKA
ILLINOIS
MISSOURI
KANSAS
COLORADO
WYOMING
MONTANA
MILWAUKEE
CHICAGO
MINNEAPOLIS
ST. PAUL
KANSAS CITY
ST. LOUIS
DENVER
Thunder Bay
Duluth
Fargo
Bismarck
Pierre
Rapid City
Sioux Falls
Sioux City
Omaha
Lincoln
Des Moines
Cedar Rapids
Madison
Green Bay
Topeka
Cheyenne
Colorado Springs
Pueblo
Springfield
Peoria
Mississippi
Missouri
Sand Hills
Black Hills
Laramie Mountains
Smoky Hills
Coteau des Prairies
Badlands
VOYAGEURS NAT. PARK
ISLE ROYALE NAT. PARK
THEODORE ROOSEVELT NAT. PARK
BADLANDS NAT. PARK

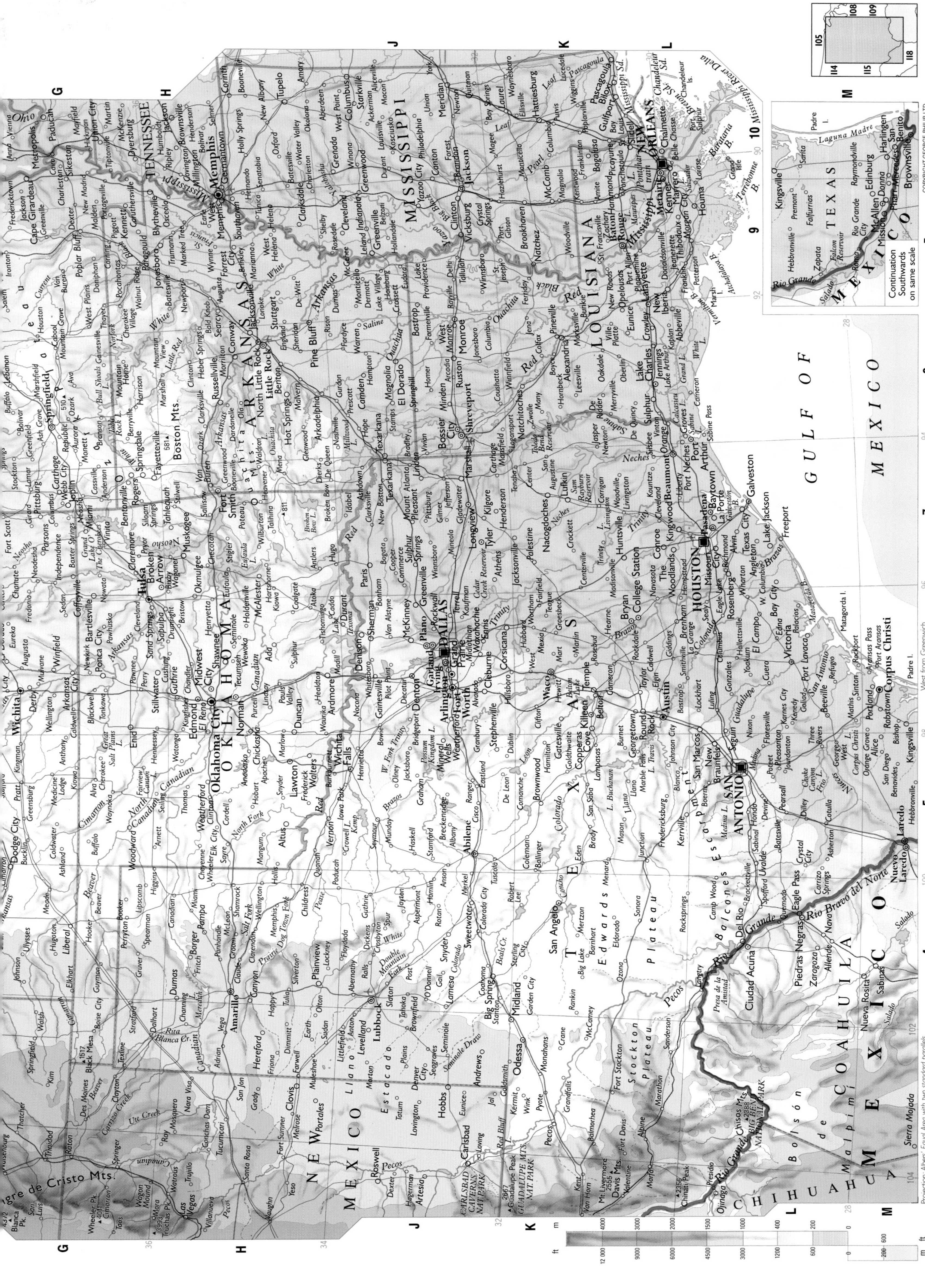

Map

States / Regions: TENNESSEE, MISSISSIPPI, LOUISIANA, ARKANSAS, OKLAHOMA, TEXAS, NEW MEXICO, MEXICO, COAHUILA, CHIHUAHUA

Water bodies: GULF OF MEXICO, Laguna Madre, Mississippi River Delta

Projection: Albers' Equal Area with two standard parallels

COPYRIGHT. GEORGE PHILIP LTD.

West from Greenwich

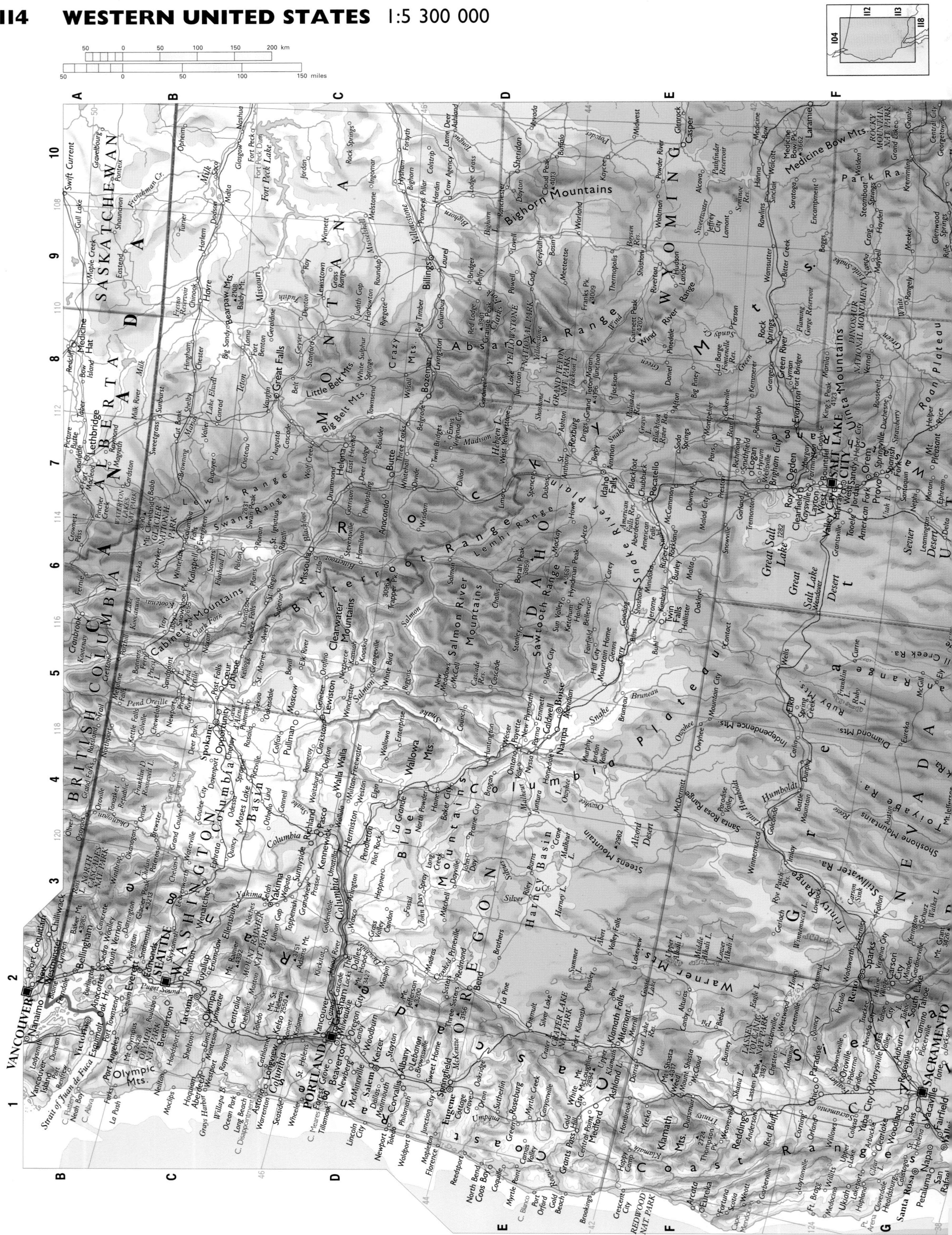
50 0 50 100 150 200 km
50 0 50 100 150 miles
104
112
113
118
BRITISH COLUMBIA
ALBERTA
SASKATCHEWAN
CANADA
WASHINGTON
OREGON
IDAHO
MONTANA
WYOMING
NEVADA
SEATTLE
PORTLAND
SPOKANE
BOISE
SALT LAKE CITY
SACRAMENTO
VANCOUVER
Great Falls
Billings
Helena
Missoula
Butte
Bozeman
Casper
Cheyenne
Laramie
Ogden
Pocatello
Idaho Falls
Twin Falls
Reno
Carson City
Eugene
Salem
Medford
Klamath Falls
Bend
Yakima
Tacoma
Olympia
Great Salt Lake
Great Salt Lake Desert
Bighorn Mountains
Salmon River Mountains
Sawtooth Range
Blue Mountains
Wind River Range
Uinta Mountains
Absaroka Range
Bitterroot Range
Lewis Range
Cabinet Mountains
Clearwater Mountains
Columbia Basin
Snake River Plain
Columbia Plateau
Great Basin
Cascade Range
Coast Ranges
Klamath Mts.
Olympic Mts.
Rocky Mountains
Puget Sound
Strait of Juan de Fuca
Harney Basin
Alvord Desert
YELLOWSTONE NATIONAL PARK
GRAND TETON NAT. PARK
GLACIER NATIONAL PARK
CRATER LAKE NAT. PARK
LASSEN VOLCANIC NAT. PARK
REDWOOD NAT. PARK
DINOSAUR NATIONAL MONUMENT

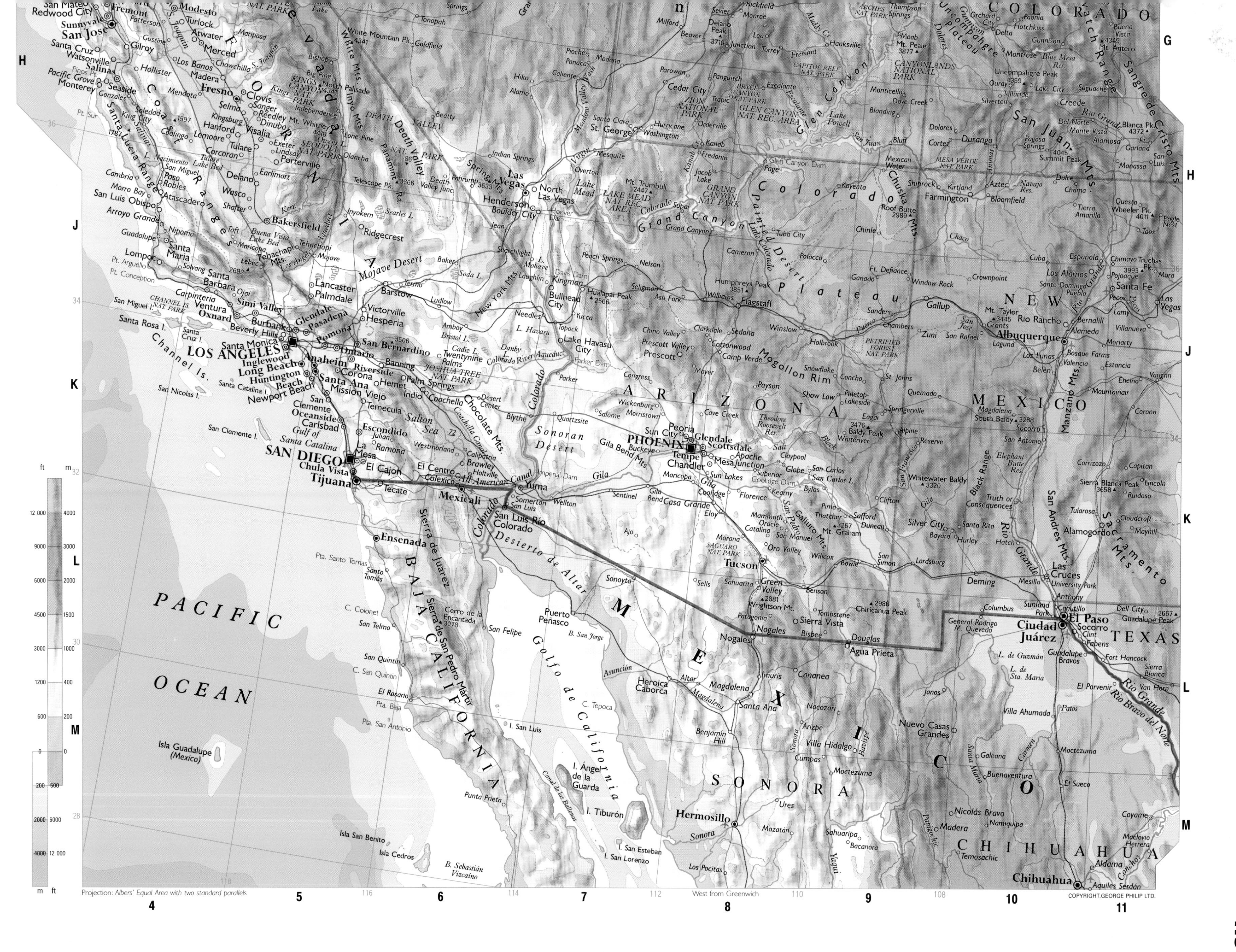

Projection: Albers' Equal Area with two standard parallels

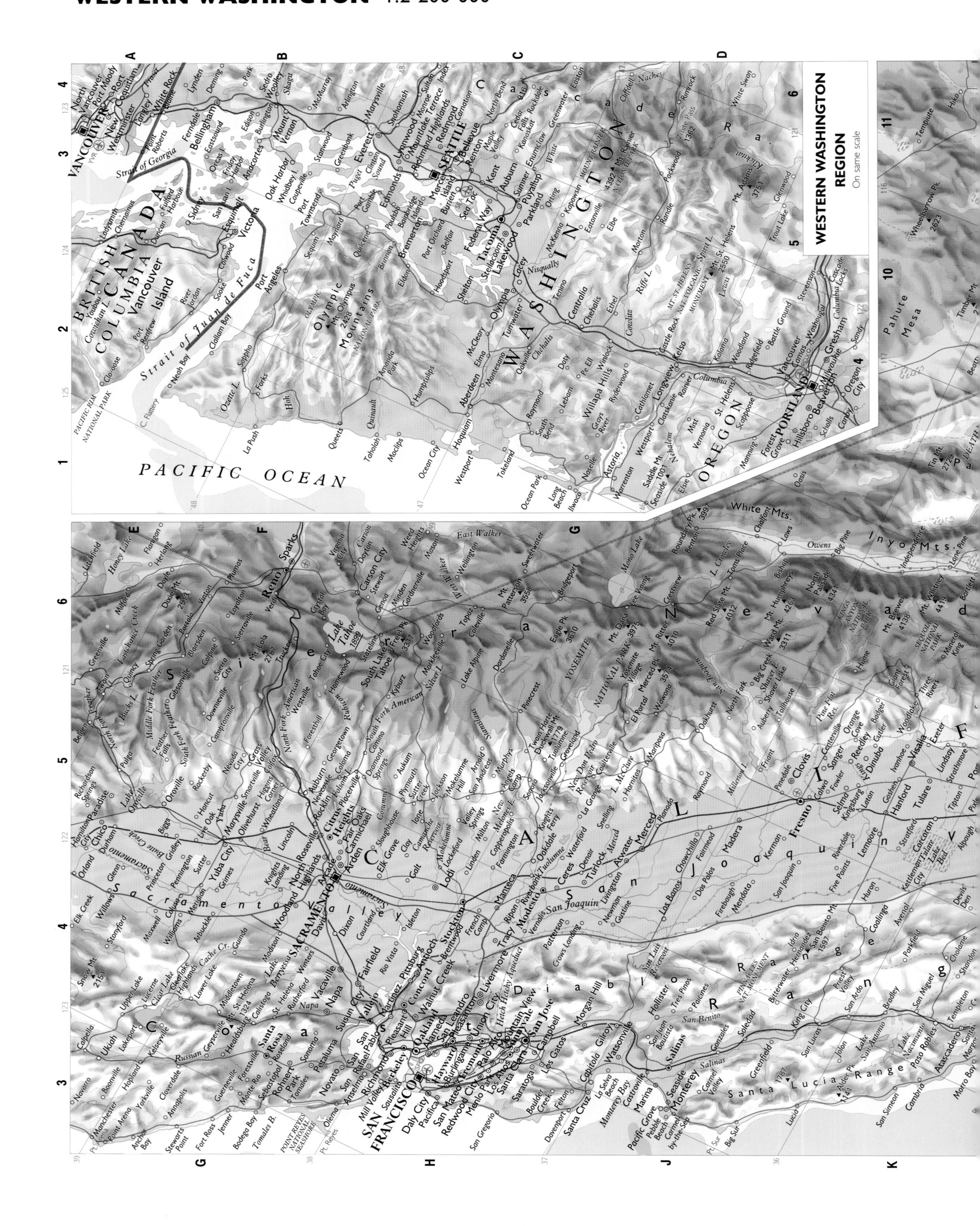

WESTERN WASHINGTON REGION On same scale

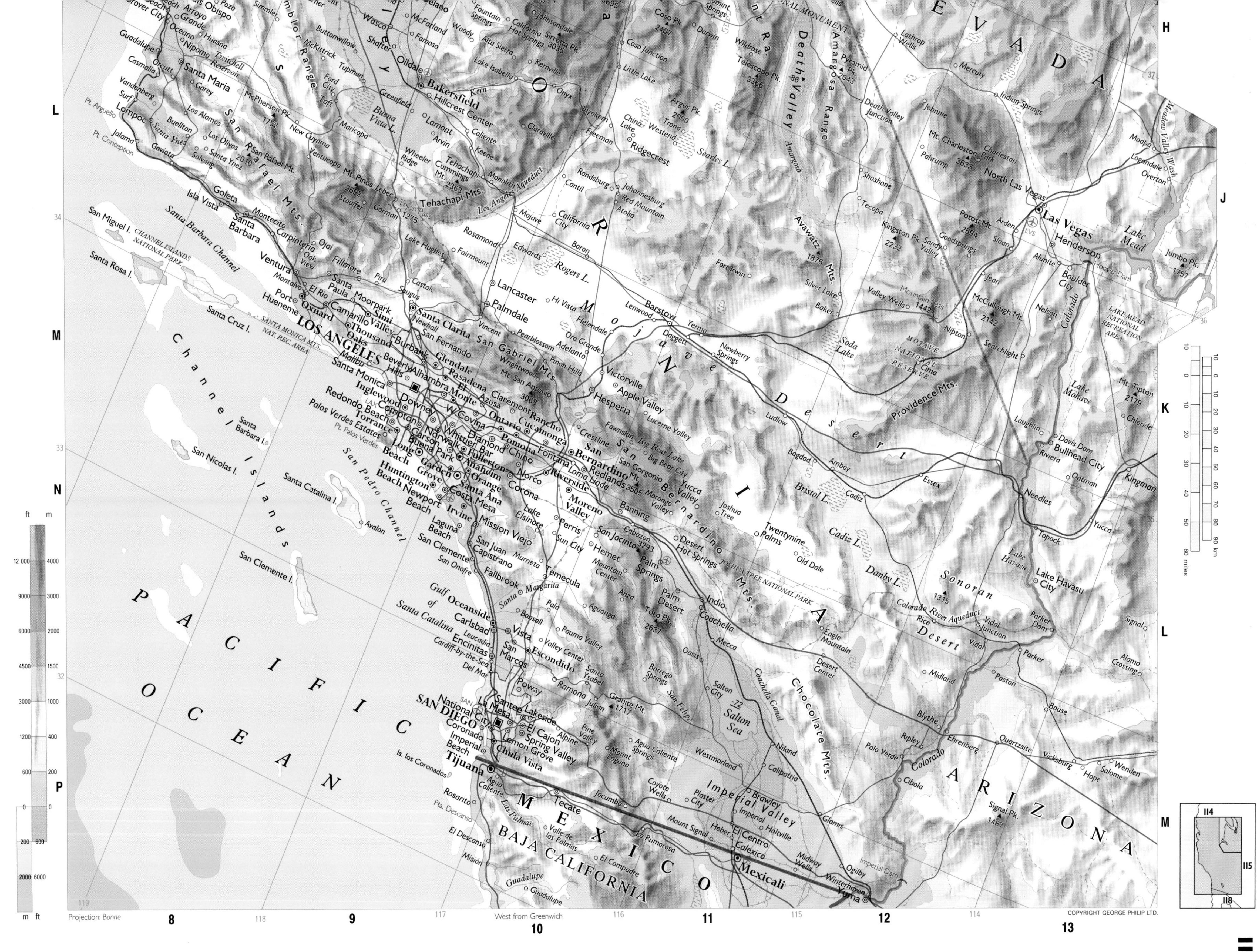

COPYRIGHT GEORGE PHILIP LTD.

Projection: Bonne

NEVADA
ARIZONA
CALIFORNIA
MEXICO
BAJA CALIFORNIA
PACIFIC OCEAN
Mojave Desert
Sonoran Desert
Channel Islands
Las Vegas
Henderson
North Las Vegas
Boulder City
Lake Mead
Lake Mohave
Colorado
Kingman
Bullhead City
Needles
Lake Havasu City
Parker
Blythe
Quartzsite
Yuma
Mexicali
Calexico
El Centro
Brawley
Imperial Valley
Salton Sea
Chocolate Mts.
Coachella Canal
Indio
Palm Springs
Palm Desert
Twentynine Palms
San Bernardino Mts.
Barstow
Victorville
Hesperia
Lancaster
Palmdale
Bakersfield
Tehachapi Mts.
Death Valley
Amargosa Range
Avawatz Mts.
Providence Mts.
Soda Lake
Bristol L.
Cadiz L.
Danby L.
Ridgecrest
San Bernardino
Riverside
Moreno Valley
Hemet
Temecula
Escondido
Oceanside
SAN DIEGO
Chula Vista
Tijuana
Tecate
Rosarito
El Descanso
LOS ANGELES
Santa Monica
Long Beach
Huntington Beach
Santa Ana
Anaheim
Irvine
Oxnard
Ventura
Santa Barbara
Santa Maria
Lompoc
San Pedro Channel
Santa Barbara Channel
Gulf of Santa Catalina
Santa Catalina I.
San Clemente I.
San Nicolas I.
Santa Cruz I.
Santa Rosa I.
San Miguel I.
Pt. Conception
Pt. Arguello
Is. los Coronados
West from Greenwich

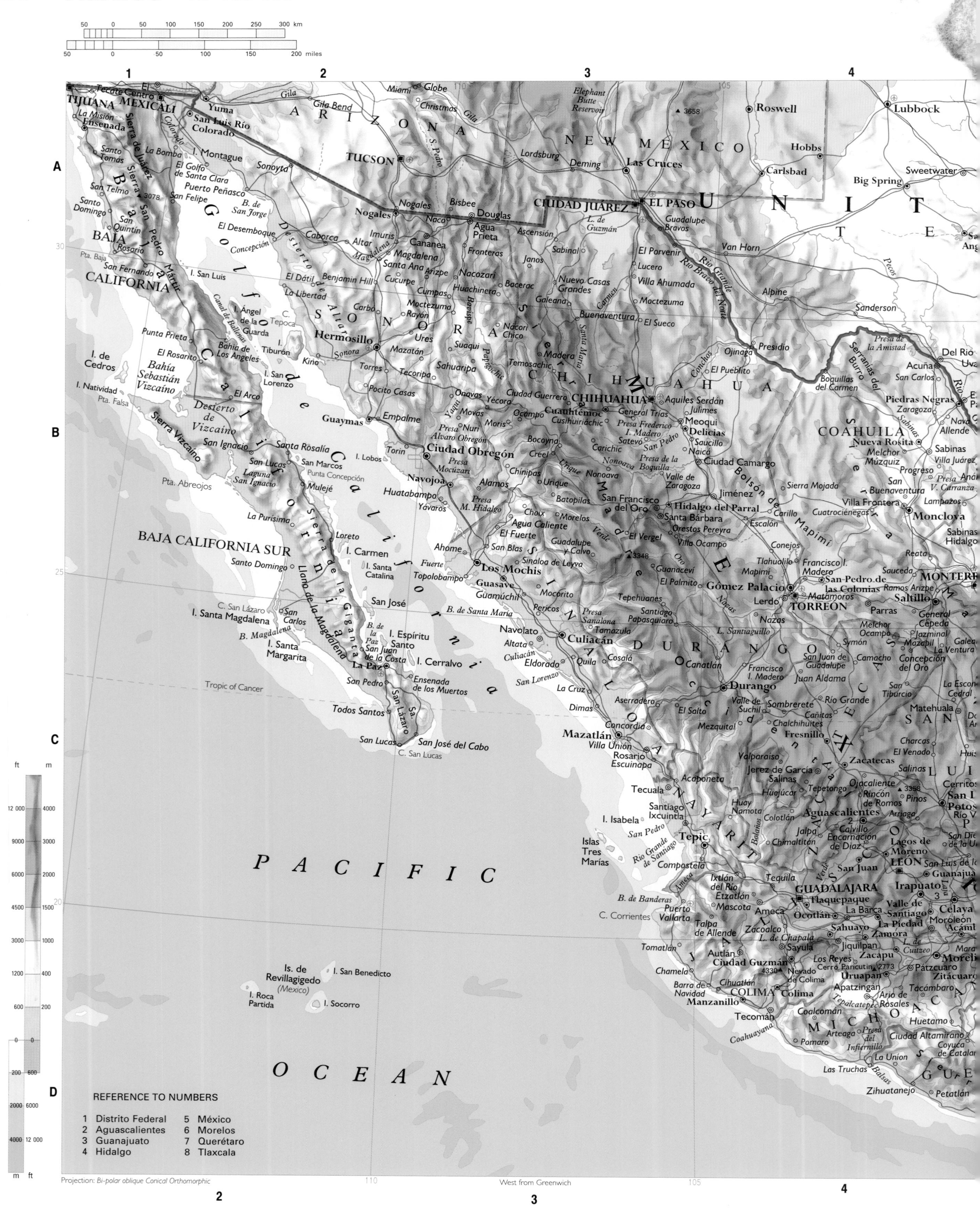

50 0 50 100 150 200 250 300 km
50 0 50 100 150 200 miles
1 2 3 4
A B C D
ft m
12 000 4000
9000 3000
6000 2000
4500 1500
3000 1000
1200 400
600 200
0 0
200 600
2000 6000
4000 12 000
m ft
REFERENCE TO NUMBERS
1 Distrito Federal
2 Aguascalientes
3 Guanajuato
4 Hidalgo
5 México
6 Morelos
7 Querétaro
8 Tlaxcala
Projection: Bi-polar oblique Conical Orthomorphic
West from Greenwich
110
105
PACIFIC OCEAN
Golfo de California
BAJA CALIFORNIA
BAJA CALIFORNIA SUR
SONORA
CHIHUAHUA
COAHUILA
DURANGO
SINALOA
NAYARIT
ZACATECAS
JALISCO
COLIMA
MICHOACÁN
ARIZONA
NEW MEXICO
Sierra Madre Occidental
Sierra de San Pedro Mártir
Sierra de la Giganta
Desierto de Altar
Desierto de Vizcaíno
Bolsón de Mapimí
Tropic of Cancer
TIJUANA
MEXICALI
Ensenada
Tecate
Yuma
San Luis Río Colorado
TUCSON
Nogales
Douglas
Agua Prieta
Lordsburg
Deming
Las Cruces
CIUDAD JUÁREZ
EL PASO
Roswell
Lubbock
Hobbs
Carlsbad
Big Spring
Sweetwater
Van Horn
Ojinaga
Presidio
Del Rio
Acuña
Piedras Negras
Nuevo Casas Grandes
Hermosillo
Guaymas
Ciudad Obregón
Navojoa
Los Mochis
Culiacán
Mazatlán
CHIHUAHUA
Cuauhtémoc
Delicias
Hidalgo del Parral
Ciudad Camargo
Jiménez
Monclova
Gómez Palacio
TORREÓN
Saltillo
Durango
Zacatecas
Fresnillo
Tepic
Puerto Vallarta
GUADALAJARA
Tlaquepaque
Aguascalientes
LEÓN
Irapuato
Celaya
Lagos de Moreno
Ciudad Guzmán
Manzanillo
COLIMA
Uruapan
Zamora
La Paz
San José del Cabo
Cabo San Lucas
Santa Rosalía
Mulegé
Loreto
I. de Cedros
Bahía Sebastián Vizcaíno
I. Tiburón
I. Ángel de la Guarda
I. Santa Magdalena
I. Santa Margarita
Islas Tres Marías
Is. de Revillagigedo (Mexico)
I. San Benedicto
I. Socorro
I. Roca Partida
Zihuatanejo
Petatlán

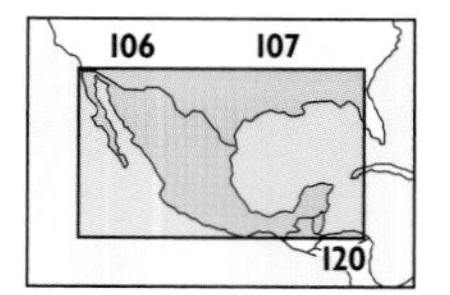

106
107
120

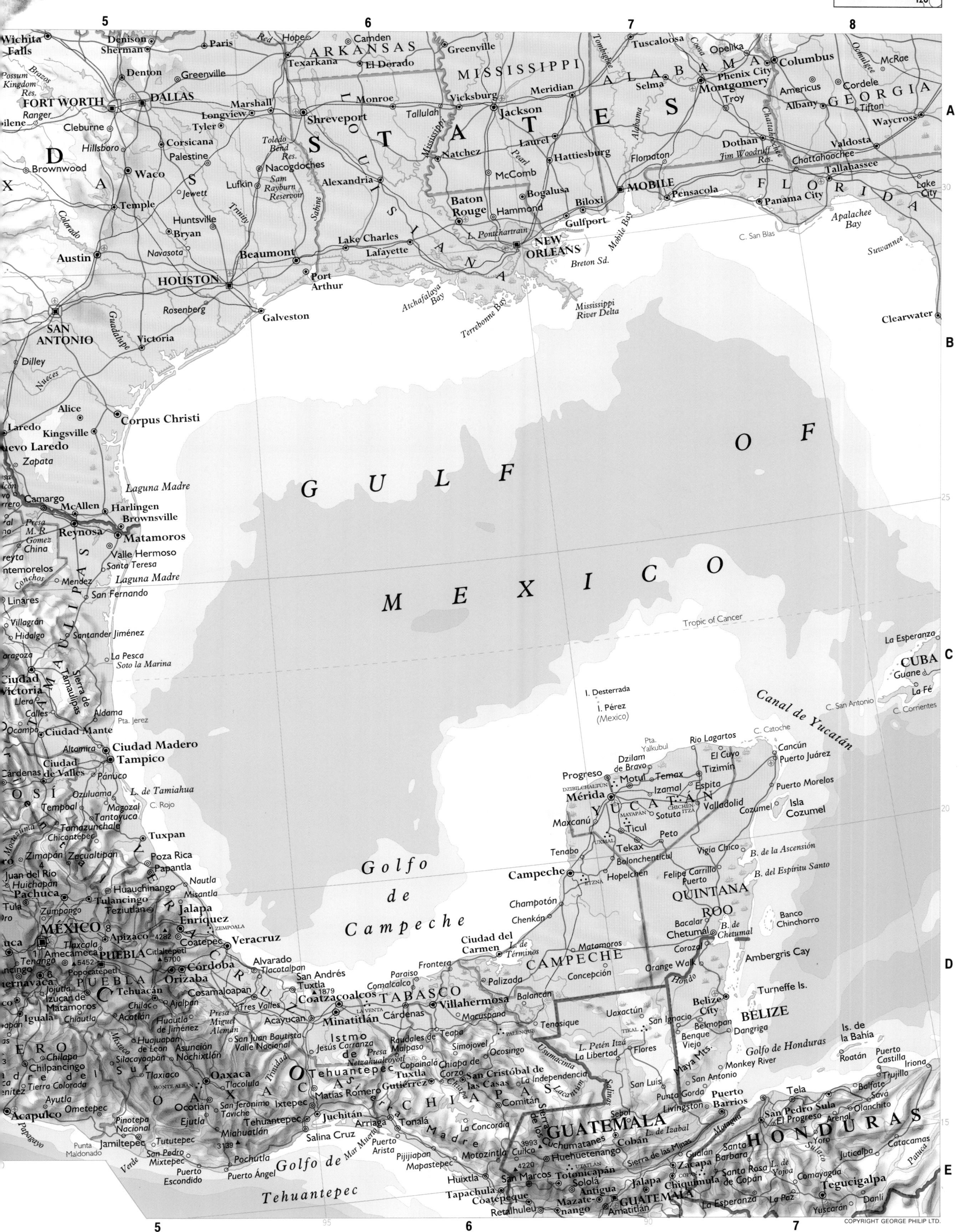

5
6
7
8
A
B
C
D
E
ARKANSAS
MISSISSIPPI
ALABAMA
GEORGIA
LOUISIANA
FLORIDA
STATES
Wichita Falls
Denison
Sherman
Paris
Hope
Camden
Texarkana
El Dorado
Greenville
Tuscaloosa
Opelika
Columbus
McRae
Denton
Greenville
Phenix City
Montgomery
Selma
Meridian
Americus
Cordele
FORT WORTH
DALLAS
Marshall
Monroe
Vicksburg
Jackson
Troy
Albany
Tifton
Ranger
Longview
Tyler
Shreveport
Tallulah
Waycross
Cleburne
Corsicana
Hillsboro
Palestine
Toledo Bend Res.
Natchez
Laurel
Hattiesburg
Dothan
Valdosta
Brownwood
Waco
Nacogdoches
Sam Rayburn Reservoir
Alexandria
McComb
Flomaton
Chattahoochee
Tallahassee
Lufkin
Jewett
Bogalusa
MOBILE
Pensacola
Panama City
Lake City
Temple
Baton Rouge
Hammond
Biloxi
Gulfport
Huntsville
Bryan
Apalachee Bay
Austin
Navasota
Beaumont
Lake Charles
Lafayette
L. Pontchartrain
NEW ORLEANS
Mobile Bay
C. San Blas
HOUSTON
Port Arthur
Breton Sd.
Suwannee
Rosenberg
Galveston
Atchafalaya Bay
Terrebonne Bay
Mississippi River Delta
Clearwater
SAN ANTONIO
Victoria
Dilley
Nueces
Alice
Corpus Christi
Laredo
Kingsville
Nuevo Laredo
Zapata
Laguna Madre
GULF OF MEXICO
Camargo
McAllen
Harlingen
Brownsville
Reynosa
Matamoros
Valle Hermoso
Santa Teresa
Laguna Madre
Mendez
San Fernando
Linares
Villagrán
Hidalgo
Santander Jiménez
La Pesca
Soto la Marina
Tropic of Cancer
La Esperanza
CUBA
Guane
La Fé
C. Corrientes
C. San Antonio
Canal de Yucatán
Ciudad Victoria
Sierra de Tamaulipas
Aldama
Pta. Jerez
I. Desterrada
I. Pérez (Mexico)
Ocampo
Ciudad Mante
C. Catoche
Pta. Yalkubul
Rio Lagartos
El Cuyo
Cancún
Puerto Juárez
Ciudad Madero
Tampico
Altamira
Ciudad de Valles
Pánuco
Progreso
Dzilam de Bravo
Motul
Temax
Tizimín
Izamal
Espita
Puerto Morelos
L. de Tamiahua
C. Rojo
Mérida
YUCATÁN
Valladolid
Isla Cozumel
Cozumel
Tempoal
Tantoyuca
Tamazunchale
Maxcanú
Sotuta
Ticul
Peto
Tuxpan
Poza Rica
Papantla
Tenabo
Tekax
Vigía Chico
B. de la Ascensión
Golfo de Campeche
Campeche
Hopelchén
Felipe Carrillo Puerto
B. del Espíritu Santo
Pachuca
Tulancingo
Huauchinango
Nautla
Misantla
QUINTANA ROO
Champotón
Chenkán
Banco Chinchorro
Jalapa Enríquez
Teziutlán
MÉXICO
Apizaco
Veracruz
Bacalar
Chetumal
B. de Chetumal
Ciudad del Carmen
L. de Términos
Matamoros
Corozal
PUEBLA
Coatepec
Alvarado
Tlacotalpan
CAMPECHE
Ambergris Cay
Córdoba
Orizaba
San Andrés Tuxtla
Paraíso
Frontera
Concepción
Orange Walk
Tehuacán
Cosamaloapan
Coatzacoalcos
Comalcalco
TABASCO
Palizada
Hondo
Turneffe Is.
Villahermosa
Balancán
Belize City
Belmopan
BELIZE
Tres Valles
Acayucan
Minatitlán
Cárdenas
Macuspana
Tenosique
Uaxactún
San Ignacio
Iguala
Acatlán
Huajuapan de León
Oaxaca
Istmo de Tehuantepec
Teapa
Simojovel
Ocosingo
L. Petén Itzá
La Libertad
Flores
Benque Viejo
Dangriga
Is. de la Bahía
Golfo de Honduras
Roatán
Puerto Castilla
Chilapa
Chilpancingo
Tlaxiaco
Tuxtla Gutiérrez
San Cristóbal de las Casas
La Independencia
Maya Mts.
Monkey River
Trujillo
Iriona
Acapulco
Ometepec
OAXACA
Matías Romero
CHIAPAS
Comitán
San Luis
San Antonio
Punta Gorda
Puerto Barrios
Tela
Ixtepec
Juchitán
Tehuantepec
Arriaga
Tonalá
La Concordia
Livingston
San Pedro Sula
El Progreso
HONDURAS
Pinotepa Nacional
Salina Cruz
GUATEMALA
Cobán
L. de Izabal
Huehuetenango
Jamiltepec
Pochutla
Puerto Ángel
Golfo de Tehuantepec
Puerto Arista
Pijijiapan
Mapastepec
Motozintla
Zacapa
Santa Bárbara
Yoro
Catacamas
Puerto Escondido
Huixtla
Tapachula
San Marcos
Totonicapán
Sololá
Antigua
Jalapa
Chiquimula
Santa Rosa de Copán
Comayagua
Tegucigalpa
Coatepeque
Retalhuleu
Mazatenango
GUATEMALA
Amatitlán
La Esperanza
La Paz
Yuscarán
Danlí
5
6
7

1:7 100 000

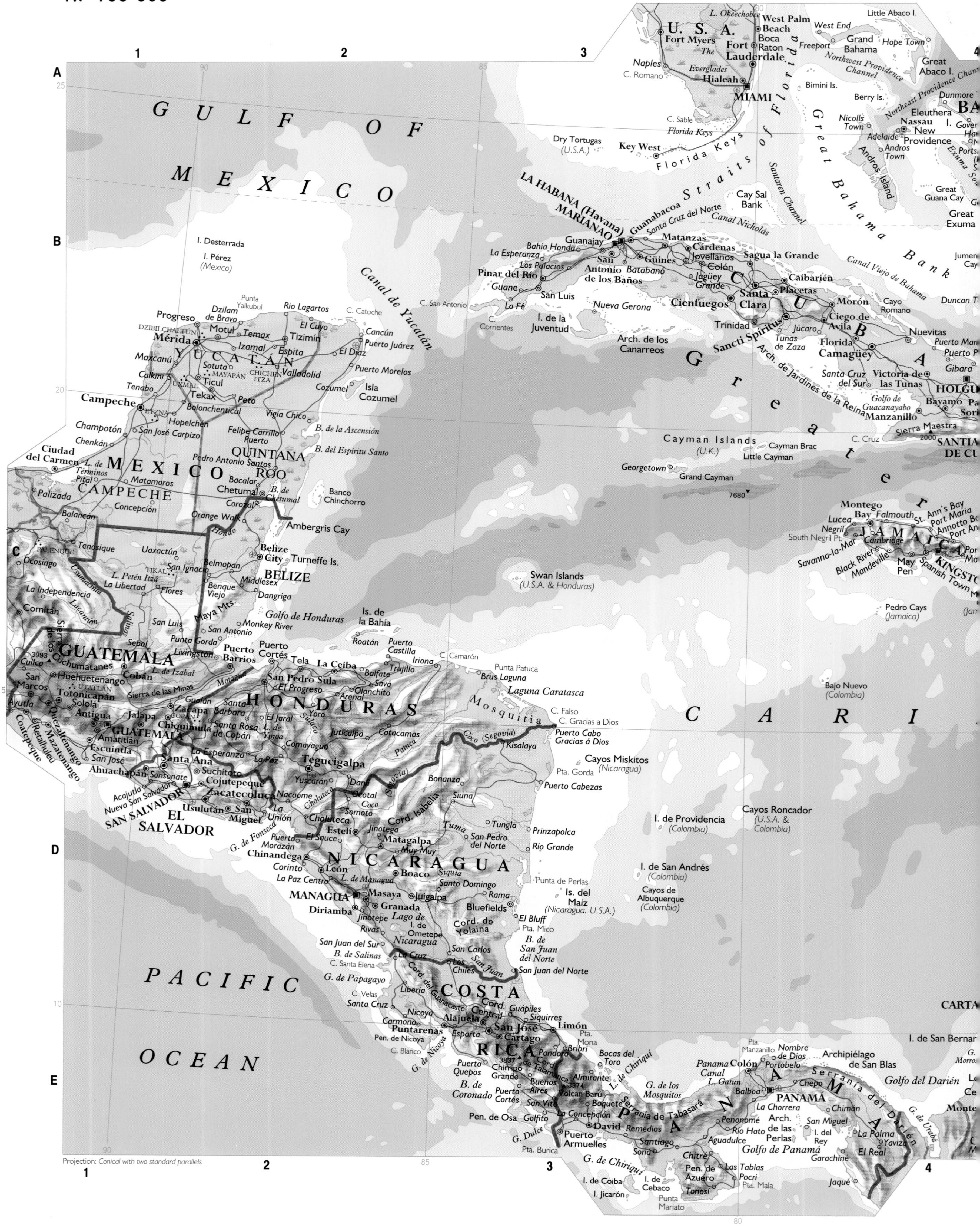

GULF OF MEXICO

PACIFIC OCEAN

U.S.A.
Fort Myers · Naples · C. Romano · Everglades · Hialeah · MIAMI · C. Sable · Florida Keys · Key West · Dry Tortugas (U.S.A.)
West Palm Beach · Fort Lauderdale · Boca Raton · Bimini Is. · West End · Freeport · Grand Bahama · Hope Town · Little Abaco I. · Great Abaco I.
Northwest Providence Channel · Nicolls Town · Nassau · Adelaide · New Providence · Andros Town · Andros Island
BAHAMA · Eleuthera I. · Governor's · Dunmore · Great Guana Cay · Great Exuma · Exuma · Jumen · Berry Is.
Northeast Providence Channel

Straits of Florida · Santaren Channel · Cay Sal Bank · Canal Nicholas · Canal Viejo de Bahama

LA HABANA (Havana) · MARIANAO · Guanabacoa · Santa Cruz del Norte · Bahía Honda · Guanajay · Matanzas · Cárdenas · Jovellanos · Sagua la Grande · Caibarién
La Esperanza · San Antonio de los Baños · Güines · Colón · Santa Clara · Placetas · Morón · Cayo Romano · Duncan I.
Los Palacios · Batabanó · Jagüey Grande · Cienfuegos · Trinidad · Sancti Spíritus · Júcaro · Ciego de Ávila · Nuevitas
Pinar del Río · San Luis · Nueva Gerona · Corrientes · I. de la Juventud · Arch. de los Canarreos · Tunas de Zaza · Florida · Camagüey · Puerto P
Guane · La Fé · C. San Antonio · Santa Cruz del Sur · Arch. de Jardines de la Reina · Victoria de las Tunas · Gibara · HOLG
CUBA · Golfo de Guacanayabo · Bayamo · Manzanillo · Sierra Maestra · 2000 · SANTIA DE CU · C. Cruz

Cayman Islands (U.K.) · Georgetown · Grand Cayman · Cayman Brac · Little Cayman · 7680

JAMAICA · Montego Bay · Lucea · Negril · Falmouth · St. Ann's Bay · Port Maria · Annotto Ba · Port An
South Negril Pt. · Savanna-la-Mar · Cambridge · Black River · Mandeville · May Pen · KINGSTON · Spanish Town · Por Mo
Pedro Cays (Jamaica) · Jan

Canal de Yucatán

MEXICO
I. Desterrada · I. Pérez (Mexico) · Punta Yalkubul · Dzilam de Bravo · Río Lagartos · C. Catoche · C. San Antonio
Progreso · Motul · Temax · El Cuyo · Tizimín · Cancún
DZIBILCHALTUN · Mérida · Izamal · Espita · Valladolid · Puerto Juárez
Maxcanú · Sotuta · MAYAPÁN · CHICHEN ITZA · Cozumel · Isla Cozumel
YUCATÁN · Calkiní · Ticul · Peto · Vigía Chico
Campeche · Tenabo · UXMAL · Tekax · Bolonchenticul · Felipe Carrillo Puerto · B. de la Ascensión
Champotón · Chenkán · Hopelchén · B. del Espíritu Santo
Ciudad del Carmen · I. de Términos · CAMPECHE · Pedro Antonio Santos · QUINTANA ROO · Banco Chinchorro
Palizada · Matamoros · Bacalar · Chetumal · B. de Chetumal
Balancán · Concepción · Orange Walk · Corozal
PALENQUE · Tenosique · Uaxactún · Ambergris Cay
Ocosingo · L. Petén Itzá · TIKAL · San Ignacio · Belmopan · Belize City · Turneffe Is.
La Independencia · La Libertad · Flores · Benque Viejo · BELIZE · Middlesex · Dangriga
Comitán · Lacanjá · Sayaxché · Maya Mts. · Monkey River
GUATEMALA · Sebol · Punta Gorda · San Antonio · Golfo de Honduras · Is. de la Bahía
Cuilco · Cuchumatanes · Cobán · L. de Izabal · Livingston · Puerto Barrios · Puerto Cortés · Roatán · Puerto Castilla
3993 · Huehuetenango · Sierra de las Minas · Tela · La Ceiba · Trujillo · Iriona · C. Camarón
San Marcos · UTATLÁN · Totonicapán · Sololá · Salamá · Santa Bárbara · San Pedro Sula · Balfate · Punta Patuca
Ayutla · Quetzaltenango · Antigua · GUATEMALA · Chiquimula · Santa Rosa de Copán · El Progreso · Olanchito · Brus Laguna
Retalhuleu · Amatitlán · Zacapa · L. de Yojoa · Yoro · Laguna Caratasca
Mazatenango · Escuintla · San José · **HONDURAS** · Comayagua · Juticalpa · Catacamas · Mosquitia
Coatepeque · Ahuachapán · Santa Ana · Suchitoto · La Esperanza · La Paz · Tegucigalpa · Panca · C. Falso · C. Gracias a Dios
Acajutla · Sonsonate · Cojutepeque · Yuscarán · Dani · Coco (Segovia) · Puerto Cabo Gracias á Dios
Nueva San Salvador · SAN SALVADOR · Zacatecoluca · Nacaóme · Ocotal · Kisalaya
EL SALVADOR · Usulután · San Miguel · La Unión · Choluteca · Somoto · Cord. Isabela · Cayos Miskitos (Nicaragua)
G. de Fonseca · Puerto Morazán · El Sauce · Estelí · Jinotega · Segovia · Bonanza · Pta. Gorda
Chinandega · Chichigalpa · León · Matagalpa · Muy Muy · Tuma · Siuna · Puerto Cabezas
Corinto · La Paz Centro · Boaco · San Pedro del Norte · Tungla · Prinzapolca · Bajo Nuevo (Colombia)
NICARAGUA · L. de Managua · Río Grande · I. de Providencia (Colombia)
MANAGUA · Masaya · Juigalpa · Siquia · Santo Domingo · Rama · Bluefields · I. de San Andrés (Colombia)
Diriamba · Granada · Jinotepe · Lago de Nicaragua · Cord. de Yolaina · El Bluff · Cayos de Albuquerque (Colombia)
San Juan del Sur · Rivas · I. de Ometepe · B. de San Juan del Norte · Is. del Maíz (Nicaragua, U.S.A.) · Cayos Roncador (U.S.A. & Colombia)
B. de Salinas · La Cruz · Los Chiles · San Carlos · San Juan · San Juan del Norte · Punta de Perlas
Sta. Elena · Liberia · G. de Papagayo · Cord. Central · Guápiles · Pta. Mico
C. Velas · Santa Cruz · Nicoya · Cord. de Talamanca · Siquirres · Limón
G. de Nicoya · Carmona · Puntarenas · Alajuela · San José · Cartago · Pta. Mona
C. Blanco · Pen. de Nicoya · Esparta · **COSTA RICA** · Bribri · Bocas del Toro · Nombre de Dios · Archipiélago de San Blas
Puerto Quepos · Chirripó Grande · 3837 · Pandora · Almirante · L. de Chiriquí · Panamá Canal · Colón · Portobelo · Serranía de San Blas
B. de Coronado · Buenos Aires · 3374 · Volcán Barú · Boquete · Penonomé · Serranía del Darién
Puerto Cortés · San Vito · La Concepción · David · Remedios · Aguadulce · San Miguel · I. del Rey · Golfo del Darién
Pen. de Osa · Golfito · G. Dulce · Puerto Armuelles · **PANAMA** · PANAMÁ · La Chorrera · Chepo · Chimán · La Palma · Yaviza
Pta. Burica · G. de Chiriquí · I. de Coiba · I. de Cebaco · Santiago · Soná · Chitré · Las Tablas · Golfo de Panamá · El Real
Pta. Mala · I. Jicarón · Punta Mariato · Pen. de Azuero · Pocrí · Tonosí · Jaqué

CARTA · I. de San Bernar · I. de San Bernardo · Morro · Garachine

CARIBBEAN

Swan Islands (U.S.A. & Honduras)

Projection: Conical with two standard parallels

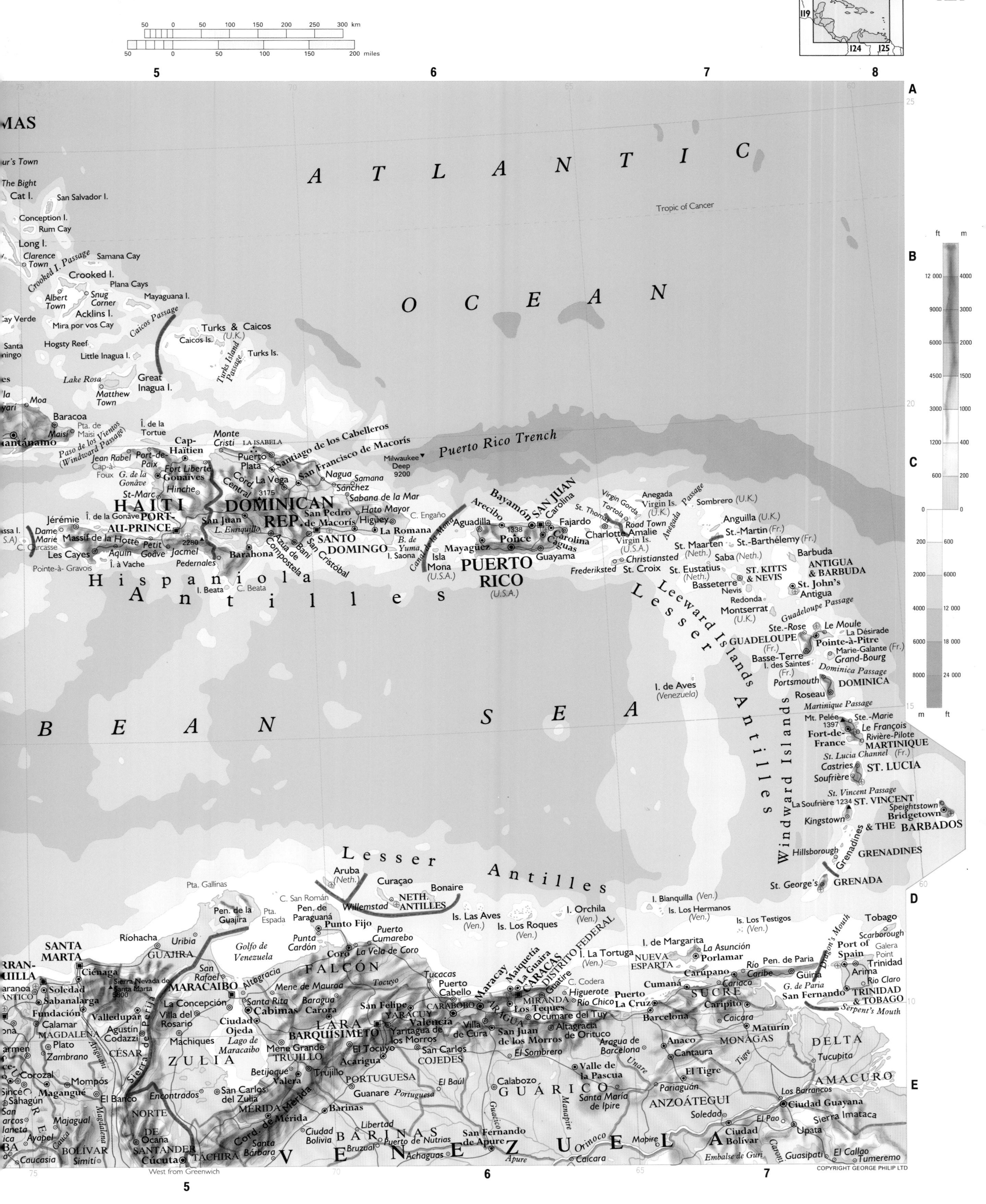

A

A T L A N T I C

Tropic of Cancer

O C E A N

MAS

ur's Town

The Bight
Cat I.

Conception I.
Rum Cay

Long I.
Clarence Town
Samana Cay

Crooked I. Passage

Albert Town
Snug Corner
Crooked I.
Plana Cays

Cay Verde
Mira por vos Cay
Acklins I.

Santa
ming
Hogsty Reef
Little Inagua I.
Turks & Caicos
Caicos Is.
Caicos Passage
(U.K.)

Lake Rosa
Great Inagua I.
Turks Island Passage
Turks Is.

la
yari
Moa
Matthew Town

ntanamo
Baracoa
Pta. de Maisi
Î. de la Tortue
Monte Cristi
LA ISABELA
Santiago de los Cabelleros
San Francisco de Macorís
Milwaukee Deep 9200

Paso de los Vientos
(Windward Passage)
Jean Rabel
Port-de-Paix
Cap-Haïtien
Puerto Plata
La Vega
Nagua
Samana
Sánchez

Cap-à-Foux
Fort Liberté
Cord. Central
Hinche
Sabana de la Mar
Hato Mayor
C. Engaño

Puerto Rico Trench

B

C

Jérémie
Î. de la Gonâve
Gonaives
St-Marc
3175
HAITI
DOMINICAN REP.
San Pedro de Macorís
Higüey
Bayamón
SAN JUAN
Carolina
Virgin Gorda
Tortola
Anegada
Virgin Is. (U.K.)
Sombrero (U.K.)

Dame Marie
G. de la Gonâve
PORT-AU-PRINCE
San Juan
L. Enriquillo
SANTO DOMINGO
La Romana
Aguadilla
Arecibo
1338
St. Thomas
Road Town
Anguilla (U.K.)
St.-Martin (Fr.)

Les Cayes
Aquin
Goâve
Jacmel
2280
Barahona
Agua Dulce
San Cristóbal
B. de Yuma
Mayagüez
Ponce
Caguas
Charlotte Amalie
Virgin Is. (U.S.A.)
St. Maarten (Neth.)
St.-Barthélemy (Fr.)

Pointe-à-Gravois
Aquin
Î. à Vache
Pedernales
Compostela
I. Saona
Isla Mona (U.S.A.)
PUERTO RICO (U.S.A.)
Guayama
Christiansted
Frederiksted
St. Croix
St. Eustatius (Neth.)
Saba (Neth.)
ST. KITTS & NEVIS
Basseterre
Nevis
Redonda
Barbuda
ANTIGUA & BARBUDA
St. John's
Antigua

I. Beata
C. Beata
Hispaniola
Antilles
Montserrat (U.K.)
Guadeloupe Passage
Ste.-Rose
Le Moule
La Désirade

Antilles
Lesser
GUADELOUPE (Fr.)
Pointe-à-Pitre
Marie-Galante (Fr.)
Grand-Bourg

ssa I.
(.S.A.)
C. Carcasse
Leeward Islands
Basse-Terre
I. des Saintes (Fr.)
Dominica Passage
Portsmouth
Roseau
DOMINICA

I. de Aves (Venezuela)
Martinique Passage
Mt. Pelée 1397
Ste.-Marie

BEAN
SEA
Windward Islands
Fort-de-France
MARTINIQUE
Le François
Rivière-Pilote

B E A N
St. Lucia Channel (Fr.)
Castries
Soufrière
ST. LUCIA

St. Vincent Passage
La Soufrière 1234
ST. VINCENT
Speightstown
Bridgetown
Kingstown
BARBADOS

Lesser
Antilles
Hillsborough
GRENADINES
Grenadines

Aruba (Neth.)
Curaçao
Bonaire
St. George's
GRENADA

Pta. Gallinas
C. San Román
Pen. de Paraguaná
Willemstad
NETH. ANTILLES
Is. Las Aves (Ven.)
I. Blanquilla (Ven.)
I. Los Hermanos (Ven.)
Is. Los Testigos (Ven.)
Tobago
Scarborough

D

SANTA MARTA
Ríohacha
Uribia
GUAJIRA
Pen. de la Guajira
Pta. Espada
Punta Cardón
Punto Fijo
Coro
La Vela de Coro
Puerto Cumarebo
Is. Los Roques (Ven.)
I. Orchila (Ven.)
I. de Margarita
La Asunción
NUEVA ESPARTA
Porlamar
Pen. de Paria
Río Caribe
Güiria
Galera Point
Arima
Port of Spain
Rio Claro

RRAN-
UILLA
ANTICO
C;énaga
San Rafael
Altagracia
Golfo de Venezuela
FALCÓN
Tucacas
Puerto Cabello
Maracay
Maiquetía
LA GUAIRA
CARACAS
DISTRITO FEDERAL
C. Codera
Higuerote
I. La Tortuga (Ven.)
Cumaná
Cariaco
Carúpano
SUCRE
Caripito
TRINIDAD & TOBAGO
San Fernando
Serpent's Mouth

aranoa
arcos
Soledad
Sabanalarga
Fundación
Calamar
Plato
Zambrano
MAGDALENA
Valledupar
Agustín Codazzi
La Concepción
Santa Rita
Villa del Rosario
Ciudad Ojeda
MARACAIBO
Cabimas
Carora
Mene de Mauroa
San Felipe
Baragua
YARACUY
CARABOBO
Valencia
Villa de Cura
MIRANDA
Los Teques
Ocumare del Tuy
Río Chico
Puerto La Cruz
Barcelona
Caicara
Anaco
Cantaura
MONAGAS
Maturín
DELTA
Tucupita
G. de Paria

marca
caneta
Plato
CÉSAR
Machiques
Lago de Maracaibo
Mene Grande
TRUJILLO
El Tocuyo
LARA
BARQUISIMETO
Acarigua
San Carlos
COJEDES
San Juan de los Morros
Yaritagua
Valle de la Pascua
El Tigre
AMACURO
Los Barrancos

San
arcos
ca
Ayapel
Majagual
Mompós
Magangué
El Banco
BOLÍVAR
Simiti
NORTE
DE
OCAÑA
Encontrados
ZULIA
Betijoque
Valera
MÉRIDA
Barinas
Santa Bárbara
Ciudad Bolivia
B A R I N A S
San Fernando de Apure
Libertad
Puerto de Nutrias
Santa María de Ipire
GUÁRICO
Pariaguán
ANZOÁTEGUI
Soledad
El Pao
Sierra Imataca
Ciudad Guayana
Ciudad Bolívar
Upata

Caucasia
Simiti
SANTANDER
Cúcuta
TACHIRA
Trujillo
Guanare
PORTUGUESA
El Baúl
Calabozo
Guárico
Manapire
Apure
Caicara
Embalse de Guri
Guasipati
El Callao
Tumeremo

V E N E Z U E L A
Bruzual
Achaguas
Orinoco

West from Greenwich

COPYRIGHT GEORGE PHILIP LTD

ft m

12 000 — 4000

9000 — 3000

6000 — 2000

4500 — 1500

3000 — 1000

1200 — 400

600 — 200

0 — 0

200 — 600

2000 — 6000

4000 — 12 000

6000 — 18 000

8000 — 24 000

m — ft

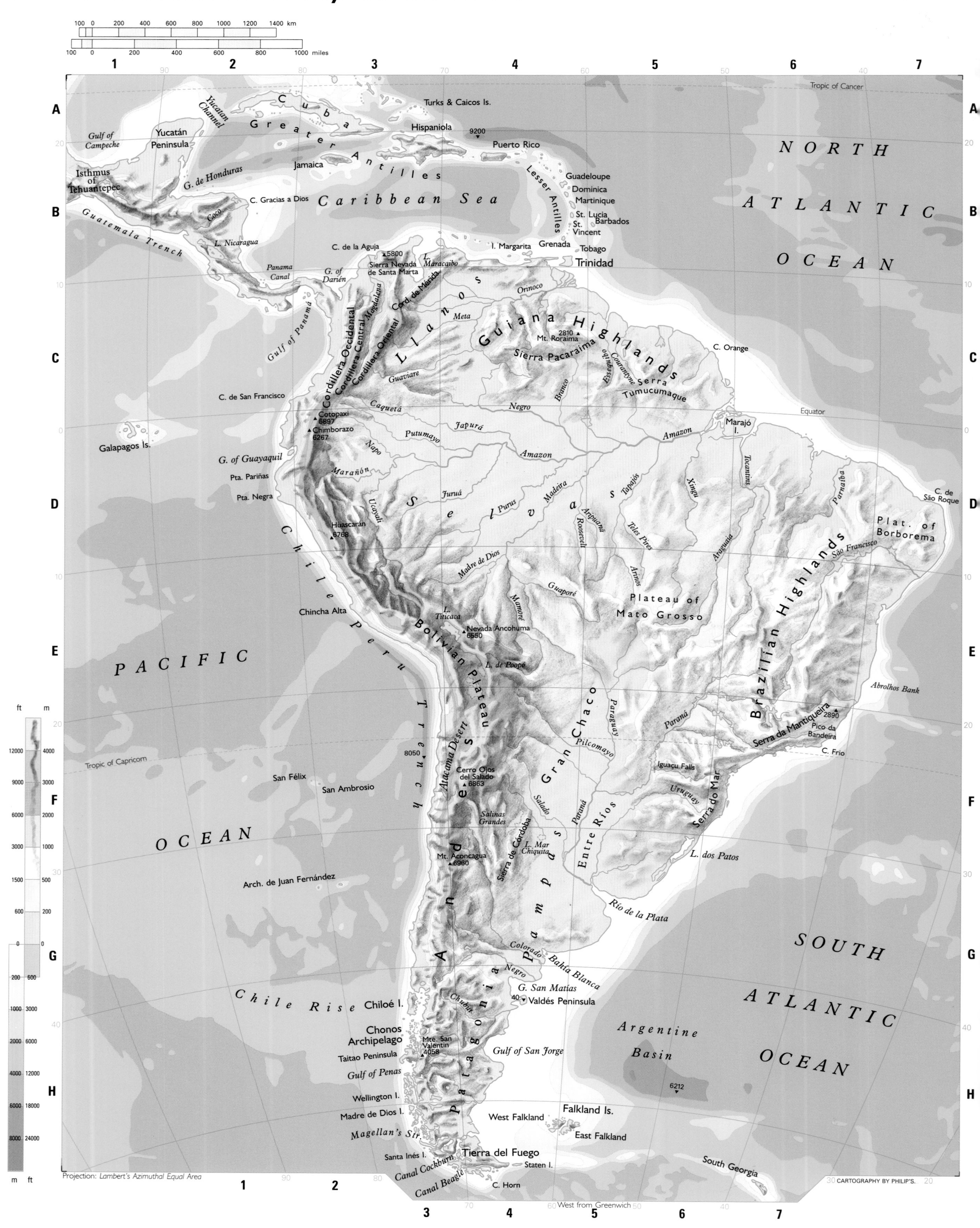

100 0 200 400 600 800 1000 1200 1400 km
100 0 200 400 600 800 1000 miles

Projection: Lambert's Azimuthal Equal Area

ft   m
12000   4000
9000   3000
6000   2000
3000   1000
1500   500
600   200
0   0
200   600
1000   3000
2000   6000
4000   12000
6000   18000
8000   24000
m   ft

North Atlantic Ocean
Tropic of Cancer
Gulf of Campeche
Yucatán Peninsula
Yucatán Channel
Cuba
Greater Antilles
Turks & Caicos Is.
Hispaniola
9200
Puerto Rico
Jamaica
G. de Honduras
C. Gracias a Dios
Caribbean Sea
Lesser Antilles
Guadeloupe
Dominica
Martinique
St. Lucia
St. Vincent
Barbados
Grenada
Tobago
Trinidad
I. Margarita
Isthmus of Tehuantepec
Guatemala Trench
Coco
L. Nicaragua
Panama Canal
C. de la Aguja
5800
Sierra Nevada de Santa Marta
L. Maracaibo
G. of Darién
Cord. de Mérida
Orinoco
Llanos
Meta
Guiana Highlands
Mt. Roraima 2810
C. Orange
Sierra Pacaraima
Serra Tumucumaque
Cordillera Occidental
Cordillera Central
Cordillera Oriental
Magdalena
C. de San Francisco
Guaviare
Caquetá
Branco
Negro
Uaupés
Equator
Cotopaxi 5897
Chimborazo 6267
Putumayo
Japurá
Amazon
Amazon
Marajó I.
Galapagos Is.
G. of Guayaquil
Pta. Pariñas
Pta. Negra
Napo
Marañón
Juruá
Purus
Madeira
Tapajós
Xingu
Tocantins
Parnaíba
C. de São Roque
Selvas
Ucayali
Huascarán 6768
Madre de Dios
Roosevelt
Aripuanã
Teles Pires
Araguaia
Arinos
São Francisco
Plat. of Borborema
Chincha Alta
L. Titicaca
Nevada Ancohuma 6550
Guaporé
Mamoré
Plateau of Mato Grosso
Brazilian Highlands
Bolivian Plateau
L. de Poopó
Atacama Desert
Gran Chaco
Paraguay
Paraná
2890 Pico da Bandeira
Serra da Mantiqueira
Abrolhos Bank
Tropic of Capricorn
San Félix
San Ambrosio
8050
Cerro Ojos del Salado 6863
Pilcomayo
Entre Rios
Paraná
Iguaçu Falls
Uruguay
Serra do Mar
C. Frio
Salinas Grandes
Salado
Arch. de Juan Fernández
Mt. Aconcagua 6960
Sierra de Córdoba
L. Mar Chiquita
Rio de la Plata
L. dos Patos
Andes
Pampas
Colorado
Bahía Blanca
Negro
G. San Matías
Valdés Peninsula 40
South Atlantic Ocean
Chile Rise
Chiloé I.
Chonos Archipelago
Taitao Peninsula
Gulf of Penas
Mte. San Valentín 4058
Gulf of San Jorge
Argentine Basin
6212
Wellington I.
Madre de Dios I.
West Falkland
East Falkland
Falkland Is.
Patagonia
Magellan's Str.
Santa Inés I.
Canal Cockburn
Canal Beagle
Tierra del Fuego
Staten I.
C. Horn
South Georgia
Pacific Ocean
Chile Peru Trench

CARTOGRAPHY BY PHILIP'S

West from Greenwich

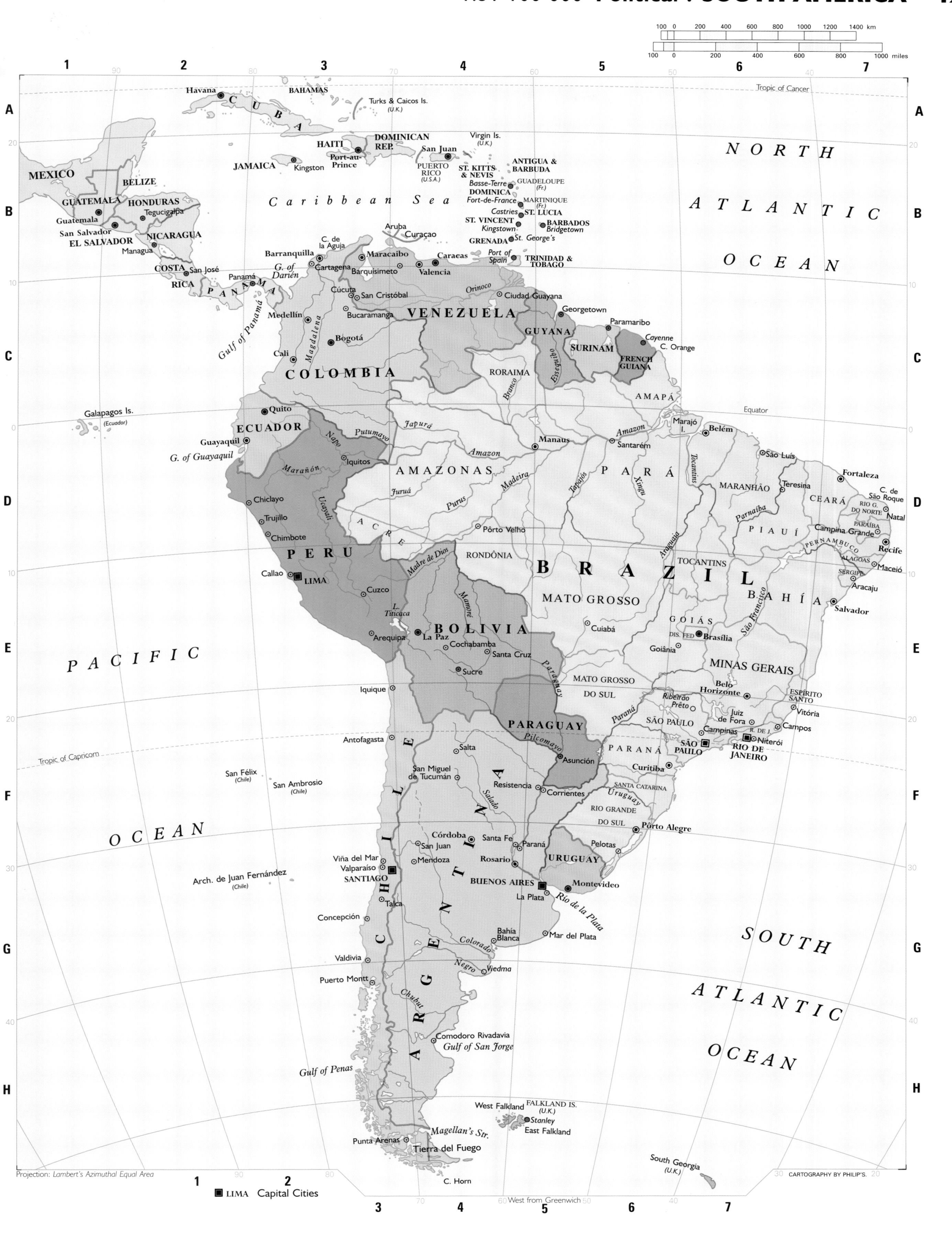

100 0 200 400 600 800 1000 1200 1400 km
100 0 200 400 600 800 1000 miles

CARTOGRAPHY BY PHILIP'S.

■ LIMA Capital Cities

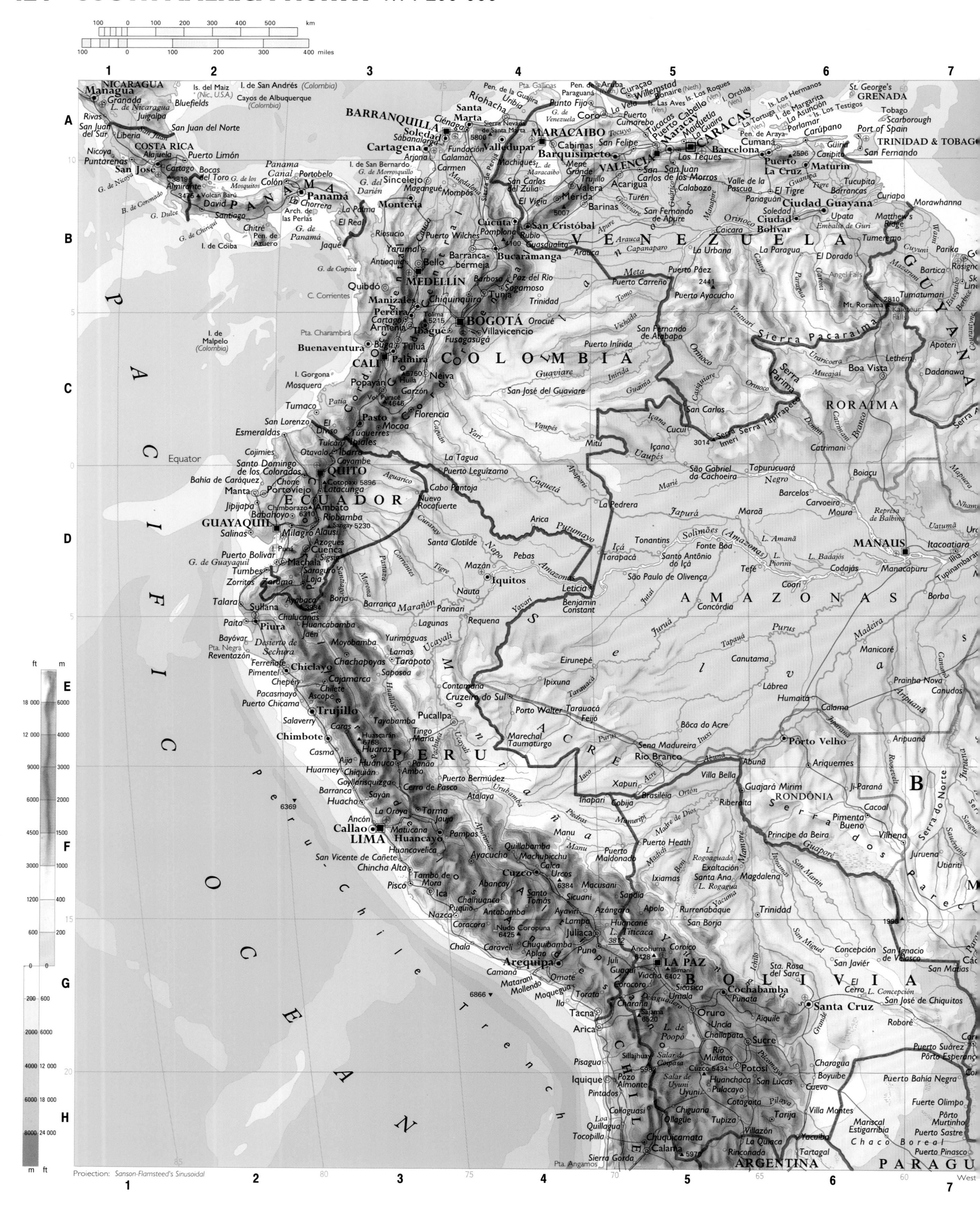

100 0 100 200 300 400 500 km
100 0 100 200 300 400 miles
NICARAGUA
Managua
COSTA RICA
San José
PANAMA
Panamá
BARRANQUILLA
Cartagena
MARACAIBO
Barquisimeto
VALENCIA
CARACAS
Barcelona
Ciudad Guayana
TRINIDAD & TOBAGO
GRENADA
V E N E Z U E L A
GUYANA
Medellín
BOGOTÁ
C O L O M B I A
CALI
Sierra Pacaraima
RORAIMA
Equator
QUITO
ECUADOR
GUAYAQUIL
Iquitos
Manaus
A M A Z O N A S
P E R U
Trujillo
Chimbote
LIMA
Callao
Cuzco
Arequipa
L. Titicaca
LA PAZ
B O L I V I A
Cochabamba
Santa Cruz
Sucre
Potosí
Oruro
CHILE
Arica
Iquique
Antofagasta
ARGENTINA
PARAGUAY
ACRE
RONDÔNIA
Porto Velho
Rio Branco
Peru-Chile Trench
P A C I F I C O C E A N
Projection: Sanson-Flamsteed's Sinusoidal

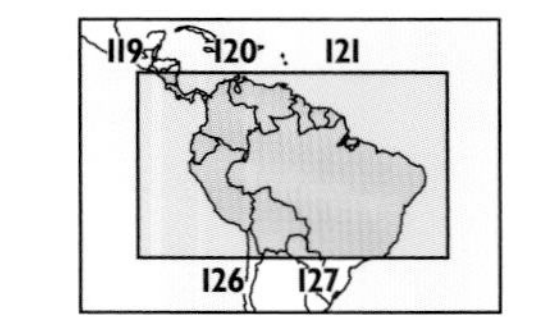

A T L A N T I C

O C E A N

Equator

Fernando de Noronha
(Braz.)

São Paulo
(Braz.)

Trindade
(Braz.)

FRENCH GUIANA

AMAPÁ

P A R Á

MARANHÃO

CEARÁ

RIO GRANDE DO NORTE

PIAUÍ

PARAÍBA

PERNAMBUCO

ALAGOAS

SERGIPE

B A H I A

TOCANTINS

GOIÁS

MINAS GERAIS

BELÉM

São Luis

FORTALEZA

Teresina

Natal

RECIFE

Olinda

Maceió

Aracaju

SALVADOR

BRASÍLIA

Goiânia

BELO HORIZONTE

Vitória

RIO DE JANEIRO

COPYRIGHT GEORGE PHILIP LTD.

6059 ▾

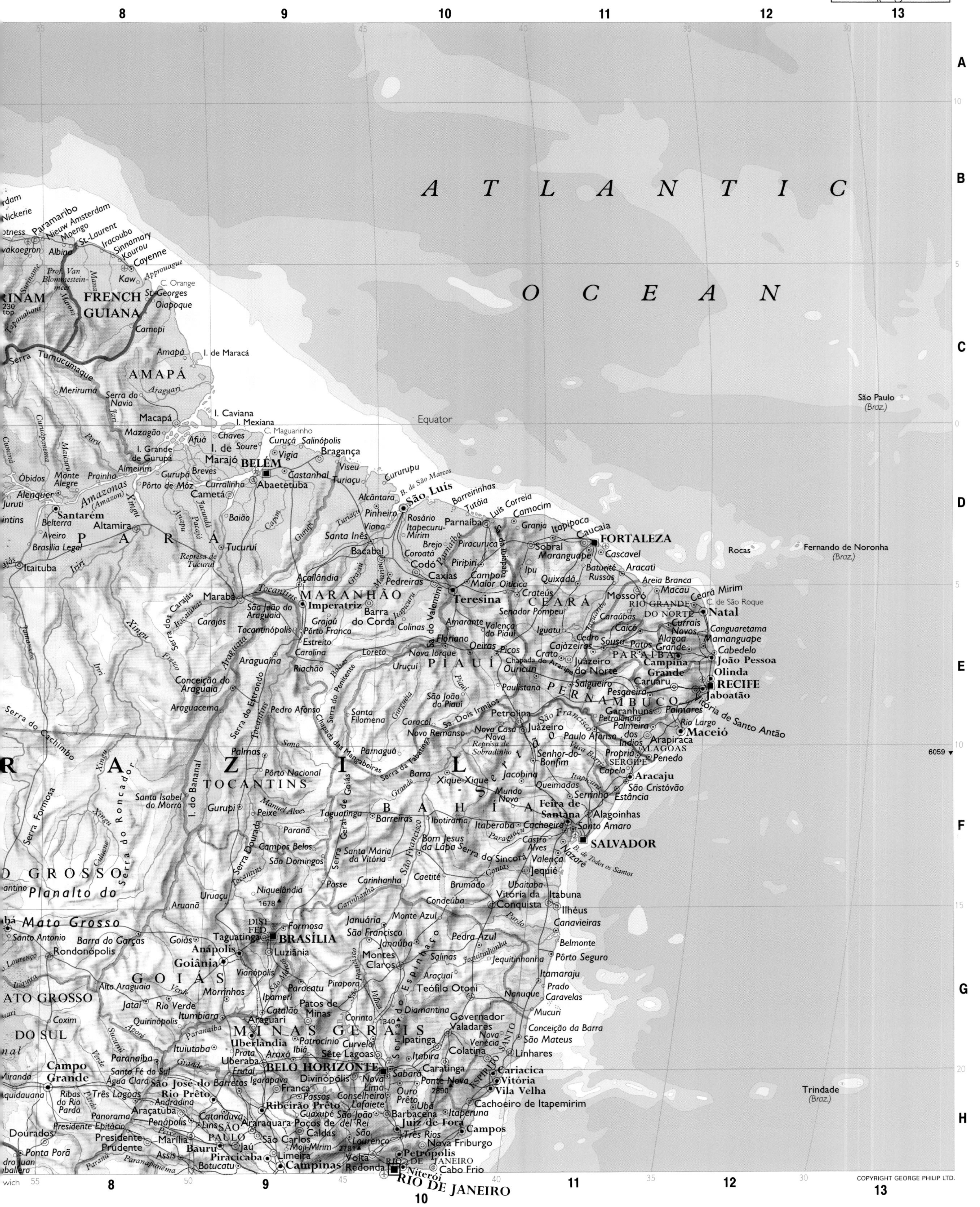

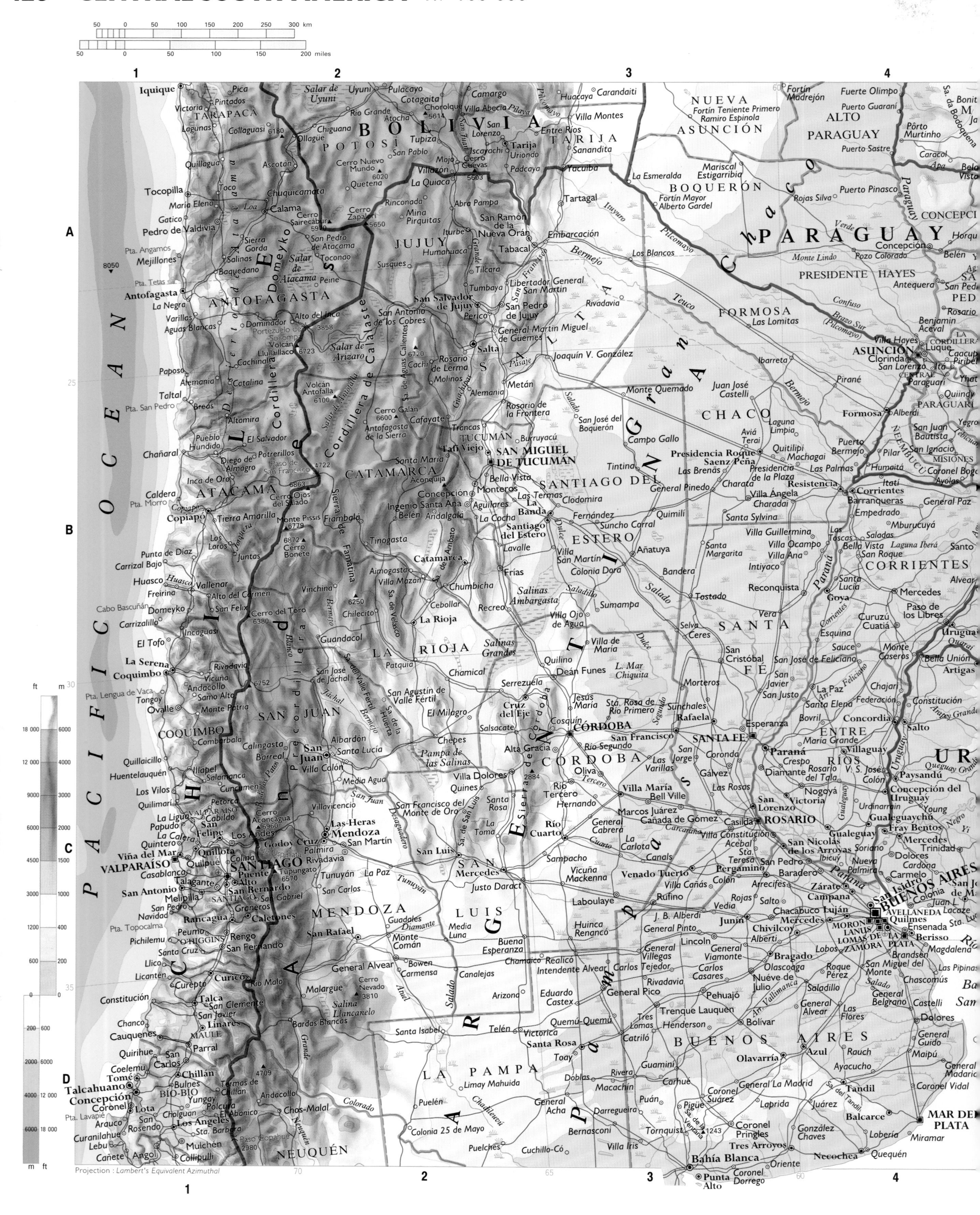

50 0 50 100 150 200 250 300 km
50 0 50 100 150 200 miles
PACIFIC OCEAN
BOLIVIA
PARAGUAY
ARGENTINA
CHILE
Gran Chaco
ALTO PARAGUAY
PRESIDENTE HAYES
BOQUERÓN
NUEVA ASUNCIÓN
TARAPACÁ
ANTOFAGASTA
ATACAMA
COQUIMBO
VALPARAÍSO
SANTIAGO
O'HIGGINS
MAULE
BIO-BIO
POTOSÍ
TARIJA
JUJUY
SALTA
TUCUMÁN
CATAMARCA
SANTIAGO DEL ESTERO
LA RIOJA
SAN JUAN
MENDOZA
SAN LUIS
CÓRDOBA
SANTA FÉ
CHACO
FORMOSA
CORRIENTES
ENTRE RÍOS
BUENOS AIRES
LA PAMPA
NEUQUÉN
MISIONES
Cordillera Domeyko
Desierto de Atacama
Cordillera de Calalaste
Sierra de Famatina
Sierras de Córdoba
Pampa de las Salinas
Salinas Grandes
Salar de Uyuni
Salar de Atacama
Salar de Arizaro
Iquique
Antofagasta
Calama
Tocopilla
Copiapó
La Serena
Coquimbo
Valparaíso
Santiago
Rancagua
Talca
Concepción
Talcahuano
Chillán
Los Angeles
Tarija
Potosí
Uyuni
Yacuiba
Asunción
Concepción
San Salvador de Jujuy
Salta
San Miguel de Tucumán
Santiago del Estero
Catamarca
La Rioja
San Juan
Mendoza
San Luis
Córdoba
Santa Fé
Paraná
Rosario
Resistencia
Corrientes
Formosa
Buenos Aires
La Plata
Mar del Plata
Bahía Blanca
Santa Rosa
Río Cuarto
Villa María
Paysandú
Salto
Aconcagua 6960
Ojos del Salado 6863
Monte Pissis 6779
Tupungato 6570
Llullaillaco 6723
Cerro Bonete 6872
Projection : Lambert's Equivalent Azimuthal

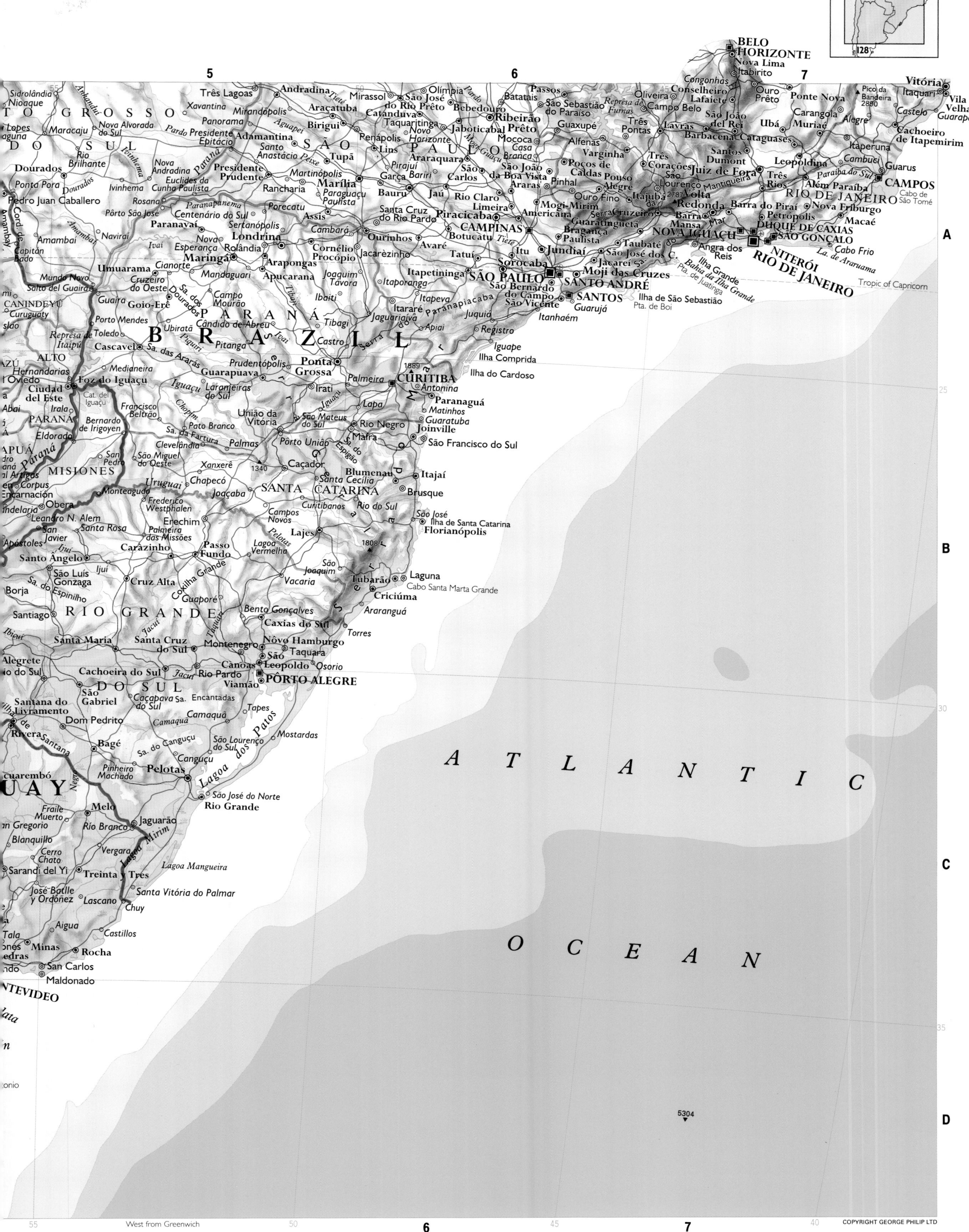

5   6   7

BELO
HORIZONTE
Nova Lima
Itabirito
Congonhas
Conselheiro
Lafaiete
Ouro
Prêto
Ponte Nova
Vitória
Itaquari
Vila
Velha
Guarapari

TO GROSSO

DO SUL

Sidrolândia
Nioaque
Lopes
Laguna
Maracaju
Nova Alvorada
do Sul
Dourados
Rio
Brilhante
Ponta Porã
Pedro Juan Caballero
Dourados
Amambaí
Capitán
Bado
Mundo Novo
Salto del Guairá

Três Lagoas
Xavantina
Mirandópolis
Andradina
Aguapeí
Nova
Andradina
Santo
Anastácio
Presidente
Epitácio
Adamantina
Nova
Euclides da
Cunha Paulista
Presidente
Prudente
Rosana
Ivinhema
Paranavaí
Nova
Esperança
Umuarama
Cruzeiro
do Oeste
Cianorte
Maringá
Mandaguari
Goio-Erê
Porto Mendes
Guaíra
Campo
Mourão
Cascavel
Medianeira

Andradina
Araçatuba
Birigui
Penápolis
Martinópolis
Rancharia
Assis
Paraguaçu
Paulista
Cambará
Londrina
Rolândia
Arapongas
Apucarana
Joaquim
Távora
Ibaiti
Tibagi

Mirassol
Catanduva
Taquaritinga
Lins
Tupã
Marília
Bauru
Sertanópolis
Cornélio
Procópio
Jacarèzinho
Ibaiti

São José
do Rio Prêto
Novo
Horizonte
Pirajuí
Garça
Bariri
Jaú
Botucatu
Avaré
Tatuí

Olímpia
Bebedouro
Jaboticabal
Mococa
Araraquara
São
Carlos
Rio Claro
Piracicaba
Santa Cruz
do Rio Pardo
Ourinhos

Batatais
Ribeirão
Prêto
Casa
Branca
São João
da Boa Vista
Araras
Limeira
Americana
CAMPINAS
Itu
Sorocaba
Itapetininga

Passos
São Sebastião
do Paraíso
Guaxupé
Poços de
Caldas
Mogi-Mirim
Jundiaí
SÃO PAULO
São Bernardo
do Campo
São Vicente

Oliveira
Campo Belo
Alfenas
Varginha
Três
Corações
Pouso
Alegre
Bragança
Moji das Cruzes
SANTO ANDRÉ
SANTOS
Guarujá

Congonhas
Conselheiro
Lafaiete
Campo Belo
Lavras
São João
del Rei
Ubá
Barbacena
Cataguases
Juiz de Fora
Leopoldina
Além Paraíba
Três
Rios
Paraíba do Sul
Petrópolis

Ouro
Prêto
Ponte Nova
Carangola
Muriaé
Itaperuna
Cambuci
RIO DE JANEIRO
CAMPOS
Cabo de
São Tomé

Ponta
Grossa
Prudentópolis
Palmeira
Castro
Guarapuava
Laranjeiras
do Sul
Iguaçu
União
da Vitória
Pato Branco
Palmas
Pôrto União
Cruzeiro
do Oeste
Francisco
Beltrão
Chopim
São Mateus
do Sul
Rio Negro
Mafra
Caçador
Xanxerê
Clevelândia
Concórdia
Chapecó
Joaçaba

CURITIBA
Antonina
Paranaguá
Matinhos
Guaratuba
Joinville
São Francisco do Sul
Itajaí
Blumenau
Brusque

PARANÁ
BRAZIL
SANTA CATARINA
Campos
Novos
Curitibanos
Rio do Sul
São José
Ilha de Santa Catarina
Florianópolis

MISIONES
RIO GRANDE
DO SUL

São Pedro
do Oeste
São Miguel
do Oeste
Frederico
Westphalen
Erechim
Palmeira
das Missões
Passo
Fundo
Carazinho
Cruz Alta
Ijuí
Vacaria
São
Joaquim
Lajes

Caxias do Sul
Bento Gonçalves
Guaporé
Montenegro
Nôvo Hamburgo
São
Leopoldo
Canoas
PÔRTO ALEGRE
Viamão
Osorio
Torres
Araranguá
Criciúma
Tubarão
Laguna
Cabo Santa Marta Grande

Santa
Maria
Santa Cruz
do Sul
São
Gabriel
Dom Pedrito
Bagé
Pinheiro
Machado
Pelotas
Canguçu
Rio Grande
São José do Norte
Mostardas
Tapes
Camaquã

ATLANTIC

OCEAN

UAY

Melo
Jaguarão
Rio Branco
Vergara
Treinta y Trés
Santa Vitória do Palmar
Lagoa Mirim
Lagoa Mangueira
Chuy

Tropic of Capricorn

25

30

35

5304

A

B

C

D

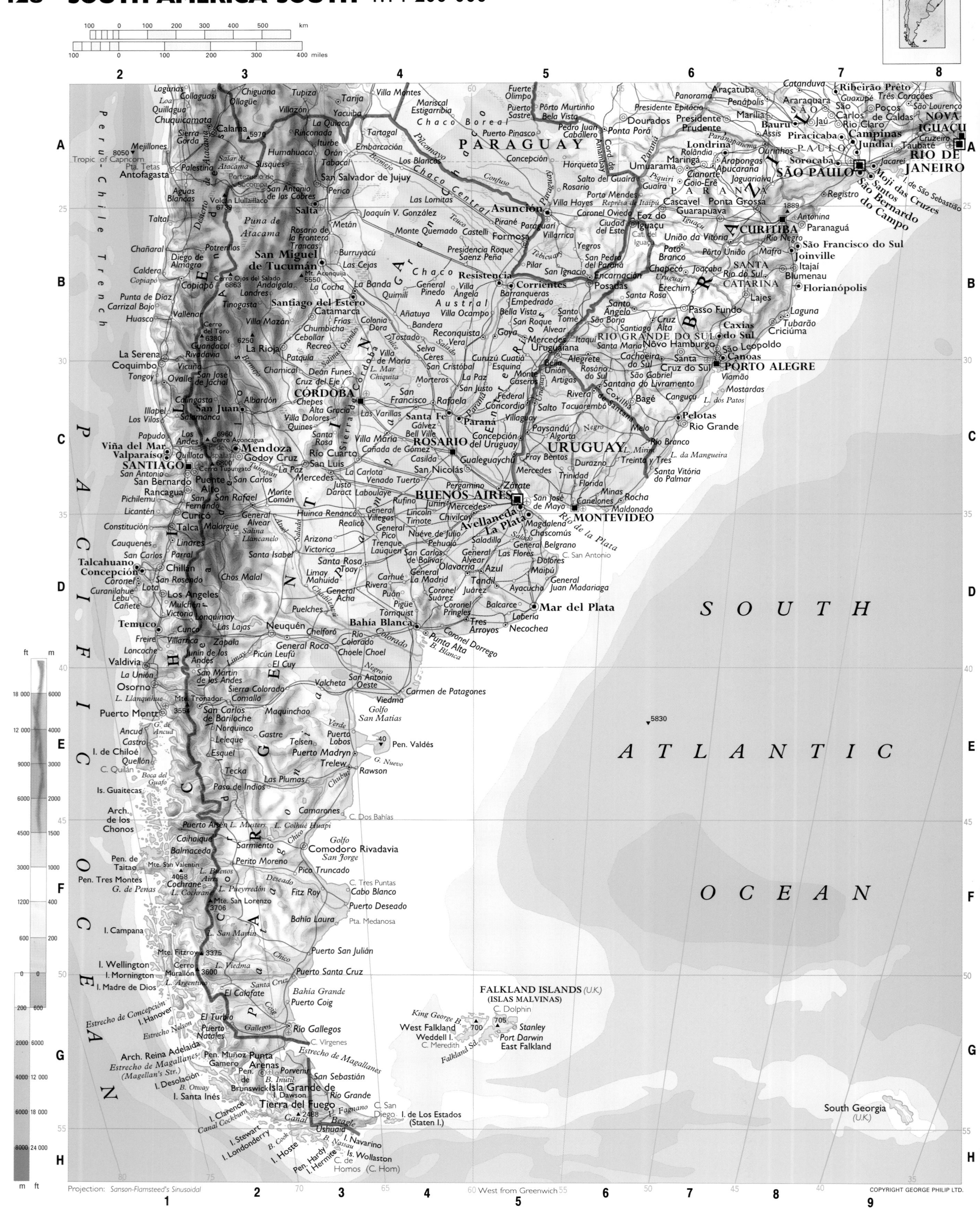

Projection: Sanson-Flamsteed's Sinusoidal

West from Greenwich

INDEX

The index contains the names of all the principal places and features shown on the World Maps. Each name is followed by an additional entry in italics giving the country or region within which it is located. The alphabetical order of names composed of two or more words is governed primarily by the first word and then by the second. This is an example of the rule:

Mīr Kūh, *Iran*	**71**	**E8**
Mīr Shahdād, *Iran*	**71**	**E8**
Mira, *Italy*	**29**	**C9**
Mira por vos Cay, *Bahamas*	**121**	**B5**
Miraj, *India*	**66**	**79**

Physical features composed of a proper name (Erie) and a description (Lake) are positioned alphabetically by the proper name. The description is positioned after the proper name and is usually abbreviated:

Erie, L., *N. Amer.* **110 D4**

Where a description forms part of a settlement or administrative name however, it is always written in full and put in its true alphabetic position:

Mount Morris, *U.S.A.* **110 D7**

Names beginning with M' and Mc are indexed as if they were spelled Mac. Names beginning St. are alphabetised under Saint, but Sankt, Sint, Sant', Santa and San are all spelt in full and are

alphabetised accordingly. If the same place name occurs two or more times in the index and all are in the same country, each is followed by the name of the administrative subdivision in which it is located. The names are placed in the alphabetical order of the subdivisions. For example:

Jackson, *Ky., U.S.A.*	**108**	**G4**
Jackson, *Mich., U.S.A.*	**108**	**D3**
Jackson, *Minn., U.S.A.*	**112**	**D7**

The number in bold type which follows each name in the index refers to the number of the map page where that feature or place will be found. This is usually the largest scale at which the place or feature appears.

The letter and figure which are in bold type immediately after the page number give the grid square on the map page, within which the feature is situated. The letter represents the latitude and the figure the longitude.

In some cases the feature itself may fall within the specified square, while the name is outside. This is usually the case only with features which are larger than a grid square.

Rivers are indexed to their mouths or confluences, and carry the symbol → after their names. A solid square ■ follows the name of a country, while an open square □ refers to a first order administrative area.

ABBREVIATIONS USED IN THE INDEX

A.C.T. – Australian Capital Territory
A.R. – Autonomous Region
Afghan. – Afghanistan
Afr. – Africa
Ala. – Alabama
Alta. – Alberta
Amer. – America(n)
Arch. – Archipelago
Ariz. – Arizona
Ark. – Arkansas
Atl. Oc. – Atlantic Ocean
B. – Baie, Bahía, Bay, Bucht, Bugt
B.C. – British Columbia
Bangla. – Bangladesh
Barr. – Barrage
Bos.-H. – Bosnia-Herzegovina
C. – Cabo, Cap, Cape, Coast
C.A.R. – Central African Republic
C. Prov. – Cape Province
Calif. – California
Cat. – Catarata
Cent. – Central
Chan. – Channel
Colo. – Colorado
Conn. – Connecticut
Cord. – Cordillera
Cr. – Creek
Czech. – Czech Republic
D.C. – District of Columbia
Del. – Delaware
Dem. – Democratic
Dep. – Dependency
Des. – Desert
Dét. – Détroit
Dist. – District
Dj. – Djebel
Domin. – Dominica

Dom. Rep. – Dominican Republic
E. – East
E. Salv. – El Salvador
Eq. Guin. – Equatorial Guinea
Est. – Estrecho
Falk. Is. – Falkland Is.
Fd. – Fjord
Fla. – Florida
Fr. – French
G. – Golfe, Golfo, Gulf, Guba, Gebel
Ga. – Georgia
Gt. – Great, Greater
Guinea-Biss. – Guinea-Bissau
H.K. – Hong Kong
H.P. – Himachal Pradesh
Hants. – Hampshire
Harb. – Harbor, Harbour
Hd. – Head
Hts. – Heights
I.(s). – Île, Ilha, Insel, Isla, Island, Isle
Ill. – Illinois
Ind. – Indiana
Ind. Oc. – Indian Ocean
Ivory C. – Ivory Coast
J. – Jabal, Jebel
Jaz. – Jazīrah
Junc. – Junction
K. – Kap, Kapp
Kans. – Kansas
Kep. – Kepulauan
Ky. – Kentucky
L. – Lac, Lacul, Lago, Lagoa, Lake, Limni, Loch, Lough
La. – Louisiana
Ld. – Land
Liech. – Liechtenstein
Lux. – Luxembourg

Mad. P. – Madhya Pradesh
Madag. – Madagascar
Man. – Manitoba
Mass. – Massachusetts
Md. – Maryland
Me. – Maine
Medit. S. – Mediterranean Sea
Mich. – Michigan
Minn. – Minnesota
Miss. – Mississippi
Mo. – Missouri
Mont. – Montana
Mozam. – Mozambique
Mt.(s) – Mont, Montaña, Mountain
Mte. – Monte
Mti. – Monti
N. – Nord, Norte, North, Northern, Nouveau
N.B. – New Brunswick
N.C. – North Carolina
N. Cal. – New Caledonia
N. Dak. – North Dakota
N.H. – New Hampshire
N.I. – North Island
N.J. – New Jersey
N. Mex. – New Mexico
N.S. – Nova Scotia
N.S.W. – New South Wales
N.W.T. – North West Territory
N.Y. – New York
N.Z. – New Zealand
Nat. – National
Nebr. – Nebraska
Neths. – Netherlands
Nev. – Nevada
Nfld. – Newfoundland
Nic. – Nicaragua
O. – Oued, Ouadi
Occ. – Occidentale

Okla. – Oklahoma
Ont. – Ontario
Or. – Orientale
Oreg. – Oregon
Os. – Ostrov
Oz. – Ozero
P. – Pass, Passo, Pasul, Pulau
P.E.I. – Prince Edward Island
Pa. – Pennsylvania
Pac. Oc. – Pacific Ocean
Papua N.G. – Papua New Guinea
Pass. – Passage
Peg. – Pegunungan
Pen. – Peninsula, Péninsule
Phil. – Philippines
Pk. – Peak
Plat. – Plateau
Prov. – Province, Provincial
Pt. – Point
Pta. – Ponta, Punta
Pte. – Pointe
Qué. – Québec
Queens. – Queensland
R. – Rio, River
R.I. – Rhode Island
Ra. – Range
Raj. – Rajasthan
Recr. – Recreational, Récréatif
Reg. – Region
Rep. – Republic
Res. – Reserve, Reservoir
Rhld-Pfz. – Rheinland-Pfalz
S. – South, Southern, Sur
Si. Arabia – Saudi Arabia
S.C. – South Carolina
S. Dak. – South Dakota
S.I. – South Island
S. Leone – Sierra Leone
Sa. – Serra, Sierra

Sask. – Saskatchewan
Scot. – Scotland
Sd. – Sound
Sev. – Severnaya
Sib. – Siberia
Sprs. – Springs
St. – Saint
Sta. – Santa
Ste. – Sainte
Sto. – Santo
Str. – Strait, Stretto
Switz. – Switzerland
Tas. – Tasmania
Tenn. – Tennessee
Terr. – Territory, Territoire
Tex. – Texas
Tg. – Tanjung
Trin. & Tob. – Trinidad & Tobago
U.A.E. – United Arab Emirates
U.K. – United Kingdom
U.S.A. – United States of America
Ut. P. – Uttar Pradesh
Va. – Virginia
Vdkhr. – Vodokhranilishche
Vdskh. – Vodoskhovyshche
Vf. – Vírful
Vic. – Victoria
Vol. – Volcano
Vt. – Vermont
W. – Wadi, West
W. Va. – West Virginia
Wall. & F. Is. – Wallis and Futuna Is.
Wash. – Washington
Wis. – Wisconsin
Wlkp. – Wielkopolski
Wyo. – Wyoming
Yorks. – Yorkshire
Yug. – Yugoslavia

A Baña

A

A Baña, *Spain* 34 C2
A Cañiza, *Spain* 34 C2
A Coruña, *Spain* 34 B2
A Estrada, *Spain* 34 C2
A Fonsagrada, *Spain* 34 B3
A Guarda, *Spain* 34 D2
A Gudiña, *Spain* 34 C3
A Rúa, *Spain* 34 C3
Aachen, *Germany* 24 E2
Aalborg = Ålborg, *Denmark* 11 G3
Aalen, *Germany* 25 G6
A'âli an Nîl □, *Sudan* 81 F3
Aalst, *Belgium* 17 D4
Aalten, *Neths.* 17 C6
Aalter, *Belgium* 17 C3
Äänekoski, *Finland* 9 E21
Aarau, *Switz.* 25 H4
Aarberg, *Switz.* 25 H3
Aare ➤, *Switz.* 25 H4
Aargau □, *Switz.* 25 H4
Aarhus = Århus, *Denmark* 11 H4
Aarschot, *Belgium* 17 D4
Aba, *China* 58 A3
Aba, *Dem. Rep. of the Congo* 86 B3
Aba, *Nigeria* 83 D6
Âbâ, Jazîrat, *Sudan* 81 E3
Abadab, J., *Sudan* 80 D4
Ābādān, *Iran* 71 D6
Abade, *Ethiopia* 81 F4
Ābādeh, *Iran* 71 D7
Abadin, *Spain* 34 B3
Abadla, *Algeria* 78 B5
Abaetetuba, *Brazil* 125 D9
Abagnar Qi, *China* 56 C9
Abai, *Paraguay* 127 B4
Abak, *Nigeria* 83 E6
Abakaliki, *Nigeria* 83 D6
Abakan, *Russia* 51 D10
Abala, *Niger* 83 C5
Abalak, *Niger* 83 B6
Abalemma, *Niger* 83 B6
Abana, *Turkey* 72 B6
Abancay, *Peru* 124 F4
Abano Terme, *Italy* 29 C8
Abarán, *Spain* 33 G3
Abariringa, *Kiribati* 96 H10
Abarqū, *Iran* 71 D7
Abashiri, *Japan* 54 B12
Abashiri-Wan, *Japan* 54 C12
Abaújszántó, *Hungary* 42 B6
Abava ➤, *Latvia* 44 A8
Ābay = Nîl el Azraq ➤, *Sudan* 81 D3
Abay, *Kazakstan* 50 E8
Abaya, L., *Ethiopia* 81 F4
Abaza, *Russia* 50 D9
Abbadia San Salvatore, *Italy* 29 F8
'Abbāsābād, *Iran* 71 C8
Abbay = Nîl el Azraq ➤, *Sudan* 81 D3
Abbaye, Pt., *U.S.A.* 108 B1
Abbé, L., *Ethiopia* 81 E5
Abbeville, *France* 19 B8
Abbeville, *Ala., U.S.A.* 109 K3
Abbeville, *La., U.S.A.* 113 L8
Abbeville, *S.C., U.S.A.* 109 H4
Abbiategrasso, *Italy* 28 C5
Abbot Ice Shelf, *Antarctica* 5 D16
Abbottabad, *Pakistan* 68 B5
Abd al Kūrī, *Ind. Oc.* 74 E5
Ābdar, *Iran* 71 D7
'Abdolābād, *Iran* 71 C8
Abdulpur, *Bangla.* 69 G13
Abéché, *Chad* 79 F10
Abejar, *Spain* 32 D2
Abekr, *Sudan* 81 E2
Abengourou, *Ivory C.* 82 D4
Abenójar, *Spain* 35 G6
Åbenrå, *Denmark* 11 J3
Abensberg, *Germany* 25 G7
Abeokuta, *Nigeria* 83 D5
Aber, *Uganda* 86 B3
Aberaeron, *U.K.* 13 E3
Aberayron = Aberaeron, *U.K.* 13 E3
Aberchirder, *U.K.* 14 D6
Abercorn = Mbala, *Zambia* 87 D3
Abercorn, *Australia* 95 D5
Aberdare, *U.K.* 13 F4
Aberdare Ra., *Kenya* 86 C4
Aberdeen, *Australia* 95 E5
Aberdeen, *Canada* 105 C7
Aberdeen, *S. Africa* 88 E3
Aberdeen, *U.K.* 14 D6
Aberdeen, *Ala., U.S.A.* 109 J1
Aberdeen, *Idaho, U.S.A.* 114 E7
Aberdeen, *Md., U.S.A.* 108 F7
Aberdeen, *S. Dak., U.S.A.* 112 C5
Aberdeen, *Wash., U.S.A.* 116 D3
Aberdeen, City of □, *U.K.* 14 D6
Aberdeenshire □, *U.K.* 14 D6
Aberdovey = Aberdyfi, *U.K.* 13 E3
Aberdyfi, *U.K.* 13 E3
Aberfeldy, *U.K.* 14 E5
Abergavenny, *U.K.* 13 F4
Abergele, *U.K.* 12 D4
Abernathy, *U.S.A.* 113 J4
Abert, L., *U.S.A.* 114 E3
Aberystwyth, *U.K.* 13 E3
Abhā, *Si. Arabia* 74 D3
Abhar, *Iran* 71 B6
Abhayapuri, *India* 69 F14
Abia □, *Nigeria* 83 D6
Abide, *Turkey* 39 C11
Abidiya, *Sudan* 80 D3
Abidjan, *Ivory C.* 82 D4
Abilene, *Kans., U.S.A.* 112 F6
Abilene, *Tex., U.S.A.* 113 J5
Abingdon, *U.K.* 13 F6
Abingdon, *U.S.A.* 109 G5
Abington Reef, *Australia* 94 B4
Abitau ➤, *Canada* 105 B7
Abitibi ➤, *Canada* 102 B3
Abitibi, L., *Canada* 102 C4
Abiy Adi, *Ethiopia* 81 E4
Abkhaz Republic = Abkhazia □, *Georgia* 49 J5
Abkhazia □, *Georgia* 49 J5
Abminga, *Australia* 95 D1
Abnûb, *Egypt* 80 B3
Åbo = Turku, *Finland* 9 F20
Abocho, *Nigeria* 83 D6
Abohar, *India* 68 D6
Aboisso, *Ivory C.* 82 D4
Abomey, *Benin* 83 D5
Abong-Mbang, *Cameroon* 84 D2
Abonnema, *Nigeria* 83 E6
Abony, *Hungary* 42 C5
Aboso, *Ghana* 82 D4
Abou-Deïa, *Chad* 79 F9
Aboyne, *U.K.* 14 D6
Abra Pampa, *Argentina* 126 A2
Abraham L., *Canada* 104 C5
Abrantes, *Portugal* 35 F2
Abreojos, Pta., *Mexico* 118 B2
Abri, *Esh Shamâliya, Sudan* 80 C3
Abri, *Janub Kordofân, Sudan* 81 E3
Abrud, *Romania* 42 D8
Abruzzo □, *Italy* 29 F10
Absaroka Range, *U.S.A.* 114 D9
Abtenau, *Austria* 26 D6
Abu, *India* 68 G5
Abū al Abyad, *U.A.E.* 71 E7
Abū al Khaṣīb, *Iraq* 71 D6
Abū 'Alī, *Si. Arabia* 71 E6
Abū 'Alī ➤, *Lebanon* 75 A4
Abu Ballas, *Egypt* 80 C2
Abu Deleiq, *Sudan* 81 D3
Abu Dhabi = Abū Ẓāby, *U.A.E.* 71 E7
Abu Dis, *Sudan* 80 D3
Abu Dom, *Sudan* 81 D3
Abū Du'ān, *Syria* 70 B3
Abu el Gairi, W. ➤, *Egypt* 75 F2
Abu Fatma, Ras, *Sudan* 80 C4
Abu Gabra, *Sudan* 81 E2
Abu Ga'da, W. ➤, *Egypt* 75 F1
Abu Gelba, *Sudan* 81 E3
Abu Gubeiha, *Sudan* 81 E3
Abu Habl, Khawr ➤, *Sudan* 81 E3
Abū Ḥadrīyah, *Si. Arabia* 71 E6
Abu Hamed, *Sudan* 80 D3
Abu Haraz, *An Nîl el Azraq, Sudan* 80 D3
Abu Haraz, *El Gezira, Sudan* 81 E3
Abu Haraz, *Esh Shamâliya, Sudan* 80 D3
Abu Higar, *Sudan* 81 E3
Abū Kamāl, *Syria* 70 C4
Abu Kuleiwat, *Sudan* 81 E2
Abū Madd, Ra's, *Si. Arabia* 70 E3
Abu Matariq, *Sudan* 81 E2
Abu Mendi, *Ethiopia* 81 E4
Abū Mūsā, *U.A.E.* 71 E7
Abū Qaṣr, *Si. Arabia* 70 D3
Abu Qir, *Egypt* 80 H7
Abu Qireiya, *Egypt* 80 C4
Abu Qurqâs, *Egypt* 80 B3
Abu Şafât, W. ➤, *Jordan* 75 E5
Abu Shagara, Ras, *Sudan* 80 C4
Abu Shanab, *Sudan* 81 E2
Abu Simbel, *Egypt* 80 C3
Abū Şukhayr, *Iraq* 70 D5
Abu Sultân, *Egypt* 80 H8
Abu Tabari, *Sudan* 80 D2
Abu Tig, *Egypt* 80 B3
Abu Tiga, *Sudan* 81 E3
Abu Tineitin, *Sudan* 81 E3
Abu Uruq, *Sudan* 81 D3
Abu Zabad, *Sudan* 81 E2
Abū Ẓāby, *U.A.E.* 71 E7
Abū Zeydābād, *Iran* 71 C6
Abuja, *Nigeria* 83 D6
Abukuma-Gawa ➤, *Japan* 54 E10
Abukuma-Sammyaku, *Japan* 54 F10
Abunã, *Brazil* 124 E5
Abunã ➤, *Brazil* 124 E5
Abune Yosef, *Ethiopia* 81 E4
Aburo, *Dem. Rep. of the Congo* 86 B3
Abut Hd., *N.Z.* 91 K3
Abuye Meda, *Ethiopia* 81 E4
Abwong, *Sudan* 81 F3
Åby, *Sweden* 11 F10
Aby, Lagune, *Ivory C.* 82 D4
Abyad, *Sudan* 81 E2
Åbybro, *Denmark* 11 G3
Acadia National Park, *U.S.A.* 109 C11
Açailândia, *Brazil* 125 D9
Acajutla, *El Salv.* 120 D2
Acámbaro, *Mexico* 118 D4
Acanthus, *Greece* 40 F7
Acaponeta, *Mexico* 118 C3
Acapulco, *Mexico* 119 D5
Acarai, Serra, *Brazil* 124 C7
Acarigua, *Venezuela* 124 B5
Acatlán, *Mexico* 119 D5
Acayucan, *Mexico* 119 D6
Accéglio, *Italy* 28 D4
Accomac, *U.S.A.* 108 G8
Accous, *France* 20 E3
Accra, *Ghana* 83 D4
Accrington, *U.K.* 12 D5
Acebal, *Argentina* 126 C3
Aceh □, *Indonesia* 62 D1
Acerra, *Italy* 31 B7
Aceuchal, *Spain* 35 G4
Achalpur, *India* 66 J10
Acheng, *China* 57 B14
Achenkirch, *Austria* 26 D4
Achensee, *Austria* 26 D4
Acher, *India* 68 H5
Achern, *Germany* 25 G4
Achill Hd., *Ireland* 15 C1
Achill I., *Ireland* 15 C1
Achim, *Germany* 24 B5
Achinsk, *Russia* 51 D10
Acıgöl, *Turkey* 39 D11
Acıpayam, *Turkey* 39 D11
Acireale, *Italy* 31 E8
Ackerman, *U.S.A.* 113 J10
Acklins I., *Bahamas* 121 B5
Acme, *Canada* 104 C6
Acme, *U.S.A.* 110 F5
Aconcagua, Cerro, *Argentina* 126 C2
Aconquija, Mt., *Argentina* 126 B2
Açores, Is. dos = Azores, *Atl. Oc.* 78 A1
Acornhoek, *S. Africa* 89 C5
Acquapendente, *Italy* 29 F8
Acquasanta Terme, *Italy* 29 F10
Acquasparta, *Italy* 29 F9
Acquaviva delle Fonti, *Italy* 31 B9
Ácqui Terme, *Italy* 28 D5
Acraman, L., *Australia* 95 E2
Acre = 'Akko, *Israel* 75 C4
Acre □, *Brazil* 124 E4
Acre ➤, *Brazil* 124 E5
Acri, *Italy* 31 C9
Acs, *Hungary* 42 C3
Actium, *Greece* 38 C2
Acton, *Canada* 110 C4
Acuña, *Mexico* 118 B4
Ad Dammām, *Si. Arabia* 71 E6
Ad Dāmūr, *Lebanon* 75 B4
Ad Dawādimī, *Si. Arabia* 70 E5
Ad Dawḥah, *Qatar* 71 E6
Ad Dawr, *Iraq* 70 C4
Ad Dir'īyah, *Si. Arabia* 70 E5
Ad Dīwānīyah, *Iraq* 70 D5
Ad Dujayl, *Iraq* 70 C5
Ad Duwayd, *Si. Arabia* 70 D4
Ada, *Ghana* 83 D5
Ada, *Serbia, Yug.* 42 E5
Ada, *Minn., U.S.A.* 112 B6
Ada, *Okla., U.S.A.* 113 H6
Adabiya, *Egypt* 75 F1
Adair, C., *Canada* 101 A12
Adaja ➤, *Spain* 34 D6
Adak I., *U.S.A.* 100 C2
Adamaoua, Massif de l', *Cameroon* 83 D7
Adamawa □, *Nigeria* 83 D7
Adamawa Highlands = Adamaoua, Massif de l', *Cameroon* 83 D7
Adamello, Mte., *Italy* 28 B7
Adami Tulu, *Ethiopia* 81 F4
Adaminaby, *Australia* 95 F4
Adams, *Mass., U.S.A.* 111 D11
Adams, *N.Y., U.S.A.* 111 C8
Adams, *Wis., U.S.A.* 112 D10
Adam's Bridge, *Sri Lanka* 66 Q11
Adams L., *Canada* 104 C5
Adams Mt., *U.S.A.* 116 D5
Adam's Peak, *Sri Lanka* 66 R12
Adamuz, *Spain* 35 G6
Adana, *Turkey* 70 B2
Adanero, *Spain* 34 E6
Adapazarı = Sakarya, *Turkey* 72 B4
Adar Gwagwa, J., *Sudan* 80 C4
Adarama, *Sudan* 81 D3
Adare, C., *Antarctica* 5 D11
Adarte, *Eritrea* 81 E5
Adaut, *Indonesia* 63 F8
Adavale, *Australia* 95 D3
Adda ➤, *Italy* 28 C6
Addis Ababa = Addis Abeba, *Ethiopia* 81 F4
Addis Abeba, *Ethiopia* 81 F4
Addis Alem, *Ethiopia* 81 F4
Addis Zemen, *Ethiopia* 81 E4
Addison, *U.S.A.* 110 D7
Addo, *S. Africa* 88 E4
Adebour, *Niger* 83 C7
Ādeh, *Iran* 70 B5
Adel, *U.S.A.* 109 K4
Adelaide, *Australia* 95 E2
Adelaide, *Bahamas* 120 A4
Adelaide, *S. Africa* 88 E4
Adelaide I., *Antarctica* 5 C17
Adelaide Pen., *Canada* 100 B10
Adelaide River, *Australia* 92 B5
Adelanto, *U.S.A.* 117 L9
Adele I., *Australia* 92 C3
Adélie, Terre, *Antarctica* 5 C10
Adélie Land = Adélie, Terre, *Antarctica* 5 C10
Ademuz, *Spain* 32 E3
Aden = Al 'Adan, *Yemen* 74 E4
Aden, G. of, *Asia* 74 E4
Adendorp, *S. Africa* 88 E3
Aderbissinat, *Niger* 83 B6
Adh Dhayd, *U.A.E.* 71 E7
Adhoi, *India* 68 H4
Adi, *Indonesia* 63 E8
Adi Arkai, *Ethiopia* 81 E4
Adi Daro, *Ethiopia* 81 E4
Adi Keyih, *Eritrea* 81 E4
Adi Kwala, *Eritrea* 81 E4
Adi Ugri, *Eritrea* 81 E4
Adieu, C., *Australia* 93 F5
Adieu Pt., *Australia* 92 C3
Adigala, *Ethiopia* 81 E5
Adige ➤, *Italy* 29 C9
Adigrat, *Ethiopia* 81 E4
Adıgüzel Barajı, *Turkey* 39 C11
Adilabad, *India* 66 K11
Adilcevaz, *Turkey* 73 C10
Adirondack Mts., *U.S.A.* 111 C10
Adıyaman, *Turkey* 73 D8
Adjohon, *Benin* 83 D5
Adjud, *Romania* 43 D12
Adjumani, *Uganda* 86 B3
Adlavik Is., *Canada* 103 A8
Adler, *Russia* 49 J4
Admer, *Algeria* 83 A6
Admiralty G., *Australia* 92 B4
Admiralty I., *U.S.A.* 104 B2
Admiralty Is., *Papua N. G.* 96 H6
Ado, *Nigeria* 83 D5
Ado-Ekiti, *Nigeria* 83 D6
Adok, *Sudan* 81 F3
Adola, *Ethiopia* 81 E5
Adonara, *Indonesia* 63 F6
Adoni, *India* 66 M10
Adony, *Hungary* 42 C3
Adour ➤, *France* 20 E2
Adra, *India* 69 H12
Adra, *Spain* 35 J7
Adrano, *Italy* 31 E7
Adrar, *Mauritania* 78 D3
Adrar des Iforas, *Algeria* 78 C5
Ádria, *Italy* 29 C9
Adrian, *Mich., U.S.A.* 108 E3
Adrian, *Tex., U.S.A.* 113 H3
Adriatic Sea, *Medit. S.* 6 G9
Adua, *Indonesia* 63 E7
Adwa, *Ethiopia* 81 E4
Adygea □, *Russia* 49 H5
Adzhar Republic = Ajaria □, *Georgia* 49 K6
Adzopé, *Ivory C.* 82 D4
Ægean Sea, *Medit. S.* 39 C7
Aerhtai Shan, *Mongolia* 60 B4
Ærø, *Denmark* 11 K4
Ærøskøbing, *Denmark* 11 K4
Aëtós, *Greece* 38 D3
'Afak, *Iraq* 70 C5
Afándou, *Greece* 36 C10
Afghanistan ■, *Asia* 66 C4
Afikpo, *Nigeria* 83 D6
Aflou, *Algeria* 78 B6
Afragóla, *Italy* 31 B7
Afram ➤, *Ghana* 83 D4
Afrera, *Ethiopia* 81 E5
Africa 76 E6
'Afrīn, *Syria* 70 B3
Afşin, *Turkey* 72 C7
Afton, *N.Y., U.S.A.* 111 D9
Afton, *Wyo., U.S.A.* 114 E8
Afuá, *Brazil* 125 D8
'Afula, *Israel* 75 C4
Afyon, *Turkey* 39 C12
Afyon □, *Turkey* 39 C12
Afyonkarahisar = Afyon, *Turkey* 39 C12
Aga, *Egypt* 80 H7
Agadès = Agadez, *Niger* 83 B6
Agadez, *Niger* 83 B6
Agadir, *Morocco* 78 B4
Agaete, *Canary Is.* 37 F4
Agaie, *Nigeria* 83 D6
Again, *Sudan* 81 F2
Ağapınar, *Turkey* 39 B12
Agar, *India* 68 H7
Agaro, *Ethiopia* 81 F4
Agartala, *India* 67 H17
Agăş, *Romania* 43 D11
Agassiz, *Canada* 104 D4
Agats, *Indonesia* 63 F9
Agawam, *U.S.A.* 111 D12
Agbélouvé, *Togo* 83 D5
Agboville, *Ivory C.* 82 D4
Ağcabädi, *Azerbaijan* 49 K8
Ağdam, *Azerbaijan* 49 L8
Ağdaş, *Azerbaijan* 49 K8
Agde, *France* 20 E7
Agde, C. d', *France* 20 E7
Agdzhabedi = Ağcabädi, *Azerbaijan* 49 K8
Agen, *France* 20 D4
Agerbæk, *Denmark* 11 J2
Agersø, *Denmark* 11 J5
Ageyevo, *Russia* 46 E9
Āgh Kand, *Iran* 71 B6
Aghireşu, *Romania* 43 D8
Aginskoye, *Russia* 51 D12
Ağlasun, *Turkey* 39 D12
Agly ➤, *France* 20 F7
Agnew, *Australia* 93 E3
Agnibilékrou, *Ivory C.* 82 D4
Agnita, *Romania* 43 E9
Agnone, *Italy* 29 G11
Agofie, *Ghana* 83 D5
Agogna ➤, *Italy* 28 C5
Agogo, *Sudan* 81 F2
Agön, *Sweden* 10 C11
Agon Coutainville, *France* 18 C5
Ágordo, *Italy* 29 B9
Agori, *India* 69 G10
Agouna, *Benin* 83 D5
Agout ➤, *France* 20 E5
Agra, *India* 68 F7
Agrakhanskiy Poluostrov, *Russia* 49 J8
Agramunt, *Spain* 32 D6
Agreda, *Spain* 32 D3
Ağri, *Turkey* 73 C10
Agri ➤, *Italy* 31 B9
Ağrı Dağı, *Turkey* 70 B5
Ağri Karakose = Ağri, *Turkey* 73 C10
Agriá, *Greece* 38 B5
Agrigento, *Italy* 30 E6
Agrínion, *Greece* 38 C3
Agrópoli, *Italy* 31 B7
Ağstafa, *Azerbaijan* 49 K7
Agua Caliente, *Baja Calif., Mexico* 117 N10
Agua Caliente, *Sinaloa, Mexico* 118 B3
Agua Caliente Springs, *U.S.A.* 117 N10
Água Clara, *Brazil* 125 H8
Agua Hechicero, *Mexico* 117 N10
Agua Prieta, *Mexico* 118 A3
Aguadilla, *Puerto Rico* 121 C6
Aguadulce, *Panama* 120 E3
Aguanga, *U.S.A.* 117 M10
Aguanish, *Canada* 103 B7
Aguanus ➤, *Canada* 103 B7
Aguapey ➤, *Argentina* 126 B4
Aguaray Guazú ➤, *Paraguay* 126 A4
Aguarico ➤, *Ecuador* 124 D3
Aguas ➤, *Spain* 32 D4
Aguas Blancas, *Chile* 126 A2
Aguas Calientes, Sierra de, *Argentina* 126 B2
Aguascalientes, *Mexico* 118 C4
Aguascalientes □, *Mexico* 118 C4
Agudo, *Spain* 35 G6
Águeda, *Portugal* 34 E2
Agueda ➤, *Spain* 34 D4
Aguelhok, *Mali* 83 B5
Aguié, *Niger* 83 C6
Aguilafuente, *Spain* 34 D6
Aguilar, *Spain* 35 H6
Aguilar de Campóo, *Spain* 34 C6
Aguilares, *Argentina* 126 B2
Aguilas, *Spain* 33 H3
Agüimes, *Canary Is.* 37 G4
Aguja, C. de la, *Colombia* 122 B3
Agulaa, *Ethiopia* 81 E4
Agulhas, C., *S. Africa* 88 E3
Agulo, *Canary Is.* 37 F2
Agung, *Indonesia* 62 F5
Agur, *Uganda* 86 B3
Agusan ➤, *Phil.* 61 G6
Ağva, *Turkey* 41 E13
Agvali, *Russia* 49 J8
Aha Mts., *Botswana* 88 B3
Ahaggar, *Algeria* 78 D7
Ahamansu, *Ghana* 83 D5
Ahar, *Iran* 70 B5
Ahat, *Turkey* 39 C11
Ahaus, *Germany* 24 C2
Ahipara B., *N.Z.* 91 F4
Ahir Dağı, *Turkey* 39 C12
Ahiri, *India* 66 K12
Ahlat, *Turkey* 73 C10
Ahlen, *Germany* 24 D3
Ahmad Wal, *Pakistan* 68 E1
Ahmadabad, *India* 68 H5
Aḥmadābād, *Khorāsān, Iran* 71 C9
Aḥmadābād, *Khorāsān, Iran* 71 C8
Aḥmadī, *Iran* 71 E8
Ahmadnagar, *India* 66 K9
Ahmadpur, *Pakistan* 68 E4
Ahmadpur Lamma, *Pakistan* 68 E4
Ahmar, *Ethiopia* 81 F5
Ahmedabad = Ahmadabad, *India* 68 H5
Ahmednagar = Ahmadnagar, *India* 66 K9
Ahmetbey, *Turkey* 41 E11
Ahmetler, *Turkey* 39 C11
Ahmetli, *Turkey* 39 C9
Ahoada, *Nigeria* 83 D6
Ahome, *Mexico* 118 B3
Ahoskie, *U.S.A.* 109 G7
Ahr ➤, *Germany* 24 E3
Ahram, *Iran* 71 D6
Ahrax Pt., *Malta* 36 D1
Ahrensbök, *Germany* 24 A6
Ahrensburg, *Germany* 24 B6
Āhū, *Iran* 71 C6
Ahuachapán, *El Salv.* 120 D2
Ahun, *France* 19 F9
Åhus, *Sweden* 11 J8
Ahvāz, *Iran* 71 D6
Ahvenanmaa = Åland, *Finland* 9 F19
Aḥwar, *Yemen* 74 E4
Ahzar ➤, *Mali* 83 B5
Ai ➤, *India* 69 F14
Ai-Ais, *Namibia* 88 D2
Aichach, *Germany* 25 G7
Aichi □, *Japan* 55 G8
Aigle, *Switz.* 25 J2
Aignay-le-Duc, *France* 19 E11
Aigoual, Mt., *France* 20 D7
Aigre, *France* 20 C4
Aigua, *Uruguay* 127 C5
Aigueperse, *France* 19 F10
Aigues ➤, *France* 21 D8
Aigues-Mortes, *France* 21 E8
Aigues-Mortes, G. d', *France* 21 E8
Aiguilles, *France* 21 D10
Aiguillon, *France* 20 D4
Aigurande, *France* 19 F8
Aihui, *China* 60 A7
Aija, *Peru* 124 E3
Aikawa, *Japan* 54 E9
Aiken, *U.S.A.* 109 J5
Ailao Shan, *China* 58 F3
Aileron, *Australia* 94 C1
Aillant-sur-Tholon, *France* 19 E10
Aillik, *Canada* 103 A8
Ailsa Craig, *U.K.* 14 F3
'Ailūn, *Jordan* 75 C4
Aim, *Russia* 51 D14

Aimere, *Indonesia* 63 F6
Aimogasta, *Argentina* 126 B2
Ain □, *France* 19 F12
Ain →, *France* 21 C9
Aïn Ben Tili, *Mauritania* 78 C4
Ain Dalla, *Egypt* 80 B2
Ain el Mafki, *Egypt* 80 B2
Ain Girba, *Egypt* 80 B2
Ain Murr, *Sudan* 80 C2
Ain Qeiqab, *Egypt* 80 B1
Aïn Sefra, *Algeria* 78 B5
Ain Sheikh Murzûk, *Egypt* 80 B2
Ain Sudr, *Egypt* 75 F2
Ain Sukhna, *Egypt* 80 J8
Ain Zeitûn, *Egypt* 80 B2
Ainaži, *Latvia* 9 H21
Aínos Óros, *Greece* 38 C2
Ainsworth, *U.S.A.* 112 D5
Aiquile, *Bolivia* 124 G5
Aïr, *Niger* 83 B6
Air Force I., *Canada* 101 B12
Air Hitam, *Malaysia* 65 M4
Airaines, *France* 19 C8
Airdrie, *Canada* 104 C6
Airdrie, *U.K.* 14 F5
Aire →, *France* 19 C11
Aire →, *U.K.* 12 D7
Aire, I. de l', *Spain* 37 B11
Aire-sur-la-Lys, *France* 19 B9
Aire-sur-l'Adour, *France* 20 E3
Airlie Beach, *Australia* 94 C4
Airvault, *France* 18 F6
Aisch →, *Germany* 25 F6
Aisne □, *France* 19 C10
Aisne →, *France* 19 C9
Ait, *India* 69 G8
Aitana, Sierra de, *Spain* 33 G4
Aitkin, *U.S.A.* 112 B8
Aitolía Kai Akarnanía □, *Greece* 38 C3
Aitolikón, *Greece* 38 C3
Aiud, *Romania* 43 D8
Aix-en-Provence, *France* 21 E9
Aix-la-Chapelle = Aachen, *Germany* 24 E2
Aix-les-Bains, *France* 21 C9
Aixe-sur-Vienne, *France* 20 C5
Áíyina, *Greece* 38 D5
Aiyínion, *Greece* 40 F6
Aíyion, *Greece* 38 C4
Aizawl, *India* 67 H18
Aizenay, *France* 18 F5
Aizkraukle, *Latvia* 9 H21
Aizpute, *Latvia* 9 H19
Aizuwakamatsu, *Japan* 54 F9
Ajaccio, *France* 21 G12
Ajaccio, G. d', *France* 21 G12
Ajaigarh, *India* 69 G9
Ajalpan, *Mexico* 119 D5
Ajanta Ra., *India* 66 J9
Ajari Rep. = Ajaria □, *Georgia* 49 K6
Ajaria □, *Georgia* 49 K6
Ajax, *Canada* 110 C5
Ajdābiyā, *Libya* 79 B10
Ajdovščina, *Slovenia* 29 C10
Ajibar, *Ethiopia* 81 E4
Ajka, *Hungary* 42 C2
'Ajmān, *U.A.E.* 71 E7
Ajmer, *India* 68 F6
Ajnala, *India* 68 D6
Ajo, *U.S.A.* 115 K7
Ajo, C. de, *Spain* 34 B7
Ajok, *Sudan* 81 F2
Ajuy, *Phil.* 61 F5
Ak Dağ, *Turkey* 39 E11
Ak Dağları, *Muğla, Turkey* 39 E11
Ak Dağları, *Sivas, Turkey* 72 C7
Akaba, *Togo* 83 D5
Akabira, *Japan* 54 C11
Akaki Beseka, *Ethiopia* 81 F4
Akala, *Sudan* 81 D4
Akamas □, *Cyprus* 36 D11
Akanthou, *Cyprus* 36 D12
Akarca, *Turkey* 39 C11
Akaroa, *N.Z.* 91 K4
Akasha, *Sudan* 80 C3
Akashi, *Japan* 55 G7
Akbarpur, *Bihar, India* 69 G10
Akbarpur, *Ut. P., India* 69 F10
Akçaabat, *Turkey* 73 B8
Akçadağ, *Turkey* 72 C7
Akçakale, *Turkey* 73 D8
Akçakoca, *Turkey* 72 B4
Akçaova, *Turkey* 41 E13
Akçay, *Turkey* 39 E11
Akçay →, *Turkey* 39 D10
Akdağ, *Turkey* 39 C8
Akdağmadeni, *Turkey* 72 C6
Akelamo, *Indonesia* 63 D7
Åkers styckebruk, *Sweden* 10 E11
Åkersberga, *Sweden* 10 E12
Aketi, *Dem. Rep. of the Congo* 84 D4
Akhaïa □, *Greece* 38 C3
Akhalkalaki, *Georgia* 49 K6
Akhaltsikhe, *Georgia* 49 K6
Akharnaí, *Greece* 38 C5
Akhelóös →, *Greece* 38 C3
Akhendriá, *Greece* 39 G7
Akhisar, *Turkey* 39 C9
Akhladhókambos, *Greece* 38 D4
Akhmîm, *Egypt* 80 B3
Akhnur, *India* 69 C6
Akhtopol, *Bulgaria* 41 D11
Akhtuba →, *Russia* 49 G8
Akhtubinsk, *Russia* 49 F8
Akhty, *Russia* 49 K8
Akhtyrka = Okhtyrka, *Ukraine* 47 G8
Aki, *Japan* 55 H6
Akimiski I., *Canada* 102 B3
Akimovka, *Ukraine* 47 J8
Åkirkeby, *Denmark* 11 J8
Akita, *Japan* 54 E10
Akita □, *Japan* 54 E10
Akjoujt, *Mauritania* 82 B2
Akka, *Mali* 82 B4
Akkaya Tepesi, *Turkey* 39 D11
Akkeshi, *Japan* 54 C12
'Akko, *Israel* 75 C4
Akköy, *Turkey* 39 D9
Aklampa, *Benin* 83 D5
Aklavik, *Canada* 100 B6
Aklera, *India* 68 G7
Akmenė, *Lithuania* 44 B9
Akmenrags, *Latvia* 44 B8
Akmolinsk = Astana, *Kazakstan* 50 D8
Akmonte = Almonte, *Spain* 35 H4
Akō, *Japan* 55 G7
Ako, *Nigeria* 83 C7
Akôbô, *Sudan* 81 F3
Akobo →, *Ethiopia* 81 F3
Akola, *India* 66 J10
Akonolinga, *Cameroon* 83 E7
Akor, *Mali* 82 C3
Akordat, *Eritrea* 81 D4
Akosombo Dam, *Ghana* 83 D5
Akot, *Sudan* 81 F3
Akoupé, *Ivory C.* 82 D4
Akpatok I., *Canada* 101 B13
Åkrahamn, *Norway* 9 G11
Akranes, *Iceland* 8 D2
Akreïjit, *Mauritania* 82 B3
Akrítas Venétiko, Ákra, *Greece* 38 E3
Akron, *Colo., U.S.A.* 112 E3
Akron, *Ohio, U.S.A.* 110 E3
Akrotiri, *Cyprus* 36 E11
Akrotíri, Ákra, *Greece* 41 F9
Akrotiri Bay, *Cyprus* 36 E12
Aksai Chin, *India* 69 B8
Aksaray, *Turkey* 70 B2
Aksay, *Kazakstan* 50 D6
Akşehir, *Turkey* 70 B1
Akşehir Gölü, *Turkey* 72 C4
Akstafa = Ağstafa, *Azerbaijan* 49 K7
Aksu, *China* 60 B3
Aksu →, *Turkey* 72 D4
Aksum, *Ethiopia* 81 E4
Aktash, *Russia* 48 C11
Aktogay, *Kazakstan* 50 E8
Aktsyabrski, *Belarus* 47 F5
Aktyubinsk = Aqtöbe, *Kazakstan* 50 D6
Aku, *Nigeria* 83 D6
Akure, *Nigeria* 83 D6
Akureyri, *Iceland* 8 D4
Akuseki-Shima, *Japan* 55 K4
Akusha, *Russia* 49 J8
Akwa-Ibom □, *Nigeria* 83 E6
Akyab = Sittwe, *Burma* 67 J18
Akyazı, *Turkey* 72 B4
Al 'Adan, *Yemen* 74 E4
Al Aḩsā = Hasa □, *Si. Arabia* 71 E6
Al Ajfar, *Si. Arabia* 70 E4
Al Amādīyah, *Iraq* 70 B4
Al 'Amārah, *Iraq* 70 D5
Al 'Aqabah, *Jordan* 75 F4
Al Arak, *Syria* 70 C3
Al 'Aramah, *Si. Arabia* 70 E5
Al Arţāwīyah, *Si. Arabia* 70 E5
Al 'Āşimah = 'Ammān □, *Jordan* 75 D5
Al 'Assāfīyah, *Si. Arabia* 70 D3
Al 'Ayn, *Oman* 71 E7
Al 'Ayn, *Si. Arabia* 70 E3
Al 'Azamīyah, *Iraq* 70 C5
Al 'Azīzīyah, *Iraq* 70 C5
Al Bāb, *Syria* 70 B3
Al Bad', *Si. Arabia* 70 D2
Al Bādī, *Iraq* 70 C4
Al Baḩrah, *Kuwait* 70 D5
Al Baḩral Mayyit = Dead Sea, *Asia* 75 D4
Al Balqā' □, *Jordan* 75 C4
Al Bārūk, J., *Lebanon* 75 B4
Al Başrah, *Iraq* 70 D5
Al Baţḩā, *Iraq* 70 D5
Al Batrūn, *Lebanon* 75 A4
Al Bayḑā, *Libya* 79 B10
Al Biqā, *Lebanon* 75 A5
Al Bi'r, *Si. Arabia* 70 D3
Al Burayj, *Syria* 75 A5
Al Faḑilī, *Si. Arabia* 71 E6
Al Fallūjah, *Iraq* 70 C4
Al Fāw, *Iraq* 71 D6
Al Fujayrah, *U.A.E.* 71 E8
Al Ghadaf, W. →, *Jordan* 75 D5
Al Ghammās, *Iraq* 70 D5
Al Ghazālah, *Si. Arabia* 70 E4
Al Ḩadīthah, *Iraq* 70 C4
Al Ḩadīthah, *Si. Arabia* 75 D6
Al Ḩaḑr, *Iraq* 70 C4
Al Ḩājānah, *Syria* 75 B5
Al Hajar al Gharbi, *Oman* 71 E8
Al Hāmad, *Si. Arabia* 70 D3
Al Hamdānīyah, *Syria* 70 C3
Al Ḩamīdīyah, *Syria* 75 A4
Al Ḩammār, *Iraq* 70 D5
Al Ḩamrā', *Si. Arabia* 70 E3
Al Ḩanākīyah, *Si. Arabia* 70 E4
Al Harīr, W. →, *Syria* 75 C4
Al Hasā, W. →, *Jordan* 75 D4
Al Ḩasakah, *Syria* 70 B4
Al Haydān, W. →, *Jordan* 75 D4
Al Ḩayy, *Iraq* 70 C5
Al Ḩijarah, *Asia* 70 D4
Al Ḩillah, *Iraq* 70 C5
Al Ḩillah, *Si. Arabia* 74 B4
Al Hindīyah, *Iraq* 70 C5
Al Hirmil, *Lebanon* 75 A5
Al Hoceïma, *Morocco* 78 A5
Al Ḩudaydah, *Yemen* 74 E3
Al Hufūf, *Si. Arabia* 71 E6
Al Ḩumayḑah, *Si. Arabia* 70 D2
Al Ḩunayy, *Si. Arabia* 71 E6
Al Īsāwīyah, *Si. Arabia* 70 D3
Al Jafr, *Jordan* 75 E5
Al Jāfūrah, *Si. Arabia* 71 E7
Al Jaghbūb, *Libya* 79 C10
Al Jahrah, *Kuwait* 70 D5
Al Jalāmīd, *Si. Arabia* 70 D3
Al Jamalīyah, *Qatar* 71 E6
Al Janūb □, *Lebanon* 75 B4
Al Jawf, *Libya* 79 D10
Al Jawf, *Si. Arabia* 70 D3
Al Jazirah, *Iraq* 70 C5
Al Jithāmīyah, *Si. Arabia* 70 E4
Al Jubayl, *Si. Arabia* 71 E6
Al Jubaylah, *Si. Arabia* 70 E5
Al Jubb, *Si. Arabia* 70 E4
Al Junaynah, *Sudan* 79 F10
Al Kabā'ish, *Iraq* 70 D5
Al Karak, *Jordan* 75 D4
Al Karak □, *Jordan* 75 E5
Al Kāzim Tyah, *Iraq* 70 C5
Al Khābūra, *Oman* 71 F8
Al Khafji, *Si. Arabia* 71 E6
Al Khalīl, *West Bank* 75 D4
Al Khāliş, *Iraq* 70 C5
Al Kharsānīyah, *Si. Arabia* 71 E6
Al Khaşab, *Oman* 71 E8
Al Khawr, *Qatar* 71 E6
Al Khiḑr, *Iraq* 70 D5
Al Khiyām, *Lebanon* 75 B4
Al Kiswah, *Syria* 75 B5
Al Kūfah, *Iraq* 70 C5
Al Kufrah, *Libya* 79 D10
Al Kuhayfīyah, *Si. Arabia* 70 E4
Al Kūt, *Iraq* 70 C5
Al Kuwayt, *Kuwait* 70 D5
Al Labwah, *Lebanon* 75 A5
Al Lādhiqīyah, *Syria* 70 C2
Al Līth, *Si. Arabia* 74 C3
Al Liwā', *Oman* 71 E8
Al Luḩayyah, *Yemen* 74 D3
Al Madīnah, *Iraq* 70 D5
Al Madīnah, *Si. Arabia* 70 E3
Al Mafraq, *Jordan* 75 C5
Al Maḩmūdīyah, *Iraq* 70 C5
Al Majma'ah, *Si. Arabia* 70 E5
Al Makhruq, W. →, *Jordan* 75 D6
Al Makḩūl, *Si. Arabia* 70 E4
Al Manāmah, *Bahrain* 71 E6
Al Maqwa', *Kuwait* 70 D5
Al Marj, *Libya* 79 B10
Al Maţlā, *Kuwait* 70 D5
Al Mawjib, W. →, *Jordan* 75 D4
Al Mawşil, *Iraq* 70 B4
Al Mayādin, *Syria* 70 C4
Al Mazār, *Jordan* 75 D4
Al Midhnab, *Si. Arabia* 70 E5
Al Minā', *Lebanon* 75 A4
Al Miqdādīyah, *Iraq* 70 C5
Al Mubarraz, *Si. Arabia* 71 E6
Al Mudawwarah, *Jordan* 75 F5
Al Mughayrā', *U.A.E.* 71 E7
Al Muḩarraq, *Bahrain* 71 E6
Al Mukallā, *Yemen* 74 E4
Al Mukhā, *Yemen* 74 E3
Al Musayjīd, *Si. Arabia* 70 E3
Al Musayyib, *Iraq* 70 C5
Al Muwayh, *Si. Arabia* 80 C5
Al Muwayliḩ, *Si. Arabia* 70 E2
Al Owuho = Otukpa, *Nigeria* 83 D6
Al Qā'im, *Iraq* 70 C4
Al Qalībah, *Si. Arabia* 70 D3
Al Qāmishlī, *Syria* 70 B4
Al Qaryatayn, *Syria* 75 A6
Al Qaşīm, *Si. Arabia* 70 E4
Al Qaţ'ā, *Syria* 70 C4
Al Qaţīf, *Si. Arabia* 71 E6
Al Qatrānah, *Jordan* 75 D5
Al Qaţrūn, *Libya* 79 D9
Al Qayşūmah, *Si. Arabia* 70 D5
Al Quds = Jerusalem, *Israel* 75 D4
Al Qunayţirah, *Syria* 75 C4
Al Qunfudhah, *Si. Arabia* 80 D5
Al Qurnah, *Iraq* 70 D5
Al Quşayr, *Iraq* 70 D5
Al Quşayr, *Syria* 75 A5
Al Qutayfah, *Syria* 75 B5
Al 'Ubaylah, *Si. Arabia* 74 C5
Al 'Uḑaylīyah, *Si. Arabia* 71 E6
Al 'Ulā, *Si. Arabia* 70 E3
Al 'Uqayr, *Si. Arabia* 71 E6
Al 'Uwaynid, *Si. Arabia* 70 E5
Al 'Uwayqīlah, *Si. Arabia* 70 D4
Al 'Uyūn, *Ḩijāz, Si. Arabia* 70 E3
Al 'Uyūn, *Najd, Si. Arabia* 70 E4
Al 'Uzayr, *Iraq* 70 D5
Al Wajh, *Si. Arabia* 70 E3
Al Wakrah, *Qatar* 71 E6
Al Waqbah, *Si. Arabia* 70 D5
Al Wari'āh, *Si. Arabia* 70 E5
Ala, *Italy* 28 C8
Ala Dağ, *Turkey* 70 B2
Ala Dağları, *Turkey* 73 C10
Alabama □, *U.S.A.* 109 J2
Alabama →, *U.S.A.* 109 K2
Alabaster, *U.S.A.* 109 J2
Alaca, *Turkey* 72 B6
Alacaatlı, *Turkey* 39 B10
Alaçam, *Turkey* 72 B6
Alaçam Dağları, *Turkey* 39 B10
Alaçatı, *Turkey* 39 C8
Alachua, *U.S.A.* 109 L4
Alaejos, *Spain* 34 D5
Alaérma, *Greece* 36 C9
Alagir, *Russia* 49 J7
Alagna Valsésia, *Italy* 28 C4
Alagoa Grande, *Brazil* 125 E11
Alagoas □, *Brazil* 125 E11
Alagoinhas, *Brazil* 125 F11
Alagón, *Spain* 32 D3
Alagón →, *Spain* 34 F4
Alaior, *Spain* 37 B11
Alajero, *Canary Is.* 37 F2
Alajuela, *Costa Rica* 120 D3
Alakamisy, *Madag.* 89 C8
Alaknanda →, *India* 69 D8
Alakol, Ozero, *Kazakstan* 60 B3
Alamarvdasht, *Iran* 71 E7
Alamata, *Ethiopia* 81 E4
Alameda, *Calif., U.S.A.* 116 H4
Alameda, *N. Mex., U.S.A.* 115 J10
Alaminos, *Phil.* 61 C3
Alamo, *U.S.A.* 117 J11
Alamo Crossing, *U.S.A.* 117 L13
Alamogordo, *U.S.A.* 115 K11
Alamos, *Mexico* 118 B3
Alamosa, *U.S.A.* 115 H11
Åland, *Finland* 9 F19
Alandroal, *Portugal* 35 G3
Ålands hav, *Sweden* 9 F18
Alange, Presa de, *Spain* 35 G4
Alania = North Ossetia □, *Russia* 49 J7
Alanís, *Spain* 35 G5
Alanya, *Turkey* 70 B1
Alaotra, Farihin', *Madag.* 89 B8
Alapayevsk, *Russia* 50 D7
Alappuzha = Alleppey, *India* 66 Q10
Alar del Rey, *Spain* 34 C6
Alaraz, *Spain* 34 E5
Alarcón, Embalse de, *Spain* 32 F2
Alarobia-Vohiposa, *Madag.* 89 C8
Alaşehir, *Turkey* 39 C10
Alaska □, *U.S.A.* 100 B5
Alaska, G. of, *Pac. Oc.* 100 C5
Alaska Peninsula, *U.S.A.* 100 C4
Alaska Range, *U.S.A.* 100 B4
Alássio, *Italy* 28 E5
Älät, *Azerbaijan* 49 L9
Alatri, *Italy* 29 G10
Alatyr, *Russia* 48 C8
Alatyr →, *Russia* 48 C8
Alausi, *Ecuador* 124 D3
Álava □, *Spain* 32 C2
Alava, C., *U.S.A.* 114 B1
Alaverdi, *Armenia* 49 K7
Alavus, *Finland* 9 E20
Alawoona, *Australia* 95 E3
'Alayh, *Lebanon* 75 B4
Alazani →, *Azerbaijan* 49 K8
Alba, *Italy* 28 D5
Alba □, *Romania* 43 D8
Alba Adriática, *Italy* 29 F10
Alba de Tormes, *Spain* 34 E5
Alba-Iulia, *Romania* 43 D8
Albac, *Romania* 42 D7
Albacete, *Spain* 33 F3
Albacete □, *Spain* 33 G3
Albacutya, L., *Australia* 95 F3
Ålbæk, *Denmark* 11 G4
Ålbæk Bugt, *Denmark* 11 G4
Albaida, *Spain* 33 G4
Albalate de las Nogueras, *Spain* 32 E2
Albalate del Arzobispo, *Spain* 32 D4
Alban, *France* 20 E6
Albanel, L., *Canada* 102 B5
Albania ■, *Europe* 40 E4
Albano Laziale, *Italy* 29 G9
Albany, *Australia* 93 G2
Albany, *Ga., U.S.A.* 109 K3
Albany, *N.Y., U.S.A.* 111 D11
Albany, *Oreg., U.S.A.* 114 D2
Albany, *Tex., U.S.A.* 113 J5
Albany →, *Canada* 102 B3
Albardón, *Argentina* 126 C2
Albarracín, *Spain* 32 E3
Albarracín, Sierra de, *Spain* 32 E3
Albatera, *Spain* 33 G4
Albatross B., *Australia* 94 A3
Albegna →, *Italy* 29 F8
Albemarle, *U.S.A.* 109 H5
Albemarle Sd., *U.S.A.* 109 H7
Albenga, *Italy* 28 D5
Alberche →, *Spain* 34 F6
Alberdi, *Paraguay* 126 B4
Albères, Mts., *France* 20 F6
Ålberga, *Sweden* 11 F10
Albersdorf, *Germany* 24 A5
Albert, *France* 19 C9
Albert, L., *Africa* 86 B3
Albert, L., *Australia* 95 F2
Albert Edward Ra., *Australia* 92 C4
Albert Lea, *U.S.A.* 112 D8
Albert Nile →, *Uganda* 86 B3
Albert Town, *Bahamas* 121 B5
Alberta □, *Canada* 104 C6
Alberti, *Argentina* 126 D3
Albertinia, *S. Africa* 88 E3
Albertirsa, *Hungary* 42 C4
Alberton, *Canada* 103 C7
Albertville = Kalemie, *Dem. Rep. of the Congo* 86 D2
Albertville, *France* 21 C10
Albertville, *U.S.A.* 109 H2
Albi, *France* 20 E6
Albia, *U.S.A.* 112 E8
Albina, *Surinam* 125 B8
Albina, Ponta, *Angola* 88 B1
Albino, *Italy* 28 C6
Albion, *Mich., U.S.A.* 108 D3
Albion, *Nebr., U.S.A.* 112 E6
Albion, *Pa., U.S.A.* 110 E4
Albocácer, *Spain* 32 E5
Albolote, *Spain* 35 H7
Alborán, *Medit. S.* 35 K7
Alborea, *Spain* 33 F3
Ålborg, *Denmark* 11 G3
Ålborg Bugt, *Denmark* 11 H4
Alborz, Reshteh-ye Kūhhā-ye, *Iran* 71 C7
Albox, *Spain* 33 H2
Albufeira, *Portugal* 35 H2
Albula →, *Switz.* 25 J5
Albuñol, *Spain* 35 J7
Albuquerque, *U.S.A.* 115 J10
Albuquerque, Cayos de, *Caribbean* 120 D3
Alburg, *U.S.A.* 111 B11
Alburno, Mte., *Italy* 31 B8
Alburquerque, *Spain* 35 F4
Albury = Albury-Wodonga, *Australia* 95 F4
Albury-Wodonga, *Australia* 95 F4
Alcácer do Sal, *Portugal* 35 G2
Alcáçovas, *Portugal* 35 G2
Alcalá de Chivert, *Spain* 32 E5
Alcalá de Guadaira, *Spain* 35 H5
Alcalá de Henares, *Spain* 34 E7
Alcalá de los Gazules, *Spain* 35 J5
Alcalá del Júcar, *Spain* 33 F3
Alcalá del Río, *Spain* 35 H5
Alcalá del Valle, *Spain* 35 J5
Alcalá la Real, *Spain* 35 H7
Álcamo, *Italy* 30 E5
Alcanadre, *Spain* 32 C2
Alcanadre →, *Spain* 32 D4
Alcanar, *Spain* 32 E5
Alcanede, *Portugal* 35 F2
Alcanena, *Portugal* 35 F2
Alcañices, *Spain* 34 D4
Alcañiz, *Spain* 32 D4
Alcântara, *Brazil* 125 D10
Alcántara, *Spain* 34 F4
Alcántara, Embalse de, *Spain* 34 F4
Alcantarilla, *Spain* 33 H3
Alcaracejos, *Spain* 35 G6
Alcaraz, *Spain* 33 G2
Alcaraz, Sierra de, *Spain* 33 G2
Alcaudete, *Spain* 35 H6
Alcázar de San Juan, *Spain* 35 F7
Alchevsk, *Ukraine* 47 H10
Alcira = Alzira, *Spain* 33 F4
Alcobaça, *Portugal* 35 F2
Alcobendas, *Spain* 34 E7
Alcolea del Pinar, *Spain* 32 D2
Alcora, *Spain* 32 E4
Alcorcón, *Spain* 34 E7
Alcoutim, *Portugal* 35 H3
Alcova, *U.S.A.* 114 E10
Alcoy, *Spain* 33 G4
Alcubierre, Sierra de, *Spain* 32 D4
Alcublas, *Spain* 32 F4
Alcúdia, *Spain* 37 B10
Alcúdia, B. d', *Spain* 37 B10
Alcudia, Sierra de la, *Spain* 35 G6
Aldabra Is., *Seychelles* 77 G8
Aldama, *Mexico* 119 C5
Aldan, *Russia* 51 D13
Aldan →, *Russia* 51 C13
Aldea, Pta. de la, *Canary Is.* 37 G4
Aldeburgh, *U.K.* 13 E9
Alder Pk., *U.S.A.* 116 K5
Alderney, *U.K.* 13 H5
Aldershot, *U.K.* 13 F7
Åled, *Sweden* 11 H6
Aledo, *U.S.A.* 112 E9
Alefa, *Ethiopia* 81 E4
Aleg, *Mauritania* 82 B2
Alegranza, *Canary Is.* 37 E6
Alegranza, I., *Canary Is.* 37 E6
Alegre, *Brazil* 127 A7
Alegrete, *Brazil* 127 B4
Aleisk, *Russia* 50 D9
Aleksandriya = Oleksandriya, *Kirovohrad, Ukraine* 47 H7
Aleksandriya = Oleksandriya, *Rivne, Ukraine* 47 G4
Aleksandriyskaya, *Russia* 49 J8
Aleksandrov, *Russia* 46 D10
Aleksandrov Gay, *Russia* 48 E9
Aleksandrovac, *Serbia, Yug.* 40 C5
Aleksandrovac, *Serbia, Yug.* 40 B5
Aleksandrovka = Oleksandrovka, *Ukraine* 47 H7
Aleksandrovo, *Bulgaria* 41 C8
Aleksandrovsk-Sakhalinskiy, *Russia* 51 D15
Aleksandrów Kujawski, *Poland* 45 F5
Aleksandrów Łódźki, *Poland* 45 G6
Alekseyevka, *Samara, Russia* 48 D10
Alekseyevka, *Voronezh, Russia* 47 G10
Aleksin, *Russia* 46 E9
Aleksinac, *Serbia, Yug.* 40 C5
Além Paraíba, *Brazil* 127 A7
Alemania, *Argentina* 126 B2
Alemania, *Chile* 126 B2
Alençon, *France* 18 D7
Alenquer, *Brazil* 125 D8
Alenuihaha Channel, *U.S.A.* 106 H17
Alépé, *Ivory C.* 82 D4
Aleppo = Ḩalab, *Syria* 70 B3
Aléria, *France* 21 F13
Alès, *France* 21 D8
Aleşd, *Romania* 42 C7

Alessándria

Alessándria, *Italy* 28 D5
Ålestrup, *Denmark* 11 H3
Ålesund, *Norway* 9 E12
Alet-les-Bains, *France* 20 F6
Aletschhorn, *Switz.* 25 J4
Aleutian Is., *Pac. Oc.* 100 C2
Aleutian Trench, *Pac. Oc.* 96 C10
Alexander, *U.S.A.* 112 B3
Alexander, Mt., *Australia* 93 E3
Alexander Arch., *U.S.A.* 100 C6
Alexander Bay, *S. Africa* 88 D2
Alexander City, *U.S.A.* 109 J3
Alexander I., *Antarctica* 5 C17
Alexandra, *Australia* 95 F4
Alexandra, *N.Z.* 91 L2
Alexandra Falls, *Canada* 104 A5
Alexandria = El Iskandarîya, *Egypt* 80 H7
Alexandria, *B.C., Canada* 104 C4
Alexandria, *Ont., Canada* 102 C5
Alexandria, *Romania* 43 G10
Alexandria, *S. Africa* 88 E4
Alexandria, *U.K.* 14 F4
Alexandria, *La., U.S.A.* 113 K8
Alexandria, *Minn., U.S.A.* 112 C7
Alexandria, *S. Dak., U.S.A.* 112 D6
Alexandria, *Va., U.S.A.* 108 F7
Alexandria Bay, *U.S.A.* 111 B9
Alexandrina, L., *Australia* 95 F2
Alexandroúpolis, *Greece* 41 F9
Alexis →, *Canada* 103 B8
Alexis Creek, *Canada* 104 C4
Alfabia, *Spain* 37 B9
Alfambra, *Spain* 32 E3
Alfândega da Fé, *Portugal* 34 D4
Alfaro, *Spain* 32 C3
Alfatar, *Bulgaria* 41 C11
Alfaz del Pi, *Spain* 33 G4
Alfeld, *Germany* 24 D5
Alfenas, *Brazil* 127 A6
Alfiós →, *Greece* 38 D3
Alföld, *Hungary* 42 D5
Alfonsine, *Italy* 29 D9
Alford, *Aberds., U.K.* 14 D6
Alford, *Lincs., U.K.* 12 D8
Alfred, *Maine, U.S.A.* 111 C14
Alfred, *N.Y., U.S.A.* 110 D7
Alfreton, *U.K.* 12 D6
Alfta, *Sweden* 10 C10
Alga, *Kazakstan* 50 E6
Algaida, *Spain* 37 B9
Algar, *Spain* 35 J5
Ålgård, *Norway* 9 G11
Algarinejo, *Spain* 35 H6
Algarve, *Portugal* 35 J2
Algeciras, *Spain* 35 J5
Algemesí, *Spain* 33 F4
Alger, *Algeria* 78 A6
Algeria ■, *Africa* 78 C6
Alghero, *Italy* 30 B1
Älghult, *Sweden* 11 G9
Algiers = Alger, *Algeria* 78 A6
Algoa B., *S. Africa* 88 E4
Algodonales, *Spain* 35 J5
Algodor →, *Spain* 34 F7
Algoma, *U.S.A.* 108 C2
Algona, *U.S.A.* 112 D7
Algonac, *U.S.A.* 110 D2
Algonquin Prov. Park, *Canada* 102 C4
Algorta, *Uruguay* 128 C5
Alhama de Almería, *Spain* 35 J8
Alhama de Aragón, *Spain* 32 D3
Alhama de Granada, *Spain* 35 H7
Alhama de Murcia, *Spain* 33 H3
Alhambra, *U.S.A.* 117 L8
Alhaurín el Grande, *Spain* 35 J6
Alhucemas = Al Hoceïma, *Morocco* 78 A5
'Alī al Gharbī, *Iraq* 70 C5
'Alī ash Sharqī, *Iraq* 70 C5
Äli Bayramlı, *Azerbaijan* 49 L9
'Alī Khēl, *Afghan.* 68 C3
Ali Sahîh, *Djibouti* 81 E5
Alī Shāh, *Iran* 70 B5
Ália, *Italy* 30 E6
'Alīābād, *Khorāsān, Iran* 71 C8
'Alīābād, *Kordestān, Iran* 70 C5
'Alīābād, *Yazd, Iran* 71 D7
Aliaga, *Spain* 32 E4
Aliağa, *Turkey* 39 C8
Aliákmon →, *Greece* 40 F6
Alibo, *Ethiopia* 81 F4
Alibori →, *Benin* 83 C5
Alibunar, *Serbia, Yug.* 42 E5
Alicante, *Spain* 33 G4
Alicante □, *Spain* 33 G4
Alice, *S. Africa* 88 E4
Alice, *U.S.A.* 113 M5
Alice →, *Queens., Australia* 94 C3
Alice →, *Queens., Australia* 94 B3
Alice, Punta, *Italy* 31 C10
Alice Arm, *Canada* 104 B3
Alice Springs, *Australia* 94 C1
Alicedale, *S. Africa* 88 E4
Aliceville, *U.S.A.* 109 J1
Alicudi, *Italy* 31 D7
Aliganj, *India* 69 F8
Aligarh, *Raj., India* 68 G7
Aligarh, *Ut. P., India* 68 F8
Alīgūdarz, *Iran* 71 C6
Alijó, *Portugal* 34 D3
Alimnía, *Greece* 36 C9
Alingsås, *Sweden* 11 G6
Alipur, *Pakistan* 68 E4
Alipur Duar, *India* 67 F16
Aliquippa, *U.S.A.* 110 F4
Alishan, *Taiwan* 59 F13
Aliste →, *Spain* 34 D5
Alitus = Alytus, *Lithuania* 9 J21
Alivérion, *Greece* 38 C6
Aliwal North, *S. Africa* 88 E4
Alix, *Canada* 104 C6
Aljezur, *Portugal* 35 H2
Aljustrel, *Portugal* 35 H2
Alkamari, *Niger* 83 C7
Alkmaar, *Neths.* 17 B4
All American Canal, *U.S.A.* 115 K6
Allada, *Benin* 83 D5
Allagash →, *U.S.A.* 109 B11
Allah Dad, *Pakistan* 68 G2
Allahabad, *India* 69 G9
Allan, *Canada* 105 C7
Allanche, *France* 20 C6
Allanridge, *S. Africa* 88 D4
Allaqi, Wadi →, *Egypt* 80 C3
Allariz, *Spain* 34 C3
Allassac, *France* 20 C5
Ålleberg, *Sweden* 11 F7
Allegany, *U.S.A.* 110 D6
Allegheny →, *U.S.A.* 110 F5
Allegheny Mts., *U.S.A.* 108 G6
Allegheny Reservoir, *U.S.A.* 110 E6
Allègre, *France* 20 C7
Allen, Bog of, *Ireland* 15 C5
Allen, L., *Ireland* 15 B3
Allendale, *U.S.A.* 109 J5
Allende, *Mexico* 118 B4
Allentown, *U.S.A.* 111 F9
Allentsteig, *Austria* 26 C8
Alleppey, *India* 66 Q10
Allepuz, *Spain* 32 E4
Aller →, *Germany* 24 C5
Alliance, *Nebr., U.S.A.* 112 D3
Alliance, *Ohio, U.S.A.* 110 F3
Allier □, *France* 19 F9
Allier →, *France* 19 F10
Alliford Bay, *Canada* 104 C2
Allinge, *Denmark* 11 J8
Alliston, *Canada* 102 D4
Alloa, *U.K.* 14 E5
Allones, *France* 18 D8
Allora, *Australia* 95 D5
Allos, *France* 21 D10
Alluitsup Paa, *Greenland* 4 C5
Alma, *Canada* 103 C5
Alma, *Ga., U.S.A.* 109 K4
Alma, *Kans., U.S.A.* 112 F6
Alma, *Mich., U.S.A.* 108 D3
Alma, *Nebr., U.S.A.* 112 E5
Alma Ata = Almaty, *Kazakstan* 50 E8
Almacelles, *Spain* 32 D5
Almada, *Portugal* 35 G1
Almaden, *Australia* 94 B3
Almadén, *Spain* 35 G6
Almanor, L., *U.S.A.* 114 F3
Almansa, *Spain* 33 G3
Almanza, *Spain* 34 C5
Almanzor, Pico, *Spain* 34 E5
Almanzora →, *Spain* 33 H3
Almaş, Munţii, *Romania* 42 F7
Almassora, *Spain* 32 F4
Almaty, *Kazakstan* 50 E8
Almazán, *Spain* 32 D2
Almeirim, *Brazil* 125 D8
Almeirim, *Portugal* 35 F2
Almelo, *Neths.* 17 B6
Almenar de Soria, *Spain* 32 D2
Almenara, *Spain* 32 F4
Almenara, Sierra de la, *Spain* 33 H3
Almendra, Embalse de, *Spain* 34 D4
Almendralejo, *Spain* 35 G4
Almere-Stad, *Neths.* 17 B5
Almería, *Spain* 35 J8
Almería □, *Spain* 33 H2
Almería, G. de, *Spain* 33 J2
Almetyevsk, *Russia* 48 C11
Älmhult, *Sweden* 11 H8
Almirante, *Panama* 120 E3
Almiropótamos, *Greece* 38 C6
Almirós, *Greece* 38 B4
Almiroú, Kólpos, *Greece* 36 D6
Almodôvar, *Portugal* 35 H2
Almodóvar del Campo, *Spain* 35 G6
Almodóvar del Río, *Spain* 35 H5
Almond, *U.S.A.* 110 D7
Almont, *U.S.A.* 110 D1
Almonte, *Canada* 111 A8
Almonte, *Spain* 35 H4
Almora, *India* 69 E8
Almoradí, *Spain* 33 G4
Almorox, *Spain* 34 E6
Almoustarat, *Mali* 83 B5
Älmsta, *Sweden* 10 E12
Almudévar, *Spain* 32 C4
Almuñécar, *Spain* 35 J7
Almunge, *Sweden* 10 E12
Almuradiel, *Spain* 35 G7
Alness, *U.K.* 14 D4
Alnmouth, *U.K.* 12 B6
Alnwick, *U.K.* 12 B6
Aloi, *Uganda* 86 B3
Alon, *Burma* 67 H19
Alor, *Indonesia* 63 F6
Alor Setar, *Malaysia* 65 J3
Álora, *Spain* 35 J6
Alosno, *Spain* 35 H3
Alot, *India* 68 H6
Aloysius, Mt., *Australia* 93 E4
Alpaugh, *U.S.A.* 116 K7
Alpedrinha, *Portugal* 34 E3
Alpena, *U.S.A.* 108 C4
Alpes-de-Haute-Provence □, *France* 21 D10
Alpes-Maritimes □, *France* 21 E11
Alpha, *Australia* 94 C4
Alphen aan den Rijn, *Neths.* 17 B4
Alpiarça, *Portugal* 35 F2
Alpine, *Ariz., U.S.A.* 115 K9
Alpine, *Calif., U.S.A.* 117 N10
Alpine, *Tex., U.S.A.* 113 K3
Alps, *Europe* 6 F7
Alpu, *Turkey* 72 C4
Alqueta, Barragem do, *Portugal* 35 G3
Alrø, *Denmark* 11 J4
Als, *Denmark* 11 K3
Alsace, *France* 19 D14
Alsask, *Canada* 105 C7
Alsasua, *Spain* 32 C2
Alsek →, *U.S.A.* 104 B1
Alsfeld, *Germany* 24 E5
Alsten, *Norway* 8 D15
Alstermo, *Sweden* 11 H9
Alston, *U.K.* 12 C5
Alta, *Norway* 8 B20
Alta, Sierra, *Spain* 32 E3
Alta Gracia, *Argentina* 126 C3
Alta Sierra, *U.S.A.* 117 K8
Altaelva →, *Norway* 8 B20
Altafjorden, *Norway* 8 A20
Altai = Aerhtai Shan, *Mongolia* 60 B4
Altamaha →, *U.S.A.* 109 K5
Altamira, *Brazil* 125 D8
Altamira, *Chile* 126 B2
Altamira, *Mexico* 119 C5
Altamira, Cuevas de, *Spain* 34 B6
Altamont, *U.S.A.* 111 D10
Altamura, *Italy* 31 B9
Altanbulag, *Mongolia* 60 A5
Altar, *Mexico* 118 A2
Altar, Desierto de, *Mexico* 118 B2
Altata, *Mexico* 118 C3
Altavista, *U.S.A.* 108 G6
Altay, *China* 60 B3
Altdorf, *Switz.* 25 J4
Alte Mellum, *Germany* 24 B4
Altea, *Spain* 33 G4
Altenberg, *Germany* 24 E9
Altenbruch, *Germany* 24 B4
Altenburg, *Germany* 24 E8
Altenkirchen, *Mecklenburg-Vorpommern, Germany* 24 A9
Altenkirchen, *Rhld-Pfz., Germany* 24 E3
Altenmarkt, *Austria* 26 D7
Alter do Chão, *Portugal* 35 F3
Altınoluk, *Turkey* 39 B8
Altınova, *Turkey* 39 B8
Altıntaş, *Turkey* 39 B12
Altınyaka, *Turkey* 39 E12
Altınyayla, *Turkey* 39 D11
Altiplano = Bolivian Plateau, *S. Amer.* 122 E4
Altkirch, *France* 19 E14
Altmark, *Germany* 24 C7
Altmühl →, *Germany* 25 G7
Altmunster, *Austria* 26 D6
Alto Adige = Trentino-Alto Adige □, *Italy* 29 B8
Alto Araguaia, *Brazil* 125 G8
Alto Cuchumatanes = Cuchumatanes, Sierra de los, *Guatemala* 120 C1
Alto del Carmen, *Chile* 126 B1
Alto del Inca, *Chile* 126 A2
Alto Ligonha, *Mozam.* 87 F4
Alto Molocue, *Mozam.* 87 F4
Alto Paraguay □, *Paraguay* 126 A4
Alto Paraná □, *Paraguay* 127 B5
Alton, *Canada* 110 C4
Alton, *U.K.* 13 F7
Alton, *Ill., U.S.A.* 112 F9
Alton, *N.H., U.S.A.* 111 C13
Altoona, *U.S.A.* 110 F6
Altötting, *Germany* 25 G8
Altstätten, *Switz.* 25 H5
Altūn Kūprī, *Iraq* 70 C5
Altun Shan, *China* 60 C3
Alturas, *U.S.A.* 114 F3
Altus, *U.S.A.* 113 H5
Alubijid, *Phil.* 61 G6
Alucra, *Turkey* 73 B8
Aluk, *Sudan* 81 F2
Alūksne, *Latvia* 9 H22
Alunda, *Sweden* 10 D12
Alunite, *U.S.A.* 117 K12
Aluoro →, *Ethiopia* 81 F3
Alupka, *Ukraine* 47 K8
Alushta, *Ukraine* 47 K8
Alusi, *Indonesia* 63 F8
Alustante, *Spain* 32 E3
Alva, *U.S.A.* 113 G5
Alvaiázere, *Portugal* 34 F2
Älvängen, *Sweden* 11 G6
Alvarado, *Mexico* 119 D5
Alvarado, *U.S.A.* 113 J6
Alvaro Obregón, Presa, *Mexico* 118 B3
Älvdalen, *Sweden* 10 C8
Alvear, *Argentina* 126 B4
Alverca, *Portugal* 35 G1
Alvesta, *Sweden* 11 H8
Alvin, *U.S.A.* 113 L7
Alvinston, *Canada* 110 D3
Alvito, *Portugal* 35 G3
Älvkarleby, *Sweden* 10 D11
Alvord Desert, *U.S.A.* 114 E4
Älvros, *Sweden* 10 B8
Älvsbyn, *Sweden* 8 D19
Alwar, *India* 68 F7
Alxa Zuoqi, *China* 56 E3
Alyangula, *Australia* 94 A2
Alyata = Älät, *Azerbaijan* 49 L9
Alyth, *U.K.* 14 E5
Alytus, *Lithuania* 9 J21
Alzada, *U.S.A.* 112 C2
Alzey, *Germany* 25 F4
Alzira, *Spain* 33 F4
Am Timan, *Chad* 79 F10
Amadeus, L., *Australia* 93 D5
Amadi, *Dem. Rep. of the Congo* 86 B2
Amâdi, *Sudan* 81 F3
Amadjuak L., *Canada* 101 B12
Amadora, *Portugal* 35 G1
Amagansett, *U.S.A.* 111 F12
Amagasaki, *Japan* 55 G7
Amager, *Denmark* 11 J6
Amagunze, *Nigeria* 83 D6
Amahai, *Indonesia* 63 E7
Amakusa-Shotō, *Japan* 55 H5
Åmål, *Sweden* 10 E6
Amalfi, *Italy* 31 B7
Amaliás, *Greece* 38 D3
Amalner, *India* 66 J9
Amamapare, *Indonesia* 63 E9
Amambaí, *Brazil* 127 A4
Amambaí →, *Brazil* 127 A5
Amambay □, *Paraguay* 127 A4
Amambay, Cordillera de, *S. Amer.* 127 A4
Amami-Guntō, *Japan* 55 L4
Amami-Ō-Shima, *Japan* 55 L4
Amaná, L., *Brazil* 124 D6
Amanat →, *India* 69 G11
Amanda Park, *U.S.A.* 116 C3
Amangeldy, *Kazakstan* 50 D7
Amantea, *Italy* 31 C9
Amapá, *Brazil* 125 C8
Amapá □, *Brazil* 125 C8
Amara, *Sudan* 81 E3
Amarante, *Brazil* 125 E10
Amarante, *Portugal* 34 D2
Amaranth, *Canada* 105 C9
Amareleja, *Portugal* 35 G3
Amargosa →, *U.S.A.* 117 J10
Amargosa Range, *U.S.A.* 117 J10
Amári, *Greece* 36 D6
Amarillo, *U.S.A.* 113 H4
Amarkantak, *India* 69 H9
Amârna, Tell el', *Sudan* 80 B3
Amaro, Mte., *Italy* 29 F11
Amarpur, *India* 69 G12
Amarti, *Eritrea* 81 E5
Amarwara, *India* 69 H8
Amasra, *Turkey* 72 B5
Amassama, *Nigeria* 83 D6
Amasya, *Turkey* 72 B6
Amata, *Australia* 93 E5
Amatikulu, *S. Africa* 89 D5
Amatitlán, *Guatemala* 120 D1
Amatrice, *Italy* 29 F10
Amay, *Belgium* 17 D5
Amazon = Amazonas →, *S. Amer.* 122 D5
Amazonas □, *Brazil* 124 E6
Amazonas →, *S. Amer.* 122 D5
Amba Ferit, *Ethiopia* 81 E4
Ambah, *India* 68 F8
Ambahakily, *Madag.* 89 C7
Ambahita, *Madag.* 89 C8
Ambala, *India* 68 D7
Ambalavao, *Madag.* 89 C8
Ambanja, *Madag.* 89 A8
Ambararata, *Madag.* 89 B8
Ambarchik, *Russia* 51 C17
Ambarijeby, *Madag.* 89 A8
Ambaro, Helodranon', *Madag.* 89 A8
Ambato, *Ecuador* 124 D3
Ambato, *Madag.* 89 A8
Ambato, Sierra de, *Argentina* 126 B2
Ambato Boeny, *Madag.* 89 B8
Ambatofinandrahana, *Madag.* 89 C8
Ambatolampy, *Madag.* 89 B8
Ambatomainty, *Madag.* 89 B8
Ambatomanoina, *Madag.* 89 B8
Ambatondrazaka, *Madag.* 89 B8
Ambatosoratra, *Madag.* 89 B8
Ambelón, *Greece* 38 B4
Ambenja, *Madag.* 89 B8
Amberg, *Germany* 25 F7
Ambergris Cay, *Belize* 119 D7
Ambérieu-en-Bugey, *France* 21 C9
Amberley, *N.Z.* 91 K4
Ambert, *France* 20 C7
Ambidédi, *Mali* 82 C2
Ambikapur, *India* 69 H10
Ambikol, *Sudan* 80 C3
Ambilobé, *Madag.* 89 A8
Ambinanindrano, *Madag.* 89 C8
Ambinanitelo, *Madag.* 89 B8
Ambinda, *Madag.* 89 B8
Amble, *U.K.* 12 B6
Ambleside, *U.K.* 12 C5
Ambo, *Peru* 124 F3
Amboahangy, *Madag.* 89 C8
Ambodifototra, *Madag.* 89 B8
Ambodilazana, *Madag.* 89 B8
Ambodiriana, *Madag.* 89 B8
Ambohidratrimo, *Madag.* 89 B8
Ambohidray, *Madag.* 89 B8
Ambohimahamasina, *Madag.* 89 C8
Ambohimahasoa, *Madag.* 89 C8
Ambohimanga, *Madag.* 89 C8
Ambohimitombo, *Madag.* 89 C8
Ambohitra, *Madag.* 89 A8
Amboise, *France* 18 E8
Ambon, *Indonesia* 63 E7
Ambondro, *Madag.* 89 D8
Amboseli, L., *Kenya* 86 C4
Ambositra, *Madag.* 89 C8
Ambovombe, *Madag.* 89 D8
Amboy, *U.S.A.* 117 L11
Amboyna Cay, *S. China Sea* 62 C4
Ambridge, *U.S.A.* 110 F4
Ambriz, *Angola* 84 F2
Amchitka I., *U.S.A.* 100 C1
Amderma, *Russia* 50 C7
Amdhi, *India* 69 H9
Ameca, *Mexico* 118 C4
Ameca →, *Mexico* 118 C3
Amecameca, *Mexico* 119 D5
Ameland, *Neths.* 17 A5
Amélia, *Italy* 29 F9
Amendolara, *Italy* 31 C9
Amenia, *U.S.A.* 111 E11
American Falls, *U.S.A.* 114 E7
American Falls Reservoir, *U.S.A.* 114 E7
American Fork, *U.S.A.* 114 F8
American Highland, *Antarctica* 5 D6
American Samoa ■, *Pac. Oc.* 91 B13
Americana, *Brazil* 127 A6
Americus, *U.S.A.* 109 K3
Amersfoort, *Neths.* 17 B5
Amersfoort, *S. Africa* 89 D4
Amery Ice Shelf, *Antarctica* 5 C6
Ames, *Spain* 34 C2
Ames, *U.S.A.* 112 E8
Amesbury, *U.S.A.* 111 D14
Amet, *India* 68 G5
Amfíklia, *Greece* 38 C4
Amfilokhía, *Greece* 38 C3
Amfípolis, *Greece* 40 F7
Ámfissa, *Greece* 38 C4
Amga, *Russia* 51 C14
Amga →, *Russia* 51 C14
Amgu, *Russia* 51 E14
Amgun →, *Russia* 51 D14
Amherst, *Canada* 103 C7
Amherst, *Mass., U.S.A.* 111 D12
Amherst, *N.Y., U.S.A.* 110 D6
Amherst, *Ohio, U.S.A.* 110 E2
Amherst I., *Canada* 111 B8
Amherstburg, *Canada* 102 D3
Amiata, Mte., *Italy* 29 F8
Amidon, *U.S.A.* 112 B3
Amiens, *France* 19 C9
Amindaion, *Greece* 40 F5
Åminne, *Sweden* 11 G7
Amino, *Ethiopia* 81 G5
Aminuis, *Namibia* 88 C2
Amīrābād, *Iran* 70 C5
Amirante Is., *Seychelles* 52 K9
Amisk L., *Canada* 105 C8
Amistad, Presa de la, *Mexico* 118 B4
Amite, *U.S.A.* 113 K9
Amla, *India* 68 J8
Amlia I., *U.S.A.* 100 C2
Amlwch, *U.K.* 12 D3
Amm Adam, *Sudan* 81 D4
'Ammān, *Jordan* 75 D4
'Ammān □, *Jordan* 75 D5
Ammanford, *U.K.* 13 F4
Ammassalik = Tasiilaq, *Greenland* 4 C6
Ammerån →, *Sweden* 10 A10
Ammersee, *Germany* 25 G7
Ammon, *U.S.A.* 114 E8
Amnat Charoen, *Thailand* 64 E5
Amnura, *Bangla.* 69 G13
Amo Jiang →, *China* 58 F3
Āmol, *Iran* 71 B7
Amorgós, *Greece* 39 E7
Amory, *U.S.A.* 109 J1
Amos, *Canada* 102 C4
Åmot, *Norway* 9 G13
Åmotfors, *Sweden* 10 E6
Amoy = Xiamen, *China* 59 E12
Ampanavoana, *Madag.* 89 B9
Ampang, *Malaysia* 65 L3
Ampangalana, Lakandranon', *Madag.* 89 C8
Ampanihy, *Madag.* 89 C7
Amparafaravola, *Madag.* 89 B8
Ampasinambo, *Madag.* 89 C8
Ampasindava, Helodranon', *Madag.* 89 A8
Ampasindava, Saikanosy, *Madag.* 89 A8
Ampenan, *Indonesia* 62 F5
Amper, *Nigeria* 83 D6
Amper →, *Germany* 25 G7
Ampezzo, *Italy* 29 B9
Ampitsikinana, *Réunion* 89 A8
Ampombiantambo, *Madag.* 89 A8
Amposta, *Spain* 32 E5
Ampotaka, *Madag.* 89 D7
Ampoza, *Madag.* 89 C7
Amqui, *Canada* 103 C6
Amravati, *India* 66 J10
Amreli, *India* 68 J4
Amritsar, *India* 68 D6
Amroha, *India* 69 E8
Amrum, *Germany* 24 A4
Amsterdam, *Neths.* 17 B4
Amsterdam, *U.S.A.* 111 D10
Amsterdam, I. = Nouvelle-Amsterdam, I., *Ind. Oc.* 3 F13
Amstetten, *Austria* 26 C7
Amudarya →, *Uzbekistan* 50 E6
Amundsen Gulf, *Canada* 100 A7
Amundsen Sea, *Antarctica* 5 D15
Amungen, *Sweden* 10 C9
Amuntai, *Indonesia* 62 E5
Amur →, *Russia* 51 D15
Amur, W. →, *Sudan* 80 D3

Amurang, *Indonesia* 63 D6
Amurrio, *Spain* 32 B1
Amursk, *Russia* 51 D14
Amusco, *Spain* 34 C6
Amvrakikós Kólpos, *Greece* 38 C2
Amvrosiyivka, *Ukraine* 47 J10
Amyderya = Amudarya →, *Uzbekistan* 50 E6
An Bien, *Vietnam* 65 H5
An Hoa, *Vietnam* 64 E7
An Nabatīyah at Tahta, *Lebanon* 75 B4
An Nabk, *Si. Arabia* 70 D3
An Nabk, *Syria* 75 A5
An Nafūd, *Si. Arabia* 70 D4
An Najaf, *Iraq* 70 C5
An Nāṣirīyah, *Iraq* 70 D5
An Nhon, *Vietnam* 64 F7
An Nîl □, *Sudan* 80 D3
An Nîl el Abyad □, *Sudan* 81 E3
An Nîl el Azraq □, *Sudan* 81 E3
An Nu'ayrīyah, *Si. Arabia* 71 E6
An Nu'mānīyah, *Iraq* 73 F11
An Nuwayb'ī, W. →, *Si. Arabia* 75 F3
An Thoi, Dao, *Vietnam* 65 H4
An Uaimh, *Ireland* 15 C5
Anabar →, *Russia* 51 B12
'Anabtā, *West Bank* 75 C4
Anaconda, *U.S.A.* 114 C7
Anacortes, *U.S.A.* 116 B4
Anacuao, Mt., *Phil.* 61 C4
Anadarko, *U.S.A.* 113 H5
Anadia, *Portugal* 34 E2
Anadolu, *Turkey* 72 C5
Anadyr, *Russia* 51 C18
Anadyr →, *Russia* 51 C18
Anadyrskiy Zaliv, *Russia* 51 C19
Anáfi, *Greece* 39 E7
Anafópoulo, *Greece* 39 E7
Anaga, Pta. de, *Canary Is.* 37 F3
Anagni, *Italy* 29 G10
'Ānah, *Iraq* 70 C4
Anaheim, *U.S.A.* 117 M9
Anahim Lake, *Canada* 104 C3
Anáhuac, *Mexico* 118 B4
Anakapalle, *India* 67 L13
Anakie, *Australia* 94 C4
Anaklia, *Georgia* 49 J5
Analalava, *Madag.* 89 A8
Analavoka, *Madag.* 89 C8
Análipsis, *Greece* 36 A3
Anambar →, *Pakistan* 68 D3
Anambas, Kepulauan, *Indonesia* 65 L6
Anambas Is. = Anambas, Kepulauan, *Indonesia* 65 L6
Anambra □, *Nigeria* 83 D6
Anamosa, *U.S.A.* 112 D9
Anamur, *Turkey* 70 B2
Anamur Burnu, *Turkey* 72 D5
Anan, *Japan* 55 H7
Anand, *India* 68 H5
Anánes, *Greece* 38 E6
Anantnag, *India* 69 C6
Ananyiv, *Ukraine* 47 J5
Anapa, *Russia* 47 K9
Anapodháris →, *Greece* 36 E7
Anápolis, *Brazil* 125 G9
Anapu →, *Brazil* 125 D8
Anār, *Iran* 71 D7
Anārak, *Iran* 71 C7
Anarisfjällen, *Sweden* 10 A7
Anas →, *India* 68 H5
Anatolia = Anadolu, *Turkey* 72 C5
Anatsogno, *Madag.* 89 C7
Añatuya, *Argentina* 126 B3
Anaunethad L., *Canada* 105 A8
Anbyŏn, *N. Korea* 57 E14
Ancares, Sierra de, *Spain* 34 C4
Ancaster, *Canada* 110 C5
Ancenis, *France* 18 E5
Anchor Bay, *U.S.A.* 116 G3
Anchorage, *U.S.A.* 100 B5
Anci, *China* 56 E9
Ancohuma, Nevada, *Bolivia* 122 E4
Ancón, *Peru* 124 F3
Ancona, *Italy* 29 E10
Ancud, *Chile* 128 E2
Ancud, G. de, *Chile* 128 E2
Ancy-le-Franc, *France* 19 E11
Andacollo, *Argentina* 126 D1
Andacollo, *Chile* 126 C1
Andaingo, *Madag.* 89 B8
Andalgalá, *Argentina* 126 B2
Åndalsnes, *Norway* 9 E12
Andalucía □, *Spain* 35 H6
Andalusia = Andalucía □, *Spain* 35 H6
Andalusia, *U.S.A.* 109 K2
Andaman Is., *Ind. Oc.* 52 H13
Andaman Sea, *Ind. Oc.* 62 B1
Andamooka Opal Fields, *Australia* 95 E2
Andapa, *Madag.* 89 A8
Andara, *Namibia* 88 B3
Andelot-Blancheville, *France* 19 D12
Andenes, *Norway* 8 B17
Andenne, *Belgium* 17 D5
Andéranboukane, *Mali* 83 B5
Andermatt, *Switz.* 25 J4
Andernach, *Germany* 24 E3
Andernos-les-Bains, *France* 20 D2
Anderslöv, *Sweden* 11 J7
Anderson, *Alaska, U.S.A.* 100 B5
Anderson, *Calif., U.S.A.* 114 F2
Anderson, *Ind., U.S.A.* 108 E3
Anderson, *Mo., U.S.A.* 113 G7
Anderson, *S.C., U.S.A.* 109 H4
Anderson →, *Canada* 100 B7
Anderstorp, *Sweden* 11 G7
Andes, *U.S.A.* 111 D10
Andes, Cord. de los, *S. Amer.* 122 F4
Andfjorden, *Norway* 8 B17
Andhra Pradesh □, *India* 66 L11
Andijon, *Uzbekistan* 50 E8
Andikíthira, *Greece* 38 F5
Andilamena, *Madag.* 89 B8
Andīmeshk, *Iran* 71 C6
Andímilos, *Greece* 38 E6
Andíparos, *Greece* 39 D7
Andípaxoi, *Greece* 38 B2
Andípsara, *Greece* 39 C7
Andírrion, *Greece* 38 C3
Andizhan = Andijon, *Uzbekistan* 50 E8
Andoain, *Spain* 32 B2
Andoany, *Madag.* 89 A8
Andong, *S. Korea* 57 F15
Andongwei, *China* 57 G10
Andoom, *Australia* 94 A3
Andorra, *Spain* 32 E4
Andorra ■, *Europe* 20 F5
Andorra La Vella, *Andorra* 20 F5
Andover, *U.K.* 13 F6
Andover, *Maine, U.S.A.* 111 B14
Andover, *Mass., U.S.A.* 111 D13
Andover, *N.J., U.S.A.* 111 F10
Andover, *N.Y., U.S.A.* 110 D7
Andover, *Ohio, U.S.A.* 110 E4
Andøya, *Norway* 8 B16
Andradina, *Brazil* 125 H8
Andrahary, Mt., *Madag.* 89 A8
Andramasina, *Madag.* 89 B8
Andranopasy, *Madag.* 89 C7
Andranovory, *Madag.* 89 C7
Andratx, *Spain* 37 B9
Andreanof Is., *U.S.A.* 100 C2
Andreapol, *Russia* 46 D7
Andrews, *S.C., U.S.A.* 109 J6
Andrews, *Tex., U.S.A.* 113 J3
Andreyevka, *Russia* 48 D10
Ándria, *Italy* 31 A9
Andriamena, *Madag.* 89 B8
Andriandampy, *Madag.* 89 C8
Andriba, *Madag.* 89 B8
Andrijevica, *Montenegro, Yug.* 40 D3
Andrítsaina, *Greece* 38 D3
Androka, *Madag.* 89 C7
Andropov = Rybinsk, *Russia* 46 C10
Ándros, *Greece* 38 D6
Andros I., *Bahamas* 120 B4
Andros Town, *Bahamas* 120 B4
Androscoggin →, *U.S.A.* 111 C14
Andrychów, *Poland* 45 J6
Andselv, *Norway* 8 B18
Andújar, *Spain* 35 G6
Andulo, *Angola* 84 G3
Aneby, *Sweden* 11 G8
Anegada I., *U.S. Virgin Is.* 121 C7
Anegada Passage, *W. Indies* 121 C7
Anécho, *Togo* 83 D5
Anenni-Noi, *Moldova* 43 D14
Aneto, Pico de, *Spain* 32 C5
Anfu, *China* 59 D10
Ang Thong, *Thailand* 64 E3
Angamos, Punta, *Chile* 126 A1
Angara →, *Russia* 51 D10
Angara-Débou, *Benin* 83 C5
Angarab, *Ethiopia* 81 E4
Angarbaka, *Sudan* 81 F1
Angarsk, *Russia* 51 D11
Angas Hills, *Australia* 92 D4
Angaston, *Australia* 95 E2
Angaur I., *Pac. Oc.* 63 C8
Ånge, *Sweden* 10 B9
Ángel, Salto = Angel Falls, *Venezuela* 124 B6
Ángel de la Guarda, I., *Mexico* 118 B2
Angel Falls, *Venezuela* 124 B6
Angeles, *Phil.* 61 D4
Ängelholm, *Sweden* 11 H6
Angels Camp, *U.S.A.* 116 G6
Ängelsberg, *Sweden* 10 E10
Anger →, *Ethiopia* 81 F4
Angereb →, *Ethiopia* 81 E4
Ångermanälven →, *Sweden* 10 B11
Ångermanland, *Sweden* 8 E18
Angermünde, *Germany* 24 B9
Angers, *Canada* 111 A9
Angers, *France* 18 E6
Angerville, *France* 19 D9
Ängesån →, *Sweden* 8 C20
Angikuni L., *Canada* 105 A9
Angkor, *Cambodia* 64 F4
Anglès, *Spain* 32 D7
Anglesey, Isle of □, *U.K.* 12 D3
Anglet, *France* 20 E2
Angleton, *U.S.A.* 113 L7
Anglin →, *France* 20 B4
Anglisidhes, *Cyprus* 36 E12
Anglure, *France* 19 D10
Angmagssalik = Tasiilaq, *Greenland* 4 C6
Ango, *Dem. Rep. of the Congo* 86 B2
Angoche, *Mozam.* 87 F4
Angoche, I., *Mozam.* 87 F4
Angol, *Chile* 126 D1
Angola, *Ind., U.S.A.* 108 E3
Angola, *N.Y., U.S.A.* 110 D5
Angola ■, *Africa* 85 G3
Angoulême, *France* 20 C4
Angoumois, *France* 20 C4
Angra dos Reis, *Brazil* 127 A7
Angren, *Uzbekistan* 50 E8
Angtassom, *Cambodia* 65 G5
Angu, *Dem. Rep. of the Congo* 86 B1
Anguang, *China* 57 B12
Anguilla ■, *W. Indies* 121 C7
Anguo, *China* 56 E8
Angurugu, *Australia* 94 A2
Angus □, *U.K.* 14 E6
Angwa →, *Zimbabwe* 89 B5
Anhanduí →, *Brazil* 127 A5
Anholt, *Denmark* 11 H5
Anhua, *China* 59 C8
Anhui □, *China* 59 B11
Anhwei = Anhui □, *China* 59 B11
Anichab, *Namibia* 88 C1
Ánidhros, *Greece* 39 E7
Anié, *Togo* 83 D5
Animas →, *U.S.A.* 115 H9
Anina, *Romania* 42 E6
Aninoasa, *Romania* 43 F9
Anivorano, *Madag.* 89 B8
Anjalankoski, *Finland* 9 F22
Anjar, *India* 68 H4
Anji, *China* 59 B12
Anjou, *France* 18 E6
Anjozorobe, *Madag.* 89 B8
Anju, *N. Korea* 57 E13
Anka, *Nigeria* 83 C6
Ankaboa, Tanjona, *Madag.* 89 C7
Ankang, *China* 56 H5
Ankara, *Turkey* 72 C5
Ankaramena, *Madag.* 89 C8
Ankaratra, *Madag.* 85 H9
Ankarsrum, *Sweden* 11 G10
Ankasakasa, *Madag.* 89 B7
Ankavandra, *Madag.* 89 B8
Ankazoabo, *Madag.* 89 C7
Ankazobe, *Madag.* 89 B8
Ankeny, *U.S.A.* 112 E8
Ankilimalinika, *Madag.* 89 C7
Ankilizato, *Madag.* 89 C8
Ankisabe, *Madag.* 89 B8
Anklam, *Germany* 24 B9
Ankober, *Ethiopia* 81 F4
Ankoro, *Dem. Rep. of the Congo* 86 D2
Ankororoka, *Madag.* 89 D8
Anlong, *China* 58 E5
Anlu, *China* 59 B9
Anmyŏn-do, *S. Korea* 57 F14
Ånn, *Sweden* 10 A6
Ann, C., *U.S.A.* 111 D14
Ann Arbor, *U.S.A.* 108 D4
Anna, *Russia* 48 E5
Anna, *U.S.A.* 113 G10
Annaba, *Algeria* 78 A7
Annaberg-Buchholz, *Germany* 24 E9
Annalee →, *Ireland* 15 B4
Annam, *Vietnam* 64 E7
Annamitique, Chaîne, *Asia* 64 D6
Annan, *U.K.* 14 G5
Annan →, *U.K.* 14 G5
Annapolis, *U.S.A.* 108 F7
Annapolis Royal, *Canada* 103 D6
Annapurna, *Nepal* 69 E10
Annean, L., *Australia* 93 E2
Anneberg, *Sweden* 11 G8
Annecy, *France* 21 C10
Annecy, Lac d', *France* 21 C10
Annemasse, *France* 19 F13
Annenskiy Most, *Russia* 46 B9
Anning, *China* 58 E4
Anniston, *U.S.A.* 109 J3
Annobón, *Atl. Oc.* 77 G4
Annonay, *France* 21 C8
Annot, *France* 21 E10
Annotto Bay, *Jamaica* 120 C4
Ånnsjön, *Sweden* 10 A6
Annville, *U.S.A.* 111 F8
Annweiler, *Germany* 25 F3
Áno Arkhánai, *Greece* 39 F7
Áno Porróia, *Greece* 40 E7
Áno Síros, *Greece* 38 D6
Áno Viánnos, *Greece* 36 D7
Anorotsangana, *Madag.* 89 A8
Anosibe, *Madag.* 89 B8
Anou Mellene, *Mali* 83 B5
Anoumaba, *Ivory C.* 82 D4
Anóyia, *Greece* 36 D6
Anping, *Hebei, China* 56 E8
Anping, *Liaoning, China* 57 D12
Anpu Gang, *China* 58 G7
Anqing, *China* 59 B11
Anqiu, *China* 57 F10
Anren, *China* 59 D9
Ansager, *Denmark* 11 J2
Ansai, *China* 56 F5
Ansbach, *Germany* 25 F6
Anseba →, *Eritrea* 81 D4
Ansfelden, *Austria* 26 C7
Anshan, *China* 57 D12
Anshun, *China* 58 D5
Ansião, *Portugal* 34 F2
Ansley, *U.S.A.* 112 E5
Ansó, *Spain* 32 C4
Ansoain, *Spain* 32 C3
Anson, *U.S.A.* 113 J5
Anson B., *Australia* 92 B5
Ansongo, *Mali* 83 B5
Ansonia, *U.S.A.* 111 E11
Anstruther, *U.K.* 14 E6
Ansudu, *Indonesia* 63 E9
Antabamba, *Peru* 124 F4
Antakya, *Turkey* 70 B3
Antalaha, *Madag.* 89 A9
Antalya, *Turkey* 72 D4
Antalya □, *Turkey* 39 E12
Antalya Körfezi, *Turkey* 72 D4
Antambohobe, *Madag.* 89 C8
Antanambao-Manampotsy, *Madag.* 89 B8
Antanambe, *Madag.* 89 B8
Antananarivo, *Madag.* 89 B8
Antananarivo □, *Madag.* 89 B8
Antanifotsy, *Madag.* 89 B8
Antanimbaribe, *Madag.* 89 C7
Antanimora, *Madag.* 89 C8
Antarctic Pen., *Antarctica* 5 C18
Antarctica 5 E3
Antelope, *Zimbabwe* 87 G2
Antequera, *Paraguay* 126 A4
Antequera, *Spain* 35 H6
Antero, Mt., *U.S.A.* 115 G10
Antevamena, *Madag.* 89 C7
Anthemoús, *Greece* 40 F7
Anthony, *Kans., U.S.A.* 113 G5
Anthony, *N. Mex., U.S.A.* 115 K10
Anti Atlas, *Morocco* 78 C4
Anti-Lebanon = Ash Sharqi, Al Jabal, *Lebanon* 75 B5
Antibes, *France* 21 E11
Antibes, C. d', *France* 21 E11
Anticosti, Î. d', *Canada* 103 C7
Antifer, C. d', *France* 18 C7
Antigo, *U.S.A.* 112 C10
Antigonish, *Canada* 103 C7
Antigua, *Canary Is.* 37 F5
Antigua, *W. Indies* 121 C7
Antigua & Barbuda ■, *W. Indies* 121 C7
Antigua Guatemala, *Guatemala* 120 D1
Antilla, *Cuba* 120 B4
Antilles = West Indies, *Cent. Amer.* 121 D7
Antioch, *U.S.A.* 116 G5
Antioche, Pertuis d', *France* 20 B2
Antioquia, *Colombia* 124 B3
Antipodes Is., *Pac. Oc.* 96 M9
Antlers, *U.S.A.* 113 H7
Antoetra, *Madag.* 89 C8
Antofagasta, *Chile* 126 A1
Antofagasta □, *Chile* 126 A2
Antofagasta de la Sierra, *Argentina* 126 B2
Antofalla, *Argentina* 126 B2
Antofalla, Salar de, *Argentina* 126 B2
Anton, *U.S.A.* 113 J3
Antongila, Helodrano, *Madag.* 89 B8
Antonibé, *Madag.* 89 B8
Antonibé, Presqu'île d', *Madag.* 89 A8
Antonina, *Brazil* 127 B6
Antrain, *France* 18 D5
Antrim, *U.K.* 15 B5
Antrim, *U.S.A.* 110 F3
Antrim □, *U.K.* 15 B5
Antrim, Mts. of, *U.K.* 15 A5
Antrim Plateau, *Australia* 92 C4
Antrodoco, *Italy* 29 F10
Antropovo, *Russia* 48 A6
Antsakabary, *Madag.* 89 B8
Antsalova, *Madag.* 89 B7
Antsenavolo, *Madag.* 89 C8
Antsiafabositra, *Madag.* 89 B8
Antsirabe, *Antananarivo, Madag.* 89 B8
Antsirabe, *Antsiranana, Madag.* 89 A8
Antsirabe, *Mahajanga, Madag.* 89 B8
Antsiranana, *Madag.* 89 A8
Antsiranana □, *Madag.* 89 A8
Antsohihy, *Madag.* 89 A8
Antsohimbondrona Seranana, *Madag.* 89 A8
Antu, *China* 57 C15
Antwerp = Antwerpen, *Belgium* 17 C4
Antwerp, *U.S.A.* 111 B9
Antwerpen, *Belgium* 17 C4
Antwerpen □, *Belgium* 17 C4
Anupgarh, *India* 68 E5
Anuppur, *India* 69 H9
Anuradhapura, *Sri Lanka* 66 Q12
Anveh, *Iran* 71 E7
Anvers = Antwerpen, *Belgium* 17 C4
Anvers I., *Antarctica* 5 C17
Anwen, *China* 59 C13
Anxi, *Fujian, China* 59 E12
Anxi, *Gansu, China* 60 B4
Anxian, *China* 58 B5
Anxiang, *China* 59 C9
Anxious B., *Australia* 95 E1
Anyama, *Ivory C.* 82 D4
Anyang, *China* 56 F8
Anyer-Kidul, *Indonesia* 63 G11
Anyi, *Jiangxi, China* 59 C10
Anyi, *Shanxi, China* 56 G6
Anyuan, *China* 59 E10
Anyue, *China* 58 B5
Anza, *U.S.A.* 117 M10
Anze, *China* 56 F7
Anzhero-Sudzhensk, *Russia* 50 D9
Ánzio, *Italy* 30 A5
Aoga-Shima, *Japan* 55 H9
Aoiz, *Spain* 32 C3
Aomen = Macau □, *China* 59 F9
Aomori, *Japan* 54 D10
Aomori □, *Japan* 54 D10
Aonla, *India* 69 E8
Aoraki Mount Cook, *N.Z.* 91 K3
Aosta, *Italy* 28 C4
Aoudéras, *Niger* 83 B6
Aoukâr, *Mauritania* 82 B3
Apa →, *S. Amer.* 126 A4
Apache, *U.S.A.* 113 H5
Apache Junction, *U.S.A.* 115 K8
Apalachee B., *U.S.A.* 109 L4
Apalachicola, *U.S.A.* 109 L3
Apalachicola →, *U.S.A.* 109 L3
Apam, *Ghana* 83 D4
Apapa, *Nigeria* 83 D5
Apaporis →, *Colombia* 124 D5
Aparri, *Phil.* 61 B4
Apateu, *Romania* 42 D6
Apatin, *Serbia, Yug.* 42 E4
Apatity, *Russia* 50 C4
Apatzingán, *Mexico* 118 D4
Apeldoorn, *Neths.* 17 B5
Apen, *Germany* 24 B3
Apennines = Appennini, *Italy* 28 E7
Aphrodisias, *Turkey* 39 D10
Apia, *Samoa* 91 A13
Apiacás, Serra dos, *Brazil* 124 E7
Apies →, *S. Africa* 89 D4
Apizaco, *Mexico* 119 D5
Aplao, *Peru* 124 G4
Apo, Mt., *Phil.* 63 C7
Apolakkiá, *Greece* 36 C9
Apolakkiá, Órmos, *Greece* 36 C9
Apolda, *Germany* 24 D7
Apollonia, *Greece* 38 E6
Apolo, *Bolivia* 124 F5
Aporé →, *Brazil* 125 G8
Apostle Is., *U.S.A.* 112 B9
Apóstoles, *Argentina* 127 B4
Apostolos Andreas, C., *Cyprus* 36 D13
Apostolovo, *Ukraine* 47 J7
Apoteri, *Guyana* 124 C7
Appalachian Mts., *U.S.A.* 108 G6
Äppelbo, *Sweden* 10 D8
Appennini, *Italy* 28 E7
Appennino Ligure, *Italy* 28 D6
Appenzell-Ausser Rhoden □, *Switz.* 25 H5
Appenzell-Inner Rhoden □, *Switz.* 25 H5
Appiano, *Italy* 29 B8
Apple Hill, *Canada* 111 A10
Apple Valley, *U.S.A.* 117 L9
Appleby-in-Westmorland, *U.K.* 12 C5
Appleton, *U.S.A.* 108 C1
Approuague →, *Fr. Guiana* 125 C8
Apricena, *Italy* 29 G12
Aprília, *Italy* 30 A5
Apsheronsk, *Russia* 49 H4
Apsley, *Canada* 110 B6
Apt, *France* 21 E9
Apuane, Alpi, *Italy* 28 D7
Apucarana, *Brazil* 127 A5
Apulia = Púglia □, *Italy* 31 A9
Apure →, *Venezuela* 124 B5
Apurimac →, *Peru* 124 F4
Apuseni, Munţii, *Romania* 42 D7
Āqā Jarī, *Iran* 71 D6
Aqaba = Al 'Aqabah, *Jordan* 75 F4
Aqaba, G. of, *Red Sea* 70 D2
'Aqabah, Khalīj al = Aqaba, G. of, *Red Sea* 70 D2
'Aqdā, *Iran* 71 C7
Aqîq, *Sudan* 80 D4
Aqîq, Khalîg, *Sudan* 80 D4
Aqmola = Astana, *Kazakstan* 50 D8
'Aqrah, *Iraq* 70 B4
Aqtaū, *Kazakstan* 50 E6
Aqtöbe, *Kazakstan* 50 D6
Aquidauana, *Brazil* 125 H7
Aquiles Serdán, *Mexico* 118 B3
Aquin, *Haiti* 121 C5
Aquitaine □, *France* 20 D3
Aqviligjuaq = Pelly Bay, *Canada* 101 B11
Ar Rachidiya = Er Rachidia, *Morocco* 78 B5
Ar Rafīd, *Syria* 75 C4
Ar Raḥḥālīyah, *Iraq* 70 C4
Ar Ramādī, *Iraq* 70 C4
Ar Ramthā, *Jordan* 75 C5
Ar Raqqah, *Syria* 70 C3
Ar Rass, *Si. Arabia* 70 E4
Ar Rawshān, *Si. Arabia* 80 C5
Ar Rifā'ī, *Iraq* 70 D5
Ar Riyāḍ, *Si. Arabia* 70 E5
Ar Ru'ays, *Qatar* 71 E6
Ar Rukhaymīyah, *Iraq* 70 D5
Ar Ruṣāfah, *Syria* 70 C3
Ar Ruṭbah, *Iraq* 70 C4
Ara, *India* 69 G11
Ara Goro, *Ethiopia* 81 F5
Ara Tera, *Ethiopia* 81 F5
'Arab, *U.S.A.* 109 H2
'Arab, Bahr el →, *Sudan* 81 F2
Arab, Khalîg el, *Egypt* 80 A2
Arab, Shatt al →, *Asia* 71 D6
'Araba, W. →, *Egypt* 80 J8
'Arabābād, *Iran* 71 C8
Araban, *Turkey* 72 D7
Arabatskaya Strelka, *Ukraine* 47 K8
Arabba, *Italy* 29 B8
Arabia, *Asia* 52 G8
Arabian Desert = Es Sahrâ' Esh Sharqîya, *Egypt* 80 B3
Arabian Gulf = Gulf, The, *Asia* 71 E6
Arabian Sea, *Ind. Oc.* 52 H10
Araç, *Turkey* 72 B5
Aracaju, *Brazil* 125 F11
Aracati, *Brazil* 125 D11
Araçatuba, *Brazil* 127 A5
Aracena, *Spain* 35 H4
Aracena, Sierra de, *Spain* 35 H4
Aračinovo, *Macedonia* 40 D5
Araçuaí, *Brazil* 125 G10
'Arad, *Israel* 75 D4
Arad, *Romania* 42 D6
Arad □, *Romania* 42 D6
Arādān, *Iran* 71 C7
Aradhippou, *Cyprus* 36 E12
Arafura Sea, *E. Indies* 52 K17
Aragats, *Armenia* 49 K7
Aragón □, *Spain* 32 D4
Aragón →, *Spain* 32 C3
Aragona, *Italy* 30 E6

Araguacema, *Brazil* 125 E9
Araguaia →, *Brazil* 122 D6
Araguaína, *Brazil* 125 E9
Araguari, *Brazil* 125 G9
Araguari →, *Brazil* 125 C9
Arain, *India* 68 F6
Arak, *Algeria* 78 C6
Arāk, *Iran* 71 C6
Araka, *Sudan* 81 G3
Arakan Coast, *Burma* 67 K19
Arakan Yoma, *Burma* 67 K19
Arákhova, *Greece* 38 C4
Arakli, *Turkey* 73 B8
Araks = Aras, Rūd-e →, *Asia* 49 K9
Aral, *Kazakstan* 50 E7
Aral Sea, *Asia* 50 E7
Aral Tengizi = Aral Sea, *Asia* 50 E7
Aralsk = Aral, *Kazakstan* 50 E7
Aralskoye More = Aral Sea, *Asia* 50 E7
Aralsor, Ozero, *Kazakstan* 49 F9
Aramac, *Australia* 94 C4
Aran I., *Ireland* 15 A3
Aran Is., *Ireland* 15 C2
Aranda de Duero, *Spain* 34 D7
Arandān, *Iran* 70 C5
Aranđelovac, *Serbia, Yug.* 40 B4
Aranjuez, *Spain* 34 E7
Aranos, *Namibia* 88 C2
Aransas Pass, *U.S.A.* 113 M6
Aranyaprathet, *Thailand* 64 F4
Araouane, *Mali* 82 B4
Arapahoe, *U.S.A.* 112 E5
Arapey Grande →, *Uruguay* 126 C4
Arapgir, *Turkey* 70 B3
Arapiraca, *Brazil* 125 E11
Arapongas, *Brazil* 127 A5
Ar'ar, *Si. Arabia* 70 D4
Araranguá, *Brazil* 127 B6
Araraquara, *Brazil* 125 H9
Ararás, Serra das, *Brazil* 127 B5
Ararat, *Armenia* 73 C11
Ararat, *Australia* 95 F3
Ararat, Mt. = Ağrı Dağı, *Turkey* 70 B5
Araria, *India* 69 F12
Araripe, Chapada do, *Brazil* 125 E11
Araruama, L. de, *Brazil* 127 A7
Aras, Rūd-e →, *Asia* 49 K9
Aratāne, *Mauritania* 82 B3
Arauca, *Colombia* 124 B4
Arauca →, *Venezuela* 124 B5
Arauco, *Chile* 126 D1
Arawa, *Ethiopia* 81 F5
Araxá, *Brazil* 125 G9
Araya, Pen. de, *Venezuela* 124 A6
Arba Gugu, *Ethiopia* 81 F5
Arba Minch, *Ethiopia* 81 F4
Arbat, *Iraq* 70 C5
Árbatax, *Italy* 30 C2
Arbi, *Ethiopia* 81 F4
Arbīl, *Iraq* 70 B5
Arboga, *Sweden* 10 E9
Arbois, *France* 19 F12
Arbore, *Ethiopia* 81 F4
Arboréa, *Italy* 30 C1
Arborfield, *Canada* 105 C8
Arborg, *Canada* 105 C9
Arbre du Ténéré, *Niger* 83 B7
Arbroath, *U.K.* 14 E6
Arbuckle, *U.S.A.* 116 F4
Arbus, *Italy* 30 C1
Arc →, *France* 21 C10
Arc-lès-Gray, *France* 19 E12
Arcachon, *France* 20 D2
Arcachon, Bassin d', *France* 20 D2
Arcade, *Calif., U.S.A.* 117 L8
Arcade, *N.Y., U.S.A.* 110 D6
Arcadia, *Fla., U.S.A.* 109 M5
Arcadia, *La., U.S.A.* 113 J8
Arcadia, *Pa., U.S.A.* 110 F6
Arcata, *U.S.A.* 114 F1
Arcévia, *Italy* 29 E9
Archangel = Arkhangelsk, *Russia* 50 C5
Archar, *Bulgaria* 40 C6
Archbald, *U.S.A.* 111 E9
Archena, *Spain* 33 G3
Archer →, *Australia* 94 A3
Archer B., *Australia* 94 A3
Archers Post, *Kenya* 86 B4
Arches National Park, *U.S.A.* 115 G9
Archidona, *Spain* 35 H6
Arci, Mte., *Italy* 30 C1
Arcidosso, *Italy* 29 F8
Arcis-sur-Aube, *France* 19 D11
Arckaringa Cr. →, *Australia* 95 D2
Arco, *Italy* 28 C7
Arco, *U.S.A.* 114 E7
Arcos = Arcos de Jalón, *Spain* 32 D2
Arcos de Jalón, *Spain* 32 D2
Arcos de la Frontera, *Spain* 35 J5
Arcos de Valdevez, *Portugal* 34 D2
Arcot, *India* 66 N11
Arcozelo, *Portugal* 34 E3
Arctic Bay, *Canada* 101 A11
Arctic Ocean, *Arctic* 4 B18
Arctic Red River = Tsiigehtchic, *Canada* 100 B6
Arda →, *Bulgaria* 41 E10
Arda →, *Italy* 28 C7
Ardabīl, *Iran* 71 B6
Ardahan, *Turkey* 73 B10
Ardakān = Sepīdān, *Iran* 71 D7
Ardakān, *Iran* 71 C7
Ardala, *Sweden* 11 F7
Ardales, *Spain* 35 J6
Ardèche □, *France* 21 D8
Ardèche →, *France* 21 D8
Ardee, *Ireland* 15 C5
Arden, *Canada* 110 B8
Arden, *Denmark* 11 H3
Arden, *Calif., U.S.A.* 116 G5
Arden, *Nev., U.S.A.* 117 J11
Ardenne, *Belgium* 6 F7
Ardennes = Ardenne, *Belgium* 6 F7
Ardennes □, *France* 19 C11
Ardentes, *France* 19 F8
Arderin, *Ireland* 15 C4
Ardeşen, *Turkey* 73 B9
Ardestān, *Iran* 71 C7
Árdhas →, *Greece* 41 E10
Ardhéa, *Greece* 40 F6
Ardila →, *Portugal* 35 G3
Ardino, *Bulgaria* 41 E9
Ardivachar Pt., *U.K.* 14 D1
Ardlethan, *Australia* 95 E4
Ardmore, *Okla., U.S.A.* 113 H6
Ardmore, *Pa., U.S.A.* 111 G9
Ardnamurchan, Pt. of, *U.K.* 14 E2
Ardnave Pt., *U.K.* 14 F2
Ardon, *Russia* 49 J7
Ardore, *Italy* 31 D9
Ardres, *France* 19 B8
Ardrossan, *Australia* 95 E2
Ardrossan, *U.K.* 14 F4
Ards Pen., *U.K.* 15 B6
Arduan, *Sudan* 80 D3
Ardud, *Romania* 42 C7
Åre, *Sweden* 10 A7
Arecibo, *Puerto Rico* 121 C6
Areia Branca, *Brazil* 125 E11
Arena, Pt., *U.S.A.* 116 G3
Arenal, *Honduras* 120 C2
Arenas = Las Arenas, *Spain* 34 B6
Arenas de San Pedro, *Spain* 34 E5
Arendal, *Norway* 9 G13
Arendsee, *Germany* 24 C7
Arenys de Mar, *Spain* 32 D7
Arenzano, *Italy* 28 D5
Areópolis, *Greece* 38 E4
Arequipa, *Peru* 124 G4
Arero, *Ethiopia* 81 G4
Arès, *France* 20 D2
Arévalo, *Spain* 34 D6
Arezzo, *Italy* 29 E8
Arga, *Turkey* 70 B3
Arga →, *Spain* 32 C3
Argalastí, *Greece* 38 B5
Argamasilla de Alba, *Spain* 35 F7
Argamasilla de Calatrava, *Spain* 35 G6
Arganda, *Spain* 34 E7
Arganil, *Portugal* 34 E2
Argedeb, *Ethiopia* 81 F5
Argelès-Gazost, *France* 20 E3
Argelès-sur-Mer, *France* 20 F7
Argens →, *France* 21 E10
Argent-sur-Sauldre, *France* 19 E9
Argenta, *Canada* 104 C5
Argenta, *Italy* 29 D8
Argentan, *France* 18 D6
Argentário, Mte., *Italy* 29 F8
Argentat, *France* 20 C5
Argentera, *Italy* 28 D4
Argenteuil, *France* 19 D9
Argentia, *Canada* 103 C9
Argentiera, C. dell', *Italy* 30 B1
Argentina ■, *S. Amer.* 128 D3
Argentina Is., *Antarctica* 5 C17
Argentino, L., *Argentina* 128 G2
Argenton-Château, *France* 18 F6
Argenton-sur-Creuse, *France* 19 F8
Argeş □, *Romania* 43 F9
Argeş →, *Romania* 43 F11
Arghandab →, *Afghan.* 68 D1
Argheile, *Ethiopia* 81 F5
Argo, *Sudan* 80 D3
Argolikós Kólpos, *Greece* 38 D4
Argolís □, *Greece* 38 D4
Argonne, *France* 19 C12
Árgos, *Greece* 38 D4
Árgos Orestikón, *Greece* 40 F5
Argostólion, *Greece* 38 C2
Arguedas, *Spain* 32 C3
Arguello, Pt., *U.S.A.* 117 L6
Arguineguín, *Canary Is.* 37 G4
Argun, *Russia* 49 J7
Argun →, *Russia* 51 D13
Argungu, *Nigeria* 83 C5
Argus Pk., *U.S.A.* 117 K9
Argyle, L., *Australia* 92 C4
Argyll & Bute □, *U.K.* 14 E3
Arhavi, *Turkey* 73 B9
Århus, *Denmark* 11 H4
Århus Amtskommune □, *Denmark* 11 H4
Ariadnoye, *Russia* 54 B7
Ariamsvlei, *Namibia* 88 D2
Ariano Irpino, *Italy* 31 A8
Aribinda, *Burkina Faso* 83 C4
Arica, *Chile* 124 G4
Arica, *Colombia* 124 D4
Arico, *Canary Is.* 37 F3
Arid, C., *Australia* 93 F3
Arida, *Japan* 55 G7
Ariège □, *France* 20 F5
Ariège →, *France* 20 E5
Arieş →, *Romania* 43 D8
Arihā, *Israel* 80 A4
Arilje, *Serbia, Yug.* 40 C4
Arílla, Ákra, *Greece* 36 A3
Arima, *Trin. & Tob.* 121 D7
Arinos →, *Brazil* 122 E5
Ario de Rosales, *Mexico* 118 D4
Ariogala, *Lithuania* 44 C10
Aripuanã, *Brazil* 124 E6
Aripuanã →, *Brazil* 122 D4
Ariquemes, *Brazil* 124 E6
Arisaig, *U.K.* 14 E3
Arîsh, W. el →, *Egypt* 80 A3
Arissa, *Ethiopia* 81 E5
Aristazabal I., *Canada* 104 C3
Arivonimamo, *Madag.* 89 B8
Ariza, *Spain* 32 D2
Arizaro, Salar de, *Argentina* 126 A2
Arizona, *Argentina* 126 D2
Arizona □, *U.S.A.* 115 J8
Arizpe, *Mexico* 118 A2
Årjäng, *Sweden* 10 E6
Arjeplog, *Sweden* 8 D18
Arjona, *Colombia* 124 A3
Arjona, *Spain* 35 H6
Arjuna, *Indonesia* 63 G15
Arka, *Russia* 51 C15
Arkadak, *Russia* 48 E6
Arkadelphia, *U.S.A.* 113 H8
Arkadhía □, *Greece* 38 D4
Arkaig, L., *U.K.* 14 E3
Arkalyk = Arqalyk, *Kazakstan* 50 D7
Arkansas □, *U.S.A.* 113 H8
Arkansas →, *U.S.A.* 113 J9
Arkansas City, *U.S.A.* 113 G6
Arkaroola, *Australia* 95 E2
Árkathos →, *Greece* 38 B3
Arkhángelos, *Greece* 36 C10
Arkhangelsk, *Russia* 50 C5
Arkhangelskoye, *Russia* 48 E5
Arki, *India* 68 D7
Arkiko, *Eritrea* 81 D4
Arklow, *Ireland* 15 D5
Árkoi, *Greece* 39 D8
Arkona, Kap, *Germany* 24 A9
Arkösund, *Sweden* 11 F10
Arkoúdhi, *Greece* 38 C2
Arkport, *U.S.A.* 110 D7
Arkticheskiy, Mys, *Russia* 51 A10
Arkul, *Russia* 48 B10
Arkville, *U.S.A.* 111 D10
Årla, *Sweden* 10 E10
Arlanza →, *Spain* 34 C6
Arlanzón →, *Spain* 34 C6
Arlbergpass, *Austria* 26 D3
Arles, *France* 21 E8
Arlington, *S. Africa* 89 D4
Arlington, *N.Y., U.S.A.* 111 E11
Arlington, *Oreg., U.S.A.* 114 D3
Arlington, *S. Dak., U.S.A.* 112 C6
Arlington, *Tex., U.S.A.* 113 J6
Arlington, *Va., U.S.A.* 108 F7
Arlington, *Vt., U.S.A.* 111 C11
Arlington, *Wash., U.S.A.* 116 B4
Arlington Heights, *U.S.A.* 108 D2
Arlit, *Niger* 78 E7
Arlon, *Belgium* 17 E5
Arltunga, *Australia* 94 C1
Arly, *Burkina Faso* 83 C5
Armagh, *U.K.* 15 B5
Armagh □, *U.K.* 15 B5
Armagnac, *France* 20 E4
Armançon →, *France* 19 E10
Armavir, *Russia* 49 H5
Armenia, *Colombia* 124 C3
Armenia ■, *Asia* 49 K7
Armeniş, *Romania* 42 E7
Armenistís, Ákra, *Greece* 36 C9
Armentières, *France* 19 B9
Armidale, *Australia* 95 E5
Armilla, *Spain* 35 H7
Armour, *U.S.A.* 112 D5
Armstrong, *B.C., Canada* 104 C5
Armstrong, *Ont., Canada* 102 B2
Armutlu, *Bursa, Turkey* 41 F12
Armutlu, *İzmir, Turkey* 39 C9
Arnaía, *Greece* 40 F7
Arnarfjörður, *Iceland* 8 D2
Arnaud →, *Canada* 101 B12
Arnauti, C., *Cyprus* 36 D11
Arnay-le-Duc, *France* 19 E11
Arnedillo, *Spain* 32 C2
Arnedo, *Spain* 32 C2
Arnett, *U.S.A.* 113 G5
Arnhem, *Neths.* 17 C5
Arnhem, C., *Australia* 94 A2
Arnhem B., *Australia* 94 A2
Arnhem Land, *Australia* 94 A1
Árnissa, *Greece* 40 F5
Arno →, *Italy* 28 E7
Arno Bay, *Australia* 95 E2
Arnold, *U.K.* 12 D6
Arnold, *U.S.A.* 116 G6
Arnoldstein, *Austria* 26 E6
Arnon →, *France* 19 E9
Arnot, *Canada* 105 B9
Arnøy, *Norway* 8 A19
Arnprior, *Canada* 102 C4
Arnsberg, *Germany* 24 D4
Arnstadt, *Germany* 24 E6
Aroab, *Namibia* 88 D2
Aroánia Óri, *Greece* 38 D4
Aroche, *Spain* 35 H4
Arochuku, *Nigeria* 83 D6
Arolsen, *Germany* 24 D5
Aron, *India* 68 G6
Aron →, *France* 19 F10
Arona, *Italy* 28 C5
Aroroy, *Phil.* 61 E5
Arosa, Ría de, *Spain* 34 C2
Arpajon, *France* 19 D9
Arpajon-sur-Cère, *France* 20 D6
Arpaşu de Jos, *Romania* 43 E9
Arqalyk, *Kazakstan* 50 D7
Arrah = Ara, *India* 69 G11
Arrah, *Ivory C.* 82 D4
Arraiolos, *Portugal* 35 G3
Arran, *U.K.* 14 F3
Arras, *France* 19 B9
Arrasate, *Spain* 32 B2
Arrats →, *France* 20 D4
Arreau, *France* 20 F4
Arrecife, *Canary Is.* 37 F6
Arrecifes, *Argentina* 126 C3
Arrée, Mts. d', *France* 18 D3
Arresø, *Denmark* 11 J6
Arriaga, *Chiapas, Mexico* 119 D6
Arriaga, *San Luis Potosí, Mexico* 118 C4
Arrilalah, *Australia* 94 C3
Arrino, *Australia* 93 E2
Arriondas, *Spain* 34 B5
Arromanches-les-Bains, *France* 18 C6
Arronches, *Portugal* 35 F3
Arros →, *France* 20 E3
Arrow, L., *Ireland* 15 B3
Arrowhead, L., *U.S.A.* 117 L9
Arrowtown, *N.Z.* 91 L2
Arroyo de la Luz, *Spain* 35 F4
Arroyo Grande, *U.S.A.* 117 K6
Års, *Denmark* 11 H3
Ars, *Iran* 70 B5
Ars-sur-Moselle, *France* 19 C13
Arsenault L., *Canada* 105 B7
Arsenev, *Russia* 54 B6
Arsi □, *Ethiopia* 81 F4
Arsiero, *Italy* 29 C8
Arsin, *Turkey* 73 B8
Arsk, *Russia* 48 B9
Årsunda, *Sweden* 10 D10
Árta, *Greece* 38 B3
Artà, *Spain* 37 B10
Árta □, *Greece* 38 B3
Arteaga, *Mexico* 118 D4
Arteche, *Phil.* 61 E6
Arteijo = Arteixo, *Spain* 34 B2
Arteixo, *Spain* 34 B2
Artem = Artyom, *Azerbaijan* 49 K10
Artem, *Russia* 54 C6
Artemovsk, *Russia* 51 D10
Artemovsk, *Ukraine* 47 H9
Artemovskiy, *Russia* 49 G5
Artenay, *France* 19 D8
Artern, *Germany* 24 D7
Artesa de Segre, *Spain* 32 D6
Artesia = Mosomane, *Botswana* 88 C4
Artesia, *U.S.A.* 113 J2
Arthington, *Liberia* 82 D2
Arthur, *Canada* 110 C4
Arthur →, *Australia* 94 G3
Arthur Cr. →, *Australia* 94 C2
Arthur Pt., *Australia* 94 C5
Arthur River, *Australia* 93 F2
Arthur's Pass, *N.Z.* 91 K3
Arthur's Town, *Bahamas* 121 B4
Artigas, *Uruguay* 126 C4
Artik, *Armenia* 49 K6
Artillery L., *Canada* 105 A7
Artois, *France* 19 B9
Artotína, *Greece* 38 C4
Artrutx, C. de, *Spain* 37 B10
Artsyz, *Ukraine* 47 J5
Artvin, *Turkey* 73 B9
Artyom, *Azerbaijan* 49 K10
Aru, Kepulauan, *Indonesia* 63 F8
Aru Is. = Aru, Kepulauan, *Indonesia* 63 F8
Arua, *Uganda* 86 B3
Aruanã, *Brazil* 125 F8
Aruba ■, *W. Indies* 121 D6
Arucas, *Canary Is.* 37 F4
Arudy, *France* 20 E3
Arun →, *Nepal* 69 F12
Arun →, *U.K.* 13 G7
Arunachal Pradesh □, *India* 67 F19
Arusha, *Tanzania* 86 C4
Arusha □, *Tanzania* 86 C4
Arusha Chini, *Tanzania* 86 C4
Aruwimi →, *Dem. Rep. of the Congo* 86 B1
Arvada, *Colo., U.S.A.* 112 F2
Arvada, *Wyo., U.S.A.* 114 D10
Arve →, *France* 19 F13
Árvi, *Greece* 36 E7
Arviat, *Canada* 105 A10
Arvidsjaur, *Sweden* 8 D18
Arvika, *Sweden* 10 E6
Arvin, *U.S.A.* 117 K8
Arwal, *India* 69 G11
Arxan, *China* 60 B6
Åryd, *Sweden* 11 H8
Aryirádhes, *Greece* 36 B3
Aryiroúpolis, *Greece* 36 D6
Arys, *Kazakstan* 50 E7
Arzachena, *Italy* 30 A2
Arzamas, *Russia* 48 C6
Arzgir, *Russia* 49 H7
Arzignano, *Italy* 29 C8
Arzúa, *Spain* 34 C2
Aš, *Czech Rep.* 26 A5
Ås, *Sweden* 10 A8
As Pontes de García Rodríguez, *Spain* 34 B3
Aş Şafā, *Syria* 75 B6
As Saffānīyah, *Si. Arabia* 71 E6
As Safīrah, *Syria* 70 B3
Aş Şahm, *Oman* 71 E8
As Sājir, *Si. Arabia* 70 E5
As Salamīyah, *Syria* 70 C3
As Salmān, *Iraq* 70 D5
As Salṭ, *Jordan* 75 C4
As Sal'w'a, *Qatar* 71 E6
As Samāwah, *Iraq* 70 D5
As Sanamayn, *Syria* 75 B5
As Sohar = Şuḩār, *Oman* 71 E8
As Sukhnah, *Syria* 70 C3
As Sulaymānīyah, *Iraq* 70 C5
As Sulaymī, *Si. Arabia* 70 E4
As Sulayyil, *Si. Arabia* 74 C4
As Summān, *Si. Arabia* 70 E5
As Suwaydā', *Syria* 75 C5
As Suwaydā' □, *Syria* 75 C5
As Suwayq, *Oman* 71 F8
As Şuwayrah, *Iraq* 70 C5
Åsa, *Sweden* 11 G6
Asab, *Namibia* 88 D2
Asaba, *Nigeria* 83 D6
Asad, Buḩayrat al, *Syria* 70 C3
Asadābād, *Iran* 73 E13
Asafo, *Ghana* 82 D4
Asahi-Gawa →, *Japan* 55 G6
Asahigawa, *Japan* 54 C11
Asale, L., *Ethiopia* 81 E5
Asamankese, *Ghana* 83 D4
Asan →, *India* 69 F8
Asansol, *India* 69 H12
Åsarna, *Sweden* 10 B8
Asayita, *Ethiopia* 81 E5
Asbe Teferi, *Ethiopia* 81 F5
Asbesberge, *S. Africa* 88 D3
Asbestos, *Canada* 103 C5
Asbury Park, *U.S.A.* 111 F10
Ascea, *Italy* 31 B8
Ascensión, *Mexico* 118 A3
Ascensión, B. de la, *Mexico* 119 D7
Ascension I., *Atl. Oc.* 77 G2
Aschach an der Donau, *Austria* 26 C7
Aschaffenburg, *Germany* 25 F5
Aschendorf, *Germany* 24 B3
Aschersleben, *Germany* 24 D7
Asciano, *Italy* 29 E8
Áscoli Piceno, *Italy* 29 F10
Áscoli Satriano, *Italy* 31 A8
Ascope, *Peru* 124 E3
Ascotán, *Chile* 126 A2
Aseb, *Eritrea* 81 E5
Åseda, *Sweden* 11 G9
Asela, *Ethiopia* 81 F4
Åsen, *Sweden* 10 C7
Asenovgrad, *Bulgaria* 41 D8
Aserradero, *Mexico* 118 C3
Asfeld, *France* 19 C11
Asfûn el Matâ'na, *Egypt* 80 B3
Asgata, *Cyprus* 36 E12
Ash Fork, *U.S.A.* 115 J7
Ash Grove, *U.S.A.* 113 G8
Ash Shabakah, *Iraq* 70 D4
Ash Shamāl □, *Lebanon* 75 A5
Ash Shāmīyah, *Iraq* 70 D5
Ash Shāriqah, *U.A.E.* 71 E7
Ash Sharmah, *Si. Arabia* 70 D2
Ash Sharqāt, *Iraq* 70 C4
Ash Sharqi, Al Jabal, *Lebanon* 75 B5
Ash Shaṭrah, *Iraq* 70 D5
Ash Shawbak, *Jordan* 70 D2
Ash Shawmari, J., *Jordan* 75 E5
Ash Shināfīyah, *Iraq* 70 D5
Ash Shu'bah, *Si. Arabia* 70 D5
Ash Shumlūl, *Si. Arabia* 70 E5
Ash Shūr'a, *Iraq* 70 C4
Ash Shurayf, *Si. Arabia* 70 E3
Ash Shuwayfāt, *Lebanon* 75 B4
Ashanti □, *Ghana* 83 D4
Ashau, *Vietnam* 64 D6
Ashbourne, *U.K.* 12 D6
Ashburn, *U.S.A.* 109 K4
Ashburton, *N.Z.* 91 K3
Ashburton →, *Australia* 92 D1
Ashcroft, *Canada* 104 C4
Ashdod, *Israel* 75 D3
Ashdown, *U.S.A.* 113 J7
Asheboro, *U.S.A.* 109 H6
Ashern, *Canada* 105 C9
Asherton, *U.S.A.* 113 L5
Asheville, *U.S.A.* 109 H4
Ashewat, *Pakistan* 68 D3
Asheweig →, *Canada* 102 B2
Ashford, *Australia* 95 D5
Ashford, *U.K.* 13 F8
Ashgabat, *Turkmenistan* 50 F6
Ashibetsu, *Japan* 54 C11
Ashikaga, *Japan* 55 F9
Ashington, *U.K.* 12 B6
Ashizuri-Zaki, *Japan* 55 H6
Ashkarkot, *Afghan.* 68 C2
Ashkhabad = Ashgabat, *Turkmenistan* 50 F6
Āshkhāneh, *Iran* 71 B8
Ashland, *Kans., U.S.A.* 113 G5
Ashland, *Ky., U.S.A.* 108 F4
Ashland, *Mont., U.S.A.* 114 D10
Ashland, *Ohio, U.S.A.* 110 F2
Ashland, *Oreg., U.S.A.* 114 E2
Ashland, *Pa., U.S.A.* 111 F8
Ashland, *Va., U.S.A.* 108 G7
Ashland, *Wis., U.S.A.* 112 B9
Ashley, *N. Dak., U.S.A.* 112 B5
Ashley, *Pa., U.S.A.* 111 E9
Ashmore Reef, *Australia* 92 B3
Ashmûn, *Egypt* 80 H7
Ashmyany, *Belarus* 9 J21
Ashokan Reservoir, *U.S.A.* 111 E10
Ashqelon, *Israel* 75 D3
Ashta, *India* 68 H7
Ashtabula, *U.S.A.* 110 E4
Ashton, *S. Africa* 88 E3
Ashton, *U.S.A.* 114 D8
Ashuanipi, L., *Canada* 103 B6
Ashville, *U.S.A.* 110 F6
'Āṣī →, *Asia* 72 D6

Asia 52 E11
Asia, Kepulauan, *Indonesia* 63 D8
Āsīā Bak, *Iran* 71 C6
Asiago, *Italy* 29 C8
Asifabad, *India* 66 K11
Asinara, *Italy* 30 A1
Asinara, G. dell', *Italy* 30 A1
Asino, *Russia* 50 D9
Asipovichy, *Belarus* 46 F5
'Asīr □, *Si. Arabia* 74 D3
Asir, Ras, *Somali Rep.* 74 E5
Aşkale, *Turkey* 73 C9
Askersund, *Sweden* 11 F8
Askham, *S. Africa* 88 D3
Askim, *Norway* 9 G14
Askja, *Iceland* 8 D5
Askøy, *Norway* 9 F11
Asl, *Egypt* 80 B3
Aslan Burnu, *Turkey* 39 C8
Aslanapa, *Turkey* 39 B11
Asmara = Asmera, *Eritrea* 81 D4
Asmera, *Eritrea* 81 D4
Asnæs, *Denmark* 11 J4
Åsnen, *Sweden* 11 H8
Asola, *Italy* 28 C7
Asosa, *Ethiopia* 81 E3
Asoteriba, Jebel, *Sudan* 80 C4
Aspe, *Spain* 33 G4
Aspen, *U.S.A.* 115 G10
Aspendos, *Turkey* 72 D4
Aspermont, *U.S.A.* 113 J4
Aspet, *France* 20 E4
Aspiring, Mt., *N.Z.* 91 L2
Aspres-sur-Buëch, *France* 21 D9
Asprókavos, Ákra, *Greece* 36 B4
Aspromonte, *Italy* 31 D9
Aspur, *India* 68 H6
Asquith, *Canada* 105 C7
Assâba, Massif de l', *Mauritania* 82 B2
Assaikio, *Nigeria* 83 D6
Assal, L., *Djibouti* 81 E5
Assam □, *India* 67 G18
Assamakka, *Niger* 83 B6
Asse, *Belgium* 17 D4
Assémini, *Italy* 30 C1
Assen, *Neths.* 17 A6
Assens, *Denmark* 11 J3
Assini, *Ivory C.* 82 D4
Assiniboia, *Canada* 105 D7
Assiniboine →, *Canada* 105 D9
Assiniboine, Mt., *Canada* 104 C5
Assis, *Brazil* 127 A5
Assisi, *Italy* 29 E9
Ássos, *Greece* 38 C2
Assynt, L., *U.K.* 14 C3
Astaffort, *France* 20 D4
Astakidha, *Greece* 39 F8
Astakós, *Greece* 38 C3
Astana, *Kazakstan* 50 D8
Āstāneh, *Iran* 71 B6
Astara, *Azerbaijan* 71 B6
Āstārā, *Iran* 73 C13
Asteroúsia, *Greece* 36 E7
Asti, *Italy* 28 D5
Astipálaia, *Greece* 39 E8
Astorga, *Spain* 34 C4
Astoria, *U.S.A.* 116 D3
Åstorp, *Sweden* 11 H6
Astrakhan, *Russia* 49 G9
Astudillo, *Spain* 34 C6
Asturias □, *Spain* 34 B5
Asunción, *Paraguay* 126 B4
Asunción Nochixtlán, *Mexico* 119 D5
Åsunden, *Sweden* 11 F9
Asutri, *Sudan* 81 D4
Aswa →, *Uganda* 86 B3
Aswad, Ra's al, *Si. Arabia* 80 C4
Aswân, *Egypt* 80 C3
Aswân High Dam = Sadd el Aali, *Egypt* 80 C3
Asyût, *Egypt* 80 B3
Asyûti, Wadi →, *Egypt* 80 B3
Aszód, *Hungary* 42 C4
At Ţafīlah, *Jordan* 75 E4
Aţ Ţā'if, *Si. Arabia* 74 C3
Aţ Ţirāq, *Si. Arabia* 70 E5
Aţ Ţubayq, *Si. Arabia* 70 D3
Atabey, *Turkey* 39 D12
Atacama □, *Chile* 126 B2
Atacama, Desierto de, *Chile* 126 A2
Atacama, Salar de, *Chile* 126 A2
Atakpamé, *Togo* 83 D5
Atalándi, *Greece* 38 C4
Atalaya, *Peru* 124 F4
Atalaya de Femes, *Canary Is.* 37 F6
Atami, *Japan* 55 G9
Atapupu, *Indonesia* 63 F6
Atâr, *Mauritania* 78 D3
Atarfe, *Spain* 35 H7
Atari, *Pakistan* 68 D6
Atascadero, *U.S.A.* 116 K6
Atasu, *Kazakstan* 50 E8
Atatürk Barajı, *Turkey* 73 D8
Atauro, *Indonesia* 63 F7
'Atbara, *Sudan* 80 D3
'Atbara, Nahr →, *Sudan* 80 D3
Atbasar, *Kazakstan* 50 D7
Atça, *Turkey* 39 D10
Atchafalaya B., *U.S.A.* 113 L9
Atchison, *U.S.A.* 112 F7
Atebubu, *Ghana* 83 D4
Ateca, *Spain* 32 D3
Aterno →, *Italy* 29 F10
Āteshān, *Iran* 71 C7
Atesine, Alpi, *Italy* 29 B8
Atessa, *Italy* 29 F11
Atfîh, *Egypt* 80 J7
Ath, *Belgium* 17 D3
Athabasca, *Canada* 104 C6
Athabasca →, *Canada* 105 B6
Athabasca, L., *Canada* 105 B7
Athboy, *Ireland* 15 C5
Athenry, *Ireland* 15 C3
Athens = Athínai, *Greece* 38 D5
Athens, *Ala., U.S.A.* 109 H2
Athens, *Ga., U.S.A.* 109 J4
Athens, *N.Y., U.S.A.* 111 D11
Athens, *Ohio, U.S.A.* 108 F4
Athens, *Pa., U.S.A.* 111 E8
Athens, *Tenn., U.S.A.* 109 H3
Athens, *Tex., U.S.A.* 113 J7
Atherley, *Canada* 110 B5
Atherton, *Australia* 94 B4
Athiéme, *Benin* 83 D5
Athienou, *Cyprus* 36 D12
Athínai, *Greece* 38 D5
Athlone, *Ireland* 15 C4
Athna, *Cyprus* 36 D12
Athol, *U.S.A.* 111 D12
Atholl, Forest of, *U.K.* 14 E5
Atholville, *Canada* 103 C6
Áthos, *Greece* 41 F8
Athy, *Ireland* 15 C5
Ati, *Chad* 79 F9
Ati, *Sudan* 81 E2
Atiak, *Uganda* 86 B3
Atienza, *Spain* 32 D2
Atiit, *Sudan* 81 F3
Atik L., *Canada* 105 B9
Atikameg →, *Canada* 102 B3
Atikokan, *Canada* 102 C1
Atikonak L., *Canada* 103 B7
Atimonan, *Phil.* 61 E4
Atka, *Russia* 51 C16
Atka I., *U.S.A.* 100 C2
Atkarsk, *Russia* 48 E7
Atkinson, *U.S.A.* 112 D5
Atlanta, *Ga., U.S.A.* 109 J3
Atlanta, *Tex., U.S.A.* 113 J7
Atlantic, *U.S.A.* 112 E7
Atlantic City, *U.S.A.* 108 F8
Atlantic Ocean 2 E9
Atlas Mts. = Haut Atlas, *Morocco* 78 B4
Atlin, *Canada* 104 B2
Atlin, L., *Canada* 104 B2
Atlin Prov. Park, *Canada* 104 B2
Atmore, *U.S.A.* 109 K2
Atoka, *U.S.A.* 113 H6
Átokos, *Greece* 38 C2
Atolia, *U.S.A.* 117 K9
Atrai →, *Bangla.* 69 G13
Atrak = Atrek →, *Turkmenistan* 71 B8
Ätran, *Sweden* 11 G6
Ätran →, *Sweden* 11 H6
Atrauli, *India* 68 E8
Atrek →, *Turkmenistan* 71 B8
Atri, *Italy* 29 F10
Atsikí, *Greece* 39 B7
Atsoum, Mts., *Cameroon* 83 D7
Atsuta, *Japan* 54 C10
Attalla, *U.S.A.* 109 H2
Attapu, *Laos* 64 E6
Attáviros, *Greece* 36 C9
Attawapiskat, *Canada* 102 B3
Attawapiskat →, *Canada* 102 B3
Attawapiskat L., *Canada* 102 B2
Attersee, *Austria* 26 D6
Attica, *Ind., U.S.A.* 108 E2
Attica, *Ohio, U.S.A.* 110 E2
Attichy, *France* 19 C10
Attigny, *France* 19 C11
Attika = Attikí □, *Greece* 38 D5
Attikamagen L., *Canada* 103 B6
Attikí □, *Greece* 38 D5
Attleboro, *U.S.A.* 111 E13
Attock, *Pakistan* 68 C5
Attopeu = Attapu, *Laos* 64 E6
Attu I., *U.S.A.* 100 C1
Attur, *India* 66 P11
Atuel →, *Argentina* 126 D2
Åtvidaberg, *Sweden* 11 F10
Atwater, *U.S.A.* 116 H6
Atwood, *Canada* 110 C3
Atwood, *U.S.A.* 112 F4
Atyraū, *Kazakstan* 50 E6
Au Sable, *U.S.A.* 110 B1
Au Sable →, *U.S.A.* 108 C4
Au Sable Forks, *U.S.A.* 111 B11
Au Sable Pt., *U.S.A.* 110 B1
Aubagne, *France* 21 E9
Aubarca, C. d', *Spain* 37 B7
Aube □, *France* 19 D11
Aube →, *France* 19 D10
Aubenas, *France* 21 D8
Aubenton, *France* 19 C11
Auberry, *U.S.A.* 116 H7
Aubigny-sur-Nère, *France* 19 E9
Aubin, *France* 20 D6
Aubrac, Mts. d', *France* 20 D7
Auburn, *Ala., U.S.A.* 109 J3
Auburn, *Calif., U.S.A.* 116 G5
Auburn, *Ind., U.S.A.* 108 E3
Auburn, *Maine, U.S.A.* 109 C10
Auburn, *N.Y., U.S.A.* 111 D8
Auburn, *Nebr., U.S.A.* 112 E7
Auburn, *Pa., U.S.A.* 111 F8
Auburn, *Wash., U.S.A.* 116 C4
Auburn Ra., *Australia* 95 D5
Auburndale, *U.S.A.* 109 L5
Aubusson, *France* 20 C6
Auce, *Latvia* 44 B9
Auch, *France* 20 E4
Auchi, *Nigeria* 83 D6
Auckland, *N.Z.* 91 G5
Auckland Is., *Pac. Oc.* 96 N8
Aude □, *France* 20 E6
Aude →, *France* 20 E7
Auden, *Canada* 102 B2
Auderville, *France* 18 C5
Audierne, *France* 18 D2
Audincourt, *France* 19 E13
Audo, *Ethiopia* 81 F5
Audubon, *U.S.A.* 112 E7
Aue, *Germany* 24 E8
Auerbach, *Germany* 24 E8
Augathella, *Australia* 95 D4
Aughnacloy, *U.K.* 15 B5
Augrabies Falls, *S. Africa* 88 D3
Augsburg, *Germany* 25 G6
Augusta, *Australia* 93 F2
Augusta, *Italy* 31 E8
Augusta, *Ark., U.S.A.* 113 H9
Augusta, *Ga., U.S.A.* 109 J5
Augusta, *Kans., U.S.A.* 113 G6
Augusta, *Maine, U.S.A.* 101 D13
Augusta, *Mont., U.S.A.* 114 C7
Augustenborg, *Denmark* 11 K3
Augustów, *Poland* 44 E9
Augustus, Mt., *Australia* 93 D2
Augustus I., *Australia* 92 C3
Aukan, *Eritrea* 81 D5
Aukum, *U.S.A.* 116 G6
Auld, L., *Australia* 92 D3
Aulla, *Italy* 28 D6
Aulnay, *France* 20 B3
Aulne →, *France* 18 D2
Aulnoye-Aymeries, *France* 19 B10
Ault, *France* 18 B8
Ault, *U.S.A.* 112 E2
Aulus-les-Bains, *France* 20 F5
Aumale, *France* 19 C8
Aumont-Aubrac, *France* 20 D7
Auna, *Nigeria* 83 C5
Auning, *Denmark* 11 H4
Aunis, *France* 20 B3
Auponhia, *Indonesia* 63 E7
Aups, *France* 21 E10
Aur, Pulau, *Malaysia* 65 L5
Auraiya, *India* 69 F8
Aurangabad, *Bihar, India* 69 G11
Aurangabad, *Maharashtra, India* 66 K9
Auray, *France* 18 E4
Aurich, *Germany* 24 B3
Aurillac, *France* 20 D6
Auronzo di Cadore, *Italy* 29 B9
Aurora, *Canada* 110 C5
Aurora, *S. Africa* 88 E2
Aurora, *Colo., U.S.A.* 112 F2
Aurora, *Ill., U.S.A.* 108 E1
Aurora, *Mo., U.S.A.* 113 G8
Aurora, *N.Y., U.S.A.* 111 D8
Aurora, *Nebr., U.S.A.* 112 E6
Aurora, *Ohio, U.S.A.* 110 E3
Aurukun, *Australia* 94 A3
Aus, *Namibia* 88 D2
Ausable →, *Canada* 110 C3
Auschwitz = Oświęcim, *Poland* 45 H6
Austerlitz = Slavkov u Brna, *Czech Rep.* 27 B9
Austin, *Minn., U.S.A.* 112 D8
Austin, *Nev., U.S.A.* 114 G5
Austin, *Pa., U.S.A.* 110 E6
Austin, *Tex., U.S.A.* 113 K6
Austin, L., *Australia* 93 E2
Austin I., *Canada* 105 A10
Austra, *Norway* 8 D14
Austral Is. = Tubuai Is., *Pac. Oc.* 97 K13
Austral Seamount Chain, *Pac. Oc.* 97 K13
Australia ■, *Oceania* 96 K5
Australian Capital Territory □, *Australia* 95 F4
Australind, *Australia* 93 F2
Austria ■, *Europe* 26 E7
Austvågøy, *Norway* 8 B16
Auterive, *France* 20 E5
Authie →, *France* 19 B8
Authon-du-Perche, *France* 18 D7
Autlán, *Mexico* 118 D4
Autun, *France* 19 F11
Auvergne, *France* 20 C7
Auvergne, Mts. d', *France* 20 C6
Auvézère →, *France* 20 C4
Auxerre, *France* 19 E10
Auxi-le-Château, *France* 19 B9
Auxonne, *France* 19 E12
Auzances, *France* 19 F9
Ava, *U.S.A.* 113 G8
Avallon, *France* 19 E10
Avalon, *U.S.A.* 117 M8
Avalon Pen., *Canada* 103 C9
Avanos, *Turkey* 70 B2
Avaré, *Brazil* 127 A6
Ávas, *Greece* 41 F9
Avawatz Mts., *U.S.A.* 117 K10
Avdan Dağı, *Turkey* 41 F13
Aveiro, *Brazil* 125 D7
Aveiro, *Portugal* 34 E2
Aveiro □, *Portugal* 34 E2
Āvej, *Iran* 71 C6
Avellaneda, *Argentina* 126 C4
Avellino, *Italy* 31 B7
Avenal, *U.S.A.* 116 K6
Aversa, *Italy* 31 B7
Avery, *U.S.A.* 114 C6
Aves, Is. las, *Venezuela* 121 D6
Avesnes-sur-Helpe, *France* 19 B10
Avesta, *Sweden* 10 D10
Aveyron □, *France* 20 D6
Aveyron →, *France* 20 D5
Avezzano, *Italy* 29 F10
Avgó, *Greece* 39 F7
Aviá Terai, *Argentina* 126 B3
Aviano, *Italy* 29 B9
Aviemore, *U.K.* 14 D5
Avigliana, *Italy* 28 C4
Avigliano, *Italy* 31 B8
Avignon, *France* 21 E8
Ávila, *Spain* 34 E6
Ávila □, *Spain* 34 E6
Ávila, Sierra de, *Spain* 34 E5
Avila Beach, *U.S.A.* 117 K6
Avilés, *Spain* 34 B5
Avintes, *Portugal* 34 D2
Avionárion, *Greece* 38 C6
Avis, *Portugal* 35 F3
Avis, *U.S.A.* 110 E7
Avísio →, *Italy* 28 B8
Aviz = Avis, *Portugal* 35 F3
Avize, *France* 19 D11
Avlum, *Denmark* 11 H2
Avoca, *U.S.A.* 110 D7
Avoca →, *Australia* 95 F3
Avoca →, *Ireland* 15 D5
Avola, *Canada* 104 C5
Avola, *Italy* 31 F8
Avon, *U.S.A.* 110 D7
Avon →, *Australia* 93 F2
Avon →, *Bristol, U.K.* 13 F5
Avon →, *Dorset, U.K.* 13 G6
Avon →, *Warks., U.K.* 13 E5
Avon Park, *U.S.A.* 109 M5
Avondale, *Zimbabwe* 87 F3
Avonlea, *Canada* 105 D8
Avonmore, *Canada* 111 A10
Avramov, *Bulgaria* 41 D10
Avranches, *France* 18 D5
Avre →, *France* 18 D8
Avrig, *Romania* 43 E9
Avrillé, *France* 18 E6
Avtovac, *Bos.-H.* 40 C2
Awag el Baqar, *Sudan* 81 E3
A'waj →, *Syria* 75 B5
Awaji-Shima, *Japan* 55 G7
'Awālī, *Bahrain* 71 E6
Awantipur, *India* 69 C6
Awasa, *Ethiopia* 81 F4
Awasa, L., *Ethiopia* 81 F4
Awash, *Ethiopia* 81 F5
Awash →, *Ethiopia* 81 E5
Awaso, *Ghana* 82 D4
Awatere →, *N.Z.* 91 J5
Awbārī, *Libya* 79 C8
Awe, L., *U.K.* 14 E3
Aweil, *Sudan* 81 F2
Awgu, *Nigeria* 83 D6
Awjilah, *Libya* 79 C10
Awka, *Nigeria* 83 D6
Ax-les-Thermes, *France* 20 F5
Axat, *France* 20 F6
Axe →, *U.K.* 13 F5
Axel Heiberg I., *Canada* 4 B3
Axim, *Ghana* 82 E4
Axintele, *Romania* 43 F11
Axiós →, *Greece* 40 F6
Axminster, *U.K.* 13 G4
Axvall, *Sweden* 11 F7
Ay, *France* 19 C11
Ayabaca, *Peru* 124 D3
Ayabe, *Japan* 55 G7
Ayacucho, *Argentina* 126 D4
Ayacucho, *Peru* 124 F4
Ayaguz, *Kazakstan* 50 E9
Ayamé, *Ivory C.* 82 D4
Ayamonte, *Spain* 35 H3
Ayan, *Russia* 51 D14
Ayancık, *Turkey* 72 B6
Ayas, *Turkey* 72 B5
Ayaviri, *Peru* 124 F4
Aybastı, *Turkey* 72 B7
Aydın, *Turkey* 72 D2
Aydin □, *Turkey* 39 D9
Aydin Dağları, *Turkey* 39 D10
Ayelu, *Ethiopia* 81 E5
Ayenngré, *Togo* 83 D5
Ayer, *U.S.A.* 111 D13
Ayerbe, *Spain* 32 C4
Ayer's Cliff, *Canada* 111 A12
Ayers Rock, *Australia* 93 E5
Ayiá, *Greece* 38 B4
Ayia Aikateríni, Ákra, *Greece* 36 A3
Ayía Ánna, *Greece* 38 C5
Ayia Dhéka, *Greece* 36 D6
Ayia Gálini, *Greece* 36 D6
Ayía Marína, *Kásos, Greece* 39 F8
Ayía Marína, *Léros, Greece* 39 D8
Áyia Napa, *Cyprus* 36 E13
Ayía Paraskeví, *Greece* 39 B8
Áyia Phyla, *Cyprus* 36 E12
Ayía Rouméli, *Greece* 38 F5
Ayia Varvára, *Greece* 36 D7
Ayiássos, *Greece* 39 B8
Áyioi Theódhoroi, *Greece* 38 D5
Áyion Óros □, *Greece* 41 F8
Áyios Amvrósios, *Cyprus* 36 D12
Áyios Andréas, *Greece* 38 D4
Áyios Evstrátios, *Greece* 38 B6
Áyios Ioánnis, Ákra, *Greece* 36 D7
Áyios Isidhoros, *Greece* 36 C9
Áyios Kiríkos, *Greece* 39 D8
Áyios Matthaíos, *Greece* 36 B3
Áyios Mírono, *Greece* 39 F7
Áyios Nikólaos, *Greece* 36 D7
Áyios Pétros, *Greece* 38 C2
Áyios Seryios, *Cyprus* 36 D12
Áyios Theodhoros, *Cyprus* 36 D13
Áyios Yeóryios, *Greece* 38 D5
Aykathonisi, *Greece* 39 D8
Aykirikçi, *Turkey* 39 B12
Aylesbury, *U.K.* 13 F7
Aylmer, *Canada* 110 D4
Aylmer, L., *Canada* 100 B8
'Ayn, Wādī al, *Oman* 71 F7
Ayn Dār, *Si. Arabia* 71 E7
Ayn Zālah, *Iraq* 70 B4
Ayna, *Spain* 33 G2
Ayod, *Sudan* 81 F3
Ayolas, *Paraguay* 126 B4
Ayom, *Sudan* 81 F2
Ayon, Ostrov, *Russia* 51 C17
Ayora, *Spain* 33 F3
Ayorou, *Niger* 83 C5
'Ayoûn el 'Atroûs, *Mauritania* 82 B3
Ayr, *Australia* 94 B4
Ayr, *Canada* 110 C4
Ayr, *U.K.* 14 F4
Ayr →, *U.K.* 14 F4
Ayrancı, *Turkey* 72 D5
Ayrancılar, *Turkey* 39 C9
Ayre, Pt. of, *U.K.* 12 C3
Aysha, *Ethiopia* 81 E5
Ayton, *Australia* 94 B4
Aytos, *Bulgaria* 41 D11
Aytoska Planina, *Bulgaria* 41 D11
Ayu, Kepulauan, *Indonesia* 63 D8
Ayutla, *Guatemala* 120 D1
Ayutla, *Mexico* 119 D5
Ayvacık, *Turkey* 72 C2
Ayvalık, *Turkey* 39 B8
Az Zabadānī, *Syria* 75 B5
Az̧ Z̧āhirīyah, *West Bank* 75 D3
Az̧ Z̧ahrān, *Si. Arabia* 71 E6
Az Zarqā, *Jordan* 75 C5
Az Zarqā', *U.A.E.* 71 E7
Az Zībār, *Iraq* 70 B5
Az Zilfī, *Si. Arabia* 70 E5
Az Zubayr, *Iraq* 70 D5
Az Zuqur, *Yemen* 81 E5
Azambuja, *Portugal* 35 F2
Azamgarh, *India* 69 F10
Azangaro, *Peru* 124 F4
Azaoua, *Niger* 83 B5
Azaouad, *Mali* 82 B4
Azaouak, Vallée de l', *Mali* 83 B5
Āzār Shahr, *Iran* 70 B5
Azara, *Nigeria* 83 D6
Azarān, *Iran* 70 B5
Azärbayjan = Azerbaijan ■, *Asia* 49 K9
Āzarbāyjān-e Gharbī □, *Iran* 70 B5
Āzarbāyjān-e Sharqī □, *Iran* 70 B5
Azare, *Nigeria* 83 C7
Azay-le-Rideau, *France* 18 E7
A'zāz, *Syria* 70 B3
Azbine = Aïr, *Niger* 83 B6
Azerbaijan ■, *Asia* 49 K9
Azerbaijchan = Azerbaijan ■, *Asia* 49 K9
Azezo, *Ethiopia* 81 E4
Azimganj, *India* 69 G13
Aznalcóllar, *Spain* 35 H4
Azogues, *Ecuador* 124 D3
Azores, *Atl. Oc.* 78 A1
Azov, *Russia* 49 G4
Azov, Sea of, *Europe* 47 J9
Azovskoye More = Azov, Sea of, *Europe* 47 J9
Azpeitia, *Spain* 32 B2
Azraq ash Shīshān, *Jordan* 75 D5
Aztec, *U.S.A.* 115 H10
Azúa de Compostela, *Dom. Rep.* 121 C5
Azuaga, *Spain* 35 G5
Azuara, *Spain* 32 D4
Azuer →, *Spain* 35 F7
Azuero, Pen. de, *Panama* 120 E3
Azuga, *Romania* 43 E10
Azul, *Argentina* 126 D4
Azusa, *U.S.A.* 117 L9
Azzano Décimo, *Italy* 29 C9

B

Ba Don, *Vietnam* 64 D6
Ba Dong, *Vietnam* 65 H6
Ba Ngoi = Cam Lam, *Vietnam* 65 G7
Ba Tri, *Vietnam* 65 G6
Ba Xian = Bazhou, *China* 56 E9
Baa, *Indonesia* 63 F6
Baamonde, *Spain* 34 B3
Baarle-Nassau, *Belgium* 17 C4
Bab el Mandeb, *Red Sea* 74 E3
Baba, *Bulgaria* 40 D7
Bābā, Koh-i-, *Afghan.* 66 B5
Baba Burnu, *Turkey* 39 B8
Baba dag, *Azerbaijan* 49 K9
Bābā Kalū, *Iran* 71 D6
Babadag, *Romania* 43 F13
Babadağ, *Turkey* 39 D10
Babadayhan, *Turkmenistan* 50 F7
Babaeski, *Turkey* 41 E11
Babahoyo, *Ecuador* 124 D3
Babai = Sarju →, *India* 69 F9
Babana, *Nigeria* 83 C5
Babanusa, *Sudan* 81 E2
Babar, *Indonesia* 63 F7
Babar, *Pakistan* 68 D3
Babarkach, *Pakistan* 68 E3
Babayevo, *Russia* 46 C8
Babb, *U.S.A.* 114 B7
Babelthuap, *Pac. Oc.* 63 C8
Babenhausen, *Germany* 25 F4
Băbeni, *Romania* 43 F9

Baberu, *India* 69 G9
Babi Besar, Pulau, *Malaysia* 65 L4
Babia Gora, *Europe* 45 J6
Babian Jiang →, *China* 58 F3
Babile, *Ethiopia* 81 F5
Babimost, *Poland* 45 F2
Babinda, *Australia* 94 B4
Babine, *Canada* 104 B3
Babine →, *Canada* 104 B3
Babine L., *Canada* 104 C3
Babo, *Indonesia* 63 E8
Babócsa, *Hungary* 42 D2
Bābol, *Iran* 71 B7
Bābol Sar, *Iran* 71 B7
Baborów, *Poland* 45 H5
Babruysk, *Belarus* 47 F5
Babuhri, *India* 68 F3
Babuna, *Macedonia* 40 E5
Babura, *Nigeria* 83 C6
Babusar Pass, *Pakistan* 69 B5
Babushkin, *Russia* 60 A5
Babušnica, *Serbia, Yug.* 40 C6
Babuyan Chan., *Phil.* 61 B4
Babylon, *Iraq* 70 C5
Bač, *Serbia, Yug.* 42 E4
Bâc →, *Moldova* 43 D14
Bac Can, *Vietnam* 58 F5
Bac Giang, *Vietnam* 58 G6
Bac Lieu, *Vietnam* 65 H5
Bac Ninh, *Vietnam* 58 G6
Bac Phan, *Vietnam* 64 B5
Bac Quang, *Vietnam* 58 F5
Bacabal, *Brazil* 125 D10
Bacalar, *Mexico* 119 D7
Bacan, Kepulauan, *Indonesia* 63 E7
Bacarra, *Phil.* 61 B4
Bacău, *Romania* 43 D11
Bacău □, *Romania* 43 D11
Baccarat, *France* 19 D13
Bacerac, *Mexico* 118 A3
Băceşti, *Romania* 43 D12
Bach Long Vi, Dao, *Vietnam* 64 B6
Bacharach, *Germany* 25 E3
Bachelina, *Russia* 50 D7
Bachhwara, *India* 69 G11
Bachuma, *Ethiopia* 81 F4
Bačina, *Serbia, Yug.* 40 C5
Back →, *Canada* 100 B9
Bačka Palanka, *Serbia, Yug.* 42 E4
Bačka Topola, *Serbia, Yug.* 42 E4
Bäckebo, *Sweden* 11 H10
Bäckefors, *Sweden* 11 F6
Bäckhammar, *Sweden* 10 E8
Bački Petrovac, *Serbia, Yug.* 42 E4
Backnang, *Germany* 25 G5
Baco, Mt., *Phil.* 61 E4
Bacolod, *Phil.* 61 F5
Bacqueville-en-Caux, *France* 18 C8
Bács-Kiskun □, *Hungary* 42 D4
Bácsalmás, *Hungary* 42 D4
Bacuag = Placer, *Phil.* 61 G6
Bacuk, *Malaysia* 65 J4
Bād, *Iran* 71 C7
Bad →, *U.S.A.* 112 C4
Bad Aussee, *Austria* 26 D6
Bad Axe, *U.S.A.* 110 C2
Bad Bergzabern, *Germany* 25 F3
Bad Berleburg, *Germany* 24 D4
Bad Bevensen, *Germany* 24 B6
Bad Bramstedt, *Germany* 24 B5
Bad Brückenau, *Germany* 25 E5
Bad Doberan, *Germany* 24 A7
Bad Driburg, *Germany* 24 D5
Bad Ems, *Germany* 25 E3
Bad Frankenhausen, *Germany* 24 D7
Bad Freienwalde, *Germany* 24 C10
Bad Goisern, *Austria* 26 D6
Bad Harzburg, *Germany* 24 D6
Bad Hersfeld, *Germany* 24 E5
Bad Hofgastein, *Austria* 26 D6
Bad Homburg, *Germany* 25 E4
Bad Honnef, *Germany* 24 E3
Bad Iburg, *Germany* 24 C4
Bad Ischl, *Austria* 26 D6
Bad Kissingen, *Germany* 25 E6
Bad Königshofen, *Germany* 25 E6
Bad Kreuznach, *Germany* 25 F3
Bad Krozingen, *Germany* 25 H3
Bad Laasphe, *Germany* 24 E4
Bad Lands, *U.S.A.* 112 D3
Bad Langensalza, *Germany* 24 D6
Bad Lauterberg, *Germany* 24 D6
Bad Leonfelden, *Austria* 26 C7
Bad Liebenwerda, *Germany* 24 D9
Bad Mergentheim, *Germany* 25 F5
Bad Münstereifel, *Germany* 24 E2
Bad Nauheim, *Germany* 25 E4
Bad Neuenahr-Ahrweiler, *Germany* 24 E3
Bad Neustadt, *Germany* 25 E6
Bad Oeynhausen, *Germany* 24 C4
Bad Oldesloe, *Germany* 24 B6
Bad Orb, *Germany* 25 E5
Bad Pyrmont, *Germany* 24 D5
Bad Reichenhall, *Germany* 25 H8
Bad Säckingen, *Germany* 25 H3
Bad Salzuflen, *Germany* 24 C4
Bad Salzungen, *Germany* 24 E6
Bad Schwartau, *Germany* 24 B6
Bad Segeberg, *Germany* 24 B6
Bad St. Leonhard, *Austria* 26 E7
Bad Tölz, *Germany* 25 H7
Bad Urach, *Germany* 25 G5
Bad Vöslau, *Austria* 27 D9
Bad Waldsee, *Germany* 25 H5
Bad Wildungen, *Germany* 24 D5
Bad Wimpfen, *Germany* 25 F5
Bad Windsheim, *Germany* 25 F6
Bad Zwischenahn, *Germany* 24 B4
Bada Barabil, *India* 69 H11
Badagara, *India* 66 P9
Badagri, *Nigeria* 83 D5
Badajós, L., *Brazil* 124 D6
Badajoz, *Spain* 35 G4
Badajoz □, *Spain* 35 G4
Badakhshān □, *Afghan.* 66 A7
Badalona, *Spain* 32 D7
Badalzai, *Afghan.* 68 E1
Badampahar, *India* 67 H15
Badanah, *Si. Arabia* 70 D4
Badarinath, *India* 69 D8
Badas, Kepulauan, *Indonesia* 62 D3
Baddo →, *Pakistan* 66 F4
Bade, *Indonesia* 63 F9
Badeggi, *Nigeria* 83 D6
Badéguichéri, *Niger* 83 C6
Baden, *Austria* 27 C9
Baden, *Switz.* 25 H4
Baden, *U.S.A.* 110 F4
Baden-Baden, *Germany* 25 G4
Baden-Württemberg □, *Germany* 25 G4
Badgastein, *Austria* 26 D6
Badger, *Canada* 103 C8
Badger, *U.S.A.* 116 J7
Bādghīs □, *Afghan.* 66 B3
Badgom, *India* 69 B6
Badia Polésine, *Italy* 29 C8
Badin, *Pakistan* 68 G3
Badlands National Park, *U.S.A.* 112 D3
Badogo, *Mali* 82 C3
Badoumbé, *Mali* 82 C2
Badrah, *Iraq* 70 C5
Badrinath, *India* 69 D8
Badulla, *Sri Lanka* 66 R12
Baena, *Spain* 35 H6
Baeza, *Spain* 35 H7
Bafang, *Cameroon* 83 D7
Bafatá, *Guinea-Biss.* 82 C2
Baffin B., *Canada* 101 A13
Baffin I., *Canada* 101 B12
Bafia, *Cameroon* 83 E7
Bafilo, *Togo* 83 D5
Bafing →, *Mali* 82 C2
Bafliyūn, *Syria* 70 B3
Bafoulabé, *Mali* 82 C2
Bafoussam, *Cameroon* 83 D7
Bāfq, *Iran* 71 D7
Bafra, *Turkey* 72 B6
Bafra Burnu, *Turkey* 72 B7
Bāft, *Iran* 71 D8
Bafut, *Cameroon* 83 D7
Bafwasende, *Dem. Rep. of the Congo* 86 B2
Bagam, *Niger* 83 B6
Bagamoyo, *Tanzania* 86 D4
Bagan Datoh, *Malaysia* 65 L3
Bagan Serai, *Malaysia* 65 K3
Baganga, *Phil.* 61 H7
Bagani, *Namibia* 88 B3
Bagansiapiapi, *Indonesia* 62 D2
Bagasra, *India* 68 J4
Bagaud, *India* 68 H6
Bagawi, *Sudan* 81 E3
Bagbag, *Sudan* 81 D3
Bagdad, *U.S.A.* 117 L11
Bagdarin, *Russia* 51 D12
Bagé, *Brazil* 127 C5
Bagenalstown = Muine Bheag, *Ireland* 15 D5
Baggs, *U.S.A.* 114 F10
Bagh, *Pakistan* 69 C5
Baghain →, *India* 69 G9
Baghdād, *Iraq* 70 C5
Bagheria, *Italy* 30 D6
Baghlān, *Afghan.* 66 A6
Baghlān □, *Afghan.* 66 B6
Bagley, *U.S.A.* 112 B7
Bagnara Cálabra, *Italy* 31 D8
Bagnasco, *Italy* 28 D5
Bagnères-de-Bigorre, *France* 20 E4
Bagnères-de-Luchon, *France* 20 F4
Bagni di Lucca, *Italy* 28 D7
Bagno di Romagna, *Italy* 29 E8
Bagnoles-de-l'Orne, *France* 18 D6
Bagnols-sur-Cèze, *France* 21 D8
Bagnorégio, *Italy* 29 F9
Bago = Pegu, *Burma* 67 L20
Bagodar, *India* 69 G11
Bagrationovsk, *Russia* 9 J19
Bagrdan, *Serbia, Yug.* 40 B5
Baguio, *Phil.* 61 C4
Bağyurdu, *Turkey* 39 C9
Bagzane, Monts, *Niger* 83 B6
Bah, *India* 69 F8
Bahabón de Esgueva, *Spain* 34 D7
Bahadurganj, *India* 69 F12
Bahadurgarh, *India* 68 E7
Bahama, Canal Viejo de, *W. Indies* 120 B4
Bahamas ■, *N. Amer.* 121 B5
Bahār, *Iran* 73 E13
Baharampur, *India* 69 G13
Baharîya, El Wâhât al, *Egypt* 80 B2
Bahawalnagar, *Pakistan* 68 E5
Bahawalpur, *Pakistan* 68 E4
Bahçe, *Turkey* 72 D7
Bahçecik, *Turkey* 41 F13
Baheri, *India* 69 E8
Bahgul →, *India* 69 F8
Bahi, *Tanzania* 86 D4
Bahi Swamp, *Tanzania* 86 D4
Bahía = Salvador, *Brazil* 125 F11
Bahía □, *Brazil* 125 F10
Bahía, Is. de la, *Honduras* 120 C2
Bahía Blanca, *Argentina* 126 D3
Bahía de Caráquez, *Ecuador* 124 D2
Bahía Honda, *Cuba* 120 B3
Bahía Laura, *Argentina* 128 F3
Bahía Negra, *Paraguay* 124 H7
Bahir Dar, *Ethiopia* 81 E4
Bahmanzād, *Iran* 71 D6
Bahr el Ahmar □, *Sudan* 80 D4
Bahr el Ghazâl □, *Sudan* 81 F2
Bahr el Jabal □, *Sudan* 81 G3
Bahr Yûsef →, *Egypt* 80 B3
Bahraich, *India* 69 F9
Bahrain ■, *Asia* 71 E6
Bahror, *India* 68 F7
Bāhū Kalāt, *Iran* 71 E9
Bai, *Mali* 82 C4
Bai Bung, Mui = Ca Mau, Mui, *Vietnam* 65 H5
Bai Duc, *Vietnam* 64 C5
Bai Thuong, *Vietnam* 64 C5
Baia de Aramă, *Romania* 42 E7
Baia Mare, *Romania* 43 C8
Baia-Sprie, *Romania* 43 C8
Baião, *Brazil* 125 D9
Baïbokoum, *Chad* 79 G9
Baicheng, *China* 57 B12
Băicoi, *Romania* 43 E10
Baidoa, *Somali Rep.* 74 G3
Baie Comeau, *Canada* 103 C6
Baie-St-Paul, *Canada* 103 C5
Baie Trinité, *Canada* 103 C6
Baie Verte, *Canada* 103 C8
Baignes-Ste-Radegonde, *France* 20 C3
Baigneux-les-Juifs, *France* 19 E11
Baihar, *India* 69 H9
Baihe, *China* 56 H6
Ba'ījī, *Iraq* 70 C4
Baijnath, *India* 69 E8
Baikal, L. = Baykal, Oz., *Russia* 51 D11
Baikunthpur, *India* 69 H10
Baile Atha Cliath = Dublin, *Ireland* 15 C5
Băile Govora, *Romania* 43 E9
Băile Herculane, *Romania* 42 F7
Băile Olăneşti, *Romania* 43 E9
Băile Tuşnad, *Romania* 43 D10
Bailén, *Spain* 35 G7
Băileşti, *Romania* 43 F8
Baima, *China* 58 A3
Bain-de-Bretagne, *France* 18 E5
Bainbridge, *Ga., U.S.A.* 109 K3
Bainbridge, *N.Y., U.S.A.* 111 D9
Baing, *Indonesia* 63 F6
Bainiu, *China* 56 H7
Baiona, *Spain* 34 C2
Bā'ir, *Jordan* 75 E5
Bairin Youqi, *China* 57 C10
Bairin Zuoqi, *China* 57 C10
Bairnsdale, *Australia* 95 F4
Bais, *Phil.* 61 G5
Baisha, *China* 56 G7
Baissa, *Nigeria* 83 D7
Baitadi, *Nepal* 69 E9
Baiyin, *China* 56 F3
Baiyü, *China* 58 B2
Baiyu Shan, *China* 56 F4
Baiyuda, *Sudan* 80 D3
Baj Baj, *India* 69 H13
Baja, *Hungary* 42 D3
Baja, Pta., *Mexico* 118 B1
Baja California, *Mexico* 118 A1
Baja California □, *Mexico* 118 B2
Baja California Sur □, *Mexico* 118 B2
Bajag, *India* 69 H9
Bajamar, *Canary Is.* 37 F3
Bajana, *India* 68 H4
Bājgīrān, *Iran* 71 B8
Bajimba, Mt., *Australia* 95 D5
Bajina Bašta, *Serbia, Yug.* 40 C3
Bajmok, *Serbia, Yug.* 42 E4
Bajo Nuevo, *Caribbean* 120 C4
Bajoga, *Nigeria* 83 C7
Bajool, *Australia* 94 C5
Bak, *Hungary* 42 D1
Bakar, *Croatia* 29 C11
Bakel, *Senegal* 82 C2
Baker, *Calif., U.S.A.* 117 K10
Baker, *Mont., U.S.A.* 112 B2
Baker, L., *Canada* 100 B10
Baker City, *U.S.A.* 114 D5
Baker I., *Pac. Oc.* 96 G10
Baker I., *U.S.A.* 104 B2
Baker L., *Australia* 93 E4
Baker Lake, *Canada* 100 B10
Baker Mt., *U.S.A.* 114 B3
Bakers Creek, *Australia* 94 C4
Baker's Dozen Is., *Canada* 102 A4
Bakersfield, *Calif., U.S.A.* 117 K8
Bakersfield, *Vt., U.S.A.* 111 B12
Bakhchysaray, *Ukraine* 47 K7
Bakhmach, *Ukraine* 47 G7
Bākhtarān, *Iran* 70 C5
Bākhtarān □, *Iran* 70 C5
Bakı, *Azerbaijan* 49 K9
Bakır →, *Turkey* 39 C9
Bakırdağı, *Turkey* 72 C6
Bakkafjörður, *Iceland* 8 C6
Baklan, *Turkey* 39 C11
Bako, *Ethiopia* 81 F4
Bako, *Ivory C.* 82 D3
Bakony, *Hungary* 42 C2
Bakony Forest = Bakony, *Hungary* 42 C2
Bakori, *Nigeria* 83 C6
Bakouma, *C.A.R.* 84 C4
Baksan, *Russia* 49 J6
Bakswaho, *India* 69 G8
Baku = Bakı, *Azerbaijan* 49 K9
Bakundi, *Nigeria* 83 D7
Bakutis Coast, *Antarctica* 5 D15
Baky = Bakı, *Azerbaijan* 49 K9
Bala, *Canada* 110 A5
Bala, *Senegal* 82 C2
Bâlâ, *Turkey* 72 C5
Bala, *U.K.* 12 E4
Bala, L., *U.K.* 12 E4
Balabac I., *Phil.* 62 C5
Balabac Str., *E. Indies* 62 C5
Balabagh, *Afghan.* 68 B4
Ba'labakk, *Lebanon* 75 B5
Balabalangan, Kepulauan, *Indonesia* 62 E5
Bălăciţa, *Romania* 43 F8
Balad, *Iraq* 70 C5
Balad Rūz, *Iraq* 70 C5
Bālādeh, *Fārs, Iran* 71 D6
Bālādeh, *Māzandaran, Iran* 71 B6
Balaghat, *India* 66 J12
Balaghat Ra., *India* 66 K10
Balaguer, *Spain* 32 D5
Balakhna, *Russia* 48 B6
Balaklava, *Ukraine* 47 K7
Balakliya, *Ukraine* 47 H9
Balakovo, *Russia* 48 D8
Balamau, *India* 69 F9
Bălan, *Romania* 43 D10
Balancán, *Mexico* 119 D6
Balashov, *Russia* 48 E6
Balasinor, *India* 68 H5
Balasore = Baleshwar, *India* 67 J15
Balassagyarmat, *Hungary* 42 B4
Balât, *Egypt* 80 B2
Balaton, *Hungary* 42 D2
Balatonboglár, *Hungary* 42 D2
Balatonfüred, *Hungary* 42 D2
Balatonszentgyörgy, *Hungary* 42 D2
Balayan, *Phil.* 61 E4
Balazote, *Spain* 33 G2
Balbieriškis, *Lithuania* 44 D10
Balbigny, *France* 21 C8
Balbina, Reprêsa de, *Brazil* 124 D7
Balboa, *Panama* 120 E4
Balbriggan, *Ireland* 15 C5
Balcarce, *Argentina* 126 D4
Balcarres, *Canada* 105 C8
Bălceşti, *Romania* 43 F8
Balchik, *Bulgaria* 41 C12
Balclutha, *N.Z.* 91 M2
Balcones Escarpment, *U.S.A.* 113 L5
Balçova, *Turkey* 39 C9
Bald Hd., *Australia* 93 G2
Bald I., *Australia* 93 F2
Bald Knob, *U.S.A.* 113 H9
Baldock L., *Canada* 105 B9
Baldwin, *Mich., U.S.A.* 108 D3
Baldwin, *Pa., U.S.A.* 110 F5
Baldwinsville, *U.S.A.* 111 C8
Baldy Mt., *U.S.A.* 114 B9
Baldy Peak, *U.S.A.* 115 K9
Bale, *Croatia* 29 C10
Bale, *Ethiopia* 81 F5
Bale □, *Ethiopia* 81 F5
Baleares, Is., *Spain* 37 B10
Balearic Is. = Baleares, Is., *Spain* 37 B10
Baleine = Whale →, *Canada* 103 A6
Băleni, *Romania* 43 E12
Baler, *Phil.* 61 D4
Baler Bay, *Phil.* 61 D4
Baleshare, *U.K.* 14 D1
Baleshwar, *India* 67 J15
Balezino, *Russia* 48 B11
Balfate, *Honduras* 120 C2
Bali, *Cameroon* 83 D7
Balí, *Greece* 36 D6
Bali, *India* 68 G5
Bali, *Indonesia* 62 F4
Bali □, *Indonesia* 62 F5
Bali, Selat, *Indonesia* 63 H16
Balia, *S. Leone* 82 D2
Baliapal, *India* 69 J12
Baligród, *Poland* 45 J9
Balıkeşir, *Turkey* 39 B9
Balıkeşir □, *Turkey* 39 B9
Balıklıçeşme, *Turkey* 41 F11
Balikpapan, *Indonesia* 62 E5
Balimbing, *Phil.* 63 C5
Baling, *Malaysia* 65 K3
Balingen, *Germany* 25 G4
Balinţ, *Romania* 42 E6
Balintang Channel, *Phil.* 61 B4
Balipara, *India* 67 F18
Balkan Mts. = Stara Planina, *Bulgaria* 40 C7
Balkhash = Balqash, *Kazakstan* 50 E8
Balkhash, Ozero = Balqash Köl, *Kazakstan* 50 E8
Balla, *Bangla.* 67 G17
Ballachulish, *U.K.* 14 E3
Balladonia, *Australia* 93 F3
Ballaghaderreen, *Ireland* 15 C3
Ballarat, *Australia* 95 F3
Ballard, L., *Australia* 93 E3
Ballater, *U.K.* 14 D5
Ballé, *Mali* 82 B3
Ballenas, Canal de, *Mexico* 118 B2
Balleny Is., *Antarctica* 5 C11
Balleroy, *France* 18 C6
Ballerup, *Denmark* 11 J6
Ballı, *Turkey* 41 F11
Ballia, *India* 69 G11
Ballina, *Australia* 95 D5
Ballina, *Ireland* 15 B2
Ballinasloe, *Ireland* 15 C3
Ballinger, *U.S.A.* 113 K5
Ballinrobe, *Ireland* 15 C2
Ballinskelligs B., *Ireland* 15 E1
Ballon, *France* 18 D7
Ballsh, *Albania* 40 F3
Ballston Spa, *U.S.A.* 111 D11
Ballycastle, *U.K.* 15 A5
Ballyclare, *U.K.* 15 B5
Ballyhaunis, *Ireland* 15 C3
Ballymena, *U.K.* 15 B5
Ballymoney, *U.K.* 15 A5
Ballymote, *Ireland* 15 B3
Ballynahinch, *U.K.* 15 B6
Ballyquintin Pt., *U.K.* 15 B6
Ballyshannon, *Ireland* 15 B3
Balmaceda, *Chile* 128 F2
Balmaseda, *Spain* 32 B1
Balmazújváros, *Hungary* 42 C6
Balmertown, *Canada* 105 C10
Balmoral, *Australia* 95 F3
Balmorhea, *U.S.A.* 113 K3
Balonne →, *Australia* 95 D4
Balotra, *India* 68 G5
Balqash, *Kazakstan* 50 E8
Balqash Köl, *Kazakstan* 50 E8
Balrampur, *India* 69 F10
Balranald, *Australia* 95 E3
Balş, *Romania* 43 F9
Balsas, *Mexico* 119 D5
Balsas →, *Brazil* 125 E9
Balsas →, *Mexico* 118 D4
Bålsta, *Sweden* 10 E11
Balston Spa, *U.S.A.* 111 D11
Balta, *Romania* 42 F7
Balta, *Ukraine* 47 H5
Baltanás, *Spain* 34 D6
Bălţi, *Moldova* 43 C12
Baltic Sea, *Europe* 9 H18
Baltîm, *Egypt* 80 H7
Baltimore, *Ireland* 15 E2
Baltimore, *Md., U.S.A.* 108 F7
Baltimore, *Ohio, U.S.A.* 110 G2
Baltit, *Pakistan* 69 A6
Baltiysk, *Russia* 9 J18
Baltrum, *Germany* 24 B3
Baluchistan □, *Pakistan* 66 F4
Balurghat, *India* 69 G13
Balvi, *Latvia* 9 H22
Balya, *Turkey* 39 B9
Bam, *Iran* 71 D8
Bama, *China* 58 E6
Bama, *Nigeria* 83 C7
Bamaga, *Australia* 94 A3
Bamaji L., *Canada* 102 B1
Bamako, *Mali* 82 C3
Bamba, *Mali* 83 B4
Bambara Maoundé, *Mali* 82 B4
Bambari, *C.A.R.* 84 C4
Bambaroo, *Australia* 94 B4
Bambaya, *Guinea* 82 D2
Bamberg, *Germany* 25 F6
Bamberg, *U.S.A.* 109 J5
Bambesi, *Ethiopia* 81 F3
Bambey, *Senegal* 82 C1
Bambili, *Dem. Rep. of the Congo* 86 B2
Bamboi, *Ghana* 82 D4
Bamenda, *Cameroon* 83 D7
Bamfield, *Canada* 104 D3
Bāmīān □, *Afghan.* 66 B5
Bamiancheng, *China* 57 C13
Bamkin, *Cameroon* 83 D7
Bampūr, *Iran* 71 E9
Ban, *Burkina Faso* 82 C4
Ban Ban, *Laos* 64 C4
Ban Bang Hin, *Thailand* 65 H2
Ban Chiang Klang, *Thailand* 64 C3
Ban Chik, *Laos* 64 D4
Ban Choho, *Thailand* 64 E4
Ban Dan Lan Hoi, *Thailand* 64 D2
Ban Don = Surat Thani, *Thailand* 65 H2
Ban Don, *Vietnam* 64 F6
Ban Don, Ao →, *Thailand* 65 H2
Ban Dong, *Thailand* 64 C3
Ban Hong, *Thailand* 64 C2
Ban Kaeng, *Thailand* 64 D3
Ban Kantang, *Thailand* 65 J2
Ban Keun, *Laos* 64 C4
Ban Khai, *Thailand* 64 F3
Ban Kheun, *Laos* 64 B3
Ban Khlong Kua, *Thailand* 65 J3
Ban Khuan Mao, *Thailand* 65 J2
Ban Ko Yai Chim, *Thailand* 65 G2
Ban Kok, *Thailand* 64 D4
Ban Laem, *Thailand* 64 F2
Ban Lao Ngam, *Laos* 64 E6
Ban Le Kathe, *Thailand* 64 E2
Ban Mae Chedi, *Thailand* 64 C2
Ban Mae Laeng, *Thailand* 64 B2
Ban Mae Sariang, *Thailand* 64 C1
Ban Mê Thuôt = Buon Ma Thuot, *Vietnam* 64 F7
Ban Mi, *Thailand* 64 E3
Ban Muong Mo, *Laos* 64 C4
Ban Na Mo, *Laos* 64 D5
Ban Na San, *Thailand* 65 H2
Ban Na Tong, *Laos* 64 B3
Ban Nam Bac, *Laos* 64 B4
Ban Nam Ma, *Laos* 64 A3
Ban Ngang, *Laos* 64 E6
Ban Nong Bok, *Laos* 64 D5
Ban Nong Boua, *Laos* 64 E6
Ban Nong Pling, *Thailand* 64 E3
Ban Pak Chan, *Thailand* 65 G2
Ban Phai, *Thailand* 64 D4
Ban Pong, *Thailand* 64 F2
Ban Ron Phibun, *Thailand* 65 H2

Batavia

Ban Sanam Chai, *Thailand* 65 **J3**
Ban Sangkha, *Thailand* 64 **E4**
Ban Tak, *Thailand* 64 **D2**
Ban Tako, *Thailand* 64 **E4**
Ban Tha Dua, *Thailand* 64 **D2**
Ban Tha Li, *Thailand* 64 **D3**
Ban Tha Nun, *Thailand* 65 **H2**
Ban Thahine, *Laos* 64 **E5**
Ban Xien Kok, *Laos* 64 **B3**
Ban Yen Nhan, *Vietnam* 64 **B6**
Banaba, *Kiribati* 96 **H8**
Banalia, *Dem. Rep. of the Congo* 86 **B2**
Banam, *Cambodia* 65 **G5**
Banamba, *Mali* 82 **C3**
Banana Is., *S. Leone* 82 **D2**
Bananal, I. do, *Brazil* 125 **F8**
Banaras = Varanasi, *India* 69 **G10**
Banas →, *Gujarat, India* 68 **H4**
Banas →, *Mad. P., India* 69 **G9**
Bânâs, Ras, *Egypt* 80 **C4**
Banaz, *Turkey* 39 **C11**
Banaz →, *Turkey* 39 **C11**
Banbridge, *U.K.* 15 **B5**
Banbury, *U.K.* 13 **E6**
Banchory, *U.K.* 14 **D6**
Banco, *Ethiopia* 81 **F4**
Bancroft, *Canada* 102 **C4**
Band, *Romania* 43 **D9**
Band Bonī, *Iran* 71 **E8**
Band Qīr, *Iran* 71 **D6**
Banda, *Mad. P., India* 69 **G8**
Banda, *Ut. P., India* 69 **G9**
Banda, Kepulauan, *Indonesia* .. 63 **E7**
Banda Aceh, *Indonesia* 62 **C1**
Banda Banda, Mt., *Australia* ... 95 **E5**
Banda Elat, *Indonesia* 63 **F8**
Banda Is. = Banda, Kepulauan, *Indonesia* 63 **E7**
Banda Sea, *Indonesia* 63 **F7**
Bandai-San, *Japan* 54 **F10**
Bandama →, *Ivory C.* 82 **D3**
Bandama Blanc →, *Ivory C.* .. 82 **D3**
Bandama Rouge →, *Ivory C.* .. 82 **D4**
Bandān, *Iran* 71 **D9**
Bandanaira, *Indonesia* 63 **E7**
Bandanwara, *India* 68 **F6**
Bandar = Machilipatnam, *India* 67 **L12**
Bandār 'Abbās, *Iran* 71 **E8**
Bandar-e Anzalī, *Iran* 71 **B6**
Bandar-e Bushehr = Būshehr, *Iran* 71 **D6**
Bandar-e Chārak, *Iran* 71 **E7**
Bandar-e Deylam, *Iran* 71 **D6**
Bandar-e Khomeynı, *Iran* 71 **D6**
Bandar-e Lengeh, *Iran* 71 **E7**
Bandar-e Maqām, *Iran* 71 **E7**
Bandar-e Ma'shur, *Iran* 71 **D6**
Bandar-e Rīg, *Iran* 71 **D6**
Bandar-e Torkeman, *Iran* 71 **B7**
Bandar Maharani = Muar, *Malaysia* 65 **L4**
Bandar Penggaram = Batu Pahat, *Malaysia* 65 **M4**
Bandar Seri Begawan, *Brunei* .. 62 **C4**
Bandar Sri Aman, *Malaysia* ... 62 **D4**
Bandawe, *Malawi* 87 **E3**
Bande, *Spain* 34 **C3**
Bandeira, Pico da, *Brazil* 127 **A7**
Bandera, *Argentina* 126 **B3**
Banderas, B. de, *Mexico* 118 **C3**
Bandhogarh, *India* 69 **H9**
Bandi →, *India* 68 **F6**
Bandiagara, *Mali* 82 **C4**
Bandikui, *India* 68 **F7**
Bandırma, *Turkey* 41 **F11**
Bandol, *France* 21 **E9**
Bandon, *Ireland* 15 **E3**
Bandon →, *Ireland* 15 **E3**
Bandula, *Mozam.* 87 **F3**
Bandundu, *Dem. Rep. of the Congo* 84 **E3**
Bandung, *Indonesia* 62 **F3**
Bané, *Burkina Faso* 83 **C4**
Băneasa, *Romania* 43 **E12**
Bāneh, *Iran* 70 **C5**
Bañeres, *Spain* 33 **G4**
Banes, *Cuba* 121 **B4**
Banff, *Canada* 104 **C5**
Banff, *U.K.* 14 **D6**
Banff Nat. Park, *Canada* 104 **C5**
Banfora, *Burkina Faso* 82 **C4**
Bang Fai →, *Laos* 64 **D5**
Bang Hieng →, *Laos* 64 **D5**
Bang Krathum, *Thailand* 64 **D3**
Bang Lamung, *Thailand* 64 **F3**
Bang Mun Nak, *Thailand* 64 **D3**
Bang Pa In, *Thailand* 64 **E3**
Bang Rakam, *Thailand* 64 **D3**
Bang Saphan, *Thailand* 65 **G2**
Bangaduni I., *India* 69 **J13**
Bangala Dam, *Zimbabwe* 87 **G3**
Bangalore, *India* 66 **N10**
Banganga →, *India* 68 **F6**
Bangangté, *Cameroon* 83 **D7**
Bangaon, *India* 69 **H13**
Bangassou, *C.A.R.* 84 **D4**
Banggai, *Indonesia* 63 **E6**
Banggai, Kepulauan, *Indonesia* 63 **E6**
Banggai Arch. = Banggai, Kepulauan, *Indonesia* 63 **E6**
Banggi, *Malaysia* 62 **C5**
Banghāzī, *Libya* 79 **B10**
Bangjang, *Sudan* 81 **E3**
Bangka, *Sulawesi, Indonesia* ... 63 **D7**
Bangka, *Sumatera, Indonesia* .. 62 **E3**
Bangka, Selat, *Indonesia* 62 **E3**
Bangkalan, *Indonesia* 63 **G15**
Bangkinang, *Indonesia* 62 **D2**
Bangko, *Indonesia* 62 **E2**
Bangkok, *Thailand* 64 **F3**
Bangladesh ■, *Asia* 67 **H17**
Bangolo, *Ivory C.* 82 **D3**
Bangong Co, *India* 69 **B8**
Bangor, *Down, U.K.* 15 **B6**
Bangor, *Gwynedd, U.K.* 12 **D3**
Bangor, *Maine, U.S.A.* 101 **D13**
Bangor, *Pa., U.S.A.* 111 **F9**
Bangued, *Phil.* 61 **C4**
Bangui, *C.A.R.* 84 **D3**
Bangui, *Phil.* 61 **B4**
Banguru, *Dem. Rep. of the Congo* 86 **B2**
Bangweulu, L., *Zambia* 87 **E3**
Bangweulu Swamp, *Zambia* ... 87 **E3**
Bani, *Dom. Rep.* 121 **C5**
Bani →, *Mali* 82 **C4**
Bani Bangou, *Niger* 83 **B5**
Banī Sa'd, *Iraq* 70 **C5**
Bania, *Ivory C.* 82 **D4**
Banihal Pass, *India* 69 **C6**
Banikoara, *Benin* 83 **C5**
Bāniyās, *Syria* 70 **C3**
Banja Luka, *Bos.-H.* 42 **F2**
Banjar, *India* 68 **D7**
Banjar →, *India* 69 **H9**
Banjarmasin, *Indonesia* 62 **E4**
Banjul, *Gambia* 82 **C1**
Banka, *India* 69 **G12**
Bankas, *Mali* 82 **C4**
Bankeryd, *Sweden* 11 **G8**
Banket, *Zimbabwe* 87 **F3**
Bankilaré, *Niger* 83 **C5**
Bankipore, *India* 67 **G14**
Banks I., *B.C., Canada* 104 **C3**
Banks I., *N.W.T., Canada* 100 **A7**
Banks Pen., *N.Z.* 91 **K4**
Banks Str., *Australia* 94 **G4**
Bankura, *India* 69 **H12**
Bankya, *Bulgaria* 40 **D7**
Banmankhi, *India* 69 **G12**
Bann →, *Arm., U.K.* 15 **B5**
Bann →, *L'derry., U.K.* 15 **A5**
Bannalec, *France* 18 **E3**
Bannang Sata, *Thailand* 65 **J3**
Banning, *U.S.A.* 117 **M10**
Banningville = Bandundu, *Dem. Rep. of the Congo* 84 **E3**
Banno, *Ethiopia* 81 **G4**
Bannockburn, *Canada* 110 **B7**
Bannockburn, *U.K.* 14 **E5**
Bannockburn, *Zimbabwe* 87 **G2**
Bannu, *Pakistan* 66 **C7**
Bano, *India* 69 **H11**
Bañolas = Banyoles, *Spain* 32 **C7**
Banon, *France* 21 **D9**
Baños de la Encina, *Spain* 35 **G7**
Baños de Molgas, *Spain* 34 **C3**
Bánovce nad Bebravou, *Slovak Rep.* 27 **C11**
Banovići, *Bos.-H.* 42 **F3**
Bansgaon, *India* 69 **F10**
Banská Bystrica, *Slovak Rep.* .. 27 **C12**
Banská Štiavnica, *Slovak Rep.* . 27 **C11**
Bansko, *Bulgaria* 40 **E7**
Banskobystrický □, *Slovak Rep.* 27 **C12**
Banswara, *India* 68 **H6**
Bantaeng, *Indonesia* 63 **F5**
Bantaji, *Nigeria* 83 **D7**
Bantayan, *Phil.* 61 **F5**
Bantry, *Ireland* 15 **E2**
Bantry B., *Ireland* 15 **E2**
Bantul, *Indonesia* 63 **G14**
Bantva, *India* 68 **J4**
Banya, *Bulgaria* 41 **D8**
Banyak, Kepulauan, *Indonesia* . 62 **D1**
Banyalbufar, *Spain* 37 **B9**
Banyo, *Cameroon* 83 **D7**
Banyoles, *Spain* 32 **C7**
Banyuls-sur-Mer, *France* 20 **F7**
Banyumas, *Indonesia* 63 **G13**
Banyuwangi, *Indonesia* 63 **H16**
Banzare Coast, *Antarctica* 5 **C9**
Banzyville = Mobayi, *Dem. Rep. of the Congo* 84 **D4**
Bao Ha, *Vietnam* 58 **F5**
Bao Lac, *Vietnam* 64 **A5**
Bao Loc, *Vietnam* 65 **G6**
Bao'an = Shenzhen, *China* 59 **F10**
Baocheng, *China* 56 **H4**
Baode, *China* 56 **E6**
Baodi, *China* 57 **E9**
Baoding, *China* 56 **E8**
Baoji, *China* 56 **G4**
Baojing, *China* 58 **C7**
Baokang, *China* 59 **B8**
Baoshan, *Shanghai, China* 59 **B13**
Baoshan, *Yunnan, China* 58 **E2**
Baotou, *China* 56 **D6**
Baoxing, *China* 58 **B4**
Baoying, *China* 57 **H10**
Bap, *India* 68 **F5**
Bapatla, *India* 67 **M12**
Bapaume, *France* 19 **B9**
Bāqerābād, *Iran* 71 **C6**
Ba'qūbah, *Iraq* 70 **C5**
Baquedano, *Chile* 126 **A2**
Bar, *Montenegro, Yug.* 40 **D3**
Bar, *Ukraine* 47 **H4**
Bar Bigha, *India* 69 **G11**
Bar Harbor, *U.S.A.* 109 **C11**
Bar-le-Duc, *France* 19 **D12**
Bar-sur-Aube, *France* 19 **D11**
Bar-sur-Seine, *France* 19 **D11**
Bara, *India* 69 **G9**
Bâra, *Romania* 43 **C12**
Bara Banki, *India* 69 **F9**
Barabai, *Indonesia* 62 **E5**
Baraboo, *U.S.A.* 112 **D10**
Baracoa, *Cuba* 121 **B5**
Baradā →, *Syria* 75 **B5**
Baradero, *Argentina* 126 **C4**
Baraga, *U.S.A.* 112 **B10**
Bărăganul, *Romania* 43 **F12**
Barah →, *India* 68 **F6**
Barahona, *Dom. Rep.* 121 **C5**
Barahona, *Spain* 32 **D2**
Barail Range, *India* 67 **G18**
Baraka, *Sudan* 81 **E2**
Baraka →, *Sudan* 80 **D4**
Barakaldo, *Spain* 32 **B2**
Barakar →, *India* 69 **G12**
Barakhola, *India* 67 **G18**
Barakot, *India* 69 **J11**
Barakpur, *India* 69 **H13**
Baralaba, *Australia* 94 **C4**
Baralla, *Spain* 34 **C3**
Baralzon L., *Canada* 105 **B9**
Barameiya, *Sudan* 80 **D4**
Baramula, *India* 69 **B6**
Baran, *India* 68 **G7**
Baran →, *Pakistan* 68 **G3**
Barañain, *Spain* 32 **C3**
Baranavichy, *Belarus* 47 **F4**
Barani, *Burkina Faso* 82 **C4**
Baranof, *U.S.A.* 104 **B2**
Baranof I., *U.S.A.* 100 **C6**
Baranów Sandomierski, *Poland* 45 **H8**
Baranya □, *Hungary* 42 **E3**
Baraolt, *Romania* 43 **D10**
Barapasi, *Indonesia* 63 **E9**
Barasat, *India* 69 **H13**
Barat Daya, Kepulauan, *Indonesia* 63 **F7**
Barataria B., *U.S.A.* 113 **L10**
Barauda, *India* 68 **H6**
Baraut, *India* 68 **E7**
Barbacena, *Brazil* 127 **A7**
Barbados ■, *W. Indies* 121 **D8**
Barban, *Croatia* 29 **C11**
Barbària, C. de, *Spain* 37 **C7**
Barbaros, *Turkey* 41 **F11**
Barbastro, *Spain* 32 **C5**
Barbate = Barbate de Franco, *Spain* 35 **J5**
Barbate de Franco, *Spain* 35 **J5**
Barberino di Mugello, *Italy* 29 **E8**
Barberton, *S. Africa* 89 **D5**
Barberton, *U.S.A.* 110 **E3**
Barbezieux-St-Hilaire, *France* . 20 **C3**
Barbosa, *Colombia* 124 **B4**
Barbourville, *U.S.A.* 109 **G4**
Barbuda, *W. Indies* 121 **C7**
Bârca, *Romania* 43 **G8**
Barcaldine, *Australia* 94 **C4**
Barcarrota, *Spain* 35 **G4**
Barcellona Pozzo di Gotto, *Italy* 31 **D8**
Barcelona, *Spain* 32 **D7**
Barcelona, *Venezuela* 124 **A6**
Barcelona □, *Spain* 32 **D7**
Barcelonette, *France* 21 **D10**
Barcelos, *Brazil* 124 **D6**
Barcin, *Poland* 45 **F4**
Barclayville, *Liberia* 82 **E3**
Barcoo →, *Australia* 94 **D3**
Barcs, *Hungary* 42 **E2**
Barczewo, *Poland* 44 **E7**
Bärdä, *Azerbaijan* 49 **K8**
Bardaï, *Chad* 79 **D9**
Bardas Blancas, *Argentina* 126 **D2**
Barddhaman, *India* 69 **H12**
Bardejov, *Slovak Rep.* 27 **B14**
Bardera, *Somali Rep.* 74 **G3**
Bardi, *Italy* 28 **D6**
Bardīyah, *Libya* 79 **B10**
Bardolino, *Italy* 28 **C7**
Bardonécchia, *Italy* 28 **C3**
Bardsey I., *U.K.* 12 **E3**
Bardstown, *U.S.A.* 108 **G3**
Bareilly, *India* 69 **E8**
Barela, *India* 69 **H9**
Barentin, *France* 18 **C7**
Barenton, *France* 18 **D6**
Barents Sea, *Arctic* 4 **B9**
Barentu, *Eritrea* 81 **D4**
Barfleur, *France* 18 **C5**
Barfleur, Pte. de, *France* 18 **C5**
Barga, *Italy* 28 **D7**
Bargara, *Australia* 94 **C5**
Bargas, *Spain* 34 **F6**
Bârgăului Bistriţa, *Romania* ... 43 **C9**
Barge, *Italy* 28 **D4**
Bargnop, *Sudan* 81 **F2**
Bargteheide, *Germany* 24 **B6**
Barguzin, *Russia* 51 **D11**
Barh, *India* 69 **G11**
Barhaj, *India* 69 **F10**
Barharwa, *India* 69 **G12**
Barhi, *India* 69 **G11**
Bari, *India* 68 **F7**
Bari, *Italy* 31 **A9**
Bari Doab, *Pakistan* 68 **D5**
Bari Sadri, *India* 68 **G6**
Bari Sardo, *Italy* 30 **C2**
Barīdī, Ra's, *Si. Arabia* 70 **E3**
Barīm, *Yemen* 76 **E8**
Barinas, *Venezuela* 124 **B4**
Baring, C., *Canada* 100 **B8**
Baringo, *Kenya* 86 **B4**
Baringo, L., *Kenya* 86 **B4**
Bârîs, *Egypt* 80 **C3**
Barisal, *Bangla.* 67 **H17**
Barisal □, *Bangla.* 67 **H17**
Barisan, Bukit, *Indonesia* 62 **E2**
Barito →, *Indonesia* 62 **E4**
Barjac, *France* 21 **D8**
Barjols, *France* 21 **E10**
Bark L., *Canada* 110 **A7**
Barka = Baraka →, *Sudan* 80 **D4**
Barkakana, *India* 69 **H11**
Barkam, *China* 58 **B4**
Barker, *U.S.A.* 110 **C6**
Barkley, L., *U.S.A.* 109 **G2**
Barkley Sound, *Canada* 104 **D3**
Barkly East, *S. Africa* 88 **E4**
Barkly Roadhouse, *Australia* .. 94 **B2**
Barkly Tableland, *Australia* ... 94 **B2**
Barkly West, *S. Africa* 88 **D3**
Barkol, Wadi →, *Sudan* 80 **D3**
Barla Dağı, *Turkey* 39 **C12**
Bârlad, *Romania* 43 **D12**
Bârlad →, *Romania* 43 **E12**
Barlee, L., *Australia* 93 **E2**
Barlee, Mt., *Australia* 93 **D4**
Barletta, *Italy* 31 **A9**
Barlinek, *Poland* 45 **F2**
Barlovento, *Canary Is.* 37 **F2**
Barlow L., *Canada* 105 **A8**
Barmedman, *Australia* 95 **E4**
Barmer, *India* 68 **G4**
Barmera, *Australia* 95 **E3**
Barmouth, *U.K.* 12 **E3**
Barmstedt, *Germany* 24 **B5**
Barna →, *India* 69 **G10**
Barnagar, *India* 68 **H6**
Barnala, *India* 68 **D6**
Barnard Castle, *U.K.* 12 **C6**
Barnaul, *Russia* 50 **D9**
Barnesville, *U.S.A.* 109 **J3**
Barnet □, *U.K.* 13 **F7**
Barneveld, *Neths.* 17 **B5**
Barneveld, *U.S.A.* 111 **C9**
Barneville-Cartevert, *France* .. 18 **C5**
Barnhart, *U.S.A.* 113 **K4**
Barnsley, *U.K.* 12 **D6**
Barnstaple, *U.K.* 13 **F3**
Barnstaple Bay = Bideford Bay, *U.K.* 13 **F3**
Barnsville, *U.S.A.* 112 **B6**
Barnwell, *U.S.A.* 109 **J5**
Baro, *Nigeria* 83 **D6**
Baro →, *Ethiopia* 81 **F3**
Baroda = Vadodara, *India* 68 **H5**
Baroda, *India* 68 **G7**
Baroe, *S. Africa* 88 **E3**
Baron Ra., *Australia* 92 **D4**
Barong, *China* 58 **B2**
Barotseland, *Zambia* 85 **H4**
Barouéli, *Mali* 82 **C3**
Barpeta, *India* 67 **F17**
Barques, Pt. Aux, *U.S.A.* 110 **B2**
Barquísimeto, *Venezuela* 124 **A5**
Barr, Ras el, *Egypt* 80 **H7**
Barr Smith Range, *Australia* ... 93 **E3**
Barra, *Brazil* 125 **F10**
Barra, *U.K.* 14 **E1**
Barra, Sd. of, *U.K.* 14 **D1**
Barra de Navidad, *Mexico* 118 **D4**
Barra do Corda, *Brazil* 125 **E9**
Barra do Piraí, *Brazil* 127 **A7**
Barra Falsa, Pta. da, *Mozam.* .. 89 **C6**
Barra Hd., *U.K.* 14 **E1**
Barra Mansa, *Brazil* 127 **A7**
Barraba, *Australia* 95 **E5**
Barrackpur = Barakpur, *India* . 69 **H13**
Barradale Roadhouse, *Australia* 92 **D1**
Barrafranca, *Italy* 31 **E7**
Barraigh = Barra, *U.K.* 14 **E1**
Barranca, *Lima, Peru* 124 **F3**
Barranca, *Loreto, Peru* 124 **D3**
Barrancabermeja, *Colombia* ... 124 **B4**
Barrancas, *Venezuela* 124 **B6**
Barrancos, *Portugal* 35 **G4**
Barranqueras, *Argentina* 126 **B4**
Barranquilla, *Colombia* 124 **A4**
Barraute, *Canada* 102 **C4**
Barre, *Mass., U.S.A.* 111 **D12**
Barre, *Vt., U.S.A.* 111 **B12**
Barreal, *Argentina* 126 **C2**
Barreiras, *Brazil* 125 **F10**
Barreirinhas, *Brazil* 125 **D10**
Barreiro, *Portugal* 35 **G1**
Barrême, *France* 21 **E10**
Barren, Nosy, *Madag.* 89 **B7**
Barretos, *Brazil* 125 **H9**
Barrhead, *Canada* 104 **C6**
Barrie, *Canada* 102 **D4**
Barrier Ra., *Australia* 95 **E3**
Barrière, *Canada* 104 **C4**
Barrington, *U.S.A.* 111 **E13**
Barrington L., *Canada* 105 **B8**
Barrington Tops, *Australia* ... 95 **E5**
Barringun, *Australia* 95 **D4**
Barro do Garças, *Brazil* 125 **G8**
Barron, *U.S.A.* 112 **C9**
Barrow, *U.S.A.* 100 **A4**
Barrow →, *Ireland* 15 **D5**
Barrow, Pt., *U.S.A.* 98 **B4**
Barrow Creek, *Australia* 94 **C1**
Barrow I., *Australia* 92 **D2**
Barrow-in-Furness, *U.K.* 12 **C4**
Barrow Pt., *Australia* 94 **A3**
Barrow Ra., *Australia* 93 **E4**
Barrow Str., *Canada* 4 **B3**
Barruecopardo, *Spain* 34 **D4**
Barruelo de Santullán, *Spain* .. 34 **C6**
Barry, *U.K.* 13 **F4**
Barry's Bay, *Canada* 102 **C4**
Barsalogho, *Burkina Faso* 83 **C4**
Barsat, *Pakistan* 69 **A5**
Barsham, *Syria* 70 **C4**
Barsi, *India* 66 **K9**
Barsinghausen, *Germany* 24 **C5**
Barsoi, *India* 67 **G15**
Barstow, *U.S.A.* 117 **L9**
Barth, *Germany* 24 **A8**
Barthélemy, Col, *Vietnam* 64 **C5**
Bartica, *Guyana* 124 **B7**
Bartin, *Turkey* 72 **B5**
Bartlesville, *U.S.A.* 113 **G7**
Bartlett, *U.S.A.* 116 **J8**
Bartlett, L., *Canada* 104 **A5**
Bartolomeu Dias, *Mozam.* 87 **G4**
Barton, *U.S.A.* 111 **B12**
Barton upon Humber, *U.K.* ... 12 **D7**
Bartoszyce, *Poland* 44 **D7**
Bartow, *U.S.A.* 109 **M5**
Barú, Volcan, *Panama* 120 **E3**
Barumba, *Dem. Rep. of the Congo* 86 **B1**
Baruth, *Germany* 24 **C9**
Baruunsuu, *Mongolia* 56 **C3**
Barvinkove, *Ukraine* 47 **H9**
Barwani, *India* 68 **H6**
Barwice, *Poland* 44 **E3**
Barycz →, *Poland* 45 **G3**
Barysaw, *Belarus* 46 **E5**
Barysh, *Russia* 48 **D8**
Barzān, *Iraq* 70 **B5**
Bârzava, *Romania* 42 **D6**
Bas-Rhin □, *France* 19 **D14**
Bašaid, *Serbia, Yug.* 42 **E5**
Bāsa'idū, *Iran* 71 **E7**
Basal, *Pakistan* 68 **C5**
Basankusa, *Dem. Rep. of the Congo* 84 **D3**
Basarabeasca, *Moldova* 43 **D13**
Basarabi, *Romania* 43 **F13**
Basauri, *Spain* 32 **B2**
Basawa, *Afghan.* 68 **B4**
Bascuñán, C., *Chile* 126 **B1**
Basel, *Switz.* 25 **H3**
Basel-Landschaft □, *Switz.* 25 **H3**
Basento →, *Italy* 31 **B9**
Bashākerd, Kūhhā-ye, *Iran* 71 **E8**
Bashaw, *Canada* 104 **C6**
Bāshī, *Iran* 71 **D6**
Bashkir Republic = Bashkortostan □, *Russia* 50 **D6**
Bashkortostan □, *Russia* 50 **D6**
Basibasy, *Madag.* 89 **C7**
Basilan I., *Phil.* 61 **H5**
Basilan Str., *Phil.* 61 **H5**
Basildon, *U.K.* 13 **F8**
Basile, *Eq. Guin.* 83 **E6**
Basilicata □, *Italy* 31 **B9**
Basim = Washim, *India* 66 **J10**
Basin, *U.S.A.* 114 **D9**
Basingstoke, *U.K.* 13 **F6**
Baška, *Croatia* 29 **D11**
Başkale, *Turkey* 73 **C10**
Baskatong, Rés., *Canada* 102 **C4**
Basle = Basel, *Switz.* 25 **H3**
Başmakçı, *Turkey* 39 **D12**
Basoda, *India* 68 **H7**
Basoka, *Dem. Rep. of the Congo* 86 **B1**
Basque, Pays, *France* 20 **E2**
Basque Provinces = País Vasco □, *Spain* 32 **C2**
Basra = Al Başrah, *Iraq* 70 **D5**
Bass Str., *Australia* 94 **F4**
Bassano, *Canada* 104 **C6**
Bassano del Grappa, *Italy* 29 **C8**
Bassar, *Togo* 83 **D5**
Bassas da India, *Ind. Oc.* 85 **J7**
Basse-Normandie □, *France* ... 18 **D6**
Basse Santa-Su, *Gambia* 82 **C2**
Basse-Terre, *Guadeloupe* 121 **C7**
Bassein, *Burma* 67 **L19**
Basseterre, *St. Kitts & Nevis* ... 121 **C7**
Bassett, *U.S.A.* 112 **D5**
Bassi, *India* 68 **D7**
Bassigny, *France* 19 **E12**
Bassikounou, *Mauritania* 82 **B3**
Bassila, *Benin* 83 **D5**
Bassum, *Germany* 24 **C4**
Båstad, *Sweden* 11 **H6**
Bastak, *Iran* 71 **E7**
Baştām, *Iran* 71 **B7**
Bastar, *India* 67 **K12**
Bastelica, *France* 21 **F13**
Basti, *India* 69 **F10**
Bastia, *France* 21 **F13**
Bastogne, *Belgium* 17 **D5**
Bastrop, *La., U.S.A.* 113 **J9**
Bastrop, *Tex., U.S.A.* 113 **K6**
Bat Yam, *Israel* 75 **C3**
Bata, *Eq. Guin.* 84 **D1**
Bata, *Romania* 42 **D7**
Bataan □, *Phil.* 61 **D4**
Batabanó, *Cuba* 120 **B3**
Batabanó, G. de, *Cuba* 120 **B3**
Batac, *Phil.* 61 **B4**
Batagai, *Russia* 51 **C14**
Batajnica, *Serbia, Yug.* 40 **B4**
Batak, *Bulgaria* 41 **E8**
Batala, *India* 68 **D6**
Batalha, *Portugal* 34 **F2**
Batama, *Dem. Rep. of the Congo* 86 **B2**
Batamay, *Russia* 51 **C13**
Batang, *China* 58 **B2**
Batang, *Indonesia* 63 **G13**
Batangas, *Phil.* 61 **E4**
Batanta, *Indonesia* 63 **E8**
Batatais, *Brazil* 127 **A6**
Batavia, *U.S.A.* 110 **D6**

Bataysk, *Russia* 47 J10
Batchelor, *Australia* 92 B5
Batdambang, *Cambodia* 64 F4
Batemans B., *Australia* 95 F5
Batemans Bay, *Australia* 95 F5
Bates Ra., *Australia* 93 E3
Batesburg-Leesville, *U.S.A.* 109 J5
Batesville, *Ark., U.S.A.* 113 H9
Batesville, *Miss., U.S.A.* 113 H10
Batesville, *Tex., U.S.A.* 113 L5
Bath, *Canada* 111 B8
Bath, *U.K.* 13 F5
Bath, *Maine, U.S.A.* 109 D11
Bath, *N.Y., U.S.A.* 110 D7
Bath & North East Somerset □, *U.K.* 13 F5
Batheay, *Cambodia* 65 G5
Bathurst = Banjul, *Gambia* 82 C1
Bathurst, *Australia* 95 E4
Bathurst, *Canada* 103 C6
Bathurst, *S. Africa* 88 E4
Bathurst, C., *Canada* 100 A7
Bathurst B., *Australia* 94 A3
Bathurst Harb., *Australia* 94 G4
Bathurst I., *Australia* 92 B5
Bathurst I., *Canada* 4 B2
Bathurst Inlet, *Canada* 100 B9
Bati, *Ethiopia* 81 E5
Batie, *Burkina Faso* 82 D4
Batlow, *Australia* 95 F4
Batman, *Turkey* 70 B4
Baṭn al Ghūl, *Jordan* 75 F4
Batna, *Algeria* 78 A7
Batobato = San Isidro, *Phil.* 61 H7
Batočina, *Serbia, Yug.* 40 B5
Batoka, *Zambia* 87 F2
Baton Rouge, *U.S.A.* 113 K9
Batong, Ko, *Thailand* 65 J2
Bátonyterenye, *Hungary* 42 C4
Batopilas, *Mexico* 118 B3
Batouri, *Cameroon* 84 D2
Båtsfjord, *Norway* 8 A23
Battambang = Batdambang, *Cambodia* 64 F4
Batticaloa, *Sri Lanka* 66 R12
Battipáglia, *Italy* 31 B7
Battle, *U.K.* 13 G8
Battle →, *Canada* 105 C7
Battle Creek, *U.S.A.* 108 D3
Battle Ground, *U.S.A.* 116 E4
Battle Harbour, *Canada* 103 B8
Battle Lake, *U.S.A.* 112 B7
Battle Mountain, *U.S.A.* 114 F5
Battlefields, *Zimbabwe* 87 F2
Battleford, *Canada* 105 C7
Battonya, *Hungary* 42 D6
Batu, *Ethiopia* 81 F4
Batu, Kepulauan, *Indonesia* 62 E1
Batu Caves, *Malaysia* 65 L3
Batu Gajah, *Malaysia* 65 K3
Batu Is. = Batu, Kepulauan, *Indonesia* 62 E1
Batu Pahat, *Malaysia* 65 M4
Batuata, *Indonesia* 63 F6
Batumi, *Georgia* 49 K5
Baturaja, *Indonesia* 62 E2
Baturité, *Brazil* 125 D11
Bau, *Malaysia* 62 D4
Baubau, *Indonesia* 63 F6
Bauchi, *Nigeria* 83 C6
Bauchi □, *Nigeria* 83 C7
Baud, *France* 18 E3
Baudette, *U.S.A.* 112 A7
Bauer, C., *Australia* 95 E1
Bauhinia, *Australia* 94 C4
Baukau, *E. Timor* 63 F7
Bauld, C., *Canada* 101 C14
Baume-les-Dames, *France* 19 E13
Baunatal, *Germany* 24 D5
Baunei, *Italy* 30 B2
Baure, *Nigeria* 83 C6
Bauru, *Brazil* 127 A6
Bausi, *India* 69 G12
Bauska, *Latvia* 9 H21
Bautino, *Kazakstan* 49 H10
Bautzen, *Germany* 24 D10
Bauya, *S. Leone* 82 D2
Bavānāt, *Iran* 71 D7
Bavanište, *Serbia, Yug.* 42 F5
Bavaria = Bayern □, *Germany* 25 G7
Båven, *Sweden* 10 E10
Bavispe →, *Mexico* 118 B3
Bawdwin, *Burma* 67 H20
Bawean, *Indonesia* 62 F4
Bawku, *Ghana* 83 C4
Bawlake, *Burma* 67 K20
Bawolung, *China* 58 C3
Baxley, *U.S.A.* 109 K4
Baxoi, *China* 58 B1
Baxter, *U.S.A.* 112 B7
Baxter Springs, *U.S.A.* 113 G7
Bay, L. de, *Phil.* 61 D4
Bay City, *Mich., U.S.A.* 108 D4
Bay City, *Tex., U.S.A.* 113 L7
Bay Minette, *U.S.A.* 109 K2
Bay Roberts, *Canada* 103 C9
Bay St. Louis, *U.S.A.* 113 K10
Bay Springs, *U.S.A.* 113 K10
Bay View, *N.Z.* 91 H6
Baya, *Dem. Rep. of the Congo* 87 E2
Bayamo, *Cuba* 120 B4
Bayamón, *Puerto Rico* 121 C6
Bayan Har Shan, *China* 60 C4
Bayan Hot = Alxa Zuoqi, *China* 56 E3
Bayan Obo, *China* 56 D5
Bayan-Ovoo = Erdenetsogt, *Mongolia* 56 C4
Bayana, *India* 68 F7
Bayanaūyl, *Kazakstan* 50 D8
Bayandalay, *Mongolia* 56 C2
Bayanhongor, *Mongolia* 60 B5
Bayard, *N. Mex., U.S.A.* 115 K9
Bayard, *Nebr., U.S.A.* 112 E3
Bayawan, *Phil.* 61 G5
Baybay, *Phil.* 61 F6
Bayburt, *Turkey* 73 B9
Bayelsa □, *Nigeria* 83 E6
Bayerische Alpen, *Germany* 25 H7
Bayerischer Wald, *Germany* 25 G8
Bayern □, *Germany* 25 G7
Bayeux, *France* 18 C6
Bayfield, *Canada* 110 C3
Bayfield, *U.S.A.* 112 B9
Bayındır, *Turkey* 39 C9
Baykal, Oz., *Russia* 51 D11
Baykan, *Turkey* 70 B4
Baykonur = Bayqongyr, *Kazakstan* 50 E7
Baynes Mts., *Namibia* 88 B1
Bayombong, *Phil.* 61 C4
Bayon, *France* 19 D13
Bayona = Baiona, *Spain* 34 C2
Bayonne, *France* 20 E2
Bayonne, *U.S.A.* 111 F10
Bayovar, *Peru* 124 E2
Bayqongyr, *Kazakstan* 50 E7
Bayram-Ali = Bayramaly, *Turkmenistan* 50 F7
Bayramaly, *Turkmenistan* 50 F7
Bayramiç, *Turkey* 39 B8
Bayreuth, *Germany* 25 F7
Bayrischzell, *Germany* 25 H8
Bayrūt, *Lebanon* 75 B4
Bays, L. of, *Canada* 110 A5
Baysville, *Canada* 110 A5
Bayt Lahm, *West Bank* 75 D4
Baytown, *U.S.A.* 113 L7
Bayzo, *Niger* 83 C5
Baza, *Spain* 35 H8
Bazar Dyuzi, *Russia* 49 K8
Bazardüzü = Bazar Dyuzi, *Russia* 49 K8
Bazarny Karabulak, *Russia* 48 D8
Bazarnyy Syzgan, *Russia* 48 D8
Bazaruto, I. do, *Mozam.* 89 C6
Bazas, *France* 20 D3
Bazhong, *China* 58 B6
Bazhou, *China* 56 E9
Bazmān, Kūh-e, *Iran* 71 D9
Beach, *U.S.A.* 112 B3
Beach City, *U.S.A.* 110 F3
Beachport, *Australia* 95 F3
Beachy Hd., *U.K.* 13 G8
Beacon, *Australia* 93 F2
Beacon, *U.S.A.* 111 E11
Beaconsfield, *Australia* 94 G4
Beagle, Canal, *S. Amer.* 122 J4
Beagle Bay, *Australia* 92 C3
Bealanana, *Madag.* 89 A8
Beals Cr. →, *U.S.A.* 113 J4
Beamsville, *Canada* 110 C5
Bear →, *Calif., U.S.A.* 116 G5
Bear →, *Utah, U.S.A.* 106 B4
Béar, C., *France* 20 F7
Bear I., *Ireland* 15 E2
Bear L., *Canada* 105 B9
Bear L., *U.S.A.* 114 F8
Beardmore, *Canada* 102 C2
Beardmore Glacier, *Antarctica* 5 E11
Beardstown, *U.S.A.* 112 F9
Bearma →, *India* 69 G8
Béarn, *France* 20 E3
Bearpaw Mts., *U.S.A.* 114 B9
Bearskin Lake, *Canada* 102 B1
Beas →, *India* 68 D6
Beas de Segura, *Spain* 35 G8
Beasain, *Spain* 32 B2
Beata, C., *Dom. Rep.* 121 C5
Beata, I., *Dom. Rep.* 121 C5
Beatrice, *U.S.A.* 112 E6
Beatrice, *Zimbabwe* 87 F3
Beatrice, C., *Australia* 94 A2
Beatton →, *Canada* 104 B4
Beatton River, *Canada* 104 B4
Beatty, *U.S.A.* 116 J10
Beaucaire, *France* 21 E8
Beauce, Plaine de la, *France* 19 D8
Beauceville, *Canada* 103 C5
Beaudesert, *Australia* 95 D5
Beaufort, *France* 21 C10
Beaufort, *Malaysia* 62 C5
Beaufort, *N.C., U.S.A.* 109 H7
Beaufort, *S.C., U.S.A.* 109 J5
Beaufort Sea, *Arctic* 4 B1
Beaufort West, *S. Africa* 88 E3
Beaugency, *France* 19 E8
Beauharnois, *Canada* 111 A11
Beaujeu, *France* 19 F11
Beaujolais, *France* 19 F11
Beaulieu →, *Canada* 104 A6
Beaulieu-sur-Dordogne, *France* 20 D5
Beaulieu-sur-Mer, *France* 21 E11
Beauly, *U.K.* 14 D4
Beauly →, *U.K.* 14 D4
Beaumaris, *U.K.* 12 D3
Beaumont, *Belgium* 17 D4
Beaumont, *France* 20 D4
Beaumont, *U.S.A.* 113 K7
Beaumont-de-Lomagne, *France* 20 E5
Beaumont-le-Roger, *France* 18 C7
Beaumont-sur-Sarthe, *France* 18 D7
Beaune, *France* 19 E11
Beaune-la-Rolande, *France* 19 D9
Beaupré, *Canada* 103 C5
Beaupréau, *France* 18 E6
Beauraing, *Belgium* 17 D4
Beaurepaire, *France* 21 C9
Beauséjour, *Canada* 105 C9
Beauvais, *France* 19 C9
Beauval, *Canada* 105 B7
Beauvoir-sur-Mer, *France* 18 F4
Beauvoir-sur-Niort, *France* 20 B3
Beaver, *Okla., U.S.A.* 113 G4
Beaver, *Pa., U.S.A.* 110 F4
Beaver, *Utah, U.S.A.* 115 G7
Beaver →, *B.C., Canada* 104 B4
Beaver →, *Ont., Canada* 102 A2
Beaver →, *Sask., Canada* 105 B7
Beaver →, *U.S.A.* 113 G5
Beaver City, *U.S.A.* 112 E5
Beaver Creek, *Canada* 100 B5
Beaver Dam, *U.S.A.* 112 D10
Beaver Falls, *U.S.A.* 110 F4
Beaver Hill L., *Canada* 105 C10
Beaver I., *U.S.A.* 108 C3
Beaverhill L., *Canada* 104 C6
Beaverlodge, *Canada* 104 B5
Beaverstone →, *Canada* 102 B2
Beaverton, *Canada* 110 B5
Beaverton, *U.S.A.* 116 E4
Beawar, *India* 68 F6
Bebedouro, *Brazil* 127 A6
Beboa, *Madag.* 89 B7
Bebra, *Germany* 24 E5
Beccles, *U.K.* 13 E9
Bečej, *Serbia, Yug.* 42 E5
Beceni, *Romania* 43 E11
Becerreá, *Spain* 34 C3
Béchar, *Algeria* 78 B5
Bechyně, *Czech Rep.* 26 B7
Beckley, *U.S.A.* 108 G5
Beckum, *Germany* 24 D4
Beclean, *Romania* 43 C9
Bečov nad Teplou, *Czech Rep.* 26 A5
Bečva →, *Czech Rep.* 27 B10
Bédar, *Spain* 33 H3
Bédarieux, *France* 20 E7
Beddouza, Ras, *Morocco* 78 B4
Bedele, *Ethiopia* 81 F4
Bederkesa, *Germany* 24 B4
Bedeso, *Ethiopia* 81 F5
Bedford, *Canada* 111 A12
Bedford, *S. Africa* 88 E4
Bedford, *U.K.* 13 E7
Bedford, *Ind., U.S.A.* 108 F2
Bedford, *Iowa, U.S.A.* 112 E7
Bedford, *Ohio, U.S.A.* 110 E3
Bedford, *Pa., U.S.A.* 110 F6
Bedford, *Va., U.S.A.* 108 G6
Bedford, C., *Australia* 94 B4
Bedfordshire □, *U.K.* 13 E7
Będków, *Poland* 45 G6
Bednja →, *Croatia* 29 B13
Bednodemyanovsk, *Russia* 48 D6
Bedónia, *Italy* 28 D6
Bedourie, *Australia* 94 C2
Bedum, *Neths.* 17 A6
Będzin, *Poland* 45 H6
Beebe Plain, *Canada* 111 A12
Beech Creek, *U.S.A.* 110 E7
Beelitz, *Germany* 24 C8
Beenleigh, *Australia* 95 D5
Be'er Menuḥa, *Israel* 70 D2
Be'er Sheva, *Israel* 75 D3
Beersheba = Be'er Sheva, *Israel* 75 D3
Beeskow, *Germany* 24 C10
Beestekraal, *S. Africa* 89 D4
Beeston, *U.K.* 12 E6
Beetzendorf, *Germany* 24 C7
Beeville, *U.S.A.* 113 L6
Befale, *Dem. Rep. of the Congo* 84 D4
Befandriana, *Mahajanga, Madag.* 89 B8
Befandriana, *Toliara, Madag.* 89 C7
Befasy, *Madag.* 89 C7
Befotaka, *Antsiranana, Madag.* 89 A8
Befotaka, *Fianarantsoa, Madag.* 89 C8
Bega, *Australia* 95 F4
Bega, Canalul, *Romania* 42 E5
Bégard, *France* 18 D3
Beğendik, *Turkey* 41 F10
Begoro, *Ghana* 83 D4
Begusarai, *India* 69 G12
Behābād, *Iran* 71 C8
Behala, *India* 69 H13
Behara, *Madag.* 89 C8
Behbehān, *Iran* 71 D6
Behm Canal, *U.S.A.* 104 B2
Behshahr, *Iran* 71 B7
Bei Jiang →, *China* 59 F9
Bei'an, *China* 60 B7
Beibei, *China* 58 C6
Beichuan, *China* 58 B5
Beihai, *China* 58 G7
Beijing, *China* 56 E9
Beijing □, *China* 56 E9
Beilen, *Neths.* 17 B6
Beiliu, *China* 59 F8
Beilngries, *Germany* 25 F7
Beilpajah, *Australia* 95 E3
Beilul, *Eritrea* 81 E5
Beinn na Faoghla = Benbecula, *U.K.* 14 D1
Beipan Jiang, *China* 58 E5
Beipiao, *China* 57 D11
Beira, *Mozam.* 87 F3
Beirut = Bayrūt, *Lebanon* 75 B4
Beiseker, *Canada* 104 C6
Beitaolaizhao, *China* 57 B13
Beitbridge, *Zimbabwe* 87 G3
Beiuş, *Romania* 42 D7
Beizhen = Binzhou, *China* 57 F10
Beizhen, *China* 57 D11
Beizhengzhen, *China* 57 B12
Beja, *Portugal* 35 G3
Béja, *Tunisia* 79 A7
Beja □, *Portugal* 35 H3
Bejaïa, *Algeria* 78 A7
Béjar, *Spain* 34 E5
Bejestān, *Iran* 71 C8
Bekçiler, *Turkey* 39 E11
Békés, *Hungary* 42 D6
Békés □, *Hungary* 42 D6
Békéscsaba, *Hungary* 42 D6
Bekilli, *Turkey* 39 C11
Bekily, *Madag.* 89 C8
Bekisopa, *Madag.* 89 C8
Bekitro, *Madag.* 89 C8
Bekodoka, *Madag.* 89 B8
Bekoji, *Ethiopia* 81 F4
Bekok, *Malaysia* 65 L4
Bekopaka, *Madag.* 89 B7
Bekwai, *Ghana* 83 D4
Bela, *India* 69 G10
Bela, *Pakistan* 68 F2
Bela Crkva, *Serbia, Yug.* 42 F6
Bela Palanka, *Serbia, Yug.* 40 C6
Bela Vista, *Brazil* 126 A4
Bela Vista, *Mozam.* 89 D5
Bélâbre, *France* 20 B5
Belalcázar, *Spain* 35 G5
Belan →, *India* 69 G9
Belanovica, *Serbia, Yug.* 40 B4
Belarus ■, *Europe* 46 F4
Belau = Palau ■, *Pac. Oc.* 52 J17
Belavenona, *Madag.* 89 C8
Belawan, *Indonesia* 62 D1
Belaya, *Ethiopia* 81 E4
Belaya Glina, *Russia* 49 G5
Belaya Kalitva, *Russia* 49 F5
Belaya Tserkov = Bila Tserkva, *Ukraine* 47 H6
Belceşti, *Romania* 43 C12
Bełchatów, *Poland* 45 G6
Belcher Is., *Canada* 102 A3
Belchite, *Spain* 32 D4
Belden, *U.S.A.* 116 E5
Belém, *Brazil* 125 D9
Belén, *Argentina* 126 B2
Belén, *Paraguay* 126 A4
Belen, *U.S.A.* 115 J10
Belene, *Bulgaria* 41 C9
Beleni, *Turkey* 72 D7
Bélesta, *France* 20 F5
Belet Uen, *Somali Rep.* 74 G4
Belev, *Russia* 46 F9
Belevi, *Turkey* 39 C9
Belfair, *U.S.A.* 116 C4
Belfast, *S. Africa* 89 D5
Belfast, *U.K.* 15 B6
Belfast, *Maine, U.S.A.* 109 C11
Belfast, *N.Y., U.S.A.* 110 D6
Belfast L., *U.K.* 15 B6
Belfield, *U.S.A.* 112 B3
Belfort, *France* 19 E13
Belfort, Territoire de □, *France* 19 E13
Belfry, *U.S.A.* 114 D9
Belgaum, *India* 66 M9
Belgioioso, *Italy* 28 C6
Belgium ■, *Europe* 17 D4
Belgodère, *France* 21 F13
Belgorod, *Russia* 47 G9
Belgorod-Dnestrovskiy = Bilhorod-Dnistrovskyy, *Ukraine* 47 J6
Belgrade = Beograd, *Serbia, Yug.* 40 B4
Belgrade, *U.S.A.* 114 D8
Belhaven, *U.S.A.* 109 H7
Beli Drim →, *Europe* 40 D4
Beli Manastir, *Croatia* 42 E3
Beli Timok →, *Serbia, Yug.* 40 C6
Bélice →, *Italy* 30 E5
Belinskiy, *Russia* 48 D6
Belinyu, *Indonesia* 62 E3
Beliton Is. = Belitung, *Indonesia* 62 E3
Belitung, *Indonesia* 62 E3
Beliu, *Romania* 42 D6
Belize ■, *Cent. Amer.* 119 D7
Belize City, *Belize* 119 D7
Beljakovci, *Macedonia* 40 D5
Beljanica, *Serbia, Yug.* 40 B5
Belkovskiy, Ostrov, *Russia* 51 B14
Bell →, *Canada* 102 C4
Bell I., *Canada* 103 B8
Bell-Irving →, *Canada* 104 B3
Bell Peninsula, *Canada* 101 B11
Bell Ville, *Argentina* 126 C3
Bella, *Italy* 31 B8
Bella Bella, *Canada* 104 C3
Bella Coola, *Canada* 104 C3
Bella Unión, *Uruguay* 126 C4
Bella Vista, *Corrientes, Argentina* 126 B4
Bella Vista, *Tucuman, Argentina* 126 B2
Bellac, *France* 20 B5
Bellágio, *Italy* 28 C6
Bellaire, *U.S.A.* 110 F4
Bellária, *Italy* 29 D9
Bellary, *India* 66 M10
Bellata, *Australia* 95 D4
Belle-Chasse, *U.S.A.* 113 L10
Belle Fourche, *U.S.A.* 112 C3
Belle Fourche →, *U.S.A.* 112 C3
Belle Glade, *U.S.A.* 109 M5
Belle-Île, *France* 18 E3
Belle Isle, *Canada* 103 B8
Belle Isle, Str. of, *Canada* 103 B8
Belle Plaine, *U.S.A.* 112 E8
Belle Yella, *Liberia* 82 D3
Belledonne, *France* 21 C10
Bellefontaine, *U.S.A.* 108 E4
Bellefonte, *U.S.A.* 110 F7
Bellegarde, *France* 19 E9
Bellegarde-en-Marche, *France* 20 C6
Bellegarde-sur-Valserine, *France* 19 F12
Bellême, *France* 18 D7
Belleoram, *Canada* 103 C8
Belleville, *Canada* 102 D4
Belleville, *France* 19 F11
Belleville, *Ill., U.S.A.* 112 F10
Belleville, *Kans., U.S.A.* 112 F6
Belleville, *N.Y., U.S.A.* 111 C8
Belleville-sur-Vie, *France* 18 F5
Bellevue, *Canada* 104 D6
Bellevue, *Idaho, U.S.A.* 114 E6
Bellevue, *Nebr., U.S.A.* 112 E7
Bellevue, *Ohio, U.S.A.* 110 E2
Bellevue, *Wash., U.S.A.* 116 C4
Belley, *France* 21 C9
Bellin = Kangirsuk, *Canada* 101 B13
Bellinge, *Denmark* 11 J4
Bellingen, *Australia* 95 E5
Bellingham, *U.S.A.* 100 D7
Bellingshausen Sea, *Antarctica* 5 C17
Bellinzona, *Switz.* 25 J5
Bello, *Colombia* 124 B3
Bellows Falls, *U.S.A.* 111 C12
Bellpat, *Pakistan* 68 E3
Bellpuig d'Urgell, *Spain* 32 D6
Belluno, *Italy* 29 B9
Bellwood, *U.S.A.* 110 F6
Bélmez, *Spain* 35 G5
Belmont, *Canada* 110 D3
Belmont, *S. Africa* 88 D3
Belmont, *U.S.A.* 110 D6
Belmonte, *Brazil* 125 G11
Belmonte, *Portugal* 34 E3
Belmonte, *Spain* 33 F2
Belmopan, *Belize* 119 D7
Belmullet, *Ireland* 15 B2
Belo Horizonte, *Brazil* 125 G10
Belo-sur-Mer, *Madag.* 89 C7
Belo-Tsiribihina, *Madag.* 89 B7
Belogorsk = Bilohirsk, *Ukraine* 47 K8
Belogorsk, *Russia* 51 D13
Belogradchik, *Bulgaria* 40 C6
Belogradets, *Bulgaria* 41 C11
Beloha, *Madag.* 89 D8
Beloit, *Kans., U.S.A.* 112 F5
Beloit, *Wis., U.S.A.* 112 D10
Belokorovichi, *Ukraine* 47 G5
Belomorsk, *Russia* 50 C4
Belonia, *India* 67 H17
Belopolye = Bilopillya, *Ukraine* 47 G8
Belorechensk, *Russia* 49 H4
Belorussia = Belarus ■, *Europe* 46 F4
Beloslav, *Bulgaria* 41 C11
Belovo, *Bulgaria* 41 D8
Belovo, *Russia* 50 D9
Belovodsk, *Ukraine* 47 H10
Beloye, Ozero, *Russia* 46 B9
Beloye More, *Russia* 50 C4
Belozem, *Bulgaria* 41 D9
Belozersk, *Russia* 46 B9
Belpasso, *Italy* 31 E7
Belpre, *U.S.A.* 108 F5
Belrain, *India* 69 E9
Belt, *U.S.A.* 114 C8
Beltana, *Australia* 95 E2
Belterra, *Brazil* 125 D8
Beltinci, *Slovenia* 29 B13
Belton, *U.S.A.* 113 K6
Belton L., *U.S.A.* 113 K6
Beltsy = Bălţi, *Moldova* 43 C12
Belturbet, *Ireland* 15 B4
Belukha, *Russia* 50 E9
Beluran, *Malaysia* 62 C5
Beluša, *Slovak Rep.* 27 B11
Belušić, *Serbia, Yug.* 40 C5
Belvedere Maríttimo, *Italy* 31 C8
Belvès, *France* 20 D5
Belvidere, *Ill., U.S.A.* 112 D10
Belvidere, *N.J., U.S.A.* 111 F9
Belvis de la Jara, *Spain* 34 F6
Belyando →, *Australia* 94 C4
Belyy, *Russia* 46 E7
Belyy, Ostrov, *Russia* 50 B8
Belyy Yar, *Russia* 50 D9
Bełżec, *Poland* 45 H10
Belzig, *Germany* 24 C8
Belzoni, *U.S.A.* 113 J9
Bełżyce, *Poland* 45 G9
Bemaraha, Lembalemban' i, *Madag.* 89 B7
Bemarivo, *Madag.* 89 C7
Bemarivo →, *Antsiranana, Madag.* 89 A9
Bemarivo →, *Mahajanga, Madag.* 89 B8
Bemavo, *Madag.* 89 C8
Bembéréke, *Benin* 83 C5
Bembesi, *Zimbabwe* 87 G2
Bembesi →, *Zimbabwe* 87 F2
Bembézar →, *Spain* 35 H5
Bembibre, *Spain* 34 C4
Bemetara, *India* 69 J9
Bemidji, *U.S.A.* 112 B7
Bemolanga, *Madag.* 89 B8
Ben, *Iran* 71 C6
Ben Cruachan, *U.K.* 14 E3
Ben Dearg, *U.K.* 14 D4
Ben Hope, *U.K.* 14 C4
Ben Lawers, *U.K.* 14 E4
Ben Lomond, *N.S.W., Australia* 95 E5

Ben Lomond, *Tas., Australia* .. 94 G4
Ben Lomond, *U.K.* 14 E4
Ben Luc, *Vietnam* 65 G6
Ben Macdhui, *U.K.* 14 D5
Ben Mhor, *U.K.* 14 D1
Ben More, *Arg. & Bute, U.K.* .. 14 E2
Ben More, *Stirl., U.K.* 14 E4
Ben More Assynt, *U.K.* 14 C4
Ben Nevis, *U.K.* 14 E3
Ben Quang, *Vietnam* 64 D6
Ben Vorlich, *U.K.* 14 E4
Ben Wyvis, *U.K.* 14 D4
Bena, *Nigeria* 83 C6
Benāb, *Iran* 73 D12
Benalla, *Australia* 95 F4
Benalmádena, *Spain* 35 J6
Benares = Varanasi, *India* 69 G10
Bénat, C., *France* 21 E10
Benavente, *Portugal* 35 G2
Benavente, *Spain* 34 C5
Benavides, *U.S.A.* 113 M5
Benavides de Órbigo, *Spain* ... 34 C5
Benbecula, *U.K.* 14 D1
Benbonyathe, *Australia* 95 E2
Bend, *U.S.A.* 114 D3
Bender Beila, *Somali Rep.* 74 F5
Bendery = Tighina, *Moldova* .. 43 D14
Bendigo, *Australia* 95 F3
Bendorf, *Germany* 24 E3
Benē Beraq, *Israel* 75 C3
Bénéna, *Mali* 82 C4
Benenitra, *Madag.* 89 C8
Benešov, *Czech Rep.* 26 B7
Benevento, *Italy* 31 A7
Benfeld, *France* 19 D14
Benga, *Mozam.* 87 F3
Bengal, Bay of, *Ind. Oc.* 67 M17
Bengbis, *Cameroon* 83 E7
Bengbu, *China* 57 H9
Benghazi = Banghāzī, *Libya* ... 79 B10
Bengkalis, *Indonesia* 62 D2
Bengkulu, *Indonesia* 62 E2
Bengkulu □, *Indonesia* 62 E2
Bengough, *Canada* 105 D7
Bengtsfors, *Sweden* 10 E6
Benguela, *Angola* 85 G2
Benguérua, I., *Mozam.* 89 C6
Benha, *Egypt* 80 H7
Beni, *Dem. Rep. of the Congo* . 86 B2
Beni →, *Bolivia* 124 F5
Beni Mazâr, *Egypt* 80 B3
Beni Mellal, *Morocco* 78 B4
Beni Suef, *Egypt* 80 J7
Beniah L., *Canada* 104 A6
Benicarló, *Spain* 32 E5
Benicássim, *Spain* 32 E5
Benicia, *U.S.A.* 116 G4
Benidorm, *Spain* 33 G4
Benin ■, *Africa* 83 D5
Benin →, *Nigeria* 83 D6
Benin, Bight of, *W. Afr.* 83 E5
Benin City, *Nigeria* 83 D6
Benisa, *Spain* 33 G5
Benitses, *Greece* 36 A3
Benjamin Aceval, *Paraguay* ... 126 A4
Benjamin Constant, *Brazil* 124 D4
Benjamin Hill, *Mexico* 118 A2
Benkelman, *U.S.A.* 112 E4
Benkovac, *Croatia* 29 D12
Bennett, *Canada* 104 B2
Bennett, L., *Australia* 92 D5
Bennetta, Ostrov, *Russia* 51 B15
Bennettsville, *U.S.A.* 109 H6
Bennichchāb, *Mauritania* 82 B1
Bennington, *N.H., U.S.A.* 111 D11
Bennington, *Vt., U.S.A.* 111 D11
Bénodet, *France* 18 E2
Benoni, *S. Africa* 89 D4
Benque Viejo, *Belize* 119 D7
Bensheim, *Germany* 25 F4
Benson, *Ariz., U.S.A.* 115 L8
Benson, *Minn., U.S.A.* 112 C7
Bent, *Iran* 71 E8
Benteng, *Indonesia* 63 F6
Bentinck I., *Australia* 94 B2
Bentiu, *Sudan* 81 F2
Bento Gonçalves, *Brazil* 127 B5
Benton, *Ark., U.S.A.* 113 H8
Benton, *Calif., U.S.A.* 116 H8
Benton, *Ill., U.S.A.* 112 G10
Benton, *Pa., U.S.A.* 111 E8
Benton Harbor, *U.S.A.* 108 D2
Bentonville, *U.S.A.* 113 G7
Bentu Liben, *Ethiopia* 81 F4
Bentung, *Malaysia* 65 L3
Benue □, *Nigeria* 83 D6
Benue →, *Nigeria* 83 D6
Benxi, *China* 57 D12
Beo, *Indonesia* 63 D7
Beograd, *Serbia, Yug.* 40 B4
Beoumi, *Ivory C.* 82 D3
Bepan Jiang →, *China* 58 E6
Beppu, *Japan* 55 H5
Beqaa Valley = Al Biqā, *Lebanon* 75 A5
Ber Mota, *India* 68 H3
Berach →, *India* 68 G6
Beraketa, *Madag.* 89 C7
Berane, *Montenegro, Yug.* 40 D3
Berat, *Albania* 40 F3
Berau, Teluk, *Indonesia* 63 E8
Beravina, *Madag.* 89 B8
Berber, *Sudan* 80 D3
Berbera, *Somali Rep.* 74 E4
Berbérati, *C.A.R.* 84 D3
Berbice →, *Guyana* 124 B7
Berceto, *Italy* 28 D6
Berchidda, *Italy* 30 B2
Berchtesgaden, *Germany* 25 H8
Berck, *France* 19 B8
Berdichev = Berdychiv, *Ukraine* 47 H5
Berdsk, *Russia* 50 D9
Berdyansk, *Ukraine* 47 J9
Berdychiv, *Ukraine* 47 H5
Berea, *U.S.A.* 108 G3
Berebere, *Indonesia* 63 D7
Bereda, *Somali Rep.* 74 E5
Berehove, *Ukraine* 47 H2
Berekum, *Ghana* 82 D4
Berenice, *Egypt* 80 C4
Berens →, *Canada* 105 C9
Berens I., *Canada* 105 C9
Berens River, *Canada* 105 C9
Beresford, *U.S.A.* 112 D6
Berestechko, *Ukraine* 47 G3
Bereşti, *Romania* 43 D12
Beretău →, *Romania* 42 C6
Berettyó →, *Hungary* 42 D6
Berettyóújfalu, *Hungary* 42 C6
Berevo, *Mahajanga, Madag.* ... 89 B7
Berevo, *Toliara, Madag.* 89 B7
Bereza = Byaroza, *Belarus* 47 F3
Berezhany, *Ukraine* 47 H3
Berezina = Byarezina →, *Belarus* 47 F6
Berezivka, *Ukraine* 47 J6
Berezna, *Ukraine* 47 G6
Berezniki, *Russia* 50 C5
Berezniki, *Russia* 50 D6
Berezovo, *Russia* 50 C7
Berga, *Spain* 32 C6
Berga, *Sweden* 11 G10
Bergama, *Turkey* 39 B9
Bergamo, *Italy* 28 C6
Bergara, *Spain* 32 B2
Bergby, *Sweden* 10 D11
Bergedorf, *Germany* 24 B6
Bergeforsen, *Sweden* 10 B11
Bergen, *Mecklenburg-Vorpommern, Germany* 24 A9
Bergen, *Niedersachsen, Germany* 24 C5
Bergen, *Neths.* 17 B4
Bergen, *Norway* 9 F11
Bergen, *U.S.A.* 110 C7
Bergen op Zoom, *Neths.* 17 C4
Bergerac, *France* 20 D4
Bergheim, *Germany* 24 E2
Bergholz, *U.S.A.* 110 F4
Bergisch Gladbach, *Germany* .. 17 D7
Bergkamen, *Germany* 24 D3
Bergkvara, *Sweden* 11 H10
Bergshamra, *Sweden* 10 E12
Bergsjö, *Sweden* 10 C11
Bergues, *France* 19 B9
Bergviken, *Sweden* 10 C10
Bergville, *S. Africa* 89 D4
Berhala, Selat, *Indonesia* 62 E2
Berhampore = Baharampur, *India* 69 G13
Berhampur = Brahmapur, *India* 67 K14
Berheci →, *Romania* 43 E12
Bering Sea, *Pac. Oc.* 100 C1
Bering Strait, *Pac. Oc.* 100 B3
Beringovskiy, *Russia* 51 C18
Berisso, *Argentina* 126 C4
Berja, *Spain* 35 J8
Berkeley, *U.S.A.* 116 H4
Berkner I., *Antarctica* 5 D18
Berkovitsa, *Bulgaria* 40 C7
Berkshire, *U.S.A.* 111 D8
Berkshire Downs, *U.K.* 13 F6
Berlanga, *Spain* 35 G5
Berlenga, I., *Portugal* 35 F1
Berlin, *Germany* 24 C9
Berlin, *Md., U.S.A.* 108 F8
Berlin, *N.H., U.S.A.* 111 B13
Berlin, *N.Y., U.S.A.* 111 D11
Berlin, *Wis., U.S.A.* 108 D1
Berlin □, *Germany* 24 C9
Berlin L., *U.S.A.* 110 E4
Bermeja, Sierra, *Spain* 35 J5
Bermejo →, *Formosa, Argentina* 126 B4
Bermejo →, *San Juan, Argentina* 126 C2
Bermen, L., *Canada* 103 B6
Bermeo, *Spain* 32 B2
Bermillo de Sayago, *Spain* 34 D4
Bermuda ■, *Atl. Oc.* 98 F13
Bern, *Switz.* 25 J3
Bern □, *Switz.* 25 J3
Bernalda, *Italy* 31 B9
Bernalillo, *U.S.A.* 115 J10
Bernardo de Irigoyen, *Argentina* 127 B5
Bernardo O'Higgins □, *Chile* .. 126 C1
Bernardsville, *U.S.A.* 111 F10
Bernasconi, *Argentina* 126 D3
Bernau, *Bayern, Germany* 25 H8
Bernau, *Brandenburg, Germany* 24 C9
Bernay, *France* 18 C7
Bernburg, *Germany* 24 D7
Berndorf, *Austria* 26 D9
Berne = Bern, *Switz.* 25 J3
Berne = Bern □, *Switz.* 25 J3
Berner Alpen, *Switz.* 25 J3
Berneray, *U.K.* 14 D1
Bernier I., *Australia* 93 D1
Bernina, Piz, *Switz.* 25 J5
Bernkastel-Kues, *Germany* 25 F3
Beroroha, *Madag.* 89 C8
Béroubouay, *Benin* 83 C5
Beroun, *Czech Rep.* 26 B7
Berounka →, *Czech Rep.* 26 B7
Berovo, *Macedonia* 40 E6
Berre, Étang de, *France* 21 E9
Berre-l'Étang, *France* 21 E9
Berri, *Australia* 95 E3
Berriane, *Algeria* 78 B6
Berry, *Australia* 95 E5
Berry, *France* 19 F8
Berry Is., *Bahamas* 120 A4
Berryessa L., *U.S.A.* 116 G4
Berryville, *U.S.A.* 113 G8
Berseba, *Namibia* 88 D2
Bersenbrück, *Germany* 24 C3
Bershad, *Ukraine* 47 H5
Berthold, *U.S.A.* 112 A4
Berthoud, *U.S.A.* 112 E2
Bertincourt, *France* 19 B9
Bertoua, *Cameroon* 84 D2
Bertraghboy B., *Ireland* 15 C2
Berwick, *U.S.A.* 111 E8
Berwick-upon-Tweed, *U.K.* 12 B6
Berwyn Mts., *U.K.* 12 E4
Beryslav, *Ukraine* 47 J7
Berzasca, *Romania* 42 F6
Berzence, *Hungary* 42 D2
Besal, *Pakistan* 69 B5
Besalampy, *Madag.* 89 B7
Besançon, *France* 19 E13
Besar, *Indonesia* 62 E5
Beshenkovichi, *Belarus* 46 E5
Beška, *Serbia, Yug.* 42 E5
Beslan, *Russia* 49 J7
Besna Kobila, *Serbia, Yug.* 40 D6
Besnard L., *Canada* 105 B7
Besni, *Turkey* 70 B3
Besor, N. →, *Egypt* 75 D3
Bessarabiya, *Moldova* 47 J5
Bessarabka = Basarabeasca, *Moldova* 43 D13
Bessèges, *France* 21 D8
Bessemer, *Ala., U.S.A.* 109 J2
Bessemer, *Mich., U.S.A.* 112 B9
Bessemer, *Pa., U.S.A.* 110 F4
Bessin, *France* 18 C6
Bessines-sur-Gartempe, *France* 20 B5
Beswick, *Australia* 92 B5
Bet She'an, *Israel* 75 C4
Bet Shemesh, *Israel* 75 D4
Betafo, *Madag.* 89 B8
Betancuria, *Canary Is.* 37 F5
Betanzos, *Spain* 34 B2
Bétaré Oya, *Cameroon* 84 C2
Betatao, *Madag.* 89 B8
Bétera, *Spain* 33 F4
Bétérou, *Benin* 83 D5
Bethal, *S. Africa* 89 D4
Bethanien, *Namibia* 88 D2
Bethany, *Canada* 110 B6
Bethany, *U.S.A.* 112 E7
Bethel, *Alaska, U.S.A.* 100 B3
Bethel, *Conn., U.S.A.* 111 E11
Bethel, *Maine, U.S.A.* 111 B14
Bethel, *Vt., U.S.A.* 111 C12
Bethel Park, *U.S.A.* 110 F4
Béthenville, *France* 19 C11
Bethlehem = Bayt Lahm, *West Bank* 75 D4
Bethlehem, *S. Africa* 89 D4
Bethlehem, *U.S.A.* 111 F9
Bethulie, *S. Africa* 88 E4
Béthune, *France* 19 B9
Béthune →, *France* 18 C8
Betioky, *Madag.* 89 C7
Betong, *Thailand* 65 K3
Betoota, *Australia* 94 D3
Betor, *Ethiopia* 81 E4
Betroka, *Madag.* 89 C8
Betsiamites, *Canada* 103 C6
Betsiamites →, *Canada* 103 C6
Betsiboka →, *Madag.* 89 B8
Bettendorf, *U.S.A.* 112 E9
Bettiah, *India* 69 F11
Bettna, *Sweden* 11 F10
Bèttola, *Italy* 28 D6
Betul, *India* 66 J10
Betung, *Malaysia* 62 D4
Betws-y-Coed, *U.K.* 12 D4
Betxi, *Spain* 32 F4
Betzdorf, *Germany* 24 E3
Beuil, *France* 21 D10
Beulah, *Mich., U.S.A.* 108 C2
Beulah, *N. Dak., U.S.A.* 112 B4
Beuvron →, *France* 18 E8
Beveren, *Belgium* 17 C4
Beverley, *Australia* 93 F2
Beverley, *U.K.* 12 D7
Beverley Hills, *U.S.A.* 109 L4
Beverly, *U.S.A.* 111 D14
Beverly Hills, *U.S.A.* 117 L8
Beverungen, *Germany* 24 D5
Bevoalavo, *Madag.* 89 D7
Bewas →, *India* 69 H8
Bex, *Switz.* 25 J3
Bexhill, *U.K.* 13 G8
Bey Dağları, *Turkey* 39 E12
Beyānlū, *Iran* 70 C5
Beyazköy, *Turkey* 41 E11
Beyçayırı, *Turkey* 41 F10
Beydağ, *Turkey* 39 C10
Beyeğaç, *Turkey* 39 D10
Beyin, *Ghana* 82 D4
Beykoz, *Turkey* 41 E13
Beyla, *Guinea* 82 D3
Beynat, *France* 20 C5
Beyneu, *Kazakstan* 50 E6
Beyoba, *Turkey* 39 C9
Beyoğlu, *Turkey* 41 E12
Beypazarı, *Turkey* 72 B4
Beyşehir, *Turkey* 72 D4
Beyşehir Gölü, *Turkey* 70 B1
Beytüşşebap, *Turkey* 73 D10
Bezdan, *Serbia, Yug.* 42 E3
Bezhetsk, *Russia* 46 D9
Béziers, *France* 20 E7
Bezwada = Vijayawada, *India* . 67 L12
Bhabua, *India* 69 G10
Bhachau, *India* 66 H7
Bhadar →, *Gujarat, India* 68 H5
Bhadar →, *Gujarat, India* 68 J3
Bhadarwah, *India* 69 C6
Bhadohi, *India* 69 G10
Bhadra, *India* 68 E6
Bhadrakh, *India* 67 J15
Bhadran, *India* 68 H5
Bhadravati, *India* 66 N9
Bhag, *Pakistan* 68 E2
Bhagalpur, *India* 69 G12
Bhagirathi →, *Ut. P., India* 69 D8
Bhagirathi →, *W. Bengal, India* 69 H13
Bhakkar, *Pakistan* 68 D4
Bhakra Dam, *India* 68 D7
Bhamo, *Burma* 67 G20
Bhandara, *India* 66 J11
Bhanpura, *India* 68 G6
Bhanrer Ra., *India* 69 H8
Bhaptiahi, *India* 69 F12
Bharat = India ■, *Asia* 66 K11
Bharatpur, *Mad. P., India* 69 H9
Bharatpur, *Raj., India* 68 F7
Bharno, *India* 69 H11
Bhatinda, *India* 68 D6
Bhatpara, *India* 69 H13
Bhattu, *India* 68 E6
Bhaun, *Pakistan* 68 C5
Bhaunagar = Bhavnagar, *India* . 66 J8
Bhavnagar, *India* 66 J8
Bhawari, *India* 68 G5
Bhayavadar, *India* 68 J4
Bhera, *Pakistan* 68 C5
Bhikangaon, *India* 68 J6
Bhilsa = Vidisha, *India* 68 H7
Bhilwara, *India* 68 G6
Bhima →, *India* 66 L10
Bhimbar, *Pakistan* 69 C6
Bhind, *India* 69 F8
Bhinga, *India* 69 F9
Bhinmal, *India* 68 G5
Bhiwandi, *India* 66 K8
Bhiwani, *India* 68 E7
Bhogava →, *India* 68 H5
Bhola, *Bangla.* 67 H17
Bholari, *Pakistan* 68 G3
Bhopal, *India* 68 H7
Bhubaneshwar, *India* 67 J14
Bhuj, *India* 68 H3
Bhusaval, *India* 66 J9
Bhutan ■, *Asia* 67 F17
Biafra, B. of = Bonny, Bight of, *Africa* 83 E6
Biak, *Indonesia* 63 E9
Biała, *Poland* 45 H4
Biała →, *Poland* 45 H7
Biała Piska, *Poland* 44 E9
Biała Podlaska, *Poland* 45 F10
Biała Rawska, *Poland* 45 G7
Białobrzegi, *Poland* 45 G7
Białogard, *Poland* 44 D2
Białowieża, *Poland* 45 F10
Biały Bór, *Poland* 44 E3
Białystok, *Poland* 45 E10
Biancavilla, *Italy* 31 E7
Bianco, *Italy* 31 D9
Biankouma, *Ivory C.* 82 D3
Biaora, *India* 68 H7
Bīārjmand, *Iran* 71 B7
Biaro, *Indonesia* 63 D7
Biarritz, *France* 20 E2
Biasca, *Switz.* 25 J4
Biba, *Egypt* 80 J7
Bibai, *Japan* 54 C10
Bibbiena, *Italy* 29 E8
Bibby I., *Canada* 105 A10
Bibel →, *Spain* 34 C3
Biberach, *Germany* 25 G5
Bibiani, *Ghana* 82 D4
Bibungwa, *Dem. Rep. of the Congo* 86 C2
Bic, *Canada* 103 C6
Bicaj, *Albania* 40 E4
Bicaz, *Romania* 43 D11
Bicazu Ardelean, *Romania* 43 D10
Biccari, *Italy* 31 A8
Bicester, *U.K.* 13 F6
Bichena, *Ethiopia* 81 E4
Bicheno, *Australia* 94 G4
Bichia, *India* 69 H9
Bichvinta, *Georgia* 49 J5
Bickerton I., *Australia* 94 A2
Bicske, *Hungary* 42 C3
Bida, *Nigeria* 83 D6
Bidar, *India* 66 L10
Biddeford, *U.S.A.* 109 D10
Biddwara, *Ethiopia* 81 F4
Bideford, *U.K.* 13 F3
Bideford Bay, *U.K.* 13 F3
Bidhuna, *India* 69 F8
Bidor, *Malaysia* 65 K3
Bie, *Sweden* 10 E10
Bié, Planalto de, *Angola* 85 G3
Bieber, *U.S.A.* 114 F3
Biebrza →, *Poland* 45 E9
Biecz, *Poland* 45 J8
Biel, *Switz.* 25 H3
Bielawa, *Poland* 45 H3
Bielefeld, *Germany* 24 C4
Bielersee, *Switz.* 25 H3
Biella, *Italy* 28 C5
Bielsk Podlaski, *Poland* 45 F10
Bielsko-Biała, *Poland* 45 J6
Bien Hoa, *Vietnam* 65 G6
Bienne = Biel, *Switz.* 25 H3
Bienvenida, *Spain* 35 G4
Bienville, L., *Canada* 102 A5
Bierné, *France* 18 E6
Bierun, *Poland* 45 H6
Bierutów, *Poland* 45 G4
Biescas, *Spain* 32 C4
Biese →, *Germany* 24 C7
Biesiesfontein, *S. Africa* 88 E2
Bietigheim-Bissingen, *Germany* 25 G5
Bieżuń, *Poland* 45 F6
Biferno →, *Italy* 29 G12
Big →, *Canada* 103 B8
Big B., *Canada* 103 A7
Big Bear City, *U.S.A.* 117 L10
Big Bear Lake, *U.S.A.* 117 L10
Big Belt Mts., *U.S.A.* 114 C8
Big Bend, *Swaziland* 89 D5
Big Bend National Park, *U.S.A.* 113 L3
Big Black →, *U.S.A.* 113 K9
Big Blue →, *U.S.A.* 112 F6
Big Creek, *U.S.A.* 116 H7
Big Cypress National Preserve, *U.S.A.* 109 M5
Big Cypress Swamp, *U.S.A.* ... 109 M5
Big Falls, *U.S.A.* 112 A8
Big Fork →, *U.S.A.* 112 A8
Big Horn Mts. = Bighorn Mts., *U.S.A.* 114 D10
Big I., *Canada* 104 A5
Big Lake, *U.S.A.* 113 K4
Big Moose, *U.S.A.* 111 C10
Big Muddy Cr. →, *U.S.A.* 112 A2
Big Pine, *U.S.A.* 116 H8
Big Piney, *U.S.A.* 114 E8
Big Rapids, *U.S.A.* 108 D3
Big Rideau L., *Canada* 111 B8
Big River, *Canada* 105 C7
Big Run, *U.S.A.* 110 F6
Big Sable Pt., *U.S.A.* 108 C2
Big Salmon →, *Canada* 104 A2
Big Sand L., *Canada* 105 B9
Big Sandy, *U.S.A.* 114 B8
Big Sandy →, *U.S.A.* 108 F4
Big Sandy Cr. →, *U.S.A.* 112 F3
Big Sioux →, *U.S.A.* 112 D6
Big Spring, *U.S.A.* 113 J4
Big Stone City, *U.S.A.* 112 C6
Big Stone Gap, *U.S.A.* 109 G4
Big Stone L., *U.S.A.* 112 C6
Big Sur, *U.S.A.* 116 J5
Big Timber, *U.S.A.* 114 D9
Big Trout L., *Canada* 102 B2
Big Trout Lake, *Canada* 102 B2
Biğa, *Turkey* 41 F11
Biga →, *Turkey* 41 F11
Bigadiç, *Turkey* 39 B10
Biganos, *France* 20 D3
Biggar, *Canada* 105 C7
Biggar, *U.K.* 14 F5
Bigge I., *Australia* 92 B4
Biggenden, *Australia* 95 D5
Biggleswade, *U.K.* 13 E7
Biggs, *U.S.A.* 116 F5
Bighorn, *U.S.A.* 114 C10
Bighorn →, *U.S.A.* 114 C10
Bighorn L., *U.S.A.* 114 D9
Bighorn Mts., *U.S.A.* 114 D10
Bignona, *Senegal* 82 C1
Bigorre, *France* 20 E4
Bigstone L., *Canada* 105 C9
Biguglia, Étang de, *France* 21 F13
Bigwa, *Tanzania* 86 D4
Bihać, *Bos.-H.* 29 D12
Bihar, *India* 69 G11
Bihar □, *India* 69 G12
Biharamulo, *Tanzania* 86 C3
Bihariganj, *India* 69 G12
Biharkeresztes, *Hungary* 42 C6
Bihor □, *Romania* 42 D7
Bihor, Munţii, *Romania* 42 D7
Bijagós, Arquipélago dos, *Guinea-Biss.* 82 C1
Bijaipur, *India* 68 F7
Bijapur, *Karnataka, India* 66 L9
Bijapur, *Mad. P., India* 67 K12
Bījār, *Iran* 70 C5
Bijawar, *India* 69 G8
Bijeljina, *Bos.-H.* 42 F4
Bijelo Polje, *Montenegro, Yug.* . 40 C3
Bijie, *China* 58 D5
Bijnor, *India* 68 E8
Bikaner, *India* 68 E5
Bikapur, *India* 69 F10
Bikeqi, *China* 56 D6
Bikfayyā, *Lebanon* 75 B4
Bikin, *Russia* 51 E14
Bikin →, *Russia* 54 A7
Bikini Atoll, *Marshall Is.* 96 F8
Bikita, *Zimbabwe* 89 C5
Bikoué, *Cameroon* 83 E7
Bila Tserkva, *Ukraine* 47 H6
Bilanga, *Burkina Faso* 83 C4
Bilara, *India* 68 F5
Bilaspur, *Mad. P., India* 69 H10
Bilaspur, *Punjab, India* 68 D7
Biläsuvar, *Azerbaijan* 73 C13
Bilauk Taungdan, *Thailand* ... 64 F2
Bilbao, *Spain* 32 B2
Bilbeis, *Egypt* 80 H7
Bilbo = Bilbao, *Spain* 32 B2
Bilbor, *Romania* 43 C10
Bilciureşti, *Romania* 43 F10

Bíldudalur, *Iceland* 8 D2
Bílé Karpaty, *Europe* 27 B11
Bileća, *Bos.-H.* 40 D2
Bilecik, *Turkey* 72 B4
Biłgoraj, *Poland* 45 H9
Bilgram, *India* 69 F9
Bilhaur, *India* 69 F9
Bilhorod-Dnistrovskyy, *Ukraine* 47 J6
Bilibino, *Russia* 51 C17
Bilibiza, *Mozam.* 87 E5
Bilisht, *Albania* 40 F5
Billabalong Roadhouse, *Australia* 93 E2
Billdal, *Sweden* 11 G5
Billiluna, *Australia* 92 C4
Billings, *U.S.A.* 114 D9
Billiton Is. = Belitung, *Indonesia* 62 E3
Billsta, *Sweden* 10 A12
Billund, *Denmark* 11 J3
Bilma, *Niger* 79 E8
Bilo Gora, *Croatia* 42 E2
Biloela, *Australia* 94 C5
Bilohirsk, *Ukraine* 47 K8
Bilopillya, *Ukraine* 47 G8
Biloxi, *U.S.A.* 113 K10
Bilpa Morea Claypan, *Australia* 94 D3
Biltine, *Chad* 79 F10
Bilyarsk, *Russia* 48 C10
Bima, *Indonesia* 63 F5
Bimban, *Egypt* 80 C3
Bimbila, *Ghana* 83 D5
Bimini Is., *Bahamas* 120 A4
Bin Xian, *Heilongjiang, China* 57 B14
Bin Xian, *Shaanxi, China* 56 G5
Bin Yauri, *Nigeria* 83 C5
Bina-Etawah, *India* 68 G8
Bināb, *Iran* 71 B6
Binalbagan, *Phil.* 61 F5
Binalong, *Australia* 95 E4
Bīnālūd, Kūh-e, *Iran* 71 B8
Binatang = Bintangor, *Malaysia* 62 D4
Binche, *Belgium* 17 D4
Binchuan, *China* 58 E3
Binder, *Chad* 83 D7
Bindki, *India* 69 F9
Bindslev, *Denmark* 11 G4
Bindura, *Zimbabwe* 87 F3
Binefar, *Spain* 32 D5
Bingara, *Australia* 95 D5
Bingen, *Germany* 25 F3
Bingerville, *Ivory C.* 82 D4
Bingham, *U.S.A.* 109 C11
Binghamton, *U.S.A.* 111 D9
Bingöl, *Turkey* 70 B4
Bingöl Dağları, *Turkey* 73 C9
Bingsjö, *Sweden* 10 C9
Binh Dinh = An Nhon, *Vietnam* 64 F7
Binh Khe, *Vietnam* 64 F7
Binh Son, *Vietnam* 64 E7
Binhai, *China* 57 G10
Binic, *France* 18 D4
Binisatua, *Spain* 37 B11
Binjai, *Indonesia* 62 D3
Binji, *Nigeria* 83 C5
Binnaway, *Australia* 95 E4
Binongko, *Indonesia* 63 F6
Binscarth, *Canada* 105 C8
Bint Goda, *Sudan* 81 E3
Bintan, *Indonesia* 62 D2
Bintangor, *Malaysia* 62 D4
Bintulu, *Malaysia* 62 D4
Bintuni, *Indonesia* 63 E8
Binyang, *China* 58 F7
Binz, *Germany* 24 A9
Binzert = Bizerte, *Tunisia* 79 A7
Binzhou, *China* 57 F10
Bío Bío □, *Chile* 126 D1
Biograd na Moru, *Croatia* 29 E12
Bioko, *Eq. Guin.* 83 E6
Biokovo, *Croatia* 29 E14
Bipindi, *Cameroon* 83 E7
Bir, *India* 66 K9
Bir, Ras, *Djibouti* 81 E5
Bîr Abu Hashim, *Egypt* 80 C3
Bîr Abu Minqar, *Egypt* 80 B2
Bîr Abu Muḩammad, *Egypt* 75 F3
Bi'r ad Dabbāghāt, *Jordan* 75 E4
Bîr Adal Deib, *Sudan* 80 C4
Bi'r al Butayyihāt, *Jordan* 75 F4
Bi'r al Mārī, *Jordan* 75 E4
Bi'r al Qattār, *Jordan* 75 F4
Bîr 'Asal, *Egypt* 80 B3
Bir Atrun, *Sudan* 80 D2
Bîr Beiḍa, *Egypt* 75 E3
Bîr Diqnash, *Egypt* 80 A2
Bîr el 'Abd, *Egypt* 75 D2
Bîr el Basur, *Egypt* 80 B2
Bîr el Biarât, *Egypt* 75 F3
Bîr el Duweidar, *Egypt* 75 E1
Bîr el Garârât, *Egypt* 75 D2
Bîr el Gellaz, *Egypt* 80 A2
Bîr el Heisi, *Egypt* 75 F3
Bîr el Jafir, *Egypt* 75 E1
Bîr el Mâlḩi, *Egypt* 75 E2
Bîr el Shaqqa, *Egypt* 80 A2
Bîr el Thamâda, *Egypt* 75 E2
Bîr Fuad, *Egypt* 80 A2
Bîr Gebeil Ḩişn, *Egypt* 75 E2
Bi'r Ghadīr, *Syria* 75 A6
Bîr Haimur, *Egypt* 80 C3
Bîr Ḩasana, *Egypt* 75 E2
Bîr Hôôker, *Egypt* 80 H7
Bîr Kanayis, *Egypt* 80 C3
Bîr Kaseiba, *Egypt* 75 E2
Bîr Kerawein, *Egypt* 80 B2
Bîr Lahfân, *Egypt* 75 E2
Bîr Madkûr, *Egypt* 75 E1
Bîr Maql, *Egypt* 80 C3
Bîr Mîneiga, *Sudan* 80 C4
Bîr Misaha, *Egypt* 80 C2
Bîr Mogreïn, *Mauritania* 78 C3
Bîr Murr, *Egypt* 80 C3
Bi'r Muṭribah, *Kuwait* 70 D5
Bîr Nakheila, *Egypt* 80 C3
Bîr Qaṭia, *Egypt* 75 E1
Bîr Qatrani, *Egypt* 80 A2
Bîr Ranga, *Egypt* 80 C4
Bîr Sahara, *Egypt* 80 C2
Bîr Seiyâla, *Egypt* 80 B3
Bîr Shalatein, *Egypt* 80 C4
Bîr Shebb, *Egypt* 80 C2
Bîr Shût, *Egypt* 80 C4
Bîr Terfawi, *Egypt* 80 C2
Bîr Umm Qubûr, *Egypt* 80 C3
Bîr Ungât, *Egypt* 80 C3
Bîr Za'farâna, *Egypt* 80 J8
Bîr Zeidûn, *Egypt* 80 B3
Biramféro, *Guinea* 82 C3
Biratnagar, *Nepal* 69 F12
Birawa, *Dem. Rep. of the Congo* 86 C2
Birch →, *Canada* 104 B6
Birch Hills, *Canada* 105 C7
Birch I., *Canada* 105 C9
Birch L., *N.W.T., Canada* 104 A5
Birch L., *Ont., Canada* 102 B1
Birch Mts., *Canada* 104 B6
Birch River, *Canada* 105 C8
Birchip, *Australia* 95 F3
Birchiş, *Romania* 42 E7
Bird, *Canada* 105 B10
Bird I. = Las Aves, Is., *W. Indies* 121 C7
Birdsville, *Australia* 94 D2
Birdum Cr. →, *Australia* 92 C5
Birecik, *Turkey* 70 B3
Birein, *Israel* 75 E3
Bireuen, *Indonesia* 62 C1
Biri →, *Sudan* 81 F2
Birifo, *Gambia* 82 C2
Birigui, *Brazil* 127 A5
Birjand, *Iran* 71 C8
Birkenfeld, *Germany* 25 F3
Birkenhead, *U.K.* 12 D4
Birkerød, *Denmark* 11 J6
Birket Qârûn, *Egypt* 80 J7
Birkfeld, *Austria* 26 D8
Bîrlad = Bârlad, *Romania* 43 D12
Birmingham, *U.K.* 13 E6
Birmingham, *U.S.A.* 109 J2
Birmitrapur, *India* 67 H14
Birni Ngaouré, *Niger* 83 C5
Birni Nkonni, *Niger* 83 C6
Birnin Gwari, *Nigeria* 83 C6
Birnin Kebbi, *Nigeria* 83 C5
Birnin Kudu, *Nigeria* 83 C6
Birobidzhan, *Russia* 51 E14
Birr, *Ireland* 15 C4
Birrie →, *Australia* 95 D4
Birsilpur, *India* 68 E5
Birsk, *Russia* 50 D6
Birštonas, *Lithuania* 44 D11
Birtle, *Canada* 105 C8
Birur, *India* 66 N9
Biryuchiy, *Ukraine* 47 J8
Biržai, *Lithuania* 9 H21
Birzebbugga, *Malta* 36 D2
Bisa, *Indonesia* 63 E7
Bisáccia, *Italy* 31 A8
Bisacquino, *Italy* 30 E6
Bisalpur, *India* 69 E8
Bisbee, *U.S.A.* 115 L9
Biscarrosse, *France* 20 D2
Biscarrosse et de Parentis, Étang de, *France* 20 D2
Biscay, B. of, *Atl. Oc.* 6 F5
Biscayne B., *U.S.A.* 109 N5
Biscéglie, *Italy* 31 A9
Bischheim, *France* 19 D14
Bischofshofen, *Austria* 26 D6
Bischofswerda, *Germany* 24 D10
Bischwiller, *France* 19 D14
Biscoe Bay, *Antarctica* 5 D13
Biscoe Is., *Antarctica* 5 C17
Biscostasing, *Canada* 102 C3
Biševo, *Croatia* 29 F13
Bisha, *Eritrea* 81 D4
Bishah, W. →, *Si. Arabia* 80 C5
Bishan, *China* 58 C6
Bishkek, *Kyrgyzstan* 50 E8
Bishnupur, *India* 69 H12
Bisho, *S. Africa* 89 E4
Bishop, *Calif., U.S.A.* 116 H8
Bishop, *Tex., U.S.A.* 113 M6
Bishop Auckland, *U.K.* 12 C6
Bishop's Falls, *Canada* 103 C8
Bishop's Stortford, *U.K.* 13 F8
Bisignano, *Italy* 31 C9
Bisina, L., *Uganda* 86 B3
Biskra, *Algeria* 78 B7
Biskupiec, *Poland* 44 E7
Bismarck, *U.S.A.* 112 B4
Bismarck Arch., *Papua N. G.* 96 H7
Bismark, *Germany* 24 C7
Bismil, *Turkey* 73 D9
Biso, *Uganda* 86 B3
Bison, *U.S.A.* 112 C3
Bīsotūn, *Iran* 70 C5
Bispgården, *Sweden* 10 A10
Bissagos = Bijagós, Arquipélago dos, *Guinea-Biss.* 82 C1
Bissau, *Guinea-Biss.* 82 C1
Bissaula, *Nigeria* 83 D7
Bissikrima, *Guinea* 82 C2
Bissorã, *Guinea-Biss.* 82 C1
Bistcho L., *Canada* 104 B5
Bistreț, *Romania* 43 G8
Bistrica = Ilirska-Bistrica, *Slovenia* 29 C11
Bistrița, *Romania* 43 C9
Bistrița →, *Romania* 43 D11
Bistrița Năsăud □, *Romania* 43 C9
Bistriței, Munții, *Romania* 43 C10
Biswan, *India* 69 F9
Bisztynek, *Poland* 44 D7
Bitburg, *Germany* 25 F2
Bitche, *France* 19 C14
Bithynia, *Turkey* 72 B4
Bitlis, *Turkey* 70 B4
Bitola, *Macedonia* 40 E5
Bitolj = Bitola, *Macedonia* 40 E5
Bitonto, *Italy* 31 A9
Bitter Creek, *U.S.A.* 114 F9
Bitter L. = Buheirat-Murrat-el-Kubra, *Egypt* 80 H8
Bitterfeld, *Germany* 24 D8
Bitterfontein, *S. Africa* 88 E2
Bitterroot →, *U.S.A.* 114 C6
Bitterroot Range, *U.S.A.* 114 D6
Bitterwater, *U.S.A.* 116 J6
Bitti, *Italy* 30 B2
Bittou, *Burkina Faso* 83 C4
Biu, *Nigeria* 83 C7
Bivolari, *Romania* 43 C12
Bivolu, Vf., *Romania* 43 C10
Biwa-Ko, *Japan* 55 G8
Biwabik, *U.S.A.* 112 B8
Bixad, *Romania* 43 C8
Bixby, *U.S.A.* 113 H7
Biyang, *China* 56 H7
Biysk, *Russia* 50 D9
Bizana, *S. Africa* 89 E4
Bizen, *Japan* 55 G7
Bizerte, *Tunisia* 79 A7
Bjargtangar, *Iceland* 8 D1
Bjärnum, *Sweden* 11 H7
Bjästa, *Sweden* 10 A12
Bjelasica, *Montenegro, Yug.* 40 D3
Bjelašnica, *Bos.-H.* 42 G3
Bjelovar, *Croatia* 29 C13
Bjerringbro, *Denmark* 11 H3
Björbo, *Sweden* 10 D8
Björklinge, *Sweden* 10 D11
Björneborg, *Sweden* 10 E8
Bjørnevatn, *Norway* 8 B23
Bjørnøya, *Arctic* 4 B8
Bjursås, *Sweden* 10 D9
Bjuv, *Sweden* 11 H6
Bla, *Mali* 82 C3
Blace, *Serbia, Yug.* 40 C5
Blachownia, *Poland* 45 H5
Black = Da →, *Vietnam* 58 G5
Black →, *Canada* 110 B5
Black →, *Ariz., U.S.A.* 115 K8
Black →, *Ark., U.S.A.* 113 H9
Black →, *Mich., U.S.A.* 110 D2
Black →, *N.Y., U.S.A.* 111 C8
Black →, *Wis., U.S.A.* 112 D9
Black Bay Pen., *Canada* 102 C2
Black Birch L., *Canada* 105 B7
Black Diamond, *Canada* 104 C6
Black Duck →, *Canada* 102 A2
Black Forest = Schwarzwald, *Germany* 25 G4
Black Forest, *U.S.A.* 112 F2
Black Hd., *Ireland* 15 C2
Black Hills, *U.S.A.* 112 D3
Black I., *Canada* 105 C9
Black L., *Canada* 105 B7
Black L., *Mich., U.S.A.* 108 C3
Black L., *N.Y., U.S.A.* 111 B9
Black Lake, *Canada* 105 B7
Black Mesa, *U.S.A.* 113 G3
Black Mt. = Mynydd Du, *U.K.* 13 F4
Black Mts., *U.K.* 13 F4
Black Range, *U.S.A.* 115 K10
Black River, *Jamaica* 120 C4
Black River Falls, *U.S.A.* 112 C9
Black Sea, *Eurasia* 6 G12
Black Tickle, *Canada* 103 B8
Black Volta →, *Africa* 82 D4
Black Warrior →, *U.S.A.* 109 J2
Blackall, *Australia* 94 C4
Blackball, *N.Z.* 91 K3
Blackbull, *Australia* 94 B3
Blackburn, *U.K.* 12 D5
Blackburn with Darwen □, *U.K.* 12 D5
Blackfoot, *U.S.A.* 114 E7
Blackfoot →, *U.S.A.* 114 C7
Blackfoot River Reservoir, *U.S.A.* 114 E8
Blackpool, *U.K.* 12 D4
Blackpool □, *U.K.* 12 D4
Blackriver, *U.S.A.* 110 B1
Blacks Harbour, *Canada* 103 C6
Blacksburg, *U.S.A.* 108 G5
Blacksod B., *Ireland* 15 B1
Blackstone, *U.S.A.* 108 G7
Blackstone Ra., *Australia* 93 E4
Blackwater, *Australia* 94 C4
Blackwater →, *Meath, Ireland* 15 C4
Blackwater →, *Waterford, Ireland* 15 D4
Blackwater →, *U.K.* 15 B5
Blackwell, *U.S.A.* 113 G6
Blackwells Corner, *U.S.A.* 117 K7
Blaenau Ffestiniog, *U.K.* 12 E4
Blaenau Gwent □, *U.K.* 13 F4
Blagaj, *Bos.-H.* 40 C1
Blagnac, *France* 20 E5
Blagodarnoye = Blagodarnyy, *Russia* 49 H6
Blagodarnyy, *Russia* 49 H6
Blagoevgrad, *Bulgaria* 40 D7
Blagoveshchensk, *Russia* 51 D13
Blain, *France* 18 E5
Blain, *U.S.A.* 110 F7
Blaine, *Minn., U.S.A.* 112 C8
Blaine, *Wash., U.S.A.* 116 B4
Blaine Lake, *Canada* 105 C7
Blair, *U.S.A.* 112 E6
Blair Athol, *Australia* 94 C4
Blair Atholl, *U.K.* 14 E5
Blairgowrie, *U.K.* 14 E5
Blairsden, *U.S.A.* 116 F6
Blairsville, *U.S.A.* 110 F5
Blaj, *Romania* 43 D8
Blake Pt., *U.S.A.* 112 A10
Blakely, *Ga., U.S.A.* 109 K3
Blakely, *Pa., U.S.A.* 111 E9
Blâmont, *France* 19 D13
Blanc, C., *Spain* 37 B9
Blanc, Mont, *Alps* 21 C10
Blanc-Sablon, *Canada* 103 B8
Blanca, B., *Argentina* 122 G4
Blanca Peak, *U.S.A.* 115 H11
Blanche, C., *Australia* 95 E1
Blanche, L., *S. Austral., Australia* 95 D2
Blanche, L., *W. Austral., Australia* 92 D3
Blanco, *S. Africa* 88 E3
Blanco, *U.S.A.* 113 K5
Blanco →, *Argentina* 126 C2
Blanco, C., *Costa Rica* 120 E2
Blanco, C., *U.S.A.* 114 E1
Blanda →, *Iceland* 8 D3
Blandford Forum, *U.K.* 13 G5
Blanding, *U.S.A.* 115 H9
Blanes, *Spain* 32 D7
Blangy-sur-Bresle, *France* 19 C8
Blanice →, *Czech Rep.* 26 B7
Blankaholm, *Sweden* 11 G10
Blankenberge, *Belgium* 17 C3
Blankenburg, *Germany* 24 D6
Blanquefort, *France* 20 D3
Blanquilla, I., *Venezuela* 121 D7
Blanquillo, *Uruguay* 127 C4
Blansko, *Czech Rep.* 27 B9
Blantyre, *Malawi* 87 F4
Blarney, *Ireland* 15 E3
Blasdell, *U.S.A.* 110 D6
Błaszki, *Poland* 45 G5
Blatná, *Czech Rep.* 26 B6
Blato, *Croatia* 29 F13
Blaubeuren, *Germany* 25 G5
Blaustein, *Germany* 25 G5
Blåvands Huk, *Denmark* 11 J2
Blaydon, *U.K.* 12 C6
Blaye, *France* 20 C3
Blaye-les-Mines, *France* 20 D6
Blayney, *Australia* 95 E4
Blaze, Pt., *Australia* 92 B5
Błażowa, *Poland* 45 J9
Bleckede, *Germany* 24 B6
Bled, *Slovenia* 29 B11
Bleiburg, *Austria* 26 E7
Blejeşti, *Romania* 43 F10
Blekinge, *Sweden* 9 H16
Blekinge län □, *Sweden* 11 H9
Blenheim, *Canada* 110 D3
Blenheim, *N.Z.* 91 J4
Bléone →, *France* 21 D10
Blérancourt, *France* 19 C10
Bletchley, *U.K.* 13 F7
Blida, *Algeria* 78 A6
Blidö, *Sweden* 10 E12
Blidsberg, *Sweden* 11 G7
Blieskastel, *Germany* 25 F3
Bligh Sound, *N.Z.* 91 L1
Blind River, *Canada* 102 C3
Blinisht, *Albania* 40 E3
Bliss, *Idaho, U.S.A.* 114 E6
Bliss, *N.Y., U.S.A.* 110 D6
Blissfield, *U.S.A.* 110 F3
Blitar, *Indonesia* 63 H15
Blitta, *Togo* 83 D5
Block I., *U.S.A.* 111 E13
Block Island Sd., *U.S.A.* 111 E13
Blodgett Iceberg Tongue, *Antarctica* 5 C9
Bloemfontein, *S. Africa* 88 D4
Bloemhof, *S. Africa* 88 D4
Blois, *France* 18 E8
Blomskog, *Sweden* 10 E6
Blomstermåla, *Sweden* 11 H10
Blönduós, *Iceland* 8 D3
Błonie, *Poland* 45 F7
Bloodvein →, *Canada* 105 C9
Bloody Foreland, *Ireland* 15 A3
Bloomer, *U.S.A.* 112 C9
Bloomfield, *Canada* 110 C7
Bloomfield, *Iowa, U.S.A.* 112 E8
Bloomfield, *N. Mex., U.S.A.* 115 H10
Bloomfield, *Nebr., U.S.A.* 112 D6
Bloomington, *Ill., U.S.A.* 112 E10
Bloomington, *Ind., U.S.A.* 108 F2
Bloomington, *Minn., U.S.A.* 112 C8
Bloomsburg, *U.S.A.* 111 F8
Blora, *Indonesia* 63 G14
Blossburg, *U.S.A.* 110 E7
Blouberg, *S. Africa* 89 C4
Blountstown, *U.S.A.* 109 K3
Bludenz, *Austria* 26 D2
Blue Earth, *U.S.A.* 112 D8
Blue Mesa Reservoir, *U.S.A.* 115 G10
Blue Mountain Lake, *U.S.A.* 111 C10
Blue Mts., *Maine, U.S.A.* 111 B14
Blue Mts., *Oreg., U.S.A.* 114 D4
Blue Mts., *Pa., U.S.A.* 111 F8
Blue Mud B., *Australia* 94 A2
Blue Nile = Nîl el Azraq →, *Sudan* 81 D3
Blue Rapids, *U.S.A.* 112 F6
Blue Ridge Mts., *U.S.A.* 109 G5
Blue River, *Canada* 104 C5
Bluefield, *U.S.A.* 108 G5
Bluefields, *Nic.* 120 D3
Bluff, *Australia* 94 C4
Bluff, *N.Z.* 91 M2
Bluff, *U.S.A.* 115 H9
Bluff Knoll, *Australia* 93 F2
Bluff Pt., *Australia* 93 E1
Bluffton, *U.S.A.* 108 E3
Blumenau, *Brazil* 127 B6
Blunt, *U.S.A.* 112 C5
Bly, *U.S.A.* 114 E3
Blyth, *Canada* 110 C3
Blyth, *U.K.* 12 B6
Blythe, *U.S.A.* 117 M12
Blytheville, *U.S.A.* 113 H10
Bo, *S. Leone* 82 D2
Bo Duc, *Vietnam* 65 G6
Bo Hai, *China* 57 E10
Bo Xian = Bozhou, *China* 56 H8
Boa Vista, *Brazil* 124 C6
Boac, *Phil.* 61 E4
Boaco, *Nic.* 120 D2
Bo'ai, *China* 56 G7
Boal, *Spain* 34 B4
Boalsburg, *U.S.A.* 110 F7
Boane, *Mozam.* 89 D5
Boardman, *U.S.A.* 110 E4
Bobadah, *Australia* 95 E4
Bobai, *China* 58 F7
Bobbili, *India* 67 K13
Bóbbio, *Italy* 28 D6
Bobcaygeon, *Canada* 102 D4
Böblingen, *Germany* 25 G5
Bobo-Dioulasso, *Burkina Faso* 82 C4
Bobolice, *Poland* 44 E3
Boboshevo, *Bulgaria* 40 D7
Bobov Dol, *Bulgaria* 40 D6
Bóbr →, *Poland* 45 F2
Bobraomby, Tanjon' i, *Madag.* 89 A8
Bobrinets, *Ukraine* 47 H7
Bobrov, *Russia* 48 E5
Bobrovitsa, *Ukraine* 47 G6
Bobruysk = Babruysk, *Belarus* 47 F5
Boby, Pic, *Madag.* 85 J9
Bôca do Acre, *Brazil* 124 E5
Boca Raton, *U.S.A.* 109 M5
Bocanda, *Ivory C.* 82 D4
Bocas del Toro, *Panama* 120 E3
Boceguillas, *Spain* 34 D7
Bochnia, *Poland* 45 J7
Bocholt, *Germany* 24 D2
Bochum, *Germany* 24 D3
Bockenem, *Germany* 24 C6
Boćki, *Poland* 45 F10
Bocognano, *France* 21 F13
Bocoyna, *Mexico* 118 B3
Bocşa, *Romania* 42 E6
Böda, *Dalarnas, Sweden* 10 C9
Böda, *Kalmar, Sweden* 11 G11
Boda, *Västernorrland, Sweden* 10 B10
Bodafors, *Sweden* 11 G8
Bodaybo, *Russia* 51 D12
Boddam, *U.K.* 14 B7
Boddington, *Australia* 93 F2
Bode Sadu, *Nigeria* 83 D5
Bodega Bay, *U.S.A.* 116 G3
Boden, *Sweden* 8 D19
Bodensee, *Europe* 25 H5
Bodenteich, *Germany* 24 C6
Bodhan, *India* 66 K10
Bodinga, *Nigeria* 83 C6
Bodmin, *U.K.* 13 G3
Bodmin Moor, *U.K.* 13 G3
Bodø, *Norway* 8 C16
Bodrog →, *Hungary* 42 B6
Bodrum, *Turkey* 39 D9
Bódva →, *Hungary* 42 B5
Boën, *France* 21 C8
Boende, *Dem. Rep. of the Congo* 84 E4
Boerne, *U.S.A.* 113 L5
Boesmans →, *S. Africa* 88 E4
Boffa, *Guinea* 82 C2
Bogalusa, *U.S.A.* 113 K10
Bogan →, *Australia* 95 D4
Bogan Gate, *Australia* 95 E4
Bogandé, *Burkina Faso* 83 C4
Bogantungan, *Australia* 94 C4
Bogata, *U.S.A.* 113 J7
Bogatić, *Serbia, Yug.* 40 B3
Boğazkale, *Turkey* 72 B6
Boğazlıyan, *Turkey* 72 C6
Bogen, *Sweden* 10 D6
Bogense, *Denmark* 11 J4
Bogetići, *Montenegro, Yug.* 40 D2
Boggabilla, *Australia* 95 D5
Boggabri, *Australia* 95 E5
Boggeragh Mts., *Ireland* 15 D3
Boglan = Solhan, *Turkey* 70 B4
Bognor Regis, *U.K.* 13 G7
Bogo, *Phil.* 61 F6
Bogodukhov = Bohodukhiv, *Ukraine* 47 G8
Bogol Manya, *Ethiopia* 81 G5
Bogong, Mt., *Australia* 95 F4
Bogor, *Indonesia* 62 F3
Bogoroditsk, *Russia* 46 F10
Bogorodsk, *Russia* 48 B6
Bogoso, *Ghana* 82 D4
Bogotá, *Colombia* 124 C4
Bogotol, *Russia* 50 D9
Bogou, *Togo* 83 C5

Bogra, *Bangla.* 67 G16
Boguchany, *Russia* 51 D10
Boguchar, *Russia* 48 F5
Bogué, *Mauritania* 82 B2
Boguslav, *Ukraine* 47 H6
Boguszów-Gorce, *Poland* 45 H3
Bohain-en-Vermandois, *France* 19 C10
Bohemian Forest = Böhmerwald, *Germany* 25 F9
Bohinjska Bistrica, *Slovenia* 29 B11
Böhmerwald, *Germany* 25 F9
Bohmte, *Germany* 24 C4
Bohodukhiv, *Ukraine* 47 G8
Bohol □, *Phil.* 61 G6
Bohol Sea, *Phil.* 63 C6
Bohongou, *Burkina Faso* 83 C5
Böhönye, *Hungary* 42 D2
Bohuslän, *Sweden* 11 F5
Boi, *Nigeria* 83 D6
Boi, Pta. de, *Brazil* 127 A6
Boiaçu, *Brazil* 124 D6
Boileau, C., *Australia* 92 C3
Boing'o, *Sudan* 81 F3
Boiro, *Spain* 34 C2
Boise, *U.S.A.* 114 E5
Boise City, *U.S.A.* 113 G3
Boissevain, *Canada* 105 D8
Bóite →, *Italy* 29 B9
Boitzenburg, *Germany* 24 B9
Boizenburg, *Germany* 24 B6
Bojador C., *W. Sahara* 78 C3
Bojana →, *Albania* 40 E3
Bojano, *Italy* 31 A7
Bojanowo, *Poland* 45 G3
Bøjden, *Denmark* 11 J4
Bojnūrd, *Iran* 71 B8
Bojonegoro, *Indonesia* 63 G14
Boju, *Nigeria* 83 D6
Boka, *Serbia, Yug.* 42 E5
Boka Kotorska, *Montenegro, Yug.* 40 D2
Bokala, *Ivory C.* 82 D4
Bokani, *Nigeria* 83 D6
Bokaro, *India* 69 H11
Boké, *Guinea* 82 C2
Bokhara →, *Australia* 95 D4
Bokkos, *Nigeria* 83 D6
Boknafjorden, *Norway* 9 G11
Bokoro, *Chad* 79 F9
Bokpyin, *Burma* 65 G2
Boksitogorsk, *Russia* 46 C7
Bol, *Croatia* 29 E13
Bolama, *Guinea-Biss.* 82 C1
Bolan →, *Pakistan* 68 E2
Bolan Pass, *Pakistan* 66 E5
Bolaños →, *Mexico* 118 C4
Bolaños de Calatrava, *Spain* 35 G7
Bolayır, *Turkey* 41 F10
Bolbec, *France* 18 C7
Boldājī, *Iran* 71 D6
Boldeşti-Scăeni, *Romania* 43 E11
Bole, *China* 60 B3
Bole, *Ethiopia* 81 F4
Bole, *Ghana* 82 D4
Bolekhiv, *Ukraine* 47 H2
Bolesławiec, *Poland* 45 G2
Bolgatanga, *Ghana* 83 C4
Bolgrad = Bolhrad, *Ukraine* 47 K5
Bolhrad, *Ukraine* 47 K5
Bolinao, *Phil.* 61 C3
Bolintin-Vale, *Romania* 43 F10
Bolívar, *Argentina* 126 D3
Bolivar, *Mo., U.S.A.* 113 G8
Bolivar, *N.Y., U.S.A.* 110 D6
Bolivar, *Tenn., U.S.A.* 113 H10
Bolivia ■, *S. Amer.* 124 G6
Bolivian Plateau, *S. Amer.* 122 E4
Boljevac, *Serbia, Yug.* 40 C5
Bolkhov, *Russia* 46 F9
Bolków, *Poland* 45 H3
Bollebygd, *Sweden* 11 G6
Bollène, *France* 21 D8
Bollnäs, *Sweden* 10 C10
Bollon, *Australia* 95 D4
Bollstabruk, *Sweden* 10 B11
Bolmen, *Sweden* 11 H7
Bolobo, *Dem. Rep. of the Congo* 84 E3
Bologna, *Italy* 29 D8
Bologoye, *Russia* 46 D8
Bolon, Ozero, *Russia* 60 B8
Bolonchenticul, *Mexico* 119 D7
Bolótana, *Italy* 30 B1
Boloven, Cao Nguyen, *Laos* 64 E6
Bolpur, *India* 69 H12
Bolsena, *Italy* 29 F8
Bolsena, L. di, *Italy* 29 F8
Bolshaya Chernigovka, *Russia* 48 D10
Bolshaya Glushitsa, *Russia* 48 D10
Bolshaya Martynovka, *Russia* 49 G5
Bolshaya Vradiyevka, *Ukraine* 47 J6
Bolshevik, Ostrov, *Russia* 51 B11
Bolshoi Kavkas = Caucasus Mountains, *Eurasia* 49 J7
Bolshoy Anyuy →, *Russia* 51 C17
Bolshoy Begichev, Ostrov, *Russia* 51 B12
Bolshoy Lyakhovskiy, Ostrov, *Russia* 51 B15
Bolshoy Tokmak = Tokmak, *Ukraine* 47 J8
Bolshoy Tyuters, Ostrov, *Russia* 9 G22
Bolsward, *Neths.* 17 A5
Bolt Head, *U.K.* 13 G4
Boltaña, *Spain* 32 C5
Boltigen, *Switz.* 25 J3
Bolton, *Canada* 110 C5
Bolton, *U.K.* 12 D5
Bolton Landing, *U.S.A.* 111 C11
Bolu, *Turkey* 72 B4
Bolungavík, *Iceland* 8 C2
Boluo, *China* 59 F10
Bolvadin, *Turkey* 70 B1
Bolzano, *Italy* 29 B8
Bom Jesus da Lapa, *Brazil* 125 F10
Boma, *Dem. Rep. of the Congo* 84 F2
Bombala, *Australia* 95 F4
Bombarral, *Portugal* 35 F1
Bombay = Mumbai, *India* 66 K8
Bomboma, *Dem. Rep. of the Congo* 84 D3
Bombombwa, *Dem. Rep. of the Congo* 86 B2
Bomi Hills, *Liberia* 82 D2
Bomili, *Dem. Rep. of the Congo* 86 B2
Bømlo, *Norway* 9 G11
Bomokandi →, *Dem. Rep. of the Congo* 86 B2
Bomu →, *C.A.R.* 84 D4
Bon, C., *Tunisia* 76 C5
Bon Sar Pa, *Vietnam* 64 F6
Bonaigarh, *India* 69 J11
Bonaire, *Neth. Ant.* 121 D6
Bonang, *Australia* 95 F4
Bonanza, *Nic.* 120 D3
Bonaparte Arch., *Australia* 92 B3
Boñar, *Spain* 34 C5
Bonaventure, *Canada* 103 C6
Bonavista, *Canada* 103 C9
Bonavista, C., *Canada* 103 C9
Bonavista B., *Canada* 103 C9
Bondeno, *Italy* 29 D8
Bondo, *Dem. Rep. of the Congo* 86 B1
Bondoukou, *Ivory C.* 82 D4
Bondowoso, *Indonesia* 63 G15
Bone, Teluk, *Indonesia* 63 E6
Bonerate, *Indonesia* 63 F6
Bonerate, Kepulauan, *Indonesia* 63 F6
Bo'ness, *U.K.* 14 E5
Bonete, Cerro, *Argentina* 126 B2
Bong Son = Hoai Nhon, *Vietnam* 64 E7
Bonga, *Ethiopia* 81 F4
Bongabong, *Phil.* 61 E4
Bongor, *Chad* 79 F9
Bongouanou, *Ivory C.* 82 D4
Bonham, *U.S.A.* 113 J6
Boni, *Mali* 82 B4
Bonifacio, *France* 21 G13
Bonifacio, Bouches de, *Medit. S.* 30 A2
Bonin Is. = Ogasawara Gunto, *Pac. Oc.* 52 G18
Bonke, *Ethiopia* 81 F4
Bonkoukou, *Niger* 83 C5
Bonn, *Germany* 24 E3
Bonnat, *France* 19 F8
Bonne Terre, *U.S.A.* 113 G9
Bonners Ferry, *U.S.A.* 114 B5
Bonnétable, *France* 18 D7
Bonneval, *Eure-et-Loir, France* 18 D8
Bonneval, *Savoie, France* 21 C11
Bonneville, *France* 19 F13
Bonney, L., *Australia* 95 F3
Bonnie Rock, *Australia* 93 F2
Bonny, *Nigeria* 83 E6
Bonny →, *Nigeria* 83 E6
Bonny, Bight of, *Africa* 83 E6
Bonny-sur-Loire, *France* 19 E9
Bonnyrigg, *U.K.* 14 F5
Bonnyville, *Canada* 105 C6
Bono, *Italy* 30 B2
Bonoi, *Indonesia* 63 E9
Bonorva, *Italy* 30 B1
Bonsall, *U.S.A.* 117 M9
Bontang, *Indonesia* 62 D5
Bonthe, *S. Leone* 82 D2
Bontoc, *Phil.* 61 C4
Bonyeri, *Ghana* 82 D4
Bonyhád, *Hungary* 42 D3
Bonython Ra., *Australia* 92 D4
Bookabie, *Australia* 93 F5
Booker, *U.S.A.* 113 G4
Boola, *Guinea* 82 D3
Boolaboolka L., *Australia* 95 E3
Booligal, *Australia* 95 E3
Boonah, *Australia* 95 D5
Boone, *Iowa, U.S.A.* 112 D8
Boone, *N.C., U.S.A.* 109 G5
Booneville, *Ark., U.S.A.* 113 H8
Booneville, *Miss., U.S.A.* 109 H1
Boonville, *Calif., U.S.A.* 116 F3
Boonville, *Ind., U.S.A.* 108 F2
Boonville, *Mo., U.S.A.* 112 F8
Boonville, *N.Y., U.S.A.* 111 C9
Boorindal, *Australia* 95 E4
Boorowa, *Australia* 95 E4
Boothia, Gulf of, *Canada* 101 A11
Boothia Pen., *Canada* 100 A10
Bootle, *U.K.* 12 D4
Booué, *Gabon* 84 E2
Boppard, *Germany* 25 E3
Boquete, *Panama* 120 E3
Boquilla, Presa de la, *Mexico* 118 B3
Boquillas del Carmen, *Mexico* 118 B4
Bor, *Czech Rep.* 26 B5
Bor, *Russia* 48 B7
Bor, *Serbia, Yug.* 40 B6
Bôr, *Sudan* 81 F3
Bor, *Sweden* 11 G8
Bor, *Turkey* 72 D6
Bor Mashash, *Israel* 75 D3
Borah Peak, *U.S.A.* 114 D7
Borang, *Sudan* 81 G3
Borås, *Sweden* 11 G6
Borāzjān, *Iran* 71 D6
Borba, *Brazil* 124 D7
Borba, *Portugal* 35 G3
Borborema, Planalto da, *Brazil* 122 D7
Borcea, *Romania* 43 F12
Borçka, *Turkey* 73 B9
Bord Khūn-e Now, *Iran* 71 D6
Borda, C., *Australia* 95 F2
Bordeaux, *France* 20 D3
Borden, *Australia* 93 F2
Borden, *Canada* 103 C7
Borden I., *Canada* 4 B2
Borden Pen., *Canada* 101 A11
Borders = Scottish Borders □, *U.K.* 14 F6
Bordertown, *Australia* 95 F3
Borðeyri, *Iceland* 8 D3
Bordighera, *Italy* 28 E4
Bordj Fly Ste. Marie, *Algeria* 78 C5
Bordj-in-Eker, *Algeria* 78 D7
Bordj Omar Driss, *Algeria* 78 C7
Bore, *Ethiopia* 81 G4
Borehamwood, *U.K.* 13 F7
Borek Wielkopolski, *Poland* 45 G4
Borensberg, *Sweden* 11 F9
Borgå = Porvoo, *Finland* 9 F21
Borgarfjörður, *Iceland* 8 D7
Borgarnes, *Iceland* 8 D3
Børgefjellet, *Norway* 8 D15
Borger, *Neths.* 17 B6
Borger, *U.S.A.* 113 H4
Borgholm, *Sweden* 11 H10
Bórgia, *Italy* 31 D9
Borgo San Dalmazzo, *Italy* 28 D4
Borgo San Lorenzo, *Italy* 29 E8
Borgo Val di Taro, *Italy* 28 D6
Borgo Valsugana, *Italy* 29 B8
Borgomanero, *Italy* 28 C5
Borgorose, *Italy* 29 F10
Borgosésia, *Italy* 28 C5
Borhoyn Tal, *Mongolia* 56 C6
Bori, *Nigeria* 83 E6
Borikhane, *Laos* 64 C4
Borisoglebsk, *Russia* 48 E6
Borisov = Barysaw, *Belarus* 46 E5
Borisovka, *Russia* 47 G9
Borja, *Peru* 124 D3
Borja, *Spain* 32 D3
Borjas Blancas = Les Borges Blanques, *Spain* 32 D5
Borjomi, *Georgia* 49 K6
Børkop, *Denmark* 11 J3
Borkou, *Chad* 79 E9
Borkum, *Germany* 24 B2
Borlänge, *Sweden* 10 D9
Borley, C., *Antarctica* 5 C5
Borlu, *Turkey* 39 C10
Bormida →, *Italy* 28 D5
Bórmio, *Italy* 28 B7
Borna, *Germany* 24 D8
Borne Sulinowo, *Poland* 44 E3
Borneo, *E. Indies* 62 D5
Bornholm, *Denmark* 11 J8
Bornholms Amtskommune □, *Denmark* 11 J8
Bornholmsgatt, *Europe* 11 J8
Borno □, *Nigeria* 83 C7
Bornos, *Spain* 35 J5
Bornova, *Turkey* 39 C9
Bornu Yassa, *Nigeria* 83 C7
Boro →, *Sudan* 81 F2
Borodino, *Russia* 46 E8
Borogontsy, *Russia* 51 C14
Boromo, *Burkina Faso* 82 C4
Boron, *U.S.A.* 117 L9
Borongan, *Phil.* 61 F6
Borotangba Mts., *C.A.R.* 81 F2
Borotou, *Ivory C.* 82 D3
Borovan, *Bulgaria* 40 C7
Borovichi, *Russia* 46 C7
Borovsk, *Russia* 46 E9
Borrby, *Sweden* 11 J8
Borrego Springs, *U.S.A.* 117 M10
Borriol, *Spain* 32 E4
Borroloola, *Australia* 94 B2
Borşa, *Cluj, Romania* 43 D8
Borşa, *Maramureş, Romania* 43 C9
Borsad, *India* 68 H5
Borsec, *Romania* 43 D10
Borsod-Abaúj-Zemplén □, *Hungary* 42 B6
Bort-les-Orgues, *France* 20 C6
Borth, *U.K.* 13 E3
Börtnan, *Sweden* 10 B7
Borūjerd, *Iran* 71 C6
Boryslav, *Ukraine* 47 H2
Boryspil, *Ukraine* 47 G6
Borzhomi = Borjomi, *Georgia* 49 K6
Borzna, *Ukraine* 47 G7
Borzya, *Russia* 51 D12
Bosa, *Italy* 30 B1
Bosanska Dubica, *Bos.-H.* 29 C13
Bosanska Gradiška, *Bos.-H.* 42 E2
Bosanska Kostajnica, *Bos.-H.* 29 C13
Bosanska Krupa, *Bos.-H.* 29 D13
Bosanski Brod, *Bos.-H.* 42 E2
Bosanski Novi, *Bos.-H.* 29 C13
Bosanski Petrovac, *Bos.-H.* 29 D13
Bosanski Šamac, *Bos.-H.* 42 E3
Bosansko Grahovo, *Bos.-H.* 29 D13
Bosaso, *Somali Rep.* 74 E4
Boscastle, *U.K.* 13 G3
Bose, *China* 58 F6
Boshan, *China* 57 F9
Boshof, *S. Africa* 88 D4
Boshrūyeh, *Iran* 71 C8
Bosilegrad, *Serbia, Yug.* 40 D6
Boskovice, *Czech Rep.* 27 B9
Bosna →, *Bos.-H.* 42 E3
Bosna i Hercegovina = Bosnia-Herzegovina ■, *Europe* 42 G2
Bosnia-Herzegovina ■, *Europe* 42 G2
Bosnik, *Indonesia* 63 E9
Bosobolo, *Dem. Rep. of the Congo* 84 D3
Bosporus = İstanbul Boğazı, *Turkey* 41 E13
Bosque Farms, *U.S.A.* 115 J10
Bossangoa, *C.A.R.* 84 C3
Bossé Bangou, *Niger* 83 C5
Bossier City, *U.S.A.* 113 J8
Bosso, *Niger* 83 C7
Bosso, Dallol →, *Niger* 83 C5
Bostan, *Pakistan* 68 D2
Bostānābād, *Iran* 70 B5
Bosten Hu, *China* 60 B3
Boston, *U.K.* 12 E7
Boston, *U.S.A.* 111 D13
Boston Bar, *Canada* 104 D4
Boston Mts., *U.S.A.* 113 H8
Bosut →, *Croatia* 42 E3
Boswell, *Canada* 104 D5
Boswell, *U.S.A.* 110 F5
Botad, *India* 68 H4
Botan →, *Turkey* 73 D10
Botene, *Laos* 64 D3
Botev, *Bulgaria* 41 D8
Botevgrad, *Bulgaria* 40 D7
Bothaville, *S. Africa* 88 D4
Bothnia, G. of, *Europe* 8 E19
Bothwell, *Australia* 94 G4
Bothwell, *Canada* 110 D3
Boticas, *Portugal* 34 D3
Botletle →, *Botswana* 88 C3
Botlikh, *Russia* 49 J8
Botna →, *Moldova* 43 D14
Botoroaga, *Romania* 43 F10
Botoşani, *Romania* 43 C11
Botoşani □, *Romania* 43 C11
Botou, *Burkina Faso* 83 C5
Botricello, *Italy* 31 D9
Botro, *Ivory C.* 82 D3
Botswana ■, *Africa* 88 C3
Bottineau, *U.S.A.* 112 A4
Bottnaryd, *Sweden* 11 G7
Bottrop, *Germany* 17 C6
Botucatu, *Brazil* 127 A6
Botwood, *Canada* 103 C8
Bou Djébéha, *Mali* 82 B4
Boû Rjeïmât, *Mauritania* 82 B1
Bouaflé, *Ivory C.* 82 D3
Bouaké, *Ivory C.* 82 D3
Bouar, *C.A.R.* 84 C3
Bouârfa, *Morocco* 78 B5
Boucaut B., *Australia* 94 A1
Bouches-du-Rhône □, *France* 21 E9
Bougainville, C., *Australia* 92 B4
Bougainville I., *Papua N. G.* 96 H7
Bougainville Reef, *Australia* 94 B4
Bougie = Bejaïa, *Algeria* 78 A7
Bougouni, *Mali* 82 C3
Bouillon, *Belgium* 17 E5
Boukombé, *Benin* 83 C5
Boulal, *Mali* 82 B3
Boulazac, *France* 20 C4
Boulder, *Colo., U.S.A.* 112 E2
Boulder, *Mont., U.S.A.* 114 C7
Boulder City, *U.S.A.* 117 K12
Boulder Creek, *U.S.A.* 116 H4
Boulder Dam = Hoover Dam, *U.S.A.* 117 K12
Bouli, *Mauritania* 82 B2
Boulia, *Australia* 94 C2
Bouligny, *France* 19 C12
Boulogne →, *France* 18 E5
Boulogne-sur-Gesse, *France* 20 E4
Boulogne-sur-Mer, *France* 19 B8
Bouloire, *France* 18 E7
Boulouli, *Mali* 82 B3
Boulsa, *Burkina Faso* 83 C4
Boultoum, *Niger* 83 C7
Boûmdeïd, *Mauritania* 82 B2
Boun Neua, *Laos* 64 B3
Boun Tai, *Laos* 64 B3
Bouna, *Ivory C.* 82 D4
Boundary Peak, *U.S.A.* 116 H8
Boundiali, *Ivory C.* 82 D3
Bountiful, *U.S.A.* 114 F8
Bounty Is., *Pac. Oc.* 96 M9
Boura, *Mali* 82 C4
Bourbon-Lancy, *France* 19 F10
Bourbon-l'Archambault, *France* 19 F10
Bourbonnais, *France* 19 F10
Bourbonne-les-Bains, *France* 19 E12
Bourbourg, *France* 19 B9
Bourdel L., *Canada* 102 A5
Bourem, *Mali* 83 B4
Bourg, *France* 20 C3
Bourg-Argental, *France* 21 C8
Bourg-de-Péage, *France* 21 C9
Bourg-en-Bresse, *France* 19 F12
Bourg-Lastic, *France* 20 C6
Bourg-Madame, *France* 20 F5
Bourg-St-Andéol, *France* 21 D8
Bourg-St-Maurice, *France* 21 C10
Bourganeuf, *France* 20 C5
Bourges, *France* 19 E9
Bourget, *Canada* 111 A9
Bourget, Lac du, *France* 21 C9
Bourgneuf, B. de, *France* 18 E4
Bourgneuf-en-Retz, *France* 18 E5
Bourgogne, *France* 19 F11
Bourgoin-Jallieu, *France* 21 C9
Bourgueil, *France* 18 E7
Bourke, *Australia* 95 E4
Bourne, *U.K.* 12 E7
Bournemouth, *U.K.* 13 G6
Bournemouth □, *U.K.* 13 G6
Bouroum, *Burkina Faso* 83 C4
Bouse, *U.S.A.* 117 M13
Boussac, *France* 19 F9
Boussé, *Burkina Faso* 83 C4
Boussouma, *Burkina Faso* 83 C4
Boutilimit, *Mauritania* 82 B2
Boutonne →, *France* 20 C3
Bouvet I. = Bouvetøya, *Antarctica* 3 G10
Bouvetøya, *Antarctica* 3 G10
Bouxwiller, *France* 19 D14
Bouza, *Niger* 83 C6
Bouzonville, *France* 19 C13
Bova Marina, *Italy* 31 E8
Bovalino Marina, *Italy* 31 D9
Bovec, *Slovenia* 29 B10
Bovill, *U.S.A.* 114 C5
Bovino, *Italy* 31 A8
Bovril, *Argentina* 126 C4
Bow →, *Canada* 104 C6
Bow Island, *Canada* 104 D6
Bowbells, *U.S.A.* 112 A3
Bowdle, *U.S.A.* 112 C5
Bowelling, *Australia* 93 F2
Bowen, *Argentina* 126 D2
Bowen, *Australia* 94 C4
Bowen Mts., *Australia* 95 F4
Bowie, *Ariz., U.S.A.* 115 K9
Bowie, *Tex., U.S.A.* 113 J6
Bowkān, *Iran* 70 B5
Bowland, Forest of, *U.K.* 12 D5
Bowling Green, *Ky., U.S.A.* 108 G2
Bowling Green, *Ohio, U.S.A.* 108 E4
Bowling Green, C., *Australia* 94 B4
Bowman, *U.S.A.* 112 B3
Bowman I., *Antarctica* 5 C8
Bowmanville, *Canada* 110 C6
Bowmore, *U.K.* 14 F2
Bowral, *Australia* 95 E5
Bowraville, *Australia* 95 E5
Bowron →, *Canada* 104 C4
Bowron Lake Prov. Park, *Canada* 104 C4
Bowser L., *Canada* 104 B3
Bowsman, *Canada* 105 C8
Bowwood, *Zambia* 87 F2
Box Cr. →, *Australia* 95 E3
Boxholm, *Sweden* 11 F9
Boxmeer, *Neths.* 17 C5
Boxtel, *Neths.* 17 C5
Boyabat, *Turkey* 72 B6
Boyalıca, *Turkey* 41 F13
Boyang, *China* 59 C11
Boyce, *U.S.A.* 113 K8
Boyd L., *Canada* 102 B4
Boyle, *Canada* 104 C6
Boyle, *Ireland* 15 C3
Boyne →, *Ireland* 15 C5
Boyne City, *U.S.A.* 108 C3
Boynitsa, *Bulgaria* 40 C6
Boynton Beach, *U.S.A.* 109 M5
Boyolali, *Indonesia* 63 G14
Boyoma, Chutes, *Dem. Rep. of the Congo* 86 B2
Boysen Reservoir, *U.S.A.* 114 E9
Boyuibe, *Bolivia* 124 G6
Boyup Brook, *Australia* 93 F2
Boz Burun, *Turkey* 41 F12
Boz Dağ, *Turkey* 39 D11
Boz Dağları, *Turkey* 39 C10
Bozburun, *Turkey* 39 E10
Bozcaada, *Turkey* 72 C2
Bozdoğan, *Turkey* 39 D10
Bozeman, *U.S.A.* 114 D8
Bozen = Bolzano, *Italy* 29 B8
Boževac, *Serbia, Yug.* 40 B5
Bozhou, *China* 56 H8
Bozkır, *Turkey* 72 D5
Bozkurt, *Turkey* 39 D11
Bozouls, *France* 20 D6
Bozoum, *C.A.R.* 84 C3
Bozova, *Antalya, Turkey* 39 D12
Bozova, *Sanliurfa, Turkey* 73 D8
Bozovici, *Romania* 42 F7
Bozüyük, *Turkey* 39 B12
Bra, *Italy* 28 D4
Braås, *Sweden* 11 G9
Brabant □, *Belgium* 17 D4
Brabant L., *Canada* 105 B8
Brabrand, *Denmark* 11 H4
Brač, *Croatia* 29 E13
Bracadale, L., *U.K.* 14 D2
Bracciano, *Italy* 29 F9
Bracciano, L. di, *Italy* 29 F9
Bracebridge, *Canada* 102 C4
Brach, *Libya* 79 C8
Bracieux, *France* 18 E8
Bräcke, *Sweden* 10 B9
Brackettville, *U.S.A.* 113 L4
Brački Kanal, *Croatia* 29 E13
Bracknell, *U.K.* 13 F7
Bracknell Forest □, *U.K.* 13 F7
Brad, *Romania* 42 D7
Brádano →, *Italy* 31 B9
Bradenton, *U.S.A.* 109 M4
Bradford, *Canada* 110 B5
Bradford, *U.K.* 12 D6
Bradford, *Pa., U.S.A.* 110 E6
Bradford, *Vt., U.S.A.* 111 C12
Bradley, *Ark., U.S.A.* 113 J8
Bradley, *Calif., U.S.A.* 116 K6
Bradley Institute, *Zimbabwe* 87 F3
Brady, *U.S.A.* 113 K5
Brædstrup, *Denmark* 11 J3
Braeside, *Canada* 111 A8

Braga, *Portugal* 34 D2
Braga □, *Portugal* 34 D2
Bragadiru, *Romania* 43 G10
Bragado, *Argentina* 126 D3
Bragança, *Brazil* 125 D9
Bragança, *Portugal* 34 D4
Bragança □, *Portugal* 34 D4
Bragança Paulista, *Brazil* 127 A6
Brahmanbaria, *Bangla.* 67 H17
Brahmani →, *India* 67 J15
Brahmapur, *India* 67 K14
Brahmaputra →, *India* 69 H13
Braich-y-pwll, *U.K.* 12 E3
Braidwood, *Australia* 95 F4
Brăila, *Romania* 43 E12
Brăila □, *Romania* 43 E12
Brainerd, *U.S.A.* 112 B7
Braintree, *U.K.* 13 F8
Braintree, *U.S.A.* 111 D14
Brak →, *S. Africa* 88 D3
Brake, *Germany* 24 B4
Brakel, *Germany* 24 D5
Bräkne-Hoby, *Sweden* 11 H9
Brakwater, *Namibia* 88 C2
Brålanda, *Sweden* 11 F6
Bramberg, *Germany* 25 E6
Bramdrupdam, *Denmark* 11 J3
Bramming, *Denmark* 11 J2
Brämön, *Sweden* 10 B11
Brampton, *Canada* 102 D4
Brampton, *U.K.* 12 C5
Bramsche, *Germany* 24 C3
Branco →, *Brazil* 122 D4
Brandberg, *Namibia* 88 B2
Brande, *Denmark* 11 J3
Brandenburg =
Neubrandenburg, *Germany* 24 B9
Brandenburg, *Germany* 24 C8
Brandenburg □, *Germany* 24 C9
Brandfort, *S. Africa* 88 D4
Brando, *France* 21 F13
Brandon, *Canada* 105 D9
Brandon, *U.S.A.* 111 C11
Brandon B., *Ireland* 15 D1
Brandon Mt., *Ireland* 15 D1
Brandsen, *Argentina* 126 D4
Brandvlei, *S. Africa* 88 E3
Brandýs nad Labem, *Czech Rep.* 26 A7
Brăneşti, *Romania* 43 F11
Branford, *U.S.A.* 111 E12
Braniewo, *Poland* 44 D6
Bransfield Str., *Antarctica* 5 C18
Brańsk, *Poland* 45 F9
Branson, *U.S.A.* 113 G8
Brantford, *Canada* 102 D3
Brantôme, *France* 20 C4
Branzi, *Italy* 28 B6
Bras d'Or L., *Canada* 103 C7
Brasher Falls, *U.S.A.* 111 B10
Brasil, Planalto, *Brazil* 122 E6
Brasiléia, *Brazil* 124 F5
Brasília, *Brazil* 125 G9
Brasília Legal, *Brazil* 125 D7
Braslaw, *Belarus* 9 J22
Braslovče, *Slovenia* 29 B12
Braşov, *Romania* 43 E10
Braşov □, *Romania* 43 E10
Brass, *Nigeria* 83 E6
Brass →, *Nigeria* 83 E6
Brassac-les-Mines, *France* 20 C7
Brasschaat, *Belgium* 17 C4
Brassey, Banjaran, *Malaysia* 62 D5
Brassey Ra., *Australia* 93 E3
Brasstown Bald, *U.S.A.* 109 H4
Brastad, *Sweden* 11 F5
Brastavăţu, *Romania* 43 G9
Bratan = Morozov, *Bulgaria* 41 D9
Brateş, *Romania* 43 E11
Bratislava, *Slovak Rep.* 27 C10
Bratislavský □, *Slovak Rep.* 27 C10
Bratsigovo, *Bulgaria* 41 D8
Bratsk, *Russia* 51 D11
Brattleboro, *U.S.A.* 111 D12
Bratunac, *Bos.-H.* 42 F4
Braunau, *Austria* 26 C6
Braunschweig, *Germany* 24 C6
Braunton, *U.K.* 13 F3
Bravicea, *Moldova* 43 C13
Bråviken, *Sweden* 11 F10
Bravo del Norte, Rio = Grande,
Rio →, *U.S.A.* 113 N6
Brawley, *U.S.A.* 117 N11
Bray, *Ireland* 15 C5
Bray, Mt., *Australia* 94 A1
Bray-sur-Seine, *France* 19 D10
Brazeau →, *Canada* 104 C5
Brazil, *U.S.A.* 108 F2
Brazil ■, *S. Amer.* 125 F9
Brazilian Highlands = Brasil,
Planalto, *Brazil* 122 E6
Brazo Sur →, *S. Amer.* 126 B4
Brazos →, *U.S.A.* 113 L7
Brazzaville, *Congo* 84 E3
Brčko, *Bos.-H.* 42 F3
Brda →, *Poland* 45 E5
Brdy, *Czech Rep.* 26 B6
Breaden, L., *Australia* 93 E4
Breaksea Sd., *N.Z.* 91 L1
Bream B., *N.Z.* 91 F5
Bream Hd., *N.Z.* 91 F5
Breas, *Chile* 126 B1
Breaza, *Romania* 43 E10
Brebes, *Indonesia* 63 G13
Brechin, *Canada* 110 B5
Brechin, *U.K.* 14 E6
Brecht, *Belgium* 17 C4
Breckenridge, *Colo., U.S.A.* 114 G10
Breckenridge, *Minn., U.S.A.* 112 B6
Breckenridge, *Tex., U.S.A.* 113 J5
Breckland, *U.K.* 13 E8
Břeclav, *Czech Rep.* 27 C9
Brecon, *U.K.* 13 F4
Brecon Beacons, *U.K.* 13 F4
Breda, *Neths.* 17 C4
Bredaryd, *Sweden* 11 G7
Bredasdorp, *S. Africa* 88 E3
Bredebro, *Denmark* 11 J2
Bredstedt, *Germany* 24 A4
Bree, *Belgium* 17 C5
Bregalnica →, *Macedonia* 40 E6
Bregenz, *Austria* 26 D2
Bregovo, *Bulgaria* 40 B6
Bréhal, *France* 18 D5
Bréhat, Î. de, *France* 18 D4
Breiðafjörður, *Iceland* 8 D2
Breil-sur-Roya, *France* 21 E11
Breisach, *Germany* 25 G3
Brejo, *Brazil* 125 D10
Bremen, *Germany* 24 B4
Bremen □, *Germany* 24 B4
Bremer Bay, *Australia* 93 F2
Bremer I., *Australia* 94 A2
Bremerhaven, *Germany* 24 B4
Bremerton, *U.S.A.* 116 C4
Bremervörde, *Germany* 24 B5
Brenes, *Spain* 35 H5
Brenham, *U.S.A.* 113 K6
Brenne, *France* 20 B5
Brennerpass, *Austria* 26 D4
Breno, *Italy* 28 C7
Brent, *U.S.A.* 109 J2
Brenta →, *Italy* 29 C9
Brentwood, *U.K.* 13 F8
Brentwood, *Calif., U.S.A.* 116 H5
Brentwood, *N.Y., U.S.A.* 111 F11
Bréscia, *Italy* 28 C7
Breskens, *Neths.* 17 C3
Breslau = Wrocław, *Poland* 45 G4
Bresle →, *France* 18 B8
Bressanone, *Italy* 29 B8
Bressay, *U.K.* 14 A7
Bresse, *France* 19 F12
Bressuire, *France* 18 F6
Brest, *Belarus* 47 F2
Brest, *France* 18 D2
Brest-Litovsk = Brest, *Belarus* 47 F2
Bretagne, *France* 18 D3
Bretçu, *Romania* 43 D11
Bretenoux, *France* 20 D5
Breteuil, *Eure, France* 18 D7
Breteuil, *Oise, France* 19 C9
Breton, *Canada* 104 C6
Breton, Pertuis, *France* 20 B2
Breton Sd., *U.S.A.* 113 L10
Brett, C., *N.Z.* 91 F5
Bretten, *Germany* 25 F4
Breuil-Cervínia, *Italy* 28 C4
Brevard, *U.S.A.* 109 H4
Breves, *Brazil* 125 D8
Brewarrina, *Australia* 95 E4
Brewer, *U.S.A.* 109 C11
Brewer, Mt., *U.S.A.* 116 J8
Brewerville, *Liberia* 82 D2
Brewster, *N.Y., U.S.A.* 111 E11
Brewster, *Ohio, U.S.A.* 110 F3
Brewster, *Wash., U.S.A.* 114 B4
Brewster, Kap = Kangikajik,
Greenland 4 B6
Brewton, *U.S.A.* 109 K2
Breyten, *S. Africa* 89 D5
Breza, *Bos.-H.* 42 F3
Brezhnev = Naberezhnyye
Chelny, *Russia* 48 C11
Brežice, *Slovenia* 29 C12
Březnice, *Czech Rep.* 26 B6
Breznik, *Bulgaria* 40 D6
Brezno, *Slovak Rep.* 27 C12
Brezoi, *Romania* 43 E9
Brezovica, *Kosovo, Yug.* 40 D5
Brezovo, *Bulgaria* 41 D9
Briançon, *France* 21 D10
Briare, *France* 19 E9
Briático, *Italy* 31 D9
Bribie I., *Australia* 95 D5
Bribri, *Costa Rica* 120 E3
Briceni, *Moldova* 43 B12
Bricquebec, *France* 18 C5
Bridgehampton, *U.S.A.* 111 F12
Bridgend, *U.K.* 13 F4
Bridgend □, *U.K.* 13 F4
Bridgeport, *Calif., U.S.A.* 116 G7
Bridgeport, *Conn., U.S.A.* 111 E11
Bridgeport, *Nebr., U.S.A.* 112 E3
Bridgeport, *Tex., U.S.A.* 113 J6
Bridger, *U.S.A.* 114 D9
Bridgeton, *U.S.A.* 108 F8
Bridgetown, *Australia* 93 F2
Bridgetown, *Barbados* 121 D8
Bridgetown, *Canada* 103 D6
Bridgewater, *Canada* 103 D7
Bridgewater, *Mass., U.S.A.* 111 E14
Bridgewater, *N.Y., U.S.A.* 111 D9
Bridgewater, C., *Australia* 95 F3
Bridgewater-Gagebrook,
Australia 94 G4
Bridgnorth, *U.K.* 13 E5
Bridgton, *U.S.A.* 111 B14
Bridgwater, *U.K.* 13 F5
Bridgwater B., *U.K.* 13 F4
Bridlington, *U.K.* 12 C7
Bridlington B., *U.K.* 12 C7
Bridport, *Australia* 94 G4
Bridport, *U.K.* 13 G5
Briec, *France* 18 D2
Brienne-le-Château, *France* 19 D11
Brienon-sur-Armançon, *France* 19 E10
Brienz, *Switz.* 25 J4
Brienzersee, *Switz.* 25 J3
Brig, *Switz.* 25 J3
Brigg, *U.K.* 12 D7
Brigham City, *U.S.A.* 114 F7
Bright, *Australia* 95 F4
Brighton, *Australia* 95 F2
Brighton, *Canada* 110 B7
Brighton, *U.K.* 13 G7
Brighton, *Colo., U.S.A.* 112 F2
Brighton, *N.Y., U.S.A.* 110 C7
Brignogan-Plage, *France* 18 D2
Brignoles, *France* 21 E10
Brihuega, *Spain* 32 E2
Brikama, *Gambia* 82 C1
Brilliant, *U.S.A.* 110 F4
Brilon, *Germany* 24 D4
Bríndisi, *Italy* 31 B10
Brinje, *Croatia* 29 D12
Brinkley, *U.S.A.* 113 H9
Brinnon, *U.S.A.* 116 C4
Brion, I., *Canada* 103 C7
Brionne, *France* 18 C7
Brionski, *Croatia* 29 D10
Brioude, *France* 20 C7
Briouze, *France* 18 D6
Brisbane, *Australia* 95 D5
Brisbane →, *Australia* 95 D5
Brisighella, *Italy* 29 D8
Bristol, *U.K.* 13 F5
Bristol, *Conn., U.S.A.* 111 E12
Bristol, *Pa., U.S.A.* 111 F10
Bristol, *R.I., U.S.A.* 111 E13
Bristol, *Tenn., U.S.A.* 109 G4
Bristol, City of □, *U.K.* 13 F5
Bristol B., *U.S.A.* 100 C4
Bristol Channel, *U.K.* 13 F3
Bristol I., *Antarctica* 5 B1
Bristol L., *U.S.A.* 115 J5
Bristow, *U.S.A.* 113 H6
Britain = Great Britain, *Europe* 6 E5
British Columbia □, *Canada* 104 C3
British Indian Ocean Terr. =
Chagos Arch., *Ind. Oc.* 52 K11
British Isles, *Europe* 6 E5
Brits, *S. Africa* 89 D4
Britstown, *S. Africa* 88 E3
Britt, *Canada* 102 C3
Brittany = Bretagne, *France* 18 D3
Britton, *U.S.A.* 112 C6
Brive-la-Gaillarde, *France* 20 C5
Briviesca, *Spain* 34 C7
Brixen = Bressanone, *Italy* 29 B8
Brixham, *U.K.* 13 G4
Brnaze, *Croatia* 29 E13
Brnenský □, *Czech Rep.* 27 B9
Brno, *Czech Rep.* 27 B9
Broad →, *U.S.A.* 109 J5
Broad Arrow, *Australia* 93 F3
Broad B., *U.K.* 14 C2
Broad Haven, *Ireland* 15 B2
Broad Law, *U.K.* 14 F5
Broad Sd., *Australia* 94 C4
Broadalbin, *U.S.A.* 111 C10
Broadback →, *Canada* 102 B4
Broadhurst Ra., *Australia* 92 D3
Broads, The, *U.K.* 12 E9
Broadus, *U.S.A.* 112 C2
Broager, *Denmark* 11 K3
Broby, *Sweden* 11 H8
Broceni, *Latvia* 44 B9
Brochet, *Canada* 105 B8
Brochet, L., *Canada* 105 B8
Brocken, *Germany* 24 D6
Brockport, *U.S.A.* 110 C7
Brockton, *U.S.A.* 111 D13
Brockville, *Canada* 102 D4
Brockway, *Mont., U.S.A.* 112 B2
Brockway, *Pa., U.S.A.* 110 E6
Brocton, *U.S.A.* 110 D5
Brod, *Macedonia* 40 E5
Brodarevo, *Serbia, Yug.* 40 C3
Brodeur Pen., *Canada* 101 A11
Brodhead, Mt., *U.S.A.* 110 E7
Brodick, *U.K.* 14 F3
Brodnica, *Poland* 45 E6
Brody, *Ukraine* 47 G3
Brogan, *U.S.A.* 114 D5
Broglie, *France* 18 C7
Brok, *Poland* 45 F8
Broken Arrow, *U.S.A.* 113 G7
Broken Bow, *Nebr., U.S.A.* 112 E5
Broken Bow, *Okla., U.S.A.* 113 H7
Broken Bow Lake, *U.S.A.* 113 H7
Broken Hill = Kabwe, *Zambia* 87 E2
Broken Hill, *Australia* 95 E3
Brokind, *Sweden* 11 F9
Bromley □, *U.K.* 13 F8
Bromölla, *Sweden* 11 H8
Bromsgrove, *U.K.* 13 E5
Brønderslev, *Denmark* 11 G3
Brong-Ahafo □, *Ghana* 82 D4
Broni, *Italy* 28 C6
Bronkhorstspruit, *S. Africa* 89 D4
Brønnøysund, *Norway* 8 D15
Bronte, *Italy* 31 E7
Brook Park, *U.S.A.* 110 E4
Brookhaven, *U.S.A.* 113 K9
Brookings, *Oreg., U.S.A.* 114 E1
Brookings, *S. Dak., U.S.A.* 112 C6
Brooklin, *Canada* 110 C6
Brooklyn Park, *U.S.A.* 112 C8
Brooks, *Canada* 104 C6
Brooks Range, *U.S.A.* 100 B5
Brooksville, *U.S.A.* 109 L4
Brookton, *Australia* 93 F2
Brookville, *U.S.A.* 110 E5
Broom, L., *U.K.* 14 D3
Broome, *Australia* 92 C3
Broons, *France* 18 D4
Brora, *U.K.* 14 C5
Brora →, *U.K.* 14 C5
Brørup, *Denmark* 11 J2
Brösarp, *Sweden* 11 J8
Brosna →, *Ireland* 15 C4
Broşteni, *Mehedinţi, Romania* 42 F7
Broşteni, *Suceava, Romania* 43 C10
Brothers, *U.S.A.* 114 E3
Brou, *France* 18 D8
Brouage, *France* 20 C2
Brough, *U.K.* 12 C5
Brough Hd., *U.K.* 14 B5
Broughton Island =
Qikiqtarjuaq, *Canada* 101 B13
Broumov, *Czech Rep.* 27 A9
Brovary, *Ukraine* 47 G6
Brovst, *Denmark* 11 G3
Brown, L., *Australia* 93 F2
Brown, Pt., *Australia* 95 E1
Brown City, *U.S.A.* 110 C2
Brown Willy, *U.K.* 13 G3
Brownfield, *U.S.A.* 113 J3
Browning, *U.S.A.* 114 B7
Brownsville, *Oreg., U.S.A.* 114 D2
Brownsville, *Pa., U.S.A.* 110 F5
Brownsville, *Tenn., U.S.A.* 113 H10
Brownsville, *Tex., U.S.A.* 113 N6
Brownville, *U.S.A.* 111 C9
Brownwood, *U.S.A.* 113 K5
Browse I., *Australia* 92 B3
Bruas, *Malaysia* 65 K3
Bruay-la-Buissière, *France* 19 B9
Bruce, Mt., *Australia* 92 D2
Bruce Pen., *Canada* 110 B3
Bruce Rock, *Australia* 93 F2
Bruche →, *France* 19 D14
Bruchsal, *Germany* 25 F4
Bruck an der Leitha, *Austria* 27 C9
Bruck an der Mur, *Austria* 26 D8
Brue →, *U.K.* 13 F5
Bruges = Brugge, *Belgium* 17 C3
Brugg, *Switz.* 25 H4
Brugge, *Belgium* 17 C3
Bruin, *U.S.A.* 110 E5
Brûlé, *Canada* 104 C5
Brûlon, *France* 18 E6
Brumado, *Brazil* 125 F10
Brumath, *France* 19 D14
Brumunddal, *Norway* 9 F14
Bruneau, *U.S.A.* 114 E6
Bruneau →, *U.S.A.* 114 E6
Bruneck = Brunico, *Italy* 29 B8
Brunei = Bandar Seri Begawan,
Brunei 62 C4
Brunei ■, *Asia* 62 D4
Brunflo, *Sweden* 10 A8
Brunico, *Italy* 29 B8
Brunna, *Sweden* 10 E11
Brunnen, *Switz.* 25 J4
Brunner, L., *N.Z.* 91 K3
Brunsbüttel, *Germany* 24 B5
Brunssum, *Neths.* 17 D5
Brunswick = Braunschweig,
Germany 24 C6
Brunswick, *Ga., U.S.A.* 109 K5
Brunswick, *Maine, U.S.A.* 109 D11
Brunswick, *Md., U.S.A.* 108 F7
Brunswick, *Mo., U.S.A.* 112 F8
Brunswick, *Ohio, U.S.A.* 110 E3
Brunswick, Pen. de, *Chile* 128 G2
Brunswick B., *Australia* 92 C3
Brunswick Junction, *Australia* 93 F2
Bruntál, *Czech Rep.* 27 B10
Bruny I., *Australia* 94 G4
Brus Laguna, *Honduras* 120 C3
Brusartsi, *Bulgaria* 40 C7
Brush, *U.S.A.* 112 E3
Brushton, *U.S.A.* 111 B10
Brusio, *Switz.* 25 J6
Brusque, *Brazil* 127 B6
Brussel, *Belgium* 17 D4
Brussels = Brussel, *Belgium* 17 D4
Brussels, *Canada* 110 C3
Brusy, *Poland* 44 E4
Bruthen, *Australia* 95 F4
Bruxelles = Brussel, *Belgium* 17 D4
Bruyères, *France* 19 D13
Bruz, *France* 18 D5
Brwinów, *Poland* 45 F7
Bryagovo, *Bulgaria* 41 E9
Bryan, *Ohio, U.S.A.* 108 E3
Bryan, *Tex., U.S.A.* 113 K6
Bryan, Mt., *Australia* 95 E2
Bryanka, *Ukraine* 47 H10
Bryansk, *Bryansk, Russia* 47 F8
Bryansk, *Dagestan, Russia* 49 H8
Bryanskoye = Bryansk, *Russia* 49 H8
Bryce Canyon National Park,
U.S.A. 115 H7
Bryne, *Norway* 9 G11
Bryson City, *U.S.A.* 109 H4
Bryukhovetskaya, *Russia* 47 K10
Brza Palanka, *Serbia, Yug.* 40 B6
Brzeg, *Poland* 45 H4
Brzeg Dolny, *Poland* 45 G3
Brześć Kujawski, *Poland* 45 F5
Brzesko, *Poland* 45 J7
Brzeziny, *Poland* 45 G6
Brzozów, *Poland* 45 J9
Bsharri, *Lebanon* 75 A5
Bū Baqarah, *U.A.E.* 71 E8
Bu Craa, *W. Sahara* 78 C3
Bū Ḩasā, *U.A.E.* 71 F7
Bua, *Sweden* 11 G6
Bua Yai, *Thailand* 64 E4
Buapinang, *Indonesia* 63 E6
Buba, *Guinea-Biss.* 82 C2
Bubanza, *Burundi* 86 C2
Bubaque, *Guinea-Biss.* 82 C1
Bube, *Ethiopia* 81 F4
Būbiyān, *Kuwait* 71 D6
Buca, *Turkey* 39 C9
Bucak, *Turkey* 39 D12
Bucaramanga, *Colombia* 124 B4
Bucas Grande I., *Phil.* 61 G6
Bucasia, *Australia* 94 C4
Buccaneer Arch., *Australia* 92 C3
Buccino, *Italy* 31 B8
Bucecea, *Romania* 43 C11
Buchach, *Ukraine* 47 H3
Buchan, *U.K.* 14 D6
Buchan Ness, *U.K.* 14 D7
Buchanan, *Canada* 105 C8
Buchanan, *Liberia* 82 D2
Buchanan, L., *Queens., Australia* 94 C4
Buchanan, L., *W. Austral.,*
Australia 93 E3
Buchanan, L., *U.S.A.* 113 K5
Buchanan Cr. →, *Australia* 94 B2
Buchans, *Canada* 103 C8
Bucharest = Bucureşti, *Romania* 43 F11
Buchen, *Germany* 25 F5
Buchholz, *Germany* 24 B5
Buchloe, *Germany* 25 G6
Buchon, Pt., *U.S.A.* 116 K6
Buciumi, *Romania* 42 C8
Buck Hill Falls, *U.S.A.* 111 E9
Bückeburg, *Germany* 24 C5
Buckeye, *U.S.A.* 115 K7
Buckeye Lake, *U.S.A.* 110 G2
Buckhannon, *U.S.A.* 108 F5
Buckhaven, *U.K.* 14 E5
Buckhorn L., *Canada* 110 B6
Buckie, *U.K.* 14 D6
Buckingham, *Canada* 102 C4
Buckingham, *U.K.* 13 F7
Buckingham B., *Australia* 94 A2
Buckinghamshire □, *U.K.* 13 F7
Buckle Hd., *Australia* 92 B4
Buckleboo, *Australia* 95 E2
Buckley, *U.K.* 12 D4
Buckley →, *Australia* 94 C2
Bucklin, *U.S.A.* 113 G5
Bucks L., *U.S.A.* 116 F5
Bucquoy, *France* 19 B9
Buctouche, *Canada* 103 C7
Bucureşti, *Romania* 43 F11
Bucyrus, *U.S.A.* 108 E4
Budacu, Vf., *Romania* 43 C10
Budalin, *Burma* 67 H19
Budaörs, *Hungary* 42 C3
Budapest, *Hungary* 42 C4
Budapest □, *Hungary* 42 C4
Budaun, *India* 69 E8
Budd Coast, *Antarctica* 5 C8
Buddusò, *Italy* 30 B2
Bude, *U.K.* 13 G3
Budennovsk, *Russia* 49 H7
Budeşti, *Romania* 43 F11
Budge Budge = Baj Baj, *India* 69 H13
Budgewoi, *Australia* 95 E5
Budia, *Spain* 32 E2
Büdingen, *Germany* 25 E5
Budjala, *Dem. Rep. of the Congo* 84 D3
Budoni, *Italy* 30 B2
Búdrio, *Italy* 29 D8
Budva, *Montenegro, Yug.* 40 D2
Budzyń, *Poland* 45 F3
Buea, *Cameroon* 83 E6
Buellton, *U.S.A.* 117 L6
Buena Esperanza, *Argentina* 126 C2
Buena Park, *U.S.A.* 117 M9
Buena Vista, *Colo., U.S.A.* 115 G10
Buena Vista, *Va., U.S.A.* 108 G6
Buena Vista Lake Bed, *U.S.A.* 117 K7
Buenaventura, *Colombia* 124 C3
Buenaventura, *Mexico* 118 B3
Buendía, Embalse de, *Spain* 32 E2
Buenos Aires, *Argentina* 126 C4
Buenos Aires, *Costa Rica* 120 E3
Buenos Aires □, *Argentina* 126 D4
Buenos Aires, L., *Chile* 128 F2
Buffalo, *Mo., U.S.A.* 113 G8
Buffalo, *N.Y., U.S.A.* 110 D6
Buffalo, *Okla., U.S.A.* 113 G5
Buffalo, *S. Dak., U.S.A.* 112 C3
Buffalo, *Wyo., U.S.A.* 114 D10
Buffalo →, *Canada* 104 A5
Buffalo →, *S. Africa* 89 D5
Buffalo Head Hills, *Canada* 104 B5
Buffalo L., *Alta., Canada* 104 C6
Buffalo L., *N.W.T., Canada* 104 A5
Buffalo Narrows, *Canada* 105 B7
Buffels →, *S. Africa* 88 D2
Buford, *U.S.A.* 109 H4
Bug = Buh →, *Ukraine* 47 J6
Bug →, *Poland* 45 F8
Buga, *Colombia* 124 C3
Buganda, *Uganda* 86 C3
Buganga, *Uganda* 86 C3
Bugasong, *Phil.* 61 F5
Bugeat, *France* 20 C5
Bugel, Tanjung, *Indonesia* 63 G14
Bugibba, *Malta* 36 D1
Bugojno, *Bos.-H.* 42 F2
Bugsuk, *Phil.* 62 C5
Buguma, *Nigeria* 83 E6
Bugun Shara, *Mongolia* 60 B5
Buguruslan, *Russia* 50 D6

Buh →, *Ukraine* 47 J6
Buharkent, *Turkey* 39 D10
Buheirat-Murrat-el-Kubra, *Egypt* 80 H8
Buhera, *Zimbabwe* 89 B5
Bühl, *Germany* 25 G4
Buhl, *U.S.A.* 114 E6
Buhuşi, *Romania* 43 D11
Builth Wells, *U.K.* 13 E4
Buinsk, *Russia* 48 C9
Buir Nur, *Mongolia* 60 B6
Buis-les-Baronnies, *France* 21 D9
Buitrago = Buitrago del Lozoya, *Spain* 34 E7
Buitrago del Lozoya, *Spain* 34 E7
Bujalance, *Spain* 35 H6
Bujanovac, *Serbia, Yug.* 40 D5
Bujaraloz, *Spain* 32 D4
Buje, *Croatia* 29 C10
Bujumbura, *Burundi* 86 C2
Bük, *Hungary* 42 C1
Buk, *Poland* 45 F3
Bukachacha, *Russia* 51 D12
Bukama, *Dem. Rep. of the Congo* 87 D2
Bukavu, *Dem. Rep. of the Congo* 86 C2
Bukene, *Tanzania* 86 C3
Bukhara = Bukhoro, *Uzbekistan* 50 F7
Bukhoro, *Uzbekistan* 50 F7
Bukima, *Tanzania* 86 C3
Bukit Mertajam, *Malaysia* 65 K3
Bukittinggi, *Indonesia* 62 E2
Bükk, *Hungary* 42 B5
Bukoba, *Tanzania* 86 C3
Bukuru, *Nigeria* 83 D6
Bukuya, *Uganda* 86 B3
Būl, Kuh-e, *Iran* 71 D7
Bula, *Guinea-Biss.* 82 C1
Bula, *Indonesia* 63 E8
Bülach, *Switz.* 25 H4
Bulahdelah, *Australia* 95 E5
Bulan, *Phil.* 61 E5
Bulancak, *Turkey* 73 B8
Bulandshahr, *India* 68 E7
Bulanık, *Turkey* 73 C10
Bûlâq, *Egypt* 80 B3
Bulawayo, *Zimbabwe* 87 G2
Buldan, *Turkey* 39 C10
Bulgar, *Russia* 48 C9
Bulgaria ■, *Europe* 41 D9
Bulgheria, Monte, *Italy* 31 B8
Bulgurca, *Turkey* 39 C9
Buli, Teluk, *Indonesia* 63 D7
Buliluyan, C., *Phil.* 61 G2
Bulki, *Ethiopia* 81 F4
Bulkley →, *Canada* 104 B3
Bull Shoals L., *U.S.A.* 113 G8
Bullaque →, *Spain* 35 G6
Bullas, *Spain* 33 G3
Bulle, *Switz.* 25 J3
Bullhead City, *U.S.A.* 117 K12
Büllingen, *Belgium* 17 D6
Bullock Creek, *Australia* 94 B3
Bulloo →, *Australia* 95 D3
Bulloo L., *Australia* 95 D3
Bulls, *N.Z.* 91 J5
Bully-les-Mines, *France* 19 B9
Bulnes, *Chile* 126 D1
Bulqizë, *Albania* 40 E4
Bulsar = Valsad, *India* 66 J8
Bultfontein, *S. Africa* 88 D4
Bulukumba, *Indonesia* 63 F6
Bulun, *Russia* 51 B13
Bumba, *Dem. Rep. of the Congo* 84 D4
Bumbeşti-Jiu, *Romania* 43 E8
Bumbiri I., *Tanzania* 86 C3
Bumbuna, *S. Leone* 82 D2
Bumhpa Bum, *Burma* 67 F20
Bumi →, *Zimbabwe* 87 F2
Buna, *Kenya* 86 B4
Bunawan, *Phil.* 61 G6
Bunazi, *Tanzania* 86 C3
Bunbury, *Australia* 93 F2
Bunclody, *Ireland* 15 D5
Buncrana, *Ireland* 15 A4
Bundaberg, *Australia* 95 C5
Bünde, *Germany* 24 C4
Bundey →, *Australia* 94 C2
Bundi, *India* 68 G6
Bundoran, *Ireland* 15 B3
Bundukia, *Sudan* 81 F3
Bung Kan, *Thailand* 64 C4
Bunga →, *Nigeria* 83 C6
Bungay, *U.K.* 13 E9
Bungil Cr. →, *Australia* 95 D4
Bungo-Suidō, *Japan* 55 H6
Bungoma, *Kenya* 86 B3
Bungotakada, *Japan* 55 H5
Bungu, *Tanzania* 86 D4
Bunia, *Dem. Rep. of the Congo* 86 B3
Bunji, *Pakistan* 69 B6
Bunkie, *U.S.A.* 113 K8
Bunnell, *U.S.A.* 109 L5
Buñol, *Spain* 33 F4
Bunsuru, *Nigeria* 83 C5
Buntok, *Indonesia* 62 E4
Bununu Dass, *Nigeria* 83 C6
Bununu Kasa, *Nigeria* 83 D6
Bünyan, *Turkey* 72 C6
Bunyu, *Indonesia* 62 D5
Bunza, *Nigeria* 83 C5
Buol, *Indonesia* 63 D6
Buon Brieng, *Vietnam* 64 F7
Buon Ma Thuot, *Vietnam* 64 F7
Buong Long, *Cambodia* 64 F6
Buorkhaya, Mys, *Russia* 51 B14
Buqayq, *Si. Arabia* 71 E6
Buqbuq, *Egypt* 80 A2
Bur Acaba, *Somali Rep.* 74 G3
Bûr Fuad, *Egypt* 80 H8
Bûr Safâga, *Egypt* 70 E2
Bûr Sa'îd, *Egypt* 80 H8
Bûr Sûdân, *Sudan* 80 D4
Bûr Taufiq, *Egypt* 80 J8
Bura, *Kenya* 86 C4
Burakin, *Australia* 93 F2
Buram, *Sudan* 81 E2
Burao, *Somali Rep.* 74 F4
Burāq, *Syria* 75 B5
Buraydah, *Si. Arabia* 70 E4
Burbank, *U.S.A.* 117 L8
Burda, *India* 68 G6
Burdekin →, *Australia* 94 B4
Burdur, *Turkey* 39 D12
Burdur □, *Turkey* 39 D12
Burdur Gölü, *Turkey* 39 D12
Burdwan = Barddhaman, *India* 69 H12
Bure, *Gojam, Ethiopia* 81 E4
Bure, *Ilubabor, Ethiopia* 81 F4
Bure →, *U.K.* 12 E9
Büren, *Germany* 24 D4
Bureya →, *Russia* 51 E13
Burford, *Canada* 110 C4
Burg, *Germany* 24 C7
Burg auf Fehmarn, *Germany* 24 A7
Burg el Arab, *Egypt* 80 H6
Burg et Tuyur, *Sudan* 80 C2
Burg Stargard, *Germany* 24 B9
Burgas, *Bulgaria* 41 D11
Burgas □, *Bulgaria* 41 D10
Burgaski Zaliv, *Bulgaria* 41 D11
Burgdorf, *Germany* 24 C6
Burgdorf, *Switz.* 25 H3
Burgenland □, *Austria* 27 D9
Burgeo, *Canada* 103 C8
Burgersdorp, *S. Africa* 88 E4
Burges, Mt., *Australia* 93 F3
Burghausen, *Germany* 25 G8
Búrgio, *Italy* 30 E6
Burglengenfeld, *Germany* 25 F8
Burgohondo, *Spain* 34 E6
Burgos, *Spain* 34 C7
Burgos □, *Spain* 34 C7
Burgstädt, *Germany* 24 E8
Burgsvik, *Sweden* 11 G12
Burguillos del Cerro, *Spain* 35 G4
Burgundy = Bourgogne, *France* 19 F11
Burhaniye, *Turkey* 39 B8
Burhanpur, *India* 66 J10
Burhi Gandak →, *India* 69 G12
Burhner →, *India* 69 H9
Buri Pen., *Eritrea* 81 D4
Burias I., *Phil.* 61 E5
Burica, Pta., *Costa Rica* 120 E3
Burien, *U.S.A.* 116 C4
Burigi, L., *Tanzania* 86 C3
Burin, *Canada* 103 C8
Buriram, *Thailand* 64 E4
Burj Sāfitā, *Syria* 70 C3
Burji, *Ethiopia* 81 F4
Burkburnett, *U.S.A.* 113 H5
Burke →, *Australia* 94 C2
Burke Chan., *Canada* 104 C3
Burketown, *Australia* 94 B2
Burkina Faso ■, *Africa* 82 C4
Burk's Falls, *Canada* 102 C4
Burlada, *Spain* 32 C3
Burleigh Falls, *Canada* 110 B6
Burley, *U.S.A.* 114 E7
Burlingame, *U.S.A.* 116 H4
Burlington, *Canada* 102 D4
Burlington, *Colo., U.S.A.* 112 F3
Burlington, *Iowa, U.S.A.* 112 E9
Burlington, *Kans., U.S.A.* 112 F7
Burlington, *N.C., U.S.A.* 109 G6
Burlington, *N.J., U.S.A.* 111 F10
Burlington, *Vt., U.S.A.* 111 B11
Burlington, *Wash., U.S.A.* 116 B4
Burlington, *Wis., U.S.A.* 108 D1
Burlyu-Tyube, *Kazakstan* 50 E8
Burma ■, *Asia* 67 J20
Burnaby I., *Canada* 104 C2
Burnet, *U.S.A.* 113 K5
Burney, *U.S.A.* 114 F3
Burnham, *U.S.A.* 110 F7
Burnham-on-Sea, *U.K.* 13 F5
Burnie, *Australia* 94 G4
Burnley, *U.K.* 12 D5
Burns, *U.S.A.* 114 E4
Burns Lake, *Canada* 104 C3
Burnside →, *Canada* 100 B9
Burnside, L., *Australia* 93 E3
Burnsville, *U.S.A.* 112 C8
Burnt L., *Canada* 103 B7
Burnt River, *Canada* 110 B6
Burntwood →, *Canada* 105 B9
Burntwood L., *Canada* 105 B8
Burqān, *Kuwait* 70 D5
Burra, *Australia* 95 E2
Burra, *Nigeria* 83 C6
Burray, *U.K.* 14 C6
Burrel, *Albania* 40 E4
Burren Junction, *Australia* 95 E4
Burriana, *Spain* 32 F4
Burrinjuck Res., *Australia* 95 F4
Burro, Serranías del, *Mexico* 118 B4
Burrow Hd., *U.K.* 14 G4
Burruyacú, *Argentina* 126 B3
Burry Port, *U.K.* 13 F3
Bursa, *Turkey* 41 F13
Burseryd, *Sweden* 11 G7
Burstall, *Canada* 105 C7
Burton, *Ohio, U.S.A.* 110 E3
Burton, *S.C., U.S.A.* 109 J5
Burton, L., *Canada* 102 B4
Burton upon Trent, *U.K.* 12 E6
Buru, *Indonesia* 63 E7
Burullus, Bahra el, *Egypt* 80 H7
Burûn, Râs, *Egypt* 75 D2
Burundi ■, *Africa* 86 C3
Bururi, *Burundi* 86 C2
Burutu, *Nigeria* 83 D6
Burwell, *U.S.A.* 112 E5
Burwick, *U.K.* 14 C5
Bury, *U.K.* 12 D5
Bury St. Edmunds, *U.K.* 13 E8
Buryatia □, *Russia* 51 D11
Buryn, *Ukraine* 47 G7
Burzenin, *Poland* 45 G5
Busalla, *Italy* 28 D5
Busango Swamp, *Zambia* 87 E2
Buşayrah, *Syria* 70 C4
Busca, *Italy* 28 D4
Bushat, *Albania* 40 E3
Büshehr, *Iran* 71 D6
Büshehr □, *Iran* 71 D6
Bushell, *Canada* 105 B7
Bushenyi, *Uganda* 86 C3
Bushire = Büshehr, *Iran* 71 D6
Busie, *Ghana* 82 C4
Businga, *Dem. Rep. of the Congo* 84 D4
Busko-Zdrój, *Poland* 45 H7
Busovača, *Bos.-H.* 42 F2
Buşra ash Shām, *Syria* 75 C5
Busselton, *Australia* 93 F2
Busseri →, *Sudan* 81 F2
Busseto, *Italy* 28 D7
Bussière-Badil, *France* 20 C4
Bussolengo, *Italy* 28 C7
Bussum, *Neths.* 17 B5
Buşteni, *Romania* 43 E10
Busto, C., *Spain* 34 B4
Busto Arsízio, *Italy* 28 C5
Busu-Djanoa, *Dem. Rep. of the Congo* 84 D4
Busuanga I., *Phil.* 61 E3
Büsum, *Germany* 24 A4
Buta, *Dem. Rep. of the Congo* 86 B1
Butare, *Rwanda* 86 C2
Butaritari, *Kiribati* 96 G9
Bute, *U.K.* 14 F3
Bute Inlet, *Canada* 104 C4
Butemba, *Uganda* 86 B3
Butembo, *Dem. Rep. of the Congo* 86 B2
Buteni, *Romania* 42 D7
Butera, *Italy* 31 E7
Butha Qi, *China* 60 B7
Butiaba, *Uganda* 86 B3
Butler, *Mo., U.S.A.* 112 F7
Butler, *Pa., U.S.A.* 110 F5
Buton, *Indonesia* 63 E6
Butte, *Mont., U.S.A.* 114 C7
Butte, *Nebr., U.S.A.* 112 D5
Butte Creek →, *U.S.A.* 116 F5
Butterworth = Gcuwa, *S. Africa* 89 E4
Butterworth, *Malaysia* 65 K3
Buttevant, *Ireland* 15 D3
Buttfield, Mt., *Australia* 93 D4
Button B., *Canada* 105 B10
Buttonwillow, *U.S.A.* 117 K7
Butty Hd., *Australia* 93 F3
Butuan, *Phil.* 61 G6
Butuku-Luba, *Eq. Guin.* 83 E6
Butung = Buton, *Indonesia* 63 E6
Buturlinovka, *Russia* 48 E5
Butzbach, *Germany* 25 E4
Bützow, *Germany* 24 B7
Buxa Duar, *India* 69 F13
Buxar, *India* 69 G10
Buxtehude, *Germany* 24 B5
Buxton, *U.K.* 12 D6
Buxy, *France* 19 F11
Buy, *Russia* 48 A5
Buynaksk, *Russia* 49 J8
Buyo, *Ivory C.* 82 D3
Buyo, L. de, *Ivory C.* 82 D3
Büyük Menderes →, *Turkey* 39 D9
Büyükçekmece, *Turkey* 41 E12
Büyükkariştiran, *Turkey* 41 E11
Büyükkemikli Burnu, *Turkey* 41 F10
Büyükorhan, *Turkey* 39 B10
Büyükyoncalı, *Turkey* 41 E11
Buzançais, *France* 18 F8
Buzău, *Romania* 43 E11
Buzău □, *Romania* 43 E11
Buzău →, *Romania* 43 E12
Buzău, Pasul, *Romania* 43 E11
Buzen, *Japan* 55 H5
Buzet, *Croatia* 29 C10
Buzi →, *Mozam.* 87 F3
Buziaş, *Romania* 42 E6
Buzuluk, *Russia* 50 D6
Buzuluk →, *Russia* 48 E6
Buzzards B., *U.S.A.* 111 E14
Buzzards Bay, *U.S.A.* 111 E14
Bwana Mkubwe, *Dem. Rep. of the Congo* 87 E2
Byala, *Ruse, Bulgaria* 41 C9
Byala, *Varna, Bulgaria* 41 D11
Byala Slatina, *Bulgaria* 40 C7
Byarezina →, *Belarus* 47 F6
Byaroza, *Belarus* 47 F3
Bychawa, *Poland* 45 G9
Byczyna, *Poland* 45 G5
Bydgoszcz, *Poland* 45 E5
Byelarus = Belarus ■, *Europe* 46 F4
Byelorussia = Belarus ■, *Europe* 46 F4
Byers, *U.S.A.* 112 F2
Byesville, *U.S.A.* 110 G3
Byford, *Australia* 93 F2
Bykhaw, *Belarus* 46 F6
Bykhov = Bykhaw, *Belarus* 46 F6
Bykovo, *Russia* 48 F7
Bylas, *U.S.A.* 115 K8
Bylot, *Canada* 105 B10
Bylot I., *Canada* 101 A12
Byrd, C., *Antarctica* 5 C17
Byrock, *Australia* 95 E4
Byron Bay, *Australia* 95 D5
Byrranga, Gory, *Russia* 51 B11
Byrranga Mts. = Byrranga, Gory, *Russia* 51 B11
Byrum, *Denmark* 11 G5
Byske, *Sweden* 8 D19
Byske älv →, *Sweden* 8 D19
Bystrzyca →, *Dolnośląskie, Poland* 45 G3
Bystrzyca →, *Lubelskie, Poland* 45 G9
Bystrzyca Kłodzka, *Poland* 45 H3
Bytča, *Slovak Rep.* 27 B11
Bytom, *Poland* 45 H5
Bytom Odrzański, *Poland* 45 G2
Bytów, *Poland* 44 D4
Byumba, *Rwanda* 86 C3
Bzenec, *Czech Rep.* 27 C10
Bzura →, *Poland* 45 F7

C

Ca →, *Vietnam* 64 C5
Ca Mau, *Vietnam* 65 H5
Ca Mau, Mui, *Vietnam* 65 H5
Ca Na, *Vietnam* 65 G7
Caacupé, *Paraguay* 126 B4
Caála, *Angola* 85 G3
Caamano Sd., *Canada* 104 C3
Caazapá, *Paraguay* 126 B4
Caazapá □, *Paraguay* 127 B4
Cabadbaran, *Phil.* 61 G6
Cabalian = San Juan, *Phil.* 61 F6
Cabana, *Spain* 34 B2
Cabañaquinta, *Spain* 34 B5
Cabanatuan, *Phil.* 61 D4
Cabanes, *Spain* 32 E5
Cabano, *Canada* 103 C6
Čabar, *Croatia* 29 C11
Cabazon, *U.S.A.* 117 M10
Cabedelo, *Brazil* 125 E12
Cabeza del Buey, *Spain* 35 G5
Cabezón de la Sal, *Spain* 34 B6
Cabildo, *Chile* 126 C1
Cabimas, *Venezuela* 124 A4
Cabinda, *Angola* 84 F2
Cabinda □, *Angola* 84 F2
Cabinet Mts., *U.S.A.* 114 C6
Cabo Blanco, *Argentina* 128 F3
Cabo Frio, *Brazil* 127 A7
Cabo Pantoja, *Peru* 124 D3
Cabonga, Réservoir, *Canada* 102 C4
Cabool, *U.S.A.* 113 G8
Caboolture, *Australia* 95 D5
Cabora Bassa Dam = Cahora Bassa, Représa de, *Mozam.* 87 F3
Caborca, *Mexico* 118 A2
Cabot, Mt., *U.S.A.* 111 B13
Cabot Hd., *Canada* 110 A3
Cabot Str., *Canada* 103 C8
Cabra, *Spain* 35 H6
Cabra del Santo Cristo, *Spain* 35 H7
Cábras, *Italy* 30 C1
Cabrera, *Spain* 37 B9
Cabrera, Sierra, *Spain* 34 C4
Cabri, *Canada* 105 C7
Cabriel →, *Spain* 33 F3
Cabugao, *Phil.* 61 C4
Cacabelos, *Spain* 34 C4
Caçador, *Brazil* 127 B5
Čačak, *Serbia, Yug.* 40 C4
Caçapava do Sul, *Brazil* 127 C5
Cáccamo, *Italy* 30 E6
Cacém, *Portugal* 35 G1
Cáceres, *Brazil* 124 G7
Cáceres, *Spain* 35 F4
Cáceres □, *Spain* 34 F5
Cache Bay, *Canada* 102 C4
Cache Cr. →, *U.S.A.* 116 G5
Cache Creek, *Canada* 104 C4
Cacheu, *Guinea-Biss.* 82 C1
Cachi, *Argentina* 126 B2
Cachimbo, Serra do, *Brazil* 125 E7
Cachinal de la Sierra, *Chile* 126 A2
Cachoeira, *Brazil* 125 F11
Cachoeira do Sul, *Brazil* 127 C5
Cachoeiro de Itapemirim, *Brazil* 127 A7
Cachopo, *Portugal* 35 H3
Cacine, *Guinea-Biss.* 82 C1
Cacoal, *Brazil* 124 F6
Cacólo, *Angola* 84 G3
Caconda, *Angola* 85 G3
Čadca, *Slovak Rep.* 27 B11
Caddo, *U.S.A.* 113 H6
Cader Idris, *U.K.* 13 E4
Cadereyta, *Mexico* 118 B5
Cadí, Sierra del, *Spain* 32 C6
Cadibarrawirracanna, L., *Australia* 95 D2
Cadillac, *France* 20 D3
Cadillac, *U.S.A.* 108 C3
Cadiz, *Phil.* 61 F5
Cádiz, *Spain* 35 J4
Cadiz, *Calif., U.S.A.* 117 L11
Cadiz, *Ohio, U.S.A.* 110 F4
Cádiz □, *Spain* 35 J5
Cádiz, G. de, *Spain* 35 J3
Cadiz L., *U.S.A.* 115 J6
Cadney Park, *Australia* 95 D1
Cadomin, *Canada* 104 C5
Cadotte Lake, *Canada* 104 B5
Cadours, *France* 20 E5
Cadoux, *Australia* 93 F2
Caen, *France* 18 C6
Caernarfon, *U.K.* 12 D3
Caernarfon B., *U.K.* 12 D3
Caernarvon = Caernarfon, *U.K.* 12 D3
Caerphilly, *U.K.* 13 F4
Caerphilly □, *U.K.* 13 F4
Caesarea, *Israel* 75 C3
Caetité, *Brazil* 125 F10
Cafayate, *Argentina* 126 B2
Cafu, *Angola* 88 B2
Cagayan →, *Phil.* 61 B4
Cagayan de Oro, *Phil.* 61 G6
Cagayan Is., *Phil.* 61 G4
Cagayan Sulu I., *Phil.* 61 H3
Cagli, *Italy* 29 E9
Cágliari, *Italy* 30 C2
Cágliari, G. di, *Italy* 30 C2
Cagnano Varano, *Italy* 29 G12
Cagnes-sur-Mer, *France* 21 E11
Caguán →, *Colombia* 124 D4
Caguas, *Puerto Rico* 121 C6
Caha Mts., *Ireland* 15 E2
Cahama, *Angola* 88 B1
Caher, *Ireland* 15 D4
Caherciveen, *Ireland* 15 E1
Cahora Bassa, Représa de, *Mozam.* 87 F3
Cahore Pt., *Ireland* 15 D5
Cahors, *France* 20 D5
Cahul, *Moldova* 43 E13
Cai Bau, Dao, *Vietnam* 58 G6
Cai Nuoc, *Vietnam* 65 H5
Caia, *Mozam.* 87 F4
Caianda, *Angola* 87 E1
Caibarién, *Cuba* 120 B4
Caibiran, *Phil.* 61 F6
Caicara, *Venezuela* 124 B5
Caicó, *Brazil* 125 E11
Caicos Is., *Turks & Caicos* 121 B5
Caicos Passage, *W. Indies* 121 B5
Caidian, *China* 59 B10
Căinari, *Moldova* 43 D14
Caird Coast, *Antarctica* 5 D1
Cairn Gorm, *U.K.* 14 D5
Cairngorm Mts., *U.K.* 14 D5
Cairnryan, *U.K.* 14 G3
Cairns, *Australia* 94 B4
Cairns L., *Canada* 105 C10
Cairo = El Qâhira, *Egypt* 80 H7
Cairo, *Ga., U.S.A.* 109 K3
Cairo, *Ill., U.S.A.* 113 G10
Cairo, *N.Y., U.S.A.* 111 D11
Cairo Montenotte, *Italy* 28 D5
Caithness, Ord of, *U.K.* 14 C5
Cajamarca, *Peru* 124 E3
Cajarc, *France* 20 D5
Cajàzeiras, *Brazil* 125 E11
Čajetina, *Serbia, Yug.* 40 C3
Çakirgol, *Turkey* 73 B8
Çakırlar, *Turkey* 39 E12
Čakovec, *Croatia* 29 B13
Çal, *Turkey* 39 C11
Cala, *Spain* 35 H4
Cala →, *Spain* 35 H4
Cala Cadolar, Punta de = Rotja, Pta., *Spain* 33 G6
Cala d'Or, *Spain* 37 B10
Cala en Porter, *Spain* 37 B11
Cala Figuera, C. de, *Spain* 37 B9
Cala Forcat, *Spain* 37 B10
Cala Major, *Spain* 37 B9
Cala Mezquida = Sa Mesquida, *Spain* 37 B11
Cala Millor, *Spain* 37 B10
Cala Ratjada, *Spain* 37 B10
Cala Santa Galdana, *Spain* 37 B10
Calabanga, *Phil.* 61 E5
Calabar, *Nigeria* 83 E6
Calabogie, *Canada* 111 A8
Calabozo, *Venezuela* 124 B5
Calábria □, *Italy* 31 C9
Calaburras, Pta. de, *Spain* 35 J6
Calaceite, *Spain* 32 D5
Calacuccia, *France* 21 F13
Calafat, *Romania* 42 G7
Calafate, *Argentina* 128 G2
Calafell, *Spain* 32 D6
Calahorra, *Spain* 32 C3
Calais, *France* 19 B8
Calais, *U.S.A.* 109 C12
Calalaste, Cord. de, *Argentina* 126 B2
Calama, *Brazil* 124 E6
Calama, *Chile* 126 A2
Calamar, *Colombia* 124 A4
Calamian Group, *Phil.* 61 F3
Calamocha, *Spain* 32 E3
Calamonte, *Spain* 35 G4
Călan, *Romania* 42 E7
Calañas, *Spain* 35 H4
Calanda, *Spain* 32 E4
Calang, *Indonesia* 62 D1
Calangiánus, *Italy* 30 B2
Calapan, *Phil.* 61 E4
Călărasi, *Moldova* 43 C13
Călăraşi, *Romania* 43 F12
Călăraşi □, *Romania* 43 F12
Calasparra, *Spain* 33 G3
Calatafimi, *Italy* 30 E5
Calatayud, *Spain* 32 D3
Călăţele, *Romania* 42 D8
Calato = Kálathos, *Greece* 39 E10
Calauag, *Phil.* 61 E5

Calavà, C., *Italy* 31 D7
Calavite, C., *Phil.* 61 E4
Calayan, *Phil.* 61 B4
Calbayog, *Phil.* 61 E6
Calca, *Peru* 124 F4
Calcasieu L., *U.S.A.* 113 L8
Calcutta = Kolkata, *India* 69 H13
Calcutta, *U.S.A.* 110 F4
Caldaro, *Italy* 29 B8
Caldas da Rainha, *Portugal* 35 F1
Caldas de Reis, *Spain* 34 C2
Calder →, *U.K.* 12 D6
Caldera, *Chile* 126 B1
Caldwell, *Idaho, U.S.A.* 114 E5
Caldwell, *Kans., U.S.A.* 113 G6
Caldwell, *Tex., U.S.A.* 113 K6
Caledon, *S. Africa* 88 E2
Caledon →, *S. Africa* 88 E4
Caledon B., *Australia* 94 A2
Caledonia, *Canada* 110 C5
Caledonia, *U.S.A.* 110 D7
Calella, *Spain* 32 D7
Calemba, *Angola* 88 B2
Calen, *Australia* 94 C4
Calenzana, *France* 21 F12
Caletones, *Chile* 126 C1
Calexico, *U.S.A.* 117 N11
Calf of Man, *U.K.* 12 C3
Calgary, *Canada* 104 C6
Calheta, *Madeira* 37 D2
Calhoun, *U.S.A.* 109 H3
Cali, *Colombia* 124 C3
Calicut, *India* 66 P9
Caliente, *U.S.A.* 115 H6
California, *Mo., U.S.A.* 112 F8
California, *Pa., U.S.A.* 110 F5
California □, *U.S.A.* 116 H7
California, Baja, *Mexico* 118 A1
California, Baja, T.N. = Baja California □, *Mexico* 118 B2
California, Baja, T.S. = Baja California Sur □, *Mexico* 118 B2
California, G. de, *Mexico* 118 B2
California City, *U.S.A.* 117 K9
California Hot Springs, *U.S.A.* 117 K8
Călimăneşti, *Romania* 43 E9
Călimani, Munţii, *Romania* 43 C10
Calingasta, *Argentina* 126 C2
Calipatria, *U.S.A.* 117 M11
Calistoga, *U.S.A.* 116 G4
Calitri, *Italy* 31 B8
Calitzdorp, *S. Africa* 88 E3
Callabonna, L., *Australia* 95 D3
Callac, *France* 18 D3
Callan, *Ireland* 15 D4
Callander, *U.K.* 14 E4
Callao, *Peru* 124 F3
Calles, *Mexico* 119 C5
Callicoon, *U.S.A.* 111 E9
Calling Lake, *Canada* 104 B6
Calliope, *Australia* 94 C5
Callosa de Ensarriá, *Spain* 33 G4
Callosa de Segura, *Spain* 33 G4
Calne, *U.K.* 13 F6
Calola, *Angola* 88 B2
Calolbon = San Andres, *Phil.* 61 E6
Calonge, *Spain* 32 D8
Caloocan, *Phil.* 61 D4
Calore →, *Italy* 31 A7
Caloundra, *Australia* 95 D5
Calpe, *Spain* 33 G5
Calpella, *U.S.A.* 116 F3
Calpine, *U.S.A.* 116 F6
Calstock, *Canada* 102 C3
Caltabellotta, *Italy* 30 E6
Caltagirone, *Italy* 31 E7
Caltanissetta, *Italy* 31 E7
Çaltılıbük, *Turkey* 41 G12
Caluire-et-Cuire, *France* 19 G11
Calulo, *Angola* 84 G2
Caluso, *Italy* 28 C4
Calvados □, *France* 18 C6
Calvert →, *Australia* 94 B2
Calvert I., *Canada* 104 C3
Calvert Ra., *Australia* 92 D3
Calvi, *France* 21 F12
Calviá, *Spain* 33 F7
Calvillo, *Mexico* 118 C4
Calvinia, *S. Africa* 88 E2
Calvo = Calvo, Mte., *Italy* 29 G12
Calvo, Mte., *Italy* 29 G12
Calwa, *U.S.A.* 116 J7
Calzada Almuradiel = Almuradiel, *Spain* 35 G7
Calzada de Calatrava, *Spain* 35 G7
Cam →, *U.K.* 13 E8
Cam Lam, *Vietnam* 65 G7
Cam Pha, *Vietnam* 58 G6
Cam Ranh, *Vietnam* 65 G7
Cam Xuyen, *Vietnam* 64 C6
Camabatela, *Angola* 84 F3
Camacha, *Madeira* 37 D3
Camacho, *Mexico* 118 C4
Camacupa, *Angola* 85 G3
Camagüey, *Cuba* 120 B4
Camaiore, *Italy* 28 E7
Camaná, *Peru* 124 G4
Camanche Reservoir, *U.S.A.* 116 G6
Camaquã, *Brazil* 127 C5
Camaquã →, *Brazil* 127 C5
Câmara de Lobos, *Madeira* 37 D3
Camarat, C., *France* 21 E10
Camarès, *France* 20 E6
Camaret-sur-Mer, *France* 18 D2
Camargo, *Mexico* 119 B5
Camargue, *France* 21 E8
Camarillo, *U.S.A.* 117 L7
Camariñas, *Spain* 34 B1
Camarón, C., *Honduras* 120 C2
Camarones, *Argentina* 128 E3
Camas, *Spain* 35 H4
Camas, *U.S.A.* 116 E4
Camas Valley, *U.S.A.* 114 E2
Camballin, *Australia* 92 C3
Cambará, *Brazil* 127 A5
Cambay = Khambhat, *India* 68 H5
Cambay, G. of = Khambhat, G. of, *India* 66 J8
Cambil, *Spain* 35 H7
Cambo-les-Bains, *France* 20 E2
Cambodia ■, *Asia* 64 F5
Camborne, *U.K.* 13 G2
Cambrai, *France* 19 B10
Cambre, *Spain* 34 B2
Cambria, *U.S.A.* 116 K5
Cambrian Mts., *U.K.* 13 E4
Cambridge, *Canada* 102 D3
Cambridge, *Jamaica* 120 C4
Cambridge, *N.Z.* 91 G5
Cambridge, *U.K.* 13 E8
Cambridge, *Mass., U.S.A.* 111 D13
Cambridge, *Minn., U.S.A.* 112 C8
Cambridge, *N.Y., U.S.A.* 111 C11
Cambridge, *Nebr., U.S.A.* 112 E4
Cambridge, *Ohio, U.S.A.* 110 F3
Cambridge Bay = Ikaluktutiak, *Canada* 100 B9
Cambridge G., *Australia* 92 B4
Cambridge Springs, *U.S.A.* 110 E4
Cambridgeshire □, *U.K.* 13 E7
Cambrils, *Spain* 32 D6
Cambuci, *Brazil* 127 A7
Cambundi-Catembo, *Angola* 84 G3
Camden, *Ala., U.S.A.* 109 K2
Camden, *Ark., U.S.A.* 113 J8
Camden, *Maine, U.S.A.* 109 C11
Camden, *N.J., U.S.A.* 111 G9
Camden, *N.Y., U.S.A.* 111 C9
Camden, *S.C., U.S.A.* 109 H5
Camden Sd., *Australia* 92 C3
Camdenton, *U.S.A.* 113 F8
Çameli, *Turkey* 39 D11
Camenca, *Moldova* 43 B13
Camerino, *Italy* 29 E10
Cameron, *Ariz., U.S.A.* 115 J8
Cameron, *La., U.S.A.* 113 L8
Cameron, *Mo., U.S.A.* 112 F7
Cameron, *Tex., U.S.A.* 113 K6
Cameron Highlands, *Malaysia* 65 K3
Cameron Hills, *Canada* 104 B5
Cameroon ■, *Africa* 84 C2
Camerota, *Italy* 31 B8
Cameroun →, *Cameroon* 83 E6
Cameroun, Mt., *Cameroon* 83 E6
Cametá, *Brazil* 125 D9
Çamiçi Gölü, *Turkey* 39 D9
Camiguin □, *Phil.* 61 G6
Camiguin I., *Phil.* 61 B4
Camiling, *Phil.* 61 D4
Camilla, *U.S.A.* 109 K3
Caminha, *Portugal* 34 D2
Camino, *U.S.A.* 116 G6
Camira Creek, *Australia* 95 D5
Cammal, *U.S.A.* 110 E7
Cammarata, *Italy* 30 E6
Camocim, *Brazil* 125 D10
Camooweal, *Australia* 94 B2
Camopi, *Fr. Guiana* 125 C8
Camotes Is., *Phil.* 61 F6
Camotes Sea, *Phil.* 61 F6
Camp Borden, *Canada* 110 B5
Camp Hill, *U.S.A.* 110 F8
Camp Nelson, *U.S.A.* 117 J8
Camp Pendleton, *U.S.A.* 117 M9
Camp Verde, *U.S.A.* 115 J8
Camp Wood, *U.S.A.* 113 L5
Campagna, *Italy* 31 B8
Campana, *Argentina* 126 C4
Campana, I., *Chile* 128 F1
Campanário, *Madeira* 37 D2
Campanario, *Spain* 35 G5
Campània □, *Italy* 31 B7
Campbell, *S. Africa* 88 D3
Campbell, *Calif., U.S.A.* 116 H5
Campbell, *Ohio, U.S.A.* 110 E4
Campbell I., *Pac. Oc.* 96 N8
Campbell L., *Canada* 105 A7
Campbell River, *Canada* 104 C3
Campbell Town, *Australia* 94 G4
Campbellford, *Canada* 110 B7
Campbellpur, *Pakistan* 68 C5
Campbellsville, *U.S.A.* 108 G3
Campbellton, *Canada* 103 C6
Campbelltown, *Australia* 95 E5
Campbeltown, *U.K.* 14 F3
Campeche, *Mexico* 119 D6
Campeche □, *Mexico* 119 D6
Campeche, Golfo de, *Mexico* 119 D6
Campello, *Spain* 33 G4
Câmpeni, *Romania* 42 D8
Camperdown, *Australia* 95 F3
Camperville, *Canada* 105 C8
Campi Salentina, *Italy* 31 B11
Câmpia Turzii, *Romania* 43 D8
Campidano, *Italy* 30 C1
Campíglia Marittima, *Italy* 28 E7
Campillo de Altobuey, *Spain* 33 F3
Campillos, *Spain* 35 H6
Câmpina, *Romania* 43 E10
Campina Grande, *Brazil* 125 E11
Campinas, *Brazil* 127 A6
Campli, *Italy* 29 F10
Campo, *Spain* 32 C5
Campo de Criptana, *Spain* 35 F7
Campo de Gibraltar, *Spain* 35 J5
Campo Grande, *Brazil* 125 H8
Campo Maíor, *Brazil* 125 D10
Campo Maior, *Portugal* 35 F3
Campo Mourão, *Brazil* 127 A5
Campo Túres, *Italy* 29 B8
Campobasso, *Italy* 31 A7
Campobello di Licata, *Italy* 30 E6
Campobello di Mazara, *Italy* 30 E5
Campofelice di Roccella, *Italy* 30 E6
Campomarino, *Italy* 29 G12
Camporeale, *Italy* 30 E6
Camporrobles, *Spain* 32 F3
Campos, *Brazil* 127 A7
Campos Belos, *Brazil* 125 F9
Campos del Puerto, *Spain* 37 B10
Campos Novos, *Brazil* 127 B5
Camprodón, *Spain* 32 C7
Camptonville, *U.S.A.* 116 F5
Camptown, *U.S.A.* 111 E8
Câmpulung, *Argeş, Romania* 43 E10
Câmpulung, *Suceava, Romania* 43 C10
Câmpuri, *Romania* 43 D11
Camrose, *Canada* 104 C6
Camsell Portage, *Canada* 105 B7
Çamyuva, *Turkey* 39 E12
Çan, *Turkey* 41 F11
Can Clavo, *Spain* 37 C7
Can Creu, *Spain* 37 C7
Can Gio, *Vietnam* 65 G6
Can Tho, *Vietnam* 65 G5
Canaan, *U.S.A.* 111 D11
Canada ■, *N. Amer.* 100 C10
Cañada de Gómez, *Argentina* 126 C3
Canadian, *U.S.A.* 113 H4
Canadian →, *U.S.A.* 113 H7
Canajoharie, *U.S.A.* 111 D10
Çanakkale, *Turkey* 41 F10
Çanakkale □, *Turkey* 41 F10
Çanakkale Boğazı, *Turkey* 41 F10
Canal Flats, *Canada* 104 C5
Canalejas, *Argentina* 126 D2
Canals, *Argentina* 126 C3
Canals, *Spain* 33 G4
Canandaigua, *U.S.A.* 110 D7
Canandaigua L., *U.S.A.* 110 D7
Cananea, *Mexico* 118 A2
Canarias, Is., *Atl. Oc.* 37 F4
Canarreos, Arch. de los, *Cuba* 120 B3
Canary Is. = Canarias, Is., *Atl. Oc.* 37 F4
Canaseraga, *U.S.A.* 110 D7
Canatlán, *Mexico* 118 C4
Canaveral, C., *U.S.A.* 109 L5
Cañaveruelas, *Spain* 32 E2
Canavieiras, *Brazil* 125 G11
Canberra, *Australia* 95 F4
Canby, *Calif., U.S.A.* 114 F3
Canby, *Minn., U.S.A.* 112 C6
Canby, *Oreg., U.S.A.* 116 E4
Cancale, *France* 18 D5
Canche →, *France* 19 B8
Cancún, *Mexico* 119 C7
Candanchu, *Spain* 32 C4
Çandarlı, *Turkey* 39 C8
Çandarlı Körfezi, *Turkey* 39 C8
Candas, *Spain* 34 B5
Candé, *France* 18 E5
Candela, *Italy* 31 A8
Candelaria, *Argentina* 127 B4
Candelaria, *Canary Is.* 37 F3
Candeleda, *Spain* 34 E5
Candelo, *Australia* 95 F4
Candia = Iráklion, *Greece* 36 D7
Candia, Sea of = Crete, Sea of, *Greece* 39 E7
Candle L., *Canada* 105 C7
Candlemas I., *Antarctica* 5 B1
Cando, *U.S.A.* 112 A5
Candon, *Phil.* 61 C4
Canea = Khaniá, *Greece* 36 D6
Canelli, *Italy* 28 D5
Canelones, *Uruguay* 127 C4
Canet-Plage, *France* 20 F7
Cañete, *Chile* 126 D1
Cañete, *Peru* 124 F3
Cañete, *Spain* 32 E3
Cañete de las Torres, *Spain* 35 H6
Cangas, *Spain* 34 C2
Cangas de Narcea, *Spain* 34 B4
Cangas de Onís, *Spain* 34 B5
Cangnan, *China* 59 D13
Canguaretama, *Brazil* 125 E11
Canguçu, *Brazil* 127 C5
Canguçu, Serra do, *Brazil* 127 C5
Cangwu, *China* 59 F8
Cangxi, *China* 58 B5
Cangyuan, *China* 58 F2
Cangzhou, *China* 56 E9
Caniapiscau →, *Canada* 103 A6
Caniapiscau, Rés. de, *Canada* 103 B6
Canicattì, *Italy* 30 E6
Canicattini Bagni, *Italy* 31 E8
Caniles, *Spain* 35 H8
Canim Lake, *Canada* 104 C4
Canindeyu □, *Paraguay* 127 A5
Canino, *Italy* 29 F8
Canisteo, *U.S.A.* 110 D7
Canisteo →, *U.S.A.* 110 D7
Cañitas, *Mexico* 118 C4
Cañizal, *Spain* 34 D5
Canjáyar, *Spain* 35 H8
Çankırı, *Turkey* 72 B5
Cankuzo, *Burundi* 86 C3
Canmore, *Canada* 104 C5
Cann River, *Australia* 95 F4
Canna, *U.K.* 14 D2
Cannanore, *India* 66 P9
Cannes, *France* 21 E11
Canning Town = Port Canning, *India* 69 H13
Cannington, *Canada* 110 B5
Cannóbio, *Italy* 28 B5
Cannock, *U.K.* 13 E5
Cannon Ball →, *U.S.A.* 112 B4
Cannondale Mt., *Australia* 94 D4
Cannonsville Reservoir, *U.S.A.* 111 D9
Cannonvale, *Australia* 94 C4
Canoas, *Brazil* 127 B5
Canoe L., *Canada* 105 B7
Canon City, *U.S.A.* 112 F2
Canora, *Canada* 105 C8
Canosa di Púglia, *Italy* 31 A9
Canowindra, *Australia* 95 E4
Canso, *Canada* 103 C7
Cantabria □, *Spain* 34 B7
Cantabria, Sierra de, *Spain* 32 C2
Cantabrian Mts. = Cantábrica, Cordillera, *Spain* 34 C5
Cantábrica, Cordillera, *Spain* 34 C5
Cantal □, *France* 20 C6
Cantal, Plomb du, *France* 20 C6
Cantanhede, *Portugal* 34 E2
Cantavieja, *Spain* 32 E4
Čantavir, *Serbia, Yug.* 42 E4
Cantemir, *Moldova* 43 D13
Canterbury, *Australia* 94 D3
Canterbury, *U.K.* 13 F9
Canterbury Bight, *N.Z.* 91 L3
Canterbury Plains, *N.Z.* 91 K3
Cantil, *U.S.A.* 117 K9
Cantillana, *Spain* 35 H5
Canton = Guangzhou, *China* 59 F9
Canton, *Ga., U.S.A.* 109 H3
Canton, *Ill., U.S.A.* 112 E9
Canton, *Miss., U.S.A.* 113 J9
Canton, *Mo., U.S.A.* 112 E9
Canton, *N.Y., U.S.A.* 111 B9
Canton, *Ohio, U.S.A.* 110 F3
Canton, *Pa., U.S.A.* 110 E8
Canton, *S. Dak., U.S.A.* 112 D6
Canton L., *U.S.A.* 113 G5
Cantù, *Italy* 28 C6
Canudos, *Brazil* 124 E7
Canumã →, *Brazil* 124 D7
Canutama, *Brazil* 124 E6
Canutillo, *U.S.A.* 115 L10
Canvey, *U.K.* 13 F8
Canyon, *U.S.A.* 113 H4
Canyonlands National Park, *U.S.A.* 115 G9
Canyonville, *U.S.A.* 114 E2
Cao Bang, *Vietnam* 58 F6
Cao He →, *China* 57 D13
Cao Lanh, *Vietnam* 65 G5
Cao Xian, *China* 56 G8
Cáorle, *Italy* 29 C9
Cap-aux-Meules, *Canada* 103 C7
Cap-Chat, *Canada* 103 C6
Cap-de-la-Madeleine, *Canada* 102 C5
Cap-Haïtien, *Haiti* 121 C5
Capac, *U.S.A.* 110 C2
Capáccio, *Italy* 31 B8
Capaci, *Italy* 30 D6
Capanaparo →, *Venezuela* 124 B5
Capánnori, *Italy* 28 E7
Capbreton, *France* 20 E2
Capdenac, *France* 20 D6
Capdepera, *Spain* 32 F8
Cape →, *Australia* 94 C4
Cape Barren I., *Australia* 94 G4
Cape Breton Highlands Nat. Park, *Canada* 103 C7
Cape Breton I., *Canada* 103 C7
Cape Charles, *U.S.A.* 108 G8
Cape Coast, *Ghana* 83 D4
Cape Coral, *U.S.A.* 109 M5
Cape Dorset, *Canada* 101 B12
Cape Fear →, *U.S.A.* 109 H6
Cape Girardeau, *U.S.A.* 113 G10
Cape May, *U.S.A.* 108 F8
Cape May Point, *U.S.A.* 108 F8
Cape Province, *S. Africa* 85 L3
Cape Tormentine, *Canada* 103 C7
Cape Town, *S. Africa* 88 E2
Cape Verde Is. ■, *Atl. Oc.* 77 E1
Cape Vincent, *U.S.A.* 111 B8
Cape York Peninsula, *Australia* 94 A3
Capela, *Brazil* 125 F11
Capella, *Australia* 94 C4
Capendu, *France* 20 E6
Capestang, *France* 20 E7
Capim →, *Brazil* 125 D9
Capistrello, *Italy* 29 G10
Capitan, *U.S.A.* 115 K11
Capitol Reef National Park, *U.S.A.* 115 G8
Capitola, *U.S.A.* 116 J5
Capizzi, *Italy* 31 E7
Capoche →, *Mozam.* 87 F3
Capoterra, *Italy* 30 C1
Cappadocia, *Turkey* 72 C6
Capraia, *Italy* 28 E6
Caprara, Pta., *Italy* 30 A1
Caprarola, *Italy* 29 F9
Capreol, *Canada* 102 C3
Caprera, *Italy* 30 A2
Capri, *Italy* 31 B7
Capricorn Group, *Australia* 94 C5
Capricorn Ra., *Australia* 92 D2
Caprino Veronese, *Italy* 28 C7
Caprivi Strip, *Namibia* 88 B3
Captain's Flat, *Australia* 95 F4
Captieux, *France* 20 D3
Caquetá →, *Colombia* 122 D4
Caracal, *Romania* 43 F9
Caracas, *Venezuela* 124 A5
Caracol, *Mato Grosso do Sul, Brazil* 126 A4
Caracol, *Piauí, Brazil* 125 E10
Caráglio, *Italy* 28 D4
Carajas, *Brazil* 125 E8
Carajás, Serra dos, *Brazil* 125 E8
Carangola, *Brazil* 127 A7
Caransebeş, *Romania* 42 E7
Carantec, *France* 18 D3
Caraquet, *Canada* 103 C6
Caras, *Peru* 124 E3
Caraş Severin □, *Romania* 42 E7
Caraşova, *Romania* 42 E6
Caratasca, L., *Honduras* 120 C3
Caratinga, *Brazil* 125 G10
Caraúbas, *Brazil* 125 E11
Caravaca = Caravaca de la Cruz, *Spain* 33 G3
Caravaca de la Cruz, *Spain* 33 G3
Caravággio, *Italy* 28 C6
Caravela, *Guinea-Biss.* 82 C1
Caravelas, *Brazil* 125 G11
Caraveli, *Peru* 124 G4
Caràzinho, *Brazil* 127 B5
Carballino = O Carballiño, *Spain* 34 C2
Carballo, *Spain* 34 B2
Carberry, *Canada* 105 D9
Carbó, *Mexico* 118 B2
Carbonara, C., *Italy* 30 C2
Carbondale, *Colo., U.S.A.* 114 G10
Carbondale, *Ill., U.S.A.* 113 G10
Carbondale, *Pa., U.S.A.* 111 E9
Carbonear, *Canada* 103 C9
Carboneras, *Spain* 33 J3
Carboneras de Guadazaón, *Spain* 32 F3
Carbónia, *Italy* 30 C1
Carcabuey, *Spain* 35 H6
Carcagente = Carcaixent, *Spain* 33 F4
Carcaixent, *Spain* 33 F4
Carcajou, *Canada* 104 B5
Carcar, *Phil.* 61 F5
Carcarana →, *Argentina* 126 C3
Carcasse, C., *Haiti* 121 C5
Carcassonne, *France* 20 E6
Carcross, *Canada* 104 A2
Çardak, *Çanakkale, Turkey* 41 F10
Çardak, *Denizli, Turkey* 39 D11
Cardamon Hills, *India* 66 Q10
Cardeña, *Spain* 35 G6
Cárdenas, *Cuba* 120 B3
Cárdenas, *San Luis Potosí, Mexico* 119 C5
Cárdenas, *Tabasco, Mexico* 119 D6
Cardenete, *Spain* 32 F3
Cardiff, *U.K.* 13 F4
Cardiff □, *U.K.* 13 F4
Cardiff-by-the-Sea, *U.S.A.* 117 M9
Cardigan, *U.K.* 13 E3
Cardigan B., *U.K.* 13 E3
Cardinal, *Canada* 111 B9
Cardona, *Spain* 32 D6
Cardona, *Uruguay* 126 C4
Cardoner →, *Spain* 32 D6
Cardoso, Ilha do, *Brazil* 127 B5
Cardston, *Canada* 104 D6
Cardwell, *Australia* 94 B4
Careen L., *Canada* 105 B7
Carei, *Romania* 42 C7
Careme = Ciremai, *Indonesia* 63 G13
Carentan, *France* 18 C5
Carey, *U.S.A.* 114 E7
Carey, L., *Australia* 93 E3
Carey L., *Canada* 105 A8
Careysburg, *Liberia* 82 D2
Cargèse, *France* 21 F12
Carhaix-Plouguer, *France* 18 D3
Carhué, *Argentina* 126 D3
Caria, *Turkey* 39 D10
Cariacica, *Brazil* 125 H10
Cariati, *Italy* 31 C9
Caribbean Sea, *W. Indies* 121 D5
Cariboo Mts., *Canada* 104 C4
Caribou, *U.S.A.* 109 B12
Caribou →, *Man., Canada* 105 B10
Caribou →, *N.W.T., Canada* 104 A3
Caribou I., *Canada* 102 C2
Caribou Is., *Canada* 104 A6
Caribou L., *Man., Canada* 105 B9
Caribou L., *Ont., Canada* 102 B2
Caribou Mts., *Canada* 104 B5
Carichic, *Mexico* 118 B3
Carigara, *Phil.* 61 F6
Carignan, *France* 19 C12
Carignano, *Italy* 28 D4
Carillo, *Mexico* 118 B4
Carinda, *Australia* 95 E4
Cariñena, *Spain* 32 D3
Carinhanha, *Brazil* 125 F10
Carinhanha →, *Brazil* 125 F10
Carini, *Italy* 30 D6
Cariño, *Spain* 34 B3
Carínola, *Italy* 30 A6
Carinthia = Kärnten □, *Austria* 26 E6
Caripito, *Venezuela* 124 A6
Carlbrod = Dimitrovgrad, *Serbia, Yug.* 40 C6
Carlet, *Spain* 33 F4
Carleton, Mt., *Canada* 103 C6
Carleton Place, *Canada* 102 C4
Carletonville, *S. Africa* 88 D4
Cărlibaba, *Romania* 43 C10
Carlin, *U.S.A.* 114 F5
Carlingford L., *U.K.* 15 B5

Carlinville, *U.S.A.* 112 F10
Carlisle, *U.K.* 12 C5
Carlisle, *U.S.A.* 110 F7
Carlit, Pic, *France* 20 F5
Carloforte, *Italy* 30 C1
Carlos Casares, *Argentina* 126 D3
Carlos Tejedor, *Argentina* 126 D3
Carlow, *Ireland* 15 D5
Carlow □, *Ireland* 15 D5
Carlsbad, *Calif., U.S.A.* 117 M9
Carlsbad, *N. Mex., U.S.A.* 113 J2
Carlsbad Caverns National Park, *U.S.A.* 113 J2
Carluke, *U.K.* 14 F5
Carlyle, *Canada* 105 D8
Carmacks, *Canada* 100 B6
Carmagnola, *Italy* 28 D4
Carman, *Canada* 105 D9
Carmarthen, *U.K.* 13 F3
Carmarthen B., *U.K.* 13 F3
Carmarthenshire □, *U.K.* 13 F3
Carmaux, *France* 20 D6
Carmel, *U.S.A.* 111 E11
Carmel-by-the-Sea, *U.S.A.* 116 J5
Carmel Valley, *U.S.A.* 116 J5
Carmelo, *Uruguay* 126 C4
Carmen, *Colombia* 124 B3
Carmen, *Paraguay* 127 B4
Carmen →, *Mexico* 118 A3
Carmen, I., *Mexico* 118 B2
Carmen de Patagones, *Argentina* 128 E4
Cármenes, *Spain* 34 C5
Carmensa, *Argentina* 126 D2
Carmi, *Canada* 104 D5
Carmi, *U.S.A.* 108 F1
Carmichael, *U.S.A.* 116 G5
Carmila, *Australia* 94 C4
Carmona, *Costa Rica* 120 E2
Carmona, *Spain* 35 H5
Carn Ban, *U.K.* 14 D4
Carn Eige, *U.K.* 14 D3
Carnamah, *Australia* 93 E2
Carnarvon, *Australia* 93 D1
Carnarvon, *S. Africa* 88 E3
Carnarvon Ra., *Queens., Australia* 94 D4
Carnarvon Ra., *W. Austral., Australia* 93 E3
Carnation, *U.S.A.* 116 C5
Carndonagh, *Ireland* 15 A4
Carnduff, *Canada* 105 D8
Carnegie, *U.S.A.* 110 F4
Carnegie, L., *Australia* 93 E3
Carnic Alps = Karnische Alpen, *Europe* 26 E6
Carniche Alpi = Karnische Alpen, *Europe* 26 E6
Carnot, *C.A.R.* 84 D3
Carnot, C., *Australia* 95 E2
Carnot B., *Australia* 92 C3
Carnoustie, *U.K.* 14 E6
Carnsore Pt., *Ireland* 15 D5
Caro, *U.S.A.* 108 D4
Carol City, *U.S.A.* 109 N5
Carolina, *Brazil* 125 E9
Carolina, *Puerto Rico* 121 C6
Carolina, *S. Africa* 89 D5
Caroline I., *Kiribati* 97 H12
Caroline Is., *Micronesia* 52 J17
Caroni →, *Venezuela* 124 B6
Caronie = Nébrodi, Monti, *Italy* 31 E7
Caroona, *Australia* 95 E5
Carpathians, *Europe* 6 F10
Carpaţii Meridionali, *Romania* 43 E9
Carpentaria, G. of, *Australia* 94 A2
Carpentras, *France* 21 D9
Carpi, *Italy* 28 D7
Cărpineni, *Moldova* 43 D13
Carpinteria, *U.S.A.* 117 L7
Carpio, *Spain* 34 D5
Carr Boyd Ra., *Australia* 92 C4
Carrabelle, *U.S.A.* 109 L3
Carral, *Spain* 34 B2
Carranza, Presa V., *Mexico* 118 B4
Carrara, *Italy* 28 D7
Carrascal, *Phil.* 61 G6
Carrascosa del Campo, *Spain* 32 E2
Carrauntoohill, *Ireland* 15 D2
Carrick-on-Shannon, *Ireland* 15 C3
Carrick-on-Suir, *Ireland* 15 D4
Carrickfergus, *U.K.* 15 B6
Carrickmacross, *Ireland* 15 C5
Carrieton, *Australia* 95 E2
Carrington, *U.S.A.* 112 B5
Carrión →, *Spain* 34 D6
Carrión de los Condes, *Spain* 34 C6
Carrizal Bajo, *Chile* 126 B1
Carrizalillo, *Chile* 126 B1
Carrizo Cr. →, *U.S.A.* 113 G3
Carrizo Springs, *U.S.A.* 113 L5
Carrizozo, *U.S.A.* 115 K11
Carroll, *U.S.A.* 112 D7
Carrollton, *Ga., U.S.A.* 109 J3
Carrollton, *Ill., U.S.A.* 112 F9
Carrollton, *Ky., U.S.A.* 108 F3
Carrollton, *Mo., U.S.A.* 112 F8
Carrollton, *Ohio, U.S.A.* 110 F3
Carron →, *U.K.* 14 D4
Carron, L., *U.K.* 14 D3
Carrot →, *Canada* 105 C8
Carrot River, *Canada* 105 C8
Carrouges, *France* 18 D6
Carrù, *Italy* 28 D4
Carruthers, *Canada* 105 C7
Carsa Dek, *Ethiopia* 81 F4
Çarşamba, *Turkey* 72 B7
Carsóli, *Italy* 29 F10
Carson, *Calif., U.S.A.* 117 M8
Carson, *N. Dak., U.S.A.* 112 B4
Carson →, *U.S.A.* 116 F8
Carson City, *U.S.A.* 116 F7
Carson Sink, *U.S.A.* 114 G4
Cartagena, *Colombia* 124 A3
Cartagena, *Spain* 33 H4
Cartago, *Colombia* 124 C3
Cartago, *Costa Rica* 120 E3
Cártama, *Spain* 35 J6
Cartaxo, *Portugal* 35 F2
Cartaya, *Spain* 35 H3
Cartersville, *U.S.A.* 109 H3
Carterton, *N.Z.* 91 J5
Carthage, *Tunisia* 30 F3
Carthage, *Ill., U.S.A.* 112 E9
Carthage, *Mo., U.S.A.* 113 G7
Carthage, *N.Y., U.S.A.* 108 D8
Carthage, *Tex., U.S.A.* 113 J7
Cartier I., *Australia* 92 B3
Cartwright, *Canada* 103 B8
Caruaru, *Brazil* 125 E11
Carúpano, *Venezuela* 124 A6
Caruthersville, *U.S.A.* 113 G10
Carvin, *France* 19 B9
Carvoeiro, *Brazil* 124 D6
Carvoeiro, C., *Portugal* 35 F1
Cary, *U.S.A.* 109 H6
Casa Branca, *Portugal* 35 G2
Casa Grande, *U.S.A.* 115 K8
Casablanca, *Chile* 126 C1
Casablanca, *Morocco* 78 B4
Casacalenda, *Italy* 29 G11
Casalbordino, *Italy* 29 F11
Casale Monferrato, *Italy* 28 C5
Casalmaggiore, *Italy* 28 D7
Casalpusterlengo, *Italy* 28 C6
Casamance →, *Senegal* 82 C1
Casarano, *Italy* 31 B11
Casares, *Spain* 35 J5
Casas Ibáñez, *Spain* 33 F3
Casasimarro, *Spain* 33 F2
Casatejada, *Spain* 34 F5
Casavieja, *Spain* 34 E6
Cascade, *Idaho, U.S.A.* 114 D5
Cascade, *Mont., U.S.A.* 114 C8
Cascade Locks, *U.S.A.* 116 E5
Cascade Ra., *U.S.A.* 116 D5
Cascade Reservoir, *U.S.A.* 114 D5
Cascais, *Portugal* 35 G1
Cascavel, *Brazil* 127 A5
Cáscina, *Italy* 28 E7
Casco B., *U.S.A.* 109 D10
Caselle Torinese, *Italy* 28 C4
Caserta, *Italy* 31 A7
Cashel, *Ireland* 15 D4
Casiguran, *Phil.* 61 C5
Casilda, *Argentina* 126 C3
Casimcea, *Romania* 43 F13
Casino, *Australia* 95 D5
Casiquiare →, *Venezuela* 124 C5
Čáslav, *Czech Rep.* 26 B8
Casma, *Peru* 124 E3
Casmalia, *U.S.A.* 117 L6
Cásola Valsénio, *Italy* 29 D8
Cásoli, *Italy* 29 F11
Caspe, *Spain* 32 D4
Casper, *U.S.A.* 114 E10
Caspian Depression, *Eurasia* 49 G9
Caspian Sea, *Eurasia* 50 E6
Cass Lake, *U.S.A.* 112 B7
Cassà de la Selva, *Spain* 32 D7
Cassadaga, *U.S.A.* 110 D5
Cassano allo Iónio, *Italy* 31 C9
Casse, Grande, *France* 21 C10
Cassel, *France* 19 B9
Casselman, *Canada* 111 A9
Casselton, *U.S.A.* 112 B6
Cassiar, *Canada* 104 B3
Cassiar Mts., *Canada* 104 B2
Cassino, *Italy* 30 A6
Cassis, *France* 21 E9
Cassville, *U.S.A.* 113 G8
Castagneto Carducci, *Italy* 28 E7
Castaic, *U.S.A.* 117 L8
Castalia, *U.S.A.* 110 E2
Castanhal, *Brazil* 125 D9
Castéggio, *Italy* 28 C6
Castejón de Monegros, *Spain* 32 D4
Castèl di Sangro, *Italy* 29 G11
Castèl San Giovanni, *Italy* 28 C6
Castèl San Pietro Terme, *Italy* 29 D8
Castelbuono, *Italy* 31 E7
Castelfidardo, *Italy* 29 E10
Castelfiorentino, *Italy* 28 E7
Castelfranco Emília, *Italy* 28 D8
Castelfranco Véneto, *Italy* 29 C8
Casteljaloux, *France* 20 D4
Castellabate, *Italy* 31 B7
Castellammare, G. di, *Italy* 30 D5
Castellammare del Golfo, *Italy* 30 D5
Castellammare di Stábia, *Italy* 31 B7
Castellamonte, *Italy* 28 C4
Castellane, *France* 21 E10
Castellaneta, *Italy* 31 B9
Castelli, *Argentina* 126 D4
Castelló de la Plana, *Spain* 32 F4
Castellón de la Plana □, *Spain* 32 E4
Castellote, *Spain* 32 E4
Castelmáuro, *Italy* 29 G11
Castelnau-de-Médoc, *France* 20 C3
Castelnau-Magnoac, *France* 20 E4
Castelnaudary, *France* 20 E5
Castelnovo ne' Monti, *Italy* 28 D7
Castelnuovo di Val di Cécina, *Italy* 28 E7
Castelo, *Brazil* 127 A7
Castelo Branco, *Portugal* 34 F3
Castelo Branco □, *Portugal* 34 F3
Castelo de Paiva, *Portugal* 34 D2
Castelo de Vide, *Portugal* 35 F3
Castelsardo, *Italy* 30 B1
Castelsarrasin, *France* 20 D5
Casteltérmini, *Italy* 30 E6
Castelvetrano, *Italy* 30 E5
Casterton, *Australia* 95 F3
Castets, *France* 20 E2
Castiglion Fiorentino, *Italy* 29 E8
Castiglione del Lago, *Italy* 29 E9
Castiglione della Pescáia, *Italy* 28 F7
Castiglione delle Stiviere, *Italy* 28 C7
Castilblanco, *Spain* 35 F5
Castile, *U.S.A.* 110 D6
Castilla, Playa de, *Spain* 35 J4
Castilla-La Mancha □, *Spain* 6 H5
Castilla y Leon □, *Spain* 34 D6
Castillo de Locubín, *Spain* 35 H7
Castillon-en-Couserans, *France* 20 F5
Castillonès, *France* 20 D4
Castillos, *Uruguay* 127 C5
Castle Dale, *U.S.A.* 114 G8
Castle Douglas, *U.K.* 14 G5
Castle Rock, *Colo., U.S.A.* 112 F2
Castle Rock, *Wash., U.S.A.* 116 D4
Castlebar, *Ireland* 15 C2
Castleblaney, *Ireland* 15 B5
Castlederg, *U.K.* 15 B4
Castleford, *U.K.* 12 D6
Castlegar, *Canada* 104 D5
Castlemaine, *Australia* 95 F3
Castlepollard, *Ireland* 15 C4
Castlerea, *Ireland* 15 C3
Castlereagh →, *Australia* 95 E4
Castlereagh B., *Australia* 94 A2
Castleton, *U.S.A.* 111 C11
Castletown, *U.K.* 12 C3
Castletown Bearhaven, *Ireland* 15 E2
Castor, *Canada* 104 C6
Castor →, *Canada* 102 B4
Castorland, *U.S.A.* 111 C9
Castres, *France* 20 E6
Castricum, *Neths.* 17 B4
Castries, *St. Lucia* 121 D7
Castril, *Spain* 35 H8
Castro, *Brazil* 127 A6
Castro, *Chile* 128 E2
Castro Alves, *Brazil* 125 F11
Castro del Río, *Spain* 35 H6
Castro-Urdiales, *Spain* 34 B7
Castro Verde, *Portugal* 35 H2
Castrojeriz, *Spain* 34 C6
Castropol, *Spain* 34 B4
Castroreale, *Italy* 31 D8
Castrovíllari, *Italy* 31 C9
Castroville, *U.S.A.* 116 J5
Castuera, *Spain* 35 G5
Çat, *Turkey* 73 C9
Cat Ba, Dao, *Vietnam* 64 B6
Cat I., *Bahamas* 121 B4
Cat L., *Canada* 102 B1
Cat Lake, *Canada* 102 B1
Čata, *Slovak Rep.* 27 D11
Catacamas, *Honduras* 120 D2
Cataguases, *Brazil* 127 A7
Çatak, *Turkey* 73 C10
Catalão, *Brazil* 125 G9
Çatalca, *Turkey* 41 E12
Catalina, *Canada* 103 C9
Catalina, *Chile* 126 B2
Catalina, *U.S.A.* 115 K8
Catalonia = Cataluña □, *Spain* 32 D6
Cataluña □, *Spain* 32 D6
Çatalzeytin, *Turkey* 72 B6
Catamarca, *Argentina* 126 B2
Catamarca □, *Argentina* 126 B2
Catanauan, *Phil.* 61 E5
Catanduanes □, *Phil.* 61 E6
Catanduva, *Brazil* 127 A6
Catánia, *Italy* 31 E8
Catánia, G. di, *Italy* 31 E8
Catanzaro, *Italy* 31 D9
Catarman, *Phil.* 61 E6
Catbalogan, *Phil.* 61 F6
Cateel, *Phil.* 61 H7
Catembe, *Mozam.* 89 D5
Caterham, *U.K.* 13 F7
Cathcart, *S. Africa* 88 E4
Cathlamet, *U.S.A.* 116 D3
Catio, *Guinea-Biss.* 82 C1
Catlettsburg, *U.S.A.* 108 F4
Çatma Dağı, *Turkey* 39 C11
Catoche, C., *Mexico* 119 C7
Cátria, Mte., *Italy* 29 E9
Catriló, *Argentina* 126 D3
Catrimani, *Brazil* 124 C6
Catrimani →, *Brazil* 124 C6
Catskill, *U.S.A.* 111 D11
Catskill Mts., *U.S.A.* 111 D10
Catt, Mt., *Australia* 94 A1
Cattaraugus, *U.S.A.* 110 D6
Cattólica, *Italy* 29 E9
Cattólica Eraclea, *Italy* 30 E6
Catuala, *Angola* 88 B2
Catuane, *Mozam.* 89 D5
Catur, *Mozam.* 87 E4
Catwick Is., *Vietnam* 65 G7
Cauca →, *Colombia* 124 B4
Caucaia, *Brazil* 125 D11
Caucasus Mountains, *Eurasia* 49 J7
Caudete, *Spain* 33 G3
Caudry, *France* 19 B10
Caulnes, *France* 18 D4
Caulónia, *Italy* 31 D9
Caungula, *Angola* 84 F3
Cauquenes, *Chile* 126 D1
Caura →, *Venezuela* 124 B6
Cauresi →, *Mozam.* 87 F3
Căuşani, *Moldova* 43 D14
Causapscal, *Canada* 103 C6
Caussade, *France* 20 D5
Causse-Méjean, *France* 20 D7
Cauterets, *France* 20 F3
Cauvery →, *India* 66 P11
Caux, Pays de, *France* 18 C7
Cava de' Tirreni, *Italy* 31 B7
Cávado →, *Portugal* 34 D2
Cavaillon, *France* 21 E9
Cavalaire-sur-Mer, *France* 21 E10
Cavalese, *Italy* 29 B8
Cavalier, *U.S.A.* 112 A6
Cavalla = Cavally →, *Africa* 82 E3
Cavalleria, C. de, *Spain* 37 A11
Cavallo, I. de, *France* 21 G13
Cavally →, *Africa* 82 E3
Cavan, *Ireland* 15 B4
Cavan □, *Ireland* 15 C4
Cavárzere, *Italy* 29 C9
Çavdarhisar, *Turkey* 39 B11
Çavdır, *Turkey* 39 D11
Cave Creek, *U.S.A.* 115 K7
Cavenagh Ra., *Australia* 93 E4
Cavendish, *Australia* 95 F3
Caviana, I., *Brazil* 125 C8
Cavite, *Phil.* 61 D4
Cavnic, *Romania* 43 C8
Cavour, *Italy* 28 D4
Cavtat, *Croatia* 40 D2
Cawndilla L., *Australia* 95 E3
Cawnpore = Kanpur, *India* 69 F9
Caxias, *Brazil* 125 D10
Caxias do Sul, *Brazil* 127 B5
Çay, *Turkey* 72 C4
Cay Sal Bank, *Bahamas* 120 B4
Cayambe, *Ecuador* 124 C3
Çaycuma, *Turkey* 72 B5
Çayeli, *Turkey* 73 B9
Cayenne, *Fr. Guiana* 125 B8
Caygören Barajı, *Turkey* 39 B10
Cayiralan, *Turkey* 72 C6
Caylus, *France* 20 D5
Cayman Brac, *Cayman Is.* 120 C4
Cayman Is. ■, *W. Indies* 120 C3
Cayo Romano, *Cuba* 120 B4
Cayres, *France* 20 D7
Cayuga, *Canada* 110 D5
Cayuga, *U.S.A.* 111 D8
Cayuga L., *U.S.A.* 111 D8
Cazalla de la Sierra, *Spain* 35 H5
Căzăneşti, *Romania* 43 F12
Cazaubon, *France* 20 E3
Cazaux et de Sanguinet, Étang de, *France* 20 D2
Cazenovia, *U.S.A.* 111 D9
Cazères, *France* 20 E5
Cazin, *Bos.-H.* 29 D12
Čazma, *Croatia* 29 C13
Cazombo, *Angola* 85 G4
Cazorla, *Spain* 35 H7
Cazorla, Sierra de, *Spain* 35 G8
Cea →, *Spain* 34 C5
Ceamurlia de Jos, *Romania* 43 F13
Ceanannus Mor, *Ireland* 15 C5
Ceará = Fortaleza, *Brazil* 125 D11
Ceará □, *Brazil* 125 E11
Ceará Mirim, *Brazil* 125 E11
Ceauru, L., *Romania* 43 F8
Cebaco, I. de, *Panama* 120 E3
Cebollar, *Argentina* 126 B2
Cebollera, Sierra de, *Spain* 32 D2
Cebreros, *Spain* 34 E6
Cebu, *Phil.* 61 F5
Čečava, *Bos.-H.* 42 F2
Ceccano, *Italy* 30 A6
Cece, *Hungary* 42 D3
Cechi, *Ivory C.* 82 D4
Cecil Plains, *Australia* 95 D5
Cécina, *Italy* 28 E7
Cécina →, *Italy* 28 E7
Ceclavín, *Spain* 34 F4
Cedar →, *U.S.A.* 112 E9
Cedar City, *U.S.A.* 115 H7
Cedar Creek Reservoir, *U.S.A.* 113 J6
Cedar Falls, *Iowa, U.S.A.* 112 D8
Cedar Falls, *Wash., U.S.A.* 116 C5
Cedar Key, *U.S.A.* 109 L4
Cedar L., *Canada* 105 C9
Cedar Rapids, *U.S.A.* 112 E9
Cedartown, *U.S.A.* 109 H3
Cedarvale, *Canada* 104 B3
Cedarville, *S. Africa* 89 E4
Cedeira, *Spain* 34 B2
Cedral, *Mexico* 118 C4
Cedrino →, *Italy* 30 B2
Cedro, *Brazil* 125 E11
Cedros, I. de, *Mexico* 118 B1
Ceduna, *Australia* 95 E1
Cedynia, *Poland* 45 F1
Cée, *Spain* 34 C1
Cefalù, *Italy* 31 D7
Cega →, *Spain* 34 D6
Cegléd, *Hungary* 42 C4
Céglie Messápico, *Italy* 31 B10
Cehegín, *Spain* 33 G3
Ceheng, *China* 58 E5
Cehu-Silvaniei, *Romania* 43 C8
Ceica, *Romania* 42 D7
Ceira →, *Portugal* 34 E2
Čelákovice, *Czech Rep.* 26 A7
Celano, *Italy* 29 F10
Celanova, *Spain* 34 C3
Celaya, *Mexico* 118 C4
Celebes Sea, *Indonesia* 63 D6
Čelić, *Bos.-H.* 42 F3
Celina, *U.S.A.* 108 E3
Celinac, *Bos.-H.* 42 F2
Celje, *Slovenia* 29 B12
Celldömölk, *Hungary* 42 C2
Celle, *Germany* 24 C6
Celorico da Beira, *Portugal* 34 E3
Çeltikçi, *Turkey* 39 D12
Çemişgezek, *Turkey* 73 C8
Cenderwasih, Teluk, *Indonesia* 63 E9
Cengong, *China* 58 D7
Ceno →, *Italy* 28 D7
Centallo, *Italy* 28 D4
Centelles, *Spain* 32 D7
Center, *N. Dak., U.S.A.* 112 B4
Center, *Tex., U.S.A.* 113 K7
Centerburg, *U.S.A.* 110 F2
Centerville, *Calif., U.S.A.* 116 J7
Centerville, *Iowa, U.S.A.* 112 E8
Centerville, *Pa., U.S.A.* 110 F5
Centerville, *Tenn., U.S.A.* 109 H2
Centerville, *Tex., U.S.A.* 113 K7
Cento, *Italy* 29 D8
Central □, *Ghana* 83 D4
Central □, *Kenya* 86 C4
Central □, *Malawi* 87 E3
Central □, *Zambia* 87 E2
Central, Cordillera, *Colombia* 122 C3
Central, Cordillera, *Costa Rica* 120 D3
Central, Cordillera, *Dom. Rep.* 121 C5
Central, Cordillera, *Phil.* 61 C4
Central African Rep. ■, *Africa* 84 C4
Central America, *America* 98 H11
Central Butte, *Canada* 105 C7
Central City, *Colo., U.S.A.* 114 G11
Central City, *Ky., U.S.A.* 108 G2
Central City, *Nebr., U.S.A.* 112 E6
Central I., *Kenya* 86 B4
Central Makran Range, *Pakistan* 66 F4
Central Patricia, *Canada* 102 B1
Central Point, *U.S.A.* 114 E2
Central Russian Uplands, *Europe* 6 E13
Central Siberian Plateau, *Russia* 52 C14
Central Square, *U.S.A.* 111 C8
Centralia, *Ill., U.S.A.* 112 F10
Centralia, *Mo., U.S.A.* 112 F8
Centralia, *Wash., U.S.A.* 116 D4
Cenxi, *China* 59 F8
Čeotina →, *Bos.-H.* 40 C2
Cephalonia = Kefallinía, *Greece* 38 C2
Čepin, *Croatia* 42 E3
Ceprano, *Italy* 30 A6
Ceptura, *Romania* 43 E11
Cepu, *Indonesia* 63 G14
Ceram = Seram, *Indonesia* 63 E7
Ceram Sea = Seram Sea, *Indonesia* 63 E7
Cerbère, *France* 20 F7
Cerbicales, Is., *France* 21 G13
Cercal, *Portugal* 35 H2
Cerdaña, *Spain* 32 C6
Cère →, *France* 20 D5
Cerea, *Italy* 29 C8
Ceredigion □, *U.K.* 13 E3
Ceres, *Argentina* 126 B3
Ceres, *S. Africa* 88 E2
Ceres, *U.S.A.* 116 H6
Céret, *France* 20 F6
Cergy, *France* 19 C9
Cerignola, *Italy* 31 A8
Cerigo = Kíthira, *Greece* 38 E5
Cérilly, *France* 19 F9
Cerisiers, *France* 19 D10
Cerizay, *France* 18 F6
Çerkeş, *Turkey* 72 B5
Çerkezköy, *Turkey* 41 E12
Cerknica, *Slovenia* 29 C11
Cerkovica, *Bulgaria* 41 C8
Cermerno, *Serbia, Yug.* 40 C4
Çermik, *Turkey* 73 C8
Cerna, *Romania* 43 E13
Cerna →, *Romania* 43 F8
Cernavodă, *Romania* 43 F13
Cernay, *France* 19 E14
Cernik, *Croatia* 42 E2
Cerralvo, I., *Mexico* 118 C3
Cërrik, *Albania* 40 E3
Cerritos, *Mexico* 118 C4
Cerro Chato, *Uruguay* 127 C4
Certaldo, *Italy* 28 E8
Cervaro →, *Italy* 31 A8
Cervati, Monte, *Italy* 31 B8
Cerventes, *Australia* 93 F2
Cervera, *Spain* 32 D6
Cervera de Pisuerga, *Spain* 34 C6
Cervera del Río Alhama, *Spain* 32 C3
Cervéteri, *Italy* 29 F9
Cérvia, *Italy* 29 D9
Cervignano del Friuli, *Italy* 29 C10
Cervinara, *Italy* 31 A7
Cervione, *France* 21 F13
Cervo, *Spain* 34 B3
Cesarò, *Italy* 31 E7
Cesena, *Italy* 29 D9
Cesenático, *Italy* 29 D9
Cēsis, *Latvia* 9 H21
Česká Lípa, *Czech Rep.* 26 A7
Česká Třebová, *Czech Rep.* 27 B9
České Budějovice, *Czech Rep.* 26 C7
České Velenice, *Czech Rep.* 26 C7
Českobudějovický □, *Czech Rep.* 26 B7
Českomoravská Vrchovina, *Czech Rep.* 26 B8
Český Brod, *Czech Rep.* 26 A7

Český Krumlov, *Czech Rep.* 26 C7
Český Těšín, *Czech Rep.* 27 B11
Česma →, *Croatia* 29 C13
Çeşme, *Turkey* 39 C8
Cessnock, *Australia* 95 E5
Cesson-Sévigné, *France* 18 D5
Cestas, *France* 20 D3
Cestos →, *Liberia* 82 D3
Cetate, *Romania* 42 F8
Cetin Grad, *Croatia* 29 C12
Cetina →, *Croatia* 29 E13
Cetinje, *Montenegro, Yug.* 40 D2
Cetraro, *Italy* 31 C8
Ceuta, *N. Afr.* 78 A4
Ceva, *Italy* 28 D5
Cévennes, *France* 20 D7
Ceyhan, *Turkey* 70 B2
Ceyhan →, *Turkey* 72 D6
Ceylânpınar, *Turkey* 73 D9
Ceylon = Sri Lanka ■, *Asia* 66 R12
Cèze →, *France* 21 D8
Cha-am, *Thailand* 64 F2
Cha Pa, *Vietnam* 64 A4
Chabanais, *France* 20 C4
Chabeuil, *France* 21 D9
Chablais, *France* 19 F13
Chablis, *France* 19 E10
Chacabuco, *Argentina* 126 C3
Chachapoyas, *Peru* 124 E3
Chachoengsao, *Thailand* 64 F3
Chachran, *Pakistan* 66 E7
Chachro, *Pakistan* 68 G4
Chaco □, *Argentina* 126 B3
Chaco □, *Paraguay* 126 B4
Chaco →, *U.S.A.* 115 H9
Chaco Austral, *S. Amer.* 128 B4
Chaco Boreal, *S. Amer.* 124 H6
Chaco Central, *S. Amer.* 128 A4
Chacon, C., *U.S.A.* 104 C2
Chad ■, *Africa* 79 F8
Chad, L. = Tchad, L., *Chad* 79 F8
Chadan, *Russia* 51 D10
Chadileuvú →, *Argentina* 126 D2
Chadiza, *Zambia* 87 E3
Chadron, *U.S.A.* 112 D3
Chadyr-Lunga = Ciadâr-Lunga, *Moldova* 43 D13
Chae Hom, *Thailand* 64 C2
Chaem →, *Thailand* 64 C2
Chaeryŏng, *N. Korea* 57 E13
Chagai Hills = Chāh Gay, *Afghan.* 66 E3
Chagda, *Russia* 51 D14
Chaghcharān, *Afghan.* 66 B4
Chagny, *France* 19 F11
Chagoda, *Russia* 46 C8
Chagos Arch., *Ind. Oc.* 52 K11
Chagrin Falls, *U.S.A.* 110 E3
Chāh Ākhvor, *Iran* 71 C8
Chāh Bahar, *Iran* 71 E9
Chāh-e Kavīr, *Iran* 71 C8
Chāh Gay, *Afghan.* 66 E3
Chahar Burjak, *Afghan.* 66 D3
Chahār Mahāll va Bakhtīarī □, *Iran* 71 C6
Chaibasa, *India* 67 H14
Chaillé-les-Marais, *France* 20 B2
Chainat, *Thailand* 64 E3
Chaiya, *Thailand* 65 H2
Chaj Doab, *Pakistan* 68 C5
Chajari, *Argentina* 126 C4
Chak Amru, *Pakistan* 68 C6
Chaka, *Sudan* 81 G3
Chakar →, *Pakistan* 68 E3
Chakari, *Zimbabwe* 89 B4
Chake Chake, *Tanzania* 86 D4
Chakhānsūr, *Afghan.* 66 D3
Chakonipau, L., *Canada* 103 A6
Chakradharpur, *India* 69 H11
Chakrata, *India* 68 D7
Chakwal, *Pakistan* 68 C5
Chala, *Peru* 124 G4
Chalais, *France* 20 C4
Chalchihuites, *Mexico* 118 C4
Chalcis = Khalkís, *Greece* 38 C5
Châlette-sur-Loing, *France* 19 D9
Chaleur B., *Canada* 103 C6
Chalfant, *U.S.A.* 116 H8
Chalhuanca, *Peru* 124 F4
Chalindrey, *France* 19 E12
Chaling, *China* 59 D9
Chalisgaon, *India* 66 J9
Chalk River, *Canada* 102 C4
Chalky Inlet, *N.Z.* 91 M1
Challans, *France* 18 F5
Challapata, *Bolivia* 124 G5
Challis, *U.S.A.* 114 D6
Chalmette, *U.S.A.* 113 L10
Chalon-sur-Saône, *France* 19 F11
Chalonnes-sur-Loire, *France* 18 E6
Châlons-en-Champagne, *France* 19 D11
Châlus, *France* 20 C4
Chalyaphum, *Thailand* 64 E4
Cham, *Germany* 25 F8
Cham, Cu Lao, *Vietnam* 64 E7
Chama, *U.S.A.* 115 H10
Chamaicó, *Argentina* 126 D3
Chaman, *Pakistan* 66 D5
Chamba, *India* 68 C7
Chamba, *Tanzania* 87 E4
Chambal →, *India* 69 F8
Chamberlain, *U.S.A.* 112 D5
Chamberlain →, *Australia* 92 C4
Chamberlain L., *U.S.A.* 109 B11
Chambers, *U.S.A.* 115 J9
Chambersburg, *U.S.A.* 108 F7
Chambéry, *France* 21 C9
Chambeshi →, *Zambia* 84 G6
Chambly, *Canada* 111 A11
Chambord, *Canada* 103 C5
Chamboulive, *France* 20 C5
Chamchamal, *Iraq* 70 C5
Chamela, *Mexico* 118 D3
Chamical, *Argentina* 126 C2
Chamkar Luong, *Cambodia* 65 G4
Chamoli, *India* 69 D8
Chamonix-Mont Blanc, *France* 21 C10
Chamouchouane →, *Canada* 102 C5
Champa, *India* 69 H10
Champagne, *Canada* 104 A1
Champagne, *France* 19 D11
Champagnole, *France* 19 F12
Champaign, *U.S.A.* 108 E1
Champassak, *Laos* 64 E5
Champaubert, *France* 19 D10
Champawat, *India* 69 E9
Champdeniers-St-Denis, *France* 20 B3
Champdoré, L., *Canada* 103 A6
Champeix, *France* 20 C7
Champion, *U.S.A.* 110 E4
Champlain, *U.S.A.* 111 B11
Champlain, L., *U.S.A.* 111 B11
Champlitte, *France* 19 E12
Champotón, *Mexico* 119 D6
Champua, *India* 69 H11
Chamusca, *Portugal* 35 F2
Chana, *Thailand* 65 J3
Chañaral, *Chile* 126 B1
Chanārān, *Iran* 71 B8
Chanasma, *India* 68 H5
Chanco, *Chile* 126 D1
Chand, *India* 69 J8
Chandan, *India* 69 G12
Chandan Chauki, *India* 69 E9
Chandannagar, *India* 69 H13
Chandausi, *India* 69 E8
Chandeleur Is., *U.S.A.* 113 L10
Chandeleur Sd., *U.S.A.* 113 L10
Chandigarh, *India* 68 D7
Chandil, *India* 69 H12
Chandler, *Australia* 95 D1
Chandler, *Canada* 103 C7
Chandler, *Ariz., U.S.A.* 115 K8
Chandler, *Okla., U.S.A.* 113 H6
Chandod, *India* 68 J5
Chandpur, *Bangla.* 67 H17
Chandrapur, *India* 66 K11
Chānf, *Iran* 71 E9
Chang, *Pakistan* 68 F3
Chang, Ko, *Thailand* 65 F4
Ch'ang Chiang = Chang Jiang →, *China* 59 B13
Chang Jiang →, *China* 59 B13
Changa, *India* 69 C7
Changanacheri, *India* 66 Q10
Changane →, *Mozam.* 89 C5
Changbai, *China* 57 D15
Changbai Shan, *China* 57 C15
Changchiak'ou = Zhangjiakou, *China* 56 D8
Ch'angchou = Changzhou, *China* 59 B12
Changchun, *China* 57 C13
Changchunling, *China* 57 B13
Changde, *China* 59 C8
Changdo-ri, *N. Korea* 57 E14
Changfeng, *China* 59 A11
Changhai = Shanghai, *China* 59 B13
Changhua, *China* 59 B12
Changhua, *Taiwan* 59 E13
Changhŭng, *S. Korea* 57 G14
Changhŭngni, *N. Korea* 57 D15
Changjiang, *China* 64 C7
Changjin, *N. Korea* 57 D14
Changjin-chŏsuji, *N. Korea* 57 D14
Changle, *China* 59 E12
Changli, *China* 57 E10
Changling, *China* 57 B12
Changlun, *Malaysia* 65 J3
Changning, *Hunan, China* 59 D9
Changning, *Sichuan, China* 58 C5
Changning, *Yunnan, China* 58 E2
Changping, *China* 56 D9
Changsha, *China* 59 C9
Changshan, *China* 59 C12
Changshu, *China* 59 B13
Changshun, *China* 58 D6
Changtai, *China* 59 E11
Changting, *China* 59 E11
Changwu, *China* 56 G4
Changxing, *China* 59 B12
Changyang, *China* 59 B8
Changyi, *China* 57 F10
Changyŏn, *N. Korea* 57 E13
Changyuan, *China* 56 G8
Changzhi, *China* 56 F7
Changzhou, *China* 59 B12
Chanhanga, *Angola* 88 B1
Chanlar = Xanlar, *Azerbaijan* 49 K8
Channapatna, *India* 66 N10
Channel Is., *U.K.* 13 H5
Channel Is., *U.S.A.* 117 M7
Channel Islands National Park, *U.S.A.* 117 M8
Channel-Port aux Basques, *Canada* 103 C8
Channel Tunnel, *Europe* 13 F9
Channing, *U.S.A.* 113 H3
Chantada, *Spain* 34 C3
Chanthaburi, *Thailand* 64 F4
Chantilly, *France* 19 C9
Chantonnay, *France* 18 F5
Chantrey Inlet, *Canada* 100 B10
Chanute, *U.S.A.* 113 G7
Chanza →, *Spain* 35 H3
Chao Hu, *China* 59 B11
Chao Phraya →, *Thailand* 64 F3
Chao Phraya Lowlands, *Thailand* 64 E3
Chaocheng, *China* 56 F8
Chaohu, *China* 59 B11
Chaoyang, *Guangdong, China* 59 F11
Chaoyang, *Liaoning, China* 57 D11
Chaozhou, *China* 59 F11
Chapais, *Canada* 102 C5
Chapala, *Mozam.* 87 F4
Chapala, L. de, *Mexico* 118 C4
Chapayev, *Kazakstan* 48 E10
Chapayevsk, *Russia* 48 D9
Chapecó, *Brazil* 127 B5
Chapel Hill, *U.S.A.* 109 H6
Chapleau, *Canada* 102 C3
Chaplin, *Canada* 105 C7
Chaplin L., *Canada* 105 C7
Chaplino, *Ukraine* 47 H9
Chaplygin, *Russia* 46 F11
Chappell, *U.S.A.* 112 E3
Chapra = Chhapra, *India* 69 G11
Chara, *Russia* 51 D12
Charadai, *Argentina* 126 B4
Charagua, *Bolivia* 124 G6
Charambirá, Punta, *Colombia* 124 C3
Charaña, *Bolivia* 124 G5
Charantsavan, *Armenia* 49 K7
Charanwala, *India* 68 F5
Charata, *Argentina* 126 B3
Charcas, *Mexico* 118 C4
Chard, *U.K.* 13 G5
Chardon, *U.S.A.* 110 E3
Chardzhou = Chärjew, *Turkmenistan* 50 F7
Charente □, *France* 20 C4
Charente →, *France* 20 C2
Charente-Maritime □, *France* 20 C3
Charenton-du-Cher, *France* 19 F9
Chari →, *Chad* 79 F8
Chārīkār, *Afghan.* 66 B6
Chariton →, *U.S.A.* 112 F8
Chärjew, *Turkmenistan* 50 F7
Charkhari, *India* 69 G8
Charkhi Dadri, *India* 68 E7
Charleroi, *Belgium* 17 D4
Charleroi, *U.S.A.* 110 F5
Charles, C., *U.S.A.* 108 G8
Charles City, *U.S.A.* 112 D8
Charles L., *Canada* 105 B6
Charles Town, *U.S.A.* 108 F7
Charleston, *Ill., U.S.A.* 108 F1
Charleston, *Miss., U.S.A.* 113 H9
Charleston, *Mo., U.S.A.* 113 G10
Charleston, *S.C., U.S.A.* 109 J6
Charleston, *W. Va., U.S.A.* 108 F5
Charleston L., *Canada* 111 B9
Charleston Peak, *U.S.A.* 117 J11
Charlestown, *Ireland* 15 C3
Charlestown, *S. Africa* 89 D4
Charlestown, *Ind., U.S.A.* 108 F3
Charlestown, *N.H., U.S.A.* 111 C12
Charleville = Rath Luirc, *Ireland* 15 D3
Charleville, *Australia* 95 D4
Charleville-Mézières, *France* 19 C11
Charlevoix, *U.S.A.* 108 C3
Charlieu, *France* 19 F11
Charlotte, *Mich., U.S.A.* 108 D3
Charlotte, *N.C., U.S.A.* 109 H5
Charlotte, *Vt., U.S.A.* 111 B11
Charlotte Amalie, *U.S. Virgin Is.* 121 C7
Charlotte Harbor, *U.S.A.* 109 M4
Charlotte L., *Canada* 104 C3
Charlottenberg, *Sweden* 10 E6
Charlottesville, *U.S.A.* 108 F6
Charlottetown, *Nfld., Canada* 103 B8
Charlottetown, *P.E.I., Canada* 103 C7
Charlton, *Australia* 95 F3
Charlton, *U.S.A.* 112 E8
Charlton I., *Canada* 102 B4
Charmes, *France* 19 D13
Charny, *Canada* 103 C5
Charolles, *France* 19 F11
Chârost, *France* 19 F9
Charre, *Mozam.* 87 F4
Charroux, *France* 20 B4
Charsadda, *Pakistan* 68 B4
Charters Towers, *Australia* 94 C4
Chartres, *France* 18 D8
Chascomús, *Argentina* 126 D4
Chasefu, *Zambia* 87 E3
Chashma Barrage, *Pakistan* 68 C4
Chasseneuil-sur-Bonnieure, *France* 20 C4
Chāt, *Iran* 71 B7
Chatal Balkan = Udvoy Balkan, *Bulgaria* 41 D10
Château-Arnoux, *France* 21 D10
Château-Chinon, *France* 19 E10
Château-d'Olonne, *France* 20 B2
Château-du-Loir, *France* 18 E7
Château-Gontier, *France* 18 E6
Château-la-Vallière, *France* 18 E7
Château-Landon, *France* 19 D9
Château-Renault, *France* 18 E7
Château-Salins, *France* 19 D13
Château-Thierry, *France* 19 C10
Châteaubourg, *France* 18 D5
Châteaubriant, *France* 18 E5
Châteaudun, *France* 18 D8
Chateaugay, *U.S.A.* 111 B10
Châteaugiron, *France* 18 D5
Châteauguay, L., *Canada* 103 A5
Châteaulin, *France* 18 D2
Châteaumeillant, *France* 19 F9
Châteauneuf-du-Faou, *France* 18 D3
Châteauneuf-sur-Charente, *France* 20 C3
Châteauneuf-sur-Cher, *France* 19 F9
Châteauneuf-sur-Loire, *France* 19 E9
Châteaurenard, *Bouches-du-Rhône, France* 21 E8
Châteaurenard, *Loiret, France* 19 E9
Châteauroux, *France* 19 F8
Châteauvillain, *France* 19 D11
Châtelaillon-Plage, *France* 20 B2
Châtelguyon, *France* 20 C7
Châtellerault, *France* 18 F7
Châtelus-Malvaleix, *France* 19 F9
Chatham = Miramichi, *Canada* 103 C6
Chatham, *Canada* 102 D3
Chatham, *U.K.* 13 F8
Chatham, *U.S.A.* 111 D11
Chatham Is., *Pac. Oc.* 96 M10
Châtillon, *Italy* 28 C4
Châtillon-Coligny, *France* 19 E9
Châtillon-en-Diois, *France* 21 D9
Châtillon-sur-Indre, *France* 18 F8
Châtillon-sur-Loire, *France* 19 E9
Châtillon-sur-Seine, *France* 19 E11
Chatmohar, *Bangla.* 69 G13
Chatra, *India* 69 G11
Chatrapur, *India* 67 K14
Chats, L. des, *Canada* 111 A8
Chatsu, *India* 68 F6
Chatsworth, *Canada* 110 B4
Chatsworth, *Zimbabwe* 87 F3
Chattahoochee, *U.S.A.* 109 K3
Chattahoochee →, *U.S.A.* 109 K3
Chattanooga, *U.S.A.* 109 H3
Chatteris, *U.K.* 13 E8
Chaturat, *Thailand* 64 E3
Chau Doc, *Vietnam* 65 G5
Chaudes-Aigues, *France* 20 D7
Chauffailles, *France* 19 F11
Chaukan Pass, *Burma* 67 F20
Chaumont, *France* 19 D12
Chaumont, *U.S.A.* 111 B8
Chaumont-en-Vexin, *France* 19 C8
Chaumont-sur-Loire, *France* 18 E8
Chaunay, *France* 20 B4
Chauny, *France* 19 C10
Chausey, Îs., *France* 18 D5
Chaussin, *France* 19 F12
Chautauqua L., *U.S.A.* 110 D5
Chauvigny, *France* 18 F7
Chauvin, *Canada* 105 C6
Chavanges, *France* 19 D11
Chaves, *Brazil* 125 D9
Chaves, *Portugal* 34 D3
Chawang, *Thailand* 65 H2
Chazelles-sur-Lyon, *France* 21 C8
Chazy, *U.S.A.* 111 B11
Cheb, *Czech Rep.* 26 A5
Cheboksarskoye Vdkhr., *Russia* 48 B8
Cheboksary, *Russia* 48 B8
Cheboygan, *U.S.A.* 108 C3
Chebsara, *Russia* 46 C10
Chech, Erg, *Africa* 78 D5
Chechen, Ostrov, *Russia* 49 H8
Chechenia □, *Russia* 49 J7
Checheno-Ingush Republic = Chechenia □, *Russia* 49 J7
Chechnya = Chechenia □, *Russia* 49 J7
Chech'ŏn, *S. Korea* 57 F15
Chęciny, *Poland* 45 H7
Checotah, *U.S.A.* 113 H7
Chedabucto B., *Canada* 103 C7
Cheduba I., *Burma* 67 K18
Cheepie, *Australia* 95 D4
Chef-Boutonne, *France* 20 B3
Chegdomyn, *Russia* 51 D14
Chegga, *Mauritania* 78 C4
Chegutu, *Zimbabwe* 87 F3
Chehalis, *U.S.A.* 116 D4
Chehalis →, *U.S.A.* 116 D3
Cheiron, Mt., *France* 21 E10
Cheju do, *S. Korea* 57 H14
Chekalin, *Russia* 46 E9
Chekiang = Zhejiang □, *China* 59 C13
Chel = Kuru, Bahr el →, *Sudan* 81 F2
Chela, Sa. da, *Angola* 88 B1
Chelan, *U.S.A.* 114 C4
Chelan, L., *U.S.A.* 114 B3
Cheleken, *Turkmenistan* 50 F6
Cheleken Yarymadasy, *Turkmenistan* 71 B7
Chelforó, *Argentina* 128 D3
Chelkar = Shalqar, *Kazakstan* 50 E6
Chelkar Tengiz, Solonchak, *Kazakstan* 50 E7
Chella, *Ethiopia* 81 F4
Chelles, *France* 19 D9
Chełm, *Poland* 45 G10
Chełmno, *Poland* 45 E5
Chelmsford, *U.K.* 13 F8
Chełmża, *Poland* 45 E5
Chelsea, *U.S.A.* 111 C12
Cheltenham, *U.K.* 13 F5
Chelva, *Spain* 32 F4
Chelyabinsk, *Russia* 50 D7
Chelyuskin, C., *Russia* 52 B14
Chemainus, *Canada* 116 B3
Chemba, *Mozam.* 85 H6
Chembar = Belinskiy, *Russia* 48 D6
Chemillé, *France* 18 E6
Chemnitz, *Germany* 24 E8
Chemult, *U.S.A.* 114 E3
Chen, Gora, *Russia* 51 C15
Chenab →, *Pakistan* 68 D4
Chenango Forks, *U.S.A.* 111 D9
Chencha, *Ethiopia* 81 F4
Chenchiang = Zhenjiang, *China* 59 A12
Cheney, *U.S.A.* 114 C5
Cheng Xian, *China* 56 H3
Chengbu, *China* 59 D8
Chengcheng, *China* 56 G5
Chengchou = Zhengzhou, *China* 56 G7
Chengde, *China* 57 D9
Chengdong Hu, *China* 59 A11
Chengdu, *China* 58 B5
Chenggong, *China* 58 E4
Chenggu, *China* 56 H4
Chenghai, *China* 59 F11
Chengjiang, *China* 58 E4
Chengkou, *China* 58 B7
Ch'engmai, *China* 64 C7
Ch'engtu = Chengdu, *China* 58 B5
Chengwu, *China* 56 G8
Chengxi Hu, *China* 59 A11
Chengyang, *China* 57 F11
Chenjiagang, *China* 57 G10
Chenkán, *Mexico* 119 D6
Chennai, *India* 66 N12
Chenôve, *France* 19 E12
Chenxi, *China* 59 C8
Chenzhou, *China* 59 E9
Cheo Reo, *Vietnam* 62 B3
Cheom Ksan, *Cambodia* 64 E5
Chepelare, *Bulgaria* 41 E8
Chepén, *Peru* 124 E3
Chepes, *Argentina* 126 C2
Chepo, *Panama* 120 E4
Chepstow, *U.K.* 13 F5
Cheptulil, Mt., *Kenya* 86 B4
Chequamegon B., *U.S.A.* 112 B9
Cher □, *France* 19 E9
Cher →, *France* 18 E7
Chéradi, *Italy* 31 B10
Cherasco, *Italy* 28 D4
Cheraw, *U.S.A.* 109 H6
Cherbourg, *France* 18 C5
Cherdakly, *Russia* 48 C9
Cherdyn, *Russia* 50 C6
Cheremkhovo, *Russia* 51 D11
Cherepanovo, *Russia* 50 D9
Cherepovets, *Russia* 46 C9
Chergui, Chott ech, *Algeria* 78 B6
Cherikov = Cherykaw, *Belarus* 46 F6
Cherkasy, *Ukraine* 47 H7
Cherkessk, *Russia* 49 H6
Cherlak, *Russia* 50 D8
Chernaya, *Russia* 51 B9
Cherni, *Bulgaria* 40 D7
Chernigov = Chernihiv, *Ukraine* 47 G6
Chernihiv, *Ukraine* 47 G6
Chernivtsi, *Ukraine* 47 H3
Chernobyl = Chornobyl, *Ukraine* 47 G6
Chernogorsk, *Russia* 51 D10
Chernomorskoye = Chornomorske, *Ukraine* 47 K7
Chernovtsy = Chernivtsi, *Ukraine* 47 H3
Chernyakhovsk, *Russia* 9 J19
Chernyanka, *Russia* 47 G9
Chernysheyskiy, *Russia* 51 C12
Chernyye Zemli, *Russia* 49 H8
Cherokee, *Iowa, U.S.A.* 112 D7
Cherokee, *Okla., U.S.A.* 113 G5
Cherokee Village, *U.S.A.* 113 G9
Cherokees, Grand Lake O' The, *U.S.A.* 113 G7
Cherrapunji, *India* 67 G17
Cherry Valley, *Calif., U.S.A.* 117 M10
Cherry Valley, *N.Y., U.S.A.* 111 D10
Cherskiy, *Russia* 51 C17
Cherskogo Khrebet, *Russia* 51 C15
Chertkovo, *Russia* 47 H11
Cherven, *Belarus* 46 F5
Cherven-Bryag, *Bulgaria* 41 C8
Chervonohrad, *Ukraine* 47 G3
Cherwell →, *U.K.* 13 F6
Cherykaw, *Belarus* 46 F6
Chesapeake, *U.S.A.* 108 G7
Chesapeake B., *U.S.A.* 108 G7
Cheshire □, *U.K.* 12 D5
Cheshskaya Guba, *Russia* 50 C5
Cheshunt, *U.K.* 13 F7
Chesil Beach, *U.K.* 13 G5
Chesley, *Canada* 110 B3
Cheste, *Spain* 33 F4
Chester, *U.K.* 12 D5
Chester, *Calif., U.S.A.* 114 F3
Chester, *Ill., U.S.A.* 113 G10
Chester, *Mont., U.S.A.* 114 B8
Chester, *Pa., U.S.A.* 108 F8
Chester, *S.C., U.S.A.* 109 H5
Chester, *Vt., U.S.A.* 111 C12
Chester, *W. Va., U.S.A.* 110 F4
Chester-le-Street, *U.K.* 12 C6
Chesterfield, *U.K.* 12 D6
Chesterfield, Is., *N. Cal.* 96 J7
Chesterfield Inlet, *Canada* 100 B10
Chesterton Ra., *Australia* 95 D4
Chestertown, *U.S.A.* 111 C11
Chesterville, *Canada* 111 A9
Chestnut Ridge, *U.S.A.* 110 F5
Chesuncook L., *U.S.A.* 109 C11
Chéticamp, *Canada* 103 C7
Chetrosu, *Moldova* 43 B12
Chetumal, *Mexico* 119 D7
Chetumal, B. de, *Mexico* 119 D7
Chetwynd, *Canada* 104 B4
Chevanceaux, *France* 20 C3
Cheviot, The, *U.K.* 12 B5
Cheviot Hills, *U.K.* 12 B5
Cheviot Ra., *Australia* 94 D3
Chew Bahir, *Ethiopia* 81 G4
Chewelah, *U.S.A.* 114 B5

Cheyenne, *Okla., U.S.A.* 113 H5
Cheyenne, *Wyo., U.S.A.* 112 E2
Cheyenne →, *U.S.A.* 112 C4
Cheyenne Wells, *U.S.A.* 112 F3
Cheyne B., *Australia* 93 F2
Chhabra, *India* 68 G7
Chhaktala, *India* 68 H6
Chhapra, *India* 69 G11
Chhata, *India* 68 F7
Chhatarpur, *Bihar, India* 69 G11
Chhatarpur, *Mad. P., India* 69 G8
Chhattisgarh □, *India* 69 J10
Chhep, *Cambodia* 64 F5
Chhindwara, *Mad. P., India* 69 H8
Chhindwara, *Mad. P., India* 69 H8
Chhlong, *Cambodia* 65 F5
Chhota Tawa →, *India* 68 H7
Chhoti Kali Sindh →, *India* 68 G6
Chhuikhadan, *India* 69 J9
Chhuk, *Cambodia* 65 G5
Chi →, *Thailand* 64 E5
Chiai, *Taiwan* 59 F13
Chiali, *Taiwan* 59 F13
Chiamboni, *Somali Rep.* 84 E8
Chiamussu = Jiamusi, *China* 60 B8
Chianciano Terme, *Italy* 29 E8
Chiang Dao, *Thailand* 64 C2
Chiang Kham, *Thailand* 64 C3
Chiang Khan, *Thailand* 64 D3
Chiang Khong, *Thailand* 58 G3
Chiang Mai, *Thailand* 64 C2
Chiang Rai, *Thailand* 58 H2
Chiang Saen, *Thailand* 58 G3
Chiapa →, *Mexico* 119 D6
Chiapa de Corzo, *Mexico* 119 D6
Chiapas □, *Mexico* 119 D6
Chiaramonte Gulfi, *Italy* 31 E7
Chiaravalle, *Italy* 29 E10
Chiaravalle Centrale, *Italy* 31 D9
Chiari, *Italy* 28 C6
Chiatura, *Georgia* 49 J6
Chiautla, *Mexico* 119 D5
Chiávari, *Italy* 28 D6
Chiavenna, *Italy* 28 B6
Chiba, *Japan* 55 G10
Chiba □, *Japan* 55 G10
Chibabava, *Mozam.* 89 C5
Chibemba, *Cunene, Angola* 85 H2
Chibemba, *Huila, Angola* 88 B2
Chibi, *Zimbabwe* 89 C5
Chibia, *Angola* 85 H2
Chibougamau, *Canada* 102 C5
Chibougamau, L., *Canada* 102 C5
Chibuk, *Nigeria* 83 C7
Chibuto, *Mozam.* 89 C5
Chic-Chocs, Mts., *Canada* 103 C6
Chicacole = Srikakulam, *India* 67 K13
Chicago, *U.S.A.* 108 E2
Chicago Heights, *U.S.A.* 108 E2
Chichagof I., *U.S.A.* 100 C6
Chichén-Itzá, *Mexico* 119 C7
Chicheng, *China* 56 D8
Chichester, *U.K.* 13 G7
Chichester Ra., *Australia* 92 D2
Chichibu, *Japan* 55 F9
Ch'ich'ihaerh = Qiqihar, *China* 51 E13
Chicholi, *India* 68 H8
Chickasha, *U.S.A.* 113 H6
Chiclana de la Frontera, *Spain* 35 J4
Chiclayo, *Peru* 124 E3
Chico, *U.S.A.* 116 F5
Chico →, *Chubut, Argentina* 128 E3
Chico →, *Santa Cruz, Argentina* 128 G3
Chicomo, *Mozam.* 89 C5
Chicontepec, *Mexico* 119 C5
Chicopee, *U.S.A.* 111 D12
Chicoutimi, *Canada* 103 C5
Chicualacuala, *Mozam.* 89 C5
Chidambaram, *India* 66 P11
Chidenguele, *Mozam.* 89 C5
Chidley, C., *Canada* 101 B13
Chiducuane, *Mozam.* 89 C5
Chiede, *Angola* 88 B2
Chiefs Pt., *Canada* 110 B3
Chiem Hoa, *Vietnam* 64 A5
Chiemsee, *Germany* 25 H8
Chiengi, *Zambia* 87 D2
Chiengmai = Chiang Mai, *Thailand* 64 C2
Chienti →, *Italy* 29 E10
Chieri, *Italy* 28 C4
Chiers →, *France* 19 C11
Chiesa in Valmalenco, *Italy* 28 B6
Chiese →, *Italy* 28 C7
Chieti, *Italy* 29 F11
Chifeng, *China* 57 C10
Chigirin, *Ukraine* 47 H7
Chignecto B., *Canada* 103 C7
Chiguana, *Bolivia* 126 A2
Chigwell, *U.K.* 13 F8
Chiha-ri, *N. Korea* 57 E14
Chihli, G. of = Bo Hai, *China* 57 E10
Chihuahua, *Mexico* 118 B3
Chihuahua □, *Mexico* 118 B3
Chiili = Shīeli, *Kazakstan* 50 E7
Chik Bollapur, *India* 66 N10
Chikmagalur, *India* 66 N9
Chikwawa, *Malawi* 87 F3
Chilac, *Mexico* 119 D5
Chilam Chavki, *Pakistan* 69 B6
Chilanga, *Zambia* 87 F2
Chilapa, *Mexico* 119 D5
Chilas, *Pakistan* 69 B6
Chilaw, *Sri Lanka* 66 R11
Chilcotin →, *Canada* 104 C4
Childers, *Australia* 95 D5
Childress, *U.S.A.* 113 H4
Chile ■, *S. Amer.* 128 D2
Chile Rise, *Pac. Oc.* 97 L18
Chilecito, *Argentina* 126 B2
Chilete, *Peru* 124 E3
Chilia, Braţul →, *Romania* 43 E14
Chililabombwe, *Zambia* 87 E2
Chilin = Jilin, *China* 57 C14
Chilka L., *India* 67 K14
Chilko →, *Canada* 104 C4
Chilko L., *Canada* 104 C4
Chillagoe, *Australia* 94 B3
Chillán, *Chile* 126 D1
Chillicothe, *Ill., U.S.A.* 112 E10
Chillicothe, *Mo., U.S.A.* 112 F8
Chillicothe, *Ohio, U.S.A.* 108 F4
Chilliwack, *Canada* 104 D4
Chilo, *India* 68 F5
Chiloane, I., *Mozam.* 89 C5
Chiloé, I. de, *Chile* 122 H3
Chilpancingo, *Mexico* 119 D5
Chiltern Hills, *U.K.* 13 F7
Chilton, *U.S.A.* 108 C1
Chilubi, *Zambia* 87 E2
Chilubula, *Zambia* 87 E3
Chilumba, *Malawi* 87 E3
Chilung, *Taiwan* 59 E13
Chilwa, L., *Malawi* 87 F4
Chimaltitán, *Mexico* 118 C4
Chimán, *Panama* 120 E4
Chimanimani, *Zimbabwe* 89 B5
Chimay, *Belgium* 17 D4
Chimayo, *U.S.A.* 115 H11
Chimbay, *Uzbekistan* 50 E6
Chimborazo, *Ecuador* 122 D3
Chimbote, *Peru* 124 E3
Chimkent = Shymkent, *Kazakstan* 50 E7
Chimoio, *Mozam.* 87 F3
Chimpembe, *Zambia* 87 D2
Chin □, *Burma* 67 J18
Chin Ling Shan = Qinling Shandi, *China* 56 H5
China, *Mexico* 119 B5
China ■, *Asia* 60 D6
China Lake, *U.S.A.* 117 K9
Chinan = Jinan, *China* 56 F9
Chinandega, *Nic.* 120 D2
Chinati Peak, *U.S.A.* 113 L2
Chincha Alta, *Peru* 122 E3
Chinchaga →, *Canada* 104 B5
Chinchilla, *Australia* 95 D5
Chinchilla de Monte Aragón, *Spain* 33 G3
Chinchorro, Banco, *Mexico* 119 D7
Chinchou = Jinzhou, *China* 57 D11
Chincoteague, *U.S.A.* 108 G8
Chinde, *Mozam.* 87 F4
Chindo, *S. Korea* 57 G14
Chindwin →, *Burma* 67 J19
Chineni, *India* 69 C6
Chinga, *Mozam.* 87 F4
Chingola, *Zambia* 87 E2
Chingole, *Malawi* 87 E3
Ch'ingtao = Qingdao, *China* 57 F11
Chinguetti, *Mauritania* 78 D3
Chingune, *Mozam.* 89 C5
Chinhae, *S. Korea* 57 G15
Chinhanguanine, *Mozam.* 89 D5
Chinhoyi, *Zimbabwe* 87 F3
Chini, *India* 68 D8
Chiniot, *Pakistan* 68 D5
Chínipas, *Mexico* 118 B3
Chinji, *Pakistan* 68 C5
Chinju, *S. Korea* 57 G15
Chinle, *U.S.A.* 115 H9
Chinmen, *Taiwan* 59 E13
Chinmen Tao, *Taiwan* 59 E12
Chinnampo = Namp'o, *N. Korea* 57 E13
Chino, *Japan* 55 G9
Chino, *U.S.A.* 117 L9
Chino Valley, *U.S.A.* 115 J7
Chinon, *France* 18 E7
Chinook, *U.S.A.* 114 B9
Chinsali, *Zambia* 87 E3
Chióggia, *Italy* 29 C9
Chíos = Khíos, *Greece* 39 C8
Chipata, *Zambia* 87 E3
Chiperceni, *Moldova* 43 C13
Chipinge, *Zimbabwe* 87 G3
Chipiona, *Spain* 35 J4
Chipley, *U.S.A.* 109 K3
Chipman, *Canada* 103 C6
Chipoka, *Malawi* 87 E3
Chippenham, *U.K.* 13 F5
Chippewa →, *U.S.A.* 112 C8
Chippewa Falls, *U.S.A.* 112 C9
Chipping Norton, *U.K.* 13 F6
Chiprovtsi, *Bulgaria* 40 C6
Chiputneticook Lakes, *U.S.A.* 109 C11
Chiquián, *Peru* 124 F3
Chiquimula, *Guatemala* 120 D2
Chiquinquira, *Colombia* 124 B4
Chir →, *Russia* 49 F6
Chirala, *India* 66 M12
Chiramba, *Mozam.* 87 F3
Chirawa, *India* 68 E6
Chirchiq, *Uzbekistan* 50 E7
Chiredzi, *Zimbabwe* 89 C5
Chiricahua Peak, *U.S.A.* 115 L9
Chiriquí, G. de, *Panama* 120 E3
Chiriquí, L. de, *Panama* 120 E3
Chirivira Falls, *Zimbabwe* 87 G3
Chirmiri, *India* 67 H13
Chirnogi, *Romania* 43 F11
Chirpan, *Bulgaria* 41 D9
Chirripó Grande, Cerro, *Costa Rica* 120 E3
Chirundu, *Zimbabwe* 89 B4
Chisamba, *Zambia* 87 E2
Chisapani Garhi, *Nepal* 67 F14
Chisasibi, *Canada* 102 B4
Ch'ishan, *Taiwan* 59 F13
Chisholm, *Canada* 104 C6
Chisholm, *U.S.A.* 112 B8
Chishtian Mandi, *Pakistan* 68 E5
Chishui, *China* 58 C5
Chishui He →, *China* 58 C5
Chisimaio, *Somali Rep.* 77 G8
Chisimba Falls, *Zambia* 87 E3
Chişinău, *Moldova* 43 C13
Chişineu Criş, *Romania* 42 D6
Chisone →, *Italy* 28 D4
Chisos Mts., *U.S.A.* 113 L3
Chistopol, *Russia* 48 C10
Chita, *Russia* 51 D12
Chitipa, *Malawi* 87 D3
Chitose, *Japan* 54 C10
Chitral, *Pakistan* 66 B7
Chitré, *Panama* 120 E3
Chittagong, *Bangla.* 67 H17
Chittagong □, *Bangla.* 67 G17
Chittaurgarh, *India* 68 G6
Chittoor, *India* 66 N11
Chitungwiza, *Zimbabwe* 87 F3
Chiusi, *Italy* 29 E8
Chiva, *Spain* 33 F4
Chivasso, *Italy* 28 C4
Chivhu, *Zimbabwe* 87 F3
Chivilcoy, *Argentina* 126 C4
Chiwanda, *Tanzania* 87 E3
Chixi, *China* 59 G9
Chizera, *Zambia* 87 E2
Chkalov = Orenburg, *Russia* 50 D6
Chkolovsk, *Russia* 48 B6
Chloride, *U.S.A.* 117 K12
Chlumec nad Cidlinou, *Czech Rep.* 26 A8
Chmielnik, *Poland* 45 H7
Cho Bo, *Vietnam* 58 G5
Cho-do, *N. Korea* 57 E13
Cho Phuoc Hai, *Vietnam* 65 G6
Choba, *Kenya* 86 B4
Chobe National Park, *Botswana* 88 B4
Choch'iwŏn, *S. Korea* 57 F14
Chocianów, *Poland* 45 G2
Chociwel, *Poland* 44 E2
Chocolate Mts., *U.S.A.* 117 M11
Choctawhatchee →, *U.S.A.* 109 K3
Chodecz, *Poland* 45 F6
Chodov, *Czech Rep.* 26 A5
Chodziez, *Poland* 45 F3
Choele Choel, *Argentina* 128 D3
Choix, *Mexico* 118 B3
Chojna, *Poland* 45 F1
Chojnice, *Poland* 44 E4
Chojnów, *Poland* 45 G2
Chōkai-San, *Japan* 54 E10
Choke, *Ethiopia* 81 E4
Choke Canyon L., *U.S.A.* 113 L5
Chokurdakh, *Russia* 51 B15
Cholame, *U.S.A.* 116 K6
Cholet, *France* 18 E6
Cholguan, *Chile* 126 D1
Choluteca, *Honduras* 120 D2
Choluteca →, *Honduras* 120 D2
Chom Bung, *Thailand* 64 F2
Chom Thong, *Thailand* 64 C2
Choma, *Zambia* 87 F2
Chomen Swamp, *Ethiopia* 81 F4
Chomun, *India* 68 F6
Chomutov, *Czech Rep.* 26 A6
Chon Buri, *Thailand* 64 F3
Chon Thanh, *Vietnam* 65 G6
Ch'onan, *S. Korea* 57 F14
Chone, *Ecuador* 124 D3
Chong Kai, *Cambodia* 64 F4
Chong Mek, *Thailand* 64 E5
Chongde, *China* 59 B13
Chŏngdo, *S. Korea* 57 G15
Chŏngha, *S. Korea* 57 F15
Chŏngjin, *N. Korea* 57 D15
Chŏngjiu, *S. Korea* 57 F14
Chŏngju, *N. Korea* 57 E13
Chongli, *China* 56 D8
Chongming, *China* 59 B13
Chongming Dao, *China* 59 B13
Chongqing, *Chongqing, China* 58 C6
Chongqing, *Sichuan, China* 58 B4
Chongqing Shi □, *China* 58 C6
Chongren, *China* 59 D11
Chonguene, *Mozam.* 89 C5
Chŏngŭp, *S. Korea* 57 G14
Chongyi, *China* 59 E10
Chongzuo, *China* 58 F6
Chŏnju, *S. Korea* 57 G14
Chonos, Arch. de los, *Chile* 122 H3
Chop, *Ukraine* 47 H2
Chopim →, *Brazil* 127 B5
Chor, *Pakistan* 68 G3
Chorbat La, *India* 69 B7
Chorley, *U.K.* 12 D5
Chornobyl, *Ukraine* 47 G6
Chornomorske, *Ukraine* 47 K7
Chorolque, Cerro, *Bolivia* 126 A2
Choroszcz, *Poland* 45 E9
Chorregon, *Australia* 94 C3
Chortkiv, *Ukraine* 47 H3
Ch'ŏrwon, *S. Korea* 57 E14
Chorzele, *Poland* 45 E7
Chorzów, *Poland* 45 H5
Chos-Malal, *Argentina* 126 D1
Ch'osan, *N. Korea* 57 D13
Choszczno, *Poland* 45 E2
Choteau, *U.S.A.* 114 C7
Chotěboř, *Czech Rep.* 26 B8
Chotila, *India* 68 H4
Chotta Udepur, *India* 68 H6
Chowchilla, *U.S.A.* 116 H6
Choybalsan, *Mongolia* 60 B6
Christchurch, *N.Z.* 91 K4
Christchurch, *U.K.* 13 G6
Christian I., *Canada* 110 B4
Christiana, *S. Africa* 88 D4
Christiansfeld, *Denmark* 11 J3
Christiansted, *U.S. Virgin Is.* 121 C7
Christie B., *Canada* 105 A6
Christina →, *Canada* 105 B6
Christmas Cr. →, *Australia* 92 C4
Christmas I. = Kiritimati, *Kiribati* 97 G12
Christmas I., *Ind. Oc.* 96 J2
Christopher L., *Australia* 93 D4
Chrudim, *Czech Rep.* 26 B8
Chrzanów, *Poland* 45 H6
Chtimba, *Malawi* 87 E3
Chu = Shū, *Kazakstan* 50 E8
Chu →, *Vietnam* 64 C5
Chu Lai, *Vietnam* 64 E7
Ch'uanchou = Quanzhou, *China* 59 E12
Chuankou, *China* 56 G6
Chubbuck, *U.S.A.* 114 E7
Chūbu □, *Japan* 55 F8
Chubut →, *Argentina* 122 H4
Chuchi L., *Canada* 104 B4
Chuda, *India* 68 H4
Chudovo, *Russia* 46 C6
Chudskoye, Ozero, *Russia* 9 G22
Chūgoku □, *Japan* 55 G6
Chūgoku-Sanchi, *Japan* 55 G6
Chuguyev = Chuhuyiv, *Ukraine* 47 H9
Chugwater, *U.S.A.* 112 E2
Chuhuyiv, *Ukraine* 47 H9
Chukchi Sea, *Russia* 51 C19
Chukotskoye Nagorye, *Russia* 51 C18
Chula Vista, *U.S.A.* 117 N9
Chulucanas, *Peru* 124 E2
Chulym →, *Russia* 50 D9
Chum Phae, *Thailand* 64 D4
Chum Saeng, *Thailand* 64 E3
Chumar, *India* 69 C8
Chumbicha, *Argentina* 126 B2
Chumerna, *Bulgaria* 41 D9
Chumikan, *Russia* 51 D14
Chumphon, *Thailand* 65 G2
Chumuare, *Mozam.* 87 E3
Chumunjin, *S. Korea* 57 F15
Chuna →, *Russia* 51 D10
Chun'an, *China* 59 C12
Ch'unch'ŏn, *S. Korea* 57 F14
Chunchura, *India* 69 H13
Chunga, *Zambia* 87 F2
Chunggang-ŭp, *N. Korea* 57 D14
Chunghwa, *N. Korea* 57 E13
Ch'ungju, *S. Korea* 57 F14
Chungking = Chongqing, *China* 58 C6
Chungli, *Taiwan* 59 E13
Ch'ungmu, *S. Korea* 57 G15
Chungt'iaoshan = Zhongtiao Shan, *China* 56 G6
Chungyang Shanmo, *Taiwan* 59 F13
Chunian, *Pakistan* 68 D6
Chunya, *Tanzania* 87 D3
Chunyang, *China* 57 C15
Chuquibamba, *Peru* 124 G4
Chuquicamata, *Chile* 126 A2
Chur, *Switz.* 25 J5
Churachandpur, *India* 67 G18
Churchill, *Canada* 105 B10
Churchill →, *Man., Canada* 105 B10
Churchill →, *Nfld., Canada* 103 B7
Churchill, C., *Canada* 105 B10
Churchill Falls, *Canada* 103 B7
Churchill L., *Canada* 105 B7
Churchill Pk., *Canada* 104 B3
Churki, *India* 69 H10
Churu, *India* 68 E6
Churún Merú = Angel Falls, *Venezuela* 124 B6
Chushal, *India* 69 C8
Chuska Mts., *U.S.A.* 115 H9
Chusovoy, *Russia* 50 D6
Chute-aux-Outardes, *Canada* 103 C6
Chuuronjang, *N. Korea* 57 D15
Chuvash Republic = Chuvashia □, *Russia* 48 C8
Chuvashia □, *Russia* 48 C8
Chuwārtah, *Iraq* 70 C5
Chuxiong, *China* 58 E3
Chūy = Shū →, *Kazakstan* 52 E10
Chuy, *Uruguay* 127 C5
Chuzhou, *China* 59 A12
Ci Xian, *China* 56 F8
Ciacova, *Romania* 42 E6
Ciadâr-Lunga, *Moldova* 43 D13
Ciamis, *Indonesia* 63 G13
Cianjur, *Indonesia* 63 G12
Cianorte, *Brazil* 127 A5
Cibola, *U.S.A.* 117 M12
Cicero, *U.S.A.* 108 E2
Cidacos →, *Spain* 32 C3
Cide, *Turkey* 72 B5
Ciechanów, *Poland* 45 F7
Ciechanowiec, *Poland* 45 F9
Ciechocinek, *Poland* 45 F5
Ciego de Avila, *Cuba* 120 B4
Ciénaga, *Colombia* 124 A4
Cienfuegos, *Cuba* 120 B3
Cierp, *France* 20 F4
Cíes, Is., *Spain* 34 C2
Cieszanów, *Poland* 45 H10
Cieszyn, *Poland* 45 J5
Cieza, *Spain* 33 G3
Çifteler, *Turkey* 72 C4
Cifuentes, *Spain* 32 E2
Cihanbeyli, *Turkey* 72 C5
Cihuatlán, *Mexico* 118 D4
Cijara, Embalse de, *Spain* 35 F6
Cijulang, *Indonesia* 63 G13
Cilacap, *Indonesia* 63 G13
Çıldır, *Turkey* 73 B10
Çıldır Gölü, *Turkey* 73 B10
Cili, *China* 59 C8
Cilibia, *Romania* 43 E12
Cilicia, *Turkey* 72 D5
Cill Chainnigh = Kilkenny, *Ireland* 15 D4
Cilo Dağı, *Turkey* 73 D10
Cima, *U.S.A.* 117 K11
Cimarron, *Kans., U.S.A.* 113 G4
Cimarron, *N. Mex., U.S.A.* 113 G2
Cimarron →, *U.S.A.* 113 G6
Cimişlia, *Moldova* 43 D13
Cimone, Mte., *Italy* 28 D7
Çinar, *Turkey* 73 D9
Çınarcık, *Turkey* 41 F13
Cinca →, *Spain* 32 D5
Cincar, *Bos.-H.* 42 G2
Cincinnati, *U.S.A.* 108 F3
Cincinnatus, *U.S.A.* 111 D9
Çine, *Turkey* 39 D10
Ciney, *Belgium* 17 D5
Cíngoli, *Italy* 29 E10
Cinigiano, *Italy* 29 F8
Cinto, Mte., *France* 21 F12
Cintruénigo, *Spain* 32 C3
Ciocile, *Romania* 43 F12
Ciolăneşti din Deal, *Romania* 43 F10
Ciorani, *Romania* 43 F11
Čiovo, *Croatia* 29 E13
Circeo, Mte., *Italy* 30 A6
Çirçir, *Turkey* 72 C7
Circle, *Alaska, U.S.A.* 100 B5
Circle, *Mont., U.S.A.* 112 B2
Circleville, *U.S.A.* 108 F4
Cirebon, *Indonesia* 62 F3
Ciremai, *Indonesia* 63 G13
Cirencester, *U.K.* 13 F6
Cireşu, *Romania* 42 F7
Cirey-sur-Vezouze, *France* 19 D13
Ciriè, *Italy* 28 C4
Cirium, *Cyprus* 36 E11
Cirò, *Italy* 31 C10
Cirò Marina, *Italy* 31 C10
Ciron →, *France* 20 D3
Cisco, *U.S.A.* 113 J5
Cislău, *Romania* 43 E11
Cisna, *Poland* 45 J9
Cisnădie, *Romania* 43 E9
Cisterna di Latina, *Italy* 30 A5
Cisternino, *Italy* 31 B10
Cistierna, *Spain* 34 C5
Citeli-Ckaro = Tsiteli-Tsqaro, *Georgia* 49 K8
Citlaltépetl, *Mexico* 119 D5
Citrus Heights, *U.S.A.* 116 G5
Citrusdal, *S. Africa* 88 E2
Città della Pieve, *Italy* 29 F9
Città di Castello, *Italy* 29 E9
Città Sant' Angelo, *Italy* 29 F11
Cittadella, *Italy* 29 C8
Cittaducale, *Italy* 29 F9
Cittanova, *Italy* 31 D9
Ciuc, Munţii, *Romania* 43 D11
Ciucaş, Vf., *Romania* 43 E10
Ciucea, *Romania* 42 D7
Ciuciulea, *Moldova* 43 C12
Ciuciuleni, *Moldova* 43 C13
Ciudad Altamirano, *Mexico* 118 D4
Ciudad Bolívar, *Venezuela* 124 B6
Ciudad Camargo, *Mexico* 118 B3
Ciudad de Valles, *Mexico* 119 C5
Ciudad del Carmen, *Mexico* 119 D6
Ciudad del Este, *Paraguay* 127 B5
Ciudad Delicias = Delicias, *Mexico* 118 B3
Ciudad Guayana, *Venezuela* 124 B6
Ciudad Guerrero, *Mexico* 118 B3
Ciudad Guzmán, *Mexico* 118 D4
Ciudad Juárez, *Mexico* 118 A3
Ciudad Madero, *Mexico* 119 C5
Ciudad Mante, *Mexico* 119 C5
Ciudad Obregón, *Mexico* 118 B3
Ciudad Real, *Spain* 35 G7
Ciudad Real □, *Spain* 35 G7
Ciudad Rodrigo, *Spain* 34 E4
Ciudad Trujillo = Santo Domingo, *Dom. Rep.* 121 C6
Ciudad Victoria, *Mexico* 119 C5
Ciudadela, *Spain* 37 B10
Ciulniţa, *Romania* 43 F12
Ciumeghiu, *Romania* 42 D6
Ciuperceni, *Romania* 42 F8
Civa Burnu, *Turkey* 72 B7
Cividale del Friuli, *Italy* 29 B10
Civita Castellana, *Italy* 29 F9
Civitanova Marche, *Italy* 29 E10
Civitavécchia, *Italy* 29 F8
Civray, *France* 20 B4
Çivril, *Turkey* 39 C11
Cixerri →, *Italy* 30 C1
Cixi, *China* 59 B13
Cizre, *Turkey* 70 B4
Cizur Mayor, *Spain* 32 C3
Clackmannanshire □, *U.K.* 14 E5
Clacton-on-Sea, *U.K.* 13 F9
Clain →, *France* 18 F7
Claire, L., *Canada* 104 B6
Clairton, *U.S.A.* 110 F5

Clairvaux-les-Lacs, *France* 19 F12
Claise →, *France* 20 B5
Clallam Bay, *U.S.A.* 116 B2
Clamecy, *France* 19 E10
Clanton, *U.S.A.* 109 J2
Clanwilliam, *S. Africa* 88 E2
Clara, *Ireland* 15 C4
Claraville, *U.S.A.* 117 K8
Clare, *Australia* 95 E2
Clare, *U.S.A.* 108 D3
Clare □, *Ireland* 15 D3
Clare →, *Ireland* 15 C2
Clare I., *Ireland* 15 C1
Claremont, *Calif., U.S.A.* 117 L9
Claremont, *N.H., U.S.A.* 111 C12
Claremont Pt., *Australia* 94 A3
Claremore, *U.S.A.* 113 G7
Claremorris, *Ireland* 15 C3
Clarence →, *Australia* 95 D5
Clarence →, *N.Z.* 91 K4
Clarence, I., *Chile* 128 G2
Clarence I., *Antarctica* 5 C18
Clarence Str., *Australia* 92 B5
Clarence Town, *Bahamas* 121 B5
Clarendon, *Pa., U.S.A.* 110 E5
Clarendon, *Tex., U.S.A.* 113 H4
Clarenville, *Canada* 103 C9
Claresholm, *Canada* 104 D6
Clarie Coast, *Antarctica* 5 C9
Clarinda, *U.S.A.* 112 E7
Clarion, *Iowa, U.S.A.* 112 D8
Clarion, *Pa., U.S.A.* 110 E5
Clarion →, *U.S.A.* 110 E5
Clark, *U.S.A.* 112 C6
Clark, Pt., *Canada* 110 B3
Clark Fork, *U.S.A.* 114 B5
Clark Fork →, *U.S.A.* 114 B5
Clarkdale, *U.S.A.* 115 J7
Clarke City, *Canada* 103 B6
Clarke I., *Australia* 94 G4
Clarke Ra., *Australia* 94 C4
Clark's Fork →, *U.S.A.* 114 D9
Clark's Harbour, *Canada* 103 D6
Clarks Hill L., *U.S.A.* 109 J4
Clarks Summit, *U.S.A.* 111 E9
Clarksburg, *U.S.A.* 108 F5
Clarksdale, *U.S.A.* 113 H9
Clarksville, *Ark., U.S.A.* 113 H8
Clarksville, *Tenn., U.S.A.* 109 G2
Clarksville, *Tex., U.S.A.* 113 J7
Clatskanie, *U.S.A.* 116 D3
Claude, *U.S.A.* 113 H4
Claveria, *Phil.* 61 B4
Clay, *U.S.A.* 116 G5
Clay Center, *U.S.A.* 112 F6
Claypool, *U.S.A.* 115 K8
Claysburg, *U.S.A.* 110 F6
Claysville, *U.S.A.* 110 F4
Clayton, *N. Mex., U.S.A.* 113 G3
Clayton, *N.Y., U.S.A.* 111 B8
Clear, C., *Ireland* 15 E2
Clear, L., *Canada* 110 A7
Clear Hills, *Canada* 104 B5
Clear I., *Ireland* 15 E2
Clear L., *U.S.A.* 116 F4
Clear Lake, *Iowa, U.S.A.* 112 D8
Clear Lake, *S. Dak., U.S.A.* 112 C6
Clear Lake Reservoir, *U.S.A.* 114 F3
Clearfield, *Pa., U.S.A.* 110 E6
Clearfield, *Utah, U.S.A.* 114 F8
Clearlake, *U.S.A.* 114 G2
Clearlake Highlands, *U.S.A.* 116 G4
Clearwater, *Canada* 104 C4
Clearwater, *U.S.A.* 109 M4
Clearwater →, *Alta., Canada* 104 C6
Clearwater →, *Alta., Canada* 105 B6
Clearwater L., *Canada* 105 C9
Clearwater Mts., *U.S.A.* 114 C6
Clearwater Prov. Park, *Canada* 105 C8
Clearwater River Prov. Park, *Canada* 105 B7
Cleburne, *U.S.A.* 113 J6
Clee Hills, *U.K.* 13 E5
Cleethorpes, *U.K.* 12 D7
Cleeve Cloud, *U.K.* 13 F6
Clelles, *France* 21 D9
Clemson, *U.S.A.* 109 H4
Clerke Reef, *Australia* 92 C2
Clermont, *Australia* 94 C4
Clermont, *France* 19 C9
Clermont, *U.S.A.* 109 L5
Clermont-en-Argonne, *France* 19 C12
Clermont-Ferrand, *France* 20 C7
Clermont-l'Hérault, *France* 20 E7
Clerval, *France* 19 E13
Clervaux, *Lux.* 17 D6
Cles, *Italy* 28 B8
Clevedon, *U.K.* 13 F5
Cleveland, *Miss., U.S.A.* 113 J9
Cleveland, *Ohio, U.S.A.* 110 E3
Cleveland, *Okla., U.S.A.* 113 G6
Cleveland, *Tenn., U.S.A.* 109 H3
Cleveland, *Tex., U.S.A.* 113 K7
Cleveland, C., *Australia* 94 B4
Cleveland, Mt., *U.S.A.* 114 B7
Cleveland Heights, *U.S.A.* 110 E3
Clevelândia, *Brazil* 127 B5
Clew B., *Ireland* 15 C2
Clewiston, *U.S.A.* 109 M5
Clifden, *Ireland* 15 C1
Clifden, *N.Z.* 91 M1
Cliffdell, *U.S.A.* 116 D5
Cliffy Hd., *Australia* 93 G2
Clifton, *Australia* 95 D5
Clifton, *Ariz., U.S.A.* 115 K9
Clifton, *Colo., U.S.A.* 115 G9
Clifton, *Tex., U.S.A.* 113 K6
Clifton Beach, *Australia* 94 B4
Climax, *Canada* 105 D7
Clinch →, *U.S.A.* 109 H3
Clingmans Dome, *U.S.A.* 109 H4
Clint, *U.S.A.* 115 L10
Clinton, *B.C., Canada* 104 C4
Clinton, *Ont., Canada* 102 D3
Clinton, *N.Z.* 91 M2
Clinton, *Ark., U.S.A.* 113 H8
Clinton, *Conn., U.S.A.* 111 E12
Clinton, *Ill., U.S.A.* 112 E10
Clinton, *Ind., U.S.A.* 108 F2
Clinton, *Iowa, U.S.A.* 112 E9
Clinton, *Mass., U.S.A.* 111 D13
Clinton, *Miss., U.S.A.* 113 J9
Clinton, *Mo., U.S.A.* 112 F8
Clinton, *N.C., U.S.A.* 109 H6
Clinton, *Okla., U.S.A.* 113 H5
Clinton, *S.C., U.S.A.* 109 H5
Clinton, *Tenn., U.S.A.* 109 G3
Clinton, *Wash., U.S.A.* 116 C4
Clinton C., *Australia* 94 C5
Clinton Colden L., *Canada* 100 B9
Clintonville, *U.S.A.* 112 C10
Clipperton, I., *Pac. Oc.* 97 F17
Clisham, *U.K.* 14 D2
Clisson, *France* 18 E5
Clitheroe, *U.K.* 12 D5
Clo-oose, *Canada* 116 B2
Cloates, Pt., *Australia* 92 D1
Clocolan, *S. Africa* 89 D4
Clodomira, *Argentina* 126 B3
Clogher Hd., *Ireland* 15 C5
Clonakilty, *Ireland* 15 E3
Clonakilty B., *Ireland* 15 E3
Cloncurry, *Australia* 94 C3
Cloncurry →, *Australia* 94 B3
Clondalkin, *Ireland* 15 C5
Clones, *Ireland* 15 B4
Clonmel, *Ireland* 15 D4
Cloppenburg, *Germany* 24 C4
Cloquet, *U.S.A.* 112 B8
Clorinda, *Argentina* 126 B4
Cloud Bay, *Canada* 102 C2
Cloud Peak, *U.S.A.* 114 D10
Cloudcroft, *U.S.A.* 115 K11
Cloverdale, *U.S.A.* 116 G4
Clovis, *Calif., U.S.A.* 116 J7
Clovis, *N. Mex., U.S.A.* 113 H3
Cloyes-sur-le-Loir, *France* 18 E8
Cloyne, *Canada* 110 B7
Cluj □, *Romania* 43 D8
Cluj-Napoca, *Romania* 43 D8
Clunes, *Australia* 95 F3
Cluny, *France* 19 F11
Cluses, *France* 19 F13
Clusone, *Italy* 28 C6
Clutha →, *N.Z.* 91 M2
Clwyd →, *U.K.* 12 D4
Clyde, *Canada* 104 C6
Clyde, *N.Z.* 91 L2
Clyde, *U.S.A.* 110 C8
Clyde →, *U.K.* 14 F4
Clyde, Firth of, *U.K.* 14 F3
Clyde River, *Canada* 101 A13
Clydebank, *U.K.* 14 F4
Clymer, *N.Y., U.S.A.* 110 D5
Clymer, *Pa., U.S.A.* 110 D5
Ćmielów, *Poland* 45 H8
Côa →, *Portugal* 34 D3
Coachella, *U.S.A.* 117 M10
Coachella Canal, *U.S.A.* 117 N12
Coahoma, *U.S.A.* 113 J4
Coahuayana →, *Mexico* 118 D4
Coahuila □, *Mexico* 118 B4
Coal →, *Canada* 104 B3
Coalane, *Mozam.* 87 F4
Coalcomán, *Mexico* 118 D4
Coaldale, *Canada* 104 D6
Coalgate, *U.S.A.* 113 H6
Coalinga, *U.S.A.* 116 J6
Coalisland, *U.K.* 15 B5
Coalville, *U.K.* 12 E6
Coalville, *U.S.A.* 114 F8
Coari, *Brazil* 124 D6
Coast □, *Kenya* 86 C4
Coast Mts., *Canada* 104 C3
Coast Ranges, *U.S.A.* 116 G4
Coatbridge, *U.K.* 14 F4
Coatepec, *Mexico* 119 D5
Coatepeque, *Guatemala* 120 D1
Coatesville, *U.S.A.* 108 F8
Coaticook, *Canada* 103 C5
Coats I., *Canada* 101 B11
Coats Land, *Antarctica* 5 D1
Coatzacoalcos, *Mexico* 119 D6
Cobadin, *Romania* 43 F13
Cobalt, *Canada* 102 C4
Cobán, *Guatemala* 120 C1
Çobanlar, *Turkey* 39 C12
Cobar, *Australia* 95 E4
Cóbh, *Ireland* 15 E3
Cobija, *Bolivia* 124 F5
Cobleskill, *U.S.A.* 111 D10
Coboconk, *Canada* 110 B6
Cobourg, *Canada* 102 D4
Cobourg Pen., *Australia* 92 B5
Cobram, *Australia* 95 F4
Cóbué, *Mozam.* 87 E3
Coburg, *Germany* 25 E6
Coca, *Spain* 34 D6
Cocanada = Kakinada, *India* 67 L13
Cocentaina, *Spain* 33 G4
Cochabamba, *Bolivia* 124 G5
Cochem, *Germany* 25 E3
Cochemane, *Mozam.* 87 F3
Cochin, *India* 66 Q10
Cochin China = Nam-Phan, *Vietnam* 65 G6
Cochran, *U.S.A.* 109 J4
Cochrane, *Alta., Canada* 104 C6
Cochrane, *Ont., Canada* 102 C3
Cochrane, *Chile* 128 F2
Cochrane →, *Canada* 105 B8
Cochrane, L., *Chile* 128 F2
Cochranton, *U.S.A.* 110 E4
Cockburn, *Australia* 95 E3
Cockburn, Canal, *Chile* 122 J3
Cockburn I., *Canada* 102 C3
Cockburn Ra., *Australia* 92 C4
Cockermouth, *U.K.* 12 C4
Cocklebiddy, *Australia* 93 F4
Coco →, *Cent. Amer.* 120 D3
Coco, I. del, *Pac. Oc.* 97 G19
Cocoa, *U.S.A.* 109 L5
Cocobeach, *Gabon* 84 D1
Cocora, *Romania* 43 F12
Cocos Is., *Ind. Oc.* 96 J1
Cod, C., *U.S.A.* 108 D10
Codajás, *Brazil* 124 D6
Codigoro, *Italy* 29 D9
Codlea, *Romania* 43 E10
Codó, *Brazil* 125 D10
Codogno, *Italy* 28 C6
Codróipo, *Italy* 29 C10
Codru, Munții, *Romania* 42 D7
Cody, *U.S.A.* 114 D9
Coe Hill, *Canada* 110 B7
Coelemu, *Chile* 126 D1
Coen, *Australia* 94 A3
Coesfeld, *Germany* 24 D3
Cœur d'Alene, *U.S.A.* 114 C5
Cœur d'Alene L., *U.S.A.* 114 C5
Coevorden, *Neths.* 17 B6
Cofete, *Canary Is.* 37 F5
Coffeyville, *U.S.A.* 113 G7
Coffin B., *Australia* 95 E2
Coffin Bay, *Australia* 95 E2
Coffin Bay Peninsula, *Australia* 95 E2
Coffs Harbour, *Australia* 95 E5
Cofrentes, *Spain* 33 F3
Cogalnic →, *Moldova* 43 E14
Cogealac, *Romania* 43 F13
Coghinas →, *Italy* 30 B1
Coghinas, L. del, *Italy* 30 B2
Cognac, *France* 20 C3
Cogne, *Italy* 28 C4
Cogolin, *France* 21 E10
Cogolludo, *Spain* 32 E1
Cohocton, *U.S.A.* 110 D7
Cohocton →, *U.S.A.* 110 D7
Cohoes, *U.S.A.* 111 D11
Cohuna, *Australia* 95 F3
Coiba, I., *Panama* 120 E3
Coig →, *Argentina* 128 G3
Coigeach, Rubha, *U.K.* 14 C3
Coihaique, *Chile* 128 F2
Coimbatore, *India* 66 P10
Coimbra, *Brazil* 124 G7
Coimbra, *Portugal* 34 E2
Coimbra □, *Portugal* 34 E2
Coín, *Spain* 35 J6
Coipasa, Salar de, *Bolivia* 124 G5
Cojimies, *Ecuador* 124 C3
Cojocna, *Romania* 43 D8
Cojutepequé, *El Salv.* 120 D2
Čoka, *Serbia, Yug.* 42 E5
Cokeville, *U.S.A.* 114 E8
Colac, *Australia* 95 F3
Colatina, *Brazil* 125 G10
Colbeck, C., *Antarctica* 5 D13
Colborne, *Canada* 110 C7
Colby, *U.S.A.* 112 F4
Colchester, *U.K.* 13 F8
Cold L., *Canada* 105 C7
Coldstream, *Canada* 104 C5
Coldstream, *U.K.* 14 F6
Coldwater, *Canada* 110 B5
Coldwater, *Kans., U.S.A.* 113 G5
Coldwater, *Mich., U.S.A.* 108 E3
Colebrook, *U.S.A.* 111 B13
Coleman, *U.S.A.* 113 K5
Coleman →, *Australia* 94 B3
Colenso, *S. Africa* 89 D4
Coleraine, *Australia* 95 F3
Coleraine, *U.K.* 15 A5
Coleridge, L., *N.Z.* 91 K3
Colesberg, *S. Africa* 88 E4
Coleville, *U.S.A.* 116 G7
Colfax, *Calif., U.S.A.* 116 F6
Colfax, *La., U.S.A.* 113 K8
Colfax, *Wash., U.S.A.* 114 C5
Colhué Huapi, L., *Argentina* 128 F3
Colibași, *Moldova* 43 E13
Colibași, *Romania* 43 F9
Cólico, *Italy* 28 B6
Coligny, *France* 19 F12
Coligny, *S. Africa* 89 D4
Colima, *Mexico* 118 D4
Colima □, *Mexico* 118 D4
Colima, Nevado de, *Mexico* 118 D4
Colina, *Chile* 126 C1
Colina do Norte, *Guinea-Biss.* 82 C2
Colinas, *Brazil* 125 E10
Colindres, *Spain* 34 B7
Coll, *U.K.* 14 E2
Collaguasi, *Chile* 126 A2
Collarada, Peña, *Spain* 32 C4
Collarenebri, *Australia* 95 D4
Colle di Val d'Elsa, *Italy* 28 E8
Collécchio, *Italy* 28 D7
Colleen Bawn, *Zimbabwe* 87 G2
College Park, *U.S.A.* 109 J3
College Station, *U.S.A.* 113 K6
Collesalvetti, *Italy* 28 E7
Collie, *Australia* 93 F2
Collier B., *Australia* 92 C3
Collier Ra., *Australia* 93 D2
Collina, Passo di, *Italy* 28 D7
Collingwood, *Canada* 102 D3
Collingwood, *N.Z.* 91 J4
Collins, *Canada* 102 B2
Collinsville, *Australia* 94 C4
Collipulli, *Chile* 126 D1
Collooney, *Ireland* 15 B3
Colmar, *France* 19 D14
Colmars, *France* 21 D10
Colmenar, *Spain* 35 J6
Colmenar de Oreja, *Spain* 34 E7
Colmenar Viejo, *Spain* 34 E7
Colo →, *Australia* 95 E5
Cologne = Köln, *Germany* 24 E2
Colom, I. d'en, *Spain* 37 B11
Coloma, *U.S.A.* 116 G6
Colomb-Béchar = Béchar, *Algeria* 78 B5
Colombey-les-Belles, *France* 19 D12
Colombey-les-Deux-Églises, *France* 19 D11
Colombia ■, *S. Amer.* 124 C4
Colombian Basin, *S. Amer.* 98 H12
Colombo, *Sri Lanka* 66 R11
Colomiers, *France* 20 E5
Colón, *Buenos Aires, Argentina* 126 C3
Colón, *Entre Ríos, Argentina* 126 C4
Colón, *Cuba* 120 B3
Colón, *Panama* 120 E4
Colonia de Sant Jordi, *Spain* 37 B9
Colonia del Sacramento, *Uruguay* 126 C4
Colonia Dora, *Argentina* 126 B3
Colonial Beach, *U.S.A.* 108 F7
Colonie, *U.S.A.* 111 D11
Colonna, C., *Italy* 31 C10
Colonsay, *Canada* 105 C7
Colonsay, *U.K.* 14 E2
Colorado □, *U.S.A.* 115 G10
Colorado →, *Argentina* 128 D4
Colorado →, *N. Amer.* 115 L6
Colorado →, *U.S.A.* 113 L7
Colorado City, *U.S.A.* 113 J4
Colorado Plateau, *U.S.A.* 115 H8
Colorado River Aqueduct, *U.S.A.* 117 L12
Colorado Springs, *U.S.A.* 112 F2
Colorno, *Italy* 28 D7
Colotlán, *Mexico* 118 C4
Colstrip, *U.S.A.* 114 D10
Colton, *U.S.A.* 111 B10
Columbia, *Ky., U.S.A.* 108 G3
Columbia, *La., U.S.A.* 113 J8
Columbia, *Miss., U.S.A.* 113 K10
Columbia, *Mo., U.S.A.* 112 F8
Columbia, *Pa., U.S.A.* 111 F8
Columbia, *S.C., U.S.A.* 109 J5
Columbia, *Tenn., U.S.A.* 109 H2
Columbia →, *N. Amer.* 116 D2
Columbia, C., *Canada* 4 A4
Columbia, District of □, *U.S.A.* 108 F7
Columbia, Mt., *Canada* 104 C5
Columbia Basin, *U.S.A.* 114 C4
Columbia Falls, *U.S.A.* 114 B6
Columbia Mts., *Canada* 104 C5
Columbia Plateau, *U.S.A.* 114 D5
Columbiana, *U.S.A.* 110 F4
Columbretes, Is., *Spain* 32 F5
Columbus, *Ga., U.S.A.* 109 J3
Columbus, *Ind., U.S.A.* 108 F3
Columbus, *Kans., U.S.A.* 113 G7
Columbus, *Miss., U.S.A.* 109 J1
Columbus, *Mont., U.S.A.* 114 D9
Columbus, *N. Mex., U.S.A.* 115 L10
Columbus, *Nebr., U.S.A.* 112 E6
Columbus, *Ohio, U.S.A.* 108 F4
Columbus, *Tex., U.S.A.* 113 L6
Colunga, *Spain* 34 B5
Colusa, *U.S.A.* 116 F4
Colville, *U.S.A.* 114 B5
Colville →, *U.S.A.* 100 A4
Colville, C., *N.Z.* 91 G5
Colwood, *Canada* 116 B3
Colwyn Bay, *U.K.* 12 D4
Coma, *Ethiopia* 81 F4
Comácchio, *Italy* 29 D9
Comalcalco, *Mexico* 119 D6
Comallo, *Argentina* 128 E2
Comana, *Romania* 43 F11
Comanche, *U.S.A.* 113 K5
Comănești, *Romania* 43 D11
Comarnic, *Romania* 43 E10
Comayagua, *Honduras* 120 D2
Combahee →, *U.S.A.* 109 J5
Combarbalá, *Chile* 126 C1
Combeaufontaine, *France* 19 E12
Comber, *Canada* 110 D2
Comber, *U.K.* 15 B6
Combermere, *Canada* 110 A7
Comblain-au-Pont, *Belgium* 17 D5
Combourg, *France* 18 D5
Combrailles, *France* 19 F9
Combronde, *France* 20 C7
Comeragh Mts., *Ireland* 15 D4
Comet, *Australia* 94 C4
Comilla, *Bangla.* 67 H17
Comino, *Malta* 36 C1
Comino, C., *Italy* 30 B2
Cómiso, *Italy* 31 F7
Comitán, *Mexico* 119 D6
Commentry, *France* 19 F9
Commerce, *Ga., U.S.A.* 109 H4
Commerce, *Tex., U.S.A.* 113 J7
Commercy, *France* 19 D12
Committee B., *Canada* 101 B11
Commonwealth B., *Antarctica* 5 C10
Commoron Cr. →, *Australia* 95 D5
Communism Pk. = Kommunizma, Pik, *Tajikistan* 50 F8
Como, *Italy* 28 C6
Como, Lago di, *Italy* 28 B6
Comodoro Rivadavia, *Argentina* 128 F3
Comorâște, *Romania* 42 E6
Comorin, C., *India* 66 Q10
Comoro Is. = Comoros ■, *Ind. Oc.* 77 H8
Comoros ■, *Ind. Oc.* 77 H8
Comox, *Canada* 104 D4
Compiègne, *France* 19 C9
Comporta, *Portugal* 35 G2
Compostela, *Mexico* 118 C4
Comprida, I., *Brazil* 127 A6
Compton, *Canada* 111 A13
Compton, *U.S.A.* 117 M8
Comrat, *Moldova* 43 D13
Con Cuong, *Vietnam* 64 C5
Con Son, *Vietnam* 65 H6
Conakry, *Guinea* 82 D2
Conara, *Australia* 94 G4
Concarneau, *France* 18 E3
Conceição, *Mozam.* 87 F4
Conceição da Barra, *Brazil* 125 G11
Conceição do Araguaia, *Brazil* 125 E9
Concepción, *Argentina* 126 B2
Concepción, *Bolivia* 124 G6
Concepción, *Chile* 126 D1
Concepción, *Mexico* 119 D6
Concepción, *Paraguay* 126 A4
Concepción □, *Chile* 126 D1
Concepción →, *Mexico* 118 A2
Concepción, Est. de, *Chile* 128 G2
Concepción, L., *Bolivia* 124 G6
Concepción, Punta, *Mexico* 118 B2
Concepción del Oro, *Mexico* 118 C4
Concepción del Uruguay, *Argentina* 126 C4
Conception, Pt., *U.S.A.* 117 L6
Conception B., *Canada* 103 C9
Conception B., *Namibia* 88 C1
Conception I., *Bahamas* 121 B4
Concession, *Zimbabwe* 87 F3
Conchas Dam, *U.S.A.* 113 H2
Conches-en-Ouche, *France* 18 D7
Concho, *U.S.A.* 115 J9
Concho →, *U.S.A.* 113 K5
Conchos →, *Chihuahua, Mexico* 118 B4
Conchos →, *Tamaulipas, Mexico* 119 B5
Concord, *Calif., U.S.A.* 116 H4
Concord, *N.C., U.S.A.* 109 H5
Concord, *N.H., U.S.A.* 111 C13
Concordia, *Argentina* 126 C4
Concórdia, *Brazil* 124 D5
Concordia, *Mexico* 118 C3
Concordia, *U.S.A.* 112 F6
Concrete, *U.S.A.* 114 B3
Condamine, *Australia* 95 D5
Condat, *France* 20 C6
Conde, *U.S.A.* 112 C5
Condé-sur-Noireau, *France* 18 D6
Condeúba, *Brazil* 125 F10
Condobolin, *Australia* 95 E4
Condom, *France* 20 E4
Condon, *U.S.A.* 114 D3
Conegliano, *Italy* 29 C9
Conejera, I. = Conills, I. des, *Spain* 37 B9
Conejos, *Mexico* 118 B4
Confolens, *France* 20 B4
Confuso →, *Paraguay* 126 B4
Congaz, *Moldova* 43 D13
Conghua, *China* 59 F9
Congjiang, *China* 58 E7
Congleton, *U.K.* 12 D5
Congo (Kinshasa) = Congo, Dem. Rep. of the ■, *Africa* 84 E4
Congo ■, *Africa* 84 E3
Congo →, *Africa* 84 F2
Congo, Dem. Rep. of the ■, *Africa* 84 E4
Congo Basin, *Africa* 84 E4
Congonhas, *Brazil* 127 A7
Congress, *U.S.A.* 115 J7
Conil = Conil de la Frontera, *Spain* 35 J4
Conil de la Frontera, *Spain* 35 J4
Conills, I. des, *Spain* 37 B9
Coniston, *Canada* 102 C3
Conjeeveram = Kanchipuram, *India* 66 N11
Conklin, *Canada* 105 B6
Conklin, *U.S.A.* 111 D9
Conn, L., *Ireland* 15 B2
Connacht □, *Ireland* 15 C2
Conneaut, *U.S.A.* 110 E4
Connecticut □, *U.S.A.* 111 E12
Connecticut →, *U.S.A.* 111 E12
Connell, *U.S.A.* 114 C4
Connellsville, *U.S.A.* 110 F5
Connemara, *Ireland* 15 C2
Connemaugh →, *U.S.A.* 110 F5
Connerré, *France* 18 D7
Connersville, *U.S.A.* 108 F3
Connors Ra., *Australia* 94 C4
Conques, *France* 20 D6
Conquest, *Canada* 105 C7
Conrad, *U.S.A.* 114 B8
Conran, C., *Australia* 95 F4
Conroe, *U.S.A.* 113 K7
Consecon, *Canada* 110 C7

Conselheiro Lafaiete, *Brazil* 127 A7
Conselve, *Italy* 29 C8
Consett, *U.K.* 12 C6
Consort, *Canada* 105 C6
Constance = Konstanz, *Germany* 25 H5
Constance, L. = Bodensee, *Europe* 25 H5
Constanţa, *Romania* 43 F13
Constanţa □, *Romania* 43 F13
Constantia, *U.S.A.* 111 C8
Constantina, *Spain* 35 H5
Constantine, *Algeria* 78 A7
Constitución, *Chile* 126 D1
Constitución, *Uruguay* 126 C4
Consuegra, *Spain* 35 F7
Consul, *Canada* 105 D7
Contact, *U.S.A.* 114 F6
Contai, *India* 69 J12
Contamana, *Peru* 124 E4
Contarina, *Italy* 29 C9
Contas →, *Brazil* 125 F11
Contes, *France* 21 E11
Contoocook, *U.S.A.* 111 C13
Contra Costa, *Mozam.* 89 D5
Contres, *France* 18 E8
Contrexéville, *France* 19 D12
Contwoyto L., *Canada* 100 B8
Conversano, *Italy* 31 B10
Conway = Conwy, *U.K.* 12 D4
Conway = Conwy →, *U.K.* 12 D4
Conway, *Ark., U.S.A.* 113 H8
Conway, *N.H., U.S.A.* 111 C13
Conway, *S.C., U.S.A.* 109 J6
Conway, L., *Australia* 95 D2
Conwy, *U.K.* 12 D4
Conwy □, *U.K.* 12 D4
Conwy →, *U.K.* 12 D4
Coober Pedy, *Australia* 95 D1
Cooch Behar = Koch Bihar, *India* 67 F16
Cooinda, *Australia* 92 B5
Cook, *Australia* 93 F5
Cook, *U.S.A.* 112 B8
Cook, B., *Chile* 128 H3
Cook, C., *Canada* 104 C3
Cook, Mt. = Aoraki Mount Cook, *N.Z.* 91 K3
Cook Inlet, *U.S.A.* 100 C4
Cook Is., *Pac. Oc.* 97 J12
Cook Strait, *N.Z.* 91 J5
Cookeville, *U.S.A.* 109 G3
Cookhouse, *S. Africa* 88 E4
Cookshire, *Canada* 111 A13
Cookstown, *U.K.* 15 B5
Cooksville, *Canada* 110 C5
Cooktown, *Australia* 94 B4
Coolabah, *Australia* 95 E4
Cooladdi, *Australia* 95 D4
Coolah, *Australia* 95 E4
Coolamon, *Australia* 95 E4
Coolgardie, *Australia* 93 F3
Coolidge, *U.S.A.* 115 K8
Coolidge Dam, *U.S.A.* 115 K8
Cooma, *Australia* 95 F4
Coon Rapids, *U.S.A.* 112 C8
Coonabarabran, *Australia* 95 E4
Coonamble, *Australia* 95 E4
Coonana, *Australia* 93 F3
Coondapoor, *India* 66 N9
Cooninie, L., *Australia* 95 D2
Cooper, *U.S.A.* 113 J7
Cooper Cr. →, *Australia* 95 D2
Cooperstown, *N. Dak., U.S.A.* 112 B5
Cooperstown, *N.Y., U.S.A.* 111 D10
Coorabie, *Australia* 93 F5
Coorong, The, *Australia* 95 F2
Coorow, *Australia* 93 E2
Cooroy, *Australia* 95 D5
Coos Bay, *U.S.A.* 114 E1
Coosa →, *U.S.A.* 109 J2
Cootamundra, *Australia* 95 E4
Cootehill, *Ireland* 15 B4
Copahue Paso, *Argentina* 126 D1
Copainalá, *Mexico* 119 D6
Copake Falls, *U.S.A.* 111 D11
Copalnic Mănăştur, *Romania* 43 C8
Copán, *Honduras* 120 D2
Cope, *U.S.A.* 112 F3
Cope, C., *Spain* 33 H3
Copenhagen = København, *Denmark* 11 J6
Copenhagen, *U.S.A.* 111 C9
Copertino, *Italy* 31 B11
Copiapó, *Chile* 126 B1
Copiapó →, *Chile* 126 B1
Coplay, *U.S.A.* 111 F9
Copp L., *Canada* 104 A6
Copparo, *Italy* 29 D8
Coppename →, *Surinam* 125 B7
Copper Harbor, *U.S.A.* 108 B2
Copper Queen, *Zimbabwe* 87 F2
Copperas Cove, *U.S.A.* 113 K6
Copperbelt □, *Zambia* 87 E2
Coppermine = Kugluktuk, *Canada* 100 B8
Coppermine →, *Canada* 100 B8
Copperopolis, *U.S.A.* 116 H6
Copşa Mică, *Romania* 43 D9
Coquet →, *U.K.* 12 B6
Coquille, *U.S.A.* 114 E1
Coquimbo, *Chile* 126 C1
Coquimbo □, *Chile* 126 C1
Corabia, *Romania* 43 G9
Coracora, *Peru* 124 G4
Coraki, *Australia* 95 D5
Coral, *U.S.A.* 110 F5
Coral Gables, *U.S.A.* 109 N5
Coral Harbour = Salliq, *Canada* 101 B11
Coral Sea, *Pac. Oc.* 96 J7
Coral Springs, *U.S.A.* 109 M5
Coraopolis, *U.S.A.* 110 F4
Corato, *Italy* 31 A9
Corbeil-Essonnes, *France* 19 D9
Corbie, *France* 19 C9
Corbières, *France* 20 F6
Corbigny, *France* 19 E10
Corbin, *U.S.A.* 108 G3
Corbones →, *Spain* 35 H5
Corbu, *Romania* 43 F13
Corby, *U.K.* 13 E7
Corcaigh = Cork, *Ireland* 15 E3
Corcoran, *U.S.A.* 116 J7
Cordele, *U.S.A.* 109 K4
Cordell, *U.S.A.* 113 H5
Cordenòns, *Italy* 29 C9
Cordes, *France* 20 D5
Córdoba, *Argentina* 126 C3
Córdoba, *Mexico* 119 D5
Córdoba, *Spain* 35 H6
Córdoba □, *Argentina* 126 C3
Córdoba □, *Spain* 35 G6
Córdoba, Sierra de, *Argentina* 126 C3
Cordon, *Phil.* 61 C4
Cordova, *U.S.A.* 100 B5
Corella, *Spain* 32 C3
Corella →, *Australia* 94 B3
Corfield, *Australia* 94 C3
Corfu = Kérkira, *Greece* 36 A3
Corfu, Str. of, *Greece* 36 A4
Corgo = O Corgo, *Spain* 34 C3
Cori, *Italy* 30 A5
Coria, *Spain* 34 F4
Coria del Río, *Spain* 35 H4
Corigliano Cálabro, *Italy* 31 C9
Coringa Is., *Australia* 94 B4
Corinth = Kórinthos, *Greece* 38 D4
Corinth, *Miss., U.S.A.* 109 H1
Corinth, *N.Y., U.S.A.* 111 C11
Corinth, G. of = Korinthiakós Kólpos, *Greece* 38 C4
Corinth Canal, *Greece* 38 D4
Corinto, *Brazil* 125 G10
Corinto, *Nic.* 120 D2
Cork, *Ireland* 15 E3
Cork □, *Ireland* 15 E3
Cork Harbour, *Ireland* 15 E3
Corlay, *France* 18 D3
Corleone, *Italy* 30 E6
Corleto Perticara, *Italy* 31 B9
Çorlu, *Turkey* 41 E11
Cormack L., *Canada* 104 A4
Cormòns, *Italy* 29 C10
Cormorant, *Canada* 105 C8
Cormorant L., *Canada* 105 C8
Corn Is. = Maiz, Is. del, *Nic.* 120 D3
Cornélio Procópio, *Brazil* 127 A5
Corner Brook, *Canada* 103 C8
Corneşti, *Moldova* 43 C13
Corníglio, *Italy* 28 D7
Corning, *Ark., U.S.A.* 113 G9
Corning, *Calif., U.S.A.* 114 G2
Corning, *Iowa, U.S.A.* 112 E7
Corning, *N.Y., U.S.A.* 110 D7
Corno Grande, *Italy* 29 F10
Cornwall, *Canada* 102 C5
Cornwall, *U.S.A.* 111 F8
Cornwall □, *U.K.* 13 G3
Corny Pt., *Australia* 95 E2
Coro, *Venezuela* 124 A5
Coroatá, *Brazil* 125 D10
Corocoro, *Bolivia* 124 G5
Coroico, *Bolivia* 124 G5
Coromandel, *N.Z.* 91 G5
Coromandel Coast, *India* 66 N12
Corona, *Calif., U.S.A.* 117 M9
Corona, *N. Mex., U.S.A.* 115 J11
Coronach, *Canada* 105 D7
Coronado, *U.S.A.* 117 N9
Coronado, B. de, *Costa Rica* 120 E3
Coronados, Is. los, *U.S.A.* 117 N9
Coronation, *Canada* 104 C6
Coronation Gulf, *Canada* 100 B8
Coronation I., *Antarctica* 5 C18
Coronation Is., *Australia* 92 B3
Coronda, *Argentina* 126 C3
Coronel, *Chile* 126 D1
Coronel Bogado, *Paraguay* 126 B4
Coronel Dorrego, *Argentina* 126 D3
Coronel Oviedo, *Paraguay* 126 B4
Coronel Pringles, *Argentina* 126 D3
Coronel Suárez, *Argentina* 126 D3
Coronel Vidal, *Argentina* 126 D4
Coropuna, Nevado, *Peru* 124 G4
Çorovodë, *Albania* 40 F4
Corowa, *Australia* 95 F4
Corozal, *Belize* 119 D7
Corps, *France* 21 D9
Corpus, *Argentina* 127 B4
Corpus Christi, *U.S.A.* 113 M6
Corpus Christi, L., *U.S.A.* 113 L6
Corral de Almaguer, *Spain* 34 F7
Corralejo, *Canary Is.* 37 F6
Corraun Pen., *Ireland* 15 C2
Corréggio, *Italy* 28 D7
Correntes, C. das, *Mozam.* 89 C6
Corrèze □, *France* 20 C5
Corrèze →, *France* 20 C5
Corrib, L., *Ireland* 15 C2
Corridónia, *Italy* 29 E10
Corrientes, *Argentina* 126 B4
Corrientes □, *Argentina* 126 B4
Corrientes →, *Argentina* 126 C4
Corrientes →, *Peru* 124 D4
Corrientes, C., *Colombia* 124 B3
Corrientes, C., *Cuba* 120 B3
Corrientes, C., *Mexico* 118 C3
Corrigan, *U.S.A.* 113 K7
Corrigin, *Australia* 93 F2
Corry, *U.S.A.* 110 E5
Corse, *France* 21 G13
Corse, C., *France* 21 E13
Corse-du-Sud □, *France* 21 G13
Corsica = Corse, *France* 21 G13
Corsicana, *U.S.A.* 113 J6
Corte, *France* 21 F13
Corte Pinto, *Portugal* 35 H3
Cortegana, *Spain* 35 H4
Cortez, *U.S.A.* 115 H9
Cortina d'Ampezzo, *Italy* 29 B9
Cortland, *N.Y., U.S.A.* 111 D8
Cortland, *Ohio, U.S.A.* 110 E4
Cortona, *Italy* 29 E8
Corubal →, *Guinea-Biss.* 82 C2
Coruche, *Portugal* 35 G2
Çoruh →, *Turkey* 49 K5
Çorum, *Turkey* 72 B6
Corumbá, *Brazil* 124 G7
Corund, *Romania* 43 D10
Corunna = A Coruña, *Spain* 34 B2
Corvallis, *U.S.A.* 114 D2
Corvette, L. de la, *Canada* 102 B5
Corydon, *U.S.A.* 112 E8
Cosalá, *Mexico* 118 C3
Cosamaloapan, *Mexico* 119 D5
Cosenza, *Italy* 31 C9
Coşereni, *Romania* 43 F11
Coshocton, *U.S.A.* 110 F3
Cosmo Newberry, *Australia* 93 E3
Cosne-Cours-sur-Loire, *France* 19 E9
Coso Junction, *U.S.A.* 117 J9
Coso Pk., *U.S.A.* 117 J9
Cospeito, *Spain* 34 B3
Cosquín, *Argentina* 126 C3
Cossato, *Italy* 28 C5
Cossé-le-Vivien, *France* 18 E6
Cosson →, *France* 18 E8
Costa Blanca, *Spain* 33 G4
Costa Brava, *Spain* 32 D8
Costa del Sol, *Spain* 35 J6
Costa Dorada, *Spain* 32 D6
Costa Mesa, *U.S.A.* 117 M9
Costa Rica ■, *Cent. Amer.* 120 E3
Costa Smeralda, *Italy* 30 A2
Costeşti, *Romania* 43 F9
Costigliole d'Asti, *Italy* 28 D5
Cosumnes →, *U.S.A.* 116 G5
Coswig, *Sachsen, Germany* 24 D9
Coswig, *Sachsen-Anhalt, Germany* 24 D8
Cotabato, *Phil.* 61 H6
Cotagaita, *Bolivia* 126 A2
Côte d'Azur, *France* 21 E11
Côte-d'Ivoire = Ivory Coast ■, *Africa* 82 D4
Côte d'Or, *France* 19 E11
Côte-d'Or □, *France* 19 E11
Coteau des Prairies, *U.S.A.* 112 C6
Coteau du Missouri, *U.S.A.* 112 B4
Coteau Landing, *Canada* 111 A10
Cotentin, *France* 18 C5
Côtes-d'Armor □, *France* 18 D4
Côtes de Meuse, *France* 19 C12
Côtes-du-Nord = Côtes-d'Armor □, *France* 18 D4
Cotiella, *Spain* 32 C5
Cotillo, *Canary Is.* 37 F5
Cotiujeni, *Moldova* 43 C13
Cotonou, *Benin* 83 D5
Cotopaxi, *Ecuador* 122 D3
Cotronei, *Italy* 31 C9
Cotswold Hills, *U.K.* 13 F5
Cottage Grove, *U.S.A.* 114 E2
Cottbus, *Germany* 24 D10
Cottonwood, *U.S.A.* 115 J7
Cotulla, *U.S.A.* 113 L5
Coubre, Pte. de la, *France* 20 C2
Couches, *France* 19 F11
Couço, *Portugal* 35 G2
Coudersport, *U.S.A.* 110 E6
Couedic, C. du, *Australia* 95 F2
Couëron, *France* 18 E5
Couesnon →, *France* 18 D5
Couhé, *France* 20 B4
Coulanges-sur-Yonne, *France* 19 E10
Coulee City, *U.S.A.* 114 C4
Coulman I., *Antarctica* 5 D11
Coulommiers, *France* 19 D10
Coulon →, *France* 21 E9
Coulonge →, *Canada* 102 C4
Coulonges-sur-l'Autize, *France* 20 B3
Coulounieix-Chamiers, *France* 20 C4
Coulterville, *U.S.A.* 116 H6
Council, *U.S.A.* 114 D5
Council Bluffs, *U.S.A.* 112 E7
Council Grove, *U.S.A.* 112 F6
Coupeville, *U.S.A.* 116 B4
Courantyne →, *S. Amer.* 122 C5
Courcelles, *Belgium* 17 D4
Courçon, *France* 20 B3
Courmayeur, *Italy* 28 C3
Couronne, C., *France* 21 E9
Cours-la-Ville, *France* 19 F11
Coursan, *France* 20 E7
Courseulles-sur-Mer, *France* 18 C6
Courtenay, *Canada* 104 D4
Courtenay, *France* 19 D10
Courtland, *U.S.A.* 116 G5
Courtrai = Kortrijk, *Belgium* 17 D3
Courtright, *Canada* 110 D2
Coushatta, *U.S.A.* 113 J8
Coutances, *France* 18 C5
Coutras, *France* 20 C3
Coutts Crossing, *Australia* 95 D5
Couvin, *Belgium* 17 D4
Covarrubias, *Spain* 34 C7
Covasna, *Romania* 43 E11
Covasna □, *Romania* 43 E10
Cove I., *Canada* 110 A3
Coventry, *U.K.* 13 E6
Covilhã, *Portugal* 34 E3
Covington, *Ga., U.S.A.* 109 J4
Covington, *Ky., U.S.A.* 108 F3
Covington, *Okla., U.S.A.* 113 G6
Covington, *Tenn., U.S.A.* 113 H10
Covington, *Va., U.S.A.* 108 G5
Cowal, L., *Australia* 95 E4
Cowan, L., *Australia* 93 F3
Cowan L., *Canada* 105 C7
Cowangie, *Australia* 95 F3
Cowansville, *Canada* 102 C5
Coward Springs, *Australia* 95 D2
Cowcowing Lakes, *Australia* 93 F2
Cowdenbeath, *U.K.* 14 E5
Cowell, *Australia* 95 E2
Cowes, *U.K.* 13 G6
Cowichan L., *Canada* 116 B2
Cowlitz →, *U.S.A.* 116 D4
Cowra, *Australia* 95 E4
Cox, *Spain* 33 G4
Coxilha Grande, *Brazil* 127 B5
Coxim, *Brazil* 125 G8
Cox's Bazar, *Bangla.* 67 J17
Coyote Wells, *U.S.A.* 117 N11
Coyuca de Benítez, *Mexico* 119 D4
Coyuca de Catalan, *Mexico* 118 D4
Cozad, *U.S.A.* 112 E5
Cozes, *France* 20 C3
Cozumel, *Mexico* 119 C7
Cozumel, Isla, *Mexico* 119 C7
Cracow = Kraków, *Poland* 45 H6
Cracow, *Australia* 95 D5
Cradock, *Australia* 95 E2
Cradock, *S. Africa* 88 E4
Craig, *U.S.A.* 114 F10
Craigavon, *U.K.* 15 B5
Craigmore, *Zimbabwe* 89 G3
Craik, *Canada* 105 C7
Crailsheim, *Germany* 25 F6
Craiova, *Romania* 43 F8
Cramsie, *Australia* 94 C3
Cranberry L., *U.S.A.* 111 B10
Cranberry Portage, *Canada* 105 C8
Cranbrook, *Australia* 93 F2
Cranbrook, *Canada* 104 D5
Crandon, *U.S.A.* 112 C10
Crane, *Oreg., U.S.A.* 114 E4
Crane, *Tex., U.S.A.* 113 K3
Cranston, *U.S.A.* 111 E13
Craon, *France* 18 E6
Craonne, *France* 19 C10
Craponne-sur-Arzon, *France* 20 C7
Crasna, *Romania* 43 D12
Crasna →, *Romania* 42 C7
Crasnei, Munţii, *Romania* 43 C8
Crater L., *U.S.A.* 114 E2
Crater Lake National Park, *U.S.A.* 114 E2
Crateús, *Brazil* 125 E10
Crati →, *Italy* 31 C9
Crato, *Brazil* 125 E11
Crato, *Portugal* 35 F3
Craven, L., *Canada* 102 B4
Crawford, *U.S.A.* 112 D3
Crawfordsville, *U.S.A.* 108 E2
Crawley, *U.K.* 13 F7
Crazy Mts., *U.S.A.* 114 C8
Crean L., *Canada* 105 C7
Crécy-en-Ponthieu, *France* 19 B8
Crediton, *Canada* 110 C3
Cree →, *Canada* 105 B7
Cree →, *U.K.* 14 G4
Cree L., *Canada* 105 B7
Creede, *U.S.A.* 115 H10
Creekside, *U.S.A.* 110 F5
Creel, *Mexico* 118 B3
Creemore, *Canada* 110 B4
Creighton, *Canada* 105 C8
Creighton, *U.S.A.* 112 D6
Creil, *France* 19 C9
Crema, *Italy* 28 C6
Cremona, *Italy* 28 C7
Crepaja, *Serbia, Yug.* 42 E5
Crépy, *France* 19 C10
Crépy-en-Valois, *France* 19 C9
Cres, *Croatia* 29 D11
Crescent City, *U.S.A.* 114 F1
Crescentino, *Italy* 28 C5
Crespo, *Argentina* 126 C3
Cresson, *U.S.A.* 110 F6
Crest, *France* 21 D9
Cresta, Mt., *Phil.* 61 C5
Crestline, *Calif., U.S.A.* 117 L9
Crestline, *Ohio, U.S.A.* 110 F2
Creston, *Canada* 104 D5
Creston, *Calif., U.S.A.* 116 K6
Creston, *Iowa, U.S.A.* 112 E7
Crestview, *Calif., U.S.A.* 116 H8
Crestview, *Fla., U.S.A.* 109 K2
Crêt de la Neige, *France* 19 F12
Crete = Kriti, *Greece* 36 D7
Crete, *U.S.A.* 112 E6
Crete, Sea of, *Greece* 39 E7
Créteil, *France* 19 D9
Creus, C. de, *Spain* 32 C8
Creuse □, *France* 19 F9
Creuse →, *France* 20 B4
Creutzwald, *France* 19 C13
Creuzburg, *Germany* 24 D6
Crèvecœur-le-Grand, *France* 19 C9
Crevillente, *Spain* 33 G4
Crewe, *U.K.* 12 D5
Crewkerne, *U.K.* 13 G5
Criciúma, *Brazil* 127 B6
Cricova, *Moldova* 43 C13
Crieff, *U.K.* 14 E5
Crikvenica, *Croatia* 29 C11
Crimea □, *Ukraine* 47 K8
Crimean Pen. = Krymskyy Pivostriv, *Ukraine* 47 K8
Crimmitschau, *Germany* 24 E8
Cristuru Secuiesc, *Romania* 43 D10
Crişul Alb →, *Romania* 42 D6
Crişul Negru →, *Romania* 42 D6
Crişul Repede →, *Romania* 42 D5
Criuleni, *Moldova* 43 C14
Crivitz, *Germany* 24 B7
Crna →, *Macedonia* 40 E5
Crna Gora = Montenegro □, *Yugoslavia* 40 D3
Crna Gora, *Macedonia* 40 D5
Crna Reka = Crna →, *Macedonia* 40 E5
Crna Trava, *Serbia, Yug.* 40 D6
Crni Drim →, *Macedonia* 40 E4
Crni Timok →, *Serbia, Yug.* 40 C6
Crnoljeva Planina, *Kosovo, Yug.* 40 D5
Črnomelj, *Slovenia* 29 C12
Croagh Patrick, *Ireland* 15 C2
Croatia ■, *Europe* 29 C13
Crocker, Banjaran, *Malaysia* 62 C5
Crockett, *U.S.A.* 113 K7
Crocodile = Krokodil →, *Mozam.* 89 D5
Crocodile Is., *Australia* 94 A1
Crocq, *France* 20 C6
Crodo, *Italy* 28 B5
Crohy Hd., *Ireland* 15 B3
Croisette, C., *France* 21 E9
Croisic, Pte. du, *France* 18 E4
Croix, L. La, *Canada* 102 C1
Croker, C., *Australia* 92 B5
Croker, C., *Canada* 110 B4
Croker I., *Australia* 92 B5
Cromarty, *U.K.* 14 D4
Cromer, *U.K.* 12 E9
Cromwell, *N.Z.* 91 L2
Cromwell, *U.S.A.* 111 E12
Cronat, *France* 19 F10
Crook, *U.K.* 12 C6
Crooked →, *Canada* 104 C4
Crooked →, *U.S.A.* 114 D3
Crooked I., *Bahamas* 121 B5
Crooked Island Passage, *Bahamas* 121 B5
Crookston, *Minn., U.S.A.* 112 B6
Crookston, *Nebr., U.S.A.* 112 D4
Crookwell, *Australia* 95 E4
Crosby, *U.K.* 12 D4
Crosby, *N. Dak., U.S.A.* 112 A3
Crosby, *Pa., U.S.A.* 110 E6
Crosbyton, *U.S.A.* 113 J4
Crosía, *Italy* 31 C9
Cross →, *Nigeria* 83 E6
Cross City, *U.S.A.* 109 L4
Cross Fell, *U.K.* 12 C5
Cross L., *Canada* 105 C9
Cross Lake, *Canada* 105 C9
Cross River □, *Nigeria* 83 D6
Cross Sound, *U.S.A.* 100 C6
Crossett, *U.S.A.* 113 J9
Crosshaven, *Ireland* 15 E3
Crossville, *U.S.A.* 109 G3
Croswell, *U.S.A.* 110 C2
Croton-on-Hudson, *U.S.A.* 111 E11
Crotone, *Italy* 31 C10
Crow →, *Canada* 104 B4
Crow Agency, *U.S.A.* 114 D10
Crow Hd., *Ireland* 15 E1
Crowell, *U.S.A.* 113 J5
Crowley, *U.S.A.* 113 K8
Crowley, L., *U.S.A.* 116 H8
Crown Point, *Ind., U.S.A.* 108 E2
Crown Point, *N.Y., U.S.A.* 111 C11
Crownpoint, *U.S.A.* 115 J9
Crows Landing, *U.S.A.* 116 H5
Crows Nest, *Australia* 95 D5
Crowsnest Pass, *Canada* 104 D6
Croydon, *Australia* 94 B3
Croydon □, *U.K.* 13 F7
Crozet, Is., *Ind. Oc.* 3 G12
Crozon, *France* 18 D2
Cruz, C., *Cuba* 120 C4
Cruz Alta, *Brazil* 127 B5
Cruz de Incio, *Spain* 34 C3
Cruz del Eje, *Argentina* 126 C3
Cruzeiro, *Brazil* 127 A7
Cruzeiro do Oeste, *Brazil* 127 A5
Cruzeiro do Sul, *Brazil* 124 E4
Cry L., *Canada* 104 B3
Crystal Bay, *U.S.A.* 116 F7
Crystal Brook, *Australia* 95 E2
Crystal City, *U.S.A.* 113 L5
Crystal Falls, *U.S.A.* 108 B1
Crystal River, *U.S.A.* 109 L4
Crystal Springs, *U.S.A.* 113 K9
Csenger, *Hungary* 42 C7
Csongrád, *Hungary* 42 D5
Csongrád □, *Hungary* 42 D5
Csorna, *Hungary* 42 C2
Csurgo, *Hungary* 42 D2
Cu Lao Hon, *Vietnam* 65 G7
Cua Rao, *Vietnam* 64 C5
Cuácua →, *Mozam.* 87 F4
Cuamato, *Angola* 88 B2
Cuamba, *Mozam.* 87 E4

Cuando →, *Angola* 85 H4
Cuando Cubango □, *Angola* 88 B3
Cuangar, *Angola* 88 B2
Cuango = Kwango →, *Dem. Rep. of the Congo* 84 E3
Cuanza →, *Angola* 84 F2
Cuarto →, *Argentina* 126 C3
Cuatrociénegas, *Mexico* 118 B4
Cuauhtémoc, *Mexico* 118 B3
Cuba, *Portugal* 35 G3
Cuba, *N. Mex., U.S.A.* 115 J10
Cuba, *N.Y., U.S.A.* 110 D6
Cuba ■, *W. Indies* 120 B4
Cubango →, *Africa* 88 B3
Çubuk, *Turkey* 72 B5
Cuchumatanes, Sierra de los, *Guatemala* 120 C1
Cuckfield, *U.K.* 13 F7
Cucuí, *Brazil* 124 C5
Cucurpe, *Mexico* 118 A2
Cúcuta, *Colombia* 124 B4
Cudalbi, *Romania* 43 E12
Cuddalore, *India* 66 P11
Cuddapah, *India* 66 M11
Cuddapan, L., *Australia* 94 D3
Cudillero, *Spain* 34 B4
Cue, *Australia* 93 E2
Cuéllar, *Spain* 34 D6
Cuenca, *Ecuador* 124 D3
Cuenca, *Spain* 32 E2
Cuenca □, *Spain* 32 F3
Cuenca, Serranía de, *Spain* 32 F3
Cuerdo del Pozo, Embalse de la, *Spain* 32 D2
Cuernavaca, *Mexico* 119 D5
Cuero, *U.S.A.* 113 L6
Cuers, *France* 21 E10
Cuevas del Almanzora, *Spain* 33 H3
Cuevo, *Bolivia* 124 H6
Cugir, *Romania* 43 E8
Cugnaux, *France* 20 E5
Cuhai-Bakony →, *Hungary* 42 C2
Cuiabá, *Brazil* 125 G7
Cuiabá →, *Brazil* 125 G7
Cuijk, *Neths.* 17 C5
Cuilco, *Guatemala* 120 C1
Cuillin Hills, *U.K.* 14 D2
Cuillin Sd., *U.K.* 14 D2
Cuiseaux, *France* 19 F12
Cuito →, *Angola* 88 B3
Cuitzeo, L. de, *Mexico* 118 D4
Cujmir, *Romania* 42 F7
Cukai, *Malaysia* 65 K4
Culbertson, *U.S.A.* 112 A2
Culcairn, *Australia* 95 F4
Culebra, Sierra de la, *Spain* 34 D4
Culfa, *Azerbaijan* 73 C11
Culgoa →, *Australia* 95 D4
Culiacán, *Mexico* 118 C3
Culiacán →, *Mexico* 118 C3
Culion, *Phil.* 61 F4
Cúllar, *Spain* 35 H8
Cullarin Ra., *Australia* 95 E4
Cullen, *U.K.* 14 D6
Cullen Pt., *Australia* 94 A3
Cullera, *Spain* 33 F4
Cullman, *U.S.A.* 109 H2
Culoz, *France* 21 C9
Culpeper, *U.S.A.* 108 F7
Culuene →, *Brazil* 125 F8
Culver, Pt., *Australia* 93 F3
Culverden, *N.Z.* 91 K4
Cumaná, *Venezuela* 124 A6
Cumaovası, *Turkey* 39 C9
Cumberland, *B.C., Canada* 104 D4
Cumberland, *Ont., Canada* 111 A9
Cumberland, *U.S.A.* 108 F6
Cumberland →, *U.S.A.* 109 G2
Cumberland, L., *U.S.A.* 109 G3
Cumberland I., *U.S.A.* 109 K5
Cumberland Is., *Australia* 94 C4
Cumberland L., *Canada* 105 C8
Cumberland Pen., *Canada* 101 B13
Cumberland Plateau, *U.S.A.* 109 H3
Cumberland Sd., *Canada* 101 B13
Cumbernauld, *U.K.* 14 F5
Cumborah, *Australia* 95 D4
Cumbres Mayores, *Spain* 35 G4
Cumbria □, *U.K.* 12 C5
Cumbrian Mts., *U.K.* 12 C5
Cumbum, *India* 66 M11
Cuminá →, *Brazil* 125 D7
Cummings Mt., *U.S.A.* 117 K8
Cummins, *Australia* 95 E2
Cumnock, *Australia* 95 E4
Cumnock, *U.K.* 14 F4
Cumpas, *Mexico* 118 B3
Cumplida, Pta., *Canary Is.* 37 F2
Çumra, *Turkey* 72 D5
Cunco, *Chile* 128 D2
Cuncumén, *Chile* 126 C1
Cunderdin, *Australia* 93 F2
Cunene →, *Angola* 88 B1
Cúneo, *Italy* 28 D4
Çüngüş, *Turkey* 70 B3
Cunillera, I. = Sa Conillera, *Spain* 37 C7
Cunlhat, *France* 20 C7
Cunnamulla, *Australia* 95 D4
Cuorgnè, *Italy* 28 C4
Cupar, *Canada* 105 C8
Cupar, *U.K.* 14 E5
Cupcini, *Moldova* 43 B12
Cupica, G. de, *Colombia* 124 B3
Ćuprija, *Serbia, Yug.* 40 C5
Curaçao, *Neth. Ant.* 121 D6
Curanilahue, *Chile* 126 D1
Curaray →, *Peru* 124 D4
Cure →, *France* 19 E10
Curepto, *Chile* 126 D1
Curiapo, *Venezuela* 124 B6
Curicó, *Chile* 126 C1
Curinga, *Italy* 31 D9
Curitiba, *Brazil* 127 B6
Curitibanos, *Brazil* 127 B5
Currabubula, *Australia* 95 E5
Currais Novos, *Brazil* 125 E11
Curralinho, *Brazil* 125 D9
Currant, *U.S.A.* 114 G6
Current →, *U.S.A.* 113 G9
Currie, *Australia* 94 F3
Currie, *U.S.A.* 114 F6
Curtea de Argeş, *Romania* 43 E9
Curtici, *Romania* 42 D6
Curtis, *U.S.A.* 112 E4
Curtis Group, *Australia* 94 F4
Curtis I., *Australia* 94 C5
Curuápanema →, *Brazil* 125 D7
Curuçá, *Brazil* 125 D9
Curuguaty, *Paraguay* 127 A4
Curup, *Indonesia* 62 E2
Cururupu, *Brazil* 125 D10
Curuzú Cuatiá, *Argentina* 126 B4
Curvelo, *Brazil* 125 G10
Cushing, *U.S.A.* 113 H6
Cushing, Mt., *Canada* 104 B3
Cusihuiriáchic, *Mexico* 118 B3
Cusna, Mte., *Italy* 28 D7
Cusset, *France* 19 F10
Custer, *U.S.A.* 112 D3
Cut Bank, *U.S.A.* 114 B7
Cutchogue, *U.S.A.* 111 E12
Cuthbert, *U.S.A.* 109 K3
Cutler, *U.S.A.* 116 J7
Cutro, *Italy* 31 C9
Cuttaburra →, *Australia* 95 D3
Cuttack, *India* 67 J14
Cuvier, C., *Australia* 93 D1
Cuvier I., *N.Z.* 91 G5
Cuxhaven, *Germany* 24 B4
Cuyahoga Falls, *U.S.A.* 110 E3
Cuyapo, *Phil.* 61 D4
Cuyo, *Phil.* 61 F4
Cuyo East Pass, *Phil.* 61 F4
Cuyo West Pass, *Phil.* 61 F4
Cuyuni →, *Guyana* 124 B7
Cuzco, *Bolivia* 124 H5
Cuzco, *Peru* 124 F4
Čvrsnica, *Bos.-H.* 42 G2
Cwmbran, *U.K.* 13 F4
Cyangugu, *Rwanda* 86 C2
Cybinka, *Poland* 45 F1
Cyclades = Kikládhes, *Greece* 38 E6
Cygnet, *Australia* 94 G4
Cynthiana, *U.S.A.* 108 F3
Cypress Hills, *Canada* 105 D7
Cypress Hills Prov. Park, *Canada* 105 D7
Cyprus ■, *Asia* 36 E12
Cyrenaica, *Libya* 79 C10
Czaplinek, *Poland* 44 E3
Czar, *Canada* 105 C6
Czarna →, *Łódzkie, Poland* 45 G6
Czarna →, *Świętokrzyskie, Poland* 45 H8
Czarna Białostocka, *Poland* 45 E10
Czarna Woda, *Poland* 44 E5
Czarne, *Poland* 44 E3
Czarnków, *Poland* 45 F3
Czech Rep. ■, *Europe* 26 B8
Czechowice-Dziedzice, *Poland* 45 J5
Czempiń, *Poland* 45 F3
Czeremcha, *Poland* 45 F10
Czerniejewo, *Poland* 45 F4
Czersk, *Poland* 44 E4
Czerwieńsk, *Poland* 45 F2
Czerwionka-Leszczyny, *Poland* 45 H5
Częstochowa, *Poland* 45 H6
Człopa, *Poland* 45 E3
Człuchów, *Poland* 44 E4
Czyżew-Osada, *Poland* 45 F9

D

Da →, *Vietnam* 58 G5
Da Hinggan Ling, *China* 60 B7
Da Lat, *Vietnam* 65 G7
Da Nang, *Vietnam* 64 D7
Da Qaidam, *China* 60 C4
Da Yunhe →, *China* 57 G11
Da'an, *China* 57 B13
Dab'a, Ras el, *Egypt* 80 H6
Daba Shan, *China* 58 B7
Dabai, *Nigeria* 83 C6
Dabakala, *Ivory C.* 82 D4
Dabas, *Hungary* 42 C4
Dabat, *Ethiopia* 81 E4
Dabbagh, Jabal, *Si. Arabia* 70 E2
Dabhoi, *India* 68 H5
Dąbie, *Poland* 45 F5
Dabie Shan, *China* 59 B10
Dabilda, *Cameroon* 83 C7
Dabnou, *Niger* 83 C6
Dabo = Pasirkuning, *Indonesia* 62 E2
Dabola, *Guinea* 82 C2
Dabou, *Ivory C.* 82 D4
Daboya, *Ghana* 83 D4
Dąbrowa Białostocka, *Poland* 44 E10
Dąbrowa Górnicza, *Poland* 45 H6
Dąbrowa Tarnowska, *Poland* 45 H7
Dabu, *China* 59 E11
Dabung, *Malaysia* 65 K4
Dabus →, *Ethiopia* 81 E4
Dacato →, *Ethiopia* 81 F5
Dacca = Dhaka, *Bangla.* 69 H14
Dacca = Dhaka □, *Bangla.* 69 G14
Dachau, *Germany* 25 G7
Dachstein, Hoher, *Austria* 26 D6
Dačice, *Czech Rep.* 26 B8
Dadanawa, *Guyana* 124 C7
Daday, *Turkey* 72 B5
Dade City, *U.S.A.* 109 L4
Dadhar, *Pakistan* 68 E2
Dadiya, *Nigeria* 83 D7
Dadra & Nagar Haveli □, *India* 66 J8
Dadri = Charkhi Dadri, *India* 68 E7
Dadu, *Pakistan* 68 F2
Dadu He →, *China* 58 C4
Daet, *Phil.* 61 D5
Dafang, *China* 58 D5
Dağ, *Turkey* 39 D12
Dagana, *Senegal* 82 B1
Dagash, *Sudan* 80 D3
Dagestan □, *Russia* 49 J8
Dagestanskiye Ogni, *Russia* 49 J9
Daggett, *U.S.A.* 117 L10
Daghestan Republic = Dagestan □, *Russia* 49 J8
Daghfeli, *Sudan* 80 D3
Dağlıq Qarabağ = Nagorno-Karabakh, *Azerbaijan* 70 B5
Dagö = Hiiumaa, *Estonia* 9 G20
Dagu, *China* 57 E9
Daguan, *China* 58 D4
Dagupan, *Phil.* 61 C4
Daguragu, *Australia* 92 C5
Dahab, *Egypt* 80 B3
Dahlak Kebir, *Eritrea* 81 D5
Dahlenburg, *Germany* 24 B6
Dahlonega, *U.S.A.* 109 H4
Dahme, *Germany* 24 D9
Dahod, *India* 68 H6
Dahomey = Benin ■, *Africa* 83 D5
Dahong Shan, *China* 59 B9
Dahra, *Senegal* 82 B1
Dahshûr, *Egypt* 80 J7
Dahūk, *Iraq* 70 B3
Dai Hao, *Vietnam* 64 C6
Dai-Sen, *Japan* 55 G6
Dai Shan, *China* 59 B14
Dai Xian, *China* 56 E7
Daicheng, *China* 56 E9
Daimiel, *Spain* 35 F7
Daingean, *Ireland* 15 C4
Dainkog, *China* 58 A1
Daintree, *Australia* 94 B4
Daiō-Misaki, *Japan* 55 G8
Dair, J. ed, *Sudan* 81 E3
Dairût, *Egypt* 80 B3
Daisetsu-Zan, *Japan* 54 C11
Dajarra, *Australia* 94 C2
Dajin Chuan →, *China* 58 B3
Dak Dam, *Cambodia* 64 F6
Dak Nhe, *Vietnam* 64 E6
Dak Pek, *Vietnam* 64 E6
Dak Song, *Vietnam* 65 F6
Dak Sui, *Vietnam* 64 E6
Dakar, *Senegal* 82 C1
Dakhla, *W. Sahara* 78 D2
Dakhla, El Wâhât el-, *Egypt* 80 B2
Dakingari, *Nigeria* 83 C5
Dakor, *India* 68 H5
Dakoro, *Niger* 83 C6
Dakota City, *U.S.A.* 112 D6
Đakovica, *Kosovo, Yug.* 40 D4
Đakovo, *Croatia* 42 E3
Dalaba, *Guinea* 82 C2
Dalachi, *China* 56 F3
Dalai Nur, *China* 56 C9
Dālakī, *Iran* 71 D6
Dalälven →, *Sweden* 10 D10
Dalaman, *Turkey* 39 E10
Dalaman →, *Turkey* 39 E10
Dalandzadgad, *Mongolia* 56 C3
Dalap-Uliga-Darrit, *Marshall Is.* 96 G9
Dalarna, *Sweden* 10 D8
Dalarnas län □, *Sweden* 10 C8
Dālbandīn, *Pakistan* 66 E4
Dalbeattie, *U.K.* 14 G5
Dalbeg, *Australia* 94 C4
Dalbosjön, *Sweden* 11 F6
Dalby, *Australia* 95 D5
Dalby, *Sweden* 11 J7
Dale City, *U.S.A.* 108 F7
Dale Hollow L., *U.S.A.* 109 G3
Dalga, *Egypt* 80 B3
Dalgān, *Iran* 71 E8
Dalhart, *U.S.A.* 113 G3
Dalhousie, *Canada* 103 C6
Dalhousie, *India* 68 C6
Dali, *Shaanxi, China* 56 G5
Dali, *Yunnan, China* 58 E3
Dalian, *China* 57 E11
Daliang Shan, *China* 58 D4
Daling He →, *China* 57 D11
Dāliyat el Karmel, *Israel* 75 C4
Dalj, *Croatia* 42 E3
Dalkeith, *U.K.* 14 F5
Dallas, *Oreg., U.S.A.* 114 D2
Dallas, *Tex., U.S.A.* 113 J6
Dallol, *Ethiopia* 81 E5
Dalmā, *U.A.E.* 71 E7
Dalmacija, *Croatia* 29 E13
Dalmas, L., *Canada* 103 B5
Dalmatia = Dalmacija, *Croatia* 29 E13
Dalmau, *India* 69 F9
Dalmellington, *U.K.* 14 F4
Dalnegorsk, *Russia* 51 E14
Dalnerechensk, *Russia* 51 E14
Daloa, *Ivory C.* 82 D3
Dalou Shan, *China* 58 C6
Dalry, *U.K.* 14 F4
Dalrymple, L., *Australia* 94 C4
Dals Långed, *Sweden* 11 F6
Dalsjöfors, *Sweden* 11 G7
Dalsland, *Sweden* 11 F6
Daltenganj, *India* 69 H11
Dalton, *Ga., U.S.A.* 109 H3
Dalton, *Mass., U.S.A.* 111 D11
Dalton, *Nebr., U.S.A.* 112 E3
Dalton Iceberg Tongue, *Antarctica* 5 C9
Dalton-in-Furness, *U.K.* 12 C4
Dalupiri I., *Phil.* 61 B4
Dalvík, *Iceland* 8 D4
Dalwallinu, *Australia* 93 F2
Daly →, *Australia* 92 B5
Daly City, *U.S.A.* 116 H4
Daly L., *Canada* 105 B7
Daly River, *Australia* 92 B5
Daly Waters, *Australia* 94 B1
Dalyan, *Turkey* 39 E10
Dam Doi, *Vietnam* 65 H5
Dam Ha, *Vietnam* 64 B6
Daman, *India* 66 J8
Dāmaneh, *Iran* 71 C6
Damanhûr, *Egypt* 80 H7
Damant L., *Canada* 105 A7
Damanzhuang, *China* 56 E9
Damar, *Indonesia* 63 F7
Damaraland, *Namibia* 88 C2
Damascus = Dimashq, *Syria* 75 B5
Damaturu, *Nigeria* 83 C7
Damāvand, *Iran* 71 C7
Damāvand, Qolleh-ye, *Iran* 71 C7
Damba, *Angola* 84 F3
Dâmboviţa □, *Romania* 43 F10
Dâmboviţa →, *Romania* 43 F11
Dâmbovnic →, *Romania* 43 F10
Dame Marie, *Haiti* 121 C5
Dāmghān, *Iran* 71 B7
Dămienesti, *Romania* 43 D11
Damietta = Dumyât, *Egypt* 80 H7
Daming, *China* 56 F8
Damīr Qābū, *Syria* 70 B4
Dammam = Ad Dammām, *Si. Arabia* 71 E6
Dammarie-les-Lys, *France* 19 D9
Dammartin-en-Goële, *France* 19 C9
Damme, *Germany* 24 C4
Damodar →, *India* 69 H12
Damoh, *India* 69 H8
Dampier, *Australia* 92 D2
Dampier, Selat, *Indonesia* 63 E8
Dampier Arch., *Australia* 92 D2
Damrei, Chuor Phnum, *Cambodia* 65 G4
Damvillers, *France* 19 C12
Dan-Gulbi, *Nigeria* 83 C6
Dan Xian, *China* 64 C7
Dana, *Indonesia* 63 F6
Dana, L., *Canada* 102 B4
Dana, Mt., *U.S.A.* 116 H7
Danakil Desert, *Ethiopia* 81 E5
Danané, *Ivory C.* 82 D3
Danao, *Phil.* 61 F6
Danau Poso, *Indonesia* 63 E6
Danba, *China* 58 B3
Danbury, *U.S.A.* 111 E11
Danby L., *U.S.A.* 115 J6
Dand, *Afghan.* 68 D1
Dandeldhura, *Nepal* 69 E9
Dandeli, *India* 66 M9
Dandenong, *Australia* 95 F4
Dandîl, *Egypt* 80 J7
Dandong, *China* 57 D13
Danfeng, *China* 56 H6
Dangan Liedao, *China* 59 F10
Dangé-St-Romain, *France* 20 B4
Dângeni, *Romania* 43 C11
Danger Is. = Pukapuka, *Cook Is.* 97 J11
Danger Pt., *S. Africa* 88 E2
Dangla, *Ethiopia* 81 E4
Dangla Shan = Tanggula Shan, *China* 60 C4
Dangora, *Nigeria* 83 C6
Dangouadougou, *Burkina Faso* 82 D4
Dangrek, Phnom, *Thailand* 64 E5
Dangriga, *Belize* 119 D7
Dangshan, *China* 56 G9
Dangtu, *China* 59 B12
Dangyang, *China* 59 B8
Dani, *Burkina Faso* 83 C4
Daniel, *U.S.A.* 114 E8
Daniel's Harbour, *Canada* 103 B8
Danielskuil, *S. Africa* 88 D3
Danielson, *U.S.A.* 111 E13
Danilov, *Russia* 46 C11
Danilovgrad, *Montenegro, Yug.* 40 D3
Danilovka, *Russia* 48 E7
Daning, *China* 56 F6
Danissa, *Kenya* 86 B5
Danja, *Nigeria* 83 C6
Danjiangkou, *China* 59 A8
Danjiangkou Shuiku, *China* 59 A8
Dạnk, *Oman* 71 F8
Dankalwa, *Nigeria* 83 C7
Dankama, *Nigeria* 83 C6
Dankhar Gompa, *India* 66 C11
Dankov, *Russia* 46 F10
Danleng, *China* 58 B4
Danlí, *Honduras* 120 D2
Dannemora, *U.S.A.* 111 B11
Dannenberg, *Germany* 24 B7
Dannevirke, *N.Z.* 91 J6
Dannhauser, *S. Africa* 89 D5
Dansville, *U.S.A.* 110 D7
Danta, *India* 68 G5
Dantan, *India* 69 J12
Dante, *Somali Rep.* 74 E5
Danube = Dunărea →, *Europe* 43 E14
Danvers, *U.S.A.* 111 D14
Danville, *Ill., U.S.A.* 108 E2
Danville, *Ky., U.S.A.* 108 G3
Danville, *Pa., U.S.A.* 111 F8
Danville, *Va., U.S.A.* 109 G6
Danville, *Vt., U.S.A.* 111 B12
Danyang, *China* 59 B12
Danzhai, *China* 58 D6
Danzig = Gdańsk, *Poland* 44 D5
Dão →, *Portugal* 34 E2
Dao Xian, *China* 59 E8
Daocheng, *China* 58 C3
Daoukro, *Ivory C.* 82 D4
Dapaong, *Togo* 83 C5
Dapchi, *Nigeria* 83 C7
Dapitan, *Phil.* 61 G5
Daqing Shan, *China* 56 D6
Daqu Shan, *China* 59 B14
Dar Banda, *Africa* 76 F6
Dar el Beida = Casablanca, *Morocco* 78 B4
Dar es Salaam, *Tanzania* 86 D4
Dar Mazār, *Iran* 71 D8
Dar'ā, *Syria* 75 C5
Dar'ā □, *Syria* 75 C5
Dārāb, *Iran* 71 D7
Daraban, *Pakistan* 68 D4
Darabani, *Romania* 43 B11
Daraina, *Madag.* 89 A8
Daraj, *Libya* 79 B8
Dārān, *Iran* 71 C6
Daravica, *Kosovo, Yug.* 40 D4
Daraw, *Egypt* 80 C3
Dārayyā, *Syria* 75 B5
Darazo, *Nigeria* 83 C7
Darband, *Pakistan* 68 B5
Darband, Kūh-e, *Iran* 71 D8
Darbhanga, *India* 69 F11
D'Arcy, *Canada* 104 C4
Darda, *Croatia* 42 E3
Dardanelle, *Ark., U.S.A.* 113 H8
Dardanelle, *Calif., U.S.A.* 116 G7
Dardanelles = Çanakkale Boğazı, *Turkey* 41 F10
Dare →, *Ethiopia* 81 F5
Darende, *Turkey* 72 C7
Dārestān, *Iran* 71 D8
Darfo, *Italy* 28 C7
Dârfûr, *Sudan* 79 F10
Dargai, *Pakistan* 68 B4
Dargan Ata, *Turkmenistan* 50 E7
Dargaville, *N.Z.* 91 F4
Dargol, *Niger* 83 C5
Darhan Muminggan Lianheqi, *China* 56 D6
Dari, *Sudan* 81 F3
Darıca, *Turkey* 72 B3
Darién, G. del, *Colombia* 122 C3
Dariganga = Ovoot, *Mongolia* 56 B7
Darinskoye, *Kazakstan* 48 E10
Darjeeling = Darjiling, *India* 69 F13
Darjiling, *India* 69 F13
Darkan, *Australia* 93 F2
Darkhana, *Pakistan* 68 D5
Darkhazīneh, *Iran* 71 D6
Darkot Pass, *Pakistan* 69 A5
Darling Downs, *Australia* 95 D5
Darling Ra., *Australia* 93 F2
Darlington, *U.K.* 12 C6
Darlington, *U.S.A.* 109 H6
Darlington □, *U.K.* 12 C6
Darlington, L., *S. Africa* 88 E4
Darlot, L., *Australia* 93 E3
Darłowo, *Poland* 44 D3
Dărmăneşti, *Bacău, Romania* 43 D11
Dărmăneşti, *Suceava, Romania* 43 C11
Darmstadt, *Germany* 25 F4
Darnah, *Libya* 79 B10
Darnall, *S. Africa* 89 D5
Darney, *France* 19 D13
Darnley, C., *Antarctica* 5 C6
Darnley B., *Canada* 100 B7
Daroca, *Spain* 32 D3
Darou-Mousti, *Senegal* 82 B1
Darr →, *Australia* 94 C3
Darra Pezu, *Pakistan* 68 C4
Darrequeira, *Argentina* 126 D3
Darrington, *U.S.A.* 114 B3
Darsser Ort, *Germany* 24 A8
Dart →, *U.K.* 13 G4
Dart, C., *Antarctica* 5 D14
Dartford, *U.K.* 13 F8
Dartmoor, *U.K.* 13 G4
Dartmouth, *Canada* 103 D7
Dartmouth, *U.K.* 13 G4
Dartmouth, L., *Australia* 95 D4
Dartmouth Res., *Australia* 95 D4
Dartuch, C. = Artrutx, C. de, *Spain* 37 B10
Daruvar, *Croatia* 42 E2
Darvaza, *Turkmenistan* 50 E6
Darvel, Teluk = Lahad Datu, Teluk, *Malaysia* 63 D5
Darwen, *U.K.* 12 D5
Darwendale, *Zimbabwe* 89 B5
Darwha, *India* 66 J10
Darwin, *Australia* 92 B5
Darwin, *U.S.A.* 117 J9
Darya Khan, *Pakistan* 68 D4
Daryoi Amu = Amudarya →, *Uzbekistan* 50 E6
Dās, *U.A.E.* 71 E7

Dashen, Ras, *Ethiopia* 81 E4
Dashetai, *China* 56 D5
Dashhowuz, *Turkmenistan* 50 E6
Dashkesan = Daşkäsän, *Azerbaijan* 49 K7
Dashköpri, *Turkmenistan* 71 B9
Dasht, *Iran* 71 B8
Dasht →, *Pakistan* 66 G2
Daska, *Pakistan* 68 C6
Daşkäsän, *Azerbaijan* 49 K7
Dassa, *Benin* 83 D5
Dasuya, *India* 68 D6
Datça, *Turkey* 39 E9
Datia, *India* 69 G8
Datian, *China* 59 E11
Datong, *Anhui, China* 59 B11
Datong, *Shanxi, China* 56 D7
Dattakhel, *Pakistan* 68 C3
Datteln, *Germany* 24 D3
Datu, Tanjung, *Indonesia* 62 D3
Datu Piang, *Phil.* 61 H6
Datuk, Tanjong = Datu, Tanjung, *Indonesia* 62 D3
Daud Khel, *Pakistan* 68 C4
Daudnagar, *India* 69 G11
Daugava →, *Latvia* 9 H21
Daugavpils, *Latvia* 9 J22
Daulpur, *India* 68 F7
Daun, *Germany* 25 E2
Dauphin, *Canada* 105 C8
Dauphin, *U.S.A.* 110 F8
Dauphin L., *Canada* 105 C9
Dauphiné, *France* 21 C9
Daura, *Borno, Nigeria* 83 C7
Daura, *Katsina, Nigeria* 83 C6
Dausa, *India* 68 F7
Däväçi, *Azerbaijan* 49 K9
Davangere, *India* 66 M9
Davao, *Phil.* 61 H6
Davao G., *Phil.* 61 H6
Dāvar Panāh, *Iran* 71 E9
Davenport, *Calif., U.S.A.* 116 H4
Davenport, *Iowa, U.S.A.* 112 E9
Davenport, *Wash., U.S.A.* 114 C4
Davenport Ra., *Australia* 94 C1
Daventry, *U.K.* 13 E6
David, *Panama* 120 E3
David City, *U.S.A.* 112 E6
David Gorodok = Davyd Haradok, *Belarus* 47 F4
Davidson, *Canada* 105 C7
Davis, *U.S.A.* 116 G5
Davis Dam, *U.S.A.* 117 K12
Davis Inlet, *Canada* 103 A7
Davis Mts., *U.S.A.* 113 K2
Davis Sea, *Antarctica* 5 C7
Davis Str., *N. Amer.* 101 B14
Davo →, *Ivory C.* 82 D3
Davos, *Switz.* 25 J5
Davutlar, *Turkey* 39 D9
Davy L., *Canada* 105 B7
Davyd Haradok, *Belarus* 47 F4
Dawa →, *Ethiopia* 81 G5
Dawaki, *Bauchi, Nigeria* 83 D6
Dawaki, *Kano, Nigeria* 83 C6
Dawei, *Burma* 64 E2
Dawes Ra., *Australia* 94 C5
Dawlish, *U.K.* 13 G4
Dawna Ra., *Burma* 64 D2
Dawros Hd., *Ireland* 15 B3
Dawson, *Canada* 100 B6
Dawson, *U.S.A.* 109 K3
Dawson, I., *Chile* 128 G2
Dawson B., *Canada* 105 C8
Dawson Creek, *Canada* 104 B4
Dawson Inlet, *Canada* 105 A10
Dawson Ra., *Australia* 94 C4
Dawu, *Hubei, China* 59 B9
Dawu, *Sichuan, China* 58 B3
Dax, *France* 20 E2
Daxian, *China* 58 B6
Daxin, *China* 58 F6
Daxindian, *China* 57 F11
Daxinggou, *China* 57 C15
Daxue Shan, *Sichuan, China* 58 B3
Daxue Shan, *Yunnan, China* 58 F2
Dayao, *China* 58 E3
Daye, *China* 59 B10
Dayet en Naharat, *Mali* 82 B4
Dayi, *China* 58 B4
Daylesford, *Australia* 95 F3
Dayong, *China* 59 C8
Dayr az Zawr, *Syria* 70 C4
Daysland, *Canada* 104 C6
Dayton, *Nev., U.S.A.* 116 F7
Dayton, *Ohio, U.S.A.* 108 F3
Dayton, *Pa., U.S.A.* 110 F5
Dayton, *Tenn., U.S.A.* 109 H3
Dayton, *Wash., U.S.A.* 114 C4
Dayton, *Wyo., U.S.A.* 114 D10
Daytona Beach, *U.S.A.* 109 L5
Dayu, *China* 59 E10
Dayville, *U.S.A.* 114 D4
Dazhu, *China* 58 B6
Dazkırı, *Turkey* 39 D11
Dazu, *China* 58 C5
De Aar, *S. Africa* 88 E3
De Funiak Springs, *U.S.A.* 109 K2
De Grey →, *Australia* 92 D2
De Haan, *Belgium* 17 C3
De Kalb, *U.S.A.* 112 E10
De Land, *U.S.A.* 109 L5
De Leon, *U.S.A.* 113 J5
De Panne, *Belgium* 17 C2
De Pere, *U.S.A.* 108 C1
De Queen, *U.S.A.* 113 H7
De Quincy, *U.S.A.* 113 K8
De Ridder, *U.S.A.* 113 K8
De Smet, *U.S.A.* 112 C6
De Soto, *U.S.A.* 112 F9
De Tour Village, *U.S.A.* 108 C4
De Witt, *U.S.A.* 113 H9
Dead Sea, *Asia* 75 D4
Deadwood, *U.S.A.* 112 C3
Deadwood L., *Canada* 104 B3
Deal, *U.K.* 13 F9
Deal I., *Australia* 94 F4
Dealesville, *S. Africa* 88 D4
De'an, *China* 59 C10
Dean →, *Canada* 104 C3
Dean, Forest of, *U.K.* 13 F5
Dean Chan., *Canada* 104 C3
Deán Funes, *Argentina* 126 C3
Dease →, *Canada* 104 B3
Dease L., *Canada* 104 B2
Dease Lake, *Canada* 104 B2
Death Valley, *U.S.A.* 117 J10
Death Valley Junction, *U.S.A.* 117 J10
Death Valley National Park, *U.S.A.* 117 J10
Deauville, *France* 18 C7
Deba, *Spain* 32 B2
Deba Habe, *Nigeria* 83 C7
Debaltsevo, *Ukraine* 47 H10
Debao, *China* 58 F6
Debar, *Macedonia* 40 E4
Debden, *Canada* 105 C7
Dębica, *Poland* 45 H8
Dęblin, *Poland* 45 G8
Dębno, *Poland* 45 F1
Débo, L., *Mali* 82 B4
Debolt, *Canada* 104 B5
Deborah East, L., *Australia* 93 F2
Deborah West, L., *Australia* 93 F2
Debrc, *Serbia, Yug.* 40 B3
Debre Birhan, *Ethiopia* 81 F4
Debre Markos, *Ethiopia* 81 E4
Debre May, *Ethiopia* 81 E4
Debre Sina, *Ethiopia* 81 F4
Debre Tabor, *Ethiopia* 81 E4
Debre Zevit, *Ethiopia* 81 F4
Debre Zeyit, *Ethiopia* 81 E4
Debrecen, *Hungary* 42 C6
Debrzno, *Poland* 44 E4
Dečani, *Kosovo, Yug.* 40 D4
Decatur, *Ala., U.S.A.* 109 H2
Decatur, *Ga., U.S.A.* 109 J3
Decatur, *Ill., U.S.A.* 112 F10
Decatur, *Ind., U.S.A.* 108 E3
Decatur, *Tex., U.S.A.* 113 J6
Decazeville, *France* 20 D6
Deccan, *India* 66 L11
Deception Bay, *Australia* 95 D5
Deception L., *Canada* 105 B8
Dechang, *China* 58 D4
Dechhu, *India* 68 F5
Děčín, *Czech Rep.* 26 A7
Decize, *France* 19 F10
Deckerville, *U.S.A.* 110 C2
Decollatura, *Italy* 31 C9
Decorah, *U.S.A.* 112 D9
Deda, *Romania* 43 D9
Dedéagach = Alexandroúpolis, *Greece* 41 F9
Deder, *Ethiopia* 81 F5
Dedham, *U.S.A.* 111 D13
Dédougou, *Burkina Faso* 82 C4
Dedovichi, *Russia* 46 D5
Dedza, *Malawi* 87 E3
Dee →, *Aberds., U.K.* 14 D6
Dee →, *Dumf. & Gall., U.K.* 14 G4
Dee →, *Wales, U.K.* 12 D4
Deep B., *Canada* 104 A5
Deepwater, *Australia* 95 D5
Deer →, *Canada* 105 B10
Deer L., *Canada* 105 C10
Deer Lake, *Nfld., Canada* 103 C8
Deer Lake, *Ont., Canada* 105 C10
Deer Lodge, *U.S.A.* 114 C7
Deer Park, *U.S.A.* 114 C5
Deer River, *U.S.A.* 112 B8
Deeragun, *Australia* 94 B4
Deerdepoort, *S. Africa* 88 C4
Deferiet, *U.S.A.* 111 B9
Defiance, *U.S.A.* 108 E3
Degana, *India* 68 F6
Dêgê, *China* 58 B2
Degebe →, *Portugal* 35 G3
Degeberga, *Sweden* 11 J8
Dégelis, *Canada* 103 C6
Degema, *Nigeria* 83 E6
Degerfors, *Sweden* 10 E8
Degerhamn, *Sweden* 11 H10
Deggendorf, *Germany* 25 G8
Degh →, *Pakistan* 68 D5
Değirmendere, *Turkey* 41 F13
Deh Bīd, *Iran* 71 D7
Deh-e Shīr, *Iran* 71 D7
Dehaj, *Iran* 71 D7
Dehak, *Iran* 71 E9
Dehdez, *Iran* 71 D6
Dehej, *India* 68 J5
Dehestān, *Iran* 71 D7
Dehgolān, *Iran* 70 C5
Dehibat, *Tunisia* 79 B8
Dehlorān, *Iran* 70 C5
Dehnow-e Kūhestān, *Iran* 71 E8
Dehra Dun, *India* 68 D8
Dehri, *India* 69 G11
Dehua, *China* 59 E12
Dehui, *China* 57 B13
Deim Zubeir, *Sudan* 81 F2
Deinze, *Belgium* 17 D3
Dej, *Romania* 43 C8
Deje, *Sweden* 10 E7
Dejiang, *China* 58 C7
Deka →, *Zimbabwe* 88 B4
Dekemhare, *Eritrea* 81 D4
Dekese, *Dem. Rep. of the Congo* 84 E4
Del Mar, *U.S.A.* 117 N9
Del Norte, *U.S.A.* 115 H10
Del Rio, *U.S.A.* 113 L4
Delai, *Sudan* 80 D4
Delambre I., *Australia* 92 D2
Delami, *Sudan* 81 E3
Delano, *U.S.A.* 117 K7
Delano Peak, *U.S.A.* 115 G7
Delareyville, *S. Africa* 88 D4
Delaronde L., *Canada* 105 C7
Delavan, *U.S.A.* 112 D10
Delaware, *U.S.A.* 108 E4
Delaware □, *U.S.A.* 108 F8
Delaware →, *U.S.A.* 111 G9
Delaware B., *U.S.A.* 108 F8
Delay →, *Canada* 103 A5
Delbrück, *Germany* 24 D4
Delčevo, *Macedonia* 40 E6
Delegate, *Australia* 95 F4
Delémont, *Switz.* 25 H3
Delevan, *U.S.A.* 110 D6
Delft, *Neths.* 17 B4
Delfzijl, *Neths.* 17 A6
Delgado, C., *Mozam.* 87 E5
Delgerhet, *Mongolia* 56 B6
Delgo, *Sudan* 80 C3
Delhi, *Canada* 110 D4
Delhi, *India* 68 E7
Delhi, *La., U.S.A.* 113 J9
Delhi, *N.Y., U.S.A.* 111 D10
Deli Jovan, *Serbia, Yug.* 40 B6
Delia, *Canada* 104 C6
Delice, *Turkey* 72 C6
Delicias, *Mexico* 118 B3
Delījān, *Iran* 71 C6
Déline, *Canada* 100 B7
Delisle, *Canada* 105 C7
Delitzsch, *Germany* 24 D8
Dell City, *U.S.A.* 115 L11
Dell Rapids, *U.S.A.* 112 D6
Delle, *France* 19 E14
Delmar, *U.S.A.* 111 D11
Delmenhorst, *Germany* 24 B4
Delnice, *Croatia* 29 C11
Delonga, Ostrova, *Russia* 51 B15
Deloraine, *Australia* 94 G4
Deloraine, *Canada* 105 D8
Delphi, *Greece* 38 C4
Delphi, *U.S.A.* 108 E2
Delphos, *U.S.A.* 108 E3
Delportshoop, *S. Africa* 88 D3
Delray Beach, *U.S.A.* 109 M5
Delsbo, *Sweden* 10 C10
Delta, *Colo., U.S.A.* 115 G9
Delta, *Utah, U.S.A.* 114 G7
Delta □, *Nigeria* 83 D6
Delta Junction, *U.S.A.* 100 B5
Deltona, *U.S.A.* 109 L5
Delungra, *Australia* 95 D5
Delvada, *India* 68 J4
Delvinákion, *Greece* 38 B2
Delvinë, *Albania* 40 G4
Demak, *Indonesia* 63 G14
Demanda, Sierra de la, *Spain* 32 C2
Demavand = Damāvand, *Iran* 71 C7
Dembecha, *Ethiopia* 81 E4
Dembi, *Ethiopia* 81 F4
Dembia, *Dem. Rep. of the Congo* 86 B2
Dembidolo, *Ethiopia* 81 F3
Demchok, *India* 69 C8
Demer →, *Belgium* 17 D4
Demetrias, *Greece* 38 B5
Demidov, *Russia* 46 E6
Deming, *N. Mex., U.S.A.* 115 K10
Deming, *Wash., U.S.A.* 116 B4
Demini →, *Brazil* 124 D6
Demirci, *Turkey* 39 B10
Demirköprü Barajı, *Turkey* 39 C10
Demirköy, *Turkey* 41 E11
Demmin, *Germany* 24 B9
Demonte, *Italy* 28 D4
Demopolis, *U.S.A.* 109 J2
Dempo, *Indonesia* 62 E2
Demyansk, *Russia* 46 D7
Den Burg, *Neths.* 17 A4
Den Chai, *Thailand* 64 D3
Den Haag = 's-Gravenhage, *Neths.* 17 B4
Den Helder, *Neths.* 17 B4
Den Oever, *Neths.* 17 B5
Denain, *France* 19 B10
Denair, *U.S.A.* 116 H6
Denau, *Uzbekistan* 50 F7
Denbigh, *Canada* 110 A7
Denbigh, *U.K.* 12 D4
Denbighshire □, *U.K.* 12 D4
Dendang, *Indonesia* 62 E3
Dendermonde, *Belgium* 17 C4
Deneba, *Ethiopia* 81 F4
Dengchuan, *China* 58 E3
Denge, *Nigeria* 83 C6
Dengfeng, *China* 56 G7
Dengi, *Nigeria* 83 D6
Dengkou, *China* 56 D4
Dengzhou, *China* 59 A9
Denham, *Australia* 93 E1
Denham Ra., *Australia* 94 C4
Denham Sd., *Australia* 93 E1
Denholm, *Canada* 105 C7
Denia, *Spain* 33 G5
Denial B., *Australia* 95 E1
Deniliquin, *Australia* 95 F3
Denison, *Iowa, U.S.A.* 112 E7
Denison, *Tex., U.S.A.* 113 J6
Denison Plains, *Australia* 92 C4
Denizli, *Turkey* 39 D11
Denizli □, *Turkey* 39 D11
Denman Glacier, *Antarctica* 5 C7
Denmark, *Australia* 93 F2
Denmark ■, *Europe* 11 J3
Denmark Str., *Atl. Oc.* 4 C6
Dennison, *U.S.A.* 110 F3
Denny, *U.K.* 14 E5
Denpasar, *Indonesia* 62 F5
Denton, *Mont., U.S.A.* 114 C9
Denton, *Tex., U.S.A.* 113 J6
D'Entrecasteaux, Pt., *Australia* 93 F2
Denu, *Ghana* 83 D5
Denver, *Colo., U.S.A.* 112 F2
Denver, *Pa., U.S.A.* 111 F8
Denver City, *U.S.A.* 113 J3
Deoband, *India* 68 E7
Deogarh, *India* 68 G5
Deoghar, *India* 69 G12
Deolali, *India* 66 K8
Deoli = Devli, *India* 68 G6
Déols, *France* 19 F8
Deora, *India* 68 F4
Deori, *India* 69 H8
Deoria, *India* 69 F10
Deosai Mts., *Pakistan* 69 B6
Deosri, *India* 69 F14
Depalpur, *India* 68 H6
Deping, *China* 57 F9
Deposit, *U.S.A.* 111 D9
Depuch I., *Australia* 92 D2
Deputatskiy, *Russia* 51 C14
Dêqên, *China* 58 C2
Deqing, *China* 59 F8
Dera Ghazi Khan, *Pakistan* 68 D4
Dera Ismail Khan, *Pakistan* 68 D4
Derabugti, *Pakistan* 68 E3
Derawar Fort, *Pakistan* 68 E4
Derbent, *Russia* 49 J9
Derbent, *Turkey* 39 C10
Derby, *Australia* 92 C3
Derby, *U.K.* 12 E6
Derby, *Conn., U.S.A.* 111 E11
Derby, *Kans., U.S.A.* 113 G6
Derby, *N.Y., U.S.A.* 110 D6
Derby City □, *U.K.* 12 E6
Derby Line, *U.S.A.* 111 B12
Derbyshire □, *U.K.* 12 D6
Derecske, *Hungary* 42 C6
Dereköy, *Turkey* 41 E11
Dereli, *Turkey* 73 B8
Derg →, *U.K.* 15 B4
Derg, L., *Ireland* 15 D3
Dergachi = Derhaci, *Ukraine* 47 G9
Dergaon, *India* 67 F19
Derhaci, *Ukraine* 47 G9
Derik, *Turkey* 73 D9
Derinkuyu, *Turkey* 72 C6
Dermantsi, *Bulgaria* 41 C8
Dermott, *U.S.A.* 113 J9
Dêrong, *China* 58 C2
Derry = Londonderry, *U.K.* 15 B4
Derry = Londonderry □, *U.K.* 15 B4
Derry, *N.H., U.S.A.* 111 D13
Derry, *Pa., U.S.A.* 110 F5
Derryveagh Mts., *Ireland* 15 B3
Derudub, *Sudan* 80 D4
Derval, *France* 18 E5
Dervéni, *Greece* 38 C4
Derventa, *Bos.-H.* 42 F2
Derwent →, *Cumb., U.K.* 12 C4
Derwent →, *Derby, U.K.* 12 E6
Derwent →, *N. Yorks., U.K.* 12 D7
Derwent Water, *U.K.* 12 C4
Des Moines, *Iowa, U.S.A.* 112 E8
Des Moines, *N. Mex., U.S.A.* 113 G3
Des Moines →, *U.S.A.* 112 E9
Desa, *Romania* 42 G8
Desaguadero →, *Argentina* 126 C2
Desaguadero →, *Bolivia* 124 G5
Descanso, Pta., *Mexico* 117 N9
Descartes, *France* 20 B4
Deschaillons, *Canada* 103 C5
Deschambault L., *Canada* 105 C8
Deschutes →, *U.S.A.* 114 D3
Dese, *Ethiopia* 81 E4
Deseado →, *Argentina* 128 F3
Desenzano del Garda, *Italy* 28 C7
Desert Center, *U.S.A.* 117 M11
Desert Hot Springs, *U.S.A.* 117 M10
Deshnok, *India* 68 F5
Desna →, *Ukraine* 47 G6
Desnătui →, *Romania* 43 G8
Desolación, I., *Chile* 128 G2
Despeñaperros, Paso, *Spain* 35 G7
Despotovac, *Serbia, Yug.* 40 B5
Dessau, *Germany* 24 D8
Dessye = Dese, *Ethiopia* 81 E4
D'Estrees B., *Australia* 95 F2
Desuri, *India* 68 G5
Desvres, *France* 19 B8
Det Udom, *Thailand* 64 E5
Deta, *Romania* 42 E6
Dete, *Zimbabwe* 88 B4
Đetinja →, *Serbia, Yug.* 40 C4
Detmold, *Germany* 24 D4
Detour, Pt., *U.S.A.* 108 C2
Detroit, *U.S.A.* 110 D1
Detroit Lakes, *U.S.A.* 112 B7
Detva, *Slovak Rep.* 27 C12
Deurne, *Neths.* 17 C5
Deutsche Bucht, *Germany* 24 A4
Deutschlandsberg, *Austria* 26 E8
Deux-Sèvres □, *France* 18 F6
Deva, *Romania* 42 E7
Devakottai, *India* 66 Q11
Devaprayag, *India* 69 D8
Dévaványa, *Hungary* 42 C5
Deveci Dağları, *Turkey* 72 B7
Devecikonağı, *Turkey* 41 G12
Devecser, *Hungary* 42 C2
Develi, *Turkey* 72 C6
Deventer, *Neths.* 17 B6
Deveron →, *U.K.* 14 D6
Devesel, *Romania* 42 F7
Devgadh Bariya, *India* 68 H5
Devikot, *India* 68 F4
Devils Den, *U.S.A.* 116 K7
Devils Lake, *U.S.A.* 112 A5
Devils Paw, *Canada* 104 B2
Devils Tower Junction, *U.S.A.* 112 C2
Devin, *Bulgaria* 41 E8
Devine, *U.S.A.* 113 L5
Devizes, *U.K.* 13 F6
Devli, *India* 68 G6
Devnya, *Bulgaria* 41 C11
Devoll →, *Albania* 40 F4
Devon, *Canada* 104 C6
Devon □, *U.K.* 13 G4
Devon I., *Canada* 4 B3
Devonport, *Australia* 94 G4
Devonport, *N.Z.* 91 G5
Devrek, *Turkey* 72 B4
Devrekâni, *Turkey* 72 B5
Devrez →, *Turkey* 72 B6
Dewas, *India* 68 H7
Dewetsdorp, *S. Africa* 88 D4
Dexing, *China* 59 C11
Dexter, *Maine, U.S.A.* 109 C11
Dexter, *Mo., U.S.A.* 113 G10
Dexter, *N. Mex., U.S.A.* 113 J2
Dey-Dey, L., *Australia* 93 E5
Deyang, *China* 58 B5
Deyhūk, *Iran* 71 C8
Deyyer, *Iran* 71 E6
Dezadeash L., *Canada* 104 A1
Dezfūl, *Iran* 71 C6
Dezhneva, Mys, *Russia* 51 C19
Dezhou, *China* 56 F9
Dhadhar →, *India* 69 G11
Dháfni, *Kríti, Greece* 36 D7
Dháfni, *Pelóponnisos, Greece* 38 D4
Dhahabān, *Si. Arabia* 80 C4
Dhahiriya = Az̧ Z̧āhirīyah, *West Bank* 75 D3
Dhahran = Az̧ Z̧ahrān, *Si. Arabia* 71 E6
Dhak, *Pakistan* 68 C5
Dhaka, *Bangla.* 69 H14
Dhaka □, *Bangla.* 69 G14
Dhali, *Cyprus* 36 D12
Dhamási, *Greece* 38 B4
Dhampur, *India* 69 E8
Dhamtari, *India* 67 J12
Dhanbad, *India* 69 H12
Dhangarhi, *Nepal* 67 E12
Dhankuta, *Nepal* 69 F12
Dhar, *India* 68 H6
Dharampur, *India* 68 H6
Dharamsala = Dharmsala, *India* 68 C7
Dhariwal, *India* 68 D6
Dharla →, *Bangla.* 69 G13
Dharmapuri, *India* 66 N11
Dharmjaygarh, *India* 69 H10
Dharmsala, *India* 68 C7
Dharni, *India* 68 J7
Dharwad, *India* 66 M9
Dhasan →, *India* 69 G8
Dhaulagiri, *Nepal* 69 E10
Dhebar, L., *India* 68 G6
Dheftera, *Cyprus* 36 D12
Dhenkanal, *India* 67 J14
Dhenoúsa, *Greece* 39 D7
Dherinia, *Cyprus* 36 D12
Dheskáti, *Greece* 40 G5
Dhespotikó, *Greece* 38 E6
Dhestina, *Greece* 38 C4
Dhiarrizos →, *Cyprus* 36 E11
Dhībān, *Jordan* 75 D4
Dhidhimótikhon, *Greece* 41 E10
Dhíkti Óros, *Greece* 36 D7
Dhilianáta, *Greece* 38 C2
Dhílos, *Greece* 39 D7
Dhilwan, *India* 68 D6
Dhimarkhera, *India* 69 H9
Dhimitsána, *Greece* 38 D4
Dhírfis Óros, *Greece* 38 C5
Dhodhekánisos, *Greece* 39 E8
Dhodhekánisos □, *Greece* 39 E8
Dhokós, *Greece* 38 D5
Dholiana, *Greece* 38 B2
Dholka, *India* 68 H5
Dhomokós, *Greece* 38 B4
Dhoraji, *India* 68 J4
Dhoxáton, *Greece* 41 E8
Dhragonísi, *Greece* 39 D7
Dhráhstis, Ákra, *Greece* 36 A3
Dhrangadhra, *India* 68 H4
Dhrápanon, Ákra, *Greece* 36 D6
Dhriopís, *Greece* 38 D6
Dhrol, *India* 68 H4
Dhuburi, *India* 67 F16
Dhule, *India* 66 J9
Di-ib, W. →, *Sudan* 80 C4
Di Linh, *Vietnam* 65 G7
Di Linh, Cao Nguyen, *Vietnam* 65 G7
Día, *Greece* 36 D7
Diabakania, *Guinea* 82 C2
Diablo, Mt., *U.S.A.* 116 H5
Diablo Range, *U.S.A.* 116 J5
Diafarabé, *Mali* 82 C4

Diala

Diala, *Mali* 82 C3
Dialakoro, *Mali* 82 C3
Dialakoto, *Senegal* 82 C2
Diallassagou, *Mali* 82 C4
Diamante, *Argentina* 126 C3
Diamante, *Italy* 31 C8
Diamante →, *Argentina* 126 C2
Diamantina, *Brazil* 125 G10
Diamantina →, *Australia* 95 D2
Diamantino, *Brazil* 125 F7
Diamond Bar, *U.S.A.* 117 L9
Diamond Harbour, *India* 69 H13
Diamond Is., *Australia* 94 B5
Diamond Mts., *U.S.A.* 114 G6
Diamond Springs, *U.S.A.* 116 G6
Dian Chi, *China* 58 E4
Dianalund, *Denmark* 11 J5
Dianbai, *China* 59 G8
Diancheng, *China* 59 G8
Dianjiang, *China* 58 B6
Diano Marina, *Italy* 28 E5
Dianra, *Ivory C.* 82 D3
Diapaga, *Burkina Faso* 83 C5
Diapangou, *Burkina Faso* 83 C5
Diariguila, *Guinea* 82 C2
Dībā, *Oman* 71 E8
Dibai, *India* 68 E8
Dibaya-Lubue, *Dem. Rep. of the Congo* 84 E3
Dibete, *Botswana* 88 C4
Dibrugarh, *India* 67 F19
Dickens, *U.S.A.* 113 J4
Dickinson, *U.S.A.* 112 B3
Dickson = Dikson, *Russia* 50 B9
Dickson, *U.S.A.* 109 G2
Dickson City, *U.S.A.* 111 E9
Dicle Nehri →, *Turkey* 73 D9
Dicomano, *Italy* 29 E8
Didesa, W. →, *Ethiopia* 81 E4
Didi, *Sudan* 81 F3
Didiéni, *Mali* 82 C3
Didsbury, *Canada* 104 C6
Didwana, *India* 68 F6
Die, *France* 21 D9
Diébougou, *Burkina Faso* 82 C4
Diecke, *Guinea* 82 D3
Diefenbaker, L., *Canada* 105 C7
Diego de Almagro, *Chile* 126 B1
Diego Garcia, *Ind. Oc.* 3 E13
Diekirch, *Lux.* 17 E6
Diéma, *Mali* 82 C3
Diembéring, *Senegal* 82 C1
Dien Ban, *Vietnam* 64 E7
Dien Bien, *Vietnam* 58 G4
Dien Khanh, *Vietnam* 65 F7
Diepholz, *Germany* 24 C4
Dieppe, *France* 18 C8
Dierks, *U.S.A.* 113 H8
Diest, *Belgium* 17 D5
Dietikon, *Switz.* 25 H4
Dieulefit, *France* 21 D9
Dieuze, *France* 19 D13
Dif, *Somali Rep.* 74 G3
Differdange, *Lux.* 17 E5
Dig, *India* 68 F7
Digba, *Dem. Rep. of the Congo* 86 B2
Digby, *Canada* 103 D6
Diggi, *India* 68 F6
Dighinala, *Bangla.* 67 H18
Dighton, *U.S.A.* 112 F4
Digna, *Mali* 82 C3
Digne-les-Bains, *France* 21 D10
Digoin, *France* 19 F11
Digor, *Turkey* 73 B10
Digos, *Phil.* 61 H6
Digranes, *Iceland* 8 C6
Digul →, *Indonesia* 63 F9
Dihang →, *India* 67 F19
Dijlah, Nahr →, *Asia* 70 D5
Dijon, *France* 19 E12
Dikhil, *Djibouti* 81 E5
Dikili, *Turkey* 39 B8
Dikirnis, *Egypt* 80 H7
Dikkil = Dikhil, *Djibouti* 81 E5
Dikodougou, *Ivory C.* 82 D3
Diksmuide, *Belgium* 17 C2
Dikson, *Russia* 50 B9
Dikwa, *Nigeria* 83 C7
Dila, *Ethiopia* 81 F4
Dili, *E. Timor* 63 F7
Dilijan, *Armenia* 49 K7
Dilizhan = Dilijan, *Armenia* 49 K7
Dilj, *Croatia* 42 E3
Dillenburg, *Germany* 24 E4
Dilley, *U.S.A.* 113 L5
Dilling, *Sudan* 81 E2
Dillingen, *Bayern, Germany* 25 G6
Dillingen, *Saarland, Germany* 25 F2
Dillingham, *U.S.A.* 100 C4
Dillon, *Canada* 105 B7
Dillon, *Mont., U.S.A.* 114 D7
Dillon, *S.C., U.S.A.* 109 H6
Dillon →, *Canada* 105 B7
Dillsburg, *U.S.A.* 110 F7
Dilly, *Mali* 82 C3
Dilolo, *Dem. Rep. of the Congo* 84 G4
Dimas, *Mexico* 118 C3
Dimashq, *Syria* 75 B5
Dimashq □, *Syria* 75 B5
Dimbaza, *S. Africa* 89 E4
Dimbokro, *Ivory C.* 82 D4
Dimboola, *Australia* 95 F3
Dîmbovița = Dâmbovița →, *Romania* 43 F11
Dimbulah, *Australia* 94 B4
Dimitrovgrad, *Bulgaria* 41 D9
Dimitrovgrad, *Russia* 48 C9
Dimitrovgrad, *Serbia, Yug.* 40 C6
Dimitrovo = Pernik, *Bulgaria* 40 D7
Dimmitt, *U.S.A.* 113 H3
Dimo, *Sudan* 81 F2
Dimona, *Israel* 75 D4
Dimovo, *Bulgaria* 40 C6
Dinagat, *Phil.* 61 F6
Dinajpur, *Bangla.* 67 G16
Dinan, *France* 18 D4
Dīnān Āb, *Iran* 71 C8
Dinant, *Belgium* 17 D4
Dinapur, *India* 69 G11
Dinar, *Turkey* 39 C12
Dīnār, Kūh-e, *Iran* 71 D6
Dinara Planina, *Croatia* 29 D13
Dinard, *France* 18 D4
Dinaric Alps = Dinara Planina, *Croatia* 29 D13
Dindanko, *Mali* 82 C3
Dinder, Nahr ed →, *Sudan* 81 E3
Dindigul, *India* 66 P11
Dindori, *India* 69 H9
Ding Xian = Dingzhou, *China* 56 E8
Dinga, *Pakistan* 68 G2
Dingalan, *Phil.* 61 D4
Dingbian, *China* 56 F4
Dingelstädt, *Germany* 24 D6
Dingle, *Ireland* 15 D1
Dingle, *Sweden* 11 F5
Dingle B., *Ireland* 15 D1
Dingmans Ferry, *U.S.A.* 111 E10
Dingnan, *China* 59 E10
Dingo, *Australia* 94 C4
Dingolfing, *Germany* 25 G8
Dingtao, *China* 56 G8
Dinguira, *Mali* 82 C2
Dinguiraye, *Guinea* 82 C2
Dingwall, *U.K.* 14 D4
Dingxi, *China* 56 G3
Dingxiang, *China* 56 E7
Dingyuan, *China* 59 A11
Dingzhou, *China* 56 E8
Dinh, Mui, *Vietnam* 65 G7
Dinh Lap, *Vietnam* 58 G6
Dinokwe, *Botswana* 88 C4
Dinorwic, *Canada* 105 D10
Dinosaur National Monument, *U.S.A.* 114 F9
Dinosaur Prov. Park, *Canada* 104 C6
Dinuba, *U.S.A.* 116 J7
Diö, *Sweden* 11 H8
Dioïla, *Mali* 82 C3
Dioka, *Mali* 82 C2
Diongoï, *Mali* 82 C3
Diósgyör, *Hungary* 42 B5
Diosig, *Romania* 42 C7
Diougani, *Mali* 82 C4
Diouloulou, *Senegal* 82 C1
Dioura, *Mali* 82 C3
Diourbel, *Senegal* 82 C1
Dipalpur, *Pakistan* 68 D5
Diplo, *Pakistan* 68 G3
Dipolog, *Phil.* 61 G5
Dir, *Pakistan* 66 B7
Diré, *Mali* 82 B4
Dire Dawa, *Ethiopia* 81 F5
Diriamba, *Nic.* 120 D2
Dirk Hartog I., *Australia* 93 E1
Dirranbandi, *Australia* 95 D4
Disa, *India* 68 G5
Disa, *Sudan* 81 E3
Disappointment, C., *U.S.A.* 114 C2
Disappointment, L., *Australia* 92 D3
Disaster B., *Australia* 95 F4
Discovery B., *Australia* 95 F3
Disentis Muster, *Switz.* 25 J4
Dishna, *Egypt* 80 B3
Disina, *Nigeria* 83 C6
Disko = Qeqertarsuaq, *Greenland* 101 B5
Disko Bugt, *Greenland* 4 C5
Disna = Dzisna →, *Belarus* 46 E5
Diss, *U.K.* 13 E9
Disteghil Sar, *Pakistan* 69 A6
Distrito Federal □, *Brazil* 125 G9
Distrito Federal □, *Mexico* 119 D5
Disūq, *Egypt* 80 H7
Diu, *India* 68 J4
Dīvāndarreh, *Iran* 70 C5
Dives →, *France* 18 C6
Dives-sur-Mer, *France* 18 C6
Divichi = Däväçi, *Azerbaijan* 49 K9
Divide, *U.S.A.* 114 D7
Dividing Ra., *Australia* 93 E2
Divinópolis, *Brazil* 125 H10
Divjake, *Albania* 40 F3
Divnoye, *Russia* 49 H6
Divo, *Ivory C.* 82 D3
Divriği, *Turkey* 73 C8
Dīwāl Kol, *Afghan.* 68 B2
Dixie Mt., *U.S.A.* 116 F6
Dixon, *Calif., U.S.A.* 116 G5
Dixon, *Ill., U.S.A.* 112 E10
Dixon Entrance, *U.S.A.* 100 C6
Dixville, *Canada* 111 A13
Diyadin, *Turkey* 73 C10
Diyālā →, *Iraq* 70 C5
Diyarbakır, *Turkey* 70 B4
Diyodar, *India* 68 G4
Djakarta = Jakarta, *Indonesia* 62 F3
Djamba, *Angola* 88 B1
Djambala, *Congo* 84 E2
Djanet, *Algeria* 78 D7
Djawa = Jawa, *Indonesia* 62 F3
Djelfa, *Algeria* 78 B6
Djema, *C.A.R.* 86 A2
Djenné, *Mali* 82 C4
Djerba, I. de, *Tunisia* 79 B8
Djerid, Chott, *Tunisia* 78 B7
Djibo, *Burkina Faso* 83 C4
Djibouti, *Djibouti* 81 E5
Djibouti ■, *Africa* 81 E5
Djolu, *Dem. Rep. of the Congo* 84 D4
Djougou, *Benin* 83 D5
Djoum, *Cameroon* 84 D2
Djourab, Erg du, *Chad* 79 E9
Djugu, *Dem. Rep. of the Congo* 86 B3
Djúpivogur, *Iceland* 8 D6
Djurås, *Sweden* 10 D9
Djursland, *Denmark* 11 H4
Dmitriya Lapteva, Proliv, *Russia* 51 B15
Dmitriyev Lgovskiy, *Russia* 47 F8
Dmitrov, *Russia* 46 D9
Dmitrovsk-Orlovskiy, *Russia* 47 F8
Dnepr → = Dnipro →, *Ukraine* 47 J7
Dneprodzerzhinsk = Dniprodzerzhynsk, *Ukraine* 47 H8
Dneprodzerzhinskoye Vdkhr. = Dniprodzerzhynske Vdskh., *Ukraine* 47 H8
Dnepropetrovsk = Dnipropetrovsk, *Ukraine* 47 H8
Dneprorudnoye = Dniprorudne, *Ukraine* 47 J8
Dnestr → = Dnister →, *Europe* 47 J6
Dnestrovski = Belgorod, *Russia* 47 G9
Dnieper = Dnipro →, *Ukraine* 47 J7
Dniester = Dnister →, *Europe* 47 J6
Dnipro →, *Ukraine* 47 J7
Dniprodzerzhynsk, *Ukraine* 47 H8
Dniprodzerzhynske Vdskh., *Ukraine* 47 H8
Dnipropetrovsk, *Ukraine* 47 H8
Dniprorudne, *Ukraine* 47 J8
Dnister →, *Europe* 47 J6
Dnistrovskyy Lyman, *Ukraine* 47 J6
Dno, *Russia* 46 D5
Dnyapro = Dnipro →, *Ukraine* 47 J7
Doaktown, *Canada* 103 C6
Doan Hung, *Vietnam* 58 G5
Doany, *Madag.* 89 A8
Doba, *Chad* 79 G9
Dobandi, *Pakistan* 68 D2
Dobbiaco, *Italy* 29 B9
Dobbyn, *Australia* 94 B3
Dobczyce, *Poland* 45 J7
Dobele, *Latvia* 9 H20
Dobele □, *Latvia* 44 B10
Döbeln, *Germany* 24 D9
Doberai, Jazirah, *Indonesia* 63 E8
Dobiegniew, *Poland* 45 F2
Doblas, *Argentina* 126 D3
Dobo, *Indonesia* 63 F8
Doboj, *Bos.-H.* 42 F3
Dobra, *Wielkopolskie, Poland* 45 G5
Dobra, *Zachodnio-Pomorskie, Poland* 44 E2
Dobra, *Dîmbovita, Romania* 43 F10
Dobra, *Hunedoara, Romania* 42 E7
Dobre Miasto, *Poland* 44 E7
Dobrești, *Romania* 42 D7
Dobrich, *Bulgaria* 41 C11
Dobrinishta, *Bulgaria* 40 E7
Dobříš, *Czech Rep.* 26 B7
Dobrodzień, *Poland* 45 H5
Dobropole, *Ukraine* 47 H9
Dobruja, *Europe* 43 F13
Dobrush, *Belarus* 47 F6
Dobrzany, *Poland* 44 E2
Dobrzyń nad Wisłą, *Poland* 45 F6
Doc, Mui, *Vietnam* 64 D6
Docker River, *Australia* 93 D4
Docksta, *Sweden* 10 A12
Doctor Arroyo, *Mexico* 118 C4
Doda, *India* 69 C6
Doda, L., *Canada* 102 C4
Dodecanese = Dhodhekánisos, *Greece* 39 E8
Dodge City, *U.S.A.* 113 G5
Dodge L., *Canada* 105 B7
Dodgeville, *U.S.A.* 112 D9
Dodo, *Cameroon* 83 D7
Dodo, *Sudan* 81 F2
Dodola, *Ethiopia* 81 F4
Dodoma, *Tanzania* 86 D4
Dodoma □, *Tanzania* 86 D4
Dodona, *Greece* 38 B2
Dodsland, *Canada* 105 C7
Dodson, *U.S.A.* 114 B9
Dodurga, *Turkey* 39 B11
Doesburg, *Neths.* 17 B6
Doetinchem, *Neths.* 17 C6
Dog Creek, *Canada* 104 C4
Dog L., *Man., Canada* 105 C9
Dog L., *Ont., Canada* 102 C2
Doğanşehir, *Turkey* 72 C7
Dogliani, *Italy* 28 D4
Dogondoutchi, *Niger* 83 C5
Dogran, *Pakistan* 68 D5
Doğubayazıt, *Turkey* 70 B5
Doguéraoua, *Niger* 83 C6
Doha = Ad Dawḩah, *Qatar* 71 E6
Dohazari, *Bangla.* 67 H18
Dohrighat, *India* 69 F10
Doi, *Indonesia* 63 D7
Doi Luang, *Thailand* 64 C3
Doi Saket, *Thailand* 64 C2
Dois Irmãos, Sa., *Brazil* 125 E10
Dojransko Jezero, *Macedonia* 40 E6
Dokkum, *Neths.* 17 A5
Dokri, *Pakistan* 68 F3
Dokuchayevsk, *Ukraine* 47 J9
Dol-de-Bretagne, *France* 18 D5
Dolac, *Kosovo, Yug.* 40 D4
Dolak, Pulau, *Indonesia* 63 F9
Dolbeau, *Canada* 103 C5
Dole, *France* 19 E12
Doleib, Wadi →, *Sudan* 81 E3
Dolenji Logatec, *Slovenia* 29 C11
Dolgellau, *U.K.* 12 E4
Dolgelley = Dolgellau, *U.K.* 12 E4
Dolhasca, *Romania* 43 C11
Dolianova, *Italy* 30 C2
Dolinskaya = Dolynska, *Ukraine* 47 H7
Dolj □, *Romania* 43 F8
Dollard, *Neths.* 17 A7
Dolna Banya, *Bulgaria* 40 D7
Dolni Chiflik, *Bulgaria* 41 D11
Dolni Dŭbnik, *Bulgaria* 41 C8
Dolnośląskie □, *Poland* 45 G3
Dolný Kubín, *Slovak Rep.* 27 B12
Dolo, *Ethiopia* 81 G5
Dolo, *Italy* 29 C9
Dolomites = Dolomiti, *Italy* 29 B8
Dolomiti, *Italy* 29 B8
Dolores, *Argentina* 126 D4
Dolores, *Uruguay* 126 C4
Dolores, *U.S.A.* 115 H9
Dolores →, *U.S.A.* 115 G9
Dolovo, *Serbia, Yug.* 42 F5
Dolphin, C., *Falk. Is.* 128 G5
Dolphin and Union Str., *Canada* 100 B8
Dolsk, *Poland* 45 G4
Dolynska, *Ukraine* 47 H7
Dolzhanskaya, *Russia* 47 J9
Dom Pedrito, *Brazil* 127 C5
Doma, *Nigeria* 83 D6
Domaniç, *Turkey* 39 B11
Domariaganj →, *India* 69 F10
Domasi, *Malawi* 87 F4
Domažlice, *Czech Rep.* 26 B5
Dombarovskiy, *Russia* 50 D6
Dombås, *Norway* 9 E13
Dombasle-sur-Meurthe, *France* 19 D13
Dombes, *France* 21 C9
Dombóvár, *Hungary* 42 D3
Dombrád, *Hungary* 42 B6
Domel I. = Letsôk-aw Kyun, *Burma* 65 G2
Domérat, *France* 19 F9
Domeyko, *Chile* 126 B1
Domeyko, Cordillera, *Chile* 126 A2
Domfront, *France* 18 D6
Dominador, *Chile* 126 A2
Dominica ■, *W. Indies* 121 C7
Dominica Passage, *W. Indies* 121 C7
Dominican Rep. ■, *W. Indies* 121 C5
Dömitz, *Germany* 24 B7
Domme, *France* 20 D5
Domnești, *Romania* 43 E9
Domodóssola, *Italy* 28 B5
Dompaire, *France* 19 D13
Dompierre-sur-Besbre, *France* 19 F10
Dompim, *Ghana* 82 D4
Domrémy-la-Pucelle, *France* 19 D12
Domville, Mt., *Australia* 95 D5
Domvraína, *Greece* 38 C4
Domžale, *Slovenia* 29 B11
Don →, *Russia* 47 J10
Don →, *Aberds., U.K.* 14 D6
Don →, *S. Yorks., U.K.* 12 D7
Don, C., *Australia* 92 B5
Don Benito, *Spain* 35 G5
Dona Ana = Nhamaabué, *Mozam.* 87 F4
Doña Mencía, *Spain* 35 H6
Donaghadee, *U.K.* 15 B6
Donald, *Australia* 95 F3
Donaldsonville, *U.S.A.* 113 K9
Donalsonville, *U.S.A.* 109 K3
Donau = Dunărea →, *Europe* 43 E14
Donau →, *Austria* 17 D3
Donaueschingen, *Germany* 25 H4
Donauwörth, *Germany* 25 G6
Doncaster, *U.K.* 12 D6
Dondo, *Mozam.* 87 F3
Dondo, Teluk, *Indonesia* 63 D6
Dondra Head, *Sri Lanka* 66 S12
Donduşeni, *Moldova* 43 B12
Donegal, *Ireland* 15 B3
Donegal □, *Ireland* 15 B4
Donegal B., *Ireland* 15 B3
Donets →, *Russia* 49 G5
Donetsk, *Ukraine* 47 J9
Dong Ba Thin, *Vietnam* 65 F7
Dong Dang, *Vietnam* 58 G6
Dong Giam, *Vietnam* 64 C5
Dong Ha, *Vietnam* 64 D6
Dong Hene, *Laos* 64 D5
Dong Hoi, *Vietnam* 64 D6
Dong Jiang →, *China* 59 F10
Dong Khe, *Vietnam* 64 A6
Dong Ujimqin Qi, *China* 56 B9
Dong Van, *Vietnam* 64 A5
Dong Xoai, *Vietnam* 65 G6
Donga, *Nigeria* 83 D7
Donga →, *Nigeria* 83 D7
Dong'an, *China* 59 D8
Dongara, *Australia* 93 E1
Dongbei, *China* 57 D13
Dongchuan, *China* 58 D4
Donges, *France* 18 E4
Dongfang, *China* 64 C7
Dongfeng, *China* 57 C13
Donggala, *Indonesia* 63 E5
Donggan, *China* 58 F5
Donggou, *China* 57 E13
Dongguan, *China* 59 F9
Dongguang, *China* 56 F9
Donghai Dao, *China* 59 G8
Dongjingcheng, *China* 57 B15
Dongkou, *China* 59 D8
Donglan, *China* 58 E6
Dongliu, *China* 59 B11
Dongmen, *China* 58 F6
Dongning, *China* 57 B16
Dongnyi, *China* 58 C3
Dongola, *Sudan* 80 D3
Dongping, *China* 56 G9
Dongshan, *China* 59 F11
Dongsheng, *China* 56 E6
Dongtai, *China* 57 H11
Dongting Hu, *China* 59 C9
Dongtou, *China* 59 D13
Dongxiang, *China* 59 C11
Dongxing, *China* 58 G7
Dongyang, *China* 59 C13
Dongzhi, *China* 59 B11
Donington, C., *Australia* 95 E2
Doniphan, *U.S.A.* 113 G9
Donja Stubica, *Croatia* 29 C12
Donji Dušnik, *Serbia, Yug.* 40 C6
Donji Miholjac, *Croatia* 42 E3
Donji Milanovac, *Serbia, Yug.* 40 B6
Donji Vakuf, *Bos.-H.* 42 F2
Dønna, *Norway* 8 C15
Donna, *U.S.A.* 113 M5
Donnaconna, *Canada* 103 C5
Donnelly's Crossing, *N.Z.* 91 F4
Donnybrook, *Australia* 93 F2
Donnybrook, *S. Africa* 89 D4
Donora, *U.S.A.* 110 F5
Donostia = Donostia-San Sebastián, *Spain* 32 B3
Donostia-San Sebastián, *Spain* 32 B3
Donskoy, *Russia* 46 F10
Donsol, *Phil.* 61 E5
Donzère, *France* 21 D8
Donzy, *France* 19 E10
Doon →, *U.K.* 14 F4
Dora, L., *Australia* 92 D3
Dora Báltea →, *Italy* 28 C5
Dora Ripária →, *Italy* 28 C4
Doran L., *Canada* 105 A7
Dorchester, *U.K.* 13 G5
Dorchester, C., *Canada* 101 B12
Dordabis, *Namibia* 88 C2
Dordogne □, *France* 20 C4
Dordogne →, *France* 20 C3
Dordrecht, *Neths.* 17 C4
Dordrecht, *S. Africa* 88 E4
Dore →, *France* 20 C7
Dore, Mts., *France* 20 C6
Doré L., *Canada* 105 C7
Doré Lake, *Canada* 105 C7
Dorfen, *Germany* 25 G8
Dorgali, *Italy* 30 B2
Dori, *Burkina Faso* 83 C4
Doring →, *S. Africa* 88 E2
Doringbos, *S. Africa* 88 E2
Dorion, *Canada* 111 A10
Dormaa-Ahenkro, *Ghana* 82 D4
Dormans, *France* 19 C10
Dormo, Ras, *Eritrea* 81 E5
Dornbirn, *Austria* 26 D2
Dornes, *France* 19 F10
Dornești, *Romania* 43 C11
Dornie, *U.K.* 14 D3
Dornoch, *U.K.* 14 D4
Dornoch Firth, *U.K.* 14 D4
Dornogovĭ □, *Mongolia* 56 C6
Doro, *Mali* 83 B4
Dorog, *Hungary* 42 C3
Dorogobuzh, *Russia* 46 E7
Dorohoi, *Romania* 43 C11
Döröö Nuur, *Mongolia* 60 B4
Dorr, *Iran* 71 C6
Dorre I., *Australia* 93 E1
Dorrigo, *Australia* 95 E5
Dorris, *U.S.A.* 114 F3
Dorset, *Canada* 110 A6
Dorset, *U.S.A.* 110 E4
Dorset □, *U.K.* 13 G5
Dorsten, *Germany* 24 D2
Dortmund, *Germany* 24 D3
Dortmund-Ems-Kanal →, *Germany* 24 D3
Dörtyol, *Turkey* 72 D7
Dorum, *Germany* 24 B4
Doruma, *Dem. Rep. of the Congo* 86 B2
Dorūneh, *Iran* 71 C8
Dos Bahías, C., *Argentina* 128 E3
Dos Hermanas, *Spain* 35 H5
Dos Palos, *U.S.A.* 116 J6
Döşemealtı, *Turkey* 39 D12
Dosso, *Niger* 83 C5
Dothan, *U.S.A.* 109 K3
Doty, *U.S.A.* 116 D3
Douai, *France* 19 B10
Douako, *Guinea* 82 D2
Douala, *Cameroon* 83 E6
Douarnenez, *France* 18 D2
Doubabougou, *Mali* 82 C3
Double Island Pt., *Australia* 95 D5
Double Mountain Fork →, *U.S.A.* 113 J4
Doubrava →, *Czech Rep.* 26 A8
Doubs □, *France* 19 E13
Doubs →, *France* 19 F12
Doubtful Sd., *N.Z.* 91 L1
Doubtless B., *N.Z.* 91 F4
Doudeville, *France* 18 C7
Doué-la-Fontaine, *France* 18 E6
Douentza, *Mali* 82 C4
Douglas, *S. Africa* 88 D3
Douglas, *U.K.* 12 C3
Douglas, *Ariz., U.S.A.* 115 L9

Douglas, *Ga., U.S.A.* 109 K4
Douglas, *Wyo., U.S.A.* 112 D2
Douglas Chan., *Canada* 104 C3
Douglas Pt., *Canada* 110 B3
Douglasville, *U.S.A.* 109 J3
Doukáton, Ákra, *Greece* 38 C2
Doulevant-le-Château, *France* 19 D11
Doullens, *France* 19 B9
Doumen, *China* 59 F9
Douna, *Mali* 82 C3
Douna, *Mali* 83 C4
Dounreay, *U.K.* 14 C5
Dourada, Serra, *Brazil* 125 F9
Dourados, *Brazil* 127 A5
Dourados →, *Brazil* 127 A5
Dourados, Serra dos, *Brazil* 127 A5
Dourdan, *France* 19 D9
Douro →, *Europe* 34 D2
Douvaine, *France* 19 F13
Douvres-la-Délivrande, *France* 18 C6
Douze →, *France* 20 E3
Dove →, *U.K.* 12 E6
Dove Creek, *U.S.A.* 115 H9
Dover, *Australia* 94 G4
Dover, *U.K.* 13 F9
Dover, *Del., U.S.A.* 108 F8
Dover, *N.H., U.S.A.* 111 C14
Dover, *N.J., U.S.A.* 111 F10
Dover, *Ohio, U.S.A.* 110 F3
Dover, Pt., *Australia* 93 F4
Dover, Str. of, *Europe* 13 G9
Dover-Foxcroft, *U.S.A.* 109 C11
Dover Plains, *U.S.A.* 111 E11
Dovey = Dyfi →, *U.K.* 13 E3
Dovrefjell, *Norway* 9 E13
Dow Rūd, *Iran* 71 C6
Dowa, *Malawi* 87 E3
Dowagiac, *U.S.A.* 108 E2
Dowerin, *Australia* 93 F2
Dowgha'i, *Iran* 71 B8
Dowlatābād, *Iran* 71 D8
Down □, *U.K.* 15 B5
Downey, *Calif., U.S.A.* 117 M8
Downey, *Idaho, U.S.A.* 114 E7
Downham Market, *U.K.* 13 E8
Downieville, *U.S.A.* 116 F6
Downpatrick, *U.K.* 15 B6
Downpatrick Hd., *Ireland* 15 B2
Downsville, *U.S.A.* 111 D10
Downton, Mt., *Canada* 104 C4
Dowsārī, *Iran* 71 D8
Doyle, *U.S.A.* 116 E6
Doylestown, *U.S.A.* 111 F9
Dozois, Rés., *Canada* 102 C4
Dra Khel, *Pakistan* 68 F2
Drac →, *France* 21 C9
Dračevo, *Macedonia* 40 E5
Drachten, *Neths.* 17 A6
Drăgănești, *Moldova* 43 C13
Drăgănești-Olt, *Romania* 43 F9
Drăgănești-Vlașca, *Romania* 43 F10
Dragaš, *Kosovo, Yug.* 40 D4
Drăgășani, *Romania* 43 F9
Dragichyn, *Belarus* 47 F3
Dragocvet, *Serbia, Yug.* 40 C5
Dragovishtitsa, *Bulgaria* 40 D6
Draguignan, *France* 21 E10
Drain, *U.S.A.* 114 E2
Drake, *U.S.A.* 112 B4
Drake Passage, *S. Ocean* 5 B17
Drakensberg, *S. Africa* 89 D4
Dráma, *Greece* 41 E8
Dráma □, *Greece* 41 E8
Drammen, *Norway* 9 G14
Drangajökull, *Iceland* 8 C2
Dranov, Ostrov, *Romania* 43 F14
Dras, *India* 69 B6
Drau = Drava →, *Croatia* 42 E3
Drava →, *Croatia* 42 E3
Dravograd, *Slovenia* 29 B12
Drawa →, *Poland* 45 F2
Drawno, *Poland* 45 E2
Drawsko Pomorskie, *Poland* 44 E2
Drayton Valley, *Canada* 104 C6
Dreieich, *Germany* 25 E4
Dren, *Kosovo, Yug.* 40 C4
Drenthe □, *Neths.* 17 B6
Drepanum, C., *Cyprus* 36 E11
Dresden, *Canada* 110 D2
Dresden, *Germany* 24 D9
Dreux, *France* 18 D8
Drezdenko, *Poland* 45 F2
Driffield, *U.K.* 12 C7
Driftwood, *U.S.A.* 110 E6
Driggs, *U.S.A.* 114 E8
Drin →, *Albania* 40 D3
Drin i Zi →, *Albania* 40 E4
Drina →, *Bos.-H.* 40 B3
Drincea →, *Romania* 42 F7
Drinjača →, *Bos.-H.* 42 F4
Drissa = Vyerkhnyadzvinsk, *Belarus* 46 E4
Drniš, *Croatia* 29 E13
Drøbak, *Norway* 9 G14
Drobeta-Turnu Severin, *Romania* 42 F7
Drobin, *Poland* 45 F6
Drochia, *Moldova* 43 B12
Drogheda, *Ireland* 15 C5
Drogichin = Dragichyn, *Belarus* 47 F3
Drogobych = Drohobych, *Ukraine* 47 H2
Drohiczyn, *Poland* 45 F9
Drohobych, *Ukraine* 47 H2
Droichead Atha = Drogheda, *Ireland* 15 C5
Droichead Nua, *Ireland* 15 C5
Droitwich, *U.K.* 13 E5
Drôme □, *France* 21 D9
Drôme →, *France* 21 D8
Dromedary, C., *Australia* 95 F5
Dromore, *U.K.* 15 B4
Dromore West, *Ireland* 15 B3
Dronero, *Italy* 28 D4
Dronfield, *U.K.* 12 D6
Dronne →, *France* 20 C3
Dronninglund, *Denmark* 11 G4
Dronten, *Neths.* 17 B5
Dropt →, *France* 20 D3
Drosendorf, *Austria* 26 C8
Droué, *France* 18 D8
Drumbo, *Canada* 110 C4
Drumheller, *Canada* 104 C6
Drummond, *U.S.A.* 114 C7
Drummond I., *U.S.A.* 108 C4
Drummond Pt., *Australia* 95 E2
Drummond Ra., *Australia* 94 C4
Drummondville, *Canada* 102 C5
Drumright, *U.S.A.* 113 H6
Druskininkai, *Lithuania* 9 J20
Drut →, *Belarus* 47 F6
Druya, *Belarus* 46 E4
Druzhba, *Bulgaria* 41 C12
Druzhina, *Russia* 51 C15
Drvar, *Bos.-H.* 29 D13
Drvenik, *Croatia* 29 E13
Drwęca →, *Poland* 45 E5
Dry Tortugas, *U.S.A.* 120 B3
Dryanovo, *Bulgaria* 41 D9
Dryden, *Canada* 105 D10
Dryden, *U.S.A.* 111 D8
Drygalski I., *Antarctica* 5 C7
Drysdale →, *Australia* 92 B4
Drysdale I., *Australia* 94 A2
Drzewica, *Poland* 45 G7
Drzewiczka →, *Poland* 45 G7
Dschang, *Cameroon* 83 D7
Du Bois, *U.S.A.* 110 E6
Du Gué →, *Canada* 102 A5
Du He, *China* 59 A8
Du Quoin, *U.S.A.* 112 G10
Du'an, *China* 58 F7
Duanesburg, *U.S.A.* 111 D10
Duaringa, *Australia* 94 C4
Dubā, *Si. Arabia* 70 E2
Dubai = Dubayy, *U.A.E.* 71 E7
Dubăsari, *Moldova* 43 C14
Dubăsari Vdkhr., *Moldova* 43 C13
Dubawnt →, *Canada* 105 A8
Dubawnt, L., *Canada* 105 A8
Dubayy, *U.A.E.* 71 E7
Dubbo, *Australia* 95 E4
Dubele, *Dem. Rep. of the Congo* 86 B2
Dübendorf, *Switz.* 25 H4
Dubica, *Croatia* 29 C13
Dublin, *Ireland* 15 C5
Dublin, *Ga., U.S.A.* 109 J4
Dublin, *Tex., U.S.A.* 113 J5
Dublin □, *Ireland* 15 C5
Dubna, *Russia* 46 D9
Dubnica nad Váhom, *Slovak Rep.* 27 C11
Dubno, *Ukraine* 47 G3
Dubois, *U.S.A.* 114 D7
Dubossary = Dubăsari, *Moldova* 43 C14
Dubossary Vdkhr. = Dubăsari Vdkhr., *Moldova* 43 C13
Dubovka, *Russia* 49 F7
Dubovskoye, *Russia* 49 G6
Dubrajpur, *India* 69 H12
Dubréka, *Guinea* 82 D2
Dubrovitsa = Dubrovytsya, *Ukraine* 47 G4
Dubrovnik, *Croatia* 40 D2
Dubrovytsya, *Ukraine* 47 G4
Dubuque, *U.S.A.* 112 D9
Dubysa →, *Lithuania* 44 C10
Duchang, *China* 59 C11
Duchesne, *U.S.A.* 114 F8
Duchess, *Australia* 94 C2
Ducie I., *Pac. Oc.* 97 K15
Duck →, *U.S.A.* 109 G2
Duck Cr. →, *Australia* 92 D2
Duck Lake, *Canada* 105 C7
Duck Mountain Prov. Park, *Canada* 105 C8
Duckwall, Mt., *U.S.A.* 116 H6
Duderstadt, *Germany* 24 D6
Dudhi, *India* 67 G13
Dudinka, *Russia* 51 C9
Dudley, *U.K.* 13 E5
Dudwa, *India* 69 E9
Duékoué, *Ivory C.* 82 D3
Dueñas, *Spain* 34 D6
Duero = Douro →, *Europe* 34 D2
Dufftown, *U.K.* 14 D5
Dufourspitz, *Switz.* 25 K3
Dūghī Kalā, *Afghan.* 66 C3
Dugi Otok, *Croatia* 29 D11
Dugo Selo, *Croatia* 29 C13
Duifken Pt., *Australia* 94 A3
Duisburg, *Germany* 24 D2
Duiwelskloof, *S. Africa* 89 C5
Dujiangyan, *China* 58 B4
Duk Fadiat, *Sudan* 81 F3
Duk Faiwil, *Sudan* 81 F3
Dukat, *Albania* 40 F3
Dūkdamīn, *Iran* 71 C8
Dukelský Průsmyk, *Slovak Rep.* 27 B14
Dukhān, *Qatar* 71 E6
Dukhovshchina, *Russia* 46 E7
Duki, *Pakistan* 66 D6
Dukla, *Poland* 45 J8
Duku, *Bauchi, Nigeria* 83 C7
Duku, *Sokoto, Nigeria* 83 C5
Dulag, *Phil.* 61 F6
Dulce, *U.S.A.* 115 H10
Dulce →, *Argentina* 126 C3
Dulce, G., *Costa Rica* 120 E3
Dulf, *Iraq* 70 C5
Dŭlgopol, *Bulgaria* 41 C11
Dulit, Banjaran, *Malaysia* 62 D4
Duliu, *China* 56 E9
Dullewala, *Pakistan* 68 D4
Dullstroom, *S. Africa* 89 D5
Dülmen, *Germany* 24 D3
Dulovo, *Bulgaria* 41 C11
Dulq Maghār, *Syria* 70 B3
Duluth, *U.S.A.* 112 B8
Dum Dum, *India* 69 H13
Dum Duma, *India* 67 F19
Dūmā, *Syria* 75 B5
Dumaguete, *Phil.* 61 G5
Dumai, *Indonesia* 62 D2
Dumaran, *Phil.* 61 F3
Dumas, *Ark., U.S.A.* 113 J9
Dumas, *Tex., U.S.A.* 113 H4
Dumayr, *Syria* 75 B5
Dumbarton, *U.K.* 14 F4
Ďumbier, *Slovak Rep.* 27 C12
Dumbleyung, *Australia* 93 F2
Dumboa, *Nigeria* 83 C7
Dumbrăveni, *Romania* 43 D9
Dumfries, *U.K.* 14 F5
Dumfries & Galloway □, *U.K.* 14 F5
Dumitrești, *Romania* 43 E11
Dumka, *India* 69 G12
Dumlupınar, *Turkey* 39 C12
Dümmer, *Germany* 24 C4
Dumoine →, *Canada* 102 C4
Dumoine, L., *Canada* 102 C4
Dumraon, *India* 69 G11
Dumyât, *Egypt* 80 H7
Dumyât, Masabb, *Egypt* 80 H7
Dún Dealgan = Dundalk, *Ireland* 15 B5
Dun Laoghaire, *Ireland* 15 C5
Dun-le-Palestel, *France* 19 F8
Dun-sur-Auron, *France* 19 F9
Dun-sur-Meuse, *France* 19 C12
Duna = Dunărea →, *Europe* 43 E14
Duna →, *Hungary* 42 E3
Duna-völgyi-főcsatorna, *Hungary* 42 D4
Dunaföldvár, *Hungary* 42 D3
Dunagiri, *India* 69 D8
Dunaj = Dunărea →, *Europe* 43 E14
Dunaj →, *Slovak Rep.* 27 D11
Dunajec →, *Poland* 45 H7
Dunajská Streda, *Slovak Rep.* 27 C10
Dunakeszi, *Hungary* 42 C4
Dunapataj, *Hungary* 42 D4
Dunărea →, *Europe* 43 E14
Dunaszekcső, *Hungary* 42 D3
Dunaújváros, *Hungary* 42 D3
Dunav = Dunărea →, *Europe* 43 E14
Dunavațu de Jos, *Romania* 43 F14
Dunavtsi, *Bulgaria* 40 C6
Dunay, *Russia* 54 C6
Dunback, *N.Z.* 91 L3
Dunbar, *U.K.* 14 E6
Dunblane, *U.K.* 14 E5
Duncan, *Canada* 104 D4
Duncan, *Ariz., U.S.A.* 115 K9
Duncan, *Okla., U.S.A.* 113 H6
Duncan, L., *Canada* 102 B4
Duncan L., *Canada* 104 A6
Duncan Town, *Bahamas* 120 B4
Duncannon, *U.S.A.* 110 F7
Duncansby Head, *U.K.* 14 C5
Duncansville, *U.S.A.* 110 F6
Dundaga, *Latvia* 44 A9
Dundalk, *Canada* 110 B4
Dundalk, *Ireland* 15 B5
Dundalk, *U.S.A.* 108 F7
Dundalk Bay, *Ireland* 15 C5
Dundas, *Canada* 110 C5
Dundas, L., *Australia* 93 F3
Dundas I., *Canada* 104 C2
Dundas Str., *Australia* 92 B5
Dundee, *S. Africa* 89 D5
Dundee, *U.K.* 14 E6
Dundee, *U.S.A.* 110 D8
Dundee City □, *U.K.* 14 E6
Dundgovĭ □, *Mongolia* 56 B4
Dundrum, *U.K.* 15 B6
Dundrum B., *U.K.* 15 B6
Dunedin, *N.Z.* 91 L3
Dunedin, *U.S.A.* 109 L4
Dunfermline, *U.K.* 14 E5
Dungannon, *Canada* 110 C3
Dungannon, *U.K.* 15 B5
Dungarpur, *India* 68 H5
Dungarvan, *Ireland* 15 D4
Dungarvan Harbour, *Ireland* 15 D4
Dungeness, *U.K.* 13 G8
Dungo, L. do, *Angola* 88 B2
Dungog, *Australia* 95 E5
Dungu, *Dem. Rep. of the Congo* 86 B2
Dungun, *Malaysia* 65 K4
Dungunâb, *Sudan* 80 C4
Dungunâb, Khalij, *Sudan* 80 C4
Dunhua, *China* 57 C15
Dunhuang, *China* 60 B4
Dunk I., *Australia* 94 B4
Dunkassa, *Benin* 83 C5
Dunkeld, *Australia* 95 E4
Dunkeld, *U.K.* 14 E5
Dunkerque, *France* 19 A9
Dunkery Beacon, *U.K.* 13 F4
Dunkirk = Dunkerque, *France* 19 A9
Dunkirk, *U.S.A.* 110 D5
Dunkuj, *Sudan* 81 E3
Dunkwa, *Central, Ghana* 82 D4
Dunkwa, *Central, Ghana* 83 D4
Dúnleary = Dun Laoghaire, *Ireland* 15 C5
Dunleer, *Ireland* 15 C5
Dunmanus B., *Ireland* 15 E2
Dunmanway, *Ireland* 15 E2
Dunmara, *Australia* 94 B1
Dunmore, *U.S.A.* 111 E9
Dunmore Hd., *Ireland* 15 D1
Dunmore Town, *Bahamas* 120 A4
Dunn, *U.S.A.* 109 H6
Dunnellon, *U.S.A.* 109 L4
Dunnet Hd., *U.K.* 14 C5
Dunning, *U.S.A.* 112 E4
Dunnville, *Canada* 110 D5
Dunolly, *Australia* 95 F3
Dunoon, *U.K.* 14 F4
Dunphy, *U.S.A.* 114 F5
Dunqul, *Egypt* 80 C3
Duns, *U.K.* 14 F6
Dunseith, *U.S.A.* 112 A4
Dunsmuir, *U.S.A.* 114 F2
Dunstable, *U.K.* 13 F7
Dunstan Mts., *N.Z.* 91 L2
Dunster, *Canada* 104 C5
Dunvegan L., *Canada* 105 A7
Duolun, *China* 56 C9
Duong Dong, *Vietnam* 65 G4
Dupree, *U.S.A.* 112 C4
Dupuyer, *U.S.A.* 114 B7
Duque de Caxias, *Brazil* 127 A7
Durack →, *Australia* 92 C4
Durack Ra., *Australia* 92 C4
Durağan, *Turkey* 72 B6
Durak, *Turkey* 39 B10
Đurakovac, *Kosovo, Yug.* 40 D4
Durance →, *France* 21 E8
Durand, *U.S.A.* 112 C9
Durango, *Mexico* 118 C4
Durango, *U.S.A.* 115 H10
Durango □, *Mexico* 118 C4
Durankulak, *Bulgaria* 41 C12
Durant, *Miss., U.S.A.* 113 J10
Durant, *Okla., U.S.A.* 113 J6
Duratón →, *Spain* 34 D6
Durazno, *Uruguay* 126 C4
Durazzo = Durrës, *Albania* 40 E3
Durban, *France* 20 F6
Durban, *S. Africa* 89 D5
Durbuy, *Belgium* 17 D5
Dúrcal, *Spain* 35 J7
Đurđevac, *Croatia* 42 D2
Düren, *Germany* 24 E2
Durg, *India* 67 J12
Durgapur, *India* 69 H12
Durham, *Canada* 102 D3
Durham, *U.K.* 12 C6
Durham, *Calif., U.S.A.* 116 F5
Durham, *N.C., U.S.A.* 109 H6
Durham, *N.H., U.S.A.* 111 C14
Durham □, *U.K.* 12 C6
Durlești, *Moldova* 43 C13
Durmā, *Si. Arabia* 70 E5
Durmitor, *Montenegro, Yug.* 40 C2
Durness, *U.K.* 14 C4
Durrës, *Albania* 40 E3
Durrow, *Ireland* 15 D4
Dursey I., *Ireland* 15 E1
Dursunbey, *Turkey* 39 B10
Durtal, *France* 18 E6
Duru, *Dem. Rep. of the Congo* 86 B2
Duru Gölü, *Turkey* 41 E12
Durusu, *Turkey* 41 E12
Durūz, Jabal ad, *Jordan* 75 C5
D'Urville, Tanjung, *Indonesia* 63 E9
D'Urville I., *N.Z.* 91 J4
Duryea, *U.S.A.* 111 E9
Dûsh, *Egypt* 80 C3
Dushak, *Turkmenistan* 50 F7
Dushan, *China* 58 E6
Dushanbe, *Tajikistan* 50 F7
Dusheti, *Georgia* 49 J7
Dushore, *U.S.A.* 111 E8
Dusky Sd., *N.Z.* 91 L1
Dussejour, C., *Australia* 92 B4
Düsseldorf, *Germany* 24 D2
Duszniki-Zdrój, *Poland* 45 H3
Dutch Harbor, *U.S.A.* 100 C3
Dutlwe, *Botswana* 88 C3
Dutsan Wai, *Nigeria* 83 C6
Dutton, *Canada* 110 D3
Dutton →, *Australia* 94 C3
Duved, *Sweden* 10 A6
Düvertepe, *Turkey* 39 B10
Duwayhin, Khawr, *U.A.E.* 71 E6
Duyun, *China* 58 D6
Düzağac, *Turkey* 39 C12
Düzce, *Turkey* 72 B4
Duzdab = Zāhedān, *Iran* 71 D9
Dve Mogili, *Bulgaria* 41 C9
Dvina, Severnaya →, *Russia* 50 C5
Dvinsk = Daugavpils, *Latvia* 9 J22
Dvor, *Croatia* 29 C13
Dvůr Králové nad Labem, *Czech Rep.* 26 A8
Dwarka, *India* 68 H3
Dwellingup, *Australia* 93 F2
Dwight, *Canada* 110 A5
Dwight, *U.S.A.* 108 E1
Dyatkovo, *Russia* 46 F8
Dyatlovo = Dzyatlava, *Belarus* 46 F3
Dyce, *U.K.* 14 D6
Dyer, C., *Canada* 101 B13
Dyer Bay, *Canada* 110 A3
Dyer Plateau, *Antarctica* 5 D17
Dyersburg, *U.S.A.* 113 G10
Dyfi →, *U.K.* 13 E3
Dyje →, *Czech Rep.* 27 C9
Dymer, *Ukraine* 47 G6
Dynów, *Poland* 45 J9
Dysart, *Australia* 94 C4
Dzamin Üüd = Borhoyn Tal, *Mongolia* 56 C6
Dzerzhinsk, *Russia* 48 B6
Dzhalinda, *Russia* 51 D13
Dzhambul = Taraz, *Kazakstan* 50 E8
Dzhankoy, *Ukraine* 47 K8
Dzhanybek, *Kazakstan* 48 F8
Dzharylhach, Ostriv, *Ukraine* 47 J7
Dzhezkazgan = Zhezqazghan, *Kazakstan* 50 E7
Dzhizak = Jizzakh, *Uzbekistan* 50 E7
Dzhugdzur, Khrebet, *Russia* 51 D14
Dzhvari = Jvari, *Georgia* 49 J6
Działdowo, *Poland* 45 E7
Działoszyce, *Poland* 45 H7
Działoszyn, *Poland* 45 G5
Dzibilchaltun, *Mexico* 119 C7
Dzierzgoń, *Poland* 44 E6
Dzierżoniów, *Poland* 45 H3
Dzilam de Bravo, *Mexico* 119 C7
Dzisna, *Belarus* 46 E5
Dzisna →, *Belarus* 46 E5
Dziwnów, *Poland* 44 D1
Dzungaria = Junggar Pendi, *China* 60 B3
Dzuumod, *Mongolia* 60 B5
Dzyarzhynsk, *Belarus* 46 F4
Dzyatlava, *Belarus* 46 F3

E

Eabamet L., *Canada* 102 B2
Eads, *U.S.A.* 112 F3
Eagar, *U.S.A.* 115 J9
Eagle, *Alaska, U.S.A.* 100 B5
Eagle, *Colo., U.S.A.* 114 G10
Eagle →, *Canada* 103 B8
Eagle Butte, *U.S.A.* 112 C4
Eagle Grove, *U.S.A.* 112 D8
Eagle L., *Canada* 105 D10
Eagle L., *Calif., U.S.A.* 114 F3
Eagle L., *Maine, U.S.A.* 109 B11
Eagle Lake, *Canada* 110 A6
Eagle Lake, *Maine, U.S.A.* 109 B11
Eagle Lake, *Tex., U.S.A.* 113 L6
Eagle Mountain, *U.S.A.* 117 M11
Eagle Nest, *U.S.A.* 115 H11
Eagle Pass, *U.S.A.* 113 L4
Eagle Pk., *U.S.A.* 116 G7
Eagle Pt., *Australia* 92 C3
Eagle River, *Mich., U.S.A.* 108 B1
Eagle River, *Wis., U.S.A.* 112 C10
Eaglehawk, *Australia* 95 F3
Eagles Mere, *U.S.A.* 111 E8
Ealing □, *U.K.* 13 F7
Ear Falls, *Canada* 105 C10
Earle, *U.S.A.* 113 H9
Earlimart, *U.S.A.* 117 K7
Earn →, *U.K.* 14 E5
Earn, L., *U.K.* 14 E4
Earnslaw, Mt., *N.Z.* 91 L2
Earth, *U.S.A.* 113 H3
Easley, *U.S.A.* 109 H4
East Anglia, *U.K.* 12 E9
East Angus, *Canada* 103 C5
East Aurora, *U.S.A.* 110 D6
East Ayrshire □, *U.K.* 14 F4
East Bengal, *Bangla.* 67 H17
East Beskids = Vychodné Beskydy, *Europe* 27 B15
East Brady, *U.S.A.* 110 F5
East C., *N.Z.* 91 G7
East Chicago, *U.S.A.* 108 E2
East China Sea, *Asia* 60 C7
East Coulee, *Canada* 104 C6
East Dereham, *U.K.* 13 E8
East Dunbartonshire □, *U.K.* 14 F4
East Falkland, *Falk. Is.* 122 J5
East Grand Forks, *U.S.A.* 112 B6
East Greenwich, *U.S.A.* 111 E13
East Grinstead, *U.K.* 13 F8
East Hartford, *U.S.A.* 111 E12
East Helena, *U.S.A.* 114 C8
East Indies, *Asia* 52 K15
East Kilbride, *U.K.* 14 F4
East Lansing, *U.S.A.* 108 D3
East Liverpool, *U.S.A.* 110 F4
East London, *S. Africa* 89 E4
East Lothian □, *U.K.* 14 F6
East Main = Eastmain, *Canada* 102 B4
East Northport, *U.S.A.* 111 F11
East Orange, *U.S.A.* 111 F10
East Pacific Ridge, *Pac. Oc.* 97 J17
East Palestine, *U.S.A.* 110 F4
East Pine, *Canada* 104 B4
East Point, *U.S.A.* 109 J3
East Providence, *U.S.A.* 111 E13
East Pt., *Canada* 103 C7
East Renfrewshire □, *U.K.* 14 F4
East Retford = Retford, *U.K.* 12 D7
East Riding of Yorkshire □, *U.K.* 12 D7
East Rochester, *U.S.A.* 110 C7
East St. Louis, *U.S.A.* 112 F9
East Schelde = Oosterschelde →, *Neths.* 17 C4
East Sea = Japan, Sea of, *Asia* 54 E7
East Siberian Sea, *Russia* 51 B17

East Stroudsburg

East Stroudsburg, U.S.A. 111 E9
East Sussex □, U.K. 13 G8
East Tawas, U.S.A. 108 C4
East Timor ■, Asia 63 F7
East Toorale, Australia 95 E4
East Walker →, U.S.A. 116 G7
East Windsor, U.S.A. 111 F10
Eastbourne, N.Z. 91 J5
Eastbourne, U.K. 13 G8
Eastend, Canada 105 D7
Easter I. = Pascua, I. de, Pac. Oc. 97 K17
Eastern □, Ghana 83 D4
Eastern □, Kenya 86 C4
Eastern Cape □, S. Africa 88 E4
Eastern Cr. →, Australia 94 C3
Eastern Ghats, India 66 N11
Eastern Group = Lau Group, Fiji 91 C9
Eastern Group, Australia 93 F3
Eastern Province □, S. Leone 82 D2
Eastern Transvaal = Mpumalanga □, S. Africa 89 B5
Easterville, Canada 105 C9
Easthampton, U.S.A. 111 D12
Eastlake, U.S.A. 110 E3
Eastland, U.S.A. 113 J5
Eastleigh, U.K. 13 G6
Eastmain, Canada 102 B4
Eastmain →, Canada 102 B4
Eastman, Canada 111 A12
Eastman, U.S.A. 109 J4
Easton, Md., U.S.A. 108 F7
Easton, Pa., U.S.A. 111 F9
Easton, Wash., U.S.A. 116 C5
Eastpointe, U.S.A. 110 D2
Eastport, U.S.A. 109 C12
Eastsound, U.S.A. 116 B4
Eaton, U.S.A. 112 E2
Eatonia, Canada 105 C7
Eatonton, U.S.A. 109 J4
Eatontown, U.S.A. 111 F10
Eatonville, U.S.A. 116 D4
Eau Claire, U.S.A. 112 C9
Eau Claire, L. à l', Canada 102 A5
Eauze, France 20 E4
Eban, Nigeria 83 D5
Ebbw Vale, U.K. 13 F4
Ebeltoft, Denmark 11 H4
Ebeltoft Vig, Denmark 11 H4
Ebensburg, U.S.A. 110 F6
Ebensee, Austria 26 D6
Eber Gölü, Turkey 72 C4
Eberbach, Germany 25 F4
Eberswalde-Finow, Germany 24 C9
Ebetsu, Japan 54 C10
Ebian, China 58 C4
Ebingen, Germany 25 G5
Éboli, Italy 31 B8
Ebolowa, Cameroon 83 E7
Ebonyi □, Nigeria 83 D6
Ebrach, Germany 25 F6
Ébrié, Lagune, Ivory C. 82 D4
Ebro →, Spain 32 E5
Ebro, Embalse del, Spain 34 C7
Ebstorf, Germany 24 B6
Eceabat, Turkey 41 F10
Ech Cheliff, Algeria 78 A6
Echigo-Sammyaku, Japan 55 F9
Échirolles, France 21 C9
Echizen-Misaki, Japan 55 G7
Echmiadzin = Yejmiadzin, Armenia 49 K7
Echo Bay, N.W.T., Canada 100 B8
Echo Bay, Ont., Canada 102 C3
Echoing →, Canada 102 B1
Echternach, Lux. 17 E6
Echuca, Australia 95 F3
Ecija, Spain 35 H5
Eckental, Germany 25 F7
Eckernförde, Germany 24 A5
Eclipse Is., Australia 92 B4
Eclipse Sd., Canada 101 A11
Écommoy, France 18 E7
Écouché, France 18 D6
Ecuador ■, S. Amer. 124 D3
Écueillé, France 18 E8
Ed, Sweden 11 F5
Ed Dabbura, Sudan 80 D3
Ed Da'ein, Sudan 81 E2
Ed Damazin, Sudan 79 F12
Ed Dâmer, Sudan 80 D3
Ed Debba, Sudan 80 D3
Ed-Déffa, Egypt 80 A2
Ed Deim, Sudan 81 E2
Ed Dueim, Sudan 81 E3
Edam, Canada 105 C7
Edam, Neths. 17 B5
Edane, Sweden 10 E6
Eday, U.K. 14 B6
Edd, Eritrea 81 E5
Eddrachillis B., U.K. 14 C3
Eddystone Pt., Australia 94 G4
Ede, Neths. 17 B5
Ede, Nigeria 83 D5
Edéa, Cameroon 83 E7
Edebäck, Sweden 10 D7
Edehon L., Canada 105 A9
Edelény, Hungary 42 B5
Eden, Australia 95 F4
Eden, N.C., U.S.A. 109 G6
Eden, N.Y., U.S.A. 110 D6
Eden, Tex., U.S.A. 113 K5
Eden →, U.K. 12 C4
Edenburg, S. Africa 88 D4
Edendale, S. Africa 89 D5
Edenderry, Ireland 15 C4
Edenton, U.S.A. 109 G7
Edenville, S. Africa 89 D4
Eder →, Germany 24 D5
Eder-Stausee, Germany 24 D4
Edewecht, Germany 24 B3
Edgar, U.S.A. 112 E6
Edgartown, U.S.A. 111 E14
Edge Hill, U.K. 13 E6
Edgefield, U.S.A. 109 J5
Edgeley, U.S.A. 112 B5
Edgemont, U.S.A. 112 D3
Edgeøya, Svalbard 4 B9
Édhessa, Greece 40 F6
Edievale, N.Z. 91 L2
Edina, Liberia 82 D2
Edina, U.S.A. 112 E8
Edinboro, U.S.A. 110 E4
Edinburg, U.S.A. 113 M5
Edinburgh, U.K. 14 F5
Edinburgh, City of □, U.K. 14 F5
Edineţ, Moldova 43 B12
Edirne, Turkey 41 E10
Edirne □, Turkey 41 E10
Edison, U.S.A. 116 B4
Edithburgh, Australia 95 F2
Edmeston, U.S.A. 111 D9
Edmond, U.S.A. 113 H6
Edmonds, U.S.A. 116 C4
Edmonton, Australia 94 B4
Edmonton, Canada 104 C6
Edmund L., Canada 102 B1
Edmundston, Canada 103 C6
Edna, U.S.A. 113 L6
Edo □, Nigeria 83 D6
Edolo, Italy 28 B7
Edremit, Turkey 39 B9
Edremit Körfezi, Turkey 39 B8
Edsbro, Sweden 10 E12
Edsbyn, Sweden 10 C9
Edson, Canada 104 C5
Eduardo Castex, Argentina 126 D3
Edward →, Australia 95 F3
Edward, L., Africa 86 C2
Edward River, Australia 94 A3
Edward VII Land, Antarctica 5 E13
Edwards, Calif., U.S.A. 117 L9
Edwards, N.Y., U.S.A. 111 B9
Edwards Air Force Base, U.S.A. 117 L9
Edwards Plateau, U.S.A. 113 K4
Edwardsville, U.S.A. 111 E9
Edzo, Canada 104 A5
Eeklo, Belgium 17 C3
Eferding, Austria 26 C7
Effingham, U.S.A. 108 F1
Eforie, Romania 43 F13
Ega →, Spain 32 C3
Égadi, Ísole, Italy 30 E5
Egan Range, U.S.A. 114 G6
Eganville, Canada 102 C4
Eger = Cheb, Czech Rep. 26 A5
Eger, Hungary 42 C5
Eger →, Hungary 42 C5
Egersund, Norway 9 G12
Egg L., Canada 105 B7
Eggenburg, Austria 26 C8
Eggenfelden, Germany 25 G8
Éghezée, Belgium 17 D4
Égletons, France 20 C6
Egmont, Canada 104 D4
Egmont, C., N.Z. 91 H4
Egmont, Mt. = Taranaki, Mt., N.Z. 91 H5
Egra, India 69 J12
Eğridir, Turkey 72 D4
Eğridir Gölü, Turkey 70 B1
Egtved, Denmark 11 J3
Egume, Nigeria 83 D6
Éguzon-Chantôme, France 19 F8
Egvekinot, Russia 51 C19
Egyek, Hungary 42 C5
Egypt ■, Africa 80 B3
Eha Amufu, Nigeria 83 D6
Ehime □, Japan 55 H6
Ehingen, Germany 25 G5
Ehrenberg, U.S.A. 117 M12
Ehrwald, Austria 26 D3
Eibar, Spain 32 B2
Eichstätt, Germany 25 G7
Eider →, Germany 24 A4
Eidsvold, Australia 95 D5
Eidsvoll, Norway 9 F14
Eifel, Germany 25 E2
Eiffel Flats, Zimbabwe 87 F3
Eiger, Switz. 28 B5
Eigg, U.K. 14 E2
Eighty Mile Beach, Australia 92 C3
Eil, Somali Rep. 74 F4
Eil, L., U.K. 14 E3
Eildon, L., Australia 95 F4
Eilenburg, Germany 24 D8
Ein el Luweiqa, Sudan 81 E3
Einasleigh, Australia 94 B3
Einasleigh →, Australia 94 B3
Einbeck, Germany 24 D5
Eindhoven, Neths. 17 C5
Einsiedeln, Switz. 25 H4
Eire = Ireland ■, Europe 15 C4
Eiríksjökull, Iceland 8 D3
Eirunepé, Brazil 124 E5
Eiseb →, Namibia 88 C2
Eisenach, Germany 24 E6
Eisenberg, Germany 24 E7
Eisenerz, Austria 26 D7
Eisenhüttenstadt, Germany 24 C10
Eisenkappel, Austria 26 E7
Eisenstadt, Austria 27 D9
Eisfeld, Germany 25 E6
Eisleben, Germany 24 D7
Eislingen, Germany 25 G5
Eivissa, Spain 37 C7
Eixe, Serra do, Spain 34 C4
Ejea de los Caballeros, Spain 32 C3
Ejeda, Madag. 89 C7
Ejura, Ghana 83 D4
Ejutla, Mexico 119 D5
Ekalaka, U.S.A. 112 C2
Ekenässjön, Sweden 11 G9
Ekerö, Sweden 10 E11
Eket, Nigeria 83 E6
Eketahuna, N.Z. 91 J5
Ekhínos, Greece 41 E9
Ekibastuz, Kazakstan 50 D8
Ekiti □, Nigeria 83 D6
Ekoli, Dem. Rep. of the Congo 86 C1
Ekoln, Sweden 10 E11
Ekshärad, Sweden 10 D7
Eksjö, Sweden 11 G8
Ekuma →, Namibia 88 B2
Ekwan →, Canada 102 B3
Ekwan Pt., Canada 102 B3
El Aaiún, W. Sahara 78 C3
El Abanico, Chile 126 D1
El Abbasiya, Sudan 81 E3
El 'Agrûd, Egypt 75 E3
El Ait, Sudan 81 E2
El 'Aiyat, Egypt 80 J7
El Alamein, Egypt 80 A2
El 'Aqaba, W. →, Egypt 75 E2
El 'Arag, Egypt 80 B2
El Arahal, Spain 35 H5
El Arīḩā, West Bank 75 D4
El 'Arîsh, Egypt 75 D2
El 'Arîsh, W. →, Egypt 75 D2
El Asnam = Ech Cheliff, Algeria 78 A6
El Astillero, Spain 34 B7
El Badâri, Egypt 80 B3
El Bahrein, Egypt 80 B2
El Ballâs, Egypt 80 B3
El Balyana, Egypt 80 B3
El Baqeir, Sudan 80 D3
El Barco de Ávila, Spain 34 E5
El Barco de Valdeorras = O Barco, Spain 34 C4
El Bauga, Sudan 80 D3
El Bawiti, Egypt 80 B2
El Bayadh, Algeria 78 B6
El Bierzo, Spain 34 C4
El Bluff, Nic. 120 D3
El Bonillo, Spain 33 G2
El Brûk, W. →, Egypt 75 E2
El Buheirat □, Sudan 81 F3
El Burgo de Osma, Spain 32 D1
El Cajon, U.S.A. 117 N10
El Campo, U.S.A. 113 L6
El Centro, U.S.A. 117 N11
El Cerro, Bolivia 124 G6
El Cerro de Andévalo, Spain 35 H4
El Compadre, Mexico 117 N10
El Coronil, Spain 35 H5
El Cuy, Argentina 128 D3
El Cuyo, Mexico 119 C7
El Dab'a, Egypt 80 H6
El Daheir, Egypt 75 D3
El Dátil, Mexico 118 B2
El Deir, Egypt 80 B3
El Dere, Somali Rep. 74 G4
El Descanso, Mexico 117 N10
El Desemboque, Mexico 118 A2
El Dilingat, Egypt 80 H7
El Diviso, Colombia 124 C3
El Djouf, Mauritania 78 D4
El Dorado, Ark., U.S.A. 113 J8
El Dorado, Kans., U.S.A. 113 G6
El Dorado, Venezuela 124 B6
El 'Ein, Sudan 81 D2
El Ejido, Spain 35 J8
El Escorial, Spain 34 E6
El Espinar, Spain 34 D6
El Faiyûm, Egypt 80 J7
El Fâsher, Sudan 81 E2
El Fashn, Egypt 80 J7
El Ferrol = Ferrol, Spain 34 B2
El Fifi, Sudan 81 E2
El Fuerte, Mexico 118 B3
El Ga'a, Sudan 81 E2
El Gal, Somali Rep. 74 E5
El Garef, Sudan 81 E3
El Gebir, Sudan 81 E2
El Gedida, Egypt 80 B2
El Geneina = Al Junaynah, Sudan 79 F10
El Geteina, Sudan 81 E3
El Gezira □, Sudan 81 E3
El Gir, Sudan 80 D2
El Gîza, Egypt 80 J7
El Goléa, Algeria 78 B6
El Grau, Spain 33 G4
El Hagiz, Sudan 81 D4
El Hâi, Egypt 80 J7
El Hammam, Egypt 80 A2
El Hawata, Sudan 81 E3
El Heiz, Egypt 80 B2
El Hideib, Sudan 81 E3
El Hilla, Sudan 81 E2
El 'Idisât, Egypt 80 B3
El Iskandarîya, Egypt 80 H7
El Istiwa'iya, Sudan 79 G11
El Jadida, Morocco 78 B4
El Jardal, Honduras 120 D2
El Jebelein, Sudan 81 E3
El Kab, Sudan 80 D3
El Kabrît, G., Egypt 75 F2
El Kafr el Sharqi, Egypt 80 H7
El Kamlin, Sudan 81 D3
El Karaba, Sudan 80 D3
El Kere, Ethiopia 81 F5
El Khandaq, Sudan 80 D3
El Khârga, Egypt 80 B3
El Khartûm, Sudan 81 D3
El Khartûm □, Sudan 81 D3
El Khartûm Bahrî, Sudan 81 D3
El Kuntilla, Egypt 75 E3
El Laqâwa, Sudan 81 E2
El Laqeita, Egypt 80 B3
El Leh, Ethiopia 81 G4
El Leiya, Sudan 81 D4
El Maestrazgo, Spain 32 E4
El Mafâza, Sudan 81 E3
El Maghra, Egypt 80 A2
El Mahalla el Kubra, Egypt 80 H7
El Mahârîq, Egypt 80 B3
El Maîmûn, Egypt 80 J7
El Maks el Bahari, Egypt 80 C3
El Manshâh, Egypt 80 B3
El Mansûra, Egypt 80 H7
El Manzala, Egypt 80 H7
El Marâgha, Egypt 80 B3
El Masid, Sudan 81 D3
El Masnou, Spain 32 D7
El Matariya, Egypt 80 H8
El Meda, Ethiopia 81 F5
El Medano, Canary Is. 37 F3
El Metemma, Sudan 81 D3
El Milagro, Argentina 126 C2
El Minyâ, Egypt 80 B3
El Monte, U.S.A. 117 L8
El Montseny, Spain 32 D7
El Mreyye, Mauritania 82 B3
El Niybo, Ethiopia 81 G4
El Obeid, Sudan 81 E3
El Odaiya, Sudan 81 E2
El Oro, Mexico 119 D4
El Oued, Algeria 78 B7
El Palmito, Presa, Mexico 118 B3
El Paso, U.S.A. 115 L10
El Paso Robles, U.S.A. 116 K6
El Pedernoso, Spain 33 F2
El Pedroso, Spain 35 H5
El Pobo de Dueñas, Spain 32 E3
El Portal, U.S.A. 116 H7
El Porvenir, Mexico 118 A3
El Prat de Llobregat, Spain 32 D7
El Progreso, Honduras 120 C2
El Pueblito, Mexico 118 B3
El Pueblo, Canary Is. 37 F2
El Puente del Arzobispo, Spain 34 F5
El Puerto de Santa María, Spain 35 J4
El Qâhira, Egypt 80 H7
El Qantara, Egypt 75 E1
El Qasr, Egypt 80 B2
El Qubâbât, Egypt 80 J7
El Quseima, Egypt 75 E3
El Qusîya, Egypt 80 B3
El Râshda, Egypt 80 B2
El Real, Panama 124 B3
El Reno, U.S.A. 113 H6
El Rîdisiya, Egypt 80 C3
El Rio, U.S.A. 117 L7
El Ronquillo, Spain 35 H4
El Roque, Pta., Canary Is. 37 F4
El Rosarito, Mexico 118 B2
El Rubio, Spain 35 H5
El Saff, Egypt 80 J7
El Saheira, W. →, Egypt 75 E2
El Salto, Mexico 118 C3
El Salvador ■, Cent. Amer. 120 D2
El Sauce, Nic. 120 D2
El Saucejo, Spain 35 H5
El Shallal, Egypt 80 C3
El Simbillawein, Egypt 80 H7
El Sueco, Mexico 118 B3
El Suweis, Egypt 80 J8
El Tabbîn, Egypt 80 J7
El Tamarâni, W. →, Egypt 75 E3
El Thamad, Egypt 75 F3
El Tigre, Venezuela 124 B6
El Tîh, Gebal, Egypt 75 F2
El Tîna, Egypt 80 H8
El Tîna, Khalîg, Egypt 75 D1
El Tofo, Chile 126 B1
El Tránsito, Chile 126 B1
El Tûr, Egypt 70 D2
El Turbio, Argentina 128 G2
El Uqsur, Egypt 80 B3
El Venado, Mexico 118 C4
El Vendrell, Spain 32 D6
El Vergel, Mexico 118 B3
El Vigía, Venezuela 124 B4
El Viso del Alcor, Spain 35 H5
El Wabeira, Egypt 75 F2
El Wak, Kenya 86 B5
El Waqf, Egypt 80 B3
El Weguet, Ethiopia 81 F5
El Wuz, Sudan 81 D3
Elafónisos, Greece 38 E4
Élancourt, France 19 D8
Élassa, Greece 39 F8
Elassón, Greece 38 B4
Elat, Israel 75 F3
Eláthia, Greece 38 C4
Elâzığ, Turkey 70 B3
Elba, Italy 28 F7
Elba, U.S.A. 109 K2
Elbasan, Albania 40 E4
Elbe, U.S.A. 116 D4
Elbe →, Europe 24 B4
Elbe-Seitenkanal, Germany 24 C6
Elbert, Mt., U.S.A. 115 G10
Elberton, U.S.A. 109 H4
Elbeuf, France 18 C8
Elbidtan, Turkey 70 B3
Elbing = Elbląg, Poland 44 D6
Elbistan, Turkey 72 C7
Elbląg, Poland 44 D6
Elbow, Canada 105 C7
Elbrus, Asia 49 J6
Elburz Mts. = Alborz, Reshteh-ye Kūhhā-ye, Iran 71 C7
Elche, Spain 33 G4
Elche de la Sierra, Spain 33 G2
Elcho I., Australia 94 A2
Elda, Spain 33 G4
Elde →, Germany 24 B7
Eldon, Mo., U.S.A. 112 F8
Eldon, Wash., U.S.A. 116 C3
Eldora, U.S.A. 112 D8
Eldorado, Argentina 127 B5
Eldorado, Canada 110 B7
Eldorado, Mexico 118 C3
Eldorado, Ill., U.S.A. 108 G1
Eldorado, Tex., U.S.A. 113 K4
Eldorado Springs, U.S.A. 113 G8
Eldoret, Kenya 86 B4
Eldred, U.S.A. 110 E6
Elea, C., Cyprus 36 D13
Eleanora, Pk., Australia 93 F3
Elefantes →, Mozam. 89 C5
Elektrogorsk, Russia 46 E10
Elektrostal, Russia 46 E10
Elele, Nigeria 83 D6
Elena, Bulgaria 41 D9
Elephant Butte Reservoir, U.S.A. 115 K10
Elephant I., Antarctica 5 C18
Eleshnitsa, Bulgaria 40 E7
Eleşkirt, Turkey 73 C10
Eleuthera, Bahamas 120 B4
Elevsís, Greece 38 C5
Elevtheroúpolis, Greece 41 F8
Elgin, Canada 111 B8
Elgin, U.K. 14 D5
Elgin, Ill., U.S.A. 108 D1
Elgin, N. Dak., U.S.A. 112 B4
Elgin, Oreg., U.S.A. 114 D5
Elgin, Tex., U.S.A. 113 K6
Elgoibar, Spain 32 B2
Elgon, Mt., Africa 86 B3
Eliase, Indonesia 63 F8
Elikón, Greece 38 C4
Elim, Namibia 88 B2
Elim, S. Africa 88 E2
Elin Pelin, Bulgaria 40 D7
Elista, Russia 49 G7
Elizabeth, Australia 95 E2
Elizabeth, N.J., U.S.A. 111 F10
Elizabeth, N.J., U.S.A. 111 F10
Elizabeth City, U.S.A. 109 G7
Elizabethton, U.S.A. 109 G4
Elizabethtown, Ky., U.S.A. 108 G3
Elizabethtown, N.Y., U.S.A. 111 B11
Elizabethtown, Pa., U.S.A. 111 F8
Elizondo, Spain 32 B3
Ełk, Poland 44 E9
Elk →, Canada 104 C5
Ełk →, Poland 44 E9
Elk →, U.S.A. 109 H2
Elk City, U.S.A. 113 H5
Elk Creek, U.S.A. 116 F4
Elk Grove, U.S.A. 116 G5
Elk Island Nat. Park, Canada 104 C6
Elk Lake, Canada 102 C3
Elk Point, Canada 105 C6
Elk River, Idaho, U.S.A. 114 C5
Elk River, Minn., U.S.A. 112 C8
Elkedra →, Australia 94 C2
Elkhart, Ind., U.S.A. 108 E3
Elkhart, Kans., U.S.A. 113 G4
Elkhorn, Canada 105 D8
Elkhorn →, U.S.A. 112 E6
Elkhovo, Bulgaria 41 D10
Elkin, U.S.A. 109 G5
Elkins, U.S.A. 108 F6
Elkland, U.S.A. 110 E7
Elko, Canada 104 D5
Elko, U.S.A. 114 F6
Elkton, U.S.A. 110 C1
Ell, L., Australia 93 E4
Ellef Ringnes I., Canada 4 B2
Ellen, Mt., U.S.A. 111 B12
Ellenburg, U.S.A. 111 B11
Ellendale, U.S.A. 112 B5
Ellensburg, U.S.A. 114 C3
Ellenville, U.S.A. 111 E10
Ellery, Mt., Australia 95 F4
Ellesmere, L., N.Z. 91 M4
Ellesmere I., Canada 4 B4
Ellesmere Port, U.K. 12 D5
Ellice Is. = Tuvalu ■, Pac. Oc. 96 H9
Ellicottville, U.S.A. 110 D6
Elliot, Australia 94 B1
Elliot, S. Africa 89 E4
Elliot Lake, Canada 102 C3
Elliotdale = Xhora, S. Africa 89 E4
Ellis, U.S.A. 112 F5
Elliston, Australia 95 E1
Ellisville, U.S.A. 113 K10
Ellon, U.K. 14 D6
Ellore = Eluru, India 67 L12
Ellsworth, Kans., U.S.A. 112 F5
Ellsworth, Maine, U.S.A. 109 C11
Ellsworth Land, Antarctica 5 D16
Ellsworth Mts., Antarctica 5 D16
Ellwangen, Germany 25 G6
Ellwood City, U.S.A. 110 F4
Elm, Switz. 25 J5
Elma, Canada 105 D9
Elma, U.S.A. 116 D3
Elmadağ, Turkey 72 C5

Elmalı, *Turkey* 39 **E11**
Elmhurst, *U.S.A.* 108 **E2**
Elmina, *Ghana* 83 **D4**
Elmira, *Canada* 110 **C4**
Elmira, *U.S.A.* 110 **D8**
Elmira Heights, *U.S.A.* 110 **D8**
Elmore, *Australia* 95 **F3**
Elmore, *U.S.A.* 117 **M11**
Elmshorn, *Germany* 24 **B5**
Elmvale, *Canada* 110 **B5**
Elne, *France* 20 **F6**
Elora, *Canada* 110 **C4**
Elos, *Greece* 38 **E4**
Eloúnda, *Greece* 36 **D7**
Eloy, *U.S.A.* 115 **K8**
Éloyes, *France* 19 **D13**
Elrose, *Canada* 105 **C7**
Elsdorf, *Germany* 24 **E2**
Elsie, *U.S.A.* 116 **E3**
Elsinore = Helsingør, *Denmark* 11 **H6**
Elster →, *Germany* 24 **D7**
Elsterwerda, *Germany* 24 **D9**
Eltham, *N.Z.* 91 **H5**
Elton, *Russia* 49 **F8**
Elton, Ozero, *Russia* 49 **F8**
Eltville, *Germany* 25 **E4**
Eluru, *India* 67 **L12**
Elvas, *Portugal* 35 **G3**
Elven, *France* 18 **E4**
Elverum, *Norway* 9 **F14**
Elvire →, *Australia* 92 **C4**
Elvire, Mt., *Australia* 93 **E2**
Elvo →, *Italy* 28 **C5**
Elwell, L., *U.S.A.* 114 **B8**
Elwood, *Ind., U.S.A.* 108 **E3**
Elwood, *Nebr., U.S.A.* 112 **E5**
Elx = Elche, *Spain* 33 **G4**
Ely, *U.K.* 13 **E8**
Ely, *Minn., U.S.A.* 112 **B9**
Ely, *Nev., U.S.A.* 114 **G6**
Elyria, *U.S.A.* 110 **E2**
Elyrus, *Greece* 38 **F5**
Elz →, *Germany* 25 **G3**
Emådalen, *Sweden* 10 **C8**
Emāmrūd, *Iran* 71 **B7**
Emån →, *Sweden* 11 **G10**
Emba, *Kazakstan* 50 **E6**
Emba →, *Kazakstan* 50 **E6**
Embarcación, *Argentina* 126 **A3**
Embarras Portage, *Canada* 105 **B6**
Embetsu, *Japan* 54 **B10**
Embi = Emba, *Kazakstan* 50 **E6**
Embi = Emba →, *Kazakstan* 50 **E6**
Embóna, *Greece* 36 **C9**
Embrun, *France* 21 **D10**
Embu, *Kenya* 86 **C4**
Emden, *Germany* 24 **B3**
Emecik, *Turkey* 39 **E9**
Emerald, *Australia* 94 **C4**
Emerson, *Canada* 105 **D9**
Emet, *Turkey* 39 **B11**
Emi Koussi, *Chad* 79 **E9**
Emília-Romagna □, *Italy* 28 **D8**
Emilius, Mte., *Italy* 28 **C4**
Eminabad, *Pakistan* 68 **C6**
Emine, Nos, *Bulgaria* 41 **D11**
Emirdağ, *Turkey* 72 **C4**
Emlenton, *U.S.A.* 110 **E5**
Emlichheim, *Germany* 24 **C2**
Emmaboda, *Sweden* 11 **H9**
Emmaus, *S. Africa* 88 **D4**
Emmaus, *U.S.A.* 111 **F9**
Emme →, *Switz.* 25 **H3**
Emmeloord, *Neths.* 17 **B5**
Emmen, *Neths.* 17 **B6**
Emmen, *Switz.* 25 **H4**
Emmendingen, *Germany* 25 **G3**
Emmental, *Switz.* 25 **J3**
Emmerich, *Germany* 24 **D2**
Emmet, *Australia* 94 **C3**
Emmetsburg, *U.S.A.* 112 **D7**
Emmett, *Idaho, U.S.A.* 114 **E5**
Emmett, *Mich., U.S.A.* 110 **D2**
Emmonak, *U.S.A.* 100 **B3**
Emo, *Canada* 105 **D10**
Emőd, *Hungary* 42 **C5**
Emona, *Bulgaria* 41 **D11**
Empalme, *Mexico* 118 **B2**
Empangeni, *S. Africa* 89 **D5**
Empedrado, *Argentina* 126 **B4**
Emperor Seamount Chain, *Pac. Oc.* 96 **D9**
Empoli, *Italy* 28 **E7**
Emporia, *Kans., U.S.A.* 112 **F6**
Emporia, *Va., U.S.A.* 109 **G7**
Emporium, *U.S.A.* 110 **E6**
Empress, *Canada* 105 **C7**
Empty Quarter = Rub' al Khālī, *Si. Arabia* 74 **D4**
Ems →, *Germany* 24 **B3**
Emsdale, *Canada* 110 **A5**
Emsdetten, *Germany* 24 **C3**
Emu, *China* 57 **C15**
Emu Park, *Australia* 94 **C5**
'En 'Avrona, *Israel* 75 **F4**
En Nahud, *Sudan* 81 **E2**
En Nofalab, *Sudan* 81 **D3**
Ena, *Japan* 55 **G8**
Enana, *Namibia* 88 **B2**
Enånger, *Sweden* 10 **C11**
Enard B., *U.K.* 14 **C3**
Enare = Inarijärvi, *Finland* 8 **B22**
Enarotali, *Indonesia* 63 **E9**
Encampment, *U.S.A.* 114 **F10**
Encantadas, Serra, *Brazil* 127 **C5**
Encarnación, *Paraguay* 127 **B4**
Encarnación de Diaz, *Mexico* 118 **C4**
Enchi, *Ghana* 82 **D4**
Encinitas, *U.S.A.* 117 **M9**
Encino, *U.S.A.* 115 **J11**
Encounter B., *Australia* 95 **F2**
Encs, *Hungary* 42 **B6**
Endako, *Canada* 104 **C3**
Ende, *Indonesia* 63 **F6**
Endeavour Str., *Australia* 94 **A3**
Endelave, *Denmark* 11 **J4**
Enderbury I., *Kiribati* 96 **H10**
Enderby, *Canada* 104 **C5**
Enderby I., *Australia* 92 **D2**
Enderby Land, *Antarctica* 5 **C5**
Enderlin, *U.S.A.* 112 **B6**
Endicott, *U.S.A.* 111 **D8**
Endwell, *U.S.A.* 111 **D8**
Endyalgout I., *Australia* 92 **B5**
Eneabba, *Australia* 93 **E2**
Enewetak Atoll, *Marshall Is.* 96 **F8**
Enez, *Turkey* 41 **F10**
Enfield, *Canada* 103 **D7**
Enfield, *Conn., U.S.A.* 111 **E12**
Enfield, *N.H., U.S.A.* 111 **C12**
Engadin, *Switz.* 25 **J6**
Engaño, C., *Dom. Rep.* 121 **C6**
Engaño, C., *Phil.* 63 **A6**
Engaru, *Japan* 54 **B11**
Engcobo, *S. Africa* 89 **E4**
Engelberg, *Switz.* 25 **J4**
Engels, *Russia* 48 **E8**
Engemann L., *Canada* 105 **B7**
Engershatu, *Eritrea* 81 **D4**
Enggano, *Indonesia* 62 **F2**
England, *U.S.A.* 113 **H9**
England □, *U.K.* 12 **D7**
Englee, *Canada* 103 **B8**
Englehart, *Canada* 102 **C4**
Englewood, *U.S.A.* 112 **F2**
English →, *Canada* 105 **C10**
English Bazar = Ingraj Bazar, *India* 69 **G13**
English Channel, *Europe* 13 **G6**
English River, *Canada* 102 **C1**
Engures ezers, *Latvia* 44 **A10**
Enguri →, *Georgia* 49 **J5**
Enid, *U.S.A.* 113 **G6**
Enipévs →, *Greece* 38 **B4**
Enkhuizen, *Neths.* 17 **B5**
Enköping, *Sweden* 10 **E11**
Enle, *China* 58 **F3**
Enna, *Italy* 31 **E7**
Ennadai, *Canada* 105 **A8**
Ennadai L., *Canada* 105 **A8**
Ennedi, *Chad* 79 **E10**
Enngonia, *Australia* 95 **D4**
Ennigerloh, *Germany* 24 **D4**
Ennis, *Ireland* 15 **D3**
Ennis, *Mont., U.S.A.* 114 **D8**
Ennis, *Tex., U.S.A.* 113 **J6**
Enniscorthy, *Ireland* 15 **D5**
Enniskillen, *U.K.* 15 **B4**
Ennistimon, *Ireland* 15 **D2**
Enns, *Austria* 26 **C7**
Enns →, *Austria* 26 **C7**
Enontekiö, *Finland* 8 **B20**
Enosburg Falls, *U.S.A.* 111 **B12**
Enping, *China* 59 **F9**
Enriquillo, L., *Dom. Rep.* 121 **C5**
Enschede, *Neths.* 17 **B6**
Ensenada, *Argentina* 126 **C4**
Ensenada, *Mexico* 118 **A1**
Ensenada de los Muertos, *Mexico* 118 **C2**
Enshi, *China* 58 **B7**
Ensiola, Pta. de n', *Spain* 37 **B9**
Ensisheim, *France* 19 **E14**
Entebbe, *Uganda* 86 **B3**
Enterprise, *Canada* 104 **A5**
Enterprise, *Ala., U.S.A.* 109 **K3**
Enterprise, *Oreg., U.S.A.* 114 **D5**
Entraygues-sur-Truyère, *France* 20 **D6**
Entre Ríos, *Bolivia* 126 **A3**
Entre Ríos □, *Argentina* 126 **C4**
Entrepeñas, Embalse de, *Spain* 32 **E2**
Entroncamento, *Portugal* 35 **F2**
Enugu, *Nigeria* 83 **D6**
Enugu □, *Nigeria* 83 **D6**
Enugu Ezike, *Nigeria* 83 **D6**
Enumclaw, *U.S.A.* 116 **C5**
Envermeu, *France* 18 **C8**
Enviken, *Sweden* 10 **D9**
Enying, *Hungary* 42 **D3**
Enza →, *Italy* 28 **D7**
Eólie, Ís., *Italy* 31 **D7**
Epanomí, *Greece* 40 **F6**
Epe, *Neths.* 17 **B5**
Epe, *Nigeria* 83 **D5**
Épernay, *France* 19 **C10**
Épernon, *France* 19 **D8**
Ephesus, *Turkey* 39 **D9**
Ephraim, *U.S.A.* 114 **G8**
Ephrata, *Pa., U.S.A.* 111 **F8**
Ephrata, *Wash., U.S.A.* 114 **C4**
Epidaurus Limera, *Greece* 38 **E5**
Épila, *Spain* 32 **D3**
Épinac, *France* 19 **F11**
Épinal, *France* 19 **D13**
Episkopi, *Cyprus* 36 **E11**
Episkopí, *Greece* 36 **D6**
Episkopi Bay, *Cyprus* 36 **E11**
Epitálion, *Greece* 38 **D3**
Eppan = Appiano, *Italy* 29 **B8**
Eppingen, *Germany* 25 **F4**
Epsom, *U.K.* 13 **F7**
Epukiro, *Namibia* 88 **C2**
Equatorial Guinea ■, *Africa* 84 **D1**
Er Hai, *China* 58 **E3**
Er Rachidia, *Morocco* 78 **B5**
Er Rahad, *Sudan* 81 **E3**
Er Rif, *Morocco* 78 **A5**
Er Rogel, *Sudan* 80 **D4**
Er Roseires, *Sudan* 81 **E3**
Er Rua'at, *Sudan* 81 **E3**
Eraclea, *Italy* 29 **C9**
Erāwadī Myit = Irrawaddy →, *Burma* 67 **M19**
Erāwadī Myitwanya = Irrawaddy, Mouths of the, *Burma* 67 **M19**
Erba, *Italy* 28 **C6**
Erba, *Sudan* 80 **D4**
Erba, J., *Sudan* 80 **C4**
Erbaa, *Turkey* 72 **B7**
Erbeskopf, *Germany* 25 **F3**
Erbil = Arbīl, *Iraq* 70 **B5**
Erbu, *Ethiopia* 81 **E3**
Erçek, *Turkey* 70 **B4**
Erçis, *Turkey* 73 **C10**
Erciyaş Dağı, *Turkey* 70 **B2**
Érd, *Hungary* 42 **C3**
Erdao Jiang →, *China* 57 **C14**
Erdek, *Turkey* 41 **F11**
Erdemli, *Turkey* 72 **D6**
Erdene = Ulaan-Uul, *Mongolia* 56 **B6**
Erdenetsogt, *Mongolia* 56 **C4**
Erding, *Germany* 25 **G7**
Erdre →, *France* 18 **E5**
Erebus, Mt., *Antarctica* 5 **D11**
Erechim, *Brazil* 127 **B5**
Ereğli, *Konya, Turkey* 70 **B2**
Ereğli, *Zonguldak, Turkey* 72 **B4**
Erei, Monti, *Italy* 31 **E7**
Erenhot, *China* 56 **C7**
Eresma →, *Spain* 34 **D6**
Eressós, *Greece* 39 **B7**
Erfenisdam, *S. Africa* 88 **D4**
Erfstadt, *Germany* 24 **E2**
Erft →, *Germany* 24 **D2**
Erfurt, *Germany* 24 **E7**
Erg Iguidi, *Africa* 78 **C4**
Ergani, *Turkey* 70 **B3**
Ergel, *Mongolia* 56 **C5**
Ergene →, *Turkey* 41 **E10**
Ergeni Vozvyshennost, *Russia* 49 **G7**
Ērgli, *Latvia* 9 **H21**
Erhlin, *Taiwan* 59 **F13**
Eria →, *Spain* 34 **C5**
Eriba, *Sudan* 81 **D4**
Eriboll, L., *U.K.* 14 **C4**
Érice, *Italy* 30 **D5**
Erie, *U.S.A.* 110 **D4**
Erie, L., *N. Amer.* 110 **D4**
Erie Canal, *U.S.A.* 110 **C7**
Erieau, *Canada* 110 **D3**
Erigavo, *Somali Rep.* 74 **E4**
Erikoúsa, *Greece* 36 **A3**
Eriksdale, *Canada* 105 **C9**
Erímanthos, *Greece* 38 **D3**
Erimo-misaki, *Japan* 54 **D11**
Erinpura, *India* 68 **G5**
Eriskay, *U.K.* 14 **D1**
Erithraí, *Greece* 38 **C5**
Eritrea ■, *Africa* 81 **E4**
Erjas →, *Portugal* 34 **F3**
Erkelenz, *Germany* 24 **D2**
Erkner, *Germany* 24 **C9**
Erlangen, *Germany* 25 **F6**
Erldunda, *Australia* 94 **D1**
Ermelo, *Neths.* 17 **B5**
Ermelo, *S. Africa* 89 **D4**
Ermenek, *Turkey* 70 **B2**
Ermil, *Sudan* 81 **E2**
Ermióni, *Greece* 38 **D5**
Ermones, *Greece* 36 **A3**
Ermoúpolis = Síros, *Greece* 38 **D6**
Ernakulam = Cochin, *India* 66 **Q10**
Erne →, *Ireland* 15 **B3**
Erne, Lower L., *U.K.* 15 **B4**
Erne, Upper L., *U.K.* 15 **B4**
Ernée, *France* 18 **D6**
Ernest Giles Ra., *Australia* 93 **E3**
Ernstberg, *Germany* 25 **E2**
Erode, *India* 66 **P10**
Eromanga, *Australia* 95 **D3**
Erongo, *Namibia* 88 **C2**
Erquy, *France* 18 **D4**
Erramala Hills, *India* 66 **M11**
Errer →, *Ethiopia* 81 **F5**
Errigal, *Ireland* 15 **A3**
Erris Hd., *Ireland* 15 **B1**
Ersekë, *Albania* 40 **F4**
Erskine, *U.S.A.* 112 **B7**
Erstein, *France* 19 **D14**
Ertholmene, *Denmark* 11 **J9**
Ertil, *Russia* 48 **E5**
Ertis = Irtysh →, *Russia* 50 **C7**
Eruh, *Turkey* 73 **D10**
Eruwa, *Nigeria* 83 **D5**
Ervy-le-Châtel, *France* 19 **D10**
Erwin, *U.S.A.* 109 **G4**
Eryuan, *China* 58 **D2**
Erzgebirge, *Germany* 24 **E8**
Erzin, *Russia* 51 **D10**
Erzincan, *Turkey* 70 **B3**
Erzurum, *Turkey* 70 **B4**
Es Caló, *Spain* 37 **C8**
Es Canar, *Spain* 37 **B8**
Es Mercadal, *Spain* 37 **B11**
Es Migjorn Gran, *Spain* 37 **B11**
Es Safiya, *Sudan* 81 **D3**
Es Sahrâ' Esh Sharqîya, *Egypt* 80 **B3**
Es Sînâ', *Egypt* 75 **F3**
Es Sûkî, *Sudan* 81 **E3**
Es Vedrà, *Spain* 37 **C7**
Esambo, *Dem. Rep. of the Congo* 86 **C1**
Esan-Misaki, *Japan* 54 **D10**
Esashi, *Hokkaidō, Japan* 54 **B11**
Esashi, *Hokkaidō, Japan* 54 **D10**
Esbjerg, *Denmark* 11 **J2**
Escalante, *U.S.A.* 115 **H8**
Escalante →, *U.S.A.* 115 **H8**
Escalón, *Mexico* 118 **B4**
Escambia →, *U.S.A.* 109 **K2**
Escanaba, *U.S.A.* 108 **C2**
Esch-sur-Alzette, *Lux.* 17 **E6**
Eschede, *Germany* 24 **C6**
Eschwege, *Germany* 24 **D6**
Eschweiler, *Germany* 24 **E2**
Escondido, *U.S.A.* 117 **M9**
Escravos →, *Nigeria* 83 **D6**
Escuinapa, *Mexico* 118 **C3**
Escuintla, *Guatemala* 120 **D1**
Eséka, *Cameroon* 83 **E7**
Eşen →, *Turkey* 39 **E11**
Esenguly, *Turkmenistan* 50 **F6**
Esens, *Germany* 24 **B3**
Esenyurt, *Turkey* 41 **E12**
Esera →, *Spain* 32 **C5**
Eşfahān, *Iran* 71 **C6**
Eşfahān □, *Iran* 71 **C6**
Esfarāyen, *Iran* 71 **B8**
Esfīdeh, *Iran* 71 **C8**
Esgueva →, *Spain* 34 **D6**
Esh Sham = Dimashq, *Syria* 75 **B5**
Esh Shamâlîya □, *Sudan* 80 **D2**
Esha Ness, *U.K.* 14 **A7**
Eshan, *China* 58 **E4**
Esher, *U.K.* 13 **F7**
Eshowe, *S. Africa* 89 **D5**
Esiama, *Ghana* 82 **E4**
Esigodini, *Zimbabwe* 89 **C4**
Esil = Ishim →, *Russia* 50 **D8**
Esino →, *Italy* 29 **E10**
Esira, *Madag.* 89 **C8**
Esk →, *Cumb., U.K.* 14 **G5**
Esk →, *N. Yorks., U.K.* 12 **C7**
Eskān, *Iran* 71 **E9**
Esker, *Canada* 103 **B6**
Eskifjörður, *Iceland* 8 **D7**
Eskilsäter, *Sweden* 11 **F7**
Eskilstuna, *Sweden* 10 **E10**
Eskimalatya, *Turkey* 73 **C8**
Eskimo Pt., *Canada* 100 **B10**
Eskişehir, *Turkey* 39 **B12**
Eskişehir □, *Turkey* 39 **B12**
Esla →, *Spain* 34 **D4**
Eslāmābād-e Gharb, *Iran* 70 **C5**
Eslāmshahr, *Iran* 71 **C6**
Eslöv, *Sweden* 11 **J7**
Eşme, *Turkey* 39 **C10**
Esmeraldas, *Ecuador* 124 **C3**
Esnagi L., *Canada* 102 **C3**
Espalion, *France* 20 **D6**
Espanola, *Canada* 102 **C3**
Espanola, *U.S.A.* 115 **H10**
Esparreguera, *Spain* 32 **D6**
Esparta, *Costa Rica* 120 **E3**
Espelkamp, *Germany* 24 **C4**
Esperance, *Australia* 93 **F3**
Esperance B., *Australia* 93 **F3**
Esperanza, *Argentina* 126 **C3**
Esperanza, *Phil.* 61 **G6**
Espéraza, *France* 20 **F6**
Espichel, C., *Portugal* 35 **G1**
Espiel, *Spain* 35 **G5**
Espigão, Serra do, *Brazil* 127 **B5**
Espinazo, Sierra del = Espinhaço, Serra do, *Brazil* 125 **G10**
Espinhaço, Serra do, *Brazil* 125 **G10**
Espinho, *Portugal* 34 **D2**
Espinilho, Serra do, *Brazil* 127 **B5**
Espinosa de los Monteros, *Spain* 34 **B7**
Espírito Santo □, *Brazil* 125 **H10**
Espíritu Santo, *Vanuatu* 96 **J8**
Espíritu Santo, B. del, *Mexico* 119 **D7**
Espíritu Santo, I., *Mexico* 118 **C2**
Espita, *Mexico* 119 **C7**
Espiye, *Turkey* 73 **B8**
Espluga de Francolí, *Spain* 32 **D6**
Espoo, *Finland* 9 **F21**
Espuña, Sierra de, *Spain* 33 **H3**
Espungabera, *Mozam.* 89 **C5**
Esquel, *Argentina* 128 **E2**
Esquimalt, *Canada* 104 **D4**
Esquina, *Argentina* 126 **C4**
Essaouira, *Morocco* 78 **B4**
Essebie, *Dem. Rep. of the Congo* 86 **B3**
Essen, *Belgium* 17 **C4**
Essen, *Germany* 24 **D3**
Essendon, Mt., *Australia* 93 **E3**
Essequibo →, *Guyana* 122 **C5**
Essex, *Canada* 110 **D2**
Essex, *Calif., U.S.A.* 117 **L11**
Essex, *N.Y., U.S.A.* 111 **B11**
Essex □, *U.K.* 13 **F8**
Essex Junction, *U.S.A.* 111 **B11**
Esslingen, *Germany* 25 **G5**
Essonne □, *France* 19 **D9**
Estaca de Bares, C. de, *Spain* 34 **B3**
Estadilla, *Spain* 32 **C5**
Estados, I. de Los, *Argentina* 122 **J4**
Estagel, *France* 20 **F6**
Eştahbānāt, *Iran* 71 **D7**
Estância, *Brazil* 125 **F11**
Estancia, *U.S.A.* 115 **J10**
Estārm, *Iran* 71 **D8**
Estarreja, *Portugal* 34 **E2**
Estats, Pic d', *Spain* 32 **C6**
Estcourt, *S. Africa* 89 **D4**
Este, *Italy* 29 **C8**
Estelí, *Nic.* 120 **D2**
Estella, *Spain* 32 **C2**
Estellencs, *Spain* 37 **B9**
Estena →, *Spain* 35 **F6**
Estepa, *Spain* 35 **H6**
Estepona, *Spain* 35 **J5**
Esterhazy, *Canada* 105 **C8**
Esternay, *France* 19 **D10**
Esterri d'Aneu, *Spain* 32 **C6**
Estevan, *Canada* 105 **D8**
Estevan Group, *Canada* 104 **C3**
Estherville, *U.S.A.* 112 **D7**
Estissac, *France* 19 **D10**
Eston, *Canada* 105 **C7**
Estonia ■, *Europe* 9 **G21**
Estoril, *Portugal* 35 **G1**
Estouk, *Mali* 83 **B5**
Estreito, *Brazil* 125 **E9**
Estrela, Serra da, *Portugal* 34 **E3**
Estrella, *Spain* 35 **G7**
Estremoz, *Portugal* 35 **G3**
Estrondo, Serra do, *Brazil* 125 **E9**
Esztergom, *Hungary* 42 **C3**
Et Tîdra, *Mauritania* 82 **B1**
Etah, *India* 69 **F8**
Étain, *France* 19 **C12**
Étampes, *France* 19 **D9**
Etanga, *Namibia* 88 **B1**
Étaples, *France* 19 **B8**
Etawah, *India* 69 **F8**
Etawney L., *Canada* 105 **B9**
Ete, *Nigeria* 83 **D6**
Ethel, *U.S.A.* 116 **D4**
Ethelbert, *Canada* 105 **C8**
Ethiopia ■, *Africa* 74 **F3**
Ethiopian Highlands, *Ethiopia* 52 **J7**
Etili, *Turkey* 41 **G10**
Etive, L., *U.K.* 14 **E3**
Etna, *Italy* 31 **E7**
Etoile, *Dem. Rep. of the Congo* 87 **E2**
Etosha Nat. Park, *Namibia* 88 **B2**
Etosha Pan, *Namibia* 88 **B2**
Etowah, *U.S.A.* 109 **H3**
Étréchy, *France* 19 **D9**
Étrépagny, *France* 19 **C8**
Étretat, *France* 18 **C7**
Etropole, *Bulgaria* 41 **D8**
Ettelbruck, *Lux.* 17 **E6**
Ettlingen, *Germany* 25 **G4**
Ettrick Water →, *U.K.* 14 **F6**
Etuku, *Dem. Rep. of the Congo* 86 **C2**
Etulia, *Moldova* 43 **E13**
Etzatlán, *Mexico* 118 **C4**
Etzná, *Mexico* 119 **D6**
Eu, *France* 18 **B8**
Euboea = Évvoia, *Greece* 38 **C6**
Eucla, *Australia* 93 **F4**
Euclid, *U.S.A.* 110 **E3**
Eucumbene, L., *Australia* 95 **F4**
Eudora, *U.S.A.* 113 **J9**
Eufaula, *Ala., U.S.A.* 109 **K3**
Eufaula, *Okla., U.S.A.* 113 **H7**
Eufaula L., *U.S.A.* 113 **H7**
Eugene, *U.S.A.* 114 **E2**
Eugowra, *Australia* 95 **E4**
Eulo, *Australia* 95 **D4**
Eunice, *La., U.S.A.* 113 **K8**
Eunice, *N. Mex., U.S.A.* 113 **J3**
Eupen, *Belgium* 17 **D6**
Euphrates = Furāt, Nahr al →, *Asia* 70 **D5**
Eure □, *France* 18 **C8**
Eure →, *France* 18 **C8**
Eure-et-Loir □, *France* 18 **D8**
Eureka, *Canada* 4 **B3**
Eureka, *Calif., U.S.A.* 114 **F1**
Eureka, *Kans., U.S.A.* 113 **G6**
Eureka, *Mont., U.S.A.* 114 **B6**
Eureka, *Nev., U.S.A.* 114 **G5**
Eureka, *S. Dak., U.S.A.* 112 **C5**
Eureka, Mt., *Australia* 93 **E3**
Euroa, *Australia* 95 **F4**
Europa, Île, *Ind. Oc.* 85 **J8**
Europa, Picos de, *Spain* 34 **B6**
Europa, Pta. de, *Gib.* 35 **J5**
Europe 6 **E10**
Europoort, *Neths.* 17 **C4**
Euskirchen, *Germany* 24 **E2**
Eustis, *U.S.A.* 109 **L5**
Eutin, *Germany* 24 **A6**
Eutsuk L., *Canada* 104 **C3**
Evale, *Angola* 88 **B2**
Evans, *U.S.A.* 112 **E2**
Evans, L., *Canada* 102 **B4**
Evans City, *U.S.A.* 110 **F4**
Evans Head, *Australia* 95 **D5**
Evans Mills, *U.S.A.* 111 **B9**
Evansburg, *Canada* 104 **C5**
Evanston, *Ill., U.S.A.* 108 **E2**
Evanston, *Wyo., U.S.A.* 114 **F8**
Evansville, *U.S.A.* 108 **G2**
Évaux-les-Bains, *France* 19 **F9**
Evaz, *Iran* 71 **E7**
Evciler, *Afyon, Turkey* 39 **C11**
Evciler, *Çanakkale, Turkey* 39 **B8**
Eveleth, *U.S.A.* 112 **B8**
Evensk, *Russia* 51 **C16**
Everard, L., *Australia* 95 **E2**
Everard Ranges, *Australia* 93 **E5**
Everest, Mt., *Nepal* 69 **E12**
Everett, *Pa., U.S.A.* 110 **F6**
Everett, *Wash., U.S.A.* 116 **C4**
Everglades, The, *U.S.A.* 109 **N5**
Everglades City, *U.S.A.* 109 **N5**
Everglades National Park, *U.S.A.* 109 **N5**
Evergreen, *Ala., U.S.A.* 109 **K2**

Evergreen, *Mont., U.S.A.* 114 B6
Everöd, *Sweden* 11 J8
Evertsberg, *Sweden* 10 C7
Evesham, *U.K.* 13 E6
Évian-les-Bains, *France* 19 F13
Évinos →, *Greece* 38 C3
Évisa, *France* 21 F12
Evje, *Norway* 9 G12
Évora, *Portugal* 35 G3
Évora □, *Portugal* 35 G3
Evowghlī, *Iran* 70 B5
Évreux, *France* 18 C8
Evritanía □, *Greece* 38 B3
Évron, *France* 18 D6
Évros □, *Greece* 41 E10
Évros →, *Greece* 72 B2
Evrótas →, *Greece* 38 E4
Évry, *France* 19 D9
Évvoia, *Greece* 38 C6
Évvoia □, *Greece* 38 C5
Evxinoúpolis, *Greece* 38 B4
Ewe, L., *U.K.* 14 D3
Ewing, *U.S.A.* 112 D5
Ewo, *Congo* 84 E2
Exaltación, *Bolivia* 124 F5
Excelsior Springs, *U.S.A.* 112 F7
Excideuil, *France* 20 C5
Exe →, *U.K.* 13 G4
Exeter, *Canada* 110 C3
Exeter, *U.K.* 13 G4
Exeter, *Calif., U.S.A.* 116 J7
Exeter, *N.H., U.S.A.* 111 D14
Exmoor, *U.K.* 13 F4
Exmouth, *Australia* 92 D1
Exmouth, *U.K.* 13 G4
Exmouth G., *Australia* 92 D1
Expedition Ra., *Australia* 94 C4
Extremadura □, *Spain* 35 F4
Exuma Sound, *Bahamas* 120 B4
Eyasi, L., *Tanzania* 86 C4
Eye Pen., *U.K.* 14 C2
Eyemouth, *U.K.* 14 F6
Eygurande, *France* 19 G9
Eyjafjörður, *Iceland* 8 C4
Eymet, *France* 20 D4
Eymoutiers, *France* 20 C5
Eynesil, *Turkey* 73 B8
Eyre (North), L., *Australia* 95 D2
Eyre (South), L., *Australia* 95 D2
Eyre Mts., *N.Z.* 91 L2
Eyre Pen., *Australia* 95 E2
Eysturoy, *Færoe Is.* 8 E9
Eyvānkī, *Iran* 71 C6
Ez Zeidab, *Sudan* 80 D3
Ezcaray, *Spain* 32 C1
Ežerėlis, *Lithuania* 44 D10
Ezhou, *China* 59 B10
Ezine, *Turkey* 39 B8
Ezouza →, *Cyprus* 36 E11

F

F.Y.R.O.M. = Macedonia ■, *Europe* 40 E5
Fabala, *Guinea* 82 D3
Fabens, *U.S.A.* 115 L10
Fabero, *Spain* 34 C4
Fåborg, *Denmark* 11 J4
Fabriano, *Italy* 29 E9
Făcăeni, *Romania* 43 F12
Fachi, *Niger* 79 E8
Fada, *Chad* 79 E10
Fada-n-Gourma, *Burkina Faso* 83 C5
Fadd, *Hungary* 42 D3
Faddeyevskiy, Ostrov, *Russia* 51 B15
Faddor, *Sudan* 81 F3
Fadghāmī, *Syria* 70 C4
Fadlab, *Sudan* 80 D3
Faenza, *Italy* 29 D8
Færoe Is. = Føroyar, *Atl. Oc.* 8 F9
Fafa, *Mali* 83 B5
Fafe, *Portugal* 34 D2
Fagam, *Nigeria* 83 C7
Făgăras, *Romania* 43 E9
Făgăras, Munţii, *Romania* 43 E9
Fågelmara, *Sweden* 11 H9
Fagerhult, *Sweden* 11 G9
Fagersta, *Sweden* 10 D9
Făget, *Romania* 42 E7
Făget, Munţii, *Romania* 43 C8
Fagnano, L., *Argentina* 128 G3
Fagnières, *France* 19 D11
Faguibine, L., *Mali* 82 B4
Fahlīān, *Iran* 71 D6
Fahraj, *Kermān, Iran* 71 D8
Fahraj, *Yazd, Iran* 71 D7
Fai Tsi Long Archipelago, *Vietnam* 58 G6
Faial, *Madeira* 37 D3
Fair Haven, *U.S.A.* 108 D9
Fair Hd., *U.K.* 15 A5
Fair Oaks, *U.S.A.* 116 G5
Fairbanks, *U.S.A.* 100 B5
Fairbury, *U.S.A.* 112 E6
Fairfax, *U.S.A.* 111 B11
Fairfield, *Ala., U.S.A.* 109 J2
Fairfield, *Calif., U.S.A.* 116 G4
Fairfield, *Conn., U.S.A.* 111 E11
Fairfield, *Idaho, U.S.A.* 114 E6
Fairfield, *Ill., U.S.A.* 108 F1
Fairfield, *Iowa, U.S.A.* 112 E9
Fairfield, *Tex., U.S.A.* 113 K7
Fairford, *Canada* 105 C9
Fairhope, *U.S.A.* 109 K2
Fairlie, *N.Z.* 91 L3
Fairmead, *U.S.A.* 116 H6
Fairmont, *Minn., U.S.A.* 112 D7
Fairmont, *W. Va., U.S.A.* 108 F5
Fairmount, *Calif., U.S.A.* 117 L8
Fairmount, *N.Y., U.S.A.* 111 C8
Fairplay, *U.S.A.* 115 G11
Fairport, *U.S.A.* 110 C7
Fairport Harbor, *U.S.A.* 110 E3
Fairview, *Canada* 104 B5
Fairview, *Mont., U.S.A.* 112 B2
Fairview, *Okla., U.S.A.* 113 G5
Fairweather, Mt., *U.S.A.* 104 B1
Faisalabad, *Pakistan* 68 D5
Faith, *U.S.A.* 112 C3
Faizabad, *India* 69 F10
Fajardo, *Puerto Rico* 121 C6
Fajr, W. →, *Si. Arabia* 70 D3
Fakenham, *U.K.* 12 E8
Fåker, *Sweden* 10 A8
Fakfak, *Indonesia* 63 E8
Fakiya, *Bulgaria* 41 D11
Fakobli, *Ivory C.* 82 D3
Fakse, *Denmark* 11 J6
Fakse Bugt, *Denmark* 11 J6
Fakse Ladeplads, *Denmark* 11 J6
Faku, *China* 57 C12
Falaba, *S. Leone* 82 D2
Falaise, *France* 18 D6
Falaise, Mui, *Vietnam* 64 C5
Falakrón Óros, *Greece* 40 E7
Falam, *Burma* 67 H18
Falces, *Spain* 32 C3
Fălciu, *Romania* 43 D13
Falcó, C. des, *Spain* 37 C7
Falcón, Presa, *Mexico* 119 B5
Falcon Lake, *Canada* 105 D9
Falcon Reservoir, *U.S.A.* 113 M5
Falconara Maríttima, *Italy* 29 E10
Falcone, C. del, *Italy* 30 B1
Falconer, *U.S.A.* 110 D5
Faléa, *Mali* 82 C2
Falémé →, *Senegal* 82 C2
Falerum, *Sweden* 11 F10
Faleshty = Făleşti, *Moldova* 43 C12
Făleşti, *Moldova* 43 C12
Falfurrias, *U.S.A.* 113 M5
Falher, *Canada* 104 B5
Falirakí, *Greece* 36 C10
Falkenberg, *Germany* 24 D9
Falkenberg, *Sweden* 11 H6
Falkensee, *Germany* 24 C9
Falkirk, *U.K.* 14 F5
Falkirk □, *U.K.* 14 F5
Falkland, *U.K.* 14 E5
Falkland Is. □, *Atl. Oc.* 128 G5
Falkland Sd., *Falk. Is.* 128 G5
Falkonéra, *Greece* 38 E5
Falköping, *Sweden* 11 F7
Fall River, *U.S.A.* 111 E13
Fallbrook, *U.S.A.* 117 M9
Fallon, *U.S.A.* 114 G4
Falls City, *U.S.A.* 112 E7
Falls Creek, *U.S.A.* 110 E6
Falmouth, *Jamaica* 120 C4
Falmouth, *U.K.* 13 G2
Falmouth, *U.S.A.* 111 E14
Falsa, Pta., *Mexico* 118 B1
False B., *S. Africa* 88 E2
Falso, C., *Honduras* 120 C3
Falster, *Denmark* 11 K5
Falsterbo, *Sweden* 9 J15
Fălticeni, *Romania* 43 C11
Falun, *Sweden* 10 D9
Famagusta, *Cyprus* 36 D12
Famagusta Bay, *Cyprus* 36 D13
Famalé, *Niger* 78 F6
Famatina, Sierra de, *Argentina* 126 B2
Family L., *Canada* 105 C9
Famoso, *U.S.A.* 117 K7
Fan Xian, *China* 56 G8
Fana, *Mali* 82 C3
Fanad Hd., *Ireland* 15 A4
Fanárion, *Greece* 38 B3
Fandriana, *Madag.* 89 C8
Fang, *Thailand* 58 H2
Fang Xian, *China* 59 A8
Fangaga, *Sudan* 80 D4
Fangak, *Sudan* 81 F3
Fangchang, *China* 59 B12
Fangcheng, *China* 56 H7
Fangchenggang, *China* 58 G7
Fangliao, *Taiwan* 59 F13
Fangshan, *China* 56 E6
Fangzi, *China* 57 F10
Fani i Madh →, *Albania* 40 E4
Fanjakana, *Madag.* 89 C8
Fanjiatun, *China* 57 C13
Fannich, L., *U.K.* 14 D4
Fannūj, *Iran* 71 E8
Fanø, *Denmark* 11 J2
Fano, *Italy* 29 E10
Fanshi, *China* 56 E7
Fao = Al Fāw, *Iraq* 71 D6
Faqirwali, *Pakistan* 68 E5
Fâqûs, *Egypt* 80 H7
Fara in Sabina, *Italy* 29 F9
Faradje, *Dem. Rep. of the Congo* 86 B2
Farafangana, *Madag.* 89 C8
Farâfra, El Wâhât el-, *Egypt* 80 B2
Farāh, *Afghan.* 66 C3
Farāh □, *Afghan.* 66 C3
Farahalana, *Madag.* 89 A9
Faraid, Gebel, *Egypt* 80 C4
Farako, *Ivory C.* 82 D4
Faramana, *Burkina Faso* 82 C4
Faranah, *Guinea* 82 C2
Farasān, Jazā'ir, *Si. Arabia* 74 D3
Farasan Is. = Farasān, Jazā'ir, *Si. Arabia* 74 D3
Faratsiho, *Madag.* 89 B8
Fardes →, *Spain* 35 H7
Fareham, *U.K.* 13 G6
Farewell, C., *N.Z.* 91 J4
Farewell C. = Nunap Isua, *Greenland* 101 C15
Färgelanda, *Sweden* 11 F5
Farghona, *Uzbekistan* 50 E8
Fargo, *U.S.A.* 112 B6
Fār'iah, W. al →, *West Bank* 75 C4
Faribault, *U.S.A.* 112 C8
Faridabad, *India* 68 E6
Faridkot, *India* 68 D6
Faridpur, *Bangla.* 69 H13
Faridpur, *India* 69 E8
Färila, *Sweden* 10 C9
Farim, *Guinea-Biss.* 82 C1
Farīmān, *Iran* 71 C8
Farina, *Australia* 95 E2
Fariones, Pta., *Canary Is.* 37 E6
Fâriskûr, *Egypt* 80 H7
Färjestaden, *Sweden* 11 H10
Farkadhón, *Greece* 38 B4
Farmakonisi, *Greece* 39 D9
Farmerville, *U.S.A.* 113 J8
Farmingdale, *U.S.A.* 111 F10
Farmington, *Canada* 104 B4
Farmington, *Calif., U.S.A.* 116 H6
Farmington, *Maine, U.S.A.* 109 C10
Farmington, *Mo., U.S.A.* 113 G9
Farmington, *N.H., U.S.A.* 111 C13
Farmington, *N. Mex., U.S.A.* 115 H9
Farmington, *Utah, U.S.A.* 114 F8
Farmington →, *U.S.A.* 111 E12
Farmville, *U.S.A.* 108 G6
Färnäs, *Sweden* 10 D8
Farne Is., *U.K.* 12 B6
Farnham, *Canada* 111 A12
Farnham, Mt., *Canada* 104 C5
Faro, *Brazil* 125 D7
Faro, *Canada* 100 B6
Faro, *Portugal* 35 H3
Fårö, *Sweden* 9 H18
Faro □, *Portugal* 35 H2
Fårösund, *Sweden* 11 G13
Farquhar, C., *Australia* 93 D1
Farrars Cr. →, *Australia* 94 D3
Farrāshband, *Iran* 71 D7
Farrell, *U.S.A.* 110 E4
Farrokhī, *Iran* 71 C8
Farruch, C. = Ferrutx, C., *Spain* 37 B10
Fārs □, *Iran* 71 D7
Fársala, *Greece* 38 B4
Farsø, *Denmark* 11 H3
Farson, *U.S.A.* 114 E9
Farsund, *Norway* 9 G12
Fartak, Râs, *Si. Arabia* 70 D2
Fartak, Ra's, *Yemen* 74 D5
Fârţăneşti, *Romania* 43 E12
Fartura, Serra da, *Brazil* 127 B5
Faru, *Nigeria* 83 C6
Fārūj, *Iran* 71 B8
Fårup, *Denmark* 11 H3
Farvel, Kap = Nunap Isua, *Greenland* 101 C15
Farwell, *U.S.A.* 113 H3
Fāryāb □, *Afghan.* 66 B4
Fasā, *Iran* 71 D7
Fasano, *Italy* 31 B10
Fashoda, *Sudan* 81 F3
Fassa, *Mali* 82 C3
Fastiv, *Ukraine* 47 G5
Fastov = Fastiv, *Ukraine* 47 G5
Fatagar, Tanjung, *Indonesia* 63 E8
Fatehabad, *Haryana, India* 68 E6
Fatehabad, *Ut. P., India* 68 F8
Fatehgarh, *India* 69 F8
Fatehpur, *Bihar, India* 69 G11
Fatehpur, *Raj., India* 68 F6
Fatehpur, *Ut. P., India* 69 G9
Fatehpur, *Ut. P., India* 69 F9
Fatehpur Sikri, *India* 68 F6
Fatesh, *Russia* 47 F8
Fathai, *Sudan* 81 F3
Fatick, *Senegal* 82 C1
Fatima, *Canada* 103 C7
Fátima, *Portugal* 35 F2
Fatoya, *Guinea* 82 C3
Fatsa, *Turkey* 72 B7
Faucille, Col de la, *France* 19 F13
Faulkton, *U.S.A.* 112 C5
Faulquemont, *France* 19 C13
Faure I., *Australia* 93 E1
Făurei, *Romania* 43 E12
Fauresmith, *S. Africa* 88 D4
Fauske, *Norway* 8 C16
Favara, *Italy* 30 E6
Faváritx, C. de, *Spain* 37 B11
Faverges, *France* 21 C10
Favignana, *Italy* 30 E5
Favignana, I., *Italy* 30 E5
Fawcett, Pt., *Australia* 92 B5
Fawn →, *Canada* 102 A2
Fawnskin, *U.S.A.* 117 L10
Faxaflói, *Iceland* 8 D2
Faxälven →, *Sweden* 10 A10
Faya-Largeau, *Chad* 79 E9
Fayd, *Si. Arabia* 70 E4
Fayence, *France* 21 E10
Fayette, *Ala., U.S.A.* 109 J2
Fayette, *Mo., U.S.A.* 112 F8
Fayetteville, *Ark., U.S.A.* 113 G7
Fayetteville, *N.C., U.S.A.* 109 H6
Fayetteville, *Tenn., U.S.A.* 109 H2
Fayied, *Egypt* 80 H8
Fayón, *Spain* 32 D5
Fazilka, *India* 68 D6
Fazilpur, *Pakistan* 68 E4
Fdérik, *Mauritania* 78 D3
Feale →, *Ireland* 15 D2
Fear, C., *U.S.A.* 109 J7
Feather →, *U.S.A.* 114 G3
Feather Falls, *U.S.A.* 116 F5
Featherston, *N.Z.* 91 J5
Featherstone, *Zimbabwe* 87 F3
Fécamp, *France* 18 C7
Fedala = Mohammedia, *Morocco* 78 B4
Federación, *Argentina* 126 C4
Féderal, *Argentina* 128 C5
Federal Capital Terr. □, *Nigeria* 83 D6
Federal Way, *U.S.A.* 116 C4
Fedeshkūh, *Iran* 71 D7
Fehérgyarmat, *Hungary* 42 C7
Fehmarn, *Germany* 24 A7
Fehmarn Bælt, *Europe* 11 K5
Fehmarn Belt = Fehmarn Bælt, *Europe* 11 K5
Fei Xian, *China* 57 G9
Feijó, *Brazil* 124 E4
Feilding, *N.Z.* 91 J5
Feira de Santana, *Brazil* 125 F11
Feixi, *China* 59 B11
Feixiang, *China* 56 F8
Fejér □, *Hungary* 42 C3
Fejø, *Denmark* 11 K5
Feke, *Turkey* 72 D6
Fekete →, *Hungary* 42 E3
Felanitx, *Spain* 37 B10
Feldbach, *Austria* 26 E8
Feldberg, *Baden-W., Germany* 25 H3
Feldberg, *Mecklenburg-Vorpommern, Germany* 24 B9
Feldkirch, *Austria* 26 D2
Feldkirchen, *Austria* 26 E7
Felipe Carrillo Puerto, *Mexico* 119 D7
Felixburg, *Zimbabwe* 89 B5
Felixstowe, *U.K.* 13 F9
Felletin, *France* 20 C6
Fellingsbro, *Sweden* 10 E9
Felton, *U.S.A.* 116 H4
Feltre, *Italy* 29 B8
Femer Bælt = Fehmarn Bælt, *Europe* 11 K5
Femø, *Denmark* 11 K5
Femunden, *Norway* 9 E14
Fen He →, *China* 56 G6
Fene, *Spain* 34 B2
Fenelon Falls, *Canada* 110 B6
Fener Burnu, *Turkey* 39 E9
Feneroa, *Ethiopia* 81 E4
Feng Xian, *Jiangsu, China* 56 G9
Feng Xian, *Shaanxi, China* 56 H4
Fengári, *Greece* 41 F9
Fengcheng, *Jiangxi, China* 59 C10
Fengcheng, *Liaoning, China* 57 D13
Fengfeng, *China* 56 F8
Fenggang, *China* 58 D6
Fenghua, *China* 59 C13
Fenghuang, *China* 58 D7
Fengkai, *China* 59 F8
Fengkang, *Taiwan* 59 F13
Fengle, *China* 59 B9
Fenglin, *Taiwan* 59 F13
Fengning, *China* 56 D9
Fengqing, *China* 58 E2
Fengqiu, *China* 56 G8
Fengrun, *China* 57 E10
Fengshan, *Guangxi Zhuangzu, China* 58 E7
Fengshan, *Guangxi Zhuangzu, China* 58 E6
Fengshan, *Taiwan* 59 F13
Fengshun, *China* 59 F11
Fengtai, *Anhui, China* 59 A11
Fengtai, *Beijing, China* 56 E9
Fengxian, *China* 59 B13
Fengxiang, *China* 56 G4
Fengxin, *China* 59 C10
Fengyang, *China* 57 H9
Fengyi, *China* 58 E3
Fengyüan, *Taiwan* 59 E13
Fengzhen, *China* 56 D7
Feno, C. de, *France* 21 G12
Fenoarivo, *Fianarantsoa, Madag.* 89 C8
Fenoarivo, *Fianarantsoa, Madag.* 89 C8
Fenoarivo Afovoany, *Madag.* 89 B8
Fenoarivo Atsinanana, *Madag.* 89 B8
Fens, The, *U.K.* 12 E7
Fensmark, *Denmark* 11 J5
Fenton, *U.S.A.* 108 D4
Fenxi, *China* 56 F6
Fenyang, *China* 56 F6
Fenyi, *China* 59 D10
Feodosiya, *Ukraine* 47 K8
Ferdows, *Iran* 71 C8
Fère-Champenoise, *France* 19 D10
Fère-en-Tardenois, *France* 19 C10
Ferentino, *Italy* 29 G10
Ferfer, *Somali Rep.* 74 F4
Fergana = Farghona, *Uzbekistan* 50 E8
Fergus, *Canada* 110 C4
Fergus Falls, *U.S.A.* 112 B6
Feričanci, *Croatia* 42 E2
Ferkéssédougou, *Ivory C.* 82 D3
Ferlach, *Austria* 26 E7
Ferland, *Canada* 102 B2
Ferlo, Vallée du, *Senegal* 82 B2
Fermanagh □, *U.K.* 15 B4
Fermo, *Italy* 29 E10
Fermont, *Canada* 103 B6
Fermoselle, *Spain* 34 D4
Fermoy, *Ireland* 15 D3
Fernán Nuñéz, *Spain* 35 H6
Fernández, *Argentina* 126 B3
Fernandina Beach, *U.S.A.* 109 K5
Fernando de Noronha, *Brazil* 125 D12
Fernando Póo = Bioko, *Eq. Guin.* 83 E6
Ferndale, *U.S.A.* 116 B4
Fernie, *Canada* 104 D5
Fernlees, *Australia* 94 C4
Fernley, *U.S.A.* 114 G4
Ferozepore = Firozpur, *India* 68 D6
Férrai, *Greece* 41 F10
Ferrandina, *Italy* 31 B9
Ferrara, *Italy* 29 D8
Ferrato, C., *Italy* 30 C2
Ferreira do Alentejo, *Portugal* 35 G2
Ferreñafe, *Peru* 124 E3
Ferrerías, *Spain* 37 B11
Ferret, C., *France* 20 D2
Ferrette, *France* 19 E14
Ferriday, *U.S.A.* 113 K9
Ferriere, *Italy* 28 D6
Ferrières, *France* 19 D9
Ferro, Capo, *Italy* 30 A2
Ferrol, *Spain* 34 B2
Ferron, *U.S.A.* 115 G8
Ferrutx, C., *Spain* 37 B10
Ferryland, *Canada* 103 C9
Fertile, *U.S.A.* 112 B6
Fertőszentmiklós, *Hungary* 42 C1
Fès, *Morocco* 78 B5
Fessenden, *U.S.A.* 112 B5
Festus, *U.S.A.* 112 F9
Feté Bowé, *Senegal* 82 C2
Feteşti, *Romania* 43 F12
Fethiye, *Turkey* 39 E11
Fethiye Körfezi, *Turkey* 39 E10
Fetlar, *U.K.* 14 A8
Feuilles →, *Canada* 101 C12
Feurs, *France* 21 C8
Fez = Fès, *Morocco* 78 B5
Fezzan, *Libya* 79 C8
Fiambalá, *Argentina* 126 B2
Fianarantsoa, *Madag.* 89 C8
Fianarantsoa □, *Madag.* 89 B8
Fiche, *Ethiopia* 81 F4
Fichtelgebirge, *Germany* 25 E7
Ficksburg, *S. Africa* 89 D4
Fidenza, *Italy* 28 D7
Fiditi, *Nigeria* 83 D5
Field →, *Australia* 94 C2
Field I., *Australia* 92 B5
Fieni, *Romania* 43 E10
Fier, *Albania* 40 F3
Fierzë, *Albania* 40 D4
Fife □, *U.K.* 14 E5
Fife Ness, *U.K.* 14 E6
Fifth Cataract, *Sudan* 80 D3
Figari, *France* 21 G13
Figeac, *France* 20 D6
Figeholm, *Sweden* 11 G10
Figline Valdarno, *Italy* 29 E8
Figtree, *Zimbabwe* 87 G2
Figueira Castelo Rodrigo, *Portugal* 34 E4
Figueira da Foz, *Portugal* 34 E2
Figueiró dos Vinhos, *Portugal* 34 F2
Figueres, *Spain* 32 C7
Figuig, *Morocco* 78 B5
Fihaonana, *Madag.* 89 B8
Fiherenana, *Madag.* 89 B8
Fiherenana →, *Madag.* 89 C7
Fiji ■, *Pac. Oc.* 91 C8
Fik, *Ethiopia* 81 F5
Fika, *Nigeria* 83 C7
Filabres, Sierra de los, *Spain* 35 H8
Filabusi, *Zimbabwe* 89 C4
Filadélfia, *Italy* 31 D9
Fil'akovo, *Slovak Rep.* 27 C12
Filey, *U.K.* 12 C7
Filey B., *U.K.* 12 C7
Filfla, *Malta* 36 D1
Filiaşi, *Romania* 43 F8
Filiátes, *Greece* 38 B2
Filiatrá, *Greece* 38 D3
Filicudi, *Italy* 31 D7
Filingué, *Niger* 83 C5
Filiourí →, *Greece* 41 E9
Filipstad, *Sweden* 10 E8
Filisur, *Switz.* 25 J5
Fillmore, *Calif., U.S.A.* 117 L8
Fillmore, *Utah, U.S.A.* 115 G7
Filótion, *Greece* 39 D7
Filottrano, *Italy* 29 E10
Filtu, *Ethiopia* 81 F5
Finale Emília, *Italy* 29 D8
Finale Lígure, *Italy* 28 D5
Fiñana, *Spain* 35 H8
Finch, *Canada* 111 A9
Findhorn →, *U.K.* 14 D5
Findlay, *U.S.A.* 108 E4
Finger L., *Canada* 102 B1
Finger Lakes, *U.S.A.* 111 D8
Fíngoè, *Mozam.* 87 E3
Finike, *Turkey* 39 E12
Finike Körfezi, *Turkey* 39 E12
Finiq, *Albania* 40 G4
Finistère □, *France* 18 D3
Finisterre = Fisterra, *Spain* 34 C1
Finisterre, C. = Fisterra, C., *Spain* 34 C1
Finke, *Australia* 94 D1
Finland ■, *Europe* 8 E22
Finland, G. of, *Europe* 9 G21
Finlay →, *Canada* 104 B3

Finley, *Australia* 95 F4
Finley, *U.S.A.* 112 B6
Finn →, *Ireland* 15 B4
Finnerödja, *Sweden* 11 F8
Finnigan, Mt., *Australia* 94 B4
Finniss, C., *Australia* 95 E1
Finnmark, *Norway* 8 B20
Finnsnes, *Norway* 8 B18
Finspång, *Sweden* 11 F9
Finsteraarhorn, *Switz.* 25 J4
Finsterwalde, *Germany* 24 D9
Fiora →, *Italy* 29 F8
Fiorenzuola d'Arda, *Italy* 28 D6
Fiq, *Syria* 75 C4
Firat = Furāt, Nahr al →, *Asia* 70 D5
Firebag →, *Canada* 105 B6
Firebaugh, *U.S.A.* 116 J6
Firedrake L., *Canada* 105 A8
Firenze, *Italy* 29 E8
Firenzuola, *Italy* 29 D8
Firk →, *Iraq* 70 D5
Firmi, *France* 20 D6
Firminy, *France* 21 C8
Firozabad, *India* 69 F8
Firozpur, *India* 68 D6
Firozpur-Jhirka, *India* 68 F7
Fīrūzābād, *Iran* 71 D7
Fīrūzkūh, *Iran* 71 C7
Firvale, *Canada* 104 C3
Fish →, *Namibia* 88 D2
Fish →, *S. Africa* 88 E3
Fish River Canyon, *Namibia* 88 D2
Fisher, *Australia* 93 F5
Fisher B., *Canada* 105 C9
Fishers I., *U.S.A.* 111 E13
Fishguard, *U.K.* 13 E3
Fishing L., *Canada* 105 C9
Fishkill, *U.S.A.* 111 E11
Fismes, *France* 19 C10
Fisterra, *Spain* 34 C1
Fisterra, C., *Spain* 34 C1
Fitchburg, *U.S.A.* 111 D13
Fitz Roy, *Argentina* 128 F3
Fitzgerald, *Canada* 104 B6
Fitzgerald, *U.S.A.* 109 K4
Fitzmaurice →, *Australia* 92 B5
Fitzroy →, *Queens., Australia* 94 C5
Fitzroy →, *W. Austral., Australia* 92 C3
Fitzroy, Mte., *Argentina* 128 F2
Fitzroy Crossing, *Australia* 92 C4
Fitzwilliam I., *Canada* 110 A3
Fiuggi, *Italy* 29 G10
Fiume = Rijeka, *Croatia* 29 C11
Five Points, *U.S.A.* 116 J6
Fivizzano, *Italy* 28 D7
Fizi, *Dem. Rep. of the Congo* 86 C2
Fjällbacka, *Sweden* 11 F5
Fjärdhundra, *Sweden* 10 E10
Fjellerup, *Denmark* 11 H4
Fjerritslev, *Denmark* 11 G3
Fjugesta, *Sweden* 10 E8
Flagstaff, *U.S.A.* 115 J8
Flagstaff L., *U.S.A.* 109 C10
Flaherty I., *Canada* 102 A4
Flåm, *Norway* 9 F12
Flambeau →, *U.S.A.* 112 C9
Flamborough Hd., *U.K.* 12 C7
Fläming, *Germany* 24 C8
Flaming Gorge Reservoir, *U.S.A.* 114 F9
Flamingo, Teluk, *Indonesia* 63 F9
Flanders = Flandre, *Europe* 19 B9
Flandre, *Europe* 19 B9
Flandre Occidentale = West-Vlaanderen □, *Belgium* 17 D2
Flandre Orientale = Oost-Vlaanderen □, *Belgium* 17 C3
Flandreau, *U.S.A.* 112 C6
Flanigan, *U.S.A.* 116 E7
Flannan Is., *U.K.* 14 C1
Flåsjön, *Sweden* 8 D16
Flat →, *Canada* 104 A3
Flathead L., *U.S.A.* 114 C7
Flattery, C., *Australia* 94 A4
Flattery, C., *U.S.A.* 116 B2
Flatwoods, *U.S.A.* 108 F4
Fleetwood, *U.K.* 12 D4
Fleetwood, *U.S.A.* 111 F9
Flekkefjord, *Norway* 9 G12
Flemington, *U.S.A.* 110 E7
Flen, *Sweden* 10 E10
Flensburg, *Germany* 24 A5
Flers, *France* 18 D6
Flesherton, *Canada* 110 B4
Flesko, Tanjung, *Indonesia* 63 D6
Fleurance, *France* 20 E4
Fleurier, *Switz.* 25 J2
Fleurieu Pen., *Australia* 95 F2
Flevoland □, *Neths.* 17 B5
Flin Flon, *Canada* 105 C8
Flinders →, *Australia* 94 B3
Flinders B., *Australia* 93 F2
Flinders Group, *Australia* 94 A3
Flinders I., *S. Austral., Australia* 95 E1
Flinders I., *Tas., Australia* 94 G4
Flinders Ranges, *Australia* 95 E2
Flinders Reefs, *Australia* 94 B4
Flint, *U.K.* 12 D4
Flint, *U.S.A.* 108 D4
Flint →, *U.S.A.* 109 K3
Flint I., *Kiribati* 97 J12
Flintshire □, *U.K.* 12 D4
Fliseryd, *Sweden* 11 G10
Flix, *Spain* 32 D5
Flixecourt, *France* 19 B9
Floby, *Sweden* 11 F7
Floda, *Sweden* 11 G6
Flodden, *U.K.* 12 B5
Flogny-la-Chapelle, *France* 19 E10
Floodwood, *U.S.A.* 112 B8
Flora, *U.S.A.* 108 F1
Florac, *France* 20 D7
Florala, *U.S.A.* 109 K2
Florence = Firenze, *Italy* 29 E8
Florence, *Ala., U.S.A.* 109 H2
Florence, *Ariz., U.S.A.* 115 K8
Florence, *Colo., U.S.A.* 112 F2
Florence, *Oreg., U.S.A.* 114 E1
Florence, *S.C., U.S.A.* 109 H6
Florence, L., *Australia* 95 D2
Florencia, *Colombia* 124 C3
Florennes, *Belgium* 17 D4
Florensac, *France* 20 E7
Florenville, *Belgium* 17 E5
Flores, *Guatemala* 120 C2
Flores, *Indonesia* 63 F6
Flores I., *Canada* 104 D3
Flores Sea, *Indonesia* 63 F6
Floreşti, *Moldova* 43 C13
Floresville, *U.S.A.* 113 L5
Floriano, *Brazil* 125 E10
Florianópolis, *Brazil* 127 B6
Florida, *Cuba* 120 B4
Florida, *Uruguay* 127 C4
Florida □, *U.S.A.* 109 L5
Florida, Straits of, *U.S.A.* 120 B4
Florida B., *U.S.A.* 120 B3
Florida Keys, *U.S.A.* 109 N5
Florídia, *Italy* 31 E8
Flórina, *Greece* 40 F5
Flórina □, *Greece* 40 F5
Florø, *Norway* 9 F11
Flower Station, *Canada* 111 A8
Flowerpot I., *Canada* 110 A3
Floydada, *U.S.A.* 113 J4
Fluk, *Indonesia* 63 E7
Flúmen →, *Spain* 32 D4
Flumendosa →, *Italy* 30 C2
Fluminimaggiore, *Italy* 30 C1
Flushing = Vlissingen, *Neths.* 17 C3
Fluviá →, *Spain* 32 C8
Flying Fish, C., *Antarctica* 5 D15
Foam Lake, *Canada* 105 C8
Foča, *Bos.-H.* 40 C2
Foça, *Turkey* 39 C8
Focşani, *Romania* 43 E12
Fodécontéa, *Guinea* 82 C2
Fogang, *China* 59 F9
Fóggia, *Italy* 31 A8
Foggo, *Nigeria* 83 C6
Foglia →, *Italy* 29 E9
Fogo, *Canada* 103 C9
Fogo I., *Canada* 103 C9
Fohnsdorf, *Austria* 26 D7
Föhr, *Germany* 24 A4
Foia, *Portugal* 35 H2
Foix, *France* 20 E5
Fojnica, *Bos.-H.* 42 G2
Fokino, *Russia* 46 F8
Fokís □, *Greece* 38 C4
Fokku, *Nigeria* 83 C5
Folda, *Nord-Trøndelag, Norway* 8 D14
Folda, *Nordland, Norway* 8 C16
Földeák, *Hungary* 42 D5
Folégandros, *Greece* 38 E6
Foley, *Botswana* 88 C4
Foley, *U.S.A.* 109 K2
Foleyet, *Canada* 102 C3
Folgefonni, *Norway* 9 F12
Foligno, *Italy* 29 F9
Folkestone, *U.K.* 13 F9
Folkston, *U.S.A.* 109 K5
Follansbee, *U.S.A.* 110 F4
Follónica, *Italy* 28 F7
Follónica, G. di, *Italy* 28 F7
Folsom L., *U.S.A.* 116 G5
Folteşti, *Romania* 43 E13
Fond-du-Lac, *Canada* 105 B7
Fond du Lac, *U.S.A.* 112 D10
Fond-du-Lac →, *Canada* 105 B7
Fonda, *U.S.A.* 111 D10
Fondi, *Italy* 30 A6
Fonfría, *Spain* 34 D4
Fongafale, *Tuvalu* 96 H9
Fonni, *Italy* 30 B2
Fonsagrada = A Fonsagrada, *Spain* 34 B3
Fonseca, G. de, *Cent. Amer.* 120 D2
Font-Romeu, *France* 20 F5
Fontaine-Française, *France* 19 E12
Fontainebleau, *France* 19 D9
Fontana, *U.S.A.* 117 L9
Fontas →, *Canada* 104 B4
Fonte Boa, *Brazil* 124 D5
Fontem, *Cameroon* 83 D6
Fontenay-le-Comte, *France* 20 B3
Fontenelle Reservoir, *U.S.A.* 114 E8
Fontur, *Iceland* 8 C6
Fonyód, *Hungary* 42 D2
Foochow = Fuzhou, *China* 59 D12
Foping, *China* 56 H5
Forbach, *France* 19 C13
Forbes, *Australia* 95 E4
Forbesganj, *India* 69 F12
Forcados, *Nigeria* 83 D6
Forcados →, *Nigeria* 83 D6
Forcalquier, *France* 21 E9
Forchheim, *Germany* 25 F7
Ford City, *Calif., U.S.A.* 117 K7
Ford City, *Pa., U.S.A.* 110 F5
Førde, *Norway* 9 F11
Ford's Bridge, *Australia* 95 D4
Fordyce, *U.S.A.* 113 J8
Forécariah, *Guinea* 82 D2
Forel, Mt., *Greenland* 4 C6
Foremost, *Canada* 104 D6
Forest, *Canada* 110 C3
Forest, *U.S.A.* 113 J10
Forest City, *Iowa, U.S.A.* 112 D8
Forest City, *N.C., U.S.A.* 109 H5
Forest City, *Pa., U.S.A.* 111 E9
Forest Grove, *U.S.A.* 116 E3
Forestburg, *Canada* 104 C6
Foresthill, *U.S.A.* 116 F6
Forestier Pen., *Australia* 94 G4
Forestville, *Canada* 103 C6
Forestville, *Calif., U.S.A.* 116 G4
Forestville, *N.Y., U.S.A.* 110 D5
Forez, Mts. du, *France* 20 C7
Forfar, *U.K.* 14 E6
Forks, *U.S.A.* 116 C2
Forksville, *U.S.A.* 111 E8
Forlì, *Italy* 29 D9
Forman, *U.S.A.* 112 B6
Formazza, *Italy* 28 B5
Formby Pt., *U.K.* 12 D4
Formentera, *Spain* 37 C7
Formentor, C. de, *Spain* 37 B10
Former Yugoslav Republic of Macedonia = Macedonia ■, *Europe* 40 E5
Fórmia, *Italy* 30 A6
Formígine, *Italy* 28 D7
Formosa = Taiwan ■, *Asia* 59 F13
Formosa, *Argentina* 126 B4
Formosa, *Brazil* 125 G9
Formosa □, *Argentina* 126 B4
Formosa, Serra, *Brazil* 125 F8
Formosa Bay, *Kenya* 86 C5
Formosa Strait = Taiwan Strait, *Asia* 59 E12
Fornells, *Spain* 37 A11
Fornos de Algodres, *Portugal* 34 E3
Fornovo di Taro, *Italy* 28 D7
Føroyar, *Atl. Oc.* 8 F9
Forres, *U.K.* 14 D5
Forrest, *Australia* 93 F4
Forrest, Mt., *Australia* 93 D4
Forrest City, *U.S.A.* 113 H9
Fors, *Sweden* 10 D10
Forsayth, *Australia* 94 B3
Forshaga, *Sweden* 10 E7
Förslöv, *Sweden* 11 H6
Forsmo, *Sweden* 10 A11
Forssa, *Finland* 9 F20
Forst, *Germany* 24 D10
Forsvik, *Sweden* 11 F8
Forsyth, *U.S.A.* 114 C10
Fort Abbas, *Pakistan* 68 E5
Fort Albany, *Canada* 102 B3
Fort Ann, *U.S.A.* 111 C11
Fort Assiniboine, *Canada* 104 C6
Fort Augustus, *U.K.* 14 D4
Fort Beaufort, *S. Africa* 88 E4
Fort Benton, *U.S.A.* 114 C8
Fort Bragg, *U.S.A.* 114 G2
Fort Bridger, *U.S.A.* 114 F8
Fort Chipewyan, *Canada* 105 B6
Fort Collins, *U.S.A.* 112 E2
Fort-Coulonge, *Canada* 102 C4
Fort Covington, *U.S.A.* 111 B10
Fort Davis, *U.S.A.* 113 K3
Fort-de-France, *Martinique* 121 D7
Fort Defiance, *U.S.A.* 115 J9
Fort Dodge, *U.S.A.* 112 D7
Fort Edward, *U.S.A.* 111 C11
Fort Erie, *Canada* 110 D6
Fort Fairfield, *U.S.A.* 109 B12
Fort Frances, *Canada* 105 D10
Fort Garland, *U.S.A.* 115 H11
Fort George = Chisasibi, *Canada* 102 B4
Fort Good-Hope, *Canada* 100 B7
Fort Hancock, *U.S.A.* 115 L11
Fort Hertz = Putao, *Burma* 67 F20
Fort Hope, *Canada* 102 B2
Fort Irwin, *U.S.A.* 117 K10
Fort Kent, *U.S.A.* 109 B11
Fort Klamath, *U.S.A.* 114 E3
Fort Laramie, *U.S.A.* 112 D2
Fort Lauderdale, *U.S.A.* 109 M5
Fort Liard, *Canada* 104 A4
Fort Liberté, *Haiti* 121 C5
Fort Lupton, *U.S.A.* 112 E2
Fort Mackay, *Canada* 104 B6
Fort Macleod, *Canada* 104 D6
Fort McMurray, *Canada* 104 B6
Fort McPherson, *Canada* 100 B6
Fort Madison, *U.S.A.* 112 E9
Fort Meade, *U.S.A.* 109 M5
Fort Morgan, *U.S.A.* 112 E3
Fort Myers, *U.S.A.* 109 M5
Fort Nelson, *Canada* 104 B4
Fort Nelson →, *Canada* 104 B4
Fort Norman = Tulita, *Canada* 100 B7
Fort Payne, *U.S.A.* 109 H3
Fort Peck, *U.S.A.* 114 B10
Fort Peck Dam, *U.S.A.* 114 C10
Fort Peck L., *U.S.A.* 114 C10
Fort Pierce, *U.S.A.* 109 M5
Fort Pierre, *U.S.A.* 112 C4
Fort Pierre Bordes = Ti-n-Zaouatene, *Algeria* 83 B5
Fort Plain, *U.S.A.* 111 D10
Fort Portal, *Uganda* 86 B3
Fort Providence, *Canada* 104 A5
Fort Qu'Appelle, *Canada* 105 C8
Fort Resolution, *Canada* 104 A6
Fort Rixon, *Zimbabwe* 87 G2
Fort Ross, *U.S.A.* 116 G3
Fort Rupert = Waskaganish, *Canada* 102 B4
Fort St. James, *Canada* 104 C4
Fort St. John, *Canada* 104 B4
Fort Saskatchewan, *Canada* 104 C6
Fort Scott, *U.S.A.* 113 G7
Fort Severn, *Canada* 102 A2
Fort Shevchenko, *Kazakstan* 49 H10
Fort Simpson, *Canada* 104 A4
Fort Smith, *Canada* 104 B6
Fort Smith, *U.S.A.* 113 H7
Fort Stockton, *U.S.A.* 113 K3
Fort Sumner, *U.S.A.* 113 H2
Fort Thompson, *U.S.A.* 112 C5
Fort Valley, *U.S.A.* 109 J4
Fort Vermilion, *Canada* 104 B5
Fort Walton Beach, *U.S.A.* 109 K2
Fort Wayne, *U.S.A.* 108 E3
Fort William, *U.K.* 14 E3
Fort Worth, *U.S.A.* 113 J6
Fort Yates, *U.S.A.* 112 B4
Fort Yukon, *U.S.A.* 100 B5
Fortaleza, *Brazil* 125 D11
Forteau, *Canada* 103 B8
Fortescue →, *Australia* 92 D2
Forth →, *U.K.* 14 E5
Forth, Firth of, *U.K.* 14 E6
Fortore →, *Italy* 29 G12
Fortrose, *U.K.* 14 D4
Fortuna, *Spain* 33 G3
Fortuna, *Calif., U.S.A.* 114 F1
Fortuna, *N. Dak., U.S.A.* 112 A3
Fortune, *Canada* 103 C8
Fortune B., *Canada* 103 C8
Forūr, *Iran* 71 E7
Fos-sur-Mer, *France* 21 E8
Foshan, *China* 59 F9
Fosna, *Norway* 8 E14
Fosnavåg, *Norway* 9 E11
Foso, *Ghana* 83 D4
Fossano, *Italy* 28 D4
Fossil, *U.S.A.* 114 D3
Fossombrone, *Italy* 29 E9
Foster, *Canada* 111 A12
Foster →, *Canada* 105 B7
Fosters Ra., *Australia* 94 C1
Fostoria, *U.S.A.* 108 E4
Fotadrevo, *Madag.* 89 C8
Fouesnant, *France* 18 E2
Fougères, *France* 18 D5
Foul Pt., *Sri Lanka* 66 Q12
Foula, *U.K.* 14 A6
Foulalaba, *Mali* 82 C3
Foulness I., *U.K.* 13 F8
Foulpointe, *Madag.* 89 B8
Foulweather, C., *U.S.A.* 106 B2
Foumban, *Cameroon* 83 D7
Foumbot, *Cameroon* 83 D7
Foundiougne, *Senegal* 82 C1
Fountain, *U.S.A.* 112 F2
Fountain Springs, *U.S.A.* 117 K8
Fourchambault, *France* 19 E10
Fouriesburg, *S. Africa* 88 D4
Fourmies, *France* 19 B11
Fournás, *Greece* 38 B3
Foúrnoi, *Greece* 39 D8
Fours, *France* 19 F10
Fourth Cataract, *Sudan* 80 D3
Fouta Djalon, *Guinea* 82 C2
Foux, Cap-à-, *Haiti* 121 C5
Foveaux Str., *N.Z.* 91 M2
Fowey, *U.K.* 13 G3
Fowler, *Calif., U.S.A.* 116 J7
Fowler, *Colo., U.S.A.* 112 F3
Fowlers B., *Australia* 93 F5
Fowman, *Iran* 71 B6
Fox →, *Canada* 105 B10
Fox Creek, *Canada* 104 C5
Fox Lake, *Canada* 104 B6
Fox Valley, *Canada* 105 C7
Foxboro, *U.S.A.* 111 D13
Foxe Basin, *Canada* 101 B12
Foxe Chan., *Canada* 101 B11
Foxe Pen., *Canada* 101 B12
Foxen, *Sweden* 10 E5
Foxton, *N.Z.* 91 J5
Foyle, Lough, *U.K.* 15 A4
Foynes, *Ireland* 15 D2
Foz, *Spain* 34 B3
Foz do Cunene, *Angola* 88 B1
Foz do Iguaçu, *Brazil* 127 B5
Frackville, *U.S.A.* 111 F8
Fraga, *Spain* 32 D5
Fraile Muerto, *Uruguay* 127 C5
Framingham, *U.S.A.* 111 D13
Frampol, *Poland* 45 H9
Franca, *Brazil* 125 H9
Francavilla al Mare, *Italy* 29 F11
Francavilla Fontana, *Italy* 31 B10
France ■, *Europe* 7 F6
Frances, *Australia* 95 F3
Frances →, *Canada* 104 A3
Frances L., *Canada* 104 A3
Franceville, *Gabon* 84 E2
Franche-Comté, *France* 19 F12
Francis Case, L., *U.S.A.* 112 D5
Francisco Beltrão, *Brazil* 127 B5
Francisco I. Madero, *Coahuila, Mexico* 118 B4
Francisco I. Madero, *Durango, Mexico* 118 C4
Francistown, *Botswana* 89 C4
Francofonte, *Italy* 31 E7
François, *Canada* 103 C8
François L., *Canada* 104 C3
Franeker, *Neths.* 17 A5
Frankado, *Djibouti* 81 E5
Frankenberg, *Germany* 24 D4
Frankenwald, *Germany* 25 E7
Frankford, *Canada* 110 B7
Frankfort, *S. Africa* 89 D4
Frankfort, *Ind., U.S.A.* 108 E2
Frankfort, *Kans., U.S.A.* 112 F6
Frankfort, *Ky., U.S.A.* 108 F3
Frankfort, *N.Y., U.S.A.* 111 C9
Frankfurt, *Brandenburg, Germany* 24 C10
Frankfurt, *Hessen, Germany* 25 E4
Fränkische Alb, *Germany* 25 F7
Fränkische Rezat →, *Germany* 25 F7
Fränkische Saale →, *Germany* 25 E5
Fränkische Schweiz, *Germany* 25 F7
Frankland →, *Australia* 93 G2
Franklin, *Ky., U.S.A.* 109 G2
Franklin, *La., U.S.A.* 113 L9
Franklin, *Mass., U.S.A.* 111 D13
Franklin, *N.H., U.S.A.* 111 C13
Franklin, *Nebr., U.S.A.* 112 E5
Franklin, *Pa., U.S.A.* 110 E5
Franklin, *Va., U.S.A.* 109 G7
Franklin, *W. Va., U.S.A.* 108 F6
Franklin B., *Canada* 100 B7
Franklin D. Roosevelt L., *U.S.A.* 114 B4
Franklin I., *Antarctica* 5 D11
Franklin L., *U.S.A.* 114 F6
Franklin Mts., *Canada* 100 B7
Franklin Str., *Canada* 100 A10
Franklinton, *U.S.A.* 113 K9
Franklinville, *U.S.A.* 110 D6
Franks Pk., *U.S.A.* 114 E9
Frankston, *Australia* 95 F4
Frånö, *Sweden* 10 B11
Fransfontein, *Namibia* 88 C2
Fränsta, *Sweden* 10 B10
Frantsa Iosifa, Zemlya, *Russia* 50 A6
Franz, *Canada* 102 C3
Franz Josef Land = Frantsa Iosifa, Zemlya, *Russia* 50 A6
Franzburg, *Germany* 24 A8
Frascati, *Italy* 29 G9
Fraser, *U.S.A.* 110 D2
Fraser →, *B.C., Canada* 104 D4
Fraser →, *Nfld., Canada* 103 A7
Fraser, Mt., *Australia* 93 E2
Fraser I., *Australia* 95 D5
Fraser Lake, *Canada* 104 C4
Fraserburg, *S. Africa* 88 E3
Fraserburgh, *U.K.* 14 D6
Fraserdale, *Canada* 102 C3
Frashër, *Albania* 40 F4
Frasne, *France* 19 F13
Frăteşti, *Romania* 43 G10
Frauenfeld, *Switz.* 25 H4
Fray Bentos, *Uruguay* 126 C4
Frechilla, *Spain* 34 C6
Fredericia, *Denmark* 11 J3
Frederick, *Md., U.S.A.* 108 F7
Frederick, *Okla., U.S.A.* 113 H5
Frederick, *S. Dak., U.S.A.* 112 C5
Fredericksburg, *Pa., U.S.A.* 111 F8
Fredericksburg, *Tex., U.S.A.* 113 K5
Fredericksburg, *Va., U.S.A.* 108 F7
Fredericktown, *Mo., U.S.A.* 113 G9
Fredericktown, *Ohio, U.S.A.* 110 F2
Frederico I. Madero, Presa, *Mexico* 118 B3
Frederico Westphalen, *Brazil* 127 B5
Fredericton, *Canada* 103 C6
Fredericton Junction, *Canada* 103 C6
Frederiksborg Amtskommune □, *Denmark* 11 J6
Frederikshåb = Paamiut, *Greenland* 4 C5
Frederikshavn, *Denmark* 11 G4
Frederikssund, *Denmark* 11 J6
Frederiksted, *U.S. Virgin Is.* 121 C7
Frederiksværk, *Denmark* 11 J6
Fredonia, *Ariz., U.S.A.* 115 H7
Fredonia, *Kans., U.S.A.* 113 G7
Fredonia, *N.Y., U.S.A.* 110 D5
Fredriksberg, *Sweden* 10 D8
Fredrikstad, *Norway* 9 G14
Free State □, *S. Africa* 88 D4
Freehold, *U.S.A.* 111 F10
Freel Peak, *U.S.A.* 116 G7
Freeland, *U.S.A.* 111 E9
Freels, C., *Canada* 103 C9
Freeman, *Calif., U.S.A.* 117 K9
Freeman, *S. Dak., U.S.A.* 112 D6
Freeport, *Bahamas* 120 A4
Freeport, *Ill., U.S.A.* 112 D10
Freeport, *N.Y., U.S.A.* 111 F11
Freeport, *Ohio, U.S.A.* 110 F3
Freeport, *Pa., U.S.A.* 110 F5
Freeport, *Tex., U.S.A.* 113 L7
Freetown, *S. Leone* 82 D2
Frégate, L., *Canada* 102 B5
Fregenal de la Sierra, *Spain* 35 G4
Fregene, *Italy* 29 G9
Fréhel, C., *France* 18 D4
Freiberg, *Germany* 24 E9
Freibourg = Fribourg, *Switz.* 25 J3
Freiburg, *Baden-W., Germany* 25 H3
Freiburg, *Niedersachsen, Germany* 24 B5
Freilassing, *Germany* 25 H8
Freire, *Chile* 128 D2
Freirina, *Chile* 126 B1
Freising, *Germany* 25 G7
Freistadt, *Austria* 26 C7
Freital, *Germany* 24 D9
Fréjus, *France* 21 E10
Fremantle, *Australia* 93 F2

Fremont, *Calif., U.S.A.* 116 H4
Fremont, *Mich., U.S.A.* 108 D3
Fremont, *Nebr., U.S.A.* 112 E6
Fremont, *Ohio, U.S.A.* 108 E4
Fremont →, *U.S.A.* 115 G8
French Camp, *U.S.A.* 116 H5
French Creek →, *U.S.A.* 110 E5
French Guiana ■, *S. Amer.* 125 C8
French Polynesia ■, *Pac. Oc.* 97 K13
Frenchman Cr. →, *N. Amer.* 114 B10
Frenchman Cr. →, *U.S.A.* 112 E4
Frenštát pod Radhoštěm, *Czech Rep.* 27 B11
Fresco, *Ivory C.* 82 D3
Fresco →, *Brazil* 125 E8
Freshfield, C., *Antarctica* 5 C10
Fresnay-sur-Sarthe, *France* 18 D7
Fresnillo, *Mexico* 118 C4
Fresno, *U.S.A.* 116 J7
Fresno Alhandiga, *Spain* 34 E5
Fresno Reservoir, *U.S.A.* 114 B9
Freudenstadt, *Germany* 25 G4
Frévent, *France* 19 B9
Frew →, *Australia* 94 C2
Frewsburg, *U.S.A.* 110 D5
Freycinet Pen., *Australia* 94 G4
Freyming-Merlebach, *France* 19 C13
Freyung, *Germany* 25 G9
Fria, *Guinea* 82 C2
Fria, C., *Namibia* 88 B1
Friant, *U.S.A.* 116 J7
Frías, *Argentina* 126 B2
Fribourg, *Switz.* 25 J3
Fribourg □, *Switz.* 25 J3
Fridafors, *Sweden* 11 H8
Friday Harbor, *U.S.A.* 116 B3
Friedberg, *Bayern, Germany* 25 G6
Friedberg, *Hessen, Germany* 25 E4
Friedens, *U.S.A.* 110 F6
Friedland, *Germany* 24 B9
Friedrichshafen, *Germany* 25 H5
Friedrichskoog, *Germany* 24 A4
Friedrichstadt, *Germany* 24 A5
Friendly Is. = Tonga ■, *Pac. Oc.* 91 D11
Friendship, *U.S.A.* 110 D6
Friesach, *Austria* 26 E7
Friesack, *Germany* 24 C8
Friesland □, *Neths.* 17 A5
Friesoythe, *Germany* 24 B3
Friggesund, *Sweden* 10 C10
Frillesås, *Sweden* 11 G6
Frinnaryd, *Sweden* 11 G8
Frio →, *U.S.A.* 113 L5
Frio, C., *Brazil* 122 F6
Friol, *Spain* 34 B3
Friona, *U.S.A.* 113 H3
Fristad, *Sweden* 11 G6
Fritch, *U.S.A.* 113 H4
Fritsla, *Sweden* 11 G6
Fritzlar, *Germany* 24 D5
Friuli-Venézia Giulia □, *Italy* 29 B9
Frobisher B., *Canada* 101 B13
Frobisher Bay = Iqaluit, *Canada* 101 B13
Frobisher L., *Canada* 105 B7
Frohavet, *Norway* 8 E13
Frohnleiten, *Austria* 26 D8
Frolovo, *Russia* 48 F6
Frombork, *Poland* 44 D6
Frome, *U.K.* 13 F5
Frome →, *U.K.* 13 G5
Frome, L., *Australia* 95 E2
Frómista, *Spain* 34 C6
Front Range, *U.S.A.* 106 C5
Front Royal, *U.S.A.* 108 F6
Fronteira, *Portugal* 35 F3
Frontera, *Canary Is.* 37 G2
Frontera, *Mexico* 119 D6
Fronteras, *Mexico* 118 A3
Frontignan, *France* 20 E7
Frosinone, *Italy* 30 A6
Frostburg, *U.S.A.* 108 F6
Frostisen, *Norway* 8 B17
Frouard, *France* 19 D13
Frövi, *Sweden* 10 E9
Frøya, *Norway* 8 E13
Frumoasa, *Romania* 43 D10
Frunze = Bishkek, *Kyrgyzstan* 50 E8
Fruška Gora, *Serbia, Yug.* 42 E4
Frutal, *Brazil* 125 H9
Frutigen, *Switz.* 25 J3
Frýdek-Místek, *Czech Rep.* 27 B11
Frýdlant, *Czech Rep.* 26 A8
Fryeburg, *U.S.A.* 111 B14
Fryvaldov = Jeseník, *Czech Rep.* 27 A10
Fthiótis □, *Greece* 38 C4
Fu Jiang →, *China* 58 C6
Fu Xian = Wafangdian, *China* 57 E11
Fu Xian, *China* 56 G5
Fu'an, *China* 59 D12
Fubian, *China* 58 B4
Fucécchio, *Italy* 28 E7
Fucheng, *China* 56 F9
Fuchou = Fuzhou, *China* 59 D12
Fuchū, *Japan* 55 G6
Fuchuan, *China* 59 E8
Fuchun Jiang →, *China* 59 B13
Fúcino, Piana del, *Italy* 29 F10
Fuding, *China* 59 D13
Fuencaliente, *Canary Is.* 37 F2
Fuencaliente, *Spain* 35 G6
Fuencaliente, Pta., *Canary Is.* 37 F2
Fuengirola, *Spain* 35 J6
Fuenlabrada, *Spain* 34 E7
Fuensalida, *Spain* 34 E6
Fuente-Álamo, *Spain* 33 G3
Fuente-Álamo de Murcia, *Spain* 33 H3
Fuente de Cantos, *Spain* 35 G4
Fuente del Maestre, *Spain* 35 G4
Fuente el Fresno, *Spain* 35 F7
Fuente Obejuna, *Spain* 35 G5
Fuente Palmera, *Spain* 35 H5
Fuentes de Andalucía, *Spain* 35 H5
Fuentes de Ebro, *Spain* 32 D4
Fuentes de León, *Spain* 35 G4
Fuentes de Oñoro, *Spain* 34 E4
Fuentesaúco, *Spain* 34 D5
Fuerte →, *Mexico* 118 B3
Fuerte Olimpo, *Paraguay* 126 A4
Fuerteventura, *Canary Is.* 37 F6
Fufeng, *China* 56 G5
Fuga I., *Phil.* 61 B4
Fugong, *China* 58 D2
Fugou, *China* 56 G8
Fugu, *China* 56 E6
Fuhai, *China* 60 B3
Fuḩaymī, *Iraq* 70 C4
Fuji, *Japan* 55 G9
Fuji-San, *Japan* 55 G9
Fuji-Yoshida, *Japan* 55 G9
Fujian □, *China* 59 E12
Fujinomiya, *Japan* 55 G9
Fujisawa, *Japan* 55 G9
Fujiyama, Mt. = Fuji-San, *Japan* 55 G9
Fukien = Fujian □, *China* 59 E12
Fukuchiyama, *Japan* 55 G7
Fukue-Shima, *Japan* 55 H4
Fukui, *Japan* 55 F8
Fukui □, *Japan* 55 G8
Fukuoka, *Japan* 55 H5
Fukuoka □, *Japan* 55 H5
Fukushima, *Japan* 54 F10
Fukushima □, *Japan* 54 F10
Fukuyama, *Japan* 55 G6
Fulacunda, *Guinea-Biss.* 82 C1
Fulda, *Germany* 24 E5
Fulda →, *Germany* 24 D5
Fulford Harbour, *Canada* 116 B3
Fuliang, *China* 59 C11
Fullerton, *Calif., U.S.A.* 117 M9
Fullerton, *Nebr., U.S.A.* 112 E6
Fulongquan, *China* 57 B13
Fülöpszállás, *Hungary* 42 D4
Fulton, *Mo., U.S.A.* 112 F9
Fulton, *N.Y., U.S.A.* 111 C8
Fuluälven →, *Sweden* 10 C7
Fulufjället, *Sweden* 10 C6
Fumay, *France* 19 C11
Fumel, *France* 20 D4
Fumin, *China* 58 E4
Funabashi, *Japan* 55 G10
Funafuti = Fongafale, *Tuvalu* 96 H9
Funäsdalen, *Sweden* 10 B6
Funchal, *Madeira* 37 D3
Fundación, *Colombia* 124 A4
Fundão, *Portugal* 34 E3
Fundu Moldovei, *Romania* 43 C10
Fundulea, *Romania* 43 F11
Fundy, B. of, *Canada* 103 D6
Funhalouro, *Mozam.* 89 C5
Funing, *Hebei, China* 57 E10
Funing, *Jiangsu, China* 57 H10
Funing, *Yunnan, China* 58 F5
Funiu Shan, *China* 56 H7
Funsi, *Ghana* 82 C4
Funtua, *Nigeria* 83 C6
Fuping, *Hebei, China* 56 E8
Fuping, *Shaanxi, China* 56 G5
Fuqing, *China* 59 E12
Fuquan, *China* 58 D6
Furano, *Japan* 54 C11
Furāt, Nahr al →, *Asia* 70 D5
Fürg, *Iran* 71 D7
Furmanov, *Russia* 48 B5
Furmanovo, *Kazakstan* 48 F9
Furnás, *Spain* 37 B8
Furnas, Represa de, *Brazil* 127 A6
Furneaux Group, *Australia* 94 G4
Furqlus, *Syria* 75 A6
Fürstenau, *Germany* 24 C3
Fürstenberg, *Germany* 24 B9
Fürstenfeld, *Austria* 26 D9
Fürstenfeldbruck, *Germany* 25 G7
Fürstenwalde, *Germany* 24 C10
Fürth, *Germany* 25 F6
Furth im Wald, *Germany* 25 F8
Furtwangen, *Germany* 25 G4
Furudal, *Sweden* 10 C9
Furukawa, *Japan* 54 E10
Furulund, *Sweden* 11 J7
Fury and Hecla Str., *Canada* 101 B11
Fusagasuga, *Colombia* 124 C4
Fuscaldo, *Italy* 31 C9
Fushan, *Shandong, China* 57 F11
Fushan, *Shanxi, China* 56 G6
Fushë Arrëz, *Albania* 40 D4
Fushë-Krujë, *Albania* 40 E3
Fushun, *Liaoning, China* 57 D12
Fushun, *Sichuan, China* 58 C5
Fusong, *China* 57 C14
Füssen, *Germany* 25 H6
Fusui, *China* 58 F6
Futog, *Yugoslavia* 42 E4
Futuna, *Wall. & F. Is.* 91 B8
Fuwa, *Egypt* 80 H7
Fuxian Hu, *China* 58 E4
Fuxin, *China* 57 C11
Fuyang, *Anhui, China* 56 H8
Fuyang, *Zhejiang, China* 59 B12
Fuyang He →, *China* 56 E9
Fuying Dao, *China* 59 D13
Fuyu, *China* 57 B13
Fuyuan, *China* 58 E5
Füzesgyarmat, *Hungary* 42 C6
Fuzhou, *China* 59 D12
Fylde, *U.K.* 12 D5
Fyn, *Denmark* 11 J4
Fyne, L., *U.K.* 14 F3
Fyns Amtskommune □, *Denmark* 11 J4
Fynshav, *Denmark* 11 K3

G

Ga, *Ghana* 82 D4
Gaanda, *Nigeria* 83 C7
Gabarin, *Nigeria* 83 C7
Gabas →, *France* 20 E3
Gabela, *Angola* 84 G2
Gabès, *Tunisia* 79 B8
Gabès, G. de, *Tunisia* 79 B8
Gabgaba, W. →, *Egypt* 80 C3
Gąbin, *Poland* 45 F6
Gabon ■, *Africa* 84 E2
Gaborone, *Botswana* 88 C4
Gabriels, *U.S.A.* 111 B10
Gābrīk, *Iran* 71 E8
Gabrovo, *Bulgaria* 41 D9
Gacé, *France* 18 D7
Gāch Sār, *Iran* 71 B6
Gachsārān, *Iran* 71 D6
Gacko, *Bos.-H.* 40 C2
Gadag, *India* 66 M9
Gadamai, *Sudan* 81 D4
Gadap, *Pakistan* 68 G2
Gadarwara, *India* 69 H8
Gadebusch, *Germany* 24 B7
Gadein, *Sudan* 81 F2
Gadhada, *India* 68 J4
Gádor, Sierra de, *Spain* 35 J8
Gadra, *Pakistan* 68 G4
Gadsden, *U.S.A.* 109 H3
Gadwal, *India* 66 L10
Gadyach = Hadyach, *Ukraine* 47 G8
Găeşti, *Romania* 43 F10
Gaeta, *Italy* 30 A6
Gaeta, G. di, *Italy* 30 A6
Gaffney, *U.S.A.* 109 H5
Gafsa, *Tunisia* 78 B7
Gagarawa, *Nigeria* 83 C6
Gagaria, *India* 68 G4
Gagarin, *Russia* 46 E8
Gaggenau, *Germany* 25 G4
Gaghamni, *Sudan* 81 E2
Gagino, *Russia* 48 C7
Gagliano del Capo, *Italy* 31 C11
Gagnef, *Sweden* 10 D9
Gagnoa, *Ivory C.* 82 D3
Gagnon, *Canada* 103 B6
Gagnon, L., *Canada* 105 A6
Gagra, *Georgia* 49 J5
Gahini, *Rwanda* 86 C3
Gahmar, *India* 69 G10
Gai Xian = Gaizhou, *China* 57 D12
Gaïdhouronísi, *Greece* 36 E7
Gail, *U.S.A.* 113 J4
Gail →, *Austria* 26 E6
Gaillac, *France* 20 E5
Gaillimh = Galway, *Ireland* 15 C2
Gaillon, *France* 18 C8
Gaines, *U.S.A.* 110 E7
Gainesville, *Fla., U.S.A.* 109 L4
Gainesville, *Ga., U.S.A.* 109 H4
Gainesville, *Mo., U.S.A.* 113 G8
Gainesville, *Tex., U.S.A.* 113 J6
Gainsborough, *U.K.* 12 D7
Gairdner, L., *Australia* 95 E2
Gairloch, L., *U.K.* 14 D3
Gaizhou, *China* 57 D12
Gaj, *Croatia* 42 E2
Gaj →, *Pakistan* 68 F2
Gakuch, *Pakistan* 69 A5
Galala, Gebel el, *Egypt* 80 J8
Galán, Cerro, *Argentina* 126 B2
Galana →, *Kenya* 86 C5
Galanta, *Slovak Rep.* 27 C10
Galapagar, *Spain* 34 E7
Galápagos, *Pac. Oc.* 122 D1
Galashiels, *U.K.* 14 F6
Galatás, *Greece* 38 D5
Galaţi, *Romania* 43 E13
Galaţi □, *Romania* 43 E12
Galatia, *Turkey* 72 C5
Galatina, *Italy* 31 B11
Galátone, *Italy* 31 B11
Galax, *U.S.A.* 109 G5
Galaxídhion, *Greece* 38 C4
Galcaio, *Somali Rep.* 74 F4
Galdhøpiggen, *Norway* 9 F12
Galeana, *Chihuahua, Mexico* 118 A3
Galeana, *Nuevo León, Mexico* 118 A3
Galegu, *Sudan* 81 E4
Galela, *Indonesia* 63 D7
Galena, *U.S.A.* 100 B4
Galera, *Spain* 33 H2
Galera Pt., *Trin. & Tob.* 121 D7
Galesburg, *U.S.A.* 112 E9
Galeton, *U.S.A.* 110 E7
Galga, *Ethiopia* 81 F4
Gali, *Georgia* 49 J5
Galicea Mare, *Romania* 43 F8
Galich, *Russia* 48 A6
Galiche, *Bulgaria* 40 C7
Galicia □, *Spain* 34 C3
Galilee = Hagalil, *Israel* 75 C4
Galilee, L., *Australia* 94 C4
Galilee, Sea of = Yam Kinneret, *Israel* 75 C4
Galim, *Cameroon* 83 D7
Galinoporni, *Cyprus* 36 D13
Galion, *U.S.A.* 110 F2
Galiuro Mts., *U.S.A.* 115 K8
Galiwinku, *Australia* 94 A2
Gallabat, *Sudan* 81 E4
Gallan Hd., *U.K.* 14 C1
Gallarate, *Italy* 28 C5
Gallatin, *U.S.A.* 109 G2
Galle, *Sri Lanka* 66 R12
Gállego →, *Spain* 32 D4
Gallegos →, *Argentina* 128 G3
Galletti →, *Ethiopia* 81 F5
Galley Hd., *Ireland* 15 E3
Galliate, *Italy* 28 C5
Gallinas, Pta., *Colombia* 124 A4
Gallipoli = Gelibolu, *Turkey* 41 F10
Gallípoli, *Italy* 31 B10
Gallipolis, *U.S.A.* 108 F4
Gällivare, *Sweden* 8 C19
Gallneukirchen, *Austria* 26 C7
Gällö, *Sweden* 10 B9
Gallo, C., *Italy* 30 D6
Gallocanta, L. de, *Spain* 32 E3
Galloo I., *U.S.A.* 111 C8
Galloway, *U.K.* 14 F4
Galloway, Mull of, *U.K.* 14 G4
Gallup, *U.S.A.* 115 J9
Gallur, *Spain* 32 D3
Galoya, *Sri Lanka* 66 Q12
Galt, *U.S.A.* 116 G5
Galten, *Denmark* 11 H3
Galtür, *Austria* 26 E3
Galty Mts., *Ireland* 15 D3
Galtymore, *Ireland* 15 D3
Galva, *U.S.A.* 112 E9
Galve de Sorbe, *Spain* 32 D1
Galveston, *U.S.A.* 113 L7
Galveston B., *U.S.A.* 113 L7
Gálvez, *Argentina* 126 C3
Galway, *Ireland* 15 C2
Galway □, *Ireland* 15 C2
Galway B., *Ireland* 15 C2
Gam →, *Vietnam* 64 B5
Gamagōri, *Japan* 55 G8
Gamari, L., *Ethiopia* 81 E5
Gamawa, *Nigeria* 83 C7
Gamay, *Phil.* 61 E6
Gambaga, *Ghana* 83 C4
Gambat, *Pakistan* 68 F3
Gambela, *Ethiopia* 81 F3
Gambhir →, *India* 68 F6
Gambia ■, *W. Afr.* 82 C1
Gambia →, *W. Afr.* 82 C1
Gambier, *U.S.A.* 110 F2
Gambier, C., *Australia* 92 B5
Gambier Is., *Australia* 95 F2
Gambo, *Canada* 103 C9
Gamboli, *Pakistan* 68 E3
Gamboma, *Congo* 84 E3
Gamka →, *S. Africa* 88 E3
Gamkab →, *Namibia* 88 D2
Gamla Uppsala, *Sweden* 10 E11
Gamlakarleby = Kokkola, *Finland* 8 E20
Gamleby, *Sweden* 11 G10
Gammon →, *Canada* 105 C9
Gamo-Gofa □, *Ethiopia* 81 F4
Gamou, *Niger* 83 C6
Gamtoos →, *S. Africa* 88 E4
Gan, *France* 20 E3
Gan Goriama, Mts., *Cameroon* 83 D7
Gan Jiang →, *China* 59 C11
Ganado, *U.S.A.* 115 J9
Gananita, *Sudan* 80 D3
Gananoque, *Canada* 102 D4
Ganāveh, *Iran* 71 D6
Gäncä, *Azerbaijan* 49 K8
Gancheng, *China* 64 C7
Gand = Gent, *Belgium* 17 C3
Ganda, *Angola* 85 G2
Gandajika, *Dem. Rep. of the Congo* 84 F4
Gandak →, *India* 69 G11
Gandava, *Pakistan* 68 E2
Gander, *Canada* 103 C9
Gander L., *Canada* 103 C9
Ganderkesee, *Germany* 24 B4
Ganderowe Falls, *Zimbabwe* 87 F2
Gandesa, *Spain* 32 D5
Gandhi Sagar, *India* 68 G6
Gandhinagar, *India* 68 H5
Gandi, *Nigeria* 83 C6
Gandía, *Spain* 33 G4
Gandino, *Italy* 28 C6
Gando, Pta., *Canary Is.* 37 G4
Gandole, *Nigeria* 83 D7
Gâneb, *Mauritania* 82 B2
Ganedidalem = Gani, *Indonesia* 63 E7
Ganetti, *Sudan* 80 D3
Ganga →, *India* 69 H14
Ganga Sagar, *India* 69 J13
Gangafani, *Mali* 82 C4
Gangan →, *India* 69 E8
Ganganagar, *India* 68 E5
Gangapur, *India* 68 F7
Gangara, *Niger* 83 C6
Gangaw, *Burma* 67 H19
Gangdisê Shan, *China* 67 D12
Ganges = Ganga →, *India* 69 H14
Ganges, *Canada* 104 D4
Ganges, *France* 20 E7
Ganges, Mouths of the, *India* 69 J14
Gånghester, *Sweden* 11 G7
Gangi, *Italy* 31 E7
Gângiova, *Romania* 43 G8
Gangoh, *India* 68 E7
Gangroti, *India* 69 D8
Gangtok, *India* 67 F16
Gangu, *China* 56 G3
Gangyao, *China* 57 B14
Gani, *Indonesia* 63 E7
Ganj, *India* 69 F8
Ganluc, *China* 58 C4
Gannat, *France* 19 F10
Gannett Peak, *U.S.A.* 114 E9
Ganquan, *China* 56 F5
Gänserdorf, *Austria* 27 C9
Ganshui, *China* 58 C6
Gansu □, *China* 56 G3
Ganta, *Liberia* 82 D3
Gantheaume, C., *Australia* 95 F2
Gantheaume B., *Australia* 93 E1
Gantsevichi = Hantsavichy, *Belarus* 47 F4
Ganye, *Nigeria* 83 D7
Ganyem = Genyem, *Indonesia* 63 E10
Ganyu, *China* 57 G10
Ganyushkino, *Kazakstan* 49 G9
Ganzhou, *China* 59 E10
Gao, *Mali* 83 B4
Gao Xian, *China* 58 C5
Gao'an, *China* 59 C10
Gaochun, *China* 59 B12
Gaohe, *China* 59 F9
Gaohebu, *China* 59 B11
Gaokeng, *China* 59 D9
Gaolan Dao, *China* 59 G9
Gaoligong Shan, *China* 58 E2
Gaomi, *China* 57 F10
Gaoming, *China* 59 F9
Gaoping, *China* 56 G7
Gaotang, *China* 56 F9
Gaoua, *Burkina Faso* 82 C4
Gaoual, *Guinea* 82 C2
Gaoxiong = Kaohsiung, *Taiwan* 59 F13
Gaoyang, *China* 56 E8
Gaoyao, *China* 59 F9
Gaoyou, *China* 59 A12
Gaoyou Hu, *China* 57 H10
Gaoyuan, *China* 57 F9
Gaozhou, *China* 59 G8
Gap, *France* 21 D10
Gapan, *Phil.* 61 D4
Gapat →, *India* 69 G10
Gapuwiyak, *Australia* 94 A2
Gar, *China* 60 C2
Garabogazköl Aylagy, *Turkmenistan* 50 E6
Garachico, *Canary Is.* 37 F3
Garachiné, *Panama* 120 E4
Garafia, *Canary Is.* 37 F2
Garah, *Australia* 95 D4
Garajonay, *Canary Is.* 37 F2
Garango, *Burkina Faso* 83 C4
Garanhuns, *Brazil* 125 E11
Garautha, *India* 69 G8
Garawe, *Liberia* 82 E3
Garba Tula, *Kenya* 86 B4
Garberville, *U.S.A.* 114 F2
Garbiyang, *India* 69 D9
Garbsen, *Germany* 24 C5
Gard □, *France* 21 D8
Gard →, *France* 21 E8
Garda, L. di, *Italy* 28 C7
Gardanne, *France* 21 E9
Gårdby, *Sweden* 11 H10
Garde L., *Canada* 105 A7
Gardelegen, *Germany* 24 C7
Garden City, *Ga., U.S.A.* 109 J5
Garden City, *Kans., U.S.A.* 113 G4
Garden City, *Tex., U.S.A.* 113 K4
Garden Grove, *U.S.A.* 117 M9
Gardēz, *Afghan.* 68 C3
Gardhíki, *Greece* 38 C3
Gardiner, *Maine, U.S.A.* 109 C11
Gardiner, *Mont., U.S.A.* 114 D8
Gardiners I., *U.S.A.* 111 E12
Gardner, *U.S.A.* 111 D13
Gardner Canal, *Canada* 104 C3
Gardnerville, *U.S.A.* 116 G7
Gardno, Jezioro, *Poland* 44 D4
Gardo, *Somali Rep.* 74 F4
Gardone Val Trómpia, *Italy* 28 C7
Gárdony, *Hungary* 42 C3
Garešnica, *Croatia* 29 C13
Garéssio, *Italy* 28 D5
Garey, *U.S.A.* 117 L6
Garfield, *U.S.A.* 114 C5
Garforth, *U.K.* 12 D6
Gargaliánoi, *Greece* 38 D3
Gargan, Mt., *France* 20 C5
Gargouna, *Mali* 83 B5
Gargždai, *Lithuania* 44 C8
Garibaldi Prov. Park, *Canada* 104 D4
Gariep, L., *S. Africa* 88 E4
Garies, *S. Africa* 88 E2
Garigliano →, *Italy* 30 A6
Garissa, *Kenya* 86 C4
Garkida, *Nigeria* 83 C7
Garko, *Nigeria* 83 C6
Garland, *Tex., U.S.A.* 113 J6
Garland, *Utah, U.S.A.* 114 F7
Garlasco, *Italy* 28 C5
Garliava, *Lithuania* 44 D10
Garlin, *France* 20 E3
Garm, *Tajikistan* 50 F8
Garmāb, *Iran* 71 C8
Garmisch-Partenkirchen, *Germany* 25 H7
Garmo, Qullai = Kommunizma, Pik, *Tajikistan* 50 F8
Garmsār, *Iran* 71 C7
Garner, *U.S.A.* 112 D8
Garnett, *U.S.A.* 112 F7

Garo Hills, *India* 69 G14
Garoe, *Somali Rep.* 74 F4
Garonne →, *France* 20 C3
Garonne, Canal Latéral à la, *France* 20 D4
Garot, *India* 68 G6
Garoua, *Cameroon* 83 D7
Garpenberg, *Sweden* 10 D10
Garphyttan, *Sweden* 10 E8
Garrauli, *India* 69 G8
Garrel, *Germany* 24 C4
Garrigue = Garrigues, *France* 20 E7
Garrigues, *France* 20 E7
Garrison, *Mont., U.S.A.* 114 C7
Garrison, *N. Dak., U.S.A.* 112 B4
Garrison Res. = Sakakawea, L., *U.S.A.* 112 B4
Garron Pt., *U.K.* 15 A6
Garrovillas, *Spain* 35 F4
Garrucha, *Spain* 33 H3
Garry →, *U.K.* 14 E5
Garry, L., *Canada* 100 B9
Garsen, *Kenya* 86 C5
Gärsnäs, *Sweden* 11 J8
Garson L., *Canada* 105 B6
Gartempe →, *France* 20 B4
Gartz, *Germany* 24 B10
Garu, *Ghana* 83 C4
Garu, *India* 69 H11
Garub, *Namibia* 88 D2
Garut, *Indonesia* 63 G12
Garvão, *Portugal* 35 H2
Garvie Mts., *N.Z.* 91 L2
Garwa = Garoua, *Cameroon* 83 D7
Garwa, *India* 69 G10
Garwolin, *Poland* 45 G8
Gary, *U.S.A.* 108 E2
Garz, *Germany* 24 A9
Garzê, *China* 58 B3
Garzón, *Colombia* 124 C3
Gas-San, *Japan* 54 E10
Gasan Kuli = Esenguly, *Turkmenistan* 50 F6
Gascogne, *France* 20 E4
Gascogne, G. de, *Europe* 20 E2
Gascony = Gascogne, *France* 20 E4
Gascoyne →, *Australia* 93 D1
Gascoyne Junction, *Australia* 93 E2
Gascueña, *Spain* 32 E2
Gash, Wadi →, *Ethiopia* 81 D4
Gashagar, *Nigeria* 83 C7
Gashaka, *Nigeria* 83 D7
Gasherbrum, *Pakistan* 69 B7
Gashua, *Nigeria* 83 C7
Gaspé, *Canada* 103 C7
Gaspé, C. de, *Canada* 103 C7
Gaspé, Pén. de, *Canada* 103 C6
Gaspésie, Parc de Conservation de la, *Canada* 103 C6
Gassan, *Burkina Faso* 82 C4
Gassol, *Nigeria* 83 D7
Gasteiz = Vitoria-Gasteiz, *Spain* 32 C2
Gastonia, *U.S.A.* 109 H5
Gastoúni, *Greece* 38 D3
Gastoúri, *Greece* 38 B1
Gastre, *Argentina* 128 E3
Gästrikland, *Sweden* 10 D10
Gata, C., *Cyprus* 36 E12
Gata, C. de, *Spain* 33 J2
Gata, Sierra de, *Spain* 34 E4
Gataga →, *Canada* 104 B3
Gătaia, *Romania* 42 E6
Gatchina, *Russia* 46 C6
Gatehouse of Fleet, *U.K.* 14 G4
Gates, *U.S.A.* 110 C7
Gateshead, *U.K.* 12 C6
Gatesville, *U.S.A.* 113 K6
Gaths, *Zimbabwe* 87 G3
Gatico, *Chile* 126 A1
Gâtinais, *France* 19 D9
Gâtine, Hauteurs de, *France* 20 B3
Gatineau, *Canada* 111 A9
Gatineau →, *Canada* 102 C4
Gatineau, Parc Nat. de la, *Canada* 102 C4
Gattaran, *Phil.* 61 B4
Gattinara, *Italy* 28 C5
Gatton, *Australia* 95 D5
Gatun, L., *Panama* 120 E4
Gatyana, *S. Africa* 89 E4
Gau, *Fiji* 91 D8
Gaucín, *Spain* 35 J5
Gauer L., *Canada* 105 B9
Gauhati, *India* 67 F17
Gauja →, *Latvia* 9 H21
Gaula →, *Norway* 8 E14
Gauri Phanta, *India* 69 E9
Gausta, *Norway* 9 G13
Gauteng □, *S. Africa* 89 D4
Gāv Koshī, *Iran* 71 D8
Gāvakān, *Iran* 71 D7
Gavarnie, *France* 20 F3
Gavāter, *Iran* 71 E9
Gāvbandī, *Iran* 71 E7
Gavdhopoúla, *Greece* 36 E6
Gávdhos, *Greece* 36 E6
Gavi, *Italy* 28 D5
Gavião, *Portugal* 35 F3
Gaviota, *U.S.A.* 117 L6
Gāvkhūnī, Bāṭlāq-e, *Iran* 71 C7
Gävle, *Sweden* 10 D11
Gävleborgs län □, *Sweden* 10 C10
Gävlebukten, *Sweden* 10 D11
Gavorrano, *Italy* 28 F7
Gavray, *France* 18 D5
Gavrilov Yam, *Russia* 46 D10
Gávrion, *Greece* 38 D6
Gawachab, *Namibia* 88 D2
Gawilgarh Hills, *India* 66 J10
Gawler, *Australia* 95 E2
Gawu, *Nigeria* 83 D6
Gaxun Nur, *China* 60 B5
Gaya, *India* 69 G11
Gaya, *Niger* 83 C5
Gaya, *Nigeria* 83 C6
Gayéri, *Burkina Faso* 83 C5
Gaylord, *U.S.A.* 108 C3
Gayndah, *Australia* 95 D5
Gaysin = Haysyn, *Ukraine* 47 H5
Gayvoron = Hayvoron, *Ukraine* 47 H5
Gaza, *Gaza Strip* 75 D3
Gaza □, *Mozam.* 89 C5
Gaza Strip □, *Asia* 75 D3
Gazanjyk, *Turkmenistan* 71 B7
Gazaoua, *Niger* 83 C6
Gāzbor, *Iran* 71 D8
Gazi, *Dem. Rep. of the Congo* 86 B1
Gaziantep, *Turkey* 70 B3
Gazipaşa, *Turkey* 72 D5
Gbarnga, *Liberia* 82 D3
Gbekebo, *Nigeria* 83 D5
Gboko, *Nigeria* 83 D6
Gbongan, *Nigeria* 83 D5
Gcoverega, *Botswana* 88 B3
Gcuwa, *S. Africa* 89 E4
Gdańsk, *Poland* 44 D5
Gdańska, Zatoka, *Poland* 44 D6
Gdov, *Russia* 9 G22
Gdynia, *Poland* 44 D5
Geba →, *Guinea-Biss.* 82 C1
Gebe, *Indonesia* 63 D7
Gebeciler, *Turkey* 39 C12
Gebeit Mine, *Sudan* 80 C4
Gebel Abyad, *Sudan* 80 D2
Gebel Iweibid, *Egypt* 80 H8
Gebze, *Turkey* 41 F13
Gecha, *Ethiopia* 81 F4
Gedaref, *Sudan* 81 E4
Gedaref □, *Sudan* 81 E4
Gediz, *Turkey* 39 B11
Gediz →, *Turkey* 39 C8
Gedo, *Ethiopia* 81 F4
Gèdre, *France* 20 F4
Gedser, *Denmark* 11 K5
Geegully Cr. →, *Australia* 92 C3
Geel, *Belgium* 17 C4
Geelong, *Australia* 95 F3
Geelvink B. = Cenderwasih, Teluk, *Indonesia* 63 E9
Geelvink Chan., *Australia* 93 E1
Geesthacht, *Germany* 24 B6
Geidam, *Nigeria* 83 C7
Geikie →, *Canada* 105 B8
Geilenkirchen, *Germany* 24 E2
Geili, *Sudan* 81 D3
Geisingen, *Germany* 25 H4
Geislingen, *Germany* 25 G5
Geistown, *U.S.A.* 110 F6
Geita, *Tanzania* 86 C3
Gejiu, *China* 58 F4
Gel →, *Sudan* 81 F2
Gel, Meydān-e, *Iran* 71 D7
Gel River, *Sudan* 81 F2
Gela, *Italy* 31 E7
Gela, G. di, *Italy* 31 F7
Gelahun, *Liberia* 82 D2
Gelderland □, *Neths.* 17 B6
Geldern, *Germany* 24 D2
Geldrop, *Neths.* 17 C5
Geleen, *Neths.* 17 D5
Gelehun, *S. Leone* 82 D2
Gelembe, *Turkey* 39 B9
Gelemso, *Ethiopia* 81 F5
Gelendost, *Turkey* 72 C4
Gelendzhik, *Russia* 47 K10
Gelibolu, *Turkey* 41 F10
Gelibolu Yarımadası, *Turkey* 41 F10
Gelidonya Burnu, *Turkey* 72 D4
Gelnhausen, *Germany* 25 E5
Gelnica, *Slovak Rep.* 27 C13
Gelsenkirchen, *Germany* 24 D3
Gelting, *Germany* 24 A5
Gemas, *Malaysia* 65 L4
Gembloux, *Belgium* 17 D4
Gembu, *Nigeria* 83 D7
Gemena, *Dem. Rep. of the Congo* 84 D3
Gemerek, *Turkey* 70 B3
Gemla, *Sweden* 11 H8
Gemlik, *Turkey* 41 F13
Gemlik Körfezi, *Turkey* 41 F12
Gemona del Friuli, *Italy* 29 B10
Gemsa, *Egypt* 80 B3
Gemünden, *Germany* 25 E5
Genale →, *Ethiopia* 81 F4
Genç, *Turkey* 73 C9
Gençay, *France* 20 B4
Geneina, Gebel, *Egypt* 80 B3
General Acha, *Argentina* 126 D3
General Alvear, *Buenos Aires, Argentina* 126 D4
General Alvear, *Mendoza, Argentina* 126 D2
General Artigas, *Paraguay* 126 B4
General Belgrano, *Argentina* 126 D4
General Cabrera, *Argentina* 126 C3
General Cepeda, *Mexico* 118 B4
General Guido, *Argentina* 126 D4
General Juan Madariaga, *Argentina* 126 D4
General La Madrid, *Argentina* 126 D3
General MacArthur, *Phil.* 61 F6
General Martin Miguel de Güemes, *Argentina* 126 A3
General Paz, *Argentina* 126 B4
General Pico, *Argentina* 126 D3
General Pinedo, *Argentina* 126 B3
General Pinto, *Argentina* 126 C3
General Roca, *Argentina* 128 D3
General Santos, *Phil.* 61 H6
General Toshevo, *Bulgaria* 41 C12
General Trevino, *Mexico* 119 B5
General Trías, *Mexico* 118 B3
General Viamonte, *Argentina* 126 D3
General Villegas, *Argentina* 126 D3
Genesee, *Idaho, U.S.A.* 114 C5
Genesee, *Pa., U.S.A.* 110 E7
Genesee →, *U.S.A.* 110 C7
Geneseo, *Ill., U.S.A.* 112 E9
Geneseo, *N.Y., U.S.A.* 110 D7
Geneva = Genève, *Switz.* 25 J2
Geneva, *Ala., U.S.A.* 109 K3
Geneva, *N.Y., U.S.A.* 110 D8
Geneva, *Nebr., U.S.A.* 112 E6
Geneva, *Ohio, U.S.A.* 110 E4
Geneva, L. = Léman, L., *Europe* 19 F13
Geneva, L., *U.S.A.* 108 D1
Genève, *Switz.* 25 J2
Gengenbach, *Germany* 25 G4
Gengma, *China* 58 F2
Genichesk = Henichesk, *Ukraine* 47 J8
Genil →, *Spain* 35 H5
Genk, *Belgium* 17 D5
Genlis, *France* 19 E12
Gennargentu, Mti. del, *Italy* 30 B2
Gennes, *France* 18 E6
Genoa = Génova, *Italy* 28 D5
Genoa, *Australia* 95 F4
Genoa, *N.Y., U.S.A.* 111 D8
Genoa, *Nebr., U.S.A.* 112 E6
Genoa, *Nev., U.S.A.* 116 F7
Génova, *Italy* 28 D5
Génova, G. di, *Italy* 28 E6
Genriyetty, Ostrov, *Russia* 51 B16
Gent, *Belgium* 17 C3
Genteng, *Indonesia* 63 G12
Genthin, *Germany* 24 C8
Genyem, *Indonesia* 63 E10
Genzano di Lucánia, *Italy* 31 B9
Genzano di Roma, *Italy* 29 G9
Geoagiu, *Romania* 43 E8
Geographe B., *Australia* 93 F2
Geographe Chan., *Australia* 93 D1
Geokchay = Göyçay, *Azerbaijan* 49 K8
Georga, Zemlya, *Russia* 50 A5
George, *S. Africa* 88 E3
George →, *Canada* 103 A6
George, L., *N.S.W., Australia* 95 F4
George, L., *S. Austral., Australia* 95 F3
George, L., *W. Austral., Australia* 92 D3
George, L., *Uganda* 86 B3
George, L., *Fla., U.S.A.* 109 L5
George, L., *N.Y., U.S.A.* 111 C11
George Gill Ra., *Australia* 92 D5
George River = Kangiqsualujjuaq, *Canada* 101 C13
George Sound, *N.Z.* 91 L1
George Town, *Australia* 94 G4
George Town, *Bahamas* 120 B4
George Town, *Cayman Is.* 120 C3
George Town, *Malaysia* 65 K3
George V Land, *Antarctica* 5 C10
George VI Sound, *Antarctica* 5 D17
George West, *U.S.A.* 113 L5
Georgetown, *Australia* 94 B3
Georgetown, *Ont., Canada* 102 D4
Georgetown, *P.E.I., Canada* 103 C7
Georgetown, *Gambia* 82 C2
Georgetown, *Guyana* 124 B7
Georgetown, *Calif., U.S.A.* 116 G6
Georgetown, *Colo., U.S.A.* 114 G11
Georgetown, *Ky., U.S.A.* 108 F3
Georgetown, *N.Y., U.S.A.* 111 D9
Georgetown, *Ohio, U.S.A.* 108 F4
Georgetown, *S.C., U.S.A.* 109 J6
Georgetown, *Tex., U.S.A.* 113 K6
Georgia □, *U.S.A.* 109 K5
Georgia ■, *Asia* 49 J6
Georgia, Str. of, *Canada* 104 D4
Georgian B., *Canada* 102 C3
Georgina →, *Australia* 94 C2
Georgina I., *Canada* 110 B5
Georgiu-Dezh = Liski, *Russia* 47 G10
Georgiyevsk, *Russia* 49 H6
Georgsmarienhütte, *Germany* 24 C4
Gera, *Germany* 24 E8
Geraardsbergen, *Belgium* 17 D3
Geral, Serra, *Brazil* 127 B6
Geral de Goiás, Serra, *Brazil* 125 F9
Geraldine, *U.S.A.* 114 C8
Geraldton, *Australia* 93 E1
Geraldton, *Canada* 102 C2
Gérardmer, *France* 19 D13
Gercüş, *Turkey* 73 D9
Gerede, *Turkey* 72 B5
Gerês, Sierra do, *Portugal* 34 D3
Gereshk, *Afghan.* 66 D4
Geretsried, *Germany* 25 H7
Gérgal, *Spain* 33 H2
Gerik, *Malaysia* 65 K3
Gering, *U.S.A.* 112 E3
Gerlach, *U.S.A.* 114 F4
Gerlachovský štit, *Slovak Rep.* 27 B13
German Planina, *Macedonia* 40 D6
Germansen Landing, *Canada* 104 B4
Germantown, *U.S.A.* 113 M10
Germany ■, *Europe* 24 E6
Germencik, *Turkey* 39 D9
Germering, *Germany* 25 G7
Germersheim, *Germany* 25 F4
Germī, *Iran* 71 B6
Germiston, *S. Africa* 89 D4
Gernika-Lumo, *Spain* 32 B2
Gernsheim, *Germany* 25 F4
Gero, *Japan* 55 G8
Gerolzhofen, *Germany* 25 F6
Gerona = Girona, *Spain* 32 D7
Gerrard, *Canada* 104 C5
Gers □, *France* 20 E4
Gers →, *France* 20 D4
Gersfeld, *Germany* 24 E5
Gersthofen, *Germany* 25 G6
Gerzat, *France* 20 C7
Gerze, *Turkey* 72 B6
Geseke, *Germany* 24 D4
Geser, *Indonesia* 63 E8
Gesso →, *Italy* 28 D4
Gestro, Wabi →, *Ethiopia* 81 G5
Getafe, *Spain* 34 E7
Getinge, *Sweden* 11 H6
Gettysburg, *Pa., U.S.A.* 108 F7
Gettysburg, *S. Dak., U.S.A.* 112 C5
Getxo, *Spain* 32 B2
Getz Ice Shelf, *Antarctica* 5 D14
Gevaş, *Turkey* 73 C10
Gévaudan, *France* 20 D7
Gevgelija, *Macedonia* 40 E6
Gévora →, *Spain* 35 G4
Gewani, *Ethiopia* 81 E5
Gex, *France* 19 F13
Geyikli, *Turkey* 39 B8
Geyser, *U.S.A.* 114 C8
Geyserville, *U.S.A.* 116 G4
Geyve, *Turkey* 72 B4
Ghâbat el Arab = Wang Kai, *Sudan* 81 F2
Ghabeish, *Sudan* 81 E2
Ghaggar →, *India* 68 E6
Ghaghara →, *India* 69 G11
Ghaghat →, *Bangla.* 69 G13
Ghagra, *India* 69 H11
Ghagra →, *India* 69 F9
Ghalla, Wadi el →, *Sudan* 81 E2
Ghana ■, *W. Afr.* 83 D4
Ghansor, *India* 69 H9
Ghanzi, *Botswana* 88 C3
Gharb el Istiwa'iya □, *Sudan* 81 G3
Gharb Kordofân, *Sudan* 81 E2
Gharbîya, Es Sahrâ el, *Egypt* 80 B2
Ghardaïa, *Algeria* 78 B6
Ghârib, G., *Egypt* 80 B3
Gharig, *Sudan* 81 E2
Gharyān, *Libya* 79 B8
Ghat, *Libya* 79 D8
Ghatal, *India* 69 H12
Ghatampur, *India* 69 F9
Ghatsila, *India* 69 H12
Ghaṭṭī, *Si. Arabia* 70 D3
Ghawdex = Gozo, *Malta* 36 C1
Ghazal, Bahr el →, *Chad* 79 F9
Ghazâl, Bahr el →, *Sudan* 81 F3
Ghaziabad, *India* 68 E7
Ghazipur, *India* 69 G10
Ghaznī, *Afghan.* 68 C3
Ghaznī □, *Afghan.* 66 C6
Ghedi, *Italy* 28 C7
Ghelari, *Romania* 42 E7
Ghent = Gent, *Belgium* 17 C3
Gheorghe Gheorghiu-Dej = Oneşti, *Romania* 43 D11
Gheorgheni, *Romania* 43 D10
Gherla, *Romania* 43 C8
Ghidigeni, *Romania* 43 D12
Ghilarza, *Italy* 30 B1
Ghimeş-Făget, *Romania* 43 D11
Ghīnah, Wādī al →, *Si. Arabia* 70 D3
Ghisonaccia, *France* 21 F13
Ghisoni, *France* 21 F13
Ghizao, *Afghan.* 68 C1
Ghizar →, *Pakistan* 69 A5
Ghot Ogrein, *Egypt* 80 A2
Ghotaru, *India* 68 F4
Ghotki, *Pakistan* 68 E3
Ghowr □, *Afghan.* 66 C4
Ghudaf, W. al →, *Iraq* 70 C4
Ghudāmis, *Libya* 77 C4
Ghughri, *India* 69 H9
Ghugus, *India* 66 K11
Ghulam Mohammad Barrage, *Pakistan* 68 G3
Ghūrīān, *Afghan.* 66 B2
Gia Dinh, *Vietnam* 65 G6
Gia Lai = Plei Ku, *Vietnam* 64 F7
Gia Nghia, *Vietnam* 65 G6
Gia Ngoc, *Vietnam* 64 E7
Gia Vuc, *Vietnam* 64 E7
Giannutri, *Italy* 28 F8
Giant Forest, *U.S.A.* 116 J8
Giant Mts. = Krkonoše, *Czech Rep.* 26 A8
Giants Causeway, *U.K.* 15 A5
Giarabub = Al Jaghbūb, *Libya* 79 C10
Giarre, *Italy* 31 E8
Giaveno, *Italy* 28 C4
Gibara, *Cuba* 120 B4
Gibb River, *Australia* 92 C4
Gibbon, *U.S.A.* 112 E5
Gibe →, *Ethiopia* 81 F4
Gibellina Nuova, *Italy* 30 E5
Gibeon, *Namibia* 88 D2
Gibraleón, *Spain* 35 H4
Gibraltar ■, *Europe* 35 J5
Gibraltar, Str. of, *Medit. S.* 35 K5
Gibson Desert, *Australia* 92 D4
Gibsons, *Canada* 104 D4
Gibsonville, *U.S.A.* 116 F6
Giddings, *U.S.A.* 113 K6
Gidole, *Ethiopia* 81 F4
Giebnegáisi = Kebnekaise, *Sweden* 8 C18
Gien, *France* 19 E9
Giengen, *Germany* 25 G6
Giessen, *Germany* 24 E4
Gīfān, *Iran* 71 B8
Gifatin, Geziret, *Egypt* 80 B3
Gifhorn, *Germany* 24 C6
Gift Lake, *Canada* 104 B5
Gifu, *Japan* 55 G8
Gifu □, *Japan* 55 G8
Gigant, *Russia* 49 G5
Giganta, Sa. de la, *Mexico* 118 B2
Gigen, *Bulgaria* 41 C8
Gigha, *U.K.* 14 F3
Gíglio, *Italy* 28 F7
Gignac, *France* 20 E7
Gigüela →, *Spain* 35 F7
Gijón, *Spain* 34 B5
Gil I., *Canada* 104 C3
Gila →, *U.S.A.* 115 K6
Gila Bend, *U.S.A.* 115 K7
Gila Bend Mts., *U.S.A.* 115 K7
Gīlān □, *Iran* 71 B6
Gilău, *Romania* 43 D8
Gilbert →, *Australia* 94 B3
Gilbert Is., *Kiribati* 96 G9
Gilbert River, *Australia* 94 B3
Gilead, *U.S.A.* 111 B14
Gilf el Kebîr, Hadabat el, *Egypt* 80 C2
Gilford I., *Canada* 104 C3
Gilgandra, *Australia* 95 E4
Gilgil, *Kenya* 86 C4
Gilgit, *India* 69 B6
Gilgit →, *Pakistan* 69 B6
Giljeva Planina, *Serbia, Yug.* 40 C3
Gillam, *Canada* 105 B10
Gilleleje, *Denmark* 11 H6
Gillen, L., *Australia* 93 E3
Gilles, L., *Australia* 95 E2
Gillette, *U.S.A.* 112 C2
Gilliat, *Australia* 94 C3
Gillingham, *U.K.* 13 F8
Gilmer, *U.S.A.* 113 J7
Gilmore, L., *Australia* 93 F3
Gilo →, *Ethiopia* 81 F3
Gilort →, *Romania* 43 F8
Gilroy, *U.S.A.* 116 H5
Gimbi, *Ethiopia* 81 F4
Gimli, *Canada* 105 C9
Gimo, *Sweden* 10 D12
Gimone →, *France* 20 E5
Gimont, *France* 20 E4
Gin Gin, *Australia* 95 D5
Ginâh, *Egypt* 80 B3
Gineifa, *Egypt* 80 H8
Gingin, *Australia* 93 F2
Gingindlovu, *S. Africa* 89 D5
Ginir, *Ethiopia* 81 F5
Ginosa, *Italy* 31 B9
Ginzo de Limia = Xinzo de Limia, *Spain* 34 C3
Gióia, G. di, *Italy* 31 D8
Gióia del Colle, *Italy* 31 B9
Gióia Táuro, *Italy* 31 D8
Gioiosa Iónica, *Italy* 31 D9
Gioiosa Marea, *Italy* 31 D7
Gióna, Óros, *Greece* 38 C4
Giovi, Passo dei, *Italy* 28 D5
Giovinazzo, *Italy* 31 A9
Gir Hills, *India* 68 J4
Girab, *India* 68 F4
Girâfi, W. →, *Egypt* 75 F3
Giraltovce, *Slovak Rep.* 27 B14
Girard, *Kans., U.S.A.* 113 G7
Girard, *Ohio, U.S.A.* 110 E4
Girard, *Pa., U.S.A.* 110 E4
Girdle Ness, *U.K.* 14 D6
Giresun, *Turkey* 73 B8
Girga, *Egypt* 80 B3
Giri →, *India* 68 D7
Giridih, *India* 69 G12
Girifalco, *Italy* 31 D9
Girne = Kyrenia, *Cyprus* 36 D12
Giro, *Nigeria* 83 C5
Giromagny, *France* 19 E13
Girona, *Spain* 32 D7
Girona □, *Spain* 32 C7
Gironde □, *France* 20 D3
Gironde →, *France* 20 C2
Gironella, *Spain* 32 C6
Giru, *Australia* 94 B4
Girvan, *U.K.* 14 F4
Gisborne, *N.Z.* 91 H7
Gisenyi, *Rwanda* 86 C2
Gislaved, *Sweden* 11 G7
Gisors, *France* 19 C8
Gitega, *Burundi* 86 C2
Giuba →, *Somali Rep.* 74 G3
Giugliano in Campania, *Italy* 31 B7
Giulianova, *Italy* 29 F10
Giurgeni, *Romania* 43 F12
Giurgiu, *Romania* 43 G10
Giurgiu □, *Romania* 43 F10
Giurgiuleşti, *Moldova* 43 E13
Give, *Denmark* 11 J3
Givet, *France* 19 B11
Givors, *France* 21 C8
Givry, *France* 19 F11
Giyon, *Ethiopia* 81 F4
Giza = El Gîza, *Egypt* 80 J7
Gizhiga, *Russia* 51 C17
Gizhiginskaya Guba, *Russia* 51 C16
Giżycko, *Poland* 44 D8
Gizzeria, *Italy* 31 D9
Gjalicë e Lumës, Mal., *Albania* 40 D4

Gjegjan, *Albania* 40 E4
Gjirokastër, *Albania* 40 F4
Gjoa Haven, *Canada* 100 B10
Gjøvik, *Norway* 9 F14
Gjuhës, Kep i, *Albania* 40 F3
Glace Bay, *Canada* 103 C8
Glacier Bay National Park and Preserve, *U.S.A.* 104 B1
Glacier National Park, *Canada* 104 C5
Glacier National Park, *U.S.A.* 114 B7
Glacier Peak, *U.S.A.* 114 B3
Gladewater, *U.S.A.* 113 J7
Gladstone, *Queens., Australia* 94 C5
Gladstone, *S. Austral., Australia* 95 E2
Gladstone, *Canada* 105 C9
Gladstone, *U.S.A.* 108 C2
Gladwin, *U.S.A.* 108 D3
Glafsfjorden, *Sweden* 10 E6
Głagów Małapolski, *Poland* 45 H8
Glåma = Glomma →, *Norway* 9 G14
Gláma, *Iceland* 8 D2
Glamis, *U.S.A.* 117 N11
Glamoč, *Bos.-H.* 29 D13
Glamsbjerg, *Denmark* 11 J4
Glarus, *Switz.* 25 H5
Glarus □, *Switz.* 25 J5
Glasco, *Kans., U.S.A.* 112 F6
Glasco, *N.Y., U.S.A.* 111 D11
Glasgow, *U.K.* 14 F4
Glasgow, *Ky., U.S.A.* 108 G3
Glasgow, *Mont., U.S.A.* 114 B10
Glasgow, City of □, *U.K.* 14 F4
Glaslyn, *Canada* 105 C7
Glastonbury, *U.K.* 13 F5
Glastonbury, *U.S.A.* 111 E12
Glauchau, *Germany* 24 E8
Glava, *Sweden* 10 E6
Glavice, *Croatia* 29 E13
Glazov, *Russia* 48 A11
Gleichen, *Canada* 104 C6
Gleisdorf, *Austria* 26 D8
Gleiwitz = Gliwice, *Poland* 45 H5
Glen, *U.S.A.* 111 B13
Glen Affric, *U.K.* 14 D3
Glen Canyon, *U.S.A.* 115 H8
Glen Canyon Dam, *U.S.A.* 115 H8
Glen Canyon National Recreation Area, *U.S.A.* 115 H8
Glen Coe, *U.K.* 14 E3
Glen Cove, *U.S.A.* 111 F11
Glen Garry, *U.K.* 14 D3
Glen Innes, *Australia* 95 D5
Glen Lyon, *U.S.A.* 111 E8
Glen Mor, *U.K.* 14 D4
Glen Moriston, *U.K.* 14 D4
Glen Robertson, *Canada* 111 A10
Glen Spean, *U.K.* 14 E4
Glen Ullin, *U.S.A.* 112 B4
Glénan, Îs. de, *France* 18 E3
Glencoe, *Canada* 110 D3
Glencoe, *S. Africa* 89 D5
Glencoe, *U.S.A.* 112 C7
Glendale, *Ariz., U.S.A.* 115 K7
Glendale, *Calif., U.S.A.* 117 L8
Glendale, *Zimbabwe* 87 F3
Glendive, *U.S.A.* 112 B2
Glendo, *U.S.A.* 112 D2
Glenelg →, *Australia* 95 F3
Glenfield, *U.S.A.* 111 C9
Glengarriff, *Ireland* 15 E2
Glenmont, *U.S.A.* 110 F2
Glenmorgan, *Australia* 95 D4
Glenn, *U.S.A.* 116 F4
Glennallen, *U.S.A.* 100 B5
Glennamaddy, *Ireland* 15 C3
Glenns Ferry, *U.S.A.* 114 E6
Glenore, *Australia* 94 B3
Glenreagh, *Australia* 95 E5
Glenrock, *U.S.A.* 114 E11
Glenrothes, *U.K.* 14 E5
Glens Falls, *U.S.A.* 111 C11
Glenside, *U.S.A.* 111 F9
Glenties, *Ireland* 15 B3
Glenville, *U.S.A.* 108 F5
Glenwood, *Canada* 103 C9
Glenwood, *Ark., U.S.A.* 113 H8
Glenwood, *Iowa, U.S.A.* 112 E7
Glenwood, *Minn., U.S.A.* 112 C7
Glenwood, *Wash., U.S.A.* 116 D5
Glenwood Springs, *U.S.A.* 114 G10
Glettinganes, *Iceland* 8 D7
Glifádha, *Greece* 38 D5
Glimåkra, *Sweden* 11 H8
Glina, *Croatia* 29 C13
Glinojeck, *Poland* 45 F7
Gliwice, *Poland* 45 H5
Globe, *U.S.A.* 115 K8
Glodeanu Siliştea, *Romania* 43 F11
Glodeni, *Moldova* 43 C12
Glödnitz, *Austria* 26 E7
Gloggnitz, *Austria* 26 D8
Głogów, *Poland* 45 G3
Głogówek, *Poland* 45 H4
Glomma →, *Norway* 9 G14
Glorieuses, Is., *Ind. Oc.* 89 A8
Glóssa, *Greece* 38 B5
Glossop, *U.K.* 12 D6
Gloucester, *Australia* 95 E5
Gloucester, *U.K.* 13 F5
Gloucester, *U.S.A.* 111 D14
Gloucester I., *Australia* 94 C4
Gloucester Point, *U.S.A.* 108 G7
Gloucestershire □, *U.K.* 13 F5
Gloversville, *U.S.A.* 111 C10
Glovertown, *Canada* 103 C9
Głowno, *Poland* 45 G6
Głubczyce, *Poland* 45 H4
Glubokiy, *Russia* 49 F5
Glubokoye = Hlybokaye, *Belarus* 46 E4
Głuchołazy, *Poland* 45 H4
Glücksburg, *Germany* 24 A5
Glückstadt, *Germany* 24 B5
Glukhov = Hlukhiv, *Ukraine* 47 G7
Glusk, *Belarus* 47 F5
Głuszyca, *Poland* 45 H3
Glyngøre, *Denmark* 11 H2
Gmünd, *Kärnten, Austria* 26 E6
Gmünd, *Niederösterreich, Austria* 26 C8
Gmunden, *Austria* 26 D6
Gnarp, *Sweden* 10 B11
Gnesta, *Sweden* 10 E11
Gniew, *Poland* 44 E5
Gniewkowo, *Poland* 45 F5
Gniezno, *Poland* 45 F4
Gnjilane, *Kosovo, Yug.* 40 D5
Gnoien, *Germany* 24 B8
Gnosjö, *Sweden* 11 G7
Gnowangerup, *Australia* 93 F2
Go Cong, *Vietnam* 65 G6
Gō-no-ura, *Japan* 55 H4
Goa, *India* 66 M8
Goa □, *India* 66 M8
Goalen Hd., *Australia* 95 F5
Goalpara, *India* 67 F17
Goaltor, *India* 69 H12
Goalundo Ghat, *Bangla.* 69 H13
Goaso, *Ghana* 82 D4
Goat Fell, *U.K.* 14 F3
Goba, *Ethiopia* 81 F4
Goba, *Mozam.* 89 D5
Gobabis, *Namibia* 88 C2
Göbel, *Turkey* 41 F12
Gobi, *Asia* 56 C6
Gobō, *Japan* 55 H7
Gobo, *Sudan* 81 F3
Göçbeyli, *Turkey* 39 B9
Goch, *Germany* 24 D2
Gochas, *Namibia* 88 C2
Godavari →, *India* 67 L13
Godavari Pt., *India* 67 L13
Godbout, *Canada* 103 C6
Godda, *India* 69 G12
Godech, *Bulgaria* 40 C7
Goderich, *Canada* 102 D3
Goderville, *France* 18 C7
Godfrey Ra., *Australia* 93 D2
Godhavn = Qeqertarsuaq, *Greenland* 4 C5
Godhra, *India* 68 H5
Gödöllő, *Hungary* 42 C4
Godoy Cruz, *Argentina* 126 C2
Gods →, *Canada* 102 A1
Gods L., *Canada* 102 B1
Gods River, *Canada* 105 C10
Godthåb = Nuuk, *Greenland* 101 B14
Godwin Austen = K2, *Pakistan* 69 B7
Goeie Hoop, Kaap die = Good Hope, C. of, *S. Africa* 88 E2
Goéland, L. au, *Canada* 102 C4
Goeree, *Neths.* 17 C3
Goes, *Neths.* 17 C3
Goffstown, *U.S.A.* 111 C13
Gogama, *Canada* 102 C3
Gogebic, L., *U.S.A.* 112 B10
Goggetti, *Ethiopia* 81 F4
Gogolin, *Poland* 45 H5
Gogonou, *Benin* 83 C5
Gogra = Ghaghara →, *India* 69 G11
Gogriâl, *Sudan* 81 F2
Gogti, *Ethiopia* 81 E5
Gohana, *India* 68 E7
Goharganj, *India* 68 H7
Goi →, *India* 68 H6
Goiânia, *Brazil* 125 G9
Goiás, *Brazil* 125 G8
Goiás □, *Brazil* 125 F9
Goio-Erê, *Brazil* 127 A5
Góis, *Portugal* 34 E2
Gojam □, *Ethiopia* 81 E4
Gojeb, Wabi →, *Ethiopia* 81 F4
Gojō, *Japan* 55 G7
Gojra, *Pakistan* 68 D5
Gökçeada, *Turkey* 41 F9
Gökçedağ, *Turkey* 39 B10
Gökçen, *Turkey* 39 C9
Gökçeören, *Turkey* 39 C10
Gökçeyazı, *Turkey* 39 B9
Gökırmak →, *Turkey* 72 B6
Gökova, *Turkey* 39 D10
Gökova Körfezi, *Turkey* 39 E9
Göksu →, *Turkey* 72 D6
Göksun, *Turkey* 72 C7
Gokteik, *Burma* 67 H20
Göktepe, *Turkey* 39 D10
Gokurt, *Pakistan* 68 E2
Gokwe, *Zimbabwe* 89 B4
Gola, *India* 69 E9
Golakganj, *India* 69 F13
Golan Heights = Hagolan, *Syria* 75 C4
Gołańcz, *Poland* 45 F4
Golāshkerd, *Iran* 71 E8
Golaya Pristen = Hola Pristan, *Ukraine* 47 J7
Gölbaşı, *Adiyaman, Turkey* 72 D7
Gölbaşı, *Ankara, Turkey* 72 C5
Golchikha, *Russia* 4 B12
Golconda, *U.S.A.* 114 F5
Gölcük, *Kocaeli, Turkey* 41 F13
Gölcük, *Niğde, Turkey* 72 C6
Gold, *U.S.A.* 110 E7
Gold Beach, *U.S.A.* 114 E1
Gold Coast, *W. Afr.* 83 E4
Gold Hill, *U.S.A.* 114 E2
Gold River, *Canada* 104 D3
Gołdap, *Poland* 44 D9
Goldberg, *Germany* 24 B8
Golden, *Canada* 104 C5
Golden B., *N.Z.* 91 J4
Golden Gate, *U.S.A.* 114 H2
Golden Hinde, *Canada* 104 D3
Golden Lake, *Canada* 110 A7
Golden Vale, *Ireland* 15 D3
Goldendale, *U.S.A.* 114 D3
Goldfield, *U.S.A.* 115 H5
Goldsand L., *Canada* 105 B8
Goldsboro, *U.S.A.* 109 H7
Goldsmith, *U.S.A.* 113 K3
Goldsworthy, *Australia* 92 D2
Goldthwaite, *U.S.A.* 113 K5
Golegã, *Portugal* 35 F2
Goleniów, *Poland* 44 E1
Golestānak, *Iran* 71 D7
Goleta, *U.S.A.* 117 L7
Golfito, *Costa Rica* 120 E3
Golfo Aranci, *Italy* 30 B2
Gölgeli Dağları, *Turkey* 39 D10
Gölhisar, *Turkey* 39 D11
Goliad, *U.S.A.* 113 L6
Golija, *Montenegro, Yug.* 40 C2
Golija, *Serbia, Yug.* 40 C4
Golina, *Poland* 45 F5
Gölköy, *Turkey* 72 B7
Göllersdorf, *Austria* 26 C9
Gölmarmara, *Turkey* 39 C9
Golo →, *France* 21 F13
Gölova, *Turkey* 39 E12
Golpāyegān, *Iran* 71 C6
Gölpazarı, *Turkey* 72 B4
Golra, *Pakistan* 68 C5
Golspie, *U.K.* 14 D5
Golub-Dobrzyń, *Poland* 45 E6
Golubac, *Serbia, Yug.* 40 B5
Golyam Perelik, *Bulgaria* 41 E8
Golyama Kamchiya →, *Bulgaria* 41 C11
Goma, *Dem. Rep. of the Congo* 86 C2
Gomal Pass, *Pakistan* 68 D3
Gomati →, *India* 69 G10
Gombari, *Dem. Rep. of the Congo* 86 B2
Gombe, *Nigeria* 83 C7
Gömbe, *Turkey* 39 E11
Gombe □, *Nigeria* 83 C7
Gombe →, *Tanzania* 86 C3
Gombi, *Nigeria* 83 C7
Gomel = Homyel, *Belarus* 47 F6
Gomera, *Canary Is.* 37 F2
Gómez Palacio, *Mexico* 118 B4
Gomīshān, *Iran* 71 B7
Gommern, *Germany* 24 C7
Gomogomo, *Indonesia* 63 F8
Gomoh, *India* 67 H15
Gomotartsi, *Bulgaria* 40 B6
Gompa = Ganta, *Liberia* 82 D3
Gomphi, *Greece* 38 B3
Gonābād, *Iran* 71 C8
Gonaïves, *Haiti* 121 C5
Gonâve, G. de la, *Haiti* 121 C5
Gonâve, I. de la, *Haiti* 121 C5
Gonbad-e Kāvūs, *Iran* 71 B7
Gönc, *Hungary* 42 B6
Gonda, *India* 69 F9
Gondal, *India* 68 J4
Gonder, *Ethiopia* 81 E4
Gonder □, *Ethiopia* 81 E4
Gondia, *India* 66 J12
Gondola, *Mozam.* 87 F3
Gondomar, *Portugal* 34 D2
Gondrecourt-le-Château, *France* 19 D12
Gönen, *Balıkesir, Turkey* 41 F11
Gönen, *Isparta, Turkey* 39 D12
Gönen →, *Turkey* 41 F11
Gong Xian, *China* 58 C5
Gong'an, *China* 59 B9
Gongcheng, *China* 59 E8
Gongga Shan, *China* 58 C3
Gongguan, *China* 58 G7
Gonghe, *China* 60 C5
Gongola →, *Nigeria* 83 D7
Gongolgon, *Australia* 95 E4
Gongshan, *China* 58 D2
Gongtan, *China* 58 C7
Gongzhuling, *China* 57 C13
Goniadz, *Poland* 44 E9
Goniri, *Nigeria* 83 C7
Gonjo, *China* 58 B2
Gonnesa, *Italy* 30 C1
Gónnos, *Greece* 38 B4
Gonnosfanádiga, *Italy* 30 C1
Gonzaga, *Phil.* 61 B5
Gonzales, *Calif., U.S.A.* 116 J5
Gonzales, *Tex., U.S.A.* 113 L6
González Chaves, *Argentina* 126 D3
Good Hope, C. of, *S. Africa* 88 E2
Gooderham, *Canada* 110 B6
Goodhouse, *S. Africa* 88 D2
Gooding, *U.S.A.* 114 E6
Goodland, *U.S.A.* 112 F4
Goodlow, *Canada* 104 B4
Goodooga, *Australia* 95 D4
Goodsprings, *U.S.A.* 117 K11
Goole, *U.K.* 12 D7
Goolgowi, *Australia* 95 E4
Goomalling, *Australia* 93 F2
Goomeri, *Australia* 95 D5
Goonda, *Mozam.* 87 F3
Goondiwindi, *Australia* 95 D5
Goongarrie, L., *Australia* 93 F3
Goonyella, *Australia* 94 C4
Goose →, *Canada* 103 B7
Goose Creek, *U.S.A.* 109 J5
Goose L., *U.S.A.* 114 F3
Gop, *India* 66 H6
Gopalganj, *India* 69 F11
Göppingen, *Germany* 25 G5
Gor, *Spain* 35 H8
Góra, *Dolnośląskie, Poland* 45 G3
Góra, *Mazowieckie, Poland* 45 F7
Góra Kalwaria, *Poland* 45 G8
Gorakhpur, *India* 69 F10
Goražde, *Bos.-H.* 42 G3
Gorbatov, *Russia* 48 B6
Gorbea, Peña, *Spain* 32 B2
Gorda, *U.S.A.* 116 K5
Gorda, Pta., *Canary Is.* 37 F2
Gorda, Pta., *Nic.* 120 D3
Gordan B., *Australia* 92 B5
Gördes, *Turkey* 39 C10
Gordon, *U.S.A.* 112 D3
Gordon →, *Australia* 94 G4
Gordon L., *Alta., Canada* 105 B6
Gordon L., *N.W.T., Canada* 104 A6
Gordonvale, *Australia* 94 B4
Gore, *Ethiopia* 81 F4
Gore, *N.Z.* 91 M2
Gore Bay, *Canada* 102 C3
Görele, *Turkey* 73 B8
Goreme, *Turkey* 72 C6
Gorey, *Ireland* 15 D5
Gorg, *Iran* 71 D8
Gorgān, *Iran* 71 B7
Gorgona, *Italy* 28 E6
Gorgona, I., *Colombia* 124 C3
Gorgora, *Ethiopia* 81 E4
Gorgoram, *Nigeria* 83 C7
Gorham, *U.S.A.* 111 B13
Gori, *Georgia* 49 J7
Goriganga →, *India* 69 E9
Gorinchem, *Neths.* 17 C4
Goris, *Armenia* 73 C12
Goritsy, *Russia* 46 D9
Gorízia, *Italy* 29 C10
Gorj □, *Romania* 43 E8
Gorki = Horki, *Belarus* 46 E6
Gorki = Nizhniy Novgorod, *Russia* 48 B7
Gorkiy = Nizhniy Novgorod, *Russia* 48 B7
Gorkovskoye Vdkhr., *Russia* 48 B6
Gorlice, *Poland* 45 J8
Görlitz, *Germany* 24 D10
Gorlovka = Horlivka, *Ukraine* 47 H10
Gorman, *U.S.A.* 117 L8
Gorna Dzhumayo = Blagoevgrad, *Bulgaria* 40 D7
Gorna Oryakhovitsa, *Bulgaria* 41 C9
Gornja Radgona, *Slovenia* 29 B13
Gornja Tuzla, *Bos.-H.* 42 F3
Gornji Grad, *Slovenia* 29 B11
Gornji Milanovac, *Serbia, Yug.* 40 B4
Gornji Vakuf, *Bos.-H.* 42 G2
Gorno Ablanovo, *Bulgaria* 41 C9
Gorno-Altay □, *Russia* 50 D9
Gorno-Altaysk, *Russia* 50 D9
Gornyatskiy, *Russia* 49 F5
Gornyy, *Saratov, Russia* 48 E9
Gornyy, *Sib., Russia* 54 B6
Gorodenka = Horodenka, *Ukraine* 47 H3
Gorodets, *Russia* 48 B6
Gorodishche = Horodyshche, *Ukraine* 47 H6
Gorodishche, *Russia* 48 D7
Gorodnya = Horodnya, *Ukraine* 47 G6
Gorodok = Haradok, *Belarus* 46 E6
Gorodok = Horodok, *Ukraine* 47 H2
Gorodovikovsk, *Russia* 49 G5
Gorokhov = Horokhiv, *Ukraine* 47 G3
Gorokhovets, *Russia* 48 B6
Gorom Gorom, *Burkina Faso* 83 C4
Goromonzi, *Zimbabwe* 87 F3
Gorong, Kepulauan, *Indonesia* 63 E8
Gorongose →, *Mozam.* 89 C5
Gorongoza, *Mozam.* 87 F3
Gorongoza, Sa. da, *Mozam.* 87 F3
Gorontalo, *Indonesia* 63 D6
Goronyo, *Nigeria* 83 C6
Górowo Iławeckie, *Poland* 44 D7
Gorron, *France* 18 D6
Gorshechnoye, *Russia* 47 G10
Gort, *Ireland* 15 C3
Gortis, *Greece* 36 D6
Góry Bystrzyckie, *Poland* 45 H3
Goryachiy Klyuch, *Russia* 49 H4
Gorzkowice, *Poland* 45 G6
Górzno, *Poland* 45 E6
Gorzów Śląski, *Poland* 45 G5
Gorzów Wielkopolski, *Poland* 45 F2
Gosford, *Australia* 95 E5
Goshen, *Calif., U.S.A.* 116 J7
Goshen, *Ind., U.S.A.* 108 E3
Goshen, *N.Y., U.S.A.* 111 E10
Goshogawara, *Japan* 54 D10
Goslar, *Germany* 24 D6
Gospič, *Croatia* 29 D12
Gosport, *U.K.* 13 G6
Gossas, *Senegal* 82 C1
Gosse →, *Australia* 94 B1
Gossi, *Mali* 83 B4
Gossinga, *Sudan* 81 F2
Gostivar, *Macedonia* 40 E4
Gostyń, *Poland* 45 G4
Gostynin, *Poland* 45 F6
Göta älv →, *Sweden* 11 G5
Göta kanal, *Sweden* 11 F9
Götaland, *Sweden* 11 G8
Göteborg, *Sweden* 11 G5
Götene, *Sweden* 11 F7
Goteşti, *Moldova* 43 D13
Gotha, *Germany* 24 E6
Gothenburg = Göteborg, *Sweden* 11 G5
Gothenburg, *U.S.A.* 112 E4
Gothèye, *Niger* 83 C5
Gotland, *Sweden* 11 G12
Gotlands län □, *Sweden* 11 G12
Gotō-Rettō, *Japan* 55 H4
Gotse Delchev, *Bulgaria* 40 E7
Gotska Sandön, *Sweden* 9 G18
Gōtsu, *Japan* 55 G6
Gott Pk., *Canada* 104 C4
Góttero, Monte, *Italy* 28 D6
Göttingen, *Germany* 24 D5
Gottwald = Zmiyev, *Ukraine* 47 H9
Gottwaldov = Zlín, *Czech Rep.* 27 B10
Goubangzi, *China* 57 D11
Gouda, *Neths.* 17 B4
Goúdhoura, Ákra, *Greece* 36 E8
Goudiry, *Senegal* 82 C2
Goudoumaria, *Niger* 83 C7
Gouéké, *Guinea* 82 D3
Gough I., *Atl. Oc.* 2 G9
Gouin, Rés., *Canada* 102 C5
Gouitafla, *Ivory C.* 82 D3
Goulburn, *Australia* 95 E4
Goulburn Is., *Australia* 94 A1
Goulia, *Ivory C.* 82 C3
Goulimine, *Morocco* 78 C3
Goumbou, *Mali* 82 B3
Gouménissa, *Greece* 40 F6
Goundam, *Mali* 82 B4
Goúra, *Greece* 38 D4
Gourbassi, *Mali* 82 C2
Gourdon, *France* 20 D5
Gouré, *Niger* 83 C7
Gourin, *France* 18 D3
Gourits →, *S. Africa* 88 E3
Gourma-Rharous, *Mali* 83 B4
Goúrnais, *Greece* 36 D7
Gournay-en-Bray, *France* 19 C8
Goursi, *Burkina Faso* 82 C4
Gouverneur, *U.S.A.* 111 B9
Gouviá, *Greece* 36 A3
Gouzon, *France* 19 F9
Governador Valadares, *Brazil* 125 G10
Governor's Harbour, *Bahamas* 120 A4
Govindgarh, *India* 69 G9
Gowan Ra., *Australia* 94 D4
Gowanda, *U.S.A.* 110 D6
Gower, *U.K.* 13 F3
Gowna, L., *Ireland* 15 C4
Goya, *Argentina* 126 B4
Göyçay, *Azerbaijan* 49 K8
Goyder Lagoon, *Australia* 95 D2
Goyllarisquisga, *Peru* 124 F3
Göynük, *Antalya, Turkey* 39 E12
Göynük, *Bolu, Turkey* 72 B4
Goz Beïda, *Chad* 79 F10
Goz Regeb, *Sudan* 81 D4
Gozdnica, *Poland* 45 G2
Gozo, *Malta* 36 C1
Graaff-Reinet, *S. Africa* 88 E3
Grabo, *Ivory C.* 82 D3
Grabow, *Germany* 24 B7
Grabów nad Prosną, *Poland* 45 G5
Gračac, *Croatia* 29 D12
Gračanica, *Bos.-H.* 42 F3
Graçay, *France* 19 E8
Gracias a Dios, C., *Honduras* 120 D3
Graciosa, I., *Canary Is.* 37 E6
Grad Sofiya □, *Bulgaria* 40 D7
Gradac, *Montenegro, Yug.* 40 C3
Gradačac, *Bos.-H.* 42 F3
Gradeška Planina, *Macedonia* 40 E6
Gradets, *Bulgaria* 41 D10
Gradišče, *Slovenia* 29 B12
Grădiştea de Munte, *Romania* 43 E8
Grado, *Italy* 29 C10
Grado, *Spain* 34 B4
Grady, *U.S.A.* 113 H3
Graeca, Lacul, *Romania* 43 F11
Grafenau, *Germany* 25 G9
Gräfenberg, *Germany* 25 F7
Grafham Water, *U.K.* 13 E7
Grafton, *Australia* 95 D5
Grafton, *N. Dak., U.S.A.* 112 A6
Grafton, *W. Va., U.S.A.* 108 F5
Graham, *Canada* 102 C1
Graham, *U.S.A.* 113 J5
Graham, Mt., *U.S.A.* 115 K9
Graham Bell, Ostrov = Greem-Bell, Ostrov, *Russia* 50 A7
Graham I., *Canada* 104 C2
Graham Land, *Antarctica* 5 C17
Grahamstown, *S. Africa* 88 E4
Grahamsville, *U.S.A.* 111 E10
Grahovo, *Montenegro, Yug.* 40 D2
Graie, Alpi, *Europe* 21 C11
Grain Coast, *W. Afr.* 82 E3
Grajaú, *Brazil* 125 E9
Grajaú →, *Brazil* 125 D10
Grajewo, *Poland* 44 E9
Gramada, *Bulgaria* 40 C6
Gramat, *France* 20 D5
Grammichele, *Italy* 31 E7
Grámmos, Óros, *Greece* 40 F4
Grampian, *U.S.A.* 110 F6
Grampian Highlands = Grampian Mts., *U.K.* 14 E5
Grampian Mts., *U.K.* 14 E5
Grampians, The, *Australia* 95 F3
Gramsh, *Albania* 40 F4
Gran Canaria, *Canary Is.* 37 G4
Gran Chaco, *S. Amer.* 126 B3

Gran Paradiso, *Italy* 28 C4
Gran Sasso d'Itália, *Italy* 29 F10
Granada, *Nic.* 120 D2
Granada, *Spain* 35 H7
Granada, *U.S.A.* 113 F3
Granada □, *Spain* 35 H7
Granadilla de Abona, *Canary Is.* 37 F3
Granard, *Ireland* 15 C4
Granbury, *U.S.A.* 113 J6
Granby, *Canada* 102 C5
Granby, *U.S.A.* 114 F11
Grand →, *Canada* 110 D5
Grand →, *Mo., U.S.A.* 112 F8
Grand →, *S. Dak., U.S.A.* 112 C4
Grand Bahama, *Bahamas* 120 A4
Grand Bank, *Canada* 103 C8
Grand Bassam, *Ivory C.* 82 D4
Grand Béréby, *Ivory C.* 82 E3
Grand-Bourg, *Guadeloupe* 121 C7
Grand Canal = Yun Ho →, *China* 57 E9
Grand Canyon, *U.S.A.* 115 H7
Grand Canyon National Park, *U.S.A.* 115 H7
Grand Cayman, *Cayman Is.* 120 C3
Grand Centre, *Canada* 105 C6
Grand Cess, *Liberia* 82 E3
Grand Coulee, *U.S.A.* 114 C4
Grand Coulee Dam, *U.S.A.* 114 C4
Grand Erg Occidental, *Algeria* 78 B6
Grand Erg Oriental, *Algeria* 78 B7
Grand Falls, *Canada* 103 C6
Grand Falls-Windsor, *Canada* 103 C8
Grand Forks, *Canada* 104 D5
Grand Forks, *U.S.A.* 112 B6
Grand Gorge, *U.S.A.* 111 D10
Grand Haven, *U.S.A.* 108 D2
Grand I., *Mich., U.S.A.* 108 B2
Grand I., *N.Y., U.S.A.* 110 D6
Grand Island, *U.S.A.* 112 E5
Grand Isle, *La., U.S.A.* 113 L9
Grand Isle, *Vt., U.S.A.* 111 B11
Grand Junction, *U.S.A.* 115 G9
Grand L., *N.B., Canada* 103 C6
Grand L., *Nfld., Canada* 103 C8
Grand L., *Nfld., Canada* 103 B7
Grand L., *U.S.A.* 113 L8
Grand Lahou, *Ivory C.* 82 D3
Grand Lake, *U.S.A.* 114 F11
Grand-Lieu, L. de, *France* 18 E5
Grand Manan I., *Canada* 103 D6
Grand Marais, *Canada* 112 B9
Grand Marais, *U.S.A.* 108 B3
Grand-Mère, *Canada* 102 C5
Grand Popo, *Benin* 83 D5
Grand Portage, *U.S.A.* 112 B10
Grand Prairie, *U.S.A.* 113 J6
Grand Rapids, *Canada* 105 C9
Grand Rapids, *Mich., U.S.A.* 108 D2
Grand Rapids, *Minn., U.S.A.* 112 B8
Grand St-Bernard, Col du, *Europe* 25 K3
Grand Teton, *U.S.A.* 114 E8
Grand Teton National Park, *U.S.A.* 114 D8
Grand Union Canal, *U.K.* 13 E7
Grand View, *Canada* 105 C8
Grandas de Salime, *Spain* 34 B4
Grande →, *Jujuy, Argentina* 126 A2
Grande →, *Mendoza, Argentina* 126 D2
Grande →, *Bolivia* 124 G6
Grande →, *Bahia, Brazil* 125 F10
Grande →, *Minas Gerais, Brazil* 125 H8
Grande, B., *Argentina* 128 G3
Grande, Rio →, *U.S.A.* 113 N6
Grande Baleine, R. de la →, *Canada* 102 A4
Grande Cache, *Canada* 104 C5
Grande-Entrée, *Canada* 103 C7
Grande Prairie, *Canada* 104 B5
Grande-Rivière, *Canada* 103 C7
Grande-Vallée, *Canada* 103 C6
Grandfalls, *U.S.A.* 113 K3
Grândola, *Portugal* 35 G2
Grandpré, *France* 19 C11
Grandview, *U.S.A.* 114 C4
Grandvilliers, *France* 19 C8
Graneros, *Chile* 126 C1
Grangemouth, *U.K.* 14 E5
Granger, *U.S.A.* 114 F9
Grängesberg, *Sweden* 10 D9
Grangeville, *U.S.A.* 114 D5
Granisle, *Canada* 104 C3
Granite City, *U.S.A.* 112 F9
Granite Falls, *U.S.A.* 112 C7
Granite L., *Canada* 103 C8
Granite Mt., *U.S.A.* 117 M10
Granite Pk., *U.S.A.* 114 D9
Graniteville, *U.S.A.* 111 B12
Granitola, C., *Italy* 30 E5
Granity, *N.Z.* 91 J3
Granja, *Brazil* 125 D10
Granja de Moreruela, *Spain* 34 D5
Granja de Torrehermosa, *Spain* 35 G5
Gränna, *Sweden* 11 F8
Granollers, *Spain* 32 D7
Gransee, *Germany* 24 B9
Grant, *U.S.A.* 112 E4
Grant, Mt., *U.S.A.* 114 G4
Grant City, *U.S.A.* 112 E7
Grant I., *Australia* 92 B5
Grant Range, *U.S.A.* 115 G6
Grantham, *U.K.* 12 E7
Grantown-on-Spey, *U.K.* 14 D5
Grants, *U.S.A.* 115 J10
Grants Pass, *U.S.A.* 114 E2
Grantsville, *U.S.A.* 114 F7
Granville, *France* 18 D5
Granville, *N. Dak., U.S.A.* 112 A4
Granville, *N.Y., U.S.A.* 111 C11
Granville, *Ohio, U.S.A.* 110 F2
Granville L., *Canada* 105 B8
Graskop, *S. Africa* 89 C5
Gräsö, *Sweden* 10 D12
Grass →, *Canada* 105 B9
Grass Range, *U.S.A.* 114 C9
Grass River Prov. Park, *Canada* 105 C8
Grass Valley, *Calif., U.S.A.* 116 F6
Grass Valley, *Oreg., U.S.A.* 114 D3
Grassano, *Italy* 31 B9
Grasse, *France* 21 E10
Grassflat, *U.S.A.* 110 F6
Grasslands Nat. Park, *Canada* 105 D7
Grassy, *Australia* 94 G3
Gråsten, *Denmark* 11 K3
Grästorp, *Sweden* 11 F6
Gratkorn, *Austria* 26 D8
Graubünden □, *Switz.* 25 J5
Graulhet, *France* 20 E5
Graus, *Spain* 32 C5
Grave, Pte. de, *France* 20 C2
Gravelbourg, *Canada* 105 D7
Gravelines, *France* 19 A9
's-Gravenhage, *Neths.* 17 B4
Gravenhurst, *Canada* 102 D4
Gravesend, *Australia* 95 D5
Gravesend, *U.K.* 13 F8
Gravina in Púglia, *Italy* 31 B9
Gravois, Pointe-à-, *Haiti* 121 C5
Gravone →, *France* 21 G12
Gray, *France* 19 E12
Grayling, *U.S.A.* 108 C3
Grays Harbor, *U.S.A.* 114 C1
Grays L., *U.S.A.* 114 E8
Grays River, *U.S.A.* 116 D3
Grayvoron, *Russia* 47 G8
Graz, *Austria* 26 D8
Grdelica, *Serbia, Yug.* 40 D6
Greasy L., *Canada* 104 A4
Great Abaco I., *Bahamas* 120 A4
Great Artesian Basin, *Australia* 94 C3
Great Australian Bight, *Australia* 93 F5
Great Bahama Bank, *Bahamas* 120 B4
Great Barrier I., *N.Z.* 91 G5
Great Barrier Reef, *Australia* 94 B4
Great Barrington, *U.S.A.* 111 D11
Great Basin, *U.S.A.* 114 G5
Great Basin Nat. Park, *U.S.A.* 114 G6
Great Bear →, *Canada* 100 B7
Great Bear L., *Canada* 100 B7
Great Belt = Store Bælt, *Denmark* 11 J4
Great Bend, *Kans., U.S.A.* 112 F5
Great Bend, *Pa., U.S.A.* 111 E9
Great Blasket I., *Ireland* 15 D1
Great Britain, *Europe* 6 E5
Great Codroy, *Canada* 103 C8
Great Dividing Ra., *Australia* 94 C4
Great Driffield = Driffield, *U.K.* 12 C7
Great Exuma I., *Bahamas* 120 B4
Great Falls, *U.S.A.* 114 C8
Great Fish = Groot Vis →, *S. Africa* 88 E4
Great Guana Cay, *Bahamas* 120 B4
Great Inagua I., *Bahamas* 121 B5
Great Indian Desert = Thar Desert, *India* 68 F5
Great Karoo, *S. Africa* 88 E3
Great Lake, *Australia* 94 G4
Great Lakes, *N. Amer.* 98 E11
Great Malvern, *U.K.* 13 E5
Great Miami →, *U.S.A.* 108 F3
Great Ormes Head, *U.K.* 12 D4
Great Ouse →, *U.K.* 12 E8
Great Palm I., *Australia* 94 B4
Great Plains, *N. Amer.* 106 A6
Great Ruaha →, *Tanzania* 86 D4
Great Sacandaga Res., *U.S.A.* 111 C10
Great Saint Bernard Pass = Grand St-Bernard, Col du, *Europe* 25 K3
Great Salt L., *U.S.A.* 114 F7
Great Salt Lake Desert, *U.S.A.* 114 F7
Great Salt Plains L., *U.S.A.* 113 G5
Great Sandy Desert, *Australia* 92 D3
Great Sangi = Sangihe, Pulau, *Indonesia* 63 D7
Great Scarcies →, *S. Leone* 82 D2
Great Skellig, *Ireland* 15 E1
Great Slave L., *Canada* 104 A5
Great Smoky Mts. Nat. Park, *U.S.A.* 109 H4
Great Snow Mt., *Canada* 104 B4
Great Stour = Stour →, *U.K.* 13 F9
Great Victoria Desert, *Australia* 93 E4
Great Wall, *China* 56 E5
Great Whernside, *U.K.* 12 C6
Great Yarmouth, *U.K.* 13 E9
Greater Antilles, *W. Indies* 121 C5
Greater London □, *U.K.* 13 F7
Greater Manchester □, *U.K.* 12 D5
Greater Sunda Is., *Indonesia* 62 F4
Grebbestad, *Sweden* 11 F5
Grebenka = Hrebenka, *Ukraine* 47 G7
Greco, C., *Cyprus* 36 E13
Greco, Mte., *Italy* 29 G10
Gredos, Sierra de, *Spain* 34 E6
Greece, *U.S.A.* 110 C7
Greece ■, *Europe* 38 B3
Greeley, *Colo., U.S.A.* 112 E2
Greeley, *Nebr., U.S.A.* 112 E5
Greem-Bell, Ostrov, *Russia* 50 A7
Green, *U.S.A.* 114 E2
Green →, *Ky., U.S.A.* 108 G2
Green →, *Utah, U.S.A.* 115 G9
Green B., *U.S.A.* 108 C2
Green Bay, *U.S.A.* 108 C2
Green C., *Australia* 95 F5
Green Cove Springs, *U.S.A.* 109 L5
Green Lake, *Canada* 105 C7
Green Mts., *U.S.A.* 111 C12
Green River, *Utah, U.S.A.* 115 G8
Green River, *Wyo., U.S.A.* 114 F9
Green Valley, *U.S.A.* 115 L8
Greenbank, *U.S.A.* 116 B4
Greenbush, *Mich., U.S.A.* 110 B1
Greenbush, *Minn., U.S.A.* 112 A6
Greencastle, *U.S.A.* 108 F2
Greene, *U.S.A.* 111 D9
Greenfield, *Calif., U.S.A.* 116 J5
Greenfield, *Calif., U.S.A.* 117 K8
Greenfield, *Ind., U.S.A.* 108 F3
Greenfield, *Iowa, U.S.A.* 112 E7
Greenfield, *Mass., U.S.A.* 111 D12
Greenfield, *Mo., U.S.A.* 113 G8
Greenfield Park, *Canada* 111 A11
Greenland ■, *N. Amer.* 4 C5
Greenland Sea, *Arctic* 4 B7
Greenock, *U.K.* 14 F4
Greenore, *Ireland* 15 B5
Greenore Pt., *Ireland* 15 D5
Greenough, *Australia* 93 E1
Greenough →, *Australia* 93 E1
Greenough Pt., *Canada* 110 B3
Greenport, *U.S.A.* 111 E12
Greensboro, *Ga., U.S.A.* 109 J4
Greensboro, *N.C., U.S.A.* 109 G6
Greensboro, *Vt., U.S.A.* 111 B12
Greensburg, *Ind., U.S.A.* 108 F3
Greensburg, *Kans., U.S.A.* 113 G5
Greensburg, *Pa., U.S.A.* 110 F5
Greenstone Pt., *U.K.* 14 D3
Greenvale, *Australia* 94 B4
Greenville, *Liberia* 82 D3
Greenville, *Ala., U.S.A.* 109 K2
Greenville, *Calif., U.S.A.* 116 E6
Greenville, *Maine, U.S.A.* 109 C11
Greenville, *Mich., U.S.A.* 108 D3
Greenville, *Miss., U.S.A.* 113 J9
Greenville, *Mo., U.S.A.* 113 G9
Greenville, *N.C., U.S.A.* 109 H7
Greenville, *N.H., U.S.A.* 111 D13
Greenville, *N.Y., U.S.A.* 111 D10
Greenville, *Ohio, U.S.A.* 108 E3
Greenville, *Pa., U.S.A.* 110 E4
Greenville, *S.C., U.S.A.* 109 H4
Greenville, *Tenn., U.S.A.* 109 G4
Greenville, *Tex., U.S.A.* 113 J6
Greenwater Lake Prov. Park, *Canada* 105 C8
Greenwich, *Conn., U.S.A.* 111 E11
Greenwich, *N.Y., U.S.A.* 111 C11
Greenwich, *Ohio, U.S.A.* 110 E2
Greenwich □, *U.K.* 13 F8
Greenwood, *Canada* 104 D5
Greenwood, *Ark., U.S.A.* 113 H7
Greenwood, *Ind., U.S.A.* 108 F2
Greenwood, *Miss., U.S.A.* 113 J9
Greenwood, *S.C., U.S.A.* 109 H4
Greenwood, Mt., *Australia* 92 B5
Gregbe, *Ivory C.* 82 D3
Gregory, *U.S.A.* 112 D5
Gregory →, *Australia* 94 B2
Gregory, L., *S. Austral., Australia* 95 D2
Gregory, L., *W. Austral., Australia* 93 E2
Gregory Downs, *Australia* 94 B2
Gregory L., *Australia* 92 D4
Gregory Ra., *Queens., Australia* 94 B3
Gregory Ra., *W. Austral., Australia* 92 D3
Greiffenberg, *Germany* 24 B9
Greifswald, *Germany* 24 A9
Greifswalder Bodden, *Germany* 24 A9
Grein, *Austria* 26 C7
Greiz, *Germany* 24 E8
Gremikha, *Russia* 50 C4
Grenå, *Denmark* 11 H4
Grenada, *U.S.A.* 113 J10
Grenada ■, *W. Indies* 121 D7
Grenade, *France* 20 E5
Grenadier I., *U.S.A.* 111 B8
Grenadines, *St. Vincent* 121 D7
Grenchen, *Switz.* 25 H3
Grenen, *Denmark* 11 G4
Grenfell, *Australia* 95 E4
Grenfell, *Canada* 105 C8
Grenoble, *France* 21 C9
Grenville, C., *Australia* 94 A3
Grenville Chan., *Canada* 104 C3
Gréoux-les-Bains, *France* 21 E9
Gresham, *U.S.A.* 116 E4
Gresik, *Indonesia* 63 G15
Gretna, *U.K.* 14 F5
Greven, *Germany* 24 C3
Grevená, *Greece* 40 F5
Grevená □, *Greece* 40 F5
Grevenbroich, *Germany* 24 D2
Grevenmacher, *Lux.* 17 E6
Grevesmühlen, *Germany* 24 B7
Grevestrand, *Denmark* 11 J6
Grey →, *Canada* 103 C8
Grey →, *N.Z.* 91 K3
Grey, C., *Australia* 94 A2
Grey Ra., *Australia* 95 D3
Greybull, *U.S.A.* 114 D9
Greymouth, *N.Z.* 91 K3
Greystones, *Ireland* 15 C5
Greytown, *N.Z.* 91 J5
Greytown, *S. Africa* 89 D5
Gribanovskiy, *Russia* 48 E5
Gribbell I., *Canada* 104 C3
Gribës, Mal i, *Albania* 40 F3
Gridley, *U.S.A.* 116 F5
Griekwastad, *S. Africa* 88 D3
Griesheim, *Germany* 25 F4
Grieskirchen, *Austria* 26 C6
Griffin, *U.S.A.* 109 J3
Griffith, *Australia* 95 E4
Griffith, *Canada* 110 A7
Griffith I., *Canada* 110 B4
Grignols, *France* 20 D3
Grigoriopol, *Moldova* 43 C14
Grimaylov = Hrymayliv, *Ukraine* 47 H4
Grimes, *U.S.A.* 116 F5
Grimma, *Germany* 24 D8
Grimmen, *Germany* 24 A9
Grimsay, *U.K.* 14 D1
Grimsby, *Canada* 110 C5
Grimsby, *U.K.* 12 D7
Grímsey, *Iceland* 8 C5
Grimshaw, *Canada* 104 B5
Grimslöv, *Sweden* 11 H8
Grimstad, *Norway* 9 G13
Grindelwald, *Switz.* 25 J4
Grindsted, *Denmark* 11 J2
Grindstone I., *Canada* 111 B8
Grindu, *Romania* 43 F11
Grinnell, *U.S.A.* 112 E8
Grintavec, *Slovenia* 29 B11
Gris-Nez, C., *France* 19 B8
Grisolles, *France* 20 E5
Grisons = Graubünden □, *Switz.* 25 J5
Grisslehamn, *Sweden* 10 D12
Grmeč Planina, *Bos.-H.* 29 D13
Groais I., *Canada* 103 B8
Grobiņa, *Latvia* 44 B8
Groblersdal, *S. Africa* 89 D4
Grobming, *Austria* 26 D6
Grocka, *Serbia, Yug.* 40 B4
Gródek, *Poland* 45 E10
Grodków, *Poland* 45 H4
Grodno = Hrodna, *Belarus* 46 F2
Grodzisk Mazowiecki, *Poland* 45 F7
Grodzisk Wielkopolski, *Poland* 45 F3
Grodzyanka = Hrodzyanka, *Belarus* 46 F5
Groesbeck, *U.S.A.* 113 K6
Groix, *France* 18 E3
Groix, Î. de, *France* 18 E3
Grójec, *Poland* 45 G7
Gronau, *Niedersachsen, Germany* 24 C5
Gronau, *Nordrhein-Westfalen, Germany* 24 C3
Grong, *Norway* 8 D15
Grönhögen, *Sweden* 11 H10
Groningen, *Neths.* 17 A6
Groningen □, *Neths.* 17 A6
Groom, *U.S.A.* 113 H4
Groot →, *S. Africa* 88 E3
Groot Berg →, *S. Africa* 88 E2
Groot-Brakrivier, *S. Africa* 88 E3
Groot Karasberge, *Namibia* 88 D2
Groot-Kei →, *S. Africa* 89 E4
Groot Vis →, *S. Africa* 88 E4
Grootdrink, *S. Africa* 88 D3
Groote Eylandt, *Australia* 94 A2
Grootfontein, *Namibia* 88 B2
Grootlaagte →, *Africa* 88 C3
Grootvloer →, *S. Africa* 88 E3
Gros C., *Canada* 104 A6
Gros Morne Nat. Park, *Canada* 103 C8
Grósio, *Italy* 28 B7
Grosne →, *France* 19 F11
Grossa, Pta., *Spain* 37 B8
Grossenbrode, *Germany* 24 A7
Grossenhain, *Germany* 24 D9
Grosser Arber, *Germany* 25 F9
Grosser Plöner See, *Germany* 24 A6
Grosseto, *Italy* 29 F8
Grossgerungs, *Austria* 26 C7
Grossglockner, *Austria* 26 D5
Groswater B., *Canada* 103 B8
Groton, *Conn., U.S.A.* 111 E12
Groton, *N.Y., U.S.A.* 111 D8
Groton, *S. Dak., U.S.A.* 112 C5
Grottáglie, *Italy* 31 B10
Grottaminarda, *Italy* 31 A8
Grottammare, *Italy* 29 F10
Grouard Mission, *Canada* 104 B5
Grouin, Pte. du, *France* 18 D5
Groundhog →, *Canada* 102 C3
Grouw, *Neths.* 17 A5
Grove City, *U.S.A.* 110 E4
Grove Hill, *U.S.A.* 109 K2
Groveland, *U.S.A.* 116 H6
Grover City, *U.S.A.* 117 K6
Groves, *U.S.A.* 113 L8
Groveton, *U.S.A.* 111 B13
Grožnjan, *Croatia* 29 C10
Groznyy, *Russia* 49 J7
Grubišno Polje, *Croatia* 42 E2
Grudovo, *Bulgaria* 41 D11
Grudusk, *Poland* 45 E7
Grudziądz, *Poland* 44 E5
Gruinard B., *U.K.* 14 D3
Gruissan, *France* 20 E7
Grumo Áppula, *Italy* 31 A9
Grums, *Sweden* 10 E7
Grünberg, *Germany* 24 E4
Gründau, *Germany* 25 E5
Grundy Center, *U.S.A.* 112 D8
Grünstadt, *Germany* 25 F4
Gruvberget, *Sweden* 10 C10
Gruver, *U.S.A.* 113 G4
Gruyères, *Switz.* 25 J3
Gruža, *Serbia, Yug.* 40 C4
Gryazi, *Russia* 47 F10
Gryazovets, *Russia* 46 C11
Grybów, *Poland* 45 J7
Grycksbo, *Sweden* 10 D9
Gryfice, *Poland* 44 E2
Gryfino, *Poland* 45 E1
Gryfów Śląski, *Poland* 45 G2
Grythyttan, *Sweden* 10 E8
Gstaad, *Switz.* 25 J3
Gua, *India* 67 H14
Gua Musang, *Malaysia* 65 K3
Guacanayabo, G. de, *Cuba* 120 B4
Guachípas →, *Argentina* 126 B2
Guadajoz →, *Spain* 35 H6
Guadalajara, *Mexico* 118 C4
Guadalajara, *Spain* 32 E1
Guadalajara □, *Spain* 32 E2
Guadalcanal, *Solomon Is.* 96 H8
Guadalcanal, *Spain* 35 G5
Guadalén →, *Spain* 35 G7
Guadales, *Argentina* 126 C2
Guadalete →, *Spain* 35 J4
Guadalimar →, *Spain* 35 G7
Guadalmena →, *Spain* 35 G8
Guadalmez →, *Spain* 35 G5
Guadalope →, *Spain* 32 D4
Guadalquivir →, *Spain* 35 J4
Guadalupe = Guadeloupe ■, *W. Indies* 121 C7
Guadalupe, *Mexico* 117 N10
Guadalupe, *Spain* 35 F5
Guadalupe, *U.S.A.* 117 L6
Guadalupe →, *Mexico* 117 N10
Guadalupe →, *U.S.A.* 113 L6
Guadalupe, Sierra de, *Spain* 35 F5
Guadalupe Bravos, *Mexico* 118 A3
Guadalupe I., *Pac. Oc.* 98 G8
Guadalupe Mts. Nat. Park, *U.S.A.* 113 K2
Guadalupe Peak, *U.S.A.* 113 K2
Guadalupe y Calvo, *Mexico* 118 B3
Guadarrama, Sierra de, *Spain* 34 E7
Guadauta, *Georgia* 49 J5
Guadeloupe ■, *W. Indies* 121 C7
Guadeloupe Passage, *W. Indies* 121 C7
Guadiamar →, *Spain* 35 J4
Guadiana →, *Portugal* 35 H3
Guadiana Menor →, *Spain* 35 H7
Guadiaro →, *Spain* 35 J5
Guadiato →, *Spain* 35 H5
Guadiela →, *Spain* 32 E2
Guadix, *Spain* 35 H7
Guafo, Boca del, *Chile* 128 E2
Guainía →, *Colombia* 124 C5
Guaíra, *Brazil* 127 A5
Guaíra □, *Paraguay* 126 B4
Guaitecas, Is., *Chile* 128 E2
Guajará-Mirim, *Brazil* 124 F5
Guajira, Pen. de la, *Colombia* 124 A4
Gualán, *Guatemala* 120 C2
Gualdo Tadino, *Italy* 29 E9
Gualeguay, *Argentina* 126 C4
Gualeguaychú, *Argentina* 126 C4
Gualequay →, *Argentina* 126 C4
Guam ■, *Pac. Oc.* 96 F6
Guaminí, *Argentina* 126 D3
Guamúchil, *Mexico* 118 B3
Guanabacoa, *Cuba* 120 B3
Guanacaste, Cordillera del, *Costa Rica* 120 D2
Guanaceví, *Mexico* 118 B3
Guanahani = San Salvador I., *Bahamas* 121 B5
Guanajay, *Cuba* 120 B3
Guanajuato, *Mexico* 118 C4
Guanajuato □, *Mexico* 118 C4
Guandacol, *Argentina* 126 B2
Guane, *Cuba* 120 B3
Guang'an, *China* 58 B6
Guangchang, *China* 59 D11
Guangde, *China* 59 B12
Guangdong □, *China* 59 F9
Guangfeng, *China* 59 C12
Guanghan, *China* 58 B5
Guangling, *China* 56 E8
Guangnan, *China* 58 E5
Guangning, *China* 59 F9
Guangrao, *China* 57 F10
Guangshui, *China* 59 B9
Guangshun, *China* 58 D6
Guangwu, *China* 56 F3
Guangxi Zhuangzu Zizhiqu □, *China* 58 F7
Guangyuan, *China* 58 A5
Guangze, *China* 59 D11
Guangzhou, *China* 59 F9
Guanipa →, *Venezuela* 124 B6
Guanling, *China* 58 E5
Guannan, *China* 57 G10
Guantánamo, *Cuba* 121 B4
Guantao, *China* 56 F8
Guanyang, *China* 59 E8
Guanyun, *China* 57 G10
Guápiles, *Costa Rica* 120 D3
Guaporé, *Brazil* 127 B5
Guaporé →, *Brazil* 122 E4
Guaqui, *Bolivia* 124 G5
Guara, Sierra de, *Spain* 32 C4
Guarapari, *Brazil* 127 A7
Guarapuava, *Brazil* 127 B5
Guaratinguetá, *Brazil* 127 A6
Guaratuba, *Brazil* 127 B6
Guarda, *Portugal* 34 E3
Guarda □, *Portugal* 34 E3
Guardafui, C. = Asir, Ras,

Somali Rep. 74 E5
Guardamar del Segura, *Spain* 33 G4
Guardavalle, *Italy* 31 D9
Guárdia Sanframondi, *Italy* 31 A7
Guardiagrele, *Italy* 29 F11
Guardo, *Spain* 34 C6
Guareña, *Spain* 35 G4
Guareña →, *Spain* 34 D5
Guárico □, *Venezuela* 124 B5
Guarujá, *Brazil* 127 A6
Guarus, *Brazil* 127 A7
Guasave, *Mexico* 118 B3
Guasdualito, *Venezuela* 124 B4
Guastalla, *Italy* 28 D7
Guatemala, *Guatemala* 120 D1
Guatemala ■, *Cent. Amer.* 120 C1
Guaviare →, *Colombia* 122 C4
Guaxupé, *Brazil* 127 A6
Guayama, *Puerto Rico* 121 C6
Guayaquil, *Ecuador* 124 D3
Guayaquil, G. de, *Ecuador* 122 D2
Guaymas, *Mexico* 118 B2
Guba, *Dem. Rep. of the Congo* 87 E2
Guba, *Ethiopia* 81 E4
Gûbâl, Madîq, *Egypt* 80 B3
Gubat, *Phil.* 61 E6
Gúbbio, *Italy* 29 E9
Guben, *Germany* 24 D10
Gubin, *Poland* 45 G1
Gubio, *Nigeria* 83 C7
Gubkin, *Russia* 47 G9
Guča, *Serbia, Yug.* 40 C4
Gucheng, *China* 59 A8
Gudata = Guadauta, *Georgia* 49 J5
Gudbrandsdalen, *Norway* 9 F14
Guddu Barrage, *Pakistan* 66 E6
Gudenå →, *Denmark* 11 H4
Gudermes, *Russia* 49 J8
Gudhjem, *Denmark* 11 J8
Gudur, *India* 66 M11
Guebwiller, *France* 19 E14
Guecho = Getxo, *Spain* 32 B2
Guékédou, *Guinea* 82 D2
Guéle Mendouka, *Cameroon* 83 E7
Guelph, *Canada* 102 D3
Guéméné-Penfao, *France* 18 E5
Guéméné-sur-Scorff, *France* 18 D3
Guéné, *Benin* 83 C5
Guer, *France* 18 E4
Guérande, *France* 18 E4
Guéret, *France* 19 F8
Guérigny, *France* 19 E10
Guerneville, *U.S.A.* 116 G4
Guernica = Gernika-Lumo, *Spain* 32 B2
Guernsey, *U.K.* 13 H5
Guernsey, *U.S.A.* 112 D2
Guerrero □, *Mexico* 119 D5
Guessou-Sud, *Benin* 83 C5
Gueugnon, *France* 19 F11
Guéyo, *Ivory C.* 82 D3
Gughe, *Ethiopia* 81 F4
Gügher, *Iran* 71 D8
Guglionesi, *Italy* 29 G11
Guhakolak, Tanjung, *Indonesia* 63 G11
Gui Jiang →, *China* 59 F8
Guia, *Canary Is.* 37 F4
Guia de Isora, *Canary Is.* 37 F3
Guia Lopes da Laguna, *Brazil* 127 A4
Guiana, *S. Amer.* 122 C4
Guibéroua, *Ivory C.* 82 D3
Guichi, *China* 59 B11
Guider, *Cameroon* 83 D7
Guidiguir, *Niger* 83 C6
Guidimouni, *Niger* 83 C6
Guiding, *China* 58 D6
Guidong, *China* 59 D9
Guidónia-Montecélio, *Italy* 29 F9
Guiers, L. de, *Senegal* 82 B1
Guigang, *China* 58 F7
Guiglo, *Ivory C.* 82 D3
Guihulñgan, *Phil.* 61 F5
Guijá, *Mozam.* 89 C5
Guijuelo, *Spain* 34 E5
Guildford, *U.K.* 13 F7
Guilford, *U.S.A.* 111 E12
Guilin, *China* 59 E8
Guillaume-Delisle L., *Canada* 102 A4
Guillaumes, *France* 21 D10
Guillestre, *France* 21 D10
Guilvinec, *France* 18 E2
Güimar, *Canary Is.* 37 F3
Guimarães, *Portugal* 34 D2
Guimaras □, *Phil.* 61 F5
Guinda, *U.S.A.* 116 G4
Guinea, *Africa* 76 F4
Guinea ■, *W. Afr.* 82 C2
Guinea, Gulf of, *Atl. Oc.* 83 E5
Guinea-Bissau ■, *Africa* 82 C2
Güines, *Cuba* 120 B3
Guingamp, *France* 18 D3
Guinguinéo, *Senegal* 82 C1
Guipavas, *France* 18 D2
Guiping, *China* 59 F8
Guipúzcoa □, *Spain* 32 B2
Guir, *Mali* 82 B4
Guirel, *Mauritania* 82 B3
Güiria, *Venezuela* 124 A6
Guiscard, *France* 19 C10
Guise, *France* 19 C10
Guitiriz, *Spain* 34 B3
Guitri, *Ivory C.* 82 D3
Guiuan, *Phil.* 61 F6
Guixi, *China* 59 C11
Guiyang, *Guizhou, China* 58 D6
Guiyang, *Hunan, China* 59 E9
Guizhou □, *China* 58 D6
Gujan-Mestras, *France* 20 D2
Gujar Khan, *Pakistan* 68 C5
Gujarat □, *India* 68 H4
Gujiang, *China* 59 D10
Gujranwala, *Pakistan* 68 C6
Gujrat, *Pakistan* 68 C6
Gukovo, *Russia* 49 F5
Gulbarga, *India* 66 L10
Gulbene, *Latvia* 9 H22
Gulf, The, *Asia* 71 E6
Gulfport, *U.S.A.* 113 K10
Gulgong, *Australia* 95 E4
Gulin, *China* 58 C5
Gulistan, *Pakistan* 68 D2
Gull Lake, *Canada* 105 C7
Gullbrandstorp, *Sweden* 11 H6
Gullspång, *Sweden* 11 F8
Güllük, *Turkey* 39 D9
Güllük Korfezi, *Turkey* 39 D9
Gulma, *Nigeria* 83 C5
Gulmarg, *India* 69 B6
Gülnar, *Turkey* 72 D5
Gülpınar, *Turkey* 39 B8
Gülşehir, *Turkey* 72 C6
Gulshad, *Kazakstan* 50 E8
Gulu, *Uganda* 86 B3
Gŭlŭbovo, *Bulgaria* 41 D9
Gulud, J., *Sudan* 81 E2
Gulwe, *Tanzania* 86 D4
Gulyaypole = Hulyaypole, *Ukraine* 47 J9
Gumal →, *Pakistan* 68 D4
Gumbaz, *Pakistan* 68 D3
Gumel, *Nigeria* 83 C6
Gumiel de Hizán, *Spain* 34 D7
Gumla, *India* 69 H11
Gumlu, *Australia* 94 B4
Gumma □, *Japan* 55 F9
Gummersbach, *Germany* 24 D3
Gummi, *Nigeria* 83 C6
Gümüldür, *Turkey* 39 C9
Gümüşçay, *Turkey* 41 F11
Gümüşhaciköy, *Turkey* 72 B6
Gümüşhane, *Turkey* 73 B8
Gümüşsu, *Turkey* 39 C11
Gumzai, *Indonesia* 63 F8
Guna, *Ethiopia* 81 F4
Guna, *India* 68 G7
Gundelfingen, *Germany* 25 G6
Güney, *Burdur, Turkey* 39 D11
Güney, *Denizli, Turkey* 39 C11
Güneydoğu Toroslar, *Turkey* 73 C9
Gunisao →, *Canada* 105 C9
Gunisao L., *Canada* 105 C9
Gunjyal, *Pakistan* 68 C4
Günlüce, *Turkey* 39 E10
Gunnarskog, *Sweden* 10 E6
Gunnbjørn Fjeld, *Greenland* 4 C6
Gunnebo, *Sweden* 11 G10
Gunnedah, *Australia* 95 E5
Gunnewin, *Australia* 95 D4
Gunningbar Cr. →, *Australia* 95 E4
Gunnison, *Colo., U.S.A.* 115 G10
Gunnison, *Utah, U.S.A.* 114 G8
Gunnison →, *U.S.A.* 115 G9
Gunpowder, *Australia* 94 B2
Guntakal, *India* 66 M10
Guntersville, *U.S.A.* 109 H2
Guntong, *Malaysia* 65 K3
Guntur, *India* 67 L12
Gunungapi, *Indonesia* 63 F7
Gunungsitoli, *Indonesia* 62 D1
Günz →, *Germany* 25 G6
Gunza, *Angola* 84 G2
Günzburg, *Germany* 25 G6
Gunzenhausen, *Germany* 25 F6
Guo He →, *China* 57 H9
Guoyang, *China* 56 H9
Gupis, *Pakistan* 69 A5
Gura Humorului, *Romania* 43 C10
Gura-Teghii, *Romania* 43 E11
Gurag, *Ethiopia* 81 F4
Gurahonţ, *Romania* 42 D7
Gurdaspur, *India* 68 C6
Gurdon, *U.S.A.* 113 J8
Güre, *Balıkesir, Turkey* 39 B8
Güre, *Uşak, Turkey* 39 C11
Gurgaon, *India* 68 E7
Gürgentepe, *Turkey* 72 B7
Gurghiu, Munţii, *Romania* 43 D10
Gurgueia →, *Brazil* 125 E10
Gurha, *India* 68 G4
Guri, Embalse de, *Venezuela* 124 B6
Gurin, *Nigeria* 83 D7
Gurjaani, *Georgia* 49 K7
Gurk →, *Austria* 26 E7
Gurkha, *Nepal* 69 E11
Gurley, *Australia* 95 D4
Gurnet Point, *U.S.A.* 111 D14
Gürpınar, *Ist., Turkey* 41 F12
Gürpınar, *Van, Turkey* 73 C10
Gürsu, *Turkey* 41 F13
Gurué, *Mozam.* 87 F4
Gurun, *Malaysia* 65 K3
Gürün, *Turkey* 72 C7
Gurupá, *Brazil* 125 D8
Gurupá, I. Grande de, *Brazil* 125 D8
Gurupi, *Brazil* 125 F9
Gurupi →, *Brazil* 125 D9
Guruwe, *Zimbabwe* 89 B5
Guryev = Atyraū, *Kazakstan* 50 E6
Gus-Khrustalnyy, *Russia* 48 C5
Gusau, *Nigeria* 83 C6
Gusev, *Russia* 9 J20
Gushan, *China* 57 E12
Gushgy, *Turkmenistan* 50 F7
Gushi, *China* 59 A10
Gushiago, *Ghana* 83 D4
Gusinje, *Montenegro, Yug.* 40 D3
Gusinoozersk, *Russia* 51 D11
Gúspini, *Italy* 30 C1
Güssing, *Austria* 27 D9
Gustavsberg, *Sweden* 10 E12
Gustavus, *U.S.A.* 104 B1
Gustine, *U.S.A.* 116 H6
Güstrow, *Germany* 24 B8
Gusum, *Sweden* 11 F10
Guta = Kolárovo, *Slovak Rep.* 27 D10
Gütersloh, *Germany* 24 D4
Gutha, *Australia* 93 E2
Guthalungra, *Australia* 94 B4
Guthrie, *Okla., U.S.A.* 113 H6
Guthrie, *Tex., U.S.A.* 113 J4
Gutian, *China* 59 D12
Guttenberg, *U.S.A.* 112 D9
Gutu, *Zimbabwe* 89 B5
Guyana ■, *S. Amer.* 124 C7
Guyane française = French Guiana ■, *S. Amer.* 125 C8
Guyang, *China* 56 D6
Guyenne, *France* 20 D4
Guymon, *U.S.A.* 113 G4
Guyra, *Australia* 95 E5
Guyuan, *Hebei, China* 56 D8
Guyuan, *Ningxia Huizu, China* 56 G4
Güzelbahçe, *Turkey* 39 C8
Guzhang, *China* 58 C7
Guzhen, *China* 57 H9
Guzmán, L. de, *Mexico* 118 A3
Gvardeysk, *Russia* 9 J19
Gvardeyskoye, *Ukraine* 47 K8
Gwa, *Burma* 67 L19
Gwaai, *Zimbabwe* 87 F2
Gwabegar, *Australia* 95 E4
Gwadabawa, *Nigeria* 83 C6
Gwādar, *Pakistan* 66 G3
Gwagwada, *Nigeria* 83 C6
Gwalior, *India* 68 F8
Gwanara, *Nigeria* 83 D5
Gwanda, *Zimbabwe* 87 G2
Gwandu, *Nigeria* 83 C5
Gwane, *Dem. Rep. of the Congo* 86 B2
Gwaram, *Nigeria* 83 C7
Gwarzo, *Nigeria* 83 C6
Gwasero, *Nigeria* 83 D5
Gwda →, *Poland* 45 E3
Gweebarra B., *Ireland* 15 B3
Gweedore, *Ireland* 15 A3
Gweru, *Zimbabwe* 87 F2
Gwi, *Nigeria* 83 D6
Gwinn, *U.S.A.* 108 B2
Gwio Kura, *Nigeria* 83 C7
Gwoza, *Nigeria* 83 C7
Gwydir →, *Australia* 95 D4
Gwynedd □, *U.K.* 12 E3
Gyandzha = Gäncä, *Azerbaijan* 49 K8
Gyaring Hu, *China* 60 C4
Gydanskiy Poluostrov, *Russia* 50 C8
Gympie, *Australia* 95 D5
Gyomaendrőd, *Hungary* 42 D5
Gyöngyös, *Hungary* 42 C4
Győr, *Hungary* 42 C2
Győr-Moson-Sopron □, *Hungary* 42 C2
Gypsum Pt., *Canada* 104 A6
Gypsumville, *Canada* 105 C9
Gyueshevo, *Bulgaria* 40 D6
Gyula, *Hungary* 42 D6
Gyumri, *Armenia* 49 K6
Gyzylarbat, *Turkmenistan* 50 F6
Gyzyletrek, *Turkmenistan* 71 B7
Gzhatsk = Gagarin, *Russia* 46 E8

H

Ha 'Arava →, *Israel* 75 E4
Ha Coi, *Vietnam* 58 G6
Ha Dong, *Vietnam* 58 G5
Ha Giang, *Vietnam* 58 F5
Ha Tien, *Vietnam* 65 G5
Ha Tinh, *Vietnam* 64 C5
Ha Trung, *Vietnam* 64 C5
Haaksbergen, *Neths.* 17 B6
Haapsalu, *Estonia* 9 G20
Haarlem, *Neths.* 17 B4
Haast →, *N.Z.* 91 K2
Haast Bluff, *Australia* 92 D5
Hab →, *Pakistan* 68 G3
Hab Nadi Chauki, *Pakistan* 68 G2
Habaswein, *Kenya* 86 B4
Habay, *Canada* 104 B5
Ḥabbānīyah, *Iraq* 70 C4
Ḥabbānīyah, Hawr al, *Iraq* 73 F10
Habo, *Sweden* 11 G8
Haboro, *Japan* 54 B10
Ḥabshān, *U.A.E.* 71 F7
Hachenburg, *Germany* 24 E3
Hachijō-Jima, *Japan* 55 H9
Hachinohe, *Japan* 54 D10
Hachiōji, *Japan* 55 G9
Hachŏn, *N. Korea* 57 D15
Hacıbektaş, *Turkey* 72 C6
Hacılar, *Turkey* 72 C6
Hackås, *Sweden* 10 B8
Hackensack, *U.S.A.* 111 F10
Hackettstown, *U.S.A.* 111 F10
Hadali, *Pakistan* 68 C5
Hadarba, Ras, *Sudan* 80 C4
Hadarom □, *Israel* 75 E4
Hadd, Ra's al, *Oman* 74 C6
Hadejia, *Nigeria* 83 C7
Hadejia →, *Nigeria* 83 C7
Ḥadera, *Israel* 75 C3
Ḥadera, N. →, *Israel* 75 C3
Haderslev, *Denmark* 11 J3
Hadhramaut = Ḥaḍramawt, *Yemen* 74 D4
Hadibu, *Yemen* 74 E5
Hadım, *Turkey* 72 D5
Hadong, *S. Korea* 57 G14
Ḥaḍramawt, *Yemen* 74 D4
Ḥadrānīyah, *Iraq* 70 C4
Hadrian's Wall, *U.K.* 12 B5
Hadsten, *Denmark* 11 H4
Hadsund, *Denmark* 11 H4
Hadyach, *Ukraine* 47 G8
Haeju, *N. Korea* 57 E13
Haenam, *S. Korea* 57 G14
Haenertsburg, *S. Africa* 89 C4
Haerhpin = Harbin, *China* 57 B14
Hafar al Bāţin, *Si. Arabia* 70 D5
Hafik, *Turkey* 72 C7
Ḥafīrat al 'Aydā, *Si. Arabia* 70 E3
Ḥafit, *Oman* 71 F7
Hafizabad, *Pakistan* 68 C5
Haflong, *India* 67 G18
Hafnarfjörður, *Iceland* 8 D3
Haft Gel, *Iran* 71 D6
Hafun, Ras, *Somali Rep.* 74 E5
Hagalil, *Israel* 75 C4
Hagby, *Sweden* 11 H10
Hagen, *Germany* 24 D3
Hagenow, *Germany* 24 B7
Hagerman, *U.S.A.* 113 J2
Hagerstown, *U.S.A.* 108 F7
Hagersville, *Canada* 110 D4
Hagetmau, *France* 20 E3
Hagfors, *Sweden* 10 D7
Hagi, *Japan* 55 G5
Hagolan, *Syria* 75 C4
Hagondange, *France* 19 C13
Hags Hd., *Ireland* 15 D2
Hague, C. de la, *France* 18 C5
Hague, The = 's-Gravenhage, *Neths.* 17 B4
Haguenau, *France* 19 D14
Hai Duong, *Vietnam* 58 G6
Hai'an, *Guangdong, China* 59 G8
Hai'an, *Jiangsu, China* 59 A13
Haicheng, *Fujian, China* 59 E11
Haicheng, *Liaoning, China* 57 D12
Haidar Khel, *Afghan.* 68 C3
Haidargarh, *India* 69 F9
Haifa = Ḥefa, *Israel* 75 C4
Haifeng, *China* 59 F10
Haiger, *Germany* 24 E4
Haikou, *China* 60 D6
Ḥā'il, *Si. Arabia* 70 E4
Hailar, *China* 60 B6
Hailey, *U.S.A.* 114 E6
Haileybury, *Canada* 102 C4
Hailin, *China* 57 B15
Hailing Dao, *China* 59 G8
Hailong, *China* 57 C13
Hailuoto, *Finland* 8 D21
Haimen, *Guangdong, China* 59 F11
Haimen, *Jiangsu, China* 59 B13
Hainan □, *China* 60 E5
Hainaut □, *Belgium* 17 D4
Hainburg, *Austria* 27 C9
Haines, *Alaska, U.S.A.* 104 B1
Haines, *Oreg., U.S.A.* 114 D5
Haines City, *U.S.A.* 109 L5
Haines Junction, *Canada* 104 A1
Hainfeld, *Austria* 26 C8
Haining, *China* 59 B13
Haiphong, *Vietnam* 58 G6
Haitan Dao, *China* 59 E12
Haiti ■, *W. Indies* 121 C5
Haiya, *Sudan* 80 D4
Haiyan, *China* 59 B13
Haiyang, *China* 57 F11
Haiyuan, *Guangxi Zhuangzu, China* 58 F6
Haiyuan, *Ningxia Huizu, China* 56 F3
Haizhou, *China* 57 G10
Haizhou Wan, *China* 57 G10
Hajdú-Bihar □, *Hungary* 42 C6
Hajdúböszörmény, *Hungary* 42 C6
Hajdúdorog, *Hungary* 42 C6
Hajdúhadház, *Hungary* 42 C6
Hajdúnánás, *Hungary* 42 C6
Hajdúsámson, *Hungary* 42 C6
Hajdúszoboszló, *Hungary* 42 C6
Hajipur, *India* 69 G11
Ḥājjī Muḥsin, *Iraq* 70 C5
Ḥājjīābād, *Iran* 71 D7
Ḥājjīābād-e Zarrīn, *Iran* 71 C7
Hajnówka, *Poland* 45 F10
Hakansson, Mts., *Dem. Rep. of the Congo* 87 D2
Hakkâri, *Turkey* 70 B4
Hakkâri Dağları, *Turkey* 73 C10
Hakken-Zan, *Japan* 55 G7
Hakodate, *Japan* 54 D10
Hakos, *Namibia* 88 C2
Håksberg, *Sweden* 10 D9
Haku-San, *Japan* 55 F8
Hakui, *Japan* 55 F8
Hala, *Pakistan* 66 G6
Ḥalab, *Syria* 70 B3
Ḥalabjah, *Iraq* 70 C5
Halaib, *Sudan* 80 C4
Halasa, *Sudan* 81 E3
Hālat 'Ammār, *Si. Arabia* 70 D3
Halbā, *Lebanon* 75 A5
Halberstadt, *Germany* 24 D7
Halcombe, *N.Z.* 91 J5
Halcon, *Phil.* 63 B6
Halden, *Norway* 9 G14
Haldensleben, *Germany* 24 C7
Haldia, *India* 67 H16
Haldwani, *India* 69 E8
Hale →, *Australia* 94 C2
Halesowen, *U.K.* 13 E5
Haleyville, *U.S.A.* 109 H2
Half Assini, *Ghana* 82 D4
Halfmoon Bay, *N.Z.* 91 M2
Halfway →, *Canada* 104 B4
Halia, *India* 69 G10
Haliburton, *Canada* 102 C4
Halifax, *Australia* 94 B4
Halifax, *Canada* 103 D7
Halifax, *U.K.* 12 D6
Halifax, *U.S.A.* 110 F8
Halifax B., *Australia* 94 B4
Halifax I., *Namibia* 88 D2
Halīl →, *Iran* 71 E8
Halkirk, *U.K.* 14 C5
Hall Beach = Sanirajak, *Canada* 101 B11
Hall in Tirol, *Austria* 26 D4
Hall Pen., *Canada* 101 B13
Hall Pt., *Australia* 92 C3
Hallabro, *Sweden* 11 H9
Halland, *Sweden* 9 H15
Hallands län □, *Sweden* 11 H6
Hallands Väderö, *Sweden* 11 H6
Hallandsås, *Sweden* 11 H7
Hällbybrunn, *Sweden* 10 E10
Halle, *Belgium* 17 D4
Halle, *Nordrhein-Westfalen, Germany* 24 C4
Halle, *Sachsen-Anhalt, Germany* 24 D7
Hällefors, *Sweden* 10 E8
Hälleforsnäs, *Sweden* 10 E10
Hallein, *Austria* 26 D6
Hällekis, *Sweden* 11 F7
Hallen, *Sweden* 10 A8
Hallett, *Australia* 95 E2
Hallettsville, *U.S.A.* 113 L6
Hallim, *S. Korea* 57 H14
Hallingdalselvi →, *Norway* 9 F13
Hallock, *U.S.A.* 112 A6
Halls Creek, *Australia* 92 C4
Hallsberg, *Sweden* 10 E9
Hallstahammar, *Sweden* 10 E10
Hallstatt, *Austria* 26 D6
Hallstavik, *Sweden* 10 D12
Hallstead, *U.S.A.* 111 E9
Halmahera, *Indonesia* 63 D7
Halmeu, *Romania* 42 C8
Halmstad, *Sweden* 11 H6
Hals, *Denmark* 11 H4
Hälsingborg = Helsingborg, *Sweden* 11 H6
Hälsingland, *Sweden* 10 C10
Halstead, *U.K.* 13 F8
Haltern, *Germany* 24 D3
Halti, *Finland* 8 B19
Halton □, *U.K.* 12 D5
Haltwhistle, *U.K.* 12 C5
Ḥalul, *Qatar* 71 E7
Halvad, *India* 68 H4
Ḥalvān, *Iran* 71 C8
Ham, *France* 19 C10
Ham Tan, *Vietnam* 65 G6
Ham Yen, *Vietnam* 64 A5
Hamab, *Namibia* 88 D2
Hamad, *Sudan* 81 D3
Hamada, *Japan* 55 G6
Hamadān, *Iran* 71 C6
Hamadān □, *Iran* 71 C6
Hamāh, *Syria* 70 C3
Hamamatsu, *Japan* 55 G8
Hamar, *Norway* 9 F14
Hamâta, Gebel, *Egypt* 70 E2
Hambantota, *Sri Lanka* 66 R12
Hamber Prov. Park, *Canada* 104 C5
Hamburg, *Germany* 24 B5
Hamburg, *Ark., U.S.A.* 113 J9
Hamburg, *N.Y., U.S.A.* 110 D6
Hamburg, *Pa., U.S.A.* 111 F9
Hamburg □, *Germany* 24 B5
Ḥamḍ, W. al →, *Si. Arabia* 70 E3
Hamden, *U.S.A.* 111 E12
Hamdibey, *Turkey* 39 B9
Häme, *Finland* 9 F20
Hämeenlinna, *Finland* 9 F21
Hamélé, *Ghana* 82 C4
Hamelin Pool, *Australia* 93 E1
Hameln, *Germany* 24 C5
Hamerkaz □, *Israel* 75 C3
Hamersley Ra., *Australia* 92 D2
Hamhung, *N. Korea* 57 E14
Hami, *China* 60 B4
Hamilton, *Australia* 95 F3
Hamilton, *Canada* 102 D4
Hamilton, *N.Z.* 91 G5
Hamilton, *U.K.* 14 F4
Hamilton, *Ala., U.S.A.* 109 H1
Hamilton, *Mont., U.S.A.* 114 C6
Hamilton, *N.Y., U.S.A.* 111 D9
Hamilton, *Ohio, U.S.A.* 108 F3
Hamilton, *Tex., U.S.A.* 113 K5
Hamilton →, *Australia* 94 C2
Hamilton City, *U.S.A.* 116 F4
Hamilton Inlet, *Canada* 103 B8
Hamilton Mt., *U.S.A.* 111 C10
Hamina, *Finland* 9 F22
Hamirpur, *H.P., India* 68 D7
Hamirpur, *Ut. P., India* 69 G9
Hamitabat, *Turkey* 41 E11
Hamlet, *U.S.A.* 109 H6
Hamley Bridge, *Australia* 95 E2
Hamlin = Hameln, *Germany* 24 C5

Hamlin, *N.Y., U.S.A.* 110 C7
Hamlin, *Tex., U.S.A.* 113 J4
Hamm, *Germany* 24 D3
Ḥammār, Hawr al, *Iraq* 70 D5
Hammarstrand, *Sweden* 10 A10
Hammelburg, *Germany* 25 E5
Hammeren, *Denmark* 11 J8
Hammerfest, *Norway* 8 A20
Hammerum, *Denmark* 11 H3
Hamminkeln, *Germany* 24 D2
Hammond, *Ind., U.S.A.* 108 E2
Hammond, *La., U.S.A.* 113 K9
Hammond, *N.Y., U.S.A.* 111 B9
Hammondsport, *U.S.A.* 110 D7
Hammonton, *U.S.A.* 108 F8
Hamneda, *Sweden* 11 H7
Hamoyet, Jebel, *Sudan* 80 D4
Hampden, *N.Z.* 91 L3
Hampshire □, *U.K.* 13 F6
Hampshire Downs, *U.K.* 13 F6
Hampton, *N.B., Canada* 103 C6
Hampton, *Ont., Canada* 110 C6
Hampton, *Ark., U.S.A.* 113 J8
Hampton, *Iowa, U.S.A.* 112 D8
Hampton, *N.H., U.S.A.* 111 D14
Hampton, *S.C., U.S.A.* 109 J5
Hampton, *Va., U.S.A.* 108 G7
Hampton Bays, *U.S.A.* 111 F12
Hampton Tableland, *Australia* 93 F4
Hamra, *Sweden* 10 C8
Hamrat esh Sheykh, *Sudan* 81 E2
Hamur, *Turkey* 73 C10
Hamyang, *S. Korea* 57 G14
Han Jiang →, *China* 59 F11
Han Shui, *China* 58 A7
Han Shui →, *China* 59 B10
Hanak, *Si. Arabia* 70 E3
Hanamaki, *Japan* 54 E10
Hanang, *Tanzania* 86 C4
Hanau, *Germany* 25 E4
Hanbogd = Ihbulag, *Mongolia* 56 C4
Hançalar, *Turkey* 39 C11
Hânceşti, *Moldova* 43 D13
Hancheng, *China* 56 G6
Hanchuan, *China* 59 B9
Hancock, *Mich., U.S.A.* 112 B10
Hancock, *N.Y., U.S.A.* 111 E9
Handa, *Japan* 55 G8
Handan, *China* 56 F8
Handeni, *Tanzania* 86 D4
Handlová, *Slovak Rep.* 27 C11
Handub, *Sudan* 80 D4
Handwara, *India* 69 B6
Hanegev, *Israel* 75 E4
Hanford, *U.S.A.* 116 J7
Hang Chat, *Thailand* 64 C2
Hang Dong, *Thailand* 64 C2
Hangang →, *S. Korea* 57 F14
Hangayn Nuruu, *Mongolia* 60 B4
Hangchou = Hangzhou, *China* 59 B13
Hanggin Houqi, *China* 56 D4
Hanggin Qi, *China* 56 E5
Hangu, *China* 57 E9
Hangzhou, *China* 59 B13
Hangzhou Wan, *China* 59 B13
Hanhongor, *Mongolia* 56 C3
Ḥanīdh, *Si. Arabia* 71 E6
Ḥanīsh, *Yemen* 74 E3
Haniska, *Slovak Rep.* 27 C14
Hanjiang, *China* 59 E12
Hankinson, *U.S.A.* 112 B6
Hanko, *Finland* 9 G20
Hankou, *China* 59 B10
Hanksville, *U.S.A.* 115 G8
Hanle, *India* 69 C8
Hanmer Springs, *N.Z.* 91 K4
Hann →, *Australia* 92 C4
Hann, Mt., *Australia* 92 C4
Hanna, *Canada* 104 C6
Hanna, *U.S.A.* 114 F10
Hannah B., *Canada* 102 B4
Hannibal, *Mo., U.S.A.* 112 F9
Hannibal, *N.Y., U.S.A.* 111 C8
Hannik, *Sudan* 80 D3
Hannover, *Germany* 24 C5
Hanö, *Sweden* 11 H8
Hanöbukten, *Sweden* 11 J8
Hanoi, *Vietnam* 58 G5
Hanover = Hannover, *Germany* 24 C5
Hanover, *Canada* 102 D3
Hanover, *S. Africa* 88 E3
Hanover, *N.H., U.S.A.* 111 C12
Hanover, *Ohio, U.S.A.* 110 F2
Hanover, *Pa., U.S.A.* 108 F7
Hanover, I., *Chile* 128 G2
Hansdiha, *India* 69 G12
Hanshou, *China* 59 C8
Hansi, *India* 68 E6
Hanson, L., *Australia* 95 E2
Hanstholm, *Denmark* 11 G2
Hantsavichy, *Belarus* 47 F4
Hanumangarh, *India* 68 E6
Hanyin, *China* 58 A7
Hanyuan, *China* 58 C4
Hanzhong, *China* 56 H4
Hanzhuang, *China* 57 G9
Haora, *India* 69 H13
Haoxue, *China* 59 B9
Haparanda, *Sweden* 8 D21
Happy, *U.S.A.* 113 H4
Happy Camp, *U.S.A.* 114 F2
Happy Valley-Goose Bay, *Canada* 103 B7
Hapsu, *N. Korea* 57 D15
Hapur, *India* 68 E7
Ḥaql, *Si. Arabia* 75 F3
Har, *Indonesia* 63 F8
Har-Ayrag, *Mongolia* 56 B5
Har Hu, *China* 60 C4
Har Us Nuur, *Mongolia* 60 B4
Har Yehuda, *Israel* 75 D3
Ḥaraḍ, *Si. Arabia* 74 C4
Haradok, *Belarus* 46 E6
Häradsbäck, *Sweden* 11 H8
Haranomachi, *Japan* 54 F10
Harare, *Zimbabwe* 87 F3
Harat, *Eritrea* 81 D4
Harbin, *China* 57 B14
Harbiye, *Turkey* 72 D7
Harbo, *Sweden* 10 D11
Harboør, *Denmark* 11 H2
Harbor Beach, *U.S.A.* 110 C2
Harbour Breton, *Canada* 103 C8
Harbour Deep, *Canada* 103 B8
Harburg, *Germany* 24 B5
Hårby, *Denmark* 11 J4
Harda, *India* 68 H7
Hardangerfjorden, *Norway* 9 F12
Hardangervidda, *Norway* 9 F12
Hardap Dam, *Namibia* 88 C2
Hardenberg, *Neths.* 17 B6
Harderwijk, *Neths.* 17 B5
Hardey →, *Australia* 92 D2
Hardin, *U.S.A.* 114 D10
Harding, *S. Africa* 89 E4
Harding Ra., *Australia* 92 C3
Hardisty, *Canada* 104 C6
Hardoi, *India* 69 F9
Hardwar = Haridwar, *India* 68 E8
Hardwick, *U.S.A.* 111 B12
Hardy, Pen., *Chile* 128 H3
Hare B., *Canada* 103 B8
Hareid, *Norway* 9 E12
Haren, *Germany* 24 C3
Harer, *Ethiopia* 81 F5
Harerge □, *Ethiopia* 81 F5
Hareto, *Ethiopia* 81 F4
Harfleur, *France* 18 C7
Hargeisa, *Somali Rep.* 74 F3
Harghita □, *Romania* 43 D10
Harghita, Munţii, *Romania* 43 D10
Hargshamn, *Sweden* 10 D12
Hari →, *Indonesia* 62 E2
Haria, *Canary Is.* 37 E6
Haridwar, *India* 68 E8
Harim, Jabal al, *Oman* 71 E8
Haringhata →, *Bangla.* 67 J16
Harīrūd →, *Asia* 66 A2
Härjedalen, *Sweden* 10 B7
Harlan, *Iowa, U.S.A.* 112 E7
Harlan, *Ky., U.S.A.* 109 G4
Hârlău, *Romania* 43 C11
Harlech, *U.K.* 12 E3
Harlem, *U.S.A.* 114 B9
Hårlev, *Denmark* 11 J6
Harlingen, *Neths.* 17 A5
Harlingen, *U.S.A.* 113 M6
Harlow, *U.K.* 13 F8
Harlowton, *U.S.A.* 114 C9
Harmancık, *Turkey* 39 B11
Harmånger, *Sweden* 10 C11
Harmil, *Eritrea* 81 D5
Harnai, *Pakistan* 68 D2
Harney Basin, *U.S.A.* 114 E4
Harney L., *U.S.A.* 114 E4
Harney Peak, *U.S.A.* 112 D3
Härnön, *Sweden* 10 B12
Härnösand, *Sweden* 10 B11
Haro, *Spain* 32 C2
Haroldswick, *U.K.* 14 A8
Harp L., *Canada* 103 A7
Harper, *Liberia* 82 E3
Harplinge, *Sweden* 11 H6
Harr, *Mauritania* 82 B2
Harrai, *India* 69 H8
Harrand, *Pakistan* 68 E4
Ḥarrat Khaybar, *Si. Arabia* 80 B5
Ḥarrat Nawāşīf, *Si. Arabia* 80 C5
Harricana →, *Canada* 102 B4
Harriman, *U.S.A.* 109 H3
Harrington Harbour, *Canada* 103 B8
Harris, *U.K.* 14 D2
Harris, Sd. of, *U.K.* 14 D1
Harris L., *Australia* 95 E2
Harris Pt., *Canada* 110 C2
Harrisburg, *Ill., U.S.A.* 113 G10
Harrisburg, *Nebr., U.S.A.* 112 E3
Harrisburg, *Pa., U.S.A.* 110 F8
Harrismith, *S. Africa* 89 D4
Harrison, *Ark., U.S.A.* 113 G8
Harrison, *Maine, U.S.A.* 111 B14
Harrison, *Nebr., U.S.A.* 112 D3
Harrison, C., *Canada* 103 B8
Harrison L., *Canada* 104 D4
Harrisonburg, *U.S.A.* 108 F6
Harrisonville, *U.S.A.* 112 F7
Harriston, *Canada* 110 C4
Harrisville, *Mich., U.S.A.* 110 B1
Harrisville, *N.Y., U.S.A.* 111 B9
Harrisville, *Pa., U.S.A.* 110 E5
Harrodsburg, *U.S.A.* 108 G3
Harrogate, *U.K.* 12 C6
Harrow □, *U.K.* 13 F7
Harrowsmith, *Canada* 111 B8
Harry S. Truman Reservoir, *U.S.A.* 112 F7
Harsefeld, *Germany* 24 B5
Harsewinkel, *Germany* 24 D4
Harsīn, *Iran* 70 C5
Hârşova, *Romania* 43 F12
Harstad, *Norway* 8 B17
Harsud, *India* 68 H7
Hart, *U.S.A.* 108 D2
Hart, L., *Australia* 95 E2
Hartbees →, *S. Africa* 88 D3
Hartberg, *Austria* 26 D8
Hartford, *Conn., U.S.A.* 111 E12
Hartford, *Ky., U.S.A.* 108 G2
Hartford, *S. Dak., U.S.A.* 112 D6
Hartford, *Wis., U.S.A.* 112 D10
Hartford City, *U.S.A.* 108 E3
Hartland, *Canada* 103 C6
Hartland Pt., *U.K.* 13 F3
Hartlepool, *U.K.* 12 C6
Hartlepool □, *U.K.* 12 C6
Hartley Bay, *Canada* 104 C3
Hartmannberge, *Namibia* 88 B1
Hartney, *Canada* 105 D8
Hârtop, *Moldova* 43 D13
Harts →, *S. Africa* 88 D3
Hartselle, *U.S.A.* 109 H2
Hartshorne, *U.S.A.* 113 H7
Hartstown, *U.S.A.* 110 E4
Hartsville, *U.S.A.* 109 H5
Hartswater, *S. Africa* 88 D3
Hartwell, *U.S.A.* 109 H4
Harunabad, *Pakistan* 68 E5
Harvand, *Iran* 71 D7
Harvey, *Australia* 93 F2
Harvey, *Ill., U.S.A.* 108 E2
Harvey, *N. Dak., U.S.A.* 112 B5
Harwich, *U.K.* 13 F9
Haryana □, *India* 68 E7
Haryn →, *Belarus* 47 F4
Harz, *Germany* 24 D6
Harzgerode, *Germany* 24 D7
Hasa □, *Si. Arabia* 71 E6
Hasaheisa, *Sudan* 81 E3
Ḥasanābād, *Iran* 71 C7
Hasdo →, *India* 69 J10
Haselünne, *Germany* 24 C3
Hashimoto, *Japan* 55 G7
Hashtjerd, *Iran* 71 C6
Haskell, *U.S.A.* 113 J5
Hasköy, *Turkey* 41 E10
Haslach, *Germany* 25 G4
Hasle, *Denmark* 11 J8
Haslemere, *U.K.* 13 F7
Haslev, *Denmark* 11 J5
Hasparren, *France* 20 E2
Hassa, *Turkey* 72 D7
Hassela, *Sweden* 10 B10
Hasselt, *Belgium* 17 D5
Hassfurt, *Germany* 25 E6
Hassi Messaoud, *Algeria* 78 B7
Hässleholm, *Sweden* 11 H7
Hassloch, *Germany* 25 F4
Hästholmen, *Sweden* 11 F8
Hastings, *N.Z.* 91 H6
Hastings, *U.K.* 13 G8
Hastings, *Mich., U.S.A.* 108 D3
Hastings, *Minn., U.S.A.* 112 C8
Hastings, *Nebr., U.S.A.* 112 E5
Hastings Ra., *Australia* 95 E5
Hästveda, *Sweden* 11 H7
Hat Yai, *Thailand* 65 J3
Hatanbulag = Ergel, *Mongolia* 56 C5
Hatay = Antalya, *Turkey* 72 D4
Hatch, *U.S.A.* 115 K10
Hatchet L., *Canada* 105 B8
Haţeg, *Romania* 42 E7
Hateruma-Shima, *Japan* 55 M1
Hatfield P.O., *Australia* 95 E3
Hatgal, *Mongolia* 60 A5
Hathras, *India* 68 F8
Hatia, *Bangla.* 67 H17
Ḥāṭibah, Ra's, *Si. Arabia* 80 C4
Hato Mayor, *Dom. Rep.* 121 C6
Hatta, *India* 69 G8
Hattah, *Australia* 95 E3
Hatteras, C., *U.S.A.* 109 H8
Hattiesburg, *U.S.A.* 113 K10
Hatvan, *Hungary* 42 C4
Hau Bon = Cheo Reo, *Vietnam* 62 B3
Hau Duc, *Vietnam* 64 E7
Haugesund, *Norway* 9 G11
Haukipudas, *Finland* 8 D21
Haultain →, *Canada* 105 B7
Hauraki G., *N.Z.* 91 G5
Hausruck, *Austria* 26 C6
Haut Atlas, *Morocco* 78 B4
Haut-Rhin □, *France* 19 E14
Haut-Zaïre = Orientale □, *Dem. Rep. of the Congo* 86 B2
Haute-Corse □, *France* 21 F13
Haute-Garonne □, *France* 20 E5
Haute-Loire □, *France* 20 C7
Haute-Marne □, *France* 19 D12
Haute-Normandie □, *France* 18 C7
Haute-Saône □, *France* 19 E13
Haute-Savoie □, *France* 21 C10
Haute-Vienne □, *France* 20 C5
Hautes-Alpes □, *France* 21 D10
Hautes Fagnes = Hohe Venn, *Belgium* 17 D6
Hautes-Pyrénées □, *France* 20 F4
Hauteville-Lompnès, *France* 21 C9
Hautmont, *France* 19 B10
Hauts-de-Seine □, *France* 19 D9
Hauts Plateaux, *Algeria* 76 C4
Hauzenberg, *Germany* 25 G9
Havana = La Habana, *Cuba* 120 B3
Havana, *U.S.A.* 112 E9
Havant, *U.K.* 13 G7
Havârna, *Romania* 43 B11
Havasu, L., *U.S.A.* 117 L12
Havdhem, *Sweden* 11 G12
Havel →, *Germany* 24 C8
Havelian, *Pakistan* 68 B5
Havelock, *Canada* 102 D4
Havelock, *N.Z.* 91 J4
Havelock, *U.S.A.* 109 H7
Haverfordwest, *U.K.* 13 F3
Haverhill, *U.S.A.* 111 D13
Haverstraw, *U.S.A.* 111 E11
Håverud, *Sweden* 11 F6
Havirga, *Mongolia* 56 B7
Havířov, *Czech Rep.* 27 B11
Havlíčkův Brod, *Czech Rep.* 26 B8
Havneby, *Denmark* 11 J2
Havran, *Turkey* 39 B9
Havre, *U.S.A.* 114 B9
Havre-Aubert, *Canada* 103 C7
Havre-St.-Pierre, *Canada* 103 B7
Havsa, *Turkey* 41 E10
Havza, *Turkey* 72 B6
Haw →, *U.S.A.* 109 H6
Hawaii □, *U.S.A.* 106 H16
Hawaii I., *Pac. Oc.* 106 J17
Hawaiian Is., *Pac. Oc.* 106 H17
Hawaiian Ridge, *Pac. Oc.* 97 E11
Hawarden, *U.S.A.* 112 D6
Hawea, L., *N.Z.* 91 L2
Hawera, *N.Z.* 91 H5
Hawick, *U.K.* 14 F6
Hawk Junction, *Canada* 102 C3
Hawke B., *N.Z.* 91 H6
Hawker, *Australia* 95 E2
Hawkesbury, *Canada* 102 C5
Hawkesbury I., *Canada* 104 C3
Hawkesbury Pt., *Australia* 94 A1
Hawkinsville, *U.S.A.* 109 J4
Hawley, *Minn., U.S.A.* 112 B6
Hawley, *Pa., U.S.A.* 111 E9
Ḥawrān, W. →, *Iraq* 70 C4
Hawsh Müssá, *Lebanon* 75 B4
Hawthorne, *U.S.A.* 114 G4
Hay, *Australia* 95 E3
Hay →, *Australia* 94 C2
Hay →, *Canada* 104 A5
Hay, C., *Australia* 92 B4
Hay I., *Canada* 110 B4
Hay L., *Canada* 104 B5
Hay-on-Wye, *U.K.* 13 E4
Hay River, *Canada* 104 A5
Hay Springs, *U.S.A.* 112 D3
Haya = Tehoru, *Indonesia* 63 E7
Hayachine-San, *Japan* 54 E10
Hayange, *France* 19 C13
Haydarlı, *Turkey* 39 C12
Hayden, *U.S.A.* 114 F10
Haydon, *Australia* 94 B3
Hayes, *U.S.A.* 112 C4
Hayes →, *Canada* 102 A1
Hayes Creek, *Australia* 92 B5
Hayle, *U.K.* 13 G2
Hayling I., *U.K.* 13 G7
Haymana, *Turkey* 72 C5
Hayrabolu, *Turkey* 41 E11
Hays, *Canada* 104 C6
Hays, *U.S.A.* 112 F5
Haysyn, *Ukraine* 47 H5
Hayvoron, *Ukraine* 47 H5
Hayward, *Calif., U.S.A.* 116 H4
Hayward, *Wis., U.S.A.* 112 B9
Haywards Heath, *U.K.* 13 G7
Hazafon □, *Israel* 75 C4
Hazārān, Kūh-e, *Iran* 71 D8
Hazard, *U.S.A.* 108 G4
Hazaribag, *India* 69 H11
Hazaribag Road, *India* 69 G11
Hazebrouck, *France* 19 B9
Hazelton, *Canada* 104 B3
Hazelton, *U.S.A.* 112 B4
Hazen, *U.S.A.* 112 B4
Hazlehurst, *Ga., U.S.A.* 109 K4
Hazlehurst, *Miss., U.S.A.* 113 K9
Hazlet, *U.S.A.* 111 F10
Hazleton, *U.S.A.* 111 F9
Hazlett, L., *Australia* 92 D4
Hazro, *Turkey* 70 B4
He Xian, *Anhui, China* 59 B12
He Xian, *Guangxi Zhuangzu, China* 59 E8
Head of Bight, *Australia* 93 F5
Headlands, *Zimbabwe* 87 F3
Healdsburg, *U.S.A.* 116 G4
Healdton, *U.S.A.* 113 H6
Healesville, *Australia* 95 F4
Heany Junction, *Zimbabwe* 89 C4
Heard I., *Ind. Oc.* 3 G13
Hearne, *U.S.A.* 113 K6
Hearst, *Canada* 102 C3
Heart →, *U.S.A.* 112 B4
Heart's Content, *Canada* 103 C9
Heath Pt., *Canada* 103 C7
Heavener, *U.S.A.* 113 H7
Hebbronville, *U.S.A.* 113 M5
Hebei □, *China* 56 E9
Hebel, *Australia* 95 D4
Heber, *U.S.A.* 117 N11
Heber City, *U.S.A.* 114 F8
Heber Springs, *U.S.A.* 113 H9
Hebert, *Canada* 105 C7
Hebgen L., *U.S.A.* 114 D8
Hebi, *China* 56 G8
Hebrides, *U.K.* 6 D4
Hebrides, Sea of the, *U.K.* 14 D2
Hebron = Al Khalīl, *West Bank* 75 D4
Hebron, *Canada* 101 C13
Hebron, *N. Dak., U.S.A.* 112 B3
Hebron, *Nebr., U.S.A.* 112 E6
Heby, *Sweden* 10 E10
Hecate Str., *Canada* 104 C2
Heceta I., *U.S.A.* 104 B2
Hechi, *China* 58 E7
Hechingen, *Germany* 25 G4
Hechuan, *China* 58 B6
Hecla, *U.S.A.* 112 C5
Hecla I., *Canada* 105 C9
Hédé, *France* 18 D5
Hede, *Sweden* 10 B7
Hedemora, *Sweden* 10 D9
Hedensted, *Denmark* 11 J3
Hedesunda, *Sweden* 10 D10
Heerde, *Neths.* 17 B6
Heerenveen, *Neths.* 17 B5
Heerhugowaard, *Neths.* 17 B4
Heerlen, *Neths.* 17 D5
Ḥefa, *Israel* 75 C4
Ḥefa □, *Israel* 75 C4
Hefei, *China* 59 B11
Hefeng, *China* 59 C8
Hegalig, *Sudan* 81 E3
Hegang, *China* 60 B8
Heiban, *Sudan* 81 E3
Heichengzhen, *China* 56 F4
Heide, *Germany* 24 A5
Heidelberg, *Germany* 25 F4
Heidelberg, *S. Africa* 88 E3
Heidenau, *Germany* 24 E9
Heidenheim, *Germany* 25 G6
Heijing, *China* 58 E3
Heilbad Heiligenstadt, *Germany* 24 D6
Heilbron, *S. Africa* 89 D4
Heilbronn, *Germany* 25 F5
Heiligenblut, *Austria* 26 D5
Heiligenhafen, *Germany* 24 A6
Heilongjiang □, *China* 60 B7
Heilunkiang = Heilongjiang □, *China* 60 B7
Heimaey, *Iceland* 8 E3
Heinola, *Finland* 9 F22
Heinsberg, *Germany* 24 D2
Heinze Kyun, *Burma* 64 E1
Heishan, *China* 57 D12
Heishui, *Liaoning, China* 57 C10
Heishui, *Sichuan, China* 58 A4
Hejaz = Ḥijāz □, *Si. Arabia* 70 E3
Hejian, *China* 56 E9
Hejiang, *China* 58 C5
Hejin, *China* 56 G6
Hekimhan, *Turkey* 70 B3
Hekla, *Iceland* 8 E4
Hekou, *Guangdong, China* 59 F9
Hekou, *Yunnan, China* 58 F4
Hel, *Poland* 44 D5
Helagsfjället, *Sweden* 10 B6
Helan Shan, *China* 56 E3
Helechosa, *Spain* 35 F6
Helen Atoll, *Pac. Oc.* 63 D8
Helena, *Ark., U.S.A.* 113 H9
Helena, *Mont., U.S.A.* 114 C7
Helendale, *U.S.A.* 117 L9
Helensburgh, *U.K.* 14 E4
Helensville, *N.Z.* 91 G5
Helenvale, *Australia* 94 B4
Helgasjön, *Sweden* 11 H8
Helgeland, *Norway* 8 C15
Helgoland, *Germany* 24 A3
Heligoland = Helgoland, *Germany* 24 A3
Heligoland B. = Deutsche Bucht, *Germany* 24 A4
Heliopolis, *Egypt* 80 H7
Hella, *Iceland* 8 E3
Hellertown, *U.S.A.* 111 F9
Hellespont = Çanakkale Boğazı, *Turkey* 41 F10
Hellevoetsluis, *Neths.* 17 C4
Hellín, *Spain* 33 G3
Helmand □, *Afghan.* 66 D4
Helmand →, *Afghan.* 66 D2
Helme →, *Germany* 24 D7
Helmeringhausen, *Namibia* 88 D2
Helmond, *Neths.* 17 C5
Helmsdale, *U.K.* 14 C5
Helmsdale →, *U.K.* 14 C5
Helmstedt, *Germany* 24 C7
Helong, *China* 57 C15
Helper, *U.S.A.* 114 G8
Helsingborg, *Sweden* 11 H6
Helsinge, *Denmark* 11 H6
Helsingfors = Helsinki, *Finland* 9 F21
Helsingør, *Denmark* 11 H6
Helsinki, *Finland* 9 F21
Helska, Mierzeja, *Poland* 44 D5
Helston, *U.K.* 13 G2
Helvellyn, *U.K.* 12 C4
Helwân, *Egypt* 80 J7
Hemel Hempstead, *U.K.* 13 F7
Hemet, *U.S.A.* 117 M10
Hemingford, *U.S.A.* 112 D3
Hemmingford, *Canada* 111 A11
Hempstead, *U.S.A.* 113 K6
Hemse, *Sweden* 11 G12
Hemsön, *Sweden* 10 B12
Henån, *Sweden* 11 F5
Henan □, *China* 56 H8
Henares →, *Spain* 34 E7
Henashi-Misaki, *Japan* 54 D9
Hendaye, *France* 20 E2
Hendek, *Turkey* 72 B4
Henderson, *Argentina* 126 D3
Henderson, *Ky., U.S.A.* 108 G2
Henderson, *N.C., U.S.A.* 109 G6
Henderson, *Nev., U.S.A.* 117 J12
Henderson, *Tenn., U.S.A.* 109 H1
Henderson, *Tex., U.S.A.* 113 J7
Hendersonville, *N.C., U.S.A.* 109 H4
Hendersonville, *Tenn., U.S.A.* 109 G2
Hendījān, *Iran* 71 D6
Hendorābī, *Iran* 71 E7
Heng Jiang, *China* 58 C5
Heng Xian, *China* 58 F7

Hengcheng

Hengcheng, China 56 E4
Hëngchun, Taiwan 59 F13
Hengdaohezi, China 57 B15
Hengelo, Neths. 17 B6
Hengfeng, China 59 C10
Hengshan, Hunan, China 59 D9
Hengshan, Shaanxi, China 56 F5
Hengshui, China 56 F8
Hengyang, China 59 D9
Henichesk, Ukraine 47 J8
Hénin-Beaumont, France 19 B9
Henlopen, C., U.S.A. 108 F8
Hennan, Sweden 10 B9
Hennebont, France 18 E3
Hennenman, S. Africa 88 D4
Hennessey, U.S.A. 113 G6
Hennigsdorf, Germany 24 C9
Henrietta, U.S.A. 113 J5
Henrietta, Ostrov = Genriyetty, Ostrov, Russia 51 B16
Henrietta Maria, C., Canada 102 A3
Henry, U.S.A. 112 E10
Henryetta, U.S.A. 113 H7
Henryville, Canada 111 A11
Hensall, Canada 110 C3
Henstedt-Ulzburg, Germany 24 B6
Hentiesbaai, Namibia 88 C1
Hentiyn Nuruu, Mongolia 60 B5
Henty, Australia 95 F4
Henzada, Burma 67 L19
Hephaestia, Greece 39 B7
Heping, China 59 E10
Heppner, U.S.A. 114 D4
Hepu, China 58 G7
Hepworth, Canada 110 B3
Heqing, China 58 D3
Hequ, China 56 E6
Héraðsflói, Iceland 8 D6
Héraðsvötn →, Iceland 8 D4
Herald Cays, Australia 94 B4
Herāt, Afghan. 66 B3
Herāt □, Afghan. 66 B3
Hérault □, France 20 E7
Hérault →, France 20 E7
Herbault, France 18 E8
Herbert →, Australia 94 B4
Herberton, Australia 94 B4
Herbertsdale, S. Africa 88 E3
Herbignac, France 18 E4
Herborn, Germany 24 E4
Herby, Poland 45 H5
Herceg-Novi, Montenegro, Yug. 40 D2
Herchmer, Canada 105 B10
Herðubreið, Iceland 8 D5
Hereford, U.K. 13 E5
Hereford, U.S.A. 113 H3
Herefordshire □, U.K. 13 E5
Hereke, Turkey 41 F13
Herencia, Spain 35 F7
Herentals, Belgium 17 C4
Herford, Germany 24 C4
Héricourt, France 19 E13
Herington, U.S.A. 112 F6
Herisau, Switz. 25 H5
Hérisson, France 19 F9
Herkimer, U.S.A. 111 D10
Herlong, U.S.A. 116 E6
Herm, U.K. 13 H5
Hermann, U.S.A. 112 F9
Hermannsburg, Australia 92 D5
Hermannsburg, Germany 24 C6
Hermanus, S. Africa 88 E2
Herment, France 20 C6
Hermidale, Australia 95 E4
Hermiston, U.S.A. 114 D4
Hermite, I., Chile 128 H3
Hermon, U.S.A. 111 B9
Hermon, Mt. = Shaykh, J. ash, Lebanon 75 B4
Hermosillo, Mexico 118 B2
Hernád →, Hungary 42 C6
Hernandarias, Paraguay 127 B5
Hernandez, U.S.A. 116 J6
Hernando, Argentina 126 C3
Hernando, U.S.A. 113 H10
Hernani, Spain 32 B3
Herndon, U.S.A. 110 F8
Herne, Germany 17 C7
Herne Bay, U.K. 13 F9
Herning, Denmark 11 H2
Heroica = Caborca, Mexico 118 A2
Heroica Nogales = Nogales, Mexico 118 A2
Heron Bay, Canada 102 C2
Herradura, Pta. de la, Canary Is. 37 F5
Herreid, U.S.A. 112 C4
Herrenberg, Germany 25 G4
Herrera, Spain 35 H6
Herrera de Alcántara, Spain 35 F3
Herrera de Pisuerga, Spain 34 C6
Herrera del Duque, Spain 35 F5
Herrestad, Sweden 11 F5
Herrin, U.S.A. 113 G10
Herriot, Canada 105 B8
Herrljunga, Sweden 11 F7
Hersbruck, Germany 25 F7
Hershey, U.S.A. 111 F8
Hersonissos, Greece 36 D7
Herstal, Belgium 17 D5
Hertford, U.K. 13 F7
Hertfordshire □, U.K. 13 F7
's-Hertogenbosch, Neths. 17 C5
Hertzogville, S. Africa 88 D4
Hervás, Spain 34 E5
Hervey B., Australia 94 C5
Herzberg, Brandenburg, Germany 24 D9
Herzberg, Niedersachsen, Germany 24 D6
Herzliyya, Israel 75 C3
Herzogenburg, Austria 26 C8
Ḥeṣār, Fārs, Iran 71 D6
Ḥeṣār, Markazī, Iran 71 C6
Hesdin, France 19 B9
Heshan, China 58 F7
Heshui, China 56 G5
Heshun, China 56 F7
Hesperia, U.S.A. 117 L9
Hesse = Hessen □, Germany 24 E4
Hessen □, Germany 24 E4
Hestra, Sweden 11 G7
Hetch Hetchy Aqueduct, U.S.A. 116 H5
Hettinger, U.S.A. 112 C3
Hettstedt, Germany 24 D7
Heuvelton, U.S.A. 111 B9
Heves, Hungary 42 C5
Heves □, Hungary 42 C5
Hewitt, U.S.A. 113 K6
Hexham, U.K. 12 C5
Hexi, Yunnan, China 58 E4
Hexi, Zhejiang, China 59 D12
Hexigten Qi, China 57 C9
Ḥeydarābād, Iran 71 D7
Heysham, U.K. 12 C5
Heyuan, China 59 F10
Heywood, Australia 95 F3
Heze, China 56 G8
Hezhang, China 58 D5
Hi Vista, U.S.A. 117 L9
Hialeah, U.S.A. 109 N5
Hiawatha, U.S.A. 112 F7
Hibbing, U.S.A. 112 B8
Hibbs B., Australia 94 G4
Hibernia Reef, Australia 92 B3
Hickman, U.S.A. 113 G10
Hickory, U.S.A. 109 H5
Hicks, Pt., Australia 95 F4
Hicks L., Canada 105 A9
Hicksville, U.S.A. 111 F11
Hida, Romania 43 C8
Hida-Gawa →, Japan 55 G8
Hida-Sammyaku, Japan 55 F8
Hidaka-Sammyaku, Japan 54 C11
Hidalgo, Mexico 119 C5
Hidalgo □, Mexico 119 C5
Hidalgo, Presa M., Mexico 118 B3
Hidalgo, Pta. del, Canary Is. 37 F3
Hidalgo del Parral, Mexico 118 B3
Hiddensee, Germany 24 A9
Hieflau, Austria 26 D7
Hiendelaencina, Spain 32 D2
Hierro, Canary Is. 37 G1
Higashiajima-San, Japan 54 F10
Higashiōsaka, Japan 55 G7
Higgins, U.S.A. 113 G4
Higgins Corner, U.S.A. 116 F5
High Atlas = Haut Atlas, Morocco 78 B4
High Bridge, U.S.A. 111 F10
High Level, Canada 104 B5
High Point, U.S.A. 109 H6
High Prairie, Canada 104 B5
High River, Canada 104 C6
High Tatra = Tatry, Slovak Rep. 27 B13
High Veld, Africa 76 J6
High Wycombe, U.K. 13 F7
Highland □, U.K. 14 D4
Highland Park, U.S.A. 108 D2
Highmore, U.S.A. 112 C5
Highrock L., Man., Canada 105 B8
Highrock L., Sask., Canada 105 B7
Higüey, Dom. Rep. 121 C6
Hihya, Egypt 80 H7
Hiiumaa, Estonia 9 G20
Híjar, Spain 32 D4
Ḥijāz □, Si. Arabia 70 E3
Hijo = Tagum, Phil. 61 H6
Hikari, Japan 55 H5
Hikmak, Ras el, Egypt 80 A2
Hiko, U.S.A. 116 H11
Hikone, Japan 55 G8
Hikurangi, N.Z. 91 F5
Hikurangi, Mt., N.Z. 91 H6
Hildburghausen, Germany 24 E6
Hildesheim, Germany 24 C5
Hill →, Australia 93 F2
Hill City, Idaho, U.S.A. 114 E6
Hill City, Kans., U.S.A. 112 F5
Hill City, S. Dak., U.S.A. 112 D3
Hill Island L., Canada 105 A7
Hillared, Sweden 11 G7
Hillcrest Center, U.S.A. 117 K8
Hillegom, Neths. 17 B4
Hillerød, Denmark 11 J6
Hillerstorp, Sweden 11 G7
Hillsboro, Kans., U.S.A. 112 F6
Hillsboro, N. Dak., U.S.A. 112 B6
Hillsboro, N.H., U.S.A. 111 C13
Hillsboro, Ohio, U.S.A. 108 F4
Hillsboro, Oreg., U.S.A. 116 E4
Hillsboro, Tex., U.S.A. 113 J6
Hillsborough, Grenada 121 D7
Hillsdale, Mich., U.S.A. 108 E3
Hillsdale, N.Y., U.S.A. 111 D11
Hillsport, Canada 102 C2
Hillston, Australia 95 E4
Hilo, U.S.A. 106 J17
Hilton, U.S.A. 110 C7
Hilton Head Island, U.S.A. 109 J5
Hilvan, Turkey 73 D8
Hilversum, Neths. 17 B5
Himachal Pradesh □, India 68 D7
Himalaya, Asia 69 E11
Himamaylan, Phil. 61 F5
Himarë, Albania 40 F3
Himatnagar, India 66 H8
Himeji, Japan 55 G7
Himi, Japan 55 F8
Himmerland, Denmark 11 H3
Ḥimş, Syria 75 A5
Ḥimş □, Syria 75 A6
Hinche, Haiti 121 C5
Hinchinbrook I., Australia 94 B4
Hinckley, U.K. 13 E6
Hinckley, U.S.A. 112 B8
Hindaun, India 68 F7
Hindmarsh, L., Australia 95 F3
Hindsholm, Denmark 11 J4
Hindu Bagh, Pakistan 68 D2
Hindu Kush, Asia 66 B7
Hindubagh, Pakistan 66 D5
Hindupur, India 66 N10
Hines Creek, Canada 104 B5
Hinesville, U.S.A. 109 K5
Hinganghat, India 66 J11
Hingham, U.S.A. 114 B8
Hingir, India 69 J10
Hingoli, India 66 K10
Hinigaran, Phil. 61 F5
Hinis, Turkey 73 C9
Hinna = Imi, Ethiopia 81 F5
Hinna, Nigeria 83 C7
Hinnerup, Denmark 11 H4
Hinnøya, Norway 8 B16
Hinojosa del Duque, Spain 35 G5
Hinsdale, U.S.A. 111 D12
Hinterrhein →, Switz. 25 J5
Hinton, Canada 104 C5
Hinton, U.S.A. 108 G5
Hınzır Burnu, Turkey 72 D6
Hirado, Japan 55 H4
Hirakud Dam, India 67 J13
Hiran →, India 69 H8
Hirapur, India 69 G8
Hiratsuka, Japan 55 G9
Hirfanlı Barajı, Turkey 72 C5
Hiroo, Japan 54 C11
Hirosaki, Japan 54 D10
Hiroshima, Japan 55 G6
Hiroshima □, Japan 55 G6
Hirson, France 19 C11
Hirtshals, Denmark 11 G3
Hisar, India 68 E6
Hisarcık, Turkey 39 B11
Hisarya, Bulgaria 41 D8
Hisb →, Iraq 70 D5
Ḥismá, Si. Arabia 70 D3
Hispaniola, W. Indies 121 C5
Hīt, Iraq 70 C4
Hita, Japan 55 H5
Hitachi, Japan 55 F10
Hitchin, U.K. 13 F7
Hitoyoshi, Japan 55 H5
Hitra, Norway 8 E13
Hitzacker, Germany 24 B7
Hixon, Canada 104 C4
Ḥiyyon, N. →, Israel 75 E4
Hjalmar L., Canada 105 A7
Hjälmaren, Sweden 10 E9
Hjältevad, Sweden 11 G9
Hjo, Sweden 11 F8
Hjørring, Denmark 11 G3
Hjortkvarn, Sweden 11 F9
Hkakabo Razi, Burma 67 E20
Hlinsko, Czech Rep. 26 B8
Hlobane, S. Africa 89 D5
Hlohovec, Slovak Rep. 27 C10
Hlučín, Czech Rep. 27 B11
Hluhluwe, S. Africa 89 D5
Hlukhiv, Ukraine 47 G7
Hlyboka, Ukraine 47 H3
Hlybokaye, Belarus 46 E4
Hnúšťa, Slovak Rep. 27 C12
Ho, Ghana 83 D5
Ho Chi Minh City = Thanh Pho Ho Chi Minh, Vietnam 65 G6
Ho Thuong, Vietnam 64 C5
Hoa Binh, Vietnam 58 G5
Hoa Da, Vietnam 65 G7
Hoa Hiep, Vietnam 65 G5
Hoai Nhon, Vietnam 64 E7
Hoang Lien Son, Vietnam 58 F4
Hoanib →, Namibia 88 B2
Hoare B., Canada 101 B13
Hoarusib →, Namibia 88 B2
Hobart, Australia 94 G4
Hobart, U.S.A. 113 H5
Hobbs, U.S.A. 113 J3
Hobbs Coast, Antarctica 5 D14
Hobe Sound, U.S.A. 109 M5
Hoboken, U.S.A. 111 F10
Hobro, Denmark 11 H3
Hoburgen, Sweden 11 H12
Hocalar, Turkey 39 C11
Hochfeld, Namibia 88 C2
Hochschwab, Austria 26 D8
Höchstadt, Germany 25 F6
Hockenheim, Germany 25 F4
Hodaka-Dake, Japan 55 F8
Hodgeville, Canada 105 C7
Hodgson, Canada 105 C9
Hódmezővásárhely, Hungary 42 D5
Hodna, Chott el, Algeria 78 A6
Hodonín, Czech Rep. 27 C10
Hoeamdong, N. Korea 57 C16
Hœdic, Î. de, France 18 E4
Hoek van Holland, Neths. 17 C4
Hoengsŏng, S. Korea 57 F14
Hoeryong, N. Korea 57 C15
Hoeyang, N. Korea 57 E14
Hof, Germany 25 E7
Hofgeismar, Germany 24 D5
Hofheim, Germany 25 E4
Hofmeyr, S. Africa 88 E4
Höfn, Iceland 8 D6
Hofors, Sweden 10 D10
Hofsjökull, Iceland 8 D4
Hōfu, Japan 55 G5
Hogan Group, Australia 95 F4
Höganäs, Sweden 11 H6
Hogarth, Mt., Australia 94 C2
Hoggar = Ahaggar, Algeria 78 D7
Högsäter, Sweden 11 F6
Högsby, Sweden 11 G10
Högsjö, Sweden 10 E9
Hogsty Reef, Bahamas 121 B5
Hoh →, U.S.A. 116 C2
Hohe Acht, Germany 25 E3
Hohe Tauern, Austria 26 D5
Hohe Venn, Belgium 17 D6
Hohenau, Austria 27 C9
Hohenems, Austria 26 D2
Hohenloher Ebene, Germany 25 F5
Hohenwald, U.S.A. 109 H2
Hohenwestedt, Germany 24 A5
Hoher Rhön = Rhön, Germany 24 E5
Hohhot, China 56 D6
Hóhlakas, Greece 36 D9
Hohoe, Ghana 83 D5
Hoi An, Vietnam 64 E7
Hoi Xuan, Vietnam 58 G5
Hoisington, U.S.A. 112 F5
Højer, Denmark 11 K2
Hōjō, Japan 55 H6
Hok, Sweden 11 G8
Hökensås, Sweden 11 G8
Hökerum, Sweden 11 G7
Hokianga Harbour, N.Z. 91 F4
Hokitika, N.Z. 91 K3
Hokkaidō □, Japan 54 C11
Hol-Hol, Djibouti 81 E5
Hola Pristan, Ukraine 47 J7
Holbæk, Denmark 11 J5
Holbrook, Australia 95 F4
Holbrook, U.S.A. 115 J8
Holden, U.S.A. 114 G7
Holdenville, U.S.A. 113 H6
Holdrege, U.S.A. 112 E5
Holešov, Czech Rep. 27 B10
Holguín, Cuba 120 B4
Holíč, Slovak Rep. 27 C10
Holice, Czech Rep. 26 A8
Höljes, Sweden 10 D6
Hollabrunn, Austria 26 C9
Hollams Bird I., Namibia 88 C1
Holland, Mich., U.S.A. 108 D2
Holland, N.Y., U.S.A. 110 D6
Hollandale, U.S.A. 113 J9
Hollandia = Jayapura, Indonesia 63 E10
Holley, U.S.A. 110 C6
Hollfeld, Germany 25 F7
Hollidaysburg, U.S.A. 110 F6
Hollis, U.S.A. 113 H5
Hollister, Calif., U.S.A. 116 J5
Hollister, Idaho, U.S.A. 114 E6
Höllviken = Höllviksnäs, Sweden 11 J6
Höllviksnäs, Sweden 11 J6
Holly Hill, U.S.A. 109 L5
Holly Springs, U.S.A. 113 H10
Hollywood, U.S.A. 109 N5
Holman, Canada 100 A8
Hólmavík, Iceland 8 D3
Holmen, U.S.A. 112 D9
Holmes Reefs, Australia 94 B4
Holmsjö, Sweden 11 H9
Holmsjön, Västernorrland, Sweden 10 B10
Holmsjön, Västernorrland, Sweden 10 B9
Holmsland Klit, Denmark 11 J2
Holmsund, Sweden 8 E19
Holod, Romania 42 D7
Holroyd →, Australia 94 A3
Holstebro, Denmark 11 H2
Holsworthy, U.K. 13 G3
Holton, Canada 103 B8
Holton, U.S.A. 112 F7
Holtville, U.S.A. 117 N11
Holwerd, Neths. 17 A5
Holy I., Angl., U.K. 12 D3
Holy I., Northumb., U.K. 12 B6
Holyhead, U.K. 12 D3
Holyoke, Colo., U.S.A. 112 E3
Holyoke, Mass., U.S.A. 111 D12
Holyrood, Canada 103 C9
Holzkirchen, Germany 25 H7
Holzminden, Germany 24 D5
Homa Bay, Kenya 86 C3
Homalin, Burma 67 G19
Homand, Iran 71 C8
Homathko →, Canada 104 C4
Homberg, Germany 24 D5
Hombori, Mali 83 B4
Homburg, Germany 25 F3
Home B., Canada 101 B13
Home Hill, Australia 94 B4
Homedale, U.S.A. 114 E5
Homer, Alaska, U.S.A. 100 C4
Homer, La., U.S.A. 113 J8
Homer City, U.S.A. 110 F5
Homestead, Australia 94 C4
Homestead, U.S.A. 109 N5
Homewood, U.S.A. 116 F6
Homoine, Mozam. 89 C6
Homoljske Planina, Serbia, Yug. 40 B5
Homorod, Romania 43 D10
Homs = Ḥimş, Syria 75 A5
Homyel, Belarus 47 F6
Hon Chong, Vietnam 65 G5
Hon Me, Vietnam 64 C5
Honan = Henan □, China 56 H8
Honaz, Turkey 39 D11
Honbetsu, Japan 54 C11
Honcut, U.S.A. 116 F5
Honda Bay, Phil. 61 G3
Hondarribia, Spain 32 B3
Hondeklipbaai, S. Africa 88 E2
Hondo, Japan 55 H5
Hondo, U.S.A. 113 L5
Hondo →, Belize 119 D7
Honduras ■, Cent. Amer. 120 D2
Honduras, G. de, Caribbean 120 C2
Hønefoss, Norway 9 F14
Honesdale, U.S.A. 111 E9
Honey L., U.S.A. 116 E6
Honfleur, France 18 C7
Høng, Denmark 11 J5
Hong →, Vietnam 58 F5
Hong Gai, Vietnam 58 G6
Hong He →, China 56 H8
Hong Hu, China 59 C9
Hong Kong □, China 59 F10
Hong'an, China 59 B10
Hongch'ŏn, S. Korea 57 F14
Honghai Wan, China 59 F10
Honghe, China 58 F4
Honghu, China 59 C9
Hongjiang, China 58 D7
Hongliu He →, China 56 F5
Hongor, Mongolia 56 B7
Hongsa, Laos 64 C3
Hongshui He →, China 58 F7
Hongsŏng, S. Korea 57 F14
Hongtong, China 56 F6
Honguedo, Détroit d', Canada 103 C7
Hongwon, N. Korea 57 E14
Hongya, China 58 C4
Hongyuan, China 58 A4
Hongze Hu, China 57 H10
Honiara, Solomon Is. 96 H7
Honiton, U.K. 13 G4
Honjō, Japan 54 E10
Honkorâb, Ras, Egypt 80 C4
Honningsvåg, Norway 8 A21
Hönö, Sweden 11 G5
Honolulu, U.S.A. 106 H16
Hontoria del Pinar, Spain 32 D1
Hood, Mt., U.S.A. 114 D3
Hood, Pt., Australia 93 F2
Hood River, U.S.A. 114 D3
Hoodsport, U.S.A. 116 C3
Hooge, Germany 24 A4
Hoogeveen, Neths. 17 B6
Hoogezand-Sappemeer, Neths. 17 A6
Hooghly = Hugli →, India 69 J13
Hooghly-Chinsura = Chunchura, India 69 H13
Hook Hd., Ireland 15 D5
Hook I., Australia 94 C4
Hook of Holland = Hoek van Holland, Neths. 17 C4
Hooker, U.S.A. 113 G4
Hooker Creek, Australia 92 C5
Hoonah, U.S.A. 104 B1
Hooper Bay, U.S.A. 100 B3
Hoopeston, U.S.A. 108 E2
Hoopstad, S. Africa 88 D4
Höör, Sweden 11 J7
Hoorn, Neths. 17 B5
Hoover, U.S.A. 109 J2
Hoover Dam, U.S.A. 117 K12
Hooversville, U.S.A. 110 F6
Hop Bottom, U.S.A. 111 E9
Hopa, Turkey 73 B9
Hope, Canada 104 D4
Hope, Ariz., U.S.A. 117 M13
Hope, Ark., U.S.A. 113 J8
Hope, L., S. Austral., Australia 95 D2
Hope, L., W. Austral., Australia 93 F3
Hope I., Canada 110 B4
Hope Town, Bahamas 120 A4
Hopedale, Canada 103 A7
Hopedale, U.S.A. 111 D13
Hopefield, S. Africa 88 E2
Hopei = Hebei □, China 56 E9
Hopelchén, Mexico 119 D7
Hopetoun, Vic., Australia 95 F3
Hopetoun, W. Austral., Australia 93 F3
Hopetown, S. Africa 88 D3
Hopevale, Australia 94 B4
Hopewell, U.S.A. 108 G7
Hopfgarten, Austria 26 D5
Hopkins, L., Australia 92 D4
Hopkinsville, U.S.A. 109 G2
Hopland, U.S.A. 116 G3
Hoquiam, U.S.A. 116 D3
Horasan, Turkey 73 B10
Horažďovice, Czech Rep. 26 B6
Horb, Germany 25 G4
Hörby, Sweden 11 J7
Horcajo de Santiago, Spain 32 F1
Horden Hills, Australia 92 D5
Horezu, Romania 43 E8
Horgen, Switz. 25 H4
Horgoš, Serbia, Yug. 42 D4
Hořice, Czech Rep. 26 A8
Horinger, China 56 D6
Horki, Belarus 46 E6
Horlick Mts., Antarctica 5 E15
Horlivka, Ukraine 47 H10
Hormak, Iran 71 D9
Hormoz, Iran 71 E7
Hormoz, Jaz.-ye, Iran 71 E8
Hormozgān □, Iran 71 E8
Hormuz, Kūh-e, Iran 71 E7

Hormuz, Str. of, *The Gulf* 71 E8
Horn, *Austria* 26 C8
Horn, *Iceland* 8 C2
Horn, *Sweden* 11 G9
Horn →, *Canada* 104 A5
Horn, Cape = Hornos, C. de, *Chile* 122 J4
Horn Head, *Ireland* 15 A3
Horn I., *Australia* 94 A3
Horn Mts., *Canada* 104 A5
Hornachuelos, *Spain* 35 H5
Hornavan, *Sweden* 8 C17
Hornbeck, *U.S.A.* 113 K8
Hornbrook, *U.S.A.* 114 F2
Hornburg, *Germany* 24 C6
Horncastle, *U.K.* 12 D7
Horndal, *Sweden* 10 D10
Hornell, *U.S.A.* 110 D7
Hornell L., *Canada* 104 A5
Hornepayne, *Canada* 102 C3
Horní Planá, *Czech Rep.* 26 C7
Hornings Mills, *Canada* 110 B4
Hornitos, *U.S.A.* 116 H6
Hornos, C. de, *Chile* 122 J4
Hornoy-le-Bourg, *France* 19 C8
Hornsea, *U.K.* 12 D7
Hornslandet, *Sweden* 10 C11
Hörnum, *Germany* 24 A4
Horobetsu, *Japan* 54 C10
Horodenka, *Ukraine* 47 H3
Horodnya, *Ukraine* 47 G6
Horodok, *Khmelnytskyy, Ukraine* 47 H4
Horodok, *Lviv, Ukraine* 47 H2
Horodyshche, *Ukraine* 47 H6
Horokhiv, *Ukraine* 47 G3
Horovice, *Czech Rep.* 26 B6
Horqin Youyi Qianqi, *China* 57 A12
Horqueta, *Paraguay* 126 A4
Horred, *Sweden* 11 G6
Horse Creek, *U.S.A.* 112 E3
Horse Is., *Canada* 103 B8
Horsefly L., *Canada* 104 C4
Horseheads, *U.S.A.* 110 D8
Horsens, *Denmark* 11 J3
Horsham, *Australia* 95 F3
Horsham, *U.K.* 13 F7
Horšovský Týn, *Czech Rep.* 26 B5
Horten, *Norway* 9 G14
Hortobágy →, *Hungary* 42 C6
Horton, *U.S.A.* 112 F7
Horton →, *Canada* 100 B7
Horwood L., *Canada* 102 C3
Hosaina, *Ethiopia* 81 F4
Hose, Gunung-Gunung, *Malaysia* 62 D4
Ḩoseynābād, *Khuzestān, Iran* 71 C6
Ḩoseynābād, *Kordestān, Iran* 70 C5
Hoshangabad, *India* 68 H7
Hoshiarpur, *India* 68 D6
Hospet, *India* 66 M10
Hoste, I., *Chile* 128 H3
Hostens, *France* 20 D3
Hot, *Thailand* 64 C2
Hot Creek Range, *U.S.A.* 114 G6
Hot Springs, *Ark., U.S.A.* 113 H8
Hot Springs, *S. Dak., U.S.A.* 112 D3
Hotagen, *Sweden* 8 E16
Hotan, *China* 60 C2
Hotazel, *S. Africa* 88 D3
Hotchkiss, *U.S.A.* 115 G10
Hotham, C., *Australia* 92 B5
Hoting, *Sweden* 8 D17
Hotolisht, *Albania* 40 E4
Hotte, Massif de la, *Haiti* 121 C5
Hottentotsbaai, *Namibia* 88 D1
Houat, Î. de, *France* 18 E4
Houdan, *France* 19 D8
Houei Sai, *Laos* 58 G3
Houeillès, *France* 20 D4
Houffalize, *Belgium* 17 D5
Houghton, *Mich., U.S.A.* 112 B10
Houghton, *N.Y., U.S.A.* 110 D6
Houghton L., *U.S.A.* 108 C3
Houhora Heads, *N.Z.* 91 F4
Houlton, *U.S.A.* 109 B12
Houma, *U.S.A.* 113 L9
Houndé, *Burkina Faso* 82 C4
Hourtin, *France* 20 C2
Hourtin-Carcans, Étang d', *France* 20 C2
Housatonic →, *U.S.A.* 111 E11
Houston, *Canada* 104 C3
Houston, *Mo., U.S.A.* 113 G9
Houston, *Tex., U.S.A.* 113 L7
Hout →, *S. Africa* 89 C4
Houtkraal, *S. Africa* 88 E3
Houtman Abrolhos, *Australia* 93 E1
Hovd, *Mongolia* 60 B4
Hove, *U.K.* 13 G7
Hoveyzeh, *Iran* 71 D6
Hovmantorp, *Sweden* 11 H9
Hövsgöl, *Mongolia* 56 C5
Hövsgöl Nuur, *Mongolia* 60 A5
Hovsta, *Sweden* 10 E9
Howakil, *Eritrea* 81 D5
Howar, Wadi →, *Sudan* 81 D2
Howard, *Australia* 95 D5
Howard, *Pa., U.S.A.* 110 F7
Howard, *S. Dak., U.S.A.* 112 C6
Howe, *U.S.A.* 114 E7
Howe, C., *Australia* 95 F5
Howe I., *Canada* 111 B8
Howell, *U.S.A.* 108 D4
Howick, *Canada* 111 A11
Howick, *S. Africa* 89 D5
Howick Group, *Australia* 94 A4
Howitt, L., *Australia* 95 D2
Howland I., *Pac. Oc.* 96 G10
Howrah = Haora, *India* 69 H13
Howth Hd., *Ireland* 15 C5
Höxter, *Germany* 24 D5
Hoy, *U.K.* 14 C5
Hoya, *Germany* 24 C5
Høyanger, *Norway* 9 F12
Hoyerswerda, *Germany* 24 D10
Hoylake, *U.K.* 12 D4
Hoyos, *Spain* 34 E4
Hpa-an = Pa-an, *Burma* 67 L20
Hpungan Pass, *Burma* 67 F20
Hradec Králové, *Czech Rep.* 26 A8
Hrádek, *Czech Rep.* 27 C9
Hranice, *Czech Rep.* 27 B10
Hrazdan, *Armenia* 49 K7
Hrebenka, *Ukraine* 47 G7
Hrodna, *Belarus* 46 F2
Hrodzyanka, *Belarus* 46 F5
Hron →, *Slovak Rep.* 27 D11
Hrubieszów, *Poland* 45 H10
Hrubý Jeseník, *Czech Rep.* 27 A10
Hrvatska = Croatia ■, *Europe* 29 C13
Hrymayliv, *Ukraine* 47 H4
Hsenwi, *Burma* 67 H20
Hsiamen = Xiamen, *China* 59 E12
Hsian = Xi'an, *China* 56 G5
Hsinchu, *Taiwan* 59 E13
Hsinhailien = Lianyungang, *China* 57 G10
Hsinying, *Taiwan* 59 F13
Hsopket, *Burma* 58 F2
Hsüchou = Xuzhou, *China* 57 G9
Hu Xian, *China* 56 G5
Hua Hin, *Thailand* 64 F2
Hua Xian, *Henan, China* 56 G8
Hua Xian, *Shaanxi, China* 56 G5
Hua'an, *China* 59 E11
Huab →, *Namibia* 88 B2
Huacheng, *China* 59 E10
Huachinera, *Mexico* 118 A3
Huacho, *Peru* 124 F3
Huade, *China* 56 D7
Huadian, *China* 57 C14
Huadu, *China* 59 F9
Huai He →, *China* 59 A12
Huai Yot, *Thailand* 65 J2
Huai'an, *Hebei, China* 56 D8
Huai'an, *Jiangsu, China* 57 H10
Huaibei, *China* 56 G9
Huaibin, *China* 59 A10
Huaide = Gongzhuling, *China* 57 C13
Huaidezhen, *China* 57 C13
Huaihua, *China* 58 D7
Huaiji, *China* 59 F9
Huainan, *China* 59 A11
Huaining, *China* 59 B11
Huairen, *China* 56 E7
Huairou, *China* 56 D9
Huaiyang, *China* 56 H8
Huaiyin, *China* 57 H10
Huaiyuan, *Anhui, China* 57 H9
Huaiyuan, *Guangxi Zhuangzu, China* 58 E7
Huajianzi, *China* 57 D13
Huajuapan de Leon, *Mexico* 119 D5
Hualapai Peak, *U.S.A.* 115 J7
Hualien, *Taiwan* 59 E13
Huallaga →, *Peru* 124 E3
Huambo, *Angola* 85 G3
Huan Jiang →, *China* 56 G5
Huan Xian, *China* 56 F4
Huancabamba, *Peru* 124 E3
Huancane, *Peru* 124 G5
Huancavelica, *Peru* 124 F3
Huancayo, *Peru* 124 F3
Huanchaca, *Bolivia* 124 H5
Huang Hai = Yellow Sea, *China* 57 G12
Huang He →, *China* 57 F10
Huang Xian, *China* 57 F11
Huangchuan, *China* 59 A10
Huanggang, *China* 59 B10
Huangguoshu, *China* 58 E5
Huangling, *China* 56 G5
Huanglong, *China* 56 G5
Huanglongtan, *China* 59 A8
Huangmei, *China* 59 B10
Huangpi, *China* 59 B10
Huangping, *China* 58 D6
Huangshan, *China* 59 C12
Huangshi, *China* 59 B10
Huangsongdian, *China* 57 C14
Huangyan, *China* 59 C13
Huangyangsi, *China* 59 D8
Huaning, *China* 58 E4
Huanjiang, *China* 58 E7
Huantai, *China* 57 F9
Huánuco, *Peru* 124 E3
Huaping, *China* 58 D3
Huaraz, *Peru* 124 E3
Huarmey, *Peru* 124 F3
Huarong, *China* 59 C9
Huascarán, *Peru* 122 D3
Huasco, *Chile* 126 B1
Huasco →, *Chile* 126 B1
Huasna, *U.S.A.* 117 K6
Huatabampo, *Mexico* 118 B3
Huauchinango, *Mexico* 119 C5
Huautla de Jiménez, *Mexico* 119 D5
Huaxi, *China* 58 D6
Huay Namota, *Mexico* 118 C4
Huayin, *China* 56 G6
Huayuan, *China* 58 C7
Huayun, *China* 58 B6
Huazhou, *China* 59 G8
Hubbard, *Ohio, U.S.A.* 110 E4
Hubbard, *Tex., U.S.A.* 113 K6
Hubbart Pt., *Canada* 105 B10
Hubei □, *China* 59 B9
Huch'ang, *N. Korea* 57 D14
Hucknall, *U.K.* 12 D6
Huddersfield, *U.K.* 12 D6
Hude, *Germany* 24 B4
Hudi, *Sudan* 80 D3
Hudiksvall, *Sweden* 10 C11
Hudson, *Canada* 102 B1
Hudson, *Mass., U.S.A.* 111 D13
Hudson, *N.Y., U.S.A.* 111 D11
Hudson, *Wis., U.S.A.* 112 C8
Hudson, *Wyo., U.S.A.* 114 E9
Hudson →, *U.S.A.* 111 F10
Hudson Bay, *Nunavut, Canada* 101 C11
Hudson Bay, *Sask., Canada* 105 C8
Hudson Falls, *U.S.A.* 111 C11
Hudson Mts., *Antarctica* 5 D16
Hudson Str., *Canada* 101 B13
Hudson's Hope, *Canada* 104 B4
Hue, *Vietnam* 64 D6
Huebra →, *Spain* 34 D4
Huedin, *Romania* 42 D8
Huehuetenango, *Guatemala* 120 C1
Huejúcar, *Mexico* 118 C4
Huélamo, *Spain* 32 E3
Huelgoat, *France* 18 D3
Huelma, *Spain* 35 H7
Huelva, *Spain* 35 H4
Huelva □, *Spain* 35 H4
Huelva →, *Spain* 35 H5
Huentelauquén, *Chile* 126 C1
Huércal-Overa, *Spain* 33 H3
Huerta, Sa. de la, *Argentina* 126 C2
Huertas, C. de las, *Spain* 33 G4
Huerva →, *Spain* 32 D4
Huesca, *Spain* 32 C4
Huesca □, *Spain* 32 C5
Huéscar, *Spain* 33 H2
Huetamo, *Mexico* 118 D4
Huete, *Spain* 32 E2
Hugh →, *Australia* 94 D1
Hughenden, *Australia* 94 C3
Hughes, *Australia* 93 F4
Hughesville, *U.S.A.* 111 E8
Hugli →, *India* 69 J13
Hugo, *Colo., U.S.A.* 112 F3
Hugo, *Okla., U.S.A.* 113 H7
Hugoton, *U.S.A.* 113 G4
Hui Xian = Huixian, *China* 56 G7
Hui Xian, *China* 56 H4
Hui'an, *China* 59 E12
Hui'anbu, *China* 56 F4
Huichang, *China* 59 E10
Huichapán, *Mexico* 119 C5
Huidong, *Guangdong, China* 59 F10
Huidong, *Sichuan, China* 58 D4
Huifa He →, *China* 57 C14
Huila, Nevado del, *Colombia* 124 C3
Huilai, *China* 59 F11
Huili, *China* 58 D4
Huimin, *China* 57 F9
Huinan, *China* 57 C14
Huinca Renancó, *Argentina* 126 C3
Huining, *China* 56 G3
Huinong, *China* 56 E4
Huisache, *Mexico* 118 C4
Huishui, *China* 58 D6
Huisne →, *France* 18 E7
Huiting, *China* 56 G9
Huitong, *China* 58 D7
Huixian, *China* 56 G7
Huixtla, *Mexico* 119 D6
Huize, *China* 58 D4
Huizhou, *China* 59 F10
Hukawng Valley, *Burma* 67 F20
Hukou, *China* 59 C11
Hukuntsi, *Botswana* 88 C3
Ḩulayfā', *Si. Arabia* 70 E4
Huld = Ulaanjirem, *Mongolia* 56 B3
Hulin He →, *China* 57 B12
Hull = Kingston upon Hull, *U.K.* 12 D7
Hull, *Canada* 102 C4
Hull →, *U.K.* 12 D7
Hulst, *Neths.* 17 C4
Hultsfred, *Sweden* 11 G9
Hulun Nur, *China* 60 B6
Hulyaypole, *Ukraine* 47 J9
Humahuaca, *Argentina* 126 A2
Humaitá, *Brazil* 124 E6
Humaitá, *Paraguay* 126 B4
Humansdorp, *S. Africa* 88 E3
Humara, J., *Sudan* 81 D3
Humbe, *Angola* 88 B1
Humber →, *U.K.* 12 D7
Humboldt, *Canada* 105 C7
Humboldt, *Iowa, U.S.A.* 112 D7
Humboldt, *Tenn., U.S.A.* 113 H10
Humboldt →, *U.S.A.* 114 F4
Humboldt Gletscher, *Greenland* 4 B4
Hume, *U.S.A.* 116 J8
Hume, L., *Australia* 95 F4
Humenné, *Slovak Rep.* 27 C14
Hummelsta, *Sweden* 10 E10
Humphreys, Mt., *U.S.A.* 116 H8
Humphreys Peak, *U.S.A.* 115 J8
Humpolec, *Czech Rep.* 26 B8
Humptulips, *U.S.A.* 116 C3
Hūn, *Libya* 79 C9
Hun Jiang →, *China* 57 D13
Húnaflói, *Iceland* 8 D3
Hunan □, *China* 59 D9
Hunchun, *China* 57 C16
Hundested, *Denmark* 11 J5
Hundewali, *Pakistan* 68 D5
Hundred Mile House, *Canada* 104 C4
Hunedoara, *Romania* 42 E7
Hunedoara □, *Romania* 42 E7
Hünfeld, *Germany* 24 E5
Hung Yen, *Vietnam* 58 G6
Hungary ■, *Europe* 27 D12
Hungary, Plain of, *Europe* 6 F10
Hungerford, *Australia* 95 D3
Hŭngnam, *N. Korea* 57 E14
Hungt'ou Hsü, *Taiwan* 59 G13
Huni Valley, *Ghana* 82 D4
Hunneberg, *Sweden* 11 F6
Hunnebostrand, *Sweden* 11 F5
Hunsberge, *Namibia* 88 D2
Hunsrück, *Germany* 25 F3
Hunstanton, *U.K.* 12 E8
Hunte →, *Germany* 24 B4
Hunter, *U.S.A.* 111 D10
Hunter I., *Australia* 94 G3
Hunter I., *Canada* 104 C3
Hunter Ra., *Australia* 95 E5
Hunters Road, *Zimbabwe* 87 F2
Hunterville, *N.Z.* 91 H5
Huntingburg, *U.S.A.* 108 F2
Huntingdon, *Canada* 102 C5
Huntingdon, *U.K.* 13 E7
Huntingdon, *U.S.A.* 110 F6
Huntington, *Ind., U.S.A.* 108 E3
Huntington, *Oreg., U.S.A.* 114 D5
Huntington, *Utah, U.S.A.* 114 G8
Huntington, *W. Va., U.S.A.* 108 F4
Huntington Beach, *U.S.A.* 117 M9
Huntington Station, *U.S.A.* 111 F11
Huntly, *N.Z.* 91 G5
Huntly, *U.K.* 14 D6
Huntsville, *Canada* 102 C4
Huntsville, *Ala., U.S.A.* 109 H2
Huntsville, *Tex., U.S.A.* 113 K7
Hunyani →, *Zimbabwe* 87 F3
Hunyuan, *China* 56 E7
Hunza →, *India* 69 B6
Huo Xian = Huozhou, *China* 56 F6
Huong Hoa, *Vietnam* 64 D6
Huong Khe, *Vietnam* 64 C5
Huonville, *Australia* 94 G4
Huoqiu, *China* 59 A11
Huoshan, *Anhui, China* 59 A12
Huoshan, *Anhui, China* 59 B11
Huoshao Dao = Lü-Tao, *Taiwan* 59 F13
Huozhou, *China* 56 F6
Hupeh = Hubei □, *China* 59 B9
Ḩūr, *Iran* 71 D8
Hurbanovo, *Slovak Rep.* 27 D11
Hurd, C., *Canada* 110 A3
Hure Qi, *China* 57 C11
Hurezani, *Romania* 43 F8
Hurghada, *Egypt* 80 B3
Hurley, *N. Mex., U.S.A.* 115 K9
Hurley, *Wis., U.S.A.* 112 B9
Huron, *Calif., U.S.A.* 116 J6
Huron, *Ohio, U.S.A.* 110 E2
Huron, *S. Dak., U.S.A.* 112 C5
Huron, L., *U.S.A.* 110 B2
Hurricane, *U.S.A.* 115 H7
Hurso, *Ethiopia* 81 F5
Hurunui →, *N.Z.* 91 K4
Hurup, *Denmark* 11 H2
Húsavík, *Iceland* 8 C5
Huşi, *Romania* 43 D13
Huskvarna, *Sweden* 11 G8
Hustadvika, *Norway* 8 E12
Hustontown, *U.S.A.* 110 F6
Hustopeče, *Czech Rep.* 27 C9
Husum, *Germany* 24 A5
Husum, *Sweden* 10 A13
Hutchinson, *Kans., U.S.A.* 113 F6
Hutchinson, *Minn., U.S.A.* 112 C7
Hutte Sauvage, L. de la, *Canada* 103 A7
Hüttenberg, *Austria* 26 E7
Hutton, Mt., *Australia* 95 D4
Huwun, *Ethiopia* 81 G5
Huy, *Belgium* 17 D5
Huzhou, *China* 59 B13
Hvalpsund, *Denmark* 11 H3
Hvammstangi, *Iceland* 8 D3
Hvar, *Croatia* 29 E13
Hvarski Kanal, *Croatia* 29 E13
Hvítá →, *Iceland* 8 D3
Hwachŏn-chŏsuji, *S. Korea* 57 E14
Hwang Ho = Huang He →, *China* 57 F10
Hwange, *Zimbabwe* 87 F2
Hwange Nat. Park, *Zimbabwe* 88 B4
Hyannis, *Mass., U.S.A.* 108 E10
Hyannis, *Nebr., U.S.A.* 112 E4
Hyargas Nuur, *Mongolia* 60 B4
Hybo, *Sweden* 10 C10
Hydaburg, *U.S.A.* 104 B2
Hyde Park, *U.S.A.* 111 E11
Hyden, *Australia* 93 F2
Hyder, *U.S.A.* 104 B2
Hyderabad, *India* 66 L11
Hyderabad, *Pakistan* 68 G3
Hyères, *France* 21 E10
Hyères, Îs. d', *France* 21 F10
Hyesan, *N. Korea* 57 D15
Hyland →, *Canada* 104 B3
Hyltebruk, *Sweden* 11 H7
Hymia, *India* 69 C8
Hyndman Peak, *U.S.A.* 114 E6
Hyōgo □, *Japan* 55 G7
Hyrum, *U.S.A.* 114 F8
Hysham, *U.S.A.* 114 C10
Hythe, *U.K.* 13 F9
Hyūga, *Japan* 55 H5
Hyvinge = Hyvinkää, *Finland* 9 F21
Hyvinkää, *Finland* 9 F21

I

I-n-Gall, *Niger* 83 B6
I-n-Oudad, *Algeria* 83 A5
I-n-Ouzzal, *Algeria* 83 A5
I-n-Tadreft, *Niger* 83 B6
Iablaniţa, *Romania* 42 F7
Iaco →, *Brazil* 124 E5
Iacobeni, *Romania* 43 C10
Iakora, *Madag.* 89 C8
Ialomiţa □, *Romania* 43 F12
Ialomiţa →, *Romania* 43 F12
Ialoveni, *Moldova* 43 D13
Ialpug →, *Moldova* 43 E13
Ianca, *Romania* 43 E12
Iara, *Romania* 43 D8
Iarda, *Ethiopia* 81 E4
Iargara, *Moldova* 43 D13
Iaşi, *Romania* 43 C12
Iaşi □, *Romania* 43 C12
Íasmos, *Greece* 41 E9
Ib →, *India* 69 J10
Iba, *Phil.* 61 D3
Ibadan, *Nigeria* 83 D5
Ibagué, *Colombia* 124 C3
Iballë, *Albania* 40 D4
Ibăneşti, *Botoşani, Romania* 43 B11
Ibăneşti, *Mureş, Romania* 43 D9
Ibar →, *Serbia, Yug.* 40 C4
Ibaraki □, *Japan* 55 F10
Ibarra, *Ecuador* 124 C3
Ibba, *Sudan* 81 G2
Ibba, Bahr el →, *Sudan* 81 F2
Ibbenbüren, *Germany* 24 C3
Ibembo, *Dem. Rep. of the Congo* 86 B1
Ibera, L., *Argentina* 126 B4
Iberian Peninsula, *Europe* 6 H5
Iberville, *Canada* 102 C5
Iberville, Lac d', *Canada* 102 A5
Ibi, *Nigeria* 83 D6
Ibi, *Spain* 33 G4
Ibiá, *Brazil* 125 G9
Ibiapaba, Sa. da, *Brazil* 125 D10
Ibicuí →, *Brazil* 127 B4
Ibicuy, *Argentina* 126 C4
Ibiza = Eivissa, *Spain* 37 C7
Íblei, Monti, *Italy* 31 E7
Ibo, *Mozam.* 87 E5
Ibonma, *Indonesia* 63 E8
Ibotirama, *Brazil* 125 F10
Ibrāhīm →, *Lebanon* 75 A4
'Ibrī, *Oman* 71 F8
İbriktepe, *Turkey* 41 E10
Ibshawâi, *Egypt* 80 J7
Ibu, *Indonesia* 63 D7
Ibusuki, *Japan* 55 J5
Ica, *Peru* 124 F3
Iça →, *Brazil* 124 D5
Içana, *Brazil* 124 C5
Içana →, *Brazil* 124 C5
İçel = Mersin, *Turkey* 70 B2
Iceland ■, *Europe* 8 D4
Ich'ang = Yichang, *China* 59 B8
Ichchapuram, *India* 67 K14
Ichhawar, *India* 68 H7
Ichihara, *Japan* 55 G10
Ichikawa, *Japan* 55 G9
Ichilo →, *Bolivia* 124 G6
Ichinohe, *Japan* 54 D10
Ichinomiya, *Japan* 55 G8
Ichinoseki, *Japan* 54 E10
Ichnya, *Ukraine* 47 G7
Icod, *Canary Is.* 37 F3
Ida Grove, *U.S.A.* 112 D7
Idabel, *U.S.A.* 113 J7
Idaga Hamus, *Ethiopia* 81 E4
Idah, *Nigeria* 83 D6
Idaho □, *U.S.A.* 114 D7
Idaho City, *U.S.A.* 114 E6
Idaho Falls, *U.S.A.* 114 E7
Idanha-a-Nova, *Portugal* 34 F3
Idar-Oberstein, *Germany* 25 F3
Idfû, *Egypt* 80 C3
Ídhi Óros, *Greece* 36 D6
Ídhra, *Greece* 38 D5
Idi, *Indonesia* 62 C1
Idiofa, *Dem. Rep. of the Congo* 84 E3
Idkerberget, *Sweden* 10 D9
Idku, Bahra el, *Egypt* 80 H7
Idlib, *Syria* 70 C3
Idre, *Sweden* 10 C6
Idria, *U.S.A.* 116 J6
Idrija, *Slovenia* 29 C11
Idritsa, *Russia* 46 D5
Idutywa, *S. Africa* 89 E4
Ieper, *Belgium* 17 D2
Ierápetra, *Greece* 36 E7
Ierissós, *Greece* 40 F7
Ierissóu Kólpos, *Greece* 40 F7
Iernut, *Romania* 43 D9
Iesi, *Italy* 29 E10
Iésolo, *Italy* 29 C9
Ifach, Peñón de, *Spain* 33 G5
Ifakara, *Tanzania* 84 F7
'Ifāl, W. al →, *Si. Arabia* 70 D2
Ifanadiana, *Madag.* 89 C8
Ife, *Nigeria* 83 D5
Iférouâne, *Niger* 83 B6
Iffley, *Australia* 94 B3
Ifon, *Nigeria* 83 D6
Iforas, Adrar des, *Africa* 83 B5
Ifould, L., *Australia* 93 F5
Iganga, *Uganda* 86 B3
Igarapava, *Brazil* 125 H9
Igarka, *Russia* 50 C9
Igatimi, *Paraguay* 127 A4

Igbetti, *Nigeria* 83 D5
Igbo-Ora, *Nigeria* 83 D5
Igboho, *Nigeria* 83 D5
Igbor, *Nigeria* 83 D6
Iğdır, *Turkey* 73 C11
Igelfors, *Sweden* 11 F9
Iggesund, *Sweden* 10 C11
Iglésias, *Italy* 30 C1
Igloolik, *Canada* 101 B11
Igluligaarjuk, *Canada* 101 B10
Iglulik = Igloolik, *Canada* 101 B11
'Igma, Gebel el, *Egypt* 80 B3
Ignace, *Canada* 102 C1
İğneada, *Turkey* 41 E11
İğneada Burnu, *Turkey* 41 E12
Igoumenítsa, *Greece* 38 B2
Igra, *Russia* 48 B11
Iguaçu →, *Brazil* 127 B5
Iguaçu, Cat. del, *Brazil* 127 B5
Iguaçu Falls = Iguaçu, Cat. del, *Brazil* 127 B5
Iguala, *Mexico* 119 D5
Igualada, *Spain* 32 D6
Iguassu = Iguaçu →, *Brazil* 127 B5
Iguatu, *Brazil* 125 E11
Iharana, *Madag.* 89 A9
Ihbulag, *Mongolia* 56 C4
Iheya-Shima, *Japan* 55 L3
Ihiala, *Nigeria* 83 D6
Ihosy, *Madag.* 89 C8
Ihotry, Farihy, *Madag.* 89 C7
Ihugh, *Nigeria* 83 D6
Ii, *Finland* 8 D21
Ii-Shima, *Japan* 55 L3
Iida, *Japan* 55 G8
Iijoki →, *Finland* 8 D21
Iisalmi, *Finland* 8 E22
Iiyama, *Japan* 55 F9
Iizuka, *Japan* 55 H5
Ijebu-Igbo, *Nigeria* 83 D5
Ijebu-Ode, *Nigeria* 83 D5
IJmuiden, *Neths.* 17 B4
IJssel →, *Neths.* 17 B5
IJsselmeer, *Neths.* 17 B5
Ijuí, *Brazil* 127 B5
Ijuí →, *Brazil* 127 B4
Ikalamavony, *Madag.* 89 C8
Ikale, *Nigeria* 83 D6
Ikaluktutiak, *Canada* 100 B9
Ikang, *Nigeria* 83 E6
Ikara, *Nigeria* 83 C6
Ikare, *Nigeria* 83 D6
Ikaría, *Greece* 39 D8
Ikast, *Denmark* 11 H3
Ikeda, *Japan* 55 G6
Ikeja, *Nigeria* 83 D5
Ikela, *Dem. Rep. of the Congo* 84 E4
Ikerre-Ekiti, *Nigeria* 83 D6
Ikhtiman, *Bulgaria* 40 D7
Iki, *Japan* 55 H4
Ikimba L., *Tanzania* 86 C3
Ikire, *Nigeria* 83 D5
İkizdere, *Turkey* 73 B9
Ikom, *Nigeria* 83 D6
Ikongo, *Madag.* 89 C8
Ikopa →, *Madag.* 89 B8
Ikot Ekpene, *Nigeria* 83 D6
Ikungu, *Tanzania* 86 C3
Ikurun, *Nigeria* 83 D5
Ila, *Nigeria* 83 D5
Ilagan, *Phil.* 61 C4
Ilaka, *Madag.* 89 B8
Īlām, *Iran* 70 C5
Ilam, *Nepal* 69 F12
Ilam □, *Iran* 70 C5
Ilan, *Taiwan* 59 E13
Ilanskiy, *Russia* 51 D10
Ilaro, *Nigeria* 83 D5
Ilatane, *Niger* 83 B5
Iława, *Poland* 44 E6
Ile →, *Kazakstan* 50 E8
Ile-à-la-Crosse, *Canada* 105 B7
Ile-à-la-Crosse, Lac, *Canada* 105 B7
Île-de-France □, *France* 19 D9
Ileanda, *Romania* 43 C8
Ilebo, *Dem. Rep. of the Congo* 84 E4
Ilek, *Russia* 50 D6
Ilero, *Nigeria* 83 D5
Ilesha, *Kwara, Nigeria* 83 D5
Ilesha, *Oyo, Nigeria* 83 D5
Ilford, *Canada* 105 B9
Ilfracombe, *Australia* 94 C3
Ilfracombe, *U.K.* 13 F3
Ilgaz, *Turkey* 72 B5
Ilgaz Dağları, *Turkey* 72 B5
Ilgın, *Turkey* 72 C4
Ílhavo, *Portugal* 34 E2
Ilhéus, *Brazil* 125 F11
Ili = Ile →, *Kazakstan* 50 E8
Ilia, *Romania* 42 E7
Ilia □, *Greece* 38 D3
Iliamna L., *U.S.A.* 100 C4
Iliç, *Turkey* 73 C8
Ilıca, *Turkey* 39 B9
Ilichevsk, *Azerbaijan* 73 C11
Iligan, *Phil.* 61 G6
Iligan Bay, *Phil.* 61 G6
Ilíkí, L., *Greece* 38 C5
Ilin I., *Phil.* 61 E4
Iliodhrómia, *Greece* 38 B5
Ilion, *U.S.A.* 111 D9
Ilirska-Bistrica, *Slovenia* 29 C11
Ilkeston, *U.K.* 12 E6
Ilkley, *U.K.* 12 D6
Illampu = Ancohuma, Nevada, *Bolivia* 122 E4
Illana B., *Phil.* 61 H5
Illapel, *Chile* 126 C1
Ille-et-Vilaine □, *France* 18 D5
Ille-sur-Têt, *France* 20 F6
Illéla, *Niger* 83 C6
Iller →, *Germany* 25 G5
Illertissen, *Germany* 25 G6
Illescas, *Spain* 34 E7
Illetas, *Spain* 37 B9
Illichivsk, *Ukraine* 47 J6
Illiers-Combray, *France* 18 D8
Illimani, Nevado, *Bolivia* 124 G5
Illinois □, *U.S.A.* 112 E10
Illinois →, *U.S.A.* 107 C8
Illium = Troy, *Turkey* 39 B8
Illizi, *Algeria* 78 C7
Illkirch-Graffenstaden, *France* 19 D14
Íllora, *Spain* 35 H7
Ilm →, *Germany* 24 D7
Ilmajoki, *Finland* 9 E20
Ilmen, Ozero, *Russia* 46 C6
Ilmenau, *Germany* 24 E6
Ilo, *Peru* 124 G4
Ilobu, *Nigeria* 83 D5
Iloilo, *Phil.* 61 F5
Ilora, *Nigeria* 83 D5
Ilorin, *Nigeria* 83 D5
Ilovatka, *Russia* 48 E7
Ilovlya, *Russia* 49 F7
Ilovlya →, *Russia* 49 F7
Iłowa, *Poland* 45 G2
Ilubabor □, *Ethiopia* 81 F4
Ilva Mică, *Romania* 43 C9
Ilwaco, *U.S.A.* 116 D2
Ilwaki, *Indonesia* 63 F7
Ilyichevsk = Illichivsk, *Ukraine* 47 J6
Iłża, *Poland* 45 G8
Iłzanka →, *Poland* 45 G8
Imabari, *Japan* 55 G6
Imaloto →, *Madag.* 89 C8
Imamoğlu, *Turkey* 72 D6
Imandra, Ozero, *Russia* 50 C4
Imanombo, *Madag.* 89 C8
Imari, *Japan* 55 H4
Imasa, *Sudan* 80 D4
Imathía □, *Greece* 40 F6
Imatra, *Finland* 46 B5
Imbil, *Australia* 95 D5
Iménas, *Mali* 83 B5
imeni 26 Bakinskikh Komissarov = Neftçala, *Azerbaijan* 71 B6
imeni 26 Bakinskikh Komissarov, *Turkmenistan* 71 B7
Imeri, Serra, *Brazil* 124 C5
Imerimandroso, *Madag.* 89 B8
Imi, *Ethiopia* 81 F5
Imishly = Imişli, *Azerbaijan* 49 L9
Imişli, *Azerbaijan* 49 L9
Imlay, *U.S.A.* 114 F4
Imlay City, *U.S.A.* 110 D1
Immaseri, *Sudan* 81 D2
Immenstadt, *Germany* 25 H6
Immingham, *U.K.* 12 D7
Immokalee, *U.S.A.* 109 M5
Imo □, *Nigeria* 83 D6
Imo →, *Nigeria* 83 E6
Ímola, *Italy* 29 D8
Imotski, *Croatia* 29 E14
Imperatriz, *Brazil* 125 E9
Impéria, *Italy* 28 E5
Imperial, *Canada* 105 C7
Imperial, *Calif., U.S.A.* 117 N11
Imperial, *Nebr., U.S.A.* 112 E4
Imperial Beach, *U.S.A.* 117 N9
Imperial Dam, *U.S.A.* 117 N12
Imperial Reservoir, *U.S.A.* 117 N12
Imperial Valley, *U.S.A.* 117 N11
Imperieuse Reef, *Australia* 92 C2
Impfondo, *Congo* 84 D3
Imphal, *India* 67 G18
Imphy, *France* 19 F10
Imranlı, *Turkey* 73 C8
Imroz = Gökçeada, *Turkey* 41 F9
Imroz, *Turkey* 41 F9
Imst, *Austria* 26 D3
Imuris, *Mexico* 118 A2
Imuruan B., *Phil.* 63 B5
In Akhmed, *Mali* 83 B4
In Aleï, *Mali* 82 B4
In Delimane, *Mali* 83 B5
In Guezzam, *Algeria* 83 B6
In Koufi, *Mali* 83 B5
In Salah, *Algeria* 78 C6
In Tallak, *Mali* 83 B5
In Tebezas, *Mali* 83 B5
Ina, *Japan* 55 G8
Inangahua, *N.Z.* 91 J3
Inanwatan, *Indonesia* 63 E8
Iñapari, *Peru* 124 F5
Inari, *Finland* 8 B22
Inarijärvi, *Finland* 8 B22
Inawashiro-Ko, *Japan* 54 F10
Inca, *Spain* 37 B9
Inca de Oro, *Chile* 126 B2
Incaguasi, *Chile* 126 B1
İnce Burun, *Turkey* 72 A6
İncekum Burnu, *Turkey* 72 D5
İncesu, *Turkey* 70 B2
Inch'ŏn, *S. Korea* 57 F14
Incio = Cruz de Incio, *Spain* 34 C3
Incirliova, *Turkey* 39 D9
Incline Village, *U.S.A.* 114 G4
Incomáti →, *Mozam.* 89 D5
Inda Silase, *Ethiopia* 81 E4
Indal, *Sweden* 10 B11
Indalsälven →, *Sweden* 10 B11
Indaw, *Burma* 67 G20
Indbir, *Ethiopia* 81 F4
Independence, *Calif., U.S.A.* 116 J8
Independence, *Iowa, U.S.A.* 112 D9
Independence, *Kans., U.S.A.* 113 G7
Independence, *Ky., U.S.A.* 108 F3
Independence, *Mo., U.S.A.* 112 F7
Independence Fjord, *Greenland* 4 A6
Independence Mts., *U.S.A.* 114 F5
Independența, *Romania* 43 E12
Index, *U.S.A.* 116 C5
India ■, *Asia* 66 K11
Indian →, *U.S.A.* 109 M5
Indian Cabins, *Canada* 104 B5
Indian Harbour, *Canada* 103 B8
Indian Head, *Canada* 105 C8
Indian Lake, *U.S.A.* 111 C10
Indian Ocean 52 K11
Indian Springs, *U.S.A.* 117 J11
Indiana, *U.S.A.* 110 F5
Indiana □, *U.S.A.* 108 F3
Indianapolis, *U.S.A.* 108 F2
Indianola, *Iowa, U.S.A.* 112 E8
Indianola, *Miss., U.S.A.* 113 J9
Indigirka →, *Russia* 51 B15
Inđija, *Serbia, Yug.* 42 E5
Indio, *U.S.A.* 117 M10
Indo-China, *Asia* 52 H14
Indonesia ■, *Asia* 62 F5
Indore, *India* 68 H6
Indramayu, *Indonesia* 63 G13
Indravati →, *India* 67 K12
Indre □, *France* 19 F8
Indre →, *France* 18 E7
Indre-et-Loire □, *France* 18 E7
Indulkana, *Australia* 95 D1
Indus →, *Pakistan* 68 G2
Indus, Mouth of the, *Pakistan* 68 H3
İnebolu, *Turkey* 72 B5
İnecik, *Turkey* 41 F11
İnegöl, *Turkey* 41 F13
Ineu, *Romania* 42 D6
Infantes = Villanueva de los Infantes, *Spain* 35 G7
Infiernillo, Presa del, *Mexico* 118 D4
Infiesto, *Spain* 34 B5
Ingelstad, *Sweden* 11 H8
Ingenio, *Canary Is.* 37 G4
Ingenio Santa Ana, *Argentina* 126 B2
Ingersoll, *Canada* 102 D3
Ingham, *Australia* 94 B4
Ingleborough, *U.K.* 12 C5
Inglewood, *Queens., Australia* 95 D5
Inglewood, *Vic., Australia* 95 F3
Inglewood, *N.Z.* 91 H5
Inglewood, *U.S.A.* 117 M8
Ingólfshöfði, *Iceland* 8 E5
Ingolstadt, *Germany* 25 G7
Ingomar, *U.S.A.* 114 C10
Ingonish, *Canada* 103 C7
Ingore, *Guinea-Biss.* 82 C1
Ingraj Bazar, *India* 69 G13
Ingrid Christensen Coast, *Antarctica* 5 C6
Ingul → = Inhul →, *Ukraine* 47 J7
Ingulec = Inhulec, *Ukraine* 47 J7
Ingulets → = Inhulets →, *Ukraine* 47 J7
Inguri → = Enguri →, *Georgia* 49 J5
Ingushetia □, *Russia* 49 J7
Ingwavuma, *S. Africa* 89 D5
Inhaca, *Mozam.* 89 D5
Inhafenga, *Mozam.* 89 C5
Inhambane, *Mozam.* 89 C6
Inhambane □, *Mozam.* 89 C5
Inhaminga, *Mozam.* 87 F4
Inharrime, *Mozam.* 89 C6
Inharrime →, *Mozam.* 89 C6
Inhisar, *Turkey* 39 A12
Inhul →, *Ukraine* 47 J7
Inhulec, *Ukraine* 47 J7
Inhulets →, *Ukraine* 47 J7
Iniesta, *Spain* 33 F3
Ining = Yining, *China* 50 E9
Inírida →, *Colombia* 124 C5
Inishbofin, *Ireland* 15 C1
Inisheer, *Ireland* 15 C2
Inishfree B., *Ireland* 15 A3
Inishkea North, *Ireland* 15 B1
Inishkea South, *Ireland* 15 B1
Inishmaan, *Ireland* 15 C2
Inishmore, *Ireland* 15 C2
Inishowen Pen., *Ireland* 15 A4
Inishshark, *Ireland* 15 C1
Inishturk, *Ireland* 15 C1
Inishvickillane, *Ireland* 15 D1
Injibara, *Ethiopia* 81 E4
Injune, *Australia* 95 D4
Inklin →, *Canada* 104 B2
Inland Sea = Setonaikai, *Japan* 55 G6
Inle L., *Burma* 67 J20
Inlet, *U.S.A.* 111 C10
Inn →, *Austria* 26 C6
Innamincka, *Australia* 95 D3
Inner Hebrides, *U.K.* 14 E2
Inner Mongolia = Nei Monggol Zizhiqu □, *China* 56 D7
Inner Sound, *U.K.* 14 D3
Innerkip, *Canada* 110 C4
Innetalling I., *Canada* 102 A4
Innisfail, *Australia* 94 B4
Innisfail, *Canada* 104 C6
In'noshima, *Japan* 55 G6
Innsbruck, *Austria* 26 D4
Innviertel, *Austria* 26 C6
Inny →, *Ireland* 15 C4
Inongo, *Dem. Rep. of the Congo* 84 E3
İnönü, *Turkey* 39 B12
Inoucdjouac = Inukjuak, *Canada* 101 C12
Inowrocław, *Poland* 45 F5
Inpundong, *N. Korea* 57 D14
Inscription, C., *Australia* 93 E1
Insein, *Burma* 67 L20
Insjön, *Sweden* 10 D9
Ińsko, *Poland* 44 E2
Însurăței, *Romania* 43 F12
Inta, *Russia* 50 C6
Intendente Alvear, *Argentina* 126 D3
İntepe, *Turkey* 39 A8
Interlaken, *Switz.* 25 J3
Interlaken, *U.S.A.* 111 D8
International Falls, *U.S.A.* 112 A8
Intiyaco, *Argentina* 126 B3
Întorsura Buzăului, *Romania* 43 E11
Inukjuak, *Canada* 101 C12
Inútil, B., *Chile* 128 G2
Inuvik, *Canada* 100 B6
Inveraray, *U.K.* 14 E3
Inverbervie, *U.K.* 14 E6
Invercargill, *N.Z.* 91 M2
Inverclyde □, *U.K.* 14 F4
Inverell, *Australia* 95 D5
Invergordon, *U.K.* 14 D4
Inverloch, *Australia* 95 F4
Invermere, *Canada* 104 C5
Inverness, *Canada* 103 C7
Inverness, *U.K.* 14 D4
Inverness, *U.S.A.* 109 L4
Inverurie, *U.K.* 14 D6
Investigator Group, *Australia* 95 E1
Investigator Str., *Australia* 95 F2
Inya, *Russia* 50 D9
Inyanga, *Zimbabwe* 87 F3
Inyangani, *Zimbabwe* 87 F3
Inyantue, *Zimbabwe* 88 B4
Inyo Mts., *U.S.A.* 116 J9
Inyokern, *U.S.A.* 117 K9
Inza, *Russia* 48 D8
Inzhavino, *Russia* 48 D6
Iō-Jima, *Japan* 55 J5
Ioánnina, *Greece* 38 B2
Ioánnina □, *Greece* 38 B2
Iola, *U.S.A.* 113 G7
Ion Corvin, *Romania* 43 F12
Iona, *U.K.* 14 E2
Ione, *U.S.A.* 116 G6
Ionia, *U.S.A.* 108 D3
Ionian Is. = Iónioi Nísoi, *Greece* 38 C2
Ionian Sea, *Medit. S.* 6 H9
Iónioi Nísoi, *Greece* 38 C2
Iónioi Nísoi □, *Greece* 38 C2
Íos, *Greece* 39 E7
Iowa □, *U.S.A.* 112 D8
Iowa →, *U.S.A.* 112 E9
Iowa City, *U.S.A.* 112 E9
Iowa Falls, *U.S.A.* 112 D8
Iowa Park, *U.S.A.* 113 J5
Ipala, *Tanzania* 86 C3
Ipameri, *Brazil* 125 G9
Ipáti, *Greece* 38 C4
Ipatinga, *Brazil* 125 G10
Ipatovo, *Russia* 49 H6
Ipel' →, *Europe* 27 D11
Ipiales, *Colombia* 124 C3
Ipin = Yibin, *China* 58 C5
Ípiros □, *Greece* 38 B2
Ipixuna, *Brazil* 124 E4
Ipoh, *Malaysia* 65 K3
Ippy, *C.A.R.* 84 C4
Ipsala, *Turkey* 41 F10
Ipsárion, Óros, *Greece* 41 F8
Ipswich, *Australia* 95 D5
Ipswich, *U.K.* 13 E9
Ipswich, *Mass., U.S.A.* 111 D14
Ipswich, *S. Dak., U.S.A.* 112 C5
Ipu, *Brazil* 125 D10
Iqaluit, *Canada* 101 B13
Iquique, *Chile* 124 H4
Iquitos, *Peru* 124 D4
Irabu-Jima, *Japan* 55 M2
Iracoubo, *Fr. Guiana* 125 B8
Īrafshān, *Iran* 71 E9
Irahuan, *Phil.* 61 G3
Iráklia, *Kikládhes, Greece* 39 E7
Iráklia, *Sérrai, Greece* 40 E7
Iráklion, *Greece* 36 D7
Iráklion □, *Greece* 36 D7
Irala, *Paraguay* 127 B5
Iran ■, *Asia* 71 C7
Iran, Gunung-Gunung, *Malaysia* 62 D4
Iran, Plateau of, *Asia* 52 F9
Iran Ra. = Iran, Gunung-Gunung, *Malaysia* 62 D4
Īrānshahr, *Iran* 71 E9
Irapuato, *Mexico* 118 C4
Iraq ■, *Asia* 70 C5
Irati, *Brazil* 127 B5
Irbes saurums, *Latvia* 44 A9
Irbid, *Jordan* 75 C4
Irbid □, *Jordan* 75 C5
Iregua →, *Spain* 32 C7
Ireland ■, *Europe* 15 C4
Irele, *Nigeria* 83 D6
Irgiz, Bolshaya →, *Russia* 48 D9
Irhyangdong, *N. Korea* 57 D15
Iri, *S. Korea* 57 G14
Irian Jaya □, *Indonesia* 63 E9
Irié, *Guinea* 82 D3
Iriga, *Phil.* 61 E5
Iringa, *Tanzania* 86 D4
Iringa □, *Tanzania* 86 D4
Iriomote-Jima, *Japan* 55 M1
Iriona, *Honduras* 120 C2
Iriri →, *Brazil* 125 D8
Irish Republic ■, *Europe* 15 C3
Irish Sea, *U.K.* 12 D3
Irkutsk, *Russia* 51 D11
Irlığanlı, *Turkey* 39 D11
Irma, *Canada* 105 C6
Irō-Zaki, *Japan* 55 G9
Iroise, Mer d', *France* 18 D2
Iron Baron, *Australia* 95 E2
Iron Gate = Portile de Fier, *Europe* 42 F7
Iron Knob, *Australia* 95 E2
Iron Mountain, *U.S.A.* 108 C1
Iron River, *U.S.A.* 112 B10
Irondequoit, *U.S.A.* 110 C7
Ironton, *Mo., U.S.A.* 113 G9
Ironton, *Ohio, U.S.A.* 108 F4
Ironwood, *U.S.A.* 112 B9
Iroquois, *Canada* 111 B9
Iroquois Falls, *Canada* 102 C3
Irosin, *Phil.* 61 E6
Irpin, *Ukraine* 47 G6
Irrara Cr. →, *Australia* 95 D4
Irrawaddy □, *Burma* 67 L19
Irrawaddy →, *Burma* 67 M19
Irrawaddy, Mouths of the, *Burma* 67 M19
Irricana, *Canada* 104 C6
Irsina, *Italy* 31 B9
Irtysh →, *Russia* 50 C7
Irumu, *Dem. Rep. of the Congo* 86 B2
Irún, *Spain* 32 B3
Irunea = Pamplona, *Spain* 32 C3
Irurzun, *Spain* 32 C3
Irvine, *U.K.* 14 F4
Irvine, *Calif., U.S.A.* 117 M9
Irvine, *Ky., U.S.A.* 108 G4
Irvinestown, *U.K.* 15 B4
Irving, *U.S.A.* 113 J6
Irvona, *U.S.A.* 110 F6
Irwin →, *Australia* 93 E1
Irymple, *Australia* 95 E3
Is, Jebel, *Sudan* 80 C4
Is-sur-Tille, *France* 19 E12
Isa, *Nigeria* 83 C6
Isa Khel, *Pakistan* 68 C4
Isaac →, *Australia* 94 C4
Isabel, *U.S.A.* 112 C4
Isabela, *Phil.* 61 H5
Isabela, I., *Mexico* 118 C3
Isabelia, Cord., *Nic.* 120 D2
Isabella Ra., *Australia* 92 D3
Isaccea, *Romania* 43 E13
Ísafjarðardjúp, *Iceland* 8 C2
Ísafjörður, *Iceland* 8 C2
Isagarh, *India* 68 G7
Isahaya, *Japan* 55 H5
Isaka, *Tanzania* 86 C3
Isakly, *Russia* 48 C10
Işalnița, *Romania* 43 F8
Isan →, *India* 69 F9
Isana = Içana →, *Brazil* 124 C5
Isanlu Makutu, *Nigeria* 83 D6
Isar →, *Germany* 25 G8
Isarco →, *Italy* 29 B8
Ísari, *Greece* 38 D3
Íscar, *Spain* 34 D6
İscehisar, *Turkey* 39 C12
Íschia, *Italy* 30 B6
Isdell →, *Australia* 92 C3
Ise, *Japan* 55 G8
Ise-Wan, *Japan* 55 G8
Isefjord, *Denmark* 11 J5
Isel →, *Austria* 26 E5
Iseo, *Italy* 28 C7
Iseo, L. d', *Italy* 28 C7
Iseramagazi, *Tanzania* 86 C3
Isère □, *France* 21 C9
Isère →, *France* 21 D8
Iserlohn, *Germany* 24 D3
Isérnia, *Italy* 31 A7
Iseyin, *Nigeria* 83 D5
Isfahan = Eşfahān, *Iran* 71 C6
Ishëm, *Albania* 40 E3
Ishigaki-Shima, *Japan* 55 M2
Ishikari-Gawa →, *Japan* 54 C10
Ishikari-Sammyaku, *Japan* 54 C11
Ishikari-Wan, *Japan* 54 C10
Ishikawa □, *Japan* 55 F8
Ishim, *Russia* 50 D7
Ishim →, *Russia* 50 D8
Ishinomaki, *Japan* 54 E10
Ishioka, *Japan* 55 F10
Ishkuman, *Pakistan* 69 A5
Ishpeming, *U.S.A.* 108 B2
Isigny-sur-Mer, *France* 18 C5
Isıklar Dağı, *Turkey* 41 F11
Işıklı, *Turkey* 39 C11
Isil Kul, *Russia* 50 D8
Ísili, *Italy* 30 C2
Isiolo, *Kenya* 86 B4
Isiro, *Dem. Rep. of the Congo* 86 B2
Isisford, *Australia* 94 C3
İskenderun, *Turkey* 70 B3
İskenderun Körfezi, *Turkey* 72 D6
İskilip, *Turkey* 72 B6
Iskŭr →, *Bulgaria* 41 C8
Iskŭr, Yazovir, *Bulgaria* 40 D7
Iskut →, *Canada* 104 B2
Isla →, *U.K.* 14 E5
Isla Cristina, *Spain* 35 H3
Isla Vista, *U.S.A.* 117 L7
İslâhiye, *Turkey* 72 D7
Islam Headworks, *Pakistan* 68 E5
Islamabad, *Pakistan* 68 C5
Islamgarh, *Pakistan* 68 F4
Islamkot, *Pakistan* 68 G4
Islampur, *India* 69 G11
Island L., *Canada* 105 C10

Island Lagoon, *Australia* 95 E2
Island Pond, *U.S.A.* 111 B13
Islands, B. of, *Canada* 103 C8
Islands, B. of, *N.Z.* 91 F5
Islay, *U.K.* 14 F2
Isle →, *France* 20 D3
Isle aux Morts, *Canada* 103 C8
Isle of Wight □, *U.K.* 13 G6
Isle Royale, *U.S.A.* 112 B10
Isle Royale National Park, *U.S.A.* 112 B10
Isleton, *U.S.A.* 116 G5
Ismail = Izmayil, *Ukraine* 47 K5
Ismâ'ilîya, *Egypt* 80 H8
Ismaning, *Germany* 25 G7
Isna, *Egypt* 80 B3
Isoanala, *Madag.* 89 C8
Isogstalo, *India* 69 B8
Ísola del Liri, *Italy* 29 G10
Ísola della Scala, *Italy* 28 C7
Ísola di Capo Rizzuto, *Italy* 31 D10
Isparta, *Turkey* 39 D12
Isperikh, *Bulgaria* 41 C10
Ispica, *Italy* 31 F7
Israel ■, *Asia* 75 D3
Isratu, *Eritrea* 81 D4
Issia, *Ivory C.* 82 D3
Issoire, *France* 20 C7
Issoudun, *France* 19 F8
Issyk-Kul, Ozero = Ysyk-Köl, *Kyrgyzstan* 50 E8
Ist, *Croatia* 29 D11
Istállós-kő, *Hungary* 42 B5
İstanbul, *Turkey* 41 E12
İstanbul □, *Turkey* 41 E12
İstanbul Boğazı, *Turkey* 41 E13
Istiaía, *Greece* 38 C5
Istok, *Kosovo, Yug.* 40 D4
Istokpoga, L., *U.S.A.* 109 M5
Istra, *Croatia* 29 C10
Istres, *France* 21 E8
Istria = Istra, *Croatia* 29 C10
Itá, *Paraguay* 126 B4
Itaberaba, *Brazil* 125 F10
Itabira, *Brazil* 125 G10
Itabirito, *Brazil* 127 A7
Itabuna, *Brazil* 125 F11
Itacaunas →, *Brazil* 125 E9
Itacoatiara, *Brazil* 124 D7
Itaipú, Reprêsa de, *Brazil* 127 B5
Itaituba, *Brazil* 125 D7
Itajaí, *Brazil* 127 B6
Itajubá, *Brazil* 127 A6
Itaka, *Tanzania* 87 D3
Italy ■, *Europe* 7 G8
Itamaraju, *Brazil* 125 G11
Itampolo, *Madag.* 89 C7
Itandrano, *Madag.* 89 C8
Itapecuru-Mirim, *Brazil* 125 D10
Itaperuna, *Brazil* 127 A7
Itapetininga, *Brazil* 127 A6
Itapeva, *Brazil* 127 A6
Itapicuru →, *Bahia, Brazil* 125 F11
Itapicuru →, *Maranhão, Brazil* 125 D10
Itapipoca, *Brazil* 125 D11
Itapuá □, *Paraguay* 127 B4
Itaquari, *Brazil* 127 A7
Itaquí, *Brazil* 126 B4
Itararé, *Brazil* 127 A6
Itarsi, *India* 68 H7
Itatí, *Argentina* 126 B4
Itbayat, *Phil.* 61 A4
Itchen →, *U.K.* 13 G6
Itéa, *Greece* 38 C4
Itezhi Tezhi, L., *Zambia* 87 F2
Ithaca = Itháki, *Greece* 38 C2
Ithaca, *U.S.A.* 111 D8
Itháki, *Greece* 38 C2
Itiquira →, *Brazil* 125 G7
Itō, *Japan* 55 G9
Itoigawa, *Japan* 55 F8
Iton →, *France* 18 C8
Itonamas →, *Bolivia* 124 F6
Itri, *Italy* 30 A6
Itsa, *Egypt* 80 J7
Ittiri, *Italy* 30 B1
Ittoqqortoormiit, *Greenland* 4 B6
Itu, *Brazil* 127 A6
Itu, *Nigeria* 83 D6
Itu Aba I., *S. China Sea* 62 B4
Ituiutaba, *Brazil* 125 G9
Itumbiara, *Brazil* 125 G9
Ituna, *Canada* 105 C8
Itunge Port, *Tanzania* 87 D3
Iturbe, *Argentina* 126 A2
Ituri →, *Dem. Rep. of the Congo* 86 B2
Iturup, Ostrov, *Russia* 51 E15
Ituxi →, *Brazil* 124 E6
Ituyuro →, *Argentina* 126 A3
Itzehoe, *Germany* 24 B5
Ivahona, *Madag.* 89 C8
Ivaí →, *Brazil* 127 A5
Ivalo, *Finland* 8 B22
Ivalojoki →, *Finland* 8 B22
Ivanava, *Belarus* 47 F3
Ivančice, *Czech Rep.* 27 B9
Ivănești, *Romania* 43 D12
Ivangorod, *Russia* 46 C5
Ivanhoe, *Australia* 95 E3
Ivanhoe, *Calif., U.S.A.* 116 J7
Ivanhoe, *Minn., U.S.A.* 112 C6
Ivanić Grad, *Croatia* 29 C13
Ivanjica, *Serbia, Yug.* 40 C4
Ivanjska, *Bos.-H.* 42 F2
Ivankoyskoye Vdkhr., *Russia* 46 D9
Ivano-Frankivsk, *Ukraine* 47 H3
Ivano-Frankovsk = Ivano-Frankivsk, *Ukraine* 47 H3
Ivanovo = Ivanava, *Belarus* 47 F3
Ivanovo, *Russia* 46 D11
Ivanšćica, *Croatia* 29 B13
Ivato, *Madag.* 89 C8
Ivatsevichy, *Belarus* 47 F3
Ivaylovgrad, *Bulgaria* 41 E10
Ivinheima →, *Brazil* 127 A5
Ivinhema, *Brazil* 127 A5
Ivohibe, *Madag.* 89 C8
Ivory Coast, *W. Afr.* 82 E4
Ivory Coast ■, *Africa* 82 D4
Ivösjön, *Sweden* 11 H8
Ivrea, *Italy* 28 C4
İvrindi, *Turkey* 39 B9
Ivujivik, *Canada* 101 B12
Ivybridge, *U.K.* 13 G4
Iwaizumi, *Japan* 54 E10
Iwaki, *Japan* 55 F10
Iwakuni, *Japan* 55 G6
Iwamizawa, *Japan* 54 C10
Iwanai, *Japan* 54 C10
Iwata, *Japan* 55 G8
Iwate □, *Japan* 54 E10
Iwate-San, *Japan* 54 E10
Iwo, *Nigeria* 83 D5
Iwonicz-Zdrój, *Poland* 45 J8
Ixiamas, *Bolivia* 124 F5
Ixopo, *S. Africa* 89 E5
Ixtepec, *Mexico* 119 D5
Ixtlán del Río, *Mexico* 118 C4
Iyal Bakhit, *Sudan* 81 E2
Iyo, *Japan* 55 H6
Izabal, L. de, *Guatemala* 120 C2
Izamal, *Mexico* 119 C7
Izberbash, *Russia* 49 J8
Izbica, *Poland* 45 H10
Izbica Kujawska, *Poland* 45 F5
Izbiceni, *Romania* 43 G9
Izena-Shima, *Japan* 55 L3
Izgrev, *Bulgaria* 41 C10
Izhevsk, *Russia* 50 D6
Izmayil, *Ukraine* 47 K5
İzmir, *Turkey* 39 C9
İzmir □, *Turkey* 39 C9
İzmir Körfezi, *Turkey* 39 C8
İzmit = Kocaeli, *Turkey* 41 F13
Iznájar, *Spain* 35 H6
Iznalloz, *Spain* 35 H7
İznik, *Turkey* 72 B3
İznik Gölü, *Turkey* 41 F13
Izobil'nyy, *Russia* 49 H5
Izola, *Slovenia* 29 C10
Izra, *Syria* 75 C5
Iztochni Rodopi, *Bulgaria* 41 E9
Izu-Shotō, *Japan* 55 G10
Izúcar de Matamoros, *Mexico* 119 D5
Izumi-Sano, *Japan* 55 G7
Izumo, *Japan* 55 G6
Izyaslav, *Ukraine* 47 G4
Izyum, *Ukraine* 47 H9

J

Jaba, *Ethiopia* 81 F4
Jabal at Tā'ir, *Red Sea* 81 D5
Jabalón →, *Spain* 35 G6
Jabalpur, *India* 69 H8
Jabbūl, *Syria* 70 B3
Jabiru, *Australia* 92 B5
Jablah, *Syria* 70 C3
Jablanac, *Croatia* 29 D11
Jablanica, *Bos.-H.* 42 G2
Jablonec nad Nisou, *Czech Rep.* 26 A8
Jablonica, *Slovak Rep.* 27 C10
Jabłonowo Pomorskie, *Poland* 44 E6
Jablunkov, *Czech Rep.* 27 B11
Jaboatão, *Brazil* 125 E11
Jaboticabal, *Brazil* 127 A6
Jabukovac, *Serbia, Yug.* 40 B6
Jaca, *Spain* 32 C4
Jacareí, *Brazil* 127 A6
Jacarèzinho, *Brazil* 127 A6
Jackman, *U.S.A.* 109 C10
Jacksboro, *U.S.A.* 113 J5
Jackson, *Ala., U.S.A.* 109 K2
Jackson, *Calif., U.S.A.* 116 G6
Jackson, *Ky., U.S.A.* 108 G4
Jackson, *Mich., U.S.A.* 108 D3
Jackson, *Minn., U.S.A.* 112 D7
Jackson, *Miss., U.S.A.* 113 J9
Jackson, *Mo., U.S.A.* 113 G10
Jackson, *N.H., U.S.A.* 111 B13
Jackson, *Ohio, U.S.A.* 108 F4
Jackson, *Tenn., U.S.A.* 109 H1
Jackson, *Wyo., U.S.A.* 114 E8
Jackson B., *N.Z.* 91 K2
Jackson L., *U.S.A.* 114 E8
Jacksons, *N.Z.* 91 K3
Jackson's Arm, *Canada* 103 C8
Jacksonville, *Ala., U.S.A.* 109 J3
Jacksonville, *Ark., U.S.A.* 113 H8
Jacksonville, *Calif., U.S.A.* 116 H6
Jacksonville, *Fla., U.S.A.* 109 K5
Jacksonville, *Ill., U.S.A.* 112 F9
Jacksonville, *N.C., U.S.A.* 109 H7
Jacksonville, *Tex., U.S.A.* 113 K7
Jacksonville Beach, *U.S.A.* 109 K5
Jacmel, *Haiti* 121 C5
Jacob Lake, *U.S.A.* 115 H7
Jacobabad, *Pakistan* 68 E3
Jacobina, *Brazil* 125 F10
Jacques Cartier, Dét. de, *Canada* 103 C7
Jacques Cartier, Mt., *Canada* 103 C6
Jacques Cartier, Parc Prov., *Canada* 103 C5
Jacqueville, *Ivory C.* 82 D4
Jacuí →, *Brazil* 127 C5
Jacumba, *U.S.A.* 117 N10
Jacundá →, *Brazil* 125 D8
Jade, *Germany* 24 B4
Jadebusen, *Germany* 24 B4
Jadotville = Likasi, *Dem. Rep. of the Congo* 87 E2
Jadovnik, *Serbia, Yug.* 40 C3
Jadraque, *Spain* 32 E2
Jaén, *Peru* 124 E3
Jaén, *Spain* 35 H7
Jaén □, *Spain* 35 H7
Jafarabad, *India* 68 J4
Jaffa = Tel Aviv-Yafo, *Israel* 75 C3
Jaffa, C., *Australia* 95 F2
Jaffna, *Sri Lanka* 66 Q12
Jaffrey, *U.S.A.* 111 D12
Jagadhri, *India* 68 D7
Jagadishpur, *India* 69 G11
Jagdalpur, *India* 67 K13
Jagersfontein, *S. Africa* 88 D4
Jaghīn →, *Iran* 71 E8
Jagodina, *Serbia, Yug.* 40 B5
Jagraon, *India* 66 D9
Jagst →, *Germany* 25 F5
Jagtial, *India* 66 K11
Jaguariaíva, *Brazil* 127 A6
Jaguaribe →, *Brazil* 125 D11
Jagüey Grande, *Cuba* 120 B3
Jahanabad, *India* 69 G11
Jahazpur, *India* 68 G6
Jahrom, *Iran* 71 D7
Jaijon, *India* 68 D7
Jailolo, *Indonesia* 63 D7
Jailolo, Selat, *Indonesia* 63 D7
Jaipur, *India* 68 F6
Jais, *India* 69 F9
Jaisalmer, *India* 68 F4
Jaisinghnagar, *India* 69 H8
Jaitaran, *India* 68 F5
Jaithari, *India* 69 H8
Jājarm, *Iran* 71 B8
Jajce, *Bos.-H.* 42 F2
Jakam →, *India* 68 H6
Jakarta, *Indonesia* 62 F3
Jakhal, *India* 68 E6
Jakhau, *India* 68 H3
Jakobstad = Pietarsaari, *Finland* 8 E20
Jakupica, *Macedonia* 40 E5
Jal, *U.S.A.* 113 J3
Jalālābād, *Afghan.* 68 B4
Jalalabad, *India* 69 F8
Jalalpur Jattan, *Pakistan* 68 C6
Jalama, *U.S.A.* 117 L6
Jalapa, *Guatemala* 120 D2
Jalapa Enríquez, *Mexico* 119 D5
Jalasjärvi, *Finland* 9 E20
Jalaun, *India* 69 F8
Jaldhaka →, *Bangla.* 69 F13
Jalesar, *India* 68 F8
Jaleswar, *Nepal* 69 F11
Jalgaon, *India* 66 J9
Jalībah, *Iraq* 70 D5
Jalingo, *Nigeria* 83 D7
Jalisco □, *Mexico* 118 D4
Jalkot, *Pakistan* 69 B5
Jallas →, *Spain* 34 C1
Jalna, *India* 66 K9
Jalón →, *Spain* 32 D3
Jalor, *India* 68 G5
Jalpa, *Mexico* 118 C4
Jalpaiguri, *India* 67 F16
Jaluit I., *Marshall Is.* 96 G8
Jalūlā, *Iraq* 70 C5
Jamaari, *Nigeria* 83 C6
Jamaica ■, *W. Indies* 120 C4
Jamalpur, *Bangla.* 67 G16
Jamalpur, *India* 69 G12
Jamalpurganj, *India* 69 H13
Jamanxim →, *Brazil* 125 D7
Jambi, *Indonesia* 62 E2
Jambi □, *Indonesia* 62 E2
Jambusar, *India* 68 H5
James →, *S. Dak., U.S.A.* 112 D6
James →, *Va., U.S.A.* 108 G7
James B., *Canada* 102 B3
James Ranges, *Australia* 92 D5
James Ross I., *Antarctica* 5 C18
Jamesabad, *Pakistan* 68 G3
Jamestown, *Australia* 95 E2
Jamestown, *S. Africa* 88 E4
Jamestown, *N. Dak., U.S.A.* 112 B5
Jamestown, *N.Y., U.S.A.* 110 D5
Jamestown, *Pa., U.S.A.* 110 E4
Jamīlābād, *Iran* 71 C6
Jamiltepec, *Mexico* 119 D5
Jamira →, *India* 69 J13
Jämjö, *Sweden* 11 H9
Jamkhandi, *India* 66 L9
Jammerbugt, *Denmark* 11 G3
Jammu, *India* 68 C6
Jammu & Kashmir □, *India* 69 B7
Jamnagar, *India* 68 H4
Jamni →, *India* 69 G8
Jampur, *Pakistan* 68 E4
Jamrud, *Pakistan* 68 C4
Jämsä, *Finland* 9 F21
Jamshedpur, *India* 69 H12
Jamtara, *India* 69 H12
Jämtland, *Sweden* 8 E15
Jämtlands län □, *Sweden* 10 B7
Jan L., *Canada* 105 C8
Jan Mayen, *Arctic* 4 B7
Janakkala, *Finland* 9 F21
Janaúba, *Brazil* 125 G10
Jand, *Pakistan* 68 C5
Jandaq, *Iran* 71 C7
Jandia, *Canary Is.* 37 F5
Jandia, Pta. de, *Canary Is.* 37 F5
Jandola, *Pakistan* 68 C4
Jandowae, *Australia* 95 D5
Jándula →, *Spain* 35 G6
Janesville, *U.S.A.* 112 D10
Janga, *Ghana* 83 C4
Jangamo, *Mozam.* 89 C6
Janghai, *India* 69 G10
Janikowo, *Poland* 45 F5
Janīn, *West Bank* 75 C4
Janinà = Ioánnina □, *Greece* 38 B2
Janja, *Bos.-H.* 42 F4
Janjevo, *Kosovo, Yug.* 40 D5
Janjgir, *India* 69 J10
Janjina, *Croatia* 29 F14
Janjina, *Madag.* 89 C8
Janos, *Mexico* 118 A3
Jánoshalma, *Hungary* 42 D4
Jánosháza, *Hungary* 42 C2
Jánossomorja, *Hungary* 42 C2
Janów, *Poland* 45 H6
Janów Lubelski, *Poland* 45 H9
Janów Podlaski, *Poland* 45 F10
Janowiec Wielkopolski, *Poland* 45 F4
Januária, *Brazil* 125 G10
Janub Dârfûr □, *Sudan* 81 E2
Janub Kordofân □, *Sudan* 81 E3
Janûb Sînî □, *Egypt* 75 F2
Janubio, *Canary Is.* 37 F6
Janville, *France* 19 D8
Janzé, *France* 18 E5
Jaora, *India* 68 H6
Japan ■, *Asia* 55 G8
Japan, Sea of, *Asia* 54 E7
Japan Trench, *Pac. Oc.* 52 F18
Japen = Yapen, *Indonesia* 63 E9
Japla, *India* 69 G11
Japurá →, *Brazil* 122 D4
Jaquarão, *Brazil* 127 C5
Jaqué, *Panama* 120 E4
Jarābulus, *Syria* 70 B3
Jaraicejo, *Spain* 35 F5
Jaraíz de la Vera, *Spain* 34 E5
Jarama →, *Spain* 34 E7
Jaramānah, *Syria* 72 F7
Jarandilla, *Spain* 34 E5
Jaranwala, *Pakistan* 68 D5
Jarash, *Jordan* 75 C4
Järbo, *Sweden* 10 D10
Jardim, *Brazil* 126 A4
Jardín →, *Spain* 33 G2
Jardines de la Reina, Arch. de los, *Cuba* 120 B4
Jargalang, *China* 57 C12
Jargalant = Hovd, *Mongolia* 60 B4
Jari →, *Brazil* 125 D8
Jarīr, W. al →, *Si. Arabia* 70 E4
Järlåsa, *Sweden* 10 E11
Jarmen, *Germany* 24 B9
Järna, *Dalarnas, Sweden* 10 D8
Järna, *Stockholm, Sweden* 10 E11
Jarnac, *France* 20 C3
Jarny, *France* 19 C12
Jarocin, *Poland* 45 G4
Jaroměř, *Czech Rep.* 26 A8
Jarosław, *Poland* 45 H9
Järpås, *Sweden* 11 F6
Järpen, *Sweden* 10 A7
Jarrahdale, *Australia* 93 F2
Jarrahi →, *Iran* 71 D6
Jarres, Plaine des, *Laos* 64 C4
Jarso, *Ethiopia* 81 F4
Jartai, *China* 56 E3
Jarud Qi, *China* 57 B11
Järvenpää, *Finland* 9 F21
Jarvis, *Canada* 110 D4
Jarvis I., *Pac. Oc.* 97 H12
Jarvorník, *Czech Rep.* 27 A10
Järvsö, *Sweden* 10 C10
Jarwa, *India* 69 F10
Jaša Tomić, *Serbia, Yug.* 42 E5
Jasdan, *India* 68 H4
Jashpurnagar, *India* 69 H11
Jasidih, *India* 69 G12
Jasień, *Poland* 45 G2
Jāsimīyah, *Iraq* 70 C5
Jasin, *Malaysia* 65 L4
Jāsk, *Iran* 71 E8
Jasło, *Poland* 45 J8
Jasmund, *Germany* 24 A9
Jaso, *India* 69 G9
Jasper, *Alta., Canada* 104 C5
Jasper, *Ont., Canada* 111 B9
Jasper, *Ala., U.S.A.* 109 J2
Jasper, *Fla., U.S.A.* 109 K4
Jasper, *Ind., U.S.A.* 108 F2
Jasper, *Tex., U.S.A.* 113 K8
Jasper Nat. Park, *Canada* 104 C5
Jasrasar, *India* 68 F5
Jastarnia, *Poland* 44 D5
Jastrebarsko, *Croatia* 29 C12
Jastrowie, *Poland* 44 E3
Jastrzębie Zdrój, *Poland* 45 J5
Jász-Nagykun-Szolnok □, *Hungary* 42 C5
Jászapáti, *Hungary* 42 C5
Jászárokszállás, *Hungary* 42 C4
Jászberény, *Hungary* 42 C4
Jászkisér, *Hungary* 42 C5
Jászladány, *Hungary* 42 C5
Jataí, *Brazil* 125 G8
Jati, *Pakistan* 68 G3
Jatibarang, *Indonesia* 63 G13
Jatinegara, *Indonesia* 63 G12
Játiva = Xátiva, *Spain* 33 G4
Jättendal, *Sweden* 10 C11
Jaú, *Brazil* 127 A6
Jauja, *Peru* 124 F3
Jaunpur, *India* 69 G10
Java = Jawa, *Indonesia* 62 F3
Java Barat □, *Indonesia* 63 G12
Java Sea, *Indonesia* 62 E3
Java Tengah □, *Indonesia* 63 G14
Java Timur □, *Indonesia* 63 G15
Java Trench, *Ind. Oc.* 62 F3
Javalambre, Sa. de, *Spain* 32 E4
Jávea, *Spain* 33 G5
Javhlant = Ulyasutay, *Mongolia* 60 B4
Jawa, *Indonesia* 62 F3
Jawad, *India* 68 G6
Jawor, *Poland* 45 G3
Jaworzno, *Poland* 45 H6
Jaworzyna Śląska, *Poland* 45 H3
Jay Peak, *U.S.A.* 111 B12
Jaya, Puncak, *Indonesia* 63 E9
Jayanti, *India* 67 F16
Jayapura, *Indonesia* 63 E10
Jayawijaya, Pegunungan, *Indonesia* 63 E9
Jaynagar, *India* 67 F15
Jayrūd, *Syria* 70 C3
Jayton, *U.S.A.* 113 J4
Jāz Mūrīān, Hāmūn-e, *Iran* 71 E8
Jazīreh-ye Shīf, *Iran* 71 D6
Jazminal, *Mexico* 118 C4
Jazzīn, *Lebanon* 75 B4
Jean, *U.S.A.* 117 K11
Jean Marie River, *Canada* 104 A4
Jean Rabel, *Haiti* 121 C5
Jeanerette, *U.S.A.* 113 L9
Jeanette, Ostrov = Zhannetty, Ostrov, *Russia* 51 B16
Jeannette, *U.S.A.* 110 F5
Jebāl Bārez, Kūh-e, *Iran* 71 D8
Jebba, *Nigeria* 83 D5
Jebel, Bahr el →, *Sudan* 81 F3
Jebel Dud, *Sudan* 81 E3
Jebel Qerri, *Sudan* 81 D3
Jedburgh, *U.K.* 14 F6
Jedda = Jiddah, *Si. Arabia* 74 C2
Jeddore L., *Canada* 103 C8
Jedlicze, *Poland* 45 J8
Jędrzejów, *Poland* 45 H7
Jedwabne, *Poland* 45 E9
Jeetzel →, *Germany* 24 B7
Jefferson, *Iowa, U.S.A.* 112 D7
Jefferson, *Ohio, U.S.A.* 110 E4
Jefferson, *Tex., U.S.A.* 113 J7
Jefferson, Mt., *Nev., U.S.A.* 114 G5
Jefferson, Mt., *Oreg., U.S.A.* 114 D3
Jefferson City, *Mo., U.S.A.* 112 F8
Jefferson City, *Tenn., U.S.A.* 109 G4
Jeffersontown, *U.S.A.* 108 F3
Jeffersonville, *U.S.A.* 108 F3
Jeffrey City, *U.S.A.* 114 E10
Jega, *Nigeria* 83 C5
Jēkabpils, *Latvia* 9 H21
Jekyll I., *U.S.A.* 109 K5
Jelcz-Laskowice, *Poland* 45 G4
Jelenia Góra, *Poland* 45 H2
Jelgava, *Latvia* 9 H20
Jelgava □, *Latvia* 44 B10
Jelica, *Serbia, Yug.* 40 C4
Jelli, *Sudan* 81 F3
Jelšava, *Slovak Rep.* 27 C13
Jemaja, *Indonesia* 65 L5
Jemaluang, *Malaysia* 65 L4
Jember, *Indonesia* 63 H15
Jembongan, *Malaysia* 62 C5
Jena, *Germany* 24 E7
Jena, *U.S.A.* 113 K8
Jenbach, *Austria* 26 D4
Jenkins, *U.S.A.* 108 G4
Jenner, *U.S.A.* 116 G3
Jennings, *U.S.A.* 113 K8
Jepara, *Indonesia* 63 G14
Jeparit, *Australia* 95 F3
Jequié, *Brazil* 125 F10
Jequitinhonha, *Brazil* 125 G10
Jequitinhonha →, *Brazil* 125 G11
Jerantut, *Malaysia* 65 L4
Jérémie, *Haiti* 121 C5
Jerez, Punta, *Mexico* 119 C5
Jerez de García Salinas, *Mexico* 118 C4
Jerez de la Frontera, *Spain* 35 J4
Jerez de los Caballeros, *Spain* 35 G4
Jericho = El Arīḥā, *West Bank* 75 D4
Jericho, *Australia* 94 C4
Jerichow, *Germany* 24 C8
Jerid, Chott = Djerid, Chott, *Tunisia* 78 B7
Jerilderie, *Australia* 95 F4
Jermyn, *U.S.A.* 111 E9
Jerome, *U.S.A.* 114 E6
Jerramungup, *Australia* 93 F2
Jersey, *U.K.* 13 H5
Jersey City, *U.S.A.* 111 F10
Jersey Shore, *U.S.A.* 110 E7
Jerseyville, *U.S.A.* 112 F9
Jerusalem, *Israel* 75 D4
Jervis B., *Australia* 95 F5
Jervis Inlet, *Canada* 104 C4
Jerzu, *Italy* 30 C2
Jesenice, *Slovenia* 29 B11
Jeseník, *Czech Rep.* 27 A10
Jesenké, *Slovak Rep.* 27 C13
Jesi = Iesi, *Italy* 29 E10
Jesselton = Kota Kinabalu, *Malaysia* 62 C5
Jessnitz, *Germany* 24 D8

Jessore, Bangla. 67 H16
Jesup, U.S.A. 109 K5
Jesús Carranza, Mexico 119 D5
Jesús María, Argentina 126 C3
Jetmore, U.S.A. 113 F5
Jetpur, India 68 J4
Jeumont, France 19 B11
Jevnaker, Norway 9 F14
Jewett, U.S.A. 110 F3
Jewett City, U.S.A. 111 E13
Jeyḩūnābād, Iran 71 C6
Jeypore, India 67 K13
Jeziorak, Jezioro, Poland 44 E6
Jeziorany, Poland 44 E7
Jeziorka →, Poland 45 F8
Jha Jha, India 69 G12
Jhaarkand = Jharkhand □, India 69 H11
Jhabua, India 68 H6
Jhajjar, India 68 E7
Jhal, Pakistan 68 E2
Jhal Jhao, Pakistan 66 F4
Jhalawar, India 68 G7
Jhalida, India 69 H11
Jhalrapatan, India 68 G7
Jhang Maghiana, Pakistan 68 D5
Jhansi, India 69 G8
Jhargram, India 69 H12
Jharia, India 69 H12
Jharkhand □, India 69 H11
Jharsuguda, India 67 J14
Jhelum, Pakistan 68 C5
Jhelum →, Pakistan 68 D5
Jhilmilli, India 69 H10
Jhudo, Pakistan 68 G3
Jhunjhunu, India 68 E6
Ji-Paraná, Brazil 124 F6
Ji Xian, Hebei, China 56 F8
Ji Xian, Henan, China 56 G8
Ji Xian, Shanxi, China 56 F6
Jia Xian, Henan, China 56 H7
Jia Xian, Shaanxi, China 56 E6
Jiading, China 59 B13
Jiahe, China 59 E9
Jialing Jiang →, China 58 C6
Jiamusi, China 60 B8
Ji'an, Jiangxi, China 59 D10
Ji'an, Jilin, China 57 D14
Jianchang, China 57 D11
Jianchangying, China 57 D10
Jianchuan, China 58 D2
Jiande, China 59 C12
Jiang'an, China 58 C5
Jiangbei, China 58 C6
Jiangcheng, China 58 F3
Jiangchuan, China 58 E4
Jiangdi, China 58 D4
Jiangdu, China 59 A12
Jiange, China 58 A5
Jianghua, China 59 E8
Jiangjin, China 58 C6
Jiangkou, China 58 D7
Jiangle, China 59 D11
Jiangling, China 59 B9
Jiangmen, China 59 F9
Jiangning, China 59 B12
Jiangshan, China 59 C12
Jiangsu □, China 57 H11
Jiangxi □, China 59 D11
Jiangyan, China 59 A13
Jiangyin, China 59 B13
Jiangyong, China 59 E8
Jiangyou, China 58 B5
Jianhe, China 58 D7
Jianli, China 59 C9
Jianning, China 59 D11
Jian'ou, China 59 D12
Jianshi, China 58 B7
Jianshui, China 58 F4
Jianyang, Fujian, China 59 D12
Jianyang, Sichuan, China 58 B5
Jiao Xian = Jiaozhou, China 57 F11
Jiaohe, Hebei, China 56 E9
Jiaohe, Jilin, China 57 C14
Jiaojiang, China 59 C13
Jiaoling, China 59 E11
Jiaozhou, China 57 F11
Jiaozhou Wan, China 57 F11
Jiaozuo, China 56 G7
Jiashan, China 59 B13
Jiawang, China 57 G9
Jiaxiang, China 56 G9
Jiaxing, China 59 B13
Jiayi = Chiai, Taiwan 59 F13
Jiayu, China 59 C9
Jibiya, Nigeria 83 C6
Jibou, Romania 43 C8
Jibuti = Djibouti ■, Africa 81 E5
Jicarón, I., Panama 120 E3
Jičín, Czech Rep. 26 A8
Jiddah, Si. Arabia 74 C2
Jido, India 67 E19
Jieshou, China 56 H8
Jiexiu, China 56 F6
Jieyang, China 59 F11
Jigawa □, Nigeria 83 C6
Jiggalong, Australia 92 D3
Jigni, India 69 G8
Jihlava, Czech Rep. 26 B8
Jihlava →, Czech Rep. 27 C9
Jihlavský □, Czech Rep. 26 B8
Jijiga, Ethiopia 74 F3
Jikamshi, Nigeria 83 C6
Jikau, Sudan 81 F3
Jilin, China 57 C14
Jilin □, China 57 C14
Jiloca →, Spain 32 D3
Jilong = Chilung, Taiwan 59 E13
Jim Thorpe, U.S.A. 111 F9
Jima, Ethiopia 81 F4
Jimbolia, Romania 42 E5
Jimena de la Frontera, Spain 35 J5
Jiménez, Mexico 118 B4
Jimo, China 57 F11
Jin Jiang →, China 59 C10
Jin Xian = Jinzhou, China 56 E8
Jin Xian, China 57 E11
Jinan, China 56 F9
Jincheng, China 56 G7
Jinchuan, China 58 B4
Jind, India 68 E7
Jindabyne, Australia 95 F4
Jindřichův Hradec, Czech Rep. 26 B8
Jing He →, China 56 G5
Jing Shan, China 59 B8
Jing Xian, China 59 B12
Jing'an, China 59 C10
Jingbian, China 56 F5
Jingchuan, China 56 G4
Jingde, China 59 B12
Jingdezhen, China 59 C11
Jingdong, China 58 E3
Jinggangshan, China 59 D10
Jinggu, China 58 F3
Jinghai, China 56 E9
Jinghong, China 58 G3
Jingjiang, China 59 A13
Jingle, China 56 E6
Jingmen, China 59 B9
Jingning, China 56 G3
Jingpo Hu, China 57 C15
Jingshan, China 59 B9
Jingtai, China 56 F3
Jingxi, China 58 F6
Jingxing, China 56 E8
Jingyang, China 56 G5
Jingyu, China 57 C14
Jingyuan, China 56 F3
Jingzhou, China 58 D7
Jingziguan, China 56 H6
Jinhua, China 59 C12
Jining, Nei Monggol Zizhiqu, China 56 D7
Jining, Shandong, China 56 G9
Jinja, Uganda 86 B3
Jinjang, Malaysia 65 L3
Jinji, China 56 F4
Jinjiang, Fujian, China 59 E12
Jinjiang, Yunnan, China 58 D3
Jinjini, Ghana 82 D4
Jinkou, China 59 B10
Jinkouhe, China 58 C4
Jinmen Dao, China 59 E12
Jinnah Barrage, Pakistan 66 C7
Jinning, China 58 E4
Jinotega, Nic. 120 D2
Jinotepe, Nic. 120 D2
Jinping, Guizhou, China 58 D7
Jinping, Yunnan, China 58 F4
Jinsha, China 58 D6
Jinsha Jiang →, China 58 C5
Jinshan, China 59 B13
Jinshi, China 59 C8
Jintan, China 59 B12
Jinxi, Jiangxi, China 59 D11
Jinxi, Liaoning, China 57 D11
Jinxian, China 59 C11
Jinxiang, China 56 G9
Jinyang, China 58 D4
Jinyun, China 59 C13
Jinzhai, China 59 B10
Jinzhou, Hebei, China 56 E8
Jinzhou, Liaoning, China 57 D11
Jiparaná →, Brazil 124 E6
Jipijapa, Ecuador 124 D2
Jiquilpan, Mexico 118 D4
Jishan, China 56 G6
Jishou, China 58 C7
Jishui, China 59 D10
Jisr ash Shughūr, Syria 70 C3
Jitarning, Australia 93 F2
Jitra, Malaysia 65 J3
Jiu →, Romania 43 G8
Jiudengkou, China 56 E4
Jiujiang, Guangdong, China 59 F9
Jiujiang, Jiangxi, China 59 C10
Jiuling Shan, China 59 C10
Jiulong, China 58 C3
Jiutai, China 57 B13
Jiuxincheng, China 56 E8
Jiuyuhang, China 59 B12
Jixi, Anhui, China 59 B12
Jixi, Heilongjiang, China 57 B16
Jiyang, China 57 F9
Jiyuan, China 56 G7
Jīzān, Si. Arabia 74 D3
Jize, China 56 F8
Jizera →, Czech Rep. 26 A7
Jizl, W. →, Si. Arabia 80 B4
Jizl, Wādī al, Si. Arabia 70 E3
Jizō-Zaki, Japan 55 G6
Jizzakh, Uzbekistan 50 E7
Joaçaba, Brazil 127 B5
Joal Fadiout, Senegal 82 C1
João Pessoa, Brazil 125 E12
Joaquín V. González, Argentina 126 B3
Jobat, India 68 H6
Jobourg, Nez de, France 18 C5
Jódar, Spain 35 H7
Jodhpur, India 68 F5
Jodiya, India 68 H4
Jōetsu, Japan 55 F9
Jœuf, France 19 C12
Jofane, Mozam. 89 C5
Jogbani, India 69 F12
Jõgeva, Estonia 9 G22
Jogjakarta = Yogyakarta, Indonesia 62 F4
Johannesburg, S. Africa 89 D4
Johannesburg, U.S.A. 117 K9
Johansfors, Sweden 11 H9
Johilla →, India 69 H9
John Day, U.S.A. 114 D4
John Day →, U.S.A. 114 D3
John D'Or Prairie, Canada 104 B5
John H. Kerr Reservoir, U.S.A. 109 G6
John o' Groats, U.K. 14 C5
Johnnie, U.S.A. 117 J10
John's Ra., Australia 94 C1
Johnson, Kans., U.S.A. 113 G4
Johnson, Vt., U.S.A. 111 B12
Johnson City, N.Y., U.S.A. 111 D9
Johnson City, Tenn., U.S.A. 109 G4
Johnson City, Tex., U.S.A. 113 K5
Johnsonburg, U.S.A. 110 E6
Johnsondale, U.S.A. 117 K8
Johnson's Crossing, Canada 104 A2
Johnston, L., Australia 93 F3
Johnston Falls = Mambilima Falls, Zambia 87 E2
Johnston I., Pac. Oc. 97 F11
Johnstone Str., Canada 104 C3
Johnstown, N.Y., U.S.A. 111 C10
Johnstown, Ohio, U.S.A. 110 F2
Johnstown, Pa., U.S.A. 110 F6
Johor Baharu, Malaysia 65 M4
Jõhvi, Estonia 9 G22
Joigny, France 19 E10
Joinville, Brazil 127 B6
Joinville, France 19 D12
Joinville I., Antarctica 5 C18
Jojutla, Mexico 119 D5
Jokkmokk, Sweden 8 C18
Jökulsá á Bru →, Iceland 8 D6
Jökulsá á Fjöllum →, Iceland 8 C5
Jolfā, Āzarbājān-e Sharqī, Iran 70 B5
Jolfā, Eşfahan, Iran 71 C6
Joliet, U.S.A. 108 E1
Joliette, Canada 102 C5
Jolo, Phil. 61 J4
Jolon, U.S.A. 116 K5
Jomalig I., Phil. 61 D5
Jombang, Indonesia 63 G15
Jomda, China 58 B2
Jonava, Lithuania 9 J21
Jones Sound, Canada 4 B3
Jonesboro, Ark., U.S.A. 113 H9
Jonesboro, La., U.S.A. 113 J8
Jong →, S. Leone 82 D2
Jonglei, Sudan 81 F3
Jonglei □, Sudan 81 F3
Joniškis, Lithuania 9 H20
Jönköping, Sweden 11 G8
Jönköpings län □, Sweden 11 G8
Jonquière, Canada 103 C5
Jonsered, Sweden 11 G6
Jonzac, France 20 C3
Joplin, U.S.A. 113 G7
Jora, India 68 F6
Jordan, Mont., U.S.A. 114 C10
Jordan, N.Y., U.S.A. 111 C8
Jordan ■, Asia 75 E5
Jordan →, Asia 75 D4
Jordan Valley, U.S.A. 114 E5
Jordanów, Poland 45 J6
Jorhat, India 67 F19
Jörn, Sweden 8 D19
Jorong, Indonesia 62 E4
Jørpeland, Norway 9 G11
Jorquera →, Chile 126 B2
Jos, Nigeria 83 D6
Jos Plateau, Nigeria 83 D6
Jošanička Banja, Serbia, Yug. 40 C4
José Batlle y Ordóñez, Uruguay 127 C4
Joseni, Romania 43 D10
Joseph, L., Nfld., Canada 103 B6
Joseph, L., Ont., Canada 110 A5
Joseph Bonaparte G., Australia 92 B4
Joshinath, India 69 D8
Joshua Tree, U.S.A. 117 L10
Joshua Tree National Park, U.S.A. 117 M10
Josselin, France 18 E4
Jostedalsbreen, Norway 9 F12
Jotunheimen, Norway 9 F13
Joubertberge, Namibia 88 B1
Joué-lès-Tours, France 18 E7
Jourdanton, U.S.A. 113 L5
Joutseno, Finland 46 B5
Jovellanos, Cuba 120 B3
Joyeuse, France 21 D8
Józefów, Lubelskie, Poland 45 H10
Józefów, Mazowieckie, Poland 45 F8
Ju Xian, China 57 F10
Juan Aldama, Mexico 118 C4
Juan Bautista Alberdi, Argentina 126 C3
Juan de Fuca Str., Canada 116 B3
Juan de Nova, Ind. Oc. 89 B7
Juan Fernández, Arch. de, Pac. Oc. 122 G2
Juan José Castelli, Argentina 126 B3
Juan L. Lacaze, Uruguay 126 C4
Juankoski, Finland 8 E23
Juárez, Argentina 126 D4
Juárez, Mexico 117 N11
Juárez, Sierra de, Mexico 118 A1
Juàzeiro, Brazil 125 E10
Juàzeiro do Norte, Brazil 125 E11
Juba, Sudan 81 G3
Jubayl, Lebanon 75 A4
Jubbah, Si. Arabia 70 D4
Jubbal, India 68 D7
Jubbulpore = Jabalpur, India 69 H8
Jübek, Germany 24 A5
Jubga, Russia 49 H4
Jubilee L., Australia 93 E4
Juby, C., Morocco 78 C3
Júcar = Xúquer →, Spain 33 F4
Júcaro, Cuba 120 B4
Juchitán, Mexico 119 D5
Judaea = Har Yehuda, Israel 75 D3
Judenburg, Austria 26 D7
Judith →, U.S.A. 114 C9
Judith, Pt., U.S.A. 111 E13
Judith Gap, U.S.A. 114 C9
Juelsminde, Denmark 11 J4
Jugoslavia = Yugoslavia ■, Europe 40 C4
Juigalpa, Nic. 120 D2
Juillac, France 20 C5
Juist, Germany 24 B2
Juiz de Fora, Brazil 127 A7
Jujuy □, Argentina 126 A2
Julesburg, U.S.A. 112 E3
Juli, Peru 124 G5
Julia Cr. →, Australia 94 C3
Julia Creek, Australia 94 C3
Juliaca, Peru 124 G4
Julian, U.S.A. 117 M10
Julian Alps = Julijske Alpe, Slovenia 29 B11
Julian L., Canada 102 B4
Julianatop, Surinam 125 C7
Julianehåb = Qaqortoq, Greenland 101 B6
Jülich, Germany 24 E2
Julijske Alpe, Slovenia 29 B11
Julimes, Mexico 118 B3
Jullundur, India 68 D6
Julu, China 56 F8
Jumbo, Zimbabwe 87 F3
Jumbo Pk., U.S.A. 117 J12
Jumentos Cays, Bahamas 120 B4
Jumilla, Spain 33 G3
Jumla, Nepal 69 E10
Jumna = Yamuna →, India 69 G9
Junagadh, India 68 J4
Junction, Tex., U.S.A. 113 K5
Junction, Utah, U.S.A. 115 G7
Junction B., Australia 94 A1
Junction City, Kans., U.S.A. 112 F6
Junction City, Oreg., U.S.A. 114 D2
Junction Pt., Australia 94 A1
Jundah, Australia 94 C3
Jundiaí, Brazil 127 A6
Juneau, U.S.A. 104 B2
Junee, Australia 95 E4
Jungfrau, Switz. 25 J3
Junggar Pendi, China 60 B3
Jungshahi, Pakistan 68 G2
Juniata →, U.S.A. 110 F7
Junín, Argentina 126 C3
Junín de los Andes, Argentina 128 D2
Jūniyah, Lebanon 75 B4
Junlian, China 58 C5
Juntas, Chile 126 B2
Juntura, U.S.A. 114 E4
Jur, Nahr el →, Sudan 81 F2
Jura = Jura, Mts. du, Europe 19 F13
Jura = Schwäbische Alb, Germany 25 G5
Jura, U.K. 14 F3
Jura □, France 19 F12
Jura □, Switz. 25 H3
Jūra →, Lithuania 44 C9
Jura, Mts. du, Europe 19 F13
Jura, Sd. of, U.K. 14 F3
Jurbarkas, Lithuania 9 J20
Jurien, Australia 93 F2
Jurilovca, Romania 43 F13
Jūrmala, Latvia 9 H20
Jurong, China 59 B12
Juruá →, Brazil 122 D4
Juruena, Brazil 124 F7
Juruena →, Brazil 124 E7
Juruti, Brazil 125 D7
Jussey, France 19 E12
Justo Daract, Argentina 126 C2
Jutaí →, Brazil 124 D5
Jüterbog, Germany 24 D9
Juticalpa, Honduras 120 D2
Jutland = Jylland, Denmark 11 H3
Juventud, I. de la, Cuba 120 B3
Juvigny-sous-Andaine, France 18 D6
Jūy Zar, Iran 70 C5
Juye, China 56 G9
Juzennecourt, France 19 D11
Jvari, Georgia 49 J6
Jwaneng, Botswana 85 J4
Jyderup, Denmark 11 J5
Jylland, Denmark 11 H3
Jyväskylä, Finland 9 E21

K

K2, Pakistan 69 B7
Ka →, Nigeria 83 C5
Kaap Plateau, S. Africa 88 D3
Kaapkruis, Namibia 88 C1
Kaapstad = Cape Town, S. Africa 88 E2
Kaba, Guinea 82 C2
Kabaena, Indonesia 63 F6
Kabala, S. Leone 82 D2
Kabale, Uganda 86 C3
Kabalo, Dem. Rep. of the Congo 86 D2
Kabambare, Dem. Rep. of the Congo 86 C2
Kabango, Dem. Rep. of the Congo 87 D2
Kabanjahe, Indonesia 62 D1
Kabankalan, Phil. 61 G5
Kabara, Mali 82 B4
Kabardinka, Russia 47 K10
Kabardino-Balkar Republic = Kabardino-Balkaria □, Russia 49 J6
Kabardino-Balkaria □, Russia 49 J6
Kabarega Falls = Murchison Falls, Uganda 86 B3
Kabasalan, Phil. 61 H5
Kabba, Nigeria 83 D6
Kabetogama, U.S.A. 112 A8
Kabi, Niger 83 C7
Kabin Buri, Thailand 64 F3
Kabinakagami L., Canada 102 C3
Kabinda, Dem. Rep. of the Congo 84 F4
Kabna, Sudan 80 D3
Kabompo, Zambia 87 E1
Kabompo →, Zambia 85 G4
Kabondo, Dem. Rep. of the Congo 87 D2
Kabongo, Dem. Rep. of the Congo 86 D2
Kabot, Guinea 82 C2
Kabou, Togo 83 D5
Kabr, Sudan 81 E2
Kabūd Gonbad, Iran 71 B8
Kabugao, Phil. 61 B4
Kābul, Afghan. 68 B3
Kābul □, Afghan. 66 B6
Kābul →, Pakistan 68 C5
Kabunga, Dem. Rep. of the Congo 86 C2
Kaburuang, Indonesia 63 D7
Kabushiya, Sudan 81 D3
Kabwe, Zambia 87 E2
Kačanik, Kosovo, Yug. 40 D5
Kačerginė, Lithuania 44 D10
Kachchh, Gulf of, India 68 H3
Kachchh, Rann of, India 68 H4
Kachchhidhana, India 69 J8
Kachebera, Zambia 87 E3
Kachia, Nigeria 83 D6
Kachikau, Botswana 88 B3
Kachin □, Burma 58 D1
Kachira, L., Uganda 86 C3
Kachiry, Kazakstan 50 D8
Kachisi, Ethiopia 81 F4
Kachnara, India 68 H6
Kachot, Cambodia 65 G4
Kaçkar, Turkey 73 B9
Kadan, Czech Rep. 26 A6
Kadan Kyun, Burma 64 F2
Kadanai →, Afghan. 68 D1
Kadarkút, Hungary 42 D2
Kade, Ghana 83 D4
Kadi, India 68 H5
Kadina, Australia 95 E2
Kadınhanı, Turkey 72 C5
Kadiolo, Mali 82 C3
Kadipur, India 69 F10
Kadirli, Turkey 70 B3
Kadiyevka = Stakhanov, Ukraine 47 H10
Kadodo, Sudan 81 E2
Kadoka, U.S.A. 112 D4
Kadom, Russia 48 C6
Kadoma, Zimbabwe 87 F2
Kâdugli, Sudan 81 E2
Kaduna, Nigeria 83 C6
Kaduna □, Nigeria 83 C6
Kaduy, Russia 46 C9
Kaédi, Mauritania 82 B2
Kaélé, Cameroon 83 C7
Kaeng Khoï, Thailand 64 E3
Kaesŏng, N. Korea 57 F14
Kāf, Si. Arabia 70 D3
Kafan = Kapan, Armenia 70 B5
Kafanchan, Nigeria 83 D6
Kafareti, Nigeria 83 C7
Kaffrine, Senegal 82 C1
Kafin, Nigeria 83 D6
Kafin Madaki, Nigeria 83 C6
Kafinda, Zambia 87 E3
Kafirévs, Ákra, Greece 38 C6
Kafr el Battikh, Egypt 80 H7
Kafr el Dauwâr, Egypt 80 H7
Kafr el Sheikh, Egypt 80 H7
Kafue, Zambia 87 F2
Kafue →, Zambia 85 H5
Kafue Flats, Zambia 87 F2
Kafue Nat. Park, Zambia 87 F2
Kafulwe, Zambia 87 D2
Kaga, Afghan. 68 B4
Kaga Bandoro, C.A.R. 84 C3
Kagan, Uzbekistan 50 F7
Kagarko, Nigeria 83 D6
Kagawa □, Japan 55 G7
Kagera = Ziwa Maghariba □, Tanzania 86 C3
Kagera →, Uganda 86 C3
Kağızman, Turkey 70 B4
Kagmar, Sudan 81 E3
Kagoshima, Japan 55 J5
Kagoshima □, Japan 55 J5
Kagul = Cahul, Moldova 43 E13
Kahak, Iran 71 B6
Kahama, Tanzania 86 C3
Kahan, Pakistan 68 E3
Kahang, Malaysia 65 L4
Kahayan →, Indonesia 62 E4
Kahe, Tanzania 86 C4
Kahnūj, Iran 71 E8

Kahoka, U.S.A. 112 E9
Kahoolawe, U.S.A. 106 H16
Kahramanmaraş, Turkey 70 B3
Kâhta, Turkey 73 D8
Kahuta, Pakistan 68 C5
Kai, Kepulauan, Indonesia 63 F8
Kai Besar, Indonesia 63 F8
Kai Is. = Kai, Kepulauan, Indonesia 63 F8
Kai Kecil, Indonesia 63 F8
Kai Xian, China 58 B7
Kaiama, Nigeria 83 D5
Kaiapoi, N.Z. 91 K4
Kaieteur Falls, Guyana 124 B7
Kaifeng, China 56 G8
Kaihua, China 59 C12
Kaijiang, China 58 B6
Kaikohe, N.Z. 91 F4
Kaikoura, N.Z. 91 K4
Kaikoura Ra., N.Z. 91 J4
Kailahun, S. Leone 82 D2
Kaili, China 58 D6
Kailu, China 57 C11
Kailua Kona, U.S.A. 106 J17
Kaimana, Indonesia 63 E8
Kaimanawa Mts., N.Z. 91 H5
Kaimganj, India 69 F8
Kaimur Hills, India 69 G10
Kainab →, Namibia 88 D2
Kainji Dam, Nigeria 83 D5
Kainji Res., Nigeria 83 C5
Kainuu, Finland 8 D23
Kaipara Harbour, N.Z. 91 G5
Kaiping, China 59 F9
Kaipokok B., Canada 103 B8
Kaira, India 68 H5
Kairana, India 68 E7
Kaironi, Indonesia 63 E8
Kairouan, Tunisia 79 A8
Kaiserslautern, Germany 25 F3
Kaiserstuhl, Germany 25 G3
Kaitaia, N.Z. 91 F4
Kaitangata, N.Z. 91 M2
Kaithal, India 68 E7
Kaitu →, Pakistan 68 C4
Kaiyang, China 58 D6
Kaiyuan, Liaoning, China 57 C13
Kaiyuan, Yunnan, China 58 F4
Kajaani, Finland 8 D22
Kajabbi, Australia 94 C3
Kajana = Kajaani, Finland 8 D22
Kajang, Malaysia 65 L3
Kajaran, Armenia 73 C12
Kajiado, Kenya 86 C4
Kajo Kaji, Sudan 81 G3
Kajuru, Nigeria 83 C6
Kaka, Sudan 81 E3
Kakabeka Falls, Canada 102 C2
Kakadu Nat. Park, Australia 92 B5
Kakamas, S. Africa 88 D3
Kakamega, Kenya 86 B3
Kakanj, Bos.-H. 42 F3
Kakanui Mts., N.Z. 91 L3
Kakata, Liberia 82 D2
Kakdwip, India 69 J13
Kake, Japan 55 G6
Kake, U.S.A. 104 B2
Kakegawa, Japan 55 G9
Kakeroma-Jima, Japan 55 K4
Kakhib, Russia 49 J8
Kakhovka, Ukraine 47 J7
Kakhovske Vdskh., Ukraine 47 J7
Kakinada, India 67 L13
Kakisa →, Canada 104 A5
Kakisa L., Canada 104 A5
Kakogawa, Japan 55 G7
Kakwa →, Canada 104 C5
Kāl Gūsheh, Iran 71 D8
Kal Safīd, Iran 70 C5
Kala, Nigeria 83 C7
Kalaallit Nunaat = Greenland ■, N. Amer. 4 C5
Kalabagh, Pakistan 68 C4
Kalabahi, Indonesia 63 F6
Kalabáka, Greece 38 B3
Kalabana, Mali 82 C3
Kalach, Russia 48 E5
Kalach na Donu, Russia 49 F6
Kaladan →, Burma 67 J18
Kaladar, Canada 102 D4
Kalahari, Africa 88 C3
Kalahari Gemsbok Nat. Park, S. Africa 88 D3
Kalajoki, Finland 8 D20
Kālak, Iran 71 E8
Kalakamati, Botswana 89 C4
Kalakan, Russia 51 D12
K'alak'unlun Shank'ou = Karakoram Pass, Pakistan 69 B7
Kalam, Pakistan 69 B5
Kalama, Dem. Rep. of the Congo 86 C2
Kalama, U.S.A. 116 E4
Kalámai, Greece 38 D4
Kalamariá, Greece 40 F6
Kalamata = Kalámai, Greece 38 D4
Kalamazoo, U.S.A. 108 D3
Kalamazoo →, U.S.A. 108 D2
Kalambo Falls, Tanzania 87 D3
Kálamos, Attikí, Greece 38 C5
Kálamos, Iónioi Nísoi, Greece 38 C2
Kalan, Turkey 70 B3
Kalankalan, Guinea 82 C3
Kalannie, Australia 93 F2
Kalāntarī, Iran 71 C7
Kalao, Indonesia 63 F6
Kalaotoa, Indonesia 63 F6
Kälarne, Sweden 10 B10
Kalasin, Thailand 64 D4
Kalat, Pakistan 66 E5
Kalāteh, Iran 71 B7
Kalāteh-ye Ganj, Iran 71 E8
Kálathos, Greece 39 E10
Kalaus →, Russia 49 H7
Kalávrita, Greece 38 C4
Kalbarri, Australia 93 E1
Kale, Antalya, Turkey 39 E12
Kale, Denizli, Turkey 39 D10
Kalecik, Turkey 72 B5
Kalegauk Kyun, Burma 67 M20
Kalehe, Dem. Rep. of the Congo 86 C2
Kalema, Tanzania 86 C3
Kalemie, Dem. Rep. of the Congo 86 D2
Kalety, Poland 45 H5
Kalewa, Burma 67 H19
Kaleybar, Iran 70 B5
Kalgan = Zhangjiakou, China 56 D8
Kalgoorlie-Boulder, Australia 93 F3
Kali →, India 69 F8
Kali Sindh →, India 68 G6
Kaliakra, Nos, Bulgaria 41 C12
Kalianda, Indonesia 62 F3
Kalibo, Phil. 61 F5
Kalima, Dem. Rep. of the Congo 86 C2
Kalimantan □, Indonesia 62 E4
Kalimantan Barat □, Indonesia 62 E4
Kalimantan Selatan □, Indonesia 62 E5
Kalimantan Tengah □, Indonesia 62 E4
Kalimantan Timur □, Indonesia 62 D5
Kálimnos, Greece 39 D8
Kalimpong, India 69 F13
Kalinin = Tver, Russia 46 D8
Kaliningrad, Russia 9 J19
Kalininsk, Russia 48 E7
Kalinkavichy, Belarus 47 F5
Kalinkovichi = Kalinkavichy, Belarus 47 F5
Kalinovik, Bos.-H. 40 C2
Kalipetrovo, Bulgaria 41 B11
Kaliro, Uganda 86 B3
Kalirrákhi, Greece 41 F8
Kalispell, U.S.A. 114 B6
Kalisz, Poland 45 G5
Kalisz Pomorski, Poland 45 E2
Kaliua, Tanzania 86 D3
Kalívia Thorikoú, Greece 38 D5
Kalix, Sweden 8 D20
Kalix →, Sweden 8 D20
Kalka, India 68 D7
Kalkan, Turkey 39 E11
Kalkarindji, Australia 92 C5
Kalkaska, U.S.A. 108 C3
Kalkfeld, Namibia 88 C2
Kalkfontein, Botswana 88 C3
Kalkım, Turkey 39 B9
Kalkrand, Namibia 88 C2
Kållandsö, Sweden 11 F7
Kallavesi, Finland 8 E22
Källby, Sweden 11 F7
Källered, Sweden 11 G6
Kallimasiá, Greece 39 C8
Kallinge, Sweden 11 H9
Kallithéa, Greece 38 D5
Kallmet, Albania 40 E3
Kalloní, Greece 39 B8
Kallonís, Kólpos, Greece 39 B8
Kallsjön, Sweden 8 E15
Kalmalo, Nigeria 83 C6
Kalmar, Sweden 11 H10
Kalmar län □, Sweden 11 G10
Kalmar sund, Sweden 11 H10
Kalmyk Republic = Kalmykia □, Russia 49 G8
Kalmykia □, Russia 49 G8
Kalmykovo, Kazakstan 50 E6
Kalna, India 69 H13
Kalnai, India 69 H10
Kalocsa, Hungary 42 D4
Kalofer, Bulgaria 41 D8
Kalokhorio, Cyprus 36 E12
Kaloko, Dem. Rep. of the Congo 86 D2
Kalol, Gujarat, India 68 H5
Kalol, Gujarat, India 68 H5
Kalolímnos, Greece 39 D9
Kalomo, Zambia 87 F2
Kalonerón, Greece 38 D3
Kalpi, India 69 F8
Kaltern = Caldaro, Italy 29 B8
Kaltungo, Nigeria 83 D7
Kalu, Pakistan 68 G2
Kaluga, Russia 46 E9
Kalulushi, Zambia 87 E2
Kalundborg, Denmark 11 J5
Kalush, Ukraine 47 H3
Kałuszyn, Poland 45 F8
Kalutara, Sri Lanka 66 R12
Kalvarija, Lithuania 44 D10
Kalyazin, Russia 46 D9
Kam, Albania 40 D4
Kam →, Nigeria 83 D7
Kama, Dem. Rep. of the Congo 86 C2
Kama →, Russia 50 D6
Kamachumu, Tanzania 86 C3
Kamaishi, Japan 54 E10
Kamalia, Pakistan 68 D5
Kaman, India 68 F6
Kaman, Turkey 72 C5
Kamanjab, Namibia 88 B2
Kamapanda, Zambia 87 E1
Kamaran, Yemen 74 D3
Kamativi, Zimbabwe 88 B4
Kamba, Nigeria 83 C5
Kambalda, Australia 93 F3
Kambar, Pakistan 68 F3
Kambia, S. Leone 82 D2
Kambolé, Togo 83 D5
Kambolé, Zambia 87 D3
Kambos, Cyprus 36 D11
Kambove, Dem. Rep. of the Congo 87 E2
Kamchatka, Poluostrov, Russia 51 D16
Kamchatka Pen. = Kamchatka, Poluostrov, Russia 51 D16
Kamchiya →, Bulgaria 41 C11
Kamen, Russia 50 D9
Kamen-Rybolov, Russia 54 B6
Kamenica, Serbia, Yug. 40 C6
Kamenica, Serbia, Yug. 40 B3
Kamenice nad Lipou, Czech Rep. 26 B8
Kamenjak, Rt, Croatia 29 D10
Kamenka = Kaminka, Ukraine 47 H7
Kamenka, Kazakstan 48 E10
Kamenka, Penza, Russia 48 D6
Kamenka, Voronezh, Russia 47 G10
Kamenka Bugskaya = Kamyanka-Buzka, Ukraine 47 G3
Kamenka Dneprovskaya = Kamyanka-Dniprovska, Ukraine 47 J8
Kamennomostskiy, Russia 49 H5
Kameno, Bulgaria 41 D11
Kamenolomini, Russia 49 G5
Kamensk-Shakhtinskiy, Russia 49 F5
Kamensk Uralskiy, Russia 50 D7
Kamenskiy, Russia 48 E7
Kamenskoye, Russia 51 C17
Kamenyak, Bulgaria 41 C10
Kamenz, Germany 24 D10
Kameoka, Japan 55 G7
Kamiah, U.S.A. 114 C5
Kamień Krajeński, Poland 44 E4
Kamień Pomorski, Poland 44 E1
Kamienna →, Poland 45 G8
Kamienna Góra, Poland 45 H3
Kamieńsk, Poland 45 G6
Kamieskroon, S. Africa 88 E2
Kamilukuak, L., Canada 105 A8
Kamin-Kashyrskyy, Ukraine 47 G3
Kamina, Dem. Rep. of the Congo 87 D2
Kaminak L., Canada 105 A10
Kaministiquia, Canada 102 C1
Kaminka, Ukraine 47 H7
Kaminoyama, Japan 54 E10
Kamiros, Greece 36 C9
Kamituga, Dem. Rep. of the Congo 86 C2
Kamla →, India 69 G12
Kamloops, Canada 104 C4
Kamnik, Slovenia 29 B11
Kamo, Armenia 49 K7
Kamo, Japan 54 F9
Kamoke, Pakistan 68 C6
Kamp →, Austria 26 C8
Kampala, Uganda 86 B3
Kampang Chhnang, Cambodia 65 F5
Kampar, Malaysia 65 K3
Kampar →, Indonesia 62 D2
Kampen, Neths. 17 B5
Kampene, Dem. Rep. of the Congo 84 E5
Kamphaeng Phet, Thailand 64 D2
Kampolombo, L., Zambia 87 E2
Kampong Saom, Cambodia 65 G4
Kampong Saom, Chaak, Cambodia 65 G4
Kampong To, Thailand 65 J3
Kampot, Cambodia 65 G5
Kampti, Burkina Faso 82 C4
Kampuchea = Cambodia ■, Asia 64 F5
Kampung Air Putih, Malaysia 65 K4
Kampung Jerangau, Malaysia 65 K4
Kampung Raja, Malaysia 65 K4
Kampungbaru = Tolitoli, Indonesia 63 D6
Kamrau, Teluk, Indonesia 63 E8
Kamsack, Canada 105 C8
Kamsai, Guinea 82 C2
Kamskoye Ustye, Russia 48 C9
Kamuchawie L., Canada 105 B8
Kamui-Misaki, Japan 54 C10
Kamyanets-Podilskyy, Ukraine 47 H4
Kamyanka-Buzka, Ukraine 47 G3
Kamyanka-Dniprovska, Ukraine 47 J8
Kāmyārān, Iran 70 C5
Kamyshin, Russia 48 E7
Kamyzyak, Russia 49 G9
Kan, Sudan 81 F3
Kanaaupscow, Canada 102 B4
Kanaaupscow →, Canada 101 C12
Kanab, U.S.A. 115 H7
Kanab →, U.S.A. 115 H7
Kanagi, Japan 54 D10
Kanairiktok →, Canada 103 A7
Kanália, Greece 38 B4
Kananga, Dem. Rep. of the Congo 84 F4
Kanash, Russia 48 C8
Kanaskat, U.S.A. 116 C5
Kanastraíon, Ákra = Palioúrion, Ákra, Greece 40 G7
Kanawha →, U.S.A. 108 F4
Kanazawa, Japan 55 F8
Kanchanaburi, Thailand 64 E2
Kanchenjunga, Nepal 69 F13
Kanchipuram, India 66 N11
Kańczuga, Poland 45 J9
Kandaghat, India 68 D7
Kandahar = Qandahār, Afghan. 66 D4
Kandalaksha, Russia 50 C4
Kandangan, Indonesia 62 E5
Kandanghaur, Indonesia 63 G13
Kandanos, Greece 36 D5
Kandava, Latvia 44 A9
Kandavu, Fiji 91 D8
Kandhíla, Greece 38 D4
Kandhkot, Pakistan 68 E3
Kandhla, India 68 E7
Kandi, Benin 83 C5
Kandi, India 69 H13
Kandiaro, Pakistan 68 F3
Kandıra, Turkey 72 B4
Kandla, India 68 H4
Kandos, Australia 95 E4
Kandreho, Madag. 89 B8
Kandy, Sri Lanka 66 R12
Kane, U.S.A. 110 E6
Kane Basin, Greenland 4 B4
Kanel, Senegal 82 B2
Kaneohe, U.S.A. 106 H16
Kanevskaya, Russia 49 G4
Kanfanar, Croatia 29 C10
Kang, Botswana 88 C3
Kangaba, Mali 82 C3
Kangal, Turkey 72 C7
Kangān, Fārs, Iran 71 E7
Kangān, Hormozgān, Iran 71 E8
Kangar, Malaysia 65 J3
Kangaré, Mali 82 C3
Kangaroo I., Australia 95 F2
Kangaroo Mts., Australia 94 C3
Kangasala, Finland 9 F21
Kangāvar, Iran 71 C6
Kangding, China 58 B3
Kangdong, N. Korea 57 E14
Kangean, Kepulauan, Indonesia 62 F5
Kangean Is. = Kangean, Kepulauan, Indonesia 62 F5
Kangen →, Sudan 81 F3
Kanggye, N. Korea 57 D14
Kanggyŏng, S. Korea 57 F14
Kanghwa, S. Korea 57 F14
Kangikajik, Greenland 4 B6
Kangiqsliniq = Rankin Inlet, Canada 100 B10
Kangiqsualujjuaq, Canada 101 C13
Kangiqsujuaq, Canada 101 B12
Kangiqtugaapik = Clyde River, Canada 101 A13
Kangirsuk, Canada 101 B13
Kangnŭng, S. Korea 57 F15
Kangping, China 57 C12
Kangra, India 68 C7
Kangto, India 67 F18
Kanhar →, India 69 G10
Kani, Ivory C. 82 D3
Kaniama, Dem. Rep. of the Congo 86 D1
Kaniapiskau = Caniapiscau →, Canada 103 A6
Kaniapiskau, Res. = Caniapiscau, Rés. de, Canada 103 B6
Kanin, Poluostrov, Russia 50 C5
Kanin Nos, Mys, Russia 50 C5
Kanin Pen. = Kanin, Poluostrov, Russia 50 C5
Kaninë, Albania 40 F3
Kaniva, Australia 95 F3
Kanjiža, Serbia, Yug. 42 D5
Kanjut Sar, Pakistan 69 A6
Kankaanpää, Finland 9 F20
Kankakee, U.S.A. 108 E2
Kankakee →, U.S.A. 108 E1
Kankan, Guinea 82 C3
Kankendy = Xankändi, Azerbaijan 70 B5
Kanker, India 67 J12
Kankossa, Mauritania 82 B2
Kankroli, India 68 G5
Kannapolis, U.S.A. 109 H5
Kannauj, India 69 F8
Kannod, India 66 H10
Kano, Nigeria 83 C6
Kano □, Nigeria 83 C6
Kan'onji, Japan 55 G6
Kanoroba, Ivory C. 82 D3
Kanowit, Malaysia 62 D4
Kanoya, Japan 55 J5
Kanpetlet, Burma 67 J18
Kanpur, India 69 F9
Kansas □, U.S.A. 112 F6
Kansas →, U.S.A. 112 F7
Kansas City, Kans., U.S.A. 112 F7
Kansas City, Mo., U.S.A. 112 F7
Kansenia, Dem. Rep. of the Congo 87 E2
Kansk, Russia 51 D10
Kansŏng, S. Korea 57 E15
Kansu = Gansu □, China 56 G3
Kantaphor, India 68 H7
Kantchari, Burkina Faso 83 C5
Kantché, Niger 83 C6
Kanté, Togo 83 D5
Kantemirovka, Russia 47 H10
Kantharalak, Thailand 64 E5
Kantli →, India 68 E6
Kantō □, Japan 55 F9
Kantō-Sanchi, Japan 55 G9
Kanturk, Ireland 15 D3
Kanuma, Japan 55 F9
Kanus, Namibia 88 D2
Kanye, Botswana 88 C4
Kanzenze, Dem. Rep. of the Congo 87 E2
Kanzi, Ras, Tanzania 86 D4
Kaohsiung, Taiwan 59 F13
Kaokoveld, Namibia 88 B1
Kaolack, Senegal 82 C1
Kaoshan, China 57 B13
Kapaa, U.S.A. 106 G15
Kapadvanj, India 68 H5
Kapaklı, Turkey 41 E11
Kapan, Armenia 70 B5
Kapanga, Dem. Rep. of the Congo 84 F4
Kapchagai = Qapshaghay, Kazakstan 50 E8
Kapela = Velika Kapela, Croatia 29 C12
Kapéllo, Ákra, Greece 38 E5
Kapema, Dem. Rep. of the Congo 87 E2
Kapfenberg, Austria 26 D8
Kapı Dağı, Turkey 41 F11
Kapiri Mposhi, Zambia 87 E2
Kāpīsā □, Afghan. 66 B6
Kapiskau →, Canada 102 B3
Kapit, Malaysia 62 D4
Kapiti I., N.Z. 91 J5
Kaplan, U.S.A. 113 K8
Kaplice, Czech Rep. 26 C7
Kapoe, Thailand 65 H2
Kapoeta, Sudan 81 G3
Kápolnásnyék, Hungary 42 C3
Kapos →, Hungary 42 D3
Kaposvár, Hungary 42 D2
Kapowsin, U.S.A. 116 D4
Kappeln, Germany 24 A5
Kappelshamn, Sweden 11 G12
Kapps, Namibia 88 C2
Kaprije, Croatia 29 E12
Kapsan, N. Korea 57 D15
Kapsukas = Marijampolė, Lithuania 9 J20
Kapuas →, Indonesia 62 E3
Kapuas Hulu, Pegunungan, Malaysia 62 D4
Kapuas Hulu Ra. = Kapuas Hulu, Pegunungan, Malaysia 62 D4
Kapulo, Dem. Rep. of the Congo 87 D2
Kapunda, Australia 95 E2
Kapuni, N.Z. 91 H5
Kapurthala, India 68 D6
Kapuskasing, Canada 102 C3
Kapuskasing →, Canada 102 C3
Kapustin Yar, Russia 49 F7
Kaputar, Australia 95 E5
Kaputir, Kenya 86 B4
Kapuvár, Hungary 42 C2
Kara, Russia 50 C7
Karā, W. →, Si. Arabia 80 C5
Kara Ada, Turkey 39 E9
Kara Bogaz Gol, Zaliv = Garabogazköl Aylagy, Turkmenistan 50 E6
Kara Burun, Turkey 39 E9
Kara Kalpak Republic = Qoraqalpoghistan □, Uzbekistan 50 E6
Kara Kum, Turkmenistan 50 F6
Kara Sea, Russia 50 B7
Karaadilli, Turkey 39 C12
Karabiğa, Turkey 41 F11
Karabük, Turkey 72 B5
Karaburun, Albania 40 F3
Karaburun, Turkey 39 C8
Karabutak = Qarabutaq, Kazakstan 50 E7
Karacabey, Turkey 41 F12
Karacakılavuz, Turkey 41 E11
Karacaköy, Turkey 41 E12
Karacasu, Turkey 39 D10
Karachala = Qaraçala, Azerbaijan 49 L9
Karachayevsk, Russia 49 J5
Karachev, Russia 47 F8
Karachey-Cherkessia □, Russia 49 J5
Karachi, Pakistan 68 G2
Karad, India 66 L9
Karadirek, Turkey 39 C12
Karaga, Ghana 83 D4
Karaganda = Qaraghandy, Kazakstan 50 E8
Karagayly, Kazakstan 50 E8
Karaginskiy, Ostrov, Russia 51 D17
Karagola Road, India 69 G12
Karagüney Dağları, Turkey 72 B6
Karahallı, Turkey 39 C11
Karaikal, India 66 P11
Karaikkudi, India 66 P11
Karaisali, Turkey 72 D6
Karaj, Iran 71 C6
Karak, Malaysia 65 L4
Karakalpakstan = Qoraqalpoghistan □, Uzbekistan 50 E6
Karakelong, Indonesia 63 D7
Karakitang, Indonesia 63 D7
Karaklis = Vanadzor, Armenia 49 K7
Karakoçan, Turkey 73 C9
Karakol, Kyrgyzstan 50 E8
Karakoram Pass, Pakistan 69 B7
Karakoram Ra., Pakistan 69 B7
Karakurt, Turkey 73 B10
Karakuwisa, Namibia 88 B2
Karalon, Russia 51 D12
Karama, Jordan 75 D4
Karaman, Balıkesir, Turkey 39 B9
Karaman, Konya, Turkey 70 B2
Karamanlı, Turkey 39 D11
Karamay, China 60 B3
Karambu, Indonesia 62 E5
Karamea Bight, N.Z. 91 J3
Karamnasa →, India 69 G10
Karamürsel, Turkey 41 F13

Karand, *Iran* 70 C5
Karangana, *Mali* 82 C3
Karanganyar, *Indonesia* 63 G13
Karanjia, *India* 69 J11
Karankasso, *Burkina Faso* 82 C4
Karaova, *Turkey* 39 D9
Karapınar, *Turkey* 72 D5
Karasburg, *Namibia* 88 D2
Karasino, *Russia* 50 C9
Karasjok, *Norway* 8 B21
Karasu, *Turkey* 72 B4
Karasu →, *Turkey* 39 E12
Karasuk, *Russia* 50 D8
Karasuyama, *Japan* 55 F10
Karataş, *Adana, Turkey* 72 D6
Karataş, *Manisa, Turkey* 39 C10
Karataş Burnu, *Turkey* 72 D6
Karatau, Khrebet = Qarataū, *Kazakstan* 50 E7
Karatoprak, *Turkey* 39 D9
Karatsu, *Japan* 55 H5
Karaul, *Russia* 50 B9
Karauli, *India* 68 F7
Karavastasë, L. e, *Albania* 40 F3
Karávi, *Greece* 38 E5
Karavostasi, *Cyprus* 36 D11
Karawang, *Indonesia* 63 G12
Karawanken, *Europe* 26 E7
Karayazı, *Turkey* 73 C10
Karazhal, *Kazakstan* 50 E8
Karbalā', *Iraq* 70 C5
Kårböle, *Sweden* 10 C9
Karcag, *Hungary* 42 C5
Karcha →, *Pakistan* 69 B7
Karchana, *India* 69 G9
Karczew, *Poland* 45 F8
Kardam, *Bulgaria* 41 C12
Kardeljovo = Ploče, *Croatia* 29 E14
Kardhámila, *Greece* 39 C8
Kardhamíli, *Greece* 38 E4
Kardhítsa, *Greece* 38 B3
Kardhítsa □, *Greece* 38 B3
Kärdla, *Estonia* 9 G20
Kareeberge, *S. Africa* 88 E3
Kareha →, *India* 69 G12
Kareima, *Sudan* 80 D3
Karelia □, *Russia* 50 C4
Karelian Republic = Karelia □, *Russia* 50 C4
Karera, *India* 68 G8
Kārevāndar, *Iran* 71 E9
Kargasok, *Russia* 50 D9
Kargat, *Russia* 50 D9
Kargı, *Turkey* 72 B6
Kargil, *India* 69 B7
Kargopol, *Russia* 46 B10
Kargowa, *Poland* 45 F2
Karguéri, *Niger* 83 C7
Karhal, *India* 69 F8
Kariá, *Greece* 38 C2
Kariaí, *Greece* 41 F8
Karīān, *Iran* 71 E8
Karianga, *Madag.* 89 C8
Kariba, *Zimbabwe* 87 F2
Kariba, L., *Zimbabwe* 87 F2
Kariba Dam, *Zimbabwe* 87 F2
Kariba Gorge, *Zambia* 87 F2
Karibib, *Namibia* 88 C2
Karimata, Kepulauan, *Indonesia* 62 E3
Karimata, Selat, *Indonesia* 62 E3
Karimata Is. = Karimata, Kepulauan, *Indonesia* 62 E3
Karimnagar, *India* 66 K11
Karimunjawa, Kepulauan, *Indonesia* 62 F4
Karin, *Somali Rep.* 74 E4
Káristos, *Greece* 38 C6
Karīt, *Iran* 71 C8
Kariya, *Japan* 55 G8
Kariyangwe, *Zimbabwe* 89 B4
Karjala, *Finland* 46 A5
Karkaralinsk = Qarqaraly, *Kazakstan* 50 E8
Karkheh →, *Iran* 70 D5
Karkinitska Zatoka, *Ukraine* 47 K7
Karkinitskiy Zaliv = Karkinitska Zatoka, *Ukraine* 47 K7
Karkur Tohl, *Egypt* 80 C2
Karl Liebknecht, *Russia* 47 G8
Karl-Marx-Stadt = Chemnitz, *Germany* 24 E8
Karlholmsbruk, *Sweden* 10 D11
Karlino, *Poland* 44 D2
Karlivka, *Ukraine* 47 H8
Karlobag, *Croatia* 29 D12
Karlovac, *Croatia* 29 C12
Karlovarský □, *Czech Rep.* 26 A5
Karlovka = Karlivka, *Ukraine* 47 H8
Karlovo, *Bulgaria* 41 D8
Karlovy Vary, *Czech Rep.* 26 A5
Karlsbad = Karlovy Vary, *Czech Rep.* 26 A5
Karlsborg, *Sweden* 11 F8
Karlshamn, *Sweden* 11 H8
Karlskoga, *Sweden* 10 E8
Karlskrona, *Sweden* 11 H9
Karlsruhe, *Germany* 25 F4
Karlstad, *Sweden* 10 E7
Karlstad, *U.S.A.* 112 A6
Karlstadt, *Germany* 25 F5
Karma, *Niger* 83 C5
Karmėlava, *Lithuania* 44 D11
Karmi'el, *Israel* 75 C4
Karnak, *Egypt* 79 C12
Karnal, *India* 68 E7
Karnali →, *Nepal* 69 E9
Karnaphuli Res., *Bangla.* 67 H18
Karnaprayag, *India* 69 D8
Karnataka □, *India* 66 N10
Karnes City, *U.S.A.* 113 L6
Karnische Alpen, *Europe* 26 E6
Karnobat, *Bulgaria* 41 D10
Kärnten □, *Austria* 26 E6
Karo, *Mali* 82 C4
Karoi, *Zimbabwe* 87 F2
Karonga, *Malawi* 87 D3
Karoonda, *Australia* 95 F2
Karor, *Pakistan* 68 D4
Karora, *Sudan* 80 D4
Káros, *Greece* 39 E7
Karounga, *Mali* 82 B3
Karousádhes, *Greece* 38 B1
Karpacz, *Poland* 45 H2
Karpasia □, *Cyprus* 36 D13
Kárpathos, *Greece* 39 F9
Kárpathos, Stenón, *Greece* 39 F9
Karpenísion, *Greece* 38 C3
Karpuz Burnu = Apostolos Andreas, C., *Cyprus* 36 D13
Karpuzlu, *Turkey* 39 D9
Karratha, *Australia* 92 D2
Kars, *Turkey* 73 B10
Karsakpay, *Kazakstan* 50 E7
Karsha, *Kazakstan* 48 F10
Karshi = Qarshi, *Uzbekistan* 50 F7
Karsiyang, *India* 69 F13
Karsog, *India* 68 D7
Karst = Kras, *Croatia* 29 C10
Kartal, *Turkey* 41 F13
Kartál Óros, *Greece* 41 E9
Kartaly, *Russia* 50 D7
Kartapur, *India* 68 D6
Karthaus, *U.S.A.* 110 E6
Kartuzy, *Poland* 44 D5
Karufa, *Indonesia* 63 E8
Karumba, *Australia* 94 B3
Karumo, *Tanzania* 86 C3
Karumwa, *Tanzania* 86 C3
Kārūn →, *Iran* 71 D6
Karungu, *Kenya* 86 C3
Karup, *Denmark* 11 H3
Karviná, *Czech Rep.* 27 B11
Karwan →, *India* 68 F8
Karwar, *India* 66 M9
Karwi, *India* 69 G9
Kaş, *Turkey* 39 E11
Kasaba, *Turkey* 39 E11
Kasache, *Malawi* 87 E3
Kasai →, *Dem. Rep. of the Congo* 84 E3
Kasaï-Oriental □, *Dem. Rep. of the Congo* 86 D1
Kasaji, *Dem. Rep. of the Congo* 87 E1
Kasama, *Zambia* 87 E3
Kasan-dong, *N. Korea* 57 D14
Kasane, *Namibia* 88 B3
Kasanga, *Tanzania* 87 D3
Kasar, Ras, *Sudan* 80 D4
Kasaragod, *India* 66 N9
Kasba L., *Canada* 105 A8
Kāseh Garān, *Iran* 70 C5
Kasempa, *Zambia* 87 E2
Kasenga, *Dem. Rep. of the Congo* 87 E2
Kasese, *Uganda* 86 B3
Kasewa, *Zambia* 87 E2
Kasganj, *India* 69 F8
Kashabowie, *Canada* 102 C1
Kashaf, *Iran* 71 C9
Kāshān, *Iran* 71 C6
Kashechewan, *Canada* 102 B3
Kashgar = Kashi, *China* 60 C2
Kashi, *China* 60 C2
Kashimbo, *Dem. Rep. of the Congo* 87 E2
Kashin, *Russia* 46 D9
Kashipur, *India* 69 E8
Kashira, *Russia* 46 E10
Kashiwazaki, *Japan* 55 F9
Kashk-e Kohneh, *Afghan.* 66 B3
Kashkū'īyeh, *Iran* 71 D7
Kāshmar, *Iran* 71 C8
Kashmir, *Asia* 69 C7
Kashmor, *Pakistan* 68 E3
Kashpirovka, *Russia* 48 D9
Kashun Noerh = Gaxun Nur, *China* 60 B5
Kasiari, *India* 69 H12
Kasimov, *Russia* 48 C5
Kasinge, *Dem. Rep. of the Congo* 86 D2
Kasiruta, *Indonesia* 63 E7
Kaskaskia →, *U.S.A.* 112 G10
Kaskattama →, *Canada* 105 B10
Kaskinen, *Finland* 9 E19
Kaslo, *Canada* 104 D5
Kasmere L., *Canada* 105 B8
Kasongo, *Dem. Rep. of the Congo* 86 C2
Kasongo Lunda, *Dem. Rep. of the Congo* 84 F3
Kásos, *Greece* 39 F8
Kásos, Stenón, *Greece* 39 F8
Kaspi, *Georgia* 49 K7
Kaspichan, *Bulgaria* 41 C11
Kaspiysk, *Russia* 49 J8
Kaspiyskiy, *Russia* 49 H8
Kassab ed Doleib, *Sudan* 81 E3
Kassaba, *Egypt* 80 C2
Kassalâ, *Sudan* 81 D4
Kassalâ □, *Sudan* 81 D4
Kassándra, *Greece* 40 F7
Kassándrinon, *Greece* 40 F7
Kassel, *Germany* 24 D5
Kassinger, *Sudan* 80 D3
Kassiópi, *Greece* 36 A3
Kasson, *U.S.A.* 112 C8
Kastamonu, *Turkey* 72 B5
Kastav, *Croatia* 29 C11
Kastélli, *Greece* 36 D5
Kastéllion, *Greece* 36 D7
Kastellórizon = Megiste, *Greece* 39 E11
Kástellos, *Greece* 39 E9
Kastellou, Ákra, *Greece* 39 F9
Kasterlee, *Belgium* 17 C4
Kastlösa, *Sweden* 11 H10
Kastóri, *Greece* 38 D4
Kastoría, *Greece* 40 F5
Kastoría □, *Greece* 40 F5
Kastorías, Límni, *Greece* 40 F5
Kastornoye, *Russia* 47 G10
Kastós, *Greece* 38 C2
Kastrosikiá, *Greece* 38 B2
Kastsyukovichy, *Belarus* 46 F7
Kasulu, *Tanzania* 86 C3
Kasumi, *Japan* 55 G7
Kasumkent, *Russia* 49 K9
Kasungu, *Malawi* 87 E3
Kasur, *Pakistan* 68 D6
Kataba, *Zambia* 87 F2
Katagum, *Nigeria* 83 C7
Katahdin, Mt., *U.S.A.* 109 C11
Katako Kombe, *Dem. Rep. of the Congo* 86 C1
Katákolon, *Greece* 38 D3
Katale, *Tanzania* 86 C3
Katanda, *Katanga, Dem. Rep. of the Congo* 86 D1
Katanda, *Nord-Kivu, Dem. Rep. of the Congo* 86 C2
Katanga □, *Dem. Rep. of the Congo* 86 D2
Katangi, *India* 66 J11
Katanning, *Australia* 93 F2
Katastári, *Greece* 38 D2
Katavi Swamp, *Tanzania* 86 D3
Kateríni, *Greece* 40 F6
Katghora, *India* 69 H10
Katha, *Burma* 67 G20
Katherîna, Gebel, *Egypt* 70 D2
Katherine, *Australia* 92 B5
Katherine Gorge, *Australia* 92 B5
Kathi, *India* 68 J6
Kathiawar, *India* 68 H4
Kathikas, *Cyprus* 36 E11
Kathua, *India* 68 C6
Kati, *Mali* 82 C3
Katihar, *India* 69 G12
Katima Mulilo, *Zambia* 88 B3
Katimbira, *Malawi* 87 E3
Katingan = Mendawai →, *Indonesia* 62 E4
Katiola, *Ivory C.* 82 D3
Katlanovo, *Macedonia* 40 E5
Katmandu, *Nepal* 69 F11
Katni, *India* 69 H9
Káto Akhaïa, *Greece* 38 C3
Káto Arkhánai, *Greece* 36 D7
Káto Khorió, *Greece* 36 D7
Káto Pyrgos, *Cyprus* 36 D11
Káto Stavros, *Greece* 40 F7
Katokhí, *Greece* 38 C3
Katompe, *Dem. Rep. of the Congo* 86 D2
Katonga →, *Uganda* 86 B3
Katoomba, *Australia* 95 E5
Katoúna, *Greece* 38 C3
Katowice, *Poland* 45 H6
Katrancı Dağı, *Turkey* 39 D12
Katrine, L., *U.K.* 14 E4
Katrineholm, *Sweden* 11 E10
Katsepe, *Madag.* 89 B8
Katsina, *Nigeria* 83 C6
Katsina □, *Nigeria* 83 C6
Katsina Ala, *Nigeria* 83 D6
Katsina Ala →, *Nigeria* 83 D6
Katsumoto, *Japan* 55 H4
Katsuura, *Japan* 55 G10
Katsuyama, *Japan* 55 F8
Kattaviá, *Greece* 36 D9
Kattegat, *Denmark* 11 H5
Katthammarsvik, *Sweden* 11 G12
Katul, J., *Sudan* 81 E2
Katumba, *Dem. Rep. of the Congo* 86 D2
Katungu, *Kenya* 86 C5
Katwa, *India* 69 H13
Katwijk, *Neths.* 17 B4
Kąty Wrocławskie, *Poland* 45 G3
Kauai, *U.S.A.* 106 H15
Kauai Channel, *U.S.A.* 106 H15
Kaub, *Germany* 25 E3
Kaufbeuren, *Germany* 25 H6
Kaufman, *U.S.A.* 113 J6
Kauhajoki, *Finland* 9 E20
Kaukauna, *U.S.A.* 108 C1
Kaukauveld, *Namibia* 88 C3
Kaunakakai, *U.S.A.* 106 H16
Kaunas, *Lithuania* 9 J20
Kaunia, *Bangla.* 69 G13
Kaunos, *Turkey* 39 E10
Kaura Namoda, *Nigeria* 83 C6
Kauru, *Nigeria* 83 C6
Kautokeino, *Norway* 8 B20
Kauwapur, *India* 69 F10
Kavacha, *Russia* 51 C17
Kavadarci, *Macedonia* 40 E6
Kavajë, *Albania* 40 E3
Kavak, *Turkey* 72 B7
Kavak Dağı, *Turkey* 39 D10
Kavaklı, *Turkey* 41 E11
Kavaklıdere, *Turkey* 39 D10
Kavalerovo, *Russia* 54 B7
Kavali, *India* 66 M12
Kavála, *Greece* 41 F8
Kavála □, *Greece* 41 E8
Kavála Kólpos, *Greece* 41 F8
Kavār, *Iran* 71 D7
Kavarna, *Bulgaria* 41 C12
Kavi, *India* 68 H5
Kavimba, *Botswana* 88 B3
Kavīr, Dasht-e, *Iran* 71 C7
Kavkaz, *Russia* 47 K9
Kävlinge, *Sweden* 11 J7
Kavos, *Greece* 36 B4
Kavoúsi, *Greece* 39 F7
Kaw, *Fr. Guiana* 125 C8
Kawa, *Sudan* 81 E3
Kawagama L., *Canada* 110 A6
Kawagoe, *Japan* 55 G9
Kawaguchi, *Japan* 55 G9
Kawambwa, *Zambia* 87 D2
Kawanoe, *Japan* 55 G6
Kawardha, *India* 69 J9
Kawasaki, *Japan* 55 G9
Kawasi, *Indonesia* 63 E7
Kawerau, *N.Z.* 91 H6
Kawhia Harbour, *N.Z.* 91 H5
Kawio, Kepulauan, *Indonesia* 63 D7
Kawnro, *Burma* 67 H21
Kawthaung, *Burma* 65 H2
Kawthoolei = Kayin □, *Burma* 67 L20
Kawthule = Kayin □, *Burma* 67 L20
Kaxholmen, *Sweden* 11 G8
Kaya, *Burkina Faso* 83 C4
Kayah □, *Burma* 67 K20
Kayalıköy Barajı, *Turkey* 41 E11
Kayan →, *Indonesia* 62 D5
Kaycee, *U.S.A.* 114 E10
Kayeli, *Indonesia* 63 E7
Kayenta, *U.S.A.* 115 H8
Kayes, *Mali* 82 C2
Kayı, *Turkey* 39 B12
Kayima, *S. Leone* 82 D2
Kayin □, *Burma* 67 L20
Kaymakçı, *Turkey* 39 C10
Kayoa, *Indonesia* 63 D7
Kayomba, *Zambia* 87 E1
Kaysatskoye, *Russia* 48 F8
Kayseri, *Turkey* 70 B2
Kaysville, *U.S.A.* 114 F8
Kaz Dağı, *Turkey* 39 B8
Kazachye, *Russia* 51 B14
Kazakstan ■, *Asia* 50 E7
Kazan, *Russia* 48 C9
Kazan →, *Canada* 105 A9
Kazan-Rettō, *Pac. Oc.* 96 E6
Kazanlŭk, *Bulgaria* 41 D9
Kazanskaya, *Russia* 48 F5
Kazatin = Kozyatyn, *Ukraine* 47 H5
Kazaure, *Nigeria* 83 C6
Kazbek, *Russia* 49 J7
Kāzerūn, *Iran* 71 D6
Kazi Magomed = Qazimämmäd, *Azerbaijan* 49 K9
Kazimierz Dolny, *Poland* 45 G8
Kazimierza Wielka, *Poland* 45 H7
Kazincbarcika, *Hungary* 42 B5
Kazlų Rūda, *Lithuania* 44 D10
Kaztalovka, *Kazakstan* 48 F9
Kazuno, *Japan* 54 D10
Kazym →, *Russia* 50 C7
Kcynia, *Poland* 45 F4
Ké-Macina, *Mali* 82 C3
Kéa, *Greece* 38 D6
Keady, *U.K.* 15 B5
Kearney, *U.S.A.* 112 E5
Kearny, *U.S.A.* 115 K8
Kearsarge, Mt., *U.S.A.* 111 C13
Keban, *Turkey* 73 C8
Keban Barajı, *Turkey* 70 B3
Kebbi □, *Nigeria* 83 C5
Kébi, *Ivory C.* 82 D3
Kebnekaise, *Sweden* 8 C18
Kebri Dehar, *Ethiopia* 74 F3
Kebumen, *Indonesia* 63 G13
Kecel, *Hungary* 42 D4
Kechika →, *Canada* 104 B3
Keçiborlu, *Turkey* 39 D12
Kecskemét, *Hungary* 42 D4
Kedada, *Ethiopia* 81 F4
Kėdainiai, *Lithuania* 9 J21
Kedarnath, *India* 69 D8
Kedgwick, *Canada* 103 C6
Kédhros Óros, *Greece* 36 D6
Kediri, *Indonesia* 62 F4
Kedjebi, *Ghana* 83 D5
Kédougou, *Senegal* 82 C2
Kędzierzyn-Koźle, *Poland* 45 H5
Keeler, *U.S.A.* 116 J9
Keeley L., *Canada* 105 C7
Keeling Is. = Cocos Is., *Ind. Oc.* 96 J1
Keelung = Chilung, *Taiwan* 59 E13
Keene, *Canada* 110 B6
Keene, *Calif., U.S.A.* 117 K8
Keene, *N.H., U.S.A.* 111 D12
Keene, *N.Y., U.S.A.* 111 B11
Keeper Hill, *Ireland* 15 D3
Keer-Weer, C., *Australia* 94 A3
Keeseville, *U.S.A.* 111 B11
Keetmanshoop, *Namibia* 88 D2
Keewatin, *Canada* 105 D10
Keewatin →, *Canada* 105 B8
Kefa □, *Ethiopia* 81 F4
Kefallinía, *Greece* 38 C2
Kefallinía □, *Greece* 38 C2
Kéfalos, *Greece* 39 E8
Kefamenanu, *Indonesia* 63 F6
Kefar Sava, *Israel* 75 C3
Keffi, *Nigeria* 83 D6
Keffin Hausa, *Nigeria* 83 C6
Keflavík, *Iceland* 8 D2
Keftya, *Ethiopia* 81 E4
Keg River, *Canada* 104 B5
Kegaska, *Canada* 103 B7
Keheili, *Sudan* 80 D3
Kehl, *Germany* 25 G3
Keighley, *U.K.* 12 D6
Keila, *Estonia* 9 G21
Keimoes, *S. Africa* 88 D3
Keita, *Niger* 83 C6
Keitele, *Finland* 8 E22
Keith, *Australia* 95 F3
Keith, *U.K.* 14 D6
Keizer, *U.S.A.* 114 D2
Kejimkujik Nat. Park, *Canada* 103 D6
Kejserr Franz Joseph Fd., *Greenland* 4 B6
Kekri, *India* 68 G6
Kelam, *Ethiopia* 81 G4
Kelamet, *Eritrea* 81 D4
Kelan, *China* 56 E6
Kelang, *Malaysia* 65 L3
Kelantan →, *Malaysia* 65 J4
Këlcyrë, *Albania* 40 F4
Kelekçi, *Turkey* 39 D11
Keles, *Turkey* 41 G13
Keleti-főcsatorna, *Hungary* 42 C6
Kelheim, *Germany* 25 G7
Kelkit, *Turkey* 73 B8
Kelkit →, *Turkey* 72 B7
Kellerberrin, *Australia* 93 F2
Kellett, C., *Canada* 4 B1
Kelleys I., *U.S.A.* 110 E2
Kellogg, *U.S.A.* 114 C5
Kells = Ceanannus Mor, *Ireland* 15 C5
Kelmė, *Lithuania* 44 C9
Kelokedhara, *Cyprus* 36 E11
Kelowna, *Canada* 104 D5
Kelseyville, *U.S.A.* 116 G4
Kelso, *N.Z.* 91 L2
Kelso, *U.K.* 14 F6
Kelso, *U.S.A.* 116 D4
Keluang, *Malaysia* 65 L4
Kelvington, *Canada* 105 C8
Kem, *Russia* 50 C4
Kema, *Indonesia* 63 D7
Kemah, *Turkey* 70 B3
Kemaliye, *Erzincan, Turkey* 73 C8
Kemaliye, *Manisa, Turkey* 39 C10
Kemalpaşa, *Turkey* 39 C9
Kemaman, *Malaysia* 62 D2
Kemano, *Canada* 104 C3
Kemasik, *Malaysia* 65 K4
Kembolcha, *Ethiopia* 81 E4
Kemer, *Antalya, Turkey* 39 E12
Kemer, *Burdur, Turkey* 39 D12
Kemer, *Muğla, Turkey* 39 E11
Kemer Barajı, *Turkey* 39 D10
Kemerovo, *Russia* 50 D9
Kemi, *Finland* 8 D21
Kemi älv = Kemijoki →, *Finland* 8 D21
Kemijärvi, *Finland* 8 C22
Kemijoki →, *Finland* 8 D21
Kemmerer, *U.S.A.* 114 F8
Kemmuna = Comino, *Malta* 36 C1
Kemp, L., *U.S.A.* 113 J5
Kemp Land, *Antarctica* 5 C5
Kempsey, *Australia* 95 E5
Kempt, L., *Canada* 102 C5
Kempten, *Germany* 25 H6
Kempton, *Australia* 94 G4
Kemptville, *Canada* 102 D4
Ken →, *India* 69 G9
Kenai, *U.S.A.* 100 B4
Kendai, *India* 69 H10
Kendal, *Indonesia* 63 G14
Kendal, *U.K.* 12 C5
Kendall, *Australia* 95 E5
Kendall, *U.S.A.* 109 N5
Kendall →, *Australia* 94 A3
Kendallville, *U.S.A.* 108 E3
Kendari, *Indonesia* 63 E6
Kendawangan, *Indonesia* 62 E4
Kende, *Nigeria* 83 C5
Kendrapara, *India* 67 J15
Këndrevicës, Maja e, *Albania* 40 F3
Kendrew, *S. Africa* 88 E3
Kene Thao, *Laos* 64 D3
Kenedy, *U.S.A.* 113 L6
Kenema, *S. Leone* 82 D2
Keng Kok, *Laos* 64 D5
Keng Tawng, *Burma* 67 J21
Keng Tung, *Burma* 58 G2
Kengeja, *Tanzania* 86 D4
Kenhardt, *S. Africa* 88 D3
Kéniéba, *Mali* 82 C2
Kenitra, *Morocco* 78 B4
Kenli, *China* 57 F10
Kenmare, *Ireland* 15 E2
Kenmare, *U.S.A.* 112 A3
Kenmare River, *Ireland* 15 E2
Kennebago Lake, *U.S.A.* 111 A14
Kennebec, *U.S.A.* 112 D5
Kennebec →, *U.S.A.* 109 D11
Kennebunk, *U.S.A.* 111 C14
Kennedy, *Zimbabwe* 88 B4
Kennedy Ra., *Australia* 93 D2
Kennedy Taungdeik, *Burma* 67 H18
Kenner, *U.S.A.* 113 L9
Kennet →, *U.K.* 13 F7
Kenneth Ra., *Australia* 93 D2
Kennett, *U.S.A.* 113 G9
Kennewick, *U.S.A.* 114 C4
Kenogami →, *Canada* 102 B3
Kenora, *Canada* 105 D10

Kenosha, *U.S.A.* 108 D2
Kensington, *Canada* 103 C7
Kent, *Ohio, U.S.A.* 110 E3
Kent, *Tex., U.S.A.* 113 K2
Kent, *Wash., U.S.A.* 116 C4
Kent □, *U.K.* 13 F8
Kent Group, *Australia* 94 F4
Kent Pen., *Canada* 100 B9
Kentaū, *Kazakstan* 50 E7
Kentland, *U.S.A.* 108 E2
Kenton, *U.S.A.* 108 E4
Kentucky □, *U.S.A.* 108 G3
Kentucky →, *U.S.A.* 108 F3
Kentucky L., *U.S.A.* 109 G2
Kentville, *Canada* 103 C7
Kentwood, *U.S.A.* 113 K9
Kenya ■, *Africa* 86 B4
Kenya, Mt., *Kenya* 86 C4
Keo Neua, Deo, *Vietnam* 64 C5
Keokuk, *U.S.A.* 112 E9
Keonjhargarh, *India* 69 J11
Kep, *Cambodia* 65 G5
Kep, *Vietnam* 64 B6
Kepez, *Turkey* 41 F10
Kepi, *Indonesia* 63 F9
Kępice, *Poland* 44 D3
Kępno, *Poland* 45 G4
Kepsut, *Turkey* 39 B10
Kerala □, *India* 66 P10
Kerama-Rettō, *Japan* 55 L3
Keran, *Pakistan* 69 B5
Kerang, *Australia* 95 F3
Keranyo, *Ethiopia* 81 F4
Kerao →, *Sudan* 81 E3
Keratéa, *Greece* 38 D5
Keraudren, C., *Australia* 92 C2
Kerava, *Finland* 9 F21
Kerch, *Ukraine* 47 K9
Kerchenskiy Proliv, *Black Sea* 47 K9
Kerchoual, *Mali* 83 B5
Kerempe Burnu, *Turkey* 72 A5
Keren, *Eritrea* 81 D4
Kerewan, *Gambia* 82 C1
Kerguelen, *Ind. Oc.* 3 G13
Keri, *Greece* 38 D2
Keri Kera, *Sudan* 81 E3
Kericho, *Kenya* 86 C4
Kerinci, *Indonesia* 62 E2
Kerki, *Turkmenistan* 50 F7
Kerkinítis, Límni, *Greece* 40 E7
Kérkira, *Greece* 36 A3
Kérkira □, *Greece* 38 B1
Kerkrade, *Neths.* 17 D6
Kerma, *Sudan* 80 D3
Kermadec Is., *Pac. Oc.* 96 L10
Kermadec Trench, *Pac. Oc.* 96 L10
Kermān, *Iran* 71 D8
Kerman, *U.S.A.* 116 J6
Kermān □, *Iran* 71 D8
Kermān, Bīābān-e, *Iran* 71 D8
Kermānshāh = Bākhtarān, *Iran* 70 C5
Kermen, *Bulgaria* 41 D10
Kermit, *U.S.A.* 113 K3
Kern →, *U.S.A.* 117 K7
Kernhof, *Austria* 26 D8
Kernow = Cornwall □, *U.K.* 13 G3
Kernville, *U.S.A.* 117 K8
Keroh, *Malaysia* 65 K3
Kérou, *Benin* 83 C5
Kérouane, *Guinea* 82 D3
Kerpen, *Germany* 24 E2
Kerrera, *U.K.* 14 E3
Kerrobert, *Canada* 105 C7
Kerrville, *U.S.A.* 113 K5
Kerry □, *Ireland* 15 D2
Kerry Hd., *Ireland* 15 D2
Kersa, *Ethiopia* 81 F5
Kerulen →, *Asia* 60 B6
Kerzaz, *Algeria* 78 C5
Kesagami →, *Canada* 102 B4
Kesagami L., *Canada* 102 B3
Keşan, *Turkey* 41 F10
Kesennuma, *Japan* 54 E10
Keshit, *Iran* 71 D8
Keşiş Dağ, *Turkey* 73 C8
Keskin, *Turkey* 72 C5
Kestell, *S. Africa* 89 D4
Kestenga, *Russia* 50 C4
Keswick, *U.K.* 12 C4
Keszthely, *Hungary* 42 D2
Ket →, *Russia* 50 D9
Keta, *Ghana* 83 D5
Keta Lagoon, *Ghana* 83 D5
Ketapang, *Indonesia* 62 E4
Ketchikan, *U.S.A.* 104 B2
Ketchum, *U.S.A.* 114 E6
Kete Krachi, *Ghana* 83 D4
Ketef, Khalîg Umm el, *Egypt* 70 F2
Keti Bandar, *Pakistan* 68 G2
Kétou, *Benin* 83 D5
Ketri, *India* 68 E6
Kętrzyn, *Poland* 44 D8
Kettering, *U.K.* 13 E7
Kettering, *U.S.A.* 108 F3
Kettle →, *Canada* 105 B11
Kettle Falls, *U.S.A.* 114 B4
Kettle Pt., *Canada* 110 C2
Kettleman City, *U.S.A.* 116 J7
Kęty, *Poland* 45 J6
Keuka L., *U.S.A.* 110 D7
Keuruu, *Finland* 9 E21
Kevelaer, *Germany* 24 D2
Kewanee, *U.S.A.* 112 E10
Kewaunee, *U.S.A.* 108 C2
Keweenaw B., *U.S.A.* 108 B1
Keweenaw Pen., *U.S.A.* 108 B2
Keweenaw Pt., *U.S.A.* 108 B2
Key Largo, *U.S.A.* 109 N5
Key West, *U.S.A.* 107 F10
Keyala, *Sudan* 81 G3
Keynsham, *U.K.* 13 F5
Keyser, *U.S.A.* 108 F6
Kezhma, *Russia* 51 D11
Kezi, *Zimbabwe* 89 C4
Kežmarok, *Slovak Rep.* 27 B13
Khabarovsk, *Russia* 51 E14
Khabr, *Iran* 71 D8
Khābūr →, *Syria* 70 C4
Khachmas = Xaçmaz, *Azerbaijan* 49 K9
Khachrod, *India* 68 H6
Khadari, W. el →, *Sudan* 81 E2
Khadro, *Pakistan* 68 F3
Khadyzhensk, *Russia* 49 H4
Khadzhilyangar, *India* 69 B8
Khaga, *India* 69 G9
Khagaria, *India* 69 G12
Khaipur, *Pakistan* 68 E5
Khair, *India* 68 F7
Khairabad, *India* 69 F9
Khairagarh, *India* 69 J9
Khairpur, *Pakistan* 68 F3
Khairpur Nathan Shah, *Pakistan* 68 F2
Khairwara, *India* 68 H5
Khaisor →, *Pakistan* 68 D3
Khajuri Kach, *Pakistan* 68 C3
Khakassia □, *Russia* 50 D9
Khakhea, *Botswana* 88 C3
Khalafābād, *Iran* 71 D6
Khalilabad, *India* 69 F10
Khalīlī, *Iran* 71 E7
Khalkhāl, *Iran* 71 B6
Khálki, *Dhodhekánisos, Greece* 39 E9
Khálki, *Thessalía, Greece* 38 B4
Khalkidhikí □, *Greece* 40 F7
Khalkís, *Greece* 38 C5
Khalmer-Sede = Tazovskiy, *Russia* 50 C8
Khalmer Yu, *Russia* 50 C7
Khalūf, *Oman* 74 C6
Kham Keut, *Laos* 64 C5
Khamaria, *India* 69 H9
Khambhaliya, *India* 68 H3
Khambhat, *India* 68 H5
Khambhat, G. of, *India* 66 J8
Khamilonísion, *Greece* 39 F8
Khamīr, *Iran* 71 E7
Khamir, *Yemen* 74 D3
Khamsa, *Egypt* 75 E1
Khan →, *Namibia* 88 C2
Khān Abū Shāmat, *Syria* 75 B5
Khān Azād, *Iraq* 70 C5
Khān Mujiddah, *Iraq* 70 C4
Khān Shaykhūn, *Syria* 70 C3
Khān Yūnis, *Gaza Strip* 75 D3
Khanai, *Pakistan* 68 D2
Khānaqīn, *Iraq* 70 C5
Khānbāghī, *Iran* 71 B7
Khandrá, *Greece* 39 F8
Khandwa, *India* 66 J10
Khandyga, *Russia* 51 C14
Khāneh, *Iran* 70 B5
Khanewal, *Pakistan* 68 D4
Khangah Dogran, *Pakistan* 68 D5
Khanh Duong, *Vietnam* 64 F7
Khaniá, *Greece* 36 D6
Khaniá □, *Greece* 36 D6
Khaniadhana, *India* 68 G8
Khaníon, Kólpos, *Greece* 36 D5
Khanka, L., *Asia* 51 E14
Khankendy = Xankändi, *Azerbaijan* 70 B5
Khanna, *India* 68 D7
Khanozai, *Pakistan* 68 D2
Khanpur, *Pakistan* 68 E4
Khanty-Mansiysk, *Russia* 50 C7
Khapalu, *Pakistan* 69 B7
Khapcheranga, *Russia* 51 E12
Kharabali, *Russia* 49 G8
Kharaghoda, *India* 68 H4
Kharagpur, *India* 69 H12
Khárakas, *Greece* 36 D7
Kharan Kalat, *Pakistan* 66 E4
Kharānaq, *Iran* 71 C7
Kharda, *India* 66 K9
Khardung La, *India* 69 B7
Khârga, El Wâhât-el, *Egypt* 80 B3
Khargon, *India* 66 J9
Khari →, *India* 68 G6
Kharian, *Pakistan* 68 C5
Kharit, Wadi el →, *Egypt* 80 C3
Khārk, Jazīreh-ye, *Iran* 71 D6
Kharkiv, *Ukraine* 47 H9
Kharkov = Kharkiv, *Ukraine* 47 H9
Kharmanli, *Bulgaria* 41 E9
Kharovsk, *Russia* 46 C11
Kharsawangarh, *India* 69 H11
Kharta, *Turkey* 72 B3
Khartoum = El Khartûm, *Sudan* 81 D3
Khasan, *Russia* 54 C5
Khasavyurt, *Russia* 49 J8
Khāsh, *Iran* 66 E2
Khashm el Girba, *Sudan* 81 E4
Khashum, *Sudan* 81 E2
Khashuri, *Georgia* 49 J6
Khaskovo, *Bulgaria* 41 E9
Khaskovo □, *Bulgaria* 41 E9
Khatanga, *Russia* 51 B11
Khatanga →, *Russia* 51 B11
Khatauli, *India* 68 E7
Khatra, *India* 69 H12
Khātūnābād, *Iran* 71 D7
Khatyrka, *Russia* 51 C18
Khavda, *India* 68 H3
Khaybar, Ḩarrat, *Si. Arabia* 70 E4
Khayelitsha, *S. Africa* 85 L3
Khāzimiyah, *Iraq* 70 C4
Khazzān Jabal al Awliyā, *Sudan* 81 D3
Khe Bo, *Vietnam* 64 C5
Khe Long, *Vietnam* 64 B5
Khed Brahma, *India* 66 G8
Khekra, *India* 68 E7
Khemarak Phouminville, *Cambodia* 65 G4
Khemisset, *Morocco* 78 B4
Khemmarat, *Thailand* 64 D5
Khenāmān, *Iran* 71 D8
Khenchela, *Algeria* 78 A7
Khersān →, *Iran* 71 D6
Khérson, *Greece* 40 E6
Kherson, *Ukraine* 47 J7
Khersónisos Akrotíri, *Greece* 36 D6
Kheta →, *Russia* 51 B11
Khewari, *Pakistan* 68 F3
Khilchipur, *India* 68 G7
Khiliomódhion, *Greece* 38 D4
Khilok, *Russia* 51 D12
Khimki, *Russia* 46 E9
Khíos, *Greece* 39 C8
Khíos □, *Greece* 39 C8
Khirsadoh, *India* 69 H8
Khiuma = Hiiumaa, *Estonia* 9 G20
Khiva, *Uzbekistan* 50 E7
Khīyāv, *Iran* 70 B5
Khlebarovo, *Bulgaria* 41 C10
Khlong Khlung, *Thailand* 64 D2
Khmelnik, *Ukraine* 47 H4
Khmelnitskiy = Khmelnytskyy, *Ukraine* 47 H4
Khmelnytskyy, *Ukraine* 47 H4
Khmer Rep. = Cambodia ■, *Asia* 64 F5
Khoai, Hon, *Vietnam* 65 H5
Khodoriv, *Ukraine* 47 H3
Khodzent = Khŭjand, *Tajikistan* 50 E7
Khojak Pass, *Afghan.* 68 D2
Khok Kloi, *Thailand* 65 H2
Khok Pho, *Thailand* 65 J3
Kholm, *Russia* 46 D6
Kholmsk, *Russia* 51 E15
Khomas Hochland, *Namibia* 88 C2
Khombole, *Senegal* 82 C1
Khomeyn, *Iran* 71 C6
Khomeynī Shahr, *Iran* 71 C6
Khomodino, *Botswana* 88 C3
Khon Kaen, *Thailand* 64 D4
Khong →, *Cambodia* 64 F5
Khong Sedone, *Laos* 64 E5
Khonuu, *Russia* 51 C15
Khoper →, *Russia* 48 F6
Khor el 'Atash, *Sudan* 81 E3
Khóra, *Greece* 38 D3
Khóra Sfakíon, *Greece* 36 D6
Khorāsān □, *Iran* 71 C8
Khorat = Nakhon Ratchasima, *Thailand* 64 E4
Khorat, Cao Nguyen, *Thailand* 64 E4
Khorixas, *Namibia* 88 C1
Khorol, *Ukraine* 47 H7
Khorramābād, *Khorāsān, Iran* 71 C8
Khorramābād, *Lorestān, Iran* 71 C6
Khorrāmshahr, *Iran* 71 D6
Khorugh, *Tajikistan* 50 F8
Khosravī, *Iran* 71 D6
Khosrowābād, *Khuzestān, Iran* 71 D6
Khosrowābād, *Kordestān, Iran* 70 C5
Khost, *Pakistan* 68 D2
Khosūyeh, *Iran* 71 D7
Khotyn, *Ukraine* 47 H4
Khouribga, *Morocco* 78 B4
Khowst, *Afghan.* 68 C3
Khowst □, *Afghan.* 66 C6
Khoyniki, *Belarus* 47 G5
Khrami →, *Georgia* 49 K7
Khrenovoye, *Russia* 48 E5
Khrisoúpolis, *Greece* 41 F8
Khristianá, *Greece* 39 E7
Khrysokhou B., *Cyprus* 36 D11
Khtapodhiá, *Greece* 39 D7
Khu Khan, *Thailand* 64 E5
Khudzhand = Khŭjand, *Tajikistan* 50 E7
Khuff, *Si. Arabia* 70 E5
Khūgīānī, *Afghan.* 68 D2
Khuis, *Botswana* 88 D3
Khuiyala, *India* 68 F4
Khŭjand, *Tajikistan* 50 E7
Khujner, *India* 68 H7
Khulna, *Bangla.* 67 H16
Khulna □, *Bangla.* 67 H16
Khulo, *Georgia* 49 K6
Khumago, *Botswana* 88 C3
Khūnsorkh, *Iran* 71 E8
Khunti, *India* 69 H11
Khūr, *Iran* 71 C8
Khurai, *India* 68 G8
Khurayş, *Si. Arabia* 71 E6
Khureit, *Sudan* 81 E2
Khurīyā Murīyā, Jazā'ir, *Oman* 74 D6
Khurja, *India* 68 E7
Khūrmāl, *Iraq* 70 C5
Khurr, Wādī al, *Iraq* 70 C4
Khūsf, *Iran* 71 C8
Khush, *Afghan.* 66 C3
Khushab, *Pakistan* 68 C5
Khust, *Ukraine* 47 H2
Khuzdar, *Pakistan* 68 F2
Khūzestān □, *Iran* 71 D6
Khvāf, *Iran* 71 C9
Khvājeh, *Iran* 70 B5
Khvalynsk, *Russia* 48 D9
Khvānsār, *Iran* 71 D7
Khvatovka, *Russia* 48 D8
Khvor, *Iran* 71 C7
Khvorgū, *Iran* 71 E8
Khvormūj, *Iran* 71 D6
Khvoy, *Iran* 70 B5
Khvoynaya, *Russia* 46 C8
Khyber Pass, *Afghan.* 68 B4
Kiabukwa, *Dem. Rep. of the Congo* 87 D1
Kiama, *Australia* 95 E5
Kiamba, *Phil.* 61 H6
Kiambi, *Dem. Rep. of the Congo* 86 D2
Kiambu, *Kenya* 86 C4
Kiangara, *Madag.* 89 B8
Kiangsi = Jiangxi □, *China* 59 D11
Kiangsu = Jiangsu □, *China* 57 H11
Kiáton, *Greece* 38 C4
Kibæk, *Denmark* 11 H2
Kibanga Port, *Uganda* 86 B3
Kibara, *Tanzania* 86 C3
Kibare, Mts., *Dem. Rep. of the Congo* 86 D2
Kibombo, *Dem. Rep. of the Congo* 86 C2
Kibondo, *Tanzania* 86 C3
Kibre Mengist, *Ethiopia* 81 F4
Kibumbu, *Burundi* 86 C2
Kibungo, *Rwanda* 86 C3
Kibuye, *Burundi* 86 C2
Kibuye, *Rwanda* 86 C2
Kibwesa, *Tanzania* 86 D2
Kibwezi, *Kenya* 86 C4
Kicasalih, *Turkey* 41 E10
Kičevo, *Macedonia* 40 E4
Kichha, *India* 69 E8
Kichha →, *India* 69 E8
Kicking Horse Pass, *Canada* 104 C5
Kidal, *Mali* 83 B5
Kidderminster, *U.K.* 13 E5
Kidete, *Tanzania* 86 D4
Kidira, *Senegal* 82 C2
Kidnappers, C., *N.Z.* 91 H6
Kidsgrove, *U.K.* 12 D5
Kidston, *Australia* 94 B3
Kidugallo, *Tanzania* 86 D4
Kiel, *Germany* 24 A6
Kiel Canal = Nord-Ostsee-Kanal, *Germany* 24 A5
Kielce, *Poland* 45 H7
Kielder Water, *U.K.* 12 B5
Kieler Bucht, *Germany* 24 A6
Kiembara, *Burkina Faso* 82 C4
Kien Binh, *Vietnam* 65 H5
Kien Tan, *Vietnam* 65 G5
Kienge, *Dem. Rep. of the Congo* 87 E2
Kiessé, *Niger* 83 C5
Kiev = Kyyiv, *Ukraine* 47 G6
Kifaya, *Guinea* 82 C2
Kiffa, *Mauritania* 82 B2
Kifisiá, *Greece* 38 C5
Kifissós →, *Greece* 38 C5
Kifrī, *Iraq* 70 C5
Kigali, *Rwanda* 86 C3
Kigarama, *Tanzania* 86 C3
Kigelle, *Sudan* 81 F3
Kigoma □, *Tanzania* 86 D3
Kigoma-Ujiji, *Tanzania* 86 C2
Kigomasha, Ras, *Tanzania* 86 C4
Kığzı, *Turkey* 70 B4
Kihei, *U.S.A.* 106 H16
Kihnu, *Estonia* 9 G21
Kii-Sanchi, *Japan* 55 G8
Kii-Suidō, *Japan* 55 H7
Kikaiga-Shima, *Japan* 55 K4
Kikinda, *Serbia, Yug.* 42 E5
Kikládhes, *Greece* 38 E6
Kikládhes □, *Greece* 38 D6
Kikwit, *Dem. Rep. of the Congo* 84 E3
Kil, *Sweden* 10 E7
Kilafors, *Sweden* 10 C10
Kilar, *India* 68 C7
Kilauea Crater, *U.S.A.* 106 J17
Kilbrannan Sd., *U.K.* 14 F3
Kilchu, *N. Korea* 57 D15
Kilcoy, *Australia* 95 D5
Kildare, *Ireland* 15 C5
Kildare □, *Ireland* 15 C5
Kileikli, *Sudan* 81 E2
Kilfinnane, *Ireland* 15 D3
Kilgore, *U.S.A.* 113 J7
Kilibo, *Benin* 83 D5
Kilifi, *Kenya* 86 C4
Kilimanjaro, *Tanzania* 86 C4
Kilimanjaro □, *Tanzania* 86 C4
Kilimli, *Turkey* 72 B4
Kilindini, *Kenya* 86 C4
Kilis, *Turkey* 70 B3
Kiliya, *Ukraine* 47 K5
Kilkee, *Ireland* 15 D2
Kilkeel, *U.K.* 15 B5
Kilkenny, *Ireland* 15 D4
Kilkenny □, *Ireland* 15 D4
Kilkieran B., *Ireland* 15 C2
Kilkís, *Greece* 40 F6
Kilkís □, *Greece* 40 E6
Killala, *Ireland* 15 B2
Killala B., *Ireland* 15 B2
Killaloe, *Ireland* 15 D3
Killaloe Station, *Canada* 110 A7
Killarney, *Australia* 95 D5
Killarney, *Canada* 105 D9
Killarney, *Ireland* 15 D2
Killary Harbour, *Ireland* 15 C2
Killdeer, *U.S.A.* 112 B3
Killeberg, *Sweden* 11 H8
Killeen, *U.S.A.* 113 K6
Killin, *U.K.* 14 E4
Killíni, *Ilía, Greece* 38 D3
Killíni, *Korinthía, Greece* 38 D4
Killorglin, *Ireland* 15 D2
Killybegs, *Ireland* 15 B3
Kilmarnock, *U.K.* 14 F4
Kilmez, *Russia* 48 B10
Kilmez →, *Russia* 48 B10
Kilmore, *Australia* 95 F3
Kilondo, *Tanzania* 87 D3
Kilosa, *Tanzania* 86 D4
Kilrush, *Ireland* 15 D2
Kilwa Kisiwani, *Tanzania* 87 D4
Kilwa Kivinje, *Tanzania* 87 D4
Kilwa Masoko, *Tanzania* 87 D4
Kilwinning, *U.K.* 14 F4
Kim, *U.S.A.* 113 G3
Kim →, *Cameroon* 83 D7
Kimaam, *Indonesia* 63 F9
Kimamba, *Tanzania* 86 D4
Kimba, *Australia* 95 E2
Kimball, *Nebr., U.S.A.* 112 E3
Kimball, *S. Dak., U.S.A.* 112 D5
Kimberley, *Australia* 92 C4
Kimberley, *Canada* 104 D5
Kimberley, *S. Africa* 88 D3
Kimberly, *U.S.A.* 114 E6
Kimch'aek, *N. Korea* 57 D15
Kimch'ŏn, *S. Korea* 57 F15
Kími, *Greece* 38 C6
Kimje, *S. Korea* 57 G14
Kimmirut, *Canada* 101 B13
Kímolos, *Greece* 38 E6
Kimovsk, *Moskva, Russia* 46 E9
Kimovsk, *Tula, Russia* 46 E10
Kimparana, *Mali* 82 C4
Kimpese, *Dem. Rep. of the Congo* 84 F2
Kimry, *Russia* 46 D9
Kimstad, *Sweden* 11 F9
Kinabalu, Gunong, *Malaysia* 62 C5
Kínaros, *Greece* 39 E8
Kinaskan L., *Canada* 104 B2
Kinbasket L., *Canada* 104 C5
Kincardine, *Canada* 102 D3
Kincolith, *Canada* 104 B3
Kinda, *Dem. Rep. of the Congo* 87 D2
Kindberg, *Austria* 26 D8
Kinde, *U.S.A.* 110 C2
Kinder Scout, *U.K.* 12 D6
Kindersley, *Canada* 105 C7
Kindia, *Guinea* 82 D2
Kindu, *Dem. Rep. of the Congo* 86 C2
Kinel, *Russia* 48 D10
Kineshma, *Russia* 48 B6
Kinesi, *Tanzania* 86 C3
King, L., *Australia* 93 F2
King, Mt., *Australia* 94 D4
King City, *U.S.A.* 116 J5
King Cr. →, *Australia* 94 C2
King Edward →, *Australia* 92 B4
King Frederick VI Land = Kong Frederik VI Kyst, *Greenland* 4 C5
King George B., *Falk. Is.* 128 G4
King George I., *Antarctica* 5 C18
King George Is., *Canada* 101 C11
King I. = Kadan Kyun, *Burma* 64 F2
King I., *Australia* 94 F3
King I., *Canada* 104 C3
King Leopold Ranges, *Australia* 92 C4
King of Prussia, *U.S.A.* 111 F9
King Sd., *Australia* 92 C3
King William I., *Canada* 100 B10
King William's Town, *S. Africa* 88 E4
Kingaok = Bathurst Inlet, *Canada* 100 B9
Kingaroy, *Australia* 95 D5
Kingfisher, *U.S.A.* 113 H6
Kingirbān, *Iraq* 70 C5
Kingisepp = Kuressaare, *Estonia* 9 G20
Kingisepp, *Russia* 46 C5
Kingman, *Ariz., U.S.A.* 117 K12
Kingman, *Kans., U.S.A.* 113 G5
Kingoonya, *Australia* 95 E2
Kingri, *Pakistan* 68 D3
Kings →, *U.S.A.* 116 J7
Kings Canyon National Park, *U.S.A.* 116 J8
King's Lynn, *U.K.* 12 E8
Kings Mountain, *U.S.A.* 109 H5
Kings Park, *U.S.A.* 111 F11
King's Peak, *U.S.A.* 114 F8
Kingsbridge, *U.K.* 13 G4
Kingsburg, *U.S.A.* 116 J7
Kingscote, *Australia* 95 F2
Kingscourt, *Ireland* 15 C5
Kingsford, *U.S.A.* 108 C1
Kingsland, *U.S.A.* 109 K5
Kingsley, *U.S.A.* 112 D7
Kingsport, *U.S.A.* 109 G4
Kingston, *Canada* 102 D4
Kingston, *Jamaica* 120 C4
Kingston, *N.Z.* 91 L2
Kingston, *N.H., U.S.A.* 111 D13
Kingston, *N.Y., U.S.A.* 111 E11
Kingston, *Pa., U.S.A.* 111 E9
Kingston, *R.I., U.S.A.* 111 E13
Kingston Pk., *U.S.A.* 117 K11
Kingston South East, *Australia* 95 F2
Kingston upon Hull, *U.K.* 12 D7
Kingston upon Hull □, *U.K.* 12 D7
Kingston-upon-Thames □, *U.K.* 13 F7
Kingstown, *St. Vincent* 121 D7
Kingstree, *U.S.A.* 109 J6
Kingsville, *Canada* 102 D3
Kingsville, *U.S.A.* 113 M6
Kingussie, *U.K.* 14 D4

Kingwood, *U.S.A.* 113 K7
Kınık, *Antalya, Turkey* 39 E11
Kınık, *İzmir, Turkey* 39 B9
Kinistino, *Canada* 105 C7
Kinkala, *Congo* 84 E2
Kinki □, *Japan* 55 H8
Kinleith, *N.Z.* 91 H5
Kinmount, *Canada* 110 B6
Kinna, *Sweden* 11 G6
Kinnairds Hd., *U.K.* 14 D6
Kinnared, *Sweden* 11 G7
Kinnarodden, *Norway* 6 A11
Kinnarp, *Sweden* 11 F7
Kinneviken, *Sweden* 11 F7
Kinngait = Cape Dorset, *Canada* 101 B12
Kino, *Mexico* 118 B2
Kinoje →, *Canada* 102 B3
Kinomoto, *Japan* 55 G8
Kinoni, *Uganda* 86 C3
Kinoosao, *Canada* 105 B8
Kinross, *U.K.* 14 E5
Kinsale, *Ireland* 15 E3
Kinsale, Old Hd. of, *Ireland* 15 E3
Kinsha = Chang Jiang →, *China* 59 B13
Kinshasa, *Dem. Rep. of the Congo* 84 E3
Kinsley, *U.S.A.* 113 G5
Kinsman, *U.S.A.* 110 E4
Kinston, *U.S.A.* 109 H7
Kintampo, *Ghana* 83 D4
Kintore Ra., *Australia* 92 D4
Kintyre, *U.K.* 14 F3
Kintyre, Mull of, *U.K.* 14 F3
Kinushseo →, *Canada* 102 A3
Kinuso, *Canada* 104 B5
Kinyangiri, *Tanzania* 86 C3
Kinyeti, *Sudan* 81 G3
Kinzig →, *Germany* 25 G3
Kinzua, *U.S.A.* 110 E6
Kinzua Dam, *U.S.A.* 110 E6
Kióni, *Greece* 38 C2
Kiosk, *Canada* 102 C4
Kiowa, *Kans., U.S.A.* 113 G5
Kiowa, *Okla., U.S.A.* 113 H7
Kipahigan L., *Canada* 105 B8
Kipanga, *Tanzania* 86 D4
Kiparissía, *Greece* 38 D3
Kiparissiakós Kólpos, *Greece* 38 D3
Kipawa, L., *Canada* 102 C4
Kipembawe, *Tanzania* 86 D3
Kipengere Ra., *Tanzania* 87 D3
Kipili, *Tanzania* 86 D3
Kipini, *Kenya* 86 C5
Kipling, *Canada* 105 C8
Kippure, *Ireland* 15 C5
Kipushi, *Dem. Rep. of the Congo* 87 E2
Kirane, *Mali* 82 B2
Kiranomena, *Madag.* 89 B8
Kiraz, *Turkey* 39 C10
Kirazlı, *Turkey* 41 F10
Kirchhain, *Germany* 24 E4
Kirchheim, *Germany* 25 G5
Kirchheimbolanden, *Germany* 25 F3
Kirchschlag, *Austria* 27 D9
Kireç, *Turkey* 39 B10
Kirensk, *Russia* 51 D11
Kirghizia = Kyrgyzstan ■, *Asia* 50 E8
Kirghizstan = Kyrgyzstan ■, *Asia* 50 E8
Kiribati ■, *Pac. Oc.* 96 H10
Kırıkhan, *Turkey* 72 D7
Kırıkkale, *Turkey* 72 C5
Kirillov, *Russia* 46 C10
Kirin = Jilin, *China* 57 C14
Kirishi, *Russia* 46 C7
Kiritimati, *Kiribati* 97 G12
Kırka, *Turkey* 39 B12
Kırkağaç, *Turkey* 39 B9
Kirkby, *U.K.* 12 D5
Kirkby Lonsdale, *U.K.* 12 C5
Kirkcaldy, *U.K.* 14 E5
Kirkcudbright, *U.K.* 14 G4
Kirkee, *India* 66 K8
Kirkenes, *Norway* 8 B23
Kirkfield, *Canada* 110 B6
Kirkjubæjarklaustur, *Iceland* 8 E4
Kirkkonummi, *Finland* 9 F21
Kirkland Lake, *Canada* 102 C3
Kırklareli, *Turkey* 41 E11
Kırklareli □, *Turkey* 41 E11
Kirksville, *U.S.A.* 112 E8
Kirkūk, *Iraq* 70 C5
Kirkwall, *U.K.* 14 C6
Kirkwood, *S. Africa* 88 E4
Kirn, *Germany* 25 F3
Kirov, *Kaluga, Russia* 46 E8
Kirov, *Kirov, Russia* 50 D5
Kirovabad = Gäncä, *Azerbaijan* 49 K8
Kirovakan = Vanadzor, *Armenia* 49 K7
Kirovograd = Kirovohrad, *Ukraine* 47 H7
Kirovohrad, *Ukraine* 47 H7
Kirovsk = Babadayhan, *Turkmenistan* 50 F7
Kirovskiy, *Astrakhan, Russia* 49 H9
Kirovskiy, *Kamchatka, Russia* 51 D16
Kirovskiy, *Primorsk, Russia* 54 B6
Kirriemuir, *U.K.* 14 E5
Kirsanov, *Russia* 48 D6
Kırşehir, *Turkey* 70 B2
Kirtachi, *Niger* 83 C5
Kirthar Range, *Pakistan* 68 F2
Kirtland, *U.S.A.* 115 H9
Kiruna, *Sweden* 8 C19
Kirundu, *Dem. Rep. of the Congo* 86 C2
Kirya, *Russia* 48 C8
Kiryū, *Japan* 55 F9
Kisa, *Sweden* 11 G9
Kisaga, *Tanzania* 86 C3
Kisalaya, *Nic.* 120 D3
Kisalföld, *Hungary* 42 C2
Kisámou, Kólpos, *Greece* 36 D5
Kisanga, *Dem. Rep. of the Congo* 86 B2
Kisangani, *Dem. Rep. of the Congo* 86 B2
Kisar, *Indonesia* 63 F7
Kisarawe, *Tanzania* 86 D4
Kisarazu, *Japan* 55 G9
Kisbér, *Hungary* 42 C3
Kishanganga →, *Pakistan* 69 B5
Kishanganj, *India* 69 F13
Kishangarh, *Raj., India* 68 F6
Kishangarh, *Raj., India* 68 F4
Kishi, *Nigeria* 83 D5
Kishinev = Chişinău, *Moldova* 43 C13
Kishiwada, *Japan* 55 G7
Kishtwar, *India* 69 C6
Kisielice, *Poland* 44 E6
Kisii, *Kenya* 86 C3
Kisiju, *Tanzania* 86 D4
Kisir, *Turkey* 73 B10
Kisizi, *Uganda* 86 C2
Kiskomárom = Zalakomár, *Hungary* 42 D2
Kiskőrei-víztároló, *Hungary* 42 C5
Kiskőrös, *Hungary* 42 D4
Kiskundorozsma, *Hungary* 42 D5
Kiskunfélegyháza, *Hungary* 42 D4
Kiskunhalas, *Hungary* 42 D4
Kiskunmajsa, *Hungary* 42 D4
Kislovodsk, *Russia* 49 J6
Kismayu = Chisimaio, *Somali Rep.* 77 G8
Kiso-Gawa →, *Japan* 55 G8
Kiso-Sammyaku, *Japan* 55 G8
Kisofukushima, *Japan* 55 G8
Kisoro, *Uganda* 86 C2
Kissidougou, *Guinea* 82 D2
Kissimmee, *U.S.A.* 109 L5
Kissimmee →, *U.S.A.* 109 M5
Kississing L., *Canada* 105 B8
Kissónerga, *Cyprus* 36 E11
Kissu, J., *Sudan* 80 C2
Kistanje, *Croatia* 29 E12
Kisújszállás, *Hungary* 42 C5
Kisumu, *Kenya* 86 C3
Kisvárda, *Hungary* 42 B7
Kiswani, *Tanzania* 86 C4
Kiswere, *Tanzania* 87 D4
Kit Carson, *U.S.A.* 112 F3
Kita, *Mali* 82 C3
Kitaibaraki, *Japan* 55 F10
Kitakami, *Japan* 54 E10
Kitakami-Gawa →, *Japan* 54 E10
Kitakami-Sammyaku, *Japan* 54 E10
Kitakata, *Japan* 54 F9
Kitakyūshū, *Japan* 55 H5
Kitale, *Kenya* 86 B4
Kitami, *Japan* 54 C11
Kitami-Sammyaku, *Japan* 54 B11
Kitangiri, L., *Tanzania* 86 C3
Kitaya, *Tanzania* 87 E5
Kitchener, *Canada* 102 D3
Kitee, *Finland* 46 A6
Kitega = Gitega, *Burundi* 86 C2
Kitengo, *Dem. Rep. of the Congo* 86 D1
Kitgum, *Uganda* 86 B3
Kíthira, *Greece* 38 E5
Kíthnos, *Greece* 38 D6
Kiti, *Cyprus* 36 E12
Kiti, C., *Cyprus* 36 E12
Kitimat, *Canada* 104 C3
Kitinen →, *Finland* 8 C22
Kitiyab, *Sudan* 81 D3
Kítros, *Greece* 40 F6
Kitsuki, *Japan* 55 H5
Kittakittaooloo, L., *Australia* 95 D2
Kittanning, *U.S.A.* 110 F5
Kittatinny Mts., *U.S.A.* 111 F10
Kittery, *U.S.A.* 109 D10
Kittilä, *Finland* 8 C21
Kitui, *Kenya* 86 C4
Kitwanga, *Canada* 104 B3
Kitwe, *Zambia* 87 E2
Kitzbühel, *Austria* 26 D5
Kitzbühler Alpen, *Austria* 26 D5
Kitzingen, *Germany* 25 F6
Kivarli, *India* 68 G5
Kivertsi, *Ukraine* 47 G3
Kividhes, *Cyprus* 36 E11
Kivik, *Sweden* 11 J8
Kivotós, *Greece* 40 F5
Kivu, L., *Dem. Rep. of the Congo* 86 C2
Kiyev = Kyyiv, *Ukraine* 47 G6
Kiyevskoye Vdkhr. = Kyyivske Vdskh., *Ukraine* 47 G6
Kıyıköy, *Turkey* 41 E12
Kiziguru, *Rwanda* 86 C3
Kızıl Adalar, *Turkey* 41 F13
Kızıl Irmak →, *Turkey* 72 B6
Kizil Jilga, *India* 69 B8
Kizil Yurt, *Russia* 49 J8
Kızılcabölük, *Turkey* 39 D11
Kızılcadağ, *Turkey* 39 D11
Kızılcahamam, *Turkey* 72 B5
Kızılhisar, *Turkey* 72 D3
Kızılırmak, *Turkey* 72 B5
Kızılkaya, *Turkey* 39 D12
Kızılören, *Turkey* 39 C12
Kızıltepe, *Turkey* 70 B4
Kizimkazi, *Tanzania* 86 D4
Kizlyar, *Russia* 49 J8
Kizyl-Arvat = Gyzylarbat, *Turkmenistan* 50 F6
Kjellerup, *Denmark* 11 H3
Kjölur, *Iceland* 8 D4
Kladanj, *Bos.-H.* 42 F3
Kladnica, *Serbia, Yug.* 40 C4
Kladno, *Czech Rep.* 26 A7
Kladovo, *Serbia, Yug.* 40 B6
Klaeng, *Thailand* 64 F3
Klagenfurt, *Austria* 26 E7
Klaipėda, *Lithuania* 9 J19
Klaipėda □, *Lithuania* 44 C8
Klaksvík, *Færoe Is.* 8 E9
Klamath →, *U.S.A.* 114 F1
Klamath Falls, *U.S.A.* 114 E3
Klamath Mts., *U.S.A.* 114 F2
Klamono, *Indonesia* 63 E8
Klanjec, *Croatia* 29 B12
Klappan →, *Canada* 104 B3
Klarälven →, *Sweden* 10 E7
Klässbol, *Sweden* 10 E6
Klatovy, *Czech Rep.* 26 B6
Klawer, *S. Africa* 88 E2
Klazienaveen, *Neths.* 17 B6
Klé, *Mali* 82 C3
Kłecko, *Poland* 45 F4
Kleczew, *Poland* 45 F5
Kleena Kleene, *Canada* 104 C4
Klein-Karas, *Namibia* 88 D2
Klekovača, *Bos.-H.* 29 D13
Klenoec, *Macedonia* 40 E4
Klenovec, *Slovak Rep.* 27 C12
Klerksdorp, *S. Africa* 88 D4
Kleszczele, *Poland* 45 F10
Kletnya, *Russia* 46 F7
Kletsk = Klyetsk, *Belarus* 47 F4
Kletskiy, *Russia* 49 F6
Kleve, *Germany* 24 D2
Klickitat, *U.S.A.* 114 D3
Klickitat →, *U.S.A.* 116 E5
Klidhes, *Cyprus* 36 D13
Klimovichi, *Belarus* 46 F6
Klin, *Russia* 46 D9
Klina, *Kosovo, Yug.* 40 D4
Klinaklini →, *Canada* 104 C3
Klintehamn, *Sweden* 11 G12
Klintsy, *Russia* 47 F7
Klip →, *S. Africa* 89 D4
Klipdale, *S. Africa* 88 E2
Klippan, *Sweden* 11 H7
Klipplaat, *S. Africa* 88 E3
Klisura, *Bulgaria* 41 D8
Kljajićevo, *Serbia, Yug.* 42 E4
Ključ, *Bos.-H.* 29 D13
Kłobuck, *Poland* 45 H5
Klockestrand, *Sweden* 10 B11
Kłodawa, *Poland* 45 F5
Kłodzko, *Poland* 45 H3
Klos, *Albania* 40 E4
Klosterneuburg, *Austria* 27 C9
Klosters, *Switz.* 25 J5
Klötze, *Germany* 24 C7
Klouto, *Togo* 83 D5
Kluane L., *Canada* 100 B6
Kluane Nat. Park, *Canada* 104 A1
Kluczbork, *Poland* 45 H5
Klukwan, *U.S.A.* 104 B1
Klyetsk, *Belarus* 47 F4
Klyuchevskaya, Gora, *Russia* 51 D17
Knäred, *Sweden* 11 H7
Knaresborough, *U.K.* 12 C6
Knee L., *Man., Canada* 102 A1
Knee L., *Sask., Canada* 105 B7
Knezha, *Bulgaria* 41 C8
Knić, *Serbia, Yug.* 40 C4
Knight Inlet, *Canada* 104 C3
Knighton, *U.K.* 13 E4
Knights Ferry, *U.S.A.* 116 H6
Knights Landing, *U.S.A.* 116 G5
Knin, *Croatia* 29 D13
Knislinge, *Sweden* 11 H8
Knittelfeld, *Austria* 26 D7
Knivsta, *Sweden* 10 E11
Knjaževac, *Serbia, Yug.* 40 C6
Knob, C., *Australia* 93 F2
Knock, *Ireland* 15 C3
Knockmealdown Mts., *Ireland* 15 D4
Knokke-Heist, *Belgium* 17 C3
Knossós, *Greece* 36 D7
Knowlton, *Canada* 111 A12
Knox, *U.S.A.* 108 E2
Knox Coast, *Antarctica* 5 C8
Knoxville, *Iowa, U.S.A.* 112 E8
Knoxville, *Pa., U.S.A.* 110 E7
Knoxville, *Tenn., U.S.A.* 109 H4
Knysna, *S. Africa* 88 E3
Knyszyn, *Poland* 44 E9
Ko Kha, *Thailand* 64 C2
Koartac = Quaqtaq, *Canada* 101 B13
Koba, *Indonesia* 63 F8
Kobarid, *Slovenia* 29 B10
Kobayashi, *Japan* 55 J5
Kobdo = Hovd, *Mongolia* 60 B4
Kōbe, *Japan* 55 G7
Kobelyaky, *Ukraine* 47 H8
København, *Denmark* 11 J6
Københavns Amtskommune □, *Denmark* 11 J6
Kobenni, *Mauritania* 82 B3
Kōbi-Sho, *Japan* 55 M1
Koblenz, *Germany* 25 E3
Kobo, *Ethiopia* 81 E4
Kobryn, *Belarus* 47 F3
Kobuleti, *Georgia* 49 K5
Kobylin, *Poland* 45 G4
Kobyłka, *Poland* 45 F8
Kobylkino, *Russia* 48 C6
Koca →, *Turkey* 41 F11
Kocabaş, *Turkey* 39 D11
Kocaeli, *Turkey* 41 F13
Kocaeli □, *Turkey* 41 F13
Kočane, *Serbia, Yug.* 40 C5
Kočani, *Macedonia* 40 E6
Koçarlı, *Turkey* 39 D9
Koceljevo, *Serbia, Yug.* 40 B3
Kočevje, *Slovenia* 29 C11
Koch Bihar, *India* 67 F16
Kochang, *S. Korea* 57 G14
Kochas, *India* 69 G10
Kocher →, *Germany* 25 F5
Kochi = Cochin, *India* 66 Q10
Kōchi, *Japan* 55 H6
Kōchi □, *Japan* 55 H6
Kochiu = Gejiu, *China* 58 F4
Kock, *Poland* 45 G9
Kodarma, *India* 69 G11
Kode, *Sweden* 11 G5
Kodiak, *U.S.A.* 100 C4
Kodiak I., *U.S.A.* 100 C4
Kodinar, *India* 68 J4
Kodok, *Sudan* 81 F3
Kodori →, *Georgia* 49 J5
Koedoesberge, *S. Africa* 88 E3
Koes, *Namibia* 88 D2
Kofçaz, *Turkey* 41 E11
Koffiefontein, *S. Africa* 88 D4
Kofiau, *Indonesia* 63 E7
Köflach, *Austria* 26 D8
Koforidua, *Ghana* 83 D4
Kōfu, *Japan* 55 G9
Koga, *Japan* 55 F9
Kogaluk →, *Canada* 103 A7
Køge, *Denmark* 11 J6
Køge Bugt, *Denmark* 11 J6
Kogi □, *Nigeria* 83 D6
Kogin Baba, *Nigeria* 83 D7
Koh-i-Khurd, *Afghan.* 68 C1
Koh-i-Maran, *Pakistan* 68 E2
Kohat, *Pakistan* 68 C4
Kohima, *India* 67 G19
Kohkīlūyeh va Būyer Aḥmadi □, *Iran* 71 D6
Kohler Ra., *Antarctica* 5 D15
Kohlu, *Pakistan* 68 E3
Kohtla-Järve, *Estonia* 9 G22
Koillismaa, *Finland* 8 D23
Koin-dong, *N. Korea* 57 D14
Koinare, *Bulgaria* 41 C8
Koindu, *S. Leone* 82 D2
Kojetín, *Czech Rep.* 27 B10
Kojō, *N. Korea* 57 E14
Kojonup, *Australia* 93 F2
Kojūr, *Iran* 71 B6
Koka, *Sudan* 80 C3
Kokand = Qūqon, *Uzbekistan* 50 E8
Kokas, *Indonesia* 63 E8
Kokava, *Slovak Rep.* 27 C12
Kokchetav = Kökshetaū, *Kazakstan* 50 D7
Kokemäenjoki →, *Finland* 9 F19
Kokhma, *Russia* 48 B5
Koki, *Senegal* 82 B1
Kokkola, *Finland* 8 E20
Koko, *Nigeria* 83 C5
Koko Kyunzu, *Burma* 67 M18
Kokolopozo, *Ivory C.* 82 D3
Kokomo, *U.S.A.* 108 E2
Kokoro, *Niger* 83 C5
Koksan, *N. Korea* 57 E14
Kökshetaū, *Kazakstan* 50 D7
Koksoak →, *Canada* 101 C13
Kokstad, *S. Africa* 89 E4
Kokubu, *Japan* 55 J5
Kola, *Indonesia* 63 F8
Kola Pen. = Kolskiy Poluostrov, *Russia* 50 C4
Kolachi →, *Pakistan* 68 F2
Kolahoi, *India* 69 B6
Kolahun, *Liberia* 82 D2
Kolaka, *Indonesia* 63 E6
Kolar, *India* 66 N11
Kolar Gold Fields, *India* 66 N11
Kolaras, *India* 68 G6
Kolari, *Finland* 8 C20
Kolárovo, *Slovak Rep.* 27 D10
Kolašin, *Montenegro, Yug.* 40 D3
Kolayat, *India* 66 F8
Kolbäck, *Sweden* 10 E10
Kolbäcksån →, *Sweden* 10 E10
Kolbermoor, *Germany* 25 H8
Kolbuszowa, *Poland* 45 H8
Kolchugino = Leninsk-Kuznetskiy, *Russia* 50 D9
Kolchugino, *Russia* 46 D10
Kolda, *Senegal* 82 C2
Koldegi, *Sudan* 81 E3
Kolding, *Denmark* 11 J3
Kolepom = Dolak, Pulau, *Indonesia* 63 F9
Kolguyev, Ostrov, *Russia* 50 C5
Kolhapur, *India* 66 L9
Kolia, *Ivory C.* 82 D3
Kolín, *Czech Rep.* 26 A8
Kolind, *Denmark* 11 H4
Kolkas rags, *Latvia* 9 H20
Kolkata, *India* 69 H13
Kollam = Quilon, *India* 66 Q10
Kölleda, *Germany* 24 D7
Kollum, *Neths.* 17 A6
Kolmanskop, *Namibia* 88 D2
Köln, *Germany* 24 E2
Kolno, *Poland* 44 E8
Koło, *Poland* 45 F5
Kołobrzeg, *Poland* 44 D2
Kolokani, *Mali* 82 C3
Koloko, *Burkina Faso* 82 C3
Kololo, *Ethiopia* 81 F5
Kolomna, *Russia* 46 E10
Kolomyya, *Ukraine* 47 H3
Kolondiéba, *Mali* 82 C3
Kolonodale, *Indonesia* 63 E6
Kolonowskie, *Poland* 45 H5
Kolosib, *India* 67 G18
Kolpashevo, *Russia* 50 D9
Kolpino, *Russia* 46 C6
Kolpny, *Russia* 47 F9
Kolskiy Poluostrov, *Russia* 50 C4
Kolsva, *Sweden* 10 E9
Kolubara →, *Serbia, Yug.* 40 B4
Koluszki, *Poland* 45 G6
Kolwezi, *Dem. Rep. of the Congo* 87 E2
Kolyma →, *Russia* 51 C17
Kolymskoye Nagorye, *Russia* 51 C16
Kôm Hamâda, *Egypt* 80 H7
Kôm Ombo, *Egypt* 80 C3
Komadugu Gana →, *Nigeria* 83 C7
Komandorskiye Is. = Komandorskiye Ostrova, *Russia* 51 D17
Komandorskiye Ostrova, *Russia* 51 D17
Komárno, *Slovak Rep.* 27 D11
Komárom, *Hungary* 42 C3
Komárom-Esztergom □, *Hungary* 42 C3
Komatipoort, *S. Africa* 89 D5
Komatou Yialou, *Cyprus* 36 D13
Komatsu, *Japan* 55 F8
Komatsushima, *Japan* 55 H7
Kombissiri, *Burkina Faso* 83 C4
Kombori, *Burkina Faso* 82 C4
Kombóti, *Greece* 38 B3
Komen, *Slovenia* 29 C10
Komenda, *Ghana* 83 D4
Komi □, *Russia* 50 C6
Komiža, *Croatia* 29 E13
Komló, *Hungary* 42 D3
Kommunarsk = Alchevsk, *Ukraine* 47 H10
Kommunizma, Pik, *Tajikistan* 50 F8
Komodo, *Indonesia* 63 F5
Komoé →, *Ivory C.* 82 D4
Komoran, Pulau, *Indonesia* 63 F9
Komoro, *Japan* 55 F9
Komotini, *Greece* 41 E9
Komovi, *Montenegro, Yug.* 40 D3
Kompasberg, *S. Africa* 88 E3
Kompong Bang, *Cambodia* 65 F5
Kompong Cham, *Cambodia* 65 F5
Kompong Chhnang = Kampang Chhnang, *Cambodia* 65 F5
Kompong Chikreng, *Cambodia* 64 F5
Kompong Kleang, *Cambodia* 64 F5
Kompong Luong, *Cambodia* 65 G5
Kompong Pranak, *Cambodia* 64 F5
Kompong Som = Kampong Saom, *Cambodia* 65 G4
Kompong Som, Chhung = Kampong Saom, Chaak, *Cambodia* 65 G4
Kompong Speu, *Cambodia* 65 G5
Kompong Sralao, *Cambodia* 64 E5
Kompong Thom, *Cambodia* 64 F5
Kompong Trabeck, *Cambodia* 64 F5
Kompong Trabeck, *Cambodia* 65 G5
Kompong Trach, *Cambodia* 65 G5
Kompong Tralach, *Cambodia* 65 G5
Komrat = Comrat, *Moldova* 43 D13
Komsberg, *S. Africa* 88 E3
Komsomolets, Ostrov, *Russia* 51 A10
Komsomolsk, *Amur, Russia* 51 D14
Komsomolsk, *Ivanovo, Russia* 46 D11
Komsomolskiy, *Russia* 48 C7
Kömür Burnu, *Turkey* 39 C8
Kon Tum, *Vietnam* 64 E7
Kon Tum, Plateau du, *Vietnam* 64 E7
Kona, *Mali* 82 C4
Konakovo, *Russia* 46 D9
Konarhā □, *Afghan.* 66 B7
Konārī, *Iran* 71 D6
Konch, *India* 69 G8
Konde, *Tanzania* 86 C4
Kondiá, *Greece* 39 B7
Kondinin, *Australia* 93 F2
Kondoa, *Tanzania* 86 C4
Kondókali, *Greece* 36 A3
Kondopaga, *Russia* 46 A8
Kondratyevo, *Russia* 51 D10
Kondrovo, *Russia* 46 E8
Konduga, *Nigeria* 83 C7
Köneürgench, *Turkmenistan* 50 E6
Konevo, *Russia* 46 A10
Kong = Khong →, *Cambodia* 64 F5
Kong, *Ivory C.* 82 D4
Kong, Koh, *Cambodia* 65 G4
Kong Christian IX Land, *Greenland* 4 C6
Kong Christian X Land, *Greenland* 4 B6
Kong Frederik IX Land, *Greenland* 4 C5
Kong Frederik VI Kyst, *Greenland* 4 C5
Kong Frederik VIII Land, *Greenland* 4 B6
Kong Oscar Fjord, *Greenland* 4 B6
Kongeå →, *Denmark* 11 J2
Kongerslev, *Denmark* 11 H4
Kongju, *S. Korea* 57 F14
Konglu, *Burma* 67 F20
Kongola, *Namibia* 88 B3

Kongolo, *Kasai-Or., Dem. Rep. of the Congo* 86 D1
Kongolo, *Katanga, Dem. Rep. of the Congo* 86 D2
Kongor, *Sudan* 81 F3
Kongoussi, *Burkina Faso* 83 C4
Kongsberg, *Norway* 9 G13
Kongsvinger, *Norway* 9 F15
Kongwa, *Tanzania* 86 D4
Koni, *Dem. Rep. of the Congo* 87 E2
Koni, Mts., *Dem. Rep. of the Congo* 87 E2
Koniakari, *Mali* 82 C2
Koniecpol, *Poland* 45 H6
Königs Wusterhausen, *Germany* 24 C9
Königsberg = Kaliningrad, *Russia* 9 J19
Königsbrunn, *Germany* 25 G6
Königslutter, *Germany* 24 C6
Konin, *Poland* 45 F5
Konispol, *Albania* 40 G4
Kónitsa, *Greece* 38 A2
Konjic, *Bos.-H.* 42 G2
Konkiep, *Namibia* 88 D2
Konkouré →, *Guinea* 82 D2
Könnern, *Germany* 24 D7
Kono, *S. Leone* 82 D2
Konongo, *Ghana* 83 D4
Konosha, *Russia* 46 B11
Kōnosu, *Japan* 55 F9
Konotop, *Ukraine* 47 G7
Konsankoro, *Guinea* 82 D3
Końskie, *Poland* 45 G7
Konstancin-Jeziorna, *Poland* 45 F8
Konstantinovka = Kostyantynivka, *Ukraine* 47 H9
Konstantinovsk, *Russia* 49 G5
Konstantynów Łódźki, *Poland* 45 G6
Konstanz, *Germany* 25 H5
Kont, *Iran* 71 E9
Kontagora, *Nigeria* 83 C6
Kontcha, *Cameroon* 83 D7
Konya, *Turkey* 70 B2
Konya Ovası, *Turkey* 72 C5
Konz, *Germany* 25 F2
Konza, *Kenya* 86 C4
Koocanusa, L., *Canada* 114 B6
Kookynie, *Australia* 93 E3
Koolyanobbing, *Australia* 93 F2
Koonibba, *Australia* 95 E1
Koorawatha, *Australia* 95 E4
Koorda, *Australia* 93 F2
Kooskia, *U.S.A.* 114 C6
Kootenay →, *U.S.A.* 104 D5
Kootenay L., *Canada* 104 D5
Kootenay Nat. Park, *Canada* 104 C5
Kootjieskolk, *S. Africa* 88 E3
Kopanovka, *Russia* 49 G8
Kopaonik, *Yugoslavia* 40 C4
Kópavogur, *Iceland* 8 D3
Koper, *Slovenia* 29 C10
Kopervik, *Norway* 9 G11
Kopet Dagh, *Asia* 71 B8
Kopi, *Australia* 95 E2
Köping, *Sweden* 10 E10
Köpingsvik, *Sweden* 11 H10
Kopište, *Croatia* 29 F13
Koplik, *Albania* 40 D3
Köpmanholmen, *Sweden* 10 A12
Kopparberg, *Sweden* 10 E9
Koppeh Dāgh = Kopet Dagh, *Asia* 71 B8
Koppies, *S. Africa* 89 D4
Koppom, *Sweden* 10 E6
Koprivlen, *Bulgaria* 40 E7
Koprivnica, *Croatia* 29 B13
Kopřivnice, *Czech Rep.* 27 B11
Koprivshtitsa, *Bulgaria* 41 D8
Köprübaşı, *Turkey* 39 C10
Kopychyntsi, *Ukraine* 47 H3
Korab, *Macedonia* 40 E4
Korakiána, *Greece* 36 A3
Koral, *India* 68 J5
Korarou, L., *Mali* 82 B4
Korba, *India* 69 H10
Korbach, *Germany* 24 D4
Korbu, G., *Malaysia* 65 K3
Korce = Korçë, *Albania* 40 F4
Korçë, *Albania* 40 F4
Korčula, *Croatia* 29 F13
Korčulanski Kanal, *Croatia* 29 E13
Kord Kūy, *Iran* 71 B7
Kord Sheykh, *Iran* 71 D7
Kordestān □, *Iran* 70 C5
Kordofân, *Sudan* 79 F11
Koré Mayroua, *Niger* 83 C5
Korea, North ■, *Asia* 57 E14
Korea, South ■, *Asia* 57 G15
Korea Bay, *Korea* 57 E13
Korea Strait, *Asia* 57 H15
Korem, *Ethiopia* 81 E4
Korenevo, *Russia* 47 G8
Korenovsk, *Russia* 49 H4
Korets, *Ukraine* 47 G4
Korfantów, *Poland* 45 H4
Korgan, *Turkey* 72 B7
Korgus, *Sudan* 80 D3
Korhogo, *Ivory C.* 82 D3
Koribundu, *S. Leone* 82 D2
Korienzé, *Mali* 82 B4
Korinthía □, *Greece* 38 D4
Korinthiakós Kólpos, *Greece* 38 C4
Kórinthos, *Greece* 38 D4
Korioumé, *Mali* 82 B4
Koríssa, Límni, *Greece* 36 B3
Kōriyama, *Japan* 54 F10
Korkuteli, *Turkey* 39 D12
Kormakiti, C., *Cyprus* 36 D11
Körmend, *Hungary* 42 C1
Kornat, *Croatia* 29 E12
Korneshty = Corneşti, *Moldova* 43 C13
Korneuburg, *Austria* 27 C9
Kórnik, *Poland* 45 F4
Koro, *Fiji* 91 C8
Koro, *Ivory C.* 82 D3
Koro, *Mali* 82 C4
Koro Sea, *Fiji* 91 C9
Korocha, *Russia* 47 G9
Köroğlu Dağları, *Turkey* 72 B5
Korogwe, *Tanzania* 86 D4
Koronadal, *Phil.* 61 H6
Koróni, *Greece* 38 E3
Korónia, Límni, *Greece* 40 F7
Koronís, *Greece* 39 D7
Koronowo, *Poland* 45 E4
Koror, *Palau* 63 C8
Körös →, *Hungary* 42 D5
Köröstarcsa, *Hungary* 42 D6
Korosten, *Ukraine* 47 G5
Korostyshev, *Ukraine* 47 G5
Korotoyak, *Russia* 47 G10
Korraraika, Helodranon' i, *Madag.* 89 B7
Korsakov, *Russia* 51 E15
Korsberga, *Sweden* 11 G9
Korshunovo, *Russia* 51 D12
Korsør, *Denmark* 11 J5
Korsun Shevchenkovskiy, *Ukraine* 47 H6
Korsze, *Poland* 44 D8
Korti, *Sudan* 80 D3
Kortrijk, *Belgium* 17 D3
Korucu, *Turkey* 39 B9
Korwai, *India* 68 G8
Koryakskoye Nagorye, *Russia* 51 C18
Koryŏng, *S. Korea* 57 G15
Koryukovka, *Ukraine* 47 G7
Kos, *Greece* 39 E9
Kosa, *Ethiopia* 81 F4
Kosaya Gora, *Russia* 46 E9
Kościan, *Poland* 45 F3
Kościerzyna, *Poland* 44 D4
Kosciusko, *U.S.A.* 113 J10
Kosciuszko, Mt., *Australia* 95 F4
Kösély →, *Hungary* 42 C6
Kosha, *Sudan* 80 C3
Koshava, *Bulgaria* 40 B7
K'oshih = Kashi, *China* 60 C2
Koshiki-Rettō, *Japan* 55 J4
Kosi, *India* 68 F7
Kosi →, *India* 69 E8
Košice, *Slovak Rep.* 27 C14
Košický □, *Slovak Rep.* 27 C14
Kosjerić, *Serbia, Yug.* 40 B3
Köşk, *Turkey* 39 D10
Koskhinoú, *Greece* 36 C10
Koslan, *Russia* 50 C5
Kosŏng, *N. Korea* 57 E15
Kosovo □, *Yugoslavia* 40 D4
Kosovo Polje, *Kosovo, Yug.* 40 D5
Kosovska Kamenica, *Kosovo, Yug.* 40 D5
Kosovska Mitrovica, *Kosovo, Yug.* 40 D4
Kossou, L. de, *Ivory C.* 82 D3
Kosta, *Sweden* 11 H9
Kostajnica, *Croatia* 29 C13
Kostanjevica, *Slovenia* 29 C12
Kostenets, *Bulgaria* 40 D7
Koster, *S. Africa* 88 D4
Kôstî, *Sudan* 81 E3
Kostinbrod, *Bulgaria* 40 D7
Kostolac, *Serbia, Yug.* 40 B5
Kostopil, *Ukraine* 47 G4
Kostroma, *Russia* 46 D11
Kostromskoye Vdkhr., *Russia* 46 D11
Kostrzyn, *Lubuskie, Poland* 45 F1
Kostrzyn, *Wielkopolskie, Poland* 45 F4
Kostyantynivka, *Ukraine* 47 H9
Kostyukovichi = Kastsyukovichy, *Belarus* 46 F7
Koszalin, *Poland* 44 D3
Kőszeg, *Hungary* 42 C1
Kot Addu, *Pakistan* 68 D4
Kot Kapura, *India* 68 D6
Kot Moman, *Pakistan* 68 C5
Kot Sultan, *Pakistan* 68 D4
Kota, *India* 68 G6
Kota Baharu, *Malaysia* 65 J4
Kota Barrage, *India* 68 G6
Kota Belud, *Malaysia* 62 C5
Kota Kinabalu, *Malaysia* 62 C5
Kota Kubu Baharu, *Malaysia* 65 L3
Kota Tinggi, *Malaysia* 65 M4
Kotaagung, *Indonesia* 62 F2
Kotabaru, *Indonesia* 62 E5
Kotabumi, *Indonesia* 62 E2
Kotamobagu, *Indonesia* 63 D6
Kotcho L., *Canada* 104 B4
Kotdwara, *India* 69 E8
Kotel, *Bulgaria* 41 D10
Kotelnich, *Russia* 48 A9
Kotelnikovo, *Russia* 49 G6
Kotelnyy, Ostrov, *Russia* 51 B14
Kothari →, *India* 68 G6
Köthen, *Germany* 24 D7
Kothi, *Mad. P., India* 69 H10
Kothi, *Mad. P., India* 69 G9
Kotiro, *Pakistan* 68 F2
Kotka, *Finland* 9 F22
Kotlas, *Russia* 50 C5
Kotlenska Planina, *Bulgaria* 41 D10
Kotli, *Pakistan* 68 C5
Kotma, *India* 69 H9
Kotmul, *Pakistan* 69 B6
Koton-Karifi, *Nigeria* 83 D6
Kotonkoro, *Nigeria* 83 C6
Kotor, *Montenegro, Yug.* 40 D2
Kotor Varoš, *Bos.-H.* 42 F2
Kotoriba, *Croatia* 29 B13
Kotovo, *Russia* 48 E7
Kotovsk, *Russia* 48 D5
Kotovsk, *Ukraine* 47 J5
Kotputli, *India* 68 F7
Kotri, *Pakistan* 68 G3
Kótronas, *Greece* 38 E4
Kötschach-Mauthen, *Austria* 26 E6
Kotturu, *India* 66 M10
Kotuy →, *Russia* 51 B11
Kotzebue, *U.S.A.* 100 B3
Koudougou, *Burkina Faso* 82 C4
Koufonísi, *Greece* 36 E8
Koufonísia, *Greece* 39 E7
Kougaberge, *S. Africa* 88 E3
Kouibli, *Ivory C.* 82 D3
Kouilou →, *Congo* 84 E2
Koula Moutou, *Gabon* 84 E2
Koulen = Kulen, *Cambodia* 64 F5
Koulikoro, *Mali* 82 C3
Kouloúra, *Greece* 36 A3
Koúm-bournoú, Ákra, *Greece* 36 C10
Koumala, *Australia* 94 C4
Koumankou, *Mali* 82 C3
Koumbia, *Burkina Faso* 82 C4
Koumbia, *Guinea* 82 C2
Koumboum, *Guinea* 82 C2
Koumpenntoum, *Senegal* 82 C2
Koumra, *Chad* 79 G9
Koun-Fao, *Ivory C.* 82 D4
Koundara, *Guinea* 82 C2
Koundian, *Guinea* 82 C3
Koungheul, *Senegal* 82 C2
Kounradskiy, *Kazakstan* 50 E8
Kountze, *U.S.A.* 113 K7
Koupéla, *Burkina Faso* 83 C4
Kourémalé, *Mali* 82 C3
Kouris →, *Cyprus* 36 E11
Kourou, *Fr. Guiana* 125 B8
Kourouba, *Mali* 82 C2
Kouroukoto, *Mali* 82 C2
Kourouma, *Burkina Faso* 82 C4
Kourouninkoto, *Mali* 82 C3
Kouroussa, *Guinea* 82 C3
Koussanar, *Senegal* 82 C2
Koussané, *Mali* 82 C2
Koussane, *Senegal* 82 C2
Kousseri, *Cameroon* 79 F8
Koutiala, *Mali* 82 C3
Kouto, *Ivory C.* 82 D3
Kouvé, *Togo* 83 D5
Kouvola, *Finland* 9 F22
Kovačica, *Serbia, Yug.* 42 E5
Kovel, *Ukraine* 47 G3
Kovin, *Serbia, Yug.* 42 F5
Kovrov, *Russia* 48 B5
Kowal, *Poland* 45 F6
Kowalewo Pomorskie, *Poland* 45 E5
Kowanyama, *Australia* 94 B3
Kowloon, *H.K.* 59 F10
Kowŏn, *N. Korea* 57 E14
Köyceğiz, *Turkey* 39 E10
Köyceğiz Gölü, *Turkey* 39 E10
Koyulhisar, *Turkey* 72 B7
Koyunyeri, *Turkey* 41 F10
Koza, *Japan* 55 L3
Kozak, *Turkey* 39 B9
Kozan, *Turkey* 70 B2
Kozáni, *Greece* 40 F5
Kozáni □, *Greece* 40 F5
Kozara, *Bos.-H.* 29 D14
Kozarac, *Bos.-H.* 29 D13
Kozelets, *Ukraine* 47 G6
Kozelsk, *Russia* 46 E8
Kozhikode = Calicut, *India* 66 P9
Koziegłowy, *Poland* 45 H6
Kozienice, *Poland* 45 G8
Kozje, *Slovenia* 29 B12
Kozloduy, *Bulgaria* 40 C7
Kozlovets, *Bulgaria* 41 C9
Kozlovka, *Russia* 48 C9
Kozlu, *Turkey* 72 B4
Kozluk, *Turkey* 73 C9
Koźmin, *Poland* 45 G4
Kozmodemyansk, *Russia* 48 B8
Kożuchów, *Poland* 45 G2
Kozyatyn, *Ukraine* 47 H5
Kpabia, *Ghana* 83 D4
Kpalimé, *Togo* 83 D5
Kpandae, *Ghana* 83 D4
Kpessi, *Togo* 83 D5
Kra, Isthmus of = Kra, Kho Khot, *Thailand* 65 G2
Kra, Kho Khot, *Thailand* 65 G2
Kra Buri, *Thailand* 65 G2
Kraai →, *S. Africa* 88 E4
Krabi, *Thailand* 65 H2
Kracheh, *Cambodia* 64 F6
Kragan, *Indonesia* 63 G14
Kragerø, *Norway* 9 G13
Kragujevac, *Serbia, Yug.* 40 B4
Krajenka, *Poland* 45 E3
Krajina, *Bos.-H.* 29 D13
Krakatau = Rakata, Pulau, *Indonesia* 62 F3
Krakatoa = Rakata, Pulau, *Indonesia* 62 F3
Krakor, *Cambodia* 64 F5
Kraków, *Poland* 45 H6
Kralanh, *Cambodia* 64 F4
Králíky, *Czech Rep.* 27 A9
Kraljevo, *Serbia, Yug.* 40 C4
Královéhradecký □, *Czech Rep.* 26 A8
Královský Chlmec, *Slovak Rep.* 27 C14
Kralupy nad Vltavou, *Czech Rep.* 26 A7
Kramatorsk, *Ukraine* 47 H9
Kramfors, *Sweden* 10 B11
Kraniá, *Greece* 40 G5
Kranía Elassónas, *Greece* 38 B4
Kranídhion, *Greece* 38 D5
Kranj, *Slovenia* 29 B11
Kranjska Gora, *Slovenia* 29 B10
Krankskop, *S. Africa* 89 D5
Krapina, *Croatia* 29 B12
Krapina →, *Croatia* 29 C12
Krapkowice, *Poland* 45 H4
Kras, *Croatia* 29 C10
Kraskino, *Russia* 51 E14
Krāslava, *Latvia* 46 E4
Kraslice, *Czech Rep.* 26 A5
Krasnaya Gorbatka, *Russia* 48 C5
Krasnaya Polyana, *Russia* 49 J5
Kraśnik, *Poland* 45 H9
Krasnoarmeisk, *Ukraine* 47 H9
Krasnoarmeysk, *Russia* 48 E7
Krasnoarmeyskiy, *Russia* 49 G6
Krasnobrod, *Poland* 45 H10
Krasnodar, *Russia* 49 H4
Krasnodon, *Ukraine* 47 H10
Krasnogorskiy, *Russia* 48 B9
Krasnograd = Krasnohrad, *Ukraine* 47 H8
Krasnogvardeyskoye, *Russia* 49 H5
Krasnogvardyesk, *Ukraine* 47 K8
Krasnohrad, *Ukraine* 47 H8
Krasnokutsk, *Ukraine* 47 G8
Krasnolesnyy, *Russia* 47 G10
Krasnoperekopsk, *Ukraine* 47 J7
Krasnorechenskiy, *Russia* 54 B7
Krasnoselkup, *Russia* 50 C9
Krasnoslobodsk, *Mordvinia, Russia* 48 C6
Krasnoslobodsk, *Volgograd, Russia* 49 F7
Krasnoturinsk, *Russia* 50 D7
Krasnovodsk = Türkmenbashi, *Turkmenistan* 50 E6
Krasnoyarsk, *Russia* 51 D10
Krasnoye = Krasnyy, *Russia* 46 E6
Krasnozavodsk, *Russia* 46 D10
Krasny Sulin, *Russia* 47 J11
Krasnystaw, *Poland* 45 H10
Krasnyy, *Russia* 46 E6
Krasnyy Kholm, *Russia* 46 C9
Krasnyy Kut, *Russia* 48 E8
Krasnyy Liman, *Ukraine* 47 H9
Krasnyy Luch, *Ukraine* 47 H10
Krasnyy Profintern, *Russia* 46 D11
Krasnyy Yar, *Astrakhan, Russia* 49 G9
Krasnyy Yar, *Samara, Russia* 48 D10
Krasnyy Yar, *Volgograd, Russia* 48 E7
Krasnyye Baki, *Russia* 48 B7
Krasnyyoskolske Vdskh., *Ukraine* 47 H9
Kraszna →, *Hungary* 42 B7
Kratie = Kracheh, *Cambodia* 64 F6
Kratovo, *Macedonia* 40 D6
Krau, *Indonesia* 63 E10
Kravanh, Chuor Phnum, *Cambodia* 65 G4
Krefeld, *Germany* 24 D2
Krémaston, Límni, *Greece* 38 C3
Kremen, *Croatia* 29 D12
Kremenchug = Kremenchuk, *Ukraine* 47 H7
Kremenchuk, *Ukraine* 47 H7
Kremenchuksk Vdskh., *Ukraine* 47 H7
Kremenets, *Ukraine* 47 G3
Kremennaya, *Ukraine* 47 H10
Kremges = Svitlovodsk, *Ukraine* 47 H7
Kremmen, *Germany* 24 C9
Kremmling, *U.S.A.* 114 F10
Kremnica, *Slovak Rep.* 27 C11
Krems, *Austria* 26 C8
Kremsmünster, *Austria* 26 C7
Kretinga, *Lithuania* 9 J19
Krettsy, *Russia* 46 C7
Kreuzberg, *Germany* 25 E5
Kreuztal, *Germany* 24 E4
Kría Vrísi, *Greece* 40 F6
Kribi, *Cameroon* 83 E6
Krichem, *Bulgaria* 41 D8
Krichev = Krychaw, *Belarus* 46 F6
Krim, *Slovenia* 29 C11
Kriós, Ákra, *Greece* 36 D5
Krishna →, *India* 67 M12
Krishnanagar, *India* 69 H13
Kristdala, *Sweden* 11 G10
Kristiansand, *Norway* 9 G13
Kristianstad, *Sweden* 11 H8
Kristiansund, *Norway* 8 E12
Kristiinankaupunki, *Finland* 9 E19
Kristinehamn, *Sweden* 10 E8
Kristinestad = Kristiinankaupunki, *Finland* 9 E19
Kríti, *Greece* 36 D7
Kritsá, *Greece* 36 D7
Kriva →, *Macedonia* 40 D5
Kriva Palanka, *Macedonia* 40 D6
Krivaja →, *Bos.-H.* 42 F3
Krivelj, *Serbia, Yug.* 40 B6
Krivoy Rog = Kryvyy Rih, *Ukraine* 47 J7
Križevci, *Croatia* 29 B13
Krk, *Croatia* 29 C11
Krka →, *Slovenia* 29 C12
Krkonoše, *Czech Rep.* 26 A8
Krnov, *Czech Rep.* 27 A10
Krobia, *Poland* 45 G3
Krokeaí, *Greece* 38 E4
Krokek, *Sweden* 11 F10
Krokodil →, *Mozam.* 89 D5
Krokom, *Sweden* 10 A8
Krokowa, *Poland* 44 D5
Krolevets, *Ukraine* 47 G7
Kroměříž, *Czech Rep.* 27 B10
Krompachy, *Slovak Rep.* 27 C13
Kromy, *Russia* 47 F8
Kronach, *Germany* 25 E7
Krong Kaoh Kong, *Cambodia* 62 B2
Kronobergs län □, *Sweden* 11 H8
Kronprins Olav Kyst, *Antarctica* 5 C5
Kronshtadt, *Russia* 46 C5
Kroonstad, *S. Africa* 88 D4
Kröpelin, *Germany* 24 A7
Kropotkin, *Russia* 49 H5
Kropp, *Germany* 24 A5
Krosna, *Lithuania* 44 D10
Krośniewice, *Poland* 45 F6
Krosno, *Poland* 45 J8
Krosno Odrzańskie, *Poland* 45 F2
Krotoszyn, *Poland* 45 G4
Krotovka, *Russia* 48 D10
Kroussón, *Greece* 36 D6
Krrabë, *Albania* 40 E3
Krško, *Slovenia* 29 C12
Krstača, *Serbia, Yug.* 40 D4
Kruger Nat. Park, *S. Africa* 89 C5
Krugersdorp, *S. Africa* 89 D4
Kruisfontein, *S. Africa* 88 E3
Krujë, *Albania* 40 E3
Krulevshchina = Krulyewshchyna, *Belarus* 46 E4
Krulyewshchyna, *Belarus* 46 E4
Krumbach, *Germany* 25 G6
Krumë, *Albania* 40 D4
Krumovgrad, *Bulgaria* 41 E9
Krung Thep = Bangkok, *Thailand* 64 F3
Krupanj, *Serbia, Yug.* 40 B3
Krupina, *Slovak Rep.* 27 C12
Krupinica →, *Slovak Rep.* 27 C11
Krupki, *Belarus* 46 E5
Kruševac, *Serbia, Yug.* 40 C5
Kruševo, *Macedonia* 40 E5
Kruszwica, *Poland* 45 F5
Krychaw, *Belarus* 46 F6
Krymsk, *Russia* 47 K10
Krymskiy Poluostrov = Krymskyy Pivostriv, *Ukraine* 47 K8
Krymskyy Pivostriv, *Ukraine* 47 K8
Krynica, *Poland* 45 J7
Krynica Morska, *Poland* 44 D6
Krynki, *Poland* 45 E10
Kryvyy Rih, *Ukraine* 47 J7
Krzepice, *Poland* 45 H5
Krzeszów, *Poland* 45 H9
Krzna →, *Poland* 45 F10
Krzywiń, *Poland* 45 G3
Krzyż Wielkopolski, *Poland* 45 F2
Ksar el Kebir, *Morocco* 78 B4
Ksar es Souk = Er Rachidia, *Morocco* 78 B5
Książ Wielkopolski, *Poland* 45 F4
Kstovo, *Russia* 48 B7
Ku, W. el →, *Sudan* 81 E2
Kuala Belait, *Malaysia* 62 D4
Kuala Berang, *Malaysia* 65 K4
Kuala Dungun = Dungun, *Malaysia* 65 K4
Kuala Kangsar, *Malaysia* 65 K3
Kuala Kelawang, *Malaysia* 65 L4
Kuala Kerai, *Malaysia* 65 K4
Kuala Lipis, *Malaysia* 65 K4
Kuala Lumpur, *Malaysia* 65 L3
Kuala Nerang, *Malaysia* 65 J3
Kuala Pilah, *Malaysia* 65 L4
Kuala Rompin, *Malaysia* 65 L4
Kuala Selangor, *Malaysia* 65 L3
Kuala Sepetang, *Malaysia* 65 K3
Kuala Terengganu, *Malaysia* 65 K4
Kualajelai, *Indonesia* 62 E4
Kualakapuas, *Indonesia* 62 E4
Kualakurun, *Indonesia* 62 E4
Kualapembuang, *Indonesia* 62 E4
Kualasimpang, *Indonesia* 62 D1
Kuancheng, *China* 57 D10
Kuandang, *Indonesia* 63 D6
Kuandian, *China* 57 D13
Kuangchou = Guangzhou, *China* 59 F9
Kuanshan, *Taiwan* 59 F13
Kuantan, *Malaysia* 65 L4
Kuba = Quba, *Azerbaijan* 49 K9
Kuban →, *Russia* 47 K9
Kubenskoye, Ozero, *Russia* 46 C10
Kubokawa, *Japan* 55 H6
Kubrat, *Bulgaria* 41 C10
Kučevo, *Serbia, Yug.* 40 B5
Kucha Gompa, *India* 69 B7
Kuchaman, *India* 68 F6
Kuchenspitze, *Austria* 26 D3
Kuchinda, *India* 69 J11
Kuching, *Malaysia* 62 D4
Kuchino-eruba-Jima, *Japan* 55 J5
Kuchino-Shima, *Japan* 55 K4
Kuchinotsu, *Japan* 55 H5
Kuchl, *Austria* 26 D6
Kucing = Kuching, *Malaysia* 62 D4
Kuçovë, *Albania* 40 F3
Küçükbahçe, *Turkey* 39 C8
Küçükköy, *Turkey* 39 B8
Küçükkuyu, *Turkey* 39 B8
Küçükmenderes →, *Turkey* 39 D9
Kud →, *Pakistan* 68 F2
Kuda, *India* 66 H7

Kudat, Malaysia 62 C5
Kudirkos Naumiestis, Lithuania 44 D9
Kudowa-Zdrój, Poland 45 H3
Kudus, Indonesia 63 G14
Kudymkar, Russia 50 D6
Kueiyang = Guiyang, China 58 D6
Kufra Oasis = Al Kufrah, Libya 79 D10
Kufstein, Austria 26 D5
Kugluktuk, Canada 100 B8
Kugong I., Canada 102 A4
Kūhak, Iran 66 F3
Kuhan, Pakistan 68 E2
Kūhbonān, Iran 71 D8
Kūhestak, Iran 71 E8
Kuhin, Iran 71 B6
Kūhīrī, Iran 71 E9
Kuhnsdorf, Austria 26 E7
Kūhpāyeh, Eşfahan, Iran 71 C7
Kūhpāyeh, Kermān, Iran 71 D8
Kūhrān, Kūh-e, Iran 71 E8
Kui Buri, Thailand 65 F2
Kuiseb →, Namibia 88 B2
Kuito, Angola 85 G3
Kuiu I., U.S.A. 104 B2
Kujang, N. Korea 57 E14
Kujawsko-Pomorskie □, Poland 44 E5
Kuji, Japan 54 D10
Kujū-San, Japan 55 H5
Kukavica, Serbia, Yug. 40 D5
Kukawa, Nigeria 83 C7
Kukës, Albania 40 D4
Kukmor, Russia 48 B10
Kukup, Malaysia 65 M4
Kukvidze, Russia 48 E6
Kula, Bulgaria 40 C6
Kula, Serbia, Yug. 42 E4
Kula, Turkey 39 C10
Kulachi, Pakistan 68 D4
Kulai, Malaysia 65 M4
Kulal, Mt., Kenya 86 B4
Kulaly, Ostrov, Kazakstan 49 H10
Kulasekarappattinam, India 66 Q11
Kulautuva, Lithuania 44 D10
Kuldīga, Latvia 9 H19
Kuldīga □, Latvia 44 B8
Kuldja = Yining, China 50 E9
Kuldu, Sudan 81 E2
Kulebaki, Russia 48 C6
Kulen, Cambodia 64 F5
Kulen Vakuf, Bos.-H. 29 D13
Kulgam, India 69 C6
Kulgera, Australia 94 D1
Kulim, Malaysia 65 K3
Kulin, Australia 93 F2
Kullen, Sweden 11 H6
Kulmbach, Germany 25 E7
Kŭlob, Tajikistan 50 F7
Kulp, Turkey 73 C9
Kulpawn →, Ghana 83 D4
Kulsary, Kazakstan 50 E6
Kulti, India 69 H12
Kulu, India 68 D7
Kulu, Turkey 72 C5
Kulumbura, Australia 92 B4
Kulunda, Russia 50 D8
Kulungar, Afghan. 68 C3
Kūlvand, Iran 71 D7
Kulwin, Australia 95 F3
Kulyab = Kŭlob, Tajikistan 50 F7
Kuma →, Russia 49 H8
Kumafşarı, Turkey 39 D11
Kumaganum, Nigeria 83 C7
Kumagaya, Japan 55 F9
Kumai, Indonesia 62 E4
Kumalar Dağı, Turkey 39 C12
Kumamba, Kepulauan, Indonesia 63 E9
Kumamoto, Japan 55 H5
Kumamoto □, Japan 55 H5
Kumanovo, Macedonia 40 D5
Kumara, N.Z. 91 K3
Kumarina, Australia 93 D2
Kumasi, Ghana 82 D4
Kumayri = Gyumri, Armenia 49 K6
Kumba, Cameroon 83 E6
Kumbağ, Turkey 41 F11
Kumbakonam, India 66 P11
Kumbarilla, Australia 95 D5
Kumbhraj, India 68 G7
Kumbia, Australia 95 D5
Kumbo, Cameroon 83 D7
Kŭmch'ŏn, N. Korea 57 E14
Kumdok, India 69 C8
Kume-Shima, Japan 55 L3
Kumeny, Russia 48 A9
Kumharsain, India 68 D7
Kŭmhwa, S. Korea 57 E14
Kumi, Uganda 86 B3
Kumkale, Turkey 41 G10
Kumla, Sweden 10 E9
Kumluca, Turkey 39 E12
Kummerower See, Germany 24 B8
Kumo, Nigeria 83 C7
Kumon Bum, Burma 67 F20
Kumylzhenskaya, Russia 48 F6
Kunágota, Hungary 42 D6
Kunashir, Ostrov, Russia 51 E15
Kunda, Estonia 9 G22
Kunda, India 69 G9
Kundar →, Pakistan 68 D3
Kundian, Pakistan 68 C4
Kundla, India 68 J4
Kunga →, Bangla. 69 J13
Kungälv, Sweden 11 G5
Kunghit I., Canada 104 C2
Kungrad = Qŭnghirot, Uzbekistan 50 E6
Kungsängen, Sweden 10 E11
Kungsbacka, Sweden 11 G6
Kungsgården, Sweden 10 D10
Kungshamn, Sweden 11 F5
Kungsör, Sweden 10 E10
Kungur, Russia 50 D6
Kunhar →, Pakistan 69 B5
Kunhegyes, Hungary 42 C5
Kuningan, Indonesia 63 G13
Kunlong, Burma 58 F2
Kunlun Shan, Asia 60 C3
Kunmadaras, Hungary 42 C5
Kunming, China 58 E4
Kunów, Poland 45 H8
Kunsan, S. Korea 57 G14
Kunshan, China 59 B13
Kunszentmárton, Hungary 42 D5
Kunszentmiklós, Hungary 42 C4
Kuntaur, Senegal 82 C2
Kununurra, Australia 92 C4
Kunwari →, India 69 F8
Kunya-Urgench = Köneürgench, Turkmenistan 50 E6
Künzelsau, Germany 25 F5
Kuopio, Finland 8 E22
Kupa →, Croatia 29 C13
Kupang, Indonesia 63 F6
Kupreanof I., U.S.A. 104 B2
Kupres, Bos.-H. 42 G2
Kupyansk, Ukraine 47 H9
Kupyansk-Uzlovoi, Ukraine 47 H9
Kuqa, China 60 B3
Kür →, Azerbaijan 73 C13
Kür Dili, Azerbaijan 71 B6
Kura = Kür →, Azerbaijan 73 C13
Kuranda, Australia 94 B4
Kuranga, India 68 H3
Kurashiki, Japan 55 G6
Kurayoshi, Japan 55 G6
Kürdämir, Azerbaijan 49 K9
Kurdistan, Asia 73 D10
Kŭrdzhali, Bulgaria 41 E9
Kure, Japan 55 G6
Küre, Turkey 72 B5
Küre Dağları, Turkey 72 B6
Kuressaare, Estonia 9 G20
Kurgan, Russia 50 D7
Kurganinsk, Russia 49 H5
Kurgannaya = Kurganinsk, Russia 49 H5
Kuri, India 68 F4
Kuria Maria Is. = Khurīyā Murīyā, Jazā'ir, Oman 74 D6
Kuridala, Australia 94 C3
Kurigram, Bangla. 67 G16
Kurikka, Finland 9 E20
Kuril Is. = Kurilskiye Ostrova, Russia 51 E15
Kuril Trench, Pac. Oc. 52 E19
Kurilsk, Russia 51 E15
Kurilskiye Ostrova, Russia 51 E15
Kurino, Japan 55 J5
Kurinskaya Kosa = Kür Dili, Azerbaijan 71 B6
Kurkur, Egypt 80 C3
Kurlovskiy, Russia 48 C5
Kurmuk, Sudan 81 E3
Kurnool, India 66 M11
Kuro-Shima, Kagoshima, Japan 55 J4
Kuro-Shima, Okinawa, Japan 55 M2
Kuror, J., Sudan 80 C3
Kurow, N.Z. 91 L3
Kurów, Poland 45 G9
Kurram →, Pakistan 68 C4
Kurri Kurri, Australia 95 E5
Kurrimine, Australia 94 B4
Kursavka, Russia 49 H6
Kurshskiy Zaliv, Russia 9 J19
Kursk, Russia 47 G9
Kuršumlija, Serbia, Yug. 40 C5
Kuršumlijska Banja, Serbia, Yug. 40 C5
Kurşunlu, Bursa, Turkey 41 F13
Kurşunlu, Çankırı, Turkey 72 B5
Kurtalan, Turkey 73 D9
Kurtbey, Turkey 41 E10
Kuru, Sudan 81 F2
Kuru, Bahr el →, Sudan 81 F2
Kurucaşile, Turkey 72 B5
Kuruçay, Turkey 70 B3
Kuruktag, China 60 B3
Kuruman, S. Africa 88 D3
Kuruman →, S. Africa 88 D3
Kurume, Japan 55 H5
Kurun →, Sudan 81 F3
Kurunegala, Sri Lanka 66 R12
Kurya, Russia 50 C6
Kus Gölü, Turkey 41 F11
Kuşadası, Turkey 72 D2
Kuşadası Körfezı, Turkey 39 D8
Kusatsu, Japan 55 F9
Kusawa L., Canada 104 A1
Kusel, Germany 25 F3
Kushaka, Nigeria 83 C6
Kushalgarh, India 68 H6
Kushchevskaya, Russia 49 G4
Kusheriki, Nigeria 83 C6
Kushikino, Japan 55 J5
Kushima, Japan 55 J5
Kushimoto, Japan 55 H7
Kushiro, Japan 54 C12
Kushiro-Gawa →, Japan 54 C12
Kūshk, Iran 71 D8
Kushka = Gushgy, Turkmenistan 50 F7
Kūshkī, Iran 70 C5
Kushol, India 69 C7
Kushtia, Bangla. 67 H16
Kushum →, Kazakstan 48 F10
Kuskokwim B., U.S.A. 100 C3
Kusmi, India 69 H10
Kussharo-Ko, Japan 54 C12
Kustanay = Qostanay, Kazakstan 50 D7
Kut, Ko, Thailand 65 G4
Kütahya, Turkey 39 B12
Kütahya □, Turkey 39 B11
Kutaisi, Georgia 49 J6
Kutaraja = Banda Aceh, Indonesia 62 C1
Kutch, Gulf of = Kachchh, Gulf of, India 68 H3
Kutch, Rann of = Kachchh, Rann of, India 68 H4
Kutina, Croatia 29 C13
Kutiyana, India 68 J4
Kutjevo, Croatia 42 E2
Kutkashen, Azerbaijan 49 K8
Kutná Hora, Czech Rep. 26 B8
Kutno, Poland 45 F6
Kutse, Botswana 88 C3
Kutu, Dem. Rep. of the Congo 84 E3
Kutum, Sudan 81 E1
Kúty, Slovak Rep. 27 C10
Kuujjuaq, Canada 101 C13
Kuujjuarapik, Canada 102 A4
Kuŭp-tong, N. Korea 57 D14
Kuusamo, Finland 8 D23
Kuusankoski, Finland 9 F22
Kuvshinovo, Russia 46 D8
Kuwait = Al Kuwayt, Kuwait 70 D5
Kuwait ■, Asia 70 D5
Kuwana, Japan 55 G8
Kuwana →, India 69 F10
Kuybyshev = Samara, Russia 48 D10
Kuybyshev, Russia 50 D8
Kuybyshevo, Ukraine 47 J9
Kuybyshevskoye Vdkhr., Russia 48 C9
Kuye He →, China 56 E6
Kūyeh, Iran 70 B5
Kūysanjaq, Iraq 70 B5
Kuyucak, Turkey 39 D10
Kuyumba, Russia 51 C10
Kuzey Anadolu Dağları, Turkey 72 B7
Kuzmin, Serbia, Yug. 42 E4
Kuznetsk, Russia 48 D8
Kuzomen, Russia 50 C4
Kvænangen, Norway 8 A19
Kværndrup, Denmark 11 J4
Kvaløy, Norway 8 B18
Kvänum, Sweden 11 F7
Kvareli = Qvareli, Georgia 49 K7
Kvarner, Croatia 29 D11
Kvarnerič, Croatia 29 D11
Kvicksund, Sweden 10 E10
Kvillsfors, Sweden 11 G9
Kvismare kanal, Sweden 10 E9
Kvissleby, Sweden 10 B11
Kwa-Nobuhle, S. Africa 85 L5
Kwabhaca, S. Africa 89 E4
Kwakhanai, Botswana 88 C3
Kwakoegron, Surinam 125 B7
Kwale, Kenya 86 C4
Kwale, Nigeria 83 D6
KwaMashu, S. Africa 89 D5
Kwando →, Africa 88 B3
Kwangdaeri, N. Korea 57 D14
Kwangju, S. Korea 57 G14
Kwango →, Dem. Rep. of the Congo 84 E3
Kwangsi-Chuang = Guangxi Zhuangzu Zizhiqu □, China 58 F7
Kwangtung = Guangdong □, China 59 F9
Kwara □, Nigeria 83 D6
Kwataboahegan →, Canada 102 B3
Kwatisore, Indonesia 63 E8
KwaZulu Natal □, S. Africa 89 D5
Kweichow = Guizhou □, China 58 D6
Kwekwe, Zimbabwe 87 F2
Kwidzyn, Poland 44 E5
Kwiha, Ethiopia 81 E4
Kwinana New Town, Australia 93 F2
Kwisa →, Poland 45 G2
Kwoka, Indonesia 63 E8
Kwolla, Nigeria 83 D6
Kyabra Cr. →, Australia 95 D3
Kyabram, Australia 95 F4
Kyaikto, Burma 64 D1
Kyakhta, Russia 51 D11
Kyancutta, Australia 95 E2
Kyaukpadaung, Burma 67 J19
Kyaukpyu, Burma 67 K18
Kyaukse, Burma 67 J20
Kybartai, Lithuania 44 D9
Kyburz, U.S.A. 116 G6
Kyelang, India 68 C7
Kyenjojo, Uganda 86 B3
Kyjov, Czech Rep. 27 B10
Kyle, Canada 105 C7
Kyle Dam, Zimbabwe 87 G3
Kyle of Lochalsh, U.K. 14 D3
Kyll →, Germany 25 F2
Kyllburg, Germany 25 E2
Kymijoki →, Finland 9 F22
Kyneton, Australia 95 F3
Kynuna, Australia 94 C3
Kyō-ga-Saki, Japan 55 G7
Kyoga, L., Uganda 86 B3
Kyogle, Australia 95 D5
Kyom →, Sudan 81 F2
Kyongju, S. Korea 57 G15
Kyongpyaw, Burma 67 L19
Kyŏngsŏng, N. Korea 57 D15
Kyōto, Japan 55 G7
Kyōto □, Japan 55 G7
Kyparissovouno, Cyprus 36 D12
Kyperounda, Cyprus 36 E11
Kyrenia, Cyprus 36 D12
Kyrgyzstan ■, Asia 50 E8
Kyritz, Germany 24 C8
Kyrkhult, Sweden 11 H8
Kyrönjoki →, Finland 8 E19
Kystatyam, Russia 51 C13
Kysucké Nové Mesto, Slovak Rep. 27 B11
Kythréa, Cyprus 36 D12
Kyunhla, Burma 67 H19
Kyuquot Sound, Canada 104 D3
Kyurdamir = Kürdämir, Azerbaijan 49 K9
Kyūshū, Japan 55 H5
Kyūshū □, Japan 55 H5
Kyūshū-Sanchi, Japan 55 H5
Kyustendil, Bulgaria 40 D6
Kyusyur, Russia 51 B13
Kyyiv, Ukraine 47 G6
Kyyivske Vdskh., Ukraine 47 G6
Kyzyl, Russia 51 D10
Kyzyl Kum, Uzbekistan 50 E7
Kyzyl-Kyya, Kyrgyzstan 50 E8
Kzyl-Orda = Qyzylorda, Kazakstan 50 E7

L

La Albuera, Spain 35 G4
La Alcarria, Spain 32 E2
La Almarcha, Spain 32 F2
La Almunia de Doña Godina, Spain 32 D3
La Asunción, Venezuela 124 A6
La Baie, Canada 103 C5
La Banda, Argentina 126 B3
La Bañeza, Spain 34 C5
La Barca, Mexico 118 C4
La Barge, U.S.A. 114 E8
La Bastide-Puylaurent, France 20 D7
La Baule-Escoubiac, France 18 E4
La Belle, U.S.A. 109 M5
La Biche →, Canada 104 B4
La Biche, L., Canada 104 C6
La Bisbal d'Empordà, Spain 32 D8
La Bomba, Mexico 118 A1
La Brède, France 20 D3
La Bresse, France 19 D13
La Bureba, Spain 34 C7
La Calera, Chile 126 C1
La Campiña, Spain 35 H6
La Canal = Sa Canal, Spain 37 C7
La Cañiza = A Cañiza, Spain 34 C2
La Canourgue, France 20 D7
La Capelle, France 19 C10
La Carlota, Argentina 126 C3
La Carlota, Phil. 61 F5
La Carlota, Spain 35 H6
La Carolina, Spain 35 G7
La Cavalerie, France 20 D7
La Ceiba, Honduras 120 C2
La Chaise-Dieu, France 20 C7
La Chapelle d'Angillon, France 19 E9
La Chapelle-St-Luc, France 19 D11
La Chapelle-sur-Erdre, France 18 E5
La Charité-sur-Loire, France 19 E10
La Chartre-sur-le-Loir, France 18 E7
La Châtaigneraie, France 20 B3
La Châtre, France 19 F9
La Chaux-de-Fonds, Switz. 25 H2
La Chorrera, Panama 120 E4
La Ciotat, France 21 E9
La Clayette, France 19 F11
La Cocha, Argentina 126 B2
La Concepción = Ri-Aba, Eq. Guin. 83 E6
La Concepción, Panama 120 E3
La Concordia, Mexico 119 D6
La Coruña = A Coruña, Spain 34 B2
La Coruña □, Spain 34 B2
La Côte-St-André, France 21 C9
La Courtine-le-Trucq, France 20 C6
La Crau, Bouches-du-Rhône, France 21 E8
La Crau, Var, France 21 E10
La Crescent, U.S.A. 112 D9
La Crete, Canada 104 B5
La Crosse, Kans., U.S.A. 112 F5
La Crosse, Wis., U.S.A. 112 D9
La Cruz, Costa Rica 120 D2
La Cruz, Mexico 118 C3
La Désirade, Guadeloupe 121 C7
La Escondida, Mexico 118 C5
La Esmeralda, Paraguay 126 A3
La Esperanza, Cuba 120 B3
La Esperanza, Honduras 120 D2
La Estrada = A Estrada, Spain 34 C2
La Faouët, France 18 D3
La Fayette, U.S.A. 109 H3
La Fé, Cuba 120 B3
La Fère, France 19 C10
La Ferté-Bernard, France 18 D7
La Ferté-Gaucher, France 19 D10
La Ferté-Macé, France 18 D6
La Ferté-St-Aubin, France 19 E8
La Ferté-sous-Jouarre, France 19 D10
La Ferté-Vidame, France 18 D7
La Flèche, France 18 E6
La Follette, U.S.A. 109 G3
La Fregeneda, Spain 34 E4
La Fuente de San Esteban, Spain 34 E4
La Gacilly, France 18 E4
La Gineta, Spain 33 F2
La Grand-Combe, France 21 D8
La Grande, U.S.A. 114 D4
La Grande →, Canada 102 B5
La Grande Deux, Rés., Canada 102 B4
La Grande-Motte, France 21 E8
La Grande Quatre, Rés., Canada 102 B5
La Grande Trois, Rés., Canada 102 B4
La Grange, Calif., U.S.A. 116 H6
La Grange, Ga., U.S.A. 109 J3
La Grange, Ky., U.S.A. 108 F3
La Grange, Tex., U.S.A. 113 L6
La Grave, France 21 C10
La Guaira, Venezuela 124 A5
La Guardia = A Guarda, Spain 34 D2
La Gudiña = A Gudiña, Spain 34 C3
La Guerche-de-Bretagne, France 18 E5
La Guerche-sur-l'Aubois, France 19 F9
La Habana, Cuba 120 B3
La Haye-du-Puits, France 18 C5
La Horra, Spain 34 D7
La Independencia, Mexico 119 D6
La Isabela, Dom. Rep. 121 C5
La Jonquera, Spain 32 C7
La Junta, U.S.A. 113 F3
La Laguna, Canary Is. 37 F3
La Libertad, Guatemala 120 C1
La Libertad, Mexico 118 B2
La Ligua, Chile 126 C1
La Línea de la Concepción, Spain 35 J5
La Loche, Canada 105 B7
La Londe-les-Maures, France 21 E10
La Lora, Spain 34 C7
La Loupe, France 18 D8
La Louvière, Belgium 17 D4
La Machine, France 19 F10
La Maddalena, Italy 30 A2
La Malbaie, Canada 103 C5
La Mancha, Spain 33 F2
La Mariña, Spain 34 B3
La Martre, L., Canada 104 A5
La Mesa, U.S.A. 117 N9
La Misión, Mexico 118 A1
La Mothe-Achard, France 18 F5
La Motte, France 21 D10
La Motte-Chalançon, France 21 D9
La Motte-Servolex, France 21 C9
La Moure, U.S.A. 112 B5
La Muela, Spain 32 D3
La Mure, France 21 D9
La Negra, Chile 126 A1
La Oliva, Canary Is. 37 F6
La Orotava, Canary Is. 37 F3
La Oroya, Peru 124 F3
La Pacaudière, France 19 F10
La Palma, Canary Is. 37 F2
La Palma, Panama 120 E4
La Palma del Condado, Spain 35 H4
La Paloma, Chile 126 C1
La Pampa □, Argentina 126 D2
La Paragua, Venezuela 124 B6
La Paz, Entre Ríos, Argentina 126 C4
La Paz, San Luis, Argentina 126 C2
La Paz, Bolivia 124 G5
La Paz, Honduras 120 D2
La Paz, Mexico 118 C2
La Paz, Phil. 61 D4
La Paz Centro, Nic. 120 D2
La Pedrera, Colombia 124 D5
La Pérade, Canada 103 C5
La Perouse Str., Asia 54 B11
La Pesca, Mexico 119 C5
La Piedad, Mexico 118 C4
La Pine, U.S.A. 114 E3
La Plata, Argentina 126 D4
La Pobla de Lillet, Spain 32 C6
La Pocatière, Canada 103 C5
La Pola de Gordón, Spain 34 C5
La Porta, France 21 F13
La Porte, Ind., U.S.A. 108 E2
La Porte, Tex., U.S.A. 113 L7
La Presanella, Italy 28 B7
La Puebla = Sa Pobla, Spain 32 F8
La Puebla de Cazalla, Spain 35 H5
La Puebla de los Infantes, Spain 35 H5
La Puebla de Montalbán, Spain 34 F6
La Puebla del Río, Spain 35 H4
La Puerta de Segura, Spain 35 G8
La Purísima, Mexico 118 B2
La Push, U.S.A. 116 C2
La Quiaca, Argentina 126 A2
La Réole, France 20 D3
La Restinga, Canary Is. 37 G2
La Rioja, Argentina 126 B2
La Rioja □, Argentina 126 B2
La Rioja □, Spain 32 C2
La Robla, Spain 34 C5
La Roche-Bernard, France 18 E4
La Roche-Canillac, France 20 C5
La Roche-en-Ardenne, Belgium 17 D5
La Roche-sur-Foron, France 19 F13
La Roche-sur-Yon, France 18 F5
La Rochefoucauld, France 20 C4
La Rochelle, France 20 B2
La Roda, Spain 33 F2
La Roda de Andalucía, Spain 35 H6
La Romana, Dom. Rep. 121 C6
La Ronge, Canada 105 B7
La Rumorosa, Mexico 117 N10
La Sabina = Sa Savina, Spain 37 C7
La Sagra, Spain 33 H2
La Salle, U.S.A. 112 E10
La Sanabria, Spain 34 C4
La Santa, Canary Is. 37 E6
La Sarre, Canada 102 C4
La Scie, Canada 103 C8

La Selva, *Spain* 32 C7
La Selva Beach, *U.S.A.* 116 J5
La Selva del Camp, *Spain* 32 D6
La Serena, *Chile* 126 B1
La Serena, *Spain* 35 G5
La Seu d'Urgell, *Spain* 32 C6
La Seyne-sur-Mer, *France* 21 E9
La Sila, *Italy* 31 C9
La Solana, *Spain* 35 G7
La Soufrière, *St. Vincent* 121 D7
La Souterraine, *France* 19 F8
La Spézia, *Italy* 28 D6
La Suze-sur-Sarthe, *France* 18 E7
La Tagua, *Colombia* 124 C4
La Teste, *France* 20 D2
La Tortuga, *Venezuela* 121 D6
La Tour-du-Pin, *France* 21 C9
La Tranche-sur-Mer, *France* 18 F5
La Tremblade, *France* 20 C2
La Tuque, *Canada* 102 C5
La Unión, *Chile* 128 E2
La Unión, *El Salv.* 120 D2
La Unión, *Mexico* 118 D4
La Unión, *Spain* 33 H4
La Urbana, *Venezuela* 124 B5
La Vall d'Uixó, *Spain* 32 F4
La Vecilla de Curveño, *Spain* 34 C5
La Vega, *Dom. Rep.* 121 C5
La Vela de Coro, *Venezuela* 124 A5
La Veleta, *Spain* 35 H7
La Venta, *Mexico* 119 D6
La Ventura, *Mexico* 118 C4
La Voulte-sur-Rhône, *France* 21 D8
Laa an der Thaya, *Austria* 27 C9
Laaber, Grosse →, *Germany* 25 G8
Laage, *Germany* 24 B8
Laatzen, *Germany* 24 C5
Laba →, *Russia* 49 H4
Labasa, *Fiji* 91 C8
Labason, *Phil.* 61 G5
Labastide-Murat, *France* 20 D5
Labastide-Rouairoux, *France* 20 E6
Labbézenga, *Mali* 83 B5
Labe = Elbe →, *Europe* 24 B4
Labé, *Guinea* 82 C2
Laberge, L., *Canada* 104 A1
Labin, *Croatia* 29 C11
Labinsk, *Russia* 49 H5
Labis, *Malaysia* 65 L4
Łabiszyn, *Poland* 45 F4
Labo, *Phil.* 61 D5
Laboe, *Germany* 24 A6
Laborec →, *Slovak Rep.* 27 C14
Labouheyre, *France* 20 D3
Laboulaye, *Argentina* 126 C3
Labrador, *Canada* 103 B7
Labrador City, *Canada* 103 B6
Labrador Sea, *Atl. Oc.* 101 C14
Lábrea, *Brazil* 124 E6
Labruguière, *France* 20 E6
Labuan, *Malaysia* 62 C5
Labuan, Pulau, *Malaysia* 62 C5
Labuha, *Indonesia* 63 E7
Labuhan, *Indonesia* 63 G11
Labuhanbajo, *Indonesia* 63 F6
Labuk, Telok, *Malaysia* 62 C5
Labyrinth, L., *Australia* 95 E2
Labytnangi, *Russia* 50 C7
Laç, *Albania* 40 E3
Lac Bouchette, *Canada* 103 C5
Lac Édouard, *Canada* 102 C5
Lac La Biche, *Canada* 104 C6
Lac la Martre = Wha Ti, *Canada* 100 B8
Lac La Ronge Prov. Park, *Canada* 105 B7
Lac-Mégantic, *Canada* 103 C5
Lac Thien, *Vietnam* 64 F7
Lacanau, *France* 20 D2
Lacanau, Étang de, *France* 20 D2
Lacantúm →, *Mexico* 119 D6
Lacara →, *Spain* 35 G4
Lacaune, *France* 20 E6
Lacaune, Mts. de, *France* 20 E6
Laccadive Is. = Lakshadweep Is., *India* 52 H11
Lacepede B., *Australia* 95 F2
Lacepede Is., *Australia* 92 C3
Lacerdónia, *Mozam.* 87 F4
Lacey, *U.S.A.* 116 C4
Lachhmangarh, *India* 68 F6
Lachi, *Pakistan* 68 C4
Lachine, *Canada* 102 C5
Lachlan →, *Australia* 95 E3
Lachute, *Canada* 102 C5
Lackawanna, *U.S.A.* 110 D6
Lackawaxen, *U.S.A.* 111 E10
Lacolle, *Canada* 111 A11
Lacombe, *Canada* 104 C6
Lacona, *U.S.A.* 111 C8
Láconi, *Italy* 30 C2
Laconia, *U.S.A.* 111 C13
Lacq, *France* 20 E3
Ladakh Ra., *India* 69 C8
Lądek-Zdrój, *Poland* 45 H3
Ládhon →, *Greece* 38 D3
Ladik, *Turkey* 72 B6
Ladismith, *S. Africa* 88 E3
Ladíspoli, *Italy* 29 G9
Lādīz, *Iran* 71 D9
Ladnun, *India* 68 F6
Ladoga, L. = Ladozhskoye Ozero, *Russia* 46 B6
Ladozhskoye Ozero, *Russia* 46 B6
Lady Elliott I., *Australia* 94 C5
Lady Grey, *S. Africa* 88 E4
Ladybrand, *S. Africa* 88 D4
Ladysmith, *Canada* 104 D4
Ladysmith, *S. Africa* 89 D4
Ladysmith, *U.S.A.* 112 C9
Lae, *Papua N. G.* 96 H6
Laem Ngop, *Thailand* 65 F4
Laem Pho, *Thailand* 65 J3
Læsø, *Denmark* 11 G5
Læsø Rende, *Denmark* 11 G4
Lafayette, *Colo., U.S.A.* 112 F2
Lafayette, *Ind., U.S.A.* 108 E2
Lafayette, *La., U.S.A.* 113 K9
Lafayette, *Tenn., U.S.A.* 109 G2
Laferte →, *Canada* 104 A5
Lafia, *Nigeria* 83 D6
Lafiagi, *Nigeria* 83 D6
Lafleche, *Canada* 105 D7
Lafon, *Sudan* 81 F3
Lagan, *Sweden* 11 H7
Lagan →, *Sweden* 11 H6
Lagan →, *U.K.* 15 B6
Lagarfljót →, *Iceland* 8 D6
Lage, *Germany* 24 D4
Lågen →, *Oppland, Norway* 9 F14
Lågen →, *Vestfold, Norway* 9 G14
Lägerdorf, *Germany* 24 B5
Laghouat, *Algeria* 78 B6
Lagnieu, *France* 21 C9
Lagny-sur-Marne, *France* 19 D9
Lago, *Italy* 31 C9
Lagôa, *Portugal* 35 H2
Lagoa Vermelha, *Brazil* 127 B5
Lagoaça, *Portugal* 34 D4
Lagodekhi, *Georgia* 49 K8
Lagónegro, *Italy* 31 B8
Lagonoy G., *Phil.* 61 E5
Lagos, *Nigeria* 83 D5
Lagos, *Portugal* 35 H2
Lagos □, *Nigeria* 83 D5
Lagos de Moreno, *Mexico* 118 C4
Lagrange, *Australia* 92 C3
Lagrange B., *Australia* 92 C3
Laguardia, *Spain* 32 C2
Laguépie, *France* 20 D5
Laguna, *Brazil* 127 B6
Laguna, *U.S.A.* 115 J10
Laguna Beach, *U.S.A.* 117 M9
Laguna de Duera, *Spain* 34 D6
Laguna Limpia, *Argentina* 126 B4
Lagunas, *Chile* 126 A2
Lagunas, *Peru* 124 E3
Lahad Datu, *Malaysia* 63 C5
Lahad Datu, Teluk, *Malaysia* 63 D5
Lahan Sai, *Thailand* 64 E4
Lahanam, *Laos* 64 D5
Lahar, *India* 69 F8
Laharpur, *India* 69 F9
Lahat, *Indonesia* 62 E2
Lahewa, *Indonesia* 62 D1
Lāhījān, *Iran* 71 B6
Lahn →, *Germany* 25 E3
Lahnstein, *Germany* 25 E3
Laholm, *Sweden* 11 H7
Laholmsbukten, *Sweden* 11 H6
Lahore, *Pakistan* 68 D6
Lahr, *Germany* 25 G3
Lahri, *Pakistan* 68 E3
Lahti, *Finland* 9 F21
Lahtis = Lahti, *Finland* 9 F21
Laï, *Chad* 79 G9
Lai Chau, *Vietnam* 58 F4
Lai'an, *China* 59 A12
Laibin, *China* 58 F7
Laifeng, *China* 58 C7
L'Aigle, *France* 18 D7
Laignes, *France* 19 E11
L'Aiguillon-sur-Mer, *France* 20 B2
Laila = Laylá, *Si. Arabia* 74 C4
Laingsburg, *S. Africa* 88 E3
Lainio älv →, *Sweden* 8 C20
Lairg, *U.K.* 14 C4
Laishui, *China* 56 E8
Laissac, *France* 20 D6
Láives, *Italy* 29 B8
Laiwu, *China* 57 F9
Laixi, *China* 57 F11
Laiyang, *China* 57 F11
Laiyuan, *China* 56 E8
Laizhou, *China* 57 F10
Laizhou Wan, *China* 57 F10
Laja →, *Mexico* 118 C4
Lajere, *Nigeria* 83 C7
Lajes, *Brazil* 127 B5
Lajkovac, *Serbia, Yug.* 40 B4
Lajosmizse, *Hungary* 42 C4
Lak Sao, *Laos* 64 C5
Lakaband, *Pakistan* 68 D3
Lakamané, *Mali* 82 C3
Lake Alpine, *U.S.A.* 116 G7
Lake Andes, *U.S.A.* 112 D5
Lake Arthur, *U.S.A.* 113 K8
Lake Cargelligo, *Australia* 95 E4
Lake Charles, *U.S.A.* 113 K8
Lake City, *Colo., U.S.A.* 115 G10
Lake City, *Fla., U.S.A.* 109 K4
Lake City, *Mich., U.S.A.* 108 C3
Lake City, *Minn., U.S.A.* 112 C8
Lake City, *Pa., U.S.A.* 110 D4
Lake City, *S.C., U.S.A.* 109 J6
Lake Cowichan, *Canada* 104 D4
Lake District, *U.K.* 12 C4
Lake Elsinore, *U.S.A.* 117 M9
Lake George, *U.S.A.* 111 C11
Lake Grace, *Australia* 93 F2
Lake Harbour = Kimmirut, *Canada* 101 B13
Lake Havasu City, *U.S.A.* 117 L12
Lake Hughes, *U.S.A.* 117 L8
Lake Isabella, *U.S.A.* 117 K8
Lake Jackson, *U.S.A.* 113 L7
Lake Junction, *U.S.A.* 114 D8
Lake King, *Australia* 93 F2
Lake Lenore, *Canada* 105 C8
Lake Louise, *Canada* 104 C5
Lake Mead National Recreation Area, *U.S.A.* 117 K12
Lake Mills, *U.S.A.* 112 D8
Lake Placid, *U.S.A.* 111 B11
Lake Pleasant, *U.S.A.* 111 C10
Lake Providence, *U.S.A.* 113 J9
Lake St. Peter, *Canada* 110 A6
Lake Superior Prov. Park, *Canada* 102 C3
Lake Village, *U.S.A.* 113 J9
Lake Wales, *U.S.A.* 109 M5
Lake Worth, *U.S.A.* 109 M5
Lakeba, *Fiji* 91 D9
Lakefield, *Canada* 102 D4
Lakehurst, *U.S.A.* 111 F10
Lakeland, *Australia* 94 B3
Lakeland, *U.S.A.* 109 M5
Lakeport, *Calif., U.S.A.* 116 F4
Lakeport, *Mich., U.S.A.* 110 C2
Lakes Entrance, *Australia* 95 F4
Lakeside, *Ariz., U.S.A.* 115 J9
Lakeside, *Calif., U.S.A.* 117 N10
Lakeside, *Nebr., U.S.A.* 112 D3
Lakeside, *Ohio, U.S.A.* 110 E2
Lakeview, *U.S.A.* 114 E3
Lakeville, *U.S.A.* 112 C8
Lakewood, *Colo., U.S.A.* 112 F2
Lakewood, *N.J., U.S.A.* 111 F10
Lakewood, *N.Y., U.S.A.* 110 D5
Lakewood, *Ohio, U.S.A.* 110 E3
Lakewood, *Wash., U.S.A.* 116 C4
Lakha, *India* 68 F4
Lakhaniá, *Greece* 36 D9
Lakhimpur, *India* 69 F9
Lakhnadon, *India* 69 H8
Lakhonpheng, *Laos* 64 E5
Lakhpat, *India* 68 H3
Läki, *Azerbaijan* 49 K8
Lakin, *U.S.A.* 113 G4
Lakitusaki →, *Canada* 102 B3
Lakki, *Pakistan* 68 C4
Lákkoi, *Greece* 36 D5
Lakonía □, *Greece* 38 E4
Lakonikós Kólpos, *Greece* 38 E4
Lakor, *Indonesia* 63 F7
Lakota, *Ivory C.* 82 D3
Lakota, *U.S.A.* 112 A5
Laksar, *India* 68 E8
Laksefjorden, *Norway* 8 A22
Lakselv, *Norway* 8 A21
Lakshadweep Is., *India* 52 H11
Lakshmanpur, *India* 69 H10
Lakshmikantapur, *India* 69 H13
Lala Ghat, *India* 67 G18
Lala Musa, *Pakistan* 68 C5
Lalago, *Tanzania* 86 C3
Lalapanzi, *Zimbabwe* 87 F3
Lalapaşa, *Turkey* 41 E10
Lalbenque, *France* 20 D5
L'Albufera, *Spain* 33 F4
Lalganj, *India* 69 G11
Lalgola, *India* 69 G13
Lālī, *Iran* 71 C6
Lalibela, *Ethiopia* 81 E4
Lalin, *China* 57 B14
Lalín, *Spain* 34 C2
Lalin He →, *China* 57 B13
Lalinde, *France* 20 D4
Lalitpur, *India* 69 G8
Lalkua, *India* 69 E8
Lalsot, *India* 68 F7
Lam, *Vietnam* 64 B6
Lam Pao Res., *Thailand* 64 D4
Lama Kara, *Togo* 83 D5
Lamaing, *Burma* 67 M20
Lamar, *Colo., U.S.A.* 112 F3
Lamar, *Mo., U.S.A.* 113 G7
Lamas, *Peru* 124 E3
Lamastre, *France* 21 D8
Lambach, *Austria* 26 C6
Lamballe, *France* 18 D4
Lambaréné, *Gabon* 84 E2
Lambay I., *Ireland* 15 C5
Lambert Glacier, *Antarctica* 5 D6
Lambert's Bay, *S. Africa* 88 E2
Lambesc, *France* 21 E9
Lambeth, *Canada* 110 D3
Lámbia, *Greece* 38 D3
Lambomakondro, *Madag.* 89 C7
Lambro →, *Italy* 28 C6
Lame, *Nigeria* 83 C6
Lame Deer, *U.S.A.* 114 D10
Lamego, *Portugal* 34 D3
Lamèque, *Canada* 103 C7
Lameroo, *Australia* 95 F3
Lamesa, *U.S.A.* 113 J4
Lamía, *Greece* 38 C4
Lamitan, *Phil.* 61 H5
Lammermuir Hills, *U.K.* 14 F6
Lammhult, *Sweden* 11 G8
Lamoille →, *U.S.A.* 111 B11
Lamon B., *Phil.* 61 D5
Lamont, *Canada* 104 C6
Lamont, *Calif., U.S.A.* 117 K8
Lamont, *Wyo., U.S.A.* 114 E10
Lamotte-Beuvron, *France* 19 E9
Lampa, *Peru* 124 G4
Lampang, *Thailand* 64 C2
Lampasas, *U.S.A.* 113 K5
Lampazos de Naranjo, *Mexico* 118 B4
Lampertheim, *Germany* 25 F4
Lampeter, *U.K.* 13 E3
Lampman, *Canada* 105 D8
Lamprechtshausen, *Austria* 26 D5
Lampung □, *Indonesia* 62 F2
Lamta, *India* 69 H9
Lamu, *Kenya* 86 C5
Lamy, *U.S.A.* 115 J11
Lan Xian, *China* 56 E6
Lan Yu = Hungt'ou Hsü, *Taiwan* 59 G13
Lanak La, *India* 69 B8
Lanak'o Shank'ou = Lanak La, *India* 69 B8
Lanao, L., *Phil.* 61 H6
Lanark, *Canada* 111 A8
Lanark, *U.K.* 14 F5
Lanbi Kyun, *Burma* 65 G2
Lancang, *China* 58 F2
Lancang Jiang →, *China* 58 G3
Lancashire □, *U.K.* 12 D5
Lancaster, *Canada* 111 A10
Lancaster, *U.K.* 12 C5
Lancaster, *Calif., U.S.A.* 117 L8
Lancaster, *Ky., U.S.A.* 108 G3
Lancaster, *N.H., U.S.A.* 111 B13
Lancaster, *N.Y., U.S.A.* 110 D6
Lancaster, *Ohio, U.S.A.* 108 F4
Lancaster, *Pa., U.S.A.* 111 F8
Lancaster, *S.C., U.S.A.* 109 H5
Lancaster, *Wis., U.S.A.* 112 D9
Lancaster Sd., *Canada* 101 A11
Lancelin, *Australia* 93 F2
Lanchow = Lanzhou, *China* 56 F2
Lanciano, *Italy* 29 F11
Lancun, *China* 57 F11
Łańcut, *Poland* 45 H9
Landau, *Bayern, Germany* 25 G8
Landau, *Rhld-Pfz., Germany* 25 F4
Landeck, *Austria* 26 D3
Lander, *U.S.A.* 114 E9
Lander →, *Australia* 92 D5
Landerneau, *France* 18 D2
Landeryd, *Sweden* 11 G7
Landes, *France* 20 D2
Landes □, *France* 20 E3
Landete, *Spain* 32 F3
Landi Kotal, *Pakistan* 68 B4
Landisburg, *U.S.A.* 110 F7
Landivisiau, *France* 18 D2
Landquart, *Switz.* 25 J5
Landrecies, *France* 19 B10
Land's End, *U.K.* 13 G2
Landsberg, *Germany* 25 G6
Landsborough Cr. →, *Australia* 94 C3
Landsbro, *Sweden* 11 G8
Landshut, *Germany* 25 G8
Landskrona, *Sweden* 11 J6
Landstuhl, *Germany* 25 F3
Landvetter, *Sweden* 11 G6
Lanesboro, *U.S.A.* 111 E9
Lanester, *France* 18 E3
Lanett, *U.S.A.* 109 J3
Lang Qua, *Vietnam* 64 A5
Lang Shan, *China* 56 D4
Lang Son, *Vietnam* 58 G6
Lang Suan, *Thailand* 65 H2
Langå, *Denmark* 11 H3
La'nga Co, *China* 67 D12
Langádhas, *Greece* 40 F7
Langádhia, *Greece* 38 D4
Långan →, *Sweden* 10 A8
Langano, L., *Ethiopia* 81 F4
Langar, *Iran* 71 C9
Langara I., *Canada* 104 C2
Långås, *Sweden* 11 H6
Langdai, *China* 58 D5
Langdon, *U.S.A.* 112 A5
Långe Jan = Ölands södra udde, *Sweden* 11 H10
Langeac, *France* 20 C7
Langeais, *France* 18 E7
Langeb Baraka →, *Sudan* 80 D4
Langeberg, *S. Africa* 88 E3
Langeberge, *S. Africa* 88 D3
Langeland, *Denmark* 11 K4
Langelands Bælt, *Denmark* 11 K4
Langen, *Hessen, Germany* 25 F4
Langen, *Niedersachsen, Germany* 24 B4
Langenburg, *Canada* 105 C8
Langeneß, *Germany* 24 A4
Langenlois, *Austria* 26 C8
Langeoog, *Germany* 24 B3
Langeskov, *Denmark* 11 J4
Länghem, *Sweden* 11 G7
Langhirano, *Italy* 28 D7
Langholm, *U.K.* 14 F5
Langjökull, *Iceland* 8 D3
Langkawi, Pulau, *Malaysia* 65 J2
Langklip, *S. Africa* 88 D3
Langkon, *Malaysia* 62 C5
Langlade, *St- P. & M.* 103 C8
Langley, *Canada* 116 A4
Langnau, *Switz.* 25 J3
Langogne, *France* 20 D7
Langon, *France* 20 D3
Langøya, *Norway* 8 B16
Langreo, *Spain* 34 B5
Langres, *France* 19 E12
Langres, Plateau de, *France* 19 E12
Langsa, *Indonesia* 62 D1
Långsele, *Sweden* 10 A11
Långshyttan, *Sweden* 10 D10
Langtry, *U.S.A.* 113 L4
Langu, *Thailand* 65 J2
Languedoc, *France* 20 E7
Languedoc-Roussillon □, *France* 20 E6
Langxi, *China* 59 B12
Langxiangzhen, *China* 56 E9
Langzhong, *China* 58 B5
Lanigan, *Canada* 105 C7
Lankao, *China* 56 G8
Länkäran, *Azerbaijan* 71 B6
Lanmeur, *France* 18 D3
Lannemezan, *France* 20 E4
Lannilis, *France* 18 D2
Lannion, *France* 18 D3
L'Annonciation, *Canada* 102 C5
Lanouaille, *France* 20 C5
Lanping, *China* 58 D2
Lansdale, *U.S.A.* 111 F9
Lansdowne, *Australia* 95 E5
Lansdowne, *Canada* 111 B8
Lansdowne, *India* 69 E8
Lansdowne House, *Canada* 102 B2
L'Anse, *U.S.A.* 108 B1
L'Anse au Loup, *Canada* 103 B8
L'Anse aux Meadows, *Canada* 103 B8
Lansford, *U.S.A.* 111 F9
Lanshan, *China* 59 E9
Lansing, *U.S.A.* 108 D3
Lanslebourg-Mont-Cenis, *France* 21 C10
Lanta Yai, Ko, *Thailand* 65 J2
Lantewa, *Nigeria* 83 C7
Lantian, *China* 56 G5
Lanus, *Argentina* 126 C4
Lanusei, *Italy* 30 C2
Lanuza, *Phil.* 61 G7
Lanxi, *China* 59 C12
Lanzarote, *Canary Is.* 37 F6
Lanzhou, *China* 56 F2
Lanzo Torinese, *Italy* 28 C4
Lao →, *Italy* 31 C8
Lao Bao, *Laos* 64 D6
Lao Cai, *Vietnam* 58 F4
Laoag, *Phil.* 61 B4
Laoang, *Phil.* 61 E6
Laoha He →, *China* 57 C11
Laohekou, *China* 59 A8
Laois □, *Ireland* 15 D4
Laon, *France* 19 C10
Laona, *U.S.A.* 108 C1
Laos ■, *Asia* 64 D5
Lapa, *Brazil* 127 B6
Lapai, *Nigeria* 83 D6
Lapalisse, *France* 19 F10
Lapeer, *U.S.A.* 108 D4
Lapeyrade, *France* 20 D3
Lapithos, *Cyprus* 36 D12
Lapland = Lappland, *Europe* 8 B21
Laporte, *U.S.A.* 111 E8
Lapovo, *Serbia, Yug.* 40 B5
Lappeenranta, *Finland* 9 F23
Lappland, *Europe* 8 B21
Laprida, *Argentina* 126 D3
Lapseki, *Turkey* 41 F10
Laptev Sea, *Russia* 51 B13
Lapua, *Finland* 8 E20
Lăpuş →, *Romania* 43 C8
Lapuş, Munţii, *Romania* 43 C8
Lăpuşna, *Moldova* 43 D13
Łapy, *Poland* 45 F9
Laqiya Arba'in, *Sudan* 80 C2
Laqiya Umran, *Sudan* 80 D2
L'Áquila, *Italy* 29 F10
Lār, *Āzarbājān-e Sharqī, Iran* 70 B5
Lār, *Fārs, Iran* 71 E7
Larabanga, *Ghana* 82 D4
Laragne-Montéglin, *France* 21 D9
Laramie, *U.S.A.* 112 E2
Laramie →, *U.S.A.* 114 F11
Laramie Mts., *U.S.A.* 112 E2
Laranjeiras do Sul, *Brazil* 127 B5
Larantuka, *Indonesia* 63 F6
Larat, *Indonesia* 63 F8
L'Arbresle, *France* 21 C8
Lärbro, *Sweden* 11 G12
Larde, *Mozam.* 87 F4
Larder Lake, *Canada* 102 C4
Lardhos, Ákra = Líndhos, Ákra, *Greece* 36 C10
Lardhos, Órmos, *Greece* 36 C10
Laredo, *Spain* 34 B7
Laredo, *U.S.A.* 113 M5
Laredo Sd., *Canada* 104 C3
Largentière, *France* 21 D8
L'Argentière-la-Bessée, *France* 21 D10
Largo, *U.S.A.* 109 M4
Largs, *U.K.* 14 F4
Lari, *Italy* 28 E7
Lariang, *Indonesia* 63 E5
Larimore, *U.S.A.* 112 B6
Lārīn, *Iran* 71 C7
Larino, *Italy* 29 G11
Lárisa, *Greece* 38 B4
Lárisa □, *Greece* 38 B4
Larkana, *Pakistan* 68 F3
Larnaca, *Cyprus* 36 E12
Larnaca Bay, *Cyprus* 36 E12
Larne, *U.K.* 15 B6
Larned, *U.S.A.* 112 F5
Laroquebrou, *France* 20 D6
Larose, *U.S.A.* 113 L9
Larrimah, *Australia* 92 C5
Larsen Ice Shelf, *Antarctica* 5 C17
Laruns, *France* 20 F3
Larvik, *Norway* 9 G14
Larzac, Causse du, *France* 20 E7
Las Alpujarras, *Spain* 33 J1
Las Animas, *U.S.A.* 112 F3
Las Anod, *Somali Rep.* 74 F4
Las Arenas, *Spain* 34 B6
Las Aves, Is., *W. Indies* 121 C7
Las Brenãs, *Argentina* 126 B3
Las Cabezas de San Juan, *Spain* 35 J5
Las Cejas, *Argentina* 128 B4

Las Chimeneas, *Mexico* ... 117 N10
Las Cruces, *U.S.A.* ... 115 K10
Las Flores, *Argentina* ... 126 D4
Las Heras, *Argentina* ... 126 C2
Las Lajas, *Argentina* ... 128 D2
Las Lomitas, *Argentina* ... 126 A3
Las Marismas, *Spain* ... 35 H4
Las Minas, *Spain* ... 33 G3
Las Navas de la Concepción, *Spain* ... 35 H5
Las Navas del Marqués, *Spain* ... 34 E6
Las Palmas, *Argentina* ... 126 B4
Las Palmas, *Canary Is.* ... 37 F4
Las Palmas →, *Mexico* ... 117 N10
Las Pedroñas, *Spain* ... 33 F2
Las Piedras, *Uruguay* ... 127 C4
Las Pipinas, *Argentina* ... 126 D4
Las Plumas, *Argentina* ... 128 E3
Las Rosas, *Argentina* ... 126 C3
Las Rozas, *Spain* ... 34 E7
Las Tablas, *Panama* ... 120 E3
Las Termas, *Argentina* ... 126 B3
Las Toscas, *Argentina* ... 126 B4
Las Truchas, *Mexico* ... 118 D4
Las Varillas, *Argentina* ... 126 C3
Las Vegas, *N. Mex., U.S.A.* ... 115 J11
Las Vegas, *Nev., U.S.A.* ... 117 J11
Lasarte, *Spain* ... 32 B2
Lascano, *Uruguay* ... 127 C5
Lash-e Joveyn, *Afghan.* ... 66 D2
Lashburn, *Canada* ... 105 C7
Lashio, *Burma* ... 67 H20
Lashkar, *India* ... 68 F8
Łasin, *Poland* ... 44 E6
Lasíthi, *Greece* ... 36 D7
Lasíthi □, *Greece* ... 36 D7
Lāsjerd, *Iran* ... 71 C7
Lask, *Poland* ... 45 G6
Łaskarzew, *Poland* ... 45 G8
Laško, *Slovenia* ... 29 B12
Lassay-les-Châteaux, *France* ... 18 D6
Lassen Pk., *U.S.A.* ... 114 F3
Lassen Volcanic National Park, *U.S.A.* ... 114 F3
Last Mountain L., *Canada* ... 105 C7
Lastchance Cr. →, *U.S.A.* ... 116 E5
Lastoursville, *Gabon* ... 84 E2
Lastovo, *Croatia* ... 29 F13
Lastovski Kanal, *Croatia* ... 29 F14
Lat Yao, *Thailand* ... 64 E2
Latacunga, *Ecuador* ... 124 D3
Latakia = Al Lādhiqīyah, *Syria* ... 70 C2
Latchford, *Canada* ... 102 C4
Latehar, *India* ... 69 H11
Laterza, *Italy* ... 31 B9
Latham, *Australia* ... 93 E2
Lathen, *Germany* ... 24 C3
Lathi, *India* ... 68 F4
Lathrop Wells, *U.S.A.* ... 117 J10
Latiano, *Italy* ... 31 B10
Latina, *Italy* ... 30 A5
Latisana, *Italy* ... 29 C10
Latium = Lazio □, *Italy* ... 29 F9
Laton, *U.S.A.* ... 116 J7
Latorytsya →, *Slovak Rep.* ... 27 C14
Latouche Treville, C., *Australia* ... 92 C3
Latrobe, *Australia* ... 94 G4
Latrobe, *U.S.A.* ... 110 F5
Latrónico, *Italy* ... 31 B9
Latvia ■, *Europe* ... 9 H20
Lau, *Nigeria* ... 83 D7
Lau Group, *Fiji* ... 91 C9
Lauchhammer, *Germany* ... 24 D9
Lauda-Königshofen, *Germany* ... 25 F5
Lauenburg, *Germany* ... 24 B6
Lauf, *Germany* ... 25 F7
Laughlin, *U.S.A.* ... 115 J6
Laujar de Andarax, *Spain* ... 33 H2
Laukaa, *Finland* ... 9 E21
Launceston, *Australia* ... 94 G4
Launceston, *U.K.* ... 13 G3
Laune →, *Ireland* ... 15 D2
Launglon Bok, *Burma* ... 64 F1
Laupheim, *Germany* ... 25 G5
Laura, *Australia* ... 94 B3
Laureana di Borrello, *Italy* ... 31 D9
Laurel, *Miss., U.S.A.* ... 113 K10
Laurel, *Mont., U.S.A.* ... 114 D9
Laurencekirk, *U.K.* ... 14 E6
Laurens, *U.S.A.* ... 109 H4
Laurentian Plateau, *Canada* ... 103 B6
Lauria, *Italy* ... 31 B8
Laurie, L., *Canada* ... 105 B8
Laurinburg, *U.S.A.* ... 109 H6
Laurium, *U.S.A.* ... 108 B1
Lausanne, *Switz.* ... 25 J2
Laut, *Indonesia* ... 65 K6
Laut, Pulau, *Indonesia* ... 62 E5
Laut Kecil, Kepulauan, *Indonesia* ... 62 E5
Lauterbach, *Germany* ... 24 E5
Lauterecken, *Germany* ... 25 F3
Lautoka, *Fiji* ... 91 C7
Lauzès, *France* ... 20 D5
Lavagh More, *Ireland* ... 15 B3
Lavagna, *Italy* ... 28 D6
Laval, *France* ... 18 D6
Lavalle, *Argentina* ... 126 B2
Lavant Station, *Canada* ... 111 A8
Lāvar Meydān, *Iran* ... 71 D7
Lávara, *Greece* ... 41 E10
Lavardac, *France* ... 20 D4
Lavaur, *France* ... 20 E5
Lavelanet, *France* ... 20 F5
Lavello, *Italy* ... 31 A8
Laverton, *Australia* ... 93 E3
Lavis, *Italy* ... 28 B8

Lávkos, *Greece* ... 38 B5
Lavos, *Portugal* ... 34 E2
Lavradio, *Portugal* ... 35 G1
Lavras, *Brazil* ... 127 A7
Lavre, *Portugal* ... 35 G2
Lávrion, *Greece* ... 38 D6
Lávris, *Greece* ... 36 D6
Lavumisa, *Swaziland* ... 89 D5
Lawas, *Malaysia* ... 62 D5
Lawele, *Indonesia* ... 63 F6
Lawng Pit, *Burma* ... 67 G20
Lawqah, *Si. Arabia* ... 70 D4
Lawra, *Ghana* ... 82 C4
Lawrence, *N.Z.* ... 91 L2
Lawrence, *Kans., U.S.A.* ... 112 F7
Lawrence, *Mass., U.S.A.* ... 111 D13
Lawrenceburg, *Ind., U.S.A.* ... 108 F3
Lawrenceburg, *Tenn., U.S.A.* ... 109 H2
Lawrenceville, *Ga., U.S.A.* ... 109 J4
Lawrenceville, *Pa., U.S.A.* ... 110 E7
Laws, *U.S.A.* ... 116 H8
Lawton, *U.S.A.* ... 113 H5
Lawu, *Indonesia* ... 63 G14
Lawz, J. al, *Si. Arabia* ... 80 B4
Laxå, *Sweden* ... 11 F8
Laxford, L., *U.K.* ... 14 C3
Laxou, *France* ... 19 D13
Lay →, *France* ... 20 B2
Laylá, *Si. Arabia* ... 74 C4
Laylān, *Iraq* ... 70 C5
Layon →, *France* ... 18 E6
Layton, *U.S.A.* ... 114 F7
Laytonville, *U.S.A.* ... 114 G2
Lazarevac, *Serbia, Yug.* ... 40 B4
Lazarevskoye, *Russia* ... 49 J4
Lazarivo, *Madag.* ... 89 C8
Lazdijai, *Lithuania* ... 44 D10
Lazio □, *Italy* ... 29 F9
Lazo, *Moldova* ... 43 C13
Lazo, *Russia* ... 54 C6
Le Beausset, *France* ... 21 E9
Le Blanc, *France* ... 20 B5
Le Bleymard, *France* ... 20 D7
Le Bourgneuf-la-Fôret, *France* ... 18 D6
Le Bugue, *France* ... 20 D4
Le Canourgue = La Canourgue, *France* ... 20 D7
Le Cateau Cambrésis, *France* ... 19 B10
Le Caylar, *France* ... 20 E7
Le Chambon-Feugerolles, *France* ... 21 C8
Le Châtelet, *France* ... 19 F9
Le Chesne, *France* ... 19 C11
Le Cheylard, *France* ... 21 D8
Le Conquet, *France* ... 18 D2
Le Creusot, *France* ... 19 F11
Le Croisic, *France* ... 18 E4
Le Donjon, *France* ... 19 F10
Le Dorat, *France* ... 20 B5
Le François, *Martinique* ... 121 D7
Le Grand-Lucé, *France* ... 18 E7
Le Grand-Pressigny, *France* ... 18 F7
Le Grand-Quevilly, *France* ... 18 C8
Le Havre, *France* ... 18 C7
Le Lavandou, *France* ... 21 E10
Le Lion-d'Angers, *France* ... 18 E6
Le Louroux-Béconnais, *France* ... 18 E6
Le Luc, *France* ... 21 E10
Le Lude, *France* ... 18 E7
Le Mans, *France* ... 18 E7
Le Mars, *U.S.A.* ... 112 D6
Le Mayet-de-Montagne, *France* ... 19 F10
Le Mêle-sur-Sarthe, *France* ... 18 D7
Le Monastier-sur-Gazeille, *France* ... 20 D7
Le Monêtier-les-Bains, *France* ... 21 D10
Le Mont-Dore, *France* ... 20 C6
Le Mont-St-Michel, *France* ... 18 D5
Le Moule, *Guadeloupe* ... 121 C7
Le Muy, *France* ... 21 E10
Le Palais, *France* ... 18 E3
Le Perthus, *France* ... 20 F6
Le Puy-en-Velay, *France* ... 20 C7
Le Sueur, *U.S.A.* ... 112 C8
Le Teil, *France* ... 21 D8
Le Teilleul, *France* ... 18 D6
Le Theil, *France* ... 18 D7
Le Thillot, *France* ... 19 E13
Le Thuy, *Vietnam* ... 64 D6
Le Touquet-Paris-Plage, *France* ... 19 B8
Le Tréport, *France* ... 18 B8
Le Val-d'Ajol, *France* ... 19 E13
Le Verdon-sur-Mer, *France* ... 20 C2
Le Vigan, *France* ... 20 E7
Lea →, *U.K.* ... 13 F8
Leach, *Cambodia* ... 65 F4
Lead, *U.S.A.* ... 112 C3
Leader, *Canada* ... 105 C7
Leadville, *U.S.A.* ... 115 G10
Leaf →, *U.S.A.* ... 113 K10
Leaf Rapids, *Canada* ... 105 B9
Leamington, *Canada* ... 102 D3
Leamington, *U.S.A.* ... 114 G7
Leamington Spa = Royal Leamington Spa, *U.K.* ... 13 E6
Le'an, *China* ... 59 D10
Leandro Norte Alem, *Argentina* ... 127 B4
Leane, L., *Ireland* ... 15 D2
Learmonth, *Australia* ... 92 D1
Leask, *Canada* ... 105 C7
Leatherhead, *U.K.* ... 13 F7
Leavenworth, *Kans., U.S.A.* ... 112 F7
Leavenworth, *Wash., U.S.A.* ... 114 C3
Łeba, *Poland* ... 44 D4
Łeb →, *Poland* ... 44 D4
Lebach, *Germany* ... 25 F2
Lebak, *Phil.* ... 61 H6

Lebam, *U.S.A.* ... 116 D3
Lebane, *Serbia, Yug.* ... 40 D5
Lebanon, *Ind., U.S.A.* ... 108 E2
Lebanon, *Kans., U.S.A.* ... 112 F5
Lebanon, *Ky., U.S.A.* ... 108 G3
Lebanon, *Mo., U.S.A.* ... 113 G8
Lebanon, *N.H., U.S.A.* ... 111 C12
Lebanon, *Oreg., U.S.A.* ... 114 D2
Lebanon, *Pa., U.S.A.* ... 111 F8
Lebanon, *Tenn., U.S.A.* ... 109 G2
Lebanon ■, *Asia* ... 75 B5
Lebec, *U.S.A.* ... 117 L8
Lebedyan, *Russia* ... 47 F10
Lebedyn, *Ukraine* ... 47 G8
Lebel-sur-Quévillon, *Canada* ... 102 C4
Lebomboberge, *S. Africa* ... 89 C5
Lębork, *Poland* ... 44 D4
Lebrija, *Spain* ... 35 J4
Łebsko, Jezioro, *Poland* ... 44 D4
Lebu, *Chile* ... 126 D1
Leca da Palmeira, *Portugal* ... 34 D2
Lecce, *Italy* ... 31 B11
Lecco, *Italy* ... 28 C6
Lecco, L. di, *Italy* ... 28 C6
Lécera, *Spain* ... 32 D4
Lech, *Austria* ... 26 D3
Lech →, *Germany* ... 25 G6
Lechang, *China* ... 59 E9
Lechtaler Alpen, *Austria* ... 26 D3
Lecontes Mills, *U.S.A.* ... 110 E6
Lectoure, *France* ... 20 E4
Łęczna, *Poland* ... 45 G9
Łęczyca, *Poland* ... 45 F6
Ledesma, *Spain* ... 34 D5
Ledong, *China* ... 64 C7
Leduc, *Canada* ... 104 C6
Lee, *U.S.A.* ... 111 D11
Lee →, *Ireland* ... 15 E3
Lee Vining, *U.S.A.* ... 116 H7
Leech L., *U.S.A.* ... 112 B7
Leechburg, *U.S.A.* ... 110 F5
Leeds, *U.K.* ... 12 D6
Leeds, *U.S.A.* ... 109 J2
Leek, *Neths.* ... 17 A6
Leek, *U.K.* ... 12 D5
Leeman, *Australia* ... 93 E1
Leeper, *U.S.A.* ... 110 E5
Leer, *Germany* ... 24 B3
Leesburg, *U.S.A.* ... 109 L5
Leesville, *U.S.A.* ... 113 K8
Leeton, *Australia* ... 95 E4
Leetonia, *U.S.A.* ... 110 F4
Leeu Gamka, *S. Africa* ... 88 E3
Leeuwarden, *Neths.* ... 17 A5
Leeuwin, C., *Australia* ... 93 F2
Leeward Is., *Atl. Oc.* ... 121 C7
Lefka, *Cyprus* ... 36 D11
Lefkoniko, *Cyprus* ... 36 D12
Lefroy, *Canada* ... 110 B5
Lefroy, L., *Australia* ... 93 F3
Łeg →, *Poland* ... 45 H8
Leganés, *Spain* ... 34 E7
Legazpi, *Phil.* ... 61 E5
Lège-Cap-Ferret, *France* ... 20 D2
Lege Hida, *Ethiopia* ... 81 F5
Legendre I., *Australia* ... 92 D2
Leghorn = Livorno, *Italy* ... 28 E7
Legionowo, *Poland* ... 45 F7
Legnago, *Italy* ... 29 C8
Legnano, *Italy* ... 28 C5
Legnica, *Poland* ... 45 G3
Legrad, *Croatia* ... 29 B13
Leh, *India* ... 69 B7
Lehigh Acres, *U.S.A.* ... 109 M5
Lehighton, *U.S.A.* ... 111 F9
Lehliu, *Romania* ... 43 F11
Leho, *Sudan* ... 81 F3
Lehrte, *Germany* ... 24 C5
Lehututu, *Botswana* ... 88 C3
Lei Shui →, *China* ... 59 D9
Leiah, *Pakistan* ... 68 D4
Leibnitz, *Austria* ... 26 E8
Leibo, *China* ... 58 C4
Leicester, *U.K.* ... 13 E6
Leicester City □, *U.K.* ... 13 E6
Leicestershire □, *U.K.* ... 13 E6
Leichhardt →, *Australia* ... 94 B2
Leichhardt Ra., *Australia* ... 94 C4
Leiden, *Neths.* ... 17 B4
Leie →, *Belgium* ... 17 C3
Leifers = Láives, *Italy* ... 29 B8
Leimen, *Germany* ... 25 F4
Leine →, *Germany* ... 24 C5
Leinefelde, *Germany* ... 24 D6
Leinster, *Australia* ... 93 E3
Leinster □, *Ireland* ... 15 C4
Leinster, Mt., *Ireland* ... 15 D5
Leipalingis, *Lithuania* ... 44 D10
Leipzig, *Germany* ... 24 D8
Leiria, *Portugal* ... 34 F2
Leiria □, *Portugal* ... 34 F2
Leirvik, *Norway* ... 9 G11
Leishan, *China* ... 58 D7
Leisler, Mt., *Australia* ... 92 D4
Leith, *U.K.* ... 14 F5
Leith Hill, *U.K.* ... 13 F7
Leitha →, *Europe* ... 27 D10
Leitrim, *Ireland* ... 15 B4
Leitrim □, *Ireland* ... 15 B4
Leitza, *Spain* ... 32 B3
Leiyang, *China* ... 59 D9
Leizhou, *China* ... 59 G8
Leizhou Bandao, *China* ... 58 G7
Leizhou Wan, *China* ... 59 G8
Lek →, *Neths.* ... 17 C4
Leka, *Norway* ... 8 D14
Lekáni, *Greece* ... 41 E8

Lekbibaj, *Albania* ... 40 D3
Lekeitio, *Spain* ... 32 B2
Lekhainá, *Greece* ... 38 D3
Lekoui, *Burkina Faso* ... 82 C4
Leksand, *Sweden* ... 10 D9
Lékva Óros, *Greece* ... 36 D6
Leland, *Mich., U.S.A.* ... 108 C3
Leland, *Miss., U.S.A.* ... 113 J9
Lelång, *Sweden* ... 10 E6
Leleque, *Argentina* ... 128 E2
Lelystad, *Neths.* ... 17 B5
Lem, *Denmark* ... 11 H2
Lema, *Nigeria* ... 83 C5
Lema Shilindi, *Ethiopia* ... 81 G5
Léman, L., *Europe* ... 19 F13
Lemera, *Dem. Rep. of the Congo* ... 86 C2
Lemery, *Phil.* ... 61 E4
Lemhi Ra., *U.S.A.* ... 114 D7
Lemmer, *Neths.* ... 17 B5
Lemmon, *U.S.A.* ... 112 C3
Lemon Grove, *U.S.A.* ... 117 N9
Lemoore, *U.S.A.* ... 116 J7
Lempdes, *France* ... 20 C7
Lemvig, *Denmark* ... 11 H2
Lena →, *Russia* ... 51 B13
Lenart, *Slovenia* ... 29 B12
Lenartovce, *Slovak Rep.* ... 27 C13
Lencloître, *France* ... 18 F7
Léndas, *Greece* ... 36 E6
Lendava, *Slovenia* ... 29 B13
Lendinara, *Italy* ... 29 C8
Lengerich, *Germany* ... 24 C3
Lenggong, *Malaysia* ... 65 K3
Lenggries, *Germany* ... 25 H7
Lengshuijiang, *China* ... 59 D8
Lengshuitan, *China* ... 59 D8
Lengua de Vaca, Pta., *Chile* ... 126 C1
Lengyeltóti, *Hungary* ... 42 D2
Lenhovda, *Sweden* ... 11 G9
Lenina, Kanal →, *Russia* ... 49 J7
Leninabad = Khŭjand, *Tajikistan* ... 50 E7
Leninakan = Gyumri, *Armenia* ... 49 K6
Leningrad = Sankt-Peterburg, *Russia* ... 46 C6
Lenino, *Ukraine* ... 47 K8
Leninogorsk, *Kazakstan* ... 50 D9
Leninsk, *Russia* ... 49 F7
Leninsk-Kuznetskiy, *Russia* ... 50 D9
Leninskoye, *Russia* ... 48 A8
Lenk, *Switz.* ... 25 J3
Lenkoran = Länkäran, *Azerbaijan* ... 71 B6
Lenmalu, *Indonesia* ... 63 E8
Lenne →, *Germany* ... 24 D3
Lennestadt, *Germany* ... 24 D4
Lennox, *U.S.A.* ... 112 D6
Lennoxville, *Canada* ... 111 A13
Leno, *Italy* ... 28 C7
Lenoir, *U.S.A.* ... 109 H5
Lenoir City, *U.S.A.* ... 109 H3
Lenore L., *Canada* ... 105 C8
Lenox, *U.S.A.* ... 111 D11
Lens, *France* ... 19 B9
Lensahn, *Germany* ... 24 A6
Lensk, *Russia* ... 51 C12
Lenti, *Hungary* ... 42 D1
Lentini, *Italy* ... 31 E8
Lenwood, *U.S.A.* ... 117 L9
Lenya, *Burma* ... 62 B1
Lenzen, *Germany* ... 24 B7
Léo, *Burkina Faso* ... 82 C4
Leoben, *Austria* ... 26 D8
Leodhas = Lewis, *U.K.* ... 14 C2
Leola, *U.S.A.* ... 112 C5
Leominster, *U.K.* ... 13 E5
Leominster, *U.S.A.* ... 111 D13
Léon, *France* ... 20 E2
León, *Mexico* ... 118 C4
León, *Nic.* ... 120 D2
León, *Spain* ... 34 C5
Leon, *U.S.A.* ... 112 E8
León □, *Spain* ... 34 C5
León →, *U.S.A.* ... 113 K6
León, Montes de, *Spain* ... 34 C4
Leonardtown, *U.S.A.* ... 108 F7
Leonardville, *Namibia* ... 88 C2
Leonberg, *Germany* ... 25 G5
Leonding, *Austria* ... 26 C7
Leonessa, *Italy* ... 29 F9
Leonforte, *Italy* ... 31 E7
Leongatha, *Australia* ... 95 F4
Leonídhion, *Greece* ... 38 D4
Leonora, *Australia* ... 93 E3
Leopoldina, *Brazil* ... 127 A7
Leopoldsburg, *Belgium* ... 17 C5
Leoti, *U.S.A.* ... 112 F4
Leova, *Moldova* ... 43 D13
Leoville, *Canada* ... 105 C7
Lepe, *Spain* ... 35 H3
Lepel = Lyepyel, *Belarus* ... 46 E5
Lepenoú, *Greece* ... 38 C3
Leping, *China* ... 59 C11
Lépo, L. do, *Angola* ... 88 B2
Lepontine, Alpi, *Italy* ... 28 B5
Leppävirta, *Finland* ... 9 E22
Lepsény, *Hungary* ... 42 D3
Lequeitio = Lekeitio, *Spain* ... 32 B2
Lercara Friddi, *Italy* ... 30 E6
Lerdo, *Mexico* ... 118 B4
Léré, *Chad* ... 83 D7
Léré, *Mali* ... 82 B4
Lere, *Bauchi, Nigeria* ... 83 D6
Lere, *Kaduna, Nigeria* ... 83 C6
Leribe, *Lesotho* ... 89 D4
Lérici, *Italy* ... 28 D6

Lérida = Lleida, *Spain* ... 32 D5
Lérins, Îs. de, *France* ... 21 E11
Lerma, *Spain* ... 34 C7
Léros, *Greece* ... 39 D8
Lérouville, *France* ... 19 D12
Lerum, *Sweden* ... 11 G6
Lerwick, *U.K.* ... 14 A7
Leş, *Romania* ... 42 D6
Les Abrets, *France* ... 21 C9
Les Borges Blanques, *Spain* ... 32 D5
Les Cayes, *Haiti* ... 121 C5
Les Andelys, *France* ... 18 C8
Les Essarts, *France* ... 18 F5
Les Herbiers, *France* ... 18 F5
Les Minquiers, Plateau des, *Chan. Is.* ... 18 D4
Les Pieux, *France* ... 18 C5
Les Ponts-de-Cé, *France* ... 18 E6
Les Riceys, *France* ... 19 E11
Les Sables-d'Olonne, *France* ... 20 B2
Les Vans, *France* ... 21 D8
Lesbos = Lésvos, *Greece* ... 39 B8
L'Escala, *Spain* ... 32 C8
Leshan, *China* ... 58 C4
Lésina, *Italy* ... 29 G12
Lésina, L. di, *Italy* ... 29 G12
Lesjöfors, *Sweden* ... 10 E8
Lesko, *Poland* ... 45 J9
Leskov I., *Antarctica* ... 5 B1
Leskovac, *Serbia, Yug.* ... 40 C5
Leskovik, *Albania* ... 40 F4
Leśna, *Poland* ... 45 G2
Lesneven, *France* ... 18 D2
Leśnica, *Poland* ... 45 H5
Lešnica, *Serbia, Yug.* ... 40 B3
Lesnoye, *Russia* ... 46 C9
Lesopilnoye, *Russia* ... 54 A7
Lesotho ■, *Africa* ... 89 D4
Lesozavodsk, *Russia* ... 51 E14
Lesparre-Médoc, *France* ... 20 C3
Lessay, *France* ... 18 C5
Lesse →, *Belgium* ... 17 D4
Lessebo, *Sweden* ... 11 H9
Lesser Antilles, *W. Indies* ... 121 D7
Lesser Slave L., *Canada* ... 104 B5
Lesser Sunda Is., *Indonesia* ... 63 F6
Lessines, *Belgium* ... 17 D3
Lester, *U.S.A.* ... 116 C5
Lestock, *Canada* ... 105 C8
Lesuer I., *Australia* ... 92 B4
Lésvos, *Greece* ... 39 B8
Leszno, *Poland* ... 45 G3
Letaba, *S. Africa* ... 89 C5
Letälven, *Sweden* ... 10 E8
Létavértes, *Hungary* ... 42 C6
Letchworth, *U.K.* ... 13 F7
Letea, Ostrov, *Romania* ... 43 E14
Lethbridge, *Canada* ... 104 D6
Lethem, *Guyana* ... 124 C7
Leti, Kepulauan, *Indonesia* ... 63 F7
Leti Is. = Leti, Kepulauan, *Indonesia* ... 63 F7
Letiahau →, *Botswana* ... 88 C3
Leticia, *Colombia* ... 124 D5
Leting, *China* ... 57 E10
Letjiesbos, *S. Africa* ... 88 E3
Letlhakane, *Botswana* ... 88 C4
Letlhakeng, *Botswana* ... 88 C4
Letong, *Indonesia* ... 62 D3
Letpadan, *Burma* ... 67 L19
Letpan, *Burma* ... 67 K19
Letsôk-aw Kyun, *Burma* ... 65 G2
Letterkenny, *Ireland* ... 15 B4
Leu, *Romania* ... 43 F9
Leucadia, *U.S.A.* ... 117 M9
Leucate, *France* ... 20 F7
Leucate, Étang de, *France* ... 20 F7
Leuk, *Switz.* ... 25 J3
Leuşeni, *Moldova* ... 43 D13
Leuser, G., *Indonesia* ... 62 D1
Leutkirch, *Germany* ... 25 H6
Leuven, *Belgium* ... 17 D4
Leuze-en-Hainaut, *Belgium* ... 17 D3
Lev Tolstoy, *Russia* ... 46 F10
Levádhia, *Greece* ... 38 C4
Levan, *Albania* ... 40 F3
Levanger, *Norway* ... 8 E14
Levant, Î. du, *France* ... 21 E10
Lévanto, *Italy* ... 28 D6
Lévanzo, *Italy* ... 30 D5
Levelland, *U.S.A.* ... 113 J3
Leven, *U.K.* ... 14 E6
Leven, L., *U.K.* ... 14 E5
Leven, Toraka, *Madag.* ... 89 A8
Leveque C., *Australia* ... 92 C3
Leverano, *Italy* ... 31 B10
Leverkusen, *Germany* ... 24 D2
Levice, *Slovak Rep.* ... 27 C11
Lévico Terme, *Italy* ... 29 C8
Levie, *France* ... 21 G13
Levier, *France* ... 19 F13
Levin, *N.Z.* ... 91 J5
Lévis, *Canada* ... 103 C5
Levis, L., *Canada* ... 104 A5
Lévitha, *Greece* ... 39 D8
Levittown, *N.Y., U.S.A.* ... 111 F11
Levittown, *Pa., U.S.A.* ... 111 F10
Levka, *Bulgaria* ... 41 E10
Levkás, *Greece* ... 38 C2
Levkás □, *Greece* ... 38 C2
Levkími, *Greece* ... 36 B4
Levkímmi, Ákra, *Greece* ... 36 B4
Levkôsia = Nicosia, *Cyprus* ... 36 D12
Levoča, *Slovak Rep.* ... 27 B13
Levroux, *France* ... 19 F8
Levski, *Bulgaria* ... 41 C9
Levskigrad = Karlovo, *Bulgaria* ... 41 D8

Levuka, *Fiji* 91 C8
Lewes, *U.K.* 13 G8
Lewes, *U.S.A.* 108 F8
Lewin Brzeski, *Poland* 45 H4
Lewis, *U.K.* 14 C2
Lewis →, *U.S.A.* 116 E4
Lewis, Butt of, *U.K.* 14 C2
Lewis Ra., *Australia* 92 D4
Lewis Range, *U.S.A.* 114 C7
Lewis Run, *U.S.A.* 110 E6
Lewisburg, *Pa., U.S.A.* 110 F8
Lewisburg, *Tenn., U.S.A.* 109 H2
Lewisburg, *W. Va., U.S.A.* 108 G5
Lewisporte, *Canada* 103 C8
Lewiston, *Idaho, U.S.A.* 114 C5
Lewiston, *Maine, U.S.A.* 109 C11
Lewiston, *N.Y., U.S.A.* 110 C5
Lewistown, *Mont., U.S.A.* 114 C9
Lewistown, *Pa., U.S.A.* 110 F7
Lexington, *Ill., U.S.A.* 112 E10
Lexington, *Ky., U.S.A.* 108 F3
Lexington, *Mich., U.S.A.* 110 C2
Lexington, *Mo., U.S.A.* 112 F8
Lexington, *N.C., U.S.A.* 109 H5
Lexington, *N.Y., U.S.A.* 111 D10
Lexington, *Nebr., U.S.A.* 112 E5
Lexington, *Ohio, U.S.A.* 110 F2
Lexington, *Tenn., U.S.A.* 109 H1
Lexington, *Va., U.S.A.* 108 G6
Lexington Park, *U.S.A.* 108 F7
Leyburn, *U.K.* 12 C6
Leye, *China* 58 E6
Leyland, *U.K.* 12 D5
Leyre →, *France* 20 D2
Leyte □, *Phil.* 61 F6
Leyte Gulf, *Phil.* 61 F6
Leżajsk, *Poland* 45 H9
Lezay, *France* 20 B3
Lezhë, *Albania* 40 E3
Lezhi, *China* 58 B5
Lézignan-Corbières, *France* 20 E6
Lezoux, *France* 20 C7
Lgov, *Russia* 47 G8
Lhasa, *China* 60 D4
Lhazê, *China* 60 D3
Lhokkruet, *Indonesia* 62 D1
Lhokseumawe, *Indonesia* 62 C1
L'Hospitalet de Llobregat, *Spain* 32 D7
Li, *Thailand* 64 D2
Li Shui →, *China* 59 C9
Li Xian, *Gansu, China* 56 G3
Li Xian, *Hebei, China* 56 E8
Li Xian, *Hunan, China* 59 C8
Liádhoi, *Greece* 39 E8
Liancheng, *China* 59 E11
Lianga, *Phil.* 61 G7
Liangcheng,
Nei Monggol Zizhiqu, China 56 D7
Liangcheng, *Shandong, China* 57 G10
Liangdang, *China* 56 H4
Lianghe, *China* 58 E2
Lianghekou, *China* 58 C7
Liangping, *China* 58 B6
Liangpran, *Indonesia* 62 D4
Lianhua, *China* 59 D9
Lianjiang, *Fujian, China* 59 D12
Lianjiang, *Guangdong, China* 59 G8
Lianping, *China* 59 E10
Lianshan, *China* 59 E9
Lianshanguan, *China* 57 D12
Lianshui, *China* 57 H10
Lianyuan, *China* 59 D8
Lianyungang, *China* 57 G10
Lianzhou, *China* 59 E9
Liao He →, *China* 57 D11
Liaocheng, *China* 56 F8
Liaodong Bandao, *China* 57 E12
Liaodong Wan, *China* 57 D11
Liaoning □, *China* 57 D12
Liaoyang, *China* 57 D12
Liaoyuan, *China* 57 C13
Liaozhong, *China* 57 D12
Liapádhes, *Greece* 38 B1
Liard →, *Canada* 104 A4
Liard River, *Canada* 104 B3
Liari, *Pakistan* 68 G2
Libau = Liepāja, *Latvia* 9 H19
Libby, *U.S.A.* 114 B6
Libenge, *Dem. Rep. of*
the Congo 84 D3
Liberal, *U.S.A.* 113 G4
Liberec, *Czech Rep.* 26 A8
Liberecký □, *Czech Rep.* 26 A8
Liberia, *Costa Rica* 120 D2
Liberia ■, *W. Afr.* 82 D3
Liberty, *Mo., U.S.A.* 112 F7
Liberty, *N.Y., U.S.A.* 111 E10
Liberty, *Pa., U.S.A.* 110 E7
Liberty, *Tex., U.S.A.* 113 K7
Libiąż, *Poland* 45 H6
Lîbîya, Sahrâ', *Africa* 79 C10
Libo, *China* 58 E6
Libobo, Tanjung, *Indonesia* 63 E7
Libode, *S. Africa* 89 E4
Libohovë, *Albania* 40 F4
Libourne, *France* 20 D3
Libramont, *Belgium* 17 E5
Librazhd, *Albania* 40 E4
Libreville, *Gabon* 84 D1
Libya ■, *N. Afr.* 79 C9
Libyan Desert = Lîbîya, Sahrâ',
Africa 79 C10
Libyan Plateau = Ed-Déffa,
Egypt 80 A2
Licantén, *Chile* 126 D1
Licata, *Italy* 30 E6
Lice, *Turkey* 73 C9
Licheng, *China* 56 F7
Lichfield, *U.K.* 13 E6
Lichinga, *Mozam.* 87 E4
Lichtenburg, *S. Africa* 88 D4
Lichtenfels, *Germany* 25 E7
Lichuan, *Hubei, China* 58 B7
Lichuan, *Jiangxi, China* 59 D11
Licking →, *U.S.A.* 108 F3
Licosa, Punta, *Italy* 31 B7
Lida, *Belarus* 9 K21
Liden, *Sweden* 10 B10
Lidhoríkion, *Greece* 38 C4
Lidhult, *Sweden* 11 H7
Lidköping, *Sweden* 11 F7
Lido, *Italy* 29 C9
Lido, *Niger* 83 C5
Lido di Roma = Óstia, Lido di,
Italy 29 G9
Lidzbark, *Poland* 45 E6
Lidzbark Warmiński, *Poland* 44 D7
Liebenwalde, *Germany* 24 C9
Lieberose, *Germany* 24 D10
Liebig, Mt., *Australia* 92 D5
Liebling, *Romania* 42 E6
Liechtenstein ■, *Europe* 25 H5
Liège, *Belgium* 17 D5
Liège □, *Belgium* 17 D5
Liegnitz = Legnica, *Poland* 45 G3
Lienart, *Dem. Rep. of the Congo* 86 B2
Lienyünchiangshih =
Lianyungang, *China* 57 G10
Lienz, *Austria* 26 E5
Liepāja, *Latvia* 9 H19
Liepāja □, *Latvia* 44 B8
Liepājas ezers, *Latvia* 44 B8
Lier, *Belgium* 17 C4
Liernais, *France* 19 E11
Lieşti, *Romania* 43 E12
Liévin, *France* 19 B9
Lièvre →, *Canada* 102 C4
Liezen, *Austria* 26 D7
Liffey →, *Ireland* 15 C5
Lifford, *Ireland* 15 B4
Liffré, *France* 18 D5
Lifudzin, *Russia* 54 B7
Ligao, *Phil.* 61 E5
Lightning Ridge, *Australia* 95 D4
Lignano Sabbiadoro, *Italy* 29 C10
Ligny-en-Barrois, *France* 19 D12
Ligonier, *U.S.A.* 110 F5
Ligoúrion, *Greece* 38 D5
Ligueil, *France* 18 E7
Liguria □, *Italy* 28 D5
Ligurian Sea, *Medit. S.* 6 G7
Lihou Reefs and Cays, *Australia* 94 B5
Lihue, *U.S.A.* 106 H15
Lijiang, *China* 58 D3
Likasi, *Dem. Rep. of the Congo* 87 E2
Likenäs, *Sweden* 10 D8
Likhoslavl, *Russia* 46 D8
Likhovskoy, *Russia* 47 H11
Likoma I., *Malawi* 87 E3
Likumburu, *Tanzania* 87 D4
L'Île-Bouchard, *France* 18 E7
L'Île-Rousse, *France* 21 F12
Liling, *China* 59 D9
Lilla Edet, *Sweden* 11 F6
Lille, *France* 19 B10
Lille Bælt, *Denmark* 11 J3
Lillebonne, *France* 18 C7
Lillehammer, *Norway* 9 F14
Lillesand, *Norway* 9 G13
Lillhärdal, *Sweden* 10 C8
Lillian Pt., *Australia* 93 E4
Lillo, *Spain* 34 F7
Lillooet, *Canada* 104 C4
Lillooet →, *Canada* 104 D4
Lilongwe, *Malawi* 87 E3
Liloy, *Phil.* 63 C6
Lim →, *Bos.-H.* 40 C3
Lima, *Indonesia* 63 E7
Lima, *Peru* 124 F3
Lima, *Mont., U.S.A.* 114 D7
Lima, *Ohio, U.S.A.* 108 E3
Lima →, *Portugal* 34 D2
Liman, *Indonesia* 63 G14
Liman, *Russia* 49 H8
Limanowa, *Poland* 45 J7
Limassol, *Cyprus* 36 E12
Limavady, *U.K.* 15 A5
Limay →, *Argentina* 128 D3
Limay Mahuida, *Argentina* 126 D2
Limbach-Oberfrohna, *Germany* 24 E8
Limbang, *Brunei* 62 D5
Limbara, Mte., *Italy* 30 B2
Limbaži, *Latvia* 9 H21
Limbdi, *India* 68 H4
Limbe, *Cameroon* 83 E6
Limburg, *Germany* 25 E4
Limburg □, *Belgium* 17 C5
Limburg □, *Neths.* 17 C5
Limedsforsen, *Sweden* 10 D7
Limeira, *Brazil* 127 A6
Limenária, *Greece* 41 F8
Limerick, *Ireland* 15 D3
Limerick, *U.S.A.* 111 C14
Limerick □, *Ireland* 15 D3
Limestone, *U.S.A.* 110 D6
Limestone →, *Canada* 105 B10
Limfjorden, *Denmark* 11 H3
Limia = Lima →, *Portugal* 34 D2
Limín Khersonísou, *Greece* 39 F7
Limingen, *Norway* 8 D15
Limmared, *Sweden* 11 G7
Limmen Bight, *Australia* 94 A2
Limmen Bight →, *Australia* 94 B2
Límni, *Greece* 38 C5
Límnos, *Greece* 39 B7
Limoges, *Canada* 111 A9
Limoges, *France* 20 C5
Limón, *Costa Rica* 120 E3
Limon, *U.S.A.* 112 F3
Limone Piemonte, *Italy* 28 D4
Limousin, *France* 20 C5
Limousin, Plateaux du, *France* 20 C5
Limoux, *France* 20 E6
Limpopo →, *Africa* 89 D5
Limuru, *Kenya* 86 C4
Lin Xian, *China* 56 F6
Lin'an, *China* 59 B12
Linapacan I., *Phil.* 61 F3
Linapacan Str., *Phil.* 61 F3
Linares, *Chile* 126 D1
Linares, *Mexico* 119 C5
Linares, *Spain* 35 G7
Linaro, Capo, *Italy* 29 F8
Línas Mte., *Italy* 30 C1
Lincang, *China* 58 F3
Lincheng, *China* 56 F8
Linchuan, *China* 59 D11
Lincoln, *Argentina* 126 C3
Lincoln, *N.Z.* 91 K4
Lincoln, *U.K.* 12 D7
Lincoln, *Calif., U.S.A.* 116 G5
Lincoln, *Ill., U.S.A.* 112 E10
Lincoln, *Kans., U.S.A.* 112 F5
Lincoln, *Maine, U.S.A.* 109 C11
Lincoln, *N.H., U.S.A.* 111 B13
Lincoln, *N. Mex., U.S.A.* 115 K11
Lincoln, *Nebr., U.S.A.* 112 E6
Lincoln City, *U.S.A.* 114 D1
Lincoln Hav = Lincoln Sea,
Arctic 4 A5
Lincoln Sea, *Arctic* 4 A5
Lincolnshire □, *U.K.* 12 D7
Lincolnshire Wolds, *U.K.* 12 D7
Lincolnton, *U.S.A.* 109 H5
L'Incudine, *France* 21 G13
Lind, *U.S.A.* 114 C4
Linda, *U.S.A.* 116 F5
Lindau, *Germany* 25 H5
Linden, *Guyana* 124 B7
Linden, *Ala., U.S.A.* 109 J2
Linden, *Calif., U.S.A.* 116 G5
Linden, *Tex., U.S.A.* 113 J7
Lindenhurst, *U.S.A.* 111 F11
Lindesberg, *Sweden* 10 E9
Lindesnes, *Norway* 9 H12
Líndhos, *Greece* 36 C10
Líndhos, Ákra, *Greece* 36 C10
Lindi, *Tanzania* 87 D4
Lindi □, *Tanzania* 87 D4
Lindi →, *Dem. Rep. of*
the Congo 86 B2
Lindö, *Sweden* 11 F10
Lindome, *Sweden* 11 G6
Lindoso, *Portugal* 34 D2
Lindow, *Germany* 24 C8
Lindsay, *Canada* 102 D4
Lindsay, *Calif., U.S.A.* 116 J7
Lindsay, *Okla., U.S.A.* 113 H6
Lindsborg, *U.S.A.* 112 F6
Lindsdal, *Sweden* 11 H10
Linesville, *U.S.A.* 110 E4
Linfen, *China* 56 F6
Ling Xian, *Hunan, China* 59 D9
Ling Xian, *Shandong, China* 56 F9
Lingao, *China* 64 C7
Lingayen, *Phil.* 63 A6
Lingayen G., *Phil.* 61 C4
Lingbi, *China* 57 H9
Lingbo, *Sweden* 10 C10
Lingchuan, *Guangxi Zhuangzu,*
China 59 E8
Lingchuan, *Shanxi, China* 56 G7
Lingen, *Germany* 24 C3
Lingga, *Indonesia* 62 E2
Lingga, Kepulauan, *Indonesia* 62 E2
Lingga Arch. = Lingga,
Kepulauan, *Indonesia* 62 E2
Linghem, *Sweden* 11 F9
Lingle, *U.S.A.* 112 D2
Lingqiu, *China* 56 E8
Lingshan, *China* 58 F7
Lingshi, *China* 56 F6
Lingshou, *China* 56 E8
Lingshui, *China* 64 C8
Lingtai, *China* 56 G4
Linguère, *Senegal* 82 B1
Lingui, *China* 59 E8
Lingwu, *China* 56 E4
Lingyuan, *China* 57 D10
Lingyun, *China* 58 E6
Linhai, *China* 59 C13
Linhares, *Brazil* 125 G10
Linhe, *China* 56 D4
Linjiang, *China* 57 D14
Linköping, *Sweden* 11 F9
Linkou, *China* 57 B16
Linli, *China* 59 C8
Linnhe, L., *U.K.* 14 E3
Linqi, *China* 56 G7
Linqing, *China* 56 F8
Linqu, *China* 57 F10
Linru, *China* 56 G7
Lins, *Brazil* 127 A6
Linshui, *China* 58 B6
Linta →, *Madag.* 89 D7
Linth →, *Switz.* 25 H5
Linthal, *Switz.* 25 J5
Linton, *Ind., U.S.A.* 108 F2
Linton, *N. Dak., U.S.A.* 112 B4
Lintong, *China* 56 G5
Linwood, *Canada* 110 C4
Linwu, *China* 59 E9
Linxi, *China* 57 C10
Linxia, *China* 60 C5
Linxiang, *China* 59 C9
Linyanti →, *Africa* 88 B4
Linyi, *China* 57 G10
Linz, *Austria* 26 C7
Linz, *Germany* 24 E3
Linzhenzhen, *China* 56 F5
Linzi, *China* 57 F10
Lion, G. du, *France* 20 E7
Lionárisso, *Cyprus* 36 D13
Lioni, *Italy* 31 B8
Lions, G. of = Lion, G. du,
France 20 E7
Lion's Den, *Zimbabwe* 87 F3
Lion's Head, *Canada* 110 B3
Liozno = Lyozna, *Belarus* 46 E6
Lipa, *Phil.* 61 E4
Lipali, *Mozam.* 87 F4
Lipany, *Slovak Rep.* 27 B13
Lípari, *Italy* 31 D7
Lípari, I., *Italy* 31 D7
Lípari, Is. = Eólie, Ís., *Italy* 31 D7
Lipcani, *Moldova* 43 B11
Lipetsk, *Russia* 47 F10
Lipiany, *Poland* 45 E1
Liping, *China* 58 D7
Lipkany = Lipcani, *Moldova* 43 B11
Lipljan, *Kosovo, Yug.* 40 D5
Lipník nad Bečvou, *Czech Rep.* 27 B10
Lipno, *Poland* 45 F6
Lipova, *Romania* 42 D6
Lipovcy Manzovka, *Russia* 54 B6
Lipovets, *Ukraine* 47 H5
Lippe →, *Germany* 24 D2
Lippstadt, *Germany* 24 D4
Lipscomb, *U.S.A.* 113 G4
Lipsk, *Poland* 44 E10
Lipsko, *Poland* 45 G8
Lipsói, *Greece* 39 D8
Liptovský Hrádok, *Slovak Rep.* 27 B12
Liptovský Milkuláš, *Slovak Rep.* 27 B12
Liptrap C., *Australia* 95 F4
Lipu, *China* 59 E8
Lira, *Uganda* 86 B3
Liri →, *Italy* 30 A6
Liria = Llíria, *Spain* 33 F4
Lisala, *Dem. Rep. of the Congo* 84 D4
Lisboa, *Portugal* 35 G1
Lisboa □, *Portugal* 35 F1
Lisbon = Lisboa, *Portugal* 35 G1
Lisbon, *N. Dak., U.S.A.* 112 B6
Lisbon, *N.H., U.S.A.* 111 B13
Lisbon, *Ohio, U.S.A.* 110 F4
Lisbon Falls, *U.S.A.* 109 D10
Lisburn, *U.K.* 15 B5
Liscannor B., *Ireland* 15 D2
Liscia →, *Italy* 30 A2
Lishe Jiang →, *China* 58 E3
Lishi, *China* 56 F6
Lishu, *China* 57 C13
Lishui, *Jiangsu, China* 59 B12
Lishui, *Zhejiang, China* 59 C12
Lisianski I., *Pac. Oc.* 96 E10
Lisichansk = Lysychansk,
Ukraine 47 H10
Lisieux, *France* 18 C7
Liski, *Russia* 47 G10
L'Isle-Jourdain, *Gers, France* 20 E5
L'Isle-Jourdain, *Vienne, France* 20 B4
L'Isle-sur-la-Sorgue, *France* 21 E9
Lisle-sur-Tarn, *France* 20 E5
Lismore, *Australia* 95 D5
Lismore, *Ireland* 15 D4
Lista, *Norway* 9 G12
Lister, Mt., *Antarctica* 5 D11
Liston, *Australia* 95 D5
Listowel, *Canada* 102 D3
Listowel, *Ireland* 15 D2
Lit, *Sweden* 10 A8
Lit-et-Mixe, *France* 20 D2
Litang, *Guangxi Zhuangzu,*
China 58 F7
Litang, *Sichuan, China* 58 B3
Litang Qu →, *China* 58 C3
Litani →, *Lebanon* 75 B4
Litchfield, *Calif., U.S.A.* 116 E6
Litchfield, *Conn., U.S.A.* 111 E11
Litchfield, *Ill., U.S.A.* 112 F10
Litchfield, *Minn., U.S.A.* 112 C7
Liteni, *Romania* 43 C11
Lithgow, *Australia* 95 E5
Líthinon, Ákra, *Greece* 36 E6
Lithuania ■, *Europe* 9 J20
Litija, *Slovenia* 29 B11
Lititz, *U.S.A.* 111 F8
Litókhoron, *Greece* 40 F6
Litoměřice, *Czech Rep.* 26 A7
Litomyšl, *Czech Rep.* 27 B9
Litschau, *Austria* 26 C8
Little Abaco I., *Bahamas* 120 A4
Little Barrier I., *N.Z.* 91 G5
Little Belt Mts., *U.S.A.* 114 C8
Little Blue →, *U.S.A.* 112 F6
Little Buffalo →, *Canada* 104 A6
Little Cayman, *Cayman Is.* 120 C3
Little Churchill →, *Canada* 105 B9
Little Colorado →, *U.S.A.* 115 H8
Little Current, *Canada* 102 C3
Little Current →, *Canada* 102 B3
Little Falls, *Minn., U.S.A.* 112 C7
Little Falls, *N.Y., U.S.A.* 111 C10
Little Fork →, *U.S.A.* 112 A8
Little Grand Rapids, *Canada* 105 C9
Little Humboldt →, *U.S.A.* 114 F5
Little Inagua I., *Bahamas* 121 B5
Little Karoo, *S. Africa* 88 E3
Little Lake, *U.S.A.* 117 K9
Little Laut Is. = Laut Kecil,
Kepulauan, *Indonesia* 62 E5
Little Mecatina = Petit-
Mécatina →, *Canada* 103 B8
Little Minch, *U.K.* 14 D2
Little Missouri →, *U.S.A.* 112 B3
Little Ouse →, *U.K.* 13 E9
Little Rann, *India* 68 H4
Little Red →, *U.S.A.* 113 H9
Little River, *N.Z.* 91 K4
Little Rock, *U.S.A.* 113 H8
Little Ruaha →, *Tanzania* 86 D4
Little Sable Pt., *U.S.A.* 108 D2
Little Scarcies →, *S. Leone* 82 D2
Little Sioux →, *U.S.A.* 112 E6
Little Smoky →, *Canada* 104 C5
Little Snake →, *U.S.A.* 114 F9
Little Valley, *U.S.A.* 110 D6
Little Wabash →, *U.S.A.* 108 G1
Little White →, *U.S.A.* 112 D4
Littlefield, *U.S.A.* 113 J3
Littlehampton, *U.K.* 13 G7
Littleton, *U.S.A.* 111 B13
Litvinov, *Czech Rep.* 26 A6
Liu He →, *China* 57 D11
Liu Jiang →, *China* 58 F7
Liuba, *China* 56 H4
Liucheng, *China* 58 E7
Liugou, *China* 57 D10
Liuhe, *China* 57 C13
Liuheng Dao, *China* 59 C14
Liujiang, *China* 58 E7
Liukang Tenggaja = Sabalana,
Kepulauan, *Indonesia* 63 F5
Liuli, *Tanzania* 87 E3
Liuwa Plain, *Zambia* 85 G4
Liuyang, *China* 59 C9
Liuzhou, *China* 58 E7
Liuzhuang, *China* 57 H11
Livada, *Romania* 42 C8
Livadherón, *Greece* 40 F5
Livadhia, *Cyprus* 36 E12
Livádhion, *Greece* 38 A4
Livarot, *France* 18 D7
Live Oak, *Calif., U.S.A.* 116 F5
Live Oak, *Fla., U.S.A.* 109 K4
Liveras, *Cyprus* 36 D11
Livermore, *U.S.A.* 116 H5
Livermore, Mt., *U.S.A.* 113 K2
Livermore Falls, *U.S.A.* 109 C11
Liverpool, *Canada* 103 D7
Liverpool, *U.K.* 12 D4
Liverpool, *U.S.A.* 111 C8
Liverpool Bay, *U.K.* 12 D4
Liverpool Plains, *Australia* 95 E5
Liverpool Ra., *Australia* 95 E5
Livigno, *Italy* 28 B7
Livingston, *Guatemala* 120 C2
Livingston, *U.K.* 14 F5
Livingston, *Ala., U.S.A.* 109 J1
Livingston, *Calif., U.S.A.* 116 H6
Livingston, *Mont., U.S.A.* 114 D8
Livingston, *S.C., U.S.A.* 109 J5
Livingston, *Tenn., U.S.A.* 109 G3
Livingston, *Tex., U.S.A.* 113 K7
Livingston, L., *U.S.A.* 113 K7
Livingston Manor, *U.S.A.* 111 E10
Livingstone, *Zambia* 87 F2
Livingstone Mts., *Tanzania* 87 D3
Livingstonia, *Malawi* 87 E3
Livno, *Bos.-H.* 42 G2
Livny, *Russia* 47 F9
Livonia, *Mich., U.S.A.* 108 D4
Livonia, *N.Y., U.S.A.* 110 D7
Livorno, *Italy* 28 E7
Livramento, *Brazil* 127 C4
Livron-sur-Drôme, *France* 21 D8
Liwale, *Tanzania* 87 D4
Liwiec →, *Poland* 45 F8
Lixi, *China* 58 D3
Lixian, *China* 58 B4
Lixoúrion, *Greece* 38 C2
Liyang, *China* 59 B12
Lizard I., *Australia* 94 A4
Lizard Pt., *U.K.* 13 H2
Lizzano, *Italy* 31 B10
Ljig, *Serbia, Yug.* 40 B4
Ljubija, *Bos.-H.* 29 D13
Ljubinje, *Bos.-H.* 40 D2
Ljubljana, *Slovenia* 29 B11
Ljubno, *Slovenia* 29 B11
Ljubovija, *Serbia, Yug.* 40 B3
Ljugarn, *Sweden* 11 G12
Ljung, *Sweden* 11 G7
Ljungan →, *Sweden* 10 B11
Ljungaverk, *Sweden* 10 B10
Ljungby, *Sweden* 9 H15
Ljungbyholm, *Sweden* 11 H10
Ljungdalen, *Sweden* 10 B6
Ljungsbro, *Sweden* 11 F9
Ljungskile, *Sweden* 11 F5
Ljusdal, *Sweden* 10 C10
Ljusfallshammar, *Sweden* 11 F9
Ljusnan →, *Sweden* 10 C11
Ljusne, *Sweden* 10 C11
Ljutomer, *Slovenia* 29 B13
Llagostera, *Spain* 32 D7
Llancanelo, Salina, *Argentina* 126 D2
Llandeilo, *U.K.* 13 F4
Llandovery, *U.K.* 13 F4
Llandrindod Wells, *U.K.* 13 E4
Llandudno, *U.K.* 12 D4
Llanelli, *U.K.* 13 F3
Llanes, *Spain* 34 B6
Llangollen, *U.K.* 12 E4

Llanidloes, *U.K.* 13 E4
Llano, *U.S.A.* 113 K5
Llano ➤, *U.S.A.* 113 K5
Llano Estacado, *U.S.A.* 113 J3
Llanos, *S. Amer.* 122 C3
Llanquihue, L., *Chile* 128 E1
Llanwrtyd Wells, *U.K.* 13 E4
Llebeig, C. des, *Spain* 37 B9
Lleida, *Spain* 32 D5
Lleida □, *Spain* 32 C6
Llentrisca, C., *Spain* 37 C7
Llera, *Mexico* 119 C5
Llerena, *Spain* 35 G5
Lleyn Peninsula, *U.K.* 12 E3
Llico, *Chile* 126 C1
Lliria, *Spain* 33 F4
Llobregat ➤, *Spain* 32 D7
Llodio, *Spain* 32 B2
Lloret de Mar, *Spain* 32 D7
Lloyd B., *Australia* 94 A3
Lloyd L., *Canada* 105 B7
Lloydminster, *Canada* 105 C7
Llucena del Cid, *Spain* 32 E4
Llucmajor, *Spain* 37 B9
Llullaillaco, Volcán, *S. Amer.* 126 A2
Lo ➤, *Vietnam* 64 B5
Loa, *U.S.A.* 115 G8
Loa ➤, *Chile* 126 A1
Loaita I., *S. China Sea* 62 B4
Loange ➤, *Dem. Rep. of the Congo* 84 E4
Loano, *Italy* 28 D5
Lobatse, *Botswana* 88 D4
Löbau, *Germany* 24 D10
Lobenstein, *Germany* 24 E7
Lobería, *Argentina* 126 D4
Löberöd, *Sweden* 11 J7
Łobez, *Poland* 44 E2
Lobito, *Angola* 85 G2
Lobo ➤, *Ivory C.* 82 D3
Lobos, *Argentina* 126 D4
Lobos, I., *Mexico* 118 B2
Lobos, I. de, *Canary Is.* 37 F6
Łobżenica, *Poland* 45 E4
Loc Binh, *Vietnam* 64 B6
Loc Ninh, *Vietnam* 65 G6
Locarno, *Switz.* 25 J4
Loch Baghasdail = Lochboisdale, *U.K.* 14 D1
Loch Garman = Wexford, *Ireland* 15 D5
Loch Nam Madadh = Lochmaddy, *U.K.* 14 D1
Lochaber, *U.K.* 14 E3
Locharbriggs, *U.K.* 14 F5
Lochboisdale, *U.K.* 14 D1
Loche, L. La, *Canada* 105 B7
Lochem, *Neths.* 17 B6
Loches, *France* 18 E7
Lochgilphead, *U.K.* 14 F3
Lochinver, *U.K.* 14 C3
Lochmaddy, *U.K.* 14 D1
Lochnagar, *Australia* 94 C4
Lochnagar, *U.K.* 14 E5
Łochów, *Poland* 45 F8
Lochy, L., *U.K.* 14 E4
Lock, *Australia* 95 E2
Lock Haven, *U.S.A.* 110 E7
Lockeford, *U.S.A.* 116 G5
Lockeport, *Canada* 103 D6
Lockerbie, *U.K.* 14 F5
Lockhart, *U.S.A.* 113 L6
Lockhart, L., *Australia* 93 F2
Lockhart River, *Australia* 94 A3
Lockney, *U.S.A.* 113 H4
Lockport, *U.S.A.* 110 C6
Locminé, *France* 18 E4
Locri, *Italy* 31 D9
Locronan, *France* 18 D2
Lod, *Israel* 75 D3
Lodeinoye Pole, *Russia* 46 B7
Lodève, *France* 20 E7
Lodge Bay, *Canada* 103 B8
Lodge Grass, *U.S.A.* 114 D10
Lodgepole Cr. ➤, *U.S.A.* 112 E2
Lodhran, *Pakistan* 68 E4
Lodi, *Italy* 28 C6
Lodi, *Calif., U.S.A.* 116 G5
Lodi, *Ohio, U.S.A.* 110 E3
Lodja, *Dem. Rep. of the Congo* 86 C1
Lodosa, *Spain* 32 C2
Lödöse, *Sweden* 11 F6
Lodwar, *Kenya* 86 B4
Łódź, *Poland* 45 G6
Łódzkie □, *Poland* 45 G6
Loei, *Thailand* 64 D3
Loengo, *Dem. Rep. of the Congo* 86 C2
Loeriesfontein, *S. Africa* 88 E2
Lofa ➤, *Liberia* 83 D2
Lofer, *Austria* 26 D5
Lofoten, *Norway* 8 B15
Lofsdalen, *Sweden* 10 B7
Lofsen ➤, *Sweden* 10 B7
Loftahammar, *Sweden* 11 G10
Loga, *Niger* 83 C5
Logan, *Iowa, U.S.A.* 112 E7
Logan, *Ohio, U.S.A.* 108 F4
Logan, *Utah, U.S.A.* 114 F8
Logan, *W. Va., U.S.A.* 108 G5
Logan, Mt., *Canada* 100 B5
Logandale, *U.S.A.* 117 J12
Logansport, *Ind., U.S.A.* 108 E2
Logansport, *La., U.S.A.* 113 K8
Logirim, *Sudan* 81 G3
Logo, *Sudan* 81 F3
Logone ➤, *Chad* 79 F9
Logroño, *Spain* 32 C2

Logrosán, *Spain* 35 F5
Løgstør, *Denmark* 11 H3
Løgumkloster, *Denmark* 11 J2
Lohals, *Denmark* 11 J4
Lohardaga, *India* 69 H11
Loharia, *India* 68 H6
Loharu, *India* 68 E6
Lohja, *Finland* 9 F21
Löhne, *Germany* 24 C4
Lohr, *Germany* 25 F5
Lohri Wah ➤, *Pakistan* 68 F2
Loi-kaw, *Burma* 67 K20
Loimaa, *Finland* 9 F20
Loir ➤, *France* 18 E6
Loir-et-Cher □, *France* 18 E8
Loire □, *France* 21 C8
Loire ➤, *France* 18 E4
Loire-Atlantique □, *France* 18 E5
Loiret □, *France* 19 E9
Loitz, *Germany* 24 B9
Loja, *Ecuador* 124 D3
Loja, *Spain* 35 H6
Loji = Kawasi, *Indonesia* 63 E7
Løjt Kirkeby, *Denmark* 11 J3
Lojung, *China* 58 E7
Loka, *Sudan* 81 G3
Lokandu, *Dem. Rep. of the Congo* 86 C2
Lokeren, *Belgium* 17 C3
Lokgwabe, *Botswana* 88 C3
Lokhvitsa, *Ukraine* 47 G7
Lokichokio, *Kenya* 86 B3
Lokitaung, *Kenya* 86 B4
Lokkan tekojärvi, *Finland* 8 C22
Løkken, *Denmark* 11 G3
Loknya, *Russia* 46 D6
Loko, *Nigeria* 83 D6
Lokoja, *Nigeria* 83 D6
Lokot, *Russia* 47 F8
Lol ➤, *Sudan* 81 F2
Lola, *Guinea* 82 D3
Lola, Mt., *U.S.A.* 116 F6
Lolibai, Gebel, *Sudan* 81 G3
Lolimi, *Sudan* 81 G3
Loliondo, *Tanzania* 86 C4
Lolland, *Denmark* 11 K5
Lollar, *Germany* 24 E4
Lolo, *U.S.A.* 114 C6
Lolodorf, *Cameroon* 83 E7
Lom, *Bulgaria* 40 C7
Lom ➤, *Bulgaria* 40 C7
Lom Kao, *Thailand* 64 D3
Lom Sak, *Thailand* 64 D3
Loma, *U.S.A.* 114 C8
Loma Linda, *U.S.A.* 117 L9
Lomami ➤, *Dem. Rep. of the Congo* 86 B1
Lomas de Zamóra, *Argentina* 126 C4
Lombadina, *Australia* 92 C3
Lombárdia □, *Italy* 28 C6
Lombardy = Lombárdia □, *Italy* 28 C6
Lombez, *France* 20 E4
Lomblen, *Indonesia* 63 F6
Lombok, *Indonesia* 62 F5
Lomé, *Togo* 83 D5
Lomela, *Dem. Rep. of Congo* 84 E4
Lomela ➤, *Dem. Rep. of the Congo* 84 E4
Lomianki, *Poland* 45 F7
Lomma, *Sweden* 11 J7
Lommel, *Belgium* 17 C5
Lomond, *Canada* 104 C6
Lomond, L., *U.K.* 14 E4
Lomphat, *Cambodia* 64 F6
Lompobatang, *Indonesia* 63 F5
Lompoc, *U.S.A.* 117 L6
Łomża, *Poland* 45 E9
Loncoche, *Chile* 128 D2
Londa, *India* 66 M9
Londiani, *Kenya* 86 C4
Londinières, *France* 18 C8
London, *Canada* 102 D3
London, *U.K.* 13 F7
London, *Ky., U.S.A.* 108 G3
London, *Ohio, U.S.A.* 108 F4
London, Greater □, *U.K.* 13 F7
Londonderry, *U.K.* 15 B4
Londonderry □, *U.K.* 15 B4
Londonderry, C., *Australia* 92 B4
Londonderry, I., *Chile* 128 H2
Londres, *Argentina* 128 B3
Londrina, *Brazil* 127 A5
Lone Pine, *U.S.A.* 116 J8
Lonely Mine, *Zimbabwe* 89 B4
Long B., *U.S.A.* 109 J6
Long Beach, *Calif., U.S.A.* 117 M8
Long Beach, *N.Y., U.S.A.* 111 F11
Long Beach, *Wash., U.S.A.* 116 D2
Long Branch, *U.S.A.* 111 F11
Long Creek, *U.S.A.* 114 D4
Long Eaton, *U.K.* 12 E6
Long I., *Australia* 94 C4
Long I., *Bahamas* 121 B4
Long I., *Canada* 102 B4
Long I., *Ireland* 15 E2
Long I., *U.S.A.* 111 F11
Long Island Sd., *U.S.A.* 111 E12
Long L., *Canada* 102 C2
Long Lake, *U.S.A.* 111 C10
Long Point B., *Canada* 110 D4
Long Prairie ➤, *U.S.A.* 112 C7
Long Pt., *Canada* 110 D4
Long Range Mts., *Canada* 103 C8
Long Reef, *Australia* 92 B4
Long Spruce, *Canada* 105 B10
Long Str. = Longa, Proliv, *Russia* 4 C16
Long Thanh, *Vietnam* 65 G6

Long Xian, *China* 56 G4
Long Xuyen, *Vietnam* 65 G5
Longá, *Greece* 38 E3
Longa, Proliv, *Russia* 4 C16
Long'an, *China* 58 F6
Longarone, *Italy* 29 B9
Longbenton, *U.K.* 12 B6
Longboat Key, *U.S.A.* 109 M4
Longchang, *China* 58 C5
Longchi, *China* 58 C5
Longchuan, *Guangdong, China* 59 E10
Longchuan, *Yunnan, China* 58 E1
Longde, *China* 56 F4
Longdi, *China* 58 F6
Longeau, *France* 19 E12
Longford, *Australia* 94 G4
Longford, *Ireland* 15 C4
Longford □, *Ireland* 15 C4
Longhai, *China* 59 E11
Longhua, *China* 57 D9
Longhui, *China* 59 D8
Longido, *Tanzania* 86 C4
Longiram, *Indonesia* 62 E5
Longkou, *Jiangxi, China* 59 D10
Longkou, *Shandong, China* 57 F11
Longlac, *Canada* 102 C2
Longli, *China* 58 D6
Longlin, *China* 58 E5
Longling, *China* 58 E2
Longmeadow, *U.S.A.* 111 D12
Longmen, *China* 59 F10
Longming, *China* 58 F6
Longmont, *U.S.A.* 112 E2
Longnan, *China* 59 E10
Longnawan, *Indonesia* 62 D4
Longobucco, *Italy* 31 C9
Longquan, *China* 59 C12
Longreach, *Australia* 94 C3
Longshan, *China* 58 C7
Longsheng, *China* 59 E8
Longué-Jumelles, *France* 18 E6
Longueau, *France* 19 C9
Longueuil, *Canada* 111 A11
Longuyon, *France* 19 C12
Longvic, *France* 19 E12
Longview, *Tex., U.S.A.* 113 J7
Longview, *Wash., U.S.A.* 116 D4
Longwy, *France* 19 C12
Longxi, *China* 56 G3
Longyan, *China* 59 E11
Longyou, *China* 59 C12
Longzhou, *China* 58 F6
Lonigo, *Italy* 29 C8
Löningen, *Germany* 24 C3
Lonja ➤, *Croatia* 29 C13
Lonoke, *U.S.A.* 113 H9
Lonquimay, *Chile* 128 D2
Lons-le-Saunier, *France* 19 F12
Lönsboda, *Sweden* 11 H8
Looe, *U.K.* 13 G3
Lookout, C., *Canada* 102 A3
Lookout, C., *U.S.A.* 109 H7
Loolmalasin, *Tanzania* 86 C4
Loon ➤, *Alta., Canada* 104 B5
Loon ➤, *Man., Canada* 105 B8
Loon Lake, *Canada* 105 C7
Loongana, *Australia* 93 F4
Loop Hd., *Ireland* 15 D2
Lop Buri, *Thailand* 64 E3
Lop Nor = Lop Nur, *China* 60 B4
Lop Nur, *China* 60 B4
Lopare, *Bos.-H.* 42 F3
Lopatin, *Russia* 49 J8
Lopatina, Gora, *Russia* 51 D15
Lopaye, *Sudan* 81 F3
Lopez, *Phil.* 61 E5
Lopez, *U.S.A.* 111 E8
Lopez, C., *Gabon* 84 E1
Lopphavet, *Norway* 8 A19
Lora ➤, *Afghan.* 66 D4
Lora, Hāmūn-i-, *Pakistan* 66 E4
Lora Cr. ➤, *Australia* 95 D2
Lora del Río, *Spain* 35 H5
Lorain, *U.S.A.* 110 E2
Loralai, *Pakistan* 68 D3
Lorca, *Spain* 33 H3
Lord Howe I., *Pac. Oc.* 96 L7
Lord Howe Ridge, *Pac. Oc.* 96 L8
Lordsburg, *U.S.A.* 115 K9
Lorestan □, *Iran* 71 C6
Loreto, *Brazil* 125 E9
Loreto, *Italy* 29 E10
Loreto, *Mexico* 118 B2
Lorgues, *France* 21 E10
Lorhosso, *Burkina Faso* 82 C4
Lorient, *France* 18 E3
Lőrinci, *Hungary* 42 C4
Lormi, *India* 69 H9
Lorn, *U.K.* 14 E3
Lorn, Firth of, *U.K.* 14 E3
Lorne, *Australia* 95 F3
Loronyo, *Sudan* 81 G3
Lorovouno, *Cyprus* 36 D11
Lörrach, *Germany* 25 H3
Lorraine □, *France* 19 D13
Los, *Sweden* 10 C9
Los, Îles de, *Guinea* 82 D2
Los Alamos, *Calif., U.S.A.* 117 L6
Los Alamos, *N. Mex., U.S.A.* 115 J10
Los Altos, *U.S.A.* 116 H4
Los Andes, *Chile* 126 C1
Los Angeles, *Chile* 126 D1
Los Angeles, *U.S.A.* 117 M8
Los Angeles, Bahia de, *Mexico* 118 B2
Los Angeles Aqueduct, *U.S.A.* 117 K9
Los Banos, *U.S.A.* 116 H6
Los Barrios, *Spain* 35 J5
Los Blancos, *Argentina* 126 A3

Los Chiles, *Costa Rica* 120 D3
Los Corrales de Buelna, *Spain* 34 B6
Los Cristianos, *Canary Is.* 37 F3
Los Gallardos, *Spain* 33 H3
Los Gatos, *U.S.A.* 116 H5
Los Hermanos Is., *Venezuela* 121 D7
Los Islotes, *Canary Is.* 37 E6
Los Llanos de Aridane, *Canary Is.* 37 F2
Los Loros, *Chile* 126 B1
Los Lunas, *U.S.A.* 115 J10
Los Mochis, *Mexico* 118 B3
Los Monegros, *Spain* 32 D4
Los Nietos, *Spain* 33 H4
Los Olivos, *U.S.A.* 117 L6
Los Palacios, *Cuba* 120 B3
Los Palacios y Villafranca, *Spain* 35 H5
Los Reyes, *Mexico* 118 D4
Los Roques Is., *Venezuela* 121 D6
Los Santos de Maimona, *Spain* 35 G4
Los Teques, *Venezuela* 124 A5
Los Testigos, Is., *Venezuela* 124 A6
Los Vilos, *Chile* 126 C1
Los Yébenes, *Spain* 35 F7
Łosice, *Poland* 45 F9
Loskop Dam, *S. Africa* 89 D4
Løsning, *Denmark* 11 J3
Lossiemouth, *U.K.* 14 D5
Lostwithiel, *U.K.* 13 G3
Lot □, *France* 20 D5
Lot ➤, *France* 20 D4
Lot-et-Garonne □, *France* 20 D4
Lota, *Chile* 126 D1
Lotagipi Swamp, *Sudan* 81 G3
Lotfābād, *Iran* 71 B8
Lothair, *S. Africa* 89 D5
Lotorp, *Sweden* 11 F9
Lötschbergtunnel, *Switz.* 25 J3
Löttorp, *Sweden* 11 G11
Lotung, *Taiwan* 59 E13
Loubomo, *Congo* 84 E2
Loudéac, *France* 18 D4
Loudi, *China* 59 D8
Loudonville, *U.S.A.* 110 F2
Loudun, *France* 18 E7
Loue ➤, *France* 19 E12
Louga, *Senegal* 82 B1
Loughborough, *U.K.* 12 E6
Loughrea, *Ireland* 15 C3
Loughros More B., *Ireland* 15 B3
Louhans, *France* 19 F12
Louis Trichardt, *S. Africa* 89 C4
Louis XIV, Pte., *Canada* 102 B4
Louisa, *U.S.A.* 108 F4
Louisbourg, *Canada* 103 C8
Louisburgh, *Ireland* 15 C1
Louise I., *Canada* 104 C2
Louiseville, *Canada* 102 C5
Louisiade Arch., *Papua N. G.* 96 J7
Louisiana, *U.S.A.* 112 F9
Louisiana □, *U.S.A.* 113 K9
Louisville, *Ky., U.S.A.* 108 F3
Louisville, *Miss., U.S.A.* 113 J10
Louisville, *Ohio, U.S.A.* 110 F3
Loulay, *France* 20 B3
Loulé, *Portugal* 35 H3
Louny, *Czech Rep.* 26 A6
Loup City, *U.S.A.* 112 E5
Loups Marins, Lacs des, *Canada* 102 A5
Lourdes, *France* 20 E3
Lourinhã, *Portugal* 35 F1
Lousã, *Portugal* 34 E2
Louta, *Burkina Faso* 82 C4
Louth, *Australia* 95 E4
Louth, *Ireland* 15 C5
Louth, *U.K.* 12 D7
Louth □, *Ireland* 15 C5
Loutrá Aidhipsoú, *Greece* 38 C5
Loutráki, *Greece* 38 D4
Louvain = Leuven, *Belgium* 17 D4
Louviers, *France* 18 C8
Louwsburg, *S. Africa* 89 D5
Lovat ➤, *Russia* 46 C6
Lovćen, *Montenegro, Yug.* 40 D2
Lovech, *Bulgaria* 41 C8
Lovech □, *Bulgaria* 41 C8
Loveland, *U.S.A.* 112 E2
Lovell, *U.S.A.* 114 D9
Lovelock, *U.S.A.* 114 F4
Lóvere, *Italy* 28 C7
Lövestad, *Sweden* 11 J7
Loviisa, *Finland* 9 F22
Loving, *U.S.A.* 113 J2
Lovington, *U.S.A.* 113 J3
Lovisa = Loviisa, *Finland* 9 F22
Lovosice, *Czech Rep.* 26 A7
Lovran, *Croatia* 29 C11
Lovrin, *Romania* 42 E5
Lövstabruk, *Sweden* 10 D11
Lövstabukten, *Sweden* 10 D11
Low, L., *Canada* 102 B4
Low Pt., *Australia* 93 F4
Low Tatra = Nízke Tatry, *Slovak Rep.* 27 C12
Lowa, *Dem. Rep. of the Congo* 86 C2
Lowa ➤, *Dem. Rep. of the Congo* 86 C2
Lowell, *U.S.A.* 111 D13
Lowellville, *U.S.A.* 110 E4
Löwen ➤, *Namibia* 88 D2
Lower Alkali L., *U.S.A.* 114 F3
Lower Arrow L., *Canada* 104 D5
Lower Austria = Niederösterreich □, *Austria* 26 C8
Lower California = Baja California, *Mexico* 118 A1
Lower Hutt, *N.Z.* 91 J5
Lower Lake, *U.S.A.* 116 G4

Lower Manitou L., *Canada* 105 D10
Lower Post, *Canada* 104 B3
Lower Red L., *U.S.A.* 112 B7
Lower Saxony = Niedersachsen □, *Germany* 24 C4
Lower Tunguska = Tunguska, Nizhnyaya ➤, *Russia* 51 C9
Lowestoft, *U.K.* 13 E9
Lowgar □, *Afghan.* 66 B6
Łowicz, *Poland* 45 F6
Lowville, *U.S.A.* 111 C9
Loxton, *Australia* 95 E3
Loxton, *S. Africa* 88 E3
Loyalton, *U.S.A.* 116 F6
Loyalty Is. = Loyauté, Is., *N. Cal.* 96 K8
Loyang = Luoyang, *China* 56 G7
Loyauté, Is., *N. Cal.* 96 K8
Loyev = Loyew, *Belarus* 47 G6
Loyew, *Belarus* 47 G6
Loyoro, *Uganda* 86 B3
Lož, *Slovenia* 29 C11
Lozère □, *France* 20 D7
Loznica, *Serbia, Yug.* 40 B3
Lozova, *Ukraine* 47 H9
Lü Shan, *China* 59 C11
Luachimo, *Angola* 84 F4
Luajan ➤, *India* 69 G11
Lualaba ➤, *Dem. Rep. of the Congo* 86 B2
Luampa, *Zambia* 87 F1
Lu'an, *China* 59 B11
Luan Chau, *Vietnam* 58 G4
Luan He ➤, *China* 57 E10
Luan Xian, *China* 57 E10
Luancheng, *Guangxi Zhuangzu, China* 58 F7
Luancheng, *Hebei, China* 56 F8
Luanco, *Spain* 34 B5
Luanda, *Angola* 84 F2
Luang, Thale, *Thailand* 65 J3
Luang Prabang, *Laos* 58 H4
Luangwa, *Zambia* 87 F3
Luangwa ➤, *Zambia* 87 E3
Luangwa Valley, *Zambia* 87 E3
Luanne, *China* 57 D9
Luanping, *China* 57 D9
Luanshya, *Zambia* 87 E2
Luapula □, *Zambia* 87 E2
Luapula ➤, *Africa* 87 D2
Luarca, *Spain* 34 B4
Luashi, *Dem. Rep. of the Congo* 87 E1
Luau, *Angola* 84 G4
Lubaczów, *Poland* 45 H10
Luban, *Poland* 45 G2
Lubana, Ozero = Lubānas Ezers, *Latvia* 9 H22
Lubānas Ezers, *Latvia* 9 H22
Lubang, *Phil.* 61 E4
Lubang Is., *Phil.* 63 B6
Lubartów, *Poland* 45 G9
Lubawa, *Poland* 44 E6
Lübbecke, *Germany* 24 C4
Lübben, *Germany* 24 D9
Lübbenau, *Germany* 24 D9
Lubbock, *U.S.A.* 113 J4
Lübeck, *Germany* 24 B6
Lübecker Bucht, *Germany* 24 A6
Lubefu, *Dem. Rep. of the Congo* 86 C1
Lubefu ➤, *Dem. Rep. of the Congo* 86 C1
Lubelskie □, *Poland* 45 G9
Lubero = Luofu, *Dem. Rep. of the Congo* 86 C2
Lubersac, *France* 20 C5
Lubicon L., *Canada* 104 B5
Lubień Kujawski, *Poland* 45 F6
Lubilash ➤, *Dem. Rep. of the Congo* 84 F4
Lubin, *Poland* 45 G3
Lublin, *Poland* 45 G9
Lubliniec, *Poland* 45 H5
Lubnān, Jabal, *Lebanon* 75 B4
Lubniewice, *Poland* 45 F2
Lubny, *Ukraine* 47 G7
Lubomierz, *Poland* 45 G2
Luboń, *Poland* 45 F3
Lubongola, *Dem. Rep. of the Congo* 86 C2
L'ubotín, *Slovak Rep.* 27 B13
Lubraniec, *Poland* 45 F5
Lubsko, *Poland* 45 G2
Lübtheen, *Germany* 24 B7
Lubuagan, *Phil.* 61 C4
Lubudi, *Dem. Rep. of the Congo* 84 F5
Lubudi ➤, *Dem. Rep. of the Congo* 87 D2
Lubuklinggau, *Indonesia* 62 E2
Lubuksikaping, *Indonesia* 62 D2
Lubumbashi, *Dem. Rep. of the Congo* 87 E2
Lubunda, *Dem. Rep. of the Congo* 86 D2
Lubungu, *Zambia* 87 E2
Lubuskie □, *Poland* 45 F2
Lubutu, *Dem. Rep. of the Congo* 86 C2
Luc An Chau, *Vietnam* 64 A5
Luc-en-Diois, *France* 21 D9
Lucan, *Canada* 110 C3
Lucania, Mt., *Canada* 100 B5
Lucas Channel, *Canada* 110 A3
Lucban, *Phil.* 61 D4
Lucca, *Italy* 28 E7
Lucé, *France* 18 D8
Luce Bay, *U.K.* 14 G4
Lucea, *Jamaica* 120 C4
Lucedale, *U.S.A.* 109 K1

Lucena, *Phil.* 61 E4
Lucena, *Spain* 35 H6
Lučenec, *Slovak Rep.* 27 C12
Lucera, *Italy* 31 A8
Lucerne = Luzern, *Switz.* 25 H4
Lucerne, *U.S.A.* 116 F4
Lucerne Valley, *U.S.A.* 117 L10
Lucero, *Mexico* 118 A3
Luchena →, *Spain* 33 H3
Lucheng, *China* 56 F7
Lucheringo →, *Mozam.* 87 E4
Lüchow, *Germany* 24 C7
Luchuan, *China* 59 F8
Lucia, *U.S.A.* 116 J5
Lucinda, *Australia* 94 B4
Luckau, *Germany* 24 D9
Luckenwalde, *Germany* 24 C9
Luckhoff, *S. Africa* 88 D3
Lucknow, *Canada* 110 C3
Lucknow, *India* 69 F9
Luçon, *France* 20 B2
Lüda = Dalian, *China* 57 E11
Luda Kamchiya →, *Bulgaria* 41 C11
Ludbreg, *Croatia* 29 B13
Lüdenscheid, *Germany* 24 D3
Lüderitz, *Namibia* 88 D2
Lüderitzbaai, *Namibia* 88 D2
Ludhiana, *India* 68 D6
Ludian, *China* 58 D4
Luding Qiao, *China* 58 C4
Lüdinghausen, *Germany* 24 D3
Ludington, *U.S.A.* 108 D2
Ludlow, *U.K.* 13 E5
Ludlow, *Calif., U.S.A.* 117 L10
Ludlow, *Pa., U.S.A.* 110 E6
Ludlow, *Vt., U.S.A.* 111 C12
Ludus, *Romania* 43 D9
Ludvika, *Sweden* 10 D9
Ludwigsburg, *Germany* 25 G5
Ludwigsfelde, *Germany* 24 C9
Ludwigshafen, *Germany* 25 F4
Ludwigslust, *Germany* 24 B7
Ludza, *Latvia* 46 D4
Lueki, *Dem. Rep. of the Congo* 86 C2
Luena, *Dem. Rep. of the Congo* 87 D2
Luena, *Zambia* 87 E3
Lüeyang, *China* 56 H4
Lufeng, *Guangdong, China* 59 F10
Lufeng, *Yunnan, China* 58 E4
Lufira →, *Dem. Rep. of the Congo* 87 D2
Lufkin, *U.S.A.* 113 K7
Lufupa, *Dem. Rep. of the Congo* 87 E1
Luga, *Russia* 46 C5
Luga →, *Russia* 46 C5
Lugano, *Switz.* 25 J4
Lugano, L. di, *Switz.* 28 C6
Lugansk = Luhansk, *Ukraine* 47 H10
Lugard's Falls, *Kenya* 86 C4
Lugela, *Mozam.* 87 F4
Lugenda →, *Mozam.* 87 E4
Lugh Ganana, *Somali Rep.* 74 G3
Lugnaquilla, *Ireland* 15 D5
Lugo, *Italy* 29 D8
Lugo, *Spain* 34 B3
Lugo □, *Spain* 34 C3
Lugoj, *Romania* 42 E6
Lugovoy = Qulan, *Kazakstan* 50 E8
Luhansk, *Ukraine* 47 H10
Luhe, *China* 59 A12
Luhe →, *Germany* 24 B6
Luhuo, *China* 58 B3
Luiana, *Angola* 88 B3
Luimneach = Limerick, *Ireland* 15 D3
Luing, *U.K.* 14 E3
Luino, *Italy* 28 C5
Luís Correia, *Brazil* 125 D10
Luitpold Coast, *Antarctica* 5 D1
Luiza, *Dem. Rep. of the Congo* 84 F4
Luizi, *Dem. Rep. of the Congo* 86 D2
Luján, *Argentina* 126 C4
Lujiang, *China* 59 B11
Lukang, *Taiwan* 59 E13
Lukanga Swamp, *Zambia* 87 E2
Lukavac, *Bos.-H.* 42 F3
Lukenie →, *Dem. Rep. of the Congo* 84 E3
Lukhisaral, *India* 69 G12
Lŭki, *Bulgaria* 41 E8
Lukolela, *Dem. Rep. of the Congo* 86 D1
Lukosi, *Zimbabwe* 87 F2
Lukovë, *Albania* 40 G3
Lukovit, *Bulgaria* 41 C8
Łuków, *Poland* 45 G9
Lukoyanov, *Russia* 48 C7
Lule älv →, *Sweden* 8 D19
Luleå, *Sweden* 8 D20
Lüleburgaz, *Turkey* 41 E11
Luliang, *China* 58 E4
Luling, *U.S.A.* 113 L6
Lulong, *China* 57 E10
Lulonga →, *Dem. Rep. of the Congo* 84 D3
Lulua →, *Dem. Rep. of the Congo* 84 E4
Lumajang, *Indonesia* 63 H15
Lumbala N'guimbo, *Angola* 85 G4
Lumberton, *U.S.A.* 109 H6
Lumbwa, *Kenya* 86 C4
Lumsden, *Canada* 105 C8
Lumsden, *N.Z.* 91 L2
Lumut, *Malaysia* 65 K3
Lumut, Tanjung, *Indonesia* 62 E3
Luna, *India* 68 H3
Lunan, *China* 58 E4
Lunavada, *India* 68 H5
Lunca, *Romania* 43 C10
Lunca Corbului, *Romania* 43 F9
Lund, *Sweden* 11 J7
Lundazi, *Zambia* 87 E3
Lunderskov, *Denmark* 11 J3
Lundi →, *Zimbabwe* 87 G3
Lundu, *Malaysia* 62 D3
Lundy, *U.K.* 13 F3
Lune →, *U.K.* 12 C5
Lüneburg, *Germany* 24 B6
Lüneburg Heath = Lüneburger Heide, *Germany* 24 B6
Lüneburger Heide, *Germany* 24 B6
Lunel, *France* 21 E8
Lünen, *Germany* 24 D3
Lunenburg, *Canada* 103 D7
Lunéville, *France* 19 D13
Lunga →, *Zambia* 87 E2
Lungi Airport, *S. Leone* 82 D2
Lunglei, *India* 67 H18
Luni, *India* 68 G5
Luni →, *India* 68 G4
Luninets = Luninyets, *Belarus* 47 F4
Luning, *U.S.A.* 114 G4
Lunino, *Russia* 48 D7
Luninyets, *Belarus* 47 F4
Lunkaransar, *India* 68 E5
Lunsemfwa →, *Zambia* 87 E3
Lunsemfwa Falls, *Zambia* 87 E2
Luo He →, *China* 56 G6
Luocheng, *China* 58 E7
Luochuan, *China* 56 G5
Luoci, *China* 58 E4
Luodian, *China* 58 E6
Luoding, *China* 59 F8
Luofu, *Dem. Rep. of the Congo* 86 C2
Luohe, *China* 56 H8
Luojiang, *China* 58 B5
Luonan, *China* 56 G6
Luoning, *China* 56 G6
Luoshan, *China* 59 A10
Luotian, *China* 59 B10
Luoxiao Shan, *China* 59 D10
Luoyang, *China* 56 G7
Luoyuan, *China* 59 D12
Luozigou, *China* 57 C16
Lupanshui, *China* 58 D5
Lupeni, *Romania* 43 E8
Lupilichi, *Mozam.* 87 E4
Łupków, *Poland* 45 J9
Lupoing, *China* 58 E5
Luquan, *China* 58 E4
Luque, *Paraguay* 126 B4
Lúras, *Italy* 30 B2
Luray, *U.S.A.* 108 F6
Lure, *France* 19 E13
Lurgan, *U.K.* 15 B5
Lusaka, *Zambia* 87 F2
Lusambo, *Dem. Rep. of the Congo* 86 C1
Lusangaye, *Dem. Rep. of the Congo* 86 C2
Luseland, *Canada* 105 C7
Lushan, *Henan, China* 56 H7
Lushan, *Sichuan, China* 58 B4
Lushi, *China* 56 G6
Lushnjë, *Albania* 40 F3
Lushoto, *Tanzania* 86 C4
Lushui, *China* 58 E2
Lüshun, *China* 57 E11
Lusignan, *France* 20 B4
Lusigny-sur-Barse, *France* 19 D11
Lusk, *U.S.A.* 112 D2
Lussac-les-Châteaux, *France* 20 B4
Lustenau, *Austria* 26 D2
Lūt, Dasht-e, *Iran* 71 D8
Luta = Dalian, *China* 57 E11
Lutherstadt Wittenberg, *Germany* 24 D8
Luton, *U.K.* 13 F7
Luton □, *U.K.* 13 F7
Lutselke, *Canada* 105 A6
Lutsk, *Ukraine* 47 G3
Lützow Holmbukta, *Antarctica* 5 C4
Lutzputs, *S. Africa* 88 D3
Luverne, *Ala., U.S.A.* 109 K2
Luverne, *Minn., U.S.A.* 112 D6
Luvua, *Dem. Rep. of the Congo* 87 D2
Luvua →, *Dem. Rep. of the Congo* 86 D2
Luvuvhu →, *S. Africa* 89 C5
Luwegu →, *Tanzania* 87 D4
Luwuk, *Indonesia* 63 E6
Luxembourg, *Lux.* 17 E6
Luxembourg □, *Belgium* 17 E5
Luxembourg ■, *Europe* 7 F7
Luxeuil-les-Bains, *France* 19 E13
Luxi, *Hunan, China* 59 C8
Luxi, *Yunnan, China* 58 E4
Luxi, *Yunnan, China* 58 E2
Luxor = El Uqsur, *Egypt* 80 B3
Luy-de-Béarn →, *France* 20 E3
Luy-de-France →, *France* 20 E3
Luyi, *China* 56 H8
Luz-St-Sauveur, *France* 20 F4
Luzern, *Switz.* 25 H4
Luzern □, *Switz.* 25 H3
Luzhai, *China* 58 E7
Luzhi, *China* 58 D5
Luzhou, *China* 58 C5
Luziânia, *Brazil* 125 G9
Lužnice →, *Czech Rep.* 26 B7
Luzon, *Phil.* 61 D4
Luzy, *France* 19 F10
Luzzi, *Italy* 31 C9
Lviv, *Ukraine* 47 H3
Lvov = Lviv, *Ukraine* 47 H3
Lwówek, *Poland* 45 F3
Lwówek Śląski, *Poland* 45 G2
Lyakhavichy, *Belarus* 47 F4
Lyakhovskiye, Ostrova, *Russia* 51 B15
Lyaki = Läki, *Azerbaijan* 49 K8
Lyal I., *Canada* 110 B3
Lyallpur = Faisalabad, *Pakistan* 68 D5
Lyaskovets, *Bulgaria* 41 C9
Lybster, *U.K.* 14 C5
Lycaonia, *Turkey* 72 D5
Lychen, *Germany* 24 B9
Lychkova, *Russia* 46 D7
Lycia, *Turkey* 39 E11
Lyckebyån →, *Sweden* 11 H9
Lycksele, *Sweden* 8 D18
Lycosura, *Greece* 38 D4
Lydda = Lod, *Israel* 75 D3
Lydenburg, *S. Africa* 89 D5
Lydia, *Turkey* 39 C10
Łydynia →, *Poland* 45 F7
Lyell, *N.Z.* 91 J4
Lyell I., *Canada* 104 C2
Lyepyel, *Belarus* 46 E5
Lygnern, *Sweden* 11 G6
Lykens, *U.S.A.* 111 F8
Lyman, *U.S.A.* 114 F8
Lyme B., *U.K.* 13 G4
Lyme Regis, *U.K.* 13 G5
Lymington, *U.K.* 13 G6
Łyna →, *Poland* 9 J19
Lynchburg, *U.S.A.* 108 G6
Lynd →, *Australia* 94 B3
Lynd Ra., *Australia* 95 D4
Lynden, *Canada* 110 C4
Lynden, *U.S.A.* 116 B4
Lyndhurst, *Australia* 95 E2
Lyndon →, *Australia* 93 D1
Lyndonville, *N.Y., U.S.A.* 110 C6
Lyndonville, *Vt., U.S.A.* 111 B12
Lyngen, *Norway* 8 B19
Lynher Reef, *Australia* 92 C3
Lynn, *U.S.A.* 111 D14
Lynn Lake, *Canada* 105 B8
Lynnwood, *U.S.A.* 116 C4
Lynton, *U.K.* 13 F4
Lyntupy, *Belarus* 9 J22
Lynx L., *Canada* 105 A7
Lyon, *France* 21 C8
Lyonnais, *France* 21 C8
Lyons = Lyon, *France* 21 C8
Lyons, *Ga., U.S.A.* 109 J4
Lyons, *Kans., U.S.A.* 112 F5
Lyons, *N.Y., U.S.A.* 110 C8
Lyons →, *Australia* 93 E2
Lyons Falls, *U.S.A.* 111 C9
Lyozna, *Belarus* 46 E6
Lys = Leie →, *Belgium* 17 C3
Lysá nad Labem, *Czech Rep.* 26 A7
Lysekil, *Sweden* 11 F5
Lyskovo, *Russia* 48 B7
Lystrup, *Denmark* 11 H4
Lysvik, *Sweden* 10 D7
Lysychansk, *Ukraine* 47 H10
Lytham St. Anne's, *U.K.* 12 D4
Lyttelton, *N.Z.* 91 K4
Lytton, *Canada* 104 C4
Lyuban, *Russia* 46 C6
Lyubertsy, *Russia* 46 E9
Lyubim, *Russia* 46 C11
Lyubimets, *Bulgaria* 41 E10
Lyuboml, *Ukraine* 47 G3
Lyubotyn, *Ukraine* 47 H8
Lyubytino, *Russia* 46 C7
Lyudinovo, *Russia* 46 F8

M

M.R. Gomez, Presa, *Mexico* 119 B5
Ma →, *Vietnam* 58 H5
Ma'adaba, *Jordan* 75 E4
Maamba, *Zambia* 88 B4
Ma'ān, *Jordan* 75 E4
Ma'ān □, *Jordan* 75 F5
Maanselkä, *Finland* 8 C23
Ma'anshan, *China* 59 B12
Maarianhamina, *Finland* 9 F18
Ma'arrat an Nu'mān, *Syria* 70 C3
Maas →, *Neths.* 17 C4
Maaseik, *Belgium* 17 C5
Maasin, *Phil.* 63 B6
Maastricht, *Neths.* 17 D5
Maave, *Mozam.* 89 C5
Mababe Depression, *Botswana* 88 B3
Mabalane, *Mozam.* 89 C5
Mabel L., *Canada* 104 C5
Mabenge, *Dem. Rep. of the Congo* 86 B1
Maberly, *Canada* 111 B8
Mabian, *China* 58 C4
Mabil, *Ethiopia* 81 E4
Mablethorpe, *U.K.* 12 D8
Mably, *France* 19 F11
Maboma, *Dem. Rep. of the Congo* 86 B2
Mabonto, *S. Leone* 82 D2
Mabrouk, *Mali* 83 B4
Mac Bac, *Vietnam* 65 H6
Macachín, *Argentina* 126 D3
Macaé, *Brazil* 127 A7
Macael, *Spain* 33 H2
McAlester, *U.S.A.* 113 H7
McAllen, *U.S.A.* 113 M5
MacAlpine L., *Canada* 100 B9
Macamic, *Canada* 102 C4
Macao = Macau □, *China* 59 F9
Macão, *Portugal* 35 F3
Macapá, *Brazil* 125 C8
McArthur →, *Australia* 94 B2
McArthur, Port, *Australia* 94 B2
Macau, *Brazil* 125 E11
Macau □, *China* 59 F9
McBride, *Canada* 104 C4
McCall, *U.S.A.* 114 D5
McCamey, *U.S.A.* 113 K3
McCammon, *U.S.A.* 114 E7
McCauley I., *Canada* 104 C2
McCleary, *U.S.A.* 116 C3
Macclenny, *U.S.A.* 109 K4
Macclesfield, *U.K.* 12 D5
M'Clintock Chan., *Canada* 100 A9
McClintock Ra., *Australia* 92 C4
McCloud, *U.S.A.* 114 F2
McCluer I., *Australia* 92 B5
McClure, *U.S.A.* 110 F7
McClure, L., *U.S.A.* 116 H6
M'Clure Str., *Canada* 4 B2
McClusky, *U.S.A.* 112 B4
McComb, *U.S.A.* 113 K9
McConaughy, L., *U.S.A.* 112 E4
McCook, *U.S.A.* 112 E4
McCreary, *Canada* 105 C9
McCullough Mt., *U.S.A.* 117 K11
McCusker →, *Canada* 105 B7
McDame, *Canada* 104 B3
McDermitt, *U.S.A.* 114 F5
McDonald, *U.S.A.* 110 F4
Macdonald, L., *Australia* 92 D4
McDonald Is., *Ind. Oc.* 3 G13
MacDonnell Ranges, *Australia* 92 D5
MacDowell L., *Canada* 102 B1
Macduff, *U.K.* 14 D6
Maceda, *Spain* 34 C3
Macedonia, *U.S.A.* 110 E3
Macedonia ■, *Europe* 40 E5
Maceió, *Brazil* 125 E11
Maceira, *Portugal* 34 F2
Macenta, *Guinea* 82 D3
Macerata, *Italy* 29 E10
McFarland, *U.S.A.* 117 K7
McFarlane →, *Canada* 105 B7
Macfarlane, L., *Australia* 95 E2
McGehee, *U.S.A.* 113 J9
McGill, *U.S.A.* 114 G6
Macgillycuddy's Reeks, *Ireland* 15 E2
McGraw, *U.S.A.* 111 D8
McGregor, *U.S.A.* 112 D9
McGregor Ra., *Australia* 95 D3
Mach, *Pakistan* 66 E5
Māch Kowr, *Iran* 71 E9
Machado = Jiparaná →, *Brazil* 124 E6
Machagai, *Argentina* 126 B3
Machakos, *Kenya* 86 C4
Machala, *Ecuador* 124 D3
Machanga, *Mozam.* 89 C6
Machattie, L., *Australia* 94 C2
Machault, *France* 19 C11
Machava, *Mozam.* 89 D5
Machece, *Mozam.* 87 F4
Machecoul, *France* 18 F5
Macheke, *Zimbabwe* 89 B5
Macheng, *China* 59 B10
Machero, *Spain* 35 F6
Machhu →, *India* 68 H4
Machias, *Maine, U.S.A.* 109 C12
Machias, *N.Y., U.S.A.* 110 D6
Machichi →, *Canada* 105 B10
Machico, *Madeira* 37 D3
Machilipatnam, *India* 67 L12
Machiques, *Venezuela* 124 A4
Machupicchu, *Peru* 124 F4
Machynlleth, *U.K.* 13 E4
Macia, *Mozam.* 89 D5
Maciejowice, *Poland* 45 G8
McIlwraith Ra., *Australia* 94 A3
Măcin, *Romania* 43 E13
Macina, *Mali* 82 C4
McInnes L., *Canada* 105 C10
McIntosh, *U.S.A.* 112 C4
McIntosh L., *Canada* 105 B8
Macintosh Ra., *Australia* 93 E4
Macintyre →, *Australia* 95 D5
Macizo Galaico, *Spain* 34 C3
Mackay, *Australia* 94 C4
Mackay, *U.S.A.* 114 E7
MacKay →, *Canada* 104 B6
Mackay, L., *Australia* 92 D4
McKay Ra., *Australia* 92 D3
McKeesport, *U.S.A.* 110 F5
McKellar, *Canada* 110 A5
McKenna, *U.S.A.* 116 D4
Mackenzie, *Canada* 104 B4
McKenzie, *U.S.A.* 109 G1
Mackenzie →, *Australia* 94 C4
Mackenzie →, *Canada* 100 B6
McKenzie →, *U.S.A.* 114 D2
Mackenzie Bay, *Canada* 4 B1
Mackenzie City = Linden, *Guyana* 124 B7
Mackenzie Mts., *Canada* 100 B6
Mackinaw City, *U.S.A.* 108 C3
McKinlay, *Australia* 94 C3
McKinlay →, *Australia* 94 C3
McKinley, Mt., *U.S.A.* 100 B4
McKinley Sea, *Arctic* 4 A7
McKinney, *U.S.A.* 113 J6
Mackinnon Road, *Kenya* 86 C4
McKittrick, *U.S.A.* 117 K7
Macklin, *Canada* 105 C7
Macksville, *Australia* 95 E5
McLaughlin, *U.S.A.* 112 C4
Maclean, *Australia* 95 D5
McLean, *U.S.A.* 113 H4
McLeansboro, *U.S.A.* 112 F10
Maclear, *S. Africa* 89 E4
Macleay →, *Australia* 95 E5
McLennan, *Canada* 104 B5
McLeod →, *Canada* 104 C5
MacLeod, B., *Canada* 105 A7
McLeod, L., *Australia* 93 D1
MacLeod Lake, *Canada* 104 C4
McLoughlin, Mt., *U.S.A.* 114 E2
McMechen, *U.S.A.* 110 G4
McMinnville, *Oreg., U.S.A.* 114 D2
McMinnville, *Tenn., U.S.A.* 109 H3
McMurdo Sd., *Antarctica* 5 D11
McMurray = Fort McMurray, *Canada* 104 B6
McMurray, *U.S.A.* 116 B4
Macodoene, *Mozam.* 89 C6
Macomb, *U.S.A.* 112 E9
Macomer, *Italy* 30 B1
Mâcon, *France* 19 F11
Macon, *Ga., U.S.A.* 109 J4
Macon, *Miss., U.S.A.* 109 J1
Macon, *Mo., U.S.A.* 112 F8
Macossa, *Mozam.* 87 F3
Macoun L., *Canada* 105 B8
Macovane, *Mozam.* 89 C6
McPherson, *U.S.A.* 112 F6
McPherson Pk., *U.S.A.* 117 L7
McPherson Ra., *Australia* 95 D5
Macquarie →, *Australia* 95 E4
Macquarie Harbour, *Australia* 94 G4
Macquarie Is., *Pac. Oc.* 96 N7
MacRobertson Land, *Antarctica* 5 D6
Macroom, *Ireland* 15 E3
MacTier, *Canada* 110 A5
Macubela, *Mozam.* 87 F4
Macugnaga, *Italy* 28 C4
Macuiza, *Mozam.* 87 F3
Macusani, *Peru* 124 F4
Macuse, *Mozam.* 87 F4
Macuspana, *Mexico* 119 D6
Macusse, *Angola* 88 B3
Mada →, *Nigeria* 83 D6
Madadeni, *S. Africa* 89 D5
Madagali, *Nigeria* 83 C7
Madagascar ■, *Africa* 89 C8
Madā'in Sālih, *Si. Arabia* 70 E3
Madama, *Niger* 79 D8
Madame I., *Canada* 103 C7
Madan, *Bulgaria* 41 E8
Madaoua, *Niger* 83 C6
Madara, *Nigeria* 83 C7
Madaripur, *Bangla.* 67 H17
Madauk, *Burma* 67 L20
Madawaska, *Canada* 110 A7
Madawaska →, *Canada* 102 C4
Madaya, *Burma* 67 H20
Madbar, *Sudan* 81 F3
Maddalena, *Italy* 30 A2
Maddaloni, *Italy* 31 A7
Madeira, *Atl. Oc.* 37 D3
Madeira →, *Brazil* 122 D5
Madeleine, Îs. de la, *Canada* 103 C7
Maden, *Turkey* 73 C8
Madera, *Mexico* 118 B3
Madera, *Calif., U.S.A.* 116 J6
Madera, *Pa., U.S.A.* 110 F6
Madha, *India* 66 L9
Madhavpur, *India* 68 J3
Madhepura, *India* 69 F12
Madhubani, *India* 69 F12
Madhupur, *India* 69 G12
Madhya Pradesh □, *India* 68 J8
Madidi →, *Bolivia* 124 F5
Madikeri, *India* 66 N9
Madill, *U.S.A.* 113 H6
Madimba, *Dem. Rep. of the Congo* 84 E3
Ma'din, *Syria* 70 C3
Madina, *Mali* 82 C3
Madinani, *Ivory C.* 82 D3
Madingou, *Congo* 84 E2
Madirovalo, *Madag.* 89 B8
Madison, *Calif., U.S.A.* 116 G5
Madison, *Fla., U.S.A.* 109 K4
Madison, *Ind., U.S.A.* 108 F3
Madison, *Nebr., U.S.A.* 112 E6
Madison, *Ohio, U.S.A.* 110 E3
Madison, *S. Dak., U.S.A.* 112 D6
Madison, *Wis., U.S.A.* 112 D10
Madison →, *U.S.A.* 114 D8
Madison Heights, *U.S.A.* 108 G6
Madisonville, *Ky., U.S.A.* 108 G2
Madisonville, *Tex., U.S.A.* 113 K7
Madista, *Botswana* 88 C4
Madiun, *Indonesia* 62 F4
Madoc, *Canada* 110 B7
Madol, *Sudan* 81 F2
Madon →, *France* 19 D13
Madona, *Latvia* 9 H22
Madonie, *Italy* 30 E6
Madonna di Campíglio, *Italy* 28 B7
Madra Dağı, *Turkey* 39 B9
Madrakah, Ra's al, *Oman* 74 D6
Madras = Chennai, *India* 66 N12
Madras = Tamil Nadu □, *India* 66 P10
Madras, *U.S.A.* 114 D3
Madre, Laguna, *U.S.A.* 113 M6
Madre, Sierra, *Phil.* 61 C5
Madre de Dios →, *Bolivia* 122 E4
Madre de Dios, I., *Chile* 122 J3
Madre del Sur, Sierra, *Mexico* 119 D5
Madre Occidental, Sierra, *Mexico* 118 B3
Madre Oriental, Sierra, *Mexico* 118 C5
Madri, *India* 68 G5
Madrid, *Spain* 34 E7

Madrid, *U.S.A.* 111 B9
Madrid □, *Spain* 34 E7
Madridejos, *Spain* 35 F7
Madrigal de las Altas Torres, *Spain* 34 D6
Madrona, Sierra, *Spain* 35 G6
Madroñera, *Spain* 35 F5
Madu, *Sudan* 81 E2
Madura, *Australia* 93 F4
Madura, *Indonesia* 63 G15
Madura, Selat, *Indonesia* 63 G15
Madurai, *India* 66 Q11
Madurantakam, *India* 66 N11
Madzhalis, *Russia* 49 J8
Mae Chan, *Thailand* 64 B2
Mae Hong Son, *Thailand* 64 C2
Mae Khlong →, *Thailand* 64 F3
Mae Phrik, *Thailand* 64 D2
Mae Ramat, *Thailand* 64 D2
Mae Rim, *Thailand* 64 C2
Mae Sot, *Thailand* 64 D2
Mae Suai, *Thailand* 58 H2
Mae Tha, *Thailand* 64 C2
Maebashi, *Japan* 55 F9
Maella, *Spain* 32 D5
Maesteg, *U.K.* 13 F4
Maestra, Sierra, *Cuba* 120 B4
Maevatanana, *Madag.* 89 B8
Mafeking = Mafikeng, *S. Africa* 88 D4
Mafeking, *Canada* 105 C8
Maféré, *Ivory C.* 82 D4
Mafeteng, *Lesotho* 88 D4
Maffra, *Australia* 95 F4
Mafia I., *Tanzania* 86 D4
Mafikeng, *S. Africa* 88 D4
Mafra, *Brazil* 127 B6
Mafra, *Portugal* 35 G1
Mafungabusi Plateau, *Zimbabwe* 87 F2
Magadan, *Russia* 51 D16
Magadi, *Kenya* 86 C4
Magadi, L., *Kenya* 86 C4
Magaliesburg, *S. Africa* 89 D4
Magallanes, Estrecho de, *Chile* 122 J3
Magaluf, *Spain* 33 F7
Magangué, *Colombia* 124 B4
Magaria, *Niger* 83 C6
Magburaka, *S. Leone* 82 D2
Magdalen Is. = Madeleine, Îs. de la, *Canada* 103 C7
Magdalena, *Argentina* 126 D4
Magdalena, *Bolivia* 124 F6
Magdalena, *Mexico* 118 A2
Magdalena, *U.S.A.* 115 J10
Magdalena →, *Colombia* 122 B3
Magdalena →, *Mexico* 118 A2
Magdalena, B., *Mexico* 118 C2
Magdalena, Llano de la, *Mexico* 118 C2
Magdeburg, *Germany* 24 C7
Magdelaine Cays, *Australia* 94 B5
Magdub, *Sudan* 81 E2
Magee, *U.S.A.* 113 K10
Magelang, *Indonesia* 62 F4
Magellan's Str. = Magallanes, Estrecho de, *Chile* 122 J3
Magenta, *Italy* 28 C5
Magenta, L., *Australia* 93 F2
Magerøya, *Norway* 8 A21
Maggia →, *Switz.* 25 J4
Maggiorasca, Mte., *Italy* 28 D6
Maggiore, Lago, *Italy* 28 C5
Maghâgha, *Egypt* 80 B3
Maghama, *Mauritania* 82 B2
Magherafelt, *U.K.* 15 B5
Maghreb, *N. Afr.* 78 B5
Magione, *Italy* 29 E9
Magistralnyy, *Russia* 51 D11
Maglaj, *Bos.-H.* 42 F3
Magliano in Toscana, *Italy* 29 F8
Máglie, *Italy* 31 B11
Magnac-Laval, *France* 20 B5
Magnetic Pole (North) = North Magnetic Pole, *Canada* 4 B2
Magnetic Pole (South) = South Magnetic Pole, *Antarctica* 5 C9
Magnisía □, *Greece* 38 B5
Magnitogorsk, *Russia* 50 D6
Magnolia, *Ark., U.S.A.* 113 J8
Magnolia, *Miss., U.S.A.* 113 K9
Magny-en-Vexin, *France* 19 C8
Magog, *Canada* 103 C5
Magoro, *Uganda* 86 B3
Magosa = Famagusta, *Cyprus* 36 D12
Magouládhes, *Greece* 36 A3
Magoye, *Zambia* 87 F2
Magozal, *Mexico* 119 C5
Magpie, L., *Canada* 103 B7
Magrath, *Canada* 104 D6
Magre →, *Spain* 33 F4
Magrur, *Sudan* 81 E3
Magrur, Wadi →, *Sudan* 81 D2
Magta Lahjar, *Mauritania* 82 B2
Maguan, *China* 58 F5
Maguarinho, C., *Brazil* 125 D9
Magude, *Mozam.* 89 D5
Mağusa = Famagusta, *Cyprus* 36 D12
Maguse L., *Canada* 105 A9
Maguse Pt., *Canada* 105 A10
Magvana, *India* 68 H3
Magwe, *Burma* 67 J19
Magwe, *Sudan* 81 G3
Maha Sarakham, *Thailand* 64 D4
Mahābād, *Iran* 70 B5
Mahabharat Lekh, *Nepal* 69 E10
Mahabo, *Madag.* 89 C7
Mahadeo Hills, *India* 69 H8
Mahaffey, *U.S.A.* 110 F6
Mahagi, *Dem. Rep. of the Congo* 86 B3
Mahajamba →, *Madag.* 89 B8
Mahajamba, Helodranon' i, *Madag.* 89 B8
Mahajan, *India* 68 E5
Mahajanga, *Madag.* 89 B8
Mahajanga □, *Madag.* 89 B8
Mahajilo →, *Madag.* 89 B8
Mahakam →, *Indonesia* 62 E5
Mahalapye, *Botswana* 88 C4
Maḩallāt, *Iran* 71 C6
Māhān, *Iran* 71 D8
Mahan →, *India* 69 H10
Mahanadi →, *India* 67 J15
Mahananda →, *India* 69 G12
Mahanoro, *Madag.* 89 B8
Mahanoy City, *U.S.A.* 111 F8
Maharashtra □, *India* 66 J9
Mahari Mts., *Tanzania* 86 D3
Mahasham, W. →, *Egypt* 75 E3
Mahasoa, *Madag.* 89 C8
Mahasolo, *Madag.* 89 B8
Mahattat ash Shīdīyah, *Jordan* 75 F4
Mahattat 'Unayzah, *Jordan* 75 E4
Mahavavy →, *Madag.* 89 B8
Mahaxay, *Laos* 64 D5
Mahbubnagar, *India* 66 L10
Maḩḑah, *Oman* 71 E7
Mahdia, *Tunisia* 79 A8
Mahe, *India* 69 C8
Mahendragarh, *India* 68 E7
Mahenge, *Tanzania* 87 D4
Maheno, *N.Z.* 91 L3
Mahesana, *India* 68 H5
Maheshwar, *India* 68 H6
Mahgawan, *India* 69 F8
Mahi →, *India* 68 H5
Mahia Pen., *N.Z.* 91 H6
Mahilyow, *Belarus* 46 F6
Mahmiya, *Sudan* 81 D3
Mahmud Kot, *Pakistan* 68 D4
Mahmudia, *Romania* 43 E14
Mahmudiye, *Turkey* 39 B12
Mahmutbey, *Turkey* 41 E12
Mahnomen, *U.S.A.* 112 B7
Mahoba, *India* 69 G8
Mahón = Maó, *Spain* 37 B11
Mahone Bay, *Canada* 103 D7
Mahopac, *U.S.A.* 111 E11
Mahuta, *Nigeria* 83 C5
Mahuva, *India* 68 J4
Mahya Daği, *Turkey* 41 E11
Mai-Ndombe, L., *Dem. Rep. of the Congo* 84 E3
Mai-Sai, *Thailand* 58 G2
Maia, *Portugal* 34 D2
Maia, *Spain* 32 B3
Maials, *Spain* 32 D5
Maîche, *France* 19 E13
Maicurú →, *Brazil* 125 D8
Máida, *Italy* 31 D9
Maidan Khula, *Afghan.* 68 C3
Maidenhead, *U.K.* 13 F7
Maidstone, *Canada* 105 C7
Maidstone, *U.K.* 13 F8
Maiduguri, *Nigeria* 83 C7
Măieruş, *Romania* 43 E10
Maigatari, *Nigeria* 83 C6
Maignelay Montigny, *France* 19 C9
Maigo, *Phil.* 61 G5
Maigudo, *Ethiopia* 81 F4
Maihar, *India* 69 G9
Maijdi, *Bangla.* 67 H17
Maikala Ra., *India* 67 J12
Mailani, *India* 69 E9
Maillezais, *France* 20 B3
Mailsi, *Pakistan* 68 E5
Main →, *Germany* 25 F4
Main →, *U.K.* 15 B5
Mainburg, *Germany* 25 G7
Maine, *France* 18 D6
Maine □, *U.S.A.* 109 C11
Maine →, *Ireland* 15 D2
Maine-et-Loire □, *France* 18 E6
Maïne-Soroa, *Niger* 83 C7
Maingkwan, *Burma* 67 F20
Mainit, L., *Phil.* 61 G6
Mainland, *Orkney, U.K.* 14 C5
Mainland, *Shet., U.K.* 14 A7
Mainoru, *Australia* 94 A1
Mainpuri, *India* 69 F8
Maintal, *Germany* 25 E4
Maintenon, *France* 19 D8
Maintirano, *Madag.* 89 B7
Mainz, *Germany* 25 E4
Maipú, *Argentina* 126 D4
Maiquetía, *Venezuela* 124 A5
Máira →, *Italy* 28 D4
Mairabari, *India* 67 F18
Maisí, *Cuba* 121 B5
Maisí, Pta. de, *Cuba* 121 B5
Maitland, *N.S.W., Australia* 95 E5
Maitland, *S. Austral., Australia* 95 E2
Maitland →, *Canada* 110 C3
Maiyema, *Nigeria* 83 C5
Maiyuan, *China* 59 E11
Maiz, Is. del, *Nic.* 120 D3
Maizuru, *Japan* 55 G7
Majalengka, *Indonesia* 63 G13
Majene, *Indonesia* 63 E5
Majevica, *Bos.-H.* 42 F3
Maji, *Ethiopia* 81 F4
Majiang, *China* 58 D6
Majorca = Mallorca, *Spain* 37 B10
Maka, *Senegal* 82 C2
Makaha, *Zimbabwe* 89 B5
Makak, *Cameroon* 83 E7
Makalamabedi, *Botswana* 88 C3
Makale, *Indonesia* 63 E5
Makamba, *Burundi* 86 C2
Makari, *Cameroon* 83 C7
Makarikari = Makgadikgadi Salt Pans, *Botswana* 88 C4
Makarovo, *Russia* 51 D11
Makarska, *Croatia* 29 E14
Makaryev, *Russia* 48 B6
Makasar = Ujung Pandang, *Indonesia* 63 F5
Makasar, Selat, *Indonesia* 63 E5
Makasar, Str. of = Makasar, Selat, *Indonesia* 63 E5
Makat, *Kazakstan* 50 E6
Makedonija = Macedonia ■, *Europe* 40 E5
Makeni, *S. Leone* 82 D2
Makeyevka = Makiyivka, *Ukraine* 47 H9
Makgadikgadi Salt Pans, *Botswana* 88 C4
Makhachkala, *Russia* 49 J8
Makharadze = Ozurgeti, *Georgia* 49 K5
Makhmūr, *Iraq* 70 C4
Makian, *Indonesia* 63 D7
Makindu, *Kenya* 86 C4
Makinsk, *Kazakstan* 50 D8
Makiyivka, *Ukraine* 47 H9
Makkah, *Si. Arabia* 74 C2
Makkovik, *Canada* 103 A8
Makó, *Hungary* 42 D5
Mako, *Senegal* 82 C2
Makokou, *Gabon* 84 D2
Makongo, *Dem. Rep. of the Congo* 86 B2
Makoro, *Dem. Rep. of the Congo* 86 B2
Maków Mazowiecki, *Poland* 45 F8
Maków Podhalański, *Poland* 45 J6
Makrá, *Greece* 39 E7
Makrai, *India* 66 H10
Makran Coast Range, *Pakistan* 66 G4
Makrana, *India* 68 F6
Mákri, *Greece* 41 F9
Makriyialos, *Greece* 36 D7
Mākū, *Iran* 70 B5
Makunda, *Botswana* 88 C3
Makung, *Taiwan* 59 F12
Makurazaki, *Japan* 55 J5
Makurdi, *Nigeria* 83 D6
Makūyeh, *Iran* 71 D7
Makwassie, *S. Africa* 88 D4
Makwiro, *Zimbabwe* 89 B5
Mâl, *Mauritania* 82 B2
Mal B., *Ireland* 15 D2
Mala, Pta., *Panama* 120 E3
Mala Belozërka, *Ukraine* 47 J8
Mala Kapela, *Croatia* 29 D12
Mała Panew →, *Poland* 45 H4
Mala Vyska, *Ukraine* 47 H6
Malabang, *Phil.* 61 H6
Malabar Coast, *India* 66 P9
Malabo = Rey Malabo, *Eq. Guin.* 83 E6
Malabon, *Phil.* 61 D4
Malabu, *Nigeria* 83 D7
Malacca, Str. of, *Indonesia* 65 L3
Malacky, *Slovak Rep.* 27 C10
Malad City, *U.S.A.* 114 E7
Maladeta, *Spain* 32 C5
Maladzyechna, *Belarus* 46 E4
Málaga, *Spain* 35 J6
Málaga □, *Spain* 35 J6
Malagarasi, *Tanzania* 86 D3
Malagarasi →, *Tanzania* 86 D2
Malagasy Rep. = Madagascar ■, *Africa* 89 C8
Malagón, *Spain* 35 F7
Malagón →, *Spain* 35 H3
Malahide, *Ireland* 15 C5
Malaimbandy, *Madag.* 89 C8
Malakâl, *Sudan* 81 F3
Malakand, *Pakistan* 68 B4
Malakwal, *Pakistan* 68 C5
Malamala, *Indonesia* 63 E6
Malanda, *Australia* 94 B4
Malang, *Indonesia* 62 F4
Malangen, *Norway* 8 B18
Malanje, *Angola* 84 F3
Mälaren, *Sweden* 10 E11
Malargüe, *Argentina* 126 D2
Malartic, *Canada* 102 C4
Malaryta, *Belarus* 47 G3
Malatya, *Turkey* 70 B3
Malawi ■, *Africa* 87 E3
Malawi, L. = Nyasa, L., *Africa* 87 E3
Malay Pen., *Asia* 65 J3
Malaya Belozërka = Mala Belozërka, *Ukraine* 47 J8
Malaya Vishera, *Russia* 46 C7
Malaya Viska = Mala Vyska, *Ukraine* 47 H6
Malaybalay, *Phil.* 61 G6
Malāyer, *Iran* 71 C6
Malaysia ■, *Asia* 65 K4
Malazgirt, *Turkey* 70 B4
Malbaza, *Niger* 83 C6
Malbon, *Australia* 94 C3
Malbooma, *Australia* 95 E1
Malbork, *Poland* 44 D6
Malcésine, *Italy* 28 C7
Malchin, *Germany* 24 B8
Malchow, *Germany* 24 B8
Malcolm, *Australia* 93 E3
Malcolm, Pt., *Australia* 93 F3
Malczyce, *Poland* 45 G3
Maldah, *India* 69 G13
Maldegem, *Belgium* 17 C3
Malden, *Mass., U.S.A.* 111 D13
Malden, *Mo., U.S.A.* 113 G10
Malden I., *Kiribati* 97 H12
Maldives ■, *Ind. Oc.* 52 J11
Maldonado, *Uruguay* 127 C5
Maldonado, Punta, *Mexico* 119 D5
Malè, *Italy* 28 B7
Malé, *Maldives* 53 J11
Malé Karpaty, *Slovak Rep.* 27 C10
Maléa, Ákra, *Greece* 38 E5
Malegaon, *India* 66 J9
Malei, *Mozam.* 87 F4
Malek, *Sudan* 81 F3
Malek Kandī, *Iran* 70 B5
Malela, *Dem. Rep. of the Congo* 86 C2
Malema, *Mozam.* 87 E4
Máleme, *Greece* 36 D5
Maleny, *Australia* 95 D5
Målerås, *Sweden* 11 H9
Malerkotla, *India* 68 D6
Máles, *Greece* 36 D7
Malesherbes, *France* 19 D9
Maleshevska Planina, *Europe* 40 E7
Malesína, *Greece* 38 C5
Malestroit, *France* 18 E4
Malfa, *Italy* 31 D7
Malgobek, *Russia* 49 J7
Malgomaj, *Sweden* 8 D17
Malgrat = Malgrat de Mar, *Spain* 32 D7
Malgrat de Mar, *Spain* 32 D7
Malha, *Sudan* 81 D2
Malhargarh, *India* 68 G6
Malheur →, *U.S.A.* 114 D5
Malheur L., *U.S.A.* 114 E4
Mali, *Guinea* 82 C2
Mali ■, *Africa* 82 B4
Mali →, *Burma* 67 G20
Mali Kanal, *Serbia, Yug.* 42 E4
Mali Kyun, *Burma* 64 F2
Malibu, *U.S.A.* 117 L8
Maliku, *Indonesia* 63 E6
Malili, *Indonesia* 63 E6
Målilla, *Sweden* 11 G9
Malimba, Mts., *Dem. Rep. of the Congo* 86 D2
Malin Hd., *Ireland* 15 A4
Malin Pen., *Ireland* 15 A4
Malindi, *Kenya* 86 C5
Malines = Mechelen, *Belgium* 17 C4
Malino, *Indonesia* 63 D6
Malinyi, *Tanzania* 87 D4
Malipo, *China* 58 F5
Maliq, *Albania* 40 F4
Malita, *Phil.* 63 C7
Maliwun, *Burma* 62 B1
Maliya, *India* 68 H4
Maljenik, *Serbia, Yug.* 40 C5
Malkara, *Turkey* 41 F10
Małkinia Górna, *Poland* 45 F9
Malko Tŭrnovo, *Bulgaria* 41 E11
Mallacoota Inlet, *Australia* 95 F4
Mallaig, *U.K.* 14 D3
Mallaoua, *Niger* 83 C6
Mallawan, *India* 69 F9
Mallawi, *Egypt* 80 B3
Mallemort, *France* 21 E9
Málles Venosta, *Italy* 28 B7
Mállia, *Greece* 36 D7
Mallión, Kólpos, *Greece* 36 D7
Mallorca, *Spain* 37 B10
Mallorytown, *Canada* 111 B9
Mallow, *Ireland* 15 D3
Malmbäck, *Sweden* 11 G8
Malmberget, *Sweden* 8 C19
Malmédy, *Belgium* 17 D6
Malmesbury, *S. Africa* 88 E2
Malmköping, *Sweden* 10 E10
Malmö, *Sweden* 11 J6
Malmslätt, *Sweden* 11 F9
Malmyzh, *Russia* 48 B10
Malnaş, *Romania* 43 D10
Malo Konare, *Bulgaria* 41 D8
Maloarkhangelsk, *Russia* 47 F9
Malolos, *Phil.* 63 B6
Malombe L., *Malawi* 87 E4
Małomice, *Poland* 45 G2
Malomir, *Bulgaria* 41 D10
Malone, *U.S.A.* 111 B10
Malong, *China* 58 E4
Małopolskie □, *Poland* 45 J7
Malorad, *Bulgaria* 40 C7
Måløy, *Norway* 9 F11
Maloyaroslovets, *Russia* 46 E9
Malpartida, *Spain* 35 F4
Malpaso, *Canary Is.* 37 G1
Malpelo, I. de, *Colombia* 124 C2
Malpica de Bergantiños, *Spain* 34 B2
Malpur, *India* 68 H5
Malpura, *India* 68 F6
Mals = Málles Venosta, *Italy* 28 B7
Malta, *Idaho, U.S.A.* 114 E7
Malta, *Mont., U.S.A.* 114 B10
Malta ■, *Europe* 36 D2
Maltahöhe, *Namibia* 88 C2
Maltepe, *Turkey* 41 F13
Malton, *Canada* 110 C5
Malton, *U.K.* 12 C7
Maluku, *Indonesia* 63 E7
Maluku □, *Indonesia* 63 E7
Maluku Sea = Molucca Sea, *Indonesia* 63 E6
Malumfashi, *Nigeria* 83 C6
Malung, *Sweden* 10 D7
Malungsfors, *Sweden* 10 D7
Maluwe, *Ghana* 82 D4
Malvan, *India* 66 L8
Malvern, *U.S.A.* 113 H8
Malvern Hills, *U.K.* 13 E5
Malvinas, Is. = Falkland Is. □, *Atl. Oc.* 128 G5
Malý Dunaj →, *Slovak Rep.* 27 D11
Malya, *Tanzania* 86 C3
Malyn, *Ukraine* 47 G5
Malyy Lyakhovskiy, Ostrov, *Russia* 51 B15
Mama, *Russia* 51 D12
Mamadysh, *Russia* 48 C10
Mamanguape, *Brazil* 125 E11
Mamarr Mitlā, *Egypt* 75 E1
Mamasa, *Indonesia* 63 E5
Mambasa, *Dem. Rep. of the Congo* 86 B2
Mamberamo →, *Indonesia* 63 E9
Mambilima Falls, *Zambia* 87 E2
Mambirima, *Dem. Rep. of the Congo* 87 E2
Mambo, *Tanzania* 86 C4
Mambrui, *Kenya* 86 C5
Mamburao, *Phil.* 61 E4
Mameigwess L., *Canada* 102 B2
Mamers, *France* 18 D7
Mamfé, *Cameroon* 83 D6
Mammoth, *U.S.A.* 115 K8
Mammoth Cave National Park, *U.S.A.* 108 G3
Mamoré →, *Bolivia* 122 E4
Mamou, *Guinea* 82 C2
Mampatá, *Guinea-Biss.* 82 C2
Mampikony, *Madag.* 89 B8
Mampong, *Ghana* 83 D4
Mamry, Jezioro, *Poland* 44 D8
Mamuju, *Indonesia* 63 E5
Mamuno, *Botswana* 88 C3
Mamuras, *Albania* 40 E3
Man, *Ivory C.* 82 D3
Man, I. of, *U.K.* 12 C3
Man-Bazar, *India* 69 H12
Man Na, *Burma* 67 H20
Mana →, *Fr. Guiana* 125 B8
Manaar, G. of = Mannar, G. of, *Asia* 66 Q11
Manacapuru, *Brazil* 124 D6
Manacor, *Spain* 37 B10
Manado, *Indonesia* 63 D6
Managua, *Nic.* 120 D2
Managua, L. de, *Nic.* 120 D2
Manakara, *Madag.* 89 C8
Manali, *India* 68 C7
Manama = Al Manāmah, *Bahrain* 71 E6
Manambao →, *Madag.* 89 B7
Manambato, *Madag.* 89 A8
Manambolo →, *Madag.* 89 B7
Manambolosy, *Madag.* 89 B8
Mananara, *Madag.* 89 B8
Mananara →, *Madag.* 89 C8
Mananjary, *Madag.* 89 C8
Manankoro, *Mali* 82 C3
Manantenina, *Madag.* 89 C8
Manaos = Manaus, *Brazil* 124 D7
Manapire →, *Venezuela* 124 B5
Manapouri, *N.Z.* 91 L1
Manapouri, L., *N.Z.* 91 L1
Manaqil, *Sudan* 81 E3
Manār, Jabal, *Yemen* 74 E3
Manaravolo, *Madag.* 89 C8
Manas, *China* 60 B3
Manas →, *India* 67 F17
Manaslu, *Nepal* 69 E11
Manasquan, *U.S.A.* 111 F10
Manassa, *U.S.A.* 115 H11
Manaung, *Burma* 67 K18
Manaus, *Brazil* 124 D7
Manavgat, *Turkey* 72 D4
Manawan L., *Canada* 105 B8
Manay, *Phil.* 61 H7
Manbij, *Syria* 70 B3
Mancha Real, *Spain* 35 H7
Manche □, *France* 18 C5
Manchegorsk, *Russia* 50 C4
Manchester, *U.K.* 12 D5
Manchester, *Calif., U.S.A.* 116 G3
Manchester, *Conn., U.S.A.* 111 E12
Manchester, *Ga., U.S.A.* 109 J3
Manchester, *Iowa, U.S.A.* 112 D9
Manchester, *Ky., U.S.A.* 108 G4
Manchester, *N.H., U.S.A.* 111 D13
Manchester, *N.Y., U.S.A.* 110 D7
Manchester, *Pa., U.S.A.* 111 F8
Manchester, *Tenn., U.S.A.* 109 H2
Manchester, *Vt., U.S.A.* 111 C11
Manchester L., *Canada* 105 A7
Manchhar L., *Pakistan* 68 F2
Manchuria = Dongbei, *China* 57 D13
Manchurian Plain, *China* 52 E16
Manciano, *Italy* 29 F8
Mancifa, *Ethiopia* 81 F5
Mand →, *India* 69 J10
Mand →, *Iran* 71 D7
Manda, *Ludewe, Tanzania* 87 E3
Manda, *Mbeya, Tanzania* 86 D3
Manda, *Mbeya, Tanzania* 87 D3
Mandabé, *Madag.* 89 C7
Mandaguari, *Brazil* 127 A5
Mandah = Töhöm, *Mongolia* 56 B5
Mandal, *Norway* 9 G12
Mandala, Puncak, *Indonesia* 63 E10
Mandalay, *Burma* 67 J20
Mandale = Mandalay, *Burma* 67 J20
Mandalgarh, *India* 68 G6
Mandalgovi, *Mongolia* 56 B4
Mandalī, *Iraq* 70 C5
Mandan, *U.S.A.* 112 B4
Mandaon, *Phil.* 61 E5

Mandar, Teluk, Indonesia 63 E5
Mándas, Italy 30 C2
Mandaue, Phil. 61 F5
Mandelieu-la-Napoule, France 21 E10
Mandera, Kenya 86 B5
Mandi, India 68 D7
Mandi Dabwali, India 68 E6
Mandiana, Guinea 82 C3
Mandimba, Mozam. 87 E4
Mandioli, Indonesia 63 E7
Mandla, India 69 H9
Mandø, Denmark 11 J2
Mandorah, Australia 92 B5
Mandoto, Madag. 89 B8
Mandoúdhion, Greece 38 C5
Mándra, Greece 38 C5
Mandra, Pakistan 68 C5
Mandrákhi, Greece 39 E9
Mandrare →, Madag. 89 D8
Mandritsara, Madag. 89 B8
Mandronarivo, Madag. 89 C8
Mandsaur, India 68 G6
Mandurah, Australia 93 F2
Mandúria, Italy 31 B10
Mandvi, India 68 H3
Mandya, India 66 N10
Mandzai, Pakistan 68 D2
Mané, Burkina Faso 83 C4
Maneh, Iran 71 B8
Manengouba, Mts., Cameroon 83 E6
Manera, Madag. 89 C7
Manérbio, Italy 28 C7
Maneroo Cr. →, Australia 94 C3
Manfalût, Egypt 80 B3
Manfredónia, Italy 29 G12
Manfredónia, G. di, Italy 29 G13
Manga, Burkina Faso 83 C4
Manga, Niger 83 C7
Mangabeiras, Chapada das, Brazil 125 F9
Mangalia, Romania 43 G13
Mangalore, India 66 N9
Mangan, India 69 F13
Mangaung, S. Africa 85 K5
Mangawan, India 69 G9
Mangaweka, N.Z. 91 H5
Manggar, Indonesia 62 E3
Manggawitu, Indonesia 63 E8
Mangindrano, Madag. 89 A8
Mangkalihat, Tanjung, Indonesia 63 D5
Mangla, Pakistan 68 C5
Mangla Dam, Pakistan 69 C5
Manglaur, India 68 E7
Mangnai, China 60 C4
Mango, Togo 83 C5
Mangoche, Malawi 87 E4
Mangoky →, Madag. 89 C7
Mangole, Indonesia 63 E6
Mangombe, Dem. Rep. of the Congo 86 C2
Mangonui, N.Z. 91 F4
Mangoro →, Madag. 89 B8
Mangrol, Mad. P., India 68 J4
Mangrol, Raj., India 68 G6
Mangualde, Portugal 34 E3
Mangueira, L. da, Brazil 127 C5
Mangum, U.S.A. 113 H5
Mangyshlak Poluostrov, Kazakstan 50 E6
Manhattan, U.S.A. 112 F6
Manhiça, Mozam. 89 D5
Mania →, Madag. 89 B8
Maniago, Italy 29 B9
Manica, Mozam. 89 B5
Manica □, Mozam. 89 B5
Manicaland □, Zimbabwe 87 F3
Manicoré, Brazil 124 E6
Manicouagan →, Canada 103 C6
Manicouagan, Rés., Canada 103 B6
Maniema □, Dem. Rep. of the Congo 86 C2
Manīfah, Si. Arabia 71 E6
Manifold, C., Australia 94 C5
Maniganggo, China 58 B2
Manigotagan, Canada 105 C9
Manigotagan →, Canada 105 C9
Manihari, India 69 G12
Manihiki, Cook Is. 97 J11
Manika, Plateau de la, Dem. Rep. of the Congo 87 E2
Manikpur, India 69 G9
Manila, Phil. 61 D4
Manila, U.S.A. 114 F9
Manila B., Phil. 61 D4
Manilla, Australia 95 E5
Manimpé, Mali 82 C3
Maningrida, Australia 94 A1
Maninian, Ivory C. 82 C3
Manipur □, India 67 G19
Manipur →, Burma 67 H19
Manisa, Turkey 39 C9
Manisa □, Turkey 39 C9
Manistee, U.S.A. 108 C2
Manistee →, U.S.A. 108 C2
Manistique, U.S.A. 108 C2
Manito L., Canada 105 C7
Manitoba □, Canada 105 B9
Manitoba, L., Canada 105 C9
Manitou, Canada 105 D9
Manitou, L., Canada 103 B6
Manitou Is., U.S.A. 108 C3
Manitou Springs, U.S.A. 112 F2
Manitoulin I., Canada 102 C3
Manitouwadge, Canada 102 C2
Manitowoc, U.S.A. 108 C2
Manizales, Colombia 124 B3
Manja, Madag. 89 C7
Manjacaze, Mozam. 89 C5
Manjakandriana, Madag. 89 B8
Manjhand, Pakistan 68 G3
Manjil, Iran 71 B6
Manjimup, Australia 93 F2
Manjra →, India 66 K10
Mankato, Kans., U.S.A. 112 F5
Mankato, Minn., U.S.A. 112 C8
Mankayane, Swaziland 89 D5
Mankera, Pakistan 68 D4
Mankim, Cameroon 83 D7
Mankono, Ivory C. 82 D3
Mankota, Canada 105 D7
Manlay = Üydzin, Mongolia 56 B4
Manlleu, Spain 32 C7
Manmad, India 66 J9
Mann Ranges, Australia 93 E5
Manna, Indonesia 62 E2
Mannahill, Australia 95 E3
Mannar, Sri Lanka 66 Q11
Mannar, G. of, Asia 66 Q11
Mannar I., Sri Lanka 66 Q11
Mannheim, Germany 25 F4
Manning, Canada 104 B5
Manning, Oreg., U.S.A. 116 E3
Manning, S.C., U.S.A. 109 J5
Manning Prov. Park, Canada 104 D4
Mannu →, Italy 30 C2
Mannu, C., Italy 30 B1
Mannum, Australia 95 E2
Mano, S. Leone 82 D2
Mano →, Liberia 82 D2
Mano River, Liberia 82 D2
Manoharpur, India 69 H11
Manokwari, Indonesia 63 E8
Manolás, Greece 38 C3
Manombo, Madag. 89 C7
Manono, Dem. Rep. of the Congo 86 D2
Manoppello, Italy 29 F11
Manosque, France 21 E9
Manotick, Canada 111 A9
Manouane →, Canada 103 C5
Manouane, L., Canada 103 B5
Manp'o, N. Korea 57 D14
Manpojin = Manp'o, N. Korea 57 D14
Manpur, Mad. P., India 68 H6
Manpur, Mad. P., India 69 H10
Manresa, Spain 32 D6
Mansa, Gujarat, India 68 H5
Mansa, Punjab, India 68 E6
Mansa, Zambia 87 E2
Månsåsen, Sweden 10 A8
Mansehra, Pakistan 68 B5
Mansel I., Canada 101 B11
Mansfield, Australia 95 F4
Mansfield, U.K. 12 D6
Mansfield, La., U.S.A. 113 J8
Mansfield, Mass., U.S.A. 111 D13
Mansfield, Ohio, U.S.A. 110 F2
Mansfield, Pa., U.S.A. 110 E7
Mansfield, Mt., U.S.A. 111 B12
Mansilla de las Mulas, Spain 34 C5
Mansle, France 20 C4
Mansoa, Guinea-Biss. 82 C1
Manson Creek, Canada 104 B4
Manta, Ecuador 124 D2
Mantalingajan, Mt., Phil. 61 G2
Mantare, Tanzania 86 C3
Manteca, U.S.A. 116 H5
Manteo, U.S.A. 109 H8
Mantes-la-Jolie, France 19 D8
Manthani, India 66 K11
Manti, U.S.A. 114 G8
Mantiqueira, Serra da, Brazil 127 A7
Manton, U.S.A. 108 C3
Mantorp, Sweden 11 F9
Mántova, Italy 28 C7
Mänttä, Finland 9 E21
Mantua = Mántova, Italy 28 C7
Manturovo, Russia 48 A7
Manu, Peru 124 F4
Manu →, Peru 124 F4
Manua Is., Amer. Samoa 91 B14
Manuel Alves →, Brazil 125 F9
Manui, Indonesia 63 E6
Manukau, N.Z. 91 G5
Manuripi →, Bolivia 124 F5
Many, U.S.A. 113 K8
Manyara, L., Tanzania 86 C4
Manyas, Turkey 41 F11
Manych →, Russia 49 G5
Manych-Gudilo, Ozero, Russia 49 G6
Manyonga →, Tanzania 86 C3
Manyoni, Tanzania 86 D3
Manzai, Pakistan 68 C4
Manzala, Bahra el, Egypt 80 H7
Manzanares, Spain 35 F7
Manzaneda, Spain 34 C3
Manzanillo, Cuba 120 B4
Manzanillo, Mexico 118 D4
Manzanillo, Pta., Panama 120 E4
Manzano Mts., U.S.A. 115 J10
Manzarīyeh, Iran 71 C6
Manzhouli, China 60 B6
Manzini, Swaziland 89 D5
Mao, Chad 79 F9
Maó, Spain 37 B11
Maoke, Pegunungan, Indonesia 63 E9
Maolin, China 57 C12
Maoming, China 59 G8
Maopi T'ou, China 59 G13
Maouri, Dallol →, Niger 83 C5
Maoxian, China 58 B4
Maoxing, China 57 B13
Mapam Yumco, China 60 C3
Mapastepec, Mexico 119 D6
Mapia, Kepulauan, Indonesia 63 D8
Mapimí, Mexico 118 B4
Mapimí, Bolsón de, Mexico 118 B4
Maping, China 59 B9
Mapinga, Tanzania 86 D4
Mapinhane, Mozam. 89 C6
Maple Creek, Canada 105 D7
Maple Valley, U.S.A. 116 C4
Mapleton, U.S.A. 114 D2
Mapuera →, Brazil 124 D7
Mapulanguene, Mozam. 89 C5
Maputo, Mozam. 89 D5
Maputo □, Mozam. 89 D5
Maputo, B. de, Mozam. 89 D5
Maqiaohe, China 57 B16
Maqnā, Si. Arabia 70 D2
Maqueda, Spain 34 E6
Maquela do Zombo, Angola 84 F3
Maquinchao, Argentina 128 E3
Maquoketa, U.S.A. 112 D9
Mar, Serra do, Brazil 127 B6
Mar Chiquita, L., Argentina 126 C3
Mar del Plata, Argentina 126 D4
Mar Menor, Spain 33 H4
Mara, Tanzania 86 C3
Mara □, Tanzania 86 C3
Maraã, Brazil 124 D5
Marabá, Brazil 125 E9
Maracá, I. de, Brazil 125 C8
Maracaibo, Venezuela 124 A4
Maracaibo, L. de, Venezuela 122 C3
Maracaju, Brazil 127 A4
Maracay, Venezuela 124 A5
Maracena, Spain 35 H7
Maradi, Niger 83 C6
Marāgheh, Iran 70 B5
Marāh, Si. Arabia 70 E5
Marajó, I. de, Brazil 122 D6
Marākand, Iran 70 B5
Maralal, Kenya 86 B4
Maralinga, Australia 93 F5
Maramaraereğlisi, Turkey 41 F11
Marampa, S. Leone 82 D2
Maramureş □, Romania 43 C9
Maran, Malaysia 65 L4
Marana, U.S.A. 115 K8
Maranboy, Australia 92 B5
Maranchón, Spain 32 D2
Marand, Iran 70 B5
Marang, Malaysia 65 K4
Maranguape, Brazil 125 D11
Maranhão = São Luís, Brazil 125 D10
Maranhão □, Brazil 125 E9
Marano, L. di, Italy 29 C10
Maranoa →, Australia 95 D4
Marañón →, Peru 122 D3
Marão, Mozam. 89 C5
Maraş = Kahramanmaraş, Turkey 70 B3
Mărăşeşti, Romania 43 E12
Maratea, Italy 31 C8
Marateca, Portugal 35 G2
Marathasa □, Cyprus 36 E11
Marathókambos, Greece 39 D8
Marathon, Australia 94 C3
Marathon, Canada 102 C2
Marathón, Greece 38 C5
Marathon, N.Y., U.S.A. 111 D8
Marathon, Tex., U.S.A. 113 K3
Marathóvouno, Cyprus 36 D12
Maratua, Indonesia 63 D5
Maravatío, Mexico 118 D4
Marawi City, Phil. 61 G6
Marāwih, U.A.E. 71 E7
Marbella, Spain 35 J6
Marble Bar, Australia 92 D2
Marble Falls, U.S.A. 113 K5
Marblehead, U.S.A. 111 D14
Marburg, Germany 24 E4
Marcal →, Hungary 42 C2
Marcali, Hungary 42 D2
Marcaria, Italy 28 C7
Mărcăuţi, Moldova 43 B12
March, U.K. 13 E8
Marche, France 20 B5
Marche □, Italy 29 E10
Marche-en-Famenne, Belgium 17 D5
Marchena, Spain 35 H5
Marches = Marche □, Italy 29 E10
Marciana Marina, Italy 28 F7
Marcianise, Italy 31 A7
Marcigny, France 19 F11
Marcillat-en-Combraille, France 19 F9
Marck, France 19 B8
Marckolsheim, France 19 D14
Marco, U.S.A. 109 N5
Marcos Juárez, Argentina 126 C3
Mărculeşti, Moldova 43 C13
Marcus I. = Minami-Tori-Shima, Pac. Oc. 96 E7
Marcus Necker Ridge, Pac. Oc. 96 F9
Marcy, Mt., U.S.A. 111 B11
Mardan, Pakistan 68 B5
Mardin, Turkey 70 B4
Mårdsjön, Sweden 10 A9
Marécchia →, Italy 29 D9
Maree, L., U.K. 14 D3
Mareeba, Australia 94 B4
Mareetsane, S. Africa 88 D4
Maremma, Italy 29 F8
Maréna, Mali 82 C2
Maréna, Mali 82 C3
Marengo, U.S.A. 112 E8
Marennes, France 20 C2
Marenyi, Kenya 86 C4
Marerano, Madag. 89 C7
Marèttimo, Italy 30 E5
Mareuil, France 20 C4
Marfa, U.S.A. 113 K2
Marfa Pt., Malta 36 D1
Marganets = Marhanets, Ukraine 47 J8
Margaret →, Australia 92 C4
Margaret Bay, Canada 104 C3
Margaret L., Canada 104 B5
Margaret River, Australia 93 F2
Margarita, I. de, Venezuela 122 B4
Margarítion, Greece 38 B2
Margaritovo, Russia 54 C7
Margate, S. Africa 89 E5
Margate, U.K. 13 F9
Margeride, Mts. de la, France 20 D7
Margherita di Savóia, Italy 31 A9
Marghita, Romania 42 C7
Margonin, Poland 45 F4
Margosatubig, Phil. 61 H5
Mārgow, Dasht-e, Afghan. 66 D3
Marguerite, Canada 104 C4
Marhanets, Ukraine 47 J8
Mari El □, Russia 48 B8
Mari Indus, Pakistan 68 C4
Mari Republic = Mari El □, Russia 48 B8
María, Sa. de, Spain 33 H2
María Elena, Chile 126 A2
María Grande, Argentina 126 C4
Maria I., N. Terr., Australia 94 A2
Maria I., Tas., Australia 94 G4
Maria van Diemen, C., N.Z. 91 F4
Mariager, Denmark 11 H3
Mariager Fjord, Denmark 11 H4
Mariakani, Kenya 86 C4
Marian, Australia 94 C4
Marian L., Canada 104 A5
Mariana Trench, Pac. Oc. 52 H18
Marianao, Cuba 120 B3
Marianna, Ark., U.S.A. 113 H9
Marianna, Fla., U.S.A. 109 K3
Mariannelund, Sweden 11 G9
Mariánské Lázně, Czech Rep. 26 B5
Marias →, U.S.A. 114 C8
Mariato, Punta, Panama 120 E3
Mariazell, Austria 26 D8
Maribo, Denmark 11 K5
Maribor, Slovenia 29 B12
Marico →, Africa 88 C4
Maricopa, Ariz., U.S.A. 115 K7
Maricopa, Calif., U.S.A. 117 K7
Marīdī, Sudan 81 G2
Marīdī, Wadi →, Sudan 81 F2
Marié →, Brazil 124 D5
Marie Byrd Land, Antarctica 5 D14
Marie-Galante, Guadeloupe 121 C7
Mariecourt = Kangiqsujuaq, Canada 101 B12
Mariefred, Sweden 10 E11
Marieholm, Sweden 11 J7
Mariembourg, Belgium 17 D4
Marienbad = Mariánské Lázně, Czech Rep. 26 B5
Marienberg, Germany 24 E9
Mariental, Namibia 88 C2
Marienville, U.S.A. 110 E5
Mariestad, Sweden 11 F7
Marietta, Ga., U.S.A. 109 J3
Marietta, Ohio, U.S.A. 108 F5
Marieville, Canada 111 A11
Mariga →, Nigeria 83 C6
Marignane, France 21 E9
Marihatag, Phil. 61 G7
Mariinsk, Russia 50 D9
Mariinskiy Posad, Russia 48 B8
Marijampolė, Lithuania 9 J20
Marijampolės □, Lithuania 44 D10
Marília, Brazil 127 A6
Marín, Spain 34 C2
Marina, U.S.A. 116 J5
Marinduque, Phil. 63 B6
Marine City, U.S.A. 110 D2
Marineo, Italy 30 E6
Marinette, U.S.A. 108 C2
Maringá, Brazil 127 A5
Marinha Grande, Portugal 34 F2
Marino, Italy 29 G9
Marion, Ala., U.S.A. 109 J2
Marion, Ill., U.S.A. 113 G10
Marion, Ind., U.S.A. 108 E3
Marion, Iowa, U.S.A. 112 D9
Marion, Kans., U.S.A. 112 F6
Marion, N.C., U.S.A. 109 H5
Marion, Ohio, U.S.A. 108 E4
Marion, S.C., U.S.A. 109 H6
Marion, Va., U.S.A. 109 G5
Marion, L., U.S.A. 109 J5
Mariposa, U.S.A. 116 H7
Mariscal Estigarribia, Paraguay 126 A3
Maritime Alps = Maritimes, Alpes, Europe 21 D11
Maritimes, Alpes, Europe 21 D11
Maritsa = Évros →, Greece 72 B2
Maritsá, Greece 36 C10
Mariupol, Ukraine 47 J9
Marīvān, Iran 70 C5
Marj 'Uyūn, Lebanon 75 B4
Marka, Si. Arabia 80 D5
Markam, China 58 C2
Markaryd, Sweden 11 H7
Markazī □, Iran 71 C6
Markdale, Canada 110 B4
Marked Tree, U.S.A. 113 H9
Markelsdorfer Huk, Germany 24 A7
Market Drayton, U.K. 12 E5
Market Harborough, U.K. 13 E7
Market Rasen, U.K. 12 D7
Markham, Canada 110 C5
Markham, Mt., Antarctica 5 E11
Marki, Poland 45 F8
Markkleeberg, Germany 24 D8
Markleeville, U.S.A. 116 G7
Markoupoulon, Greece 38 D5
Markovac, Serbia, Yug. 40 B5
Markovo, Russia 51 C17
Markoye, Burkina Faso 83 C5
Marks, Russia 48 E8
Marksville, U.S.A. 113 K8
Markt Schwaben, Germany 25 G7
Marktoberdorf, Germany 25 H6
Marktredwitz, Germany 25 E8
Marl, Germany 24 D3
Marla, Australia 95 D1
Marlbank, Canada 110 B7
Marlboro, Mass., U.S.A. 111 D13
Marlboro, N.Y., U.S.A. 111 E11
Marlborough, Australia 94 C4
Marlborough, U.K. 13 F6
Marlborough Downs, U.K. 13 F6
Marle, France 19 C10
Marlin, U.S.A. 113 K6
Marlow, Germany 24 A8
Marlow, U.S.A. 113 H6
Marmagao, India 66 M8
Marmande, France 20 D4
Marmara, Turkey 41 F11
Marmara, Sea of = Marmara Denizi, Turkey 41 F12
Marmara Denizi, Turkey 41 F12
Marmara Gölü, Turkey 39 C10
Marmaris, Turkey 39 E10
Marmaris Limanı, Turkey 39 E10
Marmion, Mt., Australia 93 E2
Marmion L., Canada 102 C1
Marmolada, Mte., Italy 29 B8
Marmolejo, Spain 35 G6
Marmora, Canada 102 D4
Mármora, La, Italy 30 C2
Marnay, France 19 E12
Marne, Germany 24 B5
Marne □, France 19 D11
Marne →, France 19 D9
Marneuli, Georgia 49 K7
Maroala, Madag. 89 B8
Maroantsetra, Madag. 89 B8
Maroelaboom, Namibia 88 B2
Marofandilia, Madag. 89 C7
Marolambo, Madag. 89 C8
Maromandia, Madag. 89 A8
Marondera, Zimbabwe 87 F3
Maroni →, Fr. Guiana 125 B8
Marónia, Greece 41 F9
Maronne →, France 20 C5
Maroochydore, Australia 95 D5
Maroona, Australia 95 F3
Maros →, Hungary 42 D5
Marosakoa, Madag. 89 B8
Maroseranana, Madag. 89 B8
Maróstica, Italy 29 C8
Marotandrano, Madag. 89 B8
Marotaolano, Madag. 89 A8
Maroua, Cameroon 83 C7
Marovato, Madag. 89 B8
Marovoay, Madag. 89 B8
Marquard, S. Africa 88 D4
Marquesas Is. = Marquises, Is., Pac. Oc. 97 H14
Marquette, U.S.A. 108 B2
Marquise, France 19 B8
Marquises, Is., Pac. Oc. 97 H14
Marra, Djebel, Sudan 79 F10
Marra, Gebel, Sudan 81 F2
Marracuene, Mozam. 89 D5
Marradi, Italy 29 D8
Marrakech, Morocco 78 B4
Marratxi, Spain 32 F7
Marrawah, Australia 94 G3
Marree, Australia 95 D2
Marrero, U.S.A. 113 L9
Marrimane, Mozam. 89 C5
Marromeu, Mozam. 89 B6
Marroquí, Punta, Spain 35 K5
Marrowie Cr. →, Australia 95 E4
Marrubane, Mozam. 87 F4
Marrúbiu, Italy 30 C1
Marrupa, Mozam. 87 E4
Mars Hill, U.S.A. 109 B12
Marsá 'Alam, Egypt 80 B3
Marsá Matrûh, Egypt 80 A2
Marsá Sha'b, Sudan 80 C4
Marsabit, Kenya 86 B4
Marsala, Italy 30 E5
Marsalforn, Malta 36 C1
Mârşani, Romania 43 F9
Marsberg, Germany 24 D4
Marsciano, Italy 29 F9
Marsden, Australia 95 E4
Marseillan, France 20 E7
Marseille, France 21 E9
Marseilles = Marseille, France 21 E9
Marsh I., U.S.A. 113 L9
Marshall, Liberia 82 D2
Marshall, Ark., U.S.A. 113 H8
Marshall, Mich., U.S.A. 108 D3
Marshall, Minn., U.S.A. 112 C7
Marshall, Mo., U.S.A. 112 F8
Marshall, Tex., U.S.A. 113 J7
Marshall →, Australia 94 C2
Marshall Is. ■, Pac. Oc. 96 G9
Marshalltown, U.S.A. 112 D8
Marshbrook, Zimbabwe 89 B5
Marshfield, Mo., U.S.A. 113 G8
Marshfield, Vt., U.S.A. 111 B12
Marshfield, Wis., U.S.A. 112 C9
Marshūn, Iran 71 B6

Mársico Nuovo, *Italy* 31 B8
Märsta, *Sweden* 10 E11
Marstal, *Denmark* 11 K4
Marstrand, *Sweden* 11 G5
Mart, *U.S.A.* 113 K6
Marta →, *Italy* 29 F8
Martaban, *Burma* 67 L20
Martaban, G. of, *Burma* 67 L20
Martano, *Italy* 31 B11
Martapura, *Kalimantan, Indonesia* 62 E4
Martapura, *Sumatera, Indonesia* 62 E2
Marte, *Nigeria* 83 C7
Martel, *France* 20 D5
Martelange, *Belgium* 17 E5
Martellago, *Italy* 29 C9
Martés, Sierra, *Spain* 33 F4
Martfű, *Hungary* 42 C5
Martha's Vineyard, *U.S.A.* 111 E14
Martigné-Ferchaud, *France* 18 E5
Martigny, *Switz.* 25 J3
Martigues, *France* 21 E9
Martin, *Slovak Rep.* 27 B11
Martin, *S. Dak., U.S.A.* 112 D4
Martin, *Tenn., U.S.A.* 113 G10
Martín →, *Spain* 32 D4
Martin, L., *U.S.A.* 109 J3
Martina Franca, *Italy* 31 B10
Martinborough, *N.Z.* 91 J5
Martinez, *Calif., U.S.A.* 116 G4
Martinez, *Ga., U.S.A.* 109 J4
Martinique ■, *W. Indies* 121 D7
Martinique Passage, *W. Indies* 121 C7
Martínon, *Greece* 38 C5
Martinópolis, *Brazil* 127 A5
Martins Ferry, *U.S.A.* 110 F4
Martinsberg, *Austria* 26 C8
Martinsburg, *Pa., U.S.A.* 110 F6
Martinsburg, *W. Va., U.S.A.* 108 F7
Martinsicuro, *Italy* 29 F10
Martinsville, *Ind., U.S.A.* 108 F2
Martinsville, *Va., U.S.A.* 109 G6
Marton, *N.Z.* 91 J5
Martorell, *Spain* 32 D6
Martos, *Spain* 35 H7
Martuni, *Armenia* 49 K7
Maru, *Nigeria* 83 C6
Marudi, *Malaysia* 62 D4
Maruf, *Afghan.* 66 D5
Marugame, *Japan* 55 G6
Marunga, *Angola* 88 B3
Marungu, Mts., *Dem. Rep. of the Congo* 86 D3
Marv Dasht, *Iran* 71 D7
Marvast, *Iran* 71 D7
Marvejols, *France* 20 D7
Marvel Loch, *Australia* 93 F2
Marwar, *India* 68 G5
Mary, *Turkmenistan* 50 F7
Maryborough = Port Laoise, *Ireland* 15 C4
Maryborough, *Queens., Australia* 95 D5
Maryborough, *Vic., Australia* 95 F3
Maryfield, *Canada* 105 D8
Maryland □, *U.S.A.* 108 F7
Maryland Junction, *Zimbabwe* 87 F3
Maryport, *U.K.* 12 C4
Mary's Harbour, *Canada* 103 B8
Marystown, *Canada* 103 C8
Marysville, *Canada* 104 D5
Marysville, *Calif., U.S.A.* 116 F5
Marysville, *Kans., U.S.A.* 112 F6
Marysville, *Mich., U.S.A.* 110 D2
Marysville, *Ohio, U.S.A.* 108 E4
Marysville, *Wash., U.S.A.* 116 B4
Maryville, *Mo., U.S.A.* 112 E7
Maryville, *Tenn., U.S.A.* 109 H4
Marzūq, *Libya* 79 C8
Masahunga, *Tanzania* 86 C3
Masai Steppe, *Tanzania* 86 C4
Masaka, *Uganda* 86 C3
Masalembo, Kepulauan, *Indonesia* 62 F4
Masalima, Kepulauan, *Indonesia* 62 F5
Masallı, *Azerbaijan* 73 C13
Masamba, *Indonesia* 63 E6
Masan, *S. Korea* 57 G15
Masandam, Ra's, *Oman* 71 E8
Masasi, *Tanzania* 87 E4
Masaya, *Nic.* 120 D2
Masba, *Nigeria* 83 C7
Masbate, *Phil.* 61 E5
Máscali, *Italy* 31 E8
Mascara, *Algeria* 78 A6
Mascota, *Mexico* 118 C4
Masela, *Indonesia* 63 F7
Maseru, *Lesotho* 88 D4
Mashaba, *Zimbabwe* 87 G3
Mashābih, *Si. Arabia* 70 E3
Mashan, *China* 58 F7
Mashar, *Sudan* 81 F2
Mashegu, *Nigeria* 83 D6
Masherbrum, *Pakistan* 69 B7
Mashhad, *Iran* 71 B8
Mashi, *Nigeria* 83 C6
Mashīz, *Iran* 71 D8
Māshkel, Hāmūn-i-, *Pakistan* 66 E3
Mashki Chāh, *Pakistan* 66 E3
Mashonaland, *Zimbabwe* 85 H6
Mashonaland Central □, *Zimbabwe* 89 B5
Mashonaland East □, *Zimbabwe* 89 B5
Mashonaland West □, *Zimbabwe* 89 B4
Mashrakh, *India* 69 F11
Mashtaga = Maştağa, *Azerbaijan* 49 K10
Masindi, *Uganda* 86 B3
Masindi Port, *Uganda* 86 B3
Maşīrah, *Oman* 74 C6
Maşīrah, Khalīj, *Oman* 74 C6
Masisi, *Dem. Rep. of the Congo* 86 C2
Masjed Soleyman, *Iran* 71 D6
Mask, L., *Ireland* 15 C2
Maskin, *Oman* 71 F8
Maslen Nos, *Bulgaria* 41 D11
Maslinica, *Croatia* 29 E13
Masnou = El Masnou, *Spain* 32 D7
Masoala, Tanjon' i, *Madag.* 89 B9
Masoarivo, *Madag.* 89 B7
Masohi = Amahai, *Indonesia* 63 E7
Masomeloka, *Madag.* 89 C8
Mason, *Nev., U.S.A.* 116 G7
Mason, *Tex., U.S.A.* 113 K5
Mason City, *U.S.A.* 112 D8
Maspalomas, *Canary Is.* 37 G4
Maspalomas, Pta., *Canary Is.* 37 G4
Masqat, *Oman* 74 C6
Massa, *Italy* 28 D7
Massa Maríttima, *Italy* 28 E7
Massachusetts □, *U.S.A.* 111 D13
Massachusetts B., *U.S.A.* 111 D14
Massafra, *Italy* 31 B10
Massakory, *Chad* 79 F9
Massanella, *Spain* 37 B9
Massangena, *Mozam.* 89 C5
Massango, *Angola* 84 F3
Massat, *France* 20 F5
Massawa = Mitsiwa, *Eritrea* 81 D4
Massena, *U.S.A.* 111 B10
Massénya, *Chad* 79 F9
Masset, *Canada* 104 C2
Masseube, *France* 20 E4
Massiac, *France* 20 C7
Massif Central, *France* 20 D7
Massigui, *Mali* 82 C3
Massillon, *U.S.A.* 110 F3
Massinga, *Mozam.* 89 C6
Massingir, *Mozam.* 89 C5
Mässlingen, *Sweden* 10 B6
Masson, *Canada* 111 A9
Masson I., *Antarctica* 5 C7
Maştağa, *Azerbaijan* 49 K10
Mastanli = Momchilgrad, *Bulgaria* 41 E9
Masterton, *N.Z.* 91 J5
Mastic, *U.S.A.* 111 F12
Mástikho, Ákra, *Greece* 39 C8
Mastuj, *Pakistan* 69 A5
Mastung, *Pakistan* 66 E5
Mastūrah, *Si. Arabia* 80 C4
Masty, *Belarus* 46 F3
Masuda, *Japan* 55 G5
Masvingo, *Zimbabwe* 87 G3
Masvingo □, *Zimbabwe* 87 G3
Maşyāf, *Syria* 70 C3
Maszewo, *Poland* 44 E2
Mat →, *Albania* 40 E3
Matabeleland, *Zimbabwe* 85 H5
Matabeleland North □, *Zimbabwe* 87 F2
Matabeleland South □, *Zimbabwe* 87 G2
Matachel →, *Spain* 35 G4
Matachewan, *Canada* 102 C3
Matadi, *Dem. Rep. of the Congo* 84 F2
Matagalpa, *Nic.* 120 D2
Matagami, *Canada* 102 C4
Matagami, L., *Canada* 102 C4
Matagorda B., *U.S.A.* 113 L6
Matagorda I., *U.S.A.* 113 L6
Matak, *Indonesia* 65 L6
Mátala, *Greece* 36 E6
Matam, *Senegal* 82 B2
Matameye, *Niger* 83 C6
Matamoros, *Campeche, Mexico* 119 D6
Matamoros, *Coahuila, Mexico* 118 B4
Matamoros, *Tamaulipas, Mexico* 119 B5
Ma'ţan as Sarra, *Libya* 79 D10
Matandu →, *Tanzania* 87 D3
Matane, *Canada* 103 C6
Matang, *China* 58 F5
Matankari, *Niger* 83 C5
Matanomadh, *India* 68 H3
Matanzas, *Cuba* 120 B3
Matapa, *Botswana* 88 C3
Matapan, C. = Taínaron, Ákra, *Greece* 38 E4
Matapédia, *Canada* 103 C6
Matara, *Sri Lanka* 66 S12
Mataram, *Indonesia* 62 F5
Matarani, *Peru* 124 G4
Mataranka, *Australia* 92 B5
Matarma, Râs, *Egypt* 75 E1
Mataró, *Spain* 32 D7
Matarraña →, *Spain* 32 D5
Mataruška Banja, *Serbia, Yug.* 40 C4
Matatiele, *S. Africa* 89 E4
Mataura, *N.Z.* 91 M2
Matehuala, *Mexico* 118 C4
Mateke Hills, *Zimbabwe* 87 G3
Matera, *Italy* 31 B9
Matese, Monti del, *Italy* 31 A7
Mátészalka, *Hungary* 42 C7
Matetsi, *Zimbabwe* 87 F2
Matfors, *Sweden* 10 B11
Matha, *France* 20 C3
Mathis, *U.S.A.* 113 L6
Mathráki, *Greece* 36 A3
Mathura, *India* 68 F7
Mati, *Phil.* 61 H7
Matiakoali, *Burkina Faso* 83 C5
Matiali, *India* 69 F13
Matías Romero, *Mexico* 119 D5
Matibane, *Mozam.* 87 E5
Matima, *Botswana* 88 C3
Matiri Ra., *N.Z.* 91 J4
Matjiesfontein, *S. Africa* 88 E3
Matla →, *India* 69 J13
Matlamanyane, *Botswana* 88 B4
Matli, *Pakistan* 68 G3
Matlock, *U.K.* 12 D6
Matna, *Sudan* 81 E4
Mato Grosso □, *Brazil* 125 F8
Mato Grosso, Planalto do, *Brazil* 122 E5
Mato Grosso do Sul □, *Brazil* 125 G8
Matochkin Shar, *Russia* 50 B6
Matopo Hills, *Zimbabwe* 87 G2
Matopos, *Zimbabwe* 87 G2
Matosinhos, *Portugal* 34 D2
Matour, *France* 19 F11
Matroosberg, *S. Africa* 88 E2
Maţruḩ, *Oman* 74 C6
Matsena, *Nigeria* 83 C7
Matsesta, *Russia* 49 J4
Matsu Tao, *Taiwan* 59 E13
Matsue, *Japan* 55 G6
Matsumae, *Japan* 54 D10
Matsumoto, *Japan* 55 F9
Matsusaka, *Japan* 55 G8
Matsuura, *Japan* 55 H4
Matsuyama, *Japan* 55 H6
Mattagami →, *Canada* 102 B3
Mattancheri, *India* 66 Q10
Mattawa, *Canada* 102 C4
Matterhorn, *Switz.* 25 K3
Mattersburg, *Austria* 27 D9
Matthew Town, *Bahamas* 121 B5
Matthew's Ridge, *Guyana* 124 B6
Mattice, *Canada* 102 C3
Mattituck, *U.S.A.* 111 F12
Mattō, *Japan* 55 F8
Mattoon, *U.S.A.* 108 F1
Matuba, *Mozam.* 89 C5
Matucana, *Peru* 124 F3
Matūn = Khowst, *Afghan.* 68 C3
Maturín, *Venezuela* 124 B6
Matveyev Kurgan, *Russia* 47 J10
Matxitxako, C., *Spain* 32 B2
Mau, *Mad. P., India* 69 F8
Mau, *Ut. P., India* 69 G10
Mau, *Ut. P., India* 69 G9
Mau Escarpment, *Kenya* 86 C4
Mau Ranipur, *India* 69 G8
Maubeuge, *France* 19 B10
Maubourguet, *France* 20 E4
Maud, Pt., *Australia* 92 D1
Maude, *Australia* 95 E3
Maudin Sun, *Burma* 67 M19
Maués, *Brazil* 124 D7
Mauganj, *India* 67 G12
Maughold Hd., *U.K.* 12 C3
Mauguio, *France* 20 E7
Maui, *U.S.A.* 106 H16
Maulamyaing = Moulmein, *Burma* 67 L20
Maule □, *Chile* 126 D1
Mauléon-Licharre, *France* 20 E3
Maumee, *U.S.A.* 108 E4
Maumee →, *U.S.A.* 108 E4
Maumere, *Indonesia* 63 F6
Maumusson, Pertuis de, *France* 20 C2
Maun, *Botswana* 88 C3
Mauna Kea, *U.S.A.* 106 J17
Mauna Loa, *U.S.A.* 106 J17
Maungmagan Kyunzu, *Burma* 64 E1
Maupin, *U.S.A.* 114 D3
Maure-de-Bretagne, *France* 18 E5
Maurepas, L., *U.S.A.* 113 K9
Maures, *France* 21 E10
Mauriac, *France* 20 C6
Maurice, L., *Australia* 93 E5
Mauricie, Parc Nat. de la, *Canada* 102 C5
Maurienne, *France* 21 C10
Mauritania ■, *Africa* 78 E3
Mauritius ■, *Ind. Oc.* 77 J9
Mauron, *France* 18 D4
Maurs, *France* 20 D6
Mauston, *U.S.A.* 112 D9
Mauterndorf, *Austria* 26 D6
Mauthen, *Austria* 26 E6
Mauvezin, *France* 20 E4
Mauzé-sur-le-Mignon, *France* 20 B3
Mavli, *India* 68 G5
Mavrovë, *Albania* 40 F3
Mavuradonha Mts., *Zimbabwe* 87 F3
Mawa, *Dem. Rep. of the Congo* 86 B2
Mawai, *India* 69 H9
Mawana, *India* 68 E7
Mawand, *Pakistan* 68 E3
Mawk Mai, *Burma* 67 J20
Mawlaik, *Burma* 67 H19
Mawlamyine = Moulmein, *Burma* 67 L20
Mawqaq, *Si. Arabia* 70 E4
Mawson Coast, *Antarctica* 5 C6
Max, *U.S.A.* 112 B4
Maxcanú, *Mexico* 119 C6
Maxesibeni, *S. Africa* 89 E4
Maxhamish L., *Canada* 104 B4
Maxixe, *Mozam.* 89 C6
Maxville, *Canada* 111 A10
Maxwell, *U.S.A.* 116 F4
Maxwelton, *Australia* 94 C3
May, C., *U.S.A.* 108 F8
May Pen, *Jamaica* 120 C4
Maya →, *Russia* 51 D14
Maya Mts., *Belize* 119 D7
Mayaguana, *Bahamas* 121 B5
Mayagüez, *Puerto Rico* 121 C6
Mayahi, *Niger* 83 C6
Mayals = Maials, *Spain* 32 D5
Mayāmey, *Iran* 71 B7
Mayang, *China* 58 D7
Mayanup, *Australia* 93 F2
Mayapan, *Mexico* 119 C7
Mayarí, *Cuba* 121 B4
Maybell, *U.S.A.* 114 F9
Maybole, *U.K.* 14 F4
Maychew, *Ethiopia* 81 E4
Maydān, *Iraq* 70 C5
Maydena, *Australia* 94 G4
Mayen, *Germany* 25 E3
Mayenne, *France* 18 D6
Mayenne □, *France* 18 D6
Mayenne →, *France* 18 E6
Mayer, *U.S.A.* 115 J7
Mayerthorpe, *Canada* 104 C5
Mayfield, *Ky., U.S.A.* 109 G1
Mayfield, *N.Y., U.S.A.* 111 C10
Mayhill, *U.S.A.* 115 K11
Maykop, *Russia* 49 H5
Maymyo, *Burma* 64 A1
Maynard, *Mass., U.S.A.* 111 D13
Maynard, *Wash., U.S.A.* 116 C4
Maynard Hills, *Australia* 93 E2
Mayne →, *Australia* 94 C3
Maynooth, *Ireland* 15 C5
Mayo, *Canada* 100 B6
Mayo □, *Ireland* 15 C2
Mayo Daga, *Nigeria* 83 D7
Mayo Faran, *Nigeria* 83 D7
Mayon Volcano, *Phil.* 61 E5
Mayor I., *N.Z.* 91 G6
Mayorga, *Spain* 34 C5
Mayotte, *Ind. Oc.* 85 G9
Mayraira Pt., *Phil.* 61 B4
Mayskiy, *Russia* 49 J7
Maysville, *U.S.A.* 108 F4
Mayu, *Indonesia* 63 D7
Mayville, *N. Dak., U.S.A.* 112 B6
Mayville, *N.Y., U.S.A.* 110 D5
Mayya, *Russia* 51 C14
Mazabuka, *Zambia* 87 F2
Mazagán = El Jadida, *Morocco* 78 B4
Mazagão, *Brazil* 125 D8
Mazamet, *France* 20 E6
Mazán, *Peru* 124 D4
Māzandarān □, *Iran* 71 B7
Mazapil, *Mexico* 118 C4
Mazara del Vallo, *Italy* 30 E5
Mazarrón, *Spain* 33 H3
Mazarrón, G. de, *Spain* 33 H3
Mazaruni →, *Guyana* 124 B7
Mazatán, *Mexico* 118 B2
Mazatenango, *Guatemala* 120 D1
Mazatlán, *Mexico* 118 C3
Mažeikiai, *Lithuania* 9 H20
Māzhān, *Iran* 71 C8
Mazīnān, *Iran* 71 B8
Mazoe, *Mozam.* 87 F3
Mazoe →, *Mozam.* 87 F3
Mazowe, *Zimbabwe* 87 F3
Mazowieckie □, *Poland* 45 F8
Mazrûb, *Sudan* 81 E2
Mazu Dao, *China* 59 D12
Mazurian Lakes = Mazurski, Pojezierze, *Poland* 44 E7
Mazurski, Pojezierze, *Poland* 44 E7
Mazyr, *Belarus* 47 F5
Mbaba, *Senegal* 82 C1
Mbabane, *Swaziland* 89 D5
Mbagne, *Mauritania* 82 B2
M'bahiakro, *Ivory C.* 82 D4
Mbaïki, *C.A.R.* 84 D3
Mbala, *Zambia* 87 D3
Mbalabala, *Zimbabwe* 89 C4
Mbale, *Uganda* 86 B3
Mbalmayo, *Cameroon* 83 E7
Mbam →, *Cameroon* 83 E7
Mbamba Bay, *Tanzania* 87 E3
Mbandaka, *Dem. Rep. of the Congo* 84 D3
Mbanga, *Cameroon* 83 E6
Mbanza Congo, *Angola* 84 F2
Mbanza Ngungu, *Dem. Rep. of the Congo* 84 F2
Mbarara, *Uganda* 86 C3
Mbashe →, *S. Africa* 89 E4
Mbatto, *Ivory C.* 82 D4
Mbenkuru →, *Tanzania* 87 D4
Mberengwa, *Zimbabwe* 87 G2
Mberengwa, Mt., *Zimbabwe* 87 G2
Mberubu, *Nigeria* 83 D6
Mbesuma, *Zambia* 87 E3
Mbeya, *Tanzania* 87 D3
Mbeya □, *Tanzania* 86 D3
M'bili, *Sudan* 81 F2
Mbinga, *Tanzania* 87 E4
Mbini □, *Eq. Guin.* 84 D2
Mboki, *C.A.R.* 81 F2
M'bonge, *Cameroon* 83 E6
Mboro, *Senegal* 82 B1
M'boukou Res., *Cameroon* 83 D7
Mboune, *Senegal* 82 C2
Mbour, *Senegal* 82 C1
Mbout, *Mauritania* 82 B2
Mbuji-Mayi, *Dem. Rep. of the Congo* 86 D1
Mbulu, *Tanzania* 86 C4
Mburucuyá, *Argentina* 126 B4
Mchinja, *Tanzania* 87 D4
Mchinji, *Malawi* 87 E3
Mdantsane, *S. Africa* 85 L5
Mead, L., *U.S.A.* 117 J12
Meade, *U.S.A.* 113 G4
Meadow Lake, *Canada* 105 C7
Meadow Lake Prov. Park, *Canada* 105 C7
Meadow Valley Wash →, *U.S.A.* 117 J12
Meadville, *U.S.A.* 110 E4
Meaford, *Canada* 102 D3
Mealhada, *Portugal* 34 E2
Mealy Mts., *Canada* 103 B8
Meander River, *Canada* 104 B5
Meares, C., *U.S.A.* 114 D2
Mearim →, *Brazil* 125 D10
Meath □, *Ireland* 15 C5
Meath Park, *Canada* 105 C7
Meaulne, *France* 19 F9
Meaux, *France* 19 D9
Mebechi-Gawa →, *Japan* 54 D10
Mecanhelas, *Mozam.* 87 F4
Mecca = Makkah, *Si. Arabia* 74 C2
Mecca, *U.S.A.* 117 M10
Mechanicsburg, *U.S.A.* 110 F8
Mechanicville, *U.S.A.* 111 D11
Mechara, *Ethiopia* 81 F5
Mechelen, *Belgium* 17 C4
Mecheria, *Algeria* 78 B5
Mechernich, *Germany* 24 E2
Mechetinskaya, *Russia* 49 G5
Mecidiye, *Turkey* 41 F10
Mecitözü, *Turkey* 72 B6
Mecklenburg-Vorpommern □, *Germany* 24 B8
Mecklenburger Bucht, *Germany* 24 A7
Meconta, *Mozam.* 87 E4
Mecsek, *Hungary* 42 D3
Meda, *Portugal* 34 E3
Medan, *Indonesia* 62 D1
Medanosa, Pta., *Argentina* 128 F3
Mede, *Italy* 28 C5
Médéa, *Algeria* 78 A6
Mededa, *Bos.-H.* 42 G4
Medellín, *Colombia* 124 B3
Medelpad, *Sweden* 10 B10
Medemblik, *Neths.* 17 B5
Mederdra, *Mauritania* 82 B1
Medford, *Mass., U.S.A.* 111 D13
Medford, *Oreg., U.S.A.* 114 E2
Medford, *Wis., U.S.A.* 112 C9
Medgidia, *Romania* 43 F13
Medi, *Sudan* 81 F3
Media Agua, *Argentina* 126 C2
Media Luna, *Argentina* 126 C2
Medianeira, *Brazil* 127 B5
Mediaş, *Romania* 43 D9
Medicina, *Italy* 29 D8
Medicine Bow, *U.S.A.* 114 F10
Medicine Bow Pk., *U.S.A.* 114 F10
Medicine Bow Ra., *U.S.A.* 114 F10
Medicine Hat, *Canada* 105 D6
Medicine Lake, *U.S.A.* 112 A2
Medicine Lodge, *U.S.A.* 113 G5
Medina = Al Madīnah, *Si. Arabia* 70 E3
Medina, *N. Dak., U.S.A.* 112 B5
Medina, *N.Y., U.S.A.* 110 C6
Medina, *Ohio, U.S.A.* 110 E3
Medina →, *U.S.A.* 113 L5
Medina de Pomar, *Spain* 34 C7
Medina de Ríoseco, *Spain* 34 D5
Medina del Campo, *Spain* 34 D6
Medina L., *U.S.A.* 113 L5
Medina Sidonia, *Spain* 35 J5
Medinaceli, *Spain* 32 D2
Medinipur, *India* 69 H12
Mediterranean Sea, *Europe* 6 H7
Médoc, *France* 20 C3
Medulin, *Croatia* 29 D10
Medveđa, *Serbia, Yug.* 40 D5
Medvedevo, *Russia* 48 B8
Medveditsa →, *Tver, Russia* 46 D9
Medveditsa →, *Volgograd, Russia* 48 F6
Medvedok, *Russia* 48 B10
Medvezhi, Ostrava, *Russia* 51 B17
Medvezhyegorsk, *Russia* 50 C4
Medway □, *U.K.* 13 F8
Medway →, *U.K.* 13 F8
Medzev, *Slovak Rep.* 27 C13
Medzilaborce, *Slovak Rep.* 27 B14
Medžitlija, *Macedonia* 40 F5
Meekatharra, *Australia* 93 E2
Meeker, *U.S.A.* 114 F10
Meelpaeg Res., *Canada* 103 C8
Meersburg, *Germany* 25 H5
Meerut, *India* 68 E7
Meeteetse, *U.S.A.* 114 D9
Mega, *Ethiopia* 81 G4
Megálo Khorío, *Greece* 39 E9
Megálo Petalí, *Greece* 38 D6
Megalópolis, *Greece* 38 D4
Meganísi, *Greece* 38 C2
Mégara, *Greece* 38 D5
Megasini, *India* 69 J12
Megdhova →, *Greece* 38 B3
Megève, *France* 21 C10
Meghalaya □, *India* 67 G17
Meghezez, *Ethiopia* 81 F4
Mégiscane, L., *Canada* 102 C4
Megiste, *Greece* 39 E11
Megra, *Russia* 46 B9
Mehadia, *Romania* 42 F7
Meharry, Mt., *Australia* 92 D2
Mehedeby, *Sweden* 10 D11
Mehedinţi □, *Romania* 42 F7
Meheisa, *Sudan* 80 D3
Mehlville, *U.S.A.* 112 F9
Mehndawal, *India* 69 F10
Mehr Jān, *Iran* 71 C7
Mehrābād, *Iran* 70 B5
Mehrān, *Iran* 70 C5

Milford

Mehrīz, *Iran* 71 **D7**
Mehun-sur-Yèvre, *France* 19 **E9**
Mei Jiang →, *China* 59 **E11**
Mei Xian, *China* 56 **G4**
Meicheng, *China* 59 **C12**
Meichengzhen, *China* 59 **C8**
Meichuan, *China* 59 **B10**
Meigu, *China* 58 **C4**
Meiktila, *Burma* 67 **J19**
Meinerzhagen, *Germany* 24 **D3**
Meiningen, *Germany* 24 **E6**
Meira, Serra de, *Spain* 34 **B3**
Meiringen, *Switz.* 25 **J4**
Meishan, *China* 58 **B4**
Meissen, *Germany* 24 **D9**
Meissner, *Germany* 24 **D5**
Meitan, *China* 58 **D6**
Meizhou, *China* 59 **E11**
Meja, *India* 69 **G10**
Mejillones, *Chile* 126 **A1**
Mekdela, *Ethiopia* 81 **E4**
Mekele, *Ethiopia* 81 **E4**
Mekhtar, *Pakistan* 66 **D6**
Meknès, *Morocco* 78 **B4**
Meko, *Nigeria* 83 **D5**
Mekong →, *Asia* 65 **H6**
Mekongga, *Indonesia* 63 **E6**
Mekrou →, *Benin* 83 **C5**
Mekvari = Kür →, *Azerbaijan* 73 **C13**
Mel, *Italy* 29 **B9**
Melagiri Hills, *India* 66 **N10**
Melaka, *Malaysia* 65 **L4**
Melalap, *Malaysia* 62 **C5**
Mélambes, *Greece* 36 **D6**
Melanesia, *Pac. Oc.* 96 **H7**
Melbourne, *Australia* 95 **F4**
Melbourne, *U.S.A.* 109 **L5**
Melchor Múzquiz, *Mexico* 118 **B4**
Melchor Ocampo, *Mexico* 118 **C4**
Méldola, *Italy* 29 **D9**
Meldorf, *Germany* 24 **A5**
Melegnano, *Italy* 28 **C6**
Melenci, *Serbia, Yug.* 42 **E5**
Melenki, *Russia* 48 **C5**
Mélèzes →, *Canada* 102 **A5**
Melfi, *Italy* 31 **B8**
Melfort, *Canada* 105 **C8**
Melfort, *Zimbabwe* 87 **F3**
Melgaço, *Portugal* 34 **C2**
Melgar de Fernamental, *Spain* 34 **C6**
Melhus, *Norway* 8 **E14**
Melide, *Spain* 34 **C2**
Meligalá, *Greece* 38 **D3**
Melilla, *N. Afr.* 78 **A5**
Melilli, *Italy* 31 **E8**
Melipilla, *Chile* 126 **C1**
Mélissa, Ákra, *Greece* 36 **D6**
Mélissa Óros, *Greece* 39 **D8**
Melita, *Canada* 105 **D8**
Mélito di Porto Salvo, *Italy* 31 **E8**
Melitopol, *Ukraine* 47 **J8**
Melk, *Austria* 26 **C8**
Mellan Fryken, *Sweden* 10 **E7**
Mellansel, *Sweden* 8 **E18**
Mellbystrand, *Sweden* 11 **H6**
Melle, *France* 20 **B3**
Melle, *Germany* 24 **C4**
Mellen, *U.S.A.* 112 **B9**
Mellerud, *Sweden* 11 **F6**
Mellette, *U.S.A.* 112 **C5**
Mellid = Melide, *Spain* 34 **C2**
Mellieha, *Malta* 36 **D1**
Mellit, *Sudan* 81 **E2**
Mellrichstadt, *Germany* 24 **E6**
Melnik, *Bulgaria* 40 **E7**
Mělník, *Czech Rep.* 26 **A7**
Melo, *Uruguay* 127 **C5**
Melolo, *Indonesia* 63 **F6**
Meloupry, *Cambodia* 64 **F5**
Melrose, *Australia* 95 **E4**
Melrose, *U.K.* 14 **F6**
Melrose, *Minn., U.S.A.* 112 **C7**
Melrose, *N. Mex., U.S.A.* 113 **H3**
Melstone, *U.S.A.* 114 **C10**
Melsungen, *Germany* 24 **D5**
Melton Mowbray, *U.K.* 12 **E7**
Melun, *France* 19 **D9**
Melut, *Sudan* 81 **E3**
Melville, *Canada* 105 **C8**
Melville, C., *Australia* 94 **A3**
Melville, L., *Canada* 103 **B8**
Melville B., *Australia* 94 **A2**
Melville I., *Australia* 92 **B5**
Melville I., *Canada* 4 **B2**
Melville Pen., *Canada* 101 **B11**
Mélykút, *Hungary* 42 **D4**
Memaliaj, *Albania* 40 **F3**
Memba, *Mozam.* 87 **E5**
Memboro, *Indonesia* 63 **F5**
Membrilla, *Spain* 35 **G7**
Memel = Klaipėda, *Lithuania* 9 **J19**
Memel, *S. Africa* 89 **D4**
Memmingen, *Germany* 25 **H6**
Mempawah, *Indonesia* 62 **D3**
Memphis, *Egypt* 80 **J7**
Memphis, *Mich., U.S.A.* 110 **D2**
Memphis, *Tenn., U.S.A.* 113 **H10**
Memphis, *Tex., U.S.A.* 113 **H4**
Memphremagog, L., *U.S.A.* 111 **B12**
Mena, *Ukraine* 47 **G7**
Mena, *U.S.A.* 113 **H7**
Mena →, *Ethiopia* 81 **F5**
Menai Strait, *U.K.* 12 **D3**
Ménaka, *Mali* 83 **B5**
Menan = Chao Phraya →, *Thailand* 64 **F3**
Menarandra →, *Madag.* 89 **D7**
Menard, *U.S.A.* 113 **K5**
Menawashei, *Sudan* 81 **E1**
Mendawai →, *Indonesia* 62 **E4**
Mende, *France* 20 **D7**
Mendebo, *Ethiopia* 81 **F4**
Menden, *Germany* 24 **D3**
Menderes, *Turkey* 39 **C9**
Mendez, *Mexico* 119 **B5**
Mendhar, *India* 69 **C6**
Mendi, *Ethiopia* 81 **F4**
Mendip Hills, *U.K.* 13 **F5**
Mendocino, *U.S.A.* 114 **G2**
Mendocino, C., *U.S.A.* 114 **F1**
Mendota, *Calif., U.S.A.* 116 **J6**
Mendota, *Ill., U.S.A.* 112 **E10**
Mendoza, *Argentina* 126 **C2**
Mendoza □, *Argentina* 126 **C2**
Mene Grande, *Venezuela* 124 **B4**
Menemen, *Turkey* 39 **C9**
Menen, *Belgium* 17 **D3**
Menfi, *Italy* 30 **E5**
Mengdingjie, *China* 58 **F2**
Mengeš, *Slovenia* 29 **B11**
Menggala, *Indonesia* 62 **E3**
Menghai, *China* 58 **G3**
Mengíbar, *Spain* 35 **H7**
Mengjin, *China* 56 **G7**
Mengla, *China* 58 **G3**
Menglian, *China* 58 **F2**
Mengshan, *China* 59 **E8**
Mengyin, *China* 57 **G9**
Mengzhe, *China* 58 **F3**
Mengzi, *China* 58 **F4**
Menihek, *Canada* 103 **B6**
Menihek L., *Canada* 103 **B6**
Menin = Menen, *Belgium* 17 **D3**
Menindee, *Australia* 95 **E3**
Menindee L., *Australia* 95 **E3**
Meningie, *Australia* 95 **F2**
Menlo Park, *U.S.A.* 116 **H4**
Menominee, *U.S.A.* 108 **C2**
Menominee →, *U.S.A.* 108 **C2**
Menomonie, *U.S.A.* 112 **C9**
Menongue, *Angola* 85 **G3**
Menorca, *Spain* 37 **B11**
Mentakab, *Malaysia* 65 **L4**
Mentawai, Kepulauan, *Indonesia* 62 **E1**
Menton, *France* 21 **E11**
Mentor, *U.S.A.* 110 **E3**
Menzies, *Australia* 93 **E3**
Meob B., *Namibia* 88 **B2**
Me'ona, *Israel* 75 **B4**
Meoqui, *Mexico* 118 **B3**
Mepaco, *Mozam.* 87 **F3**
Meppel, *Neths.* 17 **B6**
Meppen, *Germany* 24 **C3**
Mequinenza, *Spain* 32 **D5**
Mequinenza, Embalse de, *Spain* 32 **D5**
Mer, *France* 18 **E8**
Merabéllou, Kólpos, *Greece* 36 **D7**
Merak, *Indonesia* 63 **F12**
Meramangye, L., *Australia* 93 **E5**
Meran = Merano, *Italy* 29 **B8**
Merano, *Italy* 29 **B8**
Merate, *Italy* 28 **C6**
Merauke, *Indonesia* 63 **F10**
Merbein, *Australia* 95 **E3**
Merca, *Somali Rep.* 74 **G3**
Mercato Saraceno, *Italy* 29 **E9**
Merced, *U.S.A.* 116 **H6**
Merced →, *U.S.A.* 116 **H6**
Merced Pk., *U.S.A.* 116 **H7**
Mercedes, *Buenos Aires, Argentina* 126 **C4**
Mercedes, *Corrientes, Argentina* 126 **B4**
Mercedes, *San Luis, Argentina* 126 **C2**
Mercedes, *Uruguay* 126 **C4**
Mercedes, *U.S.A.* 113 **M6**
Merceditas, *Chile* 126 **B1**
Mercer, *N.Z.* 91 **G5**
Mercer, *U.S.A.* 110 **E4**
Mercer Island, *U.S.A.* 116 **C4**
Mercury, *U.S.A.* 117 **J11**
Mercy C., *Canada* 101 **B13**
Merdrignac, *France* 18 **D4**
Mere, *U.K.* 13 **F5**
Meredith, C., *Falk. Is.* 128 **G4**
Meredith, L., *U.S.A.* 113 **H4**
Merefa, *Ukraine* 47 **H9**
Merei, *Romania* 43 **E11**
Merga = Nukheila, *Sudan* 80 **D2**
Mergui, *Burma* 64 **F2**
Mergui Arch. = Myeik Kyunzu, *Burma* 65 **G1**
Meriç, *Turkey* 41 **E10**
Meriç →, *Turkey* 41 **F10**
Mérida, *Mexico* 119 **C7**
Mérida, *Spain* 35 **G4**
Mérida, *Venezuela* 124 **B4**
Mérida, Cord. de, *Venezuela* 122 **C3**
Meriden, *U.K.* 13 **E6**
Meriden, *U.S.A.* 111 **E12**
Meridian, *Calif., U.S.A.* 116 **F5**
Meridian, *Idaho, U.S.A.* 114 **E5**
Meridian, *Miss., U.S.A.* 109 **J1**
Mérignac, *France* 20 **D3**
Mérinaghène, *Senegal* 82 **B1**
Merinda, *Australia* 94 **C4**
Mering, *Germany* 25 **G6**
Meringa, *Nigeria* 83 **C7**
Merir, *Pac. Oc.* 63 **D8**
Merirumã, *Brazil* 125 **C8**
Merkel, *U.S.A.* 113 **J5**
Mermaid Reef, *Australia* 92 **C2**
Merowe, *Sudan* 80 **D3**
Merredin, *Australia* 93 **F2**
Merrick, *U.K.* 14 **F4**
Merrickville, *Canada* 111 **B9**
Merrill, *Oreg., U.S.A.* 114 **E3**
Merrill, *Wis., U.S.A.* 112 **C10**
Merrimack →, *U.S.A.* 111 **D14**
Merriman, *U.S.A.* 112 **D4**
Merritt, *Canada* 104 **C4**
Merritt Island, *U.S.A.* 109 **L5**
Merriwa, *Australia* 95 **E5**
Merry I., *Canada* 102 **A4**
Merryville, *U.S.A.* 113 **K8**
Mersa Fatma, *Eritrea* 81 **E5**
Mersch, *Lux.* 17 **E6**
Merse →, *Italy* 29 **E8**
Mersea I., *U.K.* 13 **F8**
Merseburg, *Germany* 24 **D7**
Mersey →, *U.K.* 12 **D4**
Merseyside □, *U.K.* 12 **D4**
Mersin, *Turkey* 70 **B2**
Mersing, *Malaysia* 65 **L4**
Merta, *India* 68 **F6**
Merta Road, *India* 68 **F5**
Merthyr Tydfil, *U.K.* 13 **F4**
Merthyr Tydfil □, *U.K.* 13 **F4**
Mértola, *Portugal* 35 **H3**
Mertzon, *U.S.A.* 113 **K4**
Méru, *France* 19 **C9**
Meru, *Kenya* 86 **B4**
Meru, *Tanzania* 86 **C4**
Merville, *France* 19 **B9**
Méry-sur-Seine, *France* 19 **D10**
Merzifon, *Turkey* 72 **B6**
Merzig, *Germany* 25 **F2**
Mesa, *U.S.A.* 115 **K8**
Mesa Verde National Park, *U.S.A.* 115 **H9**
Mesagne, *Italy* 31 **B10**
Mesanagrós, *Greece* 36 **C9**
Mesaoría □, *Cyprus* 36 **D12**
Mesarás, Kólpos, *Greece* 36 **D6**
Meschede, *Germany* 24 **D4**
Mescit, *Turkey* 73 **B9**
Mesfinto, *Ethiopia* 81 **E4**
Mesgouez, L., *Canada* 102 **B5**
Meshchovsk, *Russia* 46 **E8**
Meshed = Mashhad, *Iran* 71 **B8**
Meshoppen, *U.S.A.* 111 **E8**
Meshra er Req, *Sudan* 81 **F2**
Mesilinka →, *Canada* 104 **B4**
Mesilla, *U.S.A.* 115 **K10**
Meslay-du-Maine, *France* 18 **E6**
Mesocco, *Switz.* 25 **J5**
Mesolóngion, *Greece* 38 **C3**
Mesopotamia = Al Jazirah, *Iraq* 70 **C5**
Mesopotamia, *U.S.A.* 110 **E4**
Mesopótamon, *Greece* 38 **B2**
Mesoraca, *Italy* 31 **C9**
Mésou Volímais = Volímai, *Greece* 38 **D2**
Mesquite, *U.S.A.* 115 **H6**
Messaad, *Algeria* 78 **B6**
Messac, *France* 18 **E5**
Messalo →, *Mozam.* 87 **E4**
Méssaména, *Cameroon* 83 **E7**
Messeue, *Greece* 38 **D3**
Messina, *Italy* 31 **D8**
Messina, *S. Africa* 89 **C5**
Messina, Str. di, *Italy* 31 **D8**
Messíni, *Greece* 38 **D4**
Messínia □, *Greece* 38 **D3**
Messiniakós Kólpos, *Greece* 38 **E4**
Messkirch, *Germany* 25 **H5**
Messonghi, *Greece* 36 **B3**
Mesta →, *Bulgaria* 40 **E7**
Mestá, Ákra, *Greece* 39 **C7**
Mestanza, *Spain* 35 **G6**
Mestre, *Italy* 29 **C9**
Mesudiye, *Turkey* 72 **B7**
Meta →, *S. Amer.* 122 **C4**
Meta Incognita Peninsula, *Canada* 101 **B13**
Metabetchouan, *Canada* 103 **C5**
Metairie, *U.S.A.* 113 **L9**
Metalici, Munţii, *Romania* 42 **D7**
Metaline Falls, *U.S.A.* 114 **B5**
Metallifere, Colline, *Italy* 28 **E8**
Metán, *Argentina* 126 **B3**
Metangula, *Mozam.* 87 **E3**
Metauro →, *Italy* 29 **E10**
Metema, *Ethiopia* 81 **E4**
Metengobalame, *Mozam.* 87 **E3**
Méthana, *Greece* 38 **D5**
Methóni, *Greece* 38 **E3**
Methven, *N.Z.* 91 **K3**
Metil, *Mozam.* 87 **F4**
Metkovets, *Bulgaria* 40 **C7**
Metković, *Croatia* 29 **E14**
Metlakatla, *U.S.A.* 100 **C6**
Metlika, *Slovenia* 29 **C12**
Metropolis, *U.S.A.* 113 **G10**
Métsovon, *Greece* 38 **B3**
Metu, *Ethiopia* 81 **F4**
Metz, *France* 19 **C13**
Metzingen, *Germany* 25 **G5**
Meulaboh, *Indonesia* 62 **D1**
Meung-sur-Loire, *France* 19 **E8**
Meureudu, *Indonesia* 62 **C1**
Meurthe →, *France* 19 **D13**
Meurthe-et-Moselle □, *France* 19 **D13**
Meuse □, *France* 19 **C12**
Meuse →, *Europe* 17 **D5**
Meuselwitz, *Germany* 24 **D8**
Mexia, *U.S.A.* 113 **K6**
Mexiana, I., *Brazil* 125 **D9**
Mexicali, *Mexico* 117 **N11**
Mexican Plateau, *Mexico* 98 **G9**
Mexican Water, *U.S.A.* 115 **H9**
México, *Mexico* 119 **D5**
Mexico, *Maine, U.S.A.* 111 **B14**
Mexico, *Mo., U.S.A.* 112 **F9**
Mexico, *N.Y., U.S.A.* 111 **C8**
México □, *Mexico* 119 **D5**
Mexico ■, *Cent. Amer.* 118 **C4**
Mexico, G. of, *Cent. Amer.* 119 **C7**
Mexico B., *U.S.A.* 111 **C8**
Meydān-e Naftūn, *Iran* 71 **D6**
Meydani, Ra's-e, *Iran* 71 **E8**
Meyenburg, *Germany* 24 **B8**
Meymac, *France* 20 **C6**
Meymaneh, *Afghan.* 66 **B4**
Meyrueis, *France* 20 **D7**
Meyssac, *France* 20 **C5**
Meyzieu, *France* 21 **C8**
Mezdra, *Bulgaria* 40 **C7**
Mèze, *France* 20 **E7**
Mezen, *Russia* 50 **C5**
Mezen →, *Russia* 50 **C5**
Mézenc, Mt., *France* 21 **D8**
Mezeş, Munţii, *Romania* 42 **C8**
Mezha →, *Russia* 46 **E6**
Mezhdurechenskiy, *Russia* 50 **D7**
Mézidon-Canon, *France* 18 **C6**
Mézières-en-Brenne, *France* 20 **B5**
Mézilhac, *France* 21 **D8**
Mézin, *France* 20 **D4**
Mezőberény, *Hungary* 42 **D6**
Mezőfalva, *Hungary* 42 **D3**
Mezőhegyes, *Hungary* 42 **D5**
Mezőkövácsháza, *Hungary* 42 **D5**
Mezőkövesd, *Hungary* 42 **C5**
Mézos, *France* 20 **D2**
Mezőtúr, *Hungary* 42 **C5**
Mezquital, *Mexico* 118 **C4**
Mezzolombardo, *Italy* 28 **B8**
Mfolozi →, *S. Africa* 89 **D5**
Mgeta, *Tanzania* 87 **D4**
Mglin, *Russia* 47 **F7**
Mhlaba Hills, *Zimbabwe* 87 **F3**
Mhow, *India* 68 **H6**
Miahuatlán, *Mexico* 119 **D5**
Miajadas, *Spain* 35 **F5**
Miami, *Fla., U.S.A.* 109 **N5**
Miami, *Okla., U.S.A.* 113 **G7**
Miami, *Tex., U.S.A.* 113 **H4**
Miami Beach, *U.S.A.* 109 **N5**
Mian Xian, *China* 56 **H4**
Mianchi, *China* 56 **G6**
Mīāndarreh, *Iran* 71 **C7**
Mīāndowāb, *Iran* 70 **B5**
Miandrivazo, *Madag.* 89 **B8**
Mīāneh, *Iran* 70 **B5**
Mianning, *China* 58 **C4**
Mianwali, *Pakistan* 68 **C4**
Mianyang, *China* 58 **B5**
Mianzhu, *China* 58 **B5**
Miaoli, *Taiwan* 59 **E13**
Miarinarivo, *Antananarivo, Madag.* 89 **B8**
Miarinarivo, *Toamasina, Madag.* 89 **B8**
Miariravaratra, *Madag.* 89 **C8**
Miass, *Russia* 50 **D7**
Miasteczko Krajeńskie, *Poland* 45 **E4**
Miastko, *Poland* 44 **E3**
Mica, *S. Africa* 89 **C5**
Micăsasa, *Romania* 43 **D9**
Michalovce, *Slovak Rep.* 27 **C14**
Michigan □, *U.S.A.* 108 **C3**
Michigan, L., *U.S.A.* 108 **D2**
Michigan City, *U.S.A.* 108 **E2**
Michika, *Nigeria* 83 **C7**
Michipicoten I., *Canada* 102 **C2**
Michoacan □, *Mexico* 118 **D4**
Michurin, *Bulgaria* 41 **D11**
Michurinsk, *Russia* 48 **D5**
Mico, Pta., *Nic.* 120 **D3**
Micronesia, *Pac. Oc.* 96 **G7**
Micronesia, Federated States of ■, *Pac. Oc.* 96 **G7**
Midai, *Indonesia* 65 **L6**
Midale, *Canada* 105 **D8**
Middelburg, *Neths.* 17 **C3**
Middelburg, *Eastern Cape, S. Africa* 88 **E4**
Middelburg, *Mpumalanga, S. Africa* 89 **D4**
Middelfart, *Denmark* 11 **J3**
Middelpos, *S. Africa* 88 **E3**
Middelwit, *S. Africa* 88 **C4**
Middle Alkali L., *U.S.A.* 114 **F3**
Middle Bass I., *U.S.A.* 110 **E2**
Middle East, *Asia* 52 **F7**
Middle Fork Feather →, *U.S.A.* 116 **F5**
Middle I., *Australia* 93 **F3**
Middle Loup →, *U.S.A.* 112 **E5**
Middle Sackville, *Canada* 103 **D7**
Middleboro, *U.S.A.* 111 **E14**
Middleburg, *Fla., U.S.A.* 109 **K5**
Middleburg, *N.Y., U.S.A.* 111 **D10**
Middleburg, *Pa., U.S.A.* 110 **F7**
Middlebury, *U.S.A.* 111 **B11**
Middlemount, *Australia* 94 **C4**
Middleport, *N.Y., U.S.A.* 110 **C6**
Middleport, *Ohio, U.S.A.* 108 **F4**
Middlesboro, *U.S.A.* 109 **G4**
Middlesbrough, *U.K.* 12 **C6**
Middlesbrough □, *U.K.* 12 **C6**
Middlesex, *Belize* 120 **C2**
Middlesex, *N.J., U.S.A.* 111 **F10**
Middlesex, *N.Y., U.S.A.* 110 **D7**
Middleton, *Australia* 94 **C3**
Middleton, *Canada* 103 **D6**
Middleton Cr. →, *Australia* 94 **C3**
Middletown, *U.K.* 15 **B5**
Middletown, *Calif., U.S.A.* 116 **G4**
Middletown, *Conn., U.S.A.* 111 **E12**
Middletown, *N.Y., U.S.A.* 111 **E10**
Middletown, *Ohio, U.S.A.* 108 **F3**
Middletown, *Pa., U.S.A.* 111 **F8**
Midhurst, *U.K.* 13 **G7**
Mīdī, *Yemen* 81 **D5**
Midi, Canal du →, *France* 20 **E5**
Midi d'Ossau, Pic du, *France* 20 **F3**
Midi-Pyrénées □, *France* 20 **E5**
Midland, *Canada* 102 **D4**
Midland, *Calif., U.S.A.* 117 **M12**
Midland, *Mich., U.S.A.* 108 **D3**
Midland, *Pa., U.S.A.* 110 **F4**
Midland, *Tex., U.S.A.* 113 **K3**
Midlands □, *Zimbabwe* 87 **F2**
Midleton, *Ireland* 15 **E3**
Midlothian, *U.S.A.* 113 **J6**
Midlothian □, *U.K.* 14 **F5**
Midongy, Tangorombohitr' i, *Madag.* 89 **C8**
Midongy Atsimo, *Madag.* 89 **C8**
Midou →, *France* 20 **E3**
Midouze →, *France* 20 **E3**
Midsayap, *Phil.* 61 **H6**
Midu, *China* 58 **E3**
Midway Is., *Pac. Oc.* 96 **E10**
Midway Wells, *U.S.A.* 117 **N11**
Midwest, *U.S.A.* 114 **E10**
Midwest City, *U.S.A.* 113 **H6**
Midyat, *Turkey* 70 **B4**
Midzŏr, *Bulgaria* 40 **C6**
Mie □, *Japan* 55 **G8**
Miechów, *Poland* 45 **H7**
Miedwie, Jezioro, *Poland* 45 **E1**
Międzybórz, *Poland* 45 **G4**
Międzychód, *Poland* 45 **F2**
Międzylesie, *Poland* 45 **H3**
Międzyrzec Podlaski, *Poland* 45 **G9**
Międzyrzecz, *Poland* 45 **F2**
Międzyzdroje, *Poland* 44 **E1**
Miejska Górka, *Poland* 45 **G3**
Miélan, *France* 20 **E4**
Mielec, *Poland* 45 **H8**
Mienga, *Angola* 88 **B2**
Miercurea-Ciuc, *Romania* 43 **D10**
Miercurea Sibiului, *Romania* 43 **E8**
Mieres, *Spain* 34 **B5**
Mieroszów, *Poland* 45 **H3**
Mieso, *Ethiopia* 81 **F5**
Mieszkowice, *Poland* 45 **F1**
Mifflintown, *U.S.A.* 110 **F7**
Mifraz H̱efa, *Israel* 75 **C4**
Migennes, *France* 19 **E10**
Migliarino, *Italy* 29 **D8**
Miguel Alemán, Presa, *Mexico* 119 **D5**
Miguelturra, *Spain* 35 **G7**
Mihăileni, *Romania* 43 **C11**
Mihăileşti, *Romania* 43 **F10**
Mihailovca, *Moldova* 43 **D13**
Mihalgazi, *Turkey* 39 **A12**
Mihalıççık, *Turkey* 72 **C4**
Mihara, *Japan* 55 **G6**
Miheşu de Cîmpie, *Romania* 43 **D9**
Mijas, *Spain* 35 **J6**
Mikese, *Tanzania* 86 **D4**
Mikha-Tskhakaya = Senaki, *Georgia* 49 **J6**
Mikhailovka = Mykhaylivka, *Ukraine* 47 **J8**
Mikhaylov, *Russia* 46 **E10**
Mikhaylovgrad = Montana, *Bulgaria* 40 **C7**
Mikhaylovka, *Russia* 48 **E6**
Mikhnevo, *Russia* 46 **E9**
Mikínai, *Greece* 38 **D4**
Mikkeli, *Finland* 9 **F22**
Mikkwa →, *Canada* 104 **B6**
Mikniya, *Sudan* 81 **D3**
Mikołajki, *Poland* 44 **E8**
Míkonos, *Greece* 39 **D7**
Mikrí Préspa, Límni, *Greece* 40 **F5**
Mikrón Dhérion, *Greece* 41 **E10**
Mikstat, *Poland* 45 **G4**
Mikulov, *Czech Rep.* 27 **C9**
Mikumi, *Tanzania* 86 **D4**
Milaca, *U.S.A.* 112 **C8**
Milagro, *Ecuador* 124 **D3**
Milagros, *Phil.* 61 **E5**
Milan = Milano, *Italy* 28 **C6**
Milan, *Mo., U.S.A.* 112 **E8**
Milan, *Tenn., U.S.A.* 109 **H1**
Milange, *Mozam.* 87 **F4**
Milano, *Italy* 28 **C6**
Milanoa, *Madag.* 89 **A8**
Milâs, *Turkey* 39 **D9**
Mílatos, *Greece* 36 **D7**
Milazzo, *Italy* 31 **D8**
Milbank, *U.S.A.* 112 **C6**
Milbanke Sd., *Canada* 104 **C3**
Milden, *Canada* 105 **C7**
Mildenhall, *U.K.* 13 **E8**
Mildmay, *Canada* 110 **B3**
Mildura, *Australia* 95 **E3**
Mile, *China* 58 **E4**
Miléai, *Greece* 38 **B5**
Miles, *Australia* 95 **D5**
Miles City, *U.S.A.* 112 **B2**
Mileşti, *Moldova* 43 **C13**
Milestone, *Canada* 105 **D8**
Mileto, *Italy* 31 **D9**
Miletto, Mte., *Italy* 31 **A7**
Miletus, *Turkey* 39 **D9**
Milevsko, *Czech Rep.* 26 **B7**
Milford, *Calif., U.S.A.* 116 **E6**
Milford, *Conn., U.S.A.* 111 **E11**
Milford, *Del., U.S.A.* 108 **F8**
Milford, *Mass., U.S.A.* 111 **D13**
Milford, *N.H., U.S.A.* 111 **D13**

Milford

Milford, *Pa., U.S.A.* 111 E10
Milford, *Utah, U.S.A.* 115 G7
Milford Haven, *U.K.* 13 F2
Milford Sd., *N.Z.* 91 L1
Milḩ, Baḩr al, *Iraq* 70 C4
Milicz, *Poland* 45 G4
Milikapiti, *Australia* 92 B5
Miling, *Australia* 93 F2
Militello in Val di Catánia, *Italy* 31 E7
Milk →, *U.S.A.* 114 B10
Milk, Wadi el →, *Sudan* 80 D3
Milk River, *Canada* 104 D6
Mill I., *Antarctica* 5 C8
Mill Valley, *U.S.A.* 116 H4
Millárs →, *Spain* 32 F4
Millau, *France* 20 D7
Millbridge, *Canada* 110 B7
Millbrook, *Canada* 110 B6
Millbrook, *U.S.A.* 111 E11
Mille Lacs, L. des, *Canada* 102 C1
Mille Lacs L., *U.S.A.* 112 B8
Milledgeville, *U.S.A.* 109 J4
Millen, *U.S.A.* 109 J5
Millennium I. = Caroline I., *Kiribati* 97 H12
Miller, *U.S.A.* 112 C5
Millerovo, *Russia* 49 F5
Millersburg, *Ohio, U.S.A.* 110 F3
Millersburg, *Pa., U.S.A.* 110 F8
Millerton, *U.S.A.* 111 E11
Millerton L., *U.S.A.* 116 J7
Millevaches, Plateau de, *France* 20 C6
Millheim, *U.S.A.* 110 F7
Millicent, *Australia* 95 F3
Millington, *U.S.A.* 113 H10
Millinocket, *U.S.A.* 109 C11
Millmerran, *Australia* 95 D5
Millom, *U.K.* 12 C4
Mills L., *Canada* 104 A5
Millsboro, *U.S.A.* 110 G5
Milltown Malbay, *Ireland* 15 D2
Millville, *N.J., U.S.A.* 108 F8
Millville, *Pa., U.S.A.* 111 E8
Millwood L., *U.S.A.* 113 J8
Milna, *Croatia* 29 E13
Milne →, *Australia* 94 C2
Milo, *U.S.A.* 109 C11
Mílos, *Greece* 38 E6
Miłosław, *Poland* 45 F4
Milot, *Albania* 40 E3
Milparinka, *Australia* 95 D3
Miltenberg, *Germany* 25 F5
Milton, *N.S., Canada* 103 D7
Milton, *Ont., Canada* 110 C5
Milton, *N.Z.* 91 M2
Milton, *Calif., U.S.A.* 116 G6
Milton, *Fla., U.S.A.* 109 K2
Milton, *Pa., U.S.A.* 110 F8
Milton, *Vt., U.S.A.* 111 B11
Milton-Freewater, *U.S.A.* 114 D4
Milton Keynes, *U.K.* 13 E7
Milton Keynes □, *U.K.* 13 E7
Miluo, *China* 59 C9
Milverton, *Canada* 110 C4
Milwaukee, *U.S.A.* 108 D2
Milwaukee Deep, *Atl. Oc.* 121 C6
Milwaukie, *U.S.A.* 116 E4
Mim, *Ghana* 82 D4
Mimizan, *France* 20 D2
Mimoň, *Czech Rep.* 26 A7
Min Jiang →, *Fujian, China* 59 E12
Min Jiang →, *Sichuan, China* 58 C5
Min Xian, *China* 56 G3
Mina Pirquitas, *Argentina* 126 A2
Mīnā Su'ud, *Si. Arabia* 71 D6
Mīnā'al Aḩmadī, *Kuwait* 71 D6
Minago →, *Canada* 105 C9
Minaki, *Canada* 105 D10
Minamata, *Japan* 55 H5
Minami-Tori-Shima, *Pac. Oc.* 96 E7
Minas, *Uruguay* 127 C4
Minas, Sierra de las, *Guatemala* 120 C2
Minas Basin, *Canada* 103 C7
Minas de Rio Tinto = Minas de Riotinto, *Spain* 35 H4
Minas de Riotinto, *Spain* 35 H4
Minas Gerais □, *Brazil* 125 G9
Minatitlán, *Mexico* 119 D6
Minbu, *Burma* 67 J19
Minchinabad, *Pakistan* 68 D5
Mincio →, *Italy* 28 C7
Minčol, *Slovak Rep.* 27 B13
Mindanao, *Phil.* 61 H6
Mindanao Sea = Bohol Sea, *Phil.* 63 C6
Mindanao Trench, *Pac. Oc.* 61 F7
Mindel →, *Germany* 25 G6
Mindelheim, *Germany* 25 G6
Minden, *Canada* 110 B6
Minden, *Germany* 24 C4
Minden, *La., U.S.A.* 113 J8
Minden, *Nev., U.S.A.* 116 G7
Mindiptana, *Indonesia* 63 F10
Mindoro, *Phil.* 61 E4
Mindoro Str., *Phil.* 61 E4
Mine, *Japan* 55 G5
Minehead, *U.K.* 13 F4
Mineola, *N.Y., U.S.A.* 111 F11
Mineola, *Tex., U.S.A.* 113 J7
Mineral King, *U.S.A.* 116 J8
Mineral Wells, *U.S.A.* 113 J5
Mineralnyye Vody, *Russia* 49 H6
Minersville, *U.S.A.* 111 F8
Minerva, *U.S.A.* 110 F3
Minervino Murge, *Italy* 31 A9
Minetto, *U.S.A.* 111 C8
Mingäçevir, *Azerbaijan* 49 K8
Mingäçevir Su Anbarı, *Azerbaijan* 49 K8
Mingan, *Canada* 103 B7
Mingechaur = Mingäçevir, *Azerbaijan* 49 K8
Mingechaurskoye Vdkhr. = Mingäçevir Su Anbarı, *Azerbaijan* 49 K8
Mingela, *Australia* 94 B4
Mingenew, *Australia* 93 E2
Mingera Cr. →, *Australia* 94 C2
Minggang, *China* 59 A10
Mingguang, *China* 59 A11
Mingin, *Burma* 67 H19
Mingir, *Moldova* 43 D13
Minglanilla, *Spain* 33 F3
Minglun, *China* 58 E7
Mingo Junction, *U.S.A.* 110 F4
Mingorria, *Spain* 34 E6
Mingshan, *China* 58 B4
Mingteke Daban = Mintaka Pass, *Pakistan* 69 A6
Mingxi, *China* 59 D11
Mingyuegue, *China* 57 C15
Minho = Miño →, *Spain* 34 D2
Minhou, *China* 59 E12
Minićevo, *Serbia, Yug.* 42 G7
Minidoka, *U.S.A.* 114 E7
Minigwal, L., *Australia* 93 E3
Minilya →, *Australia* 93 D1
Minilya Roadhouse, *Australia* 93 D1
Minipi L., *Canada* 103 B7
Mink L., *Canada* 104 A5
Minkammen, *Sudan* 81 F3
Minna, *Nigeria* 83 D6
Minneapolis, *Kans., U.S.A.* 112 F6
Minneapolis, *Minn., U.S.A.* 112 C8
Minnedosa, *Canada* 105 C9
Minnesota □, *U.S.A.* 112 B8
Minnesota →, *U.S.A.* 112 C8
Minnewaukan, *U.S.A.* 112 A5
Minnipa, *Australia* 95 E2
Minnitaki L., *Canada* 102 C1
Mino, *Japan* 55 G8
Miño, *Spain* 34 B2
Miño →, *Spain* 34 D2
Minoa, *Greece* 39 F7
Minorca = Menorca, *Spain* 37 B11
Minot, *U.S.A.* 112 A4
Minqin, *China* 56 E2
Minqing, *China* 59 D12
Minsen, *Germany* 24 B3
Minsk, *Belarus* 46 F4
Mińsk Mazowiecki, *Poland* 45 F8
Mintabie, *Australia* 95 D1
Mintaka Pass, *Pakistan* 69 A6
Minto, *Canada* 103 C6
Minto, L., *Canada* 102 A5
Minton, *Canada* 105 D8
Minturn, *U.S.A.* 114 G10
Minturno, *Italy* 30 A6
Minûf, *Egypt* 80 H7
Minusinsk, *Russia* 51 D10
Minutang, *India* 67 E20
Minya el Qamh, *Egypt* 80 H7
Mionica, *Bos.-H.* 42 F3
Mionica, *Serbia, Yug.* 40 B4
Miquelon, *Canada* 102 C4
Miquelon, *St- P. & M.* 103 C8
Mir, *Niger* 83 C7
Mīr Kūh, *Iran* 71 E8
Mīr Shahdād, *Iran* 71 E8
Mira, *Italy* 29 C9
Mira, *Portugal* 34 E2
Mira →, *Portugal* 35 H2
Mira por vos Cay, *Bahamas* 121 B5
Mirabella Eclano, *Italy* 31 A7
Miraj, *India* 66 L9
Miram Shah, *Pakistan* 68 C4
Miramar, *Argentina* 126 D4
Miramar, *Mozam.* 89 C6
Miramas, *France* 21 E8
Mirambeau, *France* 20 C3
Miramichi, *Canada* 103 C6
Miramichi B., *Canada* 103 C7
Miramont-de-Guyenne, *France* 20 D4
Miranda, *Brazil* 125 H7
Miranda →, *Brazil* 124 G7
Miranda de Ebro, *Spain* 32 C2
Miranda do Corvo, *Portugal* 34 E2
Miranda do Douro, *Portugal* 34 D4
Mirande, *France* 20 E4
Mirandela, *Portugal* 34 D3
Mirándola, *Italy* 28 D8
Mirandópolis, *Brazil* 127 A5
Mirango, *Malawi* 87 E3
Mirano, *Italy* 29 C9
Miras, *Albania* 40 F4
Mirassol, *Brazil* 127 A6
Mirbāţ, *Oman* 74 D5
Mirear, *Egypt* 80 C4
Mirebeau, *Côte-d'Or, France* 19 E12
Mirebeau, *Vienne, France* 18 F7
Mirecourt, *France* 19 D13
Mirgorod = Myrhorod, *Ukraine* 47 H7
Miri, *Malaysia* 62 D4
Miriam Vale, *Australia* 94 C5
Miribel, *France* 19 G11
Mirim, L., *S. Amer.* 127 C5
Mirnyy, *Russia* 51 C12
Miroč, *Serbia, Yug.* 40 B6
Mirokhan, *Pakistan* 68 F3
Mirond L., *Canada* 105 B8
Mirosławiec, *Poland* 44 E3
Mirpur, *Pakistan* 69 C5
Mirpur Batoro, *Pakistan* 68 G3
Mirpur Bibiwari, *Pakistan* 68 E2
Mirpur Khas, *Pakistan* 68 G3
Mirpur Sakro, *Pakistan* 68 G2
Mirria, *Niger* 83 C6
Mirsk, *Poland* 45 H2
Mirtağ, *Turkey* 70 B4
Miryang, *S. Korea* 57 G15
Mirzaani, *Georgia* 49 K8
Mirzapur, *India* 69 G10
Mirzapur-cum-Vindhyachal = Mirzapur, *India* 69 G10
Misantla, *Mexico* 119 D5
Misawa, *Japan* 54 D10
Miscou I., *Canada* 103 C7
Mish'āb, Ra's al, *Si. Arabia* 71 D6
Mishan, *China* 60 B8
Mishawaka, *U.S.A.* 108 E2
Mishbih, Gebel, *Egypt* 80 C3
Mishima, *Japan* 55 G9
Misión, *Mexico* 117 N10
Misiones □, *Argentina* 127 B5
Misiones □, *Paraguay* 126 B4
Miskah, *Si. Arabia* 70 E4
Miskitos, Cayos, *Nic.* 120 D3
Miskolc, *Hungary* 42 B5
Misoke, *Dem. Rep. of the Congo* 86 C2
Misool, *Indonesia* 63 E8
Mişrātah, *Libya* 79 B9
Missanabie, *Canada* 102 C3
Missinaibi →, *Canada* 102 B3
Missinaibi L., *Canada* 102 C3
Mission, *Canada* 104 D4
Mission, *S. Dak., U.S.A.* 112 D4
Mission, *Tex., U.S.A.* 113 M5
Mission Beach, *Australia* 94 B4
Mission Viejo, *U.S.A.* 117 M9
Missirah, *Senegal* 82 C1
Missisa L., *Canada* 102 B2
Missisicabi →, *Canada* 102 B4
Mississagi →, *Canada* 102 C3
Mississauga, *Canada* 110 C5
Mississippi □, *U.S.A.* 113 J10
Mississippi →, *U.S.A.* 113 L10
Mississippi L., *Canada* 111 A8
Mississippi River Delta, *U.S.A.* 113 L9
Mississippi Sd., *U.S.A.* 113 K10
Missoula, *U.S.A.* 114 C7
Missouri □, *U.S.A.* 112 F8
Missouri →, *U.S.A.* 112 F9
Missouri City, *U.S.A.* 113 L7
Missouri Valley, *U.S.A.* 112 E7
Mist, *U.S.A.* 116 E3
Mistassibi →, *Canada* 103 B5
Mistassini, *Canada* 103 C5
Mistassini →, *Canada* 103 C5
Mistassini, L., *Canada* 102 B5
Mistastin L., *Canada* 103 A7
Mistelbach, *Austria* 27 C9
Misterbianco, *Italy* 31 E8
Mistinibi, L., *Canada* 103 A7
Mistretta, *Italy* 31 E7
Misty L., *Canada* 105 B8
Misurata = Mişrātah, *Libya* 79 B9
Mît Ghamr, *Egypt* 80 H7
Mitatib, *Sudan* 81 D4
Mitchell, *Australia* 95 D4
Mitchell, *Canada* 110 C3
Mitchell, *Nebr., U.S.A.* 112 E3
Mitchell, *Oreg., U.S.A.* 114 D3
Mitchell, *S. Dak., U.S.A.* 112 D6
Mitchell →, *Australia* 94 B3
Mitchell, Mt., *U.S.A.* 109 H4
Mitchell Ranges, *Australia* 94 A2
Mitchelstown, *Ireland* 15 D3
Mitha Tiwana, *Pakistan* 68 C5
Mithi, *Pakistan* 68 G3
Míthimna, *Greece* 39 B8
Mithrao, *Pakistan* 68 F3
Mitilíni, *Greece* 39 B8
Mitilinoí, *Greece* 39 D8
Mito, *Japan* 55 F10
Mitrofanovka, *Russia* 47 H10
Mitrovica = Kosovska Mitrovica, *Kosovo, Yug.* 40 D4
Mitsinjo, *Madag.* 89 B8
Mitsiwa, *Eritrea* 81 D4
Mitsiwa Channel, *Eritrea* 81 D5
Mitsukaidō, *Japan* 55 F9
Mittagong, *Australia* 95 E5
Mittelberg, *Austria* 26 D3
Mittelfranken □, *Germany* 25 F6
Mittellandkanal →, *Germany* 24 C4
Mittenwalde, *Germany* 24 C9
Mittersill, *Austria* 26 D5
Mitterteich, *Germany* 25 F8
Mittimatalik = Pond Inlet, *Canada* 101 A12
Mittweida, *Germany* 24 E8
Mitú, *Colombia* 124 C4
Mitumba, *Tanzania* 86 D3
Mitumba, Mts., *Dem. Rep. of the Congo* 86 D2
Mitwaba, *Dem. Rep. of the Congo* 87 D2
Mityana, *Uganda* 86 B3
Mixteco →, *Mexico* 119 D5
Miyagi □, *Japan* 54 E10
Miyāh, W. el →, *Egypt* 80 C3
Miyāh, W. el →, *Syria* 70 C3
Miyake-Jima, *Japan* 55 G9
Miyako, *Japan* 54 E10
Miyako-Jima, *Japan* 55 M2
Miyako-Rettō, *Japan* 55 M2
Miyakonojō, *Japan* 55 J5
Miyani, *India* 68 J3
Miyanoura-Dake, *Japan* 55 J5
Miyazaki, *Japan* 55 J5
Miyazaki □, *Japan* 55 H5
Miyazu, *Japan* 55 G7
Miyet, Bahr el = Dead Sea, *Asia* 75 D4
Miyi, *China* 58 D4
Miyoshi, *Japan* 55 G6
Miyun, *China* 56 D9
Miyun Shuiku, *China* 57 D9
Mizan Teferi, *Ethiopia* 81 F4
Mizdah, *Libya* 79 B8
Mizen Hd., *Cork, Ireland* 15 E2
Mizen Hd., *Wick., Ireland* 15 D5
Mizhi, *China* 56 F6
Mizil, *Romania* 43 F11
Mizoram □, *India* 67 H18
Miẓpe Ramon, *Israel* 75 E3
Mizusawa, *Japan* 54 E10
Mjällby, *Sweden* 11 H8
Mjöbäck, *Sweden* 11 G6
Mjölby, *Sweden* 11 F9
Mjörn, *Sweden* 11 G6
Mjøsa, *Norway* 9 F14
Mkata, *Tanzania* 86 D4
Mkokotoni, *Tanzania* 86 D4
Mkomazi, *Tanzania* 86 C4
Mkomazi →, *S. Africa* 89 E5
Mkulwe, *Tanzania* 87 D3
Mkumbi, Ras, *Tanzania* 86 D4
Mkushi, *Zambia* 87 E2
Mkushi River, *Zambia* 87 E2
Mkuze, *S. Africa* 89 D5
Mladá Boleslav, *Czech Rep.* 26 A7
Mladenovac, *Serbia, Yug.* 40 B4
Mlala Hills, *Tanzania* 86 D3
Mlange = Mulanje, *Malawi* 87 F4
Mlanje, Pic, *Malawi* 85 H7
Mlava →, *Serbia, Yug.* 40 B5
Mława, *Poland* 45 E7
Mlinište, *Bos.-H.* 29 D13
Mljet, *Croatia* 29 F14
Mljetski Kanal, *Croatia* 29 F14
Młynary, *Poland* 44 D6
Mmabatho, *S. Africa* 88 D4
Mme, *Cameroon* 83 D7
Mnichovo Hradiště, *Czech Rep.* 26 A7
Mo i Rana, *Norway* 8 C16
Moa, *Cuba* 121 B4
Moa, *Indonesia* 63 F7
Moa →, *S. Leone* 82 D2
Moab, *U.S.A.* 115 G9
Moala, *Fiji* 91 D8
Moama, *Australia* 95 F3
Moamba, *Mozam.* 89 D5
Moapa, *U.S.A.* 117 J12
Moate, *Ireland* 15 C4
Moba, *Dem. Rep. of the Congo* 86 D2
Mobārakābād, *Iran* 71 D7
Mobaye, *C.A.R.* 84 D4
Mobayi, *Dem. Rep. of the Congo* 84 D4
Moberley Lake, *Canada* 104 B4
Moberly, *U.S.A.* 112 F8
Mobile, *U.S.A.* 109 K1
Mobile B., *U.S.A.* 109 K2
Mobridge, *U.S.A.* 112 C4
Mobutu Sese Seko, L. = Albert, L., *Africa* 86 B3
Moc Chau, *Vietnam* 64 B5
Moc Hoa, *Vietnam* 65 G5
Mocabe Kasari, *Dem. Rep. of the Congo* 87 D2
Moçambique, *Mozam.* 87 F5
Moçâmedes = Namibe, *Angola* 85 H2
Mocanaqua, *U.S.A.* 111 E8
Mochudi, *Botswana* 88 C4
Mocimboa da Praia, *Mozam.* 87 E5
Mociu, *Romania* 43 D9
Möckeln, *Sweden* 11 H8
Mockfjärd, *Sweden* 10 D8
Moclips, *U.S.A.* 116 C2
Mocoa, *Colombia* 124 C3
Mococa, *Brazil* 127 A6
Mocorito, *Mexico* 118 B3
Moctezuma, *Mexico* 118 B3
Moctezuma →, *Mexico* 119 C5
Mocuba, *Mozam.* 87 F4
Mocúzari, Presa, *Mexico* 118 B3
Modane, *France* 21 C10
Modasa, *India* 68 H5
Modder →, *S. Africa* 88 D3
Modderrivier, *S. Africa* 88 D3
Módena, *Italy* 28 D7
Modena, *U.S.A.* 115 H7
Modesto, *U.S.A.* 116 H6
Módica, *Italy* 31 F7
Mödling, *Austria* 27 C9
Modo, *Sudan* 81 F3
Modra, *Slovak Rep.* 27 C10
Modriča, *Bos.-H.* 42 F3
Moe, *Australia* 95 F4
Moebase, *Mozam.* 87 F4
Moëlan-sur-Mer, *France* 18 E3
Moengo, *Surinam* 125 B8
Moffat, *U.K.* 14 F5
Moga, *India* 68 D6
Mogadishu = Muqdisho, *Somali Rep.* 74 G4
Mogador = Essaouira, *Morocco* 78 B4
Mogadouro, *Portugal* 34 D4
Mogalakwena →, *S. Africa* 89 C4
Mogami-Gawa →, *Japan* 54 E10
Mogán, *Canary Is.* 37 G4
Mogaung, *Burma* 67 G20
Mogente = Moixent, *Spain* 33 G4
Mogho, *Ethiopia* 81 G5
Mogi das Cruzes, *Brazil* 127 A6
Mogi-Guaçu →, *Brazil* 127 A6
Mogi-Mirim, *Brazil* 127 A6
Mogielnica, *Poland* 45 G7
Mogige, *Ethiopia* 81 F4
Mogilev = Mahilyow, *Belarus* 46 F6
Mogilev-Podolskiy = Mohyliv-Podilskyy, *Ukraine* 47 H4
Mogilno, *Poland* 45 F4
Mogincual, *Mozam.* 87 F5
Mogliano Véneto, *Italy* 29 C9
Mogocha, *Russia* 51 D12
Mogok, *Burma* 67 H20
Mogollon Rim, *U.S.A.* 115 J8
Mógoro, *Italy* 30 C1
Mograt, *Sudan* 80 D3
Moguer, *Spain* 35 H4
Mogumber, *Australia* 93 F2
Mohács, *Hungary* 42 E3
Mohales Hoek, *Lesotho* 88 E4
Mohall, *U.S.A.* 112 A4
Moḩammadābād, *Iran* 71 B8
Mohammedia, *Morocco* 78 B4
Mohana →, *India* 69 G11
Mohanlalganj, *India* 69 F9
Mohave, L., *U.S.A.* 117 K12
Mohawk →, *U.S.A.* 111 D11
Moheda, *Sweden* 11 G8
Mohenjodaro, *Pakistan* 68 F3
Mohicanville Reservoir, *U.S.A.* 110 F3
Möhne →, *Germany* 24 D3
Mohoro, *Tanzania* 86 D4
Mohyliv-Podilskyy, *Ukraine* 47 H4
Moia, *Sudan* 81 F2
Moidart, L., *U.K.* 14 E3
Moineşti, *Romania* 43 D11
Moira →, *Canada* 110 B7
Moirans, *France* 21 C9
Moirans-en-Montagne, *France* 19 F12
Moíres, *Greece* 36 D6
Moisaküla, *Estonia* 9 G21
Moisie, *Canada* 103 B6
Moisie →, *Canada* 103 B6
Moissac, *France* 20 D5
Moita, *Portugal* 35 G2
Moixent, *Spain* 33 G4
Möja, *Sweden* 10 E12
Mojácar, *Spain* 33 H3
Mojados, *Spain* 34 D6
Mojave, *U.S.A.* 117 K8
Mojave Desert, *U.S.A.* 117 L10
Mojiang, *China* 58 F3
Mojjo →, *Ethiopia* 81 F5
Mojkovac, *Montenegro, Yug.* 40 D3
Mojo, *Bolivia* 126 A2
Mojo, *Ethiopia* 81 F4
Mojokerto, *Indonesia* 63 G15
Mokai, *N.Z.* 91 H5
Mokambo, *Dem. Rep. of the Congo* 87 E2
Mokameh, *India* 69 G11
Mokau, *N.Z.* 91 H5
Mokelumne →, *U.S.A.* 116 G5
Mokelumne Hill, *U.S.A.* 116 G6
Mokhós, *Greece* 36 D7
Mokhotlong, *Lesotho* 89 D4
Möklinta, *Sweden* 10 D10
Mokokchung, *India* 67 F19
Mokolo, *Cameroon* 83 C7
Mokolo →, *S. Africa* 89 C4
Mokp'o, *S. Korea* 57 G14
Mokra Gora, *Yugoslavia* 40 D4
Mokronog, *Slovenia* 29 C12
Moksha →, *Russia* 48 C6
Mokshan, *Russia* 48 D7
Mokwa, *Nigeria* 83 D6
Mol, *Belgium* 17 C5
Mola di Bari, *Italy* 31 A10
Molale, *Ethiopia* 81 E4
Moláoi, *Greece* 38 E4
Molara, *Italy* 30 B2
Molaţ, *Croatia* 29 D11
Molchanovo, *Russia* 50 D9
Mold, *U.K.* 12 D4
Moldava nad Bodvou, *Slovak Rep.* 27 C14
Moldavia = Moldova ■, *Europe* 43 C13
Moldavia, *Romania* 43 D12
Molde, *Norway* 8 E12
Moldova ■, *Europe* 43 C13
Moldova Nouă, *Romania* 42 F6
Moldoveanu, Vf., *Romania* 43 E9
Moldoviţa, *Romania* 43 C10
Mole →, *U.K.* 13 F7
Mole Creek, *Australia* 94 G4
Molepolole, *Botswana* 88 C4
Molfetta, *Italy* 31 A9
Molina de Aragón, *Spain* 32 E3
Molina de Segura, *Spain* 33 G3
Moline, *U.S.A.* 112 E9
Molinella, *Italy* 29 D8
Molinos, *Argentina* 126 B2
Moliro, *Dem. Rep. of the Congo* 86 D3
Moliterno, *Italy* 31 B8
Molkom, *Sweden* 10 E7
Mölle, *Sweden* 11 H6
Molledo, *Spain* 34 B6
Mollendo, *Peru* 124 G4
Mollerin, L., *Australia* 93 F2
Mollerussa, *Spain* 32 D5
Mollina, *Spain* 35 H6
Mölln, *Germany* 24 B6
Mölltorp, *Sweden* 11 F8
Mölnlycke, *Sweden* 11 G6
Molochansk, *Ukraine* 47 J8
Molochnoye, Ozero, *Ukraine* 47 J8
Molodechno = Maladzyechna, *Belarus* 46 E4
Molokai, *U.S.A.* 106 H16
Molong, *Australia* 95 E4
Molopo →, *Africa* 88 D3
Mólos, *Greece* 38 C4

Molotov = Perm, *Russia* 50 D6
Molsheim, *France* 19 D14
Molson L., *Canada* 105 C9
Molteno, *S. Africa* 88 E4
Molu, *Indonesia* 63 F8
Molucca Sea, *Indonesia* 63 E6
Moluccas = Maluku, *Indonesia* 63 E7
Moma, *Dem. Rep. of the Congo* 86 C1
Moma, *Mozam.* 87 F4
Mombasa, *Kenya* 86 C4
Mombetsu, *Japan* 54 B11
Mombuey, *Spain* 34 C4
Momchilgrad, *Bulgaria* 41 E9
Momi, *Dem. Rep. of the Congo* 86 C2
Mompós, *Colombia* 124 B4
Møn, *Denmark* 11 K6
Mon □, *Burma* 67 L20
Mona, Canal de la, *W. Indies* 121 C6
Mona, Isla, *Puerto Rico* 121 C6
Mona, Pta., *Costa Rica* 120 E3
Monaca, *U.S.A.* 110 F4
Monaco ■, *Europe* 21 E11
Monadhliath Mts., *U.K.* 14 D4
Monadnock, Mt., *U.S.A.* 111 D12
Monaghan, *Ireland* 15 B5
Monaghan □, *Ireland* 15 B5
Monahans, *U.S.A.* 113 K3
Monapo, *Mozam.* 87 E5
Monar, L., *U.K.* 14 D3
Monarch Mt., *Canada* 104 C3
Monashee Mts., *Canada* 104 C5
Monasterevin, *Ireland* 15 C4
Monastir = Bitola, *Macedonia* 40 E5
Moncada, *Phil.* 61 D4
Moncalieri, *Italy* 28 D4
Moncalvo, *Italy* 28 C5
Moncão, *Portugal* 34 C2
Moncarapacho, *Portugal* 35 H3
Moncayo, Sierra del, *Spain* 32 D3
Mönchengladbach, *Germany* 24 D2
Monchique, *Portugal* 35 H2
Moncks Corner, *U.S.A.* 109 J5
Monclova, *Mexico* 118 B4
Moncontour, *France* 18 D4
Moncton, *Canada* 103 C7
Mondariz, *Spain* 34 C2
Mondego →, *Portugal* 34 E2
Mondego, C., *Portugal* 34 E2
Mondeodo, *Indonesia* 63 E6
Mondeville, *France* 18 C6
Mondolfo, *Italy* 29 E10
Mondoñedo, *Spain* 34 B3
Mondovì, *Italy* 28 D4
Mondragon, *Phil.* 61 E6
Mondragone, *Italy* 30 A6
Mondrain I., *Australia* 93 F3
Monemvasía, *Greece* 38 E5
Monessen, *U.S.A.* 110 F5
Monesterio, *Spain* 35 G4
Monestier-de-Clermont, *France* 21 D9
Monett, *U.S.A.* 113 G8
Moneymore, *U.K.* 15 B5
Monfalcone, *Italy* 29 C10
Monflanquin, *France* 20 D4
Monforte, *Portugal* 35 F3
Monforte de Lemos, *Spain* 34 C3
Mong Hsu, *Burma* 58 G2
Mong Kung, *Burma* 67 J20
Mong Nai, *Burma* 67 J20
Mong Pawk, *Burma* 67 H21
Mong Ping, *Burma* 58 G2
Mong Ton, *Burma* 67 J21
Mong Wa, *Burma* 67 J22
Mong Yai, *Burma* 67 H21
Mongalla, *Sudan* 81 F3
Mongers, L., *Australia* 93 E2
Monghyr = Munger, *India* 69 G12
Mongibello = Etna, *Italy* 31 E7
Mongo, *Chad* 79 F9
Mongo →, *S. Leone* 82 D2
Mongolia ■, *Asia* 51 E10
Mongonu, *Nigeria* 83 C7
Mongu, *Zambia* 85 H4
Mônguá, *Angola* 88 B2
Monifieth, *U.K.* 14 E6
Monistrol-sur-Loire, *France* 21 C8
Monkey Bay, *Malawi* 87 E4
Monkey Mia, *Australia* 93 E1
Monkey River, *Belize* 119 D7
Mońki, *Poland* 44 E9
Monkoto, *Dem. Rep. of the Congo* 84 E4
Monkton, *Canada* 110 C3
Monmouth, *U.K.* 13 F5
Monmouth, *Ill., U.S.A.* 112 E9
Monmouth, *Oreg., U.S.A.* 114 D2
Monmouthshire □, *U.K.* 13 F5
Mono L., *U.S.A.* 116 H7
Monolith, *U.S.A.* 117 K8
Monólithos, *Greece* 36 C9
Monongahela, *U.S.A.* 110 F5
Monópoli, *Italy* 31 B10
Monor, *Hungary* 42 C4
Monóvar, *Spain* 33 G4
Monreal del Campo, *Spain* 32 E3
Monreale, *Italy* 30 D6
Monroe, *Ga., U.S.A.* 109 J4
Monroe, *La., U.S.A.* 113 J8
Monroe, *Mich., U.S.A.* 108 E4
Monroe, *N.C., U.S.A.* 109 H5
Monroe, *N.Y., U.S.A.* 111 E10
Monroe, *Utah, U.S.A.* 115 G7
Monroe, *Wash., U.S.A.* 116 C5
Monroe, *Wis., U.S.A.* 112 D10
Monroe City, *U.S.A.* 112 F9
Monroeton, *U.S.A.* 111 E8
Monroeville, *Ala., U.S.A.* 109 K2
Monroeville, *Pa., U.S.A.* 110 F5
Monrovia, *Liberia* 82 D2
Mons, *Belgium* 17 D3
Møns Klint, *Denmark* 11 K6
Monsaraz, *Portugal* 35 G3
Monse, *Indonesia* 63 E6
Monségur, *France* 20 D4
Monsélice, *Italy* 29 C8
Mönsterås, *Sweden* 11 G10
Mont Cenis, Col du, *France* 21 C10
Mont-de-Marsan, *France* 20 E3
Mont-Joli, *Canada* 103 C6
Mont-Laurier, *Canada* 102 C4
Mont-Louis, *Canada* 103 C6
Mont-roig del Camp, *Spain* 32 D5
Mont-St-Michel, Le = Le Mont-St-Michel, *France* 18 D5
Mont Tremblant, Parc Recr. du, *Canada* 102 C5
Montabaur, *Germany* 24 E3
Montagnac, *France* 20 E7
Montagnana, *Italy* 29 C8
Montagu, *S. Africa* 88 E3
Montagu I., *Antarctica* 5 B1
Montague, *Canada* 103 C7
Montague, I., *Mexico* 118 A2
Montague Ra., *Australia* 93 E2
Montague Sd., *Australia* 92 B4
Montaigu, *France* 18 F5
Montalbán, *Spain* 32 E4
Montalbano Iónico, *Italy* 31 B9
Montalbo, *Spain* 32 F2
Montalcino, *Italy* 29 E8
Montalegre, *Portugal* 34 D3
Montalto, *Italy* 31 D8
Montalto di Castro, *Italy* 29 F8
Montalto Uffugo, *Italy* 31 C9
Montalvo, *U.S.A.* 117 L7
Montamarta, *Spain* 34 D5
Montana, *Bulgaria* 40 C7
Montaña, *Peru* 124 E4
Montana □, *Bulgaria* 40 C7
Montana □, *U.S.A.* 114 C9
Montaña Clara, I., *Canary Is.* 37 E6
Montánchez, *Spain* 35 F4
Montargil, *Portugal* 35 F2
Montargis, *France* 19 E9
Montauban, *France* 20 D5
Montauk, *U.S.A.* 111 E13
Montauk Pt., *U.S.A.* 111 E13
Montbard, *France* 19 E11
Montbarrey, *France* 19 E12
Montbéliard, *France* 19 E13
Montblanc, *Spain* 32 D6
Montbrison, *France* 21 C8
Montcalm, Pic de, *France* 20 F5
Montceau-les-Mines, *France* 19 F11
Montcenis, *France* 21 B8
Montclair, *U.S.A.* 111 F10
Montcornet, *France* 19 C11
Montcuq, *France* 20 D5
Montdidier, *France* 19 C9
Monte Albán, *Mexico* 119 D5
Monte Alegre, *Brazil* 125 D8
Monte Azul, *Brazil* 125 G10
Monte Bello Is., *Australia* 92 D2
Monte-Carlo, *Monaco* 21 E11
Monte Caseros, *Argentina* 126 C4
Monte Comán, *Argentina* 126 C2
Monte Cristi, *Dom. Rep.* 121 C5
Monte Lindo →, *Paraguay* 126 A4
Monte Patria, *Chile* 126 C1
Monte Quemado, *Argentina* 126 B3
Monte Redondo, *Portugal* 34 F2
Monte Rio, *U.S.A.* 116 G4
Monte San Giovanni Campano, *Italy* 30 A6
Monte San Savino, *Italy* 29 E8
Monte Sant' Ángelo, *Italy* 29 G12
Monte Santu, C. di, *Italy* 30 B2
Monte Vista, *U.S.A.* 115 H10
Monteagudo, *Argentina* 127 B5
Montealegre del Castillo, *Spain* 33 G3
Montebello, *Canada* 102 C5
Montebello Iónico, *Italy* 31 E8
Montebelluna, *Italy* 29 C9
Montebourg, *France* 18 C5
Montecastrilli, *Italy* 29 F9
Montecatini Terme, *Italy* 28 E7
Montecito, *U.S.A.* 117 L7
Montecristo, *Italy* 28 F7
Montefalco, *Italy* 29 F9
Montefiascone, *Italy* 29 F9
Montefrío, *Spain* 35 H7
Montegiórgio, *Italy* 29 E10
Montego Bay, *Jamaica* 120 C4
Montehermoso, *Spain* 34 E4
Montejicar, *Spain* 35 H7
Montélimar, *France* 21 D8
Montella, *Italy* 31 B8
Montellano, *Spain* 35 J5
Montello, *U.S.A.* 112 D10
Montemor-o-Novo, *Portugal* 35 G2
Montemor-o-Velho, *Portugal* 34 E2
Montemorelos, *Mexico* 119 B5
Montendre, *France* 20 C3
Montenegro, *Brazil* 127 B5
Montenegro □, *Yugoslavia* 40 D3
Montenero di Bisáccia, *Italy* 29 G11
Montepuez, *Mozam.* 87 E4
Montepuez →, *Mozam.* 87 E5
Montepulciano, *Italy* 29 E8
Montereale, *Italy* 29 F10
Montereau-Faut-Yonne, *France* 19 D9
Monterey, *U.S.A.* 116 J5
Monterey B., *U.S.A.* 116 J5
Montería, *Colombia* 124 B3
Monteros, *Argentina* 126 B2
Monterotondo, *Italy* 29 F9
Monterrey, *Mexico* 118 B4
Montes Claros, *Brazil* 125 G10
Montesano, *U.S.A.* 116 D3
Montesano sulla Marcellana, *Italy* 31 B8
Montesárchio, *Italy* 31 A7
Montescaglioso, *Italy* 31 B9
Montesilvano, *Italy* 29 F11
Montevarchi, *Italy* 29 E8
Montevideo, *Uruguay* 127 C4
Montevideo, *U.S.A.* 112 C7
Montezuma, *U.S.A.* 112 E8
Montfaucon, *France* 18 E5
Montfaucon-d'Argonne, *France* 19 C12
Montfaucon-en-Velay, *France* 21 C8
Montfort, *France* 18 D5
Montfort-le-Gesnois, *France* 18 D7
Montgenèvre, *France* 21 D10
Montgomery = Sahiwal, *Pakistan* 68 D5
Montgomery, *U.K.* 13 E4
Montgomery, *Ala., U.S.A.* 109 J2
Montgomery, *Pa., U.S.A.* 110 E8
Montgomery, *W. Va., U.S.A.* 108 F5
Montgomery City, *U.S.A.* 112 F9
Montguyon, *France* 20 C3
Monthermé, *France* 19 C11
Monthey, *Switz.* 25 J2
Monthois, *France* 19 C11
Monti, *Italy* 30 B2
Monticelli d'Ongina, *Italy* 28 C6
Monticello, *Ark., U.S.A.* 113 J9
Monticello, *Fla., U.S.A.* 109 K4
Monticello, *Ind., U.S.A.* 108 E2
Monticello, *Iowa, U.S.A.* 112 D9
Monticello, *Ky., U.S.A.* 109 G3
Monticello, *Minn., U.S.A.* 112 C8
Monticello, *Miss., U.S.A.* 113 K9
Monticello, *N.Y., U.S.A.* 111 E10
Monticello, *Utah, U.S.A.* 115 H9
Montichiari, *Italy* 28 C7
Montier-en-Der, *France* 19 D11
Montignac, *France* 20 C5
Montigny-les-Metz, *France* 19 C13
Montigny-sur-Aube, *France* 19 E11
Montijo, *Portugal* 35 G2
Montijo, *Spain* 35 G4
Montilla, *Spain* 35 H6
Montivilliers, *France* 18 C7
Montluçon, *France* 19 F9
Montmagny, *Canada* 103 C5
Montmarault, *France* 19 F9
Montmartre, *Canada* 105 C8
Montmédy, *France* 19 C12
Montmélian, *France* 21 C10
Montmirail, *France* 19 D10
Montmoreau-St-Cybard, *France* 20 C4
Montmorillon, *France* 20 B4
Montmort-Lucy, *France* 19 D10
Monto, *Australia* 94 C5
Montoire-sur-le-Loir, *France* 18 E7
Montório al Vomano, *Italy* 29 F10
Montoro, *Spain* 35 G6
Montour Falls, *U.S.A.* 110 D8
Montoursville, *U.S.A.* 110 E8
Montpelier, *Idaho, U.S.A.* 114 E8
Montpelier, *Vt., U.S.A.* 111 B12
Montpellier, *France* 20 E7
Montpezat-de-Quercy, *France* 20 D5
Montpon-Ménestérol, *France* 20 D4
Montréal, *Canada* 102 C5
Montréal, *Aude, France* 20 E6
Montréal, *Gers, France* 20 E4
Montreal →, *Canada* 102 C3
Montreal L., *Canada* 105 C7
Montreal Lake, *Canada* 105 C7
Montredon-Labessonnié, *France* 20 E6
Montrésor, *France* 18 E8
Montret, *France* 19 F12
Montreuil, *Pas-de-Calais, France* 19 B8
Montreuil, *Seine-St-Denis, France* 19 D9
Montreuil-Bellay, *France* 18 E6
Montreux, *Switz.* 25 J2
Montrevel-en-Bresse, *France* 19 F12
Montrichard, *France* 18 E8
Montrose, *U.K.* 14 E6
Montrose, *Colo., U.S.A.* 115 G10
Montrose, *Pa., U.S.A.* 111 E9
Monts, Pte. des, *Canada* 103 C6
Montsalvy, *France* 20 D6
Montsant, Serra de, *Spain* 32 D6
Montsauche-les-Settons, *France* 19 E11
Montsec, Serra del, *Spain* 32 C5
Montserrat, *Spain* 32 D6
Montserrat ■, *W. Indies* 121 C7
Montuenga, *Spain* 34 D6
Montuiri, *Spain* 37 B9
Monywa, *Burma* 67 H19
Monza, *Italy* 28 C6
Monze, *Zambia* 87 F2
Monze, C., *Pakistan* 68 G2
Monzón, *Spain* 32 D5
Mooers, *U.S.A.* 111 B11
Mooi →, *S. Africa* 89 D5
Mooi River, *S. Africa* 89 D4
Moonah →, *Australia* 94 C2
Moonda, L., *Australia* 94 D3
Moonie, *Australia* 95 D5
Moonie →, *Australia* 95 D4
Moonta, *Australia* 95 E2
Moora, *Australia* 93 F2
Moorcroft, *U.S.A.* 112 C2
Moore →, *Australia* 93 F2
Moore, L., *Australia* 93 E2
Moore Park, *Australia* 94 C5
Moore Reefs, *Australia* 94 B4
Moorefield, *U.S.A.* 108 F6
Moores Res., *U.S.A.* 111 B13
Moorfoot Hills, *U.K.* 14 F5
Moorhead, *U.S.A.* 112 B6
Moormerland, *Germany* 24 B3
Moorpark, *U.S.A.* 117 L8
Moorreesburg, *S. Africa* 88 E2
Moosburg, *Germany* 25 G7
Moose →, *Canada* 102 B3
Moose →, *U.S.A.* 111 C9
Moose Creek, *Canada* 111 A10
Moose Factory, *Canada* 102 B3
Moose Jaw, *Canada* 105 C7
Moose Jaw →, *Canada* 105 C7
Moose Lake, *Canada* 105 C8
Moose Lake, *U.S.A.* 112 B8
Moose Mountain Prov. Park, *Canada* 105 D8
Moosehead L., *U.S.A.* 109 C11
Mooselookmeguntic L., *U.S.A.* 109 C10
Moosilauke, Mt., *U.S.A.* 111 B13
Moosomin, *Canada* 105 C8
Moosonee, *Canada* 102 B3
Moosup, *U.S.A.* 111 E13
Mopane, *S. Africa* 89 C4
Mopeia Velha, *Mozam.* 87 F4
Mopipi, *Botswana* 88 C3
Mopoi, *C.A.R.* 86 A2
Mopti, *Mali* 82 C4
Moqatta, *Sudan* 81 E4
Moqor, *Afghan.* 68 C2
Moquegua, *Peru* 124 G4
Mór, *Hungary* 42 C3
Mora, *Cameroon* 83 C7
Móra, *Portugal* 35 G2
Mora, *Spain* 35 F7
Mora, *Sweden* 10 C8
Mora, *Minn., U.S.A.* 112 C8
Mora, *N. Mex., U.S.A.* 115 J11
Mora →, *U.S.A.* 113 H2
Mora de Ebro = Mòra d'Ebre, *Spain* 32 D5
Mora de Rubielos, *Spain* 32 E4
Mòra d'Ebre, *Spain* 32 D5
Mòra la Nova, *Spain* 32 D5
Morača →, *Montenegro, Yug.* 40 D3
Moradabad, *India* 69 E8
Morafenobe, *Madag.* 89 B7
Morąg, *Poland* 44 E6
Moral de Calatrava, *Spain* 35 G7
Moraleja, *Spain* 34 E4
Moramanga, *Madag.* 89 B8
Moran, *Kans., U.S.A.* 113 G7
Moran, *Wyo., U.S.A.* 114 E8
Moranbah, *Australia* 94 C4
Morano Cálabro, *Italy* 31 C9
Morant Cays, *Jamaica* 120 C4
Morant Pt., *Jamaica* 120 C4
Morar, *India* 68 F8
Morar, L., *U.K.* 14 E3
Moratalla, *Spain* 33 G3
Moratuwa, *Sri Lanka* 66 R11
Morava →, *Slovak Rep.* 27 C9
Moravia, *U.S.A.* 111 D8
Moravian Hts. = Českomoravská Vrchovina, *Czech Rep.* 26 B8
Moravica →, *Serbia, Yug.* 40 C4
Moraviţa, *Romania* 42 E6
Moravská Třebová, *Czech Rep.* 27 B9
Moravské Budějovice, *Czech Rep.* 26 B8
Morawa, *Australia* 93 E2
Morawhanna, *Guyana* 124 B7
Moray □, *U.K.* 14 D5
Moray Firth, *U.K.* 14 D5
Morbach, *Germany* 25 F3
Morbegno, *Italy* 28 B6
Morbi, *India* 68 H4
Morbihan □, *France* 18 E4
Mörbylånga, *Sweden* 11 H10
Morcenx, *France* 20 D3
Morcone, *Italy* 31 A7
Mordelles, *France* 18 D5
Morden, *Canada* 105 D9
Mordoğan, *Turkey* 39 C8
Mordovian Republic = Mordvinia □, *Russia* 48 C7
Mordovo, *Russia* 48 D5
Mordvinia □, *Russia* 48 C7
Mordy, *Poland* 45 F9
Morea, *Greece* 6 H10
Moreau →, *U.S.A.* 112 C4
Morecambe, *U.K.* 12 C5
Morecambe B., *U.K.* 12 C5
Moree, *Australia* 95 D4
Morehead, *U.S.A.* 108 F4
Morehead City, *U.S.A.* 109 H7
Morel →, *India* 68 F7
Morelia, *Mexico* 118 D4
Morella, *Australia* 94 C3
Morella, *Spain* 32 E4
Morelos, *Mexico* 118 B3
Morelos □, *Mexico* 119 D5
Morena, *India* 68 F8
Morena, Sierra, *Spain* 35 G7
Moreni, *Romania* 43 F10
Moreno Valley, *U.S.A.* 117 M10
Moresby I., *Canada* 104 C2
Morestel, *France* 21 C9
Moreton I., *Australia* 95 D5
Moreuil, *France* 19 C9
Morey, *Spain* 37 B10
Morez, *France* 19 F13
Morgan, *U.S.A.* 114 F8
Morgan City, *U.S.A.* 113 L9
Morgan Hill, *U.S.A.* 116 H5
Morganfield, *U.S.A.* 108 G2
Morganton, *U.S.A.* 109 H5
Morgantown, *U.S.A.* 108 F6
Morgenzon, *S. Africa* 89 D4
Morges, *Switz.* 25 J2
Morghak, *Iran* 71 D8
Morgongåva, *Sweden* 10 E10
Morhange, *France* 19 D13
Morhar →, *India* 69 G11
Mori, *Italy* 28 C7
Moriarty, *U.S.A.* 115 J10
Moribaya, *Guinea* 82 D3
Morice L., *Canada* 104 C3
Moriki, *Nigeria* 83 C6
Morinville, *Canada* 104 C6
Morioka, *Japan* 54 E10
Moris, *Mexico* 118 B3
Morlaàs, *France* 20 E3
Morlaix, *France* 18 D3
Mörlunda, *Sweden* 11 G9
Mormanno, *Italy* 31 C8
Mormant, *France* 19 D9
Mornington, *Australia* 95 F4
Mornington, I., *Chile* 128 F1
Mornington I., *Australia* 94 B2
Mórnos →, *Greece* 38 C3
Moro, *Pakistan* 68 F2
Moro, *Sudan* 81 E3
Moro →, *Pakistan* 68 E2
Moro G., *Phil.* 61 H5
Morocco ■, *N. Afr.* 78 B4
Morogoro, *Tanzania* 86 D4
Morogoro □, *Tanzania* 86 D4
Moroleón, *Mexico* 118 C4
Morombe, *Madag.* 89 C7
Moron, *Argentina* 126 C4
Morón, *Cuba* 120 B4
Morón de Almazán, *Spain* 32 D2
Morón de la Frontera, *Spain* 35 H5
Morona →, *Peru* 124 D3
Morondava, *Madag.* 89 C7
Morondo, *Ivory C.* 82 D3
Morongo Valley, *U.S.A.* 117 L10
Moroni, *Comoros Is.* 77 H8
Moroni, *U.S.A.* 114 G8
Moronou, *Ivory C.* 82 D4
Morotai, *Indonesia* 63 D7
Moroto, *Uganda* 86 B3
Moroto Summit, *Kenya* 86 B3
Morozov, *Bulgaria* 41 D9
Morozovsk, *Russia* 49 F5
Morpeth, *U.K.* 12 B6
Morphou, *Cyprus* 36 D11
Morphou Bay, *Cyprus* 36 D11
Morrilton, *U.S.A.* 113 H8
Morrinhos, *Brazil* 125 G9
Morrinsville, *N.Z.* 91 G5
Morris, *Canada* 105 D9
Morris, *Ill., U.S.A.* 112 E10
Morris, *Minn., U.S.A.* 112 C7
Morris, *N.Y., U.S.A.* 111 D9
Morris, *Pa., U.S.A.* 110 E7
Morris, Mt., *Australia* 93 E5
Morrisburg, *Canada* 111 B9
Morristown, *Ariz., U.S.A.* 115 K7
Morristown, *N.J., U.S.A.* 111 F10
Morristown, *N.Y., U.S.A.* 111 B9
Morristown, *Tenn., U.S.A.* 109 G4
Morrisville, *N.Y., U.S.A.* 111 D9
Morrisville, *Pa., U.S.A.* 111 F10
Morrisville, *Vt., U.S.A.* 111 B12
Morro, Pta., *Chile* 126 B1
Morro Bay, *U.S.A.* 116 K6
Morro del Jable, *Canary Is.* 37 F5
Morro Jable, Pta. de, *Canary Is.* 37 F5
Morrosquillo, G. de, *Colombia* 120 E4
Mörrum, *Sweden* 11 H8
Morrumbene, *Mozam.* 89 C6
Mörrumsån →, *Sweden* 11 H8
Mors, *Denmark* 11 H2
Morshansk, *Russia* 48 D5
Mörsil, *Sweden* 10 A7
Mortagne →, *France* 19 D13
Mortagne-au-Perche, *France* 18 D7
Mortagne-sur-Gironde, *France* 20 C3
Mortagne-sur-Sèvre, *France* 18 F6
Mortain, *France* 18 D6
Mortara, *Italy* 28 C5
Morteau, *France* 19 E13
Morteros, *Argentina* 126 C3
Mortlach, *Canada* 105 C7
Mortlake, *Australia* 95 F3
Morton, *Tex., U.S.A.* 113 J3
Morton, *Wash., U.S.A.* 116 D4
Morundah, *Australia* 95 E4
Moruya, *Australia* 95 F5
Morvan, *France* 19 E11
Morven, *Australia* 95 D4
Morvern, *U.K.* 14 E3
Morwell, *Australia* 95 F4
Moryń, *Poland* 45 F1
Morzine, *France* 19 F13
Mosalsk, *Russia* 46 E8
Mosbach, *Germany* 25 F5
Moščenice, *Croatia* 29 C11
Mosciano Sant' Ángelo, *Italy* 29 F10
Moscos Is., *Burma* 64 E1
Moscow = Moskva, *Russia* 46 E9
Moscow, *Idaho, U.S.A.* 114 C5
Moscow, *Pa., U.S.A.* 111 E9
Mosel →, *Europe* 19 B14
Moselle = Mosel →, *Europe* 19 B14
Moselle □, *France* 19 D13
Moses Lake, *U.S.A.* 114 C4
Mosgiel, *N.Z.* 91 L3
Moshaweng →, *S. Africa* 88 D3
Moshi, *Tanzania* 86 C4

Moshupa

Moshupa, *Botswana* 88 C4
Mosina, *Poland* 45 F3
Mosjøen, *Norway* 8 D15
Moskenesøya, *Norway* 8 C15
Moskenstraumen, *Norway* 8 C15
Moskva, *Russia* 46 E9
Moskva →, *Russia* 46 E10
Moslavačka Gora, *Croatia* 29 C13
Mosomane, *Botswana* 88 C4
Mosonmagyaróvár, *Hungary* 42 C2
Mošorin, *Serbia, Yug.* 42 E5
Mospino, *Ukraine* 47 J9
Mosquera, *Colombia* 124 C3
Mosquero, *U.S.A.* 113 H3
Mosqueruela, *Spain* 32 E4
Mosquitia, *Honduras* 120 C3
Mosquito Coast = Mosquitia, *Honduras* 120 C3
Mosquito Creek L., *U.S.A.* 110 E4
Mosquito L., *Canada* 105 A8
Mosquitos, G. de los, *Panama* 120 E3
Moss, *Norway* 9 G14
Moss Vale, *Australia* 95 E5
Mossbank, *Canada* 105 D7
Mossburn, *N.Z.* 91 L2
Mosselbaai, *S. Africa* 88 E3
Mossendjo, *Congo* 84 E2
Mossgiel, *Australia* 95 E3
Mössingen, *Germany* 25 G5
Mossman, *Australia* 94 B4
Mossoró, *Brazil* 125 E11
Mossuril, *Mozam.* 87 E5
Most, *Czech Rep.* 26 A6
Mosta, *Malta* 36 D1
Mostaganem, *Algeria* 78 A6
Mostar, *Bos.-H.* 42 G2
Mostardas, *Brazil* 127 C5
Mostiska = Mostyska, *Ukraine* 47 H2
Móstoles, *Spain* 34 E7
Mosty = Masty, *Belarus* 46 F3
Mostyska, *Ukraine* 47 H2
Mosul = Al Mawşil, *Iraq* 70 B4
Mosŭlpo, *S. Korea* 57 H14
Mota, *Ethiopia* 81 E4
Mota del Cuervo, *Spain* 33 F2
Mota del Marqués, *Spain* 34 D5
Motagua →, *Guatemala* 120 C2
Motala, *Sweden* 11 F9
Motaze, *Mozam.* 89 C5
Moţca, *Romania* 43 C11
Moth, *India* 69 G8
Motherwell, *U.K.* 14 F5
Motihari, *India* 69 F11
Motilla del Palancar, *Spain* 33 F3
Motnik, *Slovenia* 29 B11
Motovun, *Croatia* 29 C10
Motozintla de Mendoza, *Mexico* 119 D6
Motril, *Spain* 35 J7
Motru, *Romania* 42 F7
Motru →, *Romania* 43 F8
Mott, *U.S.A.* 112 B3
Móttola, *Italy* 31 B10
Motueka, *N.Z.* 91 J4
Motueka →, *N.Z.* 91 J4
Motul, *Mexico* 119 C7
Mouchalagane →, *Canada* 103 B6
Moúdhros, *Greece* 39 B7
Mouding, *China* 58 E3
Moudjeria, *Mauritania* 82 B2
Moudon, *Switz.* 25 J2
Mouila, *Gabon* 84 E2
Moulamein, *Australia* 95 F3
Moulianá, *Greece* 36 D7
Moulins, *France* 19 F10
Moulmein, *Burma* 67 L20
Moulouya, O. →, *Morocco* 78 B5
Moultrie, *U.S.A.* 109 K4
Moultrie, L., *U.S.A.* 109 J5
Mound City, *Mo., U.S.A.* 112 E7
Mound City, *S. Dak., U.S.A.* 112 C4
Moúnda, Ákra, *Greece* 38 C2
Moundou, *Chad* 79 G9
Moundsville, *U.S.A.* 110 G4
Moung, *Cambodia* 64 F4
Mount Airy, *U.S.A.* 109 G5
Mount Albert, *Canada* 110 B5
Mount Barker, *S. Austral., Australia* 95 F2
Mount Barker, *W. Austral., Australia* 93 F2
Mount Brydges, *Canada* 110 D3
Mount Burr, *Australia* 95 F3
Mount Carmel, *Ill., U.S.A.* 108 F2
Mount Carmel, *Pa., U.S.A.* 111 F8
Mount Charleston, *U.S.A.* 117 J11
Mount Clemens, *U.S.A.* 110 D2
Mount Coolon, *Australia* 94 C4
Mount Darwin, *Zimbabwe* 87 F3
Mount Desert I., *U.S.A.* 109 C11
Mount Dora, *U.S.A.* 109 L5
Mount Edziza Prov. Park, *Canada* 104 B2
Mount Fletcher, *S. Africa* 89 E4
Mount Forest, *Canada* 102 D3
Mount Gambier, *Australia* 95 F3
Mount Garnet, *Australia* 94 B4
Mount Holly, *U.S.A.* 111 G10
Mount Holly Springs, *U.S.A.* 110 F7
Mount Hope, *N.S.W., Australia* 95 E4
Mount Hope, *S. Austral., Australia* 95 E2
Mount Isa, *Australia* 94 C2
Mount Jewett, *U.S.A.* 110 E6
Mount Kisco, *U.S.A.* 111 E11
Mount Laguna, *U.S.A.* 117 N10
Mount Larcom, *Australia* 94 C5
Mount Lofty Ra., *Australia* 95 E2
Mount Magnet, *Australia* 93 E2
Mount Maunganui, *N.Z.* 91 G6
Mount Molloy, *Australia* 94 B4
Mount Morgan, *Australia* 94 C5
Mount Morris, *U.S.A.* 110 D7
Mount Pearl, *Canada* 103 C9
Mount Penn, *U.S.A.* 111 F9
Mount Perry, *Australia* 95 D5
Mount Pleasant, *Iowa, U.S.A.* 112 E9
Mount Pleasant, *Mich., U.S.A.* 108 D3
Mount Pleasant, *Pa., U.S.A.* 110 F5
Mount Pleasant, *S.C., U.S.A.* 109 J6
Mount Pleasant, *Tenn., U.S.A.* 109 H2
Mount Pleasant, *Tex., U.S.A.* 113 J7
Mount Pleasant, *Utah, U.S.A.* 114 G8
Mount Pocono, *U.S.A.* 111 E9
Mount Rainier Nat. Park, *U.S.A.* 116 D5
Mount Revelstoke Nat. Park, *Canada* 104 C5
Mount Robson Prov. Park, *Canada* 104 C5
Mount Selinda, *Zimbabwe* 89 C5
Mount Shasta, *U.S.A.* 114 F2
Mount Signal, *U.S.A.* 117 N11
Mount Sterling, *Ill., U.S.A.* 112 F9
Mount Sterling, *Ky., U.S.A.* 108 F4
Mount Surprise, *Australia* 94 B3
Mount Union, *U.S.A.* 110 F7
Mount Upton, *U.S.A.* 111 D9
Mount Vernon, *Ill., U.S.A.* 108 F1
Mount Vernon, *Ind., U.S.A.* 112 F10
Mount Vernon, *N.Y., U.S.A.* 111 F11
Mount Vernon, *Ohio, U.S.A.* 110 F2
Mount Vernon, *Wash., U.S.A.* 116 B4
Mountain Ash, *U.K.* 13 F4
Mountain Center, *U.S.A.* 117 M10
Mountain City, *Nev., U.S.A.* 114 F6
Mountain City, *Tenn., U.S.A.* 109 G5
Mountain Dale, *U.S.A.* 111 E10
Mountain Grove, *U.S.A.* 113 G8
Mountain Home, *Ark., U.S.A.* 113 G8
Mountain Home, *Idaho, U.S.A.* 114 E6
Mountain Iron, *U.S.A.* 112 B8
Mountain Pass, *U.S.A.* 117 K11
Mountain View, *Ark., U.S.A.* 113 H8
Mountain View, *Calif., U.S.A.* 116 H4
Mountain View, *Hawaii, U.S.A.* 106 J17
Mountainair, *U.S.A.* 115 J10
Mountlake Terrace, *U.S.A.* 116 C4
Mountmellick, *Ireland* 15 C4
Mountrath, *Ireland* 15 D4
Moura, *Australia* 94 C4
Moura, *Brazil* 124 D6
Moura, *Portugal* 35 G3
Mourão, *Portugal* 35 G3
Mourdi, Dépression du, *Chad* 79 E10
Mourdiah, *Mali* 82 C3
Mourenx, *France* 20 E3
Mouri, *Ghana* 83 D4
Mourilyan, *Australia* 94 B4
Mourmelon-le-Grand, *France* 19 C11
Mourne →, *U.K.* 15 B4
Mourne Mts., *U.K.* 15 B5
Mourniaí, *Greece* 36 D6
Mournies = Mourniaí, *Greece* 36 D6
Mouscron, *Belgium* 17 D3
Moussoro, *Chad* 79 F9
Mouthe, *France* 19 F13
Moutier, *Switz.* 25 H3
Moûtiers, *France* 21 C10
Moutong, *Indonesia* 63 D6
Mouy, *France* 19 C9
Mouzáki, *Greece* 38 B3
Mouzon, *France* 19 C12
Movas, *Mexico* 118 B3
Moville, *Ireland* 15 A4
Mowandjum, *Australia* 92 C3
Moy →, *Ireland* 15 B2
Moyale, *Kenya* 81 G4
Moyamba, *S. Leone* 82 D2
Moyen Atlas, *Morocco* 78 B4
Moyne, L. le, *Canada* 103 A6
Moyo, *Indonesia* 62 F5
Moyobamba, *Peru* 124 E3
Moyyero →, *Russia* 51 C11
Moyynty, *Kazakstan* 50 E8
Mozambique = Moçambique, *Mozam.* 87 F5
Mozambique ■, *Africa* 87 F4
Mozambique Chan., *Africa* 89 B7
Mozdok, *Russia* 49 J7
Mozdūrān, *Iran* 71 B9
Mozhaysk, *Russia* 46 E9
Mozhga, *Russia* 48 B11
Mozhnābād, *Iran* 71 C9
Mozirje, *Slovenia* 29 B11
Mozyr = Mazyr, *Belarus* 47 F5
Mpanda, *Tanzania* 86 D3
Mpésoba, *Mali* 82 C3
Mphoengs, *Zimbabwe* 89 C4
Mpika, *Zambia* 87 E3
Mpulungu, *Zambia* 87 D3
Mpumalanga, *S. Africa* 89 D5
Mpumalanga □, *S. Africa* 89 B5
Mpwapwa, *Tanzania* 86 D4
Mqanduli, *S. Africa* 89 E4
Mqinvartsveri = Kazbek, *Russia* 49 J7
Mrągowo, *Poland* 44 E8
Mramor, *Serbia, Yug.* 40 C5
Mrkonjić Grad, *Bos.-H.* 42 F2
Mrkopalj, *Croatia* 29 C11
Mrocza, *Poland* 45 E4
Msambansovu, *Zimbabwe* 87 F3
M'sila →, *Algeria* 78 A6
Msoro, *Zambia* 87 E3
Msta →, *Russia* 46 C6
Mstislavl = Mstsislaw, *Belarus* 46 E6
Mstsislaw, *Belarus* 46 E6
Mszana Dolna, *Poland* 45 J7
Mszczonów, *Poland* 45 G7
Mtama, *Tanzania* 87 E4
Mtamvuna →, *S. Africa* 89 E5
Mtilikwe →, *Zimbabwe* 87 G3
Mtsensk, *Russia* 46 F9
Mtskheta, *Georgia* 49 K7
Mtubatuba, *S. Africa* 89 D5
Mtwalume, *S. Africa* 89 E5
Mtwara-Mikindani, *Tanzania* 87 E5
Mu Gia, Deo, *Vietnam* 64 D5
Mu Us Shamo, *China* 56 E5
Muang Chiang Rai = Chiang Rai, *Thailand* 58 H2
Muang Khong, *Laos* 64 E5
Muang Lamphun, *Thailand* 64 C2
Muang Pak Beng, *Laos* 58 H3
Muar, *Malaysia* 65 L4
Muarabungo, *Indonesia* 62 E2
Muaraenim, *Indonesia* 62 E2
Muarajuloi, *Indonesia* 62 E4
Muarakaman, *Indonesia* 62 E5
Muaratebo, *Indonesia* 62 E2
Muaratembesi, *Indonesia* 62 E2
Muaratewe, *Indonesia* 62 E4
Mubarakpur, *India* 69 F10
Mubarraz = Al Mubarraz, *Si. Arabia* 71 E6
Mubende, *Uganda* 86 B3
Mubi, *Nigeria* 83 C7
Mubur, Pulau, *Indonesia* 65 L6
Mucajaí →, *Brazil* 124 C6
Muchachos, Roque de los, *Canary Is.* 37 F2
Mücheln, *Germany* 24 D7
Muchinga Mts., *Zambia* 87 E3
Muchkapskiy, *Russia* 48 E6
Muchuan, *China* 58 C5
Muck, *U.K.* 14 E2
Muckadilla, *Australia* 95 D4
Mucur, *Turkey* 72 C6
Mucuri, *Brazil* 125 G11
Mucusso, *Angola* 88 B3
Muda, *Canary Is.* 37 F6
Mudanjiang, *China* 57 B15
Mudanya, *Turkey* 41 F12
Muddy Cr. →, *U.S.A.* 115 H8
Mudgee, *Australia* 95 E4
Mudjatik →, *Canada* 105 B7
Mudurnu, *Turkey* 72 B4
Muecate, *Mozam.* 87 E4
Mueda, *Mozam.* 87 E4
Mueller Ra., *Australia* 92 C4
Muende, *Mozam.* 87 E3
Muerto, Mar, *Mexico* 119 D6
Mufu Shan, *China* 59 C10
Mufulira, *Zambia* 87 E2
Mufumbiro Range, *Africa* 86 C2
Mugardos, *Spain* 34 B2
Muge →, *Portugal* 35 F2
Múggia, *Italy* 29 C10
Mughal Sarai, *India* 69 G10
Mughayrā', *Si. Arabia* 70 D3
Mugi, *Japan* 55 H7
Mugia = Muxía, *Spain* 34 B1
Mugila, Mts., *Dem. Rep. of the Congo* 86 D2
Muğla, *Turkey* 39 D10
Muğla □, *Turkey* 39 D10
Muglad, *Sudan* 81 E2
Müglizh, *Bulgaria* 41 D9
Mugu, *Nepal* 69 E10
Muhammad, Ras, *Egypt* 70 E2
Muhammad Qol, *Sudan* 80 C4
Muhammadabad, *India* 69 F10
Muhesi →, *Tanzania* 86 D4
Mühlacker, *Germany* 25 G4
Mühldorf, *Germany* 25 G8
Mühlhausen, *Germany* 24 D6
Mühlig Hofmann fjell, *Antarctica* 5 D3
Mühlviertel, *Austria* 26 C7
Muhos, *Finland* 8 D22
Muhu, *Estonia* 9 G20
Muhutwe, *Tanzania* 86 C3
Muine Bheag, *Ireland* 15 D5
Muir, L., *Australia* 93 F2
Mujnak = Muynak, *Uzbekistan* 50 E6
Mukacheve, *Ukraine* 47 H2
Mukachevo = Mukacheve, *Ukraine* 47 H2
Mukah, *Malaysia* 62 D4
Mukandwara, *India* 68 G6
Mukawwa, Geziret, *Egypt* 80 C4
Mukawwar, *Sudan* 80 C4
Mukdahan, *Thailand* 64 D5
Mukden = Shenyang, *China* 57 D12
Mukerian, *India* 68 D6
Mukhtolovo, *Russia* 48 C6
Mukhtuya = Lensk, *Russia* 51 C12
Mukinbudin, *Australia* 93 F2
Mukishi, *Dem. Rep. of the Congo* 87 D1
Mukomuko, *Indonesia* 62 E2
Mukomwenze, *Dem. Rep. of the Congo* 86 D2
Muktsar, *India* 68 D6
Mukur = Moqor, *Afghan.* 68 C2
Mukutawa →, *Canada* 105 C9
Mukwela, *Zambia* 87 F2
Mula, *Spain* 33 G3
Mula →, *Pakistan* 68 F2
Mulange, *Dem. Rep. of the Congo* 86 C2
Mulanje, *Malawi* 87 F4
Mulchén, *Chile* 126 D1
Mulde →, *Germany* 24 D8
Mule Creek Junction, *U.S.A.* 112 D2
Muleba, *Tanzania* 86 C3
Mulejé, *Mexico* 118 B2
Muleshoe, *U.S.A.* 113 H3
Muletta, Gara, *Ethiopia* 81 F5
Mulgrave, *Canada* 103 C7
Mulhacén, *Spain* 35 H7
Mülheim, *Germany* 24 D2
Mulhouse, *France* 19 E14
Muli, *China* 58 D3
Muling, *China* 57 B16
Mull, *U.K.* 14 E3
Mull, Sound of, *U.K.* 14 E3
Mullaittivu, *Sri Lanka* 66 Q12
Mullen, *U.S.A.* 112 D4
Mullens, *U.S.A.* 108 G5
Muller, Pegunungan, *Indonesia* 62 D4
Mullet Pen., *Ireland* 15 B1
Mullewa, *Australia* 93 E2
Müllheim, *Germany* 25 H3
Mulligan →, *Australia* 94 D2
Mullingar, *Ireland* 15 C4
Mullins, *U.S.A.* 109 H6
Mullsjö, *Sweden* 11 G7
Mullumbimby, *Australia* 95 D5
Mulobezi, *Zambia* 87 F2
Mulroy B., *Ireland* 15 A4
Multan, *Pakistan* 68 D4
Mulumbe, Mts., *Dem. Rep. of the Congo* 87 D2
Mulungushi Dam, *Zambia* 87 E2
Mulvane, *U.S.A.* 113 G6
Mulwad, *Sudan* 80 D3
Mumbai, *India* 66 K8
Mumbwa, *Zambia* 87 F2
Mumra, *Russia* 49 H8
Mun →, *Thailand* 64 E5
Muna, *Indonesia* 63 F6
Munabao, *India* 68 G4
Munamagi, *Estonia* 9 H22
Münchberg, *Germany* 25 E7
Müncheberg, *Germany* 24 C10
München, *Germany* 25 G7
Munchen-Gladbach = Mönchengladbach, *Germany* 24 D2
Muncho Lake, *Canada* 104 B3
Munch'ŏn, *N. Korea* 57 E14
Muncie, *U.S.A.* 108 E3
Muncoonie, L., *Australia* 94 D2
Mundabbera, *Australia* 95 D5
Munday, *U.S.A.* 113 J5
Münden, *Germany* 24 D5
Mundiwindi, *Australia* 92 D3
Mundo →, *Spain* 33 G2
Mundo Novo, *Brazil* 125 F10
Mundra, *India* 68 H3
Mundrabilla, *Australia* 93 F4
Munera, *Spain* 33 F2
Mungallala, *Australia* 95 D4
Mungallala Cr. →, *Australia* 95 D4
Mungana, *Australia* 94 B3
Mungaoli, *India* 68 G8
Mungari, *Mozam.* 87 F3
Mungbere, *Dem. Rep. of the Congo* 86 B2
Mungeli, *India* 69 H9
Munger, *India* 69 G12
Munich = München, *Germany* 25 G7
Munising, *U.S.A.* 108 B2
Munka-Ljungby, *Sweden* 11 H6
Munkebo, *Denmark* 11 J4
Munkedal, *Sweden* 11 F5
Munkfors, *Sweden* 10 E7
Munku-Sardyk, *Russia* 51 D11
Münnerstadt, *Germany* 25 E6
Muñoz Gamero, Pen., *Chile* 128 G2
Munroe L., *Canada* 105 B9
Munsan, *S. Korea* 57 F14
Munster, *France* 19 D14
Munster, *Niedersachsen, Germany* 24 C6
Münster, *Nordrhein-Westfalen, Germany* 24 D3
Munster □, *Ireland* 15 D3
Muntadgin, *Australia* 93 F2
Muntele Mare, Vf., *Romania* 43 D8
Muntok, *Indonesia* 62 E3
Munyama, *Zambia* 87 F2
Munzur Dağları, *Turkey* 73 C8
Muong Beng, *Laos* 58 G3
Muong Boum, *Vietnam* 58 F4
Muong Et, *Laos* 64 B5
Muong Hai, *Laos* 58 G3
Muong Hiem, *Laos* 64 B4
Muong Houn, *Laos* 58 G3
Muong Hung, *Vietnam* 58 G4
Muong Kau, *Laos* 64 E5
Muong Khao, *Laos* 64 C4
Muong Khoua, *Laos* 58 G4
Muong Liep, *Laos* 64 C3
Muong May, *Laos* 64 E6
Muong Ngeun, *Laos* 58 G3
Muong Ngoi, *Laos* 58 G4
Muong Nhie, *Vietnam* 58 F4
Muong Nong, *Laos* 64 D6
Muong Ou Tay, *Laos* 58 F3
Muong Oua, *Laos* 64 C3
Muong Peun, *Laos* 58 G4
Muong Phalane, *Laos* 64 D5
Muong Phieng, *Laos* 64 C3
Muong Phine, *Laos* 64 D6
Muong Sai, *Laos* 58 G3
Muong Saiapoun, *Laos* 64 C3
Muong Sen, *Vietnam* 64 C5
Muong Sing, *Laos* 58 G3
Muong Son, *Laos* 58 G4
Muong Soui, *Laos* 64 C4
Muong Va, *Laos* 58 G4
Muong Xia, *Vietnam* 64 B5
Muonio, *Finland* 8 C20
Muonionjoki →, *Finland* 8 C20
Muping, *China* 57 F11
Mupoi, *Sudan* 81 F2
Muqaddam, Wadi →, *Sudan* 80 D3
Muqdisho, *Somali Rep.* 74 G4
Mur →, *Austria* 27 E9
Mur-de-Bretagne, *France* 18 D4
Muradiye, *Manisa, Turkey* 39 C9
Muradiye, *Van, Turkey* 73 C10
Murakami, *Japan* 54 E9
Murallón, Cerro, *Chile* 128 F2
Muranda, *Rwanda* 86 C2
Murang'a, *Kenya* 86 C4
Murashi, *Russia* 50 D5
Murat, *France* 20 C6
Murat →, *Turkey* 73 C9
Murat Dağı, *Turkey* 39 C11
Muratlı, *Turkey* 41 E11
Murato, *France* 21 F13
Murau, *Austria* 26 D7
Muravera, *Italy* 30 C2
Murayama, *Japan* 54 E10
Murça, *Portugal* 34 D3
Murchison →, *Australia* 93 E1
Murchison, Mt., *Antarctica* 5 D11
Murchison Falls, *Uganda* 86 B3
Murchison Ra., *Australia* 94 C1
Murchison Rapids, *Malawi* 87 F3
Murcia, *Spain* 33 G3
Murcia □, *Spain* 33 H3
Murdo, *U.S.A.* 112 D4
Murdoch Pt., *Australia* 94 A3
Mürefte, *Turkey* 41 F11
Mureş □, *Romania* 43 D9
Mureş →, *Romania* 42 D5
Mureşul = Mureş →, *Romania* 42 D5
Muret, *France* 20 E5
Murewa, *Zimbabwe* 89 B5
Murfreesboro, *N.C., U.S.A.* 109 G7
Murfreesboro, *Tenn., U.S.A.* 109 H2
Murgab = Murghob, *Tajikistan* 50 F8
Murgab →, *Turkmenistan* 71 B9
Murgenella, *Australia* 92 B5
Murgeni, *Romania* 43 D13
Murgha Kibzai, *Pakistan* 68 D3
Murghob, *Tajikistan* 50 F8
Murgon, *Australia* 95 D5
Muri, *India* 69 H11
Muria, *Indonesia* 63 G14
Muriaé, *Brazil* 127 A7
Murias de Paredes, *Spain* 34 C4
Muriel Mine, *Zimbabwe* 87 F3
Müritz, *Germany* 24 B8
Murka, *Kenya* 86 C4
Murliganj, *India* 69 G12
Murmansk, *Russia* 50 C4
Murnau, *Germany* 25 H7
Muro, *France* 21 F12
Muro, *Spain* 37 B10
Muro, C. de, *France* 21 G12
Muro de Alcoy, *Spain* 33 G4
Muro Lucano, *Italy* 31 B8
Murom, *Russia* 48 C6
Muroran, *Japan* 54 C10
Muros, *Spain* 34 C1
Muros y de Noya, Ría de, *Spain* 34 C1
Muroto, *Japan* 55 H7
Muroto-Misaki, *Japan* 55 H7
Murowana Goślina, *Poland* 45 F3
Murphy, *U.S.A.* 114 E5
Murphys, *U.S.A.* 116 G6
Murrat, *Sudan* 80 D2
Murrat Wells, *Sudan* 80 C3
Murray, *Ky., U.S.A.* 109 G1
Murray, *Utah, U.S.A.* 114 F8
Murray →, *Australia* 95 F2
Murray, L., *U.S.A.* 109 H5
Murray Bridge, *Australia* 95 F2
Murray Harbour, *Canada* 103 C7
Murraysburg, *S. Africa* 88 E3
Murree, *Pakistan* 68 C5
Murrieta, *U.S.A.* 117 M9
Murro di Porco, Capo, *Italy* 31 F8
Murrumbidgee →, *Australia* 95 E3
Murrumburrah, *Australia* 95 E4
Murrurundi, *Australia* 95 E5
Murshid, *Sudan* 80 C3
Murshidabad, *India* 69 G13
Murska Sobota, *Slovenia* 29 B13
Murtle L., *Canada* 104 C5
Murtoa, *Australia* 95 F3
Murtosa, *Portugal* 34 E2
Murungu, *Tanzania* 86 C3
Mururoa, *Pac. Oc.* 97 K14
Murwara, *India* 69 H9
Murwillumbah, *Australia* 95 D5
Mürz →, *Austria* 26 D8
Mürzzuschlag, *Austria* 26 D8
Muş, *Turkey* 70 B4
Mûsa, Gebel, *Egypt* 70 D2
Musa Khel, *Pakistan* 68 D3
Mūsa Qal'eh, *Afghan.* 66 C4
Musafirkhana, *India* 69 F9
Musala, *Bulgaria* 40 D7
Musala, *Indonesia* 62 D1
Musan, *N. Korea* 57 C15
Musangu, *Dem. Rep. of the Congo* 87 E1
Musasa, *Tanzania* 86 C3
Musay'īd, *Qatar* 71 E6
Muscat = Masqat, *Oman* 74 C6
Muscat & Oman = Oman ■, *Asia* 74 C6

Muscatine, U.S.A. 112 E9
Musgrave Harbour, Canada 103 C9
Musgrave Ranges, Australia 93 E5
Mushie, Dem. Rep. of the Congo 84 E3
Mushin, Nigeria 83 D5
Musi →, Indonesia 62 E2
Muskeg →, Canada 104 A4
Muskegon, U.S.A. 108 D2
Muskegon →, U.S.A. 108 D2
Muskegon Heights, U.S.A. 108 D2
Muskogee, U.S.A. 113 H7
Muskoka, L., Canada 110 B5
Muskwa →, Canada 104 B4
Muslīmiyah, Syria 70 B3
Musmar, Sudan 80 D4
Musofu, Zambia 87 E2
Musoma, Tanzania 86 C3
Musquaro, L., Canada 103 B7
Musquodoboit Harbour, Canada 103 D7
Musselburgh, U.K. 14 F5
Musselshell →, U.S.A. 114 C10
Mussidan, France 20 C4
Mussomeli, Italy 30 E6
Mussoorie, India 68 D8
Mussuco, Angola 88 B2
Mustafakemalpaşa, Turkey 41 F12
Mustang, Nepal 69 E10
Musters, L., Argentina 128 F3
Musudan, N. Korea 57 D15
Muswellbrook, Australia 95 E5
Muszyna, Poland 45 J7
Mût, Egypt 80 B2
Mut, Turkey 70 B2
Mutanda, Mozam. 89 C5
Mutanda, Zambia 87 E2
Mutare, Zimbabwe 87 F3
Muting, Indonesia 63 F10
Mutoko, Zimbabwe 89 B5
Mutoray, Russia 51 C11
Mutshatsha, Dem. Rep. of the Congo 87 E1
Mutsu, Japan 54 D10
Mutsu-Wan, Japan 54 D10
Muttaburra, Australia 94 C3
Muttalip, Turkey 39 B12
Mutton I., Ireland 15 D2
Mutuáli, Mozam. 87 E4
Mutum Biyu, Nigeria 83 D7
Muweilih, Egypt 75 E3
Muxía, Spain 34 B1
Muy Muy, Nic. 120 D2
Muyinga, Burundi 86 C3
Muynak, Uzbekistan 50 E6
Muzaffarabad, Pakistan 69 B5
Muzaffargarh, Pakistan 68 D4
Muzaffarnagar, India 68 E7
Muzaffarpur, India 69 F11
Muzafirpur, Pakistan 68 D3
Muzhi, Russia 50 C7
Muzillac, France 18 E4
Muzūra, Egypt 80 J7
Mvôlô, Sudan 81 F2
Mvuma, Zimbabwe 87 F3
Mvurwi, Zimbabwe 87 F3
Mwadui, Tanzania 86 C3
Mwambo, Tanzania 87 E5
Mwandi, Zambia 87 F1
Mwanza, Dem. Rep. of the Congo 86 D2
Mwanza, Tanzania 86 C3
Mwanza, Zambia 87 F1
Mwanza □, Tanzania 86 C3
Mwaya, Tanzania 87 D3
Mweelrea, Ireland 15 C2
Mweka, Dem. Rep. of the Congo 84 E4
Mwenezi, Zimbabwe 87 G3
Mwenezi →, Mozam. 87 G3
Mwenga, Dem. Rep. of the Congo 86 C2
Mweru, L., Zambia 87 D2
Mweza Range, Zimbabwe 87 G3
Mwilambwe, Dem. Rep. of the Congo 86 D2
Mwimbi, Tanzania 87 D3
Mwinilunga, Zambia 87 E1
My Tho, Vietnam 65 G6
Myajlar, India 68 F4
Myanaung, Burma 67 K19
Myanmar = Burma ■, Asia 67 J20
Myaungmya, Burma 67 L19
Myeik Kyunzu, Burma 65 G1
Myers Chuck, U.S.A. 104 B2
Myerstown, U.S.A. 111 F8
Myingyan, Burma 67 J19
Myitkyina, Burma 67 G20
Myjava, Slovak Rep. 27 C10
Mykhaylivka, Ukraine 47 J8
Mykines, Færoe Is. 8 E9
Mykolayiv, Ukraine 47 J7
Mymensingh, Bangla. 67 G17
Mynydd Du, U.K. 13 F4
Mýrdalsjökull, Iceland 8 E4
Myrhorod, Ukraine 47 H7
Myrtle Beach, U.S.A. 109 J6
Myrtle Creek, U.S.A. 114 E2
Myrtle Point, U.S.A. 114 E1
Myrtou, Cyprus 36 D12
Mysia, Turkey 41 G11
Myślenice, Poland 45 J6
Myślibórz, Poland 45 F1
Mysłowice, Poland 45 H6
Mysore = Karnataka □, India 66 N10
Mysore, India 66 N10
Mystic, U.S.A. 111 E13
Myszków, Poland 45 H6
Myszyniec, Poland 44 E8
Mytishchi, Russia 46 E9
Mývatn, Iceland 8 D5
Mže →, Czech Rep. 26 B6
Mzimba, Malawi 87 E3
Mzimkulu →, S. Africa 89 E5
Mzimvubu →, S. Africa 89 E4
Mzuzu, Malawi 87 E3

N

Na Hearadh = Harris, U.K. 14 D2
Na Noi, Thailand 64 C3
Na Phao, Laos 64 D5
Na Sam, Vietnam 58 F6
Na San, Vietnam 64 B5
Naab →, Germany 25 F8
Na'am, Sudan 81 F2
Na'am →, Sudan 81 F2
Naantali, Finland 9 F19
Naas, Ireland 15 C5
Nababeep, S. Africa 88 D2
Nabadwip = Navadwip, India 69 H13
Nabari, Japan 55 G8
Nabawa, Australia 93 E1
Nabberu, L., Australia 93 E3
Nabburg, Germany 25 F8
Naberezhnyye Chelny, Russia 48 C11
Nabeul, Tunisia 79 A8
Nabha, India 68 D7
Nabīd, Iran 71 D8
Nabire, Indonesia 63 E9
Nabisar, Pakistan 68 G3
Nabisipi →, Canada 103 B7
Nabiswera, Uganda 86 B3
Nablus = Nābulus, West Bank 75 C4
Naboomspruit, S. Africa 89 C4
Nabou, Burkina Faso 82 C4
Nabua, Phil. 61 E5
Nābulus, West Bank 75 C4
Nacala, Mozam. 87 E5
Nacala-Velha, Mozam. 87 E5
Nacaome, Honduras 120 D2
Nacaroa, Mozam. 87 E4
Naches, U.S.A. 114 C3
Naches →, U.S.A. 116 D6
Nachicapau, L., Canada 103 A6
Nachingwea, Tanzania 87 E4
Nachna, India 68 F4
Náchod, Czech Rep. 26 A9
Nacimiento L., U.S.A. 116 K6
Naco, Mexico 118 A3
Nacogdoches, U.S.A. 113 K7
Nácori Chico, Mexico 118 B3
Nacozari, Mexico 118 A3
Nadi, Sudan 80 D3
Nadiad, India 68 H5
Nădlac, Romania 42 D5
Nador, Morocco 78 B5
Nadur, Malta 36 C1
Nadūshan, Iran 71 C7
Nadvirna, Ukraine 47 H3
Nadvornaya = Nadvirna, Ukraine 47 H3
Nadym, Russia 50 C8
Nadym →, Russia 50 C8
Nærbø, Norway 9 G11
Næstved, Denmark 11 J5
Nafada, Nigeria 83 C7
Naft-e Safīd, Iran 71 D6
Naftshahr, Iran 70 C5
Nafud Desert = An Nafūd, Si. Arabia 70 D4
Nag Hammâdi, Egypt 80 B3
Naga, Phil. 61 E5
Nagahama, Japan 55 G8
Nagai, Japan 54 E10
Nagaland □, India 67 G19
Nagano, Japan 55 F9
Nagano □, Japan 55 F9
Nagaoka, Japan 55 F9
Nagappattinam, India 66 P11
Nagar →, Bangla. 69 G13
Nagar Parkar, Pakistan 68 G4
Nagasaki, Japan 55 H4
Nagasaki □, Japan 55 H4
Nagato, Japan 55 G5
Nagaur, India 68 F5
Nagda, India 68 H6
Nagercoil, India 66 Q10
Nagina, India 69 E8
Nagīneh, Iran 71 C8
Nagir, Pakistan 69 A6
Naglarby, Sweden 10 D9
Nagod, India 69 G9
Nagold, Germany 25 G4
Nagold →, Germany 25 G4
Nagoorin, Australia 94 C5
Nagorno-Karabakh, Azerbaijan 70 B5
Nagornyy, Russia 51 D13
Nagoya, Japan 55 G8
Nagpur, India 66 J11
Nagua, Dom. Rep. 121 C6
Nagyatád, Hungary 42 D2
Nagyecsed, Hungary 42 C7
Nagykálló, Hungary 42 C6
Nagykanizsa, Hungary 42 D2
Nagykáta, Hungary 42 C4
Nagykőrös, Hungary 42 C4
Naha, Japan 55 L3
Nahan, India 68 D7
Nahanni Butte, Canada 104 A4
Nahanni Nat. Park, Canada 104 A4
Nahargarh, Mad. P., India 68 G6
Nahargarh, Raj., India 68 G7
Nahariyya, Israel 70 C2
Nahāvand, Iran 71 C6
Nahe →, Germany 25 F3
Nahīya, W. →, Egypt 80 B3
Naicá, Mexico 118 B3
Naicam, Canada 105 C8
Naikoon Prov. Park, Canada 104 C2
Naila, Germany 25 E7
Naimisharanya, India 69 F9
Nain, Canada 103 A7
Nā'īn, Iran 71 C7
Naini Tal, India 69 E8
Nainpur, India 66 H12
Naintré, France 18 F7
Nainwa, India 68 G6
Naipu, Romania 43 F10
Nairn, U.K. 14 D5
Nairobi, Kenya 86 C4
Naissaar, Estonia 9 G21
Naita, Mt., Ethiopia 81 F4
Naivasha, Kenya 86 C4
Naivasha, L., Kenya 86 C4
Najac, France 20 D5
Najafābād, Iran 71 C6
Najd, Si. Arabia 74 B3
Nájera, Spain 32 C2
Najerilla →, Spain 32 C2
Najibabad, India 68 E8
Najin, N. Korea 57 C16
Najmah, Si. Arabia 71 E6
Naju, S. Korea 57 G14
Nakadōri-Shima, Japan 55 H4
Nakalagba, Dem. Rep. of the Congo 86 B2
Nakaminato, Japan 55 F10
Nakamura, Japan 55 H6
Nakano, Japan 55 F9
Nakano-Shima, Japan 55 K4
Nakashibetsu, Japan 54 C12
Nakfa, Eritrea 81 D4
Nakhfar al Buşayyah, Iraq 70 D5
Nakhichevan = Naxçıvan, Azerbaijan 70 B5
Nakhichevan Republic = Naxçıvan □, Azerbaijan 50 F5
Nakhl, Egypt 75 F2
Nakhl-e Taqī, Iran 71 E7
Nakhodka, Russia 51 E14
Nakhon Nayok, Thailand 64 E3
Nakhon Pathom, Thailand 64 F3
Nakhon Phanom, Thailand 64 D5
Nakhon Ratchasima, Thailand 64 E4
Nakhon Sawan, Thailand 64 E3
Nakhon Si Thammarat, Thailand 65 H3
Nakhon Thai, Thailand 64 D3
Nakhtarana, India 68 H3
Nakina, Canada 102 B2
Nakło nad Notecią, Poland 45 E4
Nako, Burkina Faso 82 C4
Nakodar, India 68 D6
Nakskov, Denmark 11 K5
Naktong →, S. Korea 57 G15
Nakuru, Kenya 86 C4
Nakuru, L., Kenya 86 C4
Nakusp, Canada 104 C5
Nal, Pakistan 68 F2
Nal →, Pakistan 68 G1
Naláži, Mozam. 89 C5
Nalchik, Russia 49 J6
Nałęczów, Poland 45 G9
Nalerigu, Ghana 83 C4
Nalgonda, India 66 L11
Nalhati, India 69 G12
Naliya, India 68 H3
Nallamalai Hills, India 66 M11
Nallıhan, Turkey 72 B4
Nalón →, Spain 34 B4
Nam Can, Vietnam 65 H5
Nam-ch'on, N. Korea 57 E14
Nam Co, China 60 C4
Nam Dinh, Vietnam 58 G6
Nam Du, Hon, Vietnam 65 H5
Nam Ngum Dam, Laos 64 C4
Nam-Phan, Vietnam 65 G6
Nam Phong, Thailand 64 D4
Nam Tha, Laos 58 G3
Nam Tok, Thailand 64 E2
Namacunde, Angola 88 B2
Namacurra, Mozam. 89 B6
Namak, Daryācheh-ye, Iran 71 C7
Namak, Kavir-e, Iran 71 C8
Namakzār, Daryācheh-ye, Iran 71 C9
Namaland, Namibia 88 C2
Namangan, Uzbekistan 50 E8
Namapa, Mozam. 87 E4
Namaqualand, S. Africa 88 E2
Namasagali, Uganda 86 B3
Namber, Indonesia 63 E8
Nambour, Australia 95 D5
Nambucca Heads, Australia 95 E5
Namche Bazar, Nepal 69 F12
Namchonjŏm = Nam-ch'on, N. Korea 57 E14
Namecunda, Mozam. 87 E4
Nameponda, Mozam. 87 F4
Náměšť nad Oslavou, Czech Rep. 27 B9
Námestovo, Slovak Rep. 27 B12
Nametil, Mozam. 87 F4
Namew L., Canada 105 C8
Namgia, India 69 D8
Namhkam, Burma 58 E1
Namib Desert, Namibia 88 C2
Namibe, Angola 85 H2
Namibe □, Angola 88 B1
Namibia ■, Africa 88 C2
Namibwoestyn = Namib Desert, Namibia 88 C2
Namīn, Iran 73 C13
Namlea, Indonesia 63 E7
Namoi →, Australia 95 E4
Nampa, U.S.A. 114 E5
Nampala, Mali 82 B3
Namp'o, N. Korea 57 E13
Nampō-Shotō, Japan 55 J10
Nampula, Mozam. 87 F4
Namrole, Indonesia 63 E7
Namse Shankou, China 67 E13
Namsen →, Norway 8 D14
Namsos, Norway 8 D14
Namtsy, Russia 51 C13
Namtu, Burma 67 H20
Namtumbo, Tanzania 87 E4
Namu, Canada 104 C3
Namur, Belgium 17 D4
Namur □, Belgium 17 D4
Namutoni, Namibia 88 B2
Namwala, Zambia 87 F2
Namwŏn, S. Korea 57 G14
Namysłów, Poland 45 G4
Nan, Thailand 64 C3
Nan →, Thailand 64 E3
Nan-ch'ang = Nanchang, China 59 C10
Nan Ling, China 59 E8
Nan Xian, China 59 C9
Nana, Romania 43 F11
Nana Kru, Liberia 82 E3
Nanaimo, Canada 104 D4
Nanam, N. Korea 57 D15
Nanan, China 59 E12
Nanango, Australia 95 D5
Nan'ao, China 59 F11
Nanao, Japan 55 F8
Nanbu, China 58 B6
Nanchang, Jiangxi, China 59 C10
Nanchang, Kiangsi, China 59 C10
Nancheng, China 59 D11
Nanching = Nanjing, China 59 A12
Nanchong, China 58 B6
Nanchuan, China 58 C6
Nancy, France 19 D13
Nanda Devi, India 69 D8
Nanda Kot, India 69 D9
Nandan, China 58 E6
Nandan, Japan 55 G7
Nanded, India 66 K10
Nandewar Ra., Australia 95 E5
Nandi, Fiji 91 C7
Nandigram, India 69 H12
Nandurbar, India 66 J9
Nandyal, India 66 M11
Nanfeng, Guangdong, China 59 F8
Nanfeng, Jiangxi, China 59 D11
Nanga-Eboko, Cameroon 83 E7
Nanga Parbat, Pakistan 69 B6
Nangade, Mozam. 87 E4
Nangapinoh, Indonesia 62 E4
Nangarhār □, Afghan. 66 B7
Nangatayap, Indonesia 62 E4
Nangeya Mts., Uganda 86 B3
Nangis, France 19 D10
Nangong, China 56 F8
Nanhua, China 58 E3
Nanhuang, China 57 F11
Nanhui, China 59 B13
Nanjeko, Zambia 87 F1
Nanji Shan, China 59 D13
Nanjian, China 58 E3
Nanjiang, China 58 A6
Nanjing, Fujian, China 59 E11
Nanjing, Jiangsu, China 59 A12
Nanjirinji, Tanzania 87 D4
Nankana Sahib, Pakistan 68 D5
Nankang, China 59 E10
Nanking = Nanjing, China 59 A12
Nankoku, Japan 55 H6
Nanling, China 59 B12
Nanning, China 58 F7
Nannup, Australia 93 F2
Nanpan Jiang →, China 58 E6
Nanpara, India 69 F9
Nanpi, China 56 E9
Nanping, Fujian, China 59 D12
Nanping, Henan, China 59 C9
Nanri Dao, China 59 E12
Nanripe, Mozam. 87 E4
Nansei-Shotō = Ryūkyū-rettō, Japan 55 M3
Nansen Sd., Canada 4 A3
Nanshan I., S. China Sea 62 B5
Nansio, Tanzania 86 C3
Nant, France 20 D7
Nanterre, France 19 D9
Nantes, France 18 E5
Nantiat, France 20 B5
Nanticoke, U.S.A. 111 E8
Nanton, Canada 104 C6
Nantong, China 59 A13
Nantou, Taiwan 59 F13
Nantua, France 19 F12
Nantucket I., U.S.A. 108 E10
Nantwich, U.K. 12 D5
Nanty Glo, U.S.A. 110 F6
Nanuque, Brazil 125 G10
Nanusa, Kepulauan, Indonesia 63 D7
Nanutarra Roadhouse, Australia 92 D2
Nanxi, China 58 C5
Nanxiong, China 59 E10
Nanyang, China 56 H7
Nanyi Hu, China 59 B12
Nanyuki, Kenya 86 B4
Nanzhang, China 59 B8
Nao, C. de la, Spain 33 G5
Naococane, L., Canada 103 B5
Náousa, Imathía, Greece 40 F6
Náousa, Kikládhes, Greece 39 D7
Naozhou Dao, China 59 G8
Napa, U.S.A. 116 G4
Napa →, U.S.A. 116 G4
Napanee, Canada 102 D4
Napanoch, U.S.A. 111 E10
Nape, Laos 64 C5
Nape Pass = Keo Neua, Deo, Vietnam 64 C5
Napier, N.Z. 91 H6
Napier Broome B., Australia 92 B4
Napier Pen., Australia 94 A2
Napierville, Canada 111 A11
Naples = Nápoli, Italy 31 B7
Naples, U.S.A. 109 M5
Napo, China 58 F5
Napo →, Peru 122 D3
Napoleon, N. Dak., U.S.A. 112 B5
Napoleon, Ohio, U.S.A. 108 E3
Nápoli, Italy 31 B7
Nápoli, G. di, Italy 31 B7
Napopo, Dem. Rep. of the Congo 86 B2
Naqâda, Egypt 80 B3
Naqadeh, Iran 73 D11
Naqb, Ra's an, Jordan 75 F4
Naqqāsh, Iran 71 C6
Nara, Japan 55 G7
Nara, Mali 82 B3
Nara □, Japan 55 G8
Nara Canal, Pakistan 68 G3
Nara Visa, U.S.A. 113 H3
Naracoorte, Australia 95 F3
Naradhan, Australia 95 E4
Naraini, India 69 G9
Narasapur, India 67 L12
Narathiwat, Thailand 65 J3
Narayanganj, Bangla. 67 H17
Narayanpet, India 66 L10
Narbonne, France 20 E7
Narcea →, Spain 34 B4
Nardīn, Iran 71 B7
Nardò, Italy 31 B11
Narembeen, Australia 93 F2
Narendranagar, India 68 D8
Nares Str., Arctic 98 A13
Naretha, Australia 93 F3
Narew →, Poland 45 F7
Nari →, Pakistan 68 F2
Narin, Afghan. 66 A6
Narindra, Helodranon' i, Madag. 89 A8
Narita, Japan 55 G10
Närke, Sweden 10 E8
Narmada →, India 68 J5
Narman, Turkey 73 B9
Narmland, Sweden 9 F15
Narnaul, India 68 E7
Narni, Italy 29 F9
Naro, Ghana 82 C4
Naro Fominsk, Russia 46 E9
Narodnaya, Russia 6 B17
Narok, Kenya 86 C4
Narón, Spain 34 B2
Narooma, Australia 95 F5
Narowal, Pakistan 68 C6
Narrabri, Australia 95 E4
Narran →, Australia 95 D4
Narrandera, Australia 95 E4
Narrogin, Australia 93 F2
Narromine, Australia 95 E4
Narrow Hills Prov. Park, Canada 105 C8
Narsimhapur, India 69 H8
Narsinghgarh, India 68 H7
Nartes, L. e, Albania 40 F3
Nartkala, Russia 49 J6
Naruto, Japan 55 G7
Narva, Estonia 46 C5
Narva →, Russia 9 G22
Narva Bay, Estonia 9 G19
Narvik, Norway 8 B17
Narvskoye Vdkhr., Russia 46 C5
Narwana, India 68 E7
Naryan-Mar, Russia 50 C6
Narym, Russia 50 D9
Naryn, Kyrgyzstan 50 E8
Nasa, Norway 8 C16
Nasarawa, Nigeria 83 D6
Năsăud, Romania 43 C9
Naseby, N.Z. 91 L3
Naselle, U.S.A. 116 D3
Naser, Buheirat en, Egypt 80 C3
Nashua, Mont., U.S.A. 114 B10
Nashua, N.H., U.S.A. 111 D13
Nashville, Ark., U.S.A. 113 J8
Nashville, Ga., U.S.A. 109 K4
Nashville, Tenn., U.S.A. 109 G2
Našice, Croatia 42 E3
Nasielsk, Poland 45 F7
Nasik, India 66 K8
Nasipit, Phil. 61 G6
Nasir, Sudan 81 F3
Nasirabad, India 68 F6
Nasirabad, Pakistan 68 E3
Naskaupi →, Canada 103 B7
Naso, Italy 31 D7
Naşrābād, Iran 71 C6
Naşriān-e Pā'īn, Iran 70 C5
Nass →, Canada 104 C3
Nassarawa □, Nigeria 83 D6
Nassau, Bahamas 120 A4
Nassau, U.S.A. 111 D11
Nassau, B., Chile 128 H3
Nasser, L. = Naser, Buheirat en, Egypt 80 C3
Nasser City = Kôm Ombo, Egypt 80 C3
Nassian, Ivory C. 82 D4
Nässjö, Sweden 11 G8
Nastapoka →, Canada 102 A4

Nastapoka, Is., *Canada* 102 A4
Nasugbu, *Phil.* 61 D4
Näsum, *Sweden* 11 H8
Näsviken, *Sweden* 10 C10
Nata, *Botswana* 88 C4
Nata →, *Botswana* 88 C4
Natal, *Brazil* 125 E11
Natal, *Indonesia* 62 D1
Natal, *S. Africa* 85 K6
Natalinci, *Serbia, Yug.* 42 F5
Naṭanz, *Iran* 71 C6
Natashquan, *Canada* 103 B7
Natashquan →, *Canada* 103 B7
Natchez, *U.S.A.* 113 K9
Natchitoches, *U.S.A.* 113 K8
Nathalia, *Australia* 95 F4
Nathdwara, *India* 68 G5
Nati, Pta., *Spain* 37 A10
Natimuk, *Australia* 95 F3
Nation →, *Canada* 104 B4
National City, *U.S.A.* 117 N9
Natitingou, *Benin* 83 C5
Natividad, I., *Mexico* 118 B1
Natkyizin, *Burma* 64 E1
Natron, L., *Tanzania* 86 C4
Natrona Heights, *U.S.A.* 110 F5
Natrûn, W. el →, *Egypt* 80 H7
Nättraby, *Sweden* 11 H9
Natukanaoka Pan, *Namibia* 88 B2
Natuna Besar, Kepulauan, *Indonesia* 65 L7
Natuna Is. = Natuna Besar, Kepulauan, *Indonesia* 65 L7
Natuna Selatan, Kepulauan, *Indonesia* 65 L7
Natural Bridge, *U.S.A.* 111 B9
Naturaliste, C., *Australia* 94 G4
Nau Qala, *Afghan.* 68 B3
Naucelle, *France* 20 D6
Nauders, *Austria* 26 E3
Nauen, *Germany* 24 C8
Naugatuck, *U.S.A.* 111 E11
Naujaat = Repulse Bay, *Canada* 101 B11
Naujoji Akmenė, *Lithuania* 44 B9
Naumburg, *Germany* 24 D7
Nā'ūr at Tunayb, *Jordan* 75 D4
Nauru ■, *Pac. Oc.* 96 H8
Naushahra = Nowshera, *Pakistan* 66 C8
Naushahro, *Pakistan* 68 F3
Naushon I., *U.S.A.* 111 E14
Nauta, *Peru* 124 D4
Nautanwa, *India* 67 F13
Nautla, *Mexico* 119 C5
Nava, *Mexico* 118 B4
Nava, *Spain* 34 B5
Nava del Rey, *Spain* 34 D5
Navadwip, *India* 69 H13
Navahermosa, *Spain* 35 F6
Navahrudak, *Belarus* 46 F3
Navajo Reservoir, *U.S.A.* 115 H10
Navalcarnero, *Spain* 34 E6
Navalmoral de la Mata, *Spain* 34 F5
Navalvillar de Pela, *Spain* 35 F5
Navan = An Uaimh, *Ireland* 15 C5
Navapolatsk, *Belarus* 46 E5
Navarino, I., *Chile* 128 H3
Navarra □, *Spain* 32 C3
Navarre, *U.S.A.* 110 F3
Navarro →, *U.S.A.* 116 F3
Navas de San Juan, *Spain* 35 G7
Navasota, *U.S.A.* 113 K6
Navassa I., *W. Indies* 121 C5
Nävekvarn, *Sweden* 11 F10
Naver →, *U.K.* 14 C4
Navia, *Spain* 34 B4
Navia →, *Spain* 34 B4
Navia de Suarna, *Spain* 34 C3
Navibandar, *India* 68 J3
Navidad, *Chile* 126 C1
Naviraí, *Brazil* 127 A5
Navlakhi, *India* 68 H4
Navlya, *Russia* 47 F8
Năvodari, *Romania* 43 F13
Navoi = Nawoiy, *Uzbekistan* 50 E7
Navojoa, *Mexico* 118 B3
Navolato, *Mexico* 118 C3
Návpaktos, *Greece* 38 C3
Návplion, *Greece* 38 D4
Navrongo, *Ghana* 83 C4
Navsari, *India* 66 J8
Nawa Kot, *Pakistan* 68 E4
Nawab Khan, *Pakistan* 68 D3
Nawabganj, *Ut. P., India* 69 F9
Nawabganj, *Ut. P., India* 69 E8
Nawabshah, *Pakistan* 68 F3
Nawada, *India* 69 G11
Nawakot, *Nepal* 69 F11
Nawalgarh, *India* 68 F6
Nawanshahr, *India* 69 C6
Nawar, Dasht-i-, *Afghan.* 68 C3
Nawi, *Sudan* 80 D3
Nawoiy, *Uzbekistan* 50 E7
Naxçıvan, *Azerbaijan* 70 B5
Naxçıvan □, *Azerbaijan* 50 F5
Náxos, *Greece* 39 D7
Nay, *France* 20 E3
Nay, Mui, *Vietnam* 62 B3
Nāy Band, *Būshehr, Iran* 71 E7
Nāy Band, *Khorāsān, Iran* 71 C8
Nayakhan, *Russia* 51 C16
Nayarit □, *Mexico* 118 C4
Nayé, *Senegal* 82 C2
Nayong, *China* 58 D5
Nayoro, *Japan* 54 B11
Nayyāl, W. →, *Si. Arabia* 70 D3
Nazaré, *Brazil* 125 F11
Nazaré, *Portugal* 35 F1
Nazareth = Naẓerat, *Israel* 75 C4
Nazareth, *U.S.A.* 111 F9
Nazas, *Mexico* 118 B4
Nazas →, *Mexico* 118 B4
Nazca, *Peru* 124 F4
Naze, The, *U.K.* 13 F9
Naẓerat, *Israel* 75 C4
Nāzīk, *Iran* 70 B5
Nazilli, *Turkey* 39 D10
Nazko, *Canada* 104 C4
Nazko →, *Canada* 104 C4
Nazret, *Ethiopia* 81 F4
Nazwá, *Oman* 74 C6
Nchanga, *Zambia* 87 E2
Ncheu, *Malawi* 87 E3
Ndala, *Tanzania* 86 C3
Ndalatando, *Angola* 84 F2
Ndali, *Benin* 83 D5
Ndareda, *Tanzania* 86 C4
Ndélé, *C.A.R.* 84 C4
Ndikinimeki, *Cameroon* 83 E7
N'Dioum, *Senegal* 82 B2
Ndjamena, *Chad* 79 F8
Ndola, *Zambia* 87 E2
Ndoto Mts., *Kenya* 86 B4
Nduguti, *Tanzania* 86 C3
Néa Alikarnassós, *Greece* 39 F7
Néa Ankhíalos, *Greece* 38 B4
Néa Epídhavros, *Greece* 38 D5
Néa Flippiás, *Greece* 38 B2
Néa Ionia, *Greece* 38 B4
Néa Kallikrátia, *Greece* 40 F7
Néa Mákri, *Greece* 38 C5
Néa Moudhaniá, *Greece* 40 F7
Néa Péramos, *Attikí, Greece* 38 C5
Néa Péramos, *Kaválla, Greece* 41 F8
Néa Víssi, *Greece* 41 E10
Néa Zíkhna, *Greece* 40 E7
Neagh, Lough, *U.K.* 15 B5
Neah Bay, *U.S.A.* 116 B2
Neale, L., *Australia* 92 D5
Neamţ □, *Romania* 43 C11
Neápolis, *Kozáni, Greece* 40 F5
Neápolis, *Kríti, Greece* 36 D7
Neápolis, *Lakonía, Greece* 38 E5
Near Is., *U.S.A.* 100 C1
Neath, *U.K.* 13 F4
Neath Port Talbot □, *U.K.* 13 F4
Nebbou, *Burkina Faso* 83 C4
Nebelat el Hagana, *Sudan* 81 E2
Nebine Cr. →, *Australia* 95 D4
Nebitdag, *Turkmenistan* 50 F6
Nebo, *Australia* 94 C4
Nebolchy, *Russia* 46 C7
Nebraska □, *U.S.A.* 112 E5
Nebraska City, *U.S.A.* 112 E7
Nébrodi, Monti, *Italy* 31 E7
Necedah, *U.S.A.* 112 C9
Nechako →, *Canada* 104 C4
Neches →, *U.S.A.* 113 L8
Neckar →, *Germany* 25 F4
Necochea, *Argentina* 126 D4
Neda, *Spain* 34 B2
Nedelino, *Bulgaria* 41 E9
Nedelišće, *Croatia* 29 B13
Nédha →, *Greece* 38 D3
Needles, *Canada* 104 D5
Needles, *U.S.A.* 117 L12
Needles, The, *U.K.* 13 G6
Ñeembucú □, *Paraguay* 126 B4
Neemuch = Nimach, *India* 68 G6
Neenah, *U.S.A.* 108 C1
Neepawa, *Canada* 105 C9
Neftçala, *Azerbaijan* 71 B6
Neftegorsk, *Russia* 49 H4
Neftekumsk, *Russia* 49 H7
Nefyn, *U.K.* 12 E3
Négala, *Mali* 82 C3
Negapatam = Nagappattinam, *India* 66 P11
Negaunee, *U.S.A.* 108 B2
Negele, *Ethiopia* 81 F4
Negev Desert = Hanegev, *Israel* 75 E4
Negoiul, Vf., *Romania* 43 E9
Negombo, *Sri Lanka* 66 R11
Negotin, *Serbia, Yug.* 40 B6
Negotino, *Macedonia* 40 E6
Negra, Peña, *Spain* 34 C4
Negra, Pta., *Peru* 122 D2
Negrais, C. = Maudin Sun, *Burma* 67 M19
Negreşti, *Romania* 43 D12
Negreşti-Oaş, *Romania* 43 C8
Negril, *Jamaica* 120 C4
Negro →, *Argentina* 122 H4
Negro →, *Brazil* 122 D4
Negro →, *Uruguay* 127 C4
Negros, *Phil.* 61 G5
Negru Vodă, *Romania* 43 G13
Neguac, *Canada* 103 C6
Nehalem →, *U.S.A.* 116 E3
Nehāvand, *Iran* 71 C6
Nehbandān, *Iran* 71 D9
Nehoiu, *Romania* 43 E11
Nei Monggol Zizhiqu □, *China* 56 D7
Neijiang, *China* 58 C5
Neillsville, *U.S.A.* 112 C9
Neilton, *U.S.A.* 114 C2
Neiqiu, *China* 56 F8
Neiva, *Colombia* 124 C3
Neixiang, *China* 56 H6
Nejanilini L., *Canada* 105 B9
Nejd = Najd, *Si. Arabia* 74 B3
Nejo, *Ethiopia* 81 F4
Nekā, *Iran* 71 B7
Nekemte, *Ethiopia* 81 F4
Nêkheb, *Egypt* 80 B3
Neksø, *Denmark* 11 J9
Nelas, *Portugal* 34 E3
Nelia, *Australia* 94 C3
Nelidovo, *Russia* 46 D7
Neligh, *U.S.A.* 112 D5
Nelkan, *Russia* 51 D14
Nellore, *India* 66 M11
Nelson, *Canada* 104 D5
Nelson, *N.Z.* 91 J4
Nelson, *U.K.* 12 D5
Nelson, *Ariz., U.S.A.* 115 J7
Nelson, *Nev., U.S.A.* 117 K12
Nelson →, *Canada* 105 C9
Nelson, C., *Australia* 95 F3
Nelson, Estrecho, *Chile* 128 G2
Nelson Forks, *Canada* 104 B4
Nelson House, *Canada* 105 B9
Nelson L., *Canada* 105 B8
Nelspoort, *S. Africa* 88 E3
Nelspruit, *S. Africa* 89 D5
Néma, *Mauritania* 82 B3
Neman, *Russia* 9 J20
Neman →, *Lithuania* 9 J19
Neméa, *Greece* 38 D4
Nemeiben L., *Canada* 105 B7
Nemërçkë, Mal, *Albania* 40 F4
Nemira, Vf., *Romania* 43 D11
Némiscau, *Canada* 102 B4
Némiscau, L., *Canada* 102 B4
Nemours, *France* 19 D9
Nemšová, *Slovak Rep.* 27 C11
Nemunas = Neman →, *Lithuania* 9 J19
Nemuro, *Japan* 54 C12
Nemuro-Kaikyō, *Japan* 54 C12
Nen Jiang →, *China* 57 B13
Nenagh, *Ireland* 15 D3
Nenasi, *Malaysia* 65 L4
Nene →, *U.K.* 13 E8
Nénita, *Greece* 39 C8
Nenjiang, *China* 60 B7
Neno, *Malawi* 87 F3
Neodesha, *U.S.A.* 113 G7
Neokhórion, *Aitolía kai Akarnanía, Greece* 38 C3
Neokhórion, *Árta, Greece* 38 B2
Néon Karlovásion, *Greece* 39 D8
Néon Petrítsi, *Greece* 40 E7
Neosho, *U.S.A.* 113 G7
Neosho →, *U.S.A.* 113 H7
Nepal ■, *Asia* 69 F11
Nepalganj, *Nepal* 69 E9
Nepalganj Road, *India* 69 E9
Nephi, *U.S.A.* 114 G8
Nephin, *Ireland* 15 B2
Nepi, *Italy* 29 F9
Nepomuk, *Czech Rep.* 26 B6
Neptune, *U.S.A.* 111 F10
Nera →, *Italy* 29 F9
Nera →, *Romania* 42 F6
Nérac, *France* 20 D4
Nerang, *Australia* 95 D5
Neratovice, *Czech Rep.* 26 A7
Nerchinsk, *Russia* 51 D12
Nereju, *Romania* 43 E11
Nerekhta, *Russia* 46 D11
Néret, L., *Canada* 103 B5
Neretvanski Kanal, *Croatia* 29 E14
Neringa, *Lithuania* 9 J19
Nerja, *Spain* 35 J7
Nerl →, *Russia* 46 D11
Nerpio, *Spain* 33 G2
Nerva, *Spain* 35 H4
Nervi, *Italy* 28 D6
Neryungri, *Russia* 51 D13
Nescopeck, *U.S.A.* 111 E8
Nesebŭr, *Bulgaria* 41 D11
Ness, L., *U.K.* 14 D4
Ness City, *U.S.A.* 112 F5
Nesterov, *Poland* 47 G2
Nestórion, *Greece* 40 F5
Néstos →, *Greece* 41 E8
Nesvady, *Slovak Rep.* 27 D11
Nesvizh = Nyasvizh, *Belarus* 47 F4
Netanya, *Israel* 75 C3
Netarhat, *India* 69 H11
Nete →, *Belgium* 17 C4
Netherdale, *Australia* 94 C4
Netherlands ■, *Europe* 17 C5
Netherlands Antilles ■, *W. Indies* 124 A5
Neto →, *Italy* 31 C10
Netrang, *India* 68 J5
Nettancourt, *France* 19 D11
Nettetal, *Germany* 24 D2
Nettilling L., *Canada* 101 B12
Nettuno, *Italy* 30 A5
Netzahualcoyotl, Presa, *Mexico* 119 D6
Neu-Isenburg, *Germany* 25 E4
Neu-Ulm, *Germany* 25 G6
Neubrandenburg, *Germany* 24 B9
Neubukow, *Germany* 24 A7
Neuburg, *Germany* 25 G7
Neuchâtel, *Switz.* 25 J2
Neuchâtel □, *Switz.* 25 J2
Neuchâtel, Lac de, *Switz.* 25 J2
Neudau, *Austria* 26 D9
Neuenhagen, *Germany* 24 C9
Neuenhaus, *Germany* 24 C2
Neuf-Brisach, *France* 19 D14
Neufahrn, *Bayern, Germany* 25 G8
Neufahrn, *Bayern, Germany* 25 G7
Neufchâteau, *Belgium* 17 E5
Neufchâteau, *France* 19 D12
Neufchâtel-en-Bray, *France* 18 C8
Neufchâtel-sur-Aisne, *France* 19 C11
Neuhaus, *Germany* 24 B6
Neuillé-Pont-Pierre, *France* 18 E7
Neuilly-St-Front, *France* 19 C10
Neukalen, *Germany* 24 B8
Neumarkt, *Germany* 25 F7
Neumünster, *Germany* 24 A5
Neung-sur-Beuvron, *France* 19 E8
Neunkirchen, *Austria* 26 D9
Neunkirchen, *Germany* 25 F3
Neuquén, *Argentina* 128 D3
Neuquén □, *Argentina* 126 D2
Neuruppin, *Germany* 24 C8
Neusäss, *Germany* 25 G6
Neuse →, *U.S.A.* 109 H7
Neusiedl, *Austria* 27 D9
Neusiedler See, *Austria* 27 D9
Neuss, *Germany* 24 D2
Neussargues-Moissac, *France* 20 C7
Neustadt, *Bayern, Germany* 25 F8
Neustadt, *Bayern, Germany* 25 G7
Neustadt, *Bayern, Germany* 25 F6
Neustadt, *Bayern, Germany* 25 E7
Neustadt, *Brandenburg, Germany* 24 C8
Neustadt, *Hessen, Germany* 24 E5
Neustadt, *Niedersachsen, Germany* 24 C5
Neustadt, *Rhld-Pfz., Germany* 25 F4
Neustadt, *Sachsen, Germany* 24 D10
Neustadt, *Schleswig-Holstein, Germany* 24 A6
Neustadt, *Thüringen, Germany* 24 E7
Neustrelitz, *Germany* 24 B9
Neuvic, *France* 20 C6
Neuville-sur-Saône, *France* 21 C8
Neuvy-le-Roi, *France* 18 E7
Neuvy-St-Sépulchre, *France* 19 F8
Neuvy-sur-Barangeon, *France* 19 E9
Neuwerk, *Germany* 24 B4
Neuwied, *Germany* 24 E3
Neva →, *Russia* 46 C6
Nevada, *Iowa, U.S.A.* 112 D8
Nevada, *Mo., U.S.A.* 113 G7
Nevada □, *U.S.A.* 114 G5
Nevada City, *U.S.A.* 116 F6
Nevado, Cerro, *Argentina* 126 D2
Nevel, *Russia* 46 D5
Nevers, *France* 19 F10
Nevertire, *Australia* 95 E4
Nevesinje, *Bos.-H.* 40 C2
Neville, *Canada* 105 D7
Nevinnomyssk, *Russia* 49 H6
Nevis, *St. Kitts & Nevis* 121 C7
Nevrokop = Gotse Delchev, *Bulgaria* 40 E7
Nevşehir, *Turkey* 70 B2
New →, *U.S.A.* 108 F5
New Aiyansh, *Canada* 104 B3
New Albany, *Ind., U.S.A.* 108 F3
New Albany, *Miss., U.S.A.* 113 H10
New Albany, *Pa., U.S.A.* 111 E8
New Amsterdam, *Guyana* 124 B7
New Angledool, *Australia* 95 D4
New Baltimore, *U.S.A.* 110 D2
New Bedford, *U.S.A.* 111 E14
New Berlin, *N.Y., U.S.A.* 111 D9
New Berlin, *Pa., U.S.A.* 110 F8
New Bern, *U.S.A.* 109 H7
New Bethlehem, *U.S.A.* 110 F5
New Bloomfield, *U.S.A.* 110 F7
New Boston, *U.S.A.* 113 J7
New Braunfels, *U.S.A.* 113 L5
New Brighton, *N.Z.* 91 K4
New Brighton, *U.S.A.* 110 F4
New Britain, *Papua N. G.* 96 H7
New Britain, *U.S.A.* 111 E12
New Brunswick, *U.S.A.* 111 F10
New Brunswick □, *Canada* 103 C6
New Bussa, *Nigeria* 83 D5
New Caledonia ■, *Pac. Oc.* 96 K8
New Castile = Castilla-La Mancha □, *Spain* 6 H5
New Castle, *Ind., U.S.A.* 108 F3
New Castle, *Pa., U.S.A.* 110 F4
New City, *U.S.A.* 111 E11
New Concord, *U.S.A.* 110 G3
New Cumberland, *U.S.A.* 110 F4
New Cuyama, *U.S.A.* 117 L7
New Delhi, *India* 68 E7
New Denver, *Canada* 104 D5
New Don Pedro Reservoir, *U.S.A.* 116 H6
New England, *U.S.A.* 112 B3
New England Ra., *Australia* 95 E5
New Forest, *U.K.* 13 G6
New Galloway, *U.K.* 14 F4
New Glasgow, *Canada* 103 C7
New Guinea, *Oceania* 52 K17
New Hamburg, *Canada* 110 C4
New Hampshire □, *U.S.A.* 111 C13
New Hampton, *U.S.A.* 112 D8
New Hanover, *S. Africa* 89 D5
New Hartford, *U.S.A.* 111 C9
New Haven, *Conn., U.S.A.* 111 E12
New Haven, *Mich., U.S.A.* 110 D2
New Hazelton, *Canada* 104 B3
New Hebrides = Vanuatu ■, *Pac. Oc.* 96 J8
New Holland, *U.S.A.* 111 F8
New Iberia, *U.S.A.* 113 K9
New Ireland, *Papua N. G.* 96 H7
New Jersey □, *U.S.A.* 108 E8
New Kensington, *U.S.A.* 110 F5
New Lexington, *U.S.A.* 108 F4
New Liskeard, *Canada* 102 C4
New London, *Conn., U.S.A.* 111 E12
New London, *Ohio, U.S.A.* 110 E2
New London, *Wis., U.S.A.* 112 C10
New Madrid, *U.S.A.* 113 G10
New Martinsville, *U.S.A.* 108 F5
New Meadows, *U.S.A.* 114 D5
New Melones L., *U.S.A.* 116 H6
New Mexico □, *U.S.A.* 115 J10
New Milford, *Conn., U.S.A.* 111 E11
New Milford, *Pa., U.S.A.* 111 E9
New Norcia, *Australia* 93 F2
New Norfolk, *Australia* 94 G4
New Orleans, *U.S.A.* 113 L9
New Philadelphia, *U.S.A.* 110 F3
New Plymouth, *N.Z.* 91 H5
New Plymouth, *U.S.A.* 114 E5
New Port Richey, *U.S.A.* 109 L4
New Providence, *Bahamas* 120 A4
New Quay, *U.K.* 13 E3
New Radnor, *U.K.* 13 E4
New Richmond, *Canada* 103 C6
New Richmond, *U.S.A.* 112 C8
New Roads, *U.S.A.* 113 K9
New Rochelle, *U.S.A.* 111 F11
New Rockford, *U.S.A.* 112 B5
New Romney, *U.K.* 13 G8
New Ross, *Ireland* 15 D5
New Salem, *U.S.A.* 112 B4
New Scone, *U.K.* 14 E5
New Siberian I. = Novaya Sibir, Ostrov, *Russia* 51 B16
New Siberian Is. = Novosibirskiye Ostrova, *Russia* 51 B15
New Smyrna Beach, *U.S.A.* 109 L5
New South Wales □, *Australia* 95 E4
New Town, *U.S.A.* 112 B3
New Tredegar, *U.K.* 13 F4
New Ulm, *U.S.A.* 112 C7
New Waterford, *Canada* 103 C7
New Westminster, *Canada* 116 A4
New York, *U.S.A.* 111 F11
New York □, *U.S.A.* 111 D9
New York Mts., *U.S.A.* 115 J6
New Zealand ■, *Oceania* 91 J6
Newaj →, *India* 68 G7
Newala, *Tanzania* 87 E4
Newark, *Del., U.S.A.* 108 F8
Newark, *N.J., U.S.A.* 111 F10
Newark, *N.Y., U.S.A.* 110 C7
Newark, *Ohio, U.S.A.* 110 F2
Newark-on-Trent, *U.K.* 12 D7
Newark Valley, *U.S.A.* 111 D8
Newberg, *U.S.A.* 114 D2
Newberry, *Mich., U.S.A.* 108 B3
Newberry, *S.C., U.S.A.* 109 H5
Newberry Springs, *U.S.A.* 117 L10
Newboro L., *Canada* 111 B8
Newbridge = Droichead Nua, *Ireland* 15 C5
Newburgh, *Canada* 110 B8
Newburgh, *U.S.A.* 111 E10
Newbury, *U.K.* 13 F6
Newbury, *N.H., U.S.A.* 111 B12
Newbury, *Vt., U.S.A.* 111 B12
Newburyport, *U.S.A.* 109 D10
Newcastle, *Australia* 95 E5
Newcastle, *N.B., Canada* 103 C6
Newcastle, *Ont., Canada* 102 D4
Newcastle, *S. Africa* 89 D4
Newcastle, *U.K.* 15 B6
Newcastle, *Calif., U.S.A.* 116 G5
Newcastle, *Wyo., U.S.A.* 112 D2
Newcastle Emlyn, *U.K.* 13 E3
Newcastle Ra., *Australia* 92 C5
Newcastle-under-Lyme, *U.K.* 12 D5
Newcastle-upon-Tyne, *U.K.* 12 C6
Newcastle Waters, *Australia* 94 B1
Newcastle West, *Ireland* 15 D2
Newcomb, *U.S.A.* 111 C10
Newcomerstown, *U.S.A.* 110 F3
Newdegate, *Australia* 93 F2
Newell, *Australia* 94 B4
Newell, *U.S.A.* 112 C3
Newfane, *U.S.A.* 110 C6
Newfield, *U.S.A.* 111 D8
Newfound L., *U.S.A.* 111 C13
Newfoundland, *Canada* 98 E14
Newfoundland, *U.S.A.* 111 E9
Newfoundland □, *Canada* 103 B8
Newhall, *U.S.A.* 117 L8
Newhaven, *U.K.* 13 G8
Newkirk, *U.S.A.* 113 G6
Newlyn, *U.K.* 13 G2
Newman, *Australia* 92 D2
Newman, *U.S.A.* 116 H5
Newmarket, *Canada* 110 B5
Newmarket, *Ireland* 15 D2
Newmarket, *U.K.* 13 E8
Newmarket, *U.S.A.* 111 C14
Newnan, *U.S.A.* 109 J3
Newport, *Ireland* 15 C2
Newport, *I. of W., U.K.* 13 G6
Newport, *Newp., U.K.* 13 F5
Newport, *Ark., U.S.A.* 113 H9
Newport, *Ky., U.S.A.* 108 F3
Newport, *N.H., U.S.A.* 111 C12
Newport, *N.Y., U.S.A.* 111 C9
Newport, *Oreg., U.S.A.* 114 D1
Newport, *Pa., U.S.A.* 110 F7
Newport, *R.I., U.S.A.* 111 E13
Newport, *Tenn., U.S.A.* 109 H4
Newport, *Vt., U.S.A.* 111 B12
Newport, *Wash., U.S.A.* 114 B5
Newport □, *U.K.* 13 F4
Newport Beach, *U.S.A.* 117 M9
Newport News, *U.S.A.* 108 G7
Newport Pagnell, *U.K.* 13 E7
Newquay, *U.K.* 13 G2

North Syracuse

Newry, *U.K.* 15 B5
Newton, *Ill., U.S.A.* 112 F10
Newton, *Iowa, U.S.A.* 112 E8
Newton, *Kans., U.S.A.* 113 F6
Newton, *Mass., U.S.A.* 111 D13
Newton, *Miss., U.S.A.* 113 J10
Newton, *N.C., U.S.A.* 109 H5
Newton, *N.J., U.S.A.* 111 E10
Newton, *Tex., U.S.A.* 113 K8
Newton Abbot, *U.K.* 13 G4
Newton Aycliffe, *U.K.* 12 C6
Newton Falls, *U.S.A.* 110 E4
Newton Stewart, *U.K.* 14 G4
Newtonmore, *U.K.* 14 D4
Newtown, *U.K.* 13 E4
Newtownabbey, *U.K.* 15 B6
Newtownards, *U.K.* 15 B6
Newtownbarry = Bunclody, *Ireland* 15 D5
Newtownstewart, *U.K.* 15 B4
Newville, *U.S.A.* 110 F7
Nexon, *France* 20 C5
Neya, *Russia* 48 A6
Neyrīz, *Iran* 71 D7
Neyshābūr, *Iran* 71 B8
Nezhin = Nizhyn, *Ukraine* 47 G6
Nezperce, *U.S.A.* 114 C5
Ngabang, *Indonesia* 62 D3
Ngabordamlu, Tanjung, *Indonesia* 63 F8
N'Gage, *Angola* 84 F3
Ngala, *Nigeria* 83 C7
Ngambé, *Cameroon* 83 D7
Ngambé, *Cameroon* 83 E7
Ngami Depression, *Botswana* 88 C3
Ngamo, *Zimbabwe* 87 F2
Ngangala, *Sudan* 81 G3
Nganglong Kangri, *China* 67 C12
Ngao, *Thailand* 64 C2
Ngaoundéré, *Cameroon* 84 C2
Ngapara, *N.Z.* 91 L3
Ngara, *Tanzania* 86 C3
Ngawi, *Indonesia* 63 G14
Nghia Lo, *Vietnam* 58 G5
Ngoboli, *Sudan* 81 G3
Ngoma, *Malawi* 87 E3
Ngomahura, *Zimbabwe* 87 G3
Ngomba, *Tanzania* 87 D3
Ngop, *Sudan* 81 F3
Ngoring Hu, *China* 60 C4
Ngorkou, *Mali* 82 B4
Ngorongoro, *Tanzania* 86 C4
Ngozi, *Burundi* 86 C2
Ngudu, *Tanzania* 86 C3
Nguigmi, *Niger* 79 F8
Nguila, *Cameroon* 83 E7
Nguiu, *Australia* 92 B5
Ngukurr, *Australia* 94 A1
Ngulu Atoll, *Pac. Oc.* 63 C9
Ngunga, *Tanzania* 86 C3
Nguru, *Nigeria* 83 C7
Nguru Mts., *Tanzania* 86 D4
Nguyen Binh, *Vietnam* 58 F5
Nha Trang, *Vietnam* 65 F7
Nhacoongo, *Mozam.* 89 C6
Nhamaabué, *Mozam.* 87 F4
Nhamundá →, *Brazil* 125 D7
Nhangulaze, L., *Mozam.* 89 C5
Nhill, *Australia* 95 F3
Nho Quan, *Vietnam* 58 G5
Nhulunbuy, *Australia* 94 A2
Nia-nia, *Dem. Rep. of the Congo* 86 B2
Niafounké, *Mali* 82 B4
Niagara Falls, *Canada* 102 D4
Niagara Falls, *U.S.A.* 110 C6
Niagara-on-the-Lake, *Canada* 110 C5
Niah, *Malaysia* 62 D4
Niamey, *Niger* 83 C5
Niandan-Koro, *Guinea* 82 C3
Nianforando, *Guinea* 82 D2
Niangara, *Dem. Rep. of the Congo* 86 B2
Niangbo, *Ivory C.* 82 D3
Niangoloko, *Burkina Faso* 82 C4
Niantic, *U.S.A.* 111 E12
Niaro, *Sudan* 81 E3
Nias, *Indonesia* 62 D1
Niassa □, *Mozam.* 87 E4
Nibāk, *Si. Arabia* 71 E7
Nibe, *Denmark* 11 H3
Nicaragua ■, *Cent. Amer.* 120 D2
Nicaragua, L. de, *Nic.* 120 D2
Nicastro, *Italy* 31 D9
Nice, *France* 21 E11
Niceville, *U.S.A.* 109 K2
Nichicun, L., *Canada* 103 B5
Nichinan, *Japan* 55 J5
Nicholás, Canal, *W. Indies* 120 B3
Nicholasville, *U.S.A.* 108 G3
Nichols, *U.S.A.* 111 D8
Nicholson, *Australia* 92 C4
Nicholson, *U.S.A.* 111 E9
Nicholson →, *Australia* 94 B2
Nicholson L., *Canada* 105 A8
Nicholson Ra., *Australia* 93 E2
Nicholville, *U.S.A.* 111 B10
Nicobar Is., *Ind. Oc.* 52 J13
Nicola, *Canada* 104 C4
Nicolls Town, *Bahamas* 120 A4
Nicopolis, *Greece* 38 B2
Nicosia, *Cyprus* 36 D12
Nicosia, *Italy* 31 E7
Nicótera, *Italy* 31 D8
Nicoya, *Costa Rica* 120 D2
Nicoya, G. de, *Costa Rica* 120 E3
Nicoya, Pen. de, *Costa Rica* 120 E2
Nidd →, *U.K.* 12 D6
Nidda, *Germany* 25 E5
Nidda →, *Germany* 25 E4
Nidwalden □, *Switz.* 25 J4
Nidzica, *Poland* 45 E7
Niebüll, *Germany* 24 A4
Nied →, *Germany* 19 C13
Niederaula, *Germany* 24 E5
Niederbayern □, *Germany* 25 G8
Niederbronn-les-Bains, *France* 19 D14
Niedere Tauern, *Austria* 26 D7
Niederlausitz, *Germany* 24 D9
Niederösterreich □, *Austria* 26 C8
Niedersachsen □, *Germany* 24 C4
Niekerkshoop, *S. Africa* 88 D3
Niellé, *Ivory C.* 82 C3
Niemba, *Dem. Rep. of the Congo* 86 D2
Niemen = Neman →, *Lithuania* 9 J19
Niemodlin, *Poland* 45 H4
Nienburg, *Germany* 24 C5
Niepołomice, *Poland* 45 H7
Niers →, *Germany* 24 D1
Niesky, *Germany* 24 D10
Nieszawa, *Poland* 45 F5
Nieu Bethesda, *S. Africa* 88 E3
Nieuw Amsterdam, *Surinam* 125 B7
Nieuw Nickerie, *Surinam* 125 B7
Nieuwoudtville, *S. Africa* 88 E2
Nieuwpoort, *Belgium* 17 C2
Nieves, Pico de las, *Canary Is.* 37 G4
Nièvre □, *France* 19 E10
Niga, *Mali* 82 C3
Niğde, *Turkey* 70 B2
Nigel, *S. Africa* 89 D4
Niger □, *Nigeria* 83 D6
Niger ■, *W. Afr.* 83 B7
Niger →, *W. Afr.* 83 D6
Niger Delta, *Africa* 83 E6
Nigeria ■, *W. Afr.* 83 D6
Nighasin, *India* 69 E9
Nightcaps, *N.Z.* 91 L2
Nigríta, *Greece* 40 F7
Nii-Jima, *Japan* 55 G9
Niigata, *Japan* 54 F9
Niigata □, *Japan* 55 F9
Niihama, *Japan* 55 H6
Niihau, *U.S.A.* 106 H14
Niimi, *Japan* 55 G6
Niitsu, *Japan* 54 F9
Nījar, *Spain* 33 J2
Nijil, *Jordan* 75 E4
Nijkerk, *Neths.* 17 B5
Nijmegen, *Neths.* 17 C5
Nijverdal, *Neths.* 17 B6
Nīk Pey, *Iran* 71 B6
Nike, *Nigeria* 83 D6
Nikiniki, *Indonesia* 63 F6
Nikísiani, *Greece* 41 F8
Nikítas, *Greece* 40 F7
Nikki, *Benin* 83 D5
Nikkō, *Japan* 55 F9
Nikolayev = Mykolayiv, *Ukraine* 47 J7
Nikolayevsk, *Russia* 48 E7
Nikolayevsk-na-Amur, *Russia* 51 D15
Nikolsk, *Russia* 48 D8
Nikolskoye, *Russia* 51 D17
Nikopol, *Bulgaria* 41 C8
Nikopol, *Ukraine* 47 J8
Niksar, *Turkey* 72 B7
Nīkshahr, *Iran* 71 E9
Nikšić, *Montenegro, Yug.* 40 D2
Nîl, Nahr en →, *Africa* 80 H7
Nîl el Abyad →, *Sudan* 81 D3
Nîl el Azraq →, *Sudan* 81 D3
Nila, *Indonesia* 63 F7
Niland, *U.S.A.* 117 M11
Nile = Nîl, Nahr en →, *Africa* 80 H7
Niles, *Mich., U.S.A.* 108 E2
Niles, *Ohio, U.S.A.* 110 E4
Nilüfer →, *Turkey* 41 F12
Nim Ka Thana, *India* 68 F6
Nimach, *India* 68 G6
Nimbahera, *India* 68 G6
Nîmes, *France* 21 E8
Nimfaíon, Ákra = Pínnes, Ákra, *Greece* 41 F8
Nimmitabel, *Australia* 95 F4
Nimule, *Sudan* 81 G3
Nin, *Croatia* 29 D12
Nīnawá, *Iraq* 70 B4
Nindigully, *Australia* 95 D4
Nineveh = Nīnawá, *Iraq* 70 B4
Ning Xian, *China* 56 G4
Ning'an, *China* 57 B15
Ningbo, *China* 59 C13
Ningcheng, *China* 57 D10
Ningde, *China* 59 D12
Ningdu, *China* 59 D10
Ninggang, *China* 59 D9
Ningguo, *China* 59 B12
Ninghai, *China* 59 C13
Ninghua, *China* 59 D11
Ningi, *Nigeria* 83 C6
Ningjin, *China* 56 F8
Ningjing Shan, *China* 58 C2
Ninglang, *China* 58 D3
Ningling, *China* 56 G8
Ningming, *China* 58 F6
Ningnan, *China* 58 D4
Ningpo = Ningbo, *China* 59 C13
Ningqiang, *China* 56 H4
Ningshan, *China* 56 H5
Ningsia Hui A.R. = Ningxia Huizu Zizhiqu □, *China* 56 F4
Ningwu, *China* 56 E7
Ningxia Huizu Zizhiqu □, *China* 56 F4
Ningxiang, *China* 59 C9
Ningyang, *China* 56 G9
Ningyuan, *China* 59 E8
Ninh Binh, *Vietnam* 58 G5
Ninh Giang, *Vietnam* 64 B6
Ninh Hoa, *Vietnam* 64 F7
Ninh Ma, *Vietnam* 64 F7
Ninove, *Belgium* 17 D4
Nioaque, *Brazil* 127 A4
Niobrara, *U.S.A.* 112 D6
Niobrara →, *U.S.A.* 112 D6
Niono, *Mali* 82 C3
Nionsamoridougou, *Guinea* 82 D3
Nioro du Rip, *Senegal* 82 C1
Nioro du Sahel, *Mali* 82 B3
Niort, *France* 20 B3
Nipawin, *Canada* 105 C8
Nipfjället, *Sweden* 10 C6
Nipigon, *Canada* 102 C2
Nipigon, L., *Canada* 102 C2
Nipishish L., *Canada* 103 B7
Nipissing, L., *Canada* 102 C4
Nipomo, *U.S.A.* 117 K6
Nipton, *U.S.A.* 117 K11
Niquelândia, *Brazil* 125 F9
Nīr, *Iran* 70 B5
Nirasaki, *Japan* 55 G9
Nirmal, *India* 66 K11
Nirmali, *India* 69 F12
Niš, *Serbia, Yug.* 40 C5
Nisa, *Portugal* 35 F3
Nişāb, *Si. Arabia* 70 D5
Nişāb, *Yemen* 74 E4
Nišava →, *Serbia, Yug.* 40 C5
Niscemi, *Italy* 31 E7
Nishinomiya, *Japan* 55 G7
Nishino'omote, *Japan* 55 J5
Nishiwaki, *Japan* 55 G7
Nísíros, *Greece* 39 E9
Niška Banja, *Serbia, Yug.* 40 C6
Niskibi →, *Canada* 102 A2
Nisko, *Poland* 45 H9
Nisporeni, *Moldova* 43 C13
Nisqually →, *U.S.A.* 116 C4
Nissáki, *Greece* 36 A3
Nissan →, *Sweden* 11 H6
Nissum Bredning, *Denmark* 11 H2
Nissum Fjord, *Denmark* 11 H2
Nistru = Dnister →, *Europe* 47 J6
Nisutlin →, *Canada* 104 A2
Nitchequon, *Canada* 103 B5
Niterói, *Brazil* 127 A7
Nith →, *Canada* 110 C4
Nith →, *U.K.* 14 F5
Nitra, *Slovak Rep.* 27 C11
Nitra →, *Slovak Rep.* 27 D11
Nitriansky □, *Slovak Rep.* 27 C11
Nittenau, *Germany* 25 F8
Niuafo'ou, *Tonga* 91 B11
Niue, *Cook Is.* 97 J11
Niulan Jiang →, *China* 58 D4
Niut, *Indonesia* 62 D4
Niutou Shan, *China* 59 C13
Niuzhuang, *China* 57 D12
Nivala, *Finland* 8 E21
Nivelles, *Belgium* 17 D4
Nivernais, *France* 19 E10
Niwas, *India* 69 H9
Nixon, *U.S.A.* 113 L6
Nizamabad, *India* 66 K11
Nizamghat, *India* 67 E19
Nizhne Kolymsk, *Russia* 51 C17
Nizhnegorskiy = Nyzhnohirskyy, *Ukraine* 47 K8
Nizhnekamsk, *Russia* 48 C10
Nizhneudinsk, *Russia* 51 D10
Nizhnevartovsk, *Russia* 50 C8
Nizhniy Chir, *Russia* 49 F6
Nizhniy Lomov, *Russia* 48 D6
Nizhniy Novgorod, *Russia* 48 B7
Nizhniy Tagil, *Russia* 50 D6
Nizhyn, *Ukraine* 47 G6
Nizina Mazowiecka, *Poland* 45 F8
Nizip, *Turkey* 70 B3
Nízké Tatry, *Slovak Rep.* 27 C12
Nízký Jeseník, *Czech Rep.* 27 B10
Nizza Monferrato, *Italy* 28 D5
Njakwa, *Malawi* 87 E3
Njanji, *Zambia* 87 E3
Njegoš, *Montenegro, Yug.* 40 D2
Njinjo, *Tanzania* 87 D4
Njombe, *Tanzania* 87 D3
Njombe →, *Tanzania* 86 D4
Njurundabommen, *Sweden* 10 B11
Nkambe, *Cameroon* 83 D7
Nkana, *Zambia* 87 E2
Nkandla, *S. Africa* 89 D5
Nkawkaw, *Ghana* 83 D4
Nkayi, *Zimbabwe* 87 F2
Nkhotakota, *Malawi* 87 E3
Nkongsamba, *Cameroon* 83 E6
Nkurenkuru, *Namibia* 88 B2
Nkwanta, *Ghana* 82 D4
Nmai →, *Burma* 58 F2
Noakhali = Maijdi, *Bangla.* 67 H17
Nobel, *Canada* 110 A4
Nobeoka, *Japan* 55 H5
Noblejas, *Spain* 34 F7
Noblesville, *U.S.A.* 108 E3
Noce →, *Italy* 28 B8
Nocera Inferiore, *Italy* 31 B7
Nocera Umbra, *Italy* 29 E9
Noci, *Italy* 31 B10
Nocona, *U.S.A.* 113 J6
Nocrich, *Romania* 43 E9
Noda, *Japan* 55 G9
Nogales, *Mexico* 118 A2
Nogales, *U.S.A.* 115 L8
Nogaro, *France* 20 E3
Nogat →, *Poland* 44 D6
Nōgata, *Japan* 55 H5
Nogent, *France* 19 D12
Nogent-le-Rotrou, *France* 18 D7
Nogent-sur-Seine, *France* 19 D10
Noggerup, *Australia* 93 F2
Noginsk, *Moskva, Russia* 46 E10
Noginsk, *Tunguska, Russia* 51 C10
Nogoa →, *Australia* 94 C4
Nogoyá, *Argentina* 126 C4
Nógrád □, *Hungary* 42 C4
Noguera Pallaresa →, *Spain* 32 D5
Noguera Ribagorzana →, *Spain* 32 D5
Nohar, *India* 68 E6
Nohfelden, *Germany* 25 F3
Nohta, *India* 69 H8
Noia, *Spain* 34 C2
Noire, Montagne, *France* 20 E6
Noires, Mts., *France* 18 D3
Noirétable, *France* 20 C7
Noirmoutier, Î. de, *France* 18 F4
Noirmoutier-en-l'Île, *France* 18 F4
Nojane, *Botswana* 88 C3
Nojima-Zaki, *Japan* 55 G9
Nok Kundi, *Pakistan* 66 E3
Nokaneng, *Botswana* 88 B3
Nokia, *Finland* 9 F20
Nokomis, *Canada* 105 C8
Nokomis L., *Canada* 105 B8
Nol, *Sweden* 11 G6
Nola, *C.A.R.* 84 D3
Nola, *Italy* 31 B7
Nolay, *France* 19 F11
Noli, C. di, *Italy* 28 D5
Nolinsk, *Russia* 48 B9
Noma Omuramba →, *Namibia* 88 B3
Nombre de Dios, *Panama* 120 E4
Nome, *U.S.A.* 100 B3
Nomo-Zaki, *Japan* 55 H4
Nonacho L., *Canada* 105 A7
Nonancourt, *France* 18 D8
Nonda, *Australia* 94 C3
None, *Italy* 28 D4
Nong Chang, *Thailand* 64 E2
Nong Het, *Laos* 64 C4
Nong Khai, *Thailand* 64 D4
Nong'an, *China* 57 B13
Nongoma, *S. Africa* 89 D5
Nonoava, *Mexico* 118 B3
Nonoava →, *Mexico* 118 B3
Nonthaburi, *Thailand* 64 F3
Nontron, *France* 20 C4
Nonza, *France* 21 F13
Noonamah, *Australia* 92 B5
Noord Brabant □, *Neths.* 17 C5
Noord Holland □, *Neths.* 17 B4
Noordbeveland, *Neths.* 17 C3
Noordoostpolder, *Neths.* 17 B5
Noordwijk, *Neths.* 17 B4
Nootka I., *Canada* 104 D3
Nopiming Prov. Park, *Canada* 105 C9
Nora, *Eritrea* 81 D5
Nora, *Sweden* 10 E9
Noralee, *Canada* 104 C3
Noranda = Rouyn-Noranda, *Canada* 102 C4
Norberg, *Sweden* 10 D9
Nórcia, *Italy* 29 F10
Norco, *U.S.A.* 117 M9
Nord □, *France* 19 B10
Nord-Kivu □, *Dem. Rep. of the Congo* 86 C2
Nord-Ostsee-Kanal, *Germany* 24 A5
Nord-Pas-de-Calais □, *France* 19 B9
Nordaustlandet, *Svalbard* 4 B9
Nordborg, *Denmark* 11 J3
Nordby, *Denmark* 11 J2
Norddeich, *Germany* 24 B3
Nordegg, *Canada* 104 C5
Norden, *Germany* 24 B3
Nordenham, *Germany* 24 B4
Norderney, *Germany* 24 B3
Norderstedt, *Germany* 24 B6
Nordfjord, *Norway* 9 F11
Nordfriesische Inseln, *Germany* 24 A4
Nordhausen, *Germany* 24 D6
Nordhorn, *Germany* 24 C3
Norðoyar, *Færoe Is.* 8 E9
Nordingrå, *Sweden* 10 B12
Nordjyllands Amtskommune □, *Denmark* 11 G4
Nordkapp, *Norway* 8 A21
Nordkapp, *Svalbard* 4 A9
Nordkinn = Kinnarodden, *Norway* 6 A11
Nordkinn-halvøya, *Norway* 8 A22
Nördlingen, *Germany* 25 G6
Nordrhein-Westfalen □, *Germany* 24 D3
Nordstrand, *Germany* 24 A4
Nordvik, *Russia* 51 B12
Nore →, *Ireland* 15 D4
Norfolk, *Nebr., U.S.A.* 112 D6
Norfolk, *Va., U.S.A.* 108 G7
Norfolk □, *U.K.* 13 E8
Norfolk I., *Pac. Oc.* 96 K8
Norfork L., *U.S.A.* 113 G8
Norilsk, *Russia* 51 C9
Norma, Mt., *Australia* 94 C3
Normal, *U.S.A.* 112 E10
Norman, *U.S.A.* 113 H6
Norman →, *Australia* 94 B3
Norman Wells, *Canada* 100 B7
Normanby →, *Australia* 94 A3
Normandin, *Canada* 102 C5
Normanhurst, Mt., *Australia* 93 E3
Normanton, *Australia* 94 B3
Normétal, *Canada* 102 C4
Norquay, *Canada* 105 C8
Norquinco, *Argentina* 128 E2
Norra Dellen, *Sweden* 10 C10
Norra Ulvön, *Sweden* 10 A12
Norrahammar, *Sweden* 11 G8
Norrbotten □, *Sweden* 8 C19
Nørre Åby, *Denmark* 11 J3
Nørre Alslev, *Denmark* 11 K5
Nørresundby, *Denmark* 11 G3
Norrhult, *Sweden* 11 G9
Norris Point, *Canada* 103 C8
Norristown, *U.S.A.* 111 F9
Norrköping, *Sweden* 11 F10
Norrland, *Sweden* 9 E16
Norrsundet, *Sweden* 10 D11
Norrtälje, *Sweden* 10 E12
Norseman, *Australia* 93 F3
Norsk, *Russia* 51 D14
Norte, Pta. del, *Canary Is.* 37 G2
Norte, Serra do, *Brazil* 124 F7
North, C., *Canada* 103 C7
North Adams, *U.S.A.* 111 D11
North Arm, *Canada* 104 A5
North Augusta, *U.S.A.* 109 J5
North Ayrshire □, *U.K.* 14 F4
North Bass I., *U.S.A.* 110 E2
North Battleford, *Canada* 105 C7
North Bay, *Canada* 102 C4
North Belcher Is., *Canada* 102 A4
North Bend, *Oreg., U.S.A.* 114 E1
North Bend, *Pa., U.S.A.* 110 E7
North Bend, *Wash., U.S.A.* 116 C5
North Bennington, *U.S.A.* 111 D11
North Berwick, *U.K.* 14 E6
North Berwick, *U.S.A.* 111 C14
North C., *Canada* 103 C7
North C., *N.Z.* 91 F4
North Canadian →, *U.S.A.* 113 H7
North Canton, *U.S.A.* 110 F3
North Cape = Nordkapp, *Norway* 8 A21
North Cape = Nordkapp, *Svalbard* 4 A9
North Caribou L., *Canada* 102 B1
North Carolina □, *U.S.A.* 109 H6
North Cascades National Park, *U.S.A.* 114 B3
North Channel, *Canada* 102 C3
North Channel, *U.K.* 14 F3
North Charleston, *U.S.A.* 109 J6
North Chicago, *U.S.A.* 108 D2
North Creek, *U.S.A.* 111 C11
North Dakota □, *U.S.A.* 112 B5
North Downs, *U.K.* 13 F8
North East, *U.S.A.* 110 D5
North East Frontier Agency = Arunachal Pradesh □, *India* 67 F19
North East Lincolnshire □, *U.K.* 12 D7
North Eastern □, *Kenya* 86 B5
North Esk →, *U.K.* 14 E6
North European Plain, *Europe* 6 E10
North Foreland, *U.K.* 13 F9
North Fork, *U.S.A.* 116 H7
North Fork American →, *U.S.A.* 116 G5
North Fork Feather →, *U.S.A.* 116 F5
North Fork Grand →, *U.S.A.* 112 C3
North Fork Red →, *U.S.A.* 113 H5
North Frisian Is. = Nordfriesische Inseln, *Germany* 24 A4
North Gower, *Canada* 111 A9
North Hd., *Australia* 93 F1
North Henik L., *Canada* 105 A9
North Highlands, *U.S.A.* 116 G5
North Horr, *Kenya* 86 B4
North I., *Kenya* 86 B4
North I., *N.Z.* 91 H5
North Kingsville, *U.S.A.* 110 E4
North Knife →, *Canada* 105 B10
North Koel →, *India* 69 G10
North Korea ■, *Asia* 57 E14
North Lakhimpur, *India* 67 F19
North Lanarkshire □, *U.K.* 14 F5
North Las Vegas, *U.S.A.* 117 J11
North Lincolnshire □, *U.K.* 12 D7
North Little Rock, *U.S.A.* 113 H8
North Loup →, *U.S.A.* 112 E5
North Magnetic Pole, *Canada* 4 B2
North Minch, *U.K.* 14 C3
North Moose L., *Canada* 105 C8
North Myrtle Beach, *U.S.A.* 109 J6
North Nahanni →, *Canada* 104 A4
North Olmsted, *U.S.A.* 110 E3
North Ossetia □, *Russia* 49 J7
North Pagai, I. = Pagai Utara, Pulau, *Indonesia* 62 E2
North Palisade, *U.S.A.* 116 H8
North Platte, *U.S.A.* 112 E4
North Platte →, *U.S.A.* 112 E4
North Pole, *Arctic* 4 A
North Portal, *Canada* 105 D8
North Powder, *U.S.A.* 114 D5
North Pt., *U.S.A.* 110 A1
North Rhine Westphalia = Nordrhein-Westfalen □, *Germany* 24 D3
North River, *Canada* 103 B8
North Ronaldsay, *U.K.* 14 B6
North Saskatchewan →, *Canada* 105 C7
North Sea, *Europe* 6 D6
North Seal →, *Canada* 105 B9
North Somerset □, *U.K.* 13 F5
North Sporades = Vóriai Sporádhes, *Greece* 38 B5
North Sydney, *Canada* 103 C7
North Syracuse, *U.S.A.* 111 C8

North Taranaki Bight, *N.Z.* 91 H5
North Thompson →, *Canada* 104 C4
North Tonawanda, *U.S.A.* 110 C6
North Troy, *U.S.A.* 111 B12
North Truchas Pk., *U.S.A.* 115 J11
North Twin I., *Canada* 102 B4
North Tyne →, *U.K.* 12 B5
North Uist, *U.K.* 14 D1
North Vancouver, *Canada* 104 D4
North Vernon, *U.S.A.* 108 F3
North Wabasca L., *Canada* 104 B6
North Walsham, *U.K.* 12 E9
North-West □, *S. Africa* 88 D4
North West C., *Australia* 92 D1
North West Christmas I. Ridge, *Pac. Oc.* 97 G11
North West Frontier □, *Pakistan* 68 C4
North West Highlands, *U.K.* 14 D4
North West River, *Canada* 103 B7
North Western □, *Zambia* 87 E2
North Wildwood, *U.S.A.* 108 F8
North York Moors, *U.K.* 12 C7
North Yorkshire □, *U.K.* 12 C6
Northallerton, *U.K.* 12 C6
Northam, *Australia* 93 F2
Northam, *S. Africa* 88 C4
Northampton, *Australia* 93 E1
Northampton, *U.K.* 13 E7
Northampton, *Mass., U.S.A.* 111 D12
Northampton, *Pa., U.S.A.* 111 F9
Northamptonshire □, *U.K.* 13 E7
Northbridge, *U.S.A.* 111 D13
Northcliffe, *Australia* 93 F2
Northeast Providence Chan., *W. Indies* 120 A4
Northeim, *Germany* 24 D6
Northern □, *Ghana* 83 D4
Northern □, *Malawi* 87 E3
Northern □, *Zambia* 87 E3
Northern Areas □, *Pakistan* 69 A5
Northern Cape □, *S. Africa* 88 D3
Northern Circars, *India* 67 L13
Northern Indian L., *Canada* 105 B9
Northern Ireland □, *U.K.* 15 B5
Northern Light L., *Canada* 102 C1
Northern Marianas ■, *Pac. Oc.* 96 F6
Northern Province □, *S. Leone* 82 D2
Northern Province □, *S. Africa* 89 C4
Northern Territory □, *Australia* 92 D5
Northfield, *Minn., U.S.A.* 112 C8
Northfield, *Vt., U.S.A.* 111 B12
Northland □, *N.Z.* 91 F4
Northome, *U.S.A.* 112 B7
Northport, *Ala., U.S.A.* 109 J2
Northport, *Wash., U.S.A.* 114 B5
Northumberland □, *U.K.* 12 B6
Northumberland, C., *Australia* 95 F3
Northumberland Is., *Australia* 94 C4
Northumberland Str., *Canada* 103 C7
Northville, *U.S.A.* 111 C10
Northwest Providence Channel, *W. Indies* 120 A4
Northwest Territories □, *Canada* 100 B9
Northwood, *Iowa, U.S.A.* 112 D8
Northwood, *N. Dak., U.S.A.* 112 B6
Norton, *U.S.A.* 112 F5
Norton, *Zimbabwe* 87 F3
Norton Sd., *U.S.A.* 100 B3
Nortorf, *Germany* 24 A5
Norwalk, *Calif., U.S.A.* 117 M8
Norwalk, *Conn., U.S.A.* 111 E11
Norwalk, *Iowa, U.S.A.* 112 E8
Norwalk, *Ohio, U.S.A.* 110 E2
Norway, *Maine, U.S.A.* 109 C10
Norway, *Mich., U.S.A.* 108 C2
Norway ■, *Europe* 8 E14
Norway House, *Canada* 105 C9
Norwegian Sea, *Atl. Oc.* 4 C8
Norwich, *Canada* 110 D4
Norwich, *U.K.* 13 E9
Norwich, *Conn., U.S.A.* 111 E12
Norwich, *N.Y., U.S.A.* 111 D9
Norwood, *Canada* 110 B7
Norwood, *U.S.A.* 111 B10
Noshiro, *Japan* 54 D10
Nosivka, *Ukraine* 47 G6
Nosovka = Nosivka, *Ukraine* 47 G6
Noşratābād, *Iran* 71 D8
Noss Hd., *U.K.* 14 C5
Nossebro, *Sweden* 11 F6
Nossob →, *S. Africa* 88 D3
Nossombougou, *Mali* 82 C3
Nosy Barren, *Madag.* 85 H8
Nosy Be, *Madag.* 85 G9
Nosy Boraha, *Madag.* 89 B8
Nosy Lava, *Madag.* 89 A8
Nosy Varika, *Madag.* 89 C8
Noteć →, *Poland* 45 F2
Notikewin →, *Canada* 104 B5
Notio Aigaio = Notios Aiyaíon □ 39 E7
Notios Aiyaíon □ 39 E7
Notios Evvoïkos Kólpos, *Greece* 38 C5
Noto, *Italy* 31 F8
Noto, G. di, *Italy* 31 F8
Notodden, *Norway* 9 G13
Notre Dame B., *Canada* 103 C8
Notre Dame de Koartac = Quaqtaq, *Canada* 101 B13
Notre-Dame-des-Bois, *Canada* 111 A13
Notre Dame d'Ivugivic = Ivujivik, *Canada* 101 B12
Notre-Dame-du-Nord, *Canada* 102 C4
Notsé, *Togo* 83 D5
Nottawasaga B., *Canada* 110 B4
Nottaway →, *Canada* 102 B4
Nottingham, *U.K.* 12 E6
Nottingham, City of □, *U.K.* 12 E6
Nottingham I., *Canada* 101 B12
Nottinghamshire □, *U.K.* 12 D6
Nottoway →, *U.S.A.* 108 G7
Notwane →, *Botswana* 88 C4
Nouâdhibou, *Mauritania* 78 D2
Nouâdhibou, Ras, *Mauritania* 78 D2
Nouakchott, *Mauritania* 82 B1
Nouâmghâr, *Mauritania* 82 B1
Nouméa, *N. Cal.* 96 K8
Nouna, *Burkina Faso* 82 C4
Noupoort, *S. Africa* 88 E3
Nouveau Comptoir = Wemindji, *Canada* 102 B4
Nouvelle-Amsterdam, I., *Ind. Oc.* 3 F13
Nouvelle-Calédonie = New Caledonia ■, *Pac. Oc.* 96 K8
Nouzonville, *France* 19 C11
Nová Baňa, *Slovak Rep.* 27 C11
Nová Bystřice, *Czech Rep.* 26 B8
Nova Casa Nova, *Brazil* 125 E10
Nova Esperança, *Brazil* 127 A5
Nova Friburgo, *Brazil* 127 A7
Nova Gaia = Cambundi-Catembo, *Angola* 84 G3
Nova Gorica, *Slovenia* 29 C10
Nova Gradiška, *Croatia* 42 E2
Nova Iguaçu, *Brazil* 127 A7
Nova Iorque, *Brazil* 125 E10
Nova Kakhovka, *Ukraine* 47 J7
Nova Lamego, *Guinea-Biss.* 82 C2
Nova Lima, *Brazil* 127 A7
Nova Lisboa = Huambo, *Angola* 85 G3
Nova Lusitânia, *Mozam.* 87 F3
Nova Mambone, *Mozam.* 89 C6
Nova Odesa, *Ukraine* 47 J6
Nová Paka, *Czech Rep.* 26 A8
Nova Pavova, *Serbia, Yug.* 42 F5
Nova Scotia □, *Canada* 103 C7
Nova Siri, *Italy* 31 B9
Nova Sofala, *Mozam.* 89 C5
Nova Varoš, *Serbia, Yug.* 40 C3
Nova Venécia, *Brazil* 125 G10
Nova Zagora, *Bulgaria* 41 D10
Novaci, *Macedonia* 40 E5
Novaci, *Romania* 43 E8
Novafeltria, *Italy* 29 E9
Novaleksandrovskaya = Novoaleksandrovsk, *Russia* 49 H5
Novannenskiy = Novoannenskiy, *Russia* 48 E6
Novar, *Canada* 110 A5
Novara, *Italy* 28 C5
Novato, *U.S.A.* 116 G4
Novaya Kakhovka = Nova Kakhovka, *Ukraine* 47 J7
Novaya Kazanka, *Kazakstan* 49 F9
Novaya Ladoga, *Russia* 46 B7
Novaya Lyalya, *Russia* 50 D7
Novaya Sibir, Ostrov, *Russia* 51 B16
Novaya Zemlya, *Russia* 50 B6
Nové Město, *Slovak Rep.* 27 C10
Nové Město na Moravě, *Czech Rep.* 26 B9
Nové Město nad Metují, *Czech Rep.* 27 A9
Nové Zámky, *Slovak Rep.* 27 C11
Novelda, *Spain* 33 G4
Novellara, *Italy* 28 D7
Noventa Vicentina, *Italy* 29 C8
Novgorod, *Russia* 46 C6
Novgorod-Severskiy = Novhorod-Siverskyy, *Ukraine* 47 G7
Novhorod-Siverskyy, *Ukraine* 47 G7
Novi Bečej, *Serbia, Yug.* 42 E5
Novi Iskar, *Bulgaria* 40 D7
Novi Kneževac, *Serbia, Yug.* 42 D5
Novi Lígure, *Italy* 28 D5
Novi Pazar, *Bulgaria* 41 C11
Novi Pazar, *Serbia, Yug.* 40 C4
Novi Sad, *Serbia, Yug.* 42 E4
Novi Slankamen, *Serbia, Yug.* 42 E5
Novi Travnik, *Bos.-H.* 42 F2
Novi Vinodolski, *Croatia* 29 C11
Novigrad, *Istra, Croatia* 29 C10
Novigrad, *Zadar, Croatia* 29 D12
Novigradsko More, *Croatia* 29 D12
Nôvo Hamburgo, *Brazil* 127 B5
Novo Mesto, *Slovenia* 29 C12
Novo Miloševo, *Serbia, Yug.* 42 E5
Novo Remanso, *Brazil* 125 E10
Novoaleksandrovsk, *Russia* 49 H5
Novoannenskiy, *Russia* 48 E6
Novoataysk, *Russia* 50 D9
Novoazovsk, *Ukraine* 47 J10
Novocheboksarsk, *Russia* 48 B8
Novocherkassk, *Russia* 49 G5
Novodevichye, *Russia* 48 D9
Novogrudok = Navahrudak, *Belarus* 46 F3
Novohrad-Volynskyy, *Ukraine* 47 G4
Novokachalinsk, *Russia* 54 B6
Novokazalinsk = Zhangaqazaly, *Kazakstan* 50 E7
Novokhopersk, *Russia* 48 E5
Novokuybyshevsk, *Russia* 48 D9
Novokuznetsk, *Russia* 50 D9
Novomirgorod, *Ukraine* 47 H6
Novomoskovsk, *Russia* 46 E10
Novomoskovsk, *Ukraine* 47 H8
Novopolotsk = Navapolatsk, *Belarus* 46 E5
Novorossiysk, *Russia* 47 K9
Novorybnoye, *Russia* 51 B11
Novorzhev, *Russia* 46 D5
Novosej, *Albania* 40 E4
Novoselytsya, *Ukraine* 47 H4
Novoshakhtinsk, *Russia* 47 J10
Novosibirsk, *Russia* 50 D9
Novosibirskiye Ostrova, *Russia* 51 B15
Novosil, *Russia* 47 F9
Novosokolniki, *Russia* 46 D6
Novotitarovskaya, *Russia* 49 H4
Novotroitsk, *Russia* 50 D6
Novoukrayinka, *Ukraine* 47 H6
Novouljanovsk, *Russia* 48 C9
Novouzensk, *Russia* 48 E9
Novovolynsk, *Ukraine* 47 G3
Novovoronezhskiy, *Russia* 47 G10
Novozybkov, *Russia* 47 F6
Novska, *Croatia* 29 C14
Novvy Urengoy, *Russia* 50 C8
Nový Bor, *Czech Rep.* 26 A7
Novy Bug = Novyy Buh, *Ukraine* 47 J7
Nový Bydžov, *Czech Rep.* 26 A8
Nový Dwór Mazowiecki, *Poland* 45 F7
Nový Jičín, *Czech Rep.* 27 B11
Novyy Afon, *Georgia* 49 J5
Novyy Buh, *Ukraine* 47 J7
Novyy Oskol, *Russia* 47 G9
Novyy Port, *Russia* 50 C8
Now Shahr, *Iran* 71 B6
Nowa Deba, *Poland* 45 H8
Nowa Ruda, *Poland* 45 H3
Nowa Sarzyna, *Poland* 45 H9
Nowa Sól, *Poland* 45 G2
Nowata, *U.S.A.* 113 G7
Nowbarān, *Iran* 71 C6
Nowe, *Poland* 44 E5
Nowe Miasteczko, *Poland* 45 G2
Nowe Miasto, *Poland* 45 G7
Nowe Miasto Lubawskie, *Poland* 44 E6
Nowe Skalmierzyce, *Poland* 45 G4
Nowe Warpno, *Poland* 44 E1
Nowghāb, *Iran* 71 C8
Nowgong, *Assam, India* 67 F18
Nowgong, *Mad. P., India* 69 G8
Nowogard, *Poland* 44 E2
Nowogród, *Poland* 45 E8
Nowogród Bobrzanski, *Poland* 45 G2
Nowogrodziec, *Poland* 45 G2
Nowra, *Australia* 95 E5
Nowshera, *Pakistan* 66 C8
Nowy Dwór Gdański, *Poland* 44 D6
Nowy Sącz, *Poland* 45 J7
Nowy Staw, *Poland* 44 D6
Nowy Targ, *Poland* 45 J7
Nowy Tomyśl, *Poland* 45 F3
Nowy Wiśnicz, *Poland* 45 J7
Noxen, *U.S.A.* 111 E8
Noxon, *U.S.A.* 114 C6
Noyabr'sk, *Russia* 50 C8
Noyant, *France* 18 E7
Noyers, *France* 19 E10
Noyon, *France* 19 C9
Noyon, *Mongolia* 56 C2
Nozay, *France* 18 E5
Nqutu, *S. Africa* 89 D5
Nsanje, *Malawi* 87 F4
Nsawam, *Ghana* 83 D4
Nsomba, *Zambia* 87 E2
Nsukka, *Nigeria* 83 D6
Ntui, *Cameroon* 83 E7
Nu Jiang →, *China* 58 E2
Nu Shan, *China* 58 E2
Nuba Mts. = Nubah, Jibalan, *Sudan* 81 E3
Nubah, Jibalan, *Sudan* 81 E3
Nubia, *Africa* 76 D7
Nubian Desert = Nûbîya, Es Sahrâ en, *Sudan* 80 C3
Nûbîya, Es Sahrâ en, *Sudan* 80 C3
Nubledo, *Spain* 34 B5
Nuboai, *Indonesia* 63 E9
Nubra →, *India* 69 B7
Nucet, *Romania* 42 D7
Nueces →, *U.S.A.* 113 M6
Nueltin L., *Canada* 105 A9
Nueva Asunción □, *Paraguay* 126 A3
Nueva Carteya, *Spain* 35 H6
Nueva Gerona, *Cuba* 120 B3
Nueva Palmira, *Uruguay* 126 C4
Nueva Rosita, *Mexico* 118 B4
Nueva San Salvador, *El Salv.* 120 D2
Nueva Tabarca, *Spain* 33 G4
Nuéve de Julio, *Argentina* 126 D3
Nuevitas, *Cuba* 120 B4
Nuevo, G., *Argentina* 128 E4
Nuevo Casas Grandes, *Mexico* 118 A3
Nuevo Guerrero, *Mexico* 119 B5
Nuevo Laredo, *Mexico* 119 B5
Nuevo León □, *Mexico* 118 C5
Nuevo Rocafuerte, *Ecuador* 124 D3
Nugget Pt., *N.Z.* 91 M2
Nugrus, Gebel, *Egypt* 80 C3
Nuhaka, *N.Z.* 91 H6
Nuits-St-Georges, *France* 19 E11
Nukey Bluff, *Australia* 95 E2
Nukheila, *Sudan* 80 D2
Nukhuyb, *Iraq* 70 C4
Nuku'alofa, *Tonga* 91 E12
Nukus, *Uzbekistan* 50 E6
Nules, *Spain* 32 F4
Nullagine, *Australia* 92 D3
Nullagine →, *Australia* 92 D3
Nullarbor, *Australia* 93 F5
Nullarbor Plain, *Australia* 93 F4
Numalla, L., *Australia* 95 D3
Numan, *Nigeria* 83 D7
Numata, *Japan* 55 F9
Numatinna →, *Sudan* 81 F2
Numazu, *Japan* 55 G9
Numbulwar, *Australia* 94 A2
Numfoor, *Indonesia* 63 E8
Numurkah, *Australia* 95 F4
Nunaksaluk I., *Canada* 103 A7
Nunap Isua, *Greenland* 101 C15
Nunavut □, *Canada* 101 B11
Nunda, *U.S.A.* 110 D7
Nungarin, *Australia* 93 F2
Nungo, *Mozam.* 87 E4
Nungwe, *Tanzania* 86 C3
Nunivak I., *U.S.A.* 100 B3
Nunkun, *India* 69 C7
Núoro, *Italy* 30 B2
Nūrābād, *Iran* 71 E8
Nure →, *Italy* 28 C6
Nuremberg = Nürnberg, *Germany* 25 F7
Nuri, *Mexico* 118 B3
Nuriootpa, *Australia* 95 E2
Nuristān □, *Afghan.* 66 B7
Nurlat, *Russia* 48 C10
Nurmes, *Finland* 8 E23
Nürnberg, *Germany* 25 F7
Nurpur, *Pakistan* 68 D4
Nurra, La, *Italy* 30 B1
Nurran, L. = Terewah, L., *Australia* 95 D4
Nurrari Lakes, *Australia* 93 E5
Nurri, *Italy* 30 C2
Nürtingen, *Germany* 25 G5
Nurzec →, *Poland* 45 F9
Nus, *Italy* 28 C4
Nusa Barung, *Indonesia* 63 H15
Nusa Kambangan, *Indonesia* 63 G13
Nusa Tenggara Barat □, *Indonesia* 62 F5
Nusa Tenggara Timur □, *Indonesia* 63 F6
Nusaybin, *Turkey* 73 D9
Nushki, *Pakistan* 68 E2
Nuuk, *Greenland* 101 B14
Nuwakot, *Nepal* 69 E10
Nuweiba', *Egypt* 70 D2
Nuwerus, *S. Africa* 88 E2
Nuweveldberge, *S. Africa* 88 E3
Nuyts, C., *Australia* 93 F5
Nuyts, Pt., *Australia* 93 G2
Nuyts Arch., *Australia* 95 E1
Nxau-Nxau, *Botswana* 88 B3
Nyaake, *Liberia* 82 E3
Nyabing, *Australia* 93 F2
Nyack, *U.S.A.* 111 E11
Nyagan, *Russia* 50 C7
Nyahanga, *Tanzania* 86 C3
Nyahua, *Tanzania* 86 D3
Nyahururu, *Kenya* 86 B4
Nyainqentanglha Shan, *China* 60 C4
Nyakanazi, *Tanzania* 86 C3
Nyakrom, *Ghana* 83 D4
Nyâlâ, *Sudan* 81 E1
Nyamandhlovu, *Zimbabwe* 87 F2
Nyambiti, *Tanzania* 86 C3
Nyamlell, *Sudan* 81 F2
Nyamwaga, *Tanzania* 86 C3
Nyandekwa, *Tanzania* 86 C3
Nyanding →, *Sudan* 81 F3
Nyandoma, *Russia* 46 B11
Nyangana, *Namibia* 88 B3
Nyanguge, *Tanzania* 86 C3
Nyankpala, *Ghana* 83 D4
Nyanza, *Rwanda* 86 C2
Nyanza □, *Kenya* 86 C3
Nyanza-Lac, *Burundi* 86 C2
Nyaponges, *Sudan* 81 F3
Nyasa, L., *Africa* 87 E3
Nyasvizh, *Belarus* 47 F4
Nyazura, *Zimbabwe* 87 F3
Nyazwidzi →, *Zimbabwe* 87 G3
Nyborg, *Denmark* 11 J4
Nybro, *Sweden* 11 H9
Nyda, *Russia* 50 C8
Nyeri, *Kenya* 86 C4
Nyerol, *Sudan* 81 F3
Nyhammar, *Sweden* 10 D8
Nyinahin, *Ghana* 82 D4
Nyíradony, *Hungary* 42 C6
Nyírbátor, *Hungary* 42 C7
Nyíregyháza, *Hungary* 42 C6
Nykøbing, *Storstrøm, Denmark* 11 K5
Nykøbing, *Vestsjælland, Denmark* 11 J5
Nykøbing, *Viborg, Denmark* 11 H2
Nyköping, *Sweden* 11 F11
Nykroppa, *Sweden* 10 E8
Nykvarn, *Sweden* 10 E11
Nyland, *Sweden* 10 A11
Nylstroom, *S. Africa* 89 C4
Nymagee, *Australia* 95 E4
Nymburk, *Czech Rep.* 26 A8
Nynäshamn, *Sweden* 11 F11
Nyngan, *Australia* 95 E4
Nyoma Rap, *India* 69 C8
Nyoman = Neman →, *Lithuania* 9 J19
Nyon, *Switz.* 25 J2
Nyong →, *Cameroon* 83 E6
Nyons, *France* 21 D9
Nyou, *Burkina Faso* 83 C4
Nýrsko, *Czech Rep.* 26 B6
Nysa, *Poland* 45 H4
Nysa →, *Europe* 24 C10
Nysa Kłodzka →, *Poland* 45 H4
Nysäter, *Sweden* 10 E6
Nyssa, *U.S.A.* 114 E5
Nysted, *Denmark* 11 K5
Nyunzu, *Dem. Rep. of the Congo* 86 D2
Nyurba, *Russia* 51 C12
Nyzhnohirskyy, *Ukraine* 47 K8
Nzébéla, *Guinea* 82 D3
Nzega, *Tanzania* 86 C3
Nzérékoré, *Guinea* 82 D3
Nzeto, *Angola* 84 F2
Nzilo, Chutes de, *Dem. Rep. of the Congo* 87 E2
Nzo →, *Ivory C.* 82 D3
Nzubuka, *Tanzania* 86 C3

O

O Barco, *Spain* 34 C4
O Carballiño, *Spain* 34 C2
O Corgo, *Spain* 34 C3
O Pino, *Spain* 34 C2
O Porriño, *Spain* 34 C2
Ō-Shima, *Japan* 55 G9
Oa, Mull of, *U.K.* 14 F2
Oacoma, *U.S.A.* 112 D5
Oahe, L., *U.S.A.* 112 C4
Oahe Dam, *U.S.A.* 112 C4
Oahu, *U.S.A.* 106 H16
Oak Harbor, *U.S.A.* 116 B4
Oak Hill, *U.S.A.* 108 G5
Oak Ridge, *U.S.A.* 109 G3
Oak View, *U.S.A.* 117 L7
Oakan-Dake, *Japan* 54 C12
Oakdale, *Calif., U.S.A.* 116 H6
Oakdale, *La., U.S.A.* 113 K8
Oakes, *U.S.A.* 112 B5
Oakesdale, *U.S.A.* 114 C5
Oakey, *Australia* 95 D5
Oakfield, *U.S.A.* 110 C6
Oakham, *U.K.* 13 E7
Oakhurst, *U.S.A.* 116 H7
Oakland, *U.S.A.* 116 H4
Oakley, *Idaho, U.S.A.* 114 E7
Oakley, *Kans., U.S.A.* 112 F4
Oakover →, *Australia* 92 D3
Oakridge, *U.S.A.* 114 E2
Oakville, *Canada* 110 C5
Oakville, *U.S.A.* 116 D3
Oamaru, *N.Z.* 91 L3
Oancea, *Romania* 43 E12
Oasis, *Calif., U.S.A.* 117 M10
Oasis, *Nev., U.S.A.* 116 H9
Oates Land, *Antarctica* 5 C11
Oatlands, *Australia* 94 G4
Oatman, *U.S.A.* 117 K12
Oaxaca, *Mexico* 119 D5
Oaxaca □, *Mexico* 119 D5
Ob →, *Russia* 50 C7
Oba, *Canada* 102 C3
Obala, *Cameroon* 83 E7
Obama, *Japan* 55 G7
Oban, *Nigeria* 83 D6
Oban, *U.K.* 14 E3
Obbia, *Somali Rep.* 74 F4
Obera, *Argentina* 127 B4
Oberammergau, *Germany* 25 H7
Oberasbach, *Germany* 25 F6
Oberbayern □, *Germany* 25 G7
Oberdrauburg, *Austria* 26 E5
Oberfranken □, *Germany* 25 E7
Oberhausen, *Germany* 24 D2
Oberkirch, *Germany* 25 G4
Oberlausitz, *Germany* 24 D10
Oberlin, *Kans., U.S.A.* 112 F4
Oberlin, *La., U.S.A.* 113 K8
Oberlin, *Ohio, U.S.A.* 110 E2
Obernai, *France* 19 D14
Oberndorf, *Germany* 25 G4
Oberon, *Australia* 95 E4
Oberösterreich □, *Austria* 26 C7
Oberpfalz □, *Germany* 25 F8
Oberpfälzer Wald, *Germany* 25 F8
Oberstdorf, *Germany* 25 H6
Oberursel, *Germany* 25 E4
Oberwart, *Austria* 27 D9
Obi, Kepulauan, *Indonesia* 63 E7
Obi Is. = Obi, Kepulauan, *Indonesia* 63 E7
Obiaruku, *Nigeria* 83 D6
Óbidos, *Brazil* 125 D7
Óbidos, *Portugal* 35 F1
Obihiro, *Japan* 54 C11
Obilatu, *Indonesia* 63 E7
Obilnoye, *Russia* 49 G7
Obing, *Germany* 25 G8
Objat, *France* 20 C5
Obluchye, *Russia* 51 E14
Obninsk, *Russia* 46 E9
Obo, *C.A.R.* 86 A2
Oboa, Mt., *Uganda* 86 B3
Obock, *Djibouti* 81 E5
Oborniki, *Poland* 45 F3
Oborniki Śląskie, *Poland* 45 G3
Oboyan, *Russia* 47 G9
Obozerskaya = Obozerskiy, *Russia* 50 C5
Obozerskiy, *Russia* 50 C5
Obrenovac, *Serbia, Yug.* 40 B4
Obrovac, *Croatia* 29 D12
Obruk, *Turkey* 72 C5
Obrzycko, *Poland* 45 F3
Observatory Inlet, *Canada* 104 B3
Obshchi Syrt, *Russia* 6 E16
Obskaya Guba, *Russia* 50 C8
Obuasi, *Ghana* 83 D4
Obubra, *Nigeria* 83 D6
Obudu, *Nigeria* 83 D6
Obwalden □, *Switz.* 25 J4
Obzor, *Bulgaria* 41 D11
Ocala, *U.S.A.* 109 L4
Ocampo, *Chihuahua, Mexico* 118 B3

Ocampo, *Tamaulipas, Mexico* 119 C5
Ocaña, *Spain* 34 F7
Ocanomowoc, *U.S.A.* 112 D10
Occidental, Cordillera, *Colombia* 122 C3
Ocean City, *Md., U.S.A.* 108 F8
Ocean City, *N.J., U.S.A.* 108 F8
Ocean City, *Wash., U.S.A.* 116 C2
Ocean Falls, *Canada* 104 C3
Ocean I. = Banaba, *Kiribati* 96 H8
Ocean Park, *U.S.A.* 116 D2
Oceano, *U.S.A.* 117 K6
Oceanport, *U.S.A.* 111 F10
Oceanside, *U.S.A.* 117 M9
Ochagavía, *Spain* 32 C3
Ochakiv, *Ukraine* 47 J6
Ochamchira, *Georgia* 49 J5
Ochil Hills, *U.K.* 14 E5
Ochsenfurt, *Germany* 25 F6
Ochsenhausen, *Germany* 25 G5
Ocilla, *U.S.A.* 109 K4
Ockelbo, *Sweden* 10 D10
Ocmulgee →, *U.S.A.* 109 K4
Ocna Mureş, *Romania* 43 D8
Ocna Sibiului, *Romania* 43 E9
Ocnele Mari, *Romania* 43 E9
Ocniţa, *Moldova* 43 B12
Oconee →, *U.S.A.* 109 K4
Oconto, *U.S.A.* 108 C2
Oconto Falls, *U.S.A.* 108 C1
Ocosingo, *Mexico* 119 D6
Ocotal, *Nic.* 120 D2
Ocotlán, *Mexico* 118 C4
Ocotlán de Morelos, *Mexico* 119 D5
Ocreza →, *Portugal* 35 F3
Ócsa, *Hungary* 42 C4
Octeville, *France* 18 C5
Oda, *Ghana* 83 D4
Ōda, *Japan* 55 G6
Oda, J., *Sudan* 80 C4
Ódáðahraun, *Iceland* 8 D5
Ödåkra, *Sweden* 11 H6
Odate, *Japan* 54 D10
Odawara, *Japan* 55 G9
Odda, *Norway* 9 F12
Odder, *Denmark* 11 J4
Odei →, *Canada* 105 B9
Odemira, *Portugal* 35 H2
Ödemiş, *Turkey* 39 C9
Odendaalsrus, *S. Africa* 88 D4
Odensbacken, *Sweden* 10 E9
Odense, *Denmark* 11 J4
Odenwald, *Germany* 25 F5
Oder →, *Europe* 24 B10
Oder-Havel Kanal, *Germany* 24 C10
Oderzo, *Italy* 29 C9
Odesa, *Ukraine* 47 J6
Ödeshög, *Sweden* 11 F8
Odessa = Odesa, *Ukraine* 47 J6
Odessa, *Canada* 111 B8
Odessa, *Tex., U.S.A.* 113 K3
Odessa, *Wash., U.S.A.* 114 C4
Odiakwe, *Botswana* 88 C4
Odiel →, *Spain* 35 H4
Odienné, *Ivory C.* 82 D3
Odintsovo, *Russia* 46 E9
Odiongan, *Phil.* 61 E4
Odobeşti, *Romania* 43 E12
Odolanów, *Poland* 45 G4
O'Donnell, *U.S.A.* 113 J4
Odorheiu Secuiesc, *Romania* 43 D10
Odoyevo, *Russia* 46 F9
Odra = Oder →, *Europe* 24 B10
Odra →, *Spain* 34 C6
Odžaci, *Serbia, Yug.* 42 E4
Odžak, *Bos.-H.* 42 E3
Odzi, *Zimbabwe* 89 B5
Odzi →, *Zimbabwe* 89 B5
Oebisfelde, *Germany* 24 C6
Oeiras, *Brazil* 125 E10
Oeiras, *Portugal* 35 G1
Oelrichs, *U.S.A.* 112 D3
Oelsnitz, *Germany* 25 E8
Oelwein, *U.S.A.* 112 D9
Oenpelli, *Australia* 92 B5
Oetz, *Austria* 26 D3
Of, *Turkey* 73 B9
Ofanto →, *Italy* 31 A9
Offa, *Nigeria* 83 D5
Offaly □, *Ireland* 15 C4
Offenbach, *Germany* 25 E4
Offenburg, *Germany* 25 G3
Offida, *Italy* 29 F10
Ofidhousa, *Greece* 39 E8
Ofotfjorden, *Norway* 8 B17
Ōfunato, *Japan* 54 E10
Oga, *Japan* 54 E9
Oga-Hantō, *Japan* 54 E9
Ogaden, *Ethiopia* 74 F3
Ōgaki, *Japan* 55 G8
Ogallala, *U.S.A.* 112 E4
Ogasawara Gunto, *Pac. Oc.* 52 G18
Ogbomosho, *Nigeria* 83 D5
Ogden, *U.S.A.* 114 F7
Ogdensburg, *U.S.A.* 111 B9
Ogeechee →, *U.S.A.* 109 K5
Ogilby, *U.S.A.* 117 N12
Oglio →, *Italy* 28 C7
Ogmore, *Australia* 94 C4
Ognon →, *France* 19 E12
Ogoja, *Nigeria* 83 D6
Ogoki, *Canada* 102 B2
Ogoki →, *Canada* 102 B2
Ogoki L., *Canada* 102 B2
Ogoki Res., *Canada* 102 B2
Ogooué →, *Gabon* 84 E1
Ogosta →, *Bulgaria* 40 C7
Ogowe = Ogooué →, *Gabon* 84 E1
Ogr = Sharafa, *Sudan* 81 E2
Ogražden, *Macedonia* 40 E6
Ogre, *Latvia* 9 H21
Ogrein, *Sudan* 80 D3
Ogulin, *Croatia* 29 C12
Ogun □, *Nigeria* 83 D5
Ogurchinskiy, Ostrov, *Turkmenistan* 71 B7
Oguta, *Nigeria* 83 D6
Ogwashi-Uku, *Nigeria* 83 D6
Ogwe, *Nigeria* 83 E6
Ohai, *N.Z.* 91 L2
Ohakune, *N.Z.* 91 H5
Ohata, *Japan* 54 D10
Ohau, L., *N.Z.* 91 L2
Ohio □, *U.S.A.* 110 F2
Ohio →, *U.S.A.* 108 G1
Ohře →, *Czech Rep.* 26 A7
Ohre →, *Germany* 24 C7
Ohrid, *Macedonia* 40 E4
Ohridsko Jezero, *Macedonia* 40 E4
Ohrigstad, *S. Africa* 89 C5
Öhringen, *Germany* 25 F5
Oi Qu, *China* 58 C2
Oiapoque, *Brazil* 125
Oikou, *China* 57 E9
Oil City, *U.S.A.* 110 E5
Oil Springs, *Canada* 110 D2
Oildale, *U.S.A.* 117 K7
Oinousa, *Greece* 39 C8
Oise □, *France* 19 C9
Oise →, *France* 19 C9
Ōita, *Japan* 55 H5
Ōita □, *Japan* 55 H5
Oiticica, *Brazil* 125 E10
Ojacaliente, *Mexico* 118 C4
Ojai, *U.S.A.* 117 L7
Ojinaga, *Mexico* 118 B4
Ojiya, *Japan* 55 F9
Ojos del Salado, Cerro, *Argentina* 126 B2
Oka →, *Russia* 48 B7
Okaba, *Indonesia* 63 F9
Okahandja, *Namibia* 88 C2
Okanagan L., *Canada* 104 D5
Okanogan, *U.S.A.* 114 B4
Okanogan →, *U.S.A.* 114 B4
Okány, *Hungary* 42 D6
Okaputa, *Namibia* 88 C2
Okara, *Pakistan* 68 D5
Okaukuejo, *Namibia* 88 B2
Okavango Swamps, *Botswana* 88 B3
Okaya, *Japan* 55 F9
Okayama, *Japan* 55 G6
Okayama □, *Japan* 55 G6
Okazaki, *Japan* 55 G8
Oke-Iho, *Nigeria* 83 D5
Okeechobee, *U.S.A.* 109 M5
Okeechobee, L., *U.S.A.* 109 M5
Okefenokee Swamp, *U.S.A.* 109 K4
Okehampton, *U.K.* 13 G4
Okene, *Nigeria* 83 D6
Oker →, *Germany* 24 C6
Okha, *India* 68 H3
Okha, *Russia* 51 D15
Ókhi Óros, *Greece* 38 C6
Okhotsk, *Russia* 51 D15
Okhotsk, Sea of, *Asia* 51 D15
Okhotskiy Perevoz, *Russia* 51 C14
Okhtyrka, *Ukraine* 47 G8
Oki-Shotō, *Japan* 55 F6
Okiep, *S. Africa* 88 D2
Okigwi, *Nigeria* 83 D6
Okija, *Nigeria* 83 D6
Okinawa □, *Japan* 55 L4
Okinawa-Guntō, *Japan* 55 L4
Okinawa-Jima, *Japan* 55 L4
Okino-erabu-Shima, *Japan* 55 L4
Okitipupa, *Nigeria* 83 D5
Oklahoma □, *U.S.A.* 113 H6
Oklahoma City, *U.S.A.* 113 H6
Okmulgee, *U.S.A.* 113 H7
Oknitsa = Ocniţa, *Moldova* 43 B12
Oko, W. →, *Sudan* 80 C4
Okolo, *Uganda* 86 B3
Okolona, *U.S.A.* 113 J10
Okombahe, *Namibia* 88 C2
Okonek, *Poland* 44 E3
Okotoks, *Canada* 104 C6
Okrika, *Nigeria* 83 E6
Oksibil, *Indonesia* 63 E10
Oktabrsk = Oktyabrsk, *Kazakstan* 50 E6
Oktyabrsk, *Kazakstan* 50 E6
Oktyabrsk, *Russia* 48 D9
Oktyabrskiy = Aktsyabrski, *Belarus* 47 F5
Oktyabrskiy, *Russia* 49 G5
Oktyabrskoy Revolyutsii, Ostrov, *Russia* 51 B10
Oktyabrskoye = Zhovtneve, *Ukraine* 47 J7
Okulovka, *Russia* 46 C7
Okuru, *N.Z.* 91 K2
Okushiri-Tō, *Japan* 54 C9
Okuta, *Nigeria* 83 D5
Okwa →, *Botswana* 88 C3
Ola, *U.S.A.* 113 H8
Ólafsfjörður, *Iceland* 8 C4
Ólafsvík, *Iceland* 8 D2
Olaine, *Latvia* 44 B10
Olancha, *U.S.A.* 117 J8
Olancha Pk., *U.S.A.* 117 J8
Olanchito, *Honduras* 120 C2
Öland, *Sweden* 11 H10
Ölands norra udde, *Sweden* 11 G11
Ölands södra udde, *Sweden* 11 H10
Olargues, *France* 20 E6
Olary, *Australia* 95 E3
Olascoaga, *Argentina* 126 D3
Olathe, *U.S.A.* 112 F7
Olavarría, *Argentina* 126 D3
Oława, *Poland* 45 H4
Olbernhau, *Germany* 24 E9
Ólbia, *Italy* 30 B2
Ólbia, G. di, *Italy* 30 B2
Olching, *Germany* 25 G7
Olcott, *U.S.A.* 110 C6
Old Bahama Chan. = Bahama, Canal Viejo de, *W. Indies* 120 B4
Old Baldy Pk. = San Antonio, Mt., *U.S.A.* 117 L9
Old Castile = Castilla y Leon □, *Spain* 34 D6
Old Crow, *Canada* 100 B6
Old Dale, *U.S.A.* 117 L11
Old Dongola, *Sudan* 80 D3
Old Forge, *N.Y., U.S.A.* 111 C10
Old Forge, *Pa., U.S.A.* 111 E9
Old Perlican, *Canada* 103 C9
Old Shinyanga, *Tanzania* 86 C3
Old Speck Mt., *U.S.A.* 111 B14
Old Town, *U.S.A.* 109 C11
Old Washington, *U.S.A.* 110 F3
Old Wives L., *Canada* 105 C7
Oldbury, *U.K.* 13 F5
Oldcastle, *Ireland* 15 C4
Oldeani, *Tanzania* 86 C4
Oldenburg, *Niedersachsen, Germany* 24 B4
Oldenburg, *Schleswig-Holstein, Germany* 24 A6
Oldenzaal, *Neths.* 17 B6
Oldham, *U.K.* 12 D5
Oldman →, *Canada* 104 D6
Oldmeldrum, *U.K.* 14 D6
Olds, *Canada* 104 C6
Oldziyt, *Mongolia* 56 B5
Olean, *U.S.A.* 110 D6
Olecko, *Poland* 44 D9
Oléggio, *Italy* 28 C5
Oleiros, *Portugal* 34 F3
Oleiros, *Spain* 34 B2
Olekma →, *Russia* 51 C13
Olekminsk, *Russia* 51 C13
Oleksandriya, *Kirovohrad, Ukraine* 47 H7
Oleksandriya, *Rivne, Ukraine* 47 G4
Oleksandrovka, *Ukraine* 47 H7
Olema, *U.S.A.* 116 G4
Olenek, *Russia* 51 C12
Olenek →, *Russia* 51 B13
Olenino, *Russia* 46 D7
Oléron, Î. d', *France* 20 C2
Oleśnica, *Poland* 45 G4
Olesno, *Poland* 45 H5
Olevsk, *Ukraine* 47 G4
Olga, *Russia* 51 E14
Olga, L., *Canada* 102 C4
Olga, Mt., *Australia* 93 E5
Ølgod, *Denmark* 11 J2
Olhão, *Portugal* 35 H3
Olib, *Croatia* 29 D11
Oliena, *Italy* 30 B2
Oliete, *Spain* 32 D4
Olifants →, *Africa* 89 C5
Olifants →, *Namibia* 88 C2
Olifantshoek, *S. Africa* 88 D3
Ólimbos, *Greece* 39 F9
Ólimbos, Óros, *Greece* 40 F6
Olímpia, *Brazil* 127 A6
Olinda, *Brazil* 125 E12
Olite, *Spain* 32 C3
Oliva, *Argentina* 126 C3
Oliva, *Spain* 33 G4
Oliva, Punta del, *Spain* 34 B5
Oliva de la Frontera, *Spain* 35 G4
Olivares, *Spain* 32 F2
Olivehurst, *U.S.A.* 116 F5
Oliveira de Azeméis, *Portugal* 34 E2
Oliveira do Douro, *Portugal* 34 D2
Olivenza, *Spain* 35 G3
Oliver, *Canada* 104 D5
Oliver L., *Canada* 105 B8
Olivet, *France* 19 E8
Olkhovka, *Russia* 48 F7
Olkusz, *Poland* 45 H6
Ollagüe, *Chile* 126 A2
Olmedo, *Spain* 34 D6
Olmeto, *France* 21 G12
Olney, *Ill., U.S.A.* 108 F1
Olney, *Tex., U.S.A.* 113 J5
Olofström, *Sweden* 11 H8
Oloma, *Cameroon* 83 E7
Olomane →, *Canada* 103 B7
Olomouc, *Czech Rep.* 27 B10
Olomoucký □, *Czech Rep.* 27 B10
Olonets, *Russia* 46 B7
Olongapo, *Phil.* 61 D4
Olonne-sur-Mer, *France* 20 B2
Oloron, Gave d' →, *France* 20 E2
Oloron-Ste-Marie, *France* 20 E3
Olot, *Spain* 32 C7
Olovo, *Bos.-H.* 42 F3
Olovyannaya, *Russia* 51 D12
Oloy →, *Russia* 51 C16
Olsberg, *Germany* 24 D4
Olshammar, *Sweden* 11 F8
Olshanka, *Ukraine* 47 H6
Olshany, *Ukraine* 47 G8
Olsztyn, *Poland* 44 E7
Olsztynek, *Poland* 44 E7
Olt □, *Romania* 43 F9
Olt →, *Romania* 43 G9
Olten, *Switz.* 25 H3
Olteniţa, *Romania* 43 F11
Olton, *U.S.A.* 113 H3
Oltu, *Turkey* 73 B9
Oluanpi, *Taiwan* 59 G13
Olula del Rio, *Spain* 33 H2
Olur, *Turkey* 73 B10
Olutanga, *Phil.* 61 H5
Olvega, *Spain* 32 D2
Olvera, *Spain* 35 J5
Olymbos, *Cyprus* 36 D12
Olympia, *Greece* 38 D3
Olympia, *U.S.A.* 116 D4
Olympic Dam, *Australia* 95 E2
Olympic Mts., *U.S.A.* 116 C3
Olympic Nat. Park, *U.S.A.* 116 C3
Olympus, *Cyprus* 36 E11
Olympus, Mt. = Ólimbos, Óros, *Greece* 40 F6
Olympus, Mt. = Uludağ, *Turkey* 41 F13
Olympus, Mt., *U.S.A.* 116 C3
Olyphant, *U.S.A.* 111 E9
Om →, *Russia* 50 D8
Om Hajer, *Eritrea* 81 E4
Om Koi, *Thailand* 64 D2
Ōma, *Japan* 54 D10
Ōmachi, *Japan* 55 F8
Omae-Zaki, *Japan* 55 G9
Ōmagari, *Japan* 54 E10
Omagh, *U.K.* 15 B4
Omagh □, *U.K.* 15 B4
Omaha, *U.S.A.* 112 E7
Omak, *U.S.A.* 114 B4
Omalos, *Greece* 36 D5
Oman ■, *Asia* 74 C6
Oman, G. of, *Asia* 71 E8
Omaruru, *Namibia* 88 C2
Omaruru →, *Namibia* 88 C1
Omate, *Peru* 124 G4
Ombai, Selat, *Indonesia* 63 F6
Omboué, *Gabon* 84 E1
Ombrone →, *Italy* 28 F8
Omdurmân, *Sudan* 81 D3
Omegna, *Italy* 28 C5
Omemee, *Canada* 110 B6
Omeonga, *Dem. Rep. of the Congo* 86 C1
Ometepe, I. de, *Nic.* 120 D2
Ometepec, *Mexico* 119 D5
Ominato, *Japan* 54 D10
Omineca →, *Canada* 104 B4
Omiš, *Croatia* 29 E13
Omišalj, *Croatia* 29 C11
Omitara, *Namibia* 88 C2
Ōmiya, *Japan* 55 G9
Omme Å →, *Denmark* 11 J2
Ommen, *Neths.* 17 B6
Ömnögovĭ □, *Mongolia* 56 C3
Omo →, *Ethiopia* 81 F4
Omodeo, L., *Italy* 30 B1
Omodhos, *Cyprus* 36 E11
Omoko, *Nigeria* 83 D6
Omolon →, *Russia* 51 C16
Omono-Gawa →, *Japan* 54 E10
Omsk, *Russia* 50 D8
Omsukchan, *Russia* 51 C16
Ōmu, *Japan* 54 B11
Omul, Vf., *Romania* 43 E10
Omulew →, *Poland* 45 E8
Ōmura, *Japan* 55 H4
Omuramba Omatako →, *Namibia* 88 B2
Omuramba Ovambo →, *Namibia* 88 B2
Omurtag, *Bulgaria* 41 C10
Ōmuta, *Japan* 55 H5
Oña, *Spain* 34 C7
Onaga, *U.S.A.* 112 F6
Onalaska, *U.S.A.* 112 D9
Onancock, *U.S.A.* 108 G8
Onang, *Indonesia* 63 E5
Onaping L., *Canada* 102 C3
Oñati, *Spain* 32 B2
Onavas, *Mexico* 118 B3
Onawa, *U.S.A.* 112 D6
Oncócua, *Angola* 88 B1
Onda, *Spain* 32 F4
Ondaejin, *N. Korea* 57 D15
Ondangwa, *Namibia* 88 B2
Ondarroa, *Spain* 32 B2
Ondava →, *Slovak Rep.* 27 C14
Ondjiva, *Angola* 88 B2
Ondo, *Nigeria* 83 D5
Ondo □, *Nigeria* 83 D6
Öndörshil, *Mongolia* 56 B5
Öndverðarnes, *Iceland* 8 D1
One Tree, *Australia* 95 E3
Onega, *Russia* 50 C4
Onega →, *Russia* 6 C13
Onega, L. = Onezhskoye Ozero, *Russia* 46 B8
Oneida, *U.S.A.* 111 C9
Oneida L., *U.S.A.* 111 C9
O'Neill, *U.S.A.* 112 D5
Onekotan, Ostrov, *Russia* 51 E16
Onema, *Dem. Rep. of the Congo* 86 C1
Oneonta, *U.S.A.* 111 D9
Oneşti, *Romania* 43 D11
Onezhskoye Ozero, *Russia* 46 B8
Ongarue, *N.Z.* 91 H5
Ongers →, *S. Africa* 88 E3
Ongerup, *Australia* 93 F2
Ongjin, *N. Korea* 57 F13
Ongkharak, *Thailand* 64 E3
Ongniud Qi, *China* 57 C10
Ongoka, *Dem. Rep. of the Congo* 86 C2
Ongole, *India* 66 M12
Ongon = Havirga, *Mongolia* 56 B7
Oni, *Georgia* 49 J6
Onida, *U.S.A.* 112 C4
Onilahy →, *Madag.* 89 C7
Onitsha, *Nigeria* 83 D6
Onoda, *Japan* 55 G5
Onpyŏng-ni, *S. Korea* 57 H14
Ons, I. de, *Spain* 34 C2
Onslow, *Australia* 92 D2
Onslow B., *U.S.A.* 109 H7
Ontake-San, *Japan* 55 G8
Ontario, *Calif., U.S.A.* 117 L9
Ontario, *Oreg., U.S.A.* 114 D5
Ontario □, *Canada* 102 B2
Ontario, L., *N. Amer.* 110 C7
Ontinyent, *Spain* 33 G4
Ontonagon, *U.S.A.* 112 B10
Ontur, *Spain* 33 G3
Onyx, *U.S.A.* 117 K8
Oodnadatta, *Australia* 95 D2
Ooldea, *Australia* 93 F5
Oombulgurri, *Australia* 92 C4
Oorindi, *Australia* 94 C3
Oost-Vlaanderen □, *Belgium* 17 C3
Oostende, *Belgium* 17 C2
Oosterhout, *Neths.* 17 C4
Oosterschelde →, *Neths.* 17 C4
Oosterwolde, *Neths.* 17 B6
Ootacamund = Udagamandalam, *India* 66 P10
Ootsa L., *Canada* 104 C3
Opaka, *Bulgaria* 41 C10
Opala, *Dem. Rep. of the Congo* 86 C1
Opalenica, *Poland* 45 F3
Opan, *Bulgaria* 41 D9
Opanake, *Sri Lanka* 66 R12
Opasatika, *Canada* 102 C3
Opasquia Prov. Park, *Canada* 102 B1
Opatija, *Croatia* 29 C11
Opatów, *Poland* 45 H8
Opava, *Czech Rep.* 27 B10
Opelika, *U.S.A.* 109 J3
Opelousas, *U.S.A.* 113 K8
Opémisca, L., *Canada* 102 C5
Opheim, *U.S.A.* 114 B10
Ophthalmia Ra., *Australia* 92 D2
Opi, *Nigeria* 83 D6
Opinaca →, *Canada* 102 B4
Opinaca, Rés., *Canada* 102 B4
Opinnagau →, *Canada* 102 B3
Opiscoteo, L., *Canada* 103 B6
Opobo, *Nigeria* 83 E6
Opochka, *Russia* 46 D5
Opoczno, *Poland* 45 G7
Opol, *Phil.* 61 G6
Opole, *Poland* 45 H4
Opole Lubelskie, *Poland* 45 G8
Opolskie □, *Poland* 45 H5
Oponono L., *Namibia* 88 B2
Oporto = Porto, *Portugal* 34 D2
Opotiki, *N.Z.* 91 H6
Opp, *U.S.A.* 109 K2
Oppdal, *Norway* 9 E13
Óppido Mamertina, *Italy* 31 D8
Opportunity, *U.S.A.* 114 C5
Oprişor, *Romania* 42 F8
Oprtalj, *Croatia* 29 C10
Opua, *N.Z.* 91 F5
Opunake, *N.Z.* 91 H4
Opuwo, *Namibia* 88 B1
Opuzen, *Croatia* 29 E14
Ora, *Cyprus* 36 E12
Oracle, *U.S.A.* 115 K8
Oradea, *Romania* 42 C6
Öræfajökull, *Iceland* 8 D5
Orahovac, *Kosovo, Yug.* 40 D4
Orahovica, *Croatia* 42 E2
Orai, *India* 69 G8
Oraison, *France* 21 E9
Oral = Zhayyq →, *Kazakstan* 50 E6
Oral, *Kazakstan* 48 E10
Oran, *Algeria* 78 A5
Orange, *Australia* 95 E4
Orange, *France* 21 D8
Orange, *Calif., U.S.A.* 117 M9
Orange, *Mass., U.S.A.* 111 D12
Orange, *Tex., U.S.A.* 113 K8
Orange, *Va., U.S.A.* 108 F6
Orange →, *S. Africa* 88 D2
Orange, C., *Brazil* 122 C5
Orange Cove, *U.S.A.* 116 J7
Orange Free State = Free State □, *S. Africa* 88 D4
Orange Grove, *U.S.A.* 113 M6
Orange Walk, *Belize* 119 D7
Orangeburg, *U.S.A.* 109 J5
Orangeville, *Canada* 102 D3
Orango, *Guinea-Biss.* 82 C1
Orani, *Phil.* 61 D4
Oranienburg, *Germany* 24 C9
Oranje = Orange →, *S. Africa* 88 D2
Oranje Vrystaat = Free State □, *S. Africa* 88 D4
Oranjemund, *Namibia* 88 D2
Oranjerivier, *S. Africa* 88 D3
Orapa, *Botswana* 85 J5
Orarak, *Sudan* 81 F3
Oras, *Phil.* 61 E6
Orašje, *Bos.-H.* 42 E3
Orăştie, *Romania* 43 E8
Oraşul Stalin = Braşov, *Romania* 43 E10
Orava →, *Slovak Rep.* 27 B12

Orava, Vodna nádriž, *Slovak Rep.* 27 B12
Oravița, *Romania* 42 E6
Orb →, *France* 20 E7
Orba →, *Italy* 28 D5
Ørbæk, *Denmark* 11 J4
Orbe, *Switz.* 25 J2
Orbec, *France* 18 C7
Orbetello, *Italy* 29 F8
Órbigo →, *Spain* 34 C5
Orbisonia, *U.S.A.* 110 F7
Orbost, *Australia* 95 F4
Örbyhus, *Sweden* 10 D11
Orcas I., *U.S.A.* 116 B4
Orce, *Spain* 33 H2
Orce →, *Spain* 33 H2
Orchard City, *U.S.A.* 115 G10
Orchies, *France* 19 B10
Orchila, I., *Venezuela* 121 D6
Órcia →, *Italy* 29 F8
Orco →, *Italy* 28 C4
Orcutt, *U.S.A.* 117 L6
Ord, *U.S.A.* 112 E5
Ord →, *Australia* 92 C4
Ord, Mt., *Australia* 92 C4
Ordenes = Ordes, *Spain* 34 B2
Orderville, *U.S.A.* 115 H7
Ordes, *Spain* 34 B2
Ording = St-Peter-Ording, *Germany* 24 A4
Ordos = Mu Us Shamo, *China* 56 E5
Ordu, *Turkey* 72 B7
Ordubad, *Azerbaijan* 73 C12
Orduña, *Álava, Spain* 32 C2
Orduña, *Granada, Spain* 35 H7
Ordway, *U.S.A.* 112 F3
Ordzhonikidze = Vladikavkaz, *Russia* 49 J7
Ordzhonikidze, *Ukraine* 47 J8
Ore, *Dem. Rep. of the Congo* 86 B2
Ore Mts. = Erzgebirge, *Germany* 24 E8
Orebić, *Croatia* 29 F14
Örebro, *Sweden* 10 E9
Örebro län □, *Sweden* 10 E8
Oregon, *U.S.A.* 112 D10
Oregon □, *U.S.A.* 114 E3
Oregon City, *U.S.A.* 116 E4
Öregrund, *Sweden* 10 D12
Öregrundsgrepen, *Sweden* 10 D12
Orekhov = Orikhiv, *Ukraine* 47 J8
Orekhovo-Zuyevo, *Russia* 46 E10
Orel, *Russia* 47 F9
Orel →, *Ukraine* 47 H8
Orellana, *Spain* 35 F5
Orellana, Canal de, *Spain* 35 F5
Orellana, Embalse de, *Spain* 35 F5
Orem, *U.S.A.* 114 F8
Ören, *Turkey* 39 D9
Orenburg, *Russia* 50 D6
Örencik, *Turkey* 39 B11
Orense = Ourense, *Spain* 34 C3
Orense □, *Spain* 34 C3
Orepuki, *N.Z.* 91 M1
Orestiás, *Greece* 41 E10
Orestos Pereyra, *Mexico* 118 B3
Øresund, *Europe* 11 J6
Orford Ness, *U.K.* 13 E9
Orgañà = Organyà, *Spain* 32 C6
Organos, Pta. de los, *Canary Is.* 37 F2
Organyà, *Spain* 32 C6
Orgaz, *Spain* 35 F7
Orgeyev = Orhei, *Moldova* 43 C13
Orhaneli, *Turkey* 41 G12
Orhaneli →, *Turkey* 41 G12
Orhangazi, *Turkey* 41 F13
Orhei, *Moldova* 43 C13
Orhon Gol →, *Mongolia* 60 A5
Ória, *Italy* 31 B10
Oriental, Cordillera, *Colombia* 122 C3
Orientale □, *Dem. Rep. of the Congo* 86 B2
Oriente, *Argentina* 126 D3
Orihuela, *Spain* 33 G4
Orihuela del Tremedal, *Spain* 32 E3
Orikhiv, *Ukraine* 47 J8
Orikum, *Albania* 40 F3
Orillia, *Canada* 102 D4
Orinoco →, *Venezuela* 122 C4
Orion, *Canada* 105 D6
Oriskany, *U.S.A.* 111 C9
Orissa □, *India* 67 K14
Orissaare, *Estonia* 9 G20
Oristano, *Italy* 30 C1
Oristano, G. di, *Italy* 30 C1
Orizaba, *Mexico* 119 D5
Orizare, *Bulgaria* 41 D11
Orjen, *Bos.-H.* 40 D2
Orjiva, *Spain* 35 J7
Orkanger, *Norway* 8 E13
Örkelljunga, *Sweden* 11 H7
Örken, *Sweden* 11 G9
Örkény, *Hungary* 42 C4
Orkla →, *Norway* 8 E13
Orkney, *S. Africa* 88 D4
Orkney □, *U.K.* 14 B5
Orkney Is., *U.K.* 14 B6
Orland, *U.S.A.* 116 F4
Orlando, *U.S.A.* 109 L5
Orlando, C. d', *Italy* 31 D7
Orléanais, *France* 19 E9
Orléans, *France* 19 E8
Orleans, *U.S.A.* 111 B12
Orléans, I. d', *Canada* 103 C5
Orlice →, *Czech Rep.* 26 A8
Orlov, *Slovak Rep.* 27 B13
Orlov Gay, *Russia* 48 E9
Orlová, *Czech Rep.* 27 B11
Orlovat, *Serbia, Yug.* 42 E5
Ormara, *Pakistan* 66 G4
Ormea, *Italy* 28 D4
Ormília, *Greece* 40 F7
Ormoc, *Phil.* 61 F6
Ormond, *N.Z.* 91 H6
Ormond Beach, *U.S.A.* 109 L5
Ormož, *Slovenia* 29 B13
Ormskirk, *U.K.* 12 D5
Ormstown, *Canada* 111 A11
Ornans, *France* 19 E13
Orne □, *France* 18 D7
Orne →, *France* 18 C6
Orneta, *Poland* 44 D7
Ornö, *Sweden* 10 E12
Örnsköldsvik, *Sweden* 10 A12
Oro, *N. Korea* 57 D14
Oro →, *Mexico* 118 B3
Oro Grande, *U.S.A.* 117 L9
Oro Valley, *U.S.A.* 115 K8
Orobie, Alpi, *Italy* 28 B6
Orocué, *Colombia* 124 C4
Orodara, *Burkina Faso* 82 C4
Orodo, *Nigeria* 83 D6
Orofino, *U.S.A.* 114 C5
Orol Dengizi = Aral Sea, *Asia* 50 E7
Oromocto, *Canada* 103 C6
Oron, *Nigeria* 83 E6
Orono, *Canada* 110 C6
Orono, *U.S.A.* 109 C11
Oronsay, *U.K.* 14 E2
Oropesa, *Spain* 34 F5
Oroquieta, *Phil.* 61 G5
Orosei, *Italy* 30 B2
Orosei, G. di, *Italy* 30 B2
Orosháza, *Hungary* 42 D5
Oroszlány, *Hungary* 42 C3
Orotukan, *Russia* 51 C16
Oroville, *Calif., U.S.A.* 116 F5
Oroville, *Wash., U.S.A.* 114 B4
Oroville, L., *U.S.A.* 116 F5
Orrefors, *Sweden* 11 H9
Orroroo, *Australia* 95 E2
Orrviken, *Sweden* 10 A8
Orrville, *U.S.A.* 110 F3
Orsa, *Sweden* 10 C8
Orsara di Púglia, *Italy* 31 A8
Orsasjön, *Sweden* 10 C8
Orsha, *Belarus* 46 E6
Örsjö, *Sweden* 11 H9
Orsk, *Russia* 50 D6
Orșova, *Romania* 42 F7
Ørsted, *Denmark* 11 H4
Örsundsbro, *Sweden* 10 E11
Orta, L. d', *Italy* 28 C5
Orta Nova, *Italy* 31 A8
Ortaca, *Turkey* 39 E10
Ortakent, *Turkey* 39 D9
Ortaklar, *Turkey* 39 D9
Ortaköy, *Çorum, Turkey* 72 B6
Ortaköy, *Niğde, Turkey* 72 C6
Orte, *Italy* 29 F9
Ortegal, C., *Spain* 34 B3
Orthez, *France* 20 E3
Ortigueira, *Spain* 34 B3
Orting, *U.S.A.* 116 C4
Ortisei, *Italy* 29 B8
Ortles, *Italy* 28 B7
Ortón →, *Bolivia* 124 F5
Ortona, *Italy* 29 F11
Ortonville, *U.S.A.* 112 C6
Orūmīyeh, *Iran* 70 B5
Orūmīyeh, Daryācheh-ye, *Iran* 70 B5
Orune, *Italy* 30 B2
Oruro, *Bolivia* 124 G5
Orust, *Sweden* 11 F5
Oruzgān □, *Afghan.* 66 C5
Orvault, *France* 18 E5
Orvieto, *Italy* 29 F9
Orwell, *N.Y., U.S.A.* 111 C9
Orwell, *Ohio, U.S.A.* 110 E4
Orwell →, *U.K.* 13 F9
Orwigsburg, *U.S.A.* 111 F8
Oryakhovo, *Bulgaria* 40 C7
Orzinuovi, *Italy* 28 C6
Orzyc →, *Poland* 45 F8
Orzysz, *Poland* 44 E8
Osa →, *Poland* 44 E5
Osa, Pen. de, *Costa Rica* 120 E3
Osage, *U.S.A.* 112 D8
Osage →, *U.S.A.* 112 F9
Osage City, *U.S.A.* 112 F7
Ōsaka, *Japan* 55 G7
Osan, *S. Korea* 57 F14
Osawatomie, *U.S.A.* 112 F7
Osborne, *U.S.A.* 112 F5
Osby, *Sweden* 11 H7
Osceola, *Ark., U.S.A.* 113 H10
Osceola, *Iowa, U.S.A.* 112 E8
Oschatz, *Germany* 24 D9
Oschersleben, *Germany* 24 C7
Óschiri, *Italy* 30 B2
Oscoda, *U.S.A.* 110 B1
Osečina, *Serbia, Yug.* 40 B3
Ösel = Saaremaa, *Estonia* 9 G20
Osery, *Russia* 46 E10
Osgoode, *Canada* 111 A9
Osh, *Kyrgyzstan* 50 E8
Oshakati, *Namibia* 85 H3
Oshawa, *Canada* 102 D4
Oshigambo, *Namibia* 88 B2
Oshkosh, *Nebr., U.S.A.* 112 E3
Oshkosh, *Wis., U.S.A.* 112 C10
Oshmyany = Ashmyany, *Belarus* 9 J21
Oshnovīyeh, *Iran* 70 B5
Oshogbo, *Nigeria* 83 D5
Oshtorīnān, *Iran* 71 C6
Oshwe, *Dem. Rep. of the Congo* 84 E3
Osi, *Nigeria* 83 D6
Osieczna, *Poland* 45 G3
Osijek, *Croatia* 42 E3
Ósilo, *Italy* 30 B1
Ósimo, *Italy* 29 E10
Osintorf, *Belarus* 46 E6
Osipenko = Berdyansk, *Ukraine* 47 J9
Osipovichi = Asipovichy, *Belarus* 46 F5
Osiyan, *India* 68 F5
Osizweni, *S. Africa* 89 D5
Oskaloosa, *U.S.A.* 112 E8
Oskarshamn, *Sweden* 11 G10
Oskarström, *Sweden* 11 H6
Oskélanéo, *Canada* 102 C4
Öskemen, *Kazakstan* 50 E9
Oskol →, *Ukraine* 47 H9
Oslo, *Norway* 9 G14
Oslob, *Phil.* 61 G5
Oslofjorden, *Norway* 9 G14
Osmanabad, *India* 66 K10
Osmancık, *Turkey* 72 B6
Osmaniye, *Turkey* 70 B3
Osmanlı, *Turkey* 41 E10
Ösmo, *Sweden* 10 F11
Osnabrück, *Germany* 24 C4
Ośno Lubuskie, *Poland* 45 F1
Osoblaha, *Czech Rep.* 27 A10
Osogovska Planina, *Macedonia* 40 D6
Osor, *Italy* 29 D11
Osorio, *Brazil* 127 B5
Osorno, *Chile* 128 E2
Osorno, *Spain* 34 C6
Osoyoos, *Canada* 104 D5
Osøyro, *Norway* 9 F11
Ospika →, *Canada* 104 B4
Osprey Reef, *Australia* 94 A4
Oss, *Neths.* 17 C5
Ossa, Mt., *Australia* 94 G4
Óssa, Óros, *Greece* 38 B4
Ossa de Montiel, *Spain* 33 G2
Ossabaw I., *U.S.A.* 109 K5
Osse →, *France* 20 D4
Osse →, *Nigeria* 83 D6
Ossi, *Italy* 30 B1
Ossining, *U.S.A.* 111 E11
Ossipee, *U.S.A.* 111 C13
Ossokmanuan L., *Canada* 103 B7
Ossora, *Russia* 51 D17
Ostashkov, *Russia* 46 D7
Östavall, *Sweden* 10 B9
Oste →, *Germany* 24 B5
Ostend = Oostende, *Belgium* 17 C2
Oster, *Ukraine* 47 G6
Osterburg, *Germany* 24 C7
Osterburg, *U.S.A.* 110 F6
Osterburken, *Germany* 25 F5
Österbybruk, *Sweden* 10 D11
Österbymo, *Sweden* 11 G9
Österdalälven, *Sweden* 10 C7
Østerdalen, *Norway* 9 F14
Österfärnebo, *Sweden* 10 D10
Österforse, *Sweden* 10 A11
Östergötlands län □, *Sweden* 11 F9
Osterholz-Scharmbeck, *Germany* 24 B4
Østerild, *Denmark* 11 G2
Osterode, *Germany* 24 D6
Östersund, *Sweden* 10 A8
Östervåla, *Sweden* 10 D11
Ostfriesische Inseln, *Germany* 24 B3
Ostfriesland, *Germany* 24 B3
Östhammar, *Sweden* 10 D12
Óstia, Lido di, *Italy* 29 G9
Ostíglia, *Italy* 29 C8
Östmark, *Sweden* 10 D6
Östra Husby, *Sweden* 11 F10
Ostrava, *Czech Rep.* 27 B11
Ostravský □, *Czech Rep.* 27 B10
Ostróda, *Poland* 44 E6
Ostrogozhsk, *Russia* 47 G10
Ostroh, *Ukraine* 47 G4
Ostrołęka, *Poland* 45 E8
Ostrov, *Bulgaria* 41 C8
Ostrov, *Czech Rep.* 26 A5
Ostrov, *Romania* 43 F12
Ostrov, *Russia* 46 D5
Ostrów Lubelski, *Poland* 45 G9
Ostrów Mazowiecka, *Poland* 45 F8
Ostrów Wielkopolski, *Poland* 45 G4
Ostrowiec-Świętokrzyski, *Poland* 45 H8
Ostrožac, *Bos.-H.* 42 G2
Ostrzeszów, *Poland* 45 G4
Ostseebad Kühlungsborn, *Germany* 24 A7
Osttirol □, *Austria* 26 E5
Ostuni, *Italy* 31 B10
Osum →, *Albania* 40 F4
Osŭm →, *Bulgaria* 41 C8
Ōsumi-Kaikyō, *Japan* 55 J5
Ōsumi-Shotō, *Japan* 55 J5
Osun □, *Nigeria* 83 D5
Osuna, *Spain* 35 H5
Oswegatchie →, *U.S.A.* 111 B9
Oswego, *U.S.A.* 111 C8
Oswego →, *U.S.A.* 111 C8
Oswestry, *U.K.* 12 E4
Oświęcim, *Poland* 45 H6
Otaci, *Moldova* 43 B12
Otago □, *N.Z.* 91 L2
Otago Harbour, *N.Z.* 91 L3
Ōtake, *Japan* 55 G6
Otaki, *N.Z.* 91 J5
Otaru, *Japan* 54 C10
Otaru-Wan = Ishikari-Wan, *Japan* 54 C10
Otava →, *Czech Rep.* 26 B7
Otavalo, *Ecuador* 124 C3
Otavi, *Namibia* 88 B2
Otchinjau, *Angola* 88 B1
Otelec, *Romania* 42 E5
Otelnuk L., *Canada* 103 A6
Oțelu Roșu, *Romania* 42 E7
Otero de Rey = Outeiro de Rei, *Spain* 34 B3
Othello, *U.S.A.* 114 C4
Othonoí, *Greece* 38 B1
Óthris, Óros, *Greece* 38 B4
Otjiwarongo, *Namibia* 88 C2
Otmuchów, *Poland* 45 H4
Otočac, *Croatia* 29 D12
Otoineppu, *Japan* 54 B11
Otok, *Croatia* 29 E13
Otorohanga, *N.Z.* 91 H5
Otoskwin →, *Canada* 102 B2
Otra →, *Norway* 9 G13
Otradnyy, *Russia* 48 D10
Otranto, *Italy* 31 B11
Otranto, C. d', *Italy* 31 B11
Otranto, Str. of, *Italy* 31 B11
Otrokovice, *Czech Rep.* 27 B10
Otse, *S. Africa* 88 D4
Ōtsu, *Japan* 55 G7
Ōtsuki, *Japan* 55 G9
Ottawa = Outaouais →, *Canada* 102 C5
Ottawa, *Canada* 102 C4
Ottawa, *Ill., U.S.A.* 112 E10
Ottawa, *Kans., U.S.A.* 112 F7
Ottawa Is., *Canada* 101 C11
Ottélé, *Cameroon* 83 E7
Ottensheim, *Austria* 26 C7
Otter Cr. →, *U.S.A.* 111 B11
Otter L., *Canada* 105 B8
Otterndorf, *Germany* 24 B4
Otterup, *Denmark* 11 J4
Otterville, *Canada* 110 D4
Ottery St. Mary, *U.K.* 13 G4
Otto Beit Bridge, *Zimbabwe* 87 F2
Ottosdal, *S. Africa* 88 D4
Ottumwa, *U.S.A.* 112 E8
Otu, *Nigeria* 83 D5
Otukpa, *Nigeria* 83 D6
Oturkpo, *Nigeria* 83 D6
Otway, B., *Chile* 128 G2
Otway, C., *Australia* 95 F3
Otwock, *Poland* 45 F8
Ötztaler Ache →, *Austria* 26 D3
Ötztaler Alpen, *Austria* 26 E3
Ou →, *Laos* 64 B4
Ou Neua, *Laos* 58 F3
Ou-Sammyaku, *Japan* 54 E10
Ouachita →, *U.S.A.* 113 K9
Ouachita, L., *U.S.A.* 113 H8
Ouachita Mts., *U.S.A.* 113 H7
Ouagadougou, *Burkina Faso* 83 C4
Ouahigouya, *Burkina Faso* 82 C4
Ouahran = Oran, *Algeria* 78 A5
Oualâta, *Mauritania* 82 B3
Ouallam, *Niger* 83 C5
Ouallene, *Algeria* 78 D6
Ouargaye, *Burkina Faso* 83 C5
Ouargla, *Algeria* 78 B7
Ouarkoye, *Burkina Faso* 82 C4
Ouarzazate, *Morocco* 78 B4
Ouassouas, *Mali* 83 B5
Ouatagouna, *Mali* 83 B5
Oubangi →, *Dem. Rep. of the Congo* 84 E3
Ouche →, *France* 19 E12
Ouddorp, *Neths.* 17 C3
Oude Rijn →, *Neths.* 17 B4
Oudeïka, *Mali* 83 B4
Oudenaarde, *Belgium* 17 D3
Oudon →, *France* 18 E6
Oudtshoorn, *S. Africa* 88 E3
Ouellé, *Ivory C.* 82 D4
Ouémé →, *Benin* 83 D5
Ouessa, *Burkina Faso* 82 C4
Ouessant, Î. d', *France* 18 D1
Ouesso, *Congo* 84 D3
Ouest, Pte. de l', *Canada* 103 C7
Ouezzane, *Morocco* 78 B4
Ougarou, *Burkina Faso* 83 C5
Oughterard, *Ireland* 15 C2
Ouidah, *Benin* 83 D5
Ouidi, *Niger* 83 C7
Ouistreham, *France* 18 C6
Oujda, *Morocco* 78 B5
Oujeft, *Mauritania* 82 A2
Oulainen, *Finland* 8 D21
Ould Yenjé, *Mauritania* 82 B2
Oullins, *France* 21 C8
Oulu, *Finland* 8 D21
Oulujärvi, *Finland* 8 D22
Oulujoki →, *Finland* 8 D21
Oulx, *Italy* 28 C3
Oum Chalouba, *Chad* 79 E10
Oum Hadjer, *Chad* 79 F9
Oumé, *Ivory C.* 82 D3
Ounasjoki →, *Finland* 8 C21
Ounguati, *Namibia* 88 C2
Ounianga Sérir, *Chad* 79 E10
Our →, *Lux.* 17 E6
Ouranópolis, *Greece* 40 F7
Ourârene, *Niger* 83 B6
Ouray, *U.S.A.* 115 G10
Ourcq →, *France* 19 C10
Ourense, *Spain* 34 C3
Ouricuri, *Brazil* 125 E10
Ourinhos, *Brazil* 127 A6
Ourique, *Portugal* 35 H2
Ouro Fino, *Brazil* 127 A6
Ouro-Ndia, *Mali* 82 B4
Ouro Prêto, *Brazil* 127 A7
Ouro Sogui, *Senegal* 82 B2
Oursi, *Burkina Faso* 83 C4
Ourthe →, *Belgium* 17 D5
Ouse →, *E. Susx., U.K.* 13 G8
Ouse →, *N. Yorks., U.K.* 12 D7
Oust, *France* 20 F5
Oust →, *France* 18 E4
Outaouais →, *Canada* 102 C5
Outardes →, *Canada* 103 C6
Outeiro de Rei, *Spain* 34 B3
Outer Hebrides, *U.K.* 14 D1
Outes = Serra de Outes, *Spain* 34 C2
Outjo, *Namibia* 88 C2
Outlook, *Canada* 105 C7
Outokumpu, *Finland* 8 E23
Outreau, *France* 19 B8
Ouvèze →, *France* 21 E8
Ouyen, *Australia* 95 F3
Ouzouer-le-Marché, *France* 19 E8
Ovada, *Italy* 28 D5
Ovalau, *Fiji* 91 C8
Ovalle, *Chile* 126 C1
Ovamboland, *Namibia* 88 B2
Ovar, *Portugal* 34 E2
Overath, *Germany* 24 E3
Overflakkee, *Neths.* 17 C4
Overijssel □, *Neths.* 17 B6
Overland Park, *U.S.A.* 112 F7
Overton, *U.S.A.* 117 J12
Övertorneå, *Sweden* 8 C20
Överum, *Sweden* 11 F10
Ovid, *U.S.A.* 111 D8
Ovidiopol, *Ukraine* 47 J6
Ovidiu, *Romania* 43 F13
Oviedo, *Spain* 34 B5
Oviksfjällen, *Sweden* 10 A7
Oviši, *Latvia* 9 H19
Ovoot, *Mongolia* 56 B7
Övör Hangay □, *Mongolia* 56 B2
Ovoro, *Nigeria* 83 D6
Øvre Årdal, *Norway* 9 F12
Övre Fryken, *Sweden* 10 E7
Ovruch, *Ukraine* 47 G5
Owaka, *N.Z.* 91 M2
Owambo = Ovamboland, *Namibia* 88 B2
Owasco L., *U.S.A.* 111 D8
Owase, *Japan* 55 G8
Owatonna, *U.S.A.* 112 C8
Owbeh, *Afghan.* 66 B3
Owego, *U.S.A.* 111 D8
Owen Falls Dam, *Uganda* 86 B3
Owen Sound, *Canada* 102 D3
Owens →, *U.S.A.* 116 J9
Owens L., *U.S.A.* 117 J9
Owensboro, *U.S.A.* 108 G2
Owerri, *Nigeria* 83 D6
Owl →, *Canada* 105 B10
Owo, *Nigeria* 83 D6
Owosso, *U.S.A.* 108 D3
Owyhee, *U.S.A.* 114 F5
Owyhee →, *U.S.A.* 114 E5
Owyhee, L., *U.S.A.* 114 E5
Ox Mts. = Slieve Gamph, *Ireland* 15 B3
Öxarfjörður, *Iceland* 8 C5
Oxbow, *Canada* 105 D8
Oxelösund, *Sweden* 11 F11
Oxford, *N.Z.* 91 K4
Oxford, *U.K.* 13 F6
Oxford, *Mass., U.S.A.* 111 D13
Oxford, *Miss., U.S.A.* 113 H10
Oxford, *N.C., U.S.A.* 109 G6
Oxford, *N.Y., U.S.A.* 111 D9
Oxford, *Ohio, U.S.A.* 108 F3
Oxford L., *Canada* 105 C9
Oxfordshire □, *U.K.* 13 F6
Oxía, *Greece* 38 C3
Oxie, *Sweden* 11 J7
Oxílithos, *Greece* 38 C6
Oxnard, *U.S.A.* 117 L7
Oxsjövålen, *Sweden* 10 B7
Oxus = Amudarya →, *Uzbekistan* 50 E6
Oya, *Malaysia* 62 D4
Oyama, *Japan* 55 F9
Oyem, *Gabon* 84 D2
Oyen, *Canada* 105 C6
Oykel →, *U.K.* 14 D4
Oymyakon, *Russia* 51 C15
Oyo, *Nigeria* 83 D5
Oyo □, *Nigeria* 83 D5
Oyonnax, *France* 19 F12
Oyster Bay, *U.S.A.* 111 F11
Ōyūbari, *Japan* 54 C11
Özalp, *Turkey* 73 C10
Ozamiz, *Phil.* 61 G5
Ozark, *Ala., U.S.A.* 109 K3
Ozark, *Ark., U.S.A.* 113 H8
Ozark, *Mo., U.S.A.* 113 G8
Ozark Plateau, *U.S.A.* 113 G9
Ozarks, L. of the, *U.S.A.* 112 F8
Ożarów, *Poland* 45 H8
Ózd, *Hungary* 42 B5
Ozernoye, *Russia* 48 E10
Ozette L., *U.S.A.* 116 B2
Ozieri, *Italy* 30 B2
Ozimek, *Poland* 45 H5
Ozinki, *Russia* 48 E9
Ozona, *U.S.A.* 113 K4
Ozorków, *Poland* 45 G6
Ozren, *Bos.-H.* 42 G3
Ozuluama, *Mexico* 119 C5
Ozun, *Romania* 43 E10
Ozurgeti, *Georgia* 49 K5

Pasaje

P

Pa, *Burkina Faso* 82 C4
Pa-an, *Burma* 67 L20
Pa Mong Dam, *Thailand* 64 D4
Pa Sak →, *Thailand* 62 B2
Paamiut, *Greenland* 4 C5
Paar →, *Germany* 25 G7
Paarl, *S. Africa* 88 E2
Pab Hills, *Pakistan* 68 F2
Pabbay, *U.K.* 14 D1
Pabianice, *Poland* 45 G6
Pabna, *Bangla.* 67 G16
Pabo, *Uganda* 86 B3
Pacaja →, *Brazil* 125 D8
Pacaraima, Sa., *S. Amer.* 122 C4
Pacasmayo, *Peru* 124 E3
Paceco, *Italy* 30 E5
Pachhar, *India* 68 G7
Pachino, *Italy* 31 F8
Pachitea →, *Peru* 124 E4
Pachmarhi, *India* 69 H8
Pachpadra, *India* 66 G8
Pachuca, *Mexico* 119 C5
Pacific, *Canada* 104 C3
Pacific-Antarctic Ridge, *Pac. Oc.* 97 M16
Pacific Grove, *U.S.A.* 116 J5
Pacific Ocean, *Pac. Oc.* 97 G14
Pacific Rim Nat. Park, *Canada* 116 B2
Pacifica, *U.S.A.* 116 H4
Pacitan, *Indonesia* 63 H14
Packwood, *U.S.A.* 116 D5
Pacov, *Czech Rep.* 26 B8
Pacy-sur-Eure, *France* 18 C8
Padaido, Kepulauan, *Indonesia* 63 E9
Padang, *Indonesia* 62 E2
Padang Endau, *Malaysia* 65 L4
Padangpanjang, *Indonesia* 62 E2
Padangsidempuan, *Indonesia* 62 D1
Padborg, *Denmark* 11 K3
Paddle Prairie, *Canada* 104 B5
Paddockwood, *Canada* 105 C7
Paderborn, *Germany* 24 D4
Padeş, Vf., *Romania* 42 E7
Padina, *Romania* 43 F12
Padma, *India* 69 G11
Pádova, *Italy* 29 C8
Padra, *India* 68 H5
Padrauna, *India* 69 F10
Padre I., *U.S.A.* 113 M6
Padrón, *Spain* 34 C2
Padstow, *U.K.* 13 G3
Padua = Pádova, *Italy* 29 C8
Paducah, *Ky., U.S.A.* 108 G1
Paducah, *Tex., U.S.A.* 113 H4
Padul, *Spain* 35 H7
Paengnyŏng-do, *S. Korea* 57 F13
Paeroa, *N.Z.* 91 G5
Paesana, *Italy* 28 D4
Pafúri, *Mozam.* 89 C5
Pag, *Croatia* 29 D12
Paga, *Ghana* 83 C4
Pagadian, *Phil.* 61 H5
Pagai Selatan, Pulau, *Indonesia* 62 E2
Pagai Utara, Pulau, *Indonesia* 62 E2
Pagalu = Annobón, *Atl. Oc.* 77 G4
Pagara, *India* 69 G9
Pagastikós Kólpos, *Greece* 38 B5
Pagatan, *Indonesia* 62 E5
Page, *U.S.A.* 115 H8
Pagėgiai, *Lithuania* 44 C8
Pago Pago, *Amer. Samoa* 91 B13
Pagosa Springs, *U.S.A.* 115 H10
Pagwa River, *Canada* 102 B2
Pahala, *U.S.A.* 106 J17
Pahang →, *Malaysia* 65 L4
Pahiatua, *N.Z.* 91 J5
Pahokee, *U.S.A.* 109 M5
Pahrump, *U.S.A.* 117 J11
Pahute Mesa, *U.S.A.* 116 H10
Pai, *Thailand* 64 C2
Paicines, *U.S.A.* 116 J5
Paide, *Estonia* 9 G21
Paignton, *U.K.* 13 G4
Paiho, *Taiwan* 59 F13
Päijänne, *Finland* 9 F21
Pailani, *India* 69 G9
Pailin, *Cambodia* 64 F4
Paimpol, *France* 18 D3
Painan, *Indonesia* 62 E2
Painesville, *U.S.A.* 110 E3
Paint Hills = Wemindji, *Canada* 102 B4
Paint L., *Canada* 105 B9
Painted Desert, *U.S.A.* 115 J8
Paintsville, *U.S.A.* 108 G4
País Vasco □, *Spain* 32 C2
Paisley, *Canada* 110 B3
Paisley, *U.K.* 14 F4
Paisley, *U.S.A.* 114 E3
Paita, *Peru* 124 E2
Paiva →, *Portugal* 34 D2
Paizhou, *China* 59 B9
Pajares, *Spain* 34 B5
Pajares, Puerto de, *Spain* 34 C5
Pajęczno, *Poland* 45 G5
Pak Lay, *Laos* 64 C3
Pak Phanang, *Thailand* 65 H3
Pak Sane, *Laos* 64 C4
Pak Song, *Laos* 64 E6
Pak Suong, *Laos* 58 H4
Pakaur, *India* 69 G12
Pakenham, *Canada* 111 A8
Pákhnes, *Greece* 36 D6
Pakhuis, *S. Africa* 88 E2
Pakistan ■, *Asia* 68 E4
Pakkading, *Laos* 64 C4
Pakokku, *Burma* 67 J19
Pakość, *Poland* 45 F5
Pakowki L., *Canada* 105 D6
Pakpattan, *Pakistan* 68 D5
Pakrac, *Croatia* 42 E2
Pakruojis, *Lithuania* 44 C10
Paks, *Hungary* 42 D3
Paktīā □, *Afghan.* 66 C6
Paktīkā □, *Afghan.* 66 C6
Pakwach, *Uganda* 86 B3
Pakxe, *Laos* 64 E5
Pal Lahara, *India* 69 J11
Pala, *Chad* 79 G9
Pala, *Dem. Rep. of the Congo* 86 D2
Pala, *U.S.A.* 117 M9
Palabek, *Uganda* 86 B3
Palacios, *U.S.A.* 113 L6
Palafrugell, *Spain* 32 D8
Palagiano, *Italy* 31 B10
Palagonía, *Italy* 31 E7
Palagruža, *Croatia* 29 F13
Palaiókastron, *Greece* 36 D8
Palaiokhóra, *Greece* 36 D5
Pálairos, *Greece* 38 C2
Palaiseau, *France* 19 D9
Palam, *India* 66 K10
Palamás, *Greece* 38 B4
Palamòs, *Spain* 32 D8
Palampur, *India* 68 C7
Palamut, *Turkey* 39 C9
Palana, *Australia* 94 F4
Palana, *Russia* 51 D16
Palanan, *Phil.* 61 C5
Palanan Pt., *Phil.* 61 C5
Palandri, *Pakistan* 69 C5
Palanga, *Lithuania* 9 J19
Palangkaraya, *Indonesia* 62 E4
Palani Hills, *India* 66 P10
Palanpur, *India* 68 G5
Palapye, *Botswana* 88 C4
Palas, *Pakistan* 69 B5
Palas de Rei, *Spain* 34 C3
Palashi, *India* 69 H13
Palasponga, *India* 69 J11
Palatka, *Russia* 51 C16
Palatka, *U.S.A.* 109 L5
Palau, *Italy* 30 A2
Palau ■, *Pac. Oc.* 52 J17
Palauk, *Burma* 64 F2
Palawan, *Phil.* 61 G3
Palayankottai, *India* 66 Q10
Palazzo, Pte., *France* 21 F12
Palazzo San Gervásio, *Italy* 31 B8
Palazzolo Acréide, *Italy* 31 E7
Paldiski, *Estonia* 9 G21
Pale, *Bos.-H.* 42 G3
Paleleh, *Indonesia* 63 D6
Palembang, *Indonesia* 62 E2
Palencia, *Spain* 34 C6
Palencia □, *Spain* 34 C6
Palenque, *Mexico* 119 D6
Paleokastrítsa, *Greece* 36 A3
Paleometokho, *Cyprus* 36 D12
Palermo, *Italy* 30 D6
Palermo, *U.S.A.* 114 G3
Palestina, *Chile* 128 A3
Palestine, *Asia* 75 D4
Palestine, *U.S.A.* 113 K7
Palestrina, *Italy* 29 G9
Paletwa, *Burma* 67 J18
Palghat, *India* 66 P10
Palgrave, Mt., *Australia* 92 D2
Pali, *India* 68 G5
Palikir, *Micronesia* 96 G7
Palinuro, *Italy* 31 B8
Palinuro, C., *Italy* 31 B8
Palioúrion, Ákra, *Greece* 40 G7
Palisades Reservoir, *U.S.A.* 114 E8
Paliseul, *Belgium* 17 E5
Palitana, *India* 68 J4
Palizada, *Mexico* 119 D6
Palk Bay, *Asia* 66 Q11
Palk Strait, *Asia* 66 Q11
Palkānah, *Iraq* 70 C5
Palkot, *India* 69 H11
Palla Road = Dinokwe, *Botswana* 88 C4
Pallanza = Verbánia, *Italy* 28 C5
Pallarenda, *Australia* 94 B4
Pallasovka, *Russia* 48 E8
Pallës, Bishti i, *Albania* 40 E3
Pallinup →, *Australia* 93 F2
Pallisa, *Uganda* 86 B3
Pallu, *India* 68 E6
Palm Bay, *U.S.A.* 109 L5
Palm Beach, *U.S.A.* 109 M6
Palm Coast, *U.S.A.* 109 L5
Palm Desert, *U.S.A.* 117 M10
Palm Is., *Australia* 94 B4
Palm Springs, *U.S.A.* 117 M10
Palma, *Mozam.* 87 E5
Palma, B. de, *Spain* 37 B9
Palma de Mallorca, *Spain* 37 B9
Palma del Río, *Spain* 35 H5
Palma di Montechiaro, *Italy* 30 E6
Palma Soriano, *Cuba* 120 B4
Palmares, *Brazil* 125 E11
Palmarola, *Italy* 30 B5
Palmas, *Brazil* 127 B5
Palmas, C., *Liberia* 82 E3
Pálmas, G. di, *Italy* 30 D1
Palmdale, *U.S.A.* 117 L8
Palmeira das Missões, *Brazil* 127 B5
Palmeira dos Índios, *Brazil* 125 E11
Palmela, *Portugal* 35 G2
Palmer, *U.S.A.* 100 B5
Palmer →, *Australia* 94 B3
Palmer Arch., *Antarctica* 5 C17
Palmer Lake, *U.S.A.* 112 F2
Palmer Land, *Antarctica* 5 D18
Palmerston, *Canada* 110 C4
Palmerston, *N.Z.* 91 L3
Palmerston North, *N.Z.* 91 J5
Palmerton, *U.S.A.* 111 F9
Palmetto, *U.S.A.* 109 M4
Palmi, *Italy* 31 D8
Palmira, *Argentina* 126 C2
Palmira, *Colombia* 124 C3
Palmyra = Tudmur, *Syria* 70 C3
Palmyra, *Mo., U.S.A.* 112 F9
Palmyra, *N.J., U.S.A.* 111 F9
Palmyra, *N.Y., U.S.A.* 110 C7
Palmyra, *Pa., U.S.A.* 111 F8
Palmyra Is., *Pac. Oc.* 97 G11
Palo Alto, *U.S.A.* 116 H4
Palo Verde, *U.S.A.* 117 M12
Paloich, *Sudan* 81 E3
Palompon, *Phil.* 61 F6
Palopo, *Indonesia* 63 E6
Palos, C. de, *Spain* 33 H4
Palos de la Frontera, *Spain* 35 H4
Palos Verdes, *U.S.A.* 117 M8
Palos Verdes, Pt., *U.S.A.* 117 M8
Pålsboda, *Sweden* 10 E9
Palu, *Indonesia* 63 E5
Palu, *Turkey* 70 B3
Paluke, *Liberia* 82 D3
Paluzza, *Italy* 29 B10
Palwal, *India* 68 E7
Pama, *Burkina Faso* 83 C5
Pamanukan, *Indonesia* 63 G12
Pamiers, *France* 20 E5
Pamir, *Tajikistan* 50 F8
Pamlico →, *U.S.A.* 109 H7
Pamlico Sd., *U.S.A.* 109 H8
Pampa, *U.S.A.* 113 H4
Pampa de las Salinas, *Argentina* 126 C2
Pampanua, *Indonesia* 63 E6
Pampas, *Argentina* 126 D3
Pampas, *Peru* 124 F4
Pamphylia, *Turkey* 72 D4
Pamplona, *Colombia* 124 B4
Pamplona, *Spain* 32 C3
Pampoenpoort, *S. Africa* 88 E3
Pamukçu, *Turkey* 39 B9
Pamukkale, *Turkey* 39 D11
Pan Xian, *China* 58 E5
Pana, *U.S.A.* 112 F10
Panabo, *Phil.* 61 H6
Panaca, *U.S.A.* 115 H6
Panagyurishte, *Bulgaria* 41 D8
Panaitan, *Indonesia* 63 G11
Panaji, *India* 66 M8
Panamá, *Panama* 120 E4
Panama ■, *Cent. Amer.* 120 E4
Panamá, G. de, *Panama* 120 E4
Panama Canal, *Panama* 120 E4
Panama City, *U.S.A.* 109 K3
Panamint Range, *U.S.A.* 117 J9
Panamint Springs, *U.S.A.* 117 J9
Panão, *Peru* 124 E3
Panaon I., *Phil.* 61 F6
Panare, *Thailand* 65 J3
Panarea, *Italy* 31 D8
Panaro →, *Italy* 29 D8
Panay, *Phil.* 61 F5
Panay, G., *Phil.* 63 B6
Pančevo, *Serbia, Yug.* 42 F5
Panch'iao, *Taiwan* 59 E13
Panciu, *Romania* 43 E12
Pancorbo, Desfiladero, *Spain* 34 C7
Pâncota, *Romania* 42 D6
Panda, *Mozam.* 89 C5
Pandan, *Antique, Phil.* 61 F5
Pandan, *Catanduanes, Phil.* 61 D6
Pandegelang, *Indonesia* 63 G12
Pandhana, *India* 68 J7
Pandharpur, *India* 66 L9
Pando, *Uruguay* 127 C4
Pando, L. = Hope, L., *Australia* 95 D2
Pandokrátor, *Greece* 36 A3
Pandora, *Costa Rica* 120 E3
Pandrup, *Denmark* 11 G3
Panevėžys, *Lithuania* 9 J21
Panfilov, *Kazakstan* 50 E8
Panfilovo, *Russia* 48 E6
Pang-Long, *Burma* 67 H21
Pang-Yang, *Burma* 67 H21
Panga, *Dem. Rep. of the Congo* 86 B2
Pangaíon Óros, *Greece* 41 F8
Pangalanes, Canal des = Ampangalana, Lakandranon', *Madag.* 89 C8
Pangani, *Tanzania* 86 D4
Pangani →, *Tanzania* 86 D4
Pangfou = Bengbu, *China* 57 H9
Pangil, *Dem. Rep. of the Congo* 86 C2
Pangkah, Tanjung, *Indonesia* 63 G15
Pangkajene, *Indonesia* 63 E5
Pangkalanbrandan, *Indonesia* 62 D1
Pangkalanbuun, *Indonesia* 62 E4
Pangkalpinang, *Indonesia* 62 E3
Pangnirtung, *Canada* 101 B13
Pangong Tso, *India* 68 B8
Panguitch, *U.S.A.* 115 H7
Pangutaran Group, *Phil.* 61 H4
Panhandle, *U.S.A.* 113 H4
Pani Mines, *India* 68 H5
Pania-Mutombo, *Dem. Rep. of the Congo* 86 D1
Panikota I., *India* 68 J4
Panipat, *India* 68 E7
Panjal Range, *India* 68 C7
Panjang, Hon, *Vietnam* 65 H4
Panjgur, *Pakistan* 66 F4
Panjim = Panaji, *India* 66 M8
Panjin, *China* 57 D12
Panjinad Barrage, *Pakistan* 66 E7
Panjnad →, *Pakistan* 68 E4
Panjwai, *Afghan.* 68 D1
Pankshin, *Nigeria* 83 D6
Panmunjŏm, *N. Korea* 57 F14
Panna, *India* 69 G9
Panna Hills, *India* 69 G9
Pannawonica, *Australia* 92 D2
Pannirtuuq = Pangnirtung, *Canada* 101 B13
Pano Akil, *Pakistan* 68 F3
Pano Lefkara, *Cyprus* 36 E12
Pano Panayia, *Cyprus* 36 E11
Panorama, *Brazil* 127 A5
Pánormon, *Greece* 36 D6
Pansemal, *India* 68 J6
Panshan = Panjin, *China* 57 D12
Panshi, *China* 57 C14
Pantanal, *Brazil* 124 H7
Pantar, *Indonesia* 63 F6
Pante Macassar, *E. Timor* 63 F6
Pante Makasar = Pante Macassar, *E. Timor* 63 F6
Pantelleria, *Italy* 30 F4
Pantón, *Spain* 34 C3
Pánuco, *Mexico* 119 C5
Panyam, *Nigeria* 83 D6
Panyu, *China* 59 F9
Panzhihua, *China* 58 D3
Páola, *Italy* 31 C9
Paola, *Malta* 36 D2
Paola, *U.S.A.* 112 F7
Paonia, *U.S.A.* 115 G10
Paoting = Baoding, *China* 56 E8
Paot'ou = Baotou, *China* 56 D6
Paoua, *C.A.R.* 84 C3
Pápa, *Hungary* 42 C2
Papa Stour, *U.K.* 14 A7
Papa Westray, *U.K.* 14 B6
Papagayo →, *Mexico* 119 D5
Papagayo, G. de, *Costa Rica* 120 D2
Papakura, *N.Z.* 91 G5
Papantla, *Mexico* 119 C5
Papar, *Malaysia* 62 C5
Pápas, Ákra, *Greece* 38 C3
Papeete, *Tahiti* 97 J13
Papenburg, *Germany* 24 B3
Paphlagonia, *Turkey* 72 B5
Paphos, *Cyprus* 36 E11
Papien Chiang = Da →, *Vietnam* 58 G5
Papigochic →, *Mexico* 118 B3
Paposo, *Chile* 126 B1
Papoutsa, *Cyprus* 36 E12
Papua New Guinea ■, *Oceania* 96 H6
Papudo, *Chile* 126 C1
Papuk, *Croatia* 42 E2
Papun, *Burma* 67 K20
Papunya, *Australia* 92 D5
Pará = Belém, *Brazil* 125 D9
Pará □, *Brazil* 125 D8
Paraburdoo, *Australia* 92 D2
Paracale, *Phil.* 61 D5
Paracatu, *Brazil* 125 G9
Paracel Is., *S. China Sea* 62 A4
Parachilna, *Australia* 95 E2
Parachinar, *Pakistan* 68 C4
Paraćin, *Serbia, Yug.* 40 C5
Paradas, *Spain* 35 H5
Paradela, *Spain* 34 C3
Paradhísi, *Greece* 36 C10
Paradip, *India* 67 J15
Paradise, *Calif., U.S.A.* 116 F5
Paradise, *Nev., U.S.A.* 117 J11
Paradise →, *Canada* 103 B8
Paradise Hill, *Canada* 105 C7
Paradise River, *Canada* 103 B8
Paradise Valley, *U.S.A.* 114 F5
Parado, *Indonesia* 63 F5
Paragould, *U.S.A.* 113 G9
Paragua →, *Venezuela* 124 B6
Paraguaçu →, *Brazil* 125 F11
Paraguaçu Paulista, *Brazil* 127 A5
Paraguaná, Pen. de, *Venezuela* 124 A5
Paraguarí, *Paraguay* 126 B4
Paraguarí □, *Paraguay* 126 B4
Paraguay ■, *S. Amer.* 126 A4
Paraguay →, *Paraguay* 126 B4
Paraíba = João Pessoa, *Brazil* 125 E12
Paraíba □, *Brazil* 125 E11
Paraíba do Sul →, *Brazil* 127 A7
Parainen, *Finland* 9 F20
Paraiso, *Mexico* 119 D6
Parak, *Iran* 71 E7
Parakhino Paddubye, *Russia* 46 C7
Parakou, *Benin* 83 D5
Paralimni, *Cyprus* 36 D12
Parálion-Astrous, *Greece* 38 D4
Paramaribo, *Surinam* 125 B7
Paramithiá, *Greece* 38 B2
Paramushir, Ostrov, *Russia* 51 D16
Paran →, *Israel* 75 E4
Paraná, *Argentina* 126 C3
Paraná, *Brazil* 125 F9
Paraná □, *Brazil* 127 A5
Paraná →, *Argentina* 126 C4
Paranaguá, *Brazil* 127 B6
Paranaíba, *Brazil* 125 G8
Paranaíba →, *Brazil* 125 H8
Paranapanema →, *Brazil* 127 A5
Paranapiacaba, Serra do, *Brazil* 127 A6
Paranas, *Phil.* 61 F6
Paranavaí, *Brazil* 127 A5
Parang, *Maguindanao, Phil.* 63 C6
Parang, *Sulu, Phil.* 61 J4
Parângul Mare, Vf., *Romania* 43 E8
Paraparaumu, *N.Z.* 91 J5
Parapóla, *Greece* 38 E5
Paraspóri, Ákra, *Greece* 39 F9
Paray-le-Monial, *France* 19 F11
Parbati →, *Mad. P., India* 68 G7
Parbati →, *Raj., India* 68 F7
Parbhani, *India* 66 K10
Parchim, *Germany* 24 B7
Parczew, *Poland* 45 G9
Pardes Hanna-Karkur, *Israel* 75 C3
Pardilla, *Spain* 34 D7
Pardo →, *Bahia, Brazil* 125 G11
Pardo →, *Mato Grosso, Brazil* 127 A5
Pardubice, *Czech Rep.* 26 A8
Pardubický □, *Czech Rep.* 26 B8
Pare, *Indonesia* 63 G15
Pare Mts., *Tanzania* 86 C4
Parecis, Serra dos, *Brazil* 124 F7
Paredes de Nava, *Spain* 34 C6
Paren, *Russia* 51 C17
Parent, *Canada* 102 C5
Parent, L., *Canada* 102 C4
Parentis-en-Born, *France* 20 D2
Parepare, *Indonesia* 63 E5
Parfino, *Russia* 46 D6
Párga, *Greece* 38 B2
Pargo, Pta. do, *Madeira* 37 D2
Pariaguán, *Venezuela* 124 B6
Paricutín, Cerro, *Mexico* 118 D4
Parigi, *Indonesia* 63 E6
Parika, *Guyana* 124 B7
Parikkala, *Finland* 46 B5
Parima, Serra, *Brazil* 124 C6
Parinari, *Peru* 124 D4
Pariñas, Pta., *S. Amer.* 122 D2
Parincea, *Romania* 43 D12
Parintins, *Brazil* 125 D7
Pariparit Kyun, *Burma* 67 M18
Paris, *Canada* 110 C4
Paris, *France* 19 D9
Paris, *Idaho, U.S.A.* 114 E8
Paris, *Ky., U.S.A.* 108 F3
Paris, *Tenn., U.S.A.* 109 G1
Paris, *Tex., U.S.A.* 113 J7
Paris, Ville de □, *France* 19 D9
Parish, *U.S.A.* 111 C8
Parishville, *U.S.A.* 111 B10
Park, *U.S.A.* 116 B4
Park City, *U.S.A.* 113 G6
Park Falls, *U.S.A.* 112 C9
Park Head, *Canada* 110 B3
Park Hills, *U.S.A.* 113 G9
Park Range, *U.S.A.* 114 G10
Park Rapids, *U.S.A.* 112 B7
Park River, *U.S.A.* 112 A6
Park Rynie, *S. Africa* 89 E5
Parkā Bandar, *Iran* 71 E8
Parkano, *Finland* 9 E20
Parker, *Ariz., U.S.A.* 117 L12
Parker, *Pa., U.S.A.* 110 E5
Parker Dam, *U.S.A.* 117 L12
Parkersburg, *U.S.A.* 108 F5
Parkes, *Australia* 95 E4
Parkfield, *U.S.A.* 116 K6
Parkhill, *Canada* 110 C3
Parkland, *U.S.A.* 116 C4
Parkston, *U.S.A.* 112 D6
Parksville, *Canada* 104 D4
Parla, *Spain* 34 E7
Pârliţa, *Moldova* 43 C12
Parma, *Italy* 28 D7
Parma, *Idaho, U.S.A.* 114 E5
Parma, *Ohio, U.S.A.* 110 E3
Parma →, *Italy* 28 D7
Parnaguá, *Brazil* 125 F10
Parnaíba, *Brazil* 125 D10
Parnaíba →, *Brazil* 122 D6
Parnassós, *Greece* 38 C4
Párnis, *Greece* 38 C5
Párnon Óros, *Greece* 38 D4
Pärnu, *Estonia* 9 G21
Paroo →, *Australia* 95 E3
Páros, *Greece* 39 D7
Parowan, *U.S.A.* 115 H7
Parpaillon, *France* 21 D10
Parral, *Chile* 126 D1
Parras, *Mexico* 118 B4
Parrett →, *U.K.* 13 F4
Parris I., *U.S.A.* 109 J5
Parrsboro, *Canada* 103 C7
Parry I., *Canada* 110 A4
Parry Is., *Canada* 4 B2
Parry Sound, *Canada* 102 C4
Parsberg, *Germany* 25 F7
Parsęta →, *Poland* 44 D2
Parsnip →, *Canada* 104 B4
Parsons, *U.S.A.* 113 G7
Parsons Ra., *Australia* 94 A2
Partanna, *Italy* 30 E5
Parthenay, *France* 18 F6
Partinico, *Italy* 30 D6
Partizánske, *Slovak Rep.* 27 C11
Partridge I., *Canada* 102 A2
Paru →, *Brazil* 125 D8
Parvān □, *Afghan.* 66 B6
Parvatipuram, *India* 67 K13
Parvatsar, *India* 68 F6
Påryd, *Sweden* 11 H9
Parys, *S. Africa* 88 D4
Pas, Pta. des, *Spain* 37 C7
Pas-de-Calais □, *France* 19 B9
Pasada, *Spain* 34 B5
Pasadena, *Canada* 103 C8
Pasadena, *Calif., U.S.A.* 117 L8
Pasadena, *Tex., U.S.A.* 113 L7
Pasaje →, *Argentina* 126 B3

Paşalimanı, *Turkey* 41 F11
Pasay, *Phil.* 61 D4
Pascagoula, *U.S.A.* 113 K10
Pascagoula →, *U.S.A.* 113 K10
Paşcani, *Romania* 43 C11
Pasco, *U.S.A.* 114 C4
Pasco, Cerro de, *Peru* 124 F3
Pasco I., *Australia* 92 D2
Pascoag, *U.S.A.* 111 E13
Pascua, I. de, *Pac. Oc.* 97 K17
Pasewalk, *Germany* 24 B9
Pasfield L., *Canada* 105 B7
Pasha →, *Russia* 46 B7
Pashmakli = Smolyan, *Bulgaria* 41 E8
Pasinler, *Turkey* 73 C9
Pasir Mas, *Malaysia* 65 J4
Pasir Putih, *Malaysia* 65 K4
Pasirian, *Indonesia* 63 H15
Pasirkuning, *Indonesia* 62 E2
Påskallavik, *Sweden* 11 G10
Pasküh, *Iran* 71 E9
Pasłęk, *Poland* 44 D6
Pasłęka →, *Poland* 44 D6
Pasley, C., *Australia* 93 F3
Pašman, *Croatia* 29 E12
Pasni, *Pakistan* 66 G3
Paso Cantinela, *Mexico* 117 N11
Paso de Indios, *Argentina* 128 E3
Paso de los Libres, *Argentina* 126 B4
Paso de los Toros, *Uruguay* 126 C4
Paso Robles, *U.S.A.* 115 J3
Paspébiac, *Canada* 103 C6
Pasrur, *Pakistan* 68 C6
Passage West, *Ireland* 15 E3
Passaic, *U.S.A.* 111 F10
Passau, *Germany* 25 G9
Passero, C., *Italy* 31 F8
Passo Fundo, *Brazil* 127 B5
Passos, *Brazil* 125 H9
Passow, *Germany* 24 B10
Passy, *France* 21 C10
Pastavy, *Belarus* 9 J22
Pastaza →, *Peru* 124 D3
Pasto, *Colombia* 124 C3
Pastrana, *Spain* 32 E2
Pasuruan, *Indonesia* 63 G15
Pasym, *Poland* 44 E7
Pásztó, *Hungary* 42 C4
Patagonia, *Argentina* 122 H4
Patagonia, *U.S.A.* 115 L8
Patambar, *Iran* 71 D9
Patan, *Gujarat, India* 66 H8
Patan, *Maharashtra, India* 68 H5
Patani, *Indonesia* 63 D7
Pătârlagele, *Romania* 43 E11
Pataudi, *India* 68 E7
Patchewollock, *Australia* 95 F3
Patchogue, *U.S.A.* 111 F11
Patea, *N.Z.* 91 H5
Pategi, *Nigeria* 83 D6
Patensie, *S. Africa* 88 E3
Paterna, *Spain* 33 F4
Paternion, *Austria* 26 E6
Paternò, *Italy* 31 E7
Pateros, *U.S.A.* 114 B4
Paterson, *U.S.A.* 111 F10
Paterson Ra., *Australia* 92 D3
Pathankot, *India* 68 C6
Pathfinder Reservoir, *U.S.A.* 114 E10
Pathiu, *Thailand* 65 G2
Pathum Thani, *Thailand* 64 E3
Pati, *Indonesia* 63 G14
Patía →, *Colombia* 124 C3
Patiala, *Punjab, India* 68 D7
Patiala, *Ut. P., India* 69 F8
Patine Kouka, *Senegal* 82 C2
Patitírion, *Greece* 38 B5
Patkai Bum, *India* 67 F19
Pátmos, *Greece* 39 D8
Patna, *India* 69 G11
Patnos, *Turkey* 73 C10
Pato Branco, *Brazil* 127 B5
Patonga, *Uganda* 86 B3
Patos, *Albania* 40 F3
Patos, *Brazil* 125 E11
Patos, L. dos, *Brazil* 127 C5
Patos, Río de los →, *Argentina* 126 C2
Patos de Minas, *Brazil* 125 G9
Patquía, *Argentina* 126 C2
Pátrai, *Greece* 38 C3
Pátraikós Kólpos, *Greece* 38 C3
Patras = Pátrai, *Greece* 38 C3
Patrocínio, *Brazil* 125 G9
Patta, *Kenya* 86 C5
Pattada, *Italy* 30 B2
Pattani, *Thailand* 65 J3
Pattaya, *Thailand* 62 B2
Patten, *U.S.A.* 109 C11
Patterson, *Calif., U.S.A.* 116 H5
Patterson, *La., U.S.A.* 113 L9
Patterson, Mt., *U.S.A.* 116 G7
Patti, *Punjab, India* 68 D6
Patti, *Ut. P., India* 69 G10
Patti, *Italy* 31 D7
Pattoki, *Pakistan* 68 D5
Patton, *U.S.A.* 110 F6
Patuakhali, *Bangla.* 67 H17
Patuanak, *Canada* 105 B7
Patuca →, *Honduras* 120 C3
Patuca, Punta, *Honduras* 120 C3
Pătulele, *Romania* 42 F7
Pátzcuaro, *Mexico* 118 D4
Pau, *France* 20 E3
Pau, Gave de →, *France* 20 E2
Pauillac, *France* 20 C3
Pauk, *Burma* 67 J19
Paul I., *Canada* 103 A7
Paul Smiths, *U.S.A.* 111 B10
Paulatuk, *Canada* 100 B7
Paulhan, *France* 20 E7
Paulis = Isiro, *Dem. Rep. of the Congo* 86 B2
Paulistana, *Brazil* 125 E10
Paulo Afonso, *Brazil* 125 E11
Paulpietersburg, *S. Africa* 89 D5
Pauls Valley, *U.S.A.* 113 H6
Pauma Valley, *U.S.A.* 117 M10
Pauri, *India* 69 D8
Päveh, *Iran* 70 C5
Pavelets, *Russia* 46 F10
Pavia, *Italy* 28 C6
Pavilion, *U.S.A.* 110 D6
Pavilly, *France* 18 C7
Pāvilosta, *Latvia* 9 H19
Pavlikeni, *Bulgaria* 41 C9
Pavlodar, *Kazakstan* 50 D8
Pavlograd = Pavlohrad, *Ukraine* 47 H8
Pavlohrad, *Ukraine* 47 H8
Pavlovo, *Russia* 48 C6
Pavlovsk, *Russia* 48 E5
Pavlovskaya, *Russia* 49 G4
Pavlovskiy-Posad, *Russia* 46 E10
Pavullo nel Frignano, *Italy* 28 D7
Pawayan, *India* 69 E9
Pawhuska, *U.S.A.* 113 G6
Pawling, *U.S.A.* 111 E11
Pawnee, *U.S.A.* 113 G6
Pawnee City, *U.S.A.* 112 E6
Pawtucket, *U.S.A.* 111 E13
Paximádhia, *Greece* 36 E6
Paxoí, *Greece* 38 B2
Paxton, *Ill., U.S.A.* 108 E1
Paxton, *Nebr., U.S.A.* 112 E4
Payakumbuh, *Indonesia* 62 E2
Payerne, *Switz.* 25 J2
Payette, *U.S.A.* 114 D5
Paymogo, *Spain* 35 H3
Payne Bay = Kangirsuk, *Canada* 101 B13
Payne L., *Canada* 101 C12
Paynes Find, *Australia* 93 E2
Paynesville, *Liberia* 82 D2
Paynesville, *U.S.A.* 112 C7
Pays de la Loire □, *France* 18 E6
Paysandú, *Uruguay* 126 C4
Payson, *U.S.A.* 115 J8
Paz →, *Guatemala* 120 D1
Paz, B. de la, *Mexico* 118 C2
Pāzanān, *Iran* 71 D6
Pazar, *Turkey* 73 B9
Pazarcık, *Turkey* 72 D7
Pazardzhik, *Bulgaria* 41 D8
Pazarköy, *Turkey* 39 B9
Pazarlar, *Turkey* 39 C11
Pazaryeri, *Turkey* 39 B11
Pazaryolu, *Turkey* 73 B9
Pazin, *Croatia* 29 C10
Pčinja →, *Macedonia* 40 E5
Pe Ell, *U.S.A.* 116 D3
Peabody, *U.S.A.* 111 D14
Peace →, *Canada* 104 B6
Peace Point, *Canada* 104 B6
Peace River, *Canada* 104 B5
Peach Springs, *U.S.A.* 115 J7
Peachland, *Canada* 104 D5
Peachtree City, *U.S.A.* 109 J3
Peak, The = Kinder Scout, *U.K.* 12 D6
Peak District, *U.K.* 12 D6
Peak Hill, *N.S.W., Australia* 95 E4
Peak Hill, *W. Austral., Australia* 93 E2
Peak Ra., *Australia* 94 C4
Peake Cr. →, *Australia* 95 D2
Peal de Becerro, *Spain* 35 H7
Peale, Mt., *U.S.A.* 115 G9
Pearblossom, *U.S.A.* 117 L9
Pearl →, *U.S.A.* 113 K10
Pearl City, *U.S.A.* 106 H16
Pearl Harbor, *U.S.A.* 106 H16
Pearl River, *U.S.A.* 111 E10
Pearsall, *U.S.A.* 113 L5
Peary Land, *Greenland* 4 A6
Pease →, *U.S.A.* 113 H5
Peawanuck, *Canada* 101 C11
Pebane, *Mozam.* 87 F4
Pebas, *Peru* 124 D4
Pebble Beach, *U.S.A.* 116 J5
Peć, *Kosovo, Yug.* 40 D4
Péccioli, *Italy* 28 E7
Pechea, *Romania* 43 E12
Pechenga, *Russia* 50 C4
Pechenizhyn, *Ukraine* 47 H3
Pechiguera, Pta., *Canary Is.* 37 F6
Pechnezhskoye Vdkhr., *Ukraine* 47 G9
Pechora, *Russia* 50 C6
Pechora →, *Russia* 50 C6
Pechorskaya Guba, *Russia* 50 C6
Pecica, *Romania* 42 D6
Pecka, *Serbia, Yug.* 40 B3
Pécora, C., *Italy* 30 C1
Pečory, *Russia* 9 H22
Pecos, *U.S.A.* 113 K3
Pecos →, *U.S.A.* 113 L3
Pécs, *Hungary* 42 D3
Pedder, L., *Australia* 94 G4
Peddie, *S. Africa* 89 E4
Pedernales, *Dom. Rep.* 121 C5
Pedieos →, *Cyprus* 36 D12
Pedirka, *Australia* 95 D2
Pedra Azul, *Brazil* 125 G10
Pedreguer, *Spain* 33 G5
Pedreiras, *Brazil* 125 D10
Pedro Afonso, *Brazil* 125 E9
Pedro Cays, *Jamaica* 120 C4
Pedro de Valdivia, *Chile* 126 A2
Pedro Juan Caballero, *Paraguay* 127 A4
Pedro Muñoz, *Spain* 35 F8
Pedrógão Grande, *Portugal* 34 F2
Pee Dee →, *U.S.A.* 109 J6
Peebinga, *Australia* 95 E3
Peebles, *U.K.* 14 F5
Peekskill, *U.S.A.* 111 E11
Peel, *U.K.* 12 C3
Peel →, *Australia* 95 E5
Peel →, *Canada* 100 B6
Peel Sound, *Canada* 100 A10
Peene →, *Germany* 24 A9
Peera Peera Poolanna L., *Australia* 95 D2
Peerless Lake, *Canada* 104 B6
Peers, *Canada* 104 C5
Pegasus Bay, *N.Z.* 91 K4
Peggau, *Austria* 26 D8
Pegnitz, *Germany* 25 F7
Pegnitz →, *Germany* 25 F6
Pego, *Spain* 33 G4
Pegu, *Burma* 67 L20
Pegu Yoma, *Burma* 67 K20
Pehčevo, *Macedonia* 40 E6
Pehlıvanköy, *Turkey* 41 E10
Pehuajó, *Argentina* 126 D3
Pei Xian = Pizhou, *China* 56 G9
Peine, *Chile* 126 A2
Peine, *Germany* 24 C6
Peip'ing = Beijing, *China* 56 E9
Peipus, L. = Chudskoye, Ozero, *Russia* 9 G22
Peissenberg, *Germany* 25 H7
Peitz, *Germany* 24 D10
Peixe, *Brazil* 125 F9
Peixe →, *Brazil* 125 H8
Pek →, *Serbia, Yug.* 40 B5
Pekalongan, *Indonesia* 62 F3
Pekan, *Malaysia* 65 L4
Pekanbaru, *Indonesia* 62 D2
Pekang, *Taiwan* 59 F13
Pekin, *U.S.A.* 112 E10
Peking = Beijing, *China* 56 E9
Péla, *Guinea* 82 D3
Pelabuhan Kelang, *Malaysia* 65 L3
Pelabuhan Ratu, Teluk, *Indonesia* 63 G12
Pelabuhanratu, *Indonesia* 63 G12
Pélagos, *Greece* 38 B6
Pelaihari, *Indonesia* 62 E4
Pelat, Mt., *France* 21 D10
Pełczyce, *Poland* 45 E2
Peleaga, Vf., *Romania* 42 E7
Pelée, Mt., *Martinique* 121 D7
Pelee, Pt., *Canada* 102 D3
Pelee I., *Canada* 102 D3
Pelekech, *Kenya* 86 B4
Peleng, *Indonesia* 63 E6
Pélézi, *Ivory C.* 82 D3
Pelhřimov, *Czech Rep.* 26 B8
Pelican, *U.S.A.* 104 B1
Pelican L., *Canada* 105 C8
Pelican Narrows, *Canada* 105 B8
Pelješac, *Croatia* 29 F14
Pelkosenniemi, *Finland* 8 C22
Pella, *Greece* 40 F6
Pella, *S. Africa* 88 D2
Pella, *U.S.A.* 112 E8
Pélla □, *Greece* 40 F6
Pello, *Finland* 8 C21
Pellworm, *Germany* 24 A4
Pelly →, *Canada* 100 B6
Pelly Bay, *Canada* 101 B11
Peloponnese = Pelopónnisos □, *Greece* 38 D4
Pelopónnisos □, *Greece* 38 D4
Peloritani, Monti, *Italy* 31 D8
Pelorus Sd., *N.Z.* 91 J4
Pelotas, *Brazil* 127 C5
Pelotas →, *Brazil* 127 B5
Pelovo, *Bulgaria* 41 C8
Pelplin, *Poland* 44 E5
Pelvoux, Massif du, *France* 21 D10
Pemalang, *Indonesia* 63 G13
Pemanggil, Pulau, *Malaysia* 65 L5
Pematangsiantar, *Indonesia* 62 D1
Pemba, *Mozam.* 87 E5
Pemba, *Zambia* 87 F2
Pemba Channel, *Tanzania* 86 D4
Pemba I., *Tanzania* 86 D4
Pemberton, *Australia* 93 F2
Pemberton, *Canada* 104 C4
Pembina, *U.S.A.* 112 A6
Pembroke, *Canada* 102 C4
Pembroke, *U.K.* 13 F3
Pembrokeshire □, *U.K.* 13 F3
Pen-y-Ghent, *U.K.* 12 C5
Peña, Sierra de la, *Spain* 32 C4
Peña de Francia, Sierra de la, *Spain* 34 E4
Penafiel, *Portugal* 34 D2
Peñafiel, *Spain* 34 D6
Peñaflor, *Spain* 35 H5
Peñalara, *Spain* 34 E7
Penamacôr, *Portugal* 34 E3
Penang = Pinang, *Malaysia* 65 K3
Penápolis, *Brazil* 127 A6
Peñaranda de Bracamonte, *Spain* 34 E5
Peñarroya, *Spain* 32 E4
Peñarroya-Pueblonuevo, *Spain* 35 G5
Penarth, *U.K.* 13 F4
Peñas, C. de, *Spain* 34 B5
Penas, G. de, *Chile* 122 H3
Peñas de San Pedro, *Spain* 33 G3
Peñas del Chache, *Canary Is.* 37 E6
Peñausende, *Spain* 34 D5
Pench'i = Benxi, *China* 57 D12
Pend Oreille →, *U.S.A.* 114 B5
Pend Oreille, L., *U.S.A.* 114 C5
Pendálofon, *Greece* 40 F5
Pendembu, *Eastern, S. Leone* 82 D2
Pendembu, *Northern, S. Leone* 82 D2
Pender B., *Australia* 92 C3
Pendik, *Turkey* 41 F13
Pendjari →, *Benin* 83 C5
Pendleton, *U.S.A.* 114 D4
Pendra, *India* 69 H9
Penedo, *Brazil* 125 F11
Penetanguishene, *Canada* 102 D4
Penfield, *U.S.A.* 110 E6
Pengalengan, *Indonesia* 63 G12
Penge, *Kasai-Or., Dem. Rep. of the Congo* 86 D1
Penge, *Sud-Kivu, Dem. Rep. of the Congo* 86 C2
Penghu, *Taiwan* 59 F12
Penglai, *China* 57 F11
Pengshan, *China* 58 B4
Pengshui, *China* 58 C7
Penguin, *Australia* 94 G4
Pengxi, *China* 58 B5
Pengze, *China* 59 C11
Penhalonga, *Zimbabwe* 87 F3
Peniche, *Portugal* 35 F1
Penicuik, *U.K.* 14 F5
Penida, *Indonesia* 62 F5
Peninnes, Alpes = Pennine, Alpi, *Alps* 25 J3
Peninsular Malaysia □, *Malaysia* 65 L4
Peñíscola, *Spain* 32 E5
Penitente, Serra do, *Brazil* 125 E9
Penkridge, *U.K.* 12 E5
Penmarch, *France* 18 E2
Penmarch, Pte. de, *France* 18 E2
Penn Hills, *U.S.A.* 110 F5
Penn Yan, *U.S.A.* 110 D7
Penna, Punta della, *Italy* 29 F11
Pennant, *Canada* 105 C7
Penne, *Italy* 29 F10
Penner →, *India* 66 M12
Pennine, Alpi, *Alps* 25 J3
Pennines, *U.K.* 12 C5
Pennington, *U.S.A.* 116 F5
Pennington →, *Nigeria* 83 E6
Pennino, Mte., *Italy* 29 E9
Pennsburg, *U.S.A.* 111 F9
Pennsylvania □, *U.S.A.* 108 E7
Penny, *Canada* 104 C4
Peno, *Russia* 46 D7
Penobscot →, *U.S.A.* 109 C11
Penobscot B., *U.S.A.* 109 C11
Penola, *Australia* 95 F3
Penong, *Australia* 93 F5
Penonomé, *Panama* 120 E3
Penrith, *Australia* 95 E5
Penrith, *U.K.* 12 C5
Penryn, *U.K.* 13 G2
Pensacola, *U.S.A.* 109 K2
Pensacola Mts., *Antarctica* 5 E1
Pense, *Canada* 105 C8
Penshurst, *Australia* 95 F3
Penticton, *Canada* 104 D5
Pentland, *Australia* 94 C4
Pentland Firth, *U.K.* 14 C5
Pentland Hills, *U.K.* 14 F5
Penza, *Russia* 48 D7
Penzance, *U.K.* 13 G2
Penzberg, *Germany* 25 H7
Penzhino, *Russia* 51 C17
Penzhinskaya Guba, *Russia* 51 C17
Penzhou, *China* 58 B4
Penzlin, *Germany* 24 B9
Peoria, *Ariz., U.S.A.* 115 K7
Peoria, *Ill., U.S.A.* 112 E10
Pepacton Reservoir, *U.S.A.* 111 D10
Pepani →, *S. Africa* 88 D3
Pepel, *S. Leone* 82 D2
Peqin, *Albania* 40 E3
Pera Hd., *Australia* 94 A3
Perabumulih, *Indonesia* 62 E2
Perak →, *Malaysia* 65 K3
Perakhóra, *Greece* 38 C4
Perales de Alfambra, *Spain* 32 E4
Perales del Puerto, *Spain* 34 E4
Pérama, *Kérkira, Greece* 36 A3
Pérama, *Kríti, Greece* 36 D6
Peräpohjola, *Finland* 8 C22
Perast, *Montenegro, Yug.* 40 D2
Percé, *Canada* 103 C7
Perche, *France* 18 D8
Perchtoldsdorf, *Austria* 27 C9
Percival Lakes, *Australia* 92 D4
Percy, *France* 18 D5
Percy Is., *Australia* 94 C5
Perdido, Mte., *Spain* 32 C5
Perdu, Mt. = Perdido, Mte., *Spain* 32 C5
Pereira, *Colombia* 124 C3
Perelazovskiy, *Russia* 49 F6
Perenjori, *Australia* 93 E2
Peresecina, *Moldova* 43 C13
Pereslavl-Zalesskiy, *Russia* 46 D10
Peretu, *Romania* 43 F10
Pereyaslav-Khmelnytskyy, *Ukraine* 47 G6
Pérez, I., *Mexico* 119 C7
Perg, *Austria* 26 C7
Pergamino, *Argentina* 126 C3
Pergau →, *Malaysia* 65 K3
Pérgine Valsugana, *Italy* 29 B8
Pérgola, *Italy* 29 E9
Perham, *U.S.A.* 112 B7
Perhentian, Kepulauan, *Malaysia* 62 C2
Periam, *Romania* 42 D5
Péribonca →, *Canada* 103 C5
Péribonca, L., *Canada* 103 B5
Perico, *Argentina* 126 A2
Pericos, *Mexico* 118 B3
Périers, *France* 18 C5
Périgord, *France* 20 D4
Périgueux, *France* 20 C4
Perijá, Sierra de, *Colombia* 124 B4
Peristéra, *Greece* 38 B5
Peristerona →, *Cyprus* 36 D12
Perito Moreno, *Argentina* 128 F2
Perivol = Dragovishtitsa, *Bulgaria* 40 D6
Perkasie, *U.S.A.* 111 F9
Perković, *Croatia* 29 E13
Perlas, Arch. de las, *Panama* 120 E4
Perlas, Punta de, *Nic.* 120 D3
Perleberg, *Germany* 24 B7
Perlez, *Serbia, Yug.* 42 E5
Perm, *Russia* 50 D6
Përmet, *Albania* 40 F4
Pernambuco = Recife, *Brazil* 125 E12
Pernambuco □, *Brazil* 125 E11
Pernatty Lagoon, *Australia* 95 E2
Pernik, *Bulgaria* 40 D7
Peron Is., *Australia* 92 B5
Peron Pen., *Australia* 93 E1
Péronne, *France* 19 C9
Perosa Argentina, *Italy* 28 D4
Perow, *Canada* 104 C3
Perpendicular Pt., *Australia* 95 E5
Perpignan, *France* 20 F6
Perris, *U.S.A.* 117 M9
Perros-Guirec, *France* 18 D3
Perry, *Fla., U.S.A.* 109 K4
Perry, *Ga., U.S.A.* 109 J4
Perry, *Iowa, U.S.A.* 112 E7
Perry, *Okla., U.S.A.* 113 G6
Perryton, *U.S.A.* 113 G4
Perryville, *U.S.A.* 113 G10
Persan, *France* 19 C9
Persberg, *Sweden* 10 E8
Perşembe, *Turkey* 72 B7
Persepolis, *Iran* 71 D7
Pershotravensk, *Ukraine* 47 G4
Persia = Iran ■, *Asia* 71 C7
Persian Gulf = Gulf, The, *Asia* 71 E6
Perstorp, *Sweden* 11 H7
Pertek, *Turkey* 73 C8
Perth, *Australia* 93 F2
Perth, *Canada* 102 D4
Perth, *U.K.* 14 E5
Perth & Kinross □, *U.K.* 14 E5
Perth Amboy, *U.S.A.* 111 F10
Perth-Andover, *Canada* 103 C6
Pertuis, *France* 21 E9
Pertusato, C., *France* 21 G13
Peru, *Ind., U.S.A.* 108 E2
Peru, *N.Y., U.S.A.* 111 B11
Peru ■, *S. Amer.* 124 D4
Peru Basin, *Pac. Oc.* 97 J18
Peru-Chile Trench, *Pac. Oc.* 124 G3
Perúgia, *Italy* 29 E9
Perušić, *Croatia* 29 D12
Pervomaysk, *Russia* 48 C6
Pervomaysk, *Ukraine* 47 H6
Pervouralsk, *Russia* 50 D6
Pésaro, *Italy* 29 E9
Pescadores = Penghu, *Taiwan* 59 F12
Pescara, *Italy* 29 F11
Pescara →, *Italy* 29 F11
Peschanokopskoye, *Russia* 49 G5
Péscia, *Italy* 28 E7
Pescina, *Italy* 29 F10
Peshawar, *Pakistan* 68 B4
Peshkopi, *Albania* 40 E4
Peshtera, *Bulgaria* 41 D8
Peshtigo, *U.S.A.* 108 C2
Peski, *Russia* 48 E6
Pêso da Régua, *Portugal* 34 D3
Pesqueira, *Brazil* 125 E11
Pessac, *France* 20 D3
Pest □, *Hungary* 42 C4
Pestovo, *Russia* 46 C8
Pestravka, *Russia* 48 D9
Péta, *Greece* 38 B3
Petah Tiqwa, *Israel* 75 C3
Petalídhion, *Greece* 38 E3
Petaling Jaya, *Malaysia* 65 L3
Petaloudhes, *Greece* 36 C10
Petaluma, *U.S.A.* 116 G4
Pétange, *Lux.* 17 E5
Petaro, *Pakistan* 68 G3
Petatlán, *Mexico* 118 D4
Petauke, *Zambia* 87 E3
Petawawa, *Canada* 102 C4
Petén Itzá, L., *Guatemala* 120 C2
Peter I.s Øy, *Antarctica* 5 C16
Peter Pond L., *Canada* 105 B7
Peterbell, *Canada* 102 C3
Peterborough, *Australia* 95 E2
Peterborough, *Canada* 102 D4
Peterborough, *U.K.* 13 E7
Peterborough, *U.S.A.* 111 D13
Peterborough □, *U.K.* 13 E7
Peterculter, *U.K.* 14 D6
Peterhead, *U.K.* 14 D7
Peterlee, *U.K.* 12 C6
Petermann Bjerg, *Greenland* 98 B17
Petermann Ranges, *Australia* 92 E5
Petersburg, *Alaska, U.S.A.* 100 C6
Petersburg, *Pa., U.S.A.* 110 F6
Petersburg, *Va., U.S.A.* 108 G7
Petersburg, *W. Va., U.S.A.* 108 F6
Petersfield, *U.K.* 13 F7
Petershagen, *Germany* 24 C4

Petília Policastro, *Italy* 31 C9
Petit Goâve, *Haiti* 121 C5
Petit Jardin, *Canada* 103 C8
Petit Lac Manicouagan, *Canada* 103 B6
Petit-Mécatina →, *Canada* 103 B8
Petit-Mécatina, I. du, *Canada* 103 B8
Petit Saint Bernard, Col du, *Italy* 21 C10
Petitcodiac, *Canada* 103 C6
Petite Baleine →, *Canada* 102 A4
Petite Saguenay, *Canada* 103 C5
Petitot →, *Canada* 104 A4
Petitsikapau L., *Canada* 103 B6
Petlad, *India* 68 H5
Peto, *Mexico* 119 C7
Petone, *N.Z.* 91 J5
Petorca, *Chile* 126 C1
Petoskey, *U.S.A.* 108 C3
Petra, *Jordan* 75 E4
Petra, *Spain* 37 B10
Petra, Ostrova, *Russia* 4 B13
Petra Velikogo, Zaliv, *Russia* 54 C6
Petrel = Petrer, *Spain* 33 G4
Petrella, Monte, *Italy* 30 A6
Petrer, *Spain* 33 G4
Petreto-Bicchisano, *France* 21 G12
Petrich, *Bulgaria* 40 E7
Petrified Forest National Park, *U.S.A.* 115 J9
Petrijanec, *Croatia* 29 B13
Petrikov = Pyetrikaw, *Belarus* 47 F5
Petrila, *Romania* 43 E8
Petrinja, *Croatia* 29 C13
Petrodvorets, *Russia* 46 C5
Petrograd = Sankt-Peterburg, *Russia* 46 C6
Petrolândia, *Brazil* 125 E11
Petrolia, *Canada* 102 D3
Petrolina, *Brazil* 125 E10
Petropavl, *Kazakstan* 50 D7
Petropavlovsk = Petropavl, *Kazakstan* 50 D7
Petropavlovsk-Kamchatskiy, *Russia* 51 D16
Petropavlovskiy = Akhtubinsk, *Russia* 49 F8
Petrópolis, *Brazil* 127 A7
Petroşani, *Romania* 43 E8
Petrova Gora, *Croatia* 29 C12
Petrovac, *Montenegro, Yug.* 40 D2
Petrovac, *Serbia, Yug.* 40 B5
Petrovaradin, *Serbia, Yug.* 42 E4
Petrovsk, *Russia* 48 D7
Petrovsk-Zabaykalskiy, *Russia* 51 D11
Petrovskaya, *Russia* 47 K9
Petrovskoye = Svetlograd, *Russia* 49 H6
Petrozavodsk, *Russia* 46 B8
Petrus Steyn, *S. Africa* 89 D4
Petrusburg, *S. Africa* 88 D4
Petzeck, *Austria* 26 E5
Peumo, *Chile* 126 C1
Peureulak, *Indonesia* 62 D1
Pevek, *Russia* 51 C18
Peveragno, *Italy* 28 D4
Peyrehorade, *France* 20 E2
Peyruis, *France* 21 D9
Pézenas, *France* 20 E7
Pezinok, *Slovak Rep.* 27 C10
Pfaffenhofen, *Germany* 25 G7
Pfarrkirchen, *Germany* 25 G8
Pfeffenhausen, *Germany* 25 G7
Pforzheim, *Germany* 25 G4
Pfullendorf, *Germany* 25 H5
Pfungstadt, *Germany* 25 F4
Phagwara, *India* 66 D9
Phaistós, *Greece* 36 D6
Phala, *Botswana* 88 C4
Phalera = Phulera, *India* 68 F6
Phalodi, *India* 68 F5
Phalsbourg, *France* 19 D14
Phan, *Thailand* 64 C2
Phan Rang, *Vietnam* 65 G7
Phan Ri = Hoa Da, *Vietnam* 65 G7
Phan Thiet, *Vietnam* 65 G7
Phanae, *Greece* 39 C7
Phanat Nikhom, *Thailand* 64 F3
Phangan, Ko, *Thailand* 65 H3
Phangnga, *Thailand* 65 H2
Phanom Sarakham, *Thailand* 64 F3
Phaphund, *India* 69 F8
Pharenda, *India* 69 F10
Pharr, *U.S.A.* 113 M5
Phatthalung, *Thailand* 65 J3
Phayao, *Thailand* 64 C2
Phelps, *U.S.A.* 110 D7
Phelps L., *Canada* 105 B8
Phenix City, *U.S.A.* 109 J3
Phet Buri, *Thailand* 64 F2
Phetchabun, *Thailand* 64 D3
Phetchabun, Thiu Khao, *Thailand* 64 E3
Phetchaburi = Phet Buri, *Thailand* 64 F2
Phi Phi, Ko, *Thailand* 65 J2
Phiafay, *Laos* 64 E6
Phibun Mangsahan, *Thailand* 64 E5
Phichai, *Thailand* 64 D3
Phichit, *Thailand* 64 D3
Philadelphia, *Miss., U.S.A.* 113 J10
Philadelphia, *N.Y., U.S.A.* 111 B9
Philadelphia, *Pa., U.S.A.* 111 G9
Philip, *U.S.A.* 112 C4
Philippeville, *Belgium* 17 D4
Philippi, *Greece* 41 E8
Philippi, *U.S.A.* 108 F5
Philippi L., *Australia* 94 C2
Philippines ■, *Asia* 61 F5
Philippolis, *S. Africa* 88 E4
Philippopolis = Plovdiv, *Bulgaria* 41 D8
Philipsburg, *Canada* 111 A11
Philipsburg, *Mont., U.S.A.* 114 C7
Philipsburg, *Pa., U.S.A.* 110 F6
Philipstown = Daingean, *Ireland* 15 C4
Philipstown, *S. Africa* 88 E3
Phillip I., *Australia* 95 F4
Phillips, *U.S.A.* 112 C9
Phillipsburg, *Kans., U.S.A.* 112 F5
Phillipsburg, *N.J., U.S.A.* 111 F9
Philmont, *U.S.A.* 111 D11
Philomath, *U.S.A.* 114 D2
Phimai, *Thailand* 64 E4
Phitsanulok, *Thailand* 64 D3
Phnom Dangrek, *Thailand* 62 B2
Phnom Penh, *Cambodia* 65 G5
Phnum Penh = Phnom Penh, *Cambodia* 65 G5
Phoenicia, *U.S.A.* 111 D10
Phoenix, *Ariz., U.S.A.* 115 K7
Phoenix, *N.Y., U.S.A.* 111 C8
Phoenix Is., *Kiribati* 96 H10
Phoenixville, *U.S.A.* 111 F9
Phon, *Thailand* 64 E4
Phon Tiou, *Laos* 64 D5
Phong →, *Thailand* 64 D4
Phong Saly, *Laos* 58 G4
Phong Tho, *Vietnam* 64 A4
Phonhong, *Laos* 64 C4
Phonum, *Thailand* 65 H2
Phosphate Hill, *Australia* 94 C2
Photharam, *Thailand* 64 F2
Phra Nakhon Si Ayutthaya, *Thailand* 64 E3
Phra Thong, Ko, *Thailand* 65 H2
Phrae, *Thailand* 64 C3
Phrom Phiram, *Thailand* 64 D3
Phrygia, *Turkey* 72 C4
Phu Dien, *Vietnam* 64 C5
Phu Loi, *Laos* 64 B4
Phu Ly, *Vietnam* 58 G5
Phu Quoc, Dao, *Vietnam* 65 G4
Phu Tho, *Vietnam* 58 G5
Phuc Yen, *Vietnam* 58 G5
Phuket, *Thailand* 65 J2
Phuket, Ko, *Thailand* 65 J2
Phul, *India* 68 D6
Phulad, *India* 68 G5
Phulchari, *Bangla.* 69 G13
Phulera, *India* 68 F6
Phulpur, *India* 69 G10
Phun Phin, *Thailand* 65 H2
Piacenza, *Italy* 28 C6
Pian Cr. →, *Australia* 95 E4
Piana, *France* 21 F12
Pianella, *Italy* 29 F11
Pianosa, *Puglia, Italy* 29 F12
Pianosa, *Toscana, Italy* 28 F7
Piapot, *Canada* 105 D7
Pias, *Portugal* 35 G3
Piaseczno, *Poland* 45 F8
Piaski, *Poland* 45 G9
Piastów, *Poland* 45 F7
Piatra, *Romania* 43 G10
Piatra Neamţ, *Romania* 43 D11
Piatra Olt, *Romania* 43 F9
Piauí □, *Brazil* 125 E10
Piauí →, *Brazil* 125 E10
Piave →, *Italy* 29 C9
Piazza Ármerina, *Italy* 31 E7
Pibor →, *Sudan* 81 F3
Pibor Post, *Sudan* 81 F3
Picardie, *France* 19 C10
Picardie, Plaine de, *France* 19 C9
Picardy = Picardie, *France* 19 C10
Picayune, *U.S.A.* 113 K10
Picerno, *Italy* 31 B8
Pichhor, *India* 69 G8
Pichilemu, *Chile* 126 C1
Pichor, *India* 68 G8
Pickerel L., *Canada* 102 C1
Pickering, *U.K.* 12 C7
Pickering, Vale of, *U.K.* 12 C7
Pickle Lake, *Canada* 102 B1
Pickwick L., *U.S.A.* 109 H1
Pico Truncado, *Argentina* 128 F3
Picos, *Brazil* 125 E10
Picton, *Australia* 95 E5
Picton, *Canada* 102 D4
Picton, *N.Z.* 91 J5
Pictou, *Canada* 103 C7
Picture Butte, *Canada* 104 D6
Picún Leufú, *Argentina* 128 D3
Pidurutalagala, *Sri Lanka* 66 R12
Piechowice, *Poland* 45 H2
Piedmont = Piemonte □, *Italy* 28 D5
Piedmont, *Ala., U.S.A.* 109 J3
Piedmont, *S.C., U.S.A.* 107 D10
Piedmonte Matese, *Italy* 31 A7
Piedra →, *Spain* 32 D3
Piedrabuena, *Spain* 35 G6
Piedrahita, *Spain* 34 E5
Piedralaves, *Spain* 34 E6
Piedras Blancas, *Spain* 34 B5
Piedras Negras, *Mexico* 118 B4
Piekary Śląskie, *Poland* 45 H5
Pieksämäki, *Finland* 9 E22
Piemonte □, *Italy* 28 D5
Pienaarsrivier, *S. Africa* 89 D4
Pieniężno, *Poland* 44 D7
Pieńsk, *Poland* 45 G2
Piercefield, *U.S.A.* 111 B10
Pierceland, *Canada* 105 C7
Piería □, *Greece* 40 F6
Pierpont, *U.S.A.* 110 E4
Pierre, *U.S.A.* 112 C4
Pierre-Buffière, *France* 20 C5
Pierre-de-Bresse, *France* 19 F12
Pierre E. Trudeau, Mt. = Logan, Mt., *Canada* 100 B5
Pierrefontaine-les-Varans, *France* 19 E13
Pierrefort, *France* 20 D6
Pierrelatte, *France* 21 D8
Piešťany, *Slovak Rep.* 27 C10
Piesting →, *Austria* 27 C9
Pieszyce, *Poland* 45 H3
Piet Retief, *S. Africa* 89 D5
Pietarsaari, *Finland* 8 E20
Pietermaritzburg, *S. Africa* 89 D5
Pietersburg, *S. Africa* 89 C4
Pietragalla, *Italy* 31 B8
Pietrasanta, *Italy* 28 E7
Pietroşiţa, *Romania* 43 E10
Pietrosul, Vf., *Maramureş, Romania* 43 C9
Pietrosul, Vf., *Suceava, Romania* 43 C10
Pieve di Cadore, *Italy* 29 B9
Pieve di Teco, *Italy* 28 D4
Pievepélago, *Italy* 28 D7
Pigadhítsa, *Greece* 40 G5
Pigeon L., *Canada* 110 B6
Piggott, *U.S.A.* 113 G9
Pigna, *Italy* 28 E4
Pigüe, *Argentina* 126 D3
Pihani, *India* 69 F9
Pihlajavesi, *Finland* 9 F23
Pijijiapan, *Mexico* 119 D6
Pikalevo, *Russia* 46 C8
Pikangikum Berens, *Canada* 105 C10
Pikes Peak, *U.S.A.* 112 F2
Piketberg, *S. Africa* 88 E2
Pikeville, *U.S.A.* 108 G4
Pikou, *China* 57 E12
Pikwitonei, *Canada* 105 B9
Piła, *Poland* 45 E3
Pila, *Spain* 33 G3
Pilaía, *Greece* 40 F6
Pilani, *India* 68 E6
Pilar, *Paraguay* 126 B4
Pilar de la Horadada, *Spain* 33 H4
Pilawa, *Poland* 45 G8
Pilaya →, *Bolivia* 124 H6
Pilbara, *Australia* 92 D2
Pilcomayo →, *Paraguay* 126 B4
Pilgrim's Rest, *S. Africa* 89 C5
Pilgrimstad, *Sweden* 10 B9
Pili, *Greece* 39 E9
Pilibhit, *India* 69 E8
Pilica →, *Poland* 45 G8
Pilion, *Greece* 38 B5
Pilis, *Hungary* 42 C4
Pilisvörösvár, *Hungary* 42 C3
Pilkhawa, *India* 68 E7
Pilliga, *Australia* 95 E4
Pílos, *Greece* 38 E3
Pilot Mound, *Canada* 105 D9
Pilot Point, *U.S.A.* 113 J6
Pilot Rock, *U.S.A.* 114 D4
Pilsen = Plzeň, *Czech Rep.* 26 B6
Pilštanj, *Slovenia* 29 B12
Piltene, *Latvia* 44 A8
Pilzno, *Poland* 45 J8
Pima, *U.S.A.* 115 K9
Pimba, *Australia* 95 E2
Pimenta Bueno, *Brazil* 124 F6
Pimentel, *Peru* 124 E3
Pina de Ebro, *Spain* 32 D4
Pinamalayan, *Phil.* 61 E4
Pinang, *Malaysia* 65 K3
Pinar, C. des, *Spain* 37 B10
Pinar del Río, *Cuba* 120 B3
Pınarbaşı, *Çanakkale, Turkey* 39 B8
Pınarbaşı, *Kayseri, Turkey* 72 C7
Pınarhisar, *Turkey* 41 E11
Pinatubo, Mt., *Phil.* 61 D3
Pincehely, *Hungary* 42 D3
Pinchang, *China* 58 B6
Pincher Creek, *Canada* 104 D6
Pinchi L., *Canada* 104 C4
Pinckneyville, *U.S.A.* 112 F10
Pińczów, *Poland* 45 H7
Pindar, *Australia* 93 E2
Pindi Gheb, *Pakistan* 68 C5
Pindiga, *Nigeria* 83 D7
Pindos Óros, *Greece* 38 B3
Pindus Mts. = Pindos Óros, *Greece* 38 B3
Pine →, *B.C., Canada* 104 B4
Pine →, *Sask., Canada* 105 B7
Pine, C., *Canada* 103 C9
Pine Bluff, *U.S.A.* 113 H9
Pine Bluffs, *U.S.A.* 112 E2
Pine City, *U.S.A.* 112 C8
Pine Cr. →, *U.S.A.* 110 E7
Pine Creek, *Australia* 92 B5
Pine Falls, *Canada* 105 C9
Pine Flat Res., *U.S.A.* 116 J7
Pine Grove, *U.S.A.* 111 F8
Pine Pass, *Canada* 104 B4
Pine Point, *Canada* 104 A6
Pine Ridge, *U.S.A.* 112 D3
Pine River, *Canada* 105 C8
Pine River, *U.S.A.* 112 B7
Pine Valley, *U.S.A.* 117 N10
Pinecrest, *U.S.A.* 116 G6
Pineda de Mar, *Spain* 32 D7
Pinedale, *Calif., U.S.A.* 116 J7
Pinedale, *Wyo., U.S.A.* 114 E9
Pinega →, *Russia* 50 C5
Pinehill, *Australia* 94 C4
Pinehouse L., *Canada* 105 B7
Pineimuta →, *Canada* 102 B1
Pinerolo, *Italy* 28 D4
Pineto, *Italy* 29 F11
Pinetop, *U.S.A.* 115 J9
Pinetown, *S. Africa* 89 D5
Pineville, *U.S.A.* 113 K8
Piney, *France* 19 D11
Ping →, *Thailand* 64 E3
Pingaring, *Australia* 93 F2
Pingba, *China* 58 D6
Pingbian, *China* 58 F4
Pingchuan, *China* 58 D3
Pingding, *China* 56 F7
Pingdingshan, *China* 56 H7
Pingdong, *Taiwan* 59 F13
Pingdu, *China* 57 F10
Pingelly, *Australia* 93 F2
Pingguo, *China* 58 F6
Pinghe, *China* 59 E11
Pinghu, *China* 59 B13
Pingjiang, *China* 59 C9
Pingle, *China* 59 E8
Pingli, *China* 58 A7
Pingliang, *China* 56 G4
Pinglu, *China* 56 E7
Pingluo, *China* 56 E4
Pingnan, *Fujian, China* 59 D12
Pingnan, *Guangxi Zhuangzu, China* 59 F8
Pingquan, *China* 57 D10
Pingrup, *Australia* 93 F2
Pingshan, *China* 58 C5
Pingtan, *China* 59 E12
Pingtang, *China* 58 E6
P'ingtung, *Taiwan* 59 F13
Pingwu, *China* 56 H3
Pingxiang, *Guangxi Zhuangzu, China* 58 F6
Pingxiang, *Jiangxi, China* 59 D9
Pingyao, *China* 56 F7
Pingyi, *China* 57 G9
Pingyin, *China* 56 F9
Pingyuan, *Guangdong, China* 59 E10
Pingyuan, *Shandong, China* 56 F9
Pingyuanjie, *China* 58 F4
Pinhal, *Brazil* 127 A6
Pinhal Novo, *Portugal* 35 G2
Pinheiro, *Brazil* 125 D9
Pinheiro Machado, *Brazil* 127 C5
Pinhel, *Portugal* 34 E3
Pini, *Indonesia* 62 D1
Piniós →, *Ilía, Greece* 38 D3
Piniós →, *Trikkala, Greece* 38 B4
Pinjarra, *Australia* 93 F2
Pink Mountain, *Canada* 104 B4
Pinkafeld, *Austria* 27 D9
Pinnacles, *U.S.A.* 116 J5
Pinnaroo, *Australia* 95 F3
Pinneberg, *Germany* 24 B5
Pínnes, Ákra, *Greece* 41 F8
Pinon Hills, *U.S.A.* 117 L9
Pinos, *Mexico* 118 C4
Pinos, Mt., *U.S.A.* 117 L7
Pinos Pt., *U.S.A.* 115 H3
Pinos Puente, *Spain* 35 H7
Pinotepa Nacional, *Mexico* 119 D5
Pinrang, *Indonesia* 63 E5
Pins, Pte. aux, *Canada* 110 D3
Pinsk, *Belarus* 47 F4
Pintados, *Chile* 124 H5
Pinyang, *China* 59 D13
Pinyug, *Russia* 50 C5
Pioche, *U.S.A.* 115 H6
Piombino, *Italy* 28 F7
Piombino, Canale di, *Italy* 28 F7
Pioner, Ostrov, *Russia* 51 B10
Pionki, *Poland* 45 G8
Piorini, L., *Brazil* 124 D6
Piotrków Trybunalski, *Poland* 45 G6
Piove di Sacco, *Italy* 29 C9
Pīp, *Iran* 71 E9
Pipar, *India* 68 F5
Pipar Road, *India* 68 F5
Piparia, *Mad. P., India* 68 H8
Piparia, *Mad. P., India* 68 J7
Pipéri, *Greece* 38 B6
Pipestone, *U.S.A.* 112 D6
Pipestone →, *Canada* 102 B2
Pipestone Cr. →, *Canada* 105 D8
Piplan, *Pakistan* 68 C4
Piploda, *India* 68 H6
Pipmuacan, Rés., *Canada* 103 C5
Pippingarra, *Australia* 92 D2
Pipriac, *France* 18 E5
Piqua, *U.S.A.* 108 E3
Piquiri →, *Brazil* 127 A5
Pīr Sohrāb, *Iran* 71 E9
Pira, *Benin* 83 D5
Piracicaba, *Brazil* 127 A6
Piracuruca, *Brazil* 125 D10
Piræus = Piraiévs, *Greece* 38 D5
Piraiévs, *Greece* 38 D5
Pirajuí, *Brazil* 127 A6
Piram I., *India* 68 J5
Piran, *Slovenia* 29 C10
Pirané, *Argentina* 126 B4
Pirano = Piran, *Slovenia* 29 C10
Pirapora, *Brazil* 125 G10
Pirawa, *India* 68 G7
Pirdop, *Bulgaria* 41 D8
Pírgos, *Ilía, Greece* 38 D3
Pírgos, *Kríti, Greece* 39 F7
Pirgovo, *Bulgaria* 41 C9
Piribebuy, *Paraguay* 126 B4
Pirimapun, *Indonesia* 63 F9
Pirin Planina, *Bulgaria* 40 E7
Pírineos = Pyrénées, *Europe* 20 F4
Piripiri, *Brazil* 125 D10
Pirmasens, *Germany* 25 F3
Pirna, *Germany* 24 E9
Pirot, *Serbia, Yug.* 40 C6
Piru, *Indonesia* 63 E7
Piru, *U.S.A.* 117 L8
Piryatin = Pyryatyn, *Ukraine* 47 G7
Piryí, *Greece* 39 C7
Pisa, *Italy* 28 E7
Pisa →, *Poland* 45 E8
Pisagne, *Italy* 28 C7
Pisagua, *Chile* 124 G4
Pisarovina, *Croatia* 29 C12
Pisco, *Peru* 124 F3
Piscu, *Romania* 43 E12
Písek, *Czech Rep.* 26 B7
Pishan, *China* 60 C2
Pīshīn, *Iran* 71 E9
Pishin, *Pakistan* 68 D2
Pishin Lora →, *Pakistan* 68 E1
Pisidia, *Turkey* 72 D4
Pising, *Indonesia* 63 F6
Pismo Beach, *U.S.A.* 117 K6
Piso, L., *Liberia* 82 D2
Pissila, *Burkina Faso* 83 C4
Pissis, Cerro, *Argentina* 126 B2
Pissos, *France* 20 D3
Pissouri, *Cyprus* 36 E11
Pisticci, *Italy* 31 B9
Pistóia, *Italy* 28 E7
Pistol B., *Canada* 105 A10
Pisuerga →, *Spain* 34 D6
Pisz, *Poland* 44 E8
Pit →, *U.S.A.* 114 F2
Pita, *Guinea* 82 C2
Pitarpunga, L., *Australia* 95 E3
Pitcairn I., *Pac. Oc.* 97 K14
Pite älv →, *Sweden* 8 D19
Piteå, *Sweden* 8 D19
Piterka, *Russia* 48 E8
Piteşti, *Romania* 43 F9
Pithapuram, *India* 67 L13
Pithara, *Australia* 93 F2
Píthion, *Greece* 41 E10
Pithiviers, *France* 19 D9
Pithoragarh, *India* 69 E9
Pithoro, *Pakistan* 68 G3
Pitigliano, *Italy* 29 F8
Pitkyaranta, *Russia* 46 B6
Pitlochry, *U.K.* 14 E5
Pitsilia □, *Cyprus* 36 E12
Pitt I., *Canada* 104 C3
Pittsburg, *Calif., U.S.A.* 116 G5
Pittsburg, *Kans., U.S.A.* 113 G7
Pittsburg, *Tex., U.S.A.* 113 J7
Pittsburgh, *U.S.A.* 110 F5
Pittsfield, *Ill., U.S.A.* 112 F9
Pittsfield, *Maine, U.S.A.* 109 C11
Pittsfield, *Mass., U.S.A.* 111 D11
Pittsfield, *N.H., U.S.A.* 111 C13
Pittston, *U.S.A.* 111 E9
Pittsworth, *Australia* 95 D5
Pituri →, *Australia* 94 C2
Piura, *Peru* 124 E2
Piva →, *Montenegro, Yug.* 40 C2
Piwniczna, *Poland* 45 J7
Pixley, *U.S.A.* 116 K7
Piyai, *Greece* 38 B3
Pizarra, *Spain* 35 J6
Pizhou, *China* 56 G9
Pizzo, *Italy* 31 D9
Placentia, *Canada* 103 C9
Placentia B., *Canada* 103 C9
Placer, *Masbate, Phil.* 61 F5
Placer, *Surigao N., Phil.* 61 G6
Placerville, *U.S.A.* 116 G6
Placetas, *Cuba* 120 B4
Plačkovica, *Macedonia* 40 E6
Plainfield, *N.J., U.S.A.* 111 F10
Plainfield, *Ohio, U.S.A.* 110 F3
Plainfield, *Vt., U.S.A.* 111 B12
Plains, *Mont., U.S.A.* 114 C6
Plains, *Tex., U.S.A.* 113 J3
Plainview, *Nebr., U.S.A.* 112 D6
Plainview, *Tex., U.S.A.* 113 H4
Plainwell, *U.S.A.* 108 D3
Plaisance, *France* 20 E4
Plaistow, *U.S.A.* 111 D13
Pláka, *Greece* 39 B7
Pláka, Ákra, *Greece* 36 D8
Plakenska Planina, *Macedonia* 40 E5
Planá, *Czech Rep.* 26 B5
Plana Cays, *Bahamas* 121 B5
Planada, *U.S.A.* 116 H6
Plancoët, *France* 18 D4
Plandište, *Serbia, Yug.* 42 E6
Plano, *U.S.A.* 113 J6
Plant City, *U.S.A.* 109 M4
Plaquemine, *U.S.A.* 113 K9
Plasencia, *Spain* 34 E4
Plaški, *Croatia* 29 C12
Plaster City, *U.S.A.* 117 N11
Plaster Rock, *Canada* 103 C6
Plastun, *Russia* 54 B8
Plasy, *Czech Rep.* 26 B6
Plata, Río de la, *S. Amer.* 126 C4
Plátani →, *Italy* 30 E6
Plátanos, *Greece* 36 D5
Plateau □, *Nigeria* 83 D6
Platí, Ákra, *Greece* 41 F8
Platte, *U.S.A.* 112 D5
Platte →, *Mo., U.S.A.* 112 F7
Platte →, *Nebr., U.S.A.* 112 E7
Platteville, *U.S.A.* 112 D9
Plattling, *Germany* 25 G8
Plattsburgh, *U.S.A.* 111 B11
Plattsmouth, *U.S.A.* 112 E7
Plau, *Germany* 24 B8

Plauen, Germany 24 E8
Plauer See, Germany 24 B8
Plav, Montenegro, Yug. 40 D3
Plavinas, Latvia 9 H21
Plavnica, Montenegro, Yug. 40 D3
Plavno, Croatia 29 D13
Plavsk, Russia 46 F9
Playa Blanca, Canary Is. 37 F6
Playa Blanca Sur, Canary Is. 37 F6
Playa de las Americas, Canary Is. 37 F3
Playa de Mogán, Canary Is. 37 G4
Playa del Inglés, Canary Is. 37 G4
Playa Esmerelda, Canary Is. 37 F5
Playgreen L., Canada 105 C9
Pleasant Bay, Canada 103 C7
Pleasant Hill, U.S.A. 116 H4
Pleasant Mount, U.S.A. 111 E9
Pleasanton, Calif., U.S.A. 116 H5
Pleasanton, Tex., U.S.A. 113 L5
Pleasantville, N.J., U.S.A. 108 F8
Pleasantville, Pa., U.S.A. 110 E5
Pléaux, France 20 C6
Plei Ku, Vietnam 64 F7
Plélan-le-Grand, France 18 D4
Pléneuf-Val-André, France 18 D4
Pleniţa, Romania 43 F8
Plenty →, Australia 94 C2
Plenty, B. of, N.Z. 91 G6
Plentywood, U.S.A. 112 A2
Plérin, France 18 D4
Plessisville, Canada 103 C5
Plestin-les-Grèves, France 18 D3
Pleszew, Poland 45 G4
Pleternica, Croatia 42 E2
Plétipi, L., Canada 103 B5
Pleven, Bulgaria 41 C8
Plevlja, Montenegro, Yug. 40 C3
Plevna, Canada 110 B8
Plješevica, Croatia 29 D12
Ploaghe, Italy 30 B1
Ploče, Croatia 29 E14
Płock, Poland 45 F6
Plöckenpass, Italy 29 B9
Plöckenstein, Germany 25 G9
Ploemeur, France 18 E3
Ploërmel, France 18 E4
Ploieşti, Romania 43 F11
Plomárion, Greece 39 C8
Plombières-les-Bains, France 19 E13
Plomin, Croatia 29 C11
Plön, Germany 24 A6
Plonge, Lac la, Canada 105 B7
Płońsk, Poland 45 F7
Plopeni, Romania 43 E10
Plopişului, Munţii, Romania 42 C7
Płoty, Poland 44 E2
Plouaret, France 18 D3
Plouay, France 18 E3
Ploučnice →, Czech Rep. 26 A7
Ploudalmézeau, France 18 D2
Plouescat, France 18 D2
Plougasnou, France 18 D3
Plougastel-Daoulas, France 18 D2
Plouguerneau, France 18 D2
Plouha, France 18 D4
Plouhinec, France 18 E2
Plovdiv, Bulgaria 41 D8
Plovdiv □, Bulgaria 41 D8
Plum, U.S.A. 110 F5
Plum I., U.S.A. 111 E12
Plumas, U.S.A. 116 F7
Plummer, U.S.A. 114 C5
Plumtree, Zimbabwe 87 G2
Plungė, Lithuania 9 J19
Pluvigner, France 18 E3
Plymouth, U.K. 13 G3
Plymouth, Calif., U.S.A. 116 G6
Plymouth, Ind., U.S.A. 108 E2
Plymouth, Mass., U.S.A. 111 E14
Plymouth, N.C., U.S.A. 109 H7
Plymouth, N.H., U.S.A. 111 C13
Plymouth, Pa., U.S.A. 111 E9
Plymouth, Wis., U.S.A. 108 D2
Plynlimon = Pumlumon Fawr, U.K. 13 E4
Plyusa, Russia 46 C5
Plyusa →, Russia 46 C5
Plyussa = Plyusa, Russia 46 C5
Plyussa → = Plyusa →, Russia 46 C5
Plzeň, Czech Rep. 26 B6
Plzeňský □, Czech Rep. 26 B6
Pniewy, Poland 45 F3
Pô, Burkina Faso 83 C4
Po →, Italy 29 D9
Po, Foci del, Italy 29 D9
Po Hai = Bo Hai, China 57 E10
Pobé, Benin 83 D5
Pobé, Burkina Faso 83 C4
Pobeda, Russia 51 C15
Pobedy, Pik, Kyrgyzstan 50 E8
Pobiedziska, Poland 45 F4
Pobla de Segur, Spain 32 C5
Pobladura del Valle, Spain 34 C5
Pobra de Trives, Spain 34 C3
Pocahontas, Ark., U.S.A. 113 G9
Pocahontas, Iowa, U.S.A. 112 D7
Pocatello, U.S.A. 114 E7
Počátky, Czech Rep. 26 B8
Pochep, Russia 47 F7
Pochinki, Russia 48 C7
Pochinok, Russia 46 E7
Pöchlarn, Austria 26 C8
Pochutla, Mexico 119 D5
Pocito Casas, Mexico 118 B2
Pocking, Germany 25 G9
Pocomoke City, U.S.A. 108 F8
Poços de Caldas, Brazil 127 A6
Podbořany, Czech Rep. 26 A6
Poddębice, Poland 45 G5
Poděbrady, Czech Rep. 26 A8
Podensac, France 20 D3
Podenzano, Italy 28 D6
Podgorač, Croatia 42 E3
Podgorica, Montenegro, Yug. 40 D3
Podgorie, Albania 40 F4
Podilska Vysochyna, Ukraine 47 H4
Podkarpackie □, Poland 45 H9
Podkova, Bulgaria 41 E9
Podlapača, Croatia 29 D12
Podlaskie □, Poland 45 E10
Podoleni, Romania 43 D11
Podolínec, Slovak Rep. 27 B13
Podolsk, Russia 46 E9
Podor, Senegal 82 B1
Podporozhye, Russia 46 B8
Podu Iloaiei, Romania 43 C12
Podu Turcului, Romania 43 D12
Podujevo, Kosovo, Yug. 40 D5
Poel, Germany 24 B6
Pofadder, S. Africa 88 D2
Poggiardo, Italy 31 B11
Poggibonsi, Italy 28 E8
Póggio Mirteto, Italy 29 F9
Pogoanele, Romania 43 F12
Pogorzela, Poland 45 G4
Pogradec, Albania 40 F4
Pogranitšnyi, Russia 54 B5
Poh, Indonesia 63 E6
P'ohang, S. Korea 57 F15
Pohjanmaa, Finland 8 E20
Pohnpei, Micronesia 96 G7
Pohorelá, Slovak Rep. 27 C13
Pohořelice, Czech Rep. 27 C9
Pohorje, Slovenia 29 B12
Pohri, India 68 G6
Poiana Mare, Romania 42 G8
Poiana Ruscăi, Munţii, Romania 42 E7
Poiana Stampei, Romania 43 C10
Poinsett, C., Antarctica 5 C8
Point Arena, U.S.A. 116 G3
Point Baker, U.S.A. 104 B2
Point Edward, Canada 102 D3
Point Hope, U.S.A. 100 B3
Point L., Canada 100 B8
Point Pedro, Sri Lanka 66 Q12
Point Pleasant, N.J., U.S.A. 111 F10
Point Pleasant, W. Va., U.S.A. 108 F4
Pointe-à-Pitre, Guadeloupe 121 C7
Pointe-Claire, Canada 111 A11
Pointe-Gatineau, Canada 111 A9
Pointe-Noire, Congo 84 E2
Poio, Spain 34 C2
Poirino, Italy 28 D4
Poisonbush Ra., Australia 92 D3
Poissonnier Pt., Australia 92 C2
Poitiers, France 18 F7
Poitou, France 20 B3
Poitou-Charentes □, France 20 B4
Poix-de-Picardie, France 19 C8
Poix-Terron, France 19 C11
Pojoaque, U.S.A. 115 J11
Pokaran, India 66 F7
Pokataroo, Australia 95 D4
Pokhara, Nepal 69 E10
Pokhvistnevo, Russia 48 D11
Poko, Dem. Rep. of the Congo 86 B2
Poko, Sudan 81 F3
Pokrov, Russia 46 E10
Pokrovsk = Engels, Russia 48 E8
Pokrovsk, Russia 51 C13
Pokrovskoye, Russia 47 J10
Pola = Pula, Croatia 29 D10
Pola, Russia 46 D7
Pola de Allande, Spain 34 B4
Pola de Lena, Spain 34 B5
Pola de Siero, Spain 34 B5
Pola de Somiedo, Spain 34 B4
Polacca, U.S.A. 115 J8
Polan, Iran 71 E9
Pol'ana, Slovak Rep. 27 C12
Poland ■, Europe 45 G3
Polanica-Zdrój, Poland 45 H3
Połaniec, Poland 45 H8
Polanów, Poland 44 D3
Polar Bear Prov. Park, Canada 102 A2
Polatlı, Turkey 72 C5
Polatsk, Belarus 46 E5
Polcura, Chile 126 D1
Połczyn-Zdrój, Poland 44 E3
Polessk, Russia 9 J19
Polesye = Pripet Marshes, Europe 47 F5
Polgar, Hungary 42 C6
Pŏlgyo-ri, S. Korea 57 G14
Poli, Cameroon 83 C7
Políaigos, Greece 38 E6
Policastro, G. di, Italy 31 C8
Police, Poland 44 E1
Polička, Czech Rep. 27 B9
Policoro, Italy 31 B9
Polignano a Mare, Italy 31 A9
Poligny, France 19 F12
Políkhnitas, Greece 39 B8
Polillo Is., Phil. 61 D4
Polillo Strait, Phil. 61 D4
Polis, Cyprus 36 D11
Polístena, Italy 31 D9
Políyiros, Greece 40 F7
Polk, U.S.A. 110 E5
Polkowice, Poland 45 G3
Polla, Italy 31 B8
Pollachi, India 66 P10
Pollença, Spain 37 B10
Pollença, B. de, Spain 37 B10
Póllica, Italy 31 B8
Pollino, Mte., Italy 31 C9
Polna, Russia 46 C5
Polnovat, Russia 50 C7
Pology, Ukraine 47 J9
Polonne, Ukraine 47 G4
Polonnoye = Polonne, Ukraine 47 G4
Polski Trŭmbesh, Bulgaria 41 C9
Polsko Kosovo, Bulgaria 41 C9
Polson, U.S.A. 114 C6
Poltár, Slovak Rep. 27 C12
Poltava, Ukraine 47 H8
Põltsamaa, Estonia 9 G21
Polunochnoye, Russia 50 C7
Põlva, Estonia 9 G22
Polynesia, Pac. Oc. 97 J11
Polynésie française = French Polynesia ■, Pac. Oc. 97 K13
Pomarance, Italy 28 E7
Pomaro, Mexico 118 D4
Pombal, Portugal 34 F2
Pómbia, Greece 36 E6
Pomene, Mozam. 89 C6
Pomeroy, Ohio, U.S.A. 108 F4
Pomeroy, Wash., U.S.A. 114 C5
Pomézia, Italy 30 A5
Pomichna, Ukraine 47 H6
Pomona, Australia 95 D5
Pomona, U.S.A. 117 L9
Pomorie, Bulgaria 41 D11
Pomorskie □, Poland 44 D5
Pomorskie, Pojezierze, Poland 44 E3
Pomos, Cyprus 36 D11
Pomos, C., Cyprus 36 D11
Pompano Beach, U.S.A. 109 M5
Pompei, Italy 31 B7
Pompey, France 19 D13
Pompeys Pillar, U.S.A. 114 D10
Pompton Lakes, U.S.A. 111 F10
Ponape = Pohnpei, Micronesia 96 G7
Ponask L., Canada 102 B1
Ponca, U.S.A. 112 D6
Ponca City, U.S.A. 113 G6
Ponce, Puerto Rico 121 C6
Ponchatoula, U.S.A. 113 K9
Poncheville, L., Canada 102 B4
Pond, U.S.A. 117 K7
Pond Inlet, Canada 101 A12
Pondicherry, India 66 P11
Ponds, I. of, Canada 103 B8
Ponferrada, Spain 34 C4
Pongo, Wadi →, Sudan 81 F2
Poniatowa, Poland 45 G9
Poniec, Poland 45 G3
Ponikva, Slovenia 29 B12
Ponnani, India 66 P9
Ponoka, Canada 104 C6
Ponorogo, Indonesia 63 G14
Pons = Ponts, Spain 32 D6
Pons, France 20 C3
Ponsul →, Portugal 34 F3
Pont-à-Mousson, France 19 D13
Pont-Audemer, France 18 C7
Pont-Aven, France 18 E3
Pont Canavese, Italy 28 C4
Pont-d'Ain, France 19 F12
Pont-de-Roide, France 19 E13
Pont-de-Salars, France 20 D6
Pont-de-Vaux, France 19 F11
Pont-de-Veyle, France 19 F11
Pont-du-Château, France 19 G10
Pont-l'Abbé, France 18 E2
Pont-l'Évêque, France 18 C7
Pont-St-Esprit, France 21 D8
Pont-St-Martin, Italy 28 C4
Pont-Ste-Maxence, France 19 C9
Pont-sur-Yonne, France 19 D10
Ponta do Sol, Madeira 37 D2
Ponta Grossa, Brazil 127 B5
Ponta Pora, Brazil 127 A4
Pontacq, France 20 E3
Pontailler-sur-Saône, France 19 E12
Pontarlier, France 19 F13
Pontassieve, Italy 29 E8
Pontaumur, France 20 C6
Pontcharra, France 21 C10
Pontchartrain L., U.S.A. 113 K10
Pontchâteau, France 18 E4
Ponte da Barca, Portugal 34 D2
Ponte de Sor, Portugal 35 F2
Ponte dell'Ólio, Italy 28 D6
Ponte di Legno, Italy 28 B7
Ponte do Lima, Portugal 34 D2
Ponte do Pungué, Mozam. 87 F3
Ponte-Leccia, France 21 F13
Ponte nelle Alpi, Italy 29 B9
Ponte Nova, Brazil 127 A7
Ponteareas, Spain 34 C2
Pontebba, Italy 29 B10
Ponteceso, Spain 34 B2
Pontecorvo, Italy 30 A6
Pontedeume, Spain 34 B2
Ponteix, Canada 105 D7
Pontevedra, Spain 34 C2
Pontevedra □, Spain 34 C2
Pontevedra, R. de →, Spain 34 C2
Pontevico, Italy 28 C7
Pontiac, Ill., U.S.A. 112 E10
Pontiac, Mich., U.S.A. 108 D4
Pontian Kecil, Malaysia 65 M4
Pontianak, Indonesia 62 E3
Pontine Is. = Ponziane, Ísole, Italy 30 B5
Pontine Mts. = Kuzey Anadolu Dağları, Turkey 72 B7
Pontínia, Italy 30 A6
Pontivy, France 18 D4
Pontoise, France 19 C9
Ponton →, Canada 104 B5
Pontorson, France 18 D5
Pontrémoli, Italy 28 D6
Pontrieux, France 18 D3
Ponts, Spain 32 D6
Pontypool, Canada 110 B6
Pontypool, U.K. 13 F4
Ponza, Italy 30 B5
Ponziane, Ísole, Italy 30 B5
Poochera, Australia 95 E1
Poole, U.K. 13 G6
Poole □, U.K. 13 G6
Poona = Pune, India 66 K8
Pooncarie, Australia 95 E3
Poopelloe L., Australia 95 E3
Poopó, L. de, Bolivia 122 E4
Popayán, Colombia 124 C3
Poperinge, Belgium 17 D2
Popilta L., Australia 95 E3
Popina, Bulgaria 41 B10
Popio L., Australia 95 E3
Poplar, U.S.A. 112 A2
Poplar →, Canada 105 C9
Poplar Bluff, U.S.A. 113 G9
Poplarville, U.S.A. 113 K10
Popocatépetl, Volcán, Mexico 119 D5
Popokabaka, Dem. Rep. of the Congo 84 F3
Pópoli, Italy 29 F10
Popovača, Croatia 29 C13
Popovo, Bulgaria 41 C10
Poppberg, Germany 25 F7
Poppi, Italy 29 E8
Poprad, Slovak Rep. 27 B13
Poprad →, Slovak Rep. 27 B13
Porali →, Pakistan 68 G2
Porbandar, India 66 J6
Porcher I., Canada 104 C2
Porcuna, Spain 35 H6
Porcupine →, Canada 105 B8
Porcupine →, U.S.A. 100 B5
Pordenone, Italy 29 C9
Pordim, Bulgaria 41 C8
Poreč, Croatia 29 C10
Poretskoye, Russia 48 C8
Pori, Finland 9 F19
Porí, Greece 38 F5
Porkhov, Russia 46 D5
Porlamar, Venezuela 124 A6
Porlezza, Italy 28 B6
Porma →, Spain 34 C5
Pornic, France 18 E4
Poronaysk, Russia 51 E15
Póros, Greece 38 D5
Poroshiri-Dake, Japan 54 C11
Poroszló, Hungary 42 C5
Poroto Mts., Tanzania 87 D3
Porpoise B., Antarctica 5 C9
Porquerolles, Î. de, France 21 F10
Porrentruy, Switz. 25 H3
Porreres, Spain 37 B10
Porsangen, Norway 8 A21
Porsgrunn, Norway 9 G13
Port Alberni, Canada 104 D4
Port Alfred, S. Africa 88 E4
Port Alice, Canada 104 C3
Port Allegany, U.S.A. 110 E6
Port Allen, U.S.A. 113 K9
Port Alma, Australia 94 C5
Port Angeles, U.S.A. 116 B3
Port Antonio, Jamaica 120 C4
Port Aransas, U.S.A. 113 M6
Port Arthur = Lüshun, China 57 E11
Port Arthur, Australia 94 G4
Port Arthur, U.S.A. 113 L8
Port au Choix, Canada 103 B8
Port au Port B., Canada 103 C8
Port-au-Prince, Haiti 121 C5
Port Augusta, Australia 95 E2
Port Austin, U.S.A. 110 B2
Port Bell, Uganda 86 B3
Port Bergé Vaovao, Madag. 89 B8
Port Blandford, Canada 103 C9
Port-Bouët, Ivory C. 82 D4
Port Bradshaw, Australia 94 A2
Port Broughton, Australia 95 E2
Port Burwell, Canada 110 D4
Port Canning, India 69 H13
Port-Cartier, Canada 103 B6
Port Chalmers, N.Z. 91 L3
Port Charlotte, U.S.A. 109 M4
Port Chester, U.S.A. 111 F11
Port Clements, Canada 104 C2
Port Clinton, U.S.A. 108 E4
Port Colborne, Canada 102 D4
Port Coquitlam, Canada 104 D4
Port Credit, Canada 110 C5
Port Curtis, Australia 94 C5
Port d'Alcúdia, Spain 37 B10
Port Dalhousie, Canada 110 C5
Port Darwin, Australia 92 B5
Port Darwin, Falk. Is. 128 G5
Port Davey, Australia 94 G4
Port-de-Bouc, France 21 E8
Port-de-Paix, Haiti 121 C5
Port de Pollença, Spain 37 B10
Port de Sóller, Spain 37 B9
Port Dickson, Malaysia 65 L3
Port Douglas, Australia 94 B4
Port Dover, Canada 110 D4
Port Edward, Canada 104 C2
Port Elgin, Canada 102 D3
Port Elizabeth, S. Africa 88 E4
Port Ellen, U.K. 14 F2
Port-en-Bessin, France 18 C6
Port Erin, U.K. 12 C3
Port Essington, Australia 92 B5
Port Etienne = Nouâdhibou, Mauritania 78 D2
Port Ewen, U.S.A. 111 E11
Port Fairy, Australia 95 F3
Port Fouâd = Bûr Fuad, Egypt 80 H8
Port Gamble, U.S.A. 116 C4
Port-Gentil, Gabon 84 E1
Port Germein, Australia 95 E2
Port Gibson, U.S.A. 113 K9
Port Glasgow, U.K. 14 F4
Port Harcourt, Nigeria 83 E6
Port Hardy, Canada 104 C3
Port Harrison = Inukjuak, Canada 101 C12
Port Hawkesbury, Canada 103 C7
Port Hedland, Australia 92 D2
Port Henry, U.S.A. 111 B11
Port Hood, Canada 103 C7
Port Hope, Canada 102 D4
Port Hope, U.S.A. 110 C2
Port Hope Simpson, Canada 103 B8
Port Hueneme, U.S.A. 117 L7
Port Huron, U.S.A. 110 D2
Port Iliç, Azerbaijan 73 C13
Port Jefferson, U.S.A. 111 F11
Port Jervis, U.S.A. 111 E10
Port-Joinville, France 18 F4
Port Katon, Russia 47 J10
Port Kelang = Pelabuhan Kelang, Malaysia 65 L3
Port Kenny, Australia 95 E1
Port-la-Nouvelle, France 20 E7
Port Lairge = Waterford, Ireland 15 D4
Port Laoise, Ireland 15 C4
Port Lavaca, U.S.A. 113 L6
Port Leyden, U.S.A. 111 C9
Port Lincoln, Australia 95 E2
Port Loko, S. Leone 82 D2
Port Louis, France 18 E3
Port Louis, Mauritius 77 H9
Port Lyautey = Kenitra, Morocco 78 B4
Port MacDonnell, Australia 95 F3
Port McNeill, Canada 104 C3
Port Macquarie, Australia 95 E5
Port Maria, Jamaica 120 C4
Port Matilda, U.S.A. 110 F6
Port Mellon, Canada 104 D4
Port-Menier, Canada 103 C7
Port Moody, Canada 116 A4
Port Morant, Jamaica 120 C4
Port Moresby, Papua N. G. 96 H6
Port Musgrave, Australia 94 A3
Port-Navalo, France 18 E4
Port Neches, U.S.A. 113 L8
Port Nolloth, S. Africa 88 D2
Port Nouveau-Québec = Kangiqsualujjuaq, Canada 101 C13
Port of Spain, Trin. & Tob. 121 D7
Port Orange, U.S.A. 109 L5
Port Orchard, U.S.A. 116 C4
Port Orford, U.S.A. 114 E1
Port Pegasus, N.Z. 91 M1
Port Perry, Canada 102 D4
Port Phillip B., Australia 95 F3
Port Pirie, Australia 95 E2
Port Radium = Echo Bay, Canada 100 B8
Port Renfrew, Canada 104 D4
Port Roper, Australia 94 A2
Port Rowan, Canada 110 D4
Port Safaga = Bûr Safâga, Egypt 70 E2
Port Said = Bûr Sa'îd, Egypt 80 H8
Port St. Joe, U.S.A. 109 L3
Port St. Johns = Umzimvubu, S. Africa 89 E4
Port-St-Louis-du-Rhône, France 21 E8
Port St. Lucie, U.S.A. 109 M5
Port-Ste-Marie, France 20 D4
Port Sanilac, U.S.A. 110 C2
Port Severn, Canada 110 B5
Port Shepstone, S. Africa 89 E5
Port Simpson, Canada 104 C2
Port Stanley = Stanley, Falk. Is. 128 G5
Port Stanley, Canada 102 D3
Port Sudan = Bûr Sûdân, Sudan 80 D4
Port Sulphur, U.S.A. 113 L10
Port-sur-Saône, France 19 E13
Port Talbot, U.K. 13 F4
Port Taufiq = Bûr Taufiq, Egypt 80 J8
Port Townsend, U.S.A. 116 B4
Port-Vendres, France 20 F7
Port Vila, Vanuatu 96 J8
Port Wakefield, Australia 95 E2
Port Washington, U.S.A. 108 D2
Port Weld = Kuala Sepetang, Malaysia 65 K3
Portadown, U.K. 15 B5
Portaferry, U.K. 15 B6
Portage, Pa., U.S.A. 110 F6
Portage, Wis., U.S.A. 112 D10
Portage La Prairie, Canada 105 D9
Portageville, U.S.A. 113 G10
Portalegre, Portugal 35 F3
Portalegre □, Portugal 35 F3
Portales, U.S.A. 113 H3
Portarlington, Ireland 15 C4
Portbou, Spain 32 C8
Portel, Portugal 35 G3
Porter L., N.W.T., Canada 105 A7
Porter L., Sask., Canada 105 B7
Porterville, S. Africa 88 E2
Porterville, U.S.A. 116 J8
Portes-lès-Valence, France 21 D8
Porthcawl, U.K. 13 F4

Porthill, *U.S.A.* **114 B5**
Porthmadog, *U.K.* **12 E3**
Portile de Fier, *Europe* **42 F7**
Portimão, *Portugal* **35 H2**
Portishead, *U.K.* **13 F5**
Portiţei, Gura, *Romania* **43 F14**
Portknockie, *U.K.* **14 D6**
Portland, *N.S.W., Australia* **95 E5**
Portland, *Vic., Australia* **95 F3**
Portland, *Canada* **111 B8**
Portland, *Conn., U.S.A.* **111 E12**
Portland, *Maine, U.S.A.* **101 D12**
Portland, *Mich., U.S.A.* **108 D3**
Portland, *Oreg., U.S.A.* **116 E4**
Portland, *Pa., U.S.A.* **111 F9**
Portland, *Tex., U.S.A.* **113 M6**
Portland, I. of, *U.K.* **13 G5**
Portland B., *Australia* **95 F3**
Portland Bill, *U.K.* **13 G5**
Portland Canal, *U.S.A.* **104 B2**
Portmadoc = Porthmadog, *U.K.* **12 E3**
Porto, *France* **21 F12**
Porto, *Portugal* **34 D2**
Porto □, *Portugal* **34 D2**
Porto, G. de, *France* **21 F12**
Pôrto Alegre, *Brazil* **127 C5**
Porto Amboim = Gunza, *Angola* **84 G2**
Porto Azzurro, *Italy* **28 F7**
Porto Cristo, *Spain* **37 B10**
Pôrto de Móz, *Brazil* **125 D8**
Porto Empédocle, *Italy* **30 E6**
Pôrto Esperança, *Brazil* **124 G7**
Pôrto Franco, *Brazil* **125 E9**
Pórto Lágos, *Greece* **41 E9**
Porto Mendes, *Brazil* **127 A5**
Porto Moniz, *Madeira* **37 D2**
Pôrto Murtinho, *Brazil* **124 H7**
Pôrto Nacional, *Brazil* **125 F9**
Porto-Novo, *Benin* **83 D5**
Porto Petro, *Spain* **37 B10**
Porto San Giórgio, *Italy* **29 E10**
Porto Sant' Elpídio, *Italy* **29 E10**
Porto Santo, I. de, *Madeira* **78 B2**
Porto Santo Stéfano, *Italy* **28 F8**
Pôrto São José, *Brazil* **127 A5**
Pôrto Seguro, *Brazil* **125 G11**
Porto Tolle, *Italy* **29 D9**
Porto Tórres, *Italy* **30 B1**
Pôrto União, *Brazil* **127 B5**
Pôrto Válter, *Brazil* **124 E4**
Porto-Vecchio, *France* **21 G13**
Pôrto Velho, *Brazil* **124 E6**
Portobelo, *Panama* **120 E4**
Portoferráio, *Italy* **28 F7**
Portogruaro, *Italy* **29 C9**
Portola, *U.S.A.* **116 F6**
Portomaggiore, *Italy* **29 D8**
Portoscuso, *Italy* **30 C1**
Portovénere, *Italy* **28 D6**
Portoviejo, *Ecuador* **124 D2**
Portpatrick, *U.K.* **14 G3**
Portree, *U.K.* **14 D2**
Portrush, *U.K.* **15 A5**
Portsmouth, *Domin.* **121 C7**
Portsmouth, *U.K.* **13 G6**
Portsmouth, *N.H., U.S.A.* **109 D10**
Portsmouth, *Ohio, U.S.A.* **108 F4**
Portsmouth, *R.I., U.S.A.* **111 E13**
Portsmouth, *Va., U.S.A.* **108 G7**
Portsmouth □, *U.K.* **13 G6**
Portsoy, *U.K.* **14 D6**
Portstewart, *U.K.* **15 A5**
Porttipahtan tekojärvi, *Finland* **8 B22**
Portugal ■, *Europe* **34 F3**
Portugalete, *Spain* **32 B1**
Portumna, *Ireland* **15 C3**
Portville, *U.S.A.* **110 D6**
Porvenir, *Chile* **128 G2**
Porvoo, *Finland* **9 F21**
Porzuna, *Spain* **35 F6**
Posada, *Italy* **30 B2**
Posada →, *Italy* **30 B2**
Posadas, *Argentina* **127 B4**
Posadas, *Spain* **35 H5**
Poschiavo, *Switz.* **25 J6**
Posets, *Spain* **32 C5**
Poshan = Boshan, *China* **57 F9**
Posht-e-Badam, *Iran* **71 C7**
Posídhion, Ákra, *Greece* **40 G7**
Posidium, *Greece* **39 F9**
Poso, *Indonesia* **63 E6**
Posong, *S. Korea* **57 G14**
Posse, *Brazil* **125 F9**
Possession I., *Antarctica* **5 D11**
Pössneck, *Germany* **24 E7**
Possum Kingdom L., *U.S.A.* **113 J5**
Post, *U.S.A.* **113 J4**
Post Falls, *U.S.A.* **114 C5**
Postavy = Pastavy, *Belarus* **9 J22**
Poste-de-la-Baleine = Kuujjuarapik, *Canada* **102 A4**
Postmasburg, *S. Africa* **88 D3**
Postojna, *Slovenia* **29 C11**
Poston, *U.S.A.* **117 M12**
Postville, *Canada* **103 B8**
Potamós, *Andikíthira, Greece* **38 F5**
Potamós, *Kíthira, Greece* **38 E4**
Potchefstroom, *S. Africa* **88 D4**
Potcoava, *Romania* **43 F9**
Poteau, *U.S.A.* **113 H7**
Poteet, *U.S.A.* **113 L5**
Potenza, *Italy* **31 B8**
Potenza →, *Italy* **29 E10**
Potenza Picena, *Italy* **29 E10**
Poteriteri, L., *N.Z.* **91 M1**
Potgietersrus, *S. Africa* **89 C4**
Poti, *Georgia* **49 J5**
Potiskum, *Nigeria* **83 C7**
Potlogi, *Romania* **43 F10**
Potomac →, *U.S.A.* **108 G7**
Potosí, *Bolivia* **124 G5**
Potosi Mt., *U.S.A.* **117 K11**
Pototan, *Phil.* **61 F5**
Potrerillos, *Chile* **126 B2**
Potsdam, *Germany* **24 C9**
Potsdam, *U.S.A.* **111 B10**
Pottenstein, *Germany* **25 F7**
Pottersville, *U.S.A.* **111 C11**
Pottery Hill = Abu Ballas, *Egypt* **80 C2**
Pottstown, *U.S.A.* **111 F9**
Pottsville, *U.S.A.* **111 F8**
Pottuvil, *Sri Lanka* **66 R12**
P'otzu, *Taiwan* **59 F13**
Pouancé, *France* **18 E5**
Pouce Coupé, *Canada* **104 B4**
Poughkeepsie, *U.S.A.* **111 E11**
Pouilly-sur-Loire, *France* **19 E9**
Poulaphouca Res., *Ireland* **15 C5**
Poulsbo, *U.S.A.* **116 C4**
Poultney, *U.S.A.* **111 C11**
Poulton-le-Fylde, *U.K.* **12 D5**
Pouso Alegre, *Brazil* **127 A6**
Pout, *Senegal* **82 C1**
Pouthisat, *Cambodia* **64 F4**
Pouzauges, *France* **18 F6**
Pova de Sta. Iria, *Portugal* **35 G1**
Považská Bystrica, *Slovak Rep.* **27 B11**
Poverty B., *N.Z.* **91 H7**
Povlen, *Serbia, Yug.* **40 B3**
Póvoa de Lanhosa, *Portugal* **34 D2**
Póvoa de Varzim, *Portugal* **34 D2**
Povorino, *Russia* **48 E6**
Povungnituk = Puvirnituq, *Canada* **101 B12**
Powassan, *Canada* **102 C4**
Poway, *U.S.A.* **117 N9**
Powder →, *U.S.A.* **112 B2**
Powder River, *U.S.A.* **114 E10**
Powell, *U.S.A.* **114 D9**
Powell, L., *U.S.A.* **115 H8**
Powell River, *Canada* **104 D4**
Powers, *U.S.A.* **108 C2**
Powys □, *U.K.* **13 E4**
Poyang Hu, *China* **59 C11**
Poyarkovo, *Russia* **51 E13**
Poysdorf, *Austria* **27 C9**
Poza de la Sal, *Spain* **34 C7**
Poza Rica, *Mexico* **119 C5**
Pozanti, *Turkey* **72 D6**
Požarevac, *Serbia, Yug.* **40 B5**
Pozazal, Puerto, *Spain* **34 C6**
Požega, *Croatia* **42 E2**
Požega, *Serbia, Yug.* **40 C4**
Poznań, *Poland* **45 F3**
Pozo, *U.S.A.* **117 K6**
Pozo Alcón, *Spain* **35 H8**
Pozo Almonte, *Chile* **124 H5**
Pozo Colorado, *Paraguay* **126 A4**
Pozoblanco, *Spain* **35 G6**
Pozzallo, *Italy* **31 F7**
Pozzomaggiore, *Italy* **30 B1**
Pozzuoli, *Italy* **31 B7**
Pra →, *Ghana* **83 D4**
Prabuty, *Poland* **44 E6**
Prača, *Bos.-H.* **42 G3**
Prachatice, *Czech Rep.* **26 B6**
Prachin Buri, *Thailand* **64 E3**
Prachuap Khiri Khan, *Thailand* **65 G2**
Pradelles, *France* **20 D7**
Prades, *France* **20 F6**
Prado, *Brazil* **125 G11**
Prado del Rey, *Spain* **35 J5**
Præstø, *Denmark* **11 J6**
Pragersko, *Slovenia* **29 B12**
Prague = Praha, *Czech Rep.* **26 A7**
Praha, *Czech Rep.* **26 A7**
Prahecq, *France* **20 B3**
Prahova □, *Romania* **43 E10**
Prahova →, *Romania* **43 F10**
Prahovo, *Serbia, Yug.* **40 B6**
Praia, *C. Verde Is.* **77 E1**
Práia a Mare, *Italy* **31 C8**
Praid, *Romania* **43 D10**
Prainha, *Amazonas, Brazil* **124 E6**
Prainha, *Pará, Brazil* **125 D8**
Prairie, *Australia* **94 C3**
Prairie City, *U.S.A.* **114 D4**
Prairie Dog Town Fork →, *U.S.A.* **113 H5**
Prairie du Chien, *U.S.A.* **112 D9**
Prairies, L. of the, *Canada* **105 C8**
Pramánda, *Greece* **38 B3**
Prampram, *Ghana* **83 D5**
Pran Buri, *Thailand* **64 F2**
Prang, *Ghana* **83 D4**
Prapat, *Indonesia* **62 D1**
Prasonísi, Ákra, *Greece* **36 D9**
Prästmon, *Sweden* **10 A11**
Praszka, *Poland* **45 G5**
Prata, *Brazil* **125 G9**
Pratabpur, *India* **69 H10**
Pratapgarh, *Raj., India* **68 G6**
Pratapgarh, *Ut. P., India* **69 G9**
Prato, *Italy* **28 E8**
Prátola Peligna, *Italy* **29 F10**
Prats-de-Mollo-la-Preste, *France* **20 F6**
Pratt, *U.S.A.* **113 G5**
Prattville, *U.S.A.* **109 J2**
Pravdinsk, *Russia* **48 B6**
Pravets, *Bulgaria* **40 D7**
Pravia, *Spain* **34 B4**
Praya, *Indonesia* **62 F5**
Pré-en-Pail, *France* **18 D6**
Precordillera, *Argentina* **126 C2**
Predáppio, *Italy* **29 D8**
Predazzo, *Italy* **29 B8**
Predeal, *Romania* **43 E10**
Predejane, *Serbia, Yug.* **40 D6**
Preeceville, *Canada* **105 C8**
Preetz, *Germany* **24 A6**
Pregrada, *Croatia* **29 B12**
Preiļi, *Latvia* **9 H22**
Preko, *Croatia* **29 D12**
Prelog, *Croatia* **29 B13**
Prémery, *France* **19 E10**
Premià de Mar, *Spain* **32 D7**
Premont, *U.S.A.* **113 M5**
Premuda, *Croatia* **29 D11**
Prentice, *U.S.A.* **112 C9**
Prenzlau, *Germany* **24 B9**
Preobrazheniye, *Russia* **54 C6**
Preparis North Channel, *Ind. Oc.* **67 M18**
Preparis South Channel, *Ind. Oc.* **67 M18**
Přerov, *Czech Rep.* **27 B10**
Prescott, *Canada* **102 D4**
Prescott, *Ariz., U.S.A.* **115 J7**
Prescott, *Ark., U.S.A.* **113 J8**
Prescott Valley, *U.S.A.* **115 J7**
Preservation Inlet, *N.Z.* **91 M1**
Preševo, *Serbia, Yug.* **40 D5**
Presho, *U.S.A.* **112 D4**
Presicce, *Italy* **31 C11**
Presidencia de la Plaza, *Argentina* **126 B4**
Presidencia Roque Saenz Peña, *Argentina* **126 B3**
Presidente Epitácio, *Brazil* **125 H8**
Presidente Hayes □, *Paraguay* **126 A4**
Presidente Prudente, *Brazil* **127 A5**
Presidio, *Mexico* **118 B4**
Presidio, *U.S.A.* **113 L2**
Preslav, *Bulgaria* **41 C10**
Preslavska Planina, *Bulgaria* **41 C10**
Prešov, *Slovak Rep.* **27 B14**
Prešovský □, *Slovak Rep.* **27 B13**
Prespa, *Bulgaria* **41 E8**
Prespa, L. = Prespansko Jezero, *Macedonia* **40 F5**
Prespansko Jezero, *Macedonia* **40 F5**
Presque I., *U.S.A.* **110 D4**
Presque Isle, *U.S.A.* **109 B12**
Prestatyn, *U.K.* **12 D4**
Prestea, *Ghana* **82 D4**
Presteigne, *U.K.* **13 E5**
Přeštice, *Czech Rep.* **26 B6**
Preston, *Canada* **110 C4**
Preston, *U.K.* **12 D5**
Preston, *Idaho, U.S.A.* **114 E8**
Preston, *Minn., U.S.A.* **112 D8**
Preston, C., *Australia* **92 D2**
Prestonburg, *U.S.A.* **108 G4**
Prestwick, *U.K.* **14 F4**
Pretoria, *S. Africa* **89 D4**
Preuilly-sur-Claise, *France* **18 F7**
Préveza, *Greece* **38 C2**
Préveza □, *Greece* **38 B2**
Prey Veng, *Cambodia* **65 G5**
Priazovskoye, *Ukraine* **47 J8**
Pribilof Is., *U.S.A.* **100 C2**
Priboj, *Serbia, Yug.* **40 C3**
Příbram, *Czech Rep.* **26 B7**
Price, *U.S.A.* **114 G8**
Price I., *Canada* **104 C3**
Prichard, *U.S.A.* **109 K1**
Priego, *Spain* **32 E2**
Priego de Córdoba, *Spain* **35 H6**
Priekule, *Latvia* **9 H19**
Prien, *Germany* **25 H8**
Prienai, *Lithuania* **9 J20**
Prieska, *S. Africa* **88 D3**
Priest L., *U.S.A.* **114 B5**
Priest River, *U.S.A.* **114 B5**
Priest Valley, *U.S.A.* **116 J6**
Prievidza, *Slovak Rep.* **27 C11**
Prignitz, *Germany* **24 B7**
Prijedor, *Bos.-H.* **29 D13**
Prijepolje, *Serbia, Yug.* **40 C3**
Prikaspiyskaya Nizmennost = Caspian Depression, *Eurasia* **49 G9**
Prikro, *Ivory C.* **82 D4**
Prikubanskaya Nizmennost, *Russia* **49 H4**
Prilep, *Macedonia* **40 E5**
Priluki = Pryluky, *Ukraine* **47 G7**
Prime Seal I., *Australia* **94 G4**
Primorsk, *Russia* **46 B5**
Primorsko, *Bulgaria* **41 D11**
Primorsko-Akhtarsk, *Russia* **47 J10**
Primorskoye, *Ukraine* **47 J9**
Primrose L., *Canada* **105 C7**
Prince Albert, *Canada* **105 C7**
Prince Albert, *S. Africa* **88 E3**
Prince Albert Mts., *Antarctica* **5 D11**
Prince Albert Nat. Park, *Canada* **105 C7**
Prince Albert Pen., *Canada* **100 A8**
Prince Albert Sd., *Canada* **100 A8**
Prince Alfred, C., *Canada* **4 B1**
Prince Charles I., *Canada* **101 B12**
Prince Charles Mts., *Antarctica* **5 D6**
Prince Edward I. □, *Canada* **103 C7**
Prince Edward Is., *Ind. Oc.* **3 G11**
Prince Edward Pt., *Canada* **110 C8**
Prince George, *Canada* **104 C4**
Prince of Wales, C., *U.S.A.* **98 C3**
Prince of Wales I., *Australia* **94 A3**
Prince of Wales I., *Canada* **100 A10**
Prince of Wales I., *U.S.A.* **100 C6**
Prince Patrick I., *Canada* **4 B2**
Prince Regent Inlet, *Canada* **4 B3**
Prince Rupert, *Canada* **104 C2**
Princess Charlotte B., *Australia* **94 A3**
Princess May Ranges, *Australia* **92 C4**
Princess Royal I., *Canada* **104 C3**
Princeton, *Canada* **104 D4**
Princeton, *Calif., U.S.A.* **116 F4**
Princeton, *Ill., U.S.A.* **112 E10**
Princeton, *Ind., U.S.A.* **108 F2**
Princeton, *Ky., U.S.A.* **108 G2**
Princeton, *Mo., U.S.A.* **112 E8**
Princeton, *N.J., U.S.A.* **111 F10**
Princeton, *W. Va., U.S.A.* **108 G5**
Principe, I. de, *Atl. Oc.* **76 F4**
Principe da Beira, *Brazil* **124 F6**
Prineville, *U.S.A.* **114 D3**
Prins Harald Kyst, *Antarctica* **5 D4**
Prinsesse Astrid Kyst, *Antarctica* **5 D3**
Prinsesse Ragnhild Kyst, *Antarctica* **5 D4**
Prinzapolca, *Nic.* **120 D3**
Prior, C., *Spain* **34 B2**
Priozersk, *Russia* **46 B6**
Pripet = Prypyat →, *Europe* **47 G6**
Pripet Marshes, *Europe* **47 F5**
Pripyat Marshes = Pripet Marshes, *Europe* **47 F5**
Pripyats = Prypyat →, *Europe* **47 G6**
Prislop, Pasul, *Romania* **43 C9**
Pristen, *Russia* **47 G9**
Priština, *Kosovo, Yug.* **40 D5**
Pritzwalk, *Germany* **24 B8**
Privas, *France* **21 D8**
Priverno, *Italy* **30 A6**
Privolzhsk, *Russia* **48 B5**
Privolzhskaya Vozvyshennost, *Russia* **48 E7**
Privolzhskiy, *Russia* **48 E8**
Privolzhye, *Russia* **48 D9**
Priyutnoye, *Russia* **49 G6**
Prizren, *Kosovo, Yug.* **40 D4**
Prizzi, *Italy* **30 E6**
Prnjavor, *Bos.-H.* **42 F2**
Probolinggo, *Indonesia* **63 G15**
Prochowice, *Poland* **45 G3**
Proctor, *U.S.A.* **111 C11**
Proddatur, *India* **66 M11**
Prodhromos, *Cyprus* **36 E11**
Proença-a-Nova, *Portugal* **34 F3**
Profítis Ilías, *Greece* **36 C9**
Profondeville, *Belgium* **17 D4**
Progreso, *Coahuila, Mexico* **118 B4**
Progreso, *Yucatán, Mexico* **119 C7**
Prokhladnyy, *Russia* **49 J7**
Prokletije, *Albania* **40 D3**
Prokopyevsk, *Russia* **50 D9**
Prokuplje, *Serbia, Yug.* **40 C5**
Proletarsk, *Russia* **49 G5**
Proletarskaya = Proletarsk, *Russia* **49 G5**
Prome = Pyè, *Burma* **67 K19**
Prophet →, *Canada* **104 B4**
Prophet River, *Canada* **104 B4**
Propriá, *Brazil* **125 F11**
Propriano, *France* **21 G12**
Proserpine, *Australia* **94 C4**
Prosna →, *Poland* **45 F4**
Prospect, *U.S.A.* **111 C9**
Prosser, *U.S.A.* **114 C4**
Prostějov, *Czech Rep.* **27 B10**
Prostki, *Poland* **44 E9**
Proston, *Australia* **95 D5**
Proszowice, *Poland* **45 H7**
Próti, *Greece* **38 D3**
Provadiya, *Bulgaria* **41 C11**
Provence, *France* **21 E9**
Provence-Alpes-Côte d'Azur □, *France* **21 D10**
Providence, *Ky., U.S.A.* **108 G2**
Providence, *R.I., U.S.A.* **111 E13**
Providence Bay, *Canada* **102 C3**
Providence Mts., *U.S.A.* **117 K11**
Providencia, I. de, *Colombia* **120 D3**
Provideniya, *Russia* **51 C19**
Provins, *France* **19 D10**
Provo, *U.S.A.* **114 F8**
Provost, *Canada* **105 C6**
Prozor, *Bos.-H.* **42 G2**
Prrenjas, *Albania* **40 E4**
Prudhoe Bay, *U.S.A.* **100 A5**
Prudhoe I., *Australia* **94 C4**
Prud'homme, *Canada* **105 C7**
Prudnik, *Poland* **45 H4**
Prüm, *Germany* **25 E2**
Prundu, *Romania* **43 F11**
Pruszcz Gdański, *Poland* **44 D5**
Pruszków, *Poland* **45 F7**
Prut →, *Romania* **43 E13**
Pruzhany, *Belarus* **47 F3**
Prvič, *Croatia* **29 D11**
Prydz B., *Antarctica* **5 C6**
Pryluky, *Ukraine* **47 G7**
Pryor, *U.S.A.* **113 G7**
Prypyat →, *Europe* **47 G6**
Przasnysz, *Poland* **45 E7**
Przedbórz, *Poland* **45 G6**
Przedecz, *Poland* **45 F5**
Przemków, *Poland* **45 G2**
Przemyśl, *Poland* **45 J9**
Przeworsk, *Poland* **45 H9**
Przewóz, *Poland* **45 G1**
Przhevalsk = Karakol, *Kyrgyzstan* **50 E8**
Przysucha, *Poland* **45 G7**
Psakhná, *Greece* **38 C5**
Psará, *Greece* **39 C7**
Psathoúra, *Greece* **38 B6**
Psel →, *Ukraine* **47 H7**
Pserimos, *Greece* **39 E9**
Psíra, *Greece* **36 D7**
Pskov, *Russia* **46 D5**
Pskovskoye, Ozero, *Russia* **46 D5**
Psunj, *Croatia* **42 E2**
Pteleón, *Greece* **38 B4**
Ptich = Ptsich →, *Belarus* **47 F5**
Ptolemaís, *Greece* **40 F5**
Ptsich →, *Belarus* **47 F5**
Ptuj, *Slovenia* **29 B12**
Ptujska Gora, *Slovenia* **29 B12**
Pu Xian, *China* **56 F6**
Pua, *Thailand* **64 C3**
Puán, *Argentina* **126 D3**
Pu'an, *China* **58 E5**
Puan, *S. Korea* **57 G14**
Pubei, *China* **58 F7**
Pucallpa, *Peru* **124 E4**
Pucheng, *China* **59 D12**
Pucheni, *Romania* **43 E10**
Puchheim, *Germany* **25 G7**
Púchov, *Slovak Rep.* **27 B11**
Pucioasa, *Romania* **43 E10**
Pučišća, *Croatia* **29 E13**
Puck, *Poland* **44 D5**
Pucka, Zatoka, *Poland* **44 D5**
Puçol, *Spain* **33 F4**
Pudasjärvi, *Finland* **8 D22**
Puding, *China* **58 D5**
Pudozh, *Russia* **46 B9**
Pudukkottai, *India* **66 P11**
Puebla, *Mexico* **119 D5**
Puebla □, *Mexico* **119 D5**
Puebla de Alcocer, *Spain* **35 G5**
Puebla de Don Fadrique, *Spain* **33 H2**
Puebla de Don Rodrigo, *Spain* **35 F6**
Puebla de Guzmán, *Spain* **35 H3**
Puebla de la Calzada, *Spain* **35 G4**
Puebla de Sanabria, *Spain* **34 C4**
Puebla de Trives = Pobra de Trives, *Spain* **34 C3**
Pueblo, *U.S.A.* **112 F2**
Pueblo Hundido, *Chile* **126 B1**
Puelches, *Argentina* **126 D2**
Puelén, *Argentina* **126 D2**
Puente Alto, *Chile* **126 C1**
Puente-Genil, *Spain* **35 H6**
Puente la Reina, *Spain* **32 C3**
Puenteareas = Ponteareas, *Spain* **34 C2**
Puentedeume = Pontedeume, *Spain* **34 B2**
Puentes de Garcia Rodriguez = As Pontes de García Rodríguez, *Spain* **34 B3**
Pu'er, *China* **58 F3**
Puerco →, *U.S.A.* **115 J10**
Puerto, *Canary Is.* **37 F2**
Puerto Aisén, *Chile* **128 F2**
Puerto Ángel, *Mexico* **119 D5**
Puerto Arista, *Mexico* **119 D6**
Puerto Armuelles, *Panama* **120 E3**
Puerto Ayacucho, *Venezuela* **124 B5**
Puerto Barrios, *Guatemala* **120 C2**
Puerto Bermejo, *Argentina* **126 B4**
Puerto Bermúdez, *Peru* **124 F4**
Puerto Bolívar, *Ecuador* **124 D3**
Puerto Cabello, *Venezuela* **124 A5**
Puerto Cabezas, *Nic.* **120 D3**
Puerto Cabo Gracias á Dios, *Nic.* **120 D3**
Puerto Carreño, *Colombia* **124 B5**
Puerto Castilla, *Honduras* **120 C2**
Puerto Chicama, *Peru* **124 E3**
Puerto Coig, *Argentina* **128 G3**
Puerto Cortés, *Costa Rica* **120 E3**
Puerto Cortés, *Honduras* **120 C2**
Puerto Cumarebo, *Venezuela* **124 A5**
Puerto de Alcudia = Port d'Alcúdia, *Spain* **37 B10**
Puerto de Andraitx, *Spain* **37 B9**
Puerto de Cabrera, *Spain* **37 B9**
Puerto de Gran Tarajal, *Canary Is.* **37 F5**
Puerto de la Cruz, *Canary Is.* **37 F3**
Puerto de Mazarrón, *Spain* **33 H3**
Puerto de Pozo Negro, *Canary Is.* **37 F6**
Puerto de Sóller = Port de Sóller, *Spain* **37 B9**
Puerto de Somosierra, *Spain* **34 D7**
Puerto del Carmen, *Canary Is.* **37 F6**
Puerto del Rosario, *Canary Is.* **37 F6**
Puerto Deseado, *Argentina* **128 F3**
Puerto Escondido, *Mexico* **119 D5**
Puerto Heath, *Bolivia* **124 F5**
Puerto Inírida, *Colombia* **124 C5**
Puerto Juárez, *Mexico* **119 C7**
Puerto La Cruz, *Venezuela* **124 A6**
Puerto Leguízamo, *Colombia* **124 D4**
Puerto Limón, *Colombia* **124 C4**
Puerto Lobos, *Argentina* **128 E3**
Puerto Lumbreras, *Spain* **33 H3**
Puerto Madryn, *Argentina* **128 E3**
Puerto Maldonado, *Peru* **124 F5**
Puerto Manotí, *Cuba* **120 B4**
Puerto Mazarrón = Puerto de Mazarrón, *Spain* **33 H3**
Puerto Montt, *Chile* **128 E2**
Puerto Morazán, *Nic.* **120 D2**
Puerto Morelos, *Mexico* **119 C7**
Puerto Natales, *Chile* **128 G2**
Puerto Padre, *Cuba* **120 B4**
Puerto Páez, *Venezuela* **124 B5**
Puerto Peñasco, *Mexico* **118 A2**
Puerto Pinasco, *Paraguay* **126 A4**
Puerto Plata, *Dom. Rep.* **121 C5**
Puerto Pollensa = Port de Pollença, *Spain* **37 B10**

Puerto Princesa, *Phil.* 61 G3
Puerto Quepos, *Costa Rica* 120 E3
Puerto Real, *Spain* 35 J4
Puerto Rico, *Canary Is.* 37 G4
Puerto Rico ■, *W. Indies* 121 C6
Puerto Rico Trench, *Atl. Oc.* 121 C6
Puerto San Julián, *Argentina* 128 F3
Puerto Sastre, *Paraguay* 126 A4
Puerto Serrano, *Spain* 35 J5
Puerto Suárez, *Bolivia* 124 G7
Puerto Vallarta, *Mexico* 118 C3
Puerto Wilches, *Colombia* 124 B4
Puertollano, *Spain* 35 G6
Pueyrredón, L., *Argentina* 128 F2
Puffin I., *Ireland* 15 E1
Pugachev, *Russia* 48 D9
Pugal, *India* 68 E5
Puge, *China* 58 D4
Puge, *Tanzania* 86 C3
Puget Sound, *U.S.A.* 114 C2
Puget-Théniers, *France* 21 E10
Púglia □, *Italy* 31 A9
Pugŏdong, *N. Korea* 57 C16
Pugu, *Tanzania* 86 D4
Pūgūnzī, *Iran* 71 E8
Pui, *Romania* 42 E8
Puieşti, *Romania* 43 D12
Puig Major, *Spain* 37 B9
Puigcerdà, *Spain* 32 C6
Puigmal, *Spain* 32 C7
Puigpunyent, *Spain* 37 B9
Puijiang, *China* 58 B4
Puisaye, Collines de la, *France* 19 E10
Puiseaux, *France* 19 D9
Pujehun, *S. Leone* 82 D2
Pujiang, *China* 59 C12
Pujols, *France* 20 D3
Pujon-chŏsuji, *N. Korea* 57 D14
Pukaki L., *N.Z.* 91 L3
Pukapuka, *Cook Is.* 97 J11
Pukaskwa Nat. Park, *Canada* 102 C2
Pukatawagan, *Canada* 105 B8
Pukchin, *N. Korea* 57 D13
Pukch'ŏng, *N. Korea* 57 D15
Pukë, *Albania* 40 D3
Pukekohe, *N.Z.* 91 G5
Pukhrayan, *India* 69 F8
Pukou, *China* 59 A12
Pula, *Croatia* 29 D10
Pula, *Italy* 30 C1
Pulacayo, *Bolivia* 124 H5
Pulandian, *China* 57 E11
Pularumpi, *Australia* 92 B5
Pulaski, *N.Y., U.S.A.* 111 C8
Pulaski, *Tenn., U.S.A.* 109 H2
Pulaski, *Va., U.S.A.* 108 G5
Pulau →, *Indonesia* 63 F9
Puławy, *Poland* 45 G8
Pulga, *U.S.A.* 116 F5
Pulicat L., *India* 66 N12
Pullman, *U.S.A.* 114 C5
Pulo-Anna, *Pac. Oc.* 63 D8
Pulog, Mt., *Phil.* 61 C4
Pułtusk, *Poland* 45 F8
Pülümür, *Turkey* 73 C8
Pumlumon Fawr, *U.K.* 13 E4
Puná, I., *Ecuador* 124 D2
Punakha, *Bhutan* 67 F16
Punasar, *India* 68 F5
Punata, *Bolivia* 124 G5
Punch, *India* 69 C6
Punch →, *Pakistan* 68 C5
Punda Maria, *S. Africa* 89 C5
Pune, *India* 66 K8
P'ungsan, *N. Korea* 57 D15
Pungue, Ponte de, *Mozam.* 87 F3
Puning, *China* 59 F11
Punjab □, *India* 68 D7
Punjab □, *Pakistan* 68 E6
Puno, *Peru* 124 G4
Punpun →, *India* 69 G11
Punta Alta, *Argentina* 128 D4
Punta Arenas, *Chile* 128 G2
Punta de Díaz, *Chile* 126 B1
Punta Gorda, *Belize* 119 D7
Punta Gorda, *U.S.A.* 109 M5
Punta Prieta, *Mexico* 118 B2
Punta Prima, *Spain* 37 B11
Punta Umbría, *Spain* 35 H4
Puntarenas, *Costa Rica* 120 E3
Punto Fijo, *Venezuela* 124 A4
Punxsatawney, *U.S.A.* 110 F6
Puqi, *China* 59 C9
Puquio, *Peru* 124 F4
Pur →, *Russia* 50 C8
Purace, Vol., *Colombia* 124 C3
Puračić, *Bos.-H.* 42 F3
Puralia = Puruliya, *India* 69 H12
Puranpur, *India* 69 E9
Purbeck, Isle of, *U.K.* 13 G6
Purcell, *U.S.A.* 113 H6
Purcell Mts., *Canada* 104 D5
Puri, *India* 67 K14
Purmerend, *Neths.* 17 B4
Purnia, *India* 69 G12
Pursat = Pouthisat, *Cambodia* 64 F4
Purukcahu, *Indonesia* 62 E4
Puruliya, *India* 69 H12
Purus →, *Brazil* 122 D4
Puruvesi, *Finland* 46 B5
Purvis, *U.S.A.* 113 K10
Pŭrvomay, *Bulgaria* 41 D9
Purwa, *India* 69 F9
Purwakarta, *Indonesia* 63 G12
Purwodadi, *Indonesia* 63 G14
Purwokerto, *Indonesia* 63 G13
Puryŏng, *N. Korea* 57 C15
Pusa, *India* 69 G11
Pusan, *S. Korea* 57 G15
Pushkin, *Russia* 46 C6
Pushkino, *Moskva, Russia* 46 D9
Pushkino, *Saratov, Russia* 48 E8
Püspökladány, *Hungary* 42 C6
Pustoshka, *Russia* 46 D5
Puszczykowo, *Poland* 45 F3
Putahow L., *Canada* 105 B8
Putao, *Burma* 67 F20
Putaruru, *N.Z.* 91 H5
Putbus, *Germany* 24 A9
Putian, *China* 59 E12
Putignano, *Italy* 31 B10
Puting, Tanjung, *Indonesia* 62 E4
Putlitz, *Germany* 24 B8
Putna, *Romania* 43 C10
Putna →, *Romania* 43 E12
Putnam, *U.S.A.* 111 E13
Putnok, *Hungary* 42 B5
Putorana, Gory, *Russia* 51 C10
Puttalam, *Sri Lanka* 66 Q11
Puttgarden, *Germany* 24 A7
Püttlingen, *Germany* 25 F2
Putumayo →, *S. Amer.* 122 D4
Putuo, *China* 59 C14
Putussibau, *Indonesia* 62 D4
Puvirnituq, *Canada* 101 B12
Puy-de-Dôme, *France* 20 C6
Puy-de-Dôme □, *France* 20 C7
Puy-l'Évêque, *France* 20 D5
Puyallup, *U.S.A.* 116 C4
Puyang, *China* 56 G8
Puylaurens, *France* 20 E6
Pūzeh Rīg, *Iran* 71 E8
Pwani □, *Tanzania* 86 D4
Pweto, *Dem. Rep. of the Congo* 87 D2
Pwllheli, *U.K.* 12 E3
Pyana →, *Russia* 48 C8
Pyapon, *Burma* 67 L19
Pyasina →, *Russia* 51 B9
Pyatigorsk, *Russia* 49 H6
Pyatykhatky, *Ukraine* 47 H7
Pydna, *Greece* 40 F6
Pyè, *Burma* 67 K19
Pyetrikaw, *Belarus* 47 F5
Pyhäjoki, *Finland* 8 D21
Pyinmana, *Burma* 67 K20
Pyla, C., *Cyprus* 36 E12
Pymatuning Reservoir, *U.S.A.* 110 E4
Pyŏktong, *N. Korea* 57 D13
Pyŏnggang, *N. Korea* 57 E14
P'yŏngt'aek, *S. Korea* 57 F14
P'yŏngyang, *N. Korea* 57 E13
Pyote, *U.S.A.* 113 K3
Pyramid L., *U.S.A.* 114 G4
Pyramid Pk., *U.S.A.* 117 J10
Pyramids, *Egypt* 80 J7
Pyrénées, *Europe* 20 F4
Pyrénées-Atlantiques □, *France* 20 E3
Pyrénées-Orientales □, *France* 20 F6
Pyryatyn, *Ukraine* 47 G7
Pyrzyce, *Poland* 45 E1
Pyskowice, *Poland* 45 H5
Pytalovo, *Russia* 46 D4
Pyu, *Burma* 67 K20
Pyzdry, *Poland* 45 F4

Q

Qaanaaq, *Greenland* 4 B4
Qabirri →, *Azerbaijan* 49 K8
Qachasnek, *S. Africa* 89 E4
Qa'el Jafr, *Jordan* 75 E5
Qa'emābād, *Iran* 71 D9
Qā'emshahr, *Iran* 71 B7
Qagan Nur, *China* 56 C8
Qahar Youyi Zhongqi, *China* 56 D7
Qahremānshahr = Bākhtarān, *Iran* 70 C5
Qaidam Pendi, *China* 60 C4
Qajarīyeh, *Iran* 71 D6
Qala, Ras il, *Malta* 36 C1
Qala-i-Jadid = Spīn Búldak, *Afghan.* 68 D2
Qala Viala, *Pakistan* 68 D2
Qala Yangi, *Afghan.* 68 B2
Qal'at al Akhḑar, *Si. Arabia* 70 E3
Qal'at Dīzah, *Iraq* 70 B5
Qal'at Şaliḩ, *Iraq* 70 D5
Qal'at Sukkar, *Iraq* 70 D5
Qalyûb, *Egypt* 80 H7
Qamani'tuaq = Baker Lake, *Canada* 100 B10
Qamdo, *China* 58 B1
Qamruddin Karez, *Pakistan* 68 D3
Qandahār, *Afghan.* 66 D4
Qandahār □, *Afghan.* 66 D4
Qapān, *Iran* 71 B7
Qapshaghay, *Kazakstan* 50 E8
Qaqortoq, *Greenland* 101 B6
Qâra, *Egypt* 80 B2
Qara Qash →, *India* 69 B8
Qarabutaq, *Kazakstan* 50 E7
Qaraçala, *Azerbaijan* 49 L9
Qaraghandy, *Kazakstan* 50 E8
Qārah, *Si. Arabia* 70 D4
Qarataū, *Kazakstan* 50 E8
Qarataū, *Kazakstan* 50 E7
Qardud, *Sudan* 81 E2
Qareh →, *Iran* 70 B5
Qareh Tekān, *Iran* 71 B6
Qarqan He →, *China* 60 C3
Qarqaraly, *Kazakstan* 50 E8
Qarrasa, *Sudan* 81 E3
Qarshi, *Uzbekistan* 50 F7
Qartabā, *Lebanon* 75 A4
Qaryat al Gharab, *Iraq* 70 D5
Qaryat al 'Ulyā, *Si. Arabia* 70 E5
Qasr 'Amra, *Jordan* 70 D3
Qaşr-e Qand, *Iran* 71 E9
Qasr Farâfra, *Egypt* 80 B2
Qatanā, *Syria* 75 B5
Qatar ■, *Asia* 71 E6
Qatlīsh, *Iran* 71 B8
Qattâra, *Egypt* 80 A2
Qattâra, Munkhafed el, *Egypt* 80 B2
Qattâra Depression = Qattâra, Munkhafed el, *Egypt* 80 B2
Qawām al Ḩamzah, *Iraq* 70 D5
Qāyen, *Iran* 71 C8
Qazaqstan = Kazakstan ■, *Asia* 50 E7
Qazimämmäd, *Azerbaijan* 49 K9
Qazvin, *Iran* 71 B6
Qeissan, *Sudan* 81 E3
Qena, *Egypt* 80 B3
Qena, W. →, *Egypt* 80 B3
Qeqertarsuaq, *Greenland* 101 B5
Qeqertarsuaq, *Greenland* 4 C5
Qeshlāq, *Iran* 70 C5
Qeshm, *Iran* 71 E8
Qeys, *Iran* 71 E7
Qezel Owzen →, *Iran* 71 B6
Qezi'ot, *Israel* 75 E3
Qi Xian, *China* 56 G8
Qian Gorlos, *China* 57 B13
Qian Xian, *China* 56 G5
Qiancheng, *China* 58 D7
Qianjiang, *Guangxi Zhuangzu, China* 58 F7
Qianjiang, *Hubei, China* 59 B9
Qianjiang, *Sichuan, China* 58 C7
Qianshan, *China* 59 B11
Qianwei, *China* 58 C4
Qianxi, *China* 58 D6
Qianyang, *Hunan, China* 59 D8
Qianyang, *Shaanxi, China* 56 G4
Qianyang, *Zhejiang, China* 59 B12
Qiaojia, *China* 58 D4
Qichun, *China* 59 B10
Qidong, *Hunan, China* 59 D9
Qidong, *Jiangsu, China* 59 B13
Qijiang, *China* 58 C6
Qikiqtarjuaq, *Canada* 101 B13
Qila Safed, *Pakistan* 66 E2
Qila Saifullāh, *Pakistan* 68 D3
Qilian Shan, *China* 60 C4
Qimen, *China* 59 C11
Qin He →, *China* 56 G7
Qin Jiang →, *Guangxi Zhuangzu, China* 58 F7
Qin Jiang →, *Jiangxi, China* 59 D10
Qin Ling = Qinling Shandi, *China* 56 H5
Qin'an, *China* 56 G3
Qing Xian, *China* 56 E9
Qingcheng, *China* 57 F9
Qingdao, *China* 57 F11
Qingfeng, *China* 56 G8
Qinghai □, *China* 60 C4
Qinghai Hu, *China* 60 C5
Qinghecheng, *China* 57 D13
Qinghemen, *China* 57 D11
Qingjian, *China* 56 F6
Qingjiang = Huaiyin, *China* 57 H10
Qingliu, *China* 59 D11
Qinglong, *China* 58 E5
Qingping, *China* 58 D6
Qingpu, *China* 59 B13
Qingshui, *China* 56 G4
Qingshuihe, *China* 56 E6
Qingtian, *China* 59 C13
Qingtongxia Shuiku, *China* 56 F3
Qingxi, *China* 58 D7
Qingxu, *China* 56 F7
Qingyang, *Anhui, China* 59 B11
Qingyang, *Gansu, China* 56 F4
Qingyi Jiang →, *China* 58 C4
Qingyuan, *Guangdong, China* 59 F9
Qingyuan, *Liaoning, China* 57 C13
Qingyuan, *Zhejiang, China* 59 D12
Qingyun, *China* 57 F9
Qingzhen, *China* 58 D6
Qinhuangdao, *China* 57 E10
Qinling Shandi, *China* 56 H5
Qinshui, *China* 56 G7
Qinyang = Jiyuan, *China* 56 G7
Qinyuan, *China* 56 F7
Qinzhou, *China* 58 G7
Qionghai, *China* 64 C8
Qionglai, *China* 58 B4
Qionglai Shan, *China* 58 B4
Qiongzhou Haixia, *China* 64 B8
Qiqihar, *China* 51 E13
Qirāīya, W. →, *Egypt* 75 E3
Qiryat Ata, *Israel* 75 C4
Qiryat Gat, *Israel* 75 D3
Qiryat Mal'akhi, *Israel* 75 D3
Qiryat Shemona, *Israel* 75 B4
Qiryat Yam, *Israel* 75 C4
Qishan, *China* 56 G4
Qitai, *China* 60 B3
Qiubei, *China* 58 E5
Qixia, *China* 57 F11
Qiyang, *China* 59 D8
Qızılağac Körfäzi, *Azerbaijan* 71 B6
Qojūr, *Iran* 70 B5
Qom, *Iran* 71 C6
Qomolangma Feng = Everest, Mt., *Nepal* 69 E12
Qomsheh, *Iran* 71 D6
Qoraqalpoghistan □, *Uzbekistan* 50 E6
Qorveh, *Iran* 73 E12
Qostanay, *Kazakstan* 50 D7
Qoţūr, *Iran* 73 C11
Qu Jiang →, *China* 58 B6
Qu Xian, *China* 58 B6
Quabbin Reservoir, *U.S.A.* 111 D12
Quairading, *Australia* 93 F2
Quakenbrück, *Germany* 24 C3
Quakertown, *U.S.A.* 111 F9
Qualicum Beach, *Canada* 104 D4
Quambatook, *Australia* 95 F3
Quambone, *Australia* 95 E4
Quamby, *Australia* 94 C3
Quan Long = Ca Mau, *Vietnam* 65 H5
Quanah, *U.S.A.* 113 H5
Quang Ngai, *Vietnam* 64 E7
Quang Tri, *Vietnam* 64 D6
Quang Yen, *Vietnam* 58 G6
Quannan, *China* 59 E10
Quantock Hills, *U.K.* 13 F4
Quanzhou, *Fujian, China* 59 E12
Quanzhou, *Guangxi Zhuangzu, China* 59 E8
Qu'Appelle, *Canada* 105 C8
Quaqtaq, *Canada* 101 B13
Quaraí, *Brazil* 126 C4
Quarré-les-Tombes, *France* 19 E11
Quarteira, *Portugal* 35 H2
Quartu Sant'Élena, *Italy* 30 C2
Quartzsite, *U.S.A.* 117 M12
Quatsino Sd., *Canada* 104 C3
Quba, *Azerbaijan* 49 K9
Qūchān, *Iran* 71 B8
Queanbeyan, *Australia* 95 F4
Québec, *Canada* 103 C5
Québec □, *Canada* 103 C6
Quedlinburg, *Germany* 24 D7
Queen Alexandra Ra., *Antarctica* 5 E11
Queen Charlotte City, *Canada* 104 C2
Queen Charlotte Is., *Canada* 104 C2
Queen Charlotte Sd., *Canada* 104 C3
Queen Charlotte Strait, *Canada* 104 C3
Queen Elizabeth Is., *Canada* 98 B10
Queen Elizabeth Nat. Park, *Uganda* 86 C3
Queen Mary Land, *Antarctica* 5 D7
Queen Maud G., *Canada* 100 B9
Queen Maud Land, *Antarctica* 5 D3
Queen Maud Mts., *Antarctica* 5 E13
Queens Chan., *Australia* 92 C4
Queenscliff, *Australia* 95 F3
Queensland □, *Australia* 94 C3
Queenstown, *Australia* 94 G4
Queenstown, *N.Z.* 91 L2
Queenstown, *S. Africa* 88 E4
Queets, *U.S.A.* 116 C2
Queguay Grande →, *Uruguay* 126 C4
Queimadas, *Brazil* 125 F11
Quelimane, *Mozam.* 87 F4
Quellón, *Chile* 128 E2
Quelpart = Cheju do, *S. Korea* 57 H14
Queluz, *Portugal* 35 G1
Quemado, *N. Mex., U.S.A.* 115 J9
Quemado, *Tex., U.S.A.* 113 L4
Quemoy = Chinmen, *Taiwan* 59 E13
Quemú-Quemú, *Argentina* 126 D3
Quequén, *Argentina* 126 D4
Querétaro, *Mexico* 118 C4
Querétaro □, *Mexico* 118 C5
Querfurt, *Germany* 24 D7
Quérigut, *France* 20 F6
Querqueville, *France* 18 C5
Quesada, *Spain* 35 H7
Queshan, *China* 56 H8
Quesnel, *Canada* 104 C4
Quesnel →, *Canada* 104 C4
Quesnel L., *Canada* 104 C4
Questa, *U.S.A.* 115 H11
Questembert, *France* 18 E4
Quetico Prov. Park, *Canada* 102 C1
Quetta, *Pakistan* 68 D2
Quezaltenango, *Guatemala* 120 D1
Quezon City, *Phil.* 61 D4
Qufār, *Si. Arabia* 70 E4
Qui Nhon, *Vietnam* 64 F7
Quibaxe, *Angola* 84 F2
Quibdo, *Colombia* 124 B3
Quiberon, *France* 18 E3
Quiberon, Presqu'île de, *France* 18 E3
Quickborn, *Germany* 24 B5
Quiet L., *Canada* 104 A2
Quiindy, *Paraguay* 126 B4
Quila, *Mexico* 118 C3
Quilán, C., *Chile* 128 E2
Quilcene, *U.S.A.* 116 C4
Quilimarí, *Chile* 126 C1
Quilino, *Argentina* 126 C3
Quill Lakes, *Canada* 105 C8
Quillabamba, *Peru* 124 F4
Quillagua, *Chile* 126 A2
Quillaicillo, *Chile* 126 C1
Quillan, *France* 20 F6
Quillota, *Chile* 126 C1
Quilmes, *Argentina* 126 C4
Quilon, *India* 66 Q10
Quilpie, *Australia* 95 D3
Quilpué, *Chile* 126 C1
Quilua, *Mozam.* 87 F4
Quimilí, *Argentina* 126 B3
Quimper, *France* 18 E2
Quimperlé, *France* 18 E3
Quinault →, *U.S.A.* 116 C2
Quincy, *Calif., U.S.A.* 116 F6
Quincy, *Fla., U.S.A.* 109 K3
Quincy, *Ill., U.S.A.* 112 F9
Quincy, *Mass., U.S.A.* 111 D14
Quincy, *Wash., U.S.A.* 114 C4
Quines, *Argentina* 126 C2
Quinga, *Mozam.* 87 F5
Quingey, *France* 19 E12
Quinns Rocks, *Australia* 93 F2
Quintana de la Serena, *Spain* 35 G5
Quintana Roo □, *Mexico* 119 D7
Quintanar de la Orden, *Spain* 35 F7
Quintanar de la Sierra, *Spain* 32 D2
Quintanar del Rey, *Spain* 33 F3
Quintero, *Chile* 126 C1
Quintin, *France* 18 D4
Quinto, *Spain* 32 D4
Quípar →, *Spain* 33 G3
Quirihue, *Chile* 126 D1
Quirindi, *Australia* 95 E5
Quirinópolis, *Brazil* 125 G8
Quiroga, *Spain* 34 C3
Quissac, *France* 21 E8
Quissanga, *Mozam.* 87 E5
Quissico, *Mozam.* 89 C5
Quitilipi, *Argentina* 126 B3
Quitman, *U.S.A.* 109 K4
Quito, *Ecuador* 124 D3
Quixadá, *Brazil* 125 D11
Quixaxe, *Mozam.* 87 F5
Qujing, *China* 58 E4
Qulan, *Kazakstan* 50 E8
Qul'ân, Jazâ'ir, *Egypt* 70 E2
Qumbu, *S. Africa* 89 E4
Quneitra, *Syria* 75 B4
Qŭnghirot, *Uzbekistan* 50 E6
Qu'nyido, *China* 58 B2
Quoin I., *Australia* 92 B4
Quoin Pt., *S. Africa* 88 E2
Quorn, *Australia* 95 E2
Qŭqon, *Uzbekistan* 50 E8
Qurein, *Sudan* 81 E3
Qurnat as Sawdā', *Lebanon* 75 A5
Qûs, *Egypt* 80 B3
Qusar, *Azerbaijan* 49 K9
Quşaybā', *Si. Arabia* 70 E4
Qusaybah, *Iraq* 70 C4
Quseir, *Egypt* 70 E2
Qūshchī, *Iran* 70 B5
Quthing, *Lesotho* 89 E4
Qūţīābād, *Iran* 71 C6
Quwo, *China* 56 G6
Quyang, *China* 56 E8
Quynh Nhai, *Vietnam* 64 B4
Quyon, *Canada* 111 A8
Quzhou, *China* 59 C12
Quzi, *China* 56 F4
Qvareli, *Georgia* 49 K7
Qytet Stalin = Kuçovë, *Albania* 40 F3
Qyzylorda, *Kazakstan* 50 E7

R

Ra, Ko, *Thailand* 65 H2
Raab, *Austria* 26 C6
Raahe, *Finland* 8 D21
Raalte, *Neths.* 17 B6
Raasay, *U.K.* 14 D2
Raasay, Sd. of, *U.K.* 14 D2
Rab, *Croatia* 29 D11
Raba, *Indonesia* 63 F5
Rába →, *Hungary* 42 C2
Raba →, *Poland* 45 H7
Rabaçal →, *Portugal* 34 D3
Rabah, *Nigeria* 83 C6
Rabai, *Kenya* 86 C4
Rabak, *Sudan* 81 E3
Rabastens, *France* 20 E5
Rabastens-de-Bigorre, *France* 20 E4
Rabat, *Malta* 36 D1
Rabat, *Morocco* 78 B4
Rabaul, *Papua N. G.* 96 H7
Rābigh, *Si. Arabia* 74 C2
Rabka, *Poland* 45 J6
Râbniţa, *Moldova* 43 C14
Rābor, *Iran* 71 D8
Rača, *Serbia, Yug.* 40 B4
Răcăciuni, *Romania* 43 D11
Răcăşdia, *Romania* 42 F6
Racconigi, *Italy* 28 D4
Race, C., *Canada* 103 C9
Rach Gia, *Vietnam* 65 G5
Rachid, *Mauritania* 82 B2
Raciąż, *Poland* 45 F7
Racibórz, *Poland* 45 H5
Racine, *U.S.A.* 108 D2
Rackerby, *U.S.A.* 116 F5
Radama, Nosy, *Madag.* 89 A8
Radama, Saikanosy, *Madag.* 89 A8
Radan, *Serbia, Yug.* 40 D5
Rădăuţi, *Romania* 43 C10
Rădăuţi-Prut, *Romania* 43 B11
Radbuza →, *Czech Rep.* 26 B6
Radcliff, *U.S.A.* 108 G3
Radeberg, *Germany* 24 D9
Radebeul, *Germany* 24 D9
Radeče, *Slovenia* 29 B12
Radekhiv, *Ukraine* 47 G3
Radekhov = Radekhiv, *Ukraine* 47 G3
Radenthein, *Austria* 26 E6
Radew →, *Poland* 44 D2
Radford, *U.S.A.* 108 G5
Radhanpur, *India* 68 H4
Radhwa, Jabal, *Si. Arabia* 70 E3
Radika →, *Macedonia* 40 E4
Radisson, *Qué., Canada* 102 B4
Radisson, *Sask., Canada* 105 C7
Radium Hot Springs, *Canada* 104 C5
Radlje ob Dravi, *Slovenia* 29 B12

Radnevo, Bulgaria 41 D9
Radnice, Czech Rep. 26 B6
Radnor Forest, U.K. 13 E4
Radolfzell, Germany 25 H4
Radom, Poland 45 G8
Radomir, Bulgaria 40 D6
Radomka →, Poland 45 G8
Radomsko, Poland 45 G6
Radomyshl, Ukraine 47 G5
Radomyśl Wielki, Poland 45 H8
Radoszyce, Poland 45 G7
Radoviš, Macedonia 40 E6
Radovljica, Slovenia 29 B11
Radstadt, Austria 26 D6
Radstock, C., Australia 95 E1
Răducăneni, Romania 43 D12
Raduša, Macedonia 40 D5
Radviliškis, Lithuania 9 J20
Radville, Canada 105 D8
Raḍwá, J., Si. Arabia 80 C4
Radymno, Poland 45 J9
Radzanów, Poland 45 F7
Radziejów, Poland 45 F5
Radzyń Chełmiński, Poland 44 E5
Radzyń Podlaski, Poland 45 G9
Rae, Canada 104 A5
Rae Bareli, India 69 F9
Rae Isthmus, Canada 101 B11
Raeren, Belgium 17 D6
Raeside, L., Australia 93 E3
Raetihi, N.Z. 91 H5
Rafaela, Argentina 126 C3
Rafah, Gaza Strip 75 D3
Rafai, C.A.R. 86 B1
Raffadali, Italy 30 E6
Raffili, Sudan 81 F2
Rafḥā, Si. Arabia 70 D4
Rafsanjān, Iran 71 D8
Raft Pt., Australia 92 C3
Râgâ, Sudan 81 F2
Raga →, Sudan 81 F2
Ragachow, Belarus 47 F6
Ragag, Sudan 81 E1
Ragama, Sri Lanka 66 R11
Ragged, Mt., Australia 93 F3
Raghunathpalli, India 69 H11
Raghunathpur, India 69 H12
Raglan, N.Z. 91 G5
Ragusa, Italy 31 F7
Raha, Indonesia 63 E6
Rahad, Nahr ed →, Sudan 81 E3
Rahaeng = Tak, Thailand 64 D2
Rahatgarh, India 69 H8
Rahden, Germany 24 C4
Raheita, Eritrea 81 E5
Rahimyar Khan, Pakistan 68 E4
Rāhjerd, Iran 71 C6
Rahon, India 68 D7
Raichur, India 66 L10
Raiganj, India 69 G13
Raigarh, India 67 J13
Raijua, Indonesia 63 F6
Raikot, India 68 D6
Railton, Australia 94 G4
Rainbow Lake, Canada 104 B5
Rainier, U.S.A. 116 D4
Rainier, Mt., U.S.A. 116 D5
Rainy L., Canada 105 D10
Rainy River, Canada 105 D10
Raippaluoto, Finland 8 E19
Raipur, India 67 J12
Ra'is, Si. Arabia 80 C4
Raisen, India 68 H8
Raisio, Finland 9 F20
Raj Nandgaon, India 67 J12
Raj Nilgiri, India 69 J12
Raja, Ujung, Indonesia 62 D1
Raja Ampat, Kepulauan, Indonesia 63 E7
Rajahmundry, India 67 L12
Rajang →, Malaysia 62 D4
Rajanpur, Pakistan 68 E4
Rajapalaiyam, India 66 Q10
Rajasthan □, India 68 F5
Rajasthan Canal, India 68 F5
Rajauri, India 69 C6
Rajgarh, Mad. P., India 68 G7
Rajgarh, Raj., India 68 F7
Rajgarh, Raj., India 68 E6
Rajgir, India 69 G11
Rajgród, Poland 44 E9
Rajkot, India 68 H4
Rajmahal Hills, India 69 G12
Rajpipla, India 66 J8
Rajpur, India 68 H6
Rajpura, India 68 D7
Rajshahi, Bangla. 67 G16
Rajshahi □, Bangla. 69 G13
Rajula, India 68 J4
Rakaia, N.Z. 91 K4
Rakaia →, N.Z. 91 K4
Rakan, Ra's, Qatar 71 E6
Rakaposhi, Pakistan 69 A6
Rakata, Pulau, Indonesia 62 F3
Rakhiv, Ukraine 47 H3
Rakhni, Pakistan 68 D3
Rakhni →, Pakistan 68 E3
Rakitnoye, Russia 54 B7
Rakitovo, Bulgaria 41 E8
Rakoniewice, Poland 45 F3
Rakops, Botswana 88 C3
Rakovica, Croatia 29 D12
Rakovník, Czech Rep. 26 A6
Rakovski, Bulgaria 41 D8
Rakvere, Estonia 9 G22
Raleigh, U.S.A. 109 H6
Ralja, Serbia, Yug. 40 B4
Ralls, U.S.A. 113 J4
Ralston, U.S.A. 110 E8
Ram →, Canada 104 A4
Rām Allāh, West Bank 75 D4
Rama, Nic. 120 D3
Ramacca, Italy 31 E7
Ramakona, India 69 J8
Ramales de la Victoria, Spain 34 B7
Raman, Thailand 65 J3
Ramanathapuram, India 66 Q11
Ramanetaka, B. de, Madag. 89 A8
Ramanujganj, India 69 H10
Ramat Gan, Israel 75 C3
Ramatlhabama, S. Africa 88 D4
Ramban, India 69 C6
Rambervillers, France 19 D13
Rambipuji, Indonesia 63 H15
Rambouillet, France 19 D8
Rame Hd., Australia 95 F4
Ramechhap, Nepal 69 F12
Ramenskoye, Russia 46 E10
Ramganga →, India 69 F8
Ramgarh, Bihar, India 69 H11
Ramgarh, Raj., India 68 F6
Ramgarh, Raj., India 68 F4
Rāmhormoz, Iran 71 D6
Ramīān, Iran 71 B7
Ramingining, Australia 94 A2
Ramla, Israel 75 D3
Ramlu, Eritrea 81 E5
Râmna →, Romania 43 E12
Ramnad = Ramanathapuram, India 66 Q11
Ramnagar, Jammu & Kashmir, India 69 C6
Ramnagar, Ut. P., India 69 E8
Ramnäs, Sweden 10 E10
Râmnicu Sărat, Romania 43 E12
Râmnicu Vâlcea, Romania 43 E9
Ramon, Russia 47 G10
Ramona, U.S.A. 117 M10
Ramonville-St-Agne, France 20 E5
Ramore, Canada 102 C3
Ramos →, Nigeria 83 D6
Ramotswa, Botswana 88 C4
Rampur, H.P., India 68 D7
Rampur, Mad. P., India 68 H5
Rampur, Ut. P., India 69 E8
Rampur Hat, India 69 G12
Rampura, India 68 G6
Ramrama Tola, India 69 J8
Ramree I., Burma 67 K19
Rāmsar, Iran 71 B6
Ramsey, U.K. 12 C3
Ramsey, U.S.A. 111 E10
Ramsey L., Canada 102 C3
Ramsgate, U.K. 13 F9
Ramsjö, Sweden 10 B9
Ramstein, Germany 25 F3
Ramtek, India 66 J11
Ramvik, Sweden 10 B11
Rana Pratap Sagar Dam, India 68 G6
Ranaghat, India 69 H13
Ranahu, Pakistan 68 G3
Ranau, Malaysia 62 C5
Rancagua, Chile 126 C1
Rance →, France 18 D5
Rancheria →, Canada 104 A3
Ranchester, U.S.A. 114 D10
Ranchi, India 69 H11
Rancho Cucamonga, U.S.A. 117 L9
Randalstown, U.K. 15 B5
Randan, France 19 F10
Randazzo, Italy 31 E7
Randers, Denmark 11 H4
Randers Fjord, Denmark 11 H4
Randfontein, S. Africa 89 D4
Randle, U.S.A. 116 D5
Randolph, Mass., U.S.A. 111 D13
Randolph, N.Y., U.S.A. 110 D6
Randolph, Utah, U.S.A. 114 F8
Randolph, Vt., U.S.A. 111 C12
Randsburg, U.S.A. 117 K9
Råne älv →, Sweden 8 D20
Rangae, Thailand 65 J3
Rangaunu B., N.Z. 91 F4
Rangeley, U.S.A. 111 B14
Rangeley L., U.S.A. 111 B14
Rangely, U.S.A. 114 F9
Ranger, U.S.A. 113 J5
Rangia, India 67 F17
Rangiora, N.Z. 91 K4
Rangitaiki →, N.Z. 91 G6
Rangitata →, N.Z. 91 K3
Rangkasbitung, Indonesia 63 G12
Rangon →, Burma 67 L20
Rangoon, Burma 67 L20
Rangpur, Bangla. 67 G16
Rangsit, Thailand 64 F3
Ranibennur, India 66 M9
Raniganj, Ut. P., India 69 F9
Raniganj, W. Bengal, India 67 H15
Ranikhet, India 69 E8
Raniwara, India 66 G8
Rāniyah, Iraq 70 B5
Ranka, India 69 H10
Ranken →, Australia 94 C2
Rankin, U.S.A. 113 K4
Rankin Inlet, Canada 100 B10
Rankins Springs, Australia 95 E4
Rankweil, Austria 26 D2
Rannoch, L., U.K. 14 E4
Rannoch Moor, U.K. 14 E4
Ranobe, Helodranon' i, Madag. 89 C7
Ranohira, Madag. 89 C8
Ranomafana, Toamasina, Madag. 89 B8
Ranomafana, Toliara, Madag. 89 C8
Ranomena, Madag. 89 C8
Ranong, Thailand 65 H2
Ranotsara Nord, Madag. 89 C8
Rānsa, Iran 71 C6
Ransiki, Indonesia 63 E8
Rantabe, Madag. 89 B8
Rantauprapat, Indonesia 62 D1
Rantemario, Indonesia 63 E5
Rantoul, U.S.A. 108 E1
Ranum, Denmark 11 H3
Ranyah, W. →, Si. Arabia 80 C5
Raon l'Étape, France 19 D13
Raoping, China 59 F11
Raoyang, China 56 E8
Rapa, Pac. Oc. 97 K13
Rapallo, Italy 28 D6
Rapar, India 68 H4
Rāpch, Iran 71 E8
Raper, C., Canada 101 B13
Rapid City, U.S.A. 112 D3
Rapid River, U.S.A. 108 C2
Rapla, Estonia 9 G21
Rapti →, India 69 F10
Rapu Rapu I., Phil. 61 E6
Raqaba ez Zarqa →, Sudan 81 F2
Raquette →, U.S.A. 111 B10
Raquette Lake, U.S.A. 111 C10
Rarotonga, Cook Is. 97 K12
Ra's al 'Ayn, Syria 70 B4
Ra's al Khaymah, U.A.E. 71 E7
Râs el Mâ, Mali 82 B4
Ras Ghârib, Egypt 80 B3
Ras Mallap, Egypt 80 B3
Rasca, Pta. de la, Canary Is. 37 G3
Răşcani, Moldova 43 C12
Raseiniai, Lithuania 9 J20
Rashad, Sudan 81 E3
Rashîd, Egypt 80 H7
Rashîd, Masabb, Egypt 80 H7
Rashmi, India 68 G6
Rasht, Iran 71 B6
Rasi Salai, Thailand 64 E5
Raška, Serbia, Yug. 40 C4
Râsnov, Romania 43 E10
Rason L., Australia 93 E3
Raşova, Romania 43 F12
Rasovo, Bulgaria 40 C7
Rasra, India 69 G10
Rasskazovo, Russia 48 D5
Rast, Romania 43 G8
Rastatt, Germany 25 G4
Rastede, Germany 24 B4
Rastolița, Romania 43 D9
Rasul, Pakistan 68 C5
Raszków, Poland 45 G4
Rat Buri, Thailand 64 F2
Rat Islands, U.S.A. 100 C1
Rat L., Canada 105 B9
Ratangarh, India 68 E6
Rätansbyn, Sweden 10 B8
Raṭāwī, Iraq 70 D5
Rath, India 69 G8
Rath Luirc, Ireland 15 D3
Rathdrum, Ireland 15 D5
Rathenow, Germany 24 C8
Rathkeale, Ireland 15 D3
Rathlin I., U.K. 15 A5
Rathmelton, Ireland 15 A4
Ratibor = Racibórz, Poland 45 H5
Rätikon, Austria 26 D2
Ratingen, Germany 24 D2
Ratlam, India 68 H6
Ratnagiri, India 66 L8
Ratodero, Pakistan 68 F3
Raton, U.S.A. 113 G2
Rattaphum, Thailand 65 J3
Ratten, Austria 26 D8
Rattray Hd., U.K. 14 D7
Rättvik, Sweden 10 D9
Ratz, Mt., Canada 104 B2
Ratzeburg, Germany 24 B6
Raub, Malaysia 65 L3
Rauch, Argentina 126 D4
Raudales de Malpaso, Mexico 119 D6
Raufarhöfn, Iceland 8 C6
Raufoss, Norway 9 F14
Raukumara Ra., N.Z. 91 H6
Rauma, Finland 9 F19
Raurkela, India 69 H11
Rausu-Dake, Japan 54 B12
Răut →, Moldova 43 C14
Rava-Ruska, Poland 47 G2
Rava Russkaya = Rava-Ruska, Poland 47 G2
Ravalli, U.S.A. 114 C6
Ravānsar, Iran 70 C5
Ravanusa, Italy 30 E6
Rāvar, Iran 71 D8
Ravena, U.S.A. 111 D11
Ravenna, Italy 29 D9
Ravenna, Nebr., U.S.A. 112 E5
Ravenna, Ohio, U.S.A. 110 E3
Ravensburg, Germany 25 H5
Ravenshoe, Australia 94 B4
Ravensthorpe, Australia 93 F3
Ravenswood, Australia 94 C4
Ravenswood, U.S.A. 108 F5
Ravi →, Pakistan 68 D4
Ravna Gora, Croatia 29 C11
Ravna Reka, Serbia, Yug. 40 B5
Ravne na Koroškem, Slovenia 29 B11
Rawa Mazowiecka, Poland 45 G7
Rawalpindi, Pakistan 68 C5
Rawāndūz, Iraq 70 B5
Rawang, Malaysia 65 L3
Rawene, N.Z. 91 F4
Rawicz, Poland 45 G3
Rawka →, Poland 45 F7
Rawlinna, Australia 93 F4
Rawlins, U.S.A. 114 F10
Rawlinson Ra., Australia 93 D4
Rawson, Argentina 128 E3
Raxaul, India 69 F11
Ray, U.S.A. 112 A3
Ray, C., Canada 103 C8
Rayadurg, India 66 M10
Rayagada, India 67 K13
Raychikhinsk, Russia 51 E13
Rāyen, Iran 71 D8
Rayleigh, U.K. 13 F8
Raymond, Canada 104 D6
Raymond, Calif., U.S.A. 116 H7
Raymond, N.H., U.S.A. 111 C13
Raymond, Wash., U.S.A. 116 D3
Raymondville, U.S.A. 113 M6
Raymore, Canada 105 C8
Rayón, Mexico 118 B2
Rayong, Thailand 64 F3
Rayville, U.S.A. 113 J9
Raz, Pte. du, France 18 D2
Razan, Iran 71 C6
Ražana, Serbia, Yug. 40 B3
Ražanj, Serbia, Yug. 40 C5
Razdelna, Bulgaria 41 C11
Razdel'naya = Rozdilna, Ukraine 47 J6
Razdolnoye, Russia 54 C5
Razdolnoye, Ukraine 47 K7
Razeh, Iran 71 C6
Razgrad, Bulgaria 41 C10
Razim, Lacul, Romania 43 F14
Razlog, Bulgaria 40 E7
Razmak, Pakistan 68 C3
Ré, Î. de, France 20 B2
Reading, U.K. 13 F7
Reading, U.S.A. 111 F9
Reading □, U.K. 13 F7
Realicó, Argentina 126 D3
Réalmont, France 20 E6
Ream, Cambodia 65 G4
Reata, Mexico 118 B4
Reay Forest, U.K. 14 C4
Rebais, France 19 D10
Rebi, Indonesia 63 F8
Rebiana, Libya 79 D10
Rebun-Tō, Japan 54 B10
Recanati, Italy 29 E10
Recaş, Romania 42 E6
Recco, Italy 28 D6
Recherche, Arch. of the, Australia 93 F3
Rechna Doab, Pakistan 68 D5
Rechytsa, Belarus 47 F6
Recife, Brazil 125 E12
Recklinghausen, Germany 17 C7
Reconquista, Argentina 126 B4
Recreo, Argentina 126 B2
Recz, Poland 45 E2
Red →, La., U.S.A. 113 K9
Red →, N. Dak., U.S.A. 100 C10
Red Bank, U.S.A. 111 F10
Red Bay, Canada 103 B8
Red Bluff, U.S.A. 114 F2
Red Bluff L., U.S.A. 113 K3
Red Cliffs, Australia 95 E3
Red Cloud, U.S.A. 112 E5
Red Creek, U.S.A. 111 C8
Red Deer, Canada 104 C6
Red Deer →, Alta., Canada 105 C7
Red Deer →, Man., Canada 105 C8
Red Deer L., Canada 105 C8
Red Hook, U.S.A. 111 E11
Red Indian L., Canada 103 C8
Red L., Canada 105 C10
Red Lake, Canada 105 C10
Red Lake Falls, U.S.A. 112 B6
Red Lake Road, Canada 105 C10
Red Lodge, U.S.A. 114 D9
Red Mountain, U.S.A. 117 K9
Red Oak, U.S.A. 112 E7
Red Rock, Canada 102 C2
Red Rock, L., U.S.A. 112 E8
Red Rocks Pt., Australia 93 F4
Red Sea, Asia 74 C2
Red Slate Mt., U.S.A. 116 H8
Red Sucker L., Canada 102 B1
Red Tower Pass = Turnu Roşu, P., Romania 43 E9
Red Wing, U.S.A. 112 C8
Reda, Poland 44 D5
Redang, Malaysia 62 C2
Redange, Lux. 17 E5
Redcar, U.K. 12 C6
Redcar & Cleveland □, U.K. 12 C7
Redcliff, Canada 105 C6
Redcliffe, Australia 95 D5
Redcliffe, Mt., Australia 93 E3
Reddersburg, S. Africa 88 D4
Redding, U.S.A. 114 F2
Redditch, U.K. 13 E6
Redfield, U.S.A. 112 C5
Redford, U.S.A. 111 B11
Redkino, Russia 46 D9
Redlands, U.S.A. 117 M9
Redmond, Oreg., U.S.A. 114 D3
Redmond, Wash., U.S.A. 116 C4
Redon, France 18 E4
Redonda, Antigua 121 C7
Redondela, Spain 34 C2
Redondo, Portugal 35 G3
Redondo Beach, U.S.A. 117 M8
Redruth, U.K. 13 G2
Redvers, Canada 105 D8
Redwater, Canada 104 C6
Redwood, U.S.A. 111 B9
Redwood City, U.S.A. 116 H4
Redwood Falls, U.S.A. 112 C7
Redwood National Park, U.S.A. 114 F1
Ree, L., Ireland 15 C3
Reed, L., Canada 105 C8
Reed City, U.S.A. 108 D3
Reedley, U.S.A. 116 J7
Reedsburg, U.S.A. 112 D9
Reedsport, U.S.A. 114 E1
Reedsville, U.S.A. 110 F7
Reefton, N.Z. 91 K3
Rees, Germany 24 D2
Reese →, U.S.A. 114 F5
Refahiye, Turkey 73 C8
Reftele, Sweden 11 G7
Refugio, U.S.A. 113 L6
Rega →, Poland 44 D2
Regalbuto, Italy 31 E7
Regen, Germany 25 G9
Regen →, Germany 25 F8
Regensburg, Germany 25 F8
Regenstauf, Germany 25 F8
Reggâne = Zaouiet Reggâne, Algeria 78 C6
Reggello, Italy 29 E8
Réggio di Calábria, Italy 31 D8
Réggio nell'Emília, Italy 28 D7
Reghin, Romania 43 D9
Regina, Canada 105 C8
Regina Beach, Canada 105 C8
Registro, Brazil 127 A6
Reguengos de Monsaraz, Portugal 35 G3
Rehar →, India 69 H10
Rehli, India 69 H8
Rehoboth, Namibia 88 C2
Rehovot, Israel 75 D3
Reichenbach, Germany 24 E8
Reid, Australia 93 F4
Reidsville, U.S.A. 109 G6
Reigate, U.K. 13 F7
Reillo, Spain 32 F3
Reims, France 19 C11
Reina Adelaida, Arch., Chile 128 G2
Reinbek, Germany 24 B6
Reindeer →, Canada 105 B8
Reindeer I., Canada 105 C9
Reindeer L., Canada 105 B8
Reinga, C., N.Z. 91 F4
Reinosa, Spain 34 B6
Reitz, S. Africa 89 D4
Reivilo, S. Africa 88 D3
Rejaf, Sudan 81 G3
Rejmyre, Sweden 11 F9
Rejowiec Fabryczny, Poland 45 G10
Reka →, Slovenia 29 C11
Rekovac, Serbia, Yug. 40 C5
Reliance, Canada 105 A7
Rémalard, France 18 D7
Remarkable, Mt., Australia 95 E2
Rembang, Indonesia 63 G14
Remedios, Panama 120 E3
Remeshk, Iran 71 E8
Remetea, Romania 43 D10
Remich, Lux. 17 E6
Remiremont, France 19 D13
Remo, Ethiopia 81 F5
Remontnoye, Russia 49 G6
Remoulins, France 21 E8
Remscheid, Germany 17 C7
Ren Xian, China 56 F8
Rende, Italy 31 C9
Rendína, Greece 38 B3
Rendsburg, Germany 24 A5
Renfrew, Canada 102 C4
Renfrewshire □, U.K. 14 F4
Rengat, Indonesia 62 E2
Rengo, Chile 126 C1
Renhua, China 59 E9
Renhuai, China 58 D6
Reni, Ukraine 47 K5
Renk, Sudan 81 E3
Renmark, Australia 95 E3
Rennell Sd., Canada 104 C2
Renner Springs, Australia 94 B1
Rennes, France 18 D5
Rennie L., Canada 105 A7
Reno, U.S.A. 116 F7
Reno →, Italy 29 D9
Renovo, U.S.A. 110 E7
Renqiu, China 56 E9
Rens, Denmark 11 K3
Renshou, China 58 C5
Rensselaer, Ind., U.S.A. 108 E2
Rensselaer, N.Y., U.S.A. 111 D11
Rentería, Spain 32 B3
Renton, U.S.A. 116 C4
Réo, Burkina Faso 82 C4
Reocín, Spain 34 B6
Reotipur, India 69 G10
Répcelak, Hungary 42 C2
Republic, Mo., U.S.A. 113 G8
Republic, Wash., U.S.A. 114 B4
Republican →, U.S.A. 112 F6
Repulse Bay, Canada 101 B11
Requena, Peru 124 E4
Requena, Spain 33 F3
Réquista, France 20 D6
Reşadiye = Datça, Turkey 39 E9
Reşadiye, Turkey 72 B7
Reşadiye Yarımadası, Turkey 39 E9
Resavica, Serbia, Yug. 40 B5
Resen, Macedonia 40 E5
Reserve, U.S.A. 115 K9
Resht = Rasht, Iran 71 B6

Resistencia, *Argentina* 126 B4
Reşiţa, *Romania* 42 E6
Resko, *Poland* 44 E2
Resolution I., *Canada* 101 B13
Resolution I., *N.Z.* 91 L1
Ressano Garcia, *Mozam.* 89 D5
Reston, *Canada* 105 D8
Reszel, *Poland* 44 D8
Retalhuleu, *Guatemala* 120 D1
Retenue, L. de, *Dem. Rep. of the Congo* 87 E2
Retezat, Munţii, *Romania* 42 E8
Retford, *U.K.* 12 D7
Rethel, *France* 19 C11
Rethem, *Germany* 24 C5
Réthímnon, *Greece* 36 D6
Réthímnon □, *Greece* 36 D6
Reti, *Pakistan* 68 E3
Retiche, Alpi, *Switz.* 25 J6
Retiers, *France* 18 E5
Retortillo, *Spain* 34 E4
Retournac, *France* 21 C8
Rétság, *Hungary* 42 C4
Réunion ■, *Ind. Oc.* 77 J9
Reus, *Spain* 32 D6
Reuterstadt Stavenhagen, *Germany* 24 B8
Reutlingen, *Germany* 25 G5
Reutte, *Austria* 26 D3
Reval = Tallinn, *Estonia* 9 G21
Revel, *France* 20 E6
Revelganj, *India* 69 G11
Revelstoke, *Canada* 104 C5
Reventazón, *Peru* 124 E2
Revigny-sur-Ornain, *France* 19 D11
Revillagigedo, Is. de, *Pac. Oc.* 118 D2
Revin, *France* 19 C11
Revúca, *Slovak Rep.* 27 C13
Revuè →, *Mozam.* 87 F3
Rewa, *India* 69 G9
Rewari, *India* 68 E7
Rexburg, *U.S.A.* 114 E8
Rey, *Iran* 71 C6
Rey, I. del, *Panama* 120 E4
Rey Malabo, *Eq. Guin.* 83 E6
Reyðarfjörður, *Iceland* 8 D6
Reyes, Pt., *U.S.A.* 116 H3
Reyhanlı, *Turkey* 72 D7
Reykjahlið, *Iceland* 8 D5
Reykjanes, *Iceland* 8 E2
Reykjavík, *Iceland* 8 D3
Reynolds Ra., *Australia* 92 D5
Reynoldsville, *U.S.A.* 110 E6
Reynosa, *Mexico* 119 B5
Rēzekne, *Latvia* 9 H22
Rezina, *Moldova* 43 C13
Rezovo, *Bulgaria* 41 D12
Rezvān, *Iran* 71 E8
Rgotina, *Serbia, Yug.* 40 B6
Rhamnus, *Greece* 38 C6
Rhayader, *U.K.* 13 E4
Rheda-Wiedenbrück, *Germany* 24 D4
Rhede, *Germany* 24 D2
Rhein →, *Europe* 17 C6
Rhein-Main-Donau-Kanal, *Germany* 25 F7
Rheinbach, *Germany* 24 E2
Rheine, *Germany* 24 C3
Rheinfelden, *Germany* 25 H3
Rheinhessen-Pfalz □, *Germany* 25 F3
Rheinland-Pfalz □, *Germany* 25 E2
Rheinsberg, *Germany* 24 B8
Rhin = Rhein →, *Europe* 17 C6
Rhine = Rhein →, *Europe* 17 C6
Rhinebeck, *U.S.A.* 111 E11
Rhineland-Palatinate = Rheinland-Pfalz □, *Germany* 25 E2
Rhinelander, *U.S.A.* 112 C10
Rhinns Pt., *U.K.* 14 F2
Rhino Camp, *Uganda* 86 B3
Rhir, Cap, *Morocco* 78 B4
Rho, *Italy* 28 C6
Rhode Island □, *U.S.A.* 111 E13
Rhodes = Ródhos, *Greece* 36 C10
Rhodesia = Zimbabwe ■, *Africa* 87 F3
Rhodope Mts. = Rhodopi Planina, *Bulgaria* 41 E8
Rhodopi Planina, *Bulgaria* 41 E8
Rhön, *Germany* 24 E5
Rhondda, *U.K.* 13 F4
Rhondda Cynon Taff □, *U.K.* 13 F4
Rhône □, *France* 21 C8
Rhône →, *France* 21 E8
Rhône-Alpes □, *France* 21 C9
Rhum, *U.K.* 14 E2
Rhyl, *U.K.* 12 D4
Ri-Aba, *Eq. Guin.* 83 E6
Riachão, *Brazil* 125 E9
Riangnom, *Sudan* 81 F3
Riaño, *Spain* 34 C6
Rians, *France* 21 E9
Riansáres →, *Spain* 35 F7
Riasi, *India* 69 C6
Riau □, *Indonesia* 62 D2
Riau, Kepulauan, *Indonesia* 62 D2
Riau Arch. = Riau, Kepulauan, *Indonesia* 62 D2
Riaza, *Spain* 34 D7
Riaza →, *Spain* 34 D7
Riba de Saelices, *Spain* 32 E2
Riba-Roja de Turia, *Spain* 33 F4
Ribadavia, *Spain* 34 C2
Ribadeo, *Spain* 34 B3
Ribadesella, *Spain* 34 B5
Ribado, *Nigeria* 83 D7
Ribao, *Cameroon* 83 D7
Ribas = Ribes de Freser, *Spain* 32 C7
Ribas do Rio Pardo, *Brazil* 125 H8
Ribble →, *U.K.* 12 D5
Ribe, *Denmark* 11 J2
Ribe Amtskommune □, *Denmark* 11 J2
Ribeauvillé, *France* 19 D14
Ribécourt-Dreslincourt, *France* 19 C9
Ribeira = Santa Uxía, *Spain* 34 C2
Ribeira Brava, *Madeira* 37 D2
Ribeirão Prêto, *Brazil* 127 A6
Ribemont, *France* 19 C10
Ribera, *Italy* 30 E6
Ribérac, *France* 20 C4
Riberalta, *Bolivia* 124 F5
Ribes de Freser, *Spain* 32 C7
Ribnica, *Slovenia* 29 C11
Ribnitz-Damgarten, *Germany* 24 A8
Ričany, *Czech Rep.* 26 B7
Riccarton, *N.Z.* 91 K4
Riccia, *Italy* 31 A7
Riccione, *Italy* 29 E9
Rice, *U.S.A.* 117 L12
Rice L., *Canada* 110 B6
Rice Lake, *U.S.A.* 112 C9
Rich, C., *Canada* 110 B4
Richard Toll, *Senegal* 82 B1
Richards Bay, *S. Africa* 89 D5
Richardson →, *Canada* 105 B6
Richardson Lakes, *U.S.A.* 108 C10
Richardson Springs, *U.S.A.* 116 F5
Riche, C., *Australia* 93 F2
Richelieu, *France* 18 E7
Richey, *U.S.A.* 112 B2
Richfield, *U.S.A.* 115 G8
Richfield Springs, *U.S.A.* 111 D10
Richford, *U.S.A.* 111 B12
Richibucto, *Canada* 103 C7
Richland, *Ga., U.S.A.* 109 J3
Richland, *Wash., U.S.A.* 114 C4
Richland Center, *U.S.A.* 112 D9
Richlands, *U.S.A.* 108 G5
Richmond, *Australia* 94 C3
Richmond, *N.Z.* 91 J4
Richmond, *U.K.* 12 C6
Richmond, *Calif., U.S.A.* 116 H4
Richmond, *Ind., U.S.A.* 108 F3
Richmond, *Ky., U.S.A.* 108 G3
Richmond, *Mich., U.S.A.* 110 D2
Richmond, *Mo., U.S.A.* 112 F8
Richmond, *Tex., U.S.A.* 113 L7
Richmond, *Utah, U.S.A.* 114 F8
Richmond, *Va., U.S.A.* 108 G7
Richmond, *Vt., U.S.A.* 111 B12
Richmond Hill, *Canada* 110 C5
Richmond Ra., *Australia* 95 D5
Richwood, *U.S.A.* 108 F5
Ricla, *Spain* 32 D3
Ridder = Leninogorsk, *Kazakstan* 50 D9
Riddlesburg, *U.S.A.* 110 F6
Ridgecrest, *U.S.A.* 117 K9
Ridgefield, *Conn., U.S.A.* 111 E11
Ridgefield, *Wash., U.S.A.* 116 E4
Ridgeland, *U.S.A.* 109 J5
Ridgetown, *Canada* 102 D3
Ridgewood, *U.S.A.* 111 F10
Ridgway, *U.S.A.* 110 E6
Riding Mountain Nat. Park, *Canada* 105 C9
Ridley, Mt., *Australia* 93 F3
Riebeek-Oos, *S. Africa* 88 E4
Ried, *Austria* 26 C6
Riedlingen, *Germany* 25 G5
Riedstadt, *Germany* 25 F4
Rienza →, *Italy* 29 B8
Riesa, *Germany* 24 D9
Riesi, *Italy* 31 E7
Riet →, *S. Africa* 88 D3
Rietavas, *Lithuania* 44 C8
Rietbron, *S. Africa* 88 E3
Rietfontein, *Namibia* 88 C3
Rieti, *Italy* 29 F9
Rieupeyroux, *France* 20 D6
Riez, *France* 21 E10
Riffe L., *U.S.A.* 116 D4
Rifle, *U.S.A.* 114 G10
Rift Valley □, *Kenya* 86 B4
Rīga, *Latvia* 9 H21
Riga, G. of, *Latvia* 9 H20
Rigacikun, *Nigeria* 83 C6
Rīgān, *Iran* 71 D8
Rīgas Jūras Līcis = Riga, G. of, *Latvia* 9 H20
Rigaud, *Canada* 111 A10
Rigby, *U.S.A.* 114 E8
Rīgestān, *Afghan.* 66 D4
Riggins, *U.S.A.* 114 D5
Rignac, *France* 20 D6
Rigolet, *Canada* 103 B8
Rihand Dam, *India* 69 G10
Riihimäki, *Finland* 9 F21
Riiser-Larsen-halvøya, *Antarctica* 5 C4
Rijau, *Nigeria* 83 C6
Rijeka, *Croatia* 29 C11
Rijeka Crnojevića, *Montenegro, Yug.* 40 D3
Rijssen, *Neths.* 17 B6
Rike, *Ethiopia* 81 E4
Rikuzentakada, *Japan* 54 E10
Rila, *Bulgaria* 40 D7
Rila Planina, *Bulgaria* 40 D7
Riley, *U.S.A.* 114 E4
Rima →, *Nigeria* 83 C6
Rimah, Wadi ar →, *Si. Arabia* 70 E4
Rimavská Sobota, *Slovak Rep.* 27 C13
Rimbey, *Canada* 104 C6
Rimbo, *Sweden* 10 E12
Rimersburg, *U.S.A.* 110 E5
Rimforsa, *Sweden* 11 F9
Rimi, *Nigeria* 83 C6
Rímini, *Italy* 29 D9
Rimouski, *Canada* 103 C6
Rimrock, *U.S.A.* 116 D5
Rinca, *Indonesia* 63 F5
Rincón de la Victoria, *Spain* 35 J6
Rincón de Romos, *Mexico* 118 C4
Rinconada, *Argentina* 126 A2
Rind →, *India* 69 G9
Ringarum, *Sweden* 11 F10
Ringas, *India* 68 F6
Ringe, *Denmark* 11 J4
Ringim, *Nigeria* 83 C6
Ringkøbing, *Denmark* 11 H2
Ringkøbing Amtskommune □, *Denmark* 11 H2
Ringkøbing Fjord, *Denmark* 11 H2
Ringsjön, *Sweden* 11 J7
Ringsted, *Denmark* 11 J5
Ringvassøy, *Norway* 8 B18
Ringwood, *U.S.A.* 111 E10
Rinía, *Greece* 39 D7
Rinjani, *Indonesia* 62 F5
Rinteln, *Germany* 24 C5
Río, Punta del, *Spain* 33 J2
Rio Branco, *Brazil* 124 E5
Río Branco, *Uruguay* 127 C5
Río Bravo del Norte →, *Mexico* 119 B5
Rio Brilhante, *Brazil* 127 A5
Rio Claro, *Brazil* 127 A6
Rio Claro, *Trin. & Tob.* 121 D7
Río Colorado, *Argentina* 128 D4
Río Cuarto, *Argentina* 126 C3
Rio das Pedras, *Mozam.* 89 C6
Rio de Janeiro, *Brazil* 127 A7
Rio de Janeiro □, *Brazil* 127 A7
Rio do Sul, *Brazil* 127 B6
Río Gallegos, *Argentina* 128 G3
Rio Grande = Grande, Rio →, *U.S.A.* 113 N6
Río Grande, *Argentina* 128 G3
Rio Grande, *Brazil* 127 C5
Río Grande, *Mexico* 118 C4
Río Grande, *Nic.* 120 D3
Rio Grande City, *U.S.A.* 113 M5
Río Grande de Santiago →, *Mexico* 118 C3
Rio Grande do Norte □, *Brazil* 125 E11
Rio Grande do Sul □, *Brazil* 127 C5
Río Hato, *Panama* 120 E3
Río Lagartos, *Mexico* 119 C7
Rio Largo, *Brazil* 125 E11
Rio Maior, *Portugal* 35 F2
Rio Marina, *Italy* 28 F7
Río Mulatos, *Bolivia* 124 G5
Río Muni = Mbini □, *Eq. Guin.* 84 D2
Rio Negro, *Brazil* 127 B6
Rio Pardo, *Brazil* 127 C5
Río Rancho, *U.S.A.* 115 J10
Río Segundo, *Argentina* 126 C3
Río Tercero, *Argentina* 126 C3
Rio Tinto, *Portugal* 34 D2
Rio Verde, *Brazil* 125 G8
Río Verde, *Mexico* 119 C5
Rio Vista, *U.S.A.* 116 G5
Ríobamba, *Ecuador* 124 D3
Ríohacha, *Colombia* 124 A4
Riom, *France* 20 C7
Riom-ès-Montagnes, *France* 20 C6
Rion-des-Landes, *France* 20 E3
Rionero in Vúlture, *Italy* 31 B8
Rioni →, *Georgia* 49 J5
Riós, *Spain* 34 D3
Ríosucio, *Colombia* 124 B3
Riou L., *Canada* 105 B7
Rioz, *France* 19 E13
Ripatransone, *Italy* 29 F10
Ripley, *Canada* 110 B3
Ripley, *Calif., U.S.A.* 117 M12
Ripley, *N.Y., U.S.A.* 110 D5
Ripley, *Tenn., U.S.A.* 113 H10
Ripley, *W. Va., U.S.A.* 108 F5
Ripoll, *Spain* 32 C7
Ripon, *U.K.* 12 C6
Ripon, *Calif., U.S.A.* 116 H5
Ripon, *Wis., U.S.A.* 108 D1
Riposto, *Italy* 31 E8
Risan, *Montenegro, Yug.* 40 D2
Riscle, *France* 20 E3
Rishā', W. ar →, *Si. Arabia* 70 E5
Rishiri-Tō, *Japan* 54 B10
Rishon le Ẕiyyon, *Israel* 75 D3
Risle →, *France* 18 C7
Rison, *U.S.A.* 113 J8
Risør, *Norway* 9 G13
Rita Blanca Cr. →, *U.S.A.* 113 H3
Riti, *Nigeria* 83 D6
Ritter, Mt., *U.S.A.* 116 H7
Rittman, *U.S.A.* 110 F3
Ritzville, *U.S.A.* 114 C4
Riva del Garda, *Italy* 28 C7
Riva Lígure, *Italy* 28 E4
Rivadavia, *Buenos Aires, Argentina* 126 D3
Rivadavia, *Mendoza, Argentina* 126 C2
Rivadavia, *Salta, Argentina* 126 A3
Rivadavia, *Chile* 126 B1
Rivarolo Canavese, *Italy* 28 C4
Rivas, *Nic.* 120 D2
Rive-de-Gier, *France* 21 C8
River Cess, *Liberia* 82 D3
River Jordan, *Canada* 116 B2
Rivera, *Argentina* 126 D3
Rivera, *Uruguay* 127 C4
Riverbank, *U.S.A.* 116 H6
Riverdale, *U.S.A.* 116 J7
Riverhead, *U.S.A.* 111 F12
Riverhurst, *Canada* 105 C7
Rivers, *Canada* 105 C8
Rivers □, *Nigeria* 83 E6
Rivers Inlet, *Canada* 104 C3
Riversdale, *S. Africa* 88 E3
Riverside, *U.S.A.* 117 M9
Riverton, *Australia* 95 E2
Riverton, *Canada* 105 C9
Riverton, *N.Z.* 91 M2
Riverton, *U.S.A.* 114 E9
Riverton Heights, *U.S.A.* 116 C4
Rives, *France* 21 C9
Rivesaltes, *France* 20 F6
Riviera, *U.S.A.* 117 K12
Riviera di Levante, *Italy* 28 D6
Riviera di Ponente, *Italy* 28 D5
Rivière-au-Renard, *Canada* 103 C7
Rivière-du-Loup, *Canada* 103 C6
Rivière-Pentecôte, *Canada* 103 C6
Rivière-Pilote, *Martinique* 121 D7
Rivière St. Paul, *Canada* 103 B8
Rivne, *Ukraine* 47 G4
Rívoli, *Italy* 28 C4
Rivoli B., *Australia* 95 F3
Rixheim, *France* 19 E14
Riyadh = Ar Riyāḍ, *Si. Arabia* 70 E5
Rize, *Turkey* 73 B9
Rizhao, *China* 57 G10
Rizokarpaso, *Cyprus* 36 D13
Rizzuto, C., *Italy* 31 D10
Rjukan, *Norway* 9 G13
Ro, *Greece* 39 E11
Roa, *Spain* 34 D7
Road Town, *Br. Virgin Is.* 121 C7
Roan Plateau, *U.S.A.* 114 G9
Roanne, *France* 19 F11
Roanoke, *Ala., U.S.A.* 109 J3
Roanoke, *Va., U.S.A.* 108 G6
Roanoke →, *U.S.A.* 109 H7
Roanoke I., *U.S.A.* 109 H8
Roanoke Rapids, *U.S.A.* 109 G7
Roatán, *Honduras* 120 C2
Robāt Sang, *Iran* 71 C8
Robbins I., *Australia* 94 G4
Róbbio, *Italy* 28 C5
Robe →, *Australia* 92 D2
Röbel, *Germany* 24 B8
Robert Lee, *U.S.A.* 113 K4
Robertsdale, *U.S.A.* 110 F6
Robertsganj, *India* 69 G10
Robertson, *S. Africa* 88 E2
Robertson I., *Antarctica* 5 C18
Robertson Ra., *Australia* 92 D3
Robertsport, *Liberia* 82 D2
Robertstown, *Australia* 95 E2
Roberval, *Canada* 103 C5
Robeson Chan., *Greenland* 4 A4
Robesonia, *U.S.A.* 111 F8
Robi, *Ethiopia* 81 F4
Robinson, *U.S.A.* 108 F2
Robinson →, *Australia* 94 B2
Robinson Ra., *Australia* 93 E2
Robinvale, *Australia* 95 E3
Robledo, *Spain* 33 G2
Roblin, *Canada* 105 C8
Roboré, *Bolivia* 124 G7
Robson, *Canada* 104 D5
Robson, Mt., *Canada* 104 C5
Robstown, *U.S.A.* 113 M6
Roca, C. da, *Portugal* 35 G1
Roca Partida, I., *Mexico* 118 D2
Rocamadour, *France* 20 D5
Rocas, I., *Brazil* 125 D12
Rocca San Casciano, *Italy* 29 D8
Roccadáspide, *Italy* 31 B8
Roccastrada, *Italy* 29 F8
Roccella Iónica, *Italy* 31 D9
Rocha, *Uruguay* 127 C5
Rochdale, *U.K.* 12 D5
Rochechouart, *France* 20 C4
Rochefort, *Belgium* 17 D5
Rochefort, *France* 20 C3
Rochefort-en-Terre, *France* 18 E4
Rochelle, *U.S.A.* 112 E10
Rocher River, *Canada* 104 A6
Rocheservière, *France* 18 F5
Rochester, *U.K.* 13 F8
Rochester, *Ind., U.S.A.* 108 E2
Rochester, *Minn., U.S.A.* 112 C8
Rochester, *N.H., U.S.A.* 111 C14
Rochester, *N.Y., U.S.A.* 110 C7
Rociu, *Romania* 43 F10
Rock →, *Canada* 104 A3
Rock Creek, *U.S.A.* 110 E4
Rock Falls, *U.S.A.* 112 E10
Rock Hill, *U.S.A.* 109 H5
Rock Island, *U.S.A.* 112 E9
Rock Rapids, *U.S.A.* 112 D6
Rock Sound, *Bahamas* 120 B4
Rock Springs, *Mont., U.S.A.* 114 C10
Rock Springs, *Wyo., U.S.A.* 114 F9
Rock Valley, *U.S.A.* 112 D6
Rockall, *Atl. Oc.* 6 D3
Rockdale, *Tex., U.S.A.* 113 K6
Rockdale, *Wash., U.S.A.* 116 C5
Rockefeller Plateau, *Antarctica* 5 E14
Rockford, *U.S.A.* 112 D10
Rockglen, *Canada* 105 D7
Rockhampton, *Australia* 94 C5
Rockingham, *Australia* 93 F2
Rockingham, *U.S.A.* 109 H6
Rockingham B., *Australia* 94 B4
Rocklake, *U.S.A.* 112 A5
Rockland, *Canada* 111 A9
Rockland, *Idaho, U.S.A.* 114 E7
Rockland, *Maine, U.S.A.* 109 C11
Rockland, *Mich., U.S.A.* 112 B10
Rocklin, *U.S.A.* 116 G5
Rockmart, *U.S.A.* 109 H3
Rockport, *Mass., U.S.A.* 111 D14
Rockport, *Mo., U.S.A.* 112 E7
Rockport, *Tex., U.S.A.* 113 L6
Rocksprings, *U.S.A.* 113 K4
Rockville, *Conn., U.S.A.* 111 E12
Rockville, *Md., U.S.A.* 108 F7
Rockwall, *U.S.A.* 113 J6
Rockwell City, *U.S.A.* 112 D7
Rockwood, *Canada* 110 C4
Rockwood, *Maine, U.S.A.* 109 C11
Rockwood, *Tenn., U.S.A.* 109 H3
Rocky Ford, *U.S.A.* 112 F3
Rocky Gully, *Australia* 93 F2
Rocky Harbour, *Canada* 103 C8
Rocky Island L., *Canada* 102 C3
Rocky Lane, *Canada* 104 B5
Rocky Mount, *U.S.A.* 109 H7
Rocky Mountain House, *Canada* 104 C6
Rocky Mountain National Park, *U.S.A.* 114 F11
Rocky Mts., *N. Amer.* 114 G10
Rocky Point, *Namibia* 88 B2
Rocroi, *France* 19 C11
Rod, *Pakistan* 66 E3
Rødby, *Denmark* 11 K5
Rødbyhavn, *Denmark* 11 K5
Roddickton, *Canada* 103 B8
Rødding, *Denmark* 11 J3
Rödeby, *Sweden* 11 H9
Rødekro, *Denmark* 11 J3
Rodenkirchen, *Germany* 24 B4
Rodez, *France* 20 D6
Rodholívas, *Greece* 40 F7
Rodhópi □, *Greece* 41 E9
Rodhopoú, *Greece* 36 D5
Ródhos, *Greece* 36 C10
Rodi Gargánico, *Italy* 29 G12
Rodna, *Romania* 43 C9
Rodnei, Munţii, *Romania* 43 C9
Rodney, *Canada* 110 D3
Rodney, C., *N.Z.* 91 G5
Rodniki, *Russia* 48 B5
Rodonit, Kepi i, *Albania* 40 E3
Rodriguez, *Ind. Oc.* 3 E13
Roe →, *U.K.* 15 A5
Roebling, *U.S.A.* 111 F10
Roebourne, *Australia* 92 D2
Roebuck B., *Australia* 92 C3
Roermond, *Neths.* 17 C6
Roes Welcome Sd., *Canada* 101 B11
Roeselare, *Belgium* 17 D3
Rogachev = Ragachow, *Belarus* 47 F6
Rogačica, *Serbia, Yug.* 40 B3
Rogagua, L., *Bolivia* 124 F5
Rogaška Slatina, *Slovenia* 29 B12
Rogatec, *Slovenia* 29 B12
Rogatica, *Bos.-H.* 42 G4
Rogatyn, *Ukraine* 47 H3
Rogdhia, *Greece* 36 D7
Rogers, *U.S.A.* 113 G7
Rogers City, *U.S.A.* 108 C4
Rogersville, *Canada* 103 C6
Roggan →, *Canada* 102 B4
Roggan L., *Canada* 102 B4
Roggeveldberge, *S. Africa* 88 E3
Roggiano Gravina, *Italy* 31 C9
Rogliano, *France* 21 F13
Rogliano, *Italy* 31 C9
Rogoaguado, L., *Bolivia* 124 F5
Rogoźno, *Poland* 45 F3
Rogue →, *U.S.A.* 114 E1
Rohan, *France* 18 D4
Róhda, *Greece* 36 A3
Rohnert Park, *U.S.A.* 116 G4
Rohri, *Pakistan* 68 F3
Rohri Canal, *Pakistan* 68 F3
Rohtak, *India* 68 E7
Roi Et, *Thailand* 64 D4
Roja, *Latvia* 9 H20
Rojas, *Argentina* 126 C3
Rojişte, *Romania* 43 F8
Rojo, C., *Mexico* 119 C5
Rokan →, *Indonesia* 62 D2
Rokel →, *S. Leone* 82 D2
Rokiškis, *Lithuania* 9 J21
Rokitno, *Russia* 47 G8
Rokycany, *Czech Rep.* 26 B6
Rolândia, *Brazil* 127 A5
Rolla, *U.S.A.* 113 G9
Rolleston, *Australia* 94 C4
Rollingstone, *Australia* 94 B4
Rom, *Sudan* 81 F3
Roma, *Australia* 95 D4
Roma, *Italy* 29 G9
Roma, *Sweden* 11 G12
Roma, *U.S.A.* 113 M5
Romain C., *U.S.A.* 109 J6
Romaine, *Canada* 103 B7
Romaine →, *Canada* 103 B7
Roman, *Bulgaria* 40 C7
Roman, *Romania* 43 D11
Roman-Kosh, Gora, *Ukraine* 47 K8
Romanche →, *France* 21 C9
Romang, *Indonesia* 63 F7
Români, *Egypt* 75 E1
Romania ■, *Europe* 43 D10
Romanija, *Bos.-H.* 42 G3
Romano, Cayo, *Cuba* 120 B4
Romanovka = Basarabeasca, *Moldova* 43 D13
Romans-sur-Isère, *France* 21 C9
Romanshorn, *Switz.* 25 H5

Rombari, *Sudan* 81 G3
Romblon, *Phil.* 61 E5
Rome = Roma, *Italy* 29 G9
Rome, *Ga., U.S.A.* 109 H3
Rome, *N.Y., U.S.A.* 111 C9
Rome, *Pa., U.S.A.* 111 E8
Rometta, *Italy* 31 D8
Romilly-sur-Seine, *France* 19 D10
Romney, *U.S.A.* 108 F6
Romney Marsh, *U.K.* 13 F8
Romny, *Ukraine* 47 G7
Rømø, *Denmark* 11 J2
Romodan, *Ukraine* 47 G7
Romodanovo, *Russia* 48 C7
Romont, *Switz.* 25 J2
Romorantin-Lanthenay, *France* 19 E8
Romsdalen, *Norway* 9 E12
Romsey, *U.K.* 13 G6
Ron, *Vietnam* 64 D6
Rona, *U.K.* 14 D3
Ronan, *U.S.A.* 114 C6
Roncador, Cayos, *Caribbean* 120 D3
Roncador, Serra do, *Brazil* 125 F8
Ronciglione, *Italy* 29 F9
Ronco →, *Italy* 29 D9
Ronda, *Spain* 35 J5
Ronda, Serranía de, *Spain* 35 J5
Rondane, *Norway* 9 F13
Rondônia □, *Brazil* 124 F6
Rondonópolis, *Brazil* 125 G8
Rong, Koh, *Cambodia* 65 G4
Rong Jiang →, *China* 58 E7
Rong Xian, *Guangxi Zhuangzu, China* 59 F8
Rong Xian, *Sichuan, China* 58 C5
Rong'an, *China* 58 E7
Rongchang, *China* 58 C5
Ronge, L. la, *Canada* 105 B7
Rongjiang, *China* 58 E7
Rongshui, *China* 58 E7
Rønne, *Denmark* 11 J8
Ronne Ice Shelf, *Antarctica* 5 D18
Ronneby, *Sweden* 11 H9
Ronnebyån →, *Sweden* 11 H9
Rönneshytta, *Sweden* 11 F9
Ronsard, C., *Australia* 93 D1
Ronse, *Belgium* 17 D3
Roodepoort, *S. Africa* 89 D4
Roof Butte, *U.S.A.* 115 H9
Rooiboklaagte →, *Namibia* 88 C3
Roorkee, *India* 68 E7
Roosendaal, *Neths.* 17 C4
Roosevelt, *U.S.A.* 114 F8
Roosevelt →, *Brazil* 122 D4
Roosevelt, Mt., *Canada* 104 B3
Roosevelt I., *Antarctica* 5 D12
Ropczyce, *Poland* 45 H8
Roper →, *Australia* 94 A2
Roper Bar, *Australia* 94 A1
Roque Pérez, *Argentina* 126 D4
Roquefort, *France* 20 D3
Roquemaure, *France* 21 D8
Roquetas de Mar, *Spain* 33 J2
Roquetes, *Spain* 32 E5
Roquevaire, *France* 21 E9
Roraima □, *Brazil* 124 C6
Roraima, Mt., *Venezuela* 122 C4
Røros, *Norway* 9 E14
Rorschach, *Switz.* 25 H5
Rosa, *Zambia* 87 D3
Rosa, L., *Bahamas* 121 B5
Rosa, Monte, *Italy* 28 C4
Rosal de la Frontera, *Spain* 35 H3
Rosalia, *U.S.A.* 114 C5
Rosamond, *U.S.A.* 117 L8
Rosans, *France* 21 D9
Rosario, *Argentina* 126 C3
Rosário, *Brazil* 125 D10
Rosario, *Baja Calif., Mexico* 118 B1
Rosario, *Sinaloa, Mexico* 118 C3
Rosario, *Paraguay* 126 A4
Rosario de la Frontera, *Argentina* 126 B3
Rosario de Lerma, *Argentina* 126 A2
Rosario del Tala, *Argentina* 126 C4
Rosário do Sul, *Brazil* 127 C5
Rosarito, *Mexico* 117 N9
Rosarno, *Italy* 31 D8
Rosas = Roses, *Spain* 32 C8
Roscoe, *U.S.A.* 111 E10
Roscoff, *France* 18 D3
Roscommon, *Ireland* 15 C3
Roscommon □, *Ireland* 15 C3
Roscrea, *Ireland* 15 D4
Rose →, *Australia* 94 A2
Rose Blanche, *Canada* 103 C8
Rose Pt., *Canada* 104 C2
Rose Valley, *Canada* 105 C8
Roseau, *Domin.* 121 C7
Roseau, *U.S.A.* 112 A7
Rosebery, *Australia* 94 G4
Rosebud, *S. Dak., U.S.A.* 112 D4
Rosebud, *Tex., U.S.A.* 113 K6
Roseburg, *U.S.A.* 114 E2
Rosedale, *U.S.A.* 113 J9
Roseland, *U.S.A.* 116 G4
Rosemary, *Canada* 104 C6
Rosenberg, *U.S.A.* 113 L7
Rosendaël, *France* 19 A9
Rosenheim, *Germany* 25 H8
Roses, *Spain* 32 C8
Roses, G. de, *Spain* 32 C8
Roseto degli Abruzzi, *Italy* 29 F11
Rosetown, *Canada* 105 C7
Rosetta = Rashîd, *Egypt* 80 H7
Roseville, *Calif., U.S.A.* 116 G5
Roseville, *Mich., U.S.A.* 110 D2
Rosewood, *Australia* 95 D5
Roshkhvār, *Iran* 71 C8
Rosières-en-Santerre, *France* 19 C9
Rosignano Maríttimo, *Italy* 28 E7
Rosignol, *Guyana* 124 B7
Roşiori de Vede, *Romania* 43 F10
Rositsa, *Bulgaria* 41 C11
Rositsa →, *Bulgaria* 41 C9
Roskilde, *Denmark* 11 J6
Roskilde Amtskommune □, *Denmark* 11 J6
Roskovec, *Albania* 40 F3
Roslavl, *Russia* 46 F7
Rosmaninhal, *Portugal* 34 F3
Rosmead, *S. Africa* 88 E4
Røsnæs, *Denmark* 11 J4
Rosolini, *Italy* 31 F7
Rosporden, *France* 18 E3
Ross, *Australia* 94 G4
Ross, *N.Z.* 91 K3
Ross Béthio, *Mauritania* 82 B1
Ross I., *Antarctica* 5 D11
Ross Ice Shelf, *Antarctica* 5 E12
Ross L., *U.S.A.* 114 B3
Ross-on-Wye, *U.K.* 13 F5
Ross River, *Australia* 94 C1
Ross River, *Canada* 104 A2
Ross Sea, *Antarctica* 5 D11
Rossall Pt., *U.K.* 12 D4
Rossan Pt., *Ireland* 15 B3
Rossano, *Italy* 31 C9
Rossburn, *Canada* 105 C8
Rosseau, *Canada* 110 A5
Rosseau L., *Canada* 110 A5
Rosses, The, *Ireland* 15 A3
Rossignol, L., *Canada* 102 B5
Rossignol Res., *Canada* 103 D6
Rossland, *Canada* 104 D5
Rosslare, *Ireland* 15 D5
Rosslau, *Germany* 24 D8
Rosso, *Mauritania* 82 B1
Rosso, C., *France* 21 F12
Rossosh, *Russia* 47 G10
Røssvatnet, *Norway* 8 D16
Røst, *Norway* 8 C15
Rosthern, *Canada* 105 C7
Rostock, *Germany* 24 A8
Rostov, *Don, Russia* 47 J10
Rostov, *Yaroslavl, Russia* 46 D10
Rostrenen, *France* 18 D3
Roswell, *Ga., U.S.A.* 109 H3
Roswell, *N. Mex., U.S.A.* 113 J2
Rota, *Spain* 35 J4
Rotan, *U.S.A.* 113 J4
Rotenburg, *Hessen, Germany* 24 E5
Rotenburg, *Niedersachsen, Germany* 24 B5
Roth, *Germany* 25 F7
Rothaargebirge, *Germany* 24 D4
Rothenburg ob der Tauber, *Germany* 25 F6
Rother →, *U.K.* 13 G8
Rotherham, *U.K.* 12 D6
Rothes, *U.K.* 14 D5
Rothesay, *Canada* 103 C6
Rothesay, *U.K.* 14 F3
Roti, *Indonesia* 63 F6
Rotja, Pta., *Spain* 33 G6
Roto, *Australia* 95 E4
Rotondo, Mte., *France* 21 F13
Rotoroa, L., *N.Z.* 91 J4
Rotorua, *N.Z.* 91 H6
Rotorua, L., *N.Z.* 91 H6
Rott →, *Germany* 25 G9
Rottenburg, *Germany* 25 G4
Rottenmann, *Austria* 26 D7
Rotterdam, *Neths.* 17 C4
Rotterdam, *U.S.A.* 111 D10
Rottne, *Sweden* 11 G8
Rottnest I., *Australia* 93 F2
Rottumeroog, *Neths.* 17 A6
Rottweil, *Germany* 25 G4
Rotuma, *Fiji* 96 J9
Roubaix, *France* 19 B10
Roudnice nad Labem, *Czech Rep.* 26 A7
Rouen, *France* 18 C8
Rouergue, *France* 20 D5
Rouillac, *France* 20 C3
Rouleau, *Canada* 105 C8
Round Mountain, *U.S.A.* 114 G5
Round Mt., *Australia* 95 E5
Round Rock, *U.S.A.* 113 K6
Roundup, *U.S.A.* 114 C9
Rousay, *U.K.* 14 B5
Rouses Point, *U.S.A.* 111 B11
Rouseville, *U.S.A.* 110 E5
Roussillon, *Isère, France* 21 C8
Roussillon, *Pyrénées-Or., France* 20 F6
Rouxville, *S. Africa* 88 E4
Rouyn-Noranda, *Canada* 102 C4
Rovaniemi, *Finland* 8 C21
Rovato, *Italy* 28 C7
Rovenki, *Ukraine* 47 H10
Rovereto, *Italy* 28 C8
Rovigo, *Italy* 29 C8
Rovinj, *Croatia* 29 C10
Rovno = Rivne, *Ukraine* 47 G4
Rovnoye, *Russia* 48 E8
Rovuma = Ruvuma →, *Tanzania* 87 E5
Row'ān, *Iran* 71 C6
Rowena, *Australia* 95 D4
Rowley Shoals, *Australia* 92 C2
Roxa, *Guinea-Biss.* 82 C1
Roxas, *Capiz, Phil.* 61 F5
Roxas, *Isabela, Phil.* 61 C4
Roxas, *Mind. Or., Phil.* 61 E4
Roxboro, *U.S.A.* 109 G6
Roxburgh, *N.Z.* 91 L2
Roxbury, *U.S.A.* 110 F7
Roxen, *Sweden* 11 F9
Roy, *Mont., U.S.A.* 114 C9
Roy, *N. Mex., U.S.A.* 113 H2
Roy, *Utah, U.S.A.* 114 F7
Royal Canal, *Ireland* 15 C4
Royal Leamington Spa, *U.K.* 13 E6
Royal Tunbridge Wells, *U.K.* 13 F8
Royan, *France* 20 C2
Roye, *France* 19 C9
Royston, *U.K.* 13 E7
Rožaj, *Montenegro, Yug.* 40 D4
Różan, *Poland* 45 F8
Rozay-en-Brie, *France* 19 D9
Rozdilna, *Ukraine* 47 J6
Rozhyshche, *Ukraine* 47 G3
Rožmitál pod Třemšínem, *Czech Rep.* 26 B6
Rožňava, *Slovak Rep.* 27 C13
Rozogi, *Poland* 44 E8
Rozoy-sur-Serre, *France* 19 C11
Rozzano, *Italy* 28 C6
Rrëshen, *Albania* 40 E3
Rrogozhine, *Albania* 40 E3
Rtanj, *Serbia, Yug.* 40 C5
Rtishchevo, *Russia* 48 D6
Rúa = A Rúa, *Spain* 34 C3
Ruacaná, *Namibia* 88 B1
Ruahine Ra., *N.Z.* 91 H6
Ruapehu, *N.Z.* 91 H5
Ruapuke I., *N.Z.* 91 M2
Ruâq, W. →, *Egypt* 75 F2
Rub' al Khālī, *Si. Arabia* 74 D4
Rubeho Mts., *Tanzania* 86 D4
Rubezhnoye = Rubizhne, *Ukraine* 47 H10
Rubh a' Mhail, *U.K.* 14 F2
Rubha Hunish, *U.K.* 14 D2
Rubha Robhanais = Lewis, Butt of, *U.K.* 14 C2
Rubi, *Spain* 32 D7
Rubicon →, *U.S.A.* 116 G5
Rubicone →, *Italy* 29 D9
Rubik, *Albania* 40 E3
Rubino, *Ivory C.* 82 D4
Rubio, *Venezuela* 124 B4
Rubizhne, *Ukraine* 47 H10
Rubtsovsk, *Russia* 50 D9
Ruby L., *U.S.A.* 114 F6
Ruby Mts., *U.S.A.* 114 F6
Rubyvale, *Australia* 94 C4
Rucheng, *China* 59 E9
Ruciane-Nida, *Poland* 44 E8
Rūd Sar, *Iran* 71 B6
Ruda, *Sweden* 11 G10
Ruda Śląska, *Poland* 45 H5
Rudall, *Australia* 95 E2
Rudall →, *Australia* 92 D3
Rüdersdorf, *Germany* 24 C9
Rudewa, *Tanzania* 87 E3
Rudkøbing, *Denmark* 11 K4
Rudna, *Poland* 45 G3
Rudnik, *Bulgaria* 41 D11
Rudnik, *Poland* 45 H9
Rudnik, *Serbia, Yug.* 40 B4
Rudnya, *Russia* 46 E6
Rudnyy, *Kazakstan* 50 D7
Rudo, *Bos.-H.* 42 G4
Rudolfa, Ostrov, *Russia* 50 A6
Rudolstadt, *Germany* 24 E7
Rudong, *China* 59 A13
Rudozem, *Bulgaria* 41 E8
Rudyard, *U.S.A.* 108 B3
Rue, *France* 19 B8
Rufa'a, *Sudan* 81 E3
Rufiji →, *Tanzania* 86 D4
Rufino, *Argentina* 126 C3
Rufisque, *Senegal* 82 C1
Rufunsa, *Zambia* 87 F2
Rugao, *China* 59 A13
Rugby, *U.K.* 13 E6
Rugby, *U.S.A.* 112 A5
Rügen, *Germany* 24 A9
Rugles, *France* 18 D7
Ruhengeri, *Rwanda* 86 C2
Ruhla, *Germany* 24 E6
Ruhland, *Germany* 24 D9
Ruhnu, *Estonia* 9 H20
Ruhr →, *Germany* 24 D2
Ruhuhu →, *Tanzania* 87 E3
Rui'an, *China* 59 D13
Ruichang, *China* 59 C10
Ruidoso, *U.S.A.* 115 K11
Ruijin, *China* 59 E10
Ruili, *China* 58 E1
Ruivo, Pico, *Madeira* 37 D3
Ruj, *Bulgaria* 40 D6
Rujen, *Macedonia* 40 D6
Rujm Tal'at al Jamā'ah, *Jordan* 75 E4
Ruk, *Pakistan* 68 F3
Rukhla, *Pakistan* 68 C4
Ruki →, *Dem. Rep. of the Congo* 84 E3
Rukwa □, *Tanzania* 86 D3
Rukwa, L., *Tanzania* 86 D3
Rulhieres, C., *Australia* 92 B4
Rum = Rhum, *U.K.* 14 E2
Rum Cay, *Bahamas* 121 B5
Rum Jungle, *Australia* 92 B5
Ruma, *Serbia, Yug.* 42 E4
Rumāḥ, *Si. Arabia* 70 E5
Rumania = Romania ■, *Europe* 43 D10
Rumaylah, *Iraq* 70 D5
Rumbêk, *Sudan* 81 F2
Rumburk, *Czech Rep.* 26 A7
Rumford, *U.S.A.* 109 C10
Rumia, *Poland* 44 D5
Rumilly, *France* 21 C9
Rumoi, *Japan* 54 C10
Rumonge, *Burundi* 86 C2
Rumson, *U.S.A.* 111 F11
Rumuruti, *Kenya* 86 B4
Runan, *China* 56 H8
Runanga, *N.Z.* 91 K3
Runaway, C., *N.Z.* 91 G6
Runcorn, *U.K.* 12 D5
Rundu, *Namibia* 88 B2
Rungwa, *Tanzania* 86 D3
Rungwa →, *Tanzania* 86 D3
Rungwe, *Tanzania* 87 D3
Rungwe, Mt., *Tanzania* 84 F6
Runka, *Nigeria* 83 C6
Runn, *Sweden* 10 D9
Runton Ra., *Australia* 92 D3
Ruokolahti, *Finland* 46 B5
Ruoqiang, *China* 60 C3
Rupa, *India* 67 F18
Rupar, *India* 68 D7
Rupat, *Indonesia* 62 D2
Rupea, *Romania* 43 D10
Rupen →, *India* 68 H4
Rupert, *U.S.A.* 114 E7
Rupert →, *Canada* 102 B4
Rupert B., *Canada* 102 B4
Rupert House = Waskaganish, *Canada* 102 B4
Rupsa, *India* 69 J12
Rur →, *Germany* 24 D1
Rurrenabaque, *Bolivia* 124 F5
Rus →, *Spain* 33 F2
Rusambo, *Zimbabwe* 87 F3
Rusape, *Zimbabwe* 87 F3
Ruschuk = Ruse, *Bulgaria* 41 C9
Ruse, *Bulgaria* 41 C9
Ruse □, *Bulgaria* 41 C10
Ruşeţu, *Romania* 43 F12
Rush, *Ireland* 15 C5
Rushan, *China* 57 F11
Rushden, *U.K.* 13 E7
Rushmore, Mt., *U.S.A.* 112 D3
Rushville, *Ill., U.S.A.* 112 E9
Rushville, *Ind., U.S.A.* 108 F3
Rushville, *Nebr., U.S.A.* 112 D3
Russas, *Brazil* 125 D11
Russell, *Canada* 105 C8
Russell, *Kans., U.S.A.* 112 F5
Russell, *N.Y., U.S.A.* 111 B9
Russell, *Pa., U.S.A.* 110 E5
Russell L., *Man., Canada* 105 B8
Russell L., *N.W.T., Canada* 104 A5
Russellkonda, *India* 67 K14
Russellville, *Ala., U.S.A.* 109 H2
Russellville, *Ark., U.S.A.* 113 H8
Russellville, *Ky., U.S.A.* 109 G2
Rüsselsheim, *Germany* 25 F4
Russi, *Italy* 29 D9
Russia ■, *Eurasia* 51 C11
Russian →, *U.S.A.* 116 G3
Russkoye Ustie, *Russia* 4 B15
Rust, *Austria* 27 D9
Rustam, *Pakistan* 68 B5
Rustam Shahr, *Pakistan* 68 F2
Rustavi, *Georgia* 49 K7
Rustenburg, *S. Africa* 88 D4
Ruston, *U.S.A.* 113 J8
Rutana, *Burundi* 86 C3
Rute, *Spain* 35 H6
Ruteng, *Indonesia* 63 F6
Ruth, *U.S.A.* 110 C2
Rutherford, *U.S.A.* 116 G4
Rutland, *U.S.A.* 111 C12
Rutland □, *U.K.* 13 E7
Rutland Water, *U.K.* 13 E7
Rutledge →, *Canada* 105 A6
Rutledge L., *Canada* 105 A6
Rutqa, W. →, *Syria* 73 E9
Rutshuru, *Dem. Rep. of the Congo* 86 C2
Ruvo di Púglia, *Italy* 31 A9
Ruvu, *Tanzania* 86 D4
Ruvu →, *Tanzania* 86 D4
Ruvuma □, *Tanzania* 87 E4
Ruvuma →, *Tanzania* 87 E5
Ruwais, *U.A.E.* 71 E7
Ruwenzori, *Africa* 86 B2
Ruya →, *Zimbabwe* 89 B5
Ruyigi, *Burundi* 86 C3
Ruyuan, *China* 59 E9
Ruzayevka, *Russia* 48 C7
Rŭzhevo Konare, *Bulgaria* 41 D8
Ružomberok, *Slovak Rep.* 27 B12
Rwanda ■, *Africa* 86 C3
Ryakhovo, *Bulgaria* 41 C10
Ryan, L., *U.K.* 14 G3
Ryazan, *Russia* 46 E10
Ryazhsk, *Russia* 46 F11
Rybache = Rybachye, *Kazakstan* 50 E9
Rybachye, *Kazakstan* 50 E9
Rybinsk, *Russia* 46 C10
Rybinskoye Vdkhr., *Russia* 46 C10
Rybnik, *Poland* 45 H5
Rybnitsa = Râbniţa, *Moldova* 43 C14
Rybnoye, *Russia* 46 E10
Rychnov nad Kněžnou, *Czech Rep.* 27 A9
Rychwał, *Poland* 45 F5
Rycroft, *Canada* 104 B5
Ryd, *Sweden* 11 H8
Rydaholm, *Sweden* 11 H8
Ryde, *U.K.* 13 G6
Ryderwood, *U.S.A.* 116 D3
Rydzyna, *Poland* 45 G3
Rye, *U.K.* 13 G8
Rye →, *U.K.* 12 C7
Rye Bay, *U.K.* 13 G8
Rye Patch Reservoir, *U.S.A.* 114 F4
Ryegate, *U.S.A.* 114 C9
Ryki, *Poland* 45 G8
Ryley, *Canada* 104 C6
Rylsk, *Russia* 47 G8
Rylstone, *Australia* 95 E4
Rymanów, *Poland* 45 J8
Ryn, *Poland* 44 E8
Ryn Peski, *Kazakstan* 49 G9
Ryōtsu, *Japan* 54 E9
Rypin, *Poland* 45 E6
Ryssby, *Sweden* 11 H8
Ryūgasaki, *Japan* 55 G10
Ryūkyū Is. = Ryūkyū-rettō, *Japan* 55 M3
Ryūkyū-rettō, *Japan* 55 M3
Rzepin, *Poland* 45 F1
Rzeszów, *Poland* 45 H8
Rzhev, *Russia* 46 D8

S

Sa, *Thailand* 64 C3
Sa Canal, *Spain* 37 C7
Sa Conillera, *Spain* 37 C7
Sa Dec, *Vietnam* 65 G5
Sa Dragonera, *Spain* 37 B9
Sa Mesquida, *Spain* 37 B11
Sa Pobla, *Spain* 32 F8
Sa Savina, *Spain* 37 C7
Sa'ādatābād, *Fārs, Iran* 71 D7
Sa'ādatābād, *Hormozgān, Iran* 71 D7
Sa'ādatābād, *Kermān, Iran* 71 D7
Saale →, *Germany* 24 D7
Saaler Bodden, *Germany* 24 A8
Saalfeld, *Germany* 24 E7
Saalfelden, *Austria* 26 D5
Saane →, *Switz.* 25 H3
Saar →, *Europe* 17 E6
Saarbrücken, *Germany* 25 F2
Saarburg, *Germany* 25 F2
Saaremaa, *Estonia* 9 G20
Saarijärvi, *Finland* 9 E21
Saariselkä, *Finland* 8 B23
Saarland □, *Germany* 25 F2
Saarlouis, *Germany* 25 F2
Sab 'Ābar, *Syria* 70 C3
Saba, *W. Indies* 121 C7
Šabac, *Serbia, Yug.* 40 B3
Sabadell, *Spain* 32 D7
Sabah □, *Malaysia* 62 C5
Sabak Bernam, *Malaysia* 65 L3
Sabalān, Kūhhā-ye, *Iran* 70 B5
Sabalana, Kepulauan, *Indonesia* 63 F5
Sábana de la Mar, *Dom. Rep.* 121 C6
Sábanalarga, *Colombia* 124 A4
Sabang, *Indonesia* 62 C1
Săbăoani, *Romania* 43 C11
Sabará, *Brazil* 125 G10
Sabarmati →, *India* 68 H5
Sabattis, *U.S.A.* 111 B10
Sabáudia, *Italy* 30 A6
Saberania, *Indonesia* 63 E9
Sabhah, *Libya* 79 C8
Sabi →, *India* 68 E7
Sabidana, J., *Sudan* 80 D4
Sabie, *S. Africa* 89 D5
Sabinal, *Mexico* 118 A3
Sabinal, *U.S.A.* 113 L5
Sabiñánigo, *Spain* 32 C4
Sabinar, Punta del, *Spain* 33 J2
Sabinas, *Mexico* 118 B4
Sabinas →, *Mexico* 118 B4
Sabinas Hidalgo, *Mexico* 118 B4
Sabine →, *U.S.A.* 113 L8
Sabine L., *U.S.A.* 113 L8
Sabine Pass, *U.S.A.* 113 L8
Sabinov, *Slovak Rep.* 27 B14
Sabinsville, *U.S.A.* 110 E7
Sabirabad, *Azerbaijan* 49 K9
Sabkhet el Bardawîl, *Egypt* 75 D2
Sablayan, *Phil.* 61 E4
Sable, *Canada* 103 A6
Sable, C., *Canada* 103 D6
Sable, C., *U.S.A.* 107 E10
Sable I., *Canada* 103 D8
Sablé-sur-Sarthe, *France* 18 E6
Sabonkafi, *Niger* 83 C6
Sabor →, *Portugal* 34 D3
Sabou, *Burkina Faso* 82 C4
Sabres, *France* 20 D3
Sabrina Coast, *Antarctica* 5 C9
Sabugal, *Portugal* 34 E3
Sabulubbek, *Indonesia* 62 E1
Sabuncu, *Turkey* 39 B12
Sabzevār, *Iran* 71 B8
Sabzvārān, *Iran* 71 D8
Sac City, *U.S.A.* 112 D7
Sacedón, *Spain* 32 E2
Săcele, *Romania* 43 E10
Sachigo →, *Canada* 102 A2
Sachigo, L., *Canada* 102 B1
Sachkhere, *Georgia* 49 J6
Sachsen □, *Germany* 24 E9
Sachsen-Anhalt □, *Germany* 24 D7
Sacile, *Italy* 29 C9
Sackets Harbor, *U.S.A.* 111 C8
Sackville, *Canada* 103 C7
Saco, *Maine, U.S.A.* 109 D10
Saco, *Mont., U.S.A.* 114 B10
Sacramento, *U.S.A.* 116 G5

Sacramento ➤, *U.S.A.* 116 G5
Sacramento Mts., *U.S.A.* 115 K11
Sacramento Valley, *U.S.A.* 116 G5
Sacratif, C., *Spain* 35 J7
Săcueni, *Romania* 42 C7
Sada, *Spain* 34 B2
Sada-Misaki, *Japan* 55 H6
Sádaba, *Spain* 32 C3
Sadabad, *India* 68 F8
Sadani, *Tanzania* 86 D4
Sadao, *Thailand* 65 J3
Sadd el Aali, *Egypt* 80 C3
Saddle Mt., *U.S.A.* 116 E3
Sade, *Nigeria* 83 C7
Sadimi, *Dem. Rep. of the Congo* 87 D1
Sadiola, *Mali* 82 C2
Sa'diyah, Hawr as, *Iraq* 73 F12
Sado, *Japan* 54 F9
Sado ➤, *Portugal* 35 G2
Sadon, *Burma* 67 G20
Sadon, *Russia* 49 J6
Sadra, *India* 68 H5
Sadri, *India* 68 G5
Sæby, *Denmark* 11 G4
Saegertown, *U.S.A.* 110 E4
Saelices, *Spain* 32 F2
Safaalan, *Turkey* 41 E12
Safaga, *Egypt* 80 B3
Safājah, *Si. Arabia* 70 E3
Šafárikovo = Tornal'a, *Slovak Rep.* 27 C13
Säffle, *Sweden* 10 E6
Safford, *U.S.A.* 115 K9
Saffron Walden, *U.K.* 13 E8
Safi, *Morocco* 78 B4
Şafiābād, *Iran* 71 B8
Safīd Dasht, *Iran* 71 C6
Safīd Kūh, *Afghan.* 66 B3
Safīd Rūd ➤, *Iran* 71 B6
Safipur, *India* 69 F9
Safonovo, *Russia* 46 E7
Safranbolu, *Turkey* 72 B5
Saft Rashîn, *Egypt* 80 J7
Safwān, *Iraq* 70 D5
Sag Harbor, *U.S.A.* 111 F12
Saga, *Japan* 55 H5
Saga □, *Japan* 55 H5
Sagae, *Japan* 54 E10
Sagala, *Mali* 82 C3
Sagamore, *U.S.A.* 110 F5
Sagar, *Karnataka, India* 66 M9
Sagar, *Mad. P., India* 69 H8
Sagara, L., *Tanzania* 86 D3
Sagay, *Phil.* 61 F5
Saginaw, *U.S.A.* 108 D4
Saginaw ➤, *U.S.A.* 108 D4
Saginaw B., *U.S.A.* 108 D4
Sagleipie, *Liberia* 82 D3
Saglouc = Salluit, *Canada* 101 B12
Sagŏ-ri, *S. Korea* 57 G14
Sagone, *France* 21 F12
Sagone, G. de, *France* 21 F12
Sagres, *Portugal* 35 J2
Sagua la Grande, *Cuba* 120 B3
Saguache, *U.S.A.* 115 G10
Saguaro Nat. Park, *U.S.A.* 115 K8
Saguenay ➤, *Canada* 103 C5
Sagunt, *Spain* 32 F4
Sagunto = Sagunt, *Spain* 32 F4
Sagwara, *India* 68 H6
Sahaba, *Sudan* 80 D3
Sahagún, *Spain* 34 C5
Saham al Jawlān, *Syria* 75 C4
Sahamandrevo, *Madag.* 89 C8
Sahand, Kūh-e, *Iran* 70 B5
Sahara, *Africa* 78 D6
Saharan Atlas = Saharien, Atlas, *Algeria* 78 B6
Saharanpur, *India* 68 E7
Saharien, Atlas, *Algeria* 78 B6
Saharsa, *India* 69 G12
Sahasinaka, *Madag.* 89 C8
Sahaswan, *India* 69 E8
Sahel, *Africa* 78 E5
Sahel, Canal du, *Mali* 82 C3
Sahibganj, *India* 69 G12
Sāḩilīyah, *Iraq* 70 C4
Sahiwal, *Pakistan* 68 D5
Şaḩneh, *Iran* 70 C5
Sahuaripa, *Mexico* 118 B3
Sahuarita, *U.S.A.* 115 L8
Sahuayo, *Mexico* 118 C4
Şahy, *Slovak Rep.* 27 C11
Sai ➤, *India* 69 G10
Sai Buri, *Thailand* 65 J3
Sa'id Bundas, *Sudan* 79 G10
Sa'īdābād, *Kermān, Iran* 71 D7
Sa'īdābād, *Semnān, Iran* 71 B7
Sa'īdīyeh, *Iran* 71 B6
Saidpur, *Bangla.* 67 G16
Saidpur, *India* 69 G10
Saidu, *Pakistan* 69 B5
Saignes, *France* 20 C6
Saigon = Thanh Pho Ho Chi Minh, *Vietnam* 65 G6
Saijō, *Japan* 55 H6
Saikanosy Masoala, *Madag.* 89 B9
Saikhoa Ghat, *India* 67 F19
Saiki, *Japan* 55 H5
Sailana, *India* 68 H6
Saillans, *France* 21 D9
Sailolof, *Indonesia* 63 E8
Saimaa, *Finland* 9 F23
Saimbeyli, *Turkey* 72 D7
Şa'in Dezh, *Iran* 70 B5
St. Abb's Head, *U.K.* 14 F6
St-Affrique, *France* 20 E6

St-Agrève, *France* 21 C8
St-Aignan, *France* 18 E8
St. Alban's, *Canada* 103 C8
St. Albans, *U.K.* 13 F7
St. Albans, *Vt., U.S.A.* 111 B11
St. Albans, *W. Va., U.S.A.* 108 F5
St. Alban's Head, *U.K.* 13 G5
St. Albert, *Canada* 104 C6
St-Amand-en-Puisaye, *France* 19 E10
St-Amand-les-Eaux, *France* 19 B10
St-Amand-Montrond, *France* 19 F9
St-Amarin, *France* 19 E14
St-Amour, *France* 19 F12
St-André-de-Cubzac, *France* 20 D3
St-André-les-Alpes, *France* 21 E10
St. Andrew's, *Canada* 103 C8
St. Andrews, *U.K.* 14 E6
St-Anicet, *Canada* 111 A10
St. Ann B., *Canada* 103 C7
St. Ann's Bay, *Jamaica* 120 C4
St. Anthony, *Canada* 103 B8
St. Anthony, *U.S.A.* 114 E8
St. Antoine, *Canada* 103 C7
St-Antonin-Noble-Val, *France* 20 D5
St. Arnaud, *Australia* 95 F3
St-Astier, *France* 20 C4
St-Aubin-du-Cormier, *France* 18 D5
St-Augustin ➤, *Canada* 103 B8
St-Augustin-Saguenay, *Canada* 103 B8
St. Augustine, *U.S.A.* 109 L5
St-Aulaye, *France* 20 C4
St. Austell, *U.K.* 13 G3
St-Avold, *France* 19 C13
St. Barbe, *Canada* 103 B8
St-Barthélemy, *W. Indies* 121 C7
St-Béat, *France* 20 F4
St. Bees Hd., *U.K.* 12 C4
St-Benoît-du-Sault, *France* 20 B5
St-Bonnet, *France* 21 D10
St-Brévin-les-Pins, *France* 18 E4
St-Brice-en-Coglès, *France* 18 D5
St. Bride's, *Canada* 103 C9
St. Brides B., *U.K.* 13 F2
St-Brieuc, *France* 18 D4
St-Calais, *France* 18 E7
St-Cast-le-Guildo, *France* 18 D4
St. Catharines, *Canada* 102 D4
St. Catherines I., *U.S.A.* 109 K5
St. Catherine's Pt., *U.K.* 13 G6
St-Céré, *France* 20 D5
St-Cergue, *Switz.* 25 J2
St-Cernin, *France* 20 C6
St-Chamond, *France* 21 C8
St. Charles, *Ill., U.S.A.* 108 E1
St. Charles, *Mo., U.S.A.* 112 F9
St. Charles, *Va., U.S.A.* 108 F7
St-Chély-d'Apcher, *France* 20 D7
St-Chinian, *France* 20 E6
St. Christopher-Nevis = St. Kitts & Nevis ■, *W. Indies* 121 C7
St-Ciers-sur-Gironde, *France* 20 C3
St. Clair, *Mich., U.S.A.* 110 D2
St. Clair, *Pa., U.S.A.* 111 F8
St. Clair ➤, *U.S.A.* 110 D2
St. Clair, L., *Canada* 102 D3
St. Clair, L., *Canada* 110 D2
St. Clairsville, *U.S.A.* 110 F4
St-Claud, *France* 20 C4
St-Claude, *Canada* 105 D9
St-Claude, *France* 19 F12
St-Clet, *Canada* 111 A10
St. Cloud, *Fla., U.S.A.* 109 L5
St. Cloud, *Minn., U.S.A.* 112 C7
St. Cricq, C., *Australia* 93 E1
St. Croix, *U.S. Virgin Is.* 121 C7
St. Croix ➤, *U.S.A.* 112 C8
St. Croix Falls, *U.S.A.* 112 C8
St-Cyprien, *France* 20 F7
St-Cyr-sur-Mer, *France* 21 E9
St. David's, *Canada* 103 C8
St. David's, *U.K.* 13 F2
St. David's Head, *U.K.* 13 F2
St-Denis, *France* 19 D9
St-Dié, *France* 19 D13
St-Dizier, *France* 19 D11
St-Égrève, *France* 21 C9
St. Elias, Mt., *U.S.A.* 100 B5
St. Elias Mts., *Canada* 104 A1
St. Elias Mts., *U.S.A.* 100 C6
St-Eloy-les-Mines, *France* 19 F9
St-Émilion, *France* 20 D3
St-Étienne, *France* 21 C8
St-Étienne-de-Tinée, *France* 21 D10
St-Étienne-du-Rouvray, *France* 18 C8
St. Eugène, *Canada* 111 A10
St. Eustatius, *W. Indies* 121 C7
St-Fargeau, *France* 19 E10
St-Félicien, *Canada* 102 C5
St-Florent, *France* 21 F13
St-Florent, G. de, *France* 21 F13
St-Florent-sur-Cher, *France* 19 F9
St-Florentin, *France* 19 E10
St-Flour, *France* 20 C7
St. Francis, *U.S.A.* 112 F4
St. Francis ➤, *U.S.A.* 113 H9
St. Francis, C., *S. Africa* 88 E3
St. Francisville, *U.S.A.* 113 K9
St-François, L., *Canada* 111 A10
St-Fulgent, *France* 18 F5
St-Gabriel, *Canada* 102 C5
St-Galmier, *France* 19 G11
St. Gallen = Sankt Gallen, *Switz.* 25 H9
St-Gaudens, *France* 20 E4
St-Gaultier, *France* 18 F8
St-Gengoux-le-National, *France* 19 F11
St-Geniez-d'Olt, *France* 20 D6
St. George, *Australia* 95 D4

St. George, *Canada* 103 C6
St. George, *S.C., U.S.A.* 109 J5
St. George, *Utah, U.S.A.* 115 H7
St. George, C., *Canada* 103 C8
St. George, C., *U.S.A.* 109 L3
St. George Ra., *Australia* 92 C4
St. George's, *Canada* 103 C8
St. George's, *Grenada* 121 D7
St. George's B., *Canada* 103 C8
St. Georges Basin, *N.S.W., Australia* 95 F5
St. Georges Basin, *W. Austral., Australia* 92 C4
St. George's Channel, *Europe* 15 E6
St. Georges Hd., *Australia* 95 F5
St-Georges-lès-Baillargeaux, *France* 20 B4
St-Germain-de-Calberte, *France* 20 D7
St-Germain-en-Laye, *France* 19 D9
St-Germain-Lembron, *France* 20 C7
St-Gervais-d'Auvergne, *France* 19 F9
St-Gervais-les-Bains, *France* 21 C10
St-Gildas, Pte. de, *France* 18 E4
St-Gilles, *France* 21 E8
St-Girons, *Ariège, France* 20 F5
St-Girons, *Landes, France* 20 E2
St. Gotthard P. = San Gottardo, P. del, *Switz.* 25 J4
St. Helena, *U.S.A.* 114 G2
St. Helena ■, *Atl. Oc.* 76 H3
St. Helena, Mt., *U.S.A.* 116 G4
St. Helena B., *S. Africa* 88 E2
St. Helens, *Australia* 94 G4
St. Helens, *U.K.* 12 D5
St. Helens, *U.S.A.* 116 E4
St. Helens, Mt., *U.S.A.* 116 D4
St. Helier, *U.K.* 13 H5
St-Herblain, *France* 18 E5
St-Hilaire-du-Harcouët, *France* 18 D5
St-Hippolyte, *France* 19 E13
St-Hippolyte-du-Fort, *France* 20 D7
St-Honoré-les-Bains, *France* 19 F10
St-Hubert, *Belgium* 17 D5
St-Hyacinthe, *Canada* 102 C5
St. Ignace, *U.S.A.* 108 C3
St. Ignace I., *Canada* 102 C2
St. Ignatius, *U.S.A.* 114 C6
St-Imier, *Switz.* 25 H2
St. Ives, *U.K.* 13 G2
St-James, *France* 18 D5
St. James, *U.S.A.* 112 D7
St-Jean ➤, *Canada* 103 B7
St-Jean, L., *Canada* 103 C5
St-Jean-d'Angély, *France* 20 C3
St-Jean-de-Braye, *France* 19 E8
St-Jean-de-Luz, *France* 20 E2
St-Jean-de-Maurienne, *France* 21 C10
St-Jean-de-Monts, *France* 18 F4
St-Jean-du-Gard, *France* 20 D7
St-Jean-en-Royans, *France* 21 C9
St-Jean-Pied-de-Port, *France* 20 E2
St-Jean-Port-Joli, *Canada* 103 C5
St-Jean-sur-Richelieu, *Canada* 102 C5
St-Jérôme, *Canada* 102 C5
St. John, *Canada* 103 C6
St. John, *U.S.A.* 113 G5
St. John ➤, *Liberia* 82 D2
St. John ➤, *U.S.A.* 109 C12
St. John, C., *Canada* 103 C8
St. John's, *Antigua* 121 C7
St. John's, *Canada* 103 C9
St. Johns, *Ariz., U.S.A.* 115 J9
St. Johns, *Mich., U.S.A.* 108 D3
St. Johns ➤, *U.S.A.* 109 K5
St. John's Pt., *Ireland* 15 B3
St. Johnsbury, *U.S.A.* 111 B12
St. Johnsville, *U.S.A.* 111 D10
St. Joseph, *La., U.S.A.* 113 K9
St. Joseph, *Mo., U.S.A.* 112 F7
St. Joseph ➤, *U.S.A.* 108 D2
St. Joseph, I., *Canada* 102 C3
St. Joseph, L., *Canada* 102 B1
St-Jovite, *Canada* 102 C5
St-Juéry, *France* 20 E6
St-Julien-Chapteuil, *France* 21 C8
St-Julien-de-Vouvantes, *France* 18 E5
St-Julien-en-Genevois, *France* 19 F13
St-Junien, *France* 20 C4
St-Just-en-Chaussée, *France* 19 C9
St-Just-en-Chevalet, *France* 20 C7
St. Kitts & Nevis ■, *W. Indies* 121 C7
St. Laurent, *Canada* 105 C9
St-Laurent-de-la-Salanque, *France* 20 F6
St-Laurent-du-Pont, *France* 21 C9
St-Laurent-en-Grandvaux, *France* 19 F12
St-Laurent-Médoc, *France* 20 C3
St. Lawrence, *Australia* 94 C4
St. Lawrence, *Canada* 103 C8
St. Lawrence ➤, *Canada* 103 C6
St. Lawrence, Gulf of, *Canada* 103 C7
St. Lawrence I., *U.S.A.* 100 B3
St. Leonard, *Canada* 103 C6
St-Léonard-de-Noblat, *France* 20 C5
St. Lewis ➤, *Canada* 103 B8
St-Lô, *France* 18 C5
St-Louis, *France* 19 E14
St. Louis, *Senegal* 82 B1
St. Louis, *U.S.A.* 112 F9
St. Louis ➤, *U.S.A.* 112 B8
St-Loup-sur-Semouse, *France* 19 E13
St. Lucia ■, *W. Indies* 121 D7
St. Lucia, L., *S. Africa* 89 D5
St. Lucia Channel, *W. Indies* 121 D7
St. Maarten, *W. Indies* 121 C7

St. Magnus B., *U.K.* 14 A7
St-Maixent-l'École, *France* 20 B3
St-Malo, *France* 18 D4
St-Malo, G. de, *France* 18 D4
St-Mandrier-sur-Mer, *France* 21 E9
St-Marc, *Haiti* 121 C5
St-Marcellin, *France* 21 C9
St-Marcouf, Îs., *France* 18 C5
St. Maries, *U.S.A.* 114 C5
St-Martin, *W. Indies* 121 C7
St-Martin, L., *Canada* 105 C9
St-Martin-de-Crau, *France* 21 E8
St-Martin-de-Ré, *France* 20 B2
St-Martin-d'Hères, *France* 21 C9
St-Martin-Vésubie, *France* 21 D11
St-Martory, *France* 20 E4
St. Mary Pk., *Australia* 95 E2
St. Marys, *Australia* 94 G4
St. Marys, *Canada* 110 C3
St. Mary's, *Corn., U.K.* 13 H1
St. Mary's, *Orkney, U.K.* 14 C6
St. Marys, *Ga., U.S.A.* 109 K5
St. Marys, *Pa., U.S.A.* 110 E6
St. Mary's, *Martinique* 121 D7
St. Mary's, C., *Canada* 103 C9
St. Mary's B., *Canada* 103 C9
St. Marys Bay, *Canada* 103 D6
St-Mathieu, Pte., *France* 18 D2
St. Matthews, I. = Zadetkyi Kyun, *Burma* 65 G1
St-Maurice ➤, *Canada* 102 C5
St-Maximin-la-Ste-Baume, *France* 21 E9
St-Médard-en-Jalles, *France* 20 D3
St-Méen-le-Grand, *France* 18 D4
St-Mihiel, *France* 19 D12
St. Moritz, *Switz.* 25 J5
St-Nazaire, *France* 18 E4
St. Neots, *U.K.* 13 E7
St-Nicolas-de-Port, *France* 19 D13
St-Niklaas, *Belgium* 17 C4
St-Omer, *France* 19 B9
St-Palais-sur-Mer, *France* 20 C2
St-Pamphile, *Canada* 103 C6
St-Pardoux-la-Rivière, *France* 20 C4
St. Pascal, *Canada* 103 C6
St. Paul, *Canada* 104 C6
St-Paul, *France* 21 D10
St. Paul, *Minn., U.S.A.* 112 C8
St. Paul, *Nebr., U.S.A.* 112 E5
St-Paul ➤, *Canada* 103 B8
St. Paul ➤, *Liberia* 82 D2
St. Paul, I., *Ind. Oc.* 3 F13
St-Paul-de-Fenouillet, *France* 20 F6
St. Paul I., *Canada* 103 C7
St-Paul-lès-Dax, *France* 20 E2
St-Péray, *France* 21 D8
St. Peter, *U.S.A.* 112 C8
St-Peter-Ording, *Germany* 24 A4
St. Peter Port, *U.K.* 13 H5
St. Peters, *N.S., Canada* 103 C7
St. Peters, *P.E.I., Canada* 103 C7
St. Petersburg = Sankt-Peterburg, *Russia* 46 C6
St. Petersburg, *U.S.A.* 109 M4
St-Philbert-de-Grand-Lieu, *France* 18 E5
St-Pie, *Canada* 111 A12
St-Pierre, *St- P. & M.* 103 C8
St-Pierre, L., *Canada* 102 C5
St-Pierre-d'Oléron, *France* 20 C2
St-Pierre-en-Port, *France* 18 C7
St-Pierre et Miquelon □, *St- P. & M.* 103 C8
St-Pierre-le-Moûtier, *France* 19 F10
St-Pierre-sur-Dives, *France* 18 C6
St-Pol-de-Léon, *France* 18 D3
St-Pol-sur-Mer, *France* 19 A9
St-Pol-sur-Ternoise, *France* 19 B9
St-Pons, *France* 20 E6
St-Pourçain-sur-Sioule, *France* 19 F10
St-Priest, *France* 21 C8
St-Quay-Portrieux, *France* 18 D4
St. Quentin, *Canada* 103 C6
St-Quentin, *France* 19 C10
St-Rambert-d'Albon, *France* 21 C8
St-Raphaël, *France* 21 E10
St. Regis, *U.S.A.* 114 C6
St-Renan, *France* 18 D2
St-Saëns, *France* 18 C8
St-Savin, *France* 20 B4
St-Savinien, *France* 20 C3
St. Sebastien, Tanjon' i, *Madag.* 89 A8
St-Seine-l'Abbaye, *France* 19 E11
St-Sernin-sur-Rance, *France* 20 E6
St-Sever, *France* 20 E3
St-Siméon, *Canada* 103 C6
St. Simons I., *U.S.A.* 109 K5
St. Simons Island, *U.S.A.* 109 K5
St. Stephen, *Canada* 103 C6
St-Sulpice, *France* 20 E5
St-Sulpice-Laurière, *France* 20 B5
St-Sulpice-les-Feuilles, *France* 20 B5
St-Syprien = St-Cyprien, *France* 20 F7
St-Thégonnec, *France* 18 D3
St. Thomas, *Canada* 102 D3
St. Thomas I., *U.S. Virgin Is.* 121 C7
St-Tite, *Canada* 102 C5
St-Tropez, *France* 21 E10
St. Troud = St. Truiden, *Belgium* 17 D5
St. Truiden, *Belgium* 17 D5
St-Vaast-la-Hougue, *France* 18 C5
St-Valery-en-Caux, *France* 18 C7
St-Valery-sur-Somme, *France* 19 B8
St-Vallier, *France* 19 F11
St-Vallier-de-Thiey, *France* 21 E10
St-Varent, *France* 18 F6

St-Vaury, *France* 20 B5
St. Vincent, G., *Australia* 28 C4
St. Vincent, G., *Australia* 95 F2
St. Vincent & the Grenadines ■, *W. Indies* 121 D7
St-Vincent-de-Tyrosse, *France* 20 E2
St. Vincent Passage, *W. Indies* 121 D7
St-Vith, *Belgium* 17 D6
St-Vivien-de-Médoc, *France* 20 C2
St. Walburg, *Canada* 105 C7
St-Yrieix-la-Perche, *France* 20 C5
Ste-Adresse, *France* 18 C7
Ste-Agathe-des-Monts, *Canada* 102 C5
Ste-Anne, L., *Canada* 103 B6
Ste-Anne-des-Monts, *Canada* 103 C6
Ste-Croix, *Switz.* 25 J2
Ste-Enimie, *France* 20 D7
Ste-Foy-la-Grande, *France* 20 D4
Ste. Genevieve, *U.S.A.* 112 G9
Ste-Hermine, *France* 20 B2
Ste-Livrade-sur-Lot, *France* 20 D4
Ste-Marguerite ➤, *Canada* 103 B6
Ste-Marie, *Martinique* 121 D7
Ste-Marie-aux-Mines, *France* 19 D14
Ste-Marie de la Madeleine, *Canada* 103 C5
Ste-Maure-de-Touraine, *France* 18 E7
Ste-Maxime, *France* 21 E10
Ste-Menehould, *France* 19 C11
Ste-Mère-Église, *France* 18 C5
Ste-Rose, *Guadeloupe* 121 C7
Ste. Rose du Lac, *Canada* 105 C9
Ste-Savine, *France* 19 D11
Ste-Sigolène, *France* 21 C8
Saintes, *France* 20 C3
Saintes, I. des, *Guadeloupe* 121 C7
Stes-Maries-de-la-Mer, *France* 21 E8
Saintfield, *U.K.* 15 B6
Saintonge, *France* 20 C3
Saipan, *Pac. Oc.* 96 F6
Sairang, *India* 67 H18
Sairecábur, Cerro, *Bolivia* 126 A2
Saitama □, *Japan* 55 F9
Saiteli = Kadınhanı, *Turkey* 72 C5
Saiți, *Moldova* 43 D14
Saiyid, *Pakistan* 68 C5
Sajama, *Bolivia* 124 G5
Sajan, *Serbia, Yug.* 42 E5
Sajó ➤, *Hungary* 42 C6
Sajószentpéter, *Hungary* 42 B6
Sajum, *India* 69 C8
Sak ➤, *S. Africa* 88 E3
Sakaba, *Nigeria* 83 C6
Sakai, *Japan* 55 G7
Sakaide, *Japan* 55 G6
Sakaiminato, *Japan* 55 G6
Sakākah, *Si. Arabia* 70 D4
Sakakawea, L., *U.S.A.* 112 B4
Sakami ➤, *Canada* 102 B4
Sakami, L., *Canada* 102 B4
Săkâne, 'Erg i-n, *Mali* 83 A4
Sakania, *Dem. Rep. of the Congo* 87 E2
Sakaraha, *Madag.* 89 C7
Sakarya, *Turkey* 72 B4
Sakarya ➤, *Turkey* 72 B4
Sakashima-Guntō, *Japan* 55 M2
Sakassou, *Ivory C.* 82 D3
Sakata, *Japan* 54 E9
Sakchu, *N. Korea* 57 D13
Sakeny ➤, *Madag.* 89 C8
Sakété, *Benin* 83 D5
Sakha □, *Russia* 51 C13
Sakhalin, *Russia* 51 D15
Sakhalinskiy Zaliv, *Russia* 51 D15
Şaki, *Azerbaijan* 49 K8
Šakiai, *Lithuania* 9 J20
Sakon Nakhon, *Thailand* 64 D5
Sakrand, *Pakistan* 68 F3
Sakri, *India* 69 F12
Sakrivier, *S. Africa* 88 E3
Sakskøbing, *Denmark* 11 K5
Sakti, *India* 69 H10
Sakuma, *Japan* 55 G8
Sakurai, *Japan* 55 G7
Saky, *Ukraine* 47 K7
Sal ➤, *Russia* 49 G5
Sala, *Eritrea* 81 D4
Sal'a, *Slovak Rep.* 27 C10
Sala, *Sweden* 10 E10
Sala ➤, *Eritrea* 81 D4
Sala Consilina, *Italy* 31 B8
Sala y Gómez, *Pac. Oc.* 97 K17
Salaberry-de-Valleyfield, *Canada* 102 C5
Saladas, *Argentina* 126 B4
Saladillo, *Argentina* 126 D4
Salado ➤, *Buenos Aires, Argentina* 126 D4
Salado ➤, *La Pampa, Argentina* 128 D3
Salado ➤, *Santa Fe, Argentina* 126 C3
Salado ➤, *Mexico* 113 M5
Salaga, *Ghana* 83 D4
Sālah, *Syria* 75 C5
Sălaj □, *Romania* 42 C7
Sălakhos, *Greece* 36 C9
Salala, *Liberia* 82 D2
Salala, *Sudan* 80 C4
Salālah, *Oman* 74 D5
Salamanca, *Chile* 126 C1
Salamanca, *Spain* 34 E5
Salamanca, *U.S.A.* 110 D6
Salamanca □, *Spain* 34 E5
Salāmatābād, *Iran* 70 C5
Salamína, *Cyprus* 36 D12
Salamis, *Greece* 38 D5
Salar de Atacama, *Chile* 126 A2
Salar de Uyuni, *Bolivia* 124 H5

San Pedro de Jujuy

Sălard, *Romania* 42 C7
Salas, *Spain* 34 B4
Salas de los Infantes, *Spain* 34 C7
Salatiga, *Indonesia* 63 G14
Salaverry, *Peru* 124 E3
Salawati, *Indonesia* 63 E8
Salaya, *India* 68 H3
Salayar, *Indonesia* 63 F6
Salazar →, *Spain* 32 C3
Salbris, *France* 19 E9
Salcia, *Romania* 43 G9
Sălciua, *Romania* 43 D8
Salcombe, *U.K.* 13 G4
Saldaña, *Spain* 34 C6
Saldanha, *S. Africa* 88 E2
Saldanha B., *S. Africa* 88 E2
Saldus, *Latvia* 9 H20
Saldus □, *Latvia* 44 B9
Sale, *Australia* 95 F4
Sale, *Italy* 28 D5
Salé, *Morocco* 78 B4
Sale, *U.K.* 12 D5
Salekhard, *Russia* 50 C7
Salem, *India* 66 P11
Salem, *Ill., U.S.A.* 108 F1
Salem, *Ind., U.S.A.* 108 F2
Salem, *Mass., U.S.A.* 111 D14
Salem, *Mo., U.S.A.* 113 G9
Salem, *N.H., U.S.A.* 111 D13
Salem, *N.J., U.S.A.* 108 F8
Salem, *N.Y., U.S.A.* 111 C11
Salem, *Ohio, U.S.A.* 110 F4
Salem, *Oreg., U.S.A.* 114 D2
Salem, *S. Dak., U.S.A.* 112 D6
Salem, *Va., U.S.A.* 108 G5
Salemi, *Italy* 30 E5
Sälen, *Sweden* 10 C7
Salernes, *France* 21 E10
Salerno, *Italy* 31 B7
Salerno, G. di, *Italy* 31 B7
Salford, *U.K.* 12 D5
Salgir →, *Ukraine* 47 K8
Salgótarján, *Hungary* 42 B4
Salgueiro, *Brazil* 125 E11
Salibabu, *Indonesia* 63 D7
Salida, *U.S.A.* 106 C5
Salies-de-Béarn, *France* 20 E3
Salihli, *Turkey* 72 C3
Salihorsk, *Belarus* 47 F4
Salima, *Malawi* 85 G6
Salina, *Italy* 31 D7
Salina, *Kans., U.S.A.* 112 F6
Salina, *Utah, U.S.A.* 115 G8
Salina Cruz, *Mexico* 119 D5
Salinas, *Brazil* 125 G10
Salinas, *Chile* 126 A2
Salinas, *Ecuador* 124 D2
Salinas, *U.S.A.* 116 J5
Salinas →, *Guatemala* 119 D6
Salinas →, *U.S.A.* 116 J5
Salinas, B. de, *Nic.* 120 D2
Salinas, Pampa de las, *Argentina* 126 C2
Salinas Ambargasta, *Argentina* 126 B3
Salinas de Hidalgo, *Mexico* 118 C4
Salinas Grandes, *Argentina* 126 C3
Saline →, *Ark., U.S.A.* 113 J8
Saline →, *Kans., U.S.A.* 112 F6
Salines, *Spain* 37 B10
Salines, C. de ses, *Spain* 37 B10
Salinópolis, *Brazil* 125 D9
Salins-les-Bains, *France* 19 F12
Salir, *Portugal* 35 H2
Salisbury = Harare, *Zimbabwe* 87 F3
Salisbury, *U.K.* 13 F6
Salisbury, *Md., U.S.A.* 108 F8
Salisbury, *N.C., U.S.A.* 109 H5
Salisbury I., *Canada* 101 B12
Salisbury Plain, *U.K.* 13 F6
Săliște, *Romania* 43 E8
Salka, *Nigeria* 83 C5
Şalkhad, *Syria* 75 C5
Salla, *Finland* 8 C23
Sallanches, *France* 21 C10
Sallent, *Spain* 32 D6
Salles, *France* 20 D3
Salles-Curan, *France* 20 D6
Salling, *Denmark* 11 H2
Salliq, *Canada* 101 B11
Sallisaw, *U.S.A.* 113 H7
Sallom Junction, *Sudan* 80 D4
Salluit, *Canada* 101 B12
Salmās, *Iran* 70 B5
Salmerón, *Spain* 32 E2
Salmo, *Canada* 104 D5
Salmon, *U.S.A.* 114 D7
Salmon →, *Canada* 104 C4
Salmon →, *U.S.A.* 114 D5
Salmon Arm, *Canada* 104 C5
Salmon Gums, *Australia* 93 F3
Salmon River Mts., *U.S.A.* 114 D6
Salo, *Finland* 9 F20
Salò, *Italy* 28 C7
Salobreña, *Spain* 35 J7
Salome, *U.S.A.* 117 M13
Salon, *India* 69 F9
Salon-de-Provence, *France* 21 E9
Salonica = Thessaloníki, *Greece* 40 F6
Salonta, *Romania* 42 D6
Salor →, *Spain* 35 F3
Salou, *Spain* 32 D6
Salou, C. de, *Spain* 32 D6
Saloum →, *Senegal* 82 C1
Salpausselkä, *Finland* 9 F22
Salsacate, *Argentina* 126 C2
Salses, *France* 20 F6
Salsk, *Russia* 49 G5
Salso →, *Italy* 30 E6
Salsomaggiore Terme, *Italy* 28 D6
Salt, *Spain* 32 D7
Salt →, *Canada* 104 B6
Salt →, *U.S.A.* 115 K7
Salt Lake City, *U.S.A.* 114 F8
Salt Range, *Pakistan* 68 C5
Salta, *Argentina* 126 A2
Salta □, *Argentina* 126 A2
Saltara, *Italy* 29 E9
Saltash, *U.K.* 13 G3
Saltburn by the Sea, *U.K.* 12 C7
Saltcoats, *U.K.* 14 F4
Saltee Is., *Ireland* 15 D5
Saltfjellet, *Norway* 8 C16
Saltfjorden, *Norway* 8 C16
Saltholm, *Denmark* 11 J6
Saltillo, *Mexico* 118 B4
Salto, *Argentina* 126 C3
Salto, *Uruguay* 126 C4
Salto del Guaíra, *Paraguay* 127 A5
Salton City, *U.S.A.* 117 M11
Salton Sea, *U.S.A.* 117 M11
Saltpond, *Ghana* 83 D4
Saltsburg, *U.S.A.* 110 F5
Saltsjöbaden, *Sweden* 10 E12
Saluda →, *U.S.A.* 109 J5
Salûm, *Egypt* 80 A2
Salûm, Khâlig el, *Egypt* 80 A2
Salur, *India* 67 K13
Saluzzo, *Italy* 28 D4
Salvador, *Brazil* 125 F11
Salvador, *Canada* 105 C7
Salvador, L., *U.S.A.* 113 L9
Salvaterra de Magos, *Portugal* 35 F2
Sálvora, I. de, *Spain* 34 C2
Salween →, *Burma* 67 L20
Salyan, *Azerbaijan* 50 F5
Salza →, *Austria* 26 D7
Salzach →, *Austria* 26 C5
Salzburg, *Austria* 26 D6
Salzburg □, *Austria* 26 D6
Salzgitter, *Germany* 24 C6
Salzkotten, *Germany* 24 D4
Salzwedel, *Germany* 24 C7
Sam, *India* 68 F4
Sam Neua, *Laos* 58 G5
Sam Ngao, *Thailand* 64 D2
Sam Rayburn Reservoir, *U.S.A.* 113 K7
Sam Son, *Vietnam* 64 C5
Sam Teu, *Laos* 64 C5
Sama de Langreo = Langreo, *Spain* 34 B5
Samagaltay, *Russia* 51 D10
Samales Group, *Phil.* 61 J4
Samâlût, *Egypt* 80 B3
Samana, *India* 68 D7
Samana Cay, *Bahamas* 121 B5
Samandağı, *Turkey* 72 D6
Samandıra, *Turkey* 41 F13
Samanga, *Tanzania* 87 D4
Samangān □, *Afghan.* 66 B5
Samangwa, *Dem. Rep. of the Congo* 86 C1
Samani, *Japan* 54 C11
Samanli Dağları, *Turkey* 41 F13
Samar, *Phil.* 61 F6
Samara, *Russia* 48 D10
Samara →, *Russia* 48 D10
Samara →, *Ukraine* 47 H8
Samaria = Shōmrōn, *West Bank* 75 C4
Samariá, *Greece* 36 D5
Samarinda, *Indonesia* 62 E5
Samarkand = Samarqand, *Uzbekistan* 50 F7
Samarqand, *Uzbekistan* 50 F7
Sāmarrā, *Iraq* 70 C4
Samastipur, *India* 69 G11
Şamaxi, *Azerbaijan* 49 K9
Samba, *Dem. Rep. of the Congo* 86 C2
Samba, *India* 69 C6
Sambalpur, *India* 67 J14
Sambar, Tanjung, *Indonesia* 62 E4
Sambas, *Indonesia* 62 D3
Sambava, *Madag.* 89 A9
Sambawizi, *Zimbabwe* 87 F2
Sambhal, *India* 69 E8
Sambhar, *India* 68 F6
Sambhar L., *India* 68 F6
Sambiase, *Italy* 31 D9
Sambir, *Ukraine* 47 H2
Sambor, *Cambodia* 64 F6
Samborombón, B., *Argentina* 126 D4
Sambuca di Sicilia, *Italy* 30 E6
Samch'ŏk, *S. Korea* 57 F15
Samch'onp'o, *S. Korea* 57 G15
Same, *Tanzania* 86 C4
Samer, *France* 19 B8
Samfya, *Zambia* 87 E2
Sámi, *Greece* 38 C2
Şämkir, *Azerbaijan* 49 K8
Şamlı, *Turkey* 39 B9
Samnah, *Si. Arabia* 70 E3
Samo Alto, *Chile* 126 C1
Samoa ■, *Pac. Oc.* 91 B13
Samobor, *Croatia* 29 C12
Samoëns, *France* 19 F13
Samokov, *Bulgaria* 40 D7
Šamorín, *Slovak Rep.* 27 C10
Samorogouan, *Burkina Faso* 82 C4
Sámos, *Greece* 39 D8
Samoš, *Serbia, Yug.* 42 E5
Samos, *Spain* 34 C3
Sámos □, *Greece* 39 D8
Samothráki = Mathráki, *Greece* 36 A3
Samothráki, *Évros, Greece* 41 F9
Samothráki, *Évros, Greece* 41 F9
Samoylovka, *Russia* 48 E6
Sampa, *Ghana* 82 D4
Sampacho, *Argentina* 126 C3
Sampang, *Indonesia* 63 G15
Samper de Calanda, *Spain* 32 D4
Sampéyre, *Italy* 28 D4
Sampit, *Indonesia* 62 E4
Sampit, Teluk, *Indonesia* 62 E4
Samrong, *Cambodia* 64 E4
Samrong, *Thailand* 64 E3
Samsø, *Denmark* 11 J4
Samsø Bælt, *Denmark* 11 J4
Samsun, *Turkey* 72 B7
Samtredia, *Georgia* 49 J6
Samui, Ko, *Thailand* 65 H3
Samur →, *Russia* 49 K9
Samurskiy Khrebet, *Russia* 49 K8
Samusole, *Dem. Rep. of the Congo* 87 E1
Samut Prakan, *Thailand* 64 F3
Samut Songkhram →, *Thailand* 62 B1
Samwari, *Pakistan* 68 E2
San, *Mali* 82 C4
San →, *Cambodia* 64 F5
San →, *Poland* 45 H8
San Adrián, *Spain* 32 C3
San Adrián, C. de, *Spain* 34 B2
San Agustin, C., *Phil.* 61 H7
San Agustín de Valle Fértil, *Argentina* 126 C2
San Ambrosio, *Pac. Oc.* 122 F3
San Andreas, *U.S.A.* 116 G6
San Andres, *Phil.* 61 E6
San Andrés, I. de, *Caribbean* 120 D3
San Andrês del Rabanedo, *Spain* 34 C5
San Andres Mts., *U.S.A.* 115 K10
San Andrés Tuxtla, *Mexico* 119 D5
San Angelo, *U.S.A.* 113 K4
San Anselmo, *U.S.A.* 116 H4
San Antonio, *Belize* 119 D7
San Antonio, *Chile* 126 C1
San Antonio, *Phil.* 61 D4
San Antonio, *N. Mex., U.S.A.* 115 K10
San Antonio, *Tex., U.S.A.* 113 L5
San Antonio →, *U.S.A.* 113 L6
San Antonio, C., *Argentina* 126 D4
San Antonio, C., *Cuba* 120 B3
San Antonio, C. de, *Spain* 33 G5
San Antonio, Mt., *U.S.A.* 117 L9
San Antonio de los Baños, *Cuba* 120 B3
San Antonio de los Cobres, *Argentina* 126 A2
San Antonio Oeste, *Argentina* 128 E4
San Arcángelo, *Italy* 31 B9
San Ardo, *U.S.A.* 116 J6
San Augustín, *Canary Is.* 37 G4
San Augustine, *U.S.A.* 113 K7
San Bartolomé, *Canary Is.* 37 F6
San Bartolomé de Tirajana, *Canary Is.* 37 G4
San Bartolomeo in Galdo, *Italy* 31 A8
San Benedetto del Tronto, *Italy* 29 F10
San Benedetto Po, *Italy* 28 C7
San Benedicto, I., *Mexico* 118 D2
San Benito, *U.S.A.* 113 M6
San Benito →, *U.S.A.* 116 J5
San Benito Mt., *U.S.A.* 116 J6
San Bernardino, *U.S.A.* 117 L9
San Bernardino Mts., *U.S.A.* 117 L10
San Bernardino Str., *Phil.* 61 E6
San Bernardo, *Chile* 126 C1
San Bernardo, I. de, *Colombia* 124 B3
San Blas, *Mexico* 118 B3
San Blas, Arch. de, *Panama* 120 E4
San Blas, C., *U.S.A.* 109 L3
San Bonifacio, *Italy* 29 C8
San Borja, *Bolivia* 124 F5
San Buenaventura, *Mexico* 118 B4
San Carlos = Butuku-Luba, *Eq. Guin.* 83 E6
San Carlos = Sant Carles, *Spain* 37 B8
San Carlos, *Argentina* 126 C2
San Carlos, *Chile* 126 D1
San Carlos, *Baja Calif. S., Mexico* 118 C2
San Carlos, *Coahuila, Mexico* 118 B4
San Carlos, *Nic.* 120 D3
San Carlos, *Neg. Occ., Phil.* 61 F5
San Carlos, *Pangasinan, Phil.* 61 D4
San Carlos, *Uruguay* 127 C5
San Carlos, *U.S.A.* 115 K8
San Carlos, *Venezuela* 124 B5
San Carlos de Bariloche, *Argentina* 128 E2
San Carlos de Bolívar, *Argentina* 128 D4
San Carlos de la Rápita = Sant Carles de la Ràpita, *Spain* 32 E5
San Carlos del Zulia, *Venezuela* 124 B4
San Carlos L., *U.S.A.* 115 K8
San Cataldo, *Italy* 30 E6
San Celoni = Sant Celoni, *Spain* 32 D7
San Clemente, *Chile* 126 D1
San Clemente, *Spain* 33 F2
San Clemente, *U.S.A.* 117 M9
San Clemente I., *U.S.A.* 117 N8
San Cristóbal = Es Migjorn Gran, *Spain* 37 B11
San Cristóbal, *Argentina* 126 C3
San Cristóbal, *Dom. Rep.* 121 C5
San Cristóbal, *Venezuela* 124 B4
San Cristóbal de la Casas, *Mexico* 119 D6
San Damiano d'Asti, *Italy* 28 D5
San Daniele del Friuli, *Italy* 29 B10
San Diego, *Calif., U.S.A.* 117 N9
San Diego, *Tex., U.S.A.* 113 M5
San Diego, C., *Argentina* 128 G3
San Diego de la Unión, *Mexico* 118 C4
San Dimitri, Ras, *Malta* 36 C1
San Donà di Piave, *Italy* 29 C9
San Estanislao, *Paraguay* 126 A4
San Esteban de Gormaz, *Spain* 32 D1
San Felice Circeo, *Italy* 30 A6
San Felice sul Panaro, *Italy* 29 D8
San Felipe, *Chile* 126 C1
San Felipe, *Mexico* 118 A2
San Felipe, *Venezuela* 124 A5
San Felipe →, *U.S.A.* 117 M11
San Felix, *Chile* 126 B1
San Félix, *Pac. Oc.* 122 F2
San Fernando = Sant Ferran, *Spain* 37 C7
San Fernando, *Chile* 126 C1
San Fernando, *Baja Calif., Mexico* 118 B1
San Fernando, *Tamaulipas, Mexico* 119 C5
San Fernando, *La Union, Phil.* 61 C4
San Fernando, *Pampanga, Phil.* 61 D4
San Fernando, *Spain* 35 J4
San Fernando, *Trin. & Tob.* 121 D7
San Fernando, *U.S.A.* 117 L8
San Fernando de Apure, *Venezuela* 124 B5
San Fernando de Atabapo, *Venezuela* 124 C5
San Fernando di Púglia, *Italy* 31 A9
San Francisco, *Argentina* 126 C3
San Francisco, *U.S.A.* 116 H4
San Francisco →, *U.S.A.* 115 K9
San Francisco, Paso de, *S. Amer.* 126 B2
San Francisco de Macorís, *Dom. Rep.* 121 C5
San Francisco del Monte de Oro, *Argentina* 126 C2
San Francisco del Oro, *Mexico* 118 B3
San Francisco Javier = Sant Francesc de Formentera, *Spain* 37 C7
San Francisco Solano, Pta., *Colombia* 122 C3
San Fratello, *Italy* 31 D7
San Gabriel, *Chile* 126 C1
San Gabriel Mts., *U.S.A.* 117 L9
San Gavino Monreale, *Italy* 30 C1
San Gimignano, *Italy* 28 E8
San Giórgio di Nogaro, *Italy* 29 C10
San Giórgio Iónico, *Italy* 31 B10
San Giovanni Bianco, *Italy* 28 C6
San Giovanni in Fiore, *Italy* 31 C9
San Giovanni in Persiceto, *Italy* 29 D8
San Giovanni Rotondo, *Italy* 29 G12
San Giovanni Valdarno, *Italy* 29 E8
San Giuliano Terme, *Italy* 28 E7
San Gorgonio Mt., *U.S.A.* 117 L10
San Gottardo, P. del, *Switz.* 25 J4
San Gregorio, *Uruguay* 127 C4
San Gregorio, *U.S.A.* 116 H4
San Guiseppe Jato, *Italy* 30 E6
San Ignacio, *Belize* 119 D7
San Ignacio, *Bolivia* 124 G6
San Ignacio, *Mexico* 118 B2
San Ignacio, *Paraguay* 120 C2
San Ignacio, L., *Mexico* 118 B2
San Ildefonso, C., *Phil.* 61 C5
San Isidro, *Argentina* 126 C4
San Isidro, *Phil.* 61 H7
San Jacinto, *U.S.A.* 117 M10
San Jaime = Sant Jaume, *Spain* 37 B11
San Javier, *Misiones, Argentina* 127 B4
San Javier, *Santa Fe, Argentina* 126 C4
San Javier, *Bolivia* 124 G6
San Javier, *Chile* 126 D1
San Javier, *Spain* 33 H4
San Jeronimo Taviche, *Mexico* 119 D5
San Joaquin, *U.S.A.* 116 J6
San Joaquin →, *U.S.A.* 116 G5
San Joaquin Valley, *U.S.A.* 116 J6
San Jon, *U.S.A.* 113 H3
San Jordi = Sant Jordi, *Spain* 37 B9
San Jorge, *Argentina* 126 C3
San Jorge, *Spain* 37 C7
San Jorge, B. de, *Mexico* 118 A2
San Jorge, G., *Argentina* 128 F3
San Jorge, G. of, *Argentina* 122 H4
San José = San Josep, *Spain* 37 C7
San José, *Costa Rica* 120 E3
San José, *Guatemala* 120 D1
San José, *Mexico* 118 C2
San Jose, *Mind. Occ., Phil.* 61 E4
San Jose, *Nueva Ecija, Phil.* 61 D4
San Jose, *U.S.A.* 116 H5
San Jose →, *U.S.A.* 115 J10
San Jose de Buenavista, *Phil.* 63 B6
San José de Chiquitos, *Bolivia* 124 G6
San José de Feliciano, *Argentina* 126 C4
San José de Jáchal, *Argentina* 126 C2
San José de Mayo, *Uruguay* 126 C4
San José del Cabo, *Mexico* 118 C3
San José del Guaviare, *Colombia* 124 C4
San Josep, *Spain* 37 C7
San Juan, *Argentina* 126 C2
San Juan, *Mexico* 118 C4
San Juan, *Phil.* 61 F6
San Juan, *Puerto Rico* 121 C6
San Juan □, *Argentina* 126 C2
San Juan →, *Argentina* 126 C2
San Juan →, *Nic.* 120 D3
San Juan →, *U.S.A.* 115 H8
San Juan Bautista = Sant Joan Baptista, *Spain* 37 B8
San Juan Bautista, *Paraguay* 126 B4
San Juan Bautista, *U.S.A.* 116 J5
San Juan Bautista Valle Nacional, *Mexico* 119 D5
San Juan Capistrano, *U.S.A.* 117 M9
San Juan Cr. →, *U.S.A.* 116 J5
San Juan de Alicante, *Spain* 33 G4
San Juan de Guadalupe, *Mexico* 118 C4
San Juan de la Costa, *Mexico* 118 C2
San Juan de los Morros, *Venezuela* 124 B5
San Juan del Norte, *Nic.* 120 D3
San Juan del Norte, B. de, *Nic.* 120 D3
San Juan del Río, *Mexico* 119 C5
San Juan del Sur, *Nic.* 120 D2
San Juan I., *U.S.A.* 116 B3
San Juan Mts., *U.S.A.* 115 H10
San Just, Sierra de, *Spain* 32 E4
San Justo, *Argentina* 126 C3
San Kamphaeng, *Thailand* 64 C2
San Lázaro, C., *Mexico* 118 C2
San Lázaro, Sa., *Mexico* 118 C3
San Leandro, *U.S.A.* 116 H4
San Leonardo de Yagüe, *Spain* 32 D1
San Lorenzo = Sant Llorenç des Cardassar, *Spain* 37 B10
San Lorenzo, *Argentina* 126 C3
San Lorenzo, *Ecuador* 124 C3
San Lorenzo, *Paraguay* 126 B4
San Lorenzo →, *Mexico* 118 C3
San Lorenzo, I., *Mexico* 118 B2
San Lorenzo, Mte., *Argentina* 128 F2
San Lorenzo de la Parrilla, *Spain* 32 F2
San Lorenzo de Morunys = Sant Llorenç de Morunys, *Spain* 32 C6
San Lucas, *Bolivia* 124 H5
San Lucas, *Baja Calif. S., Mexico* 118 C3
San Lucas, *Baja Calif. S., Mexico* 118 B2
San Lucas, *U.S.A.* 116 J5
San Lucas, C., *Mexico* 118 C3
San Lúcido, *Italy* 31 C9
San Luis, *Argentina* 126 C2
San Luis, *Cuba* 120 B3
San Luis, *Guatemala* 120 C2
San Luis, *Ariz., U.S.A.* 115 K6
San Luis, *Colo., U.S.A.* 115 H11
San Luis □, *Argentina* 126 C2
San Luis, I., *Mexico* 118 B2
San Luis, Sierra de, *Argentina* 126 C2
San Luis de la Paz, *Mexico* 118 C4
San Luis Obispo, *U.S.A.* 117 K6
San Luis Potosí, *Mexico* 118 C4
San Luis Potosí □, *Mexico* 118 C4
San Luis Reservoir, *U.S.A.* 116 H5
San Luis Río Colorado, *Mexico* 118 A2
San Manuel, *U.S.A.* 115 K8
San Marco, C., *Italy* 30 C1
San Marco Argentano, *Italy* 31 C9
San Marco in Lámis, *Italy* 29 G12
San Marcos, *Guatemala* 120 D1
San Marcos, *Mexico* 118 B2
San Marcos, *Calif., U.S.A.* 117 M9
San Marcos, *Tex., U.S.A.* 113 L6
San Marino, *San Marino* 29 E9
San Marino ■, *Europe* 29 E9
San Martín, *Argentina* 126 C2
San Martin →, *Bolivia* 124 F6
San Martín, L., *Argentina* 128 F2
San Martín de la Vega, *Spain* 34 E7
San Martin de los Andes, *Argentina* 128 E2
San Martín de Valdeiglesias, *Spain* 34 E6
San Mateo = Sant Mateu, *Baleares, Spain* 37 B7
San Mateo = Sant Mateu, *Valencia, Spain* 32 E5
San Mateo, *Phil.* 61 C4
San Mateo, *U.S.A.* 116 H4
San Matías, *Bolivia* 124 G7
San Matías, G., *Argentina* 122 H4
San Miguel = Sant Miquel, *Spain* 37 B7
San Miguel, *El Salv.* 120 D2
San Miguel, *Panama* 120 E4
San Miguel, *U.S.A.* 116 K6
San Miguel →, *Bolivia* 124 F6
San Miguel de Tucumán, *Argentina* 126 B2
San Miguel del Monte, *Argentina* 126 D4
San Miguel I., *U.S.A.* 117 L6
San Miniato, *Italy* 28 E7
San Nicolás, *Canary Is.* 37 G4
San Nicolas, *Phil.* 61 B4
San Nicolás de los Arroyas, *Argentina* 126 C3
San Nicolas I., *U.S.A.* 117 M7
San Onofre, *U.S.A.* 117 M9
San Pablo, *Bolivia* 126 A2
San Pablo, *Phil.* 61 D4
San Pablo, *U.S.A.* 116 H4
San Pàolo di Civitate, *Italy* 29 G12
San Pedro, *Buenos Aires, Argentina* 126 C4
San Pedro, *Misiones, Argentina* 127 B5
San Pedro, *Chile* 126 C1
San Pédro, *Ivory C.* 82 E3
San Pedro, *Mexico* 118 C2
San Pedro □, *Paraguay* 126 A4
San Pedro →, *Chihuahua, Mexico* 118 B3
San Pedro →, *Nayarit, Mexico* 118 C3
San Pedro →, *U.S.A.* 115 K8
San Pedro, Pta., *Chile* 126 B1
San Pedro, Sierra de, *Spain* 35 F4
San Pedro Channel, *U.S.A.* 117 M8
San Pedro de Atacama, *Chile* 126 A2
San Pedro de Jujuy, *Argentina* 126 A3

San Pedro de las Colonias, *Mexico* 118 B4
San Pedro de Macorís, *Dom. Rep.* 121 C6
San Pedro del Norte, *Nic.* 120 D3
San Pedro del Paraná, *Paraguay* 126 B4
San Pedro del Pinatar, *Spain* 33 H4
San Pedro Mártir, Sierra, *Mexico* 118 A1
San Pedro Mixtepec, *Mexico* 119 D5
San Pedro Ocampo = Melchor Ocampo, *Mexico* 118 C4
San Pedro Sula, *Honduras* 120 C2
San Pietro, *Italy* 30 C1
San Pietro Vernótico, *Italy* 31 B11
San Quintín, *Mexico* 118 A1
San Rafael, *Argentina* 126 C2
San Rafael, *Calif., U.S.A.* 116 H4
San Rafael, *N. Mex., U.S.A.* 115 J10
San Rafael Mt., *U.S.A.* 117 L7
San Rafael Mts., *U.S.A.* 117 L7
San Ramón de la Nueva Orán, *Argentina* 126 A3
San Remo, *Italy* 28 E4
San Roque, *Argentina* 126 B4
San Roque, *Spain* 35 J5
San Rosendo, *Chile* 126 D1
San Saba, *U.S.A.* 113 K5
San Salvador, *El Salv.* 120 D2
San Salvador, *Spain* 37 B10
San Salvador de Jujuy, *Argentina* 126 A3
San Salvador I., *Bahamas* 121 B5
San Salvo, *Italy* 29 F11
San Sebastián = Donostia-San Sebastián, *Spain* 32 B3
San Sebastián, *Argentina* 128 G3
San Sebastian de la Gomera, *Canary Is.* 37 F2
San Serra = Son Serra, *Spain* 37 B10
San Serverino Marche, *Italy* 29 E10
San Severo, *Italy* 29 G12
San Simeon, *U.S.A.* 116 K5
San Simon, *U.S.A.* 115 K9
San Stéfano di Cadore, *Italy* 29 B9
San Stino di Livenza, *Italy* 29 C9
San Telmo = Sant Telm, *Spain* 37 B9
San Telmo, *Mexico* 118 A1
San Tiburcio, *Mexico* 118 C4
San Valentin, Mte., *Chile* 122 H3
San Vicente de Alcántara, *Spain* 35 F3
San Vicente de la Barquera, *Spain* 34 B6
San Vincente del Raspeig, *Spain* 33 G4
San Vincenzo, *Italy* 28 E7
San Vito, *Costa Rica* 120 E3
San Vito, *Italy* 30 C2
San Vito, C., *Italy* 30 D5
San Vito al Tagliamento, *Italy* 29 C9
San Vito Chietino, *Italy* 29 F11
San Vito dei Normanni, *Italy* 31 B10
Sana', *Yemen* 74 D3
Sana →, *Bos.-H.* 29 C13
Sanaba, *Burkina Faso* 82 C4
Şanāfīr, *Si. Arabia* 80 B3
Sanaga →, *Cameroon* 83 E6
Sanaloa, Presa, *Mexico* 118 C3
Sanana, *Indonesia* 63 E7
Sanand, *India* 68 H5
Sanandaj, *Iran* 70 C5
Sanandita, *Bolivia* 126 A3
Sanary-sur-Mer, *France* 21 E9
Sanawad, *India* 68 H7
Sancellas = Sencelles, *Spain* 37 B9
Sancergues, *France* 19 E9
Sancerre, *France* 19 E9
Sancerrois, Collines du, *France* 19 E9
Sancha He →, *China* 58 D6
Sanchahe, *China* 57 B14
Sánchez, *Dom. Rep.* 121 C6
Sanchor, *India* 68 G4
Sancoins, *France* 19 F9
Sancti Spíritus, *Cuba* 120 B4
Sancy, Puy de, *France* 20 C6
Sand →, *S. Africa* 89 C5
Sand Hills, *U.S.A.* 112 D4
Sand Springs, *U.S.A.* 113 G6
Sanda, *Japan* 55 G7
Sandakan, *Malaysia* 62 C5
Sandan = Sambor, *Cambodia* 64 F6
Sandanski, *Bulgaria* 40 E7
Sandaré, *Mali* 82 C2
Sandared, *Sweden* 11 G6
Sandarne, *Sweden* 10 C11
Sanday, *U.K.* 14 B6
Sandefjord, *Norway* 9 G14
Sanders, *U.S.A.* 115 J9
Sanderson, *U.S.A.* 113 K3
Sandersville, *U.S.A.* 109 J4
Sandfire Roadhouse, *Australia* 92 C3
Sandfly L., *Canada* 105 B7
Sandfontein, *Namibia* 88 C2
Sandhammaren, C., *Sweden* 11 J8
Sandía, *Peru* 124 F5
Sandıklı, *Turkey* 39 C12
Sandila, *India* 69 F9
Sandnes, *Norway* 9 G11
Sandnessjøen, *Norway* 8 C15
Sandoa, *Dem. Rep. of the Congo* 84 F4
Sandomierz, *Poland* 45 H8
Sândominic, *Romania* 43 D10
Sandover →, *Australia* 94 C2
Sandoway, *Burma* 67 K19
Sandoy, *Færoe Is.* 8 F9
Sandpoint, *U.S.A.* 114 B5
Sandray, *U.K.* 14 E1
Sandringham, *U.K.* 12 E8
Sandstone, *Australia* 93 E2
Sandu, *China* 58 E6
Sandusky, *Mich., U.S.A.* 110 C2
Sandusky, *Ohio, U.S.A.* 110 E2
Sandvig, *Sweden* 11 J8
Sandviken, *Sweden* 10 D10
Sandwich, C., *Australia* 94 B4
Sandwich B., *Canada* 103 B8
Sandwich B., *Namibia* 88 C1
Sandy, *Oreg., U.S.A.* 116 E4
Sandy, *Pa., U.S.A.* 110 E6
Sandy, *Utah, U.S.A.* 114 F8
Sandy Bay, *Canada* 105 B8
Sandy Bight, *Australia* 93 F3
Sandy C., *Queens., Australia* 94 C5
Sandy C., *Tas., Australia* 94 G3
Sandy Cay, *Bahamas* 121 B4
Sandy Cr. →, *U.S.A.* 114 F9
Sandy L., *Canada* 102 B1
Sandy Lake, *Canada* 102 B1
Sandy Valley, *U.S.A.* 117 K11
Sanford, *Fla., U.S.A.* 109 L5
Sanford, *Maine, U.S.A.* 109 D10
Sanford, *N.C., U.S.A.* 109 H6
Sanford →, *Australia* 93 E2
Sanford, Mt., *U.S.A.* 100 B5
Sang-i-Masha, *Afghan.* 68 C2
Sanga, *Mozam.* 87 E4
Sanga →, *Congo* 84 E3
Sangamner, *India* 66 K9
Sangar, *Afghan.* 68 C1
Sangar, *Russia* 51 C13
Sangar Sarai, *Afghan.* 68 B4
Sangaredi, *Guinea* 82 C2
Sangarh →, *Pakistan* 68 D4
Sangasso, *Mali* 82 C3
Sangatte, *France* 19 B8
Sangay, *Ecuador* 124 D3
Sange, *Dem. Rep. of the Congo* 86 D2
Sangeang, *Indonesia* 63 F5
Sângeorz-Băi, *Romania* 43 C9
Sanger, *U.S.A.* 116 J7
Sângera, *Moldova* 43 D13
Sangerhausen, *Germany* 24 D7
Sanggan He →, *China* 56 E9
Sanggau, *Indonesia* 62 D4
Sanghar, *Pakistan* 68 F3
Sangihe, Kepulauan, *Indonesia* 63 D7
Sangihe, Pulau, *Indonesia* 63 D7
Sangju, *S. Korea* 57 F15
Sangkapura, *Indonesia* 62 F4
Sangkhla, *Thailand* 64 E2
Sangkulirang, *Indonesia* 62 D5
Sangla, *Pakistan* 68 D5
Sangli, *India* 66 L9
Sangmélima, *Cameroon* 83 E7
Sangod, *India* 68 G7
Sangre de Cristo Mts., *U.S.A.* 113 G2
Sangro →, *Italy* 29 F11
Sangrur, *India* 68 D6
Sangudo, *Canada* 104 C6
Sangue →, *Brazil* 124 F7
Sangüesa, *Spain* 32 C3
Sanguinaires, Îs., *France* 21 G12
Sangzhi, *China* 59 C8
Sanhala, *Ivory C.* 82 C3
Sanibel, *U.S.A.* 109 M4
Sanirajak, *Canada* 101 B11
Sanjawi, *Pakistan* 68 D3
Sanje, *Uganda* 86 C3
Sanjiang, *China* 58 E7
Sanjo, *Japan* 54 F9
Sankh →, *India* 69 H11
Sankt Andrä, *Austria* 26 E7
Sankt Augustin, *Germany* 24 E3
Sankt Blasien, *Germany* 25 H4
Sankt Gallen, *Switz.* 25 H5
Sankt Gallen □, *Switz.* 25 H5
Sankt Goar, *Germany* 25 E3
Sankt Ingbert, *Germany* 25 F3
Sankt Johann im Pongau, *Austria* 26 D6
Sankt Johann in Tirol, *Austria* 26 D5
Sankt-Peterburg, *Russia* 46 C6
Sankt Pölten, *Austria* 26 C8
Sankt Ulrich = Ortisei, *Italy* 29 B8
Sankt Valentin, *Austria* 26 C7
Sankt Veit an der Glan, *Austria* 26 E7
Sankt Wendel, *Germany* 25 F3
Sankt Wolfgang, *Austria* 26 D6
Sankuru →, *Dem. Rep. of the Congo* 84 E4
Sanliurfa, *Turkey* 70 B3
Sanlúcar de Barrameda, *Spain* 35 J4
Sanluri, *Italy* 30 C1
Sânmartin, *Romania* 43 D10
Sanmen, *China* 59 C13
Sanmenxia, *China* 56 G6
Sanming, *China* 59 D11
Sannaspos, *S. Africa* 88 D4
Sannicandro Gargánico, *Italy* 29 G12
Sânnicolau Mare, *Romania* 42 D5
Sannieshof, *S. Africa* 88 D4
Sannīn, J., *Lebanon* 75 B4
Sanniquellie, *Liberia* 82 D3
Sannûr, W. →, *Egypt* 80 B3
Sanok, *Poland* 45 J9
Sanquhar, *U.K.* 14 F5
Sansanding, *Mali* 82 C3
Sansepolcro, *Italy* 29 E9
Sansha, *China* 59 D13
Sanshui, *China* 59 F9
Sanski Most, *Bos.-H.* 29 D13
Sansui, *China* 58 D7
Sant Antoni Abat, *Spain* 37 C7
Sant Boi de Llobregat, *Spain* 32 D7
Sant Carles, *Spain* 37 B8
Sant Carles de la Ràpita, *Spain* 32 E5
Sant Celoni, *Spain* 32 D7
Sant Feliu de Guíxols, *Spain* 32 D8
Sant Feliu de Llobregat, *Spain* 32 D7
Sant Ferran, *Spain* 37 C7
Sant Francesc de Formentera, *Spain* 37 C7
Sant Jaume, *Spain* 37 B11
Sant Joan Baptista, *Spain* 37 B8
Sant Jordi, *Spain* 37 B9
Sant Jordi, G. de, *Spain* 32 E6
Sant Llorenç de Morunys, *Spain* 32 C6
Sant Llorenç des Cardassar, *Spain* 37 B10
Sant Mateu, *Baleares, Spain* 37 B7
Sant Mateu, *Valencia, Spain* 32 E5
Sant Miquel, *Spain* 37 B7
Sant Telm, *Spain* 37 B9
Sant' Ágata Militello, *Italy* 31 D7
Santa Agnés, *Spain* 37 B7
Santa Ana, *Bolivia* 124 F5
Santa Ana, *El Salv.* 120 D2
Santa Ana, *Mexico* 118 A2
Santa Ana, *U.S.A.* 117 M9
Sant' Ángelo Lodigiano, *Italy* 28 C6
Sant' Antíoco, *Italy* 30 C1
Santa Barbara, *Chile* 126 D1
Santa Barbara, *Honduras* 120 D2
Santa Bárbara, *Mexico* 118 B3
Santa Bárbara, *Spain* 32 E5
Santa Barbara, *U.S.A.* 117 L7
Santa Bárbara, Mt., *Spain* 33 H2
Santa Barbara Channel, *U.S.A.* 117 L7
Santa Barbara I., *U.S.A.* 117 M7
Santa Catalina, Gulf of, *U.S.A.* 117 N9
Santa Catalina, I., *Mexico* 118 B2
Santa Catalina I., *U.S.A.* 117 M8
Santa Catarina □, *Brazil* 127 B6
Santa Catarina, I. de, *Brazil* 127 B6
Santa Caterina di Pittinuri, *Italy* 30 B1
Santa Caterina Villarmosa, *Italy* 31 E7
Santa Cecília, *Brazil* 127 B5
Santa Clara, *Cuba* 120 B4
Santa Clara, *Calif., U.S.A.* 116 H5
Santa Clara, *Utah, U.S.A.* 115 H7
Santa Clara, El Golfo de, *Mexico* 118 A2
Santa Clara de Olimar, *Uruguay* 127 C5
Santa Clarita, *U.S.A.* 117 L8
Santa Clotilde, *Peru* 124 D4
Santa Coloma de Farners, *Spain* 32 D7
Santa Coloma de Gramenet, *Spain* 32 D7
Santa Comba, *Spain* 34 B2
Santa Croce Camerina, *Italy* 31 F7
Santa Croce di Magliano, *Italy* 29 G11
Santa Cruz, *Argentina* 128 G3
Santa Cruz, *Bolivia* 124 G6
Santa Cruz, *Chile* 126 C1
Santa Cruz, *Costa Rica* 120 D2
Santa Cruz, *Madeira* 37 D3
Santa Cruz, *Phil.* 61 D4
Santa Cruz, *U.S.A.* 116 J4
Santa Cruz →, *Argentina* 128 G3
Santa Cruz de la Palma, *Canary Is.* 37 F2
Santa Cruz de Mudela, *Spain* 35 G7
Santa Cruz de Tenerife, *Canary Is.* 37 F3
Santa Cruz del Norte, *Cuba* 120 B3
Santa Cruz del Retamar, *Spain* 34 E6
Santa Cruz del Sur, *Cuba* 120 B4
Santa Cruz do Rio Pardo, *Brazil* 127 A6
Santa Cruz do Sul, *Brazil* 127 B5
Santa Cruz I., *U.S.A.* 117 M7
Santa Cruz Is., *Solomon Is.* 96 J8
Santa Domingo, Cay, *Bahamas* 120 B4
Sant' Egídio alla Vibrata, *Italy* 29 F10
Santa Elena, *Argentina* 126 C4
Santa Elena, C., *Costa Rica* 120 D2
Sant' Eufémia, G. di, *Italy* 31 D9
Santa Eulàlia des Riu, *Spain* 37 C8
Santa Fe, *Argentina* 126 C3
Santa Fe, *Spain* 35 H7
Santa Fe, *U.S.A.* 115 J11
Santa Fé □, *Argentina* 126 C3
Santa Fé do Sul, *Brazil* 125 H8
Santa Filomena, *Brazil* 125 E9
Santa Fiora, *Italy* 29 F8
Santa Gertrudis, *Spain* 37 C7
Santa Giustina, *Italy* 29 B9
Santa Inês, *Brazil* 125 F11
Santa Inés, *Spain* 35 G5
Santa Inés, I., *Chile* 122 J3
Santa Isabel = Rey Malabo, *Eq. Guin.* 83 E6
Santa Isabel, *Argentina* 126 D2
Santa Isabel, Pico, *Eq. Guin.* 83 E6
Santa Isabel do Morro, *Brazil* 125 F8
Santa Lucía, *Corrientes, Argentina* 126 B4
Santa Lucía, *San Juan, Argentina* 126 C2
Santa Lucía, *Spain* 33 H4
Santa Lucía, *Uruguay* 126 C4
Santa Lucia Range, *U.S.A.* 116 K5
Santa Magdalena, I., *Mexico* 118 C2
Santa Margarita, *Argentina* 126 D3
Santa Margarita, *Spain* 37 B10
Santa Margarita, *U.S.A.* 116 K6
Santa Margarita →, *U.S.A.* 117 M9
Santa Margarita, I., *Mexico* 118 C2
Santa Margherita, *Italy* 30 D1
Santa Margherita Ligure, *Italy* 28 D6
Santa María, *Argentina* 126 B2
Santa Maria, *Brazil* 127 B5
Santa Maria, *Phil.* 61 C4
Santa Maria, *U.S.A.* 117 L6
Santa María →, *Mexico* 118 A3
Santa María, B. de, *Mexico* 118 B3
Santa Maria, C. de, *Portugal* 35 J3
Santa Maria Cápua Vétere, *Italy* 31 A7
Santa Maria da Feira, *Portugal* 34 E2
Santa Maria da Vitória, *Brazil* 125 F10
Santa Maria del Camí, *Spain* 37 B9
Santa Maria di Léuca, C., *Italy* 31 C11
Santa María la Real de Nieva, *Spain* 34 D6
Santa Marinella, *Italy* 29 F8
Santa Marta, *Colombia* 124 A4
Santa Marta, Sierra Nevada de, *Colombia* 122 B3
Santa Marta de Tormes, *Spain* 34 E5
Santa Marta Grande, C., *Brazil* 127 B6
Santa Marta Ortigueira, Ría de, *Spain* 34 B3
Santa Maura = Levkás, *Greece* 38 C2
Santa Monica, *U.S.A.* 117 M8
Santa Olalla, *Huelva, Spain* 35 H4
Santa Olalla, *Toledo, Spain* 34 E6
Santa Paula, *U.S.A.* 117 L7
Santa Pola, *Spain* 33 G4
Santa Ponsa, *Spain* 37 B9
Santa Rita, *U.S.A.* 115 K10
Santa Rosa, *La Pampa, Argentina* 126 D3
Santa Rosa, *San Luis, Argentina* 126 C2
Santa Rosa, *Brazil* 127 B5
Santa Rosa, *Calif., U.S.A.* 116 G4
Santa Rosa, *N. Mex., U.S.A.* 113 H2
Santa Rosa de Copán, *Honduras* 120 D2
Santa Rosa de Río Primero, *Argentina* 126 C3
Santa Rosa del Sara, *Bolivia* 124 G6
Santa Rosa I., *Calif., U.S.A.* 117 M6
Santa Rosa I., *Fla., U.S.A.* 109 K2
Santa Rosa Range, *U.S.A.* 114 F5
Santa Rosalía, *Mexico* 118 B2
Santa Sylvina, *Argentina* 126 B3
Santa Tecla = Nueva San Salvador, *El Salv.* 120 D2
Santa Teresa, *Argentina* 126 C3
Santa Teresa, *Australia* 94 C1
Santa Teresa, *Mexico* 119 B5
Santa Teresa di Riva, *Italy* 31 E8
Santa Teresa Gallura, *Italy* 30 A2
Santa Uxía, *Spain* 34 C2
Santa Vitória do Palmar, *Brazil* 127 C5
Santa Ynez →, *U.S.A.* 117 L6
Santa Ynez Mts., *U.S.A.* 117 L6
Santa Ysabel, *U.S.A.* 117 M10
Santadi, *Italy* 30 C1
Santaella, *Spain* 35 H6
Santai, *China* 58 B5
Santana, *Madeira* 37 D3
Sântana, *Romania* 42 D6
Santana, Coxilha de, *Brazil* 127 C4
Santana do Livramento, *Brazil* 127 C4
Santander, *Spain* 34 B7
Santander Jiménez, *Mexico* 119 C5
Santanyí, *Spain* 37 B10
Santaquin, *U.S.A.* 114 G8
Santarcángelo di Romagna, *Italy* 29 D9
Santarém, *Brazil* 125 D8
Santarém, *Portugal* 35 F2
Santarém □, *Portugal* 35 F2
Santaren Channel, *W. Indies* 120 B4
Santee, *U.S.A.* 117 N10
Santee →, *U.S.A.* 109 J6
Santéramo in Colle, *Italy* 31 B9
Santerno →, *Italy* 29 D8
Santhià, *Italy* 28 C5
Santiago, *Brazil* 127 B5
Santiago, *Chile* 126 C1
Santiago, *Panama* 120 E3
Santiago, *Phil.* 61 C4
Santiago □, *Chile* 126 C1
Santiago →, *Mexico* 98 G9
Santiago →, *Peru* 124 D3
Santiago, Punta de, *Eq. Guin.* 83 E6
Santiago de Compostela, *Spain* 34 C2
Santiago de Cuba, *Cuba* 120 C4
Santiago de los Cabelleros, *Dom. Rep.* 121 C5
Santiago del Estero, *Argentina* 126 B3
Santiago del Estero □, *Argentina* 126 B3
Santiago del Teide, *Canary Is.* 37 F3
Santiago do Cacém, *Portugal* 35 G2
Santiago Ixcuintla, *Mexico* 118 C3
Santiago Papasquiaro, *Mexico* 118 C3
Santiaguillo, L. de, *Mexico* 118 C4
Santiguila, *Mali* 82 C3
Santillana, *Spain* 34 B6
Santisteban del Puerto, *Spain* 35 G7
Santo Amaro, *Brazil* 125 F11
Santo Anastácio, *Brazil* 127 A5
Santo André, *Brazil* 127 A6
Santo Ângelo, *Brazil* 127 B5
Santo Antônio do Içá, *Brazil* 124 D5
Santo Antônio do Leverger, *Brazil* 125 G7
Santo Domingo, *Dom. Rep.* 121 C6
Santo Domingo, *Baja Calif., Mexico* 118 A1
Santo Domingo, *Baja Calif. S., Mexico* 118 B2
Santo Domingo, *Nic.* 120 D3
Santo Domingo de la Calzada, *Spain* 32 C2
Santo Domingo de los Colorados, *Ecuador* 124 D3
Santo Domingo Pueblo, *U.S.A.* 115 J10
Santo Stéfano di Camastro, *Italy* 31 D7
Santo Tirso, *Portugal* 34 D2
Santo Tomás, *Mexico* 118 A1
Santo Tomás, *Peru* 124 F4
Santo Tomé, *Argentina* 127 B4
Santo Tomé de Guayana = Ciudad Guayana, *Venezuela* 124 B6
Santomera, *Spain* 33 G3
Santoña, *Spain* 34 B7
Santoríni = Thíra, *Greece* 39 E7
Santos, *Brazil* 127 A6
Santos, Sierra de los, *Spain* 35 G5
Santos Dumont, *Brazil* 127 A7
Sanwer, *India* 68 H6
Sanxenxo, *Spain* 34 C2
Sanyuan, *China* 56 G5
São Bartolomeu de Messines, *Portugal* 35 H2
São Bernardo do Campo, *Brazil* 127 A6
São Borja, *Brazil* 127 B4
São Brás de Alportel, *Portugal* 35 H3
São Carlos, *Brazil* 127 A6
São Cristóvão, *Brazil* 125 F11
São Domingos, *Brazil* 125 F9
São Domingos, *Guinea-Biss.* 82 C1
São Francisco, *Brazil* 125 G10
São Francisco →, *Brazil* 122 E7
São Francisco do Sul, *Brazil* 127 B6
São Gabriel, *Brazil* 127 C5
São Gonçalo, *Brazil* 127 A7
Sao Hill, *Tanzania* 87 D4
São João, *Guinea-Biss.* 82 C1
São João da Boa Vista, *Brazil* 127 A6
São João da Madeira, *Portugal* 34 E2
São João da Pesqueira, *Portugal* 34 D3
São João del Rei, *Brazil* 127 A7
São João do Araguaia, *Brazil* 125 E9
São João do Piauí, *Brazil* 125 E10
São Joaquim, *Brazil* 127 B6
São Jorge, Pta. de, *Madeira* 37 D3
São José, *Brazil* 127 B5
São José do Norte, *Brazil* 127 C5
São José do Rio Prêto, *Brazil* 127 A6
São José dos Campos, *Brazil* 127 A6
São Leopoldo, *Brazil* 127 B5
São Lourenço, *Brazil* 127 A6
São Lourenço →, *Brazil* 125 G7
São Lourenço, Pta. de, *Madeira* 37 D3
São Lourenço do Sul, *Brazil* 127 C5
São Luís, *Brazil* 125 D10
São Luís Gonzaga, *Brazil* 127 B5
São Marcos →, *Brazil* 125 G9
São Marcos, B. de, *Brazil* 125 D10
São Martinho da Cortiça, *Portugal* 34 E2
São Mateus, *Brazil* 125 G11
São Mateus do Sul, *Brazil* 127 B5
São Miguel do Oeste, *Brazil* 127 B5
São Paulo, *Brazil* 127 A6
São Paulo □, *Brazil* 127 A6
São Paulo, I., *Atl. Oc.* 2 D8
São Paulo de Olivença, *Brazil* 124 D5
São Pedro do Sul, *Portugal* 34 E2
São Roque, *Madeira* 37 D3
São Roque, C. de, *Brazil* 122 D7
São Sebastião, I. de, *Brazil* 127 A6
São Sebastião do Paraíso, *Brazil* 127 A6
São Teotónio, *Portugal* 35 H2
São Tomé, *Atl. Oc.* 76 F4
São Tomé, C. de, *Brazil* 127 A7
São Tomé & Principe ■, *Africa* 77 F4
São Vicente, *Brazil* 127 A6
São Vicente, *Madeira* 37 D2
São Vicente, C. de, *Portugal* 35 H1
Saona, I., *Dom. Rep.* 121 C6
Saône →, *France* 19 G11
Saône-et-Loire □, *France* 19 F11
Saonek, *Indonesia* 63 E8
Sápai, *Greece* 41 E9
Sapanca, *Turkey* 72 B4
Saparua, *Indonesia* 63 E7
Sapele, *Nigeria* 83 D6
Sapelo I., *U.S.A.* 109 K5
Şaphane, *Turkey* 39 B11
Sapiéntza, *Greece* 38 E3
Sapone, *Burkina Faso* 83 C4
Saposoa, *Peru* 124 E3
Sapouy, *Burkina Faso* 83 C4
Sapozhok, *Russia* 48 D5
Sapphire, *Australia* 94 C4
Sappho, *U.S.A.* 116 B2
Sapporo, *Japan* 54 C10
Sapri, *Italy* 31 B8
Sapulpa, *U.S.A.* 113 H6
Saqqez, *Iran* 70 B5
Sar Dasht, *Iran* 71 C6
Sar-e Pol □, *Afghan.* 66 B4
Sar Gachīneh = Yāsūj, *Iran* 71 D6
Sar Planina, *Macedonia* 40 E4
Sara, *Burkina Faso* 82 C4
Sara, *Phil.* 61 F5
Sara Buri = Saraburi, *Thailand* 64 E3
Sarāb, *Iran* 70 B5
Sarabadi, *Iraq* 70 C5
Saraburi, *Thailand* 64 E3
Saradiya, *India* 68 J4
Saraféré, *Mali* 82 B4
Saragossa = Zaragoza, *Spain* 32 D4
Saraguro, *Ecuador* 124 D3
Sarai Naurang, *Pakistan* 68 C4
Saraikela, *India* 69 H11
Saraiu, *Romania* 43 F13
Sarajevo, *Bos.-H.* 42 G3
Sarakhs, *Turkmenistan* 71 B9
Saran, Gunung, *Indonesia* 62 E4
Saranac L., *U.S.A.* 111 B10
Saranac Lake, *U.S.A.* 111 B10
Saranda, *Tanzania* 86 D3
Sarandë, *Albania* 40 G3
Sarandí del Yi, *Uruguay* 127 C4
Sarandí Grande, *Uruguay* 126 C4
Sarangani B., *Phil.* 61 J6

Sarangani Is., Phil. 61 J6
Sarangarh, India 67 J13
Saransk, Russia 48 C7
Sarapul, Russia 50 D6
Sarasota, U.S.A. 109 M4
Saratoga, Calif., U.S.A. 116 H4
Saratoga, Wyo., U.S.A. 114 F10
Saratoga Springs, U.S.A. 111 C11
Saratok, Malaysia 62 D4
Saratov, Russia 48 E7
Saravane, Laos 64 E6
Sarawak □, Malaysia 62 D4
Saray, Tekirdağ, Turkey 41 E11
Saray, Van, Turkey 73 C11
Saraya, Guinea 82 C2
Saraya, Senegal 82 C2
Saraycık, Turkey 39 B11
Sarayköy, Turkey 39 D10
Saraylar, Turkey 41 F11
Sarayönü, Turkey 72 C5
Sarbāz, Iran 71 E9
Sarbīsheh, Iran 71 C8
Sárbogárd, Hungary 42 D3
Sarca →, Italy 28 C7
Sarcelles, France 19 D9
Sarda →, India 67 F12
Sardarshahr, India 68 E6
Sardegna □, Italy 30 B1
Sardhana, India 68 E7
Sardina, Pta., Canary Is. 37 F4
Sardinia = Sardegna □, Italy 30 B1
Sardis, Turkey 39 C10
Sārdūīyeh = Dar Mazār, Iran 71 D8
S'Arenal, Spain 37 B9
Sarentino, Italy 29 B8
Saréyamou, Mali 82 B4
Sargasso Sea, Atl. Oc. 97 D20
Sargodha, Pakistan 68 C5
Sarh, Chad 79 G9
Sarhala, Ivory C. 82 D3
Sārī, Iran 71 B7
Sari d'Orcino, France 21 F12
Sária, Greece 39 F9
Saria, India 69 J10
Sariab, Pakistan 68 D2
Sarıbeyler, Turkey 39 B9
Sarıgöl, Turkey 72 C3
Sarikamiş, Turkey 73 B10
Sarıkaya, Turkey 72 C6
Sarikei, Malaysia 62 D4
Sarıköy, Turkey 41 F11
Sarila, India 69 G8
Sarina, Australia 94 C4
Sariñena, Spain 32 D4
Sarita, U.S.A. 113 M6
Sariwŏn, N. Korea 57 E13
Sariyar Barajı, Turkey 72 B4
Sariyer, Turkey 41 E13
Sarju →, India 69 F9
Sark, U.K. 13 H5
Sarkad, Hungary 42 D6
Sarkari Tala, India 68 F4
Şarkışla, Turkey 72 C7
Şarköy, Turkey 41 F11
Sarlat-la-Canéda, France 20 D5
Sărmăşag, Romania 42 C7
Sărmaşu, Romania 43 D9
Sarmi, Indonesia 63 E9
Sarmiento, Argentina 128 F3
Sarmizegetusa, Romania 42 E7
Särna, Sweden 10 C7
Sarnano, Italy 29 E10
Sarnen, Switz. 25 J4
Sarnia, Canada 102 D3
Sarno, Italy 31 B7
Sarnthein = Sarentino, Italy 29 B8
Särö, Sweden 11 G5
Sarolangun, Indonesia 62 E2
Saronikós Kólpos, Greece 38 D5
Saronno, Italy 28 C6
Saros Körfezi, Turkey 41 F10
Sárospatak, Hungary 42 B6
Sarpsborg, Norway 9 G14
Sarracín, Spain 34 C7
Sarralbe, France 19 D14
Sarre = Saar →, Europe 17 E6
Sarre, Italy 28 C4
Sarre-Union, France 19 D14
Sarrebourg, France 19 D14
Sarreguemines, France 19 C14
Sarria, Spain 34 C3
Sarrión, Spain 32 E4
Sarro, Mali 82 C3
Sarstedt, Germany 24 C5
Sartène, France 21 G12
Sarthe □, France 18 D7
Sarthe →, France 18 E6
Sartilly, France 18 D5
Saruhanlı, Turkey 39 C9
Sărulești, Romania 43 F11
Saruna →, Pakistan 68 F2
Sárvár, Hungary 42 C1
Sarvar, India 68 F6
Sarvestān, Iran 71 D7
Särvfjället, Sweden 10 B7
Sárviz →, Hungary 42 D3
Sary-Tash, Kyrgyzstan 50 F8
Sarych, Mys, Ukraine 47 K7
Saryshagan, Kazakstan 50 E8
Sarzana, Italy 28 D6
Sarzeau, France 18 E4
Sasan Gir, India 68 J4
Sasaram, India 69 G11
Sasebo, Japan 55 H4
Saser, India 69 B7
Saskatchewan □, Canada 105 C7
Saskatchewan →, Canada 105 C8
Saskatoon, Canada 105 C7
Saskylakh, Russia 51 B12
Sasolburg, S. Africa 89 D4
Sasovo, Russia 48 C5
Sassandra, Ivory C. 82 E3
Sassandra →, Ivory C. 82 E3
Sássari, Italy 30 B1
Sassnitz, Germany 24 A9
Sasso Marconi, Italy 29 D8
Sassocorvaro, Italy 29 E9
Sassoferrato, Italy 29 E9
Sasstown, Liberia 82 E3
Sassuolo, Italy 28 D7
Sástago, Spain 32 D4
Sasumua Dam, Kenya 86 C4
Sasyk, Ozero, Ukraine 47 K5
Sata-Misaki, Japan 55 J5
Satadougou, Mali 82 C2
Satakunta, Finland 9 F20
Satama-Soukoura, Ivory C. 82 D4
Satara, India 66 L8
Satara, S. Africa 89 C5
Satbarwa, India 69 H11
Såtenäs, Sweden 11 F6
Säter, Sweden 10 D9
Satevó, Mexico 118 B3
Satilla →, U.S.A. 109 K5
Satmala Hills, India 66 J9
Satna, India 69 G9
Šator, Bos.-H. 29 D13
Sátoraljaújhely, Hungary 42 B6
Satpura Ra., India 66 J10
Satrup, Germany 24 A5
Satsuna-Shotō, Japan 55 K5
Sattahip, Thailand 64 F3
Satu Mare, Romania 42 C7
Satu Mare □, Romania 42 C8
Satui, Indonesia 62 E5
Satun, Thailand 65 J3
Saturnina →, Brazil 124 F7
Sauce, Argentina 126 C4
Sauceda, Mexico 118 B4
Saucillo, Mexico 118 B3
Sauda, Norway 9 G12
Sauðarkrókur, Iceland 8 D4
Saudi Arabia ■, Asia 70 B3
Saugeen →, Canada 110 B3
Saugerties, U.S.A. 111 D11
Saugues, France 20 D7
Saugus, U.S.A. 117 L8
Saujon, France 20 C3
Sauk Centre, U.S.A. 112 C7
Sauk Rapids, U.S.A. 112 C7
Saulgau, Germany 25 G5
Saulieu, France 19 E11
Sault, France 21 D9
Sault Ste. Marie, Canada 102 C3
Sault Ste. Marie, U.S.A. 101 D11
Saumlaki, Indonesia 63 F8
Saumur, France 18 E6
Saunders C., N.Z. 91 L3
Saunders I., Antarctica 5 B1
Saunders Point, Australia 93 E4
Sauri, Nigeria 83 C6
Saurimo, Angola 84 F4
Sausalito, U.S.A. 116 H4
Sauveterre-de-Béarn, France 20 E3
Sauzé-Vaussais, France 20 B4
Savá, Honduras 120 C2
Sava, Italy 31 B10
Sava →, Serbia, Yug. 42 F5
Savage, U.S.A. 112 B2
Savage I. = Niue, Cook Is. 97 J11
Savage River, Australia 94 G4
Savai'i, Samoa 91 A12
Savalou, Benin 83 D5
Savane, Mozam. 87 F4
Savanna, U.S.A. 112 D9
Savanna-la-Mar, Jamaica 120 C4
Savannah, Ga., U.S.A. 109 J5
Savannah, Mo., U.S.A. 112 F7
Savannah, Tenn., U.S.A. 109 H1
Savannah →, U.S.A. 109 J5
Savannakhet, Laos 64 D5
Savant L., Canada 102 B1
Savant Lake, Canada 102 B1
Săvârşin, Romania 42 D7
Savaştepe, Turkey 39 B9
Savé, Benin 83 D5
Save →, France 20 E5
Save →, Mozam. 89 C5
Sāveh, Iran 71 C6
Savelugu, Ghana 83 D4
Savenay, France 18 E5
Săveni, Romania 43 C11
Saverdun, France 20 E5
Saverne, France 19 D14
Savigliano, Italy 28 D4
Savigny-sur-Braye, France 18 E7
Sávio →, Italy 29 D9
Šavnik, Montenegro, Yug. 40 D3
Savo, Finland 8 E22
Savoie □, France 21 C10
Savona, Italy 28 D5
Savona, U.S.A. 110 D7
Savonlinna, Finland 46 B5
Savoy = Savoie □, France 21 C10
Şavşat, Turkey 73 B10
Sävsjö, Sweden 11 G8
Savur, Turkey 70 B4
Sawahlunto, Indonesia 62 E2
Sawai, Indonesia 63 E7
Sawai Madhopur, India 68 G7
Sawang Daen Din, Thailand 64 D4
Sawankhalok, Thailand 64 D2
Sawara, Japan 55 G10
Sawatch Range, U.S.A. 115 G10
Sawel Mt., U.K. 15 B4
Sawi, Thailand 65 G2
Sawla, Ghana 82 D4
Sawmills, Zimbabwe 87 F2
Sawtooth Range, U.S.A. 114 E6
Sawu, Indonesia 63 F6
Sawu Sea, Indonesia 63 F6
Saxby →, Australia 94 B3
Saxmundham, U.K. 13 E9
Saxony = Sachsen □, Germany 24 E9
Saxony, Lower = Niedersachsen □, Germany 24 C4
Saxton, U.S.A. 110 F6
Say, Mali 82 C4
Say, Niger 83 C5
Saya, Nigeria 83 D5
Sayabec, Canada 103 C6
Sayaboury, Laos 64 C3
Sayán, Peru 124 F3
Sayan, Vostochnyy, Russia 51 D10
Sayan, Zapadnyy, Russia 51 D10
Saydā, Lebanon 75 B4
Sayhandulaan = Oldziyt, Mongolia 56 B5
Sayhūt, Yemen 74 D5
Saykhin, Kazakstan 49 F8
Saynshand, Mongolia 60 B6
Sayre, Okla., U.S.A. 113 H5
Sayre, Pa., U.S.A. 111 E8
Sayreville, U.S.A. 111 F10
Sayula, Mexico 118 D4
Sayward, Canada 104 C3
Sazanit, Albania 40 F3
Sázava →, Czech Rep. 26 B7
Sazin, Pakistan 69 B5
Sazlika →, Bulgaria 41 E9
Scaër, France 18 D3
Scafell Pike, U.K. 12 C4
Scalea, Italy 31 C8
Scalloway, U.K. 14 A7
Scalpay, U.K. 14 D3
Scandia, Canada 104 C6
Scandiano, Italy 28 D7
Scandicci, Italy 29 E8
Scandinavia, Europe 8 E16
Scansano, Italy 29 F8
Scapa Flow, U.K. 14 C5
Scappoose, U.S.A. 116 E4
Scarámia, Capo, Italy 31 F7
Scarba, U.K. 14 E3
Scarborough, Trin. & Tob. 121 D7
Scarborough, U.K. 12 C7
Scariff I., Ireland 15 E1
Scarp, U.K. 14 C1
Scebeli, Wabi →, Somali Rep. 74 G3
Šćedro, Croatia 29 E13
Schaal See, Germany 24 B6
Schaffhausen, Switz. 25 H4
Schagen, Neths. 17 B4
Schaghticoke, U.S.A. 111 D11
Schärding, Austria 26 C6
Scharhörn, Germany 24 B4
Scheessel, Germany 24 B5
Schefferville, Canada 103 B6
Scheibbs, Austria 26 C8
Schelde →, Belgium 17 C4
Schell Creek Ra., U.S.A. 114 G6
Schellsburg, U.S.A. 110 F6
Schenectady, U.S.A. 111 D11
Schenevus, U.S.A. 111 D10
Scherfede, Germany 24 D5
Schesslitz, Germany 25 F7
Schiedam, Neths. 17 C4
Schiermonnikoog, Neths. 17 A6
Schiltigheim, France 19 D14
Schio, Italy 29 C8
Schladming, Austria 26 D6
Schlanders = Silandro, Italy 28 B7
Schlei →, Germany 24 A5
Schleiden, Germany 24 E2
Schleiz, Germany 24 E7
Schleswig, Germany 24 A5
Schleswig-Holstein □, Germany 24 A5
Schlüchtern, Germany 25 E5
Schmalkalden, Germany 24 E6
Schmölln, Germany 24 E8
Schneeberg, Austria 26 D8
Schneeberg, Germany 24 E8
Schneverdingen, Germany 24 B5
Schoharie, U.S.A. 111 D10
Schoharie →, U.S.A. 111 D10
Scholls, U.S.A. 116 E4
Schönberg, Mecklenburg-Vorpommern, Germany 24 B6
Schönberg, Schleswig-Holstein, Germany 24 A6
Schönebeck, Germany 24 C7
Schongau, Germany 25 H6
Schöningen, Germany 24 C6
Schopfheim, Germany 25 H3
Schorndorf, Germany 25 G5
Schortens, Germany 24 B3
Schouten I., Australia 94 G4
Schouten Is. = Supiori, Indonesia 63 E9
Schouwen, Neths. 17 C3
Schramberg, Germany 25 G4
Schrankogel, Austria 26 D4
Schreiber, Canada 102 C2
Schrems, Austria 26 C8
Schrobenhausen, Germany 25 G7
Schroffenstein, Namibia 88 D2
Schroon Lake, U.S.A. 111 C11
Schruns, Austria 26 D2
Schuler, Canada 105 C6
Schumacher, Canada 102 C3
Schurz, U.S.A. 114 G4
Schuyler, U.S.A. 112 E6
Schuylerville, U.S.A. 111 C11
Schuylkill →, U.S.A. 111 G9
Schuylkill Haven, U.S.A. 111 F8
Schwabach, Germany 25 F7
Schwaben □, Germany 25 G6
Schwäbisch Gmünd, Germany 25 G5
Schwäbisch Hall, Germany 25 F5
Schwäbische Alb, Germany 25 G5
Schwabmünchen, Germany 25 G6
Schwalmstadt, Germany 24 E5
Schwandorf, Germany 25 F8
Schwaner, Pegunungan, Indonesia 62 E4
Schwanewede, Germany 24 B4
Schwarmstedt, Germany 24 C5
Schwarze Elster →, Germany 24 D8
Schwarzenberg, Germany 24 E8
Schwarzrand, Namibia 88 D2
Schwarzwald, Germany 25 G4
Schwaz, Austria 26 D4
Schwechat, Austria 27 C9
Schwedt, Germany 24 B10
Schweinfurt, Germany 25 E6
Schweizer-Reneke, S. Africa 88 D4
Schwenningen = Villingen-Schwenningen, Germany 25 G4
Schwerin, Germany 24 B7
Schweriner See, Germany 24 B7
Schwetzingen, Germany 25 F4
Schwyz, Switz. 25 H4
Schwyz □, Switz. 25 H4
Sciacca, Italy 30 E6
Scicli, Italy 31 F7
Scilla, Italy 31 D8
Scilly, Isles of, U.K. 13 H1
Ścinawa, Poland 45 G3
Scione, Greece 40 G7
Scioto →, U.S.A. 108 F4
Scituate, U.S.A. 111 D14
Scobey, U.S.A. 112 A2
Scone, Australia 95 E5
Scordia, Italy 31 E7
Scoresbysund = Ittoqqortoormiit, Greenland 4 B6
Scorniceşti, Romania 43 F9
Scotia, Calif., U.S.A. 114 F1
Scotia, N.Y., U.S.A. 111 D11
Scotia Sea, Antarctica 5 B18
Scotland, Canada 110 C4
Scotland □, U.K. 14 E5
Scott, C., Australia 92 B4
Scott City, U.S.A. 112 F4
Scott Glacier, Antarctica 5 C8
Scott I., Antarctica 5 C11
Scott Is., Canada 104 C3
Scott L., Canada 105 B7
Scott Reef, Australia 92 B3
Scottburgh, S. Africa 89 E5
Scottdale, U.S.A. 110 F5
Scottish Borders □, U.K. 14 F6
Scottsbluff, U.S.A. 112 E3
Scottsboro, U.S.A. 109 H3
Scottsburg, U.S.A. 108 F3
Scottsdale, Australia 94 G4
Scottsdale, U.S.A. 115 K7
Scottsville, Ky., U.S.A. 109 G2
Scottsville, N.Y., U.S.A. 110 C7
Scottville, U.S.A. 108 D2
Scranton, U.S.A. 111 E9
Scugog, L., Canada 110 B6
Sculeni, Moldova 43 C12
Scunthorpe, U.K. 12 D7
Scuol Schuls, Switz. 25 J6
Scutari = Üsküdar, Turkey 41 F13
Seabrook, L., Australia 93 F2
Seaford, U.K. 13 G8
Seaford, U.S.A. 108 F8
Seaforth, Australia 94 C4
Seaforth, Canada 110 C3
Seaforth, L., U.K. 14 D2
Seagraves, U.S.A. 113 J3
Seaham, U.K. 12 C6
Seal →, Canada 105 B10
Seal L., Canada 103 B7
Sealy, U.S.A. 113 L6
Searchlight, U.S.A. 117 K12
Searcy, U.S.A. 113 H9
Searles L., U.S.A. 117 K9
Seascale, U.K. 12 C4
Seaside, Calif., U.S.A. 116 J5
Seaside, Oreg., U.S.A. 116 E3
Seaspray, Australia 95 F4
Seattle, U.S.A. 116 C4
Seaview Ra., Australia 94 B4
Sebago L., U.S.A. 111 C14
Sebago Lake, U.S.A. 111 C14
Sebastián Vizcaíno, B., Mexico 118 B2
Sebastopol = Sevastopol, Ukraine 47 K7
Sebastopol, U.S.A. 116 G4
Sebba, Burkina Faso 83 C5
Sebderat, Eritrea 81 D4
Sébékoro, Mali 82 C3
Seben, Turkey 72 B4
Sebeş, Romania 43 E8
Sebeşului, Munţii, Romania 43 E8
Sebewaing, U.S.A. 108 D4
Sebezh, Russia 46 D5
Sebha = Sabhah, Libya 79 C8
Sébi, Mali 82 B4
Şebinkarahisar, Turkey 73 B8
Sebiş, Romania 42 D7
Sebnitz, Germany 24 E10
Sebring, Fla., U.S.A. 109 M5
Sebring, Ohio, U.S.A. 110 F3
Sebringville, Canada 110 C3
Sebta = Ceuta, N. Afr. 78 A4
Sebuku, Indonesia 62 E5
Sebuku, Teluk, Malaysia 62 D5
Sečanj, Serbia, Yug. 42 E5
Secchia →, Italy 28 C8
Sechelt, Canada 104 D4
Sechura, Desierto de, Peru 124 E2
Seclin, France 19 B10
Secondigny, France 18 F6
Sečovce, Slovak Rep. 27 C14
Secretary I., N.Z. 91 L1
Secunderabad, India 66 L11
Security-Widefield, U.S.A. 112 F2
Sedalia, U.S.A. 112 F8
Sedan, France 19 C11
Sedan, U.S.A. 113 G6
Sedano, Spain 34 C7
Seddon, N.Z. 91 J5
Seddonville, N.Z. 91 J4
Sedé Boqér, Israel 75 E3
Sedeh, Fārs, Iran 71 D7
Sedeh, Khorāsān, Iran 71 C8
Séderon, France 21 D9
Sederot, Israel 75 D3
Sédhiou, Senegal 82 C1
Sedico, Italy 29 B9
Sedlčany, Czech Rep. 26 B7
Sedley, Canada 105 C8
Sedona, U.S.A. 115 J8
Sedova, Pik, Russia 50 B6
Sedro Woolley, U.S.A. 116 B4
Šeduva, Lithuania 44 C10
Sędziszów, Poland 45 H7
Sędziszów Małapolski, Poland 45 H8
Seebad Ahlbeck, Germany 24 B10
Seefeld in Tirol, Austria 26 D4
Seehausen, Germany 24 C7
Seeheim, Namibia 88 D2
Seeheim-Jugenheim, Germany 25 F4
Seeis, Namibia 88 C2
Seekoei →, S. Africa 88 E4
Seeley's Bay, Canada 111 B8
Seelow, Germany 24 C10
Sées, France 18 D7
Seesen, Germany 24 D6
Seevetal, Germany 24 B6
Sefadu, S. Leone 82 D2
Seferihisar, Turkey 39 C8
Séfeto, Mali 82 C3
Sefwi Bekwai, Ghana 82 D4
Segamat, Malaysia 65 L4
Şegarcea, Romania 43 F8
Ségbana, Benin 83 C5
Segbwema, S. Leone 82 D2
Seget, Indonesia 63 E8
Segonzac, France 20 C3
Segorbe, Spain 32 F4
Ségou, Mali 82 C3
Segovia = Coco →, Cent. Amer. 120 D3
Segovia, Spain 34 E6
Segovia □, Spain 34 E6
Segré, France 18 E6
Segre →, Spain 32 D5
Séguéla, Ivory C. 82 D3
Séguénéga, Burkina Faso 83 C4
Seguin, U.S.A. 113 L6
Segundo →, Argentina 126 C3
Segura →, Spain 33 G4
Segura, Sierra de, Spain 33 G2
Seh Konj, Kūh-e, Iran 71 D8
Seh Qal'eh, Iran 71 C8
Sehitwa, Botswana 88 C3
Sehore, India 68 H7
Sehwan, Pakistan 68 F2
Şeica Mare, Romania 43 D9
Seil, U.K. 14 E3
Seiland, Norway 8 A20
Seilhac, France 20 C5
Seiling, U.S.A. 113 G5
Seille →, Moselle, France 19 C13
Seille →, Saône-et-Loire, France 19 F11
Sein, Î. de, France 18 D2
Seinäjoki, Finland 9 E20
Seine →, France 18 C7
Seine, B. de la, France 18 C6
Seine-et-Marne □, France 19 D10
Seine-Maritime □, France 18 C7
Seine-St-Denis □, France 19 D9
Seini, Romania 43 C8
Seirijai, Lithuania 44 D10
Seistan = Sīstān, Asia 71 D9
Seistan, Daryācheh-ye = Sīstān, Daryācheh-ye, Iran 71 D9
Sejerø, Denmark 11 J5
Sejerø Bugt, Denmark 11 J5
Sejny, Poland 44 D10
Seka, Ethiopia 81 F4
Sekayu, Indonesia 62 E2
Seke, Tanzania 86 C3
Sekenke, Tanzania 86 C3
Seki, Turkey 39 E11
Sekondi-Takoradi, Ghana 82 E4
Sekota, Ethiopia 81 E4
Seksna, Russia 46 C10
Sekuma, Botswana 88 C3
Selah, U.S.A. 114 C3
Selama, Malaysia 65 K3
Selárgius, Italy 30 C2
Selaru, Indonesia 63 F8
Selb, Germany 25 E8
Selby, U.K. 12 D6
Selby, U.S.A. 112 C4
Selca, Croatia 29 E13
Selçuk, Turkey 39 D9
Selden, U.S.A. 112 F4
Sele →, Italy 31 B7
Selebi-Pikwe, Botswana 89 C4

Selemdzha

Selemdzha →, Russia 51 D13
Selendi, Manisa, Turkey 39 C10
Selendi, Manisa, Turkey 39 C9
Selenga = Selenge Mörön →, Asia 60 A5
Selenge Mörön →, Asia 60 A5
Selenicë, Albania 40 F3
Selenter See, Germany 24 A6
Sélestat, France 19 D14
Seletan, Tanjung, Indonesia 62 E4
Selevac, Serbia, Yug. 40 B4
Sélibabi, Mauritania 82 B2
Seliger, Ozero, Russia 46 D7
Seligman, U.S.A. 115 J7
Şelim, Turkey 73 B10
Selîma, El Wâhât el, Sudan 80 C2
Selimiye, Turkey 39 D9
Selinda Spillway →, Botswana 88 B3
Selinoús, Greece 38 D3
Selinsgrove, U.S.A. 110 F8
Selizharovo, Russia 46 D7
Selkirk, Canada 105 C9
Selkirk, U.K. 14 F6
Selkirk I., Canada 105 C9
Selkirk Mts., Canada 100 C8
Sellama, Sudan 81 E2
Selliá, Greece 36 D6
Sellières, France 19 F12
Sells, U.S.A. 115 L8
Sellye, Hungary 42 E2
Selma, Ala., U.S.A. 109 J2
Selma, Calif., U.S.A. 116 J7
Selma, N.C., U.S.A. 109 H6
Selmer, U.S.A. 109 H1
Selongey, France 19 E12
Selowandoma Falls, Zimbabwe 87 G3
Selpele, Indonesia 63 E8
Selsey Bill, U.K. 13 G7
Seltso, Russia 46 F8
Seltz, France 19 D15
Selu, Indonesia 63 F8
Sélune →, France 18 D5
Selva = La Selva del Camp, Spain 32 D6
Selva, Argentina 126 B3
Selvas, Brazil 122 D4
Selwyn L., Canada 105 B8
Selwyn Mts., Canada 100 B6
Selwyn Ra., Australia 94 C3
Seman →, Albania 40 F3
Semarang, Indonesia 62 F4
Sembabule, Uganda 86 C3
Şemdinli, Turkey 73 D11
Sémé, Senegal 82 B2
Semeih, Sudan 81 E3
Semenov, Russia 48 B7
Semenovka, Chernihiv, Ukraine 47 F7
Semenovka, Kremenchuk, Ukraine 47 H7
Semeru, Indonesia 63 H15
Semey, Kazakstan 50 D9
Semikarakorskiy, Russia 49 G5
Semiluki, Russia 47 G10
Seminoe Reservoir, U.S.A. 114 F10
Seminole, Okla., U.S.A. 113 H6
Seminole, Tex., U.S.A. 113 J3
Seminole Draw →, U.S.A. 113 J3
Semipalatinsk = Semey, Kazakstan 50 D9
Semirara Is., Phil. 61 F4
Semitau, Indonesia 62 D4
Semiyarka, Kazakstan 50 D8
Semiyarskoye = Semiyarka, Kazakstan 50 D8
Semmering P., Austria 26 D8
Semnān, Iran 71 C7
Semnān □, Iran 71 C7
Semporna, Malaysia 63 D5
Semuda, Indonesia 62 E4
Semur-en-Auxois, France 19 E11
Sen →, Cambodia 62 B3
Senā, Iran 71 D6
Sena, Mozam. 87 F4
Sena Madureira, Brazil 124 E5
Senador Pompeu, Brazil 125 E11
Senaki, Georgia 49 J6
Senanga, Zambia 85 H4
Senatobia, U.S.A. 113 H10
Sencelles, Spain 37 B9
Sendafa, Ethiopia 81 F4
Sendai, Kagoshima, Japan 55 J5
Sendai, Miyagi, Japan 54 E10
Sendai-Wan, Japan 54 E10
Senden, Bayern, Germany 25 G6
Senden, Nordrhein-Westfalen, Germany 24 D3
Sendhwa, India 68 J6
Sene →, Ghana 83 D4
Senec, Slovak Rep. 27 C10
Seneca, U.S.A. 109 H4
Seneca Falls, U.S.A. 111 D8
Seneca L., U.S.A. 110 D8
Senecaville L., U.S.A. 110 G3
Senegal ■, W. Afr. 82 C2
Sénégal →, W. Afr. 82 B1
Senegambia, Africa 76 E2
Senekal, S. Africa 89 D4
Senftenberg, Germany 24 D10
Senga Hill, Zambia 87 D3
Senge Khambab = Indus →, Pakistan 68 G2
Sengiley, Russia 48 D9
Sengua →, Zimbabwe 87 F2
Senhor-do-Bonfim, Brazil 125 F10
Senica, Slovak Rep. 27 C10
Senigállia, Italy 29 E10
Senio →, Italy 29 D9
Senirkent, Turkey 39 C12
Senise, Italy 31 B9
Senj, Croatia 29 D11
Senja, Norway 8 B17
Senkaku-Shotō, Japan 55 L1
Senlis, France 19 C9
Senmonorom, Cambodia 64 F6
Sennâr, Sudan 81 E3
Sennar □, Sudan 81 E3
Senneterre, Canada 102 C4
Senno, Belarus 46 E5
Sénnori, Italy 30 B1
Seno, Laos 64 D5
Senonches, France 18 D8
Senorbì, Italy 30 C2
Senožeče, Slovenia 29 C11
Sens, France 19 D10
Senta, Serbia, Yug. 42 E5
Sentani, Indonesia 63 E10
Sentery, Dem. Rep. of the Congo 86 D2
Sentinel, U.S.A. 115 K7
Šentjur, Slovenia 29 B12
Senya Beraku, Ghana 83 D4
Seo de Urgel = La Seu d'Urgell, Spain 32 C6
Seohara, India 69 E8
Seonath →, India 69 J10
Seondha, India 69 F8
Seoni, India 69 H8
Seoni Malwa, India 68 H8
Seoul = Sŏul, S. Korea 57 F14
Sepīdān, Iran 71 D7
Sepo-ri, N. Korea 57 E14
Sępólno Krajeńskie, Poland 44 E4
Sepone, Laos 64 D6
Sępopol, Poland 44 D8
Sept-Îles, Canada 103 B6
Septemvri, Bulgaria 41 D8
Sepúlveda, Spain 34 D7
Sequeros, Spain 34 E4
Sequim, U.S.A. 116 B3
Sequoia National Park, U.S.A. 116 J8
Serafimovich, Russia 48 F6
Seraing, Belgium 17 D5
Seraja, Indonesia 65 L7
Serakhis →, Cyprus 36 D11
Seram, Indonesia 63 E7
Seram Sea, Indonesia 63 E7
Seranantsara, Madag. 89 B8
Serang, Indonesia 63 G12
Serasan, Indonesia 65 L7
Seravezza, Italy 28 E7
Şerbettar, Turkey 41 E10
Serbia □, Yugoslavia 40 C5
Şercaia, Romania 43 E10
Serdo, Ethiopia 81 E5
Serdobsk, Russia 48 D7
Sered', Slovak Rep. 27 C10
Seredka, Russia 46 C5
Şereflikoçhisar, Turkey 72 C5
Seregno, Italy 28 C6
Seremban, Malaysia 65 L3
Serengeti Plain, Tanzania 86 C4
Serenje, Zambia 87 E3
Sereth = Siret →, Romania 43 E12
Sergach, Russia 48 C7
Sergen, Turkey 41 E11
Sergino, Russia 50 C7
Sergipe □, Brazil 125 F11
Sergiyev Posad, Russia 46 D10
Seria, Brunei 62 D4
Serian, Malaysia 62 D4
Seriate, Italy 28 C6
Seribu, Kepulauan, Indonesia 62 F3
Sérifontaine, France 19 C8
Sérifos, Greece 38 D6
Sérignan, France 20 E7
Sérigny →, Canada 103 A6
Serik, Turkey 72 D4
Seringapatam Reef, Australia 92 B3
Serinhisar, Turkey 39 D11
Sermaize-les-Bains, France 19 D11
Sermata, Indonesia 63 F7
Sérmide, Italy 29 D8
Sernovodsk, Russia 48 D10
Sernur, Russia 48 B9
Serock, Poland 45 F8
Serón, Spain 33 H2
Serós, Spain 32 D5
Serov, Russia 50 D7
Serowe, Botswana 88 C4
Serpa, Portugal 35 H3
Serpeddí, Punta, Italy 30 C2
Serpentara, Italy 30 C2
Serpentine Lakes, Australia 93 E4
Serpis →, Spain 33 G4
Serpukhov, Russia 46 E9
Serra de Outes, Spain 34 C2
Serra do Navio, Brazil 125 C8
Serra San Bruno, Italy 31 D9
Serradilla, Spain 34 F4
Sérrai, Greece 40 E7
Sérrai □, Greece 40 E7
Serramanna, Italy 30 C1
Serravalle Scrívia, Italy 28 D5
Serre-Ponçon, L. de, France 21 D10
Serres, France 21 D9
Serrezuela, Argentina 126 C2
Serrinha, Brazil 125 F11
Sersale, Italy 31 C9
Sertã, Portugal 34 F2
Sertanópolis, Brazil 127 A5
Sêrtar, China 58 A3
Serua, Indonesia 63 F8
Serui, Indonesia 63 E9
Serule, Botswana 88 C4
Sérvia, Greece 40 F6
Serzedelo, Portugal 34 D2
Sese Is., Uganda 86 C3
Sesepe, Indonesia 63 E7
Sesfontein, Namibia 88 B1
Sesheke, Zambia 88 B3
Sésia →, Italy 28 C5
Sesimbra, Portugal 35 G1
S'Espalmador, Spain 37 C7
S'Espardell, Spain 37 C7
Sessa Aurunca, Italy 30 A6
S'Estanyol, Spain 37 B9
Sestao, Spain 32 B2
Sesto Calende, Italy 28 C5
Sesto San Giovanni, Italy 28 C6
Sestri Levante, Italy 28 D6
Sestriere, Italy 28 D3
Sestroretsk, Russia 46 B6
Sestrunj, Croatia 29 D11
Sestu, Italy 30 C2
Setana, Japan 54 C9
Sète, France 20 E7
Sete Lagôas, Brazil 125 G10
Sétif, Algeria 78 A7
Seto, Japan 55 G8
Setonaikai, Japan 55 G6
Settat, Morocco 78 B4
Séttimo Torinese, Italy 28 C4
Setting L., Canada 105 C9
Settle, U.K. 12 C5
Settlement Pt., Bahamas 109 M6
Settlers, S. Africa 89 C4
Setúbal, Portugal 35 G2
Setúbal □, Portugal 35 G2
Setúbal, B. de, Portugal 35 G2
Seugne →, France 20 C3
Seul, Lac, Canada 102 B1
Seurre, France 19 F12
Sevan, Armenia 49 K7
Sevan, Ozero = Sevana Lich, Armenia 49 K7
Sevana Lich, Armenia 49 K7
Sevastopol, Ukraine 47 K7
Seven Sisters, Canada 104 C3
Sever →, Spain 35 F3
Sévérac-le-Château, France 20 D7
Severn →, Canada 102 A2
Severn →, U.K. 13 F5
Severn L., Canada 102 B1
Severnaya Zemlya, Russia 51 B10
Severo-Kurilsk, Russia 51 D16
Severo-Yeniseyskiy, Russia 51 C10
Severodonetsk = Syeverodonetsk, Ukraine 47 H10
Severodvinsk, Russia 50 C4
Sevier, U.S.A. 115 G7
Sevier →, U.S.A. 115 G7
Sevier Desert, U.S.A. 114 G7
Sevier L., U.S.A. 114 G7
Sevilla, Spain 35 H5
Sevilla □, Spain 35 H5
Seville = Sevilla, Spain 35 H5
Sevlievo, Bulgaria 41 C9
Sevnica, Slovenia 29 B12
Sèvre-Nantaise →, France 18 E5
Sèvre-Niortaise →, France 20 B3
Sevsk, Russia 47 F8
Sewa →, S. Leone 82 D2
Sewani, India 68 E6
Seward, Alaska, U.S.A. 100 B5
Seward, Nebr., U.S.A. 112 E6
Seward, Pa., U.S.A. 110 F5
Seward Peninsula, U.S.A. 100 B3
Sewell, Chile 126 C1
Sewer, Indonesia 63 F8
Sewickley, U.S.A. 110 F4
Sexsmith, Canada 104 B5
Seychelles ■, Ind. Oc. 52 K9
Seyðisfjörður, Iceland 8 D6
Seydişehir, Turkey 72 D4
Seydvān, Iran 70 B5
Seyhan →, Turkey 70 B2
Seyhan Barajı, Turkey 72 D6
Seyitgazi, Turkey 39 B12
Seyitömer, Turkey 39 B11
Seym →, Ukraine 47 G7
Seymen, Turkey 41 E11
Seymour, Australia 95 F4
Seymour, S. Africa 89 E4
Seymour, Conn., U.S.A. 111 E11
Seymour, Ind., U.S.A. 108 F3
Seymour, Tex., U.S.A. 113 J5
Seyne, France 21 D10
Seyssel, France 21 C9
Sežana, Slovenia 29 C10
Sézanne, France 19 D10
Sezze, Italy 30 A6
Sfântu Gheorghe, Covasna, Romania 43 E10
Sfântu Gheorghe, Tulcea, Romania 43 F14
Sfântu Gheorghe, Braţul →, Romania 43 F14
Sfax, Tunisia 79 B8
Sha Xi →, China 59 D12
Sha Xian, China 59 D11
Shaanxi □, China 56 G5
Shaba = Katanga □, Dem. Rep. of the Congo 86 D2
Shabla, Bulgaria 41 C12
Shabogamo L., Canada 103 B6
Shabunda, Dem. Rep. of the Congo 86 C2
Shache, China 60 C2
Shackleton Ice Shelf, Antarctica 5 C8
Shackleton Inlet, Antarctica 5 E11
Shādegān, Iran 71 D6
Shadi, China 59 D10
Shadi, India 69 C7
Shadrinsk, Russia 50 D7
Shadyside, U.S.A. 110 G4
Shaffa, Nigeria 83 C7
Shafter, U.S.A. 117 K7
Shaftesbury, U.K. 13 F5
Shagamu, Nigeria 83 D5
Shagram, Pakistan 69 A5
Shah Alizai, Pakistan 68 E2
Shah Bunder, Pakistan 68 G2
Shahabad, Punjab, India 68 D7
Shahabad, Raj., India 68 G7
Shahabad, Ut. P., India 69 F8
Shahadpur, Pakistan 68 G3
Shahba, Syria 75 C5
Shahdād, Iran 71 D8
Shahdād, Namakzār-e, Iran 71 D8
Shahdadkot, Pakistan 68 F2
Shahdol, India 69 H9
Shahe, China 56 F8
Shahganj, India 69 F10
Shahgarh, India 66 F6
Shahjahanpur, India 69 F8
Shahpur, India 68 H7
Shahpur, Baluchistan, Pakistan 68 E3
Shahpur, Punjab, Pakistan 68 C5
Shahpur Chakar, Pakistan 68 F3
Shahpura, Mad. P., India 69 H9
Shahpura, Raj., India 68 G6
Shahr-e Bābak, Iran 71 D7
Shahr-e Kord, Iran 71 C6
Shāhrakht, Iran 71 C9
Shahrig, Pakistan 68 D2
Shahukou, China 56 D7
Shaikhabad, Afghan. 68 B3
Shajapur, India 68 H7
Shakargarh, Pakistan 68 C6
Shakawe, Botswana 88 B3
Shaker Heights, U.S.A. 110 E3
Shakhty, Russia 49 G5
Shakhunya, Russia 48 B8
Shaki, Nigeria 83 D5
Shâkir, Egypt 80 B3
Shala, L., Ethiopia 81 F4
Shali, Russia 49 J7
Shallow Lake, Canada 110 B3
Shalqar, Kazakstan 50 E6
Shalskiy, Russia 46 B8
Shaluli Shan, China 58 B2
Shām, Iran 71 E8
Shām, Bādiyat ash, Asia 70 C3
Shamâl Bahr el Ghazal □, Sudan 81 F2
Shamâl Dârfûr □, Sudan 81 E2
Shamâl Kordofân □, Sudan 81 E3
Shamâl Sînî □, Egypt 75 E2
Shamattawa, Canada 102 A1
Shamattawa →, Canada 102 A2
Shambe, Sudan 81 F3
Shambu, Ethiopia 81 F4
Shamīl, Iran 71 E8
Shamkhor = Şämkir, Azerbaijan 49 K8
Shāmkūh, Iran 71 C8
Shamli, India 68 E7
Shammar, Jabal, Si. Arabia 70 E4
Shamo = Gobi, Asia 56 C6
Shamo, L., Ethiopia 81 F4
Shamokin, U.S.A. 111 F8
Shamrock, U.S.A. 113 H4
Shamva, Zimbabwe 87 F3
Shan □, Burma 67 J21
Shan Xian, China 56 G9
Shanan →, Ethiopia 81 F5
Shanchengzhen, China 57 C13
Shāndak, Iran 71 D9
Shandon, U.S.A. 116 K6
Shandong □, China 57 G10
Shandong Bandao, China 57 F11
Shang Xian = Shangzhou, China 56 H5
Shanga, Nigeria 78 F6
Shangalowe, Dem. Rep. of the Congo 87 E2
Shangani, Zimbabwe 89 B4
Shangani →, Zimbabwe 87 F2
Shangbancheng, China 57 D10
Shangcheng, China 59 B10
Shangchuan Dao, China 59 G9
Shangdu, China 56 D7
Shanggao, China 59 C10
Shanghai, China 59 B13
Shanghai Shi □, China 59 B13
Shanghang, China 59 E11
Shanghe, China 57 F9
Shanglin, China 58 F7
Shangnan, China 56 H6
Shangqiu, China 56 G8
Shangrao, China 59 C11
Shangshui, China 60 C6
Shangsi, China 58 F6
Shangyou, China 59 E10
Shangyu, China 59 B13
Shangzhi, China 57 B14
Shangzhou, China 56 H5
Shanhetun, China 57 B14
Shani, Nigeria 83 C7
Shannon, N.Z. 91 J5
Shannon →, Ireland 15 D2
Shannon, Mouth of the, Ireland 15 D2
Shannon Airport, Ireland 15 D3
Shansi = Shanxi □, China 56 F7
Shantar, Ostrov Bolshoy, Russia 51 D14
Shantipur, India 69 H13
Shantou, China 59 F11
Shantung = Shandong □, China 57 G10
Shanwei, China 59 F10
Shanxi □, China 56 F7
Shanyang, China 56 H5
Shanyin, China 56 E7
Shaodong, China 59 D8
Shaoguan, China 59 E9
Shaoshan, China 59 D9
Shaowu, China 59 D11
Shaoxing, China 59 C13
Shaoyang, Hunan, China 59 D8
Shaoyang, Hunan, China 59 D8
Shap, U.K. 12 C5
Shapinsay, U.K. 14 B6
Shaqq el Gi'eifer →, Sudan 81 D2
Shaqra', Si. Arabia 70 E5
Shaqrā', Yemen 74 E4
Sharafa, Sudan 81 E2
Sharafkhāneh, Iran 70 B5
Sharbot Lake, Canada 111 B8
Shari, Japan 54 C12
Sharjah = Ash Shāriqah, U.A.E. 71 E7
Shark B., Australia 93 E1
Sharm el Sheikh, Egypt 80 B3
Sharon, Mass., U.S.A. 111 D13
Sharon, Pa., U.S.A. 110 E4
Sharon Springs, Kans., U.S.A. 112 F4
Sharon Springs, N.Y., U.S.A. 111 D10
Sharp Pt., Australia 94 A3
Sharpe L., Canada 102 B1
Sharpsville, U.S.A. 110 E4
Sharq el Istiwa'iya □, Sudan 81 G3
Sharya, Russia 48 A7
Shasha, Ethiopia 81 F4
Shashemene, Ethiopia 81 F4
Shashi, Botswana 89 C4
Shashi, China 59 B9
Shashi →, Africa 87 G2
Shasta, Mt., U.S.A. 114 F2
Shasta L., U.S.A. 114 F2
Shatawi, Sudan 81 E3
Shatsk, Russia 48 C5
Shatt al Arab = Arab, Shatt al →, Asia 71 D6
Shatura, Russia 46 E10
Shaumyani = Shulaveri, Georgia 49 K7
Shaunavon, Canada 105 D7
Shaver L., U.S.A. 116 H7
Shaw →, Australia 92 D2
Shaw I., Australia 94 C4
Shawanaga, Canada 110 A4
Shawangunk Mts., U.S.A. 111 E10
Shawano, U.S.A. 108 C1
Shawinigan, Canada 102 C5
Shawnee, U.S.A. 113 H6
Shay Gap, Australia 92 D3
Shayang, China 59 B9
Shaybārā, Si. Arabia 70 E3
Shayib el Banat, Gebel, Egypt 80 B3
Shaykh, J. ash, Lebanon 75 B4
Shaykh Miskīn, Syria 75 C5
Shaykh Sa'īd, Iraq 70 C5
Shchekino, Russia 46 E9
Shcherbakov = Rybinsk, Russia 46 C10
Shchigry, Russia 47 G9
Shchors, Ukraine 47 G6
Shchuchinsk, Kazakstan 50 D8
She Xian, Anhui, China 59 C12
She Xian, Hebei, China 56 F7
Shebekino, Russia 47 G9
Shebele = Scebeli, Wabi →, Somali Rep. 74 G3
Sheboygan, U.S.A. 108 D2
Shebshi Mts., Nigeria 83 D7
Shediac, Canada 103 C7
Sheelin, L., Ireland 15 C4
Sheep Haven, Ireland 15 A4
Sheerness, U.K. 13 F8
Sheet Harbour, Canada 103 D7
Sheffield, U.K. 12 D6
Sheffield, Ala., U.S.A. 109 H2
Sheffield, Mass., U.S.A. 111 D11
Sheffield, Pa., U.S.A. 110 E5
Shehojele, Ethiopia 81 E4
Shehong, China 58 B5
Sheikh Idris, Sudan 81 E3
Sheikhpura, India 69 G11
Shek Hasan, Ethiopia 81 E4
Shekhupura, Pakistan 68 D5
Sheki = Şaki, Azerbaijan 49 K8
Shelburne, N.S., Canada 103 D6
Shelburne, Ont., Canada 102 D3
Shelburne, U.S.A. 111 B11
Shelburne B., Australia 94 A3
Shelburne Falls, U.S.A. 111 D12
Shelby, Mich., U.S.A. 108 D2
Shelby, Miss., U.S.A. 113 J9
Shelby, Mont., U.S.A. 114 B8
Shelby, N.C., U.S.A. 109 H5
Shelby, Ohio, U.S.A. 110 F2
Shelbyville, Ill., U.S.A. 112 F10
Shelbyville, Ind., U.S.A. 108 F3
Shelbyville, Ky., U.S.A. 108 F3
Shelbyville, Tenn., U.S.A. 109 H2
Sheldon, U.S.A. 112 D7
Sheldrake, Canada 103 B7
Shelengo, Khawr →, Sudan 81 E2
Shelikhova, Zaliv, Russia 51 D16
Shell Lakes, Australia 93 E4
Shellbrook, Canada 105 C7
Shellharbour, Australia 95 E5
Shelon →, Russia 46 C6
Shelter I, U.S.A. 111 E12
Shelton, Conn., U.S.A. 111 E11
Shelton, Wash., U.S.A. 116 C3
Shemakha = Şamaxi, Azerbaijan 49 K9
Shëmri, Albania 40 D4
Shemsi, Sudan 80 D2
Shen Xian, China 56 F8
Shenandoah, Iowa, U.S.A. 112 E7
Shenandoah, Pa., U.S.A. 111 F8
Shenandoah, Va., U.S.A. 108 F6

Shenandoah →, *U.S.A.* 108 **F7**
Shenandoah National Park, *U.S.A.* 108 **F6**
Shenchi, *China* 56 **E7**
Shendam, *Nigeria* 83 **D6**
Shendî, *Sudan* 81 **D3**
Shenge, *S. Leone* 82 **D2**
Shengfang, *China* 56 **E9**
Shëngjergj, *Albania* 40 **E4**
Shëngjin, *Albania* 40 **E3**
Shengzhou, *China* 59 **C13**
Shenjingzi, *China* 57 **B13**
Shenmu, *China* 56 **E6**
Shennongjia, *China* 59 **B8**
Shenqiu, *China* 56 **H8**
Shensi = Shaanxi □, *China* 56 **G5**
Shenyang, *China* 57 **D12**
Shenzhen, *China* 59 **F10**
Sheo, *India* 68 **F4**
Sheopur Kalan, *India* 66 **G10**
Shepetivka, *Ukraine* 47 **G4**
Shepetovka = Shepetivka, *Ukraine* 47 **G4**
Shepparton, *Australia* 95 **F4**
Sheppey, I. of, *U.K.* 13 **F8**
Shepton Mallet, *U.K.* 13 **F5**
Sheqi, *China* 56 **H7**
Sher Qila, *Pakistan* 69 **A6**
Sherab, *Sudan* 81 **E1**
Sherborne, *U.K.* 13 **G5**
Sherbro →, *S. Leone* 82 **D2**
Sherbro I., *S. Leone* 82 **D2**
Sherbrooke, *N.S., Canada* 103 **C7**
Sherbrooke, *Qué., Canada* 103 **C5**
Sherburne, *U.S.A.* 111 **D9**
Shereik, *Sudan* 80 **D3**
Shergarh, *India* 68 **F5**
Sherghati, *India* 69 **G11**
Sheridan, *Ark., U.S.A.* 113 **H8**
Sheridan, *Wyo., U.S.A.* 114 **D10**
Sheringham, *U.K.* 12 **E9**
Sherkin I., *Ireland* 15 **E2**
Sherkot, *India* 69 **E8**
Sherman, *U.S.A.* 113 **J6**
Sherpur, *India* 69 **G10**
Sherridon, *Canada* 105 **B8**
Sherwood Forest, *U.K.* 12 **D6**
Sherwood Park, *Canada* 104 **C6**
Sheslay →, *Canada* 104 **B2**
Shethanei L., *Canada* 105 **B9**
Shetland □, *U.K.* 14 **A7**
Shetland Is., *U.K.* 14 **A7**
Shetrunji →, *India* 68 **J5**
Shewa □, *Ethiopia* 81 **F4**
Shewa Gimira, *Ethiopia* 81 **F4**
Sheyenne →, *U.S.A.* 112 **B6**
Shibām, *Yemen* 74 **D4**
Shibata, *Japan* 54 **F9**
Shibecha, *Japan* 54 **C12**
Shibetsu, *Japan* 54 **B11**
Shibîn el Kôm, *Egypt* 80 **H7**
Shibîn el Qanâtir, *Egypt* 80 **H7**
Shibing, *China* 58 **D7**
Shibogama L., *Canada* 102 **B2**
Shibushi, *Japan* 55 **J5**
Shicheng, *China* 59 **D11**
Shickshinny, *U.S.A.* 111 **E8**
Shickshock Mts. = Chic-Chocs, Mts., *Canada* 103 **C6**
Shidao, *China* 57 **F12**
Shidian, *China* 58 **E2**
Shido, *Japan* 55 **G7**
Shiel, L., *U.K.* 14 **E3**
Shield, C., *Australia* 94 **A2**
Shieli, *Kazakstan* 50 **E7**
Shifang, *China* 58 **B5**
Shiga □, *Japan* 55 **G8**
Shigu, *China* 58 **D2**
Shiguaigou, *China* 56 **D6**
Shihchiachuangi = Shijiazhuang, *China* 56 **E8**
Shijak, *Albania* 40 **E3**
Shijiazhuang, *China* 56 **E8**
Shijiu Hu, *China* 59 **B12**
Shikarpur, *India* 68 **E8**
Shikarpur, *Pakistan* 68 **F3**
Shikohabad, *India* 69 **F8**
Shikoku □, *Japan* 55 **H6**
Shikoku-Sanchi, *Japan* 55 **H6**
Shiliguri, *India* 67 **F16**
Shilka, *Russia* 51 **D12**
Shilka →, *Russia* 51 **D13**
Shillelagh, *Ireland* 15 **D5**
Shillington, *U.S.A.* 111 **F9**
Shillong, *India* 67 **G17**
Shilo, *West Bank* 75 **C4**
Shilong, *China* 59 **F9**
Shilou, *China* 56 **F6**
Shilovo, *Russia* 48 **C5**
Shimabara, *Japan* 55 **H5**
Shimada, *Japan* 55 **G9**
Shimane □, *Japan* 55 **G6**
Shimanovsk, *Russia* 51 **D13**
Shimen, *China* 59 **C8**
Shimenjie, *China* 59 **C11**
Shimian, *China* 58 **C4**
Shimizu, *Japan* 55 **G9**
Shimodate, *Japan* 55 **F9**
Shimoga, *India* 66 **N9**
Shimoni, *Kenya* 86 **C4**
Shimonoseki, *Japan* 55 **H5**
Shimpuru Rapids, *Angola* 88 **B2**
Shimsk, *Russia* 46 **C6**
Shin, L., *U.K.* 14 **C4**
Shinan, *China* 58 **F7**
Shinano-Gawa →, *Japan* 55 **F9**
Shināş, *Oman* 71 **E8**
Shīndand, *Afghan.* 66 **C3**
Shinglehouse, *U.S.A.* 110 **E6**
Shingū, *Japan* 55 **H7**
Shingwidzi, *S. Africa* 89 **C5**
Shinjō, *Japan* 54 **E10**
Shinkafe, *Nigeria* 83 **C6**
Shinshār, *Syria* 75 **A5**
Shinyanga, *Tanzania* 86 **C3**
Shinyanga □, *Tanzania* 86 **C3**
Shio-no-Misaki, *Japan* 55 **H7**
Shiogama, *Japan* 54 **E10**
Shiojiri, *Japan* 55 **F8**
Shipchenski Prokhod, *Bulgaria* 41 **D9**
Shiping, *China* 58 **F4**
Shippegan, *Canada* 103 **C7**
Shippensburg, *U.S.A.* 110 **F7**
Shippenville, *U.S.A.* 110 **E5**
Shiprock, *U.S.A.* 115 **H9**
Shiqian, *China* 58 **D7**
Shiqma, N. →, *Israel* 75 **D3**
Shiquan, *China* 56 **H5**
Shiquan He = Indus →, *Pakistan* 68 **G2**
Shīr Kūh, *Iran* 71 **D7**
Shiragami-Misaki, *Japan* 54 **D10**
Shirakawa, *Fukushima, Japan* 55 **F10**
Shirakawa, *Gifu, Japan* 55 **F8**
Shirane-San, *Gumma, Japan* 55 **F9**
Shirane-San, *Yamanashi, Japan* 55 **G9**
Shiraoi, *Japan* 54 **C10**
Shīrāz, *Iran* 71 **D7**
Shirbīn, *Egypt* 80 **H7**
Shire →, *Africa* 87 **F4**
Shiretoko-Misaki, *Japan* 54 **B12**
Shirinab →, *Pakistan* 68 **D2**
Shiriya-Zaki, *Japan* 54 **D10**
Shiroishi, *Japan* 54 **F10**
Shīrvān, *Iran* 71 **B8**
Shirwa, L. = Chilwa, L., *Malawi* 87 **F4**
Shishi, *China* 59 **E12**
Shishou, *China* 59 **C9**
Shitai, *China* 59 **B11**
Shivpuri, *India* 68 **G7**
Shixian, *China* 57 **C15**
Shixing, *China* 59 **E10**
Shiyan, *China* 59 **A8**
Shiyata, *Egypt* 80 **B2**
Shizhu, *China* 58 **C7**
Shizong, *China* 58 **E5**
Shizuishan, *China* 56 **E4**
Shizuoka, *Japan* 55 **G9**
Shizuoka □, *Japan* 55 **G9**
Shklov = Shklow, *Belarus* 46 **E6**
Shklow, *Belarus* 46 **E6**
Shkoder = Shkodër, *Albania* 40 **D3**
Shkodër, *Albania* 40 **D3**
Shkumbini →, *Albania* 40 **E3**
Shmidta, Ostrov, *Russia* 51 **A10**
Shō-Gawa →, *Japan* 55 **F8**
Shoal L., *Canada* 105 **D9**
Shoal Lake, *Canada* 105 **C8**
Shōdo-Shima, *Japan* 55 **G7**
Sholapur = Solapur, *India* 66 **L9**
Shologontsy, *Russia* 51 **C12**
Shōmrōn, *West Bank* 75 **C4**
Shoreham by Sea, *U.K.* 13 **G7**
Shori →, *Pakistan* 68 **E3**
Shorkot Road, *Pakistan* 68 **D5**
Shoshone, *Calif., U.S.A.* 117 **K10**
Shoshone, *Idaho, U.S.A.* 114 **E6**
Shoshone L., *U.S.A.* 114 **D8**
Shoshone Mts., *U.S.A.* 114 **G5**
Shoshong, *Botswana* 88 **C4**
Shoshoni, *U.S.A.* 114 **E9**
Shostka, *Ukraine* 47 **G7**
Shou Xian, *China* 59 **A11**
Shouchang, *China* 59 **C12**
Shouguang, *China* 57 **F10**
Shouning, *China* 59 **D12**
Shouyang, *China* 56 **F7**
Show Low, *U.S.A.* 115 **J9**
Shpola, *Ukraine* 47 **H6**
Shreveport, *U.S.A.* 113 **J8**
Shrewsbury, *U.K.* 13 **E5**
Shri Mohangarh, *India* 68 **F4**
Shrirampur, *India* 69 **H13**
Shropshire □, *U.K.* 13 **E5**
Shū, *Kazakstan* 50 **E8**
Shū →, *Kazakstan* 52 **E10**
Shuangbai, *China* 58 **E3**
Shuangcheng, *China* 57 **B14**
Shuangfeng, *China* 59 **D9**
Shuanggou, *China* 57 **G9**
Shuangjiang, *China* 58 **F2**
Shuangliao, *China* 57 **C12**
Shuangshanzi, *China* 57 **D10**
Shuangyang, *China* 57 **C13**
Shuangyashan, *China* 60 **B8**
Shubra Khit, *Egypt* 80 **H7**
Shucheng, *China* 59 **B11**
Shugozero, *Russia* 46 **C8**
Shuguri Falls, *Tanzania* 87 **D4**
Shuiji, *China* 59 **D12**
Shuiye, *China* 56 **F8**
Shujalpur, *India* 68 **H7**
Shukpa Kunzang, *India* 69 **B8**
Shulan, *China* 57 **B14**
Shulaveri, *Georgia* 49 **K7**
Shule, *China* 60 **C2**
Shumagin Is., *U.S.A.* 100 **C4**
Shumen, *Bulgaria* 41 **C10**
Shumerlya, *Russia* 48 **C8**
Shumikha, *Russia* 50 **D7**
Shunchang, *China* 59 **D11**
Shunde, *China* 59 **F9**
Shungay, *Kazakstan* 49 **F8**
Shuo Xian = Shuozhou, *China* 56 **E7**
Shuozhou, *China* 56 **E7**
Shūr →, *Fārs, Iran* 71 **D7**
Shūr →, *Kermān, Iran* 71 **D8**
Shūr →, *Yazd, Iran* 71 **D7**
Shūr Āb, *Iran* 71 **C6**
Shūr Gaz, *Iran* 71 **D8**
Shūrāb, *Iran* 71 **C8**
Shūrjestān, *Iran* 71 **D7**
Shurugwi, *Zimbabwe* 87 **F3**
Shūsf, *Iran* 71 **D9**
Shūsh, *Iran* 73 **F13**
Shūshtar, *Iran* 71 **D6**
Shuswap L., *Canada* 104 **C5**
Shuya, *Russia* 48 **B5**
Shuyang, *China* 57 **G10**
Shūzū, *Iran* 71 **D7**
Shwebo, *Burma* 67 **H19**
Shwegu, *Burma* 67 **G20**
Shweli →, *Burma* 67 **H20**
Shymkent, *Kazakstan* 50 **E7**
Shyok, *India* 69 **B8**
Shyok →, *Pakistan* 69 **B6**
Si Chon, *Thailand* 65 **H2**
Si Kiang = Xi Jiang →, *China* 59 **F9**
Si-ngan = Xi'an, *China* 56 **G5**
Si Prachan, *Thailand* 64 **E3**
Si Racha, *Thailand* 64 **F3**
Si Xian, *China* 57 **H9**
Siahaf →, *Pakistan* 68 **E3**
Siahan Range, *Pakistan* 66 **F4**
Siaksriindrapura, *Indonesia* 62 **D2**
Sialkot, *Pakistan* 68 **C6**
Siam = Thailand ■, *Asia* 64 **E4**
Sian = Xi'an, *China* 56 **G5**
Sianów, *Poland* 44 **D3**
Siantan, *Indonesia* 62 **D3**
Sīāreh, *Iran* 71 **D9**
Siargao I., *Phil.* 61 **G7**
Siari, *Pakistan* 69 **B7**
Siasi, *Phil.* 63 **C6**
Siasi I., *Phil.* 61 **J4**
Siátista, *Greece* 40 **F5**
Siau, *Indonesia* 63 **D7**
Šiauliai, *Lithuania* 9 **J20**
Šiauliai □, *Lithuania* 44 **C10**
Siazan = Siyäzän, *Azerbaijan* 49 **K9**
Sibâi, Gebel el, *Egypt* 70 **E2**
Sibayi, L., *S. Africa* 89 **D5**
Sibdu, *Sudan* 81 **E2**
Šibenik, *Croatia* 29 **E12**
Siberia, *Russia* 4 **D13**
Siberut, *Indonesia* 62 **E1**
Sibi, *Pakistan* 68 **E2**
Sibil = Oksibil, *Indonesia* 63 **E10**
Sibiti, *Congo* 84 **E2**
Sibiu, *Romania* 43 **E9**
Sibiu □, *Romania* 43 **E9**
Sibley, *U.S.A.* 112 **D7**
Sibolga, *Indonesia* 62 **D1**
Sibsagar, *India* 67 **F19**
Sibu, *Malaysia* 62 **D4**
Sibuco, *Phil.* 61 **H5**
Sibuguey B., *Phil.* 61 **H5**
Sibut, *C.A.R.* 84 **C3**
Sibutu, *Phil.* 63 **D5**
Sibutu Group, *Phil.* 61 **J3**
Sibutu Passage, *E. Indies* 63 **D5**
Sibuyan I., *Phil.* 61 **E5**
Sibuyan Sea, *Phil.* 61 **E5**
Sic, *Romania* 43 **D8**
Sicamous, *Canada* 104 **C5**
Siccus →, *Australia* 95 **E2**
Sichuan □, *China* 58 **B5**
Sichuan Pendi, *China* 58 **B5**
Sicilia, *Italy* 31 **E7**
Sicilia □, *Italy* 31 **E7**
Sicily = Sicilia, *Italy* 31 **E7**
Sicuani, *Peru* 124 **F4**
Šid, *Serbia, Yug.* 42 **E4**
Sidamo □, *Ethiopia* 81 **G4**
Sidaouet, *Niger* 83 **B6**
Sidári, *Greece* 36 **A3**
Siddhapur, *India* 68 **H5**
Siddipet, *India* 66 **K11**
Sidensjö, *Sweden* 10 **A12**
Sidéradougou, *Burkina Faso* 82 **C4**
Siderno, *Italy* 31 **D9**
Sidhauli, *India* 69 **F9**
Sídheros, Ákra, *Greece* 36 **D8**
Sidhi, *India* 69 **G9**
Sidhirókastron, *Greece* 40 **E7**
Sîdi Abd el Rahmân, *Egypt* 80 **A2**
Sîdi Barrâni, *Egypt* 80 **A2**
Sidi-bel-Abbès, *Algeria* 78 **A5**
Sidi Haneish, *Egypt* 80 **A2**
Sidi Ifni, *Morocco* 78 **C3**
Sidi Omar, *Egypt* 80 **A1**
Sidlaw Hills, *U.K.* 14 **E5**
Sidley, Mt., *Antarctica* 5 **D14**
Sidmouth, *U.K.* 13 **G4**
Sidmouth, C., *Australia* 94 **A3**
Sidney, *Canada* 104 **D4**
Sidney, *Mont., U.S.A.* 112 **B2**
Sidney, *N.Y., U.S.A.* 111 **D9**
Sidney, *Nebr., U.S.A.* 112 **E3**
Sidney, *Ohio, U.S.A.* 108 **E3**
Sidney Lanier, L., *U.S.A.* 109 **H4**
Sido, *Mali* 82 **C3**
Sidoarjo, *Indonesia* 63 **G15**
Sidon = Saydā, *Lebanon* 75 **B4**
Sidra, G. of = Surt, Khalīj, *Libya* 79 **B9**
Siedlce, *Poland* 45 **F9**
Sieg →, *Germany* 24 **E3**
Siegburg, *Germany* 24 **E3**
Siegen, *Germany* 24 **E4**
Siem Pang, *Cambodia* 64 **E6**
Siem Reap = Siemreab, *Cambodia* 64 **F4**
Siemiatycze, *Poland* 45 **F9**
Siemreab, *Cambodia* 64 **F4**
Siena, *Italy* 29 **E8**
Sieniawa, *Poland* 45 **H9**
Sieradz, *Poland* 45 **G5**
Sieraków, *Poland* 45 **F3**
Sierck-les-Bains, *France* 19 **C13**
Sierning, *Austria* 26 **C7**
Sierpc, *Poland* 45 **F6**
Sierra Blanca, *U.S.A.* 115 **L11**
Sierra Blanca Peak, *U.S.A.* 115 **K11**
Sierra City, *U.S.A.* 116 **F6**
Sierra Colorada, *Argentina* 128 **E3**
Sierra de Yeguas, *Spain* 35 **H6**
Sierra Gorda, *Chile* 126 **A2**
Sierra Leone ■, *W. Afr.* 82 **D2**
Sierra Madre, *Mexico* 119 **D6**
Sierra Mojada, *Mexico* 118 **B4**
Sierra Nevada, *Spain* 35 **H7**
Sierra Nevada, *U.S.A.* 116 **H8**
Sierra Vista, *U.S.A.* 115 **L8**
Sierraville, *U.S.A.* 116 **F6**
Sierre, *Switz.* 25 **J3**
Sifani, *Ethiopia* 81 **E5**
Sifié, *Ivory C.* 82 **D3**
Sífnos, *Greece* 38 **E6**
Sifton, *Canada* 105 **C8**
Sifton Pass, *Canada* 104 **B3**
Sigean, *France* 20 **E6**
Sighetu-Marmaţiei, *Romania* 43 **C8**
Sighişoara, *Romania* 43 **D9**
Sigli, *Indonesia* 62 **C1**
Siglufjörður, *Iceland* 8 **C4**
Sigmaringen, *Germany* 25 **G5**
Signa, *Italy* 28 **E8**
Signakhi = Tsnori, *Georgia* 49 **K7**
Signal, *U.S.A.* 117 **L13**
Signal Pk., *U.S.A.* 117 **M12**
Signy-l'Abbaye, *France* 19 **C11**
Sigsig, *Ecuador* 124 **D3**
Sigüenza, *Spain* 32 **D2**
Siguiri, *Guinea* 82 **C3**
Sigulda, *Latvia* 9 **H21**
Sihanoukville = Kampong Saom, *Cambodia* 65 **G4**
Sihora, *India* 69 **H9**
Sihui, *China* 59 **F9**
Siikajoki →, *Finland* 8 **D21**
Siilinjärvi, *Finland* 8 **E22**
Siirt, *Turkey* 73 **D9**
Sijarira Ra., *Zimbabwe* 87 **F2**
Sika, *India* 68 **H3**
Sikao, *Thailand* 65 **J2**
Sikar, *India* 68 **F6**
Sikasso, *Mali* 82 **C3**
Sikeston, *U.S.A.* 113 **G10**
Sikhote Alin, Khrebet, *Russia* 51 **E14**
Sikhote Alin Ra. = Sikhote Alin, Khrebet, *Russia* 51 **E14**
Sikiá., *Greece* 40 **F7**
Síkinos, *Greece* 39 **E7**
Sikkani Chief →, *Canada* 104 **B4**
Sikkim □, *India* 67 **F16**
Siklós, *Hungary* 42 **E3**
Sikotu-Ko, *Japan* 54 **C10**
Sil →, *Spain* 34 **C3**
Silacayoapan, *Mexico* 119 **D5**
Šilalė, *Lithuania* 44 **C9**
Silandro, *Italy* 28 **B7**
Silawad, *India* 68 **J6**
Silay, *Phil.* 61 **F5**
Silba, *Croatia* 29 **D11**
Silchar, *India* 67 **G18**
Şile, *Turkey* 41 **E13**
Siler City, *U.S.A.* 109 **H6**
Silgarhi Doti, *Nepal* 69 **E9**
Silghat, *India* 67 **F18**
Sili, *Burkina Faso* 82 **C4**
Silifke, *Turkey* 70 **B2**
Siliguri = Shiliguri, *India* 67 **F16**
Siling Co, *China* 60 **C3**
Silistea Nouă, *Romania* 43 **F10**
Silistra, *Bulgaria* 41 **B11**
Silivri, *Turkey* 41 **E12**
Siljan, *Sweden* 10 **D8**
Siljansnäs, *Sweden* 10 **D8**
Silkeborg, *Denmark* 11 **H3**
Silkwood, *Australia* 94 **B4**
Silla, *Spain* 33 **F4**
Sillajhuay, Cordillera, *Chile* 124 **G5**
Sillamäe, *Estonia* 9 **G22**
Sillé-le-Guillaume, *France* 18 **D6**
Silleda, *Spain* 34 **C2**
Silloth, *U.K.* 12 **C4**
Sílo, *Greece* 41 **E9**
Siloam Springs, *U.S.A.* 113 **G7**
Silopi, *Turkey* 73 **D10**
Silsbee, *U.S.A.* 113 **K7**
Siluko, *Nigeria* 83 **D6**
Šilutė, *Lithuania* 9 **J19**
Silva Porto = Kuito, *Angola* 85 **G3**
Silvan, *Turkey* 73 **C9**
Silvani, *India* 69 **H8**
Silver City, *U.S.A.* 115 **K9**
Silver Cr. →, *U.S.A.* 114 **E4**
Silver Creek, *U.S.A.* 110 **D5**
Silver L., *U.S.A.* 116 **G6**
Silver Lake, *Calif., U.S.A.* 117 **K10**
Silver Lake, *Oreg., U.S.A.* 114 **E3**
Silverdalen, *Sweden* 11 **G9**
Silverton, *Colo., U.S.A.* 115 **H10**
Silverton, *Tex., U.S.A.* 113 **H4**
Silves, *Portugal* 35 **H2**
Silvi Marina, *Italy* 29 **F11**
Silvies →, *U.S.A.* 114 **E4**
Silvrettahorn, *Switz.* 28 **B7**
Silwa Bahari, *Egypt* 80 **C3**
Silz, *Austria* 26 **D3**
Simaltala, *India* 69 **G12**
Simanggang = Bandar Sri Aman, *Malaysia* 62 **D4**
Simao, *China* 58 **F3**
Simard, L., *Canada* 102 **C4**
Şīmareh →, *Iran* 73 **F12**
Simav, *Turkey* 39 **B10**
Simav →, *Turkey* 41 **F12**
Simav Dağları, *Turkey* 39 **B10**
Simba, *Tanzania* 86 **C4**
Simbach, *Germany* 25 **G9**
Simbirsk, *Russia* 48 **C9**
Simbo, *Tanzania* 86 **C2**
Simcoe, *Canada* 102 **D3**
Simcoe, L., *Canada* 102 **D4**
Simdega, *India* 69 **H11**
Simeonovgrad, *Bulgaria* 41 **D9**
Simeria, *Romania* 42 **E8**
Simeto →, *Italy* 31 **E8**
Simeulue, *Indonesia* 62 **D1**
Simferopol, *Ukraine* 47 **K8**
Sími, *Greece* 39 **E9**
Simi Valley, *U.S.A.* 117 **L8**
Simikot, *Nepal* 69 **E9**
Simitli, *Bulgaria* 40 **E7**
Simla, *India* 68 **D7**
Simlångsdalen, *Sweden* 11 **H7**
Şimleu-Silvaniei, *Romania* 42 **C7**
Simmern, *Germany* 25 **F3**
Simmie, *Canada* 105 **D7**
Simmler, *U.S.A.* 117 **K7**
Simnas, *Lithuania* 44 **D10**
Simojoki →, *Finland* 8 **D21**
Simojovel, *Mexico* 119 **D6**
Simonette →, *Canada* 104 **B5**
Simonstown, *S. Africa* 88 **E2**
Simontornya, *Hungary* 42 **D3**
Simplonpass, *Switz.* 25 **J4**
Simplontunnel, *Switz.* 25 **J4**
Simpson Desert, *Australia* 94 **D2**
Simpson Pen., *Canada* 101 **B11**
Simpungdong, *N. Korea* 57 **D15**
Simrishamn, *Sweden* 11 **J8**
Simsbury, *U.S.A.* 111 **E12**
Simushir, Ostrov, *Russia* 51 **E16**
Sin Cowe I., *S. China Sea* 62 **C4**
Sinabang, *Indonesia* 62 **D1**
Sinadogo, *Somali Rep.* 74 **F4**
Sinai = Es Sînâ', *Egypt* 75 **F3**
Sinai, Mt. = Mûsa, Gebel, *Egypt* 70 **D2**
Sinai Peninsula, *Egypt* 75 **F3**
Sinaia, *Romania* 43 **E10**
Sinaloa □, *Mexico* 118 **C3**
Sinaloa de Leyva, *Mexico* 118 **B3**
Sinalunga, *Italy* 29 **E8**
Sinan, *China* 58 **D7**
Sînandrei, *Romania* 42 **E6**
Sinarádhes, *Greece* 36 **A3**
Sincan, *Turkey* 72 **B5**
Sincanlı, *Turkey* 39 **C12**
Sincelejo, *Colombia* 124 **B3**
Sinch'ang, *N. Korea* 57 **D15**
Sinchang-ni, *N. Korea* 57 **E14**
Sinclair, *U.S.A.* 114 **F10**
Sinclair Mills, *Canada* 104 **C4**
Sinclair's B., *U.K.* 14 **C5**
Sinclairville, *U.S.A.* 110 **D5**
Sincorá, Serra do, *Brazil* 125 **F10**
Sind, *Pakistan* 68 **G3**
Sind □, *Pakistan* 68 **G3**
Sind →, *Jammu & Kashmir, India* 69 **B6**
Sind →, *Mad. P., India* 69 **F8**
Sind Sagar Doab, *Pakistan* 68 **D4**
Sindal, *Denmark* 11 **G4**
Sindangan, *Phil.* 61 **G5**
Sindangbarang, *Indonesia* 63 **G12**
Sinde, *Zambia* 87 **F2**
Sindelfingen, *Germany* 25 **G4**
Sındırgı, *Turkey* 39 **B10**
Sindou, *Burkina Faso* 82 **C3**
Sindri, *India* 69 **H12**
Sine →, *Senegal* 82 **C1**
Sinegorskiy, *Russia* 49 **G5**
Sinekli, *Turkey* 41 **E12**
Sinelnikovo = Synelnykove, *Ukraine* 47 **H8**
Sinendé, *Benin* 83 **C5**
Sines, *Portugal* 35 **H2**
Sines, C. de, *Portugal* 35 **H2**
Sineu, *Spain* 37 **B10**
Sinfra, *Ivory C.* 82 **D3**
Sing Buri, *Thailand* 64 **E3**
Singa, *Sudan* 81 **E3**
Singapore ■, *Asia* 65 **M4**
Singapore, Straits of, *Asia* 65 **M5**
Singaraja, *Indonesia* 62 **F5**
Singen, *Germany* 25 **H4**
Singida, *Tanzania* 86 **C3**
Singida □, *Tanzania* 86 **D3**
Singitikós Kólpos, *Greece* 40 **F7**
Singkaling Hkamti, *Burma* 67 **G19**
Singkang, *Indonesia* 63 **E6**
Singkawang, *Indonesia* 62 **D3**
Singkep, *Indonesia* 62 **E2**
Singleton, *Australia* 95 **E5**
Singleton, Mt., *N. Terr., Australia* 92 **D5**
Singleton, Mt., *W. Austral., Australia* 93 **E2**
Singö, *Sweden* 10 **D12**
Singoli, *India* 68 **G6**
Singora = Songkhla, *Thailand* 65 **J3**
Singosan, *N. Korea* 57 **E14**
Sinhung, *N. Korea* 57 **D14**
Siniátsikon, Óros, *Greece* 40 **F5**

Siniscóla, *Italy* 30 B2
Sinj, *Croatia* 29 E13
Sinjai, *Indonesia* 63 F6
Sinjajevina, *Montenegro, Yug.* 40 D3
Sinjār, *Iraq* 70 B4
Sinkat, *Sudan* 80 D4
Sinkiang Uighur = Xinjiang Uygur Zizhiqu □, *China* 60 B3
Sinmak, *N. Korea* 57 E14
Sínnai, *Italy* 30 C2
Sinnamary, *Fr. Guiana* 125 B8
Sinni →, *Italy* 31 B9
Sinnuris, *Egypt* 80 J7
Sinoie, Lacul, *Romania* 43 F13
Sinop, *Turkey* 72 A6
Sinor, *India* 68 J5
Sinp'o, *N. Korea* 57 E15
Sinsheim, *Germany* 25 F4
Sinsk, *Russia* 51 C13
Sintang, *Indonesia* 62 D4
Sinton, *U.S.A.* 113 L6
Sintra, *Portugal* 35 G1
Sinŭiju, *N. Korea* 57 D13
Sinyukha →, *Ukraine* 47 H6
Sinzig, *Germany* 24 E3
Sio →, *Hungary* 42 D3
Siocon, *Phil.* 61 H5
Siófok, *Hungary* 42 D3
Sion, *Switz.* 25 J3
Sion Mills, *U.K.* 15 B4
Sioux City, *U.S.A.* 112 D6
Sioux Falls, *U.S.A.* 112 D6
Sioux Lookout, *Canada* 102 B1
Sioux Narrows, *Canada* 105 D10
Sipalay, *Phil.* 61 G5
Šipan, *Croatia* 40 D1
Siping, *China* 57 C13
Sipiwesk L., *Canada* 105 B9
Šipovo, *Bos.-H.* 42 F2
Sipra →, *India* 68 H6
Sipura, *Indonesia* 62 E1
Siquia →, *Nic.* 120 D3
Siquijor, *Phil.* 61 G5
Siquirres, *Costa Rica* 120 D3
Şīr Banī Yās, *U.A.E.* 71 E7
Sir Edward Pellew Group, *Australia* 94 B2
Sir Graham Moore Is., *Australia* 92 B4
Sir James MacBrien, Mt., *Canada* 100 B7
Sira →, *Norway* 9 G12
Siracusa, *Italy* 31 E8
Sirajganj, *Bangla.* 69 G13
Sirakoro, *Mali* 82 C3
Şiran, *Turkey* 73 B8
Sirasso, *Ivory C.* 82 D3
Sirathu, *India* 69 G9
Sīrdān, *Iran* 71 B6
Sirdaryo = Syrdarya →, *Kazakstan* 50 E7
Sire, *Ethiopia* 81 F4
Siren, *U.S.A.* 112 C8
Sirer, *Spain* 37 C7
Siret, *Romania* 43 C11
Siret →, *Romania* 43 E12
Sirghāyā, *Syria* 75 B5
Şiria, *Romania* 42 D6
Sirino, Mte., *Italy* 31 B8
Sirmaur, *India* 69 G9
Sírna, *Greece* 39 E8
Şirnak, *Turkey* 73 D10
Sirohi, *India* 68 G5
Sironj, *India* 68 G7
Síros, *Greece* 38 D6
Sirretta Pk., *U.S.A.* 117 K8
Sīrrī, *Iran* 71 E7
Sirsa, *India* 68 E6
Sirsa →, *India* 69 F8
Siruela, *Spain* 35 G5
Sisak, *Croatia* 29 C13
Sisaket, *Thailand* 64 E5
Sisante, *Spain* 33 F2
Sisargas, Is., *Spain* 34 B2
Sishen, *S. Africa* 88 D3
Sishui, *Henan, China* 56 G7
Sishui, *Shandong, China* 57 G9
Sisipuk L., *Canada* 105 B8
Sisophon, *Cambodia* 64 F4
Sisseton, *U.S.A.* 112 C6
Sissonne, *France* 19 C10
Sīstān, *Asia* 71 D9
Sīstān, Daryācheh-ye, *Iran* 71 D9
Sīstān va Balūchestān □, *Iran* 71 E9
Sisteron, *France* 21 D9
Sisters, *U.S.A.* 114 D3
Siswa Bazar, *India* 69 F10
Sitakili, *Mali* 82 C2
Sitamarhi, *India* 69 F11
Sitampiky, *Madag.* 89 B8
Sitapur, *India* 69 F9
Siteki, *Swaziland* 89 D5
Sitges, *Spain* 32 D6
Sithoniá, *Greece* 40 F7
Sitía, *Greece* 36 D8
Sitka, *U.S.A.* 104 B1
Sitoti, *Botswana* 88 C3
Sitra, *Egypt* 80 B2
Sittang Myit →, *Burma* 67 L20
Sittard, *Neths.* 17 C5
Sittensen, *Germany* 24 B5
Sittingbourne, *U.K.* 13 F8
Sittona, *Eritrea* 81 E4
Sittoung = Sittang Myit →, *Burma* 67 L20
Sittwe, *Burma* 67 J18
Situbondo, *Indonesia* 63 G16
Siuna, *Nic.* 120 D3
Siuri, *India* 69 H12
Siutghiol, Lacul, *Romania* 43 F13
Sīvand, *Iran* 71 D7
Sivas, *Turkey* 70 B3
Sivaslı, *Turkey* 39 C11
Siverek, *Turkey* 70 B3
Sivrihisar, *Turkey* 72 C4
Sīwa, *Egypt* 80 B2
Sīwa, El Wâhât es, *Egypt* 80 B2
Siwa Oasis = Sīwa, El Wâhât es, *Egypt* 80 B2
Siwalik Range, *Nepal* 69 F10
Siwan, *India* 69 F11
Siwana, *India* 68 G5
Sixmilebridge, *Ireland* 15 D3
Sixth Cataract, *Sudan* 81 D3
Siyāl, Jazā'ir, *Egypt* 80 C4
Siyäzän, *Azerbaijan* 49 K9
Siziwang Qi, *China* 56 D6
Sjælland, *Denmark* 11 J5
Sjællands Odde, *Denmark* 11 J5
Sjenica, *Serbia, Yug.* 40 C3
Sjöbo, *Sweden* 11 J7
Sjötofta, *Sweden* 11 G7
Sjötorp, *Sweden* 11 F8
Sjumen = Shumen, *Bulgaria* 41 C10
Sjuntorp, *Sweden* 11 F6
Skadarsko Jezero, *Montenegro, Yug.* 40 D3
Skadovsk, *Ukraine* 47 J7
Skælskør, *Denmark* 11 J5
Skærbæk, *Denmark* 11 J2
Skaftafell, *Iceland* 8 D5
Skagafjörður, *Iceland* 8 D4
Skagastølstindane, *Norway* 9 F12
Skagaströnd, *Iceland* 8 D3
Skagen, *Denmark* 11 G4
Skagern, *Sweden* 10 F8
Skagerrak, *Denmark* 11 G2
Skagit →, *U.S.A.* 116 B4
Skagway, *U.S.A.* 100 C6
Skala-Podilska, *Ukraine* 47 H4
Skala Podolskaya = Skala-Podilska, *Ukraine* 47 H4
Skalat, *Ukraine* 47 H3
Skalbmierz, *Poland* 45 H7
Skälderviken, *Sweden* 11 H6
Skalica, *Slovak Rep.* 27 C10
Skallingen, *Denmark* 11 J2
Skalni Dol = Kamenyak, *Bulgaria* 41 C10
Skanderborg, *Denmark* 11 H3
Skåne, *Sweden* 11 J7
Skåne län □, *Sweden* 11 H7
Skaneateles, *U.S.A.* 111 D8
Skaneateles L., *U.S.A.* 111 D8
Skänninge, *Sweden* 11 F9
Skanör med Falsterbo, *Sweden* 11 J6
Skantzoúra, *Greece* 38 B6
Skara, *Sweden* 11 F7
Skärblacka, *Sweden* 11 F9
Skardu, *Pakistan* 69 B6
Skåre, *Sweden* 10 E7
Skärhamn, *Sweden* 11 G5
Skarszewy, *Poland* 44 D5
Skaryszew, *Poland* 45 G8
Skarżysko-Kamienna, *Poland* 45 G7
Skattkärr, *Sweden* 10 E7
Skattungbyn, *Sweden* 10 C8
Skawina, *Poland* 45 J6
Skebobruk, *Sweden* 10 E12
Skeena →, *Canada* 104 C2
Skeena Mts., *Canada* 104 B3
Skegness, *U.K.* 12 D8
Skeldon, *Guyana* 124 B7
Skeleton Coast Park, *Namibia* 88 C1
Skellefte älv →, *Sweden* 8 D19
Skellefteå, *Sweden* 8 D19
Skelleftehamn, *Sweden* 8 D19
Skender Vakuf, *Bos.-H.* 42 F2
Skerries, The, *U.K.* 12 D3
Skhíza, *Greece* 38 E3
Skhoinoúsa, *Greece* 39 E7
Ski, *Norway* 9 G14
Skíathos, *Greece* 38 B5
Skibbereen, *Ireland* 15 E2
Skiddaw, *U.K.* 12 C4
Skidegate, *Canada* 104 C2
Skídhra, *Greece* 40 F6
Skien, *Norway* 9 G13
Skierniewice, *Poland* 45 G7
Skikda, *Algeria* 78 A7
Skillingaryd, *Sweden* 11 G8
Skillinge, *Sweden* 11 J8
Skilloura, *Cyprus* 36 D12
Skinári, Ákra, *Greece* 38 D2
Skinnskatteberg, *Sweden* 10 E9
Skipton, *U.K.* 12 D5
Skirmish Pt., *Australia* 94 A1
Skiropoúla, *Greece* 38 C6
Skíros, *Greece* 38 C6
Skivarp, *Sweden* 11 J7
Skive, *Denmark* 11 H3
Skjálfandafljót →, *Iceland* 8 D5
Skjálfandi, *Iceland* 8 C5
Skjern, *Denmark* 11 J2
Skoczów, *Poland* 45 J5
Škofja Loka, *Slovenia* 29 B11
Skoghall, *Sweden* 10 E7
Skogstorp, *Sweden* 10 E10
Skoki, *Poland* 45 F4
Skole, *Ukraine* 47 H2
Skópelos, *Greece* 38 B5
Skopí, *Greece* 36 D8
Skopin, *Russia* 46 F10
Skopje, *Macedonia* 40 D5
Skórcz, *Poland* 44 E5
Skørping, *Denmark* 11 H3
Skövde, *Sweden* 11 F7
Skovorodino, *Russia* 51 D13
Skowhegan, *U.S.A.* 109 C11
Skradin, *Croatia* 29 E12
Skrea, *Sweden* 11 H6
Skrunda, *Latvia* 44 B9
Skrwa →, *Poland* 45 F6
Skull, *Ireland* 15 E2
Skultorp, *Sweden* 11 F7
Skultuna, *Sweden* 10 E10
Skunk →, *U.S.A.* 112 E9
Skuodas, *Lithuania* 9 H19
Skurup, *Sweden* 11 J7
Skutskär, *Sweden* 10 D11
Skvyra, *Ukraine* 47 H5
Skwierzyna, *Poland* 45 F2
Skye, *U.K.* 14 D2
Skykomish, *U.S.A.* 114 C3
Skyros = Skíros, *Greece* 38 C6
Skyttorp, *Sweden* 10 D11
Slættaratindur, *Færoe Is.* 8 E9
Slagelse, *Denmark* 11 J5
Slamet, *Indonesia* 63 G13
Slaney →, *Ireland* 15 D5
Slangberge, *S. Africa* 88 E3
Slănic, *Romania* 43 E10
Slano, *Croatia* 40 D1
Slantsy, *Russia* 46 C5
Slaný, *Czech Rep.* 26 A7
Śląskie □, *Poland* 45 H6
Slätbaken, *Sweden* 11 F10
Slate Is., *Canada* 102 C2
Slatina, *Croatia* 42 E2
Slatina, *Romania* 43 F9
Slatina Timiş, *Romania* 42 E7
Slatington, *U.S.A.* 111 F9
Slaton, *U.S.A.* 113 J4
Slave →, *Canada* 104 A6
Slave Coast, *W. Afr.* 83 D5
Slave Lake, *Canada* 104 B6
Slave Pt., *Canada* 104 A5
Slavgorod, *Russia* 50 D8
Slavinja, *Serbia, Yug.* 40 C6
Slavkov u Brna, *Czech Rep.* 27 B9
Slavonija, *Europe* 42 E2
Slavonski Brod, *Croatia* 42 E3
Slavuta, *Ukraine* 47 G4
Slavyanka, *Russia* 54 C5
Slavyanovo, *Bulgaria* 41 C8
Slavyansk = Slovyansk, *Ukraine* 47 H9
Slavyansk-na-Kubani, *Russia* 47 K10
Sława, *Poland* 45 G3
Slawharad, *Belarus* 46 F6
Sławno, *Poland* 44 D3
Sławoborze, *Poland* 44 E2
Sleaford, *U.K.* 12 D7
Sleaford B., *Australia* 95 E2
Sleat, Sd. of, *U.K.* 14 D3
Sleeper Is., *Canada* 101 C11
Sleepy Eye, *U.S.A.* 112 C7
Slemon L., *Canada* 104 A5
Ślesin, *Poland* 45 F5
Slide Mt., *U.S.A.* 111 E10
Slidell, *U.S.A.* 113 K10
Sliema, *Malta* 36 D2
Slieve Aughty, *Ireland* 15 C3
Slieve Bloom, *Ireland* 15 C4
Slieve Donard, *U.K.* 15 B6
Slieve Gamph, *Ireland* 15 B3
Slieve Gullion, *U.K.* 15 B5
Slieve Mish, *Ireland* 15 D2
Slievenamon, *Ireland* 15 D4
Sligeach = Sligo, *Ireland* 15 B3
Sligo, *Ireland* 15 B3
Sligo, *U.S.A.* 110 E5
Sligo □, *Ireland* 15 B3
Sligo B., *Ireland* 15 B3
Slippery Rock, *U.S.A.* 110 E4
Slite, *Sweden* 11 G12
Sliven, *Bulgaria* 41 D10
Slivnitsa, *Bulgaria* 40 D7
Sljeme, *Croatia* 29 C12
Sloan, *U.S.A.* 117 K11
Sloansville, *U.S.A.* 111 D10
Slobozia, *Moldova* 43 D14
Slobozia, *Argeş, Romania* 43 F10
Slobozia, *Ialomiţa, Romania* 43 F12
Slocan, *Canada* 104 D5
Słomniki, *Poland* 45 H7
Slonim, *Belarus* 47 F3
Slough, *U.K.* 13 F7
Slough □, *U.K.* 13 F7
Sloughhouse, *U.S.A.* 116 G5
Slovak Rep. ■, *Europe* 27 C13
Slovakia = Slovak Rep. ■, *Europe* 27 C13
Slovakian Ore Mts. = Slovenské Rudohorie, *Slovak Rep.* 27 C12
Slovenia ■, *Europe* 29 C11
Slovenija = Slovenia ■, *Europe* 29 C11
Slovenj Gradec, *Slovenia* 29 B12
Slovenska Bistrica, *Slovenia* 29 B12
Slovenske Konjice, *Slovenia* 29 B12
Slovenské Rudohorie, *Slovak Rep.* 27 C12
Slovyansk, *Ukraine* 47 H9
Słubice, *Poland* 45 F1
Sluch →, *Ukraine* 47 G4
Sluis, *Neths.* 17 C3
Slŭnchev Bryag, *Bulgaria* 41 D11
Slunj, *Croatia* 29 C12
Słupca, *Poland* 45 F4
Słupia →, *Poland* 44 D3
Słupsk, *Poland* 44 D4
Slurry, *S. Africa* 88 D4
Slutsk, *Belarus* 47 F4
Slyne Hd., *Ireland* 15 C1
Slyudyanka, *Russia* 51 D11
Småland, *Sweden* 11 G9
Smålandsfarvandet, *Denmark* 11 J5
Smålandsstenar, *Sweden* 11 G7
Smalltree L., *Canada* 105 A8
Smallwood Res., *Canada* 103 B7
Smarhon, *Belarus* 46 E4
Smarje, *Slovenia* 29 B12
Smartt Syndicate Dam, *S. Africa* 88 E3
Smartville, *U.S.A.* 116 F5
Smeaton, *Canada* 105 C8
Smedby, *Sweden* 11 H10
Smederevo, *Serbia, Yug.* 40 B4
Smederevska Palanka, *Serbia, Yug.* 40 B4
Smedjebacken, *Sweden* 10 D9
Smela = Smila, *Ukraine* 47 H6
Smerwick Harbour, *Ireland* 15 D1
Smethport, *U.S.A.* 110 E6
Smidovich, *Russia* 51 E14
Śmigiel, *Poland* 45 F3
Smila, *Ukraine* 47 H6
Smilyan, *Bulgaria* 41 E8
Smith, *Canada* 104 B6
Smith Center, *U.S.A.* 112 F5
Smith Sund, *Greenland* 4 B4
Smithburne →, *Australia* 94 B3
Smithers, *Canada* 104 C3
Smithfield, *S. Africa* 89 E4
Smithfield, *N.C., U.S.A.* 109 H6
Smithfield, *Utah, U.S.A.* 114 F8
Smiths Falls, *Canada* 102 D4
Smithton, *Australia* 94 G4
Smithville, *Canada* 110 C5
Smithville, *U.S.A.* 113 K6
Smoky →, *Canada* 104 B5
Smoky Bay, *Australia* 95 E1
Smoky Hill →, *U.S.A.* 112 F6
Smoky Hills, *U.S.A.* 112 F5
Smoky Lake, *Canada* 104 C6
Smøla, *Norway* 8 E13
Smolensk, *Russia* 46 E7
Smolikas, Óros, *Greece* 40 F4
Smolník, *Slovak Rep.* 27 C13
Smolyan, *Bulgaria* 41 E8
Smooth Rock Falls, *Canada* 102 C3
Smoothstone L., *Canada* 105 C7
Smorgon = Smarhon, *Belarus* 46 E4
Smulţi, *Romania* 43 E12
Smyadovo, *Bulgaria* 41 C11
Smygehamn, *Sweden* 11 J7
Smyrna = İzmir, *Turkey* 39 C9
Smyrna, *U.S.A.* 108 F8
Snæfell, *Iceland* 8 D6
Snaefell, *U.K.* 12 C3
Snæfellsjökull, *Iceland* 8 D2
Snake →, *U.S.A.* 114 C4
Snake I., *Australia* 95 F4
Snake Range, *U.S.A.* 114 G6
Snake River Plain, *U.S.A.* 114 E7
Snasahögarna, *Sweden* 10 A6
Snåsavatnet, *Norway* 8 D14
Snedsted, *Denmark* 11 H2
Sneek, *Neths.* 17 A5
Sneeuberge, *S. Africa* 88 E3
Snejbjerg, *Denmark* 11 H2
Snelling, *U.S.A.* 116 H6
Snezhnoye, *Ukraine* 47 J10
Snežnik, *Slovenia* 29 C11
Śniadowo, *Poland* 45 E8
Śniardwy, Jezioro, *Poland* 44 E8
Śnieżka, *Europe* 26 A8
Snigirevka = Snihurivka, *Ukraine* 47 J7
Snihurivka, *Ukraine* 47 J7
Snina, *Slovak Rep.* 27 C15
Snizort, L., *U.K.* 14 D2
Snøhetta, *Norway* 9 E13
Snohomish, *U.S.A.* 116 C4
Snoul, *Cambodia* 65 F6
Snow Hill, *U.S.A.* 108 F8
Snow Lake, *Canada* 105 C8
Snow Mt., *Calif., U.S.A.* 116 F4
Snow Mt., *Maine, U.S.A.* 111 A14
Snow Shoe, *U.S.A.* 110 E7
Snowbird L., *Canada* 105 A8
Snowdon, *U.K.* 12 D3
Snowdrift →, *Canada* 105 A6
Snowflake, *U.S.A.* 115 J8
Snowshoe Pk., *U.S.A.* 114 B6
Snowtown, *Australia* 95 E2
Snowville, *U.S.A.* 114 F7
Snowy →, *Australia* 95 F4
Snowy Mt., *U.S.A.* 111 C10
Snowy Mts., *Australia* 95 F4
Snug Corner, *Bahamas* 121 B5
Snyatyn, *Ukraine* 47 H3
Snyder, *Okla., U.S.A.* 113 H5
Snyder, *Tex., U.S.A.* 113 J4
Soahanina, *Madag.* 89 B7
Soalala, *Madag.* 89 B8
Soaloka, *Madag.* 89 B8
Soamanonga, *Madag.* 89 C7
Soan →, *Pakistan* 68 C4
Soanierana-Ivongo, *Madag.* 89 B8
Soanindraniny, *Madag.* 89 B8
Şoarş, *Romania* 43 E9
Soavina, *Madag.* 89 C8
Soavinandriana, *Madag.* 89 B8
Soba, *Nigeria* 83 C6
Sobat, Nahr →, *Sudan* 81 F3
Soběslav, *Czech Rep.* 26 B7
Sobhapur, *India* 68 H8
Sobinka, *Russia* 46 E11
Sobótka, *Poland* 45 H3
Sobra, *Croatia* 29 F14
Sobradinho, Reprêsa de, *Brazil* 125 E10
Sobral, *Brazil* 125 D10
Sobrance, *Slovak Rep.* 27 C15
Sobreira Formosa, *Portugal* 34 F3
Soc Giang, *Vietnam* 58 F6
Soc Trang, *Vietnam* 65 H5
Soča →, *Europe* 26 E6
Socastee, *U.S.A.* 109 J6
Sochaczew, *Poland* 45 F7
Soch'e = Shache, *China* 60 C2
Sochi, *Russia* 49 J4
Société, Is. de la, *Pac. Oc.* 97 J12
Society Is. = Société, Is. de la, *Pac. Oc.* 97 J12
Socompa, Portezuelo de, *Chile* 126 A2
Socorro, *N. Mex., U.S.A.* 115 J10
Socorro, *Tex., U.S.A.* 115 L10
Socorro, I., *Mexico* 118 D2
Socotra, *Yemen* 74 E5
Socovos, *Spain* 33 G3
Socuéllamos, *Spain* 33 F2
Soda L., *U.S.A.* 115 J5
Soda Plains, *India* 69 B8
Soda Springs, *U.S.A.* 114 E8
Sodankylä, *Finland* 8 C22
Soddy-Daisy, *U.S.A.* 109 H3
Söderala, *Sweden* 10 C10
Söderbärke, *Sweden* 10 D9
Söderfors, *Sweden* 10 D11
Söderhamn, *Sweden* 10 C11
Söderköping, *Sweden* 11 F10
Södermanland, *Sweden* 9 G17
Södermanlands län □, *Sweden* 10 E10
Södertälje, *Sweden* 10 E11
Sodiri, *Sudan* 81 E2
Sodo, *Ethiopia* 81 F4
Södra Dellen, *Sweden* 10 C10
Södra Finnskoga, *Sweden* 10 D6
Södra Sandby, *Sweden* 11 J7
Södra Ulvön, *Sweden* 10 B12
Södra Vi, *Sweden* 11 G9
Sodražica, *Slovenia* 29 C11
Sodus, *U.S.A.* 110 C7
Soekmekaar, *S. Africa* 89 C4
Soest, *Germany* 24 D4
Soest, *Neths.* 17 B5
Sofádhes, *Greece* 38 B4
Sofala □, *Mozam.* 89 B5
Sofara, *Mali* 82 C4
Sofia = Sofiya, *Bulgaria* 40 D7
Sofia →, *Madag.* 89 B8
Sofievka, *Ukraine* 47 H7
Sofikón, *Greece* 38 D5
Sofiya, *Bulgaria* 40 D7
Sofiya □, *Bulgaria* 40 D7
Sōfu-Gan, *Japan* 55 K10
Sogakofe, *Ghana* 83 D5
Sogamoso, *Colombia* 124 B4
Sogār, *Iran* 71 E8
Sögel, *Germany* 24 C3
Sogndalsfjøra, *Norway* 9 F12
Søgne, *Norway* 9 G12
Sognefjorden, *Norway* 9 F11
Söğüt, *Bilecik, Turkey* 39 A12
Söğüt, *Burdur, Turkey* 39 D11
Söğüt Dağı, *Turkey* 39 D11
Söğütköy, *Turkey* 39 E10
Sŏgwipo, *S. Korea* 57 H14
Soh, *Iran* 71 C6
Sohâg, *Egypt* 80 B3
Sohagpur, *India* 68 H8
Sŏhori, *N. Korea* 57 D15
Soignies, *Belgium* 17 D4
Soin, *Burkina Faso* 82 C4
Soira, *Eritrea* 81 E4
Soissons, *France* 19 C10
Sōja, *Japan* 55 G6
Sojat, *India* 68 G5
Sok →, *Russia* 48 D10
Sokal, *Ukraine* 47 G3
Söke, *Turkey* 39 D9
Sokelo, *Dem. Rep. of the Congo* 87 D1
Sokhós, *Greece* 40 F7
Sokhumi, *Georgia* 49 J5
Soko Banja, *Serbia, Yug.* 40 C5
Sokodé, *Togo* 83 D5
Sokol, *Russia* 46 C11
Sokolac, *Bos.-H.* 42 G3
Sokółka, *Poland* 44 E10
Sokolo, *Mali* 82 C3
Sokolo, *Mali* 82 C3
Sokolov, *Czech Rep.* 26 A5
Sokołów Małpolski, *Poland* 45 H9
Sokołów Podlaski, *Poland* 45 F9
Sokoły, *Poland* 45 F9
Sokoto, *Nigeria* 83 C6
Sokoto □, *Nigeria* 83 C6
Sokoto →, *Nigeria* 83 C5
Sol Iletsk, *Russia* 50 D6
Sola →, *Poland* 45 H6
Solai, *Kenya* 86 B4
Solan, *India* 68 D7
Solano, *Phil.* 61 C4
Solapur, *India* 66 L9
Solca, *Romania* 43 C10
Solda Gölü, *Turkey* 39 D11
Soldăneşti, *Moldova* 43 C13
Soldotna, *U.S.A.* 100 B4
Soléa □, *Cyprus* 36 D12
Solec Kujawski, *Poland* 45 E5
Soledad, *Colombia* 124 A4
Soledad, *U.S.A.* 116 J5
Soledad, *Venezuela* 124 B6
Solent, The, *U.K.* 13 G6
Solenzara, *France* 21 G13
Solesmes, *France* 19 B10
Solfonn, *Norway* 9 F12

Solhan, Turkey 70 B4
Soligorsk = Salihorsk, Belarus 47 F4
Solihull, U.K. 13 E6
Solikamsk, Russia 50 D6
Solila, Madag. 89 C8
Solimões = Amazonas →, S. Amer. 122 D5
Solin, Croatia 29 E13
Solingen, Germany 24 D3
Sollebrunn, Sweden 11 F6
Sollefteå, Sweden 10 A11
Sollentuna, Sweden 10 E11
Sóller, Spain 37 B9
Sollerön, Sweden 10 D8
Solling, Germany 24 D5
Solnechnogorsk, Russia 46 D9
Solo →, Indonesia 63 G15
Solofra, Italy 31 B7
Sologne, France 19 E8
Solok, Indonesia 62 E2
Sololá, Guatemala 120 D1
Solomon, N. Fork →, U.S.A. 112 F5
Solomon, S. Fork →, U.S.A. 112 F5
Solomon Is. ■, Pac. Oc. 96 H7
Solon, China 60 B7
Solon Springs, U.S.A. 112 B9
Solor, Indonesia 63 F6
Solotcha, Russia 46 E10
Solothurn, Switz. 25 H3
Solothurn □, Switz. 25 H3
Solsona, Spain 32 C6
Solt, Hungary 42 D4
Šolta, Croatia 29 E13
Soltānābād, Khorāsān, Iran 71 C8
Soltānābād, Khorāsān, Iran 71 B8
Soltau, Germany 24 C5
Soltsy, Russia 46 C6
Solunska Glava, Macedonia 40 E5
Solvang, U.S.A. 117 L6
Solvay, U.S.A. 111 C8
Sölvesborg, Sweden 11 H8
Solway Firth, U.K. 12 C4
Solwezi, Zambia 87 E2
Sōma, Japan 54 F10
Soma, Turkey 39 B9
Somabhula, Zimbabwe 89 B4
Somali Pen., Africa 76 F8
Somali Rep. ■, Africa 74 F4
Somalia = Somali Rep. ■, Africa 74 F4
Sombernon, France 19 E11
Sombor, Serbia, Yug. 42 E4
Sombra, Canada 110 D2
Sombrerete, Mexico 118 C4
Sombrero, Anguilla 121 C7
Şomcuta Mare, Romania 43 C8
Somdari, India 68 G5
Somers, U.S.A. 114 B6
Somerset, Ky., U.S.A. 108 G3
Somerset, Mass., U.S.A. 111 E13
Somerset, Pa., U.S.A. 110 F5
Somerset □, U.K. 13 F5
Somerset East, S. Africa 88 E4
Somerset I., Canada 100 A10
Somerset West, S. Africa 88 E2
Somersworth, U.S.A. 111 C14
Somerton, U.S.A. 115 K6
Somerville, U.S.A. 111 F10
Someş →, Romania 42 C7
Someşul Mare →, Romania 43 C8
Somme □, France 19 C9
Somme →, France 19 B8
Somme, B. de la, France 18 B8
Sommen, Jönköping, Sweden 11 F8
Sommen, Östergötland, Sweden 11 F9
Sommepy-Tahure, France 19 C11
Sömmerda, Germany 24 D7
Sommesous, France 19 D11
Sommières, France 21 E8
Somnath, India 68 J4
Somogy □, Hungary 42 D2
Somogyszob, Hungary 42 D2
Somoto, Nic. 120 D2
Sompolno, Poland 45 F5
Somport, Puerto de, Spain 32 C4
Son →, India 69 G11
Son Ha, Vietnam 64 E7
Son Hoa, Vietnam 64 F7
Son La, Vietnam 58 G4
Son Serra, Spain 37 B10
Son Servera, Spain 32 F8
Son Tay, Vietnam 58 G5
Soná, Panama 120 E3
Sonamarg, India 69 B6
Sonamukhi, India 69 H12
Sonar →, India 69 G8
Sŏnch'ŏn, N. Korea 57 E13
Sondags →, S. Africa 88 E4
Sóndalo, Italy 28 B7
Sondar, India 69 C6
Sønder Felding, Denmark 11 J2
Sønder Omme, Denmark 11 J2
Sønderborg, Denmark 11 K3
Sønderjyllands Amtskommune □, Denmark 11 J3
Sondershausen, Germany 24 D6
Sóndrio, Italy 28 B6
Sone, Mozam. 87 F3
Sonepur, India 67 J13
Song, Nigeria 83 D7
Song, Thailand 64 C3
Song Cau, Vietnam 64 F7
Song Xian, China 56 G7
Songch'ŏn, N. Korea 57 E14
Songea, Tanzania 87 E4
Songeons, France 19 C8
Songhua Hu, China 57 C14
Songhua Jiang →, China 60 B8
Songjiang, China 59 B13
Songjin, N. Korea 57 D15
Songjŏng-ni, S. Korea 57 G14
Songkan, China 58 C6
Songkhla, Thailand 65 J3
Songming, China 58 E4
Songnim, N. Korea 57 E13
Songo, Mozam. 85 H6
Songo, Sudan 79 G10
Songpan, China 58 A4
Songtao, China 58 C7
Songwe, Dem. Rep. of the Congo 86 C2
Songwe →, Africa 87 D3
Songxi, China 59 D12
Songzi, China 59 B8
Sonhat, India 69 H10
Sonid Youqi, China 56 C7
Sonipat, India 68 E7
Sonkach, India 68 H7
Sonkovo, Russia 46 D9
Sonmiani, Pakistan 68 G2
Sonmiani B., Pakistan 68 G2
Sonnino, Italy 30 A6
Sono →, Brazil 125 E9
Sonoma, U.S.A. 116 G4
Sonora, Calif., U.S.A. 116 H6
Sonora, Tex., U.S.A. 113 K4
Sonora □, Mexico 118 B2
Sonora →, Mexico 118 B2
Sonoran Desert, U.S.A. 117 L12
Sonoyta, Mexico 118 A2
Sonqor, Iran 73 E12
Sŏnsan, S. Korea 57 F15
Sonseca, Spain 35 F7
Sonsonate, El Salv. 120 D2
Sonsorol Is., Pac. Oc. 63 C8
Sonstorp, Sweden 11 F9
Sonthofen, Germany 25 H6
Soochow = Suzhou, China 59 B13
Sooke, Canada 116 B3
Sop Hao, Laos 58 G5
Sop Prap, Thailand 64 D2
Sopelana, Spain 32 B2
Sopi, Indonesia 63 D7
Sopo, Nahr →, Sudan 81 F2
Sopot, Bulgaria 41 D8
Sopot, Poland 44 D5
Sopot, Serbia, Yug. 40 B4
Sopotnica, Macedonia 40 E5
Sopron, Hungary 42 C1
Sopur, India 69 B6
Sør-Rondane, Antarctica 5 D4
Sora, Italy 29 G10
Sorah, Pakistan 68 F3
Söråker, Sweden 10 B11
Sorano, Italy 29 F8
Soraon, India 69 G9
Sorbas, Spain 33 H2
Sörbygden, Sweden 10 B10
Sore, France 20 D3
Sorel, Canada 102 C5
Soresina, Italy 28 C6
Sörforsa, Sweden 10 C10
Sórgono, Italy 30 B2
Sorgues, France 21 D8
Sorgun, Turkey 72 C6
Soria, Spain 32 D2
Soria □, Spain 32 D2
Soriano, Uruguay 126 C4
Soriano nel Cimino, Italy 29 F9
Sorkh, Kuh-e, Iran 71 C8
Sorø, Denmark 11 J5
Soro, Guinea 82 C3
Soroca, Moldova 43 B13
Sorocaba, Brazil 127 A6
Soroki = Soroca, Moldova 43 B13
Sorol Atoll, Pac. Oc. 63 C10
Sorong, Indonesia 63 E8
Soroní, Greece 36 C10
Soroti, Uganda 86 B3
Sørøya, Norway 8 A20
Sørøysundet, Norway 8 A20
Sorraia →, Portugal 35 G2
Sorrell, Australia 94 G4
Sorrento, Italy 31 B7
Sorsele, Sweden 8 D17
Sorsjön, Sweden 10 C7
Sorso, Italy 30 B1
Sorsogon, Phil. 61 E6
Sortavala, Russia 46 B6
Sortino, Italy 31 E8
Sortland, Norway 8 B16
Sorvizhi, Russia 48 B9
Sos = Sos del Rey Católico, Spain 32 C3
Sos del Rey Católico, Spain 32 C3
Sŏsan, S. Korea 57 F14
Soscumica, L., Canada 102 B4
Sösdala, Sweden 11 H7
Sosna →, Russia 47 F10
Sosnovka, Kirov, Russia 48 B10
Sosnovka, Tambov, Russia 48 D5
Sosnovyy Bor, Russia 46 C5
Sosnowiec, Poland 45 H6
Sospel, France 21 E11
Sossus Vlei, Namibia 88 C2
Šoštanj, Slovenia 29 B12
Sŏsura, N. Korea 57 C16
Sot →, India 69 F8
Sotkamo, Finland 8 D23
Soto del Barco, Spain 34 B4
Soto la Marina →, Mexico 119 C5
Soto y Amío, Spain 34 C5
Sotrondio, Spain 34 B5
Sotuta, Mexico 119 C7
Souanké, Congo 84 D2
Soubré, Ivory C. 82 D3
Souderton, U.S.A. 111 F9
Soúdha, Greece 36 D6
Soúdhas, Kólpos, Greece 36 D6
Souflíon, Greece 41 E10
Soufrière, St. Lucia 121 D7
Souillac, France 20 D5
Souilly, France 19 C12
Soukhouma, Laos 64 E5
Sŏul, S. Korea 57 F14
Soulac-sur-Mer, France 20 C2
Soulougou, Burkina Faso 83 C5
Soultz-sous-Forêts, France 19 D14
Sound, The = Øresund, Europe 11 J6
Sound, The, U.K. 13 G3
Soúnion, Ákra, Greece 38 D6
Sources, Mt. aux, Lesotho 89 D4
Soure, Brazil 125 D9
Soure, Portugal 34 E2
Souris, Man., Canada 105 D8
Souris, P.E.I., Canada 103 C7
Souris →, Canada 112 A5
Sourou →, Africa 82 C4
Soúrpi, Greece 38 B4
Sousa, Brazil 125 E11
Sousel, Portugal 35 G3
Sousse, Tunisia 79 A8
Soustons, France 20 E2
Sout →, S. Africa 88 E2
South Africa ■, Africa 88 E3
South America 122 E5
South Atlantic Ocean 122 H7
South Aulatsivik I., Canada 103 A7
South Australia □, Australia 95 E2
South Ayrshire □, U.K. 14 F4
South Baldy, U.S.A. 115 J10
South Bass I., U.S.A. 110 E2
South Bend, Ind., U.S.A. 108 E2
South Bend, Wash., U.S.A. 116 D3
South Boston, U.S.A. 109 G6
South Branch, Canada 103 C8
South Brook, Canada 103 C8
South Carolina □, U.S.A. 109 J5
South Charleston, U.S.A. 108 F5
South China Sea, Asia 62 C4
South Dakota □, U.S.A. 112 C5
South Deerfield, U.S.A. 111 D12
South Downs, U.K. 13 G7
South East C., Australia 94 G4
South East Is., Australia 93 F3
South Esk →, U.K. 14 E6
South Foreland, U.K. 13 F9
South Fork American →, U.S.A. 116 G5
South Fork Feather →, U.S.A. 116 F5
South Fork Grand →, U.S.A. 112 C3
South Fork Republican →, U.S.A. 112 E4
South Georgia, Antarctica 122 J7
South Gloucestershire □, U.K. 13 F5
South Hadley, U.S.A. 111 D12
South Haven, U.S.A. 108 D2
South Henik, L., Canada 105 A9
South Honshu Ridge, Pac. Oc. 96 E6
South Horr, Kenya 86 B4
South I., Kenya 86 B4
South I., N.Z. 91 L3
South Indian Lake, Canada 105 B9
South Invercargill, N.Z. 91 M2
South Knife →, Canada 105 B10
South Koel →, India 69 H11
South Korea ■, Asia 57 G15
South Lake Tahoe, U.S.A. 116 G6
South Lanarkshire □, U.K. 14 F5
South Loup →, U.S.A. 112 E5
South Magnetic Pole, Antarctica 5 C9
South Milwaukee, U.S.A. 108 D2
South Molton, U.K. 13 F4
South Moose L., Canada 105 C8
South Nahanni →, Canada 104 A4
South Nation →, Canada 111 A9
South Natuna Is. = Natuna Selatan, Kepulauan, Indonesia 65 L7
South Negril Pt., Jamaica 120 C4
South Orkney Is., Antarctica 5 C18
South Ossetia □, Georgia 49 J7
South Pagai, I. = Pagai Selatan, Pulau, Indonesia 62 E2
South Paris, U.S.A. 111 B14
South Pittsburg, U.S.A. 109 H3
South Platte →, U.S.A. 112 E4
South Pole, Antarctica 5 E
South Porcupine, Canada 102 C3
South Portland, U.S.A. 109 D10
South Pt., U.S.A. 110 B1
South River, Canada 102 C4
South River, U.S.A. 111 F10
South Ronaldsay, U.K. 14 C6
South Sandwich Is., Antarctica 5 B1
South Saskatchewan →, Canada 105 C7
South Seal →, Canada 105 B9
South Shetland Is., Antarctica 5 C18
South Shields, U.K. 12 C6
South Sioux City, U.S.A. 112 D6
South Taranaki Bight, N.Z. 91 H5
South Thompson →, Canada 104 C4
South Twin I., Canada 102 B4
South Tyne →, U.K. 12 C5
South Uist, U.K. 14 D1
South West Africa = Namibia ■, Africa 88 C2
South West C., Australia 94 G4
South Williamsport, U.S.A. 110 E8
South Yorkshire □, U.K. 12 D6
Southampton, Canada 102 D3
Southampton, U.K. 13 G6
Southampton, U.S.A. 111 F12
Southampton □, U.K. 13 G6
Southampton I., Canada 101 B11
Southaven, U.S.A. 113 H9
Southbank, Canada 104 C3
Southbridge, N.Z. 91 K4
Southbridge, U.S.A. 111 D12
Southend, Canada 105 B8
Southend-on-Sea, U.K. 13 F8
Southend-on-Sea □, U.K. 13 F8
Southern □, Malawi 87 F4
Southern □, S. Leone 82 D2
Southern □, Zambia 87 F2
Southern Alps, N.Z. 91 K3
Southern Cross, Australia 93 F2
Southern Indian L., Canada 105 B9
Southern Ocean, Antarctica 5 C6
Southern Pines, U.S.A. 109 H6
Southern Uplands, U.K. 14 F5
Southington, U.S.A. 111 E12
Southland □, N.Z. 91 L1
Southold, U.S.A. 111 E12
Southport, Australia 95 D5
Southport, U.K. 12 D4
Southport, Fla., U.S.A. 109 K3
Southport, N.Y., U.S.A. 110 D8
Southwest C., N.Z. 91 M1
Southwold, U.K. 13 E9
Soutpansberg, S. Africa 89 C4
Souvigny, France 19 F10
Sovata, Romania 43 D10
Soverato, Italy 31 D9
Sovetsk, Kaliningd., Russia 9 J19
Sovetsk, Kirov, Russia 48 B9
Sovetskaya Gavan = Vanino, Russia 51 E15
Sovicille, Italy 29 E8
Soweto, S. Africa 89 D4
Sōya-Kaikyō = La Perouse Str., Asia 54 B11
Sōya-Misaki, Japan 54 B10
Soyaux, France 20 C4
Sozh →, Belarus 47 F6
Sozopol, Bulgaria 41 D11
Spa, Belgium 17 D5
Spain ■, Europe 7 H5
Spalding, Australia 95 E2
Spalding, U.K. 12 E7
Spangler, U.S.A. 110 F6
Spanish, Canada 102 C3
Spanish Fork, U.S.A. 114 F8
Spanish Town, Jamaica 120 C4
Sparks, U.S.A. 116 F7
Sparreholm, Sweden 10 E10
Sparta = Spárti, Greece 38 D4
Sparta, Mich., U.S.A. 108 D3
Sparta, N.J., U.S.A. 111 E10
Sparta, Wis., U.S.A. 112 D9
Spartanburg, U.S.A. 109 H5
Spartansburg, U.S.A. 110 E5
Spárti, Greece 38 D4
Spartivento, C., Calabria, Italy 31 E9
Spartivento, C., Sard., Italy 30 D1
Sparwood, Canada 104 D6
Spas-Demensk, Russia 46 E7
Spas-Klepiki, Russia 46 E11
Spassk Dalniy, Russia 51 E14
Spassk-Ryazanskiy, Russia 46 E11
Spátha, Ákra, Greece 36 D5
Spatsizi →, Canada 104 B3
Spatsizi Plateau Wilderness Park, Canada 104 B3
Spean →, U.K. 14 E4
Spearfish, U.S.A. 112 C3
Spearman, U.S.A. 113 G4
Speculator, U.S.A. 111 C10
Speia, Moldova 43 D14
Speightstown, Barbados 121 D8
Speke Gulf, Tanzania 86 C3
Spello, Italy 29 F9
Spencer, Idaho, U.S.A. 114 D7
Spencer, Iowa, U.S.A. 112 D7
Spencer, N.Y., U.S.A. 111 D8
Spencer, Nebr., U.S.A. 112 D5
Spencer, C., Australia 95 F2
Spencer B., Namibia 88 D1
Spencer G., Australia 95 E2
Spencerville, Canada 111 B9
Spences Bridge, Canada 104 C4
Spennymoor, U.K. 12 C6
Spenser Mts., N.Z. 91 K4
Spentrup, Denmark 11 H4
Sperkhiós →, Greece 38 C4
Sperrin Mts., U.K. 15 B5
Spessart, Germany 25 F5
Spétsai, Greece 38 D5
Spey →, U.K. 14 D5
Speyer, Germany 25 F4
Spezand, Pakistan 68 E2
Spezzano Albanese, Italy 31 C9
Spiekeroog, Germany 24 B3
Spiez, Switz. 25 J3
Spíli, Greece 36 D6
Spilimbergo, Italy 29 B9
Spīn Búldak, Afghan. 68 D2
Spinalónga, Greece 36 D7
Spinazzola, Italy 31 B9
Spineni, Romania 43 F9
Spirit Lake, U.S.A. 116 D4
Spirit River, Canada 104 B5
Spiritwood, Canada 105 C7
Spišská Nová Ves, Slovak Rep. 27 C13
Spišské Podhradie, Slovak Rep. 27 B13
Spital, Austria 26 D7
Spithead, U.K. 13 G6
Spittal an der Drau, Austria 26 E6
Spitzbergen = Svalbard, Arctic 4 B8
Spjelkavik, Norway 9 E12
Split, Croatia 29 E13
Split L., Canada 105 B9
Split Lake, Canada 105 B9
Splitski Kanal, Croatia 29 E13
Splügenpass, Switz. 25 J5
Spofford, U.S.A. 113 L4
Spokane, U.S.A. 114 C5
Spoleto, Italy 29 F9
Spooner, U.S.A. 112 C9
Sporyy Navolok, Mys, Russia 50 B7
Sprague, U.S.A. 114 C5
Spratly I., S. China Sea 62 C4
Spratly Is., S. China Sea 62 C4
Spray, U.S.A. 114 D4
Spreča →, Bos.-H. 42 F3
Spree →, Germany 24 C9
Spreewald, Germany 24 D9
Spremberg, Germany 24 D10
Sprengisandur, Iceland 8 D5
Spring City, U.S.A. 111 F9
Spring Creek, U.S.A. 114 F6
Spring Garden, U.S.A. 116 F6
Spring Hill, U.S.A. 109 L4
Spring Mts., U.S.A. 115 H6
Spring Valley, U.S.A. 117 N10
Springbok, S. Africa 88 D2
Springboro, U.S.A. 110 E4
Springdale, Canada 103 C8
Springdale, U.S.A. 113 G7
Springe, Germany 24 C5
Springer, U.S.A. 113 G2
Springerville, U.S.A. 115 J9
Springfield, Canada 110 D4
Springfield, N.Z. 91 K3
Springfield, Colo., U.S.A. 113 G3
Springfield, Ill., U.S.A. 112 F10
Springfield, Mass., U.S.A. 111 D12
Springfield, Mo., U.S.A. 113 G8
Springfield, Ohio, U.S.A. 108 F4
Springfield, Oreg., U.S.A. 114 D2
Springfield, Tenn., U.S.A. 109 G2
Springfield, Vt., U.S.A. 111 C12
Springfontein, S. Africa 88 E4
Springhill, Canada 103 C7
Springhill, U.S.A. 113 J8
Springhouse, Canada 104 C4
Springs, S. Africa 89 D4
Springsure, Australia 94 C4
Springvale, U.S.A. 111 C14
Springville, Calif., U.S.A. 116 J8
Springville, N.Y., U.S.A. 110 D6
Springville, Utah, U.S.A. 114 F8
Springwater, U.S.A. 110 D7
Spruce-Creek, U.S.A. 110 F6
Spruce Mt., U.S.A. 111 B12
Spur, U.S.A. 113 J4
Spurn Hd., U.K. 12 D8
Spuž, Montenegro, Yug. 40 D3
Spuzzum, Canada 104 D4
Squam L., U.S.A. 111 C13
Squamish, Canada 104 D4
Square Islands, Canada 103 B8
Squillace, G. di, Italy 31 D9
Squinzano, Italy 31 B11
Squires, Mt., Australia 93 E4
Srbac, Bos.-H. 42 E2
Srbica, Kosovo, Yug. 40 D4
Srbija = Serbia □, Yugoslavia 40 C5
Srbobran, Serbia, Yug. 42 E4
Sre Ambel, Cambodia 65 G4
Sre Khtum, Cambodia 65 F6
Sre Umbell = Sre Ambel, Cambodia 65 G4
Srebrenica, Bos.-H. 42 F4
Sredinny Ra. = Sredinnyy Khrebet, Russia 51 D16
Sredinnyy Khrebet, Russia 51 D16
Središče, Slovenia 29 B13
Sredna Gora, Bulgaria 41 D8
Srednekolymsk, Russia 51 C16
Sredni Rodopi, Bulgaria 41 E8
Srednogorie, Bulgaria 41 D8
Śrem, Poland 45 F4
Sremska Mitrovica, Serbia, Yug. 42 F4
Sremski Karlovci, Serbia, Yug. 42 E4
Srepok →, Cambodia 64 F6
Sretensk, Russia 51 D12
Sri Lanka ■, Asia 66 R12
Srikakulam, India 67 K13
Srinagar, India 69 B6
Środa Śląska, Poland 45 G3
Środa Wielkopolski, Poland 45 F4
Srpska Crnja, Serbia, Yug. 42 E5
Srpski Itebej, Serbia, Yug. 42 E5
Staaten →, Australia 94 B3
Staberhuk, Germany 24 A7
Stade, Germany 24 B5
Stadskanaal, Neths. 17 A6
Stadtallendorf, Germany 24 E5
Stadthagen, Germany 24 C5
Stadtlohn, Germany 24 D2
Stadtroda, Germany 24 E7
Staffa, U.K. 14 E2
Staffanstorp, Sweden 11 J7
Stafford, U.K. 12 E5
Stafford, U.S.A. 113 G5
Stafford Springs, U.S.A. 111 E12
Staffordshire □, U.K. 12 E5
Stagnone, Italy 30 E5
Staines, U.K. 13 F7
Stainz, Austria 26 E8
Stakhanov, Ukraine 47 H10
Stalać, Serbia, Yug. 40 C5
Stalingrad = Volgograd, Russia 49 F7
Staliniri = Tskhinvali, Georgia 49 J7
Stalino = Donetsk, Ukraine 47 J9
Stalinogorsk = Novomoskovsk, Russia 46 E10
Stalis, Greece 36 D7

Stallarholmen, *Sweden* 10 E11
Ställdalen, *Sweden* 10 E8
Stalowa Wola, *Poland* 45 H9
Stalybridge, *U.K.* 12 D5
Stamford, *Australia* 94 C3
Stamford, *U.K.* 13 E7
Stamford, *Conn., U.S.A.* 111 E11
Stamford, *N.Y., U.S.A.* 111 D10
Stamford, *Tex., U.S.A.* 113 J5
Stampriet, *Namibia* 88 C2
Stamps, *U.S.A.* 113 J8
Stančevo = Kalipetrovo, *Bulgaria* 41 B11
Standerton, *S. Africa* 89 D4
Standish, *U.S.A.* 108 D4
Stanford, *S. Africa* 88 E2
Stanford, *U.S.A.* 114 C8
Stånga, *Sweden* 11 G12
Stanger, *S. Africa* 89 D5
Stanišić, *Serbia, Yug.* 42 E4
Stanislaus →, *U.S.A.* 116 H5
Stanislav = Ivano-Frankivsk, *Ukraine* 47 H3
Stanisławów, *Poland* 45 F8
Stanley, *Australia* 94 G4
Stanley, *Canada* 105 B8
Stanley, *Falk. Is.* 128 G5
Stanley, *U.K.* 12 C6
Stanley, *Idaho, U.S.A.* 114 D6
Stanley, *N. Dak., U.S.A.* 112 A3
Stanley, *N.Y., U.S.A.* 110 D7
Stanovoy Khrebet, *Russia* 51 D13
Stanovoy Ra. = Stanovoy Khrebet, *Russia* 51 D13
Stansmore Ra., *Australia* 92 D4
Stanthorpe, *Australia* 95 D5
Stanton, *U.S.A.* 113 J4
Stanwood, *U.S.A.* 116 B4
Staples, *U.S.A.* 112 B7
Stąporków, *Poland* 45 G7
Star City, *Canada* 105 C8
Star Lake, *U.S.A.* 111 B9
Stará L'ubovňa, *Slovak Rep.* 27 B13
Stara Moravica, *Serbia, Yug.* 42 E4
Stara Pazova, *Serbia, Yug.* 42 F5
Stara Planina, *Bulgaria* 40 C7
Stará Turá, *Slovak Rep.* 27 C10
Stara Zagora, *Bulgaria* 41 D9
Starachowice, *Poland* 45 G8
Staraya Russa, *Russia* 46 D6
Starbuck I., *Kiribati* 97 H12
Starchiojd, *Romania* 43 E11
Stargard Szczeciński, *Poland* 44 E2
Stari Bar, *Montenegro, Yug.* 40 D3
Stari Trg, *Slovenia* 29 C12
Staritsa, *Russia* 46 D8
Starke, *U.S.A.* 109 L4
Starnberg, *Germany* 25 H7
Starnberger See, *Germany* 25 H7
Starobilsk, *Ukraine* 47 H10
Starodub, *Russia* 47 F7
Starogard Gdański, *Poland* 44 E5
Starokonstantinov = Starokonstyantyniv, *Ukraine* 47 H4
Starokonstyantyniv, *Ukraine* 47 H4
Starominskaya, *Russia* 47 J10
Staroshcherbinovskaya, *Russia* 47 J10
Start Pt., *U.K.* 13 G4
Stary Sącz, *Poland* 45 J7
Staryy Biryuzyak, *Russia* 49 H8
Staryy Chartoriysk, *Ukraine* 47 G3
Staryy Krym, *Ukraine* 47 K8
Staryy Oskol, *Russia* 47 G9
Stassfurt, *Germany* 24 D7
Staszów, *Poland* 45 H8
State College, *U.S.A.* 110 F7
Stateline, *U.S.A.* 116 G7
Staten, I. = Estados, I. de Los, *Argentina* 122 J4
Staten I., *U.S.A.* 111 F10
Statesboro, *U.S.A.* 109 J5
Statesville, *U.S.A.* 109 H5
Stauffer, *U.S.A.* 117 L7
Staunton, *Ill., U.S.A.* 112 F10
Staunton, *Va., U.S.A.* 108 F6
Stavanger, *Norway* 9 G11
Staveley, *N.Z.* 91 K3
Stavelot, *Belgium* 17 D5
Stavern, *Norway* 9 G14
Stavoren, *Neths.* 17 B5
Stavropol, *Russia* 49 H6
Stavros, *Cyprus* 36 D11
Stavrós, *Greece* 36 D6
Stavrós, Ákra, *Greece* 36 D6
Stavroúpolis, *Greece* 41 E8
Stawell, *Australia* 95 F3
Stawell →, *Australia* 94 C3
Stawiski, *Poland* 44 E9
Stawiszyn, *Poland* 45 G5
Stayner, *Canada* 110 B4
Stayton, *U.S.A.* 114 D2
Steamboat Springs, *U.S.A.* 114 F10
Steblevë, *Albania* 40 E4
Steele, *U.S.A.* 112 B5
Steelton, *U.S.A.* 110 F8
Steen River, *Canada* 104 B5
Steenkool = Bintuni, *Indonesia* 63 E8
Steens Mt., *U.S.A.* 114 E4
Steenwijk, *Neths.* 17 B6
Steep Pt., *Australia* 93 E1
Steep Rock, *Canada* 105 C9
Ştefan Vodă, *Moldova* 43 D14
Ştefăneşti, *Romania* 43 C12
Stefanie L. = Chew Bahir, *Ethiopia* 81 G4
Stefansson Bay, *Antarctica* 5 C5
Stege, *Denmark* 11 K6
Ştei, *Romania* 42 D7
Steiermark □, *Austria* 26 D8
Steigerwald, *Germany* 25 F6
Steilacoom, *U.S.A.* 116 C4
Steilrandberge, *Namibia* 88 B1
Steinbach, *Canada* 105 D9
Steinfurt, *Germany* 24 C3
Steinhausen, *Namibia* 88 C2
Steinheim, *Germany* 24 D5
Steinhuder Meer, *Germany* 24 C5
Steinkjer, *Norway* 8 D14
Steinkopf, *S. Africa* 88 D2
Stellarton, *Canada* 103 C7
Stellenbosch, *S. Africa* 88 E2
Stelvio, Paso dello, *Italy* 28 B7
Stenay, *France* 19 C12
Stendal, *Germany* 24 C7
Stende, *Latvia* 44 A9
Stenhamra, *Sweden* 10 E11
Stenstorp, *Sweden* 11 F7
Stenungsund, *Sweden* 11 F5
Steornabhaigh = Stornoway, *U.K.* 14 C2
Stepanakert = Xankändi, *Azerbaijan* 70 B5
Stepanavan, *Armenia* 49 K7
Stephens Creek, *Australia* 95 E3
Stephens I., *Canada* 104 C2
Stephens L., *Canada* 105 B9
Stephenville, *Canada* 103 C8
Stephenville, *U.S.A.* 113 J5
Stepnica, *Poland* 44 E1
Stepnoi = Elista, *Russia* 49 G7
Steppe, *Asia* 52 D9
Stereá Ellas □, *Greece* 38 C4
Sterkstroom, *S. Africa* 88 E4
Sterling, *Colo., U.S.A.* 112 E3
Sterling, *Ill., U.S.A.* 112 E10
Sterling, *Kans., U.S.A.* 112 F5
Sterling City, *U.S.A.* 113 K4
Sterling Heights, *U.S.A.* 108 D4
Sterling Run, *U.S.A.* 110 E6
Sterlitamak, *Russia* 50 D6
Sternberg, *Germany* 24 B7
Šternberk, *Czech Rep.* 27 B10
Stérnes, *Greece* 36 D6
Sterzing = Vipiteno, *Italy* 29 B8
Stettin = Szczecin, *Poland* 44 E1
Stettiner Haff, *Germany* 24 B10
Stettler, *Canada* 104 C6
Steubenville, *U.S.A.* 110 F4
Stevenage, *U.K.* 13 F7
Stevens Point, *U.S.A.* 112 C10
Stevenson, *U.S.A.* 116 E5
Stevenson L., *Canada* 105 C9
Stevensville, *U.S.A.* 114 C6
Stevns Klint, *Denmark* 11 J6
Stewart, *Canada* 104 B3
Stewart, *U.S.A.* 116 F7
Stewart →, *Canada* 100 B6
Stewart, C., *Australia* 94 A1
Stewart, I., *Chile* 128 G2
Stewart I., *N.Z.* 91 M1
Stewarts Point, *U.S.A.* 116 G3
Stewartville, *U.S.A.* 112 D8
Stewiacke, *Canada* 103 C7
Steynsburg, *S. Africa* 88 E4
Steyr, *Austria* 26 C7
Steyr →, *Austria* 26 C7
Steytlerville, *S. Africa* 88 E3
Stia, *Italy* 29 E8
Stigler, *U.S.A.* 113 H7
Stigliano, *Italy* 31 B9
Stigtomta, *Sweden* 11 F10
Stikine →, *Canada* 104 B2
Stilfontein, *S. Africa* 88 D4
Stilís, *Greece* 38 C4
Stillwater, *N.Z.* 91 K3
Stillwater, *Minn., U.S.A.* 112 C8
Stillwater, *N.Y., U.S.A.* 111 D11
Stillwater, *Okla., U.S.A.* 113 G6
Stillwater Range, *U.S.A.* 114 G4
Stillwater Reservoir, *U.S.A.* 111 C9
Stilo, Pta., *Italy* 31 D9
Stilwell, *U.S.A.* 113 H7
Štip, *Macedonia* 40 E6
Stíra, *Greece* 38 C6
Stirling, *Canada* 110 B7
Stirling, *U.K.* 14 E5
Stirling □, *U.K.* 14 E4
Stirling Ra., *Australia* 93 F2
Stittsville, *Canada* 111 A9
Stjernøya, *Norway* 8 A20
Stjørdalshalsen, *Norway* 8 E14
Stockach, *Germany* 25 H5
Stockaryd, *Sweden* 11 G8
Stockerau, *Austria* 27 C9
Stockholm, *Sweden* 10 E12
Stockholms län □, *Sweden* 10 E12
Stockport, *U.K.* 12 D5
Stocksbridge, *U.K.* 12 D6
Stockton, *Calif., U.S.A.* 116 H5
Stockton, *Kans., U.S.A.* 112 F5
Stockton, *Mo., U.S.A.* 113 G8
Stockton-on-Tees, *U.K.* 12 C6
Stockton-on-Tees □, *U.K.* 12 C6
Stockton Plateau, *U.S.A.* 113 K3
Stoczek Łukowski, *Poland* 45 G8
Stöde, *Sweden* 10 B10
Stoeng Treng, *Cambodia* 64 F5
Stoer, Pt. of, *U.K.* 14 C3
Stogovo, *Macedonia* 40 E4
Stoholm, *Denmark* 11 H3
Stoke-on-Trent, *U.K.* 12 D5
Stoke-on-Trent □, *U.K.* 12 D5
Stokes Pt., *Australia* 94 G3
Stokes Ra., *Australia* 92 C5
Stokksnes, *Iceland* 8 D6
Stokmarknes, *Norway* 8 B16
Stolac, *Bos.-H.* 40 C1
Stolberg, *Germany* 24 E2
Stolbovoy, Ostrov, *Russia* 51 B14
Stolbtsy = Stowbtsy, *Belarus* 46 F4
Stolin, *Belarus* 47 G4
Stöllet, *Sweden* 10 D7
Stolnici, *Romania* 43 F9
Stomíon, *Greece* 36 D5
Ston, *Croatia* 29 F14
Stone, *U.K.* 12 E5
Stoneboro, *U.S.A.* 110 E4
Stonehaven, *U.K.* 14 E6
Stonehenge, *Australia* 94 C3
Stonehenge, *U.K.* 13 F6
Stonewall, *Canada* 105 C9
Stony L., *Man., Canada* 105 B9
Stony L., *Ont., Canada* 110 B6
Stony Point, *U.S.A.* 111 E11
Stony Pt., *U.S.A.* 111 C8
Stony Rapids, *Canada* 105 B7
Stony Tunguska = Tunguska, Podkamennaya →, *Russia* 51 C10
Stonyford, *U.S.A.* 116 F4
Stopnica, *Poland* 45 H7
Storå, *Sweden* 10 E9
Storå →, *Denmark* 11 H2
Stora Gla, *Sweden* 10 E6
Stora Le, *Sweden* 10 E5
Stora Lulevatten, *Sweden* 8 C18
Storavan, *Sweden* 8 D18
Stord, *Norway* 9 G11
Store Bælt, *Denmark* 11 J4
Store Heddinge, *Denmark* 11 J6
Storebro, *Sweden* 11 G9
Storfors, *Sweden* 10 E8
Storlien, *Sweden* 10 A6
Storm B., *Australia* 94 G4
Storm Lake, *U.S.A.* 112 D7
Stormberge, *S. Africa* 88 E4
Stormsrivier, *S. Africa* 88 E3
Stornoway, *U.K.* 14 C2
Storo, *Italy* 28 C7
Storozhinets = Storozhynets, *Ukraine* 47 H3
Storozhynets, *Ukraine* 47 H3
Storrs, *U.S.A.* 111 E12
Storsjön, *Gävleborg, Sweden* 10 D10
Storsjön, *Jämtland, Sweden* 10 B7
Storsjön, *Jämtland, Sweden* 10 A8
Storstrøms Amtskommune □, *Denmark* 11 J5
Storuman, *Sweden* 8 D17
Storuman, sjö, *Sweden* 8 D17
Storvätteshågna, *Sweden* 10 B6
Storvik, *Sweden* 10 D10
Storvreta, *Sweden* 10 E11
Stouffville, *Canada* 110 C5
Stoughton, *Canada* 105 D8
Stour →, *Dorset, U.K.* 13 G6
Stour →, *Kent, U.K.* 13 F9
Stour →, *Suffolk, U.K.* 13 F9
Stourbridge, *U.K.* 13 E5
Stout L., *Canada* 105 C10
Stove Pipe Wells Village, *U.S.A.* 117 J9
Støvring, *Denmark* 11 H3
Stow, *U.S.A.* 110 E3
Stowbtsy, *Belarus* 46 F4
Stowmarket, *U.K.* 13 E9
Strabane, *U.K.* 15 B4
Stracin, *Macedonia* 40 D6
Stradella, *Italy* 28 C6
Strahan, *Australia* 94 G4
Strajitsa, *Bulgaria* 41 C9
Strakonice, *Czech Rep.* 26 B6
Straldzha, *Bulgaria* 41 D10
Stralsund, *Germany* 24 A9
Strand, *S. Africa* 88 E2
Stranda, *Møre og Romsdal, Norway* 9 E12
Stranda, *Nord-Trøndelag, Norway* 8 E14
Strandby, *Denmark* 11 G4
Strangford L., *U.K.* 15 B6
Strängnäs, *Sweden* 10 E11
Stranraer, *U.K.* 14 G3
Strasbourg, *Canada* 105 C8
Strasbourg, *France* 19 D14
Strasburg, *Germany* 24 B9
Străşeni, *Moldova* 43 C13
Stråssa, *Sweden* 10 E9
Stratford, *Canada* 102 D3
Stratford, *N.Z.* 91 H5
Stratford, *Calif., U.S.A.* 116 J7
Stratford, *Conn., U.S.A.* 111 E11
Stratford, *Tex., U.S.A.* 113 G3
Stratford-upon-Avon, *U.K.* 13 E6
Strath Spey, *U.K.* 14 D5
Strathalbyn, *Australia* 95 F2
Strathaven, *U.K.* 14 F4
Strathcona Prov. Park, *Canada* 104 D3
Strathmore, *Canada* 104 C6
Strathmore, *U.K.* 14 E5
Strathmore, *U.S.A.* 116 J7
Strathnaver, *Canada* 104 C4
Strathpeffer, *U.K.* 14 D4
Strathroy, *Canada* 102 D3
Strathy Pt., *U.K.* 14 C4
Strattanville, *U.S.A.* 110 E5
Stratton, *U.S.A.* 111 A14
Stratton Mt., *U.S.A.* 111 C12
Straubing, *Germany* 25 G8
Straumnes, *Iceland* 8 C2
Strausberg, *Germany* 24 C9
Strawberry →, *U.S.A.* 114 F8
Strážnice, *Czech Rep.* 27 C10
Streaky B., *Australia* 95 E1
Streaky Bay, *Australia* 95 E1
Streator, *U.S.A.* 112 E10
Streetsboro, *U.S.A.* 110 E3
Streetsville, *Canada* 110 C5
Strehaia, *Romania* 43 F8
Strelcha, *Bulgaria* 41 D8
Strelka, *Russia* 51 D10
Streng →, *Cambodia* 64 F4
Stresa, *Italy* 28 C5
Streymoy, *Færoe Is.* 8 E9
Strezhevoy, *Russia* 50 C8
Stříbro, *Czech Rep.* 26 A6
Strimón →, *Greece* 40 F7
Strimonikós Kólpos, *Greece* 40 F7
Strofádhes, *Greece* 38 D3
Stroma, *U.K.* 14 C5
Strómboli, *Italy* 31 D8
Stromeferry, *U.K.* 14 D3
Stromness, *U.K.* 14 C5
Strömsbruk, *Sweden* 10 C11
Stromsburg, *U.S.A.* 112 E6
Strömsnäsbruk, *Sweden* 11 H7
Strömstad, *Sweden* 11 F5
Strömsund, *Sweden* 8 E16
Strongilí, *Greece* 39 E11
Stróngoli, *Italy* 31 C10
Strongsville, *U.S.A.* 110 E3
Stronie Śląskie, *Poland* 45 H3
Stronsay, *U.K.* 14 B6
Stropkov, *Slovak Rep.* 27 B14
Stroud, *U.K.* 13 F5
Stroud Road, *Australia* 95 E5
Stroudsburg, *U.S.A.* 111 F9
Stroumbi, *Cyprus* 36 E11
Struer, *Denmark* 11 H2
Struga, *Macedonia* 40 E4
Strugi Krasnyye, *Russia* 46 C5
Strumica, *Macedonia* 40 E6
Strumica →, *Europe* 40 E7
Struthers, *Canada* 102 C2
Struthers, *U.S.A.* 110 E4
Stryama, *Bulgaria* 41 D8
Stryker, *U.S.A.* 114 B6
Stryków, *Poland* 45 G6
Stryy, *Ukraine* 47 H2
Strzegom, *Poland* 45 H3
Strzelce Krajeńskie, *Poland* 45 F2
Strzelce Opolskie, *Poland* 45 H5
Strzelecki Cr. →, *Australia* 95 D2
Strzelin, *Poland* 45 H4
Strzelno, *Poland* 45 F5
Strzybnica, *Poland* 45 H5
Strzyżów, *Poland* 45 J8
Stuart, *Fla., U.S.A.* 109 M5
Stuart, *Nebr., U.S.A.* 112 D5
Stuart →, *Canada* 104 C4
Stuart Bluff Ra., *Australia* 92 D5
Stuart L., *Canada* 104 C4
Stuart Ra., *Australia* 95 D1
Stubbekøbing, *Denmark* 11 K6
Stuben, *Austria* 26 D3
Studen Kladenets, Yazovir, *Bulgaria* 41 E9
Studenka, *Czech Rep.* 27 B11
Stugun, *Sweden* 10 A9
Stuhr, *Germany* 24 B4
Stull L., *Canada* 102 B1
Stung Treng = Stoeng Treng, *Cambodia* 64 F5
Stupart →, *Canada* 102 A1
Stupava, *Slovak Rep.* 27 C10
Stupino, *Russia* 46 E10
Sturgeon B., *Canada* 105 C9
Sturgeon Bay, *U.S.A.* 108 C2
Sturgeon Falls, *Canada* 102 C4
Sturgeon L., *Alta., Canada* 104 B5
Sturgeon L., *Ont., Canada* 102 C1
Sturgeon L., *Ont., Canada* 110 B6
Sturgis, *Canada* 105 C8
Sturgis, *Mich., U.S.A.* 108 E3
Sturgis, *S. Dak., U.S.A.* 112 C3
Sturkö, *Sweden* 11 H9
Štúrovo, *Slovak Rep.* 27 D11
Sturt Cr. →, *Australia* 92 C4
Stutterheim, *S. Africa* 88 E4
Stuttgart, *Germany* 25 G5
Stuttgart, *U.S.A.* 113 H9
Stuyvesant, *U.S.A.* 111 D11
Stykkishólmur, *Iceland* 8 D2
Styria = Steiermark □, *Austria* 26 D8
Styrsö, *Sweden* 11 G5
Su Xian = Suzhou, *China* 56 H9
Suakin, *Sudan* 80 D4
Suan, *N. Korea* 57 E14
Suaqui, *Mexico* 118 B3
Suar, *India* 69 E8
Subang, *Indonesia* 63 G12
Subansiri →, *India* 67 F18
Subarnarekha →, *India* 69 H12
Subayhah, *Si. Arabia* 70 D3
Subcetate, *Romania* 42 E8
Subi, *Indonesia* 65 L7
Subiaco, *Italy* 29 G10
Subotica, *Serbia, Yug.* 42 D4
Suca, *Ethiopia* 81 F4
Suceava, *Romania* 43 C11
Suceava □, *Romania* 43 C10
Suceava →, *Romania* 43 C11
Sucha-Beskidzka, *Poland* 45 J6
Suchań, *Poland* 45 E2
Suchan, *Russia* 54 C6
Suchedniów, *Poland* 45 G7
Suchitoto, *El Salv.* 120 D2
Suchou = Suzhou, *China* 59 B13
Süchow = Xuzhou, *China* 57 G9
Suchowola, *Poland* 44 E10
Suck →, *Ireland* 15 C3
Sucre, *Bolivia* 124 G5
Sućuraj, *Croatia* 29 E14
Sucuriú →, *Brazil* 125 H8
Sud, Pte. du, *Canada* 103 C7
Sud-Kivu □, *Dem. Rep. of the Congo* 86 C2
Sud-Ouest, Pte. du, *Canada* 103 C7
Suda →, *Russia* 46 C9
Sudak, *Ukraine* 47 K8
Sudan, *U.S.A.* 113 H3
Sudan ■, *Africa* 81 E3
Sudbury, *Canada* 102 C3
Sudbury, *U.K.* 13 E8
Sûdd, *Sudan* 81 F3
Süderbrarup, *Germany* 24 A5
Süderlügum, *Germany* 24 A4
Süderoogsand, *Germany* 24 A4
Sudeten Mts. = Sudety, *Europe* 27 A9
Sudety, *Europe* 27 A9
Suðuroy, *Færoe Is.* 8 F9
Sudi, *Tanzania* 87 E4
Sudirman, Pegunungan, *Indonesia* 63 E9
Sudiţi, *Romania* 43 F12
Sudogda, *Russia* 48 C5
Sudr, *Egypt* 80 B3
Sudzha, *Russia* 47 G8
Sue →, *Sudan* 81 F2
Sueca, *Spain* 33 F4
Sŭedinenie, *Bulgaria* 41 D8
Suemez I., *U.S.A.* 104 B2
Suez = El Suweis, *Egypt* 80 J8
Suez, G. of = Suweis, Khalîg el, *Egypt* 80 J8
Suez Canal = Suweis, Qanâ es, *Egypt* 80 H8
Suffield, *Canada* 104 C6
Suffolk, *U.S.A.* 108 G7
Suffolk □, *U.K.* 13 E9
Şugag, *Romania* 43 E8
Sugargrove, *U.S.A.* 110 E5
Sugarive →, *India* 69 F12
Suğla Gölü, *Turkey* 72 D5
Sugluk = Salluit, *Canada* 101 B12
Suhaia, Lacul, *Romania* 43 G10
Şuḩār, *Oman* 71 E8
Sühbaatar □, *Mongolia* 56 B8
Suhl, *Germany* 24 E6
Şuhut, *Turkey* 39 C12
Sui, *Pakistan* 68 E3
Sui Xian, *China* 56 G8
Šuica, *Bos.-H.* 42 G2
Suichang, *China* 59 C12
Suichuan, *China* 59 D10
Suide, *China* 56 F6
Suifenhe, *China* 57 B16
Suihua, *China* 60 B7
Suijiang, *China* 58 C4
Suining, *Hunan, China* 59 D8
Suining, *Jiangsu, China* 57 H9
Suining, *Sichuan, China* 58 B5
Suiping, *China* 56 H7
Suippes, *France* 19 C11
Suir →, *Ireland* 15 D4
Suisun City, *U.S.A.* 116 G4
Suixi, *China* 59 G8
Suiyang, *Guizhou, China* 58 D6
Suiyang, *Heilongjiang, China* 57 B16
Suizhong, *China* 57 D11
Suizhou, *China* 59 B9
Sujangarh, *India* 68 F6
Sukabumi, *Indonesia* 63 G12
Sukadana, *Indonesia* 62 E3
Sukagawa, *Japan* 55 F10
Sukaraja, *Indonesia* 62 E4
Sukarnapura = Jayapura, *Indonesia* 63 E10
Sukch'ŏn, *N. Korea* 57 E13
Sukhindol, *Bulgaria* 41 C9
Sukhinichi, *Russia* 46 E8
Sukhona →, *Russia* 50 D4
Sukhothai, *Thailand* 64 D2
Sukhumi = Sokhumi, *Georgia* 49 J5
Sukkur, *Pakistan* 68 F3
Sukkur Barrage, *Pakistan* 68 F3
Sukovo, *Serbia, Yug.* 40 C6
Sukri →, *India* 68 G4
Sukumo, *Japan* 55 H6
Sukunka →, *Canada* 104 B4
Sula →, *Ukraine* 47 H7
Sula, Kepulauan, *Indonesia* 63 E7
Sulaco →, *Honduras* 120 C2
Sulaiman Range, *Pakistan* 68 D3
Sulak →, *Russia* 49 J8
Sūlār, *Iran* 71 D6
Sulawesi Sea = Celebes Sea, *Indonesia* 63 D6
Sulawesi Selatan □, *Indonesia* 63 E6
Sulawesi Utara □, *Indonesia* 63 D6
Sulechów, *Poland* 45 F2
Sulęcin, *Poland* 45 F2
Sulejów, *Poland* 45 G6
Sulejówek, *Poland* 45 F8
Süleymanlı, *Turkey* 39 C9
Sulima, *S. Leone* 82 D2
Sulina, *Romania* 43 E14
Sulina, Braţul →, *Romania* 43 E14
Sulingen, *Germany* 24 C4
Suliţa, *Romania* 43 C11
Sulitjelma, *Norway* 8 C17
Sułkowice, *Poland* 45 J6
Sullana, *Peru* 124 D2
Süller, *Turkey* 39 C11
Sullivan, *Ill., U.S.A.* 112 F10
Sullivan, *Ind., U.S.A.* 108 F2
Sullivan, *Mo., U.S.A.* 112 F9

Sullivan Bay, *Canada* 104 C3
Sullivan I. = Lanbi Kyun, *Burma* 65 G2
Sully-sur-Loire, *France* 19 E9
Sulmierzyce, *Poland* 45 G4
Sulmona, *Italy* 29 F10
Süloğlu, *Turkey* 41 E10
Sulphur, *La., U.S.A.* 113 K8
Sulphur, *Okla., U.S.A.* 113 H6
Sulphur Pt., *Canada* 104 A6
Sulphur Springs, *U.S.A.* 113 J7
Sultan, *Canada* 102 C3
Sultan, *U.S.A.* 116 C5
Sultan Dağları, *Turkey* 72 C4
Sultanhisar, *Turkey* 39 D10
Sultaniça, *Turkey* 41 F10
Sultaniye, *Turkey* 41 F12
Sultanpur, *Mad. P., India* 68 H8
Sultanpur, *Punjab, India* 68 D6
Sultanpur, *Ut. P., India* 69 F10
Sulu Arch., *Phil.* 61 J4
Sulu Sea, *E. Indies* 61 G4
Sülüklü, *Turkey* 72 C5
Sululta, *Ethiopia* 81 F4
Suluova, *Turkey* 72 B6
Suluq, *Libya* 79 B10
Sulzbach, *Germany* 25 F3
Sulzbach-Rosenberg, *Germany* 25 F7
Sulzberger Ice Shelf, *Antarctica* 5 D10
Sumalata, *Indonesia* 63 D6
Sumampa, *Argentina* 126 B3
Sumatera □, *Indonesia* 62 D2
Sumatera Barat □, *Indonesia* 62 E2
Sumatera Utara □, *Indonesia* 62 D1
Sumatra = Sumatera □, *Indonesia* 62 D2
Sumba, *Indonesia* 63 F5
Sumba, Selat, *Indonesia* 63 F5
Sumbawa, *Indonesia* 62 F5
Sumbawa Besar, *Indonesia* 62 F5
Sumbawanga □, *Tanzania* 84 F6
Sumbe, *Angola* 84 G2
Sumburgh Hd., *U.K.* 14 B7
Sumdeo, *India* 69 D8
Sumdo, *India* 69 B8
Sumedang, *Indonesia* 63 G12
Sümeg, *Hungary* 42 D2
Sumeih, *Sudan* 81 F2
Šumen = Shumen, *Bulgaria* 41 C10
Sumenep, *Indonesia* 63 G15
Sumgait = Sumqayıt, *Azerbaijan* 49 K9
Summer L., *U.S.A.* 114 E3
Summerland, *Canada* 104 D5
Summerside, *Canada* 103 C7
Summersville, *U.S.A.* 108 F5
Summerville, *Ga., U.S.A.* 109 H3
Summerville, *S.C., U.S.A.* 109 J5
Summit Lake, *Canada* 104 C4
Summit Peak, *U.S.A.* 115 H10
Sumner, *Iowa, U.S.A.* 112 D8
Sumner, *Wash., U.S.A.* 116 C4
Sumoto, *Japan* 55 G7
Šumperk, *Czech Rep.* 27 B9
Sumqayıt, *Azerbaijan* 49 K9
Sumter, *U.S.A.* 109 J5
Sumy, *Ukraine* 47 G8
Sun City, *Ariz., U.S.A.* 115 K7
Sun City, *Calif., U.S.A.* 117 M9
Sun City Center, *U.S.A.* 109 M4
Sun Lakes, *U.S.A.* 115 K8
Sun Valley, *U.S.A.* 114 E6
Sunagawa, *Japan* 54 C10
Sunan, *N. Korea* 57 E13
Sunart, L., *U.K.* 14 E3
Sunburst, *U.S.A.* 114 B8
Sunbury, *Australia* 95 F3
Sunbury, *U.S.A.* 111 F8
Sunchales, *Argentina* 126 C3
Suncho Corral, *Argentina* 126 B3
Sunch'ŏn, *S. Korea* 57 G14
Suncook, *U.S.A.* 111 C13
Sunda, Selat, *Indonesia* 62 F3
Sunda Is., *Indonesia* 52 K14
Sunda Str. = Sunda, Selat, *Indonesia* 62 F3
Sundance, *Canada* 105 B10
Sundance, *U.S.A.* 112 C2
Sundar Nagar, *India* 68 D7
Sundarbans, The, *Asia* 67 J16
Sundargarh, *India* 67 H14
Sundays = Sondags →, *S. Africa* 88 E4
Sunderland, *Canada* 110 B5
Sunderland, *U.K.* 12 C6
Sundre, *Canada* 104 C6
Sunds, *Denmark* 11 H3
Sundsvall, *Sweden* 10 B11
Sundsvallsbukten, *Sweden* 10 B11
Sung Hei, *Vietnam* 65 G6
Sungai Kolok, *Thailand* 65 J3
Sungai Lembing, *Malaysia* 65 L4
Sungai Petani, *Malaysia* 65 K3
Sungaigerong, *Indonesia* 62 E2
Sungailiat, *Indonesia* 62 E3
Sungaipenuh, *Indonesia* 62 E2
Sungari = Songhua Jiang →, *China* 60 B8
Sunghua Chiang = Songhua Jiang →, *China* 60 B8
Sungikai, *Sudan* 81 E2
Sungurlu, *Turkey* 72 B6
Sunja, *Croatia* 29 C13
Sunland Park, *U.S.A.* 115 L10
Sunnansjö, *Sweden* 10 D8
Sunndalsøra, *Norway* 9 E13
Sunne, *Sweden* 10 E7
Sunnemo, *Sweden* 10 E7
Sunnyside, *U.S.A.* 114 C3
Sunnyvale, *U.S.A.* 116 H4
Suntar, *Russia* 51 C12
Sunyani, *Ghana* 82 D4
Suomenselkä, *Finland* 8 E21
Suomussalmi, *Finland* 8 D23
Suoyarvi, *Russia* 46 A7
Supai, *U.S.A.* 115 H7
Supaul, *India* 69 F12
Superior, *Ariz., U.S.A.* 115 K8
Superior, *Mont., U.S.A.* 114 C6
Superior, *Nebr., U.S.A.* 112 E5
Superior, *Wis., U.S.A.* 112 B8
Superior, L., *N. Amer.* 102 C2
Supetar, *Croatia* 29 E13
Suphan Buri, *Thailand* 64 E3
Suphan Dağı, *Turkey* 70 B4
Supiori, *Indonesia* 63 E9
Supraśl, *Poland* 45 E10
Supraśl →, *Poland* 45 E9
Supung Shuiku, *China* 57 D13
Sūq Suwayq, *Si. Arabia* 70 E3
Suqian, *China* 57 H10
Sūr, *Lebanon* 75 B4
Şūr, *Oman* 74 C6
Sur, Pt., *U.S.A.* 116 J5
Sura →, *Russia* 48 C8
Surab, *Pakistan* 68 E2
Surabaja = Surabaya, *Indonesia* 62 F4
Surabaya, *Indonesia* 62 F4
Surahammar, *Sweden* 10 E10
Suraia, *Romania* 43 E12
Surakarta, *Indonesia* 62 F4
Surakhany, *Azerbaijan* 49 K10
Šurany, *Slovak Rep.* 27 C11
Surat, *Australia* 95 D4
Surat, *India* 66 J8
Surat Thani, *Thailand* 65 H2
Suratgarh, *India* 68 E5
Suraž, *Poland* 45 F9
Surazh, *Belarus* 46 E6
Surazh, *Russia* 47 F7
Surduc, *Romania* 43 C8
Surduc Pasul, *Romania* 43 E8
Surdulica, *Serbia, Yug.* 40 D6
Surendranagar, *India* 68 H4
Surf, *U.S.A.* 117 L6
Surgères, *France* 20 B3
Surgut, *Russia* 50 C8
Sùria, *Spain* 32 D6
Suriapet, *India* 66 L11
Surigao, *Phil.* 61 G6
Surigao Strait, *Phil.* 61 F6
Surin, *Thailand* 64 E4
Surin Nua, Ko, *Thailand* 65 H1
Surinam ■, *S. Amer.* 125 C7
Suriname = Surinam ■, *S. Amer.* 125 C7
Suriname →, *Surinam* 125 B7
Sūrmaq, *Iran* 71 D7
Sürmene, *Turkey* 73 B9
Surovikino, *Russia* 49 F6
Surrey □, *U.K.* 13 F7
Sursand, *India* 69 F11
Sursar →, *India* 69 F12
Sursee, *Switz.* 25 H4
Sursk, *Russia* 48 D7
Surskoye, *Russia* 48 C8
Surt, *Libya* 79 B9
Surt, Khalīj, *Libya* 79 B9
Surtanahu, *Pakistan* 68 F4
Surte, *Sweden* 11 G6
Surtsey, *Iceland* 8 E3
Sürüç, *Turkey* 73 D8
Suruga-Wan, *Japan* 55 G9
Susa, *Italy* 28 C4
Susâ →, *Denmark* 11 J5
Sušac, *Croatia* 29 F13
Susak, *Croatia* 29 D11
Susaki, *Japan* 55 H6
Süsangerd, *Iran* 71 D6
Susanville, *U.S.A.* 114 F3
Susch, *Switz.* 25 J6
Suşehri, *Turkey* 73 B8
Sušice, *Czech Rep.* 26 B6
Susleni, *Moldova* 43 C13
Susner, *India* 68 H7
Susong, *China* 59 B11
Susquehanna, *U.S.A.* 111 E9
Susquehanna →, *U.S.A.* 111 G8
Susques, *Argentina* 126 A2
Sussex, *Canada* 103 C6
Sussex, *U.S.A.* 111 E10
Sussex, E. □, *U.K.* 13 G8
Sussex, W. □, *U.K.* 13 G7
Sustut →, *Canada* 104 B3
Susuman, *Russia* 51 C15
Susunu, *Indonesia* 63 E8
Susurluk, *Turkey* 39 B10
Susuz, *Turkey* 73 B10
Susz, *Poland* 44 E6
Sütçüler, *Turkey* 72 D4
Şuţeşti, *Romania* 43 E12
Sutherland, *S. Africa* 88 E3
Sutherland, *U.S.A.* 112 E4
Sutherland Falls, *N.Z.* 91 L1
Sutherlin, *U.S.A.* 114 E2
Suthri, *India* 68 H3
Sutlej →, *Pakistan* 68 E4
Sutter, *U.S.A.* 116 F5
Sutter Creek, *U.S.A.* 116 G6
Sutton, *Canada* 111 A12
Sutton, *Nebr., U.S.A.* 112 E6
Sutton, *W. Va., U.S.A.* 108 F5
Sutton →, *Canada* 102 A3
Sutton Coldfield, *U.K.* 13 E6
Sutton in Ashfield, *U.K.* 12 D6
Sutton L., *Canada* 102 B3
Suttor →, *Australia* 94 C4
Suttsu, *Japan* 54 C10
Suva, *Fiji* 91 D8
Suva Gora, *Macedonia* 40 E5
Suva Planina, *Serbia, Yug.* 40 C6
Suva Reka, *Kosovo, Yug.* 40 D4
Suvorov, *Russia* 46 E9
Suvorov Is. = Suwarrow Is., *Cook Is.* 97 J11
Suvorovo, *Bulgaria* 41 C11
Suwałki, *Poland* 44 D9
Suwannaphum, *Thailand* 64 E4
Suwannee →, *U.S.A.* 109 L4
Suwanose-Jima, *Japan* 55 K4
Suwarrow Is., *Cook Is.* 97 J11
Suwayq aş Şuqban, *Iraq* 70 D5
Suweis, Khalîg el, *Egypt* 80 J8
Suweis, Qanâ es, *Egypt* 80 H8
Suwŏn, *S. Korea* 57 F14
Suzdal, *Russia* 46 D11
Suzhou, *Anhui, China* 56 H9
Suzhou, *Jiangsu, China* 59 B13
Suzu, *Japan* 55 F8
Suzu-Misaki, *Japan* 55 F8
Suzuka, *Japan* 55 G8
Suzzara, *Italy* 28 D7
Svalbard, *Arctic* 4 B8
Svalöv, *Sweden* 11 J7
Svaneke, *Denmark* 11 J9
Svängsta, *Sweden* 11 H8
Svanskog, *Sweden* 10 E6
Svappavaara, *Sweden* 8 C19
Svärdsjö, *Sweden* 10 D9
Svartå, *Sweden* 10 E8
Svartisen, *Norway* 8 C15
Svartvik, *Sweden* 10 B11
Svatove, *Ukraine* 47 H10
Svatovo = Svatove, *Ukraine* 47 H10
Svay Chek, *Cambodia* 64 F4
Svay Rieng, *Cambodia* 65 G5
Svealand □, *Sweden* 10 D9
Svedala, *Sweden* 11 J7
Sveg, *Sweden* 10 B8
Svendborg, *Denmark* 11 J4
Svenljunga, *Sweden* 11 G7
Svenstavik, *Sweden* 10 B8
Svenstrup, *Denmark* 11 H3
Sverdlovsk = Yekaterinburg, *Russia* 50 D7
Sverdlovsk, *Ukraine* 47 H10
Sverdrup Is., *Canada* 4 B3
Svetac, *Croatia* 29 E12
Sveti Nikola, Prokhad, *Europe* 40 C6
Sveti Nikole, *Macedonia* 40 E5
Sveti Rok, *Croatia* 29 D12
Svetlaya, *Russia* 54 A9
Svetlogorsk = Svyetlahorsk, *Belarus* 47 F5
Svetlograd, *Russia* 49 H6
Svetlovodsk = Svitlovodsk, *Ukraine* 47 H7
Svidník, *Slovak Rep.* 27 B14
Svilaja Planina, *Croatia* 29 E13
Svilajnac, *Serbia, Yug.* 40 B5
Svilengrad, *Bulgaria* 41 E10
Svir →, *Russia* 46 B7
Sviritsa, *Russia* 46 B7
Svishtov, *Bulgaria* 41 C9
Svislach, *Belarus* 47 F3
Svitava →, *Czech Rep.* 27 B9
Svitavy, *Czech Rep.* 27 B9
Svitlovodsk, *Ukraine* 47 H7
Svobodnyy, *Russia* 51 D13
Svoge, *Bulgaria* 40 D7
Svolvær, *Norway* 8 B16
Svratka →, *Czech Rep.* 27 B9
Svrljig, *Serbia, Yug.* 40 C6
Svyetlahorsk, *Belarus* 47 F5
Swabian Alps = Schwäbische Alb, *Germany* 25 G5
Swainsboro, *U.S.A.* 109 J4
Swakop →, *Namibia* 88 C2
Swakopmund, *Namibia* 88 C1
Swale →, *U.K.* 12 C6
Swan →, *Australia* 93 F2
Swan →, *Canada* 105 C8
Swan Hill, *Australia* 95 F3
Swan Hills, *Canada* 104 C5
Swan Is., *W. Indies* 120 C3
Swan L., *Canada* 105 C8
Swan Peak, *U.S.A.* 114 C7
Swan Ra., *U.S.A.* 114 C7
Swan River, *Canada* 105 C8
Swanage, *U.K.* 13 G6
Swansea, *Australia* 94 G4
Swansea, *Canada* 110 C5
Swansea, *U.K.* 13 F4
Swansea □, *U.K.* 13 F3
Swar →, *Pakistan* 69 B5
Swartberge, *S. Africa* 88 E3
Swartmodder, *S. Africa* 88 D3
Swartnossob →, *Namibia* 88 C2
Swartruggens, *S. Africa* 88 D4
Swarzędz, *Poland* 45 F4
Swastika, *Canada* 102 C3
Swatow = Shantou, *China* 59 F11
Swaziland ■, *Africa* 89 D5
Sweden ■, *Europe* 9 G16
Swedru, *Ghana* 83 D4
Sweet Home, *U.S.A.* 114 D2
Sweetgrass, *U.S.A.* 114 B8
Sweetwater, *Nev., U.S.A.* 116 G7
Sweetwater, *Tenn., U.S.A.* 109 H3
Sweetwater, *Tex., U.S.A.* 113 J4
Sweetwater →, *U.S.A.* 114 E10
Swellendam, *S. Africa* 88 E3
Świder →, *Poland* 45 F8
Świdnica, *Poland* 45 H3
Świdnik, *Poland* 45 G9
Świdwin, *Poland* 44 E2
Świebodzice, *Poland* 45 H3
Świebodzin, *Poland* 45 F2
Świecie, *Poland* 44 E5
Świerzawa, *Poland* 45 G2
Świętokrzyskie □, *Poland* 45 H7
Świętokrzyskie, Góry, *Poland* 45 H7
Swift Current, *Canada* 105 C7
Swiftcurrent →, *Canada* 105 C7
Swilly, L., *Ireland* 15 A4
Swindon, *U.K.* 13 F6
Swindon □, *U.K.* 13 F6
Swinemünde = Świnoujście, *Poland* 44 E1
Swinford, *Ireland* 15 C3
Świnoujście, *Poland* 44 E1
Switzerland ■, *Europe* 25 J4
Swords, *Ireland* 15 C5
Swoyerville, *U.S.A.* 111 E9
Syasstroy, *Russia* 46 B7
Sychevka, *Russia* 46 E8
Syców, *Poland* 45 G4
Sydenham →, *Canada* 110 D2
Sydney, *Australia* 95 E5
Sydney, *Canada* 103 C7
Sydney L., *Canada* 105 C10
Sydney Mines, *Canada* 103 C7
Sydprøven = Alluitsup Paa, *Greenland* 4 C5
Sydra, G. of = Surt, Khalīj, *Libya* 79 B9
Syeverodonetsk, *Ukraine* 47 H10
Syke, *Germany* 24 C4
Sykesville, *U.S.A.* 110 E6
Syktyvkar, *Russia* 50 C6
Sylacauga, *U.S.A.* 109 J2
Sylarna, *Sweden* 8 E15
Sylhet, *Bangla.* 67 G17
Sylhet □, *Bangla.* 67 G17
Sylt, *Germany* 24 A4
Sylvan Beach, *U.S.A.* 111 C9
Sylvan Lake, *Canada* 104 C6
Sylvania, *U.S.A.* 109 J5
Sylvester, *U.S.A.* 109 K4
Sym, *Russia* 50 C9
Symón, *Mexico* 118 C4
Synelnykove, *Ukraine* 47 H8
Synnott Ra., *Australia* 92 C4
Syracuse, *Kans., U.S.A.* 113 G4
Syracuse, *N.Y., U.S.A.* 111 C8
Syracuse, *Nebr., U.S.A.* 112 E6
Syrdarya →, *Kazakstan* 50 E7
Syria ■, *Asia* 70 C3
Syrian Desert = Shām, Bādiyat ash, *Asia* 70 C3
Sysslebäck, *Sweden* 10 D6
Syzran, *Russia* 48 D9
Szabolcs-Szatmár-Bereg □, *Hungary* 42 B6
Szadek, *Poland* 45 G5
Szamocin, *Poland* 45 E4
Szamos →, *Hungary* 42 B7
Szamotuły, *Poland* 45 F3
Száraz →, *Hungary* 42 D6
Szarvas, *Hungary* 42 D5
Százhalombatta, *Hungary* 42 C3
Szczawnica, *Poland* 45 J7
Szczebrzeszyn, *Poland* 45 H9
Szczecin, *Poland* 44 E1
Szczecinek, *Poland* 44 E3
Szczeciński, Zalew = Stettiner Haff, *Germany* 24 B10
Szczekociny, *Poland* 45 H6
Szczucin, *Poland* 45 H8
Szczuczyn, *Poland* 44 E9
Szczyrk, *Poland* 45 J6
Szczytna, *Poland* 45 H3
Szczytno, *Poland* 44 E7
Szechwan = Sichuan □, *China* 58 B5
Szécsény, *Hungary* 42 B4
Szeged, *Hungary* 42 D5
Szeghalom, *Hungary* 42 C6
Székesfehérvár, *Hungary* 42 C3
Szekszárd, *Hungary* 42 D3
Szendrő, *Hungary* 42 B5
Szentendre, *Hungary* 42 C4
Szentes, *Hungary* 42 D5
Szentgotthárd, *Hungary* 42 D1
Szentlőrinc, *Hungary* 42 D3
Szerencs, *Hungary* 42 B6
Szigetszentmiklós, *Hungary* 42 C4
Szigetvár, *Hungary* 42 D2
Szikszó, *Hungary* 42 B5
Szklarska Poreba, *Poland* 45 H2
Szkwa →, *Poland* 45 E8
Szlichtyngowa, *Poland* 45 G3
Szob, *Hungary* 42 C3
Szolnok, *Hungary* 42 C5
Szombathely, *Hungary* 42 C1
Szprotawa, *Poland* 45 G2
Sztum, *Poland* 44 E6
Sztutowo, *Poland* 44 D6
Szubin, *Poland* 45 E4
Szydłowiec, *Poland* 45 G7
Szypliszki, *Poland* 44 D10

T

Ta Khli Khok, *Thailand* 64 E3
Ta Lai, *Vietnam* 65 G6
Tab, *Hungary* 42 D3
Tabacal, *Argentina* 126 A3
Tabaco, *Phil.* 61 E5
Tabagné, *Ivory C.* 82 D4
Ţābah, *Si. Arabia* 70 E4
Tabankort, *Niger* 83 B5
Ţabas, *Khorāsān, Iran* 71 C9
Ţabas, *Khorāsān, Iran* 71 C8
Tabasará, Serranía de, *Panama* 120 E3
Tabasco □, *Mexico* 119 D6
Tabāsīn, *Iran* 71 D8
Tabatinga, Serra da, *Brazil* 125 F10
Taber, *Canada* 104 D6
Taberg, *Sweden* 11 G8
Taberg, *U.S.A.* 111 C9
Tabla, *Niger* 83 C5
Tablas I., *Phil.* 61 E5
Tablas Strait, *Phil.* 61 E4
Table B. = Tafelbaai, *S. Africa* 88 E2
Table B., *Canada* 103 B8
Table Mt., *S. Africa* 88 E2
Table Rock L., *U.S.A.* 113 G8
Tabletop, Mt., *Australia* 94 C4
Tábor, *Czech Rep.* 26 B7
Tabora, *Tanzania* 86 D3
Tabora □, *Tanzania* 86 D3
Tabou, *Ivory C.* 82 E3
Tabrīz, *Iran* 70 B5
Tabuaeran, *Kiribati* 97 G12
Tabuenca, *Spain* 32 D3
Tabūk, *Si. Arabia* 70 D3
Täby, *Sweden* 10 E12
Tacámbaro de Codallos, *Mexico* 118 D4
Tacheng, *China* 60 B3
Tach'i, *Taiwan* 59 E13
Tachia, *Taiwan* 59 E13
Tach'ing Shan = Daqing Shan, *China* 56 D6
Tachov, *Czech Rep.* 26 B5
Tácina →, *Italy* 31 D9
Tacloban, *Phil.* 61 F6
Tacna, *Peru* 124 G4
Tacoma, *U.S.A.* 116 C4
Tacuarembó, *Uruguay* 127 C4
Tademaït, Plateau du, *Algeria* 78 C6
Tadio, L., *Ivory C.* 82 D3
Tadjoura, *Djibouti* 81 E5
Tadjoura, Golfe de, *Djibouti* 81 E5
Tadmor, *N.Z.* 91 J4
Tadoule, L., *Canada* 105 B9
Tadoussac, *Canada* 103 C6
Tadzhikistan = Tajikistan ■, *Asia* 50 F8
Taechŏn-ni, *S. Korea* 57 F14
Taegu, *S. Korea* 57 G15
Taegwan, *N. Korea* 57 D13
Taejŏn, *S. Korea* 57 F14
Tafalla, *Spain* 32 C3
Tafar, *Sudan* 81 F2
Tafelbaai, *S. Africa* 88 E2
Tafermaar, *Indonesia* 63 F8
Tafí Viejo, *Argentina* 126 B2
Tafīhān, *Iran* 71 D7
Tafiré, *Ivory C.* 82 D3
Tafo, *Ghana* 83 D4
Tafresh, *Iran* 71 C6
Taft, *Iran* 71 D7
Taft, *Phil.* 61 F6
Taft, *U.S.A.* 117 K7
Taftān, Kūh-e, *Iran* 71 D9
Taga Dzong, *Bhutan* 67 F16
Taganrog, *Russia* 47 J10
Taganrogskiy Zaliv, *Russia* 47 J10
Tagânt, *Mauritania* 82 B2
Tagatay, *Phil.* 61 D4
Tagbilaran, *Phil.* 61 G5
Tággia, *Italy* 28 E4
Tagish, *Canada* 104 A2
Tagish L., *Canada* 104 A2
Tagliacozzo, *Italy* 29 F10
Tagliamento →, *Italy* 29 C10
Táglio di Po, *Italy* 29 D9
Tago, *Phil.* 61 G7
Tagomago, *Spain* 37 B8
Tagourăret, *Mauritania* 82 B3
Taguatinga, *Brazil* 125 F10
Tagudin, *Phil.* 61 C4
Tagum, *Phil.* 61 H6
Tagus = Tejo →, *Europe* 35 F2
Tahakopa, *N.Z.* 91 M2
Tahan, Gunong, *Malaysia* 65 K4
Tahat, *Algeria* 78 D7
Tāherī, *Iran* 71 E7
Tahiti, *Pac. Oc.* 97 J13
Tahlequah, *U.S.A.* 113 H7
Tahoe, L., *U.S.A.* 116 G6
Tahoe City, *U.S.A.* 116 F6
Tahoka, *U.S.A.* 113 J4
Taholah, *U.S.A.* 116 C2
Tahoua, *Niger* 83 C6
Tahrūd, *Iran* 71 D8
Tahsis, *Canada* 104 D3
Tahta, *Egypt* 80 B3
Tahtaköprü, *Turkey* 41 G13
Tahtalı Dağları, *Turkey* 72 C7
Tahulandang, *Indonesia* 63 D7
Tahuna, *Indonesia* 63 D7
Taï, *Ivory C.* 82 D3
Tai Hu, *China* 59 B12
Tai Shan, *China* 57 F9
Tai'an, *China* 57 F9
Taibei = T'aipei, *Taiwan* 59 E13
Taibique, *Canary Is.* 37 G2
Taibus Qi, *China* 56 D8
Taicang, *China* 59 B13
T'aichung, *Taiwan* 59 E13
Taieri →, *N.Z.* 91 M3
Taigu, *China* 56 F7
Taihang Shan, *China* 56 G7
Taihape, *N.Z.* 91 H5
Taihe, *Anhui, China* 56 H8
Taihe, *Jiangxi, China* 59 D10

Taihu, *China* 59 B11
Taijiang, *China* 58 D7
Taikang, *China* 56 G8
Tailem Bend, *Australia* 95 F2
Tailfingen, *Germany* 25 G5
Tailuko, *Taiwan* 59 E13
Taimyr Peninsula = Taymyr, Poluostrov, *Russia* 51 B11
Tain, *U.K.* 14 D4
T'ainan, *Taiwan* 59 F13
Taínaron, Ákra, *Greece* 38 E4
Taining, *China* 59 D11
T'aipei, *Taiwan* 59 E13
Taiping, *China* 59 B12
Taiping, *Malaysia* 65 K3
Taipingzhen, *China* 56 H6
Tairbeart = Tarbert, *U.K.* 14 D2
Taishan, *China* 59 F9
Taishun, *China* 59 D12
Taita Hills, *Kenya* 86 C4
Taitao, Pen. de, *Chile* 122 H3
T'aitung, *Taiwan* 59 F13
Taivalkoski, *Finland* 8 D23
Taiwan ■, *Asia* 59 F13
Taiwan Strait, *Asia* 59 E12
Taixing, *China* 59 A13
Taiyara, *Sudan* 81 E3
Taïyetos Óros, *Greece* 38 D4
Taiyiba, *Israel* 75 C4
Taiyuan, *China* 56 F7
Taizhong = T'aichung, *Taiwan* 59 E13
Taizhou, *China* 59 A12
Taizhou Liedao, *China* 59 C13
Ta'izz, *Yemen* 74 E3
Tājābād, *Iran* 71 D7
Tajikistan ■, *Asia* 50 F8
Tajima, *Japan* 55 F9
Tajo = Tejo →, *Europe* 35 F2
Tajrīsh, *Iran* 71 C6
Tak, *Thailand* 64 D2
Takāb, *Iran* 70 B5
Takachiho, *Japan* 55 H5
Takachu, *Botswana* 88 C3
Takada, *Japan* 55 F9
Takahagi, *Japan* 55 F10
Takaka, *N.Z.* 91 J4
Takamatsu, *Japan* 55 G7
Takaoka, *Japan* 55 F8
Takapuna, *N.Z.* 91 G5
Takasaki, *Japan* 55 F9
Takatsuki, *Japan* 55 G7
Takaungu, *Kenya* 86 C4
Takayama, *Japan* 55 F8
Take-Shima, *Japan* 55 J5
Takefu, *Japan* 55 G8
Takengon, *Indonesia* 62 D1
Takeo, *Japan* 55 H5
Tåkern, *Sweden* 11 F8
Tākestān, *Iran* 71 C6
Taketa, *Japan* 55 H5
Takev, *Cambodia* 65 G5
Takh, *India* 69 C7
Takht-Sulaiman, *Pakistan* 68 D3
Takikawa, *Japan* 54 C10
Takla L., *Canada* 104 B3
Takla Landing, *Canada* 104 B3
Takla Makan = Taklamakan Shamo, *China* 60 C3
Taklamakan Shamo, *China* 60 C3
Taku →, *Canada* 104 B2
Takum, *Nigeria* 83 D6
Tal Halāl, *Iran* 71 D7
Tala, *Uruguay* 127 C4
Talachyn, *Belarus* 46 E5
Talacogan, *Phil.* 61 G6
Talagang, *Pakistan* 68 C5
Talagante, *Chile* 126 C1
Talak, *Niger* 83 B6
Talamanca, Cordillera de, *Cent. Amer.* 120 E3
Talant, *France* 19 E11
Talara, *Peru* 124 D2
Talas, *Kyrgyzstan* 50 E8
Talas, *Turkey* 72 C6
Talâta, *Egypt* 75 E1
Talata Mafara, *Nigeria* 83 C6
Talaud, Kepulauan, *Indonesia* 63 D7
Talaud Is. = Talaud, Kepulauan, *Indonesia* 63 D7
Talavera de la Reina, *Spain* 34 F6
Talavera la Real, *Spain* 35 G4
Talayan, *Phil.* 61 H6
Talayuela, *Spain* 34 F5
Talbandh, *India* 69 H12
Talbert, Sillon de, *France* 18 D3
Talbot, C., *Australia* 92 B4
Talbragar →, *Australia* 95 E4
Talca, *Chile* 126 D1
Talcahuano, *Chile* 126 D1
Talcher, *India* 67 J14
Talcho, *Niger* 83 C5
Taldy Kurgan = Taldyqorghan, *Kazakstan* 50 E8
Taldyqorghan, *Kazakstan* 50 E8
Tālesh, *Iran* 71 B6
Tālesh, Kūhhā-ye, *Iran* 71 B6
Talguharai, *Sudan* 80 D4
Tali Post, *Sudan* 81 F3
Taliabu, *Indonesia* 63 E6
Talibon, *Phil.* 63 B6
Talibong, Ko, *Thailand* 65 J2
Talihina, *U.S.A.* 113 H7
Talisayan, *Phil.* 61 G6
Taliwang, *Indonesia* 62 F5
Tall 'Afar, *Iraq* 70 B4
Tall Kalakh, *Syria* 75 A5
Talla, *Egypt* 80 B3
Talladega, *U.S.A.* 109 J2
Tallahassee, *U.S.A.* 109 K3
Tallangatta, *Australia* 95 F4
Tallard, *France* 21 D10
Tällberg, *Sweden* 10 D9
Tallering Pk., *Australia* 93 E2
Talli, *Pakistan* 68 E3
Tallinn, *Estonia* 9 G21
Tallmadge, *U.S.A.* 110 E3
Tallulah, *U.S.A.* 113 J9
Tălmaciu, *Romania* 43 E9
Talmont-St-Hilaire, *France* 20 B2
Talne, *Ukraine* 47 H6
Talnoye = Talne, *Ukraine* 47 H6
Talodi, *Sudan* 81 E3
Talovaya, *Russia* 48 E5
Taloyoak, *Canada* 100 B10
Talpa de Allende, *Mexico* 118 C4
Talsi, *Latvia* 9 H20
Talsi □, *Latvia* 44 A9
Taltal, *Chile* 126 B1
Taltson →, *Canada* 104 A6
Talurqjuak = Taloyoak, *Canada* 100 B10
Talwood, *Australia* 95 D4
Talyawalka Cr. →, *Australia* 95 E3
Tam Chau, *Vietnam* 65 G5
Tam Ky, *Vietnam* 64 E7
Tam Quan, *Vietnam* 64 E7
Tama, *U.S.A.* 112 E8
Tamale, *Ghana* 83 D4
Taman, *Russia* 47 K9
Tamani, *Mali* 82 C3
Tamano, *Japan* 55 G6
Tamanrasset, *Algeria* 78 D7
Tamaqua, *U.S.A.* 111 F9
Tamar →, *U.K.* 13 G3
Tamarinda, *Spain* 37 B10
Tamarite de Litera, *Spain* 32 D5
Tamashima, *Japan* 55 G6
Tamási, *Hungary* 42 D3
Tamaské, *Niger* 83 C6
Tamaulipas □, *Mexico* 119 C5
Tamaulipas, Sierra de, *Mexico* 119 C5
Tamazula, *Mexico* 118 C3
Tamazunchale, *Mexico* 119 C5
Tamba-Dabatou, *Guinea* 82 C2
Tambacounda, *Senegal* 82 C2
Tambelan, Kepulauan, *Indonesia* 62 D3
Tambellup, *Australia* 93 F2
Tambo, *Australia* 94 C4
Tambo de Mora, *Peru* 124 F3
Tambohorano, *Madag.* 89 B7
Tambora, *Indonesia* 62 F5
Tambov, *Russia* 48 D5
Tambre →, *Spain* 34 C2
Tambuku, *Indonesia* 63 G15
Tamburâ, *Sudan* 81 F2
Tâmchekket, *Mauritania* 82 B2
Tâmega →, *Portugal* 34 D2
Tamenglong, *India* 67 G18
Tamgué, Massif du, *Guinea* 82 C2
Tamiahua, L. de, *Mexico* 119 C5
Tamil Nadu □, *India* 66 P10
Tamis →, *Serbia, Yug.* 42 F5
Tamluk, *India* 69 H12
Tammerfors = Tampere, *Finland* 9 F20
Tammisaari, *Finland* 9 F20
Tämnaren, *Sweden* 10 D11
Tamo Abu, Pegunungan, *Malaysia* 62 D5
Tampa, *U.S.A.* 109 M4
Tampa B., *U.S.A.* 109 M4
Tampere, *Finland* 9 F20
Tampico, *Mexico* 119 C5
Tampin, *Malaysia* 65 L4
Tamsweg, *Austria* 26 D6
Tamu, *Burma* 67 G19
Tamuja →, *Spain* 35 F4
Tamworth, *Australia* 95 E5
Tamworth, *Canada* 110 B8
Tamworth, *U.K.* 13 E6
Tamyang, *S. Korea* 57 G14
Tan An, *Vietnam* 65 G6
Tan-Tan, *Morocco* 78 C3
Tana →, *Kenya* 86 C5
Tana →, *Norway* 8 A23
Tana, L., *Ethiopia* 81 E4
Tana River, *Kenya* 86 C4
Tanabe, *Japan* 55 H7
Tanafjorden, *Norway* 8 A23
Tanaga, Pta., *Canary Is.* 37 G1
Tanahbala, *Indonesia* 62 E1
Tanahgrogot, *Indonesia* 62 E5
Tanahjampea, *Indonesia* 63 F6
Tanahmasa, *Indonesia* 62 E1
Tanahmerah, *Indonesia* 63 F10
Tanakpur, *India* 69 E9
Tanakura, *Japan* 55 F10
Tanami, *Australia* 92 C4
Tanami Desert, *Australia* 92 C5
Tanana →, *U.S.A.* 100 B4
Tananarive = Antananarivo, *Madag.* 89 B8
Tânaro →, *Italy* 28 D5
Tancheng, *China* 57 G10
Tanch'ŏn, *N. Korea* 57 D15
Tanda, *Ut. P., India* 69 F10
Tanda, *Ut. P., India* 69 E8
Tanda, *Ivory C.* 82 D4
Tandag, *Phil.* 61 G7
Tandaia, *Tanzania* 87 D3
Tăndărei, *Romania* 43 F12
Tandaué, *Angola* 88 B2
Tandil, *Argentina* 126 D4
Tandil, Sa. del, *Argentina* 126 D4
Tandlianwala, *Pakistan* 68 D5
Tando Adam, *Pakistan* 68 G3
Tando Allahyar, *Pakistan* 68 G3
Tando Bago, *Pakistan* 68 G3
Tando Mohommed Khan, *Pakistan* 68 G3
Tandou L., *Australia* 95 E3
Tandragee, *U.K.* 15 B5
Tandsjöborg, *Sweden* 10 C8
Tane-ga-Shima, *Japan* 55 J5
Taneatua, *N.Z.* 91 H6
Tanen Tong Dan = Dawna Ra., *Burma* 64 D2
Tanew →, *Poland* 45 H9
Tanezrouft, *Algeria* 78 D6
Tang, Koh, *Cambodia* 65 G4
Tang, Ra's-e, *Iran* 71 E8
Tang Krasang, *Cambodia* 64 F5
Tanga, *Tanzania* 86 D4
Tanga □, *Tanzania* 86 D4
Tanganyika, L., *Africa* 86 D3
Tangaza, *Nigeria* 83 C5
Tanger, *Morocco* 78 A4
Tangerang, *Indonesia* 63 G12
Tangerhütte, *Germany* 24 C7
Tangermünde, *Germany* 24 C7
Tanggu, *China* 57 E9
Tanggula Shan, *China* 60 C4
Tanghe, *China* 56 H7
Tangier = Tanger, *Morocco* 78 A4
Tangorin, *Australia* 94 C3
Tangorombohitr'i Makay, *Madag.* 89 C8
Tangshan, *China* 57 E10
Tangtou, *China* 57 G10
Tanguiéta, *Benin* 83 C5
Tangxi, *China* 59 C12
Tangyan He →, *China* 58 C7
Tanimbar, Kepulauan, *Indonesia* 63 F8
Tanimbar Is. = Tanimbar, Kepulauan, *Indonesia* 63 F8
Taninthari = Tenasserim □, *Burma* 64 F2
Tanjay, *Phil.* 61 G5
Tanjong Malim, *Malaysia* 65 L3
Tanjore = Thanjavur, *India* 66 P11
Tanjung, *Indonesia* 62 E5
Tanjungbalai, *Indonesia* 62 D1
Tanjungbatu, *Indonesia* 62 D5
Tanjungkarang Telukbetung, *Indonesia* 62 F3
Tanjungpandan, *Indonesia* 62 E3
Tanjungpinang, *Indonesia* 62 D2
Tanjungredeb, *Indonesia* 62 D5
Tanjungselor, *Indonesia* 62 D5
Tank, *Pakistan* 68 C4
Tankhala, *India* 68 J5
Tännäs, *Sweden* 10 B6
Tannersville, *U.S.A.* 111 E9
Tannis Bugt, *Denmark* 11 G4
Tannu-Ola, *Russia* 51 D10
Tannum Sands, *Australia* 94 C5
Tano →, *Ghana* 82 D4
Tanon Str., *Phil.* 61 F5
Tanout, *Niger* 83 C6
Tanshui, *Taiwan* 59 E13
Tansilla, *Burkina Faso* 82 C4
Tanta, *Egypt* 80 H7
Tantoyuca, *Mexico* 119 C5
Tantung = Dandong, *China* 57 D13
Tanumshede, *Sweden* 11 F5
Tanunda, *Australia* 95 E2
Tanus, *France* 20 D6
Tanzania ■, *Africa* 86 D3
Tanzilla →, *Canada* 104 B2
Tao, Ko, *Thailand* 65 G2
Tao'an = Taonan, *China* 57 B12
Tao'er He →, *China* 57 B13
Taohua Dao, *China* 59 C14
Taolanaro, *Madag.* 89 D8
Taole, *China* 56 E4
Taonan, *China* 57 B12
Taormina, *Italy* 31 E8
Taos, *U.S.A.* 115 H11
Taoudenni, *Mali* 78 D5
Taoyuan, *China* 59 C8
T'aoyüan, *Taiwan* 59 E13
Tapa, *Estonia* 9 G21
Tapa Shan = Daba Shan, *China* 58 B7
Tapachula, *Mexico* 119 E6
Tapah, *Malaysia* 65 K3
Tapajós →, *Brazil* 122 D5
Tapaktuan, *Indonesia* 62 D1
Tapanahoni →, *Surinam* 125 C8
Tapanui, *N.Z.* 91 L2
Tapauá →, *Brazil* 124 E6
Tapes, *Brazil* 127 C5
Tapeta, *Liberia* 82 D3
Taphan Hin, *Thailand* 64 D3
Tapi →, *India* 66 J8
Tapia de Casariego, *Spain* 34 B4
Tapirapecó, Serra, *Venezuela* 124 C6
Tapolca, *Hungary* 42 D2
Tapuaenuku, Mt., *N.Z.* 91 K4
Tapul Group, *Phil.* 61 J4
Tapurucuará, *Brazil* 124 D5
Taqṭaq, *Iraq* 70 C5
Taquara, *Brazil* 127 B5
Taquari →, *Brazil* 124 G7
Tara, *Australia* 95 D5
Tara, *Canada* 110 B3
Tara, *Russia* 50 D8
Tara, *Zambia* 87 F2
Tara →, *Montenegro, Yug.* 40 C2
Taraba □, *Nigeria* 83 D7
Taraba →, *Nigeria* 83 D7
Tarabagatay, Khrebet, *Kazakstan* 50 E9
Tarābulus, *Lebanon* 75 A4
Tarābulus, *Libya* 79 B8
Taraclia, *Moldova* 43 D14
Taraclia, *Moldova* 43 E13
Taradehi, *India* 69 H8
Tarajalejo, *Canary Is.* 37 F5
Tarakan, *Indonesia* 62 D5
Tarakit, Mt., *Kenya* 86 B4
Tarama-Jima, *Japan* 55 M2
Taran, Mys, *Russia* 9 J18
Taranagar, *India* 68 E6
Taranaki □, *N.Z.* 91 H5
Taranaki, Mt., *N.Z.* 91 H5
Tarancón, *Spain* 32 E1
Taransay, *U.K.* 14 D1
Táranto, *Italy* 31 B10
Táranto, G. di, *Italy* 31 B10
Tarapacá, *Colombia* 124 D5
Tarapacá □, *Chile* 126 A2
Tarapoto, *Peru* 124 E3
Tarare, *France* 21 C8
Tararua Ra., *N.Z.* 91 J5
Tarascon, *France* 21 E8
Tarascon-sur-Ariège, *France* 20 F5
Tarashcha, *Ukraine* 47 H6
Tarauacá, *Brazil* 124 E4
Tarauacá →, *Brazil* 124 E5
Taravo →, *France* 21 G12
Tarawa, *Kiribati* 96 G9
Tarawera, *N.Z.* 91 H6
Tarawera L., *N.Z.* 91 H6
Taraz, *Kazakstan* 50 E8
Tarazona, *Spain* 32 D3
Tarazona de la Mancha, *Spain* 33 F3
Tarbat Ness, *U.K.* 14 D5
Tarbela Dam, *Pakistan* 68 B5
Tarbert, *Arg. & Bute, U.K.* 14 F3
Tarbert, *W. Isles, U.K.* 14 D2
Tarbes, *France* 20 E4
Tarboro, *U.S.A.* 109 H7
Tărcău, Munţii, *Romania* 43 D11
Tarcento, *Italy* 29 B10
Tarcoola, *Australia* 95 E1
Tarcoon, *Australia* 95 E4
Tardets-Sorholus, *France* 20 E3
Tardoire →, *France* 20 C4
Taree, *Australia* 95 E5
Tarfa, W. el →, *Egypt* 80 B3
Tarfaya, *Morocco* 78 C3
Târgovişte, *Romania* 43 F10
Târgu Bujor, *Romania* 43 E12
Târgu Cărbuneşti, *Romania* 43 F8
Târgu Frumos, *Romania* 43 C12
Târgu-Jiu, *Romania* 43 E8
Târgu Lăpuş, *Romania* 43 C8
Târgu Mureş, *Romania* 43 D9
Târgu Neamţ, *Romania* 43 C11
Târgu Ocna, *Romania* 43 D11
Târgu Secuiesc, *Romania* 43 E11
Tărguşor, *Romania* 43 F13
Tărhăus, Vf., *Romania* 43 D11
Ţarif, *U.A.E.* 71 E7
Tarifa, *Spain* 35 J5
Tarija, *Bolivia* 126 A3
Tarija □, *Bolivia* 126 A3
Tariku →, *Indonesia* 63 E9
Tarim Basin = Tarim Pendi, *China* 60 C3
Tarim He →, *China* 60 C3
Tarim Pendi, *China* 60 C3
Taritatu →, *Indonesia* 63 E9
Tarka →, *S. Africa* 88 E4
Tarkastad, *S. Africa* 88 E4
Tarkhankut, Mys, *Ukraine* 47 K7
Tarko Sale, *Russia* 50 C8
Tarkwa, *Ghana* 82 D4
Tarlac, *Phil.* 61 D4
Tarm, *Denmark* 11 J2
Tarma, *Peru* 124 F3
Tarn □, *France* 20 E6
Tarn →, *France* 20 D5
Tarn-et-Garonne □, *France* 20 D5
Tarna →, *Hungary* 42 C4
Târnava Mare →, *Romania* 43 D8
Târnava Mică →, *Romania* 43 D8
Târnăveni, *Romania* 43 D9
Tarnica, *Poland* 45 J9
Tarnobrzeg, *Poland* 45 H8
Tarnogród, *Poland* 45 H9
Tarnos, *France* 20 E2
Târnova, *Moldova* 43 B12
Târnova, *Romania* 42 E6
Tarnów, *Poland* 45 H8
Tarnowskie Góry, *Poland* 45 H5
Tärnsjö, *Sweden* 10 D10
Táro →, *Italy* 28 C7
Ţārom, *Iran* 71 D7
Taroom, *Australia* 95 D4
Taroudannt, *Morocco* 78 B4
Tarp, *Germany* 24 A5
Tarpon Springs, *U.S.A.* 109 L4
Tarquínia, *Italy* 29 F8
Tarragona, *Spain* 32 D6
Tarragona □, *Spain* 32 D6
Tarraleah, *Australia* 94 G4
Tarrasa = Terrassa, *Spain* 32 D7
Tàrrega, *Spain* 32 D6
Tarrytown, *U.S.A.* 111 E11
Tårs, *Denmark* 11 G4
Tarshiha = Me'ona, *Israel* 75 B4
Tarso Emissi, *Chad* 79 D9
Tarsus, *Turkey* 70 B2
Tartagal, *Argentina* 126 A3
Tärtär, *Azerbaijan* 49 K8
Tärtär →, *Azerbaijan* 49 K8
Tartas, *France* 20 E3
Tartu, *Estonia* 9 G22
Ţarţūs, *Syria* 70 C2
Tarumizu, *Japan* 55 J5
Tarussa, *Russia* 46 E9
Tarutao, Ko, *Thailand* 65 J2
Tarutung, *Indonesia* 62 D1
Tarvísio, *Italy* 29 B10
Taseko →, *Canada* 104 C4
Tash-Kömür, *Kyrgyzstan* 50 E8
Tash-Kumyr = Tash-Kömür, *Kyrgyzstan* 50 E8
Tashauz = Dashhowuz, *Turkmenistan* 50 E6
Tashi Chho Dzong = Thimphu, *Bhutan* 67 F16
Ţashk, Daryācheh-ye, *Iran* 71 D7
Tashkent = Toshkent, *Uzbekistan* 50 E7
Tashtagol, *Russia* 50 D9
Tasiilaq, *Greenland* 4 C6
Tasikmalaya, *Indonesia* 63 G13
Tåsinge, *Denmark* 11 J4
Tåsjön, *Sweden* 8 D16
Taskan, *Russia* 51 C16
Tasker, *Niger* 83 C7
Taşköprü, *Turkey* 72 B6
Taşlâc, *Moldova* 43 C14
Tasman B., *N.Z.* 91 J4
Tasman Mts., *N.Z.* 91 J4
Tasman Pen., *Australia* 94 G4
Tasman Sea, *Pac. Oc.* 96 L8
Tasmania □, *Australia* 94 G4
Tăşnad, *Romania* 42 C7
Tassili n'Ajjer, *Algeria* 78 C7
Tassili Tin-Rerhoh, *Algeria* 83 A5
Tata, *Hungary* 42 C3
Tatabánya, *Hungary* 42 C3
Tatahouine, *Tunisia* 79 B8
Tatar Republic = Tatarstan □, *Russia* 48 C10
Tatarbunary, *Ukraine* 47 K5
Tatarsk, *Russia* 50 D8
Tatarstan □, *Russia* 48 C10
Tateyama, *Japan* 55 G9
Tathlina L., *Canada* 104 A5
Tathra, *Australia* 95 F4
Tatinnai L., *Canada* 105 A9
Tatla L., *Canada* 104 C4
Tatlısu, *Turkey* 41 F11
Tatnam, C., *Canada* 105 B10
Tatra = Tatry, *Slovak Rep.* 27 B13
Tatry, *Slovak Rep.* 27 B13
Tatshenshini →, *Canada* 104 B1
Tatsuno, *Japan* 55 G7
Tatta, *Pakistan* 68 G2
Tatuī, *Brazil* 127 A6
Tatum, *U.S.A.* 113 J3
Tat'ung = Datong, *China* 56 D7
Tatvan, *Turkey* 70 B4
Taubaté, *Brazil* 127 A6
Tauberbischofsheim, *Germany* 25 F5
Taucha, *Germany* 24 D8
Tauern-tunnel, *Austria* 26 D6
Taufikia, *Sudan* 81 F3
Taulé, *France* 18 D3
Taumarunui, *N.Z.* 91 H5
Taumaturgo, *Brazil* 124 E4
Taung, *S. Africa* 88 D3
Taungdwingyi, *Burma* 67 J19
Taunggyi, *Burma* 67 J20
Taungup, *Burma* 67 K19
Taungup Taunggya, *Burma* 67 K18
Taunsa, *Pakistan* 68 D4
Taunsa Barrage, *Pakistan* 68 D4
Taunton, *U.K.* 13 F4
Taunton, *U.S.A.* 111 E13
Taunus, *Germany* 25 E4
Taupo, *N.Z.* 91 H6
Taupo, L., *N.Z.* 91 H5
Tauragė, *Lithuania* 9 J20
Tauragė □, *Lithuania* 44 C9
Tauranga, *N.Z.* 91 G6
Tauranga Harb., *N.Z.* 91 G6
Taureau, Rés., *Canada* 102 C5
Taurianova, *Italy* 31 D9
Taurus Mts. = Toros Dağları, *Turkey* 70 B2
Tauste, *Spain* 32 D3
Tauz = Tovuz, *Azerbaijan* 49 K7
Tavas, *Turkey* 39 D11
Tavda, *Russia* 50 D7
Tavda →, *Russia* 50 D7
Tavernes de la Valldigna, *Spain* 33 F4
Taveta, *Tanzania* 86 C4
Taveuni, *Fiji* 91 C9
Taviano, *Italy* 31 C11
Tavignano →, *France* 21 F13
Tavira, *Portugal* 35 H3
Tavistock, *Canada* 110 C4
Tavistock, *U.K.* 13 G3
Tavolara, *Italy* 30 B2
Távora →, *Portugal* 34 D3
Tavoy = Dawei, *Burma* 64 E2
Tavşanlı, *Turkey* 39 B11
Taw →, *U.K.* 13 F3
Tawa →, *India* 68 H8
Tawas City, *U.S.A.* 108 C4
Tawau, *Malaysia* 62 D5
Taweisha, *Sudan* 81 E2
Tawitawi, *Phil.* 63 B6
Tawu, *Taiwan* 59 F13
Taxco de Alarcón, *Mexico* 119 D5
Taxila, *Pakistan* 68 C5
Tay →, *U.K.* 14 E5
Tay, Firth of, *U.K.* 14 E5
Tay, L., *Australia* 93 F3
Tay, L., *U.K.* 14 E4
Tay Ninh, *Vietnam* 65 G6

Tayabamba, *Peru* 124 E3
Tayabas Bay, *Phil.* 61 E4
Taylakova, *Russia* 50 D8
Taylakovy = Taylakova, *Russia* 50 D8
Taylor, *Canada* 104 B4
Taylor, *Nebr., U.S.A.* 112 E5
Taylor, *Pa., U.S.A.* 111 E9
Taylor, *Tex., U.S.A.* 113 K6
Taylor, Mt., *U.S.A.* 115 J10
Taylorville, *U.S.A.* 112 F10
Taymā, *Si. Arabia* 70 E3
Taymyr, Oz., *Russia* 51 B11
Taymyr, Poluostrov, *Russia* 51 B11
Tayport, *U.K.* 14 E6
Tayshet, *Russia* 51 D10
Taytay, *Phil.* 61 F3
Taz →, *Russia* 50 C8
Taza, *Morocco* 78 B5
Tāzah Khurmātū, *Iraq* 70 C5
Tazawa-Ko, *Japan* 54 E10
Tazin, *Canada* 105 B7
Tazin L., *Canada* 105 B7
Tazovskiy, *Russia* 50 C8
Tbilisi, *Georgia* 49 K7
Tchad = Chad ■, *Africa* 79 F8
Tchad, L., *Chad* 79 F8
Tchaourou, *Benin* 83 D5
Tch'eng-tou = Chengdu, *China* 58 B5
Tchentlo L., *Canada* 104 B4
Tchetti, *Benin* 83 D5
Tchibanga, *Gabon* 84 E2
Tchien, *Liberia* 82 D3
Tchin Tabaraden, *Niger* 83 B6
Tch'ong-k'ing = Chongqing, *China* 58 C6
Tczew, *Poland* 44 D5
Te Anau, *N.Z.* 91 L1
Te Anau, L., *N.Z.* 91 L1
Te Aroha, *N.Z.* 91 G5
Te Awamutu, *N.Z.* 91 H5
Te Kuiti, *N.Z.* 91 H5
Te-n-Dghâmcha, Sebkhet, *Mauritania* 82 B1
Te Puke, *N.Z.* 91 G6
Te Waewae B., *N.Z.* 91 M1
Teaca, *Romania* 43 D9
Teague, *U.S.A.* 113 K6
Teano, *Italy* 31 A7
Teapa, *Mexico* 119 D6
Teba, *Spain* 35 J6
Tebakang, *Malaysia* 62 D4
Teberda, *Russia* 49 J5
Tébessa, *Algeria* 78 A7
Tebicuary →, *Paraguay* 126 B4
Tebingtinggi, *Indonesia* 62 D1
Tebintingii, *Indonesia* 62 E2
Tebulos, *Georgia* 49 J7
Tecate, *Mexico* 117 N10
Tecer Dağları, *Turkey* 72 C7
Tech →, *France* 20 F7
Techiman, *Ghana* 82 D4
Techirghiol, *Romania* 43 F13
Tecka, *Argentina* 128 E2
Tecomán, *Mexico* 118 D4
Tecopa, *U.S.A.* 117 K10
Tecoripa, *Mexico* 118 B3
Tecuala, *Mexico* 118 C3
Tecuci, *Romania* 43 E12
Tecumseh, *Canada* 110 D2
Tecumseh, *Mich., U.S.A.* 108 D4
Tecumseh, *Okla., U.S.A.* 113 H6
Tedzhen = Tejen, *Turkmenistan* 50 F7
Tees →, *U.K.* 12 C6
Tees B., *U.K.* 12 C6
Teeswater, *Canada* 110 C3
Tefé, *Brazil* 124 D6
Tefenni, *Turkey* 39 D11
Tegal, *Indonesia* 62 F3
Tegernsee, *Germany* 25 H7
Teggiano, *Italy* 31 B8
Tegid, L. = Bala, L., *U.K.* 12 E4
Tegina, *Nigeria* 83 C6
Tegucigalpa, *Honduras* 120 D2
Teguidda i-n-Tessoum, *Niger* 83 B6
Tehachapi, *U.S.A.* 117 K8
Tehachapi Mts., *U.S.A.* 117 L8
Tehamiyam, *Sudan* 80 D4
Tehilla, *Sudan* 80 D4
Téhini, *Ivory C.* 82 D4
Tehoru, *Indonesia* 63 E7
Tehrān, *Iran* 71 C6
Tehri, *India* 69 D8
Tehuacán, *Mexico* 119 D5
Tehuantepec, *Mexico* 119 D5
Tehuantepec, G. de, *Mexico* 119 D5
Tehuantepec, Istmo de, *Mexico* 119 D6
Teide, *Canary Is.* 37 F3
Teifi →, *U.K.* 13 E3
Teign →, *U.K.* 13 G4
Teignmouth, *U.K.* 13 G4
Teiuş, *Romania* 43 D8
Teixeira Pinto, *Guinea-Biss.* 82 C1
Tejam, *India* 69 E9
Tejen, *Turkmenistan* 50 F7
Tejen →, *Turkmenistan* 71 B9
Tejo →, *Europe* 35 F2
Tejon Pass, *U.S.A.* 117 L8
Tekamah, *U.S.A.* 112 E6
Tekapo, L., *N.Z.* 91 K3
Tekax, *Mexico* 119 C7
Teke, *Turkey* 41 E13
Tekeli, *Kazakstan* 50 E8
Tekeze →, *Ethiopia* 81 E4
Tekija, *Serbia, Yug.* 40 B6
Tekirdağ, *Turkey* 41 F11
Tekirdağ □, *Turkey* 41 E11
Tekirova, *Turkey* 39 E12
Tekkali, *India* 67 K14
Tekke, *Turkey* 72 B7
Tekman, *Turkey* 73 C9
Tekoa, *U.S.A.* 114 C5
Tel Aviv-Yafo, *Israel* 75 C3
Tel Lakhish, *Israel* 75 D3
Tel Megiddo, *Israel* 75 C4
Tela, *Honduras* 120 C2
Telanaipura = Jambi, *Indonesia* 62 E2
Telavi, *Georgia* 49 J7
Telč, *Czech Rep.* 26 B8
Telciu, *Romania* 43 C9
Telde, *Canary Is.* 37 G4
Telegraph Creek, *Canada* 104 B2
Telekhany = Tsyelyakhany, *Belarus* 47 F3
Telemark, *Norway* 9 G12
Telén, *Argentina* 126 D2
Teleneşti, *Moldova* 43 C13
Teleng, *Iran* 71 E9
Teleño, *Spain* 34 C4
Teleorman □, *Romania* 43 G10
Teleorman →, *Romania* 43 G10
Teles Pires →, *Brazil* 122 D5
Telescope Pk., *U.S.A.* 117 J9
Teletaye, *Mali* 83 B5
Telfer Mine, *Australia* 92 C3
Telford, *U.K.* 13 E5
Telford and Wrekin □, *U.K.* 12 E5
Telfs, *Austria* 26 D4
Télimélé, *Guinea* 82 C2
Teljo, J., *Sudan* 81 E2
Telkwa, *Canada* 104 C3
Tell City, *U.S.A.* 108 G2
Tellicherry, *India* 66 P9
Telluride, *U.S.A.* 115 H10
Teloloapán, *Mexico* 119 D5
Telpos Iz, *Russia* 6 C17
Telsen, *Argentina* 128 E3
Telšiai, *Lithuania* 9 H20
Telšiai □, *Lithuania* 44 C9
Teltow, *Germany* 24 C9
Teluk Anson = Teluk Intan, *Malaysia* 65 K3
Teluk Betung = Tanjungkarang Telukbetung, *Indonesia* 62 F3
Teluk Intan, *Malaysia* 65 K3
Telukbutun, *Indonesia* 65 K7
Telukdalem, *Indonesia* 62 D1
Tema, *Ghana* 83 D5
Temax, *Mexico* 119 C7
Temba, *S. Africa* 89 D4
Tembagapura, *Indonesia* 63 E9
Tembe, *Dem. Rep. of the Congo* 86 C2
Tembleque, *Spain* 34 F7
Temblor Range, *U.S.A.* 117 K7
Teme →, *U.K.* 13 E5
Temecula, *U.S.A.* 117 M9
Temerloh, *Malaysia* 62 D2
Teminabuan, *Indonesia* 63 E8
Temir, *Kazakstan* 50 E6
Temirtau, *Kazakstan* 50 D8
Temirtau, *Russia* 50 D9
Témiscamie →, *Canada* 103 B5
Témiscaming, *Canada* 102 C4
Témiscamingue, L., *Canada* 102 C4
Temnikov, *Russia* 48 C6
Temo →, *Italy* 30 B1
Temosachic, *Mexico* 118 B3
Tempe, *U.S.A.* 115 K8
Témpio Pausánia, *Italy* 30 B2
Tempiute, *U.S.A.* 116 H11
Temple, *U.S.A.* 113 K6
Temple B., *Australia* 94 A3
Templemore, *Ireland* 15 D4
Templeton, *U.S.A.* 116 K6
Templeton →, *Australia* 94 C2
Templin, *Germany* 24 B9
Tempoal, *Mexico* 119 C5
Temryuk, *Russia* 47 K9
Temska →, *Serbia, Yug.* 40 C6
Temuco, *Chile* 128 D2
Temuka, *N.Z.* 91 L3
Tenabo, *Mexico* 119 C6
Tenaha, *U.S.A.* 113 K7
Tenakee Springs, *U.S.A.* 104 B1
Tenali, *India* 67 L12
Tenancingo, *Mexico* 119 D5
Tenango, *Mexico* 119 D5
Tenasserim, *Burma* 65 F2
Tenasserim □, *Burma* 64 F2
Tenby, *U.K.* 13 F3
Tenda, Colle di, *France* 21 D11
Tendaho, *Ethiopia* 81 E5
Tende, *France* 21 D11
Tendelti, *Sudan* 81 E3
Tendrovskaya Kosa, *Ukraine* 47 J6
Tendukhera, *India* 69 H8
Teneida, *Egypt* 80 B2
Tenenkou, *Mali* 82 C4
Ténéré, *Niger* 83 B7
Tenerife, *Canary Is.* 37 F3
Tenerife, Pico, *Canary Is.* 37 G1
Teng Xian, *Guangxi Zhuangzu, China* 59 F8
Teng Xian, *Shandong, China* 57 G9
Tengah □, *Indonesia* 63 E6
Tengah, Kepulauan, *Indonesia* 62 F5
Tengchong, *China* 58 E2
Tengchowfu = Penglai, *China* 57 F11
Tenggara □, *Indonesia* 63 E6
Tenggarong, *Indonesia* 62 E5
Tenggol, Pulau, *Malaysia* 65 K4
Tengiz, Ozero, *Kazakstan* 50 D7
Tenhult, *Sweden* 11 G8
Tenino, *U.S.A.* 116 D4
Tenkasi, *India* 66 Q10
Tenke, *Katanga, Dem. Rep. of the Congo* 87 E2
Tenke, *Katanga, Dem. Rep. of the Congo* 87 E2
Tenkodogo, *Burkina Faso* 83 C4
Tenna →, *Italy* 29 E10
Tennant Creek, *Australia* 94 B1
Tennessee □, *U.S.A.* 109 H2
Tennessee →, *U.S.A.* 108 G1
Teno, Pta. de, *Canary Is.* 37 F3
Tenom, *Malaysia* 62 C5
Tenosique, *Mexico* 119 D6
Tenryū-Gawa →, *Japan* 55 G8
Tenterden, *U.K.* 13 F8
Tenterfield, *Australia* 95 D5
Teo, *Spain* 34 C2
Teófilo Otoni, *Brazil* 125 G10
Tepa, *Indonesia* 63 F7
Tepalcatepec →, *Mexico* 118 D4
Tepecik, *Bursa, Turkey* 41 F12
Tepecik, *Kütahya, Turkey* 39 B11
Tepehuanes, *Mexico* 118 B3
Tepelenë, *Albania* 40 F4
Tepetongo, *Mexico* 118 C4
Tepic, *Mexico* 118 C4
Teplá, *Czech Rep.* 26 B5
Teplice, *Czech Rep.* 26 A6
Tepoca, C., *Mexico* 118 A2
Tequila, *Mexico* 118 C4
Ter →, *Spain* 32 C8
Ter Apel, *Neths.* 17 B7
Téra, *Niger* 83 C5
Tera →, *Spain* 34 D5
Teraina, *Kiribati* 97 G11
Terakeka, *Sudan* 81 F3
Téramo, *Italy* 29 F10
Terang, *Australia* 95 F3
Terazit, Massif de, *Niger* 83 A6
Tercan, *Turkey* 73 C9
Tercero →, *Argentina* 126 C3
Terebovlya, *Ukraine* 47 H3
Teregova, *Romania* 42 E7
Tereida, *Sudan* 81 E3
Terek →, *Russia* 49 J8
Tereshka →, *Russia* 48 E8
Teresina, *Brazil* 125 E10
Terespol, *Poland* 45 F10
Terewah, L., *Australia* 95 D4
Terges →, *Portugal* 35 H3
Tergnier, *France* 19 C10
Teridgerie Cr. →, *Australia* 95 E4
Terlizzi, *Italy* 31 A9
Terme, *Turkey* 72 B7
Termez = Termiz, *Uzbekistan* 50 F7
Términi Imerese, *Italy* 30 E6
Términos, L. de, *Mexico* 119 D6
Termiz, *Uzbekistan* 50 F7
Térmoli, *Italy* 29 F12
Ternate, *Indonesia* 63 D7
Terneuzen, *Neths.* 17 C3
Terney, *Russia* 51 E14
Terni, *Italy* 29 F9
Ternitz, *Austria* 26 D9
Ternopil, *Ukraine* 47 H3
Ternopol = Ternopil, *Ukraine* 47 H3
Terowie, *Australia* 95 E2
Terpní, *Greece* 40 F7
Terra Bella, *U.S.A.* 117 K7
Terra Nova Nat. Park, *Canada* 103 C9
Terrace, *Canada* 104 C3
Terrace Bay, *Canada* 102 C2
Terracina, *Italy* 30 A6
Terralba, *Italy* 30 C1
Terranova = Ólbia, *Italy* 30 B2
Terrasini, *Italy* 30 D6
Terrassa, *Spain* 32 D7
Terrasson-la-Villedieu, *France* 20 C5
Terre Haute, *U.S.A.* 108 F2
Terrebonne B., *U.S.A.* 113 L9
Terrell, *U.S.A.* 113 J6
Terrenceville, *Canada* 103 C9
Terry, *U.S.A.* 112 B2
Terryville, *U.S.A.* 111 E11
Terschelling, *Neths.* 17 A5
Tersko-Kumskiy Kanal →, *Russia* 49 H7
Tertenía, *Italy* 30 C2
Terter → = Tärtär →, *Azerbaijan* 49 K8
Teruel, *Spain* 32 E3
Teruel □, *Spain* 32 E4
Tervel, *Bulgaria* 41 C11
Tervola, *Finland* 8 C21
Teryaweyna L., *Australia* 95 E3
Tešanj, *Bos.-H.* 42 F3
Teseney, *Eritrea* 81 D4
Tesha →, *Russia* 48 C6
Teshio, *Japan* 54 B10
Teshio-Gawa →, *Japan* 54 B10
Tešica, *Serbia, Yug.* 40 C5
Tesiyn Gol →, *Mongolia* 60 A4
Teslić, *Bos.-H.* 42 F2
Teslin, *Canada* 104 A2
Teslin →, *Canada* 104 A2
Teslin L., *Canada* 104 A2
Tessalit, *Mali* 83 A5
Tessaoua, *Niger* 83 C6
Tessin, *Germany* 24 A8
Tessit, *Mali* 83 B5
Test →, *U.K.* 13 G6
Testa del Gargano, *Italy* 29 G13
Testigos, Is. Las, *Venezuela* 121 D7
Tét, *Hungary* 42 C2
Têt →, *France* 20 F7
Tetachuck L., *Canada* 104 C3
Tetas, Pta., *Chile* 126 A1
Tete, *Mozam.* 87 F3
Tete □, *Mozam.* 87 F3
Teterev →, *Ukraine* 47 G6
Teterow, *Germany* 24 B8
Teteven, *Bulgaria* 41 D8
Tethul →, *Canada* 104 A6
Tetiyev, *Ukraine* 47 H5
Teton →, *U.S.A.* 114 C8
Tétouan, *Morocco* 78 A4
Tetovo, *Macedonia* 40 D4
Tetyushi, *Russia* 48 C9
Teuco →, *Argentina* 126 B3
Teulada, *Italy* 30 D1
Teulon, *Canada* 105 C9
Teun, *Indonesia* 63 F7
Teutoburger Wald, *Germany* 24 C4
Tevere →, *Italy* 29 G9
Teverya, *Israel* 75 C4
Teviot →, *U.K.* 14 F6
Tewantin, *Australia* 95 D5
Tewkesbury, *U.K.* 13 F5
Texada I., *Canada* 104 D4
Texarkana, *Ark., U.S.A.* 113 J8
Texarkana, *Tex., U.S.A.* 113 J7
Texas, *Australia* 95 D5
Texas □, *U.S.A.* 113 K5
Texas City, *U.S.A.* 113 L7
Texel, *Neths.* 17 A4
Texline, *U.S.A.* 113 G3
Texoma, L., *U.S.A.* 113 J6
Teykovo, *Russia* 46 D11
Teza →, *Russia* 48 B5
Tezin, *Afghan.* 68 B3
Teziutlán, *Mexico* 119 D5
Tezpur, *India* 67 F18
Tezzeron L., *Canada* 104 C4
Tha-anne →, *Canada* 105 A10
Tha Deua, *Laos* 64 D4
Tha Deua, *Laos* 64 C3
Tha Pla, *Thailand* 64 D3
Tha Rua, *Thailand* 64 E3
Tha Sala, *Thailand* 65 H2
Tha Song Yang, *Thailand* 64 D1
Thaba Putsoa, *Lesotho* 89 D4
Thabana Ntlenyana, *Lesotho* 89 D4
Thabazimbi, *S. Africa* 89 C4
Thādiq, *Si. Arabia* 70 E5
Thai Binh, *Vietnam* 58 G6
Thai Muang, *Thailand* 65 H2
Thai Nguyen, *Vietnam* 58 G5
Thailand ■, *Asia* 64 E4
Thailand, G. of, *Asia* 65 G3
Thakhek, *Laos* 64 D5
Thal, *Pakistan* 68 C4
Thal Desert, *Pakistan* 68 D4
Thala La = Hkakabo Razi, *Burma* 67 E20
Thalabarivat, *Cambodia* 64 F5
Thallon, *Australia* 95 D4
Thalwil, *Switz.* 25 H4
Thames, *N.Z.* 91 G5
Thames →, *Canada* 102 D3
Thames →, *U.K.* 13 F8
Thames →, *U.S.A.* 111 E12
Thames Estuary, *U.K.* 13 F8
Thamesford, *Canada* 110 C4
Thamesville, *Canada* 110 D3
Than, *India* 68 H4
Than Uyen, *Vietnam* 64 B4
Thana Gazi, *India* 68 F7
Thandla, *India* 68 H6
Thane, *India* 66 K8
Thanesar, *India* 68 D7
Thanet, I. of, *U.K.* 13 F9
Thangool, *Australia* 94 C5
Thanh Hoa, *Vietnam* 64 C5
Thanh Hung, *Vietnam* 65 H5
Thanh Pho Ho Chi Minh, *Vietnam* 65 G6
Thanh Thuy, *Vietnam* 64 A5
Thanjavur, *India* 66 P11
Thann, *France* 19 E14
Thano Bula Khan, *Pakistan* 68 G2
Thaolinta L., *Canada* 105 A9
Thaon-les-Vosges, *France* 19 D13
Thap Sakae, *Thailand* 65 G2
Thap Than, *Thailand* 64 E2
Thar Desert, *India* 68 F5
Tharad, *India* 68 G4
Thargomindah, *Australia* 95 D3
Tharrawaddy, *Burma* 67 L19
Tharthār, Mileh, *Iraq* 70 C4
Tharthār, W. ath →, *Iraq* 70 C4
Thasopoúla, *Greece* 41 F8
Thásos, *Greece* 41 F8
That Khe, *Vietnam* 58 F6
Thatcher, *Ariz., U.S.A.* 115 K9
Thatcher, *Colo., U.S.A.* 113 G2
Thaton, *Burma* 67 L20
Thau, Bassin de, *France* 20 E7
Thaungdut, *Burma* 67 G19
Thayer, *U.S.A.* 113 G9
Thayetmyo, *Burma* 67 K19
Thazi, *Burma* 67 J20
The Alberga →, *Australia* 95 D2
The Bight, *Bahamas* 121 B4
The Dalles, *U.S.A.* 114 D3
The English Company's Is., *Australia* 94 A2
The Frome →, *Australia* 95 D2
The Great Divide = Great Dividing Ra., *Australia* 94 C4
The Hague = 's-Gravenhage, *Neths.* 17 B4
The Hamilton →, *Australia* 95 D2
The Macumba →, *Australia* 95 D2
The Neales →, *Australia* 95 D2
The Officer →, *Australia* 93 E5
The Pas, *Canada* 105 C8
The Range, *Zimbabwe* 87 F3
The Rock, *Australia* 95 F4
The Salt L., *Australia* 95 E3
The Sandheads, *India* 69 J13
The Stevenson →, *Australia* 95 D2
The Warburton →, *Australia* 95 D2
The Woodlands, *U.S.A.* 113 K7
Thebes = Thívai, *Greece* 38 C5
Thebes, *Egypt* 80 B3
Thedford, *Canada* 110 C3
Thedford, *U.S.A.* 112 E4
Theebine, *Australia* 95 D5
Thekulthili L., *Canada* 105 A7
Thelon →, *Canada* 105 A8
Thénezay, *France* 18 F6
Thenon, *France* 20 C5
Theodore, *Australia* 94 C5
Theodore, *Canada* 105 C8
Theodore, *U.S.A.* 109 K1
Theodore Roosevelt National Memorial Park, *U.S.A.* 112 B3
Theodore Roosevelt Res., *U.S.A.* 115 K8
Thepha, *Thailand* 65 J3
Thérain →, *France* 19 C9
Theresa, *U.S.A.* 111 B9
Thermaïkós Kólpos, *Greece* 40 F6
Thermí, *Greece* 39 B8
Thermopolis, *U.S.A.* 114 E9
Thermopylae P., *Greece* 38 C4
Thesprotía □, *Greece* 38 B2
Thessalía □, *Greece* 38 B4
Thessalon, *Canada* 102 C3
Thessaloníki, *Greece* 40 F6
Thessaloníki □, *Greece* 40 F7
Thessaloniki, Gulf of = Thermaïkós Kólpos, *Greece* 40 F6
Thessaly = Thessalía □, *Greece* 38 B4
Thetford, *U.K.* 13 E8
Thetford Mines, *Canada* 103 C5
Theun →, *Laos* 64 C5
Theunissen, *S. Africa* 88 D4
Thevenard, *Australia* 95 E1
Thiámis →, *Greece* 38 B2
Thiberville, *France* 18 C7
Thibodaux, *U.S.A.* 113 L9
Thicket Portage, *Canada* 105 B9
Thief River Falls, *U.S.A.* 112 A6
Thiel Mts., *Antarctica* 5 E16
Thiene, *Italy* 29 C8
Thiérache, *France* 19 C10
Thiers, *France* 20 C7
Thiès, *Senegal* 82 C1
Thiesi, *Italy* 30 B1
Thiet, *Sudan* 81 F2
Thika, *Kenya* 86 C4
Thikombia, *Fiji* 91 B9
Thille-Boubacar, *Senegal* 82 B1
Thimphu, *Bhutan* 67 F16
Þingvallavatn, *Iceland* 8 D3
Thionville, *France* 19 C13
Thíra, *Greece* 39 E7
Thirasía, *Greece* 39 E7
Third Cataract, *Sudan* 80 D3
Thirsk, *U.K.* 12 C6
Thiruvananthapuram = Trivandrum, *India* 66 Q10
Thisted, *Denmark* 11 H2
Thistle I., *Australia* 95 F2
Thívai, *Greece* 38 C5
Thiviers, *France* 20 C4
Thizy, *France* 19 F11
Þjórsá →, *Iceland* 8 E3
Thlewiaza →, *Man., Canada* 105 B8
Thlewiaza →, *N.W.T., Canada* 105 A10
Thmar Puok, *Cambodia* 64 F4
Tho Vinh, *Vietnam* 64 C5
Thoa →, *Canada* 105 A7
Thoen, *Thailand* 64 D2
Thoeng, *Thailand* 64 C3
Thohoyandou, *S. Africa* 85 J6
Tholdi, *Pakistan* 69 B7
Thomas, *U.S.A.* 113 H5
Thomas, L., *Australia* 95 D2
Thomaston, *U.S.A.* 109 J3
Thomasville, *Ala., U.S.A.* 109 K2
Thomasville, *Ga., U.S.A.* 109 K4
Thomasville, *N.C., U.S.A.* 109 H5
Thompson, *Canada* 105 B9
Thompson, *U.S.A.* 111 E9
Thompson →, *Canada* 104 C4
Thompson →, *U.S.A.* 112 F8
Thompson Falls, *U.S.A.* 114 C6
Thompson Pk., *U.S.A.* 114 F2
Thompson Springs, *U.S.A.* 115 G9
Thompsontown, *U.S.A.* 110 F7
Thomson, *U.S.A.* 109 J4
Thomson →, *Australia* 94 C3
Thomson's Falls = Nyahururu, *Kenya* 86 B4
Thônes, *France* 21 C10
Thonon-les-Bains, *France* 19 F13
Thorez, *Ukraine* 47 H10
Þórisvatn, *Iceland* 8 D4
Thornaby on Tees, *U.K.* 12 C6
Thornbury, *Canada* 110 B4
Thorne, *U.K.* 12 D7
Thornhill, *Canada* 104 C3
Thorold, *Canada* 110 C5
Þórshöfn, *Iceland* 8 C6
Thouarcé, *France* 18 E6
Thouars, *France* 18 F6
Thouet →, *France* 18 E6
Thouin, C., *Australia* 92 D2
Thousand Oaks, *U.S.A.* 117 L8
Thrace, *Turkey* 41 F10

Thrakikón Pélagos, *Greece* 41 F8
Three Forks, *U.S.A.* 114 D8
Three Gorges Dam, *China* 59 B8
Three Hills, *Canada* 104 C6
Three Hummock I., *Australia* .. 94 G3
Three Points, C., *Ghana* 82 E4
Three Rivers, *Calif., U.S.A.* ... 116 J8
Three Rivers, *Tex., U.S.A.* 113 L5
Three Sisters, *U.S.A.* 114 D3
Three Springs, *Australia* 93 E2
Throssell, L., *Australia* 93 E3
Throssell Ra., *Australia* 92 D3
Thuan Hoa, *Vietnam* 65 H5
Thubun Lakes, *Canada* 105 A6
Thueyts, *France* 21 D8
Thuin, *Belgium* 17 D4
Thuir, *France* 20 F6
Thule = Qaanaaq, *Greenland* .. 4 B4
Thun, *Switz.* 25 J3
Thunder B., *U.S.A.* 110 B1
Thunder Bay, *Canada* 102 C2
Thunersee, *Switz.* 25 J3
Thung Song, *Thailand* 65 H2
Thunkar, *Bhutan* 67 F17
Thuong Tra, *Vietnam* 64 D6
Thur →, *Switz.* 25 H5
Thurgau □, *Switz.* 25 H5
Thüringen □, *Germany* 24 D6
Thüringer Wald, *Germany* 24 E6
Thurles, *Ireland* 15 D4
Thurn P., *Austria* 24 D5
Thurrock □, *U.K.* 13 F8
Thursday I., *Australia* 94 A3
Thurso, *Canada* 102 C4
Thurso, *U.K.* 14 C5
Thurso →, *U.K.* 14 C5
Thurston I., *Antarctica* 5 D16
Thury-Harcourt, *France* 18 D6
Thutade L., *Canada* 104 B3
Thy, *Denmark* 11 H2
Thyborøn, *Denmark* 11 H2
Thyolo, *Malawi* 87 F4
Thysville = Mbanza Ngungu, *Dem. Rep. of the Congo* 84 F2
Ti-n-Amzi →, *Niger* 83 B5
Ti-n-Barraouene, O. →, *Africa* 83 B5
Ti-n-Zaouatene, *Algeria* 83 B5
Ti Tree, *Australia* 94 C1
Tiadiaye, *Senegal* 82 C1
Tian Shan, *Asia* 60 B3
Tianchang, *China* 59 A12
Tiandeng, *China* 58 F6
Tiandong, *China* 58 F6
Tian'e, *China* 58 E6
Tianhe, *China* 58 E7
Tianjin, *China* 57 E9
Tiankoura, *Burkina Faso* 82 C4
Tianlin, *China* 58 E6
Tianmen, *China* 59 B9
Tianquan, *China* 58 B4
Tianshui, *China* 56 G3
Tiantai, *China* 59 C13
Tianyang, *China* 58 F6
Tianzhen, *China* 56 D8
Tianzhu, *China* 58 D7
Tianzhuangtai, *China* 57 D12
Tiaret, *Algeria* 78 A6
Tiassalé, *Ivory C.* 82 D4
Tibagi, *Brazil* 127 A5
Tibagi →, *Brazil* 127 A5
Tibati, *Cameroon* 83 D7
Tibe, *Ethiopia* 81 F4
Tiber = Tevere →, *Italy* 29 G9
Tiberias = Teverya, *Israel* 75 C4
Tiberias, L. = Yam Kinneret, *Israel* 75 C4
Tibesti, *Chad* 79 D9
Tibet = Xizang Zizhiqu □, *China* 60 C3
Tibet, Plateau of, *Asia* 52 F12
Tibiao, *Phil.* 61 F5
Tibiri, *Niger* 83 C6
Ţibleş, Vf., *Romania* 43 C9
Ţibleşului, Munţii, *Romania* ... 43 C9
Tibnī, *Syria* 70 C3
Tibooburra, *Australia* 95 D3
Tibro, *Sweden* 11 F8
Tiburón, I., *Mexico* 118 B2
Ticao I., *Phil.* 61 E5
Tîchît, *Mauritania* 82 B3
Ticho, *Ethiopia* 81 F4
Ticino □, *Switz.* 25 J4
Ticino →, *Italy* 25 K5
Ticleni, *Romania* 43 F8
Ticonderoga, *U.S.A.* 111 C11
Ticul, *Mexico* 119 C7
Tidaholm, *Sweden* 11 F7
Tidan, *Sweden* 11 F8
Tiddim, *Burma* 67 H18
Tidioute, *U.S.A.* 110 E5
Tidjikja, *Mauritania* 82 B2
Tidore, *Indonesia* 63 D7
Tiébissou, *Ivory C.* 82 D3
Tiel, *Neths.* 17 C5
Tiel, *Senegal* 82 C1
Tieling, *China* 57 C12
Tielt, *Belgium* 17 C3
Tien Shan = Tian Shan, *Asia* ... 60 B3
Tien-tsin = Tianjin, *China* 57 E9
Tien Yen, *Vietnam* 64 B6
T'ienching = Tianjin, *China* ... 57 E9
Tienen, *Belgium* 17 D4
Tiénigbé, *Ivory C.* 82 D3
Tientsin = Tianjin, *China* 57 E9
Tieri, *Australia* 94 C4
Tierp, *Sweden* 10 D11
Tierra Amarilla, *Chile* 126 B1
Tierra Amarilla, *U.S.A.* 115 H10
Tierra Colorada, *Mexico* 119 D5
Tierra de Barros, *Spain* 35 G4
Tierra de Campos, *Spain* 34 C6
Tierra del Fuego, I. Gr. de, *Argentina* 122 J4
Tiétar →, *Spain* 34 F4
Tieté →, *Brazil* 127 A5
Tiffin, *U.S.A.* 108 E4
Tiflis = Tbilisi, *Georgia* 49 K7
Tifton, *U.S.A.* 109 K4
Tifu, *Indonesia* 63 E7
Tighina, *Moldova* 43 D14
Tigil, *Russia* 51 D16
Tignish, *Canada* 103 C7
Tigray □, *Ethiopia* 81 E4
Tigre →, *Peru* 124 D4
Tigre →, *Venezuela* 124 B6
Tigris = Dijlah, Nahr →, *Asia* . 70 D5
Tigveni, *Romania* 43 E9
Tigyaing, *Burma* 67 H20
Tîh, Gebel el, *Egypt* 80 B3
Tijara, *India* 68 F7
Tijuana, *Mexico* 117 N9
Tikal, *Guatemala* 120 C2
Tikamgarh, *India* 69 G8
Tikaré, *Burkina Faso* 83 C4
Tikhoretsk, *Russia* 49 H5
Tikhvin, *Russia* 46 C7
Tiko, *Cameroon* 83 E6
Tikrīt, *Iraq* 70 C4
Tiksi, *Russia* 51 B13
Tilamuta, *Indonesia* 63 D6
Tilburg, *Neths.* 17 C5
Tilbury, *Canada* 102 D3
Tilbury, *U.K.* 13 F8
Tilcara, *Argentina* 126 A2
Tilden, *U.S.A.* 112 D6
Tilemses, *Niger* 83 B5
Tilemsi, Vallée du, *Mali* 83 B5
Tilhar, *India* 69 F8
Tilichiki, *Russia* 51 C17
Tílissos, *Greece* 36 D7
Till →, *U.K.* 12 B5
Tillabéri, *Niger* 83 C5
Tillamook, *U.S.A.* 114 D2
Tillberga, *Sweden* 10 E10
Tillia, *Niger* 83 B5
Tillsonburg, *Canada* 102 D3
Tillyeria □, *Cyprus* 36 D11
Tilogne, *Senegal* 82 B2
Tílos, *Greece* 39 E9
Tilpa, *Australia* 95 E3
Tilsit = Sovetsk, *Russia* 9 J19
Tilt →, *U.K.* 14 E5
Tilton, *U.S.A.* 111 C13
Tiltonsville, *U.S.A.* 110 F4
Tim, *Denmark* 11 H2
Timagami, L., *Canada* 102 C3
Timaru, *N.Z.* 91 L3
Timashevo, *Russia* 48 D10
Timashevsk, *Russia* 49 H4
Timau, *Kenya* 86 B4
Timbákion, *Greece* 36 D6
Timbedgha, *Mauritania* 82 B3
Timber Creek, *Australia* 92 C5
Timber Lake, *U.S.A.* 112 C4
Timber Mt., *U.S.A.* 116 H10
Timbo, *Guinea* 82 C2
Timbo, *Liberia* 82 D3
Timbuktu = Tombouctou, *Mali* 82 B4
Timeiaouine, *Algeria* 83 A5
Timétrine, Mts., *Mali* 83 B4
Timfi Óros, *Greece* 38 B2
Timfristós, Óros, *Greece* 38 C3
Timi, *Cyprus* 36 E11
Tîmia, *Niger* 83 B6
Timimoun, *Algeria* 78 C6
Timirist, Râs, *Mauritania* 82 B1
Timiş = Tamis →, *Serbia, Yug.* 42 F5
Timiş □, *Romania* 42 E6
Timişoara, *Romania* 42 E6
Timmersdala, *Sweden* 11 F7
Timmins, *Canada* 102 C3
Timok →, *Serbia, Yug.* 40 B6
Timor, *Indonesia* 63 F7
Timor Sea, *Ind. Oc.* 92 B4
Timor Timur = East Timor ■, *Asia* 63 F7
Timrå, *Sweden* 10 B11
Tin Can Bay, *Australia* 95 D5
Tin Ethisane, *Mali* 83 B4
Tin Gornai, *Mali* 83 B4
Tin Mt., *U.S.A.* 116 J9
Tina →, *S. Africa* 89 E4
Tîna, Khalîg el, *Egypt* 80 A3
Tinaca Pt., *Phil.* 61 J6
Tinajo, *Canary Is.* 37 E6
Tinca, *Romania* 42 D6
Tindal, *Australia* 92 B5
Tindouf, *Algeria* 78 C4
Tinée →, *France* 21 E11
Tineo, *Spain* 34 B4
Ting Jiang →, *China* 59 E11
Tinggi, Pulau, *Malaysia* 65 L5
Tinglev, *Denmark* 11 K3
Tingo Maria, *Peru* 124 E3
Tingrela, *Ivory C.* 82 C3
Tingsryd, *Sweden* 11 H9
Tingstäde, *Sweden* 11 G12
Tinh Bien, *Vietnam* 65 G5
Tinnevelly = Tirunelveli, *India* . 66 Q10
Tinogasta, *Argentina* 126 B2
Tínos, *Greece* 39 D7
Tiñoso, C., *Spain* 33 H3
Tinpahar, *India* 69 G12
Tintina, *Argentina* 126 B3
Tintinara, *Australia* 95 F3
Tintioulé, *Guinea* 82 C3
Tinto →, *Spain* 35 H4
Tioga, *N. Dak., U.S.A.* 112 A3
Tioga, *Pa., U.S.A.* 110 E7
Tioman, Pulau, *Malaysia* 65 L5
Tione di Trento, *Italy* 28 B7
Tionesta, *U.S.A.* 110 E5
Tior, *Sudan* 81 F3
Tipongpani, *India* 67 F19
Tipperary, *Ireland* 15 D3
Tipperary □, *Ireland* 15 D4
Tipton, *Calif., U.S.A.* 116 J7
Tipton, *Iowa, U.S.A.* 112 E9
Tipton Mt., *U.S.A.* 117 K12
Tiptonville, *U.S.A.* 113 G10
Tīrān, *Iran* 71 C6
Tīrān, *Si. Arabia* 80 B3
Tiranë, *Albania* 40 E3
Tirano, *Italy* 28 B7
Tiraspol, *Moldova* 43 D14
Tirdout, *Mali* 83 B4
Tire, *Turkey* 39 C9
Tirebolu, *Turkey* 73 B8
Tiree, *U.K.* 14 E2
Tiree, Passage of, *U.K.* 14 E2
Tîrgovişte = Târgovişte, *Romania* 43 F10
Tîrgu-Jiu = Târgu-Jiu, *Romania* 43 E8
Tîrgu Mureş = Târgu Mureş, *Romania* 43 D9
Tirich Mir, *Pakistan* 66 A7
Tiriolo, *Italy* 31 D9
Tiriro, *Guinea* 82 C3
Tírnavos, *Greece* 38 B4
Tirodi, *India* 66 J11
Tirol □, *Austria* 26 D3
Tirschenreuth, *Germany* 25 F8
Tirso →, *Italy* 30 C1
Tirstrup, *Denmark* 11 H4
Tiruchchirappalli, *India* 66 P11
Tirunelveli, *India* 66 Q10
Tirupati, *India* 66 N11
Tiruppur, *India* 66 P10
Tiruvannamalai, *India* 66 N11
Tisa, *India* 68 C7
Tisa →, *Serbia, Yug.* 42 E5
Tisdale, *Canada* 105 C8
Tishomingo, *U.S.A.* 113 H6
Tisjön, *Sweden* 10 D7
Tisnaren, *Sweden* 11 F9
Tišnov, *Czech Rep.* 27 B9
Tisovec, *Slovak Rep.* 27 C12
Tisza = Tisa →, *Serbia, Yug.* .. 42 E5
Tiszaföldvár, *Hungary* 42 D5
Tiszafüred, *Hungary* 42 C5
Tiszalök, *Hungary* 42 B6
Tiszavasvári, *Hungary* 42 C6
Tit-Ary, *Russia* 51 B13
Titaguas, *Spain* 32 F3
Titao, *Burkina Faso* 83 C4
Titel, *Serbia, Yug.* 42 E5
Tithwal, *Pakistan* 69 B5
Titicaca, L., *S. Amer.* 122 E4
Titisee, *Germany* 25 H4
Titiwa, *Nigeria* 83 C7
Tito, *Italy* 31 B8
Titograd = Podgorica, *Montenegro, Yug.* 40 D3
Titova Korenica, *Croatia* 29 D12
Titu, *Romania* 43 F10
Titule, *Dem. Rep. of the Congo* 86 B2
Titusville, *Fla., U.S.A.* 109 L5
Titusville, *Pa., U.S.A.* 110 E5
Tivaouane, *Senegal* 82 C1
Tivat, *Montenegro, Yug.* 40 D2
Tiverton, *U.K.* 13 G4
Tívoli, *Italy* 29 G9
Tiyo, *Eritrea* 81 E5
Tizi-Ouzou, *Algeria* 78 A6
Tizimín, *Mexico* 119 C7
Tjæreborg, *Denmark* 11 J2
Tjällmo, *Sweden* 11 F9
Tjeggelvas, *Sweden* 8 C17
Tjirebon = Cirebon, *Indonesia* . 62 F3
Tjörn, *Sweden* 11 F5
Tkibuli = Tqibuli, *Georgia* 49 J6
Tkvarcheli = Tqvarcheli, *Georgia* 49 J5
Tlacotalpan, *Mexico* 119 D5
Tlahualilo, *Mexico* 118 B4
Tlaquepaque, *Mexico* 118 C4
Tlaxcala, *Mexico* 119 D5
Tlaxcala □, *Mexico* 119 D5
Tlaxiaco, *Mexico* 119 D5
Tlemcen, *Algeria* 78 B5
Tłuszcz, *Poland* 45 F8
Tlyarata, *Russia* 49 J8
To Bong, *Vietnam* 64 F7
Toad →, *Canada* 104 B4
Toad River, *Canada* 104 B3
Toamasina, *Madag.* 89 B8
Toamasina □, *Madag.* 89 B8
Toay, *Argentina* 126 D3
Toba, *China* 58 B1
Toba, *Japan* 55 G8
Toba, Danau, *Indonesia* 62 D1
Toba Kakar, *Pakistan* 68 D3
Toba Tek Singh, *Pakistan* 68 D5
Tobago, *Trin. & Tob.* 121 D7
Tobarra, *Spain* 33 G3
Tobelo, *Indonesia* 63 D7
Tobermory, *Canada* 102 C3
Tobermory, *U.K.* 14 E2
Tobi, *Pac. Oc.* 63 D8
Tobin, *U.S.A.* 116 F5
Tobin, L., *Australia* 92 D4
Tobin L., *Canada* 105 C8
Toblach = Dobbiaco, *Italy* 29 B9
Toboali, *Indonesia* 62 E3
Tobol →, *Russia* 50 D7
Toboli, *Indonesia* 63 E6
Tobolsk, *Russia* 50 D7
Tobor, *Senegal* 82 C1
Tobruk = Tubruq, *Libya* 79 B10
Tobyhanna, *U.S.A.* 111 E9
Tobyl = Tobol →, *Russia* 50 D7
Tocantinópolis, *Brazil* 125 E9
Tocantins □, *Brazil* 125 F9
Tocantins →, *Brazil* 122 D6
Toccoa, *U.S.A.* 109 H4
Toce →, *Italy* 28 C5
Tochi →, *Pakistan* 68 C4
Tochigi, *Japan* 55 F9
Tochigi □, *Japan* 55 F9
Tocina, *Spain* 35 H5
Töcksfors, *Sweden* 10 E5
Toconao, *Chile* 126 A2
Tocopilla, *Chile* 126 A1
Tocumwal, *Australia* 95 F4
Tocuyo →, *Venezuela* 124 A5
Todd →, *Australia* 94 C2
Todeli, *Indonesia* 63 E6
Todenyang, *Kenya* 86 B4
Todgarh, *India* 68 G5
Todi, *Italy* 29 F9
Todos os Santos, B. de, *Brazil* . 125 F11
Todos Santos, *Mexico* 118 C2
Todtnau, *Germany* 25 H3
Toe Hd., *U.K.* 14 D1
Toecé, *Burkina Faso* 83 C4
Tofield, *Canada* 104 C6
Tofino, *Canada* 104 D3
Tofua, *Tonga* 91 D11
Tōgane, *Japan* 55 G10
Togba, *Mauritania* 82 B2
Togian, Kepulauan, *Indonesia* . 63 E6
Togliatti, *Russia* 48 D9
Togo ■, *W. Afr.* 83 D5
Togtoh, *China* 56 D6
Tohma →, *Turkey* 72 C7
Tōhoku □, *Japan* 54 E10
Töhöm, *Mongolia* 56 B5
Toinya, *Sudan* 81 F2
Toiyabe Range, *U.S.A.* 114 G5
Tojikiston = Tajikistan ■, *Asia* 50 F8
Tojo, *Indonesia* 63 E6
Tōjō, *Japan* 55 G6
Tok, *U.S.A.* 100 B5
Tok-do, *Japan* 55 F5
Tokachi-Dake, *Japan* 54 C11
Tokachi-Gawa →, *Japan* 54 C11
Tokaj, *Hungary* 42 B6
Tokala, *Indonesia* 63 E6
Tōkamachi, *Japan* 55 F9
Tokanui, *N.Z.* 91 M2
Tokar, *Sudan* 80 D4
Tokara-Rettō, *Japan* 55 K4
Tokarahi, *N.Z.* 91 L3
Tokashiki-Shima, *Japan* 55 L3
Tokat, *Turkey* 72 B7
Tŏkch'ŏn, *N. Korea* 57 E14
Tokeland, *U.S.A.* 116 D3
Tokelau Is., *Pac. Oc.* 96 H10
Tokmak, *Kyrgyzstan* 50 E8
Tokmak, *Ukraine* 47 J8
Toko Ra., *Australia* 94 C2
Tokoro-Gawa →, *Japan* 54 B12
Tokuno-Shima, *Japan* 55 L4
Tokushima, *Japan* 55 G7
Tokushima □, *Japan* 55 H7
Tokuyama, *Japan* 55 G5
Tōkyō, *Japan* 55 G9
Tolaga Bay, *N.Z.* 91 H7
Tolbukhin = Dobrich, *Bulgaria* 41 C11
Toledo, *Brazil* 127 A5
Toledo, *Spain* 34 F6
Toledo, *Ohio, U.S.A.* 108 E4
Toledo, *Oreg., U.S.A.* 114 D2
Toledo, *Wash., U.S.A.* 114 C2
Toledo, Montes de, *Spain* 35 F6
Toledo Bend Reservoir, *U.S.A.* 113 K8
Tolentino, *Italy* 29 E10
Tolfa, *Italy* 29 F8
Tolga, *Australia* 94 B4
Toliara, *Madag.* 89 C7
Toliara □, *Madag.* 89 C8
Tolima, *Colombia* 124 C3
Tolitoli, *Indonesia* 63 D6
Tolkmicko, *Poland* 44 D6
Tollarp, *Sweden* 11 J7
Tollensesee, *Germany* 24 B9
Tollhouse, *U.S.A.* 116 H7
Tolmachevo, *Russia* 46 C5
Tolmezzo, *Italy* 29 B10
Tolmin, *Slovenia* 29 B10
Tolna, *Hungary* 42 D3
Tolna □, *Hungary* 42 D3
Tolo, Teluk, *Indonesia* 63 E6
Tolochin = Talachyn, *Belarus* .. 46 E5
Tolosa, *Spain* 32 B2
Tolox, *Spain* 35 J6
Toluca, *Mexico* 119 D5
Tom Burke, *S. Africa* 89 C4
Tom Price, *Australia* 92 D2
Toma, *Burkina Faso* 82 C4
Tomah, *U.S.A.* 112 D9
Tomahawk, *U.S.A.* 112 C10
Tomai, *Moldova* 43 D13
Tomakomai, *Japan* 54 C10
Tomales, *U.S.A.* 116 G4
Tomales B., *U.S.A.* 116 G3
Tomar, *Portugal* 35 F2
Tómaros, Óros, *Greece* 38 B2
Tomarza, *Turkey* 72 C6
Tomaszów Lubelski, *Poland* ... 45 H10
Tomaszów Mazowiecki, *Poland* 45 G7
Tomatlán, *Mexico* 118 D3
Tombadonkéa, *Guinea* 82 C2
Tombador, Serra do, *Brazil* ... 124 F7
Tombe, *Sudan* 81 F3
Tombigbee →, *U.S.A.* 109 K2
Tombouctou, *Mali* 82 B4
Tombstone, *U.S.A.* 115 L8
Tombua, *Angola* 88 B1
Tomé, *Chile* 126 D1
Tomelilla, *Sweden* 11 J7
Tomelloso, *Spain* 35 F7
Tomini, *Indonesia* 63 D6
Tomini, Teluk, *Indonesia* 63 E6
Tominian, *Mali* 82 C4
Tomiño, *Spain* 34 D2
Tomintoul, *U.K.* 14 D5
Tomislavgrad, *Bos.-H.* 42 G2
Tomkinson Ranges, *Australia* .. 93 E4
Tommot, *Russia* 51 D13
Tomnop Ta Suos, *Cambodia* .. 65 G5
Tomo →, *Colombia* 124 B5
Toms Place, *U.S.A.* 116 H8
Toms River, *U.S.A.* 111 G10
Tomsk, *Russia* 50 D9
Tomtabacken, *Sweden* 11 G8
Tona, *Spain* 32 D7
Tonalá, *Mexico* 119 D6
Tonale, Passo del, *Italy* 28 B7
Tonantins, *Brazil* 124 D5
Tonasket, *U.S.A.* 114 B4
Tonawanda, *U.S.A.* 110 D6
Tonbridge, *U.K.* 13 F8
Tondano, *Indonesia* 63 D6
Tondela, *Portugal* 34 E2
Tønder, *Denmark* 11 K2
Tondi Kiwindi, *Niger* 83 C5
Tondibi, *Mali* 83 B4
Tondoro, *Namibia* 88 B2
Tone →, *Australia* 93 F2
Tone-Gawa →, *Japan* 55 F9
Tonekābon, *Iran* 71 B6
Tong Xian, *China* 56 E9
Tôngâ, *Sudan* 81 F3
Tonga ■, *Pac. Oc.* 91 D11
Tonga Trench, *Pac. Oc.* 96 J10
Tongaat, *S. Africa* 89 D5
Tong'an, *China* 59 E12
Tongareva, *Cook Is.* 97 H12
Tongatapu Group, *Tonga* 91 E12
Tongbai, *China* 59 A9
Tongcheng, *Anhui, China* 59 B11
Tongcheng, *Hubei, China* 59 C9
Tongchŏn-ni, *N. Korea* 57 E14
Tongchuan, *China* 56 G5
Tongdao, *China* 58 D7
Tongeren, *Belgium* 17 D5
Tonggu, *China* 59 C10
Tongguan, *China* 56 G6
Tonghai, *China* 58 E4
Tonghua, *China* 57 D13
Tongjiang, *China* 58 B6
Tongjosŏn Man, *N. Korea* 57 E15
Tongking, G. of = Tonkin, G. of, *Asia* 60 E5
Tongliang, *China* 58 C6
Tongliao, *China* 57 C12
Tongling, *China* 59 B11
Tonglu, *China* 59 C12
Tongnae, *S. Korea* 57 G15
Tongnan = Anyue, *China* 58 B5
Tongobory, *Madag.* 89 C7
Tongoy, *Chile* 126 C1
Tongren, *China* 58 D7
Tongres = Tongeren, *Belgium* . 17 D5
Tongsa Dzong, *Bhutan* 67 F17
Tongue, *U.K.* 14 C4
Tongue →, *U.S.A.* 112 B2
Tongwei, *China* 56 G3
Tongxiang, *China* 59 B13
Tongxin, *China* 56 F3
Tongyang, *N. Korea* 57 E14
Tongyu, *China* 57 B12
Tongzi, *China* 58 C6
Tonj, *Sudan* 81 F2
Tonj →, *Sudan* 81 F2
Tonk, *India* 68 F6
Tonkawa, *U.S.A.* 113 G6
Tonkin = Bac Phan, *Vietnam* ... 64 B5
Tonkin, G. of, *Asia* 60 E5
Tonle Sap, *Cambodia* 64 F4
Tonnay-Charente, *France* 20 C3
Tonneins, *France* 20 D4
Tonnerre, *France* 19 E10
Tönning, *Germany* 24 A4
Tono, *Japan* 54 E10
Tonopah, *U.S.A.* 115 G5
Tonosí, *Panama* 120 E3
Tons →, *Haryana, India* 68 D7
Tons →, *Ut. P., India* 69 F10
Tønsberg, *Norway* 9 G14
Tonya, *Turkey* 73 B8
Toobanna, *Australia* 94 B4
Toodyay, *Australia* 93 F2
Tooele, *U.S.A.* 114 F7
Toompine, *Australia* 95 D3
Toora, *Australia* 95 F4
Toora-Khem, *Russia* 51 D10
Toowoomba, *Australia* 95 D5
Top Springs, *Australia* 92 C5
Topalu, *Romania* 43 F13
Topaz, *U.S.A.* 116 G7
Topeka, *U.S.A.* 112 F7
Topl'a →, *Slovak Rep.* 27 C14
Topley, *Canada* 104 C3
Toplica →, *Serbia, Yug.* 40 C5

Toplița, Romania 43 D10
Topocalma, Pta., Chile 126 C1
Topock, U.S.A. 117 L12
Topola, Serbia, Yug. 40 B4
Topolčani, Macedonia 40 E5
Topol'čany, Slovak Rep. 27 C11
Topolnitsa →, Bulgaria 41 D8
Topolobampo, Mexico 118 B3
Topoloveni, Romania 43 F10
Topolovgrad, Bulgaria 41 D10
Topolvățu Mare, Romania 42 E6
Toppenish, U.S.A. 114 C3
Topraisar, Romania 43 F13
Topusko, Croatia 29 C12
Torà, Spain 32 D6
Tora Kit, Sudan 81 E3
Toraka Vestale, Madag. 89 B7
Torata, Peru 124 G4
Torbalı, Turkey 39 C9
Torbat-e Heydārīyeh, Iran 71 C8
Torbat-e Jām, Iran 71 C9
Torbay, Canada 103 C9
Torbay □, U.K. 13 G4
Torbjörntorp, Sweden 11 F7
Tordesillas, Spain 34 D6
Töreboda, Sweden 11 F8
Torekov, Sweden 11 H6
Torellò, Spain 32 C7
Toreno, Spain 34 C4
Torfaen □, U.K. 13 F4
Torgau, Germany 24 D8
Torgelow, Germany 24 B10
Torhamn, Sweden 11 H9
Torhout, Belgium 17 C3
Tori, Ethiopia 81 F3
Tori-Shima, Japan 55 J10
Torigni-sur-Vire, France 18 C6
Torija, Spain 32 E1
Torin, Mexico 118 B2
Torino, Italy 28 C4
Torit, Sudan 81 G3
Torkamān, Iran 70 B5
Torkovichi, Russia 46 C6
Tormac, Romania 42 E6
Tormes →, Spain 34 D4
Tornado Mt., Canada 104 D6
Tornal'a, Slovak Rep. 27 C13
Torne älv →, Sweden 8 D21
Torneå = Tornio, Finland 8 D21
Torneträsk, Sweden 8 B18
Tornio, Finland 8 D21
Tornionjoki →, Finland 8 D21
Tornquist, Argentina 126 D3
Toro, Baleares, Spain 37 B11
Toro, Zamora, Spain 34 D5
Torö, Sweden 11 F11
Toro, Cerro del, Chile 126 B2
Toro Pk., U.S.A. 117 M10
Törökszentmiklós, Hungary 42 C5
Toroníos Kólpos, Greece 40 F7
Toronto, Canada 102 D4
Toronto, U.S.A. 110 F4
Toropets, Russia 46 D6
Tororo, Uganda 86 B3
Toros Dağları, Turkey 70 B2
Torpa, India 69 H11
Torquay, U.K. 13 G4
Torquemada, Spain 34 C6
Torrance, U.S.A. 117 M8
Torrão, Portugal 35 G2
Torre Annunziata, Italy 31 B7
Torre de Moncorvo, Portugal 34 D3
Torre del Campo, Spain 35 H7
Torre del Greco, Italy 31 B7
Torre del Mar, Spain 35 J6
Torre-Pacheco, Spain 33 H4
Torre Péllice, Italy 28 D4
Torreblanca, Spain 32 E5
Torrecampo, Spain 35 G6
Torrecilla en Cameros, Spain 32 C2
Torredembarra, Spain 32 D6
Torredonjimeno, Spain 35 H7
Torrejón de Ardoz, Spain 34 E7
Torrejoncillo, Spain 34 F4
Torrelaguna, Spain 34 E7
Torrelavega, Spain 34 B6
Torremaggiore, Italy 29 G12
Torremolinos, Spain 35 J6
Torrens, L., Australia 95 E2
Torrens Cr. →, Australia 94 C4
Torrens Creek, Australia 94 C4
Torrent, Spain 33 F4
Torrenueva, Spain 35 G7
Torreón, Mexico 118 B4
Torreperogil, Spain 35 G7
Torres, Brazil 127 B5
Torres, Mexico 118 B2
Torres Novas, Portugal 35 F2
Torres Strait, Australia 96 H6
Torres Vedras, Portugal 35 F1
Torrevieja, Spain 33 H4
Torrey, U.S.A. 115 G8
Torridge →, U.K. 13 G3
Torridon, L., U.K. 14 D3
Torrijos, Spain 34 F6
Tørring, Denmark 11 J3
Torrington, Conn., U.S.A. 111 E11
Torrington, Wyo., U.S.A. 112 D2
Torroella de Montgrì, Spain 32 C8
Torrox, Spain 35 J7
Torsås, Sweden 11 H9
Torsby, Sweden 10 D6
Torshälla, Sweden 10 E10
Tórshavn, Færoe Is. 8 E9
Torslanda, Sweden 11 G5
Torsö, Sweden 11 F7
Tortola, Br. Virgin Is. 121 C7
Tórtoles de Esgueva, Spain 34 D6
Tortolì, Italy 30 C2
Tortona, Italy 28 D5
Tortorici, Italy 31 D7
Tortosa, Spain 32 E5
Tortosa, C., Spain 32 E5
Tortosendo, Portugal 34 E3
Tortue, I. de la, Haiti 121 B5
Tortum, Turkey 73 B9
Ţorūd, Iran 71 C7
Torul, Turkey 73 B8
Toruń, Poland 45 E5
Tory I., Ireland 15 A3
Torysa →, Slovak Rep. 27 C14
Torzhok, Russia 46 D8
Torzym, Poland 45 F2
Tosa, Japan 55 H6
Tosa-Shimizu, Japan 55 H6
Tosa-Wan, Japan 55 H6
Toscana □, Italy 28 E8
Toscano, Arcipelago, Italy 28 F7
Toshkent, Uzbekistan 50 E7
Tosno, Russia 46 C6
Tossa de Mar, Spain 32 D7
Tösse, Sweden 11 F6
Tostado, Argentina 126 B3
Tostedt, Germany 24 B5
Tostón, Pta. de, Canary Is. 37 F5
Tosu, Japan 55 H5
Tosya, Turkey 72 B6
Toszek, Poland 45 H5
Totana, Spain 33 H3
Totebo, Sweden 11 G10
Toteng, Botswana 88 C3
Tôtes, France 18 C8
Tótkomlós, Hungary 42 D5
Totma, Russia 50 C5
Totnes, U.K. 13 G4
Totness, Surinam 125 B7
Toto, Nigeria 83 D6
Totonicapán, Guatemala 120 D1
Totten Glacier, Antarctica 5 C8
Tottenham, Australia 95 E4
Tottenham, Canada 110 B5
Tottori, Japan 55 G7
Tottori □, Japan 55 G7
Touaret, Niger 83 A6
Touba, Ivory C. 82 D3
Touba, Senegal 82 C1
Toubkal, Djebel, Morocco 78 B4
Toucy, France 19 E10
Tougan, Burkina Faso 82 C4
Touggourt, Algeria 78 B7
Tougouri, Burkina Faso 83 C4
Tougué, Guinea 82 C2
Toukoto, Mali 82 C3
Toul, France 19 D12
Toulepleu, Ivory C. 82 D3
Toulon, France 21 E9
Toulouse, France 20 E5
Toummo, Niger 79 D8
Toumodi, Ivory C. 82 D3
Tounan, Taiwan 59 F13
Toungo, Nigeria 83 D7
Toungoo, Burma 67 K20
Touques →, France 18 C7
Touraine, France 18 E7
Tourane = Da Nang, Vietnam 64 D7
Tourcoing, France 19 B10
Touriñán, C., Spain 34 B1
Tournai, Belgium 17 D3
Tournan-en-Brie, France 19 D9
Tournay, France 20 E4
Tournon-St-Martin, France 18 F7
Tournon-sur-Rhône, France 21 C8
Tournus, France 19 F11
Tours, France 18 E7
Toussora, Mt., C.A.R. 84 C4
Touws →, S. Africa 88 E3
Touwsrivier, S. Africa 88 E3
Tovarkovskiy, Russia 46 F10
Tovuz, Azerbaijan 49 K7
Towada, Japan 54 D10
Towada-Ko, Japan 54 D10
Towanda, U.S.A. 111 E8
Towang, India 67 F17
Tower, U.S.A. 112 B8
Towerhill Cr. →, Australia 94 C3
Towner, U.S.A. 112 A4
Townsend, U.S.A. 114 C8
Townshend I., Australia 94 C5
Townsville, Australia 94 B4
Towraghondi, Afghan. 66 B3
Towson, U.S.A. 108 F7
Towuti, Danau, Indonesia 63 E6
Toya-Ko, Japan 54 C10
Toyama, Japan 55 F8
Toyama □, Japan 55 F8
Toyama-Wan, Japan 55 F8
Toyohashi, Japan 55 G8
Toyokawa, Japan 55 G8
Toyonaka, Japan 55 G7
Toyooka, Japan 55 G7
Toyota, Japan 55 G8
Tozeur, Tunisia 78 B7
Tqibuli, Georgia 49 J6
Tqvarcheli, Georgia 49 J5
Trá Li = Tralee, Ireland 15 D2
Tra On, Vietnam 65 H5
Trabancos →, Spain 34 D5
Traben-Trarbach, Germany 25 F3
Trabzon, Turkey 73 B8
Tracadie, Canada 103 C7
Tracy, Calif., U.S.A. 116 H5
Tracy, Minn., U.S.A. 112 C7
Tradate, Italy 28 C5
Trade Town, Liberia 82 D3
Trafalgar, C., Spain 35 J4
Traian, Brăila, Romania 43 E12
Traian, Tulcea, Romania 43 E13
Trail, Canada 104 D5
Trainor L., Canada 104 A4
Trákhonas, Cyprus 36 D12
Tralee, Ireland 15 D2
Tralee B., Ireland 15 D2
Tramore, Ireland 15 D4
Tramore B., Ireland 15 D4
Tran Ninh, Cao Nguyen, Laos 64 C4
Tranås, Sweden 11 F8
Tranbjerg, Denmark 11 H4
Trancas, Argentina 126 B2
Trancoso, Portugal 34 E3
Tranebjerg, Denmark 11 J4
Tranemo, Sweden 11 G7
Trang, Thailand 65 J2
Trangahy, Madag. 89 B7
Trangan, Indonesia 63 F8
Trangie, Australia 95 E4
Trångsviken, Sweden 10 A7
Trani, Italy 31 A9
Tranoroa, Madag. 89 C8
Tranqueras, Uruguay 127 C4
Transantarctic Mts., Antarctica 5 E12
Transilvania, Romania 43 D9
Transilvanian Alps = Carpații Meridionali, Romania 43 E9
Transtrand, Sweden 10 C7
Transtrandsfjällen, Sweden 10 C6
Transvaal, S. Africa 85 K5
Transylvania = Transilvania, Romania 43 D9
Trápani, Italy 30 D5
Trapper Pk., U.S.A. 114 D6
Traralgon, Australia 95 F4
Trarza, Mauritania 82 B2
Trasacco, Italy 29 G10
Trăscău, Munții, Romania 43 D8
Trasimeno, L., Italy 29 E9
Träslövsläge, Sweden 11 G6
Trasvase Tajo-Segura, Canal de, Spain 32 E2
Trat, Thailand 65 F4
Tratani →, Pakistan 68 E3
Traun, Austria 26 C7
Traunreut, Germany 25 H8
Traunsee, Austria 26 D6
Traunstein, Germany 25 H8
Traveller's L., Australia 95 E3
Travemünde, Germany 24 B6
Travers, Mt., N.Z. 91 K4
Traverse City, U.S.A. 108 C3
Travis, L., U.S.A. 113 K5
Travnik, Bos.-H. 42 F2
Trbovlje, Slovenia 29 B12
Trébbia →, Italy 28 C6
Trebel →, Germany 24 B9
Trébeurden, France 18 D3
Třebíč, Czech Rep. 26 B8
Trebinje, Bos.-H. 40 D2
Trebisacce, Italy 31 C9
Trebišnjica →, Bos.-H. 40 D2
Trebišov, Slovak Rep. 27 C14
Trebižat →, Bos.-H. 29 E14
Trebnje, Slovenia 29 C12
Třeboň, Czech Rep. 26 B7
Trebonne, Australia 94 B4
Trebujena, Spain 35 J4
Trecate, Italy 28 C5
Tregaron, U.K. 13 E4
Tregnago, Italy 29 C8
Tregrosse Is., Australia 94 B5
Tréguier, France 18 D3
Trégunc, France 18 E3
Treherne, Canada 105 D9
Tréia, Italy 29 E10
Treignac, France 20 C5
Treinta y Tres, Uruguay 127 C5
Treis-karden, Germany 25 E3
Treklyano, Bulgaria 40 D6
Trelawney, Zimbabwe 89 B5
Trélazé, France 18 E6
Trelew, Argentina 128 E3
Trélissac, France 20 C4
Trelleborg, Sweden 11 J7
Tremadog Bay, U.K. 12 E3
Trémiti, Italy 29 F12
Tremonton, U.S.A. 114 F7
Tremp, Spain 32 C5
Trenche →, Canada 102 C5
Trenčiansky □, Slovak Rep. 27 C11
Trenčín, Slovak Rep. 27 C11
Trenggalek, Indonesia 63 H14
Trenque Lauquen, Argentina 126 D3
Trent →, Canada 110 B7
Trent →, U.K. 12 D7
Trentino-Alto Adige □, Italy 29 B8
Trento, Italy 28 B8
Trenton, Canada 102 D4
Trenton, Mo., U.S.A. 112 E8
Trenton, N.J., U.S.A. 111 F10
Trenton, Nebr., U.S.A. 112 E4
Trepassey, Canada 103 C9
Trepuzzi, Italy 31 B11
Tres Arroyos, Argentina 126 D3
Três Corações, Brazil 127 A6
Três Lagoas, Brazil 125 H8
Tres Lomas, Argentina 126 D3
Tres Marías, Islas, Mexico 118 C3
Tres Montes, C., Chile 128 F1
Tres Pinos, U.S.A. 116 J5
Três Pontas, Brazil 127 A6
Tres Puentes, Chile 126 B1
Tres Puntas, C., Argentina 128 F3
Três Rios, Brazil 127 A7
Tres Valles, Mexico 119 D5
Tresco, U.K. 13 H1
Treska →, Macedonia 40 E5
Treskavica, Bos.-H. 42 G3
Trespaderne, Spain 34 C7
Trets, France 21 E9
Treuchtlingen, Germany 25 G6
Treuenbrietzen, Germany 24 C8
Trevi, Italy 29 F9
Trevíglio, Italy 28 C6
Trevínca, Peña, Spain 34 C4
Treviso, Italy 29 C9
Trévoux, France 21 C8
Trgovište, Serbia, Yug. 40 D6
Triabunna, Australia 94 G4
Triánda, Greece 36 C10
Triangle, Zimbabwe 89 C5
Triaucourt-en-Argonne, France 19 D12
Tribal Areas □, Pakistan 68 C4
Tribsees, Germany 24 A8
Tribulation, C., Australia 94 B4
Tribune, U.S.A. 112 F4
Tricárico, Italy 31 B9
Tricase, Italy 31 C11
Trichinopoly = Tiruchchirappalli, India 66 P11
Trichur, India 66 P10
Trida, Australia 95 E4
Trier, Germany 25 F2
Trieste, Italy 29 C10
Trieste, G. di, Italy 29 C10
Trieux →, France 18 D3
Triggiano, Italy 31 A9
Triglav, Slovenia 29 B10
Trigno →, Italy 29 F11
Trigueros, Spain 35 H4
Tríkeri, Greece 38 B5
Trikhonis, Límni, Greece 38 C3
Tríkkala, Greece 38 B3
Tríkkala □, Greece 38 B3
Trikomo, Cyprus 36 D12
Trikora, Puncak, Indonesia 63 E9
Trilj, Croatia 29 E13
Trillo, Spain 32 E2
Trim, Ireland 15 C5
Trincomalee, Sri Lanka 66 Q12
Trindade, Brazil 125 G9
Trindade, I., Atl. Oc. 2 F8
Třinec, Czech Rep. 27 B11
Trinidad, Bolivia 124 F6
Trinidad, Cuba 120 B4
Trinidad, Trin. & Tob. 121 D7
Trinidad, Uruguay 126 C4
Trinidad, U.S.A. 113 G2
Trinidad →, Mexico 119 D5
Trinidad & Tobago ■, W. Indies 121 D7
Trinitápoli, Italy 31 A9
Trinity, Canada 103 C9
Trinity, U.S.A. 113 K7
Trinity →, Calif., U.S.A. 114 F2
Trinity →, Tex., U.S.A. 113 L7
Trinity B., Canada 103 C9
Trinity Is., U.S.A. 100 C4
Trinity Range, U.S.A. 114 F4
Trinkitat, Sudan 80 D4
Trino, Italy 28 C5
Trinway, U.S.A. 110 F2
Trionto, C., Italy 31 C9
Triora, Italy 28 D4
Tripoli = Tarābulus, Lebanon 75 A4
Tripoli = Tarābulus, Libya 79 B8
Trípolis, Greece 38 D4
Tripolitania, N. Afr. 79 B8
Tripura □, India 67 H18
Tripylos, Cyprus 36 E11
Trischen, Germany 24 A4
Tristan da Cunha, Atl. Oc. 77 K2
Trisul, India 69 D8
Trivandrum, India 66 Q10
Trivento, Italy 29 G11
Trnava, Slovak Rep. 27 C10
Trnavský □, Slovak Rep. 27 C10
Troarn, France 18 C6
Trochu, Canada 104 C6
Trodely I., Canada 102 B4
Troezen, Greece 38 D5
Trogir, Croatia 29 E13
Troglav, Croatia 29 E13
Tróia, Italy 31 A8
Troilus, L., Canada 102 B5
Troina, Italy 31 E7
Trois-Pistoles, Canada 103 C6
Trois-Rivières, Canada 102 C5
Troisdorf, Germany 24 E3
Troitsk, Russia 50 D7
Troitsko Pechorsk, Russia 50 C6
Trölladyngja, Iceland 8 D5
Trollhättan, Sweden 11 F6
Trollheimen, Norway 8 E13
Trombetas →, Brazil 125 D7
Tromsø, Norway 8 B18
Trona, U.S.A. 117 K9
Tronador, Mte., Argentina 128 E2
Trøndelag, Norway 8 D14
Trondheim, Norway 8 E14
Trondheimsfjorden, Norway 8 E14
Trönninge, Sweden 11 H6
Tronto →, Italy 29 F10
Troodos, Cyprus 36 E11
Troon, U.K. 14 F4
Tropea, Italy 31 D8
Tropic, U.S.A. 115 H7
Tropojë, Albania 40 D4
Trosa, Sweden 11 F11
Trostan, U.K. 15 A5
Trostberg, Germany 25 G8
Trostyanets, Ukraine 47 G8
Trout →, Canada 104 A5
Trout L., N.W.T., Canada 104 A4
Trout L., Ont., Canada 105 C10
Trout Lake, Canada 104 B6
Trout Lake, U.S.A. 116 E5
Trout River, Canada 103 C8
Trout Run, U.S.A. 110 E7
Trouville-sur-Mer, France 18 C7
Trowbridge, U.K. 13 F5
Troy, Turkey 39 B8
Troy, Ala., U.S.A. 109 K3
Troy, Kans., U.S.A. 112 F7
Troy, Mo., U.S.A. 112 F9
Troy, Mont., U.S.A. 114 B6
Troy, N.Y., U.S.A. 111 D11
Troy, Ohio, U.S.A. 108 E3
Troy, Pa., U.S.A. 111 E8
Troyan, Bulgaria 41 D8
Troyes, France 19 D11
Trpanj, Croatia 29 E14
Trstenik, Serbia, Yug. 40 C5
Trubchevsk, Russia 47 F7
Truchas Peak, U.S.A. 113 H2
Trucial States = United Arab Emirates ■, Asia 71 F7
Truckee, U.S.A. 116 F6
Trudfront, Russia 49 H8
Trudovoye, Russia 54 C6
Trujillo, Honduras 120 C2
Trujillo, Peru 124 E3
Trujillo, Spain 35 F5
Trujillo, U.S.A. 113 H2
Trujillo, Venezuela 124 B4
Truk, Micronesia 96 G7
Trumann, U.S.A. 113 H9
Trumansburg, U.S.A. 111 D8
Trumbull, Mt., U.S.A. 115 H7
Trŭn, Bulgaria 40 D6
Trun, France 18 D7
Trundle, Australia 95 E4
Trung-Phan = Annam, Vietnam 64 E7
Truro, Canada 103 C7
Truro, U.K. 13 G2
Truskavets, Ukraine 47 H2
Trŭstenik, Bulgaria 41 C8
Trustrup, Denmark 11 H4
Trutch, Canada 104 B4
Truth or Consequences, U.S.A. 115 K10
Trutnov, Czech Rep. 26 A8
Truxton, U.S.A. 111 D8
Truyère →, France 20 D6
Tryavna, Bulgaria 41 D9
Tryonville, U.S.A. 110 E5
Trzcianka, Poland 45 E3
Trzciel, Poland 45 F2
Trzcińsko Zdrój, Poland 45 F1
Trzebiatów, Poland 44 D2
Trzebiez, Poland 44 E1
Trzebnica, Poland 45 G4
Trzemeszno, Poland 45 F4
Tržič, Slovenia 29 B11
Tsagan Aman, Russia 49 G8
Tsamandás, Greece 38 B2
Tsandi, Namibia 88 B1
Tsaratanana, Madag. 89 B8
Tsaratanana, Mt. de, Madag. 89 A8
Tsarevo = Michurin, Bulgaria 41 D11
Tsarevo, Bulgaria 41 D9
Tsaritsáni, Greece 38 B4
Tsau, Botswana 88 C3
Tsebrykove, Ukraine 47 J6
Tselinograd = Astana, Kazakstan 50 D8
Tses, Namibia 88 D2
Tsetserleg, Mongolia 60 B5
Tsévié, Togo 83 D5
Tshabong, Botswana 88 D3
Tshane, Botswana 88 C3
Tshela, Dem. Rep. of the Congo 84 E2
Tshesebe, Botswana 89 C4
Tshibeke, Dem. Rep. of the Congo 86 C2
Tshibinda, Dem. Rep. of the Congo 86 C2
Tshikapa, Dem. Rep. of the Congo 84 F4
Tshilenge, Dem. Rep. of the Congo 86 D1
Tshinsenda, Dem. Rep. of the Congo 87 E2
Tshofa, Dem. Rep. of the Congo 86 D2
Tshwane, Botswana 88 C3
Tsigara, Botswana 88 C4
Tsihombe, Madag. 89 D8
Tsiigehtchic, Canada 100 B6
Tsimlyansk, Russia 49 G6
Tsimlyansk Res. = Tsimlyanskoye Vdkhr., Russia 49 F6
Tsimlyanskoye Vdkhr., Russia 49 F6
Tsinan = Jinan, China 56 F9
Tsineng, S. Africa 88 D3
Tsínga, Greece 41 E8
Tsinghai = Qinghai □, China 60 C4
Tsingtao = Qingdao, China 57 F11
Tsinjoarivo, Madag. 89 B8
Tsinjomitondraka, Madag. 89 B8
Tsiroanomandidy, Madag. 89 B8
Tsiteli-Tsqaro, Georgia 49 K8
Tsitondroina, Madag. 89 C8
Tsivilsk, Russia 48 C8
Tsivory, Madag. 89 C8
Tskhinvali, Georgia 49 J7
Tsna →, Russia 48 C6
Tsnori, Georgia 49 K7
Tso Moriri, L., India 69 C8
Tsobis, Namibia 88 B2
Tsodilo Hill, Botswana 88 B3

Tsogttsetsiy = Baruunsuu, Mongolia 56 C3
Tsolo, S. Africa 89 E4
Tsomo, S. Africa 89 E4
Tsu, Japan 55 G8
Tsu L., Canada 104 A6
Tsuchiura, Japan 55 F10
Tsuen Wan, H.K. 59 F10
Tsugaru-Kaikyō, Japan 54 D10
Tsumeb, Namibia 88 B2
Tsumis, Namibia 88 C2
Tsuruga, Japan 55 G8
Tsurugi-San, Japan 55 H7
Tsuruoka, Japan 54 E9
Tsushima, Gifu, Japan 55 G8
Tsushima, Nagasaki, Japan 55 G4
Tsuyama, Japan 55 G7
Tsvetkovo, Ukraine 47 H6
Tsyelyakhany, Belarus 47 F3
Tua →, Portugal 34 D3
Tual, Indonesia 63 F8
Tuam, Ireland 15 C3
Tuamotu Arch. = Tuamotu Is., Pac. Oc. 97 J13
Tuamotu Is., Pac. Oc. 97 J13
Tuamotu Ridge, Pac. Oc. 97 K14
Tuanfeng, China 59 B10
Tuanxi, China 58 D6
Tuao, Phil. 61 C4
Tuapse, Russia 49 H4
Tuatapere, N.Z. 91 M1
Tuba City, U.S.A. 115 H8
Tuban, Indonesia 63 G15
Tubani, Botswana 88 C3
Tubarão, Brazil 127 B6
Tūbās, West Bank 75 C4
Tubas →, Namibia 88 C2
Tübingen, Germany 25 G5
Tubruq, Libya 79 B10
Tubuai Is., Pac. Oc. 97 K13
Tuc Trung, Vietnam 65 G6
Tucacas, Venezuela 124 A5
T'uch'ang, Taiwan 59 E13
Tuchodi →, Canada 104 B4
Tuchola, Poland 44 E4
Tuchów, Poland 45 J8
Tuckanarra, Australia 93 E2
Tucson, U.S.A. 115 K8
Tucumán □, Argentina 126 B2
Tucumcari, U.S.A. 113 H3
Tucupita, Venezuela 124 B6
Tucuruí, Brazil 125 D9
Tucuruí, Reprêsa de, Brazil 125 D9
Tuczno, Poland 45 E3
Tudela, Spain 32 C3
Tudmur, Syria 70 C3
Tudor, L., Canada 103 A6
Tudora, Romania 43 C11
Tuella →, Portugal 34 D3
Tugela →, S. Africa 89 D5
Tuguegarao, Phil. 61 C4
Tugur, Russia 51 D14
Tui, Spain 34 C2
Tuineje, Canary Is. 37 F5
Tukangbesi, Kepulauan, Indonesia 63 F6
Tukarak I., Canada 102 A4
Tukayyid, Iraq 70 D5
Tûkh, Egypt 80 H7
Tukobo, Ghana 82 D4
Tuktoyaktuk, Canada 100 B6
Tukums, Latvia 9 H20
Tukums □, Latvia 44 B10
Tukuyu, Tanzania 87 D3
Tula, Hidalgo, Mexico 119 C5
Tula, Tamaulipas, Mexico 119 C5
Tula, Nigeria 83 D7
Tula, Russia 46 E9
Tulancingo, Mexico 119 C5
Tulare, Serbia, Yug. 40 D5
Tulare, U.S.A. 116 J7
Tulare Lake Bed, U.S.A. 116 K7
Tularosa, U.S.A. 115 K10
Tulbagh, S. Africa 88 E2
Tulcán, Ecuador 124 C3
Tulcea, Romania 43 E13
Tulcea □, Romania 43 E13
Tulchyn, Ukraine 47 H5
Tūleh, Iran 71 C7
Tulemalu L., Canada 105 A9
Tulgheş, Romania 43 D10
Tuli, Zimbabwe 87 G2
Tulia, U.S.A. 113 H4
Tuliszków, Poland 45 F5
Tulita, Canada 100 B7
Ţūlkarm, West Bank 75 C4
Tulla, Ireland 15 D3
Tullahoma, U.S.A. 109 H2
Tullamore, Australia 95 E4
Tullamore, Ireland 15 C4
Tulle, France 20 C5
Tulln, Austria 26 C9
Tullow, Ireland 15 D5
Tullus, Sudan 81 E1
Tully, Australia 94 B4
Tully, U.S.A. 111 D8
Tulnici, Romania 43 E11
Tulovo, Bulgaria 41 D9
Tulsa, U.S.A. 113 G7
Tulsequah, Canada 104 B2
Tulu Milki, Ethiopia 81 F4
Tulu Welel, Ethiopia 81 F3
Tulua, Colombia 124 C3
Tuluceşti, Romania 43 E13
Tulun, Russia 51 D11
Tulungagung, Indonesia 63 H14
Tuma, Russia 46 E11
Tuma →, Nic. 120 D3
Tumaco, Colombia 124 C3
Tumatumari, Guyana 124 B7
Tumba, Sweden 10 E11
Tumba, L., Dem. Rep. of the Congo 84 E3
Tumbarumba, Australia 95 F4
Tumbaya, Argentina 126 A2
Tumbes, Peru 124 D2
Tumbur, Sudan 81 G3
Tumbwe, Dem. Rep. of the Congo 87 E2
Tumby Bay, Australia 95 E2
Tumd Youqi, China 56 D6
Tumen, China 57 C15
Tumen Jiang →, China 57 C16
Tumeremo, Venezuela 124 B6
Tumkur, India 66 N10
Tump, Pakistan 66 F3
Tumpat, Malaysia 65 J4
Tumu, Ghana 82 C4
Tumucumaque, Serra, Brazil 122 C5
Tumut, Australia 95 F4
Tumwater, U.S.A. 116 C4
Tuna, India 68 H4
Tunadal, Sweden 10 B11
Tunas de Zaza, Cuba 120 B4
Tunbridge Wells = Royal Tunbridge Wells, U.K. 13 F8
Tunçbilek, Turkey 39 B11
Tunceli, Turkey 73 C8
Tuncurry, Australia 95 E5
Tundla, India 68 F8
Tundubai, Sudan 80 D2
Tunduru, Tanzania 87 E4
Tundzha →, Bulgaria 41 E10
Tungabhadra →, India 66 M11
Tungaru, Sudan 81 E3
Tungla, Nic. 120 D3
Tungsha Tao, Taiwan 59 G11
Tungshih, Taiwan 59 E13
Tungsten, Canada 104 A3
Tunguska, Nizhnyaya →, Russia 51 C9
Tunguska, Podkamennaya →, Russia 51 C10
Tunica, U.S.A. 113 H9
Tunis, Tunisia 78 A7
Tunisia ■, Africa 78 B6
Tunja, Colombia 124 B4
Tunkhannock, U.S.A. 111 E9
Tunliu, China 56 F7
Tunnsjøen, Norway 8 D15
Tunø, Denmark 11 J4
Tunungayualok I., Canada 103 A7
Tununirusiq = Arctic Bay, Canada 101 A11
Tunuyán, Argentina 126 C2
Tunuyán →, Argentina 126 C2
Tuo Jiang →, China 58 C5
Tuolumne, U.S.A. 116 H6
Tuolumne →, U.S.A. 116 H5
Tūp Āghāj, Iran 70 B5
Tupã, Brazil 127 A5
Tupelo, U.S.A. 109 H1
Tupik, Russia 46 E7
Tupinambaranas, Brazil 124 D7
Tupiza, Bolivia 126 A2
Tupižnica, Serbia, Yug. 40 C6
Tupman, U.S.A. 117 K7
Tupper, Canada 104 B4
Tupper Lake, U.S.A. 111 B10
Tupungato, Cerro, S. Amer. 126 C2
Tuquan, China 57 B11
Túquerres, Colombia 124 C3
Tura, Russia 51 C11
Turabah, Si. Arabia 70 D4
Turabah, Si. Arabia 80 C5
Tūrān, Iran 71 C8
Turan, Russia 51 D10
Ţurayf, Si. Arabia 70 D3
Turbacz, Poland 45 J7
Turbe, Bos.-H. 42 F2
Turčianske Teplice, Slovak Rep. 27 C11
Turcoaia, Romania 43 E13
Turda, Romania 43 D8
Turek, Poland 45 F5
Turen, Venezuela 124 B5
Turfan = Turpan, China 60 B3
Turfan Depression = Turpan Hami, China 52 E12
Turgeon →, Canada 102 C4
Tŭrgovishte, Bulgaria 41 C10
Turgut, Turkey 39 D10
Turgutlu, Turkey 39 C9
Turgwe →, Zimbabwe 89 C5
Turhal, Turkey 72 B7
Turia →, Spain 33 F4
Turiaçu, Brazil 125 D9
Turiaçu →, Brazil 125 D9
Turiec →, Slovak Rep. 27 B11
Turin = Torino, Italy 28 C4
Turkana, L., Africa 86 B4
Türkeli, Turkey 41 F11
Turkestan = Türkistan, Kazakstan 50 E7
Túrkeve, Hungary 42 C5
Turkey ■, Eurasia 72 C7
Turkey Creek, Australia 92 C4
Turki, Russia 48 D6
Türkistan, Kazakstan 50 E7
Türkmenbashi, Turkmenistan 50 E6
Turkmenistan ■, Asia 50 F6
Türkmenli, Turkey 39 B8
Türkoğlu, Turkey 72 D7
Turks & Caicos Is. ■, W. Indies 121 B5
Turks Island Passage, W. Indies 121 B5
Turku, Finland 9 F20
Turkwel →, Kenya 86 B4
Turlock, U.S.A. 116 H6
Turnagain →, Canada 104 B3
Turnagain, C., N.Z. 91 J6
Turneffe Is., Belize 119 D7
Turner, U.S.A. 114 B9
Turner Pt., Australia 94 A1
Turner Valley, Canada 104 C6
Turners Falls, U.S.A. 111 D12
Turnhout, Belgium 17 C4
Türnitz, Austria 26 D8
Turnor L., Canada 105 B7
Turnov, Czech Rep. 26 A8
Tŭrnovo = Veliko Tŭrnovo, Bulgaria 41 C9
Turnu Măgurele, Romania 43 G9
Turnu Roşu, P., Romania 43 E9
Turobin, Poland 45 H9
Turpan, China 60 B3
Turpan Hami, China 52 E12
Turrës, Kala e, Albania 40 E3
Turriff, U.K. 14 D6
Tursāq, Iraq 70 C5
Tursi, Italy 31 B9
Turtle Head I., Australia 94 A3
Turtle Is., S. Leone 82 D2
Turtle L., Canada 105 C7
Turtle Lake, U.S.A. 112 B4
Turtleford, Canada 105 C7
Turukhansk, Russia 51 C9
Turzovka, Slovak Rep. 27 B11
Tuscaloosa, U.S.A. 109 J2
Tuscánia, Italy 29 F8
Tuscany = Toscana □, Italy 28 E8
Tuscarawas →, U.S.A. 110 F3
Tuscarora Mt., U.S.A. 110 F7
Tuscola, Ill., U.S.A. 108 F1
Tuscola, Tex., U.S.A. 113 J5
Tuscumbia, U.S.A. 109 H2
Tuskegee, U.S.A. 109 J3
Tustin, U.S.A. 117 M9
Tuszyn, Poland 45 G6
Tutak, Turkey 73 C10
Tutayev, Russia 46 D10
Tuticorin, India 66 Q11
Tutin, Serbia, Yug. 40 D4
Tutóia, Brazil 125 D10
Tutong, Brunei 62 D4
Tutova →, Romania 43 D12
Tutrakan, Bulgaria 41 B10
Tuttle Creek L., U.S.A. 112 F6
Tuttlingen, Germany 25 H4
Tutuala, Indonesia 63 F7
Tutuila, Amer. Samoa 91 B13
Tutume, Botswana 85 J5
Tutun, Egypt 80 J7
Tututepec, Mexico 119 D5
Tuva □, Russia 51 D10
Tuvalu ■, Pac. Oc. 96 H9
Tuxer Alpen, Austria 26 D4
Tuxpan, Mexico 119 C5
Tuxtla Gutiérrez, Mexico 119 D6
Tuy = Tui, Spain 34 C2
Tuy An, Vietnam 64 F7
Tuy Duc, Vietnam 65 F6
Tuy Hoa, Vietnam 64 F7
Tuy Phong, Vietnam 65 G7
Tuya L., Canada 104 B2
Tuyen Hoa, Vietnam 64 D6
Tuyen Quang, Vietnam 58 G5
Tūysarkān, Iran 71 C6
Tuz Gölü, Turkey 72 C5
Ţūz Khurmātū, Iraq 70 C5
Tuzi, Montenegro, Yug. 40 D3
Tuzla, Bos.-H. 42 F3
Tuzlov →, Russia 47 J10
Tuzluca, Turkey 73 B10
Tvååker, Sweden 11 G6
Tvardiţa, Moldova 43 D13
Tver, Russia 46 D8
Tvrdošin, Slovak Rep. 27 B12
Tvrdošovce, Slovak Rep. 27 C11
Tvŭrditsa, Bulgaria 41 D9
Twain, U.S.A. 116 E5
Twain Harte, U.S.A. 116 G6
Twardogóra, Poland 45 G4
Tweed, Canada 110 B7
Tweed →, U.K. 14 F6
Tweed Heads, Australia 95 D5
Tweedsmuir Prov. Park, Canada 104 C3
Twentynine Palms, U.S.A. 117 L10
Twillingate, Canada 103 C9
Twin Bridges, U.S.A. 114 D7
Twin Falls, Canada 103 B7
Twin Falls, U.S.A. 114 E6
Twin Valley, U.S.A. 112 B6
Twinsburg, U.S.A. 110 E3
Twistringen, Germany 24 C4
Twitchell Reservoir, U.S.A. 117 L6
Two Harbors, U.S.A. 112 B9
Two Hills, Canada 104 C6
Two Rivers, U.S.A. 108 C2
Two Rocks, Australia 93 F2
Twofold B., Australia 95 F4
Tyachiv, Ukraine 47 H2
Tychy, Poland 45 H5
Tyczyn, Poland 45 J9
Tykocin, Poland 45 E9
Tyler, Minn., U.S.A. 112 C6
Tyler, Tex., U.S.A. 113 J7
Tyligul →, Ukraine 47 J6
Týn nad Vltavou, Czech Rep. 26 B7
Tynda, Russia 51 D13
Tyndall, U.S.A. 112 D6
Tyne →, U.K. 12 C6
Tyne & Wear □, U.K. 12 B6
Týnec nad Sázavou, Czech Rep. 26 B7
Tynemouth, U.K. 12 B6
Tyre = Sūr, Lebanon 75 B4
Tyrifjorden, Norway 9 F14
Tyringe, Sweden 11 H7
Tyrnyauz, Russia 49 J6
Tyrol = Tirol □, Austria 26 D3
Tyrone, U.S.A. 110 F6
Tyrone □, U.K. 15 B4
Tyrrell →, Australia 95 F3
Tyrrell, L., Australia 95 F3
Tyrrell L., Canada 105 A7
Tyrrhenian Sea, Medit. S. 6 G8
Tysfjorden, Norway 8 B17
Tystberga, Sweden 11 F11
Tytuvėnai, Lithuania 44 C10
Tyub Karagan, Mys, Kazakstan 49 H10
Tyuleni, Ostrova, Kazakstan 49 H10
Tyuleniy, Russia 49 H8
Tyuleniy, Mys, Azerbaijan 49 K10
Tyumen, Russia 50 D7
Tywi →, U.K. 13 F3
Tywyn, U.K. 13 E3
Tzaneen, S. Africa 89 C5
Tzermiádhes, Greece 36 D7
Tzoumérka, Óros, Greece 38 B3
Tzukong = Zigong, China 58 C5

U

U Taphao, Thailand 64 F3
U.S.A. = United States of America ■, N. Amer. 106 C7
Uatumã →, Brazil 124 D7
Uaupés, Brazil 124 D5
Uaupés →, Brazil 124 C5
Uaxactún, Guatemala 120 C2
Ub, Serbia, Yug. 40 B4
Ubá, Brazil 127 A7
Uba, Nigeria 83 C7
Ubaitaba, Brazil 125 F11
Ubangi = Oubangi →, Dem. Rep. of the Congo 84 E3
Ubauro, Pakistan 68 E3
Ubaye →, France 21 D10
Ubayyiḍ, W. al →, Iraq 70 C4
Ube, Japan 55 H5
Úbeda, Spain 35 G7
Uberaba, Brazil 125 G9
Uberlândia, Brazil 125 G9
Überlingen, Germany 25 H5
Ubiaja, Nigeria 83 D6
Ubolratna Res., Thailand 64 D4
Ubombo, S. Africa 89 D5
Ubon Ratchathani, Thailand 64 E5
Ubondo, Dem. Rep. of the Congo 86 C2
Ubort →, Belarus 47 F5
Ubrique, Spain 35 J5
Ubundu, Dem. Rep. of the Congo 86 C2
Ucayali →, Peru 122 D3
Uchab, Namibia 88 B2
Uchiura-Wan, Japan 54 C10
Uchquduq, Uzbekistan 50 E7
Uchte, Germany 24 C4
Uchur →, Russia 51 D14
Uckermark, Germany 24 B9
Ucluelet, Canada 104 D3
Uda →, Russia 51 D14
Udagamandalam, India 66 P10
Udainagar, India 68 H7
Udaipur, India 68 G5
Udaipur Garhi, Nepal 69 F12
Udala, India 69 J12
Udbina, Croatia 29 D12
Uddeholm, Sweden 10 D7
Uddevalla, Sweden 11 F5
Uddjaur, Sweden 8 D17
Uden, Neths. 17 C5
Udgir, India 66 K10
Udhampur, India 69 C6
Udi, Nigeria 83 D6
Údine, Italy 29 B10
Udmurtia □, Russia 50 D6
Udon Thani, Thailand 64 D4
Udupi, India 66 N9
Udvoy Balkan, Bulgaria 41 D10
Udzungwa Range, Tanzania 87 D4
Ueckermünde, Germany 24 B10
Ueda, Japan 55 F9
Uedineniya, Os., Russia 4 B12
Uele →, Dem. Rep. of the Congo 84 D4
Uelen, Russia 51 C19
Uelzen, Germany 24 C6
Uetersen, Germany 24 B5
Uetze, Germany 24 C6
Ufa, Russia 50 D6
Uffenheim, Germany 25 F6
Ugab →, Namibia 88 C1
Ugalla →, Tanzania 86 D3
Uganda ■, Africa 86 B3
Ugento, Italy 31 C11
Ugep, Nigeria 83 D6
Ughelli, Nigeria 83 D6
Ugie, S. Africa 89 E4
Ugíjar, Spain 35 J7
Ugine, France 21 C10
Uglegorsk, Russia 51 E15
Uglich, Russia 46 D10
Ugljan, Croatia 29 D12
Ugljane, Croatia 29 E13
Ugra →, Russia 46 E9
Ugŭrchin, Bulgaria 41 C8
Uh →, Slovak Rep. 27 C15
Uherské Hradiště, Czech Rep. 27 B10
Uherský Brod, Czech Rep. 27 B10
Úhlava →, Czech Rep. 26 B6
Uhlenhorst, Namibia 88 C2
Uhrichsville, U.S.A. 110 F3
Uibhist a Deas = South Uist, U.K. 14 D1
Uibhist a Tuath = North Uist, U.K. 14 D1
Uig, U.K. 14 D2
Uíge, Angola 84 F2
Uijŏngbu, S. Korea 57 F14
Ŭiju, N. Korea 57 D13
Uinta Mts., U.S.A. 114 F8
Uis, Namibia 88 B2
Uitenhage, S. Africa 88 E4
Uithuizen, Neths. 17 A6
Ujazd, Poland 45 H5
Újfehértó, Hungary 42 C6
Ujh →, India 68 C6
Ujhani, India 69 F8
Uji-guntō, Japan 55 J4
Ujjain, India 68 H6
Ujście, Poland 45 E3
Újszász, Hungary 42 C5
Ujung Pandang, Indonesia 63 F5
Uka, Russia 51 D17
Ukara I., Tanzania 86 C3
Uke-Shima, Japan 55 K4
Ukerewe I., Tanzania 86 C3
Ukholovo, Russia 48 D5
Ukhrul, India 67 G19
Ukhta, Russia 50 C6
Ukiah, U.S.A. 116 F3
Ukki Fort, India 69 C7
Ukmergė, Lithuania 9 J21
Ukraine ■, Europe 47 H7
Ukwi, Botswana 88 C3
Ulaan-Uul, Mongolia 56 B6
Ulaanbaatar, Mongolia 51 E11
Ulaangom, Mongolia 60 A4
Ulaanjirem, Mongolia 56 B3
Ulamba, Dem. Rep. of the Congo 87 D1
Ulan Bator = Ulaanbaatar, Mongolia 51 E11
Ulan Erge, Russia 49 G7
Ulan Khol, Russia 49 H8
Ulan Ude, Russia 51 D11
Ulanów, Poland 45 H9
Ulaş, Sivas, Turkey 72 C7
Ulaş, Tekirdağ, Turkey 41 E11
Ulaya, Morogoro, Tanzania 86 D4
Ulaya, Tabora, Tanzania 86 C3
Ulcinj, Montenegro, Yug. 40 E3
Ulco, S. Africa 88 D3
Ulefoss, Norway 9 G13
Ulëz, Albania 40 E3
Ulfborg, Denmark 11 H2
Ulhasnagar, India 66 K8
Uliastay = Ulyasutay, Mongolia 60 B4
Ulithi Atoll, Pac. Oc. 63 B9
Uljma, Serbia, Yug. 42 E6
Ulla →, Spain 34 C2
Ulladulla, Australia 95 F5
Ullapool, U.K. 14 D3
Ullared, Sweden 11 G6
Ulldecona, Spain 32 E5
Ullswater, U.K. 12 C5
Ullŭng-do, S. Korea 55 F5
Ulm, Germany 25 G5
Ulmarra, Australia 95 D5
Ulmeni, Buzău, Romania 43 E11
Ulmeni, Maramureş, Romania 43 C8
Ulonguè, Mozam. 87 E3
Ulricehamn, Sweden 11 G7
Ulrika, Sweden 11 F9
Ulsan, S. Korea 57 G15
Ulsta, U.K. 14 A7
Ulster □, U.K. 15 B5
Ulstrem, Bulgaria 41 D10
Ulubat Gölü, Turkey 41 F12
Ulubey, Turkey 39 C11
Uluborlu, Turkey 39 C12
Uluçinar, Turkey 72 D6
Uludağ, Turkey 41 F13
Uludere, Turkey 73 D10
Uluguru Mts., Tanzania 86 D4
Ulukışla, Turkey 72 D6
Ulungur He →, China 60 B3
Uluru = Ayers Rock, Australia 93 E5
Uluru Nat. Park, Australia 93 E5
Ulutau, Kazakstan 50 E7
Ulva, U.K. 14 E2
Ulverston, U.K. 12 C4
Ulverstone, Australia 94 G4
Ulya, Russia 51 D15
Ulyanovsk = Simbirsk, Russia 48 C9
Ulyasutay, Mongolia 60 B4
Ulysses, U.S.A. 113 G4
Umag, Croatia 29 C10
Umala, Bolivia 124 G5
Uman, Ukraine 47 H6
Umaria, India 67 H12
Umarkot, Pakistan 66 G6
Umarpada, India 68 J5
Umatilla, U.S.A. 114 D4
Umbagog L., U.S.A. 111 B13
Umbakumba, Australia 94 A2
Umbértide, Italy 29 E9
Umbrella Mts., N.Z. 91 L2
Umbria □, Italy 29 F9
Ume älv →, Sweden 8 E19
Umeå, Sweden 8 E19
Umera, Indonesia 63 E7
Umfuli →, Zimbabwe 87 F2
Umgusa, Zimbabwe 87 F2
Umim Urūmah, Si. Arabia 80 B4

Umka, *Serbia, Yug.* 40 B4
Umkomaas, *S. Africa* 89 E5
Umlazi, *S. Africa* 85 L6
Umm ad Daraj, J., *Jordan* 75 C4
Umm al Qaywayn, *U.A.E.* 71 E7
Umm al Qittayn, *Jordan* 75 C5
Umm Arda, *Sudan* 81 D3
Umm Bāb, *Qatar* 71 E6
Umm Badr, *Sudan* 81 E2
Umm Baiyud, *Sudan* 81 E3
Umm Bel, *Sudan* 81 E2
Umm Birkah, *Si. Arabia* 80 B4
Umm Boim, *Sudan* 81 E2
Umm Dam, *Sudan* 81 E3
Umm Debi, *Sudan* 81 E3
Umm Dubban, *Sudan* 81 D3
Umm el Fahm, *Israel* 75 C4
Umm Gafala, *Sudan* 81 E2
Umm Gimala, *Sudan* 81 E2
Umm Inderaba, *Sudan* 80 D3
Umm Keddada, *Sudan* 81 E2
Umm Koweika, *Sudan* 81 E3
Umm Lajj, *Si. Arabia* 70 E3
Umm Merwa, *Sudan* 80 D3
Umm Qantur, *Sudan* 81 E3
Umm Qurein, *Sudan* 81 F2
Umm Ruwaba, *Sudan* 81 E3
Umm Saiyala, *Sudan* 81 E3
Umm Shanqa, *Sudan* 81 E2
Umm Shutur, *Sudan* 81 F3
Umm Sidr, *Sudan* 81 E2
Umm Zehetir, *Egypt* 80 J8
Umnak I., *U.S.A.* 100 C3
Umniati →, *Zimbabwe* 87 F2
Umpqua →, *U.S.A.* 114 E1
Umreth, *India* 68 H5
Umtata, *S. Africa* 89 E4
Umuahia, *Nigeria* 83 D6
Umuarama, *Brazil* 127 A5
Umurbey, *Turkey* 41 F10
Umvukwe Ra., *Zimbabwe* 87 F3
Umzimvubu, *S. Africa* 89 E4
Umzingwane →, *Zimbabwe* 87 G2
Umzinto, *S. Africa* 89 E5
Una, *India* 68 J4
Una →, *Bos.-H.* 29 D13
Unac →, *Bos.-H.* 29 D13
Unadilla, *U.S.A.* 111 D9
Unalakleet, *U.S.A.* 100 B3
Unalaska, *U.S.A.* 100 C3
Unalaska I., *U.S.A.* 100 C3
'Unayzah, *Si. Arabia* 70 E4
'Unāzah, J., *Asia* 70 C3
Uncastillo, *Spain* 32 C3
Uncía, *Bolivia* 124 G5
Uncompahgre Peak, *U.S.A.* 115 G10
Uncompahgre Plateau, *U.S.A.* 115 G9
Unden, *Sweden* 11 F8
Underbool, *Australia* 95 F3
Undersaker, *Sweden* 10 A7
Unecha, *Russia* 47 F7
Ungarie, *Australia* 95 E4
Ungarra, *Australia* 95 E2
Ungava, Pén. d', *Canada* 101 C12
Ungava B., *Canada* 101 C13
Ungeny = Ungheni, *Moldova* 43 C12
Unggi, *N. Korea* 57 C16
Ungheni, *Moldova* 43 C12
Unguala →, *Ethiopia* 81 F5
Ungwatiri, *Sudan* 81 D4
Uni, *Russia* 48 B10
União da Vitória, *Brazil* 127 B5
Uničov, *Czech Rep.* 27 B10
Uniejów, *Poland* 45 G5
Unije, *Croatia* 29 D11
Unimak I., *U.S.A.* 100 C3
Union, *Miss., U.S.A.* 113 J10
Union, *Mo., U.S.A.* 112 F9
Union, *S.C., U.S.A.* 109 H5
Union City, *Calif., U.S.A.* 116 H4
Union City, *N.J., U.S.A.* 111 F10
Union City, *Pa., U.S.A.* 110 E5
Union City, *Tenn., U.S.A.* 113 G10
Union Gap, *U.S.A.* 114 C3
Union Springs, *U.S.A.* 109 J3
Uniondale, *S. Africa* 88 E3
Uniontown, *U.S.A.* 108 F6
Unionville, *U.S.A.* 112 E8
Unirea, *Romania* 43 F12
United Arab Emirates ■, *Asia* 71 F7
United Kingdom ■, *Europe* 7 E5
United States of America ■, *N. Amer.* 106 C7
Unity, *Canada* 105 C7
Universales, Mtes., *Spain* 32 E3
University Park, *U.S.A.* 115 K10
Unjha, *India* 68 H5
Unna, *Germany* 24 D3
Unnao, *India* 69 F9
Uno, Ilha, *Guinea-Biss.* 82 C1
Unst, *U.K.* 14 A8
Unstrut →, *Germany* 24 D7
Unterfranken □, *Germany* 25 F5
Unterschleissheim, *Germany* 25 G7
Unuk →, *Canada* 104 B2
Ünye, *Turkey* 72 B7
Unzha, *Russia* 48 A7
Unzha →, *Russia* 48 B6
Uozu, *Japan* 55 F8
Upata, *Venezuela* 124 B6
Upemba, L., *Dem. Rep. of the Congo* 87 D2
Upernavik, *Greenland* 4 B5
Upington, *S. Africa* 88 D3
Upleta, *India* 68 J4
Upolu, *Samoa* 91 A13
Upper □, *Ghana* 83 C4
Upper Alkali L., *U.S.A.* 114 F3
Upper Arrow L., *Canada* 104 C5
Upper Austria = Oberösterreich □, *Austria* 26 C7
Upper Foster L., *Canada* 105 B7
Upper Hutt, *N.Z.* 91 J5
Upper Klamath L., *U.S.A.* 114 E3
Upper Lake, *U.S.A.* 116 F4
Upper Musquodoboit, *Canada* 103 C7
Upper Red L., *U.S.A.* 112 A7
Upper Sandusky, *U.S.A.* 108 E4
Upper Volta = Burkina Faso ■, *Africa* 82 C4
Upphärad, *Sweden* 11 F6
Uppland, *Sweden* 10 E11
Upplands-Väsby, *Sweden* 10 E11
Uppsala, *Sweden* 10 E11
Uppsala län □, *Sweden* 10 D11
Upshi, *India* 69 C7
Upstart, C., *Australia* 94 B4
Upton, *U.S.A.* 112 C2
Ur, *Iraq* 70 D5
Urad Qianqi, *China* 56 D5
Urakawa, *Japan* 54 C11
Ural = Zhayyq →, *Kazakstan* 50 E6
Ural, *Australia* 95 E4
Ural Mts. = Uralskie Gory, *Eurasia* 50 D6
Uralla, *Australia* 95 E5
Uralsk = Oral, *Kazakstan* 48 E10
Uralskie Gory, *Eurasia* 50 D6
Urambo, *Tanzania* 86 D3
Urandangi, *Australia* 94 C2
Uranium City, *Canada* 105 B7
Uraricoera →, *Brazil* 124 C6
Urawa, *Japan* 55 G9
Uray, *Russia* 50 C7
'Uray'irah, *Si. Arabia* 71 E6
Urbana, *Ill., U.S.A.* 108 E1
Urbana, *Ohio, U.S.A.* 108 E4
Urbánia, *Italy* 29 E9
Urbel →, *Spain* 34 C7
Urbino, *Italy* 29 E9
Urbión, Picos de, *Spain* 32 C2
Urcos, *Peru* 124 F4
Urdinarrain, *Argentina* 126 C4
Urdos, *France* 20 F3
Urdzhar, *Kazakstan* 50 E9
Ure →, *U.K.* 12 C6
Uren, *Russia* 48 B7
Ures, *Mexico* 118 B2
Urfa = Sanliurfa, *Turkey* 70 B3
Urganch, *Uzbekistan* 50 E7
Urgench = Urganch, *Uzbekistan* 50 E7
Ürgüp, *Turkey* 70 B2
Uri, *India* 69 B6
Uri □, *Switz.* 25 J4
Uribia, *Colombia* 124 A4
Uricani, *Romania* 42 E8
Uriondo, *Bolivia* 126 A3
Urique, *Mexico* 118 B3
Urique →, *Mexico* 118 B3
Urk, *Neths.* 17 B5
Urla, *Turkey* 39 C8
Urlaţi, *Romania* 43 F11
Urmia = Orūmīyeh, *Iran* 70 B5
Urmia, L. = Orūmīyeh, Daryācheh-ye, *Iran* 70 B5
Uroševac, *Kosovo, Yug.* 40 D5
Urshult, *Sweden* 11 H8
Uruaçu, *Brazil* 125 F9
Uruapan, *Mexico* 118 D4
Urubamba →, *Peru* 124 F4
Uruçara, *Brazil* 124 D7
Uruçuí, *Brazil* 125 E10
Uruguai →, *Brazil* 127 B5
Uruguaiana, *Brazil* 126 B4
Uruguay ■, *S. Amer.* 126 C4
Uruguay →, *S. Amer.* 126 C4
Urumchi = Ürümqi, *China* 50 E9
Ürümqi, *China* 50 E9
Urup →, *Russia* 49 H5
Urup, Ostrov, *Russia* 51 E16
Uryupinsk, *Russia* 48 E5
Urzhum, *Russia* 48 B9
Urziceni, *Romania* 43 F11
Usa →, *Russia* 50 C6
Uşak, *Turkey* 39 C11
Uşak □, *Turkey* 39 C11
Usakos, *Namibia* 88 C2
Ušće, *Serbia, Yug.* 40 C4
Usedom, *Germany* 24 B10
Useless Loop, *Australia* 93 E1
'Usfān, *Si. Arabia* 80 C4
Ush-Tobe, *Kazakstan* 50 E8
Ushakova, Ostrov, *Russia* 4 A12
Ushant = Ouessant, Î. d', *France* 18 D1
Ushashi, *Tanzania* 86 C3
Ushat, *Sudan* 81 F2
'Ushayrah, *Si. Arabia* 80 C5
Ushibuka, *Japan* 55 H5
Ushuaia, *Argentina* 128 G3
Ushumun, *Russia* 51 D13
Usk, *Canada* 104 C3
Usk →, *U.K.* 13 F5
Uska, *India* 69 F10
Üsküdar, *Turkey* 41 F13
Uslar, *Germany* 24 D5
Usman, *Russia* 47 F10
Usoke, *Tanzania* 86 D3
Usolye Sibirskoye, *Russia* 51 D11
Usoro, *Nigeria* 83 D6
Uspallata, P. de, *Argentina* 126 C2
Uspenskiy, *Kazakstan* 50 E8
Ussel, *France* 20 C6
Usson-du-Poitou, *France* 20 B4
Ussuri →, *Asia* 54 A7
Ussuriysk, *Russia* 51 E14
Ussurka, *Russia* 54 B6
Ust-Aldan = Batamay, *Russia* 51 C13
Ust-Amginskoye = Khandyga, *Russia* 51 C14
Ust-Bolsheretsk, *Russia* 51 D16
Ust-Buzulukskaya, *Russia* 48 E6
Ust-Chaun, *Russia* 51 C18
Ust-Donetskiy, *Russia* 49 G5
Ust-Ilimpeya = Yukta, *Russia* 51 C11
Ust-Ilimsk, *Russia* 51 D11
Ust-Ishim, *Russia* 50 D8
Ust-Kamchatsk, *Russia* 51 D17
Ust-Kamenogorsk = Öskemen, *Kazakstan* 50 E9
Ust-Khayryuzovo, *Russia* 51 D16
Ust-Kut, *Russia* 51 D11
Ust-Kuyga, *Russia* 51 B14
Ust-Labinsk, *Russia* 49 H4
Ust-Luga, *Russia* 46 C5
Ust-Maya, *Russia* 51 C14
Ust-Mil, *Russia* 51 D14
Ust-Nera, *Russia* 51 C15
Ust-Nyukzha, *Russia* 51 D13
Ust-Olenek, *Russia* 51 B12
Ust-Omchug, *Russia* 51 C15
Ust-Port, *Russia* 50 C9
Ust-Tsilma, *Russia* 50 C6
Ust Urt = Ustyurt Plateau, *Asia* 50 E6
Ustaritz, *France* 20 E2
Ustecký □, *Czech Rep.* 26 A7
Uster, *Switz.* 25 H4
Ústí nad Labem, *Czech Rep.* 26 A7
Ústí nad Orlicí, *Czech Rep.* 27 B9
Ústica, *Italy* 30 D6
Ustinov = Izhevsk, *Russia* 50 D6
Ustka, *Poland* 44 D3
Ustroń, *Poland* 45 J5
Ustrzyki Dolne, *Poland* 45 J9
Ustyurt Plateau, *Asia* 50 E6
Ustyuzhna, *Russia* 46 C9
Usu, *China* 60 B3
Usuki, *Japan* 55 H5
Usulután, *El Salv.* 120 D2
Usumacinta →, *Mexico* 119 D6
Usumbura = Bujumbura, *Burundi* 86 C2
Usure, *Tanzania* 86 C3
Usutuo →, *Mozam.* 89 D5
Uta, *Indonesia* 63 E9
Utah □, *U.S.A.* 114 G8
Utah L., *U.S.A.* 114 F8
Utansjö, *Sweden* 10 B11
Utarni, *India* 68 F4
Utatlan, *Guatemala* 120 C1
Ute Creek →, *U.S.A.* 113 H3
Utebo, *Spain* 32 D3
Utena, *Lithuania* 9 J21
Utete, *Tanzania* 86 D4
Uthai Thani, *Thailand* 64 E3
Uthal, *Pakistan* 68 G2
Utiariti, *Brazil* 124 F7
Utica, *N.Y., U.S.A.* 111 C9
Utica, *Ohio, U.S.A.* 110 F2
Utiel, *Spain* 33 F3
Utikuma L., *Canada* 104 B5
Utö, *Sweden* 10 F12
Utopia, *Australia* 94 C1
Utraula, *India* 69 F10
Utrecht, *Neths.* 17 B5
Utrecht, *S. Africa* 89 D5
Utrecht □, *Neths.* 17 B5
Utrera, *Spain* 35 H5
Utsjoki, *Finland* 8 B22
Utsunomiya, *Japan* 55 F9
Uttar Pradesh □, *India* 69 F9
Uttaradit, *Thailand* 64 D3
Uttaranchal □, *India* 69 D8
Uttoxeter, *U.K.* 12 E6
Uummannarsuaq = Nunap Isua, *Greenland* 101 C15
Uusikaarlepyy, *Finland* 8 E20
Uusikaupunki, *Finland* 9 F19
Uva, *Russia* 48 B11
Uvac →, *Serbia, Yug.* 40 C3
Uvalde, *U.S.A.* 113 L5
Uvarovo, *Russia* 48 E6
Uvat, *Russia* 50 D7
Uvinza, *Tanzania* 86 D3
Uvira, *Dem. Rep. of the Congo* 86 C2
Uvs Nuur, *Mongolia* 60 A4
'Uwairidh, Ḥarrat al, *Si. Arabia* 70 E3
Uwajima, *Japan* 55 H6
Uweinat, Jebel, *Sudan* 80 C1
Uxbridge, *Canada* 110 B5
Uxin Qi, *China* 56 E5
Uxmal, *Mexico* 119 C7
Üydzin, *Mongolia* 56 B4
Uyo, *Nigeria* 83 D6
Üyüklü Tepe, *Turkey* 39 D9
Uyûn Mûsa, *Egypt* 75 F1
Uyuni, *Bolivia* 124 H5
Uzbekistan ■, *Asia* 50 E7
Uzen, Bolshoi →, *Kazakstan* 49 F9
Uzen, Mal →, *Kazakstan* 49 F9
Uzerche, *France* 20 C5
Uzès, *France* 21 D8
Uzh →, *Ukraine* 47 G6
Uzhgorod = Uzhhorod, *Ukraine* 47 H2
Uzhhorod, *Ukraine* 47 H2
Užice, *Serbia, Yug.* 40 C3
Uzlovaya, *Russia* 46 F10
Üzümlü, *Turkey* 39 E11
Uzunköprü, *Turkey* 41 E10
Uzunkuyu, *Turkey* 39 C8

V

Vaal →, *S. Africa* 88 D3
Vaal Dam, *S. Africa* 89 D4
Vaalwater, *S. Africa* 89 C4
Vaasa, *Finland* 8 E19
Vabre, *France* 20 E6
Vác, *Hungary* 42 C4
Vacaria, *Brazil* 127 B5
Vacaville, *U.S.A.* 116 G5
Vaccarès, Étang de, *France* 21 E8
Vach = Vakh →, *Russia* 50 C8
Vache, Î. à, *Haiti* 121 C5
Väckelsång, *Sweden* 11 H8
Väddö, *Sweden* 10 D12
Väderstad, *Sweden* 11 F8
Vadnagar, *India* 68 H5
Vado Lígure, *Italy* 28 D5
Vadodara, *India* 68 H5
Vadsø, *Norway* 8 A23
Vadstena, *Sweden* 11 F8
Vaduz, *Liech.* 25 H5
Værøy, *Norway* 8 C15
Vágar, *Færoe Is.* 8 E9
Vaggeryd, *Sweden* 11 G8
Vagney, *France* 19 D13
Vagnhärad, *Sweden* 11 F11
Vagos, *Portugal* 34 E2
Vågsfjorden, *Norway* 8 B17
Váh →, *Slovak Rep.* 27 D11
Vahsel B., *Antarctica* 5 D1
Vàï, *Greece* 36 D8
Vaigach, *Russia* 50 B6
Vaiges, *France* 18 D6
Vaihingen, *Germany* 25 G4
Vail, *U.S.A.* 106 C5
Vailly-sur-Aisne, *France* 19 C10
Vaisali →, *India* 69 F8
Vaison-la-Romaine, *France* 21 D9
Vakarel, *Bulgaria* 40 D7
Vakfikebir, *Turkey* 73 B8
Vakh →, *Russia* 50 C8
Vakhtan, *Russia* 48 B8
Vál, *Hungary* 42 C3
Val-de-Marne □, *France* 19 D9
Val-d'Isère, *France* 21 C10
Val-d'Oise □, *France* 19 C9
Val-d'Or, *Canada* 102 C4
Val Marie, *Canada* 105 D7
Valaam, *Russia* 46 B6
Valadares, *Portugal* 34 D2
Valahia, *Romania* 43 F9
Valais □, *Switz.* 25 J3
Valais, Alpes du, *Switz.* 25 J3
Valandovo, *Macedonia* 40 E6
Valašské Meziříčí, *Czech Rep.* 27 B10
Valáxa, *Greece* 38 C6
Vålberg, *Sweden* 10 E7
Valbo, *Sweden* 10 D10
Valbondione, *Italy* 28 B7
Vălcani, *Romania* 42 D5
Vâlcea □, *Romania* 43 F9
Valcheta, *Argentina* 128 E3
Valdagno, *Italy* 29 C8
Valdahon, *France* 19 E13
Valday, *Russia* 46 D7
Valdayskaya Vozvyshennost, *Russia* 46 D7
Valdeazogues →, *Spain* 35 G6
Valdecañas, Embalse de, *Spain* 34 F5
Valdemarsvik, *Sweden* 11 F10
Valdemoro, *Spain* 34 E7
Valdepeñas, *Spain* 35 G7
Valderaduey →, *Spain* 34 D5
Valdérice, *Italy* 30 D5
Valderrobres, *Spain* 32 E5
Valdés, Pen., *Argentina* 122 H4
Valdez, *U.S.A.* 100 B5
Valdivia, *Chile* 128 D2
Valdobbiádene, *Italy* 29 C8
Valdosta, *U.S.A.* 109 K4
Valdoviño, *Spain* 34 B2
Valdres, *Norway* 9 F13
Vale, *Georgia* 49 K6
Vale, *U.S.A.* 114 E5
Vale of Glamorgan □, *U.K.* 13 F4
Valea lui Mihai, *Romania* 42 C7
Valea Mărului, *Romania* 43 E12
Valemount, *Canada* 104 C5
Valença, *Brazil* 125 F11
Valença, *Portugal* 34 C2
Valença do Piauí, *Brazil* 125 E10
Valençay, *France* 19 E8
Valence = Valence d'Agen, *France* 20 D4
Valence, *France* 21 D8
Valence d'Agen, *France* 20 D4
Valencia, *Spain* 33 F4
Valencia, *U.S.A.* 115 J10
Valencia, *Venezuela* 124 A5
Valencia □, *Spain* 33 F4
Valencia, G. de, *Spain* 33 F5
Valencia de Alcántara, *Spain* 35 F3
Valencia de Don Juan, *Spain* 34 C5
Valencia I., *Ireland* 15 E1
Valenciennes, *France* 19 B10
Văleni, *Romania* 43 F9
Vălenii de Munte, *Romania* 43 E11
Valensole, *France* 21 E9
Valentigney, *France* 19 E13
Valentim, Sa. do, *Brazil* 125 E10
Valentin, *Russia* 54 C7
Valentine, *U.S.A.* 113 K2
Valenza, *Italy* 28 C5
Valera, *Venezuela* 124 B4
Valga, *Estonia* 9 H22
Valguarnera Caropepe, *Italy* 31 E7
Valier, *U.S.A.* 114 B7
Valinco, G. de, *France* 21 G12
Valjevo, *Serbia, Yug.* 40 B3
Valka, *Latvia* 9 H21
Valkeakoski, *Finland* 9 F20
Valkenswaard, *Neths.* 17 C5
Vall de Uxó = La Vall d'Uixó, *Spain* 32 F4
Valla, *Sweden* 10 E10
Valladolid, *Mexico* 119 C7
Valladolid, *Spain* 34 D6
Valladolid □, *Spain* 34 D6
Vallata, *Italy* 31 A8
Valldemossa, *Spain* 37 B9
Valle d'Aosta □, *Italy* 28 C4
Valle de Arán, *Spain* 32 C5
Valle de la Pascua, *Venezuela* 124 B5
Valle de las Palmas, *Mexico* 117 N10
Valle de Santiago, *Mexico* 118 C4
Valle de Suchil, *Mexico* 118 C4
Valle de Zaragoza, *Mexico* 118 B3
Valle Fértil, Sierra del, *Argentina* 126 C2
Valle Hermoso, *Mexico* 119 B5
Valledupar, *Colombia* 124 A4
Vallehermoso, *Canary Is.* 37 F2
Vallejo, *U.S.A.* 116 G4
Vallenar, *Chile* 126 B1
Vallentuna, *Sweden* 10 E12
Valleraugue, *France* 20 D7
Vallet, *France* 18 E5
Valletta, *Malta* 36 D2
Valley Center, *U.S.A.* 117 M9
Valley City, *U.S.A.* 112 B6
Valley Falls, *Oreg., U.S.A.* 114 E3
Valley Falls, *R.I., U.S.A.* 111 E13
Valley Springs, *U.S.A.* 116 G6
Valley View, *U.S.A.* 111 F8
Valley Wells, *U.S.A.* 117 K11
Valleyview, *Canada* 104 B5
Valli di Comácchio, *Italy* 29 D9
Vallimanca, Arroyo, *Argentina* 126 D4
Vallo della Lucánia, *Italy* 31 B8
Vallon-Pont-d'Arc, *France* 21 D8
Vallorbe, *Switz.* 25 J2
Valls, *Spain* 32 D6
Valmaseda = Balmaseda, *Spain* 32 B1
Valmiera, *Latvia* 9 H21
Valnera, *Spain* 34 B7
Valognes, *France* 18 C5
Valona = Vlorë, *Albania* 40 F3
Valongo, *Portugal* 34 D2
Valozhyn, *Belarus* 46 E4
Valpaços, *Portugal* 34 D3
Valparaíso, *Chile* 126 C1
Valparaíso, *Mexico* 118 C4
Valparaiso, *U.S.A.* 108 E2
Valparaíso □, *Chile* 126 C1
Valpovo, *Croatia* 42 E3
Valréas, *France* 21 D9
Vals, *Switz.* 25 J5
Vals →, *S. Africa* 88 D4
Vals, Tanjung, *Indonesia* 63 F9
Vals-les-Bains, *France* 21 D8
Valsad, *India* 66 J8
Valtellina, *Italy* 28 B6
Valuyki, *Russia* 47 G10
Valverde, *Canary Is.* 37 G2
Valverde del Camino, *Spain* 35 H4
Valverde del Fresno, *Spain* 34 E4
Vama, *Romania* 43 C10
Vamdrup, *Denmark* 11 J3
Våmhus, *Sweden* 10 C8
Vammala, *Finland* 9 F20
Vámos, *Greece* 36 D6
Van, *Turkey* 70 B4
Van, L. = Van Gölü, *Turkey* 70 B4
Van Alstyne, *U.S.A.* 113 J6
Van Blommestein Meer, *Surinam* 125 C7
Van Buren, *Canada* 103 C6
Van Buren, *Ark., U.S.A.* 113 H7
Van Buren, *Maine, U.S.A.* 109 B11
Van Buren, *Mo., U.S.A.* 113 G9
Van Canh, *Vietnam* 64 F7
Van Diemen, C., *N. Terr., Australia* 92 B5
Van Diemen, C., *Queens., Australia* 94 B2
Van Diemen G., *Australia* 92 B5
Van Gölü, *Turkey* 70 B4
Van Horn, *U.S.A.* 113 K2
Van Ninh, *Vietnam* 64 F7
Van Rees, Pegunungan, *Indonesia* 63 E9
Van Wert, *U.S.A.* 108 E3
Van Yen, *Vietnam* 58 G5
Vanadzor, *Armenia* 49 K7
Vanavara, *Russia* 51 C11
Vancouver, *Canada* 104 D4
Vancouver, *U.S.A.* 116 E4
Vancouver, C., *Australia* 93 G2
Vancouver I., *Canada* 104 D3
Vandalia, *Ill., U.S.A.* 112 F10
Vandalia, *Mo., U.S.A.* 112 F9
Vandenburg, *U.S.A.* 117 L6
Vanderbijlpark, *S. Africa* 89 D4
Vandergrift, *U.S.A.* 110 F5
Vanderhoof, *Canada* 104 C4
Vanderkloof Dam, *S. Africa* 88 E3
Vanderlin I., *Australia* 94 B2
Vänern, *Sweden* 11 F7
Vänersborg, *Sweden* 11 F6
Vang Vieng, *Laos* 64 C4
Vanga, *Kenya* 86 C4
Vangaindrano, *Madag.* 89 C8

Vanguard, *Canada* 105 D7
Vanino, *Russia* 51 E15
Vânju Mare, *Romania* 42 F7
Vanna, *Norway* 8 A18
Vännäs, *Sweden* 8 E18
Vannes, *France* 18 E4
Vanoise, *France* 21 C10
Vanrhynsdorp, *S. Africa* 88 E2
Vansbro, *Sweden* 10 D8
Vansittart B., *Australia* 92 B4
Vantaa, *Finland* 9 F21
Vanua Balavu, *Fiji* 91 C9
Vanua Levu, *Fiji* 91 C8
Vanuatu ■, *Pac. Oc.* 96 J8
Vanwyksvlei, *S. Africa* 88 E3
Vanzylsrus, *S. Africa* 88 D3
Vapnyarka, *Ukraine* 47 H5
Var □, *France* 21 E10
Var →, *France* 21 E11
Vara, *Sweden* 11 F6
Varades, *France* 18 E5
Varáita →, *Italy* 28 D4
Varallo, *Italy* 28 C5
Varanasi, *India* 69 G10
Varangerfjorden, *Norway* 8 A23
Varangerhalvøya, *Norway* 8 A23
Varano, Lago di, *Italy* 29 G12
Varaždin, *Croatia* 29 B13
Varazze, *Italy* 28 D5
Varberg, *Sweden* 11 G6
Vardak □, *Afghan.* 66 B6
Vardar = Axiós →, *Greece* 40 F6
Varde, *Denmark* 11 J2
Varde Å →, *Denmark* 11 J2
Vardø, *Norway* 8 A24
Varel, *Germany* 24 B4
Varella, Mui, *Vietnam* 64 F7
Varėna, *Lithuania* 9 J21
Varennes-sur-Allier, *France* 19 F10
Varennes-Vauzelles, *France* 19 E10
Vareš, *Bos.-H.* 42 F3
Varese, *Italy* 28 C5
Vârfurile, *Romania* 42 D7
Vårgårda, *Sweden* 11 F6
Varginha, *Brazil* 127 A6
Vargön, *Sweden* 11 F6
Varillas, *Chile* 126 A1
Varkaus, *Finland* 9 E22
Värmdölandet, *Sweden* 10 E12
Värmeln, *Sweden* 10 E6
Värmlands Bro, *Sweden* 10 E7
Värmlands län □, *Sweden* 10 E6
Varna, *Bulgaria* 41 C11
Varna □, *Bulgaria* 41 C11
Värnamo, *Sweden* 11 G8
Varnsdorf, *Czech Rep.* 26 A7
Várpalota, *Hungary* 42 C3
Vars, *Canada* 111 A9
Vars, *France* 21 D10
Varto, *Turkey* 73 C9
Varvarin, *Serbia, Yug.* 40 C5
Varysburg, *U.S.A.* 110 D6
Varzaneh, *Iran* 71 C7
Varzi, *Italy* 28 D6
Varzo, *Italy* 28 B5
Varzy, *France* 19 E10
Vas □, *Hungary* 42 C1
Vasa Barris →, *Brazil* 125 F11
Vásárosnamény, *Hungary* 42 B7
Vascâo →, *Portugal* 35 H3
Vașcău, *Romania* 42 D7
Vascongadas = País Vasco □, *Spain* 32 C2
Vasht = Khāsh, *Iran* 66 E2
Vasilevichi, *Belarus* 47 F5
Vasilikón, *Greece* 38 C5
Vasilkov = Vasylkiv, *Ukraine* 47 G6
Vaslui, *Romania* 43 D12
Vaslui □, *Romania* 43 D12
Väsman, *Sweden* 10 D9
Vassar, *Canada* 105 D9
Vassar, *U.S.A.* 108 D4
Västerås, *Sweden* 10 E10
Västerbotten, *Sweden* 8 D18
Västerdalälven →, *Sweden* 10 D8
Västergötland, *Sweden* 11 F7
Västerhaninge, *Sweden* 10 E12
Västervik, *Sweden* 11 G10
Västmanland, *Sweden* 9 G16
Västmanlands län □, *Sweden* 10 E10
Vasto, *Italy* 29 F11
Västra Götalands Län □, *Sweden* 11 F6
Vasvár, *Hungary* 42 C1
Vasylkiv, *Ukraine* 47 G6
Vatan, *France* 19 E8
Vatersay, *U.K.* 14 E1
Váthia, *Greece* 38 E4
Vatican City ■, *Europe* 29 G9
Vaticano, C., *Italy* 31 D8
Vatili, *Cyprus* 36 D12
Vatin, *Serbia, Yug.* 42 E6
Vatnajökull, *Iceland* 8 D5
Vatoa, *Fiji* 91 D9
Vatólakkos, *Greece* 36 D5
Vatoloha, *Madag.* 89 B8
Vatomandry, *Madag.* 89 B8
Vatra-Dornei, *Romania* 43 C10
Vatrak →, *India* 68 H5
Vättern, *Sweden* 11 F8
Vaucluse □, *France* 21 E9
Vaucouleurs, *France* 19 D12
Vaud □, *Switz.* 25 J2
Vaughn, *Mont., U.S.A.* 114 C8
Vaughn, *N. Mex., U.S.A.* 115 J11
Vaujours L., *Canada* 102 A5
Vaupés = Uaupés →, *Brazil* 124 C5
Vaupes □, *Colombia* 124 C4
Vauvert, *France* 21 E8
Vauxhall, *Canada* 104 C6
Vav, *India* 68 G4
Vavatenina, *Madag.* 89 B8
Vava'u, *Tonga* 91 D12
Vavoua, *Ivory C.* 82 D3
Vawkavysk, *Belarus* 47 F3
Vaxholm, *Sweden* 10 E12
Växjö, *Sweden* 11 H8
Våxtorp, *Sweden* 11 H7
Vaygach, Ostrov, *Russia* 50 C6
Váyia, *Greece* 38 C5
Váyia, Ákra, *Greece* 36 C10
Vechelde, *Germany* 24 C6
Vechta, *Germany* 24 C4
Vechte →, *Neths.* 17 B6
Vecsés, *Hungary* 42 C4
Veddige, *Sweden* 11 G6
Vedea →, *Romania* 43 G10
Vedia, *Argentina* 126 C3
Vedum, *Sweden* 11 F7
Veendam, *Neths.* 17 A6
Veenendaal, *Neths.* 17 B5
Vefsna →, *Norway* 8 D15
Vega, *Norway* 8 D14
Vega, *U.S.A.* 113 H3
Vegadeo, *Spain* 34 B3
Vegorrítis, Límni, *Greece* 40 F5
Vegreville, *Canada* 104 C6
Veinge, *Sweden* 11 H7
Veisiejai, *Lithuania* 44 D10
Vejbystrand, *Sweden* 11 H6
Vejen, *Denmark* 11 J3
Vejer de la Frontera, *Spain* 35 J5
Vejle, *Denmark* 11 J3
Vejle Amtskommune □, *Denmark* 11 J3
Vejle Fjord, *Denmark* 11 J3
Vela Luka, *Croatia* 29 F13
Velas, C., *Costa Rica* 120 D2
Velasco, Sierra de, *Argentina* 126 B2
Velay, Mts. du, *France* 20 D7
Velbert, *Germany* 24 D3
Velddrif, *S. Africa* 88 E2
Velebit Planina, *Croatia* 29 D12
Velebitski Kanal, *Croatia* 29 D11
Veleka →, *Bulgaria* 41 D11
Velencei-tó, *Hungary* 42 C3
Velenje, *Slovenia* 29 B12
Veles, *Macedonia* 40 E5
Velestínon, *Greece* 38 B4
Vélez-Málaga, *Spain* 35 J6
Vélez Rubio, *Spain* 33 H2
Velhas →, *Brazil* 125 G10
Velika, *Croatia* 42 E2
Velika Gorica, *Croatia* 29 C13
Velika Kapela, *Croatia* 29 C12
Velika Kladuša, *Bos.-H.* 29 C12
Velika Kruša, *Kosovo, Yug.* 40 D4
Velika Morava →, *Serbia, Yug.* 40 B5
Velika Plana, *Serbia, Yug.* 40 B5
Velikaya →, *Russia* 46 D5
Velikaya Kema, *Russia* 54 B8
Velikaya Lepetikha, *Ukraine* 47 J7
Veliké Kapušany, *Slovak Rep.* 27 C15
Velike Lašče, *Slovenia* 29 C11
Veliki Jastrebac, *Serbia, Yug.* 40 C5
Veliki Kanal, *Serbia, Yug.* 42 E4
Veliki Popović, *Serbia, Yug.* 40 B5
Velikiye Luki, *Russia* 46 D6
Veliko Gradište, *Serbia, Yug.* 40 B5
Veliko Tŭrnovo, *Bulgaria* 41 C9
Velikonda Range, *India* 66 M11
Vélingara, *Senegal* 82 C2
Vélingara, *Senegal* 82 B2
Velingrad, *Bulgaria* 40 D7
Velino, Mte., *Italy* 29 F10
Velizh, *Russia* 46 E6
Velké Karlovice, *Czech Rep.* 27 B11
Velké Meziříčí, *Czech Rep.* 26 B9
Vel'ký Javorník, *Slovak Rep.* 27 B11
Vel'ký Krtíš, *Slovak Rep.* 27 C12
Vel'ký Meder, *Slovak Rep.* 27 D10
Vel'ký Tribeč, *Slovak Rep.* 27 C11
Velletri, *Italy* 30 A5
Vellinge, *Sweden* 11 J6
Vellmar, *Germany* 24 D5
Vellore, *India* 66 N11
Velsk, *Russia* 46 B11
Velten, *Germany* 24 C9
Velva, *U.S.A.* 112 A4
Velvendós, *Greece* 40 F6
Vemb, *Denmark* 11 H2
Vemdalen, *Sweden* 10 B7
Ven, *Sweden* 11 J6
Venaco, *France* 21 F13
Venado Tuerto, *Argentina* 126 C3
Venafro, *Italy* 31 A7
Venarey-les-Laumes, *France* 19 E11
Venaría, *Italy* 28 C4
Venčane, *Serbia, Yug.* 40 B4
Vence, *France* 21 E11
Vendas Novas, *Portugal* 35 G2
Vendée □, *France* 18 F5
Vendée →, *France* 18 F5
Vendéen, Bocage, *France* 20 B2
Vendeuvre-sur-Barse, *France* 19 D11
Vendôme, *France* 18 E8
Vendrell = El Vendrell, *Spain* 32 D6
Vendsyssel, *Denmark* 11 G4
Venelles, *France* 21 E9
Véneta, L., *Italy* 29 C9
Véneto □, *Italy* 29 C9
Venev, *Russia* 46 E10
Venézia, *Italy* 29 C9
Venézia, G. di, *Italy* 29 C10
Venezuela ■, *S. Amer.* 124 B5
Venezuela, G. de, *Venezuela* 122 B3
Vengurla, *India* 66 M8
Venice = Venézia, *Italy* 29 C9
Venice, *U.S.A.* 109 M4
Vénissieux, *France* 21 C8
Venjansjön, *Sweden* 10 D8
Venkatapuram, *India* 67 K12
Venlo, *Neths.* 17 C6
Vennesla, *Norway* 9 G12
Venosa, *Italy* 31 B8
Venray, *Neths.* 17 C6
Venta, *Lithuania* 44 B9
Venta →, *Latvia* 44 A8
Venta de Baños, *Spain* 34 D6
Venta de Cardeña = Cardeña, *Spain* 35 G6
Ventana, Punta de la, *Mexico* 118 C3
Ventana, Sa. de la, *Argentina* 126 D3
Ventersburg, *S. Africa* 88 D4
Venterstad, *S. Africa* 88 E4
Ventimíglia, *Italy* 28 E4
Ventnor, *U.K.* 13 G6
Ventotène, *Italy* 30 B6
Ventoux, Mt., *France* 21 D9
Ventspils, *Latvia* 9 H19
Ventspils □, *Latvia* 44 A8
Ventuarí →, *Venezuela* 124 C5
Ventucopa, *U.S.A.* 117 L7
Ventura, *U.S.A.* 117 L7
Venus B., *Australia* 95 F4
Vera, *Argentina* 126 B3
Vera, *Spain* 33 H3
Veracruz, *Mexico* 119 D5
Veracruz □, *Mexico* 119 D5
Veraval, *India* 68 J4
Verbánia, *Italy* 28 C5
Verbicaro, *Italy* 31 C8
Verbier, *Switz.* 25 J3
Vercelli, *Italy* 28 C5
Verchovchevo, *Ukraine* 47 H8
Verdalsøra, *Norway* 8 E14
Verde →, *Argentina* 128 E3
Verde →, *Goiás, Brazil* 125 G8
Verde →, *Mato Grosso do Sul, Brazil* 125 H8
Verde →, *Chihuahua, Mexico* 118 B3
Verde →, *Oaxaca, Mexico* 119 D5
Verde →, *Veracruz, Mexico* 118 C4
Verde →, *Paraguay* 126 A4
Verde →, *U.S.A.* 106 D4
Verde, Cay, *Bahamas* 120 B4
Verde Island Pass, *Phil.* 61 E4
Verden, *Germany* 24 C5
Verdhikoúsa, *Greece* 38 B3
Verdi, *U.S.A.* 116 F7
Verdon →, *France* 21 E9
Verdun, *France* 19 C12
Verdun-sur-le-Doubs, *France* 19 F12
Vereeniging, *S. Africa* 89 D4
Verga, C., *Guinea* 82 C2
Vergara, *Uruguay* 127 C5
Vergato, *Italy* 28 D8
Vergemont Cr. →, *Australia* 94 C3
Vergennes, *U.S.A.* 111 B11
Vergt, *France* 20 C4
Verín, *Spain* 34 D3
Verkhnedvinsk = Vyerkhnyadzvinsk, *Belarus* 46 E4
Verkhnevilyuysk, *Russia* 51 C13
Verkhniy Baskunchak, *Russia* 49 F8
Verkhovye, *Russia* 47 F9
Verkhoyansk, *Russia* 51 C14
Verkhoyansk Ra. = Verkhoyanskiy Khrebet, *Russia* 51 C13
Verkhoyanskiy Khrebet, *Russia* 51 C13
Vermenton, *France* 19 E10
Vermilion, *Canada* 105 C6
Vermilion, *U.S.A.* 110 E2
Vermilion →, *Alta., Canada* 105 C6
Vermilion →, *Qué., Canada* 102 C5
Vermilion, B., *U.S.A.* 113 L9
Vermilion Bay, *Canada* 105 D10
Vermilion L., *U.S.A.* 112 B8
Vermillion, *U.S.A.* 112 D6
Vermont □, *U.S.A.* 111 C12
Vermosh, *Albania* 40 D3
Vernal, *U.S.A.* 114 F9
Vernalis, *U.S.A.* 116 H5
Vernazza, *Italy* 28 D6
Verner, *Canada* 102 C3
Verneuil-sur-Avre, *France* 18 D7
Verneukpan, *S. Africa* 88 E3
Vernier, *Switz.* 25 J2
Vérnio, *Italy* 28 D8
Vernon, *Canada* 104 C5
Vernon, *France* 18 C8
Vernon, *U.S.A.* 113 H5
Vernonia, *U.S.A.* 116 E3
Vernouillet, *France* 18 D8
Vero Beach, *U.S.A.* 109 M5
Véroia, *Greece* 40 F6
Véroli, *Italy* 29 G10
Verona, *Canada* 111 B8
Verona, *Italy* 28 C7
Verona, *U.S.A.* 112 D10
Verrès, *Italy* 28 C4
Versailles, *France* 19 D9
Versmold, *Germany* 24 C4
Vert, C., *Senegal* 82 C1
Vertou, *France* 18 E5
Vertus, *France* 19 D11
Verulam, *S. Africa* 89 D5
Verviers, *Belgium* 17 D5
Vervins, *France* 19 C10
Veržej, *Slovenia* 29 B13
Verzy, *France* 19 C11
Vescovato, *France* 21 F13
Veselí nad Lužnicí, *Czech Rep.* 26 B7
Veselie, *Bulgaria* 41 D11
Veselovskoye Vdkhr., *Russia* 49 G5
Veshenskaya, *Russia* 48 F5
Vesle →, *France* 19 C10
Vesoul, *France* 19 E13
Vessigebro, *Sweden* 11 H6
Vesterålen, *Norway* 8 B16
Vestfjorden, *Norway* 8 C15
Vestmannaeyjar, *Iceland* 8 E3
Vestsjællands Amtskommune □, *Denmark* 11 J5
Vestspitsbergen, *Svalbard* 4 B8
Vestvågøy, *Norway* 8 B15
Vesuvio, *Italy* 31 B7
Vesuvius, Mt. = Vesuvio, *Italy* 31 B7
Vesyegonsk, *Russia* 46 C9
Veszprém, *Hungary* 42 C2
Veszprém □, *Hungary* 42 C2
Vésztő, *Hungary* 42 D6
Vetlanda, *Sweden* 11 G9
Vetluga, *Russia* 48 B7
Vetlugu →, *Russia* 48 B8
Vetluzhskiy, *Kostroma, Russia* 48 A7
Vetluzhskiy, *Nizhniy Novgorod, Russia* 48 B7
Vetovo, *Bulgaria* 41 C10
Vetralla, *Italy* 29 F9
Vetren, *Bulgaria* 41 D8
Vettore, Mte., *Italy* 29 F10
Veurne, *Belgium* 17 C2
Veveno →, *Sudan* 81 F3
Vevey, *Switz.* 25 J2
Vévi, *Greece* 40 F5
Veynes, *France* 21 D9
Veys, *Iran* 71 D6
Vézelay, *France* 19 E10
Vézelise, *France* 19 D13
Vézère →, *France* 20 D4
Vezhen, *Bulgaria* 41 D8
Vezirköprü, *Turkey* 72 B6
Vezzani, *France* 21 F13
Vi Thanh, *Vietnam* 65 H5
Viacha, *Bolivia* 124 G5
Viadana, *Italy* 28 D7
Viamão, *Brazil* 127 C5
Viana, *Brazil* 125 D10
Viana, *Spain* 32 C2
Viana do Alentejo, *Portugal* 35 G3
Viana do Bolo, *Spain* 34 C3
Viana do Castelo, *Portugal* 34 D2
Viana do Castelo □, *Portugal* 34 D2
Vianden, *Lux.* 17 E6
Viangchan = Vientiane, *Laos* 64 D4
Vianópolis, *Brazil* 125 G9
Viar →, *Spain* 35 H5
Viaréggio, *Italy* 28 E7
Viaur →, *France* 20 D5
Vibble, *Sweden* 11 G12
Vibo Valéntia, *Italy* 31 D9
Viborg, *Denmark* 11 H3
Viborg Amtskommune □, *Denmark* 11 H3
Vibraye, *France* 18 D7
Vic, *Spain* 32 D7
Vic, Étang de, *France* 20 E7
Vic-en-Bigorre, *France* 20 E4
Vic-Fézensac, *France* 20 E4
Vic-le-Comte, *France* 19 G10
Vic-sur-Cère, *France* 20 D6
Vícar, *Spain* 33 J2
Vicenza, *Italy* 29 C8
Vich = Vic, *Spain* 32 D7
Vichada →, *Colombia* 124 C5
Vichuga, *Russia* 48 B5
Vichy, *France* 19 F10
Vicksburg, *Ariz., U.S.A.* 117 M13
Vicksburg, *Miss., U.S.A.* 113 J9
Vico, *France* 21 F12
Vico, L. di, *Italy* 29 F9
Vico del Gargano, *Italy* 29 G12
Vicovu de Sus, *Romania* 43 C10
Victor, *India* 68 J4
Victor, *U.S.A.* 110 D7
Victor Harbor, *Australia* 95 F2
Victoria = Labuan, *Malaysia* 62 C5
Victoria, *Argentina* 126 C3
Victoria, *Canada* 104 D4
Victoria, *Chile* 128 D2
Victoria, *Guinea* 82 C2
Victoria, *Malta* 36 C1
Victoria, *Phil.* 61 D4
Victoria, *Romania* 43 E9
Victoria, *Kans., U.S.A.* 112 F5
Victoria, *Tex., U.S.A.* 113 L6
Victoria □, *Australia* 95 F3
Victoria →, *Australia* 92 C4
Victoria, Grand L., *Canada* 102 C4
Victoria, L., *Africa* 86 C3
Victoria, L., *Australia* 95 E3
Victoria, Mt., *Burma* 67 J18
Victoria Beach, *Canada* 105 C9
Victoria de Durango = Durango, *Mexico* 118 C4
Victoria de las Tunas, *Cuba* 120 B4
Victoria Falls, *Zimbabwe* 87 F2
Victoria Harbour, *Canada* 110 B5
Victoria I., *Canada* 100 A8
Victoria L., *Canada* 103 C8
Victoria Ld., *Antarctica* 5 D11
Victoria Nile →, *Uganda* 86 B3
Victoria River, *Australia* 92 C5
Victoria Str., *Canada* 100 B9
Victoria West, *S. Africa* 88 E3
Victorias, *Phil.* 61 F5
Victoriaville, *Canada* 103 C5
Victorica, *Argentina* 126 D2
Victorville, *U.S.A.* 117 L9
Vicuña, *Chile* 126 C1
Vicuña Mackenna, *Argentina* 126 C3
Vidal, *U.S.A.* 117 L12
Vidal Junction, *U.S.A.* 117 L12
Vidalia, *U.S.A.* 109 J4
Vidauban, *France* 21 E10
Videbæk, *Denmark* 11 H2
Videle, *Romania* 43 F10
Vídho, *Greece* 36 A3
Vidigueira, *Portugal* 35 G3
Vidin, *Bulgaria* 40 C6
Vidio, C., *Spain* 34 B4
Vidisha, *India* 68 H7
Vidra, *Romania* 43 E11
Viduša, *Bos.-H.* 40 D2
Vidzy, *Belarus* 9 J22
Viechtach, *Germany* 25 F8
Viedma, *Argentina* 128 E4
Viedma, L., *Argentina* 128 F2
Vieira do Minho, *Portugal* 34 D2
Vielha, *Spain* 32 C5
Viella = Vielha, *Spain* 32 C5
Vielsalm, *Belgium* 17 D5
Vienenburg, *Germany* 24 D6
Vieng Pou Kha, *Laos* 58 G3
Vienna = Wien, *Austria* 27 C9
Vienna, *Ill., U.S.A.* 113 G10
Vienna, *Mo., U.S.A.* 112 F9
Vienne, *France* 21 C8
Vienne □, *France* 20 B4
Vienne →, *France* 18 E7
Vientiane, *Laos* 64 D4
Vientos, Paso de los, *Caribbean* 121 C5
Viernheim, *Germany* 25 F4
Viersen, *Germany* 24 D2
Vierwaldstättersee, *Switz.* 25 J4
Vierzon, *France* 19 E9
Vieste, *Italy* 29 G13
Vietnam ■, *Asia* 64 C6
Vieux-Boucau-les-Bains, *France* 20 E2
Vif, *France* 21 C9
Vigan, *Phil.* 61 C4
Vigévano, *Italy* 28 C5
Vigia, *Brazil* 125 D9
Vigía Chico, *Mexico* 119 D7
Víglas, Ákra, *Greece* 36 D9
Vignemale, *France* 20 F3
Vigneulles-lès-Hattonchâtel, *France* 19 D12
Vignola, *Italy* 28 D8
Vigo, *Spain* 34 C2
Vigo, Ría de, *Spain* 34 C2
Vigsø Bugt, *Denmark* 11 G2
Vihiers, *France* 18 E6
Vihowa, *Pakistan* 68 D4
Vihowa →, *Pakistan* 68 D4
Vijayawada, *India* 67 L12
Vijosë →, *Albania* 40 F3
Vík, *Iceland* 8 E4
Vika, *Sweden* 10 D8
Vikarbyn, *Sweden* 10 D9
Vikeke, *E. Timor* 63 F7
Viken, *Skåne, Sweden* 11 H6
Viken, *Västra Götaland, Sweden* 11 F8
Viking, *Canada* 104 C6
Vikmanshyttan, *Sweden* 10 D9
Vikna, *Norway* 8 D14
Vila da Maganja, *Mozam.* 87 F4
Vila de João Belo = Xai-Xai, *Mozam.* 89 D5
Vila de Rei, *Portugal* 34 F2
Vila do Bispo, *Portugal* 35 H2
Vila do Conde, *Portugal* 34 D2
Vila Franca de Xira, *Portugal* 35 G2
Vila Gamito, *Mozam.* 87 E3
Vila Gomes da Costa, *Mozam.* 89 C5
Vila Machado, *Mozam.* 87 F3
Vila Mouzinho, *Mozam.* 87 E3
Vila Nova de Famalicão, *Portugal* 34 D2
Vila Nova de Fos Côa, *Portugal* 34 D3
Vila Nova de Foscôa = Vila Nova de Fos Côa, *Portugal* 34 D3
Vila Nova de Gaia, *Portugal* 34 D2
Vila Nova de Ourém, *Portugal* 34 F2
Vila Pouca de Aguiar, *Portugal* 34 D3
Vila Real, *Portugal* 34 D3
Vila Real □, *Portugal* 34 D3
Vila-real de los Infantes, *Spain* 32 F4
Vila Real de Santo António, *Portugal* 35 H3
Vila Vasco da Gama, *Mozam.* 87 E3
Vila Velha, *Brazil* 127 A7
Vila Viçosa, *Portugal* 35 G3
Vilafranca del Maestrat, *Spain* 32 E4
Vilafranca del Penedès, *Spain* 32 D6
Vilagarcía de Arousa, *Spain* 34 C2
Vilaine →, *France* 18 E4
Vilanandro, Tanjona, *Madag.* 89 B7
Vilanculos, *Mozam.* 89 C6
Vilanova de Castelló, *Spain* 33 F4
Vilanova i la Geltrú, *Spain* 32 D6
Vilar Formosa, *Portugal* 34 E4
Vilaseca, *Spain* 32 D6
Vilaseca-Salou = Vilaseca, *Spain* 32 D6
Vilbjerg, *Denmark* 11 H2
Vilches, *Spain* 35 G7
Vileyka, *Belarus* 46 E4
Vilhelmina, *Sweden* 8 D17
Vilhena, *Brazil* 124 F6
Viliga, *Russia* 51 C16
Viliya →, *Lithuania* 9 J21
Viljandi, *Estonia* 9 G21
Vilkaviškis, *Lithuania* 44 D10

Wad Hamid

Vilkija, *Lithuania* 44 C10
Vilkitskogo, Proliv, *Russia* 51 B11
Vilkovo = Vylkove, *Ukraine* 47 K5
Villa Abecia, *Bolivia* 126 A2
Villa Ahumada, *Mexico* 118 A3
Villa Ana, *Argentina* 126 B4
Villa Ángela, *Argentina* 126 B3
Villa Bella, *Bolivia* 124 F5
Villa Bens = Tarfaya, *Morocco* 78 C3
Villa Cañás, *Argentina* 126 C3
Villa Cisneros = Dakhla, *W. Sahara* 78 D2
Villa Colón, *Argentina* 126 C2
Villa Constitución, *Argentina* 126 C3
Villa de María, *Argentina* 126 B3
Villa del Rio, *Spain* 35 H6
Villa Dolores, *Argentina* 126 C2
Villa Frontera, *Mexico* 118 B4
Villa Guillermina, *Argentina* 126 B4
Villa Hayes, *Paraguay* 126 B4
Villa Iris, *Argentina* 126 D3
Villa Juárez, *Mexico* 118 B4
Villa María, *Argentina* 126 C3
Villa Mazán, *Argentina* 126 B2
Villa Minozzo, *Italy* 28 D7
Villa Montes, *Bolivia* 126 A3
Villa Ocampo, *Argentina* 126 B4
Villa Ocampo, *Mexico* 118 B3
Villa Ojo de Agua, *Argentina* 126 B3
Villa San Giovanni, *Italy* 31 D8
Villa San José, *Argentina* 126 C4
Villa San Martín, *Argentina* 126 B3
Villa Santina, *Italy* 29 B9
Villa Unión, *Mexico* 118 C3
Villablino, *Spain* 34 C4
Villacarlos, *Spain* 37 B11
Villacarriedo, *Spain* 34 B7
Villacarrillo, *Spain* 35 G7
Villacastín, *Spain* 34 E6
Villach, *Austria* 26 E6
Villacidro, *Italy* 30 C1
Villada, *Spain* 34 C6
Villadiego, *Spain* 34 C6
Villadóssola, *Italy* 28 B5
Villafeliche, *Spain* 32 D3
Villafranca, *Spain* 32 C3
Villafranca de los Barros, *Spain* 35 G4
Villafranca de los Caballeros, *Baleares, Spain* 37 B10
Villafranca de los Caballeros, *Toledo, Spain* 35 F7
Villafranca del Cid = Vilafranca del Maestrat, *Spain* 32 E4
Villafranca del Panadés = Vilafranca del Penedès, *Spain* 32 D6
Villafranca di Verona, *Italy* 28 C7
Villafranca Tirrena, *Italy* 31 D8
Villagrán, *Mexico* 119 C5
Villaguay, *Argentina* 126 C4
Villaharta, *Spain* 35 G6
Villahermosa, *Mexico* 119 D6
Villahermosa, *Spain* 33 G2
Villaines-la-Juhel, *France* 18 D6
Villajoyosa, *Spain* 33 G4
Villalba, *Spain* 34 B3
Villalba de Guardo, *Spain* 34 C6
Villalón de Campos, *Spain* 34 C5
Villalpando, *Spain* 34 D5
Villaluenga, *Spain* 34 E7
Villamanán, *Spain* 34 C5
Villamartín, *Spain* 35 J5
Villamayor de Santiago, *Spain* 32 F2
Villamblard, *France* 20 C4
Villanova Monteleone, *Italy* 30 B1
Villanueva, *U.S.A.* 113 H2
Villanueva de Castellón = Vilanova de Castelló, *Spain* 33 F4
Villanueva de Córdoba, *Spain* 35 G6
Villanueva de la Fuente, *Spain* 33 G2
Villanueva de la Serena, *Spain* 35 G5
Villanueva de la Sierra, *Spain* 34 E4
Villanueva de los Castillejos, *Spain* 35 H3
Villanueva de los Infantes, *Spain* 35 G7
Villanueva del Arzobispo, *Spain* 33 G2
Villanueva del Fresno, *Spain* 35 G3
Villanueva y Geltrú = Vilanova i la Geltrú, *Spain* 32 D6
Villaputzu, *Italy* 30 C2
Villaquilambre, *Spain* 34 C5
Villar del Arzobispo, *Spain* 32 F4
Villar del Rey, *Spain* 35 F4
Villard-de-Lans, *France* 21 C9
Villarramiel, *Spain* 34 C6
Villarreal = Vila-real de los Infantes, *Spain* 32 F4
Villarrica, *Chile* 128 D2
Villarrica, *Paraguay* 126 B4
Villarrobledo, *Spain* 33 F2
Villarroya de la Sierra, *Spain* 32 D3
Villarrubia de los Ojos, *Spain* 35 F7
Villars-les-Dombes, *France* 19 F12
Villasayas, *Spain* 32 D2
Villaseca de los Gamitos = Villaseco de los Gamitos, *Spain* 34 D4
Villaseco de los Gamitos, *Spain* 34 D4
Villasimíus, *Italy* 30 C2
Villastar, *Spain* 32 E3
Villatobas, *Spain* 34 F7
Villavicencio, *Argentina* 126 C2
Villavicencio, *Colombia* 124 C4
Villaviciosa, *Spain* 34 B5
Villazón, *Bolivia* 126 A2
Ville-Marie, *Canada* 102 C4
Ville Platte, *U.S.A.* 113 K8
Villedieu-les-Poêles, *France* 18 D5
Villefort, *France* 20 D7
Villefranche-de-Lauragais, *France* 20 E5
Villefranche-de-Rouergue, *France* 20 D6
Villefranche-du-Périgord, *France* 20 D5
Villefranche-sur-Saône, *France* 21 C8
Villel, *Spain* 32 E3
Villemur-sur-Tarn, *France* 20 E5
Villena, *Spain* 33 G4
Villenauxe-la-Grande, *France* 19 D10
Villenave-d'Ornon, *France* 20 D3
Villeneuve-d'Ascq, *France* 19 B10
Villeneuve-l'Archevêque, *France* 19 D10
Villeneuve-lès-Avignon, *France* 21 E8
Villeneuve-sur-Allier, *France* 19 F10
Villeneuve-sur-Lot, *France* 20 D4
Villeneuve-sur-Yonne, *France* 19 D10
Villeréal, *France* 20 D4
Villers-Bocage, *France* 18 C6
Villers-Cotterêts, *France* 19 C10
Villers-sur-Mer, *France* 18 C6
Villersexel, *France* 19 E13
Villerupt, *France* 19 C12
Villeurbanne, *France* 21 C8
Villiers, *S. Africa* 89 D4
Villingen-Schwenningen, *Germany* 25 G4
Vilna, *Canada* 104 C6
Vilnius, *Lithuania* 9 J21
Vils, *Austria* 26 D3
Vils →, *Bayern, Germany* 25 G9
Vils →, *Bayern, Germany* 25 F7
Vilsbiburg, *Germany* 25 G8
Vilshofen, *Germany* 25 G9
Vilusi, *Montenegro, Yug.* 40 D2
Vilvoorde, *Belgium* 17 D4
Vilyuy →, *Russia* 51 C13
Vilyuysk, *Russia* 51 C13
Vimianzo, *Spain* 34 B1
Vimioso, *Portugal* 34 D4
Vimmerby, *Sweden* 11 G9
Vimoutiers, *France* 18 D7
Vimperk, *Czech Rep.* 26 B6
Viña del Mar, *Chile* 126 C1
Vinarós, *Spain* 32 E5
Vincennes, *U.S.A.* 108 F2
Vincent, *U.S.A.* 117 L8
Vinchina, *Argentina* 126 B2
Vindelälven →, *Sweden* 8 E18
Vindeln, *Sweden* 8 D18
Vinderup, *Denmark* 11 H2
Vindhya Ra., *India* 68 H7
Vineland, *U.S.A.* 108 F8
Vineuil, *France* 18
Vinga, *Romania* 42 D6
Vingåker, *Sweden* 10 E9
Vinh, *Vietnam* 64 C5
Vinh Linh, *Vietnam* 64 D6
Vinh Long, *Vietnam* 65 G5
Vinh Yen, *Vietnam* 58 G5
Vinhais, *Portugal* 34 D3
Vinica, *Croatia* 29 B13
Vinica, *Macedonia* 40 E6
Vinica, *Slovenia* 29 C12
Vinita, *U.S.A.* 113 G7
Vinkovci, *Croatia* 42 E3
Vinnitsa = Vinnytsya, *Ukraine* 47 H5
Vinnytsya, *Ukraine* 47 H5
Vinslöv, *Sweden* 11 H7
Vintjärn, *Sweden* 10 D10
Vinton, *Calif., U.S.A.* 116 F6
Vinton, *Iowa, U.S.A.* 112 D8
Vinton, *La., U.S.A.* 113 K8
Vinţu de Jos, *Romania* 43 D8
Viöl, *Germany* 24 A5
Vipava, *Slovenia* 29 C10
Vipiteno, *Italy* 29 B8
Vir, *Croatia* 29 D12
Virac, *Phil.* 61 E6
Virachei, *Cambodia* 64 F6
Virago Sd., *Canada* 104 C2
Viramgam, *India* 68 H5
Viranşehir, *Turkey* 70 B3
Virawah, *Pakistan* 68 G4
Virbalis, *Lithuania* 44 D9
Virden, *Canada* 105 D8
Vire, *France* 18 D6
Vire →, *France* 18 C5
Vírgenes, C., *Argentina* 128 G3
Virgin →, *U.S.A.* 115 H6
Virgin Gorda, *Br. Virgin Is.* 121 C7
Virgin Is. (British) ■, *W. Indies* 121 C7
Virgin Is. (U.S.) ■, *W. Indies* 121 C7
Virginia, *S. Africa* 88 D4
Virginia, *U.S.A.* 112 B8
Virginia □, *U.S.A.* 108 G7
Virginia Beach, *U.S.A.* 108 G8
Virginia City, *Mont., U.S.A.* 114 D8
Virginia City, *Nev., U.S.A.* 116 F7
Virginia Falls, *Canada* 104 A3
Virginiatown, *Canada* 102 C4
Virje, *Croatia* 29 B13
Viroqua, *U.S.A.* 112 D9
Virovitica, *Croatia* 42 E2
Virpazar, *Montenegro, Yug.* 40 D3
Virpur, *India* 68 J4
Virserum, *Sweden* 11 G9
Virton, *Belgium* 17 E5
Virudunagar, *India* 66 Q10
Vis, *Croatia* 29 E13
Visalia, *U.S.A.* 116 J7
Visayan Sea, *Phil.* 61 F5
Visby, *Sweden* 11 G12
Viscount Melville Sd., *Canada* 4 B2
Visé, *Belgium* 17 D5
Višegrad, *Bos.-H.* 42 G4
Viseu, *Brazil* 125 D9
Viseu, *Portugal* 34 E3
Viseu □, *Portugal* 34 E3
Vişeu de Sus, *Romania* 43 C9
Vishakhapatnam, *India* 67 L13
Vişina, *Romania* 43 G9
Vişineşti, *Moldova* 43 D13
Visingsö, *Sweden* 11 F8
Viskafors, *Sweden* 11 G6
Viskan →, *Sweden* 11 G6
Viški Kanal, *Croatia* 29 E13
Vislanda, *Sweden* 11 H8
Visnagar, *India* 68 H5
Višnja Gora, *Slovenia* 29 C11
Viso, Mte., *Italy* 28 D4
Viso del Marqués, *Spain* 35 G7
Visoko, *Bos.-H.* 42 G3
Visokoi I., *Antarctica* 5 B1
Visp, *Switz.* 25 J3
Vissefjärda, *Sweden* 11 H9
Visselhövede, *Germany* 24 C5
Vissenbjerg, *Denmark* 11 J4
Vista, *U.S.A.* 117 M9
Vistonikos, Ormos = Vistonís, Límni, *Greece* 41 E9
Vistonís, Límni, *Greece* 41 E9
Vistula = Wisła →, *Poland* 44 D5
Vit →, *Bulgaria* 41 C8
Vitanje, *Slovenia* 29 B12
Vitebsk = Vitsyebsk, *Belarus* 46 E6
Viterbo, *Italy* 29 F9
Vitez, *Bos.-H.* 42 F2
Viti Levu, *Fiji* 91 C7
Vitigudino, *Spain* 34 D4
Vitim, *Russia* 51 D12
Vitim →, *Russia* 51 D12
Vitina, *Bos.-H.* 29 E14
Vitína, *Greece* 38 D4
Vítkov, *Czech Rep.* 27 B10
Vitória, *Brazil* 125 H10
Vitória da Conquista, *Brazil* 125 F10
Vitória de São Antão, *Brazil* 125 E11
Vitoria-Gasteiz, *Spain* 32 C2
Vitré, *France* 18 D5
Vitry-le-François, *France* 19 D11
Vitry-sur-Seine, *France* 19 D9
Vitsand, *Sweden* 10 D7
Vitsi, Óros, *Greece* 40 F5
Vitsyebsk, *Belarus* 46 E6
Vittaryd, *Sweden* 11 H7
Vitteaux, *France* 19 E11
Vittel, *France* 19 D12
Vittória, *Italy* 31 F7
Vittório Véneto, *Italy* 29 C9
Vittsjö, *Sweden* 11 H7
Viveiro, *Spain* 34 B3
Vivian, *U.S.A.* 113 J8
Viviers, *France* 21 D8
Vivonne, *France* 20 B4
Vizcaíno, Desierto de, *Mexico* 118 B2
Vizcaíno, Sierra, *Mexico* 118 B2
Vizcaya □, *Spain* 32 B2
Vize, *Turkey* 41 E11
Vizianagaram, *India* 67 K13
Vizille, *France* 21 C9
Viziñada, *Croatia* 29 C10
Viziru, *Romania* 43 E12
Vizzini, *Italy* 31 E7
Vlaardingen, *Neths.* 17 C4
Vlădeasa, Vf., *Romania* 42 D7
Vladičin Han, *Serbia, Yug.* 40 D6
Vladikavkaz, *Russia* 49 J7
Vladimir, *Russia* 46 D11
Vladimir Volynskiy = Volodymyr-Volynskyy, *Ukraine* 47 G3
Vladimirci, *Serbia, Yug.* 40 B3
Vladimirovac, *Serbia, Yug.* 42 E5
Vladimirovka, *Russia* 49 F8
Vladimirovo, *Bulgaria* 40 C7
Vladimorvka, *Kazakstan* 48 E10
Vladislavovka, *Ukraine* 47 K8
Vladivostok, *Russia* 51 E14
Vlăhiţa, *Romania* 43 D10
Vlakhiótis, *Greece* 38 E4
Vlasenica, *Bos.-H.* 42 F3
Vlašić, *Bos.-H.* 42 F2
Vlašim, *Czech Rep.* 26 B7
Vlasinsko Jezero, *Serbia, Yug.* 40 D6
Vlasotince, *Serbia, Yug.* 40 D6
Vlieland, *Neths.* 17 A4
Vlissingen, *Neths.* 17 C3
Vlorë, *Albania* 40 F3
Vlorës, Gjiri i, *Albania* 40 F3
Vltava →, *Czech Rep.* 26 A7
Vo Dat, *Vietnam* 65 G6
Vobarno, *Italy* 28 C7
Voćin, *Croatia* 42 E2
Vöcklabruck, *Austria* 26 C6
Vodice, *Croatia* 29 E12
Vodňany, *Czech Rep.* 26 B7
Vodnjan, *Croatia* 29 D10
Voe, *U.K.* 14 A7
Vogel Pk., *Nigeria* 83 D7
Vogelkop = Doberai, Jazirah, *Indonesia* 63 E8
Vogelsberg, *Germany* 24 E5
Voghera, *Italy* 28 D6
Vohibinany, *Madag.* 89 B8
Vohilava, *Madag.* 89 C8
Vohimarina = Iharana, *Madag.* 89 A9
Vohimena, Tanjon' i, *Madag.* 89 D8
Vohipeno, *Madag.* 89 C8
Voi, *Kenya* 86 C4
Void-Vacon, *France* 19 D12
Voineşti, *Iaşi, Romania* 43 C12
Voineşti, *Prahova, Romania* 43 E10
Voïotía □, *Greece* 38 C5
Voiron, *France* 21 C9
Voisey B., *Canada* 103 A7
Voitsberg, *Austria* 26 D8
Vojens, *Denmark* 11 J3
Vojmsjön, *Sweden* 8 D17
Vojnić, *Croatia* 29 C12
Vojnik, *Italy* 29 B12
Vojvodina □, *Serbia, Yug.* 42 E5
Vokhtoga, *Russia* 46 C11
Volary, *Czech Rep.* 26 C6
Volborg, *U.S.A.* 112 C2
Volcano Is. = Kazan-Rettō, *Pac. Oc.* 96 E6
Volchansk = Vovchansk, *Ukraine* 47 G9
Volchya →, *Ukraine* 47 H8
Volda, *Norway* 9 E12
Volga, *Russia* 46 C10
Volga →, *Russia* 49 G9
Volga Hts. = Privolzhskaya Vozvyshennost, *Russia* 48 E7
Volgo-Baltiyskiy Kanal, *Russia* 46 B9
Volgo-Donskoy Kanal, *Russia* 49 F7
Volgodonsk, *Russia* 49 G6
Volgograd, *Russia* 49 F7
Volgogradskoye Vdkhr., *Russia* 48 E8
Volgorechensk, *Russia* 48 B5
Volímai, *Greece* 38 D2
Volintiri, *Moldova* 43 D14
Volissós, *Greece* 39 C7
Volkach, *Germany* 25 F6
Völkermarkt, *Austria* 26 E7
Volkhov, *Russia* 46 C7
Volkhov →, *Russia* 46 B7
Völklingen, *Germany* 25 F2
Volkovysk = Vawkavysk, *Belarus* 47 F3
Volksrust, *S. Africa* 89 D4
Volnansk, *Ukraine* 47 H8
Volnovakha, *Ukraine* 47 J9
Volochanka, *Russia* 51 B10
Volodarsk, *Russia* 48 B6
Volodymyr-Volynskyy, *Ukraine* 47 G3
Vologda, *Russia* 46 C10
Volokolamsk, *Russia* 46 D8
Volokonovka, *Russia* 47 G9
Vólos, *Greece* 38 B4
Volosovo, *Russia* 46 C5
Volovets, *Ukraine* 47 H2
Volovo, *Russia* 46 F10
Volozhin = Valozhyn, *Belarus* 46 E4
Volsk, *Russia* 48 D8
Volta □, *Ghana* 83 D5
Volta →, *Ghana* 83 D5
Volta, L., *Ghana* 83 D5
Volta Blanche = White Volta →, *Ghana* 83 D4
Volta Redonda, *Brazil* 127 A7
Voltaire, C., *Australia* 92 B4
Volterra, *Italy* 28 E7
Voltri, *Italy* 28 D5
Volturno →, *Italy* 30 A6
Vólvi, L., *Greece* 40 F7
Volyně, *Czech Rep.* 26 B6
Volzhsk, *Russia* 48 C9
Volzhskiy, *Russia* 49 F7
Vondrozo, *Madag.* 89 C8
Vónitsa, *Greece* 38 C2
Vopnafjörður, *Iceland* 8 D6
Vorarlberg □, *Austria* 26 D2
Vóras Óros, *Greece* 40 F5
Vorbasse, *Denmark* 11 J3
Vorchdorf, *Austria* 26 C6
Vorderrhein →, *Switz.* 25 J5
Vordingborg, *Denmark* 11 J5
Vorë, *Albania* 40 E3
Voreio Aigaio = Vórios Aiyaíon □, *Greece* 39 C7
Voreppe, *France* 21 C9
Vóriai Sporádhes, *Greece* 38 B5
Vórios Aiyaíon □, *Greece* 39 C7
Vórios Evvoïkos Kólpos, *Greece* 38 C5
Vorkuta, *Russia* 50 C7
Vormsi, *Estonia* 9 G20
Vorona →, *Russia* 48 E6
Voronezh, *Russia* 47 G10
Voronezh, *Ukraine* 47 G7
Voronezh →, *Russia* 47 G10
Vorontsovo-Aleksandrovskoye = Zelenokumsk, *Russia* 49 H6
Voroshilovgrad = Luhansk, *Ukraine* 47 H10
Voroshilovsk = Alchevsk, *Ukraine* 47 H10
Vórroi, *Greece* 38 F6
Vorskla →, *Ukraine* 47 H8
Võrts Järv, *Estonia* 9 G22
Võru, *Estonia* 9 H22
Vosges, *France* 19 D14
Vosges □, *France* 19 D13
Voskopojë, *Albania* 40 F4
Voskresensk, *Russia* 46 E10
Voskresenskoye, *Russia* 48 B7
Voss, *Norway* 9 F12
Vostok I., *Kiribati* 97 J12
Votice, *Czech Rep.* 26 B7
Votsuri-Shima, *Japan* 55 M1
Vouga →, *Portugal* 34 E2
Vouillé, *France* 18 F7
Voúxa, Ákra, *Greece* 36 D5
Vouzela, *Portugal* 34 E2
Vouziers, *France* 19 C11
Vovchansk, *Ukraine* 47 G9
Vozhe, Ozero, *Russia* 46 B10
Vozhega, *Russia* 46 B11
Voznesensk, *Ukraine* 47 J6
Voznesenye, *Russia* 46 B8
Vrå, *Denmark* 11 G3
Vráble, *Slovak Rep.* 27 C11
Vraćevšnica, *Serbia, Yug.* 40 B4
Vrakhnéïka, *Greece* 38 C3
Vrancea □, *Romania* 43 E11
Vrancei, Munţii, *Romania* 43 E11
Vrangelya, Ostrov, *Russia* 51 B19
Vranica, *Bos.-H.* 42 G2
Vranje, *Serbia, Yug.* 40 D5
Vranjska Banja, *Serbia, Yug.* 40 D6
Vranov nad Topl'ou, *Slovak Rep.* 27 C14
Vransko, *Slovenia* 29 B11
Vransko Jezero, *Croatia* 29 E12
Vrapčište, *Macedonia* 40 E4
Vratsa, *Bulgaria* 40 C7
Vrbas, *Serbia, Yug.* 42 E4
Vrbas →, *Bos.-H.* 42 E2
Vrbnik, *Croatia* 29 C11
Vrbovec, *Croatia* 29 C13
Vrbovsko, *Croatia* 29 C12
Vrchlabí, *Czech Rep.* 26 A8
Vrede, *S. Africa* 89 D4
Vredefort, *S. Africa* 88 D4
Vreden, *Germany* 24 C2
Vredenburg, *S. Africa* 88 E2
Vredendal, *S. Africa* 88 E2
Vretstorp, *Sweden* 10 E8
Vrgorac, *Croatia* 29 E14
Vrhnika, *Slovenia* 29 C11
Vridi, *Ivory C.* 82 D4
Vrigstad, *Sweden* 11 G8
Vrindavan, *India* 68 F7
Vríses, *Greece* 36 D6
Vrnograč, *Bos.-H.* 29 C12
Vrondádhes, *Greece* 39 C8
Vrpolje, *Croatia* 42 E3
Vršac, *Serbia, Yug.* 42 E6
Vrsacki Kanal, *Serbia, Yug.* 42 E5
Vrútky, *Slovak Rep.* 27 B11
Vryburg, *S. Africa* 88 D3
Vryheid, *S. Africa* 89 D5
Vsetín, *Czech Rep.* 27 B11
Vu Liet, *Vietnam* 64 C5
Vůcha →, *Bulgaria* 41 D8
Vučitrn, *Kosovo, Yug.* 40 D4
Vukovar, *Croatia* 42 E3
Vulcan, *Canada* 104 C6
Vulcan, *Romania* 43 E8
Vulcaneşti, *Moldova* 43 E13
Vulcano, *Italy* 31 D7
Vůlchedruma, *Bulgaria* 40 C7
Vulkaneshty = Vulcaneşti, *Moldova* 43 E13
Vunduzi →, *Mozam.* 87 F3
Vung Tau, *Vietnam* 65 G6
Vŭrbitsa, *Bulgaria* 41 D10
Vurshets, *Bulgaria* 40 C7
Vutcani, *Romania* 43 D12
Vuya, *Sudan* 81 F2
Vyartsilya, *Russia* 46 A6
Vyatka = Kirov, *Russia* 50 D5
Vyatka →, *Russia* 48 C10
Vyatskiye Polyany, *Russia* 48 B10
Vyazemskiy, *Russia* 51 E14
Vyazma, *Russia* 46 E8
Vyazniki, *Russia* 48 B6
Vyborg, *Russia* 46 B5
Vychegda →, *Russia* 50 C5
Vychodné Beskydy, *Europe* 27 B15
Vyerkhnyadzvinsk, *Belarus* 46 E4
Vyksa, *Russia* 48 C6
Vylkove, *Ukraine* 47 K5
Vynohradiv, *Ukraine* 47 H2
Vyrnwy, L., *U.K.* 12 E4
Vyshniy Volochek, *Russia* 46 D8
Vyshzha = imeni 26 Bakinskikh Komissarov, *Turkmenistan* 71 B7
Vyškov, *Czech Rep.* 27 B9
Vysoké Mýto, *Czech Rep.* 27 B9
Vysokovsk, *Russia* 46 D9
Vyšší Brod, *Czech Rep.* 26 C7
Vytegra, *Russia* 46 B9

W

W.A.C. Bennett Dam, *Canada* 104 B4
Wa, *Ghana* 82 C4
Waal →, *Neths.* 17 C5
Waalwijk, *Neths.* 17 C5
Waat, *Sudan* 81 F3
Wabana, *Canada* 103 C9
Wabasca →, *Canada* 104 B5
Wabasca-Desmarais, *Canada* 104 B6
Wabash, *U.S.A.* 108 E3
Wabash →, *U.S.A.* 108 G1
Wabi →, *Ethiopia* 81 F5
Wabigoon L., *Canada* 105 D10
Wabowden, *Canada* 105 C9
Wąbrzeźno, *Poland* 45 E5
Wabu Hu, *China* 59 A11
Wabuk Pt., *Canada* 102 A2
Wabush, *Canada* 103 B6
Wąchock, *Poland* 45 G8
Wächtersbach, *Germany* 25 E5
Waco, *U.S.A.* 113 K6
Waconichi, L., *Canada* 102 B5
Wad Ban Naqa, *Sudan* 81 D3
Wad Banda, *Sudan* 81 E2
Wad el Haddad, *Sudan* 81 E3
Wad en Nau, *Sudan* 81 E3
Wad Hamid, *Sudan* 81 D3

Wad Medanî, *Sudan* 81 E3
Wad Thana, *Pakistan* 68 F2
Wadai, *Africa* 76 E5
Wadayama, *Japan* 55 G7
Waddeneilanden, *Neths.* 17 A5
Waddenzee, *Neths.* 17 A5
Waddington, *U.S.A.* 111 B9
Waddington, Mt., *Canada* 104 C3
Waddy Pt., *Australia* 95 C5
Wadebridge, *U.K.* 13 G3
Wadena, *Canada* 105 C8
Wadena, *U.S.A.* 112 B7
Wädenswil, *Switz.* 25 H4
Wadern, *Germany* 25 F2
Wadeye, *Australia* 92 B4
Wadhams, *Canada* 104 C3
Wādī as Sir, *Jordan* 75 D4
Wadi Gemâl, *Egypt* 80 C4
Wadi Halfa, *Sudan* 80 C3
Wadian, *China* 59 A9
Wadlew, *Poland* 45 G6
Wadowice, *Poland* 45 J6
Wadsworth, *Nev., U.S.A.* ... 114 G4
Wadsworth, *Ohio, U.S.A.* ... 110 E3
Waegwan, *S. Korea* 57 G15
Wafangdian, *China* 57 E11
Wafrah, *Si. Arabia* 70 D5
Wageningen, *Neths.* 17 C5
Wager B., *Canada* 101 B11
Wagga Wagga, *Australia* 95 F4
Waghete, *Indonesia* 63 E9
Wagin, *Australia* 93 F2
Wagner, *U.S.A.* 112 D5
Wagon Mound, *U.S.A.* 113 G2
Wagoner, *U.S.A.* 113 H7
Wagrowiec, *Poland* 45 F4
Wah, *Pakistan* 68 C5
Wahai, *Indonesia* 63 E7
Wahiawa, *U.S.A.* 106 H15
Wâḥid, *Egypt* 75 E1
Wahnai, *Afghan.* 68 C1
Wahni, *Ethiopia* 81 E4
Wahoo, *U.S.A.* 112 E6
Wahpeton, *U.S.A.* 112 B6
Waiau →, *N.Z.* 91 K4
Waibeem, *Indonesia* 63 E8
Waiblingen, *Germany* 25 G5
Waidhofen an der Thaya,
   Austria 26 C8
Waidhofen an der Ybbs, *Austria* 26 D7
Waigeo, *Indonesia* 63 E8
Waihi, *N.Z.* 91 G5
Waihou →, *N.Z.* 91 G5
Waika, *Dem. Rep. of the Congo* 86 C2
Waikabubak, *Indonesia* 63 F5
Waikari, *N.Z.* 91 K4
Waikato →, *N.Z.* 91 G5
Waikerie, *Australia* 95 E3
Waikokopu, *N.Z.* 91 H6
Waikouaiti, *N.Z.* 91 L3
Wailuku, *U.S.A.* 106 H16
Waimakariri →, *N.Z.* 91 K4
Waimate, *N.Z.* 91 L3
Wainganga →, *India* 66 K11
Waingapu, *Indonesia* 63 F6
Waini →, *Guyana* 124 B7
Wainwright, *Canada* 105 C6
Waiouru, *N.Z.* 91 H5
Waipara, *N.Z.* 91 K4
Waipawa, *N.Z.* 91 H6
Waipiro, *N.Z.* 91 H7
Waipu, *N.Z.* 91 F5
Waipukurau, *N.Z.* 91 J6
Wairakei, *N.Z.* 91 H6
Wairarapa, L., *N.Z.* 91 J5
Wairoa, *N.Z.* 91 H6
Waitaki →, *N.Z.* 91 L3
Waitara, *N.Z.* 91 H5
Waitsburg, *U.S.A.* 114 C5
Waiuku, *N.Z.* 91 G5
Wajima, *Japan* 55 F8
Wajir, *Kenya* 86 B5
Waka, *Ethiopia* 81 F4
Wakasa, *Japan* 55 G7
Wakasa-Wan, *Japan* 55 G7
Wakatipu, L., *N.Z.* 91 L2
Wakaw, *Canada* 105 C7
Wakayama, *Japan* 55 G7
Wakayama □, *Japan* 55 H7
Wake Forest, *U.S.A.* 109 H6
Wake I., *Pac. Oc.* 96 F8
WaKeeney, *U.S.A.* 112 F5
Wakefield, *N.Z.* 91 J4
Wakefield, *U.K.* 12 D6
Wakefield, *Mass., U.S.A.* .. 111 D13
Wakefield, *Mich., U.S.A.* .. 112 B10
Wakkanai, *Japan* 54 B10
Wakkerstroom, *S. Africa* ... 89 D5
Wakool, *Australia* 95 F3
Wakool →, *Australia* 95 F3
Wakre, *Indonesia* 63 E8
Wakuach, L., *Canada* 103 A6
Walamba, *Zambia* 87 E2
Wałbrzych, *Poland* 45 H3
Walbury Hill, *U.K.* 13 F6
Walcha, *Australia* 95 E5
Walchen, *Neths.* 17 C3
Walcott, *U.S.A.* 114 F10
Wałcz, *Poland* 45 E3
Waldbröl, *Germany* 24 E3
Waldburg Ra., *Australia* ... 93 D2
Waldeck, *Germany* 24 D5
Walden, *Colo., U.S.A.* 114 F10
Walden, *N.Y., U.S.A.* 111 E10
Waldkirch, *Germany* 25 G3
Waldkirchen, *Germany* 25 G4
Waldkraiburg, *Germany* ... 25 G8

Waldport, *U.S.A.* 114 D1
Waldron, *U.S.A.* 113 H7
Waldviertel, *Austria* 26 C8
Walebing, *Australia* 93 F2
Walembele, *Ghana* 82 C4
Walensee, *Switz.* 25 H5
Wales □, *U.K.* 13 E3
Walewale, *Ghana* 83 C4
Walgett, *Australia* 95 E4
Walgreen Coast, *Antarctica* . 5 D15
Walker, *U.S.A.* 112 B7
Walker, L., *Canada* 103 B6
Walker L., *Canada* 105 C9
Walker L., *U.S.A.* 114 G4
Walkerston, *Australia* 94 C4
Walkerton, *Canada* 102 D3
Wall, *U.S.A.* 112 D3
Walla Walla, *U.S.A.* 114 C4
Wallace, *Idaho, U.S.A.* 114 C6
Wallace, *N.C., U.S.A.* 109 H7
Wallaceburg, *Canada* 102 D3
Wallachia = Valahia, *Romania* . 43 F9
Wallal, *Australia* 95 D4
Wallam Cr. →, *Australia* ... 95 D4
Wallambin, L., *Australia* ... 93 F2
Wallangarra, *Australia* 95 D5
Wallaroo, *Australia* 95 E2
Walldürn, *Germany* 25 F5
Wallenhorst, *Germany* 24 C4
Wallenpaupack, L., *U.S.A.* .. 111 E9
Wallingford, *U.S.A.* 111 E12
Wallis & Futuna, Is., *Pac. Oc.* 96 J10
Wallowa, *U.S.A.* 114 D5
Wallowa Mts., *U.S.A.* 114 D5
Walls, *U.K.* 14 A7
Wallula, *U.S.A.* 114 C4
Wallumbilla, *Australia* 95 D4
Walmsley, L., *Canada* 105 A7
Walney, I. of, *U.K.* 12 C4
Walnut Creek, *U.S.A.* 116 H4
Walnut Ridge, *U.S.A.* 113 G9
Walpole, *Australia* 93 F2
Walpole, *U.S.A.* 111 D13
Wals, *Austria* 26 D5
Walsall, *U.K.* 13 E6
Walsenburg, *U.S.A.* 113 G2
Walsh, *U.S.A.* 113 G3
Walsh →, *Australia* 94 B3
Walsrode, *Germany* 24 C5
Walterboro, *U.S.A.* 109 J5
Walters, *U.S.A.* 113 H5
Waltershausen, *Germany* ... 24 E6
Waltham, *U.S.A.* 111 D13
Waltman, *U.S.A.* 114 E10
Walton, *U.S.A.* 111 D9
Walton-on-the-Naze, *U.K.* .. 13 F9
Walvis Bay, *Namibia* 88 C1
Walvisbaai = Walvis Bay,
   Namibia 88 C1
Wamba, *Dem. Rep. of the Congo* 86 B2
Wamba, *Kenya* 86 B4
Wamba, *Nigeria* 83 D6
Wamego, *U.S.A.* 112 F6
Wamena, *Indonesia* 63 E9
Wamsutter, *U.S.A.* 114 F9
Wamulan, *Indonesia* 63 E7
Wan Xian, *China* 56 E8
Wana, *Pakistan* 68 C3
Wanaaring, *Australia* 95 D3
Wanaka, *N.Z.* 91 L2
Wanaka L., *N.Z.* 91 L2
Wan'an, *China* 59 D10
Wanapitei L., *Canada* 102 C3
Wandel Sea = McKinley Sea,
   Arctic 4 A7
Wandérama, *Ivory C.* 82 D4
Wanderer, *Zimbabwe* 87 F3
Wandhari, *Pakistan* 68 F2
Wanding, *China* 58 E2
Wandoan, *Australia* 95 D4
Wanfu, *China* 57 D12
Wang →, *Thailand* 64 D2
Wang Kai, *Sudan* 81 F2
Wang Noi, *Thailand* 64 E3
Wang Saphung, *Thailand* ... 64 D3
Wang Thong, *Thailand* 64 D3
Wanga, *Dem. Rep. of the Congo* 86 B2
Wangal, *Indonesia* 63 F8
Wanganella, *Australia* 95 F3
Wanganui, *N.Z.* 91 H5
Wangaratta, *Australia* 95 F4
Wangary, *Australia* 95 E2
Wangcang, *China* 58 A6
Wangcheng, *China* 59 C9
Wangdu, *China* 56 E8
Wangen, *Germany* 25 H5
Wangerooge, *Germany* 24 B3
Wangi, *Kenya* 86 C5
Wangiwangi, *Indonesia* 63 F6
Wangjiang, *China* 59 B11
Wangmo, *China* 58 E6
Wangolodougou, *Ivory C.* .. 82 D3
Wangqing, *China* 57 C15
Wankaner, *India* 68 H4
Wanless, *Canada* 105 C8
Wannian, *China* 59 C11
Wanning, *China* 64 D2
Wanon Niwat, *Thailand* ... 64 D4
Wanquan, *China* 56 D8
Wanrong, *China* 56 G6
Wanshan, *China* 58 D7
Wanshengchang, *China* 58 C6
Wantage, *U.K.* 13 F6
Wanyuan, *China* 58 A7
Wanzai, *China* 59 C10
Wapakoneta, *U.S.A.* 108 E3
Wapato, *U.S.A.* 114 C3

Wapawekka L., *Canada* 105 C8
Wapikopa L., *Canada* 102 B2
Wapiti →, *Canada* 104 B5
Wappingers Falls, *U.S.A.* .. 111 E11
Wapsipinicon →, *U.S.A.* ... 112 E9
Warab □, *Sudan* 81 F2
Warangal, *India* 66 L11
Waraseoni, *India* 69 J9
Waratah, *Australia* 94 G4
Waratah B., *Australia* 95 F4
Warburg, *Germany* 24 D5
Warburton, *Vic., Australia* . 95 F4
Warburton, *W. Austral.,
   Australia* 93 E4
Warburton Ra., *Australia* .. 93 E4
Ward, *N.Z.* 91 J5
Ward →, *Australia* 95 D4
Ward Mt., *U.S.A.* 116 H8
Warden, *S. Africa* 89 D4
Wardha, *India* 66 J11
Wardha →, *India* 66 K11
Ware, *Canada* 104 B3
Ware, *U.S.A.* 111 D12
Waregem, *Belgium* 17 D3
Wareham, *U.S.A.* 111 E14
Waremme, *Belgium* 17 D5
Waren, *Germany* 24 B8
Warendorf, *Germany* 24 D4
Warialda, *Australia* 95 D5
Wariap, *Indonesia* 63 E8
Warin Chamrap, *Thailand* .. 64 E5
Warka, *Poland* 45 G8
Warkopi, *Indonesia* 63 E8
Warm Springs, *U.S.A.* 115 G5
Warman, *Canada* 105 C7
Warmbad, *Namibia* 88 D2
Warmbad, *S. Africa* 89 C4
Warmińsko-Mazurskie □,
   Poland 44 D8
Warminster, *U.K.* 13 F5
Warminster, *U.S.A.* 111 F9
Warnemünde, *Germany* 24 A8
Warner Mts., *U.S.A.* 114 F3
Warner Robins, *U.S.A.* 109 J4
Warnow →, *Germany* 24 A8
Waroona, *Australia* 93 F2
Warracknabeal, *Australia* .. 95 F3
Warragul, *Australia* 95 F4
Warrego →, *Australia* 95 E4
Warrego Ra., *Australia* 94 C4
Warren, *Australia* 95 E4
Warren, *Ark., U.S.A.* 113 J8
Warren, *Mich., U.S.A.* 108 D4
Warren, *Minn., U.S.A.* 112 A6
Warren, *Ohio, U.S.A.* 110 E4
Warren, *Pa., U.S.A.* 110 E5
Warrenpoint, *U.K.* 15 B5
Warrensburg, *Mo., U.S.A.* . 112 F8
Warrensburg, *N.Y., U.S.A.* . 111 C11
Warrenton, *S. Africa* 88 D3
Warrenton, *U.S.A.* 116 D3
Warri, *Nigeria* 83 D6
Warrina, *Australia* 95 D2
Warrington, *U.K.* 12 D5
Warrington, *U.S.A.* 109 K2
Warrington □, *U.K.* 12 D5
Warrnambool, *Australia* ... 95 F3
Warroad, *U.S.A.* 112 A7
Warruwi, *Australia* 94 A1
Warsa, *Indonesia* 63 E9
Warsak Dam, *Pakistan* 68 B4
Warsaw = Warszawa, *Poland* . 45 F8
Warsaw, *Ind., U.S.A.* 108 E3
Warsaw, *N.Y., U.S.A.* 110 D6
Warsaw, *Ohio, U.S.A.* 110 F3
Warstein, *Germany* 24 D4
Warszawa, *Poland* 45 F8
Warta, *Poland* 45 G5
Warta →, *Poland* 45 F1
Warthe = Warta →, *Poland* . 45 F1
Waru, *Indonesia* 63 E8
Warwick, *Australia* 95 D5
Warwick, *U.K.* 13 E6
Warwick, *N.Y., U.S.A.* 111 E10
Warwick, *R.I., U.S.A.* 111 E13
Warwickshire □, *U.K.* 13 E6
Wasaga Beach, *Canada* 110 B4
Wasagaming, *Canada* 105 C9
Wasatch Ra., *U.S.A.* 114 F8
Wasbank, *S. Africa* 89 D5
Wasco, *Calif., U.S.A.* 117 K7
Wasco, *Oreg., U.S.A.* 114 D3
Wase, *Nigeria* 83 D6
Waseca, *U.S.A.* 112 C8
Wasekamio L., *Canada* 105 B7
Wash, The, *U.K.* 12 E8
Washago, *Canada* 110 B5
Washburn, *N. Dak., U.S.A.* . 112 B4
Washburn, *Wis., U.S.A.* ... 112 B9
Washim, *India* 66 J10
Washington, *U.K.* 12 C6
Washington, *D.C., U.S.A.* .. 108 F7
Washington, *Ga., U.S.A.* ... 109 J4
Washington, *Ind., U.S.A.* .. 108 F2
Washington, *Iowa, U.S.A.* . 112 E9
Washington, *Mo., U.S.A.* .. 112 F9
Washington, *N.C., U.S.A.* . 109 H7
Washington, *N.J., U.S.A.* .. 111 F10
Washington, *Pa., U.S.A.* .. 110 F4
Washington, *Utah, U.S.A.* . 115 H7
Washington □, *U.S.A.* 114 C3
Washington, *Mt., U.S.A.* .. 111 B13
Washington Court House,
   U.S.A. 108 F4
Washington I., *U.S.A.* 108 C2
Washougal, *U.S.A.* 116 E4
Wasian, *Indonesia* 63 E8

Wasilków, *Poland* 45 E10
Wasilla, *U.S.A.* 100 B5
Wasior, *Indonesia* 63 E8
Waskaganish, *Canada* 102 B4
Waskaiowaka, L., *Canada* .. 105 B9
Waskesiu Lake, *Canada* 105 C7
Wasserburg, *Germany* 25 G8
Wasserkuppe, *Germany* 24 E5
Wassy, *France* 19 D11
Waswanipi, *Canada* 102 C4
Waswanipi, L., *Canada* 102 C4
Watampone, *Indonesia* 63 E6
Water Park Pt., *Australia* .. 94 C5
Water Valley, *U.S.A.* 113 H10
Waterberge, *S. Africa* 89 C4
Waterbury, *Conn., U.S.A.* .. 111 E11
Waterbury, *Vt., U.S.A.* 111 B12
Waterbury L., *Canada* 105 B8
Waterdown, *Canada* 110 C5
Waterford, *Canada* 110 D4
Waterford, *Ireland* 15 D4
Waterford, *Calif., U.S.A.* .. 116 H6
Waterford, *Pa., U.S.A.* 110 E5
Waterford □, *Ireland* 15 D4
Waterford Harbour, *Ireland* . 15 D5
Waterhen L., *Canada* 105 C9
Wateringen, *Belgium* 17 D4
Waterloo, *Ont., Canada* ... 102 D3
Waterloo, *Qué., Canada* ... 111 A12
Waterloo, *S. Leone* 82 D2
Waterloo, *S. Africa* 89 D5
Waterloo, *Ill., U.S.A.* 112 F9
Waterloo, *Iowa, U.S.A.* ... 112 D8
Waterloo, *N.Y., U.S.A.* ... 110 D8
Watersmeet, *U.S.A.* 112 B10
Waterton Lakes Nat. Park,
   U.S.A. 114 B7
Watertown, *Conn., U.S.A.* . 111 E11
Watertown, *N.Y., U.S.A.* .. 111 C9
Watertown, *S. Dak., U.S.A.* . 112 C6
Watertown, *Wis., U.S.A.* .. 112 D10
Waterval-Boven, *S. Africa* . 89 D5
Waterville, *Canada* 111 A13
Waterville, *Maine, U.S.A.* .. 109 C11
Waterville, *N.Y., U.S.A.* .. 111 D9
Waterville, *Pa., U.S.A.* 110 E7
Waterville, *Wash., U.S.A.* . 114 C3
Watervliet, *U.S.A.* 111 D11
Wates, *Indonesia* 63 G14
Watford, *Canada* 110 D3
Watford, *U.K.* 13 F7
Watford City, *U.S.A.* 112 B3
Wathaman →, *Canada* 105 B8
Wathaman L., *Canada* 105 B8
Watheroo, *Australia* 93 F2
Wating, *China* 56 G4
Watkins Glen, *U.S.A.* 110 D8
Watling I. = San Salvador I.,
   Bahamas 121 B5
Watonga, *U.S.A.* 113 H5
Watrous, *Canada* 105 C7
Watrous, *U.S.A.* 113 H2
Watsa, *Dem. Rep. of the Congo* 86 B2
Watseka, *U.S.A.* 108 E2
Watson, *Australia* 93 F5
Watson, *Canada* 105 C8
Watson Lake, *Canada* 104 A3
Watsontown, *U.S.A.* 110 E8
Watsonville, *U.S.A.* 116 J5
Wattiwarriganna Cr. →,
   Australia 95 D2
Wattwil, *Switz.* 25 H5
Watuata = Batuata, *Indonesia* . 63 F6
Watubela, Kepulauan, *Indonesia* 63 E8
Watubela Is. = Watubela,
   Kepulauan, *Indonesia* ... 63 E8
Wau = Wâw, *Sudan* 81 F2
Waubamik, *Canada* 110 A4
Waubay, *U.S.A.* 112 C6
Wauchope, *N.S.W., Australia* . 95 E5
Wauchope, *N. Terr., Australia* . 94 C1
Wauchula, *U.S.A.* 109 M5
Waukarlycarly, L., *Australia* . 92 D3
Waukegan, *U.S.A.* 108 D2
Waukesha, *U.S.A.* 108 D1
Waukon, *U.S.A.* 112 D9
Waupaca, *U.S.A.* 112 C10
Waupun, *U.S.A.* 112 D10
Waurika, *U.S.A.* 113 H6
Wausau, *U.S.A.* 112 C10
Wautoma, *U.S.A.* 112 C10
Wauwatosa, *U.S.A.* 108 D2
Waveney →, *U.K.* 13 E9
Waverley, *N.Z.* 91 H5
Waverly, *Iowa, U.S.A.* 112 D8
Waverly, *N.Y., U.S.A.* 111 E8
Wavre, *Belgium* 17 D4
Wâw, *Sudan* 81 F2
Wâw al Kabîr, *Libya* 79 C9
Wawa, *Canada* 102 C3
Wawa, *Nigeria* 83 D5
Wawa, *Sudan* 80 C3
Wawanesa, *Canada* 105 D9
Wawona, *U.S.A.* 116 H7
Waxahachie, *U.S.A.* 113 J6
Way, L., *Australia* 93 E3
Waycross, *U.S.A.* 109 K4
Wayi, *Sudan* 81 F3
Wayland, *U.S.A.* 110 D7
Wayne, *Nebr., U.S.A.* 112 D6
Wayne, *W. Va., U.S.A.* ... 108 F4
Waynesboro, *Ga., U.S.A.* .. 109 J4
Waynesboro, *Miss., U.S.A.* . 109 K1
Waynesboro, *Pa., U.S.A.* .. 108 F7
Waynesboro, *Va., U.S.A.* .. 108 F6
Waynesburg, *U.S.A.* 108 F5
Waynesville, *U.S.A.* 109 H4
Waynoka, *U.S.A.* 113 G5

Wazirabad, *Pakistan* 68 C6
Wda →, *Poland* 44 E5
We, *Indonesia* 62 C1
Weald, The, *U.K.* 13 F8
Wear →, *U.K.* 12 C6
Weatherford, *Okla., U.S.A.* . 113 H5
Weatherford, *Tex., U.S.A.* . 113 J6
Weaverville, *U.S.A.* 114 F2
Webb City, *U.S.A.* 113 G7
Webequie, *Canada* 102 B2
Webo = Nyaake, *Liberia* ... 82 E3
Webster, *Mass., U.S.A.* ... 111 D13
Webster, *N.Y., U.S.A.* 110 C7
Webster, *S. Dak., U.S.A.* .. 112 C6
Webster City, *U.S.A.* 112 D8
Webster Springs, *U.S.A.* .. 108 F5
Weda, *Indonesia* 63 D7
Weda, Teluk, *Indonesia* ... 63 D7
Weddell I., *Falk. Is.* 128 G4
Weddell Sea, *Antarctica* ... 5 D1
Wedderburn, *Australia* 95 F3
Wedel, *Germany* 24 B5
Wedemark, *Germany* 24 C5
Wedgeport, *Canada* 103 D6
Wedza, *Zimbabwe* 87 F3
Wee Waa, *Australia* 95 E4
Weed, *U.S.A.* 114 F2
Weed Heights, *U.S.A.* 116 G7
Weedsport, *U.S.A.* 111 C8
Weedville, *U.S.A.* 110 E6
Weenen, *S. Africa* 89 D5
Weener, *Germany* 24 B3
Weert, *Neths.* 17 C5
Węgierska-Górka, *Poland* .. 45 J6
Węgliniec, *Poland* 45 G2
Węgorzewo, *Poland* 44 D8
Węgorzyno, *Poland* 44 E2
Węgrów, *Poland* 45 F9
Wehda □, *Sudan* 81 F2
Wei He →, *Hebei, China* .. 56 F8
Wei He →, *Shaanxi, China* . 56 G6
Weichang, *China* 57 D9
Weichuan, *China* 56 G7
Weida, *Germany* 24 E8
Weiden, *Germany* 25 F8
Weifang, *China* 57 F10
Weihai, *China* 57 F12
Weil, *Germany* 25 H3
Weilburg, *Germany* 24 E4
Weilheim, *Germany* 25 H7
Weimar, *Germany* 24 E7
Weinan, *China* 56 G5
Weingarten, *Germany* 25 H5
Weinheim, *Germany* 25 F4
Weining, *China* 58 D5
Weipa, *Australia* 94 A3
Weir →, *Australia* 95 D4
Weir →, *Canada* 105 B10
Weir River, *Canada* 105 B10
Weirton, *U.S.A.* 110 F4
Weiser, *U.S.A.* 114 D5
Weishan, *Shandong, China* . 57 G9
Weishan, *Yunnan, China* .. 58 E3
Weissenburg, *Germany* 25 F6
Weissenfels, *Germany* 24 D8
Weisswasser, *Germany* 24 D10
Wéitra, *Austria* 26 C7
Weixi, *China* 58 D2
Weixin, *China* 58 D5
Weiyuan, *China* 56 G3
Weiz, *Austria* 26 D8
Weizhou Dao, *China* 58 G7
Wejherowo, *Poland* 44 D5
Wekusko L., *Canada* 105 C9
Welch, *U.S.A.* 108 G5
Weldya, *Ethiopia* 81 E4
Welega □, *Ethiopia* 81 F3
Welkite, *Ethiopia* 81 F4
Welkom, *S. Africa* 88 D4
Welland, *Canada* 102 D4
Welland →, *U.K.* 13 E7
Wellesley Is., *Australia* 94 B2
Wellingborough, *U.K.* 13 E7
Wellington, *Australia* 95 E4
Wellington, *Canada* 110 C7
Wellington, *N.Z.* 91 J5
Wellington, *S. Africa* 88 E2
Wellington, *Somst., U.K.* .. 13 G4
Wellington, Telford & Wrekin,
   U.K. 13 E5
Wellington, *Colo., U.S.A.* .. 112 E2
Wellington, *Kans., U.S.A.* .. 113 G6
Wellington, *Nev., U.S.A.* .. 116 G7
Wellington, *Ohio, U.S.A.* .. 110 E2
Wellington, *Tex., U.S.A.* .. 113 H4
Wellington, I., *Chile* 122 F2
Wellington, L., *Australia* .. 95 F4
Wells, *U.K.* 13 F5
Wells, *Maine, U.S.A.* 111 C10
Wells, *Nev., U.S.A.* 114 F6
Wells, L., *Australia* 93 E3
Wells, Mt., *Australia* 92 C4
Wells Gray Prov. Park, *Canada* 104 C4
Wells-next-the-Sea, *U.K.* .. 12 E8
Wells River, *U.S.A.* 111 B12
Wellsboro, *U.S.A.* 110 E7
Wellsburg, *U.S.A.* 110 F4
Wellsville, *N.Y., U.S.A.* ... 110 D7
Wellsville, *Ohio, U.S.A.* ... 110 F4
Wellsville, *Utah, U.S.A.* ... 114 F8
Wellton, *U.S.A.* 115 K6
Welmel, Wabi →, *Ethiopia* . 81 F5
Welo □, *Ethiopia* 81 E4
Wels, *Austria* 26 C7
Welshpool, *U.K.* 13 E4
Welwyn Garden City, *U.K.* . 13 F7

Wem, U.K. 12 E5
Wembere →, Tanzania 86 C3
Wemindji, Canada 102 B4
Wen Xian, China 56 G7
Wenatchee, U.S.A. 114 C3
Wenchang, China 64 C8
Wencheng, China 59 D13
Wenchi, Ghana 82 D4
Wenchow = Wenzhou, China 59 D13
Wenchuan, China 58 B4
Wenden, U.S.A. 117 M13
Wendeng, China 57 F12
Wendesi, Indonesia 63 E8
Wendo, Ethiopia 81 F4
Wendover, U.S.A. 114 F6
Weng'an, China 58 D6
Wengcheng, China 59 E9
Wengyuan, China 59 E10
Wenjiang, China 58 B4
Wenling, China 59 C13
Wenlock →, Australia 94 A3
Wenshan, China 58 F5
Wenshang, China 56 G9
Wenshui, China 56 F7
Wensleydale, U.K. 12 C6
Wensu, China 60 B3
Wensum →, U.K. 12 E8
Wentworth, Australia 95 E3
Wentzel L., Canada 104 B6
Wenut, Indonesia 63 E8
Wenxi, China 56 G6
Wenxian, China 56 H3
Wenzhou, China 59 D13
Weott, U.S.A. 114 F2
Wepener, S. Africa 88 D4
Werda, Botswana 88 D3
Werdau, Germany 24 E8
Werder, Germany 24 C8
Werdohl, Germany 24 D3
Wereilu, Ethiopia 81 E4
Weri, Indonesia 63 E8
Werneck, Germany 25 F6
Wernigerode, Germany 24 D6
Werra →, Germany 24 D5
Werrimull, Australia 95 E3
Werris Creek, Australia 95 E5
Wertach →, Germany 25 G6
Wertheim, Germany 25 F5
Wertingen, Germany 25 G6
Wesel, Germany 24 D2
Weser →, Germany 24 B4
Weser-Ems □, Germany 24 C3
Weserbergland, Germany 24 C5
Wesiri, Indonesia 63 F7
Weslemkoon L., Canada 110 A7
Wesleyville, Canada 103 C9
Wesleyville, U.S.A. 110 D4
Wessel, C., Australia 94 A2
Wessel Is., Australia 94 A2
Wesselburen, Germany 24 A4
Wessington Springs, U.S.A. 112 C5
West, U.S.A. 113 K6
West →, U.S.A. 111 D12
West Baines →, Australia 92 C4
West Bank □, Asia 75 C4
West Bend, U.S.A. 108 D1
West Bengal □, India 69 H13
West Berkshire □, U.K. 13 F6
West Beskids = Západné Beskydy, Europe 27 B12
West Branch, U.S.A. 108 C3
West Branch Susquehanna →, U.S.A. 111 F8
West Bromwich, U.K. 13 E6
West Burra, U.K. 14 A7
West Canada Cr. →, U.S.A. 111 C10
West Cape Howe, Australia 93 G2
West Chazy, U.S.A. 111 B11
West Chester, U.S.A. 111 G9
West Columbia, U.S.A. 113 L7
West Covina, U.S.A. 117 L9
West Des Moines, U.S.A. 112 E8
West Dunbartonshire □, U.K. 14 F4
West End, Bahamas 120 A4
West Falkland, Falk. Is. 122 J4
West Fargo, U.S.A. 112 B6
West Farmington, U.S.A. 110 E4
West Fjord = Vestfjorden, Norway 8 C15
West Fork Trinity →, U.S.A. 113 J6
West Frankfort, U.S.A. 112 G10
West Hartford, U.S.A. 111 E12
West Haven, U.S.A. 111 E12
West Hazleton, U.S.A. 111 F9
West Helena, U.S.A. 113 H9
West Hurley, U.S.A. 111 E10
West Ice Shelf, Antarctica 5 C7
West Indies, Cent. Amer. 121 D7
West Jordan, U.S.A. 114 F8
West Lorne, Canada 110 D3
West Lothian □, U.K. 14 F5
West Lunga →, Zambia 87 E1
West Memphis, U.S.A. 113 H9
West Midlands □, U.K. 13 E6
West Mifflin, U.S.A. 110 F5
West Milton, U.S.A. 110 E8
West Monroe, U.S.A. 113 J8
West Newton, U.S.A. 110 F5
West Nicholson, Zimbabwe 87 G2
West Palm Beach, U.S.A. 109 M5
West Plains, U.S.A. 113 G9
West Point, N.Y., U.S.A. 111 E11
West Point, Nebr., U.S.A. 112 E6
West Point, Va., U.S.A. 108 G7
West Pt. = Ouest, Pte. de l', Canada 103 C7
West Pt., Australia 95 F2
West Road →, Canada 104 C4
West Rutland, U.S.A. 111 C11
West Schelde = Westerschelde →, Neths. 17 C3
West Seneca, U.S.A. 110 D6
West Siberian Plain, Russia 52 C11
West Sussex □, U.K. 13 G7
West-Terschelling, Neths. 17 A5
West Valley City, U.S.A. 114 F8
West Virginia □, U.S.A. 108 F5
West-Vlaanderen □, Belgium 17 D2
West Walker →, U.S.A. 116 G7
West Wyalong, Australia 95 E4
West Yellowstone, U.S.A. 114 D8
West Yorkshire □, U.K. 12 D6
Westall Pt., Australia 95 E1
Westbrook, U.S.A. 109 D10
Westbury, Australia 94 G4
Westby, U.S.A. 112 A2
Westend, U.S.A. 117 K9
Westerland, Germany 9 J13
Westerly, U.S.A. 111 E13
Western □, Ghana 82 D4
Western □, Kenya 86 B3
Western □, S. Leone 82 D2
Western □, Zambia 87 F1
Western Australia □, Australia 93 E2
Western Cape □, S. Africa 88 E3
Western Dvina = Daugava →, Latvia 9 H21
Western Ghats, India 66 N9
Western Isles □, U.K. 14 D1
Western Sahara ■, Africa 78 D3
Western Samoa = Samoa ■, Pac. Oc. 91 B13
Westernport, U.S.A. 108 F6
Westerschelde →, Neths. 17 C3
Westerstede, Germany 24 B3
Westerwald, Germany 24 E3
Westfield, Mass., U.S.A. 111 D12
Westfield, N.Y., U.S.A. 110 D5
Westfield, Pa., U.S.A. 110 E7
Westhill, U.K. 14 D6
Westhope, U.S.A. 112 A4
Westland Bight, N.Z. 91 K3
Westlock, Canada 104 C6
Westmar, Australia 95 D4
Westmeath □, Ireland 15 C4
Westminster, U.S.A. 108 F7
Westmont, U.S.A. 110 F6
Westmorland, U.S.A. 117 M11
Weston, Oreg., U.S.A. 114 D4
Weston, W. Va., U.S.A. 108 F5
Weston I., Canada 102 B4
Weston-super-Mare, U.K. 13 F5
Westover, U.S.A. 110 F6
Westport, Canada 111 B8
Westport, Ireland 15 C2
Westport, N.Z. 91 J3
Westport, N.Y., U.S.A. 111 B11
Westport, Oreg., U.S.A. 116 D3
Westport, Wash., U.S.A. 116 D2
Westray, Canada 105 C8
Westray, U.K. 14 B5
Westree, Canada 102 C3
Westville, U.S.A. 116 F6
Westwood, U.S.A. 114 F3
Wetar, Indonesia 63 F7
Wetaskiwin, Canada 104 C6
Wete, Tanzania 84 F7
Wetherby, U.K. 12 D6
Wethersfield, U.S.A. 111 E12
Wetteren, Belgium 17 D3
Wetzlar, Germany 24 E4
Wewoka, U.S.A. 113 H6
Wexford, Ireland 15 D5
Wexford □, Ireland 15 D5
Wexford Harbour, Ireland 15 D5
Weyburn, Canada 105 D8
Weyer Markt, Austria 26 D7
Weyhe, Germany 24 C4
Weyib →, Ethiopia 81 F5
Weymouth, Canada 103 D6
Weymouth, U.K. 13 G5
Weymouth, U.S.A. 111 D14
Weymouth, C., Australia 94 A3
Wha Ti, Canada 100 B8
Whakatane, N.Z. 91 G6
Whale →, Canada 103 A6
Whale Cove, Canada 105 A10
Whales, B. of, Antarctica 5 D12
Whalsay, U.K. 14 A8
Whangamomona, N.Z. 91 H5
Whangarei, N.Z. 91 F5
Whangarei Harb., N.Z. 91 F5
Wharfe →, U.K. 12 D6
Wharfedale, U.K. 12 C5
Wharton, N.J., U.S.A. 111 F10
Wharton, Pa., U.S.A. 110 E6
Wharton, Tex., U.S.A. 113 L6
Wheatland, Calif., U.S.A. 116 F5
Wheatland, Wyo., U.S.A. 112 D2
Wheatley, Canada 110 D2
Wheaton, Md., U.S.A. 108 F7
Wheaton, Minn., U.S.A. 112 C6
Wheelbarrow Pk., U.S.A. 116 H10
Wheeler, Oreg., U.S.A. 114 D2
Wheeler, Tex., U.S.A. 113 H4
Wheeler →, Canada 103 A6
Wheeler L., U.S.A. 109 H2
Wheeler Pk., N. Mex., U.S.A. 115 H11
Wheeler Pk., Nev., U.S.A. 115 G6
Wheeler Ridge, U.S.A. 117 L8
Wheeling, U.S.A. 110 F4
Whernside, U.K. 12 C5
Whiskey Jack L., Canada 105 B8
Whistleduck Cr. →, Australia 94 C2
Whistler, Canada 104 C4
Whitby, Canada 110 C6
Whitby, U.K. 12 C7
White →, Ark., U.S.A. 113 J9
White →, Ind., U.S.A. 108 F2
White →, S. Dak., U.S.A. 112 D5
White →, Tex., U.S.A. 113 J4
White →, Utah, U.S.A. 114 F9
White →, Vt., U.S.A. 111 C12
White →, Wash., U.S.A. 116 C4
White, L., Australia 92 D4
White B., Canada 103 C8
White Bird, U.S.A. 114 D5
White Butte, U.S.A. 112 B3
White City, U.S.A. 114 E2
White Cliffs, Australia 95 E3
White Hall, U.S.A. 112 F9
White Haven, U.S.A. 111 E9
White Horse, Vale of, U.K. 13 F6
White I., N.Z. 91 G6
White L., Canada 111 A8
White L., U.S.A. 113 L8
White Mountain Peak, U.S.A. 115 G4
White Mts., Calif., U.S.A. 116 H8
White Mts., N.H., U.S.A. 111 B13
White Nile = Nîl el Abyad →, Sudan 81 D3
White Nile Dam = Khazzān Jabal al Awliyā, Sudan 81 D3
White Otter L., Canada 102 C1
White Pass, U.S.A. 116 D5
White Plains, U.S.A. 111 E11
White River, Canada 102 C2
White River, S. Africa 89 D5
White River, U.S.A. 112 D4
White Rock, Canada 116 A4
White Russia = Belarus ■, Europe 46 F4
White Sea = Beloye More, Russia 50 C4
White Sulphur Springs, Mont., U.S.A. 114 C8
White Sulphur Springs, W. Va., U.S.A. 108 G5
White Swan, U.S.A. 116 D6
White Volta →, Ghana 83 D4
Whitecliffs, N.Z. 91 K3
Whitecourt, Canada 104 C5
Whiteface Mt., U.S.A. 111 B11
Whitefield, U.S.A. 111 B13
Whitefish, U.S.A. 114 B6
Whitefish L., Canada 105 A7
Whitefish Point, U.S.A. 108 B3
Whitegull, L., Canada 103 A7
Whitehall, Mich., U.S.A. 108 D2
Whitehall, Mont., U.S.A. 114 D7
Whitehall, N.Y., U.S.A. 111 C11
Whitehall, Wis., U.S.A. 112 C9
Whitehaven, U.K. 12 C4
Whitehorse, Canada 104 A1
Whitemark, Australia 94 G4
Whiteplains, Liberia 82 D2
Whiteriver, U.S.A. 115 K9
Whitesand →, Canada 104 A5
Whitesands, S. Africa 88 E3
Whitesboro, N.Y., U.S.A. 111 C9
Whitesboro, Tex., U.S.A. 113 J6
Whiteshell Prov. Park, Canada 105 D9
Whitesville, U.S.A. 110 D7
Whiteville, U.S.A. 109 H6
Whitewater, U.S.A. 108 D1
Whitewater Baldy, U.S.A. 115 K9
Whitewater L., Canada 102 B2
Whitewood, Australia 94 C3
Whitewood, Canada 105 C8
Whithorn, U.K. 14 G4
Whitianga, N.Z. 91 G5
Whitman, U.S.A. 111 D14
Whitney, Canada 102 C4
Whitney, Mt., U.S.A. 116 J8
Whitney Point, U.S.A. 111 D9
Whitstable, U.K. 13 F9
Whitsunday I., Australia 94 C4
Whittier, U.S.A. 117 M8
Whittlesea, Australia 95 F4
Wholdaia L., Canada 105 A8
Whyalla, Australia 95 E2
Wiarton, Canada 102 D3
Wiawso, Ghana 82 D4
Wiay, U.K. 14 D1
Wiązów, Poland 45 H4
Wibaux, U.S.A. 112 B2
Wichian Buri, Thailand 64 E3
Wichita, U.S.A. 113 G6
Wichita Falls, U.S.A. 113 J5
Wick, U.K. 14 C5
Wicked Pt., Canada 110 C7
Wickenburg, U.S.A. 115 K7
Wickepin, Australia 93 F2
Wickham, Australia 92 D2
Wickham, C., Australia 94 F3
Wickliffe, U.S.A. 110 E3
Wicklow, Ireland 15 D5
Wicklow □, Ireland 15 D5
Wicklow Hd., Ireland 15 D6
Wicklow Mts., Ireland 15 C5
Widawa, Poland 45 G5
Widawka →, Poland 45 G5
Widgeegoara Cr. →, Australia 95 D4
Widgiemooltha, Australia 93 F3
Widnes, U.K. 12 D5
Więcbork, Poland 45 E4
Wiehl, Germany 24 E3
Wiek, Germany 24 A9
Wielbark, Poland 44 E7
Wieleń, Poland 45 F3
Wielichowo, Poland 45 F3
Wieliczka, Poland 45 J7
Wielkopolskie □, Poland 45 F4
Wieluń, Poland 45 G5
Wien, Austria 27 C9
Wiener Neustadt, Austria 27 D9
Wieprz →, Poland 45 G8
Wieprza →, Poland 44 D3
Wieruszów, Poland 45 G5
Wiesbaden, Germany 25 E4
Wiesental, Germany 25 F4
Wiesloch, Germany 25 F4
Wiesmoor, Germany 24 B3
Wieżyca, Poland 44 D5
Wigan, U.K. 12 D5
Wiggins, Colo., U.S.A. 112 E2
Wiggins, Miss., U.S.A. 113 K10
Wight, I. of □, U.K. 13 G6
Wigry, Jezioro, Poland 44 D10
Wigston, U.K. 13 E6
Wigton, U.K. 12 C4
Wigtown, U.K. 14 G4
Wigtown B., U.K. 14 G4
Wil, Switz. 25 H5
Wilamowice, Poland 45 J6
Wilber, U.S.A. 112 E6
Wilberforce, Canada 110 A6
Wilberforce, C., Australia 94 A2
Wilburton, U.S.A. 113 H7
Wilcannia, Australia 95 E3
Wilcox, U.S.A. 110 E6
Wildbad, Germany 25 G4
Wildeshausen, Germany 24 C4
Wildon, Austria 26 E8
Wildrose, U.S.A. 117 J9
Wildspitze, Austria 26 E3
Wilga →, Poland 45 G8
Wilge →, S. Africa 89 D4
Wilhelm II Coast, Antarctica 5 C7
Wilhelmsburg, Austria 26 C8
Wilhelmshaven, Germany 24 B4
Wilhelmstal, Namibia 88 C2
Wilkes-Barre, U.S.A. 111 E9
Wilkie, Canada 105 C7
Wilkinsburg, U.S.A. 110 F5
Wilkinson Lakes, Australia 93 E5
Willandra Creek →, Australia 95 E4
Willapa B., U.S.A. 114 C2
Willapa Hills, U.S.A. 116 D3
Willard, N.Y., U.S.A. 110 D8
Willard, Ohio, U.S.A. 110 E2
Willcox, U.S.A. 115 K9
Willemstad, Neth. Ant. 121 D6
Willet, U.S.A. 111 D9
William →, Canada 105 B7
William 'Bill' Dannely Res., U.S.A. 109 J2
William Creek, Australia 95 D2
Williams, Australia 93 F2
Williams, Ariz., U.S.A. 115 J7
Williams, Calif., U.S.A. 116 F4
Williams Harbour, Canada 103 B8
Williams Lake, Canada 104 C4
Williamsburg, Ky., U.S.A. 109 G3
Williamsburg, Pa., U.S.A. 110 F6
Williamsburg, Va., U.S.A. 108 G7
Williamson, N.Y., U.S.A. 110 C7
Williamson, W. Va., U.S.A. 108 G4
Williamsport, U.S.A. 110 E7
Williamston, U.S.A. 109 H7
Williamstown, Australia 95 F3
Williamstown, Ky., U.S.A. 108 F3
Williamstown, Mass., U.S.A. 111 D11
Williamstown, N.Y., U.S.A. 111 C9
Willimantic, U.S.A. 111 E12
Willingboro, U.S.A. 108 E8
Willis Group, Australia 94 B5
Williston, S. Africa 88 E3
Williston, Fla., U.S.A. 109 L4
Williston, N. Dak., U.S.A. 112 A3
Williston L., Canada 104 B4
Willits, U.S.A. 114 G2
Willmar, U.S.A. 112 C7
Willoughby, U.S.A. 110 E3
Willow Bunch, Canada 105 D7
Willow L., Canada 104 A5
Willow Wall, The, China 57 C12
Willowick, U.S.A. 110 E3
Willowlake →, Canada 104 A4
Willowmore, S. Africa 88 E3
Willows, U.S.A. 116 F4
Willowvale = Gatyana, S. Africa 89 E4
Wills, L., Australia 92 D4
Wills Cr. →, Australia 94 C3
Willsboro, U.S.A. 111 B11
Willunga, Australia 95 F2
Wilmette, U.S.A. 108 D2
Wilmington, Australia 95 E2
Wilmington, Del., U.S.A. 108 F8
Wilmington, N.C., U.S.A. 109 H7
Wilmington, Ohio, U.S.A. 108 F4
Wilmington, Vt., U.S.A. 111 D12
Wilmslow, U.K. 12 D5
Wilpena Cr. →, Australia 95 E2
Wilsall, U.S.A. 114 D8
Wilson, N.C., U.S.A. 109 H7
Wilson, N.Y., U.S.A. 110 C6
Wilson, Pa., U.S.A. 111 F9
Wilson →, Australia 92 C4
Wilson Bluff, Australia 93 F4
Wilson Inlet, Australia 93 G2
Wilsons Promontory, Australia 95 F4
Wilster, Germany 24 B5
Wilton, U.S.A. 112 B4
Wilton →, Australia 94 A1
Wiltshire □, U.K. 13 F6
Wiltz, Lux. 17 E5
Wiluna, Australia 93 E3
Wimborne Minster, U.K. 13 G6
Wimereux, France 19 B8
Wimmera →, Australia 95 F3
Winam G., Kenya 86 C3
Winburg, S. Africa 88 D4
Winchendon, U.S.A. 111 D12
Winchester, U.K. 13 F6
Winchester, Conn., U.S.A. 111 E11
Winchester, Idaho, U.S.A. 114 C5
Winchester, Ind., U.S.A. 108 E3
Winchester, Ky., U.S.A. 108 G3
Winchester, N.H., U.S.A. 111 D12
Winchester, Nev., U.S.A. 117 J11
Winchester, Tenn., U.S.A. 109 H2
Winchester, Va., U.S.A. 108 F6
Wind →, U.S.A. 114 E9
Wind River Range, U.S.A. 114 E9
Windau = Ventspils, Latvia 9 H19
Windber, U.S.A. 110 F6
Winder, U.S.A. 109 J4
Windermere, U.K. 12 C5
Windhoek, Namibia 88 C2
Windischgarsten, Austria 26 D7
Windom, U.S.A. 112 D7
Windorah, Australia 94 D3
Window Rock, U.S.A. 115 J9
Windrush →, U.K. 13 F6
Windsor, Australia 95 E5
Windsor, N.S., Canada 103 D7
Windsor, Ont., Canada 102 D3
Windsor, U.K. 13 F7
Windsor, Colo., U.S.A. 112 E2
Windsor, Conn., U.S.A. 111 E12
Windsor, Mo., U.S.A. 112 F8
Windsor, N.Y., U.S.A. 111 D9
Windsor, Vt., U.S.A. 111 C12
Windsor & Maidenhead □, U.K. 13 F7
Windsorton, S. Africa 88 D3
Windward Is., W. Indies 121 D7
Windward Passage = Vientos, Paso de los, Caribbean 121 C5
Winefred L., Canada 105 B6
Winejok, Sudan 81 F2
Winfield, U.S.A. 113 G6
Wingate Mts., Australia 92 B5
Wingham, Australia 95 E5
Wingham, Canada 102 D3
Winisk, Canada 102 A2
Winisk →, Canada 102 A2
Winisk L., Canada 102 B2
Wink, U.S.A. 113 K3
Winkler, Canada 105 D9
Winklern, Austria 26 E5
Winlock, U.S.A. 116 D4
Winneba, Ghana 83 D4
Winnebago, L., U.S.A. 108 D1
Winnecke Cr. →, Australia 92 C5
Winnemucca, U.S.A. 114 F5
Winnemucca L., U.S.A. 114 F4
Winnett, U.S.A. 114 C9
Winnfield, U.S.A. 113 K8
Winnibigoshish, L., U.S.A. 112 B7
Winnipeg, Canada 105 D9
Winnipeg →, Canada 105 C9
Winnipeg, L., Canada 105 C9
Winnipeg Beach, Canada 105 C9
Winnipegosis, Canada 105 C9
Winnipegosis L., Canada 105 C9
Winnipesaukee, L., U.S.A. 111 C13
Winnisquam L., U.S.A. 111 C13
Winnsboro, La., U.S.A. 113 J9
Winnsboro, S.C., U.S.A. 109 H5
Winnsboro, Tex., U.S.A. 113 J7
Winokapau, L., Canada 103 B7
Winona, Minn., U.S.A. 112 C9
Winona, Miss., U.S.A. 113 J10
Winooski, U.S.A. 111 B11
Winooski →, U.S.A. 111 B11
Winschoten, Neths. 17 A7
Winsen, Germany 24 B6
Winsford, U.K. 12 D5
Winslow, Ariz., U.S.A. 115 J8
Winslow, Wash., U.S.A. 116 C4
Winsted, U.S.A. 111 E11
Winston-Salem, U.S.A. 109 G5
Winter Garden, U.S.A. 109 L5
Winter Haven, U.S.A. 109 M5
Winter Park, U.S.A. 109 L5
Winterberg, Germany 24 D4
Winterhaven, U.S.A. 117 N12
Winters, U.S.A. 116 G5
Wintersville, U.S.A. 110 F4
Winterswijk, Neths. 17 C6
Winterthur, Switz. 25 H4
Winthrop, U.S.A. 114 B3
Winton, Australia 94 C3
Winton, N.Z. 91 M2
Wipper →, Germany 24 D7
Wirrulla, Australia 95 E1
Wisbech, U.K. 13 E8
Wisconsin □, U.S.A. 112 C10
Wisconsin →, U.S.A. 112 D9
Wisconsin Rapids, U.S.A. 112 C10
Wisdom, U.S.A. 114 D7
Wishaw, U.K. 14 F5
Wishek, U.S.A. 112 B5
Wisła, Poland 45 J5
Wisła →, Poland 44 D5
Wisłok →, Poland 45 H9
Wisłoka →, Poland 45 H8
Wismar, Germany 24 B7
Wisner, U.S.A. 112 E6
Wissant, France 19 B8
Wissembourg, France 19 C14
Wisznice, Poland 45 G10
Witbank, S. Africa 89 D4
Witdraai, S. Africa 88 D3

Witham, *U.K.* 13 F8
Witham →, *U.K.* 12 E7
Withernsea, *U.K.* 12 D8
Witkowo, *Poland* 45 F4
Witney, *U.K.* 13 F6
Witnica, *Poland* 45 F1
Witnossob →, *Namibia* 88 D3
Wittdün, *Germany* 24 A4
Witten, *Germany* 24 D3
Wittenberge, *Germany* 24 B7
Wittenburg, *Germany* 24 B7
Wittenheim, *France* 19 E14
Wittenoom, *Australia* 92 D2
Wittingen, *Germany* 24 C6
Wittlich, *Germany* 25 F2
Wittmund, *Germany* 24 B3
Wittow, *Germany* 24 A9
Wittstock, *Germany* 24 B8
Witvlei, *Namibia* 88 C2
Witzenhausen, *Germany* 24 D5
Wkra →, *Poland* 45 F7
Władysławowo, *Poland* 44 D5
Wleń, *Poland* 45 G2
Wlingi, *Indonesia* 63 H15
Włocławek, *Poland* 45 F6
Włodawa, *Poland* 45 G10
Włoszczowa, *Poland* 45 H6
Woburn, *U.S.A.* 111 D13
Wodian, *China* 56 H7
Wodonga = Albury-Wodonga, *Australia* 95 F4
Wodzisław Śląski, *Poland* 45 H5
Wœrth, *France* 19 D14
Woinbogoin, *China* 58 A2
Woippy, *France* 19 C13
Wojcieszow, *Poland* 45 H2
Wokam, *Indonesia* 63 F8
Woking, *U.K.* 13 F7
Wokingham □, *U.K.* 13 F7
Wolbrom, *Poland* 45 H6
Wołczyn, *Poland* 45 G5
Woldegk, *Germany* 24 B9
Wolf →, *Canada* 104 A2
Wolf Creek, *U.S.A.* 114 C7
Wolf L., *Canada* 104 A2
Wolf Point, *U.S.A.* 112 A2
Wolfe I., *Canada* 102 D4
Wolfeboro, *U.S.A.* 111 C13
Wolfen, *Germany* 24 D8
Wolfenbüttel, *Germany* 24 C6
Wolfratshausen, *Germany* 25 H7
Wolfsberg, *Austria* 26 E7
Wolfsburg, *Germany* 24 C6
Wolgast, *Germany* 24 A9
Wolhusen, *Switz.* 25 H4
Wolin, *Poland* 44 E1
Wollaston, Is., *Chile* 128 H3
Wollaston L., *Canada* 105 B8
Wollaston Lake, *Canada* 105 B8
Wollaston Pen., *Canada* 100 B8
Wollongong, *Australia* 95 E5
Wolmaransstad, *S. Africa* 88 D4
Wolmirstedt, *Germany* 24 C7
Wołomin, *Poland* 45 F8
Wołów, *Poland* 45 G3
Wolseley, *S. Africa* 88 E2
Wolsey, *U.S.A.* 112 C5
Wolstenholme, C., *Canada* 98 C12
Wolsztyn, *Poland* 45 F3
Wolvega, *Neths.* 17 B6
Wolverhampton, *U.K.* 13 E5
Wondai, *Australia* 95 D5
Wongalarroo L., *Australia* 95 E3
Wongan Hills, *Australia* 93 F2
Wŏnju, *S. Korea* 57 F14
Wonosari, *Indonesia* 63 G14
Wonosobo, *Indonesia* 63 G13
Wonowon, *Canada* 104 B4
Wŏnsan, *N. Korea* 57 E14
Wonthaggi, *Australia* 95 F4
Wood Buffalo Nat. Park, *Canada* 104 B6
Wood Is., *Australia* 92 C3
Wood L., *Canada* 105 B8
Woodah I., *Australia* 94 A2
Woodbourne, *U.S.A.* 111 E10
Woodbridge, *Canada* 110 C5
Woodbridge, *U.K.* 13 E9
Woodburn, *U.S.A.* 114 D2
Woodenbong, *Australia* 95 D5
Woodend, *Australia* 95 F3
Woodford, *Australia* 95 D5
Woodfords, *U.S.A.* 116 G7
Woodlake, *U.S.A.* 116 J7
Woodland, *Calif., U.S.A.* 116 G5
Woodland, *Maine, U.S.A.* 109 C12
Woodland, *Pa., U.S.A.* 110 F6
Woodland, *Wash., U.S.A.* 116 E4
Woodland Caribou Prov. Park, *Canada* 105 C10
Woodridge, *Canada* 105 D9
Woodroffe, Mt., *Australia* 93 E5
Woods, L., *Australia* 94 B1
Woods, L. of the, *Canada* 105 D10
Woodstock, *Australia* 94 B4
Woodstock, *N.B., Canada* 103 C6
Woodstock, *Ont., Canada* 102 D3
Woodstock, *U.K.* 13 F6
Woodstock, *Ill., U.S.A.* 112 D10
Woodstock, *Vt., U.S.A.* 111 C12
Woodsville, *U.S.A.* 111 B13
Woodville, *N.Z.* 91 J5
Woodville, *Miss., U.S.A.* 113 K9
Woodville, *Tex., U.S.A.* 113 K7
Woodward, *U.S.A.* 113 G5
Woody, *U.S.A.* 117 K8
Woody →, *Canada* 105 C8
Woolamai, C., *Australia* 95 F4
Wooler, *U.K.* 12 B5
Woolgoolga, *Australia* 95 E5
Woomera, *Australia* 95 E2
Woonsocket, *R.I., U.S.A.* 111 E13
Woonsocket, *S. Dak., U.S.A.* 112 C5
Wooramel →, *Australia* 93 E1
Wooramel Roadhouse, *Australia* 93 E1
Wooster, *U.S.A.* 110 F3
Worcester, *S. Africa* 88 E2
Worcester, *U.K.* 13 E5
Worcester, *Mass., U.S.A.* 111 D13
Worcester, *N.Y., U.S.A.* 111 D10
Worcestershire □, *U.K.* 13 E5
Wörgl, *Austria* 26 D5
Workington, *U.K.* 12 C4
Worksop, *U.K.* 12 D6
Workum, *Neths.* 17 B5
Worland, *U.S.A.* 114 D10
Wormhout, *France* 19 B9
Worms, *Germany* 25 F4
Worsley, *Canada* 104 B5
Wörth, *Germany* 25 F8
Wortham, *U.S.A.* 113 K6
Wörther See, *Austria* 26 E7
Worthing, *U.K.* 13 G7
Worthington, *Minn., U.S.A.* 112 D7
Worthington, *Pa., U.S.A.* 110 F5
Wosi, *Indonesia* 63 E7
Wou-han = Wuhan, *China* 59 B10
Wousi = Wuxi, *China* 59 B13
Wowoni, *Indonesia* 63 E6
Wrangel I. = Vrangelya, Ostrov, *Russia* 51 B19
Wrangell, *U.S.A.* 104 B2
Wrangell Mts., *U.S.A.* 100 B5
Wrath, C., *U.K.* 14 C3
Wray, *U.S.A.* 112 E3
Wrekin, The, *U.K.* 13 E5
Wrens, *U.S.A.* 109 J4
Wrexham, *U.K.* 12 D4
Wrexham □, *U.K.* 12 D5
Wriezen, *Germany* 24 C10
Wright = Paranas, *Phil.* 61 F6
Wright, *U.S.A.* 112 D2
Wright Pt., *Canada* 110 C3
Wrightson Mt., *U.S.A.* 115 L8
Wrightwood, *U.S.A.* 117 L9
Wrigley, *Canada* 100 B7
Wrocław, *Poland* 45 G4
Wronki, *Poland* 45 F3
Września, *Poland* 45 F4
Wschowa, *Poland* 45 G3
Wu Jiang →, *China* 58 C6
Wu'an, *China* 56 F8
Wubin, *Australia* 93 F2
Wubu, *China* 56 F6
Wuchang, *China* 57 B14
Wucheng, *China* 56 F9
Wuchuan, *Guangdong, China* 59 G8
Wuchuan, *Guizhou, China* 58 C7
Wuchuan, *Nei Monggol Zizhiqu, China* 56 D6
Wudi, *China* 57 F9
Wuding, *China* 58 E4
Wuding He →, *China* 56 F6
Wudinna, *Australia* 95 E2
Wudu, *China* 56 H3
Wufeng, *China* 59 B8
Wugang, *China* 59 D8
Wugong Shan, *China* 59 D9
Wuhan, *China* 59 B10
Wuhe, *China* 57 H9
Wuhsi = Wuxi, *China* 59 B13
Wuhu, *China* 59 B12
Wujiang, *China* 59 B13
Wukari, *Nigeria* 83 D6
Wulajie, *China* 57 B14
Wulanbulang, *China* 56 D6
Wular L., *India* 69 B6
Wulehe, *Ghana* 83 D5
Wulian, *China* 57 G10
Wuliang Shan, *China* 58 E3
Wuliaru, *Indonesia* 63 F8
Wuling Shan, *China* 58 C7
Wulong, *China* 58 C6
Wulumuchi = Ürümqi, *China* 50 E9
Wum, *Cameroon* 83 D7
Wuming, *China* 58 F7
Wun Rog, *Sudan* 81 F2
Wundowie, *Australia* 93 F2
Wuning, *China* 59 C10
Wunnummin L., *Canada* 102 B2
Wunsiedel, *Germany* 25 E8
Wunstorf, *Germany* 24 C5
Wuntho, *Burma* 67 H19
Wuping, *China* 59 E11
Wuppertal, *Germany* 24 D3
Wuppertal, *S. Africa* 88 E2
Wuqing, *China* 57 E9
Wurtsboro, *U.S.A.* 111 E10
Würzburg, *Germany* 25 F5
Wurzen, *Germany* 24 D8
Wushan, *China* 56 G3
Wushishi, *Nigeria* 83 D6
Wusuli Jiang = Ussuri →, *Asia* 54 A7
Wutach →, *Germany* 25 H4
Wutai, *China* 56 E7
Wuting = Huimin, *China* 57 F9
Wutong, *China* 59 E8
Wutonghaolai, *China* 57 C11
Wutongqiao, *China* 58 C4
Wuwei, *Anhui, China* 59 B11
Wuwei, *Gansu, China* 60 C5
Wuxi, *Jiangsu, China* 59 B13
Wuxi, *Sichuan, China* 58 B7
Wuxiang, *China* 56 F7
Wuxuan, *China* 58 F7
Wuxue, *China* 59 C10
Wuyang, *China* 56 H7
Wuyi, *Hebei, China* 56 F8
Wuyi, *Zhejiang, China* 59 C12
Wuyi Shan, *China* 59 D11
Wuyishan, *China* 59 D12
Wuyo, *Nigeria* 83 C7
Wuyuan, *Jiangxi, China* 59 C11
Wuyuan, *Nei Monggol Zizhiqu, China* 56 D5
Wuzhai, *China* 56 E6
Wuzhi Shan, *China* 64 C7
Wuzhong, *China* 56 E4
Wuzhou, *China* 59 F8
Wyaaba Cr. →, *Australia* 94 B3
Wyalkatchem, *Australia* 93 F2
Wyalusing, *U.S.A.* 111 E8
Wyandotte, *U.S.A.* 108 D4
Wyandra, *Australia* 95 D4
Wyangala, L., *Australia* 95 E4
Wyara, L., *Australia* 95 D3
Wycheproof, *Australia* 95 F3
Wye →, *U.K.* 13 F5
Wyemandoo, *Australia* 93 E2
Wyk, *Germany* 24 A4
Wymondham, *U.K.* 13 E9
Wymore, *U.S.A.* 112 E6
Wyndham, *Australia* 92 C4
Wyndham, *N.Z.* 91 M2
Wynne, *U.S.A.* 113 H9
Wynyard, *Australia* 94 G4
Wynyard, *Canada* 105 C8
Wyola L., *Australia* 93 E5
Wyoming, *Canada* 110 D2
Wyoming □, *U.S.A.* 114 E10
Wyomissing, *U.S.A.* 111 F9
Wyong, *Australia* 95 E5
Wyrzysk, *Poland* 45 E4
Wyśmierzyce, *Poland* 45 G7
Wysoka, *Poland* 45 E4
Wysokie, *Poland* 45 H9
Wysokie Mazowieckie, *Poland* 45 F9
Wyszków, *Poland* 45 F8
Wyszogród, *Poland* 45 F7
Wytheville, *U.S.A.* 108 G5
Wyżyna Małopolska, *Poland* 45 H7

X

Xaçmaz, *Azerbaijan* 49 K9
Xai-Xai, *Mozam.* 89 D5
Xainza, *China* 60 C3
Xangongo, *Angola* 88 B2
Xankändi, *Azerbaijan* 70 B5
Xanlar, *Azerbaijan* 49 K8
Xanten, *Germany* 24 D2
Xánthi, *Greece* 41 E8
Xánthi □, *Greece* 41 E8
Xanthos, *Turkey* 39 E11
Xanxerê, *Brazil* 127 B5
Xapuri, *Brazil* 124 F5
Xar Moron He →, *China* 57 C11
Xarrë, *Albania* 40 G4
Xátiva, *Spain* 33 G4
Xau, L., *Botswana* 88 C3
Xavantina, *Brazil* 127 A5
Xenia, *U.S.A.* 108 F4
Xeropotamos →, *Cyprus* 36 E11
Xertigny, *France* 19 D13
Xhora, *S. Africa* 89 E4
Xhumo, *Botswana* 88 C3
Xi Jiang →, *China* 59 F9
Xi Xian, *Henan, China* 59 A10
Xi Xian, *Shanxi, China* 56 F6
Xia Xian, *China* 56 G6
Xiachengzi, *China* 57 B16
Xiachuan Dao, *China* 59 G9
Xiaguan, *China* 60 D5
Xiajiang, *China* 59 D10
Xiajin, *China* 56 F9
Xiamen, *China* 59 E12
Xi'an, *China* 56 G5
Xian Xian, *China* 56 E9
Xianfeng, *China* 58 C7
Xiang Jiang →, *China* 59 C9
Xiangcheng, *Henan, China* 56 H8
Xiangcheng, *Henan, China* 56 H7
Xiangcheng, *Sichuan, China* 58 C2
Xiangdu, *China* 58 F6
Xiangfan, *China* 59 A9
Xianggang = Hong Kong □, *China* 59 F10
Xianghuang Qi, *China* 56 C7
Xiangning, *China* 56 G6
Xiangquan, *China* 56 F7
Xiangquan He = Sutlej →, *Pakistan* 68 E4
Xiangshan, *China* 59 C13
Xiangshui, *China* 57 G10
Xiangtan, *China* 59 D9
Xiangxiang, *China* 59 D9
Xiangyin, *China* 59 C9
Xiangyun, *China* 58 E3
Xiangzhou, *China* 58 F7
Xianju, *China* 59 C13
Xianning, *China* 59 C10
Xianshui He →, *China* 58 B3
Xiantao, *China* 59 B9
Xianyang, *China* 56 G5
Xianyou, *China* 59 E12
Xiao Hinggan Ling, *China* 60 B7
Xiao Xian, *China* 56 G9
Xiaofeng, *China* 59 B12
Xiaogan, *China* 59 B9
Xiaojin, *China* 58 B4
Xiaolan, *China* 59 F9
Xiaoshan, *China* 59 B13
Xiaoyi, *China* 56 F6
Xiapu, *China* 59 D12
Xiawa, *China* 57 C11
Xiayi, *China* 56 G9
Xichang, *China* 58 D4
Xichong, *China* 58 B5
Xichou, *China* 58 E5
Xichuan, *China* 56 H6
Xide, *China* 58 C4
Xiemahe, *China* 59 B8
Xieng Khouang, *Laos* 64 C4
Xifei He →, *China* 56 H9
Xifeng, *Gansu, China* 56 G4
Xifeng, *Guizhou, China* 58 D6
Xifeng, *Liaoning, China* 57 C13
Xifengzhen = Xifeng, *China* 56 G4
Xigazê, *China* 60 D3
Xihe, *China* 56 G3
Xihua, *China* 56 H8
Xilaganí, *Greece* 41 F9
Xiliao He →, *China* 57 C12
Xilin, *China* 58 E5
Xilókastron, *Greece* 38 C4
Xime, *Guinea-Biss.* 82 C2
Ximeng, *China* 58 F2
Xin Jiang →, *China* 59 C11
Xin Xian = Xinzhou, *China* 56 E7
Xinavane, *Mozam.* 89 D5
Xinbin, *China* 57 D13
Xincai, *China* 59 A10
Xinchang, *China* 59 C13
Xincheng, *Guangxi Zhuangzu, China* 58 E7
Xincheng, *Jiangxi, China* 59 D10
Xindu, *China* 58 B5
Xinfeng, *Guangdong, China* 59 E10
Xinfeng, *Jiangxi, China* 59 D11
Xinfeng, *Jiangxi, China* 59 E10
Xinfengjiang Skuiku, *China* 59 F10
Xing Xian, *China* 56 E6
Xing'an, *Guangxi Zhuangzu, China* 59 E8
Xingan, *Jiangxi, China* 59 D10
Xingcheng, *China* 57 D11
Xingguo, *China* 59 D10
Xinghe, *China* 56 D7
Xinghua, *China* 57 H10
Xinghua Wan, *China* 59 E12
Xinglong, *China* 57 D9
Xingning, *China* 59 E10
Xingping, *China* 56 G5
Xingren, *China* 58 E5
Xingshan, *China* 59 B8
Xingtai, *China* 56 F8
Xingu →, *Brazil* 122 D5
Xingwen, *China* 58 C5
Xingyang, *China* 56 G7
Xinhe, *China* 56 F8
Xinhua, *China* 59 D8
Xinhuang, *China* 58 D7
Xinhui, *China* 59 F9
Xining, *China* 60 C5
Xinjian, *China* 59 C10
Xinjiang, *China* 56 G6
Xinjiang Uygur Zizhiqu □, *China* 60 B3
Xinjie, *China* 58 D3
Xinjin = Pulandian, *China* 57 E11
Xinjin, *China* 58 B4
Xinkai He →, *China* 57 C12
Xinle, *China* 56 E8
Xinlitun, *China* 57 D12
Xinlong, *China* 58 B3
Xinmin, *China* 57 D12
Xinning, *China* 59 D8
Xinping, *China* 58 E3
Xinshao, *China* 59 D8
Xintai, *China* 57 G9
Xintian, *China* 59 E9
Xinxian, *China* 59 B10
Xinxiang, *China* 56 G7
Xinxing, *China* 59 F9
Xinyang, *China* 59 A10
Xinye, *China* 59 A9
Xinyi, *China* 59 F8
Xinyu, *China* 59 D10
Xinzhan, *China* 57 C14
Xinzheng, *China* 56 G7
Xinzhou, *Hubei, China* 59 B10
Xinzhou, *Shanxi, China* 56 E7
Xinzo de Limia, *Spain* 34 C3
Xiongyuecheng, *China* 57 D12
Xiping, *Henan, China* 56 H8
Xiping, *Henan, China* 56 H6
Xiping, *Zhejiang, China* 59 C12
Xique-Xique, *Brazil* 125 F10
Xisha Qundao = Paracel Is., *S. China Sea* 62 A4
Xishui, *Guizhou, China* 58 C6
Xishui, *Hubei, China* 59 B10
Xitole, *Guinea-Biss.* 82 C2
Xiu Shui →, *China* 59 C10
Xiuning, *China* 59 C12
Xiuren, *China* 59 E8
Xiushan, *China* 58 C7
Xiushui, *China* 59 C10
Xiuwen, *China* 58 D6
Xiuyan, *China* 57 D12
Xixabangma Feng, *China* 67 E14
Xixia, *China* 56 H6
Xixiang, *China* 56 H4
Xiyang, *China* 56 F7
Xizang Zizhiqu □, *China* 60 C3
Xlendi, *Malta* 36 C1
Xu Jiang →, *China* 59 D11
Xuan Loc, *Vietnam* 65 G6
Xuan'en, *China* 58 C7
Xuanhan, *China* 58 B6
Xuanhua, *China* 56 D8
Xuanwei, *China* 58 C5
Xuanzhou, *China* 59 B12
Xuchang, *China* 56 G7
Xudat, *Azerbaijan* 49 K9
Xuefeng Shan, *China* 59 D8
Xuejiaping, *China* 59 B8
Xun Jiang →, *China* 59 F8
Xun Xian, *China* 56 G8
Xundian, *China* 58 E4
Xunwu, *China* 59 E10
Xunyang, *China* 56 H5
Xunyi, *China* 56 G5
Xupu, *China* 59 D8
Xúquer →, *Spain* 33 F4
Xushui, *China* 56 E8
Xuwen, *China* 59 G8
Xuyen Moc, *Vietnam* 65 G6
Xuyong, *China* 58 C5
Xuzhou, *China* 57 G9
Xylophagou, *Cyprus* 36 E12

Y

Ya Xian, *China* 64 C7
Yaamba, *Australia* 94 C5
Ya'an, *China* 58 C4
Yaapeet, *Australia* 95 F3
Yabassi, *Cameroon* 83 E6
Yabelo, *Ethiopia* 81 G4
Yablanitsa, *Bulgaria* 41 C8
Yablonovy Ra. = Yablonovyy Khrebet, *Russia* 51 D12
Yablonovyy Khrebet, *Russia* 51 D12
Yabrai Shan, *China* 56 E2
Yabrūd, *Syria* 75 B5
Yacheng, *China* 64 C7
Yacuiba, *Bolivia* 126 A3
Yacuma →, *Bolivia* 124 F5
Yadgir, *India* 66 L10
Yadkin →, *U.S.A.* 109 H5
Yadrin, *Russia* 48 C8
Yaeyama-Rettō, *Japan* 55 M1
Yagaba, *Ghana* 83 C4
Yağcılar, *Turkey* 39 B10
Yagodnoye, *Russia* 51 C15
Yahila, *Dem. Rep. of the Congo* 86 B1
Yahk, *Canada* 104 D5
Yahotyn, *Ukraine* 47 G6
Yahuma, *Dem. Rep. of the Congo* 84 D4
Yahyalı, *Turkey* 72 C6
Yaita, *Japan* 55 F9
Yaiza, *Canary Is.* 37 F6
Yajiang, *China* 58 B3
Yajua, *Nigeria* 83 C7
Yakima, *U.S.A.* 114 C3
Yakima →, *U.S.A.* 114 C3
Yako, *Burkina Faso* 82 C4
Yakobi I., *U.S.A.* 104 B1
Yakoruda, *Bulgaria* 40 D7
Yakovlevka, *Russia* 54 B6
Yaku-Shima, *Japan* 55 J5
Yakumo, *Japan* 54 C10
Yakutat, *U.S.A.* 100 C6
Yakutia = Sakha □, *Russia* 51 C13
Yakutsk, *Russia* 51 C13
Yala, *Thailand* 65 J3
Yale, *U.S.A.* 110 C2
Yalgoo, *Australia* 93 E2
Yalinga, *C.A.R.* 84 C4
Yalkubul, Punta, *Mexico* 119 C7
Yalleroi, *Australia* 94 C4
Yalobusha →, *U.S.A.* 113 J9
Yalong Jiang →, *China* 58 D3
Yalova, *Turkey* 41 F13
Yalta, *Ukraine* 47 K8
Yalu Jiang →, *China* 57 E13
Yalvaç, *Turkey* 72 C4
Yam Ha Melah = Dead Sea, *Asia* 75 D4
Yam Kinneret, *Israel* 75 C4
Yamada, *Japan* 55 H5
Yamagata, *Japan* 54 E10
Yamagata □, *Japan* 54 E10
Yamaguchi, *Japan* 55 G5
Yamaguchi □, *Japan* 55 G5
Yamal, Poluostrov, *Russia* 50 B8
Yamal Pen. = Yamal, Poluostrov, *Russia* 50 B8
Yamanashi □, *Japan* 55 G9
Yamba, *Australia* 95 D5
Yambarran Ra., *Australia* 92 C5
Yambéring, *Guinea* 82 C2
Yâmbiô, *Sudan* 81 G2
Yambol, *Bulgaria* 41 D10
Yamdena, *Indonesia* 63 F8
Yame, *Japan* 55 H5
Yamethin, *Burma* 67 J20
Yamma-Yamma, L., *Australia* 95 D3
Yamoussoukro, *Ivory C.* 82 D3
Yampa →, *U.S.A.* 114 F9
Yampi Sd., *Australia* 92 C3
Yampil, *Moldova* 47 H5
Yampol = Yampil, *Moldova* 47 H5
Yamrat, *Nigeria* 83 C6
Yamrukchal = Botev, *Bulgaria* 41 D8
Yamuna →, *India* 69 G9
Yamunanagar, *India* 68 D7
Yamzho Yumco, *China* 60 D4
Yan, *Nigeria* 83 C7

Yana →, Russia 51 B14
Yanagawa, Japan 55 H5
Yanai, Japan 55 H6
Yan'an, China 56 F5
Yanbian, China 58 D3
Yanbu 'al Baḥr, Si. Arabia 70 F3
Yanchang, China 56 F6
Yancheng, Henan, China 56 H8
Yancheng, Jiangsu, China 57 H11
Yanchep Beach, Australia 93 F2
Yanchi, China 56 F4
Yanchuan, China 56 F6
Yanco Cr. →, Australia 95 F4
Yandoon, Burma 67 L19
Yanfeng, China 58 E3
Yanfolila, Mali 82 C3
Yang Xian, China 56 H4
Yang-Yang, Senegal 82 B1
Yangambi, Dem. Rep. of the Congo 86 B1
Yangbi, China 58 E2
Yangcheng, China 56 G7
Yangch'ü = Taiyuan, China 56 F7
Yangchun, China 59 F8
Yanggao, China 56 D7
Yanggu, China 56 F8
Yangjiang, China 59 G8
Yangliuqing, China 57 E9
Yangon = Rangoon, Burma 67 L20
Yangping, China 59 B8
Yangpingguan, China 56 H4
Yangquan, China 56 F7
Yangshan, China 59 E9
Yangshuo, China 59 E8
Yangtse = Chang Jiang →, China 59 B13
Yangtze Kiang = Chang Jiang →, China 59 B13
Yangxin, China 59 C10
Yangyang, S. Korea 57 E15
Yangyuan, China 56 D8
Yangzhong, China 59 A12
Yangzhou, China 59 A12
Yanhe, China 58 C7
Yanji, China 57 C15
Yanjin, China 58 C5
Yanjing, China 58 C2
Yankton, U.S.A. 112 D6
Yanonge, Dem. Rep. of the Congo 86 B1
Yanqi, China 60 B3
Yanqing, China 56 D8
Yanshan, Hebei, China 57 E9
Yanshan, Jiangxi, China 59 C11
Yanshan, Yunnan, China 58 F5
Yanshou, China 57 B15
Yantabulla, Australia 95 D4
Yantai, China 57 F11
Yanting, China 58 B5
Yantra →, Bulgaria 41 C9
Yanwa, China 58 D2
Yanyuan, China 58 D3
Yanzhou, China 56 G9
Yao Xian, China 56 G5
Yao Yai, Ko, Thailand 65 J2
Yao'an, China 58 E3
Yaodu, China 58 A5
Yaoundé, Cameroon 83 E7
Yaowan, China 57 G10
Yap I., Pac. Oc. 96 G5
Yapen, Indonesia 63 E9
Yapen, Selat, Indonesia 63 E9
Yapero, Indonesia 63 E9
Yappar →, Australia 94 B3
Yaqui →, Mexico 118 B2
Yar-Sale, Russia 50 C8
Yaraka, Australia 94 C3
Yaransk, Russia 48 B8
Yarbasan, Turkey 39 C10
Yardımcı Burnu, Turkey 39 E12
Yare →, U.K. 13 E9
Yaremcha, Ukraine 47 H3
Yarensk, Russia 50 C5
Yarfa, Si. Arabia 80 C4
Yarí →, Colombia 124 D4
Yarkand = Shache, China 60 C2
Yarker, Canada 111 B8
Yarkhun →, Pakistan 69 A5
Yarmouth, Canada 103 D6
Yarmūk →, Syria 75 C4
Yaroslavl, Russia 46 D10
Yarqa, W. →, Egypt 75 F2
Yarra Yarra Lakes, Australia 93 E2
Yarram, Australia 95 F4
Yarraman, Australia 95 D5
Yarras, Australia 95 E5
Yartsevo, Sib., Russia 51 C10
Yartsevo, Smolensk, Russia 46 E7
Yarumal, Colombia 124 B3
Yasawa Group, Fiji 91 C7
Yaselda, Belarus 47 F4
Yashi, Nigeria 83 C6
Yashikera, Nigeria 83 D5
Yashkul, Russia 49 G7
Yasin, Pakistan 69 A5
Yasinovataya, Ukraine 47 H9
Yasinski, L., Canada 102 B4
Yasinya, Ukraine 47 H3
Yasothon, Thailand 64 E5
Yass, Australia 95 E4
Yāsūj, Iran 71 D6
Yatağan, Turkey 39 D10
Yatakala, Niger 83 C5
Yates Center, U.S.A. 113 G7
Yathkyed L., Canada 105 A9
Yatsushiro, Japan 55 H5
Yatta Plateau, Kenya 86 C4
Yavari →, Peru 124 D4
Yávaros, Mexico 118 B3
Yavatmal, India 66 J11
Yavne, Israel 75 D3
Yavoriv, Ukraine 47 H2
Yavorov = Yavoriv, Ukraine 47 H2
Yavuzeli, Turkey 72 D7
Yawatahama, Japan 55 H6
Yawri B., S. Leone 82 D2
Yaxi, China 58 D6
Yazd, Iran 71 D7
Yazd □, Iran 71 D7
Yazd-e Khvāst, Iran 71 D7
Yazıköy, Turkey 39 E9
Yazman, Pakistan 68 E4
Yazoo →, U.S.A. 113 J9
Yazoo City, U.S.A. 113 J9
Ybbs, Austria 26 C8
Yding Skovhøj, Denmark 11 J3
Ye Xian = Laizhou, China 57 F10
Ye Xian, China 56 H7
Yebyu, Burma 64 E2
Yechŏn, S. Korea 57 F15
Yecla, Spain 33 G3
Yécora, Mexico 118 B3
Yedintsy = Edineţ, Moldova 43 B12
Yedseram →, Nigeria 83 C7
Yefremov, Russia 46 F10
Yeghegnadzor, Armenia 73 C11
Yegorlyk →, Russia 49 G5
Yegorlykskaya, Russia 49 G5
Yegoryevsk, Russia 46 E10
Yegros, Paraguay 126 B4
Yehuda, Midbar, Israel 75 D4
Yei, Sudan 81 G3
Yei, Nahr →, Sudan 81 F3
Yejmiadzin, Armenia 49 K7
Yekaterinburg, Russia 50 D7
Yekaterinodar = Krasnodar, Russia 49 H4
Yelabuga, Russia 48 C11
Yelan, Russia 48 E6
Yelarbon, Australia 95 D5
Yelatma, Russia 48 C5
Yelets, Russia 47 F10
Yélimané, Mali 82 B2
Yelizavetgrad = Kirovohrad, Ukraine 47 H7
Yell, U.K. 14 A7
Yell Sd., U.K. 14 A7
Yellow Sea, China 57 G12
Yellowhead Pass, Canada 104 C5
Yellowknife, Canada 104 A6
Yellowknife →, Canada 104 A6
Yellowstone →, U.S.A. 112 B3
Yellowstone L., U.S.A. 114 D8
Yellowstone National Park, U.S.A. 114 D9
Yelnya, Russia 46 E7
Yelsk, Belarus 47 G5
Yelwa, Nigeria 83 C5
Yemen ■, Asia 74 E3
Yen Bai, Vietnam 58 G5
Yenagoa, Nigeria 83 E6
Yenakiyeve, Ukraine 47 H10
Yenakiyevo = Yenakiyeve, Ukraine 47 H10
Yenangyaung, Burma 67 J19
Yenbo = Yanbu 'al Baḥr, Si. Arabia 70 F3
Yenda, Australia 95 E4
Yende Millimou, Guinea 82 D2
Yendéré, Burkina Faso 82 C4
Yendi, Ghana 83 D4
Yéni, Niger 83 C5
Yenice, Ankara, Turkey 72 C5
Yenice, Aydın, Turkey 39 D10
Yenice, Çanakkale, Turkey 39 B9
Yenice, Edirne, Turkey 41 F10
Yenice →, Turkey 72 D6
Yenifoça, Turkey 39 C8
Yenihisar, Turkey 39 D9
Yeniköy, Bursa, Turkey 41 F13
Yeniköy, Çanakkale, Turkey 39 B8
Yeniköy, Kütahya, Turkey 39 C11
Yenipazar, Turkey 39 D10
Yenisaía, Greece 41 E8
Yenişehir, Turkey 41 F13
Yenisey →, Russia 50 B9
Yeniseysk, Russia 51 D10
Yeniseyskiy Zaliv, Russia 50 B9
Yennádhi, Greece 36 C9
Yenne, France 21 C9
Yenotayevka, Russia 49 G8
Yenyuka, Russia 51 D13
Yeo →, U.K. 13 G5
Yeo, L., Australia 93 E3
Yeo I., Canada 110 A3
Yeola, India 66 J9
Yeoryioúpolis, Greece 36 D6
Yeovil, U.K. 13 G5
Yepes, Spain 34 F7
Yeppoon, Australia 94 C5
Yeráki, Greece 38 D4
Yerbent, Turkmenistan 50 F6
Yerbogachen, Russia 51 C11
Yerevan, Armenia 49 K7
Yerington, U.S.A. 114 G4
Yerkesik, Turkey 39 D10
Yerköy, Turkey 72 C6
Yermak, Kazakstan 50 D8
Yermo, U.S.A. 117 L10
Yerólakkos, Cyprus 36 D12
Yeropol, Russia 51 C17
Yeropótamos →, Greece 36 D6
Yeroskipos, Cyprus 36 E11
Yershov, Russia 48 E9
Yerushalayim = Jerusalem, Israel 75 D4
Yerville, France 18 C7
Yes Tor, U.K. 13 G4
Yesan, S. Korea 57 F14
Yeşilhisar, Turkey 72 C6
Yeşilırmak →, Turkey 72 B7
Yeşilkent, Turkey 72 D7
Yeşilköy, Turkey 41 F12
Yeşilova, Turkey 39 D11
Yeşilyurt, Manisa, Turkey 39 C10
Yeşilyurt, Muğla, Turkey 39 D10
Yesnogorsk, Russia 46 E9
Yeso, U.S.A. 113 H2
Yessentuki, Russia 49 H6
Yessey, Russia 51 C11
Yeste, Spain 33 G2
Yetman, Australia 95 D5
Yeu, Î. d', France 18 F4
Yevlakh = Yevlax, Azerbaijan 49 K8
Yevlax, Azerbaijan 49 K8
Yevpatoriya, Ukraine 47 K7
Yeya →, Russia 47 J10
Yeysk, Russia 47 J10
Yezd = Yazd, Iran 71 D7
Yezerishche, Belarus 46 E5
Yhati, Paraguay 126 B4
Yhú, Paraguay 127 B4
Yi →, Uruguay 126 C4
Yi 'Allaq, G., Egypt 75 E2
Yi He →, China 57 G10
Yi Xian, Anhui, China 59 C11
Yi Xian, Hebei, China 56 E8
Yi Xian, Liaoning, China 57 D11
Yialí, Greece 39 E9
Yialiás →, Cyprus 36 D12
Yi'allaq, G., Egypt 80 A3
Yialousa, Cyprus 36 D13
Yiáltra, Greece 38 C4
Yianisádhes, Greece 36 D8
Yiannitsa, Greece 40 F6
Yibin, China 58 C5
Yichang, China 59 B8
Yicheng, Henan, China 59 B9
Yicheng, Shanxi, China 56 G6
Yichuan, China 56 F6
Yichun, Heilongjiang, China 60 B7
Yichun, Jiangxi, China 59 D10
Yidu, China 57 F10
Yidun, China 58 B2
Yifag, Ethiopia 81 E4
Yifeng, China 59 C10
Yihuang, China 59 D11
Yijun, China 56 G5
Yıldız Dağları, Turkey 41 E11
Yıldızeli, Turkey 72 C7
Yiliang, Yunnan, China 58 D5
Yiliang, Yunnan, China 58 E4
Yilong, China 58 B6
Yimen, China 58 E4
Yimianpo, China 57 B15
Yinchuan, China 56 E4
Yindarlgooda, L., Australia 93 F3
Ying He →, China 56 H9
Ying Xian, China 56 E7
Yingcheng, China 59 B9
Yingde, China 59 E9
Yingjiang, China 58 E1
Yingjing, China 58 C4
Yingkou, China 57 D12
Yingshan, Henan, China 59 B9
Yingshan, Hubei, China 59 B10
Yingshan, Sichuan, China 58 B6
Yingshang, China 59 A11
Yingtan, China 59 C11
Yining, China 50 E9
Yinjiang, China 58 C7
Yinmabin, Burma 67 H19
Yiofiros →, Greece 36 D7
Yioúra, Nótios Aiyaíon, Greece 38 D6
Yioúra, Thessalía, Greece 38 B6
Yipinglang, China 58 E3
Yirba Muda, Ethiopia 81 F4
Yirga Alem, Ethiopia 81 F4
Yirol, Sudan 81 F3
Yirrkala, Australia 94 A2
Yishan, China 58 E7
Yishui, China 57 G10
Yíthion, Greece 38 E4
Yitong, China 57 C13
Yiwu, China 59 C13
Yixing, China 59 B12
Yiyang, Henan, China 56 G7
Yiyang, Hunan, China 59 C9
Yiyang, Jiangxi, China 59 C11
Yizhang, China 59 E9
Yizheng, China 59 A12
Yli-Kitka, Finland 8 C23
Ylitornio, Finland 8 C20
Ylivieska, Finland 8 D21
Yngaren, Sweden 11 F10
Yoakum, U.S.A. 113 L6
Yobe □, Nigeria 83 C7
Yog Pt., Phil. 63 B6
Yogan, Togo 83 D5
Yoğuntaş, Turkey 41 E11
Yogyakarta, Indonesia 62 F4
Yoho Nat. Park, Canada 104 C5
Yojoa, L. de, Honduras 120 D2
Yŏju, S. Korea 57 F14
Yokadouma, Cameroon 84 D2
Yokkaichi, Japan 55 G8
Yoko, Cameroon 83 D7
Yokohama, Japan 55 G9
Yokosuka, Japan 55 G9
Yokote, Japan 54 E10
Yola, Nigeria 83 D7
Yolaina, Cordillera de, Nic. 120 D3
Yoloten, Turkmenistan 71 B9
Yom →, Thailand 62 A2
Yonago, Japan 55 G6
Yonaguni-Jima, Japan 55 M1
Yŏnan, N. Korea 57 F14
Yonezawa, Japan 54 F10
Yong Peng, Malaysia 65 L4
Yong Sata, Thailand 65 J2
Yongamp'o, N. Korea 57 E13
Yong'an, China 59 E11
Yongcheng, China 56 H9
Yŏngch'ŏn, S. Korea 57 G15
Yongchuan, China 58 C5
Yongchun, China 59 E12
Yongde, China 58 E2
Yongdeng, China 56 F2
Yongding, China 59 E11
Yŏngdŏk, S. Korea 57 F15
Yŏngdŭngpo, S. Korea 57 F14
Yongfeng, China 59 D10
Yongfu, China 58 E7
Yonghe, China 56 F6
Yŏnghŭng, N. Korea 57 E14
Yongji, China 56 G6
Yongjia, China 59 C13
Yŏngju, S. Korea 57 F15
Yongkang, Yunnan, China 58 E2
Yongkang, Zhejiang, China 59 C13
Yongnian, China 56 F8
Yongning, Guangxi Zhuangzu, China 58 F7
Yongning, Ningxia Huizu, China 56 E4
Yongping, China 58 E2
Yongqing, China 56 E9
Yongren, China 58 D3
Yongshan, China 58 C4
Yongsheng, China 58 D3
Yongshun, China 58 C7
Yongtai, China 59 E12
Yŏngwŏl, S. Korea 57 F15
Yongxin = Jinggangshan, China 59 D10
Yongxing, China 59 D9
Yongxiu, China 59 C10
Yongzhou, China 59 D8
Yonibana, S. Leone 82 D2
Yonkers, U.S.A. 111 F11
Yonne □, France 19 E10
Yonne →, France 19 D9
York, Australia 93 F2
York, U.K. 12 D6
York, Ala., U.S.A. 113 J10
York, Nebr., U.S.A. 112 E6
York, Pa., U.S.A. 108 F7
York, C., Australia 94 A3
York, City of □, U.K. 12 D6
York, Kap, Greenland 4 B4
York, Vale of, U.K. 12 C6
York Haven, U.S.A. 110 F8
York Sd., Australia 92 C4
Yorke Pen., Australia 95 E2
Yorkshire Wolds, U.K. 12 C7
Yorkton, Canada 105 C8
Yorkville, U.S.A. 116 G3
Yoro, Honduras 120 C2
Yoron-Jima, Japan 55 L4
Yorosso, Mali 82 C4
Yos Sudarso, Pulau = Dolak, Pulau, Indonesia 63 F9
Yosemite National Park, U.S.A. 116 H7
Yosemite Village, U.S.A. 116 H7
Yoshkar Ola, Russia 48 B8
Yŏsu, S. Korea 57 G14
Yotvata, Israel 75 F4
You Jiang →, China 58 F6
You Xian, China 59 D9
Youbou, Canada 116 B2
Youghal, Ireland 15 E4
Youghal B., Ireland 15 E4
Youkounkoun, Guinea 82 C2
Young, Australia 95 E4
Young, Canada 105 C7
Young, Uruguay 126 C4
Younghusband, L., Australia 95 E2
Younghusband Pen., Australia 95 F2
Youngstown, Canada 105 C6
Youngstown, N.Y., U.S.A. 110 C5
Youngstown, Ohio, U.S.A. 110 E4
Youngsville, U.S.A. 110 E5
Youngwood, U.S.A. 110 F5
Youxi, China 59 D12
Youyang, China 58 C7
Youyu, China 56 D7
Yozgat, Turkey 72 C6
Ypané →, Paraguay 126 A4
Yport, France 18 C7
Ypres = Ieper, Belgium 17 D2
Yreka, U.S.A. 114 F2
Yssingeaux, France 21 C8
Ystad, Sweden 11 J7
Ysyk-Köl, Kyrgyzstan 50 E8
Ythan →, U.K. 14 D7
Ytterhogdal, Sweden 10 B8
Ytyk-Kyuyel, Russia 51 C14
Yu Jiang →, China 58 F7
Yu Xian = Yuzhou, China 56 G7
Yu Xian, Hebei, China 56 E8
Yu Xian, Shanxi, China 56 E7
Yuan Jiang →, Hunan, China 59 C8
Yuan Jiang →, Yunnan, China 58 F4
Yuan'an, China 59 B8
Yuanjiang, Hunan, China 59 C9
Yuanjiang, Yunnan, China 58 F4
Yüanli, Taiwan 59 E13
Yüanlin, Taiwan 59 F13
Yuanling, China 59 C8
Yuanmou, China 58 E3
Yuanqu, China 56 G6
Yuanyang, Henan, China 56 G7
Yuanyang, Yunnan, China 58 F4
Yuba →, U.S.A. 116 F5
Yuba City, U.S.A. 116 F5
Yūbari, Japan 54 C10
Yubdo, Ethiopia 81 F4
Yūbetsu, Japan 54 B11
Yubo, Sudan 81 F2
Yucatán □, Mexico 119 C7
Yucatán, Canal de, Caribbean 120 B2
Yucatán, Península de, Mexico 98 H11
Yucatán Basin, Cent. Amer. 98 H11
Yucatan Str. = Yucatán, Canal de, Caribbean 120 B2
Yucca, U.S.A. 117 L12
Yucca Valley, U.S.A. 117 L10
Yucheng, China 56 F9
Yuci, China 56 F7
Yudu, China 59 E10
Yuechi, China 58 B6
Yuendumu, Australia 92 D5
Yueqing, China 59 C13
Yueqing Wan, China 59 D13
Yuexi, Anhui, China 59 B11
Yuexi, Sichuan, China 58 C4
Yueyang, China 59 C9
Yugan, China 59 C11
Yugoslavia ■, Europe 40 C4
Yuhuan, China 59 C13
Yuhuan Dao, China 59 C13
Yujiang, China 59 C11
Yukhnov, Russia 46 E8
Yukon →, U.S.A. 100 B3
Yukon Territory □, Canada 100 B6
Yüksekova, Turkey 73 D11
Yukta, Russia 51 C11
Yukuhashi, Japan 55 H5
Yulara, Australia 93 E5
Yule →, Australia 92 D2
Yuleba, Australia 95 D4
Yuli, Nigeria 83 D7
Yuli, Taiwan 59 F13
Yulin, Guangxi Zhuangzu, China 59 F8
Yülin, Hainan, China 65 C7
Yulin, Shaanxi, China 56 E5
Yuma, Ariz., U.S.A. 117 N12
Yuma, Colo., U.S.A. 112 E3
Yuma, B. de, Dom. Rep. 121 C6
Yumbe, Uganda 86 B3
Yumbi, Dem. Rep. of the Congo 86 C2
Yumen, China 60 C4
Yumurtalık, Turkey 72 D6
Yun Gui Gaoyuan, China 58 E3
Yun Ho →, China 57 E9
Yun Ling, China 58 D2
Yun Xian, Hubei, China 59 A8
Yun Xian, Yunnan, China 58 E3
Yuna, Australia 93 E2
Yunak, Turkey 72 C4
Yunan, China 59 F8
Yuncheng, Henan, China 56 G8
Yuncheng, Shanxi, China 56 G6
Yunfu, China 59 F9
Yungas, Bolivia 124 G5
Yungay, Chile 126 D1
Yunhe, China 59 C12
Yunkai Dashan, China 59 F8
Yunlin, Taiwan 59 F13
Yunlong, China 58 E2
Yunmeng, China 59 B9
Yunnan □, China 58 E4
Yunquera de Henares, Spain 32 E1
Yunt Dağı, Turkey 39 C9
Yunta, Australia 95 E2
Yunxi, China 56 H6
Yunxiao, China 59 F11
Yuping, China 58 D7
Yupyongdong, N. Korea 57 D15
Yuqing, China 58 D6
Yurga, Russia 50 D9
Yurimaguas, Peru 124 E3
Yuryev-Polskiy, Russia 46 D10
Yuryevets, Russia 48 B6
Yuscarán, Honduras 120 D2
Yushan, China 59 C12
Yushanzhen, China 58 C7
Yushe, China 56 F7
Yushu, Jilin, China 57 B14
Yushu, Qinghai, China 60 C4
Yusufeli, Turkey 73 B9
Yutai, China 56 G9
Yutian, China 57 E9
Yuxarı Qarabağ = Nagorno-Karabakh, Azerbaijan 70 B5
Yuxi, China 58 E4
Yuyao, China 59 B13
Yuzawa, Japan 54 E10
Yuzha, Russia 48 B6
Yuzhno-Sakhalinsk, Russia 51 E15
Yuzhou, China 56 G7
Yvelines □, France 19 D8
Yverdon-les-Bains, Switz. 25 J2
Yvetot, France 18 C7
Yzeure, France 19 F10

Z

Zaanstad, Neths. 17 B4
Zāb al Kabīr →, Iraq 70 C4
Zāb aş Şagīr →, Iraq 70 C4
Žabalj, Serbia, Yug. 42 E5
Žabari, Serbia, Yug. 40 B5
Zabarjad, Egypt 80 C4

Zabaykalsk, *Russia* 51 E12
Zabki, *Poland* 45 F8
Ząbkowice Śląskie, *Poland* 45 H3
Žabljak, *Montenegro, Yug.* 40 C3
Zabłudów, *Poland* 45 F9
Żabno, *Poland* 45 H7
Zābol, *Iran* 71 D9
Zābol □, *Afghan.* 66 D5
Zābolī, *Iran* 71 E9
Zabré, *Burkina Faso* 83 C4
Zábřeh, *Czech Rep.* 27 B9
Zabrze, *Poland* 45 H5
Zabzuga, *Ghana* 83 D5
Zacapa, *Guatemala* 120 D2
Zacapu, *Mexico* 118 D4
Zacatecas, *Mexico* 118 C4
Zacatecas □, *Mexico* 118 C4
Zacatecoluca, *El Salv.* 120 D2
Zachary, *U.S.A.* 113 K9
Zachodnio-Pomorskie □, *Poland* 44 E2
Zacoalco, *Mexico* 118 C4
Zacualtipán, *Mexico* 119 C5
Zadar, *Croatia* 29 D12
Zadawa, *Nigeria* 83 C7
Zadetkyi Kyun, *Burma* 65 G1
Zadonsk, *Russia* 47 F10
Zafarqand, *Iran* 71 C7
Zafora, *Greece* 39 E8
Zafra, *Spain* 35 G4
Żagań, *Poland* 45 G2
Zagaoua, *Chad* 79 E10
Žagarė, *Lithuania* 44 B10
Zagazig, *Egypt* 80 H7
Zāgheh, *Iran* 71 C6
Zaglivérion, *Greece* 40 F7
Zagnanado, *Benin* 83 D5
Zagorá, *Greece* 38 B5
Zagorje, *Slovenia* 29 B11
Zagórów, *Poland* 45 F4
Zagorsk = Sergiyev Posad, *Russia* 46 D10
Zagórz, *Poland* 45 J9
Zagreb, *Croatia* 29 C12
Zāgros, Kūhhā-ye, *Iran* 71 C6
Zagros Mts. = Zāgros, Kūhhā-ye, *Iran* 71 C6
Žagubica, *Serbia, Yug.* 40 B5
Zaguinaso, *Ivory C.* 82 C3
Zagyva →, *Hungary* 42 C5
Zāhedān, *Fārs, Iran* 71 D7
Zāhedān, *Sīstān va Balūchestān, Iran* 71 D9
Zahlah, *Lebanon* 75 B4
Zahna, *Germany* 24 D8
Záhony, *Hungary* 42 B7
Zainsk, *Russia* 48 C11
Zaïre = Congo →, *Africa* 84 F2
Zaječar, *Serbia, Yug.* 40 C6
Zaka, *Zimbabwe* 89 C5
Zakamensk, *Russia* 51 D11
Zakataly = Zaqatala, *Azerbaijan* 49 K8
Zakháro, *Greece* 38 D3
Zakhodnaya Dzvina = Daugava →, *Latvia* 9 H21
Zākhū, *Iraq* 70 B4
Zákinthos, *Greece* 38 D2
Zákinthos □, *Greece* 38 D2
Zakopane, *Poland* 45 J6
Zakroczym, *Poland* 45 F7
Zákros, *Greece* 36 D8
Zala, *Ethiopia* 81 F4
Zala □, *Hungary* 42 D1
Zala →, *Hungary* 42 D2
Zalaegerszeg, *Hungary* 42 D1
Zalakomár, *Hungary* 42 D2
Zalalövő, *Hungary* 42 D1
Zalamea de la Serena, *Spain* 35 G5
Zalamea la Real, *Spain* 35 H4
Zalău, *Romania* 42 C8
Žalec, *Slovenia* 29 B12
Zaleshchiki = Zalishchyky, *Ukraine* 47 H3
Zalew Wiślany, *Poland* 44 D6
Zalewo, *Poland* 44 E6
Zalingei, *Sudan* 79 F10
Zalishchyky, *Ukraine* 47 H3
Zama L., *Canada* 104 B5
Zambeke, *Dem. Rep. of the Congo* 86 B2
Zambeze →, *Africa* 87 F4
Zambezi = Zambeze →, *Africa* 87 F4
Zambezi, *Zambia* 85 G4
Zambezia □, *Mozam.* 87 F4
Zambia ■, *Africa* 87 F2
Zamboanga, *Phil.* 61 H5
Zambrów, *Poland* 45 F9
Zametchino, *Russia* 48 D6
Zamfara □, *Nigeria* 83 C6
Zamfara →, *Nigeria* 83 C5
Zamora, *Mexico* 118 D4
Zamora, *Spain* 34 D5
Zamora □, *Spain* 34 D5
Zamość, *Poland* 45 H10
Zamtang, *China* 58 A3
Zan, *Ghana* 83 D4
Záncara →, *Spain* 33 F1
Zandvoort, *Neths.* 17 B4
Zanesville, *U.S.A.* 110 G2
Zangābād, *Iran* 70 B5
Zangue →, *Mozam.* 87 F4
Zanjān, *Iran* 71 B6
Zanjān □, *Iran* 71 B6
Zanjān →, *Iran* 71 B6
Zannone, *Italy* 30 B6
Zante = Zákinthos, *Greece* 38 D2
Zanthus, *Australia* 93 F3
Zanzibar, *Tanzania* 86 D4
Zaouiet El-Kala = Bordj Omar Driss, *Algeria* 78 C7
Zaouiet Reggâne, *Algeria* 78 C6
Zaoyang, *China* 59 A9
Zaozhuang, *China* 57 G9
Zap Suyu = Zāb al Kabīr →, *Iraq* 70 C4
Zapadna Morava →, *Serbia, Yug.* 40 C5
Zapadnaya Dvina = Daugava →, *Latvia* 9 H21
Zapadnaya Dvina, *Russia* 46 D7
Západné Beskydy, *Europe* 27 B12
Zapadni Rodopi, *Bulgaria* 40 E7
Zapala, *Argentina* 128 D2
Zapaleri, Cerro, *Bolivia* 126 A2
Zapata, *U.S.A.* 113 M5
Zapatón →, *Spain* 35 F4
Zaporizhzhya, *Ukraine* 47 J8
Zaporozhye = Zaporizhzhya, *Ukraine* 47 J8
Zaqatala, *Azerbaijan* 49 K8
Zara, *Turkey* 70 B3
Zaragoza, *Coahuila, Mexico* 118 B4
Zaragoza, *Nuevo León, Mexico* 119 C5
Zaragoza, *Spain* 32 D4
Zaragoza □, *Spain* 32 D4
Zarand, *Kermān, Iran* 71 D8
Zarand, *Markazī, Iran* 71 C6
Zărandului, Munţii, *Romania* 42 D7
Zaranj, *Afghan.* 66 D2
Zarasai, *Lithuania* 9 J22
Zarate, *Argentina* 126 C4
Zarautz, *Spain* 32 B2
Zaraysk, *Russia* 46 E10
Zard, Kūh-e, *Iran* 71 C6
Zāreh, *Iran* 71 C6
Zari, *Nigeria* 83 C7
Zaria, *Nigeria* 83 C6
Żarki, *Poland* 45 H6
Zárkon, *Greece* 38 B4
Zarneh, *Iran* 70 C5
Zărneşti, *Romania* 43 E10
Zarós, *Greece* 36 D6
Żarów, *Poland* 45 H3
Zarqā', Nahr az →, *Jordan* 75 C4
Zarrīn, *Iran* 71 C7
Zaruma, *Ecuador* 124 D3
Żary, *Poland* 45 G2
Zarza de Granadilla, *Spain* 34 E4
Zarzis, *Tunisia* 79 B8
Zas, *Spain* 34 B2
Zaskar →, *India* 69 B7
Zaskar Mts., *India* 69 C7
Zastron, *S. Africa* 88 E4
Žatec, *Czech Rep.* 26 A6
Zaterechnyy, *Russia* 49 H7
Zator, *Poland* 45 J6
Zavala, *Bos.-H.* 40 D1
Zavāreh, *Iran* 71 C7
Zave, *Zimbabwe* 89 B5
Zavetnoye, *Russia* 49 G6
Zavidovići, *Bos.-H.* 42 F3
Zavitinsk, *Russia* 51 D13
Zavodovski, I., *Antarctica* 5 B1
Zavolzhsk, *Russia* 48 B6
Zavolzhye, *Russia* 48 B6
Zawadzkie, *Poland* 45 H5
Zawichost, *Poland* 45 H8
Zawidów, *Poland* 45 G2
Zawiercie, *Poland* 45 H6
Zāwiyat al Bayḑā = Al Bayḑā, *Libya* 79 B10
Zâwyet Shammas, *Egypt* 80 A2
Zâwyet Um el Rakham, *Egypt* 80 A2
Zâwyet Ungeîla, *Egypt* 80 A2
Zāyā, *Iraq* 70 C5
Zāyandeh →, *Iran* 71 C7
Zaysan, *Kazakstan* 50 E9
Zaysan, Oz., *Kazakstan* 50 E9
Zayü, *China* 58 C1
Zazafotsy, *Madag.* 89 C8
Zázrivá, *Slovak Rep.* 27 B12
Zbarazh, *Ukraine* 47 H3
Zbąszyń, *Poland* 45 F2
Zbąszynek, *Poland* 45 F2
Zblewo, *Poland* 44 E5
Žďár nad Sázavou, *Czech Rep.* 26 B8
Zdolbuniv, *Ukraine* 47 G4
Ždrelo, *Serbia, Yug.* 40 B5
Zduńska Wola, *Poland* 45 G5
Zduny, *Poland* 45 G4
Zeballos, *Canada* 104 D3
Zebediela, *S. Africa* 89 C4
Zebila, *Ghana* 83 C4
Zeebrugge, *Belgium* 17 C3
Zeehan, *Australia* 94 G4
Zeeland □, *Neths.* 17 C3
Zeerust, *S. Africa* 88 D4
Zefat, *Israel* 75 C4
Zege, *Ethiopia* 81 E4
Zeggerene, Iracher, *Mali* 83 B5
Zégoua, *Mali* 82 C3
Zehdenick, *Germany* 24 C9
Zeil, Mt., *Australia* 92 D5
Zeila, *Somali Rep.* 74 E3
Zeist, *Neths.* 17 B5
Zeitz, *Germany* 24 D8
Żelechów, *Poland* 45 G8
Zelengora, *Bos.-H.* 40 C2
Zelenodolsk, *Russia* 48 C9
Zelenogorsk, *Russia* 46 B5
Zelenograd, *Russia* 46 D9
Zelenogradsk, *Russia* 9 J19
Zelenokumsk, *Russia* 49 H6
Železná Ruda, *Czech Rep.* 26 B6
Železnik, *Serbia, Yug.* 40 B4
Zelienople, *U.S.A.* 110 F4
Želiezovce, *Slovak Rep.* 27 C11
Zelina, *Croatia* 29 C13
Zell, *Baden-W., Germany* 25 H3
Zell, *Rhld-Pfz., Germany* 25 E3
Zell am See, *Austria* 26 D5
Zella-Mehlis, *Germany* 24 E6
Zelów, *Poland* 45 G6
Zeltweg, *Austria* 26 D7
Zémio, *C.A.R.* 86 A2
Zempléni-hegység, *Hungary* 42 B6
Zemplínska šírava, *Slovak Rep.* 27 C15
Zemun, *Serbia, Yug.* 40 B4
Zengbé, *Cameroon* 83 D7
Zengcheng, *China* 59 F9
Zenica, *Bos.-H.* 42 F2
Žepče, *Bos.-H.* 42 F3
Zeraf, Bahr ez →, *Sudan* 81 F3
Zerbst, *Germany* 24 D8
Żerków, *Poland* 45 F4
Zermatt, *Switz.* 25 J3
Zernez, *Switz.* 25 J6
Zernograd, *Russia* 49 G5
Zerqan, *Albania* 40 E4
Zestaponi, *Georgia* 49 J6
Zetel, *Germany* 24 B3
Zeulenroda, *Germany* 24 E7
Zeven, *Germany* 24 B5
Zevenaar, *Neths.* 17 C6
Zévio, *Italy* 28 C8
Zeya, *Russia* 51 D13
Zeya →, *Russia* 51 D13
Zeytinbaği, *Turkey* 41 F12
Zeytindağ, *Turkey* 39 C9
Zghartā, *Lebanon* 75 A4
Zgierz, *Poland* 45 G6
Zgorzelec, *Poland* 45 G2
Zguriţa, *Moldova* 43 B13
Zhabinka, *Belarus* 47 F3
Zhailma, *Kazakstan* 50 D7
Zhambyl = Taraz, *Kazakstan* 50 E8
Zhangaly, *Kazakstan* 49 G10
Zhangaqazaly, *Kazakstan* 50 E7
Zhangbei, *China* 56 D8
Zhangguangcai Ling, *China* 57 B15
Zhangjiakou, *China* 56 D8
Zhangping, *China* 59 E11
Zhangpu, *China* 59 E11
Zhangshu, *China* 59 C10
Zhangwu, *China* 57 C12
Zhangye, *China* 60 C5
Zhangzhou, *China* 59 E11
Zhanhua, *China* 57 F10
Zhanjiang, *China* 59 G8
Zhannetty, Ostrov, *Russia* 51 B16
Zhanyi, *China* 58 E4
Zhanyu, *China* 57 B12
Zhao Xian, *China* 56 F8
Zhao'an, *China* 59 F11
Zhaocheng, *China* 56 F6
Zhaojue, *China* 58 C4
Zhaoping, *China* 59 E8
Zhaoqing, *China* 59 F9
Zhaotong, *China* 58 D4
Zhaoyuan, *Heilongjiang, China* 57 B13
Zhaoyuan, *Shandong, China* 57 F11
Zharkovskiy, *Russia* 46 E7
Zhashkiv, *Ukraine* 47 H6
Zhashui, *China* 56 H5
Zhayyq →, *Kazakstan* 50 E6
Zhdanov = Mariupol, *Ukraine* 47 J9
Zhecheng, *China* 56 G8
Zhegao, *China* 59 B11
Zhejiang □, *China* 59 C13
Zheleznogorsk, *Russia* 47 F8
Zheleznogorsk-Ilimskiy, *Russia* 51 D11
Zheltyye Vody = Zhovti Vody, *Ukraine* 47 H7
Zhen'an, *China* 56 H5
Zhenba, *China* 58 A6
Zhenfeng, *China* 58 E5
Zheng'an, *China* 58 C6
Zhengding, *China* 56 E8
Zhenghe, *China* 59 D12
Zhengyang, *China* 59 A10
Zhengyangguan, *China* 59 A11
Zhengzhou, *China* 56 G7
Zhenhai, *China* 59 C13
Zhenjiang, *China* 59 A12
Zhenkang, *China* 58 F2
Zhenlai, *China* 57 B12
Zhenning, *China* 58 D5
Zhenping, *Henan, China* 56 H7
Zhenping, *Shaanxi, China* 58 B7
Zhenxiong, *China* 58 D5
Zhenyuan, *Gansu, China* 56 G4
Zhenyuan, *Guizhou, China* 58 D7
Zherdevka, *Russia* 48 E5
Zherong, *China* 59 D12
Zhetiqara, *Kazakstan* 50 D7
Zhezqazghan, *Kazakstan* 50 E7
Zhicheng, *China* 59 B8
Zhidan, *China* 56 F5
Zhigansk, *Russia* 51 C13
Zhigulevsk, *Russia* 48 D9
Zhijiang, *Hubei, China* 59 B8
Zhijiang, *Hunan, China* 58 D7
Zhijin, *China* 58 D5
Zhilinda, *Russia* 51 C12
Zhirnovsk, *Russia* 48 E7
Zhitomir = Zhytomyr, *Ukraine* 47 G5
Zhizdra, *Russia* 46 F8
Zhlobin, *Belarus* 47 F6
Zhmerinka = Zhmerynka, *Ukraine* 47 H5
Zhmerynka, *Ukraine* 47 H5
Zhob, *Pakistan* 68 D3
Zhob →, *Pakistan* 68 C3
Zhodino = Zhodzina, *Belarus* 46 E5
Zhodzina, *Belarus* 46 E5
Zhokhova, Ostrov, *Russia* 51 B16
Zhongdian, *China* 58 D2
Zhongdong, *China* 58 F6
Zhongdu, *China* 58 E7
Zhongning, *China* 56 F3
Zhongshan, *Guangdong, China* 59 F9
Zhongshan, *Guangxi Zhuangzu, China* 59 E8
Zhongtiao Shan, *China* 56 G6
Zhongwei, *China* 56 F3
Zhongxiang, *China* 59 B9
Zhongyang, *China* 56 F6
Zhoucun, *China* 57 F9
Zhouning, *China* 59 D12
Zhoushan, *China* 59 B14
Zhoushan Dao, *China* 59 C14
Zhouzhi, *China* 56 G5
Zhovti Vody, *Ukraine* 47 H7
Zhovtneve, *Ukraine* 47 J7
Zhovtnevoye = Zhovtneve, *Ukraine* 47 J7
Zhu Jiang →, *China* 59 F9
Zhuanghe, *China* 57 E12
Zhucheng, *China* 57 G10
Zhugqu, *China* 56 H3
Zhuhai, *China* 59 F9
Zhuji, *China* 59 C13
Zhukovka, *Russia* 46 F7
Zhumadian, *China* 56 H8
Zhuo Xian = Zhuozhou, *China* 56 E8
Zhuolu, *China* 56 D8
Zhuozhou, *China* 56 E8
Zhuozi, *China* 56 D7
Zhushan, *China* 59 A8
Zhuxi, *China* 58 A7
Zhuzhou, *China* 59 D9
Zhytomyr, *Ukraine* 47 G5
Zi Shui →, *China* 59 C9
Žiar nad Hronom, *Slovak Rep.* 27 C11
Zīārān, *Iran* 71 B6
Ziarat, *Pakistan* 68 D2
Zibo, *China* 57 F10
Zichang, *China* 56 F5
Zidarovo, *Bulgaria* 41 D11
Ziębice, *Poland* 45 H4
Zielona Góra, *Poland* 45 G2
Zierikzee, *Neths.* 17 C3
Ziesar, *Germany* 24 C8
Zifta, *Egypt* 80 H7
Zigey, *Chad* 79 F9
Zigong, *China* 58 C5
Ziguinchor, *Senegal* 82 C1
Zihuatanejo, *Mexico* 118 D4
Zijin, *China* 59 F10
Zile, *Turkey* 72 B6
Žilina, *Slovak Rep.* 27 B11
Žilinský □, *Slovak Rep.* 27 B12
Zillah, *Libya* 79 C9
Zillertaler Alpen, *Austria* 26 D4
Zima, *Russia* 51 D11
Zimapán, *Mexico* 119 C5
Zimba, *Zambia* 87 F2
Zimbabwe, *Zimbabwe* 87 G3
Zimbabwe ■, *Africa* 87 F3
Zimi, *S. Leone* 82 D2
Zimnicea, *Romania* 43 G10
Zimovniki, *Russia* 49 G6
Zinder, *Niger* 83 C6
Zinga, *Tanzania* 87 D4
Zingst, *Germany* 24 A8
Ziniaré, *Burkina Faso* 83 C4
Zinnowitz, *Germany* 24 A9
Zion National Park, *U.S.A.* 115 H7
Zirbitzkogel, *Austria* 26 D7
Zirc, *Hungary* 42 C2
Žiri, *Slovenia* 29 B11
Žirje, *Croatia* 29 E12
Zirl, *Austria* 26 D4
Zirndorf, *Germany* 25 F6
Ziros, *Greece* 36 D8
Zirreh, Gowd-e, *Afghan.* 66 E3
Zisterdorf, *Austria* 27 C9
Zitácuaro, *Mexico* 118 D4
Žitava →, *Slovak Rep.* 27 C11
Žitište, *Serbia, Yug.* 42 E5
Zitong, *China* 58 B5
Zítsa, *Greece* 38 B2
Zittau, *Germany* 24 E10
Zitundo, *Mozam.* 89 D5
Živinice, *Bos.-H.* 42 F3
Ziwa Maghariba □, *Tanzania* 86 C3
Ziway, L., *Ethiopia* 81 F4
Zixi, *China* 59 D11
Zixing, *China* 59 E9
Ziyang, *Shaanxi, China* 56 H5
Ziyang, *Sichuan, China* 58 B5
Ziyuan, *China* 59 D8
Ziyun, *China* 58 E6
Zizhong, *China* 58 C5
Zlarin, *Croatia* 29 E12
Zlatar, *Croatia* 29 B13
Zlatar, *Serbia, Yug.* 40 C3
Zlataritsa, *Bulgaria* 41 C9
Zlaté Moravce, *Slovak Rep.* 27 C11
Zlatibor, *Serbia, Yug.* 40 C3
Zlatitsa, *Bulgaria* 41 D8
Zlatna, *Romania* 43 D8
Zlatna Panega, *Bulgaria* 41 C8
Zlatni Pyasŭtsi, *Bulgaria* 41 C12
Zlatograd, *Bulgaria* 41 E9
Zlatoust, *Russia* 50 D6
Zletovo, *Macedonia* 40 E6
Zlín, *Czech Rep.* 27 B10
Zlínský □, *Czech Rep.* 27 B10
Złocieniec, *Poland* 44 E3
Złoczew, *Poland* 45 G5
Zlot, *Serbia, Yug.* 40 B5
Złotoryja, *Poland* 45 G2
Złotów, *Poland* 44 E4
Zmeinogorsk, *Kazakstan* 50 D9
Żmigród, *Poland* 45 G3
Zmiyev, *Ukraine* 47 H9
Znamenka = Znamyanka, *Ukraine* 47 H7
Znamyanka, *Ukraine* 47 H7
Żnin, *Poland* 45 F4
Znojmo, *Czech Rep.* 26 C9
Zobeyrī, *Iran* 70 C5
Zobia, *Dem. Rep. of the Congo* 86 B2
Zoetermeer, *Neths.* 17 B4
Zogang, *China* 58 C1
Zogno, *Italy* 28 C6
Zogqên, *China* 58 A2
Zolochev = Zolochiv, *Ukraine* 47 H3
Zolochiv, *Ukraine* 47 H3
Zolotonosha, *Ukraine* 47 H7
Zomba, *Malawi* 87 F4
Zongo, *Dem. Rep. of the Congo* 84 D3
Zonguldak, *Turkey* 72 B4
Zongyang, *China* 59 B11
Zonqor Pt., *Malta* 36 D2
Zonza, *France* 21 G13
Zorgo, *Burkina Faso* 83 C4
Zorita, *Spain* 35 F5
Zorleni, *Romania* 43 D12
Zornitsa, *Bulgaria* 41 D10
Zorritos, *Peru* 124 D2
Żory, *Poland* 45 H5
Zorzor, *Liberia* 82 D3
Zossen, *Germany* 24 C9
Zou Xiang, *China* 56 G9
Zouan-Hounien, *Ivory C.* 82 D3
Zouar, *Chad* 79 D9
Zouérate = Zouîrât, *Mauritania* 78 D3
Zouîrât, *Mauritania* 78 D3
Zourika, *Niger* 83 B6
Zourma, *Burkina Faso* 83 C4
Zoushan Dao, *China* 59 B14
Zoutkamp, *Neths.* 17 A6
Zrenjanin, *Serbia, Yug.* 42 E5
Zuarungu, *Ghana* 83 C4
Zuba, *Nigeria* 83 D6
Zubayr, *Yemen* 81 D5
Zubtsov, *Russia* 46 D8
Zuénoula, *Ivory C.* 82 D3
Zuera, *Spain* 32 D4
Zufār, *Oman* 74 D5
Zug □, *Switz.* 25 H4
Zugdidi, *Georgia* 49 J5
Zugersee, *Switz.* 25 H4
Zugspitze, *Germany* 25 H6
Zuid-Holland □, *Neths.* 17 C4
Zuidbeveland, *Neths.* 17 C3
Zuidhorn, *Neths.* 17 A6
Zújar, *Spain* 35 H8
Zújar →, *Spain* 35 G5
Żukowo, *Poland* 44 D5
Zula, *Eritrea* 81 D4
Zülpich, *Germany* 24 E2
Zumaia, *Spain* 32 B2
Zumárraga, *Spain* 32 B2
Zumbo, *Mozam.* 87 F3
Zummo, *Nigeria* 83 D7
Zumpango, *Mexico* 119 D5
Zungeru, *Nigeria* 83 D6
Zunhua, *China* 57 D9
Zuni, *U.S.A.* 115 J9
Zunyi, *China* 58 D6
Zuo Jiang →, *China* 58 F6
Zuozhou, *China* 58 F6
Županja, *Croatia* 42 E3
Žur, *Kosovo, Yug.* 40 D4
Zurbātīyah, *Iraq* 70 C5
Zürich, *Switz.* 25 H4
Zürich □, *Switz.* 25 H4
Zürichsee, *Switz.* 25 H4
Żuromin, *Poland* 45 E6
Žut, *Croatia* 29 E12
Zutphen, *Neths.* 17 B6
Zuwārah, *Libya* 79 B8
Zūzan, *Iran* 71 C8
Žužemberk, *Slovenia* 29 C11
Zvenigorodka = Zvenyhorodka, *Ukraine* 47 H6
Zvenyhorodka, *Ukraine* 47 H6
Zverinogolovskoye, *Russia* 50 D7
Zvezdets, *Bulgaria* 41 D11
Zvishavane, *Zimbabwe* 87 G3
Zvolen, *Slovak Rep.* 27 C12
Zvonce, *Serbia, Yug.* 40 D6
Zvornik, *Bos.-H.* 42 F4
Zwedru = Tchien, *Liberia* 82 D3
Zweibrücken, *Germany* 25 F3
Zwenkau, *Germany* 24 D8
Zwettl, *Austria* 26 C8
Zwickau, *Germany* 24 E8
Zwierzyniec, *Poland* 45 H9
Zwiesel, *Germany* 25 F9
Zwoleń, *Poland* 45 G8
Zwolle, *Neths.* 17 B6
Zwolle, *U.S.A.* 113 K8
Żychlin, *Poland* 45 F6
Żyrardów, *Poland* 45 F7
Zyryan, *Kazakstan* 50 E9
Zyryanka, *Russia* 51 C16
Zyryanovsk = Zyryan, *Kazakstan* 50 E9
Żywiec, *Poland* 45 J6
Zyyi, *Cyprus* 36 E12